WEST'S LAW SCHOOL
ADVISORY BOARD

JESSE H. CHOPER
Professor of Law
University of California, Berkeley

DAVID P. CURRIE
Professor of Law, University of Chicago

YALE KAMISAR
Professor of Law, University of Michigan

MARY KAY KANE
Dean and Professor of Law, University of California,
Hastings College of the Law

WAYNE R. LaFAVE
Professor of Law, University of Illinois

ARTHUR R. MILLER
Professor of Law, Harvard University

GRANT S. NELSON
Professor of Law, University of California, Los Angeles

JAMES J. WHITE
Professor of Law, University of Michigan

CHARLES ALAN WRIGHT
Charles Alan Wright Chair in Federal Courts
The University of Texas

WEST'S LAW SCHOOL ADVISORY BOARD

JESSE H. CHOPER
Professor of Law,
University of California, Berkeley

DAVID P. CURRIE
Professor of Law, University of Chicago

YALE KAMISAR
Professor of Law, University of Michigan

MARY KAY KANE
Dean and Professor of Law, University of California,
Hastings College of the Law

WAYNE R. LaFAVE
Professor of Law, University of Illinois

ARTHUR R. MILLER
Professor of Law, Harvard University

GRANT S. NELSON
Professor of Law, University of California, Los Angeles

JAMES J. WHITE
Professor of Law, University of Michigan

CHARLES ALAN WRIGHT
Charles Alan Wright Chair in Federal Courts
The University of Texas

PROSSER AND KEETON ON THE LAW OF TORTS

Fifth Edition

W. Page Keeton
General Editor

W. Page Keeton
Holder of W. Page Keeton Chair in Tort Law
University of Texas at Austin

Dan B. Dobbs
Rosenstiel Professor of Law, University of Arizona

Robert E. Keeton
Langdell Professor Emeritus, Harvard Law School

David G. Owen
Webster Professor of Law, University of South Carolina

**HORNBOOK SERIES
STUDENT EDITION**

Hornbook Series, WESTLAW, the West Publishing Co. Logo, the key number appearing on the front cover and the WESTLAW Computer/Book design are registered trademarks of West Publishing Co. Registered in U.S. Patent and Trademark Office.

COPYRIGHT © 1941, 1955, 1964, 1971 By WEST PUBLISHING CO.
COPYRIGHT © 1984 By KEETON, DOBBS, KEETON & OWEN
       WEST PUBLISHING CO.
       610 Opperman Drive
       P.O. Box 3526
       St. Paul, Minnesota 55165

All rights reserved
Printed in the United States of America

Library of Congress Cataloging in Publication Data

Main entry under title:

Prosser & Keeton on torts.

 (Hornbook series student edition)
 Rev. ed. of: Handbook of the law of torts/William L. Prosser. 4th ed. 1971.
 Includes index.
 1. Torts—United States. I. Keeton, Page.
II. Prosser, William Lloyd, 1898–1972. Handbook of the law of torts. III. Title: Prosser and Keeton on torts.
IV. Series.
KF1250.P73 1984b 346.7303 83–19830
         347.3063

ISBN 0–314–74880–6

TEXT IS PRINTED ON 10% POST
CONSUMER RECYCLED PAPER

Prosser & Keeton Torts 5th Ed. HB

In Memory of William L. Prosser
1898–1972

The pronouns "he," "his," and "him," as used at various points in this book, are not intended to convey the masculine gender alone; this usage is employed in a generic sense so as to avoid awkward grammatical situations which would likely occur due to the limitations of the English language.

Preface

Anyone faced with the responsibility of revising a textbook of unusually high quality on an important area of the law, such as torts, that was written by another and by one who was long and universally acclaimed as a leading scholar in that field is confronted with several rather difficult kinds of decisions. That has been true about revising William L. Prosser's superb book on torts.

In the first place, those participating in the revision process should in general be sympathetic with (a) the nature and structure of the book to be revised, and (b) the major objectives of the book's original author. This influenced the general editor in the selection of those who have participated in the revision process. As a result, little change has been made in the book's basic structure. The major change of this type has been the elimination of the Chapter on Constitutional Privilege relating to the First Amendment and the torts of defamation and interference with privacy. The effect of the decisions relating to freedom of the press and freedom of speech under the First Amendment on these two torts has been discussed within the respective Chapters on Defamation and Privacy.

However distinguished the work of the original author, a reviser must perforce, in order to be intellectually honest, make some changes simply because of a difference of opinion about how best to explain the state of the law, both now and as it existed at the time the previous edition was published. Where this has been done, every effort has been made to preserve Prosser's insights so that the user can exercise his or her own informed judgment. Some changes of this kind have been made at irregular intervals, and especially in the Chapters on Intentional Interference With Property, Proximate Cause, and Nuisance.

It has been necessary to make substantial revisions in certain chapters, especially those on Products Liability and Defamation. This has been, of course, because of the vast amount of change in the law that has come about in these areas since the Fourth Edition of Prosser was published. The law relating to strict liability of those in the business of supplying products for the use of others was in its infancy at that time, and the constitutional privilege to defame has received substantially more elaboration since that date.

The volume of decisions in the field of torts continues to grow at a rapid pace. The number of citations given to support most propositions thus must necessarily be limited. Every effort has been made to retain citations of significant old cases while including citations of new cases that adopt new positions or provide new insights. Beyond that, the revisers have found it necessary to exercise much discretion.

The authors are grateful to the many competent and conscientious persons who have assisted us in numerous ways during this revision process, especially those who have, over several years, provided secretarial, citechecking, and student research assistance; unfortunately, due to the large number of persons involved, this precludes acknowledgment on an individual basis. As the general editor, I am deeply indebted to Shirley Green who has carefully and skillfully aided in the supervision and mechanics of this project and, in general, urged it along to completion. Other secretaries who assisted with this project significantly include, in alphabetical order, Barbara Clelland, Kathleen Clover, Rose Maria Hill, Laura Long, and Donna Passons.

W. Page Keeton

April, 1984

Preface to Fourth Edition

The first edition of this book, which was published in 1941, proposed only to make, within the limits permitted by available space, some reasonable selection of the law of torts which seemed particularly significant in the light of the problems of the middle of the century. The text was to be kept relatively brief and simple throughout, in order that it might be intelligible to the student making his first contact with the law in a first-year course; and the footnote material was to be developed beyond what is usual in a short text, in order to provide a convenient reference to other sources from which more information might be obtained than it was possible to set forth in so limited a number of pages. Cases decided within the last decade or two were to be preferred, not because they were necessarily better cases, or necessarily more important ones, but because they tended to show the present state of the law, and themselves, in many instances at least, adequately reviewed what had gone before.

Thirty years later this fourth edition can do no more than adhere to the original plan. The volume of decisions in the field of torts has grown by geometrical progression, even since 1941. There have been many changes to report—some of them fully accomplished, recognized, and well accepted by now, others in midstream and still a matter of some controversy, and still others merely incipient, with a case or two here or there, and an outlook for the future upon the basis of which one might venture a prediction. The shift on the whole has been heavily toward the side of the plaintiff, with expanded liability in nearly every area. The outstanding exception has been the recognition of the constitutional privilege in the fields of defamation and privacy, which must rank as the greatest victory for the defendants in this century. The current agitation in favor of compulsory automobile insurance and compensation plans has begun to bear fruit, and it may be that we are about to enter a new era in which legislation will take over and adopt the approach of the workmen's compensation acts, at least so far as automobile drivers, and conceivably that of other defendants, may be concerned. Such a book as this can at most report the arguments which have been going on, and the perhaps fleeting present state of the law.

The writer can only deplore the limitations of space that compel the condensation of so vast an amount of material into so limited a number of pages. As before, he must express his gratitude, together with his apologies, to the dozens of other able and distinguished writers whose ideas he has unblushingly appropriated. A packrat is at best a collector, and no heroic figure; and the most that can be said for him is that he sometimes chooses well.

WILLIAM L. PROSSER

San Francisco, California
April 1, 1971

WESTLAW Introduction

Prosser and Keeton on the Law of Torts offers a detailed and comprehensive treatment of the basic rules and principles of tort law. However, law students and lawyers frequently need to find additional authority. In an effort to assist with comprehensive research of the law of torts, preformulated WESTLAW references are included after each section of the text in this edition of the hornbook. The WESTLAW references are designed for use with the WESTLAW computer-assisted legal research service. By joining this publication with the extensive WESTLAW databases, the reader is able to move straight from the hornbook into WESTLAW with great speed and convenience.

Some readers may desire to use only the information supplied within the printed pages of this hornbook. Others, however, will encounter issues in tort law that require further information. Accordingly, those who opt to go beyond the material contained in the textual format into WESTLAW can rapidly and easily access WESTLAW, an electronic law library that possesses extraordinary currency and magnitude.

Appendix A gives concise, step-by-step instruction on how to coordinate WESTLAW research with this hornbook.

THE PUBLISHER

Summary of Contents

Chapter	Page
1. Introduction	1
2. Intentional Interference with the Person	33
3. Intentional Interference with Property	67
4. Defenses to Intentional Interference with Person or Property	108
5. Negligence: Standard of Conduct	160
6. Negligence: Proof	235
7. Proximate Cause	263
8. Joint Tortfeasors	322
9. Limited Duty	356
10. Owners and Occupiers of Land	386
11. Negligence: Defenses	451
12. Imputed Negligence	499
13. Strict Liability for Physical Harm to Persons and Tangible Things From Accidental Invasions	534
14. Compensation Systems	584
15. Nuisance	616
16. Tort and Contract	655
17. Products Liability	677
18. Misrepresentation and Nondisclosure	725
19. Defamation	771
20. Privacy	849
21. Misuse of Legal Procedure	870
22. Domestic Relations	901
23. Survival and Wrongful Death	940
24. Economic Relations	962
25. Immunities	1032
APPENDIX A—WESTLAW REFERENCES	1077
TABLE OF CASES	1091
INDEX	1263

Table of Contents

CHAPTER 1. INTRODUCTION

Sec.		Page
1.	What Are Torts?	1
2.	Tort and Crime and Punitive Damages	7
3.	Policy and Process	15
4.	Factors Affecting Tort Liability	20
5.	Motive	26
6.	History: Trespass and Case	28
7.	General Plan	31

CHAPTER 2. INTENTIONAL INTERFERENCE WITH THE PERSON

8.	Meaning of Intent	33
9.	Battery	39
10.	Assault	43
11.	False Imprisonment	47
12.	Infliction of Mental Distress	54

CHAPTER 3. INTENTIONAL INTERFERENCE WITH PROPERTY

13.	Trespass to Land	67
14.	Trespass to Chattels	85
15.	Conversion	88

CHAPTER 4. DEFENSES TO INTENTIONAL INTERFERENCE WITH PERSON OR PROPERTY

16.	Privilege	108
17.	Mistake	110
18.	Consent	112
19.	Self-Defense	124
20.	Defense of Others	129
21.	Defense of Property	131
22.	Recapture of Chattels	137
23.	Recapture of Land	142
24.	Necessity	145
25.	Legal Process	148
26.	Arrest Without a Warrant	153
27.	Discipline	157

CHAPTER 5. NEGLIGENCE: STANDARD OF CONDUCT

Sec.		Page
28.	History	160
29.	Unavoidable Accident	162
30.	Elements of Cause of Action	164
31.	Unreasonable Risk	169
32.	The Reasonable Person	173
33.	Application of the Standard	193
34.	Degrees of Care; Aggravated Negligence	208
35.	Rules of Law	217
36.	Violation of Statute	220

CHAPTER 6. NEGLIGENCE: PROOF

37.	Functions of Court and Jury	235
38.	Burden of Proof and Presumptions	239
39.	Circumstantial Evidence—Res Ipsa Loquitur	242
40.	Res Ipsa Loquitur—Procedural Effect	257

CHAPTER 7. PROXIMATE CAUSE

41.	Causation in Fact	263
42.	Proximate Cause: Scope of the Problem	272
43.	Unforeseeable Consequences	280
44.	Intervening Causes	301
45.	Functions of Court and Jury	319

CHAPTER 8. JOINT TORTFEASORS

46.	Concerted Action	322
47.	Joinder of Defendants	324
48.	Judgment and Satisfaction	330
49.	Release	332
50.	Contribution	336
51.	Indemnity	341
52.	Apportionment of Damages	345

CHAPTER 9. LIMITED DUTY

53.	Duty	356
54.	Mental Disturbance	359
55.	Prenatal Injuries	367
56.	Acts and Omissions	373

CHAPTER 10. OWNERS AND OCCUPIERS OF LAND

Sec.		Page
57.	Outside of the Premises	386
58.	Trespassing Adults	393
59.	Trespassing Children	399
60.	Licensees	412
61.	Invitees	419
62.	Abolition of Categories	432
63.	Lessor and Lessee	434
64.	Vendor and Vendee	446

CHAPTER 11. NEGLIGENCE: DEFENSES

65.	Contributory Negligence	451
66.	Last Clear Chance	462
67.	Comparative Negligence	468
68.	Assumption of Risk	480

CHAPTER 12. IMPUTED NEGLIGENCE

69.	Vicarious Liability	499
70.	Servants	501
71.	Independent Contractors	509
72.	Joint Enterprise	516
73.	Automobile Owners and Others	522
74.	Imputed Contributory Negligence	529

CHAPTER 13. STRICT LIABILITY

75.	Basis of Liability	534
76.	Animals	538
77.	Fire	543
78.	Abnormally Dangerous Things and Activities	545
79.	Extent of Liability	559
80.	Employers' Liability	568
81.	Other Applications	580

CHAPTER 14. COMPENSATION SYSTEMS

82.	Liability Insurance and Its Impact on Tort Law	584
83.	Deficiencies of the Tort and Liability Insurance System	597
84.	Enacted and Proposed Remedies	600
85.	Principles of Compensation in American Legal Systems	608

CHAPTER 15. NUISANCE

Sec.		Page
86.	Meaning of Nuisance—Historical Origins	616
87.	Private Nuisance: The Tort Action for Damages	619
88.	Substantial and Unreasonable Interference	626
88A.	Unreasonable Conduct and Injunctive Relief	630
88B.	Conduct of Others and the Plaintiff as Factors of Importance	633
88C.	"Absolute" Nuisance	636
89.	Remedies	637
90.	Public Nuisance: Remedies Available to the State	643
91.	Interference With Use and Enjoyment of Private Property—Negligence and Strict Liability	652

CHAPTER 16. TORT AND CONTRACT

92.	Tort and Contract Obligations as Between Parties to a Contract	655
93.	Liability of a Party to a Contract to Third Parties	667
94.	Election to Sue for Restitution	672

CHAPTER 17. PRODUCTS LIABILITY

95.	Theories of Recovery and Types of Losses	677
95A.	Warranty and Intangible Economic Losses	679
96.	Negligence and Liability for Physical Harm to Persons and Tangible Things	681
97.	Strict Liability in Warranty for Physical Harm to Persons and Tangible Things	690
98.	Strict Liability in Tort for Physical Harm to Persons and Tangible Things	692
99.	Meaning of Dangerously Defective or Unsafe Products	694
100.	Parties	703
101.	Summary—Interests Protected and Theories of Recovery	707
102.	Contributory Negligence, Misuse, and Other Intervening Misconduct	710
103.	Proof	712
104.	Other Suppliers	715
104A.	Real Estate Transactions	721

CHAPTER 18. MISREPRESENTATION AND NONDISCLOSURE

105.	Remedies for Misrepresentation	725
106.	Representation and Nondisclosure	736
107.	Basis of Responsibility	740
108.	Justifiable Reliance—Materiality	749
109.	—— Opinion and Intention	755
110.	Damages	765

CHAPTER 19. DEFAMATION

Sec.		Page
111.	Defamation	771
112.	Libel and Slander	785
113.	Basis of Liability	797
113A.	Defamatory Opinion	813
114.	Absolute Privilege	815
115.	Qualified Privilege	824
116.	Truth and Other Defenses	839
116A.	Damages and Matters in Mitigation	842

CHAPTER 20. PRIVACY

117.	Right of Privacy	849

CHAPTER 21. MISUSE OF LEGAL PROCEDURE

119.	Malicious Prosecution	870
120.	Wrongful Civil Proceedings	889
121.	Abuse of Process	897

CHAPTER 22. DOMESTIC RELATIONS

122.	Torts in the Family	901
123.	Vicarious Liability for Torts of Family	912
124.	Interference with Family Relations	915
125.	Injuries to Members of the Family	931

CHAPTER 23. SURVIVAL AND WRONGFUL DEATH

125A.	Survival and Wrongful Death	940
126.	Actions Under Survival Statutes	942
127.	Actions Under Wrongful Death Statutes	945

CHAPTER 24. ECONOMIC RELATIONS

128.	Injurious Falsehood	962
129.	Interference with Contractual Relations	978
130.	Interference with Prospective Advantage	1005

CHAPTER 25. IMMUNITIES

Sec.		Page
131.	Governmental Immunity	1032
132.	Public Officers	1056
133.	Charities	1069
134.	Infants	1071
135.	Insanity	1072

APPENDIX A—WESTLAW REFERENCES 1077
TABLE OF CASES 1091
INDEX 1263

PROSSER AND KEETON ON THE LAW OF TORTS

Fifth Edition

*

Chapter 1

INTRODUCTION

Table of Sections

Sec.
1. What Are Torts?
2. Tort, Crime, and Punitive Damages.
3. Policy and Process.
4. Factors Affecting Tort Liability.
5. Motive.
6. History: Trespass and Case.
7. General Plan.

§ 1. What Are Torts?

Not until yesterday, as legal generations go, did torts achieve recognition as a distinct branch of the law. The first treatise in English on Torts was published in 1859 by Francis Hilliard of Cambridge, Massachusetts, who was followed a year later by Addison in England. Even as late as 1871, the leading American legal periodical said that "We are inclined to think that Torts is not a proper subject for a law book."[1]

Even though tort law is now recognized as a proper subject, a really satisfactory definition of a tort is yet to be found.[2] The nu-

---

§ 1

1. 1871, 5 Am.L.Rev. 341. In 1853, when Mr. Joel Bishop proposed to write a book on the law of torts, he was assured by all the publishers that there was no call for a work on such a subject, and that "if the book were written by the most eminent and prominent author that ever lived, not a dozen copies a year could be sold." Bishop, Non-Contract Law, 1889, 2.

2. "No such definition of a tort can be offered. A tort, in English law, can only be defined in terms which really tell us nothing. A tort is a breach of a duty (other than a contractual or quasi-contractual duty) which gives rise to an action for damages. That is, obviously, a merely procedural definition, of no value to the layman. The latter wants to know the nature of those breaches of duty which give rise to an action for damages. And the only answer that can be given to him is: 'Read this and the preceding volume.' To put it briefly, there is no English Law of Tort; there is merely an English Law of Torts, i.e., a list of acts and omissions which, in certain conditions, are actionable. Any attempt to generalize further, however interesting from a speculative standpoint, would be profoundly unsafe as a practical guide." Miles, Digest of English Civil Law, 1910, Book II, pp. xiv, xv.

"The definition of a tort may be said to have baffled the text-book writers not so much on account of the inherent difficulty of the conception as because of the implication of the conception in questions of jurisdiction. It is a creation of the common law, a fact which rules out on the one side personal, rights created by equity, and on the other, rights created by ecclesiastical or admiralty law. Further, it is usual to exclude from the definition most if not all of the rights and duties arising out of the family relation—that is, as regards the immediate parties. Again, a tort is usually defined negatively in such terms as to distinguish it from breach of contract, and sometimes also from the breach of duties, vaguely described as quasi-contractual. Perhaps none of the text-books succeeds in introducing all of these limitations into its definition." Lee, Torts and Delicts, 1918, 27 Yale L.J. 721, 723.

merous attempts which have been made to define the term [3] have succeeded only in achieving language so broad that it includes other matters than torts, or else so narrow that it leaves out some torts themselves. The word is derived from the Latin "tortus" or "twisted." [4] The metaphor is apparent: a tort is conduct which is twisted, or crooked, not straight. "Tort" is found in the French language, and was at one time in common use in English as a general synonym for "wrong." [5] When it faded out of common speech, it remained in the law, and gradually acquired a technical meaning. Broadly speaking, a tort is a civil wrong, other than breach of contract, for which the court will provide a remedy in the form of an action for damages. This, of course, says nothing more than that a tort is one kind of legal wrong, for which the law will give a particular redress. But even this vague statement is inaccurate, since one important form of remedy for a tort is an injunction, granted in a court of equity, before any damage occurs. Another is the restitution of what has been wrongfully taken, and still another is self-help by the injured party. But the availability of all such remedies will depend in the first instance upon the possibility that an action for damages would lie for the wrong thus averted, and so the statement made is sufficiently accurate to serve the purpose.[6]

It might be possible to define a tort by enumerating the things that it is not. It is not crime, it is not breach of contract, it is not necessarily concerned with property rights or problems of government, but is the occupant of a large residuary field remaining if these are taken out of the law. But this again is illusory, and the conception of a sort of legal garbage-can to hold what can be put nowhere else is of no help. In the first place, tort is a field which pervades the entire law, and is so interlocked at every point with property, contract and other ac-

---

3. "* * * an act or omission, not a mere breach of contract, and producing injury to another, in the absence of any existing lawful relation of which such act or omission is a natural outgrowth or incident." Cooke, A Proposed New Definition of a Tort, 1899, 12 Harv.L.Rev. 335, 336.

"Tortious liability arises from the breach of a duty primarily fixed by the laws; such duty is toward persons generally, and its breach is redressible by an action for unliquidated damages." Winfield, Province of the Law of Tort, 1931, 32.

"A civil wrong for which the remedy is a common law action for unliquidated damages, and which is not exclusively the breach of a contract or the breach of a trust or other merely equitable obligation." Salmond, Law of Torts, 10th Ed. 1945, 13.

"* * * an injury inflicted otherwise than by a mere breach of contract; or, to be more nicely accurate, one's disturbance of another in rights which the law has created, either in the absence of contract, or in consequence of a relation which a contract has established between the parties." Bishop, Non-Contract Law, 1889, 4.

"A tort is an act or omission which unlawfully violates a person's right created by the law, and for which the appropriate remedy is a common law action for damages by the injured person." Burdick, Torts, 3d Ed. 1913, 12.

"Never did a Name so obstruct a true understanding of the Thing. To such a plight has it brought us that a favorite mode of defining a Tort is to declare merely that it is not a Contract. As if a man were to define Chemistry by pointing out that it is not Physics or Mathematics." 1 Wigmore, Select Cases on the Law of Torts, 1912, vii.

Dozens of similar passages might be cited, but they would add nothing to the foregoing. See Louisville & Nashville R. Co. v. Spinks, 1898, 104 Ga. 692, 30 S.E. 968; Smith, Tort and Absolute Liability—Suggested Changes in Classification, 1917, 30 Harv.L.Rev. 241, 319, 409.

4. "'Tort,' from the Latin 'tortus,' a French word for injury or wrong, as 'de son tort demesne,' in his own wrong." Jacob's Law Dictionary, 1811, vol. 6, p. 251. Similarly, "wrong" is derived from "wrung."

5. For example, it is found frequently in Spencer's "Faerie Queene," as in the following passage in the fourth book:

"The lyon did with the lamb consort

And eke the dove safe by the faulcons side;

No each of other feared fraud or tort

But did in safe security abide."

6. "Although an action for damages is the essential remedy for a tort, there may be and often are other remedies also. In an action for a private nuisance an injunction may be obtained in addition to damages. In an action for detention of a chattel an order for specific restitution may be obtained in certain cases instead of judgment for its value. In an action by a plaintiff dispossessed of his land he recovers the land itself, in addition to damages for the loss suffered during the period of his dispossession. But in all such cases it is solely by virtue of the right to damages that the wrong complained of is to be classed as a tort." Salmond, Law of Torts, 12th Ed. 1957, 9.

cepted classifications that, as the student of law soon discovers, the categories are quite arbitrary. In the second, there is a central theme, or basis or idea, running through the cases of what are called torts, which, although difficult to put into words, does distinguish them in greater or less degree from other types of cases.

Included under the head of torts are miscellaneous civil wrongs, ranging from simple, direct interferences with the person, such as assault, battery and false imprisonment, or with property, as in the case of trespass or conversion, up through various forms of negligence, to disturbances of intangible interests, such as those in good reputation, or commercial or social advantage. These wrongs have little in common and appear at first glance to be entirely unrelated to one another, except perhaps by the accident of historical development; and it is not easy to discover any general principle upon which they may all be based, unless it is the obvious one that injuries are to be compensated, and anti-social behavior is to be discouraged. This led Sir John Salmond, one of the greatest writers on the subject, to contend [7] as late as 1928 that there is no such thing as a law of Tort, but only a law of particular unconnected torts—that is, a set of pigeon-holes, each bearing a name, into which the act or omission of the defendant must be fitted before the law will take cognizance of it and afford a remedy.

This view has been rejected by many other writers,[8] who have felt that tort law is broader than any named categories, and that some more or less vague general principles run through it, however difficult it may be to formulate them.[9] There is no necessity whatever that a tort have a name.[10] New and nameless torts are being recognized constantly, and the progress of the common law is marked by many cases of first impression, in which the court has struck out boldly to create a new cause of action, where none had been recognized before. The intentional infliction of mental suffering,[11] the obstruction of the right to go where the plaintiff likes,[12] the invasion of the right of privacy,[13] the denial of the right to vote,[14] the conveyance of land to defeat a title,[15] the infliction of prenatal injuries,[16] the alienation of the affections of a parent,[17] and injury to a person's reputation by entering the person in a

---

7. Salmond, Law of Torts, 7th Ed. 1928, § 2, subsec. 3. To the same effect are Goodhart, The Foundation of Tortious Liability, 1938, 2 Mod.L.Rev. 1; Bradshaw, The Foundation of Tortious Liability, 1938, 1 Res Judicatae 320; Williams, The Foundation of Tortious Liability, 1938, 7 Camb.L.J. 111; James, Tort Law in Midstream: Its Challenge to the Judicial Process, 1959, 8 Buff.L.Rev. 315.

It is to be noted that Dr. Stallybrass, the learned editor of later editions of Salmond, somewhat retreated from this view, saying that "although we have not yet discovered any general principle of liability, the law is slowly but surely moving in that direction." Salmond, Law of Torts, 10th Ed. 1945, 17.

8. Pollock, Law of Torts, 14th Ed. 1939, 16–18; Winfield, The Foundation of Liability in Tort, 1927, 27 Col.L.Rev. 1; Winfield, Province of the Law of Tort, 1931, ch. III; Harper, Law of Torts, 1933, ch. 1; Wigmore, The Tripartite Division of Torts, 1894, 8 Harv.L. Rev. 200; Ward, The Tort Cause of Action, 1956, 42 Corn.L.Q. 28.

9. See, attempting to state very broad principles, Seavey, Principles of Torts, 1942, 56 Harv.L.Rev. 72, 22 Neb.L.B. 177, 21 Can.Bar Rev. 265; Fleming, Introduction to the Law of Torts, 1967. See also infra, § 85.

10. Smith, Torts Without Particular Names, 1921, 69 U.Pa.L.Rev. 91.

11. See infra, § 12.

12. Cullen v. Dickinson, 1913, 33 S.D. 27, 144 N.W. 656.

13. See infra, ch. 20.

14. Ashby v. White, 1703, 2 Ld.Raym. 938, 92 Eng. Rep. 126. A famous case, if only because of Chief Justice Holt's declaration that for every interference with a recognized legal right the law will provide a remedy. Accord: Nixon v. Herndon, 1927, 273 U.S. 536, 47 S.Ct. 446, 71 L.Ed. 759; Valdez v. Gonzales, 1946, 50 N.M. 281, 176 P.2d 173; Lane v. Mitchell, 1911, 153 Iowa 139, 133 N.W. 381.

See also Morningstar v. Lafayette Hotel Co., 1914, 211 N.Y. 465, 105 N.E. 656, to the effect that the triviality of the right is all the more reason for allowing the action.

15. Ring v. Ogden, 1878, 45 Wis. 303.

16. See infra, § 55.

17. See infra, § 118.

rigged television contest,[18] to name only a few instances, could not be fitted into any accepted classifications when they first arose, but nevertheless have been held to be torts. The law of torts is anything but static, and the limits of its development are never set. When it becomes clear that the plaintiff's interests are entitled to legal protection against the conduct of the defendant, the mere fact that the claim is novel will not of itself operate as a bar to the remedy.[19]

At the opposite extreme is the bold attempt [20] to reduce the entire law of torts to a single broad principle, that any harm done to another is a wrong, and calls for redress, unless "justification" for it can be shown. In its form such a statement is objectionable, since there are some torts, such as malicious prosecution,[21] as to which proof of the absence of justification is an indispensable part of the plaintiff's case, and others, such as libel or slander,[22] where in some cases it is the defendant who must justify the conduct or else lose the case. But even with allowance made for the difficulty of wording it, the rule does not tell us what the law will recognize as "harm" to another, or as "justification" for it. There are many interferences with the plaintiff's interests, including many instances of negligently causing mere mental suffering without physical consequences [23] or depriving the plaintiff of the benefit of a contract,[24] for which the law will give no remedy, although the defendant has been clearly at fault. On the other hand, the "justification" may be something quite different from moral exoneration.[25] Not only may a morally innocent person be held liable for the damage done, but many a scoundrel has been guilty of moral outrages, such as base ingratitude, without committing any tort. It is *legal* justification which must be looked to: the law will hold the defendant responsible for what the law regards as unjustified—and so stated, the broad rule means little, or nothing.

Characteristics of a Tort

Abandoning the attempt to find a definition, which, "strictly speaking, is nothing but an abbreviation in which the user of the term defined may please himself," [26] some writers have attempted to discover certain characteristics common to all torts, which might throw some light upon their nature.[27] As has been said,[28] a wrong is called a tort only if the harm which has resulted, or is about to result from it, is capable of being compensated in an action at law for damages, although other remedies may also be available. Beyond this, it has been said that torts consist of the breach of duties fixed and imposed upon the parties by the law itself, without regard to their consent to assume them, or their efforts to evade them. That is to say, one need not enter into the obligation of a contract with another save by one's own free will; but when a driver proceeds down the street in a car, the law imposes upon the driver an obligation to all persons in the highway, to drive it with reasonable care for their safety—and this without the driver's consent or understanding, and if necessary over the driver's vigorous protest. If the driver proceeds without reasonable care and injures another, it is a tort.

But this distinction between tort and contract obligations, however superficially at-

---

18. Morrison v. National Broadcasting Co., 1965, 24 A.D.2d 284, 266 N.Y.S.2d 406, reversed, 1967, 19 N.Y.2d 453, 280 N.Y.S.2d 641, 227 N.E.2d 572.

19. See infra, § 3.

20. Winfield, Law of Tort, 5th Ed. 1950, § 7. See Principles of Tort Law, infra, this section.

21. See infra, § 119.

22. See infra, ch. 19.

23. See infra, § 54.

24. See infra, § 123.

25. See infra, § 4.

26. Pollock, Review of Winfield, Province of the Law of Tort, 1931, 47 L.Q.Rev. 588.

27. Winfield, Law of Tort, 5th Ed. 1950, §§ 2–6. Cf. Radin, A Speculative Inquiry Into the Nature of Torts, 1943, 21 Tex.L.Rev. 697; Stone, Touchstones of Tort Liability, 1950, 2 Stan.L.Rev. 259; Seavey, Cogitations on Torts, 1954.

28. Supra, p. 2.

tractive it may be, is an illusory distinction.[29] All legal duties are of course imposed by law, and it is the modern rule that the maker of a contract is held to have the obligation, not because of intention or consent to have it, but because the law attaches such consequences to promises made and some representations objectively manifesting an intent to be bound; this legal result follows nevertheless, even when the defendant has no intention at all that it follow. Quasi-contractual duties are likewise imposed by the law, without regard to the consent of the defendant. In the same sense, the tort duty of care in driving the car arises because the law attaches that result to what has been done voluntarily. Furthermore, such tort obligations of conduct are imposed by reason of the relation in which the parties stand toward one another; and in determining that relation, the law will often take into account what has been agreed between them, either to increase the actor's responsibility [30] or to lessen it,[31] so that the tort duty finally fixed may coincide with that set by a contract, and for its breach either a contract or a tort action will lie. To say that the one obligation is voluntarily assumed in such a case, and that the other is not, is to resort to abstract fictions.

Again, it has been said [32] that tort duties are owed to persons generally, or toward general classes of persons. Or in other words, that the automobile driver is under a tort obligation of care to everyone in the driver's path and is not free, as an actor is when making a contract or accepting a trust, to single out one person only toward whom the actor will be bound. Certainly the distinction holds good in many cases: a common carrier, for example, may make a different contract with each single passenger, varying in its terms as to fare and the length of transportation, but the tort duty of reasonable care for their safety extends to all persons toward whom it stands in the relation of carrier and passenger, including those who have not contracted at all, but are riding free.[33] But again the classification cannot be carried through. The tort liability of a servant to the master, or of a bailee to the bailor, or of a converter of goods to their owner rests upon a duty owed to one person, and one only; and it can be called general only in the same sense that every person is under a general obligation to perform all of that person's contracts. Liability in tort is based upon the relations of persons with others; and those relations may arise generally, with large groups or classes of persons, or singly, with an individual.

Function of the Law of Torts

Enough has been said to indicate that definition or description of a tort in terms of generalities distinguishing it from other branches of the law is difficult, or impossible. It is somewhat easier to consider the function and purpose of the law of torts.[34] Contract liability is imposed by the law for the protection of a single, limited interest, that of having the promises of others performed. Quasi-contractual liability is created for the prevention of unjust enrichment of one person at the expense of another, and the restitution of benefits which in good conscience belong to the plaintiff. The criminal law is concerned with the protection of interests common to the public at large, as they are represented by the entity which we call the state; often it accomplishes its ends by exacting a penalty from the wrongdoer. There remains a body of law whch is directed toward the compensation of individuals, rather than the public, for losses which they have suffered within the scope of their legal-

29. Seavey, Review of Winfield, Province of the Law of Tort, 1931, 45 Harv.L.Rev. 209.

30. See infra, § 92.

31. See infra, § 68.

32. Winfield, Province of the Law of Tort, 5th Ed. 1950, § 4.

33. Cf. Philadelphia & Railroad Co. v. Derby, 1852, 55 U.S., 14 (How.) 468, 14 L.Ed. 502; Southern Railway Co. v. Lee, 1907, 30 Ky.L.Rep. 1360, 101 S.W. 307; Littlejohn v. Fitchburg Railroad Co., 1889, 148 Mass. 478, 20 N.E. 103.

34. Seavey, Review of Winfield, Province of the Law of Tort, 1931, 45 Harv.L.Rev. 209.

ly recognized interests generally, rather than one interest only, where the law considers that compensation is required.[35] This is the law of torts.

The law of torts, then, is concerned with the allocation of losses arising out of human activities; and since these cover a wide scope, so does this branch of the law. "Arising out of the various and ever-increasing clashes of the activities of persons living in a common society, carrying on business in competition with fellow members of that society, owning property whch may in any of a thousand ways affect the persons or property of others—in short, doing all the things that constitute modern living—there must of necessity be losses, or injuries of many kinds sustained as a result of the activities of others. The purpose of the law of torts is to adjust these losses, and to afford compensation for injuries sustained by one person as the result of the conduct of another."[36]

Principles of Tort Law

In so broad a field, where so many different types of individual interests are involved, and they may be invaded by so many kinds of conduct, it is not easy to find any single guiding principle which determines when such compensation is to be paid, even under tort law alone,[37] much less when other provisions for compensation in the entire legal system are considered.[38] So far as there is one central idea, it would seem that it is that liability must be based upon conduct which is socially unreasonable. The common thread woven into all torts is the idea of unreasonable interference with the interests of others. In many cases, of course, what is socially unreasonable will depend upon what is unreasonable from the point of view of the individual. The tort-feasor usually is held liable for acting with an intention that the law treats as unjustified, or acting in a way that departs from a reasonable standard of care. The endeavor to find some standard of intentional interference that others may reasonably be required to endure,[39] of unintentional interference that is reasonable under the circumstances,[40] of the reasonable use of one's own land,[41] of reasonable reliance upon representations made,[42] of risks and inconveniences, associated with the use of land, which others may reasonably be required to endure at the hands of the defendant—[43] in short, to strike some reasonable balance between the plaintiff's claim to protection against damage and the defendant's claim to freedom of action for defendant's own ends, and those of society, occupies a very large part of the tort opinions.

But socially unreasonable conduct is broader than this, and the law looks beyond the actor's own state of mind and the appearances which the actor's own conduct presented, or should have presented to the actor. Often it measures acts, and the harm an actor has done, by an objective, disinterested and social standard. It may consider that the actor's behavior, although entirely reasonable in itself from the point of view of anyone in the actor's position, has created a risk or has resulted in harm to neighbors which is so far unreasonable that the actor should nevertheless pay for harm done. Sometimes it must range rather far afield, and look primarily to the social consequences which will follow. The purchaser in good faith of a stolen horse, or the actor who trespasses on the land of another in an entirely reasonable belief that it is the actor's own, may have acted only as any reasonable person would act in those circum-

35. For further discussion of the objective of compensation as a factor in tort law, see infra, § 4.

36. Wright, Introduction to the Law of Torts, 1944, 8 Camb.L.J. 238.

37. See supra at notes 9, 20.

38. A set of three basic principles that shed light on tort and other compensation systems is discussed infra, § 85.

39. See infra, chs. 2, 3.

40. See infra, ch. 4.

41. See infra, chs. 10, 15.

42. See infra, § 108.

43. See infra, ch. 15.

stances; but the property rights of every owner would be threatened if such acts could be done with impunity, and as against the claim to exclusive possession, they are regarded as a socially unreasonable interference.[44] The innocent publisher of words which turn out to be libel may have behaved quite reasonably so far as personal conduct is concerned, but as against the helpless victim whose reputation is blasted, the act has sometimes been regarded, whether rightly or not, as a social menace, and so unreasonable in itself.[45] It is worthy of note that such cases of liability for personally reasonable acts have not gone unchallenged, and that they represent a field of present controversy. So far as they can be rationalized, it must be on the ground that the law of torts is concerned not solely with individually questionable conduct but as well with acts which are unreasonable, or socially harmful, from the point of view of the community as a whole.

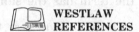 **WESTLAW REFERENCES**

379k1
topic(torts /5 general)

Characteristics of a Tort

torts /5 contract /30 differen** distinct! distinguish!
driver* /p obligation* duty duties /p pedestrian*

Function of the Law of Torts

compensat! damages /p individual* /p injur*** loss**

Principles of Tort Law

topic(torts) & reasonabl* unreasonabl* /20 interfer! /20 interest*
risk* /5 harm injury /30 neighbor*
innocent uninten! /p publish! /p libel slander defamat!

---

44. See infra, § 17.
45. See infra, § 108.

§ 2

1. Winfield, Province of the Law of Tort, 1931, ch. 8; Hall, Interrelation of Criminal Law and Torts, 1943, 43 Col.L.Rev. 753, 967.

2. Kenny, Outlines of Criminal Law, 15th Ed. 1936, ch. 1. See generally ALI Model Penal Code, 1962.

§ 2. Tort, Crime, and Punitive Damages

A tort is not the same thing as a crime, although the two sometimes have many features in common. The distinction between them lies in the interests affected and the remedy afforded by the law.[1] A crime is an offense against the public at large, for which the state, as the representative of the public, will bring proceedings in the form of a criminal prosecution. The purpose of such a proceeding is to protect and vindicate the interests of the public as a whole, by punishing, by eliminating the offender from society, either permanently or for a limited time, by reforming or rehabilitating, by teaching the offender not to repeat the offense, or by deterring others from similar conduct.[2] Although restitution is sometimes a stated condition of probation of a convicted offender, a criminal prosecution is not concerned directly with compensation of the injured individual against whom the crime is committed, and the victim's only formal part in it is that of an accuser and a witness for the state. So far as the criminal law is concerned, the victim will leave the courtroom empty-handed.

The civil action for a tort, on the other hand, is commenced and maintained by the injured person, and its primary purpose is to compensate for the damage suffered, at the expense of the wrongdoer. If successful, the plaintiff receives a judgment for a sum of money, enforceable against the defendant. The state never can sue in tort in its political or governmental capacity, although as the owner of property it may resort to the same tort actions as any individual proprietor to recover for injuries to the property,[3] or to recover the property itself.[4] It has been held, for example, that the state as a government has no cause of action against

---

3. State v. Ohio Oil Co., 1898, 150 Ind. 21, 49 N.E. 809; State v. F. W. Fitch Co., 1945, 236 Iowa 208, 17 N.W.2d 380. The same is true of a municipal corporation. Cf. Daly City v. Holbrook, 1918, 39 Cal.App. 326, 178 P. 725; City of Milwaukee v. Meyer, 1931, 204 Wis. 350, 235 N.W. 768; Mayor of Paterson v. Erie Railroad Co., 1910, 78 N.J.L. 592, 75 A. 922.

4. State v. Delesdenier, 1851, 7 Tex. 76.

an escaped convict for the expenses incurred in recapture.[5]

The same act may be both a crime against the state and a tort against an individual. In such a case, since the interests invaded are not the same, and the objects to be accomplished by the two suits are different, there may be both a civil tort action and a criminal prosecution for the same offense. The two may be conducted successively, or at the same time,[6] and, a decision for or against the defendant in one usually is not conclusive as to the other.[7] If an issue tried in a criminal action is also decisive of some aspect of a tort action, however, a conviction of the defendant in the criminal action ordinarily is preclusive in favor of the plaintiff in the tort action.[8] Except to this extent, it is the prevailing view that a conviction[9] or an acquittal[10] in the criminal case is not even admissible in evidence in the tort action. If the crime is a felony, it was the law in England that the tort is so far "merged" in the crime[11] that the civil action must be suspended or stayed until the criminal one had been completed,[12] apparently on the basis of some notion of a policy of compelling the injured party to prefer criminal charges and bring major offenders to justice. Early American decisions[13] took over the rule, but it has now been almost entirely discarded in the United States.[14]

Originally the two remedies were administered by the same court, and in the same action. Tort damages were at first awarded to the injured individual as an incident to a criminal prosecution; and as late as 1694 the defendant to a writ of trespass was still theoretically liable to a criminal fine and imprisonment.[15] Because of this common origin, it is not unusual for a tort and a crime to bear the same name, such as "assault," "battery," "trespass," or "libel," and often enough such terms will refer to the same conduct. But tort and criminal law have developed along different lines, with different ends in view, and so it does not necessarily follow that the term has the same meaning

---

5. State Highway & Public Works Commission v. Cobb, 1939, 215 N.C. 556, 2 S.E.2d 565.

6. Willliams v. Dickenson, 1891, 28 Fla. 90, 9 So. 847; White v. Fort, 1821, 10 N.C. 251; Ballew v. Alexander, 1846, 25 Tenn. (6 Humph.) 433; Austin v. Carswell, 1893, 67 Hun 579, 22 N.Y.S. 478. It is not an abuse of discretion to refuse to stay the tort action. Pettingill v. Rideout, 1833, 6 N.H. 454; Poston v. Home Insurance Co., 1939, 191 S.C. 314, 4 S.E.2d 261; State v. Schauenberg, 1924, 197 Iowa 445, 197 N.W. 295.

7. Williams v. Dickenson, 1891, 28 Fla. 90, 9 So. 847; Bundy v. Maginess, 1888, 76 Cal. 532, 18 P. 668.

8. Second Restatement of Judgments, §§ 29, 85.

9. Interstate Dry Goods Stores v. Williamson, 1922, 91 W.Va. 156, 112 S.E. 301; Blackman v. Coffin, 1938, 300 Mass. 432, 15 N.E.2d 469; Sklebar v. Downey, 1926, 220 Mo.App. 5, 285 S.W. 148; General Exchange Insurance Corp. v. Sherby, 1933, 165 Md. 1, 165 A. 809.

10. Shires v. Boggess, 1913, 72 W.Va. 109, 77 S.E. 542; Bray-Robinson Clothing Co. v. Higgins, 1925, 210 Ky. 432, 276 S.W. 129; Id. 1929, 219 Ky. 293, 293 S.W. 151; Hampton v. Westover, 1940, 137 Neb. 695, 291 N.W. 93; Harper v. Blasi, 1944, 112 Colo. 518, 151 P.2d 760.

See, generally, Griffis, Evidence of Disposition of Related Criminal Case in Subsequent Damage Suit, 1958, 25 Ins.Couns.J. 480; Note, 1941, 50 Yale L.J. 499. Cases on both conviction and acquittal are collected in the annotation in 1951, 18 A.L.R.2d 1287. See also Second Restatement of Judgments, §§ 29, 85.

11. Crosby v. Leng, 1810, 12 East 409, 104 Eng. Rep. 160; Gimson v. Woodfull, 1825, 2 C. & P. 41, 172 Eng.Rep. 19. The origin of the rule probably lay in the fact that a felon's lands were forfeited to the crown, which thus had the prior claim against them. 3 Holdsworth, History of English Law, 3d Ed. 1923, 331–333; White v. Fort, 1821, 10 N.C. 251.

12. Wells v. Abrahams, 1872, L.R. 7 Q.B. 554; Smith v. Selwyn, [1914] 3 K.B. 98.

13. Cross v. Guthery, Conn.1794, 2 Root 90; Boardman v. Gore, 1819, 15 Mass. 331. For a discussion of what, if any aspect, of the old rule survives today, see Shim v. Kikkoman International Corp., D.C.N.J.1981, 509 F.Supp. 736, affirmed, 3d Cir., 673 F.2d 1304.

14. Fidelity & Deposit Co. v. Grand National Bank, 8th Cir. 1934, 69 F.2d 177; Shim v. Kikkoman International Corp., D.C.N.J.1981, 509 F.Supp. 736, affirmed, 3d Cir., 673 F.2d 1304; Pearl Assurance Co., Limited v. National Insurance Agency, Inc., 1942, 150 Pa.Super. 265, 28 A.2d 334, affirmed 1943, 151 Pa.Super. 146, 30 A.2d 333; Quimby v. Blackey, 1884, 63 N.H. 77; Howk v. Minnick, 1869, 19 Ohio St. 462; Note, 1952, 5 Okl.L. Rev. 242. Likewise the fact that the prosecuting witness has brought suit in tort does not bar criminal prosecution. Foster v. Commonwealth, Pa.1824, 8 Watts & S. 77.

15. Pollock, Law of Torts, 15th Ed. 1951, 150; Stat. 5 & 6 W. & M., ch. 12.

in both. Thus it is entirely possible that an act may be a tort, but not a crime of the same name,[16] or that it may amount to the crime and not the tort.[17] Criminal cases may be useful as guides to the type of conduct which the law will condemn or excuse, and the existence of a criminal statute may indicate a legislative policy which the courts will further by creating tort liability.[18] But such conclusions do not always follow, and the criminal law must be regarded a a very unreliable analogy to the law of torts.

Punitive Damages

The idea of punishment, or of discouraging other offenses, usually does not enter into tort law, except in so far as it may lead the courts to weight the scales somewhat in favor of the plaintiff's interests in determining that a tort has been committed in the first place.[19] In one rather anomalous respect, however, the ideas underlying the criminal law have invaded the field of torts.

Where the defendant's wrongdoing has been intentional and deliberate, and has the character of outrage frequently associated with crime, all but a few courts[20] have permitted the jury to award in the tort action "punitive" or "exemplary" damages, or what is sometimes called "smart money." Such damages are given to the plaintiff over and above the full compensation for the injuries, for the purpose of punishing the defendant, of teaching the defendant not to do it again, and of deterring others from following the defendant's example.[21] Occasional decisions[22] have mentioned the additional purpose of reimbursing the plaintiff for elements of damage which are not legally compensable, such as wounded feelings or the expenses of suit.

Something more than the mere commission of a tort is always required for punitive damages. There must be circumstances of aggravation or outrage,[23] such as spite or

---

16. Compare the following cases (albeit from different states), in which the same type of act was held to be a tort but not a crime: Beach v. Hancock, 1853, 27 N.H. 223, with Chapman v. State, 1884, 78 Ala. 463 (assault); Malcom v. Spoor, 1847, 53 Mass. (12 Metc.) 279, with Milton v. State, 1898, 40 Fla. 251, 24 So. 60 (trespass ab initio); Basely v. Clarkson, 1681, 3 Lev. 37, 83 Eng.Rep. 565 with Garrett v. State, 1906, 49 Tex.Cr.R. 235, 91 S.W. 577. Note also that the elements of the prima facie case and the nature of recognized defenses may differ.

17. Compare Deaton v. State, 1908, 53 Tex.Cr.R. 393, 110 S.W. 69, with Robertson v. Edelstein, 1899, 104 Wis. 440, 80 N.W. 724 (abusive but not defamatory language). See Rubin, May a Person be Convicted of a Felony and Yet Escape Civil Liability Therefor, 1926, 10 Marq.L.Rev. 113. Note also that in certain circumstances consent may be a defense to a tort action but not to a criminal prosecution based on the same conduct. See infra, § 18.

18. See infra, § 36.

19. See infra, this section.

20. Some decisions have rejected punitive damages entirely. Moore v. Blanchard, 1949, 216 La. 253, 43 So. 2d 599; Boott Mills v. Boston & Maine Railroad Co., 1914, 218 Mass. 582, 106 N.E. 680; Wilfong v. Omaha & Council Bluffs Street Railway Co., 1935, 129 Neb. 600, 262 N.W. 537; Anderson v. Dalton, 1952, 40 Wn.2d 894, 246 P.2d 853. England has done away with them except where they could serve a "useful purpose," by penalizing oppressive, arbitrary and unconstitutional action by government servants, conduct calculated to make a profit for the actor, and the like. Rookes v. Barnard, [1964] A.C. 1129.

New Hampshire and Michigan have allowed such damages, regarding them as extra compensation for injured feelings or sense of outrage rather than as punishment. Bixby v. Dunlap, 1876, 56 N.H. 456; Wise v. Daniel, 1922, 221 Mich. 229, 190 N.W. 746; Veselenak v. Smith, 1982, 414 Mich. 567, 327 N.W.2d 261 (not allowed when compensatory damages for mental distress are awarded; since plaintiff would be doubly compensated for one injury). Connecticut decisions have limited punitive damages to the expenses of litigation, which must be proved. Tedesco v. Maryland Casualty Co., 1941, 127 Conn. 533, 18 A.2d 357.

21. Scott v. Donald, 1896, 165 U.S. 58, 17 S.Ct. 265, 41 L.Ed. 632; Gostkowski v. Roman Catholic Church, 1933, 262 N.Y. 320, 186 N.E. 798; Gill v. Selling, 1928, 125 Or. 587, 267 P. 812, affirmed 126 Or. 584, 270 P. 411; Kirschbaum v. Lowrey, 1925, 165 Minn. 233, 206 N.W. 171. See McCormick, Damages, 1935, § 278; Notes, 1957, 70 Harv.L.Rev. 517; 1962, 26 Albany L.J. 288.

22. Battle v. Kilcrease, 1936, 54 Ga.App. 808, 189 S.E. 573; Wright Titus, Inc. v. Swafford, Tex.Civ.App. 1939, 133 S.W.2d 287, error dismissed, judgment correct; Brewer v. Home-Stake Production Co., 1967, 200 Kan. 96, 434 P.2d 828; Cox v. Stolworthy, 1972, 94 Idaho 683, 496 P.2d 682.

23. Chiles v. Drake, 1859, 59 Ky. (2 Metc.) 146; Birmingham Waterworks Co. v. Brooks, 1017, 16 Ala.App. 209, 76 So. 515, certiorari denied 200 Ala. 697, 76 So. 995. Cf. Battle v. Kilcrease, 1936, 54 Ga.App. 808, 189

"malice," [24] or a fraudulent [25] or evil [26] motive on the part of the defendant, or such a conscious and deliberate disregard of the interests of others that the conduct may be called wilful or wanton.[27] There is general agreement that, because it lacks this element, mere negligence is not enough,[28] even though it is so extreme in degree as to be characterized as "gross," [29] a term of ill-defined content,[30] which occasionally, in a few jurisdictions, has been stretched to include the element of conscious indifference to consequences, and so to justify punitive damages.[31] Still less, of course, can such damages be charged against one who acts under an innocent mistake in engaging in conduct that nevertheless constitutes a tort.[32]

Typical of the torts for which such damages may be awarded are assault and battery,[33] libel and slander,[34] deceit,[35] seduc-

---

S.E. 573 (hit-and-run driver); Miller v. Blanton, 1948, 213 Ark. 246, 210 S.W.2d 293 (intoxication); Bucher v. Krause, 7th Cir. 1952, 200 F.2d 576, certiorari denied Krause v. Bucher, 1953, 345 U.S. 997, 73 S.Ct. 114, 97 L.Ed. 842, rehearing denied 346 U.S. 842, 74 S.Ct. 17, 98 L.Ed. 363 (cover-up activities of police).

"The jury must find that he acted with actual malice (in the sense of ill will) or conscious disregard of consequences to others. The jury may infer this from circumstances of aggravation surrounding the tortious conduct." Kelite Products, Inc. v. Binzel, 5th Cir. 1955, 224 F.2d 131, 143. See also Diapulse Corp. of America v. Birtcher Corp., 2d Cir. 1966, 362 F.2d 736, certiorari dismissed 385 U.S. 801, 87 S.Ct. 9, 17 L.Ed.2d 48; Mills v. Levine, 1956, 98 U.S.App.D.C. 137, 233 F.2d 16, certiorari denied 352 U.S. 858, 77 S.Ct. 86, 1 L.Ed.2d 67.

24. This includes a deliberate wrongful act known to be injurious to another. Cherry-Burrell Co. v. Thatcher, 9th Cir. 1940, 107 F.2d 65; Jones v. West Side Buick Co., 1936, 231 Mo.App. 187, 93 S.W.2d 1083; Morgan v. French, 1945, 70 Cal.App.2d 785, 161 P.2d 800; Bourne v. Pratt & Whitney Aircraft Corp., Mo. App.1948, 207 S.W.2d 533.

It does not include the "legal malice" implied in such torts as defamation. Corrigan v. Bobbs-Merrill Co., 1920, 228 N.Y. 58, 126 N.E. 260; Neeb v. Hope, 1886, 111 Pa. 145, 2 A. 568; Fields v. Bynum, 1911, 156 N.C. 413, 72 S.E. 449; Cottle v. Johnson, 1920, 179 N.C. 426, 102 S.E. 769 (alienation of affections).

As to the necessity of "actual" rather than "implied" malice, see Waters v. Novak, 1953, 94 Ohio App. 347, 115 N.E.2d 420.

25. Prince v. State Mutual Life Insurance Co., 1907, 77 S.C. 187, 57 S.E. 766; Treesh v. Stone, 1921, 51 Cal. App. 708, 197 P. 425; Augusta Bank & Trust v. Broomfield, 1982, 231 Kan. 52, 643 P.2d 100.

26. Eshelman v. Rawalt, 1921, 298 Ill. 192, 131 N.E. 675 (criminal conversation); Cobb v. Atlantic Coast Line Railroad Co., 1918, 175 N.C. 130, 95 S.E. 92 (blasting); Gamble v. Keyes, 1917, 39 S.D. 592, 166 N.W. 134; Hintz v. Roberts, 1923, 98 N.J.L. 768, 121 A. 711. Concerning motive generally, see infra, § 5.

27. Sebastian v. Wood, 1954, 246 Iowa 94, 66 N.W.2d 841 (drunken driving); Dorn v. Wilmarth, 1969, 254 Or. 236, 458 P.2d 942 (same); Brooks v. Wootton, 2d Cir. 1966, 355 F.2d 177 (same); Allman v. Bird, 1960, 186 Kan. 802, 353 P.2d 216; Toole v. Richardson-Merrell, Inc., 1967, 251 Cal.App.2d 689, 60 Cal.Rptr. 398 (withholding vital information in sale of drug); Cox v. Stolworthy, 1972, 94 Idaho 683, 496 P.2d 682; Bull v. McCuskey, 1980, 96 Nev. 706, 615 P.2d 957 (physician counter-suit). See also Cantrell v. Amarillo Hardware Co., 1979, 226 Kan. 681, 602 P.2d 1326 ("reckless disregard of plaintiff's rights," in products liability case involving aluminum stepladder).

28. Greyhound Corp. v. Townsend, 1959, 234 Miss. 839, 108 So.2d 208, suggestion of error sustained 234 Miss. 839, 108 So.2d 853; Wright v. Everett, 1956, 197 Va. 608, 90 S.E.2d 855; Spackman v. Ralph M. Parsons Co., 1966, 147 Mont. 500, 414 P.2d 918; Sheffield Division Armco Steel Corp. v. Jones, 1964, Tex., 376 S.W.2d 825.

29. Milwaukee & St. Paul Railroad Co. v. Arms, 1875, 91 U.S. 489, 23 L.Ed. 374; Moore v. Wilson, 1929, 180 Ark. 41, 20 S.W.2d 310; Hicks v. McCandlish, 1952, 221 S.C. 410, 70 S.E.2d 629; Eatley v. Mayer, 1931, 9 N.J.Misc. 918, 154 A. 10, affirmed 1932, 10 N.J.Misc. 219, 158 A. 411.

See, however, Arnold v. Frigid Feed Express Co., 1969, 9 Ariz.App. 472, 453 P.2d 983 (driving car at top speed through dust storm; enough that the conduct involves a risk "substantially greater than that which is necessary to make his conduct negligent.")

30. See infra, § 34.

31. Cf. Texas Pacific Coal & Oil Co. v. Robertson, 1935, 125 Tex. 4, 79 S.W.2d 830; Teche Lines v. Pope, 1936, 175 Miss. 393, 166 So. 539; Sebastian v. Wood, 1954, 246 Iowa 94, 66 N.W.2d 841.

32. Thomas v. Commercial Credit Corp., Mo.App. 1960, 335 S.W.2d 703 (repossession of wrong automobile); Calhoun v. Universal Credit Co., 1944, 106 Utah 166, 146 P.2d 284 (repossession where no default); Winn & Lovett Grocery Co. v. Archer, 1936, 126 Fla. 308, 171 So. 214 (detention of suspect in store). See also De Marasse v. Wolf, Sup.Ct.1955, 140 N.Y.S.2d 235.

33. Trogden v. Terry, 1916, 172 N.C. 540, 90 S.E. 583; Bannister v. Mitchell, 1920, 127 Va. 578, 104 S.E. 800; Maxa v. Neidlein, 1932, 163 Md. 366, 163 A. 202.

34. Reynolds v. Pegler, 2d Cir. 1955, 223 F.2d 429, certiorari denied 350 U.S. 846, 76 S.Ct. 80, 100 L.Ed. 754; Rogers v. Florence Printing Co., 1958, 233 S.C. 567, 106 S.E.2d 258; Coffin v. Brown, 1901, 94 Md. 190, 50 A. 567; Loftsgaarden v. Reiling, 1964, 267 Minn. 181, 126 N.W.2d 154, certiorari denied 379 U.S. 845, 85 S.Ct. 31, 13 L.Ed.2d 50.

tion,[36] alienation of affections,[37] malicious prosecution,[38] and intentional interferences with property such as trespass,[39] private nuisance,[40] and conversion.[41] But it is not so much the particular tort committed as the defendant's motives and conduct in committing it [42] which will be important as the basis of the award. Statutes in most states have provided punitive damages for particular torts, as in the case of multiple damages for trespass.[43]

Commencing in the 1970's, a new body of case law has developed, awarding punitive as well as compensatory damages against insurance companies on the basis of outrageous conduct in the handling of claims,[44] in some instances in association with a tort action, such as intentional infliction of severe mental distress,[45] and in other instances in association with an action for breach of an implied duty of good faith and fair dealing.[46]

The policy of giving punitive damages has been a subject of much controversy. They have been condemned [47] as undue compensation beyond the plaintiff's just deserts,[48] in the form of a criminal fine which should be paid to the state, if anyone, with the amount fixed only by the caprice of the jury and imposed without the usual safeguards thrown about criminal procedure, such as proof of guilt beyond a reasonable doubt, the privilege against self-incrimination, and even the rule against double jeopardy—since the defendant may still be prosecuted for the

35. Walker v. Sheldon, 1961, 10 N.Y.2d 401, 223 N.Y.S.2d 488, 179 N.E.2d 497; J. Truett Payne Co. v. Jackson, 1967, 281 Ala. 426, 203 So.2d 443; Saberton v. Greenwald, 1946, 146 Ohio St. 414, 66 N.E.2d 224; Augusta Bank & Trust v. Broomfield, 1982, 231 Kan. 52, 643 P.2d 100. See Note, 1962, 26 Alb.L.J. 288.

36. Reutkemeier v. Nolte, 1917, 179 Iowa 342, 161 N.W. 290.

37. Scott v. O'Brien, 1908, 129 Ky. 1, 110 S.W. 260.

38. Jackson v. American Telephone & Telegraph Co., 1905, 139 N.C. 347, 51 S.E. 1015; Brown v. McBride, 1898, 24 Misc. 235, 52 N.Y.S. 620; Bull v. McCuskey, 1980, 96 Nev. 706, 615 P.2d 957 (physician counter-suit). Cf. Seidel v. Greenberg, 1969, 108 N.J. Super. 248, 260 A.2d 863.

39. Oden v. Russell, 1952, 207 Okl. 570, 251 P.2d 184; Huling v. Henderson, 1894, 161 Pa. 553, 29 A. 276; Singer Manufacturing Co. v. Holdfodt, 1877, 86 Ill. 455; Cox v. Stolworthy, 1972, 94 Idaho 683, 496 P.2d 682.

40. Ruppel v. Ralston Purina Co., Mo.1968, 423 S.W.2d 752; Lutz v. Independent Construction Co., 1958, 183 Kan. 798, 332 P.2d 269; Corwine v. Maracaibo Oil Exploration Corp., 1959, 184 Kan. 151, 334 P.2d 419; Yazoo & Mississippi Valley Railroad Co. v. Sanders, 1906, 87 Miss. 607, 40 So. 163; Schumacher v. Shawhan Distillery Co., 1914, 178 Mo.App. 361, 165 S.W. 1142 (pollution of stream continued in defiance of injunction).

41. Watkins v. Layton, 1958, 182 Kan. 702, 324 P.2d 130; Lindgren Plumbing Co. v. Doral Country Club, Inc., Fla.App.1967, 196 So.2d 242; Jones v. Fisher, 1969, 42 Wis.2d 209, 166 N.W.2d 175 (forcible removal of dental plate as security for loan).

42. Thus punitive damages may be awarded against only one of two joint tortfeasors for the same tort. Kim v. Chinn, 1943, 56 Cal.App.2d 857, 133 P.2d 677; Hotel Riviera, Inc. v. Short, 1964, 80 Nev. 505, 396 P.2d 855; Mauk v. Brundage, 1903, 68 Ohio St. 89, 67 N.E. 152; Nelson v. Halvorson, 1912, 117 Minn. 255, 135 N.W. 818.

Cf. Heinze v. Murphy, 1942, 180 Md. 423, 24 A.2d 917 (no punitive damages for false arrest in good faith); American Oil Co. v. Colonial Oil Co., 4th Cir. 1942, 130 F.2d 72, certiorari denied 317 U.S. 679, 63 S.Ct. 159, 87 L.Ed. 545 (same as to trespass).

But punitive damages are not minimized by the value to the community of defendant's activity and its general contribution to the locality. Lampert v. Reynolds Metals Co., 9th Cir. 1967, 372 F.2d 245.

43. See for example Kelly v. Fine, 1958, 354 Mich. 384, 92 N.W.2d 511; Clark v. Sheriff, 1956, 247 Iowa 509, 74 N.W.2d 569; Louis Pizitz Dry Goods Co. v. Yeldell, 1927, 274 U.S. 112, 47 S.Ct. 509, 71 L.Ed. 952; and the cases collected in 1937, 111 A.L.R. 91.

44. An early and oft-cited case is Fletcher v. Western National Life Insurance Co., 1970, 10 Cal.App.3d 376, 89 Cal.Rptr. 78.

45. Fletcher v. Western National Life Insurance Co., 1970, 10 Cal.App.3d 376, 89 Cal.Rptr. 78; Eckenrode v. Life of America Insurance Co., 7th Cir. 1972, 470 F.2d 1 (Ill. law). See also Amsden v. Grinnel Mutual Reinsurance Co., Iowa 1972, 203 N.W.2d 252.

46. Gruenberg v. Aetna Insurance Co., 1973, 9 Cal. 3d 566, 108 Cal.Rptr. 480, 510 P.2d 1032. See also United States Fidelity & Guaranty Co. v. Peterson, 1975, 91 Nev. 617, 540 P.2d 1070.

47. Willis, Measure of Damages When Property is Wrongfully Taken by a Private Individual, 1909, 22 Harv.L.Rev. 419, 420; Walther, Punitive Damages—A Critical Analysis, 1965, 49 Marq.L.Rev. 369; Duffy, Punitive Damages: A Doctrine Which Should be Abolished, [1969] Def. Research Inst. 4; Note, 1966, 41 N.Y.U.L.Rev. 1158. See also Fay v. Parker, 1872, 53 N.H. 342; Murphy v. Hobbs, 1884, 7 Colo. 541, 5 P. 119; Spokane Truck & Dray Co. v. Hoefer, 1891, 2 Wash. 45, 25 P. 1072.

48. See the dissenting opinion in Katko v. Briney, Iowa 1971, 183 N.W.2d 657, 47 A.L.R.3d 624.

crime after being mulcted in the tort action.⁴⁹ They have been defended as a salutary method of discouraging evil motives, as a partial remedy for the defect in American civil procedure which denies compensation for actual expenses of litigation, such as counsel fees, and as an incentive to bring into court and redress a long array of petty cases of outrage and oppression which in practice escape the notice of prosecuting attorneys occupied with serious crime, and which a private individual would otherwise find not worth the trouble and expense of a lawsuit.⁵⁰ At any rate, they are an established part of our legal system, and there is no indication of any present tendency to abandon them.

One of the various controversies which have surrounded punitive damages has been over whether they may be awarded against an employer vicariously liable for the tort of a servant,⁵¹ where the employer has neither authorized nor ratified it.⁵² Following a leading federal case,⁵³ a considerable number of the courts have held that they can not,⁵⁴ laying stress upon the injustice of a punishment inflicted upon one who has been entirely innocent throughout. The Restatements of Torts and Agency take this position, subject to the additional qualification that liability is recognized also if the agent was unfit and was recklessly employed or retained, and if the agent was employed in a managerial capacity and was acting in the scope of employment.⁵⁵ It has been noted also that where the employer is a corporation, the pocket which is hit is that of the blameless stockholders, whom no one wants to punish. Where the principal is a municipal corporation, and the impact of punitive damages awards would fall on taxpayers, the majority of courts have denied liability of the principal for punitive damages.⁵⁶ This position has been reinforced by the Supreme Court's holding that punitive damages are not to be awarded against a municipal corporation in actions under 42 U.S.C. § 1983.⁵⁷

---

49. Morris v. MacNab, 1957, 25 N.J. 271, 135 A.2d 657; Pratt v. Duck, 1945, 28 Tenn.App. 502, 191 S.W.2d 562; Dubois v. Roby, 1911, 84 Vt. 465, 80 A. 150; Irby v. Wilde, 1908, 155 Ala. 388, 46 So. 454. Contra, Borkenstein v. Schrack, 1903, 31 Ind.App. 220, 67 N.E. 547. See Aldridge, The Indiana Doctrine of Exemplary Damages and Double Jeopardy, 1945, 20 Ind.L.J. 124; Wheeler, The Constitutional Case for Reforming Punitive Damages Procedures, 1983, 69 Va.L.Rev. 269.

Some courts permit a showing in mitigation of punitive damages that the defendant has been criminally punished for the same wrong. Saunders v. Gilbert, 1911, 156 N.C. 463, 72 S.E. 610; Wirsing v. Smith, 1908, 222 Pa. 8, 70 A. 906.

50. Sedgwick, Damages, 9th Ed. 1912, § 354; 1 Street, Foundations of Legal Liability, 1906, ch. XXXII; McCormick, Damages, 1935, § 77; Morris, Punitive Damages in Tort Cases, 1931, 44 Harv.L.Rev. 1173. See also Morris, Rough Justice and Some Utopian Ideas, 1930, 24 Ill.L.Rev. 730.

51. See Morris, Punitive Damages in Personal Injury Cases, 1960, 21 Ohio St.L.J. 216, Notes, 1961, 70 Yale L.J. 1296; 1967, 19 Syr.L.Rev. 189.

52. The employer's liability for punitive damages is of course clear where the employer has authorized the employee's misconduct, or has participated in it. The employer may, however, become liable for such damages by "ratification," when, with knowledge of the tort, the employer fails to take action expressing disapproval of it, as by retaining the offending servant in the employment. Haines v. Schultz, 1888, 50 N.J.L. 481, 14 A. 488; Farvour v. Geltis, 1949, 91 Cal.App.2d 603, 205 P.2d 424; Will v. Hughes, 1951, 172 Kan. 45, 238 P.2d 478; Donivan v. Manhattan Railway Co., 1893, 1 Misc. 368, 21 N.Y.S. 457; Security Aluminum Window Manufacturing Corp. v. Lehman Associates, Inc., 1970, 108 N.J.Super. 137, 260 A.2d 248.

53. Lake Shore & Michigan Southern Railway Co. v. Prentice, 1893, 147 U.S. 101, 13 S.Ct. 261, 37 L.Ed. 97. See, however, General Motors Acceptance Corp. v. Froelich, 1959, 106 U.S.App.D.C. 357, 273 F.2d 92, where the misconduct of the employees was neither directed, authorized, nor ratified, but responsibility was attributed to the corporation on the basis of its general policies.

54. Emmke v. De Silva, 8th Cir. 1923, 293 F. 17; Gates v. St. James Operating Co., 1939, 122 N.J.L. 610, 7 A.2d 632; Curtis v. Siebrand Brothers Circus & Carnival Co., 1948, 68 Idaho, 285, 194 P.2d 281; Rickman v. Safeway Stores, Inc., 1951, 124 Mont. 451, 227 P.2d 607; Parris v. St. Johnsbury Trucking Co., 2d Cir. 1968, 395 F.2d 543.

55. Second Restatement of Agency, § 217C; Second Restatement of Torts, § 909.

56. Fisher v. City of Miami, Fla.1965, 172 So.2d 455; Desforge v. City of West St. Paul, 1950, 231 Minn. 205, 42 N.W.2d 633; Rascoe v. Town of Farmington, 1956, 62 N.M. 51, 304 P.2d 575; Clarke v. City of Greer, 1957, 231 S.C. 327, 98 S.E.2d 751. See Note, 1965, 22 Wash. & Lee L.Rev. 126.

57. City of Newport v. Fact Concerts, Inc., 1981, 453 U.S. 247, 101 S.Ct. 2748, 69 L.Ed.2d 616. Such damages, however, may be assessed against individual

The majority of the courts, however, have held that the vicarious liability of the master for acts within the scope of the employment extends to punitive as well as compensatory damages, even in the absence of approval or ratification,[58] and that this is true especially in the case of corporations, who can only act through their agents.[59] They have been concerned primarily with the deterrent effect of the award of exemplary damages, and have said that if such damages will encourage employers to exercise closer control over their servants for the prevention of outrageous torts, that is sufficient ground for awarding them.[60]

A related problem, on which there is a growing body of case law, is whether punitive damages awarded against one who is insured against liability are to be paid by the insurer.[61] This involves not only construction of the terms of the contract of insurance,[62] but also the question whether the purposes of punishment and deterrence underlying the damages themselves are not only not accomplished when the insured is allowed to shift the penalty to the shoulders of an innocent party, but are actually frustrated when the wrongdoer is thus afforded protection against what is essentially a criminal punishment imposed by the law. If punitive damages are supported by any sound policy, that policy would appear to demand that they shall not be covered by liability insurance.[63] Some of the small number of decided cases, however, possibly having in mind the supposed function of punitive damages in providing a substitute for attorney's fees, have held that the liability contract effectively covers such damages.[64] A different question is presented where the claim is for coverage of the insured's vicarious liability for punitive damages. The prevailing view, at least if there is no explicit policy provision to the contrary, is that the insurance will be effective to protect the insured against any liability which is purely vicarious, although not for the insured's own wrongdoing.[65]

defendants in § 1983 actions. Smith v. Wade, 1983, ___ U.S. ___, 103 S.Ct. 1625, 75 L.Ed.2d 632.

58. Miller v. Blanton, 1948, 213 Ark. 246, 210 S.W.2d 293; Eaddy v. Greensboro-Fayetteville Bus Lines, 1939, 191 S.C. 538, 5 S.E.2d 281; Atlantic Greyhound Corp. v. Austin, 1945, 72 Ga.App. 289, 33 S.E.2d 718; Western Coach Corp. v. Vaughn, 1969, 9 Ariz. App. 336, 452 P.2d 117; Clemmons v. Life Insurance Co. of Georgia, 1968, 274 N.C. 416, 163 S.E.2d 761. See Notes, 1942, 30 Geo.L.J. 294; 1961, 70 Yale L.J. 1296.

59. Occasional courts have distinguished between corporate and individual employers, holding the latter not liable for punitive damages in the absence of approval or ratification. State ex rel. United Factories v. Hostetter, 1939, 344 Mo. 386, 126 S.W.2d 1173. Most courts make no such distinction. See State ex rel. Coffelt v. Hartford Accident & Indemnity Co., 1958, 44 Tenn.App. 405, 314 S.W.2d 161, holding a sheriff liable for punitive damages for the tort of his deputy.

60. The classic diatribe to this effect is in Goddard v. Grand Trunk Railway of Canada, 1869, 57 Me. 202.

61. See R. Keeton, Insurance Law Basic Text, 1971, §§ 5.3(f), 5.4(b); Morris, Punitive Damages in Personal Injury Cases, 1960, 21 Ohio St.L.J. 216; Long, Insurance Protection Against Punitive Damages, 1965, 32 Tenn.L.Rev. 573; Brin, Punitive Damages and Liability Insurance, 1964, 31 Ins Couns J. 265; Marks, Automobile Insurance Coverage for Punitive Damages, [1966] Ins.L.J. 480; Notes, 1966, 20 U.Miami L.Rev. 192; 1966, 39 Temp.L.Q. 459; 1966, 25 Md.L.Rev. 326.

62. Thus in Abbott v. Western National Indemnity Co., 1958, 165 Cal.App.2d 302, 331 P.2d 997, a policy excluding liability for intentional misconduct was held not to cover punitive damages for assault and battery. See R. Keeton, Insurance Law Basic Text, 1971, §§ 5.3(f), 5.4(b).

63. It was so held in Northwestern National Casualty Co. v. McNulty, 5th Cir. 1962, 307 F.2d 432; Nicholson v. American Fire & Casualty Insurance Co., Fla. App.1965, 177 So.2d 52; Lo Rocco v. New Jersey Manufacturers Indemnity Insurance Co., 1964, 82 N.J. Super. 323, 197 A.2d 591, affirmed mem. 42 N.J. 144, 199 A.2d 655; Crull v. Gleb, Mo.App.1964, 382 S.W.2d 17; American Surety Co. of New York v. Gold, 10th Cir. 1966, 375 F.2d 523.

64. Lazenby v. Universal Underwriters Insurance Co., 1964, 214 Tenn. 639, 383 S.W.2d 1; Southern Farm Bureau Casualty Insurance Co. v. Daniel, 1969, 246 Ark. 849, 440 S.W.2d 582; Carroway v. Johnson, 1965, 245 S.C. 200, 139 S.E.2d 908; Pennsylvania Threshermen & Farmers Mutual Casualty Insurance Co. v. Thornton, 4th Cir. 1957, 244 F.2d 823; General Casualty Co. of America v. Woodby, 6th Cir. 1956, 238 F.2d 452.

65. Commercial Union Insurance Co. of New York v. Reichard, S.D.Fla.1967, 273 F.Supp. 952; Sterling Insurance Co. v. Hughes, Fla.App.1966, 187 So.2d 898; Ohio Casualty Insurance Co. v. Welfare Finance Co., 8th Cir. 1934, 75 F.2d 58, certiorari denied 295 U.S. 734, 55 S.Ct. 645, 79 L.Ed. 1682.

A problem which has arisen to haunt the courts in the 20th century concerns the "mass disaster" [66] litigation, in which the defendant, as for example by discharging hazardous waste or by putting a drug or a product on the market has caused injury to a very large number of persons. How often is such a defendant to be punished? Is there no limiting rule analogous to double jeopardy? And is there any order of priority among the claimants? Confronted with this problem, in Roginsky v. Richardson-Merrell, Inc.,[67] Judge Friendly, refused, in the absence of controlling authority in the new York cases, to find a basis for punitive damages at all in the misconduct of the defendants. Such questions as these have stimulated re-examination of the policies and procedures for awarding punitive damages,[68] and can be expected to keep the controversy over punitive damages alive in the future.

It is generally agreed that punitive damages are a windfall to the plaintiff and not a matter of right, and that it is always within the discretion of the jury or trial judge to withhold them.[69] The greater number of courts have said that they are limited to cases in which actual compensatory damages are found by the jury. Sometimes this obviously means only that without a finding of such damages there is no cause of action at all, and nothing to support the award;[70] but some of these courts have gone further and have held that punitive damages cannot be sustained where a cause of action is found but only nominal damages are awarded.[71] Since it is precisely in the cases of nominal damages that the policy of providing an incentive for plaintiffs to bring petty outrages into court comes into play, the view very much to be preferred appears to be that of the minority which have held that there is sufficient support for punitive damages.[72]

It frequently is said [73] also that punitive damages must bear some reasonable proportion, or at least some undefined kind of relation, to the actual damages found, so that a

See R. Keeton, Insurance Law Basic Text, 1971, § 5.4(b); Long, Insurance Protection Against Punitive Damages, 1965, 32 Tenn.L.Rev. 573; Notes, 1966, 39 Temp.L.Q. 459; 1965, 25 Md.L.Rev. 326; 1969, 22 Sw. L.Rev. 433.

66. See the account of one such disaster in Rheingold, The MER/29 Story—An Instance of Successful Mass Disaster Litigation, 1968, 56 Cal.L.Rev. 116. The total claims for punitive damages alone ran to a total of hundreds of millions of dollars. See generally Owen, Punitive Damages in Products Liability Litigation, 1976, 74 Mich.L.Rev. 1257.

67. 2d Cir. 1967, 378 F.2d 832.

68. See Owen, Problems in Assessing Punitive Damages Against Manufacturers of Defective Products, 1982, 49 U.Chi.L.Rev. 1; Ellis, Fairness and Efficiency in the Law of Punitive Damages, 1982, 56 So.Cal.L.Rev. 1; Owen, Civil Punishment and the Public Good, 1982, 56 So.Cal.L.Rev. 103; Wheeler, The Constitutional Case for Reforming Punitive Damages Procedures, 1983, 69 Va.L.Rev. 269.

69. Hodges v. Hall, 1916, 172 N.C. 29, 89 S.E. 802; Louisville & Nashville Railroad Co. v. Logan's Administratrix, 1917, 178 Ky. 29, 198 S.W. 537; Petrey v. Liuzzi, 1945, 76 Ohio App. 19, 61 N.E.2d 158; Luke v. Mercantile Acceptance Corp., 1952, 111 Cal.App.2d 431, 244 P.2d 764. Contra, Sample v. Gulf Refining Co., 1937, 183 S.C. 399, 191 S.E. 209; Nordstrom v. Miller, 1980, 227 Kan. 59, 605 P.2d 545.

70. See for example Schippel v. Norton, 1888, 38 Kan. 567, 16 P. 804; Hoagland v. Forest Park Highlands Amusement Co., 1902, 170 Mo. 335, 70 S.W. 878.

71. Richard v. Hunter, 1949, 151 Ohio St. 185, 85 N.E.2d 109; Kroger Grocery & Baking Co. v. Reeves, 1946, 210 Ark. 178, 194 S.W.2d 876; Ennis v. Brawley, 1946, 129 W.Va. 621, 41 S.E.2d 680; Behymer v. Milgram Food Stores, 1940, 151 Kan. 921, 101 P.2d 912; Suflas v. Cleveland Wrecking Co., E.D.Pa.1963, 218 F.Supp. 289.

72. Wardman-Justice Motors v. Petrie, 1930, 59 App.D.C. 262, 39 F.2d 512; Edwards v. Nulsen, 1941, 347 Mo. 1077, 152 S.W.2d 28; Crystal Dome Oil & Gas Co. v. Savic, 1931, 51 Idaho 409, 6 P.2d 155; Barber v. Hohl, 1956, 40 N.J.Super. 526, 123 A.2d 785; Scalise v. National Utility Service, 5th Cir. 1941, 120 F.2d 938 (Florida law).

This has been carried so far as to sustain punitive damages where it is clear that there is a cause of action, but no other damages are found by the jury. Clark v. McClurg, 1932, 215 Cal. 279, 9 P.2d 505 (no finding); Fauver v. Wilkoske, 1949, 123 Mont. 228, 211 P.2d 420 (finding of no actual damages).

73. Mitchell v. Randal, 1927, 288 Pa. 518, 137 A. 171; Cotton v. Cooper, Tex.Com.App.1919, 209 S.W. 135; Luke v. Mercantile Acceptance Corp., 1952, 111 Cal.App.2d 431, 244 P.2d 764; Ogilvie v. Fotomat Corp., 8th Cir. 1981, 641 F.2d 581 (citing Mo. cases); McDonald v. Bennett, 5th Cir. 1982, 674 F.2d 1080 (Tex. law), rehearing granted 679 F.2d 415. In Wehrman v. Liberty Petroleum Co., Mo.App.1964, 382 S.W.2d 56, it was said that punitive damages must bear some relation to the injury, but need not as to damages allowed by way of compensation.

The rule resulted in setting aside such verdicts as $100 actual and $14,900 punitive damages in Bangert v.

very small award of compensation will not support a very large penalty. Apparently, however, this has meant little more than that under the particular circumstances these courts do not like the size of some verdicts; and where the enormity of the defendant's outrage calls for it, very large awards of punitive damages, ranging far out of all conceivable proportion to the amount found by way of compensation, have been sustained.[74] A few courts have repudiated outright the necessity of any ratio or relation.[75] Most courts agree that evidence of the defendant's wealth may be received as bearing on the question of the amount which will adequately punish the defendant for the conduct.[76]

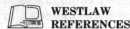
WESTLAW REFERENCES

civil tort /5 action* suit* /30 criminal /5 prosecution* /30 same single one /5 act* offense*
williams /3 dickenson /s 9 /3 847
topic(torts) & evidence /p acquit! convict! /p admissib! inadmissib!
topic(37) % topic(110)

Punitive Damages

court(ct) & punitive* exemplary /s damages
topic(negligence) /p punitive* exemplary /p damages
"alienation of affection*'' & punitive* exemplary /s damages
fletcher /s "western national" /s 10 /3 376

employer* master* /p vicarious** /p liab! /p servant* agent* /p punitive* exemplary /p damages
punitive* exemplary /5 damages /p insurer
punitive* exemplary /5 damages /p "mass disaster"

§ 3. Policy and Process

Perhaps more than any other branch of the law, the law of torts is a battleground of social theory. Its primary purpose, of course, is to make a fair adjustment of the conflicting claims of the litigating parties. But the twentieth century has brought an increasing realization of the fact that the interests of society in general may be involved in disputes in which the parties are private litigants.[1] The notion of "public policy" involved in private cases is not by any means new to tort law,[2] and doubtless has been with us ever since the troops of the sovereign first intervened in a brawl to keep the peace; but it is only in recent decades that its influence on tort law has been openly considered in judicial decisions, and not merely in commentaries on the law. The influence of public policy on tort law is apparent, and most likely to be controversial, when it comes to bear upon a proposed change that is accomplished by overruling an established precedent.[3] Although less

---

Hubbard, 1955, 127 Ind.App. 579, 126 N.E.2d 778, transfer denied, 1957, 237 Ind. 5, 143 N.E.2d 285, and $1,250 actual and $25,000 punitive in Hall Oil Co. v. Barquin, 1925, 33 Wyo. 92, 237 P. 255.

74. Reynolds v. Pegler, S.D.N.Y.1954, 123 F.Supp. 36, affirmed 2d Cir. 1954, 223 F.2d 429, certiorari denied 350 U.S. 846, 76 S.Ct. 80, 100 L.Ed. 754 (outrageous libel; nominal damages and $175,000 punitive); Toomey v. Farley, 1956, 2 N.Y.2d 71, 156 N.Y.S.2d 840, 138 N.E.2d 221 (libel; six cents actual and $5,000 punitive); Livesey v. Stock, 1929, 208 Cal. 315, 281 P. 70 (battery; $750 actual and $10,000 punitive); Seaman v. Dexter, 1921, 96 Conn. 334, 114 A. 75 ($318 actual and $5,000 punitive); Pelton v. General Motors Acceptance Corp., 1932, 139 Or. 198, 7 P.2d 263, rehearing denied 139 Or. 198, 9 P.2d 128 ($225 actual, $5,000 punitive).

75. Finney v. Lockhart, 1950, 35 Cal.2d 161, 217 P.2d 19 (unfair competition; $1 actual, $2,000 punitive); Edwards v. Nulsen, 1941, 347 Mo. 1077, 152 S.W.2d 28 (libel; $1 actual, $25,000 punitive); Malco, Inc. v. Midwest Aluminum Sales, Inc., 1961, 14 Wis.2d 57, 109 N.W.2d 516 (no arbitrary rule that punitive damages cannot be 15 times actual damages); Wegner v. Rodeo Cowboys Association, D.C.Colo.1968, 290 F.Supp. 369, affirmed, 10th Cir. 1969, 417 F.2d 881, certiorari denied 398 U.S. 903, 90 S.Ct. 1688, 26 L.Ed.2d 60; Foster v. Floyd, 1964, 276 Ala. 428, 163 So.2d 213.

76. Phelan v. Beswick, 1958, 213 Or. 612, 326 P.2d 1034; Wilson v. Oldroyd, 1954, 1 Utah 2d 362, 267 P.2d 759; Allen v. Rossi, 1929, 128 Me. 201, 146 A. 692; Johnson v. Horn, 1930, 86 Mont. 314, 283 P. 427; Charles v. Texas Co., 1942, 199 S.C. 156, 18 S.E.2d 719. Contra: Texas Public Utilities Corp. v. Edwards, Tex. Civ.App.1936, 99 S.W.2d 420, error dismissed; Blackman v. Honer, 1925, 119 Kan. 404, 239 P. 750; Taulborg v. Andresen, 1930, 119 Neb. 273, 228 N.W. 528. See Notes, 1965, 19 Ark.L.Rev. 189; 1966, 20 U.Miami L.Rev. 465.

§ 3

1. Bohlen, Fifty Years of Torts, 1937, 50 Harv.L. Rev. 725.

2. Winfield, Public Policy and the English Common Law, 1928, 42 Harv.L.Rev. 76.

3. Concerning overruling decisions, see Lawmaking by Courts, infra, this section.

apparent, the influence is no less real when a court is deciding a "case of first impression"—a case that turns on an issue not previously decided. Society has a two-fold interest in such a case. First, society has an interest in having any single dispute between individuals resolved fairly and promptly. Second, society has an interest in the outcome because of the system of precedent on which the entire common law is based. Under this system, a rule once laid down is to be followed until the courts find good reason to depart from it. Thus, others now living and even those yet unborn may be affected by a decision made today. There is good reason, therefore, to make a conscious effort to direct the law along lines which will achieve a desirable social result, both for the present and for the future.

Individuals have many interests for which they claim protection from the law, and which the law will recognize as worthy of protection. Various interesting attempts have been made [4] to classify these interests into categories, which serve at least to suggest the wide extent to which the law is concerned with human welfare. Individuals wish to be secure in their persons against harm and interference, not only as to their physical integrity, but as to their freedom to move about and their peace of mind. They want food and clothing, homes and land and goods, money, automobiles and entertainment, and they want to be secure and free from disturbance in the right to have these things, or to acquire them if they can. They want freedom to work and deal with others, and protection against interference with their private lives, their family relations, and their honor and reputation. They are concerned with freedom of thought and action, with opportunities for economic gain, and with pleasant and advantageous relations with others. The catalogue of their interests might be as long as the list of legitimate human desires; and not the least of them is the desire to do what they please, without restraint and without undue consideration for the interests and claims of others.

In any society, it is inevitable that these interests come into conflict. In cases of conflict, cultures that we choose to call "primitive" determined who should prevail with sword and club; and there is recent melancholy evidence that the law of the jungle is not yet departed from the affairs of nations. But in a civilized community, it is the law which is called upon to act as arbiter. The administration of the law becomes a process of weighing the interests for which the plaintiff demands protection against the defendant's claim to untrammeled freedom in the furtherance of defendant's desires, together with the importance of those desires themselves. When the interest of the public is thrown into the scales and allowed to swing the balance for or against the plaintiff, the result is a form of "social engineering".[5] A decisionmaker might deliberately seek to use the law as an instrument to promote the "greatest happiness of the greatest number," [6] or instead might give greater emphasis to protecting certain types of interests of individuals as fundamental entitlements central to an integrity of person that the law upholds above all else.[7] This process of weighing the interests is by no means peculiar to the law of torts, but it has been carried to its greatest lengths and has

---

4. The classic catalogue of the interests protected by the law is that of Pound, Outlines of Lectures on Jurisprudence, 1928, 60–71; III Pound, Jurisprudence, 1959, ch. 14. See also Pound, Theory of Social Interests, 1920, 4 Pub.Am.Soc.Society 15; Pound, Interests of Personality, 1915, 28 Harv.L.Rev. 343, 445; Bowman, Introduction to the Common Law, 1932, ch. 5; Harper, Law of Torts, 1933, 5; Green, Judge and Jury, 1930, ch. 1.

5. Pound, Theory of Social Interests, 1920, 4 Pub. Am.Soc.Society 15.

6. Jeremy Bentham's phrase, although an acknowledged translation from an Italian source.

7. See generally J. Rawls, A Theory of Justice, 1971, 3, 4, 27–28, observing a contrast and potential conflict between "an inviolability" that each person possesses and "the welfare of society as a whole" as assessed by "the calculus of social interests." See also C. Fried, Right and Wrong, 1978, chs. 4, 5; Keeton, Entitlement and Obligation, 1977, 46 U.Cin.L.Rev. 1, 10–13.

received its most general conscious recognition in this field.

In this process of weighing interests, and more broadly in ongoing critical evaluation of the development of tort law, the influence of writers upon the courts has been very great. Moreover, within the past half century there has been a very significant attempt at a searching and exhaustive analysis of the entire field in the American Law Institute's Restatement of the Law of Torts, which was begun in 1923, completed in 1939, and more recently revised in the Second Restatement. Some of the most eminent legal scholars have taken part in this work, with the assistance of numerous judges and lawyers.

The form of the Restatement is perhaps unfortunate, in that it seeks to reduce the law to a definite set of black-letter rules or principles, ignoring all contrary authority—since the law of torts in its present stage of development does not lend itself at all readily to such treatment. There is room for suspicion that the courts have tended to cite the Restatement when they are already in agreement with it, and to ignore it when they are not, so that the impressive list of references to it in the cases may be somewhat misleading; and there are those who have disagreed with many of its conclusions, and even denounced the whole project.[8]

It is also unfortunate that much of the immensely valuable work which was done in its preparation, together with all of the cases on which it has relied, are buried in Tentative Drafts which remain unpublished for general circulation. Nevertheless it unquestionably represents the most complete and thorough consideration which tort law ever has received.

This flood of comment and discussion, of analysis and efforts to synthesize and unify the law, has greatly speeded up its development, and the opinion may be ventured that more progress has been made in the tort field in the last three decades than in a century or two preceding.

Lawmaking by Courts

The process of weighing the various interests that may be affected by a rule of tort law is not a simple one, and the problems which arise are complex, and seldom easy of solution. It is usually far easier to describe what has been done than to give a clear reason for it, and harder still to predict what the future may hold. It is a simple matter to say that the interests of individuals are to be weighed against one another in the light of those of the general public, but far more difficult to say where the public interest may lie. Most of the writers who have pointed out the process have stopped short of telling us how it is to be done. It is easy to say that the law will require of every person reasonable conduct [9] not unduly harmful to neighbors; but what is reasonable, and what is undue harm? In determining the limits of the protection to be afforded by the law, the courts have been pulled and hauled by many conflicting considerations,[10] some of them ill defined and seldom expressed at all, no one of which can be said always to control. Often they have had chiefly in mind the justice of the individual case, even though they have had difficulty in formulating a rule of decision that coincides with the social interest in the long run.[11] If we are to have general rules, and the law is to have no

---

8. See for example Green, The Torts Restatement, 1935, 29 Ill.L.Rev. 582. Also Milner, Restatement: The Failure of a Legal Experiment, 1959, 20 U.Pitt.L. Rev. 794.

9. See supra, § 1.

10. See infra, § 4. An amusing but quite profound discussion is Cowan, The Victim of the Law of Torts, 1939, 33 Ill.L.Rev. 532. See also Williams, The Aims of the Law of Tort, 1951, 4 Curr.Leg.Prob. 137.

11. One very interesting illustration is the case of Rasmussen v. Benson, 1937, 133 Neb. 449, 275 N.W. 674, affirmed 1938, 135 Neb. 232, 280 N.W. 890, where recovery was permitted for illness and death caused by mental distress at the negligent poisoning of the decedent's cows and fear that poisoned milk had been sold to customers. It may be suggested that the decision is just and right; but even the Nebraska court recoils from the idea of any general rule permitting recovery for mental suffering at the loss of property, or at the

favorites, occasional injustice is inevitable to someone who does not fit into the rule; and the constant struggle is to make the rule sufficiently flexible to allow for the particular circumstances, and yet so rigid that lawyers may predict what the decision may be, and persons in the community may guide their conduct by that prediction. It is only by a slow, halting, confused, and often painful progress that any agreement is reached as to the best general rule. Ultimately the law must coincide with public opinion, and cannot stand against it; but when that opinion is in a state of division and flux, it is not surprising that the courts' decisions reflect the battle which is raging in the community.

Without any pretense of comprehensiveness, in another section,[12] we identify some of the factors which are to be thrown onto the scales in this process of evaluating conflicting interests.

In earlier times the role of a court in weighing the various interests at stake and determining the rules of substantive law to be applied in resolving a case before the court was often described as one of finding applicable law, even when the decisive issue was one of first impression—that is, when the issue had not previously been decided by any court and was not governed by any statute. Although controversy continues over theories of judicial action, under currently prevailing views it is commonly recognized that in deciding issues of first impression, in tort law as elsewhere, courts are making new law. Courts are constrained by limitations that do not apply to lawmaking by legislatures, but where relevant legislation does not exist, courts must by necessity decide a controversy without legislative guidance. In doing so within a common law system in which each decision is precedent, they necessarily make law. Nor is it to be assumed that all claims of types not previously recognized have been rejected by precedent. Thus, the mere fact that a claim is novel does not defeat it.[13]

Most lawmaking by courts occurs in decisions of first impression that produce evolutionary accretions to the body of existing precedents. From a very early point in the history of the common law, however, it was assumed that a court could and should occasionally overrule a precedent. This form of lawmaking has become a distinctly more frequent occurrence in American law during the last half of the twentieth century.[14] Many of these overruling decisions were handed down by divided courts, and often a dissenting opinion was grounded on the argument that even if such an abrupt change in established precedent could be justified, it should be accomplished only by a legislature and not by a court. In some instances this issue over the respective roles of courts and legislatures in making tort law occupied more of the court's attention than the clash of views over the substantive law issue.

---

peril of strangers. "If the facts are different than presented in this case, different reasoning and a different conclusion might be necessary." 135 Neb. 239, 280 N.W. 893.

12. See infra, § 4.

13. Well stated in Kujek v. Goldman, 1896, 150 N.Y. 176, 44 N.E. 773. See also Bishop v. Byrne, S.D.W.Va. 1967, 265 F.Supp. 460, and Custodio v. Bauer, 1967, 251 Cal.App.2d 303, 59 Cal.Rptr. 463, both involving damages for the birth of a child following negligent sterilization. See Smith, Torts Without Particular Names, 1921, 69 U.Pa.L.Rev. 91; Albertsworth, Recognition of New Interests in the Law of Torts, 1922, 10 Cal.L.Rev. 461; Malone, Ruminations on a New Tort, 1942, 4 La.L. Rev. 309; Heindl, A Remedy for All Injuries? 1946, 25 Chi.Kent L.Rev. 90.

See also Seidel v. Greenberg, 1969, 108 N.J.Super. 248, 260 A.2d 863.

See, however, Zepeda v. Zepeda, 1963, 41 Ill.App.2d 240, 190 N.E.2d 849, certiorari denied 1964, 379 U.S. 945, 85 S.Ct. 444, 13 L.Ed.2d 545, where a son sued his father for causing him to be born a bastard. This was said to be a tortious act; but the action was not allowed, on the basis that such a sweeping change in the existing law should be for the legislature. In accord as to the conclusion is Williams v. State, 1966, 18 N.Y.2d 481, 223 N.E.2d 343, 276 N.Y.S.2d 885, reversing 1965, 46 Misc.2d 824, 260 N.Y.S.2d 953.

14. R. Keeton, Venturing to Do Justice, 1969, 3–53, 169–179, describes this development and identifies the many tort decisions of state courts of last resort that explicitly overruled precedents during a ten-year period commencing in 1958. This accelerated pace of overruling decisions continued through the 1970's. Views differ as to the likelihood that it will continue through the 1980's.

The general practice of adherence to precedent is, of course, supported by strong policy arguments concerned with like treatment of like cases and predictability of decisions. The arguments may be overstated, however. Devotion to precedent is one thing; distrust of new ideas, quite another, which is by no means peculiar to the law but for which it often is reproached, and which has made it change slowly. There are not many rules in tort law as to which one may say that there is no better reason for their existence than that they were laid down by Lord Mildew three centuries since, at a time when the world was a very different place,[15] but they do exist.[16]

Both by the process of interstitial lawmaking in cases of first impression and by occasional overruling decisions, change and development have come, as social ideas have altered, and they are constantly continuing. The law of deceit has progressed from a point where it was assumed as a matter of course that every seller of goods will lie;[17] the law of slander at one time held that mere "brabling words" imputing harlotry to a woman were not actionable;[18] and an evolution is to be traced in the law of seduction,[19] the right of privacy,[20] and interference with contractual relations.[21] In this century,[22] courts have recognized for the first time an action for prenatal injuries,[23] an action for wrongful birth,[24] a recovery by a wife for personal injury at the hands of her husband,[25] new tort liabilities of municipal corporations,[26] and a whole new field of actions for nervous shock and mental suffering.[27] This process of development, of course, is not ended, and continues every year.

Tort law is overwhelmingly common law, developed in case-by-case decisionmaking by courts. It is also influenced, however, by statutes. Early in the development of American tort law, doctrines emerged with respect to enforcement in tort law of standards derived from criminal statutes.[28] Tort law is affected also by statutes explicitly aimed at changing substantive law rules previously developed by courts. Survival acts and wrongful death acts are examples.[29]

As statutes have increased in number and scope, in recent decades courts have addressed, more directly and openly than before, issues of process concerning the relationships between statutes and decisional law. In tort law as in other fields, courts are obliged, with exceptions founded in constitutional law, to follow statutory mandates. Every statute, however, leaves gaps or "lacunae" in its prescription of applicable law. Inevitably, it falls short of answering all questions about the subject matter it addresses. In tort law, as elsewhere,[30] the responsibility for answering the unanswered questions falls to the courts.[31] Thus, for ex-

---

15. The phrase is borrowed from A. P. Herbert, Uncommon Law, 1936, 85.

16. As instances, one may mention the distinction between libel and slander, infra, § 112, and the law as to trespass ab initio, infra, § 25.

17. See Chandelor v. Lopus, 1625, Cro.Jac. 4, 79 Eng.Rep. 3; infra, § 100.

18. See infra, § 112.

19. See infra, § 124.

20. See infra, ch. 20.

21. See infra, § 129.

22. See Albertsworth, Recognition of New Interests in the Law of Torts, 1922, 10 Cal.L.Rev. 461.

23. See infra, § 55.

24. See infra, § 55.

25. See infra, § 122.

26. See infra, § 131.

27. See infra, § 12.

28. See infra, § 36.

29. See infra, §§ 126, 127.

30. E.g., Rose v. Lundy, 1982, 455 U.S. 509, 516–18, 102 S.Ct. 1198, 1203, 71 L.Ed.2d 379, (where federal statute leaves "an hiatus," Supreme Court must supply rule of decision).

31. For suggested guidelines aimed at stating how courts proceed when not indulging in the fiction that all answers are derived from the statute itself, see R. Keeton, Venturing to Do Justice, 1969, 94–97 (courts have "obligations of fidelity to the legislature's mandate, deference to the legislature's manifestations of principle and policy, creative adaptation to the manifested principles and policies, and candid appraisal of the scope of both the mandate and the manifestations of principle and policy"). See also H. Hart & A. Sacks, 1958, The Legal Process, 1413–1417; Keeton, Statutes, Gaps, and Values in Tort Law, 1978, 44 J.Air Law &

ample, where legislation has abrogated earlier decisional law by providing for a cause of action for wrongful death in specified circumstances, courts have later determined that a right of recovery exists in other circumstances not within the scope of the legislation.[32] A court may look to statutes not only as mandates on issues directly addressed but also as sources of "establishment of policy [that] carries significance beyond the particular scope of each of the statutes involved."[33] A further problem encountered in tort law, as elsewhere, is that a statute well adapted to circumstances existing at the time of its enactment may be less apt when circumstances have materially changed. For extreme changes over a long period of time, courts sometimes, on grounds of desuetude, conclude that a clearly outmoded and probably long-forgotten statute may be disregarded. Recently, a thoughtful commentator has urged that courts should exercise a larger responsibility for reexamining potentially outmoded statutes than the narrow confines of precedents on desuetude would allow.[34]

WESTLAW REFERENCES

"public policy" /p revers! overrul! overturn! /p "stare decisis"

restatement /3 torts /3 second 2nd & date(after 1982)

Lawmaking by Courts

mental emotional /s distress suffering anguish /p loss** /3 property

rasmussen /s 275 /3 674

di desuetude

§ 4. Factors Affecting Tort Liability

Among the many considerations affecting the decision as to which of conflicting interests is to prevail, a few may be singled out for special mention, with the repeated caution that no one of them is of such supervening importance that it will control the decision of every case in which it appears.

A Recognized Need for Compensation

It is sometimes said that compensation for losses is the primary function of tort law and the primary factor influencing its development. It is perhaps more accurate to describe the primary function as one of determining when compensation is to be required.[1] Courts leave a loss where it is unless they find good reason to shift it. A recognized need for compensation is, however, a powerful factor influencing tort law. Even though, like other factors, it is not alone decisive, it nevertheless lends weight and cogency to an argument for liability that is supported also by an array of other factors.

Historical Development

The doctrine of precedent[2] inherently brings legal history to bear upon current judicial decisions. The distinctive body of precedents associated with the history of the actions of trespass and case has had a marked influence on the development of tort law, extending even into modern time. That influence is discussed in a later section.[3] Other historical developments as well continue to be significant influences on the modern law of torts. Throughout this book, in section after section, you will find references to origins of modern rules. Behind

---

Com. 1. But cf. Levi, An Introduction to Legal Reasoning, 1948, 15 U.Chi.L.Rev. 501. Materials presenting varied views on this subject appear in R. Aldisert, The Judicial Process, 1976, 170–235.

32. Moragne v. State Marine Lines, Inc., 1970, 398 U.S. 375, 90 S.Ct. 1772, 26 L.Ed.2d 339, on remand, 5th Cir. 1971, 446 F.2d 906; Gaudette v. Webb, 1972, 362 Mass. 60, 284 N.E.2d 222.

33. Boston Housing Authority v. Hemingway, 1973, 363 Mass. 184, 293 N.E.2d 831, 840, quoting Moragne v. State Marine Lines, Inc., 1970, 398 U.S. 375, 90 S.Ct. 1772, 26 L.Ed.2d 339, on remand, 5th Cir. 1971, 446 F.2d 906. See also Mailhot v. Travelers Insurance Co., 1978, 375 Mass. 342, 377 N.E.2d 681, 684.

34. Calabresi, A Common Law for the Age of Statutes, 1981.

§ 4

1. See supra, § 1.
2. See supra, § 3.
3. See infra, § 6.

the history recorded in judicial opinions lie the historical influences of the social, economic and political forces of the time. As to each of the factors discussed in this section, its influence in a particular period of time has been affected, of course, by the social attitudes and forces of that time.

Moral Aspect of Defendant's Conduct

One factor affecting the development of tort law is the moral aspect of the defendant's conduct—the moral guilt or blame [4] to be attached in the eyes of society to the defendant's acts, motives,[5] and state of mind.[6] Personal morals are of course a matter on which there may be differences of opinion; but in every community there are certain acts and motives which are generally regarded as morally right, and others which are considered morally wrong. Of course such public opinion has its effect upon the decisions of the courts. The oppressor, the perpetrator of outrage, the knave, the liar, the scandal-monger, the person who does spiteful harm for its own sake, the selfish aggressor who deliberately disregards and overrides the interests of neighbors, may expect to find that the courts of society, no less than the opinion of society itself, condemn the conduct. In a very vague general way, the law of torts reflects current ideas of morality, and when such ideas have changed, the law has tended to keep pace with them.

This has not always been true. Historians have differed as to how what we now call tort law began. There is one theory that it originated with liability based upon "actual intent and actual personal culpability," with a strong moral tinge, and slowly formulated external standards which took less account of personal fault.[7] It seems quite likely that the most flagrant wrongs would be the first to receive redress. Another, and more generally accepted theory, is that the law began by holding that action is taken at the actor's own peril, and gradually developed toward the acceptance of moral standards as the basis of liability.[8] Another suggestion is that there has been no steady progression, and the law has moved erratically, with the pendulum swinging slowly between "amoral" periods and those in which stress has been laid upon moral fault.[9]

Certainly at one time the law was not openly concerned very much with the moral responsibility of the defendant. "The thought of man shall not be tried," said Chief Justice Brian, "for the devil himself knoweth not the thought of man." [10] The courts were interested primarily in keeping the peace between individuals by providing a substitute for private vengeance,[11] and it was quite as likely that one would take the law into one's own hands when the injury was an innocent one. The person who hurt another by pure accident [12] or in self-defense [13] was required to make good the damage inflicted. "In all civil acts," it was said, "the law doth not so much regard the intent of the actor, as the loss and damage of the party suffering." [14] Even then, however,

---

4. See infra, § 85.
5. See infra, § 5.
6. See infra, § 8.
7. Holmes, The Common Law, 1881, Lecture I.
8. Wigmore, Responsibility for Tortious Acts: Its History, 1894, 7 Harv.L.Rev. 315, 383, 441; Ames, Law and Morals, 1908, 22 Harv.L.Rev. 97; 3 Holdsworth, History of English Law, 3d Ed. 1923, 375–377; 8 Holdsworth, History of English Law, 3d Ed. 1923, 446–459.
9. Isaacs, Fault and Liability, 1918, 31 Harv.L.Rev. 954, 066.
10. Y.B. 7 Edw. IV, f. 2, pl. 2.
11. Holmes, The Common Law, 1881, 2, 3.

12. "Although the defendant's intent was good, still the intent is not material, though in felony it is; as where one is shooting at butts and kills a man, it is not felony. * * * But when one shooting at butts wounds a man unintentionally, he shall be called a trespasser against his will." 1506, Y.B. 21 Hen. VII, 27, 5. See also, 1466, Y.B.Edw. IV, 7, pl. 18; Wigmore, Responsibility for Tortious Acts: Its History, 1894, 7 Harv.L.Rev. 315, 383, 441; Smith, Tort and Absolute Liability, 1917, 30 Harv.L.Rev. 241, 248; 1 Street, Foundations of Legal Liability, 1906, 76.

13. 1319, Y.B. 12 Edw. II, 381.

14. Lambert v. Bessey, 1681, T.Raym. 421, 88 Eng. Rep. 220.

there was an undercurrent of feeling that legal liability should coincide with moral blame; and it is not accurate to say that it was ever the law of England that one acts at one's peril, and is responsible for any harm that may result.[15] Liability was commonly imposed, however, without regard to the moral innocence of the defendant. From this point of view the law has moved forward toward the recognition of moral responsibility as one basis of the remedy, and at least a partial identification of tort liability with the immoral conduct which would not be expected of a good citizen.[16] Toward the close of the nineteenth century this tendency was so marked, that efforts were made by noted writers to construct a consistent theory of tort law upon the basic principle that there should be no liability without "fault," involving a large element of personal blame.[17]

Today we have retreated from this position, although perhaps somewhat less than is often stated.[18] Of course, if we say that all liability rests on "fault," then the "fault" must be "legal" or "social" fault, which may but does not necessarily coincide with personal immorality. The law finds "fault" in a failure to live up to an ideal standard of conduct which may be beyond the knowledge or capacity of the individual,[19] and in acts which are normal and usual in the community, and without moral reproach in its eyes.[20] It will impose liability for good intentions and for innocent mistakes.[21] The actor who trespasses upon the land of another in the honest, reasonable belief that it is the actor's own,[22] or buys stolen chattels in good faith,[23] or innocently publishes a statement which proves to be a libel of another,[24] is sometimes held liable without any personal guilt, because the conduct, although innocent, is still so far anti-social that the law considers that the actor should pay for the harm done. If the actor engaging in this kind of conduct is said to be "at fault," then "fault" has come to mean no more than a departure from the conduct required of the actor by society for the protection of others,[25] and it is the public and social interest which determines what is required. The twentieth century has seen the development of entire fields of liability in which the defendants are held liable for well-intentioned and entirely reasonable conduct, because it is considered to be good social policy that their enterprises should pay their way by bearing the loss they inflict.[26] In the larger sense, there is no less of a moral point of view in the rule that one who quite innocently causes loss should make it good; but it is not personal blame for the act itself which is involved. The actor may be in no way to blame, and subject to no personal reproach whatever for the act itself, considered apart from the failure to compensate for its consequences. But the act, along with the failure to compensate for its consequences, is nonetheless

---

15. "Such a proposition is merely ridiculous. Life would not be worth living on such terms. Life never has been lived on such terms in any age or in any country. If a man always acted at his peril, the whole community would be in gaol but for three obstacles. No one could legally build the gaol, no one could legally send people to it, and no one could legally keep them there." Winfield, The Myth of Absolute Liability, 1926, 42 L.Q.Rev. 37, 38. See also Isaacs, Fault and Liability, 1918, 31 Harv.L.Rev. 954.

16. Ames, Law and Morals, 1908, 22 Harv.L.Rev. 97.

17. Holmes, The Common Law, 1881, 144–163; Smith, Tort and Absolute Liability, 1917, 30 Harv.L. Rev. 241, 319, 409; Salmond, Law of Torts, 7th Ed. 1924, 11, 12.

18. See Keeton, Conditional Fault in the Law of Torts, 1959, 72 Harv.L.Rev. 401, arguing that decisions imposing strict liability, viewed almost uniformly as instances of liability without fault, are founded on a moral concept referred to as "conditional fault."

19. See infra, §§ 32, 85.

20. See infra, § 33.

21. See infra, § 17.

22. Lowenburg v. Rosenthal, 1899, 18 Or. 178, 22 P. 601; Hazelton v. Week, 1880, 49 Wis. 661, 6 N.W. 309; Perry v. Jefferies, 1901, 61 S.C. 292, 39 S.E. 515.

23. See infra, § 15.

24. See infra, § 113.

25. Seavey, Speculations as to "Respondeat Superior," Harvard Legal Essays, 1934, 433, 442.

26. See infra, ch. 13, and § 85.

out of line with what society requires, and the actor is treated accordingly by the law.

On the other hand, there are still many immoral acts which do not amount to torts, and the law has not yet enacted the golden rule. It is impossible to afford a lawsuit for every deed of unkindness or betrayal, and there is much evil in the world which must necessarily be left to other agencies of social control. The basest ingratitude is not a tort, nor is a cruel refusal of kindness or courtesy, or a denial of aid. The rich person is under no legal compulsion to feed a starving neighbor, and it may still be the law that the owners of a boat who see another person drowning before their eyes may rest on their oars and let the person drown [27]—although perhaps in so extreme a case it is a reproach to the law that it is so. Petty insults, threats, abuse and lacerated feelings must be endured in a society not many centuries removed from the law of the club.[28] To what extent the moral ideas of a future day may yet create new torts to deal with such misconduct, it is now impossible to say.

In short, it is undoubtedly true that in the great majority of the cases liability in tort rests upon some moral delinquency on the part of the individual. But quite often it is based upon considerations of public policy which have little connection with private morals. The ethical principles which underlie the law are "not the moral code of popular speech, but an artificial and somewhat sublimated morality, which is formulated by the law and is called morality only by a use of that term which is almost metaphorical." [29]

The last half century has witnessed much more willingness on the part of the courts to discard, as an absolute requirement for liability, even legal, as distinguished from moral "fault," and at least to consider and entertain the contention that the law is, or should be, primarily a question of which interest is to prevail even where no one is at "fault"; or in other words, of where society is going, and what the courts are trying to do. As a result there has been a recrudescence of the older "strict" liability, "without fault," in several areas, where new and modern ideas of policy have developed to support it; there has been legislation, and proposals for a great deal more; and the availability of liability insurance as a means of distributing a loss which might otherwise be ruinous for the individual has become a subject of much discussion. Consideration of these matters is left to a later chapter.[30]

Convenience of Administration

It does not lie within the power of any judicial system to remedy all human wrongs. The obvious limitations upon the time of the courts, the difficulty in many cases of ascertaining the real facts or of providing any effective remedy, have meant that there must be some selection of those more serious injuries which have the prior claim to redress and are dealt with most easily. Trivialities must be left to other means of settlement, and many wrongs which in themselves are flagrant—ingratitude, avarice, broken faith, brutal words, and heartless disregard of the feelings of others—are beyond any effective legal remedy, and any practical administration of the law.

The courts always have stood more or less in dread of a "flood of litigation" involving problems which they are not prepared to deal with.[31] At one time they refused to permit any inquiry as to the state of a person's knowledge, or belief or intentions, upon the ground that "they cannot be known." [32] For

---

27. See infra, § 56; Ames, Law and Morals, 1908, 22 Harv.L.Rev. 97, 112; Bohlen, The Moral Duty to Aid Others as a Basis of Tort Liability, 1908, 56 U.Pa.L. Rev. 217, 316; Bruce, Humanity and the Law, 1911, 73 Cent.L.J. 335.

28. See infra, § 12.

29. Keigwin, Cases on Torts, 1929, 19; Vold, The Functional Perspective for the Law of Torts, 1936, 14 Neb.L.B. 217.

30. See infra, § 82.

31. Green, Judge and Jury, 1930, 77–96.

32. "Upon this the plaintiff demurred and had judgment, for it appears that the fact was voluntary, and

many years they denied all recovery in cases of "mental suffering" involving fright or shock without physical impact, for fear that it would "open a wide door for unjust claims, which cannot successfully be met." [33] The refusal to extend the obligation of a contract to third parties was based upon the "infinity of actions" and the "most absurd and outrageous consequences" which might ensue,[34] and this long continued to be the chief obstacle to holding some contractors liable to third persons.[35]

The reluctance of many courts for so many years to recognize the so-called "right of privacy" rested upon the same objection,[36] and many similar instances of hesitation in the face of an expected deluge of questionable claims or troublesome problems of proof might be mentioned. Such difficulties of administration are perhaps most significant in new developments of the law, and are overcome slowly as the courts find some workable method of affording redress where it is clearly merited and justified as a matter of policy.[37]

Capacity to Bear or Distribute Loss

Another factor the courts have considered in weighing the interests before them is the relative ability of the respective parties to bear a loss which must necessarily fall upon one or the other, at least initially.[38] This is not so much a matter of their respective wealth, although certainly juries, and sometimes judges, are not indisposed to favor the poor against the rich. Rather it is a matter of their capacity to avoid the loss, or to absorb it, or to pass it along and distribute it in smaller portions among a larger group. The defendants in tort cases are to a large extent public utilities, industrial corporations, commercial enterprises, automobile owners, and others [39] who by means of rates, prices, taxes or insurance are best able to distribute to the public at large the risks and losses which are inevitable in a complex civilization. Rather than leave the loss on the shoulders of the individual plaintiff, who may be ruined by it, the courts have tended to find reasons to shift it to the defendants. Probably no small part of the general extension of the tort law to permit more frequent recovery in recent years has been due to this attitude. The development of the doctrine of

---

his intention and knowledge are not traversable; they cannot be known." Basely v. Clarkson, 1681, 3 Lev. 37, 83 Eng.Rep. 565.

33. Spade v. Lynn & Boston Railroad Co., 1897, 168 Mass. 285, 288, 47 N.E. 88, 89. "If the right of recovery in this class of cases should be once established, it would naturally result in a flood of litigation in cases where the injury complained of may be easily feigned without detection." Mitchell v. Rochester Railway Co., 1896, 151 N.Y. 107, 110, 45 N.E. 354.

This is re-echoed, as to mental distress at injury to the plaintiff's child, in Amaya v. Home Ice, Fuel & Supply Co., 1963, 59 Cal.2d 295, 29 Cal.Rptr. 33, 379 P.2d 513, where the "administrative factor" is singled out by name as the reason for the decision.

34. Winterbottom v. Wright, 1842, 10 M. & W. 109, 152 Eng.Rep. 402.

35. See H. R. Moch Co. v. Rensselaer Water Co., 1928, 247 N.Y. 160, 159 N.E. 896. See also infra, § 104.

36. "If such a principle be incorporated into the body of the law through the instrumentality of a court of equity, the attempts to logically apply the principle will necessarily result, not only in a vast amount of litigation, but in litigation bordering upon the absurd.

* * * " Roberson v. Rochester Folding Box Co., 1902, 171 N.Y. 538, 64 N.E. 442.

37. Green, Judge and Jury, 1930, 96.

38. Green, Judge and Jury, 1930, ch. 4; Feezer, Capacity to Bear Loss as a Factor in the Decision of Certain Types of Tort Cases, 1930, 78 U.Pa.L.Rev. 805, 1931, 79 U.Pa.L.Rev. 742; Morris, Hazardous Enterprises and Risk Bearing Capacity, 1952, 61 Yale L.J. 1172; Green, The Thrust of Tort Law: The Influence of Environment, 1961, 64 W.Va.L.Rev. 1; Keeton, Conditional Fault in the Law of Torts, 1959, 72 Harv.L. Rev. 401.

39. Thus a count of 672 California cases bearing on the issue of "proximate cause," made in 1950, disclosed the following list of defendants: railways, street railways and other carriers 137; other public utilities 68; automobile drivers 127; manufacturers, industrial concerns and sellers of goods 78; owners and occupiers of land 75; employers 31; municipal and other government corporations 24; contractors 39; physicians and surgeons 22; notaries and other bonded officers 13; steamship companies 8; other defendants, including several who might well have carried liability insurance, 48. See Prosser, Proximate Cause in California, 1950, 38 Cal.L.Rev. 369, 397.

strict liability "without fault" for dangerous conditions and activities has rested to some extent on this basis,[40] as has that of vicarious liability for the torts of a servant;[41] and the extension of the liability of a manufacturer to the ultimate consumer of the product was aided by the feeling that the manufacturer is best able to bear and distribute the loss.[42] The same principle, of course, underlies such statutes as the workers' compensation acts.[43]

But there are obvious limitations upon the power of a defendant to shift the loss to the public,[44] and the courts frequently have been reluctant to saddle an industry with the entire burden of the harm it may cause, for fear that it may prove ruinously heavy.[45] This is particularly true where the liability may extend to an unlimited number of unknown persons, and is incapable of being estimated or insured against in advance.[46] It is also likely to be true as to a new industry, which may be unduly hampered in its development, as was illustrated by the controversy, active especially during the early years of the aviation industry, over the liability of that industry for damage to persons or property on the ground.[47]

Beyond concerns about the ability of the defendant, or a class of persons represented by the defendant, to bear or distribute risk are concerns about the fairness of imposing this burden on the defendant and the class of persons or entities of which the defendant is one. Thus, like other factors influencing tort law, capacity to bear and distribute risk, even when plainly proved, is not alone decisive of liability. Other factors, including community notions of individual blameworthiness,[48] may help to explain why tort law has distinguished and continues to distinguish between, for example, prudent motoring, as to which strict liability is not imposed, and prudent blasting, as to which strict liability is the prevailing rule.

Prevention and Punishment

The "prophylactic" factor of preventing future harm has been quite important in the field of torts. The courts are concerned not only with compensation of the victim, but with admonition of the wrongdoer. When the decisions of the courts become known, and defendants realize that they may be held liable, there is of course a strong incentive to prevent the occurrence of the harm. Not infrequently one reason for imposing liability is the deliberate purpose of providing that incentive. The rule of vicarious liability is intended, among other things, to result in greater care in the selection and instruction of servants than would otherwise be the case;[49] the carrier which is held to the "highest practicable degree of care" toward

---

40. See Pound, The End of Law as Developed in Legal Rules and Doctrines, 1914, 27 Harv.L.Rev. 195, 233; infra, ch. 13.

41. See Seavey, Speculations, as to "Respondeat Superior," Harvard Legal Essays, 1934, 433, 450; infra, § 70.

42. Feezer, Social Justice in the Field of Torts, 1926, 11 Minn.L.Rev. 313, 323. See Traynor, J., concurring in Escola v. Coca Cola Bottling Co., 1944, 24 Cal.2d 453, 150 P.2d 436.

43. Bohlen, The Drafting of Workmen's Compensation Acts, 1912, 25 Harv.L.Rev. 544; Smith, Sequel to Workmen's Compensation Acts, 1914, 27 Harv.L.Rev. 235; see infra, § 80.

44. Douglas, Vicarious Liability and the Administration of Risk, 1928, 38 Yale L.J. 584, 720.

45. See H. R. Moch Co. v. Rensselaer Water Co., 1928, 247 N.Y. 160, 159 N.E. 896.

46. See for example the court's solicitude for the defendant's industry in Ryan v. New York Central Railroad Co., 1866, 35 N.Y. 210; Palsgraf v. Long Island Railroad Co., 1928, 248 N.Y. 339, 162 N.E. 99, reargument denied 249 N.Y. 511, 164 N.E. 564; and the case cited in the preceding footnote.

47. See Bohlen, Aviation under the Common Law, 1934, 48 Harv.L.Rev. 216; Sweeney, Adjusting the Conflicting Interests of Landowner and Aviator in Anglo-American Law, 1932, 3 J.Air Law 329, 531; Kingsley and Maugham, The Correlative Interests of the Landowner and Airman, 1932, 3 J.Air Law 374; Ewing, The Ground Rule of Torts by Aircraft at the American Law Institute, 1934, 5 Air L.Rev. 323; Proceedings of American Law Institute, vol. 11, 543–579.

48. Keeton, Conditional Fault in the Law of Torts, 1959, 72 Harv.L.Rev. 401.

49. Seavey, Speculations as to "Respondeat Superior," Harvard Legal Essays, 1934, 433, 448, 462, note 22.

its passengers will tend to observe it for their safety; the manufacturer who is made liable to the consumer for defects in a product will do what can be done to see that there are no such defects. While the idea of prevention is seldom controlling, it very often has weight as a reason for holding the defendant responsible.[50]

This idea of prevention shades into that of punishment of the offender for what the offender has already done, since one admitted purpose of punishment itself is to prevent repetition of the offense. There are those who believe [51] that punishment or retaliation is an important and proper aim of the law in assessing damages, since what is paid to the plaintiff is taken away from the defendant. However this may be, it is not often mentioned in the award of compensatory damages, which usually are treated by the courts as a mere adjustment of the loss which has occurred in accordance with responsibility. To the extent that punitive damages [52] are given, however, both prevention and retaliation become accepted objects of the administration of the law of torts.[53]

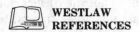 **WESTLAW REFERENCES**

A Recognized Need for Compensation
115k69

Historical Development
di trespass

Moral Aspect of Defendant's Conduct
topic(torts damages) /p self-defense
liab! damages /p innocent uninten! /p mistake*
"good faith" "bona fide" /15 purchase* buy** bought /30 stolen

Convenience of Administration
mental emotional /20 distress suffering anguish /30 physical actual /15 injury

Capacity to Bear or Distribute Loss
liab! /p manufacturer* /p ultimate end /p plaintiff* consumer* user* buyer*

Prevention and Punishment
topic(torts) & admoni! deter* deterr! punish! /p tortfeasor* wrongdoer* defendant*

§ 5. Motive

The motive or purpose underlying the defendant's conduct frequently plays a rather important part in the determination of tort liability. When an act is done, there are nearly always a number of different objectives and motivations behind it. A rather shadowy line has been drawn by the courts between the more immediate objective, which is called the actor's intent,[1] and the more remote ends, which are designated as the actor's motive. In the case of assault and battery we say that the defendant intends to strike or even to kill the plaintiff, but that the defendant's motive is one of revenge, or the gratification of rage, or self-defense, or defense of country. Similarly, if one acts to induce a third person to break a contract with the plaintiff, it is said that the actor's intent is to interfere with the contract relation, while the motive may be one of pure spite, business competition, or protection of the interests of a labor union.

The early common law, which was willing to hold the defendant liable for accidental injuries that were not even intended, took little or no account of motives. It was only by a slow process and at a later date that such justifiable motives as self-defense were recognized, and then they were accepted as defenses to acts long since established as wrongful. Conversely, a bad motive, while it might aggravate the damages, was considered of no significance unless a tort could be

---

50. There is a detailed analytical consideration of how far present rules of tort liability are consistent with a basis of deterrence, in Williams, The Aims of the Law of Tort, 1951, 4 Curr.Leg.Prob. 137.

51. Salmond, Jurisprudence, 7th Ed. 1924, 132, 424, 441; 1 Street, Foundations of Legal Liability, 1906, 477; Morris, Rough Justice and Some Utopian Ideas, 1930, 24 Ill.L.Rev. 730; Morris, Punitive Damages in Tort Cases, 1931, 44 Harv.L.Rev. 1173.

52. See supra, § 2.

53. See for example Goddard v. Grand Trunk Railway Co., 1869, 57 Me. 202.

§ 5

1. See infra, § 8, for further discussion of the distinction between motive and intent.

made out without it; and it was not until the beginning of the eighteenth century[2] that such a motive was first held to be determinative of liability.

Out of this older law there has survived the statement, repeated frequently by the courts,[3] and accepted even by so able a writer as Judge Cooley,[4] that "Malicious motives make a bad case worse, but they cannot make that wrong which is in its essence lawful." This of course merely begs the question, since unless motive is to be eliminated altogether, it must be taken into account in determining whether the act is "in its essence lawful" in the first place.[5] Equally empty is the assertion that an unlawful act resulting in damage to another is actionable unless it is "justified" by its purpose,[6] since it is the legality of the act in the light of the purpose that we seek to determine.

It is undoubtedly true that there are many questions of tortious conduct where the defendant's motive is entirely immaterial. That is because over the passage of centuries, and with the approval of custom and public opinion, the rights and privileges of the parties in the particular situation have become crystallized, standardized, definite or "absolute," so that the law looks at them with a purely objective view and applies fixed rules. Thus a defendant may use all reasonable force to exclude others from the defendant's land,[7] to eject a trespasser[8] or remove an encroachment,[9] or may revoke a license,[10] or resort to legal process to collect a valid debt[11] or to recover from a tortfeasor,[12] or may publish defamatory truth,[13] or refuse entirely to deal with another to whom one is not under contract,[14] all in the worst possible spirit of malevolent vindictiveness, and still claim immunity from all liability.

When the more modern law began to inquire into the character of the defendant's conduct, however, and to base liability upon immediate intent to interfere with the interest of the plaintiff, it was natural that underlying motives should be called into play. With recognition that the interests of the parties are to be weighed against one another has come a realization that the actor's state of mind may be an important factor in the scale. Accordingly, in many situations

---

2. The leading case is Keeble v. Hickeringill, 1707, 11 East 574, note, 11 Mod.Rep. 14, 130, 3 Salk. 9, Holt 14, 103 Eng.Rep. 1127, where the defendant repeatedly fired guns to frighten away wild fowl from the plaintiff's decoy pond, and was held liable because the act was "malicious" rather than intended to further any legitimate interest.

3. Apparently first said in Jenkins v. Fowler, 1855, 24 Pa. 308, 310, with the pious addition that "As long as a man keeps himself within the law by doing no *act* which violates it, we must leave his motives to Him who searches the heart." See also Bourlier v. Macauley, 1891, 91 Ky. 135, 15 S.W. 60; Boyson v. Thorn, 1893, 98 Cal. 578, 33 P. 492; Bohn Manufacturing Co. v. Hollis, 1893, 54 Minn. 223, 55 N.W. 1119.

See the defense of this antiquated view in Ormsby, Malice in the Law of Torts, 1892, 8 L.Q.Rev. 140.

4. Cooley, Torts, 1st Ed. 1888, 497.

5. See Ames, How Far an Act may be a Tort Because of the Wrongful Motive of the Actor, 1905, 18 Harv.L.Rev. 411. Cf. Boggs v. Duncan-Schell Furniture Co., 1913, 163 Iowa 106, 143 N.W. 482.

6. See Raycroft v. Tayntor, 1896, 68 Vt. 219, 35 A. 53; London Guarantee & Accident Co. v. Horn, 1904, 206 Ill. 493, 69 N.E. 526.

7. Rader v. Davis, 1912, 154 Iowa 306, 134 N.W. 849.

8. Kiff v. Youmans, 1881, 86 N.Y. 324; Brothers v. Morris, 1877, 49 Vt. 460. On the same basis, an unprivileged trespasser is not excused by good motives. Bruch v. Carter, 1867, 32 N.J.L. 554; Cubit v. O'Dett, 1883, 51 Mich. 347, 16 N.W. 679.

9. Smith v. Johnson, 1874, 76 Pa. 191. Cf. Jenkins v. Fowler, 1855, 24 Pa. 308; Clinton v. Myers, 1871, 46 N.Y. 511.

10. Marshfield Land & Lumber Co. v. John Week Lumber Co., 1900, 108 Wis. 268, 84 N.W. 434.

11. Morris v. Tuthill, 1878, 72 N.Y. 575; Sullivan v. Collins, 1900, 107 Wis. 291, 83 N.W. 310; Stevenson v. Newnham, 1853, 13 C.B. 285, 138 Eng.Rep. 1208; Hamilton v. Windolf, 1872, 36 Md. 301.

12. Jacobson v. Van Boening, 1896, 48 Neb. 80, 66 N.W. 993.

13. See infra, § 116.

14. McCune v. Norwich City Gas Co., 1862, 30 Conn. 521 (shutting off plaintiff's gas); Kelly v. Chicago, Milwaukee & St. Paul and Pacific Railroad Co., 1895, 93 Iowa 436, 61 N.W. 957 (refusal of free service afforded to others); see Elmore v. Atlantic Coast Line Railroad Co., 1926, 191 N.C. 182, 131 S.E. 633 (discharge of conductor).

where the interests involved are more nicely balanced, and the rights and privileges of the parties are not fixed by definite rule but are interdependent and relative, the defendant's motive may determine whether the defendant is to be held liable.[15]

One conspicuous example of this is found in the field of nuisance,[16] where the reasonableness of an interference with the plaintiff's use or enjoyment of land may depend upon the defendant's motive in causing it. Thus the erection of a spite fence, with no other purpose than the vindictive one of shutting off the plaintiff's view, or light and air, is now held by most courts [17] to be actionable as a nuisance, where the same fence serving some useful end would not. Quite in line with such cases are the modern decisions holding defendants liable for accumulating checks drawn on the plaintiff and presenting them all at once for payment,[18] or buying up a note and transferring it to a bona fide purchaser who can enforce it against the plaintiff,[19] where the sole motive is to ruin the plaintiff financially. The part played by motive where abuse of a qualified privilege is in question, in cases of defamation [20] malicious prosecution,[21] and alienation of affections,[22] is very much the same. In actions for interference with economic relations, it is now generally recognized that the defendant's motive is frequently a determining factor as to liability,[23] and sometimes it is said that bad motive is the gist of the action.[24]

The real problem underlying the question of motive remains one of weighing the conflicting interests of the parties, and determining whether the defendant's objective should prevail at the expense of the damage to the plaintiff. Whether the social value of that objective is sufficient to outweigh the gravity of the interference often becomes the question of deciding significance.

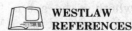

WESTLAW REFERENCES

topic(torts) /p motiv!
topic(damages) /p malicious bad evil /p motiv!
"spite fence"
interfer! /p economic financial /p motive

§ 6. History: Trespass and Case

The shadow of the past still lies rather heavily on the law of torts. When the common law first emerged, its forms of procedure were rigidly prescribed, and the plaintiff could have no cause of action without fitting the claim into the form of some existing and recognized writ. These "forms of action we have buried, but they still rule us from their graves." [1]

---

15. Terry, Malicious Torts, 1904, 20 L.Q.Rev. 10; Ames, How Far an Act may be a Tort Because of the Wrongful Motive of the Actor, 1905, 18 Harv.L.Rev. 411; Lewis, Should the Motive of the Defendant Affect the Question of His Liability, 1905, 5 Col.L.Rev. 107; Lawrence, Motive as an Element in Tort, 1919, 12 Maine L.Rev. 47; Eliot, Malice in Tort, 1919, 4 St. Louis L.Rev. 50; Duport, Disinterested Malevolence as an Actionable Wrong, 1953, 22 Ford L.Rev. 185; Fridman, Malice in the Law of Torts, 1958, 21 Mod.L.Rev. 484.

For comparison with the similar principles of the civil law, see Walton, Motive as an Element in Torts in the Common and in the Civil Law, 1909, 22 Harv.L.Rev. 501; Jenks, Theories of Tort in Modern Law, 1903, 19 L.Q.Rev. 19.

16. See infra, § 89.

17. See infra, § 89.

18. American Bank & Trust Co. v. Federal Reserve Bank, 1921, 256 U.S. 350, 41 S.Ct. 499, 65 L.Ed. 983.

19. Silliman v. Dobner, 1925, 165 Minn. 87, 205 N.W. 696. Cf. St. Charles Mercantile Co. v. Armour & Co., 1930, 156 S.C. 397, 153 S.E. 473 (alteration and premature presentation of postdated check).

20. See infra, § 115.

21. See infra, § 119.

22. See infra, § 124.

23. See infra, § 129.

24. West Virginia Transportation Co. v. Standard Oil Co., 1902, 50 W.Va. 611, 40 S.E. 591; Wheeler-Stenzel Co. v. American Window Glass Co., 1909, 202 Mass. 471, 89 N.E. 28; Globe & Rutgers Fire Insurance Co. v. Firemen's Fund Fire Insurance Co., 1910, 97 Miss. 148, 52 So. 454; S. C. Posner Co. v. Jackson, 1918, 223 N.Y. 325, 119 N.E. 573.

§ 6

1. Maitland, Forms of Action, 1936, 296. See Wilson, Writs v. Rights: An Unended Contest, 1920, 18 Mich.L.Rev. 255.

The origins of the law of torts are "secreted in the interstices of procedure."[2] The ghosts of ancient common law forms of action, long since obsolete, still walk through our courts. "In earlier days they filled the law with formalism and fiction, confusion and complexity, and though most of the mischief which they did has been buried with them, some portion of it remains inherent in the law of the present day."[3]

In the early English law, remedies for wrongs depended upon the issuance of writs to bring the defendant into court. No one could bring an action in the King's common law courts without the King's writ. The number of such writs available was very limited, and their forms were strictly prescribed; and unless the cause of action could be fitted into the form of some recognized writ, the plaintiff was without a remedy. The result was a highly formal and artificial system of procedure, which governed and controlled the law as to the substance of wrongs which might be remedied. The writs which were available for remedies that were purely tortious in character were two—that for the action of trespass, and that for the action of trespass on the case.[4]

The action of trespass, which first emerged in the thirteenth century, had a basic criminal character. It was directed at serious and forcible breaches of the King's peace, and it was upon this basis that the royal courts assumed jurisdiction over the wrong. They were concerned primarily with punishment of the crime; when convicted of trespass, the defendant was fined, and was subject to imprisonment if the fine was not paid. It was in connection with this criminal proceeding that damages first came to be awarded incidentally to the injured plaintiff.[5] What similarity remains between tort and crime is to be traced to this common beginning.

Trespass was the remedy for all forcible, direct and immediate injuries, whether to person or to property—or in other words, for the kind of conduct likely to lead to a breach of the peace by provoking immediate retaliation. Trespass on the case, or the action on the case, as it came to be called, developed somewhat later,[6] as a supplement to the parent action of trespass, designed to afford a remedy for obviously wrongful conduct resulting in injuries which were not forcible or not direct. The distinction between the two lay in the immediate application of force to the person or property of the plaintiff, as distinguished from injury through some obvious and visible secondary cause. The classic illustration of the difference between trespass and case is that of a log thrown into the highway. A person struck by the log as it fell could maintain trespass against the thrower, since the injury was direct; but one who was hurt by stumbling over it as it lay in the road could maintain, not trespass, but an action on the case.[7]

The distinction was not one between intentional and negligent conduct. The emphasis was upon the causal sequence, rather than the character of the defendant's wrong.

---

2. Maine, Early Law and Custom, 1883, 389.

3. Salmond, Observations on Trover and Conversion, 1905, 21 L.Q.Rev. 43.

4. Salmond, Law of Torts, 10th Ed. 1945, 3–4. The actions of detinue and replevin, which lay for the wrongful detention of property, were not purely delictual in character. Trover, which developed later, was a specialized form of the action on the case, modeled after detinue. 3 Street, Foundations of Legal Liability, 1906, 223.

5. Woodbine, The Origin of the Action of Trespass, 1923, 33 Yale L.J. 799, 1934, 34 Yale L.J. 343; Deiser, The Development of Principle in Trespass, 1917, 27 Yale L.J. 220; Fifoot, History and Sources of the Common Law, 1949, ch. 3.

6. Kiralfy, The Action on the Case, 1951, ch. 1; Fifoot, History and Sources of the Common Law, 1949, ch. 4; Plucknett, Case and the Statute of Westminster II, 1931, 31 Col.L.Rev. 778; Dix, The Origins of the Action of Trespass on the Case, 1937, 46 Yale L.J. 1142.

7. Reynolds v. Clarke, 1725, 1 Strange 634, 2 Ld. Raym. 1399, 92 Eng.Rep. 410; Leame v. Bray, 1802, 3 East 593, 102 Eng.Rep. 724.

Cf. Dodson v. Mock, 1838, 20 N.C. 282 (giving poison to a dog is trespass, but leaving it for him to find is case); Fleming v. Lockwood, 1907, 36 Mont. 384, 92 P. 962 (compares opening of floodgates and ditch giving way).

Trespass would lie for all direct injuries, even though they were not intended,[8] and the action on the case might be maintained for those which were intended but indirect.[9] There were, however, two significant points of difference between the two actions. Trespass, perhaps because of its criminal origin, required no proof of any actual damage, since the invasion of the plaintiff's rights was regarded as a tort in itself; however, in the action on the case, which developed purely as a tort remedy, there could ordinarily be no liability unless actual damage was proved.[10] Also, in its earlier stages trespass was identified with the view that liability might be imposed without regard to the defendant's fault,[11] but case from the beginning required proof of either a wrongful intent or negligence.[12]

Transition to Intent and Negligence

The procedural distinction between trespass and case has long been antiquated, although some vestige of it survived into modern time in states retaining common law pleading in a modified form. Modern law has almost completely abandoned the artificial classification of injuries as direct or indirect, and looks instead to the intent of the wrongdoer, or to negligence. The first step was taken when the action on the case was extended to include injuries which were not intended but were merely negligent, and were inflicted directly and immediately.[13] Because of the greater convenience of the action, it came to be used quite generally in all cases of negligence,[14] although trespass remained as the remedy for the greater number of intentional wrongs. Terms such as battery, assault and false imprisonment, which were varieties of trespass, came to be associated with intent, and negligence emerged as a separate tort.[15] The shift was a gradual one, and the courts seem to have been quite unconscious of it. When, in the nineteenth century, the old forms of action were replaced in most jurisdictions by the modern code procedure, the new classification remained. There is still some occasional confusion, and some talk of a negligent "assault and battery,"[16] but in general these terms are restricted to cases of intent.[17]

8. Day v. Edwards, 1794, 5 Term Rep. 649, 101 Eng.Rep. 361; Leame v. Bray, 1803, 3 East 593, 102 Eng.Rep. 724; Welch v. Durand, 1869, 36 Conn. 182; Edmands v. Olson, 1939, 64 R.I. 39, 9 A.2d 860.

9. Reynolds v. Clarke, 1725, 1 Stra. 634, 2 Ld.Raym. 1399, 92 Eng.Rep. 410.

10. Shipman, Common Law Pleading, 3d Ed. 1922, 211, 223.

11. 1 Street, Foundations of Legal Liability, 1906, 74–77.

12. Shipman, Common Law PLeading, 3d Ed. 1923, 216.

13. Williams v. Holland, 1833, 10 Bing. 112, 131 Eng.Rep. 848; Blin v. Campbell, N.Y.1817, 14 Johns. 432; Schuer v. Veeder, Ind.1845, 7 Blackf. 342; Clafin v. Wilcox, 1846, 18 Vt. 605.

14. The story of the change in the law is narrated in Goodhart and Winfield, Trespass and Negligence, 1933, 49 L.Q.Rev. 358, 365; Prichard, Trespass, Case, and the Rule in Williams v. Holland, [1964] Camb.L.J. 234; Millner, The Retreat of Trespass, 1965, 18 Curr. Leg.Prob. 20; Malone, Ruminations on the Role of Fault in the History of Torts, 1970, 31 La.L.Rev. 1; Gregory, Trespass to Negligence to Absolute Liability, 1951, 37 Va.L.Rev. 359; Roberts, Negligence: Blackstone to Shaw to ? 1965, 50 Corn.L.Q. 191.

15. Winfield, History of Negligence in the Law of Torts, 1926, 42 L.Q.Rev. 184.

16. See for example Anderson v. Arnold's Executor, 1881, 79 Ky. 370, where it was alleged that defendant's testator negligently and recklessly, but not intentionally, wounded plaintiff with a pistol, and it was held that the action was for "assault and battery" and so did not survive the death of the wrongdoer. Cf. Perkins v. Stein & Co., 1893, 94 Ky. 433, 22 S.W. 649, holding, without reference to the earlier case, that "to constitute an assault and battery * * * the act complained of must be done with a hostile intent."

See also Kendall v. Drake, 1892, 67 N.H. 592, 30 A. 524; Conway v. Reed, 1877, 66 Mo. 346 (allegation of assault held supported by proof of negligence). A later example of this use of an outmoded terminology is Honeycutt v. Louis Pizitz Dry Goods Co., 1938, 235 Ala. 507, 180 So. 91, which finds assault and battery where plaintiff was negligently, but not intentionally, struck by a lollipop.

17. Donner v. Graap, 1908, 134 Wis. 523, 115 N.W. 125, 126; Hackenberger v. Travelers Mutual Casualty Co., 1936, 144 Kan. 607, 62 P.2d 545; Ott v. Great Northern Railway Co., 1897, 70 Minn. 50, 72 N.W. 833; Baran v. Silverman, 1912, 34 R.I. 279, 83 A. 263.

"The intention to do harm, or an unlawful intent, is of the very essence of an assault, and without it there can be none." Raefeldt v. Koenig, 1912, 152 Wis. 459, 140 N.W. 56.

This transition was accompanied by a growing recognition that, regardless of the form of the action, there should be no liability for pure accident, and that the defendant must be found to be at fault, in the sense of being chargeable with a wrongful intent, or with negligence. As to the necessity of proving actual damage, the courts have continued the distinctions found in the older actions of trespass and case; and whether such damage is essential to the existence of a cause of action for a particular tort may depend very largely upon its ancestry in terms of the old procedure.[18]

At the beginning of the nineteenth century, the forms of action, including trespass and case, still existed, although somewhat blurred in their outlines, as the core of common law procedure. By the middle of the century they began to be modified, liberalized, and at last replaced to a great extent by the modern procedural codes. The old attitude still persisted, however, that the substance of the plaintiff's right is determined and limited by the possibility of a remedy under the common law forms. Thus even quite recently we find courts holding that blasting operations which cast rocks onto the plaintiff's land may be actionable where those which merely shake the plaintiff's house to pieces are not [19]—a position reminiscent of the old distinction between the action of trespass and the action on the case.

WESTLAW REFERENCES

writ /p trespass action /5 case
trespass /40 proof prove* liab! /40 "actual damage*"

Transition to Intent and Negligence
transition evol! chang! modern histor! /p trespass /p negligence intent battery assault "false imprisonment"

§ 7. General Plan

There are many possible approaches to the law of torts, and many different arrangements of the material to be considered have been attempted. By some odd coincidence, the classifications usually have gone by threes, and nearly everyone has found some "tripartite division." Dean Wigmore [1] arranged torts under the three general heads of the "Damage Element" (did the plaintiff suffer legal harm, or what loss or damage is actionable); the "Causation Element" (who is answerable, or was the defendant responsible for the damage); and the "Excuse Element" (what is sufficient justification or excuse for an apparent wrong). No doubt it is difficult to improve upon this as a matter of tort theory and the ultimate reasons underlying the law, but it does not assemble in any one place the questions likely to be considered by a court at the same time. Sir Frederick Pollock,[2] who has been followed by most of the text writers, classified tort into personal wrongs, wrongs to possession and property, and wrongs to person, estate and property generally. Dean Green,[3] in addition to setting forth an elaborate alignment of fact situations, has divided torts into "physical harms," "harms of appropriation," and "harms to relational interests." There are certainly many other possible categories into which the law of torts might be separated, according to the particular theory or purpose of the writer.

For no other reason than that the authors find it most convenient for what they have to say, the general plan of this book is the same as that adopted by the Restatement of Torts. The fundamental basis of tort liability may first be divided into three parts—not because that number is traditional, but because every case in which such liability has

---

18. Thus in assault and battery, false imprisonment, and trespass to land, which were derived from trespass, the action may be maintained without proof of damage. In negligence and deceit, which are descended from the action on the case, damage is the gist of the action.

19. See infra, § 13.

§ 7

1. Wigmore, The Tripartite Division of Torts, 1894, 8 Harv.L.Rev. 200; Wigmore, A General Analysis of Tort Relations, 1895, 8 Harv.L.Rev. 377; Wigmore, Select Cases on the Law of Torts, 2 vols. 1912.

2. Pollock, Law of Torts, 15th Ed. 1951, 6, 7.

3. Green, Judge and Jury, 1930, 9–13.

been imposed has rested upon one of three, and only three, grounds for imposing it. These are:

1. Intent of the defendant to interfere with the plaintiff's interests.

2. Negligence.

3. Strict liability, "without fault," where the defendant is held liable in the absence of both intent to interfere with the plaintiff's interests and negligence.

These will be considered in order, and in connection with each will be discussed those "torts," or invasions of the plaintiff's interests, which have been more or less exclusively identified with it, together with the defenses available against those torts.

This will carry the reader through Chapter 13. The remainder of the volume is devoted to a consideration of particular fields of liability which are of sufficient importance to warrant separate treatment. Usually, as in the case of liability for misrepresentation, or that of suppliers of chattels, or for defamation, these cannot be assigned to any one ground of intent, negligence or strict liability, but recovery may rest upon any of the three. The principal reason for such separate treatment, however, is not so much any difficulty of separating out the grounds of liability as the presence of problems peculiar to the particular interest invaded, which makes it desirable to consider them together.

The effort has been, wherever possible, to adhere to the terminology and the concepts which are in use in the courts, and so generally familiar to the bar. Sometimes these are not the most accurate or desirable ones that might be found, and from a theoretical point of view it might perhaps be better to refer, for example, to a "harm of appropriation" rather than to "conversion"; but any attorney approaching a court with such language would receive no very warm reception, and there are obvious advantages in preserving so far as possible the language in which lawyers must talk, even though there must necessarily be a good deal of inquiry as to its meaning.

 WESTLAW REFERENCES

topic(torts) /20 causation
topic(torts) /p "strict liability"
green /s judge /2 jury
379k1

Chapter 2

INTENTIONAL INTERFERENCE WITH THE PERSON

Table of Sections

Sec.
8. Meaning of Intent.
9. Battery.
10. Assault.
11. False Imprisonment.
12. Infliction of Mental Distress.

§ 8. Meaning of Intent

In a loose and general sense, the meaning of "intent" is easy to grasp. As Holmes observed, even a dog knows the difference between being tripped over and being kicked.[1] This is also the key distinction between two major divisions of legal liability—negligence and intentional torts—and it plays a key role in criminal law,[2] and elsewhere.[3] It is one of the most basic, organizing concepts of legal thinking.

"Intent" is also one of the most often misunderstood legal concepts. The distinction between intentional and unintentional invasions draws a bright line of separation among shadings of almost infinitely varied human experiences. As might be expected, authoritative definitions that purport to specify exactly where this bright line is to be drawn are not entirely in accord. There is even some conflict between the two major pronouncements on the subject by the American Law Institute—one in the Restatement—now the Second Restatement—of Torts[4] and the other in the Model Penal

§ 8

1. Of course, a cunning tripper might fool the dog—once, at least.

2. See, e.g., ALI Model Penal Code, 1962, § 2.02(2)(a), (b), defining "purposely" and "knowingly." The contrasting meanings of "recklessly" and "negligently" are defined, id. at (c), (d).

See also Sandstrom v. Montana, 1979, 442 U.S. 510, 99 S.Ct. 2450, 61 L.Ed.2d 39, condemning an instruction to the jury in a criminal case that "the law presumes that a person intends the ordinary consequences of his voluntary acts." Clearly distinguishable, however, is an instruction that "it is ordinarily reasonable [for the factfinder] to infer that a person intends the natural and probable consequences of acts." Hardy v. United States, 1st Cir. 1982, 691 F.2d 39. For further development of this distinction, see infra this section.

3. See infra, §§ 107, 113. See also, e.g., R. Keeton Insurance Law Basic Text, 1971, §§ 5.2–5.4, 7.6, 7.7; ALI Federal Securities Code, 1980, § 202(61)(C).

4. See §§ 8A, 13, 16, 18, 20. For an analysis of the Second Restatement's provisions on intent, with identification of some variations, in form at least, from the

Code.⁵ Still more variations appear in the great mass of statutory and judicial usages, sometimes in explicit definitions and more often among the meanings discovered as implicit when one closely examines the contexts in which statements about intent are made.

The Restatement aims at applying a single, consistent concept of intent throughout. Since the drafters were attempting to "restate" the law of torts, they were aiming for a concept consistent with the most common usage in judicial opinions in tort cases, and it seems a fair assessment that they achieved this aim. Thus, in examining the Restatement concept, we are also examining the most common, though not the only, sense in which courts use "intent" in tort cases.

The three most basic elements of this most common usage of "intent" are that (1) it is a *state of mind* (2) about *consequences* of an act (or omission)[6] and not about the act itself, and (3) it extends not only to having in the mind a purpose (or desire) to bring about given consequences but also to having in mind a belief (or knowledge) that given consequences are substantially certain[7] to result from the act. It is also essential that the state of mind of intent exist when the act occurs. Additional elements of the concept concern the extent to which the intent may relate to different persons[8] or different consequences from those at issue.[9]

Much of the confusion surrounding application of the legal requirement of intent arises from lack of a clear understanding of the relationship among act, intent, and motive.[10]

One prerequisite of liability is that the defendant act (or fail to act when there is a legal duty to act). An involuntary muscular movement of a sleeping or otherwise incapacitated person will not support liability.[11] But an "act," as that term is ordinarily used, is a voluntary contraction of the muscles, and nothing more.[12] An act is to be distinguished from its consequences.

> "Thus, if the actor, having pointed a pistol at another, pulls the trigger, the act is the pulling of the trigger and not the impingement of the bullet upon the other's person." [13]

---

first Restatement, see R. Keeton, Computer-Aided and Workbook Exercises in Tort Law, 1976, 1.14–1.23.

5. See § 2.02. Note, for example, that in the usage of the Model Penal Code a person "acts knowingly" with respect to a result of his conduct if "he is aware that it is practically certain that his conduct will cause such a result," § 2.02(2)(b), and that a requirement of knowledge is satisfied "if a person is aware of a high probability of its existence, unless he actually believes that it does not exist." § 2.02(7).

6. The Restatement speaks only of an act (not of an omission) in defining intent, in § 8A, and requires an act, as distinguished from inaction, for battery, in § 14 and comment c thereto. Also, the Restatement takes the position that purposely failing to act when there is a legal duty to act is negligence. Scope Note preceding § 13, at 24 ("failure to perform [a duty to act for the protection of others against bodily harm] constitutes negligence * * *, irrespective of whether his failure is or is not deliberate and done for the very purpose of causing the other to suffer the bodily harm from which it was the actor's duty to protect him"). This curious usage is confounding, since there is as clear a distinction (1) between purposely failing to act, in order to produce a desired consequence, and failing to act without adverting to that consequence, as (2) between purposely acting to produce a desired consequence and acting without adverting to that consequence. The confusion is aggravated by the assertion that an act is required for false imprisonment (§ 35) and that "refusal" to provide a means of escape when there is a duty to do so is a sufficient "act of confinement" (§ 45).

7. The Model Penal Code uses the phrase "practically certain," § 2.02(2)(b), in contrast with the Restatement's "substantially certain," § 8A. It seems doubtful, however, that any substantive difference was intended by the drafters or by the American Law Institute. See also supra, n. 5, as to differences that are more likely to be substantive.

8. See the discussion of "transferred intent," infra, this section.

9. For example, one who intends only to cause a harmful physical contact but succeeds only in causing apprehension that such a contact is imminent is subject to liability for assault; see infra, § 10.

10. See also supra § 5, concerning motive.

11. Slattery v. Haley, [1923] 3 Dom.L.Rep. 156, 25 Ont.L.Rep. 95; Stokes v. Carlson, 1951, 362 Mo. 93, 240 S.W.2d 132; Wishone v. Yellow Cab Co., 1936, 20 Tenn. App. 229, 97 S.W.2d 452.

12. Holmes, The Common Law, 1881, 91; Cook, Act, Intention and Motive in the Criminal Law, 1917, 26 Yale L.J. 644; Second Restatement of Torts, § 2.

13. Second Restatement of Torts, § 2, Comment c.

When "act" is used in this sense, it is tautological to speak of a "voluntary act," and self-contradictory to speak of an "involuntary act," since every act is voluntary. Nevertheless, the phrases "voluntary act" and "involuntary act" do appear in legal prose.[14] Moreover, differences may be deeper than merely a choice of terminology; one who uses the phrase "voluntary act" may be using "act" to mean something different from a mere voluntary contraction of the muscles; sometimes the phrase "voluntary act" is used to mean something closer to the concept of intent (as defined in the Restatement and in common usage), which focuses not upon the mere "act" (in the narrower sense, defined in the Restatement and in common usage) but upon volition in relation to consequences as well as volition in relation to the muscular contraction. The movement of the finger which fires a gun is the same, whether it takes place in a crowded city, or in the solitude of the Mojave Desert, and regardless of the actor's state of mind about the consequences. But the legal outcome will depend on the actor's surroundings and the actor's state of mind. The actor may move the muscles of the finger for the purpose of pulling the trigger, for the purpose of causing the bullet to strike another, for the purpose of killing the other, for the purpose of revenge, of defense of country, or of self-protection against attack. "Intent" is the word commonly used to describe the purpose to bring about *stated physical consequences;*[15] the more remote objective which inspires the act and the intent is called "motive."[16] Both intent and motive are steps removed from volition to move the muscles of the finger. Intent is concerned with consequences of that movement; motive, with reasons for desiring certain consequences. Intent is thus less removed from act than is motive. Each has its own importance in the law of torts, and a justifiable motive, such as that of self-defense, may avoid liability for the intent to kill.

Both intent and motive are states of mind. Act is a combination of muscular movement and the state of mind of volition to make that movement.

As already noted, however, intent is broader than a desire or purpose to bring about physical results. It extends not only to those consequences which are desired, but also to those which the actor believes are substantially certain to follow from what the actor does. The actor who fires a bullet into a dense crowd may fervently pray that the bullet will hit no one, but if the actor knows that it is unavoidable that the bullet will hit someone, the actor intends that consequence.

Another source of great confusion is failure to distinguish between (1) the factual elements essential to a finding of intent and (2) the elements of proof and argument that advocates and factfinders may bring to bear in addressing the question whether those

---

14. Even courts citing and following the Restatement definition of "act" have sometimes lapsed, in other passages, into using phrases such as "voluntary act" and "conscious act." See, e.g., Stokes v. Carlson, 1951, 362 Mo. 93, 240 S.W.2d 132.

Moreover, other courts and writers simply do not accept the Restatement of Torts usage. An example is the ALI Model Penal Code, § 2.01, which uses "voluntary act" and defines it in a way that appears to be very nearly if not precisely identical in meaning with "act" as defined in the Restatement of Torts.

15. See Second Restatement of Torts, § 8A, comment *a*. For a more detailed explanation of this concept, and for discussion of the failure to apply it correctly as a source of error in application of the concept of intent, see R. Keeton, Computer-Aided and Workbook Exercises in Tort Law, 1976, 1.1–1.23. One common source of confusion is failure to focus precisely on *what consequence* must be intended to meet the requirements of the legal theory at issue. In Garratt v. Dailey, 1955, 46 Wn.2d 197, 279 P.2d 1091, second appeal, 1956, 49 Wn.2d 499, 304 P.2d 681, a boy who pulled away a chair just as plaintiff was about to sit down was held liable for battery because he knew that she was substantially certain "to sit in the place where the chair had been," which, without satisfactory explanation, the court treated as the equivalent of knowing that she was substantially certain to suffer a harmful or offensive bodily contact with the ground. Might the boy not believe that she would not be hurt and that she would think it was all good fun?

16. Cook, Act, Intention and Motive in the Criminal Law, 1917, 26 Yale L.J. 644; Walton, Motive as an Element in Torts in the Common and in the Civil Law, 1909, 22 Harv.L.Rev. 501.

factual elements are present in a given case. The factfinder need not credit the actor's assertion that the actor did not intend the result in question. One of the common lines of argument against crediting the actor's assertion is (1) that, given the circumstances disclosed in the evidence, a reasonable person in the actor's position would have known that the consequence in question was substantially certain to follow the act, (2) that the evidence shows that the actor was even brighter and shrewder than most others, and (3) that the inference is therefore compelling that the actor knew even though testifying otherwise. If the factfinder credits inference (1) but not inferences (2) and (3), the finding is negligence. But if the factfinder credits all three inferences, the finding is intent to produce the consequence in question. Expressed another way the point is this: Since intent is a state of mind, it is plainly incorrect for a court to instruct a jury that an actor is presumed to intend the natural and probable consequences of the actor's conduct; but it is correct to tell the jury that, relying on circumstantial evidence, they may infer that the actor's state of mind was the same as a reasonable person's state of mind would have been.[17] Thus, when the driver who whips up horses with a loud yell while passing a neighbor's team denies intent to cause a runaway, the factfinder may discredit the driver's testimony;[18] and the defendant on a bicycle who rides down a person in full view on a sidewalk where there is ample room to pass may learn that the factfinder (judge or jury) is unwilling to credit the statement, "I didn't mean to do it."[19]

On the other hand, the mere knowledge and appreciation of a risk—something short of substantial certainty—is not intent. The defendant who acts in the belief or consciousness that the act is causing an appreciable risk of harm to another may be negligent, and if the risk is great the conduct may be characterized as reckless or wanton,[20] but it is not an intentional wrong. In such cases the distinction between intent and negligence obviously is a matter of degree. The line has been drawn by the courts at the point where the known danger ceases to be only a foreseeable risk which a reasonable person would avoid, and becomes in the mind of the actor a substantial certainty.[21]

The intent with which tort liability is concerned is not necessarily a hostile intent, or a desire to do any harm.[22] Rather it is an intent to bring about a result which will invade the interests of another in a way that the law forbids. The defendant may be liable although intending nothing more than a good-natured practical joke,[23] or honestly believing that the act would not injure the

17. Sandstrom v. Montana, 1979, 442 U.S. 510, 99 S.Ct. 2450, 61 L.Ed.2d 39; Hardy v. United States, 1st Cir. 1982, 691 F.2d 39.

18. Lambrecht v. Schreyer, 1915, 129 Minn. 271, 152 N.W. 645. See also Land v. Bachman, 1921, 223 Ill. App. 473.

19. Mercer v. Corbin, 1889, 117 Ind. 450, 20 N.E. 132. Cf. Commonwealth v. Raspa, 1939, 138 Pa.Super. 26, 9 A.2d 925.

20. See infra, § 34.

21. Hackenberger v. Travelers Mutual Casualty Co., 1936, 144 Kan. 607, 62 P.2d 545; Cook v. Kinzua Pine Mills Co., 1956, 207 Or. 34, 293 P.2d 717. See Second Restatement of Torts, § 13, Comment d; Note, 1962, 34 Rock Mt.L.Rev. 268; De Muth, A Comparison of the Conduct Required in Trespass to Chattels and Negligence, 1961, 33 Rocky Mt.L.Rev. 323.

Compare the following statement, which is somewhat at odds with the Restatement definition of "intent":

"If the manifest probability of harm is very great, and the harm follows, we say that it is done maliciously or intentionally; if not so great, but still considerable, we say that the harm is done negligently; if there is no apparent danger, we call it mischance." Holmes, Privilege, Malice and Intent, 1894, 8 Harv.L. Rev. 1.

22. Baldinger v. Banks, 1960, 26 Misc.2d 1086, 201 N.Y.S.2d 629; Restatement of Torts, § 13, Comment e.

23. Reynolds v. Pierson, 1902, 29 Ind.App. 273, 64 N.E. 484; State v. Monroe, 1897, 121 N.C. 677, 28 S.E. 547.

plaintiff,[24] or even though seeking the plaintiff's own good.[25]

More Extensive Liability for Intent

There is a definite tendency to impose greater responsibility upon a defendant whose conduct was intended to do harm, or was morally wrong.[26] More liberal rules are applied as to the consequences for which the defendant will be held liable,[27] the certainty of proof required,[28] and the type of damage for which recovery is to be permitted,[29] as well as the measure of compensation.[30] The defendant's interests have been accorded substantially less weight in opposition to the plaintiff's claim to protection when moral iniquity is thrown into the balance. Apparently the courts have more or less unconsciously worked out an irregular and poorly defined sliding scale, by which the defendant's liability is least where the conduct is merely inadvertent, greater for acts in disregard of consequences increasingly likely to follow, greater still for intentionally invading the rights of another under a mistaken belief of committing no wrong, and greatest of all where the motive is a malevolent desire to do harm.

"Transferred" Intent

One definite area in which there is more extensive liability for intent than for negligence is that covered by the curious surviving fiction of "transferred intent." The defendant who shoots or strikes at A, intending to wound or kill A, and unforeseeably hits B instead, is held liable to B for an intentional tort.[31] The intent to commit a battery upon A is pieced together with the resulting injury to B; it is "transferred" from A to B. "The intention follows the bullet." [32]

This peculiar idea appeared first in criminal cases [33] at a time when tort and crime were still merged in the old trespass form of action. It represents an established rule of the criminal law, in cases in which shooting, striking, throwing a missile or poisoning has resulted in unexpected injury to the wrong person.[34] The criminal cases have been un-

---

24. Vosburg v. Putney, 1891, 80 Wis. 523, 50 N.W. 403; Craker v. Chicago & Northwestern Railway Co., 1875, 36 Wis. 657.

25. Clayton v. New Dreamland Roller Skating Rink, 1951, 14 N.J.Super. 390, 82 A.2d 458 (plaintiff fell and broke her arm; over her protest defendant proceeded to manipulate the arm in order to set it); Johnson v. McConnel, N.Y.1878, 15 Hun 293 (defendant intervened in a scuffle to protect plaintiff and broke plaintiff's leg); Maxwell v. Maxwell, 1920, 189 Iowa 7, 177 N.W. 541, (arrest of insane person for his own protection).

26. Bauer, The Degree of Moral Fault as Affecting Defendant's Liability, 1933, 81 U.Pa.L.Rev. 586; Note, 1962, 14 Stan.L.Rev. 362.

27. "For an intended injury the law is astute to discover even very remote causation. For one which the defendant merely ought to have anticipated it has often stopped at an earlier stage of the investigation of causal connection. And as to those where there was neither knowledge nor duty to foresee, it has usually limited accountability to direct and immediate results. This is not because the defendant's act was a more immediate cause in one case than in the others, but because it has been felt to be just and reasonable that liability should extend to results further removed when certain elements of fault are present." Derosier v. New England Telephone & Telegraph Co., 1925, 81 N.H. 451, 463, 130 A. 145, 152. See infra, § 43.

See Green, Rationale of Proximate Cause, 1925, 170 ff.

28. Cases are Collected in Bauer, The Degree of Moral Fault as Affecting Defendant's Liability, 1933, 81 U.Pa.L.Rev. 586, 592–596.

29. Thus damages for mental disturbance, whether or not it results in physical injury, are more readily held to be recoverable where the wrong is intentional. See infra, §§ 12, 54.

30. Cases are collected in Bauer, The Degree of Defendant's Fault as Affecting the Administration of the Law of Excessive Compensatory Damages, 1934, 82 U.Pa.L.Rev. 583. See for example the rules applied to innocent and wilful trespassers who remove timber or minerals from land, as to the value of the property converted "in place" or after removal. McCormick, Damages, 1935, 492–496.

31. Prosser, Transferred Intent, 1967, 45 Tex.L. Rev. 650.

32. State v. Batson, 1936, 339 Mo. 298, 305, 96 S.W.2d 384, 389.

33. Regina v. Salisbury, 1553, 1 Plowd. 100, 75 Eng. Rep. 158; Queen v. Saunders and Archer, 1576, 2 Plowd. 473, 75 Eng.Rep. 706.

34. Dunaway v. People, 1884, 110 Ill. 333; State v. Williams, 1904, 122 Iowa 115, 97 N.W. 992; State v. Ochoa, 1956, 61 N.M. 225, 297 P.2d 1053; People v. Aranda, 1938, 12 Cal.2d 307, 83 P.2d 928; Coston v. State, 1939, 139 Fla. 250, 190 So. 520.

derstandably preoccupied with moral guilt, and the obvious fact that if the defendant is not convicted there is no one to hold liable for the crime. But the same rule was applied to tort cases arising in trespass.[35] This may possibly have been due to a considered feeling that the defendant could not sustain a burden of proof of freedom from fault when the defendant had at least intended to injure another person.[36] But a better explanation may lie in nothing more than the mere proximity of the criminal law to the trespass action, with its criminal tradition and the similarity of the fact situations. It is quite probable, however, that the persistence of the principle has been due to a definite feeling that the defendant is at fault, and should make good the damage. The defendant's act is characterized as "wrongful," and the fault is regarded as absolute toward all the world, rather than relative to any one person. Having departed from the social standard of conduct, the defendant is liable for the harm which follows from the act, although this harm was not intended.

The rule has been applied in a considerable number of American cases that have held the defendant liable for accidental battery to an unintended person by shooting,[37] striking,[38] or throwing,[39] where the intent was to commit a battery upon a third person. It is not, however, limited to cases of intended or resulting battery. The principle extends at least to liability for battery on one person by an act intended to cause an assault on another, and liability for assault on one person by an act intended to cause a battery on another.[40] Thus one who intended an assault, by shooting to frighten another, was held liable for battery when the bullet unexpectedly hit a stranger.[41] Possibly the principle is applicable even more broadly. The action of trespass was the progenitor not only of battery, but also of assault and false imprisonment; although the Restatement does not so state, one might reasonably argue that when the defendant intends any one of the three, the intent will be "transferred" to make the defendant liable for any of the three, at least if the harm is direct and immediate, as was required for the writ of trespass. On the other hand, where the case does not fit within the scope of the old writ of trespass, there is a lack of precedent for the "transfer" of intent. This is true where the injury is not direct and immediate, but consequential;[42] and where the plaintiff's interest which is invaded, as for example by causing pecuniary loss,[43] was one not protected by the old trespass writ.

---

35. Scott v. Shepherd, 1773, 2 Wm.Bl. 892, 96 Eng. Rep. 525; James v. Campbell, 1832, 5 C. & P. 372, 172 Eng.Rep. 1015.

36. "Originally a defendant whose act had caused bodily harm to another was prima facie liable as a trespasser unless he could exculpate himself by showing that the harm resulted from inevitable accident. To do this, he was required to show that he was innocent of fault, and it would be natural to regard it as impossible for him to do this if his conduct was intended to inflict upon even a third party an injury the same as or closely similar to that which the plaintiff had suffered." Restatement of Torts, Tentative Draft 1935, Commentary to § 10(1).

37. Lopez v. Surchia, 1952, 112 Cal.App.2d 314, 246 P.2d 111; Smith v. Moran, 1963, 43 Ill.App.2d 373, 193 N.E.2d 466; Anderson v. Arnold's Executor, 1881, 79 Ky. 370; Morrow v. Flores, Tex.Civ.App.1948, 225 S.W.2d 621, refused n.r.e.; Davis v. McKey, La.App. 1964, 167 So.2d 416, writ refused 246 La. 910, 914, 168 So.2d 822, 823.

38. Carnes v. Thompson, Mo.1932, 48 S.W.2d 903; Davis v. Collins, 1904, 69 S.C. 460, 48 S.E. 469; Bannister v. Mitchell, 1920, 127 Va. 578, 104 S.E. 800.

39. Singer v. Marx, 1956, 144 Cal.App.2d 637, 301 P.2d 440; Peterson v. Haffner, 1877, 59 Ind. 130; Talmage v. Smith, 1894, 101 Mich. 370, 59 N.W. 656; Keel v. Hainline, Okl.1958, 331 P.2d 397.

40. See Second Restatement of Torts, §§ 13, 18; Manning v. Grimsley, 1st Cir. 1981, 643 F.2d 20 (baseball thrown by warm-up pitcher in the direction of heckling fans protected by a screen broke through screen and hit plaintiff).

41. Randall v. Ridgley, La.App.1939, 185 So. 632; Brown v. Martinez, 1961, 68 N.M. 271, 361 P.2d 152; Weisbart v. Flohr, 1968, 260 Cal.App.2d 281, 67 Cal. Rptr. 114; Daingerfield v. Thompson, 1880, 74 Va. (33 Gratt.) 136.

See also Jeppsen v. Jensen, 1916, 47 Utah 536, 155 P. 429. As to damage to chattel, Vandenburgh v. Truax, N.Y.1847, 4 Denio 464.

42. Oklahoma Gas & Electric Co. v. Hofrichter, 1938, 196 Ark. 1, 116 S.W.2d 599; Commonwealth v. Campbell, 1863, 89 Mass. (7 Allen) 541; People v. Rockwell, 1878, 39 Mich. 503.

43. See, as to misrepresentation, infra, § 107. Also Mobile Life Insurance Co. v. Brame, 1877, 95 U.S. 754,

Since mental disturbance was protected only to the extent of allowing recovery for an assault, it has followed that where that tort cannot be made out, intent is not "transferred" to allow recovery for such consequences.[44]

As will be seen hereafter,[45] where the defendant's conduct is merely negligent, many courts refuse to hold the defendant liable unless the negligence can be found to be relative to the particular plaintiff, in the sense that the foreseeable risk of harm created extends to the plaintiff. The broader liability in the case of an intentional invasion of another's rights is an illustration of the general attitude of the courts as to the imposition of greater responsibility upon an intentional wrongdoer.

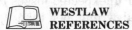
WESTLAW REFERENCES

distinction difference /s negligence /s intent! /s tort*

tort* harm invasion* /p intent! /p unintent! /p difference* distinction* define* definition*

"model penal" /3 2.202

More Extensive Liability for Intent
379k4 & court(ny)

"Transferred" Intent
"transferred intent" & topic(379) & court(ny)

§ 9. Battery

A harmful or offensive contact with a person, resulting from an act intended to cause the plaintiff or a third person to suffer such a contact, or apprehension that such a contact is imminent, is a battery.[1] With respect to the consequence for which it provides a remedy, battery thus stands in contrast with "assault," a term ordinarily used to refer to apprehension of imminent contact rather than contact itself.[2]

Although a contact of this specified type is also essential, the intent element of the cause of action is satisfied not only if the defendant intends [3] a harmful contact, or an offensive contact, upon the plaintiff, or upon a third person (all of which are battery-type consequences) but also if the defendant intends only to cause apprehension that such a contact is imminent (an assault-type consequence).[4] In this respect the intent element of the cause of action for battery is identical with the intent element of the cause of action for assault. Although the Restatement apparently limits the definition of the intent element to intending either the battery-type or assault-type consequence, there is other authority supporting an extension of the cause of action for battery somewhat more broadly—at least to cases in which the defendant's act produced a harmful or offensive contact and the defendant intended neither contact nor apprehension of contact but some other consequence, such as confinement, for which the historical writ of trespass would have provided a remedy.[5]

Protection of the interest in freedom from intentional and unpermitted contacts with the plaintiff's person extends to any part of the body,[6] or to anything which is attached to it and practically identified with it.[7] Thus, if all other requisites of a battery against the plaintiff are satisfied, contact with the plaintiff's clothing,[8] or with a

---

24 L.Ed. 580; Rockingham Mutual Fire Insurance Co. v. Bosher, 1855, 39 Me. 253; Anthony v. Slaid, 1846, 52 Mass. (11 Metc.) 290; Clark v. Gay, 1901, 112 Ga. 777, 38 S.E. 81.

44. See infra, § 12.
45. See infra, § 43.

§ 9

1. Second Restatement of Torts, § 13.
2. See infra, § 10.
3. See supra, § 8, regarding the meaning of intent.
4. Manning v. Grimsley, 1st Cir. 1981, 643 F.2d 20.

5. See Transferred Intent, supra, § 8.

6. Cole v. Turner, 1704, 6 Mod.Rep. 149, 90 Eng. Rep. 958; Mailand v. Mailand, 1901, 83 Minn. 453, 86 N.W. 445.

7. " * * * anything so closely attached thereto that it is customarily regarded as a part thereof." Second Restatement of Torts, § 18.

8. United States v. Ortega, 3d Cir., 1825, Fed.Cas. No. 15,971, 4 Wash.C.C. 531; Geraty v. Stern, N.Y. 1883, 30 Hun 426; Piggly-Wiggly Alabama Co. v. Rickles, 1925, 212 Ala. 585, 103 So. 860 (attempted search of pockets).

cane,[9] a paper,[10] or any other object held in the plaintiff's hand,[11] will be sufficient; and the same is true of the chair in which the plaintiff sits,[12] the horse[13] or the car the plaintiff rides or occupies,[14] or the person against whom the plaintiff is leaning.[15] The interest in the integrity of person includes all those things which are in contact or connected with the person.

Since the disappearance of the distinction between trespass and case, it is no longer important that the contact is not brought about by a direct application of force such as a blow, and (if other elements of the cause of action, including intent, are satisfied) it is enough that the defendant sets a force in motion which ultimately produces the result,[16] as by setting out food for the plaintiff to eat which contains a poison,[17] or digging a pitfall in the path on which the plaintiff is to walk. It is not essential that the plaintiff should be conscious of the contact at the time it occurs. Interest in personal integrity still is entitled to protection, although the plaintiff is asleep or under an anaesthetic,[18] or otherwise unaware of what is going on.[19] Proof of the technical invasion of the integrity of the plaintiff's person by even an entirely harmless, but offensive, contact entitles the plaintiff to vindication of the legal right by an award of nominal damages,[20] and the establishment of the tort cause of action entitles the plaintiff also to compensation for the resulting mental disturbance, such as fright, revulsion or humiliation.[21] The defendant's liability for the resulting harm extends, as in most other cases of intentional torts, to consequences which the defendant did not intend, and could not reasonably have foreseen,[22] upon the obvious basis that it is better for unexpected losses to fall upon the intentional wrongdoer than upon the innocent victim. Since battery usually is a matter of the worst kind of intentions, it is a tort which frequently justifies punitive dam-

9. Respublica v. De Longchamps, Pa.1784, 1 Dall. 111, 1 L.Ed. 59.

10. Dyk v. De Young, 1889, 35 Ill.App. 138, affirmed, 1890, 433 Ill. 82, 24 N.E. 520; S. H. Kress & Co. v. Brashier, Tex.Civ.App.1932, 50 S.W.2d 922.

11. Fisher v. Carrousel Motor Hotel, Inc., Tex.1967, 424 S.W.2d 627 (plate held in hand); Morgan v. Loyacomo, 1941, 190 Miss. 656, 1 So.2d 510 (package); Brodsky v. Rieser, 1921, 195 App.Div. 557, 186 N.Y.S. 841 (starting automobile of which plaintiff had hold); Wilson v. Orr, 1923, 210 Ala. 93, 97 So. 133 (opening and putting hand in box held by plaintiff); Kirkpatrick v. Crutchfield, 1919, 178 N.C. 348, 100 S.E. 602.

12. Hopper v. Reeve, 1817, 7 Taunt. 698, 129 Eng. Rep. 278. Cf. Interstate Life & Accident Insurance Co. v. Brewer, 1937, 56 Ga.App. 599, 193 S.E. 458 (bed); Singer Sewing Machine Co. v. Phipps, 1911, 49 Ind.App. 116, 94 N.E. 793 (sewing machine).

13. Riding: Dodwell v. Burford, 1669, 1 Mod.Rep. 24, 86 Eng.Rep. 703. Attached to carriage in which plaintiff riding: Clark v. Downing, 1882, 55 Vt. 259; Bull v. Colton, N.Y.1856, 22 Barb. 94.

14. Crossman v. Thurlow, 1957, 336 Mass. 252, 143 N.E.2d 814; United States v. Anderson, D.C.Md.1961, 190 F.Supp. 589; Farm Bureau Mutual Auto Insurance Co. v. Hammer, 4th Cir. 1949, 177 F.2d 793, certiorari denied 339 U.S. 914, 70 S.Ct. 575, 94 L.Ed. 1339.

15. Reynolds v. Pierson, 1902, 29 Ind.App. 273, 64 N.E. 484. Cf. State v. Davis, S.C.1833, 1 Hill 46 (slave roped to plaintiff).

16. Mooney v. Carter, 1945, 114 Colo. 267, 160 P.2d 390 (operating car so as to throw plaintifff from running board); Schmitt v. Kurrus, 1908, 234 Ill. 578, 85 N.E. 261 (striking glass door, plaintiff hit with fragments); Thomas v. Dunne, 1955, 131 Colo. 20, 279 P.2d 427 (seating plaintiff on electrified bench); Garratt v. Dailey, 1955, 46 Wn.2d 197, 279 P.2d 1091, second appeal, 1956, 49 Wn.2d 499, 304 P.2d 681 (removing chair in which plaintiff was about to sit down). Cf. Second Restatement of Torts, § 18, Comment c (daubing filth on towel plaintiff expected to use, or pulling away the chair in which he is about to sit).

17. Commonwealth v. Stratton, 1873, 114 Mass. 303 (cantharides); State v. Monroe, 1897, 121 N.C. 677, 28 S.E. 547 (croton oil).

18. Mohr v. Williams, 1905, 95 Minn. 261, 104 N.W. 12; Hively v. Higgs, 1927, 120 Or. 588, 253 P. 363. See infra, § 18.

19. Vosburg v. Putney, 1891, 80 Wis. 523, 50 N.W. 403.

20. Mason v. Wrightson, 1954, 205 Md. 481, 109 A.2d 128; Bumgart v. Bailey, 1963, 247 Miss. 604, 156 So.2d 823; Rullis v. Jacobi, 1963, 79 N.J.Super. 525, 192 A.2d 186; Marble v. Jensen, 1919, 53 Utah 226, 178 P. 66.

21. Smith v. Hubbard, 1958, 253 Minn. 215, 91 N.W.2d 756; Mecham v. Foley, 1951, 120 Utah 416, 235 P.2d 497; Glickstein v. Setzer, Fla.1955, 78 So.2d 374; Lamb v. Woodry, 1936, 154 Or. 30, 58 P.2d 1257.

22. Vosburg v. Putney, 1891, 80 Wis. 523, 50 N.W. 403; Watson v. Rheinderknecht, 1901, 82 Minn. 235, 84 N.W. 798; Trousil v. Bayer, 1909, 85 Neb. 431, 123 N.W. 445; Harris v. Hindman, 1929, 130 Or. 15, 278 P. 954; Ware v. Garvey, D.C.Mass.1956, 139 F.Supp. 71.

ages;²³ but in the comparatively infrequent case where the defendant has acted in good faith under a mistake of fact, but still has committed the tort, punitive damages are not allowed.²⁴

Character of Defendant's Act

According to classic tort law, likely to be followed in most courts even today, in order to be liable for battery, the defendant must have done some positive and affirmative act; mere passive obstruction of the plaintiff's passage, although it may constitute another tort,²⁵ does not amount to a battery.²⁶

The act must cause, and must be intended to cause, an unpermitted contact. Mere negligence, or even recklessness, which creates only a risk that the contact will result, may afford a distinct cause of action in itself, but under modern usage of the term it is not enough for battery.²⁷

The original purpose of the courts in providing the action for battery undoubtedly was to keep the peace by affording a substitute for private retribution.²⁸ The element of personal indignity involved always has been given considerable weight. Consequently, the defendant is liable not only for contacts which do actual physical harm, but also for those relatively trivial ones which are merely offensive and insulting.²⁹ Spitting in the face is a battery,³⁰ as is forcibly removing the plaintiff's hat,³¹ or any other contact brought about in a rude and insolent manner.³² "The least touching of another in anger," said Chief Justice Holt, "is a battery;"³³ and no harm or actual damage of any kind is required.³⁴ The plaintiff is entitled to demand that the defendant refrain from the offensive touching, although the contact results in no visible injury.

The defendant may be liable when intending only a joke,³⁵ or even a compliment, as where an unappreciated kiss is bestowed

---

23. See for example Rodgers v. Bryan, 1957, 82 Ariz. 143, 309 P.2d 773; Deevy v. Tassi, 1942, 21 Cal.2d 109, 130 P.2d 389; May v. Baron, 1938, 329 Pa. 65, 196 A. 866; Vaughn v. Mesch, 1939, 107 Mont. 498, 87 P.2d 177; Schlessman v. Brainard, 1939, 104 Colo. 514, 92 P.2d 749. See supra, § 2.

24. See for example Heinze v. Murphy, 1942, 180 Md. 423, 24 A.2d 917.

25. Cullen v. Dickinson, 1913, 33 S.D. 27, 144 N.W. 656; and see infra, § 11.

26. Innes v. Wylie, 1844, 1 Car. & K. 257, 174 Eng. Rep. 800.

27. Cook v. Kinzua Pine Mills Co., 1956, 207 Or. 34, 293 P.2d 717; Hackenberger v. Travelers Mutual Casualty Co., 1936, 144 Kan. 607, 62 P.2d 545. As to the persistence, in one or two states, of reference to a negligent "battery," even in criminal cases, see Note, 1942, 30 Ky.L.J. 418; supra, § 8.

28. "As to the assault, this is, perhaps, one of the kind in which the insult is more to be considered than the actual damage; for, though no great bodily pain is suffered by a blow on the palm of the hand, or the skirt of the coat, yet these are clearly within the legal definition of assault and battery, and among gentlemen too often induce duelling and terminate in murder." McKean, C.J., in Respublica v. De Longchamps, Pa. 1784, 1 Dall. 111, 114, 1 L.Ed. 59.

29. Harrigan v. Rosich, La.App.1965, 173 So.2d 880 (pushing with finger, "Go home, old man"), People v. Martinez, 1970, 3 Cal.App.3d 886, 83 Cal.Rptr. 914 (barefooted defendant kicked police officer protected by motorcycle boots); Wilson v. Orr, 1923, 210 Ala. 93, 97 So. 133; Masters v. Becker, 1964, 22 A.D.2d 118, 254 N.Y.S.2d 633.

30. Alcorn v. Mitchell, 1872, 63 Ill. 553; Draper v. Baker, 1884, 61 Wis. 450, 21 N.W. 527.

31. Seigel v. Long, 1910, 169 Ala. 79, 53 So. 753; Hull v. Bartlett, 1887, 49 Conn. 64. Cf. Piggly-Wiggly Alabama Co. v. Rickles, 1925, 212 Ala. 585, 103 So. 860 (attempted search of pockets); Forde v. Skinner, 1830, 4 C. & P. 239, 172 Eng.Rep. 687 (cutting plaintiff's hair).

32. United States v. Ortega, 3d Cir. 1825, Fed.Cas. No. 15,971, 4 Wash.C.C. 531; Crosswhite v. Barnes, 1924, 139 Va. 471, 124 S.E. 242; Singer Sewing Machine Co. v. Methvin, 1913, 184 Ala. 554, 63 So. 997; Baldinger v. Banks, 1960, 26 Misc.2d 1086, 201 N.Y.S.2d 629; Rullis v. Jacobi, 1963, 79 N.J.Super. 525, 192 A.2d 186.

33. Cole v. Turner, 1704, 6 Mod.Rep. 149, 90 Eng. 958. Cf. Mailand v. Mailand, 1901, 83 Minn. 453, 86 N.W. 445; Interstate Life & Accident Co. v. Brewer, 1937, 56 Ga.App. 599, 193 S.E. 458; Fort Wayne & Northern Indiana Traction Co. v. Ridenour, 1919, 71 Ind.App. 263, 123 N.E. 720.

34. "If Gibbs kicked plaintiff with his foot, it cannot be said as a matter of law, that there was no physical injury to him. In a legal sense, it was a physical injury, though it may have caused no physical suffering, and though the sensation resulting therefrom may have lasted but for a moment." South Brilliant Coal Co. v. Williams, 1921, 206 Ala. 637, 638, 91 So. 589, 590.

35. Newman v. Christensen, 1948, 149 Neb. 471, 31 N.W.2d 417; Moore v. El Paso Chamber of Commerce,

without consent,[36] or a misguided effort is made to render assistance.[37] The plaintiff is entitled to protection according to the usages of decent society, and offensive contacts, or those which are contrary to all good manners, need not be tolerated. At the same time, in a crowded world, a certain amount of personal contact is inevitable, and must be accepted. Absent expression to the contrary, consent is assumed to all those ordinary contacts which are customary and reasonably necessary to the common intercourse of life, such as a tap on the shoulder to attract attention,[38] a friendly grasp of the arm,[39] or a casual jostling to make a passage.[40] There is as yet no very satisfactory authority [41] as to whether even such innocuous and generally permitted contacts can become tortious if they are inflicted with knowledge that the individual plaintiff objects to them and refuses to permit them.

The time and place,[42] and the circumstances under which the act is done,[43] will necessarily affect its unpermitted character, and so will the relations between the parties. A stranger is not to be expected to tolerate liberties which would be allowed by an intimate friend.[44] But unless the defendant has special reason to believe that more or less will be permitted by the individual plaintiff, the test is what would be offensive to an ordinary person not unduly sensitive as to personal dignity.[45] The intent required is only the intent to bring about such a contact (or to cause apprehension that such a contact is imminent); given that intent, liability will depend upon whether there is a privilege, because of the plaintiff's individual consent, or otherwise.[46]

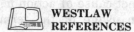

WESTLAW REFERENCES

battery /p harmful offensive /p touching contact & topic(37 379)

Tex.Civ.App.1929, 220 S.W.2d 327 (rodeo day horseplay); Markley v. Whitman, 1893, 95 Mich. 236, 54 N.W. 763; Reynolds v. Pierson, 1902, 29 Ind.App. 273, 64 N.E. 484; Keel v. Hainline, Okl.1958, 331 P.2d 397.

36. Ragsdale v. Ezell, 1899, 49 S.W. 775, 20 Ky.L. Rep. 1567; Liljegren v. United Railways Co. of St. Louis, Mo.App.1921, 227 S.W. 925; Craker v. Chicago & Northwestern Railway Co., 1875. 36 Wis. 657, 17 Am. Rep. 504.

Taking indecent liberties with a person without consent is of course a battery. Hatchett v. Blacketer, 1915, 162 Ky. 266, 172 S.W. 533; Hough v. Iderhoff, 1914, 69 Or. 568, 139 P. 931; Martin v. Jansen, 1920, 113 Wash. 290, 193 P. 674, affirmed 1921, 113 Wash. 290, 198 P. 393; Skousen v. Nidy, 1961, 90 Ariz. 215, 367 P.2d 248. Cf. Gates v. State, 1964, 110 Ga.App. 303, 138 S.E.2d 473 (slapping on buttocks).

37. Clayton v. New Dreamland Roller Skating Rink, 1951, 14 N.J.Super. 390, 82 A.2d 458 (attempt to manipulate broken arm to set it); Johnson v. McConnel, N.Y. 1878, 15 Hun 293 (intervening in scuffle to protect plaintiff).

38. Wiffin v. Kincard, 1807, 2 Bos. & P.N.R. 471, 126 Eng.Rep. 1391; Coward v. Baddeley, 1859, 4 H. & N. 478, 157 Eng.Rep. 927.

39. See United States v. Ortega, 3d Cir. 1825, Fed. Cas.No.15,971, 4 Wash.C.C. 531; Courtney v. Kneib, 1908, 131 Mo.App. 204, 110 S.W. 665. Cf. Steinman v. Baltimore Antiseptic Steam Laundry Co., 1908, 109 Md. 62, 71 A. 517 (accidental contact); State v. Hemphill, 1913, 162 N.C. 632, 78 S.E. 167 (taking hold of child to persuade); Hoffman v. Eppers, 1866, 41 Wis. 251 (assistance to an intoxicated person); Noble v. Louisville Taxicab & Transfer Co., Ky.1952, 255 S.W.2d 493 (taking hold of sick child to help).

40. Cole v. Turner, 1704, 6 Mod.Rep. 149, 90 Eng. Rep. 958.

41. The Second Restatement of Torts, § 19, leaves the question open in a Caveat. The only case approaching the matter is Richmond v. Fiske, 1893, 160 Mass. 34, 35 N.E. 103, where defendant, in violation of express instructions, entered plaintiff's room, touched him, and woke him up to present a milk bill. This was held to be a battery. It would appear, however, that this might be classified as offensive to a reasonable person, even in the absence of the instructions. See Carpenter, Intentional Invasion of Interest of Personality, 1934, 13 Or.L.Rev. 227, 231.

42. Thus horseplay which would be permissible upon the playground is out of order in the schoolroom. Vosburg v. Putney, 1891, 80 Wis. 523, 50 N.W. 403.

43. In Crawford v. Bergen, 1894, 91 Iowa 675, 60 N.W. 205, defendant, suspecting that plaintiff had set fire to a granary, touched him on the shoulder, and said, "Did you feel better after you set the fire?" It was held a question for the jury whether this was a battery. Cf. McDonald v. Franchere, 1897, 102 Iowa 496, 71 N.W. 427.

44. Reynolds v. Pierson, 1902, 29 Ind.App. 273, 64 N.E. 484. Cf. Nicholls v. Colwell, 1903, 113 Ill.App. 219.

45. Second Restatement of Torts, § 19.

46. See the discussion of consent, infra, § 18, and mistake, infra, § 17.

Character of Defendant's Act
battery /p kiss! & topic(379) & court(fl)

§ 10. Assault

The interest in freedom from apprehension of a harmful or offensive contact with the person, as distinguished from the contact itself, is protected by an action for the tort known as assault. No actual contact is necessary to it, and the plaintiff is protected against a purely mental disturbance of this distinctive kind. This action, which developed very early as a form of trespass,[1] is the first recognition of a mental, as distinct from a physical, injury. There is "a touching of the mind, if not of the body."[2] The explanation of its early appearance lies in the obvious likelihood that assaults will result in breaches of the peace, against which the action of trespass was created to enforce the criminal law.[3]

Since assault, as distinguished from battery, is essentially a mental rather than a physical invasion, it follows that the damages recoverable for it are those for the plaintiff's mental disturbance,[4] including fright, humiliation and the like, as well as any physical illness which may result from them. The establishment of the technical cause of action, even without proof of any harm, entitles the plaintiff to vindication of the legal right by an award of nominal damages.[5] Like battery, assault frequently arises out of the worst intentions, and in such cases is an appropriate tort for punitive damages,[6] which are not allowed, however, where it is committed because of an innocent mistake.

Apprehension

Any act of such a nature as to excite an apprehension of a battery may constitute an assault. It is an assault to shake a fist under another's nose,[7] to aim or strike at another with a weapon,[8] or to hold it in a threatening position,[9] to rise or advance to strike another,[10] to surround another with a display of force,[11] to chase another in a hostile manner,[12] or to lean over a woman's bed

---

§ 10

1. I de S et ux. v. W de S, 1348, Y.B.Lib.Assis. f. 99, pl. 60; 1366, Y.B. 40 Edw. III 40, pl. 19; Smith v. Newsam, 1674, 3 Keb. 283, 34 Eng.Rep. 722.

2. Kline v. Kline, 1902, 158 Ind. 602, 64 N.E. 9.

3. Carpenter, Intentional Invasion of Interest of Personality, 1934, 13 Or.L.Rev. 227, 237; Restatement of Torts, § 24, Comment c.

"The law regards these acts as breaches of the peace, because they *directly* invade that personal security, which the law guarantees to every citizen. They do not excite an apprehension that his person may be attacked on a future occasion, and thus authorize a resort to cautionary remedies against it; but they are the beginnings of an attack, excite terror of immediate personal harm or disgrace, and justify a resort to actual violence to repel the impending injury and insult." State v. Morgan, 1842, 25 N.C. (3 Ired.) 186.

4. Kline v. Kline, 1902, 158 Ind. 602, 64 N.E. 9; Ross v. Michael, 1923, 246 Mass. 126, 140 N.E. 292; Brown v. Crawford, 1944, 296 Ky. 249, 177 S.W.2d 1; Hrnicek v. Chicago, Milwaukee & St. Paul Railway Co., 1919, 187 Iowa 1145, 175 N.W. 30; John R. Thompson Co. v. Vildibill, 1924, 211 Ala. 199, 100 So. 139.

5. Walker v. L.B. Price Mercantile Co., 1932, 203 N.C. 511, 166 S.E. 391.

6. Trogden v. Terry, 1916, 172 N.C. 540, 90 S.E. 583. See supra, § 2.

7. United States v. Myers, C.C.D.C.1806, Fed.Cas. No. 15,845, 1 Cranch C.C. 310; Plonty v. Murphy, 1901, 82 Minn. 268, 84 N.W. 1005; Howell v. Winters, 1910, 58 Wash. 436, 108 P. 1077; Stockwell v. Gee, 1926, 121 Okl. 207, 249 P. 389.

8. Kline v. Kline, 1902, 158 Ind. 602, 64 N.E. 9. Cf. Nielson v. Eiler, 1929, 248 Mich. 545, 227 N.W. 688 (shooting at plaintiff); In re Cuykendalls' Estate, 1937, 223 Iowa 526, 273 N.W. 117 (same); Holdorf v. Holdorf, 1918, 185 Iowa 838, 169 N.W. 737 (threatening gesture with a club).

9. United States v. Richardson, C.C.D.C.1837, Fed. Cas.No.16,155, 5 Cranch C.C. 348; State v. Church, 1868, 63 N.C. 15; Trogdon v. Terry, 1916, 172 N.C. 540, 90 S.E. 583.

10. Stephens v. Myers, 1830, 4 C. & P. 349, 172 Eng.Rep. 735; Bishop v. Ranney, 1887, 59 Vt. 316, 7 A. 820; State v. Davis, 1840, 23 N.C. (1 Ired.) 125; Hrnicek v. Chicago, Milwaukee & St. Paul Railway Co., 1919, 187 Iowa 1145, 175 N.W. 30 (advancing on plaintiff with poker and threats).

11. Read v. Coker, 1853, 13 C.B. 850, 138 Eng.Rep. 1437.

12. Mortin v. Shoppee, 1823, 3 C. & P. 373, 172 Eng. Rep. 462; State v. Neely, 1876, 74 N.C. 425; State v. Martin, 1881, 85 N.C. 508; Townsdin v. Nutt, 1877, 19 Kan. 282 (riding toward plaintiff with intent to run her down).

and make indecent proposals, in such a way as to put her in fear.[13]

Since the interest involved is the mental one of apprehension of contact, it should follow that the plaintiff must be aware of the threat of contact, and that it is not an assault to aim a gun at one who is unaware of it.[14] Apprehension is not the same thing as fear, and the plaintiff is not deprived of an action merely because of being too courageous to be frightened or intimidated.[15] It would seem, however, that the plaintiff need not be aware that the threatened danger proceeds from a hostile human being, and that if a concealed defendant sets off an explosion which puts the plaintiff in fear of life or safety, the same interest is invaded, and in substantially the same manner, as when a visible defendant shoots at the plaintiff with a gun.

The courts have been reluctant to protect extremely timid individuals from exaggerated fears of contact, and have often stated that the apprehension must be one which would normally be aroused in the mind of a reasonable person. Perhaps, however, if the defendant has knowledge of the plaintiff's peculiar and abnormal timidity, and intends to act upon it, there should be a right to recover;[16] but there are no assault cases, and the remedy apparently has been left to the more modern tort of the infliction of mental distress.[17] But at least in the absence of such knowledge on the part of the defendant, there is no assault. It usually is held that the defendant's act must amount to an offer to use force,[18] and there must be an apparent ability and opportunity to carry out the threat immediately. There is no assault where the defendant is too far away to make contact,[19] or in mere preparation, as in bringing a gun along to an interview;[20] it is when the defendant presents the weapon in such a condition or manner as to indicate that it may immediately be made ready for use, as where all that is necessary is to cock it, that the threat becomes sufficiently imminent to constitute an assault.[21]

It is probably upon the same basis that it is said that mere words, however violent, do

---

13. Newell v. Whitcher, 1880, 53 Vt. 589. Cf. State v. Allen, 1956, 245 N.C. 185, 95 S.E.2d 526, where defendant stopped his car close to plaintiff, stared at her, and moved the lower part of his body in a "lustful" manner.

14. State v. Barry, 1912, 45 Mont. 598, 124 P. 775; Restatement of Torts, § 22. To the contrary are State v. Baker, 1897, 20 R.I. 275, 38 A. 653; People v. Pape, 1885, 66 Cal. 366, 5 P. 621; and see People v. Lilley, 1880, 43 Mich. 521, 5 N.W. 982. These cases are to be explained as involving criminal, rather than civil assault, in jurisdictions in which the crime is defined as an attempted battery. This is a deviation from the common law to which legislatures are prone. Thus Cal.Penal Code, § 240: "An assault is an unlawful attempt, coupled with a present ability, to commit a violent injury upon the person of another."

See Notes, 1909, 57 U.Pa.L.Rev. 249; 1937, 21 Minn.L.Rev. 213; 1939, 11 Rocky Mt.L.Rev. 104; 1945, 33 Ky.L.J. 189.

15. Second Restatement of Torts, § 24, Comment *b*; Brady v. Schatzel, [1911] Q.S.R. 206.

16. Second Restatement of Torts, § 27, takes the position that intended apprehension is always enough for an assault, even though it is unreasonable. Apparently there are no cases.

17. See infra, § 12.

18. State v. Daniel, 1904, 136 N.C. 571, 48 S.E. 544; Haupt v. Swenson, 1905, 125 Iowa 694, 101 N.W. 520; Alexander v. Pacholek, 1923, 222 Mich. 157, 192 N.W. 652. In Nelson v. Crawford, 1899, 122 Mich. 466, 81 N.W. 335, the defendant, known to be a harmless eccentric, appeared at plaintiff's door, dressed in woman's clothing, and followed her into the house. It was held there was no assault.

In Stearns v. Sampson, 1871, 59 Me. 568, it was held that causing physical discomfort, by removing plaintiff's doors and windows, was not an assault. Contra, Wood v. Young, 1899, 50 S.W. 541, 20 Ky.Law Rep. 1931.

19. State v. Davis, 1840, 23 N.C. (1 Ired.) 125; Fuller v. State, 1903, 44 Tex.Cr.R. 463, 72 S.W. 184 (kissing gesture at girl); Bowles v. May, 1932, 159 Va. 419, 166 S.E. 550 (shaking finger at plaintiff); Western Union Telegraph Co. v. Hill, 1933, 25 Ala.App. 540, 150 So. 709, certiorari denied 227 Ala. 469, 150 So. 711 (across counter). Cf. State v. Ingram, 1953, 237 N.C. 197, 74 S.E.2d 532 ("leering" at plaintiff not enough).

20. State v. Painter, 1877, 67 Mo. 84; Second Restatement of Torts, § 29. Cf. Lawson v. State, 1857, 30 Ala. 14 (drawing pistol without presenting it); Penny v. State, 1901, 114 Ga. 77, 39 S.E. 871 (holding rocks in hands); Lawrence v. Womack, Mo.App.1930, 23 S.W.2d 190 (picking up stick); Cucinotti v. Ortmann, 1960, 399 Pa. 26, 159 A.2d 216 (exhibiting blackjacks).

21. Osborn v. Veitch, 1858, 1 F. & F. 317, 175 Eng. Rep. 744; State v. Church, 1868, 63 N.C. 15. Contra, Woodruff v. Woodruff, 1857, 22 Ga. 237.

not amount to an assault.[22] Apparently the origin of this rule lay in nothing more than the fact that in the early days the King's courts had their hands full when they intervened at the first threatening gesture, or in other words, when the fight was about to start; and taking cognizance of all of the belligerent language which the foul mouths of merrie England could dispense was simply beyond their capacity. Threats for the future,[23] and insults for the present,[24] are simply not present breaches of the peace, and so never have fallen within the narrow boundaries of this rather antiquated tort.

It would appear, however, that too much emphasis has been placed by the courts upon the idea of motion or gesture, usually described as "some overt act." The most persuasive reason that mere words should not amount to an assault is that ordinarily they create no apprehension of immediate contact. But words are always spoken in context, and in context they may cause apprehension. When they do, there should be an assault no less than when the defendant shakes a fist. It may be suggested that a perfectly motionless highwayman, standing with pistol pointed and finger on the trigger, who cries "Stand and deliver!" or even merely appears to the plaintiff's view, commits an assault. It is the immediate physical threat which is important, rather then the manner in which it is conveyed.[25]

Words may give character to an act. A movement inoffensive in itself may be preceded or accompanied by words which give it a hostile color, as where one who has been making verbal threats of violence reaches into a pocket, so that the words and the act together create an apprehension that might otherwise not occur.[26] Likewise, the words may so far explain away the apparent intent to attack that immediate apprehension is not expectable, as where they indicate that the defendant is offering a blow in jest, or that the threat is solely for the future. "Were you not an old man, I would knock you down," so far negatives the threatening gesture that there is no assault.[27] But the defendant is not free to compel the plaintiff to buy safety by compliance with a condition which there is no legal right to impose. "Your money or your life," whether or not it does anything to allay the anxiety of the plaintiff, is an obvious invasion of the plaintiff's rights, and will not prevent an actionable assault.[28] And even a lawful demand may be made in such a violent manner, and with such a display of excessive and unreasonable force, that there may be recovery on the basis of assault.[29]

22. Kaufman v. Kansas Power & Light Co., 1936, 144 Kan. 283, 58 P.2d 1055; State v. Daniel, 1904, 136 N.C. 571, 48 S.E. 544; Gelhaus v. Eastern Air Lines, 5th Cir. 1952, 194 F.2d 774; Hixson v. Slocum, 1913, 156 Ky. 487, 161 S.W. 522; Republic Iron & Steel Co. v. Self, 1915, 192 Ala. 403, 68 So. 328; Second Restatement of Torts, § 31.

23. Cucinotti v. Ortmann, 1960, 399 Pa. 26, 159 A.2d 216; Kramer v. Ricksmeier, 1913, 159 Iowa 48, 139 N.W. 1091; Brooker v. Silverthorne, 1918, 111 S.C. 553, 99 S.E. 350.

24. Thus the mere solicitation of illicit intercourse is quite uniformly held not to amount to an assault. Prince v. Ridge, 1900, 32 Misc. 666, 66 N.Y.S. 454; Reed v. Maley, 1903, 115 Ky. 816, 74 S.W. 1079; Davis v. Richardson, 1905, 76 Ark. 348, 89 S.W. 318; Bennett v. McIntire, 1889, 121 Ind. 231, 23 N.E. 78.

25. See Seavey, Threats Inducing Emotional Reactions, 1960, 39 N.C.L.Rev. 74.

26. Hulse v. Tollman, 1893, 49 Ill.App. 490; Keep v. Quallman, 1887, 68 Wis. 451, 32 N.W. 233; Fogden v. Wade, [1945] N.Z.L.Rep. 724 (immoral suggestion to plaintiff followed by advancing towards her).

27. State v. Crow, 1841, 23 N.C. (1 Ired.) 375; Tuberville v. Savage, 1669, 1 Mod.Rep. 3, 86 Eng.Rep. 684 ("If it were not assize time, I would not take such language from you"); Commonwealth v. Eyre, Pa. 1815, 1 S. & R. 347 ("If it were not for your gray hairs, I would tear your heart out"). In State v. Hampton, 1868, 63 N.C. 13, "I have a great mind to hit you" was held not to prevent the existence of an assault.

28. Keefe v. State, 1857, 19 Ark. 190; United States v. Allison Richardson, C.C.D.C.1837, Fed.Cas.No. 16,155, 5 Cranch C.C. 348; State v. Church, 1868, 63 N.C. 15; Trogdon v. Terry, 1916, 172 N.C. 540, 90 S.E. 583.

29. Ross v. Michael, 1923, 246 Mass. 126, 140 N.E. 292 (plaintiff ordered out of defendant's house with violent words and a revolver); Ansteth v. Buffalo Railway Co., 1895, 145 N.Y. 210, 39 N.E. 708 (conductor frightened boy off of street car).

Intent

The intent element for assault is identical with that for battery.[30] There is, properly speaking, no such thing as a negligent assault.[31] But the intent need not necessarily be to inflict physical injury, and it is enough that there is an intent to arouse apprehension.[32] Thus it is an assault to fire a gun, though not aimed at the plaintiff, for the purpose of frightening the plaintiff,[33] or to point it at the plaintiff when the defendant knows that it is unloaded, and the plaintiff does not.[34] Once apprehension has been intentionally created, it is no defense that the defendant reconsidered and desisted or withdrew without doing physical harm.[35] The tort is complete with the invasion of the plaintiff's mental peace, and the failure to carry it through to battery will not prevent liability.

Assault and Battery

Assault and battery go together like ham and eggs. The difference between them is that between physical contact and the mere apprehension of it. One may exist without the other. It is a battery to strike a sleeping person, although the person struck does not discover it until afterward; it is an assault to shoot at, frighten, and miss a person. Except for this difference in the character of the invasion of the plaintiff's interests, the two are in all respects identical, and there is no apparent reason why the rules applied to battery, including the fiction of "transferred intent",[36] should not also apply to assault. In the ordinary case, both assault and battery are present; it is an assault when the defendant swings a fist to strike the plaintiff, and the plaintiff sees the movement; a battery when the fist comes in contact with the plaintiff's nose. The two terms are so closely associated in common usage that they are generally used together, or regarded as more or less synonymous.[37] Loosely drawn criminal statutes, which make use of "assault" to include attempted battery, or even battery itself, have assisted in obscuring the distinction. It is not accurate to say that "every battery includes an assault," [38] but in practice the difference between the two is often entirely ignored.

WESTLAW REFERENCES

assault /p apprehen! /p harmful offensive /p touching contact & topic(37 379)

Apprehension

word* oral** /s assault*** & topic(37 379)

Criminal statutes frequently define assault as an attempted battery, requiring present ability. This was the original criminal law meaning of assault. Under such a definition it is often held, as in People v. Sylva, 1904, 143 Cal. 62, 76 P. 814, that pointing an unloaded gun is not an assault. See the full discussion in Perkins, An Analysis of Assault and Attempts to Assault, 1962, 47 Minn.L.Rev. 71; Notes, 1945, 33 Ky.L.J. 189; 1951, 30 Tex.L.Rev. 120; 1939, 11 Rocky Mt.L.Rev. 104. Such statutes will ordinarily have no application to tort liability. Lowry v. Standard Oil Co., 1944, 63 Cal.App.2d 1, 146 P.2d 57.

---

30. See supra, § 9.

31. White v. Sander, 1897, 168 Mass. 296, 47 N.E. 90; Atchison, Topeka & Santa Fe Railway Co. v. McGinnis, 1891, 46 Kan. 109, 26 P. 453; Eckerd v. Weve, 1911, 85 Kan. 752, 118 P. 870; Second Restatement of Torts, § 21.

32. Second Restatement of Torts, § 32.

33. State v. Baker, 1897, 20 R.I. 275, 38 A. 653; State v. Triplett, 1894, 52 Kan. 678, 35 P. 815; Nelson v. State, 1955, 92 Ga.App. 738, 90 S.E.2d 38; State v. Newton, 1959, 251 N.C. 151, 110 S.E.2d 810; Burgess v. Commonwealth, 1923, 136 Va. 697, 118 S.E. 273. Contra, Degenhardt v. Heller, 1896, 93 Wis. 662, 68 N.W. 411, relying upon the criminal law definition of assault as an attempted battery (see supra, n.14, and infra, n.34, this section). The case is criticized in 1897, 10 Harv.L.Rev. 252.

34. Beach v. Hancock, 1853, 27 N.H. (7 Fost.) 223; Allen v. Hannaford, 1926, 138 Wash. 423, 244 P. 700; Burge v. Forbes, 1928, 23 Ala.App. 67, 120 So. 577, certiorari denied, 1929, 219 Ala. 700, 121 So. 915 (displaying gun); Commonwealth v. Henson, 1970, 357 Mass. 686, 259 N.E.2d 769.

35. Handy v. Johnson, 1854, 5 Md. 450; Brister v. State, 1899, 40 Tex.Cr.R. 505, 51 S.W. 393.

36. See supra, § 8.

37. See Mailand v. Mailand, 1901, 83 Minn. 453, 86 N.W. 445; Perkins v. Stein & Co., 1893, 94 Ky. 433, 22 S.W. 649.

38. As in Wood v. Commonwealth, 1927, 149 Va. 401, 140 S.E. 114; Greenman v. Smith, 1874, 20 Minn. 418. See Note, 1928, 12 Minn.L.Rev. 405.

Intent
gun /p loaded unloaded /p apprehension fright! /p assault % topic(110) & court(fl)

Assault and Battery
37k1 37k2 % topic(110) title(state people)

§ 11. False Imprisonment

The action for the tort of false imprisonment, sometimes called false arrest, is another lineal descendant of the old action of trespass. It protects the personal interest in freedom from restraint of movement. "Imprisonment," although it seems originally to have meant stone walls and iron bars, no longer signifies incarceration;[1] the plaintiff may be imprisoned when restrained in the open street,[2] or in a traveling automobile,[3] or when confined to an entire city,[4] or compelled to go along with the defendant.[5] The older idea of confinement has persisted, however, in the requirement that the restraint be a total one, rather than a mere obstruction of the right to go where the plaintiff pleases. Thus it is not imprisonment to block the plaintiff's passage in one direction only,[6] or to shut the plaintiff in a room with a reasonable exit open.[7] But it seems clear that too much emphasis has been placed upon the technical name of the tort; such interferences may invade a right which is entitled to protection, and an action may lie for them, though it is not that of false imprisonment.[8] If there is any distinction, it is that false imprisonment, being derived from the action of trespass, may be maintained without proof of actual damage, but in such other actions, proof of some damage may be required.

Since the interest is in a sense a mental one, resembling the apprehension of contact in the assault cases, the Restatement of Torts[9] has taken the position that there can be no imprisonment unless the plaintiff is aware of it at the time, arguing that the right is one of freedom to go where the

§ 11

1. It does, however, include it. St. Louis, Iron Mountain & Southern Railway Co. v. Wilson, 1902, 70 Ark. 136, 66 S.W. 661 (locking plaintiff in a room); Reese v. Julia Sport Wear, 1940, 260 App.Div. 263, 21 N.Y.S.2d 99 (locking employee in a store).

2. Lukas v. J. C. Penney Co., 1963, 233 Or. 345, 378 P.2d 717. Determined as long ago as, 1348, Y.B.Lib. Assis., f. 104, pl. 85. Cf. C. N. Robinson & Co. v. Green, 1906, 148 Ala. 434, 43 So. 797 (island).

3. Cieplinski v. Severn, 1929, 269 Mass. 261, 168 N.E. 722; Jacobson v. Sorenson, 1931, 183 Minn. 425, 236 N.W. 922. Cf. Ward v. Egan, 1935, 64 Can.C.C. 21 (moving train); Turney v. Rhodes, 1930, 42 Ga.App. 104, 155 S.E. 112 (elevator); Regina v. Macquarie, N.S.W.1875, 13 S.C.Rep. 264 (adrift in a boat).

4. Allen v. Fromme, 1910, 141 App.Div. 362, 126 N.Y.S. 520. Cases of confinement within a state, or within the United States, as by wrongful refusal of a passport, have not arisen. One may speculate that, although this may be a tort, it is not false imprisonment, since the line must obviously be drawn somewhere short of confinement to the hemisphere.

5. Brushaber v. Stegemann, 1871, 22 Mich. 266; Goodell v. Tower, 1904, 77 Vt. 61, 58 A. 790; cf. Fotheringham v. Adams Express Co., C.C.Mo.1888, 36 F. 252.

6. Bird v. Jones, 1845, 7 Ad. & El. 742, 115 Eng. Rep. 668 (obstruction of highway); Crossett v. Campbell, 1908, 122 La. 659, 48 So. 141 (expulsion from premises); Great Atlantic & Pacific Tea Co. v. Billups, 1934, 253 Ky. 126, 69 S.W.2d 5 (stopping plaintiff);

Martin v. Lincoln Park West Corp., 7th Cir. 1955, 219 F.2d 622 (locking him out of his room); Marrone v. Washington Jockey Club, 1910, 35 App.D.C. 82, affirmed 1913, 227 U.S. 633, 33 S.Ct. 401, 57 L.Ed. 679 (refusal of admission to race track); Second Restatement of Torts, § 36.

7. Wright v. Wilson, 1699, 1 Ld. Raym. 739, 91 Eng. Rep. 1394; Davis & Alcott Co. v. Boozer, 1926, 215 Ala. 116, 110 So. 28; Furlong v. German-American Press Association, Mo.1916, 189 S.W. 385, 389 ("if a way of escape is left open which is available without peril of life or limb, no imprisonment"). The Second Restatement of Torts, § 136, Comment a, regards the means of escape as unreasonable if it involves exposure of the person, material harm to the clothing, or danger of substantial harm to another.

However, a means of escape may not be a reasonable one if it is unknown to the plaintiff. Compare the debatable decision in Talcott v. National Exhibition Co., 1911, 144 App.Div 337, 128 N.Y.S. 1059.

8. Both Holt, C. J., in Wright v. Wilson, 1699, 1 Ld. Raym. 739, 91 Eng.Rep. 1394, and Patterson, J., in Bird v. Jones, 1845, 7 Ad. & El. 742, 115 Eng.Rep. 668, said that an action on the case might be maintained. Recovery was allowed in Cullen v. Dickinson, 1913, 33 S.D. 27, 144 N.W. 656, where plaintiff was prevented from entering a dance hall. Civil rights statutes have been held to afford a cause of action, as in Amos v. Prom, Inc., N.D.Iowa 1953, 115 F.Supp. 127, where a Negro was excluded from a ballroom.

9. Second Restatement of Torts, § 42. See Note, 1920, 68 U.Pa.L.Rev. 360.

plaintiff pleases, and until the plaintiff is aware of restraint there is no real interference with it; and that the mere dignitary interest in freedom from unconscious confinement is not worthy of redress. One English case [10] supports this position; but it is opposed by a later English dictum [11] as well as three American decisions in cases of children and an incompetent [12] where there was imprisonment, apparently without consciousness of it. Although very few cases ever have considered the point, it would appear that the Restatement is unduly restrictive, at least in denying recovery where, as is certainly possible, substantial damage results to the plaintiff from a confinement of which the plaintiff is unaware at the time.[13] It is at least settled that the imprisonment need not be for more than an appreciable length of time, and that it is not necessary that any damage result from it other than the confinement itself,[14] since the tort is complete with even a brief restraint of the plaintiff's freedom.

As in the case of other torts derived from the old action of trespass, the fact that there has been false imprisonment at all establishes a cause of action for at least nominal damages.[15]

The plaintiff is entitled to compensation [16] for loss of time,[17] for physical discomfort or inconvenience,[18] and for any resulting physical illness or injury to health.[19] Since the injury is in large part a mental one, the plaintiff is entitled to damages for mental suffering, humiliation, and the like.[20] The recoverable damages range farther afield, and extend also to the interruption of the plaintiff's business,[21] the harm to reputation or credit,[22] loss of the company of the plaintiff's family during imprisonment,[23] and expenses, such as attorney's fees, to which the plaintiff has been put by reason of a false arrest.[24] There may also be such special and

10. Herring v. Boyle, 1834, 1 Cr. M. & R. 377, 149 Eng.Rep. 1126.

11. In the opinion of Atkin, L. J., in Meering v. Grahame-White Aviation Co., C.A.1919, 122 L.T.R. 44, 55.

12. Barker v. Washburn, 1911, 200 N.Y. 280, 93 N.E. 958; Commonwealth v. Nickerson, 1861, 87 Mass. (5 Allen) 518; Robalina v. Armstrong, N.Y.1852, 15 Barb. 247.

13. See Prosser, False Imprisonment: Consciousness of Confinement, 1955, 55 Col.L.Rev. 847. Suppose a baby one month old is locked in a bank vault for three days, and suffers serious illness, or even dies, as a result. Is there no tort merely because the child is unaware of the confinement? And if there is a tort, what else but false imprisonment?

14. Strain v. Irwin, 1915, 195 Ala. 414, 70 So. 734 (momentary); Callahan v. Searles, 1894, 78 Hun 238, 28 N.Y.S. 904 (few minutes); Miller v. Ashcraft, 1895, 98 Ky. 314, 32 S.W. 1085, 17 Ky.Law Rep. 894; Moore v. Thompson, 1892, 92 Mich. 498, 52 N.W. 1000; Second Restatement of Torts, § 35.

15. Palmer v. Maine Central Railroad Co., 1899, 92 Me. 399, 42 A. 800; Butcher v. Adams, 1949, 310 Ky. 205, 220 S.W.2d 398; Mason v. Wrightson, 1954, 205 Md. 481, 109 A.2d 128; McLean v. Sanders, 1932, 139 Or. 144, 7 P.2d 981; Noce v. Ritchie, 1930, 109 W.Va. 391, 155 S.E. 127.

16. There are good general statements of the elements of compensatory damages in Duggan v. Baltimore & Ohio Railroad Co., 1893, 159 Pa. 248, 28 A. 182; Beckwith v. Bean, 1878, 98 U.S. 266, 25 L.Ed. 124; Gold v. Campbell, 1909, 54 Tex.Civ.App. 269, 117 S.W. 463; Oliver v. Kessler, Mo.App.1936, 95 S.W.2d 1226.

17. Goodell v. Tower, 1904, 77 Vt. 61, 58 A. 790; Young v. Gormley, 1903, 120 Iowa 372, 94 N.W. 922; Hewlett v. George, 1891, 68 Miss. 703, 9 So. 885.

18. Margaret Ann Super Markets v. Dent, Fla.1953, 64 So.2d 291; Jacques v. Parks, 1902, 96 Me. 268, 52 A. 763; Fox v. McCurnin, 1928, 205 Iowa 752, 218 N.W. 499; Paine v. Kelley, 1907, 197 Mass. 22, 83 N.E. 8.

19. Tierney v. State, 1943, 266 App.Div. 434, 42 N.Y.S.2d 877, affirmed 1944, 292 N.Y. 523, 54 N.E.2d 207; Van Dorn v. Kimball, 1916, 100 Neb. 590, 160 N.W. 953; Bailey v. Warner, 10th Cir. 1902, 118 F. 395 (nervous prostration).

20. Boies v. Raynor, 1961, 89 Ariz. 257, 361 P.2d 1; Schanafelt v. Seaboard Finance Co., 1951, 108 Cal.App. 2d 420, 239 P.2d 42; Great Atlantic & Pacific Tea Co. v. Smith, 1940, 281 Ky. 583, 136 S.W.2d 759; Burke v. Robinson, Mo.App.1925, 271 S.W. 1005; Jones v. Hebdo, 1921, 88 W.Va. 386, 106 S.E. 898.

21. Allen v. Fromme, 1910, 141 App.Div. 362, 126 N.Y.S. 520. Or the loss of particular business opportunities. Bailey v. Warner, 10 Cir. 1902, 118 F. 395; Kenyon v. Hartford Accident & Indemnity Co., 1927, 86 Cal.App. 266, 260 P. 954; Gariety v. Fleming, 1926, 121 Kan. 42, 245 P. 1054.

22. Thompson v. St. Louis & San Francisco Railroad Co., Mo.App.1928, 3 S.W.2d 1033; Hayes v. Hutchinson & Shields, 1914, 81 Wash. 394, 142 P. 865; Margaret Ann Super Markets v. Dent, Fla.1953, 64 So.2d 291.

23. Walling v. Fields, 1923, 209 Ala. 389, 96 So. 471; cf. Gariety v. Fleming, 1926, 121 Kan. 42, 245 P. 1054.

24. Worden v. Davis, 1909, 195 N.Y. 391, 88 N.E. 745; Nelson v. Kellogg, 1912, 162 Cal. 621, 123 P. 1115;

unusual consequential damages as the theft of the plaintiff's automobile when the arrest compels the plaintiff to leave it unguarded.[25] Because of the malevolent intentions which usually accompany false imprisonment, or at least the reckless disregard of the plaintiff's interests, it is usually a proper case for the award of punitive damages;[26] but where any such element of bad intent or wanton misconduct is lacking, and the imprisonment is the result of a mere mistake, either as to identity of the party or as to the propriety of arrest or imprisonment, punitive damages are denied.[27]

Character of Defendant's Act

The restraint may be by means of physical barriers,[28] or by threats of force which intimidate the plaintiff into compliance with orders.[29] It is sufficient that the plaintiff submits to an apprehension of force reasonably to be understood from the conduct of the defendant, although no force is used or even expressly threatened.[30] The plaintiff is not required to incur the risk of personal violence by resisting until it actually is used.[31] It is essential, however, that the restraint be against the plaintiff's will; and if one agrees of one's own free choice to surrender freedom of motion, as by remaining in a room or accompanying another voluntarily, to clear oneself of suspicion or to accommodate the desires of the other,[32] rather than yielding to the constraint of a threat, then there is no imprisonment.[33] This gives rise, in borderline cases, to questions of fact, turning upon the details of the testimony, as to what was reasonably to be understood and implied from the defendant's conduct, tone of voice and the like, which seldom can be reflected fully in an appellate record, and normally are for the jury.[34]

Bolton v. Vellines, 1897, 94 Va. 393, 26 S.E. 847; Schiller v. Strangis, D.Mass.1982, 540 F.Supp. 605.

25. Whitehead v. Stringer, 1919, 106 Wash. 501, 180 P. 486.

26. Atkinson v. Dixie Greyhound Lines, 5th Cir. 1944, 143 F.2d 477, certiorari denied 323 U.S. 758, 65 S.Ct. 92, 89 L.Ed. 607; Lindquist v. Friedman's, 1937, 366 Ill. 232, 8 N.E.2d 625; Sternberg v. Hogg, 1934, 254 Ky. 761, 72 S.W.2d 421; Parrott v. Bank of America National Trust & Savings Association, 1950, 97 Cal.App.2d 14, 217 P.2d 89; McAleer v. Good, 1907, 216 Pa. 473, 65 A. 934. See supra, § 2.

27. Kroger Grocery & Baking Co. v. Waller, 1945, 208 Ark. 1063, 189 S.W.2d 361; Walker v. Tucker, 1955, 131 Colo. 198, 280 P.2d 649; S. H. Kress & Co. v. Powell, 1938, 132 Fla. 471, 180 So. 757; Shelton v. Barry, 1946, 328 Ill.App. 497, 66 N.E.2d 697; Heinze v. Murphy, 1942, 180 Md. 423, 24 A.2d 917.

28. Salisbury v. Poulson, 1918, 51 Utah 552, 172 P. 315; cf. Cieplinski v. Severn, 1929, 269 Mass. 261, 168 N.E. 722 (refusal to stop moving automobile).

29. Meints v. Huntington, 8th Cir. 1921, 276 F. 245; Mahan v. Adam, 1924, 144 Md. 355, 124 A. 901; Garnier v. Squires, 1900, 62 Kan. 321, 62 P. 1005; Second Restatement of Torts, § 40.

30. Stevens v. O'Neill, 1900, 51 App.Div. 364, 64 N.Y.S. 663, affirmed 1902, 169 N.Y. 375, 62 N.E. 424; Hales v. McCrory-McLellan Corp., 1963, 260 N.C. 568, 133 S.E.2d 225; W. T. Grant Co. v. Owens, 1928, 149 Va. 906, 141 S.E. 860; Sinclair Refining Co. v. Meek, 1940, 62 Ga.App. 850, 10 S.E.2d 76; Panisko v. Dreibelbis, 1942, 113 Mont. 310, 124 P.2d 997.

One's belief that one is being restrained by another is not sufficient unless there is reasonable ground to apprehend force upon an attempt to assert liberty. Hoffman v. Clinic Hospital, 1938, 213 N.C. 669, 197 S.E. 161.

31. Brushaber v. Stegemann, 1871, 22 Mich. 266; Meints v. Huntington, 8th Cir. 1921, 276 F. 245; Halliburton–Abbott Co. v. Hodge, 1935, 172 Okl. 175, 44 P.2d 122; and see cases cited in the preceding note.

32. State for Use of Powell v. Moore, 1965, 252 Miss. 471, 174 So.2d 352; Meinecke v. Skaggs, 1950, 123 Mont. 308, 213 P.2d 237; Hunter v. Laurent, 1925, 158 La. 874, 104 So. 747; James v. MacDougall & Southwick Co., 1925, 134 Wash. 314, 235 P. 812. Cf. Great Atlantic & Pacific Tea Co. v. Billups, 1934, 253 Ky. 126, 69 S.W.2d 5.

33. Payson v. Macomber, 1861, 85 Mass. (3 Allen) 69; Sweeney v. F. W. Woolworth Co., 1924, 247 Mass. 277, 142 N.E. 50; Knowlton v. Ross, 1915, 114 Me. 18, 95 A. 281; see Powell v. Champion Fiber Co., 1908, 150 N.C. 12, 63 S.E. 159.

34. Compare Durgin v. Cohen, 1926, 168 Minn. 77, 209 N.W. 532; Lester v. Albers Super Markets, Inc., 1952, 94 Ohio App. 313, 114 N.E.2d 529; and Swetnam v. F. W. Woolworth Co., 1957, 83 Ariz. 189, 318 P.2d 364, where it was held that no implied threat of force was to be found, with Garner v. Mears, 1958, 97 Ga. App. 506, 103 S.E.2d 610, and Jacques v. Childs Dining Hall Co., 1923, 244 Mass. 438, 138 N.E. 843, where the jury were permitted to find it. Also compare, upon almost identical facts, the opposite conclusions in Weiler v. Herzfeld-Phillipson Co., 1926, 189 Wis. 554, 208 N.W. 599 (also Safeway Stores, Inc. v. Amburn, Tex.Civ.App. 1965, 388 S.W.2d 443), and Dillon v. Sears-Roebuck, Inc., 1934, 126 Neb. 357, 253 N.W. 331.

In a substantial number of cases false imprisonment was found where one's freedom of motion was surrendered because of force directed against valuable property, as where a woman remained in a store because her purse was taken,[35] or left a train because her suitcase was removed from it.[36] Beyond this the tort has not been extended, probably because of the confining scope of its origin as a branch of the action of trespass, which required direct and immediate interference with person or property, and the absence of any great necessity for the change. Moral pressure, as where one remains to clear away suspicion of theft,[37] or to avoid a scene on the street,[38] is not enough; nor, as in the case of assault, are threats for the future, as for example, to call the police and have the plaintiff arrested.[39] Any remedy for such wrongs must lie in some other theory, such as intentional infliction of mental distress.[40] It is for such reasons that the action for false imprisonment has remained relatively ineffective as a remedy, particularly for the violation of individual rights by the police.[41]

The restraint upon the plaintiff's freedom may also be imposed by the assertion of legal authority. If the plaintiff submits,[42] or if there is even a momentary taking into the custody of the law,[43] there is an arrest; and if it is without proper legal authority, it is a false arrest, and so false imprisonment.

35. Ashland Dry Goods Co. v. Wages, 1946, 302 Ky. 577, 195 S.W.2d 312. Compare the cases where plaintiff remained with his automobile rather than leave it: National Bond & Investment Co. v. Whithorn, 1938, 276 Ky. 204, 123 S.W.2d 263; Cordell v. Standard Oil Co., 1930, 131 Kan. 221, 289 P. 472; see Verstraelen v. Kellog, 1962, 60 Wn.2d 115, 372 P.2d 543. Also Schanafelt v. Seaboard Finance Co., 1951, 108 Cal.App. 2d 420, 239 P.2d 42; Harnik v. Levine, Mun.Ct.N.Y. 1951, 106 N.Y.S.2d 460, affirmed 1952, 202 Misc. 648, 115 N.Y.S.2d 25, reversed 1953, 281 App.Div. 878, 120 N.Y.S.2d 62, appeal denied 282 App.Div. 684, 122 N.Y.S.2d 817.

36. Griffin v. Clark, 1935, 55 Idaho 364, 42 P.2d 297.

37. Hershey v. O'Neill, C.C.N.Y.1888, 36 F. 168; Hunter v. Laurent, 1925, 158 La. 874, 104 So. 747; James v. MacDougall & Southwick Co., 1925, 134 Wash. 314, 235 P. 812.

38. Fitscher v. Rollman & Sons Co., 1929, 31 Ohio App. 340, 167 N.E. 469. But in Lopez v. Wigwam Department Stores No. 10, 1966, 49 Hawaii 416, 421 P.2d 289 this, under the circumstances, was held sufficient.

39. See supra, § 10. Such threats for the future were held not to constitute imprisonment in Knowlton v. Ross, 1915, 114 Me. 18, 95 A. 281; Sweeney v. F. W. Woolworth Co., 1924, 247 Mass. 277, 142 N.E. 50; Priddy v. Bunton, Tex.Civ.App.1943, 177 S.W.2d 805, error refused; Safeway Stores, Inc. v. Amburn, Tex.Civ.App. 1965, 388 S.W.2d 443; Blumenfeld v. Harris, 1957, 3 A.D.2d 219, 159 N.Y.S.2d 561, affirmed 3 N.Y.2d 905, 167 N.Y.S.2d 925, 145 N.E.2d 871, certiorari denied 356 U.S. 930, 78 S.Ct. 773, 2 L.Ed.2d 761. The case last cited also involved a threat of civil process.

40. Infra, § 12.

41. Foote, Tort Remedies for Police Violations of Individual Rights, 1955, 39 Minn.L.Rev. 493. False imprisonment, however, is often among the theories asserted in civil actions against police. See, e.g., Schiller v. Strangis, D.Mass.1982, 540 F.Supp. 605.

42. Boies v. Raynor, 1961, 89 Ariz. 257, 361 P.2d 1; Martin v. Houck, 1906, 141 N.C. 317, 54 S.E. 291; Pike v. Hanson, 1838, 9 N.H. 491; Hebrew v. Pulis, 1906, 73 N.J.L. 621, 64 A. 121; Lyons v. Worley, 1931, 152 Okl. 57, 4 P.2d 3.

43. It has been held that an arrest by a police officer was complete when the officer laid his hand on the prisoner, although the latter resisted and succeeded in escaping. See Genner v. Sparkes, 1704, 1 Salk. 79, 91 Eng.Rep. 74; Whithead v. Keyes, 1862, 85 Mass. (3 Allen) 495. In Weissengoff v. Davis, 4th Cir. 1919, 260 F. 16, certiorari denied 250 U.S. 674, 40 S.Ct. 54, 63 L.Ed. 1201, a sheriff, with a warrant for the arrest of the defendant, stepped on the running board of his automobile, informed the defendant that he was under arrest, and directed him to stop. It was held that this was as complete an arrest as if the sheriff had touched his person.

There is no arrest where the defendant does not purport to take the plaintiff into custody, but merely directs the plaintiff to appear in court at a future date. Chrestman v. State, 1927, 148 Miss. 673, 114 So. 748; Hart v. Herzig, 1955, 131 Colo. 458, 283 P.2d 177 (invalid summons for violation of game law); City of Toledo v. Lowenberg, 1955, 99 Ohio App. 165, 131 N.E.2d 682 (citation for traffic violation).

Nor is there any arrest when the plaintiff merely goes voluntarily with the officer to the police station, to clear the matter up. Pollack v. City of Newark, D.N.J.1956, 147 F.Supp. 35, affirmed 1957, 248 F.2d 543, certiorari denied 355 U.S. 964, 78 S.Ct. 554, 2 L.Ed. 2d 539, rehearing denied 1960, 362 U.S. 907, 80 S.Ct. 614, 4 L.Ed.2d 558; Foulke v. New York Consolidated Railroad Co., 1917, 180 App.Div. 848, 168 N.Y.S. 72, affirmed 1920, 228 N.Y. 269, 127 N.E. 237.

It is not necessary that the defendant have a warrant,[44] or be an officer,[45] so long as the defendant asserts the legal power to detain the plaintiff, and the plaintiff believes that the authority exists, and yields to it against the plaintiff's own will.[46] The submission may be manifested by "words only," [47] although it may be gathered from the cases that the authority must at least be asserted in the plaintiff's presence, and that a mere submission over the telephone is not enough.[48] Whether the defendant's conduct reasonably implies a claim of legal authority, and an intent to detain the plaintiff under it, is of course entirely a matter of the circumstances of the particular case. The presence of a policeman who questions the plaintiff,[49] or the bare assertion that authority to arrest exists in the defendant, without the defendant's purporting to exercise it by taking the plaintiff into custody,[50] is not imprisonment, so long as no present restraint of liberty is implied. And if the plaintiff does not submit, but seeks to resist or escape, actual force must be used before the arrest is complete.[51]

The restraint may consist in the intentional breach of a duty to take active steps to release the plaintiff from a confinement in which the plaintiff has already properly been placed—as, for example, a failure to let the plaintiff out at the end of a sentence to a term in jail,[52] or to produce the plaintiff in court promptly after an arrest.[53] Such a duty has been found in one case where the confinement was entered into voluntarily upon an assurance of release,[54] and in another where it was caused by the innocent acts of the parties.[55] It seems reasonable to say that whenever a legal duty to release another from confinement can be made out, an intentional refusal to do so is sufficient for false imprisonment;[56] but of course without such a duty there is no such tort.[57] Recovery has been denied in several cases where

44. Wood v. Lane, 1834, 6 C. & P. 774, 172 Eng. Rep. 1458.

45. Whitman v. Atchison, Topeka & Santa Fe Railway Co., 1911, 85 Kan. 150, 116 P. 234 (railroad conductor detaining plaintiff by asserion that he had authority to require a statement as to an accident); Daniel v. Phillips Petroleum Co., 1934, 229 Mo.App. 150, 73 S.W.2d 355 (filling station attendant).

46. Pike v. Hanson, 1838, 9 N.H. 491; Hebrew v. Pulis, 1906, 73 N.J.L. 621, 64 A. 121; Worden v. Davis, 1909, 195 N.Y. 391, 88 N.E. 745; Johnson v. Norfolk & Western Railway Co., 1918, 82 W.Va. 692, 97 S.E. 189; Lyons v. Worley, 1931, 152 Okl. 57, 4 P.2d 3.

47. Haskins v. Young, 1837, 19 N.C. 527; Jones v. Jones, 1852, 35 N.C. (13 Ired.) 448.

48. Second Restatement of Torts, § 41, Comment *f*.

49. Knowlton v. Ross, 1915, 114 Me. 18, 95 A. 281; Durgin v. Cohen, 1926, 168 Minn. 77, 209 N.W. 532; State ex rel. Sovine v. Stone, 1965, 149 W.Va. 310, 140 S.E.2d 801.

50. Hill v. Taylor, 1883, 50 Mich. 549, 15 N.W. 899; Simpson v. Hill, 1793, 1 Esp. 431, 170 Eng.Rep. 409.

51. Genner v. Sparkes, 1704, 1 Salk. 79, 91 Eng. Rep. 74; Russen v. Lucas, 1824, 1 Car. & P. 153, 171 Eng.Rep. 1141. Cf. Horner v. Battyn, Buller N.P. 62.

52. Withers v. Henley, 1614, Cro.Jac. 379, 79 Eng. Rep. 392; Weigel v. McCloskey, 1914, 113 Ark. 1, 166 S.W. 944; Birdsall v. Lewis, 1936, 246 App.Div. 132, 285 N.Y.S. 146, affirmed 271 N.Y. 592, 3 N.E.2d 200 (one day over sentence); Shakespeare v. City of Pasadena, 1964, 230 Cal.App.2d 375, 40 Cal.Rptr. 863 (admitted to bail); Whirl v. Kern, 5th Cir. 1969, 407 F.2d 781, certiorari denied 396 U.S. 901, 90 S.Ct. 210, 243 L.Ed.2d 177.

Cf. Geddes v. Daughters of Charity of St. Vincent De Paul, Inc., 5th Cir. 1965, 348 F.2d 144 (failure to release mental patient).

53. Thurston v. Leno, 1964, 124 Vt. 298, 204 A.2d 106; Ames v. Strain, Okl.1956, 301 P.2d 641; Lincoln v. Grazer, 1958, 163 Cal.App.2d 758, 329 P.2d 928; Doherty v. Shea, 1946, 320 Mass. 173, 68 N.E.2d 707; Kleidon v. Glascock, 1943, 215 Minn. 417, 10 N.W.2d 394. Cf. Hall v. State ex rel. Freeman, 1944, 114 Ind.App. 328, 52 N.E.2d 370 (taking to distant jail); Matovina v. Hult, 1955, 125 Ind.App. 236, 123 N.E.2d 893 (delay in obtaining warrant for further detention).

The unlawful imprisonment is a continuing trespass. Bennett v. Austro-Americana Steamship Co., 1914, 161 App.Div. 753, 147 N.Y.S. 193; Brush v. Lindsay, 1924, 210 App.Div. 361, 206 N.Y.S. 304; Note, 1925, 25 Col.L. Rev. 505.

54. Whittaker v. Sandford, 1912, 110 Me. 77, 85 A. 399; Second Restatement of Torts, § 45. Cf. Cieplinski v. Severn, 1929, 269 Mass. 261, 168 N.E. 722; C. N. Robinson & Co. v. Green, 1906, 148 Ala. 434, 43 So. 797.

55. Talcott v. National Exhibition Co., 1911, 144 App.Div. 337, 128 N.Y.S. 1059 (baseball park failing to inform business visitor of exit, after main entrance closed because of crowd).

56. As, for example, where an invitee in a department store is accidentally locked in the washroom.

57. Schichowski v. Hoffmann, 1933, 261 N.Y. 389, 185 N.E. 676 affirmed 236 App.Div. 653, 257 N.Y.S. 920

the plaintiff had good reason to know, when voluntarily entering the confinement, that the defendant did not intend to assist the plaintiff to escape.[58] For example, a workman who goes down in a mine with the understanding that there will be no opportunity to return to the surface until a definite hour, cannot complain, in the absence of some emergency that would alter the terms of the bargain, when the hoist is not operated sooner.[59]

One who participates in an unlawful arrest,[60] or procures or instigates the making of one without proper authority,[61] will be liable for the consequences; but the defendant must have taken some active part in bringing about the unlawful arrest itself, by some "affirmative direction, persuasion, request or voluntary participation." [62] There is no liability for merely giving information to legal authorities, who are left entirely free to use their own judgment,[63] or for identifying the plaintiff as the person wanted,[64] or requesting a proper arrest when an officer makes an improper one instead,[65] or swearing to a complaint before a magistrate who turns out not to have jurisdiction.[66] The remedy in such cases, if any, is by an action for malicious prosecution.[67]

Intent and Motive

Given the derivation of false imprisonment from the common law action of trespass, it seems likely that intent to cause any of the types of intrusions encompassed by the action for trespass to person (assault, battery, or confinement) will satisfy the intent element of the cause of action for false imprisonment,[68] but authority to the contrary can be found. For example, it has been said that there is no false imprisonment unless the defendant intends to cause a confinement.[69] There may, however, be liability for any negligence in such a case, if actual dam-

---

(refusal to produce corporate books to obtain plaintiff's release from confinement for contempt). See Notes, 1934, 7 So.Cal.L.Rev. 102; 1914, 23 Yale L.J. 607.

58. Spoor v. Spooner, 1847, 53 Mass. (12 Metc.) 281 (plaintiff went on boat about to sail); Moses v. Dubois, S.C. 1838, Dud. 209 (same); Balmain New Ferry Co. v. Robertson, Aust.1905, 4 Comm.L.Rep. 379 (entering ferry wharf with notice no exit until payment); Burns v. Johnston, [1916] 2 Ir.Rep. 444, affirmed [1917] 2 Ir. Rep. 137 (going to work in factory with notice no exit during working hours). Cf. Timmons v. Fulton Bag & Cotton Mills, 1932, 45 Ga.App. 670, 166 S.E. 40.

59. Herd v. Weardale Steel, Coal & Coke Co., [1913] 3 K.B. 771, [1915] A.C. 67. See Amos, Contractual Restraint of Liberty, 1928, 44 L.Q.Rev. 464.

60. Cook v. Hastings, 1907, 150 Mich. 289, 114 N.W. 71; Parker v. Roberts, 1925, 99 Vt. 219, 131 A. 21; Howard v. Burton, 1953, 338 Mich. 178, 61 N.W.2d 77; Kearley v. Cowan, 1928, 217 Ala. 295, 116 So. 145; Monk v. Ehret, 1923, 192 Cal. 186, 219 P. 452. As to participation in the detention of the mentally ill, see Note, [1966] Wash.U.L.Q. 193.

61. Minor v. Seliga, 1958, 168 Ohio St. 1, 150 N.E.2d 852; Jillson v. Caprio, 1950, 86 U.S.App.D.C. 168, 181 F.2d 523; McDermott v. W. T. Grant Co., 1943, 313 Mass. 736, 49 N.E.2d 115; Winters v. Campbell, 1964, 148 W.Va. 710, 137 S.E.2d 188; Knupp v. Esslinger, Mo.App.1962, 363 S.W.2d 210; Second Restatement of Torts § 45A.

Cf. Kettelhut v. Edwards, 1919, 65 Colo. 506, 177 P. 961 (ratification); Leon's Shoe Stores v. Hornsby, Tex. Civ.App.1957, 306 S.W.2d 402 (failure to disclose facts). See Note, 1959, 35 Ind.L.J. 80.

62. Edgar v. Omaha Public Power District, 1958, 166 Neb. 452, 89 N.W.2d 238.

63. Burlington Transportation Co. v. Josephson, 8th Cir. 1946, 153 F.2d 372; Ingo v. Koch, 2d Cir. 1942, 127 F.2d 667; Gogue v. MacDonald, 1950, 35 Cal.2d 482, 218 P.2d 542; Gooch v. Wachowiak, 1958, 352 Mich. 347, 89 N.W.2d 496; Hoock v. S. S. Kresge Co., Mo. 1950, 230 S.W.2d 758.

But one who knowingly gives false information to a police officer becomes liable for the false arrest. Jensen v. Barnett, 1965, 178 Neb. 429, 134 N.W.2d 53; Wehrman v. Liberty Petroleum Co., Mo.App.1964, 382 S.W.2d 56.

64. Miller v. Fano, 1901, 134 Cal. 103, 66 P. 183; Bisgaard v. Duvall, 1915, 169 Iowa 711, 151 N.W. 1051; Turner v. Mellon, 1953, 41 Cal.2d 45, 257 P.2d 15; Heinold v. Muntz T. V., Inc., Mo.1953, 262 S.W.2d 32.

65. Lemmon v. King, 1915, 95 Kan. 524, 148 P. 750; Central Motor Co. v. Roberson, Tex.Civ.App.1941, 154 S.W.2d 180, affirmed 1942, Burton v. Roberson, 139 Tex. 562, 164 S.W.2d 524.

66. Gifford v. Wiggins, 1892, 50 Minn. 401, 52 N.W. 904; Smith v. Clark, 1910, 37 Utah 116, 106 P. 653. Otherwise if the defendant knows or should know of the lack of jurisdiction. Pomeranz v. Class, 1927, 82 Colo. 173, 257 P. 1086; Tiede v. Fuhr, 1915, 264 Mo. 622, 175 S.W. 910.

67. See infra, § 119.

68. See supra, § 8.

69. See Wood v. Cummings, 1908, 197 Mass. 80, 83 N.E. 318; Second Restatement of Torts, § 35; also § 43, approving the rule as to transferred intent found

age results.[70] It has been held that a mere incidental confinement due to acts directed at another purpose—as, for instance, locking the door with the plaintiff inside for the sole purpose of keeping others out—[71] is not a sufficiently important invasion of the plaintiff's interests to require the protection of the law. Since in such a case the defendant is aware that the conduct is certain to result in the confinement, it can scarcely be said that the defendant did not intend it; a better justification would appear to lie not in any lack of intent, but in a privilege to proceed reasonably about the defendant's own affairs.[72]

Even if intent to confine the individual is necessary, it need not be with knowledge of who the plaintiff is; and, as in the case of other intentional interferences with person or property, an innocent, and quite reasonable, mistake of identity will not avoid liability.[73] Although intent is necessary, malice, in the sense of ill will or a desire to injure, is not.[74] There may be liability although the defendant believed in good faith that the arrest was justified,[75] or that the defendant was acting for the plaintiff's own good.[76] The presence or absence of malice may, however, be shown in aggravation[77] or mitigation[78] of damages. Nor is probable cause a defense,[79] except in so far as it may serve to validate the arrest itself,[80] or to justify a defense of person or property.[81] The defendant, merely because believing that an arrest is called for or warranted, is not permitted to take the law into the defendant's own hands, but must resort to proper legal measures.[82] Once the fact of imprisonment is established, the burden is upon the defendant to show legal justification.[83]

Distinguished from Malicious Prosecution

The kindred action of malicious prosecution protects interests closely related to

---

in the battery cases, where the intent is to imprison a third person.

70. Second Restatement of Torts, § 35, Comment h. Compare, as to negligence causing arrest: Mouse v. Central Savings & Trust Co., 1929, 120 Ohio St. 599, 167 N.E. 868; Weaver v. Bank of America National Trust & Savings Association, 1963, 59 Cal.2d 428, 30 Cal.Rptr. 4, 380 P.2d 644; Collins v. City National Bank & Trust Co. of Danbury, 1944, 131 Conn. 167, 38 A.2d 582.

71. Wood v. Cummings, 1908, 197 Mass. 80, 83 N.E. 318. Cf. Williams v. Powell, 1869, 101 Mass. 467; Spoor v. Spooner, 1847, 53 Mass. (12 Metc.) 281; Moses v. Dubois, S.C.1838, Dud. 209.

72. Suppose a custodian, whose duty it is to lock up a library at 10 o'clock to keep people out, decides to lock it up at 9 o'clock instead, and locks in those who refuse to leave. Is there any doubt that it is false imprisonment?

73. Holmes v. Blyler, 1890, 80 Iowa 365, 45 N.W. 756; West v. Cabell, 1893, 153 U.S. 78, 14 S.Ct. 752, 38 L.Ed. 643. Cf. Garvin v. Muir, Ky.1957, 306 S.W.2d 256 (jailor confining plaintiff without knowledge of absence of valid order).

74. Colter v. Lower, 1871, 35 Ind. 285; Garnier v. Squires, 1900, 62 Kan. 321, 62 P. 1005; Casserly v. Wheeler, 9th Cir. 1922, 282 F. 389; Wilson v. Lapham, 1923, 196 Iowa 745, 195 N.W. 235; Hall v. Rice, 1929, 117 Neb. 813, 223 N.W. 4. See Ashton, Motive as an Essential Element in the Crime of False Imprisonment, 1934, 38 Dick.L.Rev. 184, 187.

75. West v. Cabell, 1893, 153 U.S. 78, 14 S.Ct. 752, 38 L.Ed. 643; Holmes v. Blyler, 1890, 80 Iowa 365, 45 N.W. 756; Oxford v. Berry, 1918, 204 Mich. 197, 170 N.W. 83; Johnson v. Norfolk & Western Railway Co., 1918, 82 W.Va. 692, 97 S.E. 189.

76. Maxwell v. Maxwell, 1920, 189 Iowa 7, 177 N.W. 541; Keleher v. Putnam, 1880, 60 N.H. 30.

77. Phillips v. Morrow, 1923, 210 Ala. 34, 97 So. 130; Bolton v. Vellines, 1897, 94 Va. 393, 26 S.E. 847; Jones v. Hebdo, 1921, 88 W.Va. 386, 106 S.E. 898; Nappi v. Wilson, 1926, 22 Ohio App. 520, 155 N.E. 151, motion overruled; Note, 1927, 1 U.Cin.L.Rev. 364.

78. Roth v. Smith, 1870, 54 Ill. 431; Beckwith v. Bean, 1878, 98 U.S. 266, 25 L.Ed. 124; Landrum v. Wells, 1894, 7 Tex.Civ.App. 625, 26 S.W. 1001; Holmes v. Blyler, 1890, 80 Iowa 365, 45 N.W. 756.

79. Nelson v. Kellogg, 1912, 162 Cal. 621, 123 P. 1115; Lewis v. Montgomery Ward & Co., 1936, 144 Kan. 656, 62 P.2d 875; Titus v. Montgomery Ward & Co., 1938, 232 Mo.App. 987, 123 S.W.2d 574; Hostetler v. Carter, 1918, 73 Okl. 125, 175 P. 244; Fleischer v. Ensminger, 1922, 140 Md. 604, 118 A. 153.

80. See infra, § 26.

81. See infra, §§ 19–21.

82. Kroeger v. Passmore, 1908, 36 Mont. 504, 93 P. 805; Salisbury v. Poulson, 1918, 51 Utah 552, 172 P. 315.

83. Snead v. Bonnoil, 1901, 166 N.Y. 325, 59 N.E. 899; Joseph v. Meier & Frank Co., 1926, 120 Or. 117, 250 P. 739.

those involved in false imprisonment,[84] and sometimes the two are confused by the courts.[85] Malicious prosecution is the groundless institution of criminal proceedings against the plaintiff. False imprisonment fell within the action of trespass, as a direct interference with the plaintiff's person, while malicious prosecution was regarded as more indirect, and the remedy for it was an action on the case.[86] The distinction between the two lies in the existence of valid legal authority for the restraint imposed. If the defendant complies with the formal requirements of the law, as by swearing out a valid warrant, so that the arrest of the plaintiff is legally authorized, the defendant is not responsible for the acts of the court and its officers.[87] The defendant is therefore liable, if at all, only for a misuse of legal process to effect a valid arrest for an improper purpose. The action must be for malicious prosecution, upon proof of malice and want of probable cause,[88] as well as termination of the proceeding in favor of the plaintiff.[89] The weight of modern authority is that where the defendant has attempted to comply with legal requirements, and has failed to do so through no fault of the defendant's own, false imprisonment will not lie, and the remedy is malicious prosecution.[90] The policy is to give the defendant the privilege of making reasonable efforts to bring the case properly before the court, without liability unless the defendant's reason for doing so is an improper one.[91]

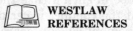

WESTLAW REFERENCES

168k1 168k2

topic(168) & car automobile auto vehicle truck /p confin! restrain! block*** stop**** % topic(110) title(state people)

Character of Defendant's Act

topic(168) & threat! apprehen! /s force restrain!

Intent and Motive

second /s restatement /s torts /s 35 & "false imprisonment"

Distinguished from Malicious Prosecution

topic(249) & malice & "probable cause" & termination result outcome /s proceeding* case /s plaintiff

---

§ 12. Infliction of Mental Distress

Notwithstanding early recognition of a cause of action in assault cases, the law has been slow to accept the interest in peace of

---

84. See Harper, Malicious Prosecution, False Imprisonment and Defamation, 1937, 15 Tex.L.Rev. 157; and see, as to malicious prosecution, infra, § 119.

85. See for example Neall v. Hart, 1886, 115 Pa. 347, 8 A. 628; Stewart v. Cooley, 1877, 23 Minn. 347. The frequency of such confusion is pointed out in Rich v. McInerny, 1894, 103 Ala. 345, 15 So. 663.

86. 1 Street Foundations of Legal Liability, 1906, 12; Kramer v. Lott, 1865, 50 Pa. 495, 498; Colter v. Lower, 1871, 35 Ind. 285.

87. Brown v. Chapman, 1848, 6 C.B. 365, 136 Eng. Rep. 1292; Sheppard v. Furniss, 1851, 19 Ala. 760; Damilitis v. Kerjas Lunch Corp., 1937, 165 Misc. 186, 300 N.Y.S. 574.

88. Nesmith v. Alford, 5th Cir. 1963, 318 F.2d 110, rehearing denied 319 F.2d 859, cert. denied 1964, 375 U.S. 975, 84 S.Ct. 489, 11 L.Ed.2d 420; Genito v. Rabinowitz, 1966, 93 N.J.Super. 225, 225 A.2d 590; S. H. Kress & Co. v. Powell, 1938, 132 Fla. 471, 180 So. 757; Riegel v. Hygrade Seed Co., W.D.N.Y.1942, 47 F.Supp. 290; Wilson v. Lapham, 1923, 196 Iowa 745, 195 N.W. 235. But in the event of an improper arrest and other proceedings, both actions may lie. Young v. Andrews Hardwood Co., 1931, 200 N.C. 310, 156 S.E. 501.

89. Frisbie v. Morris, 1903, 75 Conn. 637, 55 A. 9; Lowe v. Wartman, 1885, 47 N.J.L. 413, 1 A. 489. Such proof is not necessary in a false imprisonment action. Boesch v. Kick, 1922, 98 N.J.L. 183, 119 A. 1; Davis v. Johnson, Va.1900, 42 C.C.A. 111, 101 F. 952; Barry v. Third Avenue Railroad Co., 1900, 51 App.Div. 385, 64 N.Y.S. 615. See Note, 1923, 21 Mich.L.Rev. 704.

90. Langford v. Boston & Albany Railroad Co., 1887, 144 Mass. 431, 11 N.E. 697; Utz v. Mayes, Mo. App.1925, 267 S.W. 59, certiorari to set aside judgment and opinion quashed, 1926, 287 S.W. 606; Nelson v. Hill, 1924, 30 N.M. 288, 232 P. 526. Contra: Krause v. Spiegel, 1892, 94 Cal. 370, 29 P. 707; Satilla Manufacturing Co. v. Cason, 1895, 98 Ga. 14, 25 S.E. 909. See Notes, 1925, 34 Yale L.J. 908; 1927, 11 Minn.L.Rev. 678.

91. "This exemption of the litigant from any liability for false imprisonment extends even to cases in which the court ordering the imprisonment has acted without jurisdiction. It is the right of every litigant to bring his case before the court, and it is for the court to know the limits of its own jurisdiction and to keep within them." Salmond, Law of Torts, 13th Ed. 1961, 309, citing Carratt v. Morley, 1841, 1 Q.B. 18; West v. Smallwood, 1838, 3 M. & W. 418, 150 Eng.Rep. 1208; Brown v. Chapman, 1848, 6 C.B. 365, 136 Eng.Rep. 1292.

mind as entitled to independent legal protection, even as against intentional invasions. Not until comparatively recent decades has the infliction of mental distress served as the basis of an action, apart from any other tort. In this respect, the law is clearly in a process of growth, the ultimate limits of which cannot as yet be determined.[1]

Various reasons have been advanced for this reluctance to redress mental injuries. One is the difficulty of proof, or of measurement of the damages.[2] "Mental pain or anxiety," said Lord Wensleydale in a famous English case, "the law cannot value, and does not pretend to redress, when the unlawful act causes that alone."[3] It was regarded as something "metaphysical," "too subtle and speculative to be capable of admeasurement by any standard known to the law."[4] But mental suffering is scarcely more difficult of proof, and certainly no harder to estimate in terms of money, than the physical pain of a broken leg, which never has been denied compensation.[5] Indeed, long before the dramatic inflation of the 1970's had its impact, courts were quite willing to allow very substantial sums as damages for such "mental anguish" itself, where it accompanied a slight physical injury.[6] And it is well recognized that mental anguish may be a substantial element in an award for a severe injury.[7]

Again, it has been said that mental consequences are so evanescent, intangible, and peculiar, and vary to such an extent with the individual concerned, that they cannot be anticipated, and so lie outside the boundaries of any reasonable "proximate" connection with the act of the defendant.[8] It is not difficult to discover in the earlier opinions a distinctly masculine astonishment that any woman should ever allow herself to be

§ 12

1. The progress of the law through the first half of this century may be traced in the following series of articles: Bohlen, Right to Recover for Injury Resulting from Negligence Without Impact, 1902, 41 Am.L.Reg.,N.S., 141; Throckmorton, Damages for Fright, 1921, 34 Harv.L.Rev. 260, 57 Am.L.Rev. 828, 153 L.T. 24, 89; Goodrich, Emotional Disturbance as Legal Damage, 1922, 20 Mich.L.Rev. 497; Bohlen and Polikoff, Liability in Pennsylvania for Physical Effects of Fright, 1932, 80 U.Pa.L.Rev. 627; Bohlen and Polikoff, Liability in New York for the Physical Consequences of Emotional Disturbance, 1932, 32 Col.L.Rev. 409; Hallen, Damages for Physical Injuries Resulting from Fright or Shock, 1933, 19 Va.L.Rev. 253; Hallen, Hill v. Kimball—A Milepost in the Law, 1933, 12 Tex.L.Rev. 1; Green, "Fright" Cases, 1933, 27 Ill.L.Rev. 761, 873; Magruder, Mental and Emotional Disturbance in the Law of Torts, 1936, 49 Harv.L.Rev. 1033; Harper and McNeely, A Re-examination of the Basis for Liability for Emotional Disturbance, [1938] Wis.L.Rev. 426. See also the excellent summary in the Report of the New York State Law Revision Commission, Study Relating to Liability for Injuries Resulting from Fright or Shock, 1936, Legislative Doc.No.65(E). Also see infra, n. 25.

2. Bohlen, Right to Recover for Injury Resulting from Negligence Without Impact, 1902, 41 Am.L.Reg., N.S., 141, 143, attributes this in part to the early rule that the parties themselves were not competent witnesses.

3. Lynch v. Knight, 1861, 9 H.L.C. 577, 598, 11 Eng. Rep. 854, continuing: "Though where a material damage occurs, and is connected with it, it is impossible a jury, in estimating it, should altogether overlook the feelings of the party interested."

4. Mitchell v. Rochester Railway Co., 1896, 151 N.Y. 107, 45 N.E. 354; Cleveland, Cincinnati, Chicago & St. Louis Railway Co. v. Stewart, 1899, 24 Ind.App. 374, 56 N.E. 917; Chicago, Burlington & Quincy Railroad Co. v. Gelvin, 8th Cir. 1916, 238 F. 14.

5. McCormick, Damages, 1935, 315, 316; Pennsylvania Railroad Co. v. Allen, 1866, 53 Pa. 276; Fry v. Dubuque & Southwestern Railway Co., 1877, 45 Iowa 416. "As all pain is mental and centers in the brain, it follows that as an element of damage for personal injury the injured party is allowed to recover for actual suffering of mind and body when they are the immediate and necessary consequence of the negligent injury." Hargis v. Knoxville Power Co., 1917, 175 N.C. 31, 94 S.E. 702, 703. As to the difficulty of distinguishing the two, see Nashville, Chattanooga & St. Louis Railway Co. v. Miller, 1904, 120 Ga. 453, 47 S.E. 959.

6. Craker v. Chicago & Northwestern Railway Co., 1875, 36 Wis. 657 ($1,000 to school teacher who was kissed for "terror and anguish, her outraged feeling and insulted virtue, her mental humiliation and suffering"); Draper v. Baker, 1884, 61 Wis. 450, 21 N.W. 527 ($1,200 for spitting in the face). See Magruder, Mental and Emotional Disturbance in the Law of Torts, 1936, 49 Harv.L.Rev. 1033, 1034.

7. See Anderson v. Sears, Roebuck & Co., E.D.La. 1974, 377 F.Supp. 136.

8. See Victorian Railway Commissioners v. Coultas, 1888, 13 App.Cas. 222; Mitchell v. Rochester Railway Co., 1896, 151 N.Y. 107, 45 N.E. 354; Braun v. Craven, 1898, 175 Ill. 401, 51 N.E. 657; Chittick v. Philadelphia Rapid Transit Co., 1909, 224 Pa. 13, 73 A. 4.

frightened or shocked into a miscarriage. But medical science has recognized long since that not only fright and shock, but also grief, anxiety, rage and shame, are in themselves "physical" injuries, in the sense that they produce well marked changes in the body, and symptoms that are readily visible to the professional eye.[9] Such consequences are the normal, rather than the unusual, result of a threat of physical harm, and of many other tyes of conduct; if they are held to be beyond the scope of legal cause, the reason must be something other than unforeseeability.[10]

The most cogent objection to the protection of such interests lies in the "wide door" which might be opened, not only to fictitious claims, but to litigation in the field of trivialities and mere bad manners.[11] It would be absurd for the law to seek to secure universal peace of mind, and many interferences with it must of necessity be left to other agencies of social control. "Against a large part of the frictions and irritations and clashing of temperaments incident to participation in a community life, a certain toughening of the mental hide is a better protection than the law could ever be." [12] But this is a poor reason for denying recovery for any genuine, serious mental injury. It is the business of the law to remedy wrongs that deserve it, even at the expense of a "flood of litigation," and it is a pitiful confession of incompetence on the part of any court of justice to deny relief on such grounds.[13] That a multiplicity of actions may follow is not a persuasive objection; if injuries are multiplied, actions should be multiplied, so injured persons may have recompense.[14] So far as distinguishing true claims from false ones is concerned, what is required is rather a careful scrutiny of the evidence supporting the claim;[15] and the elimination of trivialities calls for nothing more than the same common sense which has distinguished serious from trifling injuries in other fields of the law.[16]

Type of Injury Redressed

The early cases refused all remedy for mental injury, unless it could be brought within the scope of some already recognized tort. Thus it was held that mere words, however violent, threatening or insulting, did not constitute an assault, and hence afforded no ground for redress.[17] It might

---

9. See Goodrich, Emotional Disturbance as Legal Damage, 1922, 20 Mich.L.Rev. 497, listing, upon medical authority, a variety of physical symptoms, from accelerated pulse to pyorrhea; Tibbetts, Neurasthenia, the Result of Nervous Shock, as a Ground for Damages, 1904, 59 Cent.L.J. 83; Earengey, The Legal Consequences of Shock, 1934, 2 Medico-Legal & Crim.Rec. 14; Crile, The Origin and Nature of the Emotions, 1915; Chiuchiolo v. New England Wholesale Tailors, 1930, 84 N.H. 329, 150 A. 540.

10. See infra, § 43.

11. Mitchell v. Rochester Railway Co., 1896, 151 N.Y. 107, 45 N.E. 354; Spade v. Lynn & Boston Railroad Co., 1897, 168 Mass. 285, 288, 47 N.E. 88, 89; Huston v. Freemansburg Borough, 1905, 212 Pa. 548, 61 A. 1022; Ward v. West Jersey & Sea Shore Railroad Co., 1900, 65 N.J.L. 383, 47 A. 561. See Throckmorton, Damages for Fright, 1921, 34 Harv.L.Rev. 260, 276, 57 Am.L.Rev. 828, 153 L.T. 24, 89.

12. Magruder, Mental and Emotional Disturbance in the Law of Torts, 1936, 49 Harv.L.Rev. 1033, 1035.

13. Simone v. Rhode Island Co., 1907, 28 R.I. 186, 195, 66 A. 202, 206; Kenney v. Wong Len, 1925, 81 N.H. 427, 128 A. 343; Green v. T. A. Shoemaker & Co., 1909, 111 Md. 69, 73 A. 688; Alabama Fuel & Iron Co. v. Baladoni, 1916, 15 Ala.App. 316, 73 So. 205.

14. Holt, C. J., in Ashby v. White, 1703, 2 Ld.Raym. 938, 955, 92 Eng.Rep. 126.

15. Compare the holding that substantial verdicts for personal injuries will not be sustained where the evidence consists entirely of subjective testimony on the part of the plaintiff. Johnson v. Great Northern Railway Co., 1909, 107 Minn. 285, 119 N.W. 1061; Sprogis v. Butler, 1919, 40 Cal.App. 647, 181 P. 246; Paderas v. Stauffer, 1929, 10 La.App. 50, 119 So. 757, 120 So. 886; City of Pawhuska v. Crutchfield, 1932, 155 Okl. 222, 8 P.2d 685. And see Johnson v. Sampson, 1926, 167 Minn. 203, 207, 208 N.W. 814, 816.

16. Goodrich, Emotional Disturbance as Legal Damage, 1922, 20 Mich.L.Rev. 497, 512. Compare Rogers v. Elliott, 1888, 146 Mass. 349, 15 N.E. 768, holding that a church bell is not a nuisance, even though it throws plaintiff into convulsions; and similar cases cited infra, § 89.

17. State v. Daniel, 1904, 136 N.C. 571, 48 S.E. 544; Grayson v. St. Louis Transit Co., 1903, 100 Mo.App. 60, 71 S.W. 730; Hixson v. Slocum, 1913, 156 Ky. 487, 161 S.W. 522; Kramer v. Ricksmeier, 1913, 159 Iowa 48, 139 N.W. 1091; Brooker v. Silverthorne, 1918, 111 S.C. 553, 99 S.E. 350.

well be inquired why the trespass action for assault, which was a remedy designed to keep the peace, never was extended to words which were more insulting, unendurable, and generally provocative than blows. Perhaps it was the proximity of the criminal law, with its fixed notion that assault must always be something in the nature of an attempted battery. In any event, the result was a rule which permitted recovery for a gesture that might frighten the plaintiff for a moment, and denied it for menacing words which kept the plaintiff in terror for a month. But if some independent tort, such as assault,[18] battery,[19] false imprisonment,[20] or seduction [21] could be made out, the cause of action served as a peg upon which to hang the mental damages, and recovery was freely permitted. Such "parasitic" damages were the entering wedge.[22]

It has gradually become recognized that there is no magic inherent in the name given to a tort, or in any arbitrary classification,[23] and that the infliction of mental injury may be a cause of action in itself. Its limits are as yet ill defined, but it has been extended to its greatest length in the case of intentional [24] infliction of mental suffering by conduct of a flagrant character, the enormity of which adds especial weight to the plaintiff's claim, and is in itself an important guarantee that the mental disturbance which follows is serious and not feigned.[25]

Insult and Indignity

The earliest appearance of anything like a separate cause of action for the intentional infliction of mental suffering was in cases holding a common carrier liable for insulting a passenger.[26] The justification first advanced was that of breach of an "implied contract" to be polite; [27] but the liability was soon imposed where a prospective passenger had not yet bought a ticket,[28] and the later decisions rest the liability upon the special obligation of the carrier to the public, and

---

18. Trogdon v. Terry, 1916, 172 N.C. 540, 90 S.E. 583; Kline v. Kline, 1902, 158 Ind. 602, 64 N.E. 9; Holdorf v. Holdorf, 1918, 185 Iowa 838, 169 N.W. 737; Allen v. Hannaford, 1926, 138 Wash. 423, 244 P. 700.

19. Williams v. Underhill, 1901, 63 App.Div. 223, 71 N.Y.S. 291; Draper v. Baker, 1884, 61 Wis. 450, 21 N.W. 527.

20. Gadsden General Hospital v. Hamilton, 1925, 212 Ala. 531, 103 So. 553; Fisher v. Rumler, 1927, 239 Mich. 224, 214 N.W. 310.

21. Anthony v. Norton, 1899, 60 Kan. 341, 56 P. 529; Haeissig v. Decker, 1918, 139 Minn. 422, 166 N.W. 1085.

22. "The treatment of any element of damages as a parasitic factor belongs essentially to a transitory stage of legal evolution. A factor which is today recognized as parasitic will, forsooth, tomorrow be recognized as an independent basis of liability. It is merely a question of social, economic and industrial needs as those needs are reflected in the organic law." 1 Street, Foundations of Legal Liability, 1906, 460, 470.

23. Smith, Torts Without Particular Names, 1921, 69 U.Pa.L.Rev. 91; Winfield, The Foundation of Liability in Tort, 1927, 27 Col.L.Rev. 1.

24. As to negligently caused mental disturbance, see infra, § 54.

25. The classic article on the subject is Magruder, Mental and Emotional Disturbance in the Law of Torts, 1936, 49 Harv.L.Rev. 1033. See also Prosser, Insult and Outrage, 1956, 44 Cal.L.Rev. 40; Wade, Tort Liability for Abusive and Insulting Language, 1951, 4 Vand.L.Rev. 63; Prosser, Intentional Infliction of Mental Suffering: A New Tort, 1939, 37 Mich.L.Rev. 874; Vold, Tort Recovery for Intentional Infliction of Emotional Distress, 1939, 18 Neb.L.B. 222; Borda, One's Right to Enjoy Mental Peace and Tranquillity, 1939, 28 Geo.L.J. 55; Seitz, Insults, Practical Jokes, Threats of Future Harm, 1940, 28 Ky.L.J. 411; Smith, An Independent Tort Action for Mental Suffering and Emotional Distress, 1957, 7 Drake L.Rev. 53; Notes, 1952, 52 Col.L.Rev. 939; 1952, 25 So.Cal.L.Rev. 440; Second Restatement of Torts, § 46.

26. Chamberlain v. Chandler, C.C.Mass.1823, 3 Mason 242, 5 Fed.Cas.No.2,575; Cole v. Atlanta & West Point Railroad Co., 1897, 102 Ga. 474, 31 S.E. 107; Texas & Pacific Railway Co. v. Jones, Tex.Civ.App.1897, 39 S.W. 124, error refused; Knoxville Traction Co. v. Lane, 1899, 103 Tenn. 376, 53 S.W. 557.

27. Chamberlain v. Chandler, C.C.Mass.1823, 3 Mason 242, 5 Fed.Cas.No.2,575; Knoxville Traction Co. v. Lane, 1899, 103 Tenn. 376, 53 S.W. 557; Bleecker v. Colorado & Southern Railroad Co., 1911, 50 Colo. 140, 114 P. 481. Cf. Frewen v. Page, 1921, 238 Mass. 499, 131 N.E. 475 (innkeeper).

28. Texas & Pacific Railway Co. v. Jones, Tex.Civ. App.1897, 39 S.W. 124. Accord: St. Louis-San Francisco Railroad Co. v. Clark, 1924, 104 Okl. 24, 229 P. 779; Jones v. Atlantic Coast Line Railroad Co., 1917, 108 S.C. 217, 94 S.E. 490 (in freight depot to pick up package); Moody v. Kenny, 1923, 153 La. 1007, 97 So. 21 (hotel guest not yet registered).

regard it as sounding in tort.[29] In this field the decisions have gone to considerable lengths, holding the carrier liable for language which is merely profane or indecent,[30] or grossly [31] insulting [32] to people of ordinary sensibility,[33] even though the mental disturbance is not attended by any illness or other physical consequences.[34]

The same liability has been imposed upon innkeepers, whose position toward the public is analogous to that of carriers; and a hotel detective who burst into a room crying that the occupants were unmarried, and threatening jail, made his employer liable for the mental suffering which resulted.[35] Liability has also been extended in a few cases to telegraph companies;[36] and there appears to be little doubt that it would be applied to any other public utility grossly insulting its patrons.[37] Although there has been a little indication of a desire on the part of a few courts to extend this liability for mere insult to the owners of shops and other premises held open to the public,[38] the majority of the cases[39] thus far do not support the liability,

---

29. Cole v. Atlanta & West Point Railroad Co., 1897, 102 Ga. 474, 31 S.E. 107; Goddard v. Grand Trunk Railway Co., 1869, 57 Me. 202, 2 Am.Rep. 39; cf. Boyce v. Greeley Square Hotel Co., 1920, 228 N.Y. 106, 126 N.E. 647 (hotel).

30. Birmingham Railway Light & Power Co. v. Glenn, 1912, 179 Ala. 263, 60 So. 111; Bleecker v. Colorado & Southern Railway Co., 1911, 50 Colo. 140, 114 P. 481; Fort Worth & Rio Grande Railway Co. v. Bryant, Tex.Civ.App.1918, 210 S.W. 556, error refused; St. Louis-San Francisco Railroad Co. v. Clark, 1924, 104 Okl. 24, 229 P. 779; Southeastern Greyhound Corp. v. Graham, 1943, 69 Ga.App. 621, 26 S.E.2d 371.

31. Mere discourtesy, as distinguished from gross insult, apparently is not enough. Thus a mere rough tone of voice was held not to be actionable in New York, Lake Erie & Western Railway Co. v. Bennett, 6th Cir. 1892, 50 F. 496; Crutcher v. Cleveland, Cincinnati, Chicago & St. Louis Railway Co., 1908, 132 Mo. App. 311, 111 S.W. 891; Daniels v. Florida Central & Peninsular Railroad Co., 1901, 62 S.C. 1, 39 S.E. 762; and cf. Campopiano v. Rhode Island Co., 1916, 39 R.I. 105, 97 A. 597.

The mildest insult found for which recovery was allowed was in Haile v. New Orleans Railway & Light Co., 1914, 135 La. 229, 65 So. 225: "A big fat woman like you."

32. Gillespie v. Brooklyn Heights Railroad Co., 1904, 178 N.Y. 347, 70 N.E. 857 ("deadbeat" and "swindler"); Lipman v. Atlantic Coast Line Railroad Co., 1917, 108 S.C. 151, 93 S.E. 714 ("lunatic"); Knoxville Traction Co. v. Lane, 1899, 103 Tenn. 376, 53 S.W. 557 ("whore"); Barbknecht v. Great Northern Railway Co., 1927, 55 N.D. 104, 212 N.W. 776 (opprobrious epithets and indecent proposal); Huffman v. Southern Railway Co., 1913, 163 N.C. 171, 79 S.E. 307 ("cheap, common scalawag").

33. The liability was so limited in Georgia Railway & Electric Co. v. Baker, 1907, 1 Ga.App. 832, 58 S.E. 88; Birmingham Railway Light & Power Co. v. Glenn, 1912, 179 Ala. 263, 60 So. 111.

The personality of the plaintiff is to be taken into account, and a woman or a child may recover where a man hardened to profane language might not. Fort Worth & Rio Grande Railway Co. v. Bryant, Tex.Civ. App.1918, 210 S.W. 556, error refused.

34. Lipman v. Atlantic Coast Line Railroad Co., 1917, 108 S.C. 151, 93 S.E. 714; Humphrey v. Michigan United Railways Co., 1911, 166 Mich. 645, 132 N.W. 447; Gillespie v. Brooklyn Heights Railroad Co., 1904, 178 N.Y. 347, 70 N.E. 857; Texas & Pacific Railway Co. v. Jones, Tex.Civ.App.1897, 39 S.W. 124, error refused.

35. Emmke v. De Silva, 8th Cir.1923, 293 F. 17; De Wolf v. Ford, 1908, 193 N.Y. 397, 86 N.E. 527; Dixon v. Hotel Tutwiler Operating Co., 1926, 214 Ala. 396, 108 So. 26; Frewen v. Page, 1921, 238 Mass. 499, 131 N.E 475; Milner Hotels v. Dougherty, 1943, 195 Miss. 718, 15 So.2d 358.

36. Dunn v. Western Union Telegraph Co., 1907, 2 Ga.App. 845, 59 S.E. 189 ("Go to hell with your God damn message"); Buchanan v. Western Union Telegraph Co., 1920, 115 S.C. 433, 106 S.E. 159 (indecent proposal by messenger at home); Magouirk v. Western Union Telegraph Co., 1902, 79 Miss. 632, 31 So. 206; cf. Western Union Telegraph Co. v. Watson, 1902, 82 Miss. 101, 33 So. 76; Butler v. Western Union Telegraph Co., 1901, 62 S.C. 222, 40 S.E. 162.

37. The plaintiff must qualify as a patron making use of the facilities of the carrier, innkeeper, or public utility, as such. Thus recovery was denied in Jenkins v. Kentucky Hotel, Inc., 1935, 261 Ky. 419, 87 S.W.2d 951, where plaintiff made use of defendant's hotel lobby to meet a friend; and cf. Wallace v. Shoreham Hotel Corp., Mun.App.D.C.1946, 49 A.2d 81 (customer in cocktail lounge of hotel not hotel guest).

38. Davis v. Tacoma Railway & Power Co., 1904, 35 Wash. 203, 77 P. 209 (amusement park; plaintiff ordered out, with imputation of immoral conduct); Malczewski v. New Orleans Railway & Light Co., 1924, 156 La. 830, 101 So. 213. In both cases the defendant was a carrier, but not acting as such. Other cases in which plaintiff was ejected from the premises are probably to be distinguished as involving a clear breach of contract. Weber-Stair Co. v. Fisher, Ky.1909, 119 S.W. 195 (theatre); Planchard v. Klaw & Erlanger New Orleans Theatres Co., 1928, 166 La. 235, 117 So. 132 (theatre); Aaron v. Ward, 1911, 203 N.Y. 351, 96 N.E. 736 (bathhouse); Smith v. Leo, 1895, 92 Hun. 242, 36 N.Y.S. 949 (dance hall).

39. Flowers v. Price, 1939, 190 S.C. 392, 3 S.E.2d 38 (tobacco warehouse; profanity and abuse); Wallace v.

and treat the owners of such premises upon the same footing as other defendants who are not under the special obligation of the public utility toward the public.[40]

There is virtually unanimous agreement that such ordinary defendants are not liable for mere insult, indignity, annoyance, or even threats, where the case is lacking in other circumstances of aggravation. The reasons are not far to seek. Our manners, and with them our law, have not yet progressed to the point where we are able to afford a remedy in the form of tort damages for all intended mental disturbance. Liability of course cannot be extended to every trivial indignity. There is no occasion for the law to intervene with balm for wounded feelings in every case where a flood of billingsgate is loosed in an argument over a back fence. The plaintiff must necessarily be expected and required to be hardened to a certain amount of rough language, and to acts that are definitely inconsiderate and unkind.[41] There is still, in this country at least, such a thing as liberty to express an unflattering opinion of another, however wounding it may be to the other's feelings; and in the interest not only of freedom of speech but also of avoidance of other more dangerous conduct, it is still very desirable that some safety valve be left through which irascible tempers may blow off relatively harmless steam.

There is the further, and still more significant, evident and serious danger of fictitious claims and vexatious suits in such cases. Petty insult or indignity lacks, from its very nature, any convincing assurance that the asserted mental distress is genuine, or that if genuine it is serious, and reasonable. When a citizen who has been called a son of a bitch testifies that the epithet has destroyed his slumber, ruined his digestion, wrecked his nervous system, and permanently impaired his health, other citizens who on occasion have been called the same thing without catastrophic harm may have legitimate doubts that he was really so upset, or that if he were his sufferings could possibly be so reasonable and justified under the circumstances as to be entitled to compensation.

Accordingly, it is generally held that there can be no recovery for mere profanity, obscenity, or abuse,[42] without circumstances of aggravation, or for insults,[43] indignities or threats[44] which are considered to amount to nothing more than mere annoyances. The

---

Shoreham Hotel Corp., Mun.App.D.C.1946, 49 A.2d 81 (cocktail lounge, insinuation of dishonesty); Republic Iron & Steel Co. v. Self, 1915, 192 Ala. 403, 68 So. 328 (shop; "liar," "dirty liar," and "no lady"); Miller v. Friedman's Jewelers, Inc., 1963, 107 Ga.App. 841, 131 S.E.2d 663 (shop; abuse, ordered out); Slocum v. Food Fair Stores of Florida, Inc., Fla.1958, 100 So.2d 396 ("You stink to me"); Stavnezer v. Sage-Allen & Co., 1959, 146 Conn. 460, 152 A.2d 312 (false accusation goods not paid for).

Cf. Nance v. Mayflower Tavern, Inc., 1944, 106 Utah 517, 150 P.2d 773 (restaurant refusing to serve plaintiff); Mann v. Roosevelt Shop, Fla.1949, 41 So.2d 894 (similar refusal by shop); Larson v. R. B. Wrigley Co., 1931, 183 Minn. 28, 235 N.W. 393 (restaurant refusing, plaintiff "too dirty.")

40. Thus the owner of premises, like anyone else, can be held liable for extreme outrage (see infra, this section, Extreme Outrage). Saenger Theatres Corp. v. Herndon, 1938, 180 Miss. 791, 178 So. 86 (picture theatre; schoolgirl bullied, accused of immoral conduct, threatened with arrest), Interstate Amusement Co. v. Martin, 1913, 8 Ala.App. 481, 62 So. 404 (plaintiff called upon stage of theatre and publicly humiliated); Boswell v. Barnum & Bailey, 1916, 135 Tenn. 35, 185 S.W. 692 (insult and abuse in argument over circus seats; "outrageous").

41. Magruder, Mental and Emotional Disturbance in the Law of Torts, 1936, 49 Harv.L.Rev. 1033, 1035.

42. Brooker v. Silverthorne, 1919, 111 S.C. 553, 99 S.E. 350; Ex parte Hammett, 1953, 259 Ala. 240, 66 So. 2d 600; Halliday v. Cienkowski, 1939, 333 Pa. 123, 3 A.2d 372; Atkinson v. Bibb Manufacturing Co., 1935, 50 Ga.App. 434, 178 S.E. 537; Johnson v. General Motors Acceptance Corp., 5th Cir.1955, 228 F.2d 104.

43. Slocum v. Food Fair Stores of Florida, Inc., Fla. 1958, 100 So.2d 396; Wallace v. Shoreham Hotel Corp., Mun.App.D.C.1946, 49 A.2d 81; Stavnezer v. Sage-Allen & Co., 1959, 146 Conn. 460, 152 A.2d 312; Republic Iron & Steel Co. v. Self, 1915, 192 Ala. 403, 68 So. 328; McPherson v. McCarrick, 1900, 22 Utah 232, 61 P. 1004.

44. Taft v. Taft, 1867, 40 Vt. 229; Stratton v. Posse Normal School of Gymnastics, 1928, 265 Mass. 223, 163 N.E. 905; State National Bank of Iowa Park v. Rogers, Tex.Civ.App.1935, 89 S.W.2d 825; Gefter v. Rosenthal Caterers, 1956, 384 Pa. 123, 119 A.2d 250; McKinzie v. Huckaby, D.Okl.1953, 112 F.Supp. 642.

plaintiff cannot recover merely because of hurt feelings.[45] More lenient standards of recovery apply, however, under old statutes in Mississippi, Virginia, and West Virginia,[46] which had their origin as part of an anti-dueling code, and which provide an action for "all words which from their usual construction and acceptation are considered as insults, and lead to violence and breach of the peace."

Extreme Outrage

In special situations of extreme misconduct, recovery is allowed. The leading case which first broke through the shackles of the older law was Wilkinson v. Downton,[47] in which a practical joker amused himself by telling a woman that her husband had been smashed up in an accident and was lying at The Elms at Leytonstone with both legs broken, and that she was to go at once in a cab with two pillows to fetch him home. The shock to her nervous system produced serious and permanent physical consequences, which at one time threatened her reason, and entailed weeks of suffering and incapacity. The court obviously had no love for the defendant; and as in many another hard case, the enormity of the outrage overthrew the settled rule of law.

As other outrageous cases began to accumulate, the courts continued to struggle to find some familiar and traditional basis of liability; and when it was possible without too obvious pretense, the recovery was rested upon a technical assault,[48] battery,[49] false imprisonment,[50] trespass to land,[51] nuisance,[52] or invasion of the right of privacy.[53] Gradually too many cases appeared in which no such traditional ground could be discovered; and somewhere around 1930 it began to be recognized that the intentional infliction of mental disturbance by extreme and outrageous conduct constituted a cause of action in itself.

So far as it is possible to generalize from the cases, the rule which seems to have emerged is that there is liability for conduct exceeding all bounds usually tolerated by decent society, of a nature which is especially calculated to cause, and does cause, mental distress of a very serious kind.[54] The re-

---

Cf. Meek v. Harris, 1916, 110 Miss. 805, 71 So. 1; People's Finance & Thrift Co. v. Harwell, 1938, 183 Okl. 413, 82 P.2d 994; Perati v. Atkinson, 1963, 213 Cal.App.2d 472, 28 Cal.Rptr. 898.

45. Wallace v. Shoreham Hotel Corp., Mun.App. D.C.1946, 49 A.2d 81.

46. Miss.Code Ann.1942, § 1059; Va.Code Ann. 1950, § 8–630; W.Va.Code Ann.1955, § 5471. See Landrum v. Ellington, 1929, 1523 Miss. 569, 120 So. 444; Michaelson v. Turk, 1916, 79 W.Va. 31, 90 S.E. 395; Huckabee v. Nash, 1938, 182 Miss. 754, 183 So. 500; Boyd v. Boyd, 1914, 116 Va. 326, 82 S.E. 110; Wade, Tort Liability for Abusive and Insulting Language, 1950, 4 Vand.L.Rev. 63, 82; Malone, Insult in Retaliation, 1939, 11 Miss.L.J. 333; Note, 1941, 27 Va.L.Rev. 405.

47. [1897] 2 Q.B.D. 57.

48. Atlanta Hub Co. v. Jones, 1933, 47 Ga.App. 778, 171 S.E. 470; Kurpgeweit v. Kirby, 1910, 88 Neb. 72, 129 N.W. 177; Leach v. Leach, 1895, 11 Tex.Civ.App. 699, 33 S.W. 703, error refused.

49. De May v. Roberts, 1881, 46 Mich. 160, 9 N.W. 146; Interstate Life & Accident Co. v. Brewer, 1937, 56 Ga.App. 599, 193 S.E. 458.

50. Salisbury v. Poulson, 1918, 51 Utah 552, 172 P. 315.

51. Engle v. Simmons, 1906, 148 Ala. 92, 41 So. 1023; American Security Co. v. Cook, 1934, 49 Ga.App. 723, 176 S.E. 798; Continental Casualty Co. v. Garrett, 1935, 173 Miss. 676, 161 So. 753; Watson v. Dilts, 1902, 116 Iowa 249, 89 N.W. 1068; Bouillon v. Laclede Gaslight Co., 1910, 148 Mo.App. 462, 129 S.W. 401.

52. Shellabarger v. Morris, 1905, 115 Mo.App. 566, 91 S.W. 1005. Cf. Acadia, California, Limited v. Herbert, 1960, 54 Cal.2d 328, 5 Cal.Rptr. 686, 353 P.2d 294 (refusal to supply water to desert lands).

53. Brents v. Morgan, 1927, 221 Ky. 765, 299 S.W. 967.

54. Eckenrode v. Life of America Insurance Co., 7th Cir. 1972, 470 F.2d 1; Meyer v. Nottger, Iowa 1976, 241 N.W.2d 911; Amsden v. Grinnell Mutual Reinsurance Co., Iowa 1972, 203 N.W.2d 252; Fletcher v. Western National Life Insurance Co., 1970, 10 Cal.App. 3d 376, 89 Cal.Rptr. 78. See Restatement of the Law, 1948 Supp., Torts, § 46, Comment *g*: "In short, the rule stated in this section imposes liability for intentionally causing severe emotional distress in those situations in which the actor's conduct has gone beyond all reasonable bounds of decency. The prohibited conduct is conduct which in the eyes of decent men and women in a civilized community is considered outrageous and intolerable. Generally, the case is one in which the recitation of the facts to an average member of the community would arouse his resentment against the actor and lead him to exclaim 'Outrageous!'"

quirements of the rule are rigorous, and difficult to satisfy.[55] Yet, such extreme outrage has been found, as in the leading Wilkinson case,[56] in decoying a woman suspected of insanity to a hospital by a concocted tale of an injured husband and child;[57] in spreading the false rumor that the plaintiff's son had hanged himself;[58] in bringing a mob to the plaintiff's door at night with a threat to lynch him unless he left town;[59] and in wrapping up a very gory dead rat instead of a loaf of bread, for a sensitive soul to open.[60] An invitation to illicit intercourse, insufficient in itself,[61] becomes extreme outrage when it is prolonged or repeated to the point of hounding, and accompanied by advertising in the form of indecent pictures or exposure.[62]

The extreme and outrageous nature of the conduct may arise not so much from what is done as from abuse by the defendant of some relation or position which gives the defendant actual or apparent power to damage the plaintiff's interests. The result is something very like extortion. Again the leading case is an English one, Janvier v. Sweeney,[63] where a private detective, representing himself to be a police officer, threatened to charge plaintiff with espionage unless she surrendered private letters in her possession. Not far removed from this are the cases of bullying a school girl, with threats of prison and public disgrace, unless she signed a confession of immoral misconduct,[64] and the threats of an association of rubbish collectors to beat the plaintiff up, destroy his truck, and put him out of business, unless he paid over proceeds from a territory which they had allocated to one of their members.[65]

It is on this basis that the tort action has been used as a potent counter-weapon against the more outrageous high-pressure methods of collection agencies and other creditors. These are sufficiently well known,[66] ranging from violent cursing, abuse, and accusations of dishonesty,[67] through a series of letters in lurid envelopes bearing a picture of lightning about to strike, which repeatedly threatened arrest, ruination of credit, or a suit which is never brought,[68] or telephone calls around the

---

See also Second Restatement of Torts, § 46, comment k.

Ohio held back, in Bartow v. Smith, 1948, 149 Ohio St. 301, 78 N.E.2d 735, where defendant reviled a pregnant woman on the public street. The case is commented on, in 1949, 27 Mich.L.Rev. 436; 1949, 27 Tex. L.Rev. 730 ("distinctly and inexcusably retrogressive").

55. For an illustration, see Harris v. Jones, 1977, 281 Md. 560, 380 A.2d 611.

56. Supra, this section.

57. Savage v. Boies, 1954, 77 Ariz. 355, 272 P.2d 349.

58. Bielitski v. Obadiak, 1921, 61 Dom.L.Rep. 494.

59. Wilson v. Wilkins, 1930, 181 Ark. 137, 25 S.W.2d 428. Cf. Ruiz v. Bertolotti, 1962, 37 Misc.2d 1067, 236 N.Y.S.2d 854 (threat of harm to plaintiffs, Negroes, and their children, if they moved into neighborhood); Flamm v. Van Nierop, 1968, 56 Misc.2d 1059, 291 N.Y.S.2d 189 (hounding plaintiff on the streets).

60. Great Atlantic & Pacific Tea Co. v. Roch, 1930, 160 Md. 189, 153 A. 22.

61. See supra, this section.

62. Samms v. Eccles, 1961, 11 Utah 2d 289, 358 P.2d 344; Mitran v. Williamson, 1960, 21 Misc.2d 106, 197 N.Y.S.2d 689. Cf. Webber v. Gray, 1957, 228 Ark. 289, 307 S.W.2d 80, where defendant, a former mistress of plaintiff, hounded him and his family, with incidents of aggravation, in an effort to renew the association. Also Halio v. Lurie, 1961, 15 A.D.2d 62, 222 N.Y.S.2d 759, where a man who had jilted a woman wrote her jeering verses and taunting letters; and Tate v. Canonica, 1960, 180 Cal.App.2d 898, 5 Cal.Rptr. 28, where a man was driven to suicide by threats and accusations not set forth.

63. [1919] 2 K.B. 316.

64. Johnson v. Sampson, 1926, 167 Minn. 203, 208 N.W. 814.

65. State Rubbish Collectors Association v. Siliznoff, 1952, 38 Cal.2d 330, 240 P.2d 282.

66. See Birkhead, Collection Tactics of Illegal Lenders, 1941, 8 Law & Contemp.Prob. 78; Borda, One's Right to Enjoy Mental Peace and Tranquility, 1939, 28 Geo.L.J. 55; Berger, The Bill Collector and the Law, 1968, 17 De Paul L.Rev. 327: Notes, 1939, 34 Ill.L.Rev. 505; 1957, 24 U.Chi.L.Rev. 572; 1957, 14 Wash. & Lee L.Rev. 167; 1957, 35 Chicago-Kent L.Rev. 145.

67. Kirby v. Jules Chain Stores Corp., 1936, 210 N.C. 808, 188 S.E. 625; American Security Co. v. Cook, 1934, 49 Ga.App. 723, 176 S.E. 798; American Finance & Loan Corp. v. Coots, 1962, 105 Ga.App. 849, 125 S.E.2d 689 (including pointing revolver).

68. Barnett v. Collection Service Co., 1932, 214 Iowa 1303, 242 N.W. 25; LaSalle Extension University v. Fogarty, 1934, 126 Neb. 457, 253 N.W. 424. Cf. Christensen v. Swedish Hospital, 1962, 59 Wn.2d 545, 368

clock,[69] or attempts to pile up the pressure by involving the plaintiff's employer, relatives, neighbors or the public in the controversy,[70] up to a call to a neighbor's telephone for an "emergency message" which will be a "great shock," [71] and a proposal to a woman to "take it out in trade."[72] It is seldom that any one such item of conduct is found alone in a case; and the liability usually has rested on a prolonged course of hounding by a variety of extreme methods.[73] Similar outrageous bullying tactics on the part of insurance adjusters seeking to force a settlement,[74] or evicting landlords seeking to harass unwanted tenants,[75] have been subjected to the same liability.

Still another basis on which extreme outrage can be found is the defendant's knowledge [76] that the plaintiff is especially sensitive, susceptible and vulnerable to injury through mental distress at the particular conduct. This goes back to a Louisiana case[77] in which the defendants buried a "pot of gold" for an eccentric and mentally deficient old maid to find, and when she dug it up escorted her in triumph to the city hall, where she opened the pot under circumstances of public humiliation. In line with this case there are a number of decisions in

P.2d 897 (threat of criminal prosecution); Abraham Used Car Co. v. Silva, Fla.App.1968, 208 So.2d 500 (same).

69. Moore v. Savage, Tex.Civ.App.1962, 359 S.W.2d 95, writ of error refused, n. r. e., Tex., 362 S.W.2d 298. Cf. Housh v. Peth, 1956, 165 Ohio St. 35, 133 N.E.2d 340 (held invasion of privacy). In Wiggins v. Moskins Credit Clothing Store, E.D.S.C.1956, 137 F.Supp. 764, there was continued harassing of the debtor's landlady with telephone calls. Her only remedy was held to be an action for the nusiance, since she was not the debtor.

70. Quina v. Roberts, La.App.1944, 16 So.2d 558; Barnett v. Collection Service Co., 1932, 214 Iowa 1303, 242 N.W. 25; LaSalle Extension University v. Fogarty, 1934, 126 Neb. 457, 253 N.W. 424; Moore v. Savage, Tex.Civ.App.1962, 359 S.W.2d 95, writ of error refused, n. r. e., Tex., 362 S.W.2d 298; Booty v. American Finance Corp. of Shreveport, La.App.1969, 224 So.2d 512, application denied 254 La. 782, 226 So.2d 771.

Cf. Tollefson v. Price, 1967, 247 Or. 398, 430 P.2d 990 (publication of name in list of undisputed delinquent accounts, where disputed).

71. Bowden v. Spiegel, Inc., 1950, 96 Cal.App.2d 793, 216 P.2d 571. Cf. Lyons v. Zale Jewelry Co., 1963, 246 Miss. 139, 150 So.2d 154 (swearing at woman over telephone).

72. Digsby v. Carroll Baking Co., 1948, 76 Ga.App. 656, 47 S.E.2d 203.

73. There was not much that the defendant overlooked in Duty v. General Finance Co., 1954, 154 Tex. 16, 273 S.W.2d 64. See also Advance Loan Service v. Mandik, Tex.Civ.App.1957, 306 S.W.2d 754; Salazar v. Bond Finance Co., Tex.Civ.App.1966, 410 S.W.2d 839, refused n. r. e.; Lyons v. Zale Jewelry Co., 1963, 246 Miss. 139, 150 So.2d 154; Warrem v. Parrish, Mo.1969, 436 S.W.2d 670.

Of course, reasonable attempts at collection are not actionable. Berrier v. Beneficial Finance, Inc., D.Ind. 1964, 234 F.Supp. 204; Passman v. Commercial Credit Plan of Hammond, Inc., La.App.1969, 220 So.2d 758, application denied 254 La. 287, 223 So.2d 410; Whatley v. K-Mart Discount Stores, Tex.Civ.App.1970, 451 S.W.2d 568, refused n. r. e. (wrong person).

74. Continental Casualty Co. v. Garrett, 1935, 173 Miss. 676, 161 So. 753; Pacific Mutual Life Insurance Co. v. Tetirick, 1938, 185 Okl. 37, 89 P.2d 774; National Life & Accident Insurance Co. v. Anderson, 1940, 187 Okl. 180, 102 P.2d 141; Frishett v. State Farm Mutual Automobile Insurance Co., 1966, 3 Mich.App. 688, 143 N.W.2d 612. Cf. Fletcher v. Western National Life Insurance Co., 1970, 10 Cal.App.3d 376, 89 Cal.Rptr. 78 (bad faith refusal to settle claim, to put pressure on insured); Eckenrode v. Life of America Insurance Co., 7th Cir. 1972, 470 F.2d 1; Amsden v. Grinnell Mutual Reinsurance Co., Iowa 1972, 203 N.W.2d 252; Gruenberg v. Aetna Insurance Co., 1973, 9 Cal.3d 566, 108 Cal.Rptr. 480, 510 P.2d 1032.

But coming to plaintiff's home and cajoling her into a settlement is not actionable. Cluff v. Farmers Insurance Exchange, 1969, 10 Ariz.App. 560, 460 P.2d 666.

75. Emden v. Vitz, 1948, 88 Cal.App.2d 313, 198 P.2d 696; Duncan v. Donnell, Tex.Civ.App.1928, 12 S.W.2d 811; Louisville & Nashville Railroad Co. v. Roberts, 1925, 207 Ky. 310, 269 S.W. 333; Scheman v. Schlein, 1962, 35 Misc.2d 581, 231 N.Y.S.2d 548; Kaufman v. Abramson, 4th Cir. 1966, 363 F.2d 865.

Compare, as unusual cases, Curnett v. Wolf, 1953, 244 Iowa 683, 57 N.W.2d 915 (threat to have plaintiff discharged unless he dismissed a suit); Guillory v. Godfrey, 1955, 134 Cal.App.2d 628, 286 P.2d 474 (intimidation of customers away from liquor store); Tate v. Canonica, 1960, 180 Cal.App.2d 898, 5 Cal.Rptr. 28 (driven to suicide by unspecified threats and blackmail).

76. If there is no such knowledge, conduct otherwise not sufficiently extreme leads to no liability, even though plaintiff may in fact suffer injury because of it. Braun v. Craven, 1898, 175 Ill. 401, 51 N.E. 657; Carrigan v. Henderson, 1943, 192 Okl. 254, 135 P.2d 330; Haas v. Metz, 1898, 78 Ill.App. 46; Kramer v. Ricksmeier, 1913, 159 Iowa 48, 139 N.W. 1091.

77. Nickerson v. Hodges, 1920, 146 La. 735, 84 So. 37. The pot of gold came to her heirs, in the form of $500 damages.

which sick people [78] children,[79] and pregnant women [80] have recovered, on the basis of the defendant's knowledge of their condition, for profanity and abuse, threatening letters, or other conduct which apparently would not otherwise have been sufficient to constitute a tort.

Finally, there are a great many cases involving the mishandling of dead bodies, whether by multilation,[81] disinterment,[82] interference with proper burial,[83] or other forms of intentional [84] disturbance.[85] In most of these cases the courts have talked of a somewhat dubious "property right"[86] to the body, usually in the next of kin,[87] which did not exist while the decedent was living, cannot be conveyed, can be used only for the one purpose of burial, and not only has no pecuniary value but is a source of liability for funeral expenses. It seems reasonably obvious that such "property" is something evolved out of thin air to meet the occasion, and that in reality the personal feelings of the survivors are being protected, under a fiction likely to deceive no one but a lawyer.

Some cases have avoided all of these difficulties by recognizing what is sufficiently obvious, that the tort is in reality merely the intentional infliction of mental distress.[88]

The emotional distress must in fact exist, and it must be severe. If the plaintiff is not impressed by the defendant's threatening letter, and is only sufficiently concerned to make an effort to discover who wrote it, the minor annoyanace and affront to dignity are too trivial to support a tort action.[89] Furthermore, except in cases where the defendant has knowledge of the plaintiff's peculiar susceptibility and practices upon it, the distress must be such as a reasonable person "of ordinary sensibilities" would undergo under the circumstances.[90]

---

78. Clark v. Associated Retail Credit Men, 1939, 70 App.D.C. 183, 105 F.2d 62; Continental Casualty Co. v. Garrett, 1935, 173 Miss. 676, 161 So. 753; Interstate Life & Accident Co. v. Brewer, 1937, 56 Ga.App. 599, 193 S.E. 458; Pacific Mutual Life Insurance Co. v. Tetirick, 1938, 185 Okl. 37, 89 P.2d 774; National Life & Accident Insurance Co. v. Anderson, 1940, 187 Okl. 180, 102 P.2d 141.

79. Delta Finance Co. v. Ganakas, 1956, 93 Ga.App. 297, 91 S.E.2d 383 (intimidation); Korbin v. Berlin, Fla.App.1965, 177 So.2d 551 (vilifying mother).

80. Alabama Fuel & Iron Co. v. Baladoni, 1916, 15 Ala.App. 316, 73 So. 205; Richardson v. Pridmore, 1950, 97 Cal.App.2d 124, 217 P.2d 113; Vargas v. Ruggiero, 1961, 197 Cal.App.2d 709, 17 Cal.Rptr. 568. Cf. Turner v. ABC Jalousie Co., 1968, 251 S.Ct. 92, 160 S.E.2d 528 (frightening lone woman).

81. Alderman v. Ford, 1937, 146 Kan. 698, 72 P.2d 981; Hill v. Travelers Insurance, Co., 1927, 154 Tenn. 295, 294 S.W. 1097; Crenshaw v. O'Connell, 1941, 235 Mo.App. 1085, 150 S.W.2d 489; French v. Ochsner Clinic, La.App.1967, 200 So.2d 371, writ refused 251 La. 34, 202 So.2d 652; Jackson v. Rupp, Fla.App.1969, 228 So.2d 916, writ discharged, Fla.1970, 238 So.2d 86.

82. Gostkowski v. Roman Catholic Church of Sacred Hearts of Jesus and Mary, 1933, 262 N.Y. 320, 186 N.E. 798; England v. Central Pocahontas Coal Co., 1920, 86 W.Va. 575, 104 S.E. 46; Spomer v. City of Grand Junction, 1960, 144 Colo. 207, 355 P.2d 960. Cf. Boyle v. Chandler, 1927, 33 Del. (3 W.W.Harr.) 323, 138 A. 273 (removal from casket).

83. Finley v. Atlantic Transport Co., 1917, 220 N.Y. 249, 115 N.E. 715 (burial at sea); Spiegel v. Evergreen Cemetery Co., 1936, 117 N.J.L. 90, 186 A. 585 (in absence of relatives); Kirksey v. Jernigan, Fla.1950, 45 So.2d 188 (holding unburied); Papieves v. Lawrence, 1970, 437 Pa. 373, 263 A.2d 118.

84. As to negligence, see infra, § 54.

85. Sworski v. Simons, 1940, 208 Minn. 201, 293 N.W. 309 (unauthorized embalming); Wilson v. St. Louis & San Francisco Railroad Co., 1912, 160 Mo.App. 649, 142 S.W. 775 (mishandling); Sanford v. Ware, 1950, 191 Va. 43, 60 S.E.2d 10 (misburial); Brownlee v. Pratt, 1946, 77 Ohio App. 533, 68 N.E.2d 798 (burial of intruder in lot). See Note, 1958, 19 Ohio St.L.J. 455.

86. See Note, 1934, 18 Minn.L.Rev. 204.

87. See Koerber v. Patek, 1920, 123 Wis. 453, 102 N.W. 40; Gostkowski v. Roman Catholic Church of Sacred Hearts of Jesus and Mary, 1933, 262 N.Y. 320, 186 N.E. 798; Boyle v. Chandler, 1927, 33 Del. (3 W.W. Harr.) 323, 138 A. 273; Stephens v. Waits, 1936, 53 Ga.App. 44, 184 S.E. 781. See, Generally, Green, Relational Interests, 1934, 29 Ill.L.Rev. 460, 489; Notes, 1934, 18 Minn.L.Rev. 204; 1926, 74 U.Pa.L.Rev. 404; 1933, 19 Corn.L.Q. 108.

88. See Eckenrode v. Life of America Insurance Co., 7th Cir. 1972, 470 F.2d 1; Amsden v. Grinnell Mutual Reinsurance Co., Iowa 1972, 203 N.W.2d 252; Fletcher v. Western National Life Insurance Co., 1970, 10 Cal.App.3d 376, 89 Cal.Rptr. 78; Second Restatement of Torts, § 46. For early cases, see Gadbury v. Bleitz, 1925, 133 Wash. 134, 233 P. 299; Stephens v. Waits, 1936, 53 Ga.App. 44, 184 S.E. 781.

89. Taft v. Taft, 1867, 40 Vt. 229.

90. March v. Cacioppo, 1962, 37 Ill.App.2d 235, 185 N.E.2d 397 (obtaining void judgment and garnishment of bank account, not enough); cf. Nelson v. Crawford, 1899, 122 Mich. 466, 81 N.W. 335 (hysterical fright at man dressed in woman's clothing); Oehler v. L. Bam-

In the great majority of the cases allowing recovery the genuineness of the mental disturbance has been evidenced by resulting phsyical illness of a serious character, and both the mental and the physical elements have been compensated. A few cases have said flatly that physical illness or some other nonmental damage is essential to the existence of the tort,[91] and there are other cases which look as if it were considered indispensable.[92] On the other hand, there are numerous decisions which have found liability for mere mental disturbance without any evidence of physical consequences. The mere recital, for example, of the fact that a mob came to the plaintiff's house at night with a threat to lynch him unless he left town, leaves no doubt at all that the emotional upset to which the plaintiff testifies was real.[93]

In 1948 a section of the Restatement of Torts[94] was amended to reject any absolute necessity for physical results. Probably the conclusion to be reached is that where physical harm is lacking the courts will properly tend to look for more in the way of extreme outrage as an assurance that the mental disturbance claimed is not fictitious; but that if the enormity of the outrage itself carries conviction that there has in fact been severe and serious mental distress, which is neither feigned nor trivial, bodily harm is not required.

In the great majority of the cases allowing recovery the mental distress has been inflicted intentionally, the defendant either desiring to cause it or knowing that it was substantially certain to follow from the conduct. There are, however, a few cases which indicate that liability for extreme outrage is broader and extends to situations in which there is no certainty, but merely a high degree of probability that the mental distress will follow, and the defendant goes ahead in conscious disregard of it. This is the type of conduct which commonly is called wilful or wanton, or reckless. A striking case is one in Iowa[95] in which the defendant decided that it would be a good idea to commit suicide by cutting his throat in the plaintiff's kitchen, and she returned to be confronted with his corpse, with blood all over the premises. There are other decisions[96] of the same general nature, which appear to indicate very definitely that the category of ex-

---

berger & Co., 1927, 103 N.J.L. 703, 137 A. 425, affirming 1926, 4 N.J.Misc. 1003, 135 A. 71 (stroke at repossession of vacuum cleaner).

91. Duty v. General Finance Co., 1954, 154 Tex. 16, 273 S.W.2d 64, distinguishing on this basis Harned v. E-Z Finance Co., 1953, 151 Tex. 641, 254 S.W.2d 81. But in Western Guaranty Loan Co. v. Dean, Tex.Civ. App.1958, 309 S.W.2d 857, refused n. r. e., where there was other damage in plaintiff's discharge from his employment, it was held that physical illness was not required.

92. Kirby v. Jules Chain Stores Corp., 1936, 210 N.C. 808, 188 S.E. 625; Carrigan v. Henderson, 1943, 192 Okl. 254, 135 P.2d 330; Clark v. Associated Retail Credit Men, 1939, 70 App.D.C. 183, 105 F.2d 62.

93. Wilson v. Wilkins, 1930, 181 Ark. 137, 25 S.W.2d 428. Cf. Savage v. Boies, 1954, 77 Ariz. 355, 272 P.2d 349 (police decoying plaintiff to hospital by report her husband and child were injured); Barnett v. Collection Service Co., 1932, 214 Iowa 1303, 242 N.W. 25 (extreme collection letters); La Salle Extension University v. Fogarty, 1934, 126 Neb. 457, 253 N.W. 424 (same); Delta Finance Co. v. Ganakas, 1956, 93 Ga.App. 297, 91 S.E. 2d 383 (frightening child); Samms v. Eccles, 1961, 11 Utah 2d 289, 358 P.2d 344 (invitation to illicit intercourse and indecent exposure); Mitran v. Williamson, 1960, 21 Misc.2d 106, 197 N.Y.S.2d 689 (same); Curnett v. Wolf, 1953, 244 Iowa 683, 57 N.W.2d 915 (threat to have plaintiff discharged unless he dismissed suit); State Rubbish Collectors Association v. Siliznoff, 1952, 38 Cal.2d 330, 240 P.2d 282 (threats of violence in gangster atmosphere).

94. Restatement of the Law, 1948 Supp., Torts, § 46. This has been retained, and covered by Comment k, in the Second Restatement of Torts, § 46.

95. Blakeley v. Shortal's Estate, 1945, 236 Iowa 787, 20 N.W.2d 28. Compare the appalling story in Mahnke v. Moore, 1951, 197 Md. 61, 77 A.2d 923, where, however, the shock to the child was so certain that it clearly was intentional.

96. Bielitski v. Obadiak, 1921, 15 Sask. 153, 61 Dom. L.Rep. 494 (defendant spread ruomor plaintiff's son had hanged himself, knowing that it was very likely to reach her); Price v. Yellow Pine Paper Mill Co., Tex. Civ.App.1922, 240 S.W. 588 (injured husband brought home in shocking condition and delivered abruptly to his pregnant wife); Boyle v. Chandler, 1927, 33 Del. (3 W.W.Harr.) 323, 138 A. 273 (reckless handling of dead body); Lindh v. Great Northern Railway Co., 1906, 99 Minn. 408, 109 N.W. 823 (same); Anderson v. Knox, 9th Cir. 1961, 297 F.2d 702, certiorari denied 1962, 370 U.S. 915, 82 S.Ct. 1555, 8 L.Ed.2d 498 (reckless bad advice as to insurance program). See, however, Alsteen v. Gehl, 1963, 21 Wis.2d 349, 124 N.W.2d 312, rejecting recklessness as a basis for the tort.

treme outrage is to be extended to include conduct not intended to cause mental disturbance, but wilful, wanton or reckless in its deliberate disregard of a known high degree of risk of it.

Acts Directed at a Third Person

Where the mental distress is caused by the defendant's conduct which is not directed at the plaintiff, but at a third person, other problems arise. The first possibility that comes to mind is that the doctrine of "transferred intent"[97] found in the battery cases might be applied to permit recovery. There seems to be little reason to apply it when the plaintiff suffers physical harm, and to reject it where there is mental damage. It is a strange distinction which allows damages when the plaintiff is struck by a bullet aimed at another, and denies them when it frightens the plaintiff into serious illness,[98] or finds a cause of action in mental disturbance at the mistreatment of household furniture, and none in shock at the sight of the mutilated body of a murdered sister.[99] But, probably for the simple reason that emotional distress did not fall within the framework of the old action of trespass where "transferred intent" arose, rarely does a case[1] so much as mention it by analogy in allowing recovery for fright at a battery committed upon another, even a close relative.

Other courts, rejecting "transferred intent," have rather regarded the plaintiff's mental distress as so substantially certain to follow, under the circumstances, that it must be found to be itself intended, and have allowed recovery on that basis.[2] In others stress is laid upon the foreseeability of the mental effect upon the plaintiff, and it seems to have been concluded that there was some kind of negligence toward the plaintiff,[3] which justifies the recovery. On the facts of all of these cases, it would appear that there was a very high degree of probability that the mental disturbance would follow, and that the defendant proceeded in conscious and deliberate disregard of it, so that the defendant's conduct would properly be called wilful, wanton or reckless.

There are other cases in which recovery has been denied, usually on the ground that the mental disturbance was not a thing that could reasonably have been anticipated.[4]

Ordinarily recovery in such cases is limited to plaintiffs who are not only present at the time,[5] but are known by the defendant to be present,[6] so that the mental effect can reasonably be anticipated by the defendant.

---

97. See supra, § 8.

98. Compare Corn v. Sheppard, 1930, 179 Minn. 490, 229 N.W. 869, with Renner v. Canfield, 1886, 36 Minn. 90, 30 N.W. 435.

99. Compare Rose Co. v. Lowery, 1929, 33 Ohio App. 488, 169 N.E. 716 (and see the trespass cases, supra, note 51), with Koontz v. Keller, 1936, 52 Ohio App. 265, 3 N.E.2d 694.

1. One example, however, is Lambert v. Brewster, 1924, 97 W.Va. 124, 125 S.E. 244 (battery upon plaintiff's father).

2. Jeppsen v. Jensen, 1916, 47 Utah 536, 155 P. 429 ("assault" upon the plaintiff); Rogers v. Williard, (1920) 144 Ark. 587, 223 S.W. 15 (quarrel in presence of pregnant woman); Purdy v. Woznesensky, Sask. [1937] 2 W.W.R. 116. A clear case of intent is Knierim v. Izzo, 1961, 22 Ill.2d 73, 174 N.E.2d 157, where defendant told plaintiff that he would murder her husband, and then did so. See Note, [1961] U.Ill.Law Forum 535.

3. Hill v. Kimball, 1890, 76 Tex. 210, 13 S.W. 59; Young v. Western & Atlantic Railroad Co., 1929, 39 Ga. App. 761, 148 S.E. 414; Duncan v. Donnell, Tex.Civ. App. 1929, 12 S.W.2d 811; Watson v. Dilts, 1902, 116 Iowa 249, 89 N.W. 1068. See Hallen, Hill v. Kimball— A Milepost in the Law, 1933, 12 Tex.L.Rev. 1.

4. Phillips v. Dickerson, 1877, 85 Ill. 11; Hutchinson v. Stern, 1906, 115 App.Div. 791, 101 N.Y.S. 145, dismissed 1908, 189 N.Y. 577, 82 N.E. 1128; Ellsworth v. Massacar, 1921, 215 Mich. 511, 184 N.W. 408; Reed v. Ford, 1908, 129 Ky. 471, 112 S.W. 600; Goddard v. Watters, 1914, 14 Ga.App. 722, 82 S.E. 304.

5. Magruder, Mental and Emotional Disturbance in the Law of Torts, 1936, 49 Harv.L.Rev. 1033, 1044. Recovery was denied in Koontz v. Keller, 1936, 52 Ohio App. 265, 3 N.E.2d 694 (discovery of body of murdered sister); Ellsworth v. Massacar, 1921, 215 Mich. 511, 184 N.W. 408 (later discovery of attack on husband); Knox v. Allen, 1926, 4 La.App. 223 (same as to attack on child).

With respect to liability for negligence when physical harm results, see infra, § 54.

6. Phillips v. Dickerson, 1877, 85 Ill. 11 (plaintiff in another room); Hutchinson v. Stern, 1906, 115 App. Div. 791, 101 N.Y.S. 145, dismissed 1908, 189 N.Y. 577, 82 N.E. 1128 ("present and nearby" but not in sight); Reed v. Ford, 1908, 129 Ky. 471, 112 S.W. 600 (near,

The distinction between the wife who sees her husband shot down before her eyes, and the one who hears about it five minutes later, may be a highly artificial one; but an argument in justification is the obvious necessity of drawing a line somewhere short of the widow who learns of the decease ten years afterward, when the genuineness and gravity of her distress may very reasonably be doubted.

There is the further question of whether the recovery should be limited to near relatives of the person attacked, or at least to close associates, where there is some additional guarantee that the mental disturbance is real and extreme. Nearly all of the cases allowing recovery have involved members of the immediate family; but there were at least two[7] early cases which did not. It may be suggested that when a complete stranger is asked for a match on the street and the individual who asks for it is suddenly shot down before the stranger's eyes, the mental shock may be very genuine and severe, and that a pregnant bystander who witnesses a bloody beating may suffer a real injury deserving compensation. The language of the cases themselves does not suggest any such arbitrary limitation, and it does not appear to be called for.

In short, the law appears to be moving in the direction of liability; but thus far recovery is clearly limited to the most extreme cases of violent attack, where there is some especial likelihood of fright or shock.[8]

WESTLAW REFERENCES

intentional** /5 inflict! /5 emotional mental /5 distress & mental! psychological! emotional! /s pain suffer! anguish! anxiet! damage* consequence* distress!

Type of Injury Redressed

intentional** /5 inflict! /5 emotional mental /5 distress & "mere words"

Insult and Indignity

intentional** /5 inflict! /5 emotional mental /5 distress & "common carrier*" passenger /s insult! indignit!

intentional** /5 inflict! /5 emotional mental /5 distress & mere /2 profanity obscenity abuse & court(ok)

Extreme Outrage

wilkinson /2 downton & 2 /2 57

intentional** /5 inflict! /5 emotional mental /5 distress & collection credit*** debt*** /s agent* agenc*** harass!

mishandl! /s corpse* dead

Acts Directed at a Third Person

digest(intentional** /p inflict! /p emotional mental /p distress /p third /p person party parties

synopsis,digest(intentional** /p inflict! /p emotional mental /p distress /p relative* family brother sister mother father husband wife spouse)

---

but not known to be there); Goddard v. Watters, 1914, 14 Ga.App. 722, 82 S.E. 304 (plaintiff ran out to see what was happening); Taylor v. Vallelunga, 1959, 171 Cal.App.2d 107, 339 P.2d 910 (plaintiff witnessed beating of her father; not pleaded defendant knew she was present). In Bunyan v. Jordan, Aust.1936, 57 Comm.L. Rep. 1, defendant pretended to commit suicide to frighten A, and B, who overheard but was not known to be present, was not allowed to recover.

7. Hill v. Kimball, 1890, 76 Tex. 210, 13 S.W. 59; Rogers v. Williard, 1920, 144 Ark. 587, 223 S.W. 15.

8. Thus recovery was denied in Hunt v. Calacino, D.D.C.1953, 114 F.Supp. 254 (threat of jail sentence to son); Bucknam v. Great Northern Railway Co., 1899, 76 Minn. 373, 79 N.W. 98 (violent language to husband); Sanderson v. Northern Pacific Railway Co., 1902, 88 Minn. 162, 92 N.W. 542 (putting children off of train); Ellis v. Cleveland, 1883, 55 Vt. 358 (wrongful arrest of husband); Sperier v. Ott, 1906, 116 La. 1087, 41 So. 323 (wrongful arrest of son).

Chapter 3

INTENTIONAL INTERFERENCE WITH PROPERTY

Table of Sections

Sec.
13. Trespass to Land.
14. Trespass to Chattels.
15. Conversion.

§ 13. Trespass to Land

Legal History

The term "trespass" has been used at various times during the development of modern Anglo-American tort law with different meanings. Initially, it was used to identify any tortious conduct on the part of the defendant that would subject him to liability pursuant to the common law action of trespass.[1] Thereafter, the term came to be used to describe the kind of caption of or intrusion onto tangible property, real or personal, that would give rise to recovery under the common law action of trespass.[2] Historically, the requirements for recovery for trespass to land under the common law action of trespass were an invasion (a) which interfered with the right of exclusive possession of the land, and (b) which was a direct result of some act committed by the defendant.[3] In the bundle of rights, privileges, powers, and immunities that are enjoyed by an owner of real property, perhaps the most important is the right to the exclusive "use" of the realty. An interference with this exclusive possessory interest brought about in a direct way from an act committed by the defendant was regarded legally as actionable. This was so even though the invasion caused no harm and even though the defendant was not at fault in causing the invasion. The strict and severe rules of the action of trespass, to which reference has previously been made,[4] have survived to a considerable extent until quite modern times, and the courts have been slow to modify them as in the case of injuries to the person. Some of them are only now passing out of the picture. This survival, which sometimes has resulted in distinctions between person and property that can only be described as highly artificial and unreasonable, probably was due primarily to the fact that upon the ac-

---

§ 13

1. See supra, § 7.
2. 1 Street, Foundations of Legal Liability, 1906, 19.
3. Star v. Rookesby, 1711, 1 Salk. 335, 91 Eng.Rep. 295, 3 Bl.Comm. 209; Brame v. Clark, 1908, 148 N.C. 364, 62 S.E. 418.
4. See supra, § 7.

tion of trespass was placed the burden of vindicating property rights, and claims to possession and ownership. Since in the usual case the important question was the disputed title, and any technical invasion would serve as the basis of litigation to settle it, the rules as to the character of the tort itself tended to become fixed,[5] and to remain so.

The most important of the trespass rules to survive was that which imposed liability for invasions of property which were neither intended nor negligent. The defendant was not liable so long as he had done no voluntary act, as where he was carried onto the plaintiff's land by others against his will.[6] But if, without negligence, the defendant felled a tree,[7] or dammed a stream,[8] or operated a street car [9] upon his own property, and the act resulted in the tree, stream or car going directly upon the land of another, the defendant was liable for the consequences. The same result was reached in a number of cases [10] in which the defendant, engaged in blasting operations, threw rocks or rubbish upon the plaintiff's land; and here it was perhaps justified by the highly dangerous and unusual character of the enterprise.[11]

There is no great triumph of reason in a rule which makes a street railway, whose car jumps the track, liable only for negligence to a pedestrian on the sidewalk, but absolutely liable to the owner of the plate-glass window behind him. The strict rule appears to have been repudiated in England,[12] where it was born, and it is safe to say that it is almost at its last gasp in the United States. In the famous Nitro-Glycerine Case,[13] the servants of a carrier innocently opened with a hammer a box which was leaking nitro-glycerine, and the resulting explosion damaged the plaintiff's premises. The Supreme Court refused to hold the carrier liable for trespass, in the absence of intent or negligence. Other cases, in a variety

---

5. "The law unquestionably does not prize property more than it does personal security, but at some points it has put forth more energetic efforts to protect property than it has to protect personal security. When it was once determined that a man could resort to a form of trespass to settle a matter of disputed title, the character of the trespass upon realty was fixed. Thenceforth the common law, in considering liability for intrusions upon realty, could not undertake to discriminate between the much and the little." 1 Street, Foundations of Legal Liability, 1906, 25. See also 8 Holdsworth, History of English Law, 1923, 467; Note, 1933, 5 Rocky Mt.L.Rev. 286.

6. Smith v. Stone, 1647, Style 65, 82 Eng.Rep. 533; Carter v. Thurston, 1877, 58 N.H. 104 (logs carried onto plaintiff's land by a stream). Thus one who slips and falls, or is otherwise carried onto the land by something beyond his control, is not a trespasser. Puchlopek v. Portsmouth Power Co., 1926, 82 N.H. 440, 136 A. 259; Durst v. Wareham, 1931, 132 Kan. 785, 297 P. 675; Edgarton v. H. P. Welch Co., 1947, 321 Mass. 603, 74 N.E.2d 674.

7. Newsom v. Anderson, 1841, 24 N.C. (2 Ired.) 42.

8. Lawson v. Price, 1876, 45 Md. 123; McKee v. Delaware & H. Canal Co., 1891, 125 N.Y. 353, 26 N.E. 305. This was apparently, and rather unaccountably, followed in Corrington v. Kalicak, Mo.App.1959, 319 S.W.2d 888.

9. Louisville Railway Co. v. Sweeney, 1914, 157 Ky. 620, 163 S.W. 739. Cf. Happy Coal Co. v. Smith, 1929, 229 Ky. 716, 17 S.W.2d 1008; West Virginia Cent. & P. Railway Co. v. Fuller, 1903, 96 Md. 652, 54 A. 669; Van Alstyne v. Rochester Telephone Corp., 1937, 163 Misc. 258, 296 N.Y.S. 726. These results are actually defended in Clark, Trespass Quare Clausum Fregit, 1960, 12 Ala.L.Rev. 301.

10. Hay v. Cohoes County, 1849, 2 N.Y. 159; Mulchanock v. Whitehall Cement Manufacturing Co., 1916, 253 Pa. 262, 98 A. 554; Adams & Sullivan v. Sengel, 1917, 177 Ky. 535, 197 S.W. 974; Asheville Construction Co. v. Southern Railway Co., 4 Cir.1927, 19 F.2d 32; Hakkila v. Old Colony Broken Stone & Concrete Co., 1928, 264 Mass. 447, 162 N.E. 895. Cf. Wheeler v. Norton, 1904, 92 App.Div. 368, 86 N.Y.S. 1095 (blasting resulting in flooding); Rochester Gas & Electric Co. v. Dunlop, 1933, 148 Misc. 849, 266 N.Y.S. 469 (airplane crash). See Smith, Liability for Substantial Physical Damage to Land by Blasting, 1920, 33 Harv.L.Rev. 442.

11. See § 78. Cf. United Electric Light Co. v. Deliso Construction Co., 1943, 315 Mass. 313, 52 N.E.2d 553, where the defendant constructed an underground tunnel, and forced liquid cement at high pressure against plaintiff's wires. The court found strict liability for "an improper and unreasonable use by the defendant of the space allotted to it."

12. It was rejected as to trespass to chattels, with implications as to any trespass, in National Coal Board v. J. C. Evans Co., [1951] 2 K.B. 861. The decision was at least foreshadowed in Gayler & Pope v. Davies & Son, [1924] 2 K.B. 75; and see Fowler v. Lanning, [1959] 1 Q.B. 426. See Winfield and Goodhart, Trespass and Negligence, 1933, 49 L.Q.Rev. 359.

13. Parrott v. Wells Fargo & Co., 1872, 82 U.S. (15 Wall.) 524.

of situations,[14] have agreed, and Kentucky, which was one of the strongholds of the old rule, has thrown it overboard in a case [15] where a rock was thrown up by the wheels of a truck, and onto the land of the plaintiff.

A second survival is that of the old distinction between direct and indirect invasions of the property, found in the actions of trespass and case.[16] If the defendant threw water on his neighbor's land, it was a trespass;[17] but if he merely constructed a spout,[18] or obstructed or diverted a stream so that as a result the water ultimately flowed onto the premises of the plaintiff,[19] the action was on the case. The chief importance of the distinction lay in the fact that case required proof of negligence or intent, as well as substantial damage, while trespass did not.

In a series of blasting cases,[20] a number of courts have held that injuries due to vibration or concussion, as distinguished from the actual arrival of a rock in the plaintiff's parlor, were indirect and so not actionable without proof of negligence. This distinction is now rejected by most courts,[21] and would appear to be slowly on its way to oblivion.

Trespass and Private Nuisance Distinguished

It can be said that, as of now, interests in land, as well as all other interests, are protected by three general tort theories. The three theories are intended to address these situations: (1) the defendant intended an invasion of a legally protected interest; (2) the defendant accidentally, but negligently or recklessly, brought about an invasion of a legally protected interest; and (3) the defendant accidentally caused an invasion of a legally protected interest in the course of engaging in some kind of activity, such as an abnormally dangerous activity, for which a limited strict liability is imposed. The term trespass has occasionally been used to mean any actionable entry on land [22], and the term private nuisance has occasionally been used to mean any other actionable interference with land.[23] But such usage can only lead to confusion since the rules and principles regarding matters such as the extent of liability, the importance of harm, and affirmative defenses are justifiably different for intentional and accidental invasions. Moreover, the legal doctrine related to the liability of one accidentally causing physical harm

---

14. Brown v. Collins, 1873, 53 N.H. 442 (runaway horse); Boyd v. White, 1954, 128 Cal.App.2d 641, 276 P.2d 92 (airplane crash); Wisconsin Power & Light Co. v. Columbia County, 1958, 3 Wis.2d 1, 87 N.W.2d 279 (tower caused to tilt by dirt dumped near it); Smith v. Pate, 1957, 246 N.C. 63, 97 S.E.2d 457 (automobile crashed into building); Gallin v. Poulou, 1956, 140 Cal. App.2d 638, 295 P.2d 958 (damage to building from vibration); Hawke v. Maus, 1967, 141 Ind.App. 126, 226 N.E.2d 713 (entry due to collision).

15. Randall v. Shelton, Ky.1956, 293 S.W.2d 559. See Notes, 1957, 46 Ky.L.J. 187; 1957, 14 Wash. & Lee L.Rev. 319.

16. See supra, § 7.

17. Prewitt v. Clayton, 1827, 21 Ky. (5 T.B.Mon.) 4; Wheeler v. Norton, 1904, 92 App.Div. 368, 86 N.Y.S. 1095 (breaking water pipe). Cf. Van Alstyne v. Rochester Telephone Corp., 1937, 163 Misc. 258, 296 N.Y.S. 726.

18. Reynolds v. Clarke, 1725, 1 Strange 634, 2 Ld. Raym. 1399, 93 Eng.Rep. 747. Or if water is discharged onto A's property, and then flows onto that of B, B's action is on the case. Nicholls v. Ely Beet Sugar Factory, [1931] 2 Ch. 84.

19. Suter v. Wenatchee Water Power Co., 1904, 35 Wash. 1, 76 P. 298; Butala v. Union Electric Co., 1924, 70 Mont. 580, 226 P. 899; Norwood v. Eastern Oregon Land Co., 1931, 139 Or. 25, 5 P.2d 1057, modified 1932, 139 Or. 25, 7 P.2d 996; Scheurich v. Empire District Electric Co., Mo.1916, 188 S.W. 114; Walter v. Wagner, 1928, 225 Ky. 255, 8 S.W.2d 421.

20. See infra, § 78.

21. See infra, chapter 14.

22. See, Second Restatement of Torts, § 821D, Comment d. Trespass and private nuisance are alike in that each is a field of tort liability rather than a single type of tortious conduct. Liability for either may arise from an intentional or an unintentional invasion.

23. See, Second Restatement of Torts, § 822. "General Rule.

"One is subject to liability for a private nuisance if, but only if, his conduct is a legal cause of an invasion of another's interest in the private use and enjoyment of land, and the invasion is either

(a) intentional and unreasonable, or

(b) unintentional and otherwise actionable under the rules controlling liability for negligent or reckless conduct, or for abnormally dangerous conditions or activities."

to tangible things under modern law is substantially the same as that related to the liability of those accidentally causing physical harm to the person.[24] The terms "trespass" and "private nuisance" will not, therefore, be used in this text to indicate actionable accidental invasions of interests in land; rather, these terms will be used to describe two distinct kinds of actionable intentional invasions.

Any intentional use of another's real property, without authorization and without a privilege by law to do so, is actionable as a trespass without regard to harm.[25] Except in those rare circumstances where a privilege is recognized, factors related to the amount of the harm done to the plaintiff, the utility of the defendant's conduct, and the reasonableness of the defendant's conduct without permission are immaterial. On the other hand, an intentional and nontrespassory interference with the use and enjoyment of another's real property is actionable as a private nuisance only if the interference proves to be substantial and unreasonable.[26] Thus, a defendant can, without using a plaintiff's land, become liable by maintaining a condition or engaging in an activity that unreasonably interferes with the plaintiff in the use and enjoyment of the plaintiff's land. This tort is treated in Chapter 15.

Entries as Trespasses

The historical requirement that an invasion must constitute an interference with possession in order to be actionable as a trespass has persisted.[27] It is this requirement of interference with possession and, therefore, with use, of another's property that separates the tort of trespass from the tort of private nuisance, and it is this requirement that justifies the notion that the invasion is actionable without physical harm to the land being caused.[28] One way to interfere with possession, and thereby use of property is to bring about an entry on the land. This can be done by intruding personally thereon, by causing another to so intrude, or by causing some tangible thing to be projected onto the land.[29] The right to the exclusive use of property necessarily implies the correlative right to demand that others who wish to use the property should pay for that use even though that use might involve no interference with the plaintiff in his use. It is feasible and practical to give the landowner this kind of a privilege subject to an occasional privilege of others. Various policy reasons have been given to justify the position that unprivileged and unauthorized intentional entries should be actionable without damage, including the prevention of the acquisition of a prescription right, to settle a dispute regarding title, to vindicate a property right, and to avoid breaches of the peace.[30]

Any physical entry upon the surface of the land is a trespass, whether the entry is a walking upon it, flooding it with water, casting objects upon it, or otherwise. In general, the courts, supported by the Restatement of Torts, have abandoned any distinction between direct and indirect invasions where there is an actual entry by a person or a

24. Second Restatement of Torts, § 822, Comment i.

25. See cases cited infra note 28. Keeton, 1959, Trespass, Nuisance, and Strict Liability, 59 Colum.L.Rev. 457.

26. See Chapter 15, Nuisance, Sec. 89, Private Nuisance.

27. See, Zimmerman v. Shreeve, 1882, 59 Md. 357, 362; Note, 1950, 39 Ky.L.J. 99, 102.

28. The cases are reviewed in excellent Notes in 1960, 60 Col.L.Rev. 877; 1966, 19 Okl.L.Rev. 117. Thackery v. Union Portland Cement Co., 1924, 64 Utah 437, 231 P. 813; Riblet v. Spokane-Portland Cement Co., 1952, 41 Wn.2d 249, 248 P.2d 380; Arvidson v. Reynolds Metals Co., W.D.Wash.1954, 125 F.Supp. 481, affirmed 1954, 236 F.2d 224, certiorari denied 352 U.S. 968, 77 S.Ct. 359, 1 L.Ed.2d 323; Ryan v. City of Emmetsburg, 1942, 232 Iowa 600, 4 N.W.2d 435; Waschak v. Moffatt, 1954, 379 Pa. 441, 109 A.2d 310; Bartlett v. Grasselli Chemical Co., 1922, 92 W.Va. 445, 115 S.E. 451; Davis v. Georgia-Pacific Corp., 1968, 251 Or. 239, 445 P.2d 481.

29. Second Restatement of Torts, § 158(a).

30. Morris, Torts, 1953, 18–22; Keeton, Trespass, Nuisance and Strict Liability, 1959, 59 Col.L.Rev. 457, 468.

thing.[31] The differentiation between direct and indirect results may not be absolutely dead. Some modern courts have said that the difference between trespass and nuisance is that the former must be the result of a direct infringement or invasion, while the latter is the result of an act which is not wrongful in itself, but becomes so only because of its consequences[32]. Often the court's meaning is not clear, but the position taken by Alabama in Rushing v. Hooper-McDonald, Inc.[33] is clearly representative of the modern view. In that case an adjoining landowner dumped asphalt so that in due course it entered a stream which carried it into the plaintiff's fish pond, resulting in the killing of the plaintiff's fish. In holding the defendant liable for a trespass, the court rejected the argument that the injury was not direct.

While it is generally assumed and held that a personal entry is unnecessary for a trespass, the defendant's act must result in an invasion of tangible matter.[34] Otherwise, there would be no use or interference with possession. Thus, it is not a trespass to project light, noise, or vibrations across or onto the land of another.[35] These acts may give rise to liability because of a private nuisance resulting from intentional interference with the use and enjoyment of property, or because of harm attributable to negligence, or because of liability for harm caused by an abnormally dangerous activity.[36] It is, however, reasonably clear that the mere intentional introduction onto the land of another of smoke, gas, noise, and the like, without reference to the amount thereof or other factors that are considered in connection with a private nuisance, is not actionable as a trespass. The historical requirement of an entry or a use that interferes with possession is one that is necessary, unless the very questionable position is taken that one ought to be able to use another's property without permission so long as the use does not harm the property or interfere with the owner's use.

In Martin v. Reynolds Metals Co.,[37] the court held that the projection of fluoride compounds in the form of gases and particulates onto the land of the plaintiff was a trespass. Trespassory invasions and actionable invasions constituting a private nuisance were governed by different statutes of limitations. This problem precipitated a decision that a possessor's interest in exclusive possession can be interfered with by invisible forces as well as by material things. Such a conclusion required, however, a further alteration of the tort of trespass. The court concluded that the tort of trespass involved a weighing process similar to that involved in the law of private nuisance.

There are a few additional decisions finding a trespass constituted by the entry of invisible gases and microscopic particles, but only if harm results.[38] These are, in reality,

---

31. Second Restatement of Torts, 158, Comment *h*. See infra ch. 15.

32. Arvidson v. Reynolds Metals Co., W.D.Wash. 1954, 125 F.Supp. 481, affirmed per curiam, 9th Cir. 1956, 236 F.2d 224, certiorari denied, 1957, 352 U.S. 968, 77 S.Ct. 359, 1 L.Ed.2d 323; Rinzler v. Folsom, 1953, 209 Ga. 549, 74 S.E.2d 661; Waschak v. Moffat, 1954, 379 Pa. 441, 109 A.2d 310. In Arvidson, where fluorides were being discharged upon plaintiff's land the court said: "Even though it were assumed that solids in the form of minute particulates from defendant's plants have been deposited on plaintiff's lands, the injury, if any, resulting therefrom was consequential, the action is on the case, and awards of nominal damages would not be justified by the facts or required by the law." 125 F.Supp. at 488. Cases set forth in Annot., 1927, 48 A.L.R. 1248.

33. 293 Ala. 56, 1974, 300 So.2d 94.

34. See, supra note 28.

35. Metzger v. Pennsylvania Ohio & Detroit Railroad Co., 1946, 146 Ohio St. 406, 66 N.E.2d 203 (smoke); Amphitheatres, Inc. v. Portland Meadows, 1948, 184 Or. 336, 198 P.2d 847 (light); Waschak v. Moffatt, 1954, 379 Pa. 441, 109 A.2d 310 (gas).

36. See, infra, chapters 13 and 15.

37. 1959, 221 Or. 86, 342 P.2d 790, certiorari denied, 1960, 362 U.S. 918, 80 S.Ct. 672, 4 L.Ed.2d 739.

38. Gregg v. Delhi-Taylor Oil Corp., 1961, 162 Tex. 26, 344 S.W.2d 411 (gas); Martin v. Reynolds Metals Co., 1959, 221 Or. 86, 342 P.2d 790, certiorari denied, 1960, 362 U.S. 918, 80 S.Ct. 672, 4 L.Ed.2d 739 (gas and microscopic deposit); Reynolds Metals Co. v. Martin, 9 Cir. 1964, 337 F.2d 780 (same); Hall v. De Weld Mica Corp., 1956, 244 N.C. 182, 93 S.E.2d 56 (dust); Zimmer v. Stephenson, 1965, 66 Wn.2d 477, 403 P.2d 343

examples of either the tort of private nuisance or liability for harm resulting from negligence. The historical requirement of an intrusion by a person or some tangible thing seems the sounder way to go about protecting the exclusive right to the use of property. In a recent case, a tenant of adjoining property was not permitted to recover on a trespass theory against a contractor who was excavating and thereby knowingly annoying the plaintiff by means of noise and vibrations.[39]

Invasions with Water and Liquids

Invasions of the land of another with deleterious liquids such as crude oil, salt water, gasoline, and the like have been treated both as trespassory intrusions onto the land and actionable *per se*, and as not trespassory in character and actionable only when the defendant can be said to have committed a private nuisance.[40] The resultant confusion has been reflected in the Restatement of Torts.[41] It has generally been held that a defendant commits a trespass if he constructs a dam which causes water to overflow onto the land of another from which he has acquired no easement.[42] There is much more uncertainty about the liability for known seepage or leakage from conditions that a defendant creates.[43] There are two important differences between the backwater from the dam and the seepage or leakage results from some kind of condition created by an industrial operator. First, backwater from a dam usually occupies a significant space, at least for a short period, whereas the liquid that seeps into soil or water does not. Secondly, the invasion comes about in a more indirect manner when seepage or leakage is involved. It is suggested that when liquids are intentionally caused to intrude upon the *surface* of another's land, the intrusion should be regarded as trespassory, and that subsurface invasions should not be regarded as trespassory, as pointed out infra.[44]

Character of Defendant's Act

The trespass may be committed not only by entry upon the land, or by casting objects upon it, but also by causing a third person to enter. The defendant may carry him on the land by force,[45] pursue him so that he enters through fear,[46] or lead him to enter by false

---

(spark); Martin v. Union Pacific Railroad Co., 1970, 256 Or. 563, 474 P.2d 739 (fire).

39. Celebrity Studios, Inc. v. Civetta Excavating, Inc., 1973, 72 Misc.2d 1077, 340 N.Y.S.2d 694.

40. Keeton and Jones, Tort Liability and the Oil and Gas Industry II, 1961, 39 Tex.L.Rev. 253, 260.

41. Three illustrations from the Second Restatement of Torts disclose the confusion.
Illustration 3 to Comment h of § 158 is as follows: A intentionally throws a pail of water against a wall of B's house. A is a trespasser.
Illustration 5 to Comment h of § 158 is as follows: A erects a dam across a stream, thereby intentionally causing the water to back up and flood the land of B, an upper riparian proprietor. A is a trespasser.
Illustration 1 to Comment A of section 833 is as follows: The A Railroad Company owns and is in possession of a strip of land adjacent to land owned and occupied by B. There is a natural depression across both tracts of land through which surface waters from rain and melting snow are accustomed to flow from B's land onto and across A's land. A builds an embankment across this depression, leaving no opening, and as A realizes, the surface waters accumulating from the next hard rainfall cannot escape, spread out over B's land and damage his crops. This invasion of B's interest in the use and enjoyment of his land is intentional and A's liability depends upon whether the invasion is unreasonable.

42. Winchester Water Works Co. v. Holliday, 1931, 241 Ky. 762, 45 S.W.2d 9; Bobo v. Young, 1952, 258 Ala. 222, 61 So.2d 814; Humphreys-Mexia Oil Co. v. Arseneaux, 1927, 116 Tex. 603, 297 S.W. 225.

43. Phillips v. Sun Oil Co., 1954, 307 N.Y. 328, 121 N.E.2d 249 (trespass approach); City of Barberton v. Miksch, 1934, 128 Ohio St. 169, 190 N.E. 387 (trespass approach); Burr v. Adam Eidemiller, Inc., 1956, 386 Pa. 416, 126 A.2d 403 (nuisance approach); Humble Pipe Line Co. v. Anderson, Tex.Civ.App.1966, 339 S.W.2d 259 refused, n.r.e. (nuisance approach); Healey v. Citizens Gas & Electric Co., 1924, 199 Iowa 82, 201 N.W. 118 (nuisance approach).

44. See, chapter 15, §§ 8–9.

45. Smith v. Stone, 1647, Style 65, 82 Eng.Rep. 533.

46. Vandenburgh v. Truax, 1847, 4 N.Y. (Denio) 464.

representations,[47] or by a grant of the land,[48] or other inducement.[49]

The trespass may also be committed by remaining on the land after a right of entry has terminated.[50] Thus it is a trespass to refuse to leave after a license to remain has been revoked,[51] or to fail to remove property at the end of an agreed period.[52] At common law the action must be on the case,[53] since there was no forcible invasion; but since the forms of action have been discarded, it is commonly held that there is an actionable trespass.[54]

The Intent Required

The intent required as a basis for liability as a trespasser is simply an intent to be at the place on the land where the trespass allegedly occurred.[55] The distinction to be made is between accidental and intentional entries. Accidental entries are often actionable when produced negligently or as a consequence of abnormally dangerous activities but not as trespasses.[56] Loose language over the meaning of intent has led to some confusion.

It has been said occasionally that the only requirement is that the entry be the result of an intentional act.[57] But all acts in the sense of movements of the body directed by the will are intentional. It is often difficult to know what is meant by this statement. The statement is usually made in reference to situations where the defendant intended to be where he was but did not intend the harmful consequences of his action. The point is that the defendant intended the intrusion. Thus, when a child inserted a tennis ball into a drain pipe of a swimming pool without intending to cause harm, the court held that the "intent controlling is the intent to complete the physical act" that resulted in the harm.[58] The defendant intended to intrude at a place without authorization to do

47. Kirby Lumber Corp. v. Karpel, 5th Cir. 1956, 233 F.2d 373 (inaccurate information about boundary lines).

48. Sanborn v. Sturtevant, 1882, 17 Minn. 200; Donovan v. Consolidated Coal Co., 1900, 187 Ill. 28, 58 N.E. 290; Hendrix v. Black, 1918, 132 Ark. 473, 201 S.W. 283; Murrell v. Goodwill, 1925, 159 La. 1057, 106 So. 564; Darden v. McMillian, 1956, 93 Ga.App. 892, 93 S.E.2d 169. See, however, McDermott v. Sway, 1951, 78 N.D. 521, 50 N.W.2d 235, holding that the negligent but bona fide granting of an easement does not make the grantor liable for the trespass.

49. Castleberry v. Mack, 1943, 205 Ark. XIX, 167 S.W.2d 489. Cf. State v. Lasiter, Tex.Civ.App.1961, 352 S.W.2d 915, error dismissed, where the state authorized and directed a city to trespass on the land by laying a sewer line across it.

50. Second Restatement of Torts, § 158; Wood v. Leadbitter, 1848, 13 M. & W. 838, 153 Eng.Rep. 351; People v. Weinberg, 1967, 6 Mich.App. 345, 149 N.W.2d 248; Rager v. McCloskey, 1953, 305 N.Y. 75, 111 N.E.2d 214, motion denied 305 N.Y. 924, 114 N.E.2d 476; Hubbard v. Commonwealth, 1967, 207 Va. 673, 152 S.E.2d 250; Johnson v. State, 1965, 277 Ala. 655, 173 So.2d 824.

51. Mitchell v. Mitchell, 1893, 54 Minn. 301, 55 N.W. 1134; Davis v. Stone, 1876, 120 Mass. 228. Cf. McKenzie v. Minis, 1909, 132 Ga. 323, 63 S.E. 900 (discharged servant); Emry v. Roanoke Navigation & Water Power Co., 1892, 111 N.C. 94, 16 S.E. 18 (lessee).

This is subject to the qualification that the Federal Civil Rights Act of 1964, requiring all places of public accommodation whose business affects interstate commerce to serve customers "without discrimination or segregation on the ground of race, color, religion, or national origin," is held to entitle the customer not only to enter and demand service, but to remain and insist upon it after he is ordered to leave. Hamm v. City of Rock Hill, 1964, 379 U.S. 306, 85 S.Ct. 384, 13 L.Ed.2d 300, rehearing denied, 1965, 379 U.S. 995, 85 S.Ct. 698, 13 L.Ed.2d 614; Dilworth v. Riner, 5th Cir. 1965, 343 F.2d 226.

52. Rogers v. Kent Board of County Road Commissioners, 1948, 319 Mich. 661, 30 N.W.2d 358; Ross v. Williams Manufacturing Co., 1928, 38 Ga.App. 178, 143 S.E. 448; Benjamin v. American Telephone & Telegraph Co., 1907, 196 Mass. 454, 82 N.E. 681 (failure to remove telephone pole on demand).

53. Winterbourne v. Morgan, 1809, 11 East 395, 103 Eng.Rep. 1056; Boults v. Mitchell, 1850, 15 Pa. 371; Stone v. Knapp, 1857, 29 Vt. 501.

54. Mitchell v. Mitchell, 1893, 54 Minn. 301, 55 N.W. 1134; Snedecor v. Pope, 1904, 143 Ala. 275, 39 So. 318; cf. Beers v. McGinnis, 1906, 191 Mass. 279, 77 N.E. 768.

55. Second Restatement of Torts, § 163, Comment b.

56. See infra the Chapters on Negligence, and Chapter 13, Sec. 78, on Abnormally Dangerous Activities.

57. Cleveland Park Club v. Perry, D.C.Mun.App. 1960, 165 A.2d 485; Margosian v. United States Airlines, Inc. D.C.E.D.N.Y.1955, 127 F.Supp. 464.

58. Cleveland Park Club v. Perry, supra note 57.

so, and it was for that reason a trespass. The fact that harm was not intended is immaterial.

This "volitional act" or "intentional act" language can be found in other cases, but the results can generally be explained on other grounds, or simply as novel holdings, sometimes by intermediate courts.[59] The confusion engendered by the "intentional act" language is well illustrated in Chartrand v. State of New York.[60] In that case, gas seeped from a police station operated by the State of New York and into the plaintiff's restaurant. The court said that the defendant was not liable as a trespasser because the defendant did not intend the act which produced the invasion. But he did. Still, the court went on to say that the intrusion must be the inevitable consequence of what the defendant intentionally does,[61] and so the intent to enter did not exist.

One type of recurring problem that has led to conflicting decisions is the damaging of underground cables, pipes, wires, and the like by contractors and others engaged in excavating or intruding into the subsurface of land.[62] Since there was no intent to make contact with the thing that was damaged, its presence being unknown, most courts have perhaps regarded this an an accidental intrusion, onto the thing, with liability resulting only from proof of negligence.[63] Other courts, however, have treated this as a trespassory intrusion, since there was a definite intention to intrude at the designated subgrade.[64] Even if the latter position is taken, such a decision cannot be regarded as imposing liability for accidental intrusions on a trespass theory. It is reasonably clear that the result could depend upon whether the cable or wire in place is a part of the realty or is personal property.[65]

The defendant is liable for an intentional entry although he has acted in good faith, under the mistaken belief, however reasonable, that he is committing no wrong.[66] Thus, he is a trespasser although he believes that

---

59. Phillips v. Sun Oil Co., 1954, 307 N.Y. 328, 121 N.E.2d 249 (leakage of oil from tank); Wood v. United Airlines, 1962, 32 Misc.2d 955, 223 N.Y.S.2d 692, affirmed 16 A.D.2d 659, 226 N.Y.S.2d 1022, appeal dismissed 11 N.Y.2d 1053, 230 N.Y.S.2d 207, 184 N.E.2d 180 (crash of plane out of control); First City National Bank of Houston v. Japhet, Tex.Civ.App.1965, 390 S.W.2d 70, error dismissed (motorist suffered heart attack, ran onto land).

60. App.Div.1974, 362 N.Y.S.2d 237.

61. See also, Ruiz v. Forman, Tex.Civ.App.1974, 514 S.W.2d 817, error dismissed, for a holding that probably reaches a good result for a questionable reason. There a motorist swerved off the road onto plaintiff's property to avoid a collision. The Court held that the defendant was liable even though he did not intend the invasion since he intended the act that resulted in the invasion. But he intended the invasion to escape greater harm and since he did this to prevent harm to himself he has an incomplete privilege to use plaintiff's property and must pay for any harm done.

Wood v. United Airlines, 1962, 32 Misc.2d 955, 223 N.Y.S.2d 692, affirmed 16 A.D.2d 659, 226 N.Y.S.2d 1022, appeal dismissed 11 N.Y.2d 1053, 230 N.Y.S.2d 207, 184 N.E.2d 180, draws the distinction between a forced but intentional landing, and a plane entirely out of control. In the latter case it was held that the invasion was not due to any volitional act of the defendant, as where his horse runs away with him. Cf. Gibbons v. Pepper, 1695, 1 Ld.Raym. 38, 91 Eng.Rep. 922. In the former, the invasion might be privileged to a limited extent, but the defendant might be required to pay for any damage which resulted. See infra, § 24; Notes, 1933, 33 Col.L.Rev. 1459; 1933, 47 Harv.L.Rev. 345.

See Bohlen, Aviation Under the Common Law, 1934, 45 Harv.L.Rev. 216; Vold and Wolf, Aircraft Operator's Liability for Ground Damage and Passenger Injury, 1935, 13 Neb.L.B. 373; Sweeney, Adjusting the Conflicting Interests of Landowner and Aviator in Anglo-American Law, 1932, 3 J.Air Law 329, 531.

62. Comment, Thweatt, The Defendant Broke Our Pipe Line, 1973, 6 Natural Resources Lawyer 249.

63. National Coal Board v. Evans, [1951] 2 K.B. 861; Socony-Vacuum Oil Co. v. Bailey, 1952, 202 Misc. 364, 109 N.Y.S.2d 799; Mountain States Telephone & Telegraph Co. v. Horn Tower Construction Co., 1961, 147 Colo. 166, 363 P.2d 175; Texas-New Mexico Pipeline Co. v. Allstate Construction, Inc., 1962, 70 N.M. 15, 369 P.2d 401.

64. Mountain States Telephone and Telegraph Co. v. Vowell Construction Co., 161 Tex. 432, 1960, 341 S.W.2d 148; Illinois Bell Telephone Co. v. Charles Ind Co., 1954, 3 Ill.App.2d 258, 121 N.E.2d 600; United Electric Light Co. v. Deliso Construction Co., 1943, 315 Mass. 313, 52 N.E.2d 553.

65. Infra note 77.

66. Second Restatement of Torts, § 164; State v. Cobb, 1964, 262 N.C. 262, 136 S.E.2d 674.

the land is his own,[67] or that he has the consent of the owner,[68] or the legal privilege of entry;[69] or although the defendant is a child too young to understand that what he is doing is wrong.[70] The interest of the landowner is protected at the expense of those who make innocent mistakes. But if the mistake is induced by the conduct of the owner himself, there will be no liability for the intrusion; the only possibility of recovery lies in quasi-contract, to the extent of any unjust enrichment.[71]

Necessity of Damage

The common law action of trespass could be maintained without proof of any actual damage. From every direct entry upon the soil of another, "the law infers some damage; if nothing more, the treading down grass or herbage."[72] The plaintiff recovered nominal damages where no substantial damage was shown,[73] or even where the trespass was a benefit to him.[74] The action was directed at the vindication of the legal right, without which the defendant's conduct, if repeated, might in time ripen into prescription; and there was no room for the application of the maxim that the law does not concern itself with trifles.[75]

On the other hand, the action on the case required proof of actual damage, and could not be maintained without it.[76] Here again the distinction between direct and indirect invasions is quite illogical. It seems more reasonable to limit the recovery without proof of damage to cases of intentional invasion, where the trespass action may serve an important purpose in determining and vindicating the right to exclusive possession of the property.[77] No such necessity is apparent in the case of invasions due to mere negligence or dangerous activities.[78]

---

67. Maye v. Yappen, 1863, 23 Cal. 306; Isle Royale Mining Co. v. Hertin, 1877, 37 Mich. 332; Ball & Brother Lumber Co. v. Simms Lumber Co., 1908, 121 La. 627, 46 So. 674; Alabama Great Southern Railroad Co. v. Broach, 1960, 238 Miss. 618, 119 So.2d 923; Bihm v. Hirsch, La.App.1967, 193 So.2d 865.

68. Anderson v. United States, E.D.Pa.1966, 259 F.Supp. 148; Jackson v. Pettigrew, 1908, 133 Mo.App. 508, 113 S.W. 672; Jernigan v. Clark, 1901, 134 Ala. 313, 32 So. 686; Southern Counties Ice Co. v. RKO Radio Pictures, S.D.Cal.1941, 39 F.Supp. 157; Serota v. M. & M. Utilities, Inc., 1967, 55 Misc.2d 286, 285 N.Y.S.2d 121.

69. Connor v. Greenberg, 1916, 198 Ill.App. 129; Blatt v. McBarron, 1894, 161 Mass. 21, 36 N.E. 468; Concanan v. Boynton, 1889, 76 Iowa 543, 41 N.W. 213.

70. Cleveland Park Club v. Perry, D.C.Mun.App. 1960, 165 A.2d 485; Brown v. Dellinger, Tex.Civ.App. 1962, 355 S.W.2d 742, refused n.r.e.

71. See Gunn v. Parsons, 1925, 213 Ala. 217, 104 So. 390; Merriweather v. Bell, 1900, 139 Ky. 402, 58 S.W. 987; Leach v. Fosburgh Lumber Co., 1912, 159 N.C. 532, 75 S.E. 716; Restatement of Restitution, § 129.

Contra: Holmes v. Wilson, 1839, 10 Ad. & El. 503, 113 Eng.Rep. 190; Russell v. Brown, 1874, 63 Me. 203; McGann v. Hamilton, 1890, 58 Conn. 69, 19 A. 376; Stowers v. Gilbert, 1898, 156 N.Y. 600, 51 N.E. 282. See also Fergerson v. Utilities Elkhorn Coal Co., Ky. 1958, 313 S.W.2d 395, looking to the ease of removal of the condition, as in the cases in the next succeeding note.

72. Dougherty v. Stepp, 1835, 18 N.C. 371.

73. Dixon v. Clow, N.Y.1840, 24 Wend. 188; Pfeiffer v. Grossman, 1853, 15 Ill. 53; Giddings v. Rogalewski, 1916, 192 Mich. 319, 158 N.W. 951; Fletcher v. Howard, 1928, 226 Ky. 258, 10 S.W.2d 825; Forest City Cotton Co. v. Miller, 1940, 218 N.C. 294, 10 S.E.2d 806, rehearing allowed, 1941, 219 N.C. 279, 13 S.E.2d 557.

74. Harmony Ditch Co. v. Sweeney, 1924, 31 Wyo. 1, 222 P. 577; Longenecker v. Zimmerman, 1954, 175 Kan. 719, 267 P.2d 543.

75. Norvell v. Thompson, 1834, 2 S.C. (Hill L.,) 470; Bragg v. Laraway, 1893, 65 Vt. 673, 27 A. 492; Foust v. Kinney, 1918, 202 Ala. 392, 80 So. 474; Reeves v. Jackson, 1944, 207 Ark. 1089, 184 S.W.2d 256.

76. Thompson v. Crocker, 1829, 26 Mass. (9 Pick.) 59; Cooper v. Hall, 1832, 5 Ohio 320, 321; Garrett v. McKie, 1843, 1 S.C. (Rich.) 444.

77. Second Restatement of Torts, § 163.

78. Second Restatement of Torts, § 165. One important consequence would be the effect upon the statute of limitations. In cases of intentional trespass, the cause of action is now held to accrue when the invasion occurs. Kansas Pacific Railway Co. v. Mihlman, 1876, 17 Kan. 224; Williams v. Pomeroy Coal Co., 1882, 37 Ohio St. 583; National Copper Co. v. Minnesota Mining Co., 1885, 57 Mich. 83, 23 N.W. 781. In the case of nuisance, or other indirect invasion, it usually is held to accrue only when damage results. Hempstead v. Cargill, 1891, 46 Minn. 141, 48 N.W. 558; Hooker v. Farmers' Irrigation District, 8 Cir.1921, 272 F. 600; Heckaman v. Northern Pacific Railway Co., 1933, 93 Mont. 363, 20 P.2d 258. See Note, 1937, 21 Minn.L.Rev. 334. If the view of the Restatement is adopted, the distinction would of course be between intentional and nonintentional invasions.

Furthermore, once it is determined that a trespass has been committed, the trespasser's responsibility has been carried to an extreme length as to the consequences for which he is liable. While it cannot be said that the defendant is liable for everything that follows as a result of his trespass,[79] he is held responsible, under a rule apparently derived originally from the principle of "transferred intent," [80] for any visible and tangible damage inflicted upon the land itself, although such damage is not the result of any negligent or wrongful act beyond the mere trespass, and could not reasonably have been anticipated at the time of the unlawful entry. Thus if the trespasser lights a fire in the stove, using all possible care, and the fire burns down the house, the trespasser is liable for the consequences; [81] and the same is true as to any other such damage.[82] The same liability has been extended to the person of the possessor,[83] and to his chattels on the land,[84] and even to the members of his family.[85]

So, in Wardrop v. City of Manhattan Beach,[86] the defendant was held liable on a trespass theory for causing plaintiff to develop polio by pumping contaminated water into the plaintiff's back yard. Also, in Montega Corp. v. Hazelrigs [87], the plaintiff recovered damages for the serious mental illness be suffered after the flooding of his property by the defendant in the course of carrying out a construction project on property adjacent to the plaintiff. One who trespasses upon the land of another incurs the risk of becoming liable for any bodily harm which is caused to the possessor of the land or to members of the household by any conduct of the trespasser during the continuance of the trespass.[88] It would appear that the defendant trespasser will be liable for all direct consequences of any conduct engaged in while trespassing. Quite frequently, however, the defendant has been held liable for indirect consequences, some of which have not been reasonably foreseeable, of conduct engaged in while trespassing.[89] It is important to realize that those who use another's land without permission may justifiably have

---

79. See § 14.

80. See Prosser, Transferred Intent, 1967, 45 Tex.L. Rev. 650; supra, p. 83.

81. Wyant v Crouse, 1901, 127 Mich. 158, 86 N.W. 527; Southern Counties Ice Co. v. RKO Radio Pictures, S.D.Cal.1941, 39 F.Supp. 157; Lee v. Stewart, 1940, 218 N.C. 287, 10 S.E.2d 804; Newsom v. Meyer, 1925, 102 Conn. 93, 128 A. 699; Wetzel v. Satterwhite, 1910, 59 Tex.Civ.App. 1, 125 S.W. 93.

82. Cleveland Park Club v. Perry, D.C.Mun.App. 1960, 165 A.2d 485 (drain plugged with tennis ball, simming pool damaged); Curtis v. Fruin-Colnon Contracting Co., 1952, 363 Mo. 676, 253 S.W.2d 158 (foundation cracked, building settled); City of Garland v. White, Tex.Civ.App.1963, 368 S.W.2d 12 refused, n.r.e. (shot at dog, damaged house); Whitehead v. Zeiller, Tex.Civ.App.1954, 265 S.W.2d 689 (soil removed, erosion damage to trees); Garrett v. Sewell, 1895, 108 Ala. 521, 18 So. 737 (fence removed, cattle entered).

83. Rogers v. Board of Road Commissioners for Kent County, 1948, 319 Mich. 661, 30 N.W.2d 358; Brackett v. Bellows Falls Hydro-Elec. Corp., 1934, 87 N.H. 173, 175 A. 822; Kopka v. Bell Telephone Co., 1952, 371 Pa. 444, 91 A.2d 232; Ham v. Maine-New Hampshire Interstate Bridge Authority, 1943, 92 N.H. 268, 30 A.2d 1; Mitchell v. Mitchell, 1893, 54 Minn. 301, 55 N.W. 1134.

84. Van Alstyne v. Rochester Tel. Corp., 1937, 163 Misc. 258, 296 N.Y.S. 726 (dogs swallowed dropped lead); Renaire Corp. v. Vaughn, D.C.Mun.App.1958, 142 A.2d 148 (window broken, tools stolen); Eten v. Luyster, 1875, 60 N.Y. 252 (box of money lost); Damron v. Roach, 1843, 23 Tenn. 126 (4 Humph. 134), (fence removed, cattle strayed).

85. Wardrop v. City of Manhattan Beach, 1958, 160 Cal.App.2d 779, 326 P.2d 15 (child contracting polio); St. Petersburg Coca-Cola Bottling Co. v. Cuccinello, Fla.1950, 44 So.2d 670 (child run down); Brabazon v. Joannes Bros. Co., 1939, 231 Wis. 426, 286 N.W. 21 (wife); Keesecker v. G. M. McKelvey Co., 1940, 64 Ohio App. 29, 27 N.E.2d 787, reversed on other grounds, 1941, 68 Ohio App. 505, 42 N.E.2d 223, second appeal, 1943, 141 Ohio St. 162, 47 N.E.2d 211 (child).

86. 1958, 160 Cal.App.2d 779, 326 P.2d 15.

87. 1972, 229 Ga. 126, 189 S.E.2d 421.

88. Second Restatement of Torts, § 162, Comment f.

89. Kopka v. Bell Telephone Co., 1952, 371 Pa. 444, 91 A.2d 232 (fall into hole); Rogers v. Board of Road Commissioners for Kent County, 1948, 319 Mich. 661, 30 N.W.2d 358 (fall from mowing machine); Brackett v. Bellows Falls Hydro-Electric Corp., 1934, 87 N.H. 173, 175 A. 822 (same); Van Alstyne v. Rochester Telephone Corp., 1937, 163 Misc. 258, 296 N.Y.S. 726 (dogs eating dropped lead); Keesecker v. G. M. McKelvey Co., 1940, 64 Ohio App. 29, 27 N.E.2d 787 reversed on other grounds, 1941, 68 Ohio App. 505, 42 N.E.2d 223, second appeal, 1943, 141 Ohio St. 162, 47 N.E.2d 211.

"risks of losses" allocated to them far beyond those normally imposed when liability is imposed on a negligence theory. So-called proximate cause rules adopted for fixing limits to liability for negligence are not necessarily applicable to trespasses. Even the requirement of physical harm has been relaxed to permit recovery of damages for mental distress suffered not only by the possessor of the land [90] but also by the family [91] as a consequence of a trespass.

Necessity of Possession

The action for trespass is designed to protect the interest in exclusive possession of the land in its intact physical condition. Therefore any person in the actual and exclusive possession [92] of the property may maintain the action, although the person has no legal title, and is in wrongful occupation,[93] as for example under a void lease,[94] or in mere adverse possession.[95] As against the fact of possession in the plaintiff, no defendant in a trespass action may set up the right of a third person, unless the defendant is able to connect himself with that right.[96] "Any possession is a legal possession against a wrongdoer." [97] The reason usually is stated to be that it is more conducive to the maintenance of order to protect existing, although wrongful, possession against the depredations of other wrongdoers, than to lay any one with a defective title open to such depredations without redress. But the land may of course be held through a servant; [98] and the American courts have developed the fiction that where the land is vacant and occupied by no one, the owner is deemed to be the man in possession.[99] The same policy of favoring possession operates to protect the defendant, once he is in occupancy of the land for some appreciable period of time under a colorable claim of ownership. The defendant is then no longer subject to an action of trespass on the part of the true owner, whose proper remedy is in the form of an action of ejectment.[1]

---

90. Walker v. Ingram, 1948, 251 Ala. 395, 37 So.2d 685; Kornoff v. Kingsburg Cotton Oil Co., 1955, 45 Cal.2d 265, 288 P.2d 507; Barrow v. Georgia Lightweight Aggregate Co., 1961, 103 Ga.App. 704, 120 S.E.2d 636; J. B. McCrary Co. v. Phillips, 1930, 222 Ala. 117, 130 So. 805; Sager v. Sisters of Mercy, 1927, 81 Colo. 498, 256 P. 8.

91. Engle v. Simmons, 1906, 148 Ala. 92, 41 So. 1023; American Security Co. v. Cook, 1934, 49 Ga.App. 723, 176 S.E. 798; Watson v. Dilts, 1902, 116 Iowa 249, 89 N.W. 1068; Lesch v. Great Northern Railway Co., 1906, 97 Minn. 503, 106 N.W. 955; Bouillon v. Laclede Gaslight Co., 1910, 148 Mo.App. 462, 129 S.W. 401; Second Restatement of Torts, § 162.

92. If both parties can be considered in any sense as in possession, such mixed possession inures to the benefit of the one having the legal title. Leach v. Woods, 1833, 31 Mass. (14 Pick.) 461; Abbott v. Abbott, 1863, 51 Me. 575; cf. Kentucky Land & Immigration Co. v. Crabtree, 1902, 113 Ky. 922, 70 S.W. 31.

A mere licensee, having no interest in the premises, can bring no action for trespass, or damage to the realty. Powers v. Clarkson, 1876, 17 Kan. 218; Sabine & East Texas Railway Co. v. Johnson, 1886, 65 Tex. 389; Bakersfield Religious Congregational Society v. Baker, 1843, 15 Vt. 119. The same is true of the holder of an easement. State ex rel. Green v. Gibson Circuit Court, 1965, 246 Ind. 446, 206 N.E.2d 135; Morgan v. Boyes, 1876, 65 Me. 124; Chloupek v. Perotka, 1895, 89 Wis. 551, 62 N.W. 537. See Note, 1925, 11 Va.L.Rev. 476.

93. Barstow v. Sprague, 1859, 40 N.H. 27; Nickerson v. Thacher, 1888, 146 Mass. 609, 16 N.E. 581; Langdon v. Templeton, 1894, 66 Vt. 173, 28 A. 866; Frisbee v. Town of Marshall, 1898, 122 N.C. 760, 30 S.E. 21; Southern Railway Co. v. Horine, 1904, 121 Ga. 386, 49 S.E. 285.

94. Graham v. Peat, 1801, 1 East 244, 102 Eng.Rep. 95; Brenner v. Haley, 1960, 185 Cal.App.2d 183, 8 Cal. Rptr. 224 (illegal lease in violation of zoning ordinance).

95. Catteris v. Cowper, 1812, 4 Taunt. 546, 128 Eng. Rep. 444; Evertson v. Sutton, 1830, 5 N.Y. (Wend.) 281; Langdon v. Templeton, 1894, 66 Vt. 173, 28 A. 866.

96. As in Danforth v. Briggs, 1896, 89 Me. 316, 36 A. 452; Kirk v. Cassady, 1926, 217 Ky. 87, 288 S.W. 1045.

97. Graham v. Peat, 1801, 1 East 244, 102 Eng.Rep. 95, per Lord Kenyon, C.J.

98. Bertie v. Beaumont, 1812, 16 East 33, 104 Eng. Rep. 1001.

99. Church v. Meeker, 1867, 34 Conn. 421; Miller v. Miller, 1874, 41 Md. 623; Randall v. Sanders, 1882, 87 N.Y. 578; Falejczyk v. Meo, 1961, 31 Ill.App.2d 372, 176 N.E.2d 10; Dodson v. Culp, 1963, 108 Ga.App. 408, 133 S.E.2d 631. But this fiction of "constructive possession" has no application when another is in actual possession.

1. LaRue v. Russell, 1866, 26 Ind. 386; Mosseller v. Deaver, 1890, 106 N.C. 494, 11 S.E. 529.

On the other hand, an owner who is out of possession cannot maintain trespass.[2] Thus a landlord cannot sue for a mere trespass to land in the occupation of his tenant.[3] He is not without legal remedy, in the form of an action on the case for the injury to the reversion;[4] but in order to maintain it, he must show more than the trespass—namely, actual permanent harm to the property of such sort as to affect the value of his interest.[5] The tenant may recover damages for the injury to his interest up to the end of his term, but any permanent damage beyond this is recoverable by the landlord.[6] It is the common law rule that an owner forcibly dispossessed of the property may bring trespass for the ouster, but not for damage done afterward;[7] the landlord's remedy is by way of an action for ejectment, and for mesne profits.[8]

Vertical Extent of Possession

Any physical entry upon the surface of the land is a trespass, whether it be by walking upon it,[9] flooding it with water,[10] casting objects upon it,[11] or otherwise. One may commit a trespass upon the vertical surface of another's premises, as well as the horizontal—as where he piles dirt[12] or attaches wires[13] against a boundary wall. But the interest in exclusive possession is not limited to the surfaces; it extends above and below. There is a property right in the air space above land, which may be invaded by overhanging structures,[14] or telephone wires,[15] by thrusting an arm across the boundary

---

2. Kelman v. Wilen, 1954, 283 App.Div. 1113, 131 N.Y.S.2d 679; Bacon v. Sheppard, 1830, 11 N.J.L. 197; Hawkins v. Roby, 1882, 77 Mo. 140; Ruggles v. Sands, 1879, 40 Mich. 559; Kay v. Adams, 1931, 223 Ala. 33, 134 So. 628.

This has always been subject to the exception that one who has the right to immediate possession at the time of the tort can, after entry, maintain an action for trespass. Ocean Accident Co. v. Ilford Gas Co., [1905] 2 K.B. 493.

3. Daisey v. Hudson, 1855, 5 Del. (Harr.) 320; Bascom v. Dempsey, 1887, 143 Mass. 409, 9 N.E. 744; Walden v. Conn, 1886, 84 Ky. 312, 1 S.W. 537.

Some courts have held that where the tenant in possession is merely a tenant at will, the landlord may bring trespass, as having "constructive" possession. Starr v. Jackson, 1814, 11 Mass. 519; Davis v. Nash, 1851, 32 Me. 411. Others hold that the right to immediate possession is not the equivalent of possession. Campbell v. Arnold, 1806, 1 N.Y. (Johns.) 511; Gunsolus v. Lormer, 1882, 54 Wis. 630, 12 N.W. 62.

The holder of a contract to purchase, which gives no right to possession before payment, cannot bring trespass. Greve v. Wood-Harmon Co., 1899, 173 Mass. 45, 52 N.E. 1070; Des Jardins v. Thunder Bay River Boom Co., 1893, 95 Mich. 140, 54 N.E. 718.

4. Bucki v. Cone, 1889, 25 Fla. 1, 6 So. 160; Devlin v. Snellenburg, 1890, 132 Pa. 186, 18 A. 1119; Hersey v. Chapin, 1894, 162 Mass. 176, 38 N.E. 442; Cherry v. Lake Drummond Canal & Water Co., 1906, 140 N.C. 422, 53 S.E. 138; Croasdale v. Butell, 1955, 177 Kan. 487, 280 P.2d 593.

5. Bascom v. Dempsey, 1887, 143 Mass. 409, 9 N.E. 744.

6. Gilbert v. Kennedy, 1870, 22 Mich. 5; Zimmerman Mfg. Co. v. Daffin, 1906, 149 Ala. 380, 42 So. 858.

7. Smith v. Wunderlich, 1873, 70 Ill. 426.

8. Anderson v. Radcliffe, 1860, 29 L.J.Q.B. 128.

9. Dougherty v. Stepp, 1835, 18 N.C. 371.

10. Herro v. Board of County Road Commissioners, 1962, 368 Mich. 263, 118 N.W.2d 271; Union Pacific Railroad Co. v. Vale Irrigation District, D.Or.1966, 253 F.Supp. 251; Conner v. Woodfill, 1890, 126 Ind. 85, 25 N.E. 876.

11. Prewitt v. Clayton, 1827, 21 Ky. (5 T.B.Mon.) 4 (breaking in door with stones and clubs); Clark v. Wiles, 1884, 54 Mich. 323, 20 N.W. 63 (throwing dirt).

12. Miller v. McClelland, Iowa, 1919, 173 N.W. 910; Hutchinson v. Schimmelfeder, 1861, 40 Pa. 396.

13. Boomer v. Southern California Edison Co., 1928, 91 Cal.App. 382, 267 P. 181; Wells Amusement Co. v. Eros, 1920, 204 Ala. 239, 85 So. 692; cf. Mawson v. Vess Beverage Co., Mo.App.1943, 173 S.W.2d 606 (tacking sign).

14. Smith v. Smith, 1872, 110 Mass. 302 (eaves); Puroto v. Chieppa, 1905, 78 Conn. 401, 62 A. 664 (projection of one inch held trespass for which at least nominal damages recoverable); Cumberland Telephone & Telegraph Co. v. Barnes, 1907, 30 Ky.L.Rep. 1290, 101 S.W. 301, (cross-arm of telegraph pole); Kelsen v. Imperial Tobacco Co., [1957] 2 Q.B. 334 (advertising sign). Cf. Harris v. Central Power Co., 1922, 109 Neb. 500, 191 N.W. 711.

15. Butler v. Frontier Telephone Co., 1906, 186 N.Y. 486, 79 N.E. 716; McKenzie v. Pacific Gas and Electric Co., 1962, 200 Cal.App.2d 731, 19 Cal.Rptr. 628.

line,[16] or by shooting across the land,[17] even though the bullets do not fall upon it.[18]

The upward extent of this property right has been a subject of much discussion in recent years,[19] since it has been brought into sharp relief by the progress of aviation. Lord Coke once gave utterance [20] to the statement that *"cujus est solum ejus est usque ad coelum"*—which, taken literally, means that he who has the soil owns upward unto heaven, and by analogy, downward to perdition. This dictum was repeated in many cases [21] where there was no question of anything more than the immediate space above the soil, and it remains to trouble the law of the air. No one now advocates that it be applied literally; if it were, and no way were found to evade it, it is obvious that no airplane would ever leave the ground. But the exact extent of the landowner's rights in the air column is still in process of determination.

At least four distinct theories have been advanced in the state courts to adjust the conflicting interests of the surface owner and the aviator.[22] One is the "zone" theory, which divides the airspace into two strata, with the landowner owning that contained in the lower zone, but not that in the upper. The line is drawn at the limit of the owner's "effective possession," or in other words, at so much of the space above him as is essential to the complete use and enjoyment of his land. This was the rule applied in the early case of Smith v. New England Aircraft Co.,[23] where flights at the level of one hundred feet were held to be trespasses, since the land was used for the cultivation of trees which reached that height. A few other cases have adopted the same view.[24] The height of the zone of ownership must vary according to the facts of each case,[25] and the objections to this solution are that the extent of the right is left in doubt until adjudication, and that there apparently is to be a cause of action, with nominal damages and the possibility of an injunction, for flights which do no present harm to anyone.

A second view was adopted in a decision of the Ninth Circuit,[26] where the court refused to find a trespass in flights even within five feet of the surface of unoccupied

---

16. Hannabalson v. Sessions, 1902, 116 Iowa 457, 90 N.W. 93. Cf. Ellis v. Loftus Iron Co., 1874, L.R. 10 C.P. 19 (horse kicking through fence).

17. Whittaker v. Stangvick, 1907, 100 Minn. 386, 111 N.W. 295; Munro v. Williams, 1920, 94 Conn. 377, 109 A. 129; Herrin v. Sutherland, 1925, 74 Mont. 587, 241 P. 328; Hall v. Browning, 1943, 195 Ga. 423, 24 S.E.2d 392.

18. Davies v. Bennison, 1927, 22 Tas.L.Rev. 52. This is the famous "Tasmanian cat case," in which defendant shot the cat on the roof of plaintiff's house, and the bullet remained in the cat. It was held that A could recover for trespass to his land.

19. See Hackley, Trespassers in the Sky, 1937, 21 Minn.L.Rev. 773; Hunter, The Conflicting Interests of Airport Owners and Nearby Property Owners, 1945, 11 Law & Con.Prob. 539; Mace, Ownership of Airspace, 1948, 17 U.Cin.L.Rev. 343; Calkins, Landowner and Aircraft, 1958, 25 J.Air Law 373; Anderson, Airspace Trespass, 1960, 27 J.Air Law 341; Note, 1967, 9 W. & M.L.Rev. 460.

20. Coke, Littleton, 4a. See Klein, Cujus Est Solum Ejus Est—Quousque Tandem? 1959, 26 J.Air Law & Comm. 237.

21. See for example Hannabalson v. Sessions, 1902, 116 Iowa 457, 458, 90 N.W. 93, 95: " * * * the title of the owner of the soil extends not only downward to the centre of the earth, but upward usque ad coelum, although it is, perhaps, doubtful whether owners as quarrelsome as the parties in this case will ever enjoy the usufruct of their property in the latter direction. * * * "

22. Hackley, Trespassers in the Sky, 1937, 21 Minn.L.Rev. 773; Hunter, The Conflicting Interests of Airport Owners and Nearby Property Owners, 1945, 11 Law & Con.Prob. 539; Mace, Ownership of Airspace, 1948, 17 U.Cin.L.Rev. 343; Notes, 1957, 19 U.Pitt.L.Rev. 154; 1961, 74 Harv.L.Rev. 1581. Much the best discussion is in Harvey, Landowners' Rights in the Air Age: The Airport Dilemma, 1958, 56 Mich.L.Rev. 1313.

23. 1930, 270 Mass. 511, 170 N.E. 385.

24. Burnham v. Beverly Airways, 1942, 311 Mass. 628, 42 N.E.2d 575; Delta Air Corp. v. Kersey, 1942, 193 Ga. 862, 20 S.E.2d 245; Thrasher v. City of Atlanta, 1934, 178 Ga. 514, 173 S.E. 817; Swetland v. Curtiss Airports Corp., 6 Cir.1931, 55 F.2d 201.

25. See Swetland v. Curtiss Airports Corp., D.Ohio 1930, 41 F.2d 929, 1930, U.S.Av.Rep. 21; Cory v. Physical Culture Hotel, D.C.N.Y.1936, 14 F.Supp. 977, 982 affirmed 2d Cir. 1937, 88 F.2d 411, 1936, U.S.Av.Rep. 16.

26. Hinman v. Pacific Air Transport, 9 Cir. 1936, 84 F.2d 755, certiorari denied 300 U.S. 654, 81 L.Ed. 865, discussed in Green, Trespass by Airplane, 1937, 31 Ill.L.Rev. 499. Accord, applying a Georgia statute, Wall v. Trogdon, 1959, 249 N.C. 747, 107 S.E.2d 757.

waste land. It denies any ownership of the unused airspace, and limits the owner's rights to his actual use of it, with the rule that there is no tort unless there is interference with the present enjoyment of the property. Quite a different approach is that of the Restatement of Torts.[27] Unlimited ownership of upward or outward space is there recognized, and any intrusion of space is designated a trespass, except when the intrusion is that of overflight by aircraft, and perhaps other objects, such as rockets, satellites, and missiles.[28] If the intrusion is overflight by aircraft no trespass occurs above the immediate reaches of the air space adjacent to the land. If on the other hand, the invasion or intrusion of air space is within the immediate reaches of the land, it is a trespass, but only if a substantial interference with the use and enjoyment of the land results. Thus, flying as low as five feet over waste land is not a trespass, because no interference with any use that was being made of the land follows from the overflight. This is a slightly different position from that taken in the first Restatement, which recognized as a trespass an overflight of any height.[29] However, a temporary invasion by aircraft for travel or other legitimate purpose, done in a reasonable manner and at a height, which conforms with legislative requirements, and which does not unreasonably interfere with the possessor's enjoyment of the surface of the earth and the air space above would be priviledged. This position was adopted by the Uniform State Law for Aeronautics[30] and enacted in one form or another by almost half of the states.[31] This position recognizes unlimited ownership of upward space, subject to a privilege of flight similar to the public right to make use of a navigable stream.[32] With flights now ranging into the verge of outer space, and carried on by rockets and many objects other than airplanes, this notion of private ownership of a segment of space reaching to the moon, and limited only by a privilege of flight, is now pretty well discredited. The Uniform Act was withdrawn by the Commissioners on Uniform State Laws in 1943; and while it remains on the books in a good many states, its approach is not likely to be applied so long as others are available.

Finally there is the "nuisance" theory, which is finding increasing support. It ignores arguments about ownership of the air, and gives a remedy in the form of an action for nuisance, or possibly negligence, when the flight results in actual interference with

27. Second Restatement of Torts, § 194.

28. Second Restatement of Torts, § 159.

29. First Restatement of Torts, §§ 159 and 194.

30. See Keuhnl, Uniform State Aviation Liability Legislation, [1948] Wis.L.Rev. 356.

See, applying such legislation, Capitol Airways v. Indianapolis Power & Light Co., 1939, 215 Ind. 462, 18 N.E.2d 776; Guith v. Consumers Power Co., E.D.Mich. 1940, 36 F.2d 21; Vanderslice v. Shawn, 1942, 26 Del. Ch. 225, 27 A.2d 87. In Strother v. Pacific Gas & Electric Co., 1949, 94 Cal.App.2d 525, 211 P.2d 624, the same conclusion was reached without a statute.

31. Hunter, The Conflicting Interests of Airport Owner and Nearby Property Owner, 1945, 11 Law & Con.Prob. 539, 547, gives the following list: Arizona, Arkansas, California, Colorado, Delaware, Georgia, Idaho, Indiana, Maryland, Michigan, Minnesota, Missouri, Nevada, New Jersey, North Carolina, North Dakota, Pennsylvania, South Carolina, South Dakota, Tennessee, Vermont, Wisconsin, Wyoming.

32. At lower levels, and except in the case of unreasonable activities such as "stunt" flying, the practical result would seem to be much the same as under the "zone" theory. See Eubank, Doctrine of the Airspace Zone of Effective Possession, 1932, 12 Bos.U.L.Rev. 414. One possible difference is that under the "zone" theory the landowner has the burden of proof that his zone of effective possession has been invaded; under the theory recognizing a public privilege of flight, the burden would be upon the aviator to show that his flight was privileged. See Thurston, Trespass to Airspace, Harvard Legal Essays, 1934, 521.

the use of the land,[33] but denies it unless there is such interference.[34]

All of these theories represent obvious attempts to strike a balance between the property interests of the landowner and the demands of a growing industry highly important to the public. Thus far it cannot be said that any one of them has predominated, largely because the courts have been so exceedingly cautious about committing themselves; and most of the decisions do not identify and distinguish them very clearly.

It would appear, however, that it would be a mistake to qualify the ownership of air space solely on the problems related to the flight of aircraft and other objects. There are a variety of other ways in which air space immediately above the surface of land can be occupied or used by wires, structures, and the like, absent contact with anything attached to the surface. Those who wish to occupy and use the air space immediately above the surface of land can justifiably be required to pay for the privilege of so doing. A privilege to use air space for overflight of any height could be recognized so long as the exercise of that privilege did not unreasonably interfere with the use and enjoyment of the land surface. A late Oregon decision [35] which completely jettisons trespass, and relies upon nuisance as the sole basis of liability, can therefore be regarded as achieving a desirable balancing of interests. But the same result can perhaps more appropriately be reached by recognizing ownership of the air space in the immediate reaches above land qualified by a privilege for flight.

In 1946 the Supreme Court of the United States took a hand in the matter with United States v. Causby,[36] holding that continued low-altitude flights by military aircraft, which ruined the plaintiff's poultry business, constituted a wrongful "taking" of private property, for which the Fifth Amendment required compensation. The Court began by declaring that the federal statutes, together with the regulations of the Civil Aeronautics Board, had the effect of making the airspace above the prescribed minimum altitudes a public, and a federal, domain and highway, so that is must follow that there can be no trespass in flight at such levels.[37] Apparently this has the effect of invalidating all state law to the contrary.[38] The case has left several unanswered questions. One of them is as to the extent to which Congress has occupied the field, so that state law may be precluded from allowing recovery even for flights below the minimum.[39] Another is whether there can be a "taking," or, inferentially, a trespass, in flights over the land be-

---

33. Delta Air Corp. v. Kersey, 1942, 193 Ga. 862, 20 S.E.2d 245; Warren Township School District No. 7 v. City of Detroit, 1944, 308 Mich. 460, 14 N.W.2d 134; Brandes v. Mitterling, 1948, 67 Ariz. 349, 196 P.2d 464; Hyde v. Somerset Air Service, 1948, 1 N.J.Super. 346, 61 A.2d 645; Anderson v. Souza, 1952, 38 Cal.2d 825, 243 P.2d 497.

34. See Swetland v. Curtiss Airports Corp., 6th Cir. 1931, 55 F.2d 201; Delta Air Corp. v. Kersey, 1942, 193 Ga. 862, 20 S.E.2d 245.

35. Atkinson v. Bernard, Inc., 1960, 223 Or. 624, 355 P.2d 229.

See also Cheskov v. Port of Seattle, 1960, 55 Wash. 2d 416, 348 P.2d 673; Antonik v. Chamberlain, 1947, 81 Ohio App. 465, 78 N.E.2d 752.

36. 1946, 328 U.S. 256, 66 S.Ct. 1062, 90 L.Ed. 1206. In accord is Gardner v. Allegheny County, 1955, 382 Pa. 88, 114 A.2d 491. Both decisions came before the amendment of Civil Aeronautics regulations to set minimum altitudes for glide paths in landing and taking off. See also Ackerman v. Port of Seattle, 1960, 55 Wash.2d 400, 348 P.2d 664; Wildwood Mink Ranch v. United States, D.Minn.1963, 218 F.Supp. 67.

37. This was not a new idea. In Maitland v. Twin City Aviation Corp., 1949, 254 Wis. 541, 37 N.W.2d 74, the court applied the Civil Aeronautics minimum altitude of 500 feet as a "zone" limit. This possibility was rejected in Thrasher v. City of Atlanta, 1934, 178 Ga. 514, 173 S.E. 817, as too simple a solution, since liability must depend upon the use to which the surface is put, and a single rule for all cases was regarded as too arbitrary.

38. Antonik v. Chamberlain, 1947, 81 Ohio App. 465, 78 N.E.2d 752; Cheskov v. Port of Seattle, 1960, 55 Wash.2d 416, 348 P.2d 673; Allegheny Airlines v. Village of Cedarhurst, E.D.N.Y.1955, 132 F.Supp. 871, affirmed, 2d Cir.1956, 238 F.2d 812.

39. See Note, 1961, 74 Harv.L.Rev. 1581. The Causby decision apparently has been taken to mean that Congress has occupied the field, and that any state law inconsistent with federal rules is invalidated. Antonik v. Chamberlain, 1947, 81 Ohio App. 465, 78

low the prescribed minimum altitude, but above the "immediate reaches" of the land, which do not interfere with the use of the land. Here the only federal decisions [40] since the Causby Case have said that there cannot. There is the further question of liability for flights above the minimum which do so interfere; and here the Supreme Court itself has found a "taking" in a subsequent case,[41] although apparently not upon any basis of trespass.

The common law concepts of trespass and nuisance cannot be used alone to determine which overflights by a sovereign constitute a taking. It appears that at least for this purpose, only a substantial interference constitutes a taking even if the flight is immediately above the surface of the land. This is consistent with a recognition of ownership of the air space in the immediate reaches coupled with a privilege for overflying aircraft.[42]

Subsurface Invasions

The interest in the possession of land extends also below the surface, and may present similar problems there.[43] It is a trespass to mine under another's land,[44] or to construct a tunnel and force water through it,[45] or to invade it by a projecting foundation,[46] or by driving earth under the soil.[47] But the limits of this downward right have received little consideration. In a Kentucky case,[48] notwithstanding a forceful dissenting opinion,[49] the court permitted the surface owner to recover for trespass in a cave extending laterally beneath his property three hundred and sixty feet below. Since it is quite apparent that he had no slightest practical possibility of access to the cave, either now or in the future, the decision is dog-in-the-manger law, and can only be characterized as a very bad one. Much to be preferred is the conclusion of a New York court [50] that a sewer one hundred fifty feet below the surface is not an invasion of the owner's rights. It is only where some damage to the surface results, or there is some interference with a use that can be made of the property, present or prospective, that a trespass action should be permitted in such a case.

N.E.2d 752; Cheskov v. Port of Seattle, 1960, 55 Wash. 2d 416, 348 P.2d 673; Allegheny Airlines v. Village of Cedarhurst, E.D.N.Y.1955, 132 F.Supp. 871, affirmed 2d Cir.1956, 238 F.2d 812.

40. City of Newark v. Eastern Airlines, D.N.J.1958, 159 F.Supp. 750; Freeman v. United States, W.D.Okl. 1958, 167 F.Supp. 541; Palisades Citizens Association, Inc. v. Civil Aeronautics Board, D.C.Cir.1969, 420 F.2d 188.

41. Griggs v. County of Allegheny, 1962, 369 U.S. 84, 82 S.Ct. 531, 7 L.Ed.2d 585 rehearing denied 369 U.S. 857, 82 S.Ct. 931, 8 L.Ed.2d 16, noted in 1962, 57 Nw.U.L.Rev. 346. Accord: Matson v. United States, 1959, 145 Ct.Cl. 225, 171 F.Supp. 283; Thornburg v. Port of Portland, 1962, 233 Or. 178, 376 P.2d 100. See Hill, Liability for Aircraft Noise—The Aftermath of Causby and Griggs, 1964, 19 U.Miami L.Rev. 1.

42. Thornburg v. Port of Portland, 1962, 233 Or. 178, 376 P.2d 100; Henthorn v. Oklahoma City, Okl. 1969, 453 P.2d 1013; Comment, Air Easement: Oklahoma Adopts the Trespass-Nuisance Dichotomy, 1972, 8 Tulsa L.J. 138.

43. Ball, The Vertical Extent of Ownership in Land, 1928, 76 U.Pa.L.Rev. 631, 684–689.

44. Maye v. Yappen, 1863, 23 Cal. 306; North Jellico Coal Co. v. Helton, 1920, 187 Ky. 394, 219 S.W. 185; Chartiers Block Coal Co. v. Mellon, 1893, 152 Pa. 286, 25 A. 597. In many western states, however, the miner is permitted to follow the lode, as in Bowen v. Chemi-Cote Perlite Co., 1967, 5 Ariz.App. 28, 423 P.2d 104, vacated on other grounds 102 Ariz. 423, 432 P.2d 435. As to slant drilling of oil wells, see Note, 1939, 27 Cal.L.Rev. 192.

45. City of Chicago v. Troy Laundry Machinery Co., 7 Cir. 1908, 162 F. 678.

46. Wachstein v. Christopher, 1907, 128 Ga. 229, 57 S.E. 511; Harrington v. City of Huron, 1891, 86 Mich. 46, 48 N.W. 641.

47. Costigan v. Pennsylvania Railroad Co., 1892, 54 N.J.L. 233, 23 A. 810. Cf. United Electric Light Co. v. Deliso Construction Co., 1943, 315 Mass. 313, 52 N.E.2d 553.

48. Edwards v. Lee, 1929, 230 Ky. 375, 19 S.W.2d 992; Edwards v. Sims, 1929, 232 Ky. 791, 24 S.W.2d 619; Edwards v. Lee, 1933, 250 Ky. 166, 61 S.W.2d 1049; Edwards v. Lee's Administrator, 1936, 265 Ky. 418, 96 S.W.2d 1028. The case is discussed in 1937, 31 Ill.L.Rev. 680; 1937, 37 Col.L.Rev. 503. Accord: Marengo Cave Co. v. Ross, 1937, 212 Ind. 624, 10 N.E.2d 917.

49. Logan, J., in Edwards v. Sims, 1929, 232 Ky. 791, 24 S.W.2d 619, 622.

50. Boehringer v. Montalto, 1931, 142 Misc. 560, 254 N.Y.S. 276.

Several questions can be raised about the respective rights of a surface owner and a mineral lessee of adjoining property regarding such matters as storage rights for natural gas or salt water in the underground stratum. One of the questions is whether the owner has a right of recovery on a trespass theory for the unauthorized invasion and use of the space underneath the surface. Since there is no physical damage done, and since there has been no interference with the owner's use and enjoyment of his property, there would seem to be no recovery except on a theory that the invasion being trespassory in character entitles the owner of the surface to a recovery for the value of the use that is being made of his property. Since salt water and even gas when injected under pressure are liquids, the problem is analogous to that which is involved when a riparian constructs a dam and floods the land of another. The difference of course is that the owner of the land overlying the exhausted reservoir has no more use and control over it than he has of the air a mile above his home.

Damage was regarded as a prerequisite for recovery in one case.[51] In another case, recovery for injecting water into a reservoir was regarded as depending upon whether or not the injection interfered unreasonably with any use being made of the land by the plaintiff, the owner of the surface.[52] And in a third case, it was found unnecessary to decide if recovery should be based on nuisance or trespass theory, since the injection was made at very high rates and unnecessarily close to a boundary line, and could be regarded as interfering unreasonably with an existing use of the plaintiff.[53]

Perhaps there should be no liability for subsurface invasions of water, gas, or other substances produced or employed in the production of crude oil and natural gas in the absence of proof of actual damage. The mere fact that an actor is obtaining a benefit from the subsurface use may not be justification for a quasi-contractual recovery; if so, a landowner's right should be limited to a recovery for damage caused and for the value of products unjustifiably appropriated. Moreover, it may be that a nuisance approach to all such invasions, which necessarily involves a balancing of interests, is the more desirable one.[54]

Continuing Trespass

The ordinary trespass is complete when it is committed; the cause of action accrues, and the statute of limitations begins to run at that time, although the consequence may be a permanent injury to the land.[55] But in many cases, as where the defendant erects a structure or dumps rubbish upon the land of the plaintiff, the invasion is continued by a failure to remove it. In such a case, there is a continuing wrong so long as the offending object remains.[56] A purchaser of the land may recover for the continuing trespass,[57] and a transferee of the defendant's interest in the chattel or structure may be liable.[58]

A question of considerable difficulty arises as to whether the plaintiff may maintain successive actions for such a continuing trespass, or must recover in a single action

---

51. West Edmond Salt Water Disposal Association v. Rosecrans, 1950, 204 Okl. 9, 226 P.2d 965; appeal dismissed, 1951, 340 U.S. 924, 71 S.Ct. 500, 95 L.Ed. 667.

52. Railroad Commission of Texas v. Manziel, Tex. 1962, 361 S.W.2d 560, 93 A.L.R.2d 432.

53. Tidewater Oil Co. v. Jackson, 10th Cir. 1963, 320 F.2d 157, certiorari denied 1964, 375 U.S. 942, 84 S.Ct. 347, 11 L.Ed.2d 273.

54. Keeton and Jones, Tort Liability and the Oil and Gas Industry, 1961, 39 Tex.L.Rev. 253, 269.

55. Williams v. Pomeroy Coal Co., 1882, 37 Ohio St. 583; National Copper Co. v. Minnesota Mining Co., 1885, 57 Mich. 83, 23 N.W. 781; Houston Water Works Co. v. Kennedy, 1888, 70 Tex. 233, 8 S.W. 36.

56. Second Restatement of Torts, § 161; 509 Sixth Avenue Corp. v. New York City Transit Authority, 1964, 15 N.Y.2d 48, 255 N.Y.S.2d 89, 203 N.E.2d 486.

57. Konskier v. Goodman, [1928] 1 K.B. 421; Peck v. Smith, 1814, 1 Conn. 103; Milton v. Puffer, 1911, 207 Mass. 416, 93 N.E. 634.

58. Lyons v. Fairmont Real Estate Co., 1913, 71 W.Va. 754, 77 S.E. 525; Rahn v. Milwaukee Electric Railway & Light Co., 1899, 103 Wis. 467, 79 N.W. 747; cf. Zenith Bathing Pavilion v. Fair Oaks Steamship Corp., 1925, 240 N.Y. 307, 148 N.E. 532.

for all damages, past and prospective. The first alternative may be inconvenient to the plaintiff, and compel him to harass the defendant with repeated suits over a matter which could better be disposed of in one. The second means that the statute of limitations will run from the initial trespass, and that the damages claimed may be largely speculative, or that the trespass may terminate after the judgment.

The courts are not in accord in dealing with this question. In the case of actual encroachments, as by building a structure upon the plaintiff's land, the prevailing view is that there must be a single recovery of all damages, upon the ground that the defendant is not privileged to commit a second trespass to remove it.[59] Where the trespass results from a condition on the defendant's own land, as in the case of a dam which floods the plaintiff's premises, most courts have made the solution turn upon the permanent nature of the condition, in the light of its physical durability and the likelihood that the defendant will terminate it rather than pay the plaintiff's claim.[60] In view of the uncertain and illogical nature of these distinctions, it has been suggested[61] that in all cases the plaintiff be given the option of a single recovery for all damages, or successive actions, upon the condition that he is in no way responsible for the continuance of the trespass.[62]

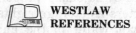

WESTLAW REFERENCES

Legal History
synopsis,digest(trespass +2 is means includes defined)
synopsis,digest(england "common law" history /6 trespass)
vibration* concussion /25 trespass

Trespass and Private Nuisance Distinguished
"private nuisance" /p trespass
invasion invad! /s element* /s trespass

Entries as Trespass
exclusive +3 possession /s trespass
invisible intangible /s trespass

Invasion with Water and Liquids
invasion invad! /5 land /p oil water liquid gasoline
seep seepage leak leakage /s trespass

Character of Defendant's Act
accident** unintentional** /s entry /s trespass % topic(110)

The Intent Required
digest(intent! intend! voluntary volition** /10 trespass) % topic(110)

Necessity of Damage
damage* /s element* /s trespass
nominal /4 damages /s trespass
consequen! /s damages /s trespass

Necessity of Possession
exclusive /s possession /s trespass
plaintiff /s possession /s trespass

---

59. Finley v. Hershey, 1875, 41 Iowa 389; Ziebarth v. Nye, 1890, 42 Minn. 541, 44 N.W. 1027; Cherry v. Lake Drummond Canal & Water Co., 1906, 140 N.C. 422, 53 S.E. 138; Blankenship v. Kansas Explorations, 1930, 325 Mo. 998, 30 S.W.2d 471.

60. Stodghill v. Chicago, Burlington & Quincy Railroad Co., 1880, 53 Iowa 341, 5 N.W. 495; Louisville, Henderson & St. Louis Railway Co. v. Roberts, 1911, 144 Ky. 820, 139 S.W. 1073; Smith v. Dallas Utility Co., 1921, 27 Ga.App. 22, 107 S.E. 381; Southern Rail Co. v. White, 1920, 128 Va. 551, 104 S.E. 865; Razzano v. Kent, 1947, 78 Cal.App.2d 254, 177 P.2d 612.

If the defendant's structure is not subject to abatement or injunction, because authorized by eminent domain statutes, many courts regard it as a "permanent nuisance," and permit a single recovery for prospective damages, Jacksonville, T. & K. W. R. Co. v. Lockwood, 1894, 33 Fla. 573, 15 So. 327; Phillips v. Postal Telegraph Cable Co., 1902, 130 N.C. 513, 41 S.E. 1022, reversed on rehearing 131 N.C. 225, 42 S.E. 587; cf. Pappenheim v. Metropolitan Elevated Railway Co., 1891, 128 N.Y. 436, 28 N.E. 518.

61. McCormick, Damages, 1935, 511–515; McCormick Damages for Anticipated Injury to Land, 1924, 37 Harv.L.Rev. 574, 593–601; Goodrich, Permanent Structure and Continuing Injuries—The Iowa Rule, 1918, 4 Iowa L.B. 65. A good case to this effect is Kornoff v. Kingsburg Cotton Oil Co., 1955, 45 Cal.2d 265, 288 P.2d 507. See also Strange v. Cleveland, Cincinnati, Chicago & St. Louis Railway Co., 1910, 245 Ill. 246, 91 N.E. 1036; City of Ottumwa v. Nicholson, 1913, 161 Iowa 473, 143 N.W. 439; Thompson v. Illinois Central Railroad Co., 1920, 191 Iowa 35, 179 N.W. 191.

62. Thus if the plaintiff refuses to permit the defendant to enter the land and remove the thing, there is no liability for the continuation of the trespass. Restatement of Torts, § 161, Comment d. If the plaintiff elects to retain the structure as a part of his land, the defendant will be liable for a second trespass if he enters to remove it. Druse v. Wheeler, 1872, 26 Mich. 189.

Vertical Extent of Possession
vertical aerial heaven airspace overflight /p nuisance trespass

Subsurface Invasions
subsurface cave tunnel*** sewer* /s trespass
reservoir /p trespass
rylands +2 fletcher

Continuing Trespass
continuing ongoing /s trespass
continuing /s trespass /p statutes* /s limitation*

§ 14. Trespass to Chattels

The earliest cases in which the action of trespass was applied to chattels involved asportation, or carrying off, and a special form of the writ, known as trespass de bonis asportatis, was devised to deal with such situations.[1] Later the action was extended to include cases where the goods were damaged but not taken—as where animals were killed[2] or beaten.[3] Later decisions extended the tort to include any direct and immediate intentional interference with a chattel in the possession of another. Thus it is a trespass to damage goods or destroy them,[4] to make an unpermitted use of them,[5] or to move them from one place to another.[6] Under the common law forms, the interference must be direct and forcible, otherwise the action must be on the case;[7] but as in the case of trespass to land, the tendency has long been to ignore any such artifical distinction.[8]

The later development of the common law action of trover, and the tort of conversion[9] provided a substitute for trespass which usually was the more convenient action. As a result trespass tended to fall more or less into disuse in the case of chattels. Some occasional confusion followed as to which was the appropriate remedy in a given case.[10] The disappearance of the forms of action has made the distinction immaterial, and the name of the tort of little consequence, in most cases of intentional interference with chattels. Its chief importance now is that there may be recovery where trespass would lie at common law, for interferences with the possession of chattels which are not sufficiently important to be classed as conversion, and so to compel the defendant to pay the full value of the thing with which he has

§ 14

1. 1 Street, Foundations of Legal Liability, 1906, 15; Ames, History of Trover, 1898, 11 Harv.L.Rev. 277, 285–286.

2. Wright v. Ramscot, 1668, 1 Wms.Saund. 108, 85 Eng.Rep. 93; Sheldrick v. Abery, 1793, 1 Esp. 55, 170 Eng.Rep. 278.

3. Dand v. Sexton, 1789, 3 Term.Rep. 37, 100 Eng. Rep. 442; Marlow v. Weekes, 1744, Barnes' Notes 452; Slater v. Swann, 1730, 2 Stra. 872, 93 Eng.Rep. 906.

4. Parker v. Mise, 1855, 27 Ala. 480 (shooting dog); Brittain v. McKay, 1840, 23 N.C. 265 (cutting crop); Cole v. Fisher, 1814, 11 Mass. 137 (frightening horse into runaway and damaging chaise); Cole v. Schweer, 1910, 159 Ill.App. 278 (releasing fish); Post v. Munn, 1818, 4 N.J.L. 61 (damaging fishing net). Cf. Bankston v. Dumont, 1949, 205 Misc. 272, 38 So.2d 721 (opening and searching purse, removing money).

5. Penfolds Wines, Limited v. Elliott, Aust.1946, 74 Comm.L.Rep. 204.

6. Kirk v. Gregory, 1876, 1 Ex.Div. 55; G. W. K., Ltd. v. Dunlop Rubber Co., K.B. (1926) 42 T.L.R. 376 (taking tire from automobile and replacing it two days later); Bruch v. Carter, 1867, 32 N.J.L. 554; Zaslow v. Kroenert, 1946, 29 Cal.2d 541, 176 P.2d 1. A fortiori if the defendant takes the goods away. Peoples v. Brown, 1894, 42 S.C. 81, 20 S.E. 24; Guttner v. Pacific Steam Whaling Co., D.Cal.1899, 96 F. 617; Danley-Evers Furniture Co. v. Cauley, 1929, 220 Ala. 542, 126 So. 844; Vaughn v. Glenn, 1932, 44 Ga.App. 426, 161 S.E. 672.

7. See Covell v. Laming, 1808, 1 Camp. 497, 170 Eng.Rep. 1034; Hopper v. Reeve, 1817, 7 Taunt. 698, 129 Eng.Rep. 278.

8. See Cole v. Fisher, 1814, 11 Mass. 137; Loubz v. Hafner, 1827, 12 N.C. 185; Waterman v. Hall, 1844, 17 Vt. 128; cf. Tennessee Coal, Iron & Railroad Co. v. Kimball, 1923, 209 Ala. 466, 96 So. 329.

9. See Ames, The History of Trover, 1898, 11 Harv. L.Rev. 374.

10. Thus it was held that trespass would lie, as well as trover, where an officer levied upon goods and took them under his legal control, although there was no physical interference with the property itself. Wintringham v. Lafoy, 1827, 7 Cow., N.Y., 735; Miller v. Baker, 1840, 42 Mass. (1 Metc.) 27.

Cf. Van Dresor v. King, 34 Pa.St. 201 (sale on execution); C. I. T. Corp. v. Brewer, 1941, 146 Fla. 247, 200 So. 910 (repossessing car).

One distinction of some importance was that trespass would not lie for a mere detention of goods rightfully acquired, without any taking or damage to them. Hartley v. Moxham, 1842, 3 Q.B. 701, 114 Eng.Rep. 675; Furlong v. Bartlett, 1838, 38 Mass. (21 Pick.) 401; Bradley v. Davis, 1836, 14 Me. 44. See infra, p. 87.

interfered.[11] Trespass to chattels survives today, in other words, largely as a little brother of conversion.

In common with other progeny of the old action of trespass, such as assault and battery,[12] trespass to chattels has become, in modern usage, exclusively a wrong of intentional interference.[13]

Pipelines, Cables and the Like—The Intent Required

The strict liability which persisted for so long in the case of trespass to land[14] did not seemingly survive to the same extent in the case of trespass to chattels. But even in this area, difficulty is encountered with the intent requirement. An intent to intrude upon or intermeddle in some way is commonly regarded as an essential requirement for recovery on the theory of a trespass.

Pipelines, cables, and the like are in general and widespread use for transmission of various substances such as oil, gas, and electricity. These instruments are often located underground, especially under the surface of public streets pursuant to an acquired easement. These cables or pipes are often unintentionally damaged or injured by contractors excavating or intruding into the area where the cable or pipe is located. There is a conflict on the result that should be reached, a conflict referred to in the section on trespass to land.[15]

The difference of opinion is over the nature of the intent required. In some states, it has been held that since the defendant intended to intrude into the precise area underground where the pipe was located, the intrusion should not be regarded as accidental, but as intentional. It would seem however that the better view is to regard the pipes and cables as personal property, and separate from the area of the land itself into which the intrusion was intentionally made. This does not mean that the defendant could not under any circumstances have intended intrusion on the cable or other chattel itself. For example, in Buckeye Pipeline Co., Inc. v. Congel-Hazard, Inc.,[16] the defendant was made aware of the approximate location of the plaintiff's pipe, but proceeded to dig, knowing that the almost inevitable consequence of what he was doing would be an intrusion on the pipe. However, in such a case the plaintiff, in the absence of his own fault for failing to take proper precautions, could recover either on a negligence, or perhaps even a strict liability, theory. While there may be liability for negligence which results in harm to the chattel, as in the case of a damaged car in an automobile collision, the remedy has been absorbed into the broader field of negligence actions,[17] leaving trespass for the intentional wrong.[18] But, as in the case of other torts derived from the old writ of trespass, the "intent" requires no wrongful motive; and it is no defense that the defendant believed the goods to be his own, so long as the defendant voluntarily interfered with them by the act which constituted the trespass.[19] As in the case of tres-

---

11. See Section 15.
12. See supra, Section 14, note 3.
13. Second Restatement of Torts, §§ 217, 222.
14. Supra, Section 14.
15. Supra, Section 14, Notes 1 and 2.
16. 1973, 41 A.D.2d 590, 340 N.Y.S.2d 263.
17. Gayler & Pope, Limited v. Davies & Son, Limited [1924] 2 K.B. 75; see Winfield and Goodhart, Trespass and Negligence, 1933, 49 L.Q.Rev. 359. As in the case of battery, there is occasional reference in the cases to a negligent "trespass," as in Percival v. Hickey, 1820, 18 N.Y. (Johns.) 257, 259; but this is obviously pure carelessness.
18. With the resulting distinction that, while mere possession of the chattel will support an action for trespass (see infra, note 25), one for negligence cannot be maintained unless the plaintiff has title, or some special property interest in the chattel, which has suffered damage. Engelman v. Bird, D.Alaska, 1955, 16 Alaska 61, 136 F.Supp. 501; Veltri v. City of Cleveland, 1957, 167 Ohio St. 90, 146 N.E.2d 442; Northern Pacific Railway Co. v. Lewis, 1895, 162 U.S. 366, 16 S.Ct. 831, 40 L.Ed. 1002; Murphy v. Sioux City & Pacific Railroad Co., 1881, 55 Iowa 473, 8 N.W. 320; Lockhart v. Western & Atlantic Railroad, 1884, 73 Ga. 472.

19. Brooks v. Olmstead, 1851, 17 Pa. 24; Dexter v. Cole, 1858, 6 Wis. 319; Hobart v. Hagget, 1835, 12 Me. 67; Shell Petroleum Corp. v. Liberty Gravel & Sand Co., Tex.Civ.App.1939, 128 S.W.2d 471. Cf. Medairy v. McAllister, 1903, 97 Md. 488, 55 A. 461 (advice of counsel as to legal right to take goods).

pass to land and conversion, the property right is protected at the expense of an innocent mistake.

Another departure from the original rule of the old writ of trespass concerns the necessity of some actual damage to the chattel before the action can be maintained. Where the defendant merely interferes without doing any harm—as where, for example, he merely lays hands upon the plaintiff's horse, or sits in his car—there has been a division of opinion among the writers, and a surprising dearth of authority. By analogy to trespass to land there might be a technical tort in such a case; and it has been contended that there is a real necessity for nominal damages to protect property from intermeddlers.[20] Such scanty authority as there is, however, has considered that the dignitary interest in the inviolability of chattels, unlike that as to land, is not sufficiently important to require any greater defense than the privilege of using reasonable force when necessary to protect them. Accordingly it has been held that nominal damages will not be awarded, and that in the absence of any actual damage the action will not lie.[21] This must be qualified, however, to the extent that any loss of possession by the plaintiff is regarded as necessarily a loss of something of value, even if only for a brief interval—so that wherever there is found to be dispossession, as in the case of seizure of goods on execution,[22] the requirement of actual damage is satisfied.[23] This qualification is hardly necessary, since almost any dispossession would give the plaintiff a right of recovery based on the theory of conversion.

The property interest protected by the old action of trespass was that of possession; and this has continued to affect the character of the action. It follows that anyone in possession of the chattel, under some colorable claim of right to it,[24] at the time of the defendant's interference, can maintain a trespass action.[25] The defendant is not permitted to set up as a defense to the plaintiff's claim the "jus tertii," which is to say the right of some third person to the chattel, superior to that of the plaintiff,[26] unless he can connect himself in his own right with that third person's claim.[27] The reason has been said to be that any other rule would be "an invitation to all the world to scramble for * * * possession;"[28] or in other words, that the maintenance of decent order requires that peaceable possession be protected against wrongdoers with no rights at all.

The original common law rule required that the plaintiff be in possession of the chattel at the time of the trespass, or the ac-

20. Pollock, Law of Torts, 13th ed. 1929, 264; Salmond, Law of Torts, 8th ed. 1934, 353; see Leitch & Co. v. Leydon [1931] A.C. 106.

21. De Marentille v. Oliver, 1808, 2 N.J.L. 379; Paul v. Slason, 1850, 22 Vt. 231; Graves v. Severens, 1868, 40 Vt. 636; Glidden v. Szybiak, 1949, 95 N.H. 318, 63 A.2d 233; Koller v. Duggan, 1963, 346 Mass. 270, 191 N.E.2d 475; J. & C. Ornamental Iron Co. v. Watkins, 1966, 114 Ga.App. 688, 152 S.E.2d 613; Second Restatement of Torts, § 218, Comment e.

22. Wintringham v. Lafoy, 1827, 7 Cow., N.Y., 735; Jaquith v. Stanger, 1957, 79 Idaho 49, 310 P.2d 805; Ohio Finance Co. v. Berry, 1941, 219 Ind. 94, 37 N.E.2d 2; Beede v. Nides Finance Corp., 1941, 209 Minn. 354, 296 N.W. 413.

23. Bankston v. Dumont, 1949, 205 Miss. 272, 38 So. 2d 721 ($10 bill taken from purse, returned shortly thereafter on request); Lowery v. McTier, 1959, 99 Ga. App. 423, 108 S.E.2d 771; Stallworth v. Doss, 1967, 280 Ala. 409, 194 So.2d 566.

24. As in the case of conversion (infra, § 15), it appears probable that a thief without colorable claim would not be allowed to recover. But trespass cases are lacking.

25. "The finder of an article may maintain trespass against any person but the real owner; and a person having an illegal possession may support this action against any person other than the true owner." Hoyt v. Gelston & Schenck, 1816, 13 N.Y. (Johns.) 141, affirmed 13 N.Y. (Johns.) 561, affirmed 3 Wheat. 246, 4 L.Ed. 381; Sewell v. Harrington, 1839, 11 Vt. 141; Browning v. Skillman, 1854, 24 N.J.L. 351; Cole v. Schweer, 1910, 159 Ill.App. 278; W. K. Syson Timber Co. v. Dickens, 1906, 146 Ala. 471, 40 So. 753; cf. Priester v. Milleman, 1947, 161 Pa.Super. 507, 55 A.2d 540; Stone v. C. I. T. Corp., 1936, 122 Pa.Super. 71, 184 A. 674.

26. Woadson v. Nawton, 1727, 2 Stra. 777, 93 Eng. Rep. 842.

27. Blades v. Higgs, 1865, 20 C.B.,N.S., 214, 144 Eng.Rep. 1087.

28. Kenyon, C. J., in Webb v. Fox, 1797, 7 Term Rep. 391, 397, 101 Eng.Rep. 1037.

tion could not be maintained.²⁹ This was relaxed slightly, at a later date, to allow trespass to be maintained by one who is entitled to possession immediately, or upon demand, as in the case of a bailor at will, or a mortgagee after default.³⁰ Furthermore, even one out of possession but entitled to it at some future time, as in the case of a bailor for a term, was not without all remedy; and while the plaintiff could not bring trespass, he might recover in an action on the case for any harm to his interest in the chattel.³¹ With the abolition of the forms of trespass and case under modern procedure, it would seem that the only distinction of any consequence is that the person entitled only to future possession recovers only to the extent of any damage to his interest.³² Complications must arise when the claims of the present possessor and of the reversioner are both asserted; but since these develop most frequently in cases of conversion,³³ the rules are identical, and there are almost no trespass cases, they are best dealt with at a later point.

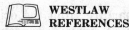

WESTLAW REFERENCES

trespass /s chattels

Pipelines, Cables and the Like—the Intent Required
trover /p trespass
pipeline* cable* /p trespass /p intent! intend!
trespass /p chattel* personal** /p possession % larceny theft

§ 15. Conversion

Conversion is a fascinating tort, although it has largely eluded the attention of legal writers.¹ Highly technical in its rules and complications, perhaps more so than any other except defamation, it almost defies definition.² The chief reason is that the hand of history, with its old common law forms of action,³ lies heavy upon this particular field.

---

29. Ward v. Macauley, 1791, 4 Term Rep. 489, 100 Eng.Rep. 1135; Putnam v. Wyley, 1811, 8 N.Y. (Johns.) 432; Winship v. Neale, 1858, 76 Mass. (10 Gray) 382; Holman v. Ketchum, 1907, 153 Ala. 360, 45 So. 206.

30. Lotan v. Cross, 1810, 2 Camp. 464, 170 Eng.Rep. 1219; Staples v. Smith, 1861, 48 Me. 470; Strong v. Adams, 1858, 30 Vt. 221. Cf. Edwards v. Edwards, 1839, 11 Vt. 587 (buyer); Roberts v. Messinger, 1890, 134 Pa. 298, 19 A. 625 (beneficiary of unadministered estate); Ker v. Bryan, 4 Cir. 1908, 163 F. 233, reversed on other grounds 222 U.S. 107, 32 S.Ct. 26, 56 L.Ed. 114 (owner of land in possession of trespasser); Manning v. Wells, 1894, 104 Ala. 383, 16 So. 23 (conditional seller after default).

31. Hall v. Pickard, 1812, 3 Camp. 186, 170 Eng. Rep. 1348; Mears v. London & S. W. R. Co., 1862, 11 C.B.,N.S., 850, 142 Eng.Rep. 1029; Devlin v. Snellenburg, 1890, 132 Pa. 186, 18 A. 1119; Perry v. Bailey, 1900, 94 Me. 50, 46 A. 789; Second Restatement of Torts, § 219.

32. Juniata Acceptance Corp. v. Hoffman, 1940, 139 Pa.Super. 87, 11 A.2d 494.

33. See infra, Section 15.

§ 15

1. The scanty literature on the subject includes Ames, History of Trover, 1898, 11 Harv.L.Rev. 277, 374; Salmond, Observations on Trover and Conversion, 1905, 21 L.Q.Rev. 43; Clark, The Test of Conversion, 1908, 21 Harv.L.Rev. 408; Warren, Qualifying as Plaintiff in an Action for a Conversion, 1936, 49 Harv.L.Rev. 1084; Rubin, Conversion of Choses in Action, 1941, 10 Ford.L.Rev. 415; Prosser, The Nature of Conversion, 1957, 42 Corn.L.Q. 168; Faust, Distinction Between Conversion and Trespass to Chattel, 1958, 37 Or.L.Rev. 256; Note, 1935, 21 Corn.L.Q. 112. See also Professor Warren's small book, Trover and Conversion, 1936.

2. The few attempts have been either so general and vague as to be quite meaningless, or so broad as to include conduct which is clearly not a conversion, or so narrow as to exclude some conduct which clearly is. See for example: "an act of wilful interference with a chattel, done without lawful justification, by which any person entitled thereto is deprived of use and possession." Salmond, Law of Torts, 10th Ed. 1945, 286. "Conversion is the unlawful and wrongful exercise of dominion, ownership or control over the property of another to the exclusion of the exercise of the same rights by the owner, either permanently or for an indefinite time." Pugh v. Hassell, 1952, 206 Okl. 290, 291, 242 P.2d 701, 702.

3. "Forms of action are dead, but their ghosts still haunt the precincts of the law. In their life they were powers of evil, and even in death they have not wholly ceased from troubling. * * * In no branch of the law is this more obvious than in that which relates to the different classes of wrongs which may be committed with respect to chattels. In particular the law of trover and conversion is a region still darkened with the mists of legal formalism, through which no man will find his way by the light of nature or with any other guide save the old learning of writs and forms of action and the mysteries of pleading." Salmond, Observations on Trover and Conversion, 1905, 21 L.Q.Rev. 43.

Although the term had made some earlier appearances,[4] conversion had its real genesis in the old common law action of trover. Trover emerged late in the fifteenth century, as a branch of the action on the case. We probably do not have the earliest examples of its use, but they were almost certainly cases in which the finder of lost goods did not return them, but used them himself, or disposed of them to someone else. The new writ was invented to fill the gap left by the action of trespass, which lay for the wrongful taking of a chattel, and detinue, which lay for its wrongful detention.[5] By 1554 the allegations of the complaint had become more or less standardized:[6] that the plaintiff was possessed of certain goods, that he casually lost them, that the defendant found them, and that the defendant did not return them, but instead "converted them to his own use." From that phrase in the pleading came the name of the tort.

Trover, as it developed, had certain definite procedural advantages over the older forms of action, not the least of which was that it avoided wager of law, a form of licensed perjury which made detinue singularly unattractive to an honest plaintiff suing a dishonest defendant. Almost from the beginning, therefore, the effort was made to expand trover into the fields occupied by the other actions. The device by which this was accomplished was that of treating, first the allegation of losing the goods, and then that of finding them, as a fiction.[7]

The defendant was not permitted to deny the losing and finding, so that the only issues to be litigated were those of the plaintiff's right to possession and the conversion itself. With losing and finding no longer essential, trover became the standard remedy for any form of interference with a chattel. It entirely replaced detinue, which fell into complete disuse; and it so far replaced trespass to chattels that that action appeared only very infrequently. For some two centuries it was said that "whenever trespass for taking goods will lie, that is, where they are taken wrongfully, trover will lie."[8] The two actions, in other words, were regarded as alternative remedies for the same wrong.

There were, however, significant differences between them, which for these two centuries passed almost entirely unremarked. One was that trover would lie for a wrongful detention of goods which had not been wrongfully taken, while trespass would not.[9] More important, however, was a basic difference in theory. The theory of trespass was that the plaintiff remained the owner of the chattel, with his possession only interrupted or interfered with, so that when it was tendered back to him the plaintiff must accept it. His recovery was limited to the damages he had sustained through loss of possession, or harm to the chattel, which were usually considerably less than its value. The theory of trover was that the defendant had appropriated the plaintiff's chattel, for which the defendant must pay. The plaintiff was therefore not required to accept it when it was tendered back to him; and the plaintiff recovered as damages the full value of the chattel at the time and place of conversion. When the defendant satisfied the judgment in trover, the title to the chattel passed to him, and the plaintiff

---

4. Simpson, The Introduction of the Action on the Case for Conversion, 1959, 75 L.Q.Rev. 364, traces it back to 1479, Y.B. 18 Edw. IV, f. 23, pl. 5, where there is reference to an earlier action on the case, in which the defendant "converted" the goods by changing their character, making clothes out of cloth of gold.

5. See Fifoot, History and Sources of the Common Law, 1949, 102–25; Ames, History of Trover, 1898, 11 Harv.L.Rev. 277, 374; Salmond, Observations on Trover and Conversion, 1905, 21 L.Q.Rev. 43.

6. Lord Mounteagle v. Countess of Worcester, 1554, 2 Dyer 121a, 73 Eng.Rep. 265.

7. Gumbleton v. Grafton, 1600, Cro.Eliz. 781, 78 Eng.Rep. 1011; Kinaston v. Moore, 1626, Cro.Car. 89, 79 Eng.Rep. 678; Ratcliff v. Davies, 1611, Cro.Jac. 244, 79 Eng.Rep. 210; Isaack v. Clark, 1614, 2 Bulst. 306, 80 Eng.Rep. 1143.

8. Lord Mansfield, in Cooper v. Chitty, 1756, 1 Burr. 20, 31, 97 Eng.Rep. 166, 172; Serjeant Williams, Note to Saunders' Reports, Wilbraham v. Snow, 1670, 2 Wms.Saund. 47aa, 85 Eng.Rep. 624.

9. Put and Hardy v. Rawsterne, 1682, T.Raym. 472, 83 Eng.Rep. 246. See supra, § 14.

had nothing more to do with it.¹⁰ The effect was that the defendant was compelled, because of his wrongful appropriation, to buy the chattel at a forced sale, of which the action of trover was the judicial instrument.¹¹

Modern Law

The modern law of conversion began when this basic difference between the theories of trespass and trover was brought into sharp focus in Fouldes v. Willoughby ¹² in England in 1841. The defendant wrongfully refused to carry plaintiff's horses on a ferry-boat, and put them off. The plaintiff remained on the boat, and as a result lost his horses. It was held that this was a trespass, but not a conversion, since there was no interference with the plaintiff's "general right of dominion" over the horses. At about the same time, in an American case,¹³ a young lawyer named Abraham Lincoln succeeded in convincing the court that there was no conversion when a horse left with the defendant to be agisted and fed was ridden, on one occasion, for a distance of fifteen miles, since it was not a sufficiently serious invasion of the owner's rights.

Following such decisions, the tort of conversion has been confined to those major interferences with the chattel, or with the plaintiff's rights in it, which are so serious, and so important, as to justify the forced judicial sale to the defendant which is the distinguishing feature of the action. Trespass remains as an occasional remedy for minor interferences, resulting in some damage, but not sufficiently serious or sufficiently important to amount to the greater tort.¹⁴ In determining the seriousness of the interference, and the justice of requiring the defendant to pay the full value, all of the relevant factors in the case are to be considered. These include the extent and duration of the defendant's exercise of control over the chattel; his intent to assert a right which is in fact inconsistent with the plaintiff's right of control; the defendant's good faith or bad intentions; the extent and duration of the resulting interference with the plaintiff's right of control; the harm done to the chattel; and the expense and inconvenience caused to the plaintiff.¹⁵ It follows that in cases of similar conduct, and similar interference, the question becomes one of degree, as to which no definite rules can be laid down—although similar cases are amazingly consistent with one another.

What May Be Converted

What property may be the subject of an action for conversion was at first determined on the basis of the fiction of losing and finding.¹⁶ Any tangible chattel could be lost and found, and so could be converted.¹⁷ Land, on the other hand, was obviously incapable of getting lost, and therefore trover would not lie for the dispossession or withholding of real property. The same was true of

---

10. Adams v. Broughton, 1737, Andrews 18, 95 Eng.Rep. 278; Gunther v. Morey Larue Laundry Co., 1943, 129 N.J.L. 345, 29 A.2d 713 affirmed, 1943, 130 N.J.L. 557, 33 A.2d 893. The mere entry of judgment, without satisfaction, did not affect the title. Hepburn v. Sewell, 1821, 5 Md. (Har. & J.) 211; Miller v. Hyde, 1894, 161 Mass. 472, 37 N.E. 760.

11. See Hale, Bailments, 1896, 188; May v. Georger, 1897, 21 Misc. 622, 47 N.Y.S. 1057.

12. 1841, 8 M. & W. 540, 151 Eng.Rep. 1153.

13. Johnson v. Weedman, 1843, 5 Ill. 495.

14. See for example Bankston v. Dumont, 1949, 205 Miss. 272, 38 So.2d 721 (opening and searching purse, removing money); Bruch v. Carter, 1867, 32 N.J.L. 554 (moving chattel); Post v. Munn, 1818, 4 N.J.L. 61 (damaging fishing net); Brittain v. McKay, 1840, 23 N.C. 265 (cutting crop). "Where the conduct complained of does not amount to a substantial interference with possession or the right thereto, but consists of intermeddling with or use of or damage to the personal property, the owner has a cause of action for trespass or case, and may recover only the actual damages suffered by reason of the impairment of the property or the loss of its use." Zaslow v. Kroenert, 1946, 29 Cal. 2d 541, 551, 176 P.2d 1, 7.

15. Second Restatement of Torts, § 222A, accepted in Mustola v. Toddy, 1969, 253 Or. 658, 456 P.2d 1004; Pearson v. Dodd, 1969, 133 U.S.App.D.C. 279, 410 F.2d 701, certiorari denied 395 U.S. 947, 89 S.Ct. 2021, 23 L.Ed.2d 465. Cases are collected in Prosser, The Nature of Conversion, 1957, 42 Corn.L.Q. 168.

16. See Ayers v. French, 1874, 41 Conn. 142.

17. Graham v. Smith, 1897, 100 Ga. 434, 28 S.E. 225 (dog); State v. Omaha National Bank, 1899, 59 Neb. 483, 81 N.W. 319 (money); Vaughn v. Wright, 1913, 139 Ga. 736, 78 S.E. 123 (tax receipts).

sand and gravel, timber, crops and fixtures, so long as they were regarded as a part of the land, so that no action of trover would lie for their severance. Once there was severance, however, such goods became personal property, and trover could be maintained for their removal from the land.[18]

Intangible rights of all kinds could not be lost or found, and the original rule was that there could be no conversion of such property. But this hoary limitation has been discarded to some extent by all of the courts.[19] The first relaxation of the rule was with respect to the conversion of a document in which intangible rights were merged, so that the one became the symbol of the other—as in the case of a promissory note,[20] a check,[21] a bond,[22] a bill of lading,[23] or a stock certificate.[24] This was then extended to include intangible rights to which a tangible object, converted by the defendant, was highly important—as in the case of a savings bank book,[25] an insurance policy,[26] a tax receipt,[27] account books,[28] or a receipted account.[29] In all of these cases the conversion of the tangible thing was held to include conversion of the intangible rights, and to carry damages for it. The final step was to find conversion of the rights themselves where there was no accompanying conversion of anything tangible—as, for example, where a corporation refuses to register a transfer of the rights of a shareholder on its books.[30]

18. Cage Bros. v. Whiteman, 1942, 139 Tex. 522, 163 S.W.2d 638; Palumbo v. Harry M. Quinn, Inc., 1944, 323 Ill.App. 404, 55 N.E.2d 825; Luhmann v. Schaefer, Mo.App.1940, 142 S.W.2d 1088; Pettigrew v. W & H Development Co., Fla.App.1960, 122 So.2d 813; Giuliano Construction Co. v. Simmons, 1960, 147 Conn. 441, 162 A.2d 511. As to the appreciated value of cut timber, see Smith v. Shiflett, 1965, 66 Wn.2d 462, 403 P.2d 364.

19. See Rubin, Conversion of Choses in Action, 1941, 10 Fordham L.Rev. 415.

20. Citizens' Bank of Madison v. Shaw, 1909, 132 Ga. 771, 65 S.E. 81; Capps v. Vasey Brothers, 1909, 23 Okl. 554, 101 P. 1043; Hoyt v. Stuart, 1915, 90 Conn. 41, 96 A. 166; Security Bank of Minnesota v. Fogg, 1889, 148 Mass. 273, 19 N.E. 378; Griggs v. Day, 1892, 136 N.Y. 152, 32 N.E. 612, rehearing denied 137 N.Y. 542, 32 N.E. 1001. In the absence of evidence, the measure of damages for conversion of a negotiable instrument usually is taken to be its face value. Allied Building Credits v. Grogan Builders Supply Co., Tex. Civ.App.1963, 365 S.W.2d 692, refused n.r.e.

21. First National Bank of Montgomery v. Montgomery Cotton Manufacturing Co., 1924, 211 Ala. 551, 101 So. 186; Bentley, Murray & Co. v. La Salle St. Trust & Savings Bank, 1916, 197 Ill.App. 322; Craven v. Wright, 1925, 114 Or. 692, 236 P. 1043; Lovell v. Hammond Co., 1895, 66 Conn. 500, 34 A. 511; Graton & Knight Manufacturing Co. v. Redelsheimer, 1902, 28 Wash. 370, 68 P. 879. Cf. Hooten v. State to Use of Cross County, 1915, 119 Ark. 334, 178 S.W. 310 (draft).

22. Knight v. Seney, 1919, 290 Ill. 11, 124 N.E. 813; Varney v. Curtis, 1913, 213 Mass. 309, 100 N.E. 650; Simon v. Reilly, 1926, 321 Ill. 431, 151 N.E. 884; Thompson v. Metropolitan Building Co., 1917, 95 Wash. 546, 164 P. 222; Chew v. Louchheim, 3d Cir., 1897, 80 F. 500.

23. Alderson v. Gulf, Colorado & Santa Fe Railway Co., Tex.Civ.App.1893, 23 S.W. 617, error refused; Market State Bank v. Farmers' Savings Bank of Me-servey, 1921, 190 Iowa 1112, 181 N.W. 486. Accord, as to warehouse receipts: Canadian Bank of Commerce v. McCrea, 1882, 106 Ill. 281; Latimer v. Stubbs, 1935, 173 Miss. 436, 159 So. 857, set aside 161 So. 869; cf. R. L. Rothstein Corp. v. Kerr S. S. Co., 1964, 21 A.D.2d 463, 251 N.Y.S.2d 81 (mate's receipt).

24. Pierpoint v. Hoyt, 1932, 260 N.Y. 26, 182 N.E. 235; United States Cities Corp. v. Sautbine, 1927, 126 Okl. 172, 259 P. 253; Pardee v. Nelson, 1922, 59 Utah 497, 205 P. 332; Reading Finance & Security Co. v. Harley, 3d Cir. 1911, 186 F. 673.

25. Stebbins v. North Adams Trust Co., 1922, 243 Mass. 69, 136 N.E. 880; Iavazzo v. Rhode Island Hospital Trust Co., 1931, 51 R.I. 459, 155 A. 407.

26. Commercial Credit Co. v. Eisenhour, 1925, 28 Ariz. 112, 236 P. 126; Hayes v. Massachusetts Mutual Life Insurance Co., 1888, 125 Ill. 626, 18 N.E. 322; Mutual Life Insurance Co. v. Allen, 1904, 212 Ill. 134, 72 N.E. 200; Handley v. Home Insurance Co. of New York, 1933, 112 Fla. 225, 150 So. 902.

27. Vaughn v. Wright, 1913, 139 Ga. 736, 78 S.E. 123.

28. Plunkett-Jarrell Grocery Co. v. Terry, 1954, 222 Ark. 784, 263 S.W.2d 229. See Note, 1954, 9 Ark.L. Rev. 72.

29. Moody v. Drown, 1876, 58 N.H. 45. Cf. Pickford Corp. v. De Luxe Laboratories, S.D.Cal.1958, 161 F.Supp. 367, supplemented, 1959, 169 F.Supp. 118, finding conversion of literary property when defendant duplicated motion picture negatives delivered to it, and turned the prints over to a television company for exhibition.

30. Herrick v. Humphrey Hardware Co., 1905, 73 Neb. 809, 103 N.W. 685; Humphreys v. Minnesota Clay Co., 1905, 94 Minn. 469, 103 N.W. 338; Mears v. Crocker First National Bank, 1948, 84 Cal.App.2d 637, 191 P.2d 501; Mastellone v. Argo Oil Corp., 1951, Del., 7 Terry 102, 82 A.2d 379; Ballenger v. Liberty National Life Insurance Co., 1957, 266 Ala. 407, 96 So.2d 728.

The process of expansion has stopped with the kind of intangible rights which are customarily merged in, or identified with some document. There is perhaps no very valid and essential reason why there might not be conversion of an ordinary debt,[31] the good will of a business,[32] or even an idea,[33] or "any species of personal property which is the subject of private ownership." [34]

The American economy has experienced an increasing use of intangible ideas. It has been urged that conversion should expand to redress interference with all properties—tangible or intangible.[35] But it would seem preferable to fashion other remedies, such as unfair competition, to protect people from having intangible values used and appropriated in unfair ways.

Character of Defendant's Act

A conversion can result only from conduct intended to affect the chattel. For merely negligent interference with it, such as failure to protect it against loss, damage or theft, the remedy is an action for negligence; but there is no conversion, and trover would not lie.[36] It usually is said that mere nonfeasance is not a conversion;[37] but it seems clear that there are situations in which a wilful omission which deprives the plaintiff of his property can serve as a foundation for the action.[38]

The intent required is not necessarily a matter of conscious wrongdoing. It is rather an intent to exercise a dominion or control over the goods which is in fact inconsistent with the plaintiff's rights.[39] A purchaser of

---

31. In Englehart v. Sage, 1925, 73 Mont. 139, 235 P. 767, and McAllaster v. Bailey, 1891, 127 N.Y. 583, 28 N.E. 591, conversion was found in the wrongful attachment of an ordinary debt. To the contrary are Rothchild v. Schwarz, 1899, 28 Misc. 521, 59 N.Y.S. 527; Wright v. School District, 1912, 36 Okl. 294, 128 P. 241; Knox v. Moskins Stores, 1941, 341 Ala. 346, 2 So.2d 449; and Petroleum Marketing Corp. v. Metropolitan Petroleum Corp., 1959, 396 Pa. 48, 151 A.2d 616.

32. No conversion: Powers v. Fisher, 1937, 279 Mich. 442, 272 N.W. 737 (names of customers); Olschewski v. Hudson, 1927, 87 Cal.App. 282, 262 P. 43 (same); Illinois Minerals Co. v. McCarty, 1943, 318 Ill. App. 423, 48 N.E.2d 424 (same); Stern v. Kaufman's Bakery, Inc., Sup.Ct.1959, 191 N.Y.S.2d 734 (bakery route); Whiteley v. Foremost Dairies, W.D.Ark.1957, 151 F.Supp. 914, affirmed, 1958, 254 F.2d 36 (milk route); Meier v. Wilkens, 1897, 15 App.Div. 97, 44 N.Y.S. 274 (right to occupy a market stall).

33. No conversion: Mackay v. Benjamin Franklin Realty & Holding Co., 1927, 288 Pa. 207, 135 A. 613; Thompson v. Mobil Producing Co., D.Mont.1958, 163 F.Supp. 402 (confidential information).

34. Vaughn v. Wright, 1913, 139 Ga. 736, 78 S.E. 123.

35. Hill, A New Found Haliday: The Conversion of Intangible Property—Re-Examination of the Action of Trover and Tort of Conversion, 1972 Utah L.Rev. 511.

36. Heald v. Carey, 1852, 11 C.B. 977, 138 Eng.Rep. 762; Dearbourn v. Union National Bank, 1870, 58 Me. 273; Wamsley v. Atlas S. S. Co., 1901, 168 N.Y. 533, 61 N.E. 896; Emmert v. United Bank & Trust Co., 1936, 14 Cal.App.2d 1, 57 P.2d 963; Armored Car Service v. First National Bank of Miami, Fla.App.1959, 114 So.2d 431.

37. Farrar v. Rollins, 1864, 37 Vt. 295; Forehand v. Jones, 1889, 84 Ga. 508, 10 S.E. 1090; Evans v. Mason, 1886, 64 N.H. 98, 5 A. 766; Bolling v. Kirby, 1889, 90 Ala. 215, 7 So. 914; Dearbourn v. Union National Bank, 1870, 58 Me. 273; Second Restatement of Torts, § 224.

38. See Donnell v. Canadian Pacific Railway Co., 1912, 109 Me. 500, 84 A. 1002. "Where B is in possession of the property, or where he has such control over it that he can readily get possession (as where he has stored it with a bailee), and A demands it, and B fails to deliver it, no modern court is going to save B from being a converter on the ground that there was only a nonfeasance." Warren, Trover and Conversion, 1936, 36.

39. See Fouldes v. Willoughby, 1841, 8 M. & W. 540, 151 Eng.Rep. 1153; Hiort v. Bott, 1874, L.R. 9 Ex. 86; Hollins v. Fowler, 1875, L.R. 7 H.L. 757; Allred v. Hinkley, 1958, 8 Utah 2d 73, 328 P.2d 726.

In Poggi v. Scott, 1914, 167 Cal. 372, 139 P. 815, defendant, on moving into a building, found in the cellar plaintiff's barrels of wine, left there for storage. Assuming that they were abandoned, he sold them for junk. He was held liable for conversion.

In Salt Springs National Bank v. Wheeler, 1872, 48 N.Y. 492, plaintiff sent three bills of exchange to defendant for acceptance. Defendant allowed them to get mixed up with other papers, which he threw into the waste basket, and the bills were burned. He was held not liable for conversion.

The difference between the two cases is that in the first, defendant intended to affect the chattels, by disposing of them, although under a mistake of fact as to what they were. In the second there was no intent to dispose of the chattels at all, although there was no doubt negligence.

stolen goods [40] or an auctioneer who sells them [41] in the utmost good faith becomes a converter, since the auctioneer's acts are an interference with the control of the property. A mistake of law or fact is no defense. "Persons deal with the property in chattels or exercise acts of ownership over them at their peril," [42] and must take the risk that there is no lawful justification for their acts. The essential problem is whether the interference is of so serious a character as to require the defendant to buy the goods.

Given the intent to affect the chattel, conversion may be committed in a number of different ways, as follows:

Acquiring Possession

The defendant may, first of all, wrongfully acquire possession of the plaintiff's chattel. The defendant may, without legal justification, take it out of the plaintiff's possession, or that of a third person. Thus conversion will lie against a trespasser,[43] or a thief.[44] It will also lie for an unjustified levy or attachment under legal process, even though possession is not otherwise disturbed, since the interference is equally serious.[45] In all such cases the taking itself is wrongful, and the tort is complete without any demand for the return of the goods.[46] The same rule has been extended to the acquisition of possession of the chattel by fraud,[47] even though title may have passed to the defendant,[48] by means of a rather fine-spun and anomalous theory which permits the plaintiff to exercise of his own motion the equitable remedy of rescission of the transaction, and thereafter to recover for the wrongful taking as if his consent to it had never been given.

Upon the same basis, a bona fide purchaser of goods from one who has stolen them, or who merely has no power to transfer them, becomes a converter when the pur-

---

40. See infra, this section on Acquiring Possession, and Note 49.

41. See infra, this section on Transferring Possession. Cf. Judkins v. Sadler-MacNeil, 1962, 61 Wash.2d 1, 376 P.2d 837 (good faith refusal to surrender goods).

42. Cleasby, B., in Hollins v. Fowler, 1874, L.R. 7 Q.B. 639. "The foundation for the action of conversion rests neither in the knowledge nor the intent of the defendant. It rests upon the unwarranted interference by defendant with the dominion over the property of the plaintiff from which injury to the latter results. Therefore neither good nor bad faith, neither care nor negligence, neither knowledge nor ignorance, are of the gist of the action." Poggi v. Scott, 1914, 167 Cal. 372, 139 P. 815. Cf. Wilson Freight Forwarding Co. v. Cleveland, Columbus & Cincinnati Highway, 1944, 74 Ohio App. 54, 57 N.E.2d 796 (wrong carrier shipped goods by mistake); McGlynn v. Schultz, 1966, 90 N.J. Super. 505, 218 A.2d 408, affirmed 95 N.J.Super. 412, 231 A.2d 386 (good faith and advice of counsel no defense); Newhart v. Pierce, 1967, 254 Cal.App.2d 783, 62 Cal.Rptr. 553.

43. Plaintiff may waive the trespass and sue for the conversion. Hunt v. City of Boston, 1903, 183 Mass. 303, 67 N.E. 244. As to the local or transitory character of the action, see American Union Telegraph Co. v. Middleton, 1880, 80 N.Y. 408; Ellenwood v. Marietta Chair Co., 1895, 158 U.S. 105, 15 S.Ct. 771, 39 L.Ed. 913; Stone v. United States, 1897, 167 U.S. 178, 17 S.Ct. 778, 42 L.Ed. 127.

44. Hutchinson v. Merchants' & Mechanics' Bank of Wheeling, 1861, 41 Pa. 42.

45. Tinkler v. Poole, 1770, 5 Burr. 2657, 98 Eng. Rep. 396; Morse v. Hurd, 1845, 17 N.H. 246; Kloos v. Gatz, 1906, 97 Minn. 167, 105 N.W. 639; Zion v. De Jonge, 1902, 39 Misc. 839, 81 N.Y.S. 491; Johnson v. Farr, 1880, 60 N.H. 426. It is not necessary that the defendant apply the property to his own use. McPheters v. Page, 1891, 83 Me. 234, 22 A. 101. See Note, 1939, 23 Minn.L.Rev. 799.

46. Bruen v. Roe, 1665, 1 Sid. 264, 82 Eng.Rep. 1095; Porell v. Cavanaugh, 1898, 69 N.H. 364, 41 A. 860; New York Central Railroad Co. v. Freedman, 1921, 240 Mass. 200, 133 N.E. 101; Atlantic Finance Corp. v. Galvam, 1942, 311 Mass. 49, 39 N.E.2d 951 (attachment of goods of wrong party).

47. Roehrich v. Holt Motor Co., 1938, 201 Minn. 586, 277 N.W. 274; McCrillis v. Allen, 1884, 57 Vt. 505; Douglas Motor Sales v. Cy Owens, Inc., 1959, 99 Ga. App. 890, 109 S.E.2d 874 (payment stopped on check); Gottesfeld v. Mechanics & Traders Insurance Co., 1961, 196 Pa.Super. 109, 173 A.2d 763. Contra, Christensen v. Pugh, 1934, 84 Utah 440, 36 P.2d 100.

48. Holland v. Bishop, 1895, 60 Minn. 23, 61 N.W. 681; Hagar v. Norton, 1905, 188 Mass. 47, 73 N.E. 1073. Since the theory of the recovery is a wrongful taking rather than wrongful detention, a demand is not essential to the cause of action. Thurston v. Blanchard, 1839, 39 Mass. (22 Pick.) 18; Yeager v. Wallace, 1868, 57 Pa. 365; Luckey v. Roberts, 1857, 25 Conn. 486; Baird v. Howard, 1894, 51 Ohio St. 57, 36 N.E. 732; Second Restatement of Torts, § 252A.

Cf. Bolton v. Stewart, Tex.Civ.App.1945, 191 S.W.2d 798 (purchase of goods from lunatic incapable of contract).

chaser takes possession to complete the transaction.[49] The courts of New York, and those of two or three other states, have held that such possession is not in itself a sufficiently serious interference with the owner's rights to amount to conversion, so that the purchaser is liable only when he refuses to return the goods on demand.[50] But the great weight of authority regards the mere acquisition of the goods under such circumstances as in itself an assertion of an adverse claim, so detrimental to the dominion of the owner that it completes the tort, and no demand is required.[51] An exception is recognized in the case of negotiable instruments, whose character protects those who rely upon them.[52] Similar rules are applied to those who in good faith take stolen goods in rental or pledge.[53]

Complications arise where there is a bona fide purchase of goods which the true owner was originally induced to sell by fraud.[54] In such a case title has passed on the sale, and there is only a right to rescind the transaction and recover back the goods. This right, although it is enforced at law, originated in equity, and is essentially equitable in character. Since it is fundamental that a bona fide purchase always cuts off equitable rights, such a purchaser is not liable to the original owner for conversion.[55] On the other hand, a purchaser with notice of the fraud obtains no better rights than the one from whom he buys, and so is liable.[56]

It is not, however, every unauthorized taking of goods from the possession of another which is sufficiently serious to amount to conversion. Intention may be good, the duration brief, the event harmless; and if so, the severe remedy of the forced sale to the defendant will not be applied. If A takes B's hat from the rack in a restaurant, immediately discovers his mistake, and returns

---

49. Second Restatement of Torts, § 229. See Newmark, Conversion by Purchase, 1881, 15 Am.L.Rev. 363.

50. Gillet v. Roberts, 1874, 57 N.Y. 28. Accord: Parker v. Middlebrook, 1855, 24 Conn. 207; see Burckhalter v. Mitchell, 1887, 27 S.C. 240, 3 S.E. 225. But demand is held to be unnecessary where it would obviously be futile, as where the defendant after knowledge of the plaintiff's rights claims to be the owner. Employers' Fire Insurance Co. v. Cotten, 1927, 245 N.Y. 102, 156 N.E. 629.

51. Hyde v. Noble, 1843, 13 N.H. 494; Hovland v. Farmers Union Elevator Co., 1936, 67 N.D. 71, 269 N.W. 842; Culp v. Signal Van & Storage Co., 1956, 142 Cal.App.2d 859, 298 P.2d 162; Lovinger v. Hix Green Buick Co., 1964, 110 Ga.App. 698, 140 S.E.2d 83; McRae v. Bandy, 1959, 270 Ala. 12, 115 So.2d 479; Second Restatement of Torts, § 229; Note, 1933, 32 Yale L.J. 292.

The purchaser is also a converter when he resells the chattel without notice that it is stolen. Rogers v. Citizens Bank, 1955, 92 Ga.App. 399, 88 S.E.2d 548; Culp v. Signal Van & Storage Co., 1956, 142 Cal.App.2d 859, 298 P.2d 162.

A fortiori if the defendant either buys or resells with notice. Fowler v. Kragel, 1956, 93 Ga.App. 403, 91 S.E.2d 794; Burns v. Commonwealth Trailer Sales, 1956, 163 Neb. 308, 79 N.W.2d 563.

52. Spooner v. Holmes, 1869, 102 Mass. 503; Pratt v. Higginson, 1918, 230 Mass. 256, 119 N.E. 661; Security-First National Bank of Los Angeles v. Lutz, 9 Cir. 1961, 297 F.2d 159. The purchaser must take in due course or he is not protected. United States Fidelity & Guaranty Co. v. Leon, 1937, 165 Misc. 549, 300 N.Y.S. 331.

53. Warner v. Martin, 1850, 49 U.S. (11 How.) 209; Bott v. McCoy & Johnson, 1852, 20 Ala. 578; O'Connell v. Chicago Park District, 1941, 376 Ill. 550, 34 N.E.2d 836; McCreary & Barlow v. Gaines, 1881, 55 Tex. 485; Thrall v. Lathrop, 1858, 30 Vt. 307. A few courts, however, represented by Varney v. Curtis, 1913, 213 Mass. 309, 100 N.E. 650, have held that the mere taking in pledge is not sufficient for conversion, and that the pledgee is not liable until demand is made upon him.

54. See infra, note 80.

55. McCullen v. Hereford State Bank, 5 Cir. 1954, 214 F.2d 185; Parr v. Helfrich, 1922, 108 Neb. 801, 189 N.W. 281; Martin v. Green, 1918, 117 Me. 138, 102 A. 977; Porell v. Cavanaugh, 1898, 69 N.H. 364, 41 A. 860; Hoffman v. Alpern, 1948, 193 Misc. 695, 85 N.Y.S.2d 561.

Where the transferee has obtained only possession by his fraud, and not title, he can convey no title, and the bona fide purchaser becomes a converter. Alexander v. Swackhamer, 1886, 105 Ind. 81, 4 N.E. 433, 5 N.E. 908; Moody v. Blake, 1874, 117 Mass. 23; Hamet v. Letcher, 1881, 37 Ohio St. 356; Ashton v. Allen, 1903, 70 N.J.L. 117, 56 A. 165; Barker v. Dinsmore, 1872, 72 Pa. 427.

56. Luckey v. Roberts, 1857, 25 Conn. 486; Traywick v. Keeble, 1890, 93 Ala. 498, 8 So. 573; Shaw v. North Pennsylvania R. Co., 1879, 101 U.S. 557, 25 L.Ed. 892; Yeomans v. Jones, 1936, 54 Ga.App. 330, 188 S.E. 62; Charles Kreisler, Inc. v. Matusow, Sup.Ct. 1955, 144 N.Y.S.2d 568.

the hat, it is clearly no conversion.[57] If A takes the hat intending to steal it,[58] or if A keeps it six months, or if a sudden gust of wind blows it off of his head into an open manhole and it is lost, the interference with the rights of the owner becomes sufficiently serious to amount to conversion.[59]

It is generally agreed that a bailee who merely receives possession of the chattel for storage, safekeeping or transportation, in ignorance of the fact that it is lost or stolen, does not thereby become liable to the owner for conversion.[60] Sometimes this is explained upon the basis that the interference with the owner's rights is not a sufficiently serious one;[61] but the rule appears in reality to be one of commercial convenience, which protects those who are needed in our society to receive such goods, against the necessity of inquiry as to the title to what is delivered to them, and so protects their patrons against the delay attending such inquiry. It may thus be regarded as in the nature of a privilege, which does not exist if the bailee receives the goods with knowledge, or reason to know that the bailor has no right to deliver them.[62]

The liability of a servant or agent who receives possession from another on behalf of his principal or master has presented more difficulty. The prevailing view is that if the agent himself has negotiated the transaction for his principal, in which the agent takes possession of the goods, the agent thereby asserts such an adverse claim, of so serious a character, that he is liable to the true owner of the goods for conversion, notwithstanding his innocence and good faith.[63] But if the agent innocently receives or transports the goods and has no other part in the transaction, he is not responsible for the conversion by the agent's principal.[64]

Removing the Chattel

The unauthorized change of the location of the chattel, without other interference with it, may or may not amount to a conversion. If there is no intent to assume any other control over it, or to deprive the owner of it, and the interference is brief in duration and otherwise harmless, it is not so serious a

---

57. Cf. Blackinton v. Pillsbury, 1927, 260 Mass. 123, 156 N.E. 895 (removal of property from locker by mistake); Hushaw v. Dunn, 1916, 62 Colo. 109, 160 P. 1037 (money taken from person of prisoner before he was locked up); Frome v. Dennis, 1883, 45 N.J.L. 515 (brief and innocent borrowing of a plow from one with no right to lend it); MacBryde v. Burnett, D.Mo.1942, 44 F.Supp. 833, affirmed, 1943, 132 F.2d 898 (trustee by mistake transferred shares of stock into his own name).

58. Cf. Lawyers' Mortgage Investment Corp. v. Paramount Laundries, 1934, 287 Mass. 357, 191 N.E. 398; Hutchinson v. Merchants' & Mechanics' Bank, 1861, 41 Pa. 42.

59. Cf. Donahue v. Shippee, 1887, 15 R.I. 453, 8 A. 541 (cutting grass, which was appropriated by third persons); and see Blackinton v. Pillsbury, 1927, 260 Mass. 123, 156 N.E. 895 (dictum, if the property were lost or destroyed there would be conversion).

60. Gurley v. Armstead, 1889, 148 Mass. 267, 19 N.E. 389; Shellnut v. Central of Georgia Railroad Co., 1908, 131 Ga. 404, 62 S.E. 294; Thomas v. D. C. Andrews & Co., 2d Cir. 1931, 54 F.2d 250; Williams v. Roberts, 1939, 59 Ga.App. 473, 1 S.E.2d 587; Manny v. Wilson, 1910, 137 App.Div. 140, 122 N.Y.S. 16, affirmed 1912, 203 N.Y. 535, 96 N.E. 1121.

61. "The carrier and the packing agent are generally held not to have converted because by their acts they merely purport to change the position of the goods and not the property." Barker v. Furlong, [1891] 2 Ch.Div. 172, 182.

62. Warder-Bushnell & Glessner Co. v. Harris, 1890, 81 Iowa 153, 46 N.W. 859; Beckwith v. Independent Transfer & Storage Co., 1928, 105 W.Va. 26, 141 S.E. 443; McAnelly v. Chapman, 1856, 18 Tex. 198; Thorp v. Burling, 1814, 11 N.Y. (11 Johns.) 285; Dodson v. Economy Equipment Co., 1936, 188 Wash. 340, 62 P.2d 708.

63. Hollins v. Fowler, 1875, L.R. 7 H.L. 757; Flannery v. Harley, 1903, 117 Ga. 483, 43 S.E. 765; Richtmyer v. Mutual Livestock Commission Co., 1932, 122 Neb. 317, 240 N.W. 315; First National Bank of Pipestone v. Siman, 1937, 65 S.D. 514, 275 N.W. 347; Nahm v. J. R. Fleming & Co., Tex.Civ.App.1938, 116 S.W.2d 1174.

64. Cases as to liability for mere receipt are few. In Burditt v. Hunt, 1885, 25 Me. 419, and Silver v. Martin, 1880, 59 N.H. 580, the agent was held not to be a converter. To the contrary are Stephens v. Elwall, 1815, 4 M. & S. 259, 105 Eng.Rep. 830, and Miller v. Wilson, 1896, 98 Ga. 567, 25 S.E. 578. See however, the cases of delivery by an agent, infra, note 89, all of which necessarily involved his receipt. If the agent receives possession with notice of the owner's rights, he is a converter. Warder-Bushnell & Glessner Co. v. Harris, 1890, 81 Iowa 153, 46 N.W. 859.

matter as to call for a forced sale to the defendant. Thus the defendant who finds in a newly purchased house the plaintiff's furniture, which the plaintiff refuses to remove, does not become a converter, although there may perhaps be trespass,[65] when the defendant sends the furniture to a storage warehouse, and informs the plaintiff where it is.[66] But if the defendant removes the furniture to a great distance,[67] or fails to notify the plaintiff or to follow the plaintiff's instructions,[68] and so puts the plaintiff to unnecessary inconvenience and expense, or if the defendant removes the furniture intending to keep it for himself,[69] or it is destroyed by fire while it is in the warehouse, there is conversion.[70]

Thus the liability of one who moves another's car upon the street will depend upon whether the person intends to steal it, or merely wants parking space for himself; and in the latter case, whether the person moves it only a few feet or locks it up in an unknown garage without informing the owner.[71] As in the case of receiving possession,[72] carriers and other bailees are protected in their transportation of stolen goods if they move them in good faith, but not if they have notice of the adverse claim.

Transferring Possession

Perhaps the most common way in which conversion is committed is by an unauthorized transfer or disposal of possession of the goods to one who is not entitled to them. Normally this is a sufficiently serious interference with the true owner's right of control, although cases are possible in which the consequences of an innocent mistake are so unimportant that conversion will not be found.[73] Ordinarily the defendant has "set the goods afloat upon a sea of strangers," and it follows that, in Professor Warren's well-known phrase, the defendant has "bought something." Thus a sale and delivery of the plaintiff's goods to another,[74] a lease,[75] a pledge,[76] a mortgage,[77] or even a gift,[78] or a mere erroneous delivery to the

---

65. See Zaslow v. Kroenert, 1946, 29 Cal.2d 541, 176 P.2d 1; Burgess v. Graffam, C.C.Mass.1883, 18 F. 251, affirmed, 1886, 117 U.S. 180, 6 S.Ct. 686, 29 L.Ed. 839; Bruch v. Carter, 1867, 32 N.J.L. 554.

66. Zaslow v. Kroenert, 1946, 29 Cal.2d 541, 176 P.2d 1; Lucas v. Durrence, (1920) 25 Ga.App. 264, 103 S.E. 36; Geisler v. David Stevenson Brewing Co., 1908, 126 App.Div. 715, 111 N.Y.S. 56; Lee Tung v. Burkhart, 1911, 59 Or. 194, 116 P. 1066; Oge v. Resolute Insurance Co., La.App.1969, 217 So.2d 738.

67. Cf. Forsdick v. Collins, 1816, 1 Stark. 173, 171 Eng.Rep. 437; Electric Power Co. v. Mayor of New York, 1899, 36 App.Div. 383, 55 N.Y.S. 460.

68. McGonigle v. Victor H. Belleisle Co., 1904, 186 Mass. 310, 71 N.E. 569; Borg & Powers Furniture Co. v. Reiling, 1943, 213 Minn. 539, 7 N.W.2d 310.

69. Hicks Rubber Distributors v. Stacy, Tex.Civ. App.1939, 133 S.W.2d 249.

70. McCurdy v. Wallblom Furniture & Carpet Co., 1905, 94 Minn. 326, 102 N.W. 873. Cf. Ryan v. Chown, 1910, 160 Mich. 204, 125 N.W. 46; Tobin v. Deal, 1884, 60 Wis. 87, 18 N.W. 634. In Egge v. West Dependable Stores, 1932, 171 Wash. 64, 17 P.2d 609, distance, intent to appropriate, and destruction by fire were all involved. Conversion was found.

71. Cf. Howard v. Deschambeault, 1959, 154 Me. 383, 148 A.2d 706; Fouldes v. Willoughby, 1841, 8 M. & W. 540, 151 Eng.Rep. 1153; Wilson v. McLaughlin, 1871, 107 Mass. 587; Mattice v. Brinkman, 1889, 74 Mich. 705, 42 N.W. 172; O. J. Gude Co. v. Farley, 1898, 25 Misc. 502, 54 N.Y.S. 998.

72. See infra, notes 93, 97.

73. For example, Gulf, Colorado & Santa Fe Railway Co. v. Wortham, Tex.Civ.App.1913, 154 S.W. 1071, where a carrier by mistake delivered plaintiff's goods to a stranger, immediately discovered the mistake, and within twenty-four hours retrieved the goods and delivered them to plaintiff. Also Brandenburg v. Northwestern Jobbers Credit Bureau, 1915, 128 Minn. 411, 151 N.W. 134, where plaintiff's furniture was delivered to a stranger with a house, and there was delay in notifying plaintiff to come and get it.

74. Poggi v. Scott, 1914, 167 Cal. 372, 139 P. 815; Miller v. Long, 1956, 126 Ind.App. 482, 131 N.E.2d 348, rehearing denied 126 Ind.App. 482, 132 N.E.2d 272; Royal-Liverpool Insurance Group v. Macarthy, 1956, 229 S.C. 72, 91 S.E.2d 881; Presley v. Cooper, 1955, 155 Tex. 168, 284 S.W.2d 138; Kenney v. Ranney, 1893, 96 Mich. 617, 55 N.W. 982.

75. Crocker v. Gullifer, 1858, 44 Me. 491.

76. Parker v. Godin, 1728, 2 Stra. 813, 93 Eng.Rep. 866; Singer Manufacturing Co. v. Clark, 1879, 5 Ex. Div. 37.

77. Stevens v. Eames, 1851, 22 N.H. 568.

78. Block v. Talge, 1943, 221 Ind.App. 658, 51 N.E.2d 81 (to junk man). See, however, Row v. Home Savings Bank, 1940, 306 Mass. 522, 29 N.E.2d 552, finding no conversion where the defendant gave away goods apparently abandoned.

wrong person,[79] will constitute a conversion. It is no answer that the defendant acted in good faith, in the honest belief that the delivery was lawful, proper, or authorized. Thus an auctioneer who sells and delivers stolen or mortgaged goods under instructions from his principal becomes liable as a converter notwithstanding his innocence,[80] and so does a carrier or other bailee who, by an innocent mistake, misdelivers the goods to the wrong party.[81] This liability has even been extended to a so-called "involuntary bailee," such as a finder,[82] or one who comes into possession of the chattel by accident or mistake,[83] and then misdelivers it to one not the owner. This has not gone without criticism,[84] and the severity and hardship of such a result can be justified only by the policy of protecting the property right, and placing the burden of tracing and retrieving goods misdelivered by mistake upon the person who made the mistake, rather than upon the equally innocent owner.

But again, as in the case of receipt of possession,[85] commercial convenience and common sense have led to some relaxation of the responsibility of bailees, agents and servants. Such a person will not be liable to his bailor, principal or master if he delivers the goods, contrary to instructions, to one who is legally entitled to possession,[86] or to an officer armed with legal process.[87] Beyond this, if he has received such possession from a thief he does not become a converter as against the true owner when, as directed and in good faith, he returns it to the thief,[88]

79. Hiort v. Bott, 1874, L.R. 9 Ex. 86; Hall v. Boston & Worcester Railroad Corp., 1867, 96 Mass. (14 Allen) 439; Knapp v. Guyer, 1909, 75 N.H. 397, 74 A. 873; Suzuki v. Small, 1925, 214 App.Div. 541, 212 N.Y.S. 589, affirmed, 1927, 243 N.Y. 590, 154 N.E. 618.

80. Morin v. Hood, 1951, 96 N.H. 485, 79 A.2d 4; United States v. Matthews, 9th Cir. 1957, 244 F.2d 626; Kearney v. Clutton, 1894, 101 Mich. 106, 59 N.W. 419; Kelly v. Lang, N.D., 1954, 62 N.W.2d 770; Sig Ellingson & Co. v. De Vries, 8th Cir. 1952, 199 F.2d 677, certiorari denied 73 S.Ct. 505, 344 U.S. 934, 97 L.Ed. 719. Cf. Swim v. Wilson, 1891, 90 Cal. 126, 27 P.2d 33 (market agent). See Notes, 1962, 41 Neb.L.Rev. 617; 1957, 45 Cal.L.Rev. 776.

81. Youl v. Harbottle, 1791, Peake 49, 170 Eng.Rep. 74; Baer v. Slater, 1927, 261 Mass. 153, 158 N.E. 328; Potomac Insurance Co. v. Nickson, 1924, 64 Utah 395, 231 P. 445; Sullivan & O'Brien v. Kennedy, 1940, 107 Ind.App. 457, 25 N.E.2d 267; Marshall & Michel Grain Co. v. Kansas City & Fort Scott & Memphis Railway Co., 1903, 176 Mo. 480, 75 S.W. 638. See Note, 1957, 45 Cal.L.Rev. 776.

82. See Dolitsky v. Dollar Bank, 1952, 203 Misc. 262, 118 N.Y.S.2d 65; and compare Ryan v. Chown, 1910, 160 Mich. 204, 125 N.W. 46; Poggi v. Scott, 1914, 167 Cal. 372, 139 P. 815.

83. Cowen v. Pressprich, 1922, 117 Misc. 663, 192 N.Y.S. 242, reversed on other grounds in 1924, 202 App.Div. 796, 194 N.Y.S. 926; Knapp v. Guyer, 1909, 75 N.H. 397, 74 A. 873; Suzuki v. Small, 1925, 214 App. Div. 541, 212 N.Y.S. 589, affirmed 1927, 243 N.Y. 590, 154 N.E. 618. Compare Hiort v. Bott, 1874, L.R. 9 Ex. 86; Helson v. McKenzies [1950] N.Z.L.Rep. 878; McCurdy v Wallblom Furniture & Carpet Co., 1905, 94 Minn. 326, 102 N.W. 873; McGonigle v. Victor H. Belleisle Co., 1904, 186 Mass. 310, 71 N.E. 569. See Note, 1922, 6 Minn.L.Rev. 579.

In New York, where a bona fide purchaser is not liable until demand and refusal, he is nevertheless liable if he has sold the goods. Pease v. Smith, 1875, 61 N.Y. 477.

84. Burnett, Conversion by Involuntary Bailee, 1960, 76 L.Q.Rev. 364; Fleming, Law of Torts, 3d ed. 1965, 58–9; 1 Harper & James, Law of Torts, 1956, 177–178. This position was taken by Elvin & Powell, Limited v. Plummer Roddie, Limited, 1934, 50 T.L.R. 158, and Morris v. Third Ave. Railroad Co., 1862, 1 Daly, N.Y., 202. Cohen v. Koster, 1909, 133 App.Div. 570, 118 N.Y.S. 142, looks like a case of doing nothing, where defendant never had come into possession. The Second Restatement of Torts, § 235, reverses the position of the First Restatement, § 236(2), and supports the text.

85. Supra, note 60.

86. Herring v. Creech, 1954, 241 N.C. 233, 84 S.E.2d 886; Farmers Union Warehouse Co. v. Barnett, 1925, 214 Ala. 202, 107 So. 46; Davis v. Donohoe-Kelly Banking Co., 1907, 152 Cal. 282, 92 P. 639; Eisiminger v. Dinwiddie, 1935, 170 Okl. 396, 40 P.2d 1029; Schrowang v. Von Hoffman Press, Mo.App.1934, 75 S.W.2d 649, affirmed 1935, 337 Mo. 522, 85 S.W.2d 417.

87. Clegg v. Boston Storage Warehouse Co., 1889, 149 Mass. 454, 21 N.E. 877; American Express Co. v. Mullins, 1909, 212 U.S. 311, 29 S.Ct. 381, 53 L.Ed. 525; Cornell v. Mahoney, 1906, 190 Mass. 265, 76 N.E. 664; Branch v. Bekins Van & Storage Co., 1930, 106 Cal. App. 623, 290 P. 146.

88. Thoms v. D. C. Andrews & Co., 2 Cir. 1931, 54 F.2d 250; Steele v. Marsicano, 1894, 102 Cal. 666, 36 P. 920; Coleman v. Francis, 1925, 102 Conn. 612, 129 A. 718; Shellnut v. Central of Georgia Railway Co., 1908, 131 Ga. 404, 62 S.E. 294; Nanson v. Jacob, 1887, 93 Mo. 331, 6 S.W. 246.

or turns the goods over to a third party.[89] The line is drawn where the agent himself negotiates the transaction by which the goods are transferred to a third party, and then makes the delivery. In such a case, unless what is transferred is negotiable paper,[90] there is general agreement that there is such a major interference with the rights of the true owner that there must be liability for conversion.[91]

Once the bailee, agent or servant has received notice of the true owner's claim, the situation is changed. There is no longer the same reason to protect the bailee, and he is required, at his peril, to avoid a wrongful delivery to a third person.[92] Even after such notice, however, the common law developed a curious rule which permitted him to redeliver the goods to his bailor without liability, so long as no demand or other claim had been made upon him by the true owner.[93] The origin of this is obscure, but it apparently rested upon the idea of a special obligation undertaken by the bailee to the bailor. Its only practical justification has been one of commercial expediency for the protection of the bailee himself. It usually has been explained upon the basis of an "estoppel" to dispute the title of the bailor; but this explanation fails when demand or other claim has been made by the true owner. The bailee then re-delivers at his peril, and is liable for conversion if he turns out to be wrong.[94] His proper course in such a case is interpleader, or deposit in court.[95]

Withholding Possession

Another very common way in which conversion may occur is by way of a refusal to surrender possession of the chattel to one who is entitled to it. Normally this is a sufficiently serious interference with the plaintiff's right of control. Here, however, as elsewhere throughout this chapter, there will obviously be occasional cases where the detention is a relatively unimportant matter, so that conversion will not be found. If a garage, even quite intentionally, delays for half an hour the return of the plaintiff's parked car, it is no conversion.[96] But if the detention is for a month, or the intent is to appropriate the car,[97] or if it is destroyed by

---

89. Ashcraft v. Tucker, 1923, 73 Colo. 363, 215 P. 877; Hodgson v. St. Paul Plow Co., 1899, 78 Minn. 172, 80 N.W. 956; Leuthold v. Fairchild, 1886, 35 Minn. 99, 27 N.W. 503, modified 35 Minn. 99, 28 N.W. 218; Walker v. First National Bank of Athena, 1903, 43 Or. 102, 72 P. 635; In re Samuel Kernan, [1945] Ch. 408.

90. Even here, where the property sold is negotiable paper, it has been held that the agent is protected by the character of the instrument, on which he is entitled to rely. Spooner v. Holmes, 1869, 102 Mass. 503; Pratt v. Higginson, 1918, 230 Mass. 256, 119 N.E. 661; First National Bank of Blairstown v. Goldberg, 1941, 340 Pa. 337, 17 A.2d 377; Gruntal v. United States Fidelity & Guaranty Co., 1930, 254 N.Y. 468, 173 N.E. 682; Second Restatement of Torts, § 233.

91. Swim v. Wilson, 1891, 90 Cal. 126, 27 P. 33; Flannery v. Harley, 1903, 117 Ga. 483, 43 S.E. 765; Richtmyer v. Mutual Live Stock Commission Co., 1932, 122 Neb. 317, 240 N.W. 315; Kelly v. Lang, N.D.1954, 62 N.W.2d 770; First National Bank of Pipestone v. Siman, 1937, 65 S.D. 514, 275 N.W. 347. See Notes, 1947, 14 U.Chi.L.Rev. 713; 1962, 41 Neb.L.Rev. 617; 1957, 45 Cal.L.Rev. 776.

92. Edwards v. Max Thieme Chevrolet Co., La.App. 1939, 191 So. 569; Thorp v. Burling, 1814, 11 N.Y. (Johns.) 285; Beckwith v. Independent Transfer & Storage Co., 1928, 105 W.Va. 26, 141 S.E. 443; Hudmon v. Du Bose, 1888, 85 Ala. 446, 5 So. 162; Dodson v. Economy Equipment Co., 1936, 188 Wash. 340, 62 P.2d 708.

93. Hill v. Hayes, 1871, 38 Conn. 532; Succession of Macon, 1922, 150 La. 1026, 91 So. 441; Rembaugh v. Phipps, 1882, 75 Mo. 422; Paccos v. Rosenthal, 1926, 137 Wash. 423, 242 P. 651. See Second Restatement of Agency, § 417.

94. Hattiesburg Auto Sales Co. v. Morrison, 1924, 136 Miss. 632, 101 So. 690; Maser v. Farmers' & Merchants' Bank, 1931, 90 Mont. 33, 300 P. 207; Bonner v. McDonald, App.Term 1916, 162 N.Y.S. 324; Roberts v. Yarboro & Wimberly, 1874, 41 Tex. 449; cf. Smith v. Bell & Stephens, 1846, 9 Mo. 873.

95. Winter v. Bancks, 1901, 84 L.T. 504; Cass v. Higenbotam, 1885, 100 N.Y. 248, 3 N.E. 189.

96. Mattice v. Brinkman, 1889, 74 Mich. 705, 42 N.W. 172; Peck v. Patterson, 1956, 119 Vt. 280, 125 A.2d 813 (brief detention of cars); Daggett v. Davis, 1884, 53 Mich. 35, 18 N.W. 548 (stock certificate). In accord are the cases in which defendant, to keep out intruders, has locked up plaintiff's goods in a building, and so delayed him in obtaining possession. Poor v. Oakman, 1870, 104 Mass. 309; Edinburg v. Allen Squire Co., 1938, 299 Mass. 206, 12 N.E.2d 718; Zaslow v. Kroenert, 1946, 29 Cal.2d 451, 176 P.2d 1.

97. Thomas v. Westbrook, 1944, 206 Ark. 841, 177 S.W.2d 931; Kirby v. Porter, 1923, 144 Md. 261, 125 A. 41; Jones v. Stone, 1917, 78 N.H. 504, 102 A. 377; Henderson v. Beggs, Tex.Civ.App.1918, 207 S.W. 565.

fire during the delay,[98] then there is clearly conversion.[99]

Where there has been no wrongful taking or disposal of the goods, and the defendant has merely come rightfully into possession and then refused to surrender them, demand and refusal are necessary to the existence of the tort.[1] When demand is made, an absolute, unqualified refusal to surrender, which puts the plaintiff to the necessity of force or a lawsuit to recover his own property, is of course a conversion.[2] Denial of possession,[3] equivocation,[4] or a lying promise to return,[5] or even continued silence and inaction for several days,[6] may amount to the same thing. Ordinarily the defendant is not required to do more than permit the plaintiff to come and get the goods,[7] but if some positive act, easily done, is called for, such as disclosure of their location or turning over a key, a failure to perform it may be a conversion.[8]

Not every failure to deliver upon demand, however, will constitute a conversion. The defendant does not become a converter when the goods are no longer in his possession or control, so that the defendant is unable to comply with the demand,[9] even though they may have been lost or destroyed through the defendant's own fault.[10] The remedy in such a case is an action for negligence. The defendant is not required to comply with a demand made at an unreasonable time or place, or in an unreasonable manner,[11] or upon an employee who has no authority to take any action.[12] And even when the defendant has possession, a qualified refusal, for a reasonable purpose and for a reasonable length of time,[13] is not a conversion. The defendant may detain the

---

98. Donnell v. Canadian Pacific Railway Co., 1912, 109 Me. 500, 84 A. 1002.

99. "The very denial of goods to him that has a right to demand them is an actual conversion, and not only evidence of it." Baldwin v. Cole, 1704, 6 Mod.Rep. 212, 87 Eng.Rep. 964; Bristol v. Burt, 1810, 7 N.Y. (7 Johns.) 254; Vilas v. Mason, 1870, 25 Wis. 310; Smith v. Durham, 1900, 127 N.C. 417, 37 S.E. 473.

1. Spackman v. Foster, 1883, 11 Q.B.Div. 99. Hence the cause of action does not accrue until demand. In the case of gratuitous bailments without a time limit, however, it has been held that the demand must be made within a reasonable time, which, in the absence of other determining factors, will be taken to be that of the statute of limitations. Lowney v. Knott, 1956, 83 R.I. 505, 120 A.2d 552; Schupp v. Taendler, 1946, 81 App.D.C. 59, 154 F.2d 849; Southward v. Foy, 1948, 65 Nev. 694, 201 P.2d 302; cf. Norwood Trust Co. v. Twenty-Four Federal Street Corp., 1936, 295 Mass. 234, 3 N.E.2d 826.

2. Singer Manufacturing Co. v. King, 1884, 14 R.I. 511; Vilas v. Mason, 1870, 25 Wis. 310; Smith v. Durham, 1900, 127 N.C. 417, 37 S.E. 473; Preble v. Hanna, 1926, 117 Or. 306, 244 P. 75 (fastening door securely, denying access); Molski v. Bendza, 1933, 116 Conn. 710, 164 A. 387 (refusal to allow plaintiff to enter premises). Even though the defendant refuses in the good faith belief that he has the right to detain the goods. Judkins v. Sadler-MacNeil, 1962, 61 Wash.2d 1, 376 P.2d 837.

3. Dunlap v. Hunting, 1846, 2 N.Y. (Denio) 643; Wright v. Frank A. Andrews Co., 1912, 212 Mass. 186, 98 N.E. 798; Russell-Vaughn Ford, Inc. v. Rouse, 1968, 281 Ala. 567, 206 So.2d 371.

4. Gray v. Frazier, 1930, 158 Md. 189, 148 A. 457 (stalling plaintiff off).

5. Lopard v. Symons, Sup.Ct.1904, 85 N.Y.S. 1025. Compare, however, Severin v. Kepple, 1803, 4 Esp. 156, 170 Eng.Rep. 674, where continued promises and excuses, apparently in good faith, were held not sufficient.

6. Willis v. Midland Finance Co., 1958, 97 Ga.App. 443, 103 S.E.2d 185.

7. Farrar v. Rollins, 1864, 37 Vt. 295; Forehand v. Jones, 1889, 84 Ga. 508, 10 S.E. 1090.

8. Donnell v. Canadian Pacific Railway Co., 1912, 109 Me. 500, 84 A. 1002; Bank of America v. McNeil, 1873, 73 Ky. (10 Bush.) 54.

9. Rushworth v. Taylor, 1842, 3 Q.B. 669, 114 Eng. Rep. 674; Dozier v. Pillot, 1891, 79 Tex. 224, 14 S.W. 1027; Nelen v. Colwell, 1924, 45 R.I. 465, 123 A. 897, reargument denied, 124 A. 257; State ex rel. Sporleder v. Staed, 1896, 65 Mo.App. 487; Magnin v. Dinsmore, 1877, 70 N.Y. 410.

10. Hawkins v. Hoffman, 1844, 6 N.Y. (Hill) 586; Dearbourn v. Union National Bank, 1870, 58 Me. 273; Wamsley v. Atlas Steamship Co., 1901, 168 N.Y. 533, 61 N.E. 896; Salt Springs National Bank v. Wheeler, 1872, 48 N.Y. 492.

11. Fifield v. Maine Central Railroad Co., 1873, 62 Me. 77; Durgin v. Gage, 1860, 40 N.H. 302; Phelps v. Gilchrist, 1854, 28 N.H. 266 (place); cf. Pantz v. Nelson, 1939, 234 Mo.App. 1043, 135 S.W.2d 397 (place); St. Louis Fixture & Show Case Co. v. F. W. Woolworth Co., 1935, 232 Mo.App. 10, 88 S.W.2d 254 (demand not specifying the chattels).

12. Mueller v. Technical Devices Corp., 1951, 8 N.J. 201, 84 A.2d 620; Fletcher v. Pump Creek Gas & Oil Syndicate, 1928, 38 Wyo. 329, 266 P. 1062.

13. Felcher v. McMillan, 1895, 103 Mich. 494, 61 N.W. 791 (24 hours); Buffington v. Clarke, 1887, 15

goods for a reasonable time to identify the plaintiff,[14] to determine his right to possession,[15] to ascertain whether charges against the goods are correct,[16] or if the defendant is an agent, to consult the principal from whom he received them.[17] All such detentions must, however, be made in good faith,[18] with the reason stated. An unqualified refusal to surrender, stating no reason,[19] or one stating the wrong reason,[20] is still a conversion, even where there are unstated justifications. And if the defendant insists upon charges,[21] or other conditions of delivery,[22] which he has no right to impose, there is conversion. After the lapse of a reasonable time for investigation, the defendant is required to make up his mind, and he becomes liable as a converter if he refuses delivery to the rightful claimant.[23] Again the defendant's way out of the difficulty is by interpleader, or deposit in court.[24]

Destruction or Alteration

If the defendant, intending to do so, completely destroys the plaintiff's chattel, as by burning a paper, there is obviously a complete interference with the plaintiff's rights, and an obvious conversion;[25] and the same must be true if the defendant so radically damages or alters it that its character is substantially changed, as by adulterating rum,[26] cutting down a fur coat so that it be-

---

R.I. 437, 8 A. 247 (12 days); St. Louis Fixture & Show Case Co. v. F. W. Woolworth Co., 1935, 232 Mo.App. 10, 88 S.W.2d 254 (22 days); Farming Corp. v. Bridgeport Bank, 1925, 113 Neb. 323, 202 N.W. 911 (30 days). An offer of indemnity may cut down the time, and require the defendant to surrender the goods or interplead promptly. Ball v. Liney, 1871, 48 N.Y. 6.

14. McEntee v. New Jersey Steamboat Co., 1871, 45 N.Y. 34; Flood v. Moore, [1933] 4 Dom.L.Rep. 392.

15. Bradley v. Roe, 1940, 282 N.Y. 525, 27 N.E.2d 35, certified questions answered 257 App.Div. 1074, 14 N.Y.S.2d 996; Buffington v. Clarke, 1887, 15 R.I. 437, 8 A. 247; Hansen v. Village of Ralston, 1945, 145 Neb. 838, 18 N.W.2d 213; Banque de France v. Equitable Trust Co., S.D.N.Y.1929, 33 F.2d 202; Wolfe v. Lewisburg Trust & Safe Deposit Co., 1931, 305 Pa. 583, 158 A. 567. Cf. Wood v. Pierson, 1881, 45 Mich. 313, 7 N.W. 888 (finder); Giacomelos v. Bank of America National Trust & Savings Association, 1965, 237 Cal.App. 2d 99, 46 Cal.Rptr. 612 (trustee).

16. Beasley v. Baltimore & Potomac Railroad Co., 1906, 27 App.D.C. 595; Stahl v. Boston & Maine Railroad Co., 1901, 71 N.H. 57, 51 A. 176; Hett v. Boston & Maine Railroad Co., 1897, 69 N.H. 139, 44 A. 910; Bolling v. Kirby, 1889, 90 Ala. 215, 7 So. 914; Felcher v. McMillan, 1895, 103 Mich. 494, 61 N.W. 791.

17. Alexander v. Southey, 1821, 5 B. & Ad. 247, 106 Eng.Rep. 1183. Cf. Beasley v. Baltimore & Potomac Railroad Co., 1906, 27 U.S.App.D.C. 595.

18. Flannery v. Brewer, 1887, 66 Mich. 509, 33 N.W. 522; Holbrook v. Wight, 1840, 24 N.Y. (Wend.) 169.

19. Boardman v. Sill, 1809, 1 Camp. 410, 170 Eng. Rep. 1003; Hanna v. Phelps, 1855, 7 Ind. 21; Clark v. Rideout, 1859, 39 N.H. 238; Williams v. Smith, 1893, 153 Pa. 462, 25 A. 1122; Rapid Sewing Center v. Sanders, 1961, 79 S.D. 373, 112 N.W.2d 233.

20. Ingalls v. Bulkley, 1853, 15 Ill. 224; Pantz v. Nelson, 1940, 234 Mo.App. 1043, 135 S.W.2d 397.

21. Jones v. Tarleton, 1842, 9 M. & W. 675, 152 Eng.Rep. 285; Semple v. Morganstern, 1922, 97 Conn. 402, 116 A. 906; Long-Lewis Hardware Co. v. Abston, 1938, 235 Ala. 599, 180 So. 261.

22. Pennsylvania Fire Insurance Co. v. Levy, 1929, 85 Colo. 565, 277 P. 779 (settlement); Herbertson v. Cohen, 1955, 132 Colo. 231, 287 P.2d 47 (complete release); Charles F. Curry & Co. v. Hedrick, Mo.1964, 378 S.W.2d 522 (waiver of all claims); Boiseau v. Morrisette, Mun.App.D.C.1951, 78 A.2d 777 (dismissal of other suit); Citizens Industrial Bank of Austin v. Oppenheim, Tex.Civ.App.1936, 92 S.W.2d 312, error dismissed (holding as security for other loans).

23. Beasley v. Baltimore & Potomac Railroad Co., 1906, 27 App.D.C. 595; Buffington v. Clarke, 1887, 15 R.I. 437, 8 A. 247.

As in the case of conversion by misdelivery, supra, p. 96, there are cases holding that a bailee is "estopped" to dispute the title of his bailor, and cannot justify refusal to surrender the chattel to him because of the claim of a third person, unless the third person has asserted the claim against the bailee. See Thorne v. Tilbury, 1858, 3 H. & N. 534, 157 Eng.Rep. 581; Biddle v. Bond, 1865, 6 Best & S. 225, 122 Eng.Rep. 1179; Ball v. Liney, 1871, 48 N.Y. 6; Powell v. Robinson, 1884, 76 Ala. 423; Flannery v. Brewer, 1887, 66 Mich. 509, 33 N.W. 522. The question may be raised, how long this antique rule for the restoration of stolen property into the hands of thieves is entitled to survive.

24. Wilson v. Anderton, 1830, 1 B. & Ad. 450, 109 Eng.Rep. 855.

25. Keyworth v. Hill, 1820, 3 B. & Ald. 684, 106 Eng.Rep. 811; Simmons v. Sikes, 1841, 24 N.C. (2 Ired.) 98.

Cf. Aschermann v. Philip Best Brewing Co., 1878, 45 Wis. 262 (melting ice). As to damages for loss of use where there is complete destruction, see Note, 1960, 33 So.Cal.L.Rev. 451.

26. Dench v. Walker, 1780, 14 Mass. 500. Cf. Richardson v. Atkinson, 1723, 1 Stra. 576, 93 Eng.Rep. 710 (drawing out part of wine and substituting water); Penfolds Wines, Limited v. Elliott, Aust.1946, 74

comes too small for the plaintiff to wear,[27] disassembling a complicated piece of machinery into many parts,[28] grinding wheat into flour,[29] or commingling the plaintiff's goods with others so that identification becomes impossible.[30] On the other hand, mere damage, falling short of destruction or material alteration, usually may be compensated without the forced purchase which is the distinguishing feature of the remedy, and so is not treated as conversion.[31] Questions of degree will of course arise. One of these may concern the destruction or removal of a part of a chattel, such as the tire of an automobile: is it conversion only of the part, or of the whole? Probably the answer is that if replacement is quick and easy, only the tire is converted; but if it is slow and difficult, with the car in the midst of a distant desert, there is conversion of the car.[32]

Using the Chattel

If the defendant has only made use of the chattel without harming it, one would expect to find much the same distinctions made. A casual and harmless use, involving no defiance of the owner's right of dominion, as where a car left to be sold is driven, on one occasion, for ten miles,[33] will not be treated as a conversion, although the defendant will of course be liable in damages for the use of the car. But if it is driven 2,000 miles,[34] or driven even the ten with the intention to steal it,[35] or if it is used for the illegal transportation of narcotics and confiscated by the government,[36] there is a conversion.

The more serious questions arise where an agent or bailee is authorized to make some use of the chattel, but exceeds or departs from what is permitted. In general, any major and serious departure will be held to be a conversion,[37] while minor ones which do no

---

Comm.L.Rep. 204, 229 (cutting seals from a deed); Colby v. Porter, 1925, 124 Me. 446, 129 A. 298 (changes in sleds).

27. Douglass v. Hart, 1925, 103 Conn. 685, 131 A. 401; May v. Georger, 1897, 21 Misc. 622, 47 N.Y.S. 1057.

28. Symphony Player Co. v. Hackstadt, 1918, 182 Ky. 546, 206 S.W. 803 (pin-cylinder organ). Cf. Jackson v. Innes, 1919, 231 Mass. 558, 121 N.E. 489.

29. Mayer v. Springer, 1901, 192 Ill. 270, 61 N.E. 348. Cf. McPheters v. Page, 1891, 83 Me. 234, 22 A. 101 (cutting up carcass of deer); Wilson Cypress Co. v. Logan, 1935, 120 Fla. 124, 162 So. 489 (sawing logs).

30. Peltola v. Western Workman's Publishing Society, 1920, 113 Wash. 283, 193 P. 691; Crane Lumber Co. v. Bellows, 1898, 116 Mich. 304, 74 N.W. 481; Martin v. Mason, 1886, 78 Me. 452, 7 A. 11; Royce v. Oakes, 1897, 20 R.I. 252, 38 A. 371; Wells v. Batts, 1893, 112 N.C. 283, 17 S.E. 417.

31. Simmons v. Lillystone, 1853, 8 Ex. 431, 155 Eng. Rep. 1417. Cf. Philpott v. Kelley, 1835, 3 Ad. & El. 106, 111 Eng.Rep. 353 (bottling wine to preserve it). Cf. Donovan v. Barkhausen Oil Co., 1929, 200 Wis. 194, 227 N.W. 940.

32. In G. W. K., Ltd. v. Dunlop Rubber Co., K.B. 1926, 42 T.L.R. 376, where a set of tires was removed from a car on exhibition in a showroom, it was held that there was no conversion of the car. Otherwise in Nielsen v. Warner, 1938, 66 S.D. 214, 281 N.W. 110, where the motor was removed. In Klam v. Koppel, 1941, 63 Idaho 171, 118 P.2d 729, some parts of a tractor were removed, others smashed with a sledge-hammer, and it was held that there was conversion of the tractor.

33. Jeffries v. Pankow, 1924, 112 Or. 439, 229 P. 903. Cf. Buice v. Campbell, 1959, 99 Ga.App. 334, 108 S.E.2d 339 (left to be repaired, driven to dealer to match parts); Johnson v. Weedman, 1843, 5 Ill. (4 Scam.) 495 (agister to feed horse rode him once for fifteen miles); Frome v. Dennis, 1883, 45 N.J.L. 515 (unauthorized borrowing of plow, used for three days); McNeill v. Brooks, 1882, 9 Tenn. 73 (horse rented for riding used once to carry goods); Donovan v. Barkhausen Oil Co., 1929, 200 Wis. 194, 227 N.W. 940 (minor repairs on automobile against orders).

34. Miller v. Uhl, 1929, 37 Ohio App. 276, 174 N.E. 591, motion overruled. Cf. E. J. Caron Enterprises v. State Operating Co., 1935, 87 N.H. 371, 179 A. 665 (theatre fixtures used in wrong theatre); West Jersey Railroad Co. v. Trenton Car Works Co., 1866, 32 N.J.L. 517 (car defendant was under duty to forward used in its own service); Schulte v. Florian, Mo.App.1963, 370 S.W.2d 623 (using plaster mixer, removing to another job, leaving it dirty).

35. Cf. Cheshire Railroad Co. v. Foster, 1871, 51 N.H. 490; Forster v. Juniata Bridge Co., 1851, 16 Pa. 393; Oakley v. Lyster, [1931] 1 K.B. 148. Cf. Lord Petre v. Heneage, 1699, 12 Mod.Rep. 519, 88 Eng.Rep. 1490; Bryant v. Wardell, 1848, 2 Exch. 479, 154 Eng. Rep. 580; Hillhouse v. Wolf, 1958, 166 Cal.App.2d Supp. 833, 333 P.2d 454; Peterson v. Wolff, 1938, 68 N.D. 354, 280 N.W. 187.

36. Vermont Acceptance Corp. v. Wiltshire, 1931, 103 Vt. 219, 153 A. 199; Moorgate Merc. Co. v. Finch, [1962] 1 Q.B. 701. Cf. Collins v. Bennett, 1871, 46 N.Y. 490 (horse used and foundered).

37. McMorris v. Simpson, 1839, 21 Wend. N.Y. 610 (sending goods to unauthorized market); Laverty v. Snethen, 1877, 68 N.Y. 522 (surrendering note without

harm will not.[38] A series of old cases concerned with the driving of rented horses beyond the agreed destination,[39] worked out the rule that if the departure is a minor one and no harm ensues, there is no conversion;[40] but that if substantial damage occurs to the chattel in the course of the deviation, even without the fault of the bailee, he is an insurer against it, and is liable as a converter.[41] This, of course, is consistent with the position taken throughout, that the severe and drastic remedy of a forced sale to the defendant is properly limited to cases where there has been an intent to deny the rights of ownership, or major interference with a substantial part of them.

Asserting Ownership

The gist of conversion is the interference with control of the property. It follows that a mere assertion of ownership, without any disturbance of possession, or any other interference with the right to it, is not sufficiently serious to be classed as conversion.[42] A sale,[43] an advertisement for sale,[44] or a purchase,[45] of the chattel by one who has no right to it, while the owner's possession remains undisturbed, does not make the defendant a converter. But obviously very little more is required. A claim of title by one who is in possession, which reasonably implies that the owner will not be permitted to obtain the goods, will be enough;[46] and so of course will any legal proceeding, such as an injunction[47] which restricts the actual control.

Plaintiff's Interest

In order to maintain the common law action of trover, the plaintiff must establish that he was in possession of the goods, or entitled to possession, at the time of the con-

---

payment); Juzeler v. Buchli, 1933, 63 N.D. 657, 249 N.W. 790 (surrendering check on compromise of collection); Maynard v. James, 1929, 109 Conn. 365, 146 A. 614 (driving car left to be washed); Regas v. Helios, 1922, 176 Wis. 56, 186 N.W. 165 (making different investment of money).

38. See cases cited this section, supra, note 66.

39. One of the minor mysteries of the law is why there are no automobile cases. This remains horse-and-buggy law, but none the less sound.

40. Wentworth v. McDuffie, 1869, 48 N.H. 402; Farkas v. Powell, 1891, 86 Ga. 800, 13 S.E. 200; Doolittle v. Shaw, 1894, 92 Iowa 348, 60 N.W. 621; Carney v. Rease, 1906, 60 W.Va. 676, 55 S.E. 729; Daugherty v. Reveal, 1915, 54 Ind.App. 71, 102 N.E. 381.

41. Palmer v. Mayo, 1907, 80 Conn. 353, 68 A. 369; Perham v. Coney, 1875, 117 Mass. 102; Baxter v. Woodward, 1916, 191 Mich. 379, 158 N.W. 137; Woodman v. Hubbard, 1862, 25 N.H. 67; Disbrow v. Tenbroeck, 1855, 4 E.D. Smith, N.Y., 397.

Cf. Ledbetter v. Thomas, 1901, 130 Ala. 299, 30 So. 342; Cartlidge v. Sloan, 1899, 124 Ala. 596, 26 So. 918; Fryer v. Cooper, 1928, 53 S.D. 286, 220 N.W. 486; De Voin v. Michigan Lumber Co., 1885, 64 Wis. 616, 25 N.W. 552. In Spooner v. Manchester, 1882, 133 Mass. 270, where the driver unintentionally deviated from the route, and the horse was injured while he was trying to get back to it, it was held that there was no conversion.

42. Hein v. Marcante, 1941, 57 Wyo. 81, 113 P.2d 940; Irish v. Cloyes, 1836, 8 Vt. 30; Jenkins v. Holly, 1920, 204 Ala. 519, 86 So. 390; Knowles v. Knowles, 1903, 25 R.I. 464, 56 A. 775; Dietzman v. Ralston Purina Co., 1967, 246 Or. 367, 425 P.2d 163 (refusal to release invalid chattel mortgage). See, 1931, 47 L.Q. Rev. 168.

Cf. Martin v. Sikes, 1951, 38 Wash.2d 274, 229 P.2d 546 (plaintiff served with criminal complaint asserting ownership, told to leave goods in status quo); Richstein v. Roesch, 1946, 71 S.D. 451, 25 N.W.2d 558 (filing and assignment of mechanic's lien).

43. Traylor v. Horrall, 1837, 4 Ind. (Blackf.) 317. But cf. Ramsby v. Beezley, 1883, 11 Or. 49, 8 P. 288, where the plaintiff apparently lost possession as a result of the sale.

44. Brandenburg v. Northwestern Jobbers' Credit Bureau, 1915, 128 Minn. 411, 151 N.W. 134; Carroll v. M. & J. Finance Corp., 1958, 233 S.C. 200, 104 S.E.2d 171.

45. Andrews v. Shattuck, 1860, 32 N.Y. (Barb.) 396; Hall v. Merchants' State Bank, 1925, 199 Iowa 483, 202 N.W. 256; Matteawan Co. v. Bentley, 1852, 13 N.Y. (Barb.) 641 (taking mortgage).

46. Baker v. Beers, 1936, 64 N.H. 102, 6 A. 35; Adams v. Mizell, 1852, 11 Ga. 106; Oakley v. Lyster, [1931] 1 K.B. 148; Laverrierre v. Casco Bank & Trust Co., 1959, 155 Me. 97, 151 A.2d 276; Gowin v. Heider, 1964, 237 Or. 266, 391 P.2d 630 (obtaining power of attorney by fraud to register car in own name).

47. Interstate National Bank v. McCormick, 1920, 67 Mont. 80, 214 P. 949. In General Finance Corp. of Jacksonville v. Sexton, Fla.App.1963, 155 So.2d 159, obtaining a transfer of title from the Motor Vehicle Commission was regarded as sufficient, apparently because of the serious disadvantages to which the plaintiff would be put.

version.⁴⁸ The early law, which was preoccupied with tangible objects and the repression of physical violence, attached an undue importance to possession, as distinguished from ownership,⁴⁹ and permitted the person in possession to recover the full value of the chattel, although the person did not own it, and might be responsible over to someone else who did. Thus a finder of goods⁵⁰ might recover or a sheriff who had seized them,⁵¹ or a bailee,⁵² or a mortgagor in default.⁵³ The rule has even been applied to permit recovery by one whose possession is wrongful, and in defiance of the owner,⁵⁴ although in all such cases the plaintiff has been in possession under some colorable claim of right. A few courts have said that the plaintiff cannot recover unless the plaintiff's possession is under such colorable claim.⁵⁵ No court ever has allowed an admitted, or even a clearly proved, thief without claim of right to recover, and it seems improbable that one ever will. Not only is all policy against giving him the money to make away with, but the case law is clear that the courts will not lend their aid by an action for conversion of property possessed for an illegal purpose.⁵⁶

The procedural method by which all this has been accomplished has been a refusal to permit the defendant in a conversion action to set up as a defense the "jus tertii," which is the claim of a third person to the chattel, superior to that of the plaintiff, unless the defendant can connect himself with that claim. The result is that the person in possession recovers the full value of the chattel, although the person may not be the full owner, or any owner at all. The original justification for this lay in the convenience of treating the possessor as the owner, and the encouragement to peace and security ex-

---

48. 1 Street, Foundations of Legal Liability, 1906, 250.

49. Ames, Disseisin of Chattels, 1890, 3 Harv.L. Rev. 23, 313, 337; Holmes, The Common Law, 1881, 163–166; Pollock and Wright, Possession in the Common Law, 1888, 91.

50. Armory v. Delamirie, 1722, 1 Stra. 505, 93 Eng. Rep. 664; Clark v. Maloney, 1839, 3 Del. (Harr.) 68; McLaughlin v. Waite, 1827, 9 N.Y. (Cow.) 670, affirmed, 1830, 5 Wend. 404; Weeks v. Hackett, 1908, 104 Me. 264, 71 A. 858. See Reisman, Possession and the Law of Finders, 1939, 52 Harv.L.Rev. 1105; Aigler, Rights of Finders, 1923, 21 Mich.L.Rev. 664, 57 Am.L. Rev. 511; Moreland, Rights of Finders of Lost Property, 1927, 16 Ky.L.J. 1; Note, 1937, 21 Minn.L.Rev. 191.

51. Wilbraham v. Snow, 1670, 2 Wms.Saund. 47, 85 Eng.Rep. 624; Barker v. Miller, 1810, 6 N.Y. (Johns.) 195; Witherspoon v. Clegg, 1880, 42 Mich. 484, 4 N.W. 209.

52. Nicolls v. Bastard, 1835, 2 Cr.M. & R. 659, 150 Eng.Rep. 279; Vining v. Baker, 1866, 53 Me. 544; Chamberlain v. West, 1887, 37 Minn. 54, 33 N.W. 114; Baker v. Troy Compress Co., 1896, 114 Ala. 415, 21 So. 496.

There was, however, a very odd little rule that a servant entrusted with the chattel by his master had only "custody" of it, with possession "constructively" in the master, so that the servant could not maintain trover, although he could be liable in such an action. The origin of this is obscure; it may have been a survival from the time when servants were slaves, or merely a device to get around some of the larceny rules of the criminal law. See Holmes, The Common Law, 1881, 227–228; Pollock and Wright Possession, 1888, 58–59; Becher v. Great Eastern Railroad Co., 1870, L.R. 5 Q.B. 241; Ludden v. Leavitt, 1812, 9 Mass. 104; Richard v. Nowlan, 1959, 19 Dom.L.Rev. 239.

It may seriously be doubted that this antique bit of lore survives in the United States. In Moore v. Robinson, 1831, 2 B. & Ad. 817, 109 Eng.Rep. 1346, the captain of a ship was held to be in such possession that he could maintain trover; and in Poole v. Symonds, 1818, 1 N.H. 289, and Thayer v. Hutchinson, 1841, 13 Vt. 504, custodians were allowed to recover because they were "responsible" for the goods and "accountable" to the owner. But is this not always true of servants? Cf. Mitchell v. Georgia & Alabama Railway Co., 1900, 111 Ga. 760, 36 S.E. 971; Gunzburger v. Rosenthal, 1910, 226 Pa. 300, 75 A. 418 (manager of business and salesman).

53. Ellis v. Snell, 1955, 44 Tenn.App. 294, 313 S.W.2d 558.

54. Jeffries v. Great Western R. Co., 1856, 5 El. & Bl. 802, 119 Eng.Rep. 680; Cook v. Patterson, 1859, 35 Ala. 102; Shaw v. Kaler, 1871, 106 Mass. 448; Wheeler v. Lawson, 1886, 103 N.Y. 40, 8 N.E. 360; Anderson v. Gouldberg, 1892, 51 Minn. 294, 53 N.W. 636.

55. Turley v. Tucker, 1840, 6 Mo. 583; Barwick v. Barwick, 1850, 33 N.C. (11 Ired.) 80; Stephenson v. Little, 1862, 10 Mich. 433; Rexroth v. Coon, 1885, 15 R.I. 35, 23 A. 37.

56. Miller v. Chicago & North Western Railroad Co., 1913, 153 Wis. 431, 141 N.W. 263 (slot machine); Du Bost v. Beresford, 1810, 2 Camp. 511, 170 Eng.Rep. 1235 (libelous portrait); Suttori v. Peckham, 1920, 48 Cal.App. 88, 191 P. 960 (fish taken in violation of law); Hofferman v. Simmons, 1943, 290 N.Y. 449, 49 N.E.2d 523 (gaming money); Carr v. Hoy, 1957, 2 N.Y.2d 185, 158 N.Y.S.2d 572, 139 N.E.2d 531 (money collected for photographing nude women).

pected to result from the protection of any possession against a wrongdoer with no rights at all. Modern law has discovered new reasons of business convenience for permitting the possessor to maintain the action, and recover the full value of the chattel. It is said that the possession is a sufficient title against the wrongdoer, because the person in possession is, of the two, the proper party to account to the true owner for the amount recovered, and to adjust with the person any question as to their respective rights.[57] But, since a full recovery by one in possession will bar any subsequent action by the true owner,[58] the disadvantages are obvious. Such a rule may result in considerable hardship where the possessor mishandles the suit,[59] or is not to be trusted with the proceeds. For these reasons it has been suggested[60] that the possessor's right to recover more than the value of the person's own interest in the chattel should be limited to cases where the person has the express or implied consent of the owner to bring the action, or the owner cannot be found; and that the proper procedure when the question of the jus tertii arises is for the court, of its own motion, to stay proceedings until the owner can be notified, and permitted to decide whether he wishes to intervene in the action, or take other measures of his own.

The common law rule was extended to permit recovery by one who had the immediate right to possession, as in the case of a bailor entitled to possession on demand,[61] or a chattel mortgagee or conditional seller after default.[62] But an owner who had neither possession nor the immediate right to it at the time of the conversion could not maintain trover.[63] The owner's remedy was an action on the case for the damage to his interest in the goods.[64] Although the distinction persists today in a good many courts,[65] it is an antique procedural survival, with nothing to recommend it. The important fact is that the person entitled only to future possession can recover, in whatever form of action, the full value of his interest in the goods which has been appropriated by the defendant, and

---

57. The Winkfield, [1902] P. 42; Warren, Qualifying as Plaintiff in an Action for a Conversion, 1936, 49 Harv.L.Rev. 1084, 1095; Warren, Trover and Conversion, 1936, 12; Note, 1938, 22 Minn.L.Rev. 863.

58. Knight v. Davis Carriage Co., 5 Cir. 1896, 71 F. 662; Lord, Stone & Co. v. Buchanan, 1897, 69 Vt. 320, 37 A. 1048.

59. As, for example, by a settlement which does not protect the owner's interests. See First National Bank v. Union Railway Co., 1926, 153 Tenn. 386, 284 S.W. 363; Ellis Motor Co. v. Hancock, 1928, 38 Ga.App. 788, 145 S.E. 518; Harris v. Seaboard Air Line Railway Co., 1925, 190 N.C. 480, 130 S.E. 319; Juniata Acceptance Corp. v. Hoffman, 1940, 139 Pa.Super. 87, 11 A.2d 494. See, 1937, 21 Minn.L.Rev. 449.

60. Warren, Qualifying as Plaintiff in an Action for a Conversion, 1936, 49 Harv.L.Rev. 1084, 1098; Warren, Trover and Conversion, 1936, 15–17; Note, 1928, 22 Minn.L.Rev. 863. The only case found which has so held is Panama Canal Co. v. Stockard & Co., 1958, 391 Pa. 374, 137 A.2d 793.

61. Manders v. Williams, 1849, 4 Ex. 339, 154 Eng. Rep. 1242; Drake v. Reddington, 1838, 9 N.H. 243; Robinson v. Bird, 1893, 158 Mass. 357, 33 N.E. 391. The wrongful act of the bailee may of course terminate the bailment and give the bailor the right to immediate possession. Sanborn v. Colman, 1832, 6 N.H. 14; Swift v. Moseley, 1838, 10 Vt. 208.

62. Nichols & Shepard Co. v. Minnesota Threshing Manufacturing Co., 1897, 70 Minn. 528, 73 N.W. 415; Worthington v. A. G. Rhodes & Son Co., 1905, 145 Ala. 656, 39 So. 614; Howard v. Burns, 1890, 44 Kan. 543, 24 P. 981; Reynolds v. Fitzpatrick, 1899, 23 Mont. 52, 57 P. 452; First National Bank of Bay Shore v. Stamper, 1966, 93 N.J.Super. 150, 225 A.2d 162 (assignee of conditional seller).

63. Gordon v. Harper, 1796, 7 Term Rep. 9, 101 Eng.Rep. 828 (landlord); Citizens' Bank of St. Louis v. Tiger Tail Mill & Land Co., 1890, 152 Mo. 145, 53 S.W. 902 (owner not in possession); Raymond Syndicate v. Guttentag, 1901, 177 Mass. 562, 59 N.E. 446 (bailor for a term); Newhall v. Kingsbury, 1881, 131 Mass. 445 (conditional seller before default); Adams & Frederick Co. v. South Omaha National Bank, 8th Cir. 1903, 123 F. 641. See Note, 1944, 19 Ohio St.L.J. 758.

64. Mears v. London & S. W. R. Co., 1862, 11 C.B.,N.S., 850, 142 Eng.Rep. 1029; Ayer v. Bartlett, 1829, 26 Mass. (9 Pick.) 156; New York, Lake Erie & Western Railroad Co. v. New Jersey Electric Ry. Co., 1897, 60 N.J.L. 338, 38 A. 828, affirmed, 1897, 61 N.J.L. 287, 41 A. 1116; Adams & Frederick Co. v. South Omaha National Bank, 8th Cir. 1903, 123 F. 641. Compare, as to a negligence action, Bell Finance Co. v. Gefter, 1958, 337 Mass. 69, 147 N.E.2d 815; Cashman v. Soulia, 1957, 120 Vt. 171, 136 A.2d 355. See Notes, 1912, 25 Harv.L.Rev. 655; 1944, 19 Ohio St.L.J. 758.

65. See for example Breault v. Merrill & Ring Lumber Co., 1898, 72 Minn. 143, 75 N.W. 122; Goebel v. Clark, 1934, 242 App.Div. 408, 275 N.Y.S. 43.

no more. If this is not to be called conversion, it is at least the same thing by another name.[66] There are a substantial number of courts which have discarded the procedural distinction, and have called the action one of conversion.[67]

Complications arise when the converter is sued both by the bailee and by the bailor. They are not peculiar to conversion, and arise also in cases of negligent destruction of the chattel, or damage to it. The bailee, using the term in the general sense of one in possession when rights to possession are outstanding, is entitled to recover the full value of the chattel,[68] being accountable to the bailor for any excess over the value of his own interest.[69] The bailor may recover the full value if he was entitled to immediate possession at the time of the conversion,[70] but if the bailor was then entitled only to future possession, he recovers only the damages the bailor can prove to his own interest in the chattel.[71]

The converter may be subjected to two of these actions, or conceivably to all three; and the mere reduction of any one of them to judgment does not bar a subsequent judgment in another. The defendant is, however, required to pay only once. The satisfaction of a judgment against the defendant by one who was in possession, or was entitled to immediate possession, and so was entitled to recover the full damages, has the effect of extinguishing all claims against the defendant, and is a complete bar to any further recovery, or any further enforcement of other judgments.[72] A settlement or release covering the full value, from the person entitled to it, has the same effect. The one whose claim is thus settled remains accountable to the other claimant to the extent of the latter's interest in the chattel, but the converter is no longer liable to anyone.[73] On the other hand, the satisfaction of a judgment, or a settlement and release, from one who was entitled only to future possession, and so not entitled to the full value of the chattel, covers only the damages for the harm to his own interest, and so does not extinguish the defendant's liability, but only

---

66. Salmond, Observations on Trover and Conversion, 1905, 21 L.Q.Rev. 43, 54. See also Warren, Qualifying as Plaintiff in an Action for a Conversion, 1936, 49 Harv.L.Rev. 1084, 1100–1109; Warren, Trover and Conversion, 1936, 19–28.

67. Morin v. Hood, 1951, 96 N.H. 485, 79 A.2d 4 (chattel mortgage); Wall v. Colvard, Inc., 1966, 268 N.C. 43, 149 S.E.2d 559; Redd Chemical & Nitrate Co. v. W. T. Clay Mercantile Co., 1929, 219 Ala. 478, 122 So. 652 (equitable lien); Moore v. Carey Bros. Oil Co., Tex.Com.App.1925, 269 S.W. 75, 272 S.W. 440 (materialmen's lien); and see Nash v. Lang, 1929, 268 Mass. 407, 414, 167 N.E. 762, 765.

68. The Winkfield, [1902] P. 42; Hopkins v. Colonial Stores, 1944, 224 N.C. 137, 29 S.E.2d 455; Hudson Transit Corp. v. Antonucci, 1948, 137 N.J.L. 704, 61 A.2d 180; Chamberlain v. West, 1887, 37 Minn. 54, 33 N.W. 114; Herries v. Bell, 1915, 220 Mass. 243, 107 N.E. 944.

69. The Winkfield, [1902] P. 42; Walsh v. United States Tent & Awning Co., 1910, 153 Ill.App. 229; Baggett v. McCormack, 1896, 73 Miss. 552, 19 So. 89; Smyth v. Fidelity & Deposit Co. of Maryland, 1937, 125 Pa.Super. 597, 190 A. 398; Fletcher v. Perry, 1932, 104 Vt. 229, 158 A. 679.

70. Clark v. Rideout, 1859, 39 N.H. 238; Knox v. Binkoski, 1923, 99 Conn. 582, 122 A. 400; Hussey v. Flanagan, 1923, 237 N.Y. 227, 142 N.E. 594; Reynolds v. Fitzpatrick, 1899, 23 Mont. 52, 57 P. 452.

71. Mears v. London & S. W. R. Co., 1862, 11 C.B.,N.S., 850, 142 Eng.Rep. 1029; Gordon v. Harper, 1796, 7 Term Rep. 9, 101 Eng.Rep. 828; White v. Griffin, 1856, 49 N.C. (4 Jones) 139.

72. Juniata Acceptance Corp. v. Hoffman, 1940, 139 Pa.Super. 87, 11 A.2d 494; Railway Express Agency v. Goodman's New York & Connecticut Express Corp., 1942, 129 Conn. 386, 28 A.2d 869; The W. C. Block, 2 Cir. 1934, 71 F.2d 682, certiorari denied Cornell Steamboat Co. v. Scholl, 293 U.S. 579, 55 S.Ct. 91, 79 L.Ed. 676; Eaton v. Schild, 1930, 8 N.J.Misc. 245, 149 A. 637; Industrial Investment Co. v. King, 1931, 159 Miss. 491, 132 So. 333.

73. Associates Discount Corp. v. Gillineau, 1948, 322 Mass. 490, 78 N.E.2d 192; Motor Finance Co. v. Noyes, 1942, 139 Me. 159, 28 A.2d 235; Jolly v. Thornton, 1940, 40 Cal.App.2d Supp. 819, 102 P.2d 467; Lowery v. Louisville & Northwest Railroad Co., 1934, 228 Ala. 137, 153 So. 467; Gas City Transfer Co. v. Miller, 1939, 107 Ind.App. 210, 21 N.E.2d 428.

In Belli v. Forsyth, 1938, 301 Mass. 203, 16 N.E.2d 656, where the settlement purported to satisfy only the bailee's own damages, it was held that further action by the bailor was not barred.

reduces it pro tanto when the person in possession seeks to recover against him.[74]

Return of the Chattel

The conversion is complete when the defendant takes, detains or disposes of the chattel. At that point, it is the traditional view that the plaintiff acquires the right to enforce a sale, and recover the full value of the property. The defendant cannot undo his wrong by forcing the goods back upon their owner, either as a bar to the action,[75] or in mitigation of damages.[76]

Such a rule is unduly severe upon comparatively innocent defendants who have converted in good faith or by mistake, and are entirely willing to restore the goods when they discover the facts. The English courts have moderated it by giving the trial judge discretion to allow the return of the goods in mitigation of damages, provided that they are uninjured, and no special damage has resulted from the detention.[77] A few American courts have recognized a similar discretion,[78] where the conversion was not intentionally wrongful,[79] and there has been no deterioration in the value of the chattel,[80] or other special damage to the plaintiff.[81] This limitation of the forced sale involved in the action of trover seems necessary to prevent occasional over-drastic remedy for relatively inoffensive legal fault.[82] In any case, return of the chattel, whether consented to by the plaintiff or compelled by the court, does not bar the action, but goes merely to reduce the damages.[83]

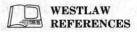

WESTLAW REFERENCES

di conversion
di trover

Modern Law
"common law" england history /p trover
trover /p conversion /p chattel*

What May Be Converted
conversion /s goodwill idea intangible*

Character of Defendant's Act
topic(conversion) /p intentional** intend***
topic(conversion) /p interference
389k1

Acquiring Possession
topic(conversion) /p possession /p wrongful unjustified
synopsis,digest(conversion /p possession /p wrongful unjustified)
conversion /s purchaser /s "bona fide" "good faith"
digest(unauthorized unintentional! /s conversion)

Removing the Chattel
bailee /s conversion

---

74. Gaines v. Briggs, 1848, 9 Ark. 46; Missouri, Kansas & Texas Railway Co. v. Hunter, Tex.Civ.App. 1919, 216 S.W. 1107; see Hudson Transit Corp. v. Antonucci, 1948, 137 N.J.L. 704, 61 A.2d 180.

75. Olivant v. Baring, 1743, 1 Wils. 23, 95 Eng.Rep. 471; De Celles v. Casey, 1914, 48 Mont. 568, 139 P. 586; Hofschulte v. Panhandle Hardware Co., Tex.Civ.App. 1899, 50 S.W. 608; Wall v. Colvard, Inc., 1966, 268 N.C. 43, 149 S.E.2d 559. The same as to repossession by the plaintiff. Schulte v. Florian, Mo.App.1963, 370 S.W.2d 623.

76. Baltimore & Ohio Railroad Co. v. O'Donnell, 1892, 49 Ohio St. 489, 32 N.E. 476; Sloan v. Butler, 1921, 148 Ark. 117, 228 S.W. 1046; West Tulsa Belt Railway Co. v. Bell, 1915, 54 Okl. 175, 153 P. 622; Ketchum v. Amsterdam Apartments Co., 1920, 94 N.J.L. 7, 110 A. 590; Gorham v. Massillon Iron & Steel Co., 1918, 284 Ill. 594, 120 N.E. 467.

77. Fisher v. Prince, 1782, 3 Burr. 1363, 97 Eng. Rep. 876; Tucker v. Wright, 1826, 3 Bing. 601, 130 Eng.Rep. 645.

78. The relief is within the discretion of the court, and there is no absolute right to it. Rutland & Washington Railroad Co. v. Bank of Middlebury, 1860, 32 Vt. 639.

79. It is not permitted where the conversion was not an innocent one. Baltimore & Ohio Railroad Co. v. O'Donnell, 1892, 49 Ohio St. 489, 32 N.E. 476; Ketchum v. Amsterdam Apartments Co., 1920, 94 N.J.L. 7, 110 A. 590; Gorham v. Massillon Iron & Steel Co., 1918, 284 Ill. 594, 120 N.E. 467.

80. It will not be granted where the goods have been damaged, or partly sold or destroyed. Magic City Steel & Metal Corp. v. Mitchell, Okl.1954, 265 P.2d 473; Hart v. Skinner, 1844, 16 Vt. 138.

81. Farr v. State Bank of Phillips, 1894, 87 Wis. 223, 58 N.W. 377; Moody v. Sindlinger, 1915, 27 Colo. App. 290, 149 P. 263; Whittler v. Sharp, 1913, 43 Utah 419, 135 P. 112; Gilbert & Miller v. Peck, 1891, 43 Mo. App. 577; Carpenter v. American Building & Loan Association, 1893, 54 Minn. 403, 56 N.W. 95.

82. Notes, 1925, 9 Minn.L.Rev. 392; 1942, 40 Mich. L.Rev. 437.

83. Cernahan v. Chrisler, 1900, 107 Wis. 645, 83 N.W. 778; Plummer v. Reeves, 1907, 83 Ark. 10, 102 S.W. 376; Jackson v. Innes, 1919, 231 Mass. 558, 121 N.E. 489; Truth Seeker Co. v. Durning, 2d Cir. 1945, 147 F.2d 54; Schulte v. Florian, Mo.App.1963, 370 S.W.2d 623 (repossession).

§ 15 CONVERSION

remove removing moved relocat! /s chattel* property personalty goods /s unauthorized permission permit! improper wrongful

Transferring Possession

conversion /p possession /s transfer! dispos! & topic(110)

deliver! dispos! transfer! /s possession /s unauthor! improper illegal unwarranted /p conversion

Withholding Possession

conversion /p withhold! /s possession

conversion /p inabil! unabl! refus! fail! /s deliver! surrender! /s possession

389K4

Destruction or Alteration

conversion /p destroy*** destruct! /s chattel* property personalty goods

389K12

Using the Chattel

digest(conversion /p use using used /p chattel* property personalty goods car auto)

topic(389) /p use

Asserting Ownership

digest(conversion /s assert! alleg! claim /s ownership "title" right)

topic(conversion) /p assert! alleg! claim /s ownership "title" right

Plaintiff's Interest

topic(conversion) /p plaintiff /p interest**

Return of the Chattel

digest(conversion /p return! /p chattel* goods property personalty)

conversion /p mitigat! /s damages

Chapter 4

DEFENSES TO INTENTIONAL INTERFERENCE WITH PERSON OR PROPERTY

Table of Sections

Sec.
16. Privilege.
17. Mistake.
18. Consent.
19. Self-Defense.
20. Defense of Others.
21. Defense of Property.
22. Recapture of Chattels.
23. Recapture of Land.
24. Necessity.
25. Legal Process.
26. Arrest Without a Warrant.
27. Discipline.

§ 16. Privilege

In the development of the law, considerations of fairness and practicality have brought about an allocation of responsibility between plaintiffs and defendants as regards the burden of pleading and proving certain matters. The plaintiff in tort actions is typically charged only with the responsibility of establishing an intentional interference with an interest of a kind that would ordinarily result in liability. It would have been manifestly unsound and impractical to require a plaintiff to negative at the outset all possible excuses or justifications. So, matters that may occasionally be asserted and established in excuse or justification for the conduct that would ordinarily be actionable are for the defendant to plead and prove. The elements allocated to the plaintiff, for establishment are referred to as the prima facie tort. Those matters that may be asserted in justification or excuse are called defenses or affirmative defenses.

The early common law classified defenses to intentional torts as "justification" or "excuse," and developed technical rules distinguishing between the two; these rules no longer have any great importance.[1] "Privi-

§ 16

1. See Beale, Justification for Injury, 1928, 41 Harv.L.Rev. 553.

"There is no justification for a tort. The so-called justification is an exceptional fact which shows that no tort was committed." Stevenson, V.C., in Booth &

lege" is the modern term applied to those considerations which avoid liability where it might otherwise follow.[2] As used in this text, it is applied to any circumstance justifying or excusing a prima facie tort, such as a battery, assault, or trespass; it signifies that the defendant has acted to further an interest of such social importance that it is entitled to protection, even at the expense of damage to the plaintiff. The defendant is allowed freedom of action because his own interests, or those of the public, require it, and because social policy will best be served by permitting it. The privilege is bounded by current ideas of what will most effectively promote the general welfare.

The question of "privilege" as a defense arises almost exclusively in connection with intentional torts. Much the same considerations have weight in negligence cases, in determining whether the defendant's conduct is reasonable under the circumstances.[3] Negligence, however, is a matter of risk and probability of harm; and where the likelihood of injury to the plaintiff is relatively slight, the defendant will necessarily be allowed greater latitude than where the harm is intended, or substantially certain to follow.[4]

The relative social value given to an interest which the defendant seeks to further can affect the nature and extent of a privilege. Occasionally, the defendant may act at his peril if he makes a mistake of fact or law;[5] at other times, an actor is justified in acting on the basis of what the facts reasonably appear to be;[6] at other times, the defendant is justified so long as he was acting in good faith;[7] or, finally, the privilege may be regarded as absolute in the sense that the court will not permit an inquiry into motive or purpose, since this could result in subjecting the honest person to harassing litigation and claims. When no inquiry is permitted into motive or purpose, it is sometimes said that defendant has an absolute privilege; at other times, it is said that he has an immunity. When defendant acts under circumstances where there is freedom from liability regardless of bad motive or any other kind of wrongful state of mind, reference to the defense as an immunity is perhaps less likely to lead to confusion. Thus, a privilege exists when it is established that the defendant acts from a justifiable motive. An immunity exists when no inquiry is permitted into motive or motives. The acts of judicial officers done under authority of law, for example, are immune, even though malicious or corrupt.[8] But when the defendant's behavior is conditioned on a proper motive, the defendant is exercising a privilege, such as the privilege of self-defense.[9] The nature of the interest to be furthered may be such as to give the defendant a limited or incomplete privilege, in the sense that the defendant may not be restrained or prevented by force from exercising the privilege, but will be liable for any economic loss or physical damage caused to person or property in the exer-

---

Brother v. Burgess, 1906, 72 N.J.Eq. 181, 188, 65 A. 226.

2. Second Restatement of Torts, § 10.

3. See infra, § 31.

4. "Even assuming that the defendant's interest is of slightly less value than that of the plaintiff, he may be permitted to do without liability an act which is certain to advance it even though it contains five chances out of a hundred of injuring a more important interest of the plaintiff, but he is not privileged to do it if the chances for and against injury reach or approach equality. Where the defendant intends to inflict the very invasion which his act causes, there is no room for such considerations. It is the bare value of the respective interests involved and the extent of the harm from which the act is intended to protect the one as compared with that which it is intended to cause to the other which determines the existence or nonexistence of the privilege." Bohlen, Incomplete Privilege to Inflict Intentional Invasions of Interests of Property and Personality, 1926, 39 Harv.L.Rev. 307, 309 note.

5. The privilege to recapture personal property is such a privilege. See § 22. Under some circumstances, and in some states, this is also true of the privilege to defend others. See § 20.

6. See, §§ 19 and 21 on the respective privileges of self-defense and defense of property.

7. This is quite often true in the case of a so-called qualified privilege to publish defamation. See chapter 19, § 115.

8. See infra, § 132.

9. See infra, § 19.

cise of the privilege.[10] The sliding scale by which the law balances the interests of the parties to accomplish a social purpose is nowhere better illustrated than in the field of privilege.

In the development of the law of the privilege to interfere intentionally with legally protected interests of persons in tangible things, the courts have dealt with three major questions:

> When will the defendant's motive or purpose be regarded as a justifiable one for intentionally interfering with the interests that were affected? What means are justified, assuming that the defendant's motive or purpose was legitimate? And under what circumstances is the defendant privileged to make a mistake as to the facts or law in carrying out his legitimate objectives in legitimate ways?

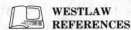

WESTLAW REFERENCES

privilege* /s intentional /s tort*
379k16
topic(379 272) /p privilege /p defense*

§ 17. Mistake

The question of mistake frequently arises in connection with privilege. There is an essential distinction between mistake and accident, which is to be considered in a later chapter.[1] The plea of unavoidable accident is that the result complained of as a wrong was not intended by the defendant, and could not have been foreseen and avoided by the exercise of reasonable care. The plea of unavoidable mistake, on the other hand, is that, although the result complained of as a wrong was intended, the defendant acted under an erroneous belief, formed upon reasonable grounds, that circumstances existed which would justify his conduct. It is an accident if the defendant's horse runs away with him and carries him upon the land of another, a mistake if he intentionally enters upon it in the belief that it is his own.[2]

When an accident is unavoidable as that term is here used, a defendant would not be subject to liability, except on the basis of a theory of strict liability, because the invasion could not be regarded as having been caused either intentionally or negligently. However, if one intentionally interferes with the interests of others, he is often subject to liability notwithstanding the invasion was made under an erroneous belief as to some fact or legal matter that would have justified the conduct. Under such circumstances, the risk of being wrong is commonly imposed on those who intentionally interfere rather than on those who are victimized by the conduct. However valid the excuse may be under the criminal law,[3] in a civil action one who intentionally interferes with the person or property of another does so at his peril, and must assume the risk that he is wrong. The line which is drawn between accident and mistake has been condemned as anomalous and unreasonable;[4] it can be justified only upon the basis of a policy which makes the defendant responsible for the physical result which he intended, and, as between two parties equally free from moral blame, places the loss upon the one who made the mistake.

A trespasser upon land who honestly believes that he is the owner,[5] or that he has authority from the owner,[6] or who has mere-

---

10. Bohlen, Incomplete Privilege to Inflict Intentional Invasions of Interests of Property and Personality, 1926, 39 Harv.L.Rev. 307. See infra, § 24.

§ 17

1. See infra, § 29.

2. Salmond, Law of Torts, 8th Ed. 1934, 27; Whittier, Mistake in the Law of Torts, 1902, 15 Harv.L.Rev. 325.

3. See Keedy, Ignorance and Mistake in the Criminal Law, 1908, 22 Harv.L.Rev. 75; Perkins, Ignorance and Mistake in Criminal Law, 1939, 88 U.Pa.L.Rev. 35.

4. Whittier, Mistake in the Law of Torts, 1902, 15 Harv.L.Rev. 335. But see Holmes, The Common Law, 1881, 96–100.

5. Perry v. Jefferies, 1901, 61 S.C. 292, 39 S.E. 515; Isle Royale Mining Co. v. Hertin, 1877, 37 Mich. 332.

6. Higginson v. York, 1809, 5 Mass. 341; Hazelton v. Week, 1880, 49 Wis. 661, 6 N.W. 309; Lowenburg v. Rosenthal, 1889, 18 Or. 178, 22 P. 601.

ly mistaken the boundary,[7] is nevertheless a trespasser, since an entry was intended. One who sells a chattel,[8] or takes possession of it, even by bona fide purchase,[9] becomes a converter, although he does not know that it is stolen property. In all of these cases, the defendant may be free from moral blame, but the rights of others are protected at his expense because there was an intention to interfere with a legally protected interest.

The law is, then, that if the defendant entertained the intent necessary for the particular tort, such as trespass to land, battery, or false imprisonment, it will be no excuse, ordinarily, that he was mistaken as to something justifying his conduct. But this generality does not apply when the defendant is regarded as having a justifiable reason for the exercise of a privilege. If, in other words, the defendant's motive or purpose is that of self-defense,[10] or defense of another,[11] then even though he may be acting under an erroneous belief as to the necessity for the exercise of this defense, he may be justified.

But such a rule must of necessity have its limitations. Although mistake as to the existence of a privilege, or a mistake of fact in itself, will not excuse the defendant, still his mistake of fact may be important in determining whether the privilege exists. One who reasonably believes that he is being attacked is privileged to defend himself by injuring another, although it turns out that he was wrong.[12] An officer armed with a warrant apparently valid on its face is privileged to make an arrest, although the warrant is in fact invalid because improperly issued;[13] or, if he mistakenly thinks that a felony has been committed, and arrests one whom he reasonably supposes to be the culprit, he is likewise privileged.[14] In such cases the interest to be protected is of such outstanding importance that the defendant is permitted greater freedom of action. The burden of the mistake is placed upon the innocent plaintiff because it is socially necessary that men be free to defend themselves against apparent attack, and that officers have leeway to make arrests.

It is not possible to state a general rule as to when the defendant will be justified in acting on the basis of a mistake of fact or law when his purpose or motive is justified.[15] The boundaries of each privilege—self-defense, recapture of property, defense of another—will be marked out in each situation based on the special reasons of policy and expediency applicable to the particular privilege.[16] A private citizen, for example, unlike a police officer, is ordinarily privileged to arrest in most states only when a crime has in fact been committed, and must take the risk that it has not, unless he is acting under a police officer's direction.[17] The reasons for this rule are that the private citizen has no public responsibility and is not trained for law enforcement tasks, and because no good

---

7. Maye v. Yappan, 1863, 23 Cal. 306; Jeffries v. Hargis, 1887, 50 Ark. 65, 6 S.W. 328. See supra, § 13.

Compare, as to trespass to chattels, Ranson v. Kitner, 1888, 31 Ill.App. 241, where defendant shot plaintiff's dog believing it to be a wolf; and see supra, § 14.

8. Hoffman v. Carow, 1839, 22 N.Y. (Wend.) 285; Kearney v. Clutton, 1894, 101 Mich. 106, 59 N.W. 419.

9. Galvin v. Bacon, 1833, 11 Me. 28; Hyde v. Noble, 1843, 13 N.H. 494; Eldred v. Oconto Co., 1873, 33 Wis. 133. See supra, § 15. Cf. Dexter v. Cole, 1858, 6 Wis. 319 (trespass).

10. Section 19.

11. Section 20.

12. Keep v. Quallman, 1887, 68 Wis. 451, 32 N.W. 233; Courvoisier v. Raymond, 1896, 23 Colo. 113, 47 P. 284; Crabtree v. Dawson, 1904, 119 Ky. 148, 83 S.W. 557. See infra, § 19.

13. Rush v. Buckley, 1905, 100 Me. 322, 61 A. 774; McIntosh v. Bullard, Earnheart & Magness, 1910, 95 Ark. 227, 129 S.W. 85; Johnson v. Scott, 1909, 134 Ky. 736, 121 S.W. 695. See infra, § 25.

14. Beckwith v. Philby, 1827, 6 B. & C. 635, 108 Eng.Rep. 585; Grau v. Forge, 1919, 183 Ky. 521, 209 S.W. 369; White v. McQueen, 1893, 96 Mich. 249, 55 N.W. 843. See infra, § 26.

15. Whittier, Mistake in the Law of Torts, 1902, 15 Harv.L.Rev. 335.

16. Smith, Tort and Absolute Liability, 1917, 30 Harv.L.Rev. 319, 326.

17. Holley v. Mix, 1829, 3 N.Y. (Wend.) 350; Reuck v. McGregor, 1866, 32 N.J.L. 70; Morley v. Chase, 1887, 143 Mass. 396, 9 N.E. 767. See infra, § 26. Most states have passed statutes setting forth the rules applicable for arrests without a warrant.

reason for encouraging private citizens to engage in such an undertaking exists.

If the mistake has been induced by the plaintiff's own conduct, it is generally held that the defendant will be absolved from any liability in tort,[18] so long as he has not acted unreasonably.[19] The plaintiff will not be heard to complain of a mistake for which he is himself responsible. If the defendant is unjustly enriched by his act, however, he may be accountable in a quasi-contract action.[20]

 WESTLAW REFERENCES

digest(mistake* "honest belief" /p defense privilege /p tort)

§ 18. Consent

Consent Ordinarily Bars Recovery

The subject of what is sometimes referred to as informed choice in the law of torts is one of the most complex and difficult in the entire area of the law. The problem discussed here is the meaning and effect of consent in relation to intentional interferences with person or property. A similar but different question relates to the questionable defense of voluntary assumption of the risk to otherwise actionable, accidental invasions giving rise to negligence, or some kind of strict liability.[1]

Consent ordinarily bars recovery for intentional interferences with person or property. It is not, strictly speaking, a privilege, or even a defense,[2] but goes to negative the existence of any tort in the first instance.[3] It is a fundamental principle of the common law that *volenti non fit injuria*—to one who is willing, no wrong is done. The attitude of the courts has not, in general, been one of paternalism. Where no public interest is contravened, they have left the individual to work out his own destiny, and are not concerned with protecting him from his own folly in permitting others to do him harm.[4] As to intentional invasions of the plaintiff's interests, his consent negatives the wrongful element of the defendant's act, and prevents the existence of a tort. "The absence of lawful consent," said Mr. Justice Holmes, "is part of the definition of an assault."[5] The same is true of false imprisonment,[6] conversion,[7] and trespass.[8]

Meaning of Consent and Justification for Non-Liability.

When it is said that consent avoids liability, consent is often used to refer to the invasion itself. At other times, consent is used to refer to the conduct that brings about the invasion. Normally, if the latter is present,

---

18. Hills v. Snell, 1870, 104 Mass. 173; Tousley v. Board of Education, 1888, 39 Minn. 419, 40 N.W. 509; Parker v. Walrod, 1836, 16 N.Y. (Wend.) 514; Cf. Row v. Home Savings Bank, 1940, 306 Mass. 522, 29 N.E.2d 552.

19. Moore v. Bowman, 1867, 47 N.H. 494.

20. Pearson v. Inlow, 1855, 20 Mo. 322.

§ 18

1. Bohlen, Voluntary Assumption of Risk, 1906, 20 Harv.L.Rev. 14, 17; see infra, § 68.

2. Except in the case of trespass to land, where by the weight of authority the burden of proving a license is upon the defendant. Sims v. Alford, 1908, 218 Ala. 216, 118 So. 395; Milton v. Puffer, 1911, 207 Mass. 416, 419, 93 N.E. 634, 635; Schiffmann v. Hickey, 1921, 101 Or. 596, 604, 200 P. 1035.

3. Lord Denman, in Christopherson v. Bare, 1848, 11 Q.B. 473, 116 Eng.Rep. 554, 556: "to say that the defendant assaulted the plaintiff by his permission * * * is a manifest contradiction in terms." It was therefore held that as a matter of pleading the consent must be shown under a general denial, and that if the defendant admitted the assault he could not defend on the ground that he did it by consent.

4. Bohlen, Consent as Affecting Civil Liability for Breaches of the Peace, 1924, 24 Col.L.Rev. 819.

5. Ford v. Ford, 1887, 143 Mass. 577, 578, 10 N.E. 474, 475. Accord: Wright v. Starr, 1919, 42 Nev. 441, 179 P. 877; Cadwell v. Farrell, 1862, 28 Ill. 438 (action must be on the case for negligence, rather than in trespass).

6. Ellis v. Cleveland, 1882, 54 Vt. 437; Kirby v. Harker, 1909, 143 Iowa 478, 121 N.W. 1071; Kirk v. Garrett, 1896, 84 Md. 383, 35 A. 1089.

7. Tousley v. Board of Education, 1888, 39 Minn. 319, 40 N.W. 509.

8. Bennett v. McIntire, 1889, 121 Ind. 231, 23 N.E. 78. But see supra, note 2.

so is the former. In any event, when the defendant by his conduct intentionally interferes with a legally protected interest of person or property, either consent to the invasion resulting from such conduct, or consent to the conduct that brought about the invasion, avoids liability. One, of course, consents to an invasion such as a sex contact if he or she wants or desires the invasion. Consent avoids recovery simply because it destroys the wrongfulness of the conduct as between the consenting parties, however harmful it might be to the interest of others, and even though it is perhaps both immoral and criminal.

But consent is regarded as present, also, when one manifests a willingness that the defendant engage in conduct and the defendant acts in response to such a manifestation.[9] This, also, normally destroys the wrongfulness of the conduct as between the parties. This manifestation of willingness can exist even when the plaintiff hopes to avoid the invasion, such as some harmful invasion in a sporting contest or a fist fight, and certainly does not want or desire any such invasion. Even so, there is a latent ambiguity about this concept of willingness that presents difficulties. The mere fact that one is willing to incur a risk that conduct in deliberate violation of the rules of a sporting contest will be committed does not mean that one is willing for such conduct to be committed. Moreover, a willingness to incur an invasion, or a willingness that the defendant should engage in conduct that brings about an invasion, may exist and be manifested only because the defendant has threatened consequences flowing from a refusal to submit. Under such circumstances the plaintiff's submission or manifestation of willingness may be coerced.

Actual willingness, established by competent evidence, will prevent liability; and, if it can ever be proved, will no doubt do so even though the plaintiff has done nothing to manifest it to the defendant.[10] But the converse is also true, that a manifestation of consent, upon which the defendant may reasonably rely, will be equally effective even though there is no willingness in fact. In our society we must perforce rely upon the overt works and acts of others, rather than upon their undisclosed minds. Consent may therefore be manifested by words, or by the kind of actions which often speak louder than words. The defendant is entitled to rely upon what any reasonable man would understand from the plaintiff's conduct. If the plaintiff expressly says, "It's all right with me," he will of course not be permitted to deny that he did consent. By the same token, if he holds up his arm without objection to be vaccinated, he will not be heard to deny that he has consented after the defendant has relied upon his action.[11] Silence and inaction may manifest consent where a reasonable person would speak if he objected. The girl who makes no protest at a proposal to kiss her in the moonlight may have mental reservations that it is without her consent, but the man who does it is none the less privileged.[12] On the other hand, of course, silence does not operate as consent where no reasonable man would so interpret it, as where one defiantly stands his ground under the threat of a blow.

The defendant is sometimes at liberty to infer consent as a matter of usage or custom, and to proceed upon the assumption

---

9. See note 10.

10. What if plaintiff writes in his secret diary, later produced in evidence, that he would be glad to have the defendant come upon his land and use his tennis court? There are no cases.

11. O'Brien v. Cunard S.S. Co., 1891, 154 Mass. 272, 28 N.E. 266. Accord: Diconzo v. Borg, 1940, 340 Pa. 305, 16 A.2d 15; Barfield v. South Highland Infirmary, 1915, 191 Ala. 553, 68 So. 30; Knowles v. Blue, 1923, 209 Ala. 27, 95 So. 481.

12. Restatement of Torts, § 50. Charley v. Cameron, 1974, 215 Kan. 750, 528 P.2d 1205 (expectant mother consented to use of forceps because of failure to object, such being a routine procedure). Otherwise where the plaintiff does not fully understand the procedure. Shulman v. Lerner, 1966, 2 Mich.App. 705, 141 N.W.2d 348 (preparation for infection).

that it is given. Thus the general habit of the community to permit strangers to enter at will upon wild land may justify a trespass;[13] consent may be assumed to the ordinary contacts of daily life,[14] and a continued course of practical joking between the parties may permit the inference that there is leave to continue it further.[15] One who enters into a sport, game or contest may be taken to consent to physical contacts consistent with the understood rules of the game.[16] It is only when notice is given that all such conduct will no longer be tolerated[17] that the defendant is no longer free to assume consent.

Consent May Not be Effective

To avoid liability, consent must be effective. Consent of a person on whom an otherwise actionable invasion is inflicted is ineffective, if (1) such person lacked capacity to consent to the conduct, (2) the consent was coerced, (3) the consenting person was mistaken about the nature and quality of the invasion intended by the conduct, or (4) the conduct was the kind of conduct to which no one can give a valid consent so as to avoid liability. These problems have arisen most frequently in connection with intentional invasions of the person.

Incapacity

Incapacity can exist because of infancy,[18] intoxication,[19] or mental incompetence.[20] The test for capacity varies with the type of problems involved. One can have capacity to commit a tort, yet lack capacity to commit a crime. Likewise, one can have capacity to consent to certain invasions, yet lack capacity to make a contract or to execute a will. So, also, one can have capacity to consent to some conduct, yet lack capacity to consent to other conduct. Generally, and except for the kinds of conduct to which consent cannot be given, one who has reached the age of majority can give an effective consent to all kinds of conduct unless the defendant knows or has reason to know of some kind of abnormality, temporary or permanent, of the consenting person. The abnormality may be temporary and attributable to sedation caused by a prescription drug, or to a condition involving severe stress and strain. It may be more or less permanent and attributable to mental defect or mental illness.[21] The abnormality must substantially impair

---

13. McKee v. Gratz, 1922, 260 U.S. 127, 43 S.Ct. 16, 67 L.Ed. 167; Marsh v. Colby, 1878, 39 Mich. 626.

14. Wiffin v. Kincard, 1807, 2 Bos. & P. 471, 126 Eng.Rep. 1391; Coward v. Baddeley, 1859, 4 H. & N. 478, 157 Eng.Rep. 927.

15. Wartman v. Swindell, 1892, 54 N.J.L. 589, 25 A. 356.

16. McAdams v. Windham, 1922, 208 Ala. 492, 94 So. 742 (boxing match); Vendrell v. School District No. 26C, 1962, 233 Or. 1, 376 P.2d 406 (football); Gibeline v. Smith, 1904, 106 Mo.App. 545, 80 S.W. 961 (friendly scuffle); Tavernier v. Maes, 1966, 242 Cal.App.2d 532, 51 Cal.Rptr. 575 (baseball); Ogden v. Rabinowitz, 1957, 294 R.I. 86, 134 A.2d 416 (college fracas); Note, 1929, 26 Mich.L.Rev. 322. Cf. Second Restatement of Torts, § 50, Comment b, to the effect that there is no liability for a violation of rules not intended for the protection of the players, but merely to further better playing of the game, such as the offside rule in football.

17. Richmond v. Fiske, 1893, 160 Mass. 34, 35 N.E. 103. Cf. Breitenbach v. Trowbridge, 1887, 64 Mich. 393, 31 N.W. 402 (revocation of license to enter place of business).

For an interesting decision involving a deliberate blow after a play was over, see Hackbart v. Cincinnati Bengals, 1977, 435 F.Supp. 352, reversed, 10th Cir. 1979, 601 F.2d 516, certiorari denied 444 U.S. 931, 100 S.Ct. 275, 62 L.Ed.2d 188. In holding for the defendant in the trial court it was said that upon all the evidence the court finds that the level of violence and frequency of outbursts in NFL football games are such that an injured player must have recognized and accepted the risk. But on appeal, the court said: "But it is highly questionable whether a professional football player consents or submits to injuries caused by conduct not within the rules, and there is no evidence which we have seen which shows this."

18. Robalina v. Armstrong, 1852, 15 N.Y. (Barb.) 247; Commonwealth v. Nickerson, 1862, 87 Mass. (5 Allen) 518.

19. McCue v. Klein, 1883, 60 Tex. 168; Ibach v. Jackson, 1934, 148 Or. 92, 35 P.2d 672; Hollerud v. Malamis, 1970, 20 Mich.App. 748, 174 N.W.2d 626; Note, 1935, 14 Or.L.Rev. 281.

20. Pratt v. Davis, 1906, 224 Ill. 300, 79 N.E. 562; Bolton v. Stewart, Tex.Civ.App.1945, 191 S.W.2d 798.

21. Gravis v. Physicians and Surgeons Hospital of Alice, Tex.1968, 427 S.W.2d 310; Demers v. Gerety, App.1973, 85 N.M. 641, 515 P.2d 645, remanded 86 N.M. 141, 520 P.2d 869, on remand App., 87 N.M. 52, 529 P.2d 278, certiorari denied 87 N.M. 47, 529 P.2d 273, appeal after remand 92 N.M. 396, 589 P.2d 180.

the plaintiff's capacity to understand and weigh the harm and risks of harm against the benefits flowing from the proposed conduct, and must reduce that capacity below the level of the average person. This can often present a difficult fact issue.

A minor acquires capacity to consent to different kinds of invasions and conduct at different stages in his development. Capacity exists when the minor has the ability of the average person to understand and weigh the risks and benefits.[22] Generally, children have been regarded as incapable of consenting to operations involving a risk of serious injury or death, commonly referred to as major operations. However, a minor female who can consent to sexual intercourse can probably give an effective consent to an abortion.[23]

Incapacity and Agency

When a person is incapable of giving consent, his consent is ineffective to avoid liability. On the other hand, it is often possible to obtain the consent of someone legally authorized to act in his behalf. Parents, as natural and legal guardians of children, have the legal capacity to make many decisions in behalf of children who are incapable of doing so.[24] Likewise, duly appointed guardians of minors and incompetents have legal capacity to consent to much conduct and to many invasions, especially medical procedures deemed to be in the interest of children and incompetents.[25] Under certain circumstances, someone regarded as the next of kin, such as a spouse or a niece, may have the capacity to consent, especially in an emergency, to a surgical procedure performed to save a life.[26] But historically, the states have exercised supervisory powers over legally authorized agents. For example, the capacity of parents and guardians to incur risks for wards is not as broad as the capacity of a normal adult in making decisions about himself.[27] There are often three legal issues in the same case. One is whether a person who presumed to consent or wishes to consent in behalf of another has the legal right to do so for any purpose. Another is the extent of the agent's authority, which is always a limited authority. A third is whether or not an appropriate trial court should make the decision, either alone and perhaps in opposition to the wishes of a parent or guardian, or in collaboration with

22. Gulf & Ship Island Railroad v. Sullivan, 1928, 155 Miss. 1, 119 So. 501, 62 A.L.R. 191.

23. Ballard v. Anderson, 1971, 4 Cal.3d 873, 95 Cal. Rptr. 1, 484 P.2d 1345. See Annotation, 1972, 42 A.L.R.3d 1406.

At least to minor operations. Bakker v. Welsh, 1906, 144 Mich. 632, 108 N.W. 94 (17 years); Gulf & Ship Island Railroad Co. v. Sullivan, 1928, 155 Miss. 1, 119 So. 501 (same); Bishop v. Shurly, 1926, 237 Mich. 76, 211 N.W. 75 (19 years); Lacey v. Laird, 1956, 166 Ohio St. 12, 139 N.E.2d 25 (18 years). The reasoning is that the minor is competent to consent, which would apply also to major operations; but there are as yet no cases so holding. See Notes, 1957, 10 Vand.L.Rev. 619; 1957, 9 West.Res.L.Rev. 101.

24. Zoski v. Gaines, 1939, 271 Mich. 1, 260 N.W. 99 (9½ years); Moss v. Rishworth, Tex.Com.App., 1920, 222 S.W. 225 (11 years); Bonner v. Moran, 1941, 75 U.S.App.D.C. 156, 126 F.2d 121 (15 years); Rogers v. Sells, 1936, 178 Okl. 103, 61 P.2d 1018 (14 years).

Where the parent unreasonably refuses consent a court may, as in other cases where it is necessary to act for the welfare of the child, remove him from the custody of the parent, and appoint a custodian, who may then consent to the operation. Matter of Brooklyn Hospital v. Torres, 1965, 45 Misc.2d 914, 258 N.Y.S.2d 621; Notes, 1955, 12 Wash. & Lee L.Rev. 239; 1953, 41 Geo.L.J. 226.

25. In re Guardianship of Pescinski, 1975, 67 Wis.2d 4, 226 N.W.2d 180; Strunk v. Strunk, Ky.1969, 445 S.W.2d 145; Ann., 35 A.L.R.3d 683. Savage, Organ Transplantations With An Incompetent Donor: Kentucky Resolves the Dilemma of Strunk v. Strunk, 1970, 58 Ky.L.J. 129; Curran, A Problem of Consent: Kidney Transplantation in Minors, 1959, 34 N.Y.U.L.Rev. 891.

26. In Pratt v. Davis, 1906, 224 Ill. 300, 79 N.E. 562, the consent of the husband was held to be required for an operation on an insane wife. But where the patient is competent to consent, and does so, consent of the spouse is not required. State to Use of Janney v. Housekeeper, 1889, 70 Md. 162, 16 A. 382; Burroughs v. Crichton, 1919, 48 App.D.C. 596; McClallen v. Adams, 1837, 36 Mass. (19 Pick.) 333. See also, In re Application of Long Island Jewish-Hillside Medical Center, 1973, 73 Misc.2d 395, 342 N.Y.S.2d 356 (consent from niece to the amputation of leg of her very old uncle was deemed proper).

27. See In re Guardianship of Pescinski, supra note 25.

a guardian or other agent or agents.[28] In the last situation, the consent of both the guardian or agent and the court would be a prerequisite to legal conduct.

In one case, an 84-year-old patient was admitted to a hospital from a nursing home. Gangrene in one leg was discovered. The patient was suffering from an arterial sclerotic disease that could have rendered him incapable of making a decision. Pursuant to an application from the hospital, the ultimate decision to amputate was made by a trial court with the approval of a niece.[29] The court sought the consent of the niece, but this is not a holding that the niece's consent would be a prerequisite to the granting of the order. Similar life and death issues have been resolved by the courts in recent years. A series of blood transfusions were given to save the life of a patient who had opposed such transfusions on religious grounds. The two reasons for the court's conclusion were: (a) the patient was near death and not competent to make a decision at the time the transfusions were administered, and (b) the patient was the mother of a seven-month-old child, and the state as "parens patriæ" would not allow the parent to abandon the child, even on religious grounds.[30] This cannot be regarded as a generally accepted view. Different views of the authority of a parent or guardian of an incompetent, alone or with the consent of the court, to authorize the transplantation of a kidney from a child or an incompetent to a brother, sister, or other close relative, when necessary to save the life of the latter, have been adopted. One view is that no surgical procedure, except those which appear to be to the financial or physical benefit of the incompetent, on a minor or an incompetent can be authorized.[31] The other view, referred to sometimes as the substituted judgment rule, is that the guardian, at least with the approval of the court, may permit what the incompetent would in all probability want done if he were competent.[32]

Just as a guardian cannot ordinarily give approval to a medical or surgical procedure that would involve a risk of serious injury or death when there is no contemplated benefit to the incompetent, so also the guardian cannot ordinarily deny a surgical or medical procedure that appears to be reasonably necessary to save life or perhaps to avoid serious bodily injury. Courts have generally granted approval for blood transfusions to minor children whose parents object on religious grounds.[33] But it is important to note that the doctor or the hospital is probably not entitled to proceed over the objection of a guardian in the absence of an emergency without obtaining the approval of the proper judicial tribunal for handling matters of this nature.[34] To proceed over the objection and without approval of a guardian would subject the doctor to liability on the theory of a battery. A much more difficult problem currently being debated is of when and by what authority artificial and extraordinary procedures to save the life of a person who is dying, or who exists only in a vegetative

---

28. Application of President & Directors of Georgetown College, Inc., D.C.Cir. 1964, 331 F.2d 1000, 1010, certiorari denied 377 U.S. 978, 84 S.Ct. 1883, 12 L.Ed.2d 746. In re Brooks' Estate, 1965, 32 Ill.2d 361, 205 N.E.2d 435; Raleigh Fitkin-Paul Morgan Memorial Hospital v. Anderson, 1964, 42 N.J. 421, 201 A.2d 537, certiorari denied 377 U.S. 985, 84 S.Ct. 1894, 12 L.Ed.2d 1032. See Notes, 1964, 51 Minn.L.Rev. 293; 1964, 77 Harv.L.Rev. 1539.

29. In re Application of Long Island Jewish-Hillside Medical Center, 1973, 73 Misc.2d 395, 342 N.Y.S.2d 356.

30. Application of the President & Directors of Georgetown College, Inc., D.C.Cir. 1964, 331 F.2d 1000, 9 A.L.R.3d 1367, certiorari denied 377 U.S. 978, 84 S.Ct. 1883, 12 L.Ed.2d 746.

31. In re Guardianship of Pescinski, 1975, 67 Wis.2d 4, 226 N.W.2d 180; In re Richardson, La.App.1973, 284 So.2d 185, application denied 284 So.2d 338.

32. Strunk v. Strunk, Ky.1969, 445 S.W.2d 145, 35 A.L.R.3d 683; Hart v. Brown, 1972, 29 Conn.Sup. 368, 289 A.2d 386.

33. State v. Perricone, 1962, 37 N.J. 463, 181 A.2d 751, certiorari denied 371 U.S. 890, 83 S.Ct. 189, 9 L.Ed. 2d 124; In the Interest of Ivey, Fla.App.1975, 319 So. 2d 53.

34. Mulloy v. Hop Sang, [1935] 1 W.W.R. 714; Schloendorff v. Society of New York Hospital, 1914, 211 N.Y. 125, 105 N.E. 92; Mohr v. Williams, 1905, 95 Minn. 261, 263, 104 N.W. 12, 13; Hively v. Higgs, 1927, 120 Or. 588, 253 P. 363; Rolater v. Strain, 1913, 39 Okl. 572, 137 P. 96.

way, can be withdrawn. Tort liability, if imposed in such a case, would probably have to be based on a negligence, rather than a battery, theory.[35] Tort liability in such a case involves a number of issues that extend beyond the scope of the present problem, including (1) when death occurs, (2) the difference between misfeasance and nonfeasance and, therefore, the difference between withholding a benefit to prolong life and doing something to hasten death, commonly regarded as euthanasia, and (3) whether the theory of recovery would be battery or negligence.

The right of a person to make decisions about his own life has been elevated in recent years to a right of privacy. While this right is not absolute, governmental intrusions into it have been regarded as requiring a clear showing not only of some compelling state interest in the absence of that person's consent but also that the means used are justified as necessary and reasonable to serve such interest. This has led to decisions greatly affecting which medical treatments can be administered to those who are incompetent, and what circumstances justify those administrations. In Price v. Sheppard,[36] the Supreme Court of Minnesota held that a medical director assuming the custody and care of a mentally ill minor pursuant to involuntary commitment would, for future cases, be subject to liability for violating the minor's constitutional right of privacy for utilizing more intrusive forms of treatment, such as psychosurgery or electroshock therapy, contrary to the wishes of the minor's natural guardian, his parent, without an order from the probate court to do so. Thus, a judicial hearing would be a prerequisite to treatments that could substantially alter one's personality.

The Emergency Privilege

The touching of another that would ordinarily be a battery in the absence of the consent of either the person touched or his legal agent can sometimes be justified in an emergency. Thus, it has often been asserted that a physician or other provider of health care has implied consent to deliver medical services, including surgical procedures, to a patient in an emergency.[37] But such lawful action is more satisfactorily explained as a privilege. There are several requirements: (a) the patient must be unconscious or without capacity to make a decision, while no one legally authorized to act as agent for the patient is available; (b) time must be of the essence, in the sense that it must reasonably appear that delay until such time as an effective consent could be obtained would subject the patient to a risk of a serious bodily injury or death which prompt action would avoid; and (3) under the circumstances, a reasonable person would consent, and the probabilities are that the patient would consent. It has often been suggested, especially in the older cases, that a "dire" emergency must exist—that death or loss of an important bodily function is likely to be the consequence. Most courts today would probably not exact such a stringent requirement unless the action to be taken itself involved the destruction of an important bodily function, such as the amputation of an arm or a leg, or the extraction of Fallopian tubes (rendering childbirth impossible). If, therefore, in the course of performing a major operation to which consent was given,

---

35. In re Quinlan, 1976, 70 N.J. 10, 355 A.2d 647, reversing 137 N.J.Super. 227, 348 A.2d 801, certiorari denied Gorger v. New Jersey, 429 U.S. 922, 97 S.Ct. 319, 50 L.Ed.2d 289.

36. Minn.1976, 239 N.W.2d 905.

37. Even in the case of a minor, where the parents cannot be reached quickly. Luka v. Lowrie, 1912, 171 Mich. 122, 136 N.W. 1106; Wells v. McGehee, La.App. 1949, 39 So.2d 196; Jackovach v. Yocom, 1931, 212 Iowa 914, 237 N.W. 444. Cf. King v. Carney, 1922, 85 Okl. 62, 204 Pa. 270; McGuire v. Rix, 1929, 118 Neb. 434, 225 N.W. 120; Delahunt v. Finton, 1928, 244 Mich. 226, 221 N.W. 168; Preston v. Hubbell, 1948, 87 Cal. App.2d 53, 196 P.2d 113; Barnett v. Bachrach, Mun. App.D.C.1943, 34 A.2d 626. See also Sullivan v. Montgomery, 1935, 155 Misc. 448, 279 N.Y.S. 575 (necessary to relieve pain).

Second Restatement of Torts, § 62. Cf. Ollet v. Pittsburgh, Cincinnati, Chicago & St. Louis Railway Co., 1902, 201 Pa. 361, 50 A. 1011, holding that emergency measures were privileged although the patient objected.

the surgeon discovers something which would likely require another operation unless the operation in progress is extended, the extension is privileged in the interest of avoiding another operation.[38] The justification is that no reasonable person would object if in a position to make a decision. If, however, an important bodily function would be destroyed by the procedure, then as a matter of law the extension would not and should not be privileged, unless death or loss of an important bodily function would likely be the result of not proceeding at once, and a reasonable person could have made the choice that the physician made in behalf of the patient.[39] However, the physician or hospital would probably not lose the privilege simply because a reasonable person could have made a different choice, so long as the choice made was a reasonable one.

Exceeding Consent

The consent is to the plaintiff's conduct, rather than to its consequences. If the plaintiff willingly engages in a boxing match, he does not of course consent to be killed, but he does consent to the defendant's striking at him, and hitting him if he can; and if death unexpectedly results, his consent to the act will defeat any action for the resulting invasion of his interests.[40] He does not, on the other hand, consent to being hit with brass knuckles, which is the same invasion by an act of a different character.

The defendant's privilege is limited to the conduct to which the plaintiff consents, or at least to acts of a substantially similar nature. A consent to a fight with fists is not a consent to an act of a different nature, such as biting off a finger,[41] or stabbing with a knife.[42] Permission to dump "a few stones" upon property is not a permission to cover it with boulders.[43] If the defendant goes beyond the consent given, and does a substantially different act, he is liable.[44]

The rule frequently is applied to surgical operations.[45] Consent to operate on the right ear is not necessarily consent to operate on the left,[46] and a patient who agrees to

---

38. Kennedy v. Parrott, 1956, 243 N.C. 355, 90 S.E.2d 754. (This was an extension of an appendectomy to include removal of a cyst).

39. Rogers v. Lumbermen's Mutual Casualty Co., La.App.1960, 119 So.2d 649.

40. McAdams v. Windham, 1922, 208 Ala. 492, 94 So. 742; cf. Nicholls v. Colwell, 1903, 113 Ill.App. 219. See Puttkammer, Consent in Criminal Assault, 1925, 19 Ill.L.Rev. 617.

It seems clear that the consent must be to the act rather than the resulting invasion of the plaintiff's interests. A consents to a boxing match with B, and unknown to A, B uses a set of brass knuckles. B punches A in the nose, inflicting exactly the same damage as if he had hit him with his fist. The consent is ineffective. On the other hand, A permits B to punch him in the chest as hard as he can. Unknown to either A or B, A has a defective heart, and drops dead. The consent is effective.

41. Milam v. Milam, 1907, 46 Wash. 468, 90 P. 595. Cf. Fitzgerald v. Cavin, 1872, 110 Mass. 153 (foul hold in wrestling match); Nicholls v. Colwell, 1903, 113 Ill.App. 219 (excessive force in scuffle).

42. Teolis v. Moscatelli, 1923, 44 R.I. 494, 119 A. 161.

43. Wheelock v. Noonan, 1888, 108 N.Y. 179, 15 N.E. 67.

44. Francis v. Sun Oil Co., 1959, 135 Mont. 307, 340 P.2d 824 (seismographic operations on plaintiff's land, too close to a spring); Shiffer v. Broadhead, 1889, 126 Pa. 260, 17 A. 592 (cutting trees below customary limit in size); Cartan v. Cruz Construction Co., 1965, 89 N.J. Super. 414, 215 A.2d 356.

This is true in particular where the consent is effectively withdrawn before or during the act. Mims v. Boland, 1964, 110 Ga.App. 477, 138 S.E.2d 902; Regina v. Miller, [1954] 2 Q.B. 282 (wife's withdrawal of consent to intercourse).

But consent to the entry of the defendants to remove heavy goods may reasonably imply consent to the entry of his servants to assist. Sterling v. Warden, 1871, 51 N.H. 217.

45. An exceptionally good discussion of the problems involved is McCoid, A Reappraisal of Liability for Unauthorized Medical Treatment, 1957, 41 Minn.L.Rev. 381. See also Straub, Antecedent Grounds of Liability in the Practice of Surgery, 1942, 14 Rocky Mt.L.Rev. 233; Smith, The Surgeon and the Unconscious Patient, 1929, 33 Law Notes 29; Kelly, The Physician, the Patient, and the Consent, 1960, 8 Kan.L.Rev. 405; Notes, 1940, 14 U.Cin.L.Rev. 161; 1946, 19 Tenn.L.Rev. 374; 1953, 42 Ky.L.J. 98; 1957, 6 Duke Bar J. 41. Cases are collected in Morris, Medical Malpractice—A Changing Picture, [1956] Ins.L.J. 318.

46. Mohr v. Williams, 1905, 95 Minn. 261, 104 N.W. 12. Cf. Moos v. United States, 8th Cir. 1955, 225 F.2d 705 (wrong leg); Hershey v. Peake, 1924, 115 Kan. 562, 223 P. 1113 (wrong tooth); Paulsen v. Gundersen, 1935,

a blood test [47] or a minor operation on his nose [48] does not thereby consent to a spinal puncture, or the removal of his tonsils. With the patient unconscious under an anaesthetic, and unable to be consulted, the mere desirability of the operation does not protect the surgeon, who becomes liable for battery—which, in addition to making him liable for at least nominal and perhaps punitive damages, renders quite immaterial any question of whether he has complied with good professional practice.[49] It is of course possible that the situation may be one of unforeseen emergency, critical in its nature, which will justify the surgeon in proceeding [50] on the assumption that the patient would consent if he were conscious and understood the situation.[51] It is also possible that the consent given will be sufficiently general in its terms to cover the particular operation, or that the surgeon may be authorized with complete freedom to do whatever he thinks best to remedy whatever he finds,[52] particularly where the patient has signed one of the written forms in common use in hospitals.[53] Such questions are matters of fact, which normally are to be determined by the jury. The general approach of the law has certainly changed from quite a rigorous one at the beginning of the century [54] to much greater liberality toward the surgeon, in the light of the conditions under which operations are now performed.[55] But it is still at least true that where an operation is found to have been prohibited,[56] the surgeon is not saved from liability by his good intentions in proceeding with it.

Mistake, Fraud and Duress

A plaintiff cannot ordinarily be regarded as actually consenting to the defendant's conduct if the plaintiff assented to the conduct while mistaken about the nature and quality of the invasion intended by the defendant.[57] Likewise, an overt manifestation of assent or willingness would not be effective apparent consent if the defendant knew, or probably if he ought to have known in the exercise of reasonable care, that the plaintiff was mistaken as to the nature and quality of the invasion intended. If the defendant, in ignorance of the fact that the candy is poisoned, gives the plaintiff a box of candy, the defendant will not be liable, because the plaintiff consented to the kind of touch intended by the defendant, and both were ignorant of the harmful nature of the invasion. If, on the other hand, the defendant knows that the candy is poisoned and that the plaintiff is unaware of the poison, the de-

---

218 Wis. 578, 260 N.W. 448; Franklyn v. Peabody, 1930, 249 Mich. 363, 228 N.W. 681.

47. Gill v. Selling, 1928, 125 Or. 587, 267 P. 812. Cf. Throne v. Wandell, 1922, 176 Wis. 97, 186 N.W. 146 (consent to examination; extraction of all teeth).

48. Hively v. Higgs, 1927, 120 Or. 588, 253 P. 363; Rolater v. Strain, 1913, 39 Okl. 572, 137 P. 96; Tabor v. Scobee, Ky.1952, 254 S.W.2d 474; Markart v. Zeimer, 1924, 67 Cal.App. 363, 227 P. 683; Wells v. Van Nort, 1919, 100 Ohio St. 101, 125 N.E. 910.

49. Perry v. Hodgson, 1929, 168 Ga. 678, 148 S.E. 659, conformed to 40 Ga.App. 117, 149 S.E. 91; Tabor v. Scobee, Ky.1952, 254 S.W.2d 474; Franklyn v. Peabody, 1930, 249 Mich. 363, 228 N.W. 681.

50. Delahunt v. Finton, 1928, 244 Mich. 226, 221 N.W. 168; Preston v. Hubbell, 1948, 87 Cal.App.2d 53, 196 P.2d 113; Barnett v. Bachrach, Mun.App.D.C.1943, 34 A.2d 626.

51. See discussion under this section on "The Emergency Privilege."

52. Bennan v. Parsonnet, 1912, 83 N.J.L. 20, 83 A. 948; Crippen v. Pulliam, 1963, 61 Wn.2d 725, 380 P.2d 475; King v. Carney, 1922, 85 Okl. 62, 204 P. 270;

Rothe v. Hull, 1944, 352 Mo. 926, 180 S.W.2d 7; Dicenzo v. Berg, 1940, 340 Pa. 305, 16 A.2d 15.

53. Danielson v. Roche, 1952, 109 Cal.App.2d 832, 241 P.2d 1028 (surgeon to "perform all treatments deemed advisable by him" during appendectomy. Held to cover removal of parts of Fallopian tubes).

54. Mohr v. Williams, 1905, 95 Minn. 261, 104 N.W. 12, is the classic case. See also Pratt v. Davis, 1906, 224 Ill. 300, 79 N.E. 562.

55. See for example Kennedy v. Parrott, 1956, 243 N.C. 355, 90 S.E.2d 754; Barnett v. Bachrach, Mun. App.D.C.1943, 34 A.2d 626; Rothe v. Hull, 1944, 352 Mo. 926, 180 S.W.2d 7; Russell v. Jackson, 1950, 37 Wn.2d 66, 221 P.2d 516.

56. Schloendorff v. Society of New York Hospital, 1914, 211 N.Y. 125, 105 N.E. 92; Chambers v. Nottebaum, Fla.App.1957, 96 So.2d 716; Corn v. French, 1955, 71 Nev. 280, 289 P.2d 173; Woodson v. Huey, Okl.1954, 261 P.2d 199. Cf. Mulloy v. Hop Sang, [1935] 1 W.W.R. 714 (amputation expressly forbidden, although necessary to save life).

57. Second Restatement of Torts, § 55.

fendant is liable, because the plaintiff did not consent to the kind of invasion which the defendant intended.[58] The decisions in this area have involved assent induced by fraud, in the sense that the defendant was either aware of the plaintiff's mistake or ignorance and failed to disclose the truth, or the defendant induced the mistake with representation which he knew was false.

Most of the conduct resulting in liability has been some kind of sexual or other intimate bodily contact with a man or a woman who submitted to the contact while mistaken about something determining the offensiveness of the contact. Thus a woman who consents to intercourse may still recover when she is infected with venereal disease, although nothing was said about it,[59] or equally when she finds that she is the victim of a mock marriage;[60] and a physician may be liable for inducing an innocent girl to submit to indecent liberties, when he knows that she is ignorant of the fact that they are unnecessary for medical treatment.[61] Apparently, however, the mistake must extend to the essential character of the act itself, which is to say that which makes it harmful or offensive,[62] rather than to some collateral matter which merely operates as an inducement. Thus consent to intercourse is still consent, although it is in return for counterfeit money, and the woman has no action for battery when she subsequently decides that she has been raped.[63] The remedy, if any, for such collateral fraud, is an action for deceit, or upon the contract for the consideration promised. It is quite possible for a court to conclude that the mistake will not vitiate consent to an offensive contact unless under the facts as they were assumed to be the touch could not be deemed to be in any way offensive or indecent, such as when a woman consents to sexual intercourse on the assumption that a mock marriage was valid. Thus, if a woman consents to sexual intercourse outside of wedlock, the fact that the consent was procured by a promise to marry which the defendant did not intend to honor would not vitiate the consent.

The question sometimes has arisen in cases involving medical or surgical treatment, where the defendant is aware that the patient does not understand the nature of the operation, or the risk of undesirable consequences involved in it.[64] Where there is active misrepresentation, this has been held to invalidate the consent, so that there is battery;[65] and the same has been held where there has been mere nondisclosure of consequences which the surgeon knew to be certain to follow.[66] Beyond this, there have been a few decisions finding battery where there was failure to disclose only a known risk of the treatment.[67]

---

58. Cf. Commonwealth v. Stratton, 1873, 114 Mass. 303; State v. Monroe, 1897, 121 N.C. 677, 28 S.E. 547; People v. Steinberg, 1947, 190 Misc. 413, 73 N.Y.S.2d 475 (pretended smallpox vaccination, with water). See Note, 1935, 14 Or.L.Rev. 281.

59. Crowell v. Crowell, 1920, 180 N.C. 516, 105 S.E. 206, rehearing denied 1921, 181 N.C. 66, 106 S.E. 149; De Vall v. Strunk, Tex.Civ.App.1936, 96 S.W.2d 245; State v. Lankford, 1917, 29 Del. 594, 102 A. 63.

60. Blossom v. Barrett, 1868, 37 N.Y. 434.

61. Bartell v. State, 1900, 106 Wis. 342, 82 N.W. 142; Commonwealth v. Gregory, 1938, 132 Pa.Super. 507, 1 A.2d 501; Bowman v. Home Life Insurance Co., 3d Cir. 1957, 243 F.2d 331. Cf. Hobbs v. Kizer, 8th Cir. 1916, 236 F. 681 (abortion represented to be other operation); People v. Steinberg, 1947, 190 Misc. 413, 73 N.Y.S.2d 475 (pretended vaccination, with water).

62. Second Restatement of Torts, §§ 55, 57.

63. Second Restatement of Torts, § 57. Cf. Oberlin v. Upson, 1911, 84 Ohio St. 111, 95 N.E. 511 (seduction under promise of marriage); Martin v. Carbide & Carbon Chemicals Corp., 1946, 184 Tenn. 166, 197 S.W.2d 798 (treatment by unlicensed physician). Compare the cases of conversion by a sale induced by fraud, supra, § 15.

64. See McCoid, The Care Required of Medical Practitioners, 1959, 12 Vand.L.Rev. 549, 586–597; Plant, An Analysis of "Informed Consent," 1968, 36 Ford.L.Rev. 639; Karchmer, Informed Consent: A Plaintiff's Malpractice "Wonder Drug," 1966, 31 Mo.L. Rev. 29; Notes, 1960, 60 Col.L.Rev. 1193; 1961, 34 So. Cal.L.Rev. 209, 1962, 75 Harv.L.Rev. 1445; 1966, 44 Tex.L.Rev. 799; 1967, 52 Iowa L.Rev. 786; 1967, 20 Okl.L.Rev. 214; 1967, 21 Sw.L.Rev. 843.

65. Paulsen v. Gundersen, 1935, 218 Wis. 578, 260 N.W. 448; Wall v. Brim, 5th Cir. 1943, 138 F.2d 478.

66. Bang v. Charles T. Miller Hospital, 1958, 251 Minn. 427, 88 N.W.2d 186 (sterilization).

67. Bang v. Charles T. Miller Hospital, 1958, 251 Minn. 427, 88 N.W.2d 186; Gray v. Grunnagle, 1966,

The greater number of decisions now regard the failure to disclose a mere risk of treatment as involving a collateral matter, and negligence rather than intent, and so have treated the question as one of negligent malpractice only, which brings into question professional standards of conduct. The matter is therefore more fully considered in connection with negligence.[68]

Relatively few cases have dealt with the problem of consent given under duress. Duress is an important defense in the criminal law,[69] and will justify rescission of a contract or other transaction, with restitution,[70] but there has been no discussion of its place in the law of torts. There are odd cases [71] which have held that duress is a tort in itself; but much more commonly it is held merely to invalidate the consent given, and so permit any other tort action which would arise if there were no consent. As to false imprisonment or battery, it is clear that yielding to a threat of force,[72] or the assertion of legal authority,[73] must be treated as no consent at all, but submission against the plaintiff's will; and the same is undoubtedly true as to trespass or conversion.[74] The same is probably true where the threat is directed against a member of the plaintiff's immediate family,[75] or his valuable property.[76] But if the threat is less direct, being merely one of future arrest,[77] or of "economic" duress such as loss of employment,[78] the courts have refused to say that the consent given, however reluctant it may be, is ineffective, so as to establish another tort. The distinction is of course one of degree. The growing tendency to recognize and extend the intentional infliction of mental suffering as an independent cause of action [79] may perhaps afford a remedy for some of the more extreme cases. In the field of contracts, duress is more generally recognized as a ground for rescission,[80] and it may in time receive more acceptance in the field of torts.

423 Pa. 144, 223 A.2d 663; Belcher v. Carter, 1967, 13 Ohio App.2d 113, 234 N.E.2d 311; Shulman v. Lerner, 1966, 2 Mich.App. 705, 141 N.W.2d 348.

68. See infra, ch. 5.

69. Newman and Weitzer, Duress, Free Will and the Criminal Law, 1957, 30 So.Cal.L.Rev. 313.

70. See Notes, 1941, 6 Mo.L.Rev. 73; 1968, 53 Iowa L.Rev. 892.

71. Neibuhr v. Gage, 1906, 99 Minn. 149, 108 N.W. 884, affirmed 1906, 99 Minn. 149, 109 N.W. 1 (duress a "form of fraud"); Smith v. Blakesburg Savings Bank, 1917, 182 Iowa 1190, 164 N.W. 762 (following case last cited); Woodham v. Allen, 1900, 130 Cal. 194, 62 P. 398 (relying upon apparently irrelevant Code provision).

72. Meints v. Huntington, 8th Cir. 1921, 276 F. 245; W.T. Grant Co. v. Owens, 1928, 149 Va. 906, 141 S.E. 860; Cordell v. Standard Oil Co., 1930, 131 Kan. 221, 289 P. 472 (false imprisonment); Miller v. Balthasser, 1875, 78 Ill. 302 (battery). But where consent to sexual intercourse is concerned, an overwhelming personality is no sufficient substitute for force. Rouse v. Creech, 1932, 203 N.C. 378, 166 S.E. 174.

73. Whitman v. Atchison, Topeka & Santa Fe Railway Co., 1911, 85 Kan. 150, 116 P. 234; Hebrew v. Pulis, 1906, 73 N.J.L. 621, 64 A. 121; Johnson v. Norfolk & Western Railway Co., 1918, 82 W.Va. 692, 97 S.E. 189.

74. Grainger v. Hill, 1838, 4 Bing.N.C. 212, 132 Eng.Rep. 769 (arrest and imprisonment); Murphy v. Hobbs, 1884, 8 Colo. 17, 5 P. 637, rehearing denied 8 Colo. 130, 11 P. 55 (threats of force); General Motors Acceptance Corp. v. Davis, 1931, 151 Okl. 255, 7 P.2d 157 (issue of warrant and threat of prosecution); see Millsap v. National Funding Corp., 1943, 57 Cal.App.2d 772, 135 P.2d 407; Saunders v. Mullinix, 1950, 195 Md. 235, 72 A.2d 720.

75. Second Restatement of Torts, § 58. See Note, 1928, 12 Minn.L.Rev. 409.

76. See supra, § 11.

77. Payson v. Macomber, 1861, 85 Mass. (3 Allen) 69; Knowlton v. Ross, 1915, 114 Me. 18, 95 A. 281; Sweeney v. F.W. Woolworth Co., 1924, 247 Mass. 277, 142 N.E. 50; Blumenfeld v. Harris, 1957, 3 App.Div.2d 219, 159 N.Y.S.2d 561, affirmed 3 N.Y.2d 905, 167 N.Y.S.2d 925, 145 N.E.2d 871, certiorari denied 356 U.S. 930, 78 S.Ct. 773, 2 L.Ed.2d 761; Priddy v. Bunton, Tex.Civ.App.1943, 177 S.W.2d 805, error refused; see Powell v. Champion Fiber Co., 1908, 150 N.C. 12, 63 S.E. 159.

78. Latter v. Braddell, 1880, 50 L.J.Q.B. 166; Weiler v. Herzfeld-Phillipson Co., 1926, 189 Wis. 554, 208 N.W. 599.

79. See supra, § 12.

80. Notes, 1925, 39 Harv.L.Rev. 108; Note 1938, 22 Minn.L.Rev. 891. As in the case of fraud (supra, note 71), any duress which will avoid a contract of sale may permit the seller to rescind and sue for conversion. General Motors Acceptance Corp. v. Davis, 1931, 151 Okl. 255, 7 P.2d 157; Borderland Hardware Co. v. Saenz, Tex.Civ.App.1928, 9 S.W.2d 1049.

Consent to Criminal Conduct

Conduct committed with the intention of inflicting a harmful or offensive contact on another is often a crime, notwithstanding that the person harmed or offended has consented to the contact. The question of what conduct between consenting parties should be regarded as so detrimental to themselves, to others, or to the general welfare as to justify punishing those who engage in it is a difficult and vexing one.[81] The further question of when, if ever, a tort action by (a) the consenting person, (b) a survivor of a consenting person (under a wrongful death statute), or (c) even some third person, such as a spouse or parent of one of the participants, seeking recovery for interference with a relational interest, should be recognized is a separate matter on which courts have not always agreed. The only issue treated here is when consent bars a tort action by the consenting party, or, if death results from a harmful invasion, a wrongful death action by a survivor. Arguably, consent should bar the tort action even though the consent is ineffective to prevent a criminal prosecution, because it destroys the wrongfulness of the conduct to the consenting party. Moreover, the plaintiff is himself a participant in an illegal enterprise and is not, for that reason, a very deserving person. But often, some of the same considerations that have motivated lawmakers to punish a defendant for engaging in consensual conduct also support a damage recovery against him by a consenting party. The considerable majority of the courts have attempted, in cases of mutual combat[82] and similar batteries,[83] to vindicate a conception of public policy by holding that the consent given will likewise not protect the defendant against a civil action for the damage inflicted. This rule has been traced[84] to a dictum in an early English case,[85] at a time when the action of trespass still had a criminal character, and the state was directly concerned in it. Its survival is due to a combination of the two notions that the interests of the state require protection by allowing a civil action, and that the parties will be deterred from fighting by the fear of liability. But the cases have been roundly criticized[86] on the grounds that no one should be rewarded with damages for his own voluntary participation in a wrong, particularly where, as is usually the case, he himself commits a crime; that the state is fully able to protect itself by a criminal prosecution; and that the parties, if they give any thought to the law at all, which is quite improbable, are quite as likely to be encouraged by the hope that if they get hurt they can still win in court. A minority,[87] with the support of the Restatement,[88] have held that the consent will defeat the civil action, except where the force used exceeds the consent.

---

81. Beale, Consent in the Criminal Law, 1895, 8 Harv.L.Rev. 317; Miller, Criminal Law, 1934, 171.

82. McNeil v. Mullin, 1905, 70 Kan. 634, 79 P. 168; Schwaller v. McFarland, 1940, 228 Iowa 405, 291 N.W. 852; Lewis v. Fountain, 1915, 168 N.C. 277, 84 S.E. 278; Condict v. Hewitt, Wyo.1962, 369 P.2d 278; Strawn v. Ingram, 1937, 118 W.Va. 603, 191 S.E. 401 (in mitigation of punitive damages only). See Notes, 1931, 17 Va.L.Rev. 374; 1949, 2 Okl.L.Rev. 108; 1949, 2 Vand.L.Rev. 301.

83. Teeters v. Frost, 1930, 145 Okl. 273, 292 P. 356 (prize fight); Gilmore v. Fuller, 1902, 198 Ill. 130, 65 N.E. 84 (unlawful charivari); Logan v. Austin, 1828, 1 Ala. (Stew.) 476; cf. Evans v. Waite, 1892, 83 Wis. 286, 53 N.W. 445.

84. Bohlen, Consent as Affecting Civil Liability for Breaches of the Peace, 1924, 24 Col.L.Rev. 819.

85. In Matthews v. Ollerton, 1693, Comb. 218, 90 Eng.Rep. 438.

86. Bohlen, Consent as Affecting Civil Liability for Breaches of the Peace, 1924, 24 Col.L.Rev. 819; Notes, 1924, 73 U.Pa.L.Rev. 74; 1931, 17 Va.L.Rev. 374; 1931, 3 Rocky Mt.L.Rev. 285; 1938, 22 Minn.L.Rev. 546.

87. Galbraith v. Fleming, 1886, 60 Mich. 408, 27 N.W. 583; Lykins v. Hamrick, 1911, 144 Ky. 80, 137 S.W. 852; Wright v. Starr, 1919, 42 Nev. 441, 179 P. 877; Hart v. Geysel, 1930, 159 Wash. 632, 294 P. 570; Dixon v. Samartino, Tex.Civ.App.1942, 163 S.W.2d 739, error refused. See also the abortion cases cited infra, note 91.

Even in such jurisdictions, the conclusion may be affected by the language of particular criminal statutes. Thus in Hudson v. Craft, 1949, 33 Cal.2d 654, 204 P.2d 1, a statute prohibiting unlicensed boxing matches was found to be filled with so many provisions for the protection of the boxers as to indicate an intention to protect them even though they consented.

88. Second Restatement of Torts, § 60.

There are certain criminal statutes, such as those fixing the age of consent to sexual intercourse, which obviously are intended to protect a limited class of persons against their own lack of judgment, and so against their own consent. In such a case, the direction of public policy has been considered to be clearly indicated, and it is generally agreed, except for one or two cases,[89] that the consent will not bar the action.[90]

Perhaps a majority of jurisdictions, prior to decisions holding statutes which criminalized solicited abortions performed during early pregnancy by licensed physicians unconstitutional, held that consent to an illegal abortion barred a tort action based on the abortion.[91] This result was due largely to the fact that, unlike the mutual combat situation, the social policy which made the consent ineffective with respect to criminality was not the protection of the consenting party, the mother.[92] Therefore, consent of the mother was regarded as effective to bar her action, or the actions of her survivors which were based on a wrongful death statute. On the other hand, the argument that the public interest demands that the plaintiff be allowed a civil action as an incentive to disclose a crime which would, otherwise, likely remain undetected has strengthened the opinions of the minority. Some of the opinions have ignored two other factors supporting a recovery. Women have often, in desperation, sought and obtained the services of a person not licensed to practice medicine; therefore that conduct could be viewed as illegal not only because it terminated the existence of life, but also because it was unreasonably dangerous to the woman. Moreover, the woman and the defendant were not in *pari delicto*, and in fact, the woman was often not guilty of any conduct addressed by the criminal abortion statute.

It is submitted that while the issues of tort liability and criminal responsibility are quite different, often the same considerations that have impelled legislatures to criminalize consensual conduct can reasonably be regarded as justifying tort liability. Three reasons are offered in support of tort liability for some consenting plaintiffs.

Arguably, no one should have the capacity to consent to conduct intended to bring about his death, or intended to bring about an invasion likely to result in his death, except when undertaken for medical reasons or for scientific or experimental purposes. Thus, a defendant was held liable to the wife of the deceased for inducing and assisting the deceased to drink three pints of whisky

---

89. Barton v. Bee Line, 1933, 238 App.Div. 501, 265 N.Y.S. 284, vigorously attacked the idea of allowing the girl to recover. See also Note, 1938, 7 Ford.L.Rev. 274, pointing out the opportunities for extortion. In Braun v. Heidrich, 1932, 62 N.D. 85, 241 N.W. 599, recovery was denied where the statute, apparently unique, expressly made the girl a criminal.

90. Bishop v. Liston, 1924, 112 Neb. 559, 199 N.W. 825; Priboth v. Haveron, 1914, 41 Okl. 692, 139 P. 973; Hough v. Iderhoff, 1914, 69 Or. 568, 139 P. 931; Glover v. Callahan, 1937, 299 Mass. 55, 12 N.E.2d 194; Gaither v. Meacham, 1926, 214 Ala. 343, 108 So. 2; Koch v. Stone, Ky.1960, 332 S.W.2d 529 (indecent liberties); Second Restatement of Torts, § 61.

91. Recovery barred: Miller v. Bennett, 1949, 190 Va. 162, 56 S.E.2d 217; Sayadoff v. Warda, 1954, 125 Cal.App.2d 626, 271 P.2d 140; Szadiwicz v. Cantor, 1926, 257 Mass. 518, 154 N.E. 251; Bowlan v. Lunsford, 1936, 176 Okl. 115, 54 P.2d 666; Martin v. Morris, 1931, 163 Tenn. 186, 42 S.W.2d 207.

Recovery allowed: Joy v. Brown, 1953, 173 Kan. 833, 252 P.2d 889; Milliken v. Heddesheimer, 1924, 110 Ohio St. 381, 144 N.E. 264; Martin v. Hardesty, 1928, 91 Ind.App. 239, 163 N.E. 610; Androws v. Coulter, 1931, 163 Wash. 429, 1 P.2d 320. See Notes, 1951, 45 Ill.L. Rev. 395; 1953, 26 So.Cal.L.Rev. 472; Wolcott v. Gaines, 1969, 225 Ga. 373, 169 S.E.2d 165 (not in pari delictur).

92. See Herman v. Turner, 1925, 117 Kan. 733, 232 P. 864.

Courts which do not bar the action for the abortion itself of course allow recovery for the damages resulting from negligence. Kimberly v. Ledbetter, 1958, 183 Kan. 644, 331 P.2d 307. But some courts which treat consent as a bar to a battery action have allowed recovery for negligence. Androws v. Coulter, 1931, 163 Wash. 429, 1 P.2d 320; True v. Older, 1948, 227 Minn. 154, 34 N.W.2d 700; Henrie v. Griffith, Okl.1964, 395 P.2d 809; Gaines v. Wolcott, 1969, 119 Ga.App. 313, 167 S.E.2d 366, affirmed 225 Ga. 373, 169 S.E.2d 165; Hunter v. Wheate, 1923, 53 App.D.C. 206, 289 F. 604; Nash v. Meyer, 1934, 54 Idaho 283, 31 P.2d 273; Castronovo v. Murawsky, 1954, 3 Ill.App.2d 168, 120 N.E.2d 871.

that caused death.[93] So, if A and B agreed to fight a duel with pistols, and A killed B, then B's wife could recover under a wrongful death statute.[94]

If the defendant's conduct is punishable as a crime primarily or substantially because of its harmful consequences to the consenting party, then there is good reason to take the position that consent will not be regarded as effective to bar a tort action, especially if the consenting party is not *pari delicto* or in equal fault, with the defendant. Most mutual combats are won by the person who was primarily responsible for provoking the fight; therefore the plaintiff may be regarded as deserving, notwithstanding his reluctant willingness to participate in an illegal affair.

Finally, the tort action may often be helpful in reducing the incidence of damaging events such as abortions performed by persons other than licensed physicians.

WESTLAW REFERENCES

Consent Ordinarily Bars Recovery
379k8.5(8)
topic(assault torts) /p consent /p defense*
"volenti non fit injuria"

Meaning of Consent and Justification for Non-Liability
di consent

Consent May Not Be Effective
consent /s effective! ineffective! /p liabili! & topic(torts negligence)
consent /s ineffective /p liability
272k105 /p consent

Incapacity
incapacit! /s intent! & negligen** tort*

Incapacity and Agency
headnote(consent! /s adult minor infant relative & topic(272 299 379)
consent /15 agent relative guardian* /p incapacity minor child infant incompet!

The Emergency Privilege
emergency /s surgery surgical & topic(272 299 379)
unconscious conscious /s patient /s consent!

Exceeding Consent
exceed! /10 consent & digest(tort* negligence assault physician*

Mistake, Fraud and Duress
consent*** /s fraud mistake duress & topic(272 299 379)

Consent to Criminal Conduct
digest(consent*** /s rape) % topic(110)

§ 19. Self-Defense

The privilege of self-defense rests upon the necessity of permitting a person who is attacked to take reasonable steps to prevent harm to himself or herself, where there is no time to resort to the law. The early English law, with its views of strict liability, did not recognize such a privilege; concerning such cases, it was said that "the man who commits homicide by misadventure or in self-defense deserves but needs a pardon."[1] But since about 1400 the privilege has been recognized,[2] and it is now undisputed, in the law of torts as well as in the criminal law. The privilege extends to the use of all reasonable force to prevent any threatened harmful or offensive bodily contact, or any confinement, whether intended or negligent.[3] Since it originated as a defense, the burden is upon the defendant to establish the facts creating the privilege.[4]

---

93. McCue v. Klein, 1883, 60 Tex. 168, 48 Am.Rep. 260.

94. But see, Lykins v. Hamrick, 1911, 144 Ky. 80, 137 S.W. 852. Second, Restatement, Torts, § 60, Illustration 3.

§ 19

1. 2 Pollock and Maitland, History of English Law, 2d ed.1898, 479. See Ames, Law and Morals, 1908, 22 Harv.L.Rev. 97; Wigmore, Responsibility for Tortious Acts: Its History, 1894, 7 Harv.L.Rev. 315.

2. Chapleyn of Greye's Inn v. , 1400, Y.B. 2 Hen. IV 8, pl. 40.

3. Second Restatement of Torts, §§ 64, 66, 68: Haeussler v. De Loretto, 1952, 109 Cal.App.2d 363, 240 P.2d 654.

There are relatively few tort cases. The tort rules are often, but not necessarily, identical with those of the criminal law. An excellent review of the latter is Perkins, Self-Defense, Re-examined, 1954, 1 U.C.L.A.L. Rev. 133.

4. Wells v. Englehart, 1905, 118 Ill.App. 217; Marriott v. Williams, 1908, 152 Cal. 705, 93 P. 875; see Note, 1928, 6 Tex.L.Rev. 553.

Apparent Necessity

The privilege to act in self-defense arises, not only where there is real danger, but also where there is a reasonable belief that it exists. The defendant is not liable where he acts under a reasonable, but mistaken, apprehension that the person advancing toward him intends to attack him,[5] or that the hand which goes to a pocket is reaching for a gun.[6] He is not required to wait until a blow is struck, for, as was quaintly observed in the earliest case, "perhaps it will come too late afterwards."[7] Undoubtedly the criminal law, with its concern with moral guilt, has had its influence in casting the loss due to an innocent mistake upon the party who is hurt; but the interest in self-protection, "the first law of nature," is perhaps sufficiently important in the mind of the public to justify the result.

Occasionally, it has been held that, in a tort action, the privilege to make a mistake does not exist unless the plaintiff acted unreasonably in creating deceptive appearances.[8] Thus, the risk of loss is placed upon the defendant who intentionally inflicted the harm rather than upon the innocent victim. There is no public good to be served by shifting the loss in such a case since the conduct is not the kind that ought or can be discouraged, unless it is believed that the defendant is morally obligated to pay for the harm that was inflicted. If so, the enforcement of this moral obligation may be justified.

The belief must, however, be one which a reasonable person would have entertained under the circumstances. The defendant is not required to behave with unusual courage,[9] but neither is he free to behave with abnormal timidity, or to be a complete fool;[10] and it is not enough that he really believes that he is about to be attacked, unless he has some reasonable ground for the belief.[11] Evidence as to his state of mind and nerves, and the threats, past conduct, and reputation of his assailant which may have induced it, is important and admissible on the issue of what was reasonable,[12] which is frequently for the jury,[13] but the standard to be applied is the external one of reasonable conduct.

Reasonable Force

The privilege is limited to the use of force which is, or reasonably appears to be,[14] necessary for protection against the threatened

---

5. Paxton v. Boyer, 1873, 67 Ill. 132; Courvoisier v. Raymond, 1896, 23 Colo. 113, 47 P. 284; Crabtree v. Dawson, 1904, 119 Ky. 148, 83 S.W. 557; Pearson v. Taylor, La.App.1959, 116 So.2d 833; Laffin v. Apalucci, 1943, 130 Conn. 153, 32 A.2d 648. As to the effect of a threat, see Hughes v. State, 1937, 212 Ind. 577, 10 N.E.2d 629.

An interesting recent application of this principle was applied to an eight-year-old child who hit a nine-year-old child allegedly in self-defense. The court held that his beliefs, impulses, and instincts as to danger were to be judged in relation to those of a reasonable person of like age. Maichle v. Jonovic, 69 Wis.2d 622, 1975, 230 N.W.2d 789.

6. Keep v. Quallman, 1887, 68 Wis. 451, 32 N.W. 233; Godwin v. Collins, 1914, 67 Fla. 197, 64 So. 752; Landry v. Hill, La.App.1957, 94 So.2d 308. The supposed assailant may be privileged in turn to defend himself, and in the resulting fracas it is entirely possible that neither party may be liable. Jamison v. Moseley, 1892, 69 Miss. 478, 10 So. 582.

7. Chapleyn of Greye's Inn v. ———, 1400, Y.B. 2 Hen. IV 8, pl. 40.

8. Chapman v. Hargrove, Tex.Civ.App.1918, 204 S.W. 379; Crabtree v. Dawson, 1904, 119 Ky. 148, 83 S.W. 557, 26 Ky.L.Rep. 1046 (the exact holding was that the defendant should have exercised the highest degree of care that was practicable, since the plaintiff was not the person the defendant thought he was).

9. Patterson v. Standley, 1900, 91 Ill.App. 671.

10. Courvoisier v. Raymond, 1896, 23 Colo. 113, 47 P. 284; Beck v. Minneapolis Union R. Co., 1905, 95 Minn. 73, 103 N.W. 746; McQuiggan v. Ladd, 1906, 79 Vt. 90, 64 A. 503; Daggs v. St. Louis-San Francisco Railway Co., 1930, 326 Mo. 555, 31 S.W.2d 769.

11. State v. Bryson, 1864, 60 N.C. (2 Winst.L.) 476; Higgins v. Minaghan, 1891, 78 Wis. 602, 47 N.W. 941; Fixico v. State, 1928, 39 Okl.Cr.App. 95, 263 P. 171.

12. Cain v. Skillin, 1929, 219 Ala. 228, 121 So. 521; Woodson v. State, 1926, 30 Ariz. 448, 247 P. 1103; State v. Mark Len, 1932, 108 N.J.L. 439, 158 A. 749; State v. Padula, 1927, 106 Conn. 454, 138 A. 456; Simms v. D'Avillier, La.App.1965, 179 So.2d 707; Notes, 1932, 18 Va.L.Rev. 794; 1940, 24 Minn.L.Rev. 426.

13. Zell v. Dunaway, 1911, 115 Md. 1, 80 A. 215.

14. Enright v. People, 1895, 155 Ill. 32, 39 N.E. 561; Shorter v. People, 1849, 2 N.Y. (2 Comst.) 193; Beck v. Minneapolis Union Railway Co., 1905, 95 Minn. 73, 103 N.W. 746. The relative size and strength of the parties is to be considered in determining what is reasonable.

injury.[15] Sometimes, it is simply held that the privilege is one to use reasonable means, and this would justify such means as a reasonable person would use even though it might involve more force than reasonably appears to be necessary. This would appear to me the more practical way to charge the jury, since the issue then is simply whether or not the defendant acted reasonably under the circumstances in protecting himself from harm. The defendant is not privileged to inflict a beating which goes beyond the real or apparent necessities of his or her own defense.[16] If he does, he is committing a tort to the extent of excessive force, and it is entirely possible that each party may have an action against the other.[17]

When it is not possible to separate the harm done by the use of unreasonable means from that which would have been privileged, the defendant will be liable for all of the harm done by the means used.[18]

There is no privilege to use violence after the assailant is disarmed or helpless, or all danger is clearly past.[19] Revenge is not a defense; for compensation, the plaintiff must look to the law. Threats and insults may give color to an act of aggression,[20] but in themselves, they do not ordinarily justify an apprehension of immediate harm,[21] and the defendant is not privileged to vindicate his outraged personal feelings at the expense of the physical safety of another.[22] Such provocation is to be considered only in mitigation of the damages; and the prevailing view, with some little authority to the contrary,[23] is that it operates only to reduce or avoid punitive, as distinguished from compensatory, damages.[24] Even though the plaintiff was the aggressor in the first instance, if he withdraws from the encounter, and clearly brings his withdrawal home to

---

Thomason v. Gray, 1886, 82 Ala. 291, 3 So. 38; Davis v. State, 1898, 152 Ind. 34, 51 N.E. 928. The same is of course true as to the number of the assailants. Thornton v. Taylor, 1899, 21 Ky.L.Rep. 1082, 54 S.W. 16; Higgins v. Minaghan, 1891, 78 Wis. 602, 47 N.W. 941. See Annotation, 1952, 25 A.L.R.2d 1215.

15. It is generally agreed that the defendant need not be threatened with death, or with "great" or "serious" bodily injury to justify an ordinary battery. Boston v. Muncy, 1951, 204 Okl. 603, 233 P.2d 300; State v. Woodward, 1937, 58 Idaho 385, 74 P.2d 92; Shires v. Boggess, 1913, 72 W.Va. 109, 77 S.E. 542.

16. Ogden v. Claycomb, 1859, 52 Ill. 365; Nichols v. Brabazon, 1896, 94 Wis. 549, 69 N.W. 342; Beavers v. Bowen, 1906, 26 Ky.L.Rep. 291, 80 S.W. 1165.

17. Elliott v. Brown, 1829, 2 N.Y. (Wend.) 497; Dole v. Erskine, 1857, 35 N.H. 503; Gutzman v. Clancy, 1902, 114 Wis. 589, 90 N.W. 1081; McCulloch v. Goodrich, 1919, 105 Kan. 1, 181 P. 556.

18. Second Restatement of Torts, § 7, Comment *b*.

19. Germolus v. Sausser, 1901, 83 Minn. 141, 85 N.W. 946; Monize v. Begaso, 1906, 190 Mass. 87, 76 N.E. 460; Custer v. Kroeger, 1922, 209 Mo.App. 450, 240 S.W. 241; Drabek v. Sabley, 1966, 31 Wis.2d 184, 142 N.W.2d 798; McCombs v. Hegarty, 1954, 205 Misc. 937, 130 N.Y.S.2d 547 (kicking man when he is down).

20. Keep v. Quallman, 1887, 68 Wis. 451, 32 N.W. 233; see Hulse v. Tollman, 1853, 49 Ill.App. 490.

21. Rippy v. State, 1858, 39 Tenn. (2 Head) 217.

22. Eisentraut v. Madden, 1915, 97 Neb. 466, 150 N.W. 627 ("Hello, Professor" does not justify battery with a shovel); Rackett v. Rackett, 1940, 5 Wash.2d 262, 105 P.2d 22; Gargotto v. Isenberg, 1932, 244 Ky. 493, 51 S.W.2d 443; Cunningham v. Reagan, Mo.1954, 273 S.W.2d 174; Prell Hotel Corp. v. Antonacci, 1970, 86 Nev. 390, 469 P.2d 399. Cf. Johnson v. Johnson, 1917, 201 Ala. 41, 77 So. 335 (the exasperating wife).

Mississippi is unique in having a statute that has been interpreted to hold that provocative words may be a complete justification for battery, if the words, under ordinary circumstances, could reasonably be expected to produce physical retaliation. Thomas v. Carter, 1927, 148 Miss. 637, 114 So. 736. See Malone, "Insult in Retaliation," 1939, 11 Miss.L.J. 333. This was also the position taken in Louisiana by judicial decision. See Note, 1944, 5 La.L.Rev. 617. However, in 1973 the Louisiana Supreme Court finally overruled the cases so holding and took the position that provocative words that are calculated to induce physical retaliation only mitigate the damages. Morneau v. American Oil Co., La.1973, 272 So.2d 313; Watts v. Aetna Casualty & Surety Co., La.App.1975, 309 So.2d 402, writ denied 313 So.2d 601; Foster v. Barker, La.App.1974, 306 So.2d 910.

23. Jackson v. Old Colony Street Railway Co., 1910, 206 Mass. 477, 92 N.E. 725; Bascom v. Hoffman, 1925, 199 Iowa 941, 203 N.W. 273; Mohler v. Owens, Tex. Civ.App.1962, 352 S.W.2d 855; Arnold v. Wiley, 1955, 39 Tenn.App. 391, 284 S.W.2d 296.

24. Heil v. Zink, 1949, 120 Colo. 481, 210 P.2d 610; Gissendanner v. Temples, 1936, 232 Ala. 608, 169 So. 231; Royer v. Belcher, 1926, 100 W.Va. 694, 131 S.E. 556; Barth v. Stewart, 1929, 229 Ky. 840, 18 S.W.2d 275; Patterson v. Henry, 1953, 72 Ohio L.Abs. 403, 136 N.E.2d 764. See Note, 1945, 14 Ford.L.Rev. 95.

the mind of his opponent,[25] there is no privilege to renew the conflict and attack him.[26]

Ordinarily the question of what is reasonable force is to be determined by the jury. Certain boundaries have, however, been marked out by the law. It is unreasonable to use force which is calculated to inflict death or serious bodily harm, such as a deadly weapon, unless one has reason to believe that he is in similar serious danger, and that there is no other safe means of defense.[27] Where a reasonably safe way of escape is open, the courts have not agreed on the rule to be applied. It is clear that the defendant may stand his ground and use force short of that likely to cause serious physical injury.[28]

The courts have generally adopted the same policy concerning civil litigation that state legislatures have followed in defining crimes. Moreover, the penal laws in many states have been or are in the process of being revised and modernized. It is therefore unsafe to rely on past decisions—one view, giving priority to the dignity and sense of honor of the individual, is to permit the person attacked to stand his ground and use deadly force against an attack which calls for it, even to the extent of killing his assailant, at least if the defender is at a place he is entitled to be.[29] Another view, giving priority to the importance of human life, is that personal honor and dignity cannot justify killing or inflicting serious bodily injury if it appears that retreat with safety is an option.[30] Of course, the obligation to retreat evaporates when the safety of doing so is no longer apparent.[31] "Detached reflection cannot be demanded in the presence of an uplifted knife," [32] and if there is any reasonable doubt, one need not run. In such states, the ancient rule that there is no obligation to retreat [33] when the defendant is attacked in his own dwelling house, "his castle," [34] has been continued. This rule is apparently based on "an instinctive feeling

---

25. People v. Button, 1895, 106 Cal. 628, 39 P. 1073 (insanity preventing). Cf. Eisentraut v. Madden, 1915, 97 Neb. 466, 150 N.W. 627.

In Ulrich v. Schwarz, 1929, 199 Wis. 24, 225 N.W. 195 it was held that evidence of provocation was admissible as bearing on the extent of plaintiff's mental suffering.

26. Rowe v. United States, 1898, 164 U.S. 546, 17 S.Ct. 172, 41 L.Ed. 547; Stoffer v. State, 1864, 15 Ohio St. 47; Allen v. State, 1859, 28 Ga. 395; McNatt v. McRae, 1903, 117 Ga. 898, 45 S.E. 248.

27. Brasseaux v. Girouard, La.App.1972, 269 So.2d 590, application denied 271 So.2d 262; Coats v. State, 1911, 101 Ark. 51, 141 S.W. 197; State v. Meyers, 1910, 57 Or. 50, 110 P. 407; State v. Clark, 1909, 64 W.Va. 625, 63 S.E. 402; Roberson v. State, 1901, 43 Fla. 156, 157, 29 So. 535; Second Restatement of Torts, § 65. See Note, 1967, 69 W.Va.L.Rev. 361.

Thus there is no privilege to kill in resisting unlawful arrest, except where it involves such serious personal danger. Creighton v. Commonwealth, 1886, 84 Ky. 103; Baxter v. State, 1955, 225 Ark. 239, 281 S.W.2d 931.

On the other hand, self-defense with fists is not limited to cases where the defendant reasonably believes that he is in danger of great bodily harm. Boston v. Muncy, 1951, 204 Okl. 603, 233 P.2d 300.

28. State v. Abbott, 1961, 36 N.J. 63, 174 A.2d 881; Beyer v. Birmingham Railway Light & Power Co., 1914, 186 Ala. 56, 64 So. 609; State v. Gough, 1919, 187 Iowa 363, 174 N.W. 279; People v. Katz, 1942, 263 App.Div. 883, 32 N.Y.S.2d 157; State v. Sherman, 1889, 16 R.I. 631, 18 A. 1040; Second Restatement of Torts, § 63.

29. Brown v. United States, 1921, 256 U.S. 335, 41 S.Ct. 501, 65 L.Ed. 961; People v. Bush, 1953, 414 Ill. 441, 111 N.E.2d 326; State v. Ellerbe, 1944, 223 N.C. 770, 28 S.E.2d 519; State v. Hiatt, 1936, 187 Wash. 226, 60 P.2d 71; People v. Ligouri, 1940, 284 N.Y. 309, 31 N.E.2d 37.

30. Beale, Retreat from Murderous Assault, 1903, 16 Harv.L.Rev. 567; Beale, Homicide in Self-Defense, 1903, 3 Col.L.Rev. 526; Restatement of Torts, § 65. Contra, Perkins, Self-Defense Re-examined, 1954, 1 U.C.L.A.L.Rev. 133.

31. King v. State, 1936, 233 Ala. 198, 171 So. 254; Ford v. State, 1953, 222 Ark. 16, 257 S.W.2d 30; State v. Cox, 1941, 138 Me. 151, 23 A.2d 634; State v. Stevenson, 1936, 8 Del. (W.W.Harr.) 105, 188 A. 750; Scholl v. State, 1927, 94 Fla. 1138, 115 So. 43.

32. Holmes, J., in Brown v. United States, 1921, 256 U.S. 335, 41 S.Ct. 501, 65 L.Ed. 961.

33. Cf. State v. Bartlett, 1902, 170 Mo. 658, 71 S.W. 148 (retreat impossible); People v. Macard, 1888, 73 Mich. 15, 40 N.W. 784; State v. Roberts, 1891, 63 Vt. 139, 21 A. 424; State v. Gardner, 1909, 96 Minn. 318, 104 N.W. 971. See Inbau, Firearms and Legal Doctrine, 1933, 7 Tul.L.Rev. 529, 531.

34. State v. Johnson, 1964, 261 N.C. 727, 136 S.E.2d 84; Crawford v. State, 1963, 231 Md. 354, 190 A.2d 538; Dunn v. State, 1957, 237 Ind. 398, 146 N.E.2d 529; State v. Preece, 1935, 116 W.Va. 176, 179 S.E. 524; Bowen v. State, 1928, 217 Ala. 574, 117 So. 204.

that a home is sacred, and that it is improper to require a man to submit to pursuit from room to room in his own house." [35] There are courts which have extended this rule to include the yard around the dwelling,[36] the defendant's place of business,[37] his club,[38] or even his automobile; [39] but such extensions have an obvious artificial air, and are scarcely to be recommended.

Perhaps the best solution to the problem of retreat is simply a rule requiring it as a condition to the use of deadly means only if it can be established that his conduct in standing his ground was unreasonable under the circumstances.[40]

Illegal Arrests

Historically, the privilege to resist unlawful arrest is subject, in general, to the same rules of reasonable conduct as that of defense against other assaults and batteries.[41] However, the use of self-help by force against one that the defendant knows or has reason to know is a public officer is calculated to escalate the affair into a serious affray and is unnecessary at a time when the rights of the accused are so well protected. The better social result is to require submission to unlawful arrests so long as unreasonable means are not used to effect the arrest.[42] The illegally arrested party does at least have a remedy by way of damages for the false imprisonment. This is the position that has been adopted in a number of states in recent Penal Code revisions.[43]

Injury to Third Person

If, in defending himself, the defendant accidentally shoots a stranger, there is no liability in the absence of some negligence,[44]

---

35. First Restatement of Torts, Tent.Draft, Commentary to § 84. Where the attack is made in the dwelling of both parties, authority is divided. See, holding that the defendant must retreat if he can safely do so: State v. Grierson, 1949, 96 N.H. 36, 69 A.2d 851; Baker v. Commonwealth, 1947, 305 Ky. 88, 202 S.W.2d 1010; Watts v. State, 1912, 177 Ala. 24, 59 So. 270; State v. Dyer, 1910, 147 Iowa 217, 124 N.W. 629. This is the position taken by the Second Restatement of Torts, § 65.

Contra: Bryant v. State, 1949, 252 Ala. 153, 39 So.2d 657; State v. Phillips, 1936, 38 Del. 24, 187 A. 721; People v. Tomlins, 1914, 213 N.Y. 240, 107 N.E. 496; State v. Gordon, 1924, 128 S.C. 422, 122 S.E. 501; People v. McGrandy, 1967, 9 Mich.App. 187, 156 N.W.2d 48.

36. State v. Frizzelle, 1955, 243 N.C. 49, 89 S.E.2d 725; cf. State v. Davis, 1948, 214 S.C. 34, 51 S.E.2d 86 (anywhere on his own premises). Contra, Brown v. Oestman, 1961, 362 Mich. 614, 107 N.W.2d 837.

37. Askew v. State, 1891, 94 Ala. 4, 10 So. 657; State v. Baratta, 1951, 242 Iowa 1308, 49 N.W.2d 866; State v. Griggs, 1950, 218 S.C. 86, 61 S.E.2d 653; State v. Turner, 1938, 95 Utah 129, 79 P.2d 46.

38. State v. Marlowe, 1922, 120 S.C. 205, 112 S.E. 921.

39. State v. Borwick, 1922, 193 Iowa 639, 187 N.W. 460. Contra, State v. McGee, 1937, 185 S.C. 184, 193 S.E. 303. As to such extensions generally, see State v. Sipes, 1926, 202 Iowa 173, 209 N.W. 458; People v. Tomlins, 1914, 213 N.Y. 240, 107 N.E. 496; Madry v. State, 1918, 201 Ala. 512, 78 So. 866; State v. Bowers, 1923, 122 S.C. 275, 115 S.E. 303; Beale, Retreat from Murderous Assault, 1903, 16 Harv.L.Rev. 567; Note, 1922, 7 Minn.L.Rev. 59.

40. See Regina v. Howe, 1058, 100 Comm.L.Rep. (Aust.) 448; Fontin v. Katapodis, 1962, 108 Comm.L. Rep. (Aust.) 117; Fleming, Law of Torts, 3d ed. 1965, 86.

41. Coats v. State, 1911, 101 Ark. 51, 141 S.W. 197; Creighton v. Commonwealth, 1886, 84 Ky. 103; Baxter v. State, 1955, 225 Ark. 239, 281 S.W.2d 931; Second Restatement of Torts, § 68.

42. In United States v. Heliczer, 2d Cir. 1967, 373 F.2d 241, 246 n. 3, certiorari denied 388 U.S. 917, 87 S.Ct. 2133, 18 L.Ed.2d 1359 Judge Learned Hand was quoted: "The idea that you may resist peaceful arrest * * * because you are in debate about whether it is lawful or not, instead of going to the authorities which can determine * * * [is] not a blow for liberty, but on the contrary, a blow for attempted anarchy."

43. See § 26, supra, for additional comments. See for an argument for the right to resist an unlawful arrest, Chevigny, "The Right to Resist an Unlawful Arrest," 1969, 78 Yale L.J. 1128, 7 Crim.L.Bull. 189 (to preserve a sense of personal liberty); and also, 1970, 2 N.C.Cent.L.J. 125 (resisting unlawful arrest is based on visceral action). Of course, the person would have the privilege to resist the use of unreasonable means to effect an arrest, lawful or unlawful. Carter v. State, Okl.Cr.1973, 507 P.2d 932; United States v. Peterson, 1973, 483 F.2d 1222, 157 U.S.App.D.C. 219, certiorari denied 414 U.S. 1007, 94 S.Ct. 367, 38 L.Ed.2d 244.

44. Morris v. Platt, 1864, 32 Conn. 75; Shaw v. Lord, 1914, 41 Okl. 347, 137 P. 885; Paxton v. Boyer, 1873, 67 Ill. 132; State v. Fielder, 1932, 330 Mo. 747, 50 S.W.2d 1031; Mayweather v. State, 1926, 29 Ariz. 460, 242 P. 864. This operates as a limitation upon the principle of "transferred intent," supra, § 9.

See, also, Grisom v. Logan, E.D.Cal.1971, 334 F.Supp. 273 (civil rights action in which baby was injured in a shoot-out; no liability); Burton v. Waller, 5th Cir. 1974, 502 F.2d 1261, certiorari denied, 1975, 420

and on the issue of negligence, the necessity of defending against the assailant must be considered in determining whether he has acted reasonably.[45] The same policy which gives the defendant the privilege of acting under a reasonable mistake protects him in such a case.

But if the injury is inflicted intentionally, as where the defendant deliberately rides another down in order to escape from a pursuer, there is a closer approach to moral blame. It may be that there is no liability in such a case for the mere technical tort, but, by analogy to a similar rule as to the invasion of property in case of "necessity,"[46] it seems reasonable to say that the privilege is qualified, and that he should be required to pay for it by making compensation for any actual damage.[47] Thus the defendant who, with a pistol held at his head, kills a third person to save his own life, is guilty at least of manslaughter,[48] as well as liable in tort for the death.

WESTLAW REFERENCES

Apparent Necessity

selfdefense /s privilege % topic(110)

selfdefense selfprotect! /p necessity /s apparent % topic(110)

selfdefense selfprotect! /p assault tort* /p necessity % topic(110 203)

Reasonable Force

selfdefense /p reasonable /s force % topic(110 203)

selfdefense /p reasonable nondeadly justifiable /s force % topic(110 203)

Illegal Arrests

illegal unlawful /10 arrest** /p selfdefense selfprotect!

Injury to Third Person

selfdefense selfprotect! /p third +3 person* party***

selfdefense selfprotect! /p innocent /s bystander* % topic(110 203)

---

§ 20. Defense of Others

Defense of Others

If the defendant's motive for inflicting harm on the plaintiff was preventing an immediate battery to or imprisonment of a third person, then his conduct may be justified as a privilege to defend another. In such a situation, there are three issues to be resolved. First, should a person have a privilege to defend another against any kind of invasion so long as the latter has a privilege of self-defense, as when a stranger intervenes in defense of a woman whose husband is forcibly removing her from a public place against her will? Second, if the defendant's purpose in intervening is to be regarded as justifiable, what is to be the effect of a mistaken but reasonable belief that he was acting in behalf of a person who had a privilege of self-defense? And third, should the answer to either of the above questions for tort liability differ from the answer for criminal responsibility?

The early common law recognized a feudal privilege in the master of the household to defend the members of his family and his servants against attack.[1] Later this was extended to permit any members of the same

---

U.S. 964, 95 S.Ct. 1356, 43 L.Ed.2d 442, rehearing denied 421 U.S. 939, 95 S.Ct. 1668, 44 L.Ed.2d 95. (Case involved injuries from gunfire of officers on Jackson State College campus; liability for negligence imposed.)

Negligence was found in Bartosh v. Banning, 1967, 251 Cal.App.2d 378, 59 Cal.Rptr. 382.

45. Shaw v. Lord, 1914, 41 Okl. 347, 137 P. 885; United States v. Jasper, 4th Cir. 1955, 222 F.2d 632.

46. See infra, § 24.

47. Cf. Regina v. Dudley, 1884, 14 Q.B.D. 273, 15 Cox C.C. 624; United States v. Holmes, 1842, Fed.Cas.

No. 15,383, 1 Wall.Jr. 1; and see Bohlen, Incomplete Privilege to Inflict Intentional Invasions of Interests of Property and Personality, 1926, 39 Harv.L.Rev. 307.

48. Arp v. State, 1893, 97 Ala. 5, 12 So. 301; People v. Repke, 1895, 103 Mich. 459, 61 N.W. 861; State v. Capaci, 1934, 179 La. 462, 154 So. 419; State v. Fisher, 1900, 23 Mont. 540, 59 P. 919; Brewer v. State, 1904, 72 Ark. 145, 78 S.W. 773.

§ 20

1. Seaman v. Cuppledick, c. 1610, Owen 150, 74 Eng.Rep. 966.

family to defend one another[2] and servants to defend their employers.[3]

All states would now recognize the privilege of anyone to go to the defense of another threatened with any kind of felonious invasion, such as rape or serious bodily injury. It has at times been suggested that the privilege should exist only when there would be a legally or socially recognized duty to intervene.[4] Thus, the driver of an automobile is permitted to defend his guest,[5] but the penal laws of most states would probably now recognize the privilege of the defendant to defend a third person against any kind of invasion against which the third person would have the privilege of self-defense, so long as the intervention appeared to be reasonably necessary.[6] There is, however, something to be said for the notion that one should "mind his own business" as regards minor dignitary invasions, because intervention can often result in the escalation of a minor disturbance into a serious one, and because the intervenor can often be mistaken about who was the aggressor. It would, however, seem questionable to give any aggressor a cause of action against an intermeddler who acted in behalf of someone who actually had a privilege of self-defense.

The privilege extends to the use of all force reasonably necessary for such defense, although there will be liability if unnecessary force is used.[7] It is said that the defender may do whatever the person attacked might do to protect himself.[8] As in the case of self-defense, the necessity must be immediate, and attacks made in the past, or threats for the future, will not justify such action.[9]

As to the effect of a mistaken but reasonable belief that intervention is necessary, or that the force used is called for, the courts have not agreed as to whether the intervenor takes the risk that the person he is defending would not be privileged to defend himself in the same manner.[10]

Most of the cases have involved criminal responsibility rather than tort liability. If the defendant makes an honest and reasona-

---

2. Martin v. Costa, 1934, 140 Cal.App. 494, 35 P.2d 362 (husband); Sheward v. Magit, 1951, 106 Cal.App.2d 163, 234 P.2d 708 (son); State v. Browers, 1947, 356 Mo. 1195, 205 S.W.2d 721 (brother); Tubbs v. Commonwealth, 1900, 22 Ky.L.Rep. 481, 57 S.W. 623 (uncle); Frew v. Teagarden, 1922, 111 Kan. 107, 205 P. 1023 (brother-in-law).

3. Barfoot v. Reynolds, 1734, 2 Strange 953, 93 Eng.Rep. 963; Malley v. Lane, 1921, 97 Conn. 133, 115 A. 674.

4. Second Restatement of Torts, § 78. The idea that the privilege is limited to the defense of relatives, servants, or at least close associates, apparently was derived from some loose language in Leward v. Baseley, 1695, 1 Ld.Raym. 62, 91 Eng.Rep. 937.

5. State v. Borwick, 1922, 193 Iowa 639, 187 N.W. 460.

6. State v. Totman, 1899, 80 Mo.App. 125; Brouster v. Fox, 1906, 117 Mo.App. 711, 93 S.W. 318; Fink v. Thomas, 1909, 66 W.Va. 487, 66 S.E. 650; Williams v. State, 1943, 70 Ga.App. 10, 27 S.E.2d 109; Beavers v. Calloway, 1946, 270 App.Div. 873, 61 N.Y.S.2d 804. "Every man has the right of defending any man by reasonable force against unlawful force." Salmond, Law of Torts, 8th ed. 1934, 44; 1962 Model Penal Code, American Law Institute, Section 3.05; Second Restatement of Torts, § 76.

There are a good many other cases in which some relation has existed, but the court has made no point of it. See for example Thompson v. State, 1954, 195 Ala. 65, 70 So.2d 282 (friend); People v. Roe, 1922, 189 Cal. 548, 209 P. 560 (friend); Johnson v. Commonwealth, 1949, 311 Ky. 182, 223 S.W.2d 741 (brother); Reeves v. State, 1949, 153 Tex.Cr. 32, 217 S.W.2d 19 (fellow officer).

7. Lopez v. Surchia, 1952, 112 Cal.App.2d 314, 246 P.2d 111.

8. People v. Forte, 1915, 269 Ill. 505, 110 N.E. 47; Roberson v. Stokes, 1921, 181 N.C. 59, 106 S.E. 151; Downs v. Jackson, Ky.1910, 128 S.W. 339.

9. People v. Cook, 1878, 39 Mich. 236; State v. Young, 1908, 52 Or. 227, 96 P. 1067; Sexton v. Commonwealth, 1922, 193 Ky. 495, 236 S.W. 956; Webb v. Snow, 1942, 102 Utah 435, 132 P.2d 114.

10. Cases holding that the intervenor takes the risk are: People v. Young, 1962, 11 N.Y.2d 274, 229 N.Y.S.2d 1, 183 N.E.2d 319; Commonwealth v. Hounchell, 1939, 280 Ky. 217, 132 S.W.2d 921; Robinson v. City of Decatur, 1947, 32 Ala.App. 654, 29 So.2d 429; State v. Melton, 1891, 102 Mo. 683, 15 S.W. 139; State v. Cook, 1907, 78 S.C. 253, 59 S.E. 862.

Cases holding that the intervenor can act on reasonable appearances are: Sloan v. Pierce, 1906, 74 Kan. 65, 85 P. 812; State v. Harper, 1899, 149 Mo. 514, 51 S.W. 89; Warnack v. State, 1908, 3 Ga.App. 590, 60 S.E. 288; Mayhew v. State, 1912, 65 Tex.Cr. 290, 144 S.W. 229; Patterson v. Kuntz, La.App.1946, 28 So.2d 278; Second Restatement of Torts, § 76; Note, 1924, 8 Minn.L.Rev. 340.

ble mistake in intervening in behalf of the wrong person, it would seem that the minority view concerning criminal responsibility is greatly to be preferred, since the defendant was guilty of no fault. It does not follow that one who was victimized by the defendant while acting in self-defense, and who was in no way to blame for the deceptive appearances, should as between the two innocent parties be required to bear the loss. Obviously, the initial aggressor is liable, but the issue is which of the two innocent parties should shoulder the risk of the aggressor's insolvency.

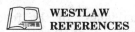 **WESTLAW REFERENCES**

Defense of Others
defense defend** protect! /s third /s privilege* % topic(110 203)
37k68
headnote(defense /2 another) % title(state people)
defense defending +5 another others % title(state people)

---

§ 21. Defense of Property

The privilege to defend the possession of property rests upon the same considerations of policy as that of self-defense.[1] The interest in peaceful possession and enjoyment justifies protection by self-help, in situations where there is usually no time to resort to the law. The limitations upon the privilege are much the same as in the case of self-defense: the force must be, or reasonably appear to be, necessary, and not excessive in view of the interest involved.

The interest to be protected is that of possession. The privilege may be exercised by anyone in possession of property who has, as against the invader, the better right to it.[2] It is the privilege to resist a trespass, by force which would otherwise amount to assault, battery or false imprisonment. It extends not only to the prevention of wrongful interference with the possession of chattels, and entry upon land, but also to the expulsion of those who have entered by right or permission whose right to remain has terminated.[3]

Apparent Necessity

As in the cases of self-defense or defense of another, the privilege to use force in defense of property does not always depend upon actual necessities. The defender may often act on the basis of reasonable appearances.[4] So, if the defendant reasonably believes that the plaintiff was about to intrude upon property, the fact that the plaintiff had no such intention will not cast the loss due to the innocent mistake on the defendant, if he had reasonable cause for believing as he did. However, as in self-defense, a reasonable argument can be made for the position that if the plaintiff was not negligent in creating the deceptive appearances and committed no other wrongful act that induced the defendant's mistake, the risk of loss should be placed on the defendant who inflicted the harm intentionally, albeit without moral fault. Quite often, the defendant's mistake has been to use force against an actual intruder who had a privilege to intrude. In such a case, the defendant acts at his peril in the sense that an erroneous belief, however reasonable, that the intruder did not have a privilege will not justify the use of force

---

§ 21

1. See also the cases as to abatement of a nuisance, infra, § 90.

2. Cole v. Rowen, 1891, 88 Mich. 219, 50 N.W. 138 (servant); Brendlin v. Beers, 1911, 144 App.Div. 403, 129 N.Y.S. 222 (janitor); Chew v. Gilliland, Tex.1965, 398 S.W.2d 98 (custodian); Moore v. Camden & Trenton Railway Co., 1907, 74 N.J.L. 498, 65 A. 1021 (wife of owner); Hoagland v. Forest Park Highlands Amusement Co., 1902, 170 Mo. 335, 70 S.W. 878 (finder).

3. Austin v. Metropolitan Life Insurance Co., 1919, 106 Wash. 371, 180 P. 134 (insurance office); Brookside-Pratt Mining Co. v. Booth, 1924, 211 Ala. 268, 100 So. 240 (merchant); Ramirez v. Chavez, 1951, 71 Ariz. 239, 226 P.2d 143 (bar); Yoder v. Yoder, 1913, 239 Pa. 12, 86 A. 523 (hotel).

4. Bunten v. Davis, 1926, 82 N.H. 304, 133 A. 16; Foster v. Shepherd, 1913, 258 Ill. 164, 101 N.E. 411; People v. Flanagan, 1881, 60 Cal. 2; Smith v. Delery, 1959, 238 La. 180, 114 So.2d 857.

against the intruder,[5] unless, perchance, the intruder intentionally or negligently caused the defendant to believe that he is not privileged.[6] Just as the defender of property acts at his peril in using force against someone who is actually privileged to intrude, so also the defender's privilege to use force against one who is not privileged to intrude is not affected by the mistaken and reasonable belief of the intruder that he had a privilege.[7] In effect, those who intrude upon property without a privilege must suffer the consequences of their mistake, and those who use force against an intruder possessing a privilege must suffer the consequences of their mistake, subject only to the qualification that this will not be so if the other party was culpably responsible for the mistake.

The use of force is not privileged when it is apparent that no immediate interference with the property is threatened,[8] or that all danger is past.[9] Ordinarily, the use of any force at all will be unreasonable unless the intruder has first been asked to desist. Blows are not justified where it is not clear that words alone would not be enough.[10] But a futile request is not required where the conduct of the intruder has indicated clearly that a request would be disregarded,[11] or where the intruder is proceeding with such violence that it is clear that a request could not be made safely or soon enough.[12]

Reasonable Force

The test to apply for the means that can be used against the person in defense of property is in general the same as that applicable in self-defense. As generally stated, it would be such means as reasonably appears necessary, although another expression sometimes used is "reasonable means," which seems preferable as a practical matter.

The reasonableness of the force used is usually a question of fact for the jury.[13] But as in the case of self-defense, the law has marked out certain limitations. The force used must be of a kind appropriate to the defense of the property.[14] A push in the right direction may be proper where a slap in the face is not,[15] and assault by a threat of force or violence may be proper where the battery itself would be excessive.[16] And, since the law has always placed a higher value upon human safety than upon mere rights in property, it is the accepted rule that there is no privilege to use any force calculated to cause death or serious bodily injury to repel the threat to land or chat-

---

5. Stuyvesant v. Wilcox, 1882, 92 Mich. 233, 52 N.W. 465; Arlowski v. Foglio, 1926, 105 Conn. 342, 135 A. 397; Second Restatement of Torts, § 77.

6. Leach v. Francis, 1868, 41 Vt. 670.

7. Second Restatement of Torts, § 78.

8. State v. Sorrentino, 1924, 31 Wyo. 129, 224 P. 420; Shea v. Cassidy, 1930, 257 Ill.App. 557; McAuley v. State, 1852, 3 G. Greene, Iowa, 435.

9. Hamilton v. Howard, 1930, 234 Ky. 321, 28 S.W.2d 7; Territory v. Drennan, 1868, 1 Mont. 41.

10. Tullay v. Reed, 1823, 1 C. & P. 6, 171 Eng.Rep. 1078; Chapell v. Schmidt, 1894, 104 Cal. 511, 38 P. 892; Emmons v. Quade, 1903, 176 Mo. 22, 75 S.W. 103; Miller v. McGuire, 1918, 202 Ala. 351, 80 So. 433; State v. Woodward, 1871, 50 N.H. 527.

11. Higgins v. Minaghan, 1891, 78 Wis. 602, 47 N.W. 941; State v. Steele, 1890, 106 N.C. 766, 11 S.E. 478.

12. State v. Cessna, 1915, 170 Iowa 726, 153 N.W. 194; Scribner v. Beach, 1847, 4 N.Y. (Denio) 448; Polkinghorn v. Wright, 1845, 8 Q.B. 197, 115 Eng.Rep. 849.

13. Hughes v. Babcock, 1944, 349 Pa. 475, 37 A.2d 551; Olesen v. Fader, 1915, 160 Wis. 473, 152 N.W. 290; Bunten v. Davis, 1926, 82 N.H. 304, 133 A. 16.

14. Collins v. Renison, 1754, Sayer 138, 96 Eng.Rep. 830 (inappropriate to overturn a ladder on which plaintiff was standing); Rowe v. Hawkins, 1858, 1 F. & F. 91, 175 Eng.Rep. 640 (force necessary to make plaintiff let go of bridle); Cunningham v. Reagan, Mo.1954, 273 S.W.2d 174 (battery not privileged where only in retaliation for insulting words).

15. Symalla v. Dusenka, 1939, 206 Minn. 280, 288 N.W. 385; Newman v. Southern Kraft Corp., La.App. 1940, 197 So. 197; Maddran v. Mullendore, 1955, 206 Md. 291, 111 A.2d 608.

16. State v. Yancey, 1876, 74 N.C. 244; Silas v. Bowen (D.S.C.1967) 277 F.Supp. 314 (shooting at the ground); cf. Daluiso v. Boone, 1968, 71 Cal.2d 484, 78 Cal.Rptr. 707, 455 P.2d 811.

tels,[17] unless there is also such a threat to the defendant's personal safety.[18]

Ambiguities permeate the concept, "calculated to cause serious bodily injury." It is not always used with consistent meaning, and this ambiguity leads to conflicting results when the means used by the defendant were not intended to cause death, but death or serious injury resulted. One view is that if the jury finds that the defendant did not intend death, or perhaps serious bodily injury, such as shooting in the direction of those suspected of attempted burglary, then the defendant is not liable unless he acted negligently or recklessly in exposing the intruder to serious bodily injury or death.[19] Since negligence and recklessness involve a weighing of interests, the mere fact that the means used exposed the intruder to an appreciable risk of death or serious bodily injury would not necessarily require a finding of negligence or recklessness; moreover, the issue would normally be for the jury to resolve. If, on the other hand, the rule is (and perhaps this is the majority view)[20] that the defendant is liable for using a means that involves an appreciable risk of serious injury, the law is taking the position that no such means can be regarded as justifiable. Normally, this can be answered as a matter of law. Another ambiguity relates to the concept "serious bodily injury." Any injury that creates a substantial risk of death or the protracted loss or impairment of the function of any bodily member or organ would commonly be regarded as serious bodily injury.[21] With these ambiguities in mind, the term "deadly means" will be used to describe the kind of means that one cannot use in the defense of property. Where the intruder is not proceeding with violence, the defendant may normally, in the first instance, use only the mildest of force, for which the old form of pleading had a phrase—"molliter manus imposuit"; he gently laid hands upon him.[22] But if the plaintiff resists, the defendant may use the force reasonably necessary to overcome his resistance and expel him,[23] and if in the process his own safety is threatened, he may defend himself, and even kill if necessary;[24] but in the first instance a mere trespass does not justify such an act. Even the tradition that a man's house is his castle, and that one may kill in defense of his dwelling, has given way in most jurisdictions[25] to the view that such force is not justified[26] unless the intrusion

---

17. McIlvoy v. Cockran, 1820, 9 Ky. (2 A.K. Marsh.) 271; Anderson v. Jenkins, 1954, 220 Miss. 145, 70 So.2d 535; Scheufele v. Newman, 1949, 187 Or. 263, 210 P.2d 573; Haworth v. Elliott, 1944, 67 Cal.App.2d 77, 153 P.2d 804; Commonwealth v. Emmons, 1945, 157 Pa. Super. 495, 43 A.2d 568.

Even assault with a deadly weapon, without battery, has been held to be excessive. People v. Doud, 1923, 223 Mich. 120, 193 N.W. 884; State v. Paxson, 1916, 6 Del. (Boyce) 249, 99 A. 46; Brown v. Martinez, 1961, 68 N.M. 271, 361 P.2d 152; Ross v. Michael, 1923, 246 Mass. 126, 140 N.E. 292.

The defendant, even when exercising reasonable force, is required to do so with reasonable care, and will be liable for any negligence which injures the plaintiff. Phillips v. Wilpers, 1869, 2 N.Y. (Lans.) 389.

18. Eldred v. Burns, 1947, 182 Or. 394, 182 P.2d 397, rehearing denied 182 Or. 394, 188 P.2d 154; Wade v. Gennaro, La.App.1942, 8 So.2d 561.

19. Foster v. Emery, Okl.1972, 495 P.2d 390; Bond v. Toriello, La.App.1972, 260 So.2d 727, application denied 262 La. 189, 262 So.2d 788.

20. Supra, this section, note 17.

21. Second Restatement of Torts, § 63, Comment b.

22. Weaver v. Bush, 1798, 8 Term Rep. 78, 101 Eng. Rep. 1276.

23. Coleman v. New York & New Haven Railroad Co., 1870, 106 Mass. 160; State v. Benson, 1959, 155 Me. 115, 151 A.2d 266; Penn v. Henderson, 1944, 174 Or. 1, 146 P.2d 760; Holley v. Kelley, Fla.1957, 91 So. 2d 862.

Considerable force may sometimes be used, as in Kent v. Southern Railway Co., 1936, 52 Ga.App. 731, 184 S.E. 638 (tear gas against strikers); State v. Goode, 1902, 130 N.C. 651, 41 S.E. 3 (indignant colored lady and the baseball bat). But the defendant will still be liable for the use of any force which does not reasonably appear to be necessary to overcome the resistance. Gosselin v. Silver, 1938, 301 Mass. 481, 17 N.E.2d 706.

24. Tipsword v. Potter, 1918, 31 Idaho 509, 174 P. 133; Eldred v. Burns, 1947, 182 Or. 394, 182 P.2d 397, 188 P.2d 154; McMurrey Corp. v. Yawn, Tex.Civ.App. 1940, 143 S.W.2d 664, error refused.

25. But see In re J.J. Hussey, Eng.1924, 18 Crim. App.Rep. 160.

26. Hamilton v. Howard, 1930, 234 Ky. 321, 28 S.W.2d 7; Hudgens v. State, 1933, 166 Tenn. 231, 60 S.W.2d 153; State v. Sorrentino, 1924, 31 Wyo. 129, 224

threatens the personal safety of the occupants.[27]

However, it should be said that state courts, in passing upon the tort liability of a defendant who has used deadly means to prevent intrusions upon property, including burglary and theft, have generally adopted the policy promulgated by their state legislatures concerning criminal responsibility. State legislatures have quite frequently sanctioned the use of deadly means to prevent the crimes of burglary and arson, and some have gone further in the direction of permitting the use of deadly means that often do not threaten bodily harm to anyone. It is quite understandable that a defendant present in a dwelling should be given a privilege to kill to prevent an entry into the dwelling when it appears that the entry is for the purpose of committing a crime. An element of personal danger is present. The same kind of immediacy of personal danger that is required as a basis for recognition of the self-defense privilege can be eliminated justifiably. However, in some states the privilege to use deadly means to prevent the escape of one who either has stolen property or has simply attempted to do so is granted. It should be apparent that the legislative policy adopted for criminal responsibility need not be followed in a tort action. However, punishing a defendant for the use of deadly means may be more justified than awarding damages to a thief or a burglar. The fact that the defendant ought to be punished for the use of a deadly weapon does not mean that the plaintiff, or his survivors, deserve to recover if death results.

In certain situations, there may be no privilege to use any force at all to expel an intruder. Just as the defendant may not kill a trespasser to eject him, he will not be privileged to put him out when he will be exposed to serious danger of physical harm. A tramp on a railway train may not be thrown off at forty miles an hour,[28] nor may a trespasser who is ill and unable to look out for himself be thrust out on a winter night,[29] unless his illness is of a contagious character which threatens the inmates of the house.[30] The necessities of the situation create a privilege to remain, which prevails over the vindication of the property right.[31]

Mechanical Devices

The defendant may not do indirectly what he could not do directly. The privilege to protect property by dangerous mechanical devices is no greater than that of defense by a personal act.[32] Barbed wire and spiked

---

P. 420, rehearing denied 31 Wyo. 499, 228 P. 283; Bradshaw v. Commonwealth, 1939, 174 Va. 391, 4 S.E.2d 752; Anderson v. Jenkins, 1954, 220 Miss. 145, 70 So.2d 535.

27. State v. Miller, 1966, 267 N.C. 409, 148 S.E.2d 279, appeal after remand 272 N.C. 243, 158 S.E.2d 47; Morrison v. State, 1963, 212 Tenn. 633, 371 S.W.2d 441; Nakashima v. Takase, 1935, 8 Cal.App.2d 35, 46 P.2d 1020; People v. Wilcox, 1927, 245 N.Y. 404, 157 N.E. 509; State v. Taylor, 1898, 143 Mo. 150, 44 S.W. 785.

Quite often this will be the case; but it is another matter entirely to say that, with a speedy remedy at law available in all jurisdictions, the occupant is justified in shooting an evicting landlord. See Notes, 1926, 25 Mich.L.Rev. 57; 1936, 9 So.Cal.L.Rev. 375.

28. Chesapeake & Ohio Railway Co. v. Ryan, 1919, 183 Ky. 428, 209 S.W. 538; Kobbe v. Chicago & North Western Railroad Co., 1928, 173 Minn. 79, 216 N.W. 543; Ansteth v. Buffalo R. Co., 1896, 145 N.Y. 210, 39 N.E. 708; Kansas City, Fort Scott & Gulf Railroad Co. v. Kelly, 1887, 36 Kan. 655, 14 P. 172; cf. Iaconio v. D'Angelo, 1928, 104 N.J.L. 506, 142 A. 46 (boy on automobile). But a verbal order to get off has been held to impose no liability where it was not accompanied by a show of force. Bjornquist v. Boston & Albany Railroad Co., 1904, 185 Mass. 130, 70 N.E. 53; Osalek v. Baltimore & Ohio Railroad Co., 1929, 295 Pa. 553, 145 A. 582; cf. Lo Castro v. Long Island Railroad Co., 1959, 6 N.Y.2d 470, 190 N.Y.S.2d 366, 160 N.E.2d 846.

29. Depue v. Flatau, 1907, 100 Minn. 299, 111 N.W. 1; Bradshaw v. Frazier, 1901, 113 Iowa 579, 85 N.W. 752; Waldrop v. Nashville, Chattanooga & St. Louis Railway Co., 1913, 183 Ala. 226, 62 So. 769; Adams v. Chicago Great Western Ry. Co., 1912, 156 Iowa 31, 135 N.W. 21. Cf. Feiges v. Racine Dry Goods Co., 1939, 231 Wis. 270, 285 N.W. 799. Also Dierkes v. Hauxhurst Land Co., 1911, 80 N.J.L. 369, 79 A. 361 (frightening trespasser over cliff with dogs); but cf. Miller v. Oscar Schmidt, Inc., 1924, 100 N.J.L. 324, 126 A. 309.

30. Tucker v. Burt, 1908, 152 Mich. 68, 115 N.W. 722.

31. See infra, § 24.

32. Bohlen and Burns, The Privilege to Protect Property by Dangerous Barriers and Mechanical Devices, 1926, 35 Yale L.J. 527; Hart, Injuries to Trespassers, 1931, 47 L.Q.Rev. 92, 101–105.

railings, which are not intended to cause serious injury, and carry their own warning by day or might reasonably be anticipated and guarded against by night, will ordinarily be privileged,[33] in the absence of some negligence in their location or construction.[34] But spring guns and other man-killing devices are not justifiable against a mere trespasser, or even a petty thief.[35] Since virtually all property, regardless of its value, can be safeguarded by insurance, the owner's economic interest in the use of deadly devices can be regarded as impermissible in all cases. A fundamental difference exists between the use of a deadly device to prevent burglarious entries of occupied dwellings and felonious entries of unoccupied buildings. The first difference involves an appreciable danger to life. The only difference between the use of a deadly mechanical device and the use of deadly means in person is that the device cannot make a prior request on the intruder to leave, and such a request would often be required before a defendant could use deadly means. So, undoubtedly, most courts would permit the use of deadly mechanical means to prevent intrusions of a general type that often involve appreciable danger to human life. But the use of deadly devices solely to protect property is highly questionable as a matter of sound policy. Even if a privilege is recognized to allow the use of deadly means by a person to prevent burglary, arson, and perhaps other felonious taking or destruction of property not involving any immediate danger to any person, that privilege exists, generally, only if no other reasonable way to prevent the intrusion is available and the intruder is first asked to leave. Moreover, using a deadly device, rather than personally directed deadly means, greatly augments the risk of killing or seriously injuring a non-intruder, or an intruder against whom such means cannot be purposely used.

There is some authority [36] that deadly devices may be utilized without liability if the intruder to whom the force is directed is the kind of intruder to whom one can personally direct deadly means. But the position adopted in the recent celebrated case of Katko v. Briney [37] would probably be the one more generally adopted, at least in tort litigation. In that case, the defendant installed a spring gun in an old, unoccupied residence for the purpose of preventing theft of household goods of no great value. The evidence that the defendant did not intend to kill or even seriously injure an intruder was considerable, but the evidence amply supported the finding that the means used involved a substantial risk of serious bodily injury and death. It is quite clear that the defendant was not the kind of intruder that would have entered an occupied dwelling or endangered human life to accomplish his objective. Since the means used involved a substantial risk of serious injury and, in fact, caused serious injury to the petty thief who broke in to steal some bottles, the majority held the defendant liable, not only for actual damages but for punitive damages as well. The

33. Quigley v. Clough, 1899, 173 Mass. 429, 53 N.E. 884; Kelly v. Bennett, 1890, 132 Pa. 218, 19 A. 69; Skaling v. Sheedy, 1924, 101 Conn. 545, 126 A. 721; Worthington v. Wade, 1891, 82 Tex. 26, 17 S.W. 520.

34. Hurd v. Lacy, 1890, 93 Ala. 427, 9 So. 378; Sisk v. Crump, 1887, 112 Ind. 504, 14 N.E. 381; cf. Kelly v. Bennett, 1890, 132 Pa. 218, 19 A. 69.

35. Bird v. Holbrook, 1828, 4 Bing. 628, 130 Eng. Rep. 911; State v. Childers, 1938, 133 Ohio St. 508, 14 N.E.2d 767; Starkey v. Dameron, 1933, 92 Colo. 420, 21 P.2d 1112, 22 P.2d 640; State v. Plumlee, 1933, 177 La. 687, 149 So. 425; State v. Beckham, 1924, 306 Mo. 566, 267 S.W. 817; Second Restatement of Torts, § 85. See Note, 1934, 18 Minn.L.Rev. 77.

36. Gray v. Combs, 1832, 7 Ky. (J.J. Marsh.) 478; Scheuermann v. Scharfenberg, 1909, 163 Ala. 337, 50 So. 335; Marquis v. Benfer, Tex.Civ.App.1957, 298 S.W.2d 601, refused n.r.e.; Pierce v. Commonwealth, 1923, 135 Va. 635, 115 S.E. 686; Second Restatement of Torts, § 85. In Allison v. Fiscus, 1951, 156 Ohio St. 120, 100 N.E.2d 237, it was held that the unreasonableness of setting a dynamite trap merely to frighten one breaking and entering on industrial premises was for the jury. As to shooting a burglar when the landowner is present in person, see supra, p. 134.

37. Iowa 1971, 183 N.W.2d 657. See Comments, 1972, 24 S.C.L.Rev. 133; and Palmer, The Iowa Spring Gun Case: A Study in American Gothic, 1971, 56 Ia.L. Rev. 1219. See, also, Posner, Killing and Wounding to Protect a Property Interest, 1971, 14 I.L. & Eco. 201; Annotation, 1973, 47 A.L.R.3d 646.

dissent took the position that if the defendant did not intend death or serious injury, there should be liability only if the defendant was negligent in the use of the device, and that negligence under the circumstances was for the jury to decide. This in reality means that if the jury concluded that the defendant did not intend serious injury while acting reasonably, no liability would attach. The difference between the positions is vast because juries might ordinarily conclude that the defendant acted just as any reasonable person who had been subjected to a series of petty thefts would have acted. As the dissent suggested, the most questionable part of the court's holding is awarding of punitive damages to the thief. The fact that the defendant ought to be punished does not mean that the plaintiff, who was guilty of criminal misconduct in the same episode, should be the recipient of the punitive fine imposed on the defendant.

In those states recognizing a privilege to use deadly means, the possibilities are several regarding the liability of the privileged user of deadly devices when injury is inflicted on someone other than the kind of person intended, against whom such means would be privileged. Probably the preferable position is that the defendant uses the device at his peril, and is subject to liability if injury is inflicted on the wrong person.[38] The commonly taken position is that liability attaches if and only if the defendant was negligent in subjecting third persons to harm.[39] Finally it has been held that the use of the device should be regarded as privileged if the defendant, had he been present, could have reasonably believed that the plaintiff was the kind of intruder whose intrusion was preventable by deadly means.[40] This last view adopts an artificial test and gives to the defendant much greater latitude in the use of deadly devices than he would have, if he were present, since he might not have believed that the intrusion could be responded to with deadly means and in all probability he would have requested the intruder to desist.

Although few cases have considered the question, and it is somewhat complicated by statutes, as well as by the common law rule of strict liability for keeping dangerous animals,[41] it would seem that a vicious watchdog is to be classed with a spring gun, and that the owner will be liable if he leaves him at large[42] to attack trespassers,[43] at least where he would not be privileged to call the dog to his assistance if he were present himself.[44]

Destruction of Property in Defense of Property

The privilege to harm or destroy property, including killing another's animals, in order to protect and defend property is clearly recognized.[45] Perhaps the generally accepted view is that one cannot use means likely to cause more harm than reasonably appears to be necessary, subject to the further qualification that the action must not be unreasonable. The conduct of the defendant in preventing the harm would be unreasonable if a reasonable person would not so act because the magnitude of the harm that would likely result from the action outweighed the benefits of the action.

---

38. Johnson v. Patterson, 1840, 14 Conn. 1; State v. Childers, 1938, 133 Ohio St. 508, 14 N.E.2d 767; Bruister v. Haney, 1958, 233 Miss. 527, 102 So.2d 806; Second Restatement of Torts, § 85.

39. Annot., 47 A.L.R.3d 646.

40. Marquis v. Benfer, Tex.Civ.App.1957, 298 S.W.2d 601, refused n.r.e.

41. See infra, § 76.

42. Otherwise if the dog is properly chained, and kept only for warning. Woodbridge v. Marks, 1897, 17 App.Div. 139, 45 N.Y.S. 156.

43. Loomis v. Terry, 1837, 17 N.Y. (Wend.) 496; Conway v. Grant, 1891, 88 Ga. 40, 13 S.E. 803; Brewer v. Furtwangler, 1933, 171 Wash. 617, 18 P.2d 837; Gerulis v. Lunecki, 1936, 284 Ill.App. 44, 1 N.E.2d 440.

44. See Woolf v. Chalker, 1862, 31 Conn. 121. Cf. Ryan v. Marren, 1914, 216 Mass. 556, 104 N.E. 353.

45. As to property other than trespassing animals, see Louisville & Nashville Railroad Co. v. Joullian, 1917, 116 Miss. 40, 76 So. 769; McKeesport Sawmill Co. v. Pennsylvania Co., C.C.Pa.1903, 122 F. 184; Berry v. Carle, 1825, 3 Me. (Green) 269; Note, 1918, 27 Yale L.J. 569.

The privilege to kill a trespassing dog in order to save property is governed by these rules. Although the dog need not be in the very act of killing the defendant's hens,[46] it has been held not reasonable to shoot the dog if there is any other reasonably available means of defense.[47] And even where there is none, the killing may not be privileged where it is obvious at the time that the value of the dog, considered with other circumstances,[48] is far in excess of the damage threatened.[49]

It is quite likely that some courts would simply say that the defendant is privileged to destroy property to protect property by acting reasonably under the circumstances. Under this kind of simple rule, two relevant factors, neither of which would be conclusive, are the apparent necessity for doing the damage and the weighing of the harm likely to be done against the benefits of the action. There is much to be said for this simpler rule, with only one issue submitted to the jury—that being whether or not the defendant acted as a reasonable person would have acted in the same situation.

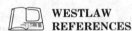 **WESTLAW REFERENCES**

Apparent Necessity

defense defend /10 property /p privilege % topic(110)

selfhelp selfdefense selfprotect! /s property & topic (torts negligence trespass assault)

Reasonable Force

defense /s property /p reasonable /s force % title(state people)

Mechanical Devices

protect! defense /p property /p "spring gun" & court(ia)

Destruction of Property in Defense of Property

sh 203 p2d 982

---

§ 22. Recapture of Chattels

The privilege of an owner dispossessed of his chattel to recapture it by force against the person differs from that of defending his possession in the first instance,[1] in that the owner is no longer maintaining the status quo and defending an existing peaceable state of affairs, but is himself an aggressor seeking to disturb the possession of another. Nevertheless, to a limited extent, the privilege has been recognized. It had its origin in cases where there was a "momentary interruption of possession," so that it was not difficult to regard the owner as still defending his original possession against one who had not got clean away.[2] Its survival, and extension to interference with the established possession of another, has been due to the recognized necessity of a speedy remedy where legal process is slow and cumbersome, and likely to be ineffective because it cannot operate in time, or cannot compel the

---

46. Hull v. Scruggs, 1941, 191 Miss. 66, 2 So.2d 543; McChesney v. Wilson, 1903, 132 Mich. 252, 93 N.W. 627; Aldrich v. Wright, 1873, 53 N.H. 398; Fisher v. Badger, 1902, 95 Mo.App. 289, 69 N.W. 26; Helsel v. Fletcher, 1924, 98 Okl. 285, 225 P. 514; cf. Brill v. Flagler, 1840, 23 N.Y. (Wend.) 354. The privilege is of course all the clearer if the dog is caught in the act. Granier v. Chagnon, 1949, 122 Mont. 327, 203 P.2d 982.

47. Leonard v. Wilkins, 1812, 9 N.Y. (Johns.) 233; Livermore v. Batchelder, 1886, 141 Mass. 179, 5 N.E. 275; Johnson v. Patterson, 1840, 14 Conn. 1; State v. Dickens, 1939, 215 N.C. 303, 1 S.E.2d 837. Thus, past depredations do not justify killing the animal. Clark v. Keliher, 1870, 107 Mass. 406 (see the poem on this case by Austin A. Martin in 1889, 1 Green Bag 292); Wells v. Head, 1831, 4 C. & P. 568, 172 Eng.Rep. 828; Brent v. Kimbell, 1871, 60 Ill. 211.

48. "* * * the value of the animal doing the mischief, the disturbance and mischief likely to be wrought, the probability of less severe measures being

successful, and the necessity for immediate action, are all elements to be considered in reaching a conclusion." Lipe v. Blackwelder, 1886, 25 Ill.App. 119; Kershaw v. McKown, 1916, 196 Ala. 123, 72 So. 47; see Nesbett v. Wilbur, 1900, 177 Mass. 200, 58 N.E. 586; O'Leary v. Wangensteen, 1928, 175 Minn. 368, 221 N.W. 430; Skog v. King, 1934, 214 Wis. 591, 254 N.W. 354.

49. Anderson v. Smith, 1880, 7 Ill.App. 354; Ex parte Minor, 1919, 203 Ala. 481, 83 So. 475; Johnston v. Wilson, 1924, 32 Ga.App. 348, 123 S.E. 222.

§ 22

1. See supra, § 21.

2. Commonwealth v. Donahue, 1889, 148 Mass. 529, 20 N.E. 171; Winter v. Atkinson, 1900, 92 Ill.App. 162; Hamilton v. Arnold, 1898, 116 Mich. 684, 75 N.W. 133; Wright v. Southern Express Co., C.C.Tenn.1897, 80 F. 85; Donnell v. Great Atlantic & Pacific Tea Co., 1934, 229 Ala. 320, 156 So. 844.

specific return of the chattel.³ One consequence, however, of the fact that the defendant is here the aggressor is that he is required to take his chances on being right as to the facts which he believes to give him the privilege; and the loss due to any mistake, however reasonable, must fall upon the one who makes it.⁴

For obvious reasons, in the interest of the preservation of order, the privilege has been restricted to those extreme cases where the emergency justifies the risk of a breach of the peace. It is properly exercised when there has been a wrongful dispossession of the property by force or fraud, and prompt action to retake it. The "momentary interruption" was extended later to situations where the wrongdoer had made his escape with the chattel, but the owner was in "fresh pursuit." ⁵ The meaning of "fresh pursuit" apparently never has been defined by any court; but it seems fairly clear that it is limited to prompt discovery of the dispossession, and prompt and persistent efforts to recover the chattel thereafter.⁶ Any undue lapse of time during which it may be said that the pursuit has come to a halt will mean that the owner no longer is privileged to fight himself back into possession, but must resort to the law.⁷ It seems quite likely that the advent of the automobile and the airplane must affect rules which developed in the days when the fastest possible pursuit was on a horse; but there are no modern cases which have considered the question.

There is the further limitation that the force used must be reasonable under the circumstances, and there will be liability for any excess. As in the case of one defending his possession, it is not reasonable to use any force calculated to inflict serious bodily harm to protect the property interest.⁸ But there is no privilege on the part of the wrongdoer to resist, and if he does, the owner may use any force required to defend his own person.⁹ Ordinarily, of course, a resort to any force at all will not be justified until a demand has been made for the return of the property.¹⁰

The privilege does not exist unless possession is taken wrongfully from the defendant.¹¹ Any wrongful taking without a

---

3. Branston, The Forcible Recaption of Chattels, 1918, 28 L.Q.Rev. 262; Notes, 1935, 19 Minn.L.Rev. 602; 1945, 34 Ky.L.J. 65.

4. Dixon v. Harrison Naval Stores, 1926, 143 Miss. 638, 109 So. 605; Dunlevy v. Wolferman, 1904, 106 Mo.App. 46, 79 S.W. 1165; S.H. Kress & Co. v. Musgrove, 1929, 153 Va. 348, 149 S.E. 453; Binder v. General Motors Acceptance Corp., 1943, 222 N.C. 512, 23 S.E.2d 894; see Estes v. Brewster Cigar Co., 1930, 156 Wash. 465, 287 P. 36; Second Restatement of Torts, § 100, Comment *d* (adding "unless the mistake was induced by the other.")

In this respect the privilege differs from that of defending possession, supra, Sec. 21.

5. State v. Elliot, 1841, 11 N.H. 540 (100 rods); Hodgeden v. Hubbard, 1846, 18 Vt. 504 (several miles); State v. Dooley, 1894, 121 Mo. 591, 26 S.W. 558; Spelina v. Sporry, 1935, 279 Ill.App. 376; McLean v. Colf, 1918, 179 Cal. 237, 176 P. 169.

6. Second Restatement of Torts, § 103. See also the definition in § 5 of the Uniform Act on the Fresh Pursuit of Criminals, drafted by the Interstate Commission on Crime, and passed to date in rather more than half of the states: "Fresh pursuit as used herein shall not necessarily imply instant pursuit, but pursuit without unreasonable delay."

7. Bobb v. Bosworth, 1808, 16 Ky. 81; Barr v. Post, 1898, 56 Neb. 698, 77 N.W. 123. Whether, even then, the owner may not act to prevent destruction of the chattel, or its removal from the jurisdiction, has not been determined. See Second Restatement of Torts, § 100, Caveat.

Some reasonable leeway is certainly permitted. Cf. People v. Pool, 1865, 27 Cal. 572 (pursuit of felons three or four hours after felony committed); White v. State, 1892, 70 Miss. 253, 11 So. 632 (felony at night, pursuit on discovery next morning).

8. Spelina v. Sporry, 1935, 279 Ill.App. 376; Carter v. Sutherland, 1884, 52 Mich. 597, 18 N.W. 375; Wingate v. Bunton, 1916, 193 Mo.App. 470, 186 S.W. 32; McLean v. Colf, 1918, 179 Cal. 237, 176 P. 169; Second Restatement of Torts, § 106. Use of a deadly weapon in a non-deadly manner may, however, be reasonable. State v. Metcalfe, 1927, 203 Iowa 155, 212 N.W. 382.

9. Gyre v. Culver, 1867, 47 Barb. N.Y. 592; Hodgeden v. Hubbard, 1846, 18 Vt. 504; Hamilton v. Barker, 1898, 116 Mich. 684, 75 N.W. 133; Curlee v. Scales, 1931, 200 N.C. 612, 158 S.E. 89.

10. Dyk v. De Young, 1889, 35 Ill.App. 138, affirmed 133 Ill. 82, 24 N.E. 520. But demand should not be required where it reasonably appears that it will be dangerous. Second Restatement of Torts, § 104.

11. Watson v. Rheinderknecht, 1901, 82 Minn. 235, 84 N.W. 798; Monson v. Lewis, 1905, 123 Wis. 583, 101 N.W. 1094; Ryerson v. Carter, 1919, 92 N.J.L. 363, 105 A. 723.

claim of right, such as theft, will suffice. Any wrongful and forcible taking, even under claim of right,[12] will also suffice. But the courts have extended the privilege beyond this, and have recognized it where the goods were obtained by fraud.[13] The owner is permitted to rescind his consent, by much the same anomalous theory which is found in actions for conversion,[14] and recover the property by his own act. The same rule is applied where the owner is induced by fraud to give temporary custody of the chattel for some particular purpose, and the wrongdoer is proceeding to make off with it.[15] It would seem that force may be used against any third person who receives the goods with notice of the circumstances under which they were taken, but not against an innocent party.[16]

If the plaintiff has come into possession rightfully in the first instance, no force may be used against him.[17] A defendant who has consented, in the absence of fraud, to part with his possession, must look to his legal remedy to recover it.[18] The question frequently arises in connection with the conditional sale of chattels. It is generally agreed that when the buyer defaults, the seller may retake possession, provided that he can do so peaceably, and without violence,[19] but not otherwise, so that if he is obstructed by the buyer he is not privileged to commit assault and battery,[20] or to resort to fraud.[21] The majority of the courts have even held that any clause in the contract which gives the seller the right to use such force against the person as may be necessary is void as inviting a breach of the peace, and so contrary to the policy of the state.[22]

Entry upon Land to Remove Chattels

The courts have experienced some difficulty with the problems which arise where an entry upon the land of another is necessary in order to take property to which the defendant is entitled to immediate possession. It is not disputed that if the goods have come upon the land through the wrongful conduct of the landowner, a privilege to enter and recover them exists.[23] The same would proba-

12. See Heminway v. Heminway, 1890, 58 Conn. 443, 19 A. 766; Cox v. Klein, 1907, 149 Mich. 162, 112 N.W. 729.

13. Hodgeden v. Hubbard, 1846, 18 Vt. 504; Anderson v. State, 1872, 65 Tenn. (6 Baxt.) 608; Commonwealth v. Donahue, 1889, 148 Mass. 529, 20 N.E. 171.

14. See supra, § 15.

15. Baldwin v. Hayden, 1827, 6 Conn. 453; Commonwealth v. Donahue, 1889, 148 Mass. 529, 20 N.E. 171; see Commonwealth v. Lynn, 1877, 123 Mass. 218.

16. See Branston, The Forcible Recaption of Chattels, 1912, 28 L.Q.Rev. 262, 266; Pollock, Law of Torts, 15th Ed. 1951, 293; Second Restatement of Torts, § 101(2)(b).

17. Bowman v. Brown, 1882, 55 Vt. 184; Shellabarger v. Morris, 1905, 115 Mo.App. 566, 91 S.W. 1005; Sabre v. Mott, C.C.Vt.1898, 88 F. 780, error dismissed 38 C.C.A. 696, 97 F. 985; Rohr v. Riedel, 1922, 112 Kan. 130, 210 P. 644.

18. Rogers v. Kabakoff, 1947, 81 Cal.App.2d 487, 184 P.2d 312; Kirby v. Foster, 1891, 17 R.I. 437, 22 A. 1111; Watson v. Rheinderknecht, 1901, 82 Minn. 235, 84 N.W. 798; Ryerson v. Carter, 1919, 92 N.J.L. 363, 105 A. 723, affirmed 1920, 93 N.J.L. 477, 108 A. 927; Monson v. Lewis, 1905, 123 Wis. 583, 101 N.W. 1094.

19. Blackford v. Neaves, 1922, 23 Ariz. 501, 205 P. 587; Westerman v. Oregon Automobile Credit Corp., 1942, 168 Or. 216, 122 P.2d 435; First National Bank & Trust Co. of Muskogee v. Winter, 1936, 176 Okl. 400, 55 P.2d 1029; Commonwealth v. Larson, 1932, 242 Ky. 317, 46 S.W.2d 82. If the seller obtains possession peaceably, he may then defend it with reasonable force against the buyer's efforts to retake it. Biggs v. Seufferlein, 1914, 164 Iowa 241, 145 N.W. 507.

20. Kensinger Acceptance Corp. v. Davis, 1954, 223 Ark. 942, 269 S.W.2d 792; Roberts v. Speck, 1932, 169 Wash. 613, 14 P.2d 33; Deevy v. Tassi, 1942, 21 Cal.2d 109, 130 P.2d 389; Lamb v. Woodry, 1936, 154 Or. 30, 58 P.2d 1257; Stowers Furniture Co. v. Brake, 1908, 158 Ala. 639, 48 So. 89.

21. Stallworth v. Doss, 1967, 280 Ala. 409, 194 So.2d 566; Barham v. Standridge, 1941, 201 Ark. 1143, 148 S.W.2d 648.

22. Fredericksen v. Singer Manufacturing Co., 1888, 38 Minn. 356, 37 N.W. 453; Abel v. M.H. Pickering Co., 1914, 58 Pa.Super. 439; Singer Sewing Machine Co. v. Phipps, 1911, 49 Ind.App. 116, 94 N.E. 793; Geissler v. Geissler, 1917, 96 Wash. 150, 164 P.2d 746, remittitur modified 96 Wn.2d 150, 166 P.2d 1119; Girard v. Anderson, 1934, 219 Iowa 142, 257 N.W. 400.

Contra: Lambert v. Robinson, 1894, 162 Mass. 34, 37 N.E. 753; W.T. Walker Furniture Co. v. Dyson, 1908, 32 App.D.C. 90. See Notes, 1935, 19 Minn.L.Rev. 602; 1933, 31 Mich.L.Rev. 987.

23. Blades v. Higgs, 1861, 10 C.B.,N.S., 713, 142 Eng.Rep. 634; Patrick v. Colerick, 1838, 3 M. & W. 483, 150 Eng.Rep. 1235; Richardson v. Anthony, 1840, 12

bly be true in the case of a wrongful taking, by a third person, of which the landowner has knowledge.[24] The entry must of course be made at a reasonable time, and in a reasonable manner, and ordinarily a demand for the surrender of the chattel must first be made.[25] It has been held that "fresh pursuit" is not necessary to justify the trespass.[26] Reasonable amounts of damage may be done, even to the extent of breaking down a fence or a door,[27] but any violence against the person of the landowner will not be justified,[28] unless resistance by the landowner threatens the personal safety of the defendant[29] or a wrongful taking which justifies the use of force against the person to recapture has occurred. The privilege is complete, and, so long as only reasonable force is used, the defendant is not liable for any damage he may do.[30]

Where the goods have come upon the land through some force of nature, such as a flood, the privilege of entry is recognized;[31] and it would seem that it should exist also where they have been placed there by a third person, either without the consent of the landowner, or with his consent but without any knowledge that they are stolen goods.[32] But in such cases, the privilege resembles that of necessity,[33] and since the plaintiff is not a wrongdoer, it seems fair to require the defendant to make good any actual damage he may do in the course of entry, if he chooses to resort to self-help instead of the law.[34]

If the chattel has come upon the land through the fault of the defendant, or with his consent, he has no privilege to enter.[35] Having put the goods where they are, he has no remedy to recover them except legal process. A conditional seller of goods may acquire, by a clause in the contract, an irrevocable license to enter the buyer's premises upon his default, and remove the property,[36]

Vt. 273; Arlowski v. Foglio, 1926, 105 Conn. 342, 135 A. 397; Wheelden v. Lowell, 1862, 50 Me. 499 (fraud).

24. See McLeod v. Jones, 1870, 105 Mass. 403; Richardson v. Anthony, 1840, 12 Vt. 273.

25. See Chambers v. Bedell, Pa.1841, 2 Watts & S. 225; Richardson v. Anthony, 1840, 12 Vt. 273; Second Restatement of Torts, § 198, Comment *d*. Contra, Salisbury v. Green, 1892, 17 R.I. 758, 24 A. 787.

26. Cunningham v. Yeomans, 1868, 7 N.S.W. 149. But see Salisbury v. Green, 1892, 17 R.I. 758, 24 A. 787.

27. Wheelden v. Lowell, 1862, 50 Me. 499; Hamilton v. Calder, 1883, 23 N.B. 373. A felonious taking will justify even breaking into a dwelling house. Madden v. Brown, 1896, 8 App.Div. 454, 40 N.Y.S. 714.

28. Barnes v. Martin, 1862, 15 Wis. 240; Huppert v. Morrison, 1870, 27 Wis. 365; cf. Churchill v. Hulbert, 1872, 110 Mass. 42.

29. Cf. Arlowski v. Foglio, 1926, 105 Conn. 342, 135 A. 397; Madden v. Brown, 1896, 8 App.Div. 454, 40 N.Y.S. 714.

30. Patrick v. Colerick, 1838, 3 M. & W. 483, 150 Eng.Rep. 1235; Wheelden v. Lowell, 1862, 50 Me. 499; Robson v. Jones, S.C.1830, 2 Bailey 4.

31. Carter v. Thurston, 1877, 58 N.H. 104; Polebitzke v. John Week Lumber Co., 1921, 173 Wis. 509, 181 N.W. 730; Pierce v. Finerty, 1910, 76 N.H. 38, 76 A. 194; Stuyvesant v. Wilcox, 1892, 92 Mich. 233, 52 N.W. 465. Cf. Shehyn v. United States, D.C.App.1969, 256 A.2d 404 (retrieving stray cat).

32. Hamilton v. Calder, 1883, 23 N.B. 373; Chapman v. Thumblethorpe, 1595, 1 Cro.Eliz. 329, 78 Eng.Rep. 579; Cunningham v. Yeomans, 1868, 7 N.S.W. 149; Salisbury v. Green, 1892, 17 R.I. 758, 24 A. 787; Richardson v. Anthony, 1840, 12 Vt. 273; Second Restatement of Torts, § 198, Comment *a*. Contra: Chess v. Kelly, Ind.1834, 3 Blackf., 438; Roach v. Damron, 1841, 21 Tenn. 425, 2 Humph. 425.

33. Infra, § 24.

34. Sheldon v. Sherman, 1870, 42 N.Y. 484. See also Anthony v. Haney, 1832, 8 Bing. 186, 131 Eng.Rep. 372; Carter v. Thurston, 1877, 58 N.H. 104; Maulsby v. Cook, 1925, 134 Wash. 133, 235 P. 23; Polebitzke v. John Week Lumber Co., 1921, 173 Wis. 509, 181 N.W. 730; Second Restatement of Torts, § 198, Comment *k*. See Bohlen, Incomplete Privilege to Inflict Intentional Invasions of Interests of Property and Personality, 1925, 39 Harv.L.Rev. 307.

35. Newkirk v. Sabler, N.Y.1850, 9 Barb. 652; Roach v. Damron, 1841, 21 Tenn. 425, 2 Humph. 425; Crocker v. Carson, 1851, 33 Me. 436; Ryerson v. Carter, 1919, 92 N.J.L. 363, 105 A. 723, affirmed, 1920, 93 N.J.L. 477, 108 A. 927; see Pierce v. Finerty, 1911, 76 N.H. 38, 76 A. 194, 79 A. 23; McGill v. Holman, 1922, 208 Ala. 9, 93 So. 848.

36. White Sewing Machine Co. v. Conner, 1901, 111 Ky. 827, 64 S.W. 841; North v. Williams, 1888, 120 Pa. 109, 13 A. 723. Such a license has been implied merely from the reservation of the right to repossess. Heath v. Randall, 1849, 58 Mass. (4 Cush.) 195; Proctor v. Tilton, 1889, 65 N.H. 3, 17 A. 638; Blackford v. Neaves, 1922, 23 Ariz. 501, 205 P. 587; C.I.T. Corp. v. Reeves, 1933, 112 Fla. 424, 150 So. 638. Cf. Plate v. Southern Bell Telephone & Telegraph Co., E.D.S.C.1951, 98 F.Supp. 355 (removing telephone); C.I.T. Corp. v.

but even such a provision gives him no right to do more than enter peaceably, at a reasonable time and in a reasonable manner,[37] and he will be liable if he uses any force to break in.[38] Even a clause in the contract authorizing him to do so has been held void as contrary to public policy.[39]

Temporary Detention for Investigation

If property is taken wrongfully, and the pursuit is fresh, the owner may use reasonable force to recover it which otherwise would amount to false imprisonment. At the same time, a private citizen has no legal authority to arrest upon the mere suspicion of a crime, and will be justified only if the crime has in fact been committed.[40] Still less has he any authority to imprison another for a debt,[41] or a civil claim for damages.[42]

It follows that a shopkeeper, who has good reason to believe that he has caught a customer in the act of stealing, of defrauding him of goods, or of sneaking out without paying for goods or services, is placed in a difficult position. He must either permit the suspected wrongdoer to walk out, and very probably say goodbye to both goods and payment, or run the risk that he will be liable for heavy damages for any detention. Many courts have held him liable for false imprisonment under an honest and reasonable mistake in such a case.[43] The problem is a major one, with theft losses ranging into many millions every year.[44]

Starting with a California case [45] in 1936, there have been a number of decisions which have permitted a businessman who reasonably [46] suspects a customer of theft,[47] or of

---

Short, 1938, 273 Ky. 190, 115 S.W.2d 899 (towing car out of garage). Contra: Kirkwood v. Hickman, 1955, 223 Miss. 372, 78 So.2d 351; Reed v. Shreveport Furniture Co., 1927, 7 La.Ann. 134.

37. Flaherty v. Ginsberg, 1907, 135 Iowa 743, 110 N.W. 1050; Drury v. Hervey, 1879, 126 Mass. 519.

38. Evers-Jordan Furniture Co. v. Hartzog, 1939, 237 Ala. 407, 187 So. 491; General Motors Acceptance Corp. v. Hicks, 1934, 189 Ark. 62, 70 S.W.2d 509; Dominick v. Rea, 1924, 226 Mich. 594, 198 N.W. 184; Wilson Motor Co. v. Dunn, 1928, 129 Okl. 211, 264 P. 194; Soulios v. Mills Novelty Co., 1941, 198 S.C. 355, 17 S.E.2d 869. See Note, 1952, 30 N.C.L.Rev. 149.

Comparatively slight force has been held to be tortious. Driver v. Commonwealth, Ky.1957, 299 S.W.2d 260 (breaking glass of car); Renaire Corp. v. Vaughn, Mun.App.D.C.1958, 142 A.2d 148 (breaking in); Lyda v. Cooper, 1933, 169 S.C. 451, 169 S.E. 236 (entering through unbroken window); M.J. Rose Co. v. Lowery, 1929, 33 Ohio App. 488, 169 N.E. 716 (opening lock with key); Commercial Credit Co. v. Spence, 1938, 185 Miss. 293, 184 So. 439 (breaking into car).

39. Girard v. Anderson, 1934, 219 Iowa 142, 257 N.W. 400; Stewart v. F.A. North Co., 1916, 65 Pa. Super. 195; Sturman v. Polito, 1936, 161 Misc. 536, 291 N.Y.S. 621.

40. See infra, § 26.

41. Gadsden General Hospital v. Hamilton, 1925, 212 Ala. 531, 105 So. 553 (hospital bill); Salisbury v. Poulson, 1918, 51 Utah 552, 172 P. 315 (dentist's bill); Bail v. Pennsylvania R. Co., 1927, 103 N.J.L. 213, 136 A. 425 (railway fare); Estes v. Brewster Cigar Co., 1930, 156 Wash. 465, 287 P. 36 (gambling debt); C.N. Robinson & Co. v. Greene, 1906, 148 Ala. 434, 43 So. 797.

42. Kearley v. Cowan, 1928, 217 Ala. 295, 116 So. 145 (automobile collision).

43. Zayre of Virginia, Inc. v. Gowdy, 1966, 207 Va. 47, 147 S.E.2d 710; Schantz v. Sears, Roebuck & Co., 1934, 12 N.J.Misc. 689, 174 A. 162, affirmed 1935, 115 N.J.L. 174, 178 A. 768; Fitscher v. Rollman & Sons Co., 1939, 31 Ohio App. 340, 343, 167 N.E. 469, 470; Mannaugh v. J.C. Penney Co., 1933, 61 S.D. 550, 250 N.W. 38; Great Atlantic & Pacific Tea Co. v. Smith, 1939, 281 Ky. 583, 136 S.W.2d 759.

44. It is discussed in Notes in 1953, 62 Yale L.J. 788; 1952, 46 Ill.L.Rev. 887, 47 Nw.U.L.Rev. 82; 1966, 17 S.C.L.Rev. 729.

45. Collyer v. S.H. Kress & Co., 1936, 5 Cal.2d 175, 54 P.2d 20, followed in Bettolo v. Safeway Stores, Inc., 1936, 11 Cal.App.2d 430, 54 P.2d 24. The California decisions are noted with approval in 1936, 25 Cal.L.Rev. 119; 1936, 10 So.Cal.L.Rev. 103; 1936, 21 Minn.L.Rev. 107; 1936, 84 U.Pa.L.Rev. 912.

46. Otherwise where there is no reasonable ground for suspicion, even though a statute authorizes detention if there is. J.C. Penney Co. v. Cox, 1963, 246 Miss. 1, 148 So.2d 679; Isaiah v. Great Atlantic & Pacific Tea Co., 1959, 111 Ohio App. 537, 174 N.E.2d 128.

47. Teel v. May Department Stores Co., 1941, 348 Mo. 696, 155 S.W.2d 74; Montgomery Ward & Co. v. Freeman, 4th Cir. 1952, 199 F.2d 720; Little Stores v. Isenberg, 1943, 26 Tenn.App. 357, 172 S.W.2d 13; Cohen v. Lit Brothers, 1950, 166 Pa.Super. 206, 70 A.2d 419; Kroger Grocery & Baking Co. v. Waller, 1945, 208 Ark. 1063, 189 S.W.2d 361.

Statutes in several states now have confirmed and regulated the privilege. See Isaiah v. Great Atlantic & Pacific Tea Co., 1959, 111 Ohio App. 537, 174 N.E.2d 128; Burnaman v. J.C. Penney Co., S.D.Tex.1960, 181 F.Supp. 633; Notes, 1958, 11 Okl.L.Rev. 102; 1965, 25 La.L.Rev. 956.

failure to pay,[48] to detain the suspected individual for a short time in order to investigate. This seems entirely reasonable, and justified by all ordinary usage among decent people: an honest person might be expected to remain voluntarily to assist in clearing up the matter. The privilege is, however, a very restricted one, confined to what is reasonably necessary for its limited purpose, of enabling the defendant to do what is possible on the spot to discover the facts. There will be liability if the detention is for a length of time beyond that which is reasonably necessary for such a short investigation,[49] or if the plaintiff is assaulted, insulted or bullied,[50] or public accusation is made against him,[51] or the privilege is exercised in an unreasonable manner;[52] and certainly if the defendant purports to make a definite arrest and take the plaintiff into legal custody,[53] or to use the detention to coerce payment,[54] or the signing of a confession.[55] In most of the decisions, the privilege apparently has been limited to detention on the defendant's premises, and does not extend to one who has left them.[56] But a Michigan decision[57] has recently allowed pursuit and detention where the plaintiff had left the store, but was in the immediate vicinity.

WESTLAW REFERENCES

Entry Upon Land to Remove Chattels
digest(immediate /s possession retak! /s property chattel* personalty /s land "real estate" realty)

Temporary Detention for Investigation
synopsis,digest("false imprisonment" /p shoplift!) % title(state people)

§ 23. Recapture of Land

The privilege of one to enter onto land, which one is entitled to the possession of, for the purpose of taking the land by self-help has been a source of longstanding confusion in the courts.[1] As in the case of recapture of chattels, it is necessary to distinguish between the privilege, if any, to use force against the person of the possessor, and the privilege, if any, to intrude upon the

---

The only recent case found which has denied the existence of the privilege is Zayre of Virginia, Inc. v. Gowdy, 1966, 207 Va. 47, 147 S.E.2d 710.

48. Standish v. Narragansett S.S. Co., 1873, 111 Mass. 512; Lynch v. Metropolitan Elevated Railway Co., 1882, 90 N.Y. 77; Jacques v. Childs Dining Hall, 1923, 244 Mass. 438, 138 N.E. 843. Cf. Cox v. Rhodes Avenue Hospital, 1916, 198 Ill.App. 82.

49. Jacques v. Childs Dining Hall, 1923, 244 Mass. 438, 138 N.E. 843 (half an hour); Herbrick v. Samardick & Co., 1960, 169 Neb. 833, 101 N.W.2d 488 (hour and a half); J.J. Newberry Co. v. Judd, 1935, 259 Ky. 309, 82 S.W.2d 359 (four or five hours); Little Stores v. Isenberg, 1943, 26 Tenn.App. 357, 172 S.W.2d 13 (after cashier stated plaintiff had paid).

50. W.T. Grant Co. v. Owens, 1928, 149 Va. 906, 141 S.E. 860; S.H. Kress & Co. v. Musgrove, 1929, 153 Va. 348, 149 S.E. 453; A. Harris & Co. v. Caldwell, Tex.Civ. App.1925, 276 S.W. 298, error dismissed; Moffatt v. Buffum's, Inc., 1937, 21 Cal.App.2d 371, 69 P.2d 424.

51. Chretien v. F.W. Woolworth Co., La.App.1964, 160 So.2d 854, writ refused 246 La. 75, 163 So.2d 356; Southwest Drug Stores of Mississippi, Inc. v. Garner, Miss.1967, 195 So.2d 837 (both under statute).

52. Lukas v. J.C. Penney Co., 1963, 233 Or. 345, 378 P.2d 717.

53. McLoughlin v. New York Edison Co., 1929, 252 N.Y. 202, 169 N.E. 277; Lindquist v. Friedman's, Inc., 1937, 366 Ill. 232, 8 N.E.2d 625; S.H. Kress & Co. v. Bradshaw, 1940, 186 Okl. 588, 99 P.2d 508; Moseley v. J.G. McCrory Co., 1926, 101 W.Va. 480, 133 S.E. 73; Martin v. Castner-Knott Dry Goods Co., 1944, 27 Tenn. App. 421, 181 S.W.2d 638.

54. Standish v. Narragansett S.S. Co., 1873, 111 Mass. 512; Lynch v. Metropolitan Elevated Railway Co., 1882, 90 N.Y. 77; Cox v. Rhodes Ave. Hospital, 1916, 198 Ill.App. 82; Sweeten v. Friedman, 1928, 9 La. App. 44, 118 So. 787.

55. Moffatt v. Buffums, Inc., 1937, 21 Cal.App.2d 371, 69 P.2d 424; Teel v. May Department Stores Co., 1941, 348 Mo. 696, 155 S.W.2d 74; W.T. Grant Co. v. Owens, 1928, 149 Va. 906, 141 S.E. 860. But a mere request to sign a statement is within the privilege. Collyer v. S.H. Kress & Co., 1936, 5 Cal.2d 175, 54 P.2d 20.

56. In McCrory Stores Corp. v. Stachell, 1925, 148 Md. 279, 129 A. 348, and Moseley v. J.G. McCrory Co., 1926, 101 W.Va. 480, 133 S.E. 73, detention on the street was held not to be privileged. In Simmons v. J.C. Penney Co., La.App.1966, 186 So.2d 358, the sidewalk in front of the store was held to be part of the premises. Cf. Montgomery Ward & Co. v. Freeman, 4th Cir. 1952, 199 F.2d 720; J.C. Penney Co. v. O'Daniell, 10th Cir. 1959, 263 F.2d 849.

57. Bonkowski v. Arlan's Department Store, 1968, 12 Mich.App. 88, 162 N.W.2d 347, reversed 1970, 383 Mich. 90, 174 N.W.2d 765.

§ 23

1. Annotation, 1966, 6 A.L.R.3d 177–223.

land itself to regain the possession one is entitled to. The whole subject continues to be of primary importance because it encompasses the privilege of a landlord to dispossess a hold-over tenant without legal process.

Perhaps a good deal of the confusion is a consequence of the adoption in 1381, under Richard II, of a statute [2] making a *forcible entry* to take possession a crime. It is clear that then, as now, the fact that conduct is a crime does not necessarily mean that it is a tort, because the conduct may not result in an invasion of an individual interest of the kind and in a manner that justifies a recovery for damages. So the fact that a forcible entry was committed ought not be determinative of the existence of a tort. Moreover, the fact that conduct is not a crime does not necessarily mean that the conduct did not result in an invasion of an individual interest of the kind and in a manner justifying a recovery for damages. So, the fact that an entry onto land was not a forcible one does not necessarily mean that locking a tenant out of an apartment or a place of business without notice ought not to be an actionable trespass. The obvious reason for making a forcible entry a crime is that a violent entry is calculated to lead to a serious brawl.

The Intrusion as an Actionable Trespass on Land.

At the outset, the English courts refused to treat this statute as a basis for a civil action of trespass to land on the ground that the plaintiff, having no right to possession, could sustain no legal injury when he was deprived of possession.[3] And most courts today deny any common law remedy for trespass [4] and permit recovery, if at all, only in the form of an action provided by statute.[5] Many states, in addition to enacting a statute similar to the criminal statute of Richard II, have provided a specific and speedy civil remedy of some kind when a forcible entry and dispossession is made.[6] The interpretation placed upon such statutes necessarily controls the rule to be adopted, and discussion of them is beyond the scope of this treatise.[7] So even if the entry was forcibly made in the sense that locks were broken, doors were knocked down, or damage of some other kind was done, no tort was committed because the intruder was entitled to the property which was damaged.

But there is some authority for the proposition that any intrusion that amounts to a forcible entry is trespassory.[8] One difficulty with this stance has to do with damages. Has the tenant suffered any harm justifying a recovery of damages? It has generally been held that the owner may await his op-

2. Statute of Forcible Entry, 5 Rich. II, c. 2.

3. Turner v. Maymott, 1823, 1 Bing. 158, 130 Eng. Rep. 64; Pollen v. Brewer, 1859, 7 C.B.,N.S., 371, 141 Eng.Rep. 860.

4. Sampson v. Henry, 1832, 13 Mass. (Pick.) 36; Weeks v. Sly, 1881, 61 N.H. 89; Levy v. McClintock, 1910, 141 Mo.App. 593, 125 S.W. 546; Gower v. Waters, 1926, 125 Me. 223, 132 A. 550; Southern Railway Co. v. Hayes, 1913, 183 Ala. 465, 62 So. 874.

Contra: Dustin v. Cowdry, 1851, 23 Vt. 631; Mosseller v. Deaver, 1890, 106 N.C. 494, 11 S.E. 529; Raniak v. Krukowski, 1924, 226 Mich. 695, 198 N.W. 190.

5. Moyer v. Gordon, 1887, 113 Ind. 282, 14 N.E.2d 476; Walker v. Chanslor, 1908, 153 Cal. 118, 94 P. 606; Wilson v. Campbell, 1907, 75 Kan. 159, 88 P. 548; Greeley v. Spratt, 1883, 19 Fla. 644.

Even here, a provision in the lease may give the landlord the privilege of entry by force, notwithstanding the statute. Princess Amusement Co. v. Smith, 1911, 174 Ala. 342, 56 So. 979; Goshen v. People, 1896, 22 Colo. 270, 44 P. 503, 504; Backus v. West, 1922, 104 Or. 129, 205 P. 533; cf. Clark v. Service Auto Co., 1926, 143 Miss. 602, 108 So. 704.

In all cases, however, he is liable for any force beyond that reasonably necessary. Gilbert v. Peck, 1912, 162 Cal. 54, 121 P. 315; Saros v. Avenue Theatre Co., 1912, 172 Mich. 238, 137 N.W. 559; Whitney v. Swett, 1850, 22 N.H. 10. Cf. Allison v. Hodo, 1951, 84 Ga. App. 790, 67 S.E.2d 606 (exposing furniture).

6. As to the New York legislation, which is more or less typical, see Wood v. Phillips, 1870, 43 N.Y. 152, 153; Fults v. Munro, 1911, 202 N.Y. 34, 95 N.E. 23.

7. See cases collected in 121 Am.St.Rep. 369; 45 A.L.R. 313; 141 A.L.R. 250. Also Sharpe, Forcible Trespass to Real Property, 1961, 39 N.C.L.Rev. 121.

8. See, Annotation, 1966, 6 A.L.R.3d 177–223; Dustin v. Cowdry, 1851, 23 Vt. 631; Mosseller v. Deaver, 1890, 106 N.C. 494, 11 S.E. 529; Raniak v. Krukowski, 1924, 226 Mich. 695, 198 N.W. 190.

portunity, and if he can regain possession peaceably, that is, without a forcible entry, he has a privilege to enter and may lawfully resist an attempt to oust him.[9] But what constitutes such "peaceable" entry, or entry without a breach of the peace, is very largely a question of the terms of the particular statute; and in some jurisdictions, unlocking a door,[10] or breaking it down,[11] is regarded as peaceable, since no force was used against the person, while in other jurisdictions, deception,[12] or a mere entry without the consent of the possessor,[13] is a violation. One trouble has been the acceptance of the notion that there must be a violation of the criminal statute in order to have a tort, but intentional interference with the possession of the tenant, resulting from difficulty over payment of his rent, could be regarded as an actionable interference with a legitimate interest of a tenant, even though the interference is not a crime. Thus, in Malcolm v. Little,[14] it was held that an apartment owner interfered with a tenant's right to maintain peaceable possession without disruption except by lawful process.

The Use of Force Against the Person and Interferences With Personal Property of Tenant

In the English case of Newton v. Harland[15] it was held that the privilege of entry of a landlord did not extend to the use of force upon the person of the occupant, and that an action for assault and battery would lie in such a case. In such a situation both a violation of the policy against forcible entries and an interference with the individual interest of the tenant in freedom from intentional invasions have occurred. This decision was overruled in 1920.[16] England adopted the position that the wrongful possessor was not entitled to damages, even though the owner committed a criminal assault to regain possession. Some courts in this country have adopted the English rule which permits the landlord or other owner to use such force as reasonably necessary to expel the occupant and his property.[17] However, the position taken in Newton v. Harland has received the greater support. So if force is used against a person by way of committing an assault or a battery, an actionable tort is committed.[18] Moreover, if an entry is forcibly made within the meaning of the statute, even though no force is used against the person, and even though an invasion of a legally protected interest of personal property of the tenant of a kind that would ordinarily constitute the tort of trespass or conversion takes place, the owner is liable.[19] No privilege to interfere intentionally with the person or the personal property of the tenant in a way that would ordinarily be actionable is recognized. The modern English view seems clearly unsound. In vir-

---

9. Winn v. State, 1892, 55 Ark. 360, 18 S.W. 375; Clarke v. Mylkes, 1921, 95 Vt. 460, 115 A. 492; Goldstein v. Webster, 1908, 7 Cal.App. 705, 95 P. 677; Mershon v. Williams, 1899, 62 N.J.L. 779, 42 A. 778; Richter v. Cordes, 1894, 100 Mich. 278, 58 N.W. 1110.

10. Smith v. Detroit Loan & Building Association, 1897, 115 Mich. 340, 73 N.W. 395.

11. Mussey v. Scott, 1859, 32 Vt. 82.

12. Pelavin v. Misner, 1928, 241 Mich. 209, 217 N.W. 36, affirmed 243 Mich. 516, 220 N.W. 665.

13. Casey v. Kitchens, 1917, 66 Okl. 169, 168 P. 812. Of course a violent entry is not peaceable. Thus where defendant, breathing curses and threats, "kicked down the door, entered the house, and fell over something, by which his leg was unfortunately broken, instead of his neck." State v. Jacobs, 1886, 94 N.C. 950.

14. Del.Sup.Ct. 1972, 295 A.2d 711.

15. 1840, 1 Man. & G. 644, 133 Eng.Rep. 490. Accord, Beddall v. Maitland, 1881, 17 Ch.Div. 174.

16. Hemmings v. Stoke Poges Golf Club, [1920] 1 K.B. 720. See Note, 1920, 36 L.Q.Rev. 205.

17. Low v. Elwell, 1876, 121 Mass. 309; Allen v. Keily, 1892, 17 R.I. 731, 24 A. 776; Shorter v. Shelton, 1945, 183 Va. 819, 33 S.E.2d 643; Gower v. Waters, 1926, 125 Me. 223, 132 A. 550; Vaughn v. Mesch, 1939, 107 Mont. 498, 87 P. 2d 177. See Annotation, 1966, 6 A.L.R.3d 177.

18. Daluiso v. Boone, 1969, 71 Cal.2d 484, 78 Cal. Rptr. 707, 455 P.2d 811; Lobdell v. Keene, 1901, 85 Minn. 90, 88 N.W. 426; Weatherly v. Manatt, 1919, 72 Okl. 138, 179 P. 470; Ray v. Dyer, Tex.Civ.App.1929, 20 S.W.2d 328, error dismissed; Mosseller v. Deaver, 1890, 106 N.C. 494, 11 S.E. 529; Second Restatement of Torts, § 185.

19. Whitney v. Brown, 1907, 75 Kan. 678, 90 P. 277; Sinclair v. Stanley, 1888, 69 Tex. 718, 7 S.W. 511.

tually all jurisdictions, a summary procedure exists by which the owner may recover possession by legal process, after only a brief delay. Few things are more likely to lead to a brawl than a landlord evicting his tenant by main force. Land cannot be sequestered or removed, and the public interest in preserving the peace would seem to justify the temporary inconvenience to the owner.

The Scrambling Possessor

The statutes of forcible entry protect only a plaintiff who is himself in peaceable possession of the property. A mere "scrambling" possession is not enough. A trespasser who ousts the owner acquires no possession which will entitle him to protection against an immediate forcible reentry, even though that reentry may involve assault and battery.[20] What is required is "something like acquiescence in the physical fact of his occupation on the part of the rightful owner."[21] Mere delay in taking effective action, even for a period of months, will not make the entry tortious, if the owner has not discovered his dispossession,[22] or has made persistent efforts to enter;[23] but acquiescence or toleration of the wrongful possession, even for a day,[24] may bring him within the statute.[25]

WESTLAW REFERENCES

privilege /3 enter /10 land*

The Intrusion as an Actionable Trespass on Land
digest(intrusion intrud! /s land realty "real estate" /p trespass)

20. Cox v. Cunningham, 1875, 77 Ill. 545; Taylor v. Adams, 1885, 58 Mich. 187, 24 N.W. 864; Hodgkins v. Price, 1882, 132 Mass. 196; O'Donohue v. Holmes, 1895, 107 Ala. 489, 18 So. 263. See cases collected in 121 Am.St.Rep. 384.

21. Pollock, Law of Torts, 13th Ed. 1929, 403.

22. Anderson v. Mills, 1882, 40 Ark. 192; Wray v. Taylor, 1876, 56 Ala. 188; Jones v. Czaza, 1935, 19 Tenn.App. 327, 86 S.W.2d 1096; Hoag v. Pierce, 1865, 28 Cal. 187; Benevides v. Lucio, Tex.Com.App.1929, 13 S.W.2d 71.

23. Bowers v. Cherokee Bob, 1873, 45 Cal. 495; Voll v. Butler, 1874, 49 Cal. 74 (nearly four years).

The Use of Force Against the Person and Interferences With Personal Property of Tenant
privilege /s retak! recaptur! reacquir! /s property chattel* personalty /s force

The Scrambling Possessor
wrongful /15 possession /p "forcible entry"

§ 24. Necessity

A defendant who acts to prevent a threatened injury from some force of nature, or some other independent cause not connected with the plaintiff, is said to be acting under necessity. The term is unfortunate, since it is broad enough to apply to any situation where it obviously is desirable to do something to avoid unpleasant consequences, including for example the cases of self-defense. The privilege considered here is in fact closely related to that of self-defense. But there is the important difference that the plaintiff is not an aggressor, or even apparently a wrongdoer, and that the defendant, instead of protecting himself against a danger created by the plaintiff, is injuring an innocent person in order to avoid a danger from another source. It follows that the plaintiff's interest has correspondingly greater weight in the scale, and the defendant's privilege may be limited accordingly.[1]

The privilege of necessity, whose basis has been said to be "a mixture of charity, the maintenance of the public good and self-protection,"[2] has been recognized in a comparatively small number of cases which have dealt with the problem. It appeared very early in a decision permitting the Crown to enter private land and dig for saltpeter to

24. Browne v. Dawson, 1840, 12 Ad. & El. 624, 113 Eng.Rep. 950.

25. Schwinn v. Perkins, 1910, 79 N.J.L. 515, 78 A. 19.

§ 24

1. Bohlen, Incomplete Privilege to Inflict Intentional Invasions of Interests of Property and Personality, 1926, 39 Harv.L.Rev. 307; Williams, The Defence of Necessity, [1953] Curr.Leg.Prob. 216.

2. Winfield, Law of Torts, 1937, 62.

make gunpowder,³ and one allowing goods to be jettisoned from a boat during a storm in order to save the passengers.⁴ Later cases permitted a traveler on a public highway to turn out to avoid a temporary obstruction, and pass over the adjoining land.⁵ But the privilege was not recognized where the way was a private one, and the interest in having it open did not extend to the public.⁶

Out of these early decisions, two lines of cases have developed involving so-called "public" and "private" necessity. Where the danger affects the entire community, or so many people that the public interest is involved,⁷ that interest serves as a complete justification to the defendant who acts to avert the peril to all. Thus, one who dynamites a house to stop the spread of a conflagration that threatens a town,⁸ or shoots a mad dog in the street,⁹ or burns clothing infected with smallpox germs,¹⁰ or in time of war, destroys property which should not be allowed to fall into the hands of the enemy,¹¹ is not liable to the owner, so long as the emergency is great enough, and he has acted reasonably under the circumstances.¹² This notion does not require the "champion of the public" to pay for the general salvation out of his own pocket. The number of persons who must be endangered in order to create a public necessity has not been determined by the courts. It would seem that the moral obligation upon the group affected to make compensation in such a case should be recognized by the law,¹³ but recovery usually has been denied.¹⁴

Thus, the position is taken in the Restatement of Torts that one has a complete privilege to destroy, damage, or use real or personal property if the actor reasonably believes it to be necessary to avert an immi-

---

3. King's Prerogative in Saltpetre, 1607, 12 Co.Rep. 12, 77 Eng.Rep. 1294. Even earlier is Maleverer v. Spinke, 1538, 1 Dyer 35b, 73 Eng.Rep. 79.

4. Mouse's Case, 1609, 12 Co.Rep. 63, 77 Eng.Rep. 1341.

5. Taylor v. Whitehead, 1781, 2 Dougl. 745, 99 Eng. Rep. 475; Campbell v. Race, 1851, 61 Mass. (7 Cush.) 408; Morey v. Fitzgerald, 1884, 56 Vt. 487; Shriver v. Marion County Court, 1910, 66 W.Va. 685, 66 S.E. 1062. Cf. Chicago & Alton Railroad Co. v. Mayer, 1904, 112 Ill.App. 149 (defendant blocking highway); Dodwell v. Missouri Pacific Railroad Co., Mo.1964, 384 S.W.2d 643 (same).

6. Williams v. Safford, 1849, 7 N.Y. (Barb.) 309; Bullard v. Harrison, 1815, 4 M. & S. 387, 105 Eng.Rep. 877. But cf. Haley v. Colcord, 1879, 59 N.H. 7; Kent v. Judkins, 1865, 53 Me. 160.

7. The act must be for the purpose of protecting the public. A private benefit to the actor is not sufficient. Newcomb v. Tisdale, 1881, 62 Cal. 575; Whalley v. Lancashire R. Co., 1884, 13 Q.B.D. 131; Grant v. Allen, 1874, 41 Conn. 156.

8. Surocco v. Geary, 1853, 3 Cal. 69; Conwell v. Emrie, 1850, 2 Ind. 35; Russell v. Mayor of New York, N.Y.1845, 2 Denio 461; American Print Works v. Lawrence, 1837, 23 N.J.L. 9, 590; Stocking v. Johnson Flying Service, 1963, 143 Mont. 61, 387 P.2d 312 (fighting forest fire).

9. Putnam v. Payne, N.Y.1816, 13 Johns. 312.

10. Seavey v. Preble, 1874, 64 Me. 120; State v. Mayor of Knoxville, 1883, 80 Tenn. (12 Lea) 146. Cf. McGuire v. Amyx, 1927, 317 Mo. 1061, 297 S.W. 968 (committing suspected smallpox patient to pesthouse).

11. Harrison v. Wisdom, 1872, 54 Tenn., 7 Heisk. 99 (liquor); United States v. Caltex, Inc., 1952, 344 U.S. 149, 73 S.Ct. 200, 97 L.Ed. 157, rehearing denied 344 U.S. 919, 73 S.Ct. 345, 97 L.Ed. 708 (stored petroleum and refinery). Cf. Juragua Iron Co. v. United States, 1909, 212 U.S. 297, 29 S.Ct. 385, 53 L.Ed. 520.

To the contrary is Burmah Oil Co. v. Lord Advocate [1962] Scot.L.T. 347, holding that when the crown does an act of confiscation which would not be open to the ordinary citizen, and justifies it under the prerogative for reasons of state, it does not have the privilege of public necessity, and must pay compensation.

See Abend, Federal Liability for Takings and Torts: An Anomalous Relationship, 1963, 31 Ford.L.Rev. 481; Note, 1964, 39 Tul.L.Rev. 133.

12. Beach v. Trudgain, 1845, 43 Va. 345, 2 Gratt. 219 (fire); Allen v. Camp, 1915, 14 Ala.App. 341, 70 So. 290 (mad dog). One who destroys property under claim of public necessity has the burden of showing an emergency which will justify the action, as distinguished from mere convenience. Hicks v. Dorn, 1870, 42 N.Y. 47.

13. Hall and Wigmore, Compensation for Property Destroyed to Stop the Spread of a Conflagration, 1907, 1 Ill.L.Rev. 501; Bishop v. Mayor, etc., of Macon, 1849, 7 Ga. 200; cf. Jarvis v. Pinckney, S.C.1836, 3 Hill 123. Many jurisdictions provide compensation by statute. See Mayor of New York v. Lord, N.Y.1837, 17 Wend. 285, affirmed 18 Wend. 126; Taylor v. Inhabitants of Plymouth, 1844, 49 Mass., 8 Metc. 462.

14. Field v. City of Des Moines, 1874, 39 Iowa 575; McDonald v. City of Red Wing, 1868, 13 Minn. 38; Bowditch v. Boston, 1879, 101 U.S. 16, 25 L.Ed. 980.

nent public disaster.[15] Actually, in virtually all of the decided cases, the property destroyed had temporarily become dangerous itself and was likely to have been destroyed anyway. That is, if the property were not destroyed, it might well have been used in a way that would promote and further disastrous results, such as buildings which were destroyed to prevent the spread of a conflagration,[16] or whisky which was destroyed to prevent it from falling into the hands of those who would seize and misuse it.[17] The denial of recovery in such a case is a far cry from asserting that one who has intentionally used or damaged property to prevent a public disaster, when such property was not endangered and was not a factor in creating the emergency, should not be held liable. For example, if a pilot of an airline, in an emergency, lands on a plaintiff's property, and in so doing destroys a barn to save the lives of the passengers, it is at least arguable that the airline should be responsible. Moreover, it is likely that if property is damaged after being seized by a public official and used to prevent a public disaster, compensation is required by the Fifth Amendment, unless the property was itself being used or likely to be used in a dangerous way.[18] It is apparently arguable, therefore, that when property is destroyed, damaged, or used even in a reasonable manner by either a private citizen or a public official to prevent a public disaster, if the property so appropriated was not a part of the menace and was not itself likely to be harmed or destroyed anyway, the owner should be compensated.

Where no public interest is involved, and the defendant acts merely to protect the private one, usually his own, the privilege is properly limited. If the emergency is sufficiently great,[19] he may trespass upon the property of another to save himself[20] or his own property,[21] or even a third person[22] or his property[23] from harm. The privilege to deviate from a blocked public highway[24] falls into this category, as the protection of the individual's private interest in going where he wants to go. In all such cases there is no liability for the technical tort, and no privilege in the landowner to resist or expel the intruder.[25] But in the leading case of Vincent v. Lake Erie Transportation Co.,[26] which has been accepted by a few other decisions,[27] and by the Restatement of

15. Second Restatement of Torts, §§ 196 and 262.

16. Surocco v. Geary, 1853, 3 Cal. 69, 58 Am.Dec. 385.

17. Harrison v. Wisdom, 1872, 54 Tenn. (7 Heisk.) 99.

18. United States v. Caltex, Inc., 1952, 344 U.S. 149, 73 S.Ct. 200, 97 L.Ed. 157, 344 U.S. 919, 73 S.Ct. 345, 97 L.Ed. 708, American Manufacturers Mutual Insurance Co. v. The United States, 1972, 197 Ct.Cl. 99, 453 F.2d 1380; Castro v. United States, 1974, 205 Ct.Cl. 534, 500 F.2d 436; Mitchell v. Harmony, 1852, 54 U.S. 115, 13 How. 115, 14 L.Ed. 75.

19. Mere convenience or advantage is not sufficient, in the absence of real emergency. Allen v. Camp, 1915, 14 Ala.App. 341, 70 So. 290 (entering to kill dog suspected of rabies); Uhlein v. Cromack, 1872, 109 Mass. 273 (same as to dog accustomed to bite); Gulf Production Co. v. Gibson, Tex.Civ.App.1921, 234 S.W. 906 (deviating from blocked highway, with other route available); Mitchell v. Oklahoma Cotton Growers' Association, 1925, 108 Okl. 200, 235 P. 597 (entering to claim reward); Currie v. Silvernale, 1919, 142 Minn. 254, 171 N.W. 782 (continued entries after emergency past).

20. Depue v. Flatau, 1907, 100 Minn. 299, 111 N.W. 1; Bradshaw v. Frazier, 1901, 113 Iowa 579, 85 N.W. 752; Rossi v. Del Duca, 1962, 344 Mass. 66, 181 N.E.2d 591 (child frightened by dog).

21. Ploof v. Putnam, 1908, 81 Vt. 471, 71 A. 188; Carter v. Thurston, 1877, 58 N.H. 104; Boutwell v. Champlain Realty Co., 1915, 89 Vt. 80, 94 A. 108. Cf. Hetfield v. Baum, 1852, 35 N.C. 394 (hauling purchased wreck over plaintiff's land).

22. People v. Roberts, 1956, 47 Cal.2d 374, 303 P.2d 721; State v. Lukus, 1967, 149 Mont. 45, 423 P.2d 49; People v. Gallmon, 1967, 19 N.Y.2d 389, 280 N.Y.S.2d 356, 227 N.E.2d 284, certiorari denied 390 U.S. 911, 88 S.Ct. 832, 19 L.Ed.2d 884.

23. Proctor v. Adams, 1873, 113 Mass. 376. Cf. Northern Assurance Co. v. New York Central Railroad Co., 1935, 271 Mich. 569, 260 N.W. 763; Metallic Compression Casting Co. v. Fitchburg Railroad Co., 1873, 109 Mass. 277.

24. Supra, § 26.

25. Ploof v. Putnam, 1908, 81 Vt. 471, 71 A. 188; Irwin v. Yeagar, 1888, 74 Iowa 174, 37 N.W. 136; Rossi v. Del Duca, 1962, 344 Mass. 66, 181 N.E.2d 591.

26. 1910, 100 Minn. 456, 124 N.W. 221.

27. Currie v. Silvernale, 1919, 142 Minn. 254, 171 N.W. 782; Swan-Finch Oil Corp. v. Warner-Quinlan Co., 1933, 11 N.J.Misc. 469, 167 A. 211, affirmed, 1934, 112 N.J.Law 519, 171 A. 800; Latta v. New Orleans &

Torts,[28] it was held that the privilege does not extend to the infliction of actual damage, and that a shipowner who kept his vessel moored to a dock during a storm must pay for the salvation of his boat by making compensation for the injury to the dock. There is, in other words, an incomplete and partial privilege, which does not extend to the infliction of any substantial harm.[29]

So far as the decisions indicate, the privilege of necessity resembles those of self-defense and defense of property,[30] in that, assuming the reasonable appearance of necessity, an honest mistake as to its existence will not destroy the privilege.[31]

The privilege to inflict death or personal harm has received very little consideration.[32] It is reasonably clear that one would not have even an incomplete privilege to kill an innocent person to save property, except perhaps to prevent destruction amounting to a public calamity, such as a nuclear disaster. There is one type of situation where one in an emergency may not be liable for intentionally destroying life or property so long as he acts reasonably in his own behalf or that of a third person. This is when, in the course of using a motor vehicle, an emergency arises and the driver is put into a dilemma of injuring the plaintiff or someone else, including perhaps himself. If the driver chooses reasonably, or as a reasonable person would choose, to injure plaintiff, the indications are there would be no liability. Thus, in order to avoid a child, a driver turned a bus towards a crowd in which the plaintiffs were standing, injuring them. Judgment for the plaintiffs was upheld, but only because the driver negligently failed to sound the horn or take proper means to stop the bus.[33]

WESTLAW REFERENCES

defense +2 necessity % topic(110 203)
reasonable /15 force /s selfprotect! selfdefens! % topic(110 203)
retreat /5 safe* % topic(110 203)
"private necessity"

§ 25. Legal Process

The privilege to interfere with person or property under legal process is merely one phase of the broader problem of the liability of public officers for their official acts [1] but because of its close relation to intentional interference with person and property, it is convenient to consider it here. A public officer, of course, cannot be held liable for doing in a proper manner an act which is commanded or authorized by a valid law.[2] The immunity of such officers, in its broader as-

---

Northwestern Railway Co., 1912, 131 La. 272, 59 So. 250. Cf. Whalley v. Lancashire & York R. Co., 1884, 13 Q.B.D. 131; Whitecross Wire & Iron Co. v. Savill, 1882, 8 Q.B.D. 653 (application of general average); Cope v. Sharpe, [1912] 1 K.B. 496.

The only case found to the contrary is Commercial Union Assurance Co. v. Pacific Gas & Electric Co., 1934, 220 Cal. 515, 31 P.2d 793, which, however, turned upon the pleading claiming negligence.

28. Second Restatement of Torts, § 263. See also Bohlen, Incomplete Privilege to Inflict Intentional Invasions of Interests of Property and Personality, 1926, 39 Harv.L.Rev. 307.

29. Compare Taylor v. Chesapeake & Ohio Railway Co., 1919, 84 W.Va. 442, 100 S.E. 218; Higgins v. New York, Lake Erie & Western Railway Co., 1894, 78 Hun 567, 29 N.Y.S. 563; Noyes v. Shepherd, 1849, 30 Me. 173; Newcomb v. Tisdale, 1881, 62 Cal. 575, in all of which a defendant who saved his own land by casting flood waters on the plaintiff's land was held liable for the damage done.

30. Supra, §§ 19 and 21.

31. Cope v. Sharpe, [1912] 1 K.B. 496; Conwell v. Emrie, 1850, 2 Ind. 35; Surocco v. Geary, 1853, 3 Cal. 69; Seavey v. Preble, 1874, 64 Me. 120, all so indicate. A striking illustration of the unwisdom of confining this privilege within too narrow limits is given in Respublica v. Sparhawk, Pa.1788, 1 Dall. 357, 1 L.Ed. 174, attributing the destruction of London by the Great Fire to the timidity of the Lord Mayor about destroying houses in its path.

32. Cf. Regina v. Dudley, 1884, 14 Q.D.B. 273, 15 Cox C.C. 273; United States v. Holmes, 1842 Fed.Cas. No.15,383, 1 Wall.Jr. 1; Phillips v. Pickwick Stages, 1927, 85 Cal.App. 571, 259 P. 968 (goes off on negligence). See also the criminal cases cited infra, § 114.

33. Phillips v. Pickwick Stages, Northern Division, Inc., 1927, 85 Cal.App. 571, 259 P. 968.

§ 25

1. See infra, § 132.

2. Burton v. Fulton, 1865, 49 Pa. 151; Highway Commissioners v. Ely, 1884, 54 Mich. 173, 19 N.W. 940; Thibodaux v. Town of Thibodeaux, 1894, 46 La.Ann.

pects, remains to be considered in a later chapter.³ As a defense to intentional torts against the person or property, it frequently arises in connection with the execution of legal process—for example, the arrest of an individual under a warrant, or the seizure of property under a writ of attachment or execution. This privilege may be considered briefly here.

Arrest under a warrant, or the levy of civil process, is considered a "ministerial act," ⁴ for which the officer will not be liable if he acts duly and properly, ⁵ but will be liable if he steps outside of his authority. If the court which issues the process is entirely without jurisdiction to do so, it is commonly held that the invalid process will afford the officer no protection.⁶ It may nevertheless be questioned whether there is any desirable policy in requiring sheriffs and constables to know, at their peril, the limitations of the power of the court whose orders they obey, particularly where those limits are likely to depend upon questions of law utterly beyond their comprehension.⁷ The rigors of the rule have been relaxed to some extent by holding that if the court has general jurisdiction to issue similar process, the officer will be protected, provided that the warrant or the writ is "fair on its face." ⁸ Any errors or irregularities in the proceedings, even though they may affect jurisdiction in the particular case, will not make him liable.⁹

The more modern and better reasoned cases,¹⁰ with many still to the contrary,¹¹ have extended this even to the protection of officers who act under statutes subsequently declared to be unconstitutional, reasoning that the mentality of the average policeman, whose life is traditionally not a happy one, should not be charged with the decisions of questions which baffle the best lawyers in the land.

Process is not "fair on its face" if the kind of examination which the reasonable officer can fairly be expected to make would show that it is not valid. The officer is required to know at least the superficial characteristics of a valid warrant; and he will be liable if it is too general in its terms,¹² fails properly to name the party wanted,¹³ or is returnable at the wrong time,¹⁴ or does not charge a

1528, 16 So. 450. See Gray, Private Wrongs of Public Servants, 1959, 47 Cal.L.Rev. 303.

3. See infra, § 132.

4. See infra, § 132.

5. Mathews v. Murray, 1960, 101 Ga.App. 216, 113 S.E.2d 232; James v. Southwestern Insurance Co., Okl. 1960, 354 P.2d 408; Bradford v. Harding, E.D.N.Y. 1959, 180 F.Supp. 855, affirmed, 2d Cir. 1959, 284 F.2d 307.

6. Warren v. Kelley, 1888, 80 Me. 512, 15 A. 49; Heller v. Clarke, 1904, 121 Wis. 71, 98 N.W. 952; Strozzi v. Wines, 1899, 24 Nev. 389, 55 P. 828, 57 P. 832; Smith v. Hilton, 1906, 147 Ala. 642, 41 So. 747; Grove v. Van Duyn, 1882, 44 N.J.L. 654.

7. See State v. McNally, 1852, 34 Me. 210; Brooks v. Mangan, 1891, 86 Mich. 576, 49 N.W. 633; Rapacz, Protection of Officers Who Act Under Unconstitutional Statutes, 1927, 11 Minn.L.Rev. 585.

8. Robinette v. Price, 1943, 214 Minn. 521, 8 N.W.2d 800; Williams v. Franzoni, 2d Cir. 1954, 217 F.2d 533; Peterson v. Lutz, 1942, 212 Minn. 307, 3 N.W.2d 489; Hansen v. Lowe, 1940, 61 Idaho 138, 100 P.2d 51; Morrill v. Hamel, 1958, 337 Mass. 83, 148 N.E.2d 283.

9. Wilbur v. Stokes, 1903, 117 Ga. 545, 43 S.E. 856 (void judgment); Bohri v. Barnett, 7th Cir. 1906, 144 F. 389 (invalid ordinance); Rush v. Buckley, 1905, 100 Me. 322, 61 A. 774 (invalid statute); Vittorio v. St. Regis Paper Co., 1924, 239 N.Y. 148, 145 N.E. 913; David v. Larochelle, 1936, 296 Mass. 302, 5 N.E.2d 571.

10. Yekhtikian v. Blessing, 1960, 90 R.I. 287, 157 A.2d 669; McCray v. City of Lake Louisville, Ky.1960, 332 S.W.2d 837; Manson v. Wabash Railroad Co., Mo. 1960, 338 S.W.2d 54; Brooks v. Mangan, 1891, 86 Mich. 576, 49 N.W. 633; Henke v. McCord, 1880, 55 Iowa 378, 7 N.W. 623. See Rapacz, Protection of Officers Who Act Under Unconstitutional Statutes, 1927, 11 Minn.L. Rev. 585; Field, The Effect of an Unconstitutional Statute in the Law of Public Officers, 1928, 77 U.Pa.L. Rev. 155; Note, 1936, 22 Va.L.Rev. 316.

11. Smith v. Costello, 1955, 77 Idaho 205, 290 P.2d 742; Sumner v. Beeler, 1875, 50 Ind. 341; Campbell v. Sherman, 1874, 35 Wis. 103; Kelly v. Bemis, 1855, 70 Mass. (4 Gray) 83; Dennison Manufacturing Co. v. Wright, 1923, 156 Ga. 789, 120 S.E. 120.

12. Commonwealth v. Crotty, 1865, 92 Mass., (10 Allen) 403; Grumon v. Raymond, 1814, 1 Conn. 40; Lynchard v. State, 1938, 183 Miss. 691, 184 So. 805; Reichman v. Harris, 6th Cir. 1918, 252 F. 371.

13. Goldberg v. Markowitz, 1904, 94 App.Div. 237, 87 N.Y.S. 1045, affirmed, 1905, 182 N.Y. 540, 75 N.E. 1129 ("John"); Harwood v. Siphers, 1880, 70 Me. 464 (no party named).

14. Toof v. Bently, N.Y.1830, 5 Wend. 276; Hussey v. Davis, 1878, 58 N.H. 317 (no return specified). Cf.

crime.[15] But so long as it is valid upon its face, the weight of authority probably is that the officer is privileged to execute it even though he has personal knowledge of facts which should prevent the arrest, and may safely leave all responsibility to the court.[16]

The officer is of course charged with the valid and lawful execution of the process placed in his hands, and will be liable if he departs from the proper procedure, no matter how excellent his intentions.[17] He will be liable if he mistakenly arrests another than the person named,[18] or seizes property not covered by the writ.[19] He is protected only if he acts with the process in his possession; it is not enough that it has been issued and is in the hands of another person.[20] He must ordinarily make known his authority, his intention to arrest, and the nature of the charge.[21] He must act at a reasonable time,[22] and use only reasonable force.[23] The execution of civil process, by long tradition, does not authorize breaking into a dwelling house without a separate court order, and such forcible entry may be resisted.[24] But there is no privilege to resist the mere seizure of goods, even under a void writ, since the property interest involved does not justify force against the person of the officer asserting legal authority, and other remedies are available.[25]

Trespass Ab Initio

One who enters upon land, seizes property, or makes an arrest by virtue of legal au-

---

Hazen v. Creller, 1910, 83 Vt. 460, 76 A. 145 (unsigned complaint).

15. Frazier v. Turner, 1890, 76 Wis. 562, 45 N.W. 411; Lueck v. Heisler, 1894, 87 Wis. 644, 58 N.W. 1101; Minor v. Seliga, 1958, 168 Ohio St. 1, 150 N.E.2d 852. The officer is not held to the standard of a trained legal mind, but merely to that of an ordinary intelligent and informed layman. Aetna Insurance Co. v. Blumenthal, 1943, 129 Conn. 545, 29 A.2d 751.

16. People v. Warren, N.Y.1843, 5 Hill 440; Watson v. Watson, 1832, 9 Conn. 140; O'Shaughnessy v. Baxter, 1876, 121 Mass. 515; Heath v. Halfhill, 1898, 106 Iowa 131, 76 N.W. 522; Rice v. Miller, 1888, 70 Tex. 613, 8 S.W. 317; Second Restatement of Torts, § 124, Comment b. Contra: Tellefsen v. Fee, 1897, 168 Mass. 188, 46 N.E. 562; Leachman v. Dougherty, 1872, 81 Ill. 324.

17. See, generally, Perkins, The Law of Arrest, 1940, 25 Iowa L.Rev. 201, 212–228.

18. Holmes v. Blyler, 1890, 80 Iowa 365, 45 N.W. 756; Walton v. Will, 1944, 66 Cal.App.2d 509, 152 P.2d 639; Jordan v. C.I.T. Corp., 1939, 302 Mass. 281, 19 N.E.2d 5; Hays v. Creary, 1883, 60 Tex. 445; Johnson v. Weiner, 1944, 155 Fla. 169, 19 So.2d 699.

The officer is liable if he arrests the person intended under a warrant bearing the wrong name. Griswold v. Sedgwick, N.Y.1826, 6 Cow. 456; West v. Cabell, 1894, 153 U.S. 78, 14 S.Ct. 752, 38 L.Ed. 643; Scheer v. Keown, 1872, 29 Wis. 586; Harris v. McReynolds, 1898, 10 Colo.App. 532, 51 P. 1016. But it has been held that an arrest in good faith of the wrong person bearing the same name is privileged. Schneider v. Kessler, 3d Cir. 1938, 97 F.2d 542; Blocker v. Clark, 1906, 126 Ga. 484, 54 S.E. 1022; Clark v. Winn, 1898, 19 Tex.Civ.App. 223, 46 S.W. 915; King v. Robertson, 1933, 227 Ala. 378, 150 So. 154.

There is no liability where the mistake is knowingly induced by the plaintiff. Dunston v. Paterson, 1857, 2 C.B.,N.S., 495, 140 Eng.Rep. 509.

19. Symonds v. Hall, 1853, 37 Me. 354; Buck v. Colbath, 1865, 70 U.S. (3 Wall.) 334, 18 L.Ed. 257 (goods of wrong party); Kane v. Hutchinson, 1892, 93 Mich. 488, 53 N.W. 624 (goods other than those specifically named).

20. Galliard v. Laxton, 1862, 2 B. & S. 363, 121 Eng. Rep. 1109; Adams v. State, 1904, 121 Ga. 163, 48 S.E. 910; People v. McLean, 1888, 68 Mich. 480, 36 N.W. 231; Webb v. State, 1889, 51 N.J.L. 189, 17 A. 113; Second Restatement of Torts, § 126. See Bohlen and Shulman, Arrest With and Without a Warrant, 1927, 75 U.Pa.L.Rev. 485, 492.

21. Hodge v. Piedmont & Northern Railway Co., 1917, 109 S.C. 62, 95 S.E. 138; State v. Phinney, 1856, 42 Me. 384; State v. Freeman, 1859, 8 Iowa 428; cf. Crosswhite v. Barnes, 1924, 139 Va. 471, 124 S.E. 242 (reading warrant). See Second Restatement of Torts, § 128; Note, 1965, 25 Md.L.Rev. 48. But such manifestation is not required where the one arrested knows the officer's authority and the charge. Wolf v. State, 1869, 19 Ohio St. 248; State v. Byrd, 1905, 72 S.C. 104, 51 S.E. 542.

22. Keith v. Tuttle, 1848, 28 Me. 326 (Sunday); Malcolmson v. Scott, 1885, 56 Mich. 459, 23 N.W. 166 (Sunday); Bryan v. Comstock, 1920, 143 Ark. 394, 220 S.W. 475 (Saturday night). An arrest for a serious offense, however, may be justified at an inconvenient time.

23. As to what is reasonable force in effecting an arrest, with or without a warrant, see infra, § 26.

24. Semayne's Case, 1604, 5 Co.Rep. 91a, 77 Eng. Rep. 194; Ilsley v. Nichols, 1831, 29 Mass. (12 Pick.) 270; Kelley v. Schuyler, 1898, 20 R.I. 432, 39 A. 893; Frothingham v. Maxim, 1928, 127 Me. 58, 141 A. 99.

25. State v. Downer, 1836, 8 Vt. 424; Faris v. State, 1854, 3 Ohio St. 159; State v. Selengut, 1915, 38 R.I. 302, 95 A. 503. Contra, Commonwealth v. Kennard, 1829, 25 Mass. (8 Pick.) 133.

thority, is of course liable for any subsequent tortious conduct. But by a curious and unique fiction, the common law courts held that his abuse of authority related back to his original act, and that he was liable as a trespasser from the beginning, however innocent of wrong he might have been up to the moment of misconduct. The fiction had its origin in the ancient law of distress of property,[26] and received its first full statement in the Six Carpenters Case,[27] in 1610. It was a procedural device, "due to the misplaced ingenuity of some medieval pleader," [28] which was designed to circumvent the rule that the action of trespass would not lie where the original entry was not wrongful.[29] It originated at a time when punitive damages were still in the far distant future, and no doubt it accomplished, in at least some outrageous cases of abuse of legal authority, much the same deterrent purpose.

Equally curious limitations were placed about the fiction. It was held that it had no application to those who entered, not by authority of law, but by a private license, upon the theory that in such a case the landowner might choose his own licensee, and should take the risk that the license might be abused.[30] It was also held that the subsequent act must be one which in itself would be tortious,[31] and that a mere omission, such as a failure to pay for drinks after entering an inn,[32] was not sufficient.[33]

Notwithstanding vigorous and unanimous denunciation on the part of all writers who have discussed it,[34] the fiction has survived, at least until recently. Since the development of punitive damages, its effect has been to pile Ossa upon Pelion by adding damages for an innocent and rightful act on top of fair compensation for the wrong plus punishment. Its commonest application has been in the case of damage done after an entry of land under authority of law,[35] or the misuse or wrongful disposition of goods seized under process,[36] where its chief importance has lain in the fact that the defendant may be required to pay greater damages such as the entire value of the chattel.[37]

26. Ames, History of Trover, 1898, 11 Harv.L.Rev. 277, 287; 7 Holdsworth, History of English Law, 1925, 499; Williams, A Strange Offspring of Trespass Ab Initio, 1936, 52 L.Q.Rev. 106.

27. 1610, 8 Co.Rep. 146a, 77 Eng.Rep. 695.

28. Salmond, Law of Torts, 8th ed. 1934, 222.

29. 1 Street, Foundations of Legal Liability, 1906, 47.

30. Page v. Town of Newbury, 1943, 113 Vt. 336, 34 A.2d 218; Cartan v. Cruz Construction Co., 1965, 89 N.J.Super. 414, 215 A.2d 356; Katsonas v. W.M. Sutherland Building and Construction Co., 1926, 104 Conn. 54, 132 A. 553; Nichols v. Sonia, 1913, 113 Me. 529, 95 A. 209; Mertz v. J.M. Covington Corp., Alaska 1970, 470 P.2d 532.

Apparently it is only ignorance of the history which has made occasional courts hold the contrary, as in Francis v. Sun Oil Co., 1959, 135 Mont. 307, 340 P.2d 824; Ercanbrack v. Clark, 1932, 79 Utah 233, 8 P.2d 1093.

31. Adams v. Rivers, N.Y.1851, 11 Barb. 390; Fullam v. Stearns, 1857, 30 Vt. 443; Ordway v. Ferrin, 1824, 3 N.H. 69; Hale v. Clark, N.Y.1838, 19 Wend. 498; Louisville & Nashville Railroad Co. v. Bartee, 1920, 204 Ala. 539, 86 So. 394 (mere words not sufficient).

32. Six Carpenters Case, 1610, 8 Co.Rep. 146a, 77 Eng.Rep. 695.

33. Waterbury v. Lockwood, Conn.1810, 4 Day 257; Gardner v. Campbell, N.Y.1818, 15 Johns 401; Fullam v. Stearns, 1857, 30 Vt. 443.

34. "It is revolting to have no better reason for a rule of law than that so it was laid down in the time of Henry IV. It is still more revolting if the grounds upon which it was laid down have vanished long since, and the rule simply persists from blind imitation of the past." Holmes, The Path of the Law, 1897, 10 Harv.L. Rev. 457, 469.

See also the denunciation in McGuire v. United States, 1927, 273 U.S. 95, 47 S.Ct. 259, 71 L.Ed. 556; also Smith, Surviving Fictions, 1918, 27 Yale L.J. 147, 164; Bohlen and Shulman, Effect of Subsequent Misconduct Upon a Lawful Arrest, 1928, 28 Col.L.Rev. 841; Salmond, Law of Torts, 6th ed. 1924, 232; Pollock, Law of Torts, 12th ed. 1923, 402.

35. Cole v. Drew, 1871, 44 Vt. 49; McClannan v. Chaplain, 1923, 136 Va. 1, 116 S.E. 495; Second Restatement of Torts, § 214.

36. Malcom v. Spoor, 1847, 53 Mass. (12 Metc.) 279; Barrett v. White, 1825, 3 N.H. 210; Walsh v. Brown, 1907, 194 Mass. 317, 80 N.E. 465.

37. Cf. Mussey v. Cahoon, 1852, 34 Me. 74; Smith v. Gates, 1838, 38 Mass. (21 Pick.) 55; Bear v. Harriss, 1896, 118 N.C. 476, 24 S.E. 364.

The reasons given by the courts for the continuance of the doctrine do not carry conviction. It is said that the abuse of the privilege creates a conclusive presumption that the actor intended from the outset to use the public authority as a cloak under which to enter for a wrongful purpose. While it may be important evidence to that effect, it scarcely justifies a rule of law.[38] The best argument in favor of the doctrine is that it affords a valuable correction for abuses by public officers; but the existence of adequate remedies for the subsequent misconduct should be sufficient.[39]

Since the turn of the century, there has been very little use of trespass ab initio in any field except that of arrest, where there has been much dispute as to its application.[40] A failure to make a return of process, even though it is only an omission, has been regarded as so identified with the arrest itself as to render it invalid, and make the defendant liable from the beginning.[41] Failure to use due diligence to bring the prisoner promptly before a magistrate has been given the same effect by many courts,[42] although there has been authority to the contrary.[43]

A release of the prisoner without any presentment before a court, over his objection, has been regarded as a trespass ab initio by some courts,[44] and not by others.[45] As to any mistreatment of the prisoner,[46] or efforts to coerce him into compliance with orders,[47] there are surprisingly few cases.

Since around 1930 there have been decisions in several jurisdictions, most of them overruling earlier cases, which have rejected the whole doctrine of trespass ab initio as applied to arrest, and have refused to hold that there is any liability for the original privileged act, unless it was intended only as a cover for the subsequent misconduct.[48] This position has received the support of the Restatement of Torts, which has rejected the doctrine of trespass ab initio in all situations.[49] For these reasons, there is good reason to expect that the entire doctrine is on its way to oblivion.

WESTLAW REFERENCES

digest(public /s official* employee* officer* /s liab! /s act*)

individual** personal** /7 liab! /s police officer /s illegal unlawful

---

38. Smith, Surviving Fictions, 1918, 27 Yale L.J. 147, 164.

39. Bohlen and Shulman, Effect of Subsequent Misconduct Upon a Lawful Arrest, 1928, 28 Col.L.Rev. 841.

40. Bohlen and Shulman, Effect of Subsequent Misconduct Upon a Lawful Arrest, 1928, 28 Col.L.Rev. 841; Notes, 1940, 28 Cal.L.Rev. 646; 1945, 6 Mont.L.Rev. 61.

41. Tubbs v. Tukey, 1893, 57 Mass. (3 Cush.) 438; Gibson v. Holmes, 1905, 78 Vt. 110, 62 A. 11; see Boston & Maine Railroad Co. v. Small, 1893, 85 Me. 462, 27 A. 349.

42. Nelson v. Eastern Air Lines, 1942, 128 N.J.L. 46, 24 A.2d 371; Bass v. State, 1949, 196 Misc. 177, 92 N.Y.S.2d 42; Peckham v. Warner Brothers Pictures, 1939, 36 Cal.App.2d 214, 97 P.2d 472; Leger v. Warren, 1900, 62 Ohio St. 500, 57 N.E. 506; Piedmont Hotel Co. v. Henderson, 1911, 9 Ga.App. 672, 72 S.E. 51.

43. Atchison, Topeka & Santa Fe Railway Co. v. Hinsdell, 1907, 76 Kan. 74, 90 P. 800; Oxford v. Berry, 1913, 204 Mich. 197, 170 N.W. 83; Mulberry v. Fuellhart, 1902, 203 Pa. 573, 53 A. 504.

44. Keefe v. Hart, 1913, 213 Mass. 476, 100 N.E. 558; Stewart v. Feeley, 1902, 118 Iowa 524, 92 N.W. 670; Newhall v. Egan, 1908, 28 R.I. 584, 68 A. 471.

45. Atchison, Topeka & Santa Fe Railway Co. v. Hinsdell, 1907, 76 Kan. 74, 90 P. 800; Harness v. Steele, 1902, 159 Ind. 286, 64 N.E. 875; Mulberry v. Fuellhart, 1902, 203 Pa. 573, 53 A. 504; Second Restatement of Torts, § 136.

46. Dumas v. Erie Railroad Co., 1935, 243 App.Div. 792, 278 N.Y.S. 197 (trespass ab initio); Grau v. Forge, 1919, 183 Ky. 521, 209 S.W. 369 (liability only for subsequent misconduct).

47. See Holley v. Mix, N.Y.1829, 3 Wend. 350; Clark v. Tilton, 1907, 74 N.H. 330, 68 A. 335; Robbins v. Swift, 1894, 86 Me. 197, 29 A. 981 (all holding trespass ab initio).

The officer's subsequent misconduct does not impose liability upon one who assisted in a valid arrest. Dehm v. Hinman, 1887, 56 Conn. 320, 15 A. 741.

48. Dragna v. White, 1955, 45 Cal.2d 469, 289 P.2d 428; Anderson v. Foster, 1953, 73 Idaho 340, 252 P.2d 199; Shaw v. Courtney, 1943, 317 Ill.App. 422, 46 N.E.2d 170, affirmed 385 Ill. 559, 53 N.E.2d 432; Cline v. Tait, 1942, 113 Mont. 475, 129 P.2d 89; Brown v. Meier & Frank Co., 1939, 160 Or. 608, 86 P.2d 79.

49. See Second Restatement of Torts, §§ 214(2), 136, 278.

Trespass Ab Initio

"trespass ab initio"
abus*** /6 legal /6 process /p trespass!

§ 26. Arrest Without a Warrant

The details of the complex rules which have grown up around arrest without a warrant might better be considered in a treatise on criminal law.[1] A distinction necessarily has been made between the authority of officers of the law,[2] charged with the official duty of enforcing it, and that of private citizens.[3] The power to arrest has been limited according to the gravity of the crime with which the wrongdoer is to be charged. Highly technical distinctions have been drawn between felonies, which in general are major crimes; breaches of the peace, which are public offenses done by violence, or likely to create public disturbance,[4] and the greater number of minor criminal violations which are mere misdemeanors. The classification of a particular offense is very largely a matter of statute, and will vary in each jurisdiction. The unfortunate officer or citizen is required to know these distinctions, or to act at his peril.[5]

Broadly speaking, either an officer or a private citizen may arrest without a warrant to prevent a felony or a breach of the peace [6] which is being committed, or reasonably appears about to be committed,[7] in his presence.[8] Once the crime has been committed, the jealous safeguards which the law always has thrown about the personal liberty of the individual have led to a restriction of the privilege. The officer, representing the state, may still arrest without legal process if he has information which affords a reasonable ground for suspicion that a felony has been committed, and that he has the right criminal.[9] The burden rests upon him

---

§ 26

1. See Perkins, The Law of Arrest, 1940, 25 Iowa L.Rev. 201; Stone, Arrest Without Warrant, [1939] Wis.L.Rev. 385; Hall, The Law of Arrest in Relation to Contemporary Social Problems, 1936, 3 U.Chi.L.Rev. 345; Waite, The Law of Arrest, 1946, 24 Tex.L.Rev. 270; Potts, The Law of Arrest, 1949, 1 Baylor L.Rev. 397; Machen, Arrest Without Warrant in Misdemeanor Cases, 1954, 33 N.C.L.Rev. 17; Notes, 1953, 41 Ky.L.J 455; 1969, 64 Nw.U.L.Rev. 229.

Also, as to particular jurisdictions, Perkins, The Tennessee Law of Arrest, 1949, 2 Vand.L.Rev. 509; Kauffman, The Law of Arrest in Maryland, 1941, 5 Md.L.Rev. 125; Miller, Arrest Without a Warrant by a Peace Officer in New York, 1946, 21 N.Y.U.L.Q.Rev. 61; Lugar, Arrest Without a Warrant in West Virginia, 1948, 48 W.Va.L.Q. 207; Note, 1956, 24 Tenn.L.Rev. 258.

2. As to the historical development of the law, as affected by the development of a professional police, see Hall, Legal and Social Aspects of Arrest Without a Warrant, 1936, 49 Harv.L.Rev. 566.

3. See Note, 1965, 65 Col.L.Rev. 502.

4. Second Restatement of Torts, § 116.

5. "The rules adopted in the American Restatement of the Law of Torts are nearly as complicated as those in our [English] law. Both systems did right in grading crimes according to their gravity so far as the criminal is concerned. Both made a cardinal blunder in making this gradation a determinant not merely of the extent of liability of the criminal, but also of the liability of an innocent third person in a collateral matter like the arrest of the offender." Winfield, Law of Tort, 1st ed. 1937, 236.

6. People v. Rounds, 1887, 67 Mich. 482, 35 N.W. 77 (officer); State v. Mancini, 1917, 91 Vt. 507, 101 A. 581 (officer); Commonwealth v. Gorman, 1934, 288 Mass. 294, 192 N.E. 618 (officer); Baltimore & Ohio Railroad Co. v. Cain, 1895, 81 Md. 87, 31 A. 801 (private person); Marcuchi v. Norfolk & Western Railway Co., 1918, 81 W.Va. 548, 94 S.E. 979 (private person).

7. Handcock v. Baker, 1800, 2 Bos. & P. 260, 120 Eng.Rep. 1270 (murder about to be committed); State v. Hughlett, 1923, 124 Wash. 366, 214 P. 841 (reasonable belief felony being committed); Malley v. Lane, 1921, 97 Conn. 133, 115 A. 674 (felony committed); State v. Hum Quock, 1931, 89 Mont. 503, 300 P. 220 (felony committed); Byrd v. Commonwealth, 1932, 158 Va. 897, 164 S.E. 400 (felony and breach of the peace).

8. "In his presence" requires that the officer shall be aware of the offense by some perception before the arrest. Snyder v. United States, 4th Cir. 1922, 285 F. 1; Black v. State, 1937, 63 Okl.Cr. 317, 74 P.2d 1172. But it is sufficient if the crime is perceived by sight, Robertson v. Commonwealth, 1923, 198 Ky. 699, 249 S.W. 1010; People v. Martin, 1955, 45 Cal.App.2d 755, 290 P.2d 855; People v. Esposito, 1922, 118 Misc. 867, 194 N.Y.S. 326; hearing, State v. Blackwelder, 1921, 182 N.C. 899, 109 S.E. 644; Davis v. Commonwealth, Ky.1955, 280 S.W.2d 714; smell, United States v. Fischer, D.Pa.1930, 38 F.2d 830; People v. Bock Leung Chew, 1956, 142 Cal.App.2d 400, 298 P.2d 118; mechanical devices, United States v. Harnish, D.Me.1934, 7 F.Supp. 305, or even a confession. State v. Gulczynski, Del.1922, 2 W.W.Harr. 120, 120 A. 88.

9. Beckwith v. Philby, 1827, 6 B. & C. 635, 108 Eng. Rep. 585; State v. Smith, 1960, 56 Wn.2d 368, 353 P.2d 155; Stephens v. United States, 1959, 106 U.S.App.D.C. 249, 271 F.2d 832; Chesapeake & Ohio Railway Co. v.

to show that he has reasonable grounds,[10] and mere suspicion, unsupported by information, is not enough.[11] The private person may arrest if a felony has in fact been committed, and he has reasonable grounds to suspect the man whom he arrests,[12] but his authority depends upon the fact of the crime, and he must take the full risk that none has been committed.[13] A reasonable mistake as to the individual will protect him, but a mistake as to the felony will not. It has even been held that the felony which has occurred must be the very one for which he purports to make the arrest.[14]

For a past breach of the peace, which is not a felony, neither the officer nor the citizen may arrest without a warrant,[15] unless the offense was committed in his presence, and he is in fresh pursuit.[16] For mere misdemeanors, the accepted common law rule is that neither the officer [17] nor the citizen [18] may arrest without a warrant, although some few jurisdictions have extended the power to an officer where the misdemeanor is committed in his presence.[19]

The person arrested must be informed of the charges against him,[20] and an arrest made upon an improper ground cannot later be justified because there was a proper one available.[21] An officer may call upon private persons to assist him in making any arrest, and those who do so will be privileged, even though the officer himself is without authority,[22] so long as he is known to be a peace officer.[23] But one who assists another pri-

Welch, 1937, 268 Ky. 93, 103 S.W.2d 698; Kirk v. Garrett, 1896, 84 Md. 383, 35 A. 1089. See Note, 1936, 24 Ky.L.J. 229.

10. Jackson v. Knowlton, 1899, 173 Mass. 94, 53 N.E. 134.

11. Laster v. Chaney, 1937, 180 Miss. 110, 177 So. 524; People v. Caruso, 1930, 339 Ill. 258, 171 N.E. 128; United States v. Gowen, 2d Cir. 1930, 40 F.2d 593; Kalkanes v. Willestoft, 1942, 13 Wn.2d 127, 124 P.2d 219.

12. Burns v. Erben, 1869, 40 N.Y. 463; Reuck v. McGregor, 1866, 32 N.J.L. 70; Davis v. United States, 1900, 16 U.S.App.D.C. 442; American Railway Express Co. v. Summers, 1922, 208 Ala. 531, 94 So. 737.

13. Carr v. State, 1884, 43 Ark. 99; Garnier v. Squires, 1900, 62 Kan. 321, 62 P. 1005; Martin v. Houck, 1906, 141 N.C. 317, 54 S.E. 291; Enright v. Gibson, 1906, 219 Ill. 550, 76 N.E. 689. A fortiori where there is no reasonable ground to suspect the plaintiff. Maliniemi v. Gronlund, 1892, 92 Mich. 222, 52 N.W. 627; Morley v. Chase, 1887, 143 Mass. 396, 9 N.E. 767.

Even where there is a felony, there may be liability for failure to take proper precautions to see that the right person is arrested. Wallner v. Fidelity & Deposit Co., 1948, 253 Wis. 66, 33 N.W.2d 215. As to the privilege of temporary detention to investigate, see supra, § 22.

14. Walters v. Smith & Sons, [1914] 1 K.B. 595.

15. State v. Lewis, 1893, 50 Ohio St. 179, 33 N.E. 405; Wahl v. Walton, 1883, 30 Minn. 506, 16 N.W. 397; John Bad Elk v. United States, 1900, 177 U.S. 529, 20 S.Ct. 729, 44 L.Ed. 874 (officers); Baynes v. Brewster, 1841, 2 Q.B. 375 (private person).

16. Curry v. Commonwealth, 1923, 199 Ky. 90, 250 S.W. 793; Wiegand v. Meade, 1932, 108 N.J.L. 471, 158 A. 825. Cf. Yates v. State, 1907, 127 Ga. 813, 56 S.E. 1017 (delay of several months).

17. State v. Mobley, 1954, 240 N.C. 476, 83 S.E.2d 100; People v. McLean, 1888, 68 Mich. 480, 36 N.W. 231; Caffini v. Hermann, 1914, 112 Me. 282, 91 A. 1009; Davids v. State, 1955, 208 Md. 377, 118 A.2d 636; McCrary v. State, 1936, 131 Tex.Cr.R. 233, 97 S.W.2d 236 (sexual intercourse in presence of officer).

18. Fox v. Gaunt, 1832, 3 B. & Ad. 798, 110 Eng. Rep. 293; Palmer v. Maine Central Railroad Co., 1899, 92 Me. 399, 42 A. 800; Union Depot & Railroad Co. v. Smith, 1891, 16 Colo. 361, 27 P. 329. Cf. Jennings v. Riddle, 1935, 20 Tenn.App. 89, 95 S.W.2d 946.

19. Coverstone v. Davies, 1952, 38 Cal.2d 315, 239 P.2d 876, certiorari denied Mock v. Davies, 344 U.S. 840, 73 S.Ct. 50, 97 L.Ed. 653; St. Clair v. Smith, Okl. 1956, 293 P.2d 597; State v. Deitz, 1925, 136 Wash. 228, 239 P. 386; State ex rel. Verdis v. Fidelity & Casualty Co., 1938, 120 W.Va. 593, 199 S.E. 884; see Carroll v. United States, 1925, 267 U.S. 132, 45 S.Ct. 280, 69 L.Ed. 543, certiorari denied 282 U.S. 873, 51 S.Ct. 78, 75 L.Ed. 771. See Bohlen and Shulman, Arrest With and Without a Warrant, 1927, 75 U.Pa.L.Rev. 485; Note, 1925, 25 So.Cal.L.Rev. 449.

20. Squadrito v. Griebsch, 1955, 1 A.D.2d 760, 147 N.Y.S.2d 553, reversed, 1956, 1 N.Y.2d 471, 154 N.Y.S.2d 37, 136 N.E.2d 504.

21. Noe v. Meadows, 1929, 299 Ky. 53, 16 S.W.2d 505 (adding that if the arrest is made on more than one ground, and justification is found for one only, the arrest is justified).

22. Watson v. State, 1887, 83 Ala. 60, 3 So. 441; Firestone v. Rice, 1888, 71 Mich. 377, 38 N.W. 885; Peterson v. Robison, 1954, 43 Cal.2d 690, 277 P.2d 19. In any case the citizen is privileged to the same extent as the officer. Byrd v. Commonwealth, 1932, 158 Va. 897, 164 S.E. 400. See Note, 1958, 13 Wyo.L.J. 72.

23. Dietrichs v. Schaw, 1873, 43 Ind. 175; Cincinnati, New Orleans & Texas Pacific Railway Co. v. Cundiff, 1915, 166 Ky. 594, 179 S.W. 615.

vate person must take the risk that there is authority for the arrest.[24]

These rules have been subjected to vigorous criticism, particularly as they allow obviously guilty criminals time to escape in a very mobile civilization, and invalidate arrests or prevent the admission of evidence, where guilt might clearly be proved.[25] They have been altered by statute in many states, and are likely to undergo further modification in the future.

The arrest and confinement of supposed lunatics, without a court order directing it, is at the risk of the person making the arrest, to the extent that the only possible justification is the apparent necessity of protecting others, or the insane person himself. It is not enough that the person arrested is believed to be insane,[26] but there must be good reason to believe that he will do serious harm to himself or another,[27] before the privilege exists.

Means Used to Effect Arrest

Since very few arrests are with the consent of the criminal, the authority to make the arrest, whether it be with or without a warrant, must necessarily carry with it the privilege of using all reasonable force to effect it. Whether the force used is reasonable is a question of fact, to be determined in the light of the circumstances of each particular case.[28] In any case the defendant can never use more force than reasonably appears to be necessary, or subject the person arrested to unnecessary risk of harm. The use of deadly force, likely to cause serious injury is a matter upon which the courts have not always agreed.[29] There is no dispute that such force may be used to prevent the commission of a felony which threatens the life or safety of a human being [30] or the burglary of a dwelling.[31] As to other felonies, the tendency of the modern cases is to find the use of deadly force unreasonable in relation to the offense.[32]

Once a crime has been committed, the chief interest is that of the state in apprehending the criminal. It is reasonable that much the same distinction should be made, although the courts have not agreed upon it: deadly force may certainly be used to maintain the arrest of a dangerous criminal whose offense has threatened human life or safety,[33] but not a thief or the like [34] whom the state never punishes with death, and sel-

---

24. Salisbury v. Commonwealth, 1908, 79 Ky. 425; Ryan v. Donnelly, 1873, 71 Ill. 100.

25. Waite, Some Inadequacies in the Law of Arrest, 1931, 29 Mich.L.Rev. 448; Waite, Public Policy and the Arrest of Felons, 1933, 31 Mich.L.Rev. 749.

26. Fletcher v. Fletcher, 1859, 28 L.J.Q.B. 134; Witte v. Haben, 1915, 131 Minn. 71, 154 N.W. 662; Crawford v. Brown, 1926, 321 Ill. 305, 151 N.E. 911; Maxwell v. Maxwell, 1920, 189 Iowa 7, 177 N.W. 541; Porter v. Ritch, 1898, 70 Conn. 235, 39 A. 169; see Note, 1950, 35 Corn.L.Q. 904. But mental irresponsibility will be sufficient, and technical insanity need not be proved. Forsythe v. Ivey, 1932, 162 Miss. 471, 139 So. 615.

27. Look v. Dean, 1871, 108 Mass. 116; Keleher v. Putnam, 1880, 60 N.H. 30; Crawford v. Brown, 1926, 321 Ill. 305, 151 N.E. 911; cf. Christiansen v. Weston, 1930, 36 Ariz. 200, 284 P. 149. But a reasonable appearance of necessity usually has been held to be enough. Babb v. Carson, 1924, 116 Kan. 690, 229 P. 76; Dyer v. Dyer, 1941, 178 Tenn. 234, 156 S.W.2d 445; Forsythe v. Ivey, 1932, 162 Miss. 471, 139 So. 615; Springer v. Steiner, 1919, 91 Or. 100, 178 P. 592; Risgaard v. Duvall, 1915, 169 Iowa 711, 151 N.W. 1051. Even here, however, it has been held that the defendant must follow the procedure prescribed by statute,

if he can. Jillson v. Caprio, 1950, 86 U.S.App.D.C. 168, 181 F.2d 523.

28. Coles v. McNamara, 1924, 131 Wash. 377, 230 P. 430; State v. Montgomery, 1910, 230 Mo. 660, 132 S.W. 232; State v. Pugh, 1888, 101 N.C. 737, 7 S.E. 757. See, generally, Perkins, The Law of Arrest, 1940, 25 Iowa L.Rev. 201, 265–289.

29. See Pearson, The Right to Kill in Making Arrests, 1930, 28 Mich.L.Rev. 957; Bohlen and Shulman, Arrest With and Without a Warrant, 1927, 75 U.Pa.L. Rev. 485, 494; Note, 1938, 24 Iowa L.Rev. 154.

30. Dill v. State, 1854, 25 Ala. 15; In re Neagle, 1890, 135 U.S. 1, 10 S.Ct. 658, 34 L.Ed. 55.

31. Cf. State v. Patterson, 1873, 45 Vt. 308; People v. Kuehn, 1892, 93 Mich. 619, 53 N.W. 721; Wright v. Commonwealth, 1887, 85 Ky. 123, 2 S.W. 904.

32. Storey v. State, 1862, 71 Ala. 329; Demato v. People, 1910, 49 Colo. 147, 111 P. 703. Cf. State v. Plumlee, 1933, 177 La. 687, 149 So. 425; State v. Beckham, 1924, 306 Mo. 566, 267 S.W. 817.

33. State v. Smith, 1905, 127 Iowa 534, 103 N.W. 944; Harvey v. City of Bonner Springs, 1917, 102 Kan. 9, 169 P. 563; Crawford v. Commonwealth, 1931, 241 Ky. 391, 44 S.W.2d 286. See the discussion in the Notes, 1950, 38 Ky.L.Rev. 609, 618.

dom with a major penalty. The only justified use of deadly means is the prevention of the escape of a person who is likely to further endanger human life. There are, however, a considerable number of decisions which have held that any felony justifies killing to enforce an arrest.[35] Arrest for a misdemeanor, it is everywhere agreed, does not justify the use of such deadly force, even though the criminal is in flight, and there is no other possible way to apprehend him.[36] If there is resistance, the arresting party may of course defend himself, and kill if it is necessary for his own protection,[37] and he is not required to retreat if a way is open, but may assert his legal authority and stand his ground.[38] But if the resistance does not threaten his safety, the better view, notwithstanding decisions in some states to the contrary,[39] is that the public interest in an arrest for a misdemeanor does not justify the use of deadly force.[40] By the same token, it is regarded as reasonable force to break in the door of a dwelling house to prevent a serious crime,[41] or to arrest after it has occurred,[42] but not to arrest for a misdemeanor,[43] unless the arrest is under a warrant.[44]

Resistance to Unlawful Arrest

If the arrest is unlawful, the traditional rule has been that it may be resisted by reasonable force.[45] But here again, the harm which is likely to be inflicted by unlawful arrest is not sufficiently important to justify the infliction of serious injury, and the use of deadly force is not reasonable, where the personal safety of the one resisting is not in danger.[46]

The modern trend has been toward requiring submission to a known peace officer, even when the arrest is unlawful, in the interest of keeping the peace. This is the position taken by the Uniform Arrest Act[47] and the Model Penal Code.[48] Some courts have

---

34. State v. Bryant, 1871, 65 N.C. 327; Storey v. State, 1882, 71 Ala. 329, 339; Thomas v. Kinkead, 1893, 55 Ark. 502, 18 S.W. 854; Donehy v. Commonwealth, 1916, 170 Ky. 474, 186 S.W. 161. See Pearson, The Right to Kill in Making Arrests, 1930, 28 Mich.L.Rev. 957, 974; Note, 1938, 24 Iowa L.Rev. 154.

35. Jones v. Marshall, 1974, 383 F.Supp. 358, affirmed 528 F.2d 132; Uraneck v. Lima, 359 Mass. 749, 1971, 269 N.E.2d 670; Stinnett v. Commonwealth, 4th Cir. 1932, 55 F.2d 644; Ex parte Warner, 10th Cir. 1927, 21 F.2d 542; Thompson v. Norfolk & Western Railway Co., 1935, 116 W.Va. 705, 182 S.E. 880; Johnson v. Chesapeake & Ohio Railway Co., 1935, 259 Ky. 789, 83 S.W.2d 521.

36. Moore v. Foster, 1938, 182 Miss. 15, 180 So. 73; Evans v. Walker, 1939, 237 Ala. 385, 187 So. 189; Padilla v. Chavez, 1957, 62 N.M. 170, 306 P.2d 1094; State ex rel. Harbin v. Dunn, 1943, 39 Tenn.App. 190, 282 S.W.2d 203; Stevens v. Adams, 1930, 181 Ark. 816, 27 S.W.2d 999; Notes, 1938, 24 Iowa L.Rev. 154; 1940, 5 Mo.L.Rev. 93.

37. Donehy v. Commonwealth, 1916, 170 Ky. 474, 186 S.W. 161; State v. Smith, 1905, 127 Iowa 534, 103 N.W. 944; People v. Hardwick, Cal.App.1928, 260 P. 946, subsequent opinion 204 Cal. 582, 269 P. 427; Gordy v. State, 1956, 93 Ga.App. 743, 92 S.E.2d 737. A fortiori where the force used is not calculated to cause death or serious injury. State v. Phillips, 1903, 119 Iowa 652, 94 N.W. 229.

38. Durham v. State, 1927, 199 Ind. 567, 159 N.E. 145; State v. Dunning, 1919, 177 N.C. 559, 98 S.E. 530; State v. Vargas, 1937, 42 N.M. 1, 74 P.2d 62.

39. State v. Dierberger, 1888, 96 Mo. 666, 10 S.W. 168; Commonwealth v. Marcum, 1909, 135 Ky. 1, 122 S.W. 215; Krueger v. State, 1920, 171 Wis. 566, 177 N.W. 917.

40. Thomas v. Kinkead, 1892, 55 Ark. 502, 18 S.W. 854; People v. Klein, 1922, 305 Ill. 141, 137 N.E. 145; Meldrum v. State, 1914, 23 Wyo. 12, 146 P. 596; People v. Newsome, 1921, 51 Cal.App. 42, 195 P. 938.

41. Handcock v. Baker, 1800, 2 Bos. & P. 260, 120 Eng.Rep. 1270; State v. Stouderman, 1851, 6 La.Ann. 286.

42. Shanley v. Wells, 1873, 71 Ill. 78; Commonwealth v. Phelps, 1911, 209 Mass. 396, 95 N.E. 868; Read v. Case, 1822, 4 Conn. 166.

43. Adair v. Williams, 1922, 24 Ariz. 422, 210 P. 853; McLennon v. Richardson, 1860, 81 Mass. (15 Gray) 74; Hughes v. State, 1922, 145 Tenn. 544, 238 S.W. 588.

44. Hawkins v. Commonwealth, 1854, 53 Ky. 14 B. Mon. 395; Commonwealth v. Reynolds, 1876, 120 Mass. 190.

45. Finch v. State, 1960, 101 Ga.App. 73, 112 S.E.2d 824; Jenkins v. State, 1963, 232 Md. 529, 194 A.2d 618; People v. Cherry, 1954, 307 N.Y. 308, 121 N.E.2d 238; State v. Morrisey, 1962, 257 N.C. 679, 127 S.E.2d 283; State v. Rousseau, 1952, 40 Wn.2d 92, 241 P.2d 447.

46. State v. Perrigo, 1895, 67 Vt. 406, 31 A. 844; State v. Gum, 1910, 68 W.Va. 105, 69 S.E. 463.

47. Uniform Arrest Act, §§ 5, 6. See Warner, The Uniform Arrest Act, 1942, 28 Va.L.Rev. 315.

48. Model Penal Code, § 3.04(2). In State v. Koonce, 1965, 89 N.J.Super. 169, 214 A.2d 428, the court accomplished the same result without a statute. See Notes, 1966, 27 U.Pitt.L.Rev. 716; 1966, 12 Wayne L.Rev. 883.

produced this result even in the absence of a controlling statute.⁴⁹

It must be said here, as has been said elsewhere, that state legislatures have in most states today prescribed the rules that are to be applied for deciding which conduct is criminal, including when an assault or battery has been committed, but these rules and principles are not binding in a civil action for damages. Normally, however, the same policies involved in balancing the public interest in the prevention of crime and the apprehension of criminals with the interest of the individual in freedom from interference at the hands of the law should be applied when reasoning about torts. Therefore, courts have generally adopted the same defenses to civil damages actions for intentional invasions of personality interests which the legislature has allowed in criminal prosecutions.

WESTLAW REFERENCES

"citizen* arrest" /p tort intentional /s interference tort
"citizen* arrest" /p false +2 arrest imprisonment
"warrantless arrest" /p false +2 arrest imprisonment

Means Used to Effect Arrest
digest(arrest /s reasonable +s force) & topic(assault)
digest(arrest /s excessive deadly +s force) & topic(assault)

Resistance to Unlawful Arrest
digest(unlawful** illegal** +s arrest** /s resist!)
unlawful** illegal** +s arrest** /s resist! /s assault***

§ 27. Discipline

In certain situations, the necessity of some degree of orderly discipline vests in persons in control of others the authority to use summary force and restraint, and they will be protected in the exercise of it, if they act in good faith, and in a reasonable manner.

A husband or father, as the head of the household, was recognized by the early law as having authority to discipline the members of his family. He might administer to his wife "moderate correction," and "restrain" her by "domestic chastisement," ¹ although there is probably no truth whatever in the legend that he was permitted to beat her with a stick no thicker than his thumb.² The altered position and independent legal status of married women in modern society has done away with any such discipline. Physical chastisement ³ or imprisonment ⁴ of a wife is everywhere a crime. As a tort, it is limited by the rule which still prevails in many jurisdictions, that one spouse may not maintain an action against the other for a personal tort.⁵ Where this rule has been abandoned, the wife may recover.⁶ The early privilege to chastise domestic servants also is no longer recognized, and the employer's only remedy is discharge, or an action for damage done.⁷

As to children, the privilege remains, despite any modern theories that to spare the rod is not to spoil the child. A parent, or one who stands in the place of a parent,⁸ may use reasonable force, including corporal punishment, for discipline and control. A

---

49. People v. Gnatz, 1972, 8 Ill.App.3d 396, 290 N.E.2d 392; Burgess v. State, Fla.App.1975, 313 So.2d 479, answer to certified questions declined, Fla., 326 So.2d 441. See, Annotation, 1972, 44 A.L.R.3d 1078.

§ 27

1. 1 Bl.Comm., 1765, 444; Stedman, Right of Husband to Chastise Wife, 1917, 3 Va.L.Reg., N.S., 241.

2. See State v. Rhodes, 1868, 61 N.C. 453. But cf. Lord Leigh's Case, 1675, 3 Keble, 433, 84 Eng.Rep. 807, saying that "the salva moderata castigatione in the register is not meant of beating, but only admonition and confinement to the house, in case of extravagance. The Court agreed, she being not as an apprentice."

3. Fulgham v. State, 1871, 46 Ala. 143; Commonwealth v. McAfee, 1871, 108 Mass. 458.

4. Regina v. Jackson, [1891] 1 Q.B. 671.

5. See infra, § 122.

6. Brown v. Brown, 1914, 88 Conn. 42, 89 A. 889; Johnson v. Johnson, 1917, 201 Ala. 41, 77 So. 335; Fiedler v. Fiedler, 1914, 42 Okl. 124, 140 P. 1022.

7. Tinkle v. Dunivant, 1886, 84 Tenn. (16 Lea) 503.

8. Steber v. Norris, 1925, 188 Wis. 366, 206 N.W. 173; Clasen v. Pruhs, 1903, 69 Neb. 278, 95 N.W. 640; Fortinberry v. Holmes, 1907, 89 Miss. 373, 42 So. 799 (one caring for child); Gorman v. State, 1875, 42 Tex. 221 (stepfather); State v. Alford, 1873, 68 N.C. 322 (paramour of mother).

school teacher has the same authority.⁹ It is sometimes said that the parent, by sending the child to school has delegated his discipline to the teacher;¹⁰ but since many children go to public schools under compulsion of law, and the child may well be punished over the objection of the parent, a sounder reason is the necessity for maintaining order in and about the school.¹¹ The teacher's authority extends to all offenses which directly and immediately affect the decorum and morale of the school,¹² including acts done away from the school premises,¹³ but not to outside misconduct by which the school is only remotely affected.¹⁴

The privilege of either parent or teacher¹⁵ extends to the infliction of any corporal punishment which is reasonable under the circumstances; but neither is privileged to use any force which goes beyond that reasonably necessary for the purpose to be accomplished.¹⁶ All of the circumstances are to be taken into consideration, including the nature of the offense, the age, sex and strength of the child, his past behavior, the kind of punishment, and the extent of the harm inflicted.¹⁷ There are some courts, particularly in the older cases, which have said that the judgment of the parent or teacher must control as to the reasonableness of the force used, so long as he acts without malice, and inflicts no serious injury,¹⁸ but the later cases have decided, it would seem more properly for the protection of the helpless at the mercy of the merciless, that the defendant is held to an external standard of what is reasonable under the circumstances.¹⁹

9. See Proehl, Tort Liability of Teachers, 1959, 12 Vand.L.Rev. 723; Notes, 1926, 11 Corn.L.Q. 266; 1964, 15 Hast.L.J. 567.

10. State v. Pendergrass, 1837, 19 N.C. 365; Cleary v. Booth, [1893] 1 Q.B. 465; Quinn v. Nolan, 1878, 7 Ohio (Dec.Repr.) 585.

11. Stevens v. Fassett, 1847, 27 Me. 266; Lander v. Seaver, 1859, 32 Vt. 114; McLeod v. Grant County School District, 1953, 42 Wash. 316, 255 P.2d 360. See Sumption, The Control of Pupil Conduct by the School, 1955, 20 Law & Con.Prob. 80; Proehl, Tort Liability of Teachers, 1959, 12 Vand.L.Rev. 723, 726–7; Note, 1932, 26 Ill.L.Rev. 815.

12. Fertich v. Michener, 1887, 111 Ind. 472, 11 N.E. 605, 14 N.E. 68; Heritage v. Dodge, 1886, 64 N.H. 297, 9 A. 722; Sheehan v. Sturges, 1885, 53 Conn. 481, 2 A. 841; Wilson v. Abilene Independent School District, Tex.Civ.App.1945, 190 S.W.2d 406 refused, for want of merit. Various kinds of rules and regulations which have been upheld are discussed in Sumption, The Control of Pupil Conduct by the School, 1955, 20 Law & Con.Prob. 80, 82–87.

13. Cleary v. Booth, [1893] 1 Q.B. 465; Lander v. Seaver, 1859, 32 Vt. 114 (insulting teacher); O'Rourke v. Walker, 1925, 102 Conn. 130, 128 A. 25 (abusing other pupils); Hutton v. State, 1887, 23 Tex.App. 386, 5 S.W. 122 (fighting); Morrison v. Lawrence, 1904, 186 Mass. 456, 72 N.E. 91 (insulting teacher); Jones v. Cody, 1902, 132 Mich. 13, 92 N.W. 495 (failure to go home from school). See Note, 1926, 11 Corn.L.Q. 266.

14. Murphy v. Board of Directors, 1870, 30 Iowa 429 (article ridiculing school board); State ex rel. Clark v. Osborne, 1887, 24 Mo.App. 309; 1888, 32 Mo.App. 536 (attending social gathering). The privilege does not extend to forcible treatment of injury or disease. Guerrieri v. Tyson, 1942, 147 Pa.Super. 239, 24 A.2d 468.

15. Suits v. Glover, 1954, 260 Ala. 449, 71 So.2d 49; Drake v. Thomas, 1941, 310 Ill.App. 57, 33 N.E.2d 889; State v. Pendergrass, 1837, 19 N.C. 365; People v. Curtiss, 1931, 116 Cal.App.Supp. 771, 300 P. 801.

16. People v. Green, 1909, 155 Mich. 524, 119 N.W. 1087; Clasen v. Pruhs, 1903, 69 Neb. 278, 95 N.W. 640; State v. Vanderbilt, 1888, 116 Ind. 11, 18 N.E. 266; Calway v. Williamson, 1944, 130 Conn. 575, 36 A.2d 377 (kneeling on stomach); Frank v. Orleans Parish School Board, La.App.1967, 195 So.2d 451, writ refused 250 La. 635, 197 So.2d 653 (lifting, shaking and dropping boy).

17. Fabian v. State, 1964, 235 Md. 306, 201 A.2d 511, certiorari denied 379 U.S. 869, 85 S.Ct. 135, 13 L.Ed.2d 72; Tinkham v. Kole, 1961, 252 Iowa 1303, 110 N.W.2d 258; Marlar v. Bill, 1944, 181 Tenn. 100, 178 S.W.2d 634 ("slight punishment with a ruler" reasonable); Fertich v. Michener, 1887, 111 Ind. 472, 11 N.E. 605, rehearing denied 14 N.E. 68 (detention after school); Patterson v. Nutter, 1886, 78 Me. 509, 7 A. 273. See Miller, Resort to Corporal Punishment in Enforcing School Discipline, 1950, 1 Syr.L.Rev. 247; Note, 1926, 11 Corn.L.Q. 266.

Considerable force may be justified in the case of an insolent or incorrigible pupil. Drake v. Thomas, 1941, 310 Ill.App. 57, 33 N.E.2d 889; Andreozzi v. Rubano, 1958, 145 Conn. 280, 141 A.2d 639.

18. State v. Pendergrass, 1837, 19 N.C. 365; Boyd v. State, 1889, 88 Ala. 169, 7 So. 268; Heritage v. Dodge, 1886, 64 N.H. 297, 9 A. 722; Dean v. State, 1890, 89 Ala. 46, 8 So. 38; People v. Green, 1909, 155 Mich. 524, 119 N.W. 1087. In other words, only good faith is required. This position is defended in Cooperrider, Child v. Parent in Tort: A Case for the Jury? 1958, 43 Minn.L.Rev. 73.

19. Patterson v. Nutter, 1886, 78 Me. 509, 7 A. 273; Steber v. Norris, 1925, 188 Wis. 366, 206 N.W. 173;

Acts of corporal punishment by public school teachers have been challenged recently with constitutional due process attacks. But in Ingraham v. Wright,[20] the Supreme Court held that there is no deprivation of substantive rights as long as disciplinary corporal punishment is within the common law privilege to use only such force as is reasonably necessary for discipline and control of the classroom. The Court went on to say that in Florida, where the case arose, the statutory procedures which must be followed and the traditional common law action for damages for excessive punishment give reasonable assurance that the risk that children will be corporally punished without cause or to excess is insufficient to require the prior administrative safeguards of a hearing.

In some jurisdictions, the old rule that a child may not maintain an action against a parent for a personal tort still prevents any civil remedy for excessive force.[21] Where the action can be brought, the child may recover.[22] The rule, of course, affords no immunity to a teacher.

For obvious reasons, military and naval officers have a power of discipline over their subordinates, which is governed by military law.[23] The necessities of the sea have established a time-honored authority in the master of a ship, not only over the crew, but also over passengers. But here again, the authority is limited, and the use of unreasonable force becomes a tort. The captain will be liable if he attacks a steward with a belaying pin for disobedience,[24] or puts a passenger in irons for calling him the landlord of a floating hotel.[25]

In many cases, the order of a superior officer has been held to protect a soldier or inferior officer from liability, where it was apparently lawful, and any want of authority was unknown to the inferior.[26] By analogy to the case of a civil officer executing a warrant "fair on its face," [27] this seems the desirable rule, notwithstanding occasional cases to the contrary.[28]

WESTLAW REFERENCES

"loco parentis" /p discipline punish! /p school* 345k169

corporal bodily physical +5 punishment /p school & tort assault

---

People v. Curtiss, 1931, 116 Cal.App.Supp. 771, 300 P. 801; Clasen v. Pruhs, 1903, 69 Neb. 278, 95 N.W. 640; State v. Fischer, 1953, 245 Iowa 170, 60 N.W.2d 105; cf. Drum v. Miller, 1904, 135 N.C. 204, 47 S.E. 421. See Note, 1932, 26 Ill.L.Rev. 815.

20. 1977, 430 U.S. 651, 97 S.Ct. 1401, 51 L.Ed.2d 711.

21. See infra, § 122.

22. Treschman v. Treschman, 1901, 28 Ind.App. 206, 61 N.E. 961. Criminal liability for battery never was affected by the immunity. Cf. State v. Black, 1950, 360 Mo. 261, 227 S.W.2d 1006.

23. See for example Keppleman v. Upston, N.D.Cal. 1949, 84 F.Supp. 478 (false imprisonment); Wright v. White, 1941, 166 Or. 136, 110 P.2d 948 (malicious prosecution).

24. Padmore v. Piltz, D.Wash.1890, 44 F. 104; Brown v. Howard, N.Y.1817, 14 Johns. 119 (brutal punishment). The flogging of sailors, upheld in Michaelson v. Denison, C.C.Conn.1808, Fed.Cas.No. 9,523, 3 Day 294, would quite certainly not be permitted today.

25. King v. Franklin, 1858, 1 F. & F. 360, 175 Eng. Rep. 764. In all cases which will admit of the delay, due inquiry should precede the act of punishment, and the party charged should be heard in his own defense. The Agincourt, 1824, 1 Hagg. 271, 166 Eng.Rep. 96.

26. Herlihy v. Donohue, 1916, 52 Mont. 601, 161 P. 164; Franks v. Smith, 1911, 142 Ky. 232, 134 S.W. 484; Trammell v. Bassett, 1866, 24 Ark. 299; cf. United States v. Clark, C.C.Mich.1887, 31 F. 710; Neu v. McCarthy, 1941, 309 Mass. 17, 33 N.E.2d 570. See Second Restatement of Torts, § 146.

27. See infra, § 132.

28. Bates v. Clark, 1877, 95 U.S. 204.

Chapter 5

NEGLIGENCE: STANDARD OF CONDUCT

Table of Sections

Sec.
28. History.
29. Unavoidable Accident.
30. Elements of Cause of Action.
31. Unreasonable Risk.
32. The Reasonable Person.
33. Application of the Standard.
34. Degrees of Care; Aggravated Negligence.
35. Rules of Law.
36. Violation of Statute.

§ 28. History

Although the strands of fault and carelessness may be traced in accident law back for centuries, negligence took shape as a separate tort only during the earlier part of the nineteenth century.[1] Prior to that time the word had been used in a very general sense to describe the breach of any legal obligation, or to designate a mental element, usually one of inadvertence or indifference, entering into the commission of other torts.[2] Some writers, in fact, once maintained that negligence was merely one way of committing any other tort, and itself had no particular legal significance,[3] just as some courts, for example, spoke occasionally of a negligent "battery."[4] But for more than a century, it has received more or less general

§ 28

1. Winfield, The History of Negligence in the Law of Torts, 1926, 42 L.Q.Rev. 184; Gregory, Trespass to Negligence to Absolute Liability, 1951, 37 Va.L.Rev. 359; Malone, Ruminations on the Role of Fault in the History of the Common Law of Torts, 1970, 31 La.L.Rev. 1; Arnold, Accident, Mistake, and Rules of Liability in the Fourteenth-Century Law of Torts, 1979, 128 U.Pa.L.Rev. 361; Rabin, The Historical Development of the Fault Principle: A Reinterpretation, 1981, 15 Ga. L.Rev. 925; Schwartz, Tort Law and the Economy in Nineteenth-Century America: A Reinterpretation, 1981, 90 Yale L.J. 1717; Roberts, Negligence: Blackstone to Shaw to? An Intellectual Escapade in a Tory Vein, 1965, 50 Cornell L.Q. 191; Donnelly, The Fault Principle: A Sketch of its Development in Tort Law During the Nineteenth Century, 1967, 18 Syr.L.Rev. 728.

2. Wigmore, Responsibility for Tortious Acts: Its History, 1894, 7 Harv.L.Rev. 315, 441, 453.

3. Salmond, Law of Torts, 6th ed. 1924, 21–26; Jenks, History of English Law, 1934, 319, 320.

4. See supra, § 6.

recognition as an independent basis of liability, with distinct features of its own, differing on the one hand from the intentional torts, and on the other from those in which strict liability is imposed.

One of the earliest appearances of what we now know as negligence was in the liability of those who professed to be competent in certain "public" callings. A carrier, an innkeeper, a blacksmith, or a surgeon, was regarded as holding oneself out to the public as one in whom confidence might be reposed, and hence as assuming an obligation to give proper service, for the breach of which, by any negligent conduct, he might be liable.[5] But in the field of trespass and nuisance, the notion also developed, thinly disguised, that there might be liability for negligence; and in later years, the action on the case produced a large, undigested group of situations in which negligence was the essence of the tort.[6] Since the early law found its hands full in dealing with the more serious forms of misbehavior, it was natural that the early cases should be concerned almost exclusively with positive acts, rather than with omissions to act, or with "misfeasance" rather than "nonfeasance." Slowly, however, the idea developed that certain relations between the parties might impose an obligation to take affirmative action, so that there might also be liability for nonfeasance.[7] Any such obligation remains to this day very largely a matter of some specific relation, by reason of which the defendant may be regarded as having undertaken a duty to act.[8]

During the first half of the nineteenth century, negligence began to gain recognition as a separate and independent basis of tort liability. Its rise coincided in a marked degree with the Industrial Revolution; and it very probably was stimulated by the rapid increase in the number of accidents caused by industrial machinery, and in particular by the invention of railways.[9] It was greatly encouraged by the disintegration of the old forms of action, and the disappearance of the distinction between direct and indirect injuries, found in trespass and case. The cause of action which at last emerged from this process of reshuffling took on, in general, the aspects of the action on the case, largely because the facts upon which the initial decisions were based fitted that action. Intentional injuries, whether direct or indirect, began to be grouped as a distinct field of liability, and negligence remained as the main basis for unintended torts. Negligence thus developed into the dominant cause of action for accidental injury in this nation today.[10]

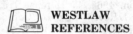 **WESTLAW REFERENCES**

272k1
di standard of care
histor! "common law" /p liab! /p nonfeasance

---

5. Winfield, The History of Negligence in the Law of Torts, 1926, 42 L.Q.Rev. 184; Ames, History of Assumpsit, 1888, 2 Harv.L.Rev. 1; Arterburn, The Origin and First Test of Public Callings, 1927, 75 U.Pa.L.Rev. 411.

6. Winfield, The History of Negligence in the Law of Torts, 1926, 42 L.Q.Rev. 184.

7. Bohlen, The Basis of Affirmative Obligations in the Law of Torts, 1905, 53 Am.L.Reg., N.S., 209, 293.

8. See infra, § 56.

9. "Perhaps one of the chief agencies in the growth of the idea is industrial machinery. Early railway trains, in particular, were notable neither for speed nor for safety. They killed any object from a Minister of State to a wandering cow, and this naturally reacted on the law." Winfield, The History of Negligence in the Law of Torts, 1926, 42 L.Q.Rev. 184, 195.

10. This is not to say that the negligence theory of liability is beyond criticism, or that it is here to stay, for it has been subjected to powerful re-examination in recent years. See generally O'Connell, Ending Insult to Injury—No-Fault Insurance for Products and Services, 1975; Atiyah, Accidents, Compensation and the Law, 3d ed., 1980, ch. 19; R. Keeton, Venturing to do Justice, 1969, ch. 9; Franklin, Replacing the Negligence Lottery: Compensation and Selective Reimbursement, 1967, 53 Va.L.Rev. 774; Epstein, A Theory of Strict Liability, 1973, 2 J.Leg.Stud. 151; Rodgers, Negligence Reconsidered: The Role of Rationality in Tort Theory, 1980, 54 So.Cal.L.Rev. 1.

§ 29. Unavoidable Accident

An unavoidable accident [1] is an occurrence which was not intended and which, under all the circumstances, could not have been foreseen or prevented by the exercise of reasonable precautions. That is, an accident is considered unavoidable or inevitable at law if it was not proximately caused by the negligence of any party to the action, or to the accident.[2] No accident, of course, is entirely inevitable, so long as it results from a voluntary human act. If the defendant rides a horse, which runs away with him and injures the plaintiff, the accident is not strictly inevitable, since the defendant intentionally rode the horse, and might have prevented all harm by keeping him in the barn. But the runaway is called "unavoidable" if it did not result from any lack of foresight or proper care in the management of the horse, because both wrongful intent and negligence are lacking. There is no liability in such a case.[3] Upon the same basis, the driver of an automobile who suddenly loses control of the car because the driver is seized with a heart attack, a stroke, a fainting spell, or an epileptic fit is not liable, unless the driver knew that he might become ill, in which case he may have been negligent in driving the car at all.[4] The same conclusions are reached when a driver strikes a child [5] or an animal [6] which darts in front of the car or when his attention is diverted by an unusual event.[7] Such rules are adopted because the

§ 29

1. Other terms include "inevitable accident," "mere accident," "pure accident," and "accident." The unavoidable accident doctrine logically subsumes the narrower doctrines of Act of God and sudden emergency. Cf. Bass v. Aetna Insurance Co., La.1979, 370 So.2d 511 (Act of God defense inapplicable to case where worshiper, "trotting under the Spirit of the Lord," collided with another worshiper praying in the aisle). See generally Rees, Unavoidable Accident—A Misunderstood Concept, 1964, 5 Ariz.L.Rev. 225; Kirchner, Sudden Illness as a Defense in Auto Accidents, 1967, 16 Clev.-Marsh.L.Rev. 523; Berry, The Unavoidable Accident Instruction, 1968, 17 Defense L.J. 259; Notes, 1976, 25 Drake L.Rev. 754 (Act of God defense); 1973, 52 Neb.L.Rev. 559; 1966, 19 Okla.L.Rev. 308; Annots., 1959, 65 A.L.R.2d 12 (auto cases); 1979, 93 A.L.R.3d 326 (auto accident from blackout or sudden unconsciousness).

2. Definitions vary from state to state, reflecting the nature and scope of the doctrine as applied in the jurisdiction. E.g., Hyatt Creek Builders-Engineers Co. v. Board of Regents, Tex.Civ.App.1980, 607 S.W.2d 258, 266, error dismissed ("an event * * * which was not proximately caused by the negligence of any party to the event"); Howard v. Howard, Ky.App.1980, 607 S.W.2d 119, 120 ("unforeseen and unexpected, occurring externally to all persons affected by it"); Zayre of Georgia, Inc. v. Haynes, 1975, 134 Ga.App. 15, 213 S.E.2d 163, 165 ("It may be an 'act of God' * * * or a pure casualty which exists without fault or carelessness on the part of either party * * * [or] an accident to the parties where * * * any negligence involved was attributable to one not a party to the suit or one too young to be legally chargeable therewith."). See also Anderton v. Montgomery, Utah 1980, 607 P.2d 828, 834 ("Unavoidable accident, rather than being a separate legal doctrine, is simply a recognition of the fact that an incident causing injury to the plaintiff does not necessarily give rise to liability in the defendant.").

3. Gibbons v. Pepper, 1695, 1 Ld.Raym. 38, 91 Eng. Rep. 922; Steudle v. Rentchler, 1872, 64 Ill. 161.

4. *Compare* Moore v. Presnell, 1977, 38 Md.App. 243, 379 A.2d 1246 (blackout unforeseeable despite hypertension medication); Cox v. Vernieuw, Wyo.1980, 604 P.2d 1353 (no reason to anticipate blackout from heart condition; yet Act of God rule inapplicable to a defendant's physical affliction); and Frechette v. Welch, 1st Cir. 1980, 621 F.2d 11 (unforeseeable blackout); *with* Reliance Insurance Co. v. Dickens, La.App. 1973, 279 So.2d 234 (epileptic attack foreseeable to driver with 8-year history of seizures). See generally Kraig, Heart Attack as a Defense in Negligence Actions, 1963, 12 Clev.-Marsh.L.Rev. 59; Kirchner, Sudden Illness as a Defense in Auto Accidents, 1967, 16 Clev.-Marsh.L.Rev. 523; Annot., 1979, 93 A.L.R.3d 326.

Although falling asleep at the wheel is often deemed negligent as a matter of law, see Annot., 1953, 28 A.L.R.2d 12, some courts permit a jury to find for the defendant in such a case if there was no prior warning of drowsiness. See Smith v. McIntyre, 1964, 20 A.D.2d 711, 247 N.Y.S.2d 361. Cf. Price v. Glosson Motor Lines, Inc., 4th Cir. 1975, 509 F.2d 1033. See generally Kaufman & Kantrowitz, The Case of the Sleeping Motorist, 1950, 25 N.Y.U.L.Q.Rev. 362; Notes, [1950] Wis. L.Rev. 334; 1944, 18 St.Johns.L.Rev. 95.

5. Compare Yarborough v. Berner, Tex.1971, 467 S.W.2d 188 (defendant entitled to unavoidable accident instruction if evidence at retrial showed 4-year-old child darted in front of car), with Alley v. Siepman, 1974, 87 S.D. 670, 214 N.W.2d 7 (defendant not entitled to instruction where accident occurred at time and place where pedestrian crossing road could well have been anticipated).

6. Rush v. State Farm Mutual Automobile Insurance Co., La.App.1973, 274 So.2d 461 (darting cow: unavoidable).

7. See Seals v. Morris, La.App.1980, 387 So.2d 1220, writ granted 393 So.2d 745 (green snake crawling on driver's shoulder: accident unavoidable), reversed 410

line must be drawn somewhere, and if the defendant is to be held liable merely because he has ridden the horse or driven the car, it would be quite as logical, at least in the eyes of the law, to hold the driver liable for owning it, or even for drawing his breath or being born.[8] To hold that a person does every voluntary act at his peril, and must insure others against all of the consequences that may occur would, in most instances, be an intolerably heavy burden upon human activity.[9]

Nevertheless, as to injuries to person or property which followed as the more direct and immediate consequences of a voluntary act, and for which an action of trespass would lie, the early common law imposed a very strict responsibility.[10] The defendant who fired a gun, and accidentally wounded the plaintiff, was held liable unless he could establish that the accident was inevitable—"judged utterly without his fault; as if a man by force take my hand and strike you—"[11] and the burden was upon the defendant to prove that such was the case.[12]

As has been stated above,[13] the progress of the law [14] generally has been away from this position. There were jurisdictions in which the rule survived well into the nineteenth century that, if the defendant voluntarily discharged the gun, he was liable for the injury.[15] But in Brown v. Kendall,[16] where the defendant, interfering in a dog fight, raised his stick and accidentally struck a man behind him, the Massachusetts court held that there was no liability in the absence of some wrongful intent or negligence. This case is now uniformly followed in the great majority of situations.[17]

Beginning principally with a California decision in 1958,[18] jury instructions on the unavoidable accident doctrine have been falling into disfavor in a growing number of jurisdictions.[19] Such an instruction, it is argued, confuses and misleads the jury because it merely restates the principles of duty, negligence and proximate causation yet appears to inject a separate issue which tends to overemphasize and favor the defendant's

So.2d 715 (driver negligently left window open under trees while fishing, permitting snake to enter). Cf. Lussan v. Grain Dealers Mutual Insurance Co., 5th Cir. 1960, 280 F.2d 491 (driver's attention diverted by a Louisiana "wasp—or a bee—it really doesn't matter"; citing cases involving a Connecticut bee and a diversity Eighth Circuit Iowa wasp).

8. See Hollingsworth v. Thomas, 1978, 148 Ga.App. 38, 250 S.E.2d 791 (milkmaid's eye injury from Granny's swishing tail was unavoidable accident; cow owner not liable). Cf. Laite v. Baxter, 1972, 126 Ga.App. 743, 191 S.E.2d 531 (13-year-old boy's slipping on rock while throwing stone in stream was "nothing more than an accident"; custodian not liable).

9. Holmes, The Common Law, 1881, 93–96.

10. 3 Holdsworth, History of English Law, 1931, 375 ff.; 1 Street, Foundations of Legal Liability, 1906, 73–85; Wigmore, Responsibility for Tortious Acts: Its History, 1884, 7 Harv.L.Rev. 315, 383, 441; Bohlen, Liability in Tort of Infants and Insane Persons, 1924, 23 Mich.L.Rev. 9. But compare Winfield, Law of Torts, 5th ed. 1950, 43–44.

11. Weaver v. Ward, 1616, Hob. 134, 80 Eng.Rep. 284.

12. Weaver v. Ward, 1616, Hob. 134, 80 Eng.Rep. 284; Dickenson v. Watson, 1682, T. Jones 205, 84 Eng. Rep. 148; Leame v. Bray, 1803, 3 East 593, 102 Eng. Rep. 724.

13. Supra, § 6.

14. See 1 Street, Foundations of Legal Liability, 1906, 73–85; Wigmore, Responsibility for Tortious Acts: Its History, 1884, 7 Harv.L.Rev. 315, 383, 441.

15. Vincent v. Stinehour, 1835, 7 Vt. 62; Wright v. Clark, 1877, 50 Vt. 130; cf. Jennings v. Fundeburg, 1827, 4 S.C. (McCord) 161; Morgan v. Cox, 1856, 22 Mo. 373.

16. 1850, 60 Mass. (6 Cush.) 292.

17. The older rule was finally put to rest in England in Fowler v. Lanning, [1959] 1 Q.B. 426. See also Letang v. Cooper, [1965] 1 Q.B. 232 (C.A.); Beals v. Hayward, [1960] N.Z.L.Rep. 131; Walmsley v. Humenick, [1954] 2 Dom.L.Rep. 232.

18. Butigan v. Yellow Cab Co., 1958, 49 Cal.2d 652, 320 P.2d 500, 65 A.L.R.2d 1 (doctrine "obsolete remnant from a time when damages * * * directly caused by a voluntary act * * * could be recovered in an action of trespass and when strict liability would be imposed unless the defendant proved * * * 'inevitable accident'"). 320 P.2d at 504.

19. "The distinct trend appears to be in the direction of extemely restricted use of this instruction if not outright disapproval." Graham v. Rolandson, 1967, 150 Mont. 270, 435 P.2d 263, 272. See Cook v. Harris, 1976, ___ W.Va. ___, 225 S.E.2d 676, 679 ("The law does not look kindly upon the concept of unavoidable accident in negligence cases [and] instructions on the subject * * * are generally regarded with disfavor and should ordinarily be refused.")

case.[20] Persuaded by arguments such as these, many courts have emphasized that the instruction should be reserved for exceptional situations where called for by the unique facts of a particular case,[21] and some have more generally disapproved the unavoidable accident instruction for use in negligence cases altogether.[22] Probably a majority of jurisdictions still permit the instruction in appropriate cases, however, and the instruction is still stoutly defended as helpful in focusing the issues in proper cases.[23] Neither the unavoidable accident doctrine nor instructions thereon should be expected to wither away completely any time soon because of the notion's underlying logical simplicity and because such instructions, properly applied, may usefully serve to translate the arcane words and concepts of the law into a common sense perspective of everyday life and experience that jurors can readily understand.[24]

 WESTLAW REFERENCES

272k140 /p "unavoidable accident"

heart coronary epilep! faint! /10 seizure* attack* & "unavoidable accident"

20. See, e.g., Butigan v. Yellow Cab Co., 1958, 49 Cal.2d 652, 320 P.2d 500, 65 A.L.R.2d 1; Graham v. Rolandson, 1967, 150 Mont. 270, 435 P.2d 263, 273.

21. See, e.g., Del Vecchio v. Lund, S.D.1980, 293 N.W.2d 474; Damron v. Hagy, 1979, 220 Va. 455, 258 S.E.2d 517, 518 (occasion for use of instruction "'rare'"; "'only where there is a reasonable theory of the evidence under which the parties involved may be held to have exercised due care'"); Guanzon v. Kalamau, 1965, 48 Hawaii 330, 402 P.2d 289.

22. Graham v. Rolandson, 1967, 150 Mont. 270, 435 P.2d 263; Miller v. Alvey, 1965, 246 Ind. 560, 207 N.E.2d 633; Koll v. Manatt's Transportation Co., Iowa 1977, 253 N.W.2d 265; Lewis v. Buckskin Joe's Inc., 1964, 156 Colo. 46, 396 P.2d 933; Fenton v. Aleshire, 1964, 238 Or. 24, 393 P.2d 217; Schaub v. Linehan, 1968, 92 Idaho 332, 442 P.2d 742; Camaras v. Moran, 1966, 100 R.I. 717, 219 A.2d 487; George v. Guerette, Me.1973, 306 A.2d 138; Alexander v. Delgado, 1973, 84 N.M. 717, 507 P.2d 778 (summarizing arguments); Vespe v. DiMarco, 1964, 43 N.J. 430, 204 A.2d 874. See also Deskin v. Brewer, Mo.App.1979, 590 S.W.2d 392, 402 (at least in auto collision cases, per M.A.I. 1.01 (2d ed.1969)); Maxwell v. Olsen, Alaska 1970, 468 P.2d 48 (semble); City of Phoenix v. Camfield, 1965, 97 Ariz. 316, 400 P.2d 115 (semble); Cox v. Vernieuw, Wyo. 1980, 604 P.2d 1353 (Act of God defense not appropriate in negligence cases).

brown /5 kendall /15 60 /5 292

jury /s instruct! /s "unavoidable accident" /s permit! permissible allow!

§ 30. Elements of Cause of Action

Negligence, as we shall see,[1] is simply one kind of conduct. But a cause of action founded upon negligence, from which liability will follow, requires more than conduct. The traditional formula for the elements necessary to such a cause of action may be stated briefly as follows:[2]

1. A duty, or obligation, recognized by the law, requiring the person to conform to a certain standard of conduct, for the protection of others against unreasonable risks.[3]

2. A failure on the person's part to conform to the standard required: a breach of the duty. These two elements go to make up what the courts usually have called negligence; but the term quite frequently is applied to the second alone. Thus it may be said that the defendant was negligent, but is not liable because he was under no duty to the plaintiff not to be.

23. See, e.g., Anderton v. Montgomery, Utah 1980, 607 P.2d 828, 835 (in light of instructions on res ipsa loquitur, it was "not only permissible but indeed proper that the need to find negligence, by one means or another, be reemphasized"); Butigan v. Yellow Cab Co., 1958, 49 Cal.2d 652, 320 P.2d 500, 508 (dissenting opinion) (instruction "can lead only to *better understanding*").

24. Indeed, even if purged, such instructions have an uncanny habit of sneaking back. See, e.g., Ernst v. Sparacino, 1978, 177 Ind.App. 610, 380 N.E.2d 1271.

§ 30

1. See infra, § 31.

2. See, e.g., Knight v. United States, E.D.Mich. 1980, 498 F.Supp. 315; Anderson v. Green Bay & Western Railroad, 1980, 99 Wisc.2d 514, 299 N.W.2d 615; Arneson v. City of Fargo, N.D.1981, 303 N.W.2d 515; ABC Builders, Inc. v. Phillips, Wyo.1981, 632 P.2d 925; Lawyers Surety Corp. v. Snell, Tex.Civ.App.1981, 617 S.W.2d 750; Quillen v. Quillen, Ala.1980, 388 So.2d 985; Beauchene v. Synanon Foundation, Inc., 1979, 88 Cal. App.3d 342, 151 Cal.Rptr. 796; Strother v. Hutchinson, 1981, 67 Ohio St.2d 282, 423 N.E.2d 467 (including element of plaintiff's freedom from contributory negligence). See generally Second Restatement of Torts, § 281.

3. See infra, ch. 9.

3. A reasonably close causal connection between the conduct and the resulting injury. This is what is commonly known as "legal cause," or "proximate cause," and which includes the notion of cause in fact.[4]

4. Actual loss or damage resulting to the interests of another.[5] Since the action for negligence developed chiefly out of the old form of action on the case, it retained the rule of that action, that proof of damage was an essential part of the plaintiff's case. Nominal damages, to vindicate a technical right, cannot be recovered in a negligence action, where no actual loss has occurred.[6] The threat of future harm, not yet realized, is not enough.[7] Negligent conduct in itself is not such an interference with the interests of the world at large that there is any right to complain of it, or to be free from it, except in the case of some individual whose interests have suffered.[8]

It follows that the statute of limitations is generally held not to begin to run against a negligence action until some damage has occurred.[9] Real difficulties have resulted where, as is frequently the case in actions for medical malpractice [10] and in products liability actions involving toxic drugs or chemicals,[11] the statute has run before the plaintiff discovers that he has suffered injury, and sometimes even before the plaintiff himself has suffered the injury. The older approach to such cases was a literal application of the statute to bar the action, regarding it as intended to protect the defendant, not only against fictitious claims, but also against the difficulty of obtaining evidence after the lapse of time even when the defendant is confronted with a genuine one—the hardship upon the plaintiff being considered as merely part of the price to be paid for such protection.[12]

---

4. See, e.g., Beauchene v. Synanon Foundation, Inc., 1979, 88 Cal.App.3d 342, 151 Cal.Rptr. 796 (stated as separate elements); Reiman Associates, Inc. v. R/A Advertising, Inc., 1981, 102 Wisc.2d 305, 306 N.W.2d 292 (legal cause comprised of two components, cause in fact and proximate cause). See infra, ch. 7.

5. See, e.g., Richards v. City of Lawton, Okl.1981, 629 P.2d 1260; Cannon v. Sears Roebuck & Co., 1978, 374 Mass. 739, 374 N.E.2d 582.

6. See Hall v. Cornett, 1952, 193 Or. 634, 240 P.2d 231; Kirby v. Carlisle, 1955, 178 Pa.Super. 389, 116 A.2d 220; Alhino v. Starr, 1980, 112 Cal.App.3d 158, 169 Cal.Rptr. 136; Second Restatement of Torts, § 907, Comment a.

7. Johnson v. Rouchleau-Ray Iron Land Co., 1918, 140 Minn. 289, 168 N.W. 1. See Alhino v. Starr, 1980, 112 Cal.App.3d 158, 169 Cal.Rptr. 136. It should be noted, however, that the danger of future harm may in itself cause present damage, as in nuisance cases, where it interferes with the enjoyment of land. See infra, ch. 15.

8. Such a statement must, however, be qualified to the extent that, as in the case of other torts, where irreparable injury is threatened, a court of equity may act by injunction to prevent the harm before it occurs. Even here the damage, even though only potential, is the basis for granting relief.

9. See, e.g., White v. Schnoebelen, 1941, 91 N.H. 273, 18 A.2d 185; Cannon v. Sears, Roebuck & Co., 1978, 374 Mass. 739, 374 N.E.2d 582; Locke v. Johns-Manville Corp., Va.1981, 275 S.E.2d 900 (asbestosis: statute runs from date of injury, which is date when cancer or lung impairment begins, rather than date of discovery or exposure). But cf. Steinhardt v. Johns-Manville Corp., 1981, 54 N.Y.2d 1008, 446 N.Y.S.2d 244, 430 N.E.2d 1297, dismissed 456 U.S. 967, 102 S.Ct. 2226, 72 L.Ed.2d 840 (asbestosis: statute runs from date of last exposure; discovery rule must come from legislature); H. Hirschfield Sons Co. v. Colt Industries Operating Corp., 1981, 107 Mich.App. 720, 309 N.W.2d 714 (statute runs from date of wrong, not damage: date of defective installation of truck scales). Compare Martin v. Edwards Laboratories, Sup.1982, 112 Misc.2d 93, 446 N.Y.S.2d 182 (cerebral hemorrhage from teflon particles in bloodstream from broken valve of artificial heart valve; injury occurred upon breakage of valve); Klein v. Dow Corning Corp., 2d Cir.1981, 661 F.2d 998 (injury occurred and statute began to run when silicone breast prosthesis burst, not when implanted).

As was observed long ago, "[i]t would be a laborious and unprofitable task to examine all the cases which have been decided on the statute of limitations." Fries v. Boisselet, Pa.1822, 9 Serg. & R. 128, 130 (Tilghman, C.J.).

10. See, e.g., Lilich, The Malpractice Statute of Limitations in New York and Other Jurisdictions, 1962, 47 Corn.L.Q. 339.

11. See Anthony v. Koppers Co., 1980, 284 Pa. Super. 81, 425 A.2d 428 (Spaeth, J.) (cancer from coke oven emissions; scholarly and exhaustive analysis), reversed, 1981, 496 Pa. 119, 436 A.2d 181. Comment, 1978, 7 Ford.Urb.L.J. 55 (asbestosis); Note, 1983, 96 Harv.L.Rev. 1683.

12. Hawks v. De Hart, 1966, 206 Va. 810, 146 S.E. 2d 187; Vaughn v. Langmack, 1964, 236 Or. 542, 390 P.2d 142; Pasquale v. Chandler, 1966, 350 Mass. 450, 215 N.E.2d 319.

The apparent injustice and illogic of this approach [13] has led to the adoption by many courts of various devices to circumvent the rule. Thus, the negligent treatment, or at least the defendant's duty, is held to continue until the relation of physician and patient has ended; [14] or the court finds fraudulent concealment of the damage or its cause, which tolls the running of the statute; [15] or, in some jurisdictions, the defendant's silence, where a confidential relationship gives rise to a duty to speak; [16] or the failure to discover and remove the sponge or other foreign object left in the plaintiff's body is held to be "continuing" negligence.[17]

Beginning in the medical malpractice area, a wave of decisions and legislative enactments has met the issue head-on by tolling the statute until the plaintiff has in fact discovered that he has suffered injury, or by the exercise of reasonable diligence should have discovered it.[18] This "discovery rule" appears infectious, and it has been spread-

---

13. "Except in topsy-turvy land, you can't die before you are conceived, or be divorced before ever you marry, or harvest a crop never planted, or burn down a house never built, or miss a train running on a non-existent railroad. For substantially similar reasons, it has always heretofore been accepted, as a sort of legal 'axiom,' that a statute of limitations does not begin to run against a cause of action before that cause of action exists, i.e., before a judicial remedy is available to the plaintiff." Frank, J., dissenting in Dincher v. Marlin Firearms Co., 2d Cir.1952, 198 F.2d 821, 823, quoted approvingly in Patterson v. Her Majesty Industries, Inc., E.D.Pa.1978, 450 F.Supp. 425, 428.

14. Samuelson v. Freeman, 1969, 75 Wn.2d 894, 454 P.2d 406; Borgia v. City of New York, 1962, 12 N.Y.2d 151, 237 N.Y.S.2d 319, 187 N.E.2d 777 (medical malpractice); Ballenger v. Crowell, 1978, 38 N.C.App. 50, 247 S.E.2d 287 (same); Wilkin v. Dana R. Pickup & Co., Sup.1973, 74 Misc.2d 1025, 347 N.Y.S.2d 122 (accountant); Greene v. Greene, 1982, 56 N.Y.2d 86, 451 N.Y.S.2d 46, 436 N.E.2d 496. See Flora's Card Shop, Inc. v. Paul Krantz & Co., Sup.1981, 111 Misc.2d 907, 445 N.Y.S.2d 392 (insurance broker: exception not applied). See generally Zepkin, Virginia's Continuing Negligent Treatment Rule: *Farley v. Goods* and *Fenton v. Danaceau*, 1981, 15 U.Rich.L.Rev. 231.

15. Brown v. Bleiberg, 1982, 32 Cal.3d 426, 186 Cal.Rptr. 228, 651 P.2d 815; Krueger v. St. Joseph's Hospital, N.D.1981, 305 N.W.2d 18; Van Bronckhorst v. Taube, 1976, 168 Ind.App. 132, 341 N.E.2d 791 (equitable fraudulent concealment doctrine, not similar statute, applied to medical malpractice claim); Alford v. Summerlin, Fla.App.1978, 362 So.2d 103 (doctor allegedly lied to father concerning cause of daughter's death).

16. Morrison v. Acton, 1948, 68 Ariz. 27, 198 P.2d 590 ("constructive fraud"); Hardin v. Farris, 1974, 87 N.M. 143, 530 P.2d 407; Garcia v. Presbyterian Hospital Center, 1979, 92 N.M. 652, 593 P.2d 487 (dissent argued that fraudulent concealment exception should not apply since no confidential relationship existed between hospital and patient); McClung v. Johnson, Tex.Civ. App.1981, 620 S.W.2d 644 (legal malpractice). But cf. Nardone v. Reynolds, Fla.1976, 333 So.2d 25, 39, conformed to, 11th Cir., 538 F.2d 1131, rehearing denied, 11th Cir., 546 F.2d 906 (duty is only "to disclose known facts and not conjecture and speculation as to possibilities"). This is said to be the minority rule, see Louisell & Williams, Medical Malpractice, 1981, ¶ 13.11, such that most courts require something more than mere silence in the way of some affirmative act or representation designed to prevent discovery of the cause of action. Urchel v. Holy Cross Hospital, 1980, 82 Ill.App. 3d 1050, 38 Ill.Dec. 314, 403 N.E.2d 545.

17. Frazor v. Osborne, 1966, 57 Tenn.App. 10, 414 S.W.2d 118, appeal after remand, 425 S.W.2d 768; Flanagan v. Mount Eden General Hospital, 1969, 301 N.Y.S.2d 23, 24 N.Y.2d 427, 248 N.E.2d 871 (clamps); Shillady v. Elliot Community Hospital, 1974, 114 N.H. 321, 320 A.2d 637; Hill v. Clarke, 1978, ___ W.Va. ___, 241 S.E.2d 572 (needle left in dishwasher's foot); Stoner v. Carr, 1976, 97 Idaho 641, 550 P.2d 259 (needle left in plaintiff's abdomen); Fox v. Passaic General Hospital, N.J.Super.1975, 135 N.J.Super. 108, 342 A.2d 859, affirmed, 1976, 71 N.J. 122, 363 A.2d 341 (drain from abdomen); Darragh v. County of Nassau, Sup.1977, 91 Misc.2d 53, 397 N.Y.S.2d 553, affirmed, 1978, 63 A.D.2d 1010, 405 N.Y.S.2d 1020 (failure to remove one IUD before inserting another one). But see Owen v. Wilson, 1976, 260 Ark. 21, 537 S.W.2d 543; Rockwell v. Ortho Pharmaceutical Co., N.D.N.Y.1981, 510 F.Supp. 266 (foreign object medical malpractice rule not extended to manufacturer of IUD in products liability action). See also Banks v. Dalbey, 1980, 245 Ga. 162, 264 S.E.2d 4 (failure to remove glass in hand; foreign object rule not applied since doctor's failure was misdiagnosis); Soto v. Greenpoint Hospital, Sup.1980, 76 A.D.2d 928, 429 N.Y.S.2d 723 (small toy in 5-year-old's esophagus; claim "founded exclusively upon diagnostic judgment or discretion"). See generally Annot., 1976, 70 A.L.R. 3d 7.

18. Franklin v. Albert, 1980, 381 Mass. 611, 411 N.E.2d 458; Moran v. Napolitano, 1976, 71 N.J. 133, 363 A.2d 346 (medical malpractice generally, including misdiagnosis); Foil v. Ballinger, Utah 1979, 601 P.2d 144; Newberry v. Tarvin, Tex.Civ.App.1980, 594 S.W.2d 204; Annot., 1961, 80 A.L.R.2d 368 (doctors and other medical practitioners). But see Alberts v. Giebink, S.D.1970, 299 N.W.2d 454; Rod v. Farrell, 1980, 96 Wis.2d 349, 291 N.W.2d 568; Robinson v. Weaver, Tex.1977, 550 S.W.2d 18 (inapplicable to misdiagnosis cases); Miller v. Duhart, Mo.App.1982, 637 S.W.2d 183. See generally Sonenshein, A Discovery Rule in Medical Malpractice: Massachusetts Joins the Fold, 1981, 3 W.New Engl.L.Rev. 433.

ing from doctors to dentists,[19] accountants,[20] architects,[21] lawyers,[22] manufacturers of defective products,[23] and a miscellany of negligence and other tort actions.[24] Yet statutes of limitations are legislative creatures, and even courts that favor the discovery rule as a general proposition are bound to follow specific legislation that mandates a different approach.[25]

The widening acceptance of the discovery rule has not been without cost, however, since the rule leaves the defendant vulnerable to suit indefinitely, sometimes decades after the event. Sparked by widening principles of liability including the discovery rule,[26] the great majority of states have enacted legislation placing an outer time limit on negligence and related claims in certain contexts where the hardship to (and perhaps the political clout of) the defendant has appeared the greatest.[27] Such statutes, called statutes of "repose," generally supplement or override the discovery accrual rule. Repose statutes were first widely applied to architects and contractors, in actions for defects in design and construction,[28] and were adapted to the medical service and chattel sale contexts in the 1970's in response to

19. See Kaufman v. Taub, 1980, 87 Ill.App.3d 134, 43 Ill.Dec. 852, 410 N.E.2d 114; Annot., 1981, 3 A.L.R.4th 418.

20. Moonie v. Lynch, 1967, 256 Cal.App.2d 361, 64 Cal.Rptr. 55; Sato v. Van Denburgh, 1979, 123 Ariz. 225, 599 P.2d 181; Annot., 1969, 26 A.L.R.3d 1438.

21. Chrischilles v. Griswold, 1967, 260 Iowa 453, 150 N.W.2d 94.

22. Anderson v. Neal, Me.1981, 428 A.2d 1189 (title search); Peters v. Simmons, 1976, 87 Wn.2d 400, 552 P.2d 1053 (drafting of business purchase agreement); Jarmillo v. Hood, 1979, 93 N.M. 433, 601 P.2d 66 (drafting and execution of will); Neel v. Magana, Olney, Levy, Cathcard & Gelfand, 1971, 6 Cal.3d 176, 98 Cal. Rptr. 837, 491 P.2d 421 (failure to serve summons within statute of limitations); Annot., 1968, 18 A.L.R.3d 978.

23. Raymond v. Eli Lilly & Co., 1977, 117 N.H. 164, 371 A.2d 170 (oral contraceptive) (Kenison,C.J.) (characteristically penetrating analysis); Nolan v. Johns-Manville Asbestos, 1981, 85 Ill.2d 161, 52 Ill.Dec. 1, 421 N.E.2d 864; Coyne v. Porter-Hayden Co., 1981, 286 Pa. Super. 1, 428 A.2d 208 (discovery rule applies to "creeping disease" such as asbestosis); Pauley v. Combustion Engineering, Inc., S.D.W.Va.1981, 528 F.Supp. 759; Louisville Trust Co. v. Johns-Manville Product Corp., Ky.1979, 580 S.W.2d 497 (asbestos); Ohler v. Tacoma General Hospital, 1979, 92 Wn.2d 507, 598 P.2d 1358 (incubator causing blindness). Cf. Dawson v. Eli Lilly & Co., D.D.C.1982, 543 F.Supp. 1330 (DES; discovery that injury resulted from defendant's wrongdoing); Clutter v. Johns-Manville Sales Corp., 6th Cir.1981 (Ohio law), 646 F.2d 1151 (asbestos: "manifestation" rule applied to asbestosis). Contra, Garrett v. Raytheon Co., Ala.1979, 368 So.2d 516 (radiation from radar system); Thornton v. Roosevelt Hospital, 1979, 47 N.Y. 2d 780, 417 N.Y.S.2d 920, 391 N.E.2d 1002 (cancer from drug). See Birnbaum, "First Breath's" Last Gasp: The Discovery Rule in Products Liability Cases, 1977, 13 Forum 279; Annots., 1979, 91 A.L.R.3d 991 (products liability generally); 1980, 1 A.L.R.4th 117 (latent industrial disease).

24. Sears, Roebuck & Co. v. Ulman, 1980, 287 Md. 397, 412 A.2d 1240 (libel to credit reputation); Friedman v. Jablonski, 1976, 371 Mass. 482, 358 N.E.2d 994 (deceit); Seelenfreund v. Terminix of Northern California, Inc., 1978, 84 Cal.App.3d 133, 148 Cal.Rptr. 307 (negligent breach of oral contract; improper termite inspection); Cain v. State Farm Mutual Automobile Insurance Co., 1976, 62 Cal.App.3d 310, 132 Cal.Rptr. 860 (invasion of privacy); Allred v. Bekins Wide World Service, Inc., 1975, 45 Cal.App.3d 984, 120 Cal.Rptr. 312 (skin rash from tiny bugs; negligence in packing and shipping household goods); Brown v. Sandwood Development Corp., 1982, 277 S.C. 581, 291 S.E.2d 375 (design and construction of concrete spillway by builder); Note, 1980, 68 Cal.L.Rev. 106 (arguing for discovery rule for all actions).

25. See, e.g., Cannon v. Sears, Roebuck & Co., 1978, 374 Mass. 739, 374 N.E.2d 582, 585.

26. Judicial adoption of the discovery rule in medical malpractice litigation appears to have been a principal cause of the enactment of statutes of repose in this context, at least in some states. See Anderson v. Wagner, 1979, 79 Ill.2d 295, 37 Ill.Dec. 558, 402 N.E.2d 560, 565, appeal dismissed 449 U.S. 807, 101 S.Ct. 54, 66 L.Ed.2d 11; Jones v. Morristown-Hamblen Hospital Association, Tenn.App.1979, 595 S.W.2d 816, 818 (noting repose legislation in 1975 following discovery opinion in 1974); S.C. Code § 15-3-545 (Supp.), enacted 1977, following Gattis v. Chavez, D.S.C.1976, 413 F.Supp. 33. Architect-contractor repose statutes may be traced to the breakdown of the privity defense, see Annot., 1979, 93 A.L.R.3d 1242, 1246, and products liability repose statutes are part of the broader reform movement in this area of the law following a decade or two of rapid expansion of liability. Compare Epstein, Products Liability: The Search for the Middle Ground, 1978, 56 N.C.L.Rev. 643; Phillips, An Analysis of Proposed Reform of Products Liability Statutes of Limitations, 1978, 56 N.C.L.Rev. 663.

27. The architect-contractor, medical malpractice, products liability, and general statutes are collected and analyzed in McGovern, The Variety, Policy and Constitutionality of Product Liability Statutes of Repose, 1981, 30 Am.U.L.Rev. 579.

28. See generally Note, 1981, 57 N.D.L.Rev. 43; Annot., 1979, 93 A.L.R.3d 1242.

perceived "crises" in the areas of medical malpractice [29] and products liability.[30]

A statute of repose generally begins to run at an earlier date and runs for a longer period of time [31] than the otherwise applicable statute of limitations unaffected by the discovery accrual rule. Repose statutes may begin to run from the time of the defendant's act or neglect, as in the medical malpractice context, or upon the occurrence of a specific and identifiable event shortly thereafter—as from the substantial completion of the structure, in actions against architects and contractors, or from the manufacture or sale of the product, in products liability cases.[32] Statutes of repose by their nature reimpose on some plaintiffs the hardship of having a claim extinguished before it is discovered, or perhaps before it even exists, and their constitutionality has been challenged on a variety of state and federal grounds.[33] Although some of the statutes have been declared unconstitutional,[34] the courts in most jurisdictions have upheld their statutes [35] and the legislatures in those that have not have sometimes reenacted new repose legislation that has withstood constitutional attack.[36] It appears quite likely that statutes of repose, at least in selected areas of tort law, are here to stay.

29. See Anderson v. Wagner, 1979, 79 Ill.2d 295, 37 Ill.Dec. 558, 402 N.E.2d 560.

30. See note 26, supra.

31. General negligence statutes of limitations for personal injury range in duration from 1–6 years, typically 2, 3 or 4 years, depending on the state. See, e.g., CCH Prod.Liab.Rep. ¶ 3420. Repose statutes typically range in length, for medical malpractice: 2–6 years; architect-contractor cases: 4–10 years; products liability: 6–12 years. See generally McGovern, supra note 27, at 625–41.

32. See generally McGovern, supra note 27, at 625–41.

33. Most frequently on equal protection, special laws, due process, and access to courts grounds. See McGovern, supra note 27, at 604; Witherspoon, Constitutionality of the Texas Statute Limiting Liability for Medical Malpractice, 1979, 10 Tex.Tech.L.Rev. 419; Note, 1981, 57 N.D.L.Rev. 43 (architect-contractors).

34. Most of these holdings have concerned the builder statutes, which have been ruled unconstitutional in some eleven states. See McGovern, supra note 27, at 587; Note 1981, 57 N.D.L.Rev. 43, 57–58; Annot., 1979, 93 A.L.R.3d 1242. E.g., Phillips v. ABC Builders, Inc., Wyo.1980, 611 P.2d 821, appeal after remand 632 P.2d 925; Overland Construction Co. v. Sirmons, Fla.1979, 369 So.2d 572; Broome v. Truluck, 1978, 270 S.C. 227, 241 S.E.2d 739; Pacific Indemnity Co. v. Thompson-Yaeger, Inc., Minn.1977, 260 N.W.2d 548; Shibuya v. Architects Hawaii, Limited, 1982, ___ Hawaii ___, 647 P.2d 276. The other states are Ala., Ill., Ky., N.H., Okla. and Wis.

Only one medical malpractice statute has been struck down, Carson v. Maurer, 1980, 120 N.H. 925, 424 A.2d 825, and four products liability statutes, although the first such product statute was passed only in 1977. Bolick v. American Barmag Corp., 1981, 54 N.C.App. 589, 284 S.E.2d 188, decision modified 306 N.C. 364, 293 S.E.2d 415; Battilla v. Allis Chalmers Manufacturing Co., Fla.1980, 392 So.2d 874 (as applied; see note 35 infra); Lankford v. Sullivan, Long & Hagerty, Ala. 1982, 416 So.2d 996; Heath v. Sears, Roebuck & Co., 1983, 123 N.H. ___, ___ A.2d ___ (Douglas, J.).

35. Architect–contractor statutes have been upheld in 20 states: Ark., Cal., Colo., Ga., La., Mass., Mich., Miss., Mont., Neb., N.J., N.M., Pa., Or., S.D., Tenn., Tex., Utah, Va. and Wash. See Anderson v. Wagner & Anderson, Inc., Miss.1981, 402 So.2d 320, 322; O'Brien v. Hazelet & Erdal, 1980, 410 Mich. 1, 299 N.W.2d 336; Freezer Storage, Inc. v. Armstrong Cork Co., 1978, 476 Pa. 270, 382 A.2d 715; Salinero v. Pon, Cal.App.1981, 177 Cal.Rptr. 204; Yarbro v. Hilton Hotels Corp., Colo.1982, 655 P.2d 822; Klein v. Catalano, 1982, 386 Mass. 701, 437 N.E.2d 514.

Medical malpractice statutes have been upheld in at least 16 states: Ala., Ariz., Ark., Colo., Del., Ga., Ill., Ind., Kan., La., Minn., Mo., Neb., N.C., Tenn., Utah, and Wash. E.g., Anderson v. Wagner, 1979, 79 Ill.2d 295, 37 Ill.Dec. 558, 402 N.E.2d 560 (scholarly and exhaustive analysis), appeal dismissed 449 U.S. 807, 101 S.Ct. 54, 66 L.Ed.2d 11; Stephens v. Snyder Clinic Association, Kan.1981, 230 Kan. 115, 631 P.2d 222; Carmichael v. Silbert, 1981, ___Ind.App.___, 422 N.E.2d 1330; Ross v. Kansas City General Hospital & Medical Center, Mo.1980, 608 S.E.2d 397.

Products liability statutes have been upheld in several decisions. See, e.g., Dague v. Piper Aircraft Corp., 1981, ___ Ind. ___, 418 N.E.2d 207; Purk v. Federal Press Co., Fla.1980, 387 So.2d 354 (where injury occurred before statute enacted and claim not abolished; but see note 34, supra); Thornton v. Mono Manufacturing Co., 1981, 99 Ill.App.3d 722, 54 Ill.Dec. 657, 425 N.E.2d 522; Buckner v. GAF Corp., E.D.Tenn.1979, 495 F.Supp. 351, affirmed without opinion, 6th Cir. 1981, 659 F.2d 1080; Scalf v. Berkel, Inc., 1983, ___ Ind.App. ___, 448 N.E.2d 1201. Compare Tyson v. Johns-Manville Sales Corp., Ala.1981, 399 So.2d 263 (discovery rule statute for asbestos injury claims upheld).

36. Five states have reenacted architect-contractor repose statutes, and none of these second-generation statutes had been stricken as of early 1981. See McGovern, supra note 27, at 587.

WESTLAW REFERENCES

272k1

fail! /s conform abide /p standard /5 care conduct /p loss** damage*

medical physician doctor /s malpractice negligen** /p "statute of limitation*" /p discover! /p injur! harm

medical physician doctor /p malpractice negligen** /p sponge* gauze "foreign object*"

statute* /5 repose

§ 31. Unreasonable Risk

Negligence is a matter or risk—that is to say, of recognizable danger of injury. It has been defined as "conduct which involves an unreasonably great risk of causing damage,"[1] or, more fully, conduct "which falls below the standard established by law for the protection of others against unreasonable risk of harm."[2] "Negligence is conduct, and not a state of mind."[3] In most instances, it is caused by heedlessness or inadvertence, by which the negligent party is unaware of the results which may follow from his act. But it may also arise where the negligent party has considered the possible consequences carefully, and has exercised his own best judgment.[4] The almost universal use of the phrase "due care" to describe conduct which is not negligent should not obscure the fact that the essence of negligence is not necessarily the absence of solicitude for those who may be adversely affected by one's actions but is instead behavior which should be recognized as involving unreasonable danger to others.[5]

The standard of conduct imposed by the law is an external one, based upon what society demands generally of its members, rather than upon the actor's personal morality or individual sense of right and wrong.[6] A failure to conform to the standard is negligence, therefore, even if it is due to clumsiness, stupidity, forgetfulness,[7] an excitable temperament, or even sheer ignorance.[8] An honest blunder, or a mistaken belief that no damage will result, may absolve the actor from moral blame, but the harm to others is still as great, and the actor's individual standards must give way in this area of the law to those of the public. In other words, society may require of a person not to be awkward or a fool.[9]

It is helpful to an understanding of the negligence concept to distinguish it from intent. In negligence, the actor does not desire to bring about the consequences which follow, nor does he know that they are substantially certain to occur, or believe that they will. There is merely a risk of such consequences, sufficiently great to lead a reasonable person in his position to anticipate them, and to guard against them.[10] If an automobile driver runs down a person in the street before him, with the desire to hit the person, or with the belief that he is certain to do so, it is an intentional battery; but if he has no such desire or belief, but merely acts unreasonably in failing to guard against a risk which he should appreciate, it is negligence. As the probability of injury to another, apparent from the facts within the acting

---

§ 31

1. Terry, Negligence, 1915, 29 Harv.L.Rev. 40.

2. Second Restatement of Torts, § 282.

3. Terry, Negligence, 1915, 29 Harv.L.Rev. 40.

4. Vaughan v. Menlove, 1837, 3 Bing.N.C. 468, 132 Eng.Rep. 490; The Germanic, 1905, 196 U.S. 589, 25 S.Ct. 317, 49 L.Ed. 610; Edgerton, Negligence, Inadvertence and Indifference, 1926, 39 Harv.L.Rev. 849.

5. Edgerton, Negligence, Inadvertence and Indifference, 1926, 39 Harv.L.Rev. 849, 860. But see Second Restatement of Torts, § 283, Comment f.

6. McNeely v. M. & M. Supermarkets, Inc., 1980, 154 Ga.App. 675, 269 S.E.2d 483; Stewart v. Jefferson Plywood Co., 1970, 255 Or. 603, 469 P.2d 783.

7. See Trowell v. United States, M.D.Fla.1981, 526 F.Supp. 1009 (having forgotten location of parking barrier, camper tripped over it at night). But cf. Soileau v. South Central Bell Telephone Co., La.1981, 406 So.2d 182 (plaintiff tripped over forgotten wire; even "reasonable man" permitted occasional lapse of memory—contributory negligence).

8. See generally infra, § 32.

9. See Vaughan v. Menlove, 1837, 3 Bing.N.C. 468, 132 Eng.Rep. 490; The Germanic, 1905, 25 S.Ct. 317, 49 L.Ed. 610, 196 U.S. 589; Teepen v. Taylor, 1910, 141 Mo.App. 282, 124 S.W. 1062; Holmes, The Common Law, 1881, 108.

10. Seavey, Negligence—Subjective or Objective, 1927, 41 Harv.L.Rev. 1, 17.

party's knowledge, becomes greater, his conduct takes on more of the attributes of intent, until it approaches and finally becomes indistinguishable from that substantial certainty of harm that underlies intent. Such intermediate mental states, based upon a recognizably great probability of harm, may still properly be classed as "negligence," [11] but are commonly called "reckless," "wanton," or even "willful." They are dealt with, in many respects, as if the harm were intended, so that they become in effect a hybrid between intent and negligence, occupying a sort of penumbra between the two. They will be dealt with in a later section.[12]

Negligence already has been defined as conduct which falls below a standard established by the law for the protection of others against unreasonable risk of harm.[13] The idea of risk in this context necessarily involves a recognizable danger, based upon some knowledge of the existing facts, and some reasonable belief that harm may possibly follow.[14] Risk, for this purpose, may then be defined as a danger which is apparent, or should be apparent, to one in the position of the actor. The actor's conduct must be judged in the light of the possibilities apparent to him at the time, and not by looking backward "with the wisdom born of the event." [15] The standard is one of conduct, rather than of consequences. It is not enough that everyone can see now that the risk was great, if it was not apparent when the conduct occurred.[16]

In the light of the recognizable risk, the conduct, to be negligent, must be unreasonable. Nearly all human acts, of course, carry some recognizable but remote possibility of harm to another. No person so much as rides a horse without some chance of a runaway, or drives a car without the risk of a broken steering gear or a heart attack. But these are not unreasonable risks. Those against which the actor is required to take precautions are those which society, in general, considers sufficiently great to demand preventive measures. No person can be expected to guard against harm from events which are not reasonably to be anticipated at all, or are so unlikely to occur that the risk, although recognizable, would commonly be disregarded.[17] An unprecedented frost [18] or flood,[19] the robbery of a customer in the parking lot of a bank,[20] a child picking up a plank with a nail in it and dropping it on his foot,[21] a pedestrian tripping on a slight im-

---

11. Terry, Negligence, 1915, 29 Harv.L.Rev. 40, 41. But see Elliott, Degrees of Negligence, 1933, 6 So.Cal. L.Rev. 91.

12. See infra, § 34.

13. See supra, p. 169.

14. Seavey, Negligence—Subjective or Objective, 1927, 41 Harv.L.Rev. 1, 5–7; Second Restatement of Torts, § 282, Comment g.

15. Cardozo, C. J., in Greene v. Sibley, Lindsay & Curr Co., 1931, 257 N.Y. 190, 177 N.E. 416. Accord: Cunis v. Brennan, 1974, 56 Ill.2d 372, 308 N.E.2d 617. "Foreseeability is an element of fault; the community deems a person to be at fault only when the injury caused by him is one which could have been anticipated because there was a reasonable likelihood that it could happen." Stewart v. Jefferson Plywood Co., 1970, 255 Or. 603, 469 P.2d 783, 786.

16. "Nothing is so easy as to be wise after the event." Branwell, B., in Cornman v. Eastern Counties R. Co., 1859, 4 H. & N. 781, 786, 157 Eng.Rep. 1050.

17. See Cunis v. Brennan, 1974, 56 Ill.2d 372, 308 N.E.2d 617 (possibility that automobile occupant in collision would be hurled 30 feet upon remains of defendant village's drainpipe, upon which his leg was impaled, requiring amputation); Hamilton v. Green, 1976, 44 Ill.App.3d 987, 3 Ill.Dec. 565, 358 N.E.2d 1250 (plaintiff fell while chasing defendant's ducks); Firestone Tire & Rubber Co. v. Lippincott, Fla.App.1980, 383 So. 2d 1181 (hernia from removing spare tire which defendant had stored upside down).

18. Blyth v. Birmingham Waterworks Co., 1856, 11 Exch. 781, 156 Eng.Rep. 1047.

19. McCauley v. Logan, 1893, 152 Pa. 202, 25 A. 499.

20. McClendon v. Citizens & Southern National Bank, 1980, 155 Ga.App. 755, 272 S.E.2d 592. See Gill v. Chicago Park District, 1980, 85 Ill.App.3d 903, 41 Ill. Dec. 173, 407 N.E.2d 671 (injury from robbery attempt in football stadium).

21. Spiering v. City of Hutchinson, 1921, 150 Minn. 305, 185 N.W. 375. Cf. Lubitz v. Wells, 1955, 19 Conn. Sup. 322, 113 A.2d 147 (boy picking up golf club, hitting other child with it); Patterson v. Weatherspoon, 1976, 225 S.E.2d 634, certiorari denied 290 N.C. 662, 228 S.E.2d 453 (same); Lance v. Senior, 1967, 36 Ill.2d 516, 224 N.E.2d 231 (child with hemophilia swallowing needle).

perfection in the sidewalk,[22] a workman being struck by ligntning,[23] —all of these things have happened, and will occur again; but they may not be so likely to do so on any particular occasion as to make it necessary to burden the freedom of human action with precautions against them.[24] Such events are, in a sense, "unavoidable accidents," [25] for which there is no liability.

On the other hand, if the risk is an appreciable one, and the possible consequences are serious, the question is not one of mathematical probability alone. The odds may be a thousand to one that no train will arrive at the very moment that an automobile is crossing a railway track, but the risk of death is nevertheless sufficiently serious to require the driver to look for the train [26] and the train to signal its approach. It may be highly improbable that lightning will strike at any given place or time; but the possibility is there, and it may require precautions for the protection of inflammables.[27] As the gravity of the possible harm increases, the apparent likelihood of its occurrence need be correspondingly less to generate a duty of precaution.[28]

Against this probability, and gravity, of the risk, must be balanced in every case the utility of the type of conduct in question. The problem is whether "the game is worth the candle." [29] While many risks are caused by simple carelessness, many other risks may reasonably be run, with the full approval of the community. To avert the risks created by heedlessness or inadvertence, the actor must only pay attention to his conduct and surroundings, a burden ordinarily considered a small and necessary price for living among one's fellows. Yet when a person's actions are deliberative, and are undertaken to promote a chosen goal, the negligence issue becomes more complex.[30] Chief among the factors which must be considered is the social value of the interest which the actor is seeking to advance. A person may be justified in dashing into the path of a train to save the life of a child, where it would be arrant folly to save a hat.[31] A railway will be permitted, or even required, to blow a whistle to warn travelers at a crossing, although it is likely to frighten horses on the highway; [32] it may be negligence to blow the same whistle without the same occasion for warning.[33] The public interest will justify the use of dangerous ma-

22. Warner v. City of Chicago, 1976, 43 Ill.App.3d 691, 3 Ill.Dec. 110, 358 N.E.2d 277, reversed, 72 Ill.2d 100, 19 Ill.Dec. 1, 378 N.E.2d 502.

23. Bennett v. Southern Railway Co., 1957, 245 N.C. 261, 96 S.E.2d 31, certiorari denied, 1957, 353 U.S. 958, 77 S.Ct. 865, 1 L.Ed.2d 900.

24. The particular circumstances are, however, always to be taken into account. Compare, as to an automobile tire throwing an object to a considerable distance, Miller v. Gonzalez, 1956, 4 Misc.2d 223, 156 N.Y.S.2d 775, reversed and held for jury, 9 Misc.2d 190, 163 N.Y.S.2d 687, and Randall v. Shelton, Ky.1956, 293 S.W.2d 559 (no negligence) with Ridley v. Grifall Trucking Co., 1955, 136 Cal.App.2d 682, 289 P.2d 31 (negligence).

25. See supra, § 29.

26. Gallagher v. Montpelier & Wells River Railroad Co., 1927, 100 Vt. 299, 137 A. 207.

27. Clark's Administrator v. Kentucky Utilities Co., 1942, 289 Ky. 225, 158 S.W.2d 134; Tex-Jersey Oil Corp. v. Beck, Tex.Civ.App.1956, 292 S.W.2d 803, affirmed in part, reversed in part, 1957, 157 Tex. 541, 305 S.W.2d 162. Cf. Helling v. Carey, 1974, 83 Wn.2d 514, 519 P.2d 981 (although risk of glaucoma to persons under forty was only 1 in 25,000, ophthalmologists were negligent in failing to give simple pressure test to such a person).

28. Tullgren v. Amoskeag Manufacturing Co., 1926, 82 N.H. 268, 133 A. 4; Gulf Refining Co. v. Williams, 1938, 183 Miss. 723, 185 So. 234; Pease v. Sinclair Refining Co., 2d Cir. 1939, 104 F.2d 183.

29. Second Restatement of Torts, § 291, Comment a. See Moning v. Alfono, 1977, 400 Mich. 425, 254 N.W.2d 759.

30. See Rodgers, Negligence Reconsidered: The Role of Rationality in Tort Theory, 1980, 54 So.Cal.L. Rev. 1; Owen, Civil Punishment and the Public Good, 1982, 56 So.Cal.L.Rev. 103.

31. See Eckert v. Long Island Railroad Co., 1871, 43 N.Y. 502; Wolfinger v. Shaw, 1940, 138 Neb. 229, 292 N.W. 731; Callais v. Furniture Showrooms, Inc., La. 1968, 213 So.2d 537. Even a rescuer, however, must act with reasonable care in the circumstances. See Rodriguez v. New York State Thruway Authority, Sup. 1981, 82 A.D.2d 853, 440 N.Y.S.2d 49.

32. Mitchell v. Central Vermont Railway Co., 1927, 261 Mass. 29, 158 N.E. 396.

33. Dugan v. St. Paul & Duluth Railroad Co., 1890, 43 Minn. 414, 45 N.W. 851.

chinery, so long as the benefits outweigh the risk,[34] and a railroad may reasonably be constructed near a highway, even at the expense of some danger to those who use it.[35]

Consideration must also be given to any alternative course open to the actor. Whether it is reasonable to travel a dangerous road may depend upon the disadvantages of another route.[36] While mere inconvenience[37] or cost[38] are often insufficient in themselves to justify proceeding in the face of danger, they will justify taking some risks which are not too extreme.[39] A county will not be required, at a ruinous expense, to build a bridge which will be safe against any accident that might be anticipated;[40] but the converse is also true, and where it can cheaply and easily post a warning, it may be required to do so.[41] A railroad need not do without a turntable because there is some chance that children will play on it and be hurt; but it is quite another matter to keep it locked.[42]

The alternative dangers and advantages to the person or property[43] of the actor himself[44] and to others[45] must be thrown into the scale, and a balance struck in which all of these elements are weighed.

---

34. Chicago, Burlington & Quincy Railroad Co. v. Krayenbuhl, 1902, 65 Neb. 889, 91 N.W. 880. Cf. Ott v. Washington Gas Light Co., D.D.C.1962, 205 F.Supp. 815, affirmed, D.C. Cir. 1963, 317 F.2d 138 (open flare pot in street, night and day); Jackson v. City of Biloxi, Miss.1973, 272 So.2d 654 (same).

35. Beatty v. Central Iowa Railway Co., 1882, 58 Iowa 242, 12 N.W. 332. Cf. Bennett v. Illinois Power & Light Corp., 1934, 355 Ill. 564, 189 N.E. 899 (spool of wire by roadside frightening horse); Beck v. Stanley Co. of America, 1947, 355 Pa. 608, 50 A.2d 306 (darkness in motion picture theater).

36. Musselman v. Borough of Hatfield, 1902, 202 Pa. 489, 52 A. 15.

37. See Bellacome v. Bailey, 1981, 121 N.H. 23, 426 A.2d 451 (crossing in middle of street rather than at crosswalk forty feet away). "The mere fact that the safe course is disagreeable is not sufficient to justify conduct which is manifestly perilous to life and limb." Williams v. East Bay Motor Coach Lines, 1936, 16 Cal. App.2d 169, 60 P.2d 320, 321. Accord, Saetz v. Braun, N.D.1962, 116 N.W.2d 628 (safe route difficult to drive, other with unsafe bridge); Johnson v. Hockessin Tractor, Inc., Del.1980, 420 A.2d 154 (adjusting tractor engine by hand without first turning off).

38. Silver Falls Timber Co. v. Eastern & Western Lumber Co., 1935, 149 Or. 126, 40 P.2d 703 (failure to shut down operation emitting sparks during dry season); Harding v. Kimwood Corp., 1976, 275 Or. 373, 551 P.2d 107 (failure to incorporate $200 anti-kickback device in design of $100,000 particleboard sanding machine).

39. Farrell v. Hidish, 1933, 132 Me. 57, 165 A. 903 (tenement child allowed to play in street); Kimbar v. Estis, 1956, 1 N.Y.2d 399, 153 N.Y.S.2d 197, 135 N.E.2d 708 (summer camp not required to floodlight woods). Cf. Roach v. Kononen, 1974, 269 Or. 457, 525 P.2d 125 (car manufacturer not required to design hoods against remote risk of flying open, at cost of $5–10 per car).

Where both alternatives appear to involve equivalent risk, the actor may reasonably choose on the basis of convenience. McManamon v. Hanover Township, 1911, 232 Pa. 439, 81 A. 440. Cf. Second Restatement of Torts, § 295, Comment a.

40. Davison v. Snohomish County, 1928, 149 Wash. 109, 270 P. 422; or to eliminate every minor defect in every sidewalk. See Warner v. City of Chicago, 1976, 43 Ill.App.3d 691, 3 Ill.Dec. 110, 358 N.E.2d 277, reversed, 72 Ill.2d 100, 19 Ill.Dec. 1, 378 N.E.2d 502.

41. Stephani v. City of Manitowoc, 1895, 89 Wis. 467, 62 N.W. 176. See Kajiya v. Dept. of Water Supply, 1981, 2 Hawaii App. 221, 629 P.2d 635 (duty to warn of hidden dangers in dangerous instrumentality is "axiomatic"); Hunt v. City Stores, Inc., La.1980, 387 So.2d 585 (aware that escalator could catch tennis shoes of small children, store had duty to warn of risk).

42. Chicago, Burlington & Quincy Railroad Co. v. Krayenbuhl, 1902, 65 Neb. 889, 91 N.W. 880. Cf. Ott v. Washington Gas Light Co., D.D.C.1962, 205 F.Supp. 815, affirmed, D.C. Cir. 1963, 317 F.2d 138 (not negligence to have open flare pot in street, but negligence in not turning off before 10 A.M.). But cf. Jackson v. City of Biloxi, Miss.1973, 272 So.2d 654 (no liability for child's burns from a "Toledo Torch" smudge pot since danger was obvious).

43. See Caldwell v. Ford Motor Co., Tenn.App.1981, 619 S.W.2d 534 (home builder injured back while hurriedly unloading materials from burning truck).

44. Thurmond v. Pepper, Tex.Civ.App.1938, 119 S.W.2d 900, error dismissed (failure to stop truck because of danger of being crushed by pipes); Indiana Consolidated Insurance Co. v. Mathew, 1980, ___ Ind.App. ___, 402 N.E.2d 1000 (failure to push burning lawnmower out of another's garage).

45. Cooley v. Public Service Co., 1940, 90 N.H. 460, 10 A.2d 673 (power line devices); Hoosac Tunnel & W. R. Co. v. New England Power Co., 1942, 311 Mass. 667, 42 N.E.2d 832 (opening sluice gates of dam in time of flood).

When either course involves danger to others, a choice either way may be reasonable, depending of course upon apparent probabilities. Second Restatement of Torts, § 295.

It thus is fundamental that the standard of conduct which is the basis of the law of negligence is usually determined upon a risk-benefit form of analysis: by balancing the risk, in the light of the social value of the interest threatened, and the probability and extent of the harm, against the value of the interest which the actor is seeking to protect, and the expedience of the course pursued.[46] For this reason, it is usually very difficult, and often simply not possible, to reduce negligence to any definite rules; it is "relative to the need and the occasion,"[47] and conduct which would be proper under some circumstances becomes negligence under others.[48]

WESTLAW REFERENCES

synopsis,digest(negligen** /5 act conduct behavior /s "unreasonable risk*" /s harm damage* injur!)

---

46. Terry, Negligence, 1915, 20 Harv.L.Rev. 40, 42; Second Restatement of Torts, §§ 291–93.

Judge Learned Hand summarized and applied these principles in two important decisions, Conway v. O'Brien, 2d Cir. 1940, 111 F.2d 611, motion denied 61 S.Ct. 610, reversed 312 U.S. 492, 61 S.Ct. 634, 85 L.Ed. 969, and United States v. Carroll Towing Co., 2d Cir. 1947, 159 F.2d 169, rehearing denied 160 F.2d 482. "Since there are occasions when every vessel will break away from her moorings, and, since, if she does, she becomes a menace to those about her, the owner's duty, as in other similar situations, to provide against resulting injuries is a function of three variables: (1) The probability that she will break away; (2) the gravity of the resulting injury, if she does; (3) the burden of adequate precautions. Possibly it serves to bring this notion into relief to state it in algebraic terms: if the probability be called P; the injury L; and the burden B; liability depends upon whether B is less than L multiplied by P; i.e., whether B [is less than] PL." 159 F.2d at 173. See generally, Posner, A Theory of Negligence, 1972, 1 J.Leg.Stud. 29; Note, 1976 Wash.U.L.Q. 447.

Some commentators have been critical of the Hand risk-benefit method for rendering safety decisions and resolving accident disputes, with its emphasis on economic efficiency and its implicit denial of "soft" or "human" variables and individual rights. See, e.g., Rodgers, Negligence Reconsidered: The Role of Rationality in Tort Theory, 1980, 54 So.Cal.L.Rev. 1; Tribe, Technology Assessment and the Fourth Discontinuity: The Limits of Instrumental Rationality, 1973, 46 So.Cal.L.Rev. 617; Hubbard, Reasonable *Human* Expectations: A Normative Model for Imposing Strict Liability for Defective Products, 1978, 29 Mercer L.Rev. 465, 468–69.

---

di due care

272k2 /p objective external reasonab! pruden** /p standard* duty criteria % "contributor! negligen**"

272k11 /p inten! /p probab! likely likelihood /p injur! harm damage* loss**

topic(272) & benefit* /s outweigh! /s risk* harm danger!

---

§ 32. The Reasonable Person

The whole theory of negligence presupposes some uniform standard of behavior. Yet the infinite variety of situations which may arise makes it impossible to fix definite rules in advance for all conceivable human conduct. The utmost that can be done is to devise something in the nature of a formula, the application of which in each particular case must be left to the jury, or to the court.[1] The standard of conduct which the community demands must be an external

---

In certain contexts, courts sometimes do appear to protect "rights" over efficiency, as, for example, by entitling an actor to rely upon the expectation that others will act with reasonable care and otherwise obey the law. Cf. Hallett v. Stone, 1975, 216 Kan. 568, 534 P.2d 232 (driver forced to brake abruptly had no duty to look to rear but could rely, instead, on duty of driver in following car to proceed with care).

47. Cardozo, C. J., in Babington v. Yellow Taxi Corp., 1928, 250 N.Y. 14, 164 N.E. 726. See Soileau v. South Central Bell Telephone Co., La.App.1981, 398 So. 2d 648, 650, reversed, 406 So.2d 182.

48. The same balance between the threatened harm and the utility of the actor's conduct appears, of course, in the various privileges, such as that of self-defense, which are recognized as defenses to intentional torts. The difference lies in the fact that, for historical reasons derived from the old action of trespass, such intentional invasions of the interests of another are regarded as prima facie wrongful, and the privilege is a matter of excuse or defense; while in negligence, which is to be traced primarily to the action on the case, it is considered that no wrong at all has occurred unless the defendant's conduct has been unreasonable in the light of the risk, and the burden is upon the plaintiff from the outset to establish the fact. See supra, § 16.

§ 32

1. Green, The Negligence Issue, 1928, 37 Yale L.J. 1029, reprinted in Green, Judge and Jury, 1930, 153, 154. "The care taken by a prudent man has always been the rule laid down [in bailment cases]; and as to the supposed difficulty of applying it, a jury has always been able to say, whether taking that rule as their guide, there has been negligence on the occasion

and objective one,[2] rather than the individual judgment, good or bad, of the particular actor;[3] and it must be, so far as possible, the same for all persons, since the law can have no favorites. At the same time, it must make proper allowance for the risk apparent to the actor, for his capacity to meet it, and for the circumstances under which he must act.

The courts have dealt with this very difficult problem by creating a fictitious person, who never has existed on land or sea: the "reasonable man of ordinary prudence."[4]

Sometimes he is described as a reasonable person,[5] or a person of ordinary prudence,[6] or a person of reasonable prudence,[7] or some other blend of reason and caution.[8] It is evident that all such phrases are intended to mean very much the same thing. The actor is required to do what such an ideal individual would be supposed to do in his place. A model of all proper qualities, with only those human shortcomings and weaknesses which the community will tolerate on the occasion, "this excellent but odious character stands like a monument in our Courts of Justice, vainly appealing to his fellow-citizens to order their lives after his own example."[9]

in question." Vaughan v. Menlove, 1837, 3 Bing.N.C. 468, 475, 132 Eng.Rep. 490, 492. See Massey v. Scripter, 1977, 401 Mich. 385, 258 N.W.2d 44.

2. "Instead, therefore, of saying that the liability for negligence should be co-extensive with the judgment of each individual, which would be as variable as the length of the foot of each individual, we ought rather to adhere to the rule which requires in all cases a regard to caution such as a man of ordinary prudence would observe." Tindal, C. J., in Vaughan v. Menlove, 1837, 3 Bing.N.C. 468, 132 Eng.Rep. 490.

"To the extent that the solution of these problems involves standardized elements, or phrasing it differently, to the extent that the actor's conduct is determined with reference to the community valuations, we may say that an objective test applies." Seavey, Negligence—Subjective or Objective, 1927, 41 Harv.L.Rev. 1, 8. See Fancher v. Southwest Missouri Truck Center, Inc., Mo.App.1981, 618 S.W.2d 271, 274: "The standard of care exacted by the law is an external and objective one and the law does not permit the defendant to make the determination * * *."

3. See supra, § 31. Thus it is error to instruct the jury that the actor was not negligent if he used his own best judgment. The Germanic, 1905, 196 U.S. 589, 25 S.Ct. 317, 49 L.Ed. 610. The actor's belief that he is using reasonable care is immaterial. Hankins v. Harvey, 1964, 248 Miss. 639, 160 So.2d 63; Hover v. Barkhoof, 1870, 44 N.Y. 113.

4. The "man of ordinary prudence" was perhaps first set as the standard in ordinary negligence cases in Vaughan v. Menlove, 1837, 3 Bing.N.C. 468, 132 Eng. Rep. 490.

5. "Negligence is the omission to do something which a reasonable man, guided upon those considerations which ordinarily regulate the conduct of human affairs, would do, or doing something which a prudent and reasonable man would not do." Alderson, B., in Blyth v. Birmingham Waterworks Co., 1856, 11 Ex. 781, 784, 156 Eng.Rep. 1047. See Second Restatement of Torts, § 283 ("a reasonable man under like circumstances"). Most recent opinions speak in terms of the reasonable "person" rather than the traditional reasonable "man." See Johnson v. Straight's, Inc., S.D.1980, 288 N.W.2d 325 ("person" and "man"); Caldwell v. Bechtel, Inc., D.C. Cir. 1980, 631 F.2d 989, 997; Walker v. Bignell, 1981, 301 Wis.2d 256, 301 N.W.2d 447; Vassos v. Roussalis, Wyo.1981, 625 P.2d 768. But cf. infra, note 9.

6. Flom v. Flom, Minn.1980, 291 N.W.2d 914; Alegria v. Payonk, 1980, 101 Idaho 617, 619 P.2d 135 ("ordinarily prudent person"); Central Transport, Inc. v. Great Dane Trailers, Inc., 1981, ___ Ind.App. ___, 423 N.E.2d 675 ("ordinary prudent person").

7. Trentacost v. Brussel, 1980, 82 N.J. 214, 412 A.2d 436 ("reasonably prudent person"); Swenson Trucking & Excavating, Inc., v. Truckweld Equipment Co., Alaska 1980, 604 P.2d 1113 (same); Canty v. Terrebonne Parish Police Jury, La.App.1981, 397 So.2d 1370 ("reasonably prudent man").

8. Knapp v. Stanford, Miss.1981, 392 So.2d 196 ("reasonable and prudent person"); Meese v. Brigham Young University, Utah 1981, 639 P.2d 720 (same); Seim v. Garavalia, Minn.1981, 306 N.W.2d 806 ("reasonable man of ordinary prudence"); Butler v. Acme Markets, Inc., 1981, 177 N.J.Super. 279, 426 A.2d 521, affirmed 89 N.J. 270, 445 A.2d 1141 ("reasonable person of ordinary prudence"); Massey v. Scripter, 1977, 401 Mich. 385, 258 N.W.2d 44 ("reasonably careful person"); St. Mary's Hosp., Inc. v. Bynum, Ark.1978, 573 S.W.2d 914 (same); Collins v. Altamaha Electric Membership Corp., 1979, 151 Ga.App. 491, 260 S.E.2d 540 ("ordinarily cautious and prudent person").

9. A. P. Herbert, Misleading Cases in the Common Law, 1930, 12–16: "He is an ideal, a standard, the embodiment of all those qualities which we demand of the good citizen. * * * He is one who invariably looks where he is going, and is careful to examine the immediate foreground before he executes a leap or a bound; who neither star-gazes nor is lost in meditation when approaching trapdoors or the margin of a dock; * * * who never mounts a moving omnibus and does not alight from any car while the train is in motion * * * and will inform himself of the history and habits of a dog before administering a caress; * * * who never drives his ball until those in front

The courts have gone to unusual pains to emphasize the abstract and hypothetical character of this mythical person. He is not to be identified with any ordinary individual, who might occasionally do unreasonable things; he is a prudent and careful person, who is always up to standard.[10] Nor is it proper to identify him with any member of the very jury which is to apply the standard;[11] he is rather a personification of a community ideal of reasonable behavior, determined by the jury's social judgment.[12]

The conduct of the reasonable person will vary with the situation with which he is confronted. The jury must therefore be instructed to take the circumstances into account; negligence is a failure to do what the reasonable person would do "under the same or similar circumstances."[13] Under the latitude of this phrase, the courts have made allowance not only for the external facts, but sometimes for certain characteristics of the actor himself, and have applied, in some respects, a more or less subjective standard. Depending on the context, therefore, the reasonable person standard may, in fact, combine in varying measure both objective and subjective ingredients.[14]

Physical Attributes

As to his physical characteristics, the reasonable person may be said to be identical with the actor.[15] The person who is blind[16]

---

of him have definitely vacated the putting-green which is his own objective; who never from one year's end to another makes an excessive demand upon his wife, his neighbors, his servants, his ox, or his ass; * * * who never swears, gambles or loses his temper; who uses nothing except in moderation, and even while he flogs his child is meditating only on the golden mean. * * * In all that mass of authorities which bears upon this branch of the law there is no single mention of a reasonable woman." Arguing that women are indeed rational beings, and that the standard of liability should be gender-free, see Collins, Language, History and the Legal Process: A Profile of the "Reasonable Man," 1977, 8 Rut.Cam.L.J. 311.

10. Reynolds v. City of Burlington, 1880, 52 Vt. 300, 308. Nevertheless, the person is "not necessarily a supercautious individual devoid of human frailties and constantly preoccupied with the idea that danger may be lurking in every direction about him at any time." Whitman v. W. T. Grant Co., 1964, 16 Utah 2d 81, 395 P.2d 918, 920; Public Service Co. of New Hampshire v. Elliott, 1st Cir. 1941, 123 F.2d 2, 7.

11. See Perry v. Fredette, 1970, 110 N.H. 114, 261 A.2d 431. Courts generally prohibit counsel from asking juries to place themselves in the position of the litigants, and the use of such a "golden rule" argument by counsel may amount to reversible error. See generally Beaumaster v. Crandall, Alaska 1978, 576 P.2d 988, 994–95 (not reversible error on facts). Nevertheless, jurors will no doubt invariably consider their own personal standards of conduct, at least to some extent: "It is inevitable that judge and jurors will still be influenced by their own life patterns and roles in deciding what a reasonable man would do." Reynolds, The Reasonable Man of Negligence Law: A Health Report on the "Odious Creature," 1970, 23 Okla.L.Rev. 410, 416; Green, The Reasonable Man: Legal Fiction or Psychosocial Reality?, 1968, 2 L. & Soc.Rev. 241.

12. See Beaumaster v. Crandall, Alaska 1978, 576 P.2d 988, 995 n. 12; B & B Insulation, Inc. v. Occupational Safety and Health Review Commission, 5th Cir. 1978, 583 F.2d 1364, 1370.

13. Second Restatement of Torts, § 283. "The rule has been repeatedly laid down that no definition is complete or correct which does not embody that element." Yerkes v. Northern Pacific Railway Co., 1901, 112 Wis. 184, 193, 88 N.W. 33, 36. See generally Johnson v. Clay, 1978, 38 N.C.App. 542, 248 S.E.2d 382; Wissman v. Wissman, Mo.App.1978, 575 S.W.2d 239; Everette v. City of New Kensington, 1978, 262 Pa.Super. 28, 396 A.2d 467.

14. "It would appear that there is no standardized man; that there is only in part an objective test; that there is no such thing as reasonable or unreasonable conduct except as viewed with reference to certain qualities of the actor—his physical attributes, his intellectual powers, probably, if superior, his knowledge and the knowledge he would have acquired had he exercised standard moral and at least average mental qualities at the time of action or at some connected time." Seavey, Negligence—Subjective or Objective, 1927, 41 Harv.L.Rev. 1, 27. See generally, Green, The Negligence Issue, 1928, 37 Yale L.J. 1029, reprinted in Green, Judge and Jury, 1930, 153, 166; James, The Qualities of the Reasonable Man in Negligence Cases, 1951, 16 Mo.L.Rev. 1; Parsons, Negligence, Contributory Negligence and the Man Who Does Not Ride the Bus to Clapham, 1958, 1 Melb.U.L.Rev. 163; Green, The Reasonable Man: Legal Fiction or Psychosocial Reality?, 1968, 2 L. & Soc.Rev. 241; Reynolds, The Reasonable Man of Negligence Law: A Health Report on the "Odious Creature," 1970, 23 Okla.L.Rev. 410.

15. tenBroek, The Right to Live in the World: The Disabled and the Law of Torts, 1966, 54 Cal.L.Rev. 841.

16. Balcom v. City of Independence, 1916, 178 Iowa 685, 160 N.W. 305; Argo v. Goodstein, 1970, 438 Pa. 468, 265 A.2d 783; Cook v. City of Winston-Salem, 1954, 241 N.C. 422, 85 S.E.2d 696; Hefferon v. Reeves, 1918, 140 Minn. 505, 167 N.W. 423; Roberts v. State, La.App.1981, 396 So.2d 566, writ granted 400 So.2d

or deaf,[17] or lame, or is otherwise physically disabled,[18] is entitled to live in the world and to have allowance made by others for his disability,[19] and the person cannot be required to do the impossible by conforming to physical standards which he cannot meet. Similar allowance has been made for the weaknesses of old age.[20] At the same time, the conduct of the handicapped individual must be reasonable in the light of the person's knowledge of his infirmity, which is treated merely as one of the circumstances under which the person acts. A blind man may be negligent in going into a place of known danger, just as one who knows that he is subject to epileptic fits, or is about to fall asleep, may be negligent in driving a car.[21] It is sometimes said that a blind man must use a greater degree of care than one who can see;[22] but it is now generally agreed that the more accurate way to state the rule is that he must take the precautions, be they more or less, which the ordinary reasonable person would take if he were blind.[23] Under the latter formulation, the standard remains essentially the same, but has added flexibility for taking the actor's physical deficiencies into account.

Mental Capacity

As to mental peculiarities of the actor, the standard remains of necessity an external one. "The law," says Mr. Justice Holmes in a much quoted passage, "takes no account of the infinite varieties of temperament, intellect, and education which make the internal character of a given act so different in different men. It does not attempt to see men as God sees them, for more than one sufficient reason."[24] The fact that the indi-

---

667, affirmed 404 So.2d 1221 (walking without cane not negligent in circumstances).

Compare, as to impaired vision, Masters v. Alexander, 1967, 424 Pa. 65, 225 A.2d 905; Bernard v. Russell, 1960, 103 N.H. 76, 164 A.2d 577; Pennington v. Southern Pacific Co., 1956, 146 Cal.App.2d 605, 304 P.2d 22; Shepherd v. Gardner Wholesale, Inc., 1972, 288 Ala. 43, 256 So.2d 877 (cataracts).

17. McCann v. Sadowski, 1926, 287 Pa. 294, 135 A. 207; Jakubiec v. Hasty, 1953, 337 Mich. 205, 59 N.W.2d 385; Rhimer v. Davis, 1923, 126 Wash. 470, 218 P. 193; Kerr v. Connecticut Co., 1928, 107 Conn. 304, 140 A. 751; Otterbeck v. Lamb, 1969, 85 Nev. 456, 456 P.2d 855.

18. Texas & New Orleans Railroad Co. v. Bean, 1909, 55 Tex.Civ.App. 341, 119 S.W. 328, error refused (club foot); Borus v. Yellow Cab Co., 1977, 52 Ill.App. 3d 194, 9 Ill.Dec. 843, 367 N.E.2d 277 (recovering from prior injuries); Memorial Hospital v. Scott, 1973, 261 Ind. 27, 300 N.E.2d 50 (multiple sclerosis); Stephens v. Dulaney, 1967, 78 N.M. 53, 428 P.2d 27 (no sense of smell; gas fumes exploded by cigarette). Cf. Sterling v. New England Fish Co., W.D.Wash.1976, 410 F.Supp. 164 (short leg). Accord, as to short stature, Mahan v. State of New York, to Use of Carr, 1937, 172 Md. 373, 191 A. 575; Singletary v. Atlantic Coast Line Railroad Co., 1950, 217 S.C. 212, 60 S.E.2d 305.

19. Thus a city must govern its excavations on sidewalks by the expectation that the blind will use them. Fletcher v. City of Aberdeen, 1959, 54 Wn.2d 174, 388 P.2d 743. See also Garbutt v. Schechter, 1959, 167 Cal. App.2d 396, 334 P.2d 225 (200 pound woman); Robinson v. Pioche, Bayerque & Co., 1885, 5 Cal. 460, 461 (drunk): "A drunken man is as much entitled to a safe street, as a sober one, and much more in need of it." Cf. Sterling v. New England Fish Co., W.D.Wash.1976, 410 F.Supp. 164 (safety of place of employment).

20. Brunner v. John, 1954, 45 Wn.2d 341, 274 P.2d 581; Kitsap County Transportation Co. v. Harvey, 9th Cir. 1927, 15 F.2d 166; Garner v. Crawford, La.App. 1973, 288 So.2d 886; Borus v. Yellow Cab Co., 1977, 52 Ill.App.3d 194, 9 Ill.Dec. 843, 367 N.E.2d 277 (dictum). But the actor's advanced age alone should not be considered unless it is shown to have impaired his abilities. See O'Connor & Raque Co. v. Bill, Ky.1971, 474 S.W.2d 344.

21. See supra, § 29. Cf. Felton v. Horner, 1896, 97 Tenn. 579, 37 S.W. 696 (aged and infirm person risking jolt of train); King v. Investment Equities, Inc., La. App.1972, 264 So.2d 297 (spastic paraplegic failed to observe large hole); Sterling v. New England Fish Co., W.D.Wash.1976, 410 F.Supp. 164 (short legged seaman should have gripped railing on steep and slippery ramp).

22. Winn v. City of Lowell, 1861, 83 Mass. (1 Allen) 177; Karl v. Juniata County, 1903, 206 Pa. 633, 56 A. 78; King v. Investment Equities, Inc., La.App.1972, 264 So.2d 297 (spastic paraplegic). See also Armstrong v. Warner Brothers Theatres, 1947, 161 Pa.Super. 385, 54 A.2d 831 (age).

23. See Second Restatement of Torts, § 283C ("a reasonable man under like disability"); Hill v. City of Glenwood, 1904, 124 Iowa 479, 100 N.W. 522; Borus v. Yellow Cab Co., 1977, 52 Ill.App.3d 194, 9 Ill.Dec. 843, 367 N.E.2d 277 (disabled); Memorial Hospital v. Scott, 1973, 261 Ind. 27, 300 N.E.2d 50 (disabled); Shepherd v. Gardner Wholesale, Inc., 1972, 288 Ala. 43, 256 So.2d 877 (impaired vision); Otterbeck v. Lamb, 1969, 85 Nev. 456, 456 P.2d 855 (deaf mute); Stephens v. Dulaney, 1967, 78 N.M. 53, 428 P.2d 27 (no sense of smell); Roberts v. State, La.App.1981, 396 So.2d 566, writ granted 400 So.2d 667, affirmed 404 So.2d 1221 (blind).

24. Holmes, The Common Law, 1881, 108. See Jolley v. Powell, Fla.App.1974, 299 So.2d 647.

vidual is a congenital fool, cursed with inbuilt bad judgment,[25] or that in the particular instance the person "did not stop to think,"[26] or that the person is merely a stupid ox, or of an excitable temperament which causes him to lose his head and get "rattled," obviously cannot be allowed to protect him from liability.[27] Apart from the very obvious difficulties of proof as to what went on in the person's head, it may be no bad policy to hold a fool according to his folly. The harm to his neighbors is quite as great, and may be greater, than if the person exhibited a modicum of brains;[28] and if the person is to live in the community, he must learn to conform to its standards or pay for what he breaks. As to all such mental deficiency of a minor nature, no allowance is made;[29] the standard of reasonable conduct is applied, and "it is not enough that the defendant did the best he knew how."[30]

As for more severe mental disabilities, including total insanity, where the actor entirely lacks the capacity to comprehend a risk or avoid an accident, one might expect a relaxation of the standard similar to the physical disability rule. Yet, for a variety of reasons, the law[31] has developed the other way, holding the mentally deranged or insane defendant accountable for his negligence as if the person were a normal, prudent person.[32] Against the apparent injustice of making persons responsible according to a standard they cannot meet,[33] several rationales have been offered to support the decision to hold mentally deranged defendants accountable for their negligence and certain other torts,[34] including the difficulty of distinguishing true incapacity from mere bad judgment, the belief that the custodians of incompetents will be encouraged by the rule to watch them more closely and keep them under control, and the perceived sense of fairness, even in the absence of moral blame, of a rule requiring mental defectives who live among the rest of society to conform to the general standards of con-

25. Fritscher v. Billiot, La.App.1959, 112 So.2d 755; Vaughan v. Menlove, 1837, 3 Bing.N.C. 467, 132 Eng. Rep. 490.

26. Cronin v. Columbian Manufacturing Co., 1909, 75 N.H. 319, 74 A. 180; Masters v. Public Service Co. of New Hampshire, 1942, 92 N.H. 85, 25 A.2d 499.

27. Cf. Crosslin v. Alsup, Tenn.1980, 594 S.W.2d 379 (plaintiff agitated and preoccupied).

28. "If, for instance, a man is born hasty and awkward, is always hurting himself or his neighbors, no doubt his congenital defects will be allowed for in the courts of Heaven, but his slips are no less troublesome to his neighbors than if they sprang from guilty neglect. His neighbors accordingly require him, at his peril, to come up to their standard, and the courts which they establish decline to take his personal equation into account." Holmes, The Common Law, 1881, 108.

29. Feldman v. Howard, 1966, 5 Ohio App.2d 65, 214 N.E.2d 235, reversed on other grounds 10 Ohio St. 2d 189, 226 N.E.2d 564; Johnson v. Texas & Pacific Railway Co., 1931, 16 La.App. 464, 133 So. 517, rehearing denied 16 La.App. 464, 135 So. 114; Riesbeck Drug Co. v. Wray, 1942, 111 Ind.App. 467, 39 N.E.2d 776.

30. Vaughan v. Menlove, 1837, 3 Bing.N.C. 468, 471, 132 Eng.Rep. 490.

31. Statutory in California, Montana, North Dakota, Oklahoma and South Dakota. "A minor, or person of unsound mind, of whatever degree, is civilly liable for a wrong done by him, but is not liable in exemplary damages unless at the time of the act he was capable of knowing that it was wrongful." West's Ann.Cal.Civ. Code § 41.

32. Kuhn v. Zabotsky, 1967, 9 Ohio St.2d 129, 224 N.E.2d 137; Johnson v. Lambotte, 1961, 147 Colo. 203, 363 P.2d 165; Jolley v. Powell, Fla.App.1974, 299 So.2d 647 (defendant shot plaintiff's intestate; acquitted in earlier homicide prosecution by reason of insanity); Schumann v. Crofoot, 1979, 43 Or.App. 53, 602 P.2d 298 (lawyer malpractice); Vosnos v. Perry, 1976, 43 Ill. App.3d 834, 2 Ill.Dec. 447, 357 N.E.2d 614 (defendant shot plaintiff's intestate). But see Fitzgerald v. Lawhorn, 1972, 29 Conn.Sup. 511, 294 A.2d 338 (defendant shot plaintiff; insanity good defense to assault claim). See generally Annot., 1973, 49 A.L.R.3d 189.

33. See generally Ague, The Liability of Insane Persons in Torts Actions, 1956, 60 Dick.L.Rev. 211; Curran, Tort Liability of the Mentally Ill and Mentally Deficient, 1960, 21 Ohio St.L.J. 52; Alexander & Szasz, Mental Illness as an Excuse for Civil Wrongs, 1967, 43 Notre Dame L.Rev. 24; Seidelson, Reasonable Expectations and Subjective Standards in Negligence Law: The Minor, the Mentally Impaired, and the Mentally Incompetent, 1981, 50 Geo.Wash.L.Rev. 17; Ellis, Tort Responsibility of Mentally Disabled Persons, 1981 Am. Bar Found.Res.J. 1079; Note, 1972, 39 Tenn.L.Rev. 705.

34. As to the tort liability of insane persons generally, see infra, § 135.

duct or pay their innocent victims for the damage they cause.³⁵

Similar to the cases involving sudden illness or unconsciousness,³⁶ there is some sentiment for treating a sudden delerium or loss of mental faculties as a "circumstance" depriving the actor of control over his conduct, thus shielding him from liability, provided that the lapse was unforeseeable.³⁷

In the case of mentally defective or insane plaintiffs, where the issue involves the contributory or comparative fault of such persons, the policy arguments outlined above lose much of their force.³⁸ In particular, the question shifts from which of two innocents should bear the loss to whether a negligent defendant should pay for the loss he has partially caused to a mentally incapacitated person incapable of properly looking after himself. Because of the obviously different equities in this situation, the great majority of courts in the contributory negligence context apply a lower standard of care and consider the plaintiff's incapacity as only one of the "circumstances" to be considered in judging the quality of his conduct.³⁹

Whether intoxication is to be regarded as a physical or a mental disability depends on how the accident occurs. On either basis, it is common enough; and it is uniformly held that voluntary⁴⁰ or negligent intoxication cannot serve as an excuse for acts done in that condition which would otherwise be negligent. One who so becomes intoxicated is held thereafter to the same standard as if he were a sober person.⁴¹ One good reason is that an excuse based on such intoxication would be far too common and too easy to assert; another is that drunkenness is so antisocial that one who indulges in it ought to be held to the consequences.⁴² Yet intoxication is not negligence in itself, and it must be shown to have caused the actor's behavior to have deviated from that of a reasonable per-

---

35. See, e.g., Jolley v. Powell, Fla.App.1974, 299 So. 2d 647; Schumann v. Crofoot, 1979, 43 Or.App. 53, 602 P.2d 298; Second Restatement of Torts, § 283B, Comment b. The rationales are critiqued in Note, 1972, 39 Tenn.L.Rev. 705.

36. See supra, § 29.

37. See Breunig v. American Family Insurance Co., 1970, 45 Wis.2d 536, 173 N.W.2d 619; Buckley & Toronto Transp. Comm'n v. Smith Transport, Ltd., [1946] Ont.L.Rep. 798, [1946] 4 Dom.L.Rep. 721. Cf. Restatement of Torts, § 283C, com. b. But see Kuhn v. Zabotsky, 1967, 9 Ohio St.2d 129, 224 N.E.2d 137.

38. See Second Restatement of Torts, § 464, Comment g.

39. Emory University v. Lee, 1958, 97 Ga.App. 680, 104 S.E.2d 234; De Martini v. Alexander Sanitarium, 1961, 192 Cal.App.2d 442, 13 Cal.Rptr. 564; Johnson v. Texas & Pacific Railway Co., 1931, 16 La.App. 464, 133 So. 517; Lynch v. Rosenthal, Mo.App.1965, 396 S.W.2d 272; Feldman v. Howard, 1966, 5 Ohio App.2d 65, 214 N.E.2d 235, reversed on other grounds, 1967, 10 Ohio St.2d 189, 226 N.E.2d 564.

Some earlier opinions held the plaintiff who was not totally insane to the same standard of safety for his own protection as a normal person. E.g., Wright v. Tate, 1967, 208 Va. 291, 156 S.E.2d 562, criticized in Note, 1968, 9 W. & M.L.Rev. 897. Recent decisions have rejected such distinctions and permit the trier of fact to determine if the plaintiff's mental condition deprived him of the ability to perceive or avoid the harm. Young v. State, 1978, 92 Misc.2d 795, 401 N.Y.S.2d 955; Miller v. Trinity Medical Center, N.D.1977, 260 N.W.2d 4; Snider v. Callahan, W.D.Mo.1966, 250 F.Supp. 1022.

40. Involuntary, non-negligent intoxication, as where the old lady who never has tasted whiskey is given a cup of "tea," is held to be treated like illness or physical disability. Cf. Davies v. Butler, 1979, 95 Nev. 763, 602 P.2d 605 (death by alcohol poisoning from forced consumption as initiation into college drinking club); Greenberg v. McCabe, E.D.Pa.1978, 453 F.Supp. 765, affirmed without opinion, 3d Cir. 1979, 594 F.2d 854 (improperly administered drugs; psychiatric malpractice action). As to the problem of the chronic alcoholic, who escapes criminal liability, see Driver v. Hinnant, 4th Cir. 1966, 356 F.2d 761; Easter v. District of Columbia, 4th Cir. 1966, 361 F.2d 50; Note, 1967, 52 Corn.L.Q. 470.

41. Hamilton v. Kinsey, Ala.1976, 337 So.2d 344; Shuman v. Mashburn, 1976, 137 Ga.App. 231, 223 S.E.2d 268; Harlow v. Connelly, Ky.App.1977, 548 S.W.2d 143; Folda v. City of Bozeman, 1978, 177 Mont. 537, 582 P.2d 767. For drug cases, see Haber v. County of Nassau, 2d Cir. 1977, 557 F.2d 322; Mikula v. Balogh, 1965, 9 Ohio App.2d 250, 224 N.E.2d 148. See generally McCoid, Intoxication and Its Effect Upon Civil Responsibility, 1956, 42 Iowa L.Rev. 38; Dooley & Mosher, Alcohol and Legal Negligence, 1978, 7 Contemp.Drug Prob. 145; Annot., 1973, 49 A.L.R.3d 189.

42. The consequences may include punitive damages. See Taylor v. Superior Ct., 1979, 2 Cal.3d 890, 157 Cal.Rptr. 693, 598 P.2d 854 (drunk driving).

Children

As to one very important group of individuals, it has been necessary, as a practical matter, to depart to a considerable extent from the objective standard of capacity. Children, although they are generally liable for their torts,[44] obviously cannot, in all instances, be held to the same standard as adults, because they often cannot in fact meet it, nor are they generally expected to.[45] It is feasible and appropriate to apply a special standard to them, because "their normal condition is one of incapacity and the state of their progress toward maturity is reasonably capable of determination,"[46] and because there is a sufficient basis of community experience, on the part of those who have been children or dealt with them, to permit the jury to apply a special standard.

Nevertheless, the capacities of children vary greatly, not only with age, but also with individuals of the same age; and it follows that no very definite statement can be made as to just what standard is to be applied to them. To a great extent it must necessarily be a subjective one. The standard which is ordinarily applied, and which is customarily given to the jury, is to measure the child's conduct against what would be reasonable to expect of a "child of like age, intelligence and experience."[47] There is something of an individual standard: the capacity of the particular child to appreciate the risk and form a reasonable judgment must be taken into account.[48] This means that more will be required of a child of superior skill or intelligence for his age,[49] and less of one who is mentally backward,[50]

---

43. See McKenna v. Volkswagenwerk A. G., 1977, 57 Hawaii 460, 558 P.2d 1018; Cain v. Houston General Insurance Co., La.App.1976, 327 So.2d 526, certiorari denied 330 So.2d 279; Haber v. County of Nassau, 2d Cir. 1977, 557 F.2d 322 (drugs). Moreover, an intoxicated person may be entitled to greater care from others. See Wilson v. City of Kotzebue, Alaska 1981, 627 P.2d 623.

44. See infra, § 134.

45. Dorais v. Paquin, 1973, 98 N.H. 159, 304 A.2d 369, 371, noting "the basic unfairness of predicating legal fault upon a standard which most children are simply incapable of meeting. Children generally do not have the same capacity to perceive, appreciate and avoid dangerous situations which is possessed by the ordinary, prudent adult." (Kenison, C. J.); DeLuca v. Bowden, 1975, 42 Ohio St.2d 268, 329 N.E.2d 109. See generally Shulman, The Standard of Care Required of Children, 1927, 37 Yale L.J. 618; Bohlen, Liability in Tort of Infants and Insane Persons, 1924, 23 Mich.L. Rev. 9; Gray, The Standard of Care for Children Revisited, 1980, 45 Mo.L.Rev. 597; Seidelson, Reasonable Expectations and Subjective Standards in Negligence Law: The Minor, the Mentally Impaired, and the Mentally Incompetent, 1981, 50 Geo.Wash.L.Rev. 17; Comment, 1978, 57 Neb.L.Rev. 763.

46. Snow, J., in Charbonneau v. MacRury, 1931, 84 N.H. 501, 153 A. 457, 463.

47. Standard v. Shine, 1982, ___ S.C. ___, 295 S.E.2d 786; Smith v. Diamond, 1981, ___ Ind.App. ___, 421 N.E.2d 1172 ("the care under the circumstances of a child of like age, knowledge, judgment and experience"); Lewis v. Northern Illinois Gas Co., 1981, 97 Ill. App.3d 227, 52 Ill.Dec. 680, 422 N.E.2d 889 ("the care and caution for his or her own safety that a child of plaintiff's age, intelligence, capacity and experience would exercise under same or similar circumstances"); Chausse v. Southland Corp., La.App.1981, 400 So.2d 1199, writ denied 404 So.2d 278 ("the self-care expected of his age, intelligence and experience under the circumstances"); Norfolk & Portsmouth Belt Line Railroad Co. v. Barker, 1981, 221 Va. 924, 275 S.E.2d 613 ("a reasonable person of like age, intelligence and experience under like circumstances," quoting Second Restatement of Torts, § 464(2)). See also Second Restatement of Torts, § 283A (same).

48. See Dorrin v. Union Electric Co., Mo.App.1979, 581 S.W.2d 852; Caradori v. Fitch, 1978, 200 Neb. 186, 263 N.W.2d 649 (standard is "that degree of care which an ordinarily prudent child of the same capacity to appreciate and avoid danger would use"); Gray, The Standard of Care for Children Revisited, 1980, 45 Mo.L. Rev. 597.

49. See Chapman v. State, 1972, 6 Wn.App. 316, 492 P.2d 607 (intelligent, college athlete performing somersault on trampoline; age 18). Cf. Pittman v. Pedro Petroleum Corp., 1974, 42 Cal.App.3d 859, 117 Cal.Rptr. 220.

50. Harris v. Indiana General Service Co., 1934, 206 Ind. 351, 189 N.E. 410 (18-year-old deaf mute with mental age of 6); Zajaczkowski v. State, 1947, 189 Misc. 299, 71 N.Y.S.2d 261 (7-year-old with mental age of 2½); Young v. Grant, La.App.1974, 290 So.2d 706; Curry v. Fruin-Colnon Contracting Co., La.App.1967, 202 So.2d 345, writ refused 251 La. 389, 204 So.2d 573 (8-year-old who was very small and "came from a poorer class of people * * * could not be held to the degree of intelligence and understanding as a child of better classes and education and intelligence"); Sherry

which is precisely what the courts have refused to do in the case of an adult.[51] But the standard is still not entirely subjective,[52] and if the conclusion is that the conduct of the child was unreasonable in view of his estimated capacity, the child may still be found negligent, even as a matter of law.[53]

Most courts have attempted to fix a minimum age, below which the child is held to be incapable of all negligence.[54] Although other limits have been set,[55] those most commonly accepted are taken over from the arbitrary rules of the criminal law, as to the age at which children are capable of crime. Below the age of seven, about a dozen states hold that the child is arbitrarily considered incapable of any intelligence.[56] Between seven and fourteen, a number of courts hold that the child is presumed to be incapable, but may be shown to be capable;[57] and that, from fourteen to majority, he is presumed to be capable, but that the contrary may be shown.[58] These multiples of seven are derived originally from the Bible, which is a poor reason for such arbitrary limits; and the analogy of the criminal law is certainly of dubious value where neither crime nor intent is in question.[59] Other courts have rejected any such fixed and arbitrary rules of delimitation, and have held that children well under the age of seven can be capable of some negligent conduct.[60] Undoubtedly there is an irreducible minimum, probably somewhere in the neighborhood of four years of age,[61] but it arguably ought not to be fixed by rules laid down in advance with-

v. Asing, 1975, 56 Hawaii 135, 531 P.2d 648 ("mentally slow" 17-year-old).

51. See supra, pp. 176–177.

52. Shulman, The Standard of Care Required of Children, 1927, 37 Yale L.J. 618.

53. Smith v. Diamond, 1981, ___ Ind.App. ___, 421 N.E.2d 1172 (12-year-old failed to look before crossing street); Hardy v. Smith, 1978, 61 Ill.App.3d 441, 19 Ill. Dec. 103, 378 N.E.2d 604 (13-year-old, same: "other than [his] desire to get to the ice cream parlor, there are no surrounding circumstances which would excuse his failure to look"); Norfolk & Portsmouth Belt Line Railroad Co. v. Barker, 1981, 221 Va. 924, 275 S.E.2d 613 (10-year-old attempted to jump on moving train).

As to the effect of a child's violation of statute, see infra, § 36.

54. Gray, The Standard of Care for Children Revisited, 1980, 45 Mo.L.Rev. 597; Note, 1966, 18 S.C.L.Rev. 648.

55. MacConnell v. Hill, Tex.Civ.App.1978, 569 S.W.2d 524 (under 5); Talley v. J. & L. Oil Co., 1978, 224 Kan. 214, 579 P.2d 706 (9 and under); Yun Jeong Koo v. St. Bernard, 1977, 89 Misc.2d 775, 392 N.Y.S.2d 815 (under 4); Bartoletti v. Kushner, 1976, 140 Ga.App. 231, 231 S.E.2d 358, certiorari dismissed 238 Ga. 688, 235 S.E.2d 8 (under 14; statutory immunity from suit in tort); Casas v. Maulhardt Buick, Inc., 1968, 258 Cal. App.2d 692, 66 Cal.Rptr. 44 (under 5); Harris v. Moriconi, Fla.App.1976, 331 So.2d 353 (under 6); Taylor v. Armiger, 1976, 277 Md. 638, 358 A.2d 883 (under 5).

56. Dunn v. Teti, 1980, 280 Pa.Super. 399, 421 A.2d 782 (5½-year-old defendant hit another child with stick; conclusive presumption "developed out of the need for a practical and simple rule to achieve expediency in the determination of capacity"); DeLuca v. Bowden, 1975, 42 Ohio St.2d 392, 329 N.E.2d 109 (BB gun), noted, 1975, 9 Akron L.Rev. 368; Bennett v. Gitzen, 1971, 29 Colo.App. 271, 484 P.2d 811 (assumption or risk and contributory negligence); Beggs v. Wilson, Del.1970, 272 A.2d 713 (rebuttable presumption); Wagner v. American Family Mutual Insurance Co., 1974, 65 Wis. 2d 243, 222 N.W.2d 652 (statute).

57. Riley v. Johnson, 1981, 98 Ill.App.3d 688, 54 Ill. Dec. 92, 424 N.E.2d 842 (8½-year-old hit by car); Hardy v. Smith, 1978, 61 Ill.App.3d 441, 19 Ill.Dec. 103, 378 N.E.2d 604 (13-year-old; same); Lewis v. Northern Illinois Gas Co., 1981, 97 Ill.App.3d 227, 52 Ill.Dec. 680, 422 N.E.2d 889 (13-year-old bicyclist hit uncovered gas valve box in sidewalk); Ross v. Vereb, 1978, 481 Pa. 446, 392 A.2d 1376 (11-year-old hit by car); Owen v. Burcham, 1979, 100 Idaho 441, 599 P.2d 1012 (presumption carries evidentiary weight). But see Williamson v. Garland, Ky.1966, 402 S.W.2d 80 (abandoning presumption).

58. Atlanta Gas Light Co. v. Brown, 1956, 94 Ga. App. 351, 94 S.E.2d 612; Welch v. Jenkins, 1967, 271 N.C. 138, 155 S.E.2d 763. Cf. Howland v. Sears, Roebuck & Co., 6th Cir. 1971, 438 F.2d 725.

59. See Johnson's Administrator v. Rutland R. Co., 1919, 93 Vt. 132, 106 A. 682.

60. Caparco v. Lambert, 1979, ___ R.I. ___, 402 A.2d 1180 (4½ years); Toetschinger v. Ihnot, 1977, 312 Minn. 59, 250 N.W.2d 204 (5½ years; comparative fault); Standard v. Shine, 1982, ___ S.C. ___, 295 S.E.2d 786 (6-year-old defendant; overruling cases based on 7-14-21 year divisions). See White v. Nicosia, La.App. 1977, 351 So.2d 234, 237: "An absolute rule setting minimum (or maximum) ages * * * has largely been discarded * * *. The more prudent method * * * is to inquire in each case whether the child's particular conduct fell below the standard reasonably expected of a [similar] child * * *."

61. Molina v. Payless Foods, Inc., Tex.Civ.App.1981, 615 S.W.2d 944 (age 2); Babin v. Zurich Ins. Co., La. App.1976, 336 So.2d 900, certiorari denied 339 So.2d 847 (3½-year-old bitten when he pulled dog's tail).

out regard to the particular case. As the age decreases, there are simply fewer possibilities of negligence, until finally, at some indeterminate point, there are none at all. There is even more reason to say that there is no arbitrary maximum age, beyond which a minor is to be held to the same standard as an adult.[62]

The great bulk of the decisions in which all these questions have been considered have involved the contributory negligence of child plaintiffs. It has been contended that where the child is a defendant no allowance should be made for the child's age, and he should in all cases be treated like an adult, for the reason that in practice children do not pay judgments against them for injuries inflicted, and such payment comes, if at all, from an adult, or from insurance paid for by an adult.[63] Whether this is universally true may perhaps be questioned; but however that may be, the case law has not sustained this point of view.[64] Instead, the courts have developed the more limited rule, which is now quite generally accepted, that whenever a child, whether as plaintiff or as defendant, engages in an activity which is normally one for adults only,[65] such as driving an automobile[66] or flying an airplane, the public interest and the public safety require that any consequences due to the child's own incapacity shall fall upon him rather than the innocent victim, and that the child must be held to the adult standard, without any allowance for his age.[67] This position has been rapidly gaining ground in recent

---

62. Older children are sometimes accorded the *child's* standard of care: Dorrin v. Union Electric Co., Mo.App.1979, 581 S.W.2d 852 (18 years); Moore v. Rose-Hulman Institute of Technology, 1975, 165 Ind. App. 165, 331 N.E.2d 462 (16½); Lehmuth v. Long Beach Unified School District, 1960, 53 Cal.2d 544, 2 Cal.Rptr. 279, 348 P.2d 887 (18); Riley v. Holcomb, 1961, 187 Kan. 711, 359 P.2d 849 (19); Goss v. Allen, 1976, 70 N.J. 442, 360 A.2d 388 (17); and sometimes held to an *adult* standard of care: Chapman v. State, 1972, 6 Wn.App. 316, 492 P.2d 607 (18 years); Atlanta Gas Light Co. v. Brown, 1956, 94 Ga.App. 351, 94 S.E.2d 612 (20); Bridges v. Arkansas-Missouri Power Co., Mo.App.1966, 410 S.W.2d 106 (16); Parzych v. Town of Branford, 1957, 20 Conn.Sup. 378, 136 A.2d 223 (15, treated like adult on particular facts); Dorais v. Paquin, 1973, 113 N.H. 187, 304 A.2d 369, 372 (17) (Kenison, C. J.): "There is no fixed age in this State when 'infants' are touched with the legal wand and suddenly bound to exercise the same degree of care as adults."

63. James, Accident Liability Reconsidered: The Impact of Liability Insurance, 1948, 57 Yale L.J. 549, 554–56; Note, 1967, 46 Neb.L.Rev. 699.

64. Dunn v. Teti, 1980, 280 Pa.Super. 399, 421 A.2d 782 (expressly rejecting double standard); Goss v. Allen, 1976, 70 N.J. 442, 360 A.2d 388 (same). Cf. Zuckerbrod v. Burch, 1965, 88 N.J.Super. 1, 210 A.2d 425; Miller v. State, Minn.1981, 306 N.W.2d 554. On contributory negligence of children, see Annot., 1961, 77 A.L.R.2d 917.

65. See Galiher, Degree of Care Required of Minors While Performing Adult Tasks, 1968, 17 Defense L.J. 657; Notes, 1970, 24 Ark.L.Rev. 379; 1967, 42 Ind.L.J. 405.

66. Miller v. State, Minn.1981, 306 N.W.2d 554 (plaintiff); Wollaston v. Burlington Northern, Inc., 1980, ___ Mont. ___, 612 P.2d 1277 (plaintiff); Gunnells v. Dethrage, Ala.1979, 366 So.2d 1104 (defendant); Constantino v. Wolverine Insurance Co., 1979, 407 Mich. 896, 284 N.W.2d 463; Reiszel v. Fontana, 1970, 35 A.D.2d 74, 312 N.Y.S.2d 988 (defendant). See Second Restatement of Torts, § 283A, Comment *c*; Annot., 1964, 97 A.L.R.2d 872. Cf. Smedley v. Piazzolla, 1977, 59 A.D.2d 940, 399 N.Y.S.2d 460 (adult standard inapplicable to 3-year-old who set car in motion).

67. An important early case was Dellwo v. Pearson, 1961, 259 Minn. 452, 107 N.W.2d 859, which involved the operation of a motorboat. The rule has been applied to *motorcycles*, Prichard v. Veterans Cab Co., 1965, 63 Cal.2d 727, 47 Cal.Rptr. 904, 408 P.2d 360; Daniels v. Evans, 1966, 107 N.H. 407, 224 A.2d 63; Davis v. Waterman, Miss.1982, 420 So.2d 1063 (motorbike); McNall v. Farmers Insurance Group, 1979, ___ Ind.App. ___, 392 N.E.2d 520; Tipton v. Mullinix, Okl.1973, 508 P.2d 1072; Fishel v. Givens, 1977, 47 Ill.App.3d 512, 5 Ill.Dec. 784, 362 N.E.2d 97 (minibike); *tractors*, Goodfellow v. Coggburn, 1977, 98 Idaho 202, 560 P.2d 873; Jackson v. McCuiston, 1969, 247 Ark. 862, 448 S.W.2d 33; *trucks*, Betzold v. Erickson, 1962, 35 Ill.App.3d 988, 182 N.E.2d 342; a *go-cart*, Ewing v. Biddle, 1966, 141 Ind.App. 25, 216 N.E.2d 863 (11-year-old); a *snowmobile*, Robinson v. Lindsay, 1979, 92 Wn.2d 410, 598 P.2d 392; and *playing golf*, Neuman v. Shlansky, 1968, 58 Misc.2d 128, 294 N.Y.S. 2d 628, affirmed, 1971, 63 Misc.2d 587, 312 N.Y.S.2d 951, affirmed 36 A.D.2d 540, 318 N.Y.S.2d 925.

But not to *bicycles,* Caradori v. Fitch, 1978, 200 Neb. 186, 263 N.W.2d 649; Davis v. Bushnell, Idaho 1970, 465 P.2d 652; Bixenman v. Hall, 1968, 251 Ind. 527, 242 N.E.2d 837; nor to *skiing,* Goss v. Allen, 1976, 70 N.J. 442, 360 A.2d 388; nor to *guns,* Thomas v. Inman, 1978, 282 Or. 279, 578 P.2d 399; Prater v. Burns, Tenn. App.1975, 525 S.W.2d 846; Purtle v. Shelton, 1972, 251 Ark. 519, 474 S.W.2d 123; Annot., 1973, 47 A.L.R.3d 620 (guns).

years,[68] and is now the rule in half the states.[69]

There are a few decisions indicating that a similar allowance is to be made at the other end of the scale, for persons at the extreme of life whose mental or physical faculties have been impaired by age [70] but the cases are few and the policy issues have yet to be thoroughly explored.

Knowledge

One of the most difficult questions in connection with negligence is that of what the actor may be required to know. Knowledge has been defined [71] as belief in the existence of a fact, which coincides with the truth. It rests upon perception of the actor's surroundings, memory of what has gone before, and a power to correlate the two with previous experience.[72] So far as perception is concerned, it seems clear that, unless his attention is legitimately distracted,[73] the actor must give to his surroundings the attention which a standard reasonable person would consider necessary under the circumstances, and that he must use such senses as he has to discover what is readily apparent. He may be negligent in failing to look,[74] or in failing to observe what is visible when he does look.[75] As to memory, a person is required to fix in his mind those matters which would make such an impression upon the standard person,[76] and, unless he is startled, or his attention is distracted for some sufficient reason,[77] to bear them in mind, at least for a reasonable length of time.[78] The real

---

68. See Robinson v. Lindsay, 1979, 92 Wn.2d 410, 598 P.2d 392 (noting trend).

69. See Gray, The Standard of Care for Children Revisited, 1980, 45 Mo.L.Rev. 597, 604–19.

70. "All that the law requires of an infant is a degree of care commensurate with its age and discretion. We think the same rule should apply to old people, whose senses are blunted, and mental faculties impaired by age." Johnson v. Saint Paul City Railway Co., 1897, 67 Minn. 260, 69 N.W. 900; LaCava v. City of New Orleans, La.App.1964, 159 So.2d 362. See supra, p. 176.

71. Seavey, Negligence—Subjective or Objective, 1927, 41 Harv.L.Rev. 1, 17. See Second Restatement of Torts, § 290, Comment *b* ("consciousness of the existence of a fact").

72. Second Restatement of Torts, § 289.

73. See Jackson Atlantic, Inc. v. Wright, 1973, 129 Ga.App. 857, 201 S.E.2d 634; Chester v. Montgomery Ward & Co., La.App.1975, 311 So.2d 572 (looking at merchandise on shelves); Lewis v. Piggly-Wiggly of Ferriday, Inc., La.App.1981, 403 So.2d 95 (same); Ellis v. McCaskill, Fla.App.1980, 382 So.2d 808 ("nearly always" a jury question); Wise v. Crown Construction Co., W.Va.1980, ___ W.Va. ___, 264 S.E.2d 463; Pensacola Restaurant Supply Co. v. Davison, Fla.App.1972, 266 So.2d 682 (thorough discussion of distraction rule).

74. See Stach v. Sears, Roebuck & Co., 1981, 102 Ill.App.3d 397, 429 N.E.2d 1242, 1249 ("a plaintiff is not excused from looking when she should look and from seeing that which is in the range of vision"; but jury could find no negligence on facts); Belcher v. City & County of San Francisco, 1945, 69 Cal.App.2d 457, 158 P.2d 996; Norwood v. Sherwin-Williams Co., 1980, 48 N.C.App. 535, 269 S.E.2d 277, reversed, 303 N.C. 462, 279 S.E.2d 559; Peck v. Olian, Mo.App.1981, 615 S.W.2d 663; Marcum v. United States, 5th Cir. 1980, 621 F.2d 142; House v. European Health Spa, 1977, 269 S.C. 644, 239 S.E.2d 653 (Rhodes, J.) (failing to look at shower floor known to be slippery, filthy and dirty).

75. "A pedestrian is held to have seen those obstructions in his pathway which would be discovered by a reasonably prudent person exercising ordinary care under the circumstances." Artigue v. South Central Bell Telephone Co., La.App.1980, 390 So.2d 211, 213, writ refused 396 So.2d 917; Hicks v. Donoho, 1979, 79 Ill.App.3d 541, 35 Ill.Dec. 304, 399 N.E.2d 138 (driver); Warren v. T. G. & Y. Stores Co., 1972, 210 Kan. 43, 499 P.2d 201 (failure to see large box in aisle of store). "[A] person is charged with seeing that which he should have seen and that which is in plain view, open and apparent." Knapp v. Stanford, Miss.1981, 392 So. 2d 196, 198. Contra, where the danger is camouflaged or otherwise difficult to see. Safeco Insurance Co. of America v. City of Watertown, D.S.D.1981, 529 F.Supp. 1220 (flock of gulls ingested in airplane engines on overcast day); Page v. Green, La.App.1975, 306 So.2d 847 (cable stretched across road in bad weather).

76. Second Restatement of Torts, § 289, Comment *f*; City of Charlottesville v. Jones, 1918, 123 Va. 682, 97 S.E. 316, 324. Cf. Deacy v. McDonnell, 1944, 131 Conn. 101, 38 A.2d 181 (not unreasonable as matter of law to forget step seen four times); Clewell v. Plummer, 1956, 384 Pa. 515, 121 A.2d 459 (otherwise occupied).

77. Beauchamp v. Los Gatos Golf Course, 1969, 273 Cal.App.2d 20, 77 Cal.Rptr. 914; Knutter v. Bakalarski, 1971, 52 Wis.2d 751, 191 N.W.2d 235 (workman). See generally Soileau v. South Central Bell Telephone Co., La.1981, 406 So.2d 182, reversing 398 So.2d 648 (even "reasonable man" permitted occasional lapse of memory—contributory negligence); Ferrie v. D'Arc, 1959, 31 N.J. 92, 155 A.2d 257 (concentration on another matter); Armagast v. Medici Gallery & Coffee House, 1977, 47 Ill.App.3d 892, 8 Ill.Dec. 208, 365 N.E.2d 446 (same). See supra, § 31.

78. Farmhand, Inc. v. Brandies, Fla.App.1976, 327 So.2d 76; O'Dell v. Cook's Market, Inc., Mo.App.1968,

difficulty lies with the question of experience. The late Henry T. Terry [79] came to the conclusion that "there are no facts whatever which every person in the community is absolutely bound at his peril to know." It seems clear, however, that there are certain things which every adult [80] with a minimum of intelligence must necessarily have learned: [81] the law of gravity,[82] the fact that fire burns and water will drown,[83] that inflammable objects will catch fire,[84] that a loose board will tip when it is trod on,[85] the ordinary features of the weather to which he is accustomed,[86] and similar phenomena of nature. A person must know in addition a few elementary facts about himself: the amount of space he occupies,[87] the principles of balance and leverage as applied to his own body,[88] the effects of his weight,[89] and, to the extent that it is reasonable to demand it of him, the limits of his own strength,[90] as well as some elementary rules of health.[91]

But beyond this, it seems clear that any individual who has led a normal existence will have learned much more: the traits of common animals,[92] the normal habits, capacities and reactions of other human beings,[93]

432 S.W.2d 382; Raflo v. Losantiville Country Club, 1973, 34 Ohio St.2d 1, 295 N.E.2d 202; Harden v. Cummings Truck Lease, Inc., Tenn.App.1972, 494 S.W.2d 512; Neusus v. Sponholtz, 7th Cir. 1966, 369 F.2d 259; Trowell v. United States, M.D.Fla.1981, 526 F.Supp. 1009; Downs v. Cammarano, 1966, 207 Pa.Super. 478, 218 A.2d 604.

79. Terry, Leading Principles of Anglo-American Law, 1884, § 200.

80. Here again a special standard based on age and capacity is applied to children. Second Restatement of Torts, § 283A.

81. See the exhaustive collection of cases in the Note, 1939, 23 Minn.L.Rev. 68. In Lange v. Hoyt, 1932, 114 Conn. 590, 159 A. 575, it was held that beliefs and theories held by a large number of reasonable and intelligent people, as for example, Christian Science, cannot be disregarded, even though the court itself might consider them unfounded.

82. See Bakunas v. Life Pack, Inc., E.D.La.1982, 531 F.Supp. 89 (stuntman falling 323 feet). For falls from ladders, see Long v. City of New Boston, 1981, 95 Ill.App.3d 430, 50 Ill.Dec. 965, 420 N.E.2d 282, judgment affirmed in part, reversed in part 91 Ill.2d 456, 64 Ill.Dec. 905, 440 N.E.2d 625 (installing Christmas lights); Quillen v. Quillen, Ala.1980, 388 So.2d 985 (erecting TV antenna); Riney v. Wray, Ky.App.1980, 594 S.W.2d 905 (painting house). Cf. McChargue v. Black Grading Contractors, Inc., 1970, 122 Ga.App. 1, 176 S.E.2d 212 (falling tree); Kopaczski v. Eastern Air Lines, Inc., 1973, 1 Mass.App.Ct. 840, 300 N.E.2d 923 (airline catering service employee stepped out of plane, while looking back over his shoulder and talking to helper, after movable stairway had been removed).

83. Gordon v. C. H. C. Corp., Miss.1970, 236 So.2d 733 (water). Cf. Herring v. R. L. Mathis Certified Dairy Co., 1970, 121 Ga.App. 373, 173 S.E.2d 716 (water), dismissed 406 U.S. 922, 91 S.Ct. 192, 27 L.Ed.2d 183.

84. Cambridge Mutual Fire Insurance Co. v. State Farm Fire & Casualty Co., La.App.1981, 405 So.2d 587 (cigarette ash ignited chair cushion); cf. Sparling v. Peabody Coal Co., 1974, 59 Ill.2d 491, 322 N.E.2d 5 (pile of slack or coal dust).

85. City of Huntingburgh v. First, 1896, 15 Ind.App. 552, 43 N.E. 17; cf. Pound v. Augusta National, Inc., 1981, 158 Ga.App. 166, 279 S.E.2d 342 (slippery rocks).

86. See Smith v. Mill Creek Court, Inc., 10th Cir. 1972, 457 F.2d 589 (ice and snow); Sea Land Industries, Inc. v. General Ship Repair Corp., D.Md.1982, 530 F.Supp. 550 (thunderstorm).

87. See Jennings v. Tacoma Railway & Motor Co., 1893, 7 Wash. 275, 34 P. 937; cf. Rapattoni v. Commercial Union Assurance Co., La.App.1979, 378 So.2d 953 (foot occupied space where marble slab would fall).

88. See Pound v. Augusta National, Inc., 1981, 158 Ga.App. 166, 279 S.E.2d 342 (slipped on rocks); cf. supra, note 74.

89. Oliver v. Aminoil, USA, Inc., 5 Cir. 1981, 662 F.2d 349, certiorari denied 456 U.S. 916, 102 S.Ct. 1770, 72 L.Ed.2d 175 (light fixture would not support welder's weight).

90. See Sweeney v. Winebaum, 1930, 84 N.H. 217, 149 A. 77; and physical condition, Carmichael v. Lexington-Fayette Urban County Government, Ky.App. 1980, 608 S.W.2d 66 (person with respiratory problem facing smoke inhalation).

91. Jurovich v. Interstate Iron Co., 1930, 181 Minn. 588, 233 N.W. 465 (working in ice water); Kroger Grocery & Baking Co. v. Woods, 1943, 205 Ark. 131, 167 S.W.2d 869 (eating moldy food). Cf. Osborn v. Leuffgen, 1943, 381 Ill. 295, 45 N.E.2d 622 (alcoholic beverages are intoxicating); Thomas v. Hanover Ins. Co., La.App.1975, 321 So.2d 30 (food particles attract mice).

92. See Arnold v. Laird, 1980, 94 Wn.2d 867, 621 P.2d 138 (dog); Farley v. M M Cattle Co., Tex.Civ.App. 1977, 549 S.W.2d 453, error refused no reversible error ("boogerish, snaky, broncish, and ill-tempered" horse); Sutton v. Sutton, 1978, 145 Ga.App. 22, 243 S.E.2d 310 ("crazy or wild" bull); cf. CeBuzz, Inc. v. Sniderman, 1970, 171 Colo. 246, 466 P.2d 457 (tarantula, lurking in bananas) (semble).

93. See Mahaffey v. Ahl, 1975, 264 S.C. 241, 214 S.E.2d 119, 123 (Ness, J.): "Children * * * are entitled to care proportioned to their inability to foresee and avoid the perils they may encounter * * *.";

including their propensities toward negligence and crime,[94] the danger involved in explosives,[95] inflammable liquids,[96] electricity,[97] moving machinery,[98] slippery surfaces [99] and firearms,[1] that worn tires will blow out,[2] and many other risks of life. Such an individual will not be excused when the individual denies knowledge of the risk; and to this extent, at least, there is a minimum standard of knowledge, based upon what is common to the community.

The few cases which have considered the question have held that when an abnormal individual who lacks the experience common to the particular community comes into it, as in the case of the old lady from the city who comes to the farm without ever having learned that a bull is a dangerous beast, the standard of ordinary knowledge will still be applied, and it is the individual who must conform to the community, rather than vice versa.[3]

Above this minimum, once it is determined, the individual will not be held to knowledge of risks which are not known or apparent to him.[4] A person may, however, know enough to be conscious of his own ignorance, and of possible danger into which it may lead him; and if that is the case, as where a layman attempts to give medical treatment,[5] or one enters a strange dark passage,[6] or an automobile driver proceeds with a mysterious wobble in his front wheels,[7] or traverses a strange town without an attempt to discover the meaning of unfamiliar purple traffic lights which suddenly confront him,[8]

Tom v. S. S. Kresge Co., App.1981, 130 Ariz. 30, 633 P.2d 439 (patrons may spill drinks on floor); F. W. Woolworth v. Kirby, 1974, 293 Ala. 248, 302 So.2d 67 (unruly nature of crowd in parking lot chasing 768 ping-pong balls containing prizes dropped from plane).

94. Second Restatement of Torts, § 290. See infra, § 33.

95. Littlehale v. E. I. duPont de Nemours & Co., S.D.N.Y.1966, 268 F.Supp. 791, affirmed, 2d Cir. 1967, 380 F.2d 274.

96. Burnett v. Amalgamated Phosphate Co., 5th Cir. 1938, 96 F.2d 974, certiorari denied 305 U.S. 647, 59 S.Ct. 153, 83 L.Ed. 418 (gasoline); Gross v. Nashville Gas Co., Tenn.App.1980, 608 S.W.2d 860 (natural gas).

97. Floyd v. Nash, 1966, 268 N.C. 547, 151 S.E.2d 1; Wood v. Southwestern Public Service Co., App.1969, 80 N.M. 164, 452 P.2d 692; Brown v. Duke Power Co., 1980, 45 N.C.App. 384, 263 S.E.2d 366, certiorari denied 300 N.C. 194, 269 S.E.2d 615.

98. Stephenson v. Dreis & Krump Manufacturing Co., 1981, 101 Ill.App.3d 380, 56 Ill.Dec. 871, 428 N.E.2d 190 (punch press); Harville v. Anchor-Wate Co., 5th Cir. 1981, 663 F.2d 598 (pipe-coating machine); Smith v. Fiber Controls Corp., 1980, 300 N.C. 669, 268 S.E.2d 504 (fine opener machine).

99. See Pound v. Augusta National, Inc., 1981, 158 Ga.App. 166, 279 S.E.2d 342 (wet gravel); Boutte v. Pennsylvania Millers Mutual Insurance Co., La.App. 1980, 386 So.2d 700 (oil spot in garage); Vidrine v. Missouri Farm Association, La.App.1976, 339 So.2d 877, writ denied 342 So.2d 216 (mud).

1. Sturm, Ruger & Co. v. Bloyd, Ky.1979, 586 S.W.2d 19; Zahrte v. Sturm, Ruger & Co., D.Mont. 1980, 498 F.Supp. 389; Wittkamp v. United States, E.D.Mich.1972, 343 F.Supp. 1075.

2. Delair v. McAdoo, 1936, 324 Pa. 392, 188 A. 181; or that overinflating a tire may cause it to explode.

See Collins v. B. F. Goodrich Co., 8th Cir. 1977, 558 F.2d 908.

3. Linnehan v. Sampson, 1879, 126 Mass. 506 (bull); Haack v. Rodenbour, 1944, 234 Iowa 368, 12 N.W.2d 861 (bull); Tolin v. Terrell, 1909, 133 Ky. 210, 117 S.W. 290 (mule); Borden v. Falk Co., 1903, 97 Mo.App. 566, 71 S.W. 478 (mule); Michigan City v. Rudolph, 1938, 104 Ind.App. 643, 12 N.E.2d 970 (deep sand on country road); Weirs v. Jones County, 1892, 86 Iowa 625, 53 N.W. 321 (inability to read English); cf. Mershon v. Gino's, Inc., 1972, 261 Md. 350, 276 A.2d 191 (elderly woman tripped over car bumper on first visit to fast food drive-in restaurant). But see Britz v. LeBase, Fla. 1971, 258 So.2d 811 (newcomer did not know about dangerous yucca, or Spanish bayonet, plants); Seavey, Negligence—Subjective or Objective, 1927, 41 Harv.L. Rev. 1, 19, arguing for a subjective standard.

4. See infra, § 43.

5. Conner v. Winton, 1856, 8 Ind. 315. Cf. Commonwealth v. Pierce, 1884, 138 Mass. 165.

6. "[D]arkness is, in itself, a warning to proceed either with extreme caution or not at all." McNally v. Liebowitz, 1980, 274 Pa.Super. 386, 418 A.2d 460, 461, reversed, 498 Pa. 163, 445 A.2d 716; Roberts v. United States, D.D.C.1981, 514 F.Supp. 712; Schoen v. Gilbert, Fla.Dist.App.1981, 404 So.2d 128; Lockwood v. Setounis, 1980, 381 Mass. 408, 408 N.E.2d 1380; cf. Beckwith v. State Farm Fire & Casualty Co., La.App. 1980, 393 So.2d 155, writ denied 399 So.2d 209 (jumping into mud "without knowing what danger lurked beneath the surface"). Although "[a] plaintiff is guilty of contributory negligence as a matter of law if he blindly ventures into the unknown without aid or direction," the particular circumstances may raise an issue of fact. Richards v. Crocker, 1967, 108 N.H. 377, 236 A.2d 692, 693 (Kenison, C. J.).

7. Prokey v. Hamm, 1941, 91 N.H. 513, 23 A.2d 327.

8. Second Restatement of Torts, § 289, Comment j.

the person may be found negligent in proceeding in the face of known ignorance.

He may, furthermore, be engaged in an activity, or stand in a relation to others, which imposes upon him an obligation to investigate and find out,[9] so that the person becomes liable not so much for being ignorant as for remaining ignorant; and this obligation may require a person to know at least enough to conduct an intelligent inquiry as to what he does not know. The occupier of premises who invites business visitors to enter,[10] the manufacturer of goods to be sold to the public,[11] the carrier who undertakes to transport passengers,[12] all are charged with the duty of the affirmative action which would be taken by a reasonable person in their position to discover dangers of which they may not be informed. As scientific knowledge advances, and more and more effective tests become available, what was excusable ignorance yesterday becomes negligent ignorance today.[13]

Superior Knowledge, Skill and Intelligence; Professional Malpractice

Thus far the question has been one of a minimum standard, below which the individual will not be permitted to fall. But if a person in fact has knowledge, skill, or even intelligence superior to that of the ordinary person, the law will demand of that person conduct consistent with it.[14] Experienced milk haulers,[15] hockey coaches,[16] expert skiers,[17] construction inspectors,[18] and doctors [19] must all use care which is reasonable in light of their superior learning and experience, and any special skills, knowledge or training they may personally have over and above what is normally possessed by persons in the field.[20]

Professional persons in general, and those who undertake any work calling for special skill, are required not only to exercise reasonable care in what they do,[21] but also to possess a standard minimum of special knowledge and ability. Most of the decided cases have dealt with surgeons and other doctors,[22] but the same is undoubtedly true of dentists,[23] pharmacists,[24] psychi-

---

9. "Where a duty to use care is imposed and where knowledge is necessary to careful conduct, voluntary ignorance is equivalent to negligence." Gobrecht v. Beckwith, 1926, 82 N.H. 415, 420, 135 A. 20, 22.

10. See infra, § 61.

11. See infra, ch. 17.

12. See Netter v. New Orleans Public Service, Inc., La.App.1977, 347 So.2d 941 (passenger slipped on vomitus); Annot., 1980, 1 A.L.R.4th 1249 (carrier's liability for injury from debris).

13. Marsh Wood Products Co. v. Babcock & Wilcox Co., 1932, 207 Wis. 209, 240 N.W. 392; Zesch v. Abrasive Co. of Philadelphia, 1944, 353 Mo. 558, 183 S.W.2d 140; Kay v. Ludwick, 1967, 87 Ill.App.2d 114, 230 N.E.2d 494, 497.

14. Seavey, Negligence—Subjective or Objective, 1927, 41 Harv.L.Rev. 1, 13; Second Restatement of Torts, § 289, Comment *m*.

15. Jewell v. Beckstine, 1978, 255 Pa.Super. 238, 386 A.2d 597.

16. Everett v. Bucky Warren, Inc., 1978, 376 Mass. 280, 380 N.E.2d 653.

17. LaVine v. Clear Creek Skiing Corp., 10th Cir. 1977, 557 F.2d 730.

18. Fisher v. United States, E.D.Pa.1969, 299 F.Supp. 1, reversed on other grounds, 3d Cir. 1971, 441 F.2d 1288.

19. See infra, p. 186.

20. See Prooth v. Wallsh, Sup.1980, 105 Misc.2d 653, 432 N.Y.S.2d 668 (doctor).

21. As to the distinction between care and skill, see Newport v. Hyde, 1962, 244 Miss. 870, 147 So.2d 113.

22. The medical malpractice literature is now voluminous. See, e.g., Louisell & Williams, Medical Malpractice, 1981; Waltz & Inbau, Medical Jurisprudence, 1971; Holder, Medical Malpractice Law, 1975; Harney, Medical Malpractice, 1973. Numerous law review articles have been written on every major aspect of the field. A good, early article is McCoid, The Care Requirement of Medical Practitioners, 1959, 12 Vand.L. Rev. 549.

23. Rice v. Jaskolski, 1981, 412 Mich. 206, 313 N.W.2d 893; Willard v. Hagemeister, 1981, 121 Cal.3d 406, 175 Cal.Rptr. 365; Simpson v. Davis, 1976, 219 Kan. 584, 549 P.2d 950; LeBeuf v. Atkins, 1981, 22 Wn. App. 50, 621 P.2d 787 (informed consent); Porubiansky v. Emory University, 1980, 156 Ga.App. 602, 275 S.E.2d 163, affirmed 248 Ga. 391, 282 S.E.2d 903.

24. French Drug Co. v. Jones, Miss.1978, 367 So.2d 431; Troppi v. Scarf, 1971, 31 Mich.App. 240, 187 N.W.2d 511 (pregnancy from druggist's negligence in filling prescription for oral contraceptive, Norinyl, with tranquilizer, Nardil); Annot., 1981, 3 A.L.R.4th 270.

atrists,[25] veterinarians,[26] lawyers,[27] architects and engineers,[28] accountants,[29] abstractors of title,[30] and many other professions and skilled trades.[31] Since, allowing for the inevitable differences in the work done, the principles applied to all of these appear to be quite similar, and since the medical cases are by far the most numerous, it will be convenient to talk only of doctors.

A doctor may, although he seldom does, contract to cure a patient, or to accomplish a particular result, in which case the doctor may be liable for breach of contract when he does not succeed.[32] In the absence of such an express agreement, the doctor does not warrant or insure either a correct diagnosis or a successful course of treatment,[33] and the doctor will not be liable for an honest mistake of judgment, where the proper course is open to reasonable doubt.[34] But by undertaking to render medical services, even

---

25. Ray v. Ameri-Care Hospital, La.App.1981, 400 So.2d 1127, writ denied 404 So.2d 277; Weatherly v. State, Ct.Cl.1981, 109 Misc.2d 1024, 441 N.Y.S.2d 319 (patient jumped out of window); Cotton v. Kambly, 1980, 101 Mich.App. 537, 300 N.W.2d 627.

26. Ruden v. Hansen, Iowa 1973, 206 N.W.2d 713; Posnien v. Rogers, Utah 1975, 533 P.2d 120; Bartlett v. MacRae, 1981, 54 Or.App. 516, 635 P.2d 666; Spilotro v. Hugi, 1981, 93 Ill.App.3d 837, 49 Ill.Dec. 239, 417 N.E.2d 1066.

27. The lawyer malpractice literature is growing rapidly. See Smith, Preventing Legal Malpractice, 1980; Mallen & Levit, Legal Malpractice, 1977; Meiselman, Attorney Malpractice: Law and Procedure, 1980; Mallen, Recognizing and Defining Legal Malpractice, 1979, 30 S.C.L.Rev. 203; Bridgman, Legal Malpractice—A Consideration of the Elements of a Strong Plaintiff's Case, 1979, 30 S.C.L.Rev. 215; Wolfram, The Code of Professional Liability as a Measure of Attorney Liability in Civil Litigation, 1979, 30 S.C.L.Rev. 281; Keeton, Professional Malpractice, 1978, 17 Washburn L.J. 445; Mallen, Legal Malpractice: The Legacy of the 1970's, 1980, 16 Forum 119; Note, 1982, 68 Va.L. Rev. 571 (suits against local counsel and specialists employed by primary attorney).

28. City of Eveleth v. Ruble, 1975, 302 Minn. 249, 225 N.W.2d 521; Cutlip v. Lucky Stores, Inc., 1974, 22 Md.App. 673, 325 A.2d 432. See Walker, Walker & Rohdenburg, Legal Pitfalls in Architecture, Engineering and Building Construction, 2d ed. 1979; Acret, Architects and Engineers—Their Professional Responsibilities, 1977; Sweet, Legal Aspects of Architecture, Engineering and the Construction Process, 2d ed. 1977; Bell, Professional Negligence of Architects and Engineers, 1959, 12 Vand.L.Rev. 711; Phillips, Judgment and Discretion in Architects' and Engineers' Professional Decisionmaking, 1980, 16 Forum 332; Notes, 1973, 58 Iowa L.Rev. 1221; 1979, 92 Harv.L.Rev. 1070; 1982, 30 Kan.L.Rev. 429; Annot., 1980, 97 A.L.R.3d 455.

29. Spherex, Inc. v. Alexander Grant & Co., 122 N.H. 898, 451 A.2d 1308; Bonhiver v. Graff, 1976, 311 Minn. 111, 248 N.W.2d 291; Seedkem, Inc. v. Safranek, D.Neb.1979, 466 F.Supp. 340; Western Surety Co. v. Loy, 1979, 3 Kan.App.2d 310, 594 P.2d 257; Aluma Kraft Manufacturing Co. v. Elmer Fox & Co., Mo.App. 1973, 493 S.W.2d 378; Kelly, An Overview of Accountants' Liability, 1980, 15 Forum 579; Dondanville, Defending Accountants' Liability: Trends and Implications, 1979, 15 Forum 173; Fiflis, Current Problems of Accountants' Responsibilities to Third Parties, 1975, 28 Vand.L.Rev. 31; Notes, 1979, 48 Fordham L.Rev. 401; 1977, 52 Notre Dame L. 838; Annots., 1979, 92 A.L.R.3d 396 (liability to client); 1972, 46 A.L.R.3d 979 (liability to third parties).

30. Adams v. Greer, W.D.Ark.1953, 114 F.Supp. 770. See Roady, Professional Liability of Abstractors, 1959, 12 Vand.L.Rev. 783.

31. Heath v. Swift Wings, Inc., 1979, 40 N.C.App. 158, 252 S.E.2d 256, certiorari denied 297 N.C. 453, 256 S.E.2d 806 (pilot); Bamert v. Central General Hospital, 1980, 77 A.D.2d 559, 430 N.Y.S.2d 336 (nurse); Chamness v. Odum, 1979, 80 Ill.App.3d 98, 35 Ill.Dec. 404, 399 N.E.2d 238 (chiropractor); Albritton v. Bossier City Hospital Commission, La.App.1972, 271 So.2d 353 (X-ray technician); Annot., 1973, 51 A.L.R.3d 1273 (optometrists and opticians); Fantini v. Alexander, App.Div. 1980, 172 N.J.Super. 105, 410 A.2d 1190 (karate teacher); cf. Josephs v. Fuller (Club Dominicus), N.J.Dist.Ct.1982, 186 N.J.Super. 47, 451 A.2d 203 (travel agent).

32. See Scarzella v. Saxon, D.C.App.1981, 436 A.2d 358; McKinney v. Nash, 1981, 120 Cal.3d 428, 174 Cal. Rptr. 642 (comment that hernia operation would be simple and without problem insufficient); Mason v. Western Pennsylvania Hospital, 1981, 286 Pa.Super. 354, 428 A.2d 1366 (pregnancy after tubal ligation). See generally Annot., 1972, 43 A.L.R.3d 1221 (liability); Annot., 1980, 99 A.L.R.3d 303 (damages).

33. See Salis v. United States, M.D.Pa.1981, 522 F.Supp. 989; Stanley v. Fisher, 1981, ___ Ind.App. ___, 417 N.E.2d 932, 937 (loss of testicle following vasectomy: "a promise to effect a cure will not be implied"); Berwald v. Kasal, 1980, 102 Mich.App. 269, 301 N.W.2d 499; Young v. Park, R.I.1980, ___ R.I. ___, 417 A.2d 889, certiorari denied, dismissed 449 U.S. 1119, 101 S.Ct. 933, 67 L.Ed.2d 106; Greenberg v. Michael Reese Hospital, 1980, 83 Ill.2d 282, 47 Ill.Dec. 385, 415 N.E.2d 390.

34. See Roberts v. Tardif, Me.1980, 417 A.2d 444; Salis v. United States, M.D.Pa.1981, 522 F.Supp. 989; Zito v. Friedman, 1980, 77 A.D.2d 514, 430 N.Y.S.2d 78. See also Woodruff v. Tomlin, 6th Cir. 1980, 616 F.2d 924, certiorari denied 449 U.S. 888, 101 S.Ct. 246, 66 L.Ed.2d 114 (en banc) (lawyer's good faith judgment on trial tactics would not support malpractice claim, although other failures might); Thomason, A Plea for

though gratuitously,[35] a doctor will ordinarily be understood to hold himself out as having standard professional skill and knowledge. The formula under which this usually is put to the jury is that the doctor must have and use the knowledge, skill and care ordinarily possessed and employed by members of the profession in good standing;[36] and a doctor will be liable if harm results because he does not have them. Sometimes this is called the skill of the "average" member of the profession;[37] but this is clearly misleading, since only those in good professional standing are to be considered; and of these it is not the middle but the minimum common skill which is to be looked to.[38] If the defendant represents himself as having greater skill than this, as where the doctor holds himself out as a specialist,[39] the standard is modified accordingly.

The courts have been compelled to recognize that there are areas in which even experts will disagree. Where there are different schools of medical thought, and alternative methods of acceptable treatment, it is held that the dispute cannot be settled by the law, and the doctor is entitled to be judged according to the tenets of the school the doctor professes to follow.[40] This does not mean, however, that any quack, charlatan or crackpot can set himself up as a "school," and so apply his individual ideas without liability. A "school" must be a recognized one within definite principles, and it must be the line of thought of a respectable minority of the profession.[41] In addition, there are minimum requirements of skill and knowledge, which anyone who holds himself out as competent to treat human ailments is required to have,[42] regardless of his personal views on medical subjects. Furthermore, the physician is required to exercise reasonable care in ascertaining the operational facts upon which his diagnosis is based, and will be liable if he fails to do so.[43]

Formerly it was generally held that allowance must be made for the type of community in which the physician carries on his practice, and for the fact, for example, that a country doctor could not be expected to have

---

Absolute Immunity for Errors in Trial Judgment, 1978, 14 Willamette L.J. 369.

35. See Sullivan v. Henry, 1982, 160 Ga.App. 791, 287 S.E.2d 652. See also Davis v. Tirrell, Sup.1981, 110 Misc.2d 889, 443 N.Y.S.2d 136; Security National Bank v. Lish, D.C.App.1973, 311 A.2d 833 (lawyer).

36. Cross v. Huttenlocher, 1981, ___ Conn. ___, 440 A.2d 952; Sullivan v. Henry, 1982, 160 Ga.App. 791, 287 S.E.2d 652; McPherson v. Ellis, 1982, 305 N.C. 266, 287 S.E.2d 892; Siebert v. Fowler, Wyo.1981, 637 P.2d 255; Young v. Park, 1980, ___ R.I. ___, 417 A.2d 889, certiorari denied, dismissed 449 U.S. 1119, 101 S.Ct. 933, 67 L.Ed.2d 106.

37. See Green v. United States, D.Wis.1982, 530 F.Supp. 633; Spike v. Sellett, 1981, 102 Ill.App.3d 270, 58 Ill.Dec. 565, 430 N.E.2d 597; Monahan v. Weichert, 1981, 82 A.D.2d 102, 442 N.Y.S.2d 295.

38. Shevak v. United States, N.D.Tex.1981, 528 F.Supp. 427; Sim v. Weeks, 1935, 7 Cal.App.2d 28, 45 P.2d 350.

39. Baker v. Story, Tex.Civ.App.1981, 621 S.W.2d 639, refused n.r.e.; Coyne v. Cirilli, 1980, 45 Or.App. 177, 607 P.2d 1383; Salis v. United States, M.D.Pa. 1981, 522 F.Supp. 989. See also Wright v. Williams, 1975, 47 Cal.App.3d 802, 121 Cal.Rptr. 194 (maritime lawyer); Schnidman & Salzler, The Legal Malpractice Dilemma: Will New Standards of Care Place Professional Liability Insurance Beyond the Reach of the Specialist?, 1976, 45 Cin.L.Rev. 541.

40. "Who shall decide when doctors disagree?" Pope, Moral Essays, 1732, Epistle III, Line 1; Force v. Gregory, 1893, 63 Conn. 167, 27 A. 1116 (homeopath); Creasey v. Hogan, 1981, 292 Or. 154, 637 P.2d 114 (podiatrist); Hersh v. Hendley, Tex.App.1981, 626 S.W.2d 151 (same); Becker v. Hidalgo, 1976, 89 N.M. 627, 556 P.2d 35 (osteopath); Roberts v. Tardif, Me.1980, 417 A.2d 444 (obstetrician).

41. See Joy v. Chau, 1978, 177 Ind.App. 29, 377 N.E.2d 670. But cf. Hood v. Phillips, Tex.1977, 554 S.W.2d 160; Hubbard v. Calvin, 1978, 83 Cal.App.3d 529, 147 Cal.Rptr. 905. See generally Brannan v. Lankenau Hospital, 1980, 490 Pa. 588, 417 A.2d 196 ("small respected body" rule inapplicable on facts); Chumbler v. McClure, 6th Cir. 1974, 505 F.2d 489.

42. Kelly v. Carroll, 1950, 36 Wn.2d 482, 219 P.2d 79, certiorari denied 340 U.S. 892, 71 S.Ct. 208, 95 L.Ed. 646 (drugless healer); Treptau v. Behrens Spa, 1945, 247 Wis. 438, 20 N.W.2d 108 (chiropractor).

43. See Momsen v. Nebraska Methodist Hospital, Neb.1981, 210 Neb. 45, 313 N.W.2d 208 (failure to go to hospital to examine patient); Larkin v. State, 1982, 84 A.D.2d 438, 446 N.Y.S.2d 818 (failure to perform spinal tap). Compare Woodruff v. Tomlin, 6th Cir. 1980, 616 F.2d 924, certiorari denied 449 U.S. 888, 101 S.Ct. 246, 66 L.Ed.2d 114 (lawyer's failure to interview persons named by client as potential witnesses).

the equipment, facilities, libraries, contacts, opportunities for learning, or experience afforded by large cities. Since the standard of the "same" locality [44] was obviously too narrow, this was commonly stated as that of "similar localities," thus including other towns of the same general type.[45] Improved facilities of communication, travel, availability of medical literature, and the like, have led some courts to abandon a fixed locality rule in favor of treating the community as merely one factor to be taken into account in applying the general professional standard.[46] In other jurisdictions the "locality rule" has been discarded outright, and a general national standard applied in all cases,[47] especially in the case of medical specialists.[48]

Since juries composed of laymen are normally incompetent to pass judgment on questions of medical science or technique, it has been held in the great majority of malpractice cases that there can be no finding of negligence in the absence of expert testimony to support it.[49] The well known reluctance of doctors to testify against one another, which has been mentioned now and then in the decisions,[50] may make this difficult or impossible to obtain, especially in a jurisdiction with a narrow locality rule, and so in some instances effectively deprive the plaintiff of any remedy for a real and grievous wrong. In recent years, however, at least some doctors appear to have become more willing to testify for plaintiffs, especially in cases where the evidence of medical negli-

44. Some courts still follow a strict "same" locality rule. See Stanely v. Fisher, 1981, ___ Ind.App. ___, 417 N.E.2d 932; Fiske v. Soland, 1968, 8 Ariz.App. 585, 448 P.2d 429; cf. Prooth v. Wallsh, 1980, 105 Misc.2d 653, 432 N.Y.S.2d 668.

45. See Gambill v. Stroud, 1976, 258 Ark. 766, 531 S.W.2d 945; Reeg v. Shaughnessy, 10th Cir. 1978, 570 F.2d 309; McPherson v. Ellis, 1982, 305 N.C. 266, 287 S.E.2d 892; Erickson v. United States, D.S.D.1980, 504 F.Supp. 646; Hirn v. Edgewater Hospital, 1980, 86 Ill. App.3d 939, 42 Ill.Dec. 261, 408 N.E.2d 970; Young v. Park, 1980, ___ R.I. ___, 417 A.2d 889, certiorari denied, dismissed 449 U.S. 1119, 101 S.Ct. 933, 67 L.Ed.2d 106.

46. Sinz v. Owens, 1949, 33 Cal.2d 749, 205 P.2d 3; Hundley v. Martinez, 1967, 151 W.Va. 977, 158 S.E.2d 159; Ruden v. Hansen, Iowa 1973, 206 N.W.2d 713 (vet); King v. Williams, 1981, 276 S.C. 478, 279 S.E.2d 618 (Littlejohn, J.); Pederson v. Dumouchel, 1967, 72 Wn.2d 73, 431 P.2d 973; Brune v. Belinkoff, 1968, 354 Mass. 102, 235 N.E.2d 793, noted, 1969, 82 Harv.L.Rev. 1781; Tallbull v. Whitney, 1977, 172 Mont. 326, 564 P.2d 162.

47. See Sullivan v. Henry, 1982, 160 Ga.App. 791, 287 S.E.2d 652; Hirschberg v. State, 1977, 91 Misc.2d 590, 398 N.Y.S.2d 470; Shilkret v. Annapolis Emergency Hospital Association, 1975, 276 Md. 187, 349 A.2d 245; Blair v. Eblen, Ky.1970, 461 S.W.2d 370; cf. Pederson v. Dumouchel, 1967, 72 Wn.2d 73, 431 P.2d 973. On the locality rule, in its various permutations, see Annot., 1980, 99 A.L.R.3d 1133.

48. Hines v. St. Paul Fire & Marine Insurance Co., La.App.1978, 365 So.2d 537; Jenkins v. Parrish, Utah 1981, 627 P.2d 533; DeWitt v. Brown, 8th Cir. 1982, 669 F.2d 516; Roberts v. Tardif, Me.1980, 417 A.2d 444; Moon v. United States, D.Nev.1981, 512 F.Supp. 140. But see Gandara v. Wilson, 1973, 85 N.M. 161, 509 P.2d 1356 (surgeon); Chapman v. Edgerton, W.D. Va.1982, 529 F.Supp. 519. See generally Annot., 1982, 18 A.L.R.4th 603.

49. "To prevail in a malpractice case the plaintiff must establish through expert testimony both the standard of care and the fact that the defendant's conduct did not measure up to that standard." Cross v. Huttenlocher, 1981, ___ Conn. ___, 440 A.2d 952, 954; Monahan v. Weichert, 1981, 82 A.D.2d 102, 442 N.Y.S.2d 295 (necessary on proximate cause); Wallace v. Garden City Osteopathic Hospital, 1981, 111 Mich. App. 212, 314 N.W.2d 557; Harvey v. Fridley Medical Center, P.A., Minn.1982, 315 N.W.2d 225; Harris v. Grizzle, Wyo.1981, 625 P.2d 747. See 530 East 89 Corp. v. Unger, 1977, 43 N.Y.2d 776, 402 N.Y.S.2d 382, 373 N.E.2d 276 (architects); Wright v. Williams, 1975, 47 Cal.App.3d 802, 121 Cal.Rptr. 194 (lawyer); O'Neil v. Bergan, D.C.App.1982, 452 A.2d 337 (lawyer); Kemmerlin v. Wingate, 1979, 274 S.C. 62, 261 S.E.2d 50 (accountants).

The necessary expert testimony may come from the defendant himself. Rice v. Jaskolski, 1981, 412 Mich. 206, 313 N.W.2d 893; Williams v. Bennett, Tex.1980, 610 S.W.2d 144; Robinson v. Pediatric Affiliates Medical Group, Inc., 1979, 98 Cal.App.3d 907, 159 Cal.Rptr. 791.

50. See Crain v. Allison, D.C.App.1982, 443 A.2d 558 (informed consent); Henning v. Parsons, App.1980, 95 N.M. 454, 623 P.2d 574 (dissent); Morgan v. Rosenberg, Mo.1963, 370 S.W.2d 685; Halldin v. Peterson, 1968, 39 Wis.2d 668, 159 N.W.2d 738; Seidelson, Medical Malpractice Cases and the Reluctant Expert, 1966, 16 Cath.U.L.Rev. 187; Markus, Conspiracy of Silence, 1965, 14 Cleve.Marsh.L.Rev. 520. Cf. Vogel & Delgado, To Tell the Truth: Physicians' Duty to Disclose Medical Mistakes, 1980, 28 U.C.L.A.L.Rev. 52. Lawyers and other professionals are similarly reluctant to testify against one another, at least in small communities. See Mallen & Levit, Legal Malpractice, 1977, 179 (lawyers); Comment, 1967, 55 Calif.L.Rev. 1361, 1363 (architects).

gence appears quite clear. Where the matter is regarded as within the common knowledge of laymen, as where the surgeon saws off the wrong leg, or there is injury to a part of the body not within the operative field,[51] it is often held that the jury may infer negligence without the aid of any expert.[52]

The cumulative effect of all of these rules has meant that the standard of conduct becomes one of "good medical practice," which is to say, what is customary and usual in the profession.[53]

It has been pointed out often enough[54] that this gives the medical profession, and also the others, the privilege, which is usually emphatically denied to other groups,[55] of setting their own legal standards of conduct, merely by adopting their own practices. It is sometimes said that this is because the physician has impliedly represented that he will follow customary methods, and so has undertaken to do so. Another explanation,[56] perhaps more valid, is the healthy respect which the courts have had for the learning of a fellow profession, and their reluctance to overburden it with liability based on uneducated judgment. It seems clear, in any case, that the result is closely tied in with the layman's ignorance of medical matters and the necessity of expert testimony, since, when the jury are considered competent to do so, they are permitted to find that a practice generally followed by the medical profession is negligent. This has frequently been done in the cases of sponges left in the patient's abdomen after an operation, where the task of keeping track of them has been delegated by the surgeon to a nurse. Although this was, and perhaps still is, universal practice, it has still been found to be negligent.[57]

A rapidly growing form of medical malpractice litigation involves the doctrine of "informed consent," which concerns the duty of the physician or surgeon to inform the patient of the risks involved in treatment or

---

51. Evans v. Roberts, 1915, 172 Iowa 653, 154 N.W. 923 (tongue cut off in removing adenoids); Steinke v. Bell, 1954, 32 N.J.Super. 67, 107 A.2d 825 (dentist pulling wrong tooth); Hyder v. Weilbaecher, 1981, 54 N.C. App. 287, 283 S.E.2d 426, review denied 304 N.C. 727, 288 S.E.2d 804 (eight inch wire left in patient during surgery); King v. Williams, 1981, 276 S.C. 478, 279 S.E.2d 618 (failure to X-ray foot for eight months despite patient's persistent pain and swelling); Clapham v. Yanga, 1980, 102 Mich.App. 47, 300 N.W.2d 727 (failure to give pregnancy test to 14-year-old patient complaining of dizzy spells and fainting); McCann v. Baton Rouge General Hospital, La.1973, 276 So.2d 259 (reproductive organs injured during treatment of elbow). Cf. Corn v. French, 1955, 71 Nev. 280, 289 P.2d 173 (cancer operation without preliminary biopsy). See generally Thode, The Unconscious Patient: Who Should Bear the Risk of Unexplained Injuries to a Healthy Part of his Body?, 1969 Utah L.Rev. 1; Annot., 1971, 37 A.L.R.3d 464 (injury to organ not operated on).

52. So, too, where a lawyer fails to follow his client's simple and explicit instructions. Olfe v. Gordon, 1980, 93 Wis.2d 173, 286 N.W.2d 573; or lets a statute of limitations run; see Watkins v. Sheppard, La.App. 1973, 278 So.2d 890; or fails to inform his client of a settlement offer. Joos v. Auto-Owners Insurance Co., 1979, 94 Mich.App. 419, 288 N.W.2d 443.

Such cases often involve the doctrine of res ipsa loquitur. See infra, § 39. See generally Eaton, Res Ipsa Loquitur and Medical Malpractice in Georgia: A Re assessment, 1982, 17 Ga.L.Rev. 33; Podell, Application of Res Ipsa Loquitur in Medical Malpractice Litigation, 1977, 44 Ins.Coun.J. 634.

53. See Hirn v. Edgewater Hospital, 1980, 86 Ill. App.3d 939, 42 Ill.Dec. 261, 408 N.E.2d 970; McPherson v. Ellis, 1982, 305 N.C. 266, 287 S.E.2d 892; Cross v. Huttenlocher, 1981, ___ Conn. ___, 440 A.2d 952; Wood v. Posthuma, Mich.App.1981, 108 Mich.App. 226, 310 N.W.2d 341. But cf. McNeill v. United States, D.S.C.1981, 519 F.Supp. 283 (custom not conclusive); Vassos v. Roussalis, Wyo.1981, 625 P.2d 768 (same). "The law generally permits the medical profession to establish its own standard of care." Toth v. Community Hospital at Glen Cove, 1968, 22 N.Y.2d 255, 292 N.Y.S.2d 440, 447, 239 N.E.2d 368, 372. See generally King, In Search of a Standard of Care for the Medical Profession: The "Accepted Practice" Formula, 1975, 28 Vand.L.Rev. 1213.

54. See for example Morris, Custom and Negligence, 1942, 42 Col.L.Rev. 1147; James, Particularizing the Standards of Conduct in Negligence Trials, 1952, 5 Vand.L.Rev. 697, 710.

55. See infra, § 33.

56. See McCoid, The Care Required of Medical Practitioners, 1959, 12 Vand.L.Rev. 549, 608.

57. See Truhitte v. French Hospital, 1982, 128 Cal. App.3d 332, 180 Cal.Rptr. 152 (sponge removal nondelegable duty of surgeon). Cf. Helling v. Carey, 1974, 83 Wn.2d 514, 519 P.2d 981 (ophthalmologists not giving glaucoma tests to persons under 40), noted, 1975, 28 Vand.L.Rev. 441, reaffirmed in Gates v. Jensen, 1979, 92 Wn.2d 246, 595 P.2d 919.

surgery. The earliest cases treated this as a matter of vitiating the consent, so that there was liability for battery.[58] Beginning around 1960, however, it began to be recognized that the matter was really one of the standard of professional conduct, and so negligence has now generally displaced battery as the basis for liability.[59]

The informed consent doctrine is based on principles of individual autonomy, and specifically on the premise that every person has the right to determine what shall be done to his own body.[60] Surgeons and other doctors are thus required to provide their patients with sufficient information to permit the patient himself to make an informed and intelligent decision on whether to submit to a proposed course of treatment or surgical procedure.[61] Such a disclosure should include the nature of the pertinent ailment or condition, the risks of the proposed treatment or procedure, and the risks of any alternative methods of treatment, including the risks of failing to undergo any treatment at all.[62] Thus, although the procedure be skillfully performed, the doctor may nevertheless be liable for an adverse consequence about which the patient was not adequately informed.[63]

In addressing the perplexing question of whether the patient needed to know about a particular undisclosed risk in order to make

---

58. See supra, § 18.

59. See Natanson v. Kline, 1960, 186 Kan. 393, 350 P.2d 1093, rehearing denied 187 Kan. 186, 354 P.2d 670. See also Salgo v. Leland Stanford, Jr., University Board of Trustees, 1957, 154 Cal.App.2d 560, 317 P.2d 170; Cobbs v. Grant, 1972, 8 Cal.3d 229, 104 Cal.Rptr. 505, 502 P.2d 1; Berroyer v. Hertz, 3d Cir. 1982, 672 F.2d 334 (dentist—no battery nor punitive damages); Woolley v. Henderson, Me.1980, 418 A.2d 1123; Trogrun v. Fruchtman, 1973, 58 Wis.2d 569, 207 N.W.2d 297. "If treatment is completely unauthorized and performed without any consent at all, there has been a battery. However, if a physician obtains a patient's consent but has breached his duty to inform, the patient has a cause of action sounding in negligence * * *." Scott v. Bradford, Okl.1979, 606 P.2d 554, 557. But cf. Congrove v. Holmes, 1973, 37 Ohio Misc. 95, 308 N.E.2d 765.

60. Schloendorff v. Society of New York Hospital, 1914, 211 N.Y. 125, 105 N.E. 92, 93; Canterbury v. Spence, D.C.Cir. 1972, 464 F.2d 772, 780, certiorari denied, 1973, 409 U.S. 1064, 93 S.Ct. 560, 34 L.Ed.2d 518; Scott v. Bradford, Okl.1979, 606 P.2d 554; Crain v. Allison, D.C.App.1982, 443 A.2d 558.

As with "medical paternalism," the notion of patient sovereignty can be carried too far: "Both positions attempt to vest exclusive moral agency, ethical wisdom, and decisionmaking authority on one side of the relationship, while assigning the other side a dependent role. * * * [N]either extreme adequately reflects the current nature and needs of health care." Making Health Care Decisions, A Report on the Ethical and Legal Implications of Informal Consent in the Patient-Practitioner Relationship, President's Commission, Oct. 1982, vol. 1, p. 36.

61. See generally McCoid, A Reappraisal of Liability for Unauthorized Medical Treatment, 1957, 41 Minn. L.Rev. 381, 424; Plant, An Analysis of "Informed Consent," 1968, 36 Ford.L.Rev. 638; Waltz & Scheuneman, Informed Consent to Therapy, 1970, 64 Nw.U.L.Rev. 628; Halligan, The Standard of Disclosure by Physicians to Patients: Competing Models of Informed Consent, 1980, 41 La.L.Rev. 9 (citing informed consent statutes at p. 59); Katz, Informed Consent—A Fairy Tale? Law's Vision, 1977, 39 U.Pitt.L.Rev. 137; Plant, Decline of "Informed Consent," 1978, 35 Wash. & Lee L.Rev. 91; King, The Standard of Care and Informed Consent Under the Tennessee Malpractice Act, 1977, 44 Tenn.L.Rev. 225; Meisel, The Expansion of Liability for Medical Accidents: From Negligence to Strict Liability by Way of Informed Consent, 1977, 56 Neb.L. Rev. 51; Notes, 1981, 76 Nw.L.Rev. 172; 1980, 55 Wash.L.Rev. 655. Other articles are cited in an excellent general piece, Meisel, The "Exceptions" to the Informed Consent Doctrine: Striking a Balance Between Competing Values in Medical Decisionmaking, 1979, Wis.L.Rev. 413 n. 3. The cases are collected in 2 Louisell & Williams, Medical Malpractice, 1981, ch. 22 (and Supp.).

62. "Where circumstances permit, the patient should be told (1) the diagnosis, (2) the general nature of the contemplated procedure, (3) the risks involved, (4) the prospects of success, (5) the prognosis if the procedure is not performed, and (6) alternative methods of treatment, if any." Louisell & Williams, Medical Malpractice, 1981, ¶ 22.01 at 594.44. See Sard v. Hardy, 1977, 281 Md. 432, 379 A.2d 1014, 1020; Miller v. Van Newkirk, Colo.App.1981, 628 P.2d 143; Crain v. Allison, D.C.App.1982, 443 A.2d 558, 562. An important recent case is Truman v. Thomas, 1980, 27 Cal.3d 285, 165 Cal.Rptr. 308, 611 P.2d 902 (4-3) (liability for nondisclosure of potentially fatal risk of failing to undergo pap smear).

63. See, e.g., Salis v. United States, M.D.Pa.1981, 522 F.Supp. 989 (renal shut-down, and gangrene in leg requiring amputation, from angiogram diagnostic procedure; 1-2% risk of serious complication); Sard v. Hardy, 1977, 281 Md. 432, 379 A.2d 1014 (2% risk of pregnancy after particular tubal ligation procedure); Miller v. Van Newkirk, Colo.App.1981, 628 P.2d 143 (risks of particular type of cataract operation); Douthitt v. United States, E.D.Mo.1980, 491 F.Supp. 891 (risk of damage to sciatic nerve during operation on thigh and buttock).

an informed decision, the courts often speak in terms of the materiality of the risk: the doctor's duty is to disclose all risks which are "material." [64] The extent of this duty to disclose has traditionally been based upon a professional medical standard—whether physicians customarily inform their patients about the type of risk involved,[65] or whether a reasonable physician would make the disclosure in the circumstances.[66] Since the use of a professional standard paternalistically leaves the right of choice to the medical community, in derogation of the patient's right of self-determination,[67] a number of recent cases have defined the duty in terms of the patient's need to know the information—based on whether a reasonable person in the patient's position would attach significance to the information.[68]

In addition to proving the doctor's failure to provide sufficient information, on whatever standard, the plaintiff must also establish a causal link between the nondisclosure and his harm, by proving that he would not have undergone the treatment had he known of the risk of harm that in fact occurred.[69] Because of the patient's obvious bias in testifying in hindsight on this hypothetical matter,[70] most courts have adopted an objective standard of causation: whether a reasonable patient in the plaintiff's position would have withheld consent to the treatment or procedure had the material risks been disclosed.[71] Other courts have adopted a subjective cau-

64. Canterbury v. Spence, D.C.Cir. 1972, 464 F.2d 772 (1% risk of paralysis from laminectomy), certiorari denied 1973, 409 U.S. 1064, 93 S.Ct. 560, 34 L.Ed.2d 518; Crain v. Allison, D.C.App.1982, 443 A.2d 558 (risk of infection from cortisone shots in finger for arthritis); Kinikin v. Heupel, Minn.1981, 305 N.W.2d 589 (risk of skin necrosis from prophylactic breast surgery—despite patient's "cancer phobia" apparently outweighing cosmetic results).

65. Rush v. Miller, 6th Cir. 1981, 648 F.2d 1075 ("in accordance with the community standards of others in the medical community"; Tennessee statute held constitutional); Fuller v. Starnes, 1980, 268 Ark. 476, 597 S.W.2d 88, 89 (adopting the "majority view" which "emphasizes the interest in the medical profession to be relatively free from vexatious and costly litigation and holds that what a patient should be told about future medical treatment is primarily a medical decision"); see Annot., 1978, 88 A.L.R.3d 1008.

66. Troy v. Long Island Jewish-Hillside Medical Center, 1982, 86 A.D.2d 631, 446 N.Y.S.2d 347 (statute); Wooley v. Henderson, Me.1980, 418 A.2d 1123; Henning v. Parsons, App.1980, 623 P.2d 574, 95 N.M. 454; see Annot., 1978, 88 A.L.R.3d 1008.

67. "Unlimited discretion in the physician is irreconcilable with the basic right of the patient to make the ultimate informed decision * * *." Cobbs v. Grant, 1972, 8 Cal.3d 229, 104 Cal.Rptr. 505, 502 P.2d 1, 10; Sard v. Hardy, 1977, 281 Md. 432, 379 A.2d 1014, 1022.

68. Crain v. Allison, D.C.App.1982, 443 A.2d 558, 562 ("the more modern rule"); Sard v. Hardy, 1977, 281 Md. 432, 379 A.2d 1014 (2% risk of another pregnancy after particular method of tubal ligation; 2 alternative methods had failure rate of less than 1/10 of 1%: jury could find material); Plutshack v. University of Minnesota Hospitals, Minn.1982, 316 N.W.2d 1; Cobbs v. Grant, 1972, 8 Cal.3d 229, 104 Cal.Rptr. 505, 502 P.2d 1; Canterbury v. Spence, D.C.Cir. 1972, 464 F.2d 772, certiorari denied 1973, 409 U.S. 1064, 93 S.Ct. 560, 34 L.Ed.2d 518; see Annot., 1978, 88 A.L.R.3d 1008. Compare In re Swine Flu Immunization Products Liability Litigation, D.Colo.1980, 533 F.Supp. 567, 576 (warning of severe or potentially fatal reaction sufficient; specific risk of neurologic disorders not significant): "the patient's right to know and consent depends upon an objective determination of what information a prudent person would require in order to make an intelligent decision. To explain all the risks * * * might be inexpedient and confusing."

Jurisdictions which have adopted a reasonable patient standard of disclosure have generally abandoned requirements for expert testimony on the scope or breach of the standard. See Cross v. Trapp, 1982, ___ W.Va. ___, 294 S.E.2d 446; Sard v. Hardy, 1977, 281 Md. 432, 379 A.2d 1014, 1023–24 (excellent summary of informed consent generally); Annot., 1973, 52 A.L.R.3d 1084.

69. See Sard v. Hardy, 1977, 281 Md. 432, 379 A.2d 1014, 1024 (jury question on evidence); Canterbury v. Spence, D.C.Cir. 1972, 464 F.2d 772, 790 (jury question on evidence, semble), certiorari denied 1973, 409 U.S. 1064, 93 S.Ct. 560, 34 L.Ed.2d 518; Kranda v. Houser-Norborg Medical Corp., 1981, ___ Ind.App. ___, 419 N.E.2d 1024, rehearing denied 424 N.E.2d 1064, appeal dismissed ___ U.S. ___, 103 S.Ct. 23, 74 L.Ed.2d 39 (no causation because no duty to disclose unexpected risk).

The plaintiff, of course, must also prove that the treatment actually caused the injury complained of. See In re Swine Flu Immunization Products Liability Litigation, N.D.Okl.1980, 533 F.Supp. 581 (failure to show GBS resulted from vaccine).

70. E.g., Sard v. Hardy, 1977, 281 Md. 432, 379 A.2d 1014, 1025.

71. Macey v. James, 1981, 139 Vt. 270, 427 A.2d 803; Wooley v. Henderson, Me.1980, 418 A.2d 1123; Cobbs v. Grant, 1972, 8 Cal.3d 229, 104 Cal.Rptr. 505, 502 P.2d 1; Canterbury v. Spence, D.C.Cir. 1972, 464 F.2d 772, certiorari denied 1973, 409 U.S. 1064, 93 S.Ct. 560, 34 L.Ed.2d 518; Hartke v. McKelway, D.C.Cir. 1983, 707 F.2d 1544.

sation test, as better protecting the essential values underlying the informed consent doctrine,[72] and so have framed the standard in terms of whether the particular plaintiff would have avoided the treatment or procedure had sufficient information been provided.[73] As a compromise, an objective-subjective mix might reasonably be adopted, substituting an "ordinary" patient for the "reasonable" one, and taking account of the patient's individual fears and beliefs in considering "the plaintiff's position."[74] Such an approach would maintain a basically objective structure for the issue, leaving it capable of reasoned adjudication, yet would also protect the basic individuality and autonomy of idiosyncratic patients who are in fact injured by insufficient disclosure.

The informed consent doctrine is circumscribed by a variety of limitations, and the physician is not required to disclose risks that are unexpected[75] or immaterial,[76] by whatever standard, nor even material risks where disclosure is precluded by an emergency situation,[77] by the patient's incapacity,[78] by the patient's waiver of his right to receive the information,[79] or where disclosure would be harmful to the patient, which gives the doctor a "therapeutic privilege" to withhold the information.[80] Nor, of course, need the doctor disclose risks that are commonly understood, obvious, or already known to the patient.[81]

The late 1960's and early 1970's witnessed a tremendous increase in the level of medical malpractice litigation, in the size of damage awards in such suits, and in the cost of medical malpractice insurance therefor. As a result of this "medical malpractice crisis," most states passed some form of legislation

---

72. MacPherson v. Ellis, 1982, 305 N.C. 266, 287 S.E.2d 892, 897 (under objective test, patient's "supposedly inviolable right to decide for himself what is to be done with his body is made subject to a standard set by others"); Scott v. Bradford, Okl.1979, 606 P.2d 554, 559 (under "reasonable man" approach, "a patient's right of self-determination is *irrevocably lost*").

73. Id.

74. Cf. Kinikin v. Heupel, Minn.1981, 305 N.W.2d 589, 595 ("to the extent a doctor is or can be aware that his patient attaches particular significance to risks not generally considered by the medical profession serious enough to require discussion with the patient, these too must be brought out").

75. Reiser v. Lohner, Utah 1982, 641 P.2d 93 (risk of cardiac arrest during amniocentesis; no prior documented cases); Kranda v. Houser-Norborg Medical Corp., 1981, ___ Ind.App. ___, 419 N.E.2d 1024, rehearing denied 424 N.E.2d 1064, appeal dismissed, ___ U.S. ___, 103 S.Ct. 23, 74 L.Ed.2d 39 (injury to rectum during gynecological surgery; never seen before by any of the expert witnesses); Hanks v. Drs. Ranson, Swan & Burch, Ltd., La.App.1978, 359 So.2d 1089, writ denied 360 So.2d 1178 (risk of error in initial diagnosis of cancer in lump in breast leading to unnecessary mastectomy; all six experts testified this was first instance of such event).

76. Masquat v. Maguire, Okl.1981, 638 P.2d 1105 (difference in reversal success rates of different tubal ligation procedures); McKinney v. Nash, 1981, 120 Cal.App.3d 428, 174 Cal.Rptr. 642 (either remote risk of contaminated spinal anesthetic solution or extremely rare idiosyncratic reaction to anesthetic); Henderson v. Milobsky, D.C.Cir. 1978, 595 F.2d 654 (1 in 100,000 chance of permanent loss of sensation in small section of face from wisdom tooth extraction).

77. Compare Keogan v. Holy Family Hospital, 1980, 95 Wn.2d 306, 622 P.2d 1246 (true emergency), with Dewes v. Indian Health Service, D.S.D.1980, 504 F.Supp. 203 (inadequate emergency).

78. As where the patient needing immediate attention is unconscious, insane, or a young child. See generally Meisel, The "Exceptions" to the Informed Consent Doctrine: Striking a Balance Between Competing Values in Medical Decisionmaking, 1979 Wis.L.Rev. 413.

Even in the case of an incompetent, however, the usual disclosures must be made to a relative, guardian or other representative if reasonably possible. See Allen v. Roark, Tex.App.1981, 625 S.W.2d 411 (to the parents in the case of a newborn infant), modified, 633 S.W.2d 804. Risks to the fetus from a pre-operative procedure need only be communicated to the prospective mother. Reiser v. Lohner, Utah 1982, 641 P.2d 93 (statute).

79. See Meisel, id.

80. Id.

81. Compare Kinikin v. Heupel, Minn.1981, 305 N.W.2d 589 (jury could find experienced patient, even after 9 or 10 operations, did not know of risk of skin necrosis); Stone v. Foster, 1980, 106 Cal.App.3d 334, 164 Cal.Rptr. 901, 910–11 (risks of tummy tuck operation, patient's tummy had been tucked before); Crain v. Allison, D.C.App.1982, 443 A.2d 558 (patient and husband knew generally of risk of infection from cortisone shots for arthritis, but did not know extent of risk); Truman v. Thomas, 1980, 27 Cal.3d 285, 165 Cal.Rptr. 308, 611 P.2d 902 (4–3) (potentially fatal risk of undetected cervical cancer from failing to undergo pap smear; issue was for jury).

affecting this type of litigation in one way or another. Among the many different types of provisions of such statutes are: various changes in statutes of limitations; creation of medical malpractice pre-litigation screening panels, composed of some combination of doctors, lawyers, judges and laymen; limitations on actual or punitive damages; modification of the collateral source rule; changes in the Good Samaritan statutes; setting arbitration guidelines; requirements of writings for warranty actions; regulation or elimination of contingent fees; and various changes in the burden of proof, the standard of care, the informed consent doctrine, and the rules of evidence.[82] As a result of such legislative modifications to the common law of medical malpractice, the statute books must carefully be consulted in every case.

WESTLAW REFERENCES

reasonable +3 man person /s "ordinary prudence"
fail! /s reasonable +3 man person /s same similar /5 circumstance*

Physical Attributes
negligen** /s reasonable /3 man person /s handicap! disab! blind! deaf! lame!

Mental Capacity
reasonable +3 man person /s foolish stupid insane deranged incompetent
court(nv) & title(butler & davies)
sh 602 p2d 605

Children
standard /p minor* child! infant* /p adult* /p activit!
minor* child! infant* /p tort! negligen** /p minimum responsib! /s age

Knowledge
distract! /s event* circumstance* occur! /s negligent**
knowledge /20 normal common /20 risk* danger*

Super Knowledge
299k18.80(9)
topic(299) /p special superior /3 knowledge skill* learning
"informed consent" /p material*** /p risk*
"good samaritan" /2 law* statute* act*

§ 33. Application of the Standard

The application of this standard of reasonable conduct is as wide as all human behavior. There is scarcely any act which, under some conceivable circumstances, may not involve an unreasonable risk of harm. Even going to sleep becomes negligence when it is done on a railway track, or at the wheel of an automobile. In so broad a field, there is space to select for consideration only a few problems, whose frequent appearance indicates that they are of sufficient importance to call for special notice.

Custom

Since the standard is a community standard, evidence of the usual and customary conduct of others under similar circumstances is normally relevant and admissible,[1] as an indication of what the community regards as proper, and a composite judgment as to the risks of the situation and the precautions required to meet them.[2] Custom also bears upon what others will expect the actor to do, and what, therefore, reasonable care may require the actor to do, upon the feasibility of taking precautions, the difficulty of change, and the actor's opportunity to learn the risks and what is called for to meet them.[3] If the actor does only what everyone else has done, there is at least an inference

---

82. See 2 Louisell & Williams, Medical Malpractice ¶ 20.07 (Supp.1981, p. 107); Probert, Nibbling at the Problems of Medical Malpractice, 1975, 28 Fla.L.Rev. 56; Comment, An Analysis of State Legislative Responses to the Medical Malpractice Crisis, 1975 Duke L.J. 1417.

§ 33

1. Coburn v. Lenox Homes, Inc., 1982, 186 Conn. 370, 441 A.2d 620; Besette v. Enderlin School District No. 22, N.D.1981, 310 N.W.2d 759; Ploetz v. Big Discount Panel Center, Inc., Fla.App.1981, 402 So.2d 64.

To be admissible, the custom must be general, and not, for example, that of a particular block in a town. Weisbart v. Flohr, 1968, 260 Cal.App.2d 281, 67 Cal. Rptr. 114.

2. 2 Wigmore, Evidence, Chadbourne Rev. ed. 1979, § 461.

3. See Morris, Custom and Negligence, 1942, 42 Col.L.Rev. 1147; James, Particularizing Standards of Conduct in Negligence Trials, 1952, 5 Vand.L.Rev. 697, 709–714; Note, 1944, 18 Tul.L.Rev. 646.

that the actor is conforming to the community's idea of reasonable behavior.[4]

In a particular case, where there is nothing in the evidence or in common experience to lead to a contrary conclusion, this inference may be so strong that it calls for a directed verdict on the issue of negligence.[5] Thus, in the absence of some special circumstances, where an automobile is driven along a private road, with no applicable highway statute, it seems quite impossible to conclude that it is negligence to drive it on the right side of the road, or that it is not negligence to drive it on the left. It should be obvious, however, that this is a matter of the custom itself, of its general acceptance by the community and the general reliance upon it, and of all of the circumstances of the case. Some few courts formerly made the effort to treat all customs in this manner, and to enlarge the normal inference into an "unbending test" of negligence, under which the ordinary usages of a business or industry became the sole criterion as to what the actor should, as a reasonable person, have done.[6]

Such an arbitrary rule proved in the long run impossible to justify. First of all, customs which are entirely reasonable under the ordinary circumstances which give rise to them in the first instance may become entirely unreasonable in the light of a single fact altering the situation in the particular case. It may become highly dangerous to follow the usual practice of bumping railroad cars together, on a day when brakemen must stand on top of cars which are covered with ice;[7] or to clean a floor with a compound which is in general use for the purpose, but quite unsuited to the particular floor.[8] But beyond this, customs and usages themselves are many and various;[9] some are the result of careful thought and decision, while others arise from the kind of inadvertence, carelessness, indifference, costparing and corner-cutting that normally is associated with negligence.[10] There can certainly be such a thing as customary negligence, as the unchecked habit of jaywalking in some communities may suggest.

Even an entire industry, by adopting such careless methods to save time, effort or money, cannot be permitted to set its own uncontrolled standard.[11] The fact that all other beverage bottlers use the same slipshod methods cannot serve as absolution for

---

4. See Ploetz v. Big Discount Panel Center, Inc., Fla.App.1981, 402 So.2d 64; Honea v. Coca Cola Bottling Co., 1944, 143 Tex. 272, 183 S.W.2d 968.

5. See Sledd v. Washington Metroplitan Area Transit Authority, D.C.App.1981, 439 A.2d 464; Westinghouse Electric Corp. v. Nutt, D.C.App.1979, 407 A.2d 606; Turner v. Manning, Maxwell & Moore, Inc., 1975, 216 Va. 245, 217 S.E.2d 863.

6. Wommack v. Orr, 1943, 352 Mo. 113, 176 S.W.2d 477; Ellis v. Louisville & Northwest Railroad Co., Ky. 1952, 251 S.W.2d 577; Titus v. Bradford, Bordell & Kinzua Railroad Co., 1890, 136 Pa. 618, 20 A. 517.

7. Texas & Pacific Railway Co. v. Behymer, 1903, 189 U.S. 468, 23 S.Ct. 622, 47 L.Ed. 905. A good opinion from the very early days of railroads is Bradley v. Boston & Maine Railroad Co., 1848, 56 Mass. (2 Cush.) 539. See Miller, The So-Called Unbending Test of Negligence, 1916, 3 Va.L.Rev. 537.

8. S. H. Kress & Co. v. Telford, 5th Cir. 1957, 240 F.2d 70.

9. See William Laurie Co. v. McCullough, 1910, 174 Ind. 477, 90 N.E. 1014, rehearing denied 1910, 174 Ind. 477, 92 N.E. 337; Annotation, 1930, 68 A.L.R. 1400, 1401. Thus in Mennis v. Cheffings, 1962, 233 Or. 215, 376 P.2d 672, a custom on a private road, by which the loaded truck was to take the inside lane, was held to be merely evidence for the jury on the issue of negligence.

10. Cf. Johnson v. Harry Jarred, Inc., La.App.1980, 391 So.2d 898 (failure to install blowout preventer on natural gas well).

11. "[I]n most cases reasonable prudence is in fact common prudence; but strictly it is never its measure; a whole calling may have unduly lagged in the adoption of new and available devices. It may never set its own tests * * *. Courts must in the end say what is required; there are precautions so imperative that even their universal disregard will not excuse their omission." The T. J. Hooper, 2d Cir. 1932, 60 F.2d 737, 740 (L. Hand, J.), certiorari denied 287 U.S. 662, 53 S.Ct. 220, 77 L.Ed. 571. See also Shafer v. H. B. Thomas Co., 1958, 53 N.J.Super. 19, 146 A.2d 483 (unchecked swinging doors); Pan American Petroleum Corp. v. Like, Wyo.1963, 381 P.2d 70; Marietta v. Cliffs Ridge, Inc., 1970, 20 Mich.App. 449, 174 N.W.2d 164, affirmed 385 Mich. 364, 189 N.W.2d 208; Johnson v. Harry Jarred, Inc., La.App.1980, 391 So.2d 898.

the bottler who is being sued.[12] And if the only test is to be what has been done before, no industry or group will ever have any great incentive to make progress in the direction of safety. Cases will no doubt be infrequent in which any defendant will be held liable for failing to do what no one in his position has ever done before; but there appears to be no doubt that they can arise.[13] Much the better view, therefore, is that of the great majority of the cases, that every custom is not conclusive merely because it is a custom, that it must meet the challenge of "learned reason," [14] and be given only the evidentiary weight which the situation deserves.[15] It follows that where common knowledge and ordinary judgment will recognize unreasonable danger, what everyone does may be found to be negligent; [16] and that there will be extreme cases where it is so clearly negligent in itself that it may even be excluded from evidence.[17]

Upon the same basis, the failure to comply with customary precaution may, in a particular case, be negligence in itself, especially where it is known that others may rely on it.[18] But, as a general rule, the fact that a thing is done in an unusual manner is merely evidence to be considered in determining negligence, and is not in itself conclusive.[19] A custom, to be relevant, must be reasonably brought home to the actor's locality,[20] and must be so general, or so well known, that the actor may be charged with knowledge of it or with negligent ignorance.[21] The actor's own record of past conduct, which is commonly called "habit" rather than custom, is no evidence of any standard of reasonable care,[22] but when the actor has departed from it, it may be used against him as indicating his knowledge of the risk and

12. Grant v. Graham Chero-Cola Bottling Co., 1918, 176 N.C. 256, 97 S.E. 27; Morrison v. Kansas City Coca Cola Bottling Co., 1953, 175 Kan. 212, 263 P.2d 217.

13. See Gryc v. Dayton-Hudson Corp., Minn.1980, 297 N.W.2d 727, certiorari denied 449 U.S. 921, 101 S.Ct. 320, 66 L.Ed.2d 149 (flame retarding cotton flannelette used for children's nightgowns); Marsh Wood Products Co. v. Babcock & Wilcox Co., 1932, 207 Wis. 209, 240 N.W. 392 (microscopic tests of steel for boiler tubes); The T. J. Hooper, 2d Cir. 1932, 60 F.2d 737, certiorari denied 287 U.S. 662, 53 S.Ct. 220, 77 L.Ed. 571 (radio sets for ocean going tugs). This was suggested as long ago as 3 Labatt, Master and Servant, 1913, § 947.

14. Allen, Learned and Unlearned Reason, 1924, 36 Jurid.Rev. 254.

15. "What usually is done may be evidence of what ought to be done, but what ought to be done is fixed by a standard of reasonable prudence, whether it usually is complied with or not." Texas & Pacific Railway Co. v. Behymer, 1903, 189 U.S. 468, 23 S.Ct. 622, 47 L.Ed. 905, per Holmes, J. Accord, Westinghouse Electric Corp. v. Nutt, D.C.App.1979, 407 A.2d 606; Forrest City Machine Works, Inc. v. Aderhold, 1981, 273 Ark. 33, 616 S.W.2d 720; Fancher v. Southwest Missouri Truck Center, Inc., Mo.App.1981, 618 S.W.2d 271.

16. MacDougall v. Pennsylvania Power & Light Co., 1932, 311 Pa. 387, 166 A. 589.

17. Mayhew v. Sullivan Mining Co., 1884, 76 Me. 100 (unguarded shafts in coal mines); Atchison & Northwest Railroad Co. v. Bailey, 1881, 11 Neb. 332, 9 N.W. 50 (leaving turntable unsecured when accessible to children); Sanchez v. J. Barron Rice, Inc., 1967, 77 N.M. 717, 427 P.2d 240 (customary violation of safety ordinance).

In rare cases, customary behavior may even be so grossly negligent as to support a punitive damages award. See Gyrc v. Dayton-Hudson Corp., Minn.1980, 297 N.W.2d 727, certiorari denied 449 U.S. 921, 101 S.Ct. 320, 66 L.Ed.2d 149; Maxey v. Freightliner Corp., 5th Cir. 1982, 665 F.2d 1367; Owen, Problems in Assessing Punitive Damages Against Manufacturers of Defective Products, 1982, 49 U.Chi.L.Rev. 1, 40–41.

18. See Roberts v. Indiana Gas & Water Co., 1966, 140 Ind.App. 409, 218 N.E.2d 556; Thropp v. Bache Halsey Stuart Shields, Inc., 6th Cir. 1981, 650 F.2d 817.

19. Coburn v. Lenox Homes, Inc., 1982, 186 Conn. 370, 441 A.2d 620; Besette v. Enderlin School District No. 22, N.D.1981, 310 N.W.2d 759; Trimarco v. Klein, 1981, 82 A.D.2d 20, 441 N.Y.S.2d 62, reversed, 88 A.D. 2d 778, 451 N.Y.S.2d 52.

20. Sprecher v. Roberts, 1933, 212 Wis. 69, 248 N.W. 795; Trimarco v. Klein, 1981, 82 A.D.2d 20, 441 N.Y.S.2d 62, reversed, 88 A.D.2d 778, 451 N.Y.S.2d 52.

21. Rhine v. Duluth, Missabe & Iron Range Railway Co., 1941, 210 Minn. 281, 297 N.W. 852; Garthe v. Ruppert, 1934, 264 N.Y. 290, 190 N.E. 643, reversed 240 App.Div. 968, 268 N.Y.S. 908, reargument denied 265 N.Y. 502, 193 N.E. 291; Beals v. Walker, 1980, 98 Mich.App. 214, 296 N.W.2d 828.

22. Bimberg v. Northern Pacific Railway Co., 1944, 217 Minn. 187, 14 N.W.2d 410, certiorari denied 323 U.S. 752, 65 S.Ct. 87, 89 L.Ed. 593; Schiro v. Oriental Realty Co., 1959, 7 Wis.2d 556, 97 N.W.2d 385.

the precautions necessary to meet it.[23] The same, in general, is true of rules made by the defendant to govern the conduct of his employees,[24] and of the safety or accident record bearing upon the particular practice.[25]

Emergency

The courts have been compelled to recognize that an actor who is confronted with an emergency is not to be held to the standard of conduct normally applied to one who is in no such situation.[26] An emergency has been defined as a sudden or unexpected event or combination of circumstances which calls for immediate action;[27] and although there are courts which have laid stress upon the "instinctive action" which usually accompanies such a situation,[28] it seems clear that the basis of the special rule is merely that the actor is left no time for adequate thought, or is reasonably so disturbed or excited that the actor cannot weigh alternative courses of action, and must make a speedy decision, based very largely upon impulse or guess.[29] Under such conditions, the actor cannot reasonably be held to the same accuracy of judgment or conduct as one who has had full opportunity to reflect, even though it later appears that the actor made the wrong decision, one which no reasonable person could possibly have made after due deliberation.[30] The actor's choice "may be mistaken and yet prudent." [31]

There are, however, a number of limitations which have hedged the "emergency" rule. It does not mean that any different standard is to be applied in the emergency. The conduct required is still that of a reasonable person under the circumstances, as they

---

23. See Thropp v. Bache Halsey Stuart Shields, Inc., 6th Cir. 1981, 650 F.2d 817; South v. National Railroad Passenger Corp. (AMTRAK), N.D.1980, 290 N.W.2d 819; James, Particularizing Standards of Conduct in Negligence Cases, 1952, 5 Vand.L.Rev. 697, 712–713.

24. Thropp v. Bache Halsey Stuart Shields, Inc., 6th Cir. 1981, 650 F.2d 817; Babcock v. Chesapeake & Ohio Railway Co., 1979, 83 Ill.App.3d 919, 38 Ill.Dec. 841, 404 N.E.2d 265; Winters, The Evidentiary Value of Defendant's Safety Rules in a Negligence Action, 1959, 38 Neb.L.Rev. 906.

25. A somewhat more complicated question, as to which see Morris, Proof of Safety History in Negligence Cases, 1948, 61 Harv.L.Rev. 205.

26. "The law takes account of the impulses of humanity when placed in dangerous positions, and does not expect thoughtful care from the persons whose lives are thus endangered." Elmore v. Des Moines City Railway Co., 1929, 207 Iowa 862, 224 N.W. 28; Pennington's Administrator v. Pure Milk Co., 1939, 279 Ky. 235, 130 S.W.2d 24.

See generally Renolds, Put Yourself in an Emergency—How Will You Be Judged?, 1974, 62 Ky.L.J. 366; Wise, The Sudden Emergency Doctrine As Applied in South Carolina, 1968, 20 S.C.L.Rev. 408; Notes, 1969, 21 U.Fla.L.Rev. 667; 1966, 19 Okla.L.Rev. 308; 1980, 51 Miss.L.J. 301 (discussing abolition of doctrine in Mississippi); Second Restatement of Torts, § 296.

27. Hunter v. Batton, 1982, 160 Ga.App. 849, 288 S.E.2d 244; Heidbreder v. Northampton Township Trustees, 1979, 64 Ohio App.2d 95, 411 N.E.2d 825 (bullet from policeman's gun ricochetted off fleeing robbers' car and hit infant plaintiff). The Texas courts formerly distinguished between "imminent peril" and "emergency" with a large measure of resulting confusion. See Thode, Imminent Peril and Emergency in Texas, 1962, 40 Tex.L.Rev. 441. The imminent peril doctrine was finally abandoned in Davila v. Sanders, Tex.1977, 557 S.W.2d 770.

28. Whicher v. Phinney, 1st Cir. 1942, 124 F.2d 929; Collette v. Boston & Maine Railroad Co., 1927, 83 N.H. 210, 140 A. 176; Cook v. Thomas, 1964, 25 Wis.2d 467, 131 N.W.2d 299.

29. Hunter v. Batton, 1982, 160 Ga.App. 849, 288 S.E.2d 244; Robertson v. Travis, La.App.1980, 393 So.2d 304, writ refused, La., 397 So.2d 805 (contributory conduct of child in traffic); Heidbreder v. Northampton Township Trustees, 1979, 64 Ohio App.2d 95, 411 N.E.2d 825 (bystander hit by bullet from police officer's gun; officer may have had time to "reflect on his course of action"); Cordas v. Peerless Transportation Co., N.Y.City 1941, 27 N.Y.S.2d 198 (cab driver leaped from moving cab after robber pointed gun at head: "the expedition of the chauffeur's violent love of his own security outran the pauser, reason, when he was suddenly confronted with unusual emergency which 'took his reason prisoner' ").

30. See Roberts v. Hooper, App.Div.1981, 181 N.J. Super. 474, 438 A.2d 351; Hunter v. Batton, 1982, 160 Ga.App. 849, 288 S.E.2d 244; Potenburg v. Varner, 1981, 284 Pa.Super. 19, 424 A.2d 1370 (auto struck person on highway). "The plaintiff had to choose at once, in agitation and with imperfect knowledge. * * * 'Errors in judgment,' however, would not count against him if they resulted 'from the excitement and confusion of the moment.' * * * The reason that was exacted of him was not the reason of the morrow. It was reason fitted and proportioned to the time and the event." Wagner v. International Railway Co., 1921, 232 N.Y. 176, 133 N.E. 437, 438 (Cardozo, J.).

31. Holmes, C. J., in Kane v. Worcester Consolidated Street Railway Co., 1902, 182 Mass. 201, 65 N.E. 54.

would appear to one who was using proper care, and the emergency is to be considered only as one of the circumstances.[32] An objective standard must still be applied, and the actor's own judgment or impulse is still not the sole criterion.[33] The actor may still be found to be negligent if, notwithstanding the emergency, his acts are found to be unreasonable.[34] The "emergency doctrine" is applied only where the situation which arises is sudden and unexpected, and such as to deprive the actor of reasonable opportunity for deliberation and considered decision.[35] Furthermore, it obviously cannot serve to excuse the actor when the emergency has been created through the actor's own negligence, since he cannot be permitted to shield himself behind a situation resulting from his own fault.[36]

A further qualification which must be made is that some "emergencies" must be anticipated, and the actor must be prepared to meet them when he engages in an activity in which they are likely to arise. Thus, under present day traffic conditions, any driver of an automobile must be prepared for the sudden appearance of obstacles and persons in the highway, and of other vehicles at intersections,[37] just as one who sees a child on the curb may be required to anticipate its sudden dash into the street, and his failure to act properly when they appear may be found to amount to negligence.[38]

Despite the basic logic and simplicity of the sudden emergency doctrine, it is all too frequently misapplied on the facts or misstated in jury instructions.[39] As a result, the model jury instructions in at least Illinois, Florida, Kansas and Missouri recommend that no such instruction be given, and Mississippi abolished the doctrine altogether in 1980.[40]

Anticipating Conduct of Others; Negligent Entrustment

There are many situations in which the hypothetical reasonable person would be expected to anticipate and guard against the conduct of others. Anyone with normal experience is required to have knowledge of

---

32. Ferrer v. Harris, 1982, 55 N.Y.2d 285, 449 N.Y.S.2d 162, 434 N.E.2d 231; Martin v. City of New Orleans, 5th Cir. 1982, 678 F.2d 1321, rehearing denied 683 F.2d 1373, certiorari denied __ U.S. __, 103 S.Ct. 1189, 75 L.Ed.2d 435 (Williams, J., J.) (2–1) (doctrine merely emphasizes the "under the circumstances" portion of general standard of "reasonable under the circumstances"); Oberempt v. Egri, 1979, 176 Conn. 652, 410 A.2d 482.

33. Gravel v. Roberge, 1926, 125 Me. 399, 134 A. 375.

34. Cook v. Thomas, 1964, 25 Wis.2d 467, 131 N.W.2d 299; Rodriguez v. New York State Thruway Authority, 1981, 82 A.D.2d 853, 440 N.Y.S.2d 49 (rescuer); Heidbreder v. Northampton Township Trustees, 1979, 64 Ohio App.2d 95, 411 N.E.2d 825 (semble); Ferrer v. Harris, 1982, 55 N.Y.2d 285, 449 N.Y.S.2d 162, 434 N.E.2d 231.

35. Lutz v. Shelby Mutual Insurance Co., 1975, 70 Wis.2d 743, 235 N.W.2d 426. Thus, blocking traffic in an intersection may be embarrassing but may not present an emergency. See Webb v. Perry, 1981, 158 Ga. App. 409, 280 S.E.2d 423. And a police officer may have time to consider the risks to bystanders before firing at a get-away car. See Heidbreder v. Northampton Township Trustees, 1979, 64 Ohio App.2d 95, 411 N.E.2d 825 (question was for jury).

36. See Kaplan v. Missouri-Pacific Railroad Co., La. App.1981, 409 So.2d 298 (plaintiff crossing railroad trestle); White v. Greer, 1982, 55 N.C.App. 450, 285 S.E.2d 848; Ratlief v. Yokum, 1981, __ W.Va. __, 280 S.E.2d 584.

Even if the plaintiff by his negligence has created the emergency, however, the defendant with the last opportunity to avoid the accident may nevertheless still be liable due to the doctrine of last clear chance. See infra, § 66; cf. Lutz v. Shelby Mutual Insurance Co., 1975, 70 Wis.2d 743, 235 N.W.2d 426.

37. See Stanek v. Swierczek, 1981, 209 Neb. 357, 307 N.W.2d 807; cf. Heidbreder v. Northampton Township Trustees, 1979, 64 Ohio App.2d 95, 411 N.E.2d 825 (suggesting that police officer should anticipate extraordinary situations); Lutz v. Shelby Mutual Insurance Co., 1975, 70 Wis.2d 743, 235 N.W.2d 426 (pedestrian crossing intersection).

38. Potts v. Krey, Ky.1962, 362 S.W.2d 726; Ennis v. Dupree, 1962, 258 N.C. 141, 128 S.E.2d 231; Kachman v. Blosberg, 1958, 251 Minn. 224, 87 N.W.2d 687; Bermudez v. Jenkins, Fla.App.1962, 144 So.2d 859; Conery v. Tackmaier, 1967, 34 Wis.2d 511, 149 N.W.2d 575 (failure to look out for children). But even in the darting children cases the doctrine may apply. Ferrer v. Harris, 1982, 55 N.Y.2d 285, 449 N.Y.S.2d 162, 434 N.E.2d 231.

39. E.g., Potenburg v. Varner, 1981, 284 Pa.Super. 19, 424 A.2d 1370. See generally Recent Decision, 1980, 51 Miss.L.J. 301.

40. Knapp v. Stanford, Miss.1980, 392 So.2d 196 (5–4), noted, 1980, 51 Miss.L.J. 301 (excellent general analysis).

the traits and habits of common animals, and of other human beings,[41] and to govern accordingly. A person may expect that horses left unattended in the road may become frightened and run away,[42] that bees disturbed may sting,[43] that a bull or a stallion will attack a man,[44] that stampeded cattle or sheep will get upon a railway track,[45] or be killed by bears in the vicinity.[46] Upon much the same basis, a person may be required to anticipate that persons who are ill or intoxicated may wander into places of danger,[47] and that human beings who are placed in a position of peril will endeavor, more or less instinctively, to escape, and may do harm to themselves or others in the attempt.[48]

But beyond this, a person is required to realize that there will be a certain amount of negligence in the world. In general, where the risk is relatively slight, a person is free to proceed upon the assumption that other people will exercise proper care. It would not be easy to move traffic if motorists could not assume that other cars will keep to the right,[49] obey stop signs [50] and stoplights,[51] and otherwise proceed with care and obey the law.[52] But when the risk becomes a serious one, either because the threatened harm is great, or because there is an especial likelihood that it will occur, reasonable care may demand precautions against "that occasional negligence which is one of the ordinary incidents of human life and therefore to be anticipated." [53] "It is not due care to depend upon the exercise of care by another when such reliance is accompanied by obvious danger." [54] Thus an automobile driver may not proceed blindly across a railway track, upon the assumption that any approaching train will sound bell and whistle,[55]

---

41. Second Restatement of Torts, §§ 290, 302.

42. Griggs v. Fleckenstein, 1869, 14 Minn. 81, 14 Gil. 62; or that Crowbar, a/k/a Cimarron, "a nervous, flighty, irritable, troublesome and contrary type of horse," might collide into the horse of another cowboy. Farley v. M M Cattle Co., Tex.Civ.App.1977, 549 S.W.2d 453, error refused no reversible error.

43. See Pehowic v. Erie Lackawanna Railroad Co., 3d Cir. 1970, 430 F.2d 697 (noting that "[i]t is also common knowledge that bees do not fly at night, unless disturbed"); Annot., 1978, 86 A.L.R.3d 829.

44. Linnehan v. Sampson, 1879, 126 Mass. 506; Sutton v. Sutton, 1978, 145 Ga.App. 22, 243 S.E.2d 310 (bull: modified one charge rule applied).

45. Sneesby v. Lancashire & York R. Co., 1874, L.R. 9 Q.B. 263.

46. Gilman v. Noyes, 1876, 57 N.H. 627.

47. Pence v. Ketchum, La.1976, 326 So.2d 831; Atchison, Topeka & Santa Fe Railway Co. v. Parry, 1903, 67 Kan. 515, 73 P. 105; Black v. New York, New Haven & Hartford Railroad Co., 1907, 193 Mass. 448, 79 N.E. 797. "A drunken man is as much entitled to a safe street, as a sober one, and much more in need of it." Robinson v. Pioche, Bayerque & Co., 1855, 5 Cal. 460, 461.

48. Ricker v. Freeman, 1870, 50 N.H. 420; Lowery v. Manhattan R. Co., 1885, 99 N.Y. 158, 1 N.E. 608; Huydts v. Dixon, 1980, 199 Colo. 260, 606 P.2d 1303 (driver forced to swerve to avoid vehicle approaching in wrong lane); Lujan v. Reed, 1967, 78 N.M. 556, 434 P.2d 378 (16-year-old girl leaped from car when two male acquaintances jumped in car and one, who had earlier tried to kiss her friend, "'gave her a smug smile, you know like "aha"'"; thereafter, every time she closed her eyes, she "'could still see that look on Bruce's face'"); cf. Byrns v. St. Louis County, Minn. 1980, 295 N.W.2d 517.

49. Bird v. Richardson, 1959, 140 Colo. 310, 344 P.2d 957; Brown v. Vinson, 1956, 198 Va. 495, 95 S.E.2d 138; Sellers v. Cayce Mill Supply Co., Ky.1961, 349 S.W.2d 677; Annot., 1956, 47 A.L.R.2d 6 (liability of driver hit by vehicle in wrong lane).

50. Kofahl v. Delgado, 1978, 63 Ill.App.3d 622, 20 Ill.Dec. 429, 380 N.E.2d 407; Williams v. Cobb, App. 1977, 90 N.M. 638, 567 P.2d 487, certiorari denied 91 N.M. 3, 569 P.2d 413.

51. Imes v. Empire Hook & Ladder Co., 1977, 247 Pa.Super. 470, 372 A.2d 922 (6–1).

52. See generally Norwood v. Sherwin Williams Co., 1981, 303 N.C. 462, 279 S.E.2d 559; Smith v. Insurance Co. of North America, 1980, ___ Ind.App. ___, 411 N.E.2d 638; Hall v. Safeco Insurance Co., La.App.1979, 374 So.2d 715; Smith v. Holst, 1976, 275 Or. 29, 549 P.2d 671 (failure to so instruct was reversible error).

53. Gibson, J., in Murphy v. Great Northern R. Co. [1897] 2 Ir.Rep. 301. See Watters v. Querry, Utah 1978, 588 P.2d 702; Garr v. Union Carbide Corp., 3d Cir. 1978, 589 F.2d 147 (plaintiff had prior knowledge of defect in sidewalk; no liability for negligent failure to repair); Wissman v. Wissman, Mo.App.1978, 575 S.W.2d 239 (contributory negligence); Second Restatement of Torts, § 302A.

54. Dragotis v. Kennedy, 1933, 190 Minn. 128, 250 N.W. 804; Tollisen v. Lehigh Valley Transportation Co., 3d Cir. 1956, 234 F.2d 121 (may not rely solely on traffic signal in crossing street).

55. Lehigh Valley Railroad Co. v. Kilmer, 2d Cir. 1916, 231 F. 628, certiorari denied 242 U.S. 627, 37 S.Ct. 13, 61 L.Ed. 535.

or into an intersection in the confidence that other vehicles will yield the right of way.[56] One who leaves another helpless in or near the highway,[57] or forces a pedestrian to walk in the street,[58] creates the risk [59] that the person will be struck by a negligently driven car. If the defendant floods the premises with gasoline, he may be negligent because of the danger that someone will cause a spark or light a match.[60]

The duty to take precautions against the negligence of others thus involves merely the usual process of multiplying the probability that such negligence will occur by the magnitude of the harm likely to result if it does, and weighing the result against the burden upon the defendant of exercising such care.[61] The duty arises, in other words, only where a reasonable person would recognize the existence of an unreasonable risk of harm to others through the intervention of such negligence.[62] It becomes most obvious when the actor has reason to know that he is dealing with persons whose characteristics make it especially likely that they will do unreasonable things. The actor may be required to guard an insane patient to prevent him from jumping from the hospital window,[63] or to refrain from putting an intoxicated person off of a train into a railroad yard,[64] or letting him have an automobile,[65] or more liquor.[66]

56. Putt v. Daussat, La.App.1980, 381 So.2d 955. One may not continue to rely on the assumption that an oncoming driver will not cross the center line once there is reason to believe that he will. See Barbieri v. Jennings, App.1976, 90 N.M. 83, 559 P.2d 1210, certiorari denied 90 N.M. 7, 558 P.2d 619.

57. Parvi v. City of Kingston, 1977, 41 N.Y.2d 553, 394 N.Y.S.2d 161, 362 N.E.2d 960; Morrison v. Medaglia, 1934, 287 Mass. 46, 191 N.E. 133.

58. McKenna v. Stephens, [1923] Ir.Rep. 2 K.B.D. 112; Donovan v. Bender, 1961, 9 N.Y.2d 854, 216 N.Y.S.2d 97, 175 N.E.2d 463.

59. This, however, is a matter of unreasonable risk. In a quiet residential thoroughfare with one-way traffic, there may be, as a matter of law, no negligence. De Luca v. Manchester Laundry & Dry Cleaning Co., 1955, 380 Pa. 484, 112 A.2d 372.

60. Watson v. Kentucky & Indiana Bridge & Railroad Co., 1910, 137 Ky. 619, 126 S.W. 146, modified 137 Ky. 619, 129 S.W. 341; Teasdale v. Beacon Oil Co., 1929, 266 Mass. 25, 164 N.E. 612; Robert R. Walker, Inc. v. Burgdorf, 1951, 150 Tex. 603, 244 S.W.2d 506 ("You know that gasoline and water will not burn.")

61. See supra, § 31.

62. Nunan v. Bennett, 1919, 184 Ky. 591, 212 S.W. 570 (tenant leaving faucets turned on); Kapphahn v. Martin Hotel Co., 1941, 230 Iowa 739, 298 N.W. 901 (hotel guest knocking out window screen); McDonald v. Fryberger, 1951, 233 Minn. 156, 46 N.W.2d 260 (employee standing on drawer of cabinet); Hendricks v. Pyramid Motor Freight Corp., 1937, 328 Pa. 570, 195 A. 907 (negligently starting truck on ferry); Rosenberg v. Hartman, 1943, 313 Mass. 54, 46 N.E.2d 406 (walking into glass door).

63. Misfeldt v. Hospital Authority of City of Marietta, 1960, 101 Ga.App. 579, 115 S.E.2d 244; Collins v. State, 1965, 23 A.D.2d 898, 258 N.Y.S.2d 938, affirmed, 1966, 17 N.Y.2d 542, 268 N.Y.S.2d 314, 215 N.E.2d 500; cf. Sneider v. Hyatt Corp., N.D.Ga.1975, 390 F.Supp. 976 (intoxicated guest committed suicide by jumping from window).

But even on the part of an insane person, there are some acts so unlikely that reasonable care does not call for guarding against them. Mesedahl v. St. Luke's Hospital Association of Duluth, 1935, 194 Minn. 198, 259 N.W. 819 (climbing out top of barred widow); Prudential Society v. Ray, 1924, 207 App.Div. 496, 202 N.Y.S. 614, affirmed, 1925, 239 N.Y. 600, 147 N.E. 212 (pawning ring); Januszko v. State, 1979, 47 N.Y.2d 774, 417 N.Y.S.2d 462, 391 N.E.2d 297 (murder). Cf. Fetzer v. Aberdeen Clinic, 1925, 48 S.D. 308, 204 N.W. 364 (patient jumping from window).

64. Fagan v. Atlantic Coast Line Railroad Co., 1917, 220 N.Y. 301, 115 N.E. 794; or placing him near a busy highway. Parvi v. City of Kingston, 1977, 41 N.Y.2d 553, 394 N.Y.S.2d 161, 362 N.E.2d 960; Pence v. Ketchum, La.1976, 326 So.2d 831.

65. Owensboro Undertaking & Livery Association v. Henderson, 1938, 273 Ky. 112, 115 S.W.2d 563; Brockett v. Kitchen Boyd Motor Co., 1968, 264 Cal.App. 2d 69, 70 Cal.Rptr. 136; Snowhite v. State, 1966, 243 Md. 291, 221 A.2d 342; Bennett v. Geblein, 1979, 71 A.D.2d 96, 421 N.Y.S.2d 487; Annot., 1968, 19 A.L.R.3d 1175. Cf. Bernethy v. Walt Failor's, Inc., 1982, 97 Wn.2d 929, 653 P.2d 280 (selling gun to intoxicated husband who shot wife).

On the negligent entrustment doctrine generally, see 1 Dooley, Modern Tort Law, 1977, ch. 23; Second Restatement of Torts §§ 308, 390. Cf. Hartford Accident & Indemnity Co. v. Abdullah, 1979, 94 Cal.App.3d 81, 156 Cal.Rptr. 254, 260 (the doctrine "is more properly resolved by application of general principles of negligence").

66. See e.g., Hutchens v. Hankins, 1983, ___ N.C. App. ___, 303 S.E.2d 584; Cantor v. Anderson, 1981, 126 Cal.App.3d 124, 178 Cal.Rptr. 540; Campbell v. Carpenter, 1977, 279 Or. 237, 566 P.2d 893; Blamey v. Brown, Minn.1978, 270 N.W.2d 884, certiorari denied 444 U.S. 1070, 100 S.Ct. 1013, 62 L.Ed.2d 751 (tavern keeper); Nazareno v. Urie, Alaska 1981, 638 P.2d 671; Linn v. Rand, 1976, 140 N.J.Super. 212, 356 A.2d 15; cf. Leppke v. Segura, Colo.App.1981, 632 P.2d 1057 (jump-starting car for drunk). Contra, Felder v. But-

And when children are in the vicinity, much is necessarily to be expected of them which would not be looked for on the part of an adult.[67] It may be anticipated that a child will dash into the street in the path of a car,[68] or meddle with a turntable.[69] It may be clear negligence to entrust him with a gun,[70] or to allow him to drive an automobile,[71] or to throw candy where a crowd of boys will scramble for it.[72] There have been a number of "pied piper" cases, in which street vendors of ice cream, and the like, which attract children into the street, have been held liable for failure to protect them against traffic.[73] Apart from providing a dangerous instrument directly to the child, it may be quite as negligent to leave the gun, or dynamite caps, where children are likely to come and can easily find them.[74] In all such cases, the question comes down essen-

ler, 1981, 292 Md. 174, 438 A.2d 494; Lewis v. Wolf, App.1979, 122 Ariz. 567, 596 P.2d 705 (no common law duty); Lowe v. Rubin, 1981, 98 Ill.App.3d 496, 53 Ill. Dec. 919, 424 N.E.2d 710 (no common law duty on social host); DeLoach v. Mayer Electric Supply Co., Ala. 1979, 378 So.2d 733. See also Cory v. Shierloh, 1981, 29 Cal.3d 430, 174 Cal.Rptr. 500, 629 P.2d 8 (reluctantly upholding constitutionality of statute immunizing from liability providers of liquor except for licensed vendors who furnish to obviously intoxicated minors). See generally Annot., 1980, 97 A.L.R.3d 528.

67. Wheeler Terrace, Inc. v. Lynott, D.C.App.1967, 234 A.2d 311 (approving instruction that fact that children "often are thoughtless and impulsive, imposes a duty to exercise proportionate vigilance and caution in those dealing with children"); Mahaffey v. Ahl, 1975, 264 S.C. 241, 214 S.E.2d 119.

68. Dufrene v. Dixie Auto Insurance Co., La.1979, 373 So.2d 162, on remand La.App., 376 So.2d 507, writ denied 378 So.2d 1390 (tricycle swerved in front of car); Bilams v. Metropolitan Transit Authority, Fla.App. 1979, 371 So.2d 693 (child dashing across street slipped under wheels of bus). See also Kilpack v. Wignall, Utah 1979, 604 P.2d 462 (child jumped off hay truck running board onto bale of hay). But a motorist is not an insurer of the safety of children playing near the street, and there may be no negligence in hitting a child who suddenly darts into the street. Lee v. Hartford, La.App.1982, 411 So.2d 704.

69. See the "attractive nuisance" cases, infra, § 59.

70. Howell v. Hairston, 1973, 261 S.C. 292, 199 S.E.2d 766 (air rifle—parents chargeable with notice of child's reputation of malicious disposition); Lichtenthal v. Gawoski, 1974, 44 A.D.2d 771, 354 N.Y.S.2d 267 (BB gun—parent); Pair v. Blakly, 1978, 160 N.J.Super. 14, 388 A.2d 1026 (BBs—storekeeper); Moning v. Alfono, 1977, 400 Mich 425, 254 N.W.2d 759 (slingshot—sellers). However, the child's age, experience, habits and other circumstances are all important variables in determining whether an entrustment is negligent. See, e.g., Prater v. Burns, Tenn.App.1975, 525 S.W.2d 846; Sabatinelli v. Butler, 1973, 363 Mass. 565, 296 N.E.2d 190.

Statutory prohibitions, and hence the doctrine of negligence per se, are often involved in such cases. In the absence of a statutory violation, a court may well not hold the seller liable. Masone v. Unishops of Modell's, Inc., 1979, 73 A.D.2d 611, 422 N.Y.S.2d 450; Jiminez v. Zayre Corp., Fla.App.1979, 374 So.2d 28. See generally infra, § 36; Annots., 1959, 68 A.L.R.2d 782 (providing or leaving gun available); 1981, 4 A.L.R.4th 331 (selling gun or ammo); 1977, 75 A.L.R.3d 825 (injury to minor or incompetent from provided gun). If the child uses the gun to murder another, the principles of proximate causation may bar recovery against the provider. See Robinson v. Howard Brothers of Jackson, Inc., Miss.1979, 372 So.2d 1074.

71. Markland v. Baltimore & Ohio Railroad Co., Del.Super.1976, 351 A.2d 89; Allen v. Toledo, 1980, 109 Cal.App.3d 415, 167 Cal.Rptr. 270 (19-year-old son with bad driving record); Keller v. Keidinger, Ala.1980, 389 So.2d 129 (but 14-year-old driver's own negligence barred recovery); James v. Franks, 1968, 15 Ohio App. 2d 215, 240 N.E.2d 508 (violation of statutory prohibition against permitting minors to operate vehicles); McDowell v. Davis, 1968, 8 Ariz.App. 33, 442 P.2d 856, reversed on other grounds, 104 Ariz. 69, 448 P.2d 869 (statutory joint and several liability with minor); Douglass v. Hartford Insurance Co., 10th Cir. 1979, 602 F.2d 934 (10-year-old on minibike); Pritchett v. Kimberling Cove, Inc., 8th Cir. 1977, 568 F.2d 570, certiorari denied 436 U.S. 922, 98 S.Ct. 2274, 56 L.Ed.2d 765 (15-year-old boy entrusted with keys to boathouse containing motorboat). Cf. Nolechek v. Gesuale, 1978, 46 N.Y.2d 332, 413 N.Y.S.2d 340, 385 N.E. 1268 (counterclaim by defendants against parents of one-eyed boy riding motorcycle). The automobile guest statutes in this context raise a variety of questions. See Rau v. Kirschenman, N.D.1973, 208 N.W.2d 1.

72. Shafer v. Keeley Ice Cream Co., 1925, 65 Utah 46, 234 P. 300. Cf. Weirum v. RKO General, Inc., 1975, 15 Cal.3d 40, 123 Cal.Rptr. 468, 539 P.2d 36 (rock radio station's contest rewarding first person to locate peripatetic disc jockey might foreseeably cause minors to drive negligently in attempting to follow disc jockey's car).

73. Roberts v. American Brewed Coffee, 1973, 40 Ohio App.2d 273, 319 N.E.2d 218; Neal v. Shiels, Inc., 1974, 166 Conn. 3, 347 A.2d 102 (despite vendor's sign warning "Caution—Watch Out for Children"); Bishop v. Hamad, 1973, 43 A.D.2d 805, 350 N.Y.S.2d 270; Ellis v. Trowen Frozen Products, Inc., 1968, 264 Cal.App.2d 499, 70 Cal.Rptr. 487; Thomas v. Goodies Ice Cream Co., 1968, 13 Ohio App.2d 67, 233 N.E.2d 876; Reid v. Swindler, 1967, 249 S.C. 483, 154 S.E.2d 910; Annot., 1978, 84 A.L.R.3d 826; Note, 1975, 26 Syr.L.Rev. 927.

74. See Gilbert v. Sabin, 1977, 76 Mich.App. 137, 256 N.W.2d 54 (gun in garage; door left open); Thomas v. Inman, 1978, 282 Or. 279, 578 P.2d 399 (gun in house); cf. Miller v. Griesel, 1974, 261 Ind. 604, 308

tially to one of whether the foreseeable risk outweighs the utility of the actor's conduct.[75] A person may be required to guard a power line pole located in a public park, but not one in the open country;[76] and whether a person must take steps to prevent children from interfering with such an object as a stationary vehicle is entirely a matter of the circumstances of the particular case.[77]

There is normally much less reason to anticipate acts on the part of others which are malicious and intentionally damaging than those which are merely negligent; and this is all the more true where, as is usually the case, such acts are criminal.[78] Under all ordinary and normal circumstances, in the absence of any reason to expect the contrary, the actor may reasonably proceed upon the assumption that others will obey the criminal law. Under such ordinary circumstances, it is not reasonably to be expected that anyone will hurl a television from an apartment building window,[79] rob and beat up a boy in a public restroom,[80] forge a check,[81] push another man into an excavation,[82] abduct a woman from a parking lot and rape her,[83] hold up a patron in the parking lot of a bank,[84] or shoot a patron in the parking lot of a restaurant.[85] Although such things do occur, as must be known to anyone who reads the daily papers, they are still so unlikely in any particular instance that the burden of taking continual precautions against them almost always exceeds the apparent risk.

There are, however, other situations, in which either a special responsibility resting upon the defendant for the protection of the plaintiff, or an especial temptation and opportunity for criminal misconduct brought about by the defendant, will call upon him to take precautions against it.[86] The responsi-

N.E.2d 701 (school not liable for negligent supervision of pupil injured by explosion of detonator cap during recess). See generally Annot., 1959, 68 A.L.R.2d 782.

75. See Bauer, The Degree of Danger and the Degree of Difficulty of Removal in "Attractive Nuisance" Cases, 1934, 18 Minn.L.Rev. 523.

76. Compare Znidersich v. Minnesota Utilities Co., 1923, 155 Minn. 293, 193 N.W. 449, with Keep v. Otter Tail Power Co., 1937, 201 Minn. 475, 277 N.W. 213.

77. No negligence: Marengo v. Roy, 1945, 318 Mass. 719, 63 N.E.2d 893; Union Carbide & Carbon Corp. v. Peters, 4th Cir. 1953, 206 F.2d 366.

Negligence: Johnson v. John Deere Plow Co., 1959, 214 Ga. 645, 106 S.E.2d 901 (tractor); Arnett v. Yeago, 1957, 247 N.C. 356, 100 S.E.2d 855 (car parked on hill).

See Glassey v. Worcester Consolidated Street Railway Co., 1904, 185 Mass. 315, 70 N.E. 199, and Second Restatement of Torts, § 302B, Illustration 14, to the effect that such acts may be anticipated on Halloween.

78. "It would be unjust to require one to anticipate that a crime will be committed unless there has been a warning or unless a previous criminal act occurred in the same premises." Brogan Cadillac-Oldsmobile Corp. v. Central Jersey Bank & Trust Co., 1981, 183 N.J.Super. 333, 443 A.2d 1108, 1110. See Watson v. Kentucky & Indiana Bridge & Railroad Co., 1910, 137 Ky. 619, 126 S.W. 146, modified 137 Ky. 619, 129 S.W. 341.

79. Trice v. Chicago Housing Authority, 1973, 14 Ill.App.3d 97, 302 N.E.2d 207 (tenant killed). Or that a trespasser will throw aluminum paint from the apartment roof upon the tenant. Gulf Reston, Inc. v. Rogers, 1974, 215 Va. 155, 207 S.E.2d 841 (tenant died from heart attack 11 days later).

80. Corbitt v. Ringley-Crockett, Inc., Tenn.App. 1973, 496 S.W.2d 914; Annot., 1977, 75 A.L.R.3d 441.

81. Citizens State Bank v. Martin, 1980, 227 Kan. 580, 609 P.2d 670. But the circumstances may make it foreseeable. Brogan Cadillac-Oldsmobile Corp. v. Central Jersey Bank & Trust Co., 1981, 183 N.J.Super. 333, 443 A.2d 1108; cf. Citizens State Bank v. Martin, 1980, 277 Kan. 580, 609 P.2d 670. See generally Annot., 1975, 67 A.L.R.3d 144 ("negligence contributing to alteration or unauthorized signature" under UCC § 3–406).

82. Alexander v. Town of New Castle, 1888, 115 Ind. 51, 17 N.E. 200.

83. Gillot v. Washington Metropolitan Area Transit Authority, D.D.C.1981, 507 F.Supp. 454.

84. McClendon v. Citizens & Southern National Bank, 1980, 155 Ga.App. 755, 272 S.E.2d 592 (two female assailants).

85. Kelly v. Retzer & Retzer, Inc., Miss.1982, 417 So.2d 556. As for the foreseeability of shooting one's former wife, see Decker v. Gibson Products Co. of Albany, Inc., M.D.Ga.1980, 505 F.Supp. 34, reversed 5th Cir., 679 F.2d 212. Compare Bradley Center, Inc. v. Wessner, 1982, 161 Ga.App. 576, 287 S.E.2d 716, affirmed 250 Ga. 199, 296 S.E.2d 693.

86. See Green v. City of Livermore, 1981, 117 Cal. App.3d 82, 172 Cal.Rptr. 461 (police left keys in car with drunks); Second Restatement of Torts, § 302B, Comments e and f. Cf. Bridges v. Kentucky Stone Co., Inc., 1980, ___ Ind.App. ___, 408 N.E.2d 575, vacated, 1981, ___ Ind. ___, 425 N.E.2d 125 (deaths from bomb made by scoundrels with stolen dynamite; claim of negligent storage by defendants).

bility for protection may arise out of a contract, by which the defendant has agreed to provide it;[87] or it may be founded upon some relation existing between the parties, such as carrier and passenger, innkeeper and guest,[88] invitor and business visitor,[89] school and pupil,[90] employer and employee,[91] landlord and tenant,[92] and no doubt others.[93] The carrier, for example, may be required to protect its passengers from third persons who have threatened them with violence,[94] or are drunk or quarrelsome,[95] or to guard or warn them against external attack[96] or look after its switches[97] in a neighborhood which is known to be frequented by criminal characters. Another possibility is that the defendant's special responsibility may arise because he is in a position to control the dan-

87. See Douglas W. Randall, Inc. v. AFA Protective Systems, Inc., E.D.Pa.1981, 516 F.Supp. 1122, affirmed, 3d Cir., 1982, 688 F.2d 820. Singer v. I.A. Durbin, Inc., Fla.App.1977, 348 So.2d 370 (installation of burglar alarm).

88. Walkoviak v. Hilton Hotels Corp., Tex.Civ.App. 1979, 580 S.W.2d 623, refused n.r.e.; Peters v. Holiday Inns, Inc., 1979, 89 Wis.2d 115, 278 N.W.2d 208; Orlando Executive Park, Inc. v. P.D.R., Fla.App.1981, 402 So.2d 442, rehearing denied, 1982, 407 So.2d 1016.

89. Nallan v. Helmsley-Spear, Inc., 1980, 50 N.Y.2d 507, 429 N.Y.S.2d 606, 407 N.E.2d 451 (union officer shot in back while signing register in lobby of office building); Butler v. Acme Markets, Inc., App.Div.1981, 177 N.J.Super. 279, 426 A.2d 521, affirmed, 1982, 89 N.J. 270, 445 A.2d 1141 (rash of recent criminal attacks); Ekberg v. Greene, 1978, 196 Colo. 494, 588 P.2d 375 (fire in service station restroom attributable to vandals); Foster v. Winston Salem Joint Venture, 1981, 303 N.C. 636, 281 S.E.2d 36 (shopping mall owners; assault in parking lot); Annot., 1979, 93 A.L.R.3d 999 (criminal attacks on shopping center patrons).

90. McLeod v. Grant County School District No. 128, 1953, 42 Wn.2d 316, 255 P.2d 360. But see Baldwin v. Zoradi, 1981, 123 Cal.App.3d 275, 176 Cal.Rptr. 809 (college had no duty to prevent students from becoming intoxicated and engaging in speed contest in which plaintiff was injured); Chavez v. Tolleson Elementary School District, App.1979, 122 Ariz. 472, 595 P.2d 1017 (young girl abducted outside school grounds and slain—unforeseeable). See generally Annot., 1980, 1 A.L.R.4th 1099; Note, 1979, 30 Hast.L.J. 1893.

91. Mike v. Borough of Aliquippa, 1980, 279 Pa. Super. 382, 421 A.2d 251 (police officer beaten by co-employees). But see Parham v. Taylor, Ala.1981, 402 So.2d 884.

92. Trentacost v. Brussel, 1980, 82 N.J. 214, 412 A.2d 436 (tenant mugged; no front door lock in high crime neighborhood); Scott v. Watson, 1976, 278 Md. 160, 359 A.2d 548; Johnston v. Harris, 1972, 387 Mich. 569, 198 N.W.2d 409; Kwaitkowski v. Superior Trading Co., 1981, 123 Cal.App.3d 324, 176 Cal.Rptr. 494; Kline v. 1500 Massachusetts Avenue Apartment Corp., D.C. Cir. 1970, 439 F.2d 477. But see Smith v. Chicago Housing Authority, 1976, 36 Ill.App.3d 967, 344 N.E.2d 536; Riley v. Marcus, 1981, 125 Cal.App.3d 103, 177 Cal.Rptr. 827. See generally Annot., 1972, 43 A.L.R.3d 331.

93. See Danielenko v. Kinney Rent A Car, Inc., 1982, 84 A.D.2d 159, 445 N.Y.S.2d 464, reversed, 1982, 57 N.Y.2d 198, 455 N.Y.S.2d 555, 441 N.E.2d 1073 (bomb under front seat of rental car); d'Hedouville v. Pioneer Hotel Co., 9th Cir. 1977, 552 F.2d 886 (products liability suit); Parness v. City of Tempe, App.1979, 123 Ariz. 460, 600 P.2d 764 (boy knocked down onto glass in negligently maintained park); Schuster v. City of New York, 1958, 5 N.Y.2d 75, 180 N.Y.S.2d 265, 145 N.E.2d 534 (city liable for failure to provide proper police protection for informer, who was murdered); Draper Mortuary v. Superior Court, 1982, 135 Cal.App.3d 533, 185 Cal.Rptr. 396 (mortuary's duty to family members of decedent whose remains were sexually assaulted by intruder into unlocked chapel).

In Liberty National Life Insurance Co. v. Weldon, 1958, 267 Ala. 171, 100 So.2d 696, a company which issued a policy insuring the life of a child to one with no insurable interest was held liable when the beneficiary murdered the child. The case relied upon a statute. See Dusenberg, Insurer's Tort Liability for Issuing Policy Without Insurance Interest, 1959, 47 Cal.L.Rev. 64; Note, 1958, 58 Col.L.Rev. 1087.

94. McPherson v. Tamiami Trail Tours, Inc., 5th Cir. 1967, 383 F.2d 527 (driver heard threats on Negro who sat in front of bus); Smith v. West Suburban Transit Lines, Inc., 1975, 27 Ill.App.3d 220, 326 N.E.2d 449 (angry motorist threatened bus driver and then assaulted church deacon).

95. German-Bey v. National Railroad Passenger Corp., 2d Cir. 1983, 703 F.2d 54; Hanback v. Seaboard Coastline Railroad, D.S.C.1975, 396 F.Supp. 80 (plaintiff raped thrice in rest room; bit intoxicated assailant during related forced act); Manfredonia v. American Airlines, Inc., 1979, 68 A.D.2d 131, 416 N.Y.S.2d 286 (plane); Watson v. Chicago Transit Authority, 1972, 52 Ill.2d 503, 288 N.E.2d 476 (bus); Watson v. Adirondack Trailways, 1974, 45 A.D.2d 504, 359 N.Y.S.2d 912 (bus terminal parking area); Annot., 1977, 76 A.L.R.3d 1218.

96. Werndli v. Greyhound Corp. Fla.App.1978, 365 So.2d 177 (failure to warn passenger of dangerous location of destination terminal); Mangini v. Southeastern Pennsylvania Transportation Authority, 1975, 235 Pa. Super. 478, 344 A.2d 621 (mob of boys hurled objects at trolley). See also Chicago South Shore & South Bend Railroad v. Brown, 1974, 162 Ind.App. 493, 320 N.E.2d 809, rehearing denied 162 Ind.App. 493, 323 N.E.2d 681 (plaintiff pushed by crowd boarding train).

97. Green v. Atlanta Charlotte Air Line Railway Co., 1925, 131 S.C. 124, 126 S.E. 441; Second Restatement of Torts, § 302B, Illustration 15.

gerous person,[98] or is in some other unique position to prevent the harm,[99] and so may be held to have an obligation to exercise reasonable care to do so.

There are other situations in which the defendant will be held liable because his affirmative conduct has greatly increased the risk of harm to the plaintiff through the criminal acts of others. The defendant may bring the plaintiff into contact with individuals of known criminal tendencies, as for example, by hiring them, under conditions in which opportunity for crime is afforded.[1] The defendant may, by his acts, defeat a protection which the plaintiff himself has set up about his own person or property, against criminal interference. Thus if valuable property is left unguarded and exposed to the public view, it may be anticipated that it will be stolen;[2] if the key is left in the lock of a jewelry store over a holiday, it is not at all unlikely that there will be a burglary;[3] if a burglar alarm is set too low, it may not detect the presence of a criminal;[4] and leaving the keys in the ignition of an unattended automobile undoubtedly enhances the possibility of its theft and perhaps reckless operation.[5] Yet the issue in such cases remains one of negligence—which is to say that the foreseeable risk of the crime is unreasonable considering the burden of taking precautions.[6]

Shifting Responsibility

A large number of negligence cases have turned on the problem of what might be called shifting responsibility—that is to say, that the defendant may not be required to take any precautions for the plaintiff's safety because the defendant is free to assume

---

98. See Sosa v. Coleman, 5th Cir. 1981, 646 F.2d 991 (sheriff let dangerous criminal escape); Daniels v. Anderson, 1975, 195 Neb. 95, 237 N.W.2d 397 (plaintiff beat up in jail "drunk tank"); Doctors Hospital, Inc. v. Kovats, 1972, 16 Ariz.App. 489, 494 P.2d 389 (one hospital patient assaulted another); Shipes v. Piggly Wiggly St. Andrews, Inc., 1977, 269 S.C. 479, 238 S.E.2d 167 (same—supermarket parking lot); Rieser v. District of Columbia, D.C.Cir. 1977, 563 F.2d 462 (inadequate control by parole officer); Annot., 1973, 48 A.L.R.3d 1288 (hospital liability for assault by patient).

99. Tarasoff v. Regents of University of California, 1976, 17 Cal.3d 425, 131 Cal.Rptr. 14, 551 P.2d 334 (therapist failed to warn person patient said he would kill); Williams v. United States, D.S.D.1978, 450 F.Supp. 1040 (VA hospital failed to notify local authorities of release of dangerous patient, contrary to prior agreement); Estate of Mathes v. Ireland, 1981, ___ Ind. App. ___, 419 N.E.2d 782 (mother and grandparents of insanely violent person, with whom he resided, and psychiatric center, which released him); Bradley Center, Inc. v. Wessner, 1982, 161 Ga.App. 576, 287 S.E.2d 716, affirmed 250 Ga. 199, 296 S.E.2d 693. See Annot., 1978, 83 A.L.R.3d 1201. See infra, § 56.

1. Estate v. Arrington v. Fields, Tex.Civ.App.1979, 578 S.W.2d 173, refused n.r.e.; Easley v. Appollo Detective Agency, Inc., 1979, 69 Ill.App.3d 920, 26 Ill. Dec. 313, 387 N.E.2d 1241 (security guard in apartment building tried to rape tenant; prior arrests and poor prior employment record, including complaint for making eyes at female employee); Comment, 1973, 52 Or.L. Rev. 296; Annot., 1973, 48 A.L.R.3d 359. Cf. Annot., 1973, 51 A.L.R.3d 983 (hospital's negligence in hiring doctor).

See generally, recognizing tort of negligent hiring or retention of incompetent, unfit, or dangerous employee, DiCosala v. Kay, 1982, 91 N.J. 159, 450 A.2d 508.

2. Morse v. Homer's, Inc., 1936, 295 Mass. 606, 4 N.E.2d 625; National Ben Franklin Insurance Co. v. Careccta, 1959, 21 Misc.2d 279, 193 N.Y.S.2d 904; cf. Orkin Exterminating Co. v. Culpepper, Fla.App.1979, 367 So.2d 1026 (burglary of house covered by exterminating tent).

3. Garceau v. Engel, 1926, 169 Minn. 62, 210 N.W. 608.

4. Douglas W. Randall, Inc. v. AFA Protective Systems, Inc., E.D.Pa.1981, 516 F.Supp. 1122, affirmed, 3d Cir. 1982, 688 F.2d 820; or, if the system is not properly installed. Singer v. I.A. Durbin, Inc., Fla.App.1977, 348 So.2d 370. See also Central Alarm of Tucson v. Ganem, App.1977, 116 Ariz. 74, 567 P.2d 1203. Cf. Klages v. General Ordinance Equipment Corp., 1976, 240 Pa.Super. 356, 367 A.2d 304 (products liability action for ineffective mace weapon).

5. Vining v. Avis Rent-A-Car Systems, Inc., Fla. 1977, 354 So.2d 54, on remand, Fla.App., 355 So.2d 226; Hill v. Yaskin, 1977, 75 N.J. 139, 380 A.2d 1107. But see Felty v. Lawton, Okl.1977, 578 P.2d 757 (police car); Lichter v. Fritsch, 1977, 77 Wis.2d 178, 252 N.W.2d 360 (on grounds of mental hospital). See generally Annot., 1972, 45 A.L.R.3d 787.

6. See, e.g., 7735 Hollywood Boulevard Venture v. Superior Court, 1981, 116 Cal.App.3d 901, 172 Cal.Rptr. 528 (landlord could not be required to provide "adequate" precautions against rape); Taylor v. Hocker, 1981, 101 Ill.App.3d 639, 57 Ill.Dec. 112, 428 N.E.2d 662 (no liability for assault in shopping mall where no prior attacks); Elliott v. Mallory Electric Corp., 1977, 93 Nev. 580, 571 P.2d 397 (foreseeability of auto theft from leaving keys in ignition depends on circumstances).

that someone else will do it or will be fully responsible in case he does not. Whether it be said that the defendant is under no duty to act in such a case, or that he has exercised reasonable care in relying upon another, the result is the same.[7]

Thus a common laborer, hired to dig a ditch in the street, may ordinarily leave it to his superiors to set out a red lantern to warn traffic,[8] and one who deposits cotton in a warehouse is not required to keep anyone from coming near the pile of bales.[9] A surgeon ordinarily may leave routine duties to competent hospital attendants,[10] and an automobile driver may of course have his car overhauled by a reliable garage, rather than do it himself.[11] A landlord who leases premises without a covenant to keep them in repair is not responsible for injuries due to defects unknown to him at the time,[12] and one who sells another a chattel in a safe condition may generally rely upon the assumption that the user will not alter or use it in an especially hazardous manner.[13] In the ordinary case, one who employs an independent contractor to do work on his premises may leave all responsibility to him, and is not liable for his negligence.[14]

Yet in many situations, where the risk is unduly great, it is not reasonable care to rely upon the responsibility of others. The operating surgeon may be required to keep an eye on the count of sponges himself, rather than leave it to the nurse.[15] If premises are leased in such condition that they are unreasonably dangerous to those outside of them,[16] or to the general public who are known to be about to be admitted to them,[17] the landlord is not free to rely upon the tenant, and even the tenant's agreement to repair will not relieve the landlord, if injury is to be anticipated before the repairs will be made.[18] The seller of a chattel which can be expected to be altered or used in a foreseeably dangerous way may be required to assume the worst and accordingly to guard against that possibility.[19] Quite apart from any question of vicarious liability, the

---

7. The question is often treated from the perspective of intervening causation. See Second Restatement of Torts, § 452; infra, § 44.

8. Jessup v. Sloneker, 1891, 142 Pa. 527, 21 A. 988; Carter v. Franklin, 1937, 234 Ala. 116, 173 So. 861.

9. Murphey v. Caralli, 1864, 3 H. & C. 461, 159 Eng. Rep. 611.

10. Su v. Perkins, 1974, 133 Ga.App. 474, 211 S.E.2d 421 (negligent injection); Adams v. Leidholdt, 1977, 38 Colo.App. 463, 563 P.2d 15, affirmed 1978, 195 Colo. 450, 579 P.2d 618 (foot paralysis from wrapping leg too tightly); Hill v. Hospital Authority of Clarke County, 1976, 137 Ga.App. 633, 224 S.E.2d 739 (respirator failure after surgery); Burke v. Pearson, 1972, 259 S.C. 288, 191 S.E.2d 721 (heating pad burn on sedated patient); Sparger v. Worley Hospital, Inc., Tex.1977, 547 S.W.2d 582, on remand, Tex.Civ.App., 552 S.W.2d 534 (sponge count).

11. Phillips v. Britannia Hygienic Laundry Co., [1923] 1 K.B. 539, affirmed [1923] 2 K.B. 832. Cf. Hackett v. Perron, 1979, 119 N.H. 419, 402 A.2d 193. But see Maloney v. Rath, 1968, 69 Cal.2d 442, 71 Cal. Rptr. 897, 445 P.2d 513 (Traynor, C.J.) (good condition of brakes is nondelegable duty under Second Restatement of Torts, §§ 423, 424). See generally Annot., 1971, 40 A.L.R.3d 9 (owner's liability for bad brakes).

12. Clarke v. Edging, 1973, 20 Ariz.App. 267, 512 P.2d 30 (child struck by clod of dirt in eroded gully); Nagel v. Landels, 1975, 271 Or. 122, 530 P.2d 1239 (slanted steps; landlord could rely on lessee); Second Restatement of Torts, § 356.

13. Hill v. General Motors Corp., Mo.App.1982, 637 S.W.2d 382 (suspension system modified by dealer); Temple v. Wean United, Inc., 1977, 50 Ohio St.2d 317, 364 N.E.2d 267 (power press operating buttons installed upside down); Union Carbide Corp. v. Holton, 1975, 136 Ga.App. 726, 222 S.E.2d 105 (disposable refrigerant cylinder illegally refilled with excessive pressure); cf. Goar v. Village of Stephen, 1923, 157 Minn. 228, 196 N.W. 171.

14. Cochran v. International Harvester Co., W.D. Ky.1975, 408 F.Supp. 598; Merritt v. Reserve Insurance Co., 1973, 34 Cal.App.3d 858, 110 Cal.Rptr. 511 (independent trial counsel's malpractice); Second Restatement of Torts, § 409; infra, § 71.

15. Burke v. Washington Hospital Center, D.C.Cir. 1973, 475 F.2d 364; Piehl v. Dalles General Hospital, 1977, 280 Or. 613, 571 P.2d 149; Truhitte v. French Hospital, 1982, 128 Cal.App.3d 332, 180 Cal.Rptr. 152; Somerset v. Hart, Ky.1977, 549 S.W.2d 814 (scalpel count).

16. See Second Restatement of Torts, § 379; infra, § 63.

17. See Second Restatement of Torts, § 359; infra, § 63.

18. See Fitchett v. Buchanan, 1970, 2 Wn.App. 965, 472 P.2d 623; Second Restatement of Torts, § 359, Comment *i*.

19. Gordon v. Niagara Machine & Tool Works, 5th Cir. 1978, 574 F.2d 1182, rehearing denied 578 F.2d 871 (foreseeable that employer would not pass on safety instructions to press operator); Cepeda v. Cumberland

employer of an independent contractor may be required to take precautions against his negligence if the work to be done is such that unreasonably dangerous conditions are likely to arise.[20] In all of these cases the defendant is not relieved, by his reliance upon another, of responsibility for a risk he has created.

It is not easy to state any general principle to govern these cases. Many factors must be taken into account: the competence and reliability of the person upon whom reliance is placed,[21] the person's understanding of the situation, the seriousness of the danger and the number of persons likely to be affected, the length of time elapsed,[22] and above all the likelihood that proper care will not be used, and the ease with which the actor himself may take precautions.[23] If an attempt must be made to generalize, it may be said that when the defendant is under a duty to act reasonably for the protection of the plaintiff, and may anticipate that a third person may fail to use proper care if the responsibility is transferred to him, and that serious harm will follow if he does not, it is not reasonable care to place reliance upon the third person.

Misrepresentation and Nondisclosure

Liability in negligence sometimes rests upon some form of misrepresentation on the part of the defendant, by which the plaintiff, or some third person, has been misled to the plaintiff's damage. The remedy of an action for deceit, which is considered elsewhere,[24] has generally been confined to cases in which the interest affected is a pecuniary one, such as sales and credit transactions. Although negligence is sometimes involved in such cases, it has been kept within somewhat more narrow limits than where the harm is to person or property. Deceit has served as an occasional remedy where there is such harm to tangible interests,[25] but for the most part cases of misrepresentation resulting in physical harm have been dealt with in an action for negligence.

If the defendant consciously misstates the facts in such a way as to lead the plaintiff to place himself or his property in danger of harm, which the defendant still does not intend, the defendant may nevertheless not be exercising proper care for the plaintiff's safety, and so be liable for his negligent use of language. But even where the defendant is not consciously misstating the facts, he may still be liable for negligence in speaking where he has not exercised proper care to ascertain the truth, or to communicate it.[26] An assurance that a bridge[27] or campus[28] is safe, or that there is no danger from blasting operations,[29] or from the location of a plane,[30] may result in liability for negligence

---

Engineering Co., Inc., 1978, 76 N.J. 152, 386 A.2d 816, overruled Suter v. San Angelo Foundry and Machine Co., 1979, 81 N.J. 150, 406 A.2d 140, 153 (that removable guard would not be replaced on hazardous machine after cleaning); see infra, ch. 17.

20. See infra, § 71.

21. Thus the defendant may be liable if he turns over his automobile to one who is intoxicated, supra, p. 200, or employs an independent contractor who is incompetent. Second Restatement of Torts, § 411.

22. See Goar v. Village of Stephen, 1923, 157 Minn. 228, 196 N.W. 171; Balido v. Improved Machinery Inc., 1972, 29 Cal.App.3d 633, 105 Cal.Rptr. 890.

23. Ulrich v. Kasco Abrasives Co., Ky.1976, 532 S.W.2d 197 (no liability); Drayton v. Jiffee Chemical Corp., N.D.Ohio 1975, 395 F.Supp. 1081, modified and affirmed, 6th Cir. 1978, 591 F.2d 352.

24. See infra, ch. 18.

25. Langridge v. Levy, 1836, 2 M. & W. 519, 150 Eng.Rep. 863, affirmed, 1838, 4 M. & W. 337, 150 Eng.Rep. 1458; Kuelling v. Roderick Lean Manufacturing Co., 1905, 183 N.Y. 78, 75 N.E. 1098; see Toole v. Richardson-Merrell, Inc., 1967, 251 Cal.App.2d 689, 60 Cal. Rptr. 398. See generally Second Restatement of Torts, § 310; infra, ch. 18.

26. See generally Second Restatement of Torts, § 311.

27. Washington & Berkeley Bridge Co. v. Pennsylvania Steel Co., 4th Cir. 1915, 226 F. 169.

28. Duarte v. State, 1978, 84 Cal.App.3d 729, 148 Cal.Rptr. 804, vacated 88 Cal.App.3d 473, 151 Cal.Rptr. 727 (student raped and murdered in university residence hall).

29. Valz v. Goodykoontz, 1911, 112 Va. 853, 72 S.E. 730; cf. Seagraves v. ABCO Manufacturing Co., 1968, 118 Ga.App. 414, 164 S.E.2d 242, appeal after remand 121 Ga.App. 224, 173 S.E.2d 416.

30. See Freeman v. United States, 6th Cir. 1975, 509 F.2d 626 (air traffic controller misinformed pilot plane was over land when actually over Lake Erie; 16 para-

when the plaintiff relies upon the assurance and suffers injury.[31] The same is true when a physician informs those in contact with the patient that the illness is not contagious, when with proper skill and care the doctor should have known better.[32] Sellers of dangerous chattels, represented to be safe, have been held liable for negligent failure to ascertain the truth.[33] The misrepresentation may be by conduct rather than by words. A driver who waves a following motorist on to pass,[34] a railroad which opens its crossing gates,[35] or a seller who paints over a stepladder to conceal its defects,[36] may become liable for negligent misrepresentation when someone is hurt as a result.

Such liability is not necessarily confined to the person to whom the false statement is made. It extends to others who may reasonably be expected to be endangered by it. Thus, the seller of a dangerous article, who misrepresents its character or assures the buyer that it is safe, may be liable to an ultimate purchaser, or to others in the vicinity of its expected use;[37] a boiler inspector who certifies that a boiler is safe without sufficient inspection may be liable to a third person who is injured when the boiler ex-

chutists drowned). Cf. Murray v. United States, D.Utah 1971, 327 F.Supp. 835, amended 10th Cir., 463 F.2d 208 (false information on aeronautical map showing runway lighting at night).

31. A false assurance by one partner that intercourse is safe, because contraceptive measures have been taken, may not give rise to liability. See Stephen K. v. Roni L., 1980, 105 Cal.App.3d 640, 164 Cal.Rptr. 618.

32. Jones v. Stanko, 1928, 118 Ohio St. 147, 160 N.E. 456; Skillings v. Allen, 1919, 143 Minn. 323, 173 N.W. 663; Edwards v. Lamb, 1899, 69 N.H. 599, 45 A. 480; cf. Boone v. Mullendore, Ala.1982, 416 So.2d 718 (healthy child born to woman whom doctor had informed was sterile; see infra, § 55).

There may be liability in the converse situation as well, for emotional distress and other damages, where the physician negligently determines that the patient is ill where in fact she is well. See Hensley v. Heavrin, 1981, 277 S.C. 86, 282 S.E.2d 854 (erroneous diagnosis that wife had syphilis; husband thereupon broke her jaw in two places); Molien v. Kaiser Foundation Hospitals, 1980, 27 Cal.3d 916, 167 Cal.Rptr. 831, 616 P.2d 813 (same; marriage dissolution proceedings begun). Cf. Ware v. United States, 5th Cir. 1980, 626 F.2d 1278 (negligent diagnosis of healthy cattle as tubercular).

33. Cunningham v. C.R. Pease House Furnishing Co., 1908, 74 N.H. 435, 69 A. 120 (inflammable stove blacking; "the warmer the stove the better it works"); Flies v. Fox Brothers Buick Co., 1928, 196 Wis. 196, 218 N.W. 855 (Owen, J.); Pabon v. Hackensack Auto Sales, Inc., 1960, 63 N.J.Super. 476, 164 A.2d 773, 784. Most of the cases are older, and typically involve car dealers. See Keeton, Owen & Montgomery, 1980, Products Liability and Safety—Cases and Materials, 88–93 (collecting the cases).

34. See Shirley Cloak & Dress Co. v. Arnold, 1956, 92 Ga.App. 885, 90 S.E.2d 622; Thelen v. Spilman, 1957, 251 Minn. 89, 86 N.W.2d 700; Armstead v. Holbert, 1961, 146 W.Va. 582, 122 S.E.2d 43. Cf. Sweet v. Ringwelski, 1961, 362 Mich. 138, 106 N.W.2d 742 (motioning child to cross); Farley v. Southeastern Pennsylvania Transportation Authority, 1980, 279 Pa.Super. 570, 421 A.2d 346 (bus signaled motorist through intersection and then smashed into him); Miller v. Watkins, Mo.1962, 355 S.W.2d 1 (waving truck driver on to pass bus). But the other motorist or pedestrian will not be relieved of his duty to maintain a proper lookout. See Government Employees Insurance Co. v. Thompson, La.App.1977, 351 So.2d 809. See also Shank v. Government Employees Insurance Co., La.App.1980, 390 So.2d 903, writ refused, La., 396 So.2d 901 (no duty or negligence on facts toward adult pedestrian); Dix v. Spampinato, 1975, 28 Ind.App. 81, 344 A.2d 155, affirmed, 1976, 278 Md. 34, 358 A.2d 237; cf. Nolde Brothers, Inc. v. Wray, 1980, 221 Va. 25, 266 S.E.2d 882 (signal could not mean safe to proceed if driver giving it not in a position to see potential danger). See generally Annots., 1956, 48 A.L.R.2d 252 (following driver); 1956, 90 A.L.R.2d 1431 (approaching driver or at intersection); 1963, 90 A.L.R.2d 1442 (pedestrian).

35. See Johnson v. Director General of Railroads, 1924, 278 Pa. 491, 123 A. 484; Zwink v. Burlington Northern, Inc., 1975, 13 Wn.App. 560, 536 P.2d 13 (flagman and mechanical signals); Churchill v. Norfolk & Western Railway Co., 1978, 73 Ill.2d 127, 23 Ill.Dec. 58, 383 N.E.2d 929, 936: "Failure of the lights and bells to function could well constitute an invitation to cross."

36. See Schubert v. J.R. Clark Co., 1892, 49 Minn. 331, 51 N.W. 1103. The misrepresentation in these cases is usually intentional and hence may amount to fraudulent concealment. See Kuelling v. Roderick Lean Manufacturing Co., 1905, 183 N.Y. 78, 75 N.E. 1098 (knothole of beam in farm machine); Woodward v. Miller & Karwisch, 1904, 119 Ga. 618, 46 S.E. 847 (crack in buggy axle covered over with grease); P. Keeton, Fraud—Concealment and Nondisclosure, 1936, 15 Tex.L.Rev. 1.

37. Waters-Pierce Oil Co. v. Deselms, 1909, 212 U.S. 159, 29 S.Ct. 270, 53 L.Ed. 453 (gasoline sold as kerosene); Wright v. Howe, 1915, 46 Utah 588, 150 P. 956; Andreotala v. Gaeta, 1927, 260 Mass. 105, 156 N.E. 731; Fort Wayne Drug Co. v. Flemion, 1931, 93 Ind.App. 40, 175 N.E. 670; Jones v. Raney Chevrolet Co., 1938, 213 N.C. 775, 197 S.E. 757; see supra, note 33.

plodes;[38] an independent testing laboratory that certifies a dangerously defective product as safe may be liable to a person injured thereby;[39] a doctor who misinforms a diabetic patient that it is safe to drive may be liable to persons injured when the patient passes out behind the wheel.[40] In such cases the basis of liability is the fact that the misrepresentation has led the person to whom it was made to forego precautions which he might otherwise have taken for the protection of the plaintiff.

In all cases of negligent misrepresentation, however, the circumstances must be such that the defendant is under a duty to the plaintiff to exercise reasonable care in giving the information, and that reliance upon what he says, with resulting danger, is reasonably to be expected.[41] An assurance from a casual bystander, asked for his opinion, that he thinks the situation is safe, involves no such duty or expectation, and has been held not to be sufficient for negligence liability.[42]

In many situations, a failure to disclose the existence of a known danger may be the equivalent of misrepresentation, where it is to be expected that another will rely upon the appearance of safety. The surgeon who remains silent when he discovers that he has left his tools in the patient's anatomy,[43] the air traffic controller who fails to warn a pilot of air turbulence,[44] the landlord who leases defective premises,[45] the landowner who permits a licensee to enter without warning of hidden perils,[46] the seller of a chattel who fails to disclose its hidden dangers,[47] the person who promises and then

38. Cleveland v. American Motorists Insurance Co., 1982, 163 Ga.App. 748, 295 S.E.2d 190; Van Winkle v. American Steam-Boiler Insurance Co., 1896, 52 N.J.L. 240, 19 A. 472. See also O'Laughlin v. Minnesota Natural Gas Co., Minn.1977, 253 N.W.2d 826 (gas furnace); Pioneer Hi-Bred Corn Co. v. Northern Illinois Gas Co., 1973, 16 Ill.App.3d 638, 306 N.E.2d 337, reversed 61 Ill. 2d 6, 329 N.E.2d 228 (gas pipes and appliances in corn processing plant); Jackson v. New Jersey Manufacturers Insurance Co., App.Div.1979, 166 N.J.Super. 448, 400 A.2d 81 (insurer liable to third persons only if it has undertaken to make safety inspections upon which insured has relied); Comment, 1977–78, 66 Ky.L.J. 910 (insurers); Annot., 1952, 26 A.L.R.2d 136 (gas companies).

39. Hanberry v. Hearst Corp., 1969, 276 Cal.App.2d 680, 81 Cal.Rptr. 519 (slippery shoes with Good Housekeeping's seal of approval); Hempstead v. General Fire Extinguisher Corp., D.Del.1967, 269 F.Supp. 109 (U.L.-approved fire extinguisher exploded); Notes, 1976, 74 Dick.L.Rev. 792; 1974, 58 Minn.L.Rev. 723; Annot., 1971, 39 A.L.R.3d 181.

40. Freese v. Lemmon, Iowa 1973, 210 N.W.2d 576.

41. "There must be knowledge, or its equivalent, that the information is desired for a serious purpose; that he to whom it is given intends to rely and act upon it; that, if false or erroneous, he will because of it be injured in person or property. Finally, the relationship of the parties, arising out of contract or otherwise, must be such that in morals and good conscience the one has the right to rely upon the other for information, and the other giving the information owes a duty to give it with care." International Products Co. v. Erie Railroad Co., 1927, 244 N.Y. 331, 155 N.E. 662, certiorari denied 275 U.S. 527, 48 S.Ct. 20, 72 L.Ed. 408. See Soto v. Frankford Hospital, E.D.Pa.1979, 478 F.Supp. 1134 (doctors misdiagnosed wife's condition as drug overdose, instead of carbon monoxide poisoning from defective heater; no liability for husband's subsequent death).

42. Avery v. Palmer, 1918, 175 N.C. 378, 95 S.E. 553 (weight of tombstone); Holt v. Kolker, 1948, 189 Md. 636, 57 A.2d 287 (safety of porch); Webb v. Cerasoli, 1949, 275 App.Div. 45, 87 N.Y.S.2d 884, affirmed 300 N.Y. 603, 90 N.E.2d 64 (owner assuring contractor in presence of workman).

43. Benson v. Dean, 1921, 232 N.Y. 52, 133 N.E. 125; Slimak v. Foster, 1927, 106 Conn. 366, 138 A. 153; Ernen v. Crofwell, 1930, 272 Mass. 172, 172 N.E. 73; Shutan v. Bloomenthal, 1939, 371 Ill. 244, 20 N.E.2d 570. Cf. Alberts v. Giebink, S.D.1980, 299 N.W.2d 454 (pin left in patient's knee). See generally Vogel & Delgado, To Tell the Truth: Physicians' Duty to Disclose Medical Mistakes, 1980, 28 U.C.L.A.L.Rev. 52.

44. See Dickens v. United States, 5th Cir. 1977, 545 F.2d 886; Himmler v. United States, E.D.Pa.1979, 474 F.Supp. 914 (failure to give weather warnings).

45. Cowen v. Sunderland, 1887, 145 Mass. 363, 14 N.E. 117 (injury to tenant); Coke v. Gutkese, 1883, 80 Ky. 598 (members of tenant's family); Rushton v. Winters, 1938, 331 Pa. 78, 200 A. 60 (licensee of tenant).

46. Campbell v. Boyd, 1883, 88 N.C. 129; Martin v. United States, C.D.Cal.1975, 392 F.Supp. 243, reversed 9th Cir., 546 F.2d 1355, certiorari denied 432 U.S. 906, 97 S.Ct. 2950, 53 L.Ed.2d 1078 (no warning of danger of grizzly bear attack in Yellowstone National Park; camper killed). Compare Rubenstein v. United States, 9th Cir. 1973, 488 F.2d 1071 (no liability where camper is given warning; legs chomped while attempting to flee).

47. E.g., Lockett v. General Electric Co., E.D.Pa. 1974, 376 F.Supp. 1201, affirmed 3d Cir., 511 F.2d 1393; Michael v. Warner/Chilcott, App.1978, 91 N.M. 651, 579 P.2d 183; Jonescue v. Jewel Home Shopping Service, 1973, 16 Ill.App.3d 339, 306 N.E.2d 312; Moran v.

fails to pass on information important to another's welfare,[48] each may be liable to the person with whom he deals, or to others to whom harm is to be expected through that person's reliance. The "something like fraud on the part of the giver,"[49] which the courts have found in these cases, consists in permitting another to rely upon a tacit assurance of safety, when it is known that there is danger.

WESTLAW REFERENCES

Custom

compliance comply! follow! conform! /p custom! /p conclusive inconclusive /p negligen!

Emergency

instruct! /s jur*** /s sudden /s emergenc!

Anticipating Conduct of Others

272k68

Shifting Responsibility

surgeon* doctor* physician* /p count*** /p sponge*

Misrepresentation

negligen! /2 misrepresent! /p surgeon* doctor* physician*

§ 34. Degrees of Care; Aggravated Negligence

The amount of care demanded by the standard of reasonable conduct must be in proportion to the apparent risk. As the danger becomes greater, the actor is required to exercise caution commensurate with it.[1] Those who deal with instrumentalities that are known to be dangerous, such as high tension electricity,[2] gas,[3] explosives,[4] elevators,[5] or wild animals,[6] must exercise a great amount of care because the risk is great. They may be required to take every reasonable precaution suggested by experience or prudence.[7] Likewise those who accept an unusual responsibility are required to act in accordance with it. Common carriers,[8] who enter into

Faberge, Inc., 1975, 273 Md. 538, 332 A.2d 11. See generally Twerski, Weinstein, Donaher & Piehler, The Use and Abuse of Warnings in Product Liability—Design Defect Litigation Comes of Age, 1976, 61 Corn.L. Rev. 495; P. Keeton, Inadequacy of Information, 1970, 48 Tex.L.Rev. 398; Kidwell, Duty to Warn: A Description of the Model of Decision, 1975, 53 Tex.L.Rev. 1375; Noel, Products Defective Because of Inadequate Directions or Warnings, 1969, 23 Sw.L.J. 256; Dillard & Hart, Product Liability: Directions for Use and the Duty to Warn, 1955, 41 Va.L.Rev. 145; Annot., 1961, 76 A.L.R.2d 9; Second Restatement of Torts, § 388; infra, ch. 17.

48. See Brown v. MacPherson's, Inc., 1975, 86 Wn. 2d 293, 545 P.2d 13 (state failed to pass on warnings from avalanche expert); Mixon v. Dobbs House, Inc., 1979, 149 Ga.App. 481, 254 S.E.2d 864 (employer failed to tell husband that wife had begun labor until husband had finished labor at end of work shift).

49. Willes, J., in Gautret v. Egerton, 1867, L.R. 2 C.P. 371.

§ 34

1. Meredith v. Reed, 1866, 26 Ind. 334 (only ordinary care required in keeping a stallion, but that is more care than in keeping a mare); Tom v. Days of '47, Inc., 1965, 16 Utah 2d 386, 401 P.2d 946 (Brahma bull at rodeo); Cowden v. Bear Country, Inc., D.S.D.1974, 382 F.Supp. 1321 (superior caution required for mountain lion).

2. Celiz & Sanchez' Estates v. Public Utility District No. 1, 1981, 30 Wn.App. 682, 638 P.2d 588; Federal Insurance Co. v. Public Service Co. of Colorado, 1977, 194 Colo. 107, 570 P.2d 239; Miller v. Lambert, La.App. 1980, 380 So.2d 695.

3. Van Hoose v. Blueflame Gas Co., Col.App.1982, 642 P.2d 36; Jones v. Hittle Service, Inc., 1976, 219 Kan. 627, 549 P.2d 1383; Mathine v. Kansas-Nebraska Natural Gas Co., Inc., 1972, 189 Neb. 247, 202 N.W.2d 191; Annot., 1972, 41 A.L.R.3d 782 (bottled gas).

4. Liber v. Flor, 1966, 160 Colo. 7, 415 P.2d 332, 35 A.L.R.3d 1165 (dynamite: "highest degree of care"); Smith v. Pennsylvania-Reading Seashore Lines, E.D. Pa.1973, 355 F.Supp. 1176, affirmed without opinion, 3d Cir.1973, 487 F.2d 1395 ("exceptionally high degree of care"); Annot., 1971, 35 A.L.R.3d 1177.

5. McGowan v. Devonshire Hall Apartments, 1980, 278 Pa.Super. 229, 420 A.2d 514; Buckel v. Maison Blanche Corp., La.App.1980, 379 So.2d 849, vacated on substantially other grounds, La., 385 So.2d 782, on remand, 386 So.2d 1385, writ refused 393 So.2d 739 (escalator); Smith v. Munger, Okl.App.1974, 532 P.2d 1202; Jardine v. Rubloff, 1978, 75 Ill.2d 31, 21 Ill.Dec. 868, 382 N.E.2d 232.

6. Cowden v. Bear Country, Inc., D.S.D.1974, 382 F.Supp. 1321 (mountain lion in animal park).

7. Koelsch v. Philadelphia Co., 1893, 152 Pa. 355, 363, 25 A. 522, 524; see Richardson v. United States, 9th Cir.1981, 645 F.2d 731 (highest degree of care human prudence equal to).

8. A few jurisdictions also apply a high standard of care to innkeepers. See Yamada v. Hilton Hotel Corp., 1978, 60 Ill.App.3d 101, 17 Ill.Dec. 228, 376 N.E.2d 227 (high degree of care); Kraaz v. La Quinta Motor Inns, Inc., La.1982, 410 So.2d 1048; cf. Shute v. Prom Motor Hotel, Inc., Mo.App.1969, 446 S.W.2d 137.

an undertaking toward the public for the benefit of all those who wish to make use of their services, must use great caution to protect passengers entrusted to their care; and this has been described as "the utmost caution characteristic of very careful prudent men," [9] or "the highest degree of vigilance, care, and precaution." [10] Where the carrier receives goods for transportation, his responsibility is even higher, and the common law made him an insurer of their safety against all hazards except an act of God and the public enemy.[11]

Although the language used by the courts sometimes seems to indicate that a special standard is being applied, it would appear that none of these cases should logically call for any departure from the usual formula. What is required is merely the conduct of the reasonable person of ordinary prudence under the circumstances, and the greater danger, or the greater responsibility, is merely one of the circumstances, demanding only an increased amount of care.[12]

A substantial number of courts, however, have dealt with some such cases by instructing the jury in terms of a higher, or the highest, "degree" of care, as for example in the case of the common carrier.[13] They thus purport to recognize a higher or lower basic standard of conduct for different defendants, or different situations. There is seldom reason to think that they mean to say anything more than that greater or less care will be required under the circumstances. Yet the "high degree" instruction is unlikely ever really to mislead the jury, and a court that fails to give one may be committing error.[14]

A different, and older, approach has recognized distinct "degrees" of negligence itself, which is to say degrees of legal fault, corresponding to required "degrees" of care. This idea was borrowed from the Roman

9. Pennsylvania Co. v. Roy, 1880, 102 U.S. 451, 456, 26 L.Ed. 141. Accord: Ware v. Yellow Cab, Inc., 1975, 193 Neb. 159, 225 N.W.2d 565; Roberts v. Trans World Airlines, 1964, 225 Cal.App.2d 344, 37 Cal.Rptr. 291.

10. Orr v. New Orleans Public Service, Inc., La. App.1977, 349 So.2d 417, 419; cf. Carson v. Boston Elevated Railway Co., 1941, 309 Mass. 32, 33 N.E.2d 701, 703. See generally Comments, 1980, 46 J.Air L. & Comm. 147 (airline liability for injuries from hijackings); 1973, 125 U.Pa.L.Rev. 1134 (airport terrorist attacks); Annot., 1976, 72 A.L.R.3d 1299 (air carrier hijacking).

11. Greenberg v. United Airlines, Inc., City Civ.Ct. 1979, 98 Misc.2d 544, 414 N.Y.S.2d 240 (loss of baggage); Convey-All Corp. v. Pacific Intermountain Express Co., Inc., 1981, 119 Cal.App.3d 577, 174 Cal.Rptr. 443; Reese v. Midland Empire Packing Co., 1981, ___ Mont. ___, 628 P.2d 289 (under Carmack Amendment to Interstate Commerce Act which codified common law rule); Ups N' Downs, Inc. v. Albina Enterprises, Inc., 1978, 61 A.D.2d 763, 402 N.Y.S.2d 194 (insurer against theft); Perlow v. AAAcon Auto Transport, Inc., 1980, 280 Pa.Super. 52, 421 A.2d 399; Albrecht v. Groat, 1978, 91 Wn.2d 257, 588 P.2d 229 (state statute); Hightower v. Bekins Van Lines Co., 1979, 267 Pa. Super. 588, 407 A.2d 397.

12. See Central Transport, Inc. v. Great Dane Trailers, Inc., 1981, ___ Ind.App. ___, 423 N.E.2d 675; People v. Brown, 1976, 40 N.Y.2d 381, 386 N.Y.S.2d 848, 353 N.E.2d 811, certiorari denied 433 U.S. 913, 97 S.Ct. 2986, 53 L.Ed.2d 1099 (electricity); Liber v. Flor, 1966, 160 Colo. 7, 415 P.2d 332 (dynamite); Thomas v. Central Geyhound Lines, Inc., 1958, 6 A.D.2d 649, 180 N.Y.S.2d 461 (carrier); Frederick v. City of Detroit, 1963, 370 Mich. 425, 121 N.W.2d 918 (carrier).

"One standard of care, that care which a reasonably prudent person would use under similar circumstances, is mandated in view of the medley of circumstances that may be presented to the trier of fact. While legal scholars and law school professors may use language intimating varying degrees of care, when charging a jury but a single standard of care is permissible." Massey v. Scripter, 1977, 401 Mich. 385, 258 N.W.2d 44, 47.

13. Widmyer v. Southeast Skyways, Inc., Alaska 1978, 584 P.2d 1; Suarez v. Trans World Airlines, 7th Cir.1974, 498 F.2d 612 (duty extended to convalescent passenger in airport who suffered heart attack from rude treatment); Lewis v. Buckskin Joe's, Inc., 1964, 156 Colo. 46, 396 P.2d 933 (stagecoach). Cf. Cowden v. Bear Country, Inc., D.S.D.1974, 382 F.Supp. 1321 (keeper of lion in animal park—highest degree of care); Sergermeister v. Recreation Corp. of America, Inc., Fla.App.1975, 314 So.2d 626 (amusement ride operator not common carrier); Pessl v. Bridger Bowl, 1974, 164 Mont. 389, 524 P.2d 1101 (ski lift operator *not* common carrier; statute); Summit County Development Corp. v. Bagnoli, 1968, 166 Colo. 27, 441 P.2d 658 (ski lift operator *is* common carrier).

14. Van Hoose v. Blueflame Gas, Inc., Colo.App.1982, 642 P.2d 36 (failure to instruct on "highest degree of care" standard was reversible error—L.P. gas); Widmyer v. Southeast Skyways, Inc., Alaska 1978, 584 P.2d 1.

law [15] in 1704 by Chief Justice Holt in a bailment case,[16] and given support by learned writers on the law of bailments.[17] It recognizes, in general, three "degrees" of negligence: slight negligence, which is failure to use great care; ordinary negligence, which is failure to use ordinary care; and gross negligence, which is failure to use even slight care.[18] The doctrine has received considerable acceptance, and is followed to some extent in the field of bailments.[19] A few courts have extended it to other situations, particularly in holding that an automobile driver is not liable to a gratuitous guest except for gross negligence.[20] Late in the nineteenth century there were experiments in Illinois [21] and Kansas,[22] which extended the doctrine to all negligence cases. These courts found themselves deluged with appeals and struggling in impossible confusion,[23] and finally repudiated and overruled the whole theory.[24]

Although the idea of "degrees of negligence" has not been without its advocates,[25] it has been condemned by most writers,[26] and, except in bailment cases,[27] rejected at common law by most courts,[28] as a distinction "vague and impracticable in [its] nature, so unfounded in principle," [29] that it adds only difficulty and confusion to the already nebulous and uncertain standards which must be given to the jury. The prevailing

---

15. See Green, The Three Degrees of Negligence, 1874, 8 Am.L.Rev. 649; Elliott, Degrees of Negligence, 1932, 6 So.Cal.L.Rev. 91.

16. Coggs v. Bernard, 1704, 2 Ld.Raym. 909, 92 Eng.Rep. 107.

17. Jones, Essay on the Law of Bailments, 3d ed. 1828, 5–36; Story, Commentaries on the Law of Bailments, 1832, 12.

18. New York Central Railroad Co. v. Lockwood, 1873, 84 U.S. (17 Wall.) 357, 21 L.Ed. 627. See Green, High Care and Gross Negligence, 1928, 23 Ill.L.Rev. 4, 62 Am.L.Rev. 545.

19. See 1 Street, Foundations of Legal Liability, 1906, 100. But the doctrine has been repudiated as to bailments in England, where it originated. Grill v. General Iron Screw Collier Co., 1866, L.R. 1 C.P. 600. And there is a trend among American courts away from the doctrine. See infra, note 27.

20. Bickford v. Nolen, 1977, 240 Ga. 255, 240 S.E.2d 24, 28 (dissenting opinion indicating that Georgia may be the only remaining state with a common law guest-passenger rule). Such rules were abandoned in McConville v. State Farm Mutual Auto Insurance Co., 1962, 15 Wis.2d 374, 113 N.W.2d 14, and Roberts v. Johnson, 1978, 91 Wn.2d 182, 588 P.2d 201.

21. Galena & Chicago Union Railroad Co. v. Jacobs, 1858, 20 Ill. 478; Illinois Cent. Railroad Co. v. Hammer, 1874, 72 Ill. 347; Wabash Railroad Co. v. Henks, 1879, 91 Ill. 406.

22. Sawyer v. Sauer, 1872, 10 Kan. 466; Union Pacific Railroad Co. v. Henry, 1883, 36 Kan. 565, 14 P. 1; Wichita & Western Railway Co. v. Davis, 1887, 37 Kan. 743, 16 P. 78.

23. Described in Chicago, Burlington & Quincy Railroad Co. v. Johnson, 1882, 103 Ill. 512; Chicago, Rock Island & Pacific Railway Co. v. Hamler, 1905, 215 Ill. 525, 74 N.E. 705. See Green, Illinois Negligence Law, 1944, 39 Ill.L.Rev. 39, 51; Malone, The Formative Era of Contributory Negligence, 1946, 41 Ill.L.Rev. 151.

24. City of Lanark v. Dougherty, 1894, 153 Ill. 163, 38 N.E. 892; Atchison, Topeka & Santa Fe Railway Co. v. Henry, 1896, 57 Kan. 154, 45 P. 576.

25. See Green, High Care and Gross Negligence, 1928, 23 Ill.L.Rev. 4, 62 Am.L.Rev. 545.

26. Heuston, Salmond on Torts, 16th ed. 1973, § 80; 1 Beven, Negligence, 4th ed. 1928, 15; Harper, Law of Torts, 1933, 176; 1 Street, Foundations of Legal Liability, 1906, 99; Elliott, Degrees of Negligence, 1932, 6 So.Cal.L.Rev. 91.

27. Even in bailment cases, there is a trend of sorts toward applying a single standard of ordinary care. See, e.g., Siverson v. Martori, App.1978, 119 Ariz. 440, 581 P.2d 285 (gratuitous bailment—reasonable care); Koennecke v. Waxwing Cedar Products, Limited, 1975, 273 Or. 639, 543 P.2d 669 (gratuitous bailee); Nash v. City of North Platte, 1980, 205 Neb. 480, 288 N.W.2d 51; United Barge Co. v. Notre Dame Fleeting & Towing Service, Inc., 8th Cir. 1978, 568 F.2d 599; English Whipple Sailyard, Limited v. Yawl Ardent, W.D.Pa. 1978, 459 F.Supp. 866; Dresser Industries, Inc. v. Foss Launch & Tug Co., Alaska 1977, 560 P.2d 393 (degree of care of a reasonably careful owner). A very few courts still hold bailees to a higher standard of care if the bailment is for the sole benefit of the bailee. Clott v. Greyhound Lines, Inc., 1971, 278 N.C. 378, 180 S.E.2d 102 (liability for slight negligence). Many, perhaps most, courts still hold a bailee liable only for gross negligence where the bailment was gratuitous and for the sole benefit of the bailor. E.g., Martin v. Bell, Fla.App.1978, 368 So.2d 600 (unpaid house sitters who left pan of grease on stove); Capezzaro v. Winfrey, App.Div.1977, 153 N.J.Super. 267, 379 A.2d 493; Linares v. Edison Parking, Inc., City Civ.1979, 97 Misc. 2d 831, 414 N.Y.S.2d 661; Jays Creations, Inc. v. Hertz Corp., 1973, 42 A.D.2d 534, 344 N.Y.S.2d 784.

28. E.g., Dickerson v. Connecticut Co., 1922, 98 Conn. 87, 118 A. 518; Thompson v. Ashba, 1951, 122 Ind.App. 58, 102 N.E.2d 519; Nadeau v. Fogg, 1950, 145 Me. 10, 70 A.2d 730.

29. Heuston, Salmond on Torts, 16th ed. 1973, § 80, at 224 n. 69.

rule in most situations is that there are no "degrees" of care or negligence, as a matter of law; there are only different amounts of care, as a matter of fact.[30] From this perspective, "gross" negligence is merely the same thing as ordinary negligence, "with the addition," as Baron Rolfe once put it, "of a vituperative epithet." [31] This much-quoted phrase may be a bit unfair, since it is not difficult to understand that there are such things as major or minor departures from reasonable conduct; but the difficulty of classification, because of the very real difficulty of drawing satisfactory lines of demarcation, together with the unhappy history, justifies the rejection of the distinctions in most situations.

Nevertheless, the idea of degrees of negligence, or at least of some kind of aggravated negligence which will result in liability where ordinary negligence will not, has been adopted in a number of judicial opinions and statutes.[32] Some of the statutes have attempted to codify the entire doctrine,[33] or apply it to particular situations such as bailments,[34] criminal negligence,[35] or others.[36] Most of them, however, are automobile guest statutes, which are discussed below.

To the extent that "degrees of negligence" survive, the distinctions most commonly made are as follows:

Slight Negligence. This has been defined as "an absence of that degree of care and vigilance which persons of extraordinary prudence and foresight are accustomed to use," or, in other words, a failure to exercise great care.[37] It finds its chief application in cases, such as those of bailments or of carriers injuring passengers, where there is an obligation to use great care, and it results in liability where lack of ordinary care would not.[38] But the term also has been used in a very general comparative sense, as contrasted with gross negligence, where the comparative negligence rule is applied.[39]

Gross Negligence. As it originally appeared, this was very great negligence, or the want of even slight or scant care.[40] It

---

30. Smith, Liability for Substantial Physical Damage to Land by Blasting, 1920, 33 Harv.L.Rev. 542, 553.

31. Wilson v. Brett, 1843, 11 M. & W. 113, 116, 152 Eng.Rep. 737. Cf. McAdoo v. Richmond & Danville Railroad Co., 1890, 105 N.C. 140, 150, 11 S.E. 316, 319 ("a mere expletive").

32. See Elliott, Degrees of Negligence, 1932, 6 So. Cal.L.Rev. 91, 127.

33. Cf. NDCC 1–01–16, 1–01–17; 25 Okl.St.Ann. §§ 3–6.

34. Cf. Cal.Civ. Code §§ 1846, 1928; S.D.Comp. Laws §§ 43–37–6, 43–39–11.

35. See Wis.Stats. § 940.06; Humes v. State, 1981, ___ Ind. ___, 426 N.E.2d 379; Moore v. State, 1981, 158 Ga.App. 579, 281 S.E.2d 322 (reckless conduct statute constitutional); Matter of Mario Y, 1980, 75 A.D.2d 954, 428 N.Y.S.2d 71 (reckless endangerment); O'Leary v. State, Alaska 1979, 604 P.2d 1099 (subjective awareness of risk unnecessary).

36. Over 40 jurisdictions have enacted statutes relieving landowners of liability for injuries to recreational users unless caused by gross negligence or wilful or malicious acts. See Barrett, Good Sports and Bad Lands: The Application of Washington's Recreational Use Statute Limiting Landowner Liability, 1977, 53 Wash.L.Rev. 1; Notes, 1980, 15 Land & Water L.Rev. 649; 1964 Wis.L.Rev. 705. See infra, § 60. Cases involving other statutes that expressly provide for liability for aggravated misconduct include: Durham v. City of Los Angeles, 1979, 91 Cal.App.3d 567, 154 Cal.Rptr. 243 (railroad liability for accidents from "hopping" trains); Vanthournout v. Burge, 1979, 69 Ill.App.3d 193, 25 Ill.Dec. 685, 387 N.E.2d 341 (parental liability for willful or malicious acts of minors); Plumbing Connections, Inc. v. Kostelnik, Com.Pl.1980, 69 Ohio Misc. 11, 430 N.E.2d 1340 (lender's improper disbursements to general contractor).

Courts sometimes construe an exception into a limited liability rule or statute for willful, wanton or reckless misconduct. E.g., Mandolidis v. Elkins Industries, Inc., W.Va.1978, ___ W.Va. ___, 246 S.E.2d 907 (workers' compensation statute); cf. Thomas v. Chicago Board of Education, 1979, 60 Ill.App.3d 729, 17 Ill.Dec. 865, 395 N.E.2d 538 (teacher immunity statute); Food Pageant, Inc. v. Consolidated Edison Co., Inc., 1981, 54 N.Y.2d 167, 445 N.Y.S.2d 60, 429 N.E.2d 738 (public utility liability).

37. Astin v. Chicago, Milwaukee & St. Paul Railway Co., 1910, 143 Wis. 477, 128 N.W. 265.

38. Putney v. Keith, 1900, 98 Ill.App. 285. See Ware v. Yellow Cab, Inc., 1975, 193 Neb. 159, 225 N.W.2d 565 (no negligence on facts).

39. See Roby v. Auker, 1949, 151 Neb. 421, 37 N.W.2d 799. Cf. Friese v. Gulbrandson, 1943, 69 S.D. 179, 8 N.W.2d 438 ("ordinary negligence, small in quantum").

40. Food Pageant, Inc. v. Consolidated Edison Co., 1981, 54 N.Y.2d 167, 445 N.Y.S.2d 60, 429 N.E.2d 738; Hanft v. Southern Bell Telephone & Telegraph Co.,

has been described as a failure to exercise even that care which a careless person would use.[41] Several courts, however, dissatisfied with a term so nebulous, and struggling to assign some more or less definite point of reference to it, have construed gross negligence as requiring willful,[42] wanton,[43] or reckless [44] misconduct, or such utter lack of all care as will be evidence thereof—sometimes on the ground that this must necessarily have been the intent of the legislature.[45] But it is still true that most courts consider that "gross negligence" falls short of a reckless disregard of the consequences, and differs from ordinary negligence only in degree, and not in kind.[46] There is, in short, no generally accepted meaning; but the probability is, when the phrase is used, that it signifies more than ordinary inadvertence or inattention,[47] but less perhaps than conscious indifference to the consequences.[48]

Willful, Wanton and Reckless. A different approach, at least in theory, looks to the actor's real or supposed state of mind. Lying between intent to do harm, which, as we have seen,[49] includes proceeding with knowledge that the harm is substantially certain to occur, and the mere unreasonable risk of harm to another involved in ordinary negligence, there is a penumbra of what has been called "quasi-intent." [50] To this area the words "willful," "wanton," or "reckless," are customarily applied; and sometimes, in a single sentence, all three. Although efforts have been made to distinguish them,[51] in practice such distinctions have consistently been ignored, and the three terms have been treated as meaning the same thing, or at least as coming out at the same legal exit. They have been grouped together as an aggravated form of negligence, differing in quality rather than in degree from ordinary lack of care.[52] These terms are in common use in the automobile guest statutes,[53] but even before such statutes, they represented an idea which had a legitimate place in the common law. They apply to conduct which

Fla.App.1981, 402 So.2d 453; Fidelity Leasing Corp. v. Dun & Bradstreet, Inc., E.D.Pa.1980, 494 F.Supp. 786; Pilot Industries v. Southern Bell Telephone & Telegraph Co., D.S.C.1979, 495 F.Supp. 356; Jones v. Foutch, 1979, 203 Neb. 246, 278 N.W.2d 572; cf. Leite v. City of Providence, D.R.I.1978, 463 F.Supp. 585 (clear and significant difference between negligence and gross negligence).

41. Louisville & Nashville Railroad Co. v. McCoy, 1883, 81 Ky. 403, 5 Ky.L.Rep. 397; Crowley v. Barto, 1962, 59 Wn.2d 280, 367 P.2d 828.

42. De Wald v. Quarnstrom, Fla.1952, 60 So.2d 919; Rideout v. Winnebago Traction Co., 1904, 123 Wis. 297, 101 N.W. 672.

43. Thompson v. Bohlken, Iowa 1981, 312 N.W.2d 501.

44. Williamson v. McKenna, 1960, 223 Or. 366, 354 P.2d 56 (very complete); In re Wright's Estate, 1951, 170 Kan. 600, 228 P.2d 911; Rokusek v. Bertsch, 1951, 78 N.D. 420, 50 N.W.2d 657. There seems at least to be no doubt that reckless conduct will satisfy a requirement of gross negligence. Desrosiers v. Cloutier, 1942, 92 N.H. 100, 25 A.2d 123.

45. See Williamson v. McKenna, 1960, 223 Or. 366, 354 P.2d 56, for complete discussion.

46. See Thompson v. Bohlken, Iowa 1981, 312 N.W.2d 501; cf. Thone v. Nicholson, 1978, 84 Mich.App. 538, 269 N.W.2d 665 (gross negligence distinguished from wilful and wanton).

47. Cf. Combined Insurance Co. of America v. Sinclair, Wyo.1978, 584 P.2d 1034, 1048 (gross negligence includes ordinary negligence); Nist v. Tudor, 1965, 67 Wn.2d 322, 407 P.2d 798 (negligence "appreciably greater than ordinary negligence").

48. See Fidelity Leasing Corp. v. Dun & Bradstreet, Inc., E.D.Pa.1980, 494 F.Supp. 786; Crowley v. Barto, 1962, 59 Wn.2d 280, 367 P.2d 828; Wyseski v. Collette, N.D.1965, 126 N.W.2d 896; Hodge v. Borden, 1966, 91 Idaho 125, 417 P.2d 75. But see Burk Royalty Co. v. Walls, Tex.1981, 616 S.W.2d 911; Schwartz v. Sears, Roebuck & Co., 5th Cir.1982, 669 F.2d 1091, 1094 ("an entire want of care indicative of conscious indifference"); Garrison v. Pacific Northwest Bell, 1980, 45 Or.App. 523, 608 P.2d 1206.

It is sometimes said that gross negligence is shown by an extreme departure from ordinary care. See Wager v. Pro, D.C.Cir.1979, 603 F.2d 1005.

49. See supra, § 8.

50. See generally Brady, Recklessness, Negligence, Indifference, and Awareness, 1980, 43 Mod.L.Rev. 381; Elliott, Degrees of Negligence, 1932, 6 So.Cal.L.Rev. 81, 143.

51. "Negligence and wilfulness are as unmixable as oil and water. 'Wilful negligence' is as self-contradictory as 'guilty innocence.'" Kelly v. Malott, 7th Cir. 1905, 135 F. 74; Neary v. Northern Pacific Railway Co., 1910, 41 Mont. 480, 490, 110 P. 226, 230.

52. Cf. Mantia v. Kaminski, 1980, 89 Ill.App.3d 932, 45 Ill.Dec. 300, 412 N.E.2d 651.

53. See infra, p. 215.

is still, at essence, negligent,[54] rather than actually intended to do harm, but which is so far from a proper state of mind that it is treated in many respects as if it were so intended. Thus it is held to justify an award of punitive damages,[55] and may justify a broader duty,[56] and more extended liability for consequences,[57] and it will avoid the defense of ordinary contributory negligence on the part of the plaintiff.[58]

The usual meaning assigned to "willful," "wanton," or "reckless," according to taste as to the word used, is that the actor has intentionally done an act of an unreasonable character in disregard of a known or obvious risk that was so great as to make it highly probable that harm would follow,[59] and which thus is usually accompanied by a conscious indifference to the consequences.[60] Since, however, it is almost never admitted, and can be proved only by the conduct and the circumstances, an objective standard must of necessity in practice be applied. The "willful" requirement, therefore, breaks down and receives at best lip service, where it is clear from the facts that the defendant, whatever his state of mind, has proceeded in disregard of a high and excessive degree of

54. See Matheson v. Pearson, Utah 1980, 619 P.2d 321 (tootsie pop dropped on plaintiff's head); DeElena v. Southern Pacific Co., 1979, 121 Ariz. 563, 592 P.2d 759; Stockman v. Marlowe, 1978, 271 S.C. 334, 247 S.E.2d 340. But see Mandolidis v. Elkins Industries, Inc., 1978, ___ W.Va. ___, 246 S.E.2d 907.

55. E.g., Dorsey v. Honda Motor Co., 5th Cir.1981, 655 F.2d 650, modified 670 F.2d 21, rehearing denied 673 F.2d 911, cert. denied, ___ U.S. ___, 103 S.Ct. 177, 74 L.Ed.2d 145 ($5 million punitive damages approved against manufacturer of car for "wantonness, willfulness or reckless indifference to the rights of others"); Grimshaw v. Ford Motor Co., 1981, 119 Cal.App.3d 757, 174 Cal.Rptr. 348 (approving $3.5 million, remitted by trial court from $125 million, for design of Pinto fuel system; "malice": "callous and conscious disregard of public safety"); Taylor v. Superior Court, 1979, 24 Cal. 3d 890, 157 Cal.Rptr. 693, 598 P.2d 854 (drunk driving). See Second Restatement of Torts, § 908(b) (punitive damages awardable for "conduct that is outrageous, because of the defendant's evil motive or his reckless indifference to the rights of others"); Owen, Punitive Damages in Products Liability Litigation, 1976, 74 Mich.L.Rev. 1257; Ellis, Fairness and Efficiency in the Law of Punitive Damages, 1982, 56 So.Cal.L.Rev. 1, 34–39. Owen, Problems in Assessing Punitive Damages Against Manufacturers of Defective Products, 1982, 49 U.Chi.L.Rev. 1.

56. See, e.g., Britt v. Allen County Community Junior College, 1982, 230 Kan. 502, 638 P.2d 914, 919 (occupier's duty to licensee). A showing of "deliberate indifference" may be required to recover damages for a civil rights violation in a § 1983 action. See Doe v. New York City Department of Social Services, 2d Cir. 1981, 649 F.2d 134. See also Grasser v. Fleming, 1977, 74 Mich.App. 338, 253 N.W.2d 757 (selling liquor to known alcoholic); Kowal v. Hofher, 1980, 181 Conn. 355, 436 A.2d 1 (sale to intoxicated patron; good analysis); Hackbart v. Cincinnati Bengals, Inc., 10th Cir. 1979, 601 F.2d 516, certiorari denied, 444 U.S. 931, 100 S.Ct. 275, 62 L.Ed.2d 188 (professional football player liable for injuries caused by reckless misconduct), noted, 1980, 15 Gonzaga L.Rev. 867; 19 Washburn L.J. 646.

57. See Derosier v. New England Telephone & Telegraph Co., 1925, 81 N.H. 451, 130 A. 145; Bremer v. Lake Erie & Western Railroad Co., 1925, 318 Ill. 11, 148 N.E. 862; Bauer, The Degree of Moral Fault as Affecting Defendant's Liability, 1933, 81 U.Pa.L.Rev. 586; Bauer, The Degree of Defendant's Fault as Affecting the Administration of the Law of Excessive Compensatory Damages, 1934, 82 U.Pa.L.Rev. 583.

58. See DeElena v. Southern Pacific Co., 1979, 121 Ariz. 563, 592 P.2d 759; infra, § 65. It may not, however, bar application of comparative fault. See Plyler v. Wheaton Van Lines, 9th Cir.1981, 640 F.2d 1091; Annot., 1981, 10 A.L.R. 4th 946.

Other defenses may also be defeated if the defendant's conduct was willful, wanton or reckless. See Catheline v. Seaboard Coast Line Railroad Co., M.D. Fla.1972, 348 F.Supp. 43 (contractual disclaimer of liability). See generally Owen, The Highly Blameworthy Manufacturer: Implications on Rules of Liability and Defense in Products Liability Actions, 1977, 10 Ind.L. Rev. 769.

59. See Second Restatement of Torts, § 500; Matkovich v. Penn Central Transportation Co., 1982, 69 Ohio St.2d 210, 431 N.E.2d 652, 654 ("failure to exercise any care whatsoever * * * under circumstances in which there is great probability that harm will result"); Thompson v. Bohlken, Iowa 1981, 312 N.W.2d 501, 504–05; Porter v. Department of Employment Security, 1981, 139 Vt. 405, 430 A.2d 450; Yalowizer v. Husky Oil Co., Wyo.1981, 629 P.2d 465.

60. See Grimshaw v. Ford Motor Co., 1981, 119 Cal. App.3d 757, 174 Cal.Rptr. 348 ("conscious disregard of public safety"); Bernesak v. Catholic Bishop of Chicago, 1980, 87 Ill.App.3d 681, 42 Ill.Dec. 672, 409 N.E.2d 287, 291 ("consciousness that an injury may probably result * * * and a reckless disregard of the consequences"); Roberts v. Brown, Ala.1980, 384 So.2d 1047; cf. Doe v. New York City Department of Social Services, 2d Cir.1981, 649 F.2d 134 (§ 1983 civil rights action: "gross negligent conduct creates a presumption of deliberate indifference"); Britt v. Allen County Community Junior College, 1982, 230 Kan. 502, 638 P.2d 914. See, however, note 62, infra.

danger, either known to him or apparent to a reasonable person in his position.[61]

The result is that "willful," "wanton," or "reckless" conduct tends to take on the aspect of highly unreasonable conduct, involving an extreme departure from ordinary care,[62] in a situation where a high degree of danger is apparent. As a result there is often no clear distinction at all between such conduct and "gross" negligence, and the two have tended to merge and take on the same meaning, of an aggravated form of negligence, differing in quality rather than in degree from ordinary lack of care.[63] It is at least clear, however, that such aggravated negligence must be more than any mere mistake resulting from inexperience, excitement, or confusion,[64] and more than mere thoughtlessness or inadvertence,[65] or simple inattention,[66] even perhaps to the extent of falling asleep at the wheel of an automobile,[67] or even of an intentional omission to perform a statutory duty,[68] except in those cases where a reasonable person in the actor's place would have been aware of great danger, and proceeding in the face of it is so entirely unreasonable as to amount to aggravated negligence.[69]

---

61. See Second Restatement of Torts, § 500, Comment c; Roberts v. Brown, Ala.1980, 384 So.2d 1047; Landers v. School District No. 203, O'Fallon, 1978, 66 Ill.App.3d 78, 22 Ill.Dec. 837, 383 N.E.2d 645; Britton v. Doehring, 1970, 286 Ala. 498, 242 So.2d 666; Catheline v. Seaboard Coast Line Railroad Co., M.D.Fla.1972, 348 F.Supp. 43. Contra, Mandolidis v. Elkins Industries, Inc., 1978, ___ W.Va. ___, 246 S.E.2d 907 (subjective).

62. Stephens v. United States, C.D.Ill.1979, 472 F.Supp. 998; Danculovich v. Brown, Wyo.1979, 593 P.2d 187; Owen, Problems in Assessing Punitive Damages Against Manufacturers of Defective Products, 1982, 49 U.Chi.L.Rev. 1, 27–28 & n. 124.

Accordingly, if the standard of liability is defined in terms of the defendant's "consciousness" of danger, it is imperative that the definition also include some notion that the danger is *excessive* and *preventable*—a consciousness that the conduct is unlawful or morally wrong—lest the defendant's mere awareness of the probability of harm generate punitive damages or other exceptional liability in all contexts, even where the conduct is reasonable and lawful notwithstanding its inherent risks. The design of automobiles for the crash environment, see infra, ch. 17, is a case in point. See Owen, supra; Owen, Crashworthiness Litigation and Punitive Damages, 1981, 4 J.Prod.Liab. 221.

63. See Britt v. Allen County Community Junior College, 1982, 230 Kan. 502, 638 P.2d 914 ("gross and wanton negligence"); Garrison v. Pacific Northwest Bell, 1980, 45 Or.App. 523, 608 P.2d 1206; DeElena v. Southern Pacific Co., 1979, 121 Ariz. 563, 592 P.2d 759.

64. Siesseger v. Puth, 1931, 213 Iowa 164, 239 N.W. 46; Willett v. Smith, 1932, 260 Mich. 101, 244 N.W. 246.

65. Shoop v. Hubbard, 1966, 259 Iowa 1362, 147 N.W.2d 51. See Stamat v. Merry, 1979, 78 Ill.App.3d 445, 33 Ill.Dec. 808, 397 N.E.2d 141. Cf. Johns-Manville Sales Corp. Private Carriage v. Workers' Compensation Appeals Board, 1979, 96 Cal.App.3d 923, 158 Cal.Rptr. 463 (employer's failure to furnish sufficient light in truck yard to avoid trips and falls).

66. Boward v. Leftwich, 1955, 197 Va. 227, 89 S.E.2d 32; cf. Thompson v. Bohlken, Iowa 1981, 312 N.W.2d 501 (plant manager's inattention to dangerous machines). See generally Danculovich v. Brown, Wyo. 1979, 593 P.2d 187.

67. Perkins v. Roberts, 1935, 272 Mich. 545, 262 N.W. 305; De Shetler v. Kordt, 1931, 43 Ohio App. 236, 183 N.E. 85.

But in Lankford v. Mong, 1968, 283 Ala. 24, 214 So. 2d 301, going to sleep while driving was held to permit a finding of wanton conduct, on the basis that the driver must have known that he was getting sleepy.

68. See Kennedy v. Carter, 1967, 249 S.C. 168, 153 S.E.2d 312 (speed limit); Mantia v. Kaminski, 1980, 89 Ill.App.3d 932, 45 Ill.Dec. 300, 412 N.E.2d 651; Bains v. Western Pacific Railway Co., 1976, 56 Cal.App.3d 902, 128 Cal.Rptr. 778 (train speed and braking statutes); Copeland v. Baltimore & Ohio Railroad Co., D.C.App. 1980, 416 A.2d 1.

69. Lewis v. Zell, 1965, 279 Ala. 33, 181 So.2d 101 (running a red light); White v. King, 1966, 244 Md. 348, 223 A.2d 763, appeal after remand, 1968, 250 Md. 192, 242 A.2d 494 (driving in danger of sleep). See generally Danculovich v. Brown, Wyo.1979, 593 P.2d 187.

A few courts have added to the confusion which surrounds the "willful and wanton" and "reckless" standards by defining the misconduct in ordinary negligence terms, as for example, as a failure to exercise ordinary care after discovery of the danger—or, in other words, ordinary negligence in the face of a known risk. See, e.g., Gammon v. Edwardsville Community Unit School District No. 7, 1980, 82 Ill.App.3d 586, 38 Ill.Dec. 28, 403 N.E.2d 43; Grimshaw v. Ford Motor Co., 1981, 119 Cal.App.3d 757, 174 Cal.Rptr. 348 ("conscious disregard" of risk). Definitions of this type have properly been condemned as unsound in principle, as allowing recovery, sometimes for punitive damages, for behavior that may have been merely negligent, or perhaps not improper at all. See supra, note 62; Owen, Problems in Assessing Punitive Damages Against Manufacturers of Defective Products, 1982, 49 U.Chi. L.Rev. 1, 20–28; Burrell, A New Approach to the Problem of Wilful and Wanton Misconduct, [1949] Ins.L.J. 716.

Automobile Guest Statutes

Beginning in Massachusetts in 1907,[70] a small minority of courts, during the early part of the century, developed a rule holding a driver to a limited standard of care to a guest passenger, based on the lower level of care assumed by a bailee in a gratuitous undertaking.[71] The state legislatures began to adopt statutes along these lines in 1927, and over the next twelve years somewhat more than half the states enacted automobile guest statutes of this type.[72] These statutes provide that the driver of an automobile [73] is liable to one riding as a gratuitous guest in his car only for gross negligence or some other form of aggravated misconduct. The definition of the proscribed misconduct varies from state to state, according to the fancy of the legislature and compromises in drawing the particular act. In addition to "gross negligence," the required form of aggravation is variously specified as "intentional," "willful," "wanton," or "reckless" misconduct, acting "in disregard of the safety of others," "intoxication," or some combination of these. There is so much individual variation in the statutes, and in their interpretation, that it may safely be said that there are as many different guest laws as there are acts.[74]

The statutes are generally acknowledged to have been the result of persistent and effective lobbying on the part of liability insurance companies.[75] Two principal rationales have been advanced for the guest statutes: (1) *hospitality protection*, and (2) *collusion prevention*.[76] The first rationale is based upon the apparent unfairness of permitting an ungrateful non-paying guest, perhaps a hitch-hiker, to force a large financial burden upon a possibly uninsured host driver, and the resulting discouragement of hospitality by motorists.[77] The second rationale looks to the interests of the insurer, who is required to pay the damages, and who is peculiarly exposed to collusion between the injured guest and his host anxious to see compensation paid, so long as he does not have to pay it—so that the truth does not come out in court, and there is a resulting increase in insurance rates.[78] The typical guest act case is that of the driver who of-

70. West v. Poor, 1907, 196 Mass. 183, 81 N.E. 960 (girl hitched ride on milk wagon). An early Australian case was decided along similar lines. Moffat v. Bateman, 1869, L.R. 3 P.C. 115. The doctrine also developed in Canada, see MacArthur, Gross Negligence and the Guest Passenger, 1960, 38 Can.Bar Rev. 47, but not in England. See Street, The Law of Torts, 6th ed. 1976, 128; Fleming, The Law of Torts, 4th ed. 1971, 399.

71. Massaletti v. Fitzroy, 1917, 228 Mass. 487, 118 N.E. 168, became the leading case. Other states judicially limiting the driver's duty included Georgia, Wisconsin (on assumption of risk grounds), Washington, Pennsylvania, and perhaps New Jersey. See Note, 1976, 43 U.Chi.L.Rev. 798, 811–14.

72. Connecticut and Iowa enacted guest statutes in 1927. See Note, 1974, 59 Corn.L.Rev. 659, 663 (setting forth both statutes).

73. The guest passenger rules are sometimes applied to airplanes. Osburn v. Pilgrim, 1980, 246 Ga. 688, 273 S.E.2d 118, on remand 157 Ga.App. 217, 276 S.E.2d 888 (common law); Middleton v. Cox, 1970, 24 Utah 2d 43, 465 P.2d 530 (statute). See Annot., 1971, 40 A.L.R.3d 1117. Delaware added boats and other vehicles to its statute in 1949. Note, 1974, 59 Corn.L. Rev. 659, 660 n. 7.

74. See, e.g., Appleman, Wilful and Wanton Conduct in Automobile Guest Cases, 1937, 13 Ind.L.J. 131;

Note, 1968, 41 So.Cal.L.Rev. 884, 899 (listing by state the standards of liability).

75. See, attacking the statutes on this basis, Allen, Why Do Courts Coddle Insurance Companies, 1927, 61 Am.L.Rev. 77; White, The Liability of an Automobile Driver to a Non-Paying Passenger, 1934, 20 Va.L.Rev. 326. See also Talbot Smith, J., in Stevens v. Stevens, 1959, 355 Mich. 363, 94 N.W.2d 858. In some states, farm groups may also have pressed for the statutes. See Pedrick, Taken for a Ride: The Automobile Guest and Assumption of Risk, 1961, 22 La.L.Rev. 90, 91.

The insurance industry reportedly made no objection when the statutes were repealed in Vermont and Florida. See Note, 1974, 59 Corn.L.Rev. 676–78.

76. The Arkansas court adds the related goal of encouraging car pooling. Davis v. Cox, 1980, 268 Ark. 78, 593 S.W.2d 180. Car pool guests are excluded from the rule under the Colorado statute. See Richardson v. Hansen, 1974, 186 Colo. 346, 527 P.2d 536.

77. The historical development and rationales behind the rules are well explored in Green, The [Excitement] of Change: A Dialogue on the Constitutionality of the Guest Statute, 1980, 14 Creighton L.Rev. 37; Notes, 1976, 43 U.Chi.L.Rev. 798; 1974, 59 Corn.L.Rev. 659.

78. See Naudzius v. Lahr, 1931, 253 Mich. 216, 234 N.W. 581.

fers his friend [79] a lift to the office or invites the friend out to dinner, negligently drives him into a collision, and fractures his skull—after which the driver and his insurance company take refuge in the statute, step out of the picture, and leave the guest to bear his own loss. If this is good social policy, it at least appears under a novel front.

There is perhaps no other group of statutes which have filled the courts with appeals on so many knotty little problems involving petty and otherwise entirely inconsequential points of law. There is first of all the question of who is a "guest." What is the effect of sharing expenses, or of the guest buying a tank of gasoline? Of an indirect, prospective, or merely remotely potential benefit to the host in the form of some business interest or hope in having the guest take the ride? Of an employer's order prohibiting the driver from taking free riders? Of the fact that the guest is not invited, but allowed to stay after he trespasses? Of the fact that the plaintiff is a child too young to know that he is a guest? Of the fact that the guest was out of the car for a moment when he was run down? Of his demand to be let out of the car? Of his assent even to the aggravated misconduct? Can the owner of the car be a guest in it when someone else is driving? And finally, what is the meaning, and application, of "gross," "willful," "wanton," "reckless," or whatever other terms the statute may adopt? [80]

The guest statutes were subjected to criticism, almost before the ink on the statute books had dried, for abrogating the traditional standard of care and for constitutional inadequacy.[81] Although a United States Supreme Court opinion upheld the constitutionality of Connecticut's statute in 1929,[82] criticism over the perceived unfairness and increasing complexity of the rules mounted over the next forty years.[83] Vermont finally broke the ice in 1969, and repealed its guest statute, and a number of other state legislatures thereafter tumbled along behind, by limiting their guest rules or abolishing them altogether.[84] Perhaps the most significant development in the recent decline of automobile guest statutes was the 1973 decision in Brown v. Merlo,[85] in which the California Supreme Court struck down its statute on equal protection grounds, reasoning that the widespread adoption of automobile insurance had undercut the hospitality-protection rationale, and that the collusion-prevention rationale was overbroad in burdening the many honest litigants in trying to reach the collusive few. A host of other constitutional challenges soon followed in other states and, within the next decade, ten other states in-

---

79. In legislative hearings there was frequent mention of the hitch-hiker, who elicited little sympathy. The hitch-hiker cases are in fact very hard to find. See Bateman v. Ursich, 1950, 36 Wn.2d 729, 220 P.2d 314; Hubble v. Brown, 1949, 227 Ind. 202, 84 N.E.2d 891; Annot., 1972, 46 A.L.R.3d 964; cf. West v. Poor, 1907, 196 Mass. 183, 81 N.E. 960.

80. No short text can hope to deal with the infinite variety of such questions and answers under the different statutes in so many states. The reader can only be referred to the law of the jurisdiction in which he may be interested, to the digests (automobiles), and to the many A.L.R. annotations on the subject.

81. See, e.g., Statute, 1929, 114 Iowa L.Rev. 342; Corish, The Automobile Guest, 1934, 14 B.U.L.Rev. 728.

82. Silver v. Silver, 1929, 280 U.S. 117, 50 S.Ct. 57, 74 L.Ed. 221. The Kentucky Supreme Court invalidated its statute under the Kentucky constitution in 1932. Ludwig v. Johnson, 1932, 243 Ky. 533, 49 S.W.2d 347. The Connecticut legislature repealed that state's statute in 1937. Act of June 8, 1927, Pub. Act 4404.

83. See, e.g., Stevens v. Stevens, 1959, 355 Mich. 363, 94 N.W.2d 858; Lascher, Hard Laws Make Bad Cases—Lots of Them (The California Guest Statute), 1968, 9 Santa Clara Law 1; Schantz, Oregon's Guest Statute, 1961, 1 Willamette L.J. 425; Notes, 1947, 1 Wyo.L.J. 182; 1959, 38 Tex.L.Rev. 110; 54 Nw.U.L.Rev. 263; 1961, 22 Ohio St.L.J. 629; 1962, 47 Iowa L.Rev. 1049; 1966, 7 W. & M. L.Rev. 321; 1968, 41 So.Cal.L.Rev. 884. The criticism continues. E.g., Vetri, The Case for Repeal of the Oregon Guest Passenger Legislation, 1976, 13 Willamette L.J. 53; Note, 1981, 33 Ala.L.Rev. 143.

84. The recent developments are chronicled in Notes, 1981, 33 Ala.L.Rev. 143; 1974, 59 Corn.L.Rev. 659. Following Vermont, repeal has occurred as follows: Ill. (1971) (restricted to hitch-hikers); Mass. (1971); Fla. (1972); Tex. (1973) (limited to close relatives); Va. (1974); Wash. (1974); Colo. (1975); Mont. (1975); Or. (1977); S.D. (1978).

85. Brown v. Merlo, 1973, 8 Cal.3d 855, 106 Cal.Rptr. 388, 506 P.2d 212.

validated their statutes on constitutional grounds.[86] Guest passenger limited duty rules now remain in only a handful of states,[87] and it may be expected that most of these will soon recognize the logic in abolishing a doctrine based upon social conditions that have long since changed.[88]

 WESTLAW REFERENCES

dangerous /2 instrumentalit! /p degree* /2 care

Slight Negligence

slight /2 negligence

Gross Negligence

headnote(gross /2 negligence /s defin! mean!)

Willful, Wanton and Reckless

willful /5 wanton /5 reckless

Automobile Guest Statutes

guest /2 statute* /p hospitality
guest /2 statute* /p collusion

§ 35. Rules of Law

The entire system of common law jurisprudence has been built upon the principle of stare decisis, that a decision of an appellate court establishes a precedent, to be followed in that jurisdiction when similar fact situations shall arise again. The principle has value in so far as it makes it possible to predict in advance the course which the administration of justice will take, it secures against bad motives or errors in judgment on the part of individual judges, and serves to prevent the sacrifice of ultimate social interests to the immediate demands of a particular case.[1] But it is not, and never has been, an ironclad and absolute principle, and such precedents may be departed from when the court subsequently concludes that they are unreasonable, or out of line with altered social conditions.[2] Nor do they control when the facts which arise are essentially different; and many writers have devoted thought to the sometimes highly artificial technique by which the facts of earlier cases are "distinguished."[3]

A decision of an appellate court that under certain circumstances a particular type of conduct is clearly negligent, or that it clearly is not negligent, or that the issue is for the jury as one on which reasonable persons may differ, establishes a precedent for other cases where the facts are identical, or substantially the same. To that extent it may define the standard of reasonable conduct which the community requires.[4] Unfortunately, the inevitable tendency to crystallize

---

86. Idaho (1974); Kan. (1974); N.D. (1974); Mich. (1975); Nev. (1975); N.M. (1975); Oh. (1975); Wyo. (1978); S.C. (1979); Iowa (1980). See Note, 1981, 33 Ala.L.Rev. 151 (citing the cases); Annot., 1975, 66 A.L.R.3d 532.

On the constitutional issue, see Green, The [Excitement] of Change: A Dialogue on the Constitutionality of the Guest Statute, 1980, 14 Creighton L.Rev. 37; Notes, 1975, B.Y.U.L.Rev. 99; 1974, 59 Corn.L.Rev. 659; 21 U.C.L.A.L.Rev. 1566; Annot., 1975, 66 A.L.R.3d 532. The constitutional issues are developed in the judicial opinions, most recently: *unconstitutional*—Bierkamp v. Rogers, Iowa 1980, 293 N.W.2d 577; Ramey v. Ramey, 1979, 273 S.C. 680, 258 S.E.2d 883, certiorari denied 1980, 444 U.S. 1078, 100 S.Ct. 1028, 62 L.Ed.2d 761; see generally Manistee Bank & Trust Co. v. McGowan, 1975, 394 Mich. 655, 232 N.W.2d 636; *constitutional*—Kreifels v. Wurtele, 1980, 206 Neb. 491, 293 N.W.2d 407 (4–3); Davis v. Cox, 1980, 268 Ark. 78, 593 S.W.2d 180 (one dissent on point); see generally Justice v. Gatchell, Del.1974, 325 A.2d 97.

87. The rule in original form now obtains in only 7 states: Ala., Ark., Del., Ga. (common law), Ind., Neb., Utah. See Note, 1981, 33 Ala.L.Rev. 143, 144 n. 5.

Rules of limited application still exist in Texas and Illinois. See supra, note 84.

88. While the guest statutes do indeed have some fairness arguments in their favor, the combination of the countervailing fairness arguments, the almost universal insurance coverage of automobile accidents, and the necessity of improving judicial efficiency in this area makes a compelling case on policy grounds for abolishing the guest statute rules.

§ 35

1. Pound, Justice According to Law, 1913, 13 Col.L. Rev. 696, 709.

2. Cardozo, The Nature of the Judicial Process, 1921, 149; Von Moschzisker, Stare Decisis in Courts of Last Resort, 1924, 37 Harv.L.Rev. 409; Aumann, Judicial Law Making and Stare Decisis, 1933, 21 Ky.L.J. 156.

3. Allen, Law in the Making, 1927, 164; Green, Judge and Jury, 1930, 274.

4. Second Restatement of Torts, § 285(c), Comments *e, h*.

the law into mechanical rules [5] has led the courts in many cases to treat such precedents as fixing definite rules of universal application. Almost invariably the rule has broken down in the face of the necessity of basing the standard upon the particular circumstances, the apparent risk, and the actor's opportunity to deal with it.

Especially noteworthy in this respect is the attempt of Mr. Justice Holmes, in Baltimore & Ohio Railway v. Goodman,[6] to "lay down a standard once for all," which would require an automobile driver approaching a railroad crossing with an obstructed view to stop, look and listen, and if he cannot be sure otherwise that no train is coming, to get out of the car. The basic idea behind this is sound enough: it is by no means proper care to cross a railroad track without taking reasonable precautions against a train, and normally such precautions will require looking, listening, and a stop, or at least slow speed, where the view is obstructed.[7] But the attempt to specify conduct for all cases virtually made it certain that there could never be a recovery for a crossing accident. A long series of cases in which gates were left open,[8] or the driver relied upon the absence of a flagman,[9] or it was clear that the conduct specified would have added nothing to the driver's safety,[10] made it quite apparent that no such inflexible rule could be applied.[11] Finally, in the subsequent case of Pokora v. Wabash Ry.,[12] where the only effective stop had to be made upon the railway tracks themselves, in a position of obvious danger, the court discarded any such uniform rule, rejecting the "get out of the car" requirement as "an uncommon precaution, likely to be futile and sometimes even dangerous," and saying that the driver need not always stop. "Illustrations such as these," said Mr. Justice Cardozo, "bear witness to the need for caution in

---

5. Pound, Mechanical Jurisprudence, 1908, 8 Col.L. Rev. 605. An interesting attempt to fix the standard of care by a rule which would very probably have strangled the automobile, if it had succeeded, is Berry, Rights and Duties of Automobile Drivers When Meeting and Passing Horse-Drawn Vehicles, 1916, 82 Cent. L.J. 315.

6. 1927, 275 U.S. 66, 48 S.Ct. 24, 72 L.Ed. 167. See Notes, 1930, 43 Harv.L.Rev. 926; 1933, 17 Minn.L.Rev. 771; 1928, 16 Cal.L.Rev. 238; 1928, 14 Va.L.Rev. 379; 1928, 4 Wis.L.Rev. 467. See generally Holmes, The Common Law, 1881, 111–29.

7. This has been applied quite consistently in Pennsylvania. See Benner v. Philadelphia & Reading Railway Co., 1918, 262 Pa. 307, 105 A. 283; Evans v. Reading Co., 1976, 242 Pa.Super. 209, 363 A.2d 1234; Note, 1951, 13 U.Pitt.L.Rev. 117. See also Hanson v. Duluth, Missabe & Northern Railway Co., 1963, 267 Minn. 24, 124 N.W.2d 486; Lundquist v. Kennecott Copper Co., 1973, 30 Utah 2d 262, 516 P.2d 1182 (statute).

8. Wabash Railroad Co. v. Glass, 6th Cir.1929, 32 F.2d 697; Canadian Pacific Railway Co. v. Slayton, 2d Cir.1928, 29 F.2d 687; Lindekugel v. Spokane, Portland & Seattle Railway Co., 1935, 149 Or. 634, 42 P.2d 907. Cf. Wabash Railroad Co. v. Walczak, 6th Cir.1931, 49 F.2d 763 (flasher signal not working); Shewmaker v. Louisville & Nashville Railroad Co., Ky.1966, 403 S.W.2d 283 (same).

9. Leuthold v. Pennsylvania Railroad Co., 6th Cir. 1929, 33 F.2d 758; cf. Weinstein v. Powell, 5th Cir. 1932, 61 F.2d 411; Malone v. St. Louis-San Francisco Railroad Co., 1926, 220 Mo.App. 9, 285 S.W. 123 (fog).

10. Torgeson v. Missouri-Kansas-Texas Railway Co., 1928, 124 Kan. 798, 262 P. 564; Swift & Co. v. St. Louis Transfer Railway Co., Mo.App.1929, 15 S.W.2d 387; Williams v. Minneapolis, St. Paul & Sault Ste. Marie Railway Co., 1928, 57 N.D. 279, 221 N.W. 42; Norfolk & Western Railway Co. v. Holbrook, C.C.A. Ky.1928, 27 F.2d 326 (heavy fog); Hoffman v. Southern Pacific Co., 1929, 101 Cal.App. 218, 281 P. 681 (same).

11. For recent cases, see, e.g., Bergeron v. Illinois Central Gulf Railroad Co., La.App.1981, 402 So.2d 184, writ denied, La., 404 So.2d 1260 (driver not negligent in failing to stop and look); Alabama Great Southern Railroad Co. v. Evans, 1972, 288 Ala. 25, 256 So.2d 861 (no absolute duty to stop, look and listen); Barclay v. Burlington Northern, Inc., 8th Cir.1976, 536 F.2d 263 (same); Connelly v. Southern Railway Co., 1967, 249 S.C. 363, 154 S.E.2d 569 (duty not inflexible but qualified by surrounding circumstances); Beasley v. Grand Trunk Western Railway Co., 1979, 90 Mich.App. 576, 282 N.W.2d 401 (same); Reiss v. Chicago, Milwaukee, St. Paul & Pacific Railroad Co., 1979, 77 Ill.App.3d 124, 32 Ill.Dec. 600, 395 N.E.2d 981 (question for jury); Lucas v. Southern Pacific Railroad, 1971, 19 Cal.App.3d 124, 96 Cal.Rptr. 356 (same); cf. Smith v. Union Pacific Railroad Co., 1977, 222 Kan. 303, 564 P.2d 514 (contributory negligence of passenger who failed to look for train was for jury).

12. 1934, 292 U.S. 98, 54 S.Ct. 580, 78 L.Ed. 1149. Accord: Doyel v. Thompson, 1948, 357 Mo. 963, 211 S.W.2d 704; Gleaton v. Southern Railway Co., 1940, 208 S.C. 507, 38 S.E.2d 710; Union Pacific Railroad Co. v. Lumbert, 10th Cir.1968, 401 F.2d 699 (Wyoming law); and cf. Macartney v. Westbrook, 1930, 132 Or. 488, 286 P. 525 (entering main highway from private road, with obstructed view).

framing standards of behavior that amount to rules of law. * * * Extraordinary situations may not wisely or fairly be subjected to tests or regulations that are fitting for the commonplace or normal."

A similar fate is overtaking the rule, which many courts have stated,[13] that it is always negligence to drive at such a speed that it is impossible to stop within the range of vision, or within the "assured clear distance ahead." Again the principle is sound enough; but universal application becomes quite impossible. The rule has proved to be much too stringent when the visibility is obscured by fog or rain,[14] when the driver is suddenly blinded by the lights of an approaching car,[15] or when unanticipated defects or obstacles suddenly appear on an apparently safe highway.[16] The reaction from the rule has been so marked that some courts have gone to the other extreme, of saying that such speed is never more than evidence of negligence for the jury.[17] Similar difficulties have arisen with the rule that a pedestrian must look when crossing a street,[18] that a driver must constantly watch the road ahead,[19] or that it is never negligent to make a product that is obviously dangerous.[20]

Such rules may be useful to fix a standard for the usual, normal case, but they are a hindrance to any just decision in the large number of unusual situations presenting new factors which may affect the standard. A standard which requires only conduct proportionate to the circumstances and the risk seldom, if ever, can be made a matter of absolute rule.[21]

---

13. The leading case is Lauson v. Town of Fond du Lac, 1909, 141 Wis. 57, 123 N.W. 629. Accord: Jones v. Spencer, 1976, 220 Kan. 445, 553 P.2d 300; Clark v. City of St. Joseph, Mo.App.1980, 606 S.W.2d 506 (statutory); Maurer v. Harper, 1981, 207 Neb. 655, 300 N.W.2d 191; Brown v. Schriver, 1978, 254 Pa.Super. 468, 386 A.2d 45. See Schmeling, The Range of Vision Rule in Nebraska, 1969, 49 Neb.L.Rev. 7. This requires that the driver at night be able to stop within the scope of his headlights. See Greenwade v. Drake, 1979, 202 Neb. 815, 277 N.W.2d 248; Johnston v. Pierce Packing Co., 9th Cir.1977, 550 F.2d 474.

14. Langill v. First National Stores, 1937, 298 Mass. 559, 11 N.E.2d 593; Timmons v. Reed, Wyo.1977, 569 P.2d 112 (fog); Black v. Davidson, 1975, 84 Wn.2d 882, 529 P.2d 1048 (dust).

15. Watson v. Southern Bus Lines, 6th Cir.1951, 186 F.2d 981; Emerson v. Bailey, 1959, 102 N.H. 360, 156 A.2d 762; Nesbit v. Everette, 5th Cir.1955, 227 F.2d 157; Winfough v. Tri-State Insurance Co., 1956, 179 Kan. 525, 297 P.2d 159; Ryan v. Cameron, 1955, 270 Wis. 325, 71 N.W.2d 408. But it may still be negligent as a matter of law not to slow down. Wolfe v. Beatty Motor Express, Inc., 1957, 143 W.Va. 238, 101 S.E.2d 81. But see Evans v. Reading Co., 1976, 242 Pa.Super. 209, 363 A.2d 1234 (sun); Beard v. Brown, Wyo.1980, 616 P.2d 726 (headlights).

16. Vanlandingham v. Vanlandingham, 1972, 212 Va. 856, 188 S.E.2d 96 (car suddenly backed into highway); cf. Timmons v. Reed, Wyo.1977, 569 P.2d 112 (unlighted vehicle in fog); Cerny v. Domer, 1968, 13 Ohio St.2d 117, 235 N.E.2d 132 (car ahead backing up).

17. Kendall v. City of Des Moines, 1918, 183 Iowa 866, 167 N.W. 684; Tresise v. Ashdown, 1928, 118 Ohio St. 307, 160 N.E. 898.

18. Knapp v. Barrett, 1915, 216 N.Y. 226, 110 N.E. 428. Cf. Albaugh v. Cooley, 1980, 88 Ill.App.3d 320, 43 Ill.Dec. 740, 410 N.E.2d 873, reversed 87 Ill.2d 241, 57 Ill.Dec. 720, 429 N.E.2d 837; Rotstain v. Lillis, Mo.App. 1977, 550 S.W.2d 879.

19. Thornton v. Pender, 1978, 268 Ind. 540, 377 N.E.2d 613; Jenkins v. Jordon, Mo.App.1979, 593 S.W.2d 236; Cleaver v. Dresser Industries, Tex.Civ. App.1978, 570 S.W.2d 479, refused n.r.e.

20. See generally Holm v. Sponco Manufacturing, Inc., Minn.1982, 324 N.W.2d 207; Micallef v. Miehle Co., 1976, 39 N.Y.2d 376, 384 N.Y.S.2d 115, 348 N.E.2d 571; Darling, The Patent Danger Rule: An Analysis and A Survey of Its Vitality, 1978, 29 Mercer L.Rev. 583; Marschall, An Obvious Wrong Does Not Make a Right: Manufacturers' Liability for Patently Dangerous Products, 1973, 48 N.Y.U.L.Rev. 1065.

21. See generally McKinney v. Yelavich, 1958, 352 Mich. 687, 90 N.W.2d 883; Nixon, Changing Rules of Liability in Automobile Accident Litigation, 1936, 3 Law & Contemp. Prob. 478; Pedrick, The Regeneration of Tort Law, 1979, Ariz.St.L.J. 143; cf. Ursin, Judicial Creativity and Tort Law, 1981, 49 Geo.Wash.L.Rev. 229. But see Henderson, Expanding the Negligence Concept: Retreat from the Rule of Law, 1976, 51 Ind. L.J. 467; Hawkins, Premises Liability After Repudiation of the Status Categories: Allocation of Judge and Jury Functions, 1981, 15 Utah L.Rev. 15.

For a judicial development against the general trend, see Helling v. Carey, 1974, 83 Wn.2d 514, 519 P.2d 981 (due care required administration of glaucoma test by ophthalmologists to patient under 40 as a matter of law); Gates v. Jensen, 1979, 92 Wn.2d 246, 595 P.2d 919 (doctrine reaffirmed in part after attempted legislative repeal). Compare Truman v. Thomas, 1980, 27 Cal.3d 285, 165 Cal.Rptr. 308, 611 P.2d 902 (jury should have determined whether doctor was negligent in not advising patient on danger of failing to undergo pap smear), vacating, 1979, 93 Cal.App.3d 304, 155 Cal. Rptr. 752 (no duty to warn of consequences as a matter of law).

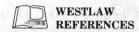
WESTLAW REFERENCES

rule* /p negligen! /p "stare decisis"

§ 36. Violation of Statute

The standard of conduct required of a reasonable person may be prescribed by legislative enactment.[1] When a statute provides that under certain circumstances particular acts shall or shall not be done, it may be interpreted as fixing a standard for all members of the community, from which it is negligence to deviate.[2] The same may be true of municipal ordinances[3] and regulations of administrative bodies.[4] The fact that such legislation is usually penal in character, and carries with it a criminal penalty, will not prevent its use in imposing civil liability,[5] and may even be a prerequisite thereto.[6]

Much ingenuity has been expended in the effort to explain why criminal legislation should result in a rule for civil liability. If there is a specific provision in the statute to that effect, there is of course no difficulty, since it is clear that that is the intent of the legislature.[7] The only questions open are whether the legislation is constitutional, whether it is applicable to the particular case, and whether it has in fact been violated. But where the statute merely declares that conduct is a crime, and makes no mention of any civil remedy, justification becomes more difficult, since the court is then obviously under no compulsion to apply the statute. Many courts have, however, purported to "find" in the statute a supposed

---

§ 36

1. Second Restatement of Torts, §§ 285, 286. See generally, Morris, The Relation of Criminal Statutes to Tort Liability, 1933, 46 Harv.L.Rev. 453; Morris, The Role of Criminal Statutes in Negligence Actions, 1949, 49 Col.L.Rev. 21; James, Statutory Standards and Negligence in Accident Cases, 1951, 11 La.L.Rev. 95; Williams, The Effect of Penal Legislation in the Law of Tort, 1960, 23 Mod.L.Rev. 232; Fricke, The Juridical Nature of the Action Upon the Statute, 1960, 76 L.Q.Rev. 240.

2. "Negligence is the breach of legal duty. It is immaterial whether the duty is one imposed by the rule of common law requiring the exercise of ordinary care not to injure another, or is imposed by a statute designed for the protection of others. * * * The only difference is that in the one case the measure of legal duty is to be determined upon common law principles, while in the other the statute fixes it, so that the violation of the statute constitutes conclusive evidence of negligence, or, in other words, negligence per se. * * * All that the statute does is to establish a fixed standard by which the fact of negligence may be determined." Mitchell, J., in Osborne v. McMasters, 1889, 40 Minn. 103, 105, 41 N.W. 543, 544.

3. District of Columbia v. White, D.C.App.1982, 442 A.2d 159; Hall v. Warren, Utah 1981, 632 P.2d 848 (housing code); Crago v. Lurie, 1980, ___ W.Va. ___, 273 S.E.2d 344 (sidewalk maintenance); Boyles v. Oklahoma Natural Gas Co., Okl.1980, 619 P.2d 613; Powell v. Village of Mount Zion, 1980, 88 Ill.App.3d 406, 43 Ill.Dec. 525, 410 N.E.2d 525; Ray v. Goldsmith, 1980, ___ Ind.App. ___, 400 N.E.2d 176 (prohibiting abandoning refrigerators accessible to children without removing doors); cf. Brown v. South Broward Hospital District, Fla.App.1981, 402 So.2d 58; Carmichael v. Lexington-Fayette Urban County Government, Ky.App.1980, 608 S.W.2d 66.

4. Davis v. Marathon Oil Co., 1976, 64 Ill.2d 380, 1 Ill.Dec. 93, 356 N.E.2d 93; Knockum v. Amoco Oil Co., La.App.1981, 402 So.2d 90 (LP gas commission); NeSmith v. Bowden, 1977, 17 Wn.App. 602, 563 P.2d 1322 (ICC maximum driving time regulations for truck drivers); cf. Lutz v. United States, 9th Cir.1982, 685 F.2d 1178 (military base regulations; state law); Koll v. Manatt's Transportation Co., Iowa 1977, 253 N.W.2d 265 (state and federal OSHA standards); Hundt v. LaCrosse Grain Co., 1981, ___ Ind.App. ___, 425 N.E.2d 687, vacated, 1983, 432 N.E.2d 71 (state building council); Beals v. Walker, 1980, 98 Mich.App. 214, 290 N.W.2d 828 (workplace safety regulations); Continental Oil Co. v. Simpson, Tex.Civ.App.1980, 604 S.W.2d 530, refused n.r.e. But cf. Distad v. Cubin, Wyo.1981, 633 P.2d 167 ("overbroad and inflexible" regulation; violation not negligence per se on facts). See Annot., 1977, 79 A.L.R.3d 962 (OSHA regulations).

5. Parker v. Barnard, 1883, 135 Mass. 116; Stehle v. Jaeger Automatic Machine Co., 1908, 220 Pa. 617, 69 A. 1116; Kavanagh v. New York, Ontario & Western Railway Co., 1921, 196 App.Div. 384, 187 N.Y.S. 859, affirmed, 1922, 233 N.Y. 597, 135 N.E. 933.

6. See Cowan v. Laughridge Construction Co., 1982, 57 N.C.App. 357, 291 S.E.2d 287 (OSHA regulations which provided only civil penalties not penal in nature).

7. For example, dog bite statutes, see Seim v. Garavalia, Minn.1981, 306 N.W.2d 806; workplace safety acts, see Norton v. Wilbur Waggoner Equipment Rental & Excavating Co., 1979, 76 Ill.2d 481, 31 Ill.Dec. 201, 394 N.E.2d 403, on remand 82 Ill.App.3d 727, 38 Ill.Dec. 93, 403 N.E.2d 108 (Structural Work Act); international airline carrier injury conventions, see Day v. Trans World Airlines, Inc., 2d Cir.1975, 528 F.2d 31, certiorari denied 429 U.S. 890, 97 S.Ct. 246, 50 L.Ed.2d 172, rehearing denied 429 U.S. 1124, 97 S.Ct. 1162, 51 L.Ed.2d 574 (Warsaw Convention); and dram shop acts, see infra, § 81.

"implied," "constructive," or "presumed" intent to provide for tort liability.⁸ This is generally the approach under federal law, where there is no doctrine of negligence per se, and where the question of whether to imply a private cause of action into a federal statute resolves to a question of Congressional intent.⁹ In the ordinary case inquiries into legislative intent are pure fiction, concocted for the purpose. The obvious conclusion must usually be that when the legislators said nothing about it, they either did not have the civil suit in mind at all, or deliberately omitted to provide for it.¹⁰ It is sometimes said that the reasonable man would obey the criminal law, and that one who does not is not acting as a reasonable person, and that he therefore must be negligent.¹¹ While this may serve to explain a decision that a breach of the statute is evidence of negligence, it is not clear that it justifies the rule under which the court must refuse to leave the issue to the jury,¹² nor does it account for the numerous violations which are held not to give rise to any civil action at all,¹³ or for the cases in which, on the basis of analogy or association, the liability has been rested upon some other tort, such as trespass, deceit, nuisance, or even strict liability.¹⁴

8. E.g., Sheehan v. Janesville Auto Transport, 1981, 102 Ill.App.3d 507, 58 Ill.Dec. 189, 430 N.E.2d 131; Board of Commissioners of Monroe County v. Hatton, 1981, ___ Ind.App. ___, 427 N.E.2d 696; Walker v. Bignell, 1981, 100 Wis.2d 256, 301 N.W.2d 447.

9. Merrill Lynch, Pierce, Fenner & Smith v. Curran, 1982, 456 U.S. 353, 102 S.Ct. 1825, 72 L.Ed.2d 182 (5–4) (Commodity Exchange Act). Texas & Pacific Railway Co. v. Rigsby, 1916, 241 U.S. 33, 36 S.Ct. 482, 60 L.Ed. 874 (Federal Safety Appliance Act), originated the federal implication doctrine, which received its modern impetus in J. I. Case Co. v. Borak, 1964, 377 U.S. 426, 84 S.Ct. 1555, 12 L.Ed.2d 423 (Securities Exchange Act of 1934, and proxy solicitation rule thereunder), and which was restated in a four factor test in Cort v. Ash, 1975, 422 U.S. 66, 95 S.Ct. 2080, 45 L.Ed.2d 26. Cases thereafter have applied the doctrine restrictively, and the Supreme Court is badly split on how compelling the evidence must be that Congress truly intended that a private right of action be allowed under the statute. "Recent Supreme Court decisions have stressed that courts should be reluctant to imply private rights of action." Riegel Textile Corp. v. Celanese Corp., 2d Cir.1981, 649 F.2d 894 (Federal Hazardous Substances Act; detailed application of *Cort* factors). See generally Frankel, Implied Rights of Action, 1981, 67 Va.L.Rev. 553; Harried, Implied Causes of Action: A Product of Statutory Construction or the Federal Common Law Power?, 1980, 51 U.Colo.L.Rev. 355; Comment, 1980 Duke L.J. 928; Annot., 1980, 61 L.Ed.2d 910. If there is no common law duty of due care applicable to the circumstances, so that the negligence per se doctrine as such is not available, state courts too will sometimes imply a private cause of action into a statute. See Bob Godfrey Pontiac, Inc. v. Roloff, Or.1981, 291 Or. 318, 630 P.2d 840 (extraordinary analysis of whole issue of statutory violations); Note, 1978, 30 Stan.L.Rev. 1243; Second Restatement of Torts, § 874A (excellent comments on both state and federal doctrines).

Independent of the federal implication doctrine, the breach of a federal statute may support a negligence per se claim as a matter of state law. E.g., Koll v. Manatt's Transportation Co., Iowa 1977, 253 N.W.2d 265 (OSHA standards); Florida Freight Terminals, Inc. v. Cabanas, Fla.App.1978, 354 So.2d 1222. On OSHA violations, see Note 1977–78, 27 Drake L.Rev. 178 (noting *Koll*); Annots., 1977, 35 A.L.R.Fed. 461; 79 A.L.R.3d 962. Thus, a federal court in a diversity case will apply the applicable state negligence per se (and implication) rules to the breach of a federal statute, not the usually more restrictive implication principles of federal law. Lowe v. General Motors Corp., 5th Cir. 1980, 624 F.2d 1373, on remand 527 F.Supp. 54 (Motor Vehicle Safety Act—excellent discussion); see Lukaszewicz v. Ortho Pharmaceutical Corp., E.D.Wis.1981, 510 F.Supp. 961, amended 532 F.Supp. 211 (FDA regulation).

10. Lowndes, Civil Liability Created by Criminal Legislation, 1932, 16 Minn.L.Rev. 361, 363; Thayer, Public Wrong and Private Action, 1913, 27 Harv.L.Rev. 317, 320.

11. Lowe v. General Motors Corp., 5th Cir.1980, 624 F.2d 1373, 1379, on remand 527 F.Supp. 54; Thayer, Public Wrong and Private Action, 1914, 27 Harv.L.Rev. 317, 322. Cf. Cardozo, J., in Martin v. Herzog, 1920, 228 N.Y. 164, 126 N.E. 814: "By the very terms of the hypothesis, to omit, willfully or heedlessly, the safeguards prescribed by law for the benefit of another that he may be preserved in life or limb, is to fall short of the standard of diligence to which those who live in organized society are under a duty to conform."

12. Lowndes, Civil Liability Created by Criminal Legislation, 1932, 16 Minn.L.Rev. 361, 367. But see Morris, The Relation of Criminal Statutes to Tort Liability, 1933, 46 Harv.L.Rev. 453, 465.

13. As to Professor Thayer's argument that the jury should not be permitted to say that a reasonable man would disobey the law, see Stevens v. Luther, 1920, 105 Neb. 184, 190, 180 N.W. 87; Walker v. Lee, 1921, 115 S.C. 495, 106 S.E. 682.

14. " * * * [W]hen a statute is passed the courts generally tend to associate it with the type of common-law liability most closely related to the statute. For example, a statute prohibiting going on property and cutting timber is thought of in the classification of a trespass statute; one prohibiting the receiving of bank deposits after insolvency as a fraud statute; one

Perhaps the most satisfactory explanation is that the courts are seeking, by something in the nature of judicial legislation, to further the ultimate policy for the protection of individuals which they find underlying the statute, and which they believe the legislature must have had in mind.[15] The statutory standard of conduct is simply adopted voluntarily, out of deference and respect for the legislature.[16] This is borne out by a considerable number of cases in which the terms of a criminal statute have been applied in a civil action, notwithstanding the fact that the statute was for some reason totally ineffective as a basis for criminal conviction—as where it had not been properly enacted,[17] or did not exactly cover the situation,[18] or the defendant was incapable of crime, and could not be prosecuted,[19] and by one or two others in which there has been flat refusal to accept a standard regarded as unreasonable.[20]

The question thus becomes one of when the court will look to a criminal statute for its negligence standard of the conduct of a reasonable person.[21]

Persons and Risks Included

It is not every provision of a criminal statute or ordinance which will be adopted by the court, in a civil action for negligence, as the standard of conduct of a reasonable person. Otherwise stated, there are statutes which are considered to create no duty of conduct toward the plaintiff, and to afford no basis for the creation of such a duty by the court.[22] The courts in such cases have been careful not to exceed the purpose which they attribute to the legislature. This judicial self-restraint is rooted in part in the theory of the separation of powers.[23]

There are many statutes, such as those directed against various activities on Sunday, which obviously are intended only to protect such interests of the state, or the community

---

prohibiting the blocking of public highways as a public nuisance statute; and one laying down rules of safety for the protection of the public or any class or group of individuals, as a negligence statute." Dart v. Pure Oil Co., 1947, 223 Minn. 526, 27 N.W.2d 555.

15. See Shroades v. Rental Homes, Inc., 1981, 68 Ohio St.2d 20, 427 N.E.2d 774 (landlord duty to repair). Compare Nazareno v. Urie, Alaska 1981, 638 P.2d 671 (tavernkeeper liable to third person for serving liquor to drunk), with Wright v. Moffitt, Del.1981, 437 A.2d 554 (tavernkeeper not liable to injured drunk). See generally Bob Godfrey Pontiac, Inc. v. Roloff, 1981, 291 Or. 318, 630 P.2d 840.

16. "We adopt the statutory test rather than that of the ordinarily prudent man as the more accurate one to determine negligence because the Legislature, by reason of its organization and investigating processes, is generally in a better position to establish such tests than are the judicial tribunals." Rudes v. Gottschalk, 1959, 159 Tex. 552, 324 S.W.2d 201.

17. Clinkscales v. Carver, 1943, 22 Cal.2d 72, 136 P.2d 777 (faulty publication); Comfort v. Penner, 1932, 166 Wash. 177, 6 P.2d 604 (municipal action contrary to statute); Sellman v. Haddock, 1959, 66 N.M. 206, 345 P.2d 416 (same); Geisking v. Sheimo, 1960, 252 Iowa 37, 105 N.W.2d 599 (same); Alviar v. Garza, Tex.Civ.App.1965, 387 S.W.2d 905, reversed on other grounds, 395 S.W.2d 821 (ordinance not complying with city charter). But see Enyart v. Blacketor, Ind.App.1976, 342 N.E.2d 654 (irregularly posted speed limit sign).

18. Black v. Stith, 1940, 164 Or. 117, 100 P.2d 485; Kern v. Autman, 1961, 54 Del. (4 Storey) 402, 177 A.2d 525. But see Hosein v. Checker Taxi Co., 1981, 95 Ill.App.3d 150, 50 Ill.Dec. 460, 419 N.E.2d 568 (requirement of bulletproof shield in taxis unconstitutionally vague).

19. Hopkins v. Droppers, 1924, 184 Wis. 400, 198 N.W. 738; Pelzer v. Lange, 1958, 254 Minn. 46, 93 N.W.2d 666.

20. Stafford v. Chippewa Valley Electric Railroad Co., 1901, 110 Wis. 331, 85 N.W. 1036; Sardo v. Herlihy, 1932, 143 Misc. 397, 256 N.Y.S. 690. The former Kentucky rule that violation of an ordinance is not even evidence of negligence may be traced to the speed limit of six miles an hour for trains in Louisville & Nashville Railroad Co. v. Dalton, 1897, 102 Ky. 290, 43 S.W. 431. See Note, 1947, 25 Tex.L.Rev. 286.

21. See generally Distad v. Cubin, Wyo.1981, 633 P.2d 167 (adopting Second Restatement of Torts, §§ 286–288C).

22. "Even if a defendant owes a duty to some one else, but does not owe it to the person injured, no action will lie. The duty must be due to the person injured. These principles are elementary, and are equally applicable, whether the duty is imposed by positive statute or is founded on general common-law principles." Mitchell, J., in Akers v. Chicago, Saint Paul, Minneapolis & Omaha Railway Co., 1894, 58 Minn. 540, 544, 60 N.W. 669, 670.

23. Cf. Merrill Lynch, Pierce, Fenner & Smith v. Curran, 1982, 456 U.S. 353, ___, 102 S.Ct. 1825, ___, 72 L.Ed.2d 182 (dissenting opinion).

at large, as public peace, morality and quiet, rather than the safety[24] of any particular class of individuals.[25] It follows that if a railroad violates such a statute, by running a train on Sunday, a private individual, as for example the owner of a cow killed on the track, cannot found an action upon that violation alone,[26] without other evidence of negligence. Likewise, ordinances which require householders to keep sidewalks in repair, or to remove snow and ice from them, are considered to be intended only for the benefit of the municipality, and not for any individual who may suffer a fall.[27] The same is often true as to the statutory duties of public officers.[28] The great weight of authority[29] has held that automobile registration statutes are for revenue purposes only and create only a public duty, and do not make the driver of an unlicensed car liable to those with whom he collides if he is otherwise exercising proper care.[30] A similar conclusion was reached by the Minnesota court in a case[31] involving a war-time speed limit intended to conserve gasoline.

The explanation quite often given in these cases is that the violation of the statute is not the proximate cause of the injury to the plaintiff.[32] In such a statement there is an obvious fallacy. In all such cases the act of the defendant has clearly caused the damage. If a train run on Sunday hits a cow, it cannot be said that the act of running the train did not have a real causal connection, and a very direct and important one, with the death of the cow; and Sunday, when the cow was there, is quite as relevant as would be, for example, the month of July or a given year. On the other hand the violation of the statute, as such, never kills a cow, since the same result would certainly follow if no statute existed.[33] When a car is driven without a license, the act of driving the car certainly causes a collision; the absence of the

---

24. See District of Columbia v. White, D.C.App. 1982, 442 A.2d 159; State of Indiana, Department of Natural Resources v. Morgan, 1982, ___ Ind.App. ___, 432 N.E.2d 59 (Strip Mining Law not a safety law); Wright v. Moffitt, Del.1981, 437 A.2d 554; Niemann v. Vermilion County Housing Authority, 1981, 101 Ill. App.3d 735, 57 Ill.Dec. 156, 428 N.E.2d 706 (housing assistance payment regulations not public safety measure); Richardson v. Dunbar, 1981, 95 Ill.App.3d 254, 50 Ill.Dec. 756, 419 N.E.2d 1205 (requirement that city officers discharge duties in good faith not a safety ordinance); Walker v. Bignell, 1981, 100 Wis.2d 256, 301 N.W.2d 447.

25. Second Restatement of Torts, § 288, Illustration 2. See Groh v. Hasencamp, Fla.App.1981, 407 So. 2d 949 (zoning ordinance; child kicked by horse).

26. Tingle v. Chicago, Burlington & Quincy Railroad Co., 1882, 60 Iowa 333, 14 N.W. 320. Cf. Platz v. City of Cohoes, 1882, 89 N.Y. 219; Hoadley v. International Paper Co., 1899, 72 Vt. 79, 47 A. 169.

27. Brown v. Kelly, 1964, 42 N.J. 362, 200 A.2d 781; Fitzwater v. Sunset Empire, Inc., 1972, 263 Or. 276, 502 P.2d 214. See Yanhko v. Fane, 1976, 70 N.J. 528, 362 A.2d 1, overruled, Stewart v. 104 Wallace St., Inc., 1981, 87 N.J. 146, 432 A.2d 881; Second Restatement of Torts, § 288, Comment b. But see Crago v. Lurie, 1980, ___ W.Va. ___, 273 S.E.2d 344 (owner, but not lessee, liable for injuries).

28. Routh v. Quinn, 1942, 20 Cal.2d 488, 127 P.2d 1; Strong v. Campbell, N.Y.1851, 11 Barb. 135. But where a ministerial duty obviously is imposed for the benefit of a particular class of persons, one within that class may found an action on the statute. Howley v. Scott, 1913, 123 Minn. 159, 143 N.W. 257; Harvey v. Board of Commissioners of Wabash County, 1981, ___ Ind.App. ___, 416 N.E.2d 1296; Indiana State Highway Commission v. Rickert, 1980, ___ Ind.App. ___, 412 N.E.2d 269, affirmed, 1981, ___ Ind. ___, 425 N.E.2d 620; Powell v. Village of Mount Zion, 1980, 88 Ill.App. 3d 406, 43 Ill.Dec. 525, 410 N.E.2d 525; Oleszczuk v. State, 1979, 124 Ariz. 373, 604 P.2d 637, 641 ("the more specific and narrow the duty required by the statute, the more likely it is that the duty has been narrowed from a general duty to the public to a specific duty to an individual").

29. Massachusetts formerly had a unique rule that the driver of an unregistered car was a "trespasser on the highway," who was liable for all injuries he caused, regardless of other fault, and could not recover himself except for injuries caused intentionally or recklessly. After Comeau v. Harrington, 1955, 333 Mass. 768, 130 N.E.2d 554, expressly disapproving of the rule, the legislature changed it in Mass.Laws 1959, c. 250.

30. Dervin v. Frenier, 1917, 91 Vt. 398, 100 A. 760; Opple v. Ray, 1935, 208 Ind. 450, 195 N.E. 81.

31. Cooper v. Hoeglund, 1946, 221 Minn. 446, 22 N.W.2d 450.

32. See Sheehan v. Janesville Auto Transport, 1981, 102 Ill.App.3d 507, 58 Ill.Dec. 189, 430 N.E.2d 131; Falvey v. Hamelburg, 1964, 347 Mass. 430, 198 N.E.2d 400; cf. Roos v. Loeser, 1918, 41 Cal.App. 782, 183 P. 204 (the case of the pampered, pedigreed, patrician Pomeranian pup).

33. Lowndes, Civil Liability Created by Criminal Legislation, 1932, 16 Minn.L.Rev. 361, 370; Green, Are There Dependable Rules of Causation, 1929, 77 U.Pa.L. Rev. 601, 618.

license, or the existence of the statute, of course does not. What the statute does, or does not do, is to condition the legality of the act, and to qualify or characterize it as negligent. Upon cause and effect it has no bearing at all. It is, of course, quite possible that the act or omission itself may have no sufficient causal connection with the result—a railway whistle means nothing to a cow.[34] But where such a connection is found, the only question concerning the statute is whether it is to be construed to afford protection against the conduct of the defendant, and so give the character of negligence to his act.

Class of Persons Protected

In many cases the evident policy of the legislature is to protect only a limited class of individuals. If so, the plaintiff must bring himself within that class in order to maintain an action based on the statute. Thus a factory act providing that dangerous machinery, or elevators, must be guarded, may be clearly intended only for the benefit of employees, and so afford no protection to others who enter the building.[35] Statutes requiring railroad trains to whistle for crossings are to protect those who are about to cross, and not parallel traffic,[36] and the ordinary rules of the highway may not be for the benefit of those on the sidewalk,[37] nor for a policeman pursuing a violator.[38] It has traditionally been held that regulations governing the condition of land or buildings are to protect only those who are rightfully upon the premises, and not trespassers.[39]

The class of persons to be protected may of course be a very broad one, extending to all those likely to be injured by the violation. Thus a statute requiring druggists to label poisons,[40] a pure food act,[41] a law prohibiting the sale of firearms to minors,[42] or an ordinance governing the servicing of gas lines,[43] must clearly be intended for the benefit of any member of the public who may be injured by the act or thing prohibited. Sometimes the courts have disagreed over a broad and a narrow construction of similar statutes, as where provisions requiring that parked cars shall be locked and the keys removed have been held to be intended,[44] and

---

34. Holman v. Chicago, Rock Island & Pacific Railway Co., 1876, 62 Mo. 562. On the causal requirement, see infra, p. 226.

35. Alsaker v. De Graff Lumber Co., 1951, 234 Minn. 280, 48 N.W.2d 431; Gibson v. Leonard, 1892, 143 Ill. 182, 32 N.E. 182. Cf. Davy v. Greenlaw, 1957, 101 N.H. 134, 135 A.2d 900; Whitman v. Campbell, Tex.Civ.App.1981, 618 S.W.2d 935 (elevator guarding rule does not require guarding open stairways).

36. Everett v. Great Northern Railway Co., 1907, 100 Minn. 309, 111 N.W. 281; Hutto v. Southern Railway Co., 1915, 100 S.C. 181, 84 S.E. 719; cf. Traylor v. Coburn, Tenn.App.1980, 597 S.W.2d 319 (requiring school bus to remain stationary until children crossed road not for benefit of child who usually did not cross road).

37. Westlund v. Iverson, 1922, 154 Minn. 52, 191 N.W. 253 (keep to right); Erickson v. Kongsli, 1952, 40 Wn.2d 79, 240 P.2d 1209 (building owner).

38. Hubbard v. Boelt, 1980, 28 Cal.3d 480, 169 Cal. Rptr. 706, 620 P.2d 156. But cf. Krueger v. City of Anaheim, 1982, 130 Cal.App.3d 166, 181 Cal.Rptr. 631 (security guard at baseball stadium injured by unruly fan included under "battery on a peace officer" criminal statute).

39. Flanagan v. Sanders, 1904, 138 Mich. 253, 101 N.W. 581; cf. Searcy v. Brown, Tex.Civ.App.1980, 607 S.W.2d 937 (dog at large statute not for benefit of uninvited person on owner's premises). Building codes are not for the protection of future owners who incur costs to bring the building into compliance. Iverson v. Solsbery, Colo.App.1982, 641 P.2d 314 (no negligence per se; but cause of action established nevertheless). But compare Ford v. Ja-Sin, Del.Super.1980, 420 A.2d 184 (landlord-tenant code should be construed broadly to cover tenant's guests).

40. Osborne v. McMasters, 1889, 40 Minn. 103, 41 N.W. 543.

41. Meshbesher v. Channellene Oil & Manufacturing Co., 1909, 107 Minn. 104, 119 N.W. 428.

42. Henningsen v. Markowitz, 1928, 132 Misc. 547, 230 N.Y.S. 313; Tamiami Gun Shop v. Klein, Fla.1959, 116 So.2d 421. But see Olson v. Ratzel, 1979, 89 Wis. 2d 227, 278 N.W.2d 238. See Note, 1960, 20 La.L.Rev. 797.

43. Knockum v. Amoco Oil Co., La.App.1981, 402 So.2d 90 (protected all persons lawfully on premises injured in explosion, not just customers of gas company).

44. Vining v. Avis Rent-A-Car Systems, Inc., Fla. 1977, 354 So.2d 54, on remand 355 So.2d 226, writ discharged 368 So.2d 346; Davis v. Thornton, 1970, 384 Mich. 138, 180 N.W.2d 11; Ney v. Yellow Cab Co., 1954, 2 Ill.2d 74, 117 N.E.2d 74.

not to be intended,[45] for the protection of a person run down by a thief escaping with a stolen car.[46]

The purpose of the legislation is of course a matter of interpretation of its terms, in the light of the evil to be remedied. The title, the provisions made, and the language used,[47] may indicate the object to be accomplished, which some courts require be quite specific,[48] and so no doubt may the records of the legislature itself.[49] The infinite variety of the statutes accounts for the typical lack of any general agreement as to their effect—as for example, as to whether OSHA regulations protect persons other than employees.[50]

Type of Risk Covered

The same limitation of the effect of the statute to accomplish only the supposed policy of the legislature is found in the overlapping requirement that the harm suffered must be of the kind which the statute was intended, in general, to prevent.[51] In the leading English case of Gorris v. Scott[52] the defendant violated a statute, obviously intended merely as a sanitation measure, which required carriers by water to provide separate pens for animals transported. As a result of this violation, the plaintiff's sheep were washed overboard during a storm at sea. It was held that, while there might have been recovery if the overcrowding had resulted in disease, no action for loss during the storm could be maintained, because "the damage is of such a nature as was not contemplated at all by the statute, and as to which it was not intended to confer any benefit on the plaintiffs."

The same principle runs through a great many cases. Statutes which limit the time during which railway trains may obstruct crossings usually are held to be intended to prevent delays of traffic, and so may give rise to an action for damages resulting from such delay,[53] but afford no protection against personal injuries caused by the position of the train.[54] Nor are railway fencing statutes designed to prevent a cow from eating

---

45. De Castro v. Boylan, La.App.1979, 367 So.2d 83, writ denied 369 So.2d 458 (policeman hit by thief); Bouldin v. Sategna, 1963, 71 N.M. 329, 378 P.2d 370; cf. Gmerek v. Rachlin, Fla.App.1980, 390 So.2d 1230 (5½ months after theft).

46. See generally Peck, An Exercise Based Upon Empirical Data: Liability for Harm Caused by Stolen Automobiles, 1969 Wis.L.Rev. 909; Annot., 1972, 45 A.L.R.3d 787 (liability for leaving key in ignition).

47. Board of Commissioners of Monroe County v. Hatton, 1981, ___ Ind.App. ___, 427 N.E.2d 696; Sheehan v. Janesville Auto Transport, 1981, 102 Ill. App.3d 507, 58 Ill.Dec. 189, 430 N.E.2d 131; see Wright v. Moffitt, Del.1981, 437 A.2d 554; Hamilton v. Green, 1976, 44 Ill.App.3d 987, 3 Ill.Dec. 565, 358 N.E.2d 1250 (plaintiff fell while chasing defendant's ducks that wandered in his yard; ducks not covered by prohibition of "geese" at large); Gerkin v. Santa Clara Valley Water District, 1979, 95 Cal.App.3d 1022, 157 Cal.Rptr. 612 (walking bike over bridge not "hiking" under recreational use statute).

48. See Reed v. Molnar, 1981, 67 Ohio St.2d 76, 423 N.E.2d 140; Nazareno v. Urie, Alaska 1981, 638 P.2d 671; Rimer v. Rockwell International Corp., 6th Cir. 1981, 641 F.2d 450, 454 (FAA directives requiring aircraft to be "airworthy" and imposing on pilot duty of determining whether "aircraft is in condition for safe flight," "provide only general standards of conduct; they do not impose a specific duty on a pilot to do a particular act," such as checking security of fuel cap);

Sego v. Mains, 1978, 41 Colo.App. 1, 578 P.2d 1069; Carter v. William Sommerville & Son, Inc., Tex.1979, 584 S.W.2d 274; District of Columbia v. White, D.C. App.1982, 442 A.2d 159.

49. Wright v. Moffitt, Del.1981, 437 A.2d 554.

50. Compare McKinnon v. Skil Corp., 1st Cir.1981, 638 F.2d 270 (not for benefit of consumers), with Dunn v. Brimer, 1976, 259 Ark. 855, 537 S.W.2d 164 (for benefit of other contractor's employees). Cf. Koll v. Manatt's Transportation Co., Iowa 1977, 253 N.W.2d 265; Annot., 1977, 79 A.L.R.3d 962.

51. Thayer, Public Wrong and Private Action, 1914, 27 Harv.L.Rev. 317, 335; Morris, The Relation of Criminal Statutes to Tort Liability, 1933, 46 Harv.L.Rev. 453, 473; Lowndes, Civil Liability Created by Criminal Legislation, 1932, 16 Minn.L.Rev. 361, 372; Second Restatement of Torts, § 286, Comment *i*.

52. 1874, L.R. 9 Ex. 125. The rule has been adopted by the Second Restatement of Torts, §§ 286, 288.

53. Patterson v. Detroit, Lansing & Northern Railroad Co., 1885, 56 Mich. 172, 22 N.W. 260; Terry v. New Orleans Great Northern Railroad Co., 1912, 103 Miss. 679, 60 So. 729.

54. Simpson v. Pere Marquette Railroad Co., 1936, 276 Mich. 653, 268 N.W. 769; Fox v. Illinois Central Railroad Co., 1941, 308 Ill.App. 367, 31 N.E.2d 805 Contra, Budkiewicz v. Elgin, Joliet & Eastern Railway Co., 1958, 238 Ind. 535, 150 N.E.2d 897. See Annot., 1962, 84 A.L.R.2d 813.

ing herself to death,[55] or regulations requiring landlords to heat premises intended to protect a child from burns from a portable electric heater.[56]

Ordinances regulating the place where vehicles may stop[57] or park[58] usually are not intended to prevent collisions or personal injuries to bus passengers, or to keep automobiles from running down pedestrians.[59] Most licensing statutes, such as those applicable to automobile drivers[60] or physicians,[61] have been construed as intended only for the protection of the public against injury at the hands of incompetents, and to create no liability where the actor is in fact competent but unlicensed. Particular statutes may, however, be construed as establishing a specific standard of competence, so that those who do not meet them are treated as negligent in acting at all.[62]

In determining whether the plaintiff's injury is within the "purpose" of the statute, three lines of approach can be discovered in the cases. Sometimes there is an exceedingly narrow and quite unreasonable interpretation, as in the Missouri case[63] where a requirement that emery wheels be hooded was held to be intended to guard only against the dust hazard, and not to prevent injuries to workmen's eyes. This sort of highly restrictive interpretation has become quite unfashionable in recent years.[64] A much more reasonable attitude is that of the New York court in a decision[65] holding that an act requiring elevator shafts to be guarded covered the risk of objects falling down the

---

55. Kansas, Oklahoma & Gulf Railway Co. v. Keirsey, Okl.1954, 266 P.2d 617.

56. Cook v. Seidenverg, 1950, 36 Wn.2d 256, 217 P.2d 799. See also Victory Sparkler & Specialty Co. v. Price, 1927, 146 Miss. 192, 111 So. 437 (sale of fireworks, eaten by child); Larrimore v. American National Insurance Co., 1939, 184 Okl. 614, 89 P.2d 340 (laying out rat poison, which exploded); Sinclair Prairie Oil Co. v. Stell, 1942, 190 Okl. 344, 124 P.2d 255 (decedent drowned in salt water from oil well); Belk v. Boyce, 1964, 263 N.C. 24, 138 S.E.2d 789 (cruelty to animals statute, man injured); Iverson v. Solsbery, Colo.App.1981, 641 P.2d 314 (building code violation, requiring subsequent owners to incur construction costs to comply); Groh v. Hasencamp, Fla.App.1981, 407 So. 2d 949 (zoning ordinance prohibiting horses; child kicked by horse).

57. Smith v. Portland Transaction Co., 1961, 226 Or. 221, 359 P.2d 899 (bus to discharge passengers at curb); Smith v. Virginia Transit Co., 1966, 206 Va. 951, 147 S.E.2d 110 (designated stopping point).

58. See Sheehan v. Janesville Auto Transport, 1981, 102 Ill.App.3d 507, 58 Ill.Dec. 189, 430 N.E.2d 131; Shelden v. Wichita Railroad & Light Co., 1928, 125 Kan. 476, 264 P. 732. Contra, Elliott v. Ditursi, 1971, 115 N.J.Super. 452, 280 A.2d 208.

59. See also Continental Oil Co. v. Simpson, Tex. Civ.App.1980, 604 S.W.2d 530, refused n.r.e. (railway commission rule requiring carrier to unload petroleum products concerned proper charge for service, not safety). Cf. Annot., 1968, 21 A.L.R.3d 989 (violation of size or weight restrictions).

60. Hertz Driv-Ur-Self System v. Hendrickson, 1942, 109 Colo. 1, 121 P.2d 483; Seaboard Coast Line R. Co. v. Zeigler, 1969, 120 Ga.App. 276, 170 S.E.2d 60; cf. Kempf v. Boehrig, 1980, 95 Wis.2d 435, 290 N.W.2d 562 (parent allowed incompetent and unlicensed child to drive). See Gregory, Breach of Criminal Licensing Statutes in Civil Litigation, 1951, 36 Corn.L.Q. 622.

Contra, Johnson v. Boston & Maine Railroad Co., 1928, 83 N.H. 350, 143 A. 516. Massachusetts refused to hold that the unlicensed driver, as distinguished from the unlicensed car, was a "trespasser on the highway," and treated such a violation merely as evidence of negligence. Bourne v. Whitman, 1911, 209 Mass. 155, 95 N.E. 404.

61. Brown v. Shyne, 1926, 242 N.Y. 176, 151 N.E. 197; Hardy v. Dahl, 1936, 210 N.C. 530, 187 S.E. 788; Janssen v. Mulder, 1925, 232 Mich. 183, 205 N.W. 159.

62. Andreen v. Escondido Citrus Union, 1928, 93 Cal.App. 182, 269 P. 556 (fumigation); Cragg v. Los Angeles Trust Co., 1908, 154 Cal. 663, 98 P. 1063 (elevator operator); Whipple v. Grandchamp, 1927, 261 Mass. 40, 158 N.E. 270 (medical); Monahan v. Devinny, 1928, 223 App.Div. 547, 229 N.Y.S. 60 (medical). Cf. Stocker v. Stitt, Colo.App.1982, 643 P.2d 793 (failure of licensed electrician to supervise unlicensed journeyman).

63. Mansfield v. Wagner Electric Manufacturing Co., 1922, 294 Mo. 235, 242 S.W. 400; Hatch v. Ford Motor Co., 1958, 163 Cal.App.2d 393, 329 P.2d 605 (prohibition of radiator ornaments on automobiles held not to protect child coming in contact with parked vehicle).

64. See, however, Christou v. Arlington Park—Washington Park Race Tracks Corp., 1982, 104 Ill.App. 3d 257, 60 Ill.Dec. 21, 432 N.E.2d 920 (care in incorporation of materials into building did not include care in selection). Sometimes the class is narrowly defined to permit an apparently deserving plaintiff to recover. See Freeman v. United States, 6th Cir.1975, 509 F.2d 626 (FAA regulation forbidding parachute jumping through clouds was for benefit of persons and property below, not parachutists; contributory negligence).

65. De Haen v. Rockwood Sprinkler Co., 1932, 258 N.Y. 350, 179 N.E. 764. See also Wildwood Mink Ranch v. United States, D.Minn. 1963, 218 F.Supp. 67 (low flight frightening mink).

shaft, to the effect that the accident need only be included within the same general risk, or class of risks, at which the statute is directed. Thus, in the absence of any other guide, a statute may well be assumed to include all risks that reasonably may be anticipated as likely to follow from its violation.[66] There are, however, occasional cases which have gone to an extreme, and apparently have included all risks which would occur to anyone as possible, following the violation.[67] A broad purpose of maximum protection, found as the basis of the statute, will of course encourage such an interpretation.[68]

Excused Violations

It is entirely possible that a criminal statute imposing no more than a small fine may be regarded as imposing an absolute duty, for the violation of which there is no recognized excuse, even in a tort action for large damages. But this is a matter of statutory interpretation. Moreover, a court may see fit to decide that strict liability in tort should be imposed on a defendant in a situation where the legislature has deemed it to be in the public interest to impose some kind of strict liability by way of the imposition of a small fine.

The legislature, within its constitutional powers, may see fit to place the burden of injuries "upon those who can measurably control their causes, instead of upon those who are in the main helpless in that regard."[69] In such a case the defendant may become liable on the mere basis of his violation of the statute. No excuse is recognized, and neither reasonable ignorance nor all proper care will avoid liability. Such a statute falls properly under the head of strict liability, rather than any basis of negligence—although the courts not infrequently continue, out of habit, to speak of the violation as "negligence per se."

Thus the Federal Safety Appliance Act, regulating the equipment of trains moving in interstate commerce, has been construed to impose such an absolute duty,[70] as have nearly all of the statutes prohibiting the employment of child labor,[71] many of the factory or scaffolding acts making specific requirements for the safety of employees,[72] various types of building regulations,[73] many of the pure food[74] cases in which the question has been decided, two or three statutes

---

66. See Note, 1935, 19 Minn.L.Rev. 666, 674.

67. See, for example, Ross v. Hartman, 1943, 78 U.S.App.D.C. 217, 139 F.2d 14; Ney v. Yellow Cab. Co., 1954, 2 Ill.2d 74, 117 N.E.2d 74.

68. See Brookins v. The Round Table, Inc., Tenn. 1981, 624 S.W.2d 547 (prohibiting sale of liquor to minors); Metropolitan Atlanta Rapid Transit v. Tuck, 1982, 163 Ga.App. 132, 292 S.E.2d 878 (public bus was "school bus," and thus required to display sign, since transporting school children was determinative factor in establishing schedule).

69. St. Louis, Iron Mountain & Southern Railway Co. v. Taylor, 1907, 210 U.S. 281, 28 S.Ct. 616, 52 L.Ed. 1061. This may be done even for criminal purposes. Cf. United States v. Park, 1975, 421 U.S. 658, 95 S.Ct. 1903, 44 L.Ed.2d 489.

70. O'Donnell v. Elgin, Joliet & Eastern Railway Co., 1949, 338 U.S. 384, 70 S.Ct. 200, 94 L.Ed.2d 187, rehearing denied 338 U.S. 984, 70 S.Ct. 427, 94 L.Ed.2d 583; Trout v. Pennsylvania Railroad Co., 3d Cir.1961, 300 F.2d 826. Accord, as to the Boiler Inspection Act, St. Louis Southwestern Railway Co. v. Williams, 5th Cir.1968, 397 F.2d 147.

71. See Vincent v. Riggi & Sons, Inc., 1972, 30 N.Y.2d 406, 334 N.Y.S.2d 380, 285 N.E.2d 380; Smith v. Uffelman, Tenn.App.1973, 509 S.W.2d 229; Second Restatement of Torts, § 288A, Comment c; Annot., 1974, 56 A.L.R.3d 1166 (lawn mowing in violation of child labor acts).

72. See Long v. Forest-Fehlhaber, Joint Venture, 1980, 74 A.D.2d 167, 427 N.Y.S.2d 649, reversed, 55 N.Y.2d 154, 448 N.Y.S.2d 132, 433 N.E.2d 115; Koenig v. Patrick Construction Corp., 1948, 298 N.Y. 313, 83 N.E.2d 133; Pankey v. Hiram Walker & Sons, S.D.Ill. 1958, 167 F.Supp. 609. But cf. Major v. Waverly & Ogden, Inc., 1960, 7 N.Y.2d 332, 197 N.Y.S.2d 165, 165 N.E.2d 181 (such effect cannot be given to administrative regulation, rather than statute).

73. Monsour v. Excelsior Tobacco Co., Mo.App. 1938, 115 S.W.2d 219. Occasionally other statutes have received a very strict construction which in effect eliminates most possible excuses. Cf. McDowell v. Federal Tea Co., 1941, 128 Conn. 437, 23 A.2d 512.

74. Coward v. Borden Foods, Inc., 1976, 267 S.C. 423, 229 S.E.2d 262; Taylor v. B. Heller & Co., 6th Cir. 1966, 364 F.2d 608.

Contra, Howson v. Foster Beef Co., 1935, 87 N.H. 200, 177 A. 656; Cheli v. Cudahy Brothers Co., 1934, 267 Mich. 690, 255 N.W. 414.

requiring effective brakes on vehicles operating on the public highway,[75] and others.[76]

These statutes are, however, the exception, and in the aggregate they make up only a very small percentage of the total safety legislation. Normally no such interpretation will be placed upon a statute, and no such conclusion reached, unless the court finds that it was clearly the purpose of the legislature.[77] In the ordinary case, all that is required is reasonable diligence to obey the statute,[78] and it frequently has been recognized that a violation of the law may be reasonable, and may be excused.[79] Although such cases often speak of a supposed intent and an "implied exception" which makes the statute inapplicable to the case even for criminal purposes,[80] they seem rather to indicate that, in the absence of a clear declaration by the legislature, the courts reserve the final authority to determine whether the civil standard of reasonable conduct will always require obedience to the criminal law.[81]

Thus it has been held not to be negligence to violate the letter of a statute because of physical circumstances beyond the driver's control, as where his lights suddenly go out on the highway at night [82] or, without prior negligence, his brakes fail[83] or his car crosses the center line of the highway.[84] The same is true where the driver's violation is due to innocent ignorance of the operative facts which make the statute applicable, as where the driver reasonably does not know that he is approaching an intersection or a railroad track.[85] Another valid excuse is that of emergency, as where one drives on the left because the right is blocked,[86] or a child dashes into the street,[87] or there is any other real necessity.[88] Undoubtedly there are even situations, such as that of the child,

---

75. Sikes v. McLean Trucking Co., La.App.1980, 383 So.2d 111; Albers v. Ottenbacher, 1962, 79 S.D. 637, 116 N.W.2d 529; Stump v. Phillians, 1965, 2 Ohio St.2d 209, 207 N.E.2d 762; Hamill v. Smith, 1964, 25 Conn. Sup. 183, 199 A.2d 343. Oregon held this in Nettleton v. James, 1958, 212 Or. 375, 319 P.2d 879, but retreated from the position in McConnell v. Herron, 1965, 240 Or. 486, 402 P.2d 726. See also Security Timber & Land Co. v. Reed, La.App.1981, 398 So.2d 174; cf. Maloney v. Rath, 1968, 69 Cal.2d 442, 71 Cal.Rptr. 897, 445 P.2d 513 (Traynor, C.J.) (no strict liability but duty was non-delegable). The great majority of states, however, allow an excuse. See Annots., 1971, 40 A.L.R.3d 9 (bad brakes); 38 A.L.R.3d 530 (violation of auto safety equipment statues).

76. See Seim v. Garavalia, Minn.1981, 306 N.W.2d 806 (dog bite statute); Zerby v. Warren, 1973, 297 Minn. 134, 210 N.W.2d 58 (sale of glue to minor).

77. Hammond v. Vestry of St. Pancras, 1874, L.R. 9 C.P. 319; Phillips v. Britannia Hygienic Laundry Co. [1923] 1 K.B. 539; Jenkins v. City of Fort Wayne, 1965, 139 Ind.App. 1, 210 N.E.2d 390.

78. Iudica v. De Nezzo, 1932, 115 Conn. 233, 161 A. 81; Romansky v. Cestaro, 1929, 109 Conn. 654, 145 A. 156.

79. See cases infra.

80. Second Restatement of Torts, § 288A; see Traynor, J., concurring in Satterlee v. Orange Glenn School District, 1947, 29 Cal.2d 581, 177 P.2d 279.

81. Morris, The Relation of Criminal Statutes to Civil Liability, 1933, 46 Harv.L.Rev. 453. Well stated in Phoenix Refining Co. v. Powell, Tex.Civ.App.1952, 251 S.W.2d 892, ref. n. r. e.

82. Brotherton v. Day & Night Fuel Co., 1937, 192 Wash. 362, 73 P.2d 788; Taber v. Smith, Tex.Civ.App. 1930, 26 S.W.2d 722.

83. Freund v. DeBuse, 1972, 264 Or. 447, 506 P.2d 491; Dayton v. Palmer, 1965, 1 Ariz.App. 184, 400 P.2d 855; Hills v. McGillvrey, 1965, 240 Or. 476, 402 P.2d 722. See Note, 1966, 45 Or.L.Rev. 156; Annots., 1971, 40 A.L.R.3d 9; 38 A.L.R.3d 530.

84. Herman v. Sladofsky, 1938, 301 Mass. 534, 17 N.E.2d 879 (skid); Wilson v. Wright, 1958, 52 Wn.2d 805, 329 P.2d 461 (hit chuck hole). Cf. Martinson v. Scherbel, 1964, 268 Minn. 509, 129 N.W.2d 802 (passing on right when car ahead stopped suddenly).

85. Winchell v. Detroit & Mackinac Railway Co., 1980, 102 Mich.App. 433, 301 N.W.2d 884 (driver did not know train approaching); Hullander v. McIntyre, 1960, 78 S.D. 453, 104 N.W.2d 40 (intersection); McEachern v. Richmond, 1957, 150 Cal.App.2d 546, 310 P.2d 122 (same); Johnson v. Chicago & Northwestern Railway Co., 1946, 71 S.D. 132, 22 N.W.2d 725 (grade crossing); cf. Gordon v. Hurtado, 1980, 96 Nev. 375, 609 P.2d 327 (reasonable person might be confused by location of traffic signals at intersection).

86. See Reuille v. Bowers, 1980, ___ Ind.App. ___, 409 N.E.2d 1144; NeSmith v. Bowden, 1977, 17 Wn.App. 602, 563 P.2d 1322.

87. Chase v. Tingdale Bros., 1914, 127 Minn. 401, 149 N.W. 654; R. & L. Transfer Co. v. State for Use of Schmidt, 1931, 160 Md. 222, 153 A. 87; cf. Byrne v. City & County of San Francisco, 1980, 113 Cal.App.3d 731, 170 Cal.Rptr. 302 (pedestrian darted from behind bus—excused).

88. Giancario v. Karabanowski, 1938, 124 Conn. 223, 198 A. 752 (useless steering gear); Seligmann v. Hammond, 1931, 205 Wis. 199, 236 N.W. 115 (blowout);

where it would be negligence as a matter of law to obey the literal terms of the statute at all.[89] There is respectable authority to the effect that at least a violation will be excused whenever it would be more dangerous to comply with the statute.[90] Although there are cases to the contrary,[91] the great majority of the cases have held that the immaturity of an infant can excuse him from a violation which would be negligence on the part of an adult.[92]

A troublesome problem is presented by the deplorable array of trivial, obsolete, or entirely unreasonable legislation, such as speed limits of six miles an hour, which persists in our statute books. Since no officer has the power to authorize a violation of the law, the fact that such a provision is not and never has been enforced,[93] or that it is customary to violate it,[94] cannot affect its validity; nor, of course, may the court declare that it is not the law. In several cases the courts have struggled hard to construe such a provision to require only reasonable conduct,[95] or have found that its unreasonableness makes it unconstitutional or otherwise invalid;[96] but in others they have considered that they had no alternative but to treat the violation as negligence.[97] But there is after all no compulsion by which a purely criminal statute must lead to any civil liability, and it is the court's own decision which brings about such a result; and, where such legislation clearly is utterly foolish, there seems to be no reason to ignore the fact that the community standard in fact permits a reasonable person to disobey it.[98]

Negligence Per Se and Evidence of Negligence

Once the statute is determined to be applicable—which is to say, once it is interpreted as designed to protect the class of persons, in which the plaintiff is included, against the

---

Martin v. Nelson, 1947, 82 Cal.App.2d 733, 187 P.2d 78 (result of collision). See also Turner v. Silver, 1978, 92 N.M. 260, 586 P.2d 1089; Porter v. Black, 1980, 205 Neb. 699, 289 N.W.2d 760 (burden of proof on unavoidability on defendant).

The emergency must of course be such that there is no reasonable opportunity to obey the statute. See Murray v. O & A Express, Inc., Tex.1982, 630 S.W.2d 633 (truck breakdown insufficient emergency to excuse failure to activate blinkers).

89. Sims v. Eleazar, 1921, 116 S.C. 41, 106 S.E. 854; Mora v. Favilla, 1921, 186 Cal. 199, 199 P. 17.

90. Hopson v. Goolsby, 1955, 196 Va. 832, 86 S.E.2d 149 (crossing street at point other than intersection); Tedla v. Ellman, 1939, 280 N.Y. 124, 19 N.E.2d 987 (walking on right side of highway where all heavy traffic on left); Cameron v. Stewart, 1957, 153 Me. 47, 134 A.2d 474 (walking on wrong side where sidewalk defective).

There is also authority that the violation will be excused where compliance with the statute would be simply foolish. Ridenhour v. Oklahoma Contracting Co., Mo.App.1932, 45 S.W.2d 108 (no lights in daylight); Sheehan v. Nims, 2d Cir.1935, 75 F.2d 293 (same); Simpson v. Miller, 1934, 97 Mont. 328, 34 P.2d 528 (no lights under street lamp).

91. See Enyart v. Blacketor, 1976, 168 Ind.App. 214, 342 N.E. 2d 654; Smith v. Diamond, 1981, ___ Ind.App. ___, 421 N.E.2d 1172; D'Ambrosio v. City of Philadelphia, 1946, 354 Pa. 403, 47 A.2d 256.

92. Rosenau v. City of Estherville, Iowa 1972, 199 N.W.2d 125; Ranard v. O'Neil, 1975, 166 Mont. 177, 531 P.2d 1000; Quillian v. Mathews, 1970, 86 Nev. 200, 467 P.2d 111; Daun v. Truax, 1961, 56 Cal.2d 647, 16 Cal.Rptr. 351, 365 P.2d 407; cf. Brookins v. The Round Table, Inc., Tenn.1981, 624 S.W.2d 547 (purchase of liquor by minor; contributory negligence). See generally Gray, The Standard of Care for Children Revisited, 1980, 45 Mo.L.Rev. 597, 604; Mertz, The Infant and Negligence Per Se in Pennsylvania, 1947, 51 Dick.L.Rev. 79.

93. Riser v. Smith, 1917, 136 Minn. 417, 162 N.W. 520; Day v. Pauly, 1925, 186 Wis. 189, 202 N.W. 363; Pitcher v. Lennon, 1896, 12 App.Div. 356, 42 N.Y.S. 156.

94. Stogdon v. Charleston Transit Co., 1944, 127 W.Va. 286, 32 S.E.2d 276; Sanchez v. J. Barron Rice, Inc., 1967, 77 N.M. 717, 427 P.2d 240. But cf. Castillo v. United States, 10th Cir.1977, 552 F.2d 1385 (may reduce evidentiary weight). See generally Annot., 1961, 77 A.L.R.2d 1327 (custom of motorists).

95. Lone Star Gas Co. v. Kelly, 1942, 140 Tex. 15, 165 S.W.2d 446, answer conformed to Tex.Civ.App., 166 S.W.2d 191; Nashville, Chattanooga & St. Louis Railway Co. v. White, 1929, 278 U.S. 456, 49 S.Ct. 189, 73 L.Ed. 452; Malloy v. New York Real Estate Association, 1898, 156 N.Y. 205, 50 N.E. 853.

96. Meyers v. Chicago, Rock Island & Pacific Railway Co., 1881, 57 Iowa 555, 10 N.W. 896. See Morris, The Role of Criminal Statutes in Negligence Actions, 1949, 49 Col.L.Rev. 21, 39–42.

97. Conrad v. Springfield Consolidated Railway Co., 1909, 240 Ill. 12, 88 N.E. 180; Riser v. Smith, 1917, 136 Minn. 417, 162 N.W. 520.

98. See Second Restatement of Torts, § 286, Comment d.

risk of the type of harm which has in fact occurred as a result of its violation—and once its breach has been established,[99] probably a majority of the courts hold that the issue of negligence is thereupon conclusively determined, in the absence of sufficient excuse, and that the court must so direct the jury.[1] The standard of conduct is taken over by the court from that fixed by the legislature, and "jurors have no dispensing power by which to relax it," [2] except insofar as the court may recognize the possibility of a valid excuse in a tort action for damages for disobedience of the criminal law. This usually is expressed by saying that the unexcused violation is negligence "per se," or in itself. The effect of such a rule is to stamp the defendant's conduct as negligence, with all of the effects of common law negligence, but with no greater effect.[3] There will still remain open such questions as the causal relation between the violation and the harm to the plaintiff,[4] and, in the ordinary case, the defenses of contributory negligence,[5] and assumption of the risk.[6] There are, however, statutes, such as the child labor laws,[7] so clearly intended to protect a particular class of persons against their own inability to protect themselves, that the policy of the legislature is interpreted to mean that even such defenses are not available.[8] California has adopted a possibly lower standard by holding that the violation creates a presumption of negligence, which may be rebutted by a showing of an adequate justification.[9]

A large number of courts have held that a violation is only evidence of negligence, or prima facie evidence thereof, which may be accepted or rejected according to all of the evidence.[10] Many courts, even some that follow the per se approach as to statutes,

---

99. See Fontanne v. Federal Paper Board Co., 1982, 105 Ill.App.3d 306, 61 Ill.Dec. 178, 434 N.E.2d 331 (contributory negligence; jury could find no violation); Salinero v. Pon, 1981, 124 Cal.App.3d 120, 177 Cal.Rptr. 204 (no violation).

1. Martin v. Herzog, 1920, 228 N.Y. 164, 126 N.E. 814; Hardaway v. Consolidated Paper Co., 1962, 366 Mich. 190, 114 N.W.2d 236; see Murray v. O & A Express, Inc., Tex.1982, 630 S.W.2d 633; Nazareno v. Urie, Alaska 1981, 638 P.2d 671; Second Restatement of Torts, § 288B.

2. Cardozo, J., in Martin v. Herzog, 1920, 228 N.Y. 164, 126 N.E. 814.

3. See generally Seim v. Garavalia, Minn.1981, 306 N.W.2d 806.

4. Peterson v. Taylor, Iowa 1982, 316 N.W.2d 869 (child played with gas not in red can; no causation); Hartenbach v. Johnson, Mo.App.1982, 628 S.W.2d 684 (whether violation of federal lighting requirements would have prevented boating collision at night; for jury); Nazareno v. Urie, Alaska 1981, 638 P.2d 671 (whether tavernkeeper sold drinks to intoxicated patron, and whether such drinks caused dance floor collision, were for jury); Board of Commissioners of Monroe County v. Hatton, 1981, ___ Ind.App. ___, 427 N.E.2d 696 (cutting weeds on blind curve would not have prevented accident); Hansen v. Washington Natural Gas Co., 1981, 95 Wn.2d 773, 632 P.2d 504 (warning sign of street construction would not have helped pedestrian who saw it anyway); Knockum v. Amoco Oil Co., La.App.1981, 402 So.2d 90 (servicing improperly installed LP gas system caused explosion); Slicer v. Quigley, 1980, 180 Conn. 252, 429 A.2d 855 (furnishing liquor to intoxicated minor driver not proximate cause of accident); Olson v. Ratzel, 1979, 89 Wis.2d 227, 278 N.W.2d 238 (sale of gun to minor; proximate cause).

5. See generally Prosser, Contributory Negligence as a Defense to Violation of a Statute, 1948, 32 Minn.L. Rev. 105; infra, § 65.

6. See infra, § 68. Cf. Armstrong v. Mailand, Minn.1979, 284 N.W.2d 343 ("primary" assumption of risk).

7. See Vincent v. Riggi & Sons, Inc., 1972, 30 N.Y.2d 406, 334 N.Y.S.2d 380, 285 N.E.2d 689; infra, § 68.

8. See John's Pass Seafood Co. v. Weber, Fla.App. 1979, 369 So.2d 616 (landlord's failure to provide fire extinguishers); Lomayestewa v. Our Lady of Mercy Hospital, Ky.1979, 589 S.W.2d 885 (failure to screen psychiatric ward window).

9. Salinero v. Pon, 1981, 124 Cal.App.3d 120, 177 Cal.Rptr. 204 (citing Evidence Code § 669, and listing the four "basic facts" that must be shown for presumption statute to apply: (1) violation; (2) violation proximate cause of injury; (3) injury of type statute designed to prevent; and (4) plaintiff as member of class statute enacted to protect). The presumption may be rebutted if the violator shows "that he did what might reasonably be expected of a person of ordinary prudence, who desired to comply with the law * * *." Byrne v. City & County of San Francisco, 1980, 113 Cal.App.3d 731, 170 Cal.Rptr. 302.

10. See Allen v. Dhuse, 1982, 104 Ill.App.3d 806, 60 Ill.Dec. 559, 433 N.E.2d 356, 360 (contributory negligence; rebuttable "by proof that the party acted reasonably under the circumstances despite the violation"); Hall v. Warren, Utah 1981, 632 P.2d 848 (violation "prima facie evidence" of negligence); Shatz v. TEC Technical Adhesives, 1980, 174 N.J.Super. 135, 415 A.2d 1188; cf. Reuille v. Bowers, 1980, ___ Ind. App. ___, 409 N.E.2d 1144; Zeni v. Anderson, 1976, 397

have held that the breach of ordinances,[11] or traffic laws,[12] or the regulations of administrative bodies,[13] even though the latter are authorized by statute, is only evidence for the jury. Such cases seem to indicate a considerable distrust of the arbitrary character of the provision, and a desire to leave some leeway for cases where its violation may not be necessarily unreasonable.[14] Even in such jurisdictions, however, it is recognized that there are cases[15] in which, merely as a matter of evidence, reasonable persons could not fail to agree that the violation is negligence.

If the statute is construed as not covering the plaintiff, or the particular type of harm, many courts have held that its violation is not even evidence of negligence, and can have no effect on liability at all.[16] Obviously such a result is called for in the case of such statutes as the Sunday blue laws, which do not purport to protect anyone, or to set any standard of care. But the existence of a statute does not prevent an action for common law negligence; and where the statute does set up standard precautions, although only for the protection of a different class of persons, or the prevention of a distinct risk, this may be a relevant fact, having proper bearing upon the conduct of a reasonable person under the circumstances, which the jury should be permitted to consider. There is, in other words, a statutory custom, which is entitled to admission as evidence.[17] Thus a statute requiring hogs to be fenced in with a fence of specified build and strength, in order to prevent misbreeding, is some indication of the kind of fence required to keep the hogs out of the way of automobiles.

The arbitrary classification of all breaches of statute as negligence per se or no negligence at all leaves too little flexibility for the standard of reasonable care.[18]

Violation by Plaintiff

Where it is the plaintiff himself who violates the statute, a slightly different problem is presented. In early cases, a few courts, influenced by the idea that no person should be permitted to base a cause of action upon his own illegal conduct,[19] held that

---

Mich. 117, 243 N.W.2d 270 (prima facie evidence—full discussion).

11. See Carlock v. Westchester Lighting Co., 1935, 268 N.Y. 345, 197 N.E. 306, reversed 242 App.Div. 778, 274 N.Y.S. 580; Brown v. South Broward Hospital District, Fla.App.1981, 402 So.2d 58; Crago v. Lurie, 1980, ___ W.Va. ___, 273 S.E.2d 344; cf. Fitch v. Adler, 1981, 51 Or.App. 845, 627 P.2d 36 (failure to comply with ordinance was nonfeasance and hence not actionable).

12. See Janssen v. Neal, Minn.1977, 256 N.W.2d 292 (statutory exception to general rule); Silvia v. Pennock, 1962, 253 Iowa 779, 113 N.W.2d 749; deJesus v. Seaboard Coast Line R. Co., Fla.1973, 281 So.2d 198 (dictum); cf. Reuille v. Bowers, 1980, ___ Ind.App. ___, 409 N.E.2d 1144; Hartman v. Brady, 1978, 201 Neb. 558, 270 N.W.2d 909. But see Stanfield v. Laccoarce, 1978, 284 Or. 651, 588 P.2d 1271 (negligence as a matter of law); Freese v. Lemmon, Iowa 1978, 267 N.W.2d 680.

13. See Castillo v. United States, 10th Cir. 1977, 552 F.2d 1385 (outmoded VA regulations); Stepanek v. Kober Construction, Mont.1981, ___ Mont. ___, 625 P.2d 51; Beals v. Walker, 1980, 98 Mich. 214, 296 N.W.2d 828; cf. Distad v. Cubin, Wyo.1981, 633 P.2d 167. Sometimes the violation is held to be negligent per se. See Weeks v. Prostrollo Sons, Inc., 1969, 84 S.D. 243, 169 N.W.2d 725; Kelley v. Howard S. Wright Construction Co., 1978, 90 Wn.2d 323, 582 P.2d 500.

Possibly the answer depends upon the importance and standing of an administrative agency. See Wilson v. Piper Aircraft Corp., 1978, 282 Or. 61, 577 P.2d 1322; Morris, The Role of Administrative Safety Measures in Negligence Actions, 1949, 28 Tex.L.Rev. 143.

14. See Morris, The Relation of Criminal Statutes to Civil Liability, 1933, 46 Harv.L.Rev. 453; James, Statutory Standards and Negligence in Accident Cases, 1950, 11 La.L.Rev. 95.

15. Cantwell v. Cermins, 1941, 347 Mo.App. 836, 149 S.W.2d 343; Wojtowicz v. Belden, 1942, 211 Minn. 461, 1 N.W.2d 409.

16. DiCaprio v. New York Central Railroad Co., 1921, 231 N.Y. 94, 131 N.E. 746; Mansfield v. Wagner Electric Manufacturing Co., 1922, 294 Mo. 235, 242 S.W. 400; Carter v. Redmond, 1920, 142 Tenn. 258, 218 S.W. 217. See Distad v. Cubin, Wyo.1981, 633 P.2d 167 (state hospital regulations).

17. See Second Restatement of Torts, § 288B(2). Compare, as to subsequent statutes, not retroactive, Geisking v. Sheimo, 1960, 252 Iowa 37, 105 N.W.2d 599; Gann v. Keith, 1952, 151 Tex. 626, 253 S.W.2d 413; Mitchell v. Emblade, 1956, 80 Ariz. 398, 298 P.2d 1034; Note, 1966, 51 Iowa L.Rev. 1148. Cf. Cowan v. Laughridge Construction Co., 1982, 57 N.C.App. 357, 291 S.E.2d 287 (OSHA regulations).

18. See Morris, The Relation of Criminal Statutes to Civil Liability, 1933, 46 Harv.L.Rev. 453.

19. See Davis, The Plaintiff's Illegal Act as a Defense in Actions of Tort, 1905, 18 Harv.L.Rev. 505; Thayer, Public Wrong and Private Action, 1914, 27

a plaintiff who was violating the criminal law, as by driving on Sunday, could not recover for any injury that the driver might sustain while so engaged.[20] The former Massachusetts rule, that the driver of an unregistered automobile was a trespasser on the highway who had no right of action, may be traced to such an early Sunday law decision.[21] But with few exceptions, the courts have long since discarded the doctrine that any violator of a statute is an outlaw with no rights against anyone, and have recognized that, except in so far as the violator must resort to an illegal contract[22] or an illegal status[23] as the basis of the defendant's duty to him, one who violates a criminal statute is not deprived of all protection against the torts of others. Thus the Sunday driver[24] or the unlicensed operator[25] of an unlicensed car,[26] although he is a criminal, can recover for his injuries if in other respects he is exercising proper care.

The accepted rule now is that a breach of statute by the plaintiff is to stand on the same footing as a violation by the defendant.[27] A few courts have held that the plaintiff's breach does not constitute contributory negligence as a matter of law, upon the ground that the statutes were enacted for the protection of others, and not of the actor himself.[28] But it seems clear that safety statutes, such as speed laws and traffic rules,[29] usually are designed for the broad purpose of preventing accidents or dangerous situations,[30] in which the plaintiff is quite as likely to be hurt as the defendant; and it is not difficult to discover a purpose to protect the plaintiff by setting up a standard of his own conduct, the unexcused violation of which is negligence per se,[31] or evidence of negligence,[32] as the jurisdiction may provide. If, as is frequently the case, the statute is found to be intended solely for the protection of other persons,[33] or the prevention of a different type of risk,[34] the breach will be irrelevant, or at best evidence of neg-

Harv.L.Rev. 317, 338; Note, 1926, 39 Harv.L.Rev. 1088.

20. Bosworth v. Inhabitants of Swansey, 1845, 51 Mass. (10 Metc.) 363; Johnson v. Irasburgh, 1874, 47 Vt. 28; Hinckley v. Penobscot, 1856, 42 Me. 89.

21. See Note, 1933, 46 Harv.L.Rev. 319; Altshuler, Use and Operation of Automobiles in Violation of Statute, 1930, 10 Boston U.L.Rev. 211.

22. Cf. McNeill v. Durham & Charlotte Railroad Co., 1903, 132 N.C. 510, 44 S.E. 34, reversed on rehearing, 1904, 135 N.C. 682, 47 S.E. 765. See Note, 1933, 13 Bos.U.L.Rev. 365.

23. Cf. Illinois Central Railroad Co. v. Messina, 1916, 240 U.S. 395, 36 S.Ct. 368, 60 L.Ed. 709; Wickenburg v. Minneapolis, St. Paul & Sault Ste. Marie Railroad Co., 1905, 94 Minn. 276, 102 N.W. 713; Texas-Louisiana Power Co. v. Daniels, 1936, 127 Tex. 126, 91 S.W.2d 302.

24. Platz v. City of Cohoes, 1882, 89 N.Y. 219; Hoadley v. International Paper Co., 1899, 72 Vt. 79, 47 A. 169. See also Bagre v. Daggett Chocolate Co., 1940, 126 Conn. 659, 13 A.2d 757 (winning candy box in bingo game does not bar recovery for negligence in manufacture).

25. Kurtz v. Morse Oil Co., 1932, 114 Conn. 336, 158 A. 906; Speight v. Simonsen, 1925, 115 Or. 618, 239 P. 542. But cf. Johnson v. Boston & Maine Railroad, 1928, 83 N.H. 350, 143 A. 516.

26. Armstead v. Lounsberry, 1915, 129 Minn. 34, 151 N.W. 542; Muller v. West Jersey & Sea Shore Railroad Co., 1923, 99 N.J.L. 186, 122 A. 693; Cobb v. Cumberland County Power & Light Co., 1918, 117 Me. 455, 104 A. 844.

27. Second Restatement of Torts, § 469; see Mechler v. McMahon, 1931, 184 Minn. 476, 239 N.W. 605, overruling a line of cases to the contrary.

28. See Dohm v. R. N. Cardozo & Bro., 1925, 165 Minn. 193, 206 N.W. 377; Watts v. Montgomery Traction Co., 1912, 175 Ala. 102, 106, 57 So. 471.

29. Henthorne v. Hopwood, 1959, 218 Or. 336, 338 P.2d 373, rehearing denied 218 Or. 336, 345 P.2d 249; Leap v. Royce, 1955, 203 Or. 566, 279 P.2d 887; see Byrne v. City and County of San Francisco, 1980, 113 Cal.App.3d 731, 170 Cal.Rptr. 302 (pedestrian leaving place of safety without precautions).

30. Second Restatement of Torts, § 469.

31. See Kimery v. Public Service Co. of Oklahoma, Okla.1980, 622 P.2d 1066; Burrow v. Jones, 1981, 51 N.C.App. 549, 277 S.E.2d 97; Carmichael v. Lexington-Fayette Urban County Government, Ky.App.1980, 608 S.W.2d 66.

32. Allen v. Dhuse, 1982, 104 Ill.App.3d 806, 60 Ill. Dec. 559, 433 N.E.2d 356.

33. Kline v. Pennsylvania Railroad Co., 6th Cir. 1925, 9 F.2d 290; Dohm v. R. N. Cardozo & Bro., 1925, 165 Minn. 193, 206 N.W. 377.

34. Salvitti v. Throppe, 1942, 343 Pa. 642, 23 A.2d 445; Chattanooga Railway & Light Co. v. Bettis, 1918, 139 Tenn. 332, 202 S.W. 70.

ligence for the jury.[35] The assertion that in such cases the breach of statute is not the proximate cause of the harm has no more validity here than in the case of a violation on the part of the defendant.[36]

Compliance with Statute

Where the violation of a criminal statute is negligence, it does not follow that compliance with it is always due care. While compliance with a statutory standard is evidence of due care, it is not conclusive on the issue. Such a standard is no more than a minimum, and it does not necessarily preclude a finding that the actor was negligent in failing to take additional precautions.[37] Thus the requirement of a hand signal on a left turn does not mean that the legislature has conferred immunity upon a driver who is otherwise negligent in making the turn, and that the driver is absolved from all obligation to slow down, keep a proper lookout, and proceed with reasonable care.[38] The same is of course true of administrative regulations.[39] Where there is a normal situation, clearly identical with that contemplated by the statute or regulation, and no special circumstances or danger are involved, it may be found, and can be ruled as a matter of law,

that the actor has done his full duty by complying with the statute, and nothing more is required. Thus a railroad may not be required to protect a country crossing, with an unobstructed view, which is little used, by anything more than the statutory warning sign.[40] But if there are unusual circumstances, or increased danger beyond the minimum which the statute was designed to meet, it may be found that there is negligence—and perhaps even recklessness [41]—in not doing more.[42]

WESTLAW REFERENCES

restatement /5 torts /5 285 286

Persons and Risks Included

snow ice /p violat! /p statute* ordinance* /p negligen!

Class of Persons Protected

minor* eighteen /p firearm* gun* /p violat! /p statute* ordinance* /p negligen!

Type of Risk Covered

rail! /p crossing* /p violat! /p statute* ordinance* /p negligen!

Excused Violation

headnote(emergen! /p violat! /p statute* ordinance* /p negligen!)

Negligence Per Se and Evidence of Negligence

di negligence per se

---

35. Corbett v. Scott, 1926, 243 N.Y. 66, 152 N.E. 467; Dohm v. R. N. Cardozo & Bro., 1925, 165 Minn. 193, 206 N.W. 377.

36. Green, Contributory Negligence and Proximate Cause, 1927, 6 N.C.L.Rev. 3, 13.

37. Christou v. Arlington Park-Washington Park Race Tracks Corp., 1982, 104 Ill.App.3d 257, 60 Ill.Dec. 21, 432 N.E.2d 920; Hill v. Husky Briquetting, Inc., 1974, 54 Mich.App. 17, 220 N.W.2d 137, affirmed 393 Mich. 136, 223 N.W.2d 290, appeal after remand 78 Mich.App. 452, 260 N.W.2d 131; Jonescue v. Jewel Home Shopping Service, 1973, 16 Ill.App.3d 339, 306 N.E.2d 312; Second Restatement of Torts, § 288C.

38. Curtis v. Perry, 1933, 171 Wash. 542, 18 P.2d 840. Cf. Mitchell v. Hotel Berry Co., 1929, 34 Ohio App. 259, 171 N.E. 39 (requirements as to hotel exits in case of fire); Caviote v. Shea, 1933, 116 Conn. 569, 165 A. 788 (parking car on highway in fog with tail light on); Peterson v. Salt River Project Agricultural Improvement & Power District, 1964, 96 Ariz. 1, 391 P.2d 567 (red flag on end of towed long pole).

39. Berkebile v. Brantley Helicopter Corp., 1971, 219 Pa.Super. 479, 281 A.2d 707; Wilson v. Piper Aircraft Corp., 1978, 282 Or. 61, 577 P.2d 1322, rehearing denied 282 Or. 411, 579 P.2d 1287; Stevens v. Parke, Davis, & Co., 1973, 9 Cal.3d 51, 107 Cal.Rptr. 45, 507 P.2d 653.

40. Leisy v. Northern Pacific Railway Co., 1950, 230 Minn. 61, 40 N.W.2d 626; Gigliotti v. New York, Chicago & St. Louis Railroad Co., 1958, 107 Ohio App. 174, 157 N.E.2d 447 (ordinary crossing with ordinary hazard). See Annot., 1949, 5 A.L.R.2d 112.

41. See Gryc v. Dayton-Hudson Corp., Minn.1980, 297 N.W.2d 727, certiorari denied 449 U.S. 921, 101 S.Ct. 320, 66 L.Ed.2d 149 (punitive damages allowed despite compliance with Flammable Fabrics Act). In most contexts, however, compliance with a statutory standard should bar liability for punitive damages. See generally Owen, Problems in Assessing Punitive Damages Against Manufacturers of Defective Products, 1982, 49 U.Chi.L.Rev. 1, 41–42.

42. Koch v. Southern Pacific Transportation Co., 1976, 274 Or. 499, 547 P.2d 589; Grand Trunk Railway Co. v. Ives, 1892, 144 U.S. 408, 12 S.Ct. 679, 36 L.Ed. 485; New York Central Railroad Co. v. Chernew, 8th Cir. 1960, 285 F.2d 189; Southern Pacific Railroad Co. v. Mitchell, 1956, 80 Ariz. 50, 292 P.2d 827. See Morris, The Role of Criminal Statutes in Negligence Actions, 1949, 49 Col.L.Rev. 21, 42.

Violation by Plaintiff
plaintiff /s violat! /s statute /s bar bars barred barring /s recovery

Compliance with Statute
comply! compliance /p statute* ordinance* /p due reasonable /2 care % fail! /5 comply! compliance

Chapter 6

NEGLIGENCE: PROOF

Table of Sections

Sec.
37. Functions of Court and Jury.
38. Burden of Proof and Presumptions.
39. Circumstantial Evidence—Res Ipsa Loquitur.
40. Res Ipsa Loquitur—Procedural Effect.

§ 37. Functions of Court and Jury

The existence of negligence in a particular case is sometimes said to be a mixed question of law and fact.[1] By this it is meant, not only that both the court and the jury have an important part to play in the determination of the issue, and that separate functions are assigned to each, but further, that these functions to some extent overlap, and that it is not easy to fix any definite line of demarcation.[2] It is said also that the court must decide questions of law, and the jury questions of fact.[3] But this means little or nothing until some method of classification is provided, by which "law" may be distinguished from "facts," and the division of functions between court and jury is a matter rather of historical origins and present policy than of any such definitions.[4]

The issue of negligence may be divided into five more or less distinct sub-issues as to which the court and the jury have separate parts to play in reaching a decision. These are as follows:

1. *The Sufficiency of the Evidence to Permit a Finding of the Facts.* Before any duty, or any standard of conduct, may be set, there must first be proof of facts which give rise to it; and once the standard is fixed, there must be proof that the actor has

§ 37

1. Parlato v. Connecticut Transit, 1980, 181 Conn. 66, 434 A.2d 322; Morgan v. Pennsylvania General Insurance Co., 1979, 87 Wis.2d 723, 275 N.W.2d 660; Waterbury v. Byron Jackson, Inc., 5th Cir. 1978, 576 F.2d 1095; Miller v. United States, 9th Cir. 1978, 587 F.2d 991.

2. Bohlen, Mixed Questions of Law and Fact, 1924, 72 U.Pa.L.Rev. 111, 112; James, Functions of Judge and Jury in Negligence Cases, 1949, 58 Yale L.J. 667. There are particularly good discussions of detail in Weiner, The Civil Jury Trial and the Law-Fact Distinction, 1966, 54 Cal.L.Rev. 1867; Baer, The Relative Roles of Legal Rules and Non-Legal Factors in Accident Litigation, 1952, 31 N.C.L.Rev. 46.

3. Stated in the negative by Lord Coke: "Ad questiones facti non respondent judices; ad questiones legis non respondent juratores." 8 Coke 308; Coke on Littleton, 1633, 295.

4. See James, Functions of Judge and Jury in Negligence Cases, 1949, 58 Yale L.J. 667; Thayer, Law and Fact in Jury Trials, 1890, 4 Harv.L.Rev. 147; Smith, Judges and Justice—The Judge's Role in Personal Injury Cases, [1962] U.Ill.L.Forum 172; Green, Juries and Justice—The Jury's Role in Personal Injury Cases, [1962] U.Ill.L.Forum 152.

235

departed from it. If it be assumed that the driver of an automobile approaching a visible intersection will be required to moderate his speed, there is still the question whether the intersection was visible, and whether the driver did in fact slow down. These are purely questions of fact, and within the recognized province of the jury as the triers of fact. But over such questions of fact the courts always have reserved a preliminary power of decision, as to whether the issue shall be submitted to the jury at all. If the evidence is such that no reasonably intelligent person would accept it as sufficient to establish the existence of a fact essential to negligence, it becomes the duty of the court to remove the issue from the jury, and to nonsuit the plaintiff, or to direct a verdict for the defendant, or to set aside a verdict once rendered.[5] This is, of course, merely a part of the law of evidence and civil procedure, and in this respect negligence cases do not differ from other cases where essential facts must be proved.

2. *The Weight of the Evidence as Establishing the Facts.* Once it is determined that reasonable persons may differ as to whether a fact has been proved, the probative value of the evidence, and the conclusions to be drawn from it, lies in the hands of the jury. They must not only decide as to the credibility of the testimony, but draw or refuse to draw any inferences from the testimony as to which there may be reasonable difference of opinion.[6] In this respect again, negligence cases do not differ from any others.

3. *The Existence of a Duty.* In other words, whether, upon the facts in evidence, such a relation exists between the parties that the community will impose a legal obligation upon one for the benefit of the other—or, more simply, whether the interest of the plaintiff which has suffered invasion was entitled to legal protection at the hands of the defendant. This is entirely a question of law, to be determined by reference to the body of statutes, rules, principles and precedents which make up the law; and it must be determined only by the court.[7] It is no part of the province of a jury to decide whether a manufacturer of goods is under any obligation for the safety of the ultimate consumer, or whether the Long Island Railroad is required to protect Mrs. Palsgraf from fireworks explosions.[8] A decision by the court that, upon any version of the facts, there is no duty, must necessarily result in judgment for the defendant. A decision that, if certain facts are found to be true, a duty exists, leaves open the other questions now under consideration.

4. *The General Standard of Conduct.* As will be seen hereafter,[9] this is the necessary complement of duty. In negligence cases, once a duty is found, the duty, in theory at least, always requires the same standard of conduct, that of a reasonable person under the same or similar circumstances [10]— except perhaps in those jurisdictions where statutory or common law modifications have recognized "degrees" of care, and a higher or lower standard in particular cases.[11] Since the standard is a legal rule, from which the jury are not free to deviate, it is a matter of law, and is to be applied by the court. Almost invariably this application takes the form of an instruction to the jury

---

5. Thayer, Preliminary Treatise on Evidence, 1898, 185, 202; Wigmore, Evidence, 3d ed. 1940, § 2494; James, Functions of Judge and Jury in Negligence Cases, 1949, 58 Yale L.J. 667, 672–675; Second Restatement of Torts, § 328B, Comment *d*.

6. Second Restatement of Torts, § 328C.

7. "Hence it becomes imperative before legal liability for conceded damages can be imposed upon a defendant, for the court in the first instance to inquire and determine the character of the duty which the law under the facts imposed upon the defendant as the basis of liability; for manifestly it cannot be conceded that the jury from their inner consciousness may evolve in every variety of tort-feasance a legal duty as the standard of liability." Minturn, J., in Morril v. Morril, 1928, 104 N.J.L. 557, 142 A. 337, 339. See Green, Judge and Jury, 1930, 55; Second Restatement of Torts, § 328B(b). But cf. Bennett v. Span Industries, Inc., Tex.Civ.App.1981, 628 S.W.2d 470.

8. See infra, § 43.

9. Infra, § 53.

10. See supra, § 32.

11. See supra, § 34.

declaring, briefly or more fully,[12] a formula such as that of the reasonable person of ordinary prudence. There is room for considerable skepticism as to how far such instructions are understood by the average jury, or have any weight with them,[13] but they represent the attempt, so far as is reasonably possible, to enlighten the layman's ignorance of the law, and to impose a social, rather than an individual, standard.[14]

5. *The Particular Standard of Conduct.* Since it is impossible to prescribe definite rules in advance for every combination of circumstances which may arise, the details of the standard must be filled in in each particular case. The question then is what the reasonable person would have done under the circumstances. Under our system of procedure, this question is to be determined in all doubtful cases by the jury, because the public insists that its conduct be judged in part by the man in the street rather than by lawyers, and the jury serves as a shock-absorber to cushion the impact of the law.[15]

The question usually is said to be one of fact, but it should be apparent that the function of the jury in fixing the standard differs from that of the judge only in that it cannot be reduced to anything approaching a definite rule.[16]

In many cases, however, the court may be required to remove the issue of the particular standard from the jury. It is possible to say, in many cases, that the conduct of the individual clearly has or has not conformed to what the community requires, and that no reasonable jury could reach a contrary conclusion. The court must then direct a verdict for the plaintiff or for the defendant, or even set aside a verdict once rendered; or, if the evidence as to the facts is in conflict, instruct the jury as to the conclusion it must draw from a particular version of the facts.[17] Thus the court may rule that it is necessarily negligence to drive across a railway track without stopping to look and listen,[18] to cross the street without looking,[19] or to walk

---

12. An early scholarly attempt at an elaborate instruction is that of Rosenberry, C. J., in Osborne v. Montgomery, 1931, 203 Wis. 223, 234 N.W. 372, inspired by the Restatement of Torts:

"Every person is negligent when, without intending to do any wrong, he does such an act or omits to take such precaution that under the circumstances he, as an ordinarily prudent person, ought reasonably to foresee that he will thereby expose the interests of another to an unreasonable risk of harm. In determining whether his conduct will subject the interests of another to an unreasonable risk of harm, a person is required to take into account such of the surrounding circumstances as would be taken into account by a reasonably prudent person and possess such knowledge as is possessed by an ordinarily reasonable person and to use such judgment and discretion as is exercised by persons of reasonable intelligence under the same or similar circumstances."

13. See Farley, Instructions to Juries—Their Role in the Judicial Process, 1932, 42 Yale L.J. 194; Elwork, Sales & Alfini, Juridic Decisions—In Ignorance of the Law or in Light of It, 1977, 1 Law & Human Behav. 163; Notes, 1980, 82 W.Va.L.Rev. 555, 574 (empirical analysis); 1981, 59 Or.L.Rev. 451. See generally The American Jury System: Final Report, 1977.

14. See Green, The Negligence Issue, 1928, 37 Yale L.J. 1029, reprinted in Green, Judge and Jury, 1930, 153–185; James, Functions of Judge and Jury in Negligence Cases, 1949, 58 Yale L.J. 667, 680–685.

15. Bohlen, Mixed Questions of Law and Fact, 1924, 72 U.Pa.L.Rev. 111, 116; Second Restatement of Torts, § 328C(b), Comment b. See Food Pageant, Inc. v. Consolidated Edison Co., Inc., 1981, 54 N.Y.2d 167, 445 N.Y.S.2d 60, 429 N.E.2d 738 (gross negligence); Havas v. Victory Paper Stock Co., 1980, 49 N.Y.2d 381, 426 N.Y.S.2d 233, 402 N.E.2d 1136, on remand 77 A.D.2d 698, 430 N.Y.S.2d 404.

16. See Bohlen, Mixed Questions of Law and Fact, 1924, 72 U.Pa.L.Rev. 111, 115, describing the function as "administrative." Also Weiner, The Civil Nonjury Trial and the Law-Fact Distinction, 1967, 55 Cal.L.Rev. 1021.

17. See Smith, The Power of a Judge to Direct a Verdict, 1924, 24 Col.L.Rev. 111; Twerski, Seizing the Middle Ground Between Rules and Standards in Design Defect Litigation: Advancing Directed Verdict Practice in the Law of Torts, 1982, 57 N.Y.U.L.Rev. 521.

18. Baltimore & Ohio Railroad Co. v. Goodman, 1927, 275 U.S. 66, 48 S.Ct. 24, 72 L.Ed. 167; Renfro v. Fox, Ky.1967, 418 S.W.2d 761; Alley v. Chicago, Rock Island & Pacific Railway Co., 1973, 213 Kan. 457, 516 P.2d 967; see supra, § 35.

19. Fennell v. Miller, 1978, 94 Nev. 528, 583 P.2d 455; Hrabik v. Gottsch, 1977, 198 Neb. 86, 251 N.W.2d 672; cf. Crawford v. Johnson, 1978, 219 Va. 9, 244 S.E.2d 752.

into the side of a passing automobile,[20] to drive at such a speed that it is impossible to stop within the range of vision,[21] or to ride with a driver who is known to be drunk;[22] or that it is not negligence to fail to take precautions which no reasonable person would consider necessary under the circumstances.[23] Particularly where the standard of conduct is taken from a statute, many courts rule that a departure from it ordinarily is negligence in itself.[24] An uneasy distrust of the jury, and of the layman's known propensity to be charitable with other people's money and to compensate any injury which has occurred, especially at the expense of corporations, has played no small part in this process by which "learned reason"[25] and the greater experience of the judge[26] are substituted for the opinion of twelve more or less good persons and true.[27]

While the function of the court, then, is primarily to determine the law, it must also decide some questions of fact, as to whether the evidence makes an issue sufficient for the jury; and the function of the jury in fixing the standard of reasonable conduct is so closely related to law that it amounts to a mere filling in of the details of the legal standard.

Courts seldom divide the issue of negligence into such separate questions. The most common statement is that if reasonable persons may differ as to the conclusion to be drawn, the issue must be left to the jury; otherwise it is for the court.[28]

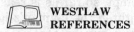

272k136(2)
topic(negligence torts "products liability") /p function purpose /9 jury
topic(negligence torts "products liability") & function /s jury /s question* /s law fact

The Sufficiency of the Evidence to Permit a Finding of the Facts
topic(272 313a 379) & opinion(sufficien** /s evidence /s finding /s facts)
topic(272 313a 379) /p province /3 jury

The Weight of the Evidence as Establishing the Facts
topic(272 313a 379 /p weight +3 evidence)

The Existence of a Duty
topic(272 313a 379) /p duty /p exist! /p relation!

The General Standard of Conduct
topic(272 313a 379) /p standard +2 conduct /p duty
topic(272 313a 379) /p degree +3 care
topic(272 313a 379) /p standard* /s reasonable +2 man

The Particular Standard of Conduct
topic(272 313a 379) /p reasonable /s person* /s differ

---

20. Iwata v. Champine, 1968, 74 Wn.2d 844, 447 P.2d 175; Leslie-Four Coal Co. v. Brock, Ky.1961, 343 S.W.2d 820.

21. Cunningham v. Baltimore & Ohio Railroad Co., 1975, 25 Md.App. 253, 334 A.2d 120; Greenwade v. Drake, 1979, 202 Neb. 815, 277 N.W.2d 248.

22. Harlow v. Connelly, Ky.App.1977, 548 S.W.2d 143.

23. See Wasson v. Brewer's Food Mart, Inc., 1982, 7 Kan.App.2d 259, 640 P.2d 352 (falling bottles); Pratt v. Freese's, Inc., Me.1981, 438 A.2d 901 (elevator closed on plaintiff's arm); Akins v. Glens Falls City School District, 1981, 53 N.Y.2d 325, 441 N.Y.S.2d 644, 424 N.E.2d 531 (4-3) (foul baseball injured spectator; limited fencing sufficient); Beals v. Walker, 1980, 98 Mich. App. 214, 296 N.W.2d 828; Seaboard Coast Line Railroad Co. v. Griffis, Fla.Dist.App.1979, 381 So.2d 1063.

24. See Wendland v. Ridgefield Construction Services, Inc., 1981, 184 Conn. 173, 439 A.2d 954; supra, § 36.

25. Allen, Learned and Unlearned Reason, 1924, 36 Jurid.Rev. 254, 262.

26. Holmes, The Common Law, 1881, 124.

27. Bohlen, Mixed Questions of Law and Fact, 1924, 72 U.Pa.L.Rev. 111, 118.

28. See Fay v. Kroblin Refrigerated Xpress, Inc., Colo.App.1981, 644 P.2d 68; Bordynoski v. Bergner, 1982, 97 Wn.2d 335, 644 P.2d 1173 (contributory negligence); Hartenbach v. Johnson, Mo.App.1982, 628 S.W.2d 684 (contributory negligence); Armstrong v. Industrial Electric & Equipment Service, App.1981, 97 N.M. 272, 639 P.2d 81; Dizco, Inc. v. Kenton, 1981, 210 Neb. 141, 313 N.W.2d 268; Lenz v. Ridgewood Associates, 1981, 55 N.C.App. 115, 284 S.E.2d 702; Brookins v. The Round Table, Inc., Tenn.1981, 624 S.W.2d 547; Donta v. Harper, 1981, ___ W.Va. ___, 283 S.E.2d 921; Graves v. North Shore Gas Co., 1981, 98 Ill.App.3d 964, 54 Ill.Dec. 376, 424 N.E.2d 1279; Eddy v. Syracuse University, 1980, 78 A.D.2d 989, 433 N.Y.S.2d 923; Hooks v. Southern California Permanente Medical Group, 1980, 107 Cal.App.3d 435, 165 Cal.Rptr. 741 (foreseeability of risk); Maxwell v. Colburn, 1980, 105 Cal.App. 3d 180, 163 Cal.Rptr. 912.

§ 38. Burden of Proof and Presumptions

Under our adversary system of litigation, which requires that all evidence be produced by the parties themselves, some method must be found to dispose of those cases in which the evidence is so inadequate, or so conflicting, that neither party can satisfy the triers of fact as to the truth of his version of the case. Someone must lose. This "risk of non-persuasion"[1] is called the burden of proof. It is of practical importance in relatively few cases, since few cases ever are so evenly balanced as to require decision on any such basis; but it often appears in instructions to the jury, based upon the possibility that such may be the case.

In civil suits, unlike criminal prosecutions, the burden of proof does not require that the jury be convinced beyond all reasonable doubt, but only that they be persuaded that a preponderance of the evidence is in favor of the party sustaining the burden.[2] This is true as to the issue of negligence, even though the act to be proved may also be a crime.[3] The burden of proof of the defendant's negligence is quite uniformly upon the plaintiff,[4] since he is asking the court for relief, and must lose if his case does not outweigh that of the defendant's. Notwithstanding a great deal of confused language in the opinions, even in bailment cases the prevailing view is that the burden of persuasion remains upon the plaintiff throughout the case, although the burden of going forward with the evidence on due care will shift to the bailee once the plaintiff has shown his delivery of the property to the bailee in good condition and its loss or return in a damaged condition.[5] So, too, does the burden of proof (as distinguished from the burden of going forward with the evidence) appear to remain on the carrier in a case brought by an injured passenger,[6] although in both carrier[7] and bailment[8] cases the plaintiff may be aided by a presumption. It is generally agreed, however, that a carrier of goods, who is an insurer against everything but a few exceptional perils, has the burden of proving its freedom from negligence and

---

§ 38

1. Wigmore, Evidence, 3d ed. 1940, § 2485. See Cleary et al., McCormick on Evidence, 2d ed. 1972, ch. 36; Dworkin, Easy Cases, Bad Law, and Burdens of Proof, 1972, 25 Vand.L.Rev. 1151; Winter, The Jury and The Risk of Nonpersuasion, 1971, 5 Law & Soc. Rev. 335; Note, 1975, 21 Loy.L.Rev. 377.

2. Cleary et al., McCormick on Evidence, 2d ed. 1972, § 339.

3. Galloway v. United Railroads of San Francisco, 1921, 51 Cal.App. 575, 197 P. 663; Grella v. Lewis Wharf Co., 1912, 211 Mass. 54, 97 N.E. 745.

4. Brantley v. Stewart Building & Hardware Supplies, Inc., 1982, 274 Ark. 555, 626 S.W.2d 943; Buckelew v. Grossbard, 1981, 87 N.J. 512, 435 A.2d 1150; Reece Construction Co., Inc., v. State Highway Commission, 1981, 6 Kan.App.2d 188, 627 P.2d 361; Smartt v. Lamar Oil Co., Colo.App.1980, 623 P.2d 73; Pickett v. First American Savings & Loan Association, 1980, 90 Ill.App.3d 245, 45 Ill.Dec. 531, 412 N.E.2d 1113.

5. See Singer Co. v. Stott & Davis Motor Express, Inc., 1981, 79 A.D.2d 227, 436 N.Y.S.2d 508; Roberts v. Mitchell Brothers Truck Lines, 1980, 289 Or. 119, 611 P.2d 297; Soby Construction, Inc. v. Skjonsby Truck Line, Inc., N.D.1979, 275 N.W.2d 336; McKissick v. R. Connelly Jewelers, Inc., 1979, 41 N.C.App. 152, 254 S.E.2d 211; Compton v. Daniels, 1978, 98 Idaho 915, 575 P.2d 1303; Nash v. City of North Platte, 1977, 198 Neb. 623, 255 N.W.2d 52, appeal after remand 1980, 205 Neb. 480, 288 N.W.2d 51. There is considerable confusion in many of the opinions between the burdens of going forward and of persuasion.

Louisiana and Georgia by statute place the burden of proof upon the bailee. See Harper v. Brown & Root, Inc., La.1980, 391 So.2d 1170, on remand, La.App.1981, 398 So.2d 94; Ga. Code Ann. § 44–12–44. Cf. Reserve Insurance Co. v. Gulf Florida Terminal Co., Fla.1980, 386 So.2d 550 (statutory burden on bailee for losses under $10,000; discussion of UCC § 7–403(1)(b)). See generally Sweet, Burden of Proof of Bailee's Negligence in Connection with His Failure to Redeliver, 1957, 8 Hast.L.J. 89; Brodkey, Practical Aspects of Bailment Proof, 1962, 45 Marq.L.Rev. 531.

6. Cf. Hunziker v. Scheidemantle, 3d Cir. 1976, 543 F.2d 489 (aircraft); Latendresse v. Marra, 1977, 49 Ill. App.3d 266, 7 Ill.Dec. 664, 364 N.E.2d 955 (taxi; no presumption of negligence); Kazales v. Minto Leasing, Inc., 1978, 61 A.D.2d 1039, 403 N.Y.S.2d 286 (burden to go forward with proof on taxi owner); Transit Casualty Co. v. Puchalski, Fla.Dist.App.1980, 382 So.2d 359 (bus); Note, 1966, 42 Wash.L.Rev. 273.

7. Transit Casualty Co. v. Puchalski, Fla.Dist.App. 1980, 382 So.2d 359 (changing rule); Dunn v. Trans World Airlines, Inc., 9th Cir. 1978, 589 F.2d 408 (Warsaw Convention).

8. New Mexico Feeding Co., Inc., v. Keck, 1981, 95 N.M. 615, 624 P.2d 1012; Compton v. Daniels, 1978, 98 Idaho 915, 575 P.2d 1303; Weinberg v. D–M Restaurant Corp., 1977, 60 A.D.2d 550, 400 N.Y.S.2d 524.

that the loss or damage to the goods falls within one of the exceptions,[9] after which the burden returns to the plaintiff to show that the carrier was actually negligent.[10]

In some types of cases, such as those of medical malpractice,[11] where laymen on the jury are not competent to judge whether the actor's conduct meets the proper standard, expert testimony may be essential, and the burden of proof cannot be sustained without it.[12]

Presumptions

The party having the burden of proof may be aided by the procedural devices known as presumptions. A presumption has been defined as "an assumption of the existence of one fact which the law requires the trier of fact to make on account of the existence of another fact or group of facts, standing alone." [13] It is, in other words, a rule of law for the determination of a question of fact, in the absence of sufficient evidence to prove the fact itself. The classic illustration of a presumption is the rule which calls for the conclusion that a person is dead when it is shown that the person has disappeared for seven years without explanation. The nature and effect of presumptions is a matter of vigorous controversy, which lies beyond the scope of this text. Courts and writers have not agreed as to the precise meaning of the term in all respects, or as to the procedural effect which is to follow when a presumption is found.[14]

There is, however, general agreement that presumptions are rules of law, and their application is for the court. Probably the greater number of presumptions are created merely for the purpose of giving effect, as a settled rule, to the normal inference or conclusion which most people would draw, if permitted, from a given set of facts, in the absence of satisfactory definite evidence as to the conclusion itself. Most of the presumptions associated with negligence are of this kind: for example, the presumptions, often stated, that a person is in possession of normal faculties and reason,[15] and that the instinct of self-preservation has made the person exercise proper care for his own safety.[16] Such presumptions require that in

---

9. Codified in the Carmack Amendment to the Interstate Commerce Act. See Plough, Inc. v. Mason & Dixon Lines, 6th Cir. 1980, 630 F.2d 468; Faribault Woolen Mill Co. v. Chicago Rock Island & Pacific Railway Co., Minn.1979, 289 N.W.2d 126; Reese v. Midland Empire Packing Co., 1981, ___ Mont. ___, 628 P.2d 289.

10. Oakland Meat Co. v. Railway Express Agency, Inc., 1964, 46 Ill.App.2d 176, 196 N.E.2d 361; Stroh Brewery Co. v. Grand Trunk Western Railway Co., E.D.Mich.1981, 513 F.Supp. 827 (Carmack Amendment). Compare Charles J. Miller, Inc. v. McClung-Logan Equipment Co., 1978, 40 Md.App. 585, 392 A.2d 1153 (bailment).

11. See supra, § 32.

12. See District of Columbia v. White, D.C.App. 1982, 442 A.2d 159 (quality of police detective's training); Bartak v. Bell-Galyardt & Wells, Inc., 8th Cir. 1980, 629 F.2d 523 (architectural malpractice). Compare Kennedy v. Ricker, 1979, 119 N.H. 827, 409 A.2d 778 (Douglas, J.) (expert funeral director testimony not required concerning necessity of giving instructions on method of carriage to carriers of handleless casket).

13. Morgan, Some Observations Concerning Presumptions, 1931, 44 Harv.L.Rev. 906.

14. Ladd, Presumptions in Civil Actions, 1977 Ariz. St.L.J. 275; Louisell, Construing Rule 301: Instructing the Jury on Presumptions in Civil Actions and Proceedings, 1977, 63 Va.L.Rev. 281; Mueller, Instructing the Jury Upon Presumptions in Civil Cases: Comparing Federal Rule 301 and Uniform Rule 301, 1977, 12 Land & Water L.Rev. 219; Cleary, Presuming and Pleading: An Essay on Juristic Immaturity, 1979 Ariz.St.L.J. 115, reprinting 1959, 12 Stan.L.Rev. 5; Hecht & Pinzler, Rebutting Presumptions: Order Out of Chaos, 19—, 58 B.U.L.Rev. 527. Note, 1981, 45 Alb.L.Rev. 1079. "One ventures the assertion that 'presumption' is the slipperiest member of the family of legal terms, except its first cousin, 'burden of proof.'" Cleary et al., McCormick on Evidence, 2d ed. 1972, § 342.

15. Brown v. Union Pacific Railroad Co., 1910, 81 Kan. 701, 106 P. 1001; Kramm v. Stockton Electric Railroad Co., 1909, 10 Cal.App. 271, 101 P. 914; cf. Fouche v. Masters, 1980, 47 Md.App. 11, 420 A.2d 1279 (statutory blood alcohol level intoxication presumptions apply only to criminal prosecutions, not to civil actions).

16. Omaha National Bank v. Omaha Public Power District, 1980, 186 Neb. 6, 180 N.W.2d 229 (only in absence of evidence); Baltimore & Potomac Railroad Co. v. Landrigan, 1903, 191 U.S. 461, 24 S.Ct. 137, 48 L.Ed. 262; see Addair v. Bryant, 1981, ___ W.Va. ___, 284 S.E.2d 374; Miller v. Fogleman Truck Lines, Inc., La. App.1981, 398 So.2d 634, writ denied, La., 401 So.2d 358 (only applicable if no eyewitnesses); Bethay v. Philadelphia Housing Authority 1979, 271 Pa.Super. 366, 413 A.2d 710; cf. Reuter v. United States, W.D.Pa. 1982, 534 F.Supp. 731 (presumption that person who was killed or lost memory acted with due care); City &

the absence of evidence to the contrary, the court must decide the issue and direct the jury. They place upon the adverse party the "burden" of going forward and offering further evidence, in the sense that a verdict will be directed against the person if he does not; but they do not affect the ultimate burden of proof, as to the preponderance of the total evidence required, once all the evidence is in. When persuasive evidence to the contrary is introduced, the occasion for the presumptions, as rules of law, is gone, and they simply cease to exist, "like bats of law flitting in the twilight, but disappering in the sunshine of actual facts." [17] All that remains is whatever inference from ordinary experience is to be drawn from the facts, which has whatever probative value the facts may justify.[18]

There are, however, other presumptions which obviously are imposed in part as a matter of policy, to compel persons in a position of special responsibility to disclose evidence within their control, under penalty of a procedural disadvantage in the case if they do not.[19] They are, in other words, "smoking out" presumptions, designed to bring about a result rather than to give effect to probabilities.[20] Such, for example, are the presumptions that when goods are delivered to a bailee in good condition, and are either not returned or returned in bad condition, the loss or damage is due to the negligence of the bailee;[21] that when a passenger is injured by a cause within the carrier's control, the carrier has been negligent;[22] and that when goods are damaged in transit over a series of carriers, the last carrier has caused the damage.[23] Quite frequently careless use of language, or genuine confusion, has led to a statement of such presumptions in terms of a "burden of proof" upon the defendant, rather than the mere "burden" of going forward with the production of evidence under penalty of a direction on the issue.[24] Some writers have contended that the policy underlying such presumptions can only be carried out by allowing them to persist in the face of contrary evidence, or by shifting the burden of proof to the adverse party and requiring a preponderance of the evidence to overthrow the presumption.[25] Others consider that the policy may be sufficiently served by instructing the jury that they must apply the presumption unless they believe the contrary evidence.[26] The

County of Denver v. De Long, 1976, 190 Colo. 219, 545 P.2d 154 (amnesia provided no contrary proof); Buckelew v. Grossbard, 1981, 87 N.J. 512, 435 A.2d 1150 (presumption against ordinary negligence); Moreno v. Herrera, 1968, 260 Cal.App.2d 418, 67 Cal.Rptr. 151 (same; amnesia victim); Annot., 1978, 88 A.L.R.3d 622 (amnesia victims).

17. Lamm, J., in Mockowik v. Kansas City, St. Joseph & Council Bluffs, Railroad Co., 1906, 196 Mo. 550, 571, 94 S.W. 256.

18. Wigmore, Evidence, 3d ed. 1940, § 2491; McGlynn v. Newark Parking Authority, 1981, 86 N.J. 551, 432 A.2d 99.

19. McGlynn v. Newark Parking Authority, 1981, 86 N.J. 551, 432 A.2d 99.

20. The basic idea is set forth at length in Jaffe, Res Ipsa Loquitur Vindicated, 1951, 1 Buff.L.Rev. 1.

21. McGlynn v. Newark Parking Authority, 1981, 86 N.J. 551, 432 A.2d 99 (car parked in enclosed garage); Garlock v. Multiple Parking Services, Inc., 1980, 103 Misc.2d 943, 427 N.Y.S.2d 670 (same); see supra, note 8.

22. Williams v. Spokane Falls & Northern Railway Co., 1905, 39 Wash. 77, 80 P. 1100, reversed 42 Wash. 597, 84 P. 1129, rehearing denied 1906, 44 Wash. 363, 87 P. 491; Galland v. New Orleans Public Service, Inc., La.1979, 377 So.2d 84; cf. Latendresse v. Marra, 1977, 49 Ill.App.3d 266, 7 Ill.Dec. 664, 364 N.E.2d 955.

23. Trans World Airlines, Inc. v. Alitalia-Linee Aeree Airlines, 1978, 85 Cal.App.3d 185, 149 Cal.Rptr. 411 (federal common law); Orient Overseas Line v. Globemaster Baltimore, Inc., 1976, 33 Md.App. 372, 365 A.2d 325.

24. Cf. Holmes v. Harden, 1957, 96 Ga.App. 365, 100 S.E.2d 101; Central Mutual Insurance Co. v. Whetstone, 1957, 249 Minn. 334, 81 N.W.2d 849. Or the converse, by characterizing the plaintiff's burden of proof on negligence in terms of a presumption. See Buckelew v. Grossbard, 1981, 87 N.J. 512, 435 A.2d 1150; Holmes v. Gamble, Colo.App.1980, 624 P.2d 905, affirmed 655 P.2d 405.

25. Morgan, Some Observations Concerning Presumptions, 1931, 44 Harv.L.Rev. 906; Bohlen, The Effect of Rebuttable Presumptions of Law Upon the Burden of Proof, 1920, 68 U.Pa.L.Rev. 307.

26. McBaine, Presumptions: Are They Evidence, 1938, 26 Cal.L.Rev. 519. Cf. McCormick, Charges on Presumptions and Burden of Proof, 1927, 5 N.C.L.Rev. 291.

writers, if not all of the courts, seem to have agreed that in any case a presumption, as a rule of law applied in the absence of evidence, is not itself evidence, and can no more be balanced against evidence than two and a half pounds of sugar can by weighed against half-past two in the afternoon.

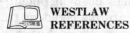
WESTLAW REFERENCES

topic(272 313a 379) /p "risk of nonpersuasion"
topic(272 313a 379) & preponderance +5 evidence

Presumptions
313ak97
topic(313a) /p "burden of proof"
272k121.1(4)
313ak75
57k89
(negligence torts "product* liability" /p statutory +3 presumption

§ 39. Circumstantial Evidence—Res Ipsa Loquitur

It is often said that negligence must be proved, and never will be presumed.[1] The mere fact that an accident or an injury has occurred, with nothing more, is not evidence of negligence on the part of anyone.[2] The fact that a man is found dead upon a railway track after a train has passed is no proof that the train was run without proper care.[3] There is of course, as a matter of speculation, sufficiently interesting in itself, always the possibility that the man may have been killed by reason of negligent operation of the train; but for a decision imposing liability to respond in damages, this is not enough. What is required is evidence, which means some form of proof; and it must be evidence from which reasonable persons may conclude that, upon the whole, it is more likely that the event was caused by negligence than that it was not. As long as the conclusion is a matter of mere speculation or conjecture,[4] or where the probabilities are at best evenly balanced between negligence and its absence,[5] it becomes the duty of the court to direct the jury that the burden of proof has not been sustained.

This does not mean, however, that there must be in every case eye-witnesses of the defendant's conduct. Negligence, like any other fact, may be proved by circumstantial evidence.[6] This is evidence of one fact, or of a set of facts, from which the existence of the fact to be determined may reasonably be inferred.[7] It involves, in addition to the assertion of witnesses as to what they have observed, a process of reasoning, or inference, by which a conclusion is drawn. Thus it may be reasonable to infer, from skid marks or other traces of an accident, that an automobile was driven at excessive speed;[8] from the usual operation of lights that they were turned out by those who had done so before;[9] or from the fact that soon after the

---

§ 39

1. Burrows v. Jacobsen, 1981, 209 Neb. 778, 311 N.W.2d 880; Northwestern Equipment Inc. v. Cudmore, N.D.1981, 312 N.W.2d 347.

2. District of Columbia v. Cooper, D.C.App.1982, 445 A.2d 652; Strick v. Stutsman, Mo.App.1982, 633 S.W.2d 148; Hamil v. Bashline, 1978, 481 Pa. 256, 392 A.2d 1280; Barcia v. Estate of Keil, La.App.1982, 413 So.2d 241; Jolley v. General Motors Corp., 1982, 55 N.C.App. 383, 285 S.E.2d 301.

3. Johnson v. Mobile & Ohio Railroad Co., 1917, 178 Ky. 108, 198 S.W. 538.

4. Haidri v. Egolf, 1982, ___ Ind.App. ___, 430 N.E.2d 429; Jones v. Tarrant Utility Co., Tex.App.1981, 626 S.W.2d 912, reversed, 638 S.W.2d 862; Jolley v. General Motors Corp., 1982, 55 N.C.App. 383, 285 S.E.2d 301.

5. Strick v. Stutsman, Mo.App.1982, 633 S.W.2d 148; American Village Corp. v. Springfield Lumber & Building Supply, 1974, 269 Or. 41, 522 P.2d 891.

6. Wigmore, Evidence, 3d ed. 1940, § 25.

7. Dixon v. Gaso Pump & Burner Manufacturing Co., 1937, 183 Okl. 249, 80 P.2d 678; Loveland v. Nelson, 1926, 235 Mich. 623, 209 N.W. 835.

8. Penzin v. Stratton, 1975, 26 Ill.App.3d 475, 325 N.E.2d 732 (length of skid marks); Yates v. Chappell, 1965, 263 N.C. 461, 139 S.E.2d 728 (position of cars, violence of impact, extent of damage); Gutierrez v. Public Service Interstate Transportation Co., 2d Cir. 1948, 168 F.2d 678 (fender of bus bent, plaintiff in gutter with torn trousers and smear of grease); cf. Silverman v. General Motors Corp., 1981, 99 Ill.App.3d 593, 54 Ill. Dec. 882, 425 N.E.2d 1099 (black residue on drum showed brakes had been applied).

9. Korel v. United States, 4th Cir. 1957, 246 F.2d 424.

passage of a train a fire started up beside the track, that it was caused by negligence in controlling sparks from the train.[10]

Defense counsel in criminal cases have long made us familiar with the weaknesses of some kinds of circumstantial evidence; but there is still no person who would not accept dog tracks in the mud against the sworn testimony of a hundred eye-witnesses that no dog has passed by. Like all other evidence, it may be strong or weak; it may be so unconvincing as to be quite worthless, or it may be irresistible and overwhelming.[11] The gist of it, and the key to it, is the inference, or process of reasoning by which the conclusion is reached. This must be based upon the evidence given, together with a sufficient background of human experience to justify the conclusion. It is not enough that plaintiff's counsel can suggest a possibility of negligence. The evidence must sustain the burden of proof by making it appear more likely than not. The inference must cover all of the necessary elements of negligence,[12] and must point to a breach of the defendant's duty. The mere fact of the presence of a banana peel on a floor may not be sufficient to show that it has been there long enough for reasonable care to require the defendant to discover and remove it,[13] but if it is "black, flattened out and gritty,"[14] the conclusion may reasonably be drawn. It is for the court to determine, in the first instance, whether reasonable persons on the jury may draw it.[15]

One type of circumstantial evidence, concerning which there has been much difference of opinion, is that which is given the name of res ipsa loquitur.[16] The Latin phrase, which means nothing more than "the thing speaks for itself," is the offspring of a casual word of Baron Pollock during argument with counsel in a case in 1863 in which a barrel of flour rolled out of a warehouse window and fell upon a passing pedestrian.[17] In its inception the principle was nothing more than a reasonable conclusion, from the circumstances of an unusual accident, that it was probably the defendant's fault. It soon became involved, however, in cases of injuries to passengers at the hands of carriers, with the aftermath of an older decision which had held that the carrier had the burden of proving that it had not been negligent.[18] The two principles, one concerned with the sufficiency of circumstantial evidence, the other with the burden of proof, gradually became confused and intermingled;[19] and from this fusion there developed an uncertain "doctrine" of res ipsa loquitur,

---

10. Viera v. Atchison, Topeka & Santa Fe Railway Co., 1909, 10 Cal.App. 267, 101 P. 690.

11. "Some circumstantial evidence is very strong, as when you find a trout in the milk." Thoreau, Journal, Nov. 11, 1850.

12. Wigmore, Evidence, 3d ed. 1940, § 2487.

13. Goddard v. Boston & Maine Railroad Co., 1901, 179 Mass. 52, 60 N.E. 486.

14. Anjou v. Boston Elevated Railway Co., 1911, 208 Mass. 273, 94 N.E. 386.

15. See James, Proof of the Breach in Negligence Cases, 1951, 37 Va.L.Rev. 179. For general reviews of slip and fall cases, see Ex parte Travis, Ala.1982, 414 So.2d 956 (plaintiff slipped on paper bag); Annots., 1980, 1 A.L.R.4th 1249 (motor carrier); 1965, 3 A.L.R.3d 938 (airport); 1975, 65 A.L.R.3d 14 (landlord); 1966, 8 A.L.R.3d 6 (gas station); 1967, 16 A.L.R.3d 1237 (hospital); 1978, 85 A.L.R.3d 1000 (store—modern status of notice requirement).

16. See generally Speiser, The Negligence Case, Res Ipsa Loquitur, 1972; Carpenter, The Doctrine of Res Ipsa Loquitur, 1934, 1 U.Chi.L.Rev. 519; Malone,

Res Ipsa Loquitur and Proof by Inference, 1941, 4 La. L.Rev. 70; Morris, Res Ipsa Loquitur in Texas, 1948, 26 Tex.L.Rev. 257, 761; Prosser, Res Ipsa Loquitur in California, 1949, 37 Cal.L.Rev. 183; James, Proof of the Breach in Negligence Cases, 1951, 37 Va.L.Rev. 179; Ghiardi, Res Ipsa Loquitur in Wisconsin, 1956, 39 Marq.L.Rev. 361; Kaye, Probability Theory Meets Res Ipsa Loquitur, 1979, 77 Mich.L.Rev. 1456; Griffith & Griffith, The Doctrine of Res Ipsa Loquitur—Old Solutions for New Problems, 1977, 48 Miss.L.J. 259; Note, 1980, 75 Nw.U.L.Rev. 147 (mathematical-logical model); Second Restatement of Torts, § 328 D.

17. Byrne v. Boadle, 1863, 2 H. & C. 722, 159 Eng. Rep. 299. Repeated, on substantially identical facts, in Hake v. George Wiedemann Brewing Co., 1970, 23 Ohio St.2d 65, 262 N.E.2d 703.

18. Christie v. Griggs, 1809, 2 Camp. 79, 170 Eng. Rep. 1088.

19. See generally Gilbert v. Korvette, Inc., 1974, 457 Pa. 602, 327 A.2d 94 (rejecting prior doctrine and adopting Second Restatement of Torts, § 328 D); Note, 1957, 33 Ind.L.J. 45.

which has been the source of some considerable trouble to the courts.[20] It is nevertheless accepted and applied by all of our courts, except in South Carolina, which still mysteriously rejects it by name,[21] while applying it as a practical matter under principles of circumstantial evidence.[22]

The statement of the doctrine most often quoted is that of Chief Justice Erle in 1865:[23]

"There must be reasonable evidence of negligence; but where the thing is shown to be under the management of the defendant or his servants, and the accident is such as in the ordinary course of things does not happen if those who have the management use proper care, it affords reasonable evidence, in the absence of explanation by the defendants, that the accident arose from want of care."

The conditions usually stated in America as necessary for the application of the principle of res ipsa loquitur were derived originally from the first edition of Wigmore on Evidence.[24] They are as follows: (1) the event must be of a kind which ordinarily does not occur in the absence of someone's negligence; (2) it must be caused by an agency or instrumentality within the exclusive control of the defendant; (3) it must not have been due to any voluntary action or contribution on the part of the plaintiff. Some courts have at least suggested a fourth condition, that evidence as to the true explanation of the event must be more readily accessible to the defendant than to the plaintiff. As will be seen, this traditional formula is neither complete nor accurate so far as it goes. The various elements of the problem remain to be considered.

Inference That Someone Was Negligent

The requirement that the occurrence be one which ordinarily does not happen without negligence is of course only another way of stating an obvious principle of circumstantial evidence: that the event must be such that in the light of ordinary experience it gives rise to an inference that someone must have been negligent. On this basis res ipsa loquitur has been applied to a wide variety of situations, and its range is as broad as the possible events which reasonably justify such a conclusion. It finds common application, for example, in the case of objects such as bricks or window panes falling from the defendant's premises,[25] falling elevators,[26] the collapse of structures,[27] live stock loose

---

20. "It adds nothing to the law, has no meaning which is not more clearly expressed for us in English, and brings confusion to our legal discussions. It does not represent a doctrine, is not a legal maxim, and is not a rule." Bond, C. J., dissenting in Potomac Edison Co. v. Johnson, 1930, 160 Md. 33, 152 A. 633. See Bond, The Use of the Phrase Res Ipsa Loquitur, 1908, 66 Cent.L.J. 386; Prosser, The Procedural Effect of Res Ipsa Loquitur, 1936, 20 Minn.L.Rev. 241, 271.

"If that phrase had not been in Latin, nobody would have called it a principle." Lord Shaw, in Ballard v. North British R. Co., [1923] Sess.Cas., H.L., 43.

21. Legette v. Smith, 1975, 265 S.C. 573, 220 S.E.2d 429; Orr v. Saylor, 1969, 253 S.C. 155, 169 S.E.2d 369 (dissent arguing forcefully for adoption of doctrine).

22. McQuillen v. Dobbs, 1974, 262 S.C. 386, 204 S.E.2d 732; Childers v. Gas Lines, Inc., 1966, 248 S.C. 316, 149 S.E.2d 761; cf. Maus v. Pickens Sentinel Co., 1972, 258 S.C. 6, 186 S.E.2d 809.

23. In Scott v. London & St. Katherine Docks Co., 1865, 3 H. & C. 596, 159 Eng.Rep. 665.

24. 4 Wigmore, Evidence, 1st ed. 1905, § 2509.

25. Kearney v. London, B. & S. C. R. Co., 1870, L.R. 5 Q.B. 411; Lipsitz v. Schechter, 1966, 377 Mich. 685,

142 N.W.2d 1; Both v. Harband, 1958, 164 Cal.App.2d 743, 331 P.2d 140; see Goodwin v. United States, E.D. N.C.1956, 141 F.Supp. 445 (practice bomb from military plane, six miles off target, hit plaintiff's fishing boat); Cortez Roofing, Inc. v. Barolo, Fla.App.1975, 323 So.2d 45 (carpet roll containing steel pipe fell off rack); Hake v. George Wiedemann Brewing Co., 1970, 23 Ohio St.2d 65, 262 N.E.2d 703 (beer keg fell on plaintiff from second story).

26. Griffen v. Manice, 1901, 166 N.Y. 188, 59 N.E. 925; Littlefield v. Laughlin, Mo.1959, 327 S.W.2d 863; Kunzie v. Leeds, Inc., 1941, 66 Ohio App. 469, 34 N.E.2d 448; cf. Montgomery Elevator Co. v. Gordon, Colo.1980, 619 P.2d 66 (door closed on passenger).

27. See Lynden Transport, Inc. v. Haragan, Alaska 1981, 623 P.2d 789 (trailer); Boyer v. Iowa High School Athletic Association, 1967, 260 Iowa 1061, 152 N.W.2d 293; Emerick v. Raleigh Hills Hospital—Newport Beach, 1982, 133 Cal.App.3d 575, 184 Cal.Rptr. 92 (bathroom sink in hospital); cf. Sabella v. Baton Rouge General Hospital, La.App.1981, 408 So.2d 382 (x-ray stretcher flipped over); Payless Discount Centers, Inc. v. 25–29 North Broadway Corp., 1981, 83 A.D.2d 960, 443 N.Y.S.2d 21 (sprinkler system in ceiling collapsed).

on the highway,[28] the escape of gas or water from mains,[29] or of electricity from wires or appliances,[30] the explosion of boilers or other objects under the defendant's control,[31] or the escape of dust or noxious gases from his premises,[32] the sudden starting of machinery,[33] the detachment of wheels from moving vehicles,[34] injuries to passengers from causes within the control of the carrier, such as derailment,[35] the sudden stop of a bus,[36] or its defective equipment,[37] some kinds of automobile accidents, such as a car suddenly leaving the highway and going into a ditch or colliding with a stationary object,[38] or starting down hill not long after it has been parked at the curb,[39] defective food in sealed containers,[40] and many other similar occurrences. There is an element of drama, and of the freakish and improbable in a good many of these cases,[41] which has led the

28. Watzig v. Tobin, 1982, 292 Or. 645, 642 P.2d 651 (motorist struck cow on highway; split in jurisdictions noted); Martinez v. Teague, App.1981, 96 N.M. 446, 631 P.2d 1314 (prior cases contra distinguished).

29. Hollywood Shop, Inc. v. Pennsylvania Gas & Water Co., 1979, 270 Pa.Super. 245, 411 A.2d 509 (water main); McWhorter v. City of New Smyrna Beach Utilities Commission, Fla.App.1981, 400 So.2d 23 (sewer blockage in city's sewer line; split in cases noted), reversed, 418 So.2d 261; Sohoro Pipeline Co. v. Harmon, Tex.App.1981, 627 S.W.2d 498 (oil pipeline). But cf. Jones v. Tarrant Utility Co., Tex.App.1981, 626 S.W.2d 912, reversed, 638 S.W.2d 862; Jennings Buick, Inc. v. City of Cincinnati, 1980, 63 Ohio St.2d 167, 406 N.E.2d 1385. See generally, Annot., 1979, 91 A.L.R.3d 186.

30. Humphrey v. Twin State Gas & Electric Co., 1927, 100 Vt. 414, 139 A. 440; Cain v. Southern Massachusetts Telephone Co., 1914, 219 Mass. 504, 107 N.E. 380; Mares v. New Mexico Public Service Co., 1938, 42 N.M. 473, 82 P.2d 257.

31. Page v. Sloan, 1971, 12 N.C.App. 433, 183 S.E.2d 813, affirmed 1972, 281 N.C. 697, 190 S.E.2d 189 (water heater); Kleinman v. Banner Laundry Co., 1921, 150 Minn. 515, 186 N.W. 123. Cf. Metz v. Central Illinois Electric & Gas Co., 1965, 32 Ill.2d 446, 207 N.E.2d 305 (gas line); Zurich Insurance Co. v. Missouri Edison Co., Mo.1964, 384 S.W.2d 623 (same); Baker v. Thompson-Hayward Chemical Co., Mo.App.1958, 316 S.W.2d 652 (chlorine plant).

32. Reynolds Metals Co. v. Yturbide, 1958, 258 F.2d 321, certiorari denied 358 U.S. 840, 79 S.Ct. 66, 3 L.Ed. 2d 76; Martin v. Reynolds Metals Co., D.Or.1952, 135 F.Supp. 379, affirmed, 258 F.2d 321, certiorari denied 358 U.S. 840, 79 S.Ct. 66, 3 L.Ed.2d 76; McKenna v. Allied Chemical & Dye Corp., 1959, 8 A.D.2d 463, 188 N.Y.S.2d 919. But cf. Marathon Oil Co. v. Sterner, Tex.1982, 632 S.W.2d 571.

33. Chiuccariello v. Campbell, 1912, 210 Mass. 532, 96 N.E. 1101; see Rose v. Port of New York Authority, 1972, 61 N.J. 129, 293 A.2d 371 (automatic electric door malfunctioned and closed on plaintiff).

34. Pitre v. Bourgeois, La.App.1979, 371 So.2d 330, writ denied, La., 374 So.2d 657; Swiney v. Malone Freight Lines, Tenn.App.1976, 545 S.W.2d 112; Annot., 1977, 79 A.L.R.3d 346.

35. Hunt v. Atlantic Coast Line Railroad Co., E.D. S.C.1956, 144 F.Supp. 877; Edgerton v. New York & Hartford Railroad Co., 1868, 39 N.Y. 227; Chicago Union Traction Co. v. Giese, 1907, 229 Ill. 260, 82 N.E. 232; Washington-Virginia Railway Co. v. Bouknight, 1912, 113 Va. 696, 75 S.E. 1032.

36. Shaw v. Pacific Greyhound Lines, 1958, 50 Cal. 2d 153, 323 P.2d 391; Mitcham v. City of Detroit, 1959, 355 Mich. 182, 94 N.W.2d 388. Blackburn v. Boise School Bus Co., 1973, 95 Idaho 323, 508 P.2d 553 (severe bump).

37. Bressler v. New York Rapid Transit Corp., 1938, 277 N.Y. 200, 13 N.E.2d 772; Chicago Union Traction Co. v. Newmiller, 1906, 215 Ill. 383, 74 N.E. 410; Hughes v. Atlantic City & Shore Railroad Co., 1914, 85 N.J.L. 212, 89 A. 769; Adam v. Los Angeles Transit Lines, 1957, 154 Cal.App.2d 535, 317 P.2d 642; cf. Gilbert v. Korvette, Inc., 1974, 457 Pa. 602, 327 A.2d 94 (child's foot caught in escalator).

38. Horowitz v. Kevah Konner, Inc., 1979, 67 A.D.2d 38, 414 N.Y.S.2d 540 (chartered bus left snowy thruway and turned over); Winter v. Scherman, 1976, 57 Hawaii 279, 554 P.2d 1137 (utility pole); Fields v. Morgan, 1978, 39 Md.App. 82, 382 A.2d 1099 (tree); Lent v. Lent, Mo.App.1976, 543 S.W.2d 312 (bridge); American Family Mutual Insurance Co. v. Dobrzynski, 1979, 88 Wis.2d 617, 277 N.W.2d 749 (plaintiff's garage door and car inside). *Contra*, Mets v. Granrud, 1980, ___ Mont. ___, 606 P.2d 1384 (telephone pole), overruled in part, Tompkins v. Northwestern Union Trust Co., 1982, ___ Mont. ___, 645 P.2d 402. Cf. Silverman v. General Motors Corp., 1981, 99 Ill.App.3d 593, 54 Ill. Dec. 882, 425 N.E.2d 1099 (doctrine inapplicable against manufacturer on facts). See generally Annot., 1961, 79 A.L.R.2d 6.

39. Gleason v. Jack Alan Enterprises, Inc., 1977, 36 Md.App. 562, 374 A.2d 408; Hill v. Thompson, Okl. 1971, 484 P.2d 513. But see Meadows v. Oates, 1980, 156 Ga.App. 242, 274 S.E.2d 634. See generally Annot., 1974, 55 A.L.R.3d 1260.

40. Richenbacher v. California Packing Corp., 1924, 250 Mass. 198, 145 N.E. 281; Dryden v. Continental Baking Co., 1938, 11 Cal.2d 33, 77 P.2d 833; cf. Shoshone Coca-Cola Bottling Co. v. Dolinski, 1966, 82 Nev. 439, 420 P.2d 855 (mouse in Squirt).

41. Carter v. Liberty Equipment Co., Inc., Mo.App. 1980, 611 S.W.2d 311 (air compressor crashed through store window and hit emloyee); Marshall v. Suburban Dairy Co., 1921, 96 N.J.L. 81, 114 A. 750 (horse leaped over hood of motor truck and arrived in cab); Guthrie v. Powell, 1955, 178 Kan. 587, 290 P.2d 834 (800 pound steer came through ceiling); Armstrong v. New Orle-

courts on occasion to say that the event must be an "unusual" one;[42] but this is not at all indispensable, and very commonplace events, such as an ordinary movement of a street car at the wrong time, will be quite enough.[43]

On the other hand there are many accidents which, as a matter of common knowledge, occur frequently enough without anyone's fault. A tumble downstairs,[44] a fall in alighting from a standing bus or street car,[45] an ordinary slip and fall,[46] a tire of an ordinary automobile which blows out,[47] a skidding car,[48] a staph infection from an operation,[49] a fire of unknown origin,[50] will not in themselves[51] justify the conclusion that negligence is the most likely explanation; and to such events res ipsa loquitur does not apply.

The earlier cases dealing with aviation took the position that there was not yet such common knowledge and experience of its hazards as to permit such a conclusion from the unexplained crash of a plane.[52] With rapid technological improvement, the position began to change; and the later cases now agree that the safety record justifies the application of res ipsa loquitur to such a crash,[53] or even to the complete disappear-

ans Public Service, La.App.1939, 188 So. 189 (uninvited street car entered restaurant); Harlow v. Standard Improvement Co., 1904, 145 Cal. 477, 78 P. 1045 (vagrant steam roller crossed lawn and crashed into house); Pillars v. R.J. Reynolds Tobacco Co., 1918, 117 Miss. 490, 78 So. 365 (human toe in chewing tobacco); Fowler v. Seaton, 1964, 61 Cal.2d 681, 39 Cal.Rptr. 881, 394 P.2d 697 (child sent to nursery school, returned with bruised head, crossed eyes and concussion); Wolfe v. Feldman, 1936, 158 Misc. 656, 286 N.Y.S. 118 (the extraordinary case of the unfortunate dentist).

42. See Strick v. Stutsman, Mo.App.1982, 633 S.W.2d 148.

43. Mudrick v. Market Street Railway Co., 1938, 11 Cal.2d 724, 81 P.2d 950. Or the tossing about of a small boat by the wakes of passing yachts. Sweeney v. Car/Puter International Corp., D.S.C.1981, 521 F.Supp. 276 (passenger injured back).

44. See Barcia v. Estate of Keil, La.App.1982, 413 So.2d 241; Hutsell v. Edens, 1961, 172 Neb. 592, 111 N.W.2d 388; Hiner v. Hubbard, 1966, 240 Cal.App.2d 63, 49 Cal.Rptr. 157.

45. Wyatt v. Pacific Electric Railway Co., 1909, 156 Cal. 170, 103 P. 892; Greeley v. Baltimore Transit Co., 1941, 180 Md. 10, 22 A.2d 460; Annot., 1979, 93 A.L.R.3d 776 (passenger boarding or alighting).

46. E.g., Winn-Dixie Montgomery, Inc. v. Rowell, Ala.Civ.App.1973, 288 So.2d 785, writ denied 292 Ala. 758, 288 So.2d 792; Dennis v. Carolina Pines Bowling Center, 1967, 248 Cal.App.2d 369, 56 Cal.Rptr. 453; Douglas v. Great Atlantic & Pacific Tea Co., Miss.1981, 405 So.2d 107 (res ipsa does not apply to slip and fall cases—"well settled rule"); Ex parte Travis, Ala.1982, 414 So.2d 956 (same); supra, note 15.

47. See Jolley v. General Motors Corp., 1982, 55 N.C.App. 383, 285 S.E.2d 301; Sears, Roebuck & Co. v. Haven Hills Farms, Inc., Ala.1981, 395 So.2d 991; Goodyear Tire & Rubber Co. v. Hughes Supply, Inc., Fla.1978, 358 So.2d 1339; Shramek v. General Motors Corp., Ill.App.1966, 69 Ill.App.2d 72, 216 N.E.2d 244.

But see Simpson v. Gray Line Co., 1961, 226 Or. 71, 358 P.2d 516, and Greyhound Corp. v. Brown, 1959, 269 Ala. 520, 113 So.2d 916, where the tire of a bus blew out, and res ipsa loquitur was applied on the basis of the carrier's extraordinary duty of care.

48. See Kuhn v. Michael, 1980, 283 Pa.Super. 101, 423 A.2d 735; Rickert v. Geppert, 1964, 64 Wn.2d 350, 391 P.2d 964; Wray v. King, Mo.App.1965, 385 S.W.2d 831; Vespe v. DiMarco, 1964, 43 N.J. 430, 204 A.2d 874; Campbell v. Fiorot, 1963, 411 Pa. 157, 191 A.2d 657; Roddy v. Chicago & Northwestern Railroad, 1977, 48 Ill.App.3d 548, 6 Ill.Dec. 536, 363 N.E.2d 65. See generally Note, 1967, 16 Buff.L.Rev. 456.

49. Roark v. St. Paul Fire & Marine Insurance Co., La.App.1982, 415 So.2d 295.

50. Lanza v. Poretti, E.D.Pa.1982, 537 F.Supp. 777; Toussant v. Guice, La.App.1982, 414 So.2d 850; DaVinci Creations, Inc. v. Nu-Frame Co., 1980, __ R.I. __, 418 A.2d 851; Annot., 1966, 8 A.L.R.3d 974; cf. Wood v. Geis Trucking Co., Wyo.1982, 639 P.2d 903 (fire in truck engine).

51. Additional facts may still justify the inference. Cf. Ruerat v. Stevens, 1931, 113 Conn. 333, 155 A. 219, where defendant was the only person to smoke on a davenport all evening; Seeley v. Combs, 1966, 65 Cal. 2d 127, 52 Cal.Rptr. 578, 416 P.2d 810 (fire started in vicinity of defendant's hot sparks and gases).

52. E.g., Wilson v. Colonial Air Transport, 1932, 278 Mass. 420, 180 N.E. 212; Morrison v. Le Tourneau Co., 5th Cir. 1943, 138 F.2d 339.

53. Higginbotham v. Mobil Oil Corp., 5th Cir. 1977, 545 F.2d 422, certiorari denied 434 U.S. 830, 98 S.Ct. 110, 54 L.Ed.2d 89, rehearing denied 434 U.S. 960, 98 S.Ct. 494, 54 L.Ed.2d 321, reversed on other grounds, 436 U.S. 618, 98 S.Ct. 2010, 56 L.Ed.2d 581, on remand 578 F.2d 565, rehearing denied 439 U.S. 884, 99 S.Ct. 232, 58 L.Ed.2d 200 (helicopter—reviewing history of doctrine); Newing v. Cheatham, 1975, 15 Cal.3d 351, 124 Cal.Rptr. 193, 540 P.2d 33; Tompkins v. Northwestern Union Trust Co., 1982, __ Mont. __, 645 P.2d 402; Widmyer v. Southeast Skyways, Inc., Alaska 1978, 584 P.2d 1; Colditz v. Eastern Airlines, Inc., S.D. N.Y.1971, 329 F.Supp. 691 (mid-air collision), noted, 1972, 40 Ford.L.Rev. 977; Newberger v. Pokrass, 1967, 33 Wis.2d 569, 148 N.W.2d 80.

ance of a plane.⁵⁴ There are, however, other kinds of aviation mishaps, such as the lurch or bump of a plane when unexpected air currents are suddenly encountered,⁵⁵ which still lead to no such conclusion.⁵⁶

There has been much the same history in the law of exploding beverage bottles, where it was at one time held that the explosion of a single bottle, which apparently then was not at all an uncommon occurrence, was no sufficient indication of negligence.⁵⁷ Both bottles and bottling methods have improved greatly since; and there is now general agreement that even a single bottle is enough to permit a finding of negligence.⁵⁸ Whether the inference may be drawn is often a matter of the details of the evidence. If minute particles of glass are found in a can of spinach, it may be that negligence cannot reasonably be inferred, since ordinary inspection might not discover them; if the particles are somewhat larger, res ipsa loquitur applies.⁵⁹

In the usual case, the basis of past experience, from which the conclusion may be drawn that such events usually do not occur without negligence, is one common to the whole community, upon which the jury are simply permitted to rely. Even where such a basis of common knowledge is lacking, however, expert testimony may provide a sufficient foundation;⁶⁰ and by the same token it may destroy an inference which would otherwise arise.⁶¹ In many cases the inference to be drawn is a double one, that the accident was caused in a particular manner, and that the defendant's conduct with reference to that cause was negligent.⁶² The inference of negligence may arise either where a definite cause is known,⁶³ or where the accident

But cf. Campbell v. First National Bank, D.N.M. 1973, 370 F.Supp. 1096 (doctrine could not apply against pilot of rented plane that might have had mechanical problems); Rathvon v. Columbia Pacific Airlines, 1981, 30 Wn.App. 193, 633 P.2d 122 (summary judgment for plaintiffs reversed). See generally McLarty, Res Ipsa Loquitur in Airline Passenger Litigation, 1951, 37 Va.L.Rev. 55; Goldin, The Doctrine of Res Ipsa Loquitur in Aviation Law, 1944, 18 So.Cal.L. Rev. 15, 124.

54. Cox v. Northwest Airlines, Inc., 7th Cir. 1967, 379 F.2d 893, certiorari denied 389 U.S. 1044, 88 S.Ct. 788, 19 L.Ed.2d 836; Haasman v. Pacific Alaska Air Express, 1951, 13 Alaska 439, 100 F.Supp. 1, affirmed, De Marais v. Beckman, 1952, 13 Alaska 745, 198 F.2d 550, certiorari denied 344 U.S. 922, 73 S.Ct. 388, 97 L.Ed. 710.

But not to the total disappearance of a car with four occupants. Hakensen v. Ennis, Alaska 1978, 584 P.2d 1138.

55. Kelly v. American Airlines, Inc., N.D.Tex.1974, 372 F.Supp. 1214, affirmed 5th Cir., 508 F.2d 1379; Cudney v. Braniff Airways, Inc., Mo.1957, 300 S.W.2d 412; Gafford v. Trans-Texas Airways, 6th Cir. 1962, 299 F.2d 60; Lazarus v. Eastern Air Lines, 1961, 110 U.S.App.D.C. 255, 292 F.2d 748; see Ness v. West Coast Airlines, Inc., 1965, 90 Idaho 111, 410 P.2d 965. Cf. Herman v. United Air Lines, Inc., D.C.Colo.1957, 157 F.Supp. 65 (murderer blew up plane).

56. But cf. Calabretta v. National Airlines, Inc., E.D.N.Y.1981, 528 F.Supp. 32 (ear injury from descent; summary judgment for defendants denied).

57. E.g., Loebig's Guardian v. Coca Cola Bottling Co., 1935, 259 Ky. 124, 81 S.W.2d 910. Even then, however, the inference could be drawn if several bottles exploded. Coca Cola Bottling Works v. Shelton, 1926, 214 Ky. 118, 282 S.W. 778; Boyd v. Marion Coca Cola Bottling Co., 1962, 240 S.C. 383, 126 S.E.2d 178.

58. See Notes, [1951] Wash.U.L.Q. 216; 1957, 24 Tenn.L.Rev. 1219; infra, note 93.

59. Compare O'Brien v. Louis K. Liggett Co., 1926, 255 Mass. 553, 152 N.E. 57, with Richenbacher v. California Packing Corp., 1924, 250 Mass. 198, 145 N.E. 281.

60. Buckelew v. Grossbard, 1981, 87 N.J. 512, 435 A.2d 1150 (medical malpractice; full discussion); Miller v. Van Newkirk, Colo.App.1980, 628 P.2d 143; Baker v. B. F. Goodrich Co., 1953, 115 Cal.App.2d 221, 252 P.2d 24 (tire exploded while being mounted); Hanaman v. New York Telephone Co., 1951, 278 App.Div. 875, 104 N.Y.S.2d 315, reargument and appeal denied 278 A.D. 986, 105 N.Y.S.2d 1007 (escape of current from telephone). See Fricke, The Use of Expert Evidence in Res Ipsa Loquitur Cases, 1959, 5 Vill.L.Rev. 59; Note, 1958, 106 U.Pa.L.Rev. 731.

61. Cf. Zeno v. Lincoln General Hospital, La.App. 1981, 404 So.2d 1337 (nerves cut during surgery); LePelley v. Grefenson, 1980, 101 Idaho 422, 614 P.2d 962 (surgeon dropped bone fragment during operation on inner ear).

62. See Terrell v. Lincoln Motel, Inc., App.Div.1982, 183 N.J.Super. 55, 443 A.2d 236 ("after they watched television for a while," plaintiff and his girlfriend entered motel shower, and plaintiff slipped and fell through door, allegedly because of sudden spurt of hot water); Zimmer v. Celebrities, Inc., 1980, 44 Colo.App. 515, 615 P.2d 76 (2-year-old suffered skull fracture in nursery; drinking fountain pipes possible cause).

63. Khanoyan v. All American Sports Enterprises, Inc., 1964, 229 Cal.App.2d 785, 40 Cal.Rptr. 596; cf. Martinez v. Teague, App.1981, 96 N.M. 446, 631 P.2d 1314.

is more or less a mystery, with no particular cause indicated. When a gasoline filling station mysteriously explodes, many possible explanations can be suggested, but the most likely one may be negligence on the part of those in charge.[64] The plaintiff is not required to eliminate with certainty all other possible causes or inferences,[65] which would mean that the plaintiff must prove a civil case beyond a reasonable doubt. All that is needed is evidence from which reasonable persons can say that on the whole it is more likely that there was negligence associated with the cause of the event than that there was not.[66] It is enough that the court cannot say that the jury could not reasonably come to that conclusion.[67] Where no such balance of probabilities in favor of negligence can reasonably be found, res ipsa loquitur does not apply.[68]

Inference the Negligence was Defendant's

It is never enough for the plaintiff to prove merely that the plaintiff has been injured by the negligence of someone unidentified. Even though there is beyond all possible doubt negligence in the air, it is still necessary to bring it home to the defendant.[69] "The purpose of this requirement is to link the defendant with the probability, already established, that the accident was negligently caused."[70] On this too the plaintiff has the burden of proof by a preponderance of the evidence; and in any case where it is clear that it is at least equally probable that the negligence was that of another, the court must direct the jury that the plaintiff has not established a case.[71] The injury must either be traced to a specific instrumentality or cause for which the defendant was responsible,[72] or it must be shown that the plaintiff was responsible for all reasonably probable causes to which the accident could be attributed.[73] Accordingly, res ipsa loquitur is held not to apply where a chair is thrown from an unidentified window in the defendant's hotel,[74] or where the presence of such an object as a bolt on a railway platform might easily have been due to the act

---

64. Nelson v. Zamboni, 1925, 164 Minn. 314, 204 N.W. 943; Hiell v. Golco Oil Co., 1940, 137 Ohio St. 180, 28 N.E.2d 561; Keck v. Bairs, Inc., 1968, 150 Mont. 562, 437 P.2d 380. Cf. Judson v. Giant Powder Co., 1895, 107 Cal. 549, 40 P. 1020 (nitroglycerine factory).

65. Wagstaff v. City of Maplewood, Mo.App.1981, 615 S.W.2d 608; National Tea Co. v. Gaylord Discount Department Stores, Inc., 1981, 100 Ill.App.3d 806, 56 Ill.Dec. 265, 427 N.E.2d 345.

66. See Sabella v. Baton Rouge General Hospital, La.App.1981, 408 So. 2d 382 (flipping over of x-ray stretcher simply does not occur when proper care is taken); Shahinian v. McCormick, 1963, 59 Cal.2d 554, 30 Cal.Rptr. 521, 381 P.2d 377.

67. Ex parte Travis, Ala.1982, 414 So.2d 956; Dunn v. Vogel Chevrolet Co., 1959, 168 Cal.App.2d 117, 335 P.2d 492.

68. Cuellar v. Garcia, Tex.Civ.App.1981, 621 S.W.2d 646, refused n.r.e. (car crashed into house); Mets v. Granrud, 1980, ___ Mont. ___, 606 P.2d 1384 (car hit telephone pole—defendant driver dead, plaintiff passenger lost memory), overruled in part, Tompkins v. Northwestern Union Trust Co., 1982, ___ Mont. ___, 645 P.2d 402; Lanza v. Poretti, E.D.Pa.1982, 537 F.Supp. 777; DaVinci Creations, Inc. v. Nu-Frame Co., 1980, ___ R.I. ___, 418 A.2d 851; Owen v. Beauchamp, 1944, 66 Cal.App.2d 750, 152 P.2d 756.

69. Marathon Oil Co. v. Sterner, Tex.1982, 632 S.W.2d 571.

70. Newing v. Cheatham, 1975, 15 Cal.App.3d 593, 124 Cal.Rptr. 193, 201, 540 P.2d 33, 41.

71. Marathon Oil Co. v. Sterner, Tex.1982, 632 S.W.2d 571; Neis v. National Super Markets, Inc., Mo. App.1982, 631 S.W.2d 690; Silverman v. General Motors Corp., 1981, 99 Ill.App.3d 593, 54 Ill.Dec. 882, 425 N.E.2d 1099; see Payne v. M. Greenberg Construction, App.1981, 130 Ariz. 338, 636 P.2d 116.

72. See Smith v. Little, Tex.App.1981, 626 S.W.2d 906 (flammable liquid that spilled on carpet, not the carpet, was relevant instrumentality in fire case; Manley v. New York Telephone Co., 1951, 303 N.Y. 18, 100 N.E.2d 113 (severe nervous shock while using telephone); Nahigian v. Belcher & Loomis Hardware Co., 1941, 66 R.I. 194, 18 A.2d 388 (injury from electric ironer not shown to be due to repairs).

73. As in Judson v. Giant Powder Co., 1895, 107 Cal. 549, 40 P. 1020, and as not in Wood v. Geis Trucking Co., Wyo.1982, 639 P.2d 903 (carrier not liable for death of sheep where cause of death might have arisen before or after carriage, or during carriage by weather beyond carrier's control). See also Lynden Transport, Inc. v. Haragan, Alaska 1981, 623 P.2d 789.

74. Larson v. St. Francis Hotel, 1948, 83 Cal.App.2d 210, 188 P.2d 513. Cf. Sipe v. Helgerson, 1944, 159 Kan. 290, 153 P.2d 934 (bottle thrown from baseball grandstand); Davidson's, Inc. v. Scott, 1965, 149 W.Va. 470, 140 S.E.2d 807 (fire in room to which several people had keys).

of a third party,[75] or where gas or water or electricity escapes from fixtures controlled in part by another.[76]

Where such other causes are in the first instance equally probable, there must be evidence which will permit the jury to eliminate them. This means, for example, that a plaintiff injured by the explosion of a beer bottle purchased from a retailer will be required to make some sufficient showing that the bottle was not cracked by mishandling after it left the defendant's plant.[77] Again, however, the evidence need not be conclusive, and only enough is required to permit a finding as to the greater probability.[78] The plaintiff is not required to do the impossible by accounting for every moment of the bottle's existence since it left the defendant's plant;[79] and it is enough if the plaintiff produces sufficient evidence of careful handling in general, and of the absence of unusual incidents, to permit reasonable persons to conclude that, more likely than not, the event was due to the defendant's negligence.[80] As to dead mice, and the like, in capped bottles, the possibility of deliberate tampering by a stranger has been ruled out as too unlikely, in the absence of some evidence to indicate it.[81] The same kind of question arises when the defendant's car, parked on the side of a hill, is found in motion shortly afterward.[82] Various explanations suggest themselves, including the same tampering stranger; but it can still be found that the most probable one is negligence in parking the car.[83]

This element usually is stated as meaning that the defendant must be in "exclusive control" of the instrumentality which has caused the accident.[84] Such control of course does serve effectively to focus any negligence upon the defendant; but the strict and literal application of the formula has led some courts to ridiculous conclusions, requiring that the defendant be in possession at the time of the plaintiff's injury—as in the Rhode Island case [85] denying recovery where a customer in a store sat down in a chair, which collapsed. Of course this is wrong: it loses sight of the real purpose of the reasoning process in an attempt to re-

75. O'Mara v. Pennsylvania Railroad Co., 6th Cir. 1938, 95 F.2d 762.

76. Jones v. Tarrant Utility Co., Tex.App.1981, 626 S.W.2d 912 (third party owned and maintained cutoff control sensors for defendant's water tanks), reversed, 638 S.W.2d 862; Barker v. Withers, 1956, 141 W.Va. 713, 92 S.E.2d 705; Hernandez v. Southern California Gas. Co., 1931, 213 Cal. 384, 2 P.2d 360; Arkansas Power & Light Co. v. Butterworth, 1953, 222 Ark. 67, 258 S.W.2d 36.

77. Keffer v. Logan Coca-Cola Bottling Works, Inc., 1956, 141 W.Va. 839, 93 S.E.2d 225; Miami Coca-Cola Bottling Co. v. Reisinger, Fla.1953, 68 So.2d 589; Trust v. Arden Farms Co., 1958, 50 Cal.2d 217, 324 P.2d 583; Joffre v. Canada Dry Ginger Ale, Inc., 1960, 222 Md. 1, 158 A.2d 631. Cf. Huggins v. John Morrell & Co., 1964, 176 Ohio St. 171, 198 N.E.2d 448 (pickled pigs' feet); Wagner v. Coca-Cola Bottling Co., S.D.1982, 319 N.W.2d 807 (bottles knocked off display by another). See generally Spangenberg, Exploding Bottles, 1963, 24 Ohio St.L.J. 516; Annot., 1962, 81 A.L.R.2d 229.

78. Weggeman v. Seven-Up Bottling Co., 1958, 5 Wis.2d 503, 93 N.W.2d 467, rehearing denied, amended 94 N.W.2d 645; Gordon v. Aztec Brewing Co., 1949, 33 Cal.2d 514, 203 P.2d 522; Honea v. Coca Cola Bottling Co., 1944, 143 Tex. 272, 183 S.W.2d 968.

79. Zarling v. La Salle Coca Cola Bottling Co., 1958, 2 Wis.2d 596, 87 N.W.2d 263; Macon Coca-Cola Bottling Co. v. Chancey, 1960, 101 Ga.App. 166, 112 S.E.2d 811, affirmed 216 Ga. 61, 114 S.E.2d 517.

80. Gordon v. Aztec Brewing Co., 1949, 33 Cal.2d 514, 203 P.2d 522; Coca Cola Bottling Works, Inc. v. Crow, 1956, 200 Tenn. 161, 291 S.W.2d 589.

81. See Shoshone Coca-Cola Bottling Co. v. Dolinski, 1966, 82 Nev. 439, 420 P.2d 855; Wichita Coca-Cola Bottling Co. v. Tyler, Tex.Civ.App.1956, 288 S.W.2d 903, refused n.r.e. Cf. Bishop, Trouble in a Bottle, 1964, 16 Baylor L.Rev. 337.

82. In Hughes v. Jolliffe, 1957, 50 Wn.2d 554, 313 P.2d 678, the lapse of several hours was held to defeat the inference of any negligence in parking. But in Gresser v. Taylor, 1967, 276 Minn. 440, 150 N.W.2d 869, and Roberts v. Ray, 1959, 45 Tenn.App. 280, 322 S.W.2d 435, res ipsa loquitur was applied notwithstanding an interval of three hours. See Meadows v. Oates, 1980, 156 Ga.App. 242, 274 S.E.2d 634 (1 or 2 hours); Annot., 1974, 55 A.L.R.3d 1260.

83. See supra, note 39.

84. Markarian v. Pagano, 1982, 87 A.D.2d 729, 449 N.Y.S.2d 335. The statement is derived from the formula stated by Wigmore, Evidence, 3d ed.1940, § 2509: "Both inspection and user must have been at the time of the injury in the control of the party charged."

85. Kilgore v. Shepard Co., 1932, 52 R.I. 151, 158 A. 720. See Note, 1952, 5 Okl.L.Rev. 99.

duce it to a fixed, mechanical and rigid rule. "Control," if it is not to be pernicious and misleading, must be a very flexible term. It may be enough that the defendant has the right or power of control, and the opportunity to exercise it,[86] as in the case of an owner who is present while another is driving the owner's car,[87] or a landowner who permits visitors to come on his premises.[88] It is enough that the defendant is under a duty which he cannot delegate to another, as in the case of a surgeon who allows a nurse to count the sponges.[89] It is enough that the defendant shares the duty and the responsibility, as in the case of the landlord of a building from which an electric sign falls into the street.[90]

There are other cases, however, in which it is clear that "control" is simply the wrong word. The plaintiff who is riding a horse is in exclusive control of it, but when the saddle slips off the inference is still that it is the fault of the defendant who put it on.[91] There is now quite general agreement that the fact that the plaintiff is sitting on the defendant's chair when it collapses,[92] or has possession of an exploding bottle,[93] or a loaf of bread with glass baked inside of it,[94] or is using an appliance, which the defendant has manufactured [95] or maintained,[96] will not prevent the application of res ipsa loquitur when the evidence reasonably eliminates other explanations than the defendant's negligence. Some courts have said that it is enough that the defendant was in exclusive control at the time of the indicated negligence.[97] It would be far better, and much confusion would be avoided, if the rigid

86. "However, if plaintiff merely shows this constructive control by defendant, the inference that the defendant's negligence caused the accident does not necessarily follow. Plaintiff must, therefore, adduce additional evidence to show defendant's responsibility." Neis v. National Super Markets, Inc., Mo.App.1982, 631 S.W.2d 690.

87. Mein v. Reed, 1938, 224 Iowa 1274, 278 N.W. 307; Price v. McDonald, 1935, 7 Cal.App.2d 77, 45 P.2d 425.

88. Pandjiris v. Oliver Cadillac Co., 1936, 339 Mo. 711, 98 S.W.2d 969. Cf. Miles v. St. Regis Paper Co., 1970, 77 Wn.2d 828, 467 P.2d 307; Payless Discount Centers, Inc. v. 25–29 North Broadway Corp., 1981, 83 A.D.2d 960, 443 N.Y.S.2d 21 (landlord, not tenant, had control of ceiling sprinkler system that collapsed).

89. Ales v. Ryan, 1936, 8 Cal.2d 82, 64 P.2d 409; Voss v. Bridwell, 1961, 188 Kan. 643, 364 P.2d 955. See supra, § 32.

90. Smith v. Claude Neon Lights, 1933, 110 N.J.L. 326, 164 A. 423; Both v. Harband, 1958, 164 Cal.App.2d 743, 331 P.2d 140. See Corcoran v. Banner Super Market, 1967, 19 N.Y.2d 425, 280 N.Y.S.2d 385, 227 N.E.2d 304, remittitur amended 21 N.Y.2d 793, 288 N.Y.S.2d 484, 235 N.E.2d 455; Decatur & Macon County Hospital Association v. Erie City Iron Works, 1966, 75 Ill. App.2d 144, 220 N.E.2d 590; Bond v. Otis Elevator Co., Tex.1965, 388 S.W.2d 681, on remand, Tex.Civ.App., 391 S.W.2d 519; Southern Indiana Gas & Electric Co. v. Indiana Insurance Co., 1978, 178 Ind.App. 505, 383 N.E.2d 387; Gilbert v. Korvette, Inc., 1974, 457 Pa. 602, 327 A.2d 94; Jones v. Harrisburg Polyclinic Hospital, 1981, 496 Pa. 465, 437 A.2d 1134 (doctors during operation). Otherwise if the responsibility or control is "divided." Lynch v. Precision Machine Shop, Ltd., 1981, 100 Ill.App.3d 771, 56 Ill.Dec. 96, 427 N.E.2d 176 (2–1), modified, 93 Ill.2d 266, 66 Ill.Dec. 643, 443 N.E.2d 569.

91. Rafter v. Dubrock's Riding Academy, 1946, 75 Cal.App.2d 621, 171 P.2d 459.

92. Gresham v. Stouffer Corp., 1978, 144 Ga.App. 553, 241 S.E.2d 451 (restaurant chair collapsed); Pear v. Labiche's, Inc., La.1974, 301 So.2d 336, on remand, La.App., 305 So.2d 740; Sweet v. Swangel, Iowa 1969, 166 N.W.2d 776; Keena v. Scales, 1964, 61 Cal.2d 779, 40 Cal.Rptr. 65, 394 P.2d 809.

93. Lee v. Crookston Coca-Cola Bottling Co., 1971, 290 Minn. 321, 188 N.W.2d 426 (waitress); Giant Food, Inc. v. Washington Coca-Cola Bottling Co., Inc., 1975, 273 Md. 592, 332 A.2d 1 (customer in store); Zentz v. Coca Cola Bottling Co., 1952, 39 Cal.2d 436, 247 P.2d 344. See generally Spangenberg, Exploding Bottles, 1963, 24 Ohio St.L.J. 516; Annot., 1962, 81 A.L.R.2d 229.

94. Dryden v. Continental Baking Co., 1938, 11 Cal. 2d 33, 77 P.2d 833.

95. Peterson v. Minnesota Power & Light Co., 1940, 207 Minn. 387, 291 N.W. 705; Bustamante v. Carborundum Co., 7th Cir. 1967, 375 F.2d 688; Ozark v. Wichita Manor, Inc., 5th Cir. 1958, 252 F.2d 671, rehearing denied 258 F.2d 805; Black v. Partridge, 1953, 115 Cal. App.2d 639, 252 P.2d 760; May v. Columbian Rope Co., 1963, 40 Ill.App.2d 264, 189 N.E.2d 394 (rope).

Otherwise when the intervening history might reasonably account for the accident. Jakubowski v. Minnesota Mining and Manufacturing, 1964, 42 N.J. 177, 199 A.2d 826 (4–3) (grinding disc brake; history of hard use); Scanlon v. General Motors Corp., 1974, 65 N.J. 582, 326 A.2d 673 (carburetor on car jammed open—possibility of improper maintenance not accounted for in strict products liability case).

96. Montgomery Elevator Co. v. Gordon, Colo.1980, 619 P.2d 66 (elevator maintenance company).

97. Mobil Chemical Co. v. Bell, Tex.1974, 517 S.W.2d 245; Escola v. Coca-Cola Bottling Co., 1944, 24

"control" test were discarded altogether, and we were to require instead that the apparent negligent cause of the accident be such that the defendant would more likely than not be responsible for it.[98]

Multiple Defendants

Some quite intricate questions arise where the plaintiff proceeds against two or more defendants.[99] Unless there is vicarious liability or shared control,[1] the logical rule usually is applied, that the plaintiff does not make out a preponderant case against either of two defendants by showing merely that the plaintiff has been injured by the negligence of one or the other.[2] The questions which arise are amply illustrated by the cases of colliding vehicles.

The courts are agreed that the mere fact of a collision of two automobiles gives rise to no inference of negligence against either driver in an action brought by the other.[3] The great majority of the decisions reach the same conclusion where the action is brought by a third party, such as a bystander, injured by the collision,[4] on the ground that neither driver is in exclusive control of the situation. It is only where one vehicle is stationary,[5] or its driver's fault is eliminated by some other specific evidence,[6] that res ipsa loquitur can apply against the other. This is true in many jurisdictions even though in the

---

Cal.2d 453, 150 P.2d 436; Gadde v. Michigan Consolidated Gas Co., 1966, 377 Mich. 117, 39 N.W.2d 722.

98. "Exclusive control is merely one fact which establishes the responsibility of the defendant; and if it can be established otherwise, exclusive control is not essential to a res ipsa loquitur case." Second Restatement of Tort, § 328 D, Comment g. This is the sound and growing view. See Tompkins v. Northwestern Union Trust Co., 1982, ___ Mont. ___, 645 P.2d 402; Sams v. Gay, 1982, 161 Ga.App. 31, 288 S.E.2d 822; Gilbert v. Korvette, Inc., 1974, 457 Pa. 602, 327 A.2d 94.

See also Watzig v. Tobin, 1982, 292 Or. 645, 642 P.2d 651, 655, where the court offered a simple reformulation of the res ipsa definition, reflecting the modern approaches of liberalizing both the "control" requirement and, in view of the doctrine of comparative fault, the plaintiff's noninvolvement requirement as well: "If exclusive control or custody is not required, and if plaintiff's voluntary participation does not bar its application, res ipsa loquitur would seem to require nothing more than evidence from which it could be concluded that the event was of a kind which does not normally occur in the absence of negligence and that the negligence which caused the event was probably that of the defendant." See also Payless Discount Centers, Inc. v. 25–29 North Broadway Corp., 1981, 83 A.D.2d 960, 443 N.Y.S.2d 21, 22 (concept of exclusive control does not require rigid application); Parrillo v. Giroux Co., Inc., 1981, ___ R.I. ___, 426 A.2d 1313.

99. See McCoid, Negligence Actions Against Multiple Defendants, 1955, 7 Stan.L.Rev. 480; Nagy, Res Ipsa Loquitur in Joint Tortfeasor Cases, 1967, 16 Cleve. Marsh.L.Rev. 550; Note, 1969, 34 Alb.L.J. 106; Annot., 1954, 38 A.L.R.2d 905.

1. See supra, note 90.

2. Turner v. North American Van Lines, Mo.App. 1956, 287 S.W.2d 384; Beakley v. Houston Oil & Minerals Corp., Tex.Civ.App.1980, 600 S.W.2d 396; Fireman's Fund American Insurance Companies v. Knobbe, 1977, 93 Nev. 201, 562 P.2d 825 (hotel fire caused by 1 of 4 smoking guests in room to which there were 18 keys).

Where, however, there is a res ipsa loquitur case against one defendant, it is not necessarily destroyed by specific evidence of negligence on the part of another. McCarty v. Hosang, W.D.Mo.1957, 154 F.Supp. 852.

3. Schofield v. King, 1957, 388 Pa. 132, 130 A.2d 93; McCarthy v. Kenosha Auto Transport Corp., 1966, 2 Ariz.App. 620, 411 P.2d 58. Even a rear-end collision, between moving vehicles. Mickelson v. Forney, 1966, 259 Iowa 91, 143 N.W.2d 390; Brehm v. Lorenz, 1955, 206 Md. 500, 112 A.2d 475; Haidri v. Egolf, 1982, ___ Ind.App. ___, 430 N.E.2d 429 ("contrary to some popular mythology"). But see Davis v. Sobik's Sandwich Shops, Inc., Fla.1977, 351 So.2d 17, appeal after remand, Fla.App., 1979, 371 So.2d 709 (3 car collision); and cf. Thrower v. Smith, 1978, 62 A.D.2d 907, 406 N.Y.S.2d 513, 517, 521–23, affirmed 46 N.Y.2d 835, 414 N.Y.S.2d 124, 386 N.E.2d 1091 (dissenting opinion arguing that burden of proof should shift to the three following drivers in a 4 car collision).

4. Diamond v. Weyerhaeuser, 1918, 178 Cal. 540, 174 P. 38; Tibbetts v. Nyberg, 1967, 276 Minn. 431, 150 N.W.2d 687. Cf. Denman v. Denman, 1961, 242 Miss. 59, 134 So.2d 457, and Denman v. Spain, 1961, 242 Miss. 431, 135 So.2d 195, where the two drivers were sued separately; Postlewaite v. Morales, La.App.1977, 352 So.2d 383 (one driver not present at trial). But see Davis v. Sobik's Sandwich Shops, Inc., Fla.1977, 351 So. 2d 17, appeal after remand, Fla.App.1979, 371 So.2d 709 (directed verdict for passenger proper in 3 vehicle collision).

5. Bondar v. Ar Jay Paint Co., 1959, 20 Misc.2d 643, 191 N.Y.S.2d 767; Ponce v. Black, 1964, 224 Cal.App.2d 159, 36 Cal.Rptr. 419; Bellere v. Madsen, Fla.1959, 114 So.2d 619.

6. Chicago City Railway Co. v. Barker, 1904, 209 Ill. 321, 70 N.E. 624 (defendant's car out of control); Hendler v. Coffey, 1932, 278 Mass. 339, 179 N.E. 801 (rear-end collision).

particular case one of the vehicles is a common carrier, and the plaintiff is its passenger.[7] But in such a case other courts have proceeded to apply res ipsa loquitur in favor of the passenger in his action against his carrier,[8] but not against the other driver,[9] and not in favor of one who is not a passenger of the defendant.[10] The reason sometimes given for this apparently freakish rule is that the carrier's duty of the highest care toward its passenger makes it more likely that the accident was due to its negligence than to that of the other driver.[11] Ingenious as this is, a better explanation would appear to be that these courts are in fact continuing the older rule which formerly [12] imposed special responsibility upon the carrier by setting up a procedural disadvantage requiring it to exonerate itself from fault or pay,[13] and that this policy has little relation to any inference of negligence, or to the principle of res ipsa loquitur as it is commonly applied.[14]

The question may legitimately be raised, however, whether all this is the reasonable and logical approach. When moving vehicles collide on the highway, whether or not one of them is a carrier, is there not a reasonable inference, based merely upon the known probabilities, that not one but *both* drivers have been negligent? There may of course be an inference that due care has not been used by someone,[15] as is demonstrated by the cases where one defendant has operated both vehicles.[16] It is not a question of assigning this fault to one or the other, but of recognizing that careful drivers do not ordinarily have collisions even with careless ones. If the driver collides with a stationary object, an inference of negligence arises; why should there be any other conclusion when the driver collides with a moving object which proper care requires him to look out for and avoid? There is a little authority to this effect;[17] but the argument has not made much headway since it was first advanced.[18]

An even more striking departure from the idea of exclusive control is found in Ybarra v. Spangard,[19] where an unconscious patient undergoing an operation for appendicitis

---

7. Yellow Cab Co. v. Hodgson, 1932, 91 Colo. 365, 14 P.2d 1081; Prosser, Res Ipsa Loquitur: Collisions of Carriers with Other Vehicles, 1936, 30 Ill.L.Rev. 980.

8. St. Clair v. McAllister, 1932, 216 Cal. 95, 13 P.2d 924; Capital Transit Co. v. Jackson, D.C.Cir.1945, 149 F.2d 839, certiorari denied 326 U.S. 762, 66 S.Ct. 143, 90 L.Ed. 459.

9. The distinction is clearly made in Capital Transit Co. v. Jackson, D.C.Cir.1945, 149 F.2d 839, certiorari denied 326 U.S. 762, 66 S.Ct. 143, 90 L.Ed. 459; Loudoun v. Eighth Avenue Railroad Co., 1900, 162 N.Y. 380, 56 N.E. 988; Kilgore v. Brown, 1928, 90 Cal.App. 555, 266 P. 297.

10. St. Clair v. McAllister, 1932, 216 Cal. 95, 13 P.2d 924; Zichler v. St. Louis Public Service Co., 1933, 332 Mo. 902, 59 S.W.2d 654.

11. See Housel v. Pacific Electric Railway Co., 1914, 167 Cal. 245, 139 P. 73; Plumb v. Richmond Light & Railroad Co., 1922, 233 N.Y. 285, 135 N.E. 504; James, Proof of the Breach in Negligence Cases, 1951, 37 Va. L.Rev. 179. Cf. Simpson v. Gray Line Co., 1961, 226 Or. 71, 358 P.2d 516, applying the same reasoning to the blowout of a bus tire.

12. In Christie v. Griggs, 1809, 2 Camp. 79, 170 Eng.Rep. 1088.

13. Cf. Greyhound Corp. v. Brown, 1959, 269 Ala. 520, 113 So.2d 916; Slife, The Iowa Doctrine of Res Ipsa Loquitur, 1950, 35 Iowa L.Rev. 393, 400.

14. See Prosser, Res Ipsa Loquitur: Collisions of Carriers with Other Vehicles, 1936, 30 Ill.L.Rev. 980.

15. Hence it has been held error to give an "unavoidable accident" instruction. Cobb v. Chubeck, 1960, 399 Pa. 201, 160 A.2d 207; McClarren v. Buck, 1955, 343 Mich. 300, 72 N.W.2d 31. Cf. Davis v. Sobik's Sandwich Shops, Inc., Fla.1977, 351 So.2d 17, appeal after remand, Fla.App. 1979, 371 So.2d 709 (directed verdict for plaintiff proper in 3 vehicle accident); Sheehan v. Allred, Fla.App.1962, 146 So.2d 760.

16. Birdsall v. Duluth-Superior Transit Co., 1936, 197 Minn. 411, 267 N.W. 363; Campbell v. Consolidated Traction Co., 1902, 201 Pa. 167, 50 A. 829; Greinke v. Chicago City Railroad Co., 1908, 234 Ill. 564, 85 N.E. 327; Niebalski v. Pennsylvania Railroad Co., 1915, 249 Pa. 530, 94 A. 1097. Cf. O'Connor v. United States, 2d Cir. 1958, 251 F.2d 939 (collision of planes).

17. La Rocco v. Fernandez, 1954, 130 Colo. 523, 277 P.2d 232; Krump v. Highlander Ice Cream Co., 1961, 30 Ill.App.2d 103, 173 N.E.2d 822; Pearlman v. W. O. King Lumber Co., 1939, 302 Ill.App. 190, 23 N.E.2d 826; Weddle v. Phelan, La.App.1937, 177 So. 407; Overstreet v. Ober, 1930, 14 La.App. 633, 130 So. 648. Contra, Dunaway v. Maroun, La.App.1937, 178 So. 710.

18. It was accepted in Phillips v. Noble, Cal.App. 1957, 313 P.2d 22, but the supreme court vacated the opinion, 1958, 50 Cal.2d 163, 323 P.2d 385.

19. 1944, 25 Cal.2d 486, 154 P.2d 687, 162 A.L.R. 1258. The outcome was judgment against all of the de-

suffered a traumatic injury to his shoulder, and res ipsa loquitur was applied against all of the doctors and hospital employees connected with the operation, although it seemed quite clear that not all of them could have been responsible. The basis of the decision appears quite definitely to have been the special responsibility for the plaintiff's safety undertaken by everyone concerned.[20] Again there is obviously a deliberate policy, similar to that found in the carrier cases, which requires the defendants to explain or pay, and goes beyond any reasonable inference from the facts; and one may surmise that this is not unconnected with the refusal of the medical profession to testify against one another.[21]

Beyond this there are a handful of sporadic decisions which have applied res ipsa loquitur against multiple defendants. Pennsylvania and Kansas[22] have done so where the bottler and the distributor of a beverage were sued together, without any such element of assumed special responsibility.[23] There are in addition odd cases[24] in which the principle has been applied against all of those who have contributed component parts to an integrated whole, apparently on the basis that they were so closely tied together that they must be treated in effect as one defendant. With these and other[25] infrequent exceptions, res ipsa loquitur is still not applied against multiple defendants, where it is inferable that only one has been negligent.[26]

fendants because they were unable, or unwilling, to explain. Ybarra v. Spangard, 1949, 93 Cal.App.2d 43, 208 P.2d 445.

The case was criticized in no very friendly vein in Seavey, Res Ipsa Loquitur: Tabula in Naufragio, 1950, 63 Harv.L.Rev. 643; Adamson, Medical Malpractice: Misuse of Res Ipsa Loquitur, 1962, 46 Minn.L.Rev. 1043.

The principle of the case was expanded in Anderson v. Somberg, 1975, 67 N.J. 291, 338 A.2d 1, certiorari denied 423 U.S. 929, 96 S.Ct. 279, 46 L.Ed.2d 258, appeal after remand 158 N.J.Super. 384, 386 A.2d 413, where the court shifted the burden of proof to the surgeon, hospital, distributor and manufacturer of the forceps which broke inside the plaintiff during an operation. See also Holliday v. Peden, La.App.1978, 359 So. 2d 640 (broken needle—doctrine applied against doctor, hospital and manufacturer).

Failure to establish the exclusive control element was held to defeat the plaintiff's claims in Stevens v. Union Memorial Hospital, 1981, 47 Md.App. 627, 424 A.2d 1118 (facial scars from tonsilectomy; operating room nurses not joined); Spannaus v. Otolaryngology Clinic, 1976, 308 Minn. 334, 242 N.W.2d 594 (anesthesiologist not joined), and O'Connor v. Bloomer, 1981, 116 Cal.App.3d 385, 172 Cal.Rptr. 128 (assistant surgeons entitled to summary judgment).

The case has been followed in a number of decisions. See, e.g., Kolakowski v. Voirs, 1980, 83 Ill.2d 388, 47 Ill.Dec. 392, 415 N.E.2d 397; Kitto v. Gilbert, 1977, 39 Colo.App. 374, 570 P.2d 544; Horner v. Northern Pacific Beneficial Association Hospitals, Inc., 1963, 62 Wn. 2d 351, 382 P.2d 518; Beaudoin v. Watertown Memorial Hospital, 1966, 32 Wis.2d 132, 145 N.W.2d 166; cf. Jones v. Harrisburg Polyclinic Hospital, 1981, 496 Pa. 465, 437 A.2d 1134. It was rejected in Rhodes v. De Haan, 1959, 184 Kan. 473, 337 P.2d 1043; Talbot v Dr. W. H. Groves' Latter-Day Saints Hospital, Inc., 1968, 21 Utah 2d 73, 440 P.2d 872. See Thode, Unconscious Patient: Who Should Bear the Risk of Unexplained Injuries to a Healthy Part of His Body, [1969] Utah L.Rev. 1.

20. The case was explained on this basis in Gobin v. Avenue Food Mart, 1960, 178 Cal.App.2d 345, 2 Cal. Rptr. 822, which refused to apply res ipsa loquitur against the retailer and wholesaler of a toy gun in a sealed container.

In Sanchez v. Rodriguez, 1964, 226 Cal.App.2d 439, 38 Cal.Rptr. 110, the court was careful to limit the rule to cases which laymen know do not usually occur without medical negligence.

21. Compare Van Zee v. Sioux Valley Hospital, S.D. 1982, 315 N.W.2d 489, where the plaintiff avoided the exclusive control problem on somewhat similar facts by suing the hospital.

22. Loch v. Confair, 1953, 372 Pa. 212, 93 A.2d 451; Nichols v. Nold, 1953, 174 Kan. 613, 258 P.2d 317.

23. Whether either state would apply res ipsa today against both defendants in such a case is unclear. Cf. Gilbert v. Korvette, Inc., 1974, 457 Pa. 602, 327 A.2d 94; Bias v. Montgomery Elevator Co. of Kansas, Inc., 1975, 216 Kan. 341, 532 P.2d 1053.

24. Dement v. Olin-Mathieson Chemical Corp., 5th Cir. 1960, 282 F.2d 76 (manufacturers of dynamite and cap); Becker v. American Airlines, Inc., S.D.N.Y.1961, 200 F.Supp. 839 (maker of plane, maker of altimeter, and air line). See also Prutch v. Ford Motor Co., Colo.1980, 618 P.2d 657, where the court in a strict products liability action shifted the burden of proof to the manufacturer and distributor to show that the product was not defective when it left their control.

25. See Tompkins v. Northwestern Union Trust Co., 1982, ___ Mont. ___, 645 P.2d 402; Stoddard v. Ling-Temco-Vought, Inc., C.D.Cal.1980, 513 F.Supp. 314.

26. The Pennsylvania-Kansas approach to exploding bottles cases was expressly rejected in Giant Foods, Inc. v. Washington Coca-Cola Bottling Co., 1975, 273 Md. 592, 332 A.2d 1, and res ipsa was held inappropri-

Eliminating the Plaintiff

Allied to the condition of exclusive control in the defendant is that of absence of any action on the part of the plaintiff contributing to the accident. Its purpose, of course, is to eliminate the possibility that it was the plaintiff who was responsible. If the boiler of a locomotive explodes while the plaintiff engineer is operating it, the inference of his own negligence is at least as great as that of the defendant, and res ipsa loquitur will not apply until the plaintiff has accounted for his own conduct.[27] But the requirement may easily be misunderstood. The plaintiff is seldom entirely static, and it is not necessary that the plaintiff be completely inactive, but merely that there be evidence removing the inference of the plaintiff's own responsibility.[28] Nor should this element of the doctrine preclude its application where the defendant's probable negligence consisted in a failure to protect the plaintiff from hurting himself.[29] Moreover, the advent of comparative fault should logically eliminate this element from the doctrine, unless the plaintiff's negligence would appear to be the sole proximate cause of the event, since comparative fault by its nature converts the plaintiff's contributing fault from its traditional function of barring liability into one of merely reducing damages.[30]

Evidence More Accessible to Defendant

Courts frequently have said, and on rare occasions have held, that res ipsa loquitur cannot be applied unless evidence of the true explanation of the accident is more accessible to the defendant than to the plaintiff.[31] Often this has been said when the inference of negligence did not arise anyway,[32] or the evidence of the plaintiff provided a complete explanation.[33]

It is difficult to believe that this factor ever can be controlling, or more than at best a makeweight. If the circumstances are such as to create a reasonable inference of the defendant's negligence, it cannot be supposed that the inference would ever be defeated by a showing that the defendant knew nothing about what had happened,[34] and if the facts give rise to no such inference, a plaintiff who has the burden of proof

---

ate in the case against the bottler, where the evidence pointed toward negligence by the retailer.

27. See O'Dell v. Whitworth, Mo.App.1981, 618 S.W.2d 681 (deceased sat on side of bed of moving pick-up truck); Brantley v. Stewart Building & Hardware Supplies, Inc., 1982, 274 Ark. 555, 626 S.W.2d 943; Simmons v. F.W. Woolworth Co., 1958, 163 Cal.App.2d 709, 329 P.2d 999; Dugas v. Coca-Cola Bottling Co., La.App.1978, 356 So.2d 1054 (bottle broke while plaintiff attempted to open it with wrench); cf. Silverman v. General Motors Corp., 1981, 99 Ill.App.3d 593, 54 Ill.Dec. 882, 425 N.E.2d 1099 (driver may not have been properly attentive).

28. Shahinian v. McCormick, 1963, 59 Cal.2d 554, 30 Cal.Rptr. 521, 381 P.2d 377.

29. See Emerick v. Raleigh Hills Hospital—Newport Beach, 1982, 133 Cal.App.3d 575, 184 Cal.Rptr. 92 (hospital patient leaned against or sat on bathroom sink which fell); cf. Jenkins v. Krieger, 1981, 67 Ohio St.2d 314, 423 N.E.2d 856, certiorari denied, 1981, 454 U.S. 1124, 102 S.Ct. 973, 71 L.Ed.2d 111 (prisoner died in fire set by matches jailers should have removed from him).

30. At least three states have so held. See Watzig v. Tobin, 1982, 292 Or. 645, 642 P.2d 651 (motorist 50% at fault in hitting defendant's wandering cow); Montgomery Elevator Co. v. Gordon, 1980, ___ Colo. ___, 619 P.2d 66, noted 1982, 53 U.Colo.L.Rev. 777 (critical);

1981, 52 U.Colo.L.Rev. 565 (approving); Turtenwald v. Aetna Casualty & Surety Co., 1972, 55 Wis.2d 659, 201 N.W.2d 1; Ghiardi, Res Ipsa Loquitur in Wisconsin, 1956, 39 Marquette L.Rev. 361; Campbell, Recent Developments in the Law of Negligence in Wisconsin, 1955 Wis.L.Rev. 1.

31. Hughes v. Jolliffe, 1957, 50 Wn.2d 554, 313 P.2d 678; Appalachian Insurance Co. v. Knutson, 8th Cir. 1966, 358 F.2d 679. See Strick v. Stutsman, Mo.App.1982, 633 S.W.2d 148; Holman v. Reliance Insurance Companies, La.App.1982, 414 So.2d 1298; Faby v. Air France, N.Y. City Small Cl.1982, 113 Misc.2d 840, 449 N.Y.S.2d 1018 (broken window from overflight); Wilson v. Stilwill, 1981, 411 Mich. 587, 309 N.W.2d 898 (stated as separate element); Buckelew v. Grossbard, 1981, 87 N.J. 512, 435 A.2d 1150, 1157 (doctrine grounded in "sound procedural policy of placing the duty of producing evidence on the party who has superior knowledge or opportunity for explanation of the causative circumstances"; medical malpractice).

32. Shinofield v. Curtis, 1954, 245 Iowa 1352, 66 N.W.2d 465; Cox v. Wilson, Ky.1954, 267 S.W.2d 83.

33. Johnson v. Ostrom, 1932, 128 Cal.App. 38, 16 P.2d 794; Collis v. Ashe, 1956, 212 Ga. 746, 95 S.E.2d 654; McKinney v. Frodsham, 1960, 57 Wash.2d 126, 356 P.2d 100, amended 360 P.2d 576.

34. Williams v. Field Transportation Co., Cal.App.1946, 166 P.2d 884, vacated 28 Cal.2d 696, 171 P.2d 722.

in the first instance could scarcely make out a case merely by proving that the plaintiff knew less about the matter than the defendant.[35]

Res ipsa loquitur has been applied where the defendant or his agent in charge is dead or vanished,[36] or it is otherwise clear from the facts in evidence that the defendant has no more information than the plaintiff.[37] It has been applied where the plaintiff himself has introduced definite evidence of negligence,[38] or has pleaded specific allegations,[39] and so has indicated that prima facie at least the plaintiff is at no disadvantage. And in a large number of cases in which there has been no consideration of the point it is apparent from the facts that the accident was a mysterious occurrence, as to which the defendant was as much in the dark as the plaintiff.[40]

The plaintiff's comparative ignorance of the facts in the type of cases under consideration no doubt provides some argument for the validity of the principle of res ipsa loquitur, and undoubtedly it has had some persuasive effect in making courts more willing to apply the doctrine.[41] It is sometimes advanced as a reason by those who seek to give the principle a greater procedural effect than that of a mere inference from circumstantial evidence.[42] But it cannot be regarded as an indispensable requirement, and there are few cases in which it can be said to have had any real importance.

Breach of Defendant's Duty

Res ipsa loquitur leads only to the conclusion that the defendant has not exercised reasonable care,[43] and is not in itself any proof that he was under a duty to do so. Thus a trespasser or a licensee injured by the condition of premises may still have no right to recover even though the facts speak for themselves.[44] In some cases the problem becomes one of whether the apparent cause of the accident lies within the scope of the defendant's obligation. Where an automobile unaccountably leaves the road and injures a guest, and under a guest statute the host is liable only for willful or wanton misconduct, or for gross negligence, res ipsa loquitur furnishes no proof of it.[45] And something slippery on the floor affords no res ipsa case against the owner of the premises, unless it is shown to have been there long

---

35. See Galbraith v. Busch, 1935, 267 N.Y. 230, 196 N.E. 36, reversed, 1934, 242 App.Div. 793, 275 N.Y.S. 655; Monkhouse v. Johns, La.App.1932, 142 So. 347.

36. Weller v. Worstall, 1934, 50 Ohio App. 11, 197 N.E. 410, affirmed, 1935, 129 Ohio St. 596, 196 N.E. 637; Burkett v. Johnston, 1955, 39 Tenn.App. 276, 282 S.W.2d 647; cf. Lane v. Dorney, 1960, 252 N.C. 90, 113 S.E.2d 33.

37. See Judson v. Giant Powder Co., 1885, 107 Cal. 549, 40 P. 1020 (explosion "scattered all the witnesses to the four winds"); Cox v. Northwest Airlines, Inc., 7th Cir. 1967, 379 F.2d 893 (airplane disappeared), certiorari denied 389 U.S. 1044, 88 S.Ct. 788, 19 L.Ed.2d 836; Widmyer v. Southeast Skyways, Inc., Alaska 1978, 584 P.2d 1 (plane crash); cf. Seffert v. Los Angeles Transit Lines, 1961, 56 Cal.2d 498, 15 Cal.Rptr. 161, 364 P.2d 337.

38. See infra, § 40.

39. See infra, § 40.

40. Nelson v. Zamboni, 1925, 164 Minn. 314, 204 N.W. 943; Hiell v. Golco Oil Co., 1940, 137 Ohio St. 180, 28 N.E.2d 561.

41. See Emerick v. Raleigh Hills Hospital—Newport Beach, 1982, 133 Cal.App.3d 575, 184 Cal.Rptr. 92; Oakdale Building Corp. v. Smithereen Co., 1944, 322 Ill.App. 222, 54 N.E.2d 231; Ybarra v. Spangard, 1944, 25 Cal.2d 486, 154 P.2d 687.

42. See infra, § 40.

43. Analogous to the res ipsa inference of negligence is the malfunction inference of defect in strict products liability. See Lee v. Crookston Coca-Cola Bottling Co., 1971, 290 Minn. 321, 188 N.W.2d 426 (Coke bottle exploded); Tweedy v. Wright Ford Sales, Inc., 1976, 64 Ill.2d 570, 2 Ill.Dec. 282, 357 N.E.2d 449 (brake failure); Greco v. Bucciconi Engineering Co., Inc., W.D.Pa.1967, 283 F.Supp. 978, affirmed, 3d Cir. 1969, 407 F.2d 87; Cassisi v. Maytag Co., Fla.Dist.App.1981, 396 So.2d 1140 (thorough discussion).

44. See Davis v. Jackson, Mo.App.1980, 604 S.W.2d 610; Beccue v. Rockford Park District, 1968, 94 Ill.App.2d 179, 236 N.E.2d 105.

Cf. Stocking v. Johnson Flying Service, 1963, 143 Mont. 61, 387 P.2d 312 (privilege of public necessity). But cf. Payne v. M. Greenberg Construction, App.1981, 130 Ariz. 338, 636 P.2d 116 (semble).

45. Johnson v. Johnson, Iowa 1970, 174 N.W.2d 444; Annot., 1969, 23 A.L.R.3d 1083.

enough so that he should have discovered and removed it.[46]

This question of duty arises frequently in cases of medical malpractice.[47] Since a physician or surgeon normally undertakes only to exercise the skill and care common to the profession,[48] there usually is not enough in a mistaken diagnosis alone,[49] or the unfortunate choice of the wrong method of treatment,[50] or the kind of accident or undesirable result which happens in spite of all reasonable precautions,[51] to show the necessary lack of skill or care. What this means is that ordinarily laymen are not qualified to say that a good doctor would not go wrong, and that expert testimony[52] is indispensable before any negligence can be found.[53] Such decisions, together with the notorious unwillingness of members of the medical profession to testify against one another, may impose an insuperable handicap upon a plaintiff who cannot obtain the proof.[54]

There are, however, some medical and surgical errors on which any layman is competent to pass judgment and conclude from common experience that such things do not happen if there has been proper skill and care. When an operation leaves a sponge or implement in the patient's interior,[55] or removes or injures an inappropriate part of his anatomy,[56] or when a tooth is dropped down his windpipe,[57] or the patient suffers a serious burn from a hot water bottle,[58] or when instruments are not sterilized,[59] the

---

46. See Spragins v. Jiffy Food Stores, Inc., Tex.Civ.App.1973, 492 S.W.2d 719; Winfrey v. S.S. Kresge Co., 1967, 6 Mich.App. 504, 149 N.W.2d 470; see supra, note 46.

47. Louisell & Williams, Medical Malpractice, 1981, §§ 14–15; Eaton, Res Ipsa Loquitur and Medical Malpractice in Georgia: A Reassessment, 1982, 17 Ga.L.Rev. 33; Podell, Application of Res Ipsa Loquitur in Medical Malpractice Litigation, 1977, 44 Ins.Coun.J. 634; Walker, Parker & Williamson, The Application of Res Ipsa Loquitur in Texas Medical Professional Liability Actions, 1975, 12 Hous.L.Rev. 1026; Thode, The Unconscious Patient: Who Should Bear the Risk of Unexplained Injuries to a Healthy Part of His Body, 1969 Utah L.Rev. 1; Johnson, Medical Malpractice—Doctrine of Res Ipsa Loquitur and Informed Consent, 1965, 37 U.Colo.Rev. 182; Notes, 1966, 60 Nw.U.L.Rev. 852; 1973, 8 U.San.F.L.Rev. 343; Annots., 1962, 82 A.L.R.2d 1262 (doctors); 1966, 9 A.L.R.3d 1315 (hospitals).

At least Florida has legislatively abolished the use of res ipsa in ordinary medical malpractice actions. Borghese v. Bartley, Fla.Dist.App.1981, 402 So.2d 475.

48. See supra, § 32.

49. Pizzalotto v. Wilson, La.App.1982, 411 So.2d 1150; Spike v. Sellett, 1981, 102 Ill.App.3d 270, 58 Ill.Dec. 565, 430 N.E.2d 597.

50. See Stringer v. Zacheis, 1982, 105 Ill.App.3d 521, 61 Ill.Dec. 113, 434 N.E.2d 50; Rodriguez v. Montgomery, Tex.App.1982, 630 S.W.2d 826.

51. See Wilson v. Stilwill, 1981, 411 Mich. 587, 309 N.W.2d 898 (post-operative infection); Stanley v. Fisher, 1981, ___ Ind.App. ___, 417 N.E.2d 932 (loss of testicle); LePelley v. Grefenson, 1980, 101 Idaho 422, 614 P.2d 962 (dropping bone fragment during operation on inner ear); cf. Zeno v. Lincoln General Hospital, La.App.1981, 404 So.2d 1337 (nerves unavoidably severed during surgery).

52. See supra, § 32.

53. Holmes v. Gamble, Colo.App.1980, 624 P.2d 905, affirmed 655 P.2d 405; Hanzlik v. Paustian, 1982, 211 Neb. 322, 318 N.W.2d 712; Harris v. Grizzle, Wyo.1981, 625 P.2d 747.

54. See generally Van Zee v. Sioux Valley Hospital, S.D.1982, 315 N.W.2d 489 (one of four doctors testifying "pierced the shroud of silence"); Jones v. Harrisburg Polyclinic Hospital, 1981, 496 Pa. 465, 437 A.2d 1134; Spidle v. Steward, 1980, 79 Ill.2d 1, 37 Ill.Dec. 326, 402 N.E.2d 216; supra, § 32.

55. Hyder v. Weilbaecher, 1981, 54 N.C.App. 287, 283 S.E.2d 426 (eight inch wire); see supra, § 32.

56. See Hurn v. Woods, 1982, 132 Cal.App.3d 896, 183 Cal.Rptr. 495 (broken rib and other injuries to parts of body not being treated by chiropractor); Horner v. Northern Pacific Beneficial Association Hospitals, Inc., 1963, 62 Wn.2d 351, 382 P.2d 518; cf. Buckelew v. Grossbard, 1981, 87 N.J. 512, 435 A.2d 1150 (surgeon cut into bladder thinking it was peritonea); Annot., 1971, 37 A.L.R.3d 464.

57. See Kim v. Anderson, Utah 1980, 610 P.2d 1270 (drill bit dropped down throat); Nelson v. Parker, 1930, 104 Cal.App. 770, 286 P. 1078; cf. Higdon v. Carlebach, 1957, 348 Mich. 363, 83 N.E.2d 296 (tongue cut); Butts v. Watts, Ky.1956, 290 S.W.2d 777 (portion of extracted tooth left in jaw).

58. Timbrell v. Suburban Hospital, 1935, 4 Cal.2d 68, 47 P.2d 737; cf. Jensen v. Linner, 1961, 260 Minn. 22, 108 N.W.2d 705; Becker v. Eisenstodt, 1960, 60 N.J.Super. 240, 158 A.2d 706; Terhune v. Margaret Hague Maternity Hospital, 1960, 63 N.J.Super. 106, 164 A.2d 75; Racer v. Utterman, Mo.App.1981, 629 S.W.2d 387 (surgical drape caught fire), certiorari denied, 1982, ___ U.S. ___, 103 S.Ct. 26, 74 L.Ed. 42. But cf. Fox v. Cohen, 1981, 160 Ga.App. 270, 287 S.E.2d 272 (burns on back).

59. See Suburban Hospital Association v. Hadary, 1974, 22 Md.App. 186, 322 A.2d 258.

thing speaks for itself without the aid of any expert's advice. Moreover, medical experts may provide a sufficient foundation for res ipsa loquitur on more complex matters, with testimony that the plaintiff's particular adverse result does not ordinarily occur when due care is used.[60]

One of the difficult questions arising in malpractice cases is that of the calculated risk, where the defendant, for perfectly sound and valid medical reasons, adopts a method of treatment which is known to produce damaging results in a small percentage of cases in spite of all the possible professional skill and care. Courts occasionally have fallen into the error of saying that because in the ordinary case no injury occurs, the jury may be permitted to conclude that there must have been negligence in the particular instance. This is clearly wrong, since at issue is the probability that an infrequent adverse result was caused by negligence, not the probability that it would happen at all.[61]

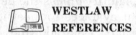
WESTLAW REFERENCES

headnote(negligen** /s circumstantial /5 evidence /p "res ipsa")

digest("res ipsa" /s infer! /s negligen** /s defendant*)

topic(272 379 313a) /p "res ipsa" & synopsis,digest (multiple numerous two three four +2 defendants)

---

60. Thompson v. Lietz, Ill.App.1981, 95 Ill.App.3d 384, 50 Ill.Dec. 915, 420 N.E.2d 232 (genital atrophy and impotence probably resulted from tightness of hernia repair that expert testified was deficient); Jones v. Harrisburg Polyclinic Hospital, 1981, 496 Pa. 465, 437 A.2d 1134 (nerve damage to arm mispositioned on operating table—good general discussion of res ipsa in medical malpractice); Buckelew v. Grossbard, N.J.1981, 87 N.J. 512, 435 A.2d 1150; see Notes, 1964, 77 Harv.L.Rev. 333; 1967, 18 Hast.L.J. 691.

61. See Wilson v. Stilwill, 1981, 411 Mich. 587, 309 N.W.2d 898 (rarity of post-operative infection alone insufficient); Brannon v. Wood, 1968, 251 Or. 349, 444 P.2d 558; Siverson v. Weber, 1962, 57 Cal.2d 834, 22 Cal.Rptr. 337, 372 P.2d 97 (overruling prior cases). A court will thus strike a res ipsa count where the plaintiff's expert testimony that the adverse result was rare and unusual is not accompanied by further evidence of specific acts of negligence. Stringer v. Zacheis, 1982, 105 Ill.App.3d 521, 61 Ill.Dec. 113, 434 N.E.2d 50; Contreras v. St. Luke's Hospital, 1978, 78 Cal.App.3d 919, 144 Cal.Rptr. 647. See generally Kaye, Probability

ybarra +3 spangard
ybarra +3 spangard & "res ipsa"
"res ipsa" /p evidence /s accessib!

---

§ 40. Res Ipsa Loquitur— Procedural Effect

There is more agreement as to the type of case to which res ipsa loquitur is applicable than as to its procedural effect when it is applied. The confusion is due in no small part to the original merger of two basic ideas in the development of the doctrine [1] and to the continued cross-purposes under which courts have sought at the same time merely to permit a conclusion to be drawn from evidence which is purely circumstantial in character, and also to make use of the principle as an instrument of policy to impose a procedural disadvantage upon certain defendants.[2]

In the ordinary case, absent special circumstances or some special relation between the parties, the great majority of the American courts regard res ipsa loquitur as no more than one form of circumstantial evidence.[3] "Where there is no direct evidence to show cause of injury, and the circumstantial evidence indicates that the negligence of the defendant is the most plausible explanation for the injury, the doctrine applies." [4]

Theory Meets Res Ipsa Loquitur, 1979, 77 Mich.L.Rev. 1456.

§ 40

1. See supra, § 39.

2. Buckelew v. Grossbard, 1981, 87 N.J. 512, 435 A.2d 1150, 1157. See generally, Heckel & Harper, Effect of the Doctrine of Res Ipsa Loquitur, 1928, 22 Ill.L.Rev. 724; Carpenter, The Doctrine of Res Ipsa Loquitur, 1934, 1 U.Chi.L.Rev. 519; Prosser, The Procedural Effect of Res Ipsa Loquitur, 1936, 20 Minn.L.Rev. 241.

3. Strick v. Stutsman, Mo.App.1982, 633 S.W.2d 148; Lanza v. Poretti, E.D.Pa.1982, 537 F.Supp. 777; Watzig v. Tobin, 1982, 292 Or. 645, 642 P.2d 651; National Tea Co. v. Gaylord Discount Department Stores, Inc., 1981, 100 Ill.App.3d 806, 56 Ill.Dec. 265, 427 N.E.2d 345.

4. Roark v. St. Paul Fire & Marine Insurance Co., La.App.1982, 415 So.2d 295.

The inference of negligence to be drawn from the circumstances is left to the jury. They are permitted, but not compelled to find it.[5] The plaintiff escapes a nonsuit, or a dismissal of his case, since there is sufficient evidence to go to the jury; but the burden of proof in most jurisdictions is not shifted to the defendant's shoulders,[6] nor is any "burden" of introducing evidence usually cast upon the defendant,[7] except in the very limited sense that if the defendant fails to do so, he runs the risk that the jury may very well find against him.[8]

The reason for this is that in the ordinary case, such as that of an automobile unaccountably leaving the highway or a stationary car starting into motion, reasonable persons may differ as to the conclusion to be drawn, both as to the probable cause of the event and as to the likelihood that negligence was associated with it. Other possibilities than negligence are in the case, which counsel should be entitled to argue to the jury; and the facts are not so definitely proved that the court can rule on them as a matter of law. In other words, many inferences are possible, and none of them is so clear that the court can say that it is compulsory.

In all such jurisdictions, however, there may be occasional cases, such as those of the human toe in the plug of chewing tobacco,[9] the collision of railway trains trying to run on the same track,[10] and perhaps a rear end collision with a stationary vehicle,[11] where the inference of negligence is so clear that no reasonable man could fail to accept it; and in such cases, if the defendant offers no explanation, a verdict should be directed for the plaintiff.[12] As a general proposition, however, the procedural effect of res ipsa may be said to be a matter of the strength of the inference to be drawn, which will vary with the circumstances of the case.

A minority of the courts, however, uniformly give res ipsa loquitur a greater effect than that of a mere permissible inference from the evidence. They have held that it shifts to the defendant the burden of going forward with the evidence, or creates a presumption which requires a directed verdict for the plaintiff unless the defendant offers sufficient evidence to meet it.[13] Louisiana, and perhaps Colorado and Mississippi,

---

5. See Lentz v. Gardin, 1978, 294 N.C. 425, 241 S.E.2d 508; Sullivan v. Crabtree, 1953, 36 Tenn.App. 469, 258 S.W.2d 782; Gilbert v. Korvette, Inc., 1974, 457 Pa. 602, 327 A.2d 94 (rejecting prior doctrine and adopting Second Restatement of Torts, § 328 D); Estate of Neal v. Friendship Manor Nursing Home, 1982, 113 Mich.App. 759, 318 N.W.2d 594. Res ipsa alone "is thus insufficient to support a summary judgment for a plaintiff unless the facts are undisputed." Rathvon v. Columbia Pacific Airlines, 1981, 30 Wn.App. 193, 633 P.2d 122.

6. Mets v. Granrud, 1980, __ Mont. __, 606 P.2d 1384, overruled in part on other grounds, Tompkins v. Northwestern Union Trust Co., 1982, __ Mont. __, 645 P.2d 402; Buckelew v. Grossbard, 1981, 87 N.J. 512, 435 A.2d 1150; Wilson v. United States, 9th Cir. 1981, 645 F.2d 728.

7. Watzig v. Tobin, 1982, 292 Or. 645, 642 P.2d 651.

8. Cf. Sweeney v. Erving, 1913, 228 U.S. 233, 33 S.Ct. 416, 57 L.Ed. 815.

9. "We can imagine no reason why, with ordinary care, human toes could not be left out of chewing tobacco, and if toes are found in chewing tobacco, it seems to us that somebody has been very careless." Cook, P. J., in Pillars v. R. J. Reynolds Tobacco Co., 1918, 117 Miss. 490, 500, 78 So. 365, 366.

10. "The time will probably never come when a collision resulting from an attempt to have two trains going at full speed, in opposite directions, pass each other, on the same track, will not be held to be negligence, in law." Rouse v. Hornsby, 8th Cir. 1895, 67 F. 219, 221, error dismissed 161 U.S. 558, 16 S.Ct. 610, 40 L.Ed. 817, certiorari denied, 1896, 163 U.S. 702, 16 S.Ct. 1205, 41 L.Ed. 320. Accord, where one train went through a red light, Moore v. Atchison, Topeka & Santa Fe Railway Co., 1961, 28 Ill.App.2d 340, 171 N.E.2d 393.

11. Gagosian v. Burdick's Television & Appliances, 1967, 254 Cal.App.2d 316, 62 Cal.Rptr. 70. But not with a moving vehicle. See supra, p. 246.

12. Horowitz v. Kevah Konner, Inc., 1979, 67 A.D.2d 38, 414 N.Y.S.2d 540 (bus left highway and turned over); Newing v. Cheatham, 1975, 15 Cal.3d 351, 124 Cal.Rptr. 193, 540 P.2d 33 (plane crash); Whitley v. Hix, 1961, 207 Tenn. 683, 343 S.W.2d 851 (driver lost control of car at curve); Annot., 1964, 97 A.L.R.2d 522.

13. See Hammond v. Scot Lad Foods, Inc., 1982, __ Ind.App. __, 436 N.E.2d 362; Hyder v. Weilbaecher, 1981, 54 N.C.App. 287, 283 S.E.2d 426 (medical malpractice); Mets v. Granrud, 1980, __ Mont. __, 606 P.2d 1384, overruled in part Tompkins v. Northwestern Union Trust Co., 1982, __ Mont. __, 645 P.2d 402;

have gone further, and have held that it shifts to the defendant the ultimate burden of proof, requiring the defendant to introduce evidence of greater weight than that of the plaintiff.[14] Such courts have sometimes been compelled to retreat from this position, either by occasional decisions to the contrary, or by recognizing, under other names, the type of res ipsa case which creates only a permissible inference of negligence. The trend has been toward viewing res ipsa loquitur as raising only a permissible inference which merely gets the plaintiff to the jury.[15]

The source of the decisions giving res ipsa greater procedural force is usually to be traced to early cases involving injuries to passengers at the hands of carriers, where it was held that the carrier had the burden of proof on the issue of negligence.[16] The partial survival of such an early attitude,[17] however, may have been due to a more or less conscious policy of requiring the defendant to produce evidence explaining the accident or pay.[18] Since at least in some cases the defendant will be unable to explain, this results in imposing upon him the losses due to such unexplainable events, and so may amount to the imposition of strict liability without fault.[19]

Such a policy seems appropriate in only certain limited classes of cases, such as perhaps those involving carriers and certain types of medical accidents, where some special responsibility assumed by the defendant toward the plaintiff justifies placing upon him the burden of proof, thus fairly requiring the defendant to exonerate himself by a preponderance of the evidence or make good the loss.[20] In such a case, the same burden should rest upon the defendant even when the plaintiff offers the direct testimony of eyewitnesses; and such a policy does not seem properly to be connected with res ipsa loquitur at all.

It has been suggested[21] that the whole procedural argument is only a tempest in a teapot, for the reason that res ipsa loquitur at least gets the plaintiff to the jury, and the jury in practice finds in his favor. Academically speaking, this may be true; but the rule to be adopted still has its importance for the trial lawyer. Not only do occasional juries find for the defendant, even though he offers no explanation,[22] but "inference," "presumption," and "burden of proof" have been involved in literally thousands of instructions, each of them replete with possibilities of reversible error.

Newing v. Cheatham, 1975, 15 Cal.3d 351, 124 Cal.Rptr. 193, 540 P.2d 33.

14. Toussant v. Guice, La.App.1982, 414 So.2d 850; Johnson v. Coca-Cola Bottling Co., 1960, 239 Miss. 759, 125 So.2d 537; Weiss v. Axler, 1958, 137 Colo. 544, 328 P.2d 88; But see Graf v. Tracy, 1977, 194 Colo. 1, 568 P.2d 467 ("rebuttable presumption," but relying on *Weiss*); Holmes v. Gamble, Colo.App.1980, 624 P.2d 905, affirmed 655 P.2d 405.

15. See supra, note 5.

16. See for example Sullivan v. Philadelphia & Reading Railway Co., 1858, 30 Pa. 234; Grignoli v. Chicago & G. E. R. Co., N.Y.1871, 4 Daly, 182; Patton v. Pickles, 1898, 50 La.Ann. 857, 24 So. 290. The origin is recognized in Klingman v. Loew's, Inc., 1941, 209 Minn. 449, 296 N.W. 528. See supra, § 39.

17. In many of the earlier cases brought by passengers against carriers, res ipsa was given an increased procedural effect in the form of a presumption or shift in the burden of proof. See Bond v. St. Louis-San Francisco Railway Co., 1926, 315 Mo. 987, 288 S.W. 777; Hartnett v. May Department Stores Co., 1935, 231 Mo.App. 1116, 85 S.W.2d 644; Ritchie v. Thomas, 1950, 190 Or. 95, 224 P.2d 543.

18. See Carpenter, The Doctrine of Res Ipsa Loquitur in California, 1937, 10 So.Cal.L.Rev. 166; Prosser, Res Ipsa Loquitur, 1937, 10 So.Cal.L.Rev. 459; Carpenter, Res Ipsa Loquitur, 1937, 10 So.Cal.L.Rev. 467; Jaffe, Res Ipsa Loquitur Vindicated, 1951, 1 Buffalo L.Rev. 1.

19. See Note, 1935, 3 U.Chi.L.Rev. 126; Bohlen, The Effect of Rebuttable Presumptions of Law Upon the Burden of Proof, 1920, 68 U.Pa.L.Rev. 307, 316.

20. This approach was rejected in Rathvon v. Columbia Pacific Airlines, 1981, 30 Wn.App. 193, 633 P.2d 122.

21. 2 Harper and James, Law of Torts, 1956, 1104.

22. See Sullivan v. Crabtree, 1953, 36 Tenn.App. 160, 258 S.W.2d 782, Tuengel v. Stobbs, 1962, 59 Wn.2d 477, 367 P.2d 1008 (decision by trial court); Simpson v. Gray Line Co., 1961, 226 Or. 71, 358 P.2d 516.

Specific Evidence Introduced by Plaintiff

Where the plaintiff introduces specific evidence of the defendant's negligence, the question arises whether he may still rely upon the inference provided by a res ipsa loquitur case. It is sometimes said that where the facts are disclosed by evidence there is no room for inference, or that by attempting specific proof the plaintiff has "waived" the benefit of the doctrine.[23]

Plaintiff is of course bound by his own evidence; but proof of some specific facts does not necessarily exclude inferences of others. When the plaintiff shows that the railway car in which he was a passenger was derailed, there is an inference that the defendant railroad has somehow been negligent. When the plaintiff goes further and shows that the derailment was caused by an open switch, the plaintiff destroys any inference of other causes; but the inference that the defendant has not used proper care in looking after its switches is not destroyed, but considerably strengthened.[24] If the plaintiff goes further still and shows that the switch was left open by a drunken switchman on duty, there is nothing left to infer; and if the plaintiff shows that the switch was thrown by an escaped convict with a grudge against the railroad, the plaintiff has proven himself out of court.[25] It is only in this sense that when the facts are known there is no inference, and res ipsa loquitur simply vanishes from the case.[26] On the basis of reasoning such as this, it is quite generally agreed that the introduction of some evidence which tends to show specific acts of negligence on the part of the defendant, but which does not purport to furnish a full and complete explanation of the occurrence, does not destroy the inferences which are consistent with the evidence, and so does not deprive the plaintiff of the benefit of res ipsa loquitur.[27]

Pleading Specific Negligence

A similar problem arises where the plaintiff has alleged specific negligence in his pleadings, and seeks to take advantage of res ipsa loquitur at the trial.[28] At least four varying positions have been taken by the courts: that the plaintiff by his specific allegations has waived or lost his right to rely on the doctrine;[29] that the plaintiff may take advantage of it if the inference of negligence to be drawn is consistent with the specific allegations;[30] that it may be applied only if the specific pleading is accompanied by a general allegation of negligence;[31] and

---

23. Jackson v. 919 Corp., 1951, 344 Ill.App. 519, 101 N.E.2d 594; Heffter v. Northern States Power Co., 1927, 173 Minn. 215, 217 N.W. 102.

24. Bolander v. Northern Pacific Railway Co., 1964, 63 Wn.2d 659, 388 P.2d 729. Cf. Citrola v. Eastern Air Lines, 2d Cir. 1959, 264 F.2d 815; Vogreg v. Shepard Ambulance Co., 1955, 47 Wn.2d 659, 289 P.2d 350; New York Chicago & St. Louis Railroad Co. v. Henderson, 1957, 237 Ind. 456, 146 N.E.2d 531, rehearing denied 237 Ind. 456, 147 N.E.2d 237.

25. Cf. Rea v. St. Louis-San Francisco Railroad Co., Mo.1967, 411 S.W.2d 96; Augspurger v. Western Auto Supply Co., 1963, 257 Iowa 777, 134 N.W.2d 913; Hill v. Hill, Mo.1966, 401 S.W.2d 438; Hall v. National Supply Co., 5th Cir. 1959, 270 F.2d 379; Tillery v. Ellison, Okl.1959, 345 P.2d 434.

26. See Mobil Chemical Co. v. Bell, Tex.1974, 517 S.W.2d 245; Racer v. Utterman, Mo.App.1981, 629 S.W.2d 387, 397, certiorari denied, 1982, ___ U.S. ___, 103 S.Ct. 26, 74 L.Ed. 42.

27. Zimmer v. Celebrities, Inc., 1980, 44 Colo.App. 515, 615 P.2d 76; Kranda v. Houser-Norborg Medical Corp., 1981, ___ Ind.App. ___, 419 N.E.2d 1024; Mobil Chemical Co. v. Bell, Tex.1974, 517 S.W.2d 245. For the effect on res ipsa of specific negligence evidence, see generally Note, 1968, 42 St. Johns L.Rev. 410; Annot., 1954, 33 A.L.R.2d 791.

28. See Mobil Chemical Co. v. Bell, Tex.1974, 517 S.W.2d 245 (full discussion). See generally Niles, Pleading Res Ipsa Loquitur, 1930, 7 N.Y.U.L.Rev. 415; Notes, 1958, 27 Ford.L.Rev. 411; 1964, 29 Mo.L.Rev. 382; Annot., 1965, 2 A.L.R.3d 1335.

29. Sankey v. Williamsen, 1966, 180 Neb. 714, 144 N.W.2d 429; Kerby v. Chicago Motor Coach Co., 1960, 28 Ill.App.2d 259, 171 N.E.2d 412; Langeland v. 78th & Park Ave. Corp., Sup.1954, 129 N.Y.S.2d 719; Annot., 1965, 2 A.L.R.3d 1335.

30. Pickwick Stages Corp. v. Messinger, 1934, 44 Ariz. 174, 36 P.2d 168; Wallace v. Norris, 1940, 310 Ky. 424, 220 S.W.2d 967; Short v. D. R. B. Logging Co., 1951, 192 Or. 383, 235 P.2d 340.

31. Whitby v. One-O-One Trailer Rental Co., 1963, 191 Kan. 653, 383 P.2d 560; Erckman v. Northern Illinois Gas Co., 1965, 61 Ill.App.2d 137, 210 N.E.2d 42; Williams v. St. Louis Public Service Co., 1952, 363 Mo. 625, 253 S.W.2d 97; Sherman v. Hartman, 1955, 137 Cal.App.2d 589, 290 P.2d 894.

that it is available without regard to the form of the pleading.[32]

The policy underlying the rule that specific pleadings limit proof is that a defendant who comes into court with notice only of a specific claim should not be required to litigate other issues, or to meet inferences based on a theory advanced for the first time at the trial. But any inferences consistent with the specific pleading should not be excluded. And if the specific allegations are accompanied by a claim of negligence in general terms, the defendant has at least received notice that the plaintiff is not relying exclusively upon the specific allegations, and can scarcely claim to have been surprised or misled.

Effect of Rebutting Evidence

When the defendant in turn offers evidence to show that the event was not due to his negligence, there is the further question of the extent to which the principle of res ipsa loquitur will survive in the face of such proof. It is generally agreed, except in one or two jurisdictions,[33] that the burden of proof is not upon the defendant, that he may not be required to introduce any evidence at all, and that any evidence he does introduce at most need only permit the jury to say that it is as probable that he was not negligent as that he was.[34] Against the defendant's evidence must be balanced any inference of negligence to be drawn from the circumstances of the case, which the jury may choose to draw or reject, and which has weight only so long as reasonable persons may still draw it from the facts in evidence.[35]

If the defendant seeks a directed verdict in his favor, he must produce evidence which will destroy any reasonable inference of negligence, or so completely contradict it that reasonable persons could no longer accept it. The evidence necessary to do this will vary with the strength of the inference. It takes more of an explanation to justify a falling elephant than a falling brick, more to account for a hundred defective bottles than for one. If the defendant shows definitely that the occurrence was caused by some outside agency over which the defendant had no control,[36] that it was of a kind which commonly occurs without negligence on the part of anyone,[37] or that it could not have been avoided by the exercise of all reasonable care,[38] the inference of negligence is no longer permissible, and the verdict is directed for the defendant. The res ipsa case has been

---

Some cases indicate that res ipsa itself must be specifically pleaded in this context before it can be relied upon at trial. Cf. Lambert v. Gearhart-Owen Industries, Inc., Tex.App.1981, 626 S.W.2d 845, 847 ("A plaintiff is not entitled to invoke the *res ipsa* doctrine when he pleads specific acts of negligence and does not give the defendant fair notice in the pleadings that he intends to rely upon the doctrine."); Mobil Chemical Co. v. Bell, Tex.1974, 517 S.W.2d 245.

32. Johnson v. Greenfield, 1946, 210 Ark. 985, 198 S.W.2d 403; Nashville Interurban Railway Co. v. Gregory, 1917, 137 Tenn. 422, 193 S.W. 1053; Briganti v. Connecticut Co., 1934, 119 Conn. 316, 175 A. 679; Loos v. Mountain Fuel Supply Co., 1940, 99 Utah 496, 108 P.2d 254. See also Creswell v. Temple Milling Co., Okl.1972, 499 P.2d 421, noted, 1973, 26 Okl.L.Rev. 100.

33. See supra, note 14.

34. See Nopson v. Wockner, 1952, 40 Wn.2d 645, 245 P.2d 1022; Micek v. Weaver-Jackson Co., 1936, 12 Cal.App.2d 19, 54 P.2d 768; Vonault v. O'Rourke, 1934, 97 Mont. 92, 33 P.2d 535.

35. Cf. Prooth v. Wallsh, Sup.1980, 105 Misc.2d 608, 432 N.Y.S.2d 666 (surgical clamp left inside heart by-pass patient; critical deterioration in condition during operation required that search be abandoned and chest closed immediately); Motiejaitis v. Johnson, 1933, 117 Conn. 631, 169 A. 606; Note, 1967, 43 N.D.L.Rev. 556.

36. Wagner v. Coca-Cola Bottling Co., S.D.1982, 319 N.W.2d 807; Lopes v. Narragansett Electric Co., 1967, 102 R.I. 128, 229 A.2d 55.

But the mere introduction of contradicted or otherwise inconclusive evidence suggesting another cause will not entitle the defendant to a directed verdict. Wood v. Indemnity Insurance Co. of North America, 1956, 273 Wis. 93, 76 N.W.2d 610; Furr v. McGrath, Okl.1959, 340 P.2d 243.

37. Strick v. Stutsman, Mo.App.1982, 633 S.W.2d 148; Town of Reasnor v. Pyland Construction Co., Iowa 1975, 229 N.W.2d 269; American Village Corp. v. Springfield Lumber & Building Supply, 1974, 269 Or. 41, 522 P.2d 891.

38. Oliver v. Union Transfer Co., 1934, 17 Tenn.App. 694, 71 S.W.2d 478. See supra, note 51.

overthrown by showing that it is not a res ipsa case.

But if the defendant merely offers evidence of his own acts and precautions amounting to reasonable care, it is seldom that a verdict can be directed in his favor.[39] The inference from the circumstances remains in the case to contradict his evidence. If the defendant testifies that he used proper care to insulate his wires,[40] to inspect his chandelier,[41] to drive his bus,[42] or to keep defunct mice and wandering insect life out of his bottled beverage,[43] the fact that electricity escaped from the wires, that the chandelier fell, that the bus went into the ditch and the bug was in the bottle, with the background of common experience that such things do not usually happen if proper care is used, may permit reasonable men to find that his witnesses are not to be believed, that the precautions described were not sufficient to conform to the standard required [44] or were not faithfully carried out,[45] and that the whole truth has not been told. It is of course not impossible that proof of proper care may be so overwhelming as to call for a directed verdict, but in the ordinary case it will not be sufficient to destroy the inference from res ipsa loquitur.[46]

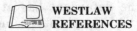

WESTLAW REFERENCES

"res ipsa" /s procedur** /2 effect
digest("res ipsa" /p rebut*** /s evidence)

---

39. Directed verdicts for defendant were upheld in Swenson v. Purity Baking Co., 1931, 183 Minn. 289, 236 N.W. 310; Dunning v. Kentucky Utilities Co., 1937, 270 Ky. 44, 109 S.W.2d 6; Nichols v. Continental Baking Co., 3d Cir. 1929, 34 F.2d 141. The correctness of these decisions seems open to question. As the defendant's evidence approaches definite proof that the defect could not be present, it is all the more clearly rebutted by the fact that the defect is there. See Prosser, The Procedural Effect of Res Ipsa Loquitur, 1936, 20 Minn.L.Rev. 241, 268; James, Proof of the Breach in Negligence Cases, 1951, 37 Va.L.Rev. 179, 227.

It is possible, however, that the evidence of due care may be found conclusively to refute the contention that the injury was traceable to the defendant, and to point to another possible cause. Cf. Rowe v. Oscar Ewing Distributing Co., Ky.1962, 357 S.W.2d 882; Rogers v. Coca Cola Bottling Co., Tex.Civ.App.1941, 156 S.W.2d 325, error refused.

40. Humphrey v. Twin State Gas & Electric Co., 1927, 100 Vt. 414, 139 A. 440. Cf. Ryan v. Zweck-Wollenberg Co., 1954, 266 Wis. 630, 64 N.W.2d 226; Reynolds Metals Co. v. Yturbide, 9th Cir. 1958, 258 F.2d 321, certiorari denied 358 U.S. 840, 79 S.Ct. 66, 3 L.Ed.2d 76; Langlinais v. Geophysical Service, Inc., 1959, 237 La. 585, 111 So.2d 781.

41. Goldstein v. Levy, 1911, 74 Misc. 463, 132 N.Y.S. 373.

42. Francisco v. Circle Tours Sightseeing Co., 1928, 125 Or. 80, 265 P. 801. Cf. Lewis v. Wolk, 1950, 312 Ky. 536, 228 S.W.2d 432; Knippenberg v. Windemuth, 1968, 249 Md. 159, 238 A.2d 915; Tarter v. Souderton Motor Co., E.D.Pa.1966, 257 F.Supp. 598.

43. Crystal Coca Cola Bottling Co. v. Cathey, 1957, 83 Ariz. 163, 317 P.2d 1094; Coca-Cola Bottling Co. v. Davidson, 1937, 193 Ark. 825, 102 S.W.2d 833; Bagre v. Daggett Chocolate Co., 1940, 126 Conn. 659, 13 A.2d 757 (tooth filling in candy); Gustafson v. Gate City Coop. Creamery, 1964, 80 S.D. 430, 126 N.W.2d 121 (glass in butter); Atlanta Coca-Cola Bottling Co. v. Burke, 1964, 109 Ga.App. 53, 134 S.E.2d 909 (exploding bottle).

44. Crigger v. Coca Cola Bottling Co., 1915, 132 Tenn. 545, 179 S.W. 155; Collins Baking Co. v. Savage, 1933, 227 Ala. 408, 150 So. 336; Minutilla v. Providence Ice Cream Co., 1929, 50 R.I. 43, 144 A. 884; Webb v. Brown & Williamson Tobacco Co., 1939, 121 W.Va. 115, 2 S.E.2d 898.

45. Richenbacher v. California Packing Corp., 1924, 250 Mass. 198, 145 N.E. 281; Try-Me Beverage Co. v. Harris, 1928, 217 Ala. 302, 116 So. 147; cf. Rozumailski v. Philadelphia Coca Cola Bottling Co., 1929, 296 Pa. 114, 145 A. 700. See Notes, 1935, 21 Va.L.Rev. 306; 1935, 23 Ky.L.J. 534.

46. Landerman v. Hamilton, 1964, 230 Cal.App.2d 782, 41 Cal.Rptr. 335. Cf. Prooth v. Wallsh, Sup.1980, 105 Misc.2d 608, 432 N.Y.S.2d 666.

Chapter 7

PROXIMATE CAUSE

Table of Sections

Sec.
41. Causation in Fact.
42. Proximate Cause: Scope of the Problem.
43. Unforeseeable Consequences.
44. Intervening Causes.
45. Functions of Court and Jury.

§ 41. Causation in Fact

An essential element of the plaintiff's cause of action for negligence, or for that matter for any other tort, is that there be some reasonable connection between the act or omission of the defendant and the damage which the plaintiff has suffered. This connection usually is dealt with by the courts in terms of what is called "proximate cause," or "legal cause." There is perhaps nothing in the entire field of law which has called forth more disagreement, or upon which the opinions are in such a welter of confusion. Nor, despite the manifold attempts which have been made to clarify the subject,[1] is there yet any general agreement as to the best approach. Much of this confusion is due to the fact that no one problem is involved, but a number of different prob-

---

§ 41

1. Green, Rationale of Proximate Cause, 1927; Bohlen, The Probable or the Natural Consequence as the Test of Liability in Negligence, 1901, 49 Am.L.Reg. 79, 148; Bingham, Some Suggestions Concerning "Legal Cause" at Common Law, 1909, 9 Col.L.Rev. 16, 136; Smith, Legal Cause in Actions of Tort, 1911, 25 Harv.L. Rev. 102, 233; Beale, The Proximate Consequences of an Act, 1920, 33 Harv.L.Rev. 633; Green, Are Negligence and "Proximate" Cause Determined by the Same Test, 1923, 1 Tex.L.Rev. 224, 423; Edgerton, Legal Cause, 1924, 72 U.Pa.L.Rev. 211, 343; McLaughlin, Proximate Cause, 1925, 39 Harv.L.Rev. 149; Green, Are There Dependable Rules of Causation, 1929, 77 U.Pa.L.Rev. 601; Carpenter, Workable Rules for Determining Proximate Cause, 1932, 20 Cal.L.Rev. 229, 396, 471; Prosser, The Minnesota Court on Proximate Cause, 1936, 21 Minn.L.Rev. 19; Campbell, Duty, Fault and Legal Cause, [1938] Wis.L.Rev. 402; Gregory, Proximate Cause in Negligence—A Retreat from Rationalization, 1938, 6 U.Chi.L.Rev. 36; Carpenter, Proximate Cause, 1940–43, 14 So.Cal.L.Rev. 1, 115, 416, 15 So.Cal.L.Rev. 187, 304, 427, 16 So.Cal.L.Rev. 1, 61, 275; Morris, Proximate Cause in Minnesota, 1950, 34 Minn. L.Rev. 185; Green, Proximate Cause in Texas Negligence Law, 1950, 28 Tex.L.Rev. 71, 621, 755; Prosser, Proximate Cause in California, 1950, 38 Cal.L.Rev. 369; James and Perry, Legal Cause, 1951, 60 Yale L.J. 761; Myers, Causation and Common Sense, 1951, 5 U.Miami L.Q. 238; Morris, Duty, Negligence and Causation, 1952, 101 U.Pa.L.Rev. 189; Pound, Causation, 1957, 67 Yale L.J. 1. Williams, Causation in the Law, [1961] Camb.L.J. 62; Green, The Causal Relation Issue in Negligence Law, 1962, 60 Mich.L.Rev. 543; R. Keeton, Legal Cause in the Law of Torts, 1963; Hart, Varieties of Legal Responsibility, 1967, 83 L.Q.Rev. 346; Thode, Tort Analysis: Duty-Risk v. Proximate Cause and the Rational Allocation of Functions Between Judge and Jury, 1977 Utah L.Rev. 1.

lems, which are not distinguished clearly, and that language appropriate to a discussion of one is carried over to cast a shadow upon the others.²

"Proximate cause"—in itself an unfortunate term—is merely the limitation which the courts have placed upon the actor's responsibility for the consequences of the actor's conduct. In a philosophical sense, the consequences of an act go forward to eternity, and the causes of an event go back to the dawn of human events, and beyond. But any attempt to impose responsibility upon such a basis would result in infinite liability for all wrongful acts, and would "set society on edge and fill the courts with endless litigation." ³ As a practical matter, legal responsibility must be limited to those causes which are so closely connected with the result and of such significance that the law is justified in imposing liability. Some boundary must be set to liability for the consequences of any act, upon the basis of some social idea of justice or policy.

This limitation is to some extent associated with the nature and degree of the connection in fact between the defendant's acts and the events of which the plaintiff complains. Often to greater extent, however, the legal limitation on the scope of liability is associated with policy—with our more or less inadequately expressed ideas of what justice demands, or of what is administratively possible and convenient. Where the defendant excavated a hole by the side of the road, and the plaintiff's runaway horse ran into it,⁴ it scarcely could be pretended that the hole was not a cause of the harm, and a very important one. If the defendant escaped responsibility, it was because the policy of the law did not require the defendant to safeguard the plaintiff against such a risk. On the same basis, if the defendant drives through the state of New Jersey at an excessive speed, and arrives in Philadelphia in time for the car to be struck by lightning,⁵ speed is a cause of the accident, since without it the car would not have been there in time; and if the defendant driver is not liable to a passenger, it is because in the eyes of the law the negligence did not extend to such a risk. The attempt to deal with such cases in the language of causation leads often to confusion.⁶

Causation as Fact

Although it is not without its complications, the simplest and most obvious problem connected with "proximate cause" is that of causation in "fact." ⁷ This question of "fact" ordinarily is one upon which all the learning, literature and lore of the law are largely lost. It is a matter upon which lay opinion is quite as competent as that of the most experienced court. For that reason, in

---

2. See Prosser, Proximate Cause in California, 1950, 38 Cal.L.Rev. 369.

3. Mitchell, J., in North v. Johnson, 1894, 58 Minn. 242, 59 N.W. 1012. The same problems arise in the criminal law, where the limits of criminal responsibility are in question; and they are dealt with, broadly speaking, in the same manner. See Note, 1962, 56 Northw. U.L.Rev. 791. As to the comparative law, see Ryu, Causation in Criminal Law, 1958, 106 U.Pa.L.Rev. 773.

4. Cf. La Londe v. Peake, 1901, 82 Minn. 124, 84 N.W. 726; Alexander v. Town of New Castle, 1888, 115 Ind. 51, 17 N.E. 200; Milostan v. City of Chicago, 1909, 148 Ill.App. 540.

5. Cf. Berry v. Sugar Notch Borough, 1899, 191 Pa. 345, 43 A. 240; Balfe v. Kramer, 1936, 249 App.Div. 746, 291 N.Y.S. 842; Doss v. Town of Big Stone Gap, 1926, 145 Va. 520, 134 S.E. 563; Lewis v. Flint & P. M. Railway Co., 1884, 54 Mich. 55, 19 N.W. 744.

6. Defendant operates an automobile over five miles of highway at a speed in excess of what is proper, and so arrives at a point in the street just at the moment that a child unexpectedly darts out from the curb. Is speed a cause of the death of the child? Cf. Dombeck v. Chicago, Milwaukee, St. Paul & Pacific Railroad Co., 1964, 24 Wis.2d 420, 129 N.W.2d 185.

Suppose that the defendant knows in advance the precise moment when the child will dash into the highway, and purposely operates the car at a carefully calculated speed, to arrive precisely at that instant, in order to kill the child. Is the speed a cause of the death? Are your answers more influenced by perceptions of causal connection in fact or by policy considerations related to differences between intent and negligence?

7. See, generally, Hart and Honoré, Causation in the Law, 1959; Becht and Miller, The Test of Factual Causation, 1961; Malone, Ruminations on Cause-in-Fact, 1956, 9 Stan.L.Rev. 60; Green, The Causal Relation Issue in Negligence Law, 1962, 60 Mich.L.Rev. 543.

the ordinary case, it is peculiarly a question for the jury.

Although we speak of this issue as one of "fact," curiously the classic test for determining cause in "fact" directs the "factfinder" to compare what did occur with what would have occurred if hypothetical, contrary-to-fact conditions had existed. Some comparison between factual and contrary-to-fact conditions is implicit in the classic formulation that a cause is a *necessary* antecedent, and in the explication that in a very real and practical sense, the term "cause in fact" embraces all things which have so far contributed to the result that without them it would not have occurred.

In a few types of cases, special difficulties arise from this inherent necessity of turning to hypothetical contrary-to-fact conditions for comparison in deciding whether a cause-in-fact relation existed.[8] In most cases, however, the general idea that a basic essential of legal cause is causal connection in fact serves well enough.

The conception of causation in fact extends not only to positive acts and active physical forces, but also to pre-existing passive conditions which have played a material part in bringing about the event.[9] In particular, it applies to the defendant's omissions as well as the defendant's acts. The failure to extinguish a fire may be quite as important in causing the destruction of a building as setting it in the first place.[10] The failure to fence a railway track may be a cause, and an important one, that a child is struck by a train.[11] It is familiar law that if such omissions are culpable they will result in liability.

The But-For and Substantial-Factor Rules

An act or an omission is not regarded as a cause of an event if the particular event would have occurred without it. A failure to fence a hole in the ice plays no part in causing the death of runaway horses which could not have been halted if the fence had been there,[12] though of course making the hole did play a part. A failure to have a lifeboat ready is not a cause of the death of a person who sinks without trace immediately upon falling into the ocean,[13] though taking the person out to sea was a cause. The failure to install a proper fire escape on a hotel is no cause of the death of a man suffocated in bed by smoke.[14] The omission of crossing signals by an approaching train is of no significance when an automobile driver runs into the sixty-eighth car.[15] The presence of a railroad embankment may be no cause of

---

8. See infra, this section, "The But-For and Substantial-Factor Rules," and "An Alternative to the Substantial-Factor Rule."

9. See infra, § 42, Proposed Formulae, Cause and Condition.

10. McNally v. Colwell, 1892, 91 Mich. 527, 52 N.W. 70; Cobb v. Twitchell, 1926, 91 Fla. 539, 108 So. 186; Musgrove v. Pandelis, [1919] 2 K.B. 43.

11. Hayes v. Michigan Central Railroad Co., 1884, 111 U.S. 228, 4 S.Ct. 369, 28 L.Ed. 410; Heiting v. Chicago, Rock Island & Pacific Railway Co., 1911, 252 Ill. 466, 96 N.E. 842.

12. Stacy v. Knickerbocker Ice Co., 1893, 84 Wis. 614, 54 N.W. 1091; Sowles v. Moore, 1893, 65 Vt. 322, 26 A. 629. Cf. Ellis v. H. S. Finke, Inc., 6th Cir. 1960, 278 F.2d 54 (fall would not have been prevented by safety device on a hoist); Southern Bell Telephone & Telegraph Co. v. Spears, 1956, 212 Ga. 537, 93 S.E.2d 659, conformed to 94 Ga.App. 329, 94 S.E.2d 514 (location of pole too close to highway; would have been hit if at proper distance); People's Service Drug Stores v. Somerville, 1931, 161 Md. 662, 158 A. 12 (poison label on prescription medicine would not have prevented too heavy a dose).

13. Ford v. Trident Fisheries Co., 1919, 232 Mass. 400, 122 N.E. 389; New York Central Railroad Co. v. Grimstad, 2d Cir. 1920, 264 F. 334; Russell v. Merchants & Miners Transportation Co., E.D.Va.1937, 19 F.Supp. 349. But cf. Kirincich v. Standard Dredging Co., 3d Cir. 1940, 112 F.2d 163, and Zinnel v. United States Shipping Board Emergency Fleet Corp., 2d Cir. 1925, 10 F.2d 47, where there was evidence that the drowning man might have been saved.

Cf. Berryhill v. Nichols, 1935, 171 Miss. 769, 158 So. 470, and Lippold v. Kidd, 1928, 126 Or. 160, 269 P. 210, where the evidence was that the best possible medical treatment would not have averted the injury.

14. Weeks v. McNulty, 1898, 101 Tenn. 495, 48 S.W. 809; Lee v. Carwile, La.App.1964, 168 So.2d 469; Smith v. The Texan, Inc., Tex.Civ.App.1944, 180 S.W.2d 1010, error refused (no showing guest made any effort to use it); Tibbits v. Crowell, Tex.Civ.App.1968, 434 S.W.2d 919 (no showing could have used it); Rosser v. Atlantic Trust & Security Co., 1937, 168 Va. 389, 191 S.E. 651 (at least two available exits).

15. Sullivan v. Boone, 1939, 205 Minn. 437, 286 N.W. 350; Wink v. Western Maryland Railway Co., 1935, 116 Pa.Super. 374, 176 A. 760. Accord: Holman

the inundation of the plaintiff's land by a cloudburst which would have flooded it in any case.[16] On similar reasoning it has been said [17] that the omission of a traffic signal to an automobile driver who could not have seen it if it had been given is not a cause of the ensuing collision.[18]

From such cases [19] many courts [20] have derived a rule, commonly known as the "but for" or "sine qua non" rule, which may be stated as follows: The defendant's conduct is a cause of the event if the event would not have occurred but for that conduct; conversely, the defendant's conduct is not a cause of the event, if the event would have occurred without it.[21] As a rule regarding legal responsibility, at most this must be a rule of exclusion: if the event would not have occurred "but for" the defendant's negligence, it still does not follow that there is liability, since other considerations remain to be discussed and may prevent liability.[22] It should be quite obvious that, once events are set in motion, there is, in terms of causation alone, no place to stop. The event without millions of causes is simply inconceivable; and the mere fact of causation, as distinguished from the nature and degree of the causal connection, can provide no clue of any kind to singling out those which are to be held legally responsible. It is for this reason that instructions to the jury that they must find the defendant's conduct to be "the sole cause," or "the dominant cause," or "the proximate cause" of the injury are rightly condemned as misleading error.[23]

Restricted to the question of causation alone, and regarded merely as a rule of exclusion, the "but for" rule serves to explain the greater number of cases; but there is one type of situation in which it fails. If two causes concur to bring about an event, and either one of them, operating alone, would have been sufficient to cause the identical result, some other test is needed. Two motorcycles simultaneously pass the plaintiff's horse, which is frightened and runs away; either one alone would have caused the fright.[24] A stabs C with a knife, and B fractures C's skull with a rock; either wound would be fatal, and C dies from the effects of both.[25] The defendant sets a fire,

v. Chicago, Rock Island & Pacific Railway Co., 1876, 62 Mo. 562 (a whistle means nothing to a cow); New Orleans & N. E. Railroad Co. v. Burge, 1941, 191 Miss. 303, 2 So.2d 825 (would not have been heard); Haire v. Brooks, 1938, 42 N.M. 634, 83 P.2d 980 (good brakes would not have stopped in time).

16. Baltimore & Ohio Railroad Co. v. Sulphur Spring Independent School District, 1880, 96 Pa. 65; City of Piqua v. Morris, 1918, 98 Ohio St. 42, 120 N.E. 300; Illinois Central Railroad Co. v. Wright, 1924, 135 Miss. 435, 100 So. 1; Cole v. Shell Petroleum Corp., 1939, 149 Kan. 25, 86 P.2d 740.

17. But see infra, this section, An Alternative to the Substantial Factor Rule.

18. Rouleau v. Blotner, 1931, 84 N.H. 539, 152 A. 916; Harvey v. Chesapeake & Potomac Telephone Co., 1956, 198 Va. 213, 93 S.E.2d 309. Accord: Gunnels v. Roach, 1963, 243 S.C. 248, 133 S.E.2d 757 (motorist inattentive, boy running into side of car); Peterson v. Nielsen, 1959, 9 Utah 2d 302, 343 P.2d 731 (slower speed would not have avoided collision); Sun Cab Co. v. Faulkner, 1932, 163 Md. 477, 163 A. 194 (same); Waugh v. Suburban Club Ginger Ale Co., 1948, 83 U.S. App.D.C. 226, 167 F.2d 758 (no lookout, but would not have seen).

19. Accord: Laidlaw v. Sage, 1899, 158 N.Y. 73, 52 N.E. 679; Powers v. Standard Oil Co., 1923, 98 N.J.L. 730, 119 A. 273, affirmed 98 N.J.L. 893, 121 A. 926; Boronkay v. Robinson & Carpenter, 1928, 247 N.Y. 365, 160 N.E. 400; Ham v. Greensboro Ice & Fuel Co., 1933, 204 N.C. 614, 169 S.E. 180; Schoonmaker v. Kaltenbach, 1940, 236 Wis. 138, 294 N.W. 794; Second Restatement of Torts, § 432(1).

20. Including the Supreme Court of the United States. See, e.g., Mt. Healthy City School District Board of Education v. Doyle, 1977, 429 U.S. 274, 285–87, 97 S.Ct. 568, 575, 50 L.Ed.2d 471.

21. See Smith, Legal Cause in Actions of Tort, 1911, 25 Harv.L.Rev. 103, 106, 109; McLaughlin, Proximate Cause, 1925, 39 Harv.L.Rev. 149, 155.

22. See Gilman v. Noyes, 1876, 57 N.H. 627, 631.

23. Barringer v. Arnold, 1960, 358 Mich. 594, 101 N.W.2d 365; Strobel v. Chicago, Rock Island, & Pacific Railway Co., 1959, 255 Minn. 201, 96 N.W.2d 195; Henthorne v. Hopwood, 1959, 218 Or. 336, 345 P.2d 249; Pigg v. Brockman, 1963, 85 Idaho 492, 381 P.2d 286; Gantt v. Sissell, 1954, 222 Ark. 902, 263 S.W.2d 916.

24. Corey v. Havener, 1902, 182 Mass. 250, 65 N.E. 69. Cf. Oulighan v. Butler, 1905, 189 Mass. 287, 75 N.E. 726; Orton v. Virginia Carolina Chemical Co., 1918, 142 La. 790, 77 So. 632; Navigazione Libera Triestina Societa Anonima v. Newtown Creek Towing Co., 2d Cir. 1938, 98 F.2d 694.

25. Wilson v. State, Tex.Cr.1893, 24 S.W. 409. Accord: Glick v. Ballentine Produce, Inc., Mo.1965, 396 S.W.2d 609, appeal dismissed 385 U.S. 5, 87 S.Ct. 44, 17

which merges with a fire from some other source; the combined fires burn the plaintiff's property, but either one would have done it alone.[26] In such cases it is quite clear that each cause has in fact played so important a part in producing the result that responsibility should be imposed upon it; and it is equally clear that neither can be absolved from that responsibility upon the ground that the identical harm would have occurred without it, or there would be no liability at all.[27]

It was in a case of this type[28] that the Minnesota court applied a broader rule, which has found general acceptance:[29] The defendant's conduct is a cause of the event if it was a material element and a substantial factor in bringing it about. Whether it was such a substantial factor is for the jury to determine, unless the issue is so clear that reasonable persons could not differ. It has been considered[30] that "substantial factor" is a phrase sufficiently intelligible to furnish an adequate guide in instructions to the jury, and that it is neither possible nor desirable to reduce it to any lower terms.

The "substantial factor" formulation is one concerning legal significance rather than factual quantum.[31] Such a formulation, which can scarcely be called a test, is an improvement over the "but for" rule for this special class of cases. It aids in the disposition of these cases and likewise of two other types of situations which have proved troublesome. One is that where a similar, but not identical result would have followed without the defendant's act;[32] the other where one defendant has made a clearly

---

L.Ed.2d 5; Thompson v. Louisville & Nashville Railroad Co., 1890, 91 Ala. 496, 8 So. 406; People v. Lewis, 1899, 124 Cal. 551, 57 P. 470. A further situation might be suggested, where no one of the acts would alone have caused the result, and no one act was essential to it—as where five persons independently beat a sixth, who dies from the effect of all of the beatings, and would have died from any three.

Cf. McAllister v. Workmen's Compensation Appeals Board, 1968, 69 Cal.2d 408, 71 Cal.Rptr. 697, 445 P.2d 313 (lung cancer from smoke inhaled in fighting fires, and from smoking cigarettes); Basko v. Sterling Drug Co., 2d Cir. 1969, 416 F.2d 417 (blindness resulting from use of two drugs).

26. Anderson v. Minneapolis, St. Paul & Sault Ste. Marie Railway Co., 1920, 146 Minn. 430, 179 N.W. 45; Seckerson v. Sinclair, 1913, 24 N.D. 625, 140 N.W. 239. Cf. Appalachian Power Co. v. Wilson, 1925, 142 Va. 468, 129 S.E. 277.

In Cook v. Minneapolis, St. Paul & Sault Ste. Marie Railway Co., 1898, 98 Wis. 624, 74 N.W. 561, the court drew a fine distinction between the case of two fires, both of responsible origin, and the case where one fire has no responsible source, holding that in the latter case there is no liability upon the responsible defendant. Later, in Kingston v. Chicago & Northwestern Railway Co., 1927, 191 Wis. 610, 211 N.W. 913, the court more or less nullified the effect of the rule by holding that the burden was upon the defendant to prove the natural origin of the other fire. The distinction has been rejected elsewhere. See Carpenter, Concurrent Causation, 1935, 83 U.Pa.L.Rev. 941.

27. An interesting occasion for application of the same principle, where the negligence of each of two parties prevents the other from being a but-for cause, is suggested by Saunders System Birmingham Co. v. Adams, 1928, 217 Ala. 621, 117 So. 72, and Rouleau v. Blotner, 1931, 84 N.H. 539, 152 A. 916, neither of which considered the point. A supplies B with a car with no brakes; B makes no attempt to apply the brakes, and C is hit. Or A fails to signal for a left turn; B is not looking; there is a collision, and C is injured.

28. Anderson v. Minneapolis, St. Paul & Sault Ste. Marie Railway Co., 1920, 146 Minn. 430, 179 N.W. 45. The court no doubt was influenced by the suggestion of the test in Smith, Legal Cause of Actions of Tort, 1911, 25 Harv.L.Rev. 103, 223, 229.

29. Carney v. Goodman, 1954, 38 Tenn.App. 55, 270 S.W.2d 572; Walton v. Blauert, 1949, 256 Wis. 125, 40 N.W.2d 545; New Orleans & N. E. Railroad Co. v. Burge, 1941, 191 Miss. 303, 2 So.2d 825; Dunham v. Village of Canisteo, 1952, 303 N.Y. 498, 104 N.E.2d 872; Edgecomb v. Great Atlantic & Pacific Tea Co., 1941, 127 Conn. 488, 18 A.2d 364; Second Restatement of Torts, §§ 431, 433. See Note, 1964, 15 West.Res.L. Rev. 807.

30. Green, Rationale of Proximate Cause, 1927, 132–141; Green, The Causal Relation Issue, 1962, 60 Mich.L.Rev. 543, 554. Hart and Honoré, Causation in the Law, 1959, 216–218, 263–266, object strongly to the phrase as undefinable. So, Green suggests, is "reasonable;" but that does not prevent its use to pose an issue for the jury.

31. McDowell v. Davis, 1969, 104 Ariz. 69, 448 P.2d 869.

As to the use of "substantial factor" in a broader sense, to include elements of "proximate" cause, see infra, § 42.

32. Thus the case put by Carpenter, Workable Rules for Determining Proximate Cause, 1932, 20 Cal. L.Rev. 229, 396, where A and B each sell a rope to C, who is bent on hanging himself, and C hangs himself with A's rope. A's act is a substantial factor in causing C's death, while B's is not. Whether A is liable is

proved but quite insignificant contribution to the result, as where he throws a lighted match into a forest fire.[33] But in the great majority of cases, it produces the same legal conclusion as the but-for test. Except in the classes of cases indicated, no case has been found where the defendant's act could be called a substantial factor when the event would have occurred without it;[34] nor will cases very often arise where it would not be such a factor when it was so indispensable a cause that without it the result would not have followed.[35]

If the defendant's conduct was a substantial factor in causing the plaintiff's injury, it follows that he will not be absolved from liability merely because other causes have contributed to the result, since such causes, innumerable, are always present. In particular, however, a defendant is not necessarily relieved of liability because the negligence of another person is also a contributing cause, and that person, too, is to be held liable.[36] Thus where two vehicles collide and injure a bystander, or a passenger in one of them, each driver may be liable for the harm inflicted.[37] The law of joint tortfeasors rests very largely upon recognition of the fact that each of two or more causes may be charged with a single result.[38]

It cannot be repeated too often that, although causation is essential to liability, it does not determine it. Other considerations, which remain to be considered, may prevent liability for results clearly caused.

An Alternative to the Substantial-Factor Rule

The substantial-factor rule was developed primarily for cases in which application of the but-for rule would allow each defendant to escape responsibility because the conduct of one or more others would have been sufficient to produce the same result.[39] It is possible—and more helpful it would seem—to apply an alternative formulation that addresses directly the need for declining to follow the but-for rule in this context. The alternative formulation is this: When the conduct of two or more actors is so related to an event that their combined conduct, viewed as a whole, is a but-for cause of the event, and application of the but-for rule to them individually would absolve all of them, the conduct of each is a cause in fact of the event.[40]

Under this alternative rule, such a grouping of the defendants is permissible only in this limited type of fact situation, which occurs relatively infrequently. These are cases in which each of the defendants bears a like relationship to the event. Each seeks to escape liability for a reason that, if recognized, would likewise protect each other defendant in the group, thus leaving the plaintiff without a remedy in the face of the fact that had none of them acted improperly [41]

---

not a question of causation, but of the effect of the intervening act of C. See infra, § 51.

33. See Golden v. Lerch Brothers, 1938, 203 Minn. 211, 281 N.W. 249; Connellan v. Coffey, 1936, 122 Conn. 136, 187 A. 901; Huey v. Milligan, 1961, 242 Ind. 93, 175 N.E.2d 698.

34. Well stated in Texas & Pacific Railway Co. v. McCleery, Tex.1967, 418 S.W.2d 494.

35. See, indicating the identity of the two rules, Schultz v. Brogan, 1947, 251 Wis. 390, 29 N.W.2d 719; New Orleans & N. E. Railroad Co. v. Burge, 1941, 191 Miss. 303, 2 So.2d 825; West Texas Utilities Co. v. Harris, Tex.Civ.App.1950, 231 S.W.2d 558, refused n. r. e.

36. Washington & G. R. Co. v. Hickey, 1897, 166 U.S. 521, 17 S.Ct. 661, 41 L.Ed. 1101; Nees Brothers v. Minneapolis Street Railway Co., 1944, 218 Minn. 532, 16 N.W.2d 758; Erie County United Bank v. Berk, 1943, 73 Ohio App. 314, 56 N.E.2d 285, motion overruled; Hill v. Edmonds, 1966, 26 A.D.2d 554, 270 N.Y.S.2d 1020.

37. Chiles v. Rohl, 1924, 47 S.D. 580, 201 N.W. 154; Kinley v. Hines, 1927, 106 Conn. 82, 137 A. 9; Peters v. Johnson, 1928, 124 Or. 237, 264 P. 459; Glazener v. Safety Transit Lines, 1929, 196 N.C. 504, 146 S.E. 134; McDonald v. Robinson, 1929, 207 Iowa 1293, 224 N.W. 820.

38. See infra, § 47.

39. See supra, this section.

40. Although no judicial opinion has approved this formulation, results reached in reported cases are almost uniformly consistent with it.

41. Of course a defendant whose conduct violated no legal standard would not be legally liable, since another element of the cause of action would be missing, even if causation in fact were established.

the plaintiff would not have suffered the harm. Candid recognition of this fact as a reason for holding that the conduct of each of such similarly situated defendants is a cause in fact of the event seems preferable to the substantial-factor rule.

Proof

On the issue of the fact of causation, as on other issues essential to the cause of action for negligence, the plaintiff, in general,[42] has the burden of proof. The plaintiff must introduce evidence which affords a reasonable basis for the conclusion that it is more likely than not that the conduct of the defendant was a cause in fact of the result. A mere possibility of such causation is not enough;[43] and when the matter remains one of pure speculation or conjecture,[44] or the probabilities are at best evenly balanced,[45] it becomes the duty of the court to direct a verdict for the defendant. Where the conclusion is not one within common knowledge, expert testimony may provide a sufficient basis for it,[46] but in the absence of such testimony it may not be drawn.[47] But on medical matters within common knowledge, no expert testimony is required to permit a conclusion as to causation.[48]

The plaintiff is not, however, required to prove the case beyond a reasonable doubt. The plaintiff need not negative entirely the possibility that the defendant's conduct was not a cause,[49] and it is enough to introduce evidence from which reasonable persons may conclude that it is more probable that the event was caused by the defendant than that it was not.[50] The fact of causation is incapable of mathematical proof, since no one can say with absolute certainty what would have occurred if the defendant had

---

42. As to the special situation of alternative tortfeasors, see infra, this section.

43. Kramer Service v. Wilkins, 1939, 184 Miss. 483, 186 So. 625; Gipson v. Memphis Street Railway Co., 1962, 51 Tenn.App. 31, 364 S.W.2d 110; Rutherford v. Modern Bakery, Ky.1958, 310 S.W.2d 274; Florig v. Sears, Roebuck & Co., 1957, 388 Pa. 419, 130 A.2d 445; Tombigbee Electric Power Association v. Gandy, 1953, 216 Miss. 444, 62 So.2d 567.

44. Wintersteen v. Semler, 1953, 197 Or. 601, 255 P.2d 138; Sears v. Mid-City Motors, Inc., 1965, 178 Neb. 175, 132 N.W.2d 361, withdrawn 179 Neb. 100, 136 N.W.2d 428; Atchison, Topeka & Santa Fe Railway Co. v. Hamilton Brothers, 8th Cir. 1951, 192 F.2d 817; Alling v. Northwestern Bell Telephone Co., 1923, 156 Minn. 60, 194 N.W. 313; Gipson v. Memphis Street Railway Co., 1962, 51 Tenn.App. 31, 364 S.W.2d 110.

45. Farmers Home Mutual Insurance Co. v. Grand Forks Implement Co., 1952, 79 N.D. 177, 55 N.W.2d 315; Lane v. Hampton, 1955, 197 Va. 46, 87 S.E.2d 803; Eckley v. Seese, 1955, 382 Pa. 425, 115 A.2d 227; Altrichter v. Shell Oil Co., D.Minn.1958, 161 F.Supp. 46; Phillips Petroleum Co. v. West, Tex.Civ.App.1955, 284 S.W.2d 196, ref. n. r. e. But where the choice is between two causes, with negligence of the defendant shown as to each, the plaintiff's case is made out. Brumm v. Goodall, 1958, 16 Ill.App.2d 212, 147 N.E.2d 699.

46. Dunham v. Village of Canisteo, 1952, 303 N.Y. 498, 104 N.E.2d 872; Pritchard v. Liggett & Myers Tobacco Co., 3d Cir. 1961, 295 F.2d 292; Lee v. Blessing, 1945, 131 Conn. 569, 41 A.2d 337; Oklahoma Natural Gas Co. v. Gray, 1951, 204 Okl. 362, 230 P.2d 256; Foley v. Pittsburgh-Des Moines Co., 1949, 363 Pa. 1, 68 A.2d 517. See Small, Gaffing at a Thing Called Cause, 1953, 31 Tex.L.Rev. 630.

As to the medical problem of cancer following traumatic injury, see Dyke, Traumatic Cancer? 1966, 15 Cleve.Marsh.L.Rev. 472; Parsons, Sufficiency of Proof in Traumatic Cancer Cases, 1961, 45 Corn.L.Q. 581; Elliott, Traumatic Cancer and "An Old Misunderstanding Between Doctors and Lawyers," 1964, 13 Kan.L.Rev. 79; Note, 1961, 46 Corn.L.Q. 581.

As to the meaning of "causation" to a doctor, see Powers, After All, Doctors Are Human, 1963, 15 U.Fla. L.Rev. 463.

47. Kramer Service v. Wilkins, 1939, 184 Miss. 483, 186 So. 625; Christensen v. Northern States Power Co., 1946, 222 Minn. 474, 25 N.W.2d 659; Blizzard v. Fitzsimmons, 1942, 193 Miss. 484, 10 So.2d 343; Blarjeske v. Thompson's Restaurant Co., 1945, 325 Ill.App. 189, 59 N.E.2d 320; Goodwin v. Misticos, 1949, 207 Miss. 361, 42 So.2d 397.

48. See for example Mitchell v. Coca Cola Bottling Co., 1960, 11 A.D.2d 579, 200 N.Y.S.2d 478, where a child drank a beverage containing an insect, immediately vomited, and was subsequently made ill.

49. Ominsky v. Charles Weinhagen & Co., 1911, 113 Minn. 422, 129 N.W. 845; Gates v. Boston & Maine Railroad Co., 1926, 255 Mass. 297, 151 N.E. 320; Cornbrooks v. Terminal Barber Shops, 1940, 282 N.Y. 217, 26 N.E.2d 25, conformed to 259 App.Div. 375, 19 N.Y.S.2d 390.

50. State of Maryland for Use of Pumphrey v. Manor Real Estate & Trust Co., 4th Cir. 1949, 176 F.2d 414; Saad v. Pappageorge, 1926, 82 N.H. 294, 133 A. 24; MacIntosh v. Great Northern Railway Co., 1922, 151 Minn. 527, 188 N.W. 551; Harmon v. Richardson, 1936, 88 N.H. 312, 188 A. 468 ("a little more probable than otherwise"); Simpson v. Logan Motor Co., Mun.App. D.C.1963, 192 A.2d 122.

acted otherwise. Proof of what we call the relation of cause and effect, that of necessary antecedent and inevitable consequence, can be nothing more than "the projection of our habit of expecting certain consequents to follow certain antecedents merely because we had observed these sequences on previous occasions." [51] If as a matter of ordinary experience a particular act or omission might be expected, under the circumstances, to produce a particular result, and that result in fact has followed, the conclusion may be permissible that the causal relation exists.

Circumstantial evidence,[52] expert testimony,[53] or common knowledge may provide a basis from which the causal sequence may be inferred. Thus it is every day experience that unlighted stairs create a danger that someone will fall. Such a condition "greatly multiplies the chances of accident, and is of a character naturally leading to its occurrence." [54] When a fat person tumbles down the steps, it is a reasonable conclusion that it is more likely than not that the fall would not have occurred but for the bad lighting.

When a child is drowned in a swimming pool, no one can say with certainty that a lifeguard would have saved the child; but the experience of the community permits the conclusion that the absence of the guard played a significant part in the drowning.[55] Such questions are peculiarly for the jury; and whether proper construction of a building would have withstood an earthquake,[56] or whether reasonable police precautions would have prevented a boy from shooting the plaintiff in the eye with an airgun,[57] are questions on which a court can seldom rule as a matter of law. And whether the defendant's negligence consists of the violation of some statutory safety regulation, or the breach of a plain common law duty of care, the court can scarcely overlook the fact that the injury which has in fact occurred is precisely the sort of thing that proper care on the part of the defendant would be intended to prevent, and accordingly allow a certain liberality to the jury in drawing its conclusion.[58]

There is one special type of situation in which the usual rule that the burden of

51. See Wolf, Causality, 5 Encyclopedia Britannica, 14th ed. 1929, 61, 62; Pearson, The Grammar of Science, 1911, 113 ff.

52. Emery v. Tilo Roofing Co., 1937, 89 N.H. 165, 195 A. 409; Paine v. Gamble Stores, 1938, 202 Minn. 462, 279 N.W. 257; Messing v. Judge & Dolph Drug Co., 1929, 322 Mo. 901, 18 S.W.2d 408; Mulligan v. Atlantic Coast Line Railroad Co., 1916, 104 S.C. 173, 88 S.E. 445, affirmed 1917, 242 U.S. 620, 37 S.Ct. 241, 61 L.Ed. 532; Casey v. Phillips Pipeline Co., 1967, 199 Kan. 538, 431 P.2d 518.

53. See supra, this section.

54. Reynolds v. Texas & Pacific Railway Co., 1885, 37 La.Ann. 694, Cf. Sullivan v. Hamacher, 1959, 339 Mass. 190, 158 N.E.2d 301; Ingersoll v. Liberty Bank, 1938, 278 N.Y. 1, 14 N.E.2d 828; Parkinson v. California Co., 10th Cir. 1956, 233 F.2d 432; Kirincich v. Standard Dredging Co., 3d Cir. 1940, 112 F.2d 163; Texas Sling Co. v. Emanuel, Tex.Civ.App.1967, 418 S.W.2d 565, affirmed in part, reversed in part, Tex., 431 S.W.2d 538.

55. Rovegno v. San Jose Knights of Columbus Hall Association, 1930, 108 Cal.App. 591, 291 P. 848. Otherwise when there is evidence indicating the person could not have been saved. Blacka v. James, 1964, 205 Va. 646, 139 S.E.2d 47.

56. Finch v. McKee, 1936, 18 Cal.App.2d 90, 62 P.2d 1380.

57. Stockwell v. Board of Trustees of Leland Stanford Jr. University, 1944, 64 Cal.App.2d 197, 148 P.2d 405. Cf. Chavira v. Carnahan, 1967, 77 N.M. 467, 423 P.2d 988; Tullgren v. Amoskeag Manufacturing Co., 1926, 82 N.H. 268, 133 A. 4; Gates v. Boston & Maine Railroad Co., 1926, 255 Mass. 297, 151 N.E. 320; Houren v. Chicago, Milwaukee & St. Paul Railway Co., 1908, 236 Ill. 620, 86 N.E. 611.

58. See for example Louisville Trust Co. v. Morgan, 1918, 180 Ky. 609, 203 S.W. 555; Kohn v. Clark, 1912, 236 Pa. 18, 84 A. 692. This is well discussed in Malone, Ruminations on Cause-in-Fact, 1956, 9 Stan.L.Rev. 60.

Two striking exceptional cases, both based on statutory policy, appear to have carried this to an extreme length. One is Pierce v. Albanese, 1957, 144 Conn. 241, 129 A.2d 606, appeal dismissed 355 U.S. 15, holding that where the Dramshop Act is violated, the defendant will not be heard to say that there is no causation of intoxication. As a constitutional exercise of the police power, there is a complete departure from "the common law precepts of proximate cause." The other is Wilson v. Hanley, 1960, 224 Or. 570, 356 P.2d 556, where apparently much the same effect is given to a regulation of the State Industrial Commission. See also Rogers v. Missouri Pacific Railroad Co., 1957, 352 U.S. 500, 77 S.Ct. 443, 1 L.Ed.2d 493, rehearing denied 353 U.S. 943, 77 S.Ct. 808, 1 L.Ed.2d 515, (plaintiff in FELA case prevails if negligence of the employer

proof as to causation is on the plaintiff has been relaxed. It may be called that of clearly established double fault and alternative liability. Where, for example, two defendants negligently shoot across a public highway at the same time, and the plaintiff is struck by one shot, which might have been fired from either gun, it is clear that both defendants were at fault, and that one of them, and only one, has caused the injury. Instead of dismissing the action against both for lack of a preponderance of proof against either, the courts have displayed some eagerness to find concert of action, and so permit recovery against both.[59]

In this situation the California supreme court solved the problem by placing the burden of proof on the issue of causation upon the two defendants.[60] There is support for this in Canadian decisions,[61] and in American automobile cases of "chain collisions," in which the plaintiff is injured by one of two or more negligently driven cars, but cannot prove which.[62] It seems a very desirable solution where negligence on the part of both defendants is clear, and it is only the issue of causation which is in doubt, so that the choice must be made between letting the loss due to failure of proof fall upon the innocent plaintiff or the culpable defendants. But where there is no evidence even as to where culpability lies, the hardship may be equally great upon an innocent defendant; and except in very special cases [63] the courts have refused to shift the burden of proof.[64]

A similar problem has arisen in products liability cases. As phrased in a leading case,[65] the question is, "[M]ay a plaintiff, injured as the result of a drug administered to her mother during pregnancy, who knows the type of drug involved but cannot identify the manufacturer of the precise product, hold liable for her injuries a maker of a drug produced from an identical formula?"[66] A divided court held that upon proof supporting liability in other respects and proof that the defendants were manufacturers of a substantial share of the drug on the market in which plaintiff's mother purchased the drug, each defendant would be liable for the proportion of plaintiff's damages represented by its share of that market unless it demonstrated that it could not have made the product which caused plaintiff's injuries. This rule, of course, goes beyond merely placing the burden of proof on the issue of causation upon two negligent actors one of whose negligent conduct was a cause in fact of plaintiff's injuries.[67] The development of further support for this rule has occurred in products liability cases.[68] It is an extension of principles underlying rules developed in cases of multiple fault and single impact upon the claimant (allowing the factfinder to

"played any part, however small, in the injury or death which is the subject of the suit").

59. Oliver v. Miles, 1927, 144 Miss. 852, 110 So. 666; Benson v. Ross, 1906, 143 Mich. 452, 106 N.W. 1120; Kuhn v. Bader, 1951, 89 Ohio App. 203, 101 N.E.2d 322; cf. Regina v. Salmon, 1880, 6 Q.B.D. 79; State v. Newberg, 1929, 129 Or. 564, 278 P. 568.

60. Summers v. Tice, 1948, 33 Cal.2d 80, 199 P.2d 1. The court merely extended the rule as to the burden of proof on the issue of apportionment of damages. See infra, § 52.

61. Cook v. Lewis, [1952] 1 Dom.L.Rep. 1, [1951] S.C.Rep. 830 (similar facts); Woodward v. Begbie, 1961, 31 Dom.L.Rev.2d 22; Saint-Pierre v. McCarthy, [1957] Que.Rep. 421 (merchants selling cartridges to boys). The first of these cases is attacked in Hogan, Cook v. Lewis Re-examined, 1961, 24 Mod.L.Rev. 331.

62. Murphy v. Taxicabs of Louisville, Inc., Ky.1959, 330 S.W.2d 395; Cummings v. Kendall, 1940, 41 Cal. App.2d 549, 107 P.2d 282; Eramdjian v. Interstate Bakery Corp., 1957, 153 Cal.App.2d 590, 315 P.2d 19;

Copley v. Putter, 1949, 93 Cal.App.2d 453, 207 P.2d 876. Cf. Micelli v. Hirsch, Ohio App.1948, 83 N.E.2d 240 (result accomplished by presumption of continuing life). See also, as to apportionment of damages, infra, § 52.

A badly confused case is Clark v. Gibbons, 1967, 66 Cal.2d 399, 58 Cal.Rptr. 125, 426 P.2d 525, where this principle apparently was applied, under the misnomer of res ipsa loquitur, to the negligence of two physicians, which might possibly have been causal.

63. See supra, § 40.

64. See supra, § 39.

65. Sindell v. Abbott Laboratories, 1980, 26 Cal.3d 588, 163 Cal.Rptr. 132, 607 P.2d 924, certiorari denied 449 U.S. 912, 101 S.Ct. 286, 66 L.Ed.2d 140. See, ch. 17, § 103 for further discussion.

66. Id.

67. This fact is acknowledged by the majority opinion in Sindell, supra n. 65.

68. See infra, § 103.

make an allocation of responsibility among defendants rather than denying all recovery to the plaintiff where the proof is sufficient to show that the conduct of each of the defendants violated a legal standard and one of them caused plaintiff's injuries) [69] and in cases of multiple fault and successive impacts.[70]

A distinctive issue of causal connection involving multiple factors arises where evidence is offered tending to show that the risk of a specified future loss has been increased by an allegedly tortious act. For example, suppose that evidence offered at trial tends to show that plaintiff's decedent, having contracted a form of cancer, had a 40% chance of cure and that defendant physician's negligent failure to make a correct diagnosis on first visit reduced the chance of cure to 25%.[71] In such a case, if we view the "death" of plaintiff's decedent, or even "death from cancer," as the relevant event, plaintiff's evidence falls short of supporting a fact finding that the negligence was, more probably than not, a but-for cause of that event.[72] More probably than not, it would have happened anyway because of the cancer. One ground for criticism of this outcome is that it does not take adequate account of the fact that in all cases death is even more certain than taxes. Only the time and cause of death may be in doubt. If evidence supports a finding that, more probably than not, negligence hastened death, ordinarily a wrongful death action lies. Should an action lie, also, when evidence supports a finding that, more probably than not, negligence reduced the patient's chance of survival? Expressed another way, the question is: should we view reduction of the patient's chance of survival as the relevant event, and allow recovery if more probably than not negligence was a cause of that event? If yes, one might argue in the hypothetical case just stated that plaintiff should recover as compensation 40% of the damages ordinarily allowable in a wrongful death action.[73] Or one might argue that only 15% of the ordinarily allowable damages should be recovered.[74] The choice between these rules would raise an issue that might be regarded as analogous to those regarding liability for aggravation of existing infirmity [75] and for proportional rather than joint liability.[76] As expert opinion evidence quantifying risk becomes more readily available, advocates will present more issues in these areas for resolution by courts and legislatures.

 WESTLAW REFERENCES

causation +2 fact

Causation as Fact
headnote(proximate /s actual** /5 caus!)

The But-For and Substantial-Factor Rules
substantial /s factor /s "proximate cause"
"proximate cause" /p "sine qua non"

An Alternative to the Substantial-Factor Rule
summers +s tice

Proof
"proximate cause" /s circumstantial
proof proving /s multiple /s caus!

§ 42. Proximate Cause: Scope of the Problem

Once it is established that the defendant's conduct has in fact been one of the causes of

---

69. See supra, this section.

70. See infra, § 52.

71. This hypothetical is a variation on Herskovits v. Group Health Cooperative of Puget Sound, 1983, 99 Wn.2d 609, 664 P.2d 474.

72. See the dissenting opinions in *Herskovits*, supra, n.71.

73. See the concurring opinion of Pearson, J., in *Herskovits*, supra, n.71. Compare Dillon v. Twin State Gas & Electric Co., 1932, 85 N.H. 449, 163 A. 111 (boy falling from bridge to substantially certain death struck defendant's wires and was electrocuted; damages allowed to compensate for value of his prospects for life and health). See infra, § 52.

74. One might view this as a logical extension of the principle of the *Dillon* case, supra, n.73.

75. See infra, § 43, Liability Beyond the Risk.

76. See infra, § 52.

the plaintiff's injury,[1] there remains the question whether the defendant should be legally responsible for the injury. Unlike the fact of causation, with which it is often hopelessly confused, this is primarily a problem of law.[2] It is sometimes said to depend on whether the conduct has been so significant and important a cause that the defendant should be legally responsible. But both significance and importance turn upon conclusions in terms of legal policy, so that they depend essentially on whether the policy of the law will extend the responsibility for the conduct to the consequences which have in fact occurred. Quite often this has been stated, and properly so, as an issue of whether the defendant is under any duty to the plaintiff, or whether the duty includes protection against such consequences. This is not a question of causation, or even a question of fact, but quite far removed from both; and the attempt to deal with it in such terms has led and can lead only to utter confusion.[3]

The term "proximate cause" is applied by the courts to those more or less undefined considerations which limit liability even where the fact of causation is clearly established. The word "proximate" is a legacy of Lord Chancellor Bacon,[4] who in his time committed other sins. The word means nothing more than near or immediate; and when it was first taken up by the courts it had connotations of proximity in time and space which have long since disappeared. It is an unfortunate word, which places an entirely wrong emphasis upon the factor of physical or mechanical closeness. For this reason "legal cause"[5] or perhaps even "responsible cause" would be a more appropriate term. There is, however, no present prospect that long ingrained practice will ever be altered by the substitution of either.

Generalizations About Proximate Cause

Before we examine in some detail the many theories of "proximate" or "legal" cause that have been advanced, and the many and diverse types of cases to which they have been applied, it may be useful to state five generalizations about this area of legal doctrine. Cross-references to these generalizations will then be used to reduce repetition as these ideas recur in different contexts throughout the treatment of legal cause.

First. Though there are countless variations of theory in this area of the law of torts, two contrasting theories of legal cause recur throughout the cases and account for most of the conflict with respect to the choice of a basic theory. One of these theories is that the scope of liability should ordinarily extend to but not beyond the scope of the "foreseeable risks"—that is, the risks by reason of which the actor's conduct is held to be negligent. The second, contrasting, theory is that the scope of liability should ordinarily extend to but not beyond all "direct" (or "directly traceable") consequences and those indirect consequences that are foreseeable.

Second. Another choice of theory concerns the question whether all limitations on the scope of liability of a negligent defendant—apart from defenses and, in some instances, requirements regarding the nature of the harm—will be dealt with under the rubric of "legal cause" (or "proximate cause") or instead some will be dealt with as issues

---

§ 42

1. See supra, § 41.

2. Well stated in Green, Proximate Cause in Texas Negligence Law, 1950, 28 Tex.L.Rev. 471, 621, 755.

3. See the odd museum collection of utterances on the subject, some of them quite profound and others quite leather-headed, in Lewis, Proximate Cause in Law, 1933, 7 U.Fla.Bar Ass'n J. 109, 138, 158.

4. "In jure non remota causa, sed proxima, spectatur. [In law the near cause is looked to, not the remote one.] It were infinite for the law to judge the cause of causes, and their impulsion of one another; therefore it contenteth itself with the immediate cause, and judgeth of acts by that, without looking to any further degree." Bacon, Maxims of the Law, Reg. I.

5. See Edgerton, Legal Cause, 1924, 72 U.Pa.L.Rev. 211; Morris, On the Teaching of Legal Cause, 1939, 39 Col.L.Rev. 1087; Second Restatement of Torts, § 431.

of "duty." This is a choice of method of analysis. But of course such a choice may have a tendency to affect outcomes, and battles over whether or not "duty" is the better, or the only "correct" analysis for certain problems have been intense.[6]

Third. A basic rule of legal cause (or of "duty," in this context) makes use of one or more flexible concepts—such as "foreseeable" or "direct"—which require that the judge (and jury, when the issue is submitted to the jury) applying the concepts to the evidence in a particular case reach an evaluative conclusion. Though often referred to as a "factfinding"—as to whether, for example, an event was "foreseeable," or injury to the plaintiff was "foreseeable," or the injury suffered was a "direct consequence"—this evaluative conclusion is distinctly not a finding of "facts" in the usual sense of answers to questions such as who was involved in the accident, when and where, and what happened. The leeway for drastically different scope of liability to be effected by different tendencies in these evaluative findings probably explains more of the differences in legal outcomes then do the different choices about basic theories of legal cause and duty.

Fourth. Adherents to either of the basic theories reach results in certain types of recurring fact situations that are more accurately characterized as exceptions to the basic rule, though often these outcomes are explained as if they were routine applications of the basic rule. This outcome is accomplished by expansive or narrow application of such flexible concepts as "foreseeable" and "direct."

Fifth. In light of the third and fourth points, predicting outcomes in pending cases is hazardous indeed if one looks only to theories. Prediction can be substantially improved, however, by close attention to apparent tendencies in cases involving fact situations as similar as one can find, before a tribunal as similar as one can find, to that in which the case will be decided. This is the principal justification for the detail with which this subject is treated here.

Relation to Duty

It is quite possible to state every question which arises in connection with "proximate cause" in the form of a single question: was the defendant under a duty to protect the plaintiff against the event which did in fact occur?[7] Such a form of statement does not, of course, provide any answer to the question, or solve anything whatever;[8] but it may be helpful since "duty"—also a legal conclusion—is perhaps less likely than "proximate cause" to be interpreted as if it were a policy-free factfinding. Thus, "duty" may serve to direct attention to the policy issues which determine the extent of the original obligation and of its continuance, rather than to the mechanical sequence of events which goes to make up causation in fact. The question whether there is a duty has most often seemed helpful in cases where the only issue is in reality whether the defendant stands in any such relation to the plaintiff as to create any legally recognized obligation of conduct for the plaintiff's benefit. Or, reverting again to the starting point, whether the interests of the plaintiff are entitled to legal protection at the defendant's hands against the invasion which has in fact occurred. Or, again reverting, whether the conduct is the "proximate cause" of the result. The circumlocution is unavoidable, since all of these questions are, in reality, one and the same.

The conclusion of no "duty" or no "proximate cause"—no legal responsibility—has

---

6. See, e.g., Restatement of Torts, § 281 Comments *e* and *ee* and Reason for Change, and § 433, Reason for Changes (1948 Supp.). But see R. Keeton, Legal Cause in the Law of Torts, 1963, 79–81.

7. Green, Rationale of Proximate Cause, 1927, 11–43; Campbell, Duty, Fault and Legal Cause, [1938] Wis.L.Rev. 402. See O'Connell, J., concurring, in Dewey v. A. F. Klaveness & Co., 1963, 233 Or. 515, 379 P.2d 560; Thode, Tort Analysis: Duty-Risk v. Proximate Cause and the Rational Allocation of Functions Between Judge and Jury, 1977 Utah L.Rev. 1.

8. Prosser, Palsgraf Revisited, 1953, 52 Mich.L.Rev. 1, reprinted in Prosser, Selected Topics on the Law of Torts, 1954, 191.

been common enough in cases where the plaintiff was outside of the zone of any obvious danger from the defendant's conduct, and so no harm to the plaintiff was to have been anticipated,[9] as where a fire set by the defendant spreads to an unusual distance,[10] or a train strikes an object on the track and throws it against a person in a position of apparent safety;[11] and likewise where harm results from a violation of a statute, such as a Sunday law, which was not designed to afford the plaintiff any protection.[12] It appears also in cases, such as those involving mental disturbance,[13] where the court is in reality saying that the particular interest invaded is not entitled to legal redress. In all such cases the causal connection between the act and the harm is usually clear and direct, and the attempt to subdivide the indivisible by way of "proximate" often proves to be an obstacle to the determination of the real issue.

In courts that use "duty" in this context, the ordinary usage has been to confine the word "duty" to questions of the existence of some relation between the defendant and the plaintiff which gives rise to the obligation of conduct in the first instance, and to deal with the connection between that obligation, once it has arisen, and the consequences which have followed in the language of "proximate cause." The usage is no doubt good enough, so long as it is not allowed to obscure the fact that identical questions are often still involved, and buried under the two terms, sometimes so deeply that a good deal of digging is called for to uncover them.

Confusion with Standard of Conduct

In other cases the standard of reasonable conduct does not require the defendant to recognize the risk, or to take precautions against it. The owner of an automobile who leaves it unattended in the street is, in some jurisdictions, not required to anticipate that other persons will move it;[14] a city need not provide all its bridges with railings sufficient to keep any car from going over the edge;[15] the owner of premises need not foresee that the wind will swing a door against a boy and put out his eye;[16] and no one is required to anticipate a storm of unprecedented violence,[17] or foresee that a cow will knock a man under a train.[18] In these cases the defendant is simply not negligent. When the courts say that his conduct is not "the proximate cause" of the harm, they not only obscure the real issue, but suggest artificial distinctions of causation which have no sound basis, and can only arise to plague them in the future.

Confusion with Defenses to Negligence Action

In many cases where the negligence of the defendant was clearly established the plaintiff (before the advent of comparative negli-

---

9. See infra, Unforeseeable Plaintiffs, § 43.

10. Cf. Ryan v. New York Central Railroad Co., 1866, 35 N.Y. 210, 91 Am.Dec. 49; Hoag & Alger v. Lake Shore & Michigan Southern Railway Co., 1877, 85 Pa. 293; Smith v. London & S. W. R. Co., 1870, L.R. 6 C.P. 14; Kuhn v. Jewett, 1880, 32 N.J.Eq. 647.

11. See Kommerstad v. Great Northern Railway Co., 1913, 120 Minn. 376, 139 N.W. 713, id., 1915, 128 Minn. 505, 151 N.W. 177.

12. Cf. Tingle v. Chicago, Burlington & Quincy Railroad Co., 1882, 60 Iowa 333, 14 N.W. 320; Dervin v. Frenier, 1917, 91 Vt. 398, 100 A. 760; Armstead v. Lounsberry, 1915, 129 Minn. 34, 151 N.W. 542; Falk v. Finkelman, 1929, 268 Mass. 524, 168 N.E. 89.

Compare also the cases of Howard v. Redden, 1919, 93 Conn. 604, 107 A. 509 (liability of building contractor where owner failed to inspect); Missouri, Kansas & Texas Railway Co. v. Merrill, 1902, 65 Kan. 436, 70 P. 358 (carrier delivering defective car to connecting line), where the decision must be supported, if at all, upon the ground that there was no duty to the plaintiff.

13. See infra, § 54.

14. Cf. Slater v. T. C. Baker Co., 1927, 261 Mass. 424, 158 N.E. 778; Squires v. Brooks, 1916, 44 App. D.C. 320; Kennedy v. Hedberg, 1924, 159 Minn. 76, 198 N.W. 302. But see infra, § 44, Foreseeable Intervening Causes.

15. Cf. Tracey v. City of Minneapolis, 1932, 185 Minn. 380, 241 N.W. 390. Compare Jones v. City of Fort Dodge, 1919, 185 Iowa 600, 171 N.W. 16.

16. Cf. Morril v. Morril, 1928, 104 N.J.L. 557, 142 A. 337, 60 A.L.R. 102.

17. Cf. Strobeck v. Bren, 1904, 93 Minn. 428, 101 N.W. 795.

18. Cf. Schreiner v. Great Northern Railway Co., 1902, 86 Minn. 245, 90 N.W. 400.

gence) was barred from recovery by contributory negligence.[19] It was said sometimes that this was because the defendant's negligence was not the proximate cause of the harm, since the plaintiff's act had intervened.[20] But certainly in the ordinary contributory negligence case, as where two automobiles collide, the causal connection is quite clear, and there is no doubt that both parties have played an important part in bringing about the result. This point is underscored when the rule that contributory negligence is a complete bar is replaced by a comparative negligence rule; it becomes an anomaly to use the proximate cause requirement as a basis for denying even partial damages.[21] The contributory negligence rule has its foundations in the common law's individualistic notions of policy; when stated as an application of proximate cause, the rule is rationalized by distorting the facts to create imaginary distinctions between causes. Similar fictitious reasoning is found as to the doctrine of the "last clear chance,"[22] the defense of assumption of risk,[23] and the rule as to avoidable consequences,[24] which bars the plaintiff from recovery for damages which the plaintiff might have avoided with reasonable care. "Proximate cause," in short, has been an extraordinarily changeable concept. "Having no integrated meaning of its own, its chameleon quality permits it to be substituted for any one of the elements of a negligence case when decision on that element becomes difficult. * * * No other formula * * * so nearly does the work of Aladdin's lamp."[25]

Proposed Formulae

The search for some test or formula which will serve as a universal solvent for all of the problems of "proximate cause" has occupied many writers. Among the dozens of touchstones and panaceas which have been proposed, the following deserve special mention:[26]

The Nearest Cause. The word "proximate," in itself, means nothing more than near, or possibly nearest. Bacon's maxim,[27] taken literally, would mean that only the antecedent which is nearest in time or space is to be regarded as the legal cause, and none other will be held responsible. Whether Bacon really meant anything of the sort is at least doubtful.[28] If he did, the courts have long since ceased to pay attention to him. It is of course obvious that if a defendant sets a fire which burns the plaintiff's house, no court in the world will deny liability upon the ground that the fire, rather than the defendant's act, was the nearest, or next cause of the destruction of the house. It is everywhere recognized that there must be some

---

19. See infra, § 65.

20. Cf. Nieboer v. Detroit Electric Railway Co., 1901, 128 Mich. 486, 489, 87 N.W. 626, 627; Henry v. St. Louis, Kansas City & N. Railway Co., 1882, 76 Mo. 288; Studer v. Southern Pacific Co., 1898, 121 Cal. 400, 53 P. 942; Curwen v. Appleton Manufacturing Co., 1916, 133 Minn. 28, 157 N.W. 899. Compare the reduction of the whole matter to a complete absurdity in Hinkle v. Minneapolis, Anoka & Cayuna Range Railway Co., 1926, 162 Minn. 112, 202 N.W. 340.

21. See infra, § 67.

See Green, Contributory Negligence and Proximate Cause, 1927, 6 North Car.L.Rev. 3; Bohlen, Contributory Negligence, 1908, 21 Harv.L.Rev. 233, 234–242; Lowndes, Contributory Negligence, 1934, 22 Georgetown L.J. 674, 675 ff.

22. Cf. Girdner v. Union Oil Co., 1932, 216 Cal. 197, 13 P.2d 915; Nehring v. Connecticut Co., 1912, 86 Conn. 109, 84 A. 301, 524; Drown v. Northern Ohio Traction Co., 1907, 76 Ohio St. 234, 81 N.E. 326. See infra, § 66.

23. Cf. Hagglund v. St. Hilaire Lumber Co., 1906, 97 Minn. 94, 106 N.W. 91; The San Onofre, [1922] P. 243. See Note, 1923, 36 Harv.L.Rev. 486.

24. Loker v. Damon, 1835, 34 Mass. (17 Pick.) 284; 1 Sedgwick, Damages, 9th ed. 1920, § 202.

25. Green, Proximate Cause in Texas Negligence Law, 1950, 28 Tex.L.Rev. 471.

26. See Smith, Legal Cause in Actions of Tort, 1911, 25 Harv.L.Rev. 103, 106–128; Carpenter, Workable Rules for Determining Proximate Cause, 1932, 20 Cal. L.Rev. 229, 235–246; James and Perry, Legal Cause, 1951, 60 Yale L.J. 761, 801–811.

27. See supra, this section.

28. See Beale, Recovery for Consequences of an Act, 1895, 9 Harv.L.Rev. 80, 81, offering the interpretation that the defendant must be *responsible* for the immediate or final cause.

degree of progression into the causal sequence. There may have been considerable confusion about this in the distant past, but the question is certainly no longer open.

The Last Human Wrongdoer. A similar formula, which has been stated and followed by some courts,[29] would place the legal responsibility upon the last culpable human actor and exempt all those antecedent in time. This rule may have been due, at least in part, to the idea, which once had some currency,[30] that the law fulfilled its function if it provided *one* legally responsible defendant, and that it was superfluous, uneconomical, and confusing to the issue to offer more. Such a rule is unworkable in two respects. The last human wrongdoer is not always responsible; one may be relieved because one's negligence did not extend to the particular risk, or by reason of unforeseen intervening forces over which one had no control.[31] And the earlier actor may be held responsible if under an obligation to protect the plaintiff against the later wrongful conduct, as in the numerous cases where the defendant is required to anticipate and safeguard the plaintiff against the negligent, or even the criminal acts of others.[32] The rule is now of purely historical interest, except for odd bits and pieces of peculiar law which survive here and there,[33] and for the influence which it has had in the development of the doctrine of the last clear chance.[34]

Cause and Condition. Many courts have sought to distinguish between the active "cause" of the harm and the existing "conditions" upon which that cause operated. If the defendant has created only a passive, static condition which made the damage possible, the defendant is said not to be liable.[35] But so far as the fact of causation is concerned, in the sense of necessary antecedents which have played an important part in producing the result, it is quite impossible to distinguish between active forces and passive situations, particularly since, as is invariably the case, the latter are the result of other active forces which have gone before.[36] The defendant who spills gasoline about the premises creates a "condition;" but the act may be culpable because of the danger of fire. When a spark ignites the gasoline, the condition has done quite as much to bring about the fire as the spark; and since that is the very risk which the defendant has created, the defendant will not escape responsibility.[37] Even the lapse of a considerable time during which the "condition" remains static will not necessarily affect liability; one who digs a trench in the highway may still be lia-

---

29. See Wharton, Negligence, 1st Ed. 1874, § 134; Vicars v. Wilcocks, 1806, 8 East 1; Singleton Abbey v. Paludina, [1927] 1 A.C. 16; Stone v. City of Philadelphia, 1931, 302 Pa. 340, 153 A. 550; Medved v. Doolittle, 1945, 220 Minn. 352, 19 N.W.2d 788; Hubbard v. Murray, 1939, 173 Va. 448, 3 S.E.2d 397. See Eldredge, Culpable Intervention as Superseding Cause, 1937, 86 U.Pa.L.Rev. 121, reprinted in Eldredge, Modern Tort Problems, 1941, 205; Note, 1928, 76 U.Pa.L. Rev. 720.

30. Bohlen, Contributory Negligence, 1908, 21 Harv.L.Rev. 232, 238; Wharton, Negligence, 1st ed. 1874, § 139.

31. See infra, § 44.

32. See infra, § 44, Foreseeable Intervening Causes.

33. See for example the exoneration of a municipality for a highway defect if the wrongful act of a third person contributed to plaintiff's injury. Hayes v. Hyde Park, 1891, 153 Mass. 514, 27 N.E. 522, Stone v. City of Philadelphia, 1930, 302 Pa. 340, 153 A. 550. See Eldredge, Culpable Intervention as Superseding Cause, 1937, 86 U.Pa.L.Rev. 121, reprinted in Eldredge, Modern Tort Problems, 1941, 205. Also such cases as Medved v. Doolittle, 1945, 220 Minn. 352, 19 N.W.2d 788; Kline v. Moyer, 1937, 325 Pa. 357, 191 A. 43; Hubbard v. Murray, 1939, 173 Va. 448, 3 S.E.2d 397, where one who negligently parks a car is held not liable because another driver has run into it.

34. See infra, § 66.

35. Gilman v. Central Vermont Railway Co., 1919, 93 Vt. 340, 107 A. 122; White v. Lang, 1880, 128 Mass. 598; Kryger v. Panaszy, 1937, 123 Conn. 353, 196 A. 795. See Green, Proximate Cause in Connecticut Negligence Law, 1950, 24 Conn.B.J. 24, 33.

36. Smith, Legal Cause in Actions of Tort, 1914, 25 Harv.L.Rev. 103, 110; Levitt, Cause, Legal Cause and Proximate Cause, 1922, 21 Mich.L.Rev. 34, 160.

37. Teasdale v. Beacon Oil Co., 1929, 266 Mass. 25, 164 N.E. 612; Watson v. Kentucky & Indiana Bridge & Railroad Co., 1910, 137 Ky. 619, 126 S.W. 146, 129 S.W. 341; Johnson v. Kosmos Portland Cement Co., 6th Cir. 1933, 64 F.2d 193, certiorari denied 290 U.S. 641, 54 S.Ct. 60, 78 L.Ed. 557; Riley v. Standard Oil Co. of Indiana, 1934, 214 Wis. 15, 252 N.W. 183.

ble to another who falls into it a month afterward.[38] "Cause" and "condition" still find occasional mention in the decisions;[39] but the distinction is now almost entirely discredited. So far as it has any validity at all, it must refer to the type of case where the forces set in operation by the defendant have come to rest in a position of apparent safety, and some new force intervenes.[40] But even in such cases, it is not the distinction between "cause" and "condition" which is important, but the nature of the risk and the character of the intervening cause.

The Substantial-Factor Test. The late Jeremiah Smith once proposed[41] as a test of proximate cause, that "the defendant's tort must have been a substantial factor in producing the damage complained of." This was picked up by the supreme court of Minnesota in a case[42] of merging fires presenting an issue of causation in fact, and was used by the court as a substitute for the obviously inapplicable "but for" rule of causation.[43] This case in turn was taken over by the Restatement of Torts, which in its original form,[44] adopted "substantial factor" as a test not only of causation, but also of the "proximate." A number of courts have followed this, apparently accepting the phrase as the answer to all prayers and some sort of universal solvent.[45] As applied to the fact of causation alone, the test though not ideal, may be thought useful.[46] But when the "substantial factor" is made to include all of the ill-defined considerations of policy which go to limit liability once causation in fact is found, it has no more definite meaning than "proximate cause," and it becomes a hindrance rather than a help. It is particularly unfortunate in so far as it suggests that the questions involved are only questions of causation, obscuring all other issues, and as it tends to leave to the jury matters which should be decided by the court.[47] Some courts which have once proclaimed adherence to it as such a general catch-all formula have been compelled to reject it later,[48] and the 1948 revision of the Restatement limited its application very definitely to cause in fact alone.[49]

Justly Attachable Cause. Professor, later Judge, Edgerton once maintained[50] that the essential question is whether the harm which has been suffered is "justly attachable" to the defendant's conduct. While this perhaps comes closer to stating the problem than anything else that has been said, it offers no solution. Justice, as every law student soon discovers, is an abstract, undefinable thing, about which people disagree. The necessity of being able to predict, to some reasonable extent at least, what the court is likely to do with any particular case, is so great that no one can be satisfied with any-

38. Pyke v. City of Jamestown, 1906, 15 N.D. 157, 107 N.W. 359; Page v. Town of Bucksport, 1874, 64 Me. 51 (defective bridge); Quaker Oats Co. v. Grice, 2d Cir. 1912, 195 F. 441 (mill permitted to become filled with dust, which exploded).

39. Briske v. Burnham, 1942, 379 Ill. 193, 39 N.E.2d 976, 979; Stewart v. Kroger Grocery Co., 1945, 198 Miss. 371, 21 So.2d 912; Oklahoma Gas & Electric Co. v. Butler, 1942, 190 Okl. 393, 124 P.2d 397, 399; Atchison v. Texas & Pacific Railway Co., 1945, 143 Tex. 466, 186 S.W.2d 228, 232.

40. See infra, § 44.

41. Smith, Legal Cause in Actions of Tort, 1911, 25 Harv.L.Rev. 103, 223, 229.

42. Anderson v. Minneapolis, St. Paul & Sault Ste. Marie Railway Co., 1920, 146 Minn. 430, 179 N.W. 45.

43. See supra, § 41.

44. First Restatement of Torts, §§ 431, 433, 435.

45. Mahoney v. Beatman, 1929, 110 Conn. 184, 147 A. 762; Hayes Freight Lines v. Wilson, 1948, 226 Ind. 1, 77 N.E.2d 580; Simon v. Hudson Coal Co., 1944, 350 Pa. 82, 38 A.2d 259; Hatch v. Smail, 1946, 249 Wis. 183, 23 N.W.2d 460; Weaver v. McClintock-Trunkey Co., 1941, 8 Wn.2d 154, 111 P.2d 570, 114 P.2d 1004.

46. See supra, § 41. See for example Schultz v. Brogan, 1947, 251 Wis. 390, 29 N.W.2d 719; Goudy v. State, 1948, 203 Miss. 366, 35 So.2d 308.

47. See Green, The Torts Restatement, 1935, 29 Ill. L.Rev. 582, 602; Prosser, The Minnesota Court on Proximate Cause, 1936, 21 Minn.L.Rev. 19.

48. See for example Seward v. Minneapolis Street Railway Co., 1946, 222 Minn. 454, 25 N.W.2d 221, retreating from Peterson v. Fulton, 1934, 192 Minn. 360, 256 N.W. 901.

49. Restatement of Torts, 1948 Supp. § 433; Second Restatement of Torts, § 433.

50. Edgerton, Legal Cause, 1924, 72 U.Pa.L.Rev. 211, 343.

thing so vague. Something more closely approaching a definite guide is possible, and essential.[51] The gist of the proposal, so far as there was anything concrete about it, was that the jury should be permitted to consider the imposition of liability upon "justly attachable" causes, on grounds of fairness and social advantage. Other writers, and the courts, have not, however, considered the jury to be a fit body to make such decisions.

Systems of Rules. At the opposite extreme are the various attempts, the most noted of which is identified with the name of Professor Carpenter,[52] to establish a fixed system of rules to cover all cases. Thus it has been said, for example, in summary, that the defendant is liable if the defendant has created a force which "remained active itself or created another force that remained active until it directly caused the result; or created a new active risk of being acted upon by the active force that caused the result."[53] Apart from the mechanical terminology used, which is more appropriate to physics than to law, such ironclad systems ignore the interplay of the various problems of policy which may arise in particular situations, and break down under the numerous obviously correct decisions which cannot be fitted into the structure erected.[54] "Proximate cause" cannot be reduced to absolute rules. No better statement ever has been made concerning the problem than that of Street: "It is always to be determined on the facts of each case upon mixed considerations of logic, common sense, justice, policy and precedent. * * * The best use that can be made of the authorities on proximate cause is merely to furnish illustrations of situations which judicious men upon careful consideration have adjudged to be on one side of the line or the other."[55]

Problems Involved

Abandoning the fruitless quest for a universal formula, it is possible to approach "proximate cause" as a series of distinct problems, more or less unrelated, to be determined upon different considerations.[56] The list, which is not necessarily exclusive, would include at least the following problems:

1. The problem of causation in fact: what part has the defendant's conduct played in bringing about the result? This has been considered above.[57]

2. The problem of apportionment of damages among causes. This will be considered below.[58]

3. The problem of liability for unforeseeable consequences: to what extent should the defendant be liable for results which the defendant could not reasonably have been expected to foresee?

4. The problem of intervening causes: should the defendant be relieved of liability by some new cause of external origin coming into operation at a time subsequent to the defendant's conduct; should the new cause be treated as superseding the defendant's responsibility?

5. The problem of shifting responsibility: is there another person to whom the defendant was free to leave the duty of protecting the plaintiff? This has been mentioned before,[59] but it becomes a factor of importance in many cases of proximate cause.

---

51. McLaughlin, Proximate Cause, 1925, 39 Harv.L. Rev. 149, 187; James and Perry, Legal Cause, 1951, 60 Yale L.J. 761, 802–803.

52. Carpenter, Workable Rules for Determining Proximate Cause, 1932, 20 Cal.L.Rev. 229, 396, 471; Carpenter, Proximate Cause, 1940–1943, 14 So.Cal.L. Rev. 1, 115, 416, 15 So.Cal.L.Rev. 187, 304, 427, 16 So. Cal.L.Rev. 1, 61, 275.

53. Beale, The Proximate Consequences of an Act, 1920, 33 Harv.L.Rev. 633.

54. See Edgerton, Legal Cause, 1924, 72 U.Pa.L. Rev. 211, 343.

55. 1 Street, Foundations of Legal Liability, 1906, 110.

56. See Green, Rationale of Proximate Cause, 1929, 77–121; Prosser, Proximate Cause in California, 1950, 38 Cal.L.Rev. 369.

57. See supra, § 41.

58. See infra, § 52.

59. See supra, § 33, Shifting Responsibility.

All these problems deal with policy issues—the last four even more than the first. The attempt to deal with all of them in terms of causation is at the bottom of much of the existing confusion.

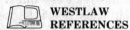
WESTLAW REFERENCES

Generalizations About Proximate Cause
headnote("proximate cause" /s jur*** /5 instruct!)
topic(torts negligence) /p "legal cause"
foresee! /3 injur*** /s jur***

Relation to Duty
topic(negligence torts) /p proximate legal /2 cause /p duty

Confusion With Standard of Conduct
automobile car /p unattended /p negligen! foresee!

Confusion With Defenses to Negligence Action
proximate /2 cause /p comparative /2 negligence

Proposed Formulae
formula* /s proximate /2 cause % formula /2 instruction

The Nearest Cause
"nearest cause" & topic(negligence torts)

The Last Human Wrongdoer
topic(negligence torts) & final last +3 wrongdoer tortfeasor

Cause and Condition
restatement +s torts +4 431 433 435

The Substantial-Factor Test
substantial /s factor /s "proximate cause"
topic(torts negligence) /p "substantial factor"

Justly Attachable Cause
"justly attachable" /s cause

Systems of Rules
topic(torts negligence) /p rule* /s determin! /s cause* causation

Problems Involved
headnote("proximate cause" /p foresee! /p risk)
topic(negligence torts) /p owe* /p duty /p protect!
topic(negligence torts) /p standard +2 conduct

§ 43. Unforeseeable Consequences

Negligence, it must be repeated, is conduct which falls below the standard established by law for the protection of others against unreasonable risk. It necessarily involves a foreseeable risk, a threatened danger of injury, and conduct unreasonable in proportion to the danger. If one could not reasonably foresee any injury as the result of one's act, or if one's conduct was reasonable in the light of what one could anticipate, there would be no negligence, and no liability.[1] But what if one does unreasonably fail to guard against harm which one should foresee, and consequences which one could in no way have anticipated in fact follow? Suppose, for example, that a defect in a railway platform offers at most the foreseeable possibility of a sprained ankle; but as a result of it a passenger dies of inflammation of the heart?[2] Or one's negligent driving threatens another with something like a broken leg, but instead causes the other to be shot?[3]

There is perhaps no other one issue in the law of torts over which so much controversy has raged, and concerning which there has been so great a deluge of legal writing.[4] At the risk of becoming wearisome, it must be repeated that the question is primarily not

§ 43

1. Stephens v. Mutual Lumber Co., 1918, 103 Wash. 1, 173 P. 1031; Mendelson v. Davis, 8th Cir., 1922, 281 F. 18; Nunan v. Bennett, 1919, 184 Ky. 591, 212 S.W. 570; Sears v. Texas & New Orleans Railroad Co., Tex. Civ.App.1923, 247 S.W. 602; Gaupin v. Murphy, 1928, 295 Pa. 214, 145 A. 123.

2. Keegan v. Minneapolis & St. Louis Railroad Co., 1899, 76 Minn. 90, 78 N.W. 965 (liable).

3. Lynch v. Fisher, La.App.1947, 34 So.2d 513 (liable). Cf. Walmsley v. Rural Telephone Association, 1917, 102 Kan. 139, 169 P. 197 (liable); Gouna v. O'Neill, Tex.Civ.App.1941, 149 S.W.2d 138 (not liable).

4. See the articles cited supra, § 41, n.1. Also Dias, The Duty Problem in Negligence, 1955, 13 Camb.L.J. 198; Dias, The Breach Problem and the Duty of Care, 1956, 30 Tulane L.Rev. 377; Fleming, The Passing of Polemis, 1961, 39 Can.Bar Rev. 489; Goodhart, The Imaginary Necktie and the Rule in Re Polemis, 1952, 68 L.Q.Rev. 514; Goodhart, Liability and Compensation, 1960, 76 L.Q.Rev. 567; Green, Foreseeability in Negligence Law, 1961, 61 Col.L.Rev. 1401; Payne, The "Direct" Consequences of a Negligent Act, 1952, 5 Curr. Leg.Prob. 189; Payne, Foreseeability and Remoteness of Damage in Negligence, 1962, 25 Mod.L.Rev. 1; Williams, The Risk Principle, 1961, 77 L.Q.Rev. 179; Wilson and Slade, A Re-examination of Remoteness, 1952, 15 Mod.L.Rev. 458; Wright, Re Polemis, 1951, 14 Mod. L.Rev. 393.

one of causation, and never arises until causation has been established. It is rather one of the fundamental policy of the law, as to whether the defendant's responsibility should extend to such results. In so far as the defendant is held liable for consequences which do not lie within the original risk which the defendant has created, a strict liability without fault is superimposed upon the liability that is logically to be attributed to the negligence itself. It is simpler, and no doubt more accurate, to state the problem in terms of legal responsibility: is the defendant legally responsible to protect the plaintiff against such unforeseeable consequences of the defendant's own negligent acts?[5] But to state the question in this manner is merely to make use of other words to ask it, and can of course provide no answer. Whether there is to be such legal responsibility is a matter of policy, of the end to be accomplished; and when we say, for example, that the defendant is or is not under a "duty" to protect the plaintiff against such consequences, "duty" is only a word with which we state our conclusion, and no more. But at least to deal with the problem in terms of causation, or to talk of the "proximate," is merely to obscure the issue. As to this problem, there are two basic, fundamental, opposing and irreconcilable views, which have been in conflict for more than a century; and each has developed complications of its own. First one will be considered, then the other, and finally, the possibility of compromise between the two.

Limitation of Liability to Risk

The first of these positions begins in 1850 with Baron Pollock,[6] who expressed the view that the same criterion of foreseeability and risk of harm which determined whether the defendant was negligent in the first instance should determine the extent of the liability for that negligence; and that no defendant should ever be held liable for consequences which no reasonable person would expect to follow from the conduct. The limitation, in other words, is to foreseeable consequences, and liability is restricted to the scope of the original risk created, with the test of responsibility for the result identical with the test for negligence.[7] In 1876, the same position was taken by Mr. Justice Strong in Milwaukee & St. Paul Railway Co. v. Kellogg,[8] which became the leading American case. It has had a great deal of support in a long line of cases,[9] although it is nowhere carried to its logical extreme of eliminating *all* damages which could not reasonably have occurred to the defendant's mind,[10] and in nearly every jurisdiction there are occasional odd cases which appear impossible to reconcile with it. It represents the rule which is almost uniformly adopted where the defendant's negligence consists of the violation of an applicable statute;[11] and here the explanation has been offered that the written rule, and the policy of strict construction

---

5. Cf. Green, Rationale of Proximate Cause, 1927, 11–43; Campbell, Duty, Fault and Legal Cause, [1938] Wisc.L.Rev. 402.

6. In Greenland v. Chaplin, 1850, 5 Ex. 243, 155 Eng.Rep. 104, and Rigby v. Hewitt, 1850, 5 Ex. 240, 155 Eng.Rep. 103.

7. "The area within which liability is imposed is that which is within the circle of reasonable foreseeability, using the original point at which the negligent act was committed or became operative, and thence looking in every direction as the semi-diameters of the circle; and those injuries which from this point could or should have been reasonably foreseen, as something likely to happen, are within the field of liability, while those which, although foreseeable, were foreseeable only as remote possibilities, those only slightly probable, are beyond and not within the circle—in all of which time, place and circumstance play their respective and important parts." Griffith, J., in Mauney v. Gulf Refining Co., 1942, 193 Miss. 421, 9 So.2d 780.

8. 1876, 94 U.S. 469, 24 L.Ed. 256.

9. Engle v. Director General of Railroads, 1921, 78 Ind.App. 547, 133 N.E. 138; Cone v. Inter County Telephone & Telegraph Co., Fla.1949, 40 So.2d 148; Dixon v. Kentucky Utilities Co., 1943, 295 Ky. 32, 174 S.W.2d 19; Shideler v. Habiger, 1952, 172 Kan. 718, 243 P.2d 211; Republic of France v. United States, 5th Cir. 1961, 290 F.2d 395 (Texas law), certiorari denied 369 U.S. 804, 82 S.Ct. 644, 7 L.Ed.2d 550.

10. See infra, Liability Beyond the Risk. As to the various tests adopted in such a state as Oklahoma, and the resulting problem of the federal court, see Hardware Mutual Insurance Co. v. Lukken, 10th Cir. 1967, 372 F.2d 8.

11. See supra, § 36.

which seeks not to go beyond legislative purpose or intent, justify the result. It is also the rule generally applied in cases of what are called intervening causes,[12] where it may be necessitated by the absence of any other place to stop, if nothing more. There are, however, so many possible factors which may interplay in any given situation, that some caution must be exercised in classifying decisions as examples of the application of the rule.

This position has been justified as more rational, since the factors which define negligence should also limit liability for negligence; as easier to administer, since it fixes the nearest thing to a definite boundary of liability which is possible; and as more just, since negligence may consist of only a slight deviation from the community standard of conduct, and even be free from all moral blame, while its consequences may be catastrophic, and out of all proportion to the fault.[13] It is, however, by no means free from difficulties, which have led, in nearly all jurisdictions, to some modification of the rule in its pristine purity.[14]

Natural and Probable Consequences. To some extent there are difficulties of language. Many courts have said that the defendant is liable only if the harm suffered is the "natural and probable" consequence of the defendant's act.[15] These words frequently appear to have been given no more definite meaning than "proximate" itself. Strictly speaking, all consequences are "natural" which occur through the operation of forces of nature, without human intervention. But the word, as used, obviously appears not to be intended to mean this at all, but to refer to consequences which are normal, not extraordinary, not surprising in the light of ordinary experience. "Probable," if it is to add anything to this, must refer to consequences which were to be anticipated at the time of the defendant's conduct.[16] The phrase therefore appears to come out as the equivalent of the test of foreseeability, of consequences within the scope of the original risk, so that the likelihood of their occurrence was a factor in making the defendant negligent in the first instance.

Time and Space. In one context, the New York courts have attempted to set an arbitary rule, in terms of what is foreseeable, by requiring that the consequences be not too far removed in time or space from the defendant's conduct. This revival of the original meaning of "proximate" originated in a case [17] in which, apparently because of the possibility of subrogation claims on the part of fire insurance companies, the court was unwilling to extend liability for a fire negligently set, beyond the first adjoining building. In later fire cases New York has retained the arbitrary rule.[18]

---

12. See infra, § 44.

13. Pollock, Liability for Consequences, 1922, 38 L.Q.Rev. 165; Goodhart, The Unforeseeable Consequences of a Negligent Act, 1930, 39 Yale L.J. 449; Seavey, Mr. Justice Cardozo and the Law of Torts, 1939, 52 Harv.L.Rev. 372, 48 Yale L.J. 390, 39 Col.L. Rev. 20; Foster, Grant and Green, The Risk Theory and Proximate Cause, 1952, 32 Neb.L.Rev. 72; Wilson, Some Thoughts About Negligence, 1949, 2 Okl.L.Rev. 275; R. Keeton, Legal Cause in the Law of Torts, 1963.

See, however, condemning the whole approach, Smith Legal Cause in Actions of Tort, 1911, 25 Harv.L. Rev. 103, 114–128; and the attack upon policy grounds in Green, Rationale of Proximate Cause, 1927, 177–185.

14. See infra, Liability Beyond the Risk.

15. In the United States this apparently originated in Milwaukee & St. Paul Railway Co. v. Kellogg, 1876, 94 U.S. 469, 24 L.Ed. 256; and the phrase was repeated from that case, and from one decision to another.

16. Bohlen, The Probable or the Natural Consequences as the Test of Liability in Negligence, 1901, 49 Am.L.Reg. 79, 85.

17. Ryan v. New York Central Railroad Co., 1866, 35 N.Y. 210.

18. See Bird v. St. Paul Fire & Marine Insurance Co., 1918, 224 N.Y. 47, 120 N.E. 86; Notes, 1932, 32 Col.L.Rev. 911; 1933, 2 Brook.L.Rev. 113. In O'Neill v. New York, Ontario & Western Railway Co., 1889, 115 N.Y. 579, 22 N.E. 217, it was suggested, but not decided that the rule did not apply to forest fires in the country (where, incidentally, there would probably be no insurance). But in Hoffman v. King, 1899, 160 N.Y. 618, 55 N.E. 401, the suggestion was repudiated, and liability for forest fires restricted to the first owner affected. The legislature then by statute changed the rule to extend liability to other lands "however distant". See Nicoll v. Long Island Railroad Co., 1931, 232 App.Div. 435, 250 N.Y.S. 366. The court has refused to apply this statute to property other than "for-

All other jurisdictions have rejected any such attempt to fix a rule.[19] Remoteness in time or space may give rise to the likelihood that other intervening causes have taken over the responsibility.[20] But when causation is found, and other factors are eliminated, it is not easy to discover any merit whatever in the contention that such physical remoteness should of itself bar recovery. The defendant who sets a bomb which explodes ten years later,[21] or mails a box of poisoned chocolates from California to Delaware,[22] has caused the result, and should obviously bear the consequences.

The "Same Hazard." Sometimes the foreseeability limitation is stated in a form which, on its face, would seem to narrow the scope of liability. It is said that the defendant's responsibility must be limited to harm which results from the realization of the particular risk or hazard which the defendant has created.[23] Just what this means is a problem, although there are decisions which have purported to apply it,[24] just as there are others which have purported to reject it.[25] The difficulty lies in the meaning to be assigned to "hazard." Does it signify the harm which is to result, and if so, does it refer to the particular harm or merely to a general class or type of damage? Does it mean the manner in which that harm is to be brought about, and if so, a broad general class of possible events, the particular details, or something undefined in between? Or does it mean merely the absence of anything very unexpected? The illustration most often given [26] is that of the child who is given a gun, and instead of being injured by a shot, suffers injury by dropping it on a toe; and the best discussion [27] gives only

est land." Rose v. Pennsylvania Railroad Co., 1923, 236 N.Y. 568, 142 N.E. 287.

The court has, however, shown some tendency to be liberal in its application of the rule. Thus recovery has been allowed to a next adjoining landowner, although the building on this property was not the first building to catch fire. Webb v. Rome, Watertown & Ogdensburgh Railroad Co., 1872, 49 N.Y. 420. Also to the first building to which the fire jumps, although it is not adjoining. Homac Corp. v. Sun Oil Co., 1932, 258 N.Y. 462, 180 N.E. 172, affirmed 1931, 233 App.Div. 890, 251 N.Y.S. 877, affirmed 137 Misc. 551, 244 N.Y.S. 51. See also Davies v. Delaware, Lackawanna & Western Railroad Co., 1915, 215 N.Y. 181, 109 N.E. 95.

19. Smith v. London & S. W. R. Co., 1870, L.R. 6 C.P. 14; Kuhn v. Jewett, 1880, 32 N.J.Eq. 647; Silver Falls Timber Co. v. Eastern & Western Lumber Co., 1935, 149 Or. 126, 40 P.2d 703; Phillips v. Durham & C.R. Co., 1905, 138 N.C. 12, 50 S.E. 462; Osborn v. City of Whittier, 1951, 103 Cal.App.2d 609, 230 P.2d 132 and cases cited infra, Liability Beyond the Risk. The New York rule was followed in Pennsylvania Railroad Co. v. Kerr, 1870, 62 Pa. 353, but was repudiated in Pennsylvania Railroad Co. v. Hope, 1876, 80 Pa. 373.

20. Thus in Firman v. Sacia, 1958, 11 Misc.2d 243, 173 N.Y.S.2d 440, affirmed, 1959, 7 A.D.2d 579, 184 N.Y.S.2d 945, where injuries inflicted by defendant drove A insane, and seven years later he was "unable to resist the impulse" to shoot B, the court refused to permit a finding that this was proximate. It said that lapse of time will not defeat recovery in itself, but it "militates against foreseeability and proximate cause of the injury. * * * The intervention of other causes is very likely to occur where the time lapse is considerable in length."

21. Cf. Western Union Telegraph Co. v. Preston, 3d Cir. 1918, 254 F. 229, certiorari denied 248 U.S. 585, 39 S.Ct. 182, 63 L.Ed. 433 (death ten years after negligence); Bishop v. St. Paul City Railway Co., 1892, 48 Minn. 26, 50 N.W. 927 (seven months); Parks v. Starks, 1955, 342 Mich. 443, 70 N.W.2d 805 (nine hours). It should, however, be noted that when the plaintiff suffers actual injury, the statute of limitations and the rule against splitting a cause of action may bar recovery for long delayed damages.

22. People v. Botkin, 1901, 132 Cal. 231, 64 P. 286. Cf. Mize v. Rocky Mountain Bell Telephone Co., 1909, 38 Mont. 521, 100 P. 971 (nine or ten miles); Chase v. Washington Water Power Co., 1941, 62 Idaho 298, 111 P.2d 872 (over a mile); Kroeger v. Safranek, 1955, 161 Neb. 182, 72 N.W.2d 831; Thornton v. Weaber, 1955, 380 Pa. 590, 112 A.2d 344.

23. Second Restatement of Torts, § 281, Comment e. Followed in Duncan v. Lumbermen's Mutual Casualty Co., 1941, 91 N.H. 349, 23 A.2d 325. Cf. New York Eskimo Pie Corp. v. Rataj, 3d Cir. 1934, 73 F.2d 184 ("substantially the manner in which it was brought about"); Harper, The Foreseeability Factor in the Law of Torts, 1932, 7 Notre Dame Lawyer 468, 470.

24. See for example Verkamp Corp. of Kentucky v. Hubbard, Ky.1956, 296 S.W.2d 740 (safety valves on gas cylinder intended to prevent explosion, not ignition of gas after release).

25. See for example Norfolk & Western Railway Co. v. Whitehurst, 1919, 125 Va. 260, 99 S.E. 568 (railroad switchman falling over unlighted switch target in the dark).

26. From Second Restatement of Torts, § 281, Illustration 3.

27. Eldredge, Modern Tort Problems, 17–24.

similar examples of unpredictable intervening causes.[28] If, as this might indicate, the significance of the "same hazard" is merely to eliminate the results of such causes, it would appear to be subject to the rule that where the result is foreseeable but the intervention is not, there is liability.[29] With such uncertainties surrounding it, the "same hazard" approach is in all probability no real aid of any kind, and merely a means of covering up or disguising somewhat complicated problems.

Unforeseeable Plaintiffs

In 1928 something of a bombshell burst upon this field, when the New York Court of Appeals, forsaking "proximate cause," stated the issue of foreseeability in terms of duty. The case was Palsgraf v. Long Island Railroad Co.,[30] which has become the most discussed and debated of all torts cases,[31] and over which the argument still goes on. It involved what may be called, instead of unforeseeable consequences, the unforeseeable plaintiff. If the defendant's conduct threatens harm, which a reasonable person would foresee, to A, and A is in fact injured, we start with negligence toward A, and the problem is purely one of the extent of liability for consequences. But what if harm results instead to B, who was in no way threatened, stood outside of the zone of all apparent danger, and to whom no harm could reasonably be foreseen? Is the defendant's duty of care limited to A, toward whom the defendant has created a foreseeable risk, or does it extend also to the plaintiff whom the defendant has in fact injured, but could not reasonably foresee? We have seen the doctrine of "transferred intent," by which one who shoots at A, and instead unexpectedly hits B, becomes liable to B.[32] Is there such a thing as "transferred negligence," which will accomplish the same result?

Actually the problem was not a new one in 1928. It had arisen before, and courts had already considered it in terms of duty,[33] as well as "proximate cause," [34] and arrived at conflicting conclusions upon either basis.

28. In addition to the boy and the gun, the following: Gorris v. Scott, 1874, L.R. 9 Ex. 125; Falk v. Finkelman, 1929, 268 Mass. 524, 168 N.E. 89; Hudson v. Lehigh Valley Railroad Co., 1913, 54 Pa.Super. 107; Bruggeman v. York, 1917, 259 Pa. 94, 102 A. 415; Hassett v. Palmer, 1940, 126 Conn. 468, 12 A.2d 646; New York, Lake Erie & Western Railway Co. v. Ball, 1891, 53 N.J.L. 283, 21 A. 1052.

29. See infra, § 44, Foreseeable Results of Unforeseeable Causes.

30. Palsgraf v. Long Island Railroad Co., 1928, 248 N.Y. 339, 162 N.E. 99, reargument denied 249 N.Y. 511, 164 N.E. 564.

31. Green, The Palsgraf Case, 1930, 30 Col.L.Rev. 789, reprinted in Green, Judge and Jury, 1930, c. 8; Goodhart, The Unforeseeable Consequences of a Negligent Act, 1930, 39 Yale L.J. 449; Campbell, Duty, Fault and Legal Cause, [1938] Wis.L.Rev. 402; Cowan, The Riddle of the Palsgraf Case, 1938, 23 Minn.L.Rev. 46; Gregory, Proximate Cause in Negligence—A Retreat from Rationalization, 1938, 6 U.Chi.L.Rev. 36; Seavey, Mr. Justice Cardozo and the Law of Torts, 1939, 52 Harv.L.Rev. 372, 48 Yale L.J. 390, 39 Col.L. Rev. 20; Ehrenzweig, Loss-Shifting and Quasi-Negligence, 1941, 8 U.Chi.L.Rev. 729; Eldredge, The Role of Foreseeable Consequences in Negligence Law, 1952, 23 Pa.B.A.Q. 158; Morris, Duty, Negligence and Causation, 1952, 101 U.Pa.L.Rev. 189; James, Scope of Duty in Negligence Cases, 1953, 47 Nev.U.L.Rev. 778; Prosser, Palsgraf Revisited, 1953, 52 Mich.L.Rev. 1, reprinted in Prosser, Selected Topics on the Law of Torts, 1954, 191; Note, 1954, 29 Ind.L.Rev. 622; R. Keeton, Legal Cause in the Law of Torts, 1963.

32. See supra, § 8.

33. Duty: Stevens v. Dudley, 1883, 56 Vt. 158; Wilson v. Northern Pacific Railway Co., 1915, 30 N.D. 456, 153 N.W. 429; Hollidge v. Duncan, 1908, 199 Mass. 121, 85 N.E. 186; Mize v. Rocky Mountain Bell Telephone Co., 1909, 38 Mont. 521, 100 P. 971; and see Poffenbarger, J., in Bond v. Baltimore & Ohio Railroad Co., 1918, 82 W.Va. 557, 96 S.E. 932.

No duty: Boyd v. City of Duluth, 1914, 126 Minn. 33, 147 N.W. 710; Goodlander Mill Co. v. Standard Oil Co., 7th Cir. 1894, 63 F. 400; Trinity & Brazos Valley Railway Co. v. Blackshear, 1915, 106 Tex. 515, 172 S.W. 544.

34. Proximate: Wolfe v. Checker Taxi Co., 1938, 299 Mass. 225, 12 N.E.2d 849; Robinson v. Standard Oil Co., 1929, 89 Ind.App. 167, 166 N.E. 160; Kommerstad v. Great Northern Railway Co., 1913, 120 Minn. 376, 139 N.W. 713, second appeal 1915, 128 Minn. 505, 151 N.W. 177; Ramsey v. Carolina-Tennessee Power Co., 1928, 195 N.C. 788, 143 S.E. 861; Walmsley v. Rural Telephone Association, 1917, 102 Kan. 139, 169 P. 197. See also the cases of fires spreading to unforeseeable distances, infra, this section.

Not proximate: Wood v. Pennsylvania Railroad Co., 1896, 177 Pa. 306, 35 A. 699; Ryan v. New York Central Railroad Co., 1866, 35 N.Y. 210.

What the Palsgraf case actually did was to submit to the nation's then most excellent state court a law professor's dream of an examination question. The factual hypothesis before the court was this: A passenger was running to catch one of the defendant's trains. The defendant's servants, trying to assist the passenger to board it, dislodged a package from the passenger's arms, and it fell upon the rails. The package contained fireworks, which exploded with some violence. The concussion overturned some scales,[35] many feet away on the platform, and they fell upon the plaintiff and injured her. The defendant's servants, who were found by the jury to have been negligent in what they did, could have foreseen harm from their clumsiness to the package, or at most to the passenger boarding the train; but no harm to the plaintiff could possibly have been anticipated.

In this situation Judge Cardozo, speaking for a majority of four, held that there was no liability, because there was no negligence toward the plaintiff. Negligence, he said, was a matter of relation between the parties, which must be founded upon the foreseeability of harm to the person in fact injured. The defendant's conduct was not a wrong toward her merely because it was negligence toward someone else. She must "sue in her own right for a wrong personal to her, and not as the vicarious beneficiary of a breach of duty to another."

Three judges dissented in the Palsgraf Case. Judge Andrews stated their contention that "Due care is a duty imposed upon each one of us to protect society from unnecessary danger, not to protect A, B or C alone. * * * Every one owes to the world at large the duty of refraining from those acts which unreasonably threaten the safety of others. * * * Not only is he wronged to whom harm might reasonably be expected to result, but he also who is in fact injured, even if he be outside what would generally be thought the danger zone."

The Restatement of Torts [36] almost immediately afterward accepted the view of the Palsgraf Case, that there is no duty, and hence no negligence, and so never any liability, to the unforeseeable plaintiff. Subsequent decisions, however, cannot be said as yet definitely to have settled the question so far as American law is concerned.[37] It has become fashionable to cite the case in connection with almost every kind of negligence problem, and most of the extensive list of references to it have no significance whatever, unless it is recognition that the decision has acquired a reputation. In particular, it has been cited in a long list of cases in which no injury to anyone was to be anticipated, and therefore there was simply no negligence at all.[38]

Even where a negligent defendant and an unforeseeable plaintiff have in fact been involved, the Palsgraf rule has become rather hopelessly entangled with other rules, and other bases of policy. Thus it has been cit-

---

35. The Record of the case is set forth in Scott and Simpson, Cases on Civil Procedure, 1950, at pp. 891–940. A study of it indicates that the event could not possibly have happened in the manner described, and that the scale must have been knocked over by a stampede of frightened passengers. See Prosser, Palsgraf Revisited, 1953, 52 Mich.L.Rev. 1, 3, reprinted in Prosser, Selected Topics on the Law of Torts, 1953, 191, 194. This would of course make no difference in the result.

36. § 281, Comment c. For the background of Cardozo's position as an Adviser in drafting the Restatement, see Prosser, Palsgraf Revisited, 1953, 52 Mich.L. Rev. 1, 4–8, reprinted in Prosser, Selected Topics on the Law of Torts, 1954, 191. For an addendum about one meeting of the Advisers, see R. Keeton, A Palsgraf Anecdote, 1978, 56 Tex.L.Rev. 513.

37. See Prosser, Palsgraf Revisited, 1953, 52 Mich. L.Rev. 1, 8–12, reprinted in Prosser, Selected Topics on the Law of Torts, 1954, 191.

38. See for example Hetrick v. Marion-Reserve Power Co., 1943, 141 Ohio St. 347, 48 N.E.2d 103; Birckhead v. Mayor and City Council of Baltimore, 1938, 174 Md. 32, 197 A. 615; Andreu v. Wellman, 1949, 144 Me. 36, 63 A.2d 926; Foreman v. Texas & New Orleans Railroad Co., 5th Cir. 1953, 205 F.2d 79; Union Carbide & Carbon Corp. v. Peters, 4th Cir. 1953, 206 F.2d 366.

ed [39] in support of the familiar rule [40] that a statute intended to protect only a particular class of persons or to guard only against a particular risk or type of harm, creates no duty to any other class or risk; but the written law and the influence of the policy of strict construction which refuses to extend its effect beyond the legislative purpose seem definitely to set this apart from any court-made rule. It has been cited [41] in holding that a railroad's duty toward drivers at crossings does not extend to its employees; but here, as in the case of the trespasser,[42] there is an element of special relationship which limits the duty. It has been relied on in holding that a contract obligation does not extend to third parties,[43] and that a contract interest is not protected against negligence toward one of the parties to the contract; [44] but here again the kind of obligation or interest involved might have been used as an adequate explanation. Finally the case has been relied on [45] in holding that a plaintiff who is in a position of safety cannot recover for mental shock and injury brought about by the sight of harm or peril to another person within the danger zone. The reluctance of the courts to enter this field even where the mental injury is clearly foreseeable, and the frequent mention of the difficulties of proof, the facility of fraud, and the problem of finding a place to stop and draw the line,[46] suggest that here it is the nature of the interest invaded and the type of damage which is the real obstacle.

It is difficult to conclude that such cases represent any general and established principle of non-liability. For each of them there are others to be found which come to the same conclusion on similar facts, but on other and better grounds. They suggest rather that the duty problem [47] is a very involved and complex one, and that the opinion of Cardozo has perhaps greatly over-simplified the whole matter. The cases which have dealt with the Palsgraf question, and which cannot be so distinguished, are few, and divided. The majority of the small number of them have accepted and followed the case.[48] There has been, however, an undercurrent of disagreement,[49] which suggests that there is something more here than meets the casual eye; and this is borne out by the conflict in the earlier decisions,[50] most of which went off on "proximate cause." It would be easy to dismiss these last opinions on the ground that they never saw the point of "duty;" but there is in them so much explicit considera-

39. Flynn v. Gordon, 1933, 86 N.H. 198, 165 A. 715; Chicago, Burlington & Quincy Railroad Co. v. Murray, 1929, 40 Wyo. 324, 277 P. 703.

40. See supra, § 36.

41. Karr v. Chicago, Rock Island & Pacific Railway Co., 1937, 341 Mo. 536, 108 S.W.2d 44.

42. Cf. Garland v. Boston & Maine Railroad Co., 1913, 76 N.H. 556, 86 A. 141; Wickenburg v. Minneapolis, St. Paul & Sault Ste. Marie Railway Co., 1905, 94 Minn. 276, 102 N.W. 713; Peterson v. South & Western Railroad Co., 1906, 143 N.C. 260, 55 S.E. 618.

43. Harris v. Lewistown Trust Co., 1937, 326 Pa. 145, 191 A. 34 (landlord's covenant to repair). See infra, § 63.

44. Sinram v. Pennsylvania Railroad Co., 2d Cir., 1932, 61 F.2d 767. As to negligent interference with contract, see infra, § 129.

45. Waube v. Warrington, 1935, 216 Wis. 603, 258 N.W. 497; Curry v. Journal Publishing Co., 1937, 41 N.M. 318, 68 P.2d 168; Blanchard v. Reliable Transfer Co., 1944, 71 Ga.App. 843, 32 S.E.2d 420; Cote v. Litawa, 1950, 96 N.H. 174, 71 A.2d 792; Resavage v. Davies, 1952, 199 Md. 479, 86 A.2d 879.

46. See infra, § 54.

47. See infra, § 53.

48. Dahlstrom v. Shrum, 1951, 368 Pa. 423, 84 A.2d 289 (A struck by bus, thrown off at an angle against B, in position of apparent safety); Radigan v. W. J. Halloran Co., 1963, 97 R.I. 122, 196 A.2d 160 (crane brought in contact with power line, resulting in gas explosion on third floor); West v. Cruz, 1952, 75 Ariz. 13, 251 P.2d 311 (motorist failed to pull to curb when siren sounded, caused collision between two other vehicles); Tucker v. Collar, 1955, 79 Ariz. 141, 285 P.2d 178 (defective machinery threatened premises of tenant, injured those of landlord); Diamond State Telephone Co. v. Atlantic Refining Co., 3d Cir. 1953, 205 F.2d 402 (barge threatened, cable injured); Geo. D. Barnard Co. v. Lane, Tex.Civ.App.1965, 392 S.W.2d 769 (collision at intersection damaging air conditioning unit in distant building).

49. Jackson v. B. Lowenstein & Brothers, 1940, 175 Tenn. 535, 136 S.W.2d 495; Pfeifer v. Standard Gateway Theater, 1952, 262 Wis. 229, 55 N.W.2d 29; Longberg v. H. L. Green Co., 1962, 15 Wis.2d 505, 113 N.W.2d 129, modified 15 Wis.2d 505, 114 N.W.2d 435.

50. See supra, this section.

tion of the bearing of foreseeability that they seem in reality to have decided it under another name.[51]

The present state of the law is, then, still one of troubled waters, in which any one may fish. The holding that duty in a negligence action extends only to those within a definite area of danger has obvious attraction. In support of it, it has been argued [52] that it simplifies the problem and facilitates administration by restricting the defendant's responsibility within some reasonable bounds—which may, however, be somewhat illusory because of the difficulties of a fragmentary analysis of the risk.[53] It has been contended that such a limitation is desirable because the negligence may consist of a momentary inadvertence, or an honest error of judgment, while the harm that results may be out of all proportion to the nature or extent of the departure from ordinary standards of conduct. The rule has been defended as more consistent with the basic theory of negligence, that of the creation of an unreasonable risk.

There is, however, something to be said for the idea of an absolute wrong adopted by the dissent. As between an entirely innocent plaintiff and a defendant who admittedly has departed from the social standard of conduct, if only toward one individual, who should bear the loss? If the result is out of all proportion to the defendant's fault, it can be no less out of proportion to the plaintiff's entire innocence. If it is unjust to the defendant to make the defendant bear a loss which the defendant could not have foreseen, it is no less unjust to the plaintiff to make the plaintiff bear a loss which the plaintiff too could not have foreseen, and which is not even due to the plaintiff's own negligence. The defendant is required to be reasonably careful, for the protection of those to whom harm can be foreseen. If we extend this liability to others, we impose upon the defendant no new obligation of conduct, and reasonable care will still protect the defendant from liability. The issue is whether the plaintiff's interests are to be afforded protection against the defendant's negligence where the consequences exceed the fault; there is nothing sacred about "duty," which is nothing more than a word, and a very indefinite one, with which we state our conclusion.

A key difficulty with this position is that it proves too much. Unlimited liability is plainly unjustified, and this approach does nothing to solve the problem of a place to stop short of infinite liability. It throws the question of any limitation back into the morass of "proximate cause," and the search for some reasonably close connection between the defendant's conduct and the injury.[54]

The real problem, and the one to which attention should be directed, would seem to be one of social policy: whether the defendants in such cases should bear the heavy negligence losses of a complex civilization, rather than the individual plaintiff.[55] Because these defendants are in large measure public utilities, governmental bodies, industries, automobile drivers, and others who by rates, prices, taxes or insurance are better able to distribute the loss to the general public, many courts may reasonably consider that the burden should rest upon them, and experience no great difficulty in finding a "duty" of protection. So far as policy is concerned, different answers might well be given in different communities, according to the view

---

51. Compare, upon essentially similar facts, Wood v. Pennsylvania Railroad Co., 1896, 177 Pa. 306, 35 A. 699 (proximate cause, no liability); Mellon v. Lehigh Valley Railroad Co., 1925, 282 Pa. 39, 127 A. 444 (proximate cause, liability); and Dahlstrom v. Shrum, 1951, 368 Pa. 423, 84 A.2d 289 (duty, no liability). Is there any difference in the analysis in the three cases, except one of terminology?

52. See for example Seavey, Mr. Justice Cardozo and the Law of Torts, 1939, 52 Harv.L.Rev. 372, 48 Yale L.J. 390, 39 Col.L.Rev. 20.

53. See infra, this section, Anatomy of Foresight.

54. See supra, § 42.

55. See Green, The Duty Problem in Negligence Cases, 1928, 28 Col.L.Rev. 1014, 1929, 29 Col.L.Rev. 255, reprinted in Green, Judge and Jury, 1930, ch. 3–4; Note, 1929, 29 Col.L.Rev. 53.

that is taken as to where the loss should fall;[56] but the issue is not to be determined by any talk of "duty," or an assumption of the conclusion. There is room for argument that the foreseeability of harm to the plaintiff should be but one factor in determining the existence of a duty, and not always conclusive,[57] and that situations will more or less inevitably arise which do not fit within any fixed and inflexible rule.[58] Also that in a field of freak accidents, which do not recur without significant differences, there should be no absolute rule as a prediction for the unpredictable; that there might well be different results not only in different jurisdictions but in different types of cases;[59] and that where there is so much dispute among lawyers the court should be rather slow to take the case from the jury.[60]

Thus, while the trend is definitely in favor of acceptance of the Palsgraf rule, it cannot be said that the issue is finally determined for all cases in the United States.

Cases of a group especially difficult to fit into the "duty" formula have been those in which a defendant has endangered one person, and has been held liable to another who is injured in an attempt to rescue.[61] The duty to the rescuer is clearly an independent one; and it has been held that the contributory negligence of the person rescued will not bar the rescuer's recovery,[62] and even that the rescuer may still recover where the imperiled person is owed no duty because of being a trespasser.[63] On the theory that anticipation of rescue, and all the more so of harm to the rescuer, unduly strains the limitation of the "foreseeable risk," these cases were formerly regarded as an exception to the rule, or at least a considerable extension of it.[64] When Cardozo himself was confronted with the question, he rationalized the apparent anomaly by declaring, as a more or less arbitrary rule, that rescuers, as a class, are always foreseeable when the defendant's negligence endangers anyone.[65] Later decisions in which the defendant's negligence

56. New York limits liability for the spread of fire to the first adjoining building. Ryan v. New York Central Railroad Co., 1866, 35 N.Y. 210, 91 Am.Dec. 49. Kansas, carrying direct causation to an extreme, holds that it extends for at least four miles. Atchison, Topeka & Santa Fe Railway Co. v. Stanford, 1874, 12 Kan. 354, 15 Am.Rep. 362. New York's prosperity depends upon railroads and heavy industry; its courts have had in mind urban communities in which nearly all property of any value carries fire insurance, and the possibility of a windfall for the insurers in the form of subrogation claims. Kansas has miles of uninsured wheat, and its community attitude toward railroads is by no means the same. Who is to say that each decision is not defensible for the jurisdiction; and what reason is there that both must come to the same conclusion?

57. Green, Judge and Jury, 1930, 71.

58. Green, Foreseeability in Negligence Law, 1961, 61 Col.L.Rev. 1401; Note, 1961, 36 N.Y.U.L.Rev. 1043. Compare the cases in which statutes have been held to call for a relaxation of rules of "proximate cause." Daggett v. Keshner, 1954, 284 App.Div. 733, 134 N.Y.S.2d 524, noted in 1955, 40 Corn.L.Q. 810; Pierce v. Albanese, 1957, 144 Conn. 241, 129 A.2d 606, appeal dismissed 355 U.S. 15, 78 S.Ct. 36, 2 L.Ed.2d 21; Kernan v. American Dredging Co., 1958, 355 U.S. 426, 78 S.Ct. 394, 2 L.Ed.2d 382.

59. See Prosser, Palsgraf Revisited, 1953, 52 Mich. L.Rev. 1, 28–32, reprinted in Prosser, Selected Topics on the Law of Torts, 1954, 191.

60. See Jackson v. B. Lowenstein & Brothers, 1940, 175 Tenn. 535, 538, 136 S.W.2d 495; Pfeifer v. Standard Gateway Theater, 1952, 262 Wis. 229, 55 N.W.2d 29.

61. Eckert v. Long Island Railroad Co., 1871, 43 N.Y. 502; Perpich v. Leetonia Mining Co., 1912, 118 Minn. 508, 137 N.W. 12; Bond v. Baltimore & Ohio Railroad Co., 1918, 82 W.Va. 557, 96 S.E. 932; Sarratt v. Holston Quarry Co., 1934, 174 S.C. 262, 177 S.E. 135; Hatch v. Globe Laundry Co., 1934, 132 Me. 379, 171 A. 387. See Tilley, The Rescue Principle, 1967, 30 Mod.L. Rev. 25; Gordon, Moral Challenge to the Legal Doctrine of Rescue, 1965, 14 Cleve.Marsh.L.Rev. 334.

62. Pittsburgh, Cincinnati, Chicago & St. Louis Railway Co. v. Lynch, 1903, 69 Ohio St. 123, 68 N.E. 703; Highland v. Wilsonian Investment Co., 1932, 171 Wash. 34, 17 P.2d 631.

63. Videan v. British Transport Commission, [1963] 2 Q.B. 650. Contra: Brady v. Chicago & Northwestern Railway Co., 1954, 265 Wis. 618, 62 N.W.2d 415; Rose v. Peters, Fla.1955, 82 So.2d 585.

64. See Bohlen, Review of Harper, Law of Torts, 1934, 47 Harv.L.Rev. 556, 557.

65. "Danger invites rescue. The cry of distress is the summons to relief. The law does not ignore these reactions of the mind in tracing conduct to its consequences. It recognizes them as normal. It places their effects within the range of the natural and probable. The wrong that imperils life is a wrong to the imperiled victim; it is a wrong also to his rescuer." Cardozo, C. J., in Wagner v. International Railway Co., 1921, 232 N.Y. 176, 133 N.E. 437.

endangered only the defendant,[66] or the defendant's own property,[67] have confirmed the rationalization, since if the defendant is under a duty to anyone, and is negligent because the defendant can foresee harm to anyone, it must be to the rescuer. One may perhaps swallow this, with a grain of salt; but when the same arbitrary rule is extended further, to hold that a rescuer of the rescuer is to be held to be foreseeable,[68] its artificial and fanciful character becomes more apparent.

Particular interest. In a dictum in the Palsgraf Case [69] Cardozo suggested a further refinement, with a distinction to be made between interests of the plaintiff as to which the defendant owes the plaintiff a duty, and those as to which the defendant does not. For example, that if only harm to the plaintiff's property is to be foreseen, there can be no recovery for injuries to the plaintiff's person which may in fact result, and vice versa. The First Restatement of Torts [70] approved this dictum also. Although it may follow logically enough from what has gone before, there is almost no authority in support of such a proposition,[71] and quite a bit to the contrary, in cases where property was threatened, and injury to the person [72] or to other property [73] has in fact been caused. Although there are writers who have approved this idea,[74] it has ter-

---

66. Carney v. Buyea, 1946, 271 App.Div. 338, 65 N.Y.S.2d 902, appeal denied 1947, 271 App.Div. 949, 68 N.Y.S.2d 446; Brugh v. Bigelow, 1944, 310 Mich. 74, 16 N.W.2d 668; Longacre v. Reddick, Tex.Civ.App.1948, 215 S.W.2d 404, mandamus overruled; Dodson v. Maddox, 1949, 359 Mo. 742, 223 S.W.2d 434; Usry v. Small, 1961, 103 Ga.App. 144, 118 S.E.2d 719. Cf. Talbert v. Talbert, 1960, 22 Misc.2d 782, 199 N.Y.S.2d 212, where the defendant attempted suicide, and his son was injured while trying to save him.

67. Rushton v. Howle, 1949, 79 Ga.App. 360, 53 S.E.2d 768; Henjum v. Bok, 1961, 261 Minn. 74, 110 N.W.2d 461; Green v. Britton, 1960, 22 Conn.Sup. 71, 160 A.2d 497; George A. Fuller Construction Co. v. Elliott, 1955, 92 Ga.App. 309, 88 S.E.2d 413.

68. Richards v. Kansas Electric Power Co., 1928, 126 Kan. 521, 268 P. 847; Brown v. Ross, 1956, 345 Mich. 54, 75 N.W.2d 68; Richardson v. United States, E.D.Okl.1965, 248 F.Supp. 99.

69. Palsgraf v. Long Island Railroad Co., 1928, 248 N.Y. 339, 346–347, 162 N.E. 99, 101, reargument denied 249 N.Y. 511, 164 N.E. 564: "There is room for argument that a distinction is to be drawn according to the diversity of interests invaded by the act, as where conduct negligent in that it threatens an insignificant invasion of an interest in property results in an unforeseeable invasion of an interest of another order, as, e.g., one of bodily security."

70. § 281, Comment *g*. In Comment *c* under the same Section, the First Restatement approved the rule of the "same hazard," this section.

71. One such case is Texas & Pacific Railway Co. v. Bigham, 1896, 90 Tex. 223, 38 S.W. 162, discussed in Green, Are Negligence and Proximate Cause Determined by the Same Test, 1923, 1 Tex.L.Rev. 399, where defendant's negligence threatened harm only to plaintiff's cattle, and the plaintiff was injured personally when they stampeded.

See also Seale v. Gulf, Colorado & Santa Fe Railway Co., 1886, 65 Tex. 274, where a railroad negligently starting a fire was held liable for loss of adjoining property, but not for death of the owner's daughter fighting the fire. This looks wrong, at least under present-day law.

The contention of the Restatement was advanced by the dissenting opinion of Jaggard, J., in Lesch v. Great Northern Railway Co., 1906, 97 Minn. 503, 106 N.W. 955, where the plaintiff recovererd for mental anguish following the invasion of her property, but it was rejected by the majority of the court.

72. Rasmussen v. Benson, 1938, 135 Neb. 232, 280 N.W. 890 (poisoning of cattle led to death of owner); Isham v. Dow's Estate, 1898, 70 Vt. 588, 41 A. 585 (harm to plaintiff's dog, resulting in personal injury); Mitchell v. Friedman, 1951, 11 N.J.Super. 344, 78 A.2d 417 (negligent failure to repair toilet, resulting in personal injury from carrying water); Chicago & Northwestern Railway Co. v. Hunerberg, 1885, 16 Ill.App. 387, (threatened harm to land, resulting personal injury); Brackett v. Bellows Falls Hydro-Electric Corp., 1934, 87 N.H. 173, 175 A. 822 (threatened harm to land, resulting personal injury); Barker v. City of Philadelphia, E.D.Pa.1955, 134 F.Supp. 231 (threatened harm to chattel, death of child) In re Guardian Casualty Co., 1938, 253 App.Div. 360, 2 N.Y.S.2d 232, affirmed 278 N.Y. 674, 16 N.E.2d 397 (damage to building, personal injury). Cf Law v. Visser, [1961] Queensland Rep. 46, where a motorist ran over an object on the highway at night, with no reason to expect it to be a man.

73. John C. Kupferle Foundry Co. v. St. Louis Merchants' Bridge Terminal Railway Co., 1918, 275 Mo. 451, 205 S.W. 57 (threatened harm to tank in street, resulting harm to factory behind it); and cf. Atherton v. Goodwin, 1947, 163 Kan. 22, 180 P.2d 296 (threatened harm to scales, resulting pecuniary loss); The Glendola, 2d Cir. 1931, 47 F.2d 206, certiorari denied 283 U.S. 857, 51 S.Ct. 650, 75 L.Ed. 1463.

74. Tilley, The English Rule as to Liability for Unintended Consequences, 1935, 33 Mich.L.Rev. 829, 848–851; Machin, Negligence and Interest, 1954, 17 Mod.L.Rev. 405.

rified others [75] with the prospect of either a whole series of hair-splitting distinctions, or else broad categories unreasonable in themselves. There is something of an analogy to the rule which does not permit the plaintiff to split a cause of action between personal injury and property damage, [76] or even between two pieces of property.[77] There is a very obvious artificiality about the whole thing. If A drops B's clock upon B's floor, it may be that A should foresee the risk of harm to the clock, and not to the floor. It may be that B's interest in the floor is not the same as B's interest in the clock, or for that matter in B's toe; and that the risk of disarranging the internal workings of the clock is distinct from the possibility of marring the varnish of the floor, or breaking the toe. These things might be; but if the floor is in fact damaged, or the toe broken, none of this is of any real aid in determining who should bear the loss—the innocent owner, or the clumsy lout who carelessly let go the clock.[78] For such reasons the Second Restatement, in the absence of case support for its proposition, has reversed it.[79]

The analogy of the cases holding that liability for the violation of a statute is limited to the particular risk covered is scarcely to be relied on, since they clearly involve the effect given to a legislative policy narrow in its scope. There are of course interests which, as a matter of policy, should not be protected against certain types of wrongful conduct,[80] but it does not follow from this that protection should always be limited to the interest which is threatened in advance.

Liability Beyond the Risk

There remains the opposing view, which has been urged from time to time by a good many writers,[81] that a defendant who is negligent must take existing circumstances as they are, and may be liable for consequences brought about by the defendant's acts, even though they were not reasonably to be anticipated. Or, as it is sometimes put, that what the defendant could foresee is important in determining whether the defendant was negligent in the first instance, but not at all decisive in determining the extent of the consequences for which, once negligent, the defendant will be liable.[82] This position ap-

---

75. "If the courts once adopt such a distinction, then we are faced with the terrifying prospect of a whole new series of cases in which it will be necessary to consider whether or not a person has the same interest in his foot and his eye, in his two adjoining houses, in his ship and the cargo which it carries. Obviously a single distinction between bodily security on the one hand and property security on the other, would be too broad." Goodhart, The Unforeseeable Consequences of a Negligent Act, 1930, 39 Yale L.J. 449, 467. See also Porter, The Measure of Damages in Contract and Tort, 1934, 5 Camb.L.J. 178, 183; Payne, Negligence and Interest, 1955, 18 Mod.L.Rev. 43.

76. See for example King v. Chicago, Milwaukee & St. Paul Railway Co., 1900, 80 Minn. 83, 82 N.W. 1113; and cases collected in the annotation, 1958, 62 A.L.R.2d 977.

77. Knowlton v. New York & New England Railroad Co., 1888, 147 Mass. 606, 18 N.E. 580; Jeffrey v. Copeland Flour Mills, [1923] 4 Dom.L.Rep. 1140.

78. See Porter, The Measure of Damages in Contract and Tort, 1934, 5 Camb.L.J. 178, 183.

79. Second Restatement of Torts, § 281, Comment j.

80. For example, the financial interests which are refused protection in Carsten v. Northern Pacific Railway Co., 1890, 44 Minn. 454, 47 N.W. 49; Northern States Contracting Co. v. Oakes, 1934, 191 Minn. 88, 253 N.W. 371. Liesbosch Dredger v. S. S. Edison, [1933] A.C. 449. See, infra, as to negligent misrepresentation, § 107, and interference with contract, § 129.

81. Bohlen, The Probable or the Natural Consequences as the Test of Liability in Negligence, 1901, 49 Am.L.Reg. 79, 148; Smith, Legal Cause in Actions of Tort, 1911, 25 Harv.L.Rev. 103, 223; Carpenter, Workable Rules for Determining Proximate Cause, 1932, 20 Cal.L.Rev. 229, 396; Myers, Causation and Common Sense, 1951, 5 Miami L.Q. 238; Hart and Honore, Causation in the Law, 1959, 151 ff.

82. "If a person had no reasonable ground to anticipate that a particular act would or might result in any injury to anybody, then, of course, the act would not be negligent at all; but if the act itself is negligent, then the person guilty of it is equally liable for all its natural and proximate consequences, whether he could have foreseen them or not. Otherwise expressed, the law is that if the act is one which the party ought, in the exercise of ordinary care, to have anticipated was liable to result in injury to others, then he is liable for any injury proximately resulting from it, although he could not have anticipated the particular injury which did happen. Consequences which follow in unbroken sequence, without an intervening efficient cause, from the original negligent act, are natural and proximate, and for such consequences the original wrongdoer is

pears to have originated in 1870 in England, in the case of Smith v. London & Southwestern Ry. Co.,[83] where it was considered unforeseeable that a fire set by the defendant on its right of way would reach the plaintiff's house. Although the present trend is definitely against it, this view still displays a great deal of vitality, and will not entirely down. Its continued prevalence has been due in no small part to the more or less instinctive feeling that, as between an entirely innocent plaintiff and a defendant who has been negligent as to results lying within the risk, the burden of the loss due to consequences beyond the risk should fall, within some quite undefined ultimate limits, upon the wrongdoer.

There are some areas in which even the courts which have been most vocal in favor of the "foreseeable risk" limitation upon liability have been forced to discard it. There is almost universal agreement upon liability beyond the risk, for quite unforeseeable consequences, when they follow an impact upon the person of the plaintiff.[84]

It is as if a magic circle were drawn about the person, and one who breaks it, even by so much as a cut on the finger, becomes liable for all resulting harm to the person, although it may be death.[85] The defendant is held liable when the defendant's negligence operates upon a concealed physical condition, such as pregnancy,[86] or a latent disease,[87] or susceptibility to disease,[88] to produce consequences which the defendant could not reasonably anticipate. The defendant is held liable for unusual results of personal injuries which are regarded as unforeseeable, such as tuberculosis,[89] paralysis,[90] pneumonia,[91] heart or kidney disease,[92] blood poisoning,[93] cancer,[94] or the loss of hair from

responsible, even though he could not have foreseen the particular result which did follow." Mitchell, J., in Christianson v. Chicago, St. Paul, Minneapolis & Omaha Railway Co., 1896, 67 Minn. 94, 69 N.W. 640. Accord: Dodge v. McArthur, 1966, 126 Vt. 81, 223 A.2d 453; Osborne v. Montgomery, 1931, 203 Wis. 223, 234 N.W. 372; Dellwo v. Pearson, 1961, 259 Minn. 452, 107 N.W.2d 859; Lynch v. Fisher, La.App.1949, 34 So.2d 513.

83. 1870, L.R. 6 C.P. 14.

84. Compare the suggestion of Burke, Rules of Legal Cause in Negligence Cases, 1926, 15 Cal.L.Rev. 1, 14, that a distinction is to be made between unforeseeable consequences following "after the first impingement of the defendant's wrong," and cases in which the "impingement" itself is of an unforeseeable character. But why the distinction, the author does not succeed in making so clear.

85. Koehler v. Waukesha Milk Co., 1926, 190 Wis. 52, 208 N.W. 901. See Notes, 1960, 43 Marq.L.Rev. 511; 1959, 34 Notre Dame Lawyer 224; 1966, 16 Drake L.Rev. 49.

86. Mann Boudoir Car Co. v. Dupre, 5th Cir. 1893, 54 F. 646; Brown v. Chicago, Milwaukee & St. Paul Railway Co., 1882, 54 Wis. 342, 11 N.W. 356, rehearing denied 54 Wis. 342, 11 N.W. 911; Malone v. Monongahela Valley Traction Co., 1927, 104 W.Va. 417, 140 S.E. 340. Cf. Thompson v. Lupone, 1948, 135 Conn. 236, 62 A.2d 861 (obesity).

87. Owen v. Dix, 1946, 210 Ark. 562, 196 S.W.2d 913; Sentilles v. Inter-Caribbean Shipping Corp., 1959, 361 U.S. 107, 80 S.Ct. 173, 4 L.Ed.2d 142; Heppner v. Atchison, Topeka & Santa Fe Railway Co., Mo.1956, 297 S.W.2d 497; City of Port Arthur v. Wallace, 1943, 141 Tex. 201, 171 S.W.2d 480; Flood v. Smith, 1940, 126 Conn. 644, 13 A.2d 677.

88. Steinhauser v. Hertz Corp., 2d Cir. 1970, 421 F.2d 1169 (psychotic tendencies); Alexander v. Knight, 1962, 197 Pa.Super. 79, 177 A.2d 142 (neurotic predisposition); Lockwood v. McCaskill, 1964, 262 N.C. 663, 138 S.E.2d 541 (predisposition to amnesia); Trascher v. Eagle Indemnity Co., La.App.1950, 48 So.2d 695 (ruptured disc); McCahill v. New York Transportation Co., 1911, 201 N.Y. 221, 94 N.E. 616 (delirium tremens).

89. Champlin Refining Co. v. Thomas, 10th Cir. 1937, 93 F.2d 133; Larson v. Boston Elevated Railway Co., 1912, 212 Mass. 262, 98 N.E. 1048; Healy v. Hoy, 1911, 115 Minn. 321, 132 N.W. 208.

90. Bishop v. St. Paul City Railway Co., 1892, 48 Minn. 26, 50 N.W. 927; Homans v. Boston Elevated Railway Co., 1902, 180 Mass. 456, 62 N.E. 737.

91. Louisville & Nashville Railroad Co. v. Jones, 1887, 83 Ala. 376, 3 So. 902; cf. Beauchamp v. Saginaw Mining Co., 1893, 50 Mich. 163, 15 N.W. 65.

92. Keegan v. Minneapolis & St. Louis Railroad Co., 1899, 76 Minn. 90, 78 N.W. 965 (endocarditis); Turner v. Minneapolis Street Railway Co., 1918, 140 Minn. 248, 167 N.W. 1041 (nephritis); Sullivan v. Boston Elevated Railway Co., 1904, 185 Mass. 602, 71 N.E. 90 (appendicitis).

93. Armstrong v. Montgomery Street Railway Co., 1899, 123 Ala. 233, 26 So. 349; Carr v. Minneapolis, St. Paul & Sault Ste. Marie Railway Co., 1919, 140 Minn.

94. See note 94 on page 292.

fright.⁹⁵ The defendant of course is liable only for the extent to which the defendant's conduct has resulted in an aggravation of the pre-existing condition, and not for the condition as it was;⁹⁶ but as to the aggravation, foreseeability is not a factor. One of the illustrations which runs through the English cases is that of the plaintiff with the "eggshell skull," who suffers death where a normal person would have had only a bump on the head;⁹⁷ and an obviously related rule is that the defendant who kills another must take the chances, as to damages for the death, that the other has a large income, although the defendant had no reason to expect it.⁹⁸

Perhaps all this might be dismissed as a more or less arbitrary rule of policy, that one who negligently inflicts any personal injury upon another is to be held liable for all the injury to the other which follows, and that the courts will refuse to attempt any division in terms of the unforeseeable. But the problem is broader than this. There have been many decisions, at one time certainly amounting to a majority rule in the United States, but now undoubtedly on the decline, which have held the defendant liable where the initial impact or harm to the plaintiff itself was unforeseeable. Thus where an object struck by a train is hurled through the air at an angle or to a distance which could not reasonably have been anticipated, and strikes a person,⁹⁹ or a fire spreads to an unanticipated distance,¹ the greater number of American decisions, never expressly overruled, hold that there is liability, although the event was to be regarded as utterly beyond foresight. There have been, in addition, a considerable number of more or less unclassifiable cases of what can only be described as freak accidents of a preposterous character, in which the fact that the defendant could not possibly have foreseen the harm to the plaintiff has been held to be no bar to recovery.²

Typical of these is the North Carolina case ³ in which a railroad over-enthusiastically shunted a freight car into a cornfield, and succeeded in killing a workman some miles

---

91, 167 N.W. 299; Koehler v. Waukesha Milk Co., 1926, 190 Wis. 52, 208 N.W. 901; Wolfe v. Checker Taxi Co., 1938, 299 Mass. 225, 12 N.E.2d 849.

94. Baltimore City Passenger Railway Co. v. Kemp, 1884, 61 Md. 74; Heppner v. Atchison, Topeka & Santa Fe Railway Co., Mo.1956, 297 S.W.2d 497.

95. Ominsky v. Charles Weinhagen & Co., 1911, 113 Minn. 422, 129 N.W. 845.

96. Schwingschlegl v. City of Monroe, 1897, 113 Mich. 683, 72 N.W. 7; Watson v. Rheinderknecht, 1901, 82 Minn. 235, 84 N.W. 798; Gates v. Fleischer, 1886, 67 Wis. 504, 30 N.W. 674.

97. This originated in Dulieu v. White, [1901] 2 K.B. 669, 679. See Williams, The Risk Principle, 1961, 77 L.Q.Rev. 179, 193–197.

98. First suggested by Blackburn, J., in Smith v. London & S. W. R. Co., 1870, L.R. 6 C.P. 14, 22–23.

99. Kommerstad v. Great Northern Railway Co., 1913, 120 Minn. 376, 139 N.W. 713, id., 1915, 128 Minn. 505, 151 N.W. 177; Alabama Great Southern Railroad Co. v. Chapman, 1886, 80 Ala. 615, 2 So. 738; Robinson v. Standard Oil Co. of Indiana, 1929, 89 Ind.App. 167, 166 N.E. 160; Wolfe v. Checker Taxi Co., 1938, 299 Mass. 225, 12 N.E.2d 849; Solomon v. Branfman, Sup. 1919, 175 N.Y.S. 835.

1. Hoyt v. Jeffers, 1874, 30 Mich. 181; Atchison, Topeka & Santa Fe Railway Co. v. Stanford, 1874, 12 Kan. 354; Poeppers v. Missouri, Kansas & Texas Railway Co., 1878, 67 Mo. 715; Kuhn v. Jewett, 1880, 32 N.J.Eq. 647; E. T. & H. K. Ide v. Boston & Maine Railroad Co., 1909, 83 Vt. 66, 74 A. 401. Contra, Hoag v. Lake Shore & Michigan Southern Railway Co., 1877, 85 Pa. 293.

It may of course be anticipated that fire will spread to a considerable distance. Cf. Gudfelder v. Pittsburgh, Cincinnati, Chicago & St. Louis Railway Co., 1904, 207 Pa. 629, 57 A. 70; Osborn v. City of Whittier, 1951, 103 Cal.App.2d 609, 230 P.2d 132. But in the foregoing cases it is assumed that the particular distance was beyond all foreseeable limits.

2. Walmsley v. Rural Telephone Association, 1917, 102 Kan. 139, 169 P. 197 (plaintiff shot because of low hanging wires); Lynch v. Fisher, La.App.1947, 34 So.2d 513 (plaintiff shot by deranged motorist because of collision); Chavers v. A. R. Blossman, Inc., La.App.1950, 45 So.2d 398 (plaintiff struck by wire severed by fire resulting from collision); Dellwo v. Pearson, 1961, 259 Minn. 452, 107 N.W.2d 859 (motorboat entangled fishline, caught and broke plaintiff's glasses, damaged her eye); Perkins v. Vermont Hydro-Electric Corp., 1934, 106 Vt. 367, 177 A. 631 (defective water diversion system and unprecedented flood); Cameron v. Bissonette, 1930, 103 Vt. 93, 152 A. 87 (mare left out in rain, drowned in brook). See also Bunting v. Hogsett, 1890, 139 Pa. 363, 21 A. 31; Osborne v. Montgomery, 1931, 203 Wis. 223, 234 N.W. 372; Pfeifer v. Standard Gateway Theater, 1952, 262 Wis. 229, 55 N.W.2d 29.

3. Ramsey v. Carolina-Tennessee Power Co., 1928, 195 N.C. 788, 143 S.E. 861.

away. On their facts many of these cases have involved the Palsgraf problem,[4] but it has been either ignored or taken in stride. The courts which have been most consistent in this rejection of foreseeability as a test of the "proximate" have been Louisiana, Vermont, and Wisconsin, and periodically Minnesota.[5]

One area in which it may be especially likely that the "foreseeability" limitation will be cast aside is that of intentional torts, as to which it has been said often enough [6] that there is more extended liability. This appears to be, however, more of a general attitude and an unexpressed tendency than anything like a concrete rule.[7]

The objection frequently has been made that such decisions may impose a ruinous liability which no private fortune could meet,[8] and which is out of all proportion to the defendant's fault. To this it has been answered that if a great loss is to be suffered, it is better that it should fall upon the wrongdoer than upon one innocent victim, or a hundred. "The simple question is, whether a loss, that must be borne somewhere, is to be visited on the head of the innocent or guilty." [9] But the difficulty lies not so much in any injustice to the defendant as in the delimitation of such liability beyond the risk.[10] It is still inconceivable that any defendant should be held liable to infinity for all of the consequences which flow from a single act, and some boundary must be set. If nothing more than "common sense" or a "rough sense of justice" is to be relied on,[11] the law becomes to that extent unpredictable, and at the mercy of whatever the court, or even the jury, may decide to do with it.

"Direct Causation" and "Directly Traceable Consequences"

The alternative to the limitation of the foreseeable risk proposed by a good many courts and writers [12] is that of "direct causation." A distinction is made, which is easier of comprehension than of any exact definition, between consequences which may be regarded as "directly traceable" from the defendant's act, or as caused "directly" by the defendant's act, and those which result from the intervention of other causes at a

4. See supra, this section, Unforeseeable Plaintiffs.

5. Concerning the cyclical development of Minnesota cases, see R. Keeton, Legal Cause in the Law of Torts, 1963, 30, and more recently the Minnesota JIGs (Jury Instruction Guides) discussed in Orwick v. Belshan, 1975, 304 Minn. 338, 231 N.W.2d 90.

6. "In determining how far the law will trace causation and afford a remedy, the facts as to the defendant's intent, his imputable knowledge, or his justifiable ignorance are often taken into account. The moral element is here the factor that has turned these cases one way or the other. For an intended injury the law is astute to discover even very remote causation. For one which the defendant merely ought to have anticipated it has often stopped at an earlier stage of the investigation of causal connection. And as to those where there was neither knowledge nor duty to foresee, it has usually limited accountability to direct and immediate results." Derosier v. New England Telephone & Telegraph Co., 1925, 81 N.H. 451, 130 A. 145. See also, Seidel v. Greenberg, 1969, 108 N.J.Super. 248, 260 A.2d 863; Bauer, The Degree of Moral Fault as Affecting Defendant's Liability, 1933, 81 U.Pa.L.Rev. 586, 592–596; Note, 1962, 14 Stan.L.Rev. 362.

7. Two cases which clearly illustrate it are Tate v. Canonica, 1960, 180 Cal.App.2d 898, 5 Cal.Rptr. 28, and Cauverian v. De Metz, 1959, 20 Misc.2d 144, 188 N.Y.S.2d 627, both cases of voluntary suicide because of an intentional and outrageous tort of the defendant. Recovery was allowed, where it would not have been for mere negligence. See infra, this section. See also criminal cases such as Regina v. Saunders, 1573, 2 Plowd. 473, 75 Eng.Rep. 706; Regina v. Mitchell, 1840, 2 Moody 120, 169 Eng.Rep. 48, where poison intended for the plaintiff was given to A, but unforeseeably administered to B. See also the cases of "transferred intent," supra, § 8, and of liability for the consequences of trespass to land, supra, § 13.

8. See Ryan v. New York Central Railroad Co., 1866, 35 N.Y. 210; Pennsylvania Railroad Co. v. Kerr, 1869, 62 Pa. 353.

9. Fent v. Toledo, Peoria & Western Railway Co., 1871, 59 Ill. 349.

10. Seavey, Mr. Justice Cardozo and the Law of Torts, 1939, 52 Harv.L.Rev. 372, 48 Yale L.J. 390, 39 Col.L.Rev. 20.

11. Cf. Andrews, J., dissenting in Palsgraf v. Long Island Railroad Co., 1928, 248 N.Y. 339, 162 N.E. 99, reargument denied 249 N.Y. 511, 164 N.E. 564.

12. Beale, The Proximate Consequences of an Act, 1920, 33 Harv.L.Rev. 633; McLaughlin, Proximate Cause, 1925, 39 Harv.L.Rev. 149; Carpenter, Proximate Cause, 1940, 14 So.Cal.L.Rev. 1, 115 ff; Myers, Causation and Common Sense, 1951, 5 Miami L.Q. 238.

later time. "Direct" consequences [13] are those which follow in sequence from the effect of the defendant's act upon conditions existing and forces already in operation at the time, without the intervention of any external forces which come into active operation later. Thus if the defendant stabs the plaintiff with a knife, the bacteria which enter the wound upon the blade of the knife may cause infection, which may cause septicemia, which may cause death.[14] No new external factor of significance intervenes. There is an analogy to knocking over the first of a row of blocks, after which all of the rest fall down without the assistance of any other force. Upon the same basis, if the defendant sets a fire with a strong wind blowing at the time, there is "direct" causation of any damage which the fire may do when the same wind blows it to any distance,[15] so long as new forces do not intervene.

It seems very likely that the ultimate origins of this distinction between the direct and the indirect sequence are to be sought in the old actions of trespass and case. Applying it, courts frequently have said that direct consequences are always proximate. The defendant is liable for all such consequences of the defendant's negligence, although they were unforeseeable, and lie entirely beyond the scope of the risk created;[16] but the defendant's liability for the intervention of new causes is limited to the risk involved in the defendant's conduct.[17]

This approach is obviously an arbitrary one, and of course not a matter of causal connection at all, but only of convenience in limiting liability. If there is any justification for it, it must rest in the fact that when a defendant acts upon a set stage, the boundaries of the direct consequences are always limited, not by foreseeability, but by the way the stage is set.[18] The defendant may be expected to take existing circumstances as they are, and be responsible for the effect of the defendant's act upon them. But the possibilities of intervening causes which may enlarge the consequences at some later time are virtually infinite, and the necessity for some restriction obviously is more imperative. It is another thing to extend the defendant's liability to cover the unlimited number of independent factors which may enter at some later moment to change the situation the defendant has created.

Artificial as it is, "direct" causation has been seized in quite a few cases as affording some way of steering a course between the alternatives of limiting all liability to the risk on the one hand, and unlimited liability on the other. But apart from the fact that it offers a mechanical solution of a problem which is primarily and essentially one of pol-

---

13. It should be noted that "direct" sometimes is used in other senses—referring, for example, to the immediate physical consequences, as distinguished from later ones. See Bauer, Confusion of the Terms "Proximate" and "Direct," 1919, 86 Cent.L.J. 226; Bauer, Confusion of the Terms "Proximate" and "Direct," 1936, 11 Notre Dame Lawyer 395; cf. Berkovitz v. American River Gravel Co., 1923, 191 Cal. 195, 215 P. 675. It is also used vaguely as a general synonym for "proximate," as in Coates v. Dewoskin, Mo.App.1964, 379 S.W.2d 146; Hamilton v. Vare, 1931, 184 Minn. 580, 239 N.W. 659. An unsatisfactory term, but it is used by the courts, and no better is at hand.

14. Cf. State v. James, 1913, 123 Minn. 487, 144 N.W. 216; McGarrahan v. New York, New Haven & Hartford Railroad Co., 1898, 171 Mass. 211, 50 N.E. 610; Koehler v. Waukesha Milk Co., 1926, 190 Wis. 52, 208 N.W. 901.

15. Burlington & M.R. Co. v. Westover, 1876, 4 Neb. 268; cf. Kuhn v. Jewett, 1880, 32 N.J.Eq. 647.

Compare, as cases of direct causation, Rich v. Finley, 1949, 325 Mass. 99, 89 N.E.2d 213 (aviation student freezing at controls); Loftus v. McCramie, Fla.1950, 47 So.2d 298 (escaped steers wandering about and doing damage); Brown v. Travelers' Indemnity Co., 1947, 251 Wis. 188, 28 N.W.2d 306 (stunned cow revived and injured plaintiff).

16. See for example Chicago, Rock Island & Pacific Railway Co. v. Goodson, 5th Cir. 1957, 242 F.2d 203 (Texas law); Dixon v. Kentucky Utilities Co., 1943, 295 Ky. 32, 37, 174 S.W.2d 19, 22; Williams v. Brennan, 1912, 213 Mass. 28, 99 N.E. 516.

17. See infra, § 44. The distinction is well stated in Nunan v. Bennett, 1919, 184 Ky. 591, 212 S.W. 570.

18. Cf. the suggestion in Winfield, Law of Torts, 1937, 80, that cases will be relatively infrequent in which direct consequences will not be foreseeable. See also, justifying the distinction, Carpenter, Proximate Cause, 1940, 14 So.Cal.L.Rev. 1, 115.

icy,[19] it is not always easy to say whether new forces have intervened—as where for example, a wind changes its direction—[20] and in nearly all cases of "direct" causation it is necessary to ignore as unimportant a number of external factors which have intervened before the result.[21] More important, however, is the objection that no really successful and satisfactory limitation is provided which will eliminate the consequences which most of us feel, more or less instinctively, to be going too far. Although direct consequences are not unlimited, they may still be fantastic; and it is not likely that any court would ever carry the direct liability to all of the extreme lengths to which it might lead. Indeed, in courts that have firmly applied the rule that liability extends to all "direct" consequences, foreseeability has come in through the back door as a factor considered in determining whether consequences were direct.[22]

The spectacular case applying the theory of direct causation is the English one of In re Polemis,[23] in which a plank dropped by defendant's workman into the hold of a ship struck out a spark, which exploded petrol vapor, and destroyed the ship and its cargo. Although the arbitrators had specifically found that this was not a foreseeable result of the negligence, recovery was allowed because it was all "direct." The case remained something of a storm center in England for forty years, with much outpouring of attack[24] and support.[25] In 1961 the decision was flatly overruled by the Privy Council in the first of two cases which have been

19. The attitude is well illustrated in Collier v. Citizens Coach Co., 1959, 231 Ark. 489, 330 S.W.2d 74, 76, where it is actually said that "proximate cause is a rule of physics and not a criterion of negligence!"

20. Compare Stephens v. Mutual Lumber Co., 1918, 103 Wash. 1, 173 P. 1031 (considered a new intervening force) with E.T. & H.K. Ide v. Boston & Maine Railroad Co., 1909, 83 Vt. 66, 74 A. 401 (considered direct).

21. "The entire assumption that the physiological disturbances which follow from a wound are part of the defendant's direct force rests upon a refusal to analyze the physiological processes. It is necessary only to note here that obvious intervening forces, such as a man's eating, may often be neglected for practical purposes in analyzing a case. Eating bacteria is so foreseeable that it would not be an isolating force, and so the question of classification as direct causation or some other type may be ignored. It must be obvious, however, that the limits of direct causation are not sharply defined." McLaughlin, Proximate Cause, 1925, 39 Harv.L.Rev. 149, 165.

22. This point is well illustrated in Minnesota. In 1961 the Supreme Court overruled intervening decisions, explicitly reaffirmed earlier precedent imposing liability for consequences of a defendant's negligent act that "follow in unbroken sequence, without an intervening efficient cause, from the original negligent act," "even though he could not have foreseen the particular results which did follow," and concluded: "It is enough to say that negligence is tested by foresight but proximate cause is determined by hindsight." Dellwo v. Pearson, 1961, 259 Minn. 452, 107 N.W.2d 859. Thereafter a committee of judges and lawyers prepared Jury Instruction Guides ("JIGs") to aid trial judges and trial lawyers in the preparation of the charge to the jury. JIG 142, defining "superseding cause," declares: "However, a cause is not a direct cause when there is a superseding cause. For a cause to be a superseding cause all the following elements must be present: * * * It must not have been reasonably foreseeable by the original wrongdoer." 4 Hetland & Adamson, Minnesota Practice, Jury Instruction Guides (2d ed.). See also Orwick v. Belshan, 1975, 304 Minn. 338, 231 N.W.2d 90.

For observations about the influence of foreseeability on determinations of "direct" cause, see Edgerton, Legal Cause, 1924, 72 U.Pa.L.Rev. 211, 343, 352; Winfield, Lewis ed. 1954, Tort 84–85; Hart and Honoré, Causation in the Law, 1959, 230; R. Keeton, Legal Cause in the Law of Torts, 1963, 41–45.

23. In re Polemis and Furness, Withy & Co., [1921] 3 K.B. 560.

24. Goodhart, The Unforeseeable Consequences of a Negligent Act, 1930, 39 Yale L.J. 449; Goodhart, The Imaginary Necktie and the Rule of Re Polemis, 1952, 68 L.Q.Rev. 514; Goodhart, Liability and Compensation, 1960, 76 L.Q.Rev. 567; Goodhart, The Brief Life Story of the Direct Consequence Rule in English Tort Law, 1967, 53 Va.L.Rev. 857.

(Among the great one-man crusades of history, that of Sir Arthur Goodhart against the Polemis rule must certainly be numbered; and there can be little doubt that its ultimate overthrow was due in large part to him).

See also Seavey, Mr. Justice Cardozo and the Law of Torts, 1939, 52 Harv.L.Rev. 372, 48 Yale L.J. 390, 39 Col.L.Rev. 20; Payne, The "Direct" Consequences of a Negligent Act, 1952, 5 Curr.Leg.Prob. 189.

25. Porter, The Measure of Damages in Contract and Tort, 1934, 5 Camb.L.J. 176; Wright, Re Polemis, 1951, 14 Mod.L.Rev. 393; Hart and Honoré, Causation in the Law, 1959, 151 ff; Wilson and Slade, A Re-examination of Remoteness, 1952, 15 Mod.L.Rev. 458.

nicknamed The Wagon Mound,[26] after the oil tanker involved. Her bunker crew negligently allowed furnace oil to overflow into Sydney harbor, where it was carried to the plaintiff's dock, some 600 feet away. It might have been expected that the oil would do minor damage to the plaintiff's slipways, which it did; but it was found that because of the high flash point of the oil it could not reasonably be foreseen that it would become ignited when spread upon the water. Molten metal falling from the dock ignited cotton waste floating on the oil, which acted as a wick, and the dock was burned. The court repudiated the "direct causation" rule, adopting a straight limitation of the liability to the foreseeable risk, and so denied recovery for the loss of the dock. The decision is the logical aftermath of Cardozo's position in the Palsgraf case,[27] since there is an obvious absurdity in holding that one who can foresee some harm to A is liable for consequences to A which he cannot foresee, but is not liable for similar consequences to B.

The decision appeared to have settled the issue for the British Commonwealth,[28] although it left a legacy of vexatious unsettled questions,[29] and the prediction was made [30] that any such flat and final rule could not possibly hold good for all situations. This was borne out by decisions holding that foreseeability was not required as to consequences following an injury to the person,[31] as in the case of the plaintiff with the "egg-shell skull," and that if the consequences themselves were foreseeable, it was not necessary to foresee the manner in which they were brought about.[32]

Six years later, in Wagon Mound II,[33] the Privy Council retreated somewhat from its earlier position. The action was for damage to ships docked at the same wharf. This time there was evidence justifying the conclusion that the defendants were, or should have been, aware that there was some slight risk that the oil on the water would be ignited, although it was very unlikely. It was held that since the conduct of the defendants had no justification or social value, they were not justified in neglecting even that slight risk, and they were therefore liable. The decision would appear to have adopted the American formula of balancing magnitude of risk and gravity of harm against utility of conduct,[34] and to have applied it to foreseeability in relation to "proximate cause." The effect comes close to letting the Polemis Case in again by the back door, since cases will obviously be quite infrequent in which there is not some recognizable slight risk of this character.

It is still a matter of speculation, what effect the Wagon Mound decisions may have in the United States.[35] Although in the be-

26. Overseas Tankship (U.K.) Ltd. v. Morts Dock & Engineering Co., Ltd., [1961] A.C. 388.

27. Supra, this section.

28. There was for a time some doubt as to whether the decision of the Privy Council would be followed as to Great Britain itself. This was finally set at rest by Doughty v. Turner Mfg. Co., Ltd., [1964] 1 Q.B. 518.

29. Two excellent articles in which the situation following Wagon Mound No. 1 is reviewed are Fleming, The Passing of Polemis, 1961, 39 Can.Bar Rev. 489, and Williams, The Risk Principle, 1961, 77 L.Q.Rev. 179. See also Morison, The Victory of Reasonable Foresight, 1961, 34 Aust.L.J. 317; Payne, Foresight and Remoteness of Damage in Negligence, 1962, 25 Mod.L.Rev. 1; Dias, Remoteness of Liability and Legal Policy, [1962] Camb.L.J. 178; see also Smith, The Limits of Tort Liability in Canada, included in Linden, Studies in Canadian Tort Law (1968).

30. Green, Foreseeability in Negligence Law, 1961, 61 Col.L.Rev. 1401.

31. Smith v. Leech Brain & Co., Ltd., [1962] 2 Q.B. 405; Oman v. McIntyre, [1962] Scot.L.T. 168.

32. Hughes v. Lord Advocate, [1963] A.C. 837.

33. Overseas Tankship (U.K.) Ltd. v. Miller Steamship Co., [1967] 1 A.C. 617. The whole story of the Wagon Mound cases is narrated in Goodhart, The Brief Life Story of the Direct Consequence Law in English Tort Law, 1967, 53 Va.L.Rev. 857; Smith, The Limits of Tort Liability in Canada, included in Linden, Studies in Canadian Tort Law (1968); Green, The Wagon Mound No. 2—Foreseeability Revisited, [1967] Utah L.Rev. 197; Dias, Trouble on Oiled Waters: Problems of the Wagon Mound (No. 2), [1967] Camb.L.J. 62.

34. See Learned Hand, in United States v. Carroll Towing Co., 2d Cir. 1947, 159 F.2d 169, rehearing denied 160 F.2d 482.

35. See Petition of Kinsman Transit Co., 2d Cir. 1964, 338 F.2d 708, certiorari denied 380 U.S. 944, 85 S.Ct. 1026, 13 L.Ed.2d 963, where Wagon Mound No. 1

ginning the American courts were much influenced by English cases,[36] in later years they have been preoccupied with the somewhat over-ample supply of American decisions, and English cases have tended to pass unremarked. The Polemis Case itself has been a subject of discussion very largely in the law schools, and its passing may very possibly have no great effect on this side of the water.

Two important decisions bearing upon the Palsgraf Case are involved in Petition of Kinsman Transit Co. In the first of these,[37] a ship negligently moored in the Buffalo River was set adrift by floating ice, collided with a bridge and overthrew it, creating an ice jam in the river, which backed up water to damage factories on the bank below the point of mooring. The court, bound by New York law, proceeded to limit the Palsgraf rule by holding that if any harm to the plaintiff was foreseeable, the defendant was liable for unforeseeable consequences to the plaintiff. In the second,[38] the action was for pecuniary loss due to the necessity of transporting ship cargoes around the jam. The court was unwilling to hold that there could be no liability for pecuniary loss caused by negligence,[39] and held instead that the connection between the negligence and these damages was too "tenuous and remote" to permit recovery. Just what this may mean would appear to be anybody's guess.

Anatomy of Foresight

From what has gone before in this chapter, the conclusion may well be drawn that, while there are still rearguard actions, and cases that do not fit, the "scope of the foreseeable risk" is on its way to ultimate victory as the criterion of what is "proximate," if it has not already achieved it. The triumph of theory has been both more easily achieved and less clearly significant because the concept of foreseeability so completely lacks all clarity and precision that it amounts to little more than a convenient formula for disposing of the case—usually by leaving it to the jury under instructions calling for "foreseeable," or "natural and probable" consequences. What, then, does foresight mean?[40]

In one sense, almost nothing is entirely unforeseeable, since there is a very slight mathematical chance, recognizable in advance, that even the most freakish accident which is possible will occur, particulary if it has ever happened in history before.[41] In another, no event whatever is entirely foreseeable, since the exact details of a sequence never can be predicted with complete omniscience and accuracy. If one takes a very broad, type-of-harm perspective in describing both the "foreseeable risk" and the "result" of which the plaintiff is complaining, very likely the result will appear to be within the foreseeable risk. If, on the other hand, one takes a mechanism-of-harm perspective, it is easy to conclude that the re-

---

was rejected, so far as the limitation to foreseeable consequences was concerned.

36. Particularly Smith v. London & Southwestern Ry. Co., 1870, L.R. 6 C.P. 14.

37. Petition of Kinsman Transit Co., 2d Cir. 1964, 338 F.2d 708, certiorari denied 380 U.S. 944, 85 S.Ct. 1026, 13 L.Ed.2d 963.

38. Petition of Kinsman Transit Co., 2d Cir. 1968, 388 F.2d 821.

39. See infra, § 129.

40. Well considered in Fleming, The Passing of Polemis, 1961, 39 Can.Bar Rev. 489, 508–529; Linden, Down with Foreseeability! Of Thin Skulls and Rescuers, 1969, 47 Can.Bar Rev. 545.

41. Compare the argument of Edgerton, Legal Cause, 1924, 72 U.Pa.L.Rev. 211, 238, that there may

be a slight chance of the particular result (as of a fire spreading several miles), which a reasonable person would recognize in advance, but which would not in itself influence conduct. When there is negligence because of other risks, recovery, says Edgerton, should be allowed for such consequences. Cf. Morey v. Lake Superior Terminal & Transfer Co., 1905, 125 Wis. 148, 103 N.W. 271; Pittsburgh Forge & Iron Co. v. Dravo Contracting Co., 1922, 272 Pa. 118, 116 A. 147.

Compare also Green, Foreseeability in Negligence Law, 1961, 61 Col.L.Rev. 1401, explaining In re Polemis, [1921] 3 K.B. 560, on the ground that blowing up the ship was just what was to be expected—despite the fact that the arbitrator specifically found, and the whole court assumed throughout, that it was quite "unforeseeable."

sult at issue is not within the foreseeable risk.⁴² What is meant must lie somewhere between the two extremes; but where? The usual answer has been that "foreseeability" means, in "proximate cause," the same thing as in negligence; and that the same considerations which determine the original culpability are to be used again to determine liability for consequences. This has a comforting sound of predictable certainty and facility of administration. But, with deference, it is submitted that both are quite illusory.

Foreseeability of consequences, or, as it is sometimes called, the risk of harm, is only one of the factors which are important in determining negligence. Into the scales with it there must also be thrown the gravity of the harm if it is to occur, and against both must be weighed the utility of the challenged conduct.⁴³ But even the risk of harm itself, when the defendant is found to be negligent, is usually an aggregate risk of many possibilities.

If a train is operated without a proper lookout, it is relatively easy to say that the total risk, made up of everything that can happen, be it probable or fantastic, is so great that the reasonable person of ordinary prudence would not do this, and therefore there is negligence. But how easy is it, by a process of fragmentation of that risk, to sort it out into particular consequences, and to say that they are, or are not, such substantial parts of the original total foreseeable risk that liability is to be attached to them? There is some likelihood that the train will collide with an automobile or a cow, or be derailed and injure its passengers; less that it will endanger a child on the track and injure its rescuer; still less that the cow will be thrown against a person a hundred feet from the track and break the person's leg, that the train wreck will start a forest fire and burn a distant village, or twist a power line pole and electrocute a person ten miles away; and what of the likelihood that the injured person's watch will be stolen, that the injured person will contract pneumonia and die of it, or will receive negligent medical treatment and be further injured? ⁴⁴

All of these things have happened, and all of them have been held "proximate" by some court. But which of them are to be called "foreseeable," in the sense that any reasonable person would really have had them in mind at the time of the operation of the train?

Recognizing these difficulties, there are courts which have thrown over the language of foreseeability, and have said outright that this becomes a matter of hindsight, which is to say of relating the consequences back into the picture of the original negligence after they have in fact occurred.⁴⁵

The Restatement of Torts ⁴⁶ has in a limited way adopted much the same approach by saying that the defendant is not to be liable for consequences which, looking backward after the event with full knowledge of all that has occurred, would appear to be "highly extraordinary." The language may be unfortunate; to one gifted with omniscience as to all existing circumstances, no result

---

42. R. Keeton, Legal Cause in the Law of Torts, 1963, 49–60.

43. See supra, § 31.

44. See Gregory, Proximate Cause in Negligence—A Retreat from Rationalization, 1938, 6 U.Chi.L.Rev. 36, 50; Prosser, Proximate Cause in California, 1950, 38 Cal.L.Rev. 369, 396.

45. Leposki v. Railway Express Agency, Inc., 3d Cir. 1962, 297 F.2d 849 is an excellent example. Defendant allowed gasoline to drip from its truck into the gutter; boys ignited it, and it burned the plaintiff's home. It was held improper to charge that defendant was not liable unless this act was foreseeable; the Pennsylvania test is whether the intervening act was extraordinary, looking back. See also Dellwo v. Pearson, 1961, 259 Minn. 452, 107 N.W.2d 859 ("Negligence is tested by foresight, but proximate cause is determined by hindsight").

46. Second Restatement of Torts, § 435(2). Cf. Wabash Railroad Co. v. Coker, 1898, 81 Ill.App. 660, affirmed 183 Ill. 223, 55 N.E. 693; Wallin v. Eastern Railway Co., 1901, 83 Minn. 149, 158, 86 N.W. 76, 79; Butts v. Anthis, 1937, 181 Okl. 276, 73 P.2d 843 (" * * * all the consequences which a prudent and experienced person, fully acquainted with the circumstances which in fact existed * * * would at the time of the negligent act have thought reasonably possible if they had occurred to his mind.")

could appear remarkable, or indeed anything but inevitable, as a matter of hindsight. Certainly no element of mystery is necessary, or of ignorance as to what has happened. Perhaps the Restatement has come close to expressing the underlying idea of a limitation of liability short of the remarkable, the preposterous, the highly unlikely, in the sometime language of the street the cock-eyed and far-fetched, even when we look at the event, as we must, after it has occurred.

The problem is in no way simplified by the quite universal agreement that what is required to be foreseeable is only the "general character" or "general type" of the event or the harm,[47] and not its "precise" nature, details, or above all manner of occurrence.[48] This goes back to two early cases in which a workman who might have been expected to be knocked down by the collision of a tug with a bridge was pinched between piles instead when the collision knocked out a brace,[49] and an engine involved in a collision was thrown out of control, traveled in a circle, and collided again with the same train.[50] Some "margin of leeway" has to be left for the unusual and the unexpected.[51] But this has opened a very wide door; and the courts have taken so much advantage of the leeway that it can scarcely be doubted that a great deal of what the ordinary person would regard as freakish, bizarre, and unpredictable has crept within the bounds of liability by the simple device of permitting the jury to foresee at least its very broad, and vague, general outlines.[52] This becomes, in the courtroom, a matter for the skill of the advocate who can lay stress upon broad, general, and very simple things, and stay away from all complications of detail.[53]

With such a background, one would expect confusion as to what is or is not foreseeable; and confusion there is. On the one hand there are limitations which appear to be amazingly short-sighted. The New York court has solemnly held that it is unforeseeable that a fire will spread beyond the first adjoining house.[54] Learned Hand, a great judge,—recognizing that his determination was one of fiat, which could not be reached by reason alone—concluded that the master of a tug, in approaching a barge, "need not have considered the possibility that if he struck her, she might be injured, that her bargee might be so slack in his care of her

47. Danner v. Arnsberg, 1961, 227 Or. 420, 362 P.2d 758 ("the same general character"); Tropea v. Shell Oil Co., 2d Cir. 1962, 307 F.2d 757 ("in a general way"); Byrnes v. Stephens, Tex.Civ.App.1961, 349 S.W.2d 611 ("such general character as might have been anticipated"); Smith v. Prater, 1966, 206 Va. 693, 146 S.E.2d 179; Nobles v. Unruh, Miss.1967, 198 So.2d 245; Thornton v. Weaber, 1955, 380 Pa. 590, 112 A.2d 344 ("some injury of the same general character"); Carey v. Pure Distributing Corp., 1939, 133 Tex. 31, 124 S.W.2d 847. Perhaps the best statement of all this is that of Magruder, J., in Marshall v. Nugent, 1st Cir. 1955, 222 F.2d 604, 58 A.L.R.2d 251.

48. Biggers v. Continental Bus System, 1957, 157 Tex. 351, 303 S.W.2d 359; Bondurant v. Holland, Mastin & Sales Co., 1960, 252 N.C. 190, 113 S.E.2d 292; Chase v. Washington Water Power Co., 1941, 62 Idaho 298, 111 P.2d 872; Foss v. Chicago, Burlington & Quincy Railroad Co., 1922, 151 Minn. 506, 187 N.W. 609; Pulaski Gas Light Co. v. McClintock, 1911, 97 Ark. 576, 134 S.W. 1189.

49. Hill v. Winsor, 1875, 118 Mass. 251.

50. Bunting v. Hogsett, 1890, 139 Pa. 363, 21 A. 31.

51. In Lady Nelson, Limited v. Creole Petroleum Corp., 2d Cir. 1955, 224 F.2d 591, certiorari denied 350 U.S. 935, 76 S.Ct. 308, 100 L.Ed. 817, this was applied even in a Palsgraf type of situation. In accord is the striking case of Petition of Kinsman Transit Co., 2d Cir. 1964, 338 F.2d 708, certiorari denied 380 U.S. 944, 85 S.Ct. 1026, 13 L.Ed.2d 963, where a negligently moored ship, drifting down a winding river amid floating ice, might have been expected to do some kind of damage to shore installations, and actually resulted in flooding several factories. See Note, 1965, 49 Minn.L. Rev. 1052.

52. See Coatney v. Southwest Tennessee Electric Membership Corp., 1956, 40 Tenn.App. 541, 292 S.W.2d 420: "some such harm of a like general character * * * almost any harm from electricity which could humanly have been avoided would render the company liable in damages."

53. Well stated in Morris, Proximate Cause in Minnesota, 1950, 34 Minn.L.Rev. 185, who attributes the decision in Hines v. Morrow, Tex.Civ.App.1922, 236 S.W. 183, error refused, to the summary of the facts in plaintiff's brief, as follows: "The case stated in its briefest form, is simply this: Appellee was on the highway using it in a lawful manner, and slipped into this hole, created by appellant's negligence, and was injured in attempting to extricate himself."

54. Ryan v. New York Central Railroad Co., 1866, 35 N.Y. 210.

as to let her be loaded without examination, and might so expose her to the danger of sinking."[55] Pennsylvania has twice held that no reasonable driver can foresee that, when a speeding vehicle strikes another, the other's body will fly off at an angle, and hit a third person not directly in the path.[56] Wisconsin has considered that when a child is run down in the street there is no sufficient recognizable risk that the mother will be somewhere in the vicinity, and will suffer severe nervous shock.[57] Opinions may differ; but surely it is permissible to say that to agree with all these things requires the faith that moveth mountains.

On the other hand, there are quite remarkable events which have been taken in stride by various courts as within the boundaries of the jury's permission to find foreseeability. The defendant negligently drives a car so that it leaves the roadway and collides with a power line pole; this shuts off power from a traffic control box, traffic signals cease to function, and two other cars collide at an intersection.[58] A power line pole breaks, falls upon a telephone wire and charges it; the plaintiff's power shovel, elevated above the ground, comes in contact with the wire.[59] A negligently driven car collides with a taxicab, which is rammed against the stone stoop of a building, where it becomes wedged among stones knocked down. While a wrecking car is attempting to remove the taxicab, a stone which has been dislodged is loosened, and falls upon a bystander.[60] Defendant parks a car and leaves it without setting the brake. Five hours later a drunken driver rams the car, shoving it into the plaintiff.[61] A mudhole is negligently left in a highway; a car gets stuck in it, and a man with a wooden leg attempts to pull the car out with a tow rope. His wooden leg becomes stuck in the mud and a loop in the tow rope lassos his good leg and breaks it.[62] It is all found to be foreseeable. Illustrations might be multiplied, but surely enough has been said to indicate the essential conflict in the cases, all of which are making use of the same words, to mean whatever they are desired to mean. With so much leeway and flexibility in "foreseeability," it is not surprising that "unforeseeable consequences" and "direct causation" are somewhat in disrepute.

It seems evident that in all of these proposed rules and formulae the courts and the writers have been groping for something that is difficult, if not impossible, to put into words: some method of limiting liability to those consequences which have some reasonably close connection with the defendant's conduct and the harm which it originally threatened, and are in themselves not so remarkable and unusual as to lead one to stop short of them. It may be questioned whether anyone has yet succeeded in devising terminology that, as a way of expressing the idea of such a reasonably close connection, will ever achieve greater acceptance in courtrooms than the despised word "proximate."

WESTLAW REFERENCES

topic(torts negligence) /p legal** /s liability responsibl***

---

55. Sinram v. Pennsylvania Railroad Co., 2d Cir. 1932, 61 F.2d 767.

56. Wood v. Pennsylvania Railroad Co., 1896, 177 Pa. 306, 35 A. 699; Dahlstrom v. Shrum, 1951, 368 Pa. 423, 84 A.2d 289. But cf. Mellon v. Lehigh Valley Railroad Co., 1925, 282 Pa. 39, 127 A. 444, which appears to contradict both.

57. Waube v. Warrington, 1935, 216 Wis. 603, 258 N.W. 497. Cf. Davis v. Shiappacossee, Fla.App.1962, 145 So.2d 758, judgment quashed, Fla., 155 So.2d 365 holding that it is not really foreseeable that when intoxicating liquor is sold to minors they will be injured in an automobile crash.

58. Ferroggiaro v. Bowline, 1957, 153 Cal.App.2d 759, 315 P.2d 446. Reference to the Record discloses that it was not even the same intersection, but one at a considerable distance.

59. Jackson v. Utica Light & Power Co., 1944, 64 Cal.App.2d 885, 149 P.2d 748.

60. In re Guardian Casualty Co., 1938, 253 App.Div. 360, 2 N.Y.S.2d 232, affirmed 278 N.Y. 674, 16 N.E.2d 397.

61. Byrnes v. Stephens, Tex.Civ.App.1961, 349 S.W.2d 611.

62. Hines v. Morrow, Tex.Civ.App.1922, 236 S.W. 183, error refused.

topic(negligence torts) /p unforeseeable /p consequence*

Limitation of Liability to Risk
topic(negligence torts) & scope /s original /s risk

Natural and Probable Consequences
foreseeab! /s "risk of harm" & topic(torts negligence)
headnote(natural /4 probable /4 consequence*) & topic(272 313a 379)

Time and Space
topic(negligence torts) & cause /s remote removed distant /s time

The "Same Hazard"
restatement /5 second 2d /5 torts /5 281 /p hazard* risk* kn*w! recogn! aware! realiz! & court(ca1 ca3)

Unforseeable Plaintiffs
topic(272 313a 379) & headnote(unforeseeab! foreseeab! /5 plaintiff*)
palsgraf
topic(negligence torts) /p policy /s liability % topic (insurance)

Particular Interest
restatement +s torts +s 281

Liability Beyond the Risk
topic(negligence torts) & liable liability /s consequence* consequential /2 injur***
topic(negligence torts) & liability liable /s limit** /s foreseeabl!

"Direct Causation" and "Directly Traceable Consequences"
topic(negligence torts) & digest(direct** /4 consequence* cause*)
272k56(1.1)

Anatomy of Foresight
"strict liability without fault"
foresight foresee! +4 require! & topic(negligence torts)

§ 44. Intervening Causes

In dealing with a large group of cases, it is convenient to adopt the language frequently used by the courts, and to speak of intervening causes, or intervening forces. On its face, the problem is one of whether the defendant is to be held liable for an injury to which the defendant has in fact made a substantial contribution, when it is brought about by a later cause of independent origin, for which the defendant is not responsible. In its essence, however, it becomes again a question of the extent of the defendant's original obligation; and once more the problem is not primarily one of causation at all, since it does not arise until cause in fact is established. It is rather one of the policy as to imposing legal responsibility. The older cases tend to ask the question, why should the defendant be held liable for harm brought about by something for which the defendant is not responsible? The later ones tend to ask instead, why should the defendant be relieved of liability for something as to which the defendant's conduct is a cause, along with other causes? For this reason, the Restatement [1] has stated the problem in terms of whether there is a "superseding cause."

"Intervening cause," like "direct causation," is a term easier of general comprehension than of any exact definition. An intervening cause is one which comes into active operation in producing the result *after* the negligence of the defendant.[2] "Intervening" is used in a time sense; it refers to later events. If the defendant sets a fire with a strong wind blowing at the time, which carries the fire to the plaintiff's property, the wind does not intervene, since it was already in operation; but if the fire is set first, and the wind springs up later, it is then an intervening cause.[3] Also, forces caused or set in motion by the operation of the defen-

§ 44

1. Second Restatement of Torts, § 440: "A superseding cause is an act of a third person or other force which by its intervention prevents the actor from being liable for harm to another which his antecedent negligence is a substantial factor in bringing about."

2. Second Restatement of Torts, § 441: "An intervening force is one which actively operates in producing harm to another after the actor's negligent act or omission has been committed."

"An intervening force is a force which is neither operating in the defendant's presence, nor at the place where the defendant's act takes effect at the time of the defendant's act, but comes into effective operation at or before the time of the damage." McLaughlin, Proximate Cause, 1925, 39 Harv.L.Rev. 149, 159.

3. Cf. Burlington & M.R. Co. v. Westover, 1876, 4 Neb. 268, and Kuhn v. Jewett, 1880, 32 N.J.Eq. 647 (direct), with Haverly v. State Line & Sullivan Railroad Co., 1890, 135 Pa. 50, 19 A. 1013 (intervening). Some confusion has arisen from an occasional use of "inter-

dant's conduct upon the existing situation—as where the defendant's spark ignites gasoline vapor already present—are not intervening causes. Their origin is not external and independent, and they are to be attributed to the defendant.[4]

It must be conceded that "intervening cause" is a highly unsatisfactory term, since we are dealing with problems of responsibility, and not physics.[5] It is used in default of a better, because it is useful in dealing with the type of case where a new and independent cause acts upon a situation once created by the defendant. In the most common usage it is meant to be understood in a very general sense that distinguishes intervening causes from concurring [6] causes of either natural or human origin, which come into active operation at a later time to change a situation resulting from the defendant's conduct.

The number and variety of causes which may intervene, after the negligence of the defendant is an accomplished fact, are obviously without any limit whatever. In the effort to hold the defendant's liability within some reasonable bounds, the courts have been compelled, out of sheer necessity and in default of anything better, to fall back upon the scope of the original foreseeable risk which the defendant has created. The question is always one of whether the defendant is to be relieved of responsibility, and the defendant's liability superseded, by the subsequent event. In general, this has been determined by asking whether the intervention of the later cause is a significant part of the risk involved in the defendant's conduct, or is so reasonably connected with it that the responsibility should not be terminated. It is therefore said that the defendant is to be held liable if, but only if, the intervening cause is "foreseeable." [7]

But here, as before,[8] this overworked and undefined word covers a multitude of sins. It is at least clear that in many cases recov-

vening" to include forces operating at the time and place of the defendant's act, as in Hoag & Alger v. Lake Shore & Michigan Southern Railway Co., 1877, 85 Pa. 293.

4. In re Polemis and Furness, Withy & Co., [1921] 3 K.B. 560. Cf. Larson v. Boston Elevated Railway Co., 1912, 212 Mass. 262, 98 N.E. 1048 (latent tuberculosis). "The new, independent intervening cause must be one not produced by the wrongful act or omission, but independent of it, and adequate to bring about the injurious result." Purcell v. St. Paul City Railway Co., 1892, 48 Minn. 134, 50 N.W. 1034.

5. "Force obviously must be a word of practical application, rather than a scientific term. Thus a spreading fire, for practical purposes, may be regarded as a continuous force, rather than a series of chemical reactions from one blade of grass to another, resulting from the interplay of many forces." Atchison, Topeka & Santa Fe Railway Co. v. Stanford, 1874, 12 Kan. 354, 375. There will of course be occasional difficulty in determining whether a "force" is to be regarded as a new one—as where the wind shifts from east to north. Compare Stephens v. Mutual Lumber Co., 1918, 103 Wash. 1, 173 P. 1031 (new force) with E.T. & H.K. Ide v. Boston & Maine Railroad Co., 1909, 83 Vt. 66, 74 A. 401 (same force). But so long as the emphasis is placed upon the risk, such questions are seldom important.

6. There is some confusion as to the meaning of "concurring causes" and "intervening causes." All causes, whether intervening or otherwise, which materially contribute to the result, may properly be called "concurring" in a causal sense, but it is generally said that only those which come into active operation later in point of time are "intervening." See Notes, 1934, 12 Tex.L.Rev. 518; 1936, 26 Georgetown L.J. 167. When "intervening" is defined with this focus on coming into "active operation" later, it is entirely possible that each of two concurring causes may be an intervening force as to the other. For example, suppose that each of two defendants leaves an automobile at the top of a hill without setting the brakes. The two cars run down hill and collide at the bottom, and one of them is deflected so that it injures the plaintiff. Although the negligent acts creating dangerous conditions may have been either simultaneous or successive, the motion of each car has intervened after the original negligence connected with the other; both are "concurring" causes. Many courts confuse the terms or use them interchangeably, or use them in other senses not clearly defined. See Johnson v. Plymouth Gypsum Plaster Co., 1916, 174 Iowa 498, 156 N.W. 721.

7. See for example Payne v. City of New York, 1938, 277 N.Y. 393, 14 N.E.2d 449 (stone in street thrown by wheel of passing car through windshield); Silver Falls Timber Co. v. Eastern & Western Lumber Co., 1935, 149 Or. 126, 40 P.2d 703 (fire carried by wind); Pease v. Sinclair Refining Co., 2d Cir. 1939, 104 F.2d 183 (mislabeled water mixed with sodium caused explosion); Royal Indemnity Co. v. Midland Counties Public Service Corp., 1919, 42 Cal.App. 628, 183 P. 960 (horse entangled in improperly insulated guy wire); Mize v. Rocky Mountain Bell Telephone Co., 1909, 38 Mont. 521, 100 P. 971 (telephone wire electrified, current carried ten miles).

8. See supra, § 43.

ery has been allowed where the intervening cause was not one which any reasonable actor could be expected to anticipate or have in mind, but it is regarded as "normal" to the situation which the actor has created.[9] In other words, although the theory of the cases is one of foreseeability, a considerable element of hindsight may have entered into its practical application.

Foreseeable Intervening Causes

If the intervening cause is one which in ordinary human experience is reasonably to be anticipated, or one which the defendant has reason to anticipate under the particular circumstances,[10] the defendant may be negligent, among other reasons, because of failing to guard against it; or the defendant may be negligent only for that reason. Thus one who sets a fire may be required to foresee that an ordinary, usual and customary wind arising later will spread it beyond the defendant's own property, and therefore to take precautions to prevent that event.[11] The person who leaves combustible or explosive material exposed in a public place may foresee the risk of fire from some independent source.[12] One who leaves uninsulated electric wires where people may come in contact with them may anticipate that they will do so as a result of their own acts.[13] A defendant who has a hole in the sidewalk may expect that some person walking by will slip or catch a foot in it.[14] An unguarded elevator shaft involves the risk that someone will fall into it;[15] unprotected dangerous machinery, that someone may get caught in it.[16] If a gun is entrusted to a child, it suggests at once to anyone with any imagination at all that someone, the child or another, is likely to be shot.[17] In all of these cases there is an intervening cause combining with the defendant's conduct to produce the result, and in each case the defendant's negligence consists in failure to protect the plaintiff against that very risk.

Obviously the defendant cannot be relieved from liability by the fact that the risk, or a substantial and important part of the risk, to which the defendant has subjected the plaintiff has indeed come to pass. Foreseeable intervening forces are within the scope of the original risk, and hence of the defendant's negligence. The courts are quite generally agreed that intervening causes which fall fairly in this category will

---

9. Second Restatement of Torts, § 435, Comment *d*.

10. Cf. Bell Lumber Co. v. Bayfield Transfer Railway Co., 1919, 169 Wis. 357, 172 N.W. 955 (notice of forest fires); Chesapeake & Ohio Railway Co. v. J. Wix & Sons, 4th Cir. 1937, 87 F.2d 257 (weather forecast of storm of great intensity); Toledo & Ohio Central Railway Co. v. S.J. Kibler & Brothers Co., 1918, 97 Ohio St. 262, 119 N.E. 733 (notice of flood); Ithaca Roller Mills v. Ann Arbor Railroad Co., 1922, 217 Mich. 348, 186 N.W. 516 (same).

11. Haverly v. State Line & Sullivan Railroad Co., 1890, 135 Pa. 50, 19 A. 1013; Olson v. Riddle, 1911, 22 N.D. 144, 132 N.W. 655; Silver Falls Timber Co. v. Eastern & Western Lumber Co., 1935, 149 Or. 126, 40 P.2d 703.

12. Watson v. Kentucky & Indiana Bridge & Railroad Co., 1910, 137 Ky. 619, 126 S.W. 146, modified 1911, 137 Ky. 619, 129 S.W. 341; Teasdale v. Beacon Oil Co., 1929, 266 Mass. 25, 164 N.E. 612; Trapp v. Standard Oil Co., 1954, 176 Kan. 39, 269 P.2d 469. Cf. Williams v. American Mutual Liability Insurance Co., La.App.1960, 121 So.2d 545; McClure v. Hoopeston Gas & Electric Co., 1922, 303 Ill. 89, 135 N.E. 43. Contrast the older attitude toward such cases, in Stone v. Boston & Albany Railroad Co., 1898, 171 Mass. 536, 51 N.E. 1.

13. Asher v. City of Independence, 1913, 177 Mo. App. 1, 163 S.W. 574; Davidson v. Otter Tail Power Co., 1921, 150 Minn. 446, 185 N.W. 644.

14. Magay v. Claflin-Sumner Coal Co., 1926, 257 Mass. 244, 153 N.E. 534. Cf. Rodgers v. Yellow Cab Co., 1959, 395 Pa. 412, 147 A.2d 611; Hastings v. F.W. Woolworth Co., 1933, 189 Minn. 523, 250 N.W. 362; Duteny v. Pennichuck Water Co., 1929, 84 N.H. 65, 146 A. 161.

15. Landy v. Olson & Serley Sash & Door Co., 1927, 171 Minn. 440, 214 N.W. 659. Cf. Mawson v. Eagle Harbor Transportation Co., 1928, 148 Wash. 258, 268 P. 595; Eggen v. Hickman, 1938, 274 Ky. 550, 119 S.W.2d 633.

16. Nelson v. William H. Ziegler Co., 1933, 190 Minn. 313, 251 N.W. 534.

17. Dixon v. Bell, 1816, 5 M. & S. 198, 105 Eng.Rep. 1023; Mautino v. Piercedale Supply Co., 1940, 338 Pa. 435, 13 A.2d 51; Milton Bradley Co. of Georgia, Inc. v. Cooper, 1949, 79 Ga.App. 302, 53 S.E.2d 761; Anderson v. Settergren, 1907, 100 Minn. 294, 111 N.W. 279. Accord: Pudlo v. Dubiel, 1930, 273 Mass. 172, 173 N.E. 536 (shot for air rifle); Allen v. Gornto, 1959, 100 Ga. App. 744, 112 S.E.2d 368 (fireworks); Rappaport v. Nichols, 1959, 31 N.J. 188, 156 A.2d 1 (liquor).

not supersede the defendant's responsibility.[18]

Thus it has been held that a defendant will be required to anticipate the usual weather of the vicinity, including all ordinary forces of nature such as usual wind or rain,[19] or snow[20] or frost[21] or fog[22] or even lightning;[23] that one who leaves an obstruction on the road[24] or a railroad track[25] should foresee that a vehicle or a train will run into it; that one who sells defective goods to a dealer should expect the dealer to resell them,[26] and that they may be passed on into the hands of those who will be injured by them;[27] that workmen who are furnished with a defective appliance may be expected to try to make it work;[28] that it may be foreseen that animals which are loose will wander into danger[29] or take fright and run away if they are left unguarded;[30] and that mosquitoes will breed in a swamp.[31]

The risk created by the defendant may include the intervention of the foreseeable negligence of others. As we have seen above,[32] the standard of reasonable conduct may require the defendant to protect the plaintiff against "that occasional negligence which is one of the ordinary incidents of human life, and therefore to be anticipated."[33] Thus a defendant who blocks the sidewalk and forces the plaintiff to walk in a street where the plaintiff will be exposed to the risks of heavy traffic becomes liable when the plaintiff is run down by a car,[34]

18. Two early decisions to this effect which have been cited frequently are Lane v. Atlantic Works, 1872, 111 Mass. 136, and Gilman v. Noyes, 1876, 57 N.H. 627.

19. Holter Hardware Co. v. Western Mortgage & Warranty Title Co., 1915, 51 Mont. 94, 149 P. 489; Kimble v. Mackintosh Hemphill Co., 1948, 359 Pa. 461, 59 A.2d 68; Fairbrother v. Wiley's, Inc., 1958, 183 Kan. 579, 331 P.2d 330; Cachick v. United States, S.D.Ill. 1958, 161 F.Supp. 15; The Mariner, 5th Cir. 1927, 17 F.2d 253.

20. Bowman v. Columbia Telephone Co., 1962, 406 Pa. 455, 179 A.2d 197; Klein v. United States, 2d Cir. 1964, 339 F.2d 512.

21. Fox v. Boston & Maine Railroad Co., 1889, 148 Mass. 220, 19 N.E. 222; Benedict Pineapple Co. v. Atlantic Coast Line Railroad Co., 1908, 55 Fla. 514, 46 So. 732. But not a frost beyond all prior experience. Blyth v. Birmingham Waterworks Co., 1856, 11 Ex. 781, 156 Eng.Rep. 1047.

22. White v. Dickerson, Inc., 1958, 248 N.C. 723, 105 S.E.2d 51.

23. Clark's Administrator v. Kentucky Utilities Co., 1942, 289 Ky. 225, 158 S.W.2d 134; Jackson v. Wisconsin Telephone Co., 1894, 88 Wis. 243, 60 N.W. 430.

24. Hyatt v. Murray, 1907, 101 Minn. 507, 112 N.W. 881; cf. Stemmler v. City of Pittsburgh, 1926, 287 Pa. 365, 135 A. 100.

25. Martin v. North Star Iron Works, 1884, 31 Minn. 407, 18 N.W. 109; cf. American Express Co. v. Risley, 1899, 179 Ill. 295, 53 N.E. 558.

26. Meshbesher v. Channellene Oil & Manufacturing Co., 1909, 107 Minn. 104, 119 N.W. 428; Farley v. Edward E. Tower & Co., 1930, 271 Mass. 230, 171 N.E. 639. Cf. Skinn v. Reutter, 1903, 135 Mich. 57, 97 N.W. 152.

27. Mossrud v. Lee, 1916, 163 Wis. 229, 157 N.W. 758; Burk v. Creamery Package Manufacturing Co., 1905, 126 Iowa 730, 102 N.W. 793; cf. Moehlenbrock v. Parke Davis & Co., 1918, 141 Minn. 154, 169 N.W. 541 (doctors administering impure ether).

28. Arko v. Shenango Furance Co., 1909, 107 Minn. 220, 119 N.W. 789; Liberty Mutual Insurance Co. v. Great Northern Railway Co., 1928, 174 Minn. 466, 219 N.W. 755; Anderson v. Baltimore & Ohio Railroad Co., 2d Cir. 1937, 89 F.2d 629, certiorari denied 302 U.S. 696, 58 S.Ct. 14, 82 L.Ed. 538; Frederick v. Goff, 1960, 251 Iowa 290, 100 N.W.2d 624 (citing numerous cases in accord).

29. Sneesby v. Lancashire & Y. R. Co., 1874, L.R. 8 Q.B. 263; Wilder v. Stanley, 1893, 65 Vt. 145, 26 A. 189. Cf. Gilman v. Noyes, 1876, 57 N.H. 627.

There has been statistical research verifying this conclusion, which may very well affect the attitude of the courts. See Davis v. Thornton, 1970, 384 Mich. 138, 180 N.W.2d 11; Gaither v. Meyers, D.C.Cir.1968, 404 F.2d 216.

30. McDonald v. Snelling, 1867, 96 Mass. (14 Allen) 290; Collins v. West Jersey Express Co., 1905, 72 N.J.L. 231, 62 A. 675; cf. Murchison v. Powell, 1967, 269 N.C. 656, 153 S.E.2d 352. But it is not foreseeable that a horse will take fright at a keg by the side of the road. Rozell v. Northern Pacific Railway Co., 1918, 39 N.D. 475, 167 N.W. 489.

31. Towaliga Falls Power Co. v. Sims, 1909, 6 Ga. App. 749, 65 S.E. 844.

32. Supra, § 33.

33. Murphy v. Great Northern Railway Co., [1897] 2 Ir.Rep. 301; Second Restatement of Torts, § 302A. Cf. McEvoy v. American Pool Corp., 1948, 32 Cal.2d 295, 195 P.2d 783; Nance v. Parks, 1966, 266 N.C. 206, 146 S.E.2d 24. See Eldredge, Culpable Intervention as Superseding Cause, 1937, 86 U.Pa.L.Rev. 121.

34. The case is of course all the clearer where there is no showing of any negligence on the part of the driver. O'Neill v. City of Port Jervis, 1930, 253 N.Y. 423, 171 N.E. 694. Cf. Brechtel v. Lopez, La.App.1962, 140

even though the car is negligently driven;[35] and one who parks an automobile on the highway without lights at night is not relieved of responsibility when another negligently drives into it.[36] By the same token, one who spills gasoline can expect it to be negligently set afire,[37] and when a drunken passenger is ejected from a bus into the midst of traffic it may be anticipated that the passenger will be negligently run down.[38] The circumstances of the particular case may of course indicate the danger of some quite unusual negligence, as when children are in the vicinity, and conduct is to be expected of them which would not be foreseen on the part of an adult.[39] The question is essentially one of the scope of the defendant's obligation, and far removed from causation.

The same is true as to those intervening intentional or criminal acts which the defendant might reasonably anticipate, and against which the defendant would be required to take precautions.[40] It must be remembered that the mere fact that misconduct on the part of another might be foreseen is not of itself sufficient to place the responsibility upon the defendant. As we have seen,[41] there are situations in which the defendant may reasonably say, "It is not my concern." But once it is determined that the defendant has a duty to anticipate the intervening misconduct, and guard against it, it cannot supersede the defendant's liability.

Even though the intervening cause may be regarded as foreseeable, the defendant is not liable unless the defendant's conduct has created or increased an unreasonable risk of harm through its intervention. A wind might be expected to blow at any time, and it might damage the plaintiff in a hundred different ways, but the defendant is not responsible for it unless the defendant has set a fire or done some other act which increases the foreseeable danger that the wind will do harm.[42] There may be an appreciable danger that the plaintiff will be struck by

So.2d 189, where a speeding driver, pursued by the police, was held liable when the police car struck a utility pole.

35. Johnson v. City of Rockford, 1962, 35 Ill.App.2d 107, 182 N.E.2d 240; Shafir v. Sieben, Mo.1921, 233 S.W. 419; O'Malley v. Laurel Line Bus Co., 1933, 311 Pa. 251, 166 A. 868. Cf. Boese v. Love, Mo.1957, 300 S.W.2d 453, where an improperly parked truck blocked the view of an automobile driver, and a boy crossing the street was run down. But cf. City of Okmulgee v. Hemphill, 1938, 183 Okl. 450, 83 P.2d 189, where, on the particular facts, the negligent driving was held to relieve the defendant.

36. Kline v. Moyer, 1937, 325 Pa. 357, 191 A. 43; Butts v. Ward, 1938, 227 Wis. 387, 279 N.W. 6; Leveillee v. Wright, 1938, 300 Mass. 382, 15 N.E.2d 247; Berry v. Visser, 1958, 354 Mich. 38, 92 N.W.2d 1; Washington v. Kemp, 1959, 99 Ga.App. 635, 109 S.E.2d 294.

37. Watson v. Kentucky & Indiana Bridge & Railroad Co., 1910, 137 Ky. 619, 126 S.W. 146, modified 137 Ky. 619, 129 S.W. 341; Teasdale v. Beacon Oil Co., 1929, 266 Mass. 25, 164 N.E. 612; Miles v. Southeastern Motor Truck Lines, 1943, 295 Ky. 156, 173 S.W.2d 990; Robert R. Walker, Inc. v. Burgdorf, 1951, 150 Tex. 603, 244 S.W.2d 506.

38. Houston v. Strickland, 1946, 184 Va. 994, 37 S.E.2d 64.

39. Such as tampering with dangerous articles left exposed to them. Vaughan v. Industrial Silica Corp., 1942, 140 Ohio St. 17, 42 N.E.2d 156; Kingsland v. Erie County Agricultural Society, 1949, 298 N.Y. 409, 84 N.E.2d 38; New York Eskimo Pie Co. v. Rataj, 3d Cir., 1934, 73 F.2d 184; Butrick v. Snyder, 1926, 236 Mich. 300, 210 N.W. 311. Cf. Shafer v. Keeley Ice Cream Co., 1925, 65 Utah 46, 234 P. 300 (scrambling for candy).

40. Wallinga v. Johnson, 1964, 269 Minn. 436, 131 N.W.2d 216; J. H. Welch & Son Contracting Co. v. Gardner, 1964, 96 Ariz. 95, 392 P.2d 567; McLeod v. Grant County School District, 1953, 42 Wash. 316, 255 P.2d 360; Hines v. Garrett, 1921, 131 Va. 125, 108 S.E. 690; Morse v. Homer's, Inc., 1936, 295 Mass. 606, 4 N.E.2d 625.

The liability is of course all the clearer where the foreseeable act of the third person, although intended to affect the plaintiff adversely, is not of itself wrongful. Thus where a bank dishonors a check, and plaintiff is arrested under a bad check law. Weaver v. Bank of America National Trust & Savings Association, 1962, 59 Cal.2d 428, 30 Cal.Rptr. 4, 380 P.2d 644; Collins v. City National Bank & Trust Co., 1944, 131 Conn. 167, 38 A.2d 582; cf. Segal v. Horwitz Brothers 1929, 32 Ohio App. 1, 167 N.E. 406 (selling plaintiff stolen goods); Wilson v. Capital Automobile Co., 1939, 59 Ga.App. 834, 2 S.E.2d 147 (failing to change registration of car in name of criminal).

41. Supra, § 33.

42. Cf. Rex v. Gill, 1719, 1 Stra. 190, 93 Eng.Rep. 465; San Antonio & Aransas Pass Railway Co. v. Behne, Tex.Comm.App.1921, 231 S.W. 354; Strong v. Granite Furniture Co., 1930, 77 Utah 292, 294 P. 303.

lightning,[43] or by an automobile in the street,[44] or a mail sack thrown from a train,[45] or that a kerosene lamp will explode in the plaintiff's face,[46] but there is no liability unless what the defendant has done has increased the risk. Railway trainmen are subject to a constant risk of falling from trains and bridges, but the railway company is not liable for such an accident unless its negligence has contributed to the danger.[47] And although the defendant's excessive speed in driving a car may be in fact a cause of the death of a child who suddenly darts out from behind a tree on a lonely road—since without it the defendant would not have been there in time for the event to occur—there is no liability if the speed is found not to have increased the risk.[48]

Normal Intervening Causes

There are other intervening causes which could scarcely have been contemplated by any reasonable person in the place of the defendant at the time of the conduct, but which are nevertheless to be regarded as normal incidents of the risks the defendant has created. Here "foreseeability" has undergone the same process of dilution and attenuation which we have encountered before,[49] but the results are even more striking. One who negligently drives a car should foresee that the car may run down a person, or collide with another car. It may be straining anticipation to the breaking point to say that the driver should have in mind the possibility that the person might be left unconscious in the highway, and be run over there by another car,[50] or that the car might be left across the highway and cause a second collision.[51] The driver might have even less reason to contemplate the possibility that if the driver endangered a child, a rescuer dashing out from the sidewalk might be injured.[52] But such events are certainly not abnormal incidents of the situation in fact created—the unconscious person, the blocked highway, or the danger to the child.

It is perhaps a pointless quibble over the meaning of a term to debate whether such normal intervening causes are to be called

43. Shell Oil Co. v. Mahler, Tex.Civ.App.1965, 385 S.W.2d 684, refused n.r.e.; Bennett v. Southern Railway Co., 1957, 245 N.C. 261, 96 S.E.2d 31, certiorari denied 353 U.S. 958, 77 S.Ct. 865, 1 L.Ed.2d 909; Alling v. Northwestern Bell Telephone Co., 1923, 156 Minn. 60, 194 N.W. 313 (no increased risk). Compare, where the risk was held to be increased; Jackson v. Wisconsin Telephone Co., 1894, 88 Wis. 243, 60 N.W. 430; Johnson v. Kosmos Portland Cement Co., 6th Cir. 1933, 64 F.2d 193, certiorari denied 290 U.S. 641, 54 S.Ct. 60, 78 L.Ed. 557.

44. Balfe v. Kramer, 1936, 249 App.Div. 746, 291 N.Y.S. 842; cf. Fulton v. Kalbach, Sup.1920, 179 N.Y.S. 604 (collision after plaintiff carried past stop on street car). Compare, where the risk was increased, O'Malley v. Laurel Line Bus Co., 1933, 311 Pa. 251, 166 A. 868, and O'Neill v. City of Port Jervis, 1930, 253 N.Y. 423, 171 N.E. 694.

45. Louisville & Nashville Railroad Co. v. Daniels, 1924, 135 Miss. 33, 99 So. 434. Cf. Berry v. Sugar Notch Borough, 1899, 191 Pa. 345, 43 A. 240.

46. Central of Georgia Railway Co. v. Price, 1898, 106 Ga. 176, 32 S.E. 77.

47. Goneau v. Minneapolis, St. Paul & Sault St. Marie Railway Co., 1922, 154 Minn. 1, 191 N.W. 279; Bohm v. Chicago, Milwaukee & St. Paul Railway Co., 1924, 161 Minn. 74, 200 N.W. 804, certiorari denied 267 U.S. 600, 45 S.Ct. 355, 69 L.Ed. 807.

48. Howk v. Anderson, 1934, 218 Iowa 358, 253 N.W. 32; Burlie v. Stephens, 1920, 113 Wash. 182, 193 P. 684; see Wallace v. Suburban Railway Co., 1894, 26 Or. 174, 177, 37 P. 477, 478. Cf. Berry v. Sugar Notch Borough, 1899, 191 Pa. 345, 43 A. 240 (struck by falling tree); Doss v. Town of Big Stone Gap, 1926, 145 Va. 520, 134 S.E. 563 (driver forced to detour, injured by crashing airplane).

49. See supra, § 43.

50. Bunda v. Hardwick, 1965, 376 Mich. 640, 138 N.W.2d 305; Morrison v. Medaglia, 1934, 287 Mass. 46, 191 N.E. 133; Thornton v. Eneroth, 1934, 177 Wash. 1, 30 P.2d 951; Adams v. Parrish, 1920, 189 Ky. 628, 225 S.W. 467; Hill v. Peres, 1934, 136 Cal.App. 132, 28 P.2d 946. Compare the even more remarkable case of Matthews v. Porter, 1962, 239 S.C. 620, 124 S.E.2d 321.

51. Sworden v. Gross, 1966, 243 Or. 83, 409 P.2d 897; Evans v. Farmer, 1963, 148 W.Va. 142, 133 S.E.2d 710; Anderson v. Jones, 1966, 66 Ill.App.2d 407, 213 N.E.2d 627; Garbe v. Halloran, 1948, 150 Ohio St. 476, 83 N.E.2d 217; Caylor v. B. C. Motor Transportation, Limited, 1937, 191 Wash. 365, 71 P.2d 162. Cf. Wedel v. Johnson, 1936, 196 Minn. 170, 264 N.W. 689 (horse); and see Note, 1949, 9 La.L.Rev. 421. See, however, Millirons v. Blue, 1934, 48 Ga.App. 483, 173 S.E. 443, where it was held unforeseeable that anyone would have collided with a car left across the road at a 45 degree angle, with all lights on and the horn continually sounding.

52. See supra, § 43.

"foreseeable." [53] They are at least foreseeable in the sense that any event which is not abnormal may reasonably be expected to occur now and then, and would be recognized as not highly unlikely if it did suggest itself to the actor's mind. They are closely and reasonably associated with the immediate consequences of the defendant's act, and form a normal part of its aftermath; and to that extent they are not foreign to the scope of the risk created by the original negligence. For the most part they have been called foreseeable by the courts; but that word obviously has traveled a long way from its original meaning in connection with the risk created by negligence.

In a large number of cases these normal intervening causes have been held not to supersede the defendant's liability. Thus defensive acts, such as the reasonable attempt of an individual threatened with harm to escape it, as by leaping from a vehicle [54] or swerving aside [55] will not relieve the original wrongdoer of liability, whether the act be instinctive [56] or after time for reflection,[57] and whether the resulting injury is to the person so seeking to escape, or to another.[58] The same is true of attempts to defend the actor's property,[59] or the actor's rights or privileges.[60]

Upon the same basis, under the "rescue doctrine," efforts to protect the personal safety of another have been held not to supersede the liability for the original negligence which has endangered it.[61] Whether or not the rescuer is to be regarded as "foreseeable," [62] it has been recognized since the early case of the crowd rushing to assist the descending balloonist [63] that the rescuer is nothing abnormal. "The risk of rescue, if

---

53. See Restatement of Torts, 1948 Supp., § 435; Bohlen, Review of Harper, Law of Torts, 1934, 47 Harv.L.Rev. 556, 557; Goodhart, Rescue and Voluntary Assumption of Risk, 1934, 5 Camb.L.J. 192, 197.

54. Jones v. Boyce, 1816, 1 Stark. 493, 171 Eng.Rep. 540. Accord: Tuttle v. Atlantic City Railroad Co., 1901, 66 N.J.L. 327, 49 A. 450; Danner v. Arnsberg, 1961, 227 Or. 420, 362 P.2d 758; Hill v. Associated Transport, Inc., 1962, 345 Mass. 55, 185 N.E.2d 642; Quigley v. Delaware & Hudson Canal Co., 1891, 142 Pa. 388, 21 A. 827.

55. Ryan v. Cameron, 1955, 270 Wis. 325, 71 N.W.2d 408; Wilson v. Goscinske, 6th Cir. 1956, 233 F.2d 759. Cf. Hall v. Macco Corp., 1961, 198 Cal.App.2d 415, 18 Cal.Rptr. 273 (crowd stampeding from fire and explosion); Sayers v. Harlow U.D.C., [1958] 2 All Eng. Rep. 342 (climbing out of lavatory to avoid inconvenience when locked in).

56. Scott v. Shepherd, 1773, 3 Wils. 403, 95 Eng. Rep. 1124; Ricker v. Freeman, 1870, 50 N.H. 420; Hill v. Associated Transport, Inc., 1962, 345 Mass. 55, 185 N.E.2d 642 (frightened when truck crashed through door of house in middle of night; leaped out of bed and fell on scatter rug). Cf. Russo v. Dinerstein, 1951, 138 Conn. 220, 83 A.2d 222 (letting child fall out of door).

57. Schumaker v. St. Paul & Duluth Railroad Co., 1891, 46 Minn. 39, 48 N.W. 559; Yazoo & Mississippi Valley Railroad Co. v. Aden, 1900, 77 Miss. 382, 27 So. 385; Reimard v. Bloomsburg & Sullivan Railroad Co., 1910, 228 Pa. 384, 77 A. 560.

But not where the plaintiff's defensive efforts are foolhardy. Fowlks v. Southern Railway Co., 1899, 96 Va. 742, 32 S.E. 464; Weeks v. Great Northern Railway Co., 1919, 43 N.D. 426, 175 N.W. 726; Brady v. Oregon Lumber Co., 1926, 117 Or. 188, 243 P. 96, rehearing denied 118 Or. 15, 245 P. 732.

58. Jackson v. Galveston, Harrisburg & San Antonio Railway Co., 1897, 90 Tex. 372, 38 S.W. 745; Griffin v. Hustis, 1919, 234 Mass. 95, 125 N.E. 387; Gedeon v. East Ohio Gas Co., 1934, 128 Ohio St. 335, 190 N.E. 924; Crow v. Colson, 1927, 123 Kan. 702, 256 P. 971; Smith v. Carlson, 1941, 209 Minn. 268, 296 N.W. 132.

59. Illinois Central Railroad Co. v. Siler, 1907, 229 Ill. 390, 82 N.E. 362; Glanz v. Chicago, Milwaukee & St. Paul Railway Co., 1903, 119 Iowa 611, 93 N.W. 575; Cooper v. Richland County, 1907, 76 S.C. 202, 56 S.E. 958; Esposito v. Christopher, 1968, 166 Colo. 361, 443 P.2d 731, appeal after remand, Colo.App., 485 P.2d 510; Lowden v. Shoffner Mercantile Co., 8th Cir. 1940, 109 F.2d 956. See Second Restatement of Torts, § 445.

A few cases to the contrary have proceeded on the ground that it is unreasonable and so contributory negligence for the plaintiff to risk serious personal injury to save property. See Cook v. Johnston, 1885, 58 Mich. 437, 25 N.W. 388; Morris v. Lake Shore & Michigan Southern Railway Co., 1896, 148 N.Y. 182, 42 N.E. 579; Taylor v. Home Telephone Co., 1910, 163 Mich. 458, 128 N.W. 728; see Note, 1935, 8 So.Cal.L.Rev. 159.

60. See Clark v. Chambers, 1878, 3 Q.B.D. 327; Cieplinski v. Severn, 1929, 269 Mass. 261, 168 N.E. 722; O'Neill v. City of Port Jervis, 1930, 253 N.Y. 423, 171 N.E. 694; Second Restatement of Torts, § 446.

61. Bond v. Baltimore & Ohio Railroad Co., 1918, 82 W.Va. 557, 96 S.E. 932; Brock v. Peabody Cooperative Equity Exchange, 1960, 186 Kan. 657, 352 P.2d 37; Mitchell v. Pettigrew, 1958, 65 N.M. 137, 333 P.2d 879; Silbernagel v. Voss, 7th Cir. 1959, 265 F.2d 390; Hatch v. Globe Laundry Co., 1934, 132 Me. 379, 171 A. 387. See Note, 1950, 3 Okl.L.Rev. 476.

62. See supra, § 43.

63. Guille v. Swan, N.Y.1822, 19 Johns. 381.

only it be not wanton, is born of the occasion. The emergency begets the man." [64] There is thus an independent duty of care owed to the rescuer,[65] which arises even when the defendant endangers no one's safety but the defendant's own.[66] The rule is not limited to spontaneous or instinctive action, but applies even when there is time for thought.[67] And whether the person injured in the attempt at rescue is the rescuer,[68] or the person rescued,[69] or a stranger,[70] the original wrongdoer is still liable.

Although there has been some disagreement,[71] the great majority of the courts now apply the same rule to one who tries to rescue the property of another,[72] even when under no duty to do so,[73] and even though the property involved is that of the defendant.[74] Even a rescuer of a rescuer of property has been allowed to recover;[75] and the same type of rule has been applied where the plaintiff seeks only to remedy a dangerous situation, such as a blocked highway, which threatens harm to person or property of those in the vicinity.[76] If any such defensive act is itself unreasonable, or done in an unreasonable manner, it may amount to contributory negligence which may affect any recovery by the actor,[77] but it will not necessarily prevent the defendant's liability to a

64. Cardozo, J., in Wagner v. International Railway Co., 1921, 232 N.Y. 176, 133 N.E. 437.

65. See supra, § 43, Unforeseeable Plaintiffs. Thus actual danger to the rescued is not essential, and it is enough that the rescuer reasonably believes that an act of rescue is necessary. Ellmaker v. Goodyear Tire & Rubber Co., Mo.App.1963, 372 S.W.2d 650.

66. Ruth v. Ruth, 1963, 213 Tenn. 82, 372 S.W.2d 285; Dodson v. Maddox, 1949, 359 Mo. 742, 223 S.W.2d 434; Provenzo v. Sam, 1968, 23 N.Y.2d 256, 296 N.Y.S.2d 322, 244 N.E.2d 26; Brugh v. Bigelow, 1944, 310 Mich. 74, 16 N.W.2d 668; Usry v. Small, 1961, 103 Ga.App. 144, 118 S.E.2d 719. Cf. Talbert v. Talbert, 1960, 22 Misc.2d 782, 199 N.Y.S.2d 212 (rescuing one attempting suicide).

67. Wagner v. International R. Co., 1921, 232 N.Y. 176, 133 N.E. 437; Luce v. Hartman, 1959, 6 N.Y.2d 786, 188 N.Y.S.2d 184, 159 N.E.2d 677, reversing, 1957, 5 A.D.2d 19, 168 N.Y.S.2d 501; Da Rin v. Casualty Co. of America, 1910, 41 Mont. 175, 108 P. 649. In Parks v. Starks, 1955, 342 Mich. 443, 70 N.W.2d 805, the lapse of nine hours after the original negligence was held not to prevent liability to the rescuer.

68. Including stress and strain. Williams v. Chick, 8th Cir. 1967, 373 F.2d 330 (death from stress); Britt v. Mangum, 1964, 261 N.C. 250, 134 S.E.2d 235 (strained back).

69. Second Restatement of Torts, § 445.

70. Guille v. Swan, N.Y.1822, 10 Johns. 381; Woodcock's Administrator v. Hallock, 1925, 98 Vt. 284, 127 A. 380; Thomas v. Casey, 1956, 49 Wn.2d 14, 297 P.2d 614.

71. Sometimes on the basis that the rescuer is a "volunteer," as in Glines v. Maine Central Railroad Co., 1947, 94 N.H. 299, 52 A.2d 298; Johnson v. Terminal Railroad Association, 1928, 320 Mo. 884, 8 S.W.2d 891, certiorari denied 278 U.S. 644, 49 S.Ct. 80, 73 L.Ed. 558. Sometimes on the basis that the "rescue doctrine" applies only to volunteers, and so not to a fireman whose duty it is to rescue. Nastasio v. Cinnamon, Mo.1956, 295 S.W.2d 117.

72. Foster v. LaPlante, Me.1968, 244 A.2d 803; George A. Fuller Construction Co. v. Elliott, 1955, 92 Ga.App. 309, 88 S.E.2d 413; Keystone-Fleming Transport v. City of Tahoka, Tex.Civ.App.1958, 315 S.W.2d 656, ref. n. r. e. (city fire equipment damaged); Henshaw v. Belyea, 1934, 220 Cal. 458, 31 P.2d 348; Stewart v. Jefferson Plywood Co., 1970, 255 Or. 603, 469 P.2d 783. See Notes, 1929, 77 U.Pa.L.Rev. 393; 1934, 23 Cal.L.Rev. 110.

73. Liming v. Illinois Central Railroad Co., 1890, 81 Iowa 246, 47 N.W. 66; Superior Oil Co. v. Richmond, 1935, 172 Miss. 407, 159 So. 850; Burnett v. Conner, 1938, 299 Mass. 604, 13 N.E.2d 417; Pike v. Grand Trunk Railway Co., 1st Cir. 1889, 39 F. 255.

74. Rushton v. Howle, 1949, 79 Ga.App. 360, 53 S.E.2d 768; Henjum v. Bok, 1961, 261 Minn. 74, 110 N.W.2d 461; Green v. Britton, 1960, 22 Conn.Sup. 71, 160 A.2d 497; Schmartz v. Harger, 1961, 22 Conn.Sup. 308, 171 A.2d 89.

75. Richards v. Kansas Electric Power Co., 1928, 126 Kan. 521, 268 P. 847; Brown v. Ross, 1956, 345 Mich. 54, 75 N.W.2d 68; Richardson v. United States, E.D.Okl.1965, 248 F.Supp. 99.

76. Marshall v. Nugent, 1st Cir. 1955, 222 F.2d 604, 58 A.L.R.2d 251 (warning traffic); Scott v. Texaco, Inc., 1966, 239 Cal.App.2d 431, 48 Cal.Rptr. 785 (same); Bilyeu v. Standard Freight Lines, 1960, 182 Cal.App.2d 536, 6 Cal.Rptr. 65 (police clearing wreckage); Rovinski v. Rowe, 6th Cir. 1942, 131 F.2d 687 (trying to move disabled truck); Hatch v. Smail, 1946, 249 Wis. 183, 23 N.W.2d 460 (trying to right overturned car).

77. Taylor v. Home Telephone Co., 1910, 163 Mich. 458, 128 N.W. 728; Hogan v. Bragg, 1918, 41 N.D. 203, 170 N.W. 324; Berg v. Great Northern Railway Co., 1897, 70 Minn. 272, 73 N.W. 648; Illinois Central Railroad Co. v. Oswald, 1930, 338 Ill. 270, 170 N.E. 247; Barnett v. Des Moines Electric Co., 8th Cir. 1925, 10 F.2d 111. See the excellent statement in Wolfinger v. Shaw, 1940, 138 Neb. 229, 292 N.W. 731.

third person who is injured.[78] The scope of the risk created may still extend to the possibility that such defensive efforts may be negligent, and so may endanger others. It is only when they are so utterly foolhardy and extraordinary that they cannot be regarded as any normal part of the original risk that they will be considered a superseding cause.[79]

A similar group of cases hold the defendant liable for the results of medical treatment of the injured victim.[80] Even where such treatment is itself negligent, because of lack of proper skill or care, recovery for its consequences is permitted.[81] It would be an undue compliment to the medical profession to say that bad surgery is no part of the risk of a broken leg.[82] So long as the plaintiff has exercised reasonable care in selecting a physician,[83] the defendant will be liable for all ordinary forms of professional negligence. There undoubtedly is a line to be drawn, short of the highly unusual varieties of medical misconduct, such as, for example, the infliction of an intentional injury,[84] or the misperformance of an entirely independent and unrelated operation,[85] which cannot fairly be regarded as normal incidents of the

---

78. Turner v. Page, 1904, 186 Mass. 600, 72 N.E. 329; Williams v. Koehler & Co., 1899, 41 App.Div. 426, 58 N.Y.S. 863; Henry v. Dennis, 1883, 93 Ind. 452; Woodcock's Administrator v. Hallock, 1925, 98 Vt. 284, 127 A. 380.

79. Atchison, Topeka & Santa Fe Railway Co. v. Calhoun, 1909, 213 U.S. 1, 29 S.Ct. 321, 53 L.Ed. 671 (injuring child in hopeless effort to catch train); Robinson v. Butler, 1948, 226 Minn. 491, 33 N.W.2d 821 (excited passenger seizing wheel); Weller v. Chicago & Northwestern Railway Co., 1952, 244 Iowa 149, 55 N.W.2d 720 (excited mother unreasonably seizing child). Compare the cases of foolhardy exposure to danger in Cone v. Inter County Telephone & Telegraph Co., Fla.1949, 40 So.2d 148; Central Wisconsin Trust Co. v. Chicago & Northwestern Railway Co., 1939, 232 Wis. 536, 287 N.W. 699.

It has been held that the rescuer may not recover where his injury is an abnormal one, not reasonably to be expected as a result of the situation. Whitman v. Mobile & Ohio Railroad Co., 1927, 217 Ala. 70, 114 So. 912 (wrenching side carrying water to extinguish fire). But compare the unusual events for which recovery was allowed in Lynch v. Fisher, La.App.1949, 41 So.2d 692; Hines v. Morrow, Tex.Civ.App.1921, 236 S.W. 183; St. Louis-San Francisco Railroad Co. v. Ginn, Okl.1954, 264 P.2d 351.

A rescuer who is partly responsible for creating the danger has been barred from recovery. Tarnowski v. Fite, 1952, 335 Mich. 267, 55 N.W.2d 824; Atlanta & Charlotte Air-Line Railway Co. v. Leach, 1893, 91 Ga. 419, 17 S.E. 619.

80. E.g., Simmons v. Lollar, 10th Cir. 1962, 304 F.2d 774, allowing recovery for death on the operating table, without negligence. In accord is Adams v. Dantin, La. App.1958, 107 So.2d 809. Also Lane v. Southern R. Co., 1926, 192 N.C. 287, 134 S.E. 855, where recovery was allowed for pain and suffering due to treatment which was proper, although not beneficial.

The familiar rule that plaintiff may recover expenses of reasonably necessary medical care rests upon the same basis. Alt v. Konkle, 1927, 237 Mich. 264, 211 N.W. 661; Dreyfus & Co. v. Wooters, 1918, 123 Va. 42, 96 S.E. 235.

81. Thompson v. Fox, 1937, 326 Pa. 209, 192 A. 107; Harris v. Brian, 10th Cir. 1958, 255 F.2d 176; Jess Edwards, Inc. v. Goergen, 10th Cir. 1958, 256 F.2d 542; Kansas City Southern Railway Co. v. Justis, 5th Cir. 1956, 232 F.2d 267, certiorari denied 352 U.S. 833, 77 S.Ct. 49, 1 L.Ed.2d 53; City of Covington v. Keal, 1939, 280 Ky. 237, 133 S.W.2d 49.

This is not limited to the negligence of physicians, but extends to that of members of plaintiff's family who are looking after the plaintiff. Ewing v. Duncan, 1935, 209 Ind. 33, 197 N.E. 901; Lange v. Hoyt, 1932, 114 Conn. 590, 159 A. 575; H. T. Whitson Lumber Co. v. Upchurch, 1923, 198 Ky. 127, 248 S.W. 243.

But in Exner Sand & Gravel Corp. v. Petterson Lighterage & Towing Corp., 2d Cir. 1958, 258 F.2d 1, the court, in a 2–1 decision, refused to extend it to the negligence of the repair crew after damage to a barge.

82. Pullman Palace Car Co. v. Bluhm, 1884, 109 Ill. 20 ("The liability to mistakes in curing is incident to a broken arm"); Thompson v. Fox, 1937, 326 Pa. 209, 192 A. 107.

83. Cf. Flint v. Connecticut Hassam Paving Co., 1918, 92 Conn. 576, 103 A. 840.

Some courts have held that there is no such liability where the negligent physician has been selected with reasonable care by the defendant, on the ground that the physician is then an independent contractor. Nall v. Alabama Utilities Co., 1931, 224 Ala. 33, 138 So. 411; Andrews v. Davis, 1930, 128 Me. 464, 148 A. 684. This is no less true where the doctor is chosen by the plaintiff, and the distinction appears quite indefensible. It was rejected in Martin v. Cunningham, 1916, 93 Wash. 517, 161 P. 355; Edmondson v. Hancock, 1929, 40 Ga.App. 587, 151 S.E. 114.

84. Second Restatement of Torts, § 457, Comment e. Cf. Brown v. New York State Training School for Girls, 1941, 285 N.Y. 37, 32 N.E.2d 783, where, to alleviate pain, the injured man took a bichloride of mercury tablet instead of the sedative prescribed by the physician.

85. Cf. Hoyt v. Independent Asphalt Paving Co., 1909, 52 Wash. 672, 101 P. 367 (operation rendered necessary not by injury but by childbirth); Upham's Case, 1923, 245 Mass. 31, 139 N.E. 433 (appendicitis).

risk; but the few cases which have approached the problem have been far from affording any very reliable guide to the location of the line.[86]

Where the injured plaintiff subsequently contracts a disease, similar principles are applied. If the injury renders the plaintiff peculiarly susceptible to the disease, as where an open wound becomes infected,[87] there is little difficulty in holding the defendant for the consequences of the disease and its treatment. Likewise where the plaintiff's weakened condition creates an especial susceptibility to such an ailment as pneumonia or tuberculosis,[88] it is not difficult to regard it as a normal intervention. Even where the disease is one such as smallpox, which appears equally likely to attack a person in good health, recovery will probably be allowed if it is found that the effects of the disease have been more serious because of the lowered vitality.[89] So also, if the plaintiff's weakened condition or physical disability subjects plaintiff, while exercising proper care,[90] to the risk of a fall or some similar mishap, the plaintiff may recover if the accident was one normally to be expected in view of the plaintiff's condition,[91] even though the second accident injures some entirely different part of the body.[92] On the other hand, if the second accident is such an abnormal consequence as drowning, because of a cast on the arm, when the plaintiff falls out of a boat, it has been held to operate as a superseding cause.[93]

Some difficulty has arisen in cases where the injured person becomes insane and commits suicide. Although there are cases to the contrary,[94] it is the prevailing view that when insanity prevents one from realizing the nature of one's act or controlling one's conduct, the suicide is to be regarded as a

86. In Purchase v. Seelye, 1918, 231 Mass. 434, 121 N.E. 413, a clerical error in a hospital, as a result of which a surgeon operated on the wrong patient, was held to be a superseding cause. This might be questioned on the ground that such a routine mistake is a normal part of the risk of going to a hospital. The same appears to be true of Corbett v. Clarke, 1948, 187 Va. 222, 46 S.E.2d 327, where a second dentist, trying to repair the ravages of a first, left a foreign substance in the cavity; and of Bush v. Commonwealth, 1880, 78 Ky. 268, where plaintiff caught scarlet fever from the physician. Contrary to this last case is Schafer & Olson v. Varney, 1926, 191 Wis. 186, 210 N.W. 359, a workmen's compensation case, where plaintiff contracted smallpox in the hospital. See Second Restatement of Torts, § 457.

On the other hand, in Lucas v. City of Juneau, D. Alaska 1955, 127 F.Supp. 730, and State ex rel. Smith v. Weinstein, Mo.App.1965, 398 S.W.2d 41, one who injured the plaintiff was held liable when the plaintiff was further injured while being transported in an ambulance.

87. Dickson v. Hollister, 1888, 123 Pa. 421, 16 A. 484; cf. Day v. Great Eastern Casualty Co., 1919, 104 Wash. 575, 177 P. 650.

88. Hazelwood v. Hodge, Ky.1961, 357 S.W.2d 711 (tuberculosis); Beauchamp v. Saginaw Mining Co., 1883, 50 Mich. 163, 15 N.W. 65 (pneumonia); Anderson v. Anderson, 1933, 188 Minn. 602, 248 N.W. 35 (same); Terre Haute & I. R. Co. v. Buck, 1884, 96 Ind. 346 (malarial fever); Wallace v. Ludwig, 1935, 292 Mass. 251, 198 N.E. 159 (streptococcus infection); see Second Restatement of Torts, § 458.

89. There are few cases. This is the conclusion in St. Louis, Iron Mountain & Southern Railway Co. v. Steel, 1915, 119 Ark. 349, 178 S.W. 320, second appeal, 1917, 129 Ark. 520, 197 S.W. 288, and in Schafer & Olson v. Varney, 1926, 191 Wis. 186, 210 N.W. 359. To the contrary is Upham's Case, 1923, 245 Mass. 31, 139 N.E. 433 (appendicitis).

90. The limitation is necessary, both from the point of view of contributory negligence, and that of proximate cause. Cf. Sporna v. Kalina, 1931, 184 Minn. 89, 237 N.W. 841; Ault v. Kuiper, 1937, 279 Mich. 1, 271 N.W. 530; S. S. Kresge Co. v. Kenney, 1936, 66 App. D.C. 274, 86 F.2d 651.

91. Wagner v. Mittendorf, 1922, 232 N.Y. 481, 134 N.E. 539; Squires v. Reynolds, 1939, 125 Conn. 366, 5 A.2d 877; Mitchell v. Legarksy, 1948, 95 N.H. 214, 60 A.2d 136; Green v. Orion Shipping & Trading Co., D.Md.1956, 139 F.Supp. 431; Wilder v. General Motorcycle Sales Co., 1919, 232 Mass. 305, 122 N.E. 319. See Second Restatement of Torts, § 460; Vance, Liability for Subsequent Injuries, 1963, 42 Tex.L.Rev. 86; Note, 1937, 22 Wash.U.L.Q. 139.

92. Bowyer v. Te-Co., Inc., Mo.1958, 310 S.W.2d 892; Eichstadt v. Underwood, Ky.1960, 337 S.W.2d 684; Eli Witt Cigar & Tobacco Co. v. Matatics, Fla.1951, 55 So.2d 549.

93. Linder v. City of Payette, 1943, 64 Idaho 656, 135 P.2d 440. Cf. Armstrong v. Bergeron, 1962, 104 N.H. 85, 178 A.2d 293 (aggravation of whiplash injury due to second rear-end collision); Koch v. Zimmermann, 1903, 85 App.Div. 370, 83 N.Y.S. 339; Ault v. Kuiper, 1937, 279 Mich. 1, 271 N.W. 530.

94. Scheffer v. Washington City, Virginia Midland & Great Southern Railroad Co., 1881, 105 U.S. 249, 26 L.Ed. 1070; Salsedo v. Palmer, 2d Cir. 1921, 278 F. 92.

direct result, and no intervening force at all, or else as a normal incident of the consequences inflicted, for which the defendant will be liable.[95] The situation is the same as if one should hurt oneself during unconsciousness or delirium brought on by the injury.[96] But if one is sane, or if the suicide is during a lucid interval, when one is in full command of all faculties, but life has become unendurable by reason of the injury, it is agreed in negligence cases [97] that the voluntary choice of suicide is an abnormal thing, which supersedes the defendant's liability.[98] An English decision, recognizing that the mental condition brought about by the original injury may still be the producing cause, has allowed recovery even in the latter case.[99]

Unforeseeable Results of Unforeseeable Causes

If the defendant can foresee neither any danger of direct injury, nor any risk from an intervening cause, the defendant is simply not negligent. Negligence cannot be predicated solely upon a failure to anticipate that extraordinary and unprecedented rainfall will flood the streets,[1] that a pedestrian will slip and fall upon an apparently safe highway,[2] that the wind will blow a door latch against the eye of a boy,[3] or that a ribbon held across a street to stop a wedding procession will cause one carriage to run into another.[4] But once the defendant's negligence is established, because injury of some kind was to be anticipated, intervening causes which could not reasonably be foreseen, and which are no normal part of the

---

95. Exxon Corp. v. Brecheen, Tex.1975, 526 S.W.2d 519; Orcutt v. Spokane County, 1961, 58 Wn.2d 846, 364 P.2d 1102; State ex rel. Richardson v. Edgeworth, Miss.1968, 214 So.2d 579; Appling v. Jones, 1967, 115 Ga.App. 301, 154 S.E.2d 406. See Daniels v. New York, New Haven & Hartford Railroad Co., 1903, 183 Mass. 393, 67 N.E. 424; Long v. Omaha & Council Bluffs Street Railway Co., 1922, 108 Neb. 342, 187 N.W. 930.

This is of course all the clearer when the defendant knows of the mental condition, and should take precautions against the suicide. Trapani v. State, 1965, 23 A.D.2d 709, 257 N.Y.S.2d 224; Muhlmichl v. State, 1964, 20 A.D.2d 837, 247 N.Y.S.2d 959.

96. Cf. Koch v. Fox, 1902, 71 App.Div. 288, 75 N.Y.S. 913; Hall v. Coble Dairies, 1951, 234 N.C. 206, 67 S.E.2d 63; Millman v. United States Mortgage & Title Guaranty Co., 1938, 121 N.J.L. 28, 1 A.2d 265.

97. Where the tort is intentional, recovery has been allowed. Tate v. Canonica, 1960, 180 Cal.App.2d 898, 5 Cal.Rptr. 28 (intentional infliction of mental disturbance by unspecified threats, apparently blackmail); Stephenson v. State, 1932, 205 Ind. 141, 179 N.E. 633, petition dismissed, 1933, 205 Ind. 141, 186 N.E. 293 (rape and torture; in its day a very famous case). See also Cauverien v. De Metz, 1959, 20 Misc.2d 144, 188 N.Y.S.2d 627, where "irresistible impulse" was alleged. See Note, 1960, 20 La.L.Rev. 791.

98. Arsnow v. Red Top Cab Co., 1930, 159 Wash. 137, 292 P. 436; Tucson Rapid Transit Co. v. Tocci, 1966, 3 Ariz.App. 330, 414 P.2d 179; Lancaster v. Montesi, 1965, 216 Tenn. 50, 390 S.W.2d 217; Stasiof v. Chicago Hoist & Body Co., 1964, 50 Ill.App.2d 115, 200 N.E.2d 88; Wallace v. Bounds, Mo.1963, 369 S.W.2d 138. See Second Restatement of Torts, § 455; Notes, 1949, 2 Vand.L.Rev. 330; 1966, 33 Tenn.L.Rev. 540.

99. Pigney v. Pointers Transport Service, [1957] 2 All Eng.Rep. 121. Contra, however, are Murdoch v. British Israel Fed., [1942] N.Z.L.Rep. 600; Cowan v. National Coal Board, [1958] Scot.L.T. (Notes) 19.

There are occasional workmen's compensation cases that have held that suicide is compensable even though it is an act of conscious volition. Harper v. Industrial Commission, 1962, 24 Ill.2d 103, 180 N.E.2d 480; Burnight v. Industrial Accident Commission, 1960, 181 Cal.App.2d 816, 5 Cal.Rptr. 786; Graver Tank & Manufacturing Co. v. Industrial Commission, 1965, 97 Ariz. 256, 399 P.2d 664.

1. Power v. Village of Hibbing, 1930, 182 Minn. 66, 233 N.W. 597; McCauley v. Logan, 1893, 152 Pa. 202, 25 A. 499; Fairmont Creamery Co. v. Thompson, 1941, 139 Neb. 677, 298 N.W. 551; Blyth v. Birmingham Waterworks Co., 1856, 11 Ex. 781, 156 Eng.Rep. 1047 (frost); Sutphen v. Hedden, 1902, 67 N.J.L. 324, 51 A. 721 (wind).

2. Missouri Pacific Railway Co. v. Richardson, 1932, 185 Ark. 472, 47 S.W.2d 794. Cf. Spiering v. City of Hutchinson, 1921, 150 Minn. 305, 185 N.W. 375 (child picked up plank with nail in it and dropped it on his foot); Smith v. Lampe, 6th Cir. 1933, 64 F.2d 201, certiorari denied 289 U.S. 751, 53 S.Ct. 695, 77 L.Ed. 1496 (sounding automobile horn which caused steamboat collision in fog); Gaupin v. Murphy, 1928, 295 Pa. 214, 145 A. 123 (defendant's automobile wheel picked up rope dropped by one child, and dragged another child into the street).

3. Morril v. Morril, 1928, 104 N.J.L. 557, 142 A. 337.

4. Simek v. Korbel, 1911, 114 Minn. 533, 131 N.W. 1134. Cf. Briglia v. City of St. Paul, 1916, 134 Minn. 97, 158 N.W. 794 (automobile going off of apparently safe highway); Tracey v. City of Minneapolis, 1932, 185 Minn. 380, 241 N.W. 390 (same).

risk created, may bring about results of an entirely different kind.

It is here at least that the line is drawn to terminate the defendant's responsibility. The courts have exhibited a more or less instinctive feeling that it would be unfair to hold the defendant liable. The virtually unanimous agreement that the liability must be limited to cover only those intervening causes which lie within the scope of the foreseeable risk, or have at least some reasonable connection with it, is based upon a recognition of the fact that the independent causes which may intervene to change the situation created by the defendant are infinite, and that as a practical matter responsibility simply cannot be carried to such lengths.

Accordingly, it has been held that the defendant is not liable for the results of unforeseeable, abnormal forces of nature, such as unpredictable storms or floods;[5] the unlikely acts of animals, such as a cow knocking a person under a train;[6] the fall of an airplane upon the plaintiff when the defendant has caused the plaintiff to make a detour;[7] and the more unpredictable behavior of irresponsible persons[8] or children[9] who get themselves into trouble or injure others. The more unusual, extraordinary forms of negligent conduct of adults, against which the defendant was under no obligation to take precautions, have been held to be superseding causes: the reckless or unusual driving of vehicles,[10] tampering with dangerous articles,[11] with stationary vehicles,[12] or other articles left unguarded,[13] the violation of express orders by workmen,[14] the unreasonable stampede of a frightened crowd,[15] abnormal mistakes in medical treatment,[16]

---

5. Gerber v. McCall, 1953, 175 Kan. 433, 264 P.2d 490; Strobeck v. Bren, 1904, 93 Minn. 428, 101 N.W. 795; Seaboard Air Line Railway Co. v. Mullin, 1915, 70 Fla. 450, 70 So. 467; see Kimble v. Mackintosh Hemphill Co., 1948, 359 Pa. 461, 59 A.2d 68. Apparently contra is Bushnell v. Telluride Power Co., 10th Cir. 1944, 145 F.2d 950.

6. Schreiner v. Great Northern Railway Co., 1902, 86 Minn. 245, 90 N.W. 400. Cf. Loiseau v. Arp, 1908, 21 S.D. 566, 114 N.W. 701; Eberhardt v. Glasco Mutual Telephone Association, 1914, 91 Kan. 763, 139 P. 416; La Londe v. Peake, 1901, 82 Minn. 124, 84 N.W. 726.

7. Doss v. Town of Big Stone Gap, 1926, 145 Va. 520, 134 S.E. 563. Cf. Dunnivant v. Nafe, 1960, 206 Tenn. 458, 334 S.W.2d 717 (brake failure after car stopped on hill by obstructed highway). See Note, 1960, 27 Tenn.L.Rev. 634.

8. Fisher v. Mutimer, 1938, 293 Ill.App. 201, 12 N.E.2d 315 (murder by discharged lunatic); Mesedahl v. St. Luke's Hospital Association, 1935, 194 Minn. 198, 259 S.W. 819 (climbing out of top of barred window); Bellows v. Worcester Storage Co., 1937, 297 Mass. 188, 7 N.E.2d 588 (insane person set fire to warehouse).

9. Leoni v. Reinhard, 1937, 327 Pa. 391, 194 A. 490 (child injuring self with lime found on highway); Dahl v. Valley Dredging Co., 1914, 125 Minn. 90, 145 N.W. 796 (heating naphtha on stove); Glassey v. Worcester Consolidated Street Railway Co., 1904, 185 Mass. 315, 70 N.E. 199 (rolling reel of wire down hill); Perry v. Rochester Lime Co., 1916, 219 N.Y. 60, 113 N.E. 529 (finding dynamite concealed in apparent safety); Paquin v. Wisconsin Central Railway Co., 1906, 99 Minn. 170, 108 N.W. 882 (starting railway cars down grade). See, as to "attractive nuisance," infra, § 59.

10. Hendricks v. Pyramid Motor Freight Corp., 1938, 328 Pa. 570, 195 A. 907; Meyette v. Canadian Pacific Railway Co., 1939, 110 Vt. 345, 6 A.2d 33; Butner v. Spease, 1940, 217 N.C. 82, 6 S.E.2d 808; Mull v. Ford Motor Co., 2d Cir. 1966, 368 F.2d 713; Batts v. Faggart, 1963, 260 N.C. 641, 133 S.E.2d 504. Cf. Salt River Valley Water Users' Association v. Cornum, 1937, 49 Ariz. 1, 63 P.2d 639; Frerichs v. Eastern Nebraska Public Power District, 1951, 154 Neb. 777, 49 N.W.2d 619; Merlo v. Public Service Co., 1942, 381 Ill. 300, 45 N.E.2d 665.

11. Larson v. Duluth, Missabe & Northern Railway Co., 1919, 142 Minn. 366, 172 N.W. 762. Cf. Spence v. American Oil Co., 1938, 171 Va. 62, 197 S.E. 468 (defendant sold watered gasoline to A; A's servant drained it into the gutter, where B threw a match into it to see whether it would burn).

12. Kinsley v. Von Atzingen, 1952, 20 N.J.Super. 378, 90 A.2d 37; Reti v. Vaniska, Inc., 1951, 14 N.J.Super. 94, 81 A.2d 377; Mars v. Delaware & Hudson Canal Co., 1889, 54 Hun. 625, 8 N.Y.S. 107.

13. Quill v. Empire State Telephone & Telegraph Co., 1899, 159 N.Y. 1, 53 N.E. 679 (telephone insulator); Schwartz v. California Gas & Electric Corp., 1912, 163 Cal. 398, 125 P. 1044 (same); Bentley v. Fischer Lumber & Manufacturing Co., 1899, 51 La.Ann. 451, 25 So. 262 (levee); cf. Bellino v. Columbus Construction Co., 1905, 188 Mass. 430, 74 N.E. 684 (workmen putting gasoline in stove).

14. Schendel v. Chicago, Milwaukee & St. Paul Railway Co., 1924, 158 Minn. 378, 197 N.W. 744.

15. Southern Transportation Co. v. Harper, 1903, 118 Ga. 672, 45 S.E. 458.

16. See supra, this section.

unlikely, foolhardy efforts to avert a threatened danger.[17]

The same is true of those intentional or criminal acts against which no reasonable standard of care would require the defendant to be on guard: unforeseeable personal attacks upon the plaintiff,[18] destructive meddling with property,[19] and the forgery of a check.[20]

Almost invariably these cases present no issue of causation, since there is no doubt whatever that the defendant has created the situation acted upon by another force to bring about the result; and to deal with them in terms of "cause" or "proximate cause" is only to avoid the real issue. The question is one of negligence and the extent of the obligation: whether the defendant's responsibility extends to such interventions, which are foreign to the risk the defendant has created. It is best stated as a problem of the scope of the legal obligation to protect the plaintiff against such an intervening cause.[21] A decision that the defendant's conduct is not the "proximate cause" of the result means only that the defendant has not been negligent at all, or that the defendant's negligence, if any, does not cover such a risk. The element of shifting responsibility[22] frequently enters. Sometimes the defendant will be free to assume that when a third person becomes aware of the danger, and is in a position to deal with it, the third person will act reasonably.[23] It is only where misconduct was to be anticipated, and taking the risk of it was unreasonable, that liability will be imposed for consequences to which such intervening acts contributed.

One recurring type of case in which the problem is well illustrated[24] is that in which the defendant parks a car, leaving the key in the ignition lock, and the plaintiff is run down and injured by a thief who has stolen the car and is making a getaway. Here a few courts have found liability at common law,[25] and others have construed legislation to create a duty to the plaintiff and impose liability.[26]

The great majority have refused to hold the defendant liable, either with[27] or with-

---

17. See supra, this section.

18. Hoff v. Public Service R. Co., 1918, 91 N.J.L. 641, 103 A. 209; Sira v. Wabash Railroad Co., 1893, 115 Mo. 127, 21 S.W. 905; Toone v. Adams, 1964, 262 N.C. 403, 137 S.E.2d 132 (baseball umpire); United States v. Shively, 5th Cir. 1965, 345 F.2d 294, certiorari denied 382 U.S. 883, 86 S.Ct. 177, 15 L.Ed.2d 124.

19. Deyo v. New York Central Railroad Co., 1865, 34 N.Y. 9; Aune v. Oregon Trunk Railway, 1935, 151 Or. 622, 51 P.2d 663; Bellows v. Worcester Storage Co., 1937, 297 Mass. 188, 7 N.E.2d 588; Stasulat v. Pacific Gas & Electric Co., 1937, 8 Cal.2d 631, 67 P.2d 678.

20. Glasscock v. First National Bank, 1924, 114 Tex. 207, 266 S.W. 393; Saugerties Bank v. Delaware & Hudson Co., 1923, 236 N.Y. 425, 141 N.E. 904; Walsh v. Hunt, 1898, 120 Cal. 46, 52 P. 115.

As to the obligation to guard against criminal acts in general, see supra, this section.

21. See Campbell, Duty, Fault and Legal Cause, [1938] Wis.L.Rev. 402. Concerning "duty" and "cause" generally, see supra, § 42.

22. See supra, § 33.

23. Cf. Rulane Gas Co. v. Montgomery Ward & Co., 1949, 231 N.C. 270, 56 S.E.2d 689; Venorick v. Revetta, 1943, 152 Pa.Super. 455, 33 A.2d 655; Ford Motor Co. v. Wagoner, 1946, 183 Tenn. 392, 192 S.W.2d 840, petition dismissed 183 Tenn. 392, 192 S.W.2d 852; Dooley v. Borough of Charleroi, 1937, 328 Pa. 57, 195 A. 6.

24. See Notes, [1951] Wis.L.Rev. 740; 1955, 43 Cal. L.Rev. 140; 1956, 21 Mo.L.Rev. 197; 1956, 24 Tenn. L.Rev. 395; 1958, 37 N.C.L.Rev. 104; 1949, 34 Iowa L.Rev. 376; 1964, 29 Mo.L.Rev. 379; 1965, 38 So.Cal.L. Rev. 125.

25. Mellish v. Cooney, 1962, 23 Conn.Sup. 350, 183 A.2d 753; Schaff v. R. W. Claxton, Inc., 1944, 79 U.S. App.D.C. 207, 144 F.2d 532, overruling Squires v. Brooks, 1916, 44 App.D.C. 320. The District of Columbia now has a statute. See the following note.

26. Ross v. Hartman, 1943, 78 App.D.C. 217, 139 F.2d 14, certiorari denied 321 U.S. 790, 64 S.Ct. 790, 88 L.Ed. 1080; Ney v. Yellow Cab Co., 1954, 2 Ill.2d 74, 117 N.E.2d 74; Garbo v. Walker, Ohio Com.Pl.1955, 129 N.E.2d 537 (ordinance).

27. Meihost v. Meihost, 1966, 29 Wis.2d 537, 139 N.W.2d 116; Galbraith v. Levin, 1948, 323 Mass. 255, 81 N.E.2d 560; Corinti v. Wittkopp, 1959, 355 Mich. 170, 93 N.W.2d 906; Hersh v. Miller, 1959, 169 Neb. 517, 99 N.W.2d 878; Anderson v. Theisen, 1950, 231 Minn. 369, 43 N.W.2d 272. Some car-locking statutes specifically provide that they shall have no effect upon civil liability. Richards v. Stanley, 1954, 43 Cal.2d 60, 271 P.2d 23; Gower v. Lamb, Mo.App.1955, 282 S.W.2d 867.

out [28] a car-locking ordinance. The opinions have run the gamut of all possible grounds, ranging from no duty through no lack of reasonable care to no proximate causation. Actually the problem appears to be a very simple one. Leaving a car unlocked certainly creates a foreseeable likelihood that it will be stolen, which endangers the interests of the owner; but is it so likely that the thief, getting away, will drive negligently, that there is any unreasonable risk of harm to anyone else? [29] When the plaintiff is run down five days after the theft, the decisions agree [30] that there is no liability, since there is nothing more than the ordinary risk of being run down by any car. Is there so much more danger while the thief is escaping that the owner is required to take precautions for the protection of those down the highway? The bulk of the decisions have said no.[31]

But when the danger is increased, as where the car is parked with the engine running and children about,[32] or there has been past experience of meddling with an enormous bulldozer left unlocked on a plateau at the top of a canyon,[33] liability is found. The same kind of distinction may be made between public authorities who have a dangerous pyromaniac in prison,[34] and those who have one merely convicted of forgery.[35]

In only one considerable group of cases [36] has the defendant been held liable where unforeseeable intervening causes have brought about unforeseeable results. It is quite often said in the cases that when the negligence of a defendant "concurs" with an act of God, which is to say an unforeseeable force of nature, the defendant is to be held liable.[37] Sometimes it is a problem what this is supposed to mean. In most of the cases

28. Richards v. Stanley, 1954, 43 Cal.2d 60, 271 P.2d 23; Liney v. Chestnut Motors, Inc., 1966, 421 Pa. 26, 218 A.2d 336; Ross v. Nutt, 1964, 177 Ohio St. 113, 203 N.E.2d 118; Williams v. Mickens, 1957, 247 N.C. 262, 100 S.E.2d 511; Kalberg v. Anderson Brothers Motor Co., 1958, 251 Minn. 458, 88 N.W.2d 197.

29. It has been contended that a thief making his getaway is likely to be the most careful of all drivers, to avoid attracting attention. See, however, Peck, An Exercise Based upon Empirical Data: Liability for Harm Caused by Stolen Automobiles, [1969] Wis.L. Rev. 909, demonstrating rather clearly that the accident rate is much higher among drivers of stolen cars.

30. Wannebo v. Gates, 1948, 227 Minn. 194, 34 N.W.2d 695; Dersookian v. Helmick, 1970, 256 Md. 627, 261 A.2d 472; see Justus v. Wood, 1961, 209 Tenn. 55, 348 S.W.2d 332, rehearing denied 209 Tenn. 55, 349 S.W.2d 793.

31. There is especially good discussion, with a dissent, in Richards v. Stanley, 1954, 43 Cal.2d 60, 271 P.2d 23.

32. Hatch v. Globe Laundry Co., 1934, 132 Me. 379, 171 A. 387; Lomano v. Ideal Towel Supply Co., 1947, 25 N.J.Misc. 162, 51 A.2d 888. Cf. Anderson v. Bushong Pontiac Co., 1961, 404 Pa. 382, 171 A.2d 771 (car keys stolen); Murray v. Wright, 1958, 166 Cal.App.2d 589, 333 P.2d 111 (many unlocked cars in open car lot); Pfaehler v. Ten Cent Taxi Co., 1942, 198 S.C. 476, 18 S.E.2d 331 (taxi left with ignition key in lock and drunken passenger on front seat).

33. Richardson v. Ham, 1955, 44 Cal.2d 772, 285 P.2d 269. Cf Hergenrether v. East, 1964, 61 Cal.2d 440, 39 Cal.Rptr. 4, 393 P.2d 164 (character of neighborhood); Anderson v. Bushong Pontiac Co., 1961, 404 Pa. 382, 171 A.2d 771; Mezyk v. National Repossessions, Inc., 1965, 241 Or. 333, 405 P.2d 840; Kacena v. George W. Bowers Co., Inc., 1965, 63 Ill.App.2d 27, 211 N.E.2d 563.

34. Austin W. Jones Co. v. State, 1923, 122 Me. 214, 119 A. 577; St. George v. State, 1953, 203 Misc. 340, 118 N.Y.S.2d 596, reversed on other grounds 283 App. Div. 245, 127 N.Y.S.2d 147, settled, 1954, 128 N.Y.S.2d 583, motion denied 307 N.Y. 689, 120 N.E.2d 860, affirmed, 1955, 308 N.Y. 681, 124 N.E.2d 320; University of Louisville v. Hammock, 1907, 127 Ky. 564, 106 S.W. 219 (delirium tremens). Cf. Missouri, Kansas & Texas Railway Co. v. Wood, 1902, 95 Tex. 223, 66 S.W. 449 (smallpox patient); Webb v. State, La.App.1956, 91 So. 2d 156 (dangerous criminal).

35. Williams v. State, 1955, 308 N.Y. 548, 127 N.E.2d 545. Accord, Green v. State through Department of Institutions, La.App.1956, 91 So.2d 153 (negligent driving by escaped inmates of state institution for youths).

36. Mention should be made, however, of Daggett v. Keshner, 1954, 284 App.Div. 733, 134 N.Y.S.2d 524, affirmed, 1950, 14 Misc.2d 154, 149 N.Y.S.2d 422, again, 304 N.Y. 968, 110 N.E.2d 892, again, 305 N.Y. 553, 111 N.E.2d 246. A statute penalizing the sale of gasoline compounds unless there was a permit or delivery into a fuel tank of a vehicle, provided a tort action for any person injured as a result of violation. This was held to make the seller liable when the gasoline was used for arson, and detectives trying to apprehend the criminals were injured. The case is noted in 1955, 40 Corn.L.Q. 810. Contrast, however, Gonzalez v. Derrington, 1961, 56 Cal.2d 130, 14 Cal.Rptr. 1, 363 P.2d 1, where violation of a statute prohibiting sale of gasoline in open cans, without provision for any tort action, was held not to make defendant liable for arson.

37. See for example Manila School District No. 15 v. Sanders, 1956, 226 Ark. 270, 289 S.W.2d 529. See

the result brought about by the act of God is the same as that threatened by the defendant's negligence, so that the defendant is held liable for the foreseeable result.[38] Where a totally different result is brought about, most cases agree that there is no liability, even though there is concurrence in causation.[39] The exceptional cases are those in which a carrier delays goods in transit, and during such delay the goods are destroyed by an unforeseeable flood or other force of nature. Here a number of courts have held the carrier liable.[40]

Here again the talk of "proximate cause" has obscured the real problem. The common law always has held a common carrier so far an insurer of the goods entrusted to its care that it is liable for all damage to them, whether caused by its negligence or entirely accidental, except that resulting from the acts of the public enemy or the act of God.[41] But when the carrier is itself guilty of misconduct, there are cases in which it forfeits even this exemption. If the carrier deviates from the prescribed route it is liable when the goods are lost by the act of God in the course of the deviation.[42] If it fails to make delivery of goods on hand to deliver, it is liable for their subsequent destruction through natural causes.[43] It is quite arguable that this strict liability, which is of course based upon the special responsibility assumed by the carrier, should be extended to cases where the delay has exposed the goods to a loss which could not have been anticipated.

Another group of courts, representing the view which has been preferred by most writers, have rejected any such extension, and have held that a carrier is not responsible for the results of a force of nature which is no part of the risk created by the delay.[44] If a flood is unforeseeable, it would of course be equally likely to occur at any time or place.[45] Upon any ordinary principles of negligence, there is no more reason to hold the carrier when it occurs during a delayed transit than if the flood should destroy the goods, with the delay still operating to keep them behind schedule, in the hands of a con-

---

also supra, § 41, for discussion of the contention that harm is not caused in fact by negligence if an "act of God" would have caused it anyway.

38. See infra, this section.

39. See cases cited supra, note 5.

40. Bibb Broom Corn Co. v. Atchison, Topeka & Santa Fe Railway Co., 1905, 94 Minn. 269, 102 N.W. 709; Green-Wheeler Shoe Co. v. Chicago Rock Island & Pacific Railway Co., 1906, 130 Iowa 123, 106 N.W. 498; Alabama Great Southern Railroad Co. v. Quarles & Couturie, 1906, 145 Ala. 436, 40 So. 120; Sunderland Brothers Co. v. Chicago, Burlington & Quincy Railroad Co., 1911, 89 Neb. 660, 131 N.W. 1047; Michaels v. New York Central Railroad Co., 1864, 30 N.Y. 564.

41. To these exceptions "native justice and the genius of our jurisprudence" have added losses due to the act of the shipper, the public authority, and the inherent nature of the goods. Dobie, Bailments and Carriers, 1914, 325. See generally, Holmes, Common Carriers and the Common Law, 1879, 13 Am.L.Rev. 609; Beale, The Carrier's Liability: Its History, 1898, 11 Harv.L.Rev. 158.

But see the strict interpretation of "act of God" in Forward v. Pittard, 1785, 1 Term Rep. 27, 99 Eng.Rep. 953 (fire of possible human origin); Schaff v. Roach, 1925, 116 Okl. 205, 243 P. 976 (sale); Leister v. Kelley, 1939, 279 Ky. 767, 132 S.W.2d 67 (confiscation of whiskey during flood); Lysaght, Limited v. Lehigh Valley Railroad Co., D.N.Y.1918, 254 F. 351 (Black Tom explosion).

42. Davis v. Garrett, 1830, 6 Bing. 716, 130 Eng. Rep. 1456; Seavey Co. v. Union Transit Co., 1900, 106 Wis. 394, 82 N.W. 285; Louisville & Cincinnati Packet Co. v. Rogers, 1898, 20 Ind.App. 594, 49 N.E. 970.

43. Richmond & Danville Railroad Co. v. Benson, 1890, 86 Ga. 203, 12 S.E. 357; East Tennessee, Virginia & Georgia Railway Co. v. Kelly, 1892, 91 Tenn. 699, 20 S.W. 312.

44. Rodgers v. Missouri Pacific Railway Co., 1907, 75 Kan. 222, 88 P. 885; Morrison v. Davis & Co., 1852, 20 Pa. 171; Seaboard Air Line Railway Co. v. Mullin, 1915, 70 Fla. 450, 70 So. 467; Yazoo & Mississippi Valley Railroad Co. v. Millsaps, 1899, 76 Miss. 855, 25 So. 672; Little Rock Packing Co. v. Chicago, Burlington & Quincy Railroad Co., W.D.Mo.1953, 116 F.Supp. 213; Second Restatement of Torts, § 451.

45. It has been suggested that there is a slight risk of the flood, which the carrier has increased by the delay. See Green, Rationale of Proximate Cause, 1927, 29; Bauer, Common Carrier's Negligent Delay Plus Act of God, 1933, 8 Notre Dame Lawyer 394. Such a suggestion overlooks the fact that the courts imposing liability have been willing to assume that the intervening force was beyond all human foresight, and in no way a normal part of the risk created by the delay, and still hold the carrier. Cf. the Bibb Broom Corn Case, supra, note 40 where it was conceded "that it was unprecedented, and beyond the reasonable anticipation of the most prudent residents of the vicinity where it occurred."

necting carrier, or even after delivery to the consignee.[46] The problem is purely one of the extent of the responsibility which the policy of the law is to impose upon the carrier. A number of federal cases have held that the carrier is not liable for such unforeseeable forces of nature.[47] The federal rule has been held to control all shipments in interstate commerce,[48] and for this reason alone it should be adopted by the state courts, since recovery should not depend upon the fortuitous circumstance that the goods did not cross a state line.[49]

Foreseeable Results of Unforeseeable Causes

Suppose that the defendant is negligent because the defendant's conduct threatens a result of a particular kind which will injure the plaintiff, and an intervening cause which could not be anticipated changes the situation, but ultimately produces the same result?[50] The very statement of the question implies a description of the "result" more generalized than would be a description in terms of how it came about. Thus, this is another illustration of the flexibility of standards or concepts, and the significant impact on outcome that flows from different degrees of generality or specificity in the ways risk and results are described.[51] The cases are more often analyzed, however, in the ways indicated in the discussion that follows. The problem is well illustrated by a well-known federal case.[52] The defendant failed to clean the residue out of an oil barge, tied to a dock, leaving it full of explosive gas. This was of course negligence, since fire or explosion, resulting in harm to any person in the vicinity, was to be anticipated from any one of several possible sources. A bolt of lightning struck the barge, exploded the gas, and injured workmen on the premises. The defendant was held liable. If it be assumed that the lightning was an unforeseeable intervening cause, still the result itself was to be anticipated, and the risk of it imposed upon the defendant the original duty to use proper care.

In such a case, the result is within the scope of the defendant's negligence. The defendant's obligation to the plaintiff was to protect the plaintiff against the risk of such an accident. It is only a slight extension of this responsibility to hold the defendant liable when the danger created is realized through external factors which could not be anticipated. An instinctive feeling of justice leads to the conclusion that the defendant is morally responsible in such a case, and that the loss should fall upon the defendant rather than upon the innocent plaintiff.

Many cases have held the defendant liable where the result which was to be foreseen was brought about by causes that were unforeseeable: a ladder left standing in the street blown down by an unforeseeable

---

46. Cf. Denny v. New York Central Railroad Co., 1859, 79 Mass. (13 Gray) 481, where the goods had arrived at destination but had not yet been delivered. Compare also Berry v. Borough of Sugar Notch, 1899, 191 Pa. 345, 43 A. 240, where the speed of the car brought it under a tree in time to be struck when it fell. Is there any real distinction?

47. Memphis & Charleston Railroad Co. v. Reeves, 1870, 77 U.S. (10 Wall.) 176, 19 L.Ed. 909.

48. Northwestern Consolidated Milling Co. v. Chicago, Burlington & Quincy Railroad Co., 1917, 135 Minn. 363, 160 N.W. 1028, certiorari denied 245 U.S. 644, 38 S.Ct. 8, 62 L.Ed. 528; Toledo & Ohio Central Railway Co. v. S. J. Kibler & Brothers Co., 1918, 97 Ohio St. 262, 119 N.E. 733, certiorari denied 248 U.S. 569, 39 S.Ct. 10, 63 L.Ed. 425; Barnet v. New York Central & Hudson River Railroad Co., 1918, 222 N.Y. 195, 118 N.E. 625; Continental Paper Bag Co. v. Maine Central Railroad Co., 1916, 115 Me. 449, 99 A. 259.

49. Second Restatement of Torts, § 451, Comment a.

50. Suppose the defendant, in dry weather, runs its train without proper spark arresters. A spark from the engine sets fire to a field of hay on the south side of the track; a cyclone blows the fire in a circle of a hundred miles, and a wheat field adjoining the right of way on the north side at the same point is burned. Is the defendant liable? See Note, 1966, 18 U.Fla.L.Rev. 538.

51. See supra, § 43, Anatomy of Foresight.

52. Johnson v. Kosmos Portland Cement Co., 6th Cir. 1933, 64 F.2d 193, certiorari denied 290 U.S. 641, 54 S.Ct. 60, 78 L.Ed. 557.

wind;[53] an obstruction in the highway with which a runaway horse collides;[54] delay upon a railway track because of the unexpected lowering of the crossing gates;[55] an insecure gas pipe bursting because it was struck by an automobile;[56] a loose pile of lumber knocked over by a stranger;[57] a termite-riddled telephone pole thrown down by an automobile which comes up on the sidewalk,[58] cattle driven from a farmyard wandering back onto a railway onto which they had escaped in the first instance because of improper fencing.[59] In all such cases the courts have taken refuge in the rule, stated to be well settled, that if the result is foreseeable, the manner in which it is brought about need not be, and is immaterial.[60]

Yet there are other cases[61] in which it seems equally clear that the defendant should not be liable. What if A knocks B down and leaves B lying unconscious in the street, where B may be run over by negligently driven automobiles, and C, a personal enemy of B, discovers B there and intentionally runs B down? When the defendant excavates a hole in the sidewalk into which someone might fall, the defendant may be liable if the plaintiff is negligently pushed into it by a stranger,[62] but what if the plaintiff is pushed deliberately?[63] Nor should the defendant be liable where a chair seat is left on a balcony railing, and it is purposely thrown down,[64] or a policeman aware of the danger of a live wire knocks it with a club against the plaintiff,[65] or a stranger imper-

53. Moore v. Townsend, 1899, 76 Minn. 64, 78 N.W. 880. Accord: O'Connor v. Chicago, Milwaukee & St. Paul Railway Co., 1916, 163 Wis. 653, 158 N.W. 343, affirmed, 1918, 248 U.S. 536, 39 S.Ct. 21, 63 L.Ed. 408 (tree and storm); Mars v. Meadville Telephone Co., 1942, 344 Pa. 29, 23 A.2d 856 (pole and cow); Mummaw v. Southwestern Telegraph & Telephone Co., Mo.App. 1918, 208 S.W. 476 (pole and fire); Blanks v. Saenger Theaters, 1932, 19 La.App. 305, 138 So. 883 (fire escape ladder tipped by child trespasser). See Second Restatement of Torts, § 442B.

It should be noted that in some cases it is possible to apportion the damages. See infra, § 52.

54. McDowell v. Village of Preston, 1908, 104 Minn. 263, 116 N.W. 470; Baldwin v. Greenwoods Turnpike Co., 1873, 40 Conn. 238.

Cf. McDermott v. McClain, Fla.App.1969, 220 So.2d 394, reversed, Fla., 232 So.2d 161, vacated 233 So.2d 453 (car parked at forbidden place, plaintiff helping to pour gasoline into it struck by drunken driver).

55. Washington & Georgetown Railroad Co. v. Hickey, 1897, 166 U.S. 521, 17 S.Ct. 661, 41 L.Ed. 1101. Cf. Munsey v. Webb, 1913, 231 U.S. 150, 34 S.Ct. 44, 58 L.Ed. 162 (passenger in unsafe elevator falling down); Teasdale v. Beacon Oil Co., 1929, 266 Mass. 25, 164 N.E. 612 (spark from unexpected source igniting gasoline); Robert R. Walker, Inc. v. Burgdorf, 1951, 150 Tex. 603, 244 S.W.2d 506 (gasoline negligently ignited).

56. Carroll v. Central Counties Gas Co., 1925, 74 Cal.App. 303, 240 P. 53. Accord: Van Cleef v. City of Chicago, 1909, 240 Ill. 318, 88 N.E. 815; Dalton v. Great Atlantic & Pacific Tea Co., 1922, 241 Mass. 400, 135 N.E. 318; Hughes v. Lord Advocate, [1963] A.C. 837.

57. Pastene v. Adams, 1874, 49 Cal. 87. Accord: Chacey v. City of Fargo, 1895, 5 N.D. 173, 64 N.W. 932.

58. Gibson v. Garcia, 1950, 96 Cal.App.2d 681, 216 P.2d 119; Friendship Tel. Co. v. Russom, 1957, 43 Tenn.App. 441, 309 S.W.2d 416; cf. Blunt v. Spears, 1956, 93 Ga.App. 623, 92 S.E.2d 573, reversed on other grounds 212 Ga. 537, 93 S.E.2d 659, conformed to 94 Ga.App. 329, 94 S.E.2d 514. Contra, Indiana Service Corp. v. Johnston, 1941, 109 Ind.App. 204, 34 N.E.2d 157.

59. Turner v. Chicago, Rock Island & Pacific Railway Co., 1917, 136 Minn. 383, 162 N.W. 469. Cf. Riley v. Standard Oil Co., 1934, 214 Wis. 15, 252 N.W. 183 (fire communicated in unexpected manner); Chase v. Washington Water Power Co., 1941, 62 Idaho 298, 111 P.2d 872 (high tension electric arc caused by fighting chicken-hawks); Billups Petroleum Co. v. Entrekin, 1950, 209 Miss. 302, 46 So.2d 781; Steele v. Rapp, 1958, 183 Kan. 371, 327 P.2d 1053. A quite extraordinary case is United Novelty Co., Inc. v. Daniels, Miss.1949, 42 So.2d 395, where fire was carried by a rat.

60. See supra, this section.

61. See Carpenter, Workable Rules for Determining Proximate Cause, 1932, 20 Cal.L.Rev. 229, 471, 515–520, contending that "probable consequences" of unforeseeable intervening forces are never "proximate."

62. Village of Carterville v. Cook, 1889, 129 Ill. 152, 22 N.E. 14.

63. Milostan v. City of Chicago, 1909, 148 Ill.App. 540; Alexander v. Town of New Castle, 1888, 115 Ind. 51, 17 N.E. 200; Miller v. Bahmmuller, 1908, 124 App. Div. 558, 108 N.Y.S. 924; Loftus v. Dehail, 1901, 133 Cal. 214, 65 P. 379.

64. Klaman v. Hitchcock, 1930, 181 Minn. 109, 231 N.W. 716.

65. Seith v. Commonwealth Electric Co., 1909, 241 Ill. 252, 89 N.E. 425. Accord: Polloni v. Ryland, 1915, 28 Cal.App. 51, 151 P. 296; and cf. Watson v. Kentucky & Indiana Bridge & Railroad Co., 1910, 137 Ky. 619, 126 S.W. 146, modified 137 Ky. 619, 129 S.W. 341 (setting fire to spilled gasoline).

sonating an elevator operator deliberately invites the plaintiff to step into an open shaft.[66]

The difference between the two groups of cases is a matter of intangible factors not easy to express. It apparently lies in the conclusion of the courts that in the latter type of case the responsibility is shifted to the second actor. Where there is a malicious or criminal act,[67] the original actor might be free to say, even if anticipating the misconduct, that it was not the actor's concern, whereas the actor might still be responsible for inadvertence or ignorant blunders.[68] Where the defendant would be relieved of responsibility even if the act were to be anticipated, the defendant should be no less relieved when it is unforeseeable.

Such a suggestion may resolve the apparent confusion surrounding two types of cases. One is that in which the defendant permits dynamite caps, or something similarly dangerous, to get into the hands of a child, and the parents of the child, after taking the caps away from the child, fail to prevent the child from obtaining possession of them again, to the child's subsequent injury. The injury, of course, is what was to be expected in the first place; and ordinarily a defendant is not free to rely upon others to avert the danger which the defendant creates. If the defendant sets a fire, the failure of a third person to extinguish it, however unreasonable, will not relieve the defendant from liability.[69] If the parents do not discover the nature of the dynamite, their failure to take it from the child, or to keep it from the child, although it may be negligent, does not end the defendant's responsibility when the risk the defendant has created is realized.[70] But once the parent becomes aware of the danger and interferes, it is at least possible to conclude that from that point forward the responsibility is the parent's rather than the defendant's.[71] Whether, in such a case, the danger is not so extreme that the defendant could not reasonably rely upon even the parent to protect the child, is a question which is open to debate.[72]

The other group of cases involve the situation in which a third person fully discovers the danger, and then proceeds, in deliberate disregard of it, to resell, pass on to employees, or continue to make use of a defective chattel bought from the defendant,[73] or otherwise to inflict upon the plaintiff the dan-

---

66. Cole v. German Savings & Loan Society, 10th Cir. 1903, 124 F. 113. But see contra, Mozer v. Semenza, Fla.App.1965, 177 So.2d 880 (arson).

67. See cases cited supra, notes 63, 66.

68. See for example The Lusitania, D.C.N.Y.1918, 251 F. 715 (published threat of German government to sink passenger liner in violation of international law); Graves v. Johnson, 1901, 179 Mass. 53, 60 N.E. 383 (liquor sold to one known to intend to make illegal resale); Beatty v. Gilbanks, 1882, 15 Cox.C.C. 138 (riot started by group known to oppose Salvation Army).

69. Wiley v. West Jersey Railroad Co., 1882, 44 N.J.L. 247. Accord: Nicholson v. Buffalo, Rochester & Pittsburgh Railway Co., 1930, 302 Pa. 41, 153 A. 128; Diehl v. Fidelity Philadelphia Trust Co., 1946, 159 Pa. Super. 513, 49 A.2d 190; Bixby v. Thurber, 1922, 80 N.H. 411, 118 A. 99; Harber v. Gledhill, 1922, 60 Utah 391, 208 P. 1111.

Nor is the defendant relieved when a third person attempts to halt the consequences, but fails. Haverly v. State Line & Sullivan Railroad Co., 1890, 135 Pa. 50, 19 A. 1013; Mathis v. Granger Brick & Tile Co., 1915, 85 Wash. 634, 149 P. 3; Clark v. E. I. Du Pont de Nemours Powder Co., 1915, 94 Kan. 268, 146 P. 320.

70. Mathis v. Granger Brick & Tile Co., 1915, 85 Wash. 634, 149 P. 3; Diehl v. A. P. Green Fire Brick Co., 1923, 299 Mo. 641, 253 S.W. 984.

71. Carter v. Towne, 1870, 103 Mass. 507; Peterson v. Martin, 1917, 138 Minn. 195, 164 N.W. 813; Pittsburg Reduction Co. v. Horton, 1908, 87 Ark. 576, 113 S.W. 647; Kingsland v. Erie County Agricultural Society, 1949, 298 N.Y. 409, 84 N.E.2d 38. Cf. Pollard v. Oklahoma City Railway Co., 1912, 36 Okl. 96, 128 P. 300.

72. See Henningsen v. Markowitz, 1928, 132 Misc. 547, 230 N.Y. 313; Clark v. E. I. Du Pont de Nemours Powder Co., 1915, 94 Kan. 268, 146 P. 320. In McGettigan v. National Bank of Washington, D.C.Cir. 1963, 320 F.2d 703, certiorari denied 375 U.S. 943, 84 S.Ct. 348, 11 L.Ed.2d 273, and Calkins v. Albi, 1967, 163 Colo. 370, 431 P.2d 17, the court refused to say as a matter of law that the negligence of the parent was a superseding cause.

73. Ford Motor Co. v. Wagoner, 1946, 183 Tenn. 392, 192 S.W.2d 840, petition dismissed 183 Tenn. 392, 192 S.W.2d 852; Foster v. Ford Motor Co., 1926, 139 Wash. 341, 246 P. 945; Ford Motor Co. v. Atcher, Ky. 1957, 310 S.W.2d 510; Stultz v. Benson Lumber Co., 1936, 6 Cal.2d 688, 59 P.2d 100; J. C. Penney Co. v.

ger which the third person has discovered.⁷⁴ Again the explanation appears to be that the responsibility is shifted, as it would be if the third party were notified of the danger in advance, and then elected to proceed. Again, however, there will be situations of extreme danger, or special relations, in which, as a matter of policy, the defendant will not be allowed to shift the responsibility, and intervening discovery of the danger will not relieve the defendant.⁷⁵

Still more difficult to explain are the occasional cases in which mere lapse of time has been held to shift the responsibility to another—as where, for example, an electric company which installed a defective transformer pole was held to be relieved by the failure of the village, for more than a year and a half, to perform its agreement to inspect and maintain the pole.⁷⁶ Such decisions are perhaps to be explained merely on the ground that there must be a terminus somewhere, short of eternity, at which the second party becomes responsible in lieu of the first. And these decisions may not be reliable indicators of where other courts, at other times, would fix that terminus.

 **WESTLAW REFERENCES**

Foreseeable Intervening Causes
topic(negligence torts & intervening /s cause* force*)

topic(negligence torts & digest(intervening /s cause* force* /p foresee!)

Unforeseeable Results of Unforeseeable Causes
topic(negligence torts) /p supersed! /s cause* factor! force*

topic(negligence torts) /p unforesee! /s result* act* consequence*

Foreseeable Results of Unforeseeable Causes
topic(negligence torts) /p foresee! /s result* act* consequence*

---

§ 45. Functions of Court and Jury

The confusion which has surrounded the whole subject of "proximate cause" has extended to the respective functions of the court and the jury. There is a decided tendency to leave every question to the bewildered jury,¹ under some vague instruction which provides no effective guide.² At the other extreme, it has been contended³ that the only question of "proximate cause" which is properly left to the jury at all is that of causation in fact, and that the limitations to be imposed upon liability are always a matter for the court.

It must be remembered that the primary function of the jury is the determination of questions of fact upon which reasonable persons might differ. The administration of rules of law, and the determination of facts upon which there could be no reasonable dif-

---

Morris, 1935, 173 Miss. 710, 163 So. 124. See Note, 1959, 48 Ky.L.J. 177.

74. Cf. Drazen v. Otis Elevator Co., 1963, 96 R.I. 114, 189 A.2d 693; Dooley v. Borough of Charleroi, 1937, 328 Pa. 57, 195 A. 6; Rulane Gas Co. v. Montgomery Ward & Co., 1949, 231 N.C. 270, 56 S.E.2d 689; Goede v. Rondorf, 1950, 231 Minn. 322, 43 N.W.2d 770; McMurdie v. Underwood, 1959, 9 Utah 2d 400, 346 P.2d 711. Otherwise where, after knowledge of the danger, the third person forgets it, instead of proceeding deliberately. Comstock v. General Motors Corp., 1959, 358 Mich. 163, 99 N.W.2d 627.

75. Clement v. Crosby & Co., 1907, 148 Mich. 293, 111 N.W. 745 (inflammable stove polish); Farley v. Edward E. Tower & Co., 1930, 271 Mass. 230, 171 N.E. 639, 86 A.L.R. 941 (inflammable beauty shop combs); Kentucky Independent Oil Co. v. Schnitzler, 1925, 208 Ky. 507, 271 S.W. 570 (gasoline in kerosene); Ferraro v. Taylor, 1936, 197 Minn. 5, 265 N.W. 829 (highly dangerous rented automobile); Trusty v. Patterson, 1930, 299 Pa. 469, 149 A. 717 (same).

76. Goar v. Village of Stephen, 1923, 157 Minn. 228, 196 N.W. 171. A very similar case is Greenwood v. Lyles & Buckner, Inc., Okl., 1958, 329 P.2d 1063.

Compare, as to putting an ill or intoxicated person off a train in a place of danger, Atchison, Topeka & Santa Fe Railway Co., v. Parry, 1903, 67 Kan. 515, 73 P. 105, with Lammers v. Pacific Electric Railway Co., 1921, 186 Cal. 379, 199 P. 523.

§ 45

1. See Green, Rationale of Proximate Cause, 1927, 122–127.

2. See Prosser, Proximate Cause in California, 1950, 38 Cal.L.Rev. 369, 419–425. Also Ray's Administrator v. Standard Oil Co., 1933, 250 Ky. 111, 61 S.W.2d 1067, to the effect that the jury should not be given any definition of "proximate cause" because the term has no definite meaning. If the courts are unable to attach a meaning to the term, what can be expected of the jury?

3. Green, Rationale of Proximate Cause, 1927, 122.

ference of opinion is in the hands of the court.[4]

To these well settled and well understood points must be added one more which is well settled but not always well understood and applied. The issue as to whether a described consequence was "foreseeable," or was "directly" caused, and the issue as to whether an intervening force was "abnormal" are to be decided as issues of fact are decided. These are not issues of fact in the sense of what happened physically, where and when, and with whose physical involvement in what ways. Rather, to decide, for example, whether a described consequence was "foreseeable" one must apply to the determined physical facts a legal standard—the concept of "foreseeability" as it is defined and explained in legal precedents. The decision to be made is an evaluative determination [5]—an evaluation of the facts as measuring up to or not measuring up to the legal standard which has been set by the precedents defining "foreseeability" as used in this legal context. Even though this evaluative determination is not a factfinding in the usual what-happened sense, it is nevertheless a question that is to be decided by a jury to the same extent, no more and no less, as fact questions are to be decided by a jury. Thus, if reasonable persons could not differ about the determination on the evidence before the court, it is decided by the trial judge, or by the appellate court. If, on the other hand, reasonable persons could differ, then the trial judge must explain the applicable legal concept to the jury, and leave to the jury the responsibility of making the evaluative determination—the application of that concept to the facts, as they find them to be. Two kinds of questions, then, are always to be decided by the jury if reasonable persons could differ about them on the evidence received at trial—first, fact questions in the usual sense and, second, evaluative applications of legal standards (such as the legal concept of "foreseeability") to the facts.

In summary, the duties of the court and jury in any case in which "proximate cause" is involved are as follows:

1. If the facts about the relationship between the plaintiff and the defendant are not in dispute, the court determines whether, given that relationship, the law imposes upon the defendant any obligation of reasonable conduct for the benefit of the plaintiff.[6] This issue is one of law and is never for the jury.

2. If the facts about the relationship between the parties are in dispute, the disputed issue as to which of various relationships existed is submitted to the jury. For example, suppose that, in a jurisdiction where it makes a difference, the plaintiff claims to have been an expense-sharing passenger in the defendant's car, and the defendant claims that the plaintiff was instead a guest passenger. The court determines (and instructs the jury about) what legal obligation applies if the plaintiff was an expense-sharing passenger, and what different legal obligation applies if the plaintiff was a guest passenger. Thus, an issue of fact as to what relationship existed is for the jury to decide; issues of law as to what legal obligations apply in each of the different relationships are for the court to decide.

3. If the facts bearing upon breach of obligation (that is, negligence) are not in dispute and reasonable persons could not differ about the application to those facts of the legal standard defining negligence, the court determines the negligence issue. But if reasonable persons might differ, either because relevant facts are in dispute or because application of the legal standard is an evaluative determination as to which reasonable persons might differ, the issue of negligence

---

4. See supra, § 37.

5. See R. Keeton, Legal Cause in the Law of Torts, 1963, 49–60.

6. See Morril v. Morril, 1922, 104 N.J.L. 557, 142 A. 337; Palsgraf v. Long Island Railroad Co., 1928, 248 N.Y. 339, 162 N.E. 99, reargument denied 249 N.Y. 511, 64 N.E. 564.

is submitted to the jury with appropriate explanation of the legal standard.

4. If the facts bearing upon the issue of causation in fact are not in dispute and reasonable persons could not differ about the application of the legal concept of causation in fact, the court determines that issue.[7] But if reasonable persons might differ, either because relevant facts are in dispute or because application of a legal concept (such as a "substantial factor" formulation)[8] is an evlauative determination as to which reasonable persons might differ, the issue is submitted to the jury[9] with appropriate instructions on the law.

5. If either party contends that elements of damages should be apportioned and in part assigned separately to different causes, the court determines whether each type of claimed damages is or is not subject to such a legal rule of apportionment.[10] If relevant facts are in dispute or if reasonable persons might differ about the amounts to be apportioned to each cause, in accordance with the legal rules determined by the court, the issue regarding apportionment is submitted to the jury.

6. If the facts bearing upon other aspects of "proximate cause" (that is, aspects other than causation in fact) are not in dispute and reasonable persons could not differ about the application to those facts of the legal concept of "proximate cause," the court determines that issue. But if reasonable persons could differ, either because relevant facts are in dispute or because application of the legal concept of "proximate cause" to the case at hand is an evaluative determination as to which reasonable persons might differ, the issue of "proximate cause" is submitted to the jury with appropriate instructions on the law.

Thus, in any case where there might be reasonable difference of opinion as to the foreseeability of a particular risk, the reasonableness of the defendant's conduct with respect to it, or the normal character of an intervening cause, the question is for the jury,[11] subject of course to suitable instructions from the court as to the legal conclusion to be drawn as the issue is determined either way. By far the greater number of the cases which have arisen have been of this description; and to this extent it may properly be said that "proximate cause is ordinarily a question of fact for the jury, to be solved by the exercise of good common sense in the consideration of the evidence of each particular case."[12]

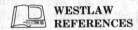
WESTLAW
REFERENCES

restatement +s torts /p jury /s function province

topic(negligence torts) /p jury /p foresee!

topic(negligence torts) /p "proximate cause" /s reasonable /s persons /s differ

---

7. Stacy v. Knickerbocker Ice Co., 1893, 84 Wis. 614, 54 N.W. 1091; Illinois Central Railroad Co. v. Wright, 1924, 135 Miss. 435, 100 So. 1.

8. See supra, § 41.

9. Reynolds v. Texas & Pacific Railway Co., 1885, 37 La.Ann. 694; Tullgren v. Amoskeag Manufacturing Co., 1926, 82 N.H. 268, 133 A. 4; Pfeifer v. Standard Gateway Theatre, 1952, 262 Wis. 229, 55 N.W.2d 29.

10. Rix v. Town of Alamogordo, 1938, 42 N.M. 325, 77 P.2d 765; Jenkins v. Pennsylvania Railroad Co., 1902, 67 N.J.L. 331, 51 A. 704; McAllister v. Pennsylvania Railroad Co., 1936, 342 Pa. 65, 187 A. 415. See infra, § 52.

11. See Gilman v. Noyes, 1876, 57 N.H. 627; Holter Hardware Co. v. Western Mortgage & Warranty Title Co., 1915, 51 Mont. 94, 149 P. 489; Henry v. City of Philadelphia, 1919, 264 Pa. 33, 107 A. 315.

12. Healy v. Hoy, 1911, 115 Minn. 321, 132 N.W. 208. There is a very good discussion of all this in Pfeifer v. Standard Gateway Theatre, 1952, 262 Wis. 229, 55 N.W.2d 29.

Chapter 8

JOINT TORTFEASORS

Table of Sections

Sec.
46. Concerted Action.
47. Joinder of Defendants.
48. Judgment and Satisfaction.
49. Release.
50. Contribution.
51. Indemnity.
52. Apportionment of Damages.

§ 46. Concerted Action

The terms "joint tort" and "joint tortfeasors" have been surrounded by no little uncertainty and confusion.[1] There have been various attempts to define them, and to propose tests [2] of one kind or another as to when they may be found to exist. An examination of the multitude of cases in which they are to be found leads to the conclusion that they have meant very different things to different courts, and often to the same court, and that much of the existing confusion is due to a failure to distinguish the different senses in which the terms are used, which often has had an unfortunate effect upon the substance of the law. Since a "joint tort" can have significance only in so far as it may involve some definite legal result, it is possible to approach the problem by distinguishing the various consequences which follow from it, and to indicate how far they are related, or unrelated, to one another.

Concerted Action

The original meaning of a "joint tort" was that of vicarious liability for concerted action. All persons who acted in concert to commit a trespass, in pursuance of a common design, were held liable for the entire

§ 46

1. See Prosser, Joint Torts and Several Liability, 1937, 25 Cal.L.Rev. 413; Jackson, Joint Torts and Several Liability, 1939, 17 Tex.L.Rev. 399.

2. Thus, the identity of a cause of action against each of two or more defendants; the existence of a common, or like, duty; whether the same evidence will support an action against each; the single, indivisible nature of the injury to the plaintiffs; identity of the facts as to time, place or result; whether the injury is direct and immediate, rather than consequential; responsibility of the defendants for the same *injuria*, as distinguished from the same *damnum*. See 1 Cooley, Torts, 4th Ed. 1932, 276–278; Clerk and Lindsell, Torts, 8th Ed. 1929, 58; Brunsden v. Humphrey, 1884, 14 Q.B.D. 141, 147; Petcoff v. Pestoret Lawrence Co., 1913, 124 Minn. 531, 144 N.W. 474; Farley v. Crystal Coal & Coke Co., 1920, 85 W.Va. 595, 102 S.E. 265; The Koursk, [1924] P. 140.

result. In such a case there was a common purpose, with mutual aid in carrying it out; in short, there was a joint enterprise, so that "all coming to do an unlawful act, and of one party, the act of one is the act of all of the same party being present." [3] Each was therefore liable for the entire damage done, although one might have battered, while another imprisoned the plaintiff, and a third stole the plaintiff's silver buttons.[4] All might be joined as defendants in the same action at law, and since each was liable for all, the jury would not be permitted to apportion the damages.[5] The rule goes back to the early days when the action of trespass was primarily a criminal action; and it has survived also in the criminal law.[6] This principle, somewhat extended beyond its original scope, is still law.[7] All those who, in pursuance of a common plan or design to commit a tortious act, actively take part in it, or further it by cooperation or request,[8] or who lend aid or encouragement to the wrongdoer,[9] or ratify and adopt the wrongdoer's acts done for their benefit,[10] are equally liable.

Express agreement is not necessary, and all that is required is that there be a tacit understanding,[11] as where two automobile drivers suddenly and without consultation decide to race their cars on the public highway.[12] There are even occasional statements that mere knowledge by each party of what the other is doing is sufficient "concert" to make each liable for the acts of the other;[13] but this seems clearly wrong. Such knowledge may very well be important evidence that a tacit understanding exists; but since there is ordinarily no duty to take affirmative steps to interfere,[14] mere pres-

3. Sir John Heydon's Case, 1613, 11 Co.Rep. 5, 77 Eng.Rep. 1150.

4. Smithson v. Garth, 1601, 3 Lev. 324, 83 Eng.Rep. 711. Cf. Clark v. Newsam, 1847, 1 Exch. 131, 154 Eng. Rep. 55; Sir Charles Stanley's Case, 1663, Kel. 86, 84 Eng.Rep. 1094.

5. Austen v. Willward, 1601, Cro.Eliz. 860, 78 Eng. Rep. 1086; Crane and Hill v. Hummerstone, 1606, Cro. Jac. 118, 79 Eng.Rep. 102; Sir John Heydon's Case, 1613, 11 Co.Rep. 5, 77 Eng.Rep. 1150; Matthews v. Coal, 1615, Cro.Jac. 384, 79 Eng.Rep. 329. Cf. Hill v. Goodchild, 1771, 5 Burr. 2790, 98 Eng.Rep. 465. A late decision to the same effect is Miller v. Singer, 1955, 131 Colo. 112, 279 P.2d 846.

6. Sir Charles Stanley's Case, 1663, Kel. 86, 84 Eng. Rep. 1094; State v. Newberg, 1929, 129 Or. 564, 278 P. 568.

7. Garrett v. Garrett, 1948, 228 N.C. 530, 46 S.E.2d 302; Moore v. Foster, 1938, 182 Miss. 15, 180 So. 73; Drake v. Keeling, 1941, 230 Iowa 1038, 299 N.W. 919; Wrabek v. Suchomel, 1920, 145 Minn. 468, 177 N.W. 764; Oliver v. Miles, 1926, 144 Miss. 852, 110 So. 666. And see the amusing opinion of Minturn, J., in Tricoli v. Centalanza, 1924, 100 N.J.L. 231, 126 A. 214, affirmed, 101 N.J.L. 170, 129 A. 923.

It makes no difference that the damage inflicted by one tortfeasor exceeds what the others might reasonably have foreseen. Thompson v. Johnson, 5th Cir. 1950, 180 F.2d 431.

8. Sourbier v. Brown, 1919, 188 Ind. 554, 123 N.E. 802; Kirby Lumber Co. v. Karpel, 5th Cir. 1956, 233 F.2d 373; Thompson v. Fehlig Brothers Box & Lumber Co., Mo.App.1941, 155 S.W.2d 279; Johnson v. Sartain, 1962, 46 Hawaii 112, 375 P.2d 229, rehearing denied, 46 Hawaii 134, 375 P.2d 856; Jaffray v. Hill, 1963, 41 Ill. App.2d 460, 191 N.E.2d 399.

9. Daingerfield v. Thompson, 1880, 74 Va. (33 Grat.) 136; Hilmes v. Stroebel, 1883, 59 Wis. 74, 17 N.W. 539; Thompson v. Johnson, 5th Cir. 1950, 180 F.2d 431; Knott v. Litton, La.App.1955, 81 So.2d 124; Thomas v. Doorley, 1959, 175 Cal.App.2d 545, 346 P.2d 491. As to what is meant by encouragement, see Bird v. Lynn, 1850, 49 Ky. (10 B.Mon.) 422; Brown v. Perkins, 1861, 83 Mass. (1 Allen) 89.

10. Stull v. Porter, 1921, 100 Or. 514, 196 P. 1116; Weinberg Co. v. Bixby, 1921, 185 Cal. 87, 196 P. 25; see Myers v. Shipley, 1922, 140 Md. 380, 116 A. 645.

11. Patnode v. Westenhaver, 1902, 114 Wis. 460, 90 N.W. 467; Stapler v. Parler, 1925, 212 Ala. 644, 103 So. 573; Troop v. Dew, 1921, 150 Ark. 560, 234 S.W. 992; Daggy v. Miller, 1917, 180 Iowa 1146, 162 N.W. 854; Larimer & Weld Irrigation Co. v. Walker, 1918, 65 Colo. 320, 176 P. 282.

12. Bierczynski v. Rogers, Del.1968, 239 A.2d 218; Nelson v. Nason, 1961, 343 Mass. 220, 177 N.E.2d 887; Lemons v. Kelly, 1964, 239 Or. 354, 397 P.2d 784; Skipper v. Hartley, 1963, 242 S.C. 221, 130 S.E.2d 486; Anderson v. Esposito, 1966, 90 N.J.Super. 170, 216 A.2d 607. Compare, as to physicians acting in concert in negligent medical treatment, Sprinkle v. Lemley, 1966, 243 Or. 521, 414 P.2d 797.

13. Moses v. Town of Morgantown, 1926, 192 N.C. 102, 133 S.E. 421; see Sloggy v. Dilworth, 1888, 38 Minn. 179, 36 N.W. 451; Bowman v. Humphrey, 1904, 124 Iowa 744, 100 N.W. 854. Knowledge of what another is doing may of course be important in determining the tortious character of the defendant's own conduct. See Folsom v. Apple River Log-Driving Co., 1877, 41 Wis. 602, McKay v. Southern Bell Telegraph & Telephone Co., 1896, 111 Ala. 337, 19 So. 695.

14. See infra, § 56.

ence at the commission of the wrong, or failure to object to it, is not enough to charge one with responsibility.[15] It is, furthermore, essential that each particular defendant who is to be charged with responsibility shall be proceeding tortiously, which is to say with the intent requisite to committing a tort, or with negligence. One who innocently, and carefully, does an act which happens to further the tortious purpose of another is not acting in concert with the other.[16]

It is in connection with such vicarious liability that the word conspiracy is often used. The original writ of conspiracy was employed only in the case of combinations of two or more persons to abuse legal procedure, and was the forerunner of the action for malicious prosecution.[17] This was replaced at a later date by an action on the case in the nature of conspiracy, and the word gradually came to be used to extend liability in tort, as well as crime, beyond the active wrongdoer to those who have merely planned, assisted or encouraged the active wrongdoer. There has been a good deal of discussion as to whether conspiracy is to be regarded as a separate tort in itself.[18] On the one hand, it is clear that the mere agreement to do a wrongful act can never alone amount to a tort, whether or not it may be a crime; and that some act must be committed by one of the parties in pursuance of the agreement, which is itself a tort.[19] "The gist of the action is not the conspiracy charged, but the tort working damage to the plaintiff."[20] It is only where means are employed,[21] or purposes are accomplished,[22] which are themselves tortious, that the conspirators who have not acted but have promoted the act will be held liable. On the other hand, it now seems generally agreed, although there has been authority to the contrary, that there are certain types of conduct, such as boycotts,[23] in which the element of combination adds such a power of coercion, undue influence or restraint of trade, that it makes unlawful, when done in combination, acts which one person alone might legitimately do. It is perhaps pointless to debate whether in such a case the combination or conspiracy becomes itself the tort, or whether it merely gives a tortious character to the acts done in furtherance of it. On either basis, it is a determining factor in liability.

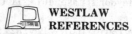
WESTLAW REFERENCES

di joint tortfeasors

Concerted Action

joint +2 tort tortfeasor* /p act*** /3 concert**
joint +2 tort tortfeasor* /s knowledge consent!

§ 47. Joinder of Defendants

A second meaning of a joint tort is that two or more persons may be joined as defendants in the same action at law. The common law rules as to joinder were ex-

---

15. Duke v. Feldman, 1967, 245 Md. 454, 226 A.2d 345; Ramirez v. Chavez, 1951, 71 Ariz. 239, 226 P.2d 143; Bukowski v. Juranek, 1948, 227 Minn. 313, 35 N.W.2d 427; Heisler v. Heisler, 1911, 151 Iowa 503, 131 N.W. 676; Rhinehart v. Whitehead, 1885, 64 Wis. 42, 24 N.W. 401.

16. Day v. Walton, 1955, 199 Tenn. 10, 281 S.W.2d 685; Knight v. Western Auto Supply Co., 1946, 239 Mo. App. 643, 193 S.W.2d 771.

17. Winfield, History of Conspiracy, 1921, ch. II.

18. See Charlesworth, Conspiracy as a Ground of Liability in Tort, 1920, 36 L.Q.Rev. 38; Burdick, Conspiracy as a Crime and as a Tort, 1907, 7 Col.L.Rev. 229; Burdick, The Tort of Conspiracy, 1908, 8 Col.L. Rev. 117.

19. Beechley v. Mulville, 1897, 102 Iowa 602, 70 N.W. 107, 71 N.W. 428, rehearing denied 102 Iowa 602, 71 N.W. 42; Delz v. Winfree, 1891, 80 Tex. 400, 16 S.W. 111; Robertson v. Parks, 1892, 76 Md. 118, 24 A. 411; City of Boston v. Simmons, 1890, 150 Mass. 461, 23 N.E. 210; Van Horn v. Van Horn, 1894, 56 N.J.L. 318, 28 A. 669.

20. James v. Evans, 3d Cir. 1906, 149 F. 136, 140.

21. Wickersham v. Johnson, 1873, 51 Mo. 313; Van Horn v. Van Horn, 1890, 52 N.J.L. 284, 20 A. 485; see Fleming v. Dane, 1939, 304 Mass. 46, 22 N.E.2d 609.

22. White v. White, 1907, 132 Wis. 121, 111 N.W. 1116; Hutton v. Watters, 1915, 132 Tenn. 527, 179 S.W. 134; Hudgens v. Chamberlain, 1911, 161 Cal. 710, 120 P. 422; Newton Co. v. Erickson, 1911, 70 Misc. 291, 126 N.Y.S. 949.

23. See infra, § 130. Cf. Gregory v. Duke of Brunswick, 1844, 6 M. & G. 205, 1 C. & K. 24, 134 Eng. Rep. 866; Collins v. Cronin, 1887, 117 Pa. 35, 11 A. 869; Morris Run Coal Co. v. Barclay Coal Co., 1871, 68 Pa. 173; Place v. Minster, 1875, 65 N.Y. 89.

tremely strict. Joinder was limited to cases of concerted action, where a mutual agency might be found. Given such joint responsibility, the identity of the cause of action against each defendant was clear.[1] The joinder was merely permitted, and was not compulsory, and the defendants might each be sued severally for the entire damages; but the plaintiff could recover only one judgment, because it was considered that the plaintiff had but one cause of action against the several parties.[2] Where the defendants did not act in concert, the English courts consistently [3] refused to allow them to be joined, even though they had done acts identical in character, which had combined in their effect to cause a single, more or less indivisible injury to the plaintiff. Thus two persons who had independently uttered the same slanderous words could not be joined,[4] nor could successive converters of the same goods,[5] nor those who separately blocked the highway with their vans and prevented access to the plaintiff's property.[6]

The early American cases adopted the same position, although they showed some tendency to liberalize it.[7] Joinder was permitted where the defendants had acted in concert,[8] but not where the acts were independent.[9] A different rule developed in equity suits, where the purpose was the prevention of a wrong, and it was not necessary for such prevention to ascertain what particular share of damage each defendant had inflicted or threatened to inflict.[10] The attitude of the American courts toward joinder of parties was materially altered, however, by the passage of the Field Code of Procedure in New York in 1848, and similar codes in a majority of the other states. The codes contained a provision, intentionally framed to permit, at law as in equity, the complete settlement of all questions connected with a transaction in a single suit,[11] to the effect that "Any person may be made a defendant

§ 47

1. Crane and Hill v. Hummerstone, 1606, Cro.Jac. 118, 79 Eng.Rep. 102; Sir John Heydon's Case, 1613, 11 Co.Rep. 5, 77 Eng.Rep. 1150; Austen v. Willward, 1601, Cro.Eliz. 860, 78 Eng.Rep. 1086; Matthews v. Coal, 1615, Cro.Jac. 384, 79 Eng.Rep. 329.

2. Brown v. Wootton, 1600, Cro.Jac. 73, 79 Eng. Rep. 62; Barlye v. Martin, 1647, Sty. 20, 82 Eng.Rep. 498; Mitchell v. Tarbutt, 1794, 5 Term Rep. 649, 101 Eng.Rep. 362; Sutton v. Clarke, 1815, 6 Taunt. 29, 128 Eng.Rep. 943; Brinsmead v. Harrison, 1872, L.R. 7 C.P. 547.

3. A servant and the master vicariously liable for the servant's acts could be joined, but of course it is obvious that each is held responsible for the same act. Cf. Wilson v. Tumman, 1843, 6 M. & G. 236, 134 Eng. Rep. 879. In Arneil v. Peterson, [1931] A.C. 560, the principle was extended to two defendants whose dogs together killed sheep; but the court was at some pains to lay stress on the fact that the dogs, if not the defendants, were acting in concert.

4. Chamberlain v. White and Goodwin, 1617, Cro. Jac. 647, 79 Eng.Rep. 558.

5. Nicoll v. Glennie, 1817, 1 M. & S. 588, 105 Eng. Rep. 220. Cf. Morris v. Robinson, 1824, 3 B. & C. 196, 107 Eng.Rep. 706.

6. Sadler v. Great Western Railroad Co., [1896] A.C. 450. Accord: Thompson v. London County Council, [1899] 1 Q.B. 840 (one defendant negligently excavated, another left its water main insufficiently stopped, and plaintiff's property was undermined); The Koursk, [1924] P. 140 (collision between two vessels, injuring a third. The court notes the occasional use of the term "joint tortfeasor" to signify nothing more than concurrent liability for the same loss).

7. Thus Wright v. Cooper, Vt.1802, 1 Tyler, 425 (two dams flooding plaintiff's land); Ellis v. Howard, 1845, 17 Vt. 330; Stone v. Dickinson, 1862, 87 (5 Allen) Mass. 29 (officers executing process on behalf of different parties).

8. Halsey v. Woodruff, 1830, 26 Mass. (9 Pick.) 555; Williams v. Sheldon, N.Y.1833, 10 Wend. 654; Fuller v. Chamberlain, 1846, 52 Mass. (11 Metc.) 503.

9. Russell v. Tomlinson, 1817, 2 Conn. 206; Adams v. Hall, 1829, 2 Vt. 9; Hopkins v. Hersey, 1841, 20 Me. 449; Webb v. Cecil, 1848, 48 Ky. (9 B.Mon.) 198; Bard v. Yohn, 1856, 26 Pa. 482.

This antique procedural rule survived as late as 1939 is Desforge v. American-Bristol Home Building Association, 1939, 63 R.I. 305, 7 A.2d 788, where the court refused to allow joinder of a lessor and a lessee through whose breach of separate duties as to the condition of the premises the plaintiff was injured.

10. Woodruff v. North Bloomfield Gravel Mining Co., C.C.Cal.1883, 8 Sawy. 628, 16 F. 25; Miller v. Highland Ditch Co., 1891, 87 Cal. 430, 25 P. 550; Kelley v. Boettcher, 8th Cir. 1898, 85 F. 55.

11. See First Report of New York Commissioners on Pleading and Practice, 1848, 124; Clark, Code Pleading, 2d Ed.1947, §§ 60, 61; Note, 1924, 33 Yale L.J. 817; Yankwich, Joinder of Parties, 1929, 2 So.Cal.L. Rev. 315; Harris, Joinder of Parties and Causes, 1930, 36 W.Va.L.Q. 192.

who has or claims an interest in the controversy adverse to the plaintiff or who is a necessary party to the complete determination or settlement of the questions involved therein."

This provision received, at the outset, most uncharitable treatment at the hands of the courts, which tended to follow the earlier precedents,[12] and to preserve the rule as to concerted action as the test of permissive joinder. The chief reason for this failure to accomplish the manifest intention of the code was the retention of the common law notion that the same "cause of action" must affect all of the joined defendants.[13] Nevertheless with the passage of time the code provision has had its effect, and joinder has been permitted in a number of situations where the acts of two defendants have combined to produce a single, indivisible result. Thus in the common case where the vehicles of two defendants collide and injure the plaintiff, it is held in most jurisdictions that there may be joinder under the codes.[14] The same liberality has been extended to other similar situations, where the negligence of both defendants has been necessary to produce a single injury which from its nature obviously cannot be apportioned.[15]

Joinder usually is permitted where it can be found that the defendants were under a common duty, as in the case of the fall of a party wall,[16] or the failure of two defendants to keep property in repair.[17] There has been much rather pointless argument as to whether, in a given case, the duties are sufficiently identical to permit joinder; and some cases, for example, refuse to allow a city and a property owner responsible for the condition of a sidewalk to be sued together.[18] If joinder is merely a matter of procedural convenience, no reason is apparent for refusing to permit it in such a case, and the modern weight of authority allows

---

12. See for example Cogswell v. Murphy, 1877, 46 Iowa 44 (trespassing cattle); Blaisdell v. Stephens, 1879, 14 Nev. 17 (flooding land); Farley v. Crystal Coal & Coke Co., 1920, 85 W.Va. 595, 102 S.E. 265 (pollution of stream); Johnson v. City of Fairmont, 1933, 188 Minn. 451, 247 N.W. 572 (same); Key v. Armour Fertilizer Works, 1916, 18 Ga.App. 472, 89 S.E. 593 (smoke nuisance).

13. Clark Code Pleading, 2d Ed.1947, § 61. Thus in Ader v. Blau, 1924, 241 N.Y. 7, 148 N.E. 771, it was held that an original tortfeasor and a surgeon who negligently treated the injured man could not be joined, since there was a distinct "cause of action" against each defendant. Accord: Bost v. Metcalfe, 1941, 219 N.C. 607, 14 S.E.2d 648; cf. Rose v. Sprague, 1933, 248 Ky. 635, 59 S.W.2d 554 (successive physicians); Kniess v. Armour & Co., 1938, 134 Ohio St. 432, 17 N.E.2d 734, (meat packer and dealer); Dorsey v. Material Service Corp., 1956, 9 Ill.App.2d 428, 133 N.E.2d 730 (damage from three different blasters). See criticisms in Notes, 1925, 35 Yale L.J. 85; 1925, 25 Col.L.Rev. 975; 1925, 11 Corn.L.Q. 113.

14. See cases cited supra, § 41. Also Tillman v. Bellamy, 1955, 242 N.C. 211, 87 S.E.2d 253; Way v. Waterloo, Cedar Falls & Northern Railroad Co., 1947, 239 Iowa 244, 29 N.W.2d 867; Meyer v. Cincinnati Street Railway Co., 1952, 157 Ohio St. 38, 104 N.E.2d 173; Sutterfield v. District Court, 1968, 165 Colo. 225, 438 P.2d 236 (chain collision). Peters v. Johnson, 1928, 124 Or. 237, 264 P. 459. Cf. Kirby Lumber Corp. v. Walters, Tex.Civ.App.1955, 277 S.W.2d 796 (several defendants putting mud on highway, plaintiff lost control); De Bardelaben v. Stallings, 4th Cir. 1955, 226 F.2d 951 (truck left on highway, motorist swerved to avoid it); Carpini v. Pittsburgh & Weirton Bus Co., 3d Cir. 1954, 216 F.2d 404 (manufacturer and operator of bus); Tracy v. Rublein, 1955, 342 Mich. 623, 70 N.W.2d 819 (truck stalled on highway, other driver).

15. Carstesen v. Town of Stratford, 1896, 67 Conn. 428, 35 A. 276 (horse fell successively into two excavations); Fleming v. Arkansas Fuel Co., 1957, 231 S.C. 42, 97 S.E.2d 76 (three successive sellers of liquid which exploded); Cassity v. Brady, 1958, 182 Kan. 381, 321 P.2d 171 (successive physicians); Robertson v. Chicago, Burlington & Quincy Railroad Co., 1922, 108 Neb. 569, 188 N.W. 190 (two defendants delaying shipment); Smith v. McDowell Furniture Co., 1941, 220 N.C. 155, 16 S.E.2d 685 (motorist blinded by steam).

16. Johnson v. Chapman, 1897, 43 W.Va. 639, 28 S.E. 744; Klauder v. McGrath, 1860, 35 Pa. 128; Simmons v. Everson, 1891, 124 N.Y. 319, 26 N.E. 911.

17. Lindsay v. Acme Cement Plaster Co., 1922, 220 Mich. 367, 190 N.W. 275. Cf. Schaffer v. Pennsylvania Railroad Co., 7th Cir. 1939, 101 F.2d 369; Wisconsin Central Railroad Co. v. Ross, 1892, 142 Ill. 9, 31 N.E. 412; Doeg v. Cook, 1899, 126 Cal. 213, 58 P. 707; Walton, Witten & Graham Co. v. Miller's Administratrix, 1909, 109 Va. 210, 63 S.E. 458; Nelson v. Illinois Central Railroad Co., 1910, 98 Miss. 295, 53 So. 619.

18. Bennett v. Fifield, 1880, 13 R.I. 139, 43 Am.Rep. 17; Morris v. Woodburn, 1897, 57 Ohio St. 330, 48 N.E. 1097; Wiest v. City of Philadelphia, 1901, 200 Pa. 148, 49 A. 891. Cf. Cole v. Lippitt, 1900, 22 R.I. 31, 46 A. 43. The reason often given is the possibility that one defendant may be entitled to indemnity from the other. But if joinder is a matter of procedural convenience, it should not bar adjustment of the rights of the defendants, among themselves. Schneider v. City Council of Augusta, 1903, 118 Ga. 610, 45 S.E. 459.

it.[19] Similarly, in modern times the joinder of a servant and the master vicariously liable for the servant's tort is generally permitted.[20]

The enactment of statutes similar to the code provisions and the adoption of liberalizing rules of procedure [21] have led to further relaxation of the earlier rule.[22] Joinder has been allowed where, even though the defendants clearly have committed separate, independent wrongs which resulted in distinct injuries, the difficulty of determining questions of fact, such as the apportionment of damages, has made joinder "necessary;" [23] other courts, however, have declined to adopt such a liberal rule of joinder.[24] It is highly unfortunate that the common law concept of the identity of a "cause of action" is carried over to defeat the obvious intent of the statutes. The advantages of joinder are obvious; [25] and the rules against misjoinder are rules of convenience and expediency, and should be construed in the light of the broader policy against multiplicity of suits.[26] It is still more unfortunate that the uncertainty of procedural rules should have affected the substantive liability of the defendants.

When joinder is permitted, it is not compelled, and each tortfeasor may be sued severally, and held responsible for the damage caused, although other wrongdoers have contributed to it. The defendant cannot compel the plaintiff to make the others parties to the action,[27] or complain because they have not been joined,[28] or because the action against one is dismissed out of court; [29] nor is it a defense that the defendant's own par-

---

19. City of Peoria v. Simpson, 1884, 110 Ill. 294; Fortmeyer v. National Biscuit Co., 1911, 116 Minn. 158, 133 N.W. 461; Scearce v. Mayor of Gainesville, 1925, 33 Ga.App. 411, 126 S.E. 883; Rowe v. Richards, 1913, 32 S.D. 66, 142 N.W. 664.

20. Daniels v. Parker, 1956, 119 Vt. 348, 126 A.2d 85; Feger v. Concrete Materials & Construction Co., 1951, 172 Kan. 75, 238 P.2d 708; Skala v. Lehon, 1931, 343 Ill. 602, 175 N.E. 832; Putnam Memorial Hospital v. Allen, 2d Cir. 1929, 34 F.2d 927; Allen v. Trester, 1924, 112 Neb. 515, 199 N.W. 841. See Notes, 1942, 26 Minn.L.Rev. 730; 1959, 44 Iowa L.Rev. 542.

21. See Fed.R.Civ.P. 18–25.

22. See for example Arnst v. Estes, 1939, 136 Me. 272, 8 A.2d 201; Carlton v. Boudar, 1916, 118 Va. 521, 88 S.E. 174; Matthews v. Delaware, Lackawanna & Western Railroad Co., 1893, 56 N.J.L. 34, 27 A. 919; Feneff v. Boston & Maine Railroad Co., 1907, 196 Mass. 575, 82 N.E. 705; Smith v. Yellow Cab Co., 1926, 285 Pa. 229, 132 A. 124.

23. For example, Gunder v. Tibbitts, 1899, 153 Ind. 591, 55 N.E. 762; Sherlock v. Manwaren, 1924, 208 App.Div. 538, 203 N.Y.S. 709. But the former case arrives at the extraordinary conclusion that the doctor who performs an abortion is liable for the original seduction!

24. McGannon v. Chicago & North Western Railroad Co., 1924, 160 Minn. 143, 199 N.W. 894; Miller v. Highland Ditch Co., 1891, 87 Cal. 430, 25 P. 550; Albrecht v. St. Hedwig's Roman Catholic Benevolent Society, 1919, 205 Mich. 395, 171 N.W. 461; Ader v. Blau, 1925, 241 N.Y. 7, 148 N.E. 771; White v. Arizona Eastern Railroad Co., 1924, 26 Ariz. 590, 229 P. 101.

25. The result of the refusal to permit joinder is that: (1) in the separate suits it is open to each defendant to prove that the other was solely responsible, or responsible for the greater part of the damage, and so defeat or minimize recovery; (2) it is equally open to the plaintiff to prove that each defendant was solely responsible, or responsible for the greater part of the damage, and so recover excessive compensation; (3) the two verdicts will seldom have any relation to one another; (4) different witnesses may be called in the two suits, or the same witness may tell different stories, so that the full truth is told in neither; (5) neither defendant may cross-examine the other, or the other's witnesses, and plaintiff may not cross-examine both in one action; (6) time and expense are doubled.

In some jurisdictions, these difficulties have been obviated by consolidation of the actions, usually at the discretion of the court. But if this is possible, why not permit joinder in the first instance, and treat it as the equivalent of consolidation? See Snow v. Rudolph, 1910, 62 Tex.Civ.App. 235, 131 S.W. 249; Note, 1920, 18 Mich.L.Rev. 708.

26. See Great Southern Life Insurance Co. v. Dolan, Tex.Civ.App.1922, 239 S.W. 236, reversed on other grounds in, Tex.Com.App.1924, 262 S.W. 475.

27. Hoosier Stone Co. v. McCain, 1892, 133 Ind. 231, 31 N.E. 956; Melichar v. Frank, 1959, 78 S.D. 58, 98 N.W.2d 345; Sox v. Hertz Corp., D.S.C.1967, 262 F.Supp. 531. Cf. Johns v. Castles, 1956, 229 S.C. 51, 91 S.E.2d 721 (having sued only one, plaintiff may not be heard to demand joinder of the others).

28. Berkson v. Kansas City Cable Railway Co., 1898, 144 Mo. 211, 45 S.W. 1119; Coleman v. Bennett, 1902, 111 Tenn. 705, 69 S.W. 734; Farmers' State Bank v. Jeske, 1924, 50 N.D. 813, 197 N.W. 854; Tower v. Camp, 1925, 103 Conn. 41, 130 A. 86.

29. Arnst v. Estes, 1939, 136 Me. 272, 8 A.2d 201; Yellow Cab Co. of Nashville v. Pewitt, 1958, 44 Tenn. App. 572, 316 S.W.2d 17; May v. Bradford, Mo.1963, 369 S.W.2d 225; Farmers' State Bank v. Jeske, 1924, 50 N.D. 813, 197 N.W. 854; Eyak River Packing Co. v.

ticipation was slight in comparison with that of others not joined.[30] Since each is severally liable, a verdict in favor of one will not discharge the others,[31] either in the same or in separate suits,[32] unless, as in the case of vicarious liability, it is clear that one cannot be discharged without also discharging the other.[33] In such a case it is common practice to accept the verdict for the defendant, and deny the plaintiff any recovery; but since the inconsistency calls into question the validity of one verdict as much as the other, much the preferable procedure is to refuse to accept the entire verdict from the jury, or if it be too late for that, to order a complete new trial.[34]

Entire Liability

Quite apart from any question of vicarious liability or joinder of defendants, the common law developed a separate principle, that a defendant might be liable for the entire loss sustained by the plaintiff, even though the defendant's act concurred or combined with that of another wrongdoer to produce the result—or, as the courts have put it, that the defendant is liable for all consequences proximately caused by the defendant's wrongful act. The rule was first applied in actions against a single defendant, where there was no concert of action, and therefore no joinder would have been possible, and there was no suggestion of a "joint tort."[35] The extent to which such entire liability has been imposed is considered elsewhere.[36]

In England, such concurrent but independent wrongdoers were not confused with joint tortfeasors because there could be no joinder in the absence of concerted action.[37] They had to be sued separately, and although each might be liable for the entire loss, factfinders were under no compulsion to return verdicts for the same amount. Under the more liberal American rules as to

---

Huglen, 1927, 143 Wash. 229, 255 P. 123, judgment affirmed on rehearing, 143 Wash. 229, 257 P. 638.

Likewise vacation or reversal of a judgment against one joint tortfeasor does not affect the judgments with respect to the others. Chmielewski v. Marich, 1954, 2 Ill.2d 568, 119 N.E.2d 247; Regent Co-op Equity Exchange v. Johnston's Fuel Liners, Inc., N.D.1964, 130 N.W.2d 165 (new trial). One alone may appeal. Wright v. Royse, 1963, 43 Ill.App.2d 267, 193 N.E.2d 340; see Note, 1966, 31 Mo.L.Rev. 141.

30. Wrabek v. Suchomel, 1920, 145 Minn. 468, 177 N.W. 764; Wisecarver & Stone v. Chicago, Rock Island & Pacific Railway Co., 1909, 141 Iowa 121, 119 N.W. 532; Riverside Cotton Mills v. Lainer, 1903, 102 Va. 148, 45 S.E. 875; City of Atlanta v. Chattanooga Foundry & Pipeworks, 6th Cir. 1903, 127 F. 23.

31. Doran v. Chicago, St. Paul, Minneapolis & Omaha Railway Co., 1915, 128 Minn. 193, 150 N.W. 800; Garrison v. Everett, 1924, 112 Neb. 230, 199 N.W. 30; Miller v. Alaska Steam Ship Co., 1926, 139 Wash. 207, 246 P. 296; Wood v. Rolfe, 1924, 128 Wash. 55, 221 P. 982; San Antonio Gas Co. v. Singleton, 1900, 24 Tex. Civ.App. 341, 59 S.W. 920, error refused.

32. Nelson v. Illinois Central Railway Co., 1910, 98 Miss. 295, 53 So. 619; City of Tulsa v. Wells, 1920, 79 Okl. 39, 191 P. 186.

33. Pangburn v. Buick Motor Co., 1914, 211 N.Y. 228, 105 N.E. 423; Walker v. St. Louis-San Francisco Railroad Co., 1926, 214 Ala. 492, 108 So. 388; Chesapeake & Ohio Railroad Co. v. Williams' Administratrix 1945, 300 Ky. 850, 190 S.W.2d 549; Eckleberry v. Kaiser Foundation Northern Hospital, 1961, 226 Or. 616, 359 P.2d 1090; Jentick v. Pacific Gas & Electric Co., 1941, 18 Cal.2d 117, 114 P.2d 343. The same principle prevents verdicts differing in amount in the same action. Goines v. Pennsylvania Railroad Co., 1957, 3 A.D.2d 307, 160 N.Y.S.2d 39, reargument denied, 4 A.D.2d 831, 166 N.Y.S.2d 303; Biel, Inc. v. Kirsch, 1958, 130 Ind.App. 46, 153 N.E.2d 140; cf. Miller v. Singer, 1955, 131 Colo. 112, 279 P.2d 846 (concerted action). See Note, 1964, 17 Okl.L.Rev. 432.

Mississippi, however, has a unique rule permitting inconsistent verdicts as to master and servant, on the ground that either could have been sued and held liable separately. Gulf Refining Co. v. Myrick, 1954, 220 Miss. 429, 71 So.2d 217; Capital Transport Co. v. McDuff, Miss.1975, 319 So.2d 658. See Note, 1955, 26 Miss.L.J. 265.

34. Monumental Motor Tours v. Eaton, 1945, 184 Va. 311, 35 S.E.2d 105; Berger v. Podolsky Brothers, 1950, 360 Mo. 239, 227 S.W.2d 695; Begin v. Liederbach Bus Co., 1926, 167 Minn. 84, 208 N.W. 546; Tolley v. Engert, 1925, 71 Cal.App. 439, 235 P. 651.

35. Dixon v. Bell, 1816, 5 M. & S. 198, 105 Eng.Rep. 1023 (defendant gave loaded gun to young servant, who negligently shot plaintiff); Illidge v. Goodwin, 1831, 5 C. & P. 190, 172 Eng.Rep. 934 (defendant left horse unguarded in street, passing stranger whipped it); Lynch v. Nurdin, 1841, 1 Q.B. 29, 113 Eng.Rep. 1041 (defendant left horse and cart in street, and boy made it move); cf. Hume v. Oldacre, 1816, 1 Stark. 351, 171 Eng.Rep. 494; King v. Moore, 1832, 3 B. & Ad. 184, 110 Eng.Rep. 68; Guille v. Swan, N.Y.1822, 19 Johns. 381.

36. See supra, § 41, and infra, § 52.

37. Sadler v. Great Western Railroad Co., [1896] A.C. 450; Thompson v. London County Council, [1899] 1 Q.B. 840; The Koursk, [1924] P. 140.

joinder, defendants whose negligence has concurred to produce a single result have been joined in one action, and by loose usage have been called joint tortfeasors.[38]

One immediate result has been to confuse joinder of parties with liability for entire damages, and to crystallize the prejudice of the courts against joinder of defendants liable for separate results. Another has been the rigid enforcement of the common law rule that a verdict for one sum must be returned against all those who are found liable in the joint action.[39] This rule, which developed in cases of concerted action, was of course reasonable where the act of one was considered the act of all, and no basis could be found to permit the jury to apportion the damages.[40] It has unfortunate results where joinder is permitted only as a matter of convenience, and it is clear that not all of those who are "necessary parties to the complete determination of the questions involved" are liable for the same damages. Thus an earlier tortfeasor may be liable for the damages inflicted by a later one, even though the later wrongdoer is not liable for the earlier damage;[41] and yet there are obvious reasons of convenience for the joinder of both defendants in a single action.[42] The rule against separate verdicts has meant either that the courts insist upon separate suits,[43] or what is even worse, that joinder is permitted and each defendant is held liable for the entire damage.[44] No reason can be found for refusing to allow joinder without making the parties "joint" for any other purpose than the convenient trial of the case.

Where the jury improperly returns verdicts for separate amounts against two or more defendants, various rules have been applied.[45] The plaintiff is permitted by some courts to take judgment against all for the higher damages,[46] and by others to enter judgment against one defendant and dismiss the action against the others.[47] A few courts have adopted the most reasonable solution, which is to return the case to the jury with instructions to render a single verdict.[48]

38. Carolina, Clinchfield & Ohio Railway Co. v. Hill, 1916, 119 Va. 416, 89 S.E. 902; Riley v. Industrial Finance Service Co., 1957, 157 Tex. 306, 302 S.W.2d 652; Tracy v. Rublein, 1955, 342 Mich. 623, 70 N.W.2d 819; De Bardelaben v. Stallings, 4th Cir. 1955, 226 F.2d 951; Carpini v. Pittsburgh & Weirton Bus Co., 3d Cir. 1954, 216 F.2d 404.

39. See Note, 1928, 14 Va.L.Rev. 677; Marriott v. Williams, 1908, 152 Cal. 705, 93 P. 875; Jordan v. Koerth, 1933, 212 Wis. 109, 248 N.W. 918; Ross v. Pennsylvania Railroad Co., 1927, 5 N.J.Misc. 811, 138 A. 383; Lake Erie & Western Railroad Co. v. Halleck, 1922, 78 Ind.App. 495, 136 N.E. 39; Hall v. McClure, 1923, 112 Kan. 752, 212 P. 875.

The length to which the rule is carried is illustrated by Fort Worth & New Orleans Railway Co. v. Enos, 1897, 15 Tex.Civ.App. 673, 39 S.W. 1095, where the power of the jury to assess damages severally was denied, even though the acts and defenses of the defendants were so distinct that each was held entitled to a separate continuance.

40. Austen v. Willward, 1601, Cro.Eliz. 860, 78 Eng. Rep. 1086; Crane and Hill v. Hummerstone, 1606, Cro. Jac. 118, 79 Eng.Rep. 102; Sir John Heydon's Case, 1613, 11 Co.Rep. 5, 77 Eng.Rep. 1150; Matthews v. Coal, 1615, Cro.Jac. 384, 79 Eng.Rep. 329; Hill v. Goodchild, 1771, 5 Burr. 2790, 98 Eng.Rep. 465.

41. See infra, § 52.

42. Compare the procedure in La Bella v. Brown, 1926, 103 N.J.L. 491, 133 A. 82, affirmed, 1927, 103 N.J.L. 491, 135 A. 918, where the actions were consolidated by agreement and separate verdicts were returned. Also Young v. Dille, 1923, 127 Wash. 398, 220 P. 782; and see Sherlock v. Manwaren, 1924, 208 App. Div. 538, 203 N.Y.S. 709.

43. Cf. Albrecht v. St. Hedwig's Roman Catholic Benevolent Society, 1919, 205 Mich. 395, 171 N.W. 461; McGannon v. Chicago & North Western Railroad Co., 1924, 160 Minn. 143, 199 N.W. 894; Schafer v. Ostmann, 1910, 148 Mo.App. 644, 129 S.W. 63; Barton v. Barton, 1906, 119 Mo.App. 507, 94 S.W. 574; Ader v. Blau, 1925, 241 N.Y. 7, 148 N.E. 771.

44. Sawdey v. R. W. Rasmussen Co., 1930, 107 Cal. App. 467, 290 P. 684; Owens v. Cerullo, 1931, 9 N.J. Misc. 776, 155 A. 759. Cf. Gunder v. Tibbitts, 1899, 153 Ind. 591, 55 N.E. 762.

45. See Notes, 1928, 14 Va.L.Rev. 677; 1938, 22 Minn.L.Rev. 569.

46. Halsey v. Woodruff, 1830, 26 Mass. (9 Pick.) 555; Kinsey v. William Spencer & Son Corp., 1937, 165 Misc. 143, 300 N.Y.S. 391; Rochester v. Anderson, 1809, 4 Ky. (1 Bibb.) 439.

47. Koltz v. Jahaaske, 1942, 312 Ill.App. 623, 38 N.E.2d 973; Whitney v. Tuttle, 1936, 178 Okl. 170, 62 P.2d 508; Warren v. Westrup, 1890, 44 Minn. 237, 46 N.W. 347; Crawford v. Morris, 1848, 46 Va. (5 Grat.) 90.

48. City of Tuscaloosa v. Fair, 1936, 232 Ala. 129, 167 So. 276; Forslund v. Swenson, 1923, 110 Neb. 188, 192 N.W. 649; Chrudinsky v. Evans, 1917, 85 Or. 548,

A defendant, however, usually is not permitted to complain at all. The reason given is that any defendant might have been sued severally, and the smaller verdict against another defendant does not relieve one of one's own liability, as determined by the jury.[49]

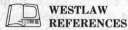

WESTLAW REFERENCES

joint +2 tort tortfeasor* /p necessary /s party parties

digest(joinder & multiple joint /s tortfeasor*)

Entire Liability

272k15

joint /s tortfeasor* /s individual** entire /s liabl!

§ 48. Judgment and Satisfaction

The English rule, until it was altered by statute[1] in 1935, was that the plaintiff could obtain but one judgment on a joint tort. Since the act of each tortfeasor was the act of all, it was considered that there was only one cause of action, which was "reduced to certainty" or merged in the judgment, and judgment against one alone, even though unsatisfied, barred any later action against another.[2] But if the defendants had not acted in concert, the tort was not joint, there were two or more causes of action, and an unsatisfied judgment against one did not prevent a later action against the others.[3] At the same time the courts developed a quite distinct principle that the plaintiff was entitled to but one compensation for the loss, and that satisfaction of the claim, even by a stranger to the action,[4] would prevent its further enforcement.[5] It is obvious that this rule is equitable in its nature,[6] and that its purpose is to prevent unjust enrichment. It is equally obvious that it applies not only to concerted wrongdoers, but also to concurrent tortfeasors not acting in concert, or even to payments made by parties who have no connection with the tort at all.[7]

American courts have sometimes confused these two rules. The first has generally been repudiated in the United States,[8] and it is now held everywhere that an unsatisfied judgment against one tortfeasor does not bar an action against another. The plaintiff may bring separate suits, pursue each to judgment, and elect to enforce either or both.[9] It has even been held[10] that the plaintiff may refuse tender of payment of

---

167 P. 562; Cullen v. City of Minneapolis, 1937, 201 Minn. 102, 275 N.W. 414.

49. Kelly v. Schneller, 1927, 148 Va. 573, 139 S.E. 275; Ohio Valley Bank v. Greenbaum Sons Bank & Trust Co., 4th Cir. 1926, 11 F.2d 87; Crawford v. Morris, 1848, 46 Va. (5 Grat.) 90; Nashville Railway & Light Co. v. Trawick, 1907, 118 Tenn. 273, 99 S.W. 695.

§ 48

1. 25 & 26 Geo. V, ch. 30, § 6(1).

2. Brown v. Wootton, 1600, Cro.Jac. 73, 79 Eng. Rep. 62; King v. Hoare, 1844, 13 M. & W. 494, 153 Eng.Rep. 206; Day v. Porter, 1838, 2 Moody & R. 151, 174 Eng.Rep. 245; Brinsmead v. Harrison, 1872, L.R. 7 C.P. 547.

3. Morris v. Robinson, 1824, 3 B. & C. 196, 107 Eng. Rep. 706; Ellis v. Stenning, [1932] 2 Ch. 81; The Koursk, [1924] P. 140.

4. Welby v. Drake, 1825, 1 C. & P. 557, 171 Eng. Rep. 1315; Belshaw v. Bush, 1851, 11 C.B. 191, 138 Eng.Rep. 444; Freshwater v. Bulmer Rayon Co., [1933] Ch. 162. See Gold, Accord and Satisfaction by a Stranger, 1941, 19 Can.Bar Rev. 165.

5. Morris v. Robinson, 1824, 3 B. & C. 196, 107 Eng. Rep. 706; Cooper v. Shepherd, 1846, 3 C.B. 266, 136 Eng.Rep. 107; Ellis v. Stenning, [1932] 2 Ch. 81.

6. See the statement in Morris v. Robinson, 1824, 3 B. & C. 196, 107 Eng.Rep. 706, that equity will prevent double satisfaction.

7. See Miller v. Beck, 1899, 108 Iowa 575, 79 N.W. 344. And cf. Schoenly v. Nashville Speedways, Inc., 1961, 208 Tenn. 107, 344 S.W.2d 349, where an award of a Board of Claims, based on the negligence of a state highway patrolman, was held to be in satisfaction, and so to bar action against other tortfeasors.

8. See Note, 1955, 68 Harv.L.Rev. 700. Virginia adopted the English rule in Petticolas v. City of Richmond, 1897, 95 Va. 456, 28 S.E. 566, but it was later changed by statute. Fitzgerald v. Campbell, 1921, 131 Va. 486, 109 S.E. 308. An early Rhode Island case, Hunt v. Bates, 1862, 7 R.I. 217, was later limited strictly to its own facts. Parmenter v. Barstow, 1899, 21 R.I. 410, 43 A. 1035. Earlier cases holding that suing out an unsatisfied execution against one bars action against another were overruled in Cleveland v. City of Bangor, 1895, 87 Me. 259, 32 A. 892; Ketelson v. Stilz, 1916, 184 Ind. 702, 111 N.E. 423; Verhoeks v. Gillivan, 1928, 244 Mich. 367, 221 N.W. 287.

9. Lovejoy v. Murray, 1866, 70 U.S. (3 Wall.) 1, 18 L.Ed. 129; Black v. Bringhurst, 1935, 7 Cal.App.2d 711, 46 P.2d 993; Irwin v. Jetter Brewing Co., 1917, 101

10. See note 10 on page 331.

the first judgment, and still proceed to speculate upon the possibility of a larger recovery by means of a second. And even a partial satisfaction of one judgment will not prevent obtaining or enforcing another, although it is everywhere agreed that the amount received must be credited pro tanto against the amount to be collected.[11] It has been held, however, that full satisfaction of a lesser judgment will extinguish a greater one, apparently on the ground that it has been adjudicated in court that the amount paid is the complete equivalent of the plaintiff's damage.[12]

The second rule, as to satisfaction itself, has become involved in the confused concept of "joint torts." [13] When payment of the judgment in full is made by the judgment debtor, there is no doubt that the plaintiff is barred from a further action against another who is liable for the same damages,[14] or from enforcement of another judgment against the other.[15] But where the plaintiff's claim, whether reduced to judgment or not, is paid in full by a stranger who is not connected with the tort at all, there are a good many cases [16] which have held that it does not discharge the plaintiff's claim against the real tortfeasor even though it has been agreed that it shall do so. Such decisions thus in effect permit double compensation. The weight of authority is now definitely to the contrary.[17] It is supported by decisions [18] as to accord and satisfaction of contracts, and appears definitely to represent the preferable view, at least where the

---

Neb. 409, 163 N.W. 470; Squire v. Ordemann, 1909, 194 N.Y. 394, 87 N.E. 435; Moss v. Jones, 1966, 93 N.J. Super. 179, 225 A.2d 369.

As to the related problem of the privity between defendants which will make a judgment in favor of one bar action against the other, see Second Restatement of Judgments, 1982, § 51; 1 Freeman, Judgments, 5th Ed. 1925, § 451; Note, 1952, 65 Harv.L.Rev. 818, 862. The problem is beyond the scope of this text.

10. Bradford v. Carson, 1931, 223 Ala. 594, 137 So. 426; Skelly Oil Co. v. Jordan, 1939, 186 Okl. 130, 96 P.2d 524; Fitzgerald v. Campbell, 1921, 131 Va. 486, 109 S.E. 308; Restatement of Torts, 1939, § 886, Comment c.

11. Laurenzi v. Vranizan, 1945, 25 Cal.2d 806, 155 P.2d 633; Meixell v. Kirkpatrick, 1883, 29 Kan. 679; McVey v. Marratt, 1890, 80 Iowa 132, 45 N.W. 548; Stusser v. Mutual Union Insurance Co., 1923, 127 Wash. 449, 221 P. 331; Boyles v. Knight, 1899, 123 Ala. 289, 26 So. 939.

12. Thomas' Administrator v. Maysville Street Railway & Transfer Co., 1910, 136 Ky. 446, 124 S.W. 398; Cox v. Smith, 1882, 10 Or. 418; Larson v. Anderson, 1919, 108 Wash. 157, 182 P. 957; cf. Simpson v. Plyler, 1963, 258 N.C. 390, 128 S.E.2d 843; Battle v. Morris, 1957, 265 Ala. 581, 93 So.2d 428. By statute in England, the plaintiff is limited to satisfaction of the *first* judgment. See Williams, Joint Torts and Contributory Negligence, 1951, 1–194; Note, 1955, 68 Harv.L.Rev. 697, 701.

13. See for example Price-Bass Co. v. Owen, 1940, 24 Tenn.App. 474, 146 S.W.2d 149.

14. City of Wetumka v. Crowell-Franklin Oil Co., 1935, 171 Okl. 565, 43 P.2d 434; Laver v. Kingston, 1956, 11 Ill.App.2d 323, 137 N.E.2d 113; Viehweg v. Mountain States Telephone & Telegraph Co., D.Idaho 1956, 141 F.Supp. 848; Theobald v. Kenney's Suburban House, Inc., 1966, 48 N.J. 203, 225 A.2d 10; Bundt v. Embro, 1965, 48 Misc.2d 802, 265 N.Y.S.2d 872.

But satisfaction of a judgment against an original tortfeasor may not bar a subsequent malpractice action against a physician aggravating the injury, where it is found that there was not satisfaction of such damages. Selby v. Kuhns, 1963, 345 Mass. 600, 188 N.E.2d 861; Knutsen v. Brown, 1966, 93 N.J.Super, 522, 226 A.2d 460, affirmed, 1967, 96 N.J.Super. 229, 232 A.2d 833. And vice versa. Mathis v. Virgin, Fla.App.1964, 167 So.2d 897.

15. Thomas' Administrator v. Maysville Street Railway & Transfer Co., 1910, 136 Ky. 446, 124 S.W. 398. In Hilbert v. Roth, 1959, 395 Pa. 270, 149 A.2d 648, this was carried to the length of refusing to permit collection of punitive damages, awarded in the second judgment but not the first.

16. Papenfus v. Shell Oil Co., 1949, 254 Wis. 233, 35 N.W.2d 920; Deatley's Administrator v. Phillips, Ky. 1951, 243 S.W.2d 918; Brimer v. Scheibel, 1926, 154 Tenn. 253, 290 S.W. 5; Carroll v. Kerrigen, 1938, 173 Md. 627, 197 A. 127; Phillips Sheet & Tin Plate Co. v. Griffith, 1918, 98 Ohio St. 73, 120 N.E. 207.

17. Latham v. Des Moines Electric Light Co., 1942, 232 Iowa 1038, 6 N.W.2d 853; Harris v. City of Roanoke, 1942, 179 Va. 1, 18 S.E.2d 303; Husky Refining Co. v. Barnes, 8th Cir. 1941, 119 F.2d 715; Jacobsen v. Woerner, 1939, 149 Kan. 598, 89 P.2d 24; Bacich v. Northland Transportation Co., 1932, 185 Minn. 544, 242 N.W. 379. See Notes, 1944, 22 N.C.L.Rev. 167; 1950, 15 Mo.L.Rev. 115; 1955, 8 Vand.L.Rev. 509.

18. Abrahamson v. Brown, 1948, 149 Neb. 267, 30 N.W.2d 675; Somers & Sons v. Le Clerc, 1939, 110 Vt. 408, 8 A.2d 663; Welsh v. Loomis, 1940, 5 Wn.2d 377, 105 P.2d 500; Restatement of Contracts, § 421. See King, Accord and Satisfaction by a Third Person, 1950, 15 Mo.L.Rev. 115; Gold, Accord and Satisfaction by a Stranger, 1941, 19 Can.Bar Rev. 165.

intent of the parties is clear that the claim shall be satisfied. The problem has been futher complicated, however, by the matter of releases, which remains to be considered.

 **WESTLAW REFERENCES**

digest(release /s one /s tortfeasor* /s all)
digest(uniform +s contribution +s joint +s tortfeasors)
topic(331) /p joint /p tort* tortfeasor*
di satisfaction

§ 49. Release

There is a genuine distinction between a satisfaction and a release. A satisfaction is an acceptance of full compensation for the injury; a release is a surrender of the cause of action, which may be gratuitous, or given for inadequate consideration.[1] Releases at common law were under seal,[2] which disposed of any possible dispute as to the adequacy of consideration. Such a release to one of two tortfeasors who had acted in concert necessarily released the other, since there was in the eyes of the law but one cause of action against the two, liable for the same acts, which was surrendered.[3] But as to independent wrongdoers, not acting in concert, who were liable for the same loss, there seems to be no reason to conclude that a release of one would release the others, except in so far as it was based upon actual satisfaction of the claim.[4]

The American courts, possibly because of the diminished effect given to the seal,[5] have rather hopelessly confused release with satisfaction. When, in turn, concurrent wrongdoers who have caused the same loss become "joint tort-feasors," for the sole reason that they can be joined, the result is still more confusion. Until quite recent decades, most of the courts continued to hold that a release to one of two concurrent tortfeasors was a complete surrender of any cause of action against the other, and a bar to any suit against the other,[6] without regard to the sufficiency of the compensation actually received.[7] This was held to be true even though the release was accompanied by an oral agreement that it should have no such effect,[8] or the agreement was inserted in the release itself.[9] No better reason was offered than that such terms are necessarily repugnant to the legal operation and effect of the instrument itself, and hence are

---

§ 49

1. See Miller v. Beck, 1899, 108 Iowa, 575, 79 N.W. 344; Ellis v. Essau, 1880, 50 Wis. 138, 6 N.W. 518; Cleveland, Cincinnati Chicago & St. Louis Railway Co. v. Hilligoss, 1908, 171 Ind. 417, 86 N.E. 485. See, generally, Havighurst, The Effect of a Settlement with One Co-obligor upon the Obligations of the Others, 1959, 45 Corn.L.Q. 1.

2. 2 Williston, Contracts, Rev.ed. 1936, § 333A.

3. Cocke v. Jenner, 1614, Hob. 66, 80 Eng.Rep. 214; Duck v. Mayeu, [1892] 2 Q.B. 511. See Winfield, Province of the Law of Tort, 1931, 40, suggesting that the rule was influenced by the fact that until 1695 the court would not interfere with an award of excessive damages.

4. Amazingly enough, the point seems never to have been presented directly to an English court; but the conclusion would seem to follow from the fact that an unsatisfied judgment was not a bar in such a case, because the causes of action were separate. See Salmond, Law of Torts, 8th Ed. 1934, 82, note; and cf. Freshwater v. Bulmer Rayon Co., [1933] Ch. 162; The Koursk, [1924] P. 140.

5. 2 Williston, Contracts Rev.ed. 1936, § 333A. So long as the seal remained conclusive as to adequate consideration, the release necessarily imported full satisfaction. Gunther v. Lee, 1876, 45 Md. 60; Carpenter v. W. H. McElwain Co., 1916, 78 N.H. 118, 97 A. 560.

6. Price v. Baker, 1959, 143 Colo. 264, 352 P.2d 90; McFarland v. News & Observer Publishing Co., 1963, 260 N.C. 397, 132 S.E.2d 752; Lucio v. Curran, 1956, 2 N.Y.2d 157, 157 N.Y.S.2d 948, 139 N.E.2d 133; Jackman v. Jones, 1953, 198 Or. 564, 258 P.2d 133; Atlantic Coast Line Railroad Co. v. Boone, Fla.1956, 85 So.2d 834.

7. The release was said to be "conclusive evidence" of full satisfaction. Greene v. Waters, 1951, 260 Wis. 40, 49 N.W.2d 919; J. E. Pinkham Lumber Co. v. Woodland State Bank, 1930, 156 Wash. 117, 286 P. 95; Hawber v. Raley, 1928, 92 Cal.App. 701, 268 P. 943.

8. Martin v. Setter, 1931, 184 Minn. 457, 239 N.W. 219; Muse v. De Vito, 1923, 243 Mass. 384, 137 N.E. 730; Colby v. Walker, 1934, 86 N.H. 568, 171 A. 774; Williams v. Le Bar, 1891, 141 Pa. 149, 21 A. 525. As to the parol evidence rule, see infra, this section.

9. Friday v. United States, 9th Cir. 1957, 239 F.2d 701; Shortt v. Hudson Supply & Equipment Co., 1950, 191 Va. 306, 60 S.E.2d 900; Morris v. Diers, 1956, 134 Colo. 39, 298 P.2d 957; Roper v. Florida Public Utilities Co., 1938, 131 Fla. 709, 179 So. 904; Bryan v. Creaves, 7th Cir. 1943, 138 F.2d 377, certiorari denied 321 U.S. 778, 88 L.Ed. 1071 (Illinois law).

void,[10] or that the cause of action is by its nature indivisible in the eyes of the law.[11]

This result has been justly condemned[12] because it compels the plaintiff either to forego any opportunity of obtaining what it is possible to get from one defendant without suit, or to give up the entire claim against the other without full compensation. Historically, and on policy grounds, it has no justification, since causes of action against mere concurrent tortfeasors not acting in concert have always been separate,[13] and their separate character should not be affected by the possibility of joinder for procedural convenience. A surrender of one therefore should not on any reasonable basis discharge the other, except to the extent that there has been full compensation. Even as applied to cases of concerted action,[14] the rule seems at best an antiquated survival of an arbitrary common law procedural concept, arising out of long forgotten semi-criminal forms of action; and it has no reasonable application at all to cases of mere concurrent negligence. The fear of double recovery[15] is unfounded, since the amount paid under the release must be credited to the second tortfeasor in any case;[16] and the argument[17] that the plaintiff should not be permitted to make piecemeal collections from different defendants is quite pointless when the plaintiff is allowed to do precisely that after judgment.[18]

Such was the original state of the American law; but the last half century has seen wholesale changes in it.[19] Statutes have been enacted in many states.[20] As is inevitable, they have not explicitly provided for all the issues that may arise, and issues of pro-

---

10. McBride v. Scott, 1903, 132 Mich. 176, 93 N.W. 243; Abb v. Northern Pacific Railroad Co., 1902, 28 Wash. 428, 68 P. 954; Price v. Baker, 1959, 143 Colo. 264, 352 P.2d 90. This reached a peak of absurdity when one who was never liable at all to the plaintiff was released, and this was held to release the real wrongdoer, upon the basis that the plaintiff was "estopped" or "precluded" from denying that they were joint tortfeasors. See for example Bittner v. Little, 3d Cir. 1959, 270 F.2d 286 (Virginia law); Connelly v. United States Steel Co., 1954, 161 Ohio St. 448, 119 N.E.2d 843; Note, 1955, 8 Vand.L.Rev. 509.

See, however, Hamm v. Thompson, 1960, 143 Colo. 298, 353 P.2d 73, holding that a release to a master does not release a servant, since the master would be entitled to indemnity over against the servant.

11. McBride v. Scott, 1903, 132 Mich. 176, 93 N.W. 243; Muse v. De Vito, 1923, 243 Mass. 384, 137 N.E. 730; Sunset Copper v. Zickrick, 1924, 125 Wash. 565, 217 P. 5; Kirkland v. Ensign-Bickford Co., D.Conn. 1920, 267 F. 472.

12. Havighurst, The Effect of a Settlement with One Co-obligor upon the Obligations of the Others, 1959, 45 Corn.L.Q. 1; Notes, 1959, 12 Vand.L.Rev. 1414; 1961, 40 N.C.L.Rev. 88; 1951, 24 So.Cal.L.Rev. 466; 1943, 28 Iowa L.Rev. 515; 1941, 3 Wash. & Lee L.Rev. 151; 1938, 22 Minn.L.Rev. 692.

13. Milwaukee Insurance Co. v. Gas Service Co., 1959, 185 Kan. 604, 347 P.2d 394. Suppose that the damages inflicted by an original wrongdoer are aggravated by the negligent treatment of a physician. If a release is given to the original wrongdoer before the malpractice occurs, does it discharge the physician before the cause of action against the physician even accrues? The answer invariably has been no. Western Express Co. v. Smeltzer, 6th Cir. 1937, 88 F.2d 94, certiorari denied 302 U.S. 698, 58 S.Ct. 17, 82 L.Ed. 539; Smith v. Golden State Hospital, 1931, 111 Cal.App. 667, 296 P. 127; De Nike v. Mowery, 1966, 69 Wn.2d 357, 418 P.2d 1010, amended, 422 P.2d 328 (discovered later). Cf. Dakin v. Allis, 1964, 25 Wis.2d 49, 130 N.W.2d 191; Lackey v. Brooks, 1963, 204 Va. 428, 132 S.E.2d 461. See Note, 1933, 18 Corn.L.Q. 257.

14. The American cases relied in general upon two early decisions of this type: Ruble v. Turner, 1808, 12 Va. (2 Hen. & M.) 38; Gunther v. Lee, 1876, 45 Md. 60.

15. See McBride v. Scott, 1903, 132 Mich. 176, 182, 93 N.W. 243, 245; J.E. Pinkham Lumber Co. v. Woodland State Bank, 1930, 156 Wash. 117, 286 P. 95.

16. See infra, this section.

17. Advanced in Price v. Baker, 1959, 143 Colo. 264, 352 P.2d 90.

18. See supra, this section.

19. But see Bland v. Warwickshire Corp., 1933, 160 Va. 131, 168 S.E. 443; Goldstein v. Gilbert, 1942, 125 W.Va. 250, 23 S.E.2d 606 (Virginia law); Rust v. Schaitzer, 1933, 175 Wash. 331, 27 P.2d 571; Haney v. Cheatham, 1941, 8 Wn.2d 310, 111 P.2d 1003. See also Price v. Baker, 1959, 143 Colo. 264, 352 P.2d 90; but the case was overruled in Cox v. Pearl Investment Co., 1969, 168 Colo. 67, 450 P.2d 60.

20. See Note, 1959, 12 Vand.L.Rev. 1414, listing then enacted statutes. Much more legislation has been enacted during intervening years. The National Conference of Commissioners on Uniform State Laws entered this field early. Relevant provisions appeared in its Uniform Contribution Among Tortfeasors Acts of 1939 and 1955. The latter Act stands "for possible use by states not adopting the principle of comparative fault," and the Uniform Comparative Fault Act, 1977, contains relevant provisions on the effect of releases for states accepting the principle of comparative fault. See 12 Uniform Laws Annotated, 1982 Pocket Part, 34.

cess as well as policy have arisen.²¹ Even in the absence of a statute on the subject, the courts have retreated, in one way or another, from the common law rule. The device commonly accepted is that of a covenant not to sue,²² by which the plaintiff does not surrender the cause of action, but merely agrees not to enforce it, and so becomes liable for an equivalent amount of damages for breaking the agreement by suing.²³ Such a covenant is held not to release other tortfeasors,²⁴ even in the absence of any reservation of rights against them,²⁵ unless it is found that there has in fact been full satisfaction of the claim.²⁶ Under this technical evasion, which is the most obvious of subterfuges for circumventing an inconvenient common law rule, the form of the instrument becomes highly important in some jurisdictions; and the drafter who uses the language of covenant has sometimes succeeded where any mention of the word release would have been fatal.²⁷ It has been said often, however, that intent governs rather than form, and that the court will look to the four corners of the instrument to determine it.²⁸

There still remain some instruments which by any fair construction are not covenants, but releases. Even as to these the common law rule has been changed in some states. Statutes have been enacted,²⁹ and even without a statute, a substantial number of jurisdictions have held that the release does not discharge the second tortfeasor if it provides in terms that it shall not do so.³⁰ Some of them even have recognized an accompanying oral agreement to that effect,³¹ and have met the objection of the parol evidence rule³² with the argument that the second tortfeasor is not a party to the instrument.³³ Still others have accomplished the same result by the short and simple method of calling a release with reservation of rights against others a covenant not to sue.³⁴

21. Concerning such issues generally, see supra, § 3.

22. Or not to proceed further, as in Hicklin v. Anders, 1953, 201 Or. 128, 253 P.2d 897; or not to enforce judgment, as in Pellett v. Sonotone Corp., 1945, 26 Cal. 2d 705, 160 P.2d 783; Whittlesea v. Farmer, 1970, 86 Nev. 347, 469 P.2d 57. A mere dismissal of the action against some defendants may have the same practical effect, although it is not satisfactory protection for the one released. Adolph Gottscho, Inc. v. American Marking Corp., 1955, 18 N.J. 467, 114 A.2d 438, certiorari denied 350 U.S. 834, 76 S.Ct. 69, 100 L.Ed. 744.

23. The effect of the convenant between the parties is well stated in Pellett v. Sonotone Corp., 1945, 26 Cal. 2d 705, 160 P.2d 783.

24. Johnson v. Harnisch, 1966, 259 Iowa 1090, 147 N.W.2d 11; Lyons v. Durocher, 1960, 341 Mass. 382, 169 N.E.2d 911; Burke v. Burnham, 1952, 97 N.H. 203, 84 A.2d 918; Southern Pacific Co. v. Raish, 9th Cir. 1953, 205 F.2d 389 (Oregon law); Boucher v. Thomsen, 1950, 328 Mich. 312, 43 N.W.2d 866.

25. Joyce v. Massachusetts Real Estate Co., 1928, 173 Minn. 310, 217 N.W. 337. The intent not to release other tortfeasors is a question of fact, and open to inquiry. Fagerburg v. Phoenix Flour Mills Co., 1937, 50 Ariz. 227, 71 P.2d 1022; Richardson v. Pacific Power & Light Co., 1941, 11 Wn.2d 288, 118 P.2d 985.

26. Daniels v. Celeste, 1939, 303 Mass. 148, 21 N.E.2d 1; Haase v. Employers Mutual Liability Insurance Co., 1947, 250 Wis. 422, 27 N.W.2d 468; Shortt v. Hudson Supply & Equipment Co., 1950, 191 Va. 306, 60 S.E.2d 900.

27. Compare Oliver v. Williams, 1935, 19 Tenn.App. 54, 83 S.W.2d 271, with Byrd v. Crowder, 1933, 166 Tenn. 215, 60 S.W.2d 171. See Note, 1964, 7 South Tex.L.Rev. 134.

28. See for example Atlantic Coast Line Railroad Co. v. Boone, Fla.1956, 85 So.2d 834; Albert's Shoes, Inc. v. Crabtree Construction Co., Fla.1956, 89 So.2d 491.

29. See supra, notes 20, 21.

30. McKenna v. Austin, 1943, 77 U.S.App.D.C. 228, 134 F.2d 659; Gronquist v. Olson, 1954, 242 Minn. 119, 64 N.W.2d 159; Jukes v. North American Van Lines, 1957, 181 Kan. 12, 309 P.2d 692; Riley v. Industrial Finance Service Co., 1957, 157 Tex. 306, 302 S.W.2d 652; Standard Sanitary Manufacturing Co. v. Brian's Administrator, 1928, 224 Ky. 419, 6 S.W.2d 491.

31. Couillard v. Charles T. Miller Hospital, 1958, 253 Minn. 418, 92 N.W.2d 96; Safety Cab Co. v. Fair, 1937, 181 Okl. 264, 74 P.2d 607; Standard Sanitary Manufacturing Co. v. Brian's Administrator, 1928, 224 Ky. 419, 6 S.W.2d 491; Fitzgerald v. Union Stock Yards Co., 1911, 89 Neb. 393, 131 N.W. 612; Weldon v. Lehmann, 1956, 226 Miss. 600, 84 So.2d 796. See also Breen v. Peck, 1958, 28 N.J. 351, 146 A.2d 665; Daily v. Somberg, 1959, 28 N.J. 372, 146 A.2d 676.

32. See Goss v. Ellison, 1884, 136 Mass. 503; Martin v. Setter, 1931, 184 Minn. 457, 239 N.W. 219; Cannon v. Pearson, Tex.1964, 383 S.W.2d 565.

33. See for example Fitzgerald v. Union Stock Yards Co., 1911, 89 Neb. 393, 131 N.W. 612.

34. Carey v. Bilby, 8th Cir. 1930, 129 F. 203; Bolton v. Ziegler, N.D.Iowa 1953, 111 F.Supp. 516; Natrona

The only desirable rule would seem to be that a plaintiff should never be deprived of a cause of action against any wrongdoer when the plaintiff has neither intentionally surrendered the cause of action nor received substantially full compensation.[35] If the statutes are taken into account, this is now the rule actually applied in most American jurisdictions. Where there has been such full satisfaction,[36] or where it is agreed that the amount paid under the release is so received,[37] no claim should remain as to any other tortfeasor; but these are questions of fact, and normally to be determined by the jury, where the amount of the claim is unliquidated.[38] The release, however, may very well be taken as a prima facie acknowledgment of satisfaction, and the burden placed upon the plaintiff to prove that it is not.[39] The requirement that an express reservation of rights against other tortfeasors be inserted in the release itself [40] seems unfortunate, when releases frequently are signed by plaintiffs ignorant of the law and without legal advice. If it is clear that the satisfaction received was understood to be only partial, it should not discharge the claim against the second tortfeasor.[41] It is commonly held, however, that a credit is allowed to diminish the amount of damages recoverable against the second tortfeasor,[42] irrespective of an

Power Co. v. Clark, 1924, 31 Wyo. 284, 225 P. 586; Cox v. Pearl Investment Co., 1969, 168 Colo. 67, 450 P.2d 60.

35. See the excellent opinion of Rutledge, J., in McKenna v. Austin, 1943, 77 U.S.App.D.C. 228, 134 F.2d 659. Also Black v. Martin, 1930, 88 Mont. 256, 292 P. 577; Aldrich v. Charles Beauregard & Sons, Inc., 1964, 105 N.H. 330, 200 A.2d 14; Gronquist v. Olson, 1954, 242 Minn. 119, 64 N.W.2d 159.

See also, holding that a release to an original tortfeasor does not necessarily release a negligent physician who aggravates the injury: Derby v. Prewitt, 1962, 12 N.Y.2d 100, 236 N.Y.S.2d 953, 187 N.E.2d 556; Smith v. Conn, Iowa 1969, 163 N.W.2d 407; Hansen v. Collett, 1963, 79 Nev. 159, 380 P.2d 301; Couillard v. Charles T. Miller Hospital, 1958, 253 Minn. 418, 92 N.W.2d 96; Galloway v. Lawrence, 1965, 263 N.C. 433, 139 S.E.2d 761.

36. Berry v. Pullman Co., 5th Cir. 1918, 249 F. 816; Cleveland, Cincinnati Chicago & St. Louis Railway Co. v. Hilligoss, 1908, 171 Ind. 417, 86 N.E. 485; Urton v. Price, 1881, 57 Cal. 270; Bowman v. Davis, 1889, 13 Colo. 297, 22 P. 507; State ex rel. Cox v. Maryland Electric Railway Co., 1915, 126 Md. 300, 95 A. 43.

37. Beedle v. Carolan, 1944, 115 Mont. 587, 148 P.2d 559; Greenhalch v. Shell Oil Co., 10th Cir. 1935, 78 F.2d 942; Fitzgerald v. Union Stock Yards Co., 1911, 89 Neb. 393, 131 N.W. 612; Hartigan v. Dickson, 1900, 81 Minn. 284, 83 N.W. 1901.

38. Ellis v. Essau, 1880, 50 Wis. 138, 6 N.W. 518; Fitzgerald v. Union Stock Yards Co., 1911, 89 Neb. 393, 131 N.W. 612; Berry v. Pullman Co., 5th Cir. 1918, 249 F. 816; O'Neil v. National Oil Co., 1918, 231 Mass. 20, 120 N.E. 107; Arnett v. Missouri Pacific Railroad Co., 1895, 64 Mo.App. 368.

39. See Dwy v. Connecticut Co., 1915, 89 Conn. 74, 92 A. 883; Smith v. Mann, 1931, 184 Minn. 485, 239 N.W. 223; Moss v. Cherdak, 1935, 114 N.J.L. 332, 176 A. 333; Tanana Trading Co. v. North American Trading & Transportation Co., 9th Cir. 1915, 220 F. 783; Snyder v. Mutual Telegraph Co., 1907, 135 Iowa 215, 112 N.W. 776. Contra Booker v. Kansas City Gas Co., 1936, 231 Mo.App. 214, 96 S.W.2d 919.

40. See supra, this section; Second Restatement of Torts, § 885.

In Young v. State, Alaska 1969, 455 P.2d 889, the court took the converse position, that a release without full compensation does not release other tortfeasors unless they are specifically named in the release.

41. Adams Express Co. v. Beckwith, 1919, 100 Ohio St. 348, 126 N.E. 300; Louisville & E. Mail Co. v. Barnes' Administrator, 1904, 117 Ky. 860, 79 S.W. 261; Kropidlowski v. Pfister & Vogel Leather Co., 1912, 149 Wis. 421, 135 N.W. 839; Robertson v. Trammell, 1904, 37 Tex.Civ.App. 53, 83 S.W. 258, error refused 98 Tex. 364, 83 S.W. 1098.

42. McKenna v. Austin, 1943, 77 U.S.App.D.C. 228, 134 F.2d 659; McNair v. Goodwin, 1964, 262 N.C. 1, 136 S.E.2d 218; Hutchinson v. Rubel Baking Co., 1939, 34 O.L.A. 15, 34 N.E.2d 472, motion overruled; Natrona Power Co. v. Clark, 1924, 31 Wyo. 284, 225 P. 586; Dwy v. Connecticut Co., 1915, 89 Conn. 74, 92 A. 883. Normally the deduction is to be made by the jury; but it may be made after judgment, by credit against the judgment. Price v. Wabash Railroad Co., 1961, 30 Ill.App.2d 115, 174 N.E.2d 5; Hardin v. New York Central Railroad Co., 1960, 145 W.Va. 676, 116 S.E.2d 697. Many statutes now require this. See Daugherty v. Hershberger, 1956, 386 Pa. 367, 126 A.2d 730; Note, 1957, 106 U.Pa.L.Rev. 311.

See Mayhew v. Berrien County Road Commission, 1982, 414 Mich. 399, 326 N.W.2d 366, holding that Michigan's adoption of comparative negligence does not implicitly repeal its contribution-release statute, under which nonsettling tortfeasor's share of liability is total amount of damages less value of settling tortfeasor's settlement (not proportionate share of fault).

A few courts, under statute or at common law, have held that there must be a pro rata reduction in the amount to be recovered, rather than a lump sum. Theobald v. Angelos, 1965, 44 N.J. 228, 208 A.2d 129; Palestine Contractors, Inc. v. Perkins, Tex.1964, 386

agreement that it shall not,[43] and regardless of whether it is received under a release or a covenant not to sue.[44] The prevailing view, with some authority to the contrary,[45] is that it must be so credited even where the person released was not in fact a joint tortfeasor, or was not liable to the plaintiff at all.[46]

WESTLAW REFERENCES

digest(release /s joint +1 tortfeasor*)
di release
pierringer +s release & "joint tortfeasor*"
release* /s joint /s tortfeasor* /s reservation*

§ 50. Contribution

Still another significance attached to a "joint tort" is the common law rule that there can be no contribution[1] among those who are regarded as "joint tortfeasors," when one has discharged the claim of the injured plaintiff.[2] The rule had its origin in 1799 in the case of Merryweather v. Nixan.[3]

There is a very meagre report of the case, but it seems clear that there had been an action for conversion and a joint judgment against two defendants, and that they had acted in concert, since they were joined at a time when joinder was not possible on any other basis. One of the two, who had been levied on for the whole judgment, sought "contribution of a moiety" from the other, on the theory of an implied promise, "as for so much money paid to his use." Lord Kenyon said that there could be no doubt that he should be nonsuit; and that he had never heard of such an action where the former judgment was for a tort. The ground of the decision would appear to have been simply the fact that the parties had acted intentionally and in concert, and the plaintiff's claim for contribution rested upon what was, in the eyes of the law, entirely the plaintiff's own deliberate wrong.[4]

Lord Kenyon expressly stated that the decision "would not affect cases of indemnity,

---

S.W.2d 764; Martello v. Hawley, 1962, 112 U.S.App. D.C. 129, 300 F.2d 721; Harvey v. Travelers Insurance Co., La.App.1964, 163 So.2d 915. See Notes, 1966, 18 Stan.L.Rev. 486; 1966, 14 Kan.L.Rev. 541; 1964, 43 Tex.L.Rev. 118.

See also Uniform Comparative Fault Act, 1977, § 6, which provides that the claim be reduced "by the amount of the released person's equitable share."

43. Home Telephone Co. v. Fields, 1907, 150 Ala. 306, 43 So. 711.

44. Ramsey v. Camp, 1961, 254 N.C. 443, 119 S.E.2d 209; Price v. Wabash Railroad Co., 1961, 30 Ill.App.2d 115, 174 N.E.2d 5; Burke v. Burnham, 1952, 97 N.H. 203, 84 A.2d 918; Bolton v. Ziegler, N.D.Iowa 1953, 111 F.Supp. 516; Harmon v. Givens, 1953, 88 Ga.App. 629, 77 S.E.2d 223. Contra, Mink v. Majors, 1954, 39 Tenn. App. 50, 279 S.W. 714, criticized in Note, 1956, 24 Tenn. L.Rev. 390.

45. Harllee v. City of Gulfport, 5th Cir. 1941, 120 F.2d 41; Herberger v. Anderson Motor Service Co., 1933, 268 Ill.App. 403; Brandstein v. Ironbound Transportation Co., 1934, 112 N.J.L. 585, 172 A. 580; Carroll v. Kerrigen, 1938, 173 Md. 627, 197 A. 127; Scoggins v. Village of Hartford, 1967, 86 Ill.App.2d 233, 229 N.E.2d 550, appeal after remand, 1969, 104 Ill.App.2d 403, 244 N.E.2d 433.

46. Holland v. Southern Pacific Utilities Co., 1935, 208 N.C. 289, 180 S.E. 592; Jacobsen v. Woerner, 1939, 149 Kan. 598, 89 P.2d 24; Husky Refining Co. v. Barnes, 8th Cir. 1941, 119 F.2d 715; Steger v. Egyud, 1959, 219 Md. 331, 149 A.2d 762; Caplan v. Caplan, 1940, 62 Ga.App. 577, 9 S.E.2d 96.

§ 50

1. With respect to distinctions between "contribution" and "indemnity" in common usage, see infra, § 51.

2. See, generally, Leflar, Contribution and Indemnity Between Tortfeasors, 1932, 81 U.Pa.L.Rev. 130; Bohlen, Contribution and Indemnity Between Tortfeasors, 1936, 21 Corn.L.Q. 552, 1937, 22 Corn.L.Q. 469; Hodges, Contribution and Indemnity Among Tortfeasors, 1947, 26 Tex.L.Rev. 150; Notes, 1931, 45 Harv.L.Rev. 349; 1947, 35 Geo.L.J. 382; 1953, 37 Minn. L.Rev. 470; 1958, 37 Neb.L.Rev. 820; 1959, 68 Yale L.J. 964; 1970, 31 Mont.L.Rev. 69.

Contribution and indemnity are generally allowed in the continental law. See Cohn, Responsibility of Joint Wrongdoers in Continental Law, 1935, 51 L.Q.Rev. 46.

3. 1799, 8 Term.Rep. 186, 101 Eng.Rep. 1337. See Reath, Contribution Between Persons Jointly Charged with Negligence—Merryweather v. Nixan, 1799, 12 Harv.L.Rev. 176; Hatcher, Battersey's Case, 1941, 47 W.Va.L.Q. 123.

4. Compare the celebrated Highwayman's Case, Everet v. Williams, Ex. 1725, reported in 1893, 9 L.Q. Rev. 197, and Costigan's Cases on Legal Ethics, 1917, 399. This was a suit by one highwayman against another for an accounting of their plunder. The bill was dismissed with costs to be paid by the defendant; the plaintiff's solicitors were attached and fined fifty pounds each for contempt. Both plaintiff and defendant were subsequently hanged. In short, contribution was not allowed.

where one man employed another to do acts, not unlawful in themselves." Later cases seized upon this limitation, and held that the rule against contribution did not apply unless the plaintiff was a wilful and conscious wrongdoer.[5] It was not until 1894 that the question was even raised in England in a case of concurrent negligence,[6] and the better English view, even before their statute,[7] appears clearly to have been that contribution is not denied in cases of mere vicarious liability, negligence, accident, mistake, or other unintentional breaches of the law.[8]

The early American cases applied the rule against contribution to cases of wilful misconduct,[9] but refused to recognize it where the tort committed by the claimant was a matter of negligence or mistake.[10] But once the door was thrown open to joinder in one action of those who had merely caused the same damage, the origin of the rule and the reason for it were lost to sight. The great majority of our courts proceeded to apply it generally, and refused to permit contribution even where independent, although concurrent, negligence had contributed to a single result.[11] Until the 1970s—for a period of more than a century—only nine American jurisdictions came to the contrary conclusion, allowing contribution without legislation.[12] Cogent criticism of the rule against contribution among tortfeasors eventually began to bear more fruit in the 1970s.

There is obvious lack of sense and justice in a rule which permits the entire burden of a loss, for which two defendants were equally, unintentionally responsible, to be shouldered onto one alone, according to the

---

5. Adamson v. Jarvis, 1827, 4 Bing. 66, 130 Eng. Rep. 693 (indemnity to an auctioneer innocently selling goods). See also Betts v. Gibbins, 1834, 2 Ad. & El. 57, 111 Eng.Rep. 22 (exception "where the act is not clearly illegal in itself"); Pearson v. Skelton, 1836, 1 M. & W. 504, 150 Eng.Rep. 533 (same).

6. Palmer v. Wick & Pultneytown Steam Shipping Co., [1894] A.C. 318, a case arising in Scotland, where a workman was killed when one defendant furnished defective tackle and the other negligently used it. Lord Herschell allowed contribution, saying that the rule did not apply to mere negligence, and in any case should not extend to Scots law. Even prior to this, in Wooley v. Batte, 1826, 2 C. & P. 417, 172 Eng.Rep. 188, contribution had been allowed between two joint proprietors of a stagecoach, not personally at fault, but held liable because of the negligence of the coachman.

7. Contribution was later provided by statute in England. See Williams, Joint Torts and Contributory Negligence, 1951, §§ 25–54.

8. Salmond, Law of Torts, 8th Ed. 1934, 86, relying on the cases cited, as well as Burrows v. Rhodes, [1899] 1 Q.B. 816; Hillen v. I. C. I., [1934] 1 K.B. 455. Contra, The Englishman and The Australia, [1895] P. 212.

9. Peck v. Ellis, N.Y.1816, 2 Johns.Ch. 131; Miller v. Fenton, N.Y.1844, 11 Paige 18; Hunt v. Lane, 1857, 9 Ind. 248; Rhea v. White, 1859, 40 Tenn. (3 Head.) 121; Atkins v. Johnson, 1870, 43 Vt. 78, 5 Am.Rep. 260; cf. Spalding v. Oakes' Administrator, 1869, 42 Vt. 343 (keeping ram known to be vicious).

10. Thweatt's Administrator v. Jones, 1825, 22 Va. (1 Rand.) 328; Horbach's Administrators v. Elder, 1851, 18 Pa. (6 Harris.) 33; Acheson v. Miller, 1853, 2 Ohio St. 203; Bailey v. Bussing, 1859, 28 Conn. 455; Armstrong County v. Clarion County, 1870, 66 Pa. 218; Nickerson v. Wheeler, 1875, 118 Mass. 295. See Reath, Contribution Between Persons Jointly Charged for Negligence, 1899, 12 Harv.L.Rev. 176, 180–182; Hatcher, Battersey's Case, 1941, 47 W.Va.L.Q. 123.

11. Union Stock Yards Co. v. Chicago Burlington & Quincy Railroad Co., 1905, 196 U.S. 217; National Trailer Convoy, Inc. v. Oklahoma Turnpike Authority, Okl.1967, 434 P.2d 238; Denneler v. Aubel Ditching Service, 1969, 203 Kan. 117, 453 P.2d 88; Riexinger v. Ashton Co., 1969, 9 Ariz.App. 406, 453 P.2d 235; Fidelity & Casualty Co. of New York v. Chapman, 1941, 167 Or. 661, 120 P.2d 223. The rule could not be evaded by the assignment of a judgment from the plaintiff to one tortfeasor. Adams v. White Bus Line, 1921, 184 Cal. 710, 195 P. 389.

12. Knell v. Feltman, 1949, 85 App.D.C. 22, 174 F.2d 662; Best v. Yerkes, 1956, 247 Iowa 800, 77 N.W.2d 23; Hawkeye-Security Insurance Co. v. Lowe Construction Co., 1959, 251 Iowa 27, 99 N.W.2d 421; Quatray v. Wicker, 1933, 178 La. 289, 151 So. 208; Linkenburger v. Owens, 5th Cir. 1950, 181 F.2d 97; Bedell v. Reagan, 1963, 159 Me. 292, 192 A.2d 24; Ankeny v. Moffett, 1887, 37 Minn. 109, 33 N.W. 320; Underwriters at Lloyds of Minneapolis v. Smith, 1926, 166 Minn. 388, 208 N.W. 13; Skaja v. Andrews Hotel Co., 1968, 281 Minn. 417, 161 N.W.2d 657. See Note, 1953, 37 Minn.L.Rev. 470; Wiener v. United Airlines, S.D.Cal.1962, 216 F.Supp. 701 (probably, concludes the federal court); Goldman v. Mitchell-Fletcher Co., 1928, 292 Pa. 354, 141 A. 231; Davis v. Broad Street Garage, 1950, 191 Tenn. 320, 232 S.W.2d 355; Huggins v. Graves, E.D.Tenn.1962, 210 F.Supp. 98 (apparently, however, some confusion of the ideas of contribution and indemnity); American Casualty Co. v. Billingsley, 1953, 195 Tenn. 448, 260 S.W.2d 173; Ellis v. Chicago & North Western Railroad Co., 1918, 167 Wis. 392, 167 N.W. 1048; Mitchell v. Raymond, 1923, 181 Wis. 591, 195 N.W. 855.

accident of a successful levy of execution, the existence of liability insurance, the plaintiff's whim or spite, or the plaintiff's collusion with the other wrongdoer,[13] while the latter goes scot free.[14] The only kind words said by any writer over the last century for the rule denying contribution[15] have been addressed to the proposition that contribution will be used chiefly to permit liability insurance companies to shift a part of the loss which they have been paid to bear to the shoulders of uninsured defendants. In reply it has been suggested[16] that if this is true it is at least odd that the insurance companies are among the most vigorous opponents of the change, and that it is by no means yet true that there will be insurance in every case.

However this may be, half a century of vigorous attack upon the original rule has had its effect in the passage of statutes in most states, which to a greater or lesser extent permit contribution among tortfeasors.[17] Some of these acts are limited to contribution between defendants against whom a joint judgment has been rendered.[18] Others are quite broad and general in scope, declaring the principle of contribution and leaving its administration to the courts.[19] Still others provide methods by which the tortfeasor from whom contribution is sought may be joined as a defendant, and subjected to liability in the original action.[20] The drafting has not been free from difficulty.[21] Since there is so much variation in the terms of the statutes, in decisions on issues not explicitly addressed by the statutes,[22] and even in the decisions in states having no statutes, we do no more here than indicate some of

---

13. As examples of such collusion, see Pennsylvania Co. v. West Penn Railways, 1924, 110 Ohio St. 516, 144 N.E. 51; Norfolk Southern Railroad Co. v. Beskin, 1924, 140 Va. 744, 125 S.E. 678.

14. Skinner v. Reed-Prentice Division Package Machinery Co., 1978, 70 Ill.2d 1, 15 Ill.Dec. 829, 374 N.E.2d 437, certiorari denied 98 S.Ct. 2849, 436 U.S. 946, 56 L.Ed.2d 787.

15. James, Contribution Among Joint Tortfeasors: A Pragmatic Criticism, 1941, 54 Harv.L.Rev. 1156; Jones, Contribution Among Tortfeasors, 1958, 11 U.Fla.L.Rev. 175.

16. The James article led to the ensuing debate: Gregory, Contribution Among Joint Tortfeasors: A Defense; James, Replication; Gregory, Rejoinder, all in 1941, 54 Harv.L.Rev. 1170 ff.

17. Jurisdictions were collected and classified in the Note, 1959, 68 Yale L.J. 964, 981–984. See, for former discussions, Gregory, Legislative Loss Distribution in Negligence Actions, 1936; Gregory, Contribution Among Tortfeasors: A Uniform Practice, [1938] Wis.L. Rev. 365; Notes, 1932, 32 Col.L.Rev. 94; 1931, 45 Harv.L.Rev. 349. The movement toward comparative fault—see infra, § 67—has accelerated the movement toward contribution, since comparative fault statutes commonly provide also for contribution. See Uniform Comparative Fault Act, 1977.

18. See for example Kahn v. Urania Lumber Co., La.App.1958, 103 So.2d 476; Powell v. Barker, 1957, 96 Ga.App. 592, 101 S.E.2d 113; State ex rel. McClure v. Dinwiddie, 1948, 358 Mo. 15, 213 S.W.2d 127; Buckner v. Foster, E.D.Mich.1952, 105 F.Supp. 279; Distefano v. Lamborn, 1951, 46 Del. (7 Terry) 195, 83 A.2d 300. See Gregory, Tort Contribution Practice in New York, 1935, 20 Corn.L.Q. 269; Note, 1950, 24 St. Johns L.Rev. 276.

19. See for example Consolidated Coach Corp. v. Burge, 1932, 245 Ky. 631, 54 S.W.2d 16; Callihan Interests, Inc. v. Duffield, Tex.Civ.App.1965, 385 S.W.2d 586, error refused.

20. See for example Brotman v. McNamara, 1942, 181 Md. 224, 29 A.2d 264. See Gregory, Procedural Aspects of Securing Contribution in the Injured Plaintiff's Action, 1933, 47 Harv.L.Rev. 209.

The original Uniform Contribution Among Tortfeasors Act, proposed by the Commissioners on Uniform State Laws in 1939, contained elaborate provisions for such joinder. It was adopted in nine jurisdictions, but was so extensively amended everywhere that there was no real uniformity. The Act was withdrawn by the Commissioners, and a new Uniform Contribution Among Tortfeasors Act was proposed in 1955. This Act avoided any attempt to deal with procedural questions such as joinder. The National Conference has left this act outstanding, although it is no longer recommended for jurisdictions that accept the principle of comparative fault. See 12 Uniform Laws Annotated, 1982 Pocket Part, 34.

21. See Wade, Uniform Comparative Fault Act— What Should It Provide? 1977, 10 U.Mich.J.L.Ref. 220; Stevens, A Proposal for Contribution Among Joint Tortfeasors in Ohio, 1951, 3 West.Res.L.Rev. 50; Jones, Contribution Among Tortfeasors, 1958, 11 U.Fla.L.Rev. 175; Note, 1936, 24 Cal.L.Rev. 546; Reports of New York Law Revision Commission, 1936, 699; 1937, 67; 1938, 65; 1939, 27; 1941, 17; 1952. An unhappy lawyer's estimate of the New Jersey statute is Orlando, The Operation of the "Joint Tortfeasors Contribution Law" in New Jersey, 1955, 22 Ins.Counsel J. 480.

22. Concerning issues of process arising when courts must answer questions not explicitly addressed in a statute, see supra, § 3.

the important questions, and how they have been dealt with.

1. It is necessary first of all to distinguish between contribution and indemnity.[23] In any case where there is a right to indemnity, contribution statutes and rules do not apply.[24]

2. Some statutes and some decisions continue the original rule that there is no contribution in favor of those who commit intentional torts,[25] but some statutes and decisions allow contribution in such cases.[26]

3. Notwithstanding arguments as to policy,[27] there appears to be general agreement,[28] that the contribution suit will lie in favor of a liability insurer who has paid the plaintiff's judgment and become subrogated to the claim.[29]

4. A more difficult question is whether a tortfeasor who has settled with the original plaintiff shall be entitled to contribution. The argument against it is that the other defendant may take no part in the settlement, violently oppose it, and regard it as outrageous, and still be held liable for a share. It is for this reason that the statutes of several jurisdictions limit contribution to those against whom judgments have been rendered, which fix both liability and amount. Where there is no such provision, it is almost invariably held that one who settles without judgment can recover contribution.[30] It is usually held, however, that in the contribution suit such a compromiser must sustain the burden of proof, not only as to the compromiser's own liability to the original plaintiff, but also as to the amount of the damages and the reasonableness of the settlement.[31]

5. The contribution defendant must be a tortfeasor, and originally liable to the plaintiff. If there was never any such liability, as where the contribution defendant has the defense of family immunity,[32] assumption of risk,[33] or the application of an automobile

23. See infra, this section and § 51.

24. See for example Melichar v. Frank, 1959, 78 S.D. 58, 98 N.W.2d 345 (master and servant); Weis v. A. T. Hipke & Sons, 1955, 271 Wis. 140, 72 N.W.2d 715. See also infra, § 51.

25. Turner v. Kirkwood, 10th Cir. 1931, 49 F.2d 590, certiorari denied, 284 U.S. 635, 52 S.Ct. 18, 76 L.Ed. 540; Jacobs v. General Accident Fire & Life Assurance Corp., 1961, 14 Wis.2d 1, 109 N.W.2d 462; Best v. Yerkes, 1956, 247 Iowa 800, 77 N.W.2d 23 ("intentional wrong, concerted action, or moral turpitude").

26. Judson v. Peoples Bank & Trust Co. of Westfield, 1954, 17 N.J. 67, 110 A.2d 24, second appeal, 1957, 25 N.J. 17, 134 A.2d 761; Brenneis v. Marley, Pa. 1955, 5 D. & C.2d 24; cf. Maryland Lumber Co. v. White, 1954, 205 Md. 180, 107 A.2d 73.

27. See supra, this section.

28. But see Lumbermen's Mutual Casualty Co. v. United States Fidelity & Guarantee Co., 1936, 211 N.C. 13, 188 S.E. 634. See Notes, 1963, 41 N.C.L.Rev. 890; 1965, 44 N.C.L.Rev. 142.

29. Coble v. Lacey, 1960, 257 Minn. 352, 101 N.W.2d 594; Hudgins v. Jones, 1964, 205 Va. 495, 138 S.E.2d 16; Zeglen v. Minkiewicz, 1963, 12 N.Y.2d 497, 240 N.Y.S.2d 965, 191 N.E.2d 450; Hawkeye-Security Insurance Co. v. Lowe Construction Co., 1959, 251 Iowa 27, 99 N.W.2d 421; State Farm Mutual Auto Insurance Co. v. Continental Casualty Co., 1953, 264 Wis. 493, 59 N.W.2d 425. See Note, 1936, 45 Yale L.J. 151.

30. Harger v. Caputo, 1966, 420 Pa. 528, 218 A.2d 108; Morris v. Kospelich, 1969, 253 La. 413, 218 So.2d 316; Huggins v. Graves, 6th Cir. 1964, 337 F.2d 486 (Tennessee law); Zontelli Brothers v. Northern Pacific Railway Co., 8th Cir. 1959, 263 F.2d 194; Hawkeye-Security Insurance Co. v. Lowe Construction Co., 1959, 251 Iowa 27, 99 N.W.2d 421.

31. Farmers Mutual Auto Insurance Co. v. Milwaukee Automobile Insurance Co., 1959, 8 Wis.2d 512, 99 N.W.2d 746. Accord: Allied Mutual Casualty Co. v. Long, 1961, 252 Iowa 829, 107 N.W.2d 682 ("The whole matter may be summed up in the statement that before there can be contribution among tortfeasors, there must be tortfeasors"); Clemmons v. King, 1965, 265 N.C. 199, 143 S.E.2d 83; Consolidated Coach Corp. v. Burge, 1932, 245 Ky. 631, 54 S.W.2d 16; McKenna v. Austin, 1943, 77 U.S.App.D.C. 228, 134 F.2d 659; Duluth, Missabe & Northern Railroad Co. v. McCarthy, 1931, 183 Minn. 414, 236 N.W. 766.

32. Yellow Cab Co. of District of Columbia v. Dreslin, 1950, 86 U.S.App.D.C. 327, 181 F.2d 626; Chamberlain v. McCleary, E.D.Tenn.1963, 217 F.Supp. 591; Blunt v. Brown, S.D.Iowa 1963, 225 F.Supp. 326; Rodgers v. Galindo, 1961, 68 N.M. 215, 360 P.2d 400; Zaccari v. United States, D.Md.1955, 130 F.Supp. 50.

There is some support, however, for allowing the contribution, on the ground that the immunity does not go to tort liability, but merely to suit. Bedell v. Reagan, 1963, 159 Me. 292, 192 A.2d 24; Zarrella v. Miller, 1966, 100 R.I. 545, 217 A.2d 673; Restifo v. McDonald, 1967, 426 Pa. 5, 230 A.2d 199; Weinberg v. Underwood, 1968, 101 N.J.Co. 448, 244 A.2d 538.

33. Shonka v. Campbell, 1967, 260 Iowa 1178, 152 N.W.2d 242; Troutman v. Modlin, 8th Cir. 1965, 353 F.2d 382; Burmeister v. Youngstrom, 1965, 81 S.D.

guest statute,[34] or the substitution of workers' compensation for common law liability,[35] then there is no liability for contribution.

6. Once liability has existed, however, there is more difficulty as to subsequent events discharging it. It is generally agreed that the fact that the statute of limitations has run against the original plaintiff's action does not bar a suit for contribution,[36] since that cause of action does not arise until payment.[37]

7. The effect of a settlement with the plaintiff by the contribution defendant, who has received a release or a covenant not to sue, has perhaps given more difficulty than any other problem. The usual holding has been that the defendant so relieved of liability is not released from contribution.[38] There has been much dissatisfaction with this because it becomes impossible for a defendant to settle the case, take a release, and close the file, since the potential liability for contribution is still open. On the other hand, the proposed solution of a pro rata reduction of the amount remaining due[39] discourages plaintiffs from accepting smaller settlements from one defendant. In either case both parties complain.[40]

8. In some jurisdictions the apportionment of liability effected by contribution is on the basis that "equality is equity," which means that each tortfeasor is required ultimately to pay a pro rata share,[41] arrived at by dividing the damages by the number of tortfeasors. In some instances, as where the owner and the driver of a car are joined as defendants, equity may require treating the two together as liable for a single share,[42] or that the share of a tortfeasor who is insolvent or absent from the jurisdiction be borne by the others.[43] In other jurisdictions, either by express provision of statute

---

578, 139 N.W.2d 226; Shrofe v. Rural Mutual Casualty Insurance Co., 1950, 258 Wis. 128, 45 N.W.2d 76.

34. Troutman v. Modlin, 8th Cir. 1965, 353 F.2d 382; Blunt v. Brown, S.D.Iowa 1963, 225 F.Supp. 326; Patterson v. Tomlinson, Tex.Civ.App.1938, 118 S.W.2d 645, error refused; Hill Hardware Corp. v. Hesson, 1956, 198 Va. 425, 94 S.E.2d 256; Downing v. Dillard, 1951, 55 N.M. 267, 232 P.2d 140.

35. Hunsucker v. High Point Bending & Chair Co., 1953, 237 N.C. 559, 75 S.E.2d 768; Bertone v. Turco Products, Inc., 3d Cir. 1958, 252 F.2d 726 (New Jersey law); Auld v. Globe Indemnity Co., W.D.La.1963, 220 F.Supp. 96; Mahone v. McGraw-Edison Co., E.D.Va. 1968, 281 F.Supp. 582; Iowa Power & Light Co. v. Abild Construction Co., 1966, 259 Iowa 314, 144 N.W.2d 303.

36. Keleket X-Ray Corp. v. United States, D.C.Cir. 1960, 275 F.2d 167; Cooper v. Philadelphia Dairy Products Co., 1955, 34 N.J.Sup. 301, 112 A.2d 308; Godfrey v. Tidewater Power Co., 1943, 223 N.C. 647, 27 S.E.2d 736; Ainsworth v. Berg, 1948, 253 Wis. 438, 35 N.W.2d 911.

37. The problem of long deferred payment has been dealt with in several of the statutes, by short limitation provisions applicable to the contribution suit itself.

38. State Farm Mutual Auto Insurance Co. v. Continental Casualty Co., 1953, 264 Wis. 493, 59 N.W.2d 425; Employers Mutual Casualty Co. v. Chicago, St. Paul, Minneapolis & Ohio Railroad Co., 1951, 235 Minn. 304, 50 N.W.2d 689; Blauvelt v. Village of Nyack, 1931, 141 Misc. 730, 252 N.Y.S. 746; Blanchard v. Wilt, 1963, 410 Pa. 356, 188 A.2d 722; Buckley v. Basford, D.Me.1960, 184 F.Supp. 870. This was the position taken by § 4 of the first Uniform Act.

39. See Larson, A Problem in Contribution: The Tortfeasor with an Individual Defense Against the Injured Party, [1940] Wis.L.Rev. 467. This was actually applied under the New Jersey statute in Judson v. Peoples Bank & Trust Co. of Westfield, 1954, 17 N.J. 67, 110 A.2d 24, but was doubted on a second appeal in 1957, 25 N.J. 17, 134 A.2d 761.

40. For the current position of the National Conference of Commissioners on Uniform State Laws, see Uniform Comparative Fault Act, 1977, § 6. See also Levi v. Montgomery, N.D.1960, 120 N.W.2d 383; Pilosky v. Dougherty, E.D.Pa.1959, 179 F.Supp. 148; Augustin v. General Accident Fire & Life Assurance Corp., 7th Cir. 1960, 283 F.2d 82; and cf. Tino v. Stout, 1967, 49 N.J. 289, 229 A.2d 793.

41. Early Settlers Insurance Co. v. Schweid, D.C. App.1966, 221 A.2d 920; Russell v. United States, D.Pa.1953, 113 F.Supp. 353; Hutcherson v. Slate, 1928, 105 W.Va. 184, 142 S.E. 444; Mulderig v. St. Louis Kansas City & Colorado Railroad Co., 1906, 116 Mo. App. 655, 94 S.W. 801.

42. See for example Larsen v. Minneapolis Gas Co., 1968, 282 Minn. 135, 163 N.W.2d 755 (independent contractor); Ramirez v. Redevelopment Agency of City & County of San Francisco, 1970, 4 Cal.App.3d 397, 84 Cal.Rptr. 356 (same); Bundy v. City of New York, 1965, 23 A.D.2d 392, 261 N.Y.S.2d 221; Zeglen v. Minkiewicz, 1963, 12 N.Y.2d 497, 240 N.Y.S.2d 965, 191 N.E.2d 450 (master and servant); and cf. Wold v. Grozalsky, 1938, 277 N.Y. 364, 14 N.E.2d 437 (joint owners of building).

43. See Moody v. Kirkpatrick, M.D.Tenn.1964, 234 F.Supp. 537; Judson v. Peoples Bank & Trust Co. of Westfield, 1957, 25 N.J. 17, 134 A.2d 761. See Notes, 1958, 12 Rut.L.Rev. 533; 1934, 47 Harv.L.Rev. 209.

or by interpretation of it, the distribution of the liability is in proportion to the comparative fault of the defendants.⁴⁴

WESTLAW REFERENCES

digest(contribution /s "joint tortfeasor*")
topic(contribution) /p "joint tortfeasor"
contribution /s statute legislation /p joint +2 tort tortfeasor*

§ 51. Indemnity

There is an important substantive difference between, first, an order distributing loss among tortfeasors by requiring others each to pay a proportionate share to one who has discharged their "joint" liability and, second, an order requiring another to reimburse in full one who has discharged a common liability. In the prevailing usage, the first is referred to as contribution; the second, as indemnity.[1] Because of either confusion or deliberate departure from prevailing usage, however, there are decisions in which full reimbursement has been allowed under the name of contribution,[2] or some form of distribution has been allowed under the name of indemnity.[3] Unless otherwise indicated, we adhere in this text to the prevailing terminology, using "contribution" to refer to an order for some form of distribution and "indemnity" to refer to an order for full reimbursement.

One of the common, and simple, bases for indemnity is a contract which provides for it.[4] The right to indemnity may, however, arise without agreement, and by operation of law to prevent a result which is regarded as unjust or unsatisfactory. Although the ancient specious argument that the courts will not aid one tortfeasor against another because no one should be permitted to found a cause of action on one's own wrong, would appear to apply quite as fully to indemnity as to contribution, the courts have been much more disposed to reject it where indemnity is involved.[5]

Thus it is generally agreed that there may be indemnity in favor of one who is held responsible solely by imputation of law because of a relation to the actual wrongdoer, as where an employer is vicariously liable for the tort of a servant[6] or an independent

---

44. Bielski v. Schulze, 1962, 16 Wis.2d 1, 114 N.W.2d 105; Mitchell v. Branch, 1961, 45 Hawaii 128, 363 P.2d 969; Little v. Miles, 1948, 213 Ark. 725, 212 S.W.2d 935. See Uniform Comparative Fault Act, 1977, § 2. Also see infra, § 51, in relation to problems of both terminology and substance arising when legislation is not explicit as to whether allocation proportional to culpability or to causal contribution is allowable.

§ 51

1. Well stated in McFall v. Compagnie Maritime Belge, 1952, 304 N.Y. 314, 107 N.E.2d 463.

2. See for example Horrabin v. City of Des Moines, 1924, 198 Iowa 549, 199 N.W. 988; Seaboard Air Line Railroad Co. v. American District Electric Protective Co., 1932, 106 Fla. 330, 143 So. 316; Preferred Accident Insurance Co. v. Musante, Berman & Steinberg, 1947, 133 Conn. 536, 52 A.2d 862; Skala v. Lehon, 1931, 343 Ill. 602, 175 N.E. 832.

3. See infra, this section, at notes 32–34.

4. A contract agreeing to indemnify a party against the consequences of that party's own negligence is not against public policy. Southern Pacific Co. v. Morrison-Knudsen Co., 1959, 216 Or. 398, 338 P.2d 665; Indemnity Insurance Co. v. Koontz-Wagner Electric Co., 7th Cir. 1956, 233 F.2d 380. But such a construction will not be put upon a contract unless it is very clearly expressed. Barrus v. Wilkinson, 1965, 16 Utah 2d 204, 398 P.2d 207. An agreement of indemnity against intentional trespass has been held to be ineffective as against public policy. Pruet v. Dugger-Holmes & Associates, 1964, 276 Ala. 403, 162 So.2d 613.

5. See Davis, Indemnity Between Negligent Tortfeasors; A Proposed Rationale, 1952, 37 Iowa L.Rev. 517; Meriam and Thornton, Indemnity Between Tort-Feasors, 1950, 25 N.Y.U.L.Rev. 845; Leflar, Contribution and Indemnity Between Tortfeasors, 1932, 81 U.Pa.L.Rev. 130; Cohlen, Contribution and Indemnity Between Tortfeasors, 1936, 21 Corn.L.Q. 552, 1937, 22 Corn.L.Q. 469; Shark, Common Law Indemnity Among Joint Tortfeasors, 1965, 7 Ariz.L.Rev. 59; Note, 1966, 33 Tenn.L.Rev. 184.

6. Canadian Indemnity Co. v. United States Fidelity & Guaranty Co., 9th Cir. 1954, 213 F.2d 658; Thomas v. Malco Refineries, 10th Cir. 1954, 214 F.2d 884; American Southern Insurance Co. v. Dime Taxi Service, 1963, 275 Ala. 51, 151 So.2d 783; McLaughlin v. Siegel, 1936, 166 Va. 374, 185 S.E. 873; Skala v. Lehon, 1931, 343 Ill. 602, 175 N.E. 832; Restatement of Restitution, § 96. See Jolowicz, The Right to Indemnity Between Master and Servant, [1956] Camb.L.J. 100.

This has been vigorously attacked as subverting the policy behind respondeat superior. Steffen, The Employer's "Indemnity" Action, 1958, 25 U.Chi.L.Rev. 465; Williams, Vicarious Liability and the Master's In-

contractor;[7] or an innocent partner[8] or carrier[9] is held liable for the acts of another, or the owner of an automobile for the conduct of the driver.[10] Likewise one who is directed or employed by another[11] to do an act not manifestly wrong,[12] or is induced to act by the misrepresentations of the other,[13] is entitled to indemnity for recovery by a third party.

The principle is not, however, limited to those who are personally free from fault. A similar rule has been applied to indemnity against a supplier of goods when a retailer[14] or user[15] of the goods incurs liability by reason of negligent reliance upon the supplier's proper care. The same is true where the owner of a building negligently relies upon a contractor who makes improvements or repairs.[16] Again, it is quite generally agreed that there may be indemnity in favor of one who was under only a secondary duty where another was primarily responsible, as where a municipal corporation, held liable for failure to keep its streets in safe condition, seeks recovery from the person who has created the condition, or a property owner who has permitted it;[17] or an owner of land held

demnity, 1957, 20 Mod.L.Rev. 220; James, Contribution, Indemnity and Subrogation, and the Efficient Distribution of Accident Losses, 1958, 21 NACCA L.J. 360, 369; Note, 1954, 63 Yale L.J. 570. In United States v. Gilman, 1953, 347 U.S. 507, 74 S.Ct. 695, 98 L.Ed. 898, it was held that the United States, held liable under the Federal Tort Claims Act, had no right to indemnity. See, however, McCrary v. United States, D.Tenn.1964, 235 F.Supp. 33; Gahagan v. State Farm Mutual Auto Insurance Co., D.La.1964, 233 F.Supp. 171.

7. Tipaldi v. Riverside Memorial Chapel, 1948, 273 App.Div. 414, 78 N.Y.S.2d 12, motion denied 297 N.Y.S.2d 1029, 80 N.E.2d 544, affirmed, 298 N.Y. 686, 82 N.E.2d 585; Waylander-Peterson Co. v. Great Northern Railway Co., 8th Cir. 1953, 201 F.2d 408; George A. Fuller Co. v. Otis Elevator Co., 1918, 245 U.S. 489, 38 S.Ct. 180, 62 L.Ed. 422; Standard Oil Co. v. Robins Dry Dock & Repair Co., 2d Cir. 1929, 32 F.2d 182; Griffiths & Son Co. v. National Fireproofing Co., 1923, 310 Ill. 331, 141 N.E. 739.

8. Farney v. Hauser, 1921, 109 Kan. 75, 198 P. 178; In re Ryan's Estate, 1914, 157 Wis. 576, 147 N.W. 993; Smith v. Ayrault, 1888, 71 Mich. 475, 39 N.W. 724.

9. Joest v. Clarendon & Rosedale Packet Co., 1916, 122 Ark. 353, 183 S.W. 759; Produce Trading Co. v. Norfolk Southern Railway Co., 1919, 178 N.C. 175, 100 S.E. 316; Orlove v. Philippine Air Lines, 2d Cir. 1958, 257 F.2d 384; Merchant Shippers Association v. Kellogg Express & Draying Co., 1946, 28 Cal.2d 594, 170 P.2d 923.

10. Fontainebleau Hotel Corp. v. Postol, Fla.App. 1962, 142 So.2d 299; Lunderberg v. Bierman, 1954, 241 Minn. 349, 63 N.W.2d 355; Traub v. Dinzler, 1955, 309 N.Y. 395, 131 N.E.2d 564. Compare, as to an original tortfeasor held liable for the negligence of a physician treating the victim, Herrero v. Atkinson, 1964, 227 Cal. App.2d 69, 38 Cal.Rptr. 490; Musco v. Conte, 1964, 22 A.D.2d 121, 254 N.Y.S.2d 589.

11. Horrabin v. City of Des Moines, 1924, 198 Iowa 549, 199 N.W. 988; Oats v. Dublin National Bank, 1936, 127 Tex. 2, 90 S.W.2d 824; Culmer v. Wilson, 1896, 13 Utah 129, 44 P. 833; Aberdeen Construction Co. v. City of Aberdeen, 1915, 84 Wash. 429, 147 P. 2; Higgins v. Russo, 1899, 72 Conn. 238, 43 A. 1050.

12. Plasikowski v. Arbus, 1919, 92 Conn. 556, 103 A. 642; Cox v. Cameron Lumber Co., 1905, 39 Wash. 562, 82 P. 116. Cf. Russell v. Walker, 1890, 150 Mass. 531, 23 N.E. 383 (sheriff attaching wrong goods).

13. Kennedy v. Colt, 1959, 216 Or. 647, 339 P.2d 450; Philadelphia, Baltimore & Washington Railroad Co. v. Roberts, 1919, 134 Md. 398, 106 A. 615; Henderson v. Sevey, 1822, 2 Me. (2 Greenl.) 139. Otherwise where the actor was not entitled to rely on the representation. Trimble v. Exchange Bank, 1901, 23 Ky.L. Rep. 367, 62 S.W. 1027.

14. Tromza v. Tecumseh Products Co., 3d Cir. 1967, 378 F.2d 601; Frank R. Jelleff, Inc. v. Pollak Brothers, N.D.Ind.1959, 171 F.Supp. 467; Popkin Brothers v. Volk's Tire Co., 1941, 20 N.J.Misc. 1, 23 A.2d 162; Busch & Latta Paint Co. v. Woermann Construction Co., 1925, 310 Mo. 419, 276 S.W. 614; Farr v. Armstrong Rubber Co., 1970, 288 Minn. 83, 179 N.W.2d 64. See Degnan and Barton, Vouching to Quality Warranty: Case Law and Commercial Code, 1963, 51 Cal.L. Rev. 471.

15. Allied Mutual Casualty Corp. v. General Motors Corp., 10th Cir. 1960, 279 F.2d 455; Blair v. Cleveland Twist Drill Co., 7th Cir. 1952, 197 F.2d 842; Crouse v. Wilbur-Ellis Co., 1954, 77 Ariz. 359, 272 P.2d 352; McFall v. Compagnie Maritime Belge, 1952, 304 N.Y. 314, 107 N.E.2d 463; Peters v. Lyons, Iowa 1969, 168 N.W.2d 759.

16. Bethlehem Shipbuilding Corp. v. Joseph Gutradt Co., 9th Cir. 1926, 10 F.2d 769; Pennsylvania Steel Co. v. Washington & Berkeley Bridge Co., D.W.Va.1912, 194 F. 1011; Georgia Power Co. v. Banning Cotton Mills Co., 1931, 42 Ga.App. 671, 157 S.E. 525; Barb v. Farmers Insurance Exchange, Mo.1955, 281 S.W.2d 297; Bond v. Otis Elevator Co., Tex.1965, 388 S.W.2d 681, on remand, Tex.Civ.App., 391 S.W.2d 519.

17. City & County of San Francisco v. Ho Sing, Cal. App.1958, 323 P.2d 1054, replaced by, 51 Cal.2d 127, 330 P.2d 802 (long list of cases); Washington Gaslight Co. v. District of Columbia, 1895, 161 U.S. 316, 16 S.Ct. 564, 40 L.Ed. 712; City of Des Moines v. Barnes, 1947, 238 Iowa 1192, 30 N.W.2d 170; City of Fort Scott v. Pen Lubric Oil Co., 1927, 122 Kan. 369, 252 P. 268;

liable for injury received upon it sues the wrongdoer who created the hazard.[18]

There is in addition considerable language in the cases to the effect that one whose negligence has consisted of mere passive neglect may have indemnity from an active wrongdoer.[19] It appears that this rule has been applied only in situations where one tortfeasor, by active conduct, has created a danger to the plaintiff, and the other has merely failed to discover or to remedy it. Certainly there is no general principle that one who has failed to turn on the lights on a parked automobile is entitled to indemnity against a driver who runs into it and injures a passenger. Moreover, the rule that a passive tortfeasor is entitled to indemnity from an active tortfeasor may be held inapplicable after the principle of comparative fault has been adopted.[20]

Carrying the idea of different kinds of fault to a possible logical conclusion, it has been suggested[21] that one who is liable merely for ordinary negligence should have indemnity from another who has been guilty of intentionally wrongful or reckless conduct. There is, however, no visible support for such a proposition, other than the obvious fact that there can be no indemnity in favor of the intentional or reckless tortfeasor,[22] and it has been firmly rejected when the question has arisen;[23] moreover, as noted in the next preceding paragraph, this rule, as well as any other rule that gives one tortious actor a right of indemnity from another tortious actor, may be held inapplicable after the principle of comparative fault has been adopted. Finally, it has even been held that the doctrine of the last clear chance[24] is to be applied to permit indemnity for the earlier liability against the later.[25] It is difficult to see any good reason why the mere difference in time which is the basis of the last clear chance rule should lead to any such conclusion as to liability between the tortfeasors themselves.

Out of all this, it is extremely difficult to state any general rule or principle as to when indemnity will be allowed and when it will not.[26] It has been said that it is permit-

---

Township of Hart v. Noret, 1916, 191 Mich. 427, 158 N.W. 17.

18. Preferred Accident Insurance Co. v. Musante, Berman & Steinberg, 1947, 133 Conn. 536, 52 A.2d 862; Middlesboro Home Telegraph Co. v. Louisville & Nashville Railroad Co., 1926, 214 Ky. 822, 284 S.W. 104; Eureka Coal Co. v. Louisville & Nashville Railroad Co., 1929, 219 Ala. 286, 122 So. 169; cf. United States v. Chicago, Rock Island & Pacific Railroad Co., 10th Cir. 1949, 171 F.2d 377.

19. Chicago Great Western Railway Co. v. Casura, 8th Cir. 1956, 234 F.2d 441; Western Casualty & Surety Co. v. Shell Oil Co., Mo.App.1967, 413 S.W.2d 550; Jackson v. Associated Dry Goods Corp., 1963, 13 N.Y.2d 112, 242 N.Y.S.2d 210, 192 N.E.2d 167; Daly v. Bergstedt, 1964, 267 Minn. 244, 126 N.W.2d 242; D'Amico v. Moriarty Meat Co., 1964, 47 Ill.App.2d 63, 197 N.E.2d 445. See Notes, 1960, 28 Ford.L.Rev. 782; 1966, 30 Mo.L.Rev. 624.

Otherwise where there is more than mere failure to discover. Kenyon v. F. M. C. Corp., 1970, 286 Minn. 283, 176 N.W.2d 69.

The converse is sometimes stated: no indemnity when plaintiff's active negligence contributed to the injury. Spivack v. Hara, 1966, 69 Ill.App.2d 22, 216 N.E.2d 173; Campbell v. Preston, Mo.1964, 379 S.W.2d 557; Miller v. Pennsylvania Railroad Co., 2d Cir. 1956, 236 F.2d 295; Public Service Electric & Gas Co. v. Waldroup, 1955, 38 N.J.Super. 419, 119 A.2d 172. See, however, Seiden v. Savings & Loan Association, 1958, 10 Misc.2d 720, 172 N.Y.S.2d 403, still allowing recovery on the basis of a difference in degree.

20. See Tolbert v. Gerber Industries, Inc., Minn. 1977, 255 N.W.2d 362.

21. Keeton, Contribution and Indemnity Among Tortfeasors, 1960, 27 Ins.Counsel J. 630, 631.

22. Cf. Padgett v. Boswell, Tex.Civ.App.1952, 250 S.W.2d 234, refused, no reversible error.

23. Jacobs v. General Accident, Fire & Life Assurance Corp., 1961, 14 Wis.2d 1, 109 N.W.2d 462; Panasuk v. Seaton, D.Mont.1968, 277 F.Supp. 979. Cf. Warner v. Capital Transit Co., D.D.C.1958, 162 F.Supp. 253 (contribution, but not indemnity, when one of the defendants violated carrier's higher duty of care). Contrary to this last case is United Airlines, Inc. v. Wiener, 9th Cir. 1964, 335 F.2d 379, certiorari dismissed, 1965, 379 U.S. 951, 85 S.Ct. 452, 13 L.Ed.2d 549.

24. See infra, § 66.

25. Nashua Iron & Steel Co. v. Worcester & Nashua Railroad Co., 1882, 62 N.H. 159; Colorado & Southern Railway Co. v. Western Light & Power Co., 1923, 73 Colo. 107, 214 P. 30; Knippenberg v. Lord & Taylor, 1920, 193 App.Div. 753, 184 N.Y.S. 785. Cf. Parchefsky v. Kroll Brothers, 1935, 267 N.Y. 410, 196 N.E. 308.

26. Two careful attempts at analysis of indemnity are Hendrickson v. Minnesota Power & Light Co., 1960, 258 Minn. 368, 104 N.W.2d 843, and Jacobs v. General Accident, Fire & Life Assurance Corp., 1961,

ted only where the indemnitor has owed a separate duty to the indemnitee;[27] that it is based on a "great difference" in the gravity of the fault of the two tortfeasors;[28] or that it rests upon a disproportion or difference in character of the duties owed by the two to the injured plaintiff.[29] Probably none of these is the complete answer, and, as is so often the case in the law of torts, no one explanation can be found which will cover all of the cases. Indemnity is a shifting of responsibility from the shoulders of one person to another; and the duty to indemnify has been recognized in cases where equities supported it. A court's view of the equities may have been based on the relation of the parties to one another, and the consequent duty owed; or it may be because of a significant difference in the kind or quality of their conduct.

Changes in the law of contribution and comparative fault may materially alter the context and the equities, thus causing courts to reconsider rules of indemnity. In the past, courts often viewed their choice as one between allocating the whole loss to one of two tortfeasors or dividing it equally between them. Adoption of comparative fault may be seen as creating another option—allocating loss according to percentages. In some contexts, this outcome may appear more equitable then either of the first two. Recognition of this option of percentage allocation has already caused some modification of the law of indemnity,[30] and further modification may be expected.[31] These changes may also produce some confusion in terminology. "Contribution," as traditionally used, refers to distribution in equal shares. Thus an allocation proportional either to culpability or to causal contribution[32] is neither contribution in the traditional sense nor indemnity in the traditional sense, and one may be tempted to attach one or the other of the traditional labels in the hope of influencing a court's response to claims for an allocation proportional to culpability or to causal contribution.[33] The substantive issues are, of course, issues that should be examined on the merits rather than being controlled by the choice of a label. Since in many states there is a statute regarding contribution and a statute regarding comparative fault, but no statute explicitly allowing or disallowing indemnity, it may be argued that courts, addressing the merits, have less freedom to modify rules of "contribution" or "comparative fault" than to modify rules of "indemnity" so as to allow percentage rather than full indemnity. Thus, resolution of claims for a form of relief that might be viewed as somewhere between traditional contribution

14 Wis.2d 1, 109 N.W.2d 462. Both arrived at a brief list, similar to the foregoing. Subsequently, the Minnesota legislature adopted a comparative fault act, and the court then held that the rule allowing a passive tortfeasor indemnity from an active tortfeasor should be deleted from the list. Tolbert v. Gerber Industries, Inc., Minn.1977, 255 N.W.2d 362.

As in the case of contribution, indemnity is not allowed against one who has a defense, such as family immunity against the original plaintiff. Chamberlain v. McCleary, E.D.Tenn.1963, 217 F.Supp. 591.

27. Humble Oil & Refining Co. v. Martin, 1949, 148 Tex. 175, 222 S.W.2d 995.

28. See United Air Lines v. Wiener, 9th Cir. 1964, 335 F.2d 379, certiorari dismissed 1965, 379 U.S. 951, 85 S.Ct. 452, 13 L.Ed.2d 549; Slattery v. Marra Bro., 2d Cir. 1951, 186 F.2d 134, certiorari denied, 341 U.S. 915, 71 S.Ct. 736, 95 L.Ed. 1351; Atchison, Topeka & Santa Fe Railroad Co. v. Lan Franco, 1968, 267 Cal.App.2d 881, 73 Cal.Rptr. 660.

29. Davis, Indemnity Between Negligent Tortfeasors: A Proposed Rationale, 1952, 37 Iowa L.Rev. 517.

30. See Tolbert v. Gerber Industries, Inc., Minn. 1977, 255 N.W.2d 362, abrogating the rule under which a passive tortfeasor obtained indemnity from an active tortfeasor, and allowing contribution in proportion to relative culpability.

31. As suggestive of reduced application of indemnity and greater application of contribution proportional either to culpability or to causal contribution, see American Motorcycle Association v. Superior Court, 1978, 20 Cal.3d 578, 146 Cal.Rptr. 182, 578 P.2d 899; Safeway Stores, Inc. v. Nest-Kart, 1978, 21 Cal.3d 322, 146 Cal.Rptr. 550, 579 P.2d 441; Skinner v. Reed-Prentice Division Package Machinery Co., 1978, 70 Ill.2d 1, 15 Ill.Dec. 829, 374 N.E.2d 437; Dole v. Dow Chemical Co., 1972, 30 N.Y.2d 143, 331 N.Y.S.2d 382, 282 N.E.2d 288, and the Annotation at 53 A.L.R.2d 184.

32. See cases cited in the next preceding footnote.

33. See Dole v. Dow Chemical Co., 1972, 30 N.Y.2d 143, 331 N.Y.S.2d 382, 282 N.E.2d 288.

and traditional indemnity is likely to involve issues of policy and process, including the respective roles of courts and legislatures, and especially the role of courts in deciding issues closely related to but not identical with those explicitly controlled by legislation.[34]

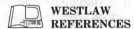
WESTLAW REFERENCES

digest(indemnity /s joint /s liability tortfeasor*)
contribution indemnity /s "comparative fault"
indemnity /5 partial percent! % topic(413)

§ 52. Apportionment of Damages

Once it is determined that the defendant's conduct has been a cause of some damage suffered by the plaintiff, a further question may arise as to the portion of the total damage sustained which may properly be assigned to the defendant, as distinguished from other causes. The question is primarily not one of the fact of causation, but of the feasibility and practical convenience of splitting up the total harm into separate parts which may be attributed to each of two or more causes.[1] Where a factual basis can be found for some rough practical apportionment, which limits a defendant's liability to that part of the harm of which that defendant's conduct has been a cause in fact, it is likely that the apportionment will be made. Where no such basis can be found, the courts generally hold the defendant for the entire loss, notwithstanding the fact that other causes have contributed to it.

The distinction is one between injuries which are reasonably capable of being separated and injuries which are not. If two defendants, struggling for a single gun, succeed in shooting the plaintiff, there is no reasonable basis for dividing the injury between them, and each will be liable for all of it. If they shoot the plaintiff independently, with separate guns, and the plaintiff dies from the effect of both wounds, there can still be no division, for death cannot be divided or apportioned except by an arbitrary rule devised for that purpose.[2] If they merely inflict separate wounds, and the plaintiff survives, a basis for division exists, because it is possible to regard the two wounds as separate injuries;[3] and the same is of course true as to wounds negligently inflicted.[4] There will be obvious difficulties of proof as to the apportionment of certain elements of damages, such as physical and mental suffering and medical expenses, but such difficulties are not insuperable, and it is better to attempt some rough division than to hold one defendant for the wound inflicted by the other. Upon the same basis, if two defendants each pollute a stream with oil, in some instances it may be possible to say that each has interfered to a separate extent with the plaintiff's rights in the water, and to make some division of the

---

34. See supra, § 3.

§ 52

1. See Prosser, Joint Torts and Several Liability, 1937, 25 Cal.L.Rev. 413; Jackson, Joint Torts and Several Liability, 1939, 17 Tex.L.Rev. 399; Conant, Recent Developments in Joint and Several Tort Liability, 1962, 14 Baylor L.Rev. 421. An analogy may be suggested to the problem of splitting a cause of action against a single defendant, in the pleading cases. See Clark, Code Pleading, 1928, 84; McCaskill, The Elusive Cause of Action, 1937, 4 U.Chi.L.Rev. 281; Gavit, The Code Cause of Action, 1930, 30 Col.L.Rev. 802; Harris, What is a Cause of Action, 1928, 16 Cal.L.Rev. 459.

2. Cf. Wilson v. State, Tex.Cr.1893, 24 S.W. 409; People v. Lewis, 1899, 124 Cal. 551, 57 P. 470; Thompson v. Louisville & Nashville Railroad Co., 1890, 91 Ala. 496, 8 So. 406; Hawkes v. Goll, 1939, 256 App.Div.

940, 9 N.Y.S.2d 924, appeal granted, 1939, 256 App.Div. 1002, 11 N.Y.S.2d 556, affirmed, 1940, 281 N.Y. 808, 24 N.E.2d 484. Upon the same basis, it has been held that insanity cannot be apportioned among several causes. Rooney v. New York, New Haven & Hartford Railroad Co., 1899, 173 Mass. 222, 53 N.E. 435.

3. Le Laurin v. Murray, 1905, 75 Ark. 232, 87 S.W. 131; Schafer v. Ostmann, 1910, 148 Mo.App. 644, 129 S.W. 63; Albrecht v. St. Hedwig's Roman Catholic Benevolent Society, 1919, 205 Mich. 395, 171 N.W. 461.

4. McAllister v. Pennsylvania Railroad Co., 1936, 324 Pa. 65, 187 A. 415; Meier v. Holt, 1956, 347 Mich. 430, 80 N.W.2d 207; Hughes v. Great American Indemnity Co., 5th Cir. 1956, 236 F.2d 71, certiorari denied 352 U.S. 989, 77 S.Ct. 386, 1 L.Ed.2d 368; Corbett v. Clarke, 1948, 187 Va. 222, 46 S.E.2d 327; De Witt v. Gerard, 1936, 274 Mich. 299, 264 N.W. 379.

damages.⁵ It is not possible if the oil is ignited, and burns the plaintiff's barn.⁶

In general, entire liability is imposed only where there is no factual basis for holding that one wrongdoer's conduct was not a cause in fact of part of the harm. Factual variations among individual cases may be quite significant, but it is possible to make a classification of the more common types of situations.⁷

Concerted Action

Where two or more persons act in concert, it is well settled both in criminal ⁸ and in civil cases that each will be liable for the entire result.⁹ Such concerted wrongdoers were considered "joint tort feasors" by the early common law.¹⁰ In legal contemplation, there is a joint enterprise, and a mutual agency, so that the act of one is the act of all,¹¹ and liability for all that is done is visited upon each.¹²

Vicarious Liability

The liability of a master for the acts of a servant,¹³ or that of a principal, in exceptional circumstances, for those of a non-servant agent,¹⁴ within the scope of the employment or agency, stands upon grounds that do not support apportionment. Under the doctrine of respondeat superior,¹⁵ the master becomes responsible for the same act for which the servant is liable, and for the same consequences. Ordinarily there is a sound basis for indemnity,¹⁶ but not for any apportionment of damages between the two.¹⁷

Common Duty

Two defendants may be under a similar duty to exercise care to prevent a particular occurrence. The most obvious illustration is the case of the fall of a party wall, which each of two adjoining landowners was required to maintain.¹⁸ So likewise two or more defendants may each be under an obligation to keep the same railway track ¹⁹ or

---

5. Watson v. Pyramid Oil Co., 1923, 198 Ky. 135, 248 S.W. 227; Snavely v. City of Goldendale, 1941, 10 Wn.2d 453, 117 P.2d 221; Farley v. Crystal Coal & Coke Co., 1920, 85 W.Va. 595, 102 S.E. 265; Johnson v. City of Fairmont, 1933, 188 Minn. 451, 247 N.W. 572.

6. Northup v. Eakes, 1918, 72 Okl. 66, 178 P. 266; Phillips Petroleum Co. v. Vandergriff, 1942, 190 Okl. 280, 122 P.2d 1020. Accord, as to poisoning livestock, Tidal Oil Co. v. Pease, 1931, 153 Okl. 137, 5 P.2d 389; as to damage to crops, Phillips Petroleum Co. v. Hardee, 5th Cir. 1951, 189 F.2d 205; Robillard v. Selah-Moxee Irrigation District, 1959, 54 Wn.2d 582, 343 P.2d 565. Cf. Neville v. Mitchell, 1902, 28 Tex.Civ.App. 89, 66 S.W. 579 (illness resulting from nuisance). On this basis Griffith v. Kerrigan, 1952, 109 Cal.App.2d 637, 241 P.2d 296, where water damaged fruit trees, appears wrongly decided.

7. See Prosser, Joint Torts and Several Liability, 1937, 25 Cal.L.Rev. 413; Notes, 1924, 24 Col.L.Rev. 891; 1931, 19 Cal.L.Rev. 630; 1937, 21 Minn.L.Rev. 616.

8. Sir Charles Stanley's Case, 1663, Kel. 86, 84 Eng. Rep. 1094; State v. Newberg, 1929, 129 Or. 564, 278 P. 568.

9. Garrett v. Garrett, 1948, 228 N.C. 530, 46 S.E.2d 302; Wrabek v. Suchomel, 1920, 145 Minn. 468, 177 N.W. 764; Bunker Hill & Sullivan Mining & Concentrating Co. v. Polak, 9th Cir. 1925, 7 F.2d 583, certiorari denied 269 U.S. 581, 46 S.Ct. 106, 70 L.Ed.2d 423; Oliver v. Miles, 1926, 144 Miss. 852, 110 So. 666; Bobich v. Dackow, 1929, 229 Ky. 830, 18 S.W.2d 280. See also the amusing opinion of Minturn, J., in Tricoli v. Centalanza, 1924, 100 N.J.L. 231, 126 A. 214, affirmed, 1925, 101 N.J.L. 570, 129 A. 923.

10. As to joinder of defendants in one action, and the meaning of "concert", see supra, § 46.

11. "* * * all coming to do an unlawful act, and of one party, the act of one is the act of all of the same party being present." Sir John Heydon's Case, 1613, 11 Co.Rep. 5, 77 Eng.Rep. 1150.

12. See Note, 1928, 14 Va.L.Rev. 677.

13. Schumpert v. Southern Railway Co., 1903, 65 S.C. 332, 43 S.E. 813; Mayberry v. Northern Pacific Railroad Co., 1907, 100 Minn. 79, 110 N.W. 356; Verlinda v. Stone & Webster Engineering Corp., 1911, 44 Mont. 223, 119 P. 573; Allen v. Trester, 1924, 112 Neb. 515, 199 N.W. 841. See Second Restatement of Agency, § 219.

14. Second Restatement of Agency, §§ 214, 250, 251. See also Bradford v. Brock, 1934, 140 Cal.App. 47, 34 P.2d 1048 (statutory agency).

15. See infra, § 70.

16. See supra, § 51.

17. As to joinder of defendants and contradictory verdicts, see supra, § 47.

18. Johnson v. Chapman, 1897, 43 W.Va. 639, 28 S.E. 744; Klauder v. McGrath, 1860, 35 Pa. 128; Simmons v. Everson, 1891, 124 N.Y. 319, 26 N.E. 911.

19. Lindsay v. Acme Cement Plaster Co., 1922, 220 Mich. 367, 190 N.W. 275; Wisconsin Central Railroad Co. v. Ross, 1892, 142 Ill. 9, 31 N.E. 412; Schaffer v. Pennsylvania Railroad Co., 7th Cir. 1939, 101 F.2d 369;

highway [20] in repair. When both defendants fail to perform their obligation, and harm results, each will be liable for the event; and here likewise there is no reasonable basis for any division of damages.

Single Indivisible Result

Certain results, by their very nature, are obviously incapable of any reasonable or practical division. Death is such a result,[21] and so is a broken leg or any single wound, the destruction of a house by fire, or the sinking of a barge.[22] No ingenuity can suggest anything more than a purely arbitrary apportionment of such harm. Where two or more causes combine to produce such a single result, incapable of any reasonable division, each may be a substantial factor in bringing about the loss, and if so, each is charged with all of it. Here again the typical case is that of two vehicles which collide and injure a third person.[23] The duties which are owed to the plaintiff by the defendants are separate, and may not be identical in character or scope,[24] but entire liability rests upon the obvious fact that each has contributed to the single result, and that no reasonable division can be made.[25]

Such entire liability is imposed both where some of the causes are innocent, as where a fire set by the defendant is carried by a wind,[26] and where two or more of the causes are culpable. It is imposed where either cause would have been sufficient in itself to bring about the result, as in the case of merging fires which burn a building,[27] and also where both were essential to the injury,

cf. Galveston, Harrisburg & San Antonio Railroad Co. v. Nass, 1900, 94 Tex. 255, 59 S.W. 870; Hoye v. Great Northern Railroad Co., C.C.Mont.1903, 120 F. 712.

20. Doeg v. Cook, 1899, 126 Cal. 213, 58 P. 707. Cf. Walton, Witten & Graham Co. v. Miller's Administratrix, 1909, 109 Va. 210, 63 S.E. 458 (employer and contractor both under duty to warn of blasting); Nelson v. Illinois Central Railroad Co., 1910, 98 Miss. 295, 53 So. 619 (railroad and Pullman company liable for loss of baggage); Woods v. Kansas City, Kaw Valley & Western Railroad Co., 1932, 134 Kan. 755, 8 P.2d 404; Economy Light & Power Co. v. Hiller, 1903, 203 Ill. 518, 68 N.E. 72.

21. Blanton v. Sisters of Charity, 1948, 82 Ohio App. 20, 79 N.E.2d 688; Bolick v. Gallagher, 1955, 268 Wis. 421, 67 N.W.2d 860; Hackworth v. Davis, 1964, 87 Idaho 98, 390 P.2d 422.

22. Cf. Brown v. Murdy, 1960, 78 S.D. 367, 102 N.W.2d 664 (loss of foot through negligence of two physicians); Watts v. Smith, 1965, 375 Mich. 120, 134 N.W.2d 194 (morning and afternoon accidents causing indivisible injury); Maddux v. Donaldson, 1961, 362 Mich. 425, 108 N.W.2d 33 (multiple collisions in quick succession; if factfinder cannot reasonably make a decision based on evidence, wrongdoers producing the indivisible injury are jointly and severally liable). But see, as to the possibility of a division on the basis of potential damage from the earlier cause, infra, this section.

23. See Arnst v. Estes, 1939, 136 Me. 272, 8 A.2d 201 (stating clearly that entire liability rests upon the absence of any logical basis for apportionment). Also Schools v. Walker, 1948, 187 Va. 619, 47 S.E.2d 418; Way v. Waterloo, Cedar Falls & Northern Railroad Co., 1947, 239 Iowa 244, 29 N.W.2d 867; Nees v. Minneapolis St. Railway Co., 1944, 218 Minn. 532, 16 N.W.2d 758. Cf. Crowe v. Domestic Loans, Inc., 1963, 242 S.C. 310, 130 S.E.2d 845 (procuring discharge of employee).

24. In Matthews v. Delaware, Lackawanna & Western Railroad Co., 1893, 56 N.J.L. 34, 27 A. 919, and Carlton v. Boudar, 1916, 118 Va. 521, 88 S.E. 174, the court specifically held this to be immaterial.

25. Except in Kentucky, where an unusual statute permits but does not require the jury to apportion the damages arbitrarily. Elpers v. Kimbel, Ky.1963, 366 S.W.2d 157; Note, 1960, 48 Ky.L.J. 606. This has been carried to the length of permitting apportionment of damages between two defendants held liable for deceit. Evola Realty Co. v. Westerfield, Ky.1952, 251 S.W.2d 298.

In Rourk v. Selvey, 1968, 252 S.C. 25, 164 S.E.2d 909, the court overruled a line of South Carolina cases which had permitted the jury to do the same thing.

26. Haverly v. State Line & Sullivan Railroad Co., 1890, 135 Pa. 50, 19 A. 1013. Cf. Holter Hardware Co. v. Western Mortgage & Warranty Title Co., 1915, 51 Mont. 94, 149 P. 489; Long v. Crystal Refrigerator Co., 1938, 134 Neb. 44, 277 N.W. 830; Jackson v. Wisconsin Telephone Co., 1894, 88 Wis. 243, 60 N.W. 430 (lightning); Fox v. Boston & Maine Railroad Co., 1889, 148 Mass. 220, 19 N.E. 222 (frost).

Obviously only culpable causes will be held responsible. Thus where a negligent automobile driver collides with an innocent one and injures a third person, only the negligent driver is liable.

27. Anderson v. Minneapolis, St. Paul & Sault Ste. Marie Railway Co., 1920, 146 Minn. 430, 179 N.W. 45; Seckerson v. Sinclair, 1913, 24 N.D. 625, 140 N.W. 239; Miller v. Northern Pacific Railway Co., 1913, 24 Idaho 567, 135 P. 845. Cf. Oulighan v. Butler, 1905, 189 Mass. 287, 75 N.E. 726; Orton v. Virginia Carolina Chemical Co., 1918, 142 La. 790, 77 So. 632; Luengene v. Consumers' Light, Heat & Power Co., 1912, 86 Kan. 866, 122 P. 1032.

as in the vehicle collision suggested above.[28] It is not necessary that the misconduct of two defendants be simultaneous. One defendant may create a situation upon which the other may act later to cause the damage. One may leave combustible material, and the other set it afire;[29] one may leave a hole in the street, and the other drive into it.[30] Liability in such a case turns not upon causation, but on the effect of the intervening agency upon culpability.[31] A defendant, if liable at all, will be liable for all the damage caused.[32]

Damage Capable of Apportionment

Certain other results, by their nature, are more capable of apportionment. If two defendants independently shoot the plaintiff at the same time, and one wounds the plaintiff in the arm and the other in the leg, the ultimate result may be a badly damaged plaintiff in the hospital, but it is still possible, as a practical matter, to regard the two wounds as separate wrongs.[33] Mere coincidence in time does not make the two one tort, nor does similarity of design or conduct, without concert.[34] Evidence may be entirely lacking upon which to apportion some elements of the damages, such as medical expenses, or permanent disability, or the plaintiff's pain and suffering; but this is not regarded as sufficient reason to hold one defendant liable for the entire harm, including damage inflicted solely by the other.[35]

There have appeared in the decisions a number of similar situations, in some of which the extent of the harm inflicted by the separate torts has been almost incapable of any definite and satisfactory proof, and has been left merely to the jury's estimate. Thus the owners of trespassing cattle,[36] or of dogs which together kill sheep,[37] are held liable only for the separate damage done by their own animals, unless there has been

---

28. Washington & Georgetown R. Co. v. Hickey, 1897, 166 U.S. 521, 17 S.Ct. 661, 14 L.Ed. 1101 (horse car driven onto railway tracks with negligent operation of crossing gates); Folsom v. Apple River Log-Driving Co., 1877, 41 Wis. 602 (dam and bridge causing flood); Drown v. New England Telephone & Telegraph Co., 1907, 80 Vt. 1, 66 A. 801 (light wires and telephone wires crossed); Ramsey v. Carolina-Tennessee Power Co., 1928, 195 N.C. 788, 143 S.E. 861 (railway shunting cars which struck negligently maintained power line pole); Barnes v. Masterson, 1899, 38 App.Div. 612, 56 N.Y.S. 939 (defendants successively deposited sand against plaintiff's wall, which collapsed).

29. Johnson v. Chicago, Milwaukee & St. Paul Railway Co., 1883, 31 Minn. 57, 16 N.W. 488. Cf. Watson v. Kentucky & Indiana Bridge & Railroad Co., 1910, 137 Ky. 619, 126 S.W. 146, modified, 137 Ky. 619, 129 S.W. 341 (defendant flooded vicinity with gasoline, another person struck a match); Oviatt v. Garretson, 1943, 205 Ark. 792, 171 S.W.2d 287 (one defendant burned leaves, another drove into smoke pall).

30. Tobin v. Seattle, 1923, 127 Wash. 664, 221 P. 583. Cf. Ethridge v. Nicholson, 1950, 80 Ga.App. 693, 57 S.E.2d 231 (dog chasing boy on bicycle into obstruction in street); Stemmler v. Pittsburgh, 1926, 287 Pa. 365, 135 A. 100 (defective street and cyclist splashing mud); Butts v. Ward, 1938, 227 Wis. 387, 279 N.W. 6 (truck parked without lights and negligently driven car); Hill v. Edmonds, 1966, 26 A.D.2d 554, 270 N.Y.S.2d 1020 (same).

31. See supra, § 45.

32. As to joinder of defendants and the possibility of contribution from one to the other, see supra, §§ 47, 50.

33. Le Laurin v. Murray, 1905, 75 Ark. 232, 87 S.W. 131; Albrecht v. St. Hedwig's Roman Catholic Benevolent Society, 1919, 205 Mich. 395, 171 N.W. 461; McAllister v. Pennsylvania Railroad Co., 1936, 324 Pa. 65, 187 A. 415; Corbett v. Clarke, 1948, 187 Va. 222, 46 S.E.2d 327; Phillips v. Gulf & South American Steamship Co., Tex.Civ.App.1959, 323 S.W.2d 631, error refused.

34. Dickson v. Yates, 1922, 194 Iowa 910, 188 N.W. 948 (battery and trespass at same time by different persons); Millard v. Miller, 1907, 39 Colo. 103, 88 P. 845 (independent appropriations of different parts of pasture).

35. As to joining defendants in one action, see supra, § 47.

36. Dooley v. Seventeen Thousand Five Hundred Head of Sheep, 1894, 4 Cal.Unrep. 479, 101 Cal. xvii, 35 P. 1011; Pacific Live Stock Co. v. Murray, 1904, 45 Or. 103, 76 P. 1079; Wood v. Snider, 1907, 187 N.Y. 28, 79 N.E. 858; Hill v. Chappel Bros. of Montana, 1933, 93 Mont. 92, 18 P.2d 1106. Cf. King v. Ruth, 1924, 136 Miss. 377, 101 So. 500.

37. Anderson v. Halverson, 1904, 126 Iowa 125, 101 N.W. 781; Nohre v. Wright, 1906, 98 Minn. 477, 108 N.W. 865; Stine v. McShane, 1927, 55 N.D. 745, 214 N.W. 906; Miller v. Prough, 1920, 203 Mo.App. 413, 221 S.W. 159.

In a number of states owners of dogs which kill sheep are made liable for the entire damage by statute. See Worcester County v. Ashworth, 1893, 160 Mass. 186, 35 N.E. 773; McAdams v. Sutton, 1873, 24 Ohio St. 333; Dole v. Hardinger, 1917, 204 Ill.App. 640.

some concerted action, such as keeping the animals in a common herd.[38] Nuisance cases, in particular, have tended to result in apportionment of the damages, largely because the interference with the plaintiff's use of land has tended to be severable in terms of quantity, percentage, or degree. Thus defendants who independently pollute the same stream,[39] or who flood the plaintiff's land from separate sources,[40] are liable only severally for the damages individually caused, and the same is true as to nuisances due to noise,[41] or pollution of the air.[42] Perhaps the most extreme example is the case of separate repetitions of the same defamatory statement,[43] or separate acts which result in alienation of affections.[44] One may speculate that the effort to apportion the damages whenever some reasonable and practical basis could be found has been due in no small measure in the past to the lack of any rule of contribution if one tortfeasor should be compelled to pay the entire damages.

The same kind of apportionment is, however, entirely possible where some part of the damage may reasonably and conveniently be assigned to an innocent cause. Thus a defendant's dam or embankment might reasonably be expected to flood the plaintiff's property in the event of any ordinary rainfall, but a quite unprecedented and unforeseeable cloudburst may cause a flood similar in kind but far greater in extent. In such cases the weight of authority [45] holds that the defendant is liable only for such portion of the total damage as may properly be attributed to the defendant's negligence. A similar distinction has been made between damages which would have followed in any case from the defendant's reasonable conduct, and those in excess which may be attributed to the defendant's negligence,[46] and likewise between those damages caused by the defendant and those by the plaintiff.[47]

---

38. Ushirohira v. Stuckey, 1921, 52 Cal.App. 526, 199 P. 339; Wilson v. White, 1906, 77 Neb. 351, 109 N.W. 367; cf. Stephens v. Schadler, 1919, 182 Ky. 833, 207 S.W. 704.

39. Chipman v. Palmer, 1879, 77 N.Y. 51; Johnson v. City of Fairmont, 1933, 188 Minn. 451, 247 N.W. 572; Farley v. Crystal Coal & Coke Co., 1920, 85 W.Va. 595, 102 S.E. 265; Somerset Villa, Inc. v. City of Lee's Summit, Mo.1969, 436 S.W.2d 658; Snavely v. City of Goldendale, 1941, 10 Wn.2d 453, 117 P.2d 221. See Note, 1953, 31 N.C.L.Rev. 237. As to indivisible consequences, see supra, this section.

40. Miller v. Highland Ditch Co., 1891, 87 Cal. 430, 23 P. 550; William Tackaberry Co. v. Sioux City Service Co., 1911, 154 Iowa 358, 132 N.W. 945, rehearing denied, 1912, 134 N.W. 1064; Verheyen v. Dewey, 1915, 27 Idaho 1, 146 P. 1116; Boulger v. Northern Pacific Railway Co., 1918, 41 N.D. 316, 171 N.W. 632; Ryan Gulch Reservoir Co. v. Swartz, 1925, 77 Colo. 60, 234 P. 1059. Cf. Connor v. Grosso, 1953, 41 Cal.2d 229, 259 P.2d 435 (trespass by dumping earth), Wm. G. Roe & Co. v. Armour & Co., 5th Cir. 1969, 414 F.2d 862 (damages to citrus crop from two sources).

41. Sherman Gas & Electric Co. v. Belden, 1909, 103 Tex. 59, 123 S.W. 119; Neville v. Mitchell, 1902, 28 Tex. Civ.App. 89, 66 S.W. 579.

42. Swain v. Tennessee Copper Co., 1903, 111 Tenn. 430, 78 S.W. 93; Key v. Armour Fertilizer Works, 1916, 18 Ga.App. 472, 89 S.E. 593; O'Neal v. Southern Carbon Co., 1949, 216 La. 96, 43 So.2d 230.

43. Harriott v. Plimpton, 1896, 166 Mass. 585, 44 N.E. 992; Yocum v. Husted, 1918, 185 Iowa 119, 167 N.W. 663; Howe v. Bradstreet Co., 1911, 135 Ga. 564, 69 S.E. 1082; Hall v. Frankel, 1924, 183 Wis. 247, 197 N.W. 820.

44. Barton v. Barton, 1906, 119 Mo.App. 507, 94 S.W. 574; Heisler v. Heisler, 1911, 151 Iowa 503, 131 N.W. 676.

45. Radburn v. Fir Tree Lumber Co., 1915, 83 Wash. 643, 145 P. 632; McAdams v. Chicago, Rock Island & Puget Sound Co., 1925, 200 Iowa 732, 205 N.W. 310; Rix v. Town of Alamogordo, 1938, 42 N.M. 325, 77 P.2d 765; Wilson v. Hagins, 1927, 116 Tex. 538, 295 S.W. 922; Brown v. Chicago, Burlington & Quincy Railroad Co., D.Neb.1912, 195 F. 1007. See Notes, 1938, 23 Minn.L.Rev. 91; 1950, 15 Mo.L.Rev. 93.

§ 450 of the First Restatement of Torts, to the contrary, has been reversed by the Second Restatement, §§ 433A and 450. It was based on Elder v. Lykens Valley Coal Co., 1893, 157 Pa. 490, 27 A. 545.

46. Jenkins v. Pennsylvania Railroad Co., 1902, 67 N.J.L. 331, 51 A. 704 (smoke nuisance); Middleton v. Melbourne Tramway Co., 1913, 16 Comm.L.Rep. (Aust.) 572 (motorist hitting pedestrian).

47. Philadelphia & Reading Railway Co. v. Smith, 3d Cir. 1894, 64 F. 679; Bowman v. Humphrey, 1906, 132 Iowa 234, 109 N.W. 714; Randolf v. Town of Bloomfield, 1889, 77 Iowa 50, 41 N.W. 562; Walters v. Prairie Oil & Gas Co., 1922, 85 Okl. 77, 204 P. 906.

Compare also the cases where a separate part of the plaintiff's suffering or disability may be found to result from a pre-existing condition not caused by the defendant. Nelson v. Twin City Motor Bus Co., 1953, 239

The difficulty of any complete and exact proof in assessing such separate damages has been noted frequently in these cases, but it has not been regarded as sufficient justification for entire liability. The emphasis is placed upon the possibility of reasonable apportionment, and the distinct and separate invasion of the plaintiff's interests which may be attributed to each cause. The difficulty of proof may have been overstated. The courts quite reasonably have been very liberal in permitting the jury to award damages where the uncertainty as to their extent arises from the nature of the wrong itself, for which the defendant, and not the plaintiff, is responsible.[48] The requirements of proof usually have been somewhat relaxed in such cases, and it has been said that no very exact evidence will be required, and that general evidence as to the proportion in which the causes contributed to the result will be sufficient to support a verdict.[49] Cases are few in which recovery has actually been denied for lack of such proof.[50] As a last resort, in the absence of anything to the contrary, damages have been divided equally between the wrongdoers.[51] The difficulty is certainly no greater than in cases where part of the damage is to be attributed to the unreasonable conduct of the plaintiff, and the rule of avoidable consequences is applied to limit recovery.[52]

There has remained, however, enough in the way of real difficulty experienced, and possible injustice feared, to lead several writers [53] to urge that in any case where two or more defendants are shown to have been negligent, and each to have caused some damage, and only the extent as to each is in question, the burden of proof should be shifted to the defendants, and each should be held liable to the extent not disproved. The justification for this rests upon the fact that a choice must be made, as to where the loss due to failure of proof shall fall, between an entirely innocent plaintiff and defendants who are clearly proved to have been at fault, and to have done harm. A few courts have accepted this position, and have placed the burden of proof as to apportionment upon the defendants in such

Minn. 276, 58 N.W.2d 561; Gates v. Fleischer, 1886, 67 Wis. 504, 30 N.W. 674; Dallas Railway & Terminal Co. v. Ector, Com.App.1938, 131 Tex. 505, 116 S.W.2d 683; Texas Coca Cola Bottling Co. v. Lovejoy, Tex.Civ.App. 1940, 138 S.W.2d 254, error refused; Pittsburgh Steamship Co. v. Palo, 6th Cir. 1933, 64 F.2d 198; O'Keefe v. Kansas City Western Railway Co., 1912, 87 Kan. 322, 124 P. 416. Cf. Gould v. McKenna, 1878, 86 Pa. 297 (part of flooding due to condition of wall).

Compare also the "last clear chance" cases, in which the plaintiff is struck by a vehicle because of plaintiff's own negligence, but after the plaintiff is helpless the defendant inflicts further injuries by negligent failure to stop the vehicle. Cleveland, Cincinnati, Chicago & St. Louis Railway Co. v. Klee, 1900, 154 Ind. 430, 56 N.E. 234; Teakle v. San Pedro, Los Angeles & Salt Lake Railroad Co., 1907, 32 Utah 276, 90 P. 402; Weitzman v. Nassau Electric Railroad Co., 1898, 33 App.Div. 585, 53 N.Y.S. 905.

48. Little Schuylkill Navigation Railroad & Coal Co. v. Richards' Administrator, 1858, 57 Pa. 142; Jenkins v. Pennsylvania Railroad Co., 1902, 67 N.J.L. 331, 51 A. 704; Inland Power & Light Co. v. Grieger, 9th Cir. 1937, 91 F.2d 811; De Witt v. Gerard, 1936, 274 Mich. 299, 264 N.W. 379; Hughes v. Great American Indemnity Co., 5th Cir. 1956, 236 F.2d 71, certiorari denied 352 U.S. 989, 77 S.Ct. 386, 1 L.Ed.2d 368.

49. Eckman v. Lehigh & Wilkes-Barre Coal Co., 1912, 50 Pa.Super. 427; William Tackaberry Co. v. Sioux City Service Co., 1911, 154 Iowa 358, 132 N.W. 945, 134 N.W. 1064; Miller v. Prough, 1920, 203 Mo. App. 413, 221 S.W. 159; Hill v. Chappel Brothers of Montana, 1933, 93 Mont. 92, 18 P.2d 1106; Sellick v. Hall, 1879, 47 Conn. 260.

50. The only cases found are Deutsch v. Connecticut Co., 1923, 98 Conn. 482, 119 A. 891; Maas v. Perkins, 1953, 42 Wn.2d 38, 253 P.2d 427; Slater v. Pacific American Oil Co., 1931, 212 Cal. 648, 300 P. 31; Tucker Oil Co. v. Matthews, Tex.Civ.App.1938, 119 S.W.2d 606. All of these cases are believed no longer to be law.

51. Wood v. Snider, 1907, 187 N.Y. 28, 79 N.E. 858; Anderson v. Halverson, 1904, 126 Iowa 125, 101 N.W. 781; Miller v. Prough, 1920, 203 Mo.App. 413, 221 S.W. 159; Powers v. Kindt, 1874, 13 Kan. 74. See also Loui v. Oakley, 1968, 50 Hawaii 260, 272, 438 P.2d 393, and supra, §§ 41, 47.

52. Cf. Bowman v. Humphrey, 1906, 132 Iowa 234, 109 N.W. 714; Randolf v. Town of Bloomfield, 1889, 77 Iowa 50, 41 N.W. 562; Philadelphia & Reading Railroad Co. v. Smith, 3d Cir. 1894, 64 F. 679; Walters v. Prairie Oil & Gas Co., 1922, 85 Okl. 77, 204 P. 906.

53. Wigmore, Joint Tortfeasors and Severance of Damages, 1923, 17 Ill.L.Rev. 458; Carpenter, Workable Rules for Determining Proximate Cause, 1932, 20 Cal. L.Rev. 306, 406; Jackson, Joint Torts and Several Liability, 1939, 17 Tex.L.Rev. 399.

cases,[54] as for example where there are chain automobile collisions, and there is doubt as to the injuries inflicted by each driver.[55] Texas decisions [56] refusing to permit apportionment because the injury is regarded as "indivisible" may be thought to mean no more than that the defendants have the burden of proving any basis for division. There are even courts [57] which have placed upon the defendant the burden of apportionment where part of the damage has been due to an innocent cause. There are, however, some cases [58] which have rejected all idea of shifting the burden of proof to the defendant.

The choice among different rules may have significant implications with respect to who bears the risk of financial irresponsibility of one or more tortfeasors. Three different types of outcomes may be identified: first, denying relief on the ground that the plaintiff has failed to meet a burden of proof on causation; second, imposing entire liability on each of two or more wrongdoers, allowing them to be sued jointly or severally;[59] or, third, apportioning liability in some manner. If entire liability is imposed on each wrongdoer, an injured person may in fact recover full damages if any one of the wrongdoers is financially responsible, even though others are not. If instead liability is apportioned, the injured person bears the risk of financial irresponsibility of each wrongdoer. In some circumstances, the effect of making each wrongdoer legally responsible for the entire harm has been challenged as imposing an excessive and unfair burden; there is limited support for a rule that when the plaintiff suffers from the consequences of a succession of injuries sustained in different vehicular accidents, the jury should be instructed to apportion damages on the basis of evidence before them, or equally among those responsible for different impacts as to which the evidence supplies no basis for a different apportionment.[60] Also, in the context of proof that one or another of the defendants before the court manufactured a drug that caused the injuries of which the plaintiff complains, there is precedent for apportioning liability according to market shares rather than ei-

54. Phillips Petroleum Co. v. Hardee, 5th Cir. 1951, 189 F.2d 205 (pollution of irrigation waters); Finnegan v. Royal Realty Co., 1950, 35 Cal.2d 409, 218 P.2d 17 (aggravation of injuries from fire because of failure to provide exit doors); De Corsey v. Purex Corp., 1949, 92 Cal.App.2d 669, 207 P.2d 616 (aggravation of injuries from exploding bottle due to deterioration of compound); cf. Colonial Insurance Co. v. Industrial Accident Commission, 1946, 29 Cal.2d 79, 172 P.2d 884 (workers' compensation, with multiple insurance carriers).

55. Maddux v. Donaldson, 1961, 362 Mich. 425, 108 N.W.2d 33; Maroulis v. Elliot, 1966, 247 Va. 503, 151 S.E.2d 339; Holtz v. Holder, 1966, 101 Ariz. 247, 418 P.2d 584; Mathews v. Mills, 1970, 288 Minn. 16, 178 N.W.2d 841; Ruud v. Grimm, 1961, 252 Iowa 1266, 110 N.W.2d 321. See Doyle, Multiple Causes and Apportionment of Damages, 1966, 43 Denv.L.Rev. 490; Notes, 1966, 44 N.C.L.Rev. 249; 1967, 9 Ariz.L.Rev. 129; 1967, 18 Syr.L.Rev. 898.

56. Landers v. East Texas Salt Water Disposal Co., 1952, 151 Tex. 251, 248 S.W.2d 731 (pollution); Burns v. Lamb, Tex.Civ.App.1958, 312 S.W.2d 730, refused, no reversible error (same); Western Guaranty Loan Co. v. Dean, Tex.Civ.App.1958, 309 S.W.2d 857, refused, no reversible error (mental distress at collection methods); Riley v. Industrial Finance Service Co., 1957, 157 Tex. 306, 302 S.W.2d 652 (same). See, as to this interpretation of these cases, Phillips v. Gulf & South American Steamship Co., Tex.Civ.App.1959, 323 S.W.2d 631, error refused. See supra, §§ 41, 47.

57. City of Oakland v. Pacific Gas & Electric Co., 1941, 47 Cal.App.2d 444, 118 P.2d 328 (increased damage to books from delay in shutting off steam); Newbury v. Vogel, 1962, 151 Colo. 520, 379 P.2d 811 (pre-existing diseased condition); Kawamoto v. Yasutake, 1966, 49 Hawaii 42, 410 P.2d 976 (same); Wise v. Carter, Fla.App.1960, 119 So.2d 40 (prior injury). See Note, 1964, 43 N.C.L.Rev. 1011.

58. Panther Coal Co. v. Looney, 1946, 185 Va. 758, 40 S.E.2d 298; Grzybowski v. Connecticut Co., 1933, 116 Conn. 292, 164 A. 632; Maas v. Perkins, 1953, 42 Wn.2d 38, 253 P.2d 427; Sweet Milk Co. v. Stanfield, 9th Cir. 1965, 353 F.2d 811.

59. See supra, § 47, regarding joinder.

60. Loui v. Oakley, 1968, 50 Hawaii 260, 272, 438 P.2d 393, where plaintiff was injured in four different accidents, widely spaced over months, and it was considered unfair to hold one defendant liable for the consequences of all four. See Successive Injuries, infra, this section. But cf. Maddux v. Donaldson, 1961, 362 Mich. 425, 108 N.W.2d 33 (multiple collisions in quick succession; if factfinder cannot reasonably make an allocation of liability based on evidence, wrongdoers producing the indivisible injury are jointly and severally liable for entire harm).

ther imposing entire liability or denying liability altogether.[61] An apportionment has been allowed in a few additional contexts despite serious difficulties of proof.[62]

Successive Injuries

Damage may be conveniently severable in point of time. If two defendants, independently operating the same plant, pollute a stream over successive periods, it is clear that each has caused separate damage, limited in time, and that neither has any responsibility for the loss caused by the other.[63] The same may be true where a worker's health is impaired by the negligence of successive employers,[64] and of course, as stated above, where successive batteries or other personal injuries are inflicted upon the plaintiff.[65]

It is important to note that there are situations in which the earlier wrongdoer will be liable for the entire damage, but the later one will not. If an automobile negligently driven by defendant A strikes the plaintiff, causing a skull fracture, and leaves the plaintiff helpless on the highway, where shortly afterward a second automobile, negligently driven by defendant B, runs over the plaintiff and breaks a leg, A will be liable for both injuries, for when the plaintiff was left in the highway, it was reasonably to be anticipated that a second car would run the plaintiff down.[66] But defendant B should be liable only for the broken leg, since B had no part in causing the fractured skull, and could not foresee or avoid it.[67] On the same basis, an original wrongdoer may be liable for the additional harm inflicted by the negligent treatment of the victim by a physician,[68] but the physician will not be liable for the original injury.[69]

In some instances, however, injuries resulting from successive impacts, as in vehic-

---

61. See supra, § 41, and infra, § 103.

62. See Spier v. Barker, 1974, 35 N.Y.2d 444, 363 N.Y.S.2d 916, 323 N.E.2d 164 (jury may, on supporting evidence, segregate injuries caused by initial collision of cars from injuries caused by failure to fasten seat belt). Also compare Mitchell v. Volkswagenwerk, A.G., 8th Cir. 1982, 669 F.2d 1199 (Minnesota law; if injuries are indivisible, absent a reasonable basis for determining which wrongdoer caused harm, manufacturer and driver are treated as joint and several tortfeasors) with Caiazzo v. Volkswagenwerk, A.G., 2d Cir. 1981, 647 F.2d 241 (New York law; lack of evidence of what would have occurred but for alleged design defect; plaintiff has not established claim of enhancement of injuries).

63. Midland Empire Packing Co. v. Yale Oil Corp., 1946, 119 Mont. 36, 169 P.2d 732; Coleman Vitrified Brick Co. v. Smith, Tex.Civ.App.1915, 175 S.W. 860, error refused; Southern Iron & Steel Co. v. Acton, 1913, 8 Ala.App. 502, 62 So. 402; Freshwater v. Bulmer Rayon Co., [1933] Ch. 162.

64. McGannon v. Chicago & North Western Railway Co., 1924, 160 Minn. 143, 199 N.W. 894; cf. Pieczonka v. Pullman Co., 2d Cir. 1937, 89 F.2d 353. Contrast the interesting case of silicosis developed three years after the latter of two successive employments, in Golden v. Lerch Brothers, 1938, 203 Minn. 211, 281 N.W. 249. The original opinion, holding each employer liable for the full damage on the ground that the injury could not be apportioned, was withdrawn on rehearing as not supported by sufficient evidence that one employer contributed substantially to the result, and remains unpublished. It is discussed in Note, 1937, 21 Minn.L.Rev. 616.

65. Supra, introductory part of this section.

66. Adams v. Parrish, 1920, 189 Ky. 628, 225 S.W. 467; Morrison v. Medaglia, 1934, 287 Mass. 46, 191 N.E. 133; Thornton v. Eneroth, 1934, 177 Wash. 1, 30 P.2d 951; Hill v. Peres, 1934, 136 Cal.App. 132, 28 P.2d 946.

67. Bowles v. Lindley, Tex.Civ.App.1967, 411 S.W.2d 751, refused, no reversible error; Grzybowski v. Connecticut Co., 1933, 116 Conn. 292, 164 A. 632; Frye v. City of Detroit, 1932, 256 Mich. 466, 239 N.W. 886; Ristan v. Frantzen, 1953, 26 N.J.Super. 225, 97 A.2d 726, affirmed, 1954, 14 N.J. 455, 102 A.2d 614; Hughes v. Great American Indemnity Co., 5th Cir. 1956, 236 F.2d 71, certiorari denied 352 U.S. 989, 77 S.Ct. 386, 1 L.Ed.2d 368.

Compare, however, Gibson v. Bodley, 1943, 156 Kan. 338, 133 P.2d 112, where the events were treated as substantially simultaneous, and entire liability was found.

68. Thompson v. Fox, 1937, 326 Pa. 209, 192 A. 107; Aubuschon v. Witt, Mo.1967, 412 S.W.2d 136; Herrero v. Atkinson, 1964, 227 Cal.App.2d 69, 38 Cal.Rptr. 490; Sauter v. New York Central & Hudson River Railroad Co., 1876, 66 N.Y. 50; Selleck v. City of Janesville, 1898, 100 Wis. 157, 75 N.W. 975.

69. See Viou v. Brooks-Scanlon Lumber Co., 1906, 99 Minn. 97, 108 N.W. 891; Pederson v. Eppard, 1930, 181 Minn. 47, 231 N.W. 393; Staehlin v. Hochdoerfer, Mo.1921, 235 S.W. 1060; Pedigo & Pedigo v. Croom, Tex.Civ.App.1931, 37 S.W.2d 1074, error refused; Notes, 1929, 29 Col.L.Rev. 630; 1933, 18 Corn.L.Q. 257.

ular collisions in quick succession, have nevertheless been regarded as indivisible.[70]

Potential Damage

Chief Justice Peaslee of New Hampshire, in an extremely interesting article,[71] pointed out that there are situations in which an apparently indivisible injury may be apportioned upon the basis of potential damage from one cause, which reduces the valuation of the loss inflicted by another. In the case which prompted the article,[72] a boy standing on the high beam of a bridge trestle lost his balance and started to fall to substantially certain death or serious injury far below. He came in contact with defendant's wires, and was electrocuted. The incipient fall was an accomplished fact before the defendant's negligence caused any harm at all. The court allowed damages only for such a sum as his prospects for life and health were worth when the defendant killed him.

In the same manner, it has been held that an existing disease[73] or a prior accident[74] which reduces the plaintiff's life expectancy will limit accordingly the value of the life in an action for wrongful death. Then what is the value of a burning house which the defendant prevents a fire engine from extinguishing,[75] or one in the path of a conflagration which the defendant destroys?[76] What damage has the plaintiff suffered when the defendant blocks the passage of the plaintiff's barge into a canal in which passage was already blocked by a landslide?[77]

Value is an estimate of worth at the time and place of the wrong. It is obvious that if such factors as these are to be considered as reducing value, they must be in operation when the defendant causes harm, and so imminent that reasonable persons would take them into account.[78] There is a clear distinction between a person who is standing in the path of an avalanche when the defendant shoots to kill, and one who is about to embark on a steamship doomed later to strike an iceberg and sink.[79] The life of the latter has value at the time, as any insurance company would agree, but that of the former has none. So a forest fire a mile away may affect the market value of a building, but one a hundred miles away will not, although it may afterwards destroy it.

So far as the feasibility of such apportionment is concerned, it is equally possible

---

70. See Single Indivisible Result, supra, this section, and Damage Capable of Apportionment, supra, this section.

71. Peaslee, Multiple Causation and Damage, 1934, 47 Harv.L.Rev. 1127. See also, adopting opposing views, Carpenter, Concurrent Causation, 1935, 83 U.Pa. L.Rev. 941.

72. Dillon v. Twin State Gas & Electric Co., 1932, 85 N.H. 449, 163 A. 111. See also last paragraph of § 41, supra.

73. Pieczonka v. Pullman Co., 2d Cir. 1937, 89 F.2d 353. Cf. Evans v. S.J. Groves & Sons Co., 2d Cir. 1963, 315 F.2d 335; Henderson v. United States, 5th Cir. 1964, 328 F.2d 502; Denman v. Johnston, 1891, 85 Mich. 387, 48 N.W. 565; Fortner v. Koch, 1935, 272 Mich. 273, 261 N.W. 762 ($25,000 reduced to $7,000).

74. Slaven v. Germain, 1892, 64 Hun 506, 19 N.Y.S. 492. Cf. Pittsburgh Steamship Co. v. Palo, 6th Cir. 1933, 64 F.2d 198.

75. Felter v. Delaware & Hudson Railroad Corp., D.Pa.1937, 19 F.Supp. 852, affirmed, 3d Cir. 1938, 98 F.2d 868 (damages for only portion of total value), discussed in, 1937, 12 Temple L.Q. 132.

76. Peaslee, Multiple Causation and Damage, 1934, 47 Harv.L.Rev. 1127, approves on this basis the decision in Cook v. Minneapolis, St. Paul & Sault Ste Marie Railway Co., 1898, 98 Wis. 624, 74 N.W. 561, where a fire set by the defendant merged with a fire of innocent origin to burn the plaintiff's property. It may be suggested that this is unsound, since any decrease in value of the property before destruction must be attributed equally to the threat of each fire.

77. Douglas Burt & Buchanan Co. v. Texas & Pacific Railway Co., 1922, 150 La. 1038, 91 So. 503 (none).

78. In Morris v. St. Paul City Railway Co., 1908, 105 Minn. 276, 117 N.W. 500, where defendant caused a miscarriage, the court refused to permit the jury to weigh against the pain suffered the pain to be expected from the normal birth of the child, saying that it was "too remote, speculative and uncertain to be taken as a basis for estimating damages." Reference to the record in the case discloses that plaintiff was pregnant only two months. But in a case where the miscarriage occurred three weeks before birth was due, the deduction was made. Hawkins v. Front Street Cable Railway Co., 1898, 3 Wash. 592, 28 P. 1021. See 1 Joyce, Damages, 1903, § 185.

79. Peaslee, Multiple Causation and Damage, 1934, 47 Harv.L.Rev. 1127, 1139.

where both causes are culpable.[80] If A shoots B and kills B instantly, two minutes after C has administered to B a slow poison for which there is no known antidote, it can still be said that B's life had little value when A killed B. But in such a case, if C is relieved of liability, A has deprived B not only of the life, but of a possible redress against C. If, because A has killed B, it is held that C has not caused B's death, and so has not become liable, as C was otherwise certain to be, then there was not only potential damage, but a potential cause of action in compensation for it, which A has destroyed. It would therefore be proper to hold A liable for the full value of B's life, in contrast to the case where B was destined to die from self-administered poison. One may, however, question the assumption that A's shooting B relieved C of liability. Should this hypothetical case be viewed as closely analogous to cases in which the but-for rule of causation produces an indefensible result when applied to two defendants individually, and leads to holding both defendants liable, jointly and severally?[81] Such questions apparently have not been considered by any court.

Acts Harmless in Themselves Which Together Cause Damage

A very troublesome question arises where the acts of each of two or more parties, standing alone, would not be wrongful, but together they cause harm to the plaintiff. If several defendants independently pollute a stream, the impurities traceable to each may be negligible and harmless, but all together may render the water entirely unfit for use. The difficulty lies in the fact that each defendant alone would have committed no tort. There would have been no negligence, and no nuisance, since the individual use of the stream would have been a reasonable use, and no harm would have resulted.

Obviously the plaintiff's interests have been invaded, and if each defendant is to escape because that defendant's contribution was harmless in itself, there will be no redress.[82] A number of courts have held that acts which individually would be innocent may be tortious if they thus combine to cause damage, in cases of pollution,[83] flooding of land,[84] diversion of water,[85] obstruction of a highway,[86] or even a noise nuisance.[87] The explanation is that the standard of reasonable conduct applicable to each defendant is governed by the circumstances, including the activities of the other defendants. Pollution of a stream to even a slight extent becomes unreasonable when similar pollution by others makes the condition of the stream approach the danger point. The single act itself becomes wrongful because it is done in the context of what others are doing.[88]

---

80. To vary slightly a case suggested by McLaughlin, Proximate Cause, 1925, 39 Harv.L.Rev. 149, 155: Suppose A is entering a desert. B secretly empties A's water keg, leaving only three days' supply. A takes the keg into the desert, where C steals it, both A and C believing that it is full. A dies of thirst. Should C be liable for the loss of more than three days of A's life?

81. See supra, § 41.

82. Hill v. Smith, 1867, 32 Cal. 166; James, L.J., in Thorpe v. Brumfitt, 1873, L.R. 8 Ch.App. 650.

83. Duke of Buccleuch v. Cowan, 1866, 5 Sess.Cas. (Macph.) 214; Woodyear v. Schaefer, 1881, 57 Md. 1, 40 Am.Rep. 419; Warren v. Parkhurst, 1904, 45 Misc. 466, 92 N.Y.S. 725, affirmed 186 N.Y. 45, 78 N.E. 579; Northup v. Eakes, 1918, 72 Okl. 66, 178 P. 266. Compare the case suggested in Blair v. Deakin, 1887, 57 L.T., N.S., 522, of two defendants each discharging a chemical harmless in itself, which combined with the other renders the water unusable.

84. Sloggy v. Dilworth, 1888, 38 Minn. 179, 36 N.W. 451; Wright v. Cooper, Vt.1802, 1 Tyler 425; Town of Sharon v. Anahama Realty Corp., 1924, 97 Vt. 336, 123 A. 192; Woodland v. Portneuf-Marsh Valley Irrigation Co., 1915, 26 Idaho 789, 146 P. 1106.

85. Hillman v. Newington, 1880, 57 Cal. 56.

86. Thorpe v. Brumfitt, 1873, L.R. 8 Ch.App. 650; Sadler v. Great Western R. Co., [1895] L.R. 2 Q.B. 688.

87. Lambton v. Mellish, [1894] 3 Ch. 163.

88. "The acts of the other company must be taken into account because it may be that the one company ought not to be doing what it was when the other company was doing what it did." Sadler v. Great Western R. Co., [1895] 2 Q.B. 688. Accord; Woodyear v. Schaefer, 1881, 57 Md. 1; Hillman v. Newington, 1880, 57 Cal. 56; United States v. Luce, C.C.Del.1905, 141 F. 385, 411; Lawton v. Herrick, 1910, 83 Conn. 417, 428, 76 A. 986, 990.

Where, as in the usual case, such liability must be based on negligence or intent rather than any abnormally dangerous activity, it would seem that there can be no tortious conduct unless the individual knows, or is at least negligent in failing to discover, that the conduct may concur with that of others to cause damage.[89] And liability need not necessarily be entire, for there is no reason why damages may not be apportioned here, to the same extent as in any other case.[90]

 WESTLAW REFERENCES

apportion! /s damages /p joint /5 tort* tortfeasor*

Concerted Action

concert** /s act*** /p joint /5 tort* tortfeasor*

concert** /s act*** /p joint /s tort* tortfeasor* & apportion! /s damages liability

Vicarious Liability

vicarious** /s liab! & apportion! /s damages

Common Duty

mutual common /6 duty /s joint /s tort* tortfeasor*

Single Indivisible Result

indivisib! division /s injury damages /p joint /5 tort* tortfeasor*

Damage Capable of Apportionment

damages /s apportion! allocat! /p successive /s injur***

Successive Injuries

damages /s apportion! /p successive /s injur!

Potential Damage

peaslee /s multiple +s causation /s 47 +s 1127

It has been said, however, that to be liable the defendant must have "contributed substantially" rather than infinitesimally. See Duke of Buccleuch v. Cowan, 1866, 5 Sess.Cas., (Macph.), 214. This may be regarded as an application of the substantial factor test of causation, discussed supra, § 41.

89. See the stress placed upon knowledge of the situation by each defendant in Warren v. Parkhurst, 1904, 45 Misc. 466, 92 N.Y.S. 725, affirmed 105 A.D. 239, 93 N.Y.S. 1009; Lambton v. Mellish, [1894] 3 Ch. 163; also the instruction approved in Folsom v. Apple River Log-Driving Co., 1877, 41 Wis. 602; cf. McKay v. Southern Bell Telephone & Telegraph Co., 1896, 111 Ala. 337, 19 So. 695.

90. Sloggy v. Dilworth, 1888, 38 Minn. 179, 36 N.W. 451; Woodland v. Portneuf-Marsh Valley Irrigation Co., 1915, 26 Idaho 789, 146 P. 1106.

Chapter 9

LIMITED DUTY

Table of Sections

Sec.
53. Duty.
54. Mental Disturbance.
55. Prenatal Injuries.
56. Acts and Omissions.

§ 53. Duty

"Duty" we have already encountered, in connection with the problem of the unforeseeable plaintiff.[1] It is quite possible, and not at all uncommon, to deal with most of the questions which arise in a negligence case in terms of "duty." Thus, the standard of conduct required of the individual may be expressed by saying that the driver of an automobile approaching an intersection is under a duty to moderate his speed, to keep a proper lookout, or to blow his horn, but that he is not under a duty to take precautions against an unexpected explosion of a manhole cover in the street. But the problems of "duty" are sufficiently complex without subdividing it in this manner to cover an endless series of details of conduct. It is better to reserve "duty" for the problem of the relation between individuals which imposes upon one a legal obligation for the benefit of the other, and to deal with particular conduct in terms of a legal standard of what is required to meet the obligation. In other words, "duty" is a question of whether the defendant is under any obligation for the benefit of the particular plaintiff; and in negligence cases, the duty is always the same—to conform to the legal standard of reasonable conduct in the light of the apparent risk. What the defendant must do, or must not do, is a question of the standard of conduct required to satisfy the duty. The distinction is one of convenience only, and it must be remembered that the two are correlative, and one cannot exist without the other.

A duty, in negligence cases, may be defined as an obligation, to which the law will give recognition and effect, to conform to a particular standard of conduct toward another. In the early English law, there was virtually no consideration of duty. Liability was imposed with no great regard even for the fault of the defendant.[2] The requirements as to conduct were absolute, and once the act was found to be wrongful, the actor was liable for the damage that might result.

§ 53
1. See supra, § 43.

2. See supra, § 4.

Such few limitations upon his responsibility as are found in the earlier cases are stated, not in any terms of duty, but of remoteness of the damage, or what we now call "proximate cause."[3] Certainly there is little trace of any notion of a relation between the parties, or an obligation to any one individual, as essential to the tort.[4] The defendant's obligation to behave properly apparently was owed to all the world, and he was liable to any person whom he might injure by his misconduct.

The conception of an absolute wrong remains in the criminal law,[5] and in the field of intentional torts, where the doctrine of "transferred intent" makes any one who attempts to injure another liable to any stranger whom he may injure instead.[6] But when negligence began to take form as a separate basis of tort liability, the courts developed the idea of duty, as a matter of some specific relation between the plaintiff and the defendant, without which there could be no liability.[7] We owe this to three English cases,[8] decided between 1837 and 1842. The rule which developed out of them was that no action could be founded upon the breach of a duty owed only to some person other than the plaintiff. He must bring himself within the scope of a definite legal obligation, so that it might be regarded as personal to him.[9] "Negligence in the air, so to speak, will not do."[10] The first cases[11] in which this idea was stated held only that the obligation of a contract could give no right of action to one who was not a contracting party; but it was soon extended to the whole field of negligence. The period during which it developed was that of the industrial revolution, and there is good reason to believe that it was a means by which the courts sought, perhaps more or less unconsciously, to limit the responsibilities of growing industry within some reasonable bounds.

This concept of a relative duty is not regarded as essential by the continental law, and it has been assailed as serving no useful purpose, and producing only confusion in ours.[12] Its artificial character is readily apparent; in the ordinary case, if the court should desire to find liability, it would be quite as easy to find the necessary "relation" in the position of the parties toward one another, and hence to extend the defendant's duty to the plaintiff.[13] The statement that there is or is not a duty begs the essential question—whether the plaintiff's interests are entitled to legal protection against the defendant's conduct.[14] It is therefore not surprising to find that the problem of

---

3. 2 Holdsworth, History of English Law, 1931, 50–54; 3 Holdsworth, History of English Law, 1931, 375–382.

4. Winfield, Duty in Tortious Negligence, 1934, 34 Col.L.Rev. 41.

5. State v. Renfrow, 1892, 111 Mo. 589, 20 S.W. 299; State v. Levelle, 1891, 34 S.C. 120, 13 S.E. 319; Commonwealth v. Mink, 1877, 123 Mass. 422; State v. Dalton, 1919, 178 N.C. 779, 101 S.E. 548.

6. See supra, § 8.

7. Winfield, Duty in Tortious Negligence, 1934, 34 Col.L.Rev. 41.

8. Vaughan v. Menlove, 1837, 3 Bing.N.C. 468, 132 Eng.Rep. 490; Langridge v. Levy, 1836, 2 M. & W. 519, 150 Eng.Rep. 863, affirmed, 1838, 4 M. & W. 337, 150 Eng.Rep. 1458; Winterbottom v. Wright, 1842, 10 M. & W. 109, 152 Eng.Rep. 402.

9. "The question of liability for negligence cannot arise at all until it is established that the man who has been negligent owed some duty to the person who seeks to make him liable for his negligence. * * * A man is entitled to be as negligent as he pleases toward the whole world if he owes no duty to them." Lord Esher, in Le Lievre v. Gould, [1893] 1 Q.B. 491, 497.

10. Pollock, Law of Torts, 13th Ed. 1920, 468. "[N]egligence does not exist in the abstract, it contemplates a legal duty owing from one party to another * * *." Tappen v. Ager, 10th Cir. 1979, 599 F.2d 376, 379 (doctor's countersuit alleging that earlier malpractice suit was frivolous; held, patient's lawyer owed no duty to doctor); Shore v. Town of Stonington, 1982, 187 Conn. 147, 444 A.2d 1379 (no duty by police officer to person killed by drunk driver who had been stopped earlier but not arrested by officer).

11. See supra, note 8.

12. Winfield, Duty in Tortious Negligence, 1934, 34 Col.L.Rev. 41; Buckland, The Duty to Take Care, 1935, 51 L.Q.Rev. 637.

13. Compare the opinions of Cardozo, C.J., in MacPherson v. Buick Motor Co., 1916, 217 N.Y. 382, 111 N.E. 1050, where a duty was found, and H.R. Moch Co. v. Rensselaer Water Co., 1928, 247 N.Y. 160, 159 N.E. 896, where it was not.

14. See Green, The Duty Problem in Negligence Cases, 1928, 28 Col.L.Rev. 1014, 1929, 29 Col.L.Rev.

duty is as broad as the whole law of negligence, and that no universal test for it ever has been formulated. It is a shorthand statement of a conclusion, rather than an aid to analysis in itself. Yet it is embedded far too firmly in our law to be discarded,[15] and no satisfactory substitute for it, by which the defendant's responsibility may be limited, has been devised.[16] But it should be recognized that "duty" is not sacrosanct in itself, but is only an expression of the sum total of those considerations of policy which lead the law to say that the plaintiff is entitled to protection.[17]

There is little analysis of the problem of duty in the courts. Frequently it is dealt with in terms of what is called "proximate cause," usually with resulting confusion. In such cases, the question of what is "proximate" and that of duty are fundamentally the same: whether the interests of the plaintiff are to be protected against the particular invasion by the defendant's conduct.

Scope of Duty

In Heaven v. Pender,[18] Brett, M.R., afterwards Lord Esher, made the first attempt to state a formula of duty. "Whenever one person," he said, "is by circumstances placed in such a position with regard to another that every one of ordinary sense who did think would at once recognize that if he did not use ordinary care and skill in his own conduct with regard to those circumstances he would cause danger of injury to the person or property of the other, a duty arises to use ordinary care and skill to avoid such danger." But this formula, which afterwards was rejected by Lord Esher himself,[19] was soon recognized as far too broad. As a general proposition to be applied in the ordinary negligence case, where the defendant has taken some affirmative action such as driving an automobile, it holds good. That is to say, that whenever the automobile driver should, as a reasonable person, foresee that his conduct will involve an unreasonable risk of harm to other drivers or to pedestrians, he is then under a duty to them to exercise the care of a reasonable person as to what he does or does not do. There are, however, a good many defendants, and a good many situations, as to which there is no such duty. In other words, the defendant is under no legal obligation toward the particular plaintiff to act with the care of a reasonable man, and he is not liable even though his conduct falls short of that standard, and the other is injured as a result.

A later attempt at a formula for duty was that of Lord Atkin in Donoghue v. Stevenson:[20]

"The rule that you are to love your neighbor becomes in law, you must not injure your neighbor; and the lawyer's question, Who is my neighbor? receives a restricted reply. You must take reasonable care to avoid acts or omissions which you can reasonably foresee would be likely to injure your neighbor. Who, then, in law is my neighbor? The answer seems to be—persons who are so closely and directly affected by my act that I ought reasonably to have them in contemplation as being so affected

255; Green, Judge and Jury, 1930, ch. 3; Prosser, Palsgraf Revisited, 1953, 52 Mich.L.Rev. 1; Earp v. Nobmann, 1981, 122 Cal.App.3d 270, 175 Cal.Rptr. 767.

15. Cf. Restatement of Torts, § 4.

16. As to the deficiencies of "remoteness of damage," or "proximate cause" as a limitation, see Green, Rationale of Proximate Cause, 1927; Edgerton, Legal Cause, 1924, 72 U.Pa.L.Rev. 211, 343; Prosser, The Minnesota Court on Proximate Cause, 1936, 21 Minn.L. Rev. 19.

17. Brennen v. City of Eugene, 1979, 285 Or. 401, 591 P.2d 719; Bigbee v. Pacific Telephone & Telegraph Co., 1982, 131 Cal.App.3d 999, 183 Cal.Rptr. 535.

18. 1883, 11 Q.B.D. 503, 509. The other members of the court stated definitely that they did not concur in this formula. Id. at 516. See Bennett v. Span Industries, Inc., Tex.App.1981, 628 S.W.2d 470; cf. King v. Avtech Aviation, Inc., 5th Cir. 1981, 655 F.2d 77.

19. In Le Lievre v. Gould, [1893] 1 Q.B. 491.

20. [1932] A.C. 562, 580. See Pollock, The Snail in the Bottle, and Thereafter, 1933, 49 L.Q.Rev. 22. The "rule" of Donoghue v. Stevenson is examined in Atiyah, Accidents, Compensation and the Law, 3d ed. 1980, 71; Street, The Law of Torts, 6th ed. 1976, 105; Heuston, Salmond on the Law of Torts, 16th ed. 1973, 197; Rogers, Winfield & Jolowicz on Tort, 11th ed. 1979, 68.

when I am directing my mind to the acts or omissions which are called in question."

As a formula this dictum is so vague as to have little meaning, and as a guide to decision it has had no value at all. Within some such undefined general limits, it may be said that the courts have merely "reacted to the situation in the way in which the great mass of mankind customarily react," [21] and that as our ideas of human relations change the law as to duties changes with them.[22] Various factors undoubtedly have been given conscious or unconscious weight,[23] including convenience of administration, capacity of the parties to bear the loss, a policy of preventing future injuries, the moral blame attached to the wrongdoer, and many others.[24] Changing social conditions lead constantly to the recognition of new duties.[25] No better general statement can be made than that the courts will find a duty where, in general, reasonable persons would recognize it and agree that it exists.

WESTLAW REFERENCES

limited /3 duty /p tort* negligen**
headnote(existence /3 duty /s tort negligen**)

21. Bohlen, Review of Green, Judge and Jury, 1932, 80 U.Pa.L.Rev. 781, 785.

22. Prosser, Palsgraf Revisited, 1953, 52 Mich.L. Rev. 1, 12–15.

23. See supra, § 4. See generally Green, The Duty Problem in Negligence Cases, 1928, 28 Col.L.Rev. 1014, 1929, 29 Col.L.Rev. 255, reprinted in Green, Judge and Jury, 1930, ch. 3–4; Thode, Tort Analysis: Duty-Risk v. Proximate Cause and the Rational Allocation of Functions Between Judge and Jury, 1977 Utah.L.Rev. 1; Reynolds, Limits on Negligence Liability: *Palsgraf* at 50, 1979, 32 Okla.L.Rev. 63.

24. "The court must balance the following factors when determining the existence of duty in each particular case: (1) foreseeability of harm to plaintiff; (2) degree of certainty that plaintiff suffered injury; (3) closeness of connection between defendant's conduct and injury suffered; (4) moral blame attached to defendant's conduct; (5) policy of preventing future harm; (6) extent of burden to defendant and the consequences to the community of imposing a duty to exercise care with resulting liability for breach; and (7) availability, cost, and prevalence of insurance for the risk involved." Vu v. Singer Co., N.D.Cal.1981, 538 F.Supp. 26, 29; Tarasoff v. Regents of University of California, 1976, 17 Cal.3d 425, 131 Cal.Rptr. 14, 22, 551 P.2d 334, 342. Compare Guy v. Liederbach, 1980, 279 Pa.Super.

Scope of Duty

topic(272 313a 379) /p standard* /s reasonable /s conduct
topic(272 313a 379) /p scope /2 duty

§ 54. Mental Disturbance

Certain types of interest, because of various difficulties they present, have been afforded relatively little protection at the hands of the law against negligent invasions. Thus, interests of a pecuniary nature, such as the right to have a contract performed,[1] the expectation of financial advantage,[2] or the integrity of the pocketbook which may be damaged by reliance upon a representation,[3] all present special problems, which are considered elsewhere in this text. In general, however, it may be said that the law gives protection against negligent acts to the interest in security of the person, and to the various interests in tangible property. In other words, negligence may result in liability for personal injury or property damage. One interest which is still a subject of substantial controversy is that in freedom from mental disturbance. No general agreement has yet been reached on many of

543, 421 A.2d 333 (duty may be owed by testator's lawyer to intended beneficiary under will), with Pelham v. Griesheimer, 1981, 93 Ill.App.3d 751, 49 Ill.Dec. 192, 417 N.E.2d 882, affirmed, 1982, 92 Ill.2d 13, 64 Ill.Dec. 544, 440 N.E.2d 96 (mother's divorce lawyer owed no duty to her children).

25. See, for example, three recent opinions allowing a cause of action for children for loss of society and companionship of a parent tortiously injured by a third party. Weitl v. Moes, Iowa 1981, 311 N.W.2d 259; Berger v. Weber, 1981, 411 Mich. 1, 303 N.W.2d 424; Ferriter v. Daniel O'Connell's Sons, Inc., 1980, 381 Mass. 507, 413 N.E.2d 690. The traditional view has been to deny such claims. See Salin v. Kloempken, Minn.1982, 322 N.W.2d 736; DeAngelis v. Lutheran Medical Center, 1981, 84 A.D.2d 17, 445 N.Y.S.2d 188; Borer v. American Airlines, Inc., 1977, 19 Cal.3d 441, 138 Cal.Rptr. 302, 563 P.2d 858. See generally Love, Tortious Interference with the Parent-Child Relationship: Loss of an Injured Person's Society and Companionship, 1976, 51 Ind.L.J. 590.

§ 54

1. See infra, § 129.
2. See infra, § 130.
3. See infra, ch. 18.

the issues involving liability for negligence resulting in fright, shock, or other mental or emotional harm, and any resulting physical consequences.[4]

Previous reference has been made to the reluctance with which the courts have recognized the interest in peace of mind, even where the interference with it is intentional.[5] This reluctance has of course been more pronounced where the defendant's conduct is merely negligent. The same objections against allowing recovery have been advanced here as well: that mental disturbance cannot be measured in terms of money, and so cannot serve in itself as a basis for the action;[6] that its physical consequences are too remote, and so not "proximately caused";[7] that there is a lack of precedent,[8] and that a vast increase in litigation would follow.[9] All these objections have been answered many times, and it is threshing old straw to deal with them.[10] Mental suffering is no more difficult to estimate in financial terms, and no less a real injury, than "physical" pain;[11] it is not an independent intervening cause, but a thing brought about by the defendant's negligence itself, and its consequences may follow in unbroken sequence from that negligence;[12] and while it may be true that its consequences are seldom very serious unless there is some predisposing physical condition,[13] the law is not for the protection of the physically sound alone.[14] It is the business of the courts to make precedent where a wrong calls for redress, even if lawsuits must be multiplied;[15] and there has long been precedent enough, and no great increase in litigation has been observed.[16]

There are at least three principal concerns, however, that continue to foster judicial caution and doctrinal limitations on recovery for emotional distress: (1) the problem of permitting legal redress for

4. See generally Second Restatement of Torts, §§ 313, 436, 436A.

5. Supra, § 12.

6. See Lynch v. Knight, 1861, 9 H.L.C. 577, 598, 11 Eng.Rep. 854; Mitchell v. Rochester Railway Co., 1896, 151 N.Y. 107, 45 N.E. 354.

7. Victorian Railways Commissioners v. Coultas, 1888, 13 A.C. 222; Mitchell v. Rochester Railway Co., 1897, 151 N.Y. 107, 45 N.E. 354; Chittick v. Philadelphia Rapid Transit Co., 1909, 224 Pa. 13, 73 A. 4.

8. Lehman v. Brooklyn City R. Co., N.Y.1888, 47 Hun, 355; Victorian Railways Commissioners v. Coultas, 1888, 13 A.C. 222.

9. Mitchell v. Rochester Railway Co., 1897, 151 N.Y. 107, 45 N.E. 354; Spade v. Lynn & Boston Railroad Co., 1896, 168 Mass. 285, 47 N.E. 88.

10. Early treatments of the topic included Bohlen, The Right to Recover for Injury Resulting from Negligence Without Impact, 1902, 41 Am.L.Reg.,N.S., 141; Goodrich, Emotional Disturbance as Legal Damage, 1922, 20 Mich.L.Rev. 497; Magruder, Mental and Emotional Disturbance in the Law of Torts, 1936, 49 Harv. L.Rev. 1033; Harper and McNeely, A Re-examination of the Basis for Liability for Emotional Distress, [1938] Wis.L.Rev. 426; Smith, Relation of Emotions to Injury and Disease, 1944, 30 Va.L.Rev. 193.

Recent articles include Pearson, Liability to Bystanders for Negligently Inflicted Emotional Harm—A Comment On the Nature of Arbitrary Rules, 1982, 34 U.Fla.L.R. 477; Simons, Psychic Injury and the Bystander: The Transcontinental Dispute Between California and New York, 1976, 51 St.John's L.Rev. 1; Leibson, Recovery of Damages for Emotional Distress Caused by Physical Injury to Another, 1976–77, 15 J.Fam.L. 163; Golden, The Development of Recovery for Negligently Inflicted Mental Distress Arising from Peril or Injury to Another: An Analysis of the American and Australian Approaches, 1979, 26 Emory L.J. 647; Langhenry, 1981, Personal Injury Law and Emotional Distress, 9 J.Psych. & Law 91; Miller, The Scope of Liability for Negligent Infliction of Emotional Distress: Making "The Punishment Fit the Crime," 1979, 1 U.Haw.L.Rev. 1; Connolly & McCall, Negligent Infliction of Emotional Distress: Liability to the Bystander—Recent Developments, 1979, 30 Mercer L.Rev. 735; Nolan & Ursin, Negligent Infliction of Emotional Distress: Coherence Emerging from Chaos, 1982, 33 Hast. L.J. 583; Notes, 1982, 4 U.Hawaii L.Rev. 207; 22 Santa Clara L.Rev. 181; 1981, 19 Am.Bus L.Rev. 214; 13 Pacif.L.J. 179; 33 Hast.L.J. 291; 10 Hofstra L.Rev. 213; 1981 Wis.L.Rev. 1089; 1975, 63 Geo.L.J. 1179; 1971, 59 Geo.L.J. 1237.

11. Goodrich, Emotional Disturbance as Legal Damage, 1922, 20 Mich.L.Rev. 497.

12. Purcell v. St. Paul City Railway Co., 1892, 48 Minn. 134, 50 N.W. 1034; Simone v. Rhode Island Co., 1907, 28 R.I. 186, 66 A. 202.

13. Havard, Reasonable Foresight of Nervous Shock, 1956, 19 Mod.L.Rev. 478.

14. See supra, § 43.

15. Chiuchiolo v. New England Wholesale Tailors, 1930, 84 N.H. 329, 150 A. 540; Alabama Fuel & Iron Co. v. Baladoni, 1916, 15 Ala.App. 316, 73 So. 205.

16. Gulf, Colorado & Santa Fe Railway Co. v. Hayter, 1900, 93 Tex. 239, 54 S.W. 944. But see Note, 1981, 19 Am.Bus.L.J. 214.

harm that is often temporary and relatively trivial; (2) the danger that claims of mental harm will be falsified or imagined; and (3) the perceived unfairness of imposing heavy and disproportionate financial burdens upon a defendant, whose conduct was only negligent, for consequences which appear remote from the "wrongful" act.[17] These problems are very real, and they must be met. Mental disturbance is easily simulated, and courts which are plagued with fraudulent personal injury claims may be unwilling to open the door to an even more dubious field. But the difficulties may not be insuperable. Not only fright and shock, but other kinds of mental injury are marked by definite physical symptoms, which are capable of medical or other objective proof.[18] It is entirely possible to allow recovery only upon satisfactory evidence and deny it when there is nothing to corroborate the claim, or to look for some guarantee of genuineness in the circumstances of the case.[19] The problem from this perspective is one of adequate proof, and it is not necessary to deny a remedy in all cases because some claims may be false. And where the concern is to avoid imposing excessive punishment upon a negligent defendant, it must be asked whether fairness will permit leaving the burden of loss instead upon the innocent victim. Such are the basic policy issues with which the courts continue to struggle in defining the limits of liability for negligently inflicted emotional harm.

Mental Disturbance Alone

Where the defendant's negligence causes only mental disturbance, without accompanying physical injury, illness or other physical consequences, and in the absence of some other independent basis for tort liability,[20] the great majority of courts still hold that in the ordinary case there can be no recovery.[21] The temporary emotion of fright,[22] so far from serious that it does no physical harm, is so evanescent a thing, so easily counterfeited, and usually so trivial, that the courts have been quite unwilling to protect the plaintiff against mere negligence, where the elements of extreme outrage and moral blame which have had such weight in the intentional tort context are lacking.[23] Other unpleasant emotions, such as the distress of a mother at being given the wrong baby by a hospital, have been dealt with on the same basis.[24] Nor may it make any difference that there has been a harmless but emotionally disturbing contact with the plaintiff's person, as where he gets a mouthful of broken glass without actually being cut.[25]

---

17. See Payton v. Abbott Labs, 1982, 386 Mass. 540, 437 N.E.2d 171, 178–81; Second Restatement of Torts, § 436A, Comment b.

18. Earengey, The Legal Consequences of Shock, 1934, 2 Medico-Leg. & Crim.Rec. 14; Smith, Relation of Emotions to Injury and Disease, 1944, 30 Va.L.Rev. 193.

19. See Molien v. Kaiser Foundation Hospitals, 1980, 27 Cal.3d 916, 167 Cal.Rptr. 831, 616 P.2d 813; cf. Payton v. Abbott Labs, 386 Mass. 540, 1982, 437 A.2d 171, 192 (dissent).

20. See Note, 1982, 22 Santa Clara L.Rev. 181, 184–85.

21. Second Restatement of Torts, § 436A. But see the recent development to the contrary, infra notes 57–60.

22. Weissman v. Wells, 1924, 306 Mo. 82, 267 S.W. 400; Logan v. St. Luke's General Hospital, 1965, 65 Wn.2d 914, 400 P.2d 296. But see Butler v. Pardue, La.App.1982, 415 So.2d 249.

To be distinguished is shock to the nervous system, which commonly is regarded as injury to the body rather than to the mind, and hence satisfies the requirement of physical injury. See, e.g., Vanoni v. Western Airlines, 1967, 247 Cal.App.2d 793, 56 Cal.Rptr. 115.

23. See supra, § 12.

24. Espionosa v. Beverly Hospital, 1952, 114 Cal. App.2d 232, 249 P.2d 843. Cf. Seidenbach's, Inc. v. Williams, Okl.1961, 361 P.2d 185 (failure to deliver wedding gown in time for wedding); Manie v. Matson Oldsmobile-Cadillac Co., 1967, 378 Mich. 650, 148 N.W.2d 779 (mental distress when stopped by police); Sears, Roebuck & Co. v. Devers, Miss.1981, 405 So.2d 898 (embarrassment at being stopped when tag on purchased sweater activated alarm).

25. Tuttle v. Meyer Dairy Products Co., 1956, 100 Ohio App. 133, 138 N.E.2d 429. Cf. Sullivan v. H.P. Hood & Sons, 1960, 341 Mass. 216, 168 N.E.2d 80 (dead mouse in milk). But cf. Way v. Tampa Coca Cola Bottling Co., Fla.App.1972, 260 So.2d 288 (plaintiff sucked on rat in Coke).

In two special groups of cases, however, there has been some movement to break away from the settled rule and allow recovery for mental disturbance alone. A number of courts have allowed recovery against a telegraph company for the negligent transmission of a message, especially one announcing death, which indicates upon its face that there is an especial likelihood that such mental distress will result.[26] The other group of cases has involved the negligent mishandling of corpses. Here the traditional rule has denied recovery for mere negligence, without circumstances of aggravation.[27] There are by now, however, a series of cases allowing recovery for negligent embalming,[28] negligent shipment,[29] running over the body,[30] and the like,[31] without such circumstances of aggravation. What all of these cases appear to have in common is an especial likelihood of genuine and serious mental distress, arising from the special circumstances, which serves as a guarantee that the claim is not spurious. There may perhaps be other such cases.[32] Where the guarantee can be found, and the mental distress is undoubtedly real and serious, there may be no good reason to deny recovery. But cases will obviously be infrequent in which "mental disturbance," not so severe as to cause physical harm, will clearly be a serious wrong worthy of redress and sufficiently attested by the circumstances of the case.

Mental Disturbance with Physical Injury

Where the defendant's negligence inflicts an immediate physical injury, such as a bro-

26. So Relle v. Western Union Telegraph Co., 1881, 55 Tex. 308; Russ v. Western Union Telegraph Co., 1943, 222 N.C. 504, 23 S.E.2d 681; Western Union Telegraph Co. v. Redding, 1930, 100 Fla. 495, 129 So. 743; cf. Johnson v. State of New York, 1975, 37 N.Y.2d 378, 372 N.Y.S.2d 638, 334 N.E.2d 590 (hospital negligently misinformed plaintiff that her mother had died).

Contra, Morton v. Western Union Telegraph Co., 1895, 53 Ohio St. 431, 41 N.E. 689; Corcoran v. Postal Telegraph Cable Co., 1917, 80 Wash. 570, 142 P. 29; Connelly v. Western Union Telegraph Co., 1900, 100 Va. 51, 40 S.E. 618; Western Union Telegraph Co. v. Speight, 1920, 254 U.S. 17, 41 S.Ct. 11, 65 L.Ed. 104; Western Union Telegraph Co. v. Junker, Tex.Civ.App. 1941, 153 S.W.2d 210. See Notes, 1956, 34 Tex.L.Rev. 487. The federal rule does, however, allow recovery where the mental disturbance results in physical illness. Kaufman v. Western Union Telegraph Co., 5th Cir. 1955, 224 F.2d 723, certiorari denied, 350 U.S. 947, 76 S.Ct. 321, 100 L.Ed. 825. See generally, Annot., 1977, 77 A.L.R.3d 501.

27. See Chisum v. Behrens, S.D.1979, 283 N.W.2d 235; Dunahoo v. Bess, 1941, 146 Fla. 182, 200 So. 541. This is said to be the majority rule. See Annot., 1973, 48 A.L.R.3d 261 (preparation); Annot., 1973, 48 A.L.R.3d (withholding corpse from relatives).

Compare Daniels v. Adkins Protective Service, Inc., Miss.1971, 247 So.2d 710 (negligent embalming—no recovery for mental distress without physical injury); Estate of Harper v. Orlando Funeral Home, Fla.App.1979, 366 So.2d 126 (no recovery absent impact where casket started falling apart while being carried from hearse to grave during funeral). See also Muniz v. United Hospital Medical Center Presbyterian Hospital, 1977, 153 N.J.Super. 79, 379 A.2d 57 ("substantial physical disability"); Corrigal v. Ball & Dodd Funeral Home, Inc., 1978, 89 Wn.App.2d 959, 577 P.2d 580 (must be manifested by objective symptoms—weight and sleep loss, and general physical deterioration, sufficient).

28. Chelini v. Nieri, 1948, 32 Cal.2d 480, 196 P.2d 915; Carey v. Lima, Salmon & Tully Mortuary, 1959, 168 Cal.App.2d 42, 335 P.2d 181; cf. Lamm v. Shingleton, 1949, 231 N.C. 10, 55 S.E.2d 810 (leaky casket); Clark v. Smith, Tex.Civ.App.1973, 494 S.W.2d 192, refused, no reversible error.

29. See Allen v. Jones, 1980, 104 Cal.App.3d 207, 163 Cal.Rptr. 445 (package supposedly containing cremated remains of plaintiff's brother arrived empty); Clemm v. Atchison, Topeka & Santa Fe Railroad Co., 1928, 126 Kan. 181, 268 P. 103; Missouri, Kansas & Texas Railway Co. v. Hawkins, 1908, 50 Tex.Civ.App. 128, 109 S.W. 221.

30. St. Louis South Western Railway Co. v. White, 1936, 192 Ark. 350, 91 S.W.2d 277; Pollard v. Phelps, 1937, 56 Ga.App. 408, 193 S.E. 102; Morrow v. Southern Railway Co., 1938, 213 N.C. 127, 195 S.E. 383; cf. Owens v. Liverpool Corp., [1939] 1 K.B. 394.

31. Torres v. State, 1962, 34 Misc.2d 488, 228 N.Y.S.2d 1005 (autopsy and unauthorized burial); Weingast v. State, 1964, 44 Misc.2d 824, 254 N.Y.S.2d 952 (confusion of bodies); Blanchard v. Brawley, La. App.1954, 75 So.2d 891 (burning body, trying to cut it out of wreck). See Note [1960] Duke L.J. 135. See also Gonzalez v. Sacramento Mem. Lawn, Cal.Super. 1982, 25 ATLA L.Rep. 348 (Oct. 1982), where 21-year-old mortuary employee, or "morgue rat," committed 20–40 acts of necrophilia on remains of plaintiff's son before driving stolen hearse and coffin into mountains where she was finally caught by police.

32. See Johnson v. State of New York, 1975, 37 N.Y.2d 378, 372 N.Y.S.2d 638, 334 N.E.2d 590 (hospital negligently misinformed plaintiff that her mother had died); Naccash v. Burger, 1982, 223 Va. 406, 290 S.E.2d 825 (wrongful birth of severely defective child); Laxton v. Orkin Exterminating Co., Tenn.1982, 639 S.W.2d 431 (consumption of water containing toxic chemical).

ken leg, none of the foregoing objections has prevented the courts from allowing compensation for the purely mental elements of damage accompanying it, such as fright at the time of the injury,[33] apprehension as to its effects,[34] nervousness,[35] or humiliation at disfigurement.[36] With a cause of action established by the physical harm, "parasitic" damages are awarded, and it is considered that there is sufficient assurance that the mental injury is not feigned.[37]

There is still some dispute, however, if the physical harm is not immediate, but follows later as a result of the plaintiff's emotional distress over the negligently caused event—as in the case of a miscarriage, which appears so frequently in these cases that it has come to typify them.[38] After England had led off by denying liability,[39] a large number of the American courts, including those of the leading industrial states,[40] refused to permit recovery for such consequences unless there had been some "impact" upon the person of the plaintiff. Apart from some quite untenable notions of causal connection,[41] the theory appears to be that the "impact" affords the desired guarantee that the mental disturbance is genuine. But the same courts have found "impact" in minor contacts with the person which often play no part in causing the real harm,[42] and in themselves can have no importance whatever. "Impact" has meant a slight blow,[43] a trifling burn[44] or electric shock,[45] a trivial jolt or jar,[46] a forcible seating on the

---

33. Bullard v. Central Vermont Railway, Inc., 1st Cir. 1977, 565 F.2d 193; Easton v. United Trade School Contracting Co., 1916, 173 Cal. 199, 159 P. 597.

34. See Judd v. Rowley's Cherry Hill Orchards, Inc., Utah 1980, 611 P.2d 1216; Ferrara v. Galluchio, 1958, 5 N.Y.2d 16, 176 N.Y.S.2d 996, 152 N.E.2d 249 (fear of cancer); Lorenc v. Chemirad Corp., 1962, 37 N.Y. 56, 179 A.2d 401 (same); Murray v. Lawson, Ky. 1969, 441 S.W.2d 136 ("phobic reaction" anxiety neurosis); Hamilan Corp. v. O'Neill, 1959, 106 U.S.App.D.C. 354, 273 F.2d 89 (worry over drinking beverage containing glass); Domenico v. Kaherl, 1964, 160 Me. 182, 200 A.2d 844 (worry over unborn child); Rennick v. Fruehauf Corp., 1978, 82 Wis.2d 793, 264 N.W.2d 264 (fear of loss of economic livelihood); cf. Laxton v. Orkin Exterminating Co., Tenn.1982, 639 S.W.2d 431 (anxiety over possible carcinogenic effects of drinking water contaminated by toxic chemical); Templin v. Erkekedis, 1949, 119 Ind.App. 171, 84 N.E.2d 728 (virgin whose hymen was ruptured).

35. Redick v. Peterson, 1918, 99 Wash. 368, 169 P. 804.

36. See generally Ceco Corp. v. Coleman, D.C.App. 1982, 441 A.2d 940; Lester v. Magic Chef, Inc., 1982, 230 Kan. 643, 641 P.2d 353; Holmquist v. Volkswagen of America, Inc., Iowa App.1977, 261 N.W.2d 516; Chmurka v. Southern Farm Bureau Insurance Co., La. App.1978, 357 So.2d 1207.

37. 1 Street, Foundations of Legal Liability, 1906, 470. The thin-skulled plaintiff rule applies to parasitic psychological injuries, so that a plaintiff with a particular susceptibility to psychological disorders may recover for her idiosyncratic emotional harm resulting from her physical injuries and the accident. Martinez v. Teague, 1981, 96 N.M. 446, 631 P.2d 1314.

38. "With few exceptions, recoveries have been restricted to women, and for the most part, pregnant women." Green, "Fright" Cases, 1933, 27 Ill.L.Rev. 761. Although miscarriages are still plentiful, there is also by now a good supply of cases of heart attacks and the like, occurring to males.

39. In Victorian Railways Commissioners v. Coultas, P.C.1888, 13 App.Cas. 222. This was subsequently rejected in Dulieu v. White, [1901] 2 K.B. 669. See generally Rogers, Winfield & Jolowicz on Tort, 11th ed. 1979, ch. 7.

40. Bosley v. Andrews, 1958, 393 Pa. 161, 142 A.2d 263; Brisboise v. Kansas City Public Service Co., Mo. 1957, 303 S.W.2d 619; Spade v. Lynn & Boston Railroad Co., 1897, 168 Mass. 285, 47 N.E. 88; Miller v. Baltimore & Ohio South Western Railroad Co., 1908, 78 Ohio St. 309, 85 N.E. 499; West Chicago St. Railroad Co. v. Liebig, 1898, 79 Ill.App. 567.

For recent statements of the rule, see Little v. Williamson, 1982, ___ Ind.App. ___, 441 N.E.2d 974; Cadillac Motor Car Division v. Brown, Fla.Dist.App.1983, 428 So.2d 301; Deutsch v. Shein, Ky.1980, 597 S.W.2d 141; Howard v. Bloodworth, 1976, 137 Ga.App. 478, 224 S.E.2d 122; see generally Annot., 1959, 64 A.L.R.2d 100.

41. See Mitchell v. Rochester Railway Co., 1896, 151 N.Y. 107, 45 N.E. 354.

42. Cf. Homans v. Boston Elevated Railway Co., 1902, 180 Mass. 456, 62 N.E. 737; Kentucky Traction & Terminal Co. v. Roman's Guardian, 1929, 232 Ky. 285, 23 S.W.2d 272.

43. Homans v. Boston Elevated Railway Co., 1902, 180 Mass. 456, 62 N.E. 737.

44. Kentucky Traction & Terminal Co. v. Roman's Guardian, 1929, 232 Ky. 285, 23 S.W.2d 272.

45. Hess v. Philadelphia Transportation Co., 1948, 358 Pa. 144, 56 A.2d 89; Clark v. Choctawhatchee Electric Cooperative, Fla.1958, 107 So.2d 609. See Deutsch v. Shein, Ky.1980, 597 S.W.2d 141 (X-rays of pregnant woman).

46. Zelinsky v. Chimics, 1961, 196 Pa.Super. 312, 175 A.2d 351 ("any degree of physical impact, however

floor,[47] dust in the eye,[48] or the inhalation of smoke.[49] The requirement has even been satisfied by a fall brought about by a faint after a collision,[50] or the plaintiff's own wrenching of her shoulder [51] in reaction to the fright. "The magic formula 'impact' is pronounced; the door opens to the full joy of a complete recovery." [52] A Georgia circus case reduced the matter to something of an absurdity by finding "impact" where the defendant's horse "evacuated his bowels" into the plaintiff's lap.[53]

The true value of the impact requirement may lie in the opportunity which is afforded to the defendant to testify that there was in fact no impact. He may be able to swear that within the period of the statute of limitations he has struck no one with his automobile, where he cannot be sure whom he may have frightened. But so far as substantial justice is concerned, it would seem that it is possible to have nearly as much assurance that the mental disturbance is genuine when the plaintiff escapes "impact" only by an inch. Starting with an early Irish decision,[54] the great majority of courts have now repudiated the requirement of "impact," regarding as sufficient the requirement that the mental distress be certified by some physical injury, illness or other objective physical manifestation.[55] There is still considerable confusion, however, as to just what conditions or symptoms should be deemed to qualify as the requisite "injury," "illness," or other physical consequence.[56]

Beginning with a Hawaii decision in 1970,[57] followed by a California case in 1980,[58] a handful of courts [59] have taken the

---

slight"); Johnson Freight Lines, Inc. v. Tallent, 1964, 53 Tenn.App. 464, 384 S.W.2d 46; Boston v. Chesapeake & Ohio Railway Co., 1945, 223 Ind. 425, 61 N.E.2d 326.

47. Driscoll v. Gaffey, 1910, 207 Mass. 102, 92 N.E. 1010. Cf. Block v. Pascucci, 1930, 111 Conn. 58, 149 A. 210.

48. Porter v. Delaware, Lackawanna Western Railroad Co., 1906, 73 N.J.L. 405, 63 A. 860.

49. Morton v. Stack, 1930, 122 Ohio St. 115, 170 N.E. 869.

50. Comstock v. Wilson, 1931, 257 N.Y. 231, 177 N.E. 431.

51. Freedman v. Eastern Mass. Street Railway Co., 1938, 299 Mass. 246, 12 N.E.2d 739.

52. Goodrich, Emotional Disturbance as Legal Damage, 1922, 20 Mich.L.Rev. 497, 504.

53. Christy Brothers Circus v. Turnage, 1928, 38 Ga.App. 581, 144 S.E. 680.

54. Bell v. Great Northern Railway, 1890, L.R. 26 Ir.Rep. 428. The parent American case was Hill v. Kimball, 1890, 76 Tex. 210, 13 S.W. 59.

55. See, e.g., Payton v. Abbott Labs, 1982, 386 Mass. 540, 437 N.E.2d 171, 181 ("physical harm manifested by objective symptomatology"); Fournell v. Usher Pest Control Co., 1981, 208 Neb. 684, 305 N.W.2d 605 ("physical injury"); Wyatt v. Gilmore, N.C. App.1982, 290 S.E.2d 790; Vicnire v. Ford Motor Credit Co., Me.1979, 401 A.2d 148, 155 ("illness or bodily harm [with] objective symptomatology"); Sears, Roebuck & Co. v. Young, Miss.1980, 384 So.2d 69, 71 ("physical injury or genuine physical consequences"); Melton v. Allen, 1978, 282 Or. 731, 580 P.2d 1019, 1022 ("physical injury or physical consequences"); Towns v. Anderson, Colo.1978, 579 P.2d 1163, 1165 ("physical or mental illness"; adopting Second Restatement of Torts, §§ 436, 436A, and Comments); Annots., 1959, 64 A.L.R.2d 100; 1970, 29 A.L.R.3d 1337.

56. See Payton v. Abbott Labs, 1982, 386 Mass. 540, 437 N.E.2d 171, 175 n. 5 (listing standards by jurisdiction); Note, 1981, 10 Hofstra L.Rev. 213 n. 3. A court can, of course, define away any requirement of "physical" harm. See Vance v. Vance, 1979, 286 Md. 490, 408 A.2d 728, 733–34 (defining "physical injury" as "mental harm capable of objective determination"). Or it can "find" an injury from any contact with a deleterious substance. Cf. Laxton v. Orkin Exterminating Co., Tenn.1982, 639 S.W.2d 431 (consumption of water containing toxic chemical).

57. Rodrigues v. State, 1970, 52 Hawaii 156, 472 P.2d 509. See Campbell v. Animal Quarantine Station, 1981, 63 Hawaii 557, 632 P.2d 1066 (family members allowed recovery for mental distress from death of dog), noted 1982, 4 U.Haw.L.Rev. 207; Miller, The Scope of Liability for Negligent Infliction of Emotional Distress: Making "The Punishment Fit the Crime," 1979, 1 U.Haw.L.Rev. 1 (thorough policy analysis).

58. Molien v. Kaiser Foundation Hospitals, 1980, 27 Cal.3d 916, 167 Cal.Rptr. 831, 616 P.2d 813. See Nolan & Ursin, Negligent Infliction of Emotional Distress: Coherence Emerging from Chaos, 1982, 33 Hast.L.J. 583; Notes, 1982, 22 Santa Clara L.Rev. 181; 1981, 13 Pacif.L.J. 179; 33 Hast.L.J. 291; 10 Hofstra L.Rev. 213.

59. Bass v. Nooney Co., Mo.1983, 646 S.W.2d 765 (trapped in elevator for 30 minutes; severe anxiety reaction); Shultz v. Barberton Glass Co., 1983, 4 Ohio St.3d 131, 447 N.E.2d 109 (vehicular accident; traumatic neurosis); Taylor v. Baptist Medical Center, Inc., Ala.1981, 400 So.2d 369; Chappetta v. Bowman Transportation, Inc., La.App.1982, 415 So.2d 1019; see Montinieri v. Southern New England Telephone Co., 1978, 175 Conn. 337, 398 A.2d 1180. Cf. Ferrara v. Galluchio, 1958, 2 N.Y.2d 16, 176 N.Y.S.2d 996, 152 N.E.2d

final step and permitted a general negligence cause of action for the infliction of serious emotional distress,[60] without regard to whether the plaintiff suffered any physical injury or illness as a result. A couple of other recent decisions, over strong dissents, have expressly refused to move this far, opting instead to retain the physical harm requirement.[61]

Peril or Harm to Another

Where the mental disturbance and its consequences are not caused by any fear for the plaintiff's own safety, but by distress at witnessing some peril or harm to another person—as in the classic and strongest case of a mother observing the death of her child—additional problems arise.[62] Those few courts which still require an "impact" upon the person would of course deny recovery,[63] although if there is an impact some of them have been willing to allow damages due in part to fear for another.[64] But even in states that have not insisted upon "impact," many of the cases until quite recently denied all recovery.[65] The reason usually assigned, as in an early, leading Wisconsin case, was that the defendant could not reasonably anticipate any harm to the plaintiff, and therefore owed her no duty of care.[66] She stands, in other words, in the position of Mrs. Palsgraf.[67] Thus, if the plaintiff herself is threatened with physical injury by the defendant's negligence, as where she is standing in the path of his vehicle, and suffers physical harm through fright at the peril to her child, it was held in the English case of Hambrook v. Stokes Brothers[68] that, with an initial breach of duty to her established, it becomes merely a matter of the unexpected manner in which the foreseeable harm has occurred, so that recovery should be allowed. Many American decisions have followed this approach and held that bystanders may recover for mental distress provided that they were personally within the "zone of danger."[69]

249; Vance v. Vance, Md.1979, 408 A.2d 728, 733–34 (defining "physical injury" as mental harm "capable of objective determination"); Naccash v. Burger, 1982, 223 Va. 406, 290 S.E.2d 825 (wrongful birth of severely defective child). A few of the bystander cases have also abandoned the physical harm or manifestation requirement. See Culbert v. Sampson's Supermarkets, Inc., Me.1982, 444 A.2d 433; Portee v. Jaffee, 1980, 84 N.J. 88, 417 A.2d 521; cf. Sinn v. Burd, Pa.1979, 404 A.2d 672 (but cf. concurring opinion). Contra, Rickey v. Chicago Transit Authority, 1983, 101 Ill.App.3d 439, 57 Ill.Dec. 46, 428 N.E.2d 596.

60. The standard applied in this context is an objective one, which excludes liability for hypersensitive mental disturbance: "serious mental distress may be found where a reasonable man, normally constituted, would be unable to adequately cope with the mental distress engendered by the circumstances of the case." Rodrigues v. State, 1970, 52 Hawaii 156, 472 P.2d 509, 520. Accord, Molien v. Kaiser Foundation Hospitals, 1980, 27 Cal.3d 916, 167 Cal.Rptr. 831, 837, 616 P.2d 813, 819–20. See Culbert v. Sampson's Supermarkets, Inc., Me.1982, 444 A.2d 433, 437. Compare the older cases denying liability for hypersensitive mental reactions. Williamson v. Bennett, 1960, 251 N.C. 498, 112 S.E.2d 48 (fear for safety of child whom plaintiff imagined she had struck); Legac v. Vietmayer Brothers, 1929, 7 N.J.Misc. 685, 147 A. 110 (made ill by sight of a bug in loaf of bread); Caputzal v. Lindsay Co., 1966, 48 N.J. 69, 222 A.2d 513 (heart attack at sight of brownish water from faucet). See Note, 1961, 39 N.C.L.Rev. 303.

61. Payton v. Abbott Labs, 1982, 386 Mass. 540, 437 N.E.2d 171 (4–3); Fournell v. Usher Pest Control Co., 1981, 208 Neb. 684, 305 N.W.2d 605 (5–2). See also Pearson, supra note 10, at 516, arguing that "valid policy reasons support the judicial reluctance to create a broad tort of negligent infliction of emotional harm."

62. See generally Annot., 1970, 29 A.L.R.3d 1337.

63. See Selfe v. Smith, Fla.App.1981, 397 So.2d 348; Carlinville National Bank v. Rhoads, 1978, 63 Ill.App. 3d 502, 20 Ill.Dec. 386, 380 N.E.2d 63.

64. Chesapeake & Ohio Railway Co. v. Robinett, 1913, 151 Ky. 778, 152 S.W. 976; Greenberg v. Stanley, 1958, 51 N.J.Super. 90, 143 A.2d 588, affirmed in part, reversed in part, 30 N.J. 485, 153 A.2d 833.

65. Tobin v. Grossman, 1969, 24 N.Y.2d 609, 301 N.Y.S.2d 554, 249 N.E.2d 419; Burroughs v. Jordan, 1970, 224 Tenn. 418, 456 S.W.2d 652; McMahon v. Bergeson, 1960, 9 Wis.2d 256, 101 N.W.2d 63.

66. Waube v. Warrington, 1935, 216 Wis. 603, 258 N.W. 497. Accord: Cote v. Litawa, 1950, 96 N.H. 174, 71 A.2d 792; Resavage v. Davies, 1952, 199 Md. 479, 86 A.2d 879.

67. See supra, § 43.

68. [1925] 1 K.B. 141.

69. E.g., Stadler v. Cross, Minn.1980, 295 N.W.2d 552; Keck v. Jackson, 1979, 122 Ariz. 114, 593 P.2d 668; Vaillancourt v. Medical Center Hospital of Vermont, Inc., 1980, 139 Vt. 138, 425 A.2d 92. See Annot., 1970, 29 A.L.R.3d 1337.

It seems sufficiently obvious that the shock of a mother at danger or harm to her child may be both a real and a serious injury. All ordinary human feelings are in favor of her action against the negligent defendant. If a duty to her requires that she herself be in some foreseeable danger, then it may fairly be argued that when a child is endangered, it is not beyond contemplation that its mother will be somewhere in the vicinity, and thus may suffer serious shock.[70] There is surely no great triumph of logic in a rule which permits recovery for distress over an unborn being, where the mother miscarries,[71] yet which denies it once the child is born. If recovery is to be permitted, however, it is also clear that there must be some limitation. It would be an entirely unreasonable burden on all human activity if the defendant who has endangered one person were to be compelled to pay for the lacerated feelings of every other person disturbed by reason of it, including every bystander shocked at an accident, and every distant relative of the person injured, as well as all his friends. And probably the danger of fictitious claims, and the necessity of some guarantee of genuineness, are even greater here than before. It is no doubt such considerations that have made the law extremely cautious in extending its protection to the bystander.

But the law in this area has begun to move. In 1968, in the case of Dillon v. Legg,[72] the California court kicked over the zone of danger rule and held that a mother who saw her child run down and killed could recover, although she was herself in a position of complete safety. The bystander may be foreseeable—and hence owed a duty—under the California rule, which may be termed the "bystander proximity" doctrine, if: (1) the bystander is located near the scene of the accident—"physical proximity"; (2) the bystander personally observes the accident—"temporal proximity";[73] and (3) the bystander is closely related to the victim—"relational proximity." A number of courts have followed or developed further upon the *Dillon* foreseeability guidelines,[74] while many others have retained their zone of danger or other more restrictive rules of bystander recovery for mental disturbance.[75] How far the rule of Dillon v. Legg may ultimately spread,[76] and whether it may even one day be swallowed up in the newly emerging "independent" cause of action for emotional distress,[77] remain for now unan-

---

70. Hallen, Damages for Physical Injuries Resulting from Fright or Shock, 1933, 19 Va.L.Rev. 253, 270. Compare the rescue cases, infra, where the mental reactions of a bystander are regarded as normal, supra § 44.

71. See supra, note 38.

72. Dillon v. Legg, 1968, 69 Cal.Rptr. 72, 80, 441 P.2d 912, 920, overruling Amaya v. Home Ice, Fuel & Supply Co., 1963, 29 Cal.Rptr. 33, 379 P.2d 513.

73. See Annots., 1981, 5 A.L.R.4th 833 (temporal proximity); 1979, 94 A.L.R.3d 486 (relational proximity); 1970, 29 A.L.R.3d 1337 (general).

74. See, e.g., Leong v. Takasaki, 1974, 55 Hawaii 398, 520 P.2d 758; D'Amicol v. Alvarez Shipping Co., 1973, 31 Conn.Sup. 164, 326 A.2d 129; Miller v. Cook, 1978, 87 Mich.App. 6, 273 N.W.2d 567; D'Ambra v. United States, 1975, 114 R.I. 643, 338 A.2d 524; General Motors Corp. v. Grizzle, Tex.Civ.App.1982, 642 S.W.2d 837; Sinn v. Burd, Pa.1979, 404 A.2d 672, noted 1980, 56 Chi.-Kent L.Rev. 1011; Corso v. Merrill, N.H. 1979, 406 A.2d 300 (see Grimes, J., dissenting: "the genie is now clearly out of the bottle and I can only hope that someone will find a way to get him back in"); Dziokonski v. Babineau, 1978, 375 Mass. 555, 380 N.E.2d 1295; Barnhill v. Davis, Iowa 1981, 300 N.W.2d 104 (see Albee, J., dissenting: "I am not a party to the opening of this 'Pandora's Box'"); Portee v. Jaffee, 1980, 84 N.J. 88, 417 A.2d 521; Culbert v. Sampson's Supermarkets, Inc., Me.1982, 444 A.2d 433 (mother watched baby gag on substance in baby food). Cf. Walker v. Clark Equipment Co., Iowa 1982, 320 N.W.2d 561 (recovery allowed in warranty and strict tort).

75. See, e.g., Tobin v. Grossman, 1969, 24 N.Y.2d 609, 301 N.Y.S.2d 554, 249 N.E.2d 419 (no duty to bystanders); Stadler v. Cross, Minn.1980, 295 N.W.2d 552 (zone of danger); Rickey v. Chicago Transit Authority, 1983, 101 Ill.App.3d 439, 57 Ill.Dec. 46, 428 N.E.2d 596; Dageforde v. Potomac Edison Co., 1977, 35 Md.App. 37, 369 A.2d 93; Madison v. Deseret Livestock Co., 10th Cir. 1978, 574 F.2d 1027; Shelton v. Russell Pipe & Foundry Co., Tenn.1978, 570 S.W.2d 861; Steele v. St. Paul Fire & Marine Insurance Co., La.App.1979, 371 So.2d 843.

76. See the review of decisions during the decade following *Dillon* in Note, 1981, 19 Am.Bus.L.J. 214 (10 states following *Dillon*, 19 opposed); Note, 1974, 25 Hast.L.J. 1248 (reaction to 1974). See also Pearson, supra note 10, arguing zone of danger rule preferable to *Dillon* rule.

77. See articles cited supra, notes 10 & 58.

swered questions in this tumultuous area of the law.[78]

 **WESTLAW REFERENCES**

digest("emotional distress" /s negligent)

Mental Disturbance Alone

headnote(duty /p "emotional distress")
topic(272 313a 379) /p mental emotional nervous /4 injur***

Mental Disturbance with Physical Injury

topic(272 313a 379) & mental emotional nervous /3 injur*** /p physical
topic(272 313a 379) & impact /10 recovery

Peril or Harm to Another

emotional mental +5 distress /s witness! /s another third
dillon +2 legg
leong +s takasaki

§ 55. Prenatal Injuries

One area where the limitation imposed by the concept of "duty" has played an especially significant role is that of prenatal injuries. There are two basic classifications into which the cases in this area may be divided: (1) those where the defendant tortiously inflicts a physical injury, through the body of the mother, upon an unborn child; and (2) those where the defendant's tortious acts or omissions result in the birth of an unwanted child.

Infliction of Harm Through Mother's Body

Prior to 1946, when a pregnant woman was injured, and her child as a result was subsequently born in an injured or deformed condition, nearly all of the decisions denied recovery to the child.[1] Two reasons were usually given: first, that the defendant could owe no duty of conduct to a person who was not in existence at the time of his action;[2] and second, that the difficulty of proving any causal connection between negligence and damage was too great, such that there was too much danger of fictitious claims.[3]

So far as duty is concerned, if existence at the time of the tortious act is necessary,[4] medical authority has long recognized that an unborn child is in existence from the moment of conception,[5] and for many purposes its existence is recognized by the law.[6] It

---

78. One interesting reform proposal deserving of consideration is to allow the *cause of action* for serious mental distress largely under ordinary negligence and foreseeability principles, but to limit the *damages* recoverable therefore to tangible economic loss. See Miller, The Scope of Liability for Negligent Infliction of Emotional Distress: Making "The Punishment Fit the Crime," 1979, U.Haw.L.Rev. 1.

For accounts of the difficulties involved in compensating absent members of a community for their mental distress following a flood disaster, see Prince v. Pittston Co., S.D.W.Va.1974, 63 F.R.D. 28, noted 1975, 63 Geo.L.J. 1179; Stern, The Buffalo Creek Disaster, 1976; Stern, The Anguish of Buffalo Creek, April, 1977, 13 Trial 41; Rabin, Dealing with Disasters: Some Thoughts on the Adequacy of the Legal System, 1978, 30 Stan.L.Rev. 281.

§ 55

1. E.g., Allaire v. St. Luke's Hospital, 1900, 184 Ill. 359, 56 N.E. 638; Drobner v. Peters, 1921, 232 N.Y. 220, 133 N.E. 567.

A fortiori, there could be no action for wrongful death of the child after its birth. Dietrich v. Inhabitants of Northampton, 1884, 138 Mass. 14; Gorman v. Budlong, 1901, 23 R.I. 169, 49 A. 704; Magnolia Coca Cola Bottling Co. v. Jordan, 1935, 124 Tex. 347, 78 S.W.2d 944; Newman v. City of Detroit, 1937, 281 Mich. 60, 274 N.W. 710.

2. See Dietrich v. Inhabitants of Northampton, 1884, 138 Mass. 14, 17.

3. "[T]here are instances in the law where rules of right are founded upon the inherent and inevitable difficulty or impossibility of proof. And it is easy to see what a boundless sea of speculation in evidence this new idea would launch us." Walker v. Great Northern Railway, [Q.B. 1891], 28 L.R.Ir. 69, 81–82 (O'Brien, J., concurring).

4. Cf. Kine v. Zuckerman, Pa.1924, 4 D. & C. 227, saying the case is the same as if the defendant had installed a dangerous apparatus in the home of the unborn child, and shortly after birth the child had been injured by it.

5. See Herzog, Medical Jurisprudence, 1931, §§ 860–975; Malloy, Legal Anatomy and Surgery, 1930, 669–687.

6. "Let us see what this non-entity can do. He may be vouched in a recovery, though it is for the purpose of making him answer over in value. He may be an executor. He may take under the Statute of Distributions. He may take by devise. He may be entitled under a charge for raising portions. He may have an injunction, and he may have a guardian." Butler, J., in Thellusson v. Woodford, 1798, 4 Ves. 227, 322, 31 Eng. Rep. 117. See Notes, 1971, 40 Notre Dame Law. 349; 56 Iowa L.Rev. 994.

has been accorded legal status for various purposes in equity,[7] criminal law,[8] property law,[9] and tort law.[10] As far as causation is concerned, there will certainly be cases in which there are difficulties of proof, but they should be no more frequent, nor the difficulties any greater, than as to many other medical problems.[11] All writers who have discussed the problem have joined in condemning the total no-duty rule and agree that the unborn child in the path of an automobile is as much a person in the street as the mother, and should be equally protected under the law.[12]

A good many years of rather devastating criticism finally had its effect. Beginning with a decision in the District of Columbia in 1946,[13] a rapid series of cases, many of them expressly overruling prior holdings,[14] brought about a rather spectacular reversal of the no-duty rule. The child, if he is born alive, is now permitted in every jurisdiction to maintain an action for the consequences of prenatal injuries,[15] and if he dies of such injuries after birth an action will lie for his wrongful death.[16]

There are, however, two problems on which there is as yet no complete agreement. One concerns the stage of development of the unborn child at the time of the original injury. Most of the cases allowing recovery have involved a fetus which was then viable, meaning capable of independent life, if only in an incubator.[17] Many of them have said, by way of dictum, that recovery must be limited to such cases,[18] and others have said that the child, if not viable, must at least be "quick."[19] But when actually faced with the issue for decision, most courts have allowed recovery, even though

---

7. Jefferson v. Griffin Spalding County Hospital Authorities, 1981, 247 Ga. 86, 274 S.E.2d 457 (requiring mother to have caesarean section contrary to her religious beliefs because fetus, viable at thirty-nine weeks, was endangered); Raleigh Fitkin-Paul Morgan Memorial Hospital v. Anderson, 1964, 42 N.J. 421, 201 A.2d 537, certiorari denied 377 U.S. 985, 84 S.Ct. 1894, 12 L.Ed.2d 1032 (ordering blood transfusion for mother to save unborn despite mother's contrary religious beliefs).

8. See West's Ann.Cal.Pen.Code § 187 ("Murder is the unlawful killing of a human being, or a fetus, with malice aforethought").

9. Deal v. Sexton, 1907, 144 N.C. 157, 56 S.E. 691; Biggs v. McCarty, 1882, 86 Ind. 352; cf. Hall v. Hancock, 1834, 32 Mass. (15 Pick.) 255.

10. After its birth, it has long been permitted to maintain a statutory action for the wrongful death of a parent. The George and Richard, [1871], 111 Eng.Rep. 491; Herndon v. St. Louis & San Francisco Railway, 1912, 37 Okl. 256, 128 P. 727.

11. "The questions of causation, reasonable certainty, etc., which will arise in these cases are no different, in kind, from the ones which have arisen in thousands of other negligence cases decided in this State, in the past." Woods v. Lancet, 1951, 303 N.Y. 349, 102 N.E.2d 691.

12. Winfield, The Unborn Child, 1942, 4 U.Toronto L.J. 278; Muse and Spinella, Right of Infant to Recover for Prenatal Injury, 1950, 36 Va.L.Rev. 611; Gordon, The Unborn Plaintiff, 1965, 12 J.For.Med. 111; Note, 1962, 110 U.Pa.L.Rev. 554.

13. Bonrest v. Kotz, D.D.C.1946, 65 F.Supp. 138. The real start of the movement was the dissenting opinion of Boggs, J., in Allaire v. St. Luke's Hospital, 1900, 184 Ill. 359, 56 N.E. 638.

14. E.g., Amann v. Faidy, 1953, 415 Ill. 422, 114 N.E.2d 412, overruling Allaire v. St. Luke's Hospital, 1900, 184 Ill. 359, 56 N.E. 638; Leal v. C.C. Pitts Sand & Gravel, Inc., Tex.1967, 419 S.W.2d 820, overruling Magnolia Coca Cola Bottling Co. v. Jordan, 1935, 124 Tex. 347, 78 S.W.2d 944.

15. See Hughson v. St. Francis Hospital, 1983, 92 A.D.2d 131, 459 N.Y.S.2d 814 (child had action against physician who failed to obtain mother's informed consent to invasive diagnostic procedure); Grodin v. Grodin, 1980, 102 Mich.App. 396, 301 N.W.2d 869 (child born with brown teeth could maintain action against mother for taking drug while pregnant); Williams v. Marion Rapid Transit Co., 1949, 152 Ohio St. 114, 87 N.E.2d 334; Woods v. Lancet, 1951, 303 N.Y. 349, 102 N.E.2d 691; Rodriquez v. Patti, 1953, 415 Ill. 496, 114 N.E.2d 271; Second Restatement of Torts, § 869. The cases are collected in Annot., 1971, 40 A.L.R.3d 1222.

16. Group Health Association, Inc. v. Blumenthal, 1983, 295 Md. 104, 453 A.2d 1198 (non-viable); Simon v. Mullin, 1977, 34 Conn.Sup. 139, 380 A.2d 1353; see Stokes v. Liberty Mutual Insurance Co., Fla.1968, 213 So.2d 695; Annot., 1971, 40 A.L.R.3d 1222.

17. "Viable: Capable of living, especially capable of living outside the uterus; said of a fetus that has reached such a stage of development that it can live outside the uterus." Dorland, American Illustrated Medical Dictionary, 21st ed. 1948, 1616.

18. New Hampshire so held in Poliquin v. MacDonald, 1957, 101 N.H. 104, 135 A.2d 249, but this was apparently overruled in Bennett v. Hymers, 1958, 101 N.H. 483, 147 A.2d 108.

19. Damasiewicz v. Gorsuch, 1951, 197 Md. 417, 79 A.2d 550.

the injury occurred during the early weeks of pregnancy, when the child was neither viable nor quick.[20]

Viability of course does not affect the question of the legal existence of the unborn, and therefore of the defendant's duty, and it is a most unsatisfactory criterion, since it is a relative matter, depending on the health of the mother and child and many other matters in addition to the stage of development.[21] Certainly the infant may be no less injured; and logic is in favor of ignoring the stage at which the injury occurs. With recent advances in embryology and medical technology,[22] medical proof of causation in these cases has become increasingly reliable, which argues for eliminating the viability or other arbitrary developmental requirement altogether.

A perplexing problem that remains in this area is whether claims should be permitted where the harmful contact with the mother occurs even before the child is conceived,[23] as from ingestion of a defective drug causing chromosomal damage to the mother's ovum,[24] or injury to her uterus during a preconception operation.[25] A small number of courts have allowed recovery,[26] but New York in a thinly reasoned case has recently ruled that a child has no cause of action for preconception torts upon the mother.[27] The reasons for denying such claims involve the problems of proof and proximate causation arising, for example, from the imposition of liability upon a chemical, drug or power company for future generations of genetically mutated children resulting from toxic chemicals or radioactive waste.[28] These are indeed staggering problems, that will have to be dealt with carefully in future toxic tort contexts such as these, but they by no means require that a blanket no-duty rule be applied in pre-conception injury cases where such problems do not exist.

The other major problem, in cases where the harmful contact is made upon the mother's body, is whether the child must be born alive, or whether an action can be maintained for its wrongful death if it is stillborn as a result of the injury.[29] The answer to this question has often turned on the construction of the particular state's wrongful death statute, as to whether such an infant is the kind of "person" intended by the legislature; but there are also obvious difficulties of proof of causation and damages, and a real possibility of double recovery, since the mother has her own action for the miscarriage.[30] For such reasons, many courts—including those in several of the larger

---

20. Sylvia v. Gobeille, 1966, 101 R.I. 76, 220 A.2d 222; Bennett v. Hymers, 1958, 101 N.H. 483, 147 A.2d 108; Sinkler v. Kneale, 1960, 401 Pa. 267, 164 A.2d 93; Smith v. Brennan, 1960, 31 N.J. 353, 157 A.2d 497. See Note, 1968, 21 Okl.L.Rev. 114.

21. Greenhill, Principles and Practice of Obstetrics, 10th ed. 1951, 391, 794. Infants born as early as the twenty-fifth week have survived. Ismach, The Smallest Patients, Sept. 14, 1981, Med.World News, 28, 29; see Note, 1982, 33 S.C.L.Rev. 797, 805.

22. Hirshhorn, Prenatal Diagnosis of Disease, in Developmental Genetics, 1976, Fenoglio, Goodman & King eds., 87, 93; Friedmann, Legal Implications of Amniocentesis, 1974, 123 U.Pa.L.Rev. 92; Goodner, Prenatal Genetic Diagnosis: Present and Future, 1976, 19 Clin.Obst. & Gyn. 965; Notes, 1978, 87 Yale L.J. 1488, 1493; 1962, 110 U.Pa.L.Rev. 554.

23. See generally Robertson, Toward Rational Boundaries of Tort Liability for Injury to the Unborn: Prenatal Injuries, Preconception Injuries and Wrongful Life, 1978 Duke L.J. 1401; Notes, 1982, 60 Wash.U.L. Q. 275; 1977, 48 U.Colo.L.Rev. 621; Annot., 1979, 91 A.L.R.3d 316.

24. See Jorgensen v. Meade Johnson Laboratories, Inc., 10th Cir. 1973, 483 F.2d 237.

25. Bergstreser v. Mitchell, 8th Cir. 1978, 577 F.2d 22.

26. See supra, notes 24 & 25; Renslow v. Mennonite Hospital, 1977, 67 Ill.2d 348, 10 Ill.Dec. 484, 367 N.E.2d 1250.

27. Albala v. City of New York, 1981, 54 N.Y.2d 269, 445 N.Y.S.2d 108, 429 N.E.2d 786 noted, 1982, 50 Tenn.L.Rev. 195; 15 Conn.L.Rev. 161.

28. See generally Notes, 1981, 26 St.Louis L.J. 105 (genetic mutation and chromosomal breakage issues); 1979, 12 U.Mich.J.L.Ref. 237 (birth defects from workplace toxins).

29. Speiser, Recovery for Wrongful Death, 2d ed. 1975, § 4:21; Kader, The Law of Tortious Prenatal Death Since Roe v. Wade, 1980, 45 Mo.L.Rev. 639; Notes, 1982, 33 S.C.L.Rev. 797; 1976, 15 J.Fam.L. 276; Annot., 1967, 15 A.L.R.3d 992.

30. Pregnant women have traditionally been given recovery for their own injuries caused by a miscarriage. Thomas v. Gates, 1899, 126 Cal. 1, 58 P. 315.

states—deny a wrongful birth action for the stillborn fetus.[31] A majority of states, however, have been more concerned with compensating for the loss, and so have allowed such claims for wrongful death.[32]

Unwanted Children—"Wrongful Birth", "Wrongful Life" and "Wrongful Pregnancy"

The last couple of decades have witnessed the rapid development of tort claims concerning a variety of issues that arise when the tortfeasor's act or omission results in the birth of an unwanted child. The defendants in these cases are typically doctors charged with negligence in failing directly to prevent the conception or birth of the child, as by negligently performing a sterilization or abortion procedure, or in failing to diagnose or inform the parents that the child might be born deformed—because of a disease contracted by the mother or a genetic condition in one of the parents—in time to permit the termination of the pregnancy.

These actions are now generally referred to as "wrongful birth" claims, when brought by the parents for their own damages, and "wrongful life" claims, when brought by or on behalf of the child for the harm of being born deformed.[33]

Following a couple of wrongful life cases denying recovery to children born into a state of illegitimacy in the early and mid-1960s,[34] New Jersey in 1967 handed down Gleitman v. Cosgrove,[35] which was destined to become the fountainhead for debate in this country[36] in cases of this type. The *Gleitman* court denied recovery, to both the child and the parents, for birth defects that resulted when the mother contracted German measles during her early pregnancy. Claiming that the defendant doctor had negligently assured her that the disease would not affect the child, the mother asserted that she might have secured an abortion had the defendant informed her of the risk of birth defects from the disease. Troubled by the philosophical difficulties of allowing the

---

The mother's action does not, however, include damages for the loss of the child. Occhipinti v. Rheem Manufacturing Co., 1965, 252 Miss. 172, 172 So.2d 186.

31. E.g., Scott v. Kopp, 1981, 494 Pa. 487, 431 A.2d 959; Weitl v. Moes, Iowa 1981, 311 N.W.2d 259; Justus v. Atchison, 1977, 19 Cal.3d 564, 139 Cal.Rptr. 97, 565 P.2d 122; Stern v. Miller, Fla.1977, 348 So.2d 303; Endresz v. Friedberg, 1969, 24 N.Y.2d 478, 301 N.Y.S.2d 65, 248 N.E.2d 901; Graf v. Taggert, 1964, 43 N.J. 303, 204 A.2d 140.

32. E.g., Volk v. Baldazo, 1982, 103 Idaho 570, 651 P.2d 11; Danos v. St. Pierre, La.1981, 402 So.2d 633; Salazar v. St. Vincent Hospital, App.1980, 95 N.M. 150, 619 P.2d 826; Vaillancourt v. Medical Center Hospital, Inc., 1980, 139 Vt. 138, 425 A.2d 92; Mone v. Greyhound Lines, Inc., 1975, 368 Mass. 354, 331 N.E.2d 916; Libbee v. Permanente Clinic, 1974, 268 Or. 258, 518 P.2d 636, rehearing denied 268 Or. 258, 520 P.2d 361, appeal after remand 269 Or. 543, 525 P.2d 1296; Chrisafogeorgis v. Brandenberg, 1973, 55 Ill.2d 268, 304 N.E.2d 88. Iowa allows such actions if brought by the parents, but not by the fetus. Dunn v. Rose Way, Inc., Iowa 1983, 333 N.W.2d 830.

33. See generally Rogers, Wrongful Life and Wrongful Birth: Medical Malpractice in Genetic Counseling and Prenatal Testing, 1982, 33 S.C.L.Rev. 713; Trotzig, The Defective Child and the Actions for Wrongful Life and Wrongful Birth, 1980, 14 Fam.L.Q. 15; Peters & Peters, Wrongful Life: Recognizing the Defective Child's Right to a Cause of Action, 1980, 18 Duq.L.Rev. 857; Capron, Tort Liability in Genetic Counseling, 1979, 79 Colum.L.Rev. 618; Morrison,

Torts Involving the Unborn—A Limited Cosmology, 1979, 31 Baylor L.Rev. 131; Kelley, Wrongful Life, Wrongful Birth, and Justice in Tort Law, 1979 Wash. U.L.Q. 919; Robertson, Toward Rational Boundaries of Tort Liability for Injury to the Unborn: Prenatal Injuries, Preconception Injuries and Wrongful Life, 1978 Duke L.J. 1401; Kashi, The Case of the Unwanted Blessing: Wrongful Life, 1977, 31 U.Miami L.Rev. 1409; Tedeschi, On Tort Liability for "Wrongful Life," 1966, 1 Israel L.Rev. 513, reprinted 1977, 7 J.Fam.L. 465; Notes, 1982, 18 Idaho L.Rev. 237 (wrongful life); 24 Ariz.L.Rev. 391 (wrongful life action against parents); 10 Fla.St.U.L.Rev. 312; 1981, 42 Ohio St.L.J. 551; 30 Buff.L.Rev. 587 (wrongful life); 50 U.Cin.L. Rev. 65; 15 U.Cal.Dav.L.Rev. 447 (wrongful life); 1980, 54 Tul.L.Rev. 480 (wrongful life); 1980 Wis.L. Rev. 782; 1979, 14 Gonz.L.Rev. 891; 20 Wm. & Mary L.Rev. 125 (wrongful life); 1978, 87 Yale L.J. 1488; 13 Val.U.L.Rev. 127 (damages); 47 Ford.L.Rev. 418; Annot., 1978, 83 A.L.R.3d 15.

34. Zepeda v. Zepeda, 1963, 41 Ill.App.2d 240, 190 N.E.2d 849, certiorari denied 379 U.S. 945, 85 S.Ct. 444, 13 L.Ed.2d 545; Williams v. State, 1966, 18 N.Y.2d 481, 276 N.Y.S.2d 885, 223 N.E.2d 343.

35. Gleitman v. Cosgrove, 1967, 49 N.J. 22, 227 A.2d 689.

36. For the law in other English-speaking countries, see Bickenbach, Damages for Wrongful Conception: *Doiron v. Orr*, 1980, 18 U.West.Ontario L.Rev. 493; Pace, Civil Liability for Pre-Natal Injuries, 1977, 40 Mod.L.Rev. 141.

child to claim that he never should have been born at all, together with the logical and practical difficulties of calculating damages for such "harm," the court denied the child's wrongful life claim: "The infant plaintiff would have us measure the difference between his life with defects against the utter void of nonexistence, but it is impossible to make such a determination." [37] Because of similar difficulties in weighing the resulting emotional and financial burdens to the parents against the "unmeasurable, and complex human benefits of motherhood and fatherhood," [38] coupled with a reluctance to sanction abortion by allowing a cause of action to be predicated upon the deprivation of "the opportunity to terminate the existence of a defective child in embryo," [39] the court further denied the parents' claim for wrongful birth.

With the exception of three lower court decisions subsequently nullified by the high courts of New York [40] and California, [41] and a close call in Pennsylvania, [42] all jurisdictions [43] that have ruled on the issue now follow *Gleitman* in denying the child a wrongful life cause of action for general damages [44] for the suffering of being born in an impaired condition. [45] On the other hand, most courts subsequent to *Gleitman* have been more receptive to the parents' wrongful birth claims, after the Supreme Court's legalization of abortion in 1973, [46] and there is by now quite general agreement that the parents should be permitted to recover at least their pecuniary losses, [47] and perhaps damages for emotional distress as well. [48] Even New Jersey has recanted, if in backward order, first by allowing the parents' claim for emotional distress, and later for the pecuniary losses attributable to the child's impaired condition. [49]

Due in part to the increasing prevalence of sterilization among both men and women,

---

37. 49 N.J. at 25, 227 A.2d at 692.

38. Id. at 693.

39. Id.

40. Becker v. Schwartz, 1978, 46 N.Y.2d 401, 413 N.Y.S.2d 895, 386 N.E.2d 807, modifying 1977, 60 A.D.2d 587, 400 N.Y.S.2d 119, and Park v. Chessin, 1977, 60 A.D.2d 80, 400 N.Y.S.2d 110.

41. Turpin v. Sortini, 1982, 31 Cal.3d 220, 182 Cal. Rptr. 337, 643 P.2d 954, effectively overruling Curlender v. Bio-Science Laboratories, 1980, 106 Cal. App.3d 811, 165 Cal.Rptr. 477.

42. Speck v. Finegold, 1981, 497 Pa. 77, 439 A.2d 110, denying the child's wrongful life claim by an evenly divided court.

43. Some states have recently enacted legislation on point. See West's Ann.Cal.Civ.Code § 43.6 (wrongful life claims against parents prohibited), construed in Turpin v. Sortini, supra note 41; Minn.Stat.Ann. § 145.424 (prohibiting wrongful life and wrongful birth actions, but allowing wrongful pregnancy actions); S.D.Cod.L. ch. 21-55 (prohibiting actions for wrongful life, wrongful birth, and perhaps wrongful pregnancy).

44. Both California and Washington now permit the child in a "wrongful life" action to recover as special damages the costs of any special training or medical care, but not general damages for his affliction. Turpin v. Sortini, 1982, 31 Cal.3d 220, 182 Cal.Rptr. 337, 643 P.2d 954; Harbeson v. Parke-Davis, Inc., 1983, 98 Wn.2d 460, 656 P.2d 483.

45. Turpin v. Sortini, 1982, 31 Cal.3d 220, 182 Cal. Rptr. 337, 643 P.2d 954; DiNatale v. Lieberman, Fla. App.1982, 409 So.2d 512; Eisbrenner v. Stanley, 1981, 106 Mich.App. 357, 308 N.W.2d 209; Speck v. Finegold, 1981, 497 Pa. 77, 439 A.2d 110 (3-3); Phillips v. United States, D.S.C.1980, 508 F.Supp. 537; Berman v. Allan, 1979, 80 N.J. 421, 404 A.2d 8; Becker v. Schwartz, 1978, 46 N.Y.2d 401, 413 N.Y.S.2d 895, 386 N.E.2d 807; Elliott v. Brown, Ala.1978, 361 So.2d 546; Dumer v. St. Michael's Hospital, 1975, 69 Wis.2d 766, 233 N.W.2d 372; Coleman v. Garrison, Del.1975, 349 A.2d 8; Annot., 1978, 83 A.L.R.3d 15.

46. Roe v. Wade, 1973, 410 U.S. 113, 93 S.Ct. 705, 35 L.Ed.2d 147, rehearing denied 410 U.S. 959, 93 S.Ct. 1409, 35 L.Ed.2d 694.

47. E.g., Robak v. United States, 7th Cir. 1981, 658 F.2d 471; Becker v. Schwartz, 1978, 46 N.Y.2d 401, 413 N.Y.S.2d 895, 386 N.E.2d 807.

48. E.g., Harbeson v. Parke-Davis, Inc., 1983, 98 Wn.2d 460, 656 P.2d 483; Naccash v. Burger, 1982, 223 Va. 406, 290 S.E.2d 825; Speck v. Finegold, 1981, 497 Pa. 77, 439 A.2d 110; Eisbrenner v. Stanley, 1981, 106 Mich.App. 357, 308 N.W.2d 209 (requiring offset of parental benefits). In the case of the wrongful birth of a severely impaired child, it would appear that the usual joys of parenthood would often be substantially overshadowed by the emotional trauma of caring for the child in such a condition, so that application of the benefit rule would appear inappropriate in this context. See Schroeder v. Perkel, 1981, 87 N.J. 53, 432 A.2d 834, 842 ("There is no joy in watching a child suffer and die from cystic fibrosis."). Cf. Robak v. United States, 7th Cir. 1981, 658 F.2d 471 (no offset of normal childrearing costs in action for wrongful birth of impaired child.)

49. Berman v. Allan, 1979, 80 N.J. 421, 404 A.2d 8 (emotional distress); Schroeder v. Perkel, 1981, 87 N.J. 53, 432 A.2d 834 (pecuniary losses allowed).

and the general availability of abortions, a growing number of "wrongful conception" or "wrongful pregnancy" cases are being brought against doctors [50] and others [51] for tortiously failing to prevent the birth of a *healthy,* but unwanted, child. The early decisions denied recovery to the parents in these cases, reasoning that the benefits from having a healthy child outweighed any detriments, as a matter of law.[52] While there is some scant continued support for this view,[53] the great majority of courts today allow the parents to recover,[54] but not the child,[55] even if he is born illegitimate.[56] Yet the question of how the parents' damages should be determined has become pregnant with controversy. While the courts are now in general agreement that the costs, expenses and pain directly attributable to the pregnancy and childbirth should be recoverable,[57] the question of whether to allow child-rearing expenses remains an issue of fertile debate. A majority of courts have refused to allow any damages for the costs of raising a normal child,[58] and this position has much in logic and philosophy to support it. A growing number of jurisdictions, however, permit the recovery of child-rearing expenses, but generally [59] require that such damages be reduced, under a sometimes strained interpretation [60] of the "benefit rule," [61] by the accompanying financial and emotional benefits that may be expected to accrue to the parents in raising a healthy

50. Most of these cases involve unsuccessfully performed vasectomy or tubal ligation procedures, but sometimes involve the failure to diagnose a pregnancy or an unsuccessful abortion. See generally Holt, Wrongful Pregnancy, 1982, 33 S.C.L.Rev. 759; Robertson, Civil Litigation Arising from "Wrongful Birth" Following an Unsuccessful Sterilization Operation, 1978, 4 Am.J.L. & Med. 130; Kashi, The Case of the Unwanted Blessing: Wrongful Life, 1977, 31 U.Miami L.Rev. 1409; Lombard, Vasectomy, 1975, 10 Suffolk U.L.Rev. 25; Notes, 1982, 68 Va. 1311 (damages); 1981, 50 U.Cin.L.Rev. 65; 1979, 44 U.Mo.L.Rev. 589; 1978, 35 Wash. & Lee L.Rev. 1065; 1976, 76 Colum.L. Rev. 1187 (failed birth control methods); 1974, 27 U.Fla.L.Rev. 158; Annot., 1978, 83 A.L.R.3d 15.

51. See Troppi v. Scarf, 1971, 31 Mich.App. 240, 187 N.W.2d 511 (pharmacist, who negligently filled birth control pills prescription with other pills); Whittington v. Eli Lilly & Co., S.D.W.Va.1971, 333 F.Supp. 98 (manufacturer of birth control pills); J.P.M. & B.M. v. Schmid Laboratories, Inc., 1981, 178 N.J.Super. 122, 428 A.2d 515 (manufacturer of condom).

52. Christensen v. Thornby, 1934, 192 Minn. 123, 255 N.W. 620; Shaheen v. Knight, Pa.1957, 11 D & C 2d 41, 45 ("to allow damages for the normal birth of a normal child is foreign to the universal public sentiment").

53. See Hickman v. Myers, Tex.App.1982, 632 S.W. 2d 869; Rieck v. Medical Protective Co. of Fort Wayne, Indiana, 1974, 64 Wis.2d 514, 219 N.W.2d 242.

54. The first case expressly so holding was Custodio v. Bauer, 1967, 251 Cal.App.2d 303, 59 Cal.Rptr. 463. See also Sherlock v. Stillwater Clinic, Minn.1977, 260 N.W.2d 169 (helpful review and analysis); Ochs v. Borrelli, 1982, 187 Conn. 253, 445 A.2d 883 (good review); see cases infra, note 59.

55. See Stribling v. deQuevedo, 1980, 288 Pa.Super. 436, 432 A.2d 239; White v. United States, D.Kan. 1981, 510 F.Supp. 146 (also denying claim by siblings).

56. See Moores v. Lucas, Fla.App.1981, 405 So.2d 1022.

57. Many courts limit damages to those losses, allowing compensation only for items such as pain and suffering, loss of consortium, lost wages, and medical expenses. See, e.g., Mason v. Western Pennsylvania Hospital, 1982, 499 Pa. 484, 453 A.2d 974; Cockrum v. Baumgartner, 1983, 95 Ill.2d 193, 69 Ill.Dec. 168, 447 N.E.2d 385 (5–2) (citing cases both ways); Beardsley v. Wierdsma, Wyo.1982, 650 P.2d 288; Wilbur v. Kerr, Ark.1982, 628 S.W.2d 568; Boone v. Mullendore, Ala. 1982, 416 So.2d 718; White v. United States, D.Kan. 1981, 510 F.Supp. 146; Maggard v. McKelvey, Ky.App. 1982, 627 S.W.2d 44; Kingsbury v. Smith, 1982, 122 N.H. 237, 442 A.2d 1003; see Mears v. Alhadeff, 1982, 88 A.D.2d 827, 451 N.Y.S.2d 133 (including interruption of education, but not humiliation from being unwed mother nor from needing welfare assistance); P. v. Portadin, 1981, 179 N.J.Super. 465, 432 A.2d 556; Ramey v. Fassoulas, Fla.App.1982, 414 So.2d 198 (but also holding special expenses of rearing substantially impaired child recoverable).

58. See supra, notes 53 and 57.

59. The lead opinion in Cockrum v. Baumgartner, 1981, 99 Ill.App.3d 271, 54 Ill.Dec. 751, 425 N.E.2d 968 (2–1), reversed 69 Ill.Dec. 168, 95 Ill.2d 193, 447 N.E.2d 385, stated that no reduction for parental benefits is required, but this opinion was expressly rejected in Pierce v. DeGracia, 1982, 103 Ill.App.3d 511, 59 Ill.Dec. 267, 431 N.E.2d 768.

60. See, e.g., Note, 1982, 68 Va.L.Rev. 1311.

61. "When the defendant's tortious conduct has caused harm to the plaintiff or his property and in so doing has conferred a special benefit to the interest of the plaintiff that was harmed, the value of the benefit conferred is considered in mitigation of damages, to the extent that it is equitable." Second Restatement of Torts, § 920.

child.[62] The cases and commentary concerning the law of prenatal torts is mounting rapidly, and the doctrine in this area will remain in ferment for at least some time.[63]

WESTLAW REFERENCES

Infliction of Harm Through Mother's Body
unborn prenatal /8 injur! /s recover*
unborn prenatal fetus embryo utero /s tort negligen**

Unwanted Children—"Wrongful Birth", "Wrongful Life" and "Wrongful Pregnancy"
"wrongful birth"
"wrongful life"
"wrongful pregnancy"
gleitman +s cosgrove

§ 56. Acts and Omissions

In the determination of the existence of a duty, there runs through much of the law a distinction between action and inaction.[1] In the early common law one who injured another by a positive, affirmative act, was held liable without any great regard even for his fault.[2] But the courts were far too much occupied with the more flagrant forms of misbehavior to be greatly concerned with one who merely did nothing, even though another might suffer harm because of his omission to act. Hence there arose very early a difference, still deeply rooted in the law of negligence, between "misfeasance" and "nonfeasance"—that is to say, between active misconduct working positive injury to others and passive inaction or a failure to take steps to protect them from harm.[3] The reason for the distinction may be said to lie in the fact that by "misfeasance" the defendant has created a new risk of harm to the plaintiff, while by "nonfeasance" he has at least made his situation no worse, and has merely failed to benefit him by interfering in his affairs.[4] The highly individualistic philosophy of the older common law had no great difficulty in working out restraints upon the commission of affirmative acts of harm, but shrank from converting the courts into an agency for forcing men to help one another.[5]

Liability for nonfeasance was therefore slow to receive recognition in the law. It first appears in the case of those engaged in "public" callings, who, by holding themselves out to the public, were regarded as having undertaken a duty to give service, for the breach of which they were liable.[6] With the development of the action of assumpsit, this principle was extended to anyone who, for a consideration, has undertaken to perform a promise—[7] or what we now call a contract. During the last century, liability for "nonfeasance" has been extended

---

62. Ochs v. Borrelli, 1982, 187 Conn. 253, 445 A.2d 883; Phillips v. United States, D.S.C.1981, 508 F.Supp. 544; Sherlock v. Stillwater Clinic, Minn.1977, 260 N.W. 2d 169. A particularly thoughtful opinion, arguing that child-rearing expenses should be allowed if the reason for sterilization was economic, but not if the reason was to protect the health of the mother, is Hartke v. McKelway, D.C.Cir. 1983, 707 F.2d 1544. See Mason v. Western Pennsylvania Hospital, 1981, 286 Pa.Super. 354, 428 A.2d 1366.

63. Well illustrated by Mason v. Western Pennsylvania Hospital, 1982, 499 Pa. 484, 453 A.2d 974, where the court was badly split on several issues, four of the court's seven judges issuing opinions.

§ 56

1. See Bohlen, The Basis of Affirmative Obligations in the Law of Tort, 1905, 44 Am.L.Reg.,N.S., 209, 273, 337; McNiece and Thornton, Affirmative Duties in Tort, 1949, 58 Yale L.J. 1272; Gregory, Gratuitous Undertakings and the Duty of Care, 1951, 1 De Paul L.Rev. 30; Seavey, Reliance on Gratuitous Promises or Other Conduct, 1951, 64 Harv.L.Rev. 913; Wright, Negligent "Acts or Omissions," 1941, 19 Can.Bar Rev. 465.

2. See supra, § 28.

3. Bohlen, The Moral Duty to Aid Others as a Basis of Tort Liability, 1908, 56 U.Pa.L.Rev. 217, 219.

4. Bohlen, The Moral Duty to Aid Others as a Basis of Tort Liability, 1908, 56 U.Pa.L.Rev. 217, 221. See Terry v. Linscott Hotel Corp., App.1980, 126 Ariz. 548, 617 P.2d 56, 61. On similar reasoning, punitive damages are less likely to be appropriate in cases of nonfeasance than misfeasance. See Owen, Civil Punishment and the Public Good, 1982, 56 So.Cal.L.Rev. 103, 108 (defendant's failure to energize power to protect plaintiff is ordinarily less culpable than purposeful activation and release of it harmfully upon the plaintiff).

5. Green, Judge and Jury, 1930, 62.

6. Arterburn, The Origin and First Test of Public Callings, 1927, 75 U.Pa.L.Rev. 411.

7. Ames, History of Assumpsit, 1888, 2 Harv.L. Rev. 1, 53; Jenks, On Negligence and Deceit in the Law of Torts, 1910, 26 L.Q.Rev. 159.

still further to a limited group of relations, in which custom, public sentiment and views of social policy have led the courts to find a duty of affirmative action. In such relationships the plaintiff is typically in some respect particularly vulnerable and dependent upon the defendant who, correspondingly, holds considerable power over the plaintiff's welfare.[8] In addition, such relations have often involved some existing or potential economic advantage to the defendant.[9] Fairness in such cases thus may require the defendant to use his power to help the plaintiff, based upon the plaintiff's expectation of protection, which itself may be based upon the defendant's expectation of financial gain. The largest single group upon whom the duty of affirmative conduct has been imposed are the owners and occupiers of land, who are to be considered later.[10]

Liability for "misfeasance," then, may extend to any person to whom harm may reasonably be anticipated as a result of the defendant's conduct, or perhaps even beyond;[11] while for "nonfeasance" it is necessary to find some definite relation between the parties, of such a character that social policy justifies the imposition of a duty to act.[12]

In theory the difference between the two is fairly clear; but in practice it is not always easy to draw the line and say whether conduct is active or passive.[13] It is clear that it is not always a matter of action or inaction as to the particular act or omission which has caused the plaintiff's damage. Failure to blow a whistle or to shut off steam,[14] although in itself inaction, is readily treated as negligent operation of a train, which is affirmative misconduct; an omission to repair a gas pipe is regarded as negligent distribution of gas;[15] and failure to supply heat for a building can easily become mismanagement of a boiler.[16] On the other hand, the discharge of an employee, which is certainly an affirmative act, may be considered to be no more than non-performance of an agreement to continue employment,[17] and

---

As to the interrelation of tort and contract, see infra, § 92.

8. See Shapo, The Duty to Act: Tort Law, Power and Public Policy, 1977; Owen, Civil Punishment and the Public Good, 1982, 56 So.Cal.L.Rev. 103, 104–08.

9. Bohlen, The Basis of Affirmative Obligations in the Law of Tort, 1905, 44 Am.L.Reg.,N.S., 209, 273, 337; McNiece and Thornton, Affirmative Duties in Tort, 1949, 58 Yale L.J. 1272.

10. See infra, ch. 10.

11. See supra, § 43.

12. Although other issues are involved as well, a governmental entity is less likely to be liable for nonfeasance than for misfeasance. Cf. Clemente v. United States, 1st Cir. 1977, 567 F.2d 1140, certiorari denied 1978, 435 U.S. 1006, 98 S.Ct. 1876, 56 L.Ed.2d 388 (FAA); Brennen v. City of Eugene, 1979, 285 Or. 401, 591 P.2d 719, 724 (dictum); Baker v. State, 1981, 97 Nev. 634, 637 P.2d 1217 (fire department went to wrong address); Bishop v. City of Chicago, 1970, 121 Ill.App.2d 33, 257 N.E.2d 152 (inadequate rescue equipment for crashes in lake by airport); Williams v. California, 1983, 34 Cal.3d 18, 192 Cal.Rptr. 233, 664 P.2d 137 (no duty on highway patrolman to investigate accident adequately or preserve evidence for civil litigation). For an interesting policy analysis of these issues in the constitutional tort area, see Wells & Eaton, Affirmative Duty and Constitutional Tort, 1982, 16 J.L.Ref. 1.

13. "So, while to use an article known to be defective is palpably misfeasance, and while a mere failure to provide protection for those who by one's bare permission use one's premises is plainly passive nonfeasance, the use of a chattel for a particular purpose without having first ascertained whether it is fit for such purpose is a compound of both. There is both action, i.e., the use of the chattel, and nonfeasance, the failure to perform the positive duty of inspecting it to ascertain if it be defective. * * * Still, the final cause of whatever injury is sustained being the use of the chattel, the tendency is to consider that the whole constitutes an act of misfeasance." Bohlen, The Moral Duty to Aid Others as a Basis of Tort Liability, 1908, 56 U.Pa.L.Rev. 217, 220.

14. Southern Railway Co. v. Grizzle, 1906, 124 Ga. 735, 53 S.E. 244.

15. Consolidated Gas Co. v. Connor, 1911, 114 Md. 140, 78 A. 725. Provided there is notice of the danger. Ruberg v. Skelly Oil Co., Minn.1980, 297 N.W.2d 746 (customer's notice of substantial, inexplicable increased usage sufficient indication of possible leak).

16. Pittsfield Cottonwear Manufacturing Co. v. Pittsfield Shoe Co., 1902, 71 N.H. 522, 53 A. 807. Cf. Hall v. Consolidated Edison Corp., 1980, 104 Misc.2d 565, 428 N.Y.S.2d 837 (power cut off without notice to tenants); Delmarva Power & Light Co. v. Burrows, Del.1981, 435 A.2d 716 (failure to insulate high voltage wires).

17. Addis v. Gramophone Co., Limited, [1909] A.C. 488; Elmore v. Atlantic Coast Line Railroad Co., 1926, 191 N.C. 182, 131 S.E. 633; Manley v. Exposition Cotton Mills, 1933, 47 Ga.App. 496, 170 S.E. 711.

a similar conclusion has been reached as to the revocation of a theater ticket and expulsion of a patron.[18] But a physician who starts to treat a patient and then neglects or abandons him is held liable in tort for breach of a duty undertaken.[19] The question appears to be essentially one of whether the defendant has gone so far in what he has actually done, and has got himself into such a relation with the plaintiff, that he has begun to affect the interests of the plaintiff adversely, as distinguished from merely failing to confer a benefit upon him.[20]

Duty to Aid One in Peril

Because of this reluctance to countenance "nonfeasance" as a basis of liability, the law has persistently refused to impose on a stranger the moral obligation of common humanity to go to the aid of another human being who is in danger, even if the other is in danger of losing his life.[21] Some of the decisions have been shocking in the extreme. The expert swimmer, with a boat and a rope at hand, who sees another drowning before his eyes, is not required to do anything at all about it, but may sit on the dock, smoke his cigarette, and watch the man drown.[22] A physician is under no duty to answer the call of one who is dying and might be saved,[23] nor is anyone required to play the part of Florence Nightingale and bind up the wounds of a stranger who is bleeding to death,[24] or to prevent a neighbor's child from hammering on a dangerous explosive,[25] or to remove a stone from the highway where it is a menace to traffic,[26] or a train from a place where it blocks a fire engine on its way to save a house,[27] or even to cry a warning to one who is walking into the jaws of a dangerous machine.[28] The remedy in such cases is left to the "higher law" and the "voice of conscience,"[29] which, in a wicked world, would seem to be singularly ineffective either to prevent the harm or to compensate the victim.

Consider, however the growing body of wrongful discharge law providing tort or contract relief for employees at will discharged for reasons contrary to public policy. Smith v. Atlas Off-Shore Boat Service, Inc., 5th Cir. 1981, 653 F.2d 1057; Tameny v. Atlantic Richfield Co., 1981, 27 Cal.3d 167, 164 Cal.Rptr. 839, 610 P.2d 1330; Pierce v. Ortho Pharmaceutical Corp., 1980, 84 N.J. 58, 417 A.2d 505; Notes, 1980, 93 Harv.L.Rev. 1816; 1975, 28 Vand.L.Rev. 805; Annot., 1981, 12 A.L.R.4th 544; Symposium, 1983, 16 U.Mich.J.L.Ref. 199.

18. Horney v. Nixon, 1905, 213 Pa. 20, 61 A. 1088; Marrone v. Washington Jockey Club, 1913, 227 U.S. 633, 33 S.Ct. 401, 57 L.Ed. 679; Boswell v. Barnum & Bailey, 1916, 135 Tenn. 35, 185 S.W. 692.

19. See Harney, Medical Malpractice, 1973, § 1.3 (B).

20. See Nallan v. Helmsley-Spear, Inc., 1980, 50 N.Y.2d 507, 429 N.Y.S.2d 606, 615, 407 N.E.2d 451, 460, quoting Cardozo, J., in H.R. Moch Co. v. Rensselaer Water Co., 1928, 247 N.Y. 160, 159 N.E. 896, 898.

21. Three states (Vt., Minn. & R.I.) and several countries have statutes, generally criminal, which impose a duty, under certain limited conditions, to rescue another in peril. See Feldbrugge, Good and Bad Samaritans: A Comparative Survey, 1967, 14 Am.J.Comp. Law, 630; Linden, Tort Liability for Criminal Nonfeasance, 1966, 44 Can.Bar Rev. 25 (Canada); Nat'l Law J., p. 5, Aug. 22, 1983; infra, notes 30–31.

22. Osterlind v. Hill, 1928, 263 Mass. 73, 160 N.E. 301. Here the defendant had even rented a canoe to the intoxicated plaintiff, who upset it. Still worse is Yania v. Bigan, 1959, 397 Pa. 316, 155 A.2d 343, where plaintiff was not a stranger but a business visitor, and defendant incited him to jump into the water and let him drown. There is also Handiboe v. McCarthy, 1966, 114 Ga.App. 541, 151 S.E.2d 905, where it was held that there ws no duty whatever to rescue a child licensee drowning in a swimming pool. It would be hard to find a more unappetizing trio of decisions. See Seavey, I Am Not My Guest's Keeper, 1960, 13 Vand.L.Rev. 699.

23. Hurley v. Eddingfield, 1901, 156 Ind. 416, 59 N.E. 1058; see Randolph's Administrator v. Snyder, 1910, 139 Ky. 159, 129 S.W. 562. As to hospitals, see Note, 1966, 18 U.Fla.L.Rev. 475.

24. Allen v. Hixson, 1900, 111 Ga. 460, 36 S.E. 810; Riley v. Gulf, Colorado & Santa Fe Railway Co., Tex. Civ.App.1913, 160 S.W. 595.

25. Sidwell v. McVay, Okl.1955, 282 P.2d 756.

26. O'Keefe v. William J. Barry Co., 1942, 311 Mass. 517, 42 N.E.2d 267.

27. Louisville & Nashville R. Co. v. Scruggs & Echols, 1909, 161 Ala. 97, 49 So. 399. But see infra, note 96.

28. See Gautret v. Egerton, 1887, L.R. 2 C.P. 381; Buch v. Amory Manufacturing Co., 1897, 69 N.H. 257, 44 A. 809; Toadvine v. Cincinnati, New Orleans & Texas Pacific Railway Co., D.Ky.1937, 20 F.Supp. 226. See also Chastain v. Fuqua Industries, Inc., 1980, 156 Ga.App. 719, 275 S.E.2d 679 (aunt had no duty to warn 11-year-old nephew of loose seat on riding power mower).

29. Union Pacific Railroad Co. v. Cappier, 1903, 66 Kan. 649, 72 P. 281.

Such decisions are revolting to any moral sense. They have been denounced with vigor by legal writers.[30] Yet thus far the difficulties of setting any standards of unselfish service to fellow men, and of making any workable rule to cover possible situations where fifty people might fail to rescue one,[31] has limited any tendency to depart from the rule to cases where some special relation between the parties has afforded a justification for the creation of a duty, without any question of setting up a rule of universal application. Thus, a carrier has been required to take reasonable affirmative steps to aid a passenger in peril,[32] and an innkeeper to aid his guest.[33] Maritime law has long recognized the duty of a ship to save its seaman who has fallen overboard;[34] and there is now quite a general tendency to extend the same duty to any employer when his employee is injured or endangered in the course of his employment.[35] There is now respectable authority imposing the same duty upon a shopkeeper to his business visitor,[36] upon a host to his social guest,[37] upon a jailer to his prisoner,[38] and upon a school to its pu-

30. See generally Shapo, The Duty to Act: Tort Law, Power and Public Policy, 1977; Ratcliffe (ed.), The Good Samaritan and the Law, 1966; Ames, Law and Morals, 1908, 22 Harv.L.Rev. 97, 112; Bohlen, The Moral Duty to Aid Others as a Basis of Tort Liability, 1908, 56 U.Pa.L.Rev. 217, 316; Seavey, I Am Not My Guest's Keeper, 1960, 13 Vand.L.Rev. 699; Rudolph, The Duty to Act: A Proposed Rule, 1965, 44 Neb.L.J. 499; Franklin, Vermont Requires Rescue: A Comment, 1972, 25 Stan.L.Rev. 51; De Kuiper, Stalking the Good Samaritan: Communists, Capitalists and the Duty to Rescue, 1976 Utah L.Rev. 529; Landes & Posner, Salvors, Finders, Good Samaritans and Other Rescuers: An Economic Study of Law and Altruism, 1978, 7 J.Leg.Stud. 83; Notes, 1952, 52 Colum.L.Rev. 631; 1972, 47 Ind.L.J. 321; Weinrib, The Case for a Duty to Rescue, 1980, 90 Yale L.J. 247, 251–258.

31. Consider the provision of the Dutch Penal Code, Art. 450: "One who, witnessing the danger of death with which another is suddenly threatened, neglects to give or furnish him such assistance as he can give or procure without reasonable fear of danger to himself, is to be punished, if the death of the person in distress follows, by a detention of three months at most and an amende of three hundred florins at most." See also Vt.Stat.Ann. tit. 12 § 519, providing a maximum fine of $100 for willful violation: "A person who knows that another is exposed to grave physical harm shall, to the extent that the same can be rendered without danger or peril to himself or without interference with important duties owed to others, give reasonable assistance to the exposed person unless that assistance or care is being provided by others." See Note, 1982, 7 Vt.L.Rev. 143. There is no duty to intervene in a fight under the statute. State v. Joyce, Vt.1981, 433 A.2d 271. Czechoslovakia, Denmark, France, Germany, Hungary, Italy, Norway, Poland, Portugal, Rumania, Russia and Turkey have similar statutes. Franklin, Vermont Requires Rescue: A Comment, 1972, 25 Stan. L.Rev. 51, 59.

32. Yu v. New York, New Haven & Hartford Railroad Co., 1958, 145 Conn. 451, 144 A.2d 56; Middleton v. Whitridge, 1915, 213 N.Y. 499, 108 N.E. 192; cf. Borus v. Yellow Cab Co., 1977, 52 Ill.App.3d 194, 9 Ill. Dec. 843, 367 N.E.2d 277.

33. At least in case of fire. Dove v. Lowden, W.D. Mo.1942, 47 F.Supp. 546; West v. Spratling, 1920, 204 Ala. 478, 86 So. 32; Stewart v. Weiner, 1922, 108 Neb. 49, 187 N.W. 121; Texas Hotel Co. of Longview v. Cosby, Tex.Civ.App.1939, 131 S.W.2d 261, error dismissed.

34. Abbott v. United States Lines, Inc., 4 Cir. 1975, 512 F.2d 118; Walsh v. Zuisei Kaiun K.K., 9th Cir. 1979, 606 F.2d 259; Cortes v. Baltimore Insular Line, 1932, 287 U.S. 367, 53 S.Ct. 173, 77 L.Ed. 368; Gardner v. National Bulk Carriers, Inc., 4th Cir. 1962, 310 F.2d 284, certiorari denied 372 U.S. 913, 83 S.Ct. 728, 9 L.Ed.2d 721, rehearing denied 372 U.S. 961, 83 S.Ct. 1012, 10 L.Ed.2d 13; Bentley, Shipowners' Responsibility for Rescue at Sea, 1972, 3 J.Mar.L. & Com. 573; Note, 1980, 5 Mar.Lawyer 81.

35. Anderson v. Atchison, Topeka & Santa Fe Railroad Co., 1948, 333 U.S. 821, 68 S.Ct. 854, 92 L.Ed. 1108; Rival v. Atchison, Topeka & Santa Fe Railroad Co., 1957, 62 N.M. 159, 306 P.2d 648; Szabo v. Pennsylvania Railroad Co., 1945, 132 N.J.L. 331, 40 A.2d 562; Carey v. Davis, 1921, 190 Iowa 720, 180 N.W. 889.

It has been held that there is no duty to an employee outside of the course of his employment. Allen v. Hixson, 1900, 111 Ga. 460, 36 S.E. 810; Matthews v. Carolina & North Western Railway Co., 1918, 175 N.C. 35, 94 S.E. 714. And of course none in the absence of reason to believe that he needs aid. Wilke v. Chicago Great Western Railway Co., 1933, 190 Minn. 89, 251 N.W. 11; Gypsy Oil Co. v. McNair, 1937, 179 Okl. 182, 64 P.2d 885.

36. L.S. Ayres & Co. v. Hicks, 1942, 220 Ind. 86, 41 N.E.2d 195, 196; Connelly v. Kaufmann & Baer Co., 1944, 349 Pa. 261, 37 A.2d 125; see Harold's Club v. Sanchez, 1954, 70 Nev. 518, 275 P.2d 384; Blizzard v. Fitzsimmons, 1942, 193 Miss. 484, 10 So.2d 343.

37. Hutchinson v. Dickie, 6th Cir. 1947, 162 F.2d 103, cert. denied, 332 U.S. 830, 68 S.Ct. 208, 92 L.Ed. 404 (on yacht); Tubbs v. Argus, 1967, 140 Ind.App. 695, 225 N.E.2d 841; Matthews v. MacLaren, [1969] 2 Ont.L.Rep. 137.

38. Iglesias v. Wells, 1982, ___ Ind.App. ___, 441 N.E.2d 1017; Farmer v. State, 1955, 224 Miss. 96, 79 So.2d 528; Dunham v. Village of Canisteo, 1952, 303 N.Y. 498, 104 N.E.2d 872; Thomas v. Williams, 1962, 105 Ga.App. 321, 124 S.E.2d 409; Smith v. Miller, 1950, 241 Iowa 625, 40 N.W.2d 597; cf. Azura v. City of Billings, Mont.1979, 596 P.2d 460.

pil.³⁹ There are undoubtedly other relations calling for the same conclusion.⁴⁰ Two that appear likely to receive early recognition are those of husband and wife, and parent and child, where the duty to aid has been established in the criminal law,⁴¹ and with the rapidly growing tendency to abrogate family immunities to suit ⁴² may be expected to be taken over into tort cases.

It also is recognized that if the defendant's own negligence has been responsible for the plaintiff's situation, a relation has arisen which imposes a duty to make a reasonable effort to give assistance, and avoid any further harm.⁴³ Where the original danger is created by innocent conduct, involving no fault on the part of the defendant, it was formerly the rule that no such duty arose; ⁴⁴ but this appears to have given way to a recognition of a duty to take action, both where the prior innocent conduct has created an unreasonable risk of harm to the plaintiff,⁴⁵ and where it has already injured him.⁴⁶ In a few states, "hit and run driver" statutes have been construed to result in civil liability for failure to stop and aid a person injured in an automobile accident, even without the fault of the driver.⁴⁷ This process of extension has been slow, and marked with extreme caution; but there is reason to think that it may continue until it approaches a general holding that the mere knowledge of serious peril, threatening death or great bodily harm to another, which an identified defendant might avoid with little inconvenience, creates a sufficient relation to impose a duty of action.⁴⁸

Where the duty to rescue is required, it is agreed that it calls for nothing more than reasonable care under the circumstances. The defendant is not liable when he neither knows nor should know of the unreasonable risk,⁴⁹ nor of the illness or injury. He is not required to give aid to one whom he has no reason to know to be ill. He will seldom be required to do more than give such first aid as he reasonably can, and take reasonable steps to turn the sick person over to a doctor or to those who will look after him until one can be brought.⁵⁰

39. See Pirkle v. Oakdale Union Grammar School District, 1953, 40 Cal.2d 207, 253 P.2d 1.

40. See Farwell v. Keaton, 1976, 396 Mich. 281, 240 N.W.2d 217 (drinking companions), infra, note 88; Pridgen v. Boston Housing Authority, 1974, 364 Mass. 696, 308 N.E.2d 467, noted 1975, 44 U.Cin.L.Rev. 124 (landowner has duty to rescue trapped trespasser).

41. Rex. v. Russell, [1933] Vict.L.Rep. 59; Rex v. Smith, 1826, 2 C. & P. 449, 172 Eng.Rep. 203; State v. Rivers, 1958, 133 Mont. 129, 320 P.2d 1004; State v. Zobel, 1965, 81 S.D. 260, 134 N.W.2d 101, certiorari denied 382 U.S. 833, 86 S.Ct. 74, 15 L.Ed.2d 76. See Linden, Tort Liability for Criminal Nonfeasance, 1966, 44 Am.Bar Rev. 25. But cf. Chastain v. Fuqua Industries, Inc., 1980, 156 Ga.App. 719, 275 S.E.2d 679 (aunt had no duty to warn young nephew).

42. See infra, § 122.

43. Parrish v. Atlantic Coast Line Railroad Co., 1942, 221 N.C. 292, 20 S.E.2d 299; Trombley v. Kolts, 1938, 29 Cal.App.2d 699, 85 P.2d 541.

44. Griswold v. Boston & Maine Railroad Co., 1903, 183 Mass. 434, 67 N.E. 354; Union Pacific Railroad Co. v. Cappier, 1903, 66 Kan. 649, 72 P. 281; Turbeville v. Mobile Light & Railroad Co., 1930, 221 Ala. 91, 127 So. 519.

45. Hollinbeck v. Downey, 1962, 261 Minn. 481, 113 N.W.2d 9 (hooked golf ball, duty to cry warning); Hardy v. Brooks, 1961, 103 Ga.App. 124, 118 S.E.2d 492 (blocked highway); Chandler v. Forsyth Royal Crown Bottling Co., 1962, 257 N.C. 245, 125 S.E.2d 584 (glass on road); Zylka v. Leikvoll, 1966, 274 Minn. 435, 144 N.W.2d 358. See Second Restatement of Torts, § 321; Note, 1966, 51 Minn.L.Rev. 362.

46. Tubbs v. Argus, 1967, 140 Ind.App. 695, 225 N.E.2d 841 (harm caused by instrumentality under defendant's control); L.S. Ayres & Co. v. Hicks, 1942, 220 Ind. 86, 40 N.E.2d 334, 41 N.E.2d 195, 196; Holland v. St. Paul Mercury Insurance Co., La.App.1961, 135 So. 2d 145; Annot., 1970, 33 A.L.R.3d 301 (duty to aid when not liable for initial injury).

Cf. Rains v. Heldenfels Brothers, Tex.Civ.App.1969, 443 S.W.2d 280, refused no reversible error (plaintiff barred by contributory negligence from recovery for original injury, but may still recover for failure to give aid after it).

47. Brumfield v. Wofford, 1958, 143 W.Va. 332, 102 S.E.2d 103; Hallman v. Cushman, 1941, 196 S.C. 402, 13 S.E.2d 498; Brooks v. E.J. Willig Truck Transportation Co., 1953, 40 Cal.2d 669, 255 P.2d 802.

48. Cf. Warshauer v. Lloyd Sabaudo S.A., 2d Cir. 1934, 71 F.2d 146, certiorari denied 293 U.S. 610, 55 S.Ct. 140, 79 L.Ed. 700 (duty to rescue ship at sea; relying on general maritime law).

49. Grimes v. Hettinger, Ky.App.1978, 566 S.W.2d 769 (guest at swimming party had already drowned when discovered missing).

50. Owl Drug Co. v. Crandall, 1938, 52 Ariz. 322, 80 P.2d 952; Shaw v. Chicago, Milwaukee & St. Paul Rail-

Affirmative Conduct

If there is no duty to go to the assistance of a person in difficulty or peril, there is at least a duty to avoid any affirmative acts which make his situation worse. When we cross the line into the field of "misfeasance," liability is far easier to find. A truck driver may be under no obligation whatever to signal to a car behind him that it may safely pass; but if he does signal, he will be liable if he fails to exercise proper care and injury results.[51] There may be no duty to take care of a man who is ill or intoxicated, and unable to look out for himself; but it is another thing entirely to eject him into the danger of a street or railroad yard; and if he is injured there will be liability.[52] But further, if the defendant does attempt to aid him, and takes charge and control of the situation, he is regarded as entering voluntarily into a relation which is attended with responsibility. The same is true, of course, of a physician who accepts a charity patient.[53] Such a defendant will then be liable for a failure to use reasonable care for the protection of the plaintiff's interests.[54] And on the same basis one who, without any legal obligation to do so, attempts to remove ice from the sidewalk, may find himself liable when he makes the situation worse.[55] The result of all this is that the good Samaritan who tries to help may find himself mulcted in damages, while the priest and the Levite who pass by on the other side go on their cheerful way rejoicing. It has been pointed out often enough that this in fact operates as a real, and serious, deterrent to the giving of needed aid. Physicians, who are so frequently called upon for needed help, have been much concerned about potential liability.[56] This led to active lobbying by medical associations, which has resulted in the adoption, in the great majority of states, of statutes absolving a doctor who gratuitously renders aid in an emergency from all liability for negligence.[57]

---

way Co., 1907, 103 Minn. 8, 114 N.W. 85; Fitzgerald v. Chesapeake & Ohio Railway Co., 1935, 116 W.Va. 239, 180 S.E. 766.

51. Shirley Cloak & Dress Co. v. Arnold, 1955, 92 Ga.App. 885, 90 S.E.2d 622; Thelen v. Spilman, 1957, 251 Minn. 89, 86 N.W.2d 700; Haralson v. Jones Truck Lines, 1954, 223 Ark. 813, 270 S.W.2d 892; see Allstate Amusement Co. of Illinois v. Pasinato, 1981, 96 Ill.App.3d 306, 51 Ill.Dec. 866, 421 N.E.2d 374 (but no causal link on facts).

52. Fagg's Administrator v. Louisville & Nashville Railroad Co., 1901, 111 Ky. 30, 31, 63 S.W. 580, 581; Cincinnati, New Orleans & Texas Pacific Railway Co. v. Marrs' Administratrix, 1905, 119 Ky. 954, 85 S.W. 188; Parvi v. City of Kingston, 1977, 41 N.Y.2d 553, 394 N.Y.S.2d 161, 362 N.E.2d 960 (police placed drunk near highway).

53. Christie v. Callahan, 1941, 75 U.S.App.D.C. 133, 124 F.2d 825; Le Juene Road Hospital, Inc. v. Watson, Fla.App.1965, 171 So.2d 102; Du Bois v. Decker, 1891, 130 N.Y. 325, 29 N.E. 313; See Notes, 1964, 31 Tenn.L. Rev. 525; 1965, 19 U.Miami L.Rev. 652; 1966, 18 U.Fla. L.Rev. 475. An extreme case of this is O'Neill v. Montefiore Hospital, 1960, 11 A.D.2d 132, 202 N.Y.S.2d 436, where a physician and a nurse attempted to give free advice over the telephone.

54. Slater v. Illinois Central Railroad Co., M.D. Tenn.1911, 209 F. 480; Devlin v. Safeway Stores, S.D. N.Y.1964, 235 F.Supp. 882; Yazoo & Mississippi Valley Railroad Co. v. Leflar, 1933, 168 Miss. 255, 150 So. 220; Bascho v. Pennsylvania Railroad Co., 1949, 3 N.J. Super. 86, 65 A.2d 613.

55. Nelson v. Schultz, 1939, 170 Misc. 681, 11 N.Y.S.2d 184; Foley v. Ulrich, 1967, 94 N.J.Super. 410, 228 A.2d 702, reversed on other grounds 50 N.J. 426, 236 A.2d 137. See also Cox v. Wagner, Fla.App.1964, 162 So.2d 527 (attempt to steady stepladder); Briere v. Lathrop Co., 1970, 22 Ohio St.2d 166, 258 N.E.2d 597 (volunteer help in moving scaffold; Roberts v. Indiana Gas & Water Co., 1966, 140 Ind.App. 409, 221 N.E.2d 693 (gas company odorized gas, discontinued the practice without warning).

56. One poll of 1209 doctors, reported in Medical Tribune, Aug. 28, 1961, p. 23, resulted in only about half of them saying that they would stop to give medical aid at the scene of an emergency. Another poll of 214 led to 16% saying they would refuse to come forward for an emergency in a theater. See Notes, 1962, 75 Harv.L.Rev. 641; 1963, 51 Cal.L.Rev. 816.

57. See the discussion of these "Good Samaritan Acts" in Hessel, Good Samaritan Laws: Bad Legislation, 1974, 2 J.Leg.Med. [No. 3] 40; Notes, 1964, 64 Col.L.Rev. 1301; 10 Vill.L.Rev. 130; [1964] Wis.L.Rev. 494; 13 De Paul L.Rev. 297; 42 Or.L.Rev. 328; 1965, 17 U.Fla.L.Rev. 586; 1966, 44 N.C.L.Rev. 508; 1979, 7 W.St.U.L.Rev. 115; Annot., 1971, 39 A.L.R.3d 222. In some states, such statutes more broadly cover defendants other than doctors alone.

Such statutes do not protect the doctor working on an emergency case in the hospital as part of his normal duties. Colby v. Schwartz, 1978, 78 Cal.App.3d 885, 144 Cal.Rptr. 624. But cf. Matts v. Homsi, 1981, 106 Mich.App. 563, 308 N.W.2d 284 (statute protected surgeon not on call). Nor do they generally protect the good Samaritan from liability for his negligent driving

This idea of voluntary assumption of a duty by affirmative conduct runs through a variety of cases. Just when the duty is undertaken, when it ends, and what conduct is required, are nowhere clearly defined, and perhaps cannot be. Following an early, leading decision in New York,[58] never overruled, a large body of case law has been built up, which holds that a mere gratuitous promise [59] to render service or assistance, with nothing more, imposes no tort obligation upon the promisor, even though the plaintiff may rely on the promise and suffer damage because of that reliance. Most of the decisions have involved only pecuniary loss, as where the promise is to obtain insurance upon a building, and the uninsured building is destroyed by fire.[60] There are, however, a good many in which reliance upon the promise has led to injury to the person,[61] or to damage to tangible property.[62]

Due to its apparent harshness, however, the old rule has served chiefly as a point of departure; and very little extra is required for the assumption of the duty. If the defendant receives the plaintiff's property or papers, and undertakes, without consideration, to obtain insurance on them,[63] to record a deed,[64] to collect a note,[65] or otherwise to act as agent,[66] he assumes the duty to use proper care in the performance of the task. The duty is of course all the more clear when he has actually entered upon performance of the promise. But such initiation of the "undertaking" is commonly found in minor acts, of no significance in themselves and without any effect of their own upon the plaintiff's interests, such as writing a let-

on the way to the hospital. See McMahon v. City of Virginia Beach, 1980, 221 Va. 102, 267 S.E.2d 130, certiorari denied 449 U.S. 954, 101 S.Ct. 361, 66 L.Ed.2d 219; Dahl v. Turner, App.1969, 80 N.M. 564, 458 P.2d 816, certiorari denied 80 N.M. 608, 458 P.2d 860. Immunity under the statutes usually is limited to actions taken in "good faith," and the immunity is lost under many of the statutes when the negligence is gross or willful and wanton. See generally 2 Louisell & Williams, Medical Malpractice, 1981, ch. 21.

58. Thorne v. Deas, N.Y.1809, 4 Johns. 84.

59. Where there is consideration for the promise, or where the doctrine of promissory estoppel is applicable, there may of course be liability for breach of contract; but the same rule, in general, is applied to bar recovery in tort. This is more conveniently dealt with in connection with the interrelation of tort and contract. See infra, § 92.

60. Brawn v. Lyford, 1907, 103 Me. 362, 69 A. 544; Northern Commercial Co. v. United Airmotive, Inc., 1951, 13 Alaska 503, 101 F.Supp. 169; Comfort v. McCorkle, 1933, 149 Misc. 826, 268 N.Y.S. 192 (proof of fire loss). Cf. Newton v. Brook, 1902, 134 Ala. 269, 32 So. 722 (preparation of corpse for shipment by certain train); Louisville & Nashville Railroad Co. v. Spinks, 1898, 104 Ga. 692, 30 S.E. 968 (transportation home if plaintiff not employed).

61. Long v. Patterson, 1945, 198 Miss. 554, 22 So.2d 490 (warn of approaching traffic); Galveston, H. & S. A.R. Co. v. Hennigan, 1903, 33 Tex.Civ.App. 314, 76 S.W. 452 (provide medical treatment); Stone v. Johnson, 1938, 89 N.H. 329, 197 A. 713 (promise to light stair; treated as case of pure nonfeasance).

62. Tomko v. Sharp, 1915, 87 N.J.L. 385, 94 A. 793 (take car to garage for repairs and bring it back; treated as case of pure nonfeasance); Houston Milling Co. v. Carlock, Tex.Civ.App.1944, 183 S.W.2d 1013 (notify when hay stored in building).

63. Siegel v. Spear & Co., 1925, 234 N.Y. 479, 138 N.E. 414; Schroeder v. Mauzy, 1911, 16 Cal.App. 443, 118 P. 459. See Arterburn, Liability for Breach of Gratuitous Promises, 1927, 22 Ill.L.Rev. 161; Shattuck, Gratuitous Promises—A New Writ, 1937, 35 Mich.L. Rev. 908.

Some courts have held that an insurance company whose agent is entrusted with an application for insurance is liable in tort for undue delay in acting on the application. There are a variety of theories, one of which is that the agent has assumed a duty of care in dealing with the application. See United States Fire Insurance Co. v. Cannon, 8th Cir. 1965, 349 F.2d 941; Travelers Insurance Co. v. Anderson, W.D.S.C.1962, 210 F.Supp. 735.

Contra: Patten v. Continental Casualty Co., 1954, 162 Ohio St. 18, 120 N.E.2d 441; Zaye v. John Hancock Mut. Life Insurance Co., 1940, 338 Pa. 426, 13 A.2d 34. See Funk, The Duty of an Insurer to Act Promptly on Applications, 1927, 75 U.Pa.L.Rev. 207; Prosser, Delay in Acting on an Application for Insurance, 1935, 3 U.Chi.L.Rev. 39; Notes, 1955, 16 Ohio St.L.J. 111; 1963, 36 Temple L.Q. 84; 1967, 18 S.C.L.Rev. 863.

64. Hyde v. Moffat, 1844, 16 Vt. 271; cf. Carr v. Maine Central Railroad Co., 1917, 78 N.H. 502, 102 A. 532 (filing claim for rebate); Melbourne & Troy v. Louisville & Nashville Railroad Co., 1889, 88 Ala. 443, 6 So. 762 (failure to notify second carrier of goods).

65. Herzig v. Herzig, 1910, 67 Misc. 250, 122 N.Y.S. 440.

66. Stockmen's National Bank v. Richardson, 1933, 45 Wyo. 306, 18 P.2d 635.

ter [67] or attending a meeting,[68] or merely accepting a general agency.[69] These decisions have so much of an air of courts seeking some kind of excuse to impose tort liability for the breach of the promise itself, that it has been urged by a couple of writers [70] that the excuse should be thrown overboard, and liability imposed outright for breach of the promise alone, when it is relied on to the plaintiff's detriment.

Actually there are a few decisions in which this has been done. The leader is the fascinating Louisiana cat case,[71] in which the defendant broke a promise to confine a cat which had bitten the plaintiff during a rabies scare, and in consequence she was compelled to undergo the Pasteur treatment. Others have involved a gratuitous promise to call for medical [72] or police [73] help, to put salt on icy steps, and an employer's promise to relay a message to an employee that his wife had gone into labor.[74] In each, the plaintiff's harm resulted from reliance on the promise.[75] These decisions may possibly represent the beginning of the overthrow of the traditional rule.

Where performance clearly has been begun, there is no doubt that there is a duty of care.[76] Thus, a landlord who makes repairs on leased premises, although he is under no obligation to do so, assumes a duty to his tenant and to those entering in the right of the tenant to exercise proper care to see that the repairs are safe, or at least that the tenant is not left in ignorance of his danger.[77] The same principle has been applied where a railway company historically has maintained a flagman or provided warning signals at a crossing; when it subsequently fails to do so without notice, it is held liable to a traveler who is injured from his reliance upon the usual practice.[78] It has also been applied to air traffic controllers supplying information to pilots,[79] to the maintenance of a light-

---

67. Evan L. Reed Manufacturing Co. v. Wurts, 1914, 187 Ill.App. 378. Cf. Warrener v. Federal Land Bank, 1936, 266 Ky. 668, 99 S.W.2d 817 (calling for and receiving insurance premium).

68. Kirby v. Brown, Wheelock, Harris, Vought & Co., 1930, 229 App.Div. 155, 241 N.Y.S. 255, reversed on other grounds, 1931, 255 N.Y. 274, 174 N.E. 652, reargument denied 255 N.Y. 632, 175 N.E. 346.

69. Phoenix Insurance Co. v. Thomas, 1927, 103 W.Va. 574, 138 S.E. 381.

70. Seavey, Reliance Upon Gratuitous Promises or Other Conduct, 1951, 64 Harv.L.Rev. 913; Gregory, Gratuitous Undertakings and the Duty of Care, 1951, 1 De Paul L.Rev. 30.

71. Marsalis v. La Salle, La.App.1957, 94 So.2d 120. See Note, 1958, 18 La.L.Rev. 585. It should be noted, however, that the case began with defendant's cat biting the plaintiff, who was an invitee, so that a duty to take care might have been imposed on either ground.

72. Dudley v. Victor Lynn Lines, 1958, 48 N.J.Super. 457, 138 A.2d 53, reversed on other grounds, 1960, 32 N.J. 479, 161 A.2d 479.

73. DeLong v. County of Erie, 1982, 89 A.D.2d 376, 455 N.Y.S.2d 887 (emergency call to 911 number; police were dispatched to wrong address and caller was killed).

74. Johnson v. Souza, 1961, 71 N.J.Super. 240, 176 A.2d 797 (icy steps); Mixon v. Dobbs Houses, Inc., 1979, 149 Ga.App. 481, 254 S.E.2d 864 (wife in labor).

75. These decisions were encouraged by the ambiguity in § 325 of the First Restatement of Torts, which stated that one who gratuitously "undertakes" to give aid to another is subject to liability, without defining "undertaking." This is replaced, but of course not clarified, by the Caveat under § 323 of the Second Restatement, expressing no opinion as to whether a bare promise can be a sufficient undertaking.

76. See for example Abresch v. Northwestern Bell Telephone Co., 1956, 246 Minn. 408, 75 N.W.2d 206 (telephone company attempting to call fire department for plaintiff); Thompson v. Southwestern Bell Telephone Co., Mo.1970, 451 S.W.2d 147 (same); Stahlin v. Hilton Hotels Corp., 7th Cir. 1973, 484 F.2d 580 (hotel undertaking to provide medical assistance must exercise care to provide qualified person); Dailey v. City of Birmingham, Ala.1979, 378 So.2d 728 (barrier beside storm sewer ditch never completed; child fell in and drowned).

77. See infra, § 63; Cross v. Wells Fargo Alarm Services, 1980, 82 Ill.2d 313, 45 Ill.Dec. 121, 412 N.E.2d 472 (same, where landlord has undertaken to provide security services).

78. Burns v. North Chicago Rolling Mill Co., 1886, 65 Wis. 312, 27 N.W. 43; Langston v. Chicago & North Western Railroad Co., 1947, 398 Ill. 248, 75 N.E.2d 363; Westaway v. Chicago, St. Paul, Minneapolis & Omaha Railway Co., 1893, 56 Minn. 28, 57 N.W. 222; Will v. Southern Pacific Co., 1941, 18 Cal.2d 468, 116 P.2d 44; cf. Teall v. City of Cudahy, 1963, 60 Cal.2d 431, 34 Cal.Rptr. 869, 386 P.2d 493 (city traffic signal).

79. Yates v. United States, 10th Cir. 1974, 497 F.2d 878 (failure to warn pilot of small plane of wake turbulence from airliner).

house by the United States government,[80] and to an emergency ward maintained by a private hospital.[81] There are a number of cases in which a liability insurer, making a voluntary inspection of premises to determine their safety for the purpose of workmen's compensation insurance, has been held liable to an injured workman, for its negligence in doing so.[82]

In most of the cases finding liability, the defendant has made the situation worse, either by increasing the danger,[83] by misleading the plaintiff into the belief that it has been removed,[84] or by depriving him of the possibility of help from other sources.[85] Many of the decisions state that some such element is necessary, and that there can be no liability where the conduct in no way aggravates the situation or misleads the plaintiff, and he is left no worse off than he was before.[86] There are, however, a number of cases, mostly involving gratuitous repairs by

---

80. Indian Towing Co. v. United States, 1955, 350 U.S. 61, 76 S.Ct. 122, 100 L.Ed. 48. Cf. Ingham v. Eastern Air Lines, Inc., 2d Cir. 1967, 373 F.2d 227, certiorari denied 389 U.S. 931, 88 S.Ct. 295, 19 L.Ed.2d 292 (weather service to aircraft); Armiger v. United States, 1964, 168 Ct.Cl. 379, 339 F.2d 625 (obtaining flight insurance for Navy band); Neal v. Bergland, 6th Cir. 1981, 646 F.2d 1178, certiorari granted 456 U.S. 988, 102 S.Ct. 2267 (negligent supervision and inspection of home by FmHA); S.A. Empresa De Viacao Aerea Rio Grandense (Varig Airlines) v. United States, 9th Cir. 1982, 692 F.2d 1205 (negligent FAA inspection of airliner); Irving v. United States, D.N.H.1982, 532 F.Supp. 840 (negligent OSHA inspection; plaintiff's hair caught in unguarded machine).

81. Wilmington General Hospital v. Manlove, 1961, 54 Del. 10, 174 A.2d 135; Stanturf v. Sipes, Mo.1969, 447 S.W.2d 558; Guerrero v. Copper Queen Hospital, 1975, 112 Ariz. 104, 537 P.2d 1329; Annot., 1971, 35 A.L.R.3d 841; Notes, 1962, 40 Tex.L.Rev. 732, 1966, 18 U.Fla.L.Rev. 475.

82. Huggins v. Aetna Casualty & Surety Co., 1980, 245 Ga. 248, 264 S.E.2d 191, on remand 154 Ga.App. 559, 269 S.E.2d 471 (providing there is reliance; adopting Second Restatement of Torts, § 324A); Thompson v. Bohlken, Iowa 1981, 312 N.W.2d 501 (adopting Second Restatement of Torts, § 324A). Cf. Adams v. State, Alaska 1976, 555 P.2d 235 (fire inspectors had duty to act reasonably to abate discovered fire hazards); Perry v. Northern Indiana Public Service Co., 1982, ___ Ind.App. ___, 433 N.E.2d 44 (workplace safety services); Heinrich v. Goodyear Tire & Rubber Co., D.Md.1982, 532 F.Supp. 1348 (same).

Many cases, however, are to the contrary. E.g., De Jesus v. Liberty Mutual Insurance Co., 1966, 423 Pa. 198, 223 A.2d 849; Williams v. United States Fidelity & Guaranty Co., 4th Cir. 1966, 358 F.2d 799; Kerner v. Employers Mutual Liability Insurance Co. of Wisconsin, 1967, 35 Wis.2d 391, 151 N.W.2d 72; Matthews v. Liberty Mutual Insurance Co., 1968, 354 Mass. 470, 238 N.E.2d 348; Scott v. City of Detroit, 1982, 113 Mich. App. 241, 318 N.W.2d 32; cf. Zabala Clemente v. United States, 1st Cir. 1977, 567 F.2d 1140 (FAA had no duty to warn of dangers in chartered aircraft); Ranger Insurance Co. v. Hartford Steam Boiler Inspection & Insurance Co., Ala.1982, 410 So.2d 40.

See Boynton and Evans, What Price Liability for Insurance Carriers Who Undertake Voluntary Safety Inspections, 1967, 43 Notre Dame L. 193; McCoid, The Third Person in the Compensation Picture, 1959, 37 Tex.L.Rev. 389; Hammond and Poust, Safety Inspection by Workmen's Compensation Insurer, 1969, 10 For the Defense No. 9, Nov. 1969; Note, 1968, 21 Vand.L. Rev. 395; Annot., 1964, 93 A.L.R.2d 598.

83. See United States v. Lawter, 5th Cir. 1955, 219 F.2d 559 (Coast Guard rescue; clumsy work with a helicopter); cf. Parvi v. City of Kingston, 1977, 41 N.Y.2d 553, 394 N.Y.S.2d 161, 362 N.E.2d 960 (police relocated drunk near highway); Cross v. Wells Fargo Alarm Services, 1980, 82 Ill.2d 313, 45 Ill.Dec. 121, 412 N.E.2d 472 (providing part-time guard service at housing project until 1 a.m. increased crime thereafter).

84. As by signaling another driver that it is safe to turn. See Allstate Amusement Co. of Illinois v. Pasinato, 1981, 96 Ill.App.3d 306, 51 Ill.Dec. 866, 421 N.E.2d 374 (but no causal link on facts); Remeikis v. Boss & Phelps, Inc., D.C.App.1980, 419 A.2d 986 (assurance by real estate broker that sales contract would protect purchaser from termite damage). Compare Coffee v. McDonnell-Douglas Corp., 1972, 8 Cal.3d 551, 105 Cal.Rptr. 358, 503 P.2d 1366 (duty of due care in preemployment physical), and James v. United States, N.C.Cal.1980, 483 F.Supp. 581 (same: lung cancer), with Dornak v. Lafayette General Hospital, La.App. 1979, 368 So.2d 1185 (no duty to inform employee of tubercular condition revealed in preemployment physical x-ray). But cf. Rose v. Sapulpa Rural Water Co., Okl.1981, 631 P.2d 752 (installation of fire hydrant imposes no duty on water company to maintain in operable condition).

85. See the stress laid on this element in United States v. Gavagan, 5th Cir. 1960, 280 F.2d 319, certiorari denied 364 U.S. 933, 81 S.Ct. 379, 5 L.Ed.2d 365 (Coast Guard rescue); Zelenko v. Gimbel Brothers, 1935, 158 Misc. 904, 287 N.Y.S. 134, affirmed 1936, 247 App.Div. 867, 287 N.Y.S. 136; Owl Drug Co. v. Crandall, 1938, 52 Ariz. 322, 80 P.2d 952; Brown v. MacPherson's, Inc., 1975, 86 Wn.2d 293, 545 P.2d 13 (defendant led avalanche expert to believe cabin owners would be warned of risk); cf. Maldonado v. Southern Pacific Transportation Co., App.1981, 129 Ariz. 165, 629 P.2d 1001 (adopting Second Restatement of Torts, § 326, but holding mere attempt to prevent aid insufficient).

86. Nallan v. Helmsley-Spear, Inc., 1980, 50 N.Y.2d 507, 429 N.Y.S.2d 606, 407 N.E.2d 451 (uncorrupted union official, shot in back in hotel lobby, must show reliance on attendant); Miller v. Arnal Corp., App.1981,

landlords,[87] in which any such requirement has been rejected, and the defendant has been held to the obligation of reasonable care in his undertaking, although the plaintiff has not been more endangered, misled, or deprived of other help.[88]

It is quite possible that this obligation of reasonable care under all the circumstances provides all the limitation that is really necessary. The defendant is never required to do more than is reasonable;[89] and he may terminate his responsibility by turning an injured man over to a doctor[90] or to his friends;[91] or he may discontinue his performance and step out of the picture altogether, upon notice of his intention[92] and disclosure of what remains undone,[93] provided that it is reasonable to do so under the circumstances.[94]

Preventing Aid by Others

Even though the defendant may be under no obligation to render assistance himself, he is at least required to take reasonable care that he does not prevent others from giving it. A railway company is liable if it negligently runs over a fire hose which is being used to put out a fire,[95] or obstructs a crossing so that the fire engines cannot arrive in time.[96] The principle has been carried even to the length of holding that there is liability for interfering with the possibility of such aid, before it is actually being given.[97] Such acts are of course "misfeasance," but the real basis of liability would appear to be the interference with the plaintiff's opportunity of obtaining assistance, and the principle might perhaps be applied to other situations.[98]

---

129 Ariz. 484, 632 P.2d 987; Raymer v. United States, 6th Cir. 1981, 660 F.2d 1136, certiorari denied 456 U.S. 944, 102 S.Ct. 2009, 72 L.Ed.2d 466 (mine inspectors); Rappenenecker v. United States, N.C.Cal.1981, 509 F.Supp. 1018 (reliance necessary; government failure to warn SS Mayaguez of possibility of seizure by Cambodian forces). See Second Restatement of Torts, § 324A.

87. Bartlett v. Taylor, 1943, 351 Mo. 1060, 174 S.W.2d 844; Janofsky v. Garland, 1941, 42 Cal.App.2d 655, 109 P.2d 750; Olsen v. Mading, 1935, 45 Ariz. 423, 45 P.2d 23; Bauer v. 141–149 Cedar Lane Holding Co., 1957, 24 N.J. 139, 130 A.2d 833; Conner v. Farmers & Merchants Bank, 1963, 243 S.C. 132, 132 S.E.2d 385.

88. Cf. Farwell v. Keaton, 1976, 396 Mich. 281, 240 N.W.2d 217, 222 (3–2) (drinking companion had duty to obtain medical assistance for friend who was beaten up: "Implicit in such a common undertaking is the understanding that one will render assistance to the other when he is in peril if he can do so without endangering himself.")

89. See Nidiffer v. Clinchfield Railroad Co., Tenn. App.1980, 600 S.W.2d 242; Owl Drug Co. v. Crandall, 1938, 52 Ariz. 322, 80 P.2d 952.

90. Baltimore & Ohio Railroad Co. v. State to Use of Woodward, 1874, 41 Md. 268; Ohio & Mississippi Railway Co. v. Early, 1894, 141 Ind. 73, 40 N.E. 257.

91. Fitzgerald v. Chesapeake & Ohio Railway Co., 1935, 116 W.Va. 239, 180 S.E. 766.

92. Backus v. Ames, 1900, 79 Minn. 145, 81 N.W. 766; Pennsylvania Railroad Co. v. Yingling, 1925, 148 Md. 169, 129 A. 36.

93. Kirshenbaum v. General Outdoor Advertising Co., 1932, 258 N.Y. 489, 180 N.E. 245, motion denied 259 N.Y. 525, 182 N.E. 165.

94. Cf. Miller v. Arnal Corp., App.1981, 129 Ariz. 484, 632 P.2d 987 (ski patrol could abandon rescue effort where stranded hiker's condition not worsened).

95. Metallic Compression Casting Co. v. Fitchburg Railroad Co., 1872, 109 Mass. 277; Phenix Insurance Co. of Brooklyn v. New York Central & Hudson River Railroad Co., 1909, 196 N.Y. 554, 90 N.E. 1164; Eclipse Lumber Co. v. Davis, 1923, 196 Iowa 1349, 195 N.W. 337.

96. Luedeke v. Chicago & North Western Railroad Co., 1930, 120 Neb. 124, 231 N.W. 695; Globe Malleable Iron & Steel Co. v. New York Central & Hudson River Railroad Co., 1919, 227 N.Y. 58, 124 N.E. 109, 5 A.L.R. 1648; Hanlon Drydock & Shipbuilding Co. v. Southern Pacific Co., 1928, 92 Cal.App. 230, 268 P. 385; Felter v. Delaware & Hudson Railway Corp., D.Pa.1937, 19 F.Supp 852, affirmed 3rd Cir. 1938, 98 F.2d 868. But see supra, note 27.

97. See Soldano v. O'Daniels, 1983, 141 Cal.App.3d 443, 190 Cal.Rptr. 310 (refusal by restaurant employee to let good samaritan use telephone to call police to protect man in nearby bar who had been threatened and was subsequently shot); Concordia Fire Insurance Co. v. Simmons Co., 1918, 167 Wis. 541, 168 N.W. 199.

98. See infra, § 130. Cf. International Products Co. v. Erie Railroad Co., 1927, 244 N.Y. 331, 155 N.E. 662 (misinformation depriving plaintiff of opportunity to obtain insurance). But see Vicenty v. Eastern Air Lines, D.Puerto Rico 1981, 528 F.Supp. 171 (no duty by guard, toward woman who suffered hernia, to let daughter into baggage area to lift heavy suitcase).

Controlling Conduct of Others

The general duty which arises in many relations to take reasonable precautions for the safety of others may include the obligation to exercise control over the conduct of third persons.[99] Certain relationships are protective by nature, requiring the defendant to guard his charge against harm from others.[1] Thus, the duty of a carrier toward its passengers may require it to maintain order in its trains and stations, and to use reasonable care to prevent not only conduct which is merely negligent,[2] but also physical attacks[3] or thefts of property[4] on the part of other passengers or strangers.[5] A similar obligation rests upon innkeepers towards their guests,[6] landlords toward their tenants,[7] employers toward their employees,[8] jailers toward their prisoners,[9] hospitals toward their patients,[10] schools toward their pupils,[11] business establishments toward their customers,[12] and landlords toward their tenants.[13] The list appears to include all those who are under an affirmative duty to render aid,[14] and may possibly include other relations.[15]

Other relationships are custodial by nature, requiring the defendant to control his charge and to guard other persons against his dangerous propensities.[16] Thus, the

---

99. Harper and Kime, The Duty to Control the Conduct of Another, 1934, 43 Yale L.J. 886, 898; Note, 1958, 19 La.L.Rev. 228; Second Restatement of Torts, § 315.

1. Second Restatement of Torts, § 320.

2. La Sota v. Philadelphia Transportation Co., 1966, 421 Pa. 386, 219 A.2d 296 (controlling unruly mob of passengers); Kuhlen v. Boston & Northern Street Railway Co., 1907, 193 Mass. 341, 79 N.E. 815.

3. McPherson v. Tamiami Trail Tours, Inc., 5th Cir. 1967, 383 F.2d 527; Bullock v. Tamiami Trail Tours, Inc., 5th Cir. 1959, 266 F.2d 326.

4. Robinson v. Southern Railway Co., 1913, 40 U.S.App.D.C. 549; Pullman Palace-Car Co. v. Adams, 1898, 120 Ala. 581, 24 So. 921.

5. Harpell v. Public Service Coordinated Transport, 1955, 20 N.J. 309, 120 A.2d 43; Melicharek v. Hill Bus Co., 1961, 70 N.J.Super. 150, 175 A.2d 238, reversed 37 N.J. 549, 182 A.2d 557.

6. Fortney v. Hotel Rancroft, 1955, 5 Ill.App.2d 327, 125 N.E.2d 544; McFadden v. Bancroft Hotel Corp., 1943, 313 Mass. 56, 46 N.E.2d 573; Miller v. Derusa, La.App.1955, 77 So.2d 748; Garzilli v. Howard Johnson's Motor Lodges, Inc., E.D.N.Y.1976, 419 F.Supp. 1210 (Connie Francis recovered $2.5 million); Jenness v. Sheraton-Cadillac Properties, Inc., 1973, 48 Mich.App. 723, 211 N.W.2d 106 (after lighting her cigarette in his room, letting her use the bathroom, and supposedly declining her proposition, hotel guest "while walking to the elevator" was struck on head with tire iron by "attractively dressed young lady" whom manager earlier had suspected of loitering in the lobby "to turn a trick"). But see Terry v. Lincscott Hotel Corp., App. 1980, 126 Ariz. 548, 617 P.2d 56 (no liability for nonfeasance for theft of jewelry; statute).

7. See infra, § 63.

8. Walker v. Rowe, N.D.Ill.1982, 535 F.Supp. 55; David v. Missouri Pacific Railway Co., 1931, 328 Mo. 437, 41 S.W.2d 179.

9. See, e.g., Taylor v. Slaughter, 1935, 171 Okl. 152, 42 P.2d 235; Breaux v. State, La.1976, 326 So.2d 481.

10. Sylvester v. Northwestern Hospital of Minneapolis, 1952, 236 Minn. 384, 53 N.W.2d 17.

11. Schultz v. Gould Academy, Me.1975, 332 A.2d 368; Brahatcek v. Millard School District, 1979, 202 Neb. 86, 273 N.W.2d 680; Landers v. School District, Ill.App.1978, 383 N.E.2d 645; cf. Wallace v. Der-Ohanian, 1962, 199 Cal.App.2d 141, 18 Cal.Rptr. 892 (children's camp). See Hauserman & Lansing, Rape on Campus: Postsecondary Institutions as Third Party Defendants, 1981–82, 8 J.Coll. & Univ.L. 182; cf. Notes, 1981, 28 Wayne L.Rev. 183 (teacher failure to report suspected child abuse); 1967, 19 Me.L.Rev. 111.

12. Winn-Dixie Stores, Inc. v. Johnstoneaux, Fla. App.1981, 395 So.2d 599; Morgan v. Bucks Associates, E.D.Pa.1977, 428 F.Supp. 546; Butler v. Acme Markets, Inc., 1982, 89 N.J. 270, 445 A.2d 1141; cf. F.W. Woolworth v. Kirby, 1974, 302 So.2d 67, 293 Ala. 248 (injury from jostling crowd assembled for ping pong ball drop from airplane). The duty may extend off the premises as well. See Coath v. Jones, 1980, 277 Pa. Super. 479, 419 A.2d 1249 (attack by former employee in plaintiff's home).

But cf. Boyd v. Racine Currency Exchange, Inc., 1973, 56 Ill.2d 95, 306 N.E.2d 39 (no duty to accede to criminal demand to protect patron taken hostage). Accord, Bence v. Crawford Savings & Loan Association, 1980, 80 Ill.App.3d 491, 35 Ill.Dec. 902, 400 N.E.2d 39. See generally Note, 1977, 19 Ariz.L.Rev. 696; Annots., 1979, 93 A.L.R.3d 999 (shopping center); 1977, 75 A.L.R.3d 441 (theater); 1976, 72 A.L.R.3d 1269 (store keeper).

13. See Annot., 1972, 43 A.L.R.3d 331; infra, § 63.

14. See supra, pp. 368–70.

15. Schuster v. City of New York, 1958, 5 N.Y.2d 75, 180 N.Y.S.2d 265, 154 N.E.2d 534 (city had duty to provide police protection to key witness in criminal case); Bartels v. Westchester County, 1980, 76 A.D.2d 517, 429 N.Y.S.2d 906 (child abuse of infant negligently placed by county with particular foster parents).

16. Second Restatement of Torts, § 319; Harper and Kime, The Duty to Control the Conduct of Anoth-

owner of an automobile is in such a position to control the conduct of one who is driving it in his presence that he is required to act reasonably to prevent negligent driving.[17] A tavern keeper must act reasonably to prevent intoxicated patrons from injuring others.[18] An employer must prevent his employees from throwing objects from his factory windows,[19] and this had been extended quite generally to include an obligation on the part of any occupier of premises to exercise reasonable care to control the conduct of any one upon them, for the protection of those outside.[20] A franchisor may be liable for negligently permitting its franchisee to cheat the customers.[21] The physician in charge of an operation may be liable for failure to prevent the negligence of his assistants.[22] A hospital may be liable for permitting an unqualified doctor to treat a patient on its premises.[23] The same rule has been applied to hospitals and psychotherapists who have charge of dangerous mental patients,[24] and to those who have charge of dangerous criminals.[25] A common application of the principle is found in the liability of parents for failure to exercise proper control over their children, which is con-

er, 1934, 43 Yale L.J. 886; Note, 1938, 36 Mich.L.Rev. 505. Cf. Brooke v. Bool, [1928] 2 K.B. 578, 585.

17. Wheeler v. Darmochwat, 1932, 280 Mass. 553, 183 N.E. 55; Parks v. Pere Marquette Railway Co., 1946, 315 Mich. 38, 23 N.W.2d 196; Second Restatement of Torts, § 318.

18. See McFarlin v. Hall, 1980, 127 Ariz. 220, 619 P.2d 729; Slawinski v. Mocettini, 1963, 217 Cal.App.2d 192, 31 Cal.Rptr. 613, appeal after remand 63 Cal.2d 70, 45 Cal.Rptr. 15, 403 P.2d 143.

19. Hogle v. H.H. Franklin Manufacturing Co., 1910, 199 N.Y. 388, 92 N.E. 794. Accord, Fletcher v. Baltimore & Potomac Railroad Co., 1897, 168 U.S. 135, 18 S.Ct. 35, 42 L.Ed. 411; Palmer v. Keene Forestry Association, 1921, 80 N.H. 68, 112 A. 798; Second Restatement of Torts, § 317. And he must restrain from sending them onto the highway in an intoxicated condition. Clark v. Otis Engineering Corp., Tex.App.1982, 633 S.W.2d 538.

20. De Ryss v. New York Central Railway Co., 1937, 275 N.Y. 85, 9 N.E.2d 788 (trespassers shooting on land); Connolly v. Nicollet Hotel, 1959, 254 Minn. 373, 95 N.W.2d 657 (rowdy conduct in hotel convention); cf. Uccello v. Laudenslayer, 1975, 44 Cal.3d 504, 118 Cal.Rptr. 741 (landlord could have evicted tenant with vicious dog).

21. Cullen v. BMW of North America, Inc., E.D. N.Y.1982, 531 F.Supp. 555, reversed (2–1), 2d Cir. 1982, 691 F.2d 1097.

22. Davis v. Potter, 1931, 51 Idaho 81, 2 P.2d 318; Morey v. Thybo, 7th Cir. 1912, 199 F. 760; Beck v. The German Klinik, 1889, 78 Iowa 696, 43 N.W. 617. See supra, p. 189.

23. See Johnson v. Misericordia Community Hospital, 1981, 90 Wis.2d 708, 301 N.W.2d 156, noted 1981, 65 Marq.L.Rev. 139; Hendrickson v. Hodkin, 1937, 276 N.Y. 252, 11 N.E.2d 899; Note, 1938, 48 Yale L.J. 81; Annot., 1982, 12 A.L.R.4th 57 (failure to supervise doctor's treatment or require consultation).

24. The leading case is Tarasoff v. Regents of University of California, 1976, 17 Cal.3d 425, 131 Cal.Rptr. 14, 551 P.2d 334, holding a therapist to a duty of reasonable care to protect the intended victim of a patient known to be dangerous. Accord, Lipari v. Sears, Roebuck & Co., D.Neb.1980, 497 F.Supp. 185; Bradley Center, Inc. v. Wessner, 1982, 250 Ga. 199, 296 S.E.2d 693 (negligent issuance of weekend pass to mental patient who killed wife); McIntosh v. Milano, L.Div.1979, 168 N.J.Super. 466, 403 A.2d 500. See also Rausch v. McVeigh, 1980, 105 Misc.2d 163, 431 N.Y.S.2d 887 (negligent supervision of autistic son who assaulted therapist); Jablonski v. United States, 9th Cir. 1983, 712 F.2d 391 (veterans hospital psychiatrist; suit allowed under FTCA). But cf. Cairl v. Minnesota, Minn.1982, 323 N.W.2d 20 (no duty to warn mother of dangerous characteristic she already knew); Furr v. Spring Grove State Hospital, 1983, 53 Md.App. 474, 454 A.2d 414 (no liability unless plaintiff is "readily identifiable victim"; see infra, note 25). See generally Stone, The *Tarasoff* Decision: Suing Psychotherapists to Safeguard Society, 1976, 90 Harv.L.Rev. 358; Fleming & Maximov, The Patient or His Victim: The Therapist's Dilemma, 1974, 62 Cal.L.Rev. 1025; Notes, 1978, 31 Stan.L.Rev. 165; 1981, 76 Nw.L.Rev. 331; 1982, 91 Yale L.J. 1430; Annot., 1978, 83 A.L.R.3d 1201.

25. Kulaga v. State, 1971, 37 A.D.2d 58, 322 N.Y.S.2d 542, affirmed 1972, 31 N.Y.2d 756, 338 N.Y.S. 2d 436, 290 N.E.2d 437; Grimm v. Arizona Board of Pardons and Paroles, 1977, 115 Ariz. 260, 564 P.2d 1227; Bergmann v. United States, E.D.Mo.1981, 526 F.Supp. 443 reversed, 8th Cir. 1982, 689 F.2d 789 (mobster participant in federal witness security program killed police officer during burglary attempt); Duarte v. City of San Jose, 1980, 100 Cal.App.3d 648, 161 Cal. Rptr. 140 (while mowing his lawn, plaintiff struck by arrestee who had stolen police car). Cf. Sosa v. Coleman, 5th Cir. 1981, 646 F.2d 991; Pamela L. v. Farmer, 1980, 112 Cal.App.3d 206, 169 Cal.Rptr. 282 (wife invited young girls to swim in pool while knowing husband was child molester). But the duty to warn may arise only if the dangerous person makes a specific threat on a specific person. Thompson v. County of Alameda, 1980, 27 Cal.3d 741, 167 Cal.Rptr. 70, 614 P.2d 728, noted, 1981, 76 Nw.L.Rev. 331. Accord, Cairl v. Minnesota, Minn.1982, 323 N.W.2d 20 (mental patient). See generally Note, 1978, 46 Ford.L.Rev. 1301 (decisions by parole board to release prisoners entitled only to qualified immunity); Annots., 1981, 6 A.L.R.4th 1155 (government liability for injuries from negligent release); 1981, 5 A.L.R.4th 773 (official immunity for same).

sidered in the chapter on domestic relations.²⁶ Yet, in the absence of the requisite relationship, there generally is no duty to protect others against harm from third persons.²⁷

In all such cases where the duty does exist, the obligation is not an absolute one to insure the plaintiff's safety, but requires only that the defendant exercise reasonable care.²⁸ There is thus no liability when such care has in fact been used,²⁹ nor where the defendant neither knows nor has reason to foresee the danger or otherwise to know that precautions are called for.³⁰

WESTLAW REFERENCES

topic(272 313a 379) /p omission* /p duty

topic(272 313a 379) /p nonfeasance misfeasance

Duty to Aid One in Peril
topic(272 379) /p duty /p peril emergency
headnote(duty /s aid /s another)
"hit and run" /s duty

Affirmative Conduct
restatement +s torts /p affirmative +s act conduct
tort negligence /p assumption +3 duty

Preventing Aid by Others
restatement /5 326 327 & aid*** /s another third

Controlling Conduct of Others
headnote(control*** /s conduct behavior /s another third) & topic(negligence torts)
control*** /s conduct behavior /s another third /p negligence torts

---

26. See infra, ch. 22.
27. See Hosein v. Checker Taxi Co., Inc., 1981, 95 Ill.App.3d 150, 50 Ill.Dec. 460, 419 N.E.2d 568 (taxi owner had no duty to protect lessee against criminal acts); Pulka v. Edelman, 1976, 40 N.Y.2d 781, 390 N.Y.S.2d 393, 358 N.E.2d 1019 (pedestrian struck by car driven from parking garage; garage-pedestrian relationship too tenuous to support duty).
28. Chicago, Rock Island & Pacific Railway Co. v. Brown, 1914, 111 Ark. 288, 163 S.W. 525; Hoff v. Public Service Co., 1915, 91 N.J.L. 641, 103 A. 209; City of Dallas v. Jackson, Tex.1970, 450 S.W.2d 62.

Nor of course is a defendant required to exercise control he does not have. Cuppy v. Bunch, 1974, 88 S.D. 22, 214 N.W.2d 786 (lead driver had no control over intoxicated following driver who hit plaintiff's car); Megeff v. Doland, 1981, 123 Cal.App.3d 251, 176 Cal.Rptr. 467 (daughter could not control father); cf. Tout v. Hartford Accident & Indemnity Co., Fla.App. 1980, 390 So.2d 155 (husband could not fairly be expected to control wife).

29. Saatzer v. Smith, 1981, 122 Cal.App.3d 512, 176 Cal.Rptr. 68 (tavern keeper stopped fight as soon as possible; no duty to obtain names of other persons in fight); Wilson v. Sponable, 1981, 81 A.D.2d 1, 439 N.Y.S.2d 549 (reasonable care does not require 24-hour-per-day supervision of suicidal prisoner).

30. See Thompson v. Ange, 1981, 83 App.Div.2d 193, 443 N.Y.S.2d 918 (school had no reason to suspect particular student might cause car accident); Cornpropst v. Sloan, Tenn.1975, 528 S.W.2d 188; Munn v. Hardee's Food Systems, Inc., 1980, 274 S.C. 529, 266 S.E.2d 414 (plaintiff's decedent knifed in spontaneous fight outside restaurant); Whitson v. Oakland Unified School District, 1981, 176 Cal.Rptr. 287, 123 Cal.App.3d 133 (janitor raped student); Wingard v. Safeway Stores, Inc., 1981, 123 Cal.App.3d 37, 176 Cal.Rptr. 320 (no previous assaults in warehouse guarded by plaintiff); Gill v. Chicago Park District, 1980, 85 Ill.App.3d 903, 41 Ill.Dec. 173, 407 N.E.2d 671 (assault at football stadium).

Chapter 10

OWNERS AND OCCUPIERS OF LAND

Table of Sections

Sec.
57. Outside of the Premises.
58. Trespassing Adults.
59. Trespassing Children.
60. Licensees.
61. Invitees.
62. Abolition of Categories.
63. Lessor and Lessee.
64. Vendor and Vendee.

§ 57. Outside of the Premises

The largest single area in which the concept of "duty" has operated as a limitation upon liability has concerned owners and occupiers of land. Largely for historical reasons, the rights and liabilities arising out of the condition of land, and activities conducted upon it, have been concerned chiefly with the possession of the land, and this has continued into the present day. This development has occurred for the obvious reason that the person in possession of property ordinarily is in the best position to discover and control its dangers, and often is responsible for creating them in the first place.[1] He has a privilege to make use of the land for his own benefit, and according to his own desires, which is an integral part of our whole system of private property; but it has been said many times that this privilege is qualified by a due regard for the interests of others who may be affected by it. The possessor's right is therefore bounded by principles of reasonableness, so as to cause no unreasonable risks of harm to others in the vicinity.[2]

His liability for a breach of this obligation may fall into any of the three categories into which tort liability has been divided. It may rest upon intent, as where he fills the air with poisonous fumes knowing that they are certain to damage the plaintiff's adjoining

---

§ 57

1. The obligation may arise from possession and control, even without legal ownership. Jacobs v. Mutual Mortgage & Investment Co., 1966, 6 Ohio St.2d 92, 216 N.E.2d 49; Trainor v. Frank Mercede & Sons, Inc., 1965, 152 Conn. 364, 207 A.2d 54. See Sprecher v. Adamson Companies, 1981, 30 Cal.3d 358, 178 Cal.Rptr. 783, 788, 636 P.2d 1121, 1126; Black v. City of Cordele, 1982, 163 Ga.App. 322, 293 S.E.2d 557 (operator-occupier of city-owned gas pipeline system).

2. Schulz v. Quintana, Utah 1978, 576 P.2d 855; Smith, Reasonable Use as a Justification for Damage to a Neighbor, 1917, 17 Col.L.Rev. 383.

land.³ It may be based upon negligence in the creation of an unreasonable risk, as when he runs a gasoline engine that frightens horses in the street,⁴ or allows a building to fall into such disrepair that it is a menace to passersby.⁵ It may be strict liability, for the keeping of animals ⁶ or for abnormal activities which, as a matter of social policy, are required to pay their way by making good the harm they do.⁷ When any of the three results in an unreasonable interference with the use and enjoyment of the land of another, it has been treated by the courts as a question of private nuisance; ⁸ and when the interference is with a public right, as in the case of a danger to the highway or a disturbance of the public morals or the peace, it has been dealt with as a public nuisance.⁹ In the great majority of other cases, particularly in those involving personal injury, the problem has been treated as one of simple negligence. The principal distinguishing feature involved is the weight which must be given to the interest in the free use of the property, which must be thrown into the scales in determining both the duty to exercise any care at all, and the reasonableness of the defendant's conduct.

The possessor of land is first of all required to exercise reasonable care, with regard to any activities which he carries on, for the protection of those outside of his premises.¹⁰ He may be liable if he blows a whistle where it will frighten horses in the street,¹¹ or operates a barrel hoist which is dangerous to adjoining property,¹² or runs a factory so that it gives out unnecessary noise or smoke.¹³ Likewise, he must use similar care as to the erection ¹⁴ or demolition ¹⁵ of structures on his land, or the digging of excavations,¹⁶ to see that they are not unreasonably dangerous to persons or property in the vicinity. In addition, he is under the affirmative duty to take reasonable steps ¹⁷ to inspect his premises and keep them in repair, and he may be liable if through his negligence a ruined house,¹⁸ a fire escape ¹⁹ or a loose sign ²⁰ falls and injures the plaintiff.

3. Vaughn v. Missouri Power & Light Co., Mo.App. 1935, 89 S.W.2d 699; Smith v. Staso Milling Co., 2d Cir. 1927, 18 F.2d 736.
4. Wolf v. Des Moines Elevator Co., 1905, 126 Iowa 659, 98 N.W. 301, affirmed 126 Iowa 659, 102 N.W. 517; Fort Wayne Cooperage Co. v. Page, 1908, 170 Ind. 585, 84 N.E. 145.
5. Mitchell v. Brady, 1907, 124 Ky. 411, 99 S.W. 266; McCarthy v. Thompson Square Theatre Co., 1926, 254 Mass. 373, 150 N.E. 170.
6. See infra, § 76.
7. See infra, § 78.
8. See infra, § 91.
9. See infra, § 90. In cases of personal injury to those on the highway, the courts have talked indiscriminately of public nuisance or negligence.
10. Second Restatement of Torts, § 371.
11. Dugan v. St. Paul & Duluth Railroad Co., 1890, 43 Minn. 414, 45 N.W. 851.
12. Weitzmann v. A. L. Barber Asphalt Co., 1908, 190 N.Y. 452, 83 N.E. 477. Cf. Cessna v. Coffeyville Racing Association, 1956, 179 Kan. 766, 298 P.2d 265 (automobile race track, insufficiently fenced).
13. See Brown v. Nebraska Public Power District, 1981, 209 Neb. 61, 306 N.W.2d 167 (smoke from burning weeds); Timmons v. Reed, Wyo.1977, 569 P.2d 112 (fog from oil treater facility covered highway); Westerman v. Stout, 1975, 232 Pa.Super. 195, 335 A.2d 741 (fog from cooling tower); infra, § 89. Or fails properly to maintain his engine, which starts a fire. Hass v. Chicago & Northwestern Railway Co., 1970, 48 Wis.2d 321, 179 N.W.2d 885 (but no duty to fireman injured while fighting the blaze). But see Yin Sang Shum v. Venell, 1975, 273 Or. 143, 539 P.2d 1085 (farmer burning field grass not liable for smoke on highway).
14. Smethurst v. Proprietors, Independent Congregational Church, 1889, 148 Mass. 261, 19 N.E. 387 (roof shedding snow); Ferris v. Board of Education, 1899, 122 Mich. 315, 81 N.W. 98 (same).
15. Alamo National Bank v. Kraus, Tex.1981, 616 S.W.2d 908.
16. See Spall v. Janota, 1980, ___ Ind.App. ___, 406 N.E.2d 378; St. Joseph Light & Power Co. v. Kaw Valley Tunneling, Inc., Mo.1979, 589 S.W.2d 260; Mile High Fence Co. v. Radovich, 1971, 175 Colo. 537, 489 P.2d 308. See infra, note 26.
17. The defendant is not an insurer of safe conditions, and is thus not liable where he has exercised reasonable care. Schell v. Second National Bank, 1869, 14 Minn. 43, 14 Gil. 34.
18. Mullen v. St. John, 1874, 57 N.Y. 567; Pope v. Reading Co., 1931, 304 Pa. 326, 156 A. 106; see Glorioso v. Chandler, La.App.1976, 337 So.2d 269.
19. McCarthy v. Thompson Square Theatre Co., 1926, 254 Mass. 373, 150 N.E. 170. Cf. Restaino v. Griggs Motor Sales, 1937, 118 N.J.L. 442, 193 A. 543 (show window); Pearson v. Ehrich, 1912, 148 App.Div. 680, 133 N.Y.S. 273 (same); Mitchell v. Brady, 1907, 124 Ky. 411, 99 S.W. 266 (downspout); Crow v. Colson, 1927, 123 Kan. 702, 256 P. 971 (screen).
20. Smith v. Claude Neon Lights, 1933, 110 N.J.L. 326, 164 A. 423. Cf. Houston v. Brush, 1894, 66 Vt.

Danger to Highway

A large proportion of the cases have involved danger to an adjacent public highway. The public right of passage carries with it, once the highway has been established,[21] an obligation upon the occupiers of abutting land to use reasonable care to see that the passage is safe.[22] They are not required to maintain or repair the highway itself,[23] but they will be liable for any unreasonable risk to those who are on it, such as an open coal hole in the sidewalk, or overhanging objects ready to fall.[24] The obligation extends also to any artificial conditions,[25] such as an excavation[26] or utility pole[27] next to the street, or a protrusion into

---

331, 29 A. 380 (iron plate falling from railway); Glasgow Realty Co. v. Metcalfe, Ky.1972, 482 S.W.2d 750 (glass from upstairs window).

21. The weight of authority is strongly with the Second Restatement of Torts, § 368, Comment c, to the effect that the responsibility for remedying a condition, such as an excavation, which exists when the highway is constructed, is upon those charged with the duty of maintaining the highway, and the adjoining landowner is not liable. City of Fort Worth v. Lee, 1945, 143 Tex. 551, 186 S.W.2d 954; Harvell v. City of Wilmington, 1939, 214 N.C. 608, 200 S.E. 367; Galiano v. Pacific Gas & Electric Co., 1937, 20 Cal.App.2d 534, 67 P.2d 388.

22. See Weber v. Madison, Iowa 1977, 251 N.W.2d 523, 527 (geese on highway; noting "strong public policy that highways must be free from obstructions and hazards"); Pindell v. Rubenstein, 1921, 139 Md. 567, 115 A. 859; De Ark v. Nashville Stone Setting Corp., 1955, 38 Tenn.App. 678, 279 S.W.2d 518.

23. Second Restatement of Torts, § 349, unless the dangerous condition is "created in the highway by him for his sole benefit subsequent to dedication" (§ 350). See Gabrielson v. City of Seattle, 1928, 150 Wash. 157, 272 P. 723, affirmed 152 Wash. 700, 278 P. 1071; Korricks Dry Goods Co. v. Kendall, 1928, 33 Ariz. 325, 264 P. 692; cf. Haas v. Firestone Tire & Rubber Co., Okl. 1976, 563 P.2d 620 (no duty to hose down tires of trucks leaving construction site to avoid accumulation of dirt on highway). See generally Annot., 1963, 88 A.L.R.2d 331 (abutting owner—condition of sidewalk).

The duty to design and maintain the public ways in a reasonably safe manner normally rests upon the government. See Wichita Falls v. Ramos, Tex.Civ.App. 1980, 596 S.W.2d 654 (uncovered water meter box in street); Annot., 1972, 45 A.L.R.3d 875 (liability for dangerous design of highway); Annot., 1983, 22 A.L.R.4th 624 (liability for failure to cut vegetation obscuring vision at crossings). Some jurisdictions hold that if the abutting landowner puts the street or sidewalk to a special use, he may have a duty of reasonable maintenance. District of Columbia v. Texaco, Inc., D.C.App. 1974, 324 A.2d 690 (portion of sidewalk used as driveway by service station); Herndon v. Arco Petroleum Co., 1975, 91 Nev. 404, 536 P.2d 1023 (same); cf. Ferrill v. Southern Railway, Tenn.App.1972, 493 S.W.2d 90 (railroad has duty to keep street in repair at crossing). A couple of jurisdictions have imposed a general duty of reasonable maintenance of sidewalks upon abutting commercial landowners. Stewart v. 104 Wallace Street, Inc., 1981, 87 N.J. 146, 432 A.2d 881, noted, 1982, 13 Rut.-Cam.L.J. 429; Nash v. Atlantic White Tower System, Inc., 1961, 404 Pa. 83, 170 A.2d 341.

24. Glascow Realty Co. v. Metcalfe, Ky.1972, 482 S.W.2d 750 (glass fell from window onto sidewalk); Magay v. Claflin-Sumner Coal Co., 1926, 257 Mass. 244, 153 N.E. 534; Feeney v. New York Waist House, 1927, 105 Conn. 647, 136 A. 554. Cf. Thompson v. White, 1963, 274 Ala. 413, 149 So.2d 797 (performing clowns on highway).

25. The rule is limited to artificial conditions. Second Restatement of Torts, § 368. Hence, it does not apply to a tree, or even a tree stump, 6 feet off a sharp turn in the highway. Paquette v. Joyce, 1977, 117 N.H. 832, 379 A.2d 207 (Kenison, C. J.) (carefully reasoned analysis); Annot., 1980, 100 A.L.R.3d 510 (trees and stumps). Nor, in most states, unless there is a statutory duty, to uncut weeds or other indigenous vegetation obstructing the vision of motorists at intersections, on land belonging to the city or state. See Walker v. Bignell, 1981, 100 Wis.2d 256, 301 N.W.2d 447 (statutory duty to cut vegetation planted by highway authorities, but no common law duty as matter of public policy; citing cases following majority rule, and Texas and Louisiana cases contra); Annot., 1955, 42 A.L.R.2d 817; Annot., 1983, 22 A.L.R.4th 624 (govt. liability for failure to cut vegetation). With respect to privately owned land, the issues are generally similar but are also analogous to the tree cases discussed below, which are in a state of flux. Compare Evans v. Southern Holding Corp., Fla.App.1980, 391 So.2d 231 (2-1) (no duty), with Savarese v. Bye, La.App.1981, 398 So.2d 1276 (duty).

26. See supra, note 16; Lacanfora v. Goldapel, 1971, 37 A.D.2d 721, 323 N.Y.S.2d 990 (12-foot drop behind door without handle in building beside sidewalk); Downes v. Silva, 1937, 57 R.I. 343, 190 A. 42; White v. Suncook Mills, 1940, 91 N.H. 92, 13 A.2d 729; Mile High Fence Co. v. Radovich, 1971, 175 Colo. 537, 489 P.2d 308 (post hole 7 inches from paving in alley); cf. Williams v. Aetna Insurance Co., La.App.1981, 402 So. 2d 192 (drop between porch and walkway was hidden trap). But not to an open mine shaft at the end of an old dirt road. Holcombe v. Harris, 1977, 143 Ga.App. 173, 237 S.E.2d 677. Nor will a municipality ordinarily be liable for maintaining a drainage ditch beside a road. Tomassi v. Town of Union, 1978, 46 N.Y.2d 91, 412 N.Y.S.2d 842, 385 N.E.2d 581 (car); Lovick v. Marion, 1975, 43 Ohio St.2d 171, 331 N.E.2d 445 (pedestrian).

27. See Weiss v. Holman, 1973, 58 Wis.2d 608, 207 N.W.2d 660 (four feet from road). But see Shapiro v. Toyota Motor Co., 1978, 38 N.C.App. 658, 248 S.E.2d 868 (one foot); Southern Bell Telephone & Telegraph Co. v. Martin, 1972, 229 Ga. 881, 194 S.E.2d 910, conformed to 128 Ga.App. 42, 195 S.E.2d 756 (utility not

it,[28] which are dangerous to those who use it.

The status of a user of the highway has been extended to those who stray a few feet from it inadvertently.[29] It has been extended also to those who deviate intentionally for some purpose reasonably connected with the travel itself, such as detouring an obstruction,[30] or stepping out to avoid others on the sidewalk,[31] or even stopping in a doorway to tie a shoelace.[32] On the other hand, one who intentionally leaves the highway for some purpose of his own not reasonably connected with travel is not regarded as a user of the highway, but becomes a trespasser, or at most a licensee.[33] And one who wanders into a pit a considerable distance from the road after traversing the adjoining land, even though he does so inadvertently, is denied such protection, and treated as a trespasser.[34] The distance would appear not to be so important in itself, but merely to bear upon the existence of a recognizable danger to the normal users of the highway.[35] On the same basis the occupier of abutting land is required to guard against the tendency of children to stray from the road, where there is a condition close to it which will be unreasonably dangerous to them if they do.[36] Likewise, if he so maintains a part of his land that it appears to be a highway, as where he paves a strip next to the street,[37] or gives a private way the appearance of a public one,[38] he must use reasonable care to see that there is no danger to those who are misled into using it. It is often said in such cases that there is an implied "invitation" to enter, but the true basis of liability seems to

---

liable where placement subject to supervision by city officials); Hyde v. County of Rensselaer, 1980, 51 N.Y.2d 927, 434 N.Y.S.2d 984, 415 N.E.2d 972 (9½ feet; no liability on facts, but noting that utility may be liable for placing poles in unreasonably dangerous location for highway travelers); Hayes v. Malkan, 1970, 26 N.Y.2d 295, 310 N.Y.S.2d 281, 258 N.E.2d 695 (7 inches) (4–3), criticized in Note, 1971, 71 Colum.L.Rev. 352. Cf. Bernier v. Boston Edison Co., 1980, 380 Mass. 372, 403 N.E.2d 391 (utility liable for unsafe design of pole that fell on pedestrians when struck by car).

28. See Ross v. Kirby, 1967, 251 Cal.App.2d 267, 59 Cal.Rptr. 601 (berm).

29. Puchlopek v. Portsmouth Power Co., 1926, 82 N.H. 440, 136 A. 259 (slip); Edgarton v. H. P. Welch Co., 1947, 321 Mass. 603, 74 N.E.2d 674 (truck out of control); Louisville & Nashville Railroad Co. v. Anderson, 5th Cir. 1930, 39 F.2d 403 (automobile missing turn); Gaylord Container Corp. v. Miley, 5th Cir. 1956, 230 F.2d 177 (drunk); Weiss v. Holman, 1973, 58 Wis.2d 608, 207 N.W.2d 660 (utility pole 4 feet from road). But see Lioni v. Marr, 1946, 320 Mass. 17, 67 N.E.2d 766; Sheets v. Burleson, Tenn.1972, 488 S.W.2d 365 (no liability for maintaining metal fence, with spear-like pointed ends on top, beside sidewalk).

30. See Bacsick v. Barnes, 1975, 234 Pa.Super. 616, 341 A.2d 157 (snow and ice on sidewalk requiring plaintiff to walk in street); Sawicki v. Connecticut Railway & Lighting Co., 1943, 129 Conn. 626, 30 A.2d 556. But see West v. Faurbo, 1978, 66 Ill.App.3d 815, 23 Ill.Dec. 663, 384 N.E.2d 457 (bicycle swerved 4 or 5 feet onto defendant's property where it hit cement blocks hidden in grass; deviation was not "ordinary incident of travel").

31. Weidman v. Consolidated Gas, Electric Light & Power Co., 1930, 158 Md. 39, 148 A. 270; Gibson v. Johnson, 1941, 69 Ohio App. 19, 42 N.E. 689.

32. Murray v. McShane, 1879, 52 Md. 217. Or to talk to a friend. Lacanfora v. Goldapel, 1971, 37 A.D.2d 721, 323 N.Y.S.2d 990. Cf. Hynes v. New York Central Railroad Co., 1921, 231 N.Y. 229, 131 N.E. 898 (using springboard to dive into navigable stream). See Note, 1938, 36 Mich.L.Rev. 159.

33. Foley v. H. F. Farnham Co., 1936, 135 Me. 29, 188 A. 708 (conversation with a friend); Racine v. Morris, 1910, 136 App.Div. 467, 121 N.Y.S. 146, affirmed 1911, 201 N.Y. 240, 94 N.E. 864 (policeman on official duty); Anderson v. Speer, 1926, 36 Ga.App. 29, 134 S.E. 811 (viewing show window); Chickering v. Thompson, 1912, 76 N.H. 311, 82 A. 839 (on way to back of lot); West v. Faurbo, 1978, 66 Ill.App.3d 815, 23 Ill. Dec. 663, 384 N.E.2d 457 (swerving onto land to avoid collision: licensee); Schulz v. Quintana, Utah 1978, 576 P.2d 855 (short cut: trespasser).

34. Hardcastle v. South Yorkshire R. & R. D. Co., 1859, 4 H. & N. 67, 157 Eng.Rep. 761; Brooks v. Logan, 1975, 134 Ga.App. 226, 213 S.E.2d 916 (child taking short cut fell into water cut-off control hole 11 feet into yard).

35. See City of Norwich v. Breed, 1852, 30 Conn. 535. But cf. Boutelje v. Tarzian, 1940, 142 Pa.Super. 275, 16 A.2d 146. But cf. Weiss v. Holman, 1973, 58 Wis.2d 608, 207 N.W.2d 660 (distance important, but four feet from highway close enough).

36. See infra, § 59.

37. Beckwith v. Somerset Theatres, 1942, 139 Me. 65, 27 A.2d 596; Williamson v. Southern Railway Co., 1930, 42 Ga.App. 9, 155 S.E. 113; Mercier v. Naugatuck Fuel Co., 1953, 139 Conn. 521, 95 A.2d 263.

38. Allen v. Yazoo & Mississippi Valley Railroad Co., 1916, 111 Miss. 267, 71 So. 386; Reddington v. Getchell, 1919, 40 R.I. 463, 101 A. 123, reargument denied 42 R.I. 439, 102 A. 88; Southern v. Cowan Stone Co., 1949, 188 Tenn. 576, 221 S.W.2d 809.

be the misrepresentation as to the character of the property.[39]

Natural Conditions

The one important limitation upon the responsibility of the possessor of land to those outside of his premises has been the traditional rule, of both the English and the American courts, that he is under no affirmative duty to remedy conditions of purely natural origin upon his land, although they may be highly dangerous or inconvenient to his neighbors.[40] The origin of this, in both countries, lay in an early day when much land, in fact most, was unsettled or uncultivated, and the burden of inspecting it and putting it in safe condition would have been not only unduly onerous, but out of all proportion to any harm likely to result. Thus it has been held that the landowner is not liable for the existence of a foul swamp,[41] for falling rocks,[42] for uncut weeds obstructing the view of motorists at an intersection,[43] for thistles growing on his land,[44] for harm done by indigenous animals,[45] or for the normal, natural flow of surface water.[46] Closely allied to this is the generally accepted holding that an abutting owner is under no duty to remove ice and snow which has fallen upon his own land or upon the highway.[47]

On the other hand, if the occupier has himself altered the condition of the premises, as by erecting a structure which discharges water upon the sidewalk,[48] setting up a parking lot upon which water will collect,[49] weakening rocks by the construction of a highway,[50] damming a stream so that it forms a malarial pond,[51] planting a row of trees next to the highway,[52] digging out part of a hill,[53] or piling sand or plowing a field so that the

---

39. See infra, § 61.

40. Second Restatement of Torts, § 363. See Noel, Nuisances from Land in its Natural Condition, 1943, 56 Harv.L.Rev. 772; Goodhart, Liability for Things Naturally on the Land, 1930, 4 Camb.L.J. 13.

41. Roberts v. Harrison, 1897, 101 Ga. 773, 28 S.E. 995.

42. Pontardawe R. D. C. v. Moore-Gwynn, [1929] 1 Ch. 656. But see Sprecher v. Adamson Companies, 1981, 30 Cal.3d 358, 178 Cal.Rptr. 783, 636 P.2d 1121 (duty of due care to prevent landslide).

43. See supra, note 25.

44. Giles v. Walker, 1890, 24 Q.B.D. 656 (thistles); cf. Salmon v. Delaware, L. & W. R. Co., 1875, 38 N.J.L. 5 (leaves); Langer v. Goode, 1911, 21 N.D. 462, 131 N.W. 258 (wild mustard).

45. Brady v. Warren, [1909] 2 Ir.Rep. 632; Stearn v. Prentice Bros., [1919] 1 K.B. 394; Seaboard Air Line Railroad Co. v. Richmond-Petersburg Turnpike Authority, 1961, 202 Va. 1029, 121 S.E.2d 499 (pigeons); Merriam v. McConnell, 1961, 31 Ill.App.2d 241, 175 N.E.2d 293 (box elder bugs). Nor, perhaps, for horses kept by a tenant. Blake v. Dunn Farms, Inc., 1980, ___ Ind. ___, 413 N.E.2d 560. Contra, perhaps, for horses kept by an employee. See Misterek v. Washington Mineral Products, Inc., 1975, 85 Wn.2d 166, 531 P.2d 805. Cf. Weber v. Madison, Iowa 1977, 251 N.W.2d 523 (geese); King v. Blue Mountain Forest Association, 1956, 100 N.H. 212, 123 A.2d 151 (wild Prussian boar, fourth or fifth generation from original imports).

46. See Keys v. Romley, 1966, 64 Cal.2d 396, 50 Cal. Rptr. 273, 412 P.2d 529; Mohr v. Gault, 1860, 10 Wis. 513; Livezey v. Schmidt, 1895, 96 Ky. 441, 29 S.W. 25.

47. Rockafellow v. Rockwell City, Iowa 1974, 217 N.W.2d 246; Bailey v. Blacker, 1929, 267 Mass. 73, 165 N.E. 699; Moore v. Gadsden, 1881, 87 N.Y. 84. Ordinances requiring the property owner to remove snow and ice usually are construed to impose no duty to any private individual. See supra, § 36.

48. See Leahan v. Cochran, 1901, 178 Mass. 566, 60 N.E. 382; Tremblay v. Harmony Mills, 1902, 171 N.Y. 598, 64 N.E. 501; Updegraff v. City of Ottumwa, 1929, 210 Iowa 382, 226 N.W. 928. Note, 1937, 21 Minn.L. Rev. 703, 713; cf. Harris v. Thompson, Ky.1973, 497 S.W.2d 422 (broken water pipe caused ice on road). But see North Little Rock Transportation Co. v. Finkbeiner, 1967, 243 Ark. 596, 420 S.W.2d 874 (Finky not liable for water in street from sprinkler system).

49. Moore v. Standard Paint & Glass Co. of Pueblo, 1960, 145 Colo. 151, 358 P.2d 33. But see Williams v. United States, E.D.Pa.1981, 507 F.Supp. 121 (no liability, under "hills and ridges" doctrine, for slippery sheet of ice with no ridges or elevations in parking lot).

50. McCarthy v. Ference, 1948, 358 Pa. 485, 58 A.2d 49.

51. Mills v. Hall, N.Y.1832, 9 Wend. 315; Towaliga Falls Power Co. v. Sims, 1909, 6 Ga.App. 749, 65 S.E. 844. Cf. Andrews v. Andrews, 1955, 242 N.C. 382, 88 S.E.2d 88 (artificial pond collecting wild geese, which destroyed plaintiff's crops).

52. Coates v. Chinn, 1958, 51 Cal.2d 304, 332 P.2d 289 (cultivated trees). Accord, Wisher v. Fowler, 1970, 7 Cal.App.3d 225, 86 Cal.Rptr. 582 (maintaining hedge). Cf. Crowhurst v. Amersham Burial Board, 1878, 4 Exch.Div. 5, 48 L.J.Ex. 109 (planting poisonous trees near boundary line). But there may be no liability for merely failing to cut weeds. See supra, note 25.

53. Fabbri v. Regis Forcier, Inc., 1975, 114 R.I. 207, 330 A.2d 807.

wind may blow it,[54] the condition is no longer to be regarded as a natural one, and he will be held liable for the damage resulting from any negligence.

The rule of non-liability for natural conditions was obviously a practical necessity in the early days, when land was very largely in a primitive state. It remains to a considerable extent a necessity in rural communities, where the burden of inspecting and improving the land is likely to be entirely disproportionate not only to any threatened harm but even to the value of the land itself. But it is scarcely suited to cities, to say that a landowner may escape all liability for serious damage to his neighbors, merely by allowing nature to take its course.[55] A different rule accordingly has been developing as to urban centers.

This is well illustrated by the cases of dangerous trees.[56] It is still the prevailing rule that the owner of rural land is not required to inspect it to make sure that every tree is safe, and will not fall over into the public highway and kill a person,[57] although there is already some little dissent even as to this[58] and, at least if the defendant knows that the tree is dangerous, he may be required to take affirmative steps.[59] But when the tree is in an urban area, and may fall into a city street, the landowner now has a duty of reasonable care, including inspection to make sure that the tree is safe.[60] Recent decisions have extended the right to reasonable protection from travelers on the street to adjoining landowners as well.[61] The tree cases may suggest that the ordinary rules as to negligence should apply generally to natural conditions, at least in urban and residential areas, so that the inquiry would focus upon such factors as the nature of the locality, the seriousness of the danger, and the ease with which it may be prevented, in the light of all the circumstances.[62]

Conduct of Others

The defendant will of course be liable for any acts of his servants within the scope of

---

54. Ettl v. Land & Loan Co., 1939, 122 N.J.L. 401, 5 A.2d 689. Accord, Haas v. Lavin, 10th Cir. 1980, 625 F.2d 1384 (blowing dust from improperly prepared farmland). But cf. Gabaldon v. Sanchez, App.1978, 92 N.M. 224, 585 P.2d 1105.

55. See Sprecher v. Adamson Companies, 1981, 30 Cal.3d 358, 178 Cal.Rptr. 783, 787, 636 P.2d 1121.

56. See Annot., 1979, 95 A.L.R.3d 778 (governmental liability for limb falling from abutting land into highway); 1979, 94 A.L.R.3d 1160 (same, private owner or occupier).

57. Chambers v. Whelen, 4th Cir. 1930, 44 F.2d 340; Zacharias v. Nesbitt, 1921, 150 Minn. 369, 185 N.W. 295; O'Brien v. United States, 9th Cir. 1960, 275 F.2d 696; Lemon v. Edwards, Ky.1961, 344 S.W.2d 822; see Hay v. Norwalk Lodge, 1951, 92 Ohio App. 14, 109 N.E.2d 481.

58. See Hensley v. Montgomery County, 1975, 25 Md.App. 361, 334 A.2d 542; Taylor v. Olsen, 1978, 282 Or. 343, 578 P.2d 779. England, thickly settled, requires reasonable care as to all trees. Davey v. Harrow Corp., [1958] 1 Q.B. 60.

59. Hay v. Norwalk Lodge, 1951, 92 Ohio App. 14, 109 N.E.2d 481. Cf. Plesko v. City of Milwaukee, 1963, 19 Wis.2d 210, 120 N.W.2d 130 (urban).

60. Husovsky v. United States, 4th Cir. 1978, 590 F.2d 944 (tree fell on highway from wooded tract in urban location); Taylor v. Olsen, 1978, 282 Or. 343, 578 P.2d 779 (motorist struck fallen tree; rejecting urban-rural distinction); Hensley v. Montgomery County, 1975, 25 Md.App. 361, 334 A.2d 542 (limb fell through windshield); Kurtigian v. City of Worcester, 1965, 348 Mass. 284, 203 N.E.2d 692. See McCleary, The Possessor's Responsibility as to Trees, 1964, 29 Mo.L.Rev. 159; Second Restatement of Torts, §§ 363, 840.

But rotten limbs falling onto the highway are not "defects" in the highway for purposes of municipal liability. Comba v. Town of Ridgefield, 1979, 177 Conn. 268, 413 A.2d 859 (tree limb with crotch rot fell on vehicle).

61. See Mahurin v. Lockhart, 1979, 71 Ill.App.3d 691, 28 Ill.Dec. 356, 390 N.E.2d 523 (dead branch fell on neighbor); Barker v. Brown, 1975, 236 Pa.Super. 75, 340 A.2d 566; Cornett v. Agee, 1977, 143 Ga.App. 55, 237 S.E.2d 522, 524 (in accord with second law of thermodynamics, energy decay, "that all in the universe, trees, human beings, plants, animals, buildings and all else are headed downward from complexity to simplicity toward decay, deterioration, decadence, and death"); cf. Sprecher v. Adamson Companies, 1981, 30 Cal.3d 358, 178 Cal.Rptr. 783, 636 P.2d 1121.

62. Mahurin v. Lockhart, 1979, 71 Ill.App.3d 691, 28 Ill.Dec. 356, 390 N.E.2d 523; Hensley v. Montgomery County, 1975, 25 Md.App. 361, 334 A.2d 542. See the very thorough analysis in Sprecher v. Adamson Companies, 1981, 30 Cal.3d 358, 178 Cal.Rptr. 783, 636 P.2d 1121, involving a landslide, where the court abrogated the traditional distinction between natural and artificial conditions and replaced it with a general duty of reasonable care.

their employment which create an unreasonable risk of harm to those outside of his premises.⁶³ In addition, his possession and control of the land may give him a power of control over the conduct of those whom he allows to enter it, which he is required to exercise for the protection of those outside. Thus he will be liable if he stands idly by and permits others on his land to throw junk upon adjoining property,⁶⁴ to shoot at neighbors or passing motorists,⁶⁵ to play golf⁶⁶ or baseball,⁶⁷ or to turn a hotel convention into a minor riot,⁶⁸ where it will be dangerous to persons on the highway. But the liability is for negligence, and he will not be liable for the damage of others that he could not foresee or prevent.⁶⁹

A large number of the cases involving liability for the torts of an independent contractor, which are to be considered later,⁷⁰ have concerned work done on the premises of the employer. The possessor of land is not free to delegate his responsibility for its condition, or for activities carried on upon it, where the work to be done is regarded as "inherently dangerous" to those outside of the land, and he remains liable for the negligence of the contractor in such a case. On the other hand, he is not liable for "collateral" or "casual" negligence in the operative details of the work, which he could not reasonably contemplate as likely to occur.

There have been surprisingly few cases dealing with liability for the conduct of trespassers and others acting without the possessor's knowledge or consent. It seems clear, however, that he is not liable for such conduct, or for conditions resulting from it, until he knows or should know of the danger,⁷¹ but that once he has had a reasonable opportunity to discover the situation he is under a duty to exercise proper care to prevent harm to others.⁷²

WESTLAW REFERENCES

outside /5 premises /p negligen** tort*
digest(owner* occupier* possessor* /6 land /s reasonable +4 care)

Danger to Highway
digest(owner* occupier* possessor* /6 land /s highway sidewalk /s duty)
200k199
highway street sidewalk footpath crosswalk /s "artificial condition" & tort* negligen**
restatement +s torts +3 364

Natural Conditions
natural /4 condition* /p adjoining adjacent abutting /s land property /p tort* negligen**
owner* occupier* possessor* /5 land premises /p inherent** /5 danger***

Conduct of Others
owner* occupier* possessor* /5 land premises /p conduct*** behavior* /6 another third

---

63. See infra, § 70.

64. Hogle v. H. H. Franklin Manufacturing Co., 1910, 199 N.Y. 388, 92 N.E. 794; Fletcher v. Baltimore & Potomac Railroad Co., 1897, 168 U.S. 135, 18 S.Ct. 35, 42 L.Ed. 411; cf. Brogan v. City of Philadelphia, 1943, 346 Pa. 208, 29 A.2d 671; De Ryss v. New York Central Railroad Co., 1937, 275 N.Y. 85, 9 N.E.2d 788.

65. Rosales v. Stewart, 1980, 113 Cal.App.3d 130, 169 Cal.Rptr. 660 (defendant's tenant shooting at neighbor's child); Drake v. State, 1979, 97 Misc.2d 1015, 416 N.Y.S.2d 734, affirmed 75 A.D.2d 1016, 432 N.Y.S.2d 676 (Mohawk Indians Warrior Society, encamped in state park, shooting at motorists).

66. Castle v. St. Augustine's Links, 1922, 38 T.L.R. 615; Gleason v. Hillcrest Golf Course, 1933, 148 Misc. 246, 265 N.Y.S. 886.

67. Harrington v. Border City Manufacturing Co., 1921, 240 Mass. 170, 132 N.E. 721. Cf. Thompson v. White, 1963, 274 Ala. 413, 149 So.2d 797 (performing clowns distracting attention of driver on highway); Rochette v. Town of Newburgh, 1982, 88 A.D.2d 614,

449 N.Y.S.2d 1013 (permitting ice sailboat racing on adjacent lake).

68. Connolly v. Nicollet Hotel, 1959, 254 Minn. 373, 95 N.W.2d 657. Cf. Stevens v. City of Pittsburgh, 1938, 329 Pa. 496, 198 A. 655 (shooting in park); De Rosa v. Fordham University, 1963, 18 A.D.2d 1056, 238 N.Y.S.2d 778 (using sledge hammer on rock).

69. See Freeman v. Kelly, Ala.Civ.App.1981, 395 So. 2d 1019 (timber cutter let tree fall on neighbor's house).

70. See infra, § 71.

71. Sanderson v. Beaugh, La.App.1978, 367 So.2d 14; Spiker v. Elkenberry, 1907, 135 Iowa 79, 110 N.W. 457.

72. De Ryss v. New York Central Railroad Co., 1937, 275 N.Y. 85, 9 N.E.2d 788; Brogan v. City of Philadelphia, 1943, 346 Pa. 208, 29 A.2d 671; Katz v. Helbing, 1932, 215 Cal. 449, 10 P.2d 1001; City of Bowie v. Hill, Tex.Civ.App.1923, 258 S.W. 568, error dismissed; Note, 1944, 18 Temple L.Q. 526.

§ 58. Trespassing Adults

Where the injury occurs on the premises of the defendant, rather than outside of them, additional factors enter the case. The result has been a set of limitations of liability in terms of duty, quite complicated in their detailed variations, and tending to be quite rigidly distinguished and enforced.[1] Those who enter upon land are divided into three fixed categories: trespassers, licensees, and invitees, and there are subdivided duties as to each.[2] They make out, as a general pattern, a rough sliding scale, by which, as the legal status of the visitor improves, the possessor of the land owes him more of an obligation of protection. This system has long made many legal writers, and some of the courts, quite unhappy because of its arbitrary and sometimes unreasonable character; and there has been some recent movement toward abolishing the distinctions, at least between invitees and licensees.[3] But the traditional entrant classification scheme is well entrenched in the great majority of jurisdictions, and so the categories must be carefully considered one by one.

Lowest in the legal scale is the trespasser, defined as "a person who enters or remains upon land in the possession of another without a privilege to do so, created by the possessor's consent or otherwise."[4] The possessor of land[5] has a legally protected interest in the exclusiveness of his possession.[6] In general, no one has any right to enter without his consent, and he is free to fix the terms on which that consent will be given. Intruders who come without his permission have no right to demand that he provide them with a safe place to trespass, or that he protect them in their wrongful use of his property. When they enter where they have no right or privilege, the responsibility is theirs, and they must assume the risk of what they may encounter,[7] and are expected to look out for themselves. Such has always been the point of view of the common law, with its traditional regard for the rights of private ownership of property. Accordingly, it is the general rule, subject to a number of qualifications which remain to be considered, that the possessor is not liable for injury to trespassers caused by his failure to exercise reasonable care to put his land in a safe condition for them, or to carry

---

§ 58

1. "What I particularly wish to emphasize is that there are the three different classes—invitees, licensees, trespassers. * * * Now the line that separates each of these three classes is an absolutely rigid line. There is no half-way house, no no-man's land between adjacent territories." Lord Dunedin, in Robert Addie & Sons v. Dumbreck, [1929] A.C. 358, 371. See Note, 1964, 31 Tenn.L.Rev. 485.

2. See Rowland v. City of Corpus Christi, Tex.Civ.App.1981, 620 S.W.2d 930, refused n. r. e.; Payne v. M. Greenberg Construction, App.1981, 130 Ariz. 338, 636 P.2d 116; Barbre v. Indianapolis Water Co., 1980, ___ Ind.App. ___, 400 N.E.2d 1142; Rennick v. Hoover, 1980, ___ Mont. ___, 606 P.2d 1079; Tjas v. Procter, Utah 1979, 591 P.2d 438; Starr v. Clapp, 1979, 40 N.C.App. 142, 252 S.E.2d 220, affirmed 298 N.C. 275, 258 S.E.2d 348; Murray v. Lane, 1982, 51 Md.App. 597, 444 A.2d 1069. See generally Annot., 1983, 22 A.L.R.4th 294 (modern status of rules based on entrant's status as trespasser, licensee or invitee).

3. See infra, § 62.

4. Second Restatement of Torts, § 329. See Murray v. Lane, 1982, 51 Md.App. 597, 444 A.2d 1069; Bovino v. Metropolitan Dade County, Fla.App.1979, 378 So.2d 50; Monterosso v. Gaudette, 1979, 8 Mass.App.Ct. 93, 391 N.E.2d 948; Yalowizer v. Husky Oil Co., Wyo.1981, 629 P.2d 465; Rowland v. City of Corpus Christi, Tex.Civ.App.1981, 620 S.W.2d 930, refused n. r. e.

5. Most of the cases have involved trespassers on land; but the same rules are applied to trespassers on personal property. See Jefferson v. King, 1929, 12 La.App. 249, 124 So. 589 (automobile); Lavallee v. Pratt, 1960, 122 Vt. 90, 166 A.2d 195 (truck); Payne v. M. Greenberg Construction, App.1981, 130 Ariz. 338, 636 P.2d 116 (scaffold); Kirby v. Hylton, 1982, 51 Md.App. 365, 443 A.2d 640 (pipe); cf. Durham v. City of Los Angeles, 1979, 91 Cal.App.3d 567, 154 Cal.Rptr. 243 (statutory immunity for harm to persons hopping trains unless conduct intentional, wanton or reckless); Murphy v. Baltimore Gas & Electric Co., 1981, 290 Md. 186, 428 A.2d 459 (electric transformer).

6. See VI-A Am. Law of Property 3 (1954).

7. McPheters v. Loomis, 1939, 125 Conn. 526, 7 A.2d 437; Sheehan v. St. Paul & Duluth Railroad Co., 7th Cir. 1896, 76 F. 201; Great Atlantic & Pacific Tea Co. v. Wilson, 1980, ___ Ind.App. ___, 408 N.E.2d 144. Cf. Petrak v. Cooke Contracting Co., 1951, 329 Mich. 564, 46 N.W.2d 574 (the principle of assumption of risk will be "conservatively applied" in trespasser cases).

on his activities in a manner which does not endanger them.[8] He thus is under no obligation to guard a concealed pitfall,[9] a pond,[10] nor a dangerous electric wire,[11] nor to repair a defective building [12] for their benefit, nor to keep a lookout for them as he operates his machinery [13] or runs his train.[14] Even involuntary trespassers, such as those who wander too far from the highway in the dark,[15] have no right to such protection.

Sometimes reasons have been given for this immunity which are difficult to support. It has been said that the presence of a trespasser is not to be anticipated, and hence that a reasonable person would not take steps to protect him. In many cases, this is no doubt true; [16] but it is common knowledge that people do trespass upon the land of others, and yet, in most jurisdictions, the foreseeability of such general trespassing is said to impose no obligation.[17] It has been said that the trespasser is contributorily negligent, or that he is a wrongdoer,[18] who may not recover for the consequences of his own wrong. But even where the trespass is complete, and the trespasser is helpless to protect himself before the defendant's conduct occurs, many of the courts which accept the doctrine of the "unconscious last clear chance" [19] still refuse to find any duty to him.[20] And so far as contributory negligence is concerned, recovery has been denied to children too young to be negligent.[21] And while it is often said that the trespasser assumes the risk of injury, this is rather a

---

8. Second Restatement of Torts, § 333. See Page, The Law of Premises Liability, 1976, ch. 2; Eldredge, Tort Liability to Trespassers, 1937, 12 Temple L.Q. 32, reprinted in Eldredge, Modern Tort Problems, 1941, 163; James, Tort Liability of Occupiers of Land: Duties Owed to Trespassers, 1953, 63 Yale L.J. 144; Green, Landowner v. Intruder; Intruder v. Landowner: Basis of Responsibility in Tort, 1923, 21 Mich.L.Rev. 495; Hughes, Duties to Trespassers: A Comparative Survey and Revaluation, 1959, 68 Yale L.J. 633.

9. Blyth v. Topham, 1607, Cro.Jac. 158, 79 Eng.Rep. 139 ("for he shows not any right why his mare should be in the said common, and the digging of the pit is lawful as against him"); Yalowizer v. Husky Oil Co., Wyo.1981, 629 P.2d 465; Champlin v. Walker, Iowa 1977, 249 N.W.2d 839 (maintaining unguarded excavation not "wanton").

10. See Barbre v. Indianapolis Water Co., 1980, ___ Ind.App. ___, 400 N.E.2d 1142; Ochampaugh v. City of Seattle, 1979, 91 Wn.2d 514, 588 P.2d 1351 (drowning); Murphy v. Baltimore, Gas & Electric Co., 1981, 290 Md. 186, 428 A.2d 459 (same); Schofield v. Merrill, 1982, 386 Mass. 244, 435 N.E.2d 339.

11. Gramlich v. Wurst, 1878, 86 Pa. 74; Susquehanna Power Co. v. Jeffress, 1930, 159 Md. 465, 150 A. 788 (or an electrical transformer); Murphy v. Baltimore Gas & Electric Co., 1981, 290 Md. 186, 428 A.2d 459. Or a wire cable stretched across a private road. Starr v. Clapp, 1979, 40 N.C.App. 142, 252 S.E.2d 220, affirmed 298 N.C. 275, 258 S.E.2d 348 (struck by motorcycle); Huyck v. Hecla Mining Co., 1980, 101 Idaho 299, 612 P.2d 142 (same).

12. Lary v. Cleveland, Columbus, Cincinnati, & Indianapolis Railway Co., 1881, 78 Ind. 323; Pittsburgh, Fort Wayne, & Chicago Railway Co. v. Bingham, 1876, 29 Ohio St. 364, followed 77 Ohio St. 628, 84 N.E. 1124.

13. Wilson v. City of Long Beach, 1945, 71 Cal.App. 2d 235, 163 P.2d 501; Woodward Iron Co. v. Goolsby, 1942, 242 Ala. 329, 6 So.2d 11.

14. Sawler v. Boston & Albany Railroad Co., 1959, 339 Mass. 34, 157 N.E.2d 516; Reasoner v. Chicago, Rock Island & Pacific Railway Co., 1960, 251 Iowa 506, 101 N.W.2d 739; Davies v. Delaware Lackawanna & Western Railroad Co., 1952, 370 Pa. 180, 87 A.2d 183; Anderson v. Green Bay & Western Railroad, 1980, 99 Wis.2d 514, 299 N.W.2d 615 (no duty to maintain continuous lookout during switching operations); Holland v. Baltimore & Ohio Railroad Co., D.C.App.1981, 431 A.2d 597.

15. See supra, § 57.

16. See Hume v. Hart, 1952, 109 Cal.App.2d 614, 241 P.2d 25; Keep v. Otter Tail Power Co., 1937, 201 Minn. 475, 277 N.W. 213. Compare also the startling accident which befell the uninvited stranger in Cleveland Electric Illuminating Co. v. Van Benshoten, 1929, 120 Ohio St. 438, 166 N.E. 374.

17. Rowland v. Byrd, 1938, 57 Ga.App. 390, 195 S.E. 458; Hanks v. Great Northern Railway Co., 1915, 131 Minn. 281, 154 N.W. 1088. "A landowner may in fact reasonably anticipate an invasion of his property, but in law he is entitled to assume that he will not be interfered with." Guinn v. Delaware & Atlantic Telephone Co., 1905, 72 N.J.L. 276, 278, 62 A. 412.

18. But not an outlaw. See infra, note 39.

19. See infra, § 66.

20. Newman v. Louisville & Nashville Railroad Co., 1925, 212 Ala. 580, 103 So. 856; Castile v. O'Keefe, 1916, 138 La. 479, 70 So. 481. See Peaslee, Duty to Seen Trespassers, 1914, 27 Harv.L.Rev. 403, 406-408.

21. See Gregory v. Johnson, 1981, 159 Ga.App. 320, 283 S.E.2d 357 (2-year-old trespasser fell in unfenced swimming pool), reversed, 1982, 249 Ga. 151, 289 S.E.2d 232; Murphy v. Baltimore Gas & Electric Co., 1981, 290 Md. 186, 428 A.2d 459 (3½ year old drowned); Connecticut v. Pennsylvania Railroad Co., 1927, 288 Pa. 494, 136 A. 779; Santora v. New York, New Haven & Hartford Railroad Co., 1912, 211 Mass. 464, 98 N.E. 90 (child of 27 months); cf. Ochampaugh v. City of Seat-

way of describing the rule and its effect than of accounting for it, since he is quite usually unaware of any risk at all.[22] The true explanation seems to be merely that, in a civilization based on private ownership, it is considered a socially desirable policy to allow a person to use his own land in his own way, without the burden of watching for and protecting those who come there without permission or right.[23]

This is indicated by the prevailing view which refuses to extend the immunity to other defendants who are not in possession of the land.[24] It is shared, of course, by members of the possessor's household,[25] by his servants in the course of their employment, and by contractors who are doing work for him on the land.[26] But other trespassers,[27] adjoining landowners,[28] and even the possessor himself when he carries his activities outside of his premises,[29] are held liable for a failure to exercise reasonable care, notwithstanding the fact that the plaintiff is a trespasser. Although there is authority to the contrary, courts have placed a similar responsibility upon gratuitous licensees,[30] invitees,[31] and the holders of easements, such as power companies stringing wires over the land.[32]

Frequent Trespass on Limited Area

Once the foregoing general rule of nonliability has been stated, the rest of the law of trespassers is a list of exceptions to it. These have developed in many states because of an increasing feeling that human safety is generally of more importance than the defendant's interest in unrestricted freedom to make use of his land as he sees fit, which usually has meant no more than his desire to be free from all burden of trouble and expense in taking precautions. If that burden is very slight, and if the risk of harm to trespassers is correspondingly very great, there may be good reason to hold the defendant liable. This has been true first of all in the case of frequent trespass upon a limited area.

Where, to the knowledge of the occupier of the land, trespassers in substantial num-

---

tle, 1979, 91 Wn.2d 514, 588 P.2d 1351 (6 and 8-year-old boys drowned in pond).

22. See infra, § 68.

23. See McPheters v. Loomis, 1939, 125 Conn. 526, 7 A.2d 437; Bagby v. Kansas City, 1936, 338 Mo. 771, 92 S.W.2d 142; Anderson v. Green Bay & Western Railroad, 1980, 99 Wis.2d 514, 299 N.W.2d 615, 617 ("If the railroad were to check between and around all cars prior to * * * its switching operation, an extremely large crew would be required."); cf. Ochampaugh v. City of Seattle, 1979, 91 Wn.2d 514, 588 P.2d 1351, 1358.

24. See Notes, 1929, 77 U.Pa.L.Rev. 506; 1937, 21 Minn.L.Rev. 333.

25. Sohn v. Katz, 1934, 112 N.J.L. 106, 169 A. 838; Second Restatement of Torts, § 382.

26. Hamakawa v. Crescent Wharf & Warehouse Co., 1935, 4 Cal.2d 499, 50 P.2d 803; Mikaelian v. Palaza, 1938, 300 Mass. 354, 15 N.E.2d 480; Ireland v. Complete Machinery & Equipment Co., 1940, 174 Misc. 91, 21 N.Y.S.2d 430; Hollett v. Dundee, Inc., D.Del. 1967, 272 F.Supp. 1.

27. Second Restatement of Torts, § 381.

28. Fitzpatrick v. Penfield, 1920, 267 Pa. 564, 109 A. 653; Wilson v. American Bridge Co., 1902, 74 App.Div. 596, 77 N.Y.S. 820.

29. Ehret v. Village of Scarsdale, 1935, 269 N.Y. 198, 199 N.E. 56 (pipes laid in street). See Notes, 1936, 84 U.Pa.L.Rev. 795; 49 Harv.L.Rev. 1010.

30. Edwards v. Kansas City, 1919, 104 Kan. 684, 180 P. 271; Law v. Railway Express Agency, 1st Cir. 1940, 111 F.2d 427. See Hart, Injuries to Trespassers, 1931, 47 L.Q.Rev. 92.

Contra, Parshall v. Lapeer Gas-Electric Co., 1924, 228 Mich. 80, 199 N.W. 599; Stansfield v. Chesapeake & Potomac Telephone Co., 1914, 123 Md. 120, 91 A. 149.

31. Lewis v. I. M. Shapiro Co., 1945, 132 Conn. 342, 44 A.2d 124; O'Gara v. Philadelphia Electric Co., 1914, 244 Pa. 156, 90 A. 529.

Contra: Louisville Trust Co. v. Horn, 1925, 209 Ky. 827, 273 S.W. 549; Kirkpatrick v. Damianakes, 1936, 15 Cal.App.2d 446, 59 P.2d 556. See Note, 1937, 21 Minn. L.Rev. 338.

32. Humphrey v. Twin State Gas & Electric Co., 1927, 100 Vt. 414, 139 A. 440; Langazo v. San Joaquin Light & Power Corp., 1939, 32 Cal.App.2d 678, 90 P.2d 825; Blackwell v. Alabama Power Co., 1963, 275 Ala. 123, 152 So.2d 670.

Contra, on the ground that the easement holder had the right to exclude the trespasser from his easement: Kesterson v. California-Oregon Power Co., 1924, 114 Or. 22, 228 P. 1092; Roe v. Narragansett Electric Co., 1933, 53 R.I. 342, 166 A. 695.

ber [33] are in the habit of entering it at a particular point, or of traversing an area of small size, the burden of looking out for them is reduced, and the risk of harm perhaps increased, so that many courts have held that there is a duty of reasonable care to discover and protect them in the course of activities which the defendant carries on.[34] The typical case is that of frequent use of a particular part of a railroad track, as where a "beaten path" crosses it, which is held to impose a duty of reasonable care as to the operation of trains.[35] While there are fewer cases, some courts have imposed a similar duty as to dangerous passive conditions known to the possessor, such as concealed high tension wires.[36] There has been some effort to explain the liability in such cases by saying that the defendant's continued toleration of the trespass amounts to permission to make use of the land, so that the plaintiff is not a trespasser but a licensee.[37] While it is undoubtedly true that a failure to object may amount to tacit permission,[38] it seems clear that the mere fact the landowner does not take burdensome and expensive precautions, which may well be futile, to keep trespassers out, does not in itself indicate that he is willing to have them enter.[39] The real basis of liability to such "tolerated intruders" would seem to be only the ordinary duty to protect another, where the harm to be anticipated from a risk for which the defendant is responsible outweighs the inconvenience of guarding against it.[40]

Discovered Trespassers

The most important exception as to the adult trespasser rule is the requirement that the occupier exercise reasonable care for his

---

33. One court which attempted to be more specific is Kentucky, which held that fewer than 150 persons a day, at a point on a railroad track, is not enough. Louisville & Nashville Railroad Co. v. Jones, 1944, 297 Ky. 528, 180 S.W.2d 555; Deitz v. Cincinnati, New Orleans & Texas Pacific Railway Co., 1943, 269 Ky. 279, 176 S.W.2d 699 (75 a day). Where larger numbers were involved, recovery was allowed, in Louisville & Nashville Railroad Co. v. Spoonamore, 1939, 278 Ky. 673, 129 S.W.2d 175. In Wise v. Chicago, Rock Island & Pacific Railway Co., 1934, 335 Mo. 1168, 76 S.W.2d 118, the presence of a path across the track was held sufficient evidence of frequent use.

34. The Second Restatement of Torts, § 334, speaks in terms of "highly dangerous" activities. Many of the earlier cases involved railroad trains, and extended the burden of precaution to any part of the land where the trespasser could be anticipated. See Pickett v. Wilmington & Weldon Railroad Co., 1895, 117 N.C. 616, 23 S.E. 264; Gulf, Colorado & Sante Fe Railway Co. v. Russell, 1935, 125 Tex. 443, 82 S.W.2d 948; Tillman v. Public Belt Railroad Commission, La.App.1949, 42 So. 2d 888; cf. Renz v. Penn Central Corp., 1981, 87 N.J. 437, 435 A.2d 540.

Most of the decisions, however, have held that the railroads should not be required to watch every mile of track for the protection of those who have no right to be there. E.g., State for Use of Anderson v. Baltimore & Ohio Railroad Co., 1924, 144 Md. 571, 125 A. 393; Capitula v. New York Central Railroad Co., 1925, 213 App.Div. 526, 210 N.Y.S. 651. See Note, 1947, 22 St. John's L.Rev. 118.

35. See id. See also Southern Railway Co. v. Campbell, 5th Cir. 1962, 309 F.2d 569; Cheslock v. Pittsburgh Railways Co., 1949, 363 Pa. 157, 69 A.2d 108; Carter v. Seaboard Air Line Railway Co., 1950, 114 S.C. 517, 104 S.E. 186.

36. Clark v. Longview Public Service Co., 1927, 143 Wash. 319, 255 P. 380. See also Imre v. Riegel Paper Corp., 1957, 24 N.J. 438, 132 A.2d 505; Franc v. Pennsylvania Railroad Co., 1967, 424 Pa. 99, 225 A.2d 528; Hanson v. Bailey, 1957, 249 Minn. 495, 83 N.W.2d 252; Wood v. State Through Dept. of Highways, La.App. 1974, 295 So.2d 78, writ denied 295 So.2d 446 (sawhorse on closed highway); Second Restatement of Torts, § 335.

But see Murphy v. Baltimore Gas & Electric Co., 1981, 290 Md. 186, 428 A.2d 459 (swimmers at abandoned quarry pond); Smith v. Goldman, 1977, 53 Ill. App.3d 632, 11 Ill.Dec. 444, 368 N.E.2d 1052 (sharp object in water: no duty).

37. Libby v. West Coast Rock Co., Fla.App.1975, 308 So.2d 602; Mentesana v. LaFranco, 1979, 73 Ill. App. 204, 29 Ill.Dec. 153, 391 N.E.2d 416 (short cut across gas station; but duty no higher to licensee than trespasser); Smith v. Philadelphia & Reading Railway Co., 1922, 274 Pa. 97, 117 A. 786.

38. See Lodge v. Pittsburgh & Lake Erie Railroad Co., 1914, 243 Pa. 10, 89 A. 790; Bosiljevac v. Ready Mixed Concrete Co., 1967, 182 Neb. 199, 153 N.W.2d 864 (implied invitation).

39. See Denton v. L. W. Vail Co., 1975, 23 Or.App. 28, 541 P.2d 511; Mentesana v. LaFranco, 1979, 73 Ill. App. 204, 29 Ill.Dec. 153, 391 N.E.2d 416 (habitual acquiescence in trespass does not raise duty to ordinary care); Earnest v. Regent Pool, Inc., 1972, 288 Ala. 63, 257 So.2d 313 (toleration of trespassers does not alter their status); Eldredge, Tort Liability to Trespassers, 1937, 12 Temple L.Q. 32, 34–38.

40. Green, Landowner v. Intruder; Intruder v. Landowner, 1923, 21 Mich.L.Rev. 495, 57 Am.L.Rev. 321.

safety once his presence is known. This is lineally descended from the older rule, that the possessor of land was not free to inflict unreasonable intentional injury upon his unwelcome visitor. A trespasser, while he may be a wrongdoer, is not an outlaw,[41] and an intentional, unprivileged battery upon him was too much to be tolerated even by the great veneration of the English courts for rights in land. The defendant was not permitted to set traps for the trespasser,[42] or to use unreasonable force to expel him from the premises.[43] Nor, in later cases, was he allowed to injure him negligently by an act specifically directed toward him,[44] or recklessly by conduct in conscious disregard of his peril.[45] Thus the rule which has come down, and which is stated often, whether the trespasser has been discovered or not, is that the landowner owes no duty to a trespasser except to refrain from injuring him by "willful or wanton" conduct.[46]

Some courts have stopped at this point, and have refused to find any liability to the trespasser, even after his presence is known, unless such "willful or wanton" conduct is found.[47] Certain of these courts have retreated from this position by the expedient, also adopted in other types of cases,[48] of questionably defining "willful or wanton" to include any failure to use ordinary care after it is discovered that the trespasser is there.[49] Other courts have discarded "willful or wanton" entirely as a limitation, and have said outright that once the presence of the trespasser is discovered, there is a duty to use ordinary care to avoid injuring him. The defendant is thereupon required to govern his active conduct, such as running a train,[50] conducting a circus,[51] or operating an elevator,[52] with the caution of a reasonable person for the trespasser's safety.[53]

41. Schofield v. Merrill, 1982, 386 Mass. 244, 435 N.E.2d 339, 343; Antoniewicz v. Reszcynski, 1975, 70 Wis.2d 836, 236 N.W.2d 1, 4.

42. See supra, § 21.

43. See supra, § 21.

44. Palmer v. Gordon, 1899, 173 Mass. 410, 53 N.E. 909; Magar v. Hammond, 1906, 183 N.Y. 387, 76 N.E. 474.

45. Aiken v. Holyoke Street Railway Co., 1903, 184 Mass. 269, 68 N.E. 238; Trico Coffee Co. v. Clemens, 1933, 168 Miss. 748, 151 So. 175. Cf. Bremer v. Lake Erie & Western Railroad Co., 1925, 318 Ill. 11, 148 N.E. 862 (reckless conduct, trespasser undiscovered).

46. E.g., Schofield v. Merrill, 1982, 386 Mass. 244, 435 N.E.2d 339; Votava v. Material Service Corp., 1979, 74 Ill.App.3d 208, 30 Ill.Dec. 113, 392 N.E.2d 768; Payne v. M. Greenberg Construction, App.1981, 130 Ariz. 338, 636 P.2d 116; Huyck v. Hecla Mining Co., 1980, 101 Idaho 299, 612 P.2d 142; Ochampaugh v. City of Seattle, 1979, 91 Wn.2d 514, 588 P.2d 1351; Hughes v. Star Homes, Miss.1980, 379 So.2d 301; Renz v. Penn Central Corp., 1981, 87 N.J. 437, 435 A.2d 540; Holland v. Baltimore & Ohio Railroad Co., D.C.App.1981, 431 A.2d 597; Murphy v. Baltimore Gas & Electric Co., 1981, 290 Md. 186, 428 A.2d 459.

The "willful or wanton" element does not necessarily require active conduct, but may be found in an omission to remedy a highly dangerous condition or to give warning of it. Blaylock v. Malernee, 1939, 185 Okl. 381, 92 P.2d 357; Romana v. Boston Elevated Railway Co., 1917, 226 Mass. 532, 116 N.E. 218.

For definitions of "willful or wanton," see Starr v. Clapp, 1979, 40 N.C.App. 142, 252 S.E.2d 220, affirmed 298 N.C. 275, 258 S.E.2d 348; Yalowizer v. Husky Oil Co., Wyo.1981, 629 P.2d 465; Coleman v. Associated Pipeline Contractors, Inc., 5th Cir. 1971, 444 F.2d 737.

47. See Nalepinski v. Durner, 1951, 259 Wis. 583, 49 N.W.2d 601; Columbus Mining Co. v. Napier's Administrator, 1931, 239 Ky. 642, 40 S.W.2d 285; Oliver v. City of Atlanta, 1978, 147 Ga.App. 790, 250 S.E.2d 519; Hughes v. Star Homes, Miss.1980, 379 So.2d 301; Earnest v. Regent Pool, Inc., 1972, 288 Ala. 63, 257 So.2d 313; Fitzgerald v. Montgomery County Board of Education, 1975, 25 Md.App. 709, 336 A.2d 795, 798.

48. See supra, § 34.

49. Frederick v. Philadelphia Rapid Transit Co., 1940, 337 Pa. 136, 10 A.2d 576; Tempfer v. Joplin & Pittsburg Railway Co., 1913, 89 Kan. 374, 131 P. 592. Compare Starr v. Clapp, 1979, 40 N.C.App. 142, 252 S.E.2d 220, affirmed, 298 N.C. 275, 258 S.E.2d 348 (jury stretched "willful and wanton" to allow recovery and court reversed).

50. Gulf & Ship Island Railroad Co. v. Williamson, 1932, 162 Miss. 726, 139 So. 601; Denver & Rio Grande Western Railroad Co. v. Clint, 10th Cir. 1956, 235 F.2d 445. Cf. McManus v. Rogers, 1959, 106 App.D.C. 369, 273 F.2d 104 (automobile); Nielsen v. Henry H. Stevens, Inc., 1960, 359 Mich. 130, 101 N.W.2d 284 (truck).

51. Herrick v. Wixom, 1899, 121 Mich. 384, 80 N.W. 117, affirmed 121 Mich. 384, 81 N.W. 333. Cf. Fernan-

52, 53. See notes 52 & 53 on page 398.

The discovered trespasser is owed the higher duty when he is perceived to be in a situation of peril or possible danger [54] — whether or not the defendant is aware that he is a trespasser, as where a boy has crawled under a circus tent and become one of the crowd.[55] But it is not essential that his presence actually be perceived. It is enough that the defendant is notified, by information which would lead a reasonable person to conclude that a person is there, or to proceed upon that assumption.[56] There is, however, some authority that the defendant must at least have reason to think that an object which he has discovered may be a human being, or valuable property,[57] so that something unidentified ahead on a railroad track which looks like a discarded bundle of waste paper will not necessarily call for slowing down,[58] unless there is something about the situation, such as its locality, to suggest a risk that the thing is a person.[59]

Whether the duty to the discovered trespasser extends to warning or otherwise protecting him against a purely passive condition of the premises was for a long time uncertain. A well-known old New Hampshire case [60] held that there was no more obligation to rescue the trespasser from peril than to rescue any other stranger. But the Restatement of Torts [61] and some courts [62] have disagreed, taking the position that possession of the land carries with it the duty to see that any artificial and dangeorus conditions do not become instruments of harm to others, and that the discovery makes requirement of a warning reasonable. Many courts now hold that the landowner has a duty of care to the discovered trespasser at least in his active conduct, including the operation of his machinery,[63] and it is now fre-

dez v. Consolidated Fisheries, 1950, 98 Cal.App.2d 91, 219 P.2d 73 (delivering fish); Lyshak v. City of Detroit, 1958, 351 Mich. 230, 88 N.W.2d 596 (driving golf ball).

52. Pridgen v. Boston Housing Authority, Mass. 1974, 364 Mass. 696, 308 N.E.2d 467; Davis' Administrator v. Ohio Valley Banking & Trust Co., 1908, 127 Ky. 800, 106 S.W. 843.

53. Scheibel v. Hillis, Mo.1976, 531 S.W.2d 285, appeal after remand 570 S.W.2d 724; Surratt v. Petrol, Inc., 1974, 160 Ind.App. 479, 316 N.E.2d 453 (active, affirmative or positive conduct); Atlanta Funtown, Inc. v. Crouch, 1966, 114 Ga.App. 702, 152 S.E.2d 583.

54. See Louisville & Nashville Railroad Co. v. Vanderpool, Ky.1973, 496 S.W.2d 349; Medi-Clean Services, Inc. v. Hill, 1977, 144 Ga.App. 389, 241 S.E.2d 290. A "position of peril" means only that the trespasser may be injured if the defendant is negligent. Beverly Bank v. Penn Central Co., 1974, 21 Ill.App.3d 77, 315 N.E.2d 110; Kakluskas v. Somers Motor Lines, 1947, 134 Conn. 35, 54 A.2d 592. "[W]here a trespasser is in a position of peril * * * and his presence becomes known, the owner then has a duty to use reasonable care * * * in the circumstances." Pridgen v. Boston Housing Authority, 1974, 364 Mass. 696, 308 N.E. 2d 467.

55. Herrick v. Wixom, 1899, 121 Mich. 384, 80 N.W. 117, affirmed 121 Mich. 384, 81 N.W. 333; Cleveland-Cliffs Iron Co. v. Metzner, 6th Cir. 1945, 150 F.2d 206.

56. Frederick v. Philadelphia Rapid Transit Co., 1940, 337 Pa. 136, 10 A.2d 576 (tripping device, and warning of man under train); Lavallee v. Pratt, 1960, 122 Vt. 90, 166 A.2d 195 (on information available defendant required to "know or apprehend"). Cf. Kumkumian v. City of New York, 1953, 305 N.Y. 167, 111 N.E.2d 865.

57. Haskins v. Grybko, 1938, 301 Mass. 322, 17 N.E.2d 146 (shooting at object believed to be a wild animal).

58. Missouri Pacific Railway Co. v. Gordon, 1939, 186 Okl. 424, 98 P.2d 39; Cochran v. Thompson, 1941, 347 Mo. 649, 148 S.W.2d 532; Southern Railway Co. v. Wahl, 1925, 196 Ind. 581, 149 N.E. 72.

59. See Jones v. Chicago, Rock Island & Pacific Railway Co., 1946, 4 La.App. 457 (locality); Hyde v. Union Pacific Railroad Co., 1891, 7 Utah 356, 26 P. 979 (place frequented by children); Owen v. Delano, Mo. App.1917, 194 S.W. 756 (locality); Norfolk & Western Railway Co. v. Henderson, 1922, 132 Va. 297, 111 S.E. 277 (locality).

60. Buch v. Amory Manufacturing Co., 1897, 69 N.H. 257, 44 A. 809. See also Carroll v. Spencer, 1954, 204 Md. 387, 104 A.2d 628 (no duty at least where the peril is not imminent). Cf. Votava v. Material Service Corp., 1979, 74 Ill.App.3d 208, 30 Ill.Dec. 113, 392 N.E.2d 768.

61. Second Restatement of Torts, § 337 (with a caveat, however, as to natural conditions).

62. See Martin v. Jones, 1953, 122 Utah 597, 253 P.2d 359, conformed to 123 Utah 603, 261 P.2d 174; Gaylord Container Corp. v. Miley, 5th Cir. 1956, 230 F.2d 177; Appling v. Stuck, Iowa 1969, 164 N.W.2d 810; Nolan v. Roberts, Fla.App.1980, 383 So.2d 945, review denied 401 So.2d 1338 (sharply pointed plant; but no duty to warn of known or obvious danger); cf. Latimer v. City of Clovis, App.1972, 83 N.M. 610, 495 P.2d 788 (swimming pool).

63. See Anderson v. Green Bay & Western Railroad, 1980, 99 Wis.2d 514, 299 N.W.2d 615 (dictum); Bethay v. Philadelphia Housing Authority, 1979, 271 Pa.Super. 366, 413 A.2d 710 (employee pushed elevator

quently stated as a general principle that the landowner has a duty to warn of hidden dangers known to the landowner but not to the trespasser.[64]

The obligation is of course only to exercise reasonable care under the circumstances.[65] Thus the engineer of a train who discovers a trespasser ahead on the track may ordinarily assume that he is in possession of his faculties, and that after proper warning he will remove himself to safety.[66] It is only when it becomes apparent that he is insensible[67] or otherwise helpless,[68] or that the warning has not been heard,[69] that something more than the whistle is required.

 WESTLAW REFERENCES

digest(owner* occupier* possessor* /5 land premises /s trespass! /s duty)

Frequent Trespass on Limited Area
frequent** /1 trespass!
headnote(trespass! /s duty /s owner* occupier* possessor*)

Discovered Trespassers
discovered /9 trespasser*
presence /3 trespasser*

§ 59. Trespassing Children

When the trespasser is a child, one important reason for the general rule of nonliability may be lacking. Because of his immaturity and want of judgment, the child may be incapable of perceiving and appreciating all of the possible dangers which he may encounter in trespassing, or of making his own intelligent decisions as to the chances he will take. While it is true that his parents or guardians are charged with the duty of looking out for him, it is obviously neither customary nor practicable for them to follow him around with a keeper, or to chain him to the bedpost. The landowner or occupier,[1] rather than the parent, is often in the best position to protect the straying child against perils on the land.[2] Also to be considered is the fundamental social interest in maintaining the safety and welfare of children. On the other hand, the burden of making the premises safe against harm to the child is usually no less than in the case of an adult, and is often a great deal heavier. But the interest in unrestricted freedom to make use of the land may be required, within reasonable limits, to give way to the greater social interest in the safety of the child. The

---

button after being informed that children were playing on top); Farrior v. Payton, 1977, 57 Hawaii 620, 562 P.2d 779; Castonguay v. Acme Knitting Machine & Needle Co., 1927, 83 N.H. 1, 136 A. 702; Second Restatement of Torts, §§ 336, 338.

Contra, in some states, as to passive or natural conditions. Odar v. Chase Manhattan Bank, 1976, 138 N.J.Super. 464, 351 A.2d 389. And recall the general rule of limited liability stated by many courts. See supra, note 45.

64. See generally Bovino v. Metropolitan Dade County, Fla.App.1980, 378 So.2d 50 (no duty to warn of danger known to trespasser); Nolan v. Roberts, Fla.App.1980, 383 So.2d 945, review denied 401 So.2d 1338 (same; passive condition); Joyce v. Nash, Mo.App. 1982, 630 S.W.2d 219, 223 n. 1 (no duty unless presence known). But cf. Rowland v. City of Corpus Christi, Tex.Civ.App.1981, 620 S.W.2d 930, refused n. r. e. (duty to warn licensees, but not trespassers, of hazards known to landowner).

65. See Joyce v. Nash, Mo.App.1982, 630 S.W.2d 219 (making customary round of commercial premises sufficient precaution against presence of trespassers before release of vicious guard dogs).

66. Campbell v. Kansas City, Ft. Scott & Memphis Railroad Co., 1895, 55 Kan. 536, 40 P. 997; Lawrence v. Bamberger Railroad Co., 1955, 3 Utah 2d 247, 282 P.2d 335.

67. Tyson v. East Carolina Railroad Co., 1914, 167 N.C. 215, 83 S.E. 318 (drunk); Bragg v. Central New England Railroad Co., 1920, 228 N.Y. 54, 126 N.E. 253 (asleep).

68. Chicago Terminal Transfer Railroad Co. v. Kotoski, 1902, 199 Ill. 383, 65 N.E. 350 (on trestle); Pollard v. Nicholls, 5th Cir. 1938, 99 F.2d 955 (on a horse).

69. Yazoo & Mississippi Valley Railroad Co. v. Lee, 1927, 148 Miss. 809, 114 So. 866; Russo v. Texas & Pacific Railway Co., 1938, 189 La. 1042, 181 So. 485.

§ 59

1. See Brady v. Skinner, App.1982, 132 Ariz. 425, 646 P.2d 310 (attractive nuisance doctrine applicable only to possessors; landlord not liable for kicking mule). But see Duggan v. Esposito, 1979, 178 Conn. 156, 422 A.2d 287 (subcontractor held to same standard of care as possessor under § 339).

2. See Pasierb v. Hanover Park Park District, 1981, 103 Ill.App.3d 806, 59 Ill.Dec. 461, 431 N.E.2d 1218. But see Campbell v. Northern Signal Co., 1981, 103 Ill. App.3d 154, 58 Ill.Dec. 638, 430 N.E.2d 670.

struggle in the courts has been to arrive at some reasonable compromise between these conflicting interests between the freedom of land use and the protection of children.[3]

Although it was foreshadowed in England,[4] the special rule as to trespassing children first appeared in 1873 in the Supreme Court of the United States,[5] where recovery was allowed, virtually without discussion, when a child trespassed on railroad land and was injured while playing with a turntable. The situation was repeated, and the rule first clearly stated, two years later in Minnesota.[6] In this second opinion the court displayed a great deal of ingenuity in inventing the theory that the child had been allured or enticed upon the land by the turntable "as a bait attracts a fish or a piece of stinking meat draws a dog,"[7] so that the defendant himself was considered responsible for the trespass, and therefore could not be allowed to use it defensively against the child. From these decisions, and others like them, the rule became known as the "turntable doctrine"; and from the second one it acquired the name of "attractive nuisance."[8]

Almost from the beginning the new rule met with vigorous opposition on the part of some of the courts, who denounced it, sometimes in quite unrestrained language,[9] as a barefaced fiction and a piece of sentimental humanitarianism, founded on sympathy rather than law or logic, which imposed an undue burden upon landowners and industry by giving the jury a free hand to express its feelings for the injured child out of the defendant's pocketbook. The number of such jurisdictions has diminished in recent years as more and more courts have embraced the attractive nuisance doctrine,[10] and today there are only three or four courts which still purport to reject the special rule with-

---

3. Smith, Liability of Landowners to Children Entering Without Permission, 1898, 11 Harv.L.Rev. 349, 434; Eldredge, Tort Liability to Trespassers, 1937, 12 Temple L.Q. 32; Green, Landowners' Responsibility to Children, 1948, 27 Tex.L.Rev. 1; James, Tort Liability of Occupiers of Land: Duties Owed to Trespassers, 1953, 63 Yale L.J. 144; Prosser, Trespassing Children, 1959, 47 Cal.L.Rev. 427; Reynolds, Attractive Nuisance: More Nuisance Than Attraction, 1973, 26 Okla. L.Rev. 342, reprinted 1973 Ins.L.J. 671; Lynch, The Landowner's Dilemma—The Infant Trespasser, 1976, 11 Trial L.Q. 26 (No. 4, Winter) New York.

4. In Lynch v. Nurdin, 1841, 1 Q.B. 29, 113 Eng. Rep. 1041, where a child was hurt as the result of tampering with a negligently loaded cart on the highway. The English courts, however, have not traditionally accorded the child trespasser special status, except in liberally finding some "implied" license or invitation that would change the child's status to a licensee or invitee. The child trespasser's status was reevaluated and improved somewhat by the House of Lords in British Railways Board v. Herrington, [1972] A.C. 877. See Rogers, Winfield & Jolowicz on Tort, 11th ed. 1979, ch. 10.

5. Sioux City & Pacific Railroad Co. v. Stout, 1873, 84 U.S. (17 Wall.) 657, 21 L.Ed. 745.

6. Keffe v. Milwaukee & St. Paul Railway Co., 1875, 21 Minn. 207.

7. 1 Thompson, Negligence, 1st ed. 1886, 305. There is an obvious effort to find an analogy to such cases as Townsend v. Wathen, 1808, 9 East 277, 103 Eng.Rep. 579, where baited traps were set for plaintiff's dogs. Cf. Buckeye Cotton Oil Co. v. Horton, 1915, 117 Ark. 1, 173 S.W. 423; Williams Estate Co. v. Nevada Wonder Mining Co., 1921, 45 Nev. 25, 196 P. 844.

8. "Nuisance" because of a supposed analogy to conditions dangerous to children in the highway or otherwise outside of the premises; "attractive" because it was thought essential that the child be allured onto the premises. Although the doctrine has generally broadened in recent years, as discussed below, most courts have retained the "attractive nuisance" terminology because it captures so much of the essence of the current doctrine. See, e.g., Barnhizer v. Paradise Valley Unified School District, 1979, 123 Ariz. 253, 599 P.2d 209 (applying principles of Second Restatement of Torts, § 339); Lister v. Campbell, Fla.App.1979, 371 So.2d 133 (same); Burk Royalty Co. v. Pace, Tex.Civ. App.1981, 620 S.W.2d 882 (same); Gerchberg v. Loney, 1978, 223 Kan. 446, 576 P.2d 593; Christians v. Homestake Enterprises, Limited, 1981, 101 Wis.2d 25, 303 N.W.2d 608, 609 (calling "attractive nuisance" a "misnomer," but retaining the phrase); Metropolitan Government of Nashville v. Counts, Tenn.1976, 541 S.W.2d 133 (same).

9. The classic denunciation is in Ryan v. Towar, 1901, 128 Mich. 463, 87 N.W. 644. See also Bottum's Administrator v. Hawks, 1911, 84 Vt. 370, 79 A. 858; Frost v. Eastern Railroad Co., 1886, 64 N.H. 220, 9 A. 790.

10. For recent examples, see Jones v. Billings, Me. 1972, 289 A.2d 39; Haddad v. First National Stores, 1971, 109 R.I. 59, 280 A.2d 93; Gregory v. Johnson, 1982, 249 Ga. 151, 289 S.E.2d 232. Massachusetts adopted a special child trespasser rule by statute in 1977. See Soule v. Massachusetts Electric Co., 1979, 378 Mass. 177, 390 N.E.2d 716.

out qualification.[11] Even some of these proceed to apply it when the child is injured while climbing on a chattel in the street,[12] usually upon the rather weak ground that he is then "where he has a right to be." Since he has no more right to be upon the truck, the power line pole, or the lumber pile than upon the land, this appears in reality to represent a half-hearted acceptance of the principle, which may in time lead to full recognition.

As a logical consequence of the "attraction" theory, the Supreme Court, in a much criticized opinion of Mr. Justice Holmes,[13] held that a child could not recover when he was not induced to trespass by the presence of the pool of poisoned water that killed him, but discovered it only after he had come upon the land. Thirteen years later the decision apparently was overruled;[14] but in the meantime this limitation on the doctrine had been accepted and followed by a number of other courts. It has now been rejected by a large majority of courts, and there remain only a handful of jurisdictions which still adhere to it.[15] Early in the twenties a different theory began to gain ground[16] as a justification for the liability to the child, which discarded the necessity of allurement, enticement or attraction onto the land, and considered that this was important only in so far as it meant that the trespass was to be anticipated.[17] The basis of the liability was thought to be little more than the foreseeability of harm to the child, and the considerations of social policy which, in other negligence cases, operate to bring about a balancing of the conflicting interests, and to curtail to a reasonable extent the defendant's privilege to act as he sees fit without regard to the effects on others. In other words, child trespasser law began to be viewed as essentially ordinary negligence law, and the fact that the child was a trespasser merely one fact to be taken into account, with others, in determining the defendant's duty, and the care required of him.[18] The result has been a compromise between the conflicting interests,[19] which gives the child trespasser much of the protection of

11. Murphy v. Baltimore Gas & Electric Co., 1981, 290 Md. 186, 428 A.2d 459; McKenzie v. Fairmont Food Co., W.D.Ohio 1969, 305 F.Supp. 163; Trudo v. Lazarus, 1950, 116 Vt. 221, 73 A.2d 306; Devost v. Twin State Gas & Electric Co., 1920, 79 N.Y. 411, 109 A. 839. But cf. Labore v. Davison Construction Co., 1957, 101 N.H. 123, 135 A.2d 591; Winslow v. Mahfuz, 1963, 105 N.H. 114, 193 A.2d 882.

Several jurisdictions have kept the special rule quite narrow and close to the original turntable doctrine, as by limiting its application to inherently "dangerous instrumentalities." E.g., Hughes v. Star Homes, Inc., Miss.1980, 379 So.2d 301; Kesner v. Trenton, 1975, ___ W.Va. ___, 216 S.E.2d 880; cf. Foster v. Alabama Power Co., Ala.1981, 395 So.2d 27; McKenzie v. Fairmont Food Co., W.D.Ohio 1969, 305 F.Supp. 163.

12. Pindell v. Rubinstein, 1921, 139 Md. 567, 115 A. 859; De Groodt v. Skrbina, 1924, 111 Ohio St. 108, 144 N.E. 601; cf. Rine v. Morris, 1925, 99 W.Va. 52, 127 S.E. 908.

13. United Zinc & Chemical Co. v. Britt, 1921, 258 U.S. 268, 42 S.Ct. 299, 66 L.Ed. 615.

14. In Best v. District of Columbia, 1934, 291 U.S. 411, 54 S.Ct. 487, 78 L.Ed. 882. The *Britt* case was cited with apparent approval, but the decision is quite inconsistent with it, and later cases have said it is overruled. See McGettigan v. National Bank of Washington, 1963, 115 App.D.C. 384, 320 F.2d 703, certiorari denied 375 U.S. 943, 84 S.Ct. 348, 11 L.Ed.2d 273.

15. See, e.g., Foster v. Alabama Power Co., Ala. 1981, 395 So.2d 27; Johnson v. Bathey, Fla.1979, 376 So.2d 848, criticized in Note, 1980, 8 Fla.St.U.L.Rev. 577; cf. Lanier v. North Carolina State Highway Commission, 1976, 31 N.C.App. 304, 229 S.E.2d 321 (dictum); Ausmer v. Sliman, Miss.1976, 336 So.2d 730. Tennessee still adheres to this requirement but ameliorates it by its "playground doctrine." See Metropolitan Government of Nashville v. Counts, Tenn.1976, 541 S.W.2d 133.

16. Largely under the impetus of two noted law review articles: Green, Landowner v. Intruder; Intruder v. Landowner: Basis of Responsibility in Tort, 1923, 21 Mich.L.Rev. 495, 57 Am.L.Rev. 321; Hudson, The Turntable Doctrine in the Federal Courts, 1923, 36 Harv.L.Rev. 826.

17. More recently, see Burk Royalty Co. v. Pace, Tex.Civ.App.1981, 620 S.W.2d 882; Glastris v. Union Electric Co., Mo.App.1976, 542 S.W.2d 65; Niemann v. Vermilion County Housing Authority, 1981, 101 Ill. App.3d 735, 57 Ill.Dec. 156, 428 N.E.2d 706.

18. See Soule v. Massachusetts Electric Co., 1979, 378 Mass. 177, 390 N.E.2d 716 (adopting duty of reasonable care); Peterson v. Taylor, Iowa 1982, 316 N.W.2d 869 (instructions on ordinary negligence, instead of attractive nuisance, sufficient).

19. Hughes v. Star Homes, Inc., Miss.1980, 379 So. 2d 301.

ordinary negligence doctrine.[20] And even if the child fails for some reason or another to qualify for special treatment under the attractive nuisance principles, the landowner or occupier will still owe the child the same limited duty owed generally to trespassers to refrain from injuring him by willful or wanton misconduct.[21]

In 1934 the Restatement of Torts, in what has proved to be one of its most effective single sections,[22] threw its support behind the special duty rules for child trespassers. It discarded the idea of allurement to trespass, and defined the "attractive nuisance" rule in general negligence terms. Section 339, as modified in the Second Restatement,[23] has been cited so frequently, and has received such general acceptance on the part of the courts, that it has become the new point of departure.[24]

"The decisions show an effort to hammer out a compromise between the interest of society in preserving the safety of its children and the legitimate interest of landowners to use their land for their own purposes with reasonable freedom, and so are naturally in a state of flux and motion." Bohlen, The Duty of a Landowner Towards Those Entering His Premises of Their Own Right, 1921, 69 U.Pa.L.Rev. 142, 237, 340, 348.

20. Cf. Ochampaugh v. City of Seattle, 1979, 91 Wn. 2d 514, 588 P.2d 1351, 1358 (but defendant not negligent on facts).

21. Partin v. Olney, App.1979, 121 Ariz. 448, 591 P.2d 74; see Ochampaugh v. City of Seattle, 1979, 91 Wn.2d 514, 588 P.2d 1351, 1359–60 (dissent); Foster v. Alabama Power Co., Ala.1981, 395 So.2d 27.

22. Restatement of Torts, § 339. See Gladstone, The Supreme Court of Pennsylvania and Section 339 of the Restatement of Torts, 1965, 113 U.Pa.L.Rev. 563.

23. Discussed, in its earlier drafting stages, in Prosser, Trespassing Children, 1959, 47 Cal.L.Rev. 427.

24. See, e.g., Gregory v. Johnson, 1982, 249 Ga. 151, 289 S.E.2d 232; Crawford v. Pacific Western Mobile Estates, Inc., Mo.App.1977, 548 S.W.2d 216 (thorough application of § 339 to facts); Christians v. Homestakes Enterprises, Limited, 1981, 101 Wis.2d 25, 303 N.W.2d 608 (abandoning prior similar doctrine and adopting § 339).

Section 339 of the Second Restatement of Torts, entitled "Artificial Conditions Highly Dangerous to Trespassing Children," provides as follows:

A possessor of land is subject to liability for physical harm to children trespassing thereon caused by an artificial condition upon the land if

Child Trespassing on Defendant's Premises

The Restatement rule is stated in terms of liability to children who are trespassers on premises occupied by the defendant, but the principle may not be so limited. In any case where the child could recover if he were a trespasser, he can recover at least as well when he is a licensee or an invitee [25] on the premises. There are also occasional cases in which the plaintiff is a third person, not upon the land at all, who is injured when the child finds something like a dynamite cap and carries it away. And in some cases the defendant is not the occupier of the premises at the time of the injury. There has been much confusion over whether general negligence principles or the attractive nuisance doctrine should be applied in these situa-

(a) the place where the condition exists is one upon which the possessor knows or has reason to know that children are likely to trespass, and

(b) the condition is one of which the possessor knows or has reason to know and which he realizes or should realize will involve an unreasonable risk of death or serious bodily harm to such children, and

(c) the children because of their youth do not discover the condition or realize the risk involved in intermeddling with it or in coming within the area made dangerous by it, and

(d) the utility to the possessor of maintaining the condition and the burden of eliminating the danger are slight as compared with the risk to children involved, and

(e) the possessor fails to exercise reasonable care to eliminate the danger or otherwise to protect the children.

25. Crawford v. Pacific Western Mobile Estates, Inc., Mo.App.1977, 548 S.W.2d 216, 218 n. 1; Kemline v. Simonds, 1965, 231 Cal.App.2d 165, 41 Cal.Rptr. 653; Gerchberg v. Loney, 1978, 223 Kan. 446, 576 P.2d 593; Gilbert v. Sabin, 1977, 76 Mich.App. 137, 256 N.W.2d 54; Grimes v. Hettinger, Ky.App.1978, 566 S.W.2d 769; Nesmith v. Starr, 1967, 115 Ga.App. 472, 155 S.E.2d 24. Cf. Bazos v. Chouinard, 1981, 96 Ill.App.3d 526, 51 Ill. Dec. 931, 421 N.E.2d 566.

Contra, Williams v. Primary School District No. 3, 1966, 3 Mich.App. 468, 142 N.W.2d 894; McIntyre v. McIntyre, Tenn.1977, 558 S.W.2d 836; Metropolitan Government of Nashville v. Counts, Tenn.1976, 541 S.W.2d 133 (also holding government immune from attractive nuisance actions).

Recreational use statutes, typically limiting liability to cases of willful or wanton misconduct, may not apply to the child at play. See Paige v. North Oaks Part-

tions.[26] Probably the most satisfactory general guideline in such novel contexts is to reserve the more specific doctrine for use in situations where the clash of interests between land use and child protection is brought into sharp relief, and to use the more general negligence principles where these particular interests do not significantly compete.

Artificial Conditions

The Restatement limits its rule to "an artificial condition upon the land." There are a number of decisions involving natural waters,[27] rocks,[28] one involving the "rolling hills" of Tennessee,[29] and a good many more in which artificial ponds and other conditions[30] have duplicated nature, and that fact has been given as one reason among others for denying liability. In all such cases, however, the condition was one which the child might be expected to understand and appreciate,[31] so that, whether natural or artificial, there could be no recovery in any event. The case of the natural condition which the child would not appreciate may not yet have arisen.[32] It is difficult to see why the origin of the condition should in itself be dispositive on liability, if the possessor could easily remove it or protect against it, and fails to do so. But, regardless of its origin, it may not be necessary to liability that the defendant personally have created the condition, or maintained it in any active sense. Accordingly, he has been held liable for conditions created by adjoining landowners,[33] oth-

---

ners, 1982, 134 Cal.App.3d 860, 184 Cal.Rptr. 867 (jumping bike over ditch in shopping center construction project); Smith v. Crown-Zellerbach, Inc., 5th Cir. 1981, 638 F.2d 883; Lacombe v. Greathouse, La.App. 1981, 407 So.2d 1346 (playing in woods); see West's Wash.Rev.Code Ann. §§ 4.24.200–.210. Contra, Wirth v. Ehly, 1980, 93 Wis.2d 433, 287 N.W.2d 140 (riding trail bike into cable across road on state land; statute had no exception for minors, and attractive nuisance doctrine inapplicable since child not a trespasser).

26. See, e.g., Katz v. Helbing, 1928, 205 Cal. 629, 271 P. 1062 (boys throwing mortar); Kahn v. James Burton Co., 1955, 5 Ill.2d 614, 126 N.E.2d 836 (child injured while playing on dangerously piled lumber on third party's land; lumber company and contractor could be liable under doctrine); Commercial Union Fire Insurance Co. v. Blocker, La.App.1956, 86 So.2d 760 (starting tractor, running it into house); Lone Star Gas Co. v. Parsons, 1932, 159 Okl. 52, 14 P.2d 369 (dynamite caps); McGettigan v. National Bank of Washington, D.C. Cir. 1963, 320 F.2d 703, certiorari denied 375 U.S. 943, 84 S.Ct. 348, 11 L.Ed.2d 273 (explosive flare); Christians v. Homestake Enterprises, Limited, 1981, 101 Wis.2d 25, 303 N.W.2d 608 (dynamite caps; adopting this position, and rejecting that of Harper & James, in well-reasoned opinion); cf. Batiste v. Boh Brothers Construction Co., La.App.1981, 404 So.2d 1348 (runaway bulldozer, started by playful boys, hit car).

27. Fitch v. Selwyn Village, 1951, 234 N.C. 632, 68 S.E.2d 255; Anneker v. Quinn-Robbins Co., 1958, 80 Idaho 1, 323 P.2d 1073; Adams v. Brookwood Country Club, 1958, 16 Ill.App.2d 263, 148 N.E.2d 39; Woolf v. City of Dallas, Tex.Civ.App.1958, 311 S.W.2d 78; Loney v. McPhillips, 1974, 268 Or. 378, 521 P.2d 340 (ocean cove); Byrd v. Melton, 1972, 259 S.C. 271, 191 S.E.2d 515 (natural stream); see infra, note 75

28. Bagby v. Kansas City, 1936, 338 Mo. 771, 92 S.W.2d 142; McComb City v. Hayman, 1920, 124 Miss. 525, 87 So. 11.

29. "While we acknowledge the picturesque beauty of the rolling hills and majestic mountains of Tennessee and agree that they are attractive, the fortunate fact that God has strewn His splendor with such a lavish hand and blessed our state with great beauty, and has made it a veritable playground, hardly affords a reason to classify any normal topographical feature as an attractive nuisance." McIntyre v. McIntyre, Tenn. 1977, 558 S.W.2d 836, 837 (motorcyclist, going over hill, collided with another). Cf. Ostroski v. Mount Prospect Shop-Rite, Inc., 1967, 94 N.J.Super. 374, 228 A.2d 545 (coasting on icy slope). See Annot., 1974, 59 A.L.R.3d 848 (trees, shrubs, etc.).

30. For artificial ponds, see infra note 75. For other conditions, see Anderson v. Reith-Riley Construction Co., 1942, 112 Ind.App. 170, 44 N.E.2d 184 (sand bank caving in); Zagar v. Union Pacific Railroad Co., 1923, 113 Kan. 240, 214 P. 107.

31. See infra, notes 93–99, 1–16.

32. See, however, Corporation of City of Glasgow v. Taylor, [1922] 1 A.C. 44, to the effect that there is no distinction between a natural poisonous bush and a planted one. See also Norton v. Black, 1970, 12 Ariz. App. 209, 469 P.2d 101; Hofer v. Meyer, S.D.1980, 295 N.W.2d 333 (horse, discussing case involving pigeons); infra, note 81; Notes 1949, 2 Okl.L.Rev. 537; 1951, 26 Ind.L.J. 266.

33. Smith v. Otto Hendrickson Post 212, American Legion, 1954, 241 Minn. 46, 62 N.W.2d 354; Halloran v. Belt Railway of Chicago, 1960, 25 Ill.App.2d 114, 166 N.E.2d 98 (condition actually on adjoining land); Chapman v. Parking, Inc., Tex.Civ.App.1959, 329 S.W.2d 439 (same); cf. Clayton v. Penn Central Transportation Co., 1978, 176 Ind.App. 544, 376 N.E.2d 524 (city-owned, unfenced playground beside railroad tracks).

er trespassers,[34] prior occupants [35] and independent contractors.[36]

Location Where Children Are Likely to Trespass

The place where the condition is found must be one upon which the possessor knows or has reason to know that children are likely to trespass.[37] The occupier, in other words, must have reason to anticipate the presence of the child at the place of danger. He is not required to take precautions when he has no reason to expect that children will come upon his land.[38] If a power line pole is located in the woods or open country, at a distance from any highway or habitation,[39] or can be climbed only with great difficulty and ingenuity,[40] there may be no duty to guard it; but if it is in or near a street,[41] or a park or playground,[42] and is easily climbed,[43] the duty may arise. It is here that the element of attractiveness to children outside of the premises plays its legitimate part.[44] Without it the presence of the children may still be foreseeable, on the basis of past trespasses,[45] proximity to places where children are likely to be,[46] accessibility of the dangerous condition,[47] or any other evidence or as-

---

34. Johnson v. Clement F. Sculley Construction Co., 1959, 255 Minn. 41, 95 N.W.2d 409; Lorusso v. De Carlo, 1957, 48 N.J.Super. 112, 136 A.2d 900; Pickens v. Southern Railway Co., E.D.Tenn.1959, 177 F.Supp. 553; cf. McGettigan v. National Bank of Washington, D.C. Cir. 1963, 320 F.2d 703, certiorari denied 375 U.S. 943, 84 S.Ct. 348, 11 L.Ed.2d 273 (person unknown). But cf. Bellflower v. Pennise, 8th Cir. 1977, 548 F.2d 776 (shack erected by trespassers; motorbike riding not artificial condition).

35. Christians v. Homestake Enterprises, Ltd., 1981, 101 Wis.2d 25, 303 N.W.2d 608; Coeur d'Alene Lumber Co. v. Thompson, 9th Cir. 1914, 215 F. 8. Contra, Calore v. Domnitch, 1957, 5 Misc.2d 895, 162 N.Y.S.2d 173.

36. Foster v. Lusk, 1917, 129 Ark. 1, 194 S.W. 855. Cf. Dehn v. S. Brand Coal & Oil Co., 1954, 241 Minn. 237, 63 N.W.2d 6 (lessee).

37. The chief application is to trespassers on land; but many of the same principles should apply to those on chattels. Browning v. Eichelman, 1968, 12 Mich. App. 408, 162 N.W.2d 898; Wytupeck v. City of Camden, 1957, 25 N.J. 450, 136 A.2d 887; Helton v. Montgomery, Ky.App.1980, 595 S.W.2d 257 (truck); Duggan v. Esposito, 1979, 178 Conn. 156, 422 A.2d 287 (pipes on truck); cf. Kirby v. Hylton, 1982, 51 Md.App. 365, 443 A.2d 640 (pipe).

38. Walker v. Sprinkle, 1966, 267 N.C. 626, 148 S.E.2d 631; Klaus v. Eden, 1962, 70 N.M. 371, 374 P.2d 129; Long v. Sutherland-Backer Co., 1967, 48 N.J. 134, 224 A.2d 321.

39. James v. Wisconsin Power & Light Co., 1954, 266 Wis. 290, 63 N.W.2d 116; Jennings v. Glen Alden Coal Co., 1952, 369 Pa. 532, 87 A.2d 206; Glastris v. Union Electric Co., Mo.App.1976, 542 S.W.2d 65. And perhaps even if people are known to frequent the area, if there is no reason to know they may be climbing the tower. Foster v. Alabama Power Co., Ala.1981, 395 So.2d 27.

40. Ross v. Sequatchie Valley Electric Co-op., 1955, 198 Tenn. 638, 281 S.W.2d 646; Tampa Electric Co. v. Larisey, Fla.App.1964, 166 So.2d 227. Cf. Slinker v. Wallner, 1960, 258 Minn. 243, 103 N.W.2d 377; Callahan v. Dearborn Developments, 1959, 57 N.J.Super. 437, 154 A.2d 865, affirmed 1960, 32 N.J. 27, 158 A.2d 830.

41. Koch v. City of Chicago, 1938, 297 Ill.App. 103, 17 N.E.2d 411; Kentucky Utilities Co. v. Garland, 1950, 314 Ky. 252, 234 S.W.2d 753; Ekdahl v. Minnesota Utilities Co., 1938, 203 Minn. 374, 281 N.W. 517.

42. Wolczek v. Public Service Co., 1931, 342 Ill. 482, 174 N.E. 577; Wytupeck v. City of Camden, 1957, 25 N.J. 450, 136 A.2d 887. Cf. Pasierb v. Hanover Park Park District, 1981, 59 Ill.Dec. 461, 431 N.E.2d 1218 (creek in park); Talley v. J & L Oil Co., 1978, 224 Kan. 214, 579 P.2d 706 (tanks near pasture where children played).

43. Bartleson v. Glen Alden Coal Co., 1949, 361 Pa. 519, 64 A.2d 846; O'Donnell v. City of Chicago, 1937, 289 Ill.App. 41, 6 N.E.2d 449.

44. Commercial Union Fire Insurance Co. v. Blocker, La.App.1956, 86 So.2d 760; Pickens v. Southern Railway Co., E.D.Tenn.1959, 177 F.Supp. 553. Clayton v. Penn Central Transportation Co., 1978, 176 Ind.App. 544, 376 N.E.2d 524, 527 ("a train which moves slowly past a children's park is sure to invite interest and attention").

45. Hofer v. Meyer, S.D.1980, 295 N.W.2d 333; Crawford v. Pacific Western Mobile Estates, Inc., Mo. App.1977, 548 S.W.2d 216, 220 (child drowned in sewage settlement tank at trailer court; manager admitted that "the kids 'were like a bunch of damn monkeys and were down there all the time'"); Duggan v. Esposito, 1979, 178 Conn. 156, 422 A.2d 287 (earlier in day children asked to leave); Bethay v. Philadelphia Housing Authority, 1979, 271 Pa.Super. 366, 413 A.2d 710.

Isolated instances of trespass, in a remote place, may not be enough to require anticipation that they will be repeated. Jennings v. Glen Alden Coal Co., 1952, 369 Pa. 532, 87 A.2d 206. In Clover Fork Coal Co. v. Daniels, Ky.1960, 340 S.W.2d 210, it was held that the children need not be shown to have been present at the exact point of danger.

46. See supra, notes 41–45.

47. Swanson v. City of Marquette, 1959, 357 Mich. 424, 98 N.W.2d 574; Healing v. Security Steel Equipment Corp., 1958, 51 N.J.Super. 123, 143 A.2d 844;

pect of the situation which would lead a reasonable person to anticipate the trespass.[48] It is generally held that the circumstances which make the trespass foreseeable must actually be known to the possessor, so that he is not required in the first instance to police his premises or make inquiry to discover whether there is a likelihood that children will enter.[49]

Knowledge of Unreasonable Danger

The condition must be one which the occupier should recognize as involving an unreasonable risk of harm to such children. Again, he must know of the dangerous condition, or at least have reason to know of it;[50] and, in the absence of any notice that something may be wrong, he generally is not required to inspect his land, or otherwise investigate, to discover whether there may be some condition on it which might harm trespassing children.[51] And even though the condition be known, if it is not one from which any unreasonable danger to children is reasonably to be anticipated, there is no negligence in failing to protect them against it, and no liability.[52]

The stress here is upon "unreasonable." There is virtually no condition upon any land with which a child may not possibly get himself into trouble. He may choke to death upon a green apple, pick up a stick and poke it into his eye,[53] or have his skull fractured by a rock found and thrown by his companion.[54] Unless the possessor is to shoulder the impossible burden of making his land completely "child-proof," which could mean razing it to the bare earth, something more is called for than the general possibility of somehow coming to some harm which follows the child everywhere throughout his daily existence. Accordingly, there is a long line of cases involving normally harmless objects, such as a sharp-pointed pole,[55] railroad spikes,[56] a wooden horse,[57] a piece of shingle

Burk Royalty Co. v. Pace, Tex.Civ.App.1981, 620 S.W.2d 882 (worn path from child's home to oil well pumping unit).

48. See Smith v. Otto Hendrickson Post 212, American Legion, 1954, 241 Minn. 46, 62 N.W.2d 354 (condition extending onto adjoining land); Gilbert v. Sabin, 1977, 76 Mich.App. 137, 256 N.W.2d 54 (young children guests might wander into garage and find loaded gun); cf. Lister v. Campbell, Fla.App.1979, 371 So.2d 133 (picnic litter and tire tracks by gravel pit pond).

49. Hickey v. Nulty, 1960, 182 Cal.App.2d 237, 5 Cal.Rptr. 914; Jones v. Louisville & Nashville Railroad Co., 1944, 297 Ky. 197, 179 S.W.2d 874; Hedgepath v. City of Durham, 1944, 223 N.C. 822, 28 S.E.2d 503.

50. See Christians v. Homestake Enterprises, Ltd., 1981, 101 Wis.2d 25, 303 N.W.2d 608, 621 (adopting "reason to know" rather than "should know" standard proposed by Professor James); Glastris v. Union Electric Co., Mo.App.1976, 542 S.W.2d 65. But see 2 Harper & James, Torts, 1956, 1458–1459.

51. See cases, id. Recovery was denied where the defendant had no knowledge at all in Rush v. Plains Township, 1952, 371 Pa. 117, 89 A.2d 200; Pocholec v. Giustina, 1960, 224 Or. 245, 355 P.2d 1104; Pier v. Schultz, 1962, 243 Ind. 200, 182 N.E.2d 255; Simmel v. New Jersey Co-op. Co., 1958, 28 N.J. 1, 143 A.2d 521.

52. Lee v. Salt River Valley Water Users' Association, 1951, 73 Ariz. 122, 238 P.2d 945 (pump house and power line pole); Giddings v. Superior Oil Co., 1951, 106 Cal.App.2d 607, 235 P.2d 843 (oil well pump); Deffland v. Spokane Portland Cement Co., 1947, 26 Wn.2d 891, 176 P.2d 311 (charged wire and pigeons in cupola); J. C. Penney Co. v. Clark, Okl.1961, 366 P.2d 637 (stool in shoe store); Bellflower v. Pennise, 8th Cir. 1977, 548 F.2d 776 (motorbike activity alone does not require investigation to find possibly explosive gasoline in shack); Norton v. City of Easton, 1977, 249 Pa.Super. 520, 378 A.2d 417 (knowledge of car on lot but not bullets in glove compartment).

53. Niemann v. Vermilion County Housing Authority, 1981, 101 Ill.App.3d 735, 57 Ill.Dec. 156, 428 N.E.2d 706 (playmate's eye).

54. Cole v. Housing Authority of La Salle County, 1979, 68 Ill.App.3d 66, 24 Ill.Dec. 470, 385 N.E.2d 382 (metal stake); Sahara v. Ragnar Benson, Inc., 1977, 52 Ill.App.3d 119, 9 Ill.Dec. 799, 367 N.E.2d 233 (stone hit eye).

55. Mail v. M. R. Smith Lumber & Shingle Co., 1955, 47 Wn.2d 447, 287 P.2d 877. Cf. Southern Bell Telephone & Telegraph Co. v. Brackin, 1959, 215 Ga. 225, 109 S.E.2d 782 (piece of wire).

56. Genovese v. New Orleans Public Service Co., La.App.1950, 45 So.2d 642. Cf. Bruce v. Housing Authority of City of Pittsburgh, 1950, 365 Pa. 571, 76 A.2d 400 (broken glass on floor, child on roller skates); Johnson v. Williams, Fla.App.1966, 192 So.2d 339 (low wire cable between trees). On the other hand, in Brittain v. Cubbon, 1963, 190 Kan. 641, 378 P.2d 141, rusty nails protruding from a plank in a razed building were held to be sufficient, as unlikely to be discovered by trespassing children.

57. Ray v. Hutchinson, 1933, 17 Tenn.App. 477, 68 S.W.2d 948. Cf. State ex rel. W. E. Callahan Construction Co. v. Hughes, 1941, 348 Mo. 1209, 159 S.W.2d 251 (bucket).

on a roof,[58] a red lantern,[59] a picnic table,[60] or even stationary vehicles,[61] which have been held to be so innocuous that as a matter of law there was no liability, unless the possessor had some special reason to anticipate injury.[62]

Struggling to characterize these cases, the courts sometimes have said that the condition must be an unusual one,[63] or that the doctrine has no application to common objects or dangers,[64] or to conditions arising from the ordinary conduct of a business,[65] or that it is limited to special and unusual conditions of modern industry.[66] But a recognizable and unreasonable risk of harm may arise from a very ordinary condition; and where there has been past meddling, a concealed danger, a special attraction to children, or any other special reason to expect harm, even so commonplace a thing as a mailbox may be found to be enough for liability.[67] While it is evident that there must be some aggravated danger to the child, greater than the ordinary risks which attend his daily life, it is equally clear that this cannot be reduced to a definite formula, and that it must be the product of all the factors bearing on the case.[68] A high degree of probability of relatively slight harm, as in the case of concealed barbed wire,[69] may be sufficient, and so may a relatively slighter probability of death, as in the case of high tension electric wires.[70] This is a matter of calculus of risk, considered further below.[71]

One very important factor is that of whether the trespassing child may reasona-

58. Massino v. Smaglick, 1958, 3 Wis.2d 607, 89 N.W.2d 223. Cf. Landman v. M. Susan & Associates, 1965, 63 Ill.App.2d 292, 211 N.E.2d 407 (pile of sand on beach); Krakowiak v. Sampson, 1967, 85 Ill.App.2d 71, 229 N.E.2d 578 (mounds of earth, tree stumps, overhanging branches).

59. Brown v. City of Minneapolis, 1917, 136 Minn. 177, 161 N.W. 503. Cf. St. Louis, Iron Mountain & Southern Railway Co. v. Waggoner, 1914, 112 Ark. 593, 166 S.W. 948 (empty alcohol barrel); Esquibel v. City and County of Denver, 1944, 112 Colo. 546, 151 P.2d 757 (old auto bodies and parts).

60. Bazos v. Chouinard, 1981, 96 Ill.App.3d 526, 51 Ill.Dec. 931, 421 N.E.2d 566 (placed under tree with good swinging limb).

61. Anderson v. B. F. Goodrich Co., 1961, 103 Ga. App. 453, 119 S.E.2d 603 (truck with hanging chain and hook); Sydenstricker v. Chicago & Northwestern Railway Co., 1969, 107 Ill.App.2d 427, 247 N.E.2d 15 (tank car); Gear v. General Casualty Insurance Co., 1953, 263 Wis. 261, 57 N.W.2d 340 (automobile); Harris v. Roberson, 1943, 78 U.S.App.D.C. 246, 139 F.2d 529 (trailer); cf. Phillips v. J. F. Martin Cartage Co., 1976, 42 Ill.App.3d 890, 1 Ill.Dec. 904, 356 N.E.2d 1237 (refuse container).

62. Britten v. City of Eau Claire, 1952, 260 Wis. 382, 51 N.W.2d 30 (past meddling); Gimmestad v. Rose Bros. Co., 1935, 194 Minn. 531, 261 N.W. 194 (way lumber was piled); Pasierb v. Hanover Park Park District, 1981, 103 Ill.App.3d 806, 59 Ill.Dec. 461, 431 N.E.2d 1218 (snow covering thin ice on creek: "an instrumentality, although not in itself dangerous, may become dangerous when joined with other nondangerous instrumentalities or surroundings"). See infra, note 67.

63. E.g., Denver Tramway Co. v. Garcia, 1964, 154 Colo. 417, 390 P.2d 952; McIntyre v. McIntyre, Tenn. 1977, 558 S.W.2d 836.

64. Corcoran v. Village of Libertyville, 1978, 73 Ill. App.3d 316, 22 Ill.Dec. 701, 383 N.E.2d 177 (open ditch); Niemann v. Vermilion County Housing Authority, 1981, 101 Ill.App.3d 735, 57 Ill.Dec. 156, 428 N.E.2d 706 (stick was "ordinarily innocuous" rather than "inherently dangerous" object; no liability for former unless combined with other objects or surroundings to make it dangerous to children); Metropolitan Government of Nashville v. Counts, Tenn.1976, 541 S.W.2d 133 (cattle pond).

65. Brown v. Rockwell City Canning Co., 1906, 132 Iowa 631, 110 N.W. 12; Holt v. Fuller Cotton Oil Co., Tex.Civ.App.1943, 175 S.W.2d 272, error refused.

66. Giannini v. Campodonico, 1917, 176 Cal. 548, 169 P. 80; San Antonio & Aransas Pass Railway Co. v. Morgan, 1898, 92 Tex. 98, 46 S.W. 28. See Green, Judge and Jury, 1930, 128–133.

67. United States v. Bernhardt, 5th Cir. 1957, 244 F.2d 154. Cf. Garcia v. Soogian, 1959, 52 Cal.2d 107, 338 P.2d 433 (stacked building materials); Hoff v. Natural Refining Products Co., 1955, 38 N.J.Super. 222, 118 A.2d 714 (refuse mound); Crutchfield v. Adams, Fla.App.1963, 152 So.2d 808 (unguarded fan belt); Eastburn v. Levin, D.C.Cir. 1940, 72 App.D.C. 190, 113 F.2d 176 (junk yard).

68. Well stated in Lone Star Gas Co. v. Parsons, 1932, 159 Okl. 52, 14 P.2d 369.

69. Cincinnati & Hammond Spring Co. v. Brown, 1903, 32 Ind.App. 58, 69 N.E. 197; cf. Holland Builders, Inc. v. Leck, Fla.App.1981, 395 So.2d 579.

70. Harris v. Indiana General Service Co., 1933, 206 Ind. 351, 189 N.E. 410; Fort Wayne & Northern Indiana Traction Co. v. Stark, 1920, 74 Ind.App. 669, 127 N.E. 460; infra, note 39. Cf. Carradine v. City of New York, 1962, 16 App.Div.2d 928, 229 N.Y.S.2d 328, reversed on other grounds, 1964, 13 N.Y.2d 291, 246 N.Y.S.2d 620, 196 N.E.2d 259 (explosives); Medlin v. United States, W.D.S.C.1965, 244 F.Supp. 403 (same).

71. See infra, notes 17–34.

bly be expected to comprehend the situation. Sometimes this is expressed by saying that the danger must be latent,[72] meaning apparently nothing more than that the child can be expected not to perceive or appreciate the peril.[73] The question here is not whether he does in fact understand, although that too has its importance;[74] it is rather what the possessor may reasonably expect of him. Here the courts have displayed a tendency to set up certain more or less arbitrary categories of conditions which trespassing children, as a matter of law, can be expected to understand. This means that the possessor is free to rely upon the assumption that any child of sufficient age to be allowed at large by his parents, and so to be at all likely to trespass, will appreciate the danger and avoid it, or at least make his own intelligent and responsible choice. The danger to which such a fixed rule most often has been applied is that of drowning in water;[75] but there are numerous cases showing a similar rigidity as to the perils of fire,[76] falling from a height[77] or into an excavation,[78] moving vehicles,[79] ordinary visible machinery in motion,[80] the natural propensities of a horse,[81] sliding or caving soil,[82] and piles of lumber, crossties, and other building material.[83]

These fixed rules have been found deficient in certain situations. One is where the possessor of the land knows or has reason to know[84] that the children who are likely to trespass are so extremely young that they cannot appreciate the danger. When an infant of three or four is known to be in the

72. Hayes v. Criterion Corp., Fla.App.1976, 337 So. 2d 1026; McIntyre v. McIntyre, Tenn.1977, 558 S.W.2d 836; see infra, note 96.

73. Montgomery Ward & Co. v. Ramirez, Tex.Civ. App.1939, 127 S.W.2d 1034.

74. See infra, notes 94–97.

75. Prince v. Wolf, 1981, 93 Ill.App.3d 505, 48 Ill. Dec. 947, 417 N.E.2d 679; Ochampaugh v. City of Seattle, 1979, 91 Wn.2d 514, 588 P.2d 1351 (thorough review); Lanier v. North Carolina State Highway Commission, 1976, 31 N.C.App. 304, 229 S.E.2d 321; Hughes v. Star Homes, Inc., Miss.1980, 379 So.2d 301 (dictum); Smith v. United States Steel Corp., Ala.1977, 351 So.2d 1369; Metropolitan Government of Nashville v. Counts, Tenn.1976, 541 S.W.2d 133. Compare Barbre v. Indianapolis Water Co., 1980, ___ Ind.App. ___, 400 N.E.2d 1142 (diving into shallow water). See Annots., 1978, 88 A.L.R.3d 1197 (liability of swimming facility operator to trespassing child); 1968, 20 A.L.R.3d 1395 (liability of owner of private pool); Note, 1967, 9 Ariz.L.Rev. 339 (swimming pools). See supra, note 27.

76. Rhodes v. City of Kansas City, 1949, 167 Kan. 719, 208 P.2d 275; Goss v. Shawnee Post No. 3204, V. F. W., Ky.1954, 265 S.W.2d 799; Hancock v. Aiken Mills, 1935, 180 S.C. 93, 185 S.E. 188; Jackson v. City of Biloxi, Miss.1973, 272 So.2d 654.

77. Bazos v. Chouinard, 1981, 96 Ill.App.3d 526, 51 Ill.Dec. 931, 421 N.E.2d 566; Phillips v. J. F. Martin Cartage Co., 1976, 42 Ill.App.3d 890, 1 Ill.Dec. 904, 356 N.E.2d 1237; Barnhizer v. Paradise Valley Unified School District, 1979, 123 Ariz. 253, 599 P.2d 209; Pittman v. Pedro Petroleum Corp., 1974, 42 Cal.App.3d 859, 117 Cal.Rptr. 220.

78. Fain v. Standard Oil Co., 1940, 284 Ky. 561, 145 S.W.2d 39; Corcoran v. Village of Libertyville, 1978, 73 Ill.2d 316, 22 Ill.Dec. 701, 383 N.E.2d 177 (2 year old).

79. Smith v. Illinois Central Railroad Co., 1952, 214 Miss. 293, 58 So.2d 812 (train); Courtright v. Southern Compress & Warehouse Co., Tex.Civ.App.1957, 299 S.W.2d 169 (trailer); Holland v. Baltimore & Ohio Railroad Co., D.C.App.1981, 431 A.2d 597 (Nebeker, J.) (train; following "overwhelming weight of authority"); Annot., 1971, 35 A.L.R.3d 9 (child injured by moving train).

80. Giddings v. Superior Oil Co., 1951, 106 Cal.App. 2d 607, 235 P.2d 843 (oil well pump); Teagarden v. Russell's Administratrix, 1947, 306 Ky. 528, 207 S.W.2d 18 (conveyor belt).

81. See Whitcanock v. Nelson, 1980, 81 Ill.App.3d 186, 36 Ill.Dec. 418, 400 N.E.2d 998 (infant trampled); cf. Brady v. Skinner, App.1982, 132 Ariz. 425, 646 P.2d 310 (child kicked by mule); Hall v. Edlefson, Tex.Civ. App.1973, 498 S.W.2d 514 (attractive nuisance doctrine inapplicable to domesticated shetland pony); Annot., 1975, 64 A.L.R.3d 1069 (animals as attractive nuisance); supra, note 32.

82. Knight v. Kaiser Co., 1957, 48 Cal.2d 778, 312 P.2d 1089; Powell v. Ligon, 1939, 334 Pa. 250, 5 A.2d 373; Hayes v. Criterion Corp., Fla.App.1976, 337 So.2d 1026.

83. Lovell v. Southern Railway Co., 1952, 257 Ala. 561, 59 So.2d 807 (steel girders); Morris v. Lewis Manufacturing Co., 1951, 331 Mich. 252, 49 N.W.2d 164 (lumber); Boyette v. Atlantic Coast Line Railroad Co., 1947, 227 N.C. 406, 42 S.E.2d 462 (ties and timbers). Contra, Kahn v. James Burton Co., 1955, 5 Ill.2d 614, 126 N.E.2d 836 (lumber).

84. Where the defendant has no reason to anticipate such very young children, recovery is denied. Davis v. Goodrich, 1959, 171 Cal.App.2d 92, 340 P.2d 48; Meyer v. General Electric Co., 1955, 46 Wn.2d 251, 280 P.2d 257.

vicinity of fire or water,[85] or other dangerous conditions,[86] it is "pure fantasy, straight from outer space"[87] to say that he will be fully able to protect himself against them. The arbitrary categories have also proved unsatisfactory in cases where there is an enhanced risk, greater than the ordinary one normally attending such a condition, as where some part of the danger is hidden,[88] or there is some special, distracting feature, such as a diving board,[89] or special reason to anticipate trespasses, such as past experience[90] or proximity to a place where children congregate.[91] There are so many of these exceptional cases that many courts have rejected such fixed and arbitrary rules, and said that each case must be considered in the light of all of its particular facts.[92]

Child's Age and Ignorance of Danger

The child, because of his immaturity, either must not discover the condition or must not in fact appreciate the danger involved.[93] Since the principal reason for the rule distinguishing trespassing children from trespassing adults is the inability of the child to protect himself, the courts have been quite firm in their insistence that if the child is fully aware of the condition, understands the risk which it carries, and is quite able to avoid it, he stands in no better position than an adult with similar knowledge and understanding.[94]

---

85. *Fire:* Louisville Trust Co. v. Nutting, Ky.1968, 437 S.W.2d 484 (3 years); Wozniczka v. McKean, 1969, 144 Ind.App. 471, 247 N.E.2d 215 (5 years); Courtell v. McEachen, 1959, 51 Cal.2d 448, 334 P.2d 870 (5 years); Ford v. Blythe Brothers Co., 1955, 242 N.C. 347, 87 S.E.2d 879 (3 years); Gerchberg v. Loney, 1977, 1 Kan. App.2d 84, 562 P.2d 464, affirmed, 1978, 223 Kan. 446, 576 P.2d 593. *Water:* Everett v. White, 1965, 245 S.C. 331, 140 S.E.2d 582 (5 years); Davies v. Land O'Lakes Racing Association, 1955, 244 Minn. 248, 69 N.W.2d 642 (5 years); Rosario v. City of Lansing, 1978, 403 Mich. 124, 268 N.W.2d 230; Gregory v. Johnson, 1982, 249 Ga. 151, 289 S.E.2d 232; see supra, note 75 (water).

86. See, e.g., Clayton v. Penn Central Transportation Co., 1978, 176 Ind.App. 544, 376 N.E.2d 524 (4 years, moving train); Peterson v. Richfield Plaza, 1958, 252 Minn. 215, 89 N.W.2d 712 (2 years, fall from balcony); Gould v. De Beve, 1964, 117 App.D.C. 360, 330 F.2d 826, 829 (2½ years, fall from window); Eaton v. R. B. George Investments, 1953, 152 Tex. 523, 260 S.W. 587 (3 years, cattle dipping vat); Hofer v. Meyer, S.D. 1980, 295 N.W.2d 333 (3 years, horse). But see Corcoran v. Village of Libertyville, 1978, 73 Ill.2d 316, 22 Ill. Dec. 701, 383 N.E.2d 177 (2-year-old fell into ditch).

87. Smith, J., in Elbert v. City of Saginaw, 1961, 363 Mich. 463, 109 N.W.2d 879.

88. Lehmkuhl v. Junction City, 1956, 179 Kan. 389, 295 P.2d 621 (deceptive surface); Ansin v. Thurston, Fla.App.1957, 98 So.2d 87, certiorari denied 101 So.2d 808 (concealed drop-off); Skaggs v. Junis, 1960, 27 Ill. App.2d 251, 169 N.E.2d 684 (concealed stump in pond); Hoff v. Natural Refining Products Co., 1955, 38 N.J. Super. 222, 118 A.2d 714 (pile of refuse caved in); Pasierb v. Hanover Park Park District, 1981, 103 Ill. App.3d 806, 59 Ill.Dec. 461, 431 N.E.2d 1218 (thin layer of ice over creek concealed by snow); cf. Novak v. C. M. S. Builders & Developers, 1980, 83 Ill.App.3d 761, 39 Ill.Dec. 327, 404 N.E.2d 918 (noting "complex synergistic relationship" between mounds of dirt, excavation and concrete foundation at construction site).

89. Smith v. Evans, 1955, 178 Kan. 259, 284 P.2d 1065. Cf. Galleher v. City of Wichita, 1956, 179 Kan. 513, 296 P.2d 1062 (deceptive water with sand beach); Cargill, Inc. v. Zimmer, 8th Cir. 1967, 374 F.2d 924 (72 foot ladder with pigeons at top); Salanski v. Enright, Mo.1970, 452 S.W.2d 143 (tree house); Crawford v. Pacific Western Mobil Estates, Inc., Mo.App.1977, 548 S.W.2d 216 (ball floating in tank with bridges across top).

90. Dickeson v. Baltimore & Ohio Chicago Terminal Railroad Co., 1965, 73 Ill.App.2d 5, 220 N.E.2d 43, affirmed, 1969, 42 Ill.2d 103, 245 N.E.2d 762 (moving trains); Nechodomu v. Lindstrom, 1956, 273 Wis. 313, 77 N.W.2d 707, rehearing denied 273 Wis. 313, 78 N.W.2d 417 (mud mixer machine); see supra, note 45.

91. Clayton v. Penn Central Transportation Co., 1978, 176 Ind.App. 544, 376 N.E.2d 524 (train passing playground); Harris v. Buckeye Irrigation Co., 1978, 118 Ariz. 498, 578 P.2d 177 (normal immunity from attractive nuisance doctrine for irrigation ditch accidents inapplicable to heavily used foot bridge over ditch near high school, baseball field and swimming pool); see supra, note 46.

92. King v. Lennen, 1959, 53 Cal.2d 340, 1 Cal.Rptr. 665, 348 P.2d 98 (swimming pool, overruling long line of cases); Pocholec v. Giustina, 1960, 224 Or. 245, 355 P.2d 1104 (pond); Elbert v. City of Saginaw, 1961, 363 Mich. 463, 109 N.W.2d 879; Kahn v. James Burton Co., 1955, 5 Ill.2d 614, 126 N.E.2d 836; but see supra, note 75.

93. See Annot., 1967, 16 A.L.R.3d 25 (age and mentality of child affecting attractive nuisance).

94. Alston v. Baltimore & Ohio Railroad Co., D.D.C. 1977, 433 F.Supp. 553, 569 (9-year-old hopping trains because it was "exciting"); Warchol v. City of Chicago, 1979, 75 Ill.App.3d 289, 30 Ill.Dec. 689, 393 N.E.2d 725 (risk of slipping while walking on top of metal fence); Lister v. Campbell, Fla.App.1979, 371 So.2d 133 (diving in shallow water); Richards v. Marlow, La.App.1977, 347 So.2d 281, 283, writ denied 350 So.2d 676 (risk of slipping while walking on wet pipe; application of doctrine "necessarily includes a finding that the injured child was too young to understand and avoid the dan-

This is not merely a matter of contributory negligence or assumption of risk,[95] but of lack of duty to the child. Thus the fact that the danger is obvious even to a child,[96] or that the child has been warned about it, may be enough to defeat his recovery, where the child was thereby made fully aware of the situation.[97] But it is appreciation of the danger which is required to bar recovery, rather than mere knowledge of the existence of the condition itself;[98] and where the child is too young to understand,[99] or not sufficiently impressed to forego the attractive hazard,[1] the warning may be found not to relieve the defendant of liability, if he could reasonably be expected to do more.

The age of the child is obviously an important factor throughout. The original turntable cases involved children of the ages of six and seven; and prior to 1925 it was very rarely that a child over twelve was allowed to recover.[2] Even today the great majority of the recoveries have been on the part of children of twelve or under; and there is a long list of decisions refusing to permit the jury to find for a plaintiff of thirteen,[3] fourteen,[4] fifteen,[5] sixteen,[6] and above.[7] It is commonly said that the special rule applies only to "young" children, or those of "tender years;" and the original rule of the Restatement of Torts was so limited.

A small number of courts have declared a fixed age limit of fourteen, after which the

ger"); cf. Grimes v. Hetlinger, Ky.App.1978, 566 S.W.2d 769 (pool).

95. Pocholec v. Giustina, 1960, 224 Or. 245, 355 P.2d 1104; Nechodomu v. Lindstrom, 1956, 273 Wis. 313, 77 N.W.2d 707, rehearing denied 273 Wis. 313, 78 N.W.2d 417. But see Larnel Builders v. Martin, Fla.1959, 110 So.2d 649. Although the same evidence may establish lack of duty, contributory negligence and assumption of risk. Richards v. Marlow, La.App.1977, 347 So.2d 281, writ denied 350 So.2d 676.

96. See Corcoran v. Village of Libertyville, 1978, 73 Ill.2d 316, 22 Ill.Dec. 701, 383 N.E.2d 177 (open ditch); Carlson v. Tucson Racquet & Swim Club, Inc., App. 1980, 127 Ariz. 247, 619 P.2d 756; Lanier v. North Carolina State Highway Commission, 1976, 31 N.C.App. 304, 229 S.E.2d 321 (excavation pit pond); Richards v. Marlow, La.App.1977, 347 So.2d 281, writ denied 350 So.2d 676 ("tightroping" wet pipe); Holland v. Baltimore & Ohio Railroad Co., D.C.App.1981, 431 A.2d 597 (moving train).

97. See Phipps v. Mitze, 1947, 116 Colo. 288, 180 P.2d 233; McCulley v. Cherokee Amusement Co., 1944, 182 Tenn. 68, 184 S.W.2d 170; Prince v. Wolf, 1981, 93 Ill.App.3d 505, 48 Ill.Dec. 947, 417 N.E.2d 679 (swimming in mudholes); Ochampaugh v. City of Seattle, 1979, 91 Wn.2d 514, 588 P.2d 1351 (same).

98. Novicki v. Blaw-Knox Co., 3d Cir. 1962, 304 F.2d 931; Helguera v. Cirone, 1960, 178 Cal.App.2d 232, 3 Cal.Rptr. 64; Talley v. J & L Oil Co., 1978, 224 Kan. 214, 579 P.2d 706 (fumes and lack of oxygen in oil tank).

99. See Missouri Pacific Railway Co. v. Lester, 1951, 219 Ark. 413, 242 S.W.2d 714; Tucker Bros. v. Menard, Fla.1956, 90 So.2d 908; cf. Bethay v. Philadelphia Housing Authority, 1979, 271 Pa.Super. 366, 413 A.2d 710 (whether 10-year-old appreciated risk of playing on elevator roof for jury).

1. See Kalinowski v. Smith, 1978, 6 Mass.App.Ct. 769, 383 N.E.2d 550 (4½-year-old on track waving at approaching train); Christians v. Homestake Enterprises, Limited, 1981, 101 Wis.2d 25, 303 N.W.2d 608 (plaintiff failed to appreciate risk that blasting caps could explode ten minutes after thrown in fire).

2. See Schulte v. Willow River Power Co., 1940, 234 Wis. 188, 290 N.W. 629, 631.

3. E.g., Barnhizer v. Paradise Valley Unified School District, 1979, 123 Ariz. 253, 599 P.2d 209; Lanier v. North Carolina State Highway Commission, 1976, 31 N.C.App. 304, 229 S.E.2d 321 (excavation pit pond); Smith v. United States Steel Corp., Ala.1977, 351 So.2d 1369; Felger v. Duquesne Light Co., 1971, 441 Pa. 421, 273 A.2d 738 (3–3).

4. E.g., Massie v. Copeland, 1950, 149 Tex. 319, 233 S.W.2d 449; Lister v. Campbell, Fla.App.1979, 371 So. 2d 133; McIntyre v. McIntyre, Tenn.1977, 558 S.W.2d 836.

5. Scheffer v. Braverman, 1965, 89 N.J.Super. 452, 215 A.2d 378; O'Keefe v. South End Rowing Club, 1966, 64 Cal.2d 729, 51 Cal.Rptr. 534, 414 P.2d 830; Prince v. Wolf, 1981, 93 Ill.App.3d 505, 48 Ill.Dec. 947, 417 N.E.2d 679; Warchol v. City of Chicago, 1979, 75 Ill.App.3d 289, 30 Ill.Dec. 689, 393 N.E.2d 725; Foster v. Alabama Power Co., Ala.1981, 395 So.2d 27.

6. E.g., Carlson v. Tucson Racquet & Swim Club, Inc., App.1980, 127 Ariz. 247, 619 P.2d 756; Cates v. Beauregard Electric Coop., Inc., La.App.1975, 316 So. 2d 367, affirmed, 1976, 328 So.2d 367, certiorari denied 429 U.S. 833, 97 S.Ct. 97, 50 L.Ed.2d 98; Haden v. Hockenberger & Chambers Co., 1975, 193 Neb. 713, 228 N.W.2d 883.

7. Barbre v. Indianapolis Water Co., 1980, ___ Ind. App. ___, 400 N.E.2d 1142 (seventeen); E. I. Du Pont de Nemours & Co. v. Edgerton, 8th Cir. 1956, 231 F.2d 430 (same); Garrett v. Arkansas Power & Light Co., 1951, 218 Ark. 575, 237 S.W.2d 895 (same); Texas Power & Light Co. v. Burt, Tex.Civ.App.1937, 104 S.W.2d 941, error refused (eighteen); Soles v. Ohio Edison Co., 1945, 144 Ohio St. 373, 59 N.E.2d 138 (nineteen).

doctrine will not apply,[8] generally borrowed from their rule as to the presumed incapacity of children under that age for contributory negligence. This authority is not, however, as impressive as it may appear, since the cases have mostly involved conditions which would have been understood and appreciated by even younger children.

On the other hand, with the increasing development of especially hazardous conditions, such as high tension wires,[9] which a boy of high school age may not fully appreciate, there are now a considerable number of cases in which such children have been allowed to recover, at the age of thirteen [10] and fourteen,[11] with a few instances of even older children.[12] No definite line is drawn, but as the age goes up the possible conditions diminish, until at some uncertain point they vanish.[13] For these reasons, the Second Restatement of Torts [14] has eliminated the limitation to "young" children originally stated. There is even a little authority that the infant's mental development is to be taken into account,[15] as in cases of contributory neligence; and on this basis, the extreme case allowing recovery was one of an eighteen-year old deaf mute with the mind of a child of six.[16]

Calculus of Risk; Negligence

The utility to the possessor of maintaining the condition must be slight as compared against the risk to children involved.[17] Here, as elsewhere,[18] negligence is to be determined by weighing the probability and the gravity of the possible harm against the utility of the defendant's conduct, and the cost and trouble of reducing the risk.[19] The public interest in the free use of land is such that the landowner or occupier will not be required to take precautions which are so burdensome or expensive as to be unreasonable in the light of the risk,[20] or to make his

8. See Hashtani v. Duke Power Co., 4th Cir. 1978, 578 F.2d 542 (Russell, J.) (14 years 2 months: doctrine inapplicable); Moseley v. City of Kansas City, 1951, 170 Kan. 585, 228 P.2d 699; cf. Foster v. Alabama Power Co., Ala.1981, 395 So.2d 27; Helton v. Montgomery, Ky.App.1980, 595 S.W.2d 257 (dictum; doctrine applied to 9 year old).

9. See Annot., 1979, 91 A.L.R.3d 616 (injury from electric wire while climbing tree).

10. E.g., Johnson v. Clement F. Sculley Construction Co., 1959, 255 Minn. 41, 95 N.W.2d 409; Hoff v. Natural Refining Products Co., 1955, 38 N.J.Super. 222, 118 A.2d 714; Talley v. J & L Oil Co., 1978, 224 Kan. 214, 579 P.2d 706; cf. Johnson v. Delmarva Power & Light Co., Del.Super.1973, 312 A.2d 634 (jury question).

11. Glastris v. Union Electric Co., Mo.App.1976, 542 S.W.2d 65; Scurti v. City of New York, 1976, 40 N.Y.2d 433, 387 N.Y.S.2d 55, 354 N.E.2d 794 (for jury); Petroski v. Northern Indiana Public Service Co., 1976, 171 Ind.App. 14, 354 N.E.2d 736; Roseneau v. City of Estherville, Iowa 1972, 199 N.W.2d 125.

12. E.g., Skaggs v. Junis, 1960, 27 Ill.App.2d 251, 169 N.E.2d 684 (sixteen, diving into pool with concealed stump); Boyer v. Guidicy Marble, Terrazzo & Tile Co., Mo.1952, 246 S.W.2d 742 (seventeen, dynamite cap); cf. Fouraker v. Mullis, Fla.App.1960, 120 So.2d 808 (seventeen, throwing wet plaster).

13. There is a very good discussion of this in Hoff v. Natural Refining Products Co., 1955, 38 N.J.Super. 222, 118 A.2d 714.

14. See supra, note 24.

15. Giacona v. Tapley, 1967, 5 Ariz.App. 494, 428 P.2d 439; Lynch v. Motel Enterprises, Inc., 1966, 248 S.C. 490, 151 S.E.2d 435; Dickeson v. Baltimore & Ohio Chicago Terminal Railroad, 1965, 73 Ill.App.2d 5, 220 N.E.2d 43, affirmed 42 Ill.2d 103, 245 N.E.2d 762; cf. Hashtani v. Duke Power Co., 4th Cir. 1978, 578 F.2d 542 (but child not dumb enough on facts). But cf. Hunter v. Evergreen Presbyterian Vocational School, La.App.1976, 338 So.2d 164. See Annot., 1967, 16 A.L.R.3d 25 (age and mentality of child affecting attractive nuisance).

16. Harris v. Indiana General Service Co., 1934, 206 Ind. 351, 189 N.E. 410.

17. See Bauer, The Degree of Danger and the Degree of Difficulty of Removal of the Danger as Factors in Attractive Nuisance Cases, 1934, 18 Minn.L.Rev. 523.

18. See supra, § 31.

19. E.g., Scibelli v. Pennsylvania Railroad Co., 1954, 379 Pa. 282, 108 A.2d 348; Courtright v. Southern Compress & Warehouse Co., Tex.Civ.App.1957, 299 S.W.2d 169; Coughlin v. United States Tool Co., 1958, 52 N.J.Super. 341, 145 A.2d 482.

20. Jesko v. Turk, 1966, 421 Pa. 434, 219 A.2d 591; McGaughey v. Haines, 1962, 189 Kan. 453, 370 P.2d 120; Cole v. Housing Authority of La Salle County, 1979, 68 Ill.App.3d 66, 24 Ill.Dec. 470, 385 N.E.2d 382 (small risk did not justify burden of assuring that all metal stakes picked up from work site every day); Metropolitan Government of Nashville v. Counts, Tenn. 1976, 541 S.W.2d 133 (drowning risk too small to demand guarding or fencing cattle pond).

premises "childproof."[21] Such things as standing freight cars[22] and moving vehicles[23] are undeniably attractive to children, but are socially useful and very difficult to safeguard, and so may call for very little in the way of care. On the other hand, dynamite caps,[24] or uninsulated wires,[25] which can easily be put away or guarded, may properly serve as a basis of liability. A railroad company may not be negligent in having a turntable where children frequently play, but may be negligent in failing to keep it locked when it is not in use.[26] At one stage of its construction an unfinished house may be practically impossible to safeguard so that children cannot get into it[27] while at a later stage it becomes possible, and reasonable, to barricade or lock the door.[28] The defendant is to be held liable only for negligence, however, which means that he is required to exercise only reasonable care, and to take only those precautions which would be taken by a reasonable person under the circumstances,[29] against risks that could reasonably be foreseen[30] and prevented.[31] Depending on the circumstances, a locked fence may be required,[32] or a warning alone may be sufficient[33] if the danger is smaller or if other precautions would be ineffectual or infeasible.[34]

 WESTLAW REFERENCES

headnote(child! infant* minor* /s trespass!) % topic(110)

---

21. McLendon v. Hampton Cotton Mills Co., 1917, 109 S.C. 238, 95 S.E. 781; Colligen v. Philadelphia Electric Co., 1930, 301 Pa. 87, 151 A. 699.

22. Dugan v. Pennsylvania Railroad Co., 1956, 387 Pa. 25, 127 A.2d 343, certiorari denied 353 U.S. 946, 77 S.Ct. 825, 1 L.Ed.2d 856; Kressine v. Janesville Traction Co., 1921, 175 Wis. 192, 184 N.W. 777.

23. See supra, note 79.

24. Mattson v. Minnesota & North Wisconsin Railroad Co., 1905, 95 Minn. 477, 104 N.W. 443; Nelson v. McLellan, 1903, 31 Wash. 208, 71 P. 747.

25. Hayes v. Southern Power Co., 1913, 95 S.C. 230, 78 S.E. 956; Meyer v. Menominee & Marinette Light & Traction Co., 1912, 151 Wis. 279, 138 N.W. 1008; see supra, note 9.

26. Chicago, Burlington & Quincy Railroad Co. v. Krayenbuhl, 1902, 65 Neb. 889, 91 N.W. 880; Louisville & Nashville Railroad Co. v. Vaughn, 1942, 292 Ky. 120, 166 S.W.2d 43; see also Chase v. Luce, 1953, 239 Minn. 364, 58 N.W.2d 565 (closing door of unfinished house); Nichols v. Consolidated Dairies, 1952, 125 Mont. 460, 239 P.2d 740, (safety catch on elevator out of repair); Talley v. J & L Oil Co., 1978, 224 Kan. 214, 579 P.2d 706 (repairing fence and bolting hatch on oil tank); cf. Bethay v. Philadelphia Housing Authority, 1979, 271 Pa.Super. 366, 413 A.2d 710 (reasonableness of requiring precautions against children playing on elevator roof for jury).

27. Puchta v. Rothman, 1950, 99 Cal.App.2d 285, 221 P.2d 744; Neal v. Home Builders, 1953, 232 Ind. 160, 111 N.E.2d 280, rehearing denied 232 Ind. 160, 111 N.E. 713; Callahan v. Dearborn Developments, 1959, 57 N.J.Super. 437, 154 A.2d 865.

28. Wilinski v. Belmont Builders, 1957, 14 Ill.App.2d 100, 143 N.E.2d 69; Greene v. De Fazio, 1961, 148 Conn. 419, 171 A.2d 411.

29. Slinker v. Wallner, 1960, 258 Minn. 243, 103 N.W.2d 377; Matheny v. Stonecutter Mills Corp., 1959, 249 N.C. 575, 107 S.E.2d 143.

30. Gordon v. Harris, 1982, 86 A.D.2d 948, 448 N.Y.S.2d 598 (fortuitous accident concerning two children at play); Rice v. Argento, 1977, 59 A.D.2d 1051, 399 N.Y.S.2d 809 (same); Bellflower v. Pennise, 8th Cir. 1977, 548 F.2d 776 (unforeseeable that teenagers would spill gasoline and explode it with firecrackers); Cole v. Housing Authority of La Salle County, 1979, 68 Ill.App.3d 66, 24 Ill.Dec. 470, 385 N.E.2d 382 (unforeseeable that one child would throw metal stake at another); Sahara v. Ragnar Benson, Inc., 1977, 52 Ill.App.3d 119, 9 Ill.Dec. 799, 367 N.E.2d 233 (same: stone); Hayes v. Criterion Corp., Fla.App.1976, 337 So.2d 1026 (unforeseeable that children would dig deep tunnel in side of drainage ditch).

31. The attractive nuisance must be the cause in fact of the child's injuries, or the landowner will not be liable. See Chapman v. Fritzche, 1979, 60 Ill.App.3d 754, 18 Ill.Dec. 155, 377 N.E.2d 308 (child held onto slide on ice in lake while standing on edge of ice reaching for ball in water).

32. See Burk Royalty Co. v. Pace, Tex.Civ.App. 1981, 620 S.W.2d 882 (unfenced oil well pumping unit); Gregory v. Johnson, 1982, 249 Ga. 151, 289 S.E.2d 232 (fence around pool may be sufficient; dictum).

Since the act of fencing may amount to an admission that the hazard might present an unreasonable risk if accessible to children, the landowner or occupier may be required periodically to inspect the fence and maintain it in a secure condition. See Crawford v. Pacific Western Mobile Estates, Inc., Mo.App.1977, 548 S.W.2d 216. But see Metropolitan Government of Nashville v. Counts, Tenn.1976, 541 S.W.2d 133.

33. McCulley v. Cherokee Amusement Co., 1944, 182 Tenn. 68, 184 S.W.2d 170; Niernberg v. Gavin, 1950, 123 Colo. 1, 224 P.2d 215; cf. Pasierb v. Hanover Park Park District, 1981, 103 Ill.App.3d 806, 59 Ill.Dec. 461, 431 N.E.2d 1218.

34. Jarvis v. Howard, 1949, 310 Ky. 38, 219 S.W.2d 958; Schock v. Ringling Brothers and Barnum & Bailey Combined Shows, 1940, 5 Wn.2d 599, 105 P.2d 838.

```
digest(trespass!  /p  minor* child! infant*)  %  topic(110)
320k359(2)
```

Child Trespassing on Defendant's Premises
```
digest(trespass!  /p  minor* child! infant*  /p  duty)
272k33(3)
```

Artificial Conditions
```
child! infant* minor*  /p  trespass  /p  artificial  /5
    condition*
```

Location Where Children are Likely to Trespass
```
child! infant* minor*  /p  trespass!  /s  frequent**
child! infant* minor*  /s  trespass!  /s  aware knew
    known
```

Knowledge of Unreasonable Danger
```
child! infant* minor*  /p  trespass!  &  unreasonabl!  /4
    danger***
child! infant* minor*  /p  trespass!  &  unreasonabl!  /9
    danger***  /s  knew known aware
```

Child's Age and Ignorance of Danger
```
child! infant* minor*  /s  realiz! underst**d appreciat!  /s
    risk  /s  trespass!  /s  age yearold
```

Calculus of Risk; Negligence
```
headnote(child! infant* minor* yearold  /p  trespass!  &
    utility)
```

---

§ 60. Licensees

In its broadest sense, the term "licensee" includes anyone who has a license, which is to say a privilege, to enter upon land.[1] It has sometimes been employed to designate any person who comes upon the land with a privilege arising from the consent of the possessor, including all invitees. But as the word is most commonly used by the courts, it is limited to those who enter with that consent and nothing more.

Such a person is not a trespasser, since he is permitted to enter; but he comes for his own purposes rather than for any purpose or interest of the possessor of the land.[2] He has only the consent to distinguish him from a trespasser; and for this reason he is sometimes unflatteringly referred to as a "bare" or a "naked" licensee.[3] He receives the use of the premises as a gift, and comes well within the old saying that one may not look a gift horse in the mouth. He has no right to demand that the land be made safe for his reception, and he must in general assume the risk of whatever he may encounter, and look out for himself.[4] The rendering of permission to enter carries with it no obligation to inspect the premises to discover dangers which are unknown to the possessor,[5] nor, a fortiori, to give warning or protection against conditions which are known or should be obvious to the licensee.[6]

Here again, as in the case of trespassers,[7] the immunity is limited to persons in possession or those acting on their behalf,[8] and it is generally held that it does not extend to trespassing third parties,[9] to other licen-

---

§ 60

1. See generally Page, The Law of Premises Liability, 1976, ch. 3; Second Restatement of Torts, § 330; Annot., 1983, 22 A.L.R.4th 294.

2. See Hundt v. LaCrosse Grain Co., 1981, ___ Ind. App. ___, 425 N.E.2d 687, 697–98 ("one who enters for his own convenience, curiosity, or entertainment"); Mazzacco v. Purcell, 1981, 303 N.C. 493, 279 S.E.2d 583; McCurry v. Young Men's Christian Association, 1981, 210 Neb. 278, 313 N.W.2d 689, 691 ("solely for his own personal pleasure, convenience, or benefit"); Socha v. Passino, 1981, 105 Mich.App. 445, 306 N.W.2d 316, 318 ("because of some personal, unshared benefit and is merely tolerated on the premises by the owner"); Rowland v. City of Corpus Christi, Tex.Civ.App.1981, 620 S.W.2d 930, 933, refused, n. r. e.); Pinal v. Ocean Ship Supply, Inc., Fla.App.1982, 410 So.2d 1007.

3. E.g., Lave v. Neumann, 1982, 211 Neb. 97, 317 N.W.2d 779; Bauer v. Harn, 1982, 223 Va. 31, 286 S.E.2d 192; see Pearce v. Illinois Central Gulf Railroad Co., 1981, 89 Ill.App.3d 22, 44 Ill.Dec. 196, 411 N.E.2d 102.

4. See James, Tort Liability of Occupiers of Land: Duties Owed to Licensees and Invitees, 1954, 63 Yale L.J. 605; Marsh, The History and Comparative Law of Invitees, Licensees and Trespassers, 1953, 69 L.Q.Rev. 182, 359; Bohlen, The Duty of a Landowner Towards Those Entering His Premises of Their Own Right, 1921, 69 U.Pa.L.Rev. 142, 237, 340.

5. Steinmeyer v. McPherson, 1951, 171 Kan. 275, 232 P.2d 236; Ford v. United States, 10th Cir. 1952, 200 F.2d 272; Rosenberger v. Consolidated Coal Co., 1943, 318 Ill.App. 8, 47 N.E.2d 491. See infra, note 60.

6. See infra, notes 58, 75 and 76.

7. See supra, § 58.

8. Ireland v. Complete Machinery & Equipment Co., 1940, 174 Misc. 91, 21 N.Y.S.2d 430 (contractor); Dishington v. A. W. Kuettel & Sons, 1959, 255 Minn. 325, 96 N.W.2d 684 (subcontractor).

9. Davoust v. City of Alameda, 1906, 149 Cal. 69, 84 P. 760; Boutlier v. City of Malden, 1917, 226 Mass. 479, 116 N.E. 251; Williams v. Springfield Gas & Electric Co., 1918, 274 Mo. 1, 202 S.W. 1.

sees,[10] or even to invitees who have paid for the privilege of entry.[11]

Persons Included

Among the more common classes of persons who enter with nothing more than consent are those taking short cuts across the property [12] or making merely permissive use of crossings and ways [13] or other parts of the premises; [14] loafers, loiterers, and people who come in only to get out of the weather; [15] those in search of their children, servants or other third persons; [16] spectators and sightseers not in any way invited to come; [17] those who enter for social visits [18] or personal business dealings with employees of the possessor of the land; [19] tourists visiting a plant at their own request; [20] those who come to borrow tools [21] or to pick up and remove refuse or chattels for their own benefit; [22] salesmen calling at the door of private homes,[23] and those soliciting money for charity; [24] and a stranger entering an office building to post a letter in a mail-box provided for the use of tenants only.[25] The permission may of course be tacit, and may be manifested by the defendant's conduct, or by the condition of the land itself.[26] It is

---

10. Constantino v. Watson Contracting Co., 1916, 219 N.Y. 443, 114 N.E. 802; Duel v. Mansfield Plumbing Co., 1914, 86 N.J.L. 582, 92 A. 367; Mullen v. Wilkes-Barre Gas & Electric Co., 1910, 229 Pa. 54, 77 A. 1108; Thompson v. Tilton Electric Light & Power Co., 1913, 77 N.H. 92, 88 A. 216. Contra: Hafey v. Dwight Manufacturing Co., 1921, 240 Mass. 155, 133 N.E. 107; New Omaha Thompson Electric Light Co. v. Anderson, 1905, 73 Neb. 84, 102 N.W. 89.

11. Barnett v. Atlantic City Electric Co., 1915, 87 N.J.L. 29, 93 A. 108; Oil Belt Power Co. v. Touchstone, Tex.Civ.App.1924, 266 S.W. 432. See generally Note, 1929, 77 U.Pa.L.Rev. 506.

12. Nicoletti v. Westcor, Inc., 1982, 131 Ariz. 140, 639 P.2d 330; Yalowizer v. Husky Oil Co., Wyo.1981, 629 P.2d 465; Hamilton v. Brown, 1974, 157 W.Va. 910, 207 S.E.2d 923. Such persons may be trespassers. See supra, § 58.

13. Barry v. New York Central & Hudson River Railroad Co., 1883, 92 N.Y. 289; Phipps v. Oregon Railroad & Navigation Co., C.C.Wash.1908, 161 F. 376; Reardon v. Thompson, 1889, 149 Mass. 267, 21 N.E. 369.

14. Standard Oil Co. of Indiana v. Meissner, 1936, 102 Ind.App. 552, 200 N.E. 445; Brinkmeyer v. United Iron & Metal Co., 1935, 168 Md. 149, 177 A. 171; McCurry v. Young Men's Christian Association, 1981, 210 Neb. 278, 313 N.W.2d 689 (non-member using outdoor YMCA basketball court).

15. Dye v. Rule, 1934, 138 Kan. 808, 28 P.2d 758; Murry Chevrolet Co. v. Cotten, 1934, 169 Miss. 521, 152 So. 657; Kneiser v. Belasco-Blackwood Co., 1913, 22 Cal.App. 205, 133 P. 989; Texas Co. v. Haggard, 1939, 23 Tenn.App. 475, 134 S.W.2d 880; Cumberland Telegraph & Telephone Co. v. Martin's Administrator, 1903, 116 Ky. 554, 76 S.W. 394, 77 S.W. 718.

16. Plummer v. Dill, 1892, 156 Mass. 426, 31 N.E. 128; Flatley v. Acme Garage, 1923, 196 Iowa 82, 194 N.W. 180; Faris v. Hoberg, 1892, 134 Ind. 269, 33 N.E. 1028.

17. Gillis v. Pennsylvania Railroad Co., 1868, 59 Pa St. 129; Midland Valley Railroad Co. v. Littlejohn, 1914, 44 Okl. 8, 143 P. 1; Poling v. Ohio River Railroad Co., 1893, 38 W.Va. 645, 18 S.E. 782.

18. Snyder v. I. Jay Realty Co., 1959, 30 N.J. 303, 153 A.2d 1; cf. Holiday Inns, Inc. v. Drew, 1982, 276 Ark. 390, 635 S.W.2d 252 (meeting friends at motel; jury question); Pinal v. Ocean Ship Supply, Inc., Fla.App. 1982, 410 So.2d 1007 (cleaning lady took grandchild to work).

19. Roadman v. C. E. Johnson Motor Sales Co., 1941, 210 Minn. 59, 297 N.W. 166; Pries v. Atlanta Enterprises, 1941, 66 Ga.App. 464, 17 S.E.2d 902. Cf. Eisen v. Sportogs, Inc., Fla.1956, 87 So.2d 44 (wife returning work to shop as accommodation to husband employee).

20. Benson v. Baltimore Traction Co., 1893, 77 Md. 535, 26 A. 973; Roe v. St. Louis Independent Packing Co., 1920, 203 Mo.App. 11, 217 S.W. 335.

21. Laporta v. New York Central Railroad Co., 1916, 224 Mass. 100, 112 N.E. 643; Aguilar v. Riverdale Cooperative Creamery Association, 1930, 104 Cal.App. 263, 285 P. 889; Forbrick v. General Electric Co., 1904, 45 Misc. 452, 92 N.Y.S. 36.

22. Cowart v. Meeks, 1938, 131 Tex. 36, 111 S.W.2d 1105; Socha v. Passino, 1981, 105 Mich.App. 445, 306 N.W.2d 316 (plaintiff picking up bed given to his aunt by defendant). Contra, where the occupier charges a fee for the removal of the waste. Gage v. Ford Motor Co., 1980, 102 Mich.App. 310, 301 N.W.2d 517 (removal of steel slag from steel plant per contract).

23. Prior v. White, 1938, 132 Fla. 1, 180 So. 347; Malatesta v. Lowry, La.App.1961, 130 So.2d 785; De Berry v. City of La Grange, 1940, 62 Ga.App. 74, 8 S.E.2d 146, followed Garrison v. City of Cartersville, 62 Ga.App. 85, 8 S.E.2d 154; Phillips v. Bush, 1961, 50 Tenn.App. 639, 363 S.W.2d 401; cf. Britt v. Allan County Community College, 1982, 230 Kan. 502, 638 P.2d 914 (using college lecture hall).

24. Jones v. Asa G. Candler, Inc., 1918, 22 Ga.App. 717, 97 S.E. 112; Ockerman v. Faulkner's Garage, Ky. 1953, 261 S.W.2d 296.

25. Brosnan v. Koufman, 1936, 294 Mass. 495, 2 N.E.2d 441.

26. Meitzner v. Baltimore & Ohio Railroad Co., 1909, 224 Pa. 352, 73 A. 434; Rooney v. Woolworth, 1905, 78 Conn. 167, 61 A. 366.

often a question for the jury. But notwithstanding occasional great liberality on the part of some courts,[27] it is generally agreed that the mere toleration of continued intrusion where objection or interference would be burdensome or likely to be futile, as in the case of habitual trespasses on railroad tracks, is not in itself and without more a manifestation of consent.[28]

Early decisions, seeking to find some justification for liability to licensees, sometimes struggled hard to find some element of invitation or allurement in the permission given.[29] While there is occasional language to this effect today, it is now very generally recognized that permission is not necessarily invitation,[30] and that, even where there is encouragement to enter or the occupier takes the initiative, it adds nothing to the permission unless the circumstances are such as to imply an assurance that the premises have been prepared and made safe for the particular visit.

Thus, nearly all of the decisions are agreed that a social guest,[31] however cordially he may have been invited and urged to come, is not in law an invitee—a distinction which has puzzled generations of law students, and even some lawyers and judges.[32] The guest is legally nothing more than a licensee, to whom the possessor owes no duty of inspection nor affirmative care to make the premises safe for his visit.[33] The fact that in the course of his visit he gratuitously performs incidental services for his host, such as picking fruit, washing the dishes, or feeding the dog, does not in most states improve his legal position.[34] The reason usually given is that the guest understands when he comes that he is to be placed on the same footing as one of the family, and must take the premises as the occupier himself uses them, without any inspection or preparation for his safety; and that he also understands that he must take his chances as to any defective conditions unknown to the occupier, and is entitled at most to a warning of hid-

27. As for example in Brinilson v. Chicago & North Western Railroad Co., 1911, 144 Wis. 614, 129 N.W. 664; Kremposky v. Mt. Jessup Coal Co., 1920, 266 Pa. 568, 109 A. 766.

28. Arkansas Short Line v. Bellars, 1928, 176 Ark. 53, 2 S.W.2d 683; Indiana Harbor Belt R. Co. v. Jones, 1942, 220 Ind. 139, 41 N.E.2d 361; Second Restatement of Torts, § 330, Comment c. But see Savignac v. Department of Transportation, Fla.App.1981, 406 So.2d 1143 (divers from bridge into canal).

29. Sweeny v. Old Colony & N. R. Co., 1865, 92 Mass. (10 Allen) 368, 87 Am.Dec. 644; Holmes v. Drew, 1890, 151 Mass. 578, 25 N.E. 22.

30. Plummer v. Dill, 1892, 156 Mass. 426, 31 N.E. 128; Branan v. Wimsatt, 1924, 54 App.D.C. 374, 298 F. 833, certiorari denied 265 U.S. 591, 68 L.Ed. 1195; Larmore v. Crown Point Iron Co., 1886, 101 N.Y. 391, 4 N.E. 752.

31. As for child social guests, see Annot., 1968, 20 A.L.R.3d 1127.

32. See dissenting opinion in Pashinian v. Haritonoff, 1980, 81 Ill.2d 377, 43 Ill.Dec. 21, 410 N.E.2d 21 (4–3); Sideman v. Guttman, 1972, 38 A.D.2d 420, 330 N.Y.S.2d 263, 273 (thorough review; opining that "'reason and a right sense of justice' cry out for the abolition by the Court of Appeals of the social guest rule").

33. Walker v. Williams, 1964, 215 Tenn. 195, 384 S.W.2d 447; Lomberg v. Renner, 1960, 121 Vt. 311, 157 A.2d 222, following on remand 121 Vt. 317, 157 A.2d 226; Cordula v. Dietrich, 1960, 9 Wis.2d 211, 101 N.W.2d 126. Contra, perhaps, for social guests of the defendant's tenants. See infra, § 61.

34. Ciaglo v. Ciaglo, 1959, 20 Ill.App.2d 360, 156 N.E.2d 376; Pearlstein v. Leeds, 1958, 52 N.J.Super. 450, 145 A.2d 650 (aiding in preparations for party); Murrell v. Handley, 1957, 245 N.C. 559, 96 S.E.2d 717 (fetching scissors); Cochran v. Abercrombie, Fla.App. 1958, 118 So.2d 636 (looking over motor); Dotson v. Haddock, 1955, 46 Wn.2d 52, 278 P.2d 338 (baby sitter).

Contra, Campbell v. Eubanks, 1963, 107 Ga.App. 527, 130 S.E.2d 832; Cozine v. Shuff, Ky.App.1964, 378 S.W.2d 635; Schlicht v. Thesing, 1964, 25 Wis.2d 436, 130 N.W.2d 763; Benedict v. Podwats, 1970, 109 N.J. Super. 402, 263 A.2d 486, affirmed 57 N.J. 219, 271 A.2d 417.

A guest who brings a gift does not become an invitee. Blackman v. Crowe, 1967, 149 Mont. 253, 425 P.2d 323; Kapka v. Urbaszewski, 1964, 47 Ill.App.2d 321, 198 N.E.2d 569.

Otherwise when the guest comes in response to a request to render gratuitous services, such as nursing—in which case he is an invitee. Murdock v. Petersen, 1958, 74 Nev. 363, 332 P.2d 649; see Maxwell v. Maxwell, 1962, 140 Mont. 59, 367 P.2d 308; Brant v. Matlin, Fla.App.1965, 172 So.2d 902; Mazzacco v. Purcell, 1981, 303 N.C. 493, 279 S.E.2d 583 (to help sister remove trees); Cornutt v. Bolin, Ala.1981, 404 So.2d 38 (to clean grandmother's loaded gun).

den dangers known to the occupier.³⁵ There has, however, been some undercurrent of dissent, as to whether this is really in accord with present social customs, under which it is contended that the guest, invited and even urged to come, rightfully expects more than mere inactivity for his safety,³⁶ and some writers ³⁷ have urged that the social guest be treated as an invitee. The prevalence of liability insurance covering injuries due to defective premises has been advanced as a reason for the change.³⁸ Thus far, however, these arguments have persuaded only a couple of jurisdictions to hold the social guest to be an invitee.³⁹

As in the case of trespassers,⁴⁰ the earlier decisions frequently said that there was no duty to a licensee except to refrain from injuring him intentionally, or by willful, wanton or reckless conduct.⁴¹ This statement of the rule is still sometimes repeated.⁴² Again, as in the case of trespassers, there is something of a tendency to find "wanton" or "reckless" conduct in what clearly appears to be nothing more than ordinary negligence.⁴³ The trend here too, however, has been toward a gradual modification of this position.⁴⁴

Recreational Use Statutes

A significant development in the opposite direction over the last couple of decades ⁴⁵ has been the enactment of "recreational use" statutes in most states,⁴⁶ passed for the purpose of encouraging landowners to hold

---

35. See Bell v. Horton, 1980, ___ Ind.App. ___, 411 N.E.2d 648, 651 ("Defects readily apparent to the victim are not 'hidden.'"); Delk v. Sellers, 1979, 149 Ga. App. 439, 254 S.E.2d 446; Zuther v. Schild, 1978, 224 Kan. 528, 581 P.2d 385 (assistant girl scout leader slipped on ice); Wright v. Caffey, 1960, 239 Miss. 470, 123 So.2d 841 (mother-in-law stepped in bowl of dog food and fell); Ransom v. Grubbs, Tenn.App.1978, 582 S.W.2d 758 (tripped on rake in grass); Preston v. Slezjak, Mich.1970, 175 N.W.2d 759, reversing 1969, 167 N.W.2d 477; Memel v. Feimer, 1975, 85 Wn.2d 685, 538 P.2d 517; Dukes v. Barkdoll, 1982, 211 Neb. 546, 319 N.W.2d 432 (mother-in-law fell down basement steps).

36. See particularly Laube v. Stevenson, 1951, 137 Conn. 469, 78 A.2d 693, and Scheibel v. Lipton, 1951, 156 Ohio St. 308, 102 N.E.2d 453. The arguments are considered at length in Wolfson v. Chelist, Mo.1955, 284 S.W.2d 447.

37. See Laube v. Stevenson, A Discussion, 1951, 25 Conn.Bar J. 123; McCleary, The Liability of a Possessor of Land in Missouri to Persons Injured While on the Land, 1936, 1 Mo.L.Rev. 45, 58; Notes, 1959, 19 La. L.Rev. 906; 1957, 22 Mo.L.Rev. 186; 1958, 12 Rutgers L.Rev. 599; 1966, 7 Wm. & M.L.Rev. 313.

38. 2 Harper and James, Torts, 1956, 1476–1478.

39. Foggin v. General Guaranty Insurance Co., La. 1967, 195 So.2d 636. Maine and Connecticut adhere to this approach by statute. See Ferguson v. Bretton, Me.1977, 375 A.2d 225; Conn.Gen.Stat.Ann. § 52–557a. See also Wood v. Camp, Fla.1973, 284 So.2d 691. Illinois just barely missed slipping into this camp in Pashinian v. Haritonoff, 1980, 81 Ill.2d 377, 410 N.E.2d 21 (4–3).

40. See supra, § 58.

41. See Kahn v. Graper, 1966, 114 Ga.App. 572, 152 S.E.2d 10. Recklessness is generally enough for liability. See Blackburn v. Colvin, 1963, 191 Kan. 239, 380 P.2d 432.

42. Pierce v. Walters, 1972, 152 Ind.App. 321, 283 N.E.2d 560 (child hunting frogs in tall weeds hit by truck); Pashinian v. Haritonoff, 1980, 81 Ill.2d 377, 410 N.E.2d 21 (guest fell down basement stairs when looking for bathroom); Frankel v. Antman, 1981, 157 Ga. App. 26, 276 S.E.2d 87 (statute; dictum); Britt v. Allen County Community Junior College, 1982, 230 Kan. 502, 638 P.2d 914 (piano overturned onto plaintiff). Delaware's premises guest statute so limits the duty of a private residential or farm owner. See Malin v. Consolidated Rail Corp., Del.1981, 438 A.2d 1221.

43. See Holcombe v. Buckland, 4th Cir. 1942, 130 F.2d 544; King v. Patrylow, 1951, 15 N.J.Super. 429, 83 A.2d 639; cf. Simpson v. United States, 9th Cir. 1981, 652 F.2d 831 (recreational use statute; accident in National Forest).

44. See, e.g., Memel v. Feimer, 1975, 85 Wn.2d 685, 538 P.2d 517 (adopting Second Restatement of Torts, § 342); Hoffman v. Planters Gin Co., Miss.1978, 358 So.2d 1008.

45. Only ten states had passed such legislation prior to the promulgation in 1965 of a model act of this type. Council of State Governments, Suggested State Legislation, 1965, Vol. 24, 150–52. Most such statutes have been enacted thereafter and have been influenced thereby. See Barrett, Good Sports and Bad Lands: The Application of Washington's Recreational Use Statute Limiting Landowner Liability, 1977, 53 Wash. L.Rev. 1, 2–3.

46. Forty-two states now have such statutes. E.g., West's Ann.Cal.Civ.Code § 846; West's Fla.Stat.Ann. § 375.251; Ill.—S.H.A. ch. 70 ¶¶ 31–37; Mass.Gen.L. Ann. ch. 21 § 17C; Mich.Comp.L.Ann. § 300.201; N.J. Stat.Ann. 2A:42A–2 to 2A:42A–5; N.Y.—McKinney's Gen.Ob.L. § 9–103; Ohio Rev.Code § 1533.181; Pa. Stat. tit. 68, §§ 477–1 to 477–8; Vernon's Ann.Texas Civ.Stat. art. 16. Utah and Montana have repealed their statutes. The other six states without such statutes are Alas., Ariz., Ind., Miss., Mo., and R.I. The latest compilation of citations to the statutes is in

open to the public their lands and waters for recreational use.[47] Although the statutes vary in their particulars from state to state, they all limit the duties of landowners[48] toward recreational users injured on the land, typically shielding the owner from liability for such injuries unless the entrant was charged a fee for admission to the premises or was injured on account of the owner's wilful or wanton misconduct. The statutes, which have been upheld against constitutional attack,[49] involve a large number of questions of statutory interpretation, including broadly the extent to which they displace the common law principles of landowner liability.[50]

Activities Dangerous to Licensees

It is now generally held that as to any active operations which the occupier carries on, there is an obligation to exercise reasonable care for the protection of a licensee.[51] He must in most jurisdictions run his train,[52] operate his machinery,[53] or back his truck[54] with due regard for the possibility that the permission given may have been accepted and the licensee may be present. The obligation is higher than that owed to a trespasser, because the possessor may be required to look out for licensees before their presence is discovered; but reasonable care will of course be affected by the probability that the licensee will come, whether he may be expected to follow a particular path,[55] the time of day,[56] and the nature of the danger. No more than reasonable care is required, and ordinarily a proper warning will be sufficient.[57] The licensee has no right to demand that the occupier change his method of conducting activities for his safety and, in

---

Knowles, Landowners' Liability Toward Recreational Users: A Critical Comment, 1982, 18 Idaho L.Rev. 59, 64 n. 25. See also Haw.Rev.Stat. §§ 520–1 to –8.

47. See generally Page, The Law of Premises Liability, 1976, §§ 5.13–.22. The most helpful article is Barrett, Good Sports and Bad Lands: The Application of Washington's Recreational Use Statute Limiting Landowner Liability, 1977, 53 Wash.L.Rev. 1. See also Note, 1980, 15 Land & Water L.R. 649.

48. Usually defined to include lessees, occupiers or those otherwise in control of the premises.

49. E.g., Simpson v. United States, 9th Cir. 1981, 652 F.2d 831 (California; no violation of equal protection); Crawford v. Consumers Power Co., 1981, 108 Mich.App. 232, 310 N.W.2d 343; Abdin v. Fischer, Fla. 1979, 374 So.2d 1379.

50. Recent cases interpreting such statutes include Rochette v. Town of Newburgh, 1982, 88 A.D.2d 614, 449 N.Y.S.2d 1013 (specification of recreational uses including "boating" did not apply to iceboat racing); Nelsen v. City of Gridley, 1980, 113 Cal.App.3d 87, 169 Cal. Rptr. 757 (statute inapplicable to state owned lands; discussing case contra); Crawford v. Consumers Power Co., 1981, 108 Mich.App. 232, 310 N.W.2d 343 (immunity did not depend on whether negligence active or passive; statute merely codifies duties owed to licensees); Wirth v. Ehly, 1980, 93 Wis.2d 433, 287 N.W.2d 140 (minor claimants not excluded from coverage); Lacombe v. Greathouse, La.App.1981, 407 So.2d 1346 (contra: statute inapplicable to minor); Paige v. North Oaks Partners, 1982, 134 Cal.App.3d 860, 184 Cal.Rptr. 867 (statute inapplicable to construction ditch in shopping center); Michalovic v. Genesee-Monroe Racing Association, Inc., 1981, 79 A.D.2d 82, 436 N.Y.S.2d 468 (relatively undeveloped lands, not asphalt parking lot, covered by statute); Harrison v. Middlesex Water Co., 1979, 80 N.J. 391, 403 A.2d 910 (act applied to recreational activities on rural lands, not to reservoir in residential area, nor to person attempting to rescue skaters who fell through ice).

51. Ragnone v. Portland School District No. 1J, 1981, 291 Or. 617, 633 P.2d 1287; Potts v. Amis, 1963, 62 Wn.2d 777, 384 P.2d 825 (swinging golf club); Blystone v. Kiesel, 1967, 247 Or. 528, 431 P.2d 262 (running to front door); Bradshaw v. Minter, 1965, 206 Va. 450, 143 S.E.2d 827 (giving guest horse). Second Restatement of Torts, § 341. Contra, Britt v. Allen County Community Junior College, 1982, 230 Kan. 502, 638 P.2d 914.

52. Louisville & Nashville Railroad Co. v. Blevins, Ky.1956, 293 S.W.2d 246; Seaboard Air Lines Railway Co. v. Branham, Fla.App.1958, 99 So.2d 621, certiorari discharged, App., 104 So.2d 356. Contra, Jackson v. Pennsylvania Railroad Co., 1939, 176 Md. 1, 3 A.2d 719.

53. Boardman v. McNeff, 1964, 177 Neb. 534, 129 N.W.2d 457 (harrow and truck). Cf. Cropanese v. Martinez, 1955, 35 N.J.Super. 118, 113 A.2d 433 (joining pipe); Draper v. Switous, 1963, 370 Mich. 468, 122 N.W.2d 698 (washing rack); Perry v. St. Jean, 1966, 100 R.I. 622, 218 A.2d 484 (providing horse to be ridden); Hoffman v. Planters Gin Co., Miss.1978, 358 So. 2d 1008 (revolving auger).

54. Cullmann v. Mumper, 1967, 83 Ill.App.2d 395, 228 N.E.2d 276; Potter Title & Trust Co. v. Young, 1951, 367 Pa. 239, 80 A.2d 76.

55. Cf. Olderman v. Bridgeport-City Trust Co., 1939, 125 Conn. 177, 4 A.2d 646; Morrison v. Carpenter, 1914, 179 Mich. 207, 146 N.W. 106.

56. Cf. Sherman v. Maine Central Railroad Co., 1913, 110 Me. 228, 85 A. 755.

57. Second Restatement of Torts, § 341, Comment c.

the usual case, if he is fully informed as to what is going on or it is obvious to him, he has all that he is entitled to expect, and assumes the risk thereafter.[58]

Dangerous Conditions Known to the Occupier

As to passive conditions on the land, it is still the settled rule that the possessor is under no obligation to the licensee with respect to anything that the possessor does not know.[59] He is not required to inspect his land for unknown dangers, nor, of course, to disclose their existence or take precautions against them.[60] But another special rule that developed in England[61] was that the occupier was not permitted to "set a trap" for the licensee. This phrase originally was used in the sense of presenting an appearance of safety where it did not exist;[62] but the significance which gradually became attached to it was not one of intent to injure, or even of any active misconduct, but merely that the possessor of the land was under an obligation to warn the licensee of any concealed dangerous conditions on the premises of which he had knowledge.[63] The theory usually advanced in support of this duty is that, by extending permission to enter the land, he represents that it is as safe as it appears to be, and when he knows that it is not there is "something like fraud"[64] in his failure to give warning.[65] The licensee may be required to accept the premises as the occupier uses them, but he is entitled to equal knowledge of the danger, and should not be expected to assume the risk of a defective bridge,[66] an uninsulated wire,[67] an unusually slippery floor,[68] or a dangerous step,[69] in the face of a misleading silence.

The duty arises only when the occupier has actual knowledge of the risk,[70] although this may be shown by circumstantial evidence, and he is held to the standard of a reasonable person in realizing the significance of what he has discovered.[71] It may

---

58. Downes v. Elmira Bridge Co., 1904, 179 N.Y. 136, 71 N.E. 743; Shafer v. Tacoma Eastern Railroad Co., 1916, 91 Wash. 164, 157 P. 485.

59. See supra, note 5.

60. Fleck v. Nickerson, 1965, 239 Or. 641, 399 P.2d 353; Brauner v. Leutz, 1943, 293 Ky. 406, 169 S.W.2d 4; Steinmeyer v. McPherson, 1951, 171 Kan. 275, 232 P.2d 236; Ford v. United States, 10th Cir. 1952, 200 F.2d 272; Gabbert v. Wood, 1954, 127 Cal.App.2d 188, 273 P.2d 319.

61. Corby v. Hill, 1858, 4 C.B.,N.S., 556, 140 Eng. Rep. 1209; Bolch v. Smith, 1862, 7 H. & N. 736, 158 Eng.Rep. 666.

62. Griffith, Licensors and "Traps," 1925, 41 L.Q. Rev. 255.

63. See Fitch v. Adler, 1981, 51 Or.App. 845, 627 P.2d 36; Savignac v. Department of Transportation, Fla.App.1981, 406 So.2d 1143; Ragnone v. Portland School District No. 1J, 1981, 291 Or. 617, 633 P.2d 1287 (dictum); Second Restatement of Torts, § 342; Annot., 1969, 26 A.L.R.3d 317 (duty to warn child licensee).

64. Willes, J., in Gautret v. Eberton, 1867, L.R. 2 C.P. 271, 36 L.J.C.P. 191. See Eldredge, Landlord's Tort Liability for Disrepair, 1936, 84 U.Pa.L.Rev. 467, 468–470.

65. See supra, § 33, as to nondisclosure as negligence.

66. Campbell v. Boyd, 1883, 88 N.C. 129; cf. Chappell v. Dwyer, Tex.Civ.App.1981, 611 S.W.2d 158 (deceptive road).

67. Smith v. Southwest Missouri Railroad Co., 1933, 333 Mo. 314, 62 S.W.2d 761. Cf. Snow v. Judy, 1968, 96 Ill.App.2d 420, 239 N.E.2d 327 (barbed wire).

68. Choate v. Carter, 1958, 98 Ga.App. 375, 105 S.E.2d 909; Newman v. Fox West Coast Theatres, 1948, 86 Cal.App.2d 428, 194 P.2d 706; Hennessey v. Hennessey, 1958, 145 Conn. 211, 140 A.2d 473.

69. Berger v. Shapiro, 1959, 30 N.J. 89, 152 A.2d 20; Haffey v. Lemieux, 1966, 154 Conn. 185, 224 A.2d 551. Accord: Miniken v. Carr, 1967, 71 Wn.2d 325, 428 P.2d 716 (two doors); Rushton v. Winters, 1938, 331 Pa. 78, 200 A. 60 (porch railing); Smith v. Benson's Wild Animal Farm, 1954, 99 N.H. 243, 109 A.2d 39 (loose pony); Maxfield v. Maxfield, 1959, 102 N.H. 101, 151 A.2d 226 (oily rags). But see Schoen v. Gilbert, Fla.App. 1981, 404 So.2d 128 (2–1) (drop between foyer and living room: no duty to warn).

70. Joyce v. Nash, Mo.App.1982, 630 S.W.2d 219; Rowland v. City of Corpus Christi, Tex.Civ.App.1981, 620 S.W.2d 930; Davis v. Jackson, Mo.App.1980, 604 S.W.2d 610; Beckwith v. State Farm Fire & Casualty Co., La.App.1980, 393 So.2d 155, writ denied, Sup., 399 So.2d 209 (sharp object in water-filled ditch); Judd v. Zupon, 1973, 297 Minn. 38, 209 N.W.2d 423 (viciousness of Siamese cats).

71. Hennessey v. Hennessey, 1958, 145 Conn. 211, 140 A.2d 473. He is not, however, required to know more than the standard reasonable man about the dangers of a situation; and if he knows of the existence of a condition, but is reasonably ignorant of its dangers, he is not liable. Schlaks v. Schlaks, 1962, 17 A.D.2d 153, 232 N.Y.S.2d 814.

include disclosure of natural [72] as well as artificial conditions, and extend to activities of third persons on the premises which may create a danger to the licensee.[73] The duty ordinarily is not to maintain the land in safe condition, but to exercise reasonable care to warn the licensee of the danger; [74] so that if it is known [75] or must be obvious [76] to him, he must look out for himself, and there is no further obligation. If, however, the possessor knows of a physical infirmity of the visitor, such as bad eyesight, which will make discovery difficult, there may be a duty to disclose even the otherwise obvious.[77] The perils of darkness usually are held to be assumed by one who voluntarily proceeds into it,[78] but if the occupier has any special reason to believe that the licensee will encounter a particular danger there, of which he is unaware, there may still be a duty to give warning.[79] In short, the duty of disclosure may arise only where a reasonable man in the position of the occupier would conclude that it is called for.[80] Account must, however, be taken of the curiosity and meddling propensities of children and their inability to protect themselves; and the doctrine of "attractive nuisance" applies to licensees as fully as to trespassers.[81]

Liability sometimes is imposed where the occupier, knowing that licensees are in the habit of entering or are likely to come, alters the condition of his premises so as to create a new danger without giving notice of the change or taking other precautions to prevent injury. Thus he may be liable if he places an obstruction in a private way or path,[82] or digs a hole,[83] installs a dangerous electric wire,[84] or sets a vicious horse [85] where licensees customarily pass, or establishes or permits some other new danger [86] where it may reasonably be expected that they will not discover it.

 WESTLAW REFERENCES

di licensee

Persons Included
digest(licensee /s includes) % topic(238) 272k32(2)

Recreational Use Statutes
375.251 & court(fl)

---

72. Windsor Reservoir & Canal Co. v. Smith, 1933, 92 Colo. 464, 21 P.2d 1116; Kittle v. State, 1935, 245 App.Div. 401, 284 N.Y.S. 657, affirmed, 1936, 272 N.Y. 420, 3 N.E.2d 850.

73. Martin v. Shea, 1982, ___ Ind.App. ___, 432 N.E.2d 46 (guests at defendant's party knocked plaintiff in swimming pool); Mangione v. Dimino, 1972, 39 A.D.2d 128, 332 N.Y.S.2d 683 (thrown in); Second Restatement of Torts, § 318.

74. Second Restatement of Torts, § 342.

75. Kopp v. R.S. Noonan, Inc., 1956, 385 Pa. 460, 123 A.2d 429; Maxfield v. Maxfield, 1959, 102 N.H. 101, 151 A.2d 226; see Annot., 1971, 35 A.L.R.3d 230.

76. See Bell v. Horton, 1980, ___ Ind.App. ___, 411 N.E.2d 648; McCurry v. Young Men's Christian Association, 1981, 210 Neb. 278, 313 N.W.2d 689; cf. Pinal v. Ocean Ship Supply, Inc., Fla.App.1982, 410 So.2d 1007 (floor fan). See generally, Keeton, Personal Injuries Resulting from Open and Obvious Conditions, 1952, 100 U.Pa.L.Rev. 629.

77. Berger v. Shapiro, 1959, 30 N.J. 89, 152 A.2d 20; Choate v. Carter, 1958, 98 Ga.App. 375, 105 S.E.2d 909.

78. Tempest v. Richardson, 1956, 5 Utah 2d 174, 299 P.2d 124; Schoen v. Gilbert, Fla.App.1981, 404 So.2d 128 (2–1); see supra, § 32.

79. See Fitch v. Adler, 1981, 51 Or.App. 845, 627 P.2d 36; cf. Frederick v. Reed, Ala.Civ.App.1982, 410 So.2d 95.

80. Birdsong v. City of Chattanooga, 1958, 204 Tenn. 264, 319 S.W.2d 233 (no duty to warn one using well defined path of dangers off path); Sokoloski v. Pugliese, 1962, 149 Conn. 299, 179 A.2d 603 (must have reason to believe plaintiff would not discover and realize risk); Mathias v. Denver Union Terminal Railway Co., 1958, 137 Colo. 224, 323 P.2d 624 (when aware licensee has embarked on dangerous course, duty to warn him).

81. See supra, § 59.

82. Nashville, Chattanooga & St. Louis Railway Co. v. Blackwell, 1918, 201 Ala. 657, 79 So. 129; Batts v. Home Telephone & Telegraph Co., 1923, 186 N.C. 120, 118 S.E. 893; Frederick v. Reed, Ala.Civ.App.1982, 410 So.2d 95 (mother-in-law tripped in dark over roll of carpet placed in her usual path in carport).

83. Morrison v. Carpenter, 1914, 179 Mich. 207, 146 N.W. 106; Oliver v. City of Worcester, 1869, 102 Mass. 489; Burton v. Western & Atlantic Railroad Co., 1896, 98 Ga. 783, 25 S.E. 736.

84. Ellsworth v. Metheney, 6th Cir. 1900, 104 F. 119.

85. Lowery v. Walker, [1911] A.C. 10.

86. Newman v. Fox West Coast Theatres, 1948, 86 Cal.App.2d 428, 194 P.2d 706; Savignac v. Department of Transportation, Fla.App.1981, 406 So.2d 1143 (excavation nearby filled in bottom of canal used for diving).

court(mi) & 300.201
landowner /s liabil! /s recreation!

Activities Dangerous to Licensees
licensee* /s danger! /s activit! % topic(223 238)
headnote(reasonable /s care /s licensee*)

Dangerous Conditions Known to the Occupier
headnote(danger! /s condition* /s licensee*)

§ 61. Invitees

The leading English case of Indermaur v. Dames[1] laid down the rule that as to those who enter premises upon business which concerns the occupier, and upon his invitation express or implied, the latter is under an affirmative duty to protect them, not only against dangers of which he knows, but also against those which with reasonable care he might discover. The case was accepted in all common law jurisdictions, and the invitee,[2] or as he is sometimes called the business visitor, is placed upon a higher footing than a licensee. The typical example, of course, is the customer in a store.[3] Patrons of restaurants,[4] taverns,[5] banks,[6] theatres,[7] bathing beaches,[8] fairs[9] and other places of amusement,[10] and other businesses open to the public[11] are included, as are drivers calling for or delivering goods purchased or sold,[12] independent contractors doing work on the premises[13] and the workmen employed by such contractors,[14] as well as a

§ 61

1. 1866, L.R. 1 C.P. 274, 35 L.J.C.P. 184, affirmed L.R. 2 C.P. 311, 36 L.J.C.P. 181.

2. See generally Page, The Law of Premises Liability, 1976, ch. 4; Second Restatement of Torts, § 332; Annot., 1983, 22 A.L.R.4th 294.

3. See Mock v. Sears, Roebuck & Co., 1981, 101 Ill.App.3d 103, 56 Ill.Dec. 540, 427 N.E.2d 872; Foster v. Winston-Salem Joint Venture, 1981, 303 N.C. 636, 281 S.E.2d 36; J.C. Penney Co. v. Chavez, Tex.Civ.App. 1981, 618 S.W.2d 399, refused, n.r.e. Lingerfelt v. Winn-Dixie Texas, Inc., Okl.1982, 645 P.2d 485; cf. Green v. Wellons, Inc., 1981, 52 N.C.App. 529, 279 S.E.2d 37 (shopping center).

4. Allgauer v. Le Bastille, Inc., 1981, 101 Ill.App.3d 978, 57 Ill.Dec. 466, 428 N.E.2d 1146; Backer v. Pizza Inn, Inc., 1982, 162 Ga.App. 682, 292 S.E.2d 562; McDonald's Corp. v. Grissom, Ala.1981, 402 So.2d 953; cf. Bishop v. Hamad, 1973, 43 A.D.2d 805, 350 N.Y.S.2d 270 (ice cream vending truck; child hit by car).

5. Frankovitch v. Burton, 1981, ___ Conn. ___, 440 A.2d 254; Prather v. H–K Corp., 1980, 282 Pa.Super. 556, 423 A.2d 385; Chadwick v. Barba Lou, Inc., 1982, 69 Ohio St.2d 222, 431 N.E.2d 660; cf. Hovermale v. Berkeley Springs Moose Lodge, 1980, ___ W.Va. ___, 271 S.E.2d 335 (private bar at Moose Lodge).

6. Sinn v. Farmers' Deposit Savings Bank, 1930, 150 A. 163, 300 Pa. 85, 150 A. 163; Howlett v. Dorchester Trust Co., 1926, 256 Mass. 544, 152 N.E. 895; Annot., 1973, 51 A.L.R.3d 711 (injury to customer in robbery).

7. Durning v. Hyman, 1926, 286 Pa. 376, 133 A. 568; Knapp v. Connecticut Theatrical Corp., 1937, 122 Conn. 413, 190 A. 291; Martin Theatres of Texas, Inc. v. Puryear, Tex.App.1982, 631 S.W.2d 600.

8. Beverly Beach Club v. Marron, 1937, 172 Md. 471, 192 A. 278; Knight v. Moore, 1942, 179 Va. 139, 18 S.E.2d 266.

9. Dunn v. Brown County Agricultural Society, 1888, 46 Ohio St. 93, 18 N.E. 496; Smith v. Cumberland County Agricultural Society, 1913, 163 N.C. 346, 79 S.E. 632; Annot., 1969, 24 A.L.R.3d 945.

10. Scott v. University of Michigan Athletic Association, 1908, 152 Mich. 684, 116 N.W. 624, motion to retax costs denied 154 Mich. 328, 117 N.W. 729 (football); Crane v. Kansas City Baseball & Exhibition Co., 1913, 168 Mo.App. 301, 153 S.W. 1076 (baseball); Brown v. Rhoades, 1927, 126 Me. 186, 137 A. 58 (amusement park); Mastad v. Swedish Brethren, 1901, 83 Minn. 40, 85 N.W. 913 (Swedish picnic); Nicholas v. Tri-State Fair & Sales Association, 1967, 82 S.D. 450, 148 N.W.2d 183 (rodeo); Duffy v. Midlothian Country Club, 1980, 92 Ill.App.3d 193, 47 Ill.Dec. 786, 415 N.E.2d 1099 (golf tournament); Pound v. Augusta National, Inc., 1981, 158 Ga.App. 166, 279 S.E.2d 342 (same); Starling v. Fisherman's Pier, Inc., Fla.App. 1981, 401 So.2d 1136 (commercial fishing pier); Schreiber v. Walt Disney World Co., Fla.App.1980, 389 So.2d 1040 (patron injured on "Flume" while "plummeting from the heights to * * * the watery depths below"); cf. Sanders v. Stutes, La.App.1981, 400 So.2d 1159 (miniature golf course).

11. Jay v. Walla Walla College, 1959, 53 Wn.2d 590, 335 P.2d 458 (college); Ilgenfritz v. Missouri Power & Light Co., 1933, 340 Mo. 648, 101 S.W.2d 723 (light company); Chatkin v. Talarski, 1937, 123 Conn. 157, 193 A. 611 (undertaker); Smith v. Mottman, 1938, 194 Wash. 100, 77 P.2d 376 (seamstress); Treadway v. Ebert Motor Co., 1981, ___ Pa.Super. ___, 436 A.2d 994 (repair garage).

12. Harvill v. Swift & Co., 1960, 102 Ga.App. 543, 117 S.E.2d 202; cf. Gage v. Ford Motor Co., 1980, 102 Mich.App. 310, 301 N.W.2d 517 (to pick up waste metal from steel plant per removal contract). See Annot., 1970, 32 A.L.R.3d 9.

13. Hundt v. LaCross Grain Co., 1981, ___ Ind.App. ___, 425 N.E.2d 687 (bird exterminator looking for bathroom); Kraustrunk v. Chicago Housing Authority, 1981, 95 Ill.App.3d 529, 51 Ill.Dec. 15, 420 N.E.2d 429 (elevator repairman criminally assaulted); Harris v.

14. See note 14 on page 420.

large and miscellaneous group of similar persons who are present in the interest of the occupier as well as of their own.

There is, however, an important conflict of opinion as to the definition of an invitee, as well as to whether certain visitors are to be included in this category.[15] The argument turns on the fundamental theory as to the basis of the special obligation which is placed upon the occupier of the land. One theory, which has received approval from a number of legal writers,[16] and was adopted by the First Restatement of Torts,[17] is that the duty of affirmative care to make the premises safe is imposed upon the person in possession as the price he must pay for the economic benefit he derives, or expects to derive, from the presence of the visitor; and that when no such benefit is to be found, he is under no such duty. On this basis, the "business" on which the visitor comes must be one of at least potential pecuniary profit to the possessor.[18]

The application of the economic benefit theory has led to a good deal of what looks like legal ingenuity. Potential gain is not difficult to find in the case of one who enters a store to make a purchase,[19] or forms such an intention after entering,[20] or one who is shopping in the hope of finding something that he wants,[21] or even one with the "vague purpose of buying something if she saw anything she took a fancy to"[22]—although obviously any such test is at the mercy of the plaintiff's own testimony as to his reasons.[23] And no doubt the customer who returns to pay a bill, or to retrieve a purse left at the store is still to be treated as on the original business.[24] But many courts which have proceeded on this basis have endeavored to find in other cases some even more tenuous economic advantage, in the form of advertising or good will, encourage-

Cool, 1981, 85 A.D.2d 921, 446 N.Y.S.2d 774 (bee-fleeing house painter struck head); Annot., 1979, 96 A.L.R.3d 1213 (actions against storekeeper for injuries during repair).

14. See Conover v. Northern States Power Co., Minn.1981, 313 N.W.2d 397; Chesapeake & Potomac Telephone Co. of Maryland v. Chesapeake Utilities Corp., Del.1981, 436 A.2d 314; Cowan v. Laughridge Construction Co., N.C.1982, 57 N.C.App. 321, 291 S.E.2d 287; cf. Wingard v. Safeway Stores, Inc., 1981, 123 Cal.App.3d 37, 176 Cal.Rptr. 320; Hewett v. First National Bank of Atlanta, 1980, 155 Ga.App. 773, 272 S.E.2d 744 (Wells Fargo security guard picking up securities at bank). But see Brown v. South Broward Hospital District, Fla.App.1981, 402 So.2d 58; Lumpkin v. Streifel, N.D.1981, 308 N.W.2d 878; Thrasher v. Gerken, Iowa 1981, 309 N.W.2d 488 (landowner relinquished control of property during construction period to construction company).

15. See Prosser, Business Visitors and Invitees, 1942, 26 Minn.L.Rev. 573, 20 Can.Bar Rev. 446; James, Tort Liability of Occupiers of Land: Duties Owed to Licensees and Invitees, 1954, 63 Yale L.J. 605; Notes, 1958, 44 Va.L.Rev. 804; 1958, 46 Ky.L.J. 501; 1966, 42 Wash.L.Rev. 299.

16. Salmond, Law of Torts, 11th ed. 1953, § 162; Harper, Law of Torts, 1933, § 98; Charlesworth, Law of Negligence, 2d ed. 1947, § 181 ff.

In the United States this theory appears to have originated with the writer of a forgotten treatise on the law of negligence, Robert Campbell, who derived it from the rather ambiguous use of the word "business" in some of the early English cases. Campbell, Law of Negligence, 2d ed. 1878, 63–64.

17. §§ 332, 343, Comment a. It should be noted that the Reporter for this part of the First Restatement was Professor Bohlen, the leading advocate of the economic benefit theory. See, e.g., Bohlen, The Duty of a Landowner Towards Those Entering His Premises of Their Own Right, 1920, 69 U.Pa.L.Rev. 142, 340. Recent examples include Richey v. Kemper, Mo.1965, 392 S.W.2d 266; Vogel v. Fetter Livestock Co., 1964, 144 Mont. 127, 394 P.2d 766.

18. See, e.g., Socha v. Passino, 1981, 105 Mich. 445, 306 N.W.2d 316, 317 (defining an "invitee" as "one who is on the owner's premise for a purpose mutually beneficial to both parties [and where] the visit may reasonably be said to confer or anticipate a business, commercial, monetary, or other tangible benefit to the occupant").

19. Kroger Co. v. Thomas, 6th Cir. 1960, 277 F.2d 854; Coston v. Skyland Hotel, 1950, 231 N.C. 546, 57 S.E.2d 793.

20. Braun v. Vallade, 1917, 33 Cal.App. 279, 164 P. 904.

21. Dickey v. Hochschild, Kohn & Co., 1929, 157 Md. 448, 146 A. 282; Nelson v. F.W. Woolworth Co., 1930, 211 Iowa 592, 231 N.W. 665; cf. Krone v. McCann, 1982, ___ Mont. ___, 638 P.2d 397 (prospective purchaser of defendant's realty).

22. MacDonough v. F.W. Woolworth Co., 1918, 91 N.J.L. 677, 103 A. 74.

23. See Shulman and James, Cases and Materials on the Law of Torts, 2d ed. 1952, 631.

24. Andrews v. Goetz, Fla.App.1958, 104 So.2d 653; Sulhoff v. Everett, 1944, 235 Iowa 396, 16 N.W.2d 737.

ment of customers to come, possible advice or assistance which might be given to another about to buy,[25] or even the chance that the plaintiff might see something that he likes,[26] which would appear to be true of any person whatever on the premises, and to exclude virtually no one, even a policeman coming to confer "benefit" upon the landowner by arresting him.

Thus children[27] and friends[28] who accompany customers with no intention of buying anything themselves, or go to visit patients in hospitals[29] or to railway stations to see people off,[30] guests in automobiles who go with drivers to garages,[31] filling stations[32] or parking lots,[33] tourists who visit factories at the invitation of the owner,[34] those who bring employees their lunch with the encouragement of the management,[35] and even possible purchasers who look at displays in shop windows,[36] or who desire on the particular occasion only to use a toilet[37] or a telephone[38] open to the public, or even the man who goes into a bank to change a five dollar bill,[39] or into a building to read a notice required by law to be posted there,[40] all have been held to be invitees. While the "mutuality of interest" is often indirect and remote

25. Sears, Roebuck & Co. v. Donovan, Mun.App. D.C.1958, 137 A.2d 716; Kennedy v. Phillips, 1928, 319 Mo. 573, 5 S.W.2d 33; cf. Fournier v. New York, New Haven & Hartford Railroad Co., 1934, 286 Mass. 7, 189 N.E. 574 (railway station).

Or that the parent might be unable to come if she must leave her child at home. Grogan v. O'Keefe's, Inc., 1929, 267 Mass. 189, 166 N.E. 721; Anderson v. Cooper, 1958, 214 Ga. 164, 104 S.E.2d 90.

26. Campbell v. Weathers, 1941, 153 Kan. 316, 111 P.2d 72; Kennedy v. Phillips, 1928, 319 Mo. 573, 5 S.W.2d 33.

27. Murphy v. Kelly, 1954, 15 N.J. 608, 105 A.2d 841; Hostick v. Hall, Okl.1963, 386 P.2d 758; Valunas v. J.J. Newberry Co., 1957, 336 Mass. 305, 145 N.E.2d 685; Jackson v. Pike, Fla.1956, 87 So.2d 410; cf. Hoffman v. Planters Gin Co., Miss.1978, 358 So.2d 1008 (son helping father at work); Radle v. Hennepin Ave. Theatre & Realty Co., 1941, 209 Minn. 415, 296 N.W. 510 (mother accompanying child entered in talent contest); Goyette v. Sousa, 1959, 90 R.I. 8, 153 A.2d 509, reargument denied 90 R.I. 8, 154 A.2d 697 (wife accompanying fisherman). But in Dunleavy v. Constant, 1964, 106 N.H. 64, 204 A.2d 236, children accompanying those on business at a private residence were held to be only licensees.

28. Smigielski v. Nowak, 1940, 124 N.J.L. 235, 11 A.2d 251; Farrier v. Levin, 1959, 176 Cal.App.2d 791, 1 Cal.Rptr. 742; Briggs v. John Yeon Co., 1942, 168 Or. 239, 122 P.2d 444.

29. Murray v. Eastern Maine Medical Center, Me. 1982, 447 A.2d 465 (slip on water on stairs); Burkowske v. Church Hospital Corp., 1982, 50 Md.App. 515, 439 A.2d 40 (bench in waiting room collapsed when plaintiff sat beside her 350 pound mother); Syas v. Nebraska Methodist Hospital Foundation, 1981, 209 Neb. 201, 307 N.W.2d 112.

30. McCann v. Anchor Line, 2d Cir. 1933, 79 F.2d 338; Powell v. Great Lakes Transit Corp., 1922, 152 Minn. 90, 188 N W 61. Cf. Mathias v. Denver Union Terminal Railway Co., 1958, 137 Colo. 224, 323 P.2d 624 (photographer in railroad station to photograph visiting celebrity).

31. De Soto Auto Hotel v. McDonough, 6th Cir. 1955, 219 F.2d 253; Pope v. Willow Garages, 1930, 274 Mass. 440, 174 N.E. 727.

32. Nave v. Hixenbaugh, 1956, 180 Kan. 370, 304 P.2d 482; Wingrove v. Home Land Co., 1938, 120 W.Va. 100, 196 S.E. 563. Contra, Morse v. Sinclair Automobile Service Co., 5th Cir. 1936, 86 F.2d 298.

33. Goldsmith v. Cody, 1958, 351 Mich. 380, 88 N.W.2d 268; Nary v. Parking Authority of Town of Dover, 1959, 58 N.J.Super. 222, 156 A.2d 42; Parking, Inc. v. Dalrymple, Tex.Civ.App.1964, 375 S.W.2d 758.

34. Gilliland v. Bondurant, Mo.App.1932, 51 S.W.2d 559, affirmed, 1933, 332 Mo. 881, 59 S.W.2d 679; Deach v. Woolner Distilling Co., 1914, 187 Ill.App. 524 ("mutuality of interest" specifically rejected).

35. Taylor v. McCowat-Mercer Printing Co., D.Tenn.1939, 27 F.Supp. 880, affirmed, 6th Cir. 1940, 115 F.2d 868; Coburn v. Village of Swanton, 1921, 95 Vt. 320, 115 A. 153.

36. Leighton v. Dean, 1917, 117 Me. 40, 102 A. 565 ("All are invited that some may be persuaded").

37. Campbell v. Weathers, 1941, 153 Kan. 316, 111 P.2d 72; Dym v. Merit Oil Corp., 1944, 130 Conn. 585, 36 A.2d 276.

38. Ward v. Avery, 1931, 113 Conn. 394, 155 A. 502; Coston v. Skyland Hotel, 1950, 231 N.C. 546, 57 S.E.2d 793. Contra, Argus v. Michler, Mo.App.1963, 349 S.W.2d 389. In Hartman v. Di Lello, 1959, 109 Ohio App. 387, 157 N.E.2d 127, the defendant apparently received payment for the use of the telephone, since the plaintiff is called a business visitor.

39. First National Bank of Birmingham v. Lowery, 1955, 263 Ala. 36, 81 So.2d 284; American National Bank v. Wolfe, 1938, 22 Tenn.App. 642, 125 S.W.2d 193. Contrast, where the place was not open for such a purpose, and the visitor was held only a licensee: Stewart v. Texas Co., Fla.1953, 67 So.2d 653 (changing bill in filling station).

40. Walker v. County of Randolph, 1960, 251 N.C. 805, 112 S.E.2d 551 (courthouse); St. Louis, Iron Mountain & Southern Railway Co. v. Fairbairn, 1886, 48 Ark. 491, 4 S.W. 50 (railroad station).

from the object of the particular visit,[41] there is at least ground for suspecting that in some of these cases, at least, it has been dredged up for the occasion.

The alternative theory, which appears to have been the earlier one,[42] is that the basis of liability is not any economic benefit to the occupier, but a representation to be implied, when he encourages others to enter to further a purpose of his own, that reasonable care has been exercised to make the place safe for those who come for that purpose.[43] This idea of course underlies the stress laid upon "invitation" in so many of the cases; but, as in the case of the social guest,[44] invitation is not enough without the circumstances which convey the implied assurance. When premises are thrown open to the public, the assurance is ordinarily given; and this generally explains the foregoing cases more satisfactorily than any indirect hope of pecuniary gain. It accounts also for decisions holding that when a strip of land abutting upon the highway is so paved that it is indistinguishable from the sidewalk,[45] or a private way is given the appearance of a public thoroughfare,[46] those who use it are to be treated as invitees. It is the implied representation made to the public, by holding the land open to them, that it has been prepared for their reception, which is the basis of the liability. There is thus a distinction between a landowner who tacitly permits the boys of the neighborhood to play ball on his vacant lot, in which case they are only licensees,[47] and the man who installs playground equipment and throws the lot open gratuitously to the children of the town as offered and provided for the purpose, in which case there is a public invitation.[48]

This second theory is now accepted by a large number of the courts which hold that many visitors, from whose presence no shadow of pecuniary benefit can be found, are invitees. The list of "public invitees"[49] has included persons attending free public lectures,[50] church services and meetings,[51]

---

41. See Knudsen v. Duffee-Freeman, Inc., 1959, 99 Ga.App. 520, 109 S.E.2d 339; cf. Frankel v. Antman, 1982, 157 Ga.App. 26, 276 S.E.2d 87 (invited guest to private home for fund-raising event of charitable women's organization).

42. The early history is traced in Prosser, Business Visitors and Invitees, 1942, 26 Minn.L.Rev. 573, 1943, 20 Can.Bar Rev. 446; Marsh, The History and Comparative Law of Invitees, Licensees and Trespassers, 1953, 69 L.Q.Rev. 182, 359.

43. "The business visitor enters landowner's premises with implied assurance of preparation and reasonable care for his protection and safety while he is there." Treadway v. Ebert Motor Co., 1981, ___ Pa.Super. ___, 436 A.2d 994.

44. See supra, § 60. But see infra, note 53.

45. Latzoni v. City of Garfield, 1956, 22 N.J. 84, 123 A.2d 531; Daisey v. Colonial Parking, Inc., 1963, 118 U.S.App.D.C. 31, 331 F.2d 777; Olsen v. Macy, 1959, 86 Ariz. 72, 340 P.2d 985.

Otherwise if the boundary line is clearly marked out so that the private land does not appear to be intended for public use. Kelley v. City of Columbus, 1884, 41 Ohio St. 263. Or if the defendant did not create the appearance or know of it. Conroy v. Allston Storage Warehouse Co., 1935, 292 Mass. 133, 197 N.E. 454.

46. Aluminum Co. of America v. Walden, 1959, 230 Ark. 337, 322 S.W.2d 696; Chronopoulos v. Gil Wyner Co., 1956, 334 Mass. 593, 137 N.E.2d 667; Malin v. Consolidated Rail Corp., Del.1981, 438 A.2d 1221 (railroad crossing; thorough analysis).

Compare, as to permissive use: Renfro Drug Co. v. Lewis, 1950, 149 Tex. 507, 235 S.W.2d 609 (short cut through drug store); Sandford v. Firestone Tire & Rubber Co., Fla.App.1962, 139 So.2d 916 (filling station next to sidewalk).

Otherwise if a notice is posted that the way is not open to the public. Bowler v. Pacific Mills, 1909, 200 Mass. 364, 86 N.E. 767; Mitchell v. Ozan-Graysonia Lumber Co., 1921, 151 Ark. 6, 235 S.W. 44.

47. Cf. Adams v. American Enka Corp., 1932, 202 N.C. 767, 164 S.E. 367; Indiana Harbor Belt Railroad Co. v. Jones, 1942, 220 Ind. 139, 41 N.E.2d 361; O'Keefe v. South End Rowing Club, 1966, 64 Cal.2d 729, 51 Cal.Rptr. 534, 414 P.2d 830.

48. Cf. Dorsey v. Chautauqua Institution, 1922, 203 App.Div. 251, 196 N.Y.S. 798; Hutzler Brothers v. Taylor, 1967, 247 Md. 228, 230 A.2d 663 (parking lot); Colonial Natural Gas Co. v. Sayers, 1981, 222 Va. 781, 284 S.E.2d 599 (tenant in common area).

49. Second Restatement of Torts, § 332(2).

50. Bunnell v. Waterbury Hospital, 1925, 103 Conn. 520, 131 A. 501; Howe v. Ohmart, 1893, 7 Ind.App. 32, 33 N.E. 466. But cf. Holiday Inns, Inc. v. Drew, 1982, 276 Ark. 390, 635 S.W.2d 252 (nonregistered guest planning to attend meeting with registered friends; jury question); Britt v. Allen County Community Jr. College, 1982, 230 Kan. 502, 638 P.2d 914 (sponsor of lecture).

51. Davis v. Central Congregational Society, 1880, 129 Mass. 367; Weigel v. Reintjes, Mo.App.1941, 154 S.W.2d 412; Price v. Central Assembly of God, 1960,

and college reunions;[52] social guests of tenants;[53] free spectators invited to public places of amusement;[54] those who enter in the reasonable expectation of buying something not sold on the premises,[55] or come in response to advertisements of something to be given away;[56] and a long array of members of the public making use of municipal parks and playgrounds,[57] swimming pools,[58] libraries,[59] comfort stations,[60] wharves,[61] golf courses,[62] community centers,[63] and state[64] and federal[65] land.

Without this element of "invitation," and the assurance that it carries, the mere potential for benefit to the occupier is not enough to make the visitor an invitee. Thus salesmen,[66] workers seeking employment,[67] or prospective purchasers[68] or tenants[69] of land are considered invitees, when they come to a place which they have good reason to believe

144 Colo. 297, 356 P.2d 240; cf. Napier v. First Congregational Church, 1937, 157 Or. 110, 70 P.2d 43 (coming to see minister for advice). Contra, McNulty v. Hurley, Fla.1957, 97 So.2d 185. There was pecuniary benefit in De Mello v. St. Thomas the Apostle Church Corp., 1960, 91 R.I. 476, 165 A.2d 500.

52. Guilford v. Yale University, 1942, 128 Conn. 449, 23 A.2d 917. Cf. American Legion, Department of Georgia, v. Simonton, 1956, 94 Ga.App. 184, 94 S.E.2d 66 (meeting of American Legion Auxiliary, at state headquarters); Rovegno v. San Jose Knights of Columbus Hall Association, 1930, 108 Cal.App. 591, 291 P. 848 (600 members regularly using swimming pool).

53. See Murray v. Lane, 1982, 51 Md.App. 597, 444 A.2d 1069; Hiller v. Harsh, 1981, 100 Ill.App.3d 332, 55 Ill.Dec. 635, 426 N.E.2d 960 (common area); cf. Davis v. Garden Services, Inc., 1980, 155 Ga.App. 34, 270 S.E.2d 228 (tenant's independent contractor); Nicoletti v. Westcor, Inc., 1982, 131 Ariz. 140, 639 P.2d 330 (employee of commercial tenant).

54. Demarest v. Palisades Realty & Amusement Co., 1925, 101 N.J.L. 66, 127 A. 536, 38 A.L.R. 352; Recreation Centre Corp. v. Zimmerman, 1937, 172 Md. 309, 191 A. 233; cf. Watford by Johnston v. Evening Star Newspaper Co., 1954, 93 App.D.C. 260, 211 F.2d 31 (soap box derby on public property).

55. Vanderdoes v. Rumore, La.App.1941, 2 So.2d 284 (sold out); Talcott v. National Exhibition Co., 1911, 144 App.Div. 337, 128 N.Y.S. 1059 (same); Schmidt v. George H. Hurd Realty Co., 1927, 170 Minn. 322, 212 N.W. 903 (not yet open); Lewis-Kures v. Edwards R. Walsh & Co., 2d Cir. 1939, 102 F.2d 42, certiorari denied 308 U.S. 596, 60 S.Ct. 132, 84 L.Ed. 499 (out of business); Rasmussen v. National Tea Co., 1940, 304 Ill.App. 353, 26 N.E.2d 523 (rummage sale, not yet open).

Otherwise where the plaintiff has no reason to think the article is sold there. Fraters v. Keeling, 1937, 20 Cal.App.2d 490, 67 P.2d 118.

56. Roper v. Commercial Fibre Co., 1928, 105 N.J.L. 10, 143 A. 741 ("Ashes and boxes given away"); Edwards v. Gulf Oil Corp., 1943, 69 Ga.App. 140, 24 S.E.2d 843 (free comic books at filling station).

57. E.g., Caldwell v. Village of Island Park, 1952, 304 N.Y. 268, 107 N.E.2d 441; Paraska v. City of Scranton, 1933, 313 Pa. 227, 169 A. 434.

58. City of Longmont v. Swearingen, 1927, 81 Colo. 246, 254 P. 1000; Ashworth v. City of Clarksburg, 1937, 118 W.Va. 476, 190 S.E. 763; City of Columbia v. Wilks, Miss.1936, 166 So. 925; Taylor v. Kansas City, Mo.App.1961, 353 S.W.2d 814, transferred to 361 S.W.2d 797.

59. Abbott v. New York Public Library, 1942, 263 App.Div. 314, 32 N.Y.S.2d 963; Nickell v. Windsor, [1927] 1 Dom.L.Rev. 379, 59 Ont.L.Rep. 618.

60. Pitman v. City of New York, 1910, 141 App.Div. 670, 125 N.Y.S. 941.

61. Hise v. City of North Ben, 1931, 138 Or. 150, 6 P.2d 30.

62. Lowe v. City of Gastonia, 1937, 211 N.C. 564, 191 S.E. 7.

63. Kelly v. Board of Education, 1920, 191 App.Div. 251, 180 N.Y.S. 796.

64. Le Roux v. State, 1954, 307 N.Y. 397, 121 N.E.2d 386 (public hunting ground); Hall v. State, 1940, 173 Misc. 903, 19 N.Y.S.2d 20, affirmed, 1943, 265 App.Div. 1037, 41 N.Y.S.2d 183 (canal lock); Surmanek v. State, 1960, 24 Misc.2d 102, 202 N.Y.S.2d 756 (beach).

65. Claypool v. United States, S.D.Cal.1951, 98 F.Supp. 702 (misunderstanding with a bear in national park); Ashley v. United States, D.Neb.1963, 215 F.Supp. 39, affirmed 8th Cir. 1964, 326 F.2d 499 (same); Adams v. United States, E.D.Okl.1965, 239 F.Supp. 503 (national park); Smith v. United States, N.D.Cal.1953, 117 F.Supp. 525 (campground); Phillips v. United States, E.D.Tenn.1952, 102 F.Supp. 943 (visitor seeking pass at Oak Ridge). See Note, 1967, 2 L. & W.Rev. 447.

66. Hartman v. Miller, 1941, 143 Pa.Super. 143, 17 A.2d 652; C.R. Anthony Co. v. Williams, 1939, 185 Okl. 564, 94 P.2d 836; Austin v. Beuttner, 1956, 211 Md. 61, 124 A.2d 793.

67. St. Louis, Iron Mountain & Southern Railway Co. v. Wirbel, 1912, 104 Ark. 236, 149 S.W. 92 (well stated); Brigman v. Fiske-Carter Construction Co., 1926, 192 N.C. 791, 136 S.E. 125.

68. Harry Poretsky & Sons v. Hurwitz, 4th Cir. 1956, 235 F.2d 295; Singleton v. Kubiak & Schmitt, 1960, 9 Wis.2d 472, 101 N.W.2d 619.

69. Ware v. Cattaneo, 1962, 69 N.M. 394, 367 P.2d 705; Tutwiler v. I. Beverally Nalle, Inc., 1943, 152 Fla. 479, 12 So.2d 163.

to be open for possible dealings with them, but not when they enter without such encouragement.[70] On the other hand, an unsuccessful canvasser calling at a private home is at most a licensee, because the place is not held open to him for the purpose,[71] although the potential for benefit to the occupier would appear to be no less. The Second Restatement of Torts[72] bowed to this spate of authority and included a separate classification for "public invitees."

It is in connection with invitations to enter private land, not held open to the public, that possible pecuniary benefit has its greatest importance—but only as justifying an expectation that the place has been prepared and made safe for the visit. Anyone invited to transact business[73] or do work[74] on private premises not open to the public normally has the assurance that the place is prepared for him; but one who comes to volunteer assistance, although he confers a benefit, is treated as a licensee,[75] unless the circumstances indicate that he has reason to expect protection in return.[76]

Area of Invitation

The special obligation toward invitees exists only while the visitor is upon the part of the premises which the occupier has thrown open to him for the purpose which makes him an invitee. This "area of invitation"[77] will of course vary with the circumstances of the case. It extends to the entrance to the property,[78] and to a safe exit after the purpose is concluded;[79] and it extends to all parts of the premises to which the purpose may reasonably be expected to take him,[80] and to those which are so arranged as to lead him reasonably to think that they are

---

70. Larmore v. Crown Point Iron Co., 1886, 101 N.Y. 391, 4 N.E. 752; Mills v. Heidingsfield, La.App. 1939, 192 So. 786; Mortgage Commission Servicing Corp. v. Brock, 1939, 60 Ga.App. 695, 4 S.E.2d 669. But if business is in fact transacted, the salesman becomes an invitee, regardless of whether the office was originally held open for the purpose. Lavitch v. Smith, 1960, 224 Or. 498, 356 P.2d 531.

71. Prior v. White, 1938, 132 Fla. 1, 180 So. 347; Malatesta v. Lowry, La.App.1961, 130 So.2d 785; Reuter v. Kenmore Building Co., 1934, 153 Misc. 646, 276 N.Y.S. 545.

72. § 332(2). Section 332(3) is the classification for "business visitors."

73. Finch v. W.R. Roach Co., 1941, 299 Mich. 703, 1 N.W.2d 46 (picking cherries purchased); Fishang v. Eyerman Contracting Co., 1933, 333 Mo. 874, 63 S.W.2d 30 (paying for privilege of dumping refuse); Sills v. Forbes, 1939, 33 Cal.App.2d 219, 91 P.2d 246 (paying for use of road by maintaining it).

74. Schlicht v. Thesing, 1964, 25 Wis. 436, 130 N.W.2d 763 (babysitter); Cozine v. Shuff, Ky.1964, 378 S.W.2d 635 (helping invalid); Speece v. Browne, 1964, 229 Cal.App.2d 487, 40 Cal.Rptr. 384 (cooking Sunday dinner); Burks v. Madyun, 1982, 105 Ill.App.3d 917, 61 Ill.Dec. 696, 435 N.E.2d 185 (babysitter). If the circumstances do not justify such an expectation, the visitor is not an invitee, notwithstanding any pecuniary benefit. Fuchs v. Mapes, 1958, 74 Nev. 366, 332 P.2d 1002.

Those entering in response to a request for gratuitous services are commonly held to be invitees. Drews v. Mason, 1961, 29 Ill.App.2d 269, 172 N.E.2d 383; Murdock v. Petersen, 1958, 74 Nev. 363, 332 P.2d 649; Brant v. Matlin, Fla.App.1965, 172 So.2d 902. See supra, § 60.

75. Davis v. Silverwood, 1953, 116 Cal.App.2d 39, 253 P.2d 83; Krantz v. Nichols, 1956, 11 Ill.App.2d 37, 135 N.E.2d 816.

76. As where he is asked to come for the sole purpose of doing the gratuitous work. Drews v. Mason, 1961, 29 Ill.App.2d 269, 172 N.E.2d 383; Cain v. Friend, 1959, 171 Cal.App.2d 806, 341 P.2d 753; Murdock v. Petersen, 1958, 74 Nev. 363, 332 P.2d 649; see Maxwell v. Maxwell, 1962, 140 Mont. 59, 367 P.2d 308.

77. Second Restatement of Torts, § 332, Comment l.

78. Hopkins v. F.W. Woolworth Co., Mass.App. 1981, 419 N.E.2d 302; Weaver v. Winn-Dixie of La., Inc., La.App.1981, 406 So.2d 792 (foot of patron, "shuffling" into store, caught under non-flat mat); cf. Stewart v. 104 Wallace St., Inc., 1981, 87 N.J. 146, 432 A.2d 881 (duty imposed on commercial landowner to maintain abutting sidewalk).

79. Chadwick v. Barba Lou, Inc., 1982, 69 Ohio St. 2d 222, 431 N.E.2d 660 (outside steps); Allgauer v. Le Bastille, Inc., 1981, 101 Ill.App.3d 978, 57 Ill.Dec. 466, 428 N.E.2d 1146 (stairway); Treadway v. Ebert Motor Co., 1981, ___ Pa.Super. ___, 436 A.2d 994 (slippery metal plate under snow outside door); cf. Butler v. Acme Markets, Inc., 1982, 89 N.J. 270, 445 A.2d 1141 (attack in parking lot); Foster v. Winston-Salem Joint Venture, 1981, 303 N.C. 636, 281 S.E.2d 36 (same); Furr's Inc. v. Patterson, Tex.Civ.App.1981, 618 S.W.2d 417 (sign obstructing exit ramp).

80. Williams v. Morristown Memorial Hospital, 1960, 59 N.J.Super. 384, 157 A.2d 840 (short cut across grass). Compare Frankovitch v. Burton, 1981, ___ Conn. ___, 440 A.2d 254 (tavern owner could be held to foresee that patron might go to back of building at night to relieve himself), with Burns v. Bradley, 1980, 120 N.H. 542, 419 A.2d 1069 (contra: trespasser).

open to him.[81] If a toilet or a telephone is provided and maintained for the use of customers, as is usual in theatres and department stores, the customer is an invitee while he makes use of it,[82] but if it is kept for the private use of the occupier and his employees, as is often the case in the corner drug store and the butcher shop, he is at most a licensee.[83]

If the customer is invited or encouraged to go to an unusual part of the premises, such as behind a counter or into a storeroom, for the purpose which has brought him, he remains an invitee;[84] but if he goes without such encouragement and solely on his own initiative, he is only a licensee if there is consent, or a trespasser if there is not.[85] Thus, as a general proposition, an invitee who exceeds the scope of his invitation is converted to a licensee or a trespasser depending on the circumstances.[86] Since the potential for benefit through a possible purchase or a satisfied customer is the same in all of these cases, they offer an additional argument against the theory of pecuniary advantage as the sole basis of liability.[87] There are similar limitations of time; and if the invitee remains on the land beyond the time reasonably necessary to accomplish the purpose for which he came, and fails to withdraw from the premises in a timely manner, he becomes at most a licensee thereafter.[88]

Care Required

The occupier is not an insurer of the safety of invitees, and his duty is only to exercise reasonable care for their protection.[89] But the obligation of reasonable care is a full one, applicable in all respects, and extending to everything that threatens the invitee with an unreasonable risk of harm. The occupier must not only use care not to injure the visitor by negligent activities,[90] and warn him of hidden dangers known to

81. Crown Cork & Seal Co. v. Kane, 1957, 213 Md. 153, 131 A.2d 470 (smoking room); Montgomery Ward & Co. v. Steele, 8th Cir. 1965, 352 F.2d 822 (warehouse aisle); Morris v. Granato, 1946, 133 Conn. 295, 50 A.2d 416 (basement door looked like toilet); Plewes v. City of Lancaster, 1952, 171 Pa.Super. 312, 90 A.2d 279 (obstructed portion of airport).

82. Dickau v. Rafala, 1954, 141 Conn. 121, 104 A.2d 214; Bass v. Hunt, 1940, 151 Kan. 740, 100 P.2d 696; McClusky v. Duncan, 1927, 216 Ala. 388, 113 So. 250; Main v. Lehman, 1922, 294 Mo. 579, 243 S.W. 91.

83. Hashim v. Chimiklis, 1941, 91 N.H. 456, 21 A.2d 166; Wesbrock v. Colby, 1942, 315 Ill.App. 494, 43 N.E.2d 405; McMullen v. M. & M. Hotel Co., 1940, 227 Iowa 1061, 290 N.W. 3; Liveright v. Max Lifsitz Furniture Co., 1936, 117 N.J.L. 243, 187 A. 583. But see Hundt v. LaCrosse Grain Co., 1981, __ Ind.App. __, 425 N.E.2d 687 (whether use of bathroom incidental to transaction of business was for jury).

84. Bullock v. Safeway Stores, 8th Cir. 1956, 236 F.2d 29 (back room); Blackburn v. Consolidated Rock Products, 1956, 140 Cal.App.2d 858, 295 P.2d 929 (truck driver motioned to area normally outside invitation); Duffy v. Stratton, 1926, 169 Minn. 136, 210 N.W. 866 (behind counter); cf. Mock v. Sears, Roebuck & Co., 1981, 101 Ill.App.3d 103, 56 Ill.Dec. 540, 427 N.E.2d 872 (loading ramp in pick-up area fell on plaintiff's foot, as he tried to lower it himself since male employee was chattering with female employee). In Stein v. Powell, 1962, 203 Va. 423, 124 S.E.2d 889, where a child got into a storeroom-dressing room, it was said that there was no apparent limitation as to what parts of the store the invitation extended to.

85. Whelan v. Van Natta, Ky.1964, 382 S.W.2d 205; Langford v. Mercurio, 1966, 254 Miss. 788, 183 So.2d 150; Campbell v. Hoffman, 1963, 51 Tenn.App. 672, 371 S.W.2d 174; Gayer v. J.C. Penney Co., Mo.App. 1959, 326 S.W.2d 413 (stock room).

86. Hoffman v. Planters Gin Co., Miss.1978, 358 So. 2d 1008; Nicolleti v. Westcor, Inc., 1982, 131 Ariz. 140, 639 P.2d 330 (short cut through shrubs).

87. See also the cases involving the liability of lessors for common passageways and premises leased for admission of the public, infra, § 63.

88. Hansen v. Cohen, 1954, 203 Or. 157, 276 P.2d 391, rehearing denied, 1955, 203 Or. 157, 278 P.2d 898; Robillard v. Tillotson, 1954, 118 Vt. 294, 108 A.2d 524.

89. Resag v. Washington National Insurance Co., 1980, 90 Ill.App.3d 971, 46 Ill.Dec. 385, 414 N.E.2d 107; Backer v. Pizza Inn, Inc., 1982, 162 Ga.App. 682, 292 S.E.2d 562; Foster v. Winston-Salem Joint Venture, 1981, 303 N.C. 636, 281 S.E.2d 36; Hovermale v. Berkeley Springs Moose Lodge, 1980, __ W.Va. __, 271 S.E.2d 335; Lingerfelt v. Winn-Dixie Texas, Inc., Okl. 1982, 645 P.2d 485.

He may, for example, await the end of a storm before removing ice and snow from church steps. Hedglin v. Church of St. Paul of Sauk Centre, 1968, 280 Minn. 119, 158 N.W.2d 269.

90. See Harris v. Cool, 1981, 85 A.D.2d 921, 446 N.Y.S.2d 774 (house painter struck head while fleeing swarm of bees angered by defendant's spraying); Potter Title & Trust Co. v. Young, 1951, 367 Pa. 239, 80 A.2d 76; Second Restatement of Torts, § 341A.

the occupier,[91] but he must also act reasonably to inspect the premises to discover possible dangerous conditions of which he does not know,[92] and take reasonable precautions to protect the invitee from dangers which are foreseeable from the arrangement[93] or use[94] of the property. The obligation extends to the original construction of the premises, where it results in a dangerous condition.[95] The occupier must also act reasonably to render first aid or other care when he knows or should know that the invitee is ill or injured.[96] The fact that the premises are open to the public must generally be considered, which may call for greater care than in the case of a visitor at a private home.[97] If the presence of children is to be expected, their meddling propensities must be anticipated; and the principle of "attractive nuisance" applies to child invitees no less than to child trespassers.[98]

On the other hand, there is no liability for harm resulting from conditions from which no unreasonable risk was to be anticipated,[99] or from those which the occupier neither knew about nor could have discovered with reasonable care.[1] The mere existence of a defect or danger is generally insufficient to establish liability,[2] unless it is shown to be of such a character or of such duration that the

---

91. See Frankovitch v. Burton, 1981, ___ Conn. ___, 440 A.2d 254 (fall off behind tavern); Treadway v. Ebert Motor Co., 1981, ___ Pa.Super. ___, 436 A.2d 994 (slippery metal plate under snow); Allgauer v. Le Bastille, Inc., 1981, 101 Ill.App.3d 978, 57 Ill.Dec. 466, 428 N.E.2d 1146 ("duty to give proper warning of hidden dangers"); Duffy v. Midlothian Country Club, 1980, 92 Ill.App.3d 193, 47 Ill.Dec. 786, 415 N.E.2d 1099 (risk of being hit with golf ball at concession stand between two fairways); Cornutt v. Bolin, Ala.1981, 404 So.2d 38 (gun to be cleaned was loaded).

92. Keller v. Schwegmann Brothers, Inc., La.App. 1981, 402 So.2d 724 (supermarket must periodically inspect aisles); Forcier v. Grand Union Stores, Inc., 1970, 128 Vt. 389, 264 A.2d 796; Second Restatement of Torts, § 343, Comments b and d.

93. Norwood v. Sherwin-Williams Co., 1981, 303 N.C. 462, 279 S.E.2d 559 (low protrusion into aisle of store); Furr's Inc. v. Patterson, Tex.Civ.App.1981, 618 S.W.2d 417 (sign in exit pathway); Lingerfelt v. Winn-Dixie Texas, Inc., Okl.1982, 645 P.2d 485 (strawberries heaped so high they might fall into aisle); cf. Green v. Wellons, Inc., 1981, 52 N.C.App. 529, 279 S.E.2d 37 (pedestrian fell on rocks from rock garden beside sidewalk).

94. Schwartzmann v. Lloyd, 1936, 65 App.D.C. 216, 82 F.2d 822 (crowd at advertised sale); Lee v. National League Baseball Club of Milwaukee, 1958, 4 Wis.2d 168, 89 N.W.2d 811 (scramble by baseball spectators for foul ball); Philpot v. Brooklyn National League Baseball Club, 1951, 303 N.Y. 116, 100 N.E.2d 164 (thrown bottle at baseball park); cf. Schreiber v. Walt Disney World Co., Fla.App.1980, 389 So.2d 1040 (failure to instruct on how best to descend the "Flume"); see infra, note 14.

95. Chadwick v. Barba Lou, Inc., 1982, 69 Ohio St. 2d 222, 431 N.E.2d 660 (no handrail on barroom steps); Allgauer v. Le Bastille, Inc., 1981, 101 Ill.App.3d 978, 57 Ill.Dec. 466, 428 N.E.2d 1146 (steep stairs with unexpected drop-off); Hundt v. LaCrosse Grain Co., 1981, ___ Ind.App. ___, 425 N.E.2d 687 (same); Williams v. Aetna Insurance Co., La.App.1981, 402 So.2d 192 (drop off from porch to walkway difficult to see).

96. Hovermale v. Berkeley Springs Moose Lodge, 1980, ___ W.Va. ___, 271 S.E.2d 335; Lloyd v. S.S. Kresge Co., 1978, 85 Wis. 296, 270 N.W.2d 423; Boles v. La Quinta Motor Inns, 5th Cir. 1982, 680 F.2d 1077 (failure to attend to known rape victim until police arrived); Personal Representative, Starling v. Fisherman's Pier, Inc., Fla.App.1981, 401 So.2d 1136 (drunk rolled off pier into ocean); see Second Restatement of Torts, § 314A; supra, § 56.

97. Criterion Theatre Corp. v. Starns, 1944, 194 Okl. 624, 154 P.2d 92.

98. See supra, § 59.

99. Greenfield v. Freedman, 1952, 328 Mass. 272, 103 N.E.2d 242 (leaves on sidewalk); Home Public Market v. Newrock, 1943, 111 Colo. 428, 142 P.2d 272 (swinging doors); Sheridan v. Great Atlantic & Pacific Tea Co., 1945, 353 Pa. 11, 44 A.2d 280 (double entrance doors); Chew v. Paramount-Richards Theatres, La. App.1943, 14 So.2d 583 (gentle slope); Resag v. Washington National Insurance Co., 1980, 90 Ill.App.3d 971, 46 Ill.Dec. 385, 414 N.E.2d 107 (unforeseeable that "pedestrian would be lifted and blown away by high velocity winds," even in Chicago area).

1. Brown v. Dorney Park Coaster Co., 3d Cir. 1948, 167 F.2d 433; Penny v. Sears, Roebuck & Co., 1934, 193 Minn. 65, 258 N.W. 522; Marinopoliski v. Irish, D.C.App.1982, 445 A.2d 339 (homeowners unaware of plywood beneath snow on which workman slipped).

2. Murray v. Lane, 1982, 51 Md.App. 597, 444 A.2d 1069 (water on stairs); Burkowske v. Church Hospital Corp., 1982, 50 Md.App. 515, 439 A.2d 40 (defective bench); Preuss v. Sambo's of Arizona, Inc., 1981, 130 Ariz. 288, 635 P.2d 1210 (rock on entrance ramp); Gold & White, Inc. v. Long, 1981, 159 Ga.App. 259, 283 S.E.2d 45 (puddle in supermarket); Martin Theatres of Texas, Inc. v. Puryear, Tex.App.1982, 631 S.W.2d 600 (slippery gop on theater floor).

But knowledge that the condition gives rise to a risk of a future hazard may be sufficient. See Lingerfelt v. Winn-Dixie Texas, Inc., Okl.1982, 645 P.2d 485 (6–3) (strawberries stacked so high they might fall into aisle; notice of risk sufficient); Bloom v. Fry's Food Stores, Inc., App.1981, 130 Ariz. 447, 636 P.2d 1229, 1232

jury may reasonably conclude that due care would have discovered it.³

Likewise, in the usual case, there is no obligation to protect the invitee against dangers which are known to him,⁴ or which are so obvious and apparent that he may reasonably be expected to discover them.⁵ Against such conditions it may normally be expected that the visitor will protect himself. It is for this reason that it is sometimes held that reasonable care requires nothing more than a warning of the danger.⁶ But this is certainly not a fixed rule, and all of the circumstances must be taken into account. In any case where the occupier as a reasonable person should anticipate an unreasonable risk of harm to the invitee notwithstanding his knowledge, warning, or the obvious nature

of the condition, something more in the way of precautions may be required.⁷ This is true, for example, where there is reason to expect that the invitee's attention will be distracted, as by goods on display,⁸ or that after a lapse of time he may forget the existence of the condition, even though he has discovered it or been warned;⁹ or where the condition is one which would not reasonably be expected, and for some reason, such as an arm full of bundles, it may be anticipated that the visitor will not be looking for it.¹⁰ In some jurisdictions, it is also true where the condition is one, such as icy steps, which cannot be negotiated with reasonable safety even though the invitee is fully aware of it, when, because the premises are held open to him for his use, it is to be expected that he will nevertheless proceed to encounter it.¹¹

(O'Connor, J.) (slip on grape that fell from loosely packed, highly stacked pile; thorough review, noting "emerging rule which in effect requires storekeepers to anticipate spillages which are likely to result from the acts of patrons"); Smith v. Safeway Stores, Inc., Colo.App.1981, 636 P.2d 1310, affirmed, Colo.1983, 658 P.2d 255 (same); Tom v. S.S. Kresge Co., App.1981, 130 Ariz. 30, 633 P.2d 439 (same, "mode of operation" rule); Annot., 1978, 85 A.L.R.3d 1000.

3. Murray v. Lane, 1982, 51 Md.App. 597, 444 A.2d 1069 (wood railing rotten and weak); Canales v. Dominick's Finer Foods, Inc., 1981, 92 Ill.App.3d 773, 48 Ill.Dec. 272, 416 N.E.2d 303 (plaintiff slipped on greasy Ben-Gay ointment from trampelled tube); J.C. Penney Co. v. Chavez, Tex.Civ.App.1981, 618 S.W.2d 399, refused, n.r.e. (classic slip and fall on banana peel: black and yellow, dark, gooey); cf. Wasson v. Brewer's Food Mart, Inc., 1982, 7 Kan.App.2d 352, 640 P.2d 352 (falling item from shelf; no proof of cause for fall).

4. Backer v. Pizza Inn, Inc., 1982, 162 Ga.App. 682, 292 S.E.2d 562 (returning to car with pizza, patron tripped over parking barrier railroad tie); Moss v. Atlanta Housing Authority, 1981, 160 Ga.App. 555, 287 S.E.2d 619; Pound v. Augusta National, Inc., 1981, 158 Ga.App. 166, 279 S.E.2d 342 (slippery gravel in parking lot); Krone v. McCann, 1982, ___ Mont. ___, 638 P.2d 397 (debris in open field); Buford v. Jitney Jungle Stores of America, Inc., Miss.1980, 388 So.2d 146 (workman tripped over pipe); cf. Nash v. Draughton Business School, La.App.1981, 397 So.2d 37 (puckered carpet). See generally Annot., 1971, 35 A.L.R.3d 230.

5. Sherman v. Platte County, Wyo.1982, 642 P.2d 787 (obvious danger no-duty rule not abrogated by adoption of comparative negligence); Flowers v. K-Mart Corp., App.1980, 126 Ariz. 495, 616 P.2d 955; Haney v. General Host Corp., La.App.1982, 413 So.2d 624. But see Zambito v. Southland Recreation Enterprises, Fla.App.1980, 383 So.2d 989 (patent or known danger is only one factor to be considered in comparative fault

evaluation). See Keeton, Personal Injuries Resulting from Open and Obvious Conditions, 1952, 100 U.Pa.L. Rev. 629.

6. Burk v. Walsh, 1902, 118 Iowa 397, 92 N.W. 65; Hordes v. Kessner, App.Term 1916, 159 N.Y.S. 891; Paubel v. Hitz, 1936, 339 Mo. 274, 96 S.W.2d 369.

7. See Second Restatement of Torts, § 343A, Comment f.

8. Norwood v. Sherwin-Williams Co., 1981, 303 N.C. 462, 279 S.E. 2d 559 (patron tripped over low protrusion in aisle where "impulse items" were placed at eye-level); cf. Guthrie v. Reliance Construction Co., Mo. App.1980, 612 S.W.2d 366 (workman fell through hole in roof during first day on job); TG&Y Stores v. Atchley, Ala.1982, 414 So.2d 912 (boxes on floor in front of display case); Jaconne v. Schwegmann Brothers Giant Super Markets, Inc., La.App.1981, 407 So.2d 513.

9. Walgreen-Texas Co. v. Shivers, 1941, 137 Tex. 493, 154 S.W.2d 625; Simpson v. Doe, 1952, 39 Wn.2d 934, 239 P.2d 1951; Allgauer v. Le Bastille, Inc., 1981, 101 Ill.App.3d 978, 57 Ill.Dec. 466, 428 N.E.2d 1146 (patron forgot dangerous characteristic of restaurant stairway during 2 hour dinner).

10. See Seng v. American Stores Co., 1956, 384 Pa. 338, 121 A.2d 123; Hanson v. Town & Country Shopping Center, Inc., 1966, 259 Iowa 542, 144 N.W.2d 870; Stofer v. Montgomery Ward & Co., 8th Cir. 1957, 249 F.2d 285; Ackerberg v. Muskegon Osteopathic Hospital, 1962, 366 Mich. 596, 115 N.W.2d 290 (hospital visitor dizzy from odors); Valdes v. Karoll's Inc., 7th Cir. 1960, 277 F.2d 637 (stairwell just inside revolving door); Furr's Inc. v. Patterson, Tex.Civ.App.1981, 618 S.W.2d 417 (writing in checkbook while leaving grocery store).

11. This is probably the growing view, known as the "Connecticut rule," which rejects the natural accumulation no-duty rule. See Geise v. Lee, 1975, 84 Wn.2d 866, 529 P.2d 1054; Hammond v. Allegretti, 1974, 262 Ind. 82, 311 N.E.2d 821; Quinlivan v. Great

The jury in such cases may be permitted to find that obviousness, warning or even knowledge is not enough.

In particular, the possessor must exercise the power of control or expulsion which his occupation of the premises gives him over the conduct of a third person who may be present, to prevent injury to the visitor at his hands.[12] He must act as a reasonable person to avoid harm from the negligence of contractors and concessionaires as to activities on the land,[13] as well as that of other persons who have entered it,[14] and even from intentional attacks on the part of such third persons.[15] He is required to take action when he has reason to believe, from what he has observed or from past experience, that the conduct of the other will be dangerous to the invitee,[16] but not if there is no reason to anticipate a problem.[17] Again, in the usual case, a warning will be a sufficient precaution,[18] unless it is apparent that, either because of lack of time or by reason of the character of the conduct to be expected on the part of the third person, it will not be effective to give protection.[19]

Public Employees, Generally

The courts have encountered considerable difficulty in dealing with those who come upon the land in the exercise of a privilege not conferred by the consent of the occupier.[20] These have consisted for the most part of public officers and employees, who enter in the performance of their public duties. Such individuals do not fit very comfortably

---

Atlantic & Pacific Tea Co., 1975, 395 Mich. 244, 235 N.W.2d 732; Kremer v. Carr's Food Center, Inc., Alaska 1969, 462 P.2d 747; cf. Murray v. Eastern Maine Medical Center, Me.1982, 447 A.2d 465 (water on stairs).

Contra, and following the "Massachusetts rule," see Smalling v. LaSalle National Bank of Chicago, 1982, 104 Ill.App.3d 894, 60 Ill.Dec. 671, 433 N.E.2d 713 (2–1) (no duty to guard against natural accumulations of snow and ice); Brandert v. Scottsbluff National Bank & Trust Co., 1975, 194 Neb. 777, 235 N.W.2d 864; Chadwick v. Barba Lou, Inc., 1982, 69 Ohio St.2d 222, 431 N.E.2d 660 (but sufficient evidence of highly dangerous, unexpected condition); cf. Sherman v. Platte County, Wyo.1982, 642 P.2d 787 (obvious or known slippery ice).

12. See Second Restatement of Torts, § 344.

13. McCordic v. Crawford, 1943, 23 Cal.2d 1, 142 P.2d 7; Thornton v. Maine State Agricultural Society, 1903, 97 Me. 108, 53 A. 979; Smith v. Cumberland County Agricultural Society, 1913, 163 N.C. 346, 79 S.E. 632; Stickel v. Riverview Sharpshooters' Park Co., 1911, 250 Ill. 452, 95 N.E. 445.

14. Moran v. Valley Forge Drive-in Theatres, Inc., 1968, 431 Pa. 432, 246 A.2d 875; Adamson v. Hand, 1955, 93 Ga.App. 5, 90 S.E.2d 669; Hill v. Merrick, 1934, 147 Or. 244, 31 P.2d 663; F.W. Woolworth v. Kirby, 1974, 293 Ala. 248, 302 So.2d 67 (elderly woman injured in parking lot stampede during promotional ping-pong ball drop from plane); cf. Duffy v. Midlothian Country Club, 1980, 92 Ill.App.3d 193, 415 N.E.2d 1099 (spectator hit by golf ball; no "fore"); Flowers v. K-Mart, App.1980, 126 Ariz. 495, 616 P.2d 955 (but no duty to provide crosswalk in front of store to protect patrons from being struck by cars).

15. See generally Bazyler, The Duty to Provide Adequate Protection: Landowners' Liability for Failure to Protect Patrons from Criminal Attack, 1979, 21 Ariz.L.Rev. 727; Note, 1982, 18 Wake Forest L.Rev. 114.

16. Butler v. Acme Markets Inc., 1982, 89 N.J. 270, 445 A.2d 1141 (history of prior attacks in parking lot; thorough review); Prather v. H–K Corp., 1980, 282 Pa.Super. 556, 423 A.2d 385 (boisterous bar patron started argument that led to fight before shooting other patron); Kraustrunk v. Chicago Housing Authority, 1981, 95 Ill.App.3d 529, 51 Ill.Dec. 15, 420 N.E.2d 429 (loiterers and criminals known to be on vacant floor where repairmen sent to work); Foster v. Winston-Salem Joint Venture, 1981, 303 N.C. 636, 281 S.E.2d 36 (29 incidents of crime in parking lot over previous year); Huyler v. Rose, 1982, 88 A.D.2d 755, 451 N.Y.S.2d 478 (parents knew that son, who pushed plaintiff into bonfire at graduation party, was intoxicated, argumentative and combative).

17. See Saatzer v. Smith, 1981, 122 Cal.App.3d 512, 176 Cal.Rptr. 68 (spontaneous barroom brawl); Burks v. Madyun, 1982, 105 Ill.App.3d 917, 61 Ill.Dec. 696, 435 N.E.2d 185 (babysitter shot by gang looking for defendant's teenage children); Hewett v. First National Bank of Atlanta, 1980, 272 Ga.App. 744, 272 S.E.2d 745 (unexpected attack on armed security guard in bank); Harvey v. Van Aelstyn, 1982, 211 Neb. 607, 319 N.W.2d 725 (sudden attack in bar; thorough review); Kohler v. Wray, Sup.1982, 452 N.Y.S.2d 831 (plaintiff punched in jaw when asked defendant's wife to dance; host only knew defendant was jealous, not combative).

18. Western Auto Supply Co. v. Campbell, Tex. 1963, 373 S.W.2d 735.

19. See Taylor v. Centennial Bowl, Inc., 1966, 65 Cal.2d 114, 52 Cal.Rptr. 561, 416 P.2d 793; Second Restatement of Torts, § 344. But see § 343A(2), suggesting that in the case of a public utility, where the customer cannot be required to forego its use, more in the way of protection may be required than in the case of an occupier of private land.

20. See generally Page, The Law of Premises Liability, 1976, ch. 5A; Notes, 1966, 19 Vand.L.Rev. 407; 1961, 47 Corn.L.Q. 119.

into any of the arbitrary categories which the law has established for the classification of visitors.[21] They are not trespassers, since they are privileged to come. The privilege is independent of any permission, consent or license of the occupier, and they would be privileged to enter, and would insist upon doing so, even if he made active objection. They normally do not come for any of the purposes for which the premises are held open to the public, and frequently, upon private premises, they do not enter for any benefit of the occupier, or under circumstances which justify any expectation that the place has been prepared to receive them. For these reasons some writers have advocated an additional and separate category for them.[22] Thus far, however, the courts have generally proceeded to cram them, with some straining at the seams, into the sack of either licensees or invitees.[23]

Where it can be found that the public employee comes for a purpose which has some connection with business transacted on the premises by the occupier, he is almost invariably treated as an invitee. Quite often, however, this has a very artificial look. It is no doubt possible to spell out pecuniary benefit to the occupier in the case of a garbage collector,[24] a city water meter reader,[25] or even a postman,[26] but it becomes quite fanciful, to say the least, in the case of sanitary[27] or building[28] inspectors, and especially so as to a tax[29] or a customs[30] collector. The courts are reduced to saying that the occupier cannot legally do business without such visits.

While this is true, pecuniary benefit on such a basis appears to be quite unrealistic. The visitor is an unsought and often resented intruder form the occupier's perspective. The freedom of choice to admit or exclude him, which is so essential to ordinary invitation, is entirely lacking, and he is a burden thrust upon the occupier as the fruit of compulsion.[31] This is not to say, however, that the duty owed to him may not properly be the same as that owed to an invitee. Since he knows that the occupier is required by law to receive him, however, he has some reason to believe that his coming is not completely unanticipated, and that the premises may thus have been made ready for him. On this basis there may be justification for holding that there is an affirmative duty of reasonable care to make the premises safe for such visitors.

Firemen and Policemen; "Fireman's Rule"

Firemen[32] and policemen,[33] on the other hand, traditionally have been held to be merely licensees, entering under a privilege

---

21. See Page, id., at 99–100.

22. Bohlen, The Duty of a Landowner Towards Those Entering His Premises of Their Own Right, 1921, 69 U.Pa.L.Rev. 142, 237, 340; Paton, The Responsibility of an Occupier to Those Who Enter as of Right, 1941, 19 Can.Bar Rev. 1; Wallis-Jones, Liability of Public Authorities as Occupiers of Dangerous Premises, 1949, 65 L.Q.Rev. 367.

23. Second Restatement of Torts, § 345.

24. Toomey v. Sanborn, 1888, 146 Mass. 28, 14 N.E. 921; Annot., 1971, 36 A.L.R.3d 610.

25. Cowan v. One Hour Valet, Inc., 1967, 151 W.Va. 941, 157 S.E.2d 843; Sheffield Co. v. Phillips, 1943, 69 Ga.App. 41, 24 S.E.2d 834; see Annot., 1965, 2 A.L.R.3d 1344.

26. Paubel v. Hitz, 1936, 339 Mo. 274, 96 S.W.2d 369; Sutton v. Penn, 1925, 238 Ill.App. 182; Annot., 1968, 21 A.L.R.3d 1009.

27. Jennings v. Industrial Paper Stock Co., Mo.App. 1952, 248 S.W.2d 43; Swift & Co. v. Schuster, 10th Cir. 1951, 192 F.2d 615.

28. Fred Howland, Inc. v. Morris, 1940, 143 Fla. 189, 196 So. 472; Miller v. Pacific Constructors, 1945, 68 Cal.App.2d 529, 157 P.2d 57; Annot., 1969, 28 A.L.R.3d 891 (building or construction inspector).

29. Anderson & Nelson Distilling Co. v. Hair, 1898, 103 Ky. 196, 44 S.W. 658; Bowers v. Schenley Distillers, Inc., Ky.1971, 469 S.W.2d 565.

30. Low v. Grand Trunk Railway Co., 1881, 72 Me. 313; Wilson v. Union Iron Works Dry Dock Co., 1914, 167 Cal. 539, 140 P. 250.

31. 2 Harper and James, Torts, 1956, 1500.

32. Lave v. Neumann, 1982, 211 Neb. 97, 317 N.W. 2d 779 (dictum); Romedy v. Johnston, Fla.App.1967, 193 So.2d 487; Pallikan v. Mark, 1975, 163 Ind.App. 178, 322 N.E.2d 398; Krauth v. Geller, 1960, 31 N.J. 270, 157 A.2d 129; Baxley v. Williams Construction Co., 1958, 98 Ga.App. 662, 106 S.E.2d 799; Roberts v. Rosenblatt, 1959, 146 Conn. 110, 148 A.2d 142.

In Mulcrone v. Wagner, 1942, 212 Minn. 478, 4 N.W. 2d 97, this was carried to the length of holding that a

---

33. See note 33 on page 430.

conferred by legal authority, toward whom there is no such duty. The occupier is still required to refrain from injuring such persons intentionally[34] or by willful and wanton misconduct,[35] and he must exercise reasonable care for their protection in carrying on his activities,[36] and give warning of hidden dangers of which he knows,[37] as in the case of other licensees; but there is in general no obligation to inspect and prepare the premises for them. And the fact that the occupier himself has been negligent[38] in starting the fire for which the fireman is called may make no difference.[39]

A number of recent cases have expanded the foundation and application of the fireman's rule, reasoning that firemen,[40] policemen[41] and other such persons[42] professional-

---

fire inspector on a back stair was a licensee only. Contra, Walsh v. Madison Park Properties, Ltd., 1968, 102 N.J.Super. 134, 245 A.2d 512.

See generally Notes, 1978, 66 Calif.L.Rev. 585; Annot., 1982, 11 A.L.R.4th 497.

33. Nared v. School District of Omaha, 1974, 191 Neb. 376, 215 N.W.2d 115; London Iron & Metal Co. v. Abney, 1980, 245 Ga. 759, 267 S.E.2d 214; Sherman v. Suburban Trust Co., 1978, 282 Md. 238, 384 A.2d 76; State v. Plummer, 1967, 5 Conn.Cir. 35, 241 A.2d 198; Hall v. Holton, Fla.App.1976, 330 So.2d 81; Cook v. Demetrakas, 1971, 108 R.I. 397, 275 A.2d 919. See generally Notes, 1981, 9 Pepper.L.Rev. 197; 1978, 66 Calif.L.Rev. 585.

34. Cf. Anton v. Lehpamer, N.D.Ill.1982, 534 F.Supp. 239 (policeman assaulted during arrest).

35. See Whitten v. Miami-Dade Water & Sewer Authority, Fla.App.1978, 357 So.2d 430 (dictum); cf. Marquart v. Toledo, Peoria & Western Railroad Co., 1975, 30 Ill.App.3d 431, 333 N.E.2d 558 (defendant's conduct not willful or wanton on facts). But see Hubbard v. Boelt, 1980, 28 Cal.3d 480, 169 Cal.Rptr. 706, 620 P.2d 156 (policeman; fireman's rule applies to reckless misconduct), criticized, 1981, 9 Pepper.L.Rev. 197; Ferraro v. Demetrakis, 1979, 167 N.J.Super. 429, 400 A.2d 1227; Grable v. Varela, App.1977, 115 Ariz. 222, 564 P.2d 911 (fireman's rule barred suit even if fire started recklessly).

36. Houston Belt & Terminal Rail Co. v. O'Leary, Tex.Civ.App.1911, 136 S.W. 601, error refused; Cameron v. Kenyon-Connell Commercial Co., 1899, 22 Mont. 312, 56 P. 358.

37. Clark v. Corby, 1977, 75 Wis.2d 292, 249 N.W.2d 567; Hall v. Holton, Fla.App.1976, 330 So.2d 81 (rotten floor). "Virtually all jurisdictions [considering the issue] have allowed recovery where the failure to warn ultimately resulted in an injury to the firefighter." Lipson v. Superior Court of Orange County, 1982, 31 Cal.3d 362, 182 Cal.Rptr. 629, 635, 644 P.2d 822 (extending liability to misrepresentations on the nature of the hazard); Rogers v. Cato Oil & Grease Co., Okl. 1964, 396 P.2d 1000; Bartels v. Continental Oil Co., Mo. 1964, 384 S.W.2d 667. There is, however, no duty to warn a fireman of dangers in a place where there is no reason to expect him to go. Anderson v. Cinnamon, 1955, 365 Mo. 304, 282 S.W.2d 445.

38. Because the fireman's rule is principally based on assumption of risk, it will also bar recovery for strict liability for conducting an ultrahazardous or abnormally dangerous activity. Lipson v. Superior Court of Orange County, 1982, 31 Cal.3d 362, 182 Cal.Rptr. 629, 644 P.2d 822; Armstrong v. Mailand, Minn.1979, 284 N.W.2d 343.

39. Giorgi v. Pacific Gas & Electric Co., 1968, 266 Cal.App.2d 355, 72 Cal.Rptr. 119; Buren v. Midwest Industries, Inc., 1964, 380 S.W.2d 96. But see infra, note 45.

40. Armstrong v. Mailand, Minn.1979, 284 N.W.2d 343 ("primary" assumption of risk); Baker v. Superior Court for County of Orange, 1982, 129 Cal.App.3d 710, 181 Cal.Rptr. 311 (thorough review); Bay Area Rapid Transit District v. Superior Court, 1980, 113 Cal.App.3d 1018, 170 Cal.Rptr. 390; Buchanan v. Prickett & Son, Inc., 1979, 203 Neb. 684, 279 N.W.2d 855; cf. Thompson v. Warehouse Corp. of America, Inc., La.App.1976, 337 So.2d 572 (fireman's duty is to save owner from his own negligence in starting fire).

41. Berko v. Freda, 1983, 93 N.J. 81, 459 A.2d 663 (4–2) (keys accidently left in stolen car that rammed pursuing officer), affirming 182 N.J.Super. 396, 442 A.2d 208; Hannah v. Jensen, Minn.1980, 298 N.W.2d 52 (7–1) (breaking up fight in bar); Christensen v. Murphy, 1982, 57 Or.App. 330, 644 P.2d 627 (2–1) (stabbed while apprehending fleeing fugitive negligently released earlier by defendant matron); Steelman v. Lind, 1981, 97 Nev. 425, 634 P.2d 666 (highway patrolman hit by truck while helping defendant reload trailer with beehives that had fallen onto roadway); Wilson v. Florida Processing Co., Fla.App.1979, 368 So.2d 609 (fireman's rule, not rescue doctrine, applied to police chief inhaling chlorine gas while evacuating residents of town); Berko v. Freda, 1980, 172 N.J.Super. 426, 412 A.2d 821 (pursuing policeman rammed by thief of defendant's stolen car); Walters v. Sloan, 1977, 20 Cal. App.3d 199, 142 Cal.Rptr. 152, 571 P.2d 609 (thorough review); Hubbard v. Boelt, 1980, 28 Cal.3d 480, 169 Cal.Rptr. 706, 620 P.2d 156 (policeman lost control while pursuing speeder in high-speed chase). But see Lave v. Neumann, 1982, 211 Neb. 97, 317 N.W.2d 779 (4–3) (rescue doctrine, allowing recovery, rather than fireman's rule, applied to policeman injured while trying to stop runaway truck).

42. See Maltman v. Sauer, 1975, 84 Wn.2d 975, 530 P.2d 254 (crash of Army rescue helicopter); cf. Carter v. Taylor Diving & Salvage Co., E.D.La.1972, 341 F.Supp. 628, affirmed mem., 5th Cir. 1973, 470 F.2d 995 (doctor suffering heart attack from having to conduct emergency operation under strenuous conditions).

ly trained[43] to deal with dangerous situations on a regular basis must be held to assume the normal, apparent risks that are to be expected in encountering such hazards,[44] whether on or off the premises. Yet the fireman's rule has been held only to apply when the firefighter or police officer is injured from the very danger, created by the defendant's act of negligence, that required his professional assistance and presence at the scene in the first place, and the rule will not shield a defendant from liability for independent acts of misconduct which otherwise cause the injury.[45]

There always has been something bothersome about these decisions. It is of course quite foolish to say that a fireman who comes to extinguish a blaze or a policeman who enters to prevent a burglary confers no pecuniary benefit upon the occupier;[46] and if invitation is called for, it is certainly present when he comes in response to a call for help. The argument sometimes offered,[47] that tort liability might deter landowners from uttering such cries of distress, is surely preposterous rubbish.[48] It is quite true that injuries to firemen and policemen are covered by disability compensation and pension funds,[49] but this may also be true of the other public employees mentioned above, and even of many private employees who are held to be invitees.

Perhaps the most legitimate basis for the distinction lies in the fact that firemen and policemen are likely to enter at unforeseeable times, upon unusual parts of the premises, and under circumstances of emergency, where care in looking after the premises, and in preparation for the visit, cannot rea-

---

43. Based on the notion of assumption of risk, volunteers as well as professionals are held subject to the limited-duty fireman's rule. Buchanan v. Prickett & Son, Inc., 1979, 203 Neb. 684, 279 N.W.2d 855 (volunteer fireman); Ferraro v. Demetrakis, 1979, 167 N.J. Super. 429, 400 A.2d 1227 (same); Baker v. Superior Court for County of Orange, 1982, 129 Cal.App.3d 710, 181 Cal.Rptr. 311 (paid-call volunteer firewomen). But see Walker Hauling Co. v. Johnson, 1964, 110 Ga.App. 620, 139 S.E.2d 496.

44. Compare Christensen v. Murphy, 1982, 57 Or. App. 330, 644 P.2d 627 (being stabbed while apprehending fleeing criminal is not "unusual, serious, hidden and totally unexpected" risk for policeman), and Bay Area Rapid Transit District v. Superior Court, 1980, 113 Cal.App.3d 1018, 170 Cal.Rptr. 390 (firemen inhaled smoke and fumes from fire), with Griffiths v. Lovelette Transfer Co., Minn.1981, 313 N.W.2d 602, 605 (policeman directing traffic at accident scene, could not be held to anticipate "the risk of being struck by a downed utility pole which was jerked into the air when a passing automobile snagged a guide wire attached to the pole"); and Lipson v. Superior Court of Orange County, 1982, 31 Cal.3d 362, 182 Cal.Rptr. 629, 644 P.2d 822, 828 ("Smoke, flames, and the collapse of a burning wall are typical risks normally associated with a fireman's occupation. * * * However, the risk that the owner of a burning building will deceive a firefighter as to the nature or existence of a hazard on the premises is not an inherent part of a firefighter's job").

45. "Since firefighting is an occupation which by its very nature exposes firemen to particular hazards, firemen cannot complain of negligent or reckless conduct which forms the basis for their being summoned." Yet, "'the fireman's rule was not intended to bar recovery for independent acts of misconduct which were not the cause of the plaintiff's presence at the accident scene.'" Lipson v. Superior Court of Orange County, 1982, 31 Cal.3d 362, 182 Cal.Rptr. 629, 832–33, 644 P.2d 822, 825–26 (defendants could be liable for negligent or intentional misrepresentation to firemen that chemicals in boilover were nontoxic). See also Malo v. Willis, 1981, 126 Cal.App.3d 543, 178 Cal.Rptr. 774 (highway patrol officer who had stopped speeding motorist suffered whiplash when vehicle struck from rear); Garcia v. City of South Tucson, App.1981, 131 Ariz. 315, 640 P.2d 1117, 1120 ("pertinent inquiry is whether or not the negligently created risk which resulted in plaintiff's injury was the reason for his being at the scene in his professional capacity"); Shaw v. Plunkett, 1982, 135 Cal.App.3d 756, 185 Cal.Rptr. 571 (while arresting prostitute in parking lot of motel, officer struck by car driven by prostitute's customer); Kocan v. Garino, 1980, 107 Cal.App.3d 291, 165 Cal.Rptr. 712 (in hot pursuit of suspect over defendant's dilapidated fence, policeman injured when fence collapsed; fireman's rule inapplicable); Trainor v. Santana, 1981, 86 N.J. 403, 432 A.2d 23 (after arresting speeding motorist, policeman struck by motorist's vehicle trying to make escape).

46. See Strong v. Seattle Stevedore Co., 1970, 1 Wn. App. 898, 466 P.2d 545 (fireman provided at least potential economic benefit).

47. Baker v. Superior Court for County of Orange, 1982, 129 Cal.App.3d 710, 181 Cal.Rptr. 311, 318; Steelman v. Lind, 1981, 97 Nev. 425, 634 P.2d 666.

48. For rubbish collectors, see supra, note 24.

49. See Baker v. Superior Court for County of Orange, 1982, 129 Cal.App.3d 710, 181 Cal.Rptr. 311; Walters v. Sloan, 1977, 20 Cal.3d 199, 142 Cal.Rptr. 152, 571 P.2d 609; cf. Steelman v. Lind, 1981, 97 Nev. 425, 634 P.2d 666; Note, 1978, 66 Calif.L.Rev. 585.

sonably be looked for.⁵⁰ A person who climbs in through a basement window in search of a fire or a thief does not expect any assurance that he will not find a bulldog in the cellar, and he is trained to be on guard for any such general dangers inherent in the profession.⁵¹ But whether this requires a blanket rule limiting liability in every case is another question. One solution would be to require the occupier to take precautions only where it is reasonable to expect him to do so. On this basis, there is obvious merit in the position, taken by a small number of courts, that such visitors are entitled to the status of invitees, and to the full duty of reasonable care, when they come under the same circumstances as other members of the public to a part of the premises held open to the public.⁵² This means that a policeman calling to make an inquiry at a business office is an invitee; and that the occupier must exercise ordinary care to see that the usual means of access to his premises are safe for a visiting fireman. The additional obligation in fact requires no more care than is already required for other invitees. Two or three states have gone even further and held that firemen and policemen will be treated generally as invitees,⁵³ although there does not appear to be any trend in this direction nor sufficient reason on balance for moving the law this far.

---

50. See Boneau v. Swift & Co., Mo.App.1934, 66 S.W.2d 172, 173; Shypulski v. Waldorf Paper Products Co., 1951, 232 Minn. 394, 397, 45 N.W.2d 549, 551; Notes, 1926, 26 Col.L.Rev. 116; 1938, 22 Minn.L.Rev. 898.

51. Steelman v. Lind, 1981, 97 Nev. 425, 634 P.2d 666; Walters v. Sloan, 1977, 20 Cal.App.3d 199, 142 Cal.Rptr. 152, 155, 571 P.2d 609; Malo v. Willis, 1981, 126 Cal.App.3d 543, 178 Cal.Rptr. 774 (dictum).

52. Mounsey v. Ellard, 1973, 363 Mass. 693, 297 N.E.2d 43; Nared v. School District of Omaha in County of Douglas, 1974, 191 Neb. 376, 215 N.W.2d 115. See also McCarthy v. Port of New York Authority, 1968, 30 A.D.2d 111, 290 N.Y.S.2d 255. Cf. Caroff v. Liberty Lumber Co., App.Div.1977, 146 N.J.Super. 353, 369 A.2d 983 (park ranger). This is the position taken in Second Restatement of Torts, § 345, Comment e.

53. See Murphy v. Ambassador East, 1977, 54 Ill. App.3d 980, 12 Ill.Dec. 501, 370 N.E.2d 124 (policeman; but no duty on particular facts); Strong v. Seattle Stevedore Co., 1970, 1 Wn.App. 898, 466 P.2d 545 (fireman); cf. Cameron v. Abatiell, 1968, 127 Vt. 111, 241 A.2d 310. But even in these jurisdictions, the underlying fireman's rule based on assumption of risk may bar recovery for the negligence in starting the fire or otherwise creating the need for professional assistance in the first place. Washington v. Atlantic Richfield Co., 1976, 66 Ill.2d 103, 5 Ill.Dec. 143, 361 N.E.2d 282 (Schaefer, J.) (5–2).

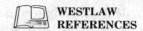

WESTLAW REFERENCES

di invitee
272k32(2.3)
376k6(3)
"public invitee*"
restatement +s torts /s invitee* /s duty

Area of Invitation
area /3 invitation

Care Required
digest(invitee* /s reasonable /5 care /s duty)
digest(invitee* /p "standard of care")

Public Employees, Generally
272k32(2.17)
"garbage collector*" garbagem*n "building inspector*" mailm*n "meter reader*" "meat inspector*" /s invitee*

Firemen and Policemen; "Fireman's Rule"
firem*n policem*n /s licensee*
"fireman's rule"

---

§ 62. Abolition of Categories

The traditional distinctions in the duties of care owed to persons entering land—based upon the entrant's status as a trespasser, licensee or invitee—have been criticized for some time as being harshly mechanical, unduly complex, and overly protective of property interests at the expense of human safety.¹ In 1957, England by statute abolished the distinction between licensees and invitees, and imposed upon the occupier a "common duty of care" toward all persons who

---

§ 62

1. See, e.g., 2 Harper & James, Law of Torts, 1956, 1430–1505; Hughes, Duties to Trespassers: A Comparative Survey and Revaluation, 1959, 68 Yale L.J. 633; McMahon, Conclusions on Judicial Behavior from a Comparative Study of Occupiers' Liability, 1975, 38 Mod.L.Rev. 39; Notes, 1977, 36 Md.L.Rev. 816; 1979, 33 Ark.L.Rev. 194.

For the modern status of these entrant classification rules, see Annot., 1983, 22 A.L.R.4th 294.

lawfully enter the premises.[2] This was followed in the United States in 1958 by a Supreme Court decision refusing to engraft the traditional distinctions onto the law of admiralty.[3] Ten years thereafter, in 1968, the Supreme Court of California in Rowland v. Christian[4] abolished the traditional duty classification scheme for trespassers, licensees and invitees, and replaced it with the ordinary negligence principles of foreseeable risk and reasonable care. Over the next ten or twelve years, eight other jurisdictions followed suit, abolishing all distinctions between entrants on land,[5] and another five jurisdictions discarded the distinctions between licensees and invitees but retained the traditional duty limitations toward trespassing adults.[6]

Although the abolition movement gathered impressive momentum through the mid-1970s, it thereafter quite abruptly lost its steam, and in 1979 it came to a screeching halt. All six courts passing on the issue from then until 1982 have reaffirmed their commitment to the traditional trespasser-licensee-invitee classification scheme.[7] It is still too early to determine whether this most recent shift in attitude toward the entrant categories will prove to be only a momentary rest stop on the long march toward a general overthrow of this entire system of legal doctrine. Instead, it may reflect a more fundamental dissatisfaction with certain developments in accident law that accelerated during the 1960s—the reduction of whole systems of legal principles to a single, perhaps simplistic, standard of reasonable care, the sometimes blind subordination of other legitimate social objectives to the goals of accident prevention and compensation, and the commensurate shifting of the decisional balance of power to the jury from

2. Occupiers' Liability Act, 5 & 6 Eliz. II, c. 31; 1 Odgers, Occupiers' Liability: A Further Comment, [1957] Camb.L.J. 39; Payne, The Occupiers' Liability Act, 1958, 21 Mod.L.Rev. 359; see Rogers, Winfield & Jolowicz on Tort, 11th ed. 1979, 195–211.

3. Kermarec v. Compagnie Generale Transatlantique, 1959, 358 U.S. 625, 79 S.Ct. 406, 3 L.Ed.2d 550. See also Judy v. Belk, Fla.App.1966, 181 So.2d 694.

4. 70 Cal.Rptr. 97, 443 P.2d 561. See Notes, 1969, 44 N.Y.U.L.Rev. 426; 23 Ark.L.Rev. 153; 41 U.Colo.L. Rev. 167; 1972, 25 Vand.L.Rev. 623. On Rowland v. Christian and its progeny, see generally Page, The Law of Premises Liability, 1976, ch. 6; Hawkins, Premises Liability After Repudiation of the Status Categories: Allocation of Judge and Jury Functions, 1981, 15 Utah L.Rev. 15; Annots., 1970, 32 A.L.R.3d 508; 1983, 22 A.L.R.4th 294.

5. Following California in abolishing the distinctions between all three categories of entrants, including trespassers, are Pickard v. City of Honolulu, 1969, 51 Hawaii 134, 452 P.2d 445; Mile High Fence Co. v. Radovich, 1971, 175 Colo. 537, 489 P.2d 308; Smith v. Arbaugh's Restaurant, Inc., D.C.Cir.1972, 469 F.2d 97, certiorari denied, 1973, 412 U.S. 939, 93 S.Ct. 2774, 37 L.Ed.2d 399, questioned and limited in Holland v. Baltimore & Ohio Railroad Co., D.C.App.1981, 431 A.2d 597 (Nebeker, J.) (retaining traditional limited duty rules for trespassers, and questioning authority of circuit court to declare common law for District of Columbia); Mariorenzi v. Joseph DiPonte, Inc., 1975, 114 R.I. 294, 333 A.2d 127; Basso v. Miller, 1976, 40 N.Y.2d 233, 386 N.Y.S.2d 564, 352 N.E.2d 868; Ouellette v. Blanchard, 1976, 116 N.H. 552, 364 A.2d 631; Cates v. Beauregard Electric Coop., La.1976, 328 So.2d 367, certiorari denied

429 U.S. 833, 97 S.Ct. 97, 50 L.Ed.2d 98; Webb v. City of Sitka, Alaska 1977, 561 P.2d 731; cf. Scheibel v. Hillis, Mo.1976, 531 S.W.2d 285, appeal after remand 570 S.W.2d 724 (once presence of visitor known, uniform duty of due care in conducting activities).

6. Abolishing the distinctions only between licensees and invitees, and retaining limited duty rules toward trespassers, are Peterson v. Balach, 1972, 294 Minn. 161, 199 N.W.2d 639; Mounsey v. Ellard, 1973, 363 Mass. 693, 297 N.E.2d 43, trespasser exclusion reaffirmed in Schofield v. Merrill, 1982, 386 Mass. 244, 435 N.E.2d 339 (4–3); Antoniewicz v. Reszcynski, 1975, 70 Wis.2d 836, 236 N.W.2d 1; O'Leary v. Coenen, N.D. 1977, 251 N.W.2d 746; Poulin v. Colby College, Me. 1979, 402 A.2d 846.

Note also the elevation of the social visitor, fireman and policeman to invitee status in a very few jurisdictions, supra, §§ 61 & 62.

7. Refusing to abandon the traditional status distinctions are Britt v. Allen County Community Junior College, 1982, 230 Kan. 502, 638 P.2d 914 (5–2) (adoption of comparative fault notwithstanding); Murphy v. Baltimore Gas & Electric Co., 1981, 290 Md. 186, 428 A.2d 459 (6–1); Yalowizer v. Husky Oil Co., Wyo.1981, 629 P.2d 465; Egede-Nissen v. Crystal Mountain, Inc., 1980, 93 Wn.2d 127, 606 P.2d 1214; Huyck v. Hecla Mining Co., 1980, 101 Idaho 299, 612 P.2d 142; Pashinian v. Haritonoff, 1980, 81 Ill.2d 377, 43 Ill.Dec. 21, 410 N.E.2d 21 (4–3). In addition, numerous cases against owners and occupiers of land were decided in the late 1970s and early 1980s based upon the traditional doctrines, without express consideration of whether those doctrines should be materially changed. See supra, §§ 57–61.

the judge.⁸ At least it appears that the courts are gaining a renewed appreciation for the considerations behind the traditional duty limitations toward trespassing adults, and that they are acquiring more generally a healthy skepticism toward invitations to jettison years of developed jurisprudence in favor of a beguiling legal panacea.

 WESTLAW REFERENCES

classification* category categories /s abolish! abolition /s licensee* trespass* invitee*

§ 63. Lessor and Lessee

When land is leased to a tenant, the law of property regards the lease as equivalent to a sale of the premises for the term.¹ The lessee acquires an estate in the land, and becomes for the time being both owner and occupier, subject to all of the responsibilities of one in possession, to those who enter upon the land and those outside of its boundaries.²

In the absence of agreement to the contrary, the lessor surrenders both possession and control of the land to the lessee, retaining only a reversionary interest; and he has no right even to enter without the permission of the lessee. Consequently, the traditional common law rule has been that he is under no obligation to anyone to look after the premises or to keep them in repair, and is not responsible, either to persons injured on ³ or off the land ⁴ for conditions which develop or are created by the tenant after possession has been transferred. Neither is he held responsible, in general, for activities which the tenant carries on upon the land after such transfer,⁵ even when they create a nuisance.⁶ Furthermore, the doctrine of *caveat emptor* has traditionally been applied

---

8. See generally Henderson, Expanding the Negligence Concept: Retreat from the Rule of Law, 1976, 51 Ind.L.J. 467, 510–14.

§ 63

1. Thomas v. Barnes, Mo.App.1982, 634 S.W.2d 554; Shackett v. Schwartz, 1977, 77 Mich.App. 518, 258 N.W.2d 543.

See generally, Page, The Law of Premises Liability, 1976, ch. 9; Harkrider, Tort Liability of a Landlord, 1928, 26 Mich.L.Rev. 260, 383; Eldredge, Landlord's Tort Liability for Disrepair, 1936, 84 U.Pa.L.Rev. 467; James, Tort Risks of Land Ownership: How Affected by Lease or Sale, 1954, 28 Conn.Bar J. 127; Quinn & Phillips, The Law of Landlord-Tenant: A Critical Evaluation of the Past with Guidelines for the Future, 1969, 38 Ford.L.Rev. 225; Love, Landlord's Liability for Defective Premises: Caveat Lessee, Negligence, or Strict Liability?, 1975 Wis.L.Rev. 19; Browder, The Taming of A Duty—The Tort Liability of Landlords, 1982, 81 Mich.L.Rev. 99; Note, 1981, 22 B.C.L.Rev. 885 (Massachusetts).

2. As in the case of a vendee, it is generally held that he is free to assume when he rents that no private nuisance exists upon the property without the consent of those in the neighborhood, and he is not liable for such a nuisance until he has at least discovered or been notified of the condition, and had a reasonable opportunity to remedy it. McDonough v. Gilman, 1861, 85 Mass. (3 Allen) 264, (request to abate required); Philadelphia & Reading Railway Co. v. Smith, 3d Cir. 1894, 64 F. 679 (same). Otherwise in the case of a public nuisance. Irvine v.Wood, 1872, 51 N.Y. 224; see infra, § 64.

3. See Thomas v. Barnes, Mo.App.1982, 634 S.W.2d 554; Seago v. Roy, 1981, 97 Ill.App.3d 6, 53 Ill.App. Dec. 849, 424 N.E.2d 640 (landlord had no duty to keep premises under tenant's control in repair, despite making occasional minor repairs); Williams v. Riley, 1982, 56 N.C.App. 427, 289 S.E.2d 102 (beach house; S.C. law); cf. Moore v. Muntzel, 1982, 231 Kan. 46, 642 P.2d 957 (fire damage; lessor retained no control); Mills v. Bonanza International Corp., 1981, 160 Ga.App. 104, 286 S.E.2d 337; Powell v. United Oil Corp., 1982, 160 Ga.App. 810, 287 S.E.2d 667 (lessor of service station not liable for plaintiff's emotional distress when she was peered at through peep hole in restroom mirror while using facilities).

4. Jackson v. 919 Corp., 1951, 344 Ill.App. 519, 101 N.E.2d 594; Spinelli v. Golda, 1950, 6 N.J. 68, 77 A.2d 233.

5. See National Tea Co. v. Gaylord Discount Department Stores, Inc., 1981, 101 Ill.App.3d 806, 56 Ill. Dec. 265, 427 N.E.2d 345; Thompson v. United States, 9th Cir. 1979, 592 F.2d 1104 (injuries during course of race on track controlled by lessee). See Second Restatement of Torts, § 379A; Note, 1964, 50 Iowa L.Rev. 648; cf. Martinez v. Lazaroff, 1979, 48 N.Y.2d 819, 424 N.Y.S.2d 126, 399 N.E.2d 1148 (landlord's failure to supply hot water not proximate cause of child's burns from boiling water spilled by tenant transporting water from alternate source); Annot. 1977, 81 A.L.R.3d 638 (tenant's vicious animal).

6. Pinnell v. Woods, 1938, 275 Ky. 290, 121 S.W.2d 679; Meloy v. City of Santa Monica, 1932, 124 Cal.App. 622, 12 P.2d 1072; Lufkin v. Zane, 1892, 157 Mass. 117, 31 N.E. 757.

to the lessee,[7] quite as much as to a vendee, so that a tenant who has not exacted an express warranty is left to inspect the land for himself, and ordinarily at common law must take it as he finds it, for better or for worse. There is therefore, as a general rule, no liability upon the landlord, either to the tenant [8] or to others entering the land [9] for defective conditions existing at the time of the lease.

Modern ideas of social policy have given rise to a number of exceptions to these general rules of nonliability of the lessor, which to a large extent swallow up the general no-duty rule. There is increasing recognition of the fact that the tenant who leases defective premises is likely to be impecunious and unable to make the necessary repairs, and that sometimes the financial burden is best placed upon the landlord, who receives a benefit from the transaction in the form of rent. This policy is expressed by statutes in a number of states which require the landlord to put and keep certain types of premises, such as tenement houses, in good condition and repair, the breach of which may be evidence of negligence or even negligence per se.[10] It is also expressed by statutes and judicial opinions in a growing minority of states holding exculpatory clauses in residential leases void and unenforceable, at least in certain contexts.[11] The shifting responsibility from tenant to landlord for defects in the premises has been perhaps most significantly expressed in the recent surge of statutes and decisions implying a warranty of habitability into residential leases.[12]

---

7. Sometimes referred to in this context as "caveat lessee," meaning that the risk of defects in the premises falls upon the tenant. This principle is the converse of the implied warranty of habitability. See infra, note 12.

8. Taylor v. Stimson, 1958, 52 Wn.2d 278, 324 P.2d 1070; Lemley v. Penner, 1981, 230 Kan. 25, 630 P.2d 1086 (tenant's child).

9. Bowles v. Mahoney, 1952, 91 App.D.C. 155, 202 F.2d 320, certiorari denied 344 U.S. 935, 73 S.Ct. 505, 97 L.Ed. 719 (invitee); Borders v. Roseberry, 1975, 216 Kan. 486, 532 P.2d 1366 (guest). See Note, 1964, 39 Wash.L.Rev. 345.

10. See Shroades v. Rental Homes, Inc., 1981, 68 Ohio St.2d 20, 427 N.E.2d 774 (4–3) (Landlords and Tenants Act); Hall v. Warren, Utah 1981, 632 P.2d 848 (Building Code); Simon v. Solomon, 1982, 385 Mass. 91, 431 N.E.2d 556 (State Sanitary Code); Allen v. Equity & Investors Management Corp., 1982, 56 N.C.App. 706, 289 S.E.2d 623; Second Restatement of Property, § 17.6 & Reporter's Note 4; cf. Turner v. Thompson, 1981, 102 Ill.App.3d 838, 58 Ill.Dec. 215, 430 N.E.2d 157 (failure to light stairs public nuisance under Municipal Code); Slusher v. State, 1982, ___ Ind.App. ___, 437 N.E.2d 97 (reckless homicide conviction of landlords, arising out of death of tenant's guest due to disrepair of landing, reversed on due process grounds). Contra, Thomas v. Barnes, Mo.App.1982, 634 S.W.2d 554.

The only states with neither a relevant statute nor a decision are Alabama, Arkansas, Colorado, Indiana, Mississippi, South Carolina and Utah. Browder, The Taming of A Duty—The Tort Liability of Landlords, 1982, 81 Mich.L.Rev. 99, 113 n. 56 (citing statutes, at 112–13 n. 55).

11. By statute in Ill., Md., Mass., and N.Y. By decision in Miss., Cal., D.C., Fla., Ind., N.H., N.J., Tex., Wash., Wis., Ga., and Ala. See Cappaert v. Junker, Miss.1982, 413 So.2d 378; Henrioulle v. Marin Ventures, Inc., 1978, 20 Cal.3d 512, 143 Cal.Rptr. 247, 573 P.2d 465; Country Club Apartments, Inc. v. Scott, 1980, 246 Ga. 443, 271 S.E.2d 841; John's Pass Seafood Co. v. Weber, Fla.App.1979, 369 So.2d 616 (violation of safety ordinance); Taylor v. Leedy & Co., Ala.1982, 412 So.2d 763 (willful failure to disclose latent defect); Annot., 1972, 49 A.L.R.3d 321.

Such clauses are effective in commercial leases, even in personal injury actions. But they are "strictly construed against a landlord who attempts to insulate himself from liability for his own fault." Ultimate Computer Services v. Biltmore Realty Co., App.Div.1982, 183 N.J.Super. 144, 443 A.2d 723, 726. See Miller v. A & R Joint Venture, 1981, 97 Nev. 580, 636 P.2d 277.

12. The issue of implied warranty of habitability typically arises in the context of a dispute surrounding the nonpayment of rent. See, e.g., Pugh v. Holmes, 1979, 486 Pa. 272, 405 A.2d 897, 901 n. 2 (citations of 40 states and D.C. having this warranty). Since the warranty is contractual in nature, it is beyond the scope of this text. See generally Annots., 1971, 40 A.L.R.3d 646 (generally); 1980, 1 A.L.R.4th 1982 (damages). A very few of the cases have involved negligence and personal injuries. See, e.g., Rivera v. Selfon Home Repairs & Improvements Co., 1982, 294 Pa.Super. 41, 439 A.2d 739; Snyder v. Moore, 1979, 72 A.D.2d 580, 421 N.Y.S.2d 25. Compare Crowell v. McCaffrey, 1979, 377 Mass. 443, 386 N.E.2d 1256 (breach of implied warranty of habitability would support action for personal injuries from collapse of porch railing that did not support plaintiff), with Auburn v. Amoco Oil Co., 1982, 106 Ill.App.3d 60, 61 Ill.Dec. 939, 435 N.E.2d 780, 783 ("no action for personal injuries can result from a breach of the implied warranty of habitability"); Segal v. Justice Court Mutual Housing Cooperative, Inc., App.1981, 108 Misc.2d 1074, 442 N.Y.S.2d 686 (same, semble; per curiam).

Concealed Dangerous Conditions Known to Lessor

One exception developed by the common law is that the lessor, like a vendor,[13] is under the obligation to disclose to the lessee concealed dangerous conditions existing when possession is transferred, of which he has knowledge.[14] There is "something like fraud" in a failure to give warning of a known hidden danger to one who enters upon the assumption that it does not exist; and the lessor will be liable to the lessee[15] or to members of his family[16] for his non-disclosure. The liability extends likewise to guests and others who enter in the right of the tenant,[17] since they have been deprived of an opportunity for protection at the hands of the tenant by the landlord's silence.

It is not necessary that the lessor shall believe the condition to be unsafe,[18] or even that he have definite knowledge of its existence, before he is under any duty in regard to it. It is enough that he be informed of facts from which a reasonable man would conclude that there is danger,[19] and the decisions run the gamut of "reasonable notice,"[20] "reason to know,"[21] or "should have known."[22] If he has such information, and it would lead a reasonable man to suspect the existence of an unreasonable risk of harm, it is his duty to communicate at least that suspicion.[23] A couple of jurisdictions have gone further and imposed upon the lessor an affirmative duty to use reasonable care to inspect the premises before transfer;[24] but the great majority of states have held that there is no obligation to inspect or investigate in the absence of some reason to believe that there is a danger.[25]

There is of course no duty to disclose conditions which are known to the tenant,[26] or which are so open and obvious that he cannot reasonably be expected to fail to discover them when he takes possession,[27] or are of a kind, such as a flight of steps, or poison ivy on a campsite,[28] which anyone might expect to encounter upon similar premises, and therefore to look out for himself.

---

13. See infra, § 64.

14. Second Restatement of Torts, § 358; Property, § 17.1.

15. See Reeves v. Property Managers, Inc., Ala. 1982, 416 So.2d 717; Hall v. Warren, Utah 1981, 632 P.2d 848; cf. Evans v. Van Kleek, 1981, 101 Mich.App. 798, 314 N.W.2d 486 (tenant's goods).

16. Younger v. United States, 9th Cir. 1981, 662 F.2d 580; Taylor v. Leedy & Co., Ala.1982, 412 So.2d 763; cf. Annot., 1972, 43 A.L.R.3d 1268 (liability for lead poisoning from peeling paint).

17. See Mansur v. Eubanks, Fla.1981, 401 So.2d 1328; Kaylor v. Magill, 6th Cir. 1950, 181 F.2d 179.

18. Murphy v. Barlow Realty Co., 1943, 214 Minn. 64, 7 N.W.2d 684; Cutter v. Hamlen, 1888, 147 Mass. 471, 18 N.E. 397.

19. See Reeves v. Property Managers, Inc., Ala. 1982, 416 So.2d 717 (landlord had noticed loose caulking in wall from which piece of brick fell on tenant).

20. Taylor v. Leedy & Co., Ala.1982, 412 So.2d 763 (prior collapse of other tenants' stoves); Evans v. Van Kleek, 1981, 110 Mich.App. 798, 314 N.W.2d 486 (where defendant created hazardous condition, not even constructive knowledge is required).

But notice of a leaking faucet is not notice of the danger of scalding. Campbell v. Hagen-Burger, 1951, 327 Mass. 159, 97 N.E.2d 409.

21. Meade v. Montrose, 1913, 173 Mo.App. 722, 160 S.W. 11 ("adequate reason to suspect"); Cummings v. Prater, Ariz.1963, 386 P.2d 27 (same).

22. Rhoades v. Seidel, 1905, 139 Mich. 608, 102 N.W. 1025 ("ought to have known"); Reckert v. Roco Petroleum Corp., Mo.1966, 411 S.W.2d 199 (same).

23. Johnson v. O'Brien, 1960, 258 Minn. 502, 105 N.W.2d 244.

24. Mansur v. Eubanks, Fla.1981, 401 So.2d 1328; Willcox v. Hines, 1898, 100 Tenn. 538, 46 S.W. 297; Kaylor v. Magill, 6th Cir. 1950, 181 F.2d 179. See Noel, Landlord's Tort Liability in Tennessee, 1963, 30 Tenn.L.Rev. 368.

25. State for Use of Bohon v. Feldstein, 1955, 207 Md. 20, 113 A.2d 100; Pyburn v. Fourseam Coal Co., 1946, 303 Ky. 443, 197 S.W.2d 921; Harrill v. Sinclair Refining Co., 1945, 225 N.C. 421, 35 S.E.2d 240.

26. See Watson v. McSoud, Okla.App.1977, 566 P.2d 171 (slippery rug remnants on steps); Lemley v. Penner, 1981, 230 Kan. 25, 630 P.2d 1086 (even if the injury is to tenant's child).

27. Hyde v. Bryant, 1966, 114 Ga.App. 535, 151 S.E.2d 925; Stover v. Fechtman, 1966, 140 Ind.App. 62, 222 N.E.2d 281; Smedberg v. Simons, 1981, 129 Ariz. 375, 631 P.2d 530. But see Younger v. United States, 9th Cir. 1981, 662 F.2d 580 (absence of smoke detector in Army residence may not have been apparent to tenant).

28. Hersch v. Anderson Acres, Ohio C.P.1957, 146 N.E.2d 648.

Conditions Dangerous to Those Outside of the Premises

A second exception is that the lessor, like a vendor, has a responsibility that continues for some time after the transfer of possession for conditions involving an unreasonable risk of harm to others outside the land.[29] Most of the cases have involved either private nuisances[30] or dangers to the highway, such as awnings likely to fall into the street,[31] or holes in the sidewalk.[32] The liability extends not only to dangerous conditions and disrepair existing at the time of the transfer, but also to conditions which are then potentially dangerous, and likely to become so in the course of the use of the land for the purpose for which it is leased.[33] The lessor's responsibility to adjoining landowners and to the public is such that he is not permitted to shift it to another, and even a covenant on the part of the lessee to repair the defect will not relieve him of liability.[34]

In a few cases the responsibility of the lessor has been carried even beyond that of a vendor,[35] and he has been held liable for a nuisance created by the activities of the tenant to which he consented at the time of the lease, and which he should have known would necessarily involve such a result. If he leases his land for a stone quarry, he cannot escape responsibility for the blasting and rock crushing carried on by the lessee.[36] But he is not responsible for activities nor for the creation of dangers which he neither consented to nor had any reason to expect.[37]

Premises Leased for Admission of the Public

A third exception arises where the land is leased for a purpose which involves the admission of the public.[38] There is quite general agreement that the lessor is under an affirmative duty to exercise reasonable care to inspect and repair the premises, before possession is transferred, to prevent any unreasonable risk of harm to the public who may enter.[39] The earliest decisions involved wharves and piers,[40] and the principle has

---

29. See Second Restatement of Torts, § 379; Property, § 18.1. As for the vendor, see infra, § 64.

30. Wofford v. Rudick, 1957, 63 N.M. 307, 318 P.2d 605; Boyle v. Pennsylvania Railroad Co., 1943, 346 Pa. 602, 31 A.2d 89 (explosion danger). See Note, 1949, 37 Ky.L.J. 322.

31. Both v. Harband, 1958, 164 Cal.App.2d 743, 331 P.2d 140 (piece of building material); City of Knoxville v. Hargis, 1946, 184 Tenn. 262, 198 S.W.2d 555; Whalen v. Shivek, 1950, 326 Mass. 142, 93 N.E.2d 393 (parapet); Kelly v. Laclede Real Estate & Investment Co., 1941, 348 Mo. 407, 155 S.W.2d 90 (portion of building wall); Barrett v. Stoneburg, 1947, 238 Iowa 1068, 29 N.W.2d 420 (ruined building).

32. See Smith v. Rengel, 1981, 97 Ill.App.3d 204, 52 Ill.Dec. 937, 422 N.E.2d 1146 (hole beside sidewalk).

33. Larson v. Calder's Park Co., 1919, 54 Utah 325, 180 P. 599 (unguarded shooting gallery); Rose v. Gunn Fruit Co., 1919, 201 Mo.App. 262, 211 S.W. 85 (potentially dangerous hole in sidewalk); Knauss v. Brua, 1884, 107 Pa. 85 (obstructed sewer pipe).

34. Whalen v. Shivek, 1950, 326 Mass. 142, 93 N.E.2d 393; Updegraff v. City of Ottumwa, 1929, 210 Iowa 382, 226 N.W. 928.

35. A possible reason for the distinction is the policy against restraints in the case of a vendor, and the greater ease with which the activities of the tenant may be restricted by a clause in the lease.

36. Benton v. Kernan, 1940, 127 N.J.Eq. 434, 13 A.2d 825, modified in 1941, 130 N.J.Eq. 193, 21 A.2d 755; City of San Angelo v. Sitas, 1944, 143 Tex. 154, 183 S.W.2d 417; State v. Monarch Chemicals, Inc., Sup. 1981, 111 Misc.2d 343, 443 N.Y.S.2d 967 modified 1982, 90 A.2d 907, 456 N.Y.S.2d 867 (storage of toxic chemicals polluting water supply); Second Restatement of Torts, § 837. Cf. Rosales v. Stewart, 1980, 113 Cal. App.3d 130, 169 Cal.Rptr. 660 (landlord might be liable for tenant's firing rifle at child playing in her own backyard); Note, 1978, 30 Stan.L.Rev. 725 (landlord's duty in selecting and retaining tenants).

37. Edgar v. Walker, 1899, 106 Ga. 454, 32 S.E. 582; Lufkin v. Zane, 1892, 157 Mass. 117, 31 N.E. 757.

38. Second Restatement of Torts, § 359; Property, § 17.2; Annot., 1968, 17 A.L.R.3d 873 (what constitutes "public" use).

39. The lessor is not an insurer, and is liable only for negligence. O'Toole v. Thousand Island Park Association, 1923, 206 App.Div. 31, 200 N.Y.S. 502. There is no obligation as to conditions which are obvious, and which the entering public may be expected to avoid. Lyman v. Herrmann, 1938, 203 Minn. 225, 280 N.W. 862. But liability is not limited to known defects, and there is an obligation to inspect. Colorado Mortgage & Investment Co. v. Giacomini, 1913, 55 Colo. 540, 136 P. 1039; Junkermann v. Tilyou Realty Co., 1915, 213 N.Y. 404, 108 N.E. 190.

40. Swords v. Edgar, 1874, 59 N.Y. 28; Campbell v. Portland Sugar Co., 1873, 62 Me. 552; Albert v. State, 1887, 66 Md. 325, 7 A. 697; Joyce v. Martin, 1887, 15 R.I. 558, 10 A. 620.

been applied to amusement parks,[41] theatres [42] and other halls of entertainment,[43] beaches,[44] hotels,[45] and baseball grandstands.[46] Various reasons for the landlord's liability have been advanced. It has been regarded as an extension of his obligation to the public outside of the land, and the defective condition has been called, quite unjustifiably, a nuisance. Some courts have said that the lessor has "invited" the public to enter, or that he has represented, or has authorized the lessee to represent, that the premises are safe for public admission. Perhaps the best explanation is merely the arbitrary one that his responsibility to the public is so great that he will not be permitted to shift it to the tenant, and he simply may not escape responsibility for the use of his land to be used in a manner involving a public, rather than a private, danger.[47] This is borne out by the decisions holding that the mere agreement of the tenant to repair or remedy the condition will not of itself relieve the landlord of liability,[48] but if the agreement is that the land is not to be open to the public until the repairs have been made, the lessor may rely on the lessee, and his responsibility is terminated.[49]

The First Restatement of Torts [50] rather unaccountably took the position that the "public use" exception applied only to places leased for the purpose of admitting the public in large numbers; and a few cases have accepted this limitation.[51] Yet there would appear to be little justification for such a limitation if the landlord's responsibility is indeed a public one; and it is now rejected by the great majority of courts. The liability thus has been found in the case of stores [52] and shops,[53] a restaurant,[54] tav-

41. Junkermann v. Tilyou Realty Co., 1915, 213 N.Y. 404, 108 N.E. 190; Larson v. Calder's Park Co., 1919, 54 Utah 325, 180 P. 599; Lyons v. Wagers, 1966, 55 Tenn.App. 667, 404 S.W.2d 270; cf. Fitchett v. Buchanan, 1970, 2 Wn.App. 965, 472 P.2d 623. But see Solmo v. Catholic Bishop of Chicago, 1967, 85 Ill.App. 2d 75, 229 N.E.2d 389 (concession stand at church festival).

42. Lang v. Stadium Purchasing Corp., 1926, 216 App.Div. 558, 215 N.Y.S. 502.

43. Camp v. Wood, 1879, 76 N.Y. 92 (dance); Johnson v. Zemel, 1932, 109 N.J.L. 197, 160 A. 356 (boxing); Brown v. Reorganization Investment Co., 1942, 350 Mo. 407, 166 S.W.2d 476 (wrestling); Friedman v. Richman, 1914, 85 Misc. 376, 147 N.Y.S. 461 (auditorium leased to religious society).

44. Barrett v. Lake Ontario Beach Improvement Co., 1903, 174 N.Y. 310, 66 N.E. 968; Martin v. City of Asbury Park, 1933, 111 N.J.L. 364, 168 A. 612.

45. Colorado Mortgage & Investment Co. v. Giacomini, 1913, 55 Colo. 540, 136 P. 1039; Copley v. Balle, 1900, 9 Kan.App. 465, 60 P. 656; see Goodman v. Harris, 1953, 40 Cal.2d 254, 253 P.2d 447.

46. Tulsa Entertainment Co. v. Greenlees, 1922, 85 Okl. 113, 205 P. 179; Folkman v. Lauer, 1914, 244 Pa. 605, 91 A. 218.

Accord, as to race tracks, Fox v. Buffalo Park, 1900, 163 N.Y. 559, 57 N.E. 1109, affirming 1897, 21 App. Div. 321, 47 N.Y.S. 488; Gibson v. Shelby County Fair Association, 1950, 241 Iowa 1349, 44 N.W.2d 362.

47. "We may say more simply, and perhaps more wisely, rejecting the fiction of invitation, that the nature of the use itself creates the duty, and that an owner is just as much bound to repair a structure that endangers travelers on a walk in an amusement park as he is to repair a structure that endangers travelers on a highway." Cardozo, J., in Junkermann v. Tilyou Realty Co., 1915, 213 N.Y. 404, 408, 409, 108 N.E. 190, 191. Accord, Fitchett v. Buchanan, 1970, 2 Wn.App. 965, 472 P.2d 623.

48. Folkman v. Lauer, 1914, 244 Pa. 605, 91 A. 218; Warner v. Lucey, 1923, 207 App.Div. 241, 201 N.Y.S. 658, affirmed, 1924, 238 N.Y. 638, 144 N.E. 924.

49. Beaman v. Grooms, 1917, 138 Tenn. 320, 197 S.W. 1090; Nickelsen v. Minneapolis, Northfield & Southern Railway Co., 1926, 168 Minn. 118, 209 N.W. 646.

In Maglin v. Peoples City Bank, 1940, 141 Pa.Super. 329, 14 A.2d 827, the lessee's covenant to repair was held to give the lessor adequate reason to believe that the public would not be admitted until repairs were made.

50. § 359. This was relied on in Zinn v. Hill Lumber & Investment Co., 1954, 176 Kan. 669, 272 P.2d 1106.

51. Hayden v. Second National Bank of Allentown, 1938, 331 Pa. 29, 199 A. 218 (garage); Warner v. Fry, 1950, 360 Mo. 496, 228 S.W.2d 729 (tavern); Marx v. Standard Oil Co., 1949, 6 N.J.Super. 39, 69 A.2d 748 (gasoline filling station); Dunlap v. Howard, Mo.App. 1982, 629 S.W.2d 664 (same).

Still less accountable is the limitation to places of amusement, as distinguished from commercial premises, found in Gentry v. Taylor, 1945, 182 Tenn. 223, 185 S.W.2d 521 (restaurant); Clark v. Chase Hotel Co., 1934, 230 Mo.App. 739, 74 S.W.2d 498 (Turkish bath); Bender v. Weber, 1913, 250 Mo. 551, 157 S.W. 570 (grocery store).

52. Schlender v. Andy Jansen Co., Okl. 1962, 380 P.2d 523; Turner v. Kent, 1932, 134 Kan. 574, 7 P.2d 513; Senner v. Danewolf, 1932, 139 Or. 93, 293 P. 599,

erns,[55] a garage,[56] gasoline filling stations,[57] a parking lot,[58] a voting precinct,[59] small meetings,[60] a doctor's office,[61] a boarding house,[62] a motel,[63] and even premises across which there is a passageway used by the public.[64] On the other hand, it is not found in the case of private dwellings,[65] a warehouse leased for private storage,[66] or a private pier.[67]

It is not necessary that the members of the public enter, or be expected to enter, as paying customers, or that they come on any business purpose of either the lessor or the lessee; and the lessor's duty arises when the land is leased for a free public lecture, piano recital, or social gathering.[68] It has been held that it is not even necessary that the lessor be paid rent, and that a gratuitous lease for the admission of the public is enough.[69] The lessor's liability extends only to those parts of the premises which are in fact thrown open to the public,[70] and to those invitees who enter for the purpose for which the place was leased.[71] Since he has no control over the land after the tenant has taken possession, he is not liable for the negligence of the tenant in maintaining the premises, once they are turned over in good condition;[72] and for the same reason he is not liable if the land is used for a public pur-

6 P.2d 240; Corrigan v. Antupit, 1944, 131 Conn. 71, 37 A.2d 697.

53. Webel v. Yale University, 1939, 125 Conn. 515, 7 A.2d 215 (beauty shop); Wood v. Prudential Insurance Co., 1942, 212 Minn. 551, 4 N.W.2d 617 (same).

54. Hilleary v. Earle Restaurant, D.D.C.1952, 109 F.Supp. 829. But cf. Blair v. Berlo Vending Corp., Del. Super.1972, 287 A.2d 696 (collapse of restaurant chair furnished per agreement by lessee).

55. Nelson v. Hokuf, 1941, 140 Neb. 290, 299 N.W. 472; Austin v. Beuttner, 1956, 211 Md. 61, 124 A.2d 793; Spain v. Kelland, 1963, 93 Ariz. 172, 379 P.2d 149.

56. Warner v. Lucey, 1923, 207 App.Div. 241, 201 N.Y.S. 658, affirmed, 1924, 238 N.Y. 638, 144 N.E. 924.

57. Hayes v. Richfield Oil Corp., 1952, 38 Cal.2d 375, 240 P.2d 580; Bluemer v. Saginaw Central Oil & Gas Service, 1959, 356 Mich. 399, 97 N.W.2d 90; Pagarigan v. Phillips Petroleum Co., 1976, 16 Wn.App. 34, 552 P.2d 1065. Contra, Dunlap v. Howard, Mo.App. 1982, 629 S.W.2d 664; Richardson v. Bulk Petroleum Corp., 1973, 11 Ill.App.3d 655, 297 N.E.2d 405.

58. Burroughs v. Ben's Auto Park, 1945, 27 Cal.2d 449, 164 P.2d 897.

59. Boothby v. Town of Yreka City, 1931, 117 Cal. App. 643, 4 P.2d 589.

60. Howe v. Jameson, 1940, 91 N.H. 55, 13 A.2d 471 (domestic science lectures); King v. New Masonic Temple Association, 1942, 51 Cal.App.2d 512, 125 P.2d 559 (woman's club and guests); Bunnell v. Waterbury Hospital, 1925, 103 Conn. 520, 131 A. 501 (Salvation Army); Rau v. Redwood City Woman's Club, 1952, 111 Cal. App.2d 546, 245 P.2d 12 (piano recital).

61. Gilligan v. Blakesley, 1933, 93 Colo. 370, 26 P.2d 808; McCarthy v. Maxon, 1947, 134 Conn. 170, 55 A.2d 912 (veterinarian).

62. Stenberg v. Wilcox, 1896, 96 Tenn. 163, 33 S.W. 917.

63. Goodman v. Harris, 1953, 40 Cal.2d 254, 253 P.2d 447.

64. Standard Oil Co. v. Decell, 1936, 175 Miss. 251, 166 So. 379.

65. Areal v. Home Owners Loan Corp., Sup.Ct.1943, 43 N.Y.S.2d 538; Patton v. Texas Co., 1951, 13 N.J. Super. 42, 80 A.2d 231. Cf. La Freda v. Woodward, 1940, 125 N.J.L. 489, 15 A.2d 798 (doctor's office in private dwelling); De Motte v. Arkell, 1926, 77 Cal.App. 610, 247 P. 254 (private lodge meeting).

66. Campbell v. Elsie S. Holding Co., 1929, 251 N.Y. 446, 167 N.E. 582; O'Brien v. Fong Wan, 1960, 185 Cal. App.2d 112, 8 Cal.Rptr. 124. Cf. Brittain v. Atlantic Refining Co., 1941, 126 N.J.L. 528, 19 A.2d 793 (workroom of gasoline filling station).

67. Lafredo v. Bush Terminal Co., 1933, 261 N.Y. 323, 185 N.E. 398, reargument denied 262 N.Y. 522, 188 N.E. 48.

68. Bunnell v. Waterbury Hospital, 1925, 103 Conn. 520, 131 A. 501; Howe v. Jameson, 1940, 91 N.H. 55, 13 A.2d 471; Rau v. Redwood City Woman's Club, 1952, 111 Cal.App.2d 546, 245 P.2d 12; King v. New Masonic Temple Association, 1942, 51 Cal.App.2d 512, 125 P.2d 559.

69. In Tulsa Entertainment Co. v. Greenlees, 1922, 85 Okl. 113, 205 P. 179, the owner was held liable where he donated the premises for the admission of the public. Accord, Second Restatement of Torts, § 359, Comment g. Contra: Davis v. Schmitt Brothers, 1922, 199 App.Div. 683, 192 N.Y.S. 15; Karlowski v. Kissock, 1931, 275 Mass. 180, 175 N.E. 500.

70. Wilson v. Dowtin, 1939, 215 N.C. 547, 2 S.E.2d 576; Van Avery v. Platte Valley Land & Investment Co., 1937, 133 Neb. 314, 275 N.W. 288; Regan v. City of Seattle, 1969, 76 Wn.2d 501, 458 P.2d 12; cf. Pagarigan v. Phillips Petroleum Co., 1976, 16 Wn.App. 34, 552 P.2d 1065 (foreseeable that service station patrons would go into lubrication room).

71. Kneiser v. Belasco-Blackwood Co., 1913, 22 Cal. App. 205, 133 P. 989; Second Restatement of Torts, § 359, Comment e.

72. Goodman v. Harris, 1953, 40 Cal.2d 254, 253 P.2d 447; Bonfield v. Blackmore, 1917, 90 N.J.L. 252, 100 A. 161; Dawson v. Kitch, 1910, 156 Ill.App. 185; Cunningham v. Rogers, 1909, 225 Pa. 132, 73 A. 1094; Rice v. Forby, Minn.1975, 228 N.W.2d 581.

pose not contemplated by the lease.⁷³ Since the basis of liability is the likelihood that the public will be permitted to enter before the dangerous condition is changed, it is logical that it should be limited to the time within which there is reason to believe that it will remain unaltered.⁷⁴

Common Areas Retained Under Landlord's Control

When different parts of a building, such as an office building or an apartment house, are leased to several tenants, the approaches and common passageways normally do not pass to the tenant, but remain in the possession and control of the landlord.⁷⁵ The tenants are permitted to make use of them but do not occupy them, and the responsibility for their condition remains upon the lessor.⁷⁶ His position is closely analogous to that of a possessor who permits visitors to enter for a purpose of his own; and those who come in the course of the expected use may be considered his invitees, as a good many courts have held.⁷⁷ He is therefore under an affirmative obligation to exercise reasonable care to inspect and repair such parts of the premises for the protection of the lessee;⁷⁸ and the duty extends also to members of the tenant's family,⁷⁹ his employees,⁸⁰ his invitees,⁸¹ his guests,⁸² and others on the land in the right of the tenant,⁸³ since their presence is a part of the normal use of the premises for which the lessor holds them open.⁸⁴ It extends also to those outside of the premises who may be injured as a result of their condition.⁸⁵ It is entirely possible that as to any of these plaintiffs the landlord may be liable where the tenant is not.⁸⁶ The duty does not extend to intruders who come for a purpose

---

73. Edwards v. New York & Harlem Railroad Co., 1885, 98 N.Y. 245.

74. Second Restatement of Torts § 359, Comment *i*. No cases definitely supporting this position have been found. See, however, Volz v. Williams, 1944, 112 Colo. 592, 152 P.2d 996; Corrigan v. Antupit, 1944, 131 Conn. 71, 37 A.2d 697; Maglin v. Peoples City Bank, 1940, 141 Pa.Super. 329, 14 A.2d 827.

75. Sawyer v. McGillicuddy, 1889, 81 Me. 318, 17 A. 124; Inglehardt v. Mueller, 1914, 156 Wis. 609, 146 N.W. 808; Looney v. McLean, 1880, 129 Mass. 33. Cf. Nunan v. Dudley Properties, 1950, 325 Mass. 551, 91 N.E.2d 840 (retained control of part of single building); Coleman v. Steinberg, 1969, 54 N.J. 58, 253 A.2d 167 (single control heating unit in two-family apartment). Contra where a stairway services only one apartment. Seago v. Roy, 1981, 97 Ill.App.3d 6, 53 Ill.Dec. 849, 424 N.E.2d 640; cf. Sargent v. Ross, 1973, 113 N.H. 388, 308 A.2d 528.

76. Second Restatement of Torts, §§ 360–61; Property, §§ 17.3–.4.

77. Murray v. Lane, 1982, 51 Md.App. 597, 444 A.2d 1069 (guest; thorough analysis); Colonial Natural Gas Co. v. Sayers, 1981, 222 Va. 781, 284 S.E.2d 599 (tenant); Rennick v. Hoover, 1980, ___ Mont. ___, 606 P.2d 1079.

78. Franklin Drug Stores v. Gur-Sil Corp., 1967, 269 N.C. 169, 152 S.E.2d 77 (property of tenant damaged); Levine v. Katz, 1968, 132 U.S.App.D.C. 173, 407 F.2d 303 (mat on polished floor of hallway); Colonial Natural Gas Co. v. Sayers, 1981, 222 Va. 781, 284 S.E.2d 599; Lenz v. Ridgewood Associates, 1981, 55 N.C.App. 115, 284 S.E.2d 702, review denied 305 N.C. 300, 290 S.E.2d 702.

79. Norwood v. Lazarus, 1982, ___ Mo.App. ___, 634 S.W.2d 584; Allen v. Equity & Investors Management Corp., 1982, 56 N.C.App. 706, 289 S.E.2d 623; Cruz v. Drezek, 1978, 175 Conn. 230, 397 A.2d 1335.

80. Lyon v. Barrett, 1982, 89 N.J. 294, 445 A.2d 1153 (employee of landlord who was tenant in his own office building); Kuhn v. General Parking Corp., 1981, 98 Ill.App.3d 570, 54 Ill.Dec. 191, 424 N.E.2d 941.

81. Chalfen v. Kraft, 1949, 324 Mass. 1, 84 N.E.2d 454; Siegel v. Detroit City Ice & Fuel Co., 1949, 324 Mich. 205, 36 N.W.2d 719; Swenson v. Slawik, 1952, 236 Minn. 403, 53 N.W.2d 107; Johnston v. De La Guerra Properties, 1946, 28 Cal.2d 394, 170 P.2d 5. Also to the property of invitees. Whellkin Coat Co. v. Long Branch Trust Co., 1938, 121 N.J.L. 106, 1 A.2d 394.

82. Murray v. Lane, 1982, 51 Md.App. 597, 444 A.2d 1069; Smith v. Rengel, 1981, 97 Ill.App.3d 204, 52 Ill. Dec. 937, 422 N.E.2d 1146.

83. See Menard v. Cashman, 1947, 94 N.H. 428, 55 A.2d 156 (licensee); Urseleo v. Rosengard, 1924, 248 Mass. 542, 143 N.E. 497 (lodger); cf. Hiller v. Harsh, 1981, 100 Ill.App.3d 332, 55 Ill.Dec. 635, 426 N.E.2d 960 (classification as invitee or licensee unnecessary, since the same duty of reasonable care is imposed upon the landlord to keep common areas reasonably safe for all lawful visitors).

84. See Slusher v. State, 1982, ___ Ind.App. ___, 437 N.E.2d 97 (dictum).

85. Washington Loan & Trust Co. v. Hickey, 1943, 78 App.D.C. 59, 137 F.2d 677; Laskowski v. Manning, 1950, 325 Mass. 393, 91 N.E.2d 231.

86. Sockett v. Gottlieb, 1960, 187 Cal.App.2d 760, 9 Cal.Rptr. 831; Snyder v. I. Jay Realty Co., 1959, 30 N.J. 303, 153 A.2d 1; Temple v. Congress Square Garage, 1950, 145 Me. 274, 75 A.2d 459. The point is strikingly illustrated in Taneian v. Meghrigian, 1954, 15 N.J. 267, 104 A.2d 689, where a lessor who lived in one

for which the building is not open and provided, and such individuals are at best licensees.[87]

The obligation is one of reasonable care [88] only, and the lessor is not liable where no injury to anyone was reasonably to be anticipated,[89] or the condition was not discoverable by reasonable inspection,[90] unless it is shown to have been of such duration as to permit the conclusion that due care would have discovered it.[91] The prevailing view is that the duty extends to conditions of purely natural origin, such as ice and snow on the steps,[92] although the rule is to the contrary in a number of jurisdictions.[93]

The lessor's obligation extends to hallways,[94] stairs,[95] elevators,[96] approaches and entrances,[97] yards,[98] basements,[99] bath-

---

unit of a multi-family house was held liable to his own social guest as a landlord, where he would not be liable as an occupier.

87. Stacy v. Shapiro, 1925, 212 App.Div. 723, 209 N.Y.S. 305 (canvasser); Reuter v. Kenmore Building Co., 1934, 153 Misc. 646, 276 N.Y.S. 545 (canvasser); Jolles v. 3720 Corp., 1937, 163 Misc. 51, 296 N.Y.S. 354 (peddler); Hart v. Cole, 1892, 156 Mass. 475, 31 N.E. 644 (uninvited interloper coming to see a wake); Medcraft v. Merchants Exchange, 1931, 211 Cal. 404, 295 P. 822 (using toilet in office building).

88. See generally Annot., 1975, 66 A.L.R.3d 202 (inadequacy of lighting).

By analogy to the rule as to trespassing children, supra, § 59, due care may require the lessor to protect children against dangerous objects attractive to them. Nesmith v. Starr, 1967, 115 Ga.App. 472, 155 S.E.2d 24. Or against the acts of other children. Mayer v. Housing Authority of Jersey City, 1964, 84 N.J.Super. 411, 202 A.2d 439, affirmed, 1965, 44 N.J. 567, 210 A.2d 617.

89. American Fire & Casualty Co. v. Jackson, 5th Cir. 1951, 187 F.2d 379, certiorari denied 342 U.S. 818, 72 S.Ct. 33, 96 L.Ed. 619; Security Building Co. v. Lewis, 1953, 127 Colo. 139, 255 P.2d 405; Anderson v. Reeder, 1953, 42 Wn.2d 45, 253 P.2d 423; Taylor v. Hocker, 1981, 101 Ill.App.3d 639, 57 Ill.Dec. 112, 428 N.E.2d 662 (criminal assault).

90. Fernandes v. Medeiros, 1950, 325 Mass. 293, 90 N.E.2d 9; C. W. Simpson Co. v. Langley, 1942, 76 U.S. App.D.C. 365, 131 F.2d 869; Revell v. Deegan, 1951, 192 Va. 428, 65 S.E.2d 543.

91. Barb v. Farmers Insurance Exchange, Mo.1955, 281 S.W.2d 297; Morris v. King Cole Stores, 1946, 132 Conn. 489, 45 A.2d 710.

92. Bostian v. Jewell, 1963, 254 Iowa 1289, 121 N.W.2d 141; Langhorne Road Apartments, Inc. v. Bisson, 1966, 207 Va. 474, 150 S.E.2d 540; Klein v. United States, 2d Cir. 1964, 339 F.2d 512; Langley Park Apartments v. Lund, 1964, 234 Md. 402, 199 A.2d 620; Skupienski v. Maly, 1958, 27 N.J. 240, 142 A.2d 220; Lenz v. Ridgewood Associates, 1981, 55 N.C.App. 115, 284 S.E.2d 702, review denied 305 N.C. 300, 290 S.E.2d 702 (sidewalk); cf. Rountree v. Lerner Development Co., 1982, 52 Md.App. 281, 447 A.2d 902 (jury issue on assumption of risk). See generally Annot., 1973, 49 A.L.R.3d 387.

Reasonable care may, however, permit the landlord to wait until the end of a storm. Reuter v. Iowa Trust & Savings Bank, 1953, 244 Iowa 939, 57 N.W.2d 225; Young v. Saroukos, 1962, 55 Del. 149, 185 A.2d 274, judgment affirmed, 1963, 56 Del. 44, 189 A.2d 437.

93. Carey v. Malley, 1951, 327 Mass. 189, 97 N.E.2d 645; Pomfret v. Fletcher, 1965, 99 R.I. 452, 208 A.2d 743; Cronin v. Brownlee, 1952, 348 Ill.App. 448, 109 N.E.2d 352; Burke v. O'Neil, 1934, 192 Minn. 492, 257 N.W. 81; Sidle v. Humphrey, 1968, 13 Ohio St.2d 45, 233 N.E.2d 589.

94. Norwood v. Lazarus, Mo.App.1982, 634 S.W.2d 584 (tenant's 2-year-old suffered lead poisoning from eating flakes of lead-based paint fallen from walls to floor); Murray v. Lane, 1982, 51 Md.App. 597, 444 A.2d 1069 (guest fell through rotten railing on second floor landing).

95. Lyon v. Barrett, 1982, 89 N.J. 294, 445 A.2d 1153; Turner v. Thompson, 1981, 102 Ill.App.3d 838, 58 Ill.Dec. 215, 430 N.E.2d 157 (failure to light, as public nuisance under municipal code); Hiller v. Harsh, 1981, 100 Ill.App.3d 332, 55 Ill.Dec. 635, 426 N.E.2d 960 (rotten, loose and slanted steps); Nicks v. Joseph, 1981, 82 A.D.2d 768, 440 N.Y.S.2d 218 (wet interior stairs); O'Neal v. Kellett, 1981, 55 N.C.App. 225, 284 S.E.2d 707 (dimly lit exterior stairs). See Annots., 1975, 67 A.L.R.3d 490 (exterior steps); 67 A.L.R.3d 587 (interior).

96. Lee v. Jerome Realty, Inc., 1958, 338 Mass. 150, 154 N.E.2d 126; Swenson v. Slawik, 1952, 236 Minn. 403, 53 N.W.2d 107; Carter v. United Novelty & Premium Co., 1957, 389 Pa. 198, 132 A.2d 202; cf. Firth v. Marhoefer, Fla.App.1981, 406 So.2d 521 (slippery condition on elevator floor).

97. Trimble v. Spears, 1958, 182 Kan. 406, 320 P.2d 1029; Arnold v. Walters, 1950, 203 Okl. 503, 224 P.2d 261; cf. Ruby v. Casello, 1964, 204 Pa.Super. 9, 201 A.2d 219 (alleyway); Cooper v. City of Philadelphia, 1955, 178 Pa.Super. 205, 115 A.2d 849 (sidewalk in front of premises); Smith v. Rengel, 1981, 97 Ill.App.3d 204, 52 Ill.Dec. 937, 422 N.E.2d 1146 (hole beside sidewalk off the premises).

98. Reek v. Lutz, 1960, 90 R.I. 340, 158 A.2d 145; Lake v. Emigh, 1948, 121 Mont. 87, 190 P.2d 550; cf. Colonial Natural Gas Co. v. Sayers, 1981, 222 Va. 781, 284 S.E.2d 599 (footpath between apartments in complex).

99. McNab v. Wallin, 1916, 133 Minn. 370, 158 N.W. 623; Wright & Taylor v. Smith, Ky.1958, 315 S.W.2d 624.

Prosser & Keeton Torts 5th Ed. HB—11

rooms,¹ common rooms,² porches,³ the roof of the building⁴ and any other parts of the premises maintained for the benefit of the tenants within the purposes of the lease.⁵ It extends also to any appliances, such as a heating plant, water system, or washing machine,⁶ over which the lessor retains control, and which he furnishes for common use by the tenants. It may even extend into the portion of the premises leased to the tenant, provided that the landlord has retained control over that aspect of the premises responsible for the injury.⁷ It does not extend, however, to parts of the premises where the tenant or his visitors may not reasonably be expected to go,⁸ or to their use for an unintended purpose.⁹ If the lessee discovers the dangerous condition, he may, but does not necessarily, assume the risk or become contributorily negligent in dealing with it;¹⁰ but his knowledge will not prevent recovery by a third party who is himself ignorant of the danger.¹¹

Prior to 1970, there was no general tort duty on landlords to protect their tenants against criminal theft or attack.¹² The situation began to change in that year, however, with the landmark decision of Kline v. 1500 Massachusetts Avenue Apartment Corp.,¹³ which imposed a duty of reasonable care upon the owner of an urban multiple unit apartment dwelling to protect its tenants from foreseeable criminal assaults. A growing number of courts have imposed similar duties of reasonable protection upon landlords to protect their tenants,¹⁴ and to pro-

1. Lennox v. White, 1949, 133 W.Va. 1, 54 S.E.2d 8; Iverson v. Quam, 1948, 226 Minn. 290, 32 N.W.2d 596 (toilet).

2. Primus v. Bellevue Apartments, 1950, 241 Iowa 1055, 44 N.W.2d 347 (laundry room).

3. Crowell v. McCaffrey, 1979, 377 Mass. 443, 386 N.E.2d 1256; Cruz v. Drezek, 1978, 175 Conn. 230, 397 A.2d 1335.

4. 2310 Madison Avenue, Inc. v. Allied Bedding Manufacturing Co., 1956, 209 Md. 399, 121 A.2d 203; Hunkins v. Amoskeag Manufacturing Co., 1933, 86 N.H. 356, 169 A. 3; Graeber v. Anderson, 1952, 237 Minn. 20, 53 N.W.2d 642 (knob on door to roof).

5. Baldwin v. McEldowney, 1936, 324 Pa. 399, 188 A. 154 (fire escape); Rowe v. Ayer & Williams, 1933, 86 N.H. 127, 164 A. 761 (same); Sezzin v. Stark, 1946, 187 Md. 241, 49 A.2d 742 (air shaft); Allen v. Equity & Investors Management Corp., 1982, 56 N.C.App. 706, 289 S.E.2d 623 (recreational area near apartment complex); Shackett v. Schwartz, 1977, 77 Mich.App. 518, 258 N.W.2d 543 (parking lot).

6. Conroy v. 10 Brewster Ave. Corp., 1967, 97 N.J. Super. 75, 234 A.2d 415 (waterheater); Shaefer v. Investors' Co. of Oregon, 1935, 150 Or. 16, 41 P.2d 440. See Annot., 1975, 66 A.L.R.3d 374 (appliances).

7. Campbell v. Harrison, 1973, 16 Ill.App.3d 570, 306 N.E.2d 643, held that a lessor could be liable for injuries from the disrepair of the tenant's walls and ceiling if he retained control over them. See also Kuhn v. General Parking Corp., 1981, 98 Ill.App.3d 570, 54 Ill.Dec. 191, 424 N.E.2d 941 (floor in tenant's office). But see Godwin v. Olshan, 1982, 161 Ga.App. 35, 288 S.E.2d 850 (shopping center owner not liable to patron shot inside sandwich shop during robbery).

8. Matthews v. Spiegel, 1956, 385 Pa. 203, 122 A.2d 696 (tenant with no right under lease to use cellar); Cohen v. Davies, 1940, 305 Mass. 152, 25 N.E.2d 223 (walking across lawn); Roessler v. O'Brien, 1949, 119 Colo. 222, 201 P.2d 901 (use of fire escape not contemplated); Toole v. Levitt, Tenn.App.1972, 492 S.W.2d 230 (tenant's guest climbed over fence and dove into pool that was closed and obviously filthy). But a female guest cannot be bound by the landlord's "no women upstairs" policy of which she is unaware. Murray v. Lane, 1982, 51 Md.App. 597, 444 A.2d 1069. But see Black v. Nelson, Utah 1975, 532 P.2d 212 (violation of "no patrons through rear door" policy).

9. Seaman v. Henriques, 1953, 139 Conn. 561, 95 A.2d 701.

10. See Rountree v. Lerner Development Co., 1982, 52 Md.App. 281, 447 A.2d 902 (jury issue on assumption of risk); Turner v. Thompson, 1981, 102 Ill.App.3d 838, 58 Ill.Dec. 215, 430 N.E.2d 157 (contributory negligence no defense to nuisance claim); Hiller v. Harsh, 1981, 100 Ill.App.3d 332, 55 Ill.Dec. 635, 426 N.E.2d 960 (evidence sustained jury finding of no contributory fault); Brooks v. Francis, 1982, 57 N.C.App. 556, 291 S.E.2d 889 (contributory negligence as a matter of law). See generally infra, ch. 11.

11. Gibson v. Hoppman, 1928, 108 Conn. 401, 143 A. 635; Hunn v. Windsor Hotel Co., 1937, 119 W.Va. 215, 193 S.E. 57.

12. On the landlord's duty to protect against criminal attacks, see generally Haines, Landlords or Tenants: Who Bears the Costs of Crime, 1981, 2 Cardozo L.Rev. 299 (thorough review and analysis); Henszey & Weisman, What Is the Landlord's Responsibility for Criminal Acts Committed on the Premises?, 1977, 6 Real Est.L.J. 104; Annot., 1972, 43 A.L.R.3d 331; Second Restatement of Property, § 17.3, Comment *l* & Reporter's Note 13.

13. D.C.Cir. 1970, 439 F.2d 477. See Notes, 1971, 71 Colum.L.Rev. 275; 59 Geo.L.J. 1153; 55 Minn.L. Rev. 1097; 1970 Duke L.J. 1046; 45 N.Y.U.L.Rev. 943.

14. See, e.g., Trentacost v. Brussel, 1980, 82 N.J. 214, 412 A.2d 436 (mugging); O'Hara v. Western Seven

tect others perhaps as well,[15] from criminal attack, provided that such assaults are reasonably foreseeable [16] and preventable.[17]

Lessor's Agreement to Repair

The effect of an agreement on the part of the lessor to keep the premises in repair has been for some time a subject of considerable dispute.[18] The older rule was that when a landlord's contract to repair was broken, the only remedy of the tenant was an action in contract for the breach.[19] It followed that no action could be maintained against the landlord by any third person, such as a member of the tenant's family or a guest, who was not a party to the contract.[20]

An increasing number of courts, however, now a majority,[21] have worked out a liability in tort for such injuries to person or property, finding a duty arising out of the contract relation.[22] This duty extends not only to the tenant,[23] but also to the members of his family,[24] his employees,[25] guests[26] and invitees,[27]

Trees Corp. Intercoast Management, 1977, 75 Cal.App. 3d 798, 142 Cal.Rptr. 487 (rape); Duarte v. State, 1979, 88 Cal.App.3d 473, 151 Cal.Rptr. 727 (rape and murder in college dormitory); Kwaitkowski v. Superior Trading Co., 1981, 123 Cal.App.3d 324, 176 Cal.Rptr. 494 (rape, assault and robbery); Johnston v. Harris, 1972, 387 Mich. 569, 198 N.W.2d 409 (assault and robbery); Smith v. General Apartment Co., 1975, 133 Ga.App. 927, 213 S.E.2d 74; Scott v. Watson, 1976, 278 Md. 160, 359 A.2d 548 (murder); Sherman v. Concourse Realty Corp., 1975, 47 A.D.2d 134, 365 N.Y.S.2d 239 (assault and robbery); Skaria v. State, 1981, 110 Misc.2d 711, 442 N.Y.S.2d 838 (rape); Day v. Castilow, La.App.1981, 407 So.2d 510 (assault); Phillips v. Chicago Housing Authority, 1982, 89 Ill.2d 122, 59 Ill.Dec. 281, 431 N.E.2d 1038 (abduction, rape, and murder); Braitman v. Overlook Terrace Corp., 1975, 68 N.J. 368, 346 A.2d 76 (theft from apartment); Prager v. City of New York Housing Authority, 1982, 112 Misc.2d 1034, 447 N.Y.S.2d 1013 (same); Vermes v. American District Telegraph Co., 1977, 312 Minn. 33, 251 N.W.2d 101 (theft from tenant's jewelry store). Contra, King v. Ilikai Properties, Inc., 1981, 2 Hawaii App. 359, 632 P.2d 657.

15. See Samson v. Saginaw Professional Building, Inc., 1975, 393 Mich. 393, 224 N.W.2d 843 (tenant's employee; landlord of commercial office building); Pippin v. Chicago Housing Authority, 1979, 78 Ill.2d 204, 35 Ill.Dec. 530, 399 N.E.2d 596 (tenant's guest); Medina v. 187th Street Apartments, Limited, Fla.App.1981, 405 So.2d 485 (tenants' escort; foreseeability of attack for jury); Haines, supra note 12, at 335 n. 127.

16. There is of course no duty to prevent criminal attacks that are unforeseeable, as where there has been no prior history of such attacks nor other reason to expect them to occur. See, e.g., Taylor v. Hocker, 1981, 101 Ill.App.3d 639, 57 Ill.Dec. 112, 428 N.E.2d 662 (first criminal assault in parking lot); Riley v. Marcus, 1981, 125 Cal.App.3d 103, 177 Cal.Rptr. 827 (no prior rapes in apartment building); 7735 Hollywood Boulevard Venture v. Superior Court, 1981, 116 Cal. App.3d 901, 172 Cal.Rptr. 528 (rape; burglary and rape in same general area within previous 6 months held insufficient).

17. Escobar v. Brent General Hospital, 1981, 106 Mich.App. 828, 308 N.W.2d 691 (no duty to provide continuous security personnel in parking lot, even in high crime area).

18. See Bohlen, Landlord and Tenant, 1922, 35 Harv.L.Rev. 633; Harkrider, Tort Liability of a Landlord, 1928, 26 Mich.L.Rev. 260, 383, 392–400; Eldredge, Landlord's Tort Liability for Disrepair, 1936, 84 U.Pa. L.Rev. 467; Notes, 1950, 48 Mich.L.Rev. 689; 1951, 49 Mich.L.Rev. 1080; 1951, 30 Tex.L.Rev. 131.

19. See, e.g., Tuttle v. George H. Gilbert Manufacturing Co., 1887, 145 Mass. 169, 13 N.E. 465; Caudill v. Gibson Fuel Co., 1946, 185 Va. 233, 38 S.E.2d 465; Berkowitz v. Winston, 1934, 128 Ohio St. 611, 193 N.E. 343.

20. Huey v. Barton, 1950, 328 Mich. 584, 44 N.W.2d 132; Soulia v. Noyes, 1940, 111 Vt. 323, 16 A.2d 173.

21. With the overruling of earlier decisions, in such cases as Reitmeyer v. Sprecher, 1968, 431 Pa. 284, 243 A.2d 395; Rampone v. Wanskuck Buildings, Inc., 1967, 102 R.I. 30, 227 A.2d 586; Putnam v. Stout, 1976, 38 N.Y.2d 607, 381 N.Y.S.2d 848, 345 N.E.2d 319; Mobil Oil Corp. v. Thorn, 1977, 401 Mich. 306, 258 N.W.2d 30; Great Atlantic & Pacific Tea Co. v. Yanofsky, 1980, 380 Mass. 326, 403 N.E.2d 370. See Annot., 1961, 78 A.L.R.2d 1238.

22. Second Restatement of Torts, § 357; Property, § 17.5.

23. Michaels v. Brookchester, Inc., 1958, 26 N.J. 379, 140 A.2d 199; 2310 Madison Avenue, Inc. v. Allied Bedding Manufacturing Co., 1956, 209 Md. 399, 121 A.2d 203; Mobil Oil Co. v. Thorn, 1977, 401 Mich. 306, 258 N.W.2d 30.

24. Faber v. Creswick, 1959, 31 N.J. 234, 156 A.2d 252; Williams v. Davis, 1961, 188 Kan. 385, 362 P.2d 641; Wallace v. Schrier, Fla.App.1958, 107 So.2d 754. See Dunson v. Friedlander Realty, Ala.1979, 369 So.2d 792 (tenant's children; failure to remove lead-based paint).

25. Ferber v. Orange Blossom Center, Inc., Fla. App.1980, 388 So.2d 1074; Nicks v. Joseph, 1981, 82 A.D.2d 768, 440 N.Y.S.2d 218.

26. Flood v. Pabst Brewing Co., 1914, 158 Wis. 626, 149 N.W. 489; Mesher v. Osborne, 1913, 75 Wash. 439, 134 P. 1092. See also Mitchell v. Moore, Ala.1981, 406 So.2d 347

27. Krieger v. Ownership Corp., 3d Cir. 1959, 270 F.2d 265 (New Jersey law); Putnam v. Stout, 1976, 38 N.Y.2d 607, 381 N.Y.S.2d 848, 345 N.E.2d 319.

to others on the land in his right,[28] and even to those outside of it who are endangered.[29]

A variety of ingenious theories have been advanced in support of this liability. An older, popular one is that under the agreement to repair the lessor retains the privilege to enter and supervise the condition of the property, and so is in "control" of it, and therefore subject to the same duties as an occupier.[30] On this basis a few courts have held him liable to persons outside of the premises where he merely reserves the right to enter and repair, without obligating himself to do so;[31] but as to persons on the land most of the courts have refused to go so far.[32] It seems obvious that the lessor's "control," even under a covenant, is a fiction devised to meet the case, since he has no power to exclude any one, or to direct the use of the land, and it is difficult to see how his privilege to enter differs in any significant respect from that of any carpenter hired to do the work.[33]

A second theory is that the landlord by his promise has induced the tenant to forego repairs of his own, and by his misleading undertaking has made himself responsible for the consequences, and that he is distinguished from other contractors by the peculiar probability that the tenant will rely on him.[34] Until quite recently, however, recovery was quite uniformly denied where such a promise was made after the lease and without consideration,[35] in which case it would appear that the tenant is no less misled. It seems clear that it is the contract itself which gives rise to the tort liability, and that it is distinguished from other contracts to enter and repair by reason of the peculiar relation existing between the parties, which gives the lessee a special reason and right to rely upon the promise. This, together with an undeclared policy which places the responsibility for harm caused by disrepair upon the party best able to bear it, and most likely to prevent the injuries, at least where he has expressed willingness to assume responsibility, is perhaps the best explanation for the result.[36]

The jurisdictions which find a tort duty usually construe the lessor's covenant, in the absence of an express provision to the contrary, to mean merely that he must repair only within a reasonable time after he has

---

28. Barron v. Liedloff, 1905, 95 Minn. 474, 104 N.W. 289 (sublessee); Hodges v. Hilton, 1935, 173 Miss. 343, 161 So. 686 (same).

29. Lommori v. Milner Hotels, 1957, 63 N.M. 342, 319 P.2d 949; Marzotto v. Gay Garment Co., 1951, 11 N.J.Super. 368, 78 A.2d 394, affirmed 7 N.J. 116, 80 A.2d 554; Second Restatement of Torts, § 378.

30. See Barron v. Liedloff, 1905, 95 Minn. 474, 104 N.W. 289; Flood v. Pabst Brewing Co., 1914, 158 Wis. 626, 149 N.W. 489. It is of course quite possible for the lessor to reserve and exercise a genuine control over the premises. See Brown v. Cleveland Baseball Co., 1952, 158 Ohio St. 1, 106 N.E.2d 632; Kuhn v. General Parking Corp., 1981, 98 Ill.App.3d 570, 54 Ill.Dec. 191, 424 N.E.2d 941.

31. Appel v. Muller, 1933, 262 N.Y. 278, 186 N.E. 785; City of Dalton v. Anderson, 1945, 72 Ga.App. 109, 33 S.E.2d 115; Fjellman v. Weller, 1942, 213 Minn. 457, 7 N.W.2d 521; Johnson v. Prange-Geussenhainer Co., 1942, 240 Wis. 363, 2 N.W.2d 723; Mitchell v. C & H Transportation Co., 1977, 90 N.M. 471, 565 P.2d 342.

32. People v. Scott 1970, 26 N.Y.2d 286, 309 N.Y.S.2d 919, 258 N.E.2d 206; Mills v. Bonanza International Corp., 160 Ga.App. 104, 1981, 286 S.E.2d 337. But cf. Noble v. Marx, 1948, 298 N.Y. 106, 81 N.E.2d 40; De Clara v. Barber S. S. Lines, 1956, 309 N.Y. 620, 132 N.E.2d 871; Kuhn v. General Parking Corp., 1981, 98 Ill.App.3d 570, 54 Ill.Dec. 191, 424 N.E.2d 941 (reservation plus making repairs).

33. See Cavalier v. Pope, [1906] A.C. 428; Harkrider, Tort Liability of a Landlord, 1928, 26 Mich.L.Rev. 260, 383, 394–398. In Strand Enterprises v. Turner, 1955, 223 Miss. 588, 78 So.2d 769, a landlord entering premises to inspect them was held to have the status of an invitee of the tenant.

34. See Merchants' Cotton Press & Storage Co. v. Miller, 1916, 135 Tenn. 187, 186 S.W. 87; Notes, 1931, 45 Harv.L.Rev. 166; 1935, 83 U.Pa.L.Rev. 1035.

35. Metcalf v. Chiprin, 1963, 217 Cal.App.2d 305, 31 Cal.Rptr. 571; Redden v. James T. McCreery Co., 1941, 123 W.Va. 367, 15 S.E.2d 150; Papallo v. Meriden Savings Bank, 1942, 128 Conn. 563, 24 A.2d 472.

Contra, Conradi v. Helvogt, 1977, 278 Or. 229, 563 P.2d 707; see also Jones v. Chicago Housing Authority, 1978, 59 Ill.App.3d 138, 17 Ill.Dec. 133, 376 N.E.2d 26 (duty to repair arose from course of conduct in gratuitously making repairs in past as needed).

36. See generally Rivera v. Selfon Home Repairs & Improvements Co., 1982, 294 Pa.Super. 41, 439 A.2d 739; Putnam v. Stout, 1976, 38 N.Y.2d 607, 381 N.Y.S.2d 848, 345 N.E.2d 319; Dean v. Hershowitz, 1935, 119 Conn. 398, 177 A. 262.

been notified of the dangerous condition, or has otherwise discovered it.[37]

Negligence in Making Repairs

When the lessor does in fact endeavor to make repairs, whether he is bound by a covenant to do so or not, and fails to exercise reasonable care,[38] there is general agreement that he is liable for resulting injuries to the tenant[39] or to members of his family[40] or others on the premises in his right.[41] It has been said that the lessor's liability does not rest upon his standing in the relation of landlord, but rather on his course of affirmative conduct[42] endangering the plaintiff. The landlord's duty is not necessarily to complete the repairs,[43] but merely to exercise due care for the safety of those on the premises, which may require no more than a warning. In most of the cases, the attempt to repair has either made the situation worse by increasing the danger,[44] or has given the tenant a deceptive assurance of safety;[45] and there are cases which have held that there is no liability when it does neither.[46] There are, however, several decisions which have rejected any such requirement, and have said that the mere failure of the lessor to exercise reasonable care under the circumstances is enough for liability.[47]

When the lessor entrusts the repairs to an independent contractor, the general weight of authority is that his duty of care in making them cannot be delegated, and he will be liable for the contractor's negligence.[48] Nearly all courts are agreed on this where the work is done on the part of the premises over which the lessor has retained control,[49] or where it is pursuant to his contract with the tenant,[50] but there is a division of opinion where no control is retained and the repairs to the leased premises are gratuitous.[51] Even here, the growing view seems to be that the tenant's right to rely on the land-

---

37. Cooper v. Roose, 1949, 151 Ohio St. 316, 85 N.E.2d 545; Second Restatement of Torts, § 357, Comment d.

The obligation is one of reasonable care only. Asheim v. Fahey, 1943, 170 Or. 330, 133 P.2d 246.

38. Second Restatement of Torts, § 362; Property, § 17.7.

39. See Barham v. Baca, 1969, 80 N.M. 502, 458 P.2d 228; Mahan-Jellico Coal Co. v. Dulling, 1940, 282 Ky. 698, 139 S.W.2d 749. Cf. Strayer v. Lindeman, 1981, 68 Ohio St.2d 32, 427 N.E.2d 781 (tenant's personal property).

40. Gill v. Middleton, 1870, 105 Mass. 477; Shaw v. Butterworth, 1931, 327 Mo. 622, 38 S.W.2d 57; Good v. Von Hemert, 1911, 114 Minn. 393, 131 N.W. 466.

41. Ginsberg v. Wineman, 1946, 314 Mich. 1, 22 N.W.2d 49 (employee); Olsen v. Mading, 1935, 45 Ariz. 423, 45 P.2d 23 (invitee); Brewer v. Bankord, 1979, 69 Ill.App.3d 196, 25 Ill.Dec. 688, 387 N.E.2d 344 (guest).

42. Holmes, J., in Riley v. Lissner, 1894, 160 Mass. 330, 35 N.E. 1130; see supra, § 56.

43. Marshall v. Mastadon, Inc., 1976, 51 A.D.2d 21, 379 N.Y.S.2d 177 (roller-skating arena); Bauer v. 141–149 Cedar Lane Holding Co., 1957, 24 N.J. 139, 130 A.2d 833.

44. See for example Buck v. Miller, 1947, 198 Okl. 617, 181 P.2d 264.

45. See Smith v. Kravitz, 1953, 173 Pa.Super. 11, 93 A.2d 889; Dunnigan v. Kirkorian, 1942, 67 R.I. 172, 25 A.2d 221.

46. E.g., Kuchynski v. Ukryn, 1938, 89 N.H. 400, 200 A. 416; Kirshenbaum v. General Outdoor Advertising Co., 1932, 258 N.Y. 489, 180 N.E. 245, motion denied, 1932, 259 N.Y. 525, 182 N.E. 165; Kearns v. Smith, 1943, 55 Cal.App.2d 532, 131 P.2d 36.

47. E.g., Bauer v. 141–149 Cedar Lane Holding Co., 1957, 24 N.J. 139, 130 A.2d 833; Conner v. Farmers & Merchants Bank, 1963, 243 S.C. 132, 132 S.E.2d 385.

48. See Second Restatement of Property, § 19.1; infra, § 71.

49. Brown v. George Pepperdine Foundation, 1943, 23 Cal.2d 256, 143 P.2d 929; Hussey v. Long Dock Railroad Co., 1924, 100 N.J.L. 380, 126 A. 314; Lebright v. Gentzlinger, 1931, 232 App.Div. 274, 249 N.Y.S. 501; Hill v. McDonald, D.C.App.1982, 442 A.2d 133 (architect; inadequate protective railing on stairs); Second Restatement of Property, § 19.2.

50. Peerless Manufacturing Co. v. Bagley, 1901, 126 Mich. 225, 85 N.W. 568; Vitale v. Duerbeck, 1933, 332 Mo. 1184, 62 S.W.2d 559. Or pursuant to a statutory requirement to keep the premises in good condition. Strayer v. Lindeman, 1981, 68 Ohio St.2d 32, 427 N.E.2d 781.

51. *Liability:* Ryce v. Whitley, 1901, 115 Iowa 784, 87 N.W. 694; Bancroft v. Godwin, 1905, 41 Wash. 253, 83 P. 189; O'Rourke v. Feist, 1899, 42 App.Div. 136, 59 N.Y.S. 157; Dalkowitz Brothers v. Schreiner, Tex.Civ. App. 1908, 110 S.W. 564.

No liability: Jefferson v. Jameson & Morse Co., 1896, 165 Ill. 138, 46 N.E. 272, Dains v. Dank, 1917, 199 Ala. 250, 74 So. 341; Eblin v. Miller's Executors, 1880, 78 Ky. 371; Schatzky v. Harber, Sup.Ct.1917, 164 N.Y.S. 610.

lord is such that the responsibility cannot be shifted.[52]

Adoption of General Negligence Principles

Discontent with the appearance of unfairness in the landlord's general immunity from tort liability, and with the artificiality and increasing complexity of the various exceptions to this seemingly archaic rule of nonliability, the New Hampshire Supreme Court in Sargent v. Ross [53] turned the rule on its head in 1973 [54] and imposed on the lessor a general tort duty of reasonable care.[55] The holding has been followed by several courts,[56] and rejected by a couple of others,[57] and it is still too early to know how broadly this restructuring of landlord tort law may extend.

 WESTLAW REFERENCES

Concealed Dangerous Conditions Known to Lessor

landlord* lessor* /s liabl! /p dangerous /s condition* /s hidden conceal** nondisclos!

landlord* lessor* /s liabl! /s defective /s condition* premises

233k164(6)

233k167(2)

Conditions Dangerous to Those Outside of the Premises

topic(233) /p dangerous /p condition* /p stairway stairwell steps

topic(233) /p dangerous /p condition* /p yard lawn sidewalk*

synopsis,digest(landlord* lessor* /p dangerous /p condition* /p yard lawn sidewalk*)

Premises Leased for Admission of the Public

public /4 admission /p landlord* lessor* /p liabl!

Common Areas Retained Under Landlord's Control

landlord* lessor* /s liabl! /p common /s area*

Lessor's Agreement to Repair

lessor* landlord /s duty agreement /s repair & topic(negligence torts)

synopsis,digest(lessor* landlord /s duty agreement /s repair /s negligen** tort)

Negligence in Making Repairs

digest(lessor* landlord /s negligen! /s repair!)

digest(lessor* landlord /s fail! /10 repair!)

233k172(3)

Adoption of General Negligence Principles

landlord* /s immun! /s tort

§ 64. Vendor and Vendee

The vendor of real property who parts with title, possession and control of it ceases to be either an owner or an occupier.[1] Ordinarily, therefore, he is permitted to step out of the picture and shift all responsibility for

---

52. E.g., Bailey v. Zlotnick, 1945, 80 App.D.C. 117, 149 F.2d 505; Rubin v. Girard Trust Co., 1944, 154 Pa. Super. 257, 35 A.2d 601; Livingston v. Essex Investment Co., 1941, 219 N.C. 416, 14 S.E.2d 489; Second Restatement of Torts, § 420; Property, § 19.3.

53. 1973, 113 N.H. 388, 308 A.2d 528 (Kenison, C.J.). See Love, Landlord's Liability for Defective Premises: Caveat Lessee, Negligence, or Strict Liability?, 1975 Wis.L.Rev. 19, 114 (thorough analysis; offering thesis that "other jurisdictions should follow New Hampshire's lead"); Notes, 1974, 59 Corn.L.Rev. 1161; 1974 Duke L.J. 185; 23 Emory L.J. 1051; 2 Ford.Urb. L.J. 647; 35 Ohio St.L.J. 212; 8 Suff.U.L.Rev. 1305; 5 Tex.Tech.L.Rev. 887; 43 U.Cin.L.Rev. 218; 1974 Wash. U.L.Q. 510; 1975, 9 Urb.L.Ann. 259; Annot., 1975, 64 A.L.R.3d 348.

54. There had been earlier rumblings. See Wilcox v. Hines, 1898, 100 Tenn. 538, 46 S.W. 297; Clarke v. O'Connor, D.C. Cir. 1970, 435 F.2d 104; Presson v. Mountain States Properties, Inc., App.1972, 18 Ariz. 176, 501 P.2d 17.

55. "Henceforth, landlords as other persons must exercise reasonable care not to subject others to an unreasonable risk of harm. A landlord must act as a reasonable person under all of the circumstances including the likelihood of injury to others, the probable seriousness of such injuries, and the burden of reducing or avoiding the risk. We think this basic principle of responsibility for landlords as for others 'best expresses the principles of justice and reasonableness upon which our law of torts is founded.'" 308 A.2d at 534.

56. Young v. Garwacki, 1980, 380 Mass. 162, 402 N.E.2d 1045; Mansur v. Eubanks, Fla.1981, 401 So.2d 1328; Pagelsdorf v. Safeco Insurance Co. of America, 1979, 91 Wis.2d 734, 284 N.W.2d 55; see Brennan v. Cockrell Investments, Inc., 1973, 35 Cal.App.3d 796, 111 Cal.Rptr. 122; Corrigan v. Janney, 1981, ___ Mont. ___, 626 P.2d 838; cf. Old Town Development Co. v. Langford, 1976, ___ Ind.App. ___, 349 N.E.2d 744, set aside after settlement, 1977, 267 Ind. 176, 369 N.E.2d 404; Hall v. Warren, Utah 1981, 632 P.2d 848.

57. See Dapkunas v. Cagle, 1976, 42 Ill.App.3d 644, 1 Ill.Dec. 387, 356 N.E.2d 575 (2–1); Francis v. Pic, N.D.1975, 226 N.W.2d 654.

§ 64

1. See generally Annot., 1973, 48 A.L.R.3d 1027; 1982, 18 A.L.R.4th 1168 (property damage).

the condition of the land to the purchaser. As to sales of land, the ancient doctrine of *caveat emptor* has lingered on to a very large extent;[2] and it is only in recent years that the implied warranties which have grown up around the sale of chattels[3] have begun to be paralleled as to land. This was perhaps for the reason that great importance is attached to the deed of conveyance, which is taken to represent the full agreement of the parties, and to exclude all other terms;[4] the lack of any standard marketable quality, or even standard use, of land;[5] and the fact that the vendee normally inspects the property before purchase, and so is assumed to have accepted it as it is.[6] Thus, in the absence of express agreement[7] or misrepresentation,[8] the purchaser is expected to make his own examination and draw his own conclusions as to the condition of the land; and the vendor is, in general, not liable for any harm resulting to him or others from any defects existing at the time of transfer.[9]

Over the years, however, an increased regard for human safety and a sadly needed improvement in bargaining ethics led to the development of two exceptions to this once universal rule, one for the benefit of persons on the land and one for persons outside.[10] The first, which finds support in the cases of lessors,[11] is that the vendor is under a duty to disclose to the vendee any hidden defects[12] which he knows or should know[13] may present an unreasonable risk of harm to persons on the premises, and which he may anticipate that the vendee will not discover.[14] If he fails to give such warnings, he becomes liable for any resulting harm to the vendee, members of his family, or others upon the land in the right of the vendee.[15]

---

2. "The common-law rule of *caveat emptor* is applied strictly to a purchaser of real property." Sosebee v. Hiott, 1981, 157 Ga.App. 768, 278 S.E.2d 700, 702; Higgenbottom v. Noreen, 9th Cir. 1978, 586 F.2d 719.

3. See infra, § 95. The classic case holding that there are no implied warranties on the sale of land is Hart v. Windsor, 1843, 12 M. & W. 68, 152 Eng.Rep. 1114.

4. See Graham v. United States, N.D.Tex.1977, 441 F.Supp. 741, 744.

5. Dunham, Vendor's Obligation as to Fitness of Land for a Particular Purpose, 1953, 37 Minn.L.Rev. 110.

6. Cf. Lake v. United States, N.D.Ill.1981, 522 F.Supp. 166.

7. As, for example, the vendor's promise to make repairs after the transfer. Martin v. United States, 9th Cir. 1981, 649 F.2d 701.

8. See Johnson v. Healy, 1978, 176 Conn. 97, 405 A.2d 54 (builder-vendor of house liable for innocent misrepresentation); infra, ch. 18.

9. Sosebee v. Hiott, 1981, 157 Ga.App. 768, 278 S.E.2d 700; Lake v. United States, N.D.Ill.1981, 522 F.Supp. 166; O'Connor v. Altus, 1973, 123 N.J.Super. 379, 303 A.2d 329, affirmed 1975, 67 N.J. 106, 335 A.2d 545, 549 (dictum); Combow v. Kansas City Ground Investment Co., 1949, 358 Mo. 934, 218 S.W.2d 539; Ramsey v. Mading, 1950, 36 Wn.2d 303, 217 P.2d 1041; Merrick v. Murphy, Sup.Ct.1975, 83 Misc.2d 39, 371 N.Y.S.2d 97 (dictum); Carlson v. Hampl, 1969, 284 Minn. 85, 169 N.W.2d 56; cf. Great Atlantic & Pacific Tea Co. v. Wilson, 1980, ___ Ind.App. ___, 408 N.E.2d 144 (former tenant not liable to prospective purchaser); Beall v. Lo-Vaca Gathering Co., Tex.Civ.App.1975, 532 S.W.2d 362, refused n.r.e. (former lessee not liable); Brock v. Rogers & Babler, Inc., Alaska 1975, 536 P.2d 778 (same). See generally Second Restatement of Torts, § 352.

Nor will he be liable, a fortiori, when dangerous conditions do not arise until after the transfer of title and possession. Neuhaus v. Daniels, Tex.Civ.App.1968, 430 S.W.2d 906; Second Restatement of Torts, § 351 (persons on the land); § 372 (off the land).

10. See Notes, 1965, 53 Cal.L.Rev. 1062; 1966, 51 Corn.L.Q. 389.

11. See supra, § 63.

12. Hence, no liability for obvious or known defects. See Carlson v. Hampl, 1969, 284 Minn. 85, 169 N.W.2d 56 (absence of handrail by steps); see also Lake v. United States, N.D.Ill.1981, 522 F.Supp. 166 (vendee had probably discovered hazardous condition).

And any duty that he may have had as owner to *cure* even an obvious hazard may carry over after the transfer as well. See Smith v. Monmaney, 1969, 127 Vt. 585, 255 A.2d 674 (former landlord, who had promised to buy pipe to make railing for icy steps, liable for fall 2 days after transfer).

13. Cf. Graham v. United States, N.D.Tex.1977, 441 F.Supp. 741 (seller, HUD, not liable since no reason to know ventilation pipe clogged by bird nest); Johnson v. Healy, 1978, 176 Conn. 97, 405 A.2d 54 (vendor had no notice of subsurface defects on house lot).

14. See generally Second Restatement of Torts, § 353.

15. See ABC Builders, Inc. v. Phillips, Wyo.1981, 632 P.2d 925 (builder-vendor liable in negligence to sub-vendee for locating house in path of landslide); Village Development Co. v. Filice, 1974, 90 Nev. 305, 526 P.2d 83 (vendor of lot in flood plain of stream); Wilson v.

The recognition of this duty of disclosure is about as far as most courts have gone in holding vendors liable in negligence to persons on the land.[16] However, there have been important developments along the lines of strict liability, both in warranty and tort,[17] which to a large extent are superseding the ground of negligence, and which remain to be considered below.[18]

The other exception to the general rule of nonliability of the vendor is found in a number of cases where the land, when it is transferred, is in such condition that it involves an unreasonable risk of harm to those outside of the premises. In many of the cases, this has amounted to either a public or a private nuisance, but this is clearly not essential. In such a case the vendor remains subject, at least for a reasonable time, to any liability he would have incurred if he had remained in possession for injuries to persons or property outside of the land, caused by such a condition.[19] The reason sometimes given is the obviously fictitious one that by selling the land in such condition he has "authorized the continuance of the nuisance." A more reasonable explanation would appear to be that the vendor's responsibility to those outside of his land is regarded as of such social importance that he is not permitted in every situation to shift it automatically upon the sale.[20] Although there was traditional support for limiting such liability to structures and other artificial conditions on the land,[21] especially if created by the vendor himself, the very sparse authority in recent years has rejected this limitation.[22]

As to both of these exceptions under which the vendor is held liable for injuries occurring after possession is transferred, it seems obvious that there must be some time limit upon the duration of the potential liability. A corporation, still in existence, can scarcely be required to pay for damages which occur a century after the grant. The

---

Thermal Energy, Inc., 1978, 21 Wn.App. 153, 583 P.2d 679; State v. Hughes, 1975, 14 Wn.App. 186, 540 P.2d 439 (attractive nuisance); cf. Farragher v. City of New York, 1966, 26 A.D.2d 494, 275 N.Y.S.2d 542, affirmed 1968, 21 N.Y.2d 756, 288 N.Y.S.2d 232, 235 N.E.2d 218; Gasteiger v. Gillenwater, 1966, 57 Tenn.App. 206, 417 S.W.2d 568; Shane v. Hoffmann, 1974, 227 Pa.Super. 176, 324 A.2d 532 (sewer periodically backed up inundating basement with human excrement); Holmes v. Worthey, 1981, 159 Ga.App. 262, 282 S.E.2d 919 affirmed 1982, 249 Ga. 104, 287 S.E.2d 9 (defectively constructed house; economic loss); Brown v. Fowler, S.D. 1979, 279 N.W.2d 907 (negligence action allowed against builder-vendor of house by subsequent purchasers for settling of basement).

16. There are, however, certain other scattered stirrings in this direction. See, e.g., Merrick v. Murphy, Sup.Ct.1975, 83 Misc.2d 39, 371 N.Y.S.2d 97 (negligence liability for *creation* of defect, analogizing to manufacture of chattel); Rogers v. Scyphers, 1968, 251 S.C. 128, 161 S.E.2d 81 (same; builder-vendor of new home liable for injuries from negligent construction); Kristek v. Catron, 1982, 7 Kan.App.2d 495, 644 P.2d 480 (home builder liable to subpurchaser in negligence for cost of repairing leaky roof).

17. See, e.g., Lantis v. Astec Industries, Inc., 7th Cir. 1981, 648 F.2d 1118 (builder-vendor of asphalt plant strictly liable in tort for death of employee who fell through hole in service platform); Kaneko v. Hilo Coast Processing Corp., Hawaii 1982, 654 P.2d 343 (prefabricated building is "product," subjecting manufacturer to strict liability); Blagg v. Fred Hunt Co., Inc., 1981, 272 Ark. 185, 612 S.W.2d 321 (subsequent purchasers of house; implied warranty and statutory strict liability for economic loss); McDonald v. Mianecki, 1979, 79 N.J. 275, 398 A.2d 1283 (implied warranty of habitability in sale of new home by builder-vendor). See generally Annot., 1969, 25 A.L.R.3d 383.

18. See infra, chapters 16 & 17.

19. Cogliati v. Ecco High Frequency Corp., App. Div.1981, 181 N.J.Super. 579, 439 A.2d 91 (fall on defective sidewalk); Narsh v. Zirbser Brothers, Inc., App. Div.1970, 111 N.J.Super. 203, 268 A.2d 46 (tree fell on car in highway); Keeley v. Manor Park Apartments, Del.Ch.1953, 99 A.2d 248; Wilks v. New York Telephone Co., 1926, 243 N.Y. 351, 153 N.E. 444; Derby v. Public Service Co., 1955, 100 N.H. 53, 119 A.2d 335; Second Restatement of Torts, § 373.

20. "The fact that the vendor may have lost the right to go on the property and make repairs is beside the point—the rule is aimed at inducing him to make inspections and guard against dangers *before* conveyance." Narsh v. Zirbser Brothers, Inc., 1970, 111 N.J. Super. 203, 268 A.2d 46, 53.

21. See Palmore v. Morris, Tasker & Co., 1897, 182 Pa. 82, 37 A. 995; Second Restatement of Torts, § 373.

22. "We find no support in reason and logic for any distinction between the liability of a vendor of land in an urban area who erects a tower on his land which later falls into the highway and injures a pedestrian, and one who maintains a rotten tree on the land which later falls with the same result." Narsh v. Zirbser Brothers, Inc., 1970, 111 N.J.Super. 203, 268 A.2d 46, 53.

emerging view is that the vendor is no longer liable once the vendee has had a reasonable time to discover and remedy the condition,[23] unless the vendor has actively concealed it,[24] in which case his liability will continue until actual discovery, and a reasonable time thereafter to take action.[25]

Vendees

The vendee to whom possession is transferred becomes himself an occupier, and subject to all of the obligations of a possessor. The most important problem which has arisen in connection with such vendees is that of liability for injuries, usually to persons outside [26] of the premises, resulting from conditions of which the vendee has no knowledge, or which he has not yet had an opportunity to remedy after entering into possession. Most of the cases have involved a private nuisance or danger existing on the land at the time of transfer.[27] The First Restatement of Torts,[28] supported by almost nothing in the way of authority,[29] took the position that the vendee is required at his peril to make full inspection before he buys, and that as to all artificial conditions which are not latent he assumes responsibility from the moment he takes possession, regardless of knowledge of the danger or of any opportunity whatever to guard against it.

The weight of authority has now developed heavily against this proposition. A long line of cases have held that the vendee becomes liable only after he acquires notice of the condition and fails within a reasonable time [30] thereafter to act reasonably to rectify it.[31]

In the private nuisance context, the rationale for giving the new vendee a reasonable time to act is that he should be permitted to assume, when he takes possession, that any existing private nuisance has the consent of the adjoining landowners, and that if compensation for it is required, it has been paid.

Where, on the other hand, the condition of the premises creates a public nuisance, it is generally agreed that there is liability as soon as the vendee knows of the condition and fails to remedy it, without any notice or

---

23. O'Connor v. Altus, 1975, 67 N.J. 106, 335 A.2d 545, 549 (9 years "much more than a reasonable time," although design defect was latent and subtle); Narsh v. Zirbser Brothers, Inc., 1970, 111 N.J.Super. 203, 268 A.2d 46 (11 months enough); Century Display Manufacturing Corp. v. D. R. Wager Construction Co., Ill. 1978, 71 Ill.2d 428, 17 Ill.Dec. 664, 376 N.E.2d 993 (3 months enough for sophisticated buyer who inspected several times); Anderson v. Cosmopolitan National Bank of Chicago, 1973, 54 Ill.2d 504, 301 N.E.2d 296 (6 days enough time for simple repairs of obvious hazard); Cogliati v. Ecco High Frequency Corp., 1981, 181 N.J.Super. 579, 439 A.2d 91.

Compare Cavanaugh v. Pappas, 1966, 91 N.J.Super. 597, 222 A.2d 34 (vendor could still be liable: 5 days after transfer); Sparling v. Peabody Coal Co., 1974, 59 Ill.2d 491, 322 N.E.2d 5 (same: 6 years; 22½ acre tract); Louisville & Jefferson Co. Metropolitan Sewer District v. City of Louisville, Ky.1970, 451 S.W.2d 172 (same: 19 years; pipe laid mostly underground).

24. And, perhaps in the case of a person off the land, if the dangerous condition was created by the vendor. Second Restatement of Torts, § 373(2). Contra, Cogliati v. Ecco High Frequency Corp., App.Div. 1981, 181 N.J.Super. 579, 439 A.2d 91 (reasonable time after sale).

25. Pavelchak v. Finn, Sup.Ct.1956, 153 N.Y.S.2d 795, affirmed 1958, 6 A.D.2d 841, 176 N.Y.S.2d 933; Narsh v. Zirbser Brothers, Inc., 1970, 111 N.J.Super. 203, 268 A.2d 46.

26. E.g., Narsh v. Zirbser Brothers, Inc., 1970, 111 N.J.Super. 203, 268 A.2d 46 (rotten tree from defendant's new lot fell on plaintiff's car in driveway). But see Farragher v. City of New York, 1966, 26 A.D.2d 494, 275 N.Y.S.2d 542, affirmed 21 N.Y.2d 756, 288 N.Y.S.2d 232, 235 N.E.2d 218.

27. On the law of nuisance, see infra, ch. 15.

28. § 366.

29. The only support found is some very dubious dictum in Harvey v. Machtig, 1925, 73 Cal.App. 667, 239 P. 78, and Palmore v. Morris, Tasker & Co., 1897, 182 Pa. 82, 37 A. 995.

30. See Narsh v. Zirbser Brothers, Inc., 1970, 111 N.J.Super. 203, 268 A.2d 46 (jury could find 8 days insufficient); Smith v. Monmaney, 1969, 127 Vt. 585, 255 A.2d 674 (same: 2 days). Compare Farragher v. City of New York, 1966, 26 A.D.2d 494, 275 N.Y.S.2d 542, affirmed 21 N.Y.2d 756, 288 N.Y.S.2d 232, 235 N.E.2d 218 (90 days insufficient time to expect vendee to install sprinkler system, and hence not liable for death of fireman), with Anderson v. Cosmopolitan National Bank of Chicago, 1973, 54 Ill.2d 504, 301 N.E.2d 296 (rejecting Farragher, and holding 6 days enough time for simple repairs).

31. Second Restatement of Torts, § 366.

request.³² This is because a public nuisance, being criminal in character and an invasion of the rights of the public, cannot reasonably be assumed by anyone to exist with public consent. The possessor is therefore required to know the condition of his land, and to take all reasonable steps to insure that it does not interfere with the public right.

32. Leahan v. Cochran, 1901, 178 Mass. 566, 60 N.E. 382; Turner v. Ridley, Mun.App.D.C.1958, 144 A.2d 269; Corby v. Ramsdell, 2d Cir. 1931, 48 F.2d 701; Bixby v. Thurber, 1922, 80 N.H. 411, 118 A. 99; Matthews v. Missouri Pacific Railway Co., 1887, 26 Mo. App. 75.

WESTLAW REFERENCES

vendor* /s liabl! /s negligen! & topic(negligence tort*)

vendor* /p liabl! /p trespass! licensee* invitee*

Vendees

vendee* /p liabl! /p trespass! licensee* invitee*

Chapter 11

NEGLIGENCE: DEFENSES

Table of Sections

Sec.
65. Contributory Negligence.
66. Last Clear Chance.
67. Comparative Negligence.
68. Assumption of Risk.

§ 65. Contributory Negligence

The two most common defenses in a negligence action are contributory negligence and assumption of risk. Since both developed at a comparatively late date in the development of the common law,[1] and since both clearly operate to the advantage of the defendant, they are commonly regarded as defenses to a tort which would otherwise be established. All courts now hold that the burden of pleading and proof of the contributory negligence of the plaintiff is on the defendant.[2]

Contributory negligence is conduct on the part of the plaintiff, contributing as a legal cause to the harm he has suffered, which falls below the standard to which he is required to conform for his own protection.[3] Unlike assumption of risk, the defense does not rest upon the idea that the defendant is relieved of any duty toward the plaintiff. Rather, although the defendant has violated his duty, has been negligent, and would oth-

---

§ 65

1. The earliest contributory negligence case is Butterfield v. Forrester, 1809, 11 East 60, 103 Eng.Rep. 926. The first American case appears to have been Smith v. Smith, 1824, 19 Mass. (2 Pick.) 621. Assumption of risk first appears in a negligence case in 1799. See infra, § 68 n. 1.

2. E.g., Wilkinson v. Hartford Accident & Indemnity Co., La.1982, 411 So.2d 22; Moodie v. Santoni, 1982, 292 Md. 582, 441 A.2d 323; Addair v. Bryant, 1981, ___ W.Va. ___, 284 S.E.2d 374; Pickett v. Parks, 1981, 208 Neb. 310, 303 N.W.2d 296; Hatton v. Chem-Haulers, Inc., Ala.1980, 393 So.2d 950; Sampson v. W. F. Enterprises, Inc., Mo.App.1980, 611 S.W.2d 333; Howard v. Howard, Ky.App.1980, 607 S.W.2d 119; cf. Reuter v. United States, W.D.Pa.1982, 534 F.Supp. 731 (presumption that person killed or suffering loss of memory was acting with due care).

Illinois and certain other jurisdictions held to the contrary for some time. See West Chicago Street Railroad Co. v. Liderman, 1900, 187 Ill. 463, 58 N.E. 367; Kotler v. Lalley, 1930, 112 Conn. 86, 151 A. 433; Dreier v. McDermott, 1913, 157 Iowa 726, 141 N.W. 315. See Green, Illinois Negligence Law II, 1944, 39 Ill.L.Rev. 116, 125–130.

3. Second Restatement of Torts, § 463. See generally, Malone, The Formative Era of Contributory Negligence, 1946, 41 Ill.L.Rev. 151; James, Contributory Negligence, 1953, 62 Yale L.J. 691; Bohlen, Contributory Negligence, 1908, 21 Harv.L.Rev. 233; Lowndes, Contributory Negligence, 1934, 22 Geo.L.J. 674; Malone, Some Ruminations on Contributory Negligence, 1981, 65 Utah L.Rev. 91; Schwartz, Contributory and Comparative Negligence: A Reappraisal, 1978, 87 Yale L.J. 697; Note, 1979, 39 La.L.Rev. 637.

erwise be liable, the plaintiff is denied recovery because his own conduct disentitles him to maintain the action. In the eyes of the law both parties are at fault; and the defense is one of the plaintiff's disability, rather than the defendant's innocence.

Many theories have been advanced to explain the defense of contributory negligence. It has been said that it has a penal basis, and that the plaintiff is denied recovery to punish him for his own misconduct.[4] Another theory, sometimes advanced,[5] has been that the plaintiff is required to come into court with "clean hands." The defense has been said to rest upon voluntary assumption of risk; but this is clearly error, since it may exist in the absence of knowledge of the risk, or any consent, other than an obviously fictitious one, to encounter it.[6]

The greater number of courts have explained it in terms of "proximate cause," saying that the plaintiff's negligence is an intervening, or insulating, cause between the defendant's negligence and the result.[7] But this cannot be supported unless a meaning is assigned to "proximate cause" which goes beyond anything applied elsewhere.[8] If two automobiles collide and injure a bystander, the negligence of one driver is not held to be an "insulating cause" which relieves the other of liability. So far as causation is concerned, it can hardly have any different effect when the action is by one driver against the other.[9] It has been said also that the rule is intended to discourage accidents, by denying recovery to those who fail to use proper care for their own safety.[10] But the assumption that the speeding motorist is, or should be, meditating on the possible failure of a lawsuit for his possible injuries appears contrary to human experience; and it might be as reasonable to say that the rule promotes accidents by encouraging the negligent defendant to hope that the person he injures will be negligent too.[11]

Probably no one theory can adequately explain the doctrine of contributory negligence. In its essence, it is an expression of the highly individualistic attitude of the common law, and its policy of making the personal interests of each party depend upon his own care and prudence.[12] Its development was at least encouraged, if not entirely explained, by three factors.[13] Chief among these was the uneasy distrust of the plaintiff-minded jury which grew upon the courts in the earlier part of the nineteenth century, and a desire to keep the liabilities of growing industry within some bounds. Another was the tendency of the courts of the day to look for some single, principal, dominant, "proximate" cause of every injury.[14] The third was the inability of the courts, apart from admiralty cases where there was no ju-

4. See Lord Halsbury, L. C., in Wakelin v. London & S. W. R. Co., 1886, 12 A.C. 41, 45.

5. Owen, C.J., in Davis v. Guarnieri, 1887, 45 Ohio St. 470, 15 N.E. 350.

6. See Bohlen, Contributory Negligence, 1908, 21 Harv.L.Rev. 233; Lowndes, Contributory Negligence, 1934, 22 Geo.L.J. 674, 679–681; Warren, Volenti Non Fit Injuria in Actions of Negligence, 1895, 8 Harv.L.Rev. 457, 458–461; James, Assumption of Risk, 1952, 61 Yale L.J. 141.

7. Bowen, L.J., in Thomas v. Quartermaine, 1897, 18 Q.B.D. 685, 697; Gilman v. Central Vermont Railway Co., 1919, 93 Vt. 340, 107 A. 122; Ware v. Saufley, 1922, 194 Ky. 53, 237 S.W. 1060; Exum v. Atlantic Coast Line Railroad Co., 1911, 154 N.C. 408, 70 S.E. 845; Chesapeake & Ohio Railroad Co. v. Wills, 1910, 111 Va. 32, 68 S.E. 395.

8. Green, Contributory Negligence and Proximate Cause, 1927, 6 North Car.L.Rev. 3; Lowndes, Contributory Negligence, 1934, 22 Georgetown L.J. 674; Bohlen, Contributory Negligence, 1908, 21 Harv.L.Rev. 233.

9. Albritton v. Hill, 1925, 190 N.C. 429, 130 S.E. 5; Etheridge v. Norfolk Southern Railway Co., 1925, 143 Va. 789, 129 S.E. 680; McDonald v. Robinson, 1929, 207 Iowa 1293, 224 N.W. 820; Fraser v. Flanders, 1924, 248 Mass. 62, 142 N.E. 836.

10. Schofield, Davies v. Mann: Theory of Contributory Negligence, 1890, 3 Harv.L.Rev. 263, 270.

11. See infra, § 67, notes 2 & 3.

12. Schofield, Davies v. Mann: Theory of Contributory Negligence, 1890, 3 Harv.L.Rev. 263, 270; Owen, C. J., in Davis v. Guarnieri, 1887, 45 Ohio St. 470, 15 N.E. 350.

13. Malone, The Formative Era of Contributory Negligence, 1947, 41 Ill.L.Rev. 151.

14. Wright, Contributory Negligence, 1950, 13 Mod. L.Rev. 2, 5.

ry, to conceive of a satisfactory method by which the damages for a single, indivisible injury could be apportioned between the parties, so that, although both were at fault, the loss simply had to fall entirely upon the negligent plaintiff or upon the negligent defendant.[15]

All this, however, is the antique heritage of an older day. Criticism of the denial of all recovery was not slow in coming, and it has been with us now for more than a century.[16] The history of the doctrine has been that of a chronic invalid who will not die. With the gradual change in social viewpoint, such that the compensation of injured persons appears to have become the dominant goal of accident law, the defense of contributory negligence has come to be looked upon with increasing disfavor by the courts,[17] and its rigors have been quite extensively modified, as will be seen below.

Compared with Negligence

It is perhaps unfortunate that contributory negligence is called negligence at all. "Contributory fault" would be a more descriptive term. Negligence as it is commonly understood is conduct which creates an undue risk of harm to others. Contributory negligence is conduct which involves an undue risk of harm to the actor himself.[18] Negligence requires a duty, an obligation of conduct to another person. Contributory negligence involves no duty,[19] unless we are to be so ingenious as to say that the plaintiff is under an obligation to protect the defendant against liability for the consequences of the plaintiff's own negligence.[20]

Nevertheless, and largely because of the long-continued process of setting one over against the other, contributory negligence, in general, is determined and governed by the same tests and rules as the negligence of the defendant. The plaintiff is required to conform to the same objective[21] standard of conduct, that of the reasonable person of ordinary prudence under like circumstances.[22] The unreasonableness of the risks which he incurs is judged by the same process of weighing the importance of the interest he is seeking to advance, and the burden of taking precautions,[23] against the

---

15. See Lowndes, Contributory Negligence, 1934, 22 Geo.L.J. 674, 683–685; Beach, Contributory Negligence, 3d ed. 1899, § 12.

16. One of the best statements of the attack on contributory negligence is found in Green, Illinois Negligence Law, 1944, 39 Ill.L.Rev. 36, 116, 197. See also Lowndes, Contributory Negligence, 1934, 22 Geo.L.J. 674; James, Last Clear Chance: A Transitional Doctrine, 1938, 47 Yale L.J. 704. A good recent analysis, also critical, is Malone, Some Ruminations on Contributory Negligence, 1981, 65 Utah L.Rev. 91, 108, opining: "It is not at all unlikely that we have a dying horse on our hands."

17. See Leflar, The Declining Defense of Contributory Negligence, 1946, 1 Ark.L.Rev. 1; James, Contributory Negligence, 1953, 62 Yale L.J. 691.

18. Second Restatement of Torts, § 463, Comment b; Pappas v. Evans, 1951, 242 Iowa 804, 48 N.W.2d 298.

19. But see, e.g., Stephen v. City of Lincoln, 1981, 209 Neb. 792, 311 N.W.2d 889 (breach of duty to protect oneself from injury); Bartlett v. MacRae, 1981, 54 Or.App. 516, 635 P.2d 666 (obligation to use ordinary care for own protection); Glenn v. Brown, 1980, 28 Wn. App. 86, 622 P.2d 1279 (duty to exercise reasonable care to avoid injury to himself).

20. See Atkin, L.J., in Ellerman Lines v. Grayson, [1919] 2 K.B. 535; Lord Parmoor, in Grayson v. Ellerman Lines, [1920] A.C. 477. See also Dean Green's attempt to deal with contributory negligence in terms of "duty," in Green, Mahoney v. Beatman: A Study in Proximate Cause, 1930, 39 Yale L.J. 532, reprinted in Green, Judge and Jury, 1930, ch. 7, and the criticism of Bohlen in his Review, 1932, 80 U.Pa.L.Rev. 781, 784.

21. Antcliff v. Datzman, 1982, ___ Ind.App. ___, 436 N.E.2d 114 (dictum).

22. Second Restatement of Torts, § 464. See, e.g., Moodie v. Santoni, 1982, 292 Md. 582, 441 A.2d 323; Wright v. O'Neal, La.App.1982, 414 So.2d 880; Martin v. Hertz Corp., 1982, 104 Ill.App.3d 592, 60 Ill.Dec. 363, 432 N.E.2d 1262; Green v. Wellons, Inc., 1981, 52 N.C. App. 529, 279 S.E.2d 37.

Custom in the plaintiff's trade is therefore evidence of due care. Fahringer v. Rinehimer, 1980, 283 Pa. Super. 93, 423 A.2d 731. See Lytell v. Hushfield, La. 1982, 408 So.2d 1344, 1349 (common practice to load forklift higher than boom).

23. Starr v. Philadelphia Transportation Co., 1960, 191 Pa.Super. 559, 159 A.2d 10; Lenz v. Ridgewood Associates, 1981, 55 N.C.App. 115, 284 S.E.2d 702 (plaintiff had to cross ice to reach car to go to college classes).

The reasonableness of an employee's actions resulting in injury is considered against the pressures upon him to perform his job. See Lundy v. Whiting Corp., 1981, 93 Ill.App.3d 244, 48 Ill.Dec. 752, 417 N.E.2d 154.

probability and probable gravity of the anticipated harm to himself. Thus it may not be contributory negligence to dash into the path of a train to save a child,[24] into a burning hotel to save a guest,[25] or to stand in the street to warn travelers of an obstruction to traffic.[26]

The same intelligence, attention,[27] memory,[28] knowledge[29] and judgment[30] are required of the actor for the protection of his own interests as for the protection of others, and the same allowance is made for his physical inferiorities,[31] and for the immaturity of children.[32] Whether the plaintiff's violation of a safety statute should be considered evidence of negligence or negligence per se also is typically treated the same as when the violation is by the defendant.[33]

The similarity of negligence and contributory negligence does not, however, necessarily mean that identical conduct is to be demanded of the plaintiff and the defendant in the same situation. Too many varying factors may affect what the standard of the reasonable person requires to permit any such rigid rule. The defendant may have

See also Fireman's Fund American Insurance Co. v. Coleman, Ala.1980, 394 So.2d 334; Cook v. Export Leaf Tobacco Co., 1980, 50 N.C.App. 89, 272 S.E.2d 883; DiSalvatore v. United States, E.D.Pa.1980, 499 F.Supp. 338; Shannon v. Howard S. Wright Co., 1979, ___ Mont. ___, 593 P.2d 438.

24. Brock v. Peabody Cooperative Equity Exchange, 1960, 186 Kan. 657, 352 P.2d 37; Brown v. Ross, 1956, 345 Mich. 54, 75 N.W.2d 68; Bond v. Baltimore & Ohio Railroad Co., 1918, 82 W.Va. 557, 96 S.E. 932; Williams v. City of Baton Rouge, La.App.1967, 200 So.2d 420, affirmed and amended, 1968, 252 La. 770, 214 So.2d 138.

25. See Altamuro v. Milner Hotel, Inc., E.D.Pa. 1982, 540 F.Supp. 870 (standard of care for rescuer is not to act rashly or imprudently).

26. Hammonds v. Haven, Mo.1955, 280 S.W.2d 814; Marshall v. Nugent, 1st Cir. 1955, 222 F.2d 604; cf. Lave v. Neumann, Neb.1982, 317 N.W.2d 779 (attempt to stop runaway truck). But cf. Rodriguez v. New York State Thruway Authority, 1981, 82 A.D.2d 853, 440 N.Y.S.2d 49 (standing in roadway while looking at stranded vehicle was contributory negligence).

27. Peck v. Olian, Mo.App.1981, 615 S.W.2d 663 (failure to observe hole in parking lot), error dismissed; Linde v. Welch, 1981, 95 Ill.App.3d 581, 51 Ill.Dec. 76, 420 N.E.2d 490 (failure to look at icy steps); Poche v. Maryland Casualty Co., La.App.1981, 407 So.2d 1237 (mother tripped again over dog restraint board in kitchen doorway); Norwood v. Sherwin-Williams Co., 1981, 303 N.C. 462, 279 S.E.2d 559 (failure to observe platform on floor).

28. Kinchen v. Missouri Pacific Railway Co., 5th Cir. 1982, 678 F.2d 619 (momentary forgetfulness doctrine); Soileau v. South Central Bell Telephone Co., La. 1981, 406 So.2d 182 (even reasonable man permitted occasional lapse of memory). Contra, Trowell v. United States, M.D.Fla.1981, 526 F.Supp. 1009.

29. Public Service Co. of New Hampshire v. Elliott, 1st Cir. 1941, 123 F.2d 2; Peterson v. Minnesota Power & Light Co., 1939, 206 Minn. 268, 288 N.W. 588; Sanders v. Wheaton, Ark.1981, 619 S.W.2d 674 (one's own strength). Cf. Hosey v. Mobil Oil Corp., S.D.Miss.1981, 542 F.Supp. 1033 (employer's knowledge of danger imputable to employee).

30. Thus, under the sudden emergency doctrine, a plaintiff confronted with a sudden emergency created by the defendant's negligence alone must thereafter act only as would a prudent person under such circumstances. See Horne v. Trivette, 1982, 58 N.C.App. 77, 293 S.E.2d 290; Baily v. State, La.App.1982, 414 So.2d 1273. Compare Preyan v. United States Fidelity & Guaranty Co., La.App.1981, 408 So.2d 1162 (worker negligent in failing to shut eyes when dust-like insulation material fell toward him). See also Allen v. Dhuse, 1982, 104 Ill.App.3d 806, 60 Ill.Dec. 559, 433 N.E.2d 356 (choosing more dangerous of two, alternative courses of action); Walsh v. A.D. Conner, Inc., 1981, 99 Ill.App.3d 427, 54 Ill.Dec. 936, 425 N.E.2d 1153 (choosing one of two equally dangerous methods). But even a rescuer must act with reasonable care toward his own safety. Rodriguez v. New York State Thruway Authority, 1981, 82 A.D.2d 853, 440 N.Y.S.2d 49.

31. See West v. United States Fidelity & Guaranty Co., La.App.1981, 405 So.2d 877 (short-legged dancer at wedding reception); Eden v. Conrail, 1981, 87 N.J. 467, 435 A.2d 556 (epileptic; comparative negligence); Second Restatement of Torts, § 464, Comments a, b; supra, § 32.

32. Shulman, The Standard of Care Required of Children, 1927, 37 Yale L.J. 618; Bohlen, Liability in Tort of Infants and Insane Persons, 1924, 23 Mich.L. Rev. 9; Wilderman, Contributory Negligence of Infants, 1935, 10 Ind.L.J. 427; Wilkens, Contributory Negligence of Very Young Children, 1971, 20 Clev.St. L.Rev. 65. See supra, § 32.

33. See, e.g., Murray v. Alabama Power Co., Ala. 1982, 413 So.2d 1109; Rex Utilities, Inc. v. Gaddy, Fla. App.1982, 413 So.2d 1232 (motorcycle helmet law; doctrine applicable to comparative negligence, but defendant must prove causal link between violation and harm); Colorado Flying Academy, Inc. v. United States, D.Colo.1981, 506 F.Supp. 1221; Kimery v. Public Service Co. of Oklahoma, Okla.1980, 622 P.2d 1066; Fontanne v. Federal Paper Board Co., 1982, 105 Ill. App.3d 306, 61 Ill.Dec. 178, 434 N.E.2d 331. For the effect of the defendant's violation of statute, see supra, § 36.

more information than the plaintiff as to the risk,[34] or by reason of the enterprise in which he is engaged may be required to obtain it;[35] or the risk of harm to others may be more apparent, or apparently more serious, than the risk to the actor himself; or he may have reasonable confidence in his own awareness of the risk, and his ability to avoid it, where he cannot reasonably have such confidence in the awareness or ability of others. He may have undertaken a responsibility toward others, which will require him to exercise an amount of care for their protection which he would not be required to exercise for his own safety.[36] Or the plaintiff may be justified in relying upon the defendant to protect him; or, even without such factors, the jury may find that in the particular situation a reasonable man would have been more careful for others than for himself.[37]

Thus the greater number of courts have recognized that a passenger in an automobile is entitled to rely upon the driver, and may take and keep his eyes off of the road,[38] and may even go to sleep,[39] where it is quite clear that the driver cannot reasonably do either. There has been so much of this differentiation in the decisions that eminent writers[40] and an occasional court[41] have advocated outright recognition of the double standard. Whether this is at all necessary, or even desirable, may seriously be questioned, in the light of the flexibility which has developed in the decided cases under the present single formula for both.

The result of all this is that, while the theory is the same, and the formula put to the jury is the same, the practical application of both may not be entirely the same for negligence and for contributory negligence. As to the latter, in part because of these differentiating factors, and in part because of the dislike that many courts have developed for this defense, the marked tendency has been to let the issue go to the jury whenever possible.[42] It is still not entirely impossible for the defendant to get a directed verdict, where the negligence of the plaintiff is beyond all dispute—as where, for example, he runs without excuse into the side of a train, and collides with a car ten feet high, painted red with bright yellow letters on the side.[43] But in the ordinary case, where enough un-

---

34. Haverly v. State Line & Sullivan Railroad Co., 1890, 135 Pa. 50, 19 A. 1013; Antcliff v. Datzman, 1982, ___ Ind.App. ___, 436 N.E.2d 114 (both intoxicated; driver guilty of "willful or wanton misconduct," but not passenger who thought driver was sober).

35. See supra, § 32.

36. Gobrecht v. Beckwith, 1926, 82 N.H. 415, 135 A. 20. Cf. Sollinger v. Himchak, 1961, 402 Pa. 232, 166 A.2d 531 (driver of car may be found negligent toward his own passengers, but not contributorily negligent in his action against driver of car with which he collided).

37. See Stubbs v. Pancake Corner of Salem, Inc., 1969, 254 Or. 220, 458 P.2d 676.

38. O'Toole v. Pittsburgh & Lake Erie Railroad Co., 1893, 158 Pa. 99, 27 A. 737; Love v. Cardwell, 8th Cir. 1966, 368 F.2d 289; Smith v. Union Pacific Railroad Co., 1977, 202 Kan. 303, 564 P.2d 514 (no duty to watch for trains). See Mechem, The Contributory Negligence of Automobile Passengers, 1930, 78 U.Pa.L.Rev. 736.

39. Ramirez v. Deters, 1976, 41 Ill.App.3d 935, 2 Ill. Dec. 379, 357 N.E.2d 546. The distinction is clearly made in Shine v. Wujick, 1959, 89 R.I. 22, 150 A.2d 1, where both driver and passenger went to sleep; cf. Annot., 1980, 1 A.L.R.4th 556 (driver's drowsiness, passenger's contributory negligence).

40. 2 Harper and James, Law of Torts, 1956, 1227–1234.

41. "[I]n order to lessen the egregious results sometimes occasioned by the operation of the defense of contributory negligence, courts apply a more restrictive definition of negligence where it bars the plaintiff's recovery than where it is used to establish the defendant's liability. * * * A plaintiff need not be a 'super-perfect' human." Peterson v. Campbell, 1982, 105 Ill.App.3d 992, 61 Ill.Dec. 572, 434 N.E.2d 1169, 1172.

42. See, e.g., Tichenor v. Lohaus, 1982, 212 Neb. 218, 322 N.W.2d 629; Merriman v. Sea Pines Plantation Co., 1982, ___ S.C. ___, 294 S.E.2d 423; McNally v. Liebowitz, Pa.1982, 445 A.2d 716; Rodriguez v. City of New Haven, 1981, 183 Conn. 473, 439 A.2d 421; Brantley v. Stewart Building & Hardware Supplies, Inc., 1982, 274 Ark. 555, 626 S.W.2d 943; Duhl v. Nash Realty Inc., 1981, 102 Ill.App.3d 483, 57 Ill.Dec. 904, 429 N.E.2d 1267 ("nearly always" for jury); Bertsch v. Brewer, 1982, 96 Wn.2d 973, 640 P.2d 711 (for jury except in "rare" cases); Wernimont v. State, Iowa 1981, 312 N.W.2d 568 (except in "very exceptional" case); Fontanne v. Federal Paper Board Co., 1982, 105 Ill. App.3d 306, 434 N.E.2d 331 ("preeminently" for jury).

43. Union Pacific Railroad Co. v. Cogburn, 1957, 136 Colo. 184, 315 P.2d 209; Jenkins v. Atlantic Coast Line Railroad Co., 1962, 258 N.C. 58, 127 S.E.2d 778 (side of engine). Cf. Sargent v. Williams, 1953, 152 Tex. 413, 258 S.W.2d 787 (riding with driver with repu-

Cause in Fact

The ordinary negligence principles of cause in fact apply with equal force to contributory negligence.[45] There is one rather curious aberration, however, which makes an apparent distinction between negligence and contributory negligence. It has been said by a number of courts [46] that the plaintiff is barred from recovery if his own negligence has contributed to his injury "in any degree, however slight." On the face of it this means that any insignificant contribution, such as the addition of a lighted match to a forest fire, would bar the action. In all probability this is nothing more than a confusion of words, which fails to distinguish slight negligence from slight contribution; and what is really meant is that the plaintiff's negligence can be a defense, no matter how slight his departure from ordinary standards of conduct.[47] The intent, in other words, is to reject any idea of comparative negligence. If so, it is a mistake peculiarly likely to mislead the jury when an instruction is given in such terms. Most courts, when the distinction has been pointed out to them, have held that the rules as to causation [48] are the same for contributory negligence as for negligence,[49] and that the plaintiff is not barred unless his negligence, of whatever degree, has been a substantial factor in causing his injury.[50]

---

tation for recklessness, who traveled 110 miles per hour); Long v. City of New Boston, 1981, 95 Ill.App.3d 430, 50 Ill.Dec. 965, 420 N.E.2d 282 (climbing unsteady ladder to string Christmas lights); Hulett v. Central Illinois Light Co., 1981, 99 Ill.App.3d 211, 54 Ill.Dec. 463, 424 N.E.2d 1366 (spraying liquid fungus remover around exposed electrical wires; summary judgment); Smith v. Diamond, 1981, __ Ind.App. __, 421 N.E.2d 1172 (failing to look before crossing street); Pound v. Augusta National, Inc., 1981, 158 Ga.App. 166, 279 S.E.2d 342 (walking on obviously wet and slippery gravel); Bigelow v. Johnson, 1981, 303 N.C. 126, 277 S.E.2d 347 (riding at night on motorcycle using flashlight as headlight).

44. "It is not disputed by appellant, that we must view the evidence in the light most favorable to plaintiff; that it is only the exceptional case in which the issue of freedom from contributory negligence should not be submitted to the jury—only where such negligence is so palpable, flagrant and manifest that reasonable minds may fairly reach no other conclusion; that if there is any evidence tending to establish plaintiff's freedom from contributory negligence, the question is one of fact for the jury, and doubts should be resolved in favor of such submission." Goman v. Benedik, 1962, 253 Iowa 719, 113 N.W.2d 738.

The Arizona constitution requires that the issue of contributory negligence always be left to the jury. See Heimke v. Munoz, 1970, 106 Ariz. 26, 470 P.2d 107.

45. See Rex Utilities, Inc. v. Gaddy, Fla.App.1982, 413 So.2d 1232 (2–1) (no showing that death of motorcycle passenger would have been prevented by helmet); Brown v. Smith, Tenn.App.1980, 604 S.W.2d 56 (failure to wear helmet irrelevant where no injuries to head); Correll v. Werner, 1981, 293 Pa.Super. 88, 437 A.2d 1004; Sea Land Industries, Inc. v. General Ship Repair Corp., D.Md.1982, 530 F.Supp. 550, 567–68; Hartenbach v. Johnson, Mo.App.1982, 628 S.W.2d 684 (stern light on boat would not have prevented accident); cf. Bigelow v. Johnson, 1981, 303 N.C. 126, 277 S.E.2d 347 (same, semble; flashlight used as motorcycle headlight); Correll v. Werner, 1981, 293 Pa.Super. 88, 437 A.2d 1004.

46. Koroniotis v. La Porte Transit, Inc., 1979, __ Ind.App. __, 397 N.E.2d 656; Crane v. Neal, 1957, 389 Pa. 329, 132 A.2d 675; Ferris v. Patch, 1956, 119 Vt. 274, 126 A.2d 114; Aitchison v. Reter, 1954, 245 Iowa 1005, 64 N.W.2d 923; Keck v. Pozorski, 1963, 135 Ind. App. 192, 191 N.E.2d 325; compare Bradley v. Appalachian Power Co., 1979, __ W.Va. __, 256 S.E.2d 879 (characterizing "slightest degree" rule as "manifestly unfair," and adopting 50% comparative rule, whereby plaintiff "substantially" contributing to his own injury is barred from all recovery).

47. Made clear in Bahm v. Pittsburgh & Lake Erie Railroad Co., 1966, 6 Ohio St.2d 192, 217 N.E.2d 217; Daigle v. Twin City Ready Mix Concrete Co., 1964, 268 Minn. 136, 128 N.W.2d 148; Bazydlo v. Placid Marcy Co., 2d Cir. 1970, 422 F.2d 842.

48. See supra, § 41.

49. Second Restatement of Torts, § 465. See Malone, Ruminations on Dixie Drive It Yourself v. American Beverage Co., 1970, 30 La.L.Rev. 363.

50. Mack v. Precast Industries, Inc., 1963, 369 Mich. 439, 120 N.W.2d 225; Bahm v. Pittsburgh & Lake Erie Railroad Co., 1966, 6 Ohio St.2d 192, 217 N.E.2d 217; Huey v. Milligan, 1961, 242 Ind. 93, 175 N.E.2d 698; Busch v. Lilly, 1960, 257 Minn. 343, 101 N.W.2d 199; McManus v. Getter Trucking Co., Wyo. 1963, 384 P.2d 974; Correll v. Werner, 1981, 293 Pa. Super. 88, 437 A.2d 1004 ("substantial factor"); Marsh v. Interstate & Ocean Transportation Co., D.Del.1981, 521 F.Supp. 1007 ("significant contributing cause"); cf. Cardwell v. Golden, Tenn.App.1981, 621 S.W.2d 774.

Proximate Cause

The usual principles of proximate cause [51] also apply to the contributory negligence defense.[52] Thus, it is generally held that contributory negligence bars recovery only when the injury results from a hazard, or risk, which made the plaintiff's conduct negligent.[53] The "clean hands" theory of contributory negligence, which induced a few early courts to deny recovery to a plaintiff whose conduct was unlawful in any way whatever, as in the case of one driving quite carefully in violation of a Sunday law,[54] was soon found to be neither just nor workable. It has long since been discarded, and there is now no doubt, for example, that one who goes upon land for the purpose of engaging in fornication [55] or gaming [56] is not an outlaw, and is not for that reason barred from recovery when he is injured on the premises; nor is an alien unlawfully in the United States, when he is run down by a car.[57] There is thus agreement for the general proposition that the plaintiff is not barred when his failure to exercise reasonable care for his own safety exposes him to a foreseeable risk of injury through one event, and he is in fact injured through another which he could not foresee.[58]

In an early leading Connecticut case,[59] in which a workman violated instructions not to work on the unguarded end of a slippery platform, and was injured by the fall of a brick wall, it was held that he might recover, since his negligence did not extend to such a risk. Upon the same basis, it has been held that a passenger riding upon the platform of a street car is not negligent with respect to a collision,[60] nor is an automobile driver who parks near a fire hydrant negligent as to any vehicle which may drive into him, except a fire engine,[61] nor is one who drives at excessive speed negligent as to a tree which falls on him.[62] In a few instances this has been carried to extreme and hair-splitting lengths, as by holding that negligence as to being hit by an eastbound train does not bar recovery when it is a westbound train on a

---

51. See generally supra, ch. 7.

52. Gomes v. Peter Scalamandre & Sons, Inc., 1981, 85 A.D.2d 594, 444 N.Y.S.2d 706 (error not to so charge). The ordinary principles of foreseeability thus apply to contributory negligence. See, e.g., Moore v. Burton Lumber & Hardware Co., Utah 1981, 631 P.2d 865; Sea Land Industries, Inc. v. General Ship Repair Corp., D.Md.1982, 530 F.Supp. 550, 568 (no duty to protect against unexpected negligence of third party); Fuentes v. Gentry, Tex.App.1981, 628 S.W.2d 458 (plaintiff could not foresee specific danger).

53. As to negligence, see supra, § 43.

54. Bosworth v. Inhabitants of Swansey, 1845, 51 Mass. (10 Metc.) 363; Johnson v. Irasburgh, 1874, 47 Vt. 28; Hinckley v. Penobscot, 1856, 42 Me. 89. See Davis, The Plaintiff's Illegal Act as a Defense in Actions of Tort, 1905, 18 Harv.L.Rev. 505; Thayer, Public Wrong and Private Action, 1914, 27 Harv.L.Rev. 317, 338.

55. Rapee v. Beacon Hotel Corp., 1944, 293 N.Y. 196, 56 N.E.2d 548; Cramer v. Tarr, D.Me.1958, 165 F.Supp. 130; Holcomb v. Meeds, 1952, 173 Kan. 321, 246 P.2d 239; Meador v. Hotel Grover, 1942, 193 Miss. 392, 9 So.2d 782. See Notes, 1945, 31 Corn.L.Q. 89; 1938, 4 U.Pitt.L.Rev. 223.

56. Manning v. Noa, 1956, 345 Mich. 130, 76 N.W.2d 75; Shiroma v. Itano, 1956, 10 Ill.App.2d 428, 135 N.E.2d 123. Cf. Bagre v. Daggett Chocolate Co., 1940, 126 Conn. 659, 13 A.2d 757 (bingo game prize); Johnson v. Thompson, 1965, 111 Ga.App. 654, 143 S.E.2d 51 (same).

57. Janusis v. Long, 1933, 284 Mass. 403, 188 N.E. 228; Mulhall v. Fallon, 1900, 176 Mass. 266, 57 N.E. 386.

58. Second Restatement of Torts, § 468. See Green, Contributory Negligence and Proximate Cause, 1927, 6 N.C.L.Rev. 3.

59. Smithwick v. Hall & Upson Co., 1890, 59 Conn. 261, 21 A. 924. Accord, Gray & Bell v. Scott, 1870, 66 Pa. 345.

60. Dewire v. Boston & Maine Railroad Co., 1889, 148 Mass. 343, 19 N.E. 523; Montambault v. Waterbury & Milldale Tramway Co., 1923, 98 Conn. 584, 120 A. 145; Webster v. Rome, Watertown & Ogdenburgh Railroad Co., 1889, 115 N.Y. 112, 21 N.E. 725; New York, Lake Erie & Western Railway Co. v. Ball, 1891, 53 N.J.L. 283, 21 A. 1052. Cf. Cosgrove v. Shusterman, 1942, 129 Conn. 1, 26 A.2d 471 (riding on running board); Guile v. Greenberg, 1934, 192 Minn. 548, 257 N.W. 649 (on fender).

61. Denson v. McDonald Brothers, 1919, 144 Minn. 252, 175 N.W. 108.

62. Nesta v. Meyer, 1968, 100 N.J.Super. 434, 242 A.2d 386; Berry v. Borough of Sugar Notch, 1899, 191 Pa. 345, 43 A. 240. Cf. Hyde v. Avalon Air Transport, Inc., 1966, 243 Cal.App.2d 88, 52 Cal.Rptr. 300 (spear fishing in city limits, struck by airplane); Graft v. Crooker, D.Mont.1967, 263 F.Supp. 941 (plane taking off in bad weather, obstruction at end of field).

second track,[63] or that the risk of falling is not the risk of falling upon a hook.[64]

Such cases frequently say that the plaintiff's negligence is not the "proximate cause" of his own damage.[65] It is, of course, quite possible that his conduct may not have been a substantial contributing factor at all, where the harm would have occurred even if he had exercised proper care.[66] But in the usual case the causal connection is clear and beyond dispute, and no problem of cause in fact is involved.[67] What is meant is that the plaintiff's conduct has not exposed him to a foreseeable risk of the particular type of injury that in fact occurred through the defendant's negligence, and that it is therefore unavailable as a defense.[68]

Distinguished from Avoidable Consequences

Somewhat similar to the doctrine of contributory negligence is the rule of "avoidable consequences," which denies recovery for any damages which could have been avoided by reasonable conduct on the part of the plaintiff. Both doctrines rest upon the same fundamental policy of making recovery depend upon the plaintiff's proper care for the protection of his own interests, and both require of him only the standard of the reasonable person under the circumstances.[69] The statement commonly made as to the distinction between the two is that contributory negligence is negligence of the plaintiff before any damage, or any invasion of his rights, has occurred, which bars all recovery. The rule of avoidable conseqences comes into play after a legal wrong has occurred, but while some damages may still be averted, and bars recovery only for such damages.[70] Thus, if the plaintiff is injured in an automobile collision, his contributorily negligent driving before the collision will prevent any recovery at all, but his failure to obtain proper medical care for his broken leg will bar only his damages for the subsequent aggravated condition of the leg.[71]

It may be suggested that the underlying basis for the distinction is merely the practical feasibility of assigning a part of the damages to the defendant's negligence alone in

---

63. Kinderavich v. Palmer, 1940, 127 Conn. 85, 15 A.2d 83. Cf. Brazel v. McMurray, 1961, 404 Pa. 188, 171 A.2d 151 (plaintiff struck by one car, left helpless in the highway, run over by a second); Fahringer v. Rinehimer, 1980, 283 Pa.Super. 93, 423 A.2d 731 (truck lurched forward, crunching worker's hand, rather than rolling backward as expected); Wainwright v. Truckenmiller, 1981, 96 Ill.App.3d 1127, 52 Ill.Dec. 163, 421 N.E.2d 1026 (pedestrian need not look for car approaching in wrong lane).

64. Furukawa v. Yoshio Ogawa, 9th Cir. 1956, 236 F.2d 272. The case is criticized, and the difficulties of defining the "particular hazard" pointed out, in Note, [1958] Wash.U.L.Q. 111.

65. See for example Garland v. Nelson, 1944, 219 Minn. 1, 17 N.W.2d 28. See Notes, 1938, 22 Minn.L. Rev. 410; 1953, 41 Ky.L.J. 317.

66. Boulfrois v. United Traction Co., 1904, 210 Pa. 263, 59 A. 1007; Travis v. Hay, Ky.1961, 352 S.W.2d 209.

67. Payne v. Chicago & Alton Railroad Co., 1895, 129 Mo. 405, 31 S.W. 885; Green, Contributory Negligence and Proximate Cause, 1927, 6 North Car.L.Rev. 3, 11; Note, 1938, 22 Minn.L.Rev. 410, 414.

68. Compare the "intervening cause" cases, as to the negligence of the defendant. See supra, § 44.

69. See McCormick, Damages, 1935, §§ 33, 35; American Railway Express Co. v. Judd, 1925, 213 Ala. 242, 104 So. 418; James B. Berry's Sons Co. v. Presnall, 1931, 183 Ark. 125, 35 S.W.2d 83; Stewart Dry Goods Co. v. Boone, 1918, 180 Ky. 199, 202 S.W. 489.

70. See McCormick, Damages, 1935, § 33; Dippold v. Cathlamet Timber Co., 1924, 111 Or. 199, 225 P. 202; Armfield v. Nash, 1856, 31 Miss. 361; Bailey v. J.L. Roebuck Co., 1929, 135 Okl. 216, 275 P. 329; Gilbert v. Mayor & Council of City of Athens, 5th Cir. 1981, 655 F.2d 73.

71. Wingrove v. Home Land Co., 1938, 120 W.Va. 100, 196 S.E. 563; Hendler Creamery Co. v. Miller, 1927, 153 Md. 264, 138 A. 1. See also Socony Vacuum Oil Co. v. Marvin, 1946, 313 Mich. 528, 21 N.W.2d 841 (preventing fire after accident); Quinones v. Public Administrator, 1975, 49 A.D.2d 889, 373 N.Y.S.2d 224 (failure to follow doctor's instructions after negligent medical treatment); Dohmann v. Richard, La.App.1973, 282 So.2d 789 (injured pedestrian need not submit to recommended electro-shock therapy to treat post-accident depression). "If a reasonably prudent person would submit to the operation, then those damages that the operation would have alleviated are not recoverable." Verrett v. McDonough Marine Service, 5th Cir. 1983, 705 F.2d 1437, 1444 (no recovery for future pain that could be avoided by "quite routine" laminectomy and lumbar fusion of disc that ruptured in collision).

the latter case. Here as elsewhere [72] the courts have been willing to apportion damages to separate causes when a logical basis may be found. In the "avoidable consequence" cases, the initial damage cannot logically be charged to the plaintiff's own negligence as a cause, while the later damages may be. If no such division can be made, the plaintiff's negligence may bar all recovery, notwithstanding that it is subsequent in point of time to that of the defendant.[73]

In a limited number of situations, the plaintiff's unreasonable conduct, although it is prior or contemporaneous, may be found to have caused only a separable part of the damage. In such a case, even though it is called contributory negligence, the apportionment will be made. This is true, for example, where plaintiff and defendant both pollute the same stream,[74] or flood the plaintiff's property,[75] or cause other damage similar in kind but capable of logical division. A more difficult problem is presented when the plaintiff's prior conduct is found to have played no part in bringing about an impact or accident, but to have aggravated the ensuing damages.[76] In such a case,[77] upon a finding that the plaintiff's excessive speed in driving was not responsible for a collision, but greatly increased the damages resulting from it, the Connecticut court refused to make any division, and held that the plaintiff could recover the entire amount. In analogous situations, however, other courts have apportioned the damages, holding that the plaintiff's recovery should be reduced to the extent that they have been aggravated by his own antecedent negligence.[78] This may be the better view, unless we are to place an artificial emphasis upon the moment of impact, and the pure mechanics of causation. Cases will be infrequent, however, in which the extent of aggravation can be determined with any reasonable degree of certainty, and a court may properly refuse to divide the damages upon the basis of mere speculation.[79]

It is suggested, therefore, that the doctrines of contributory negligence and avoidable consequences are in reality the same, and that the distinction which exists is rather one between damages which are capable of assignment to separate causes, and damages which are not.

---

72. See supra, § 52.

73. It has been held that a plaintiff seeking apportionment of damages caused by his contributory negligence and damages that would have occurred anyway has the burden of proof on the issue. Dziedzic v. St. John's Cleaners & Shirt Launderers, Inc., 1968, 99 N.J. Super. 565, 240 A.2d 697, reversed on other grounds 53 N.J. 157, 249 A.2d 382.

74. Randolf v. Town of Bloomfield, 1889, 77 Iowa 50, 41 N.W. 562; Bowman v. Humphrey, 1906, 132 Iowa 234, 109 N.W. 714.

75. Philadelphia & Reading Railway Co. v. Smith, 3d Cir. 1894, 64 F. 679; Thomas v. Kenyon, N.Y.1861, 1 Daly 132; Gould v. McKenna, 1878, 86 Pa. 297.

76. The aggravation of injuries in a car accident due to the occupant's failure to use a seat belt is the paradigm modern example of this problem. Compare Spier v. Barker, 1974, 35 N.Y.2d 444, 363 N.Y.S.2d 916, 323 N.E.2d 164 (nonuse of seatbelt relevant to damages only, not liability; thorough discussion), with McCord v. Green, D.C.App.1976, 362 A.2d 720 (not to be considered on damages either). Most courts hold that the failure to wear a seat belt will not ordinarily bar recovery entirely on grounds of contributory negligence. See Annots., 1979, 92 A.L.R.3d 9; 95 A.L.R.3d 239 (comparative negligence). Special circumstances, however, such as a defective door, may require its use. See Tempe v. Giacco, 1981, 186 Conn.Sup. 120, 442 A.2d 947. See generally Wayand, Seat Belts—A Comparative Study of the Law and Practice, 1981, 30 Intern. & Comp.L.Q. 165.

77. E.g., Mahoney v. Beatman, 1929, 110 Conn. 184, 147 A. 762. Accord: Guile v. Greenberg, 1934, 192 Minn. 548, 257 N.W. 649; Hamilton v. Boyd, 1934, 218 Iowa 885, 256 N.W. 290. See Green, Mahoney v. Beatman: A Study in Proximate Cause, 1930, 39 Yale L.J. 532; Gregory, Justice Maltbie's Dissent in Mahoney v. Beatman, 1950, 24 Conn.Bar J. 78.

78. See Wright v. Illinois & Mississippi Telephone Co., 1866, 20 Iowa 195 (plaintiff's damages from a runaway enhanced by his negligent failure to have more than one helper); O'Keefe v. Kansas City Western Railway Co., 1912, 87 Kan. 322, 124 P. 416 (plaintiff's injuries from a fall increased by his prior intoxication, which did not contribute to the fall).

79. See Schomaker v. Havey, 1927, 291 Pa. 30, 139 A. 495; cf. Rex Utilities, Inc. v. Gaddy, Fla.App.1982, 413 So.2d 1232 (2-1) (no way to know whether motorcycle helmet would have prevented death; defense disallowed).

Negligence Toward Known Danger

Contributory negligence may consist not only in a failure to discover or appreciate a risk which would be apparent to a reasonable person,[80] or an inadvertent mistake in dealing with it, but also in an intentional but unreasonable exposure to a danger of which the plaintiff is aware.[81] Thus it may be negligence, even as a matter of law, to continue to ride with a drunken automobile driver at high speed, after there is an opportunity to leave the car,[82] or to walk through a dark passage with which the plaintiff is unfamiliar without taking appropriate precautions.[83] In such cases the plaintiff's conduct may be such as to indicate his consent or willingness to encounter the danger and relieve the defendant of responsibility, and hence the controversial defense of assumption of risk may also be available as a defense, overlapping contributory negligence.[84] So far as contributory negligence itself is concerned, however, the issue is the reasonableness of the plaintiff's choice and conduct, which is determined by balancing the risks against the advantages which he is seeking.[85]

In particular, the plaintiff may not be required to surrender a valuable right or privilege merely because the defendant's conduct threatens him with what would otherwise be an unreasonable risk.[86] Because the defendant builds a powder mill[87] or runs a railroad[88] near his property, he need not abandon it, or take special precautions against fire. He should not in general be deprived of the free, ordinary and proper use of his land because his neighbor is negligent, and he ordinarily may leave the responsibility to the defendant.[89] At least this is true where the danger is still relatively slight, and the alternative means of protection expensive or burdensome. And due regard must be given to the importance of the plaintiff's interest in asserting the legal right itself. There are very definite situations, however, where insistence upon a right, such as the use of a

---

80. See, e.g., Tichenor v. Lohaus, 1982, 212 Neb. 218, 322 N.W.2d 629 (invitor; obvious danger); Skalos v. Higgins, 1982, 303 Pa.Super. 107, 449 A.2d 601; Womack v. Willis-Knighton Clinic, La.App.1982, 412 So.2d 629 (bags on sidewalk); Peck v. Olian, Mo.App.1981, 615 S.W.2d 663, error dismissed (hole in parking lot).

81. See Pound v. Augusta National Inc., 1981, 158 Ga.App. 166, 279 S.E.2d 342 (walking on slippery gravel in parking lot); Second Restatement of Torts, § 466.

But the defense may not be made out if some aspect of the danger makes it significantly greater than the plaintiff believes. See Merriman v. Sea Pines Plantation Co., 1982, __ S.C. __, 294 S.E.2d 423 (deceptively slippery oyster shell walkway).

82. See, e.g., Hutchinson v. Mitchell, 1957, 143 W.Va. 280, 101 S.E.2d 73. But not if the driver was thought to be sober upon entering the car, and there was no opportunity thereafter to leave the car or avert the accident. Cf. Antcliff v. Datzman, 1982, __ Ind. App. __, 436 N.E.2d 114.

83. Trowell v. United States, M.D.Fla.1981, 526 F.Supp. 1009; Roberts v. United States, D.D.C.1981, 514 F.Supp. 712; cf. Doggett v. Welborn, 1973, 18 N.C. App. 105, 196 S.E.2d 36, certiorari denied 283 N.C. 665, 197 S.E.2d 873; Beckwith v. State Farm Fire & Casualty Co., La.App.1980, 393 So.2d 155, writ denied 399 So. 2d 209 (leaping over ditch with bare feet without knowing what dangers might lurk beneath water). But cf. McNally v. Liebowitz, 1982, 498 Pa. 163, 445 A.2d 716 (for jury). See generally Annot., 1969, 28 A.L.R.3d 605.

84. See infra, § 68.

85. A person may act reasonably in some circumstances, however, in carefully proceeding to encounter a known danger. See Stach v. Sears, Roebuck & Co., 1981, 102 Ill.App.3d 397, 57 Ill.Dec. 879, 429 N.E.2d 1242 (dictum); Smith v. Fried, 1981, 98 Ill.App.3d 467, 53 Ill.Dec. 845, 424 N.E.2d 636 (walking over rough spot on stairway); infra, § 68.

86. See Tichenor v. Lohaus, 1982, 212 Neb. 218, 322 N.W.2d 629 (invitee).

87. Judson v. Giant Powder Co., 1895, 107 Cal. 549, 40 P. 1020. Cf. North Bend Lumber Co. v. City of Seattle, 1921, 116 Wash. 500, 199 P. 988 (dam); Spencer v. Gedney, 1927, 45 Idaho 64, 260 P. 699 (fire).

88. Leroy Fibre Co. v. Chicago, Milwaukee & St. Paul Railway Co., 1914, 232 U.S. 340, 34 S.Ct. 415, 58 L.Ed. 631; Louisville & Nashville Railroad Co. v. Malone, 1897, 116 Ala. 600, 22 So. 897; Martin v. Western Union Railroad Co., 1868, 23 Wis. 437; Donovan v. Hannibal & St. Joseph Railroad Co., 1886, 89 Mo. 147, 1 S.W. 232; Kellogg v. Chicago & North Western Railway Co., 1870, 26 Wis. 223.

89. "Unless a party has notice to the contrary, he has the right to assume others who owe him a duty of reasonable care will exercise such care." Smith v. Insurance Co. of North America, 1980, __ Ind.App. __, 411 N.E.2d 638, 641 (landowner is not required to keep watch on neighbor's trash fire to assure it does not spread to his premises).

highway,[90] or the right of way,[91] or the boarding of an overcrowded street car,[92] may clearly involve a risk out of all proportion to its value, and the plaintiff will then generally be held negligent without regard to any prior legal "right."

Scope of the Defense

Within the limits above indicated, and in the absence of modifying legislation[93] or judicial action,[94] contributory negligence of the plaintiff is a complete bar to his action for any common law negligence of the defendant.[95] Whether it is a bar to the liability of a defendant who has violated a statutory duty is a matter of the legislative purpose which the court finds in the statute. If it is found to be intended merely to establish a standard of ordinary care for the protection of the plaintiff against a risk, his contributory negligence with respect to that risk will bar his action,[96] as in the case of common law negligence. But there are certain unusual types of statutes, such as child labor acts,[97] those prohibiting the sale of dangerous articles such as firearms to minors,[98] the Federal Safety Appliance and Boiler Inspection Acts,[99] workplace safety acts,[1] and railway fencing[2] or fire[3] statutes, all of which have been construed as intended to place the entire responsibility upon the defendant, and to protect the particular class of plaintiffs against their own negligence.[4] In such a case, as in the case of the statutes involving the age of consent,[5] the object of the statute itself would be defeated if the plaintiff's

90. Wright v. City of St. Cloud, 1893, 54 Minn. 94, 55 N.W. 819; Harris v. Clinton, 1887, 64 Mich. 447, 31 N.W. 425. Cf. Holle v. Lake, 1965, 194 Kan. 200, 398 P.2d 300; Provenzo v. Sam, 1967, 27 A.D.2d 442, 280 N.Y.S.2d 308, reversed on other grounds, 1968, 23 N.Y.2d 256, 296 N.Y.S.2d 322, 244 N.E.2d 26. Or the highway shoulder. Rue v. State, Department of Highways, La.1979, 372 So.2d 1197.

91. Rosenau v. Peterson, 1920, 147 Minn. 95, 179 N.W. 647.

92. Harding v. Philadelphia Rapid Transit Co., 1907, 217 Pa. 69, 66 A. 151.

93. Many legislatures have now changed the rule. See infra, § 67.

94. Several courts have changed the rule. See infra, § 67.

95. See Smith v. Diamond, 1981, ___ Ind.App. ___, 421 N.E.2d 1172; McElroy v. Boise Cascade Corp., Tenn.App.1982, 632 S.W.2d 127; Elam v. Ethical Prescription Pharmacy, Inc., D.C.App.1980, 422 A.2d 1288; Hoover v. Gray, Mo.App.1981, 616 S.W.2d 867.

96. Dart v. Pure Oil Co., 1947, 223 Minn. 526, 27 N.W.2d 555; Wertz v. Lincoln Liberty Life Insurance Co., 1950, 152 Neb. 451, 41 N.W.2d 740; Richardson v. Fountain, Fla.App.1963, 154 So.2d 709; Carroll v. Getty Oil Co., D.Del.1980, 498 F.Supp. 409; Scoggins v. Jude, D.C.App.1980, 419 A.2d 999 (rental property housing regulations).

97. Karpeles v. Heine, 1919, 227 N.Y. 74, 124 N.E. 101; Pinoza v. Northern Chair Co., 1913, 152 Wis. 473, 140 N.W. 84; Dusha v. Virginia & Rainy Lake Co., 1920, 145 Minn. 171, 176 N.W. 482; Boyles v. Hamilton, 1965, 235 Cal.App.2d 492, 45 Cal.Rptr. 399.

98. Tamiami Gun Shop v. Klein, Fla.1959, 116 So.2d 421; McMillen v. Steele, 1923, 275 Pa. 584, 119 A. 721. Compare, as to protection of intoxicated persons, Hauth v. Sambo, 1916, 100 Neb. 160, 158 N.W. 1036; Soronen v. Olde Milford Inn, 1964, 84 N.J.Super. 372,

202 A.2d 208; Schelin v. Goldberg, 1958, 188 Pa.Super. 341, 146 A.2d 648. Also Van Gaasbeck v. Webatuck Central School District No. 1, 1968, 21 N.Y.2d 239, 287 N.Y.S.2d 77, 234 N.E.2d 243 (instructing children on school bus how to cross street); McCallie v. New York Cent. Railroad Co., 1969, 23 Ohio App.2d 152, 261 N.E.2d 179 (warning sign at grade crossing).

99. Bass v. Seaboard Airline Railway Co., 1949, 205 Ga. 458, 53 S.E.2d 895; Gowins v. Pennsylvania Railroad Co., 6th Cir. 1962, 299 F.2d 431, certiorari denied 371 U.S. 824, 83 S.Ct. 44, 9 L.Ed.2d 64.

1. See Wells v. Coulter Sales, Inc., 1981, 105 Mich. App. 107, 306 N.W.2d 411; Martin v. George Hyman Construction Co., D.C.App.1978, 395 A.2d 63; cf. Larabee v. Triangle Steel, Inc., 1982, 86 A.D.2d 289, 451 N.Y.S.2d 258 (absolute liability, and hence no contributory negligence defense, under one section of labor law, but not under another). But see Long v. Forest-Fehlhaber, 1982, 55 N.Y.2d 154, 448 N.Y.S.2d 132, 433 N.E.2d 115 (contributory and comparative negligence good defenses to breach of safe workplace regulations under labor law).

2. Welty v. Indianapolis & Vincennes Railroad Co., 1885, 105 Ind. 55, 4 N.E. 410; Atchison, Topeka & Santa Fe Railroad Co. v. Paxton, 1907, 75 Kan. 197, 88 P. 1082.

3. Matthews v. Missouri Pacific Railway Co., 1897, 142 Mo. 645, 44 S.W. 802; Peter v. Chicago & North Western Railway Co., 1899, 121 Mich. 324, 80 N.W. 295; Bowen v. Boston & Albany Railroad Co., 1901, 179 Mass. 524, 61 N.E. 141.

4. See also Vegich v. McDougal Hartmann Co., 1981, 84 Ill.2d 461, 50 Ill.Dec. 880, 419 N.E.2d 918 (Road Construction Injuries Act); Lomayestewa v. Our Lady of Mercy Hospital, Ky.1979, 589 S.W.2d 885 (absence of screen over window in mental ward).

5. See supra, § 18.

fault were a defense, and the courts refuse to recognize it.

The ordinary contributory negligence of the plaintiff is to be set over against the ordinary negligence of the defendant, to bar the action. But where the defendant's conduct is actually intended to inflict harm upon the plaintiff, there is a difference, not merely in degree but in the kind of fault; and the defense never has been extended to such intentional torts.[6] Thus it is no defense to assault or battery.[7] The same is true of that aggravated form of negligence, approaching intent, which has been characterized variously as "willful," "wanton," or "reckless,"[8] as to which all courts have held that ordinary negligence on the part of the plaintiff will not bar recovery.[9] Such conduct differs from negligence not only in degree but in kind, and in the social condemnation attached to it. Some courts have said that in such cases the plaintiff's conduct is not the "proximate cause" of the harm; but the causal connection appears to be basically the same as in any ordinary contributory negligence case. It is perhaps more a form of comparative fault, where the court is refusing to set up the lesser fault against the greater. Thus, if the plaintiff's own conduct is "willful," "wanton," or "reckless," it will be set up against similar conduct on the part of the defendant, and recognized as a bar to his action.[10]

In cases involving strict liability, not based upon wrongful intent or negligence, traditional contributory negligence is generally not available as a defense,[11] a matter discussed further below.[12]

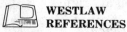
WESTLAW REFERENCES

digest("contributory negligence" /s "burden of proof")
digest("contributory negligence" /s "affirmative defense*")

Compared with Negligence
"contributory fault"
"contributory negligence" /p "standard of conduct"

Cause in Fact
"contributory negligence" /p cause +2 fact

Proximate Cause
272k82

Distinguished from Avoidable Consequences
"contributory negligence" /s avoidable /s consequence*

Negligence Toward Known Danger
digest("contributory negligence" /s known /s danger*)

Scope of the Defense
"contributory negligence" /s complete /1 bar

§ 66. Last Clear Chance

The most commonly accepted modification of the strict rule of contributory negligence is the doctrine of last clear chance. This doctrine, about which there has been little agreement and endless discussion,[1] had its

---

6. See Jackson v. Brantley, Ala.App.1979, 378 So.2d 1109, affirmed 378 So.2d 1112.

7. Jenkins v. North Carolina Department of Motor Vehicles, 1956, 244 N.C. 560, 94 S.E.2d 577; Peterson v. Campbell, 1982, 105 Ill.App.3d 992, 61 Ill.Dec. 572, 434 N.E.2d 1169 (dictum).

8. See supra, § 34.

9. Kellerman v. J.S. Durig Co., 1964, 176 Ohio St. 320, 199 N.E.2d 562; Tabor v. O'Grady, 1960, 61 N.J. Super. 446, 161 A.2d 267; Newman v. Piazza, 1967, 6 Ariz.App. 396, 433 P.2d 47; Liebhart v. Calahan, 1967, 72 Wn.2d 620, 434 P.2d 605; St. Onge v. Detroit & Mackinac Railway Co., 1982, 116 Mich.App. 128, 321 N.W.2d 865; Rimer v. Rockwell International Corp., 6th Cir. 1981, 641 F.2d 450; Second Restatement of Torts, §§ 482(1) & 503(1).

10. Second Restatement of Torts, §§ 482(2) & 503(3); Zank v. Chicago, Rock Island & Pacific Railway Co., 1959, 17 Ill.2d 473, 161 N.E.2d 848, on remand

1960, 26 Ill.App.2d 389, 168 N.E.2d 472; Ardis v. Griffin, 1962, 239 S.C. 529, 123 S.E.2d 876; Tabor v. O'Grady, 1960, 61 N.J.Super. 446, 161 A.2d 267; cf. Antcliff v. Datzman, 1982, ___ Ind.App. ___, 436 N.E.2d 114 (passenger's intoxication alone does not show contributory "willful or wanton misconduct" to bar claim against intoxicated driver guilty of willful or wanton misconduct in operating vehicle). The result may be different under pure comparative fault. See infra, § 67, note 89.

11. See, e.g., Marshall v. Ranne, Tex.1974, 511 S.W.2d 255 (vicious animal); Bringle v. Lloyd, 1975, 13 Wn.App. 844, 537 P.2d 1060 (blasting).

12. See infra, chapters 13 & 17.

§ 66

1. See generally Schofield, Davies v. Mann: Theory of Contributory Negligence, 1890, 3 Harv.L.Rev. 263; Bohlen, Contributory Negligence, 1908, 21 Harv.L.Rev.

origin in 1842 in the English case of Davies v. Mann,[2] in which the plaintiff left his ass fettered in the highway, and the defendant drove into it. It was held that the plaintiff might recover, notwithstanding any negligence of his own, if the defendant might, by proper care, have avoided injuring the animal.

No very satisfactory reason for the rule ever has been suggested. The first explanation given,[3] and the one which still is most often stated, is that if the defendant has the last clear opportunity to avoid the harm, the plaintiff's negligence[4] is not a "proximate cause" of the result.[5] While this coincides rather well with the attempt made in an older day to fix liability upon the "last human wrongdoer,"[6] it is quite out of line with the evolving ideas of proximate cause.[7] In such a case the negligence of the plaintiff undoubtedly has been a cause, and a substantial and important one, of his own damage, and it cannot be said that injury through the defendant's negligence was not fully within the risk which the plaintiff has created. If the injury should be to a third person, such as a passenger in the defendant's vehicle, the plaintiff's negligence would clearly be recognized as a responsible cause,[8] and it is an utterly artificial distinction which applies any other rule when the plaintiff himself is injured.

Other courts have said that the later negligence of the defendant involves a higher degree of fault, and that it is a rule of comparative negligence which is being applied.[9] This may be true in many cases where the defendant has discovered the plaintiff's helpless situation, or his conduct approaches reckless or intentional disregard of the danger; but it can scarcely explain many others in which the defendant's fault consists mere-

---

233; Smith, Last Clear Chance, 1916, 82 Cent.L.J. 425, 55 Am.L.Rev. 897; Lowndes, Contributory Negligence, 1934, 22 Geo.L.J. 674; James, Last Clear Chance: A Transitional Doctrine, 1938, 47 Yale L.J. 704; MacIntyre, The Rationale of Last Clear Chance, 1940, 53 Harv.L.Rev. 1225; Wittman, Optimal Pricing of Sequential Inputs: Last Clear Chance, Mitigation of Damages, and Related Doctrines in the Law, 1981, 10 J.Leg.Stud. 65; Rozas, The Last Clear Chance Doctrine in Louisiana, 1967, 27 La.L.Rev. 269; Van Dyck, Last Clear Chance in Virginia, 1954, 40 Va.L.Rev. 637; Notes, 1980, 66 Iowa L.Rev. 187; 1973, 40 Tenn.L.Rev. 782; Annot., 1970, 34 A.L.R.3d 570 (collision between moving and stopped vehicles); Second Restatement of Torts, § 479 (helpless plaintiff); § 480 (inattentive plaintiff).

2. 1842, 10 M. & W. 546, 152 Eng.Rep. 588. Hence the nickname of the "jackass doctrine," with whatever implications it may carry.

3. Dowell v. General Steam Nav. Co., 1855, 5 El. & Bl. 195, 119 Eng.Rep. 454; Tuff v. Warman, 1857, 2 C.B., N.S., 740, 140 Eng.Rep. 607, 5 C.B., N.S., 573, 141 Eng.Rep. 231.

4. The doctrine does not apply to intentional torts. Wager v. Pro, D.C.Cir. 1979, 603 F.2d 1005.

5. Hunter v. Batton, 1982, 160 Ga.App. 849, 288 S.E.2d 244; Stephens v. Mann, 1980, 50 N.C.App. 133, 272 S.E.2d 771, review denied 276 S.E.2d 919. "It applies only where the antecedent negligence of the plaintiff has become remote in the chain of causation and a mere condition of his injury. * * * It does not apply where the plaintiff's act combines and concurs with the defendant's act as a proximate cause of the injury." Brown v. George, 1982, ___ S.C. ___, 294 S.E.2d 35, 36 (Harwell, J.). "Where the plaintiff's negligence actively continues up to the time of the accident, i.e., where the negligence of two persons is contemporaneous, and the fault of each operates directly to cause the injury, neither can recover from the other." Walker v. City of New York, 1982, 88 A.D.2d 803, 450 N.Y.S.2d 814, 816.

6. Bohlen, Contributory Negligence, 1908, 21 Harv. L.Rev. 233. See supra, § 42.

7. Green, Contributory Negligence and Proximate Cause, 1927, 6 North Car.L.Rev. 3, 21.

It is of course possible that the plaintiff's negligence may have played such an insignificant part that it is not to be regarded as a substantial factor in causing the result. This is the theory relied on in Jaggers v. Southeastern Greyhound Lines, D.Tenn.1940, 34 F.Supp. 667, reversed 126 F.2d 762, and Kinderavich v. Palmer, 1940, 127 Conn. 85, 15 A.2d 83, 89, although the facts of the cases do not appear to justify it.

8. Lincoln City Lines, Inc. v. Schmidt, 8th Cir. 1957, 245 F.2d 600; Evans v. Phoenix Insurance Co., La.App. 1965, 175 So.2d 425; Atlantic Coast Line Railroad Co. v. Coxwell, 1955, 93 Ga.App. 159, 91 S.E.2d 135.

The defendant who has the last clear chance may be required to indemnify the other defendant. See Leflar, Contribution and Indemnity Between Tortfeasors, 1932, 81 U.Pa.L.Rev. 130, 152.

9. Wilson v. Southern Traction Co., 1921, 111 Tex. 361, 234 S.W. 663; Rawitzer v. St. Paul City Railway Co., 1904, 93 Minn. 84, 100 N.W. 664; Moreno v. Los Angeles Transfer Co., 1920, 44 Cal.App. 551, 186 P. 800. Contra, Stephens v. Mann, 1980, 50 N.C.App. 133, 272 S.E.2d 771.

ly in a failure to discover the danger at all,[10] or in slowness, clumsiness, inadvertence or an error in judgment in dealing with it.

The real explanation would seem to be a fundamental dislike for the harshness of the contributory negligence defense.[11]

The doctrine has been called a transitional one, a way station on the road to apportionment of damages,[12] but its effect has been to freeze the transition rather than to speed it. As a broad final solution, it is obviously inadequate, since, except in a few cases where a part of the plaintiff's damages have occurred before the "last clear chance," [13] it merely transfers from the plaintiff to the defendant an entire loss due to the fault of both.

The application of the doctrine has been attended with much confusion.[14] Virtually every possible rule has been adopted, often in a single jurisdiction.[15] Some courts have repudiated the last clear chance rule by name,[16] but have nevertheless applied it under the guise of "wantonness" or "proximate cause." [17] It is quite literally true that there are as many variant forms and applications of this doctrine as there are jurisdictions which apply it. A few courts, with something resembling billiard-parlor reverse English, have even purported to recognize a "last clear chance" doctrine in favor of the defendant, to bar the plaintiff's recovery,[18] but since this comes out at exactly the same place as the defense of contributory negligence without the doctrine at all, and is calculated only to bewilder the jury with incomprehensible instructions, most courts have rejected any such idea.[19] In such a general area of confusion and disagreement, only very general statements can be offered, and reference must of necessity be made to the law of each particular state. The situations which have arisen may be classified as follows: [20]

10. See infra, notes 31–33.

11. "[T]he doctrine of last clear chance was a judicial development to modify the harshness of the contributory negligence rule." Ratlief v. Yokum, 1981, ___ W.Va. ___, 280 S.E.2d 584, 588. Accord, Alvis v. Ribar, 1981, 85 Ill.2d 1, 52 Ill.Dec. 23, 421 N.E.2d 886; Abalos v. Oil Development Co. of Texas, Tex.1976, 544 S.W.2d 627; Mitchell v. Sigrest, La.App.1977, 345 So.2d 141. See Kirby v. Larson, 1977, 400 Mich. 585, 256 N.W.2d 400.

12. James, Last Clear Chance: A Transitional Doctrine, 1938, 47 Yale L.J. 704; MacIntyre, The Rationale of Last Clear Chance, 1940, 53 Harv.L.Rev. 1225.

13. In such cases the courts have been willing to regard the damages as divisible and apportion them. Cleveland, Cincinnati, Chicago & St. Louis Railway Co. v. Klee, 1900, 154 Ind. 430, 56 N.E. 234; Weitzman v. Nassau Electric Railroad Co., 1898, 33 App.Div. 585, 53 N.Y.S. 905; Teakle v. San Pedro, Los Angeles & Salt Lake Railroad Co., 1907, 32 Utah 276, 90 P. 402.

14. See Ratlief v. Yokum, 1981, ___ W.Va. ___, 280 S.E.2d 584 (abolishing doctrine, earlier having adopted comparative negligence); Street v. Calvert, Tenn.1976, 541 S.W.2d 576 (jettisoning decades of elaborate doctrine and adopting Second Restatement of Torts, §§ 479, 480); Massey v. Scripter, 1977, 401 Mich. 385, 258 N.W.2d 44 (same).

15. See De Muth, Derogation of the Common Law Rule of Contributory Negligence, 1935, 7 Rocky Mt.L. Rev. 161.

16. Brennan v. Public Service Railway Co., 1930, 106 N.J.L. 464, 148 A. 775; Carson, Pirie Scott & Co. v. Chicago Railways Co., 1923, 309 Ill. 346, 141 N.E. 172;

Switzer v. Detroit Investment Co., 1925, 188 Wis. 330, 206 N.W. 407; Spillers v. Griffin, 1917, 109 S.C. 78, 95 S.E. 133. The most recent case "abolishing" last clear chance in a then contributory negligence state is Stewart v. Madison, Iowa 1979, 278 N.W.2d 284, noted 1980, 66 Iowa L.Rev. 187.

17. Walldren Express & Van Co. v. Krug, 1920, 291 Ill. 472, 126 N.E. 97; Clyde v. Southern Public Utilities Co., 1918, 109 S.C. 290, 96 S.E. 116; Bryant v. Northern Pacific Co., 1946, 221 Minn. 577, 23 N.W.2d 174; Sutton v. Public Service Interstate Transportation Co., 2d Cir. 1946, 157 F.2d 947 (New Jersey law).

18. Umberger v. Koop, 1952, 194 Va. 123, 72 S.E.2d 370; Island Express v. Frederick, Del.1934, 5 W.W. Harr., 569, 171 A. 181; Louisville & Nashville Railroad Co. v. Patterson, 1948, 77 Ga.App. 406, 49 S.E.2d 218; cf. Johnson v. Powell, La.App.1977, 346 So.2d 283.

19. See Ratlief v. Yokum, 1981, ___ W.Va. ___, 280 S.E.2d 584, 588–89; Smith v. Wright, Ky.1974, 512 S.W.2d 943; Baumgartner v. State Farm Insurance Co., La.1978, 356 So.2d 400; Schlimmeyer v. Yurkiw, 1975, 50 A.D.2d 616, 374 N.Y.S.2d 427; Rollman v. Morgan, 1952, 73 Ariz. 305, 240 P.2d 1196; Durant v. Stuckey, 1952, 221 S.C. 342, 70 S.E2d 473; cf. Salter Marine, Inc. v. Conti Carriers & Terminals, Inc., 4th Cir. 1982, 677 F.2d 388. See generally Annot., 1953, 32 A.L.R.2d 543.

20. Cases are classified in Bradford & Carlson, Last Clear Chance in Automobile Negligence Cases, 1962, 11 Defense L.J. 61. Although many courts have parroted the standard classifications, many of the recent decisions ignore any distinction between the "helpless" or "inattentive" plaintiff, to the express chagrin of one re-

Plaintiff Helpless

Where the plaintiff's prior [21] negligence has placed him in a position from which he is powerless to extricate himself [22] by the exercise of any ordinary care,[23] and the defendant discovers his danger while there is still time to avoid it and then fails to do so, all of the courts, some which purport to reject the whole doctrine by name, have held that the plaintiff can recover.[24] This "conscious last clear chance," sometimes called the "doctrine of discovered peril," occasionally has been explained on the basis that negligence after the danger is known to the defendant necessarily involves a greater degree of fault, and amounts to "willful" or "wanton" misconduct, to which the ordinary negligence of the plaintiff is no defense.[25] Such an explanation does not meet a number of cases where the defendant's conduct consists of nothing more than confusion, inadvertence, or a mistake in judgment,[26] and the greater number of courts treat the issue as one of negligence only, and apply the rule of the last clear chance.[27]

There must be proof that the defendant discovered the situation,[28] that he then had the time to take action which would have saved the plaintiff,[29] and that he then failed to exercise reasonable care to avert the acci-

---

cent judge. See Kenison v. Schaeffer, 1980, 125 Ariz. 186, 608 P.2d 325, 326 (Borowiec, J., concurring).

21. Many cases hold that the doctrine does not apply where the plaintiff's negligence is active and continuous as a contributing factor up until the time of the injury. E.g., O'Connor v. G & R Packing Co., 1980, 74 A.D.2d 37, 426 N.Y.S.2d 557; Muirhead v. Gunst, 1979, 204 Neb. 1, 281 N.W.2d 207. See supra, note 5.

22. The doctrine thus is inapplicable where the plaintiff at all times is in control of the danger and simply chooses to take the risk. See Stephens v. Mann, 1980, 50 N.C.App. 133, 272 S.E.2d 771 (plaintiff, bouncing around in back of pickup truck, did not hold on, and finally bounced out). A drunken person should logically be considered helpless, to the extent he is unable to protect himself. See Brown v. George, 1982, ___ S.C. ___, 294 S.E.2d 35.

23. Including cases where the plaintiff's only effective means of escape would not be expected of a reasonable man, as in Schaaf v. Coen, 1936, 131 Ohio St. 279, 2 N.E.2d 605; Bence v. Teddy's Taxi, 1931, 112 Cal.App. 636, 297 P. 128; cf. Honeycutt v. Bess, 1979, 43 N.C.App. 684, 259 S.E.2d 798 (jury could find plaintiff was reasonable in staying in and trying to start truck stalled in intersection, rather than escaping).

24. E.g., Williams v. Spell, 1981, 51 N.C.App. 134, 275 S.E.2d 282; Barry v. Southern Pacific Railway Co., 1946, 64 Ariz. 116, 166 P.2d 825; New York Central Railroad Co. v. Thompson, 1939, 215 Ind. 652, 21 N.E.2d 625. See generally Second Restatement of Torts, § 479.

25. Esrey v. Southern Pacific Co., 1894, 103 Cal. 541, 37 P. 500; Tempfer v. Joplin & Pittsburg Railway Co., 1913, 89 Kan. 374, 131 P. 592; Labarge v. Pere Marquette Railroad Co., 1903, 134 Mich. 139, 95 N.W. 1073.

26. As, for example, in Smith v. Connecticut Railway & Lighting Co., 1907, 80 Conn. 268, 67 A. 888; Clark v. Wilmington & Weldon Railroad Co., 1891, 109 N.C. 430, 14 S.E. 43.

27. E.g., Hutchinson, Purity Ice Cream Co. v. Des Moines City Railway Co., 1915, 172 Iowa 527, 154 N.W. 890; Muskogee Electric Traction Co. v. Tanner, 1923, 93 Okl. 284, 220 P. 655; Louisville & Nashville Railroad Co. v. Harrod's Administrator, 1913, 155 Ky. 155, 159 S.W. 685.

28. "The last clear chance doctrine can be invoked only where the defendant knows of the plaintiff's perilous situation, and realizes, or has reason to realize, the plaintiff's helpless condition." Hunter v. Batton, 1982, 160 Ga.App. 849, 288 S.E.2d 244, 246; Cooper v. Driggers, 1981, 276 S.C. 299, 277 S.E.2d 893, 894 ("applicable only when and if the defendant sees that a negligent plaintiff is in a predicament from which he may not extricate himself"). Compare Georgia Southern & Florida Railway Co. v. Odom, 1980, 152 Ga.App. 664, 263 S.E.2d 469 (brakeman told engineer "Here comes another one" before train hit car at crossing), with Stephens v. Mann, 1980, 50 N.C.App. 133, 272 S.E.2d 771 (defendant could not see plaintiff bouncing around in back of truck). See also Adams v. Boyd, Ky.App.1977, 557 S.W.2d 426 (no proof defendant knew plaintiff in peril).

It is enough that the defendant has discovered that someone is in peril. Bolus v. Martin L. Adams & Son, Ky.1969, 438 S.W.2d 79; Chadwick v. City of New York, 1950, 301 N.Y. 176, 93 N.E.2d 625. Or that he may be. Kumkumian v. City of New York, 1953, 305 N.Y. 167, 111 N.E.2d 865.

29. See Brown v. George, 1982, ___ S.C. ___, 294 S.E.2d 35 (8–10 seconds insufficient time to avoid hitting drunk); Palmer v. State, La.App.1980, 393 So.2d 427, writ denied 399 So.2d 601 (2 seconds insufficient); Kenison v. Schaeffer, App.1980, 125 Ariz. 186, 608 P.2d 325, 326 ("The last clear chance doctrine implies sufficient time to think, appreciate and act, * * * and should not be applied to fast-happening accidents."—3/4 second insufficient); Crane v Banner, 1969, 93 Idaho 69, 455 P.2d 313 (6 or 7 tenths of second insufficient); Sims v. Huntington, 1979, 271 Ind. 368, 393 N.E.2d 135 (insufficient time). See infra, note 36.

dent.[30] In the absence of any one of these elements, the doctrine does not apply and the plaintiff is barred from recovery by his contributory negligence.

Where the plaintiff has become helpless, and the defendant does not discover his danger in time to avoid the injury, but is under a duty to discover it,[31] and with proper vigilance could do so in time to avoid the result, there is a division in the courts. In such an "unconscious last cear chance" situation, a number of the courts refuse to apply the doctrine, and deny recovery.[32] There has been something of a shift, however, and a considerable number have now swung over to the position that the doctrine should be applied in this context, and recovery allowed.[33] There is an astonishing lack of reasoning in the decisions to support either conclusion. Much emphasis is placed upon the time sequence of events, and the interval during which the defendant is still able to prevent the harm while the plaintiff is not, as if this in itself were a sufficient explanation not only for the absolution given the plaintiff, but for the requirement or nonrequirement of discovery of the situation. The usual "reason" given is merely that the defendant's later negligence is, or is not, the "proximate cause" of the injury, rather than that of the plaintiff.

Plaintiff Inattentive

In another group of cases, the plaintiff's situation is not one of true helplessness, and he is still in a position to escape, but his negligence consists in failure to pay attention to his surroundings and discover his own peril. If the defendant discovers his danger, and his inattentiveness, and is then negligent, most courts hold, with an occasional contrary view,[34] that the plaintiff may recover.[35] It is sometimes said that the defendant has a "conscious" and the plaintiff an "unconscious" chance, although obviously neither is "last" nor "clear." There is much the same vague talk of "wanton" conduct and comparative fault, or of proximate cause; but here all of the usual explanations and excuses for the doctrine would apear to fall particularly flat. There is the same tendency to avoid any explanation at all, and to lay stress upon the time interval during which the defendant might have done something, as if that were

---

30. "The defendant is charged with a duty of using with reasonable care and competence his *then* existing ability to avoid harming plaintiff." Hunter v. Batton, 1982, 160 Ga.App. 849, 288 S.E.2d 244, 246. See Williams v. Spell, 1981, 51 N.C.App. 134, 275 S.E.2d 282 (driver could have swerved to left or right to avoid pedestrian in highway); Georgia Southern & Florida Railway Co. v. Odom, 1980, 152 Ga.App. 664, 263 S.E.2d 469 (train crew could have slowed down, or tooted horn or whistle, once they saw car trying to cross tracks). Ordinary care does not usually require the defendant to imperil his own safety to avoid the accident. See Mercer v. Braswell, 1976, 140 Ga.App. 624, 231 S.E.2d 431.

31. Without such a duty, the doctrine does not apply. Thus in the case of trespassers, to whom the defendant owes no duty of vigilance to discover their presence, actual discovery may be necessary before the defendant can be found negligent at all. Southern Railway Co. v. Drake, 1910, 166 Ala. 540, 51 So. 996; Dyrcz v. Missouri Pacific Railway Co., 1911, 238 Mo. 33, 141 S.W. 861; Castile v. O'Keefe, 1916, 138 La. 479, 70 So. 481.

If the defendant's duty is only to exercise reasonable care to discover the danger, he may not even be negligent in failing to discover it, and so the last clear chance doctrine will not apply. See Jolivette v. City of Lafayette, La.App.1982, 408 So.2d 309 (lifeguard had other duties than watching particular location in swimming pool).

32. Cartwright v. Harris, 1980, ___ Ind.App. ___, 400 N.E.2d 1192, 1197 ("if a defendant merely might have discovered the plaintiff's predicament by proper vigilance but did not actually become aware of it, he obviously cannot be said to have had the last clear chance to avoid the accident"). See also Garcia v. Burlington Northern, Inc., Tex.Civ.App.1976, 543 S.W.2d 425, refused no reversable error.

33. See Sink v. Sumrell, 1979, 41 N.C.App. 242, 254 S.E.2d 665; French v. Mozzali, Ky.1968, 433 S.W.2d 122; Minton v. Southern Railway Co., 6th Cir. 1966, 368 F.2d 719; Letcher v. Derricott, 1963, 191 Kan. 596, 383 P.2d 533; Spenser v. Fondry, 1960, 122 Vt. 149, 167 A.2d 372; Second Restatement of Torts, § 479.

34. Middletown Trust Co. v. Armour & Co., 1937, 122 Conn. 615, 191 A. 532; Butler v. Rockland, Thomaston & Camden St. Railway Co., 1904, 99 Me. 149, 58 A. 775; Hanson v. New Hampshire Pre-Mix Concrete, Inc., 1970, 110 N.H. 377, 268 A.2d 841.

35. Burnham v. Yellow Checker Cab, Inc., 1964, 74 N.M. 125, 391 P.2d 413; Greear v. Noland Co., 1955, 197 Va. 233, 89 S.E.2d 49; Byrd v. Hawkins, D.C.App. 1979, 404 A.2d 941; Street v. Calvert, Tenn.1976, 541 S.W.2d 576 (adopting and applying Second Restatement of Torts, § 480).

a reason in itself.³⁶ As to what it is necessary for the defendant to discover, there is further disagreement. Some courts appear to hold that he must in fact realize the plaintiff's danger and his inattention; ³⁷ others apply a more objective standard, and require only that he discover the situation, and that the danger and lack of attention only be apparent to a reasonable person.³⁸ But the discovery may be proved by circumstantial evidence,³⁹ and there is in the decisions so much hair-splitting as to whether "ought to have seen" is equivalent to "saw" that the result of any particular case is likely to be unpredictable in a given jurisdiction. There is the further necessary qualification that the defendant may often reasonably assume until the last moment that the plaintiff will look out for himself, and has no reason to act until he has some notice to the contrary.⁴⁰

If the defendant does not discover the plaintiff's situation, but merely might do so by proper vigilance, it is obvious that neither party can be said to have a "last clear" chance. The plaintiff is still in a position to escape, and his lack of attention continues up to the point of the accident, without the interval of superior opportunity of the defendant,⁴¹ which has been considered so important. The plaintiff may not reasonably demand of the defendant greater care for his own protection than that which he exercises himself. Accordingly, the nearly universal rule is that there can be no recovery.⁴² The great exception is Missouri,⁴³ which has evolved a rather marvelous so-called "humanitarian doctrine," ⁴⁴ fearful and wonderful in its ramifications, which allows recovery. It appears to have begun as a distinction between a defendant operating a dangerous machine, such as a railroad train or an automobile, and a plaintiff who was not, and to have become transformed instead into a doctrine favoring the plaintiff where both parties were equally, and similarly, at fault. Unquestionably it represents an attempt to stress the greater importance of human safety over the convenience and financial interests of defendants; but its application has been marked by great confusion and many appeals.

36. In the absence of sufficient time to act, the doctrine does not apply. See supra, note 29.

37. See Dodd v. Wilson, 1980, 46 N.C.App. 601, 265 S.E.2d 449 (driver did not see pedestrian); Green v. Millsboro Fire Co., Del.Super.1978, 385 A.2d 1135, affirmed in part, reversed in part 403 A.2d 286. But such knowledge may be proved by circumstantial evidence over the defendant's denial. Arnold v. Owens, 4th Cir. 1935, 78 F.2d 495; Groves v. Webster City, 1936, 222 Iowa 849, 270 N.W. 329.

38. See Williams v. Spell, 1981, 51 N.C.App. 134, 275 S.E.2d 282; Nicholas v. Jenkins, La.App.1982, 411 So.2d 631; Menke v. Peterschmidt, 1955, 246 Iowa 722, 69 N.W.2d 65. Cf. Kumkumian v. City of New York, 1953, 305 N.Y. 167, 111 N.E.2d 865 (discovery of man on subway track by automatic tripper device).

39. E.g., Williams v. Spell, 1981, 51 N.C.App. 134, 275 S.E.2d 282.

40. See, e.g., Palmer v. State, La.App.1980, 393 So.2d 427, writ denied 399 So.2d 601; Sims v. Huntington, 1979, 271 Ind. 368, 393 N.E.2d 135; Lee v. Atlantic Coast Line Railroad Co., 1953, 237 N.C. 357, 75 S.E.2d 143.

41. It sometimes is said that the defendant's chance must be later by the amount of time it would take a normal human being to react to the situation. See Hutcheson v. Misenheimer, 1938, 169 Va. 511, 194 S.E. 665; Palmer v. State, La.App.1980, 393 So.2d 427, writ denied 399 So.2d 601. See supra, note 29.

42. See, e.g., Donahue v. Rolando, 1965, 16 Utah 2d 294, 400 P.2d 12; Hester v. Watson, 1968, 74 Wn.2d 924, 448 P.2d 320; Underwood v. Gardner, Ky.1952, 249 S.W.2d 950.

43. Virginia, North Carolina and perhaps the District of Columbia have had decisions allowing recovery. See Notes, 1954, 40 Va.L.Rev. 666; 1958, 36 N.C.L. Rev. 545. Later decisions in the first two states appear to deny it. See Anderson v. Payne, 1949, 189 Va. 712, 54 S.E.2d 82; Craighead v. Sellers, 1953, 194 Va. 920, 76 S.E.2d 212; Byrd v. Hawkins, D.C.App.1979, 404 A.2d 941 (semble). See also INA Aviation Corp. v. United States, E.D.N.Y.1979, 468 F.Supp. 695.

44. Meyers v. City of Louisiana, Mo.App.1982, 637 S.W.2d 219; Wilson v. Missouri-Kansas-Texas Railway Co., Mo.App.1980, 595 S.W.2d 41 (train severed leg of drunk asleep on tracks); Epple v. Western Auto Supply, Mo.1977, 548 S.W.2d 535, supplemented 557 S.W.2d 253. See Otis, The Humanitarian Doctrine, 1912, 46 Am.L.Rev. 381; Gaines, The Humanitarian Doctrine in Missouri, 1935, 20 St. Louis L.Rev. 113; Stryker, A Comparison—Last Clear Chance Doctrine of Kansas and Humanitarian Doctrine of Missouri, 1950, 18 Kan.Bar.A.J. 334; Note, 1964, 9 St. Louis L.Rev. 285.

Defendant's Antecedent Negligence

A further problem arises where the defendant, after discovery of the danger, does what he can to avoid the injury, but his *prior* negligence prevents his efforts from being effective—as, for example, where he tries to stop his car, but cannot do so because of defective brakes. No reason is evident in such a case for distinguishing between the antecedent negligence of the defendant and that of the plaintiff who has put himself into danger;[45] and most courts have denied recovery.[46] It was allowed in an English case,[47] upon the ground that "a last opportunity which the defendant would have had but for his own negligence is equivalent in law to one he actually had"—a line of reasoning which the court refused to apply to the plaintiff. A small number of American cases[48] reached the same result. It is difficult to justify the application of the doctrine in this situation, however, in view of the plain illogic of equating the negligence of a person in failing to have the last clear chance with the negligence of one who actually has it.

Criticism

This variety of irreconcilable rules, all purporting to be the same, and the lack of any rational fundamental theory to support them, suggest that the "last clear chance" doctrine is more a matter of dissatisfaction with the defense of contributory negligence than anything else.[49] In its application, it is not infrequent that the greater the defendant's negligence, the less likely it is that he will be held liable for the resulting harm. The driver who looks carefully and discovers the danger, and is then slow in applying the brakes, may be liable, while the one who does not look at all, or who has no effective brakes to apply, may not. Nor is it easy to defend a rule which absolves the plaintiff entirely of his own negligence, and places the whole loss upon the defendant, whose fault may be the lesser of the two. The doctrine thus appears to be a dying one, particularly in many of the jurisdictions which have adopted a system of comparative fault.[50]

 WESTLAW REFERENCES

digest("last clear chance")

Plaintiff Helpless
"last clear chance" /s helpless /s plaintiff
restatement /5 torts /5 479

Plaintiff Inattentive
"last clear chance" /p inattentive /s plaintiff
"last clear chance" /p "humanitarian doctrine"

Defendant's Antecedent Negligence
"last clear chance" /p prior antecedent /s negligen**

Criticism
critic! /s defense* /s negligen**

§ 67. Comparative Negligence

The hardship of the doctrine of contributory negligence upon the plaintiff is readily apparent. It places upon one party the en-

---

45. Suppose that A is lying drunk and unconscious in the street, and B, driving a car, sees him and endeavors to stop, but cannot do so because he has negligently failed to maintain his brakes. B runs over A's pego, and proceeds into a tree injuring his own. Are we to say that B's antecedent negligence makes him liable for A's injuries, but that A's antecedent negligence does not make him responsible for B's—or his own?

46. Andersen v. Bingham & Garfield Railway Co., 1950, 117 Utah 197, 214 P.2d 607; Johnson v. Director-General of Railroads, 1924, 81 N.H. 289, 125 A. 147; Chesapeake & Ohio Railroad Co. v. Conley's Administratrix, 1935, 261 Ky. 669, 88 S.W.2d 683; Illinois Central Railroad Co. v. Nelson, 8th Cir. 1909, 173 F. 915; Noe v. Chicago Great Western Railway Co., 1969, 130 Ill.App.2d 36, 263 N.E.2d 889, certiorari denied 402 U.S. 1009, 91 S.Ct. 2192, 29 L.Ed.2d 431 (Iowa law).

47. British Columbia Elec. R. Co. v. Loach, [1916] 1 A.C. 719. See Bohlen, The Rule in British Columbia R.R. Co. v. Loach, 1917, 66 U.Pa.L.Rev. 73.

48. Fairport, P. & E.R. Co. v. Meredith, 1933, 46 Ohio App. 457, 189 N.E. 10; Little Rock Traction & Electric Co. v. Morrison, 1901, 69 Ark. 289, 62 S.W. 1045; Dent v. Bellows Falls & Saxons River Street Railway Co., 1922, 95 Vt. 523, 116 A. 83; Neary v. Northern Pacific Railway Co., 1910, 41 Mont. 480, 110 P. 226.

49. See supra, note 12.

50. For the recent death of the doctrine in a (then) contributory negligence state, see Stewart v. Madison, Iowa 1979, 278 N.W.2d 284, noted 1980, 66 Iowa L.Rev. 187. For its death in one of a dozen or so comparative fault states, see Ratlief v. Yokum, 1981, ___ W.Va. ___, 280 S.E.2d 584, and see infra, § 67.

tire burden of a loss for which two are, by hypothesis, responsible. The negligence of the defendant has played no less a part in causing the damage; the plaintiff's deviation from the community standard of conduct may even be relatively slight, and the defendant's quite extreme. The injured person is in all probability, for the very reason of his injury, the less able of the two to bear the financial burden of his loss, and the answer of the law to all this is that the defendant goes scot free of all liability, and the plaintiff bears it all. Nor is it any answer to say that the contributory negligence rule promotes caution by making the plaintiff responsible for his own safety.[1] It is quite as reasonable to say that it encourages negligence, by giving the defendant reason to hope that he will escape the consequences.[2] Actually any such idea of deterrence is quite unrealistic. In the usual case, the negligence on both sides will consist of mere inadvertence or inattention, or an error in judgment, and it is quite unlikely that forethought of any legal liability will in fact be in the mind of either party.[3] No one supposes that an automobile driver, as he approaches an intersection, is in fact meditating upon the golden mean of the reasonable person of ordinary prudence, and the possibility of tort damages, whether for himself or for another.

There has been for many years an increasing dissatisfaction with the absolute defense of contributory negligence.[4] Courts have become more reluctant to rule that the plaintiff's conduct is negligent as a matter of law,[5] and juries are notoriously inclined to find that there has been no such negligence, or to make some more or less haphazard reduction of the plaintiff's damages in proportion to his fault. This dissatisfaction has led to a number of attempts to find some substitute method of dealing with cases where there is negligence on the part of both parties.[6]

The makeshift doctrine of the last clear chance, as discussed above,[7] was adopted to some extent in nearly all jurisdictions in an attempt to limit the harshness of the contributory negligence rule. Apart from this, both Illinois and Kansas at one time endeav-

§ 67

1. See V. Schwartz, Comparative Negligence, 1974, § 21.1, at 336; G. Schwartz, Contributory and Comparative Negligence: A Reappraisal, 1978, 87 Yale L.J. 697.

2. Lowndes, Contributory Negligence, 1934, 22 Geo. L.J. 674, 681–682.

3. See Alvis v. Ribar, 1981, 85 Ill.2d 1, 52 Ill.Dec. 23, 421 N.E.2d 886; supra, §§ 31 & 32. But cf. Epstein, Plaintiff's Conduct in Products Liability Actions: Comparative Negligence, Automatic Division and Multiple Parties, 1979, 45 J.Air L. & Com. 87.

4. "No one can appreciate more than we the hardship of depriving plaintiff of his verdict and of all right to collect damages from defendant; but the rule of contributory negligence, through no fault of ours, remains in our law and gives us no alternative other than to hold that defendant is entitled to judgment notwithstanding the verdict. It would be hard to imagine a case more illustrative of the truth that in operation the rule of comparative negligence would serve justice more faithfully than that of contributory negligence. * * * But as long as the legislature refuses to substitute the rule of comparative for that of contributory negligence, we have no option but to enforce the law in a proper case." Holt, J., in Haeg v. Sprague, Warner & Co., 1938, 202 Minn. 425, 281 N.W. 261.

5. See Rossman v. La Grega, 1971, 28 N.Y.2d 300, 321 N.Y.S.2d 588, 270 N.E.2d 313 (death case); Lazar v. Cleveland Electric Illuminating Co., 1975, 43 Ohio St. 2d 131, 331 N.E.2d 424; Scott v. Alpha Beta Co., 1980, 104 Cal.App.3d 305, 163 Cal.Rptr. 544 (fat lady's trick knee gave out); cf. Ariz. Const. art. 18, § 5.

6. On comparative negligence generally, see Schwartz, Comparative Negligence, 1974; Woods, The Negligence Case—Comparative Fault, 1978; Annot., 1977, 78 A.L.R.3d 339 (modern development of comparative negligence).

There has been an out-pouring of articles on the topic in recent years. In addition to those cited in note 34, infra, see, e.g., Wade, Comparative Negligence—Its Development in the United States and Its Present Status in Louisiana, 1980, 40 La.L.Rev. 299; Keeton, Legal Process in Comparative Negligence Cases, 1980, 17 Harv.J.Legis. 1; Symposium, 1980, 40 La.L.Rev. 289 (Malone, Wade, Johnson, Pearson, Chamallas & Plant); Fleming, Forward: Comparative Negligence Statute: An Analysis of Some Problems, 1973–74, 6 Conn.L.Rev. 207; Notes, 1981, 81 Colum.L.Rev. 1668; 1977, 51 Tul. L.Rev. 1217.

For constitutional dimensions to the issue, see Phillips, The Case for Judicial Adoption of Comparative Fault in South Carolina, 1980, 32 S.C.L.Rev. 295; Sowle & Conkle, Comparative Negligence Versus The Constitutional Guarantee of Equal Protection: A Hypothetical Judicial Decision, 1979 Duke L.J. 1083.

7. See supra, § 66.

ored to modify the rigors of contributory negligence by classifying negligence into "degrees," and providing that if the plaintiff's negligence was "ordinary" or "slight," while that of the defendant was "gross," the plaintiff might recover.[8] This approach was also unsatisfactory, since it merely shifted the entire loss from the plaintiff to the defendant, when both parties were still at fault. Moreover, it proved extremely difficult to assign any definite meaning to "gross" negligence, or to furnish the jury with any satisfactory guide as to the distinction; and the result was to fill the courts with appeals frought with confusion.[9] Both states finally abandoned the experiment,[10] and this form of "comparative negligence" is now entirely discarded at common law.[11]

Apportionment of Damages

An entirely different approach to the whole problem is to shift the focus of attention from liability to damages, and to divide the damages between the parties who are at fault. The common law courts were initially unwilling to make or permit any such division. Their reasons seldom have been given; but, in addition to judicial inertia and the survival of tradition, they appear to include the notion of the indivisibility of any single injury, the lack of any definite basis for apportionment,[12] and a marked distrust of the bias and general unreliability of the jury which would be expected to make any division. Indeed, since the apportionment of fault and damages is by nature a factual matter, virtually every case must be given to the jury, and the courts are left with very little "law" with which to look behind the jury's final verdict. These objections notwithstanding, there never has been any essential reason why such a change could not be made without a statute by the courts which made the contributory negligence rule in the first place.[13] Yet it is so sweeping an alteration of the law, affecting so many thousands of cases, that there has been an understandable reluctance by the courts, at least until quite recently, to make the change in the absence of legislative action.[14]

Many civil law jurisdictions,[15] and common law jurisdictions outside of the United States,[16] have apportioned damages in accident cases for some time, and they do not

---

8. Galena & Chicago Union Railroad Co. v. Jacobs, 1858, 20 Ill. 478; Chicago, Burlington & Quincy Railroad Co. v. Payne, 1871, 59 Ill. 534; Union Pacific Railroad Co. v. Henry, 1883, 36 Kan. 565, 14 P. 1; Wichita & Western Railway Co. v. Davis, 1887, 37 Kan. 743, 16 P. 78. See Malone, The Formative Era of Contributory Negligence, 1946, 41 Ill.L.Rev. 151. Compare Tennessee's mysterious doctrine of "remote" contributory negligence. See infra, note 49. Similar experiments in the late 1800s were tried and abandoned in Oregon, Wisconsin and Tennessee. See Prosser, Comparative Negligence, 1953, 51 Mich.L.Rev. 465, 485.

9. See supra, § 34.

10. Lake Shore & Michigan Southern Railway Co. v. Hession, 1894, 150 Ill. 546, 37 N.E. 905; City of Lanark v. Dougherty, 1894, 153 Ill. 163, 38 N.E. 892; Atchison, Topeka & Santa Fe Railway Co. v. Morgan, 1883, 31 Kan. 77, 1 P. 298.

11. The "slight"-"gross" distinction, however, has been adopted in two statutes providing for apportionment of damages. See infra, note 49. And Tennessee still appears to have its quaint doctrine of "remote" contributory negligence. See infra, note 49.

12. "The reason why, in cases of mutual concurring negligence, neither party can maintain an action against the other, is, not that the wrong of the one is set off against the wrong of the other; it is that the law cannot measure how much the damage suffered is attributable to the plaintiff's own fault. If he were allowed to recover, it might be that he would obtain from the other party compensation for his own misconduct." Heil v. Glanding, 1862, 42 Pa. 493, 499. As to avoidable consequences, see supra, § 65.

13. See Keeton, Creative Continuity in the Law of Torts, 1962, 75 Harv.L.Rev. 463; Symposium, 1968, 21 Vand.L.Rev. 889–949.

14. See, e.g., Golden v. McCurry, Ala.1980, 392 So. 2d 815; Stewart v. Madison, Iowa 1979, 278 N.W.2d 284; Steinman v. Strobel, Mo.1979, 589 S.W.2d 293; Gross v. Nashville Gas Co., Tenn.App.1980, 608 S.W.2d 860.

15. Including Switzerland, Spain, Portugal, Austria, Germany, France, China, Japan, Russia, Poland, Turkey and Quebec, Canada. See Woods, The Negligence Case—Comparative Negligence, 1978, § 1.9 at 17.

16. England has had ("pure") comparative negligence since 1945. Law Reform (Contributory Negligence) Act of 1945, 8 & 9 Geo. VI c. 28. The Act applies to Scotland and has been followed in Northern Ireland, Australia and New Zealand. Fleming, The Law of Torts, 4th ed. 1971, 219. The Canadian provinces all apply comparative negligence. See Woods, supra, note 15.

appear to have experienced any insurmountable difficulties in administration. The law of admiralty, which is derived by descent from the civil law, follows the apportionment approach even in common law countries. The original English admiralty rule divided the damages equally between the negligent parties; but in 1911 England conformed to the Brussels Maritime Convention by adopting a statute providing for a division "in proportion to the degree in which each vessel was at fault." [17] The American courts followed the equal division rule in admiralty law until 1975, when the Supreme Court overruled earlier cases [18] and adopted "pure" comparative fault.[19] The objections formerly made to this manner of apportionment do not appear to have been borne out by the subsequent experience in this area.[20]

Outside of admiralty, comparative negligence did not appear in American jurisprudence until the early twentieth century. At that time, provisions for apportionment of damages were included in several federal safety and employment statutes,[21] as well as many of the state railway [22] and labor acts.[23]

The first state to adopt a general comparative negligence act was Mississippi, which in 1910 enacted a statute applicable to all actions for personal injuries, and expanded it in 1920 to include damages to property.[24] Georgia accomplished the same result by a rather remarkable tour de force of construction by which a statute applicable only to damage inflicted by a railroad was expanded into a general act.[25] Although by the mid-1960s only seven states [26] had replaced contributory negligence with comparative fault, several states switched over in 1969, and the 1970s and early 1980s witnessed a surge of legislative [27] and judicial [28] action accomplishing the switch.[29] As of 1982, some 40 states had adopted some general form of comparative negligence.[30]

There are basically three types of comparative negligence systems: pure, modified, and slight-gross.

Pure Comparative Negligence

Probably the simplest method of allocating damages is what is commonly called

---

17. Maritime Conventions Act of 1911, 1 & 2 Geo. V, c. 57, § 1.

18. In particular, The Schooner Catharine v. Dickinson, 1854, 58 U.S. (17 How.) 170, 5 L.Ed. 233.

19. United States v. Reliable Transfer Co., 1975, 421 U.S. 397, 95 S.Ct. 1708, 44 L.Ed.2d 251, on remand, 2nd Cir., 522 F.2d 1381.

20. See, e.g., Gator Marine Service Towing, Inc. v. J. Ray McDermott & Co., 5th Cir. 1981, 651 F.2d 1096; Portacci v. Moran Towing & Transportation Co., 5th Cir. 1980, 615 F.2d 293; Curtis Bay Towing Co. v. The M/V Maryland Clipper, 4 Cir. 1979, 599 F.2d 1313.

21. E.g., Federal Employers' Liability Act, 45 U.S.C. § 53 (promulgated in 1908); Merchant Marine Act of 1920, 46 U.S.C. § 688 (Jones Act).

22. See, e.g., Louisville & Nashville Railroad Co. v. Chapman's Administratrix, 1945, 300 Ky. 835, 190 S.W.2d 542; McLean v. Andrews Hardwood Co., 1931, 200 N.C. 312, 156 S.E. 528; Boyleston v. Southern R. Co., 1947, 211 S.C. 232, 44 S.E.2d 537. See generally Wade, Crawford & Ryder, Comparative Fault in Tennessee Tort Actions: Past, Present, and Future, 1974, 41 Tenn.L.Rev. 423.

23. See, e.g., Benson v. Brady, 1960, 177 Cal.App.2d 280, 2 Cal.Rptr. 124; Tampa Electric Co. v. Bryant, 1931, 101 Fla. 204, 133 So. 887; Price v. McNeill, 1946, 237 Iowa 1120, 24 N.W.2d 464; Dierks Lumber & Coal Co. v. Noles, 1941, 201 Ark. 1088, 148 S.W.2d 650; Fitzgerald v. Oregon-Washington Railroad & Navigation Co., 1932, 141 Or. 1, 16 P.2d 27.

24. Miss.Code Ann. § 11-7-15.

25. See generally Turk, Comparative Negligence on the March, 1950, 28 Chi-Kent L.Rev. 304, 326–33.

26. Georgia, Mississippi, Nebraska, Wisconsin, South Dakota, Arkansas, and Maine.

27. See notes 31, 39, 40 & 48.

28. Beginning with Florida in 1973, eight states adopted the doctrine judicially over the next decade. Hoffman v. Jones, Fla.1973, 280 So.2d 431; Li v. Yellow Cab Co., Cal.1975, 13 Cal.3d 804, 119 Cal.Rptr. 858, 532 P.2d 1226; Kaatz v. State, Alaska 1975, 540 P.2d 1037, appeal after remand 572 P.2d 775; Placek v. City of Sterling Heights, 1979, 405 Mich. 638, 275 N.W.2d 511; Bradley v. Appalachian Power Co., W.Va.1979, 256 S.E.2d 879; Scott v. Rizzo, 1981, 96 N.M. 682, 634 P.2d 1234; Alvis v. Ribar, 1981, 85 Ill.2d 1, 52 Ill.Dec. 23, 421 N.E.2d 886, 891–92 (listing by jurisdiction each state's adopting statute or judicial decision); Goetzman v. Wichern, Iowa 1982, 327 N.W.2d 742.

29. Chronicling the development is Wade, Comparative Negligence, 1980, 40 La.L.Rev. 299.

30. As of early 1983, the ten remaining contributory negligence states were Alabama, Arizona, Delaware, Kentucky, Maryland, Missouri, North Carolina, South Carolina, Tennessee, and Virginia.

"pure" comparative negligence.[31] In this form, a plaintiff's contributory negligence does not operate to bar his recovery altogether, but does serve to reduce his damages in proportion to his fault. The system in this form is designed to compensate an injured party for all of the harm attributable to the wrongdoing of the defendant; when multiple defendants are involved, all are liable to the plaintiff for their respective shares of the loss, even though some may have been less negligent than he. Except for West Virginia,[32] all of the states which have adopted comparative negligence by judicial opinion have opted for the flexibility and relative simplicity of "pure" comparative negligence.[33] This is the form of the doctrine most widely endorsed by the commentators and as it is applied in the Uniform Comparative Fault Act.[34]

There is at least one major substantive objection to the pure system of comparative negligence,[35] and that is that by its nature it permits the major wrongdoer to recover against the minor one.[36] In cases where both plaintiff and defendant suffer injuries due to the other's negligence, a counterclaiming defendant may end up with a greater monetary recovery despite his greater negligence, simply because his injuries were more severe. Although this problem is a troublesome one, especially in cases where the plaintiff's fault is slight,[37] the result at least in theory is not entirely unfair,

---

31. In addition to the states (except for West Virginia) that judicially adopted the doctrine, see supra, note 28, the following states have adopted "pure" comparative negligence by statute: *Louisiana*, La.Civ. Code Ann. art. 2323; *Mississippi*, Miss.Code § 11–7–15; *New York*, N.Y.Civ.Prac.Law § 1411; *Rhode Island*, R.I.Gen.Laws, § 9–20–4; *Washington*, West's RCWA 4.22005.

32. Adopting the modified approach in Bradley v. Appalachian Power Co., W.Va.1979, 256 S.E.2d 879.

33. See supra, note 28.

34. See, e.g., Schwartz, Comparative Negligence, 1974, § 21.3; Keeton, Comment on *Maki v. Frelk—Comparative v. Contributory Negligence: Should the Court or Legislature Decide?*, 1968, 21 Vand.L.Rev. 906; Prosser, Comparative Negligence, 1953, 51 Mich. L.Rev. 465; Schwartz, Contributory and Comparative Negligence: A Reappraisal, 1978, 87 Yale L.J. 697; Sowle & Conkle, Comparative Negligence Versus the Constitutional Guarantee of Equal Protection: A Hypothetical Judicial Decision, 1979 Duke L.J. 1083; Fleming, Forward: Comparative Negligence At Last—By Judicial Choice, 1976, 64 Cal.L.Rev. 239.

On the uniform act, see Wade, Uniform Comparative Fault Act, 1979, 14 Forum 379; Wade, A Uniform Comparative Fault Act—What Should It Provide?, 1977, 10 U.Mich.J.Law Ref. 220.

35. A significant procedural problem may arise in the operation of the pure system, if set-off is allowed. If both plaintiff and defendant are injured, and both obtain judgments against the other, a court applying set-off will deduct the smaller from the larger verdict and enter only one judgment for the net amount. If both parties are uninsured, this approach has the same effect as entering both judgments in their full amount. But if either or both parties are insured, the insurers will receive an artificial windfall at their insureds' expense, since the recovery of the party entitled to the smaller judgment is extinguished altogether in the set-off, and the recovery of the other party is reduced by the amount of the smaller judgment. This result would be in derogation of the parties' private insurance contractual arrangements, and would deprive the insureds of their fair entitlements to compensation for their losses. "The loss would be taken from the insurance companies who were paid to carry it, and placed upon the parties who paid to have it carried." Comment on § 3 of draft Uniform Comparative Fault Act, in Wade, A Uniform Comparative Fault Act—What Should It Provide?, 1977, 10 U.Mich.J.L.Rev. 220, 230. For this reason, some states prohibit set-off, at least when one or more parties is insured. See R.I.Gen.L. § 9–20–4.1; Or.Rev.Stat. 18.490; Stuyvesant Insurance Co. v. Bournazian, Fla.1977, 342 So.2d 471; Jess v. Herrman, 1979, 26 Cal.3d 131, 161 Cal.Rptr. 87, 604 P.2d 208; cf. Uniform Comp. Fault Act § 3. See generally Pearson, Apportionment of Losses Under Comparative Fault Laws—An Analysis of the Alternatives, 1980, 40 La.L.Rev. 343, 358.

36. See Bradley v. Appalachian Power Co., W.Va. 1979, 256 S.E.2d 879; Schwartz, Comparative Negligence, 1974, § 21.3.

37. "To illustrate, a plaintiff who has sustained a moderate injury with a potential injury verdict of $20,000, and who is [only 10% at fault] may be reluctant to file suit against a defendant who is 90% at fault, but who has received severe injuries and whose case carries a potential of $800,000 in damages from a jury verdict. In this situation, even though the defendant's verdict is reduced by his 90 percent fault to $80,000, it is still far in excess of the plaintiff's potential recovery of $18,000." Bradley v. Appalachian Power Co., W.Va.1979, 256 S.E.2d 879, 883 (adopting modified in lieu of pure form). The net result of this situation is that the person only very slightly at fault, after set off, would have to pay the serious wrongdoer $62,000.

The sole proximate cause doctrine can be used to cure this problem in extreme cases. See infra, note 56.

since the plaintiff is made to pay only for those losses which his negligence has actually caused, and he is compensated for all damage to himself that can fairly be attributed to the fault of the defendant.

Modified Comparative Negligence

The most common legislative approach for apportioning fault is the modified or "50%" system, under which a plaintiff's contributory negligence does not bar recovery so long as it remains below a specified proportion of the total fault.[38] There are two varieties of the 50% comparative negligence approach. Under the "equal fault bar" approach, the plaintiff cannot recover anything if his fault is *equal to* or greater than that of the defendant; he is allowed to recover, in other words, only if his negligence is *less than* that of the defendant.[39] Under the "greater fault bar" system, the plaintiff is prevented from all recovery only if his fault *exceeds* the defendant's; he is therefore allowed to recover if his negligence is equal to or less than that of the defendant.[40] There is an understandable tendency of juries to apportion fault equally in close cases,[41] and the plaintiff in such a case will recover 50% of his damages under the "greater fault bar approach, but will take absolutely nothing under the "equal fault bar" system. This result has led to substantial criticism of the latter approach.[42] Under both systems, the plaintiff's contributory negligence operates as a complete bar, and he takes nothing,[43] if his fault exceeds the permitted threshold amount; if his negligence falls below that amount, his damages are reduced proportionately to his fault, just as if the pure system were to be applied.

A significant problem under the modified systems is determining the manner in which a plaintiff's negligence should be compared to that of multiple defendants. In some states, the plaintiff's negligence is compared with that of each individual defendant.[44] Although this approach preserves the principles of non-liability for any defendant less at fault than the plaintiff, the risk of nonrecovery for the plaintiff increases with the number of defendants involved. Thus, defendants are artificially encouraged to increase the number of nominal defendants, in the hope of avoiding liability altogether; and

---

38. See generally, Schwartz, Comparative Negligence, 1974, § 3.5 at 73–82.

39. The following states have adopted the 50% fault bar system: *Arkansas*, Ark.Stat. § 27–1765; *Colorado*, Colo.Rev.Stat. § 13–21–111; *Georgia*, Ga.Code § 105–603; *Idaho*, Idaho Code § 6–801; *Kansas*, Kan. Stat.Ann. 60–258a; *Maine*, Me.Rev.Stat.Ann. tit. 14, § 156; *North Dakota*, N.D.Cent.Code 9–10–07; *Utah*, Utah Code Ann. 78–27–37; *West Virginia*, Bradley v. Appalachian Power Co., W.Va.1979, 256 S.E.2d 879; *Wyoming*, Wyo.Stat.1977, § 1–1–109.

40. The following states have adopted the 51% fault bar system: *Connecticut*, Conn.Gen.Stat.Ann. § 52–572h; *Hawaii*, Haw.Rev.Stat. § 663.31; *Indiana*, Ind.Code § 34-4-33 (Act of 1983, eff. Jan. 1, 1985); *Massachusetts*, Mass.Gen.Laws Ann. ch. 231, § 85; *Minnesota*, Minn.Stat.Ann. § 604.01; *Montana*, Mont. Code Ann. 27–1–702; *Nevada*, Nev.Rev.Stat. 41.141; *New Hampshire*, N.H.Rev.Stat.Ann. 507a; *New Jersey*, N.J.Stat.Ann. 2A:15–5.1; *Ohio*, Ohio Rev.Code 2315.19; *Oklahoma*, Okla.Stat.Ann. tit. 23, § 13; *Oregon*, Or.Rev.Stat. 18.470; *Pennsylvania*, Pa.Stat. tit. 42, § 7102; *Texas*, Vernon's Ann.Tex.Civ.Stat. Art. 2212A; *Vermont*, Vt.Stat.Ann. tit. 12, § 1036; *Wisconsin*, Wis.Stat.Ann. 895.045.

41. See, e.g., Moyer Car Rental, Inc. v. Halliburton Co., Okla.1980, 610 P.2d 232 (equal fault; no recovery); Marier v. Memorial Rescue Serv., Inc., 1973, 296 Minn. 242, 207 N.W.2d 706 (plaintiff and both defendants each 33$\frac{1}{3}$% at fault; no recovery). See generally Pearson, Apportionment of Losses Under Comparative Fault Laws—An Analysis of the Alternatives, 1980, 40 La.L.Rev. 343, 353–54.

42. See, e.g., Campbell, Recent Developments of the Law of Negligence in Wisconsin—Part II, 1956 Wis.L. Rev. 4, 21; Keeton, Comment on *Maki v. Frelk*—Comparative v. Contributory Negligence: Should the Court or Legislature Decide?, 1968, 21 Vand.L.Rev. 906, 911; Sowle & Conkle, Comparative Negligence Versus the Constitutional Guarantee of Equal Protection: A Hypothetical Judicial Decision, 1979 Duke L.J. 1083. For the opposite view, see Gilmore, Comparative Negligence From a Viewpoint of Casualty Insurance, 1956, 10 Ark.L.Rev. 82. Some states, such as Wisconsin in 1971, have switched over from the 50% to the 51% bar system.

43. Subject to the possible application of last clear chance in a few jurisdictions. See infra, note 84.

44. See, e.g., Odenwalt v. Zaring, 1980, 102 Idaho 15, 624 P.2d 383; Van Horn v. William Blanchard Co., 1980, 88 N.J. 91, 438 A.2d 552; Board of County Commissioners v. Ridenour, Wyo.1981, 623 P.2d 1174, rehearing denied 627 P.2d 163; Wisconsin Natural Gas Co. v. Ford, 1980, 95 Wis.2d 691, 291 N.W.2d 825; Cambern v. Sioux Tools, Inc., Minn.1982, 323 N.W.2d 795.

plaintiffs are similarly discouraged from joining all potential defendants who might properly be held accountable for the loss.[45] By contrast, under the "unit rule" adopted by other states, the plaintiff's negligence is compared with the aggregate negligence of all defendants,[46] who may then through contribution adjust the loss among themselves.[47]

Slight-Gross System

Two states, Nebraska and South Dakota,[48] currently have statutes under which the plaintiff's contributory negligence is a bar to recovery unless his negligence is "slight," and the defendant's negligence by comparison is "gross."[49] The plaintiff who meets this threshold criterion still has his damages reduced by the proportion of the total negligence that is attributable to him. Because "slight" has been held to be merely a term of comparison, which varies according to the conduct of the parties,[50] the present system appears to function more satisfactorily than earlier approaches which attempted to establish absolute standards for determining whether the plaintiff's negligence was "slight."[51]

Causation

There is some debate over what is to be compared under comparative negligence, negligence or causation.[52] The problem in certain respects is one of terminology. Causation in fact is an absolute concept, which by its nature is incapable of being divided into comparative degrees—it either exists or it does not.[53] The adoption of comparative negligence, therefore, should not affect this preliminary determination.[54]

Once causation in fact has been established, however, the determination of proximate or legal cause remains a question of policy that may be susceptible to proportionate division. A court which is able to award an injured plaintiff substantially diminished damages may thus be willing to extend the traditional boundaries of proximate cause and permit a limited recovery against a remotely negligent defendant.[55] There has been too little experience and analysis to

---

45. See Schwartz, Comparative Negligence, 1974, § 3.5(C), at 79–80; Note, Comparative Negligence, 1981, 81 Colum.L.Rev. 1668, 1674.

46. See, e.g., Mountain Mobile Mix, Inc. v. Gifford, Colo.1983, 660 P.2d 883; Negley v. Massey Ferguson, Inc., 1981, 229 Kan. 465, 625 P.2d 472; Laubach v. Morgan, Okl.1978, 588 P.2d 1071; Bradley v. Appalachian Power Co., W.Va.1979, 256 S.E.2d 879. Many states have specific statutory provisions implementing the unit rule. See, e.g., Ark.Stat. § 27–1765; Haw.Rev. Stat. § 663–31; Mass.Gen.Laws Ann., ch. 231, § 85; Ohio Rev.Code § 2315.19.

47. See infra, notes 58–81.

48. Neb.Rev.Stat. § 25–1151; S.D. Compiled Laws 20–9–2.

49. Illinois and Kansas operated under a rule in the nineteenth century which used similar terms, but which did not apportion loss between the parties. See Prosser, Comparative Negligence, 1953, 51 Mich.L.Rev. 465. The only remnant of these earlier systems exists in Tennessee, where a plaintiff's contributory negligence does not bar recovery if it is "remote" in comparison to that of the defendant. See, e.g., Frady v. Smith, Tenn. 1974, 519 S.W.2d 584; Street v. Calvert, Tenn.1976, 541 S.W.2d 576. The scope of the doctrine and its relationship to comparative negligence is unclear. Wade, Crawford & Ryder, Comparative Fault in Tennessee Tort Acts: Past, Present, and Future, 1974, 41 Tenn.L. Rev. 423. It may in effect only be a "sole proximate cause" rule. See infra, notes 56 & 57.

50. See, e.g., C.C. Natvig's Sons, Inc. v. Summers, 1977, 198 Neb. 741, 255 N.W.2d 272; Nugent v. Quam, 1967, 82 S.D. 583, 152 N.W.2d 371. See also Urban v. Wait's Supermarket, Inc., S.D.1980, 294 N.W.2d 793, 796 ("comparison turns on the individual facts of each case and is not subject to any exact rule").

51. See Schwartz, Comparative Negligence, 1974, p. 67.

52. See, e.g., State v. Kaatz, Alaska 1977, 572 P.2d 775, appeal after remand 572 P.2d 775 (negligence); Amend v. Bell, 1977, 89 Wash.2d 124, 570 P.2d 138 (negligence); Cirillo v. City of Milwaukee, 1967, 34 Wis. 2d 705, 150 N.W.2d 460 (causal negligence); Prosser, Comparative Negligence 1953, 51 Mich.L.Rev. 465, 481 (negligence); Twerski, From Defect to Cause to Comparative Fault, 1977, 60 Marq.L.Rev. 297, 326 (causation). See generally Borgo, Causal Paradigms in Tort Law, 1979, 8 J.Legal Stud. 419, 448–52; Calabresi, Concerning Cause and the Law of Torts: An Essay for Harry Kalven, Jr., 1975, 43 U.Chi.L.Rev. 69, 71–73; Epstein, Defenses and Subsequent Pleas in a System of Strict Liability, 1974, 3 J.Legal Stud. 165, 179–80.

53. See supra, § 41.

54. See, e.g., Ledford v. Pittsburgh & Lake Erie Railroad Co., 1975, 236 Pa.Super. 65, 345 A.2d 218; Thomas v. Sarrett, Tex.App.1979, 505 S.W.2d 345, ref. n.r.e.

55. See, e.g., Hoyem v. Manhattan Beach City School District, 1978, 22 Cal.3d 508, 150 Cal.Rptr. 1, 585 P.2d 851.

date to assert with confidence whether the flexibility of this approach will produce more equitable results, or whether instead it should be condemned as an "unlawful" abandonment of legal principle. In any event, at either end of the fault continuum, where one party's negligence approaches one hundred percent and the other party's approaches zero, the court may rule or the jury find that the conduct of the plaintiff [56] or of the defendant [57] was the "sole proximate cause" of the plaintiff's harm, so that damages will not be awarded—or not reduced—at all.

Apportionment of Damages Among Joint Tortfeasors

Most jurisdictions which have adopted comparative negligence have retained the common law rule of joint and several liability, by which a plaintiff is entitled to recover his judgment in whole or in part from any jointly liable defendant.[58] Several states, however, have modified the common law rule and provided for several liability alone,[59] limiting an individual defendant's liability to his equitable share.[60]

The rule of joint liability favors plaintiffs, since the aggregate wealth of the defendants stands behind the judgment,[61] without regard to the proportionate responsibility of the defendants individually for the loss. The joint liability rule operates from the premise that the "blameworthy" defendant should be responsible for either joining others who may also be partially responsible for the harm or for pursuing his claim for contribution or indemnity in another forum.[62] Several liability, on the other hand, transfers to the plaintiff the principal incentive to join all potentially liable defendants. This is particularly true if the negligence of absent tortfeasors is considered in calculating the proportional fault of each participant in the occurrence. In some jurisdictions, the proportional fault of such "phantom" defendants is figured into the equation, and the percentage of responsibility of the joined defendants is reduced by that of any absent tortfeasors, against whom the plaintiff can have no judgment.[63] But the failure to consider the negligence of all tortfeasors, whether parties or not, prejudices the joined defendants who are thus required to bear a greater portion of the plaintiff's loss than is

---

56. See, e.g., Armstrong v. Industrial Electric & Equipment Service, App.1981, 97 N.M. 272, 639 P.2d 81; Korbelik v. Johnson, 1975, 193 Neb. 356, 227 N.W.2d 21 (darting child); Kroon v. Beech Aircraft Corp., 5 Cir.1980, 628 F.2d 891 (Fla. law) (airplane accident); George v. Guerette, Me.1973, 306 A.2d 138.

Indeed, a creative use of the sole proximate cause doctrine may be the most effective means of remedying the quandary of the slightly negligent plaintiff. See supra, note 37.

57. See, e.g., Mosca v. Middleton, Fla.App.1977, 342 So.2d 986.

58. See, e.g., American Motorcycle Association v. Superior Court, 1978, 20 Cal.3d 578, 146 Cal.Rptr. 182, 578 P.2d 899; Tucker v. Union Oil Co. of California, 1979, 100 Idaho 590, 603 P.2d 156; Johnston v. Billot, 1981, 109 Mich.App. 578, 311 N.W.2d 808; Maday v. Yellow Taxi Co., Minn.1981, 311 N.W.2d 849; Wisconsin Natural Gas Co. v. Ford, Bacon & Davis Construction Corp., 1980, 96 Wis.2d 314, 291 N.W.2d 825; Sieben v. Sieben, 1982, 231 Kan. 372, 646 P.2d 1036 (intentional tortfeasors). By statute in Id., Me., N.J., N.D., Utah, and Wyo. See McNichols, infra note 60, at 3 n. 11.

59. See Kan.Stat.Ann. 60-258; Ohio Rev.Code § 2315.19(A)(2); Vt.Stat.Ann. tit. 12, § 1036; Pa.Stat. tit. 42, § 7102; N.H.Rev.Stat.Ann. 507:7a; La.Civ.Code Arts. 2103, 2323.

60. See, e.g., Brown v. Keill, 1978, 224 Kan. 195, 580 P.2d 867; cf. Berry v. Empire Indemnity Insurance Co., Okl.1981, 634 P.2d 718. See generally McNichols, Judicial Elimination of Joint and Several Liability Because of Comparative Negligence—A Puzzling Choice, 1979, 32 Okla.L.Rev. 1; McNichols, The Complexities of Oklahoma's Proportionate Several Liability Doctrine of Comparative Negligence—Is Products Liability Next?, 1982, 35 Okla.L.Rev. 193; Pearson, Apportionment of Losses Under Comparative Fault Laws—An Analysis of the Alternatives, 1980, 40 La.L.Rev. 343.

61. See supra, ch. 8.

62. See generally Chamallas, Comparative Fault and Multiple Party Litigation in Louisiana, 1980, 40 La. L.Rev. 373; Comment, Comparative Negligence, Multiple Parties, and Settlements, 1977, 65 Cal.L.Rev. 1264.

63. See generally, Fleming, Forward: Comparative Negligence at Last By Judicial Choice, 1976, 64 Calif. L.Rev. 239; McNichols, Judicial Elimination of Joint and Several Liability Because of Comparative Negligence—A Puzzling Choice, 1979, 32 Okla.L.Rev. 1.

attributable to their fault. The jurisdictions have differed on how these problems should be handled.[64]

In states where joint and several liability has been retained, the issue of contribution among tortfeasors arises when one defendant pays to the plaintiff more than his equitable share of the common judgment.[65] Two basic methods have been developed for determining this equitable share: the equality rule, which apportions damages equally among the tortfeasors,[66] and comparative contribution, which apportions according to their respective fault.[67]

Certain categories of joint tortfeasors traditionally have been precluded from obtaining contribution and continue to be so even after the adoption of comparative negligence: those guilty of intentional misconduct,[68] willful and wanton negligence,[69] and those liable for punitive damages.[70] Some states preclude contribution from a defendant to whom the plaintiff gave a good faith release from liability.[71] If this approach is followed, then the remaining defendants should be entitled to a reduction in damages equal to the amount paid by,[72] or the proportional negligence of,[73] the settling defendant. Certain types of immune tortfeasors may remain exempt from contribution, for example those protected by intra-family immunities[74] and employers protected by state workers' compensation acts,[75] although the courts are split. Some courts have permitted contribution from negligent employers[76] or have reduced the plaintiff's recovery against the

64. See, e.g., American Motorcycle Association v. Superior Court, 1978, 20 Cal.3d 578, 146 Cal.Rptr. 182, 578 P.2d 899 (negligence of absent tortfeasors considered; joint and several liability); Brown v. Kiell, 1978, 224 Kan. 195, 580 P.2d 867 (negligence of all tortfeasors considered; several liability); Paul v. N.L. Industries, Okl.1980, 624 P.2d 68 (negligence of all considered; several liability); Conner v. Mertz, 1976, 274 Or. 657, 548 P.2d 975 (negligence of parties considered; joint and several liability); Albertson v. Volkswagenwerk, A.G., 1981, 230 Kan. 368, 634 P.2d 1127 (fault of all parties to occurrence considered; those not joined escape liability); Kapchuck v. Orlan, Fla.App.1976, 332 So.2d 671 (negligence considered is only that of parties joined). National Farmers Union Property & Casualty Co. v. Frackelton, Colo.1983, 662 P.2d 1056 (but joined defendants may have contribution against absent tortfeasors).

65. See generally, Berg, Comparative Contribution and Its Alternatives: The Equitable Distribution of Accident Losses, 1976, 43 Ins.Coun. 577; Fleming, Forward: Comparative Negligence at Last—By Judicial Choice, 1976, 64 Cal.L.Rev. 239; Greenstone, Spreading the Loss—Indemnity, Contribution, Comparative Negligence and Subrogation, 1977, 13 Forum 266; Griffith, Helmsley & Burr, Contribution, Indemnity, Settlements & Releases, What the Pennsylvania Comparative Negligence Statute Did Not Say, 1979, 24 Vill.L.Rev. 494; Annot., 1973, 53 A.L.R.3d 184 (contribution and indemnity).

66. See, e.g., Lincenberg v. Issen, Fla.1975, 318 So. 2d 386; Sanchez v. City of Espanola, App.1980, 94 N.M. 993, 615 P.2d 993. See also Uniform Contribution Among Tortfeasors Act, 1955, § 2(a).

67. See, e.g., Tucker v. Union Oil Co. of California, 1979, 100 Idaho 590, 603 P.2d 156; N.D.Cent.Code § 9–10–07; Vernon's Ann.Tex.Civ.Stat. art. 2212a, § 2. See also Uniform Comparative Fault Act 1979, § 2(C).

68. See, e.g., West's Ann.Cal.Civ.Proc.Code § 875(d). And the intentional joint tortfeasor may be liable to the negligent tortfeasors for "equitable indemnity." See Gardner v. Murphy, 1975, 54 Cal.App.3d 164, 126 Cal.Rptr. 302. See generally Note, Comparative Fault and Intentional Torts, 1978, 12 Loyola (LA) U.L.Rev. 179.

69. See, e.g., West's Fla.Stat.Ann. § 768.31(2)(c). But see Note, 1978, 12 Loyola (L.A.) U.L.Rev. 179, 199.

70. See State v. Cook, Mo.1966, 400 S.W.2d 39.

71. E.G., Bartels v. City of Williston, N.D.1979, 276 N.W.2d 113; Conkright v. Ballantyne of Omaha, Inc., D.Mich.1980, 496 F.Supp. 147.

72. E.g., Yost v. State, Utah 1981, 640 P.2d 1044.

73. See, e.g., Rogers v. Spady, 1977, 147 N.J.Super. 274, 371 A.2d 285; Bartels v. City of Williston, N.D. 1979, 276 N.W.2d 113. See also Uniform Comparative Fault Act § 6.

74. See e.g., Short Line, Inc. v. Perez, Del.1968, 238 A.2d 341; Welter v. Curry, Ark.1976, 539 S.W.2d 264. Contra, Shor v. Paoli, Fla.1977, 353 So.2d 825; Perchell v. District of Columbia, D.C.Cir.1971, 444 F.2d 997.

75. E.g., Jarrett v. Duncan Thecker Associates, 1980, 175 N.J.Super. 109, 417 A.2d 1064; Mulder v. Acme-Cleveland Corp., 1980, 95 Wis.2d 173, 290 N.W.2d 276. See generally 2A Larson, Workmen's Compensation Law, 1976, § 76.21.

76. See, e.g., Skinner v. Reed-Prentice Division Package Machinery Co., 1978, 70 Ill.2d 1, 15 Ill.Dec. 829, 374 N.E.2d 437, certiorari denied 436 U.S. 946, 98 S.Ct. 2849, 56 L.Ed.2d 787 (contribution to full extent of equitable share); Lambertson v. Cincinnati Corp., 1977, 312 Minn. 114, 257 N.W.2d 679 (contribution up to amount of benefits). Compare Dole v. Dow Chemical Co., 1972, 30 N.Y.2d 143, 331 N.Y.S.2d 382, 282 N.E.2d 288 (comparative "indemnity"); infra, note 81.

other party by the amount of workers' compensation benefits received.[77]

An issue closely related to contribution is that of common law indemnity, which traditionally has served to shift the entire burden of damages from the defendant who suffered the judgment to another who is under an express or implied obligation to assume responsibility for the loss.[78] Where the party seeking indemnity is in no way personally at fault, but is liable only on some derivative basis, comparative negligence should not affect the existing law of indemnity.[79] Yet where such a defendant was himself personally at fault in some respect, as often is the case when a "passively" negligent defendant seeks indemnity from an "actively" negligent party,[80] some recent decisions have applied the fault and damages apportionment principles of comparative negligence to the indemnity context, thereby adopting a form of "equitable" or "comparative" indemnity.[81]

Effect on Other Tort Doctrines

The doctrine of last clear chance, which originated as a mechanism for avoiding the harsh effects of contributory negligence, has been abolished in about a dozen jurisdictions since the adoption of comparative fault.[82] Courts in these states have reasoned that the doctrine fails to serve any further purpose and indeed conflicts with the basic principles of comparative negligence.[83] On the other hand, three or four comparative fault jurisdictions, emphasizing the doctrine's foundation in proximate causation, have held that the doctrine is still viable.[84]

The defense of assumption of risk has been merged into the comparative negligence scheme in some jurisdictions, but not in others, as discussed below.[85]

Contributory negligence never has been considered a good defense to an intentional tort such as a battery,[86] and it would likewise appear contrary to sound policy to reduce a plaintiff's damages under com-

---

77. See, e.g., Aceves v. Regal Pale Brewing Co., 1979, 24 Cal.3d 502, 156 Cal.Rptr. 41, 595 P.2d 619; Tucker v. Union Oil Co. of California, 1979, 100 Idaho 590, 603 P.2d 156. At least in the products liability context, this appears to be the best solution. See Recommendation IV, ABA Special Comm. to Study Prod. Liab., Rep. to House of Delegates, Feb. 1983; Twerski, National Product Liability Legislation: In Search for the Best of All Possible Worlds, 1982, 18 Idaho L.Rev. 411, 463. See generally Lynch, The Clash Between Strict Products Liability Doctrine and The Workers' Compensation Exclusivity Rule: The Negligent Employer and The Third Party Manufacturer, 1983 Ins. Coun.J. 35; Mitchell, Products Liability, Workmen's Compensation, and The Industrial Accident, 1976, 14 Duq.L.Rev. 349; Weisgall, Product Liability in the Workplace: The Effect of Workers' Compensation on the Rights and Liabilities of Third Parties, 1977 Wis.L. Rev. 1035; Note, 1977, 50 So.Cal.L.Rev. 1029.

78. See supra, § 51. See generally Gordon & Crowley, Indemnity Issues in Settlement of Multiparty Actions in Comparative Negligence Jurisdictions, 1981, 48 Ins.Coun. 457; Annot., 1973, 53 A.L.R.3d 184.

79. See generally Schwartz, Comparative Negligence, 1974, § 16.9. But see Southern Railway Co. v. Brunswick Pulp & Paper Co., S.D.Ga.1974, 376 F.Supp. 96.

80. See supra, § 51.

81. See, e.g., Missouri Pacific Railway Co. v. Whitehead & Kales Co., Mo.1978, 566 S.W.2d 466, noted 1979, 48 U.Mo.K.C.L.Rev. 54; Skinner v. Reed-Prentice Division Package Machinery Co., 1977, 70 Ill.2d 1, 15 Ill.Dec. 829, 374 N.E.2d 437, certiorari denied 436 U.S. 946, 98 S.Ct. 2849, 56 L.Ed.2d 787; Dole v. Dow Chemical Co., 1972, 30 N.Y.2d 143, 331 N.Y.S.2d 382, 282 N.E.2d 288; Tolbert v. Gerber Industries, Inc., Minn. 1977, 255 N.W.2d 362; Safeway Stores, Inc. v. Nest-Kart, 1978, 21 Cal.3d 322, 146 Cal.Rtpr. 550, 579 P.2d 441.

82. See, e.g., Kaatz v. State, Alaska 1975, 540 P.2d 1037, appeal after remand 572 P.2d 775; Li v. Yellow Cab Co., 1975, 13 Cal.3d 804, 119 Cal.Rptr. 858, 532 P.2d 1226; Danculovich v. Brown, Wyo.1979, 593 P.2d 187; Ratlief v. Yokum, W.Va.1981, 280 S.E.2d 584; French v. Grigsby, Tex.1978, 571 S.W.2d 867; Davies v. Butler, Nev.1979, 602 P.2d 605; Alvis v. Ribar, 1981, 85 Ill.2d 1, 52 Ill.Dec. 23, 421 N.E.2d 886. Also at least in Colo., Fla., Me., Conn. (statute) and Or. (statute).

83. See, e.g., Li v. Yellow Cab Co., 1975, 13 Cal.3d 804, 119 Cal.Rptr. 858, 532 P.2d 1226; Danculovich v. Brown, Wyo.1979, 593 P.2d 187.

84. See Conner v. Mangum, 1974, 132 Ga.App. 100, 207 S.E.2d 604; cf. Macon v. Seaward Construction Co., 1 Cir. 1977, 555 F.2d 1 (N.H. law). Also in S.D. See generally Notes, 1975, 28 Okla.L.Rev. 444; 1974, 6 Tex.Tech.L.Rev. 131.

85. See infra, § 68.

86. See supra, § 65.

parative fault for his "negligence" in encountering the defendant's deliberately inflicted harm.[87] Where the defendant's conduct is found to have been willful, wanton, reckless, or grossly negligent, the traditional rule was also to preclude the defense of contributory negligence.[88] In these cases of aggravated misconduct short of intentionally harmful behavior, however, courts in comparative fault jurisdictions where the statute is not clear have divided, some holding that the plaintiff's contributory negligence should reduce his recovery,[89] others holding that he should recover his total loss.[90]

The effect of comparative negligence on the law of strict liability in tort [91] has also differed among jurisdictions.[92] A few courts have held the doctrine to be entirely inapplicable to actions for strict products liability, reasoning that to compare a user's fault with the maker's no-fault responsibility is to mix apples with oranges, and that to reduce the user's damages would undermine the strict products liability goal of encouraging manufacturers to anticipate and protect against consumer negligence.[93] Most courts, however, have brushed aside such analytical and policy arguments, and have applied the comparative negligence apportionment principles to such actions.[94]

Finally, a few courts have even extended the damages apportionment principle to the "defense" of product misuse,[95] while other courts have rejected this approach and con-

87. Munoz v. Olin, 1977, 24 Cal.3d 629, 142 Cal. Rptr. 667 vacated 24 Cal.3d 629, 156 Cal.Rptr. 727, 596 P.2d 1143; Carman v. Heber, 1979, 43 Colo.App. 5, 601 P.2d 646; Melendres v. Soales, 1981, 105 Mich.App. 73, 306 N.W.2d 399; Stephan v. Lynch, 1978, 136 Vt. 226, 388 A.2d 376. But see Lomonte v. A & P Food Stores, 1981, 107 Misc.2d 88, 438 N.Y.S.2d 54; Comer v. Gregory, Miss.1978, 365 So.2d 1212 (assault and battery).

88. See supra, § 65.

89. See, e.g., Amoco Pipeline Co. v. Montgomery, W.D.Okl.1980, 487 F.Supp. 1268; Bielski v. Schulze, 1962, 16 Wis.2d 1, 114 N.W.2d 105; Zavala v. Regents of the University of California, 1981, 125 Cal.App.3d 646, 178 Cal.Rptr. 185 (intoxicated plaintiff still entitled to partial recovery, even though 80% at fault and guilty of willful misconduct himself); cf. Davies v. Butler, Nev.1979, 602 P.2d 605.

90. Ryan v. Foster & Marshall, Inc., 9 Cir. 1977, 556 F.2d 460 (construing Or.Rev.Stat. § 18.470); Vargus v. Pitman Mfg. Co., D.Pa.1981, 510 F.Supp. 116, affirmed 673 F.2d 1301, rehearing denied 675 F.2d 73 (construing Pa.C.Stat.Ann. § 7102(a)); Danculovich v. Brown, Wyo.1979, 593 P.2d 187; cf. Davies v. Butler, Nev. 1979, 602 P.2d 605. See generally Owen, The Highly Blameworthy Manufacturer: Implications on Rules of Liability and Defense in Products Liability Actions, 1977, 10 Ind.L.Rev. 769; Annot., 1981, 10 A.L.R. 4th 947.

91. See infra, chapters 13 & 14.

92. See generally Twerski, The Use and Abuse of Comparative Negligence in Products Liability, 1977, 10 Ind.L.Rev. 797; Fischer, Products Liability—Applicability of Comparative Negligence, 1978, 43 Mo.L.Rev. 431; Plant, Comparative Negligence and Strict Tort Liability, 1980, 40 La.L.Rev. 403; Walkowiak, Reconsidering Plaintiff's Fault in Products Liability Litigation: The Proposed Conscious Design Choice Exceptions, 1980, 33 Vand.L.Rev. 651; Thode, Some Thoughts on the Use of Comparisons in Product Liability Cases, 1981 Utah L.Rev. 3; Wade, Products Liability and Plaintiff's Fault: The Uniform Comparative Fault Act, 1978, 29 Mercer L.Rev. 373; Annot., 1981, 9 A.L.R. 4th 633.

93. See, e.g., Lewis v. Timco, Inc., 5th Cir. 1983, 697 F.2d 1252 ("simple negligence, ineptness or inadvertence"; discussing cases contra); Melia v. Ford Motor Co., 8 Cir. 1976, 534 F.2d 795; Kinard v. Coats Co. Inc., 1976, 37 Colo.App. 555, 553 P.2d 835; Kirkland v. General Motors Corp., Okla.1974, 521 P.2d 1353; Seay v. Chrysler Corp., 1980, 93 Wash.2d 319, 609 P.2d 1382. See also Daly v. General Motors Corp., 1978, 20 Cal.3d 725, 144 Cal.Rptr. 380, 403, 575 P.2d 1162, 1185 (Mosk, J., dissenting).

94. See, e.g., Caterpillar Tractor Co. v. Beck, Alaska 1979, 593 P.2d 871; Daly v. General Motors Corp., 1978, 20 Cal.3d 725, 144 Cal.Rptr. 380, 575 P.2d 1162; Albertson v. Volkswagenwerk, A.G., 1981, 230 Kan. 368, 634 P.2d 1127; Jack Frost, Inc. v. Engineered Building Components Co., Inc., Minn.1981, 304 N.W.2d 346; Keneko v. Hilo Coast Processing, Haw.1982, 654 P.2d 343, 352 ("We find that fairness and equity are more important than conceptual and semantic consistency * * * ."; Sandford v. Chevrolet Division of General Motors, 1982, 292 Or. 590, 642 P.2d 624; Suter v. San Angelo Foundry & Machine Co., 1979, 81 N.J. 150, 406 A.2d 140.

In the absence of legislative resolution, the courts have also split on the applicability of comparative negligence to claims for breach of implied warranty. See infra, note 99.

95. See, e.g., Harville v. Anchor-Wate Co., 5 Cir. 1981, 663 F.2d 598; Mulherin v. Ingersoll-Rand Co., Utah 1981, 628 P.2d 1301; General Motors v. Hopkins, Tex.1977, 548 S.W.2d 344, examined in Twerski, The Many Faces of Misuse: An Inquiry Into the Emerging Doctrine of Comparative Causation, 1978, 29 Mercer L.Rev. 403. See Fischer, Products Liability—Applicability of Comparative Negligence to Misuse and Assumption of Risk, 1978, 43 Mo.L.Rev. 643.

tinued to consider unforeseeable misuse as a complete bar to recovery, reasoning logically that the defendant in such cases has breached no duty to the plaintiff.[96]

Future of Comparative Negligence

The principle of comparative fault apportionment of damages is veritably sweeping the land, gobbling up much traditional tort doctrine as it goes. Courts need to be cautious not to become caught up by the sheer momentum of the movement, and with the facile simplicity of the doctrine,[97] but instead should apply deliberate thought to each new call for its further extension. How much of the classic principles of accident law will remain in the long run, after the forward march[98] of comparative negligence finally comes to rest, is far beyond prediction at the present time. Yet the doctrine has already markedly changed the face of accident law in this nation virtually overnight, and one should assume that much in the way of further change is still to come.[99]

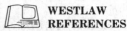
WESTLAW REFERENCES

di comparative negligence
topic("comparative negligence")

Apportionment of Damages
digest("comparative negligence" /p apportion! /p damages)

Pure Comparative Negligence
"comparative negligence" /5 pure "uniform comparative fault act"

Modified Comparative Negligence
"comparative negligence" /p 50% "comparative negligence" /5 modified
"comparative negligence" /p 51% 49%

Slight-Gross System
court(ne) & 25–1151
court(sd) & 20-9-2
digest(gross /s slight /s negligen**)

Causation
"comparative negligence" /s causation

---

96. See, e.g., Murray v. Fairbanks Morse, 3 Cir. 1979, 610 F.2d 149, 160.

97. See, e.g., Pearson, Apportionment of Losses Under Comparative Fault Laws—An Analysis of the Alternatives, 1980, 40 La.L.Rev. 343, 372 ("what is a relatively simple idea involves a great deal of complexity in translating that concept into a concrete plan for loss apportionment"); Chamallas, Comparative Fault and Multiple Party Litigation in Louisiana: A Sampling of the Problems, 1980, 40 La.L.Rev. 373 ("deceptively simple").

98. Well described as such in Turk, Comparative Negligence on the March (pts. 1-2), 1950, 28 Chi.-Kent. L.Rev. 189, 304. See also Schwartz, Comparative Negligence, 1974, p. 2 (Supp.1981), noting that the march "is now becoming a stampede."

99. A sampling of the decisions involving the effect of comparative fault on other tort doctrines shows the potential expansiveness of the doctrine. Compare Shahrokhfar v. State Farm Mutual Auto Insurance Co., Mont.1981, 634 P.2d 653 (punitive damages—comparative negligence inapplicable), with Pedernales Electric Cooperative, Inc. v. Schulz, Tex.Civ.App.1979, 583 S.W.2d 882, refused n.r.e. (punitive damages—applicable). See also Bradfield v. Trans-World Airlines, 1979, 88 Cal.App.3d 681, 152 Cal.Rptr. 172 (Wassaw Convention—applicable); Thomas v. Board of Township Trustees of Salem Township, Sedgwick County, 1978, 224 Kan. 539, 582 P.2d 271 (highway defect statute—applicable); Renz v. Penn Central Corp., 1981, 87 N.J. 437, 435 A.2d 540 (railroad immunity statute—applicable); Arredondo v. Duckwall Stores, Inc., 1980, 227 Kan. 842, 610 P.2d 1107 (statute prohibiting sale of explosives to children—applicable); Johnson v. Tilden, 1977, 278 Or. 11, 562 P.2d 1188 (auto guest statute—applicable); Evans v. Nab Construction Co., 1981, 80 A.D.2d 841, 436 N.Y.S.2d 774 (labor law—inapplicable); Sherman v. Platte County, Wyo.1982, 642 P.2d 787, noted 1983, 18 Land & Water L.Rev. 373 (obvious danger no-duty rule—inapplicable); Britt v. Allen County Community Jr. College, 1982, 230 Kan. 502, 638 P.2d 914 (land entrant status rules—inapplicable); Akermanis v. Sea-Land Service, Inc., 2 Cir. 1982, 688 F.2d 898 (apportionment of responsibility for jury; trial judge may not adjust same by remittitur); Bailey by Bailey v. Morris, Minn.1982, 323 N.W.2d 785 (strict liability statutes—inapplicable); Rex Utilities, Inc. v. Gaddy, Fla.App.1982, 413 So.2d 1232 (contributory negligence per se—applicable); Otto v. Leany, Utah 1981, 635 P.2d 410 (comparative negligence of minor driver not imputed to parents' claim for damages to car); Hannabass v. Florida Home Insurance Co., Fla.App.1981, 412 So.2d 376 (child's negligence imputed to parents—applicable). Compare also Sebring v. Colver, Alaska 1982, 649 P.2d 932 (implied warranty—good defense), and Karl v. Bryant Air Conditioning Co., 1982, 416 Mich. 558, 331 N.W.2d 456 (same), with Duff v. Bonner Building Supply, Inc., App.1982, 103 Idaho 432, 649 P.2d 391 (implied warranty—no defense).

For the effect of comparative negligence on the seat belt "defense," see, e.g., Taplin v. Clark, 1981, 6 Kan.App.2d 66, 626 P.2d 1198 (no reduction, discussing cases contra); Annot., 1979, 95 A.L.R.3d 239. On res ipsa loquitur, see, e.g., Montgomery Elevator Co. v. Gordon, Colo.1980, 619 P.2d 66 (freedom from contributory negligence element of plaintiff's res ipsa case abandoned); Emerick v. Raleigh Hills Hosp.-Newport Beach, 1982, 133 Cal.App.3d 575, 184 Cal.Rptr. 92 (no bar to recovery); Note, 1982, 53 U.Colo.L.Rev. 777; supra, page 254.

Apportionment of Damages Among Joint Tortfeasors
digest("comparative negligence" /p apportion! /s damages liability)

Effect on Other Tort Doctrines
"comparative negligence" /s defense /s "contributory negligence"
"comparative negligence" /s effect /s defense*

Future of Comparative Negligence
"comparative negligence" /s public social /s policy consideration % topic(insurance)

§ 68. Assumption of Risk

Like contributory negligence, assumption of risk developed relatively late in the development of the common law.[1]

It has been a subject of much controversy,[2] and has been surrounded by much confusion, because "assumption of risk" has been used by the courts in several different senses,[3] which traditionally have been lumped together under the one name, often without realizing that any differences exist.[4] There are even courts which have limited the use of the term "assumption of risk" to cases in which the parties stand in the relation of master and servant,[5] or at least some other contractual relation; but they have been compelled to invent other names for other cases, such as "incurred risk,"[6] or "volenti non fit injuria."[7] This appears to be largely a distinction without a difference; and most courts have made general use of the one term.

It is helpful to consider the cases in which assumption of risk has been recognized from three different perspectives, as follows:

Express Consent Perspective. In its most basic sense, assumption of risk means that the plaintiff, in advance, has given his *express* consent to relieve the defendant of an obligation of conduct toward him, and to take his chances of injury from a known risk arising from what the defendant is to do or leave undone.[8] The situation is then the same as where the plaintiff consents to the infliction of what would otherwise be an intentional tort,[9] except that the consent is to

§ 68

1. Cruden v. Fentham, 1799, 2 Esp. 685, 170 Eng. Rep. 496, is perhaps the first clearly distinguishable case. The defense received its greatest impetus from Priestley v. Fowler, 1837, 3 M. & W. 1, 150 Eng.Rep. 1030, a case of master and servant. See generally Warren, Volenti Non Fit Injuria in Actions of Negligence, 1895, 8 Harv.L.Rev. 457, 462.

2. See Bohlen, Voluntary Assumption of Risk, 1906, 20 Harv.L.Rev. 14, 91; Rice, The Automobile Guest and the Rationale of Assumption of Risk, 1943, 27 Minn.L.Rev. 33; Keeton, Assumption of Risk and the Landowner, 1942, 20 Tex.L.Rev. 562; Keeton, Personal Injuries Resulting from Open and Obvious Conditions, 1952, 100 U.Pa.L.Rev. 629; James, Assumption of Risk, 1952, 61 Yale L.J. 141; Wade, The Place of Assumption of Risk in the Law of Negligence, 1961, 22 La.L.Rev. 5; Mansfield, Informed Choice in the Law of Torts, 1961, 22 La.L.Rev. 17; Green, Assumed Risk as a Defense, 1961, 22 La.L.Rev. 77; James, Assumption of Risk: Unhappy Reincarnation, 1968, 78 Yale L.J. 185; Gaetanos, Essay—Assumption of Risk: Casuistry in the Law of Negligence, 1981, 83 W.Va.L.Rev. 471; Note, 1982, 95 Harv.L.Rev. 872 (strict products liability).

3. See Keeton, Assumption of Risk in Products Liability Cases, 1961, 22 La.L.Rev. 122, classifying assumption of risk into six different categories: express, subjectively consensual, objectively consensual, by consent to conduct or condition, associational, and imposed.

4. But the distinctions are increasingly becoming appreciated. E.g., Moore v. Burton Lumber & Hardware Co., Utah 1981, 631 P.2d 865; Blackburn v. Dorta, Fla.1977, 348 So.2d 287, on remand 350 So.2d 25; Blair v. Mt. Hood Meadows Development Corp., 1981, 291 Or. 293, 630 P.2d 827, rehearing denied and opinion modified 291 Or. 703, 634 P.2d 241.

5. "Assumption of risk is a defense which finds its roots in the employee/employer relationship. Its application to tortious conduct outside that relationship should be narrowly confined." Shahrokhfar v. State Farm Mutual Automobile Insurance Co., 1981, ___ Mont. ___, 634 P.2d 653; Ziegert v. South Chicago Community Hospital, 1981, 99 Ill.App.3d 83, 54 Ill.Dec. 585, 425 N.E.2d 450, 463 (doctrine generally "confined to cases where the parties have a contractual or employment relationship").

6. See Antcliff v. Datzman, 1982, ___ Ind.App. ___, 436 N.E.2d 114.

7. See Walsh v. West Coast Mines, 1948, 31 Wn.2d 396, 197 P.2d 233; Conrad v. Springfield Consolidated Railway Co., 1909, 240 Ill. 12, 88 N.E. 180; Emhardt v. Perry Stadium, 1943, 113 Ind.App. 197, 46 N.E.2d 704; Fletcher v. Kemp, Mo.1959, 327 S.W.2d 178; Cummins v. Halliburton Oil Well Cementing Co., Tex.Civ.App. 1958, 319 S.W.2d 379.

8. This type of assumption of risk should therefore survive the advent of comparative fault. See infra, p. 486.

9. See supra, § 18.

run the risk of unintended injury, to take a chance, rather than to accept the greater certainty of intended harm. The result is that the defendant is relieved of legal duty to the plaintiff; and being under no duty, he cannot be charged with negligence.

Duty Perspective. A second situation is where the plaintiff voluntarily enters into some relation with the defendant, with knowledge that the defendant will not protect him against one or more future risks that may arise from the relation. He may then be regarded as tacitly or *impliedly* consenting to the negligence, and agreeing to take his own chances. Thus, he may accept employment, knowing that he is expected to work with a dangerous horse; or a ride in a car with knowledge that the brakes are defective, or the driver incompetent; or he may enter a baseball park, sit in an unscreened seat, and so consent that the players may proceed with the game without taking any precautions to protect him from being hit by the ball. Again, the legal result is that the defendant is simply relieved of the duty which would otherwise exist.[10]

Misconduct Defense Perspective. In the third type of situation, the plaintiff is aware of a risk that has already been created by the negligence of the defendant, yet chooses voluntarily to proceed to encounter it—as where he has been supplied with a chattel which he knows to be unsafe, yet proceeds to use it anyway; or where he proceeds to walk over debris on the sidewalk carelessly strewn and left there by a construction contractor. If these are voluntary choices, the plaintiff may be found to have accepted the situation, and consented to relieve the defendant of his duty.

In all three of these situations the plaintiff may be acting quite reasonably, and not be at all negligent in taking the chance, because the advantages of his conduct outweigh the risk.[11] His decision may be the right one, and he may even act with unusual caution because he knows the danger he is to meet.[12] On the other hand, and particularly in the second and third situations, the plaintiff's conduct in encountering a known risk may in itself be unreasonable, because the danger is out of all proportion to the advantage which he is seeking to obtain—as where, with other transportation available, he elects to ride with a drunken automobile driver, or dashes into a burning building to save his hat. In cases such as these, his conduct is a form of contributory negligence, in which the negligence consists in making the wrong choice and voluntarily encountering a known unreasonable risk. In such cases it is clear that the defenses of assumption of risk and contributory negligence overlap, and are as intersecting circles, with a considerable area in common, where both exist and neither excludes the possibility of the other.

In this area of intersection, the traditional position of the courts has been that the defendant may at his election avail himself of either defense, or of both.[13] Since either traditionally was sufficient to bar the action, it usually made no practical difference what the defense was called, and it is not surprising that the two have not been clearly distinguished, and are quite commonly confused.[14]

---

10. This form of the doctrine, generally referred to as "primary" assumption of risk, should also survive comparative fault. See infra, p. 497.

11. See infra, note 69.

12. Miner v. Connecticut River Railroad Co., 1891, 153 Mass. 398, 26 N.E. 994; Hunn v. Windsor Hotel Co., 1937, 119 W.Va. 215, 193 S.E. 57. The unusual care exercised may itself be evidence that the plaintiff knew the risk and assumed it. Hotchkin v. Erdrich, 1906, 214 Pa. 460, 63 A. 1035.

13. See Bugh v. Webb, 1959, 231 Ark. 27, 328 S.W.2d 379; Schmidt v. Fontaine Ferry Enterprises, Ky.1958, 319 S.W.2d 468; Evans v. Johns Hopkins University, 1961, 224 Md. 234, 167 A.2d 591; Centrello v. Basky, 1955, 164 Ohio St. 41, 128 N.E.2d 80; cf. Ambrosio v. Price, D.Neb.1979, 495 F.Supp. 381.

14. See James, Assumption of Risk, 1952, 61 Yale L.J. 141; Petrone v. Margolis, 1952, 20 N.J.Super. 180, 89 A.2d 476.

The distinction in some states is now very important, where assumption of risk may continue as a total bar, while contributory negligence may only reduce the plaintiff's damages. See Schwartz, Comparative Negligence, 1974, § 9.4 (Supp.1981, at 80).

Where they have been distinguished, the traditional basis has been that assumption of risk is a matter of knowledge of the danger and voluntary acquiescence in it, while contributory negligence is a matter of some fault or departure from the standard of conduct of the reasonable person, however unaware, unwilling, or even protesting the plaintiff may be.[15] Obviously the two may coexist when the plaintiff makes an unreasonable choice to incur the risk; but either may exist without the other.

Express Agreement

It is quite possible for the parties expressly to agree in advance that the defendant is under no obligation of care for the benefit of the plaintiff, and shall not be liable for the consequences of conduct which would otherwise be negligent.[16] There is in the ordinary case no public policy which prevents the parties from contracting as they see fit, as to whether the plaintiff will undertake the responsibility of looking out for himself.[17]

Thus, one who accepts a gratuitous pass on a railway train,[18] or enters into a lease,[19] or rents a horse,[20] or employs an agent,[21] or enters into some other relation involving free and open bargaining between the parties, may agree that there shall be no obligation to take precautions, and hence no liability for negligence.

The courts have refused to uphold such agreements, however, where one party is at such obvious disadvantage in bargaining power that the effect of the contract is to put him at the mercy of the other's negligence. Thus it is generally held that a contract exempting an employer from all liability for negligence toward his employees is void as against public policy.[22] The same is true as to the efforts of public utilities to escape liability for negligence in the performance of their duty of public service.[23] A carrier who transports goods[24] or passengers for hire,[25] or a telegraph company transmitting a message,[26] may not contract away its

---

15. See infra, note 69.

16. See Arensberg, Limitation by Bailees and by Landlords of Liability for Negligent Acts, 1947, 51 Dick.L.Rev. 36; R. Keeton, Assumption of Risk in Products Liability Cases, 1961, 22 La.L.Rev. 122, 133–38; Second Restatement of Torts, § 496B; Contracts, § 337.

17. Winterstein v. Wilcom, 1972, 16 Md.App. 130, 293 A.2d 821; Second Restatement of Torts, § 496B, Comment *b*.

18. Gonzales v. Baltimore & Ohio Railroad Co., 4th Cir. 1963, 318 F.2d 294, certiorari denied 375 U.S. 911, 85 S.Ct. 208, 11 L.Ed.2d 151; Atlantic Greyhound Lines v. Skinner, 1939, 172 Va. 428, 2 S.E.2d 441; Louisville & Nashville Railroad Co. v. George, 1939, 279 Ky. 24, 129 S.W.2d 986; Thompson v. National Railroad Passenger Corp., 6th Cir. 1980, 621 F.2d 814, certiorari denied 449 U.S. 1035, 101 S.Ct. 611, 66 L.Ed.2d 497.

19. This is the classic view. See, e.g., O'Callaghan v. Waller & Beckwith Realty Co., 1958, 15 Ill.2d 436, 155 N.E.2d 545; Hartford Fire Insurance Co. v. Chicago, Milwaukee & St. Paul Railway Co., 1899, 175 U.S. 91, 20 S.Ct. 33, 44 L.Ed. 84. This view has changed for residential leases in many states. See supra, § 63 at note 36.

20. Moss v. Fortune, 1960, 207 Tenn. 426, 340 S.W.2d 902.

21. Griffiths v. Henry Broderick, Inc., 1947, 27 Wn. 2d 901, 182 P.2d 18.

22. Johnston v. Fargo, 1906, 184 N.Y. 379, 77 N.E. 388; Pittsburgh, Cincinnati Chicago & St. Louis Railway Co. v. Kinney, 1916, 95 Ohio St. 64, 115 N.E. 505; Hughes v. Warman Steel Casting Co., 1917, 174 Cal. 556, 163 P. 885; Second Restatement of Torts, § 496B, Comment *f*.

23. Restatement of Contracts, § 575(1); Collins v. Virginia Power & Electric Co., 1933, 204 N.C. 320, 168 S.E. 500; Oklahoma Natural Gas Co. v. Appel, Okla. 1954, 266 P.2d 442; Reeder v. Western Gas & Power Co., 1953, 42 Wn.2d 542, 256 P.2d 825.

24. See, e.g, Caribbean Produce Exchange, Inc. v. Sea Land Service, Inc., D.P.R.1976, 415 F.Supp. 88 (but *private* carrier may so contract); First National Bank of Girard v. Bankers Dispatch Corp., 1977, 221 Kan. 528, 562 P.2d 32; Varian Associates v. Compagnie Generale Transatlantique, 1976, 85 Cal.App.3d 369, 149 Cal.Rptr. 534. But the rule prohibiting a carrier from contracting away its liability for *negligence* may not apply to its strict liability for non-negligent loss. North American Phillips Corp. v. Emery Air Freight Corp., 2d Cir. 1978, 579 F.2d 229; Nolan v. Auto Transporters, 1979, 226 Kan. 176, 597 P.2d 614.

25. See, e.g., Richard A. Berjian, D.O., Inc. v. Ohio Bell Telephone Co., 1978, 54 Ohio St.2d 147, 375 N.E.2d 410.

26. Western Union Telegraph Co. v. James, 1896, 162 U.S. 650, 16 S.Ct. 934, 40 L.Ed. 1105; Vermilye v. Western Union Telegraph Co., 1911, 207 Mass. 401, 93 N.E. 635; Dickerson v. Western Union Telegraph Co., 1917, 114 Miss. 115, 74 So. 779. But as to interstate messages, the Interstate Commerce Act, 49 U.S.C.A. § 1 et seq., permits a limitation of liability as to unrepeated messages. Postal Telegraph-Cable Co. v. War-

public responsibility, and this is true although the agreement takes the form of a limitation of recovery to an amount less than the probable damages.[27] The contract may be sustained, however, where it represents an honest attempt to fix a value as liquidated damages in advance, and the carrier graduates its rates according to such value, so that full protection would be open to the plaintiff upon paying a higher rate.[28] The same rules apply to innkeepers [29] and public warehousemen.[30]

There has been some tendency to extend the same rule to other professional bailees who are under no public duty but deal with the public, such as garagemen and owners of parking lots,[31] and of parcel checkrooms,[32] on the ground that the indispensable need for their services deprives the customer of any real equal bargaining power. As to other private bailees for hire, the courts are divided as to the validity of a contract against liability for negligence—some holding that such a general agreement is valid,[33] while others regard it as against public policy.[34] The decision is likely to turn upon the extent to which it is considered that the public interest is involved. Where it is not, it seems the better view that there is no unfair advantage to the bailee in permitting him to set the terms upon which he will receive the goods, so long as the bailor knows about them and is free without any serious disadvantage to turn them down.[35] It is generally agreed that he may at least contract that he is not required to exercise care to protect the deposited goods against a specific limited risk.[36]

If an express agreement exempting the defendant from liability for his negligence is to be sustained, it must appear that its terms were brought home to the plaintiff; and if he did not know of the provision in his contract, and a reasonable person in his posi-

---

ren-Godwin Lumber Co., 1919, 251 U.S. 27, 40 S.Ct. 69, 64 L.Ed. 118.

27. Union Pacific Railroad Co. v. Burke, 1921, 255 U.S. 317, 41 S.Ct. 283, 65 L.Ed. 656; Adams Express Co. v. Mellichamp, 1912, 138 Ga. 443, 75 S.E. 596, answers to certified questions conformed to 11 Ga.App. 448, 75 S.E. 673. See Bikle, Agreed Valuation as Affecting the Liability of Common Carriers for Negligence, 1907, 21 Harv.L.Rev. 32.

28. Hogan Transfer & Storage Corp. v. Waymire, 1980, ___ Ind.App. ___, 399 N.E.2d 779 (availability of alternative coverage and rates essential under statute and common law). Under the Carmack Amendment to the Interstate Commerce Act, the carrier is permitted to limit liability to the declared or released value of the goods, based on a differential rate structure. See George R. Hall, Inc. v. Superior Trucking Co., N.D.Ga. 1981, 514 F.Supp. 581; Hogan Transfer & Storage Corp. v. Waymire, 1980, ___ Ind.App. ___, 399 N.E.2d 779; Trans-American Van Service, Inc. v. Shirzad, Tex. Civ.App.1980, 596 S.W.2d 587; Anton v. Greyhound Van Lines, Inc., 1st Cir. 1978, 591 F.2d 103 (limitation ineffective where shipper had no choice to pay higher rate). See also Caribbean Produce Exchange, Inc. v. Sea Land Service, Inc., D.Puerto Rico 1976, 415 F.Supp. 88 (Carriage of Goods by Sea Act). But a long delay in delivery or other fundamental breach may serve to rescind the contract. Cassidy v. Airborne Freight Corp., Okla.1977, 565 P.2d 360; Information Control Corp. v. United Airlines, 1977, 73 Cal.App.3d 630, 140 Cal.Rptr. 877.

29. Oklahoma City Hotel Co. v. Levine, 1941, 189 Okla. 331, 116 P.2d 997; see Gardner v. Jonathan Club, 1950, 35 Cal.2d 343, 317 P.2d 961.

30. George v. Bekins Van & Storage Co., 1949, 33 Cal.2d 834, 205 P.2d 1037; Inland Compress Co. v. Simmons, 1916, 59 Okla. 287, 159 P. 262.

31. See, e.g., Makower v. Kinney System, 1970, 65 Misc.2d 808, 318 N.Y.S.2d 515 (statute); System Auto Parks & Garages, Inc. v. American Economy Insurance Co., 1980, ___ Ind.App. ___, 411 N.E.2d 163. But see White v. Atlanta Parking Service Co., 1976, 139 Ga. App. 243, 228 S.E.2d 156. See generally Annots., 1982, 13 A.L.R.4th 442 (damaged car); 13 A.L.R.4th 362 (lost car).

32. Denver Union Terminal Railway Co. v. Cullinan, 1922, 72 Colo. 248, 210 P. 602; Hotels Statler Co. v. Safier, 1921, 103 Ohio St. 638, 134 N.E. 460.

In Tunkl v. Regents of University of California, 1963, 60 Cal.2d 92, 32 Cal.Rptr. 33, 383 P.2d 441, the same rule was applied to a charitable hospital accepting patients from the public, upon the ground that the "public interest" was involved.

33. Fidelity Storage Co. v. Kingsbury, 1935, 65 U.S. App.D.C. 69, 79 F.2d 705; Marlow v. Conway Iron Works, 1924, 130 S.C. 256, 125 S.E. 569.

34. Sporsem v. First National Bank, 1925, 133 Wash. 199, 233 P. 641; Downs v. Sley System Garages, 1937, 129 Pa.Super. 68, 194 A. 772. Cf. Hunter v. American Rentals, Inc., 1962, 189 Kan. 615, 371 P.2d 131 (business of renting trailers).

35. See Winterstein v. Wilcom, 1972, 16 Md.App. 130, 293 A.2d 821 (auto racetrack); Note, 1938, 86 U.Pa.L.Rev. 772.

36. See Gesford v. Star Van & Storage Co., 1920, 104 Neb. 453, 177 N.W. 794 (freezing); Nolan v. Auto Transporters, 1979, 226 Kan. 176, 597 P.2d 614.

tion would not have known of it, it is not binding upon him, and the agreement fails for want of mutual assent.[37] It is also necessary that the expressed terms of the agreement be applicable to the particular misconduct of the defendant, and the courts have strictly construed the terms of exculpatory clauses against the defendant [38] who is usually the draftsman. If the defendant seeks to use the agreement to escape responsibility for the consequences of his negligence, then it must so provide, clearly and unequivocally, as by using the word "negligence" itself.[39] Further, on the basis either of common experience as to what is intended, or of public policy to discourage aggravated wrongs, such agreements generally are not construed to cover the more extreme forms of negligence, described as willful, wanton, reckless or gross,[40] or to any conduct which constitutes an intentional tort.[41]

Implied Acceptance of Risk

In by far the greater number of cases, the consent to assume the risk has not been a matter of express agreement, but has been found to be implied from the conduct of the plaintiff under the circumstances. Although it was said in early decisions [42] that assumption of risk will not be found apart from a contract relation between the parties, it is now generally recognized that the basis of the defense is not contract but consent, and that it is available in many cases where no express agreement exists.[43] It was also early said on occasion that the plaintiff never assumes the risk of the defendant's negligence, once it exists; [44] but the case law developed to the effect that once the plaintiff is informed of such negligence, the risks arising from it may be assumed,[45] but are not necessarily so.

It is here that there is the greatest misapprehension and confusion as to assumption of risk, and its most frequent misapplication.

---

37. See, e.g., Anton v. Greyhound Van Lines, Inc., 1st Cir. 1978, 591 F.2d 103 (shipper must make absolute, deliberate and well-informed choice); Cordingley v. Allied Van Lines, Inc., 9th Cir. 1977, 563 F.2d 960; Georgakis v. Eastern Air Lines, Inc., E.D.N.Y.1981, 512 F.Supp. 330 (foreigner could not read provision on ticket); Omni Flying Club, Inc. v. Cessna Aircraft Co., 1974, 366 Mass. 154, 315 N.E.2d 885 (buried in fine print in owner's manual supplied after sale).

But a shipper will be held to the terms of the contract he signs, whether he reads them or not, unless perhaps the shipper makes representations to the contrary. See Allied Van Lines, Inc. v. Bratton, Fla.1977, 351 So.2d 344. And the shipper is held to the terms of the carrier's tariff schedule. Anton v. Greyhound Van Lines, Inc., 1st Cir. 1978, 591 F.2d 103; Marohn v. Burnham Van Services, Inc., N.D.Ill.1979, 478 F.Supp. 49.

38. See Willard Van Dyke Productions, Inc. v. Eastman Kodak Co., 1963, 12 N.Y.2d 301, 239 N.Y.S.2d 337, 189 N.E.2d 693; Galligan v. Arovitch, 1966, 421 Pa. 301, 219 A.2d 463; Rothenberg v. Aero Mayflower Transit Co., D.D.C.1980, 495 F.Supp. 399; Second Restatement of Torts § 496B, Comment d.

39. See, e.g., O'Connell v. Walt Disney World Co., Fla.App.1982, 413 So.2d 444 (stampede during trail ride on horseback); Willard Van Dyke Productions, Inc. v. Eastman Kodak Co., 1963, 12 N.Y.2d 301, 239 N.Y.S.2d 337, 189 N.E.2d 693. See also Posttape Associates v. Eastman Kodak Co., E.D.Pa.1974, 387 F.Supp. 184, reversed on other grounds, 3d Cir. 1976, 537 F.2d 751, appeal after remand 450 F.Supp. 407; Haugen v. Ford Motor Co., N.D.1974, 219 N.W.2d 462 (valid only if negligence or other fault was "plainly and precisely" covered by disclaimer); cf. Turner v. International Harvester Co., 1975, 133 N.J.Super. 277, 336 A.2d 62, 72–73 (whether "as is" sale of used truck for jury to determine whether disclaimer "was meant to serve as an intentional relinquishment of a known right").

40. Friedman v. Lockheed Aircraft Corp., E.D.N.Y. 1956, 138 F.Supp. 530; Thomas v. Atlantic Coast Line Railroad Co., 5th Cir. 1953, 201 F.2d 167; Pratt v. Western Pacific Railway Co., 1963, 213 Cal.App.2d 573, 29 Cal.Rptr. 108.

41. Cf. Sands v. American Railway Express Co., 1923, 154 Minn. 308, 193 N.W. 721, reversed, 1924, 159 Minn. 25, 198 N.W. 402.

42. See B. Shoninger Co. v. Mann, 1905, 219 Ill. 242, 76 N.E. 354; and cf. Papakalos v. Shaka, 1941, 91 N.H. 265, 18 A.2d 377. See Note, 1941, 40 Mich.L.Rev. 137.

43. Akins v. Glens Falls City School District, 1981, 53 N.Y.2d 325, 441 N.Y.S.2d 644, 424 N.E.2d 531 (4–3); Scanlon v. Wedger, 1898, 156 Mass. 462, 31 N.E. 642; Mountain v. Wheatley, 1951, 106 Cal.App.2d 333, 234 P.2d 1031; Bohnsack v. Driftmier, 1952, 243 Iowa 383, 52 N.W.2d 79. See Note, 1954, 32 N.C.L.Rev. 366.

44. See for example Jewell v. Kansas City Bolt & Nut Co., 1910, 231 Mo. 176, 132 S.W. 703.

45. Choctaw, Oklahoma & Gulf Railroad Co. v. Jones, 1906, 77 Ark. 367, 92 S.W. 244; De Kallands v. Washtenaw Home Telephone Co., 1908, 153 Mich. 25, 116 N.W. 564; Kath v. East St. Louis & Suburban Railway Co., 1908, 232 Ill. 126, 83 N.E. 533.

It is not true that in any case where the plaintiff voluntarily encounters a known danger he necessarily consents to any future negligence of the defendant. A pedestrian who walks across the street in the middle of a block, through a stream of traffic travelling at excessive speed, cannot by any stretch of the imagination be found to consent that the drivers shall not use care to watch for him and avoid running him down. On the contrary, he is insisting that they shall. This is contributory negligence pure and simple; it is not assumption of risk.[46] And if A leaves an automobile stopped at night on the travelled portion of the highway, and his passenger remains sitting in it, it can readily be found that there is consent to the prior negligence of A, whose control over the risk has terminated, but not to the subsequent negligence of B, who thereafter runs into the car from the rear.[47] In both cases, the plaintiff has exposed himself to the risk of future harm, but he has not consented to relieve the defendant of any future duty to act with reasonable care. This is a distinction which has baffled a great many law students, some judges, and unhappily a few very learned legal writers.

Implied assumption of risk has been found in a variety of cases, some where the plaintiff's conduct has apparently been quite reasonable, and others where it has amounted to contributory negligence.[48] By entering freely and voluntarily into any relation or situation where the negligence of the defendant is obvious,[49] the plaintiff may be found to accept and consent to it, and to undertake to look out for himself and relieve the defendant of the duty. Thus those who participate or sit as spectators at sports and amusements may be taken to assume the known risks of being hurt[50] by roller coasters,[51] flying baseballs,[52] hockey pucks,[53] golf

---

46. See infra, note 99, and text.

47. Suggested by Calahan v. Wood, 1970, 24 Utah 2d 8, 465 P.2d 169.

48. See supra, p. 481.

49. See infra, note 75.

50. See Moe v. Steenberg, 1966, 275 Minn. 448, 147 N.W.2d 587 (skater); Tavernier v. Maes, 1966, 242 Cal. App.2d 532, 51 Cal.Rptr. 575 (second baseman's ankle broken by runner's hard slide); Richmond v. Employers' Fire Insurance Co., La.App.1974, 298 So.2d 118, writ denied 302 So.2d 18 (flying baseball bat); McGee v. Board of Education, 1962, 16 A.D.2d 99, 226 N.Y.S.2d 329, appeal denied 19 A.D.2d 526, appeal dismissed 12 N.Y.2d 1100, 240 N.Y.S.2d 165, 190 N.E.2d 537 (flying baseball); Robillard v. P & R Racetracks, Inc., La.App.1981, 405 So.2d 1203 (stock car drag racer hit disabled vehicle). Perhaps with the exception of professional hockey, the players should not ordinarily be deemed to have consented to unsportsmanlike rule violations, not part of the game, that may recklessly or intentionally result in injury. See Nabozny v. Barnhill, 1975, 31 Ill.App.3d 212, 334 N.E.2d 258 (soccer goalkeeper kicked in head); Bourque v. Duplechin, La.App. 1976, 331 So.2d 40, writ not considered 334 So.2d 230, certiorari refused 334 So.2d 210; cf. Hackbart v. Cincinnati Bengals, Inc., D.Colo.1977, 435 F.Supp. 352, reversed 10th Cir. 1979, 601 F.2d 516, certiorari denied 444 U.S. 931, 100 S.Ct. 275, 62 L.Ed.2d 188 (one football player struck another on back of head and neck in anger and frustration after interception), noted, 1980, Duke L.J. 742. On sports injuries generally, see Weistart & Lowell, The Law of Sports, 1979, ch. 8; Hechter, The Criminal Law and Violence in Sports, 1976-77, 19 Crim.L.Q. 425; Notes, 1976, 75 Mich.L.Rev. 148 (consent, under criminal law, to sports violence); 1975 Wis. L.Rev. 771 (ice hockey); Annots., 1977, 77 A.L.R.3d 1300 (participant); 1966, 10 A.L.R.3d 446 (umpire); 1970, 33 A.L.R.3d 316 (ice skater).

51. Lumsden v. L.A. Thompson Scenic Railway Co., 1909, 130 App.Div. 209, 114 N.Y.S. 421; Sullivan v. Ridgeway Construction Co., 1920, 236 Mass. 75, 127 N.E. 543; Murphy v. Steeplechase Amusement Co., 1929, 250 N.Y. 479, 166 N.E. 173.

See McPherson v. Sunset Speedway, Inc., 8th Cir. 1979, 594 F.2d 711 (Nebraska law) (hit by race car); Provence v. Doolin, 1980, 91 Ill.App.3d 271, 46 Ill.Dec. 733, 414 N.E.2d 786 (auto racer pit member).

52. See Akins v. Glens Falls City School District, 1981, 53 N.Y.2d 325, 441 N.Y.S.2d 644, 424 N.E.2d 531 (4–3); Hudson v. Kansas City Baseball Club, 1942, 349 Mo. 1215, 164 S.W.2d 318; Hunt v. Portland Baseball Club, 1956, 207 Or. 337, 296 P.2d 495; Shaw v. Boston American League Baseball Co., 1930, 325 Mass. 419, 90 N.E.2d 840; Brisson v. Minneapolis Baseball & Athletic Association, 1932, 185 Minn. 507, 240 N.W. 903; Williams v. Houston Baseball Association, Tex.Civ.App. 1941, 154 S.W.2d 874. See Notes, [1951] Wash.U.L.Q. 434; 1952, 26 Temple L.Q. 206; Annot., 1979, 91 A.L.R.3d 24.

53. See Kennedy v. Providence Hockey Club, Inc., 1977, ___ R.I. ___, 376 A.2d 329. But see Riley v. Chicago Cougars Hockey Club, Inc., 1981, 100 Ill.App.3d 664, 56 Ill.Dec. 210, 427 N.E.2d 290 (upholding plaintiff's verdict, and distinguishing baseball cases). See generally, Annot., 1967, 14 A.L.R.3d 1018.

balls,[54] wrestlers,[55] or such things as fireworks explosions.[56] Cardozo once summarized all this quite neatly: "The timorous may stay at home."[57]

On the same basis, plaintiffs who enter business premises as invitees and discover dangerous conditions, such as slippery floors and unsafe stairways, may be found to assume the risks when they nevertheless proceed freely and voluntarily to encounter them.[58] The guest who accepts a ride with an automobile driver may assume the risk of his known incompetence,[59] or intoxication,[60] of his continued or threatened negligent driving,[61] or of known defects in the car.[62]

Likewise the user of a product supplied to him may assume the risks of its known dangerous defects.[63] In all of these cases the plaintiff may be barred by his voluntary choice to go ahead with full knowledge of the risk. In all of them, however, other factors, which remain to be considered, may affect the "voluntary choice"; and the fact that the risk *may* be assumed is by no means conclusive as to whether it has in fact been assumed.

Knowledge and Appreciation of Risk

The defense of assumption of risk is in fact quite narrowly confined and restricted

---

54. Schlenger v. Weinberg, 1930, 107 N.J.L. 130, 150 A. 434; Slotnick v. Cooley, 1933, 166 Tenn. 373, 61 S.W.2d 462; Alexander v. Wrenn, 1932, 158 Va. 486, 164 S.E. 715; Stober v. Embry, 1932, 243 Ky. 117, 47 S.W.2d 921. See Annot., 1978, 82 A.L.R.3d 1183. But see Duffy v. Midlothian Country Club, 1980, 92 Ill.App. 3d 193, 47 Ill.Dec. 786, 415 N.E.2d 1099. Cf. Douglas v. Converse, 1915, 248 Pa. 232, 93 A. 955 (polo); Ingerson v. Shattuck School, 1931, 185 Minn. 16, 239 N.W. 667 (football); Hammel v. Madison Square Garden Corp., 1935, 156 Misc. 311, 279 N.Y.S. 815 (hockey); Filler v. Stenvick, 1953, 79 N.D. 422, 56 N.W.2d 798 (skater, crack in ice).

55. Dusckiewicz v. Carter, 1947, 115 Vt. 122, 52 A.2d 419. See Annot., 1967, 14 A.L.R.3d 993 (wrestling or boxing). Cf. Annots., 1969, 24 A.L.R.3d 1447 (skiers); 1969, 8 A.L.R.3d 675 (water skiers); 1978, 82 A.L.R.2d 1183 (basketball spectators).

56. Scanlon v. Wedger, 1892, 156 Mass. 462, 31 N.E. 642. Cf. Morton v. California Sports Car Club, 1958, 163 Cal.App.2d 685, 329 P.2d 967 (wheel from car in automobile race); Johnson v. City of New York, 1906, 186 N.Y. 139, 78 N.E. 715 (automobile speed test); Shafer v. Tacoma Eastern Railroad Co., 1916, 91 Wash. 164, 157 P. 485 (raising derailed engine). See generally, Calapietro, The Promoters' Liability for Sports Spectator Injuries, 1960, 46 Corn.L.Q. 140.

57. In Murphy v. Steeplechase Amusement Co., 1929, 250 N.Y. 479, 166 N.E. 173.

58. See Moss v. Atlanta Housing Authority, 1981, 160 Ga.App. 555, 287 S.E.2d 619; Fillis v. Wahlig, 1943, 267 App.Div. 781, 45 N.Y.S.2d 609, affirmed mem. 1944, 293 N.Y. 710, 56 N.E.2d 729; Curtis v. Traders National Bank, 1951, 314 Ky. 765, 237 S.W.2d 76.

See generally Keeton, Assumption of Risk and the Landowner, 1942, 20 Tex.L.Rev. 562; Keeton, Personal Injury Resulting from Open and Obvious Conditions, 1952, 100 U.Pa.L.Rev. 629; Keeton, Assumption of Risk and the Landowner, 1961, 22 La.L.Rev. 108.

59. See Young v. Wlazik, Minn.1977, 262 N.W.2d 300 (dictum); Schubring v. Weggen, 1940, 234 Wis. 517, 291 N.W. 788; cf. Le Fleur v. Vergilia, 1952, 280 App.Div. 1035, 117 N.Y.S.2d 244 (teaching learner to drive car); Corbett v. Curtis, Me.1967, 225 A.2d 402 (same); Annot., 1980, 1 A.L.R.4th 556 (driver's drowsiness, physical defect or illness). Contra, where the passenger has no knowledge of the driver's sleepy condition. Clements v. Stephens, 1975, ___ W.Va. ___, 211 S.E.2d 110.

60. See Ambrosio v. Price, D.Neb.1979, 495 F.Supp. 381; Prestenbach v. Sentry Insurance Co., La.1976, 340 So.2d 1331; Powell v. Heck, La.App.1979, 378 So.2d 582 (motorcycle); cf. Employers Casualty Co. v. Hagendorfer, Ala.1981, 393 So.2d 999 (contributory negligence); Hamilton v. Kinsey, Ala.1976, 337 So.2d 344 (same); Harlow v. Connelly, Ky.App.1977, 548 S.W.2d 143 (contributory gross negligence); Annot., 1981, 5 A.L.R.4th 1194 (admissibility of evidence of *passenger's* blood alcohol level to show assumption of risk). Contra, when there is no knowledge of the driver's intoxicated condition. Case v. Arrow Trucking Co., La.App.1979, 372 So.2d 670; Nelson v. Nelson, Minn.1979, 283 N.W.2d 375 (contributory negligence); Amrine v. Murray, 1981, 28 Wn.App. 650, 626 P.2d 24 (same).

61. Bugh v. Webb, 1959, 231 Ark. 27, 328 S.W.2d 379 (drag racing); Sprague v. Hauck, 1958, 3 Wis.2d 616, 89 N.W.2d 226 (speed); Kelly v. Checker White Cab Co., 1948, 131 W.Va. 816, 50 S.E.2d 888 (snow and ice on road); cf. Walker v. Hamby, Tenn.1973, 503 S.W.2d 118 (dune buggy antics).

62. Clise v. Prunty, 1930, 108 W.Va. 635, 152 S.E. 201 (chains and brakes); Sloan v. Gulf Refining Co. of Louisiana, La.App.1924, 139 So. 26 (lights); Mitchell v. Heaton, 1941, 231 Iowa 269, 1 N.W.2d 284 (defective wheel bolts). See Rice, The Automobile Guest and the Rationale of Assumption of Risk, 1943, 27 Minn.L.Rev. 323; Pedrick, Taken for a Ride: The Automobile Guest and Assumption of Risk, 1961, 22 La.L.Rev. 90.

63. See, e.g., Vargus v. Pitman Manufacturing Co., E.D.Pa.1981, 510 F.Supp. 116; Campbell v. Nordco Products, 7th Cir. 1980, 629 F.2d 1258 (Ill. law). The defense has narrowed in many states, however, under the principles of strict tort liability. See generally Note, 1982, 95 Harv.L.Rev. 872; infra, ch. 17.

by two or three elements or requirements: first, the plaintiff must know that the risk is present, and he must further understand its nature; and second, his choice to incur it must be free and voluntary. Since in the ordinary case there is no conclusive evidence against the plaintiff on these issues, they are normally for the jury to decide.

"Knowledge of the risk is the watchword of assumption of risk." [64] Under ordinary circumstances the plaintiff will not be taken to assume any risk of either activities or conditions of which he has no knowledge.[65] Moreover, he must not only know of the facts which create the danger, but he must comprehend and appreciate the nature of the danger he confronts.[66] "A defect and the danger arising from it are not necessarily to be identified, and a person may know of one without appreciating the other." [67] Knowledge of the general danger may not be enough, and some courts require knowledge of the specific risk that caused the plaintiff's harm.[68] The standard to be applied is, in theory at least, a subjective one, geared to the particular plaintiff and his situation, rather than that of the reasonable person of ordinary prudence who appears in contributory negligence.[69] If, because of age [70] or lack of information or experience,[71] he does not comprehend the risk involved in a known situation, he will not be taken to consent to assume it. His failure to exercise ordinary care to discover the danger is not properly a matter of assumption of risk, but of the defense of contributory negligence.[72]

At the same time, it is evident that a purely subjective standard opens a very wide door for the plaintiff who is willing to testify that he did not know or understand the risk; [73] and there have been a good many cases in which the courts have said in effect

---

64. Cincinnati, New Orleans & Texas Pacific Railway Co. v. Thompson, 6th Cir. 1916, 236 F. 1, 9.

65. See Clements v. Stephens, 1975, ___ W.Va. ___, 211 S.E.2d 110; Meese v. Brigham Young University, Utah 1981, 639 P.2d 720; Brooks v. Douglas, 1982, 163 Ga.App. 224, 292 S.E.2d 911, certiorari granted; Colonial Natural Gas Co. v. Sayers, 1981, 222 Va. 781, 284 S.E.2d 599; Fonseca v. Marlin Marine Corp., La.1981, 410 So.2d 674.

66. Shufelberger v. Worden, 1962, 189 Kan. 379, 369 P.2d 382; Ellis v. Moore & Wardlaw, Tex.1966, 401 S.W.2d 789; Stotzheim v. Djos, 1959, 256 Minn. 316, 98 N.W.2d 129; Dean v. Martz, Ky.1959, 329 S.W.2d 371; Gilbert v. City of Los Angeles, 1967, 249 Cal.App.2d 1006, 58 Cal.Rptr. 56.

67. Errico v. Washburn Williams Co., C.C.Pa.1909, 170 F. 852, 853. Cf. Dean v. Martz, Ky.1959, 329 S.W.2d 371; Shufelberger v. Worden, 1962, 189 Kan. 379, 369 P.2d 382; Sparks v. Porcher, 1964, 109 Ga. App. 334, 136 S.E.2d 153 (knowledge that driver has been drinking not as matter of law knowledge he is too drunk to drive).

68. "A general knowledge of 'a danger' is not sufficient, but rather plaintiff must have actual knowledge of the specific risk that injured him and appreciate its magnitude." Garcia v. City of South Tucson, App. 1981, 131 Ariz. 315, 640 P.2d 1117, 1121. Accord, Maxey v. Freightliner, 5th Cir. 1982, 665 F.2d 1367 (Tex. law); Heil Co. v. Grant, Tex.Civ.App.1976, 534 S.W.2d 916, refused no reversible error; Klein v. R. D. Werner Co., 1982, 98 Wn.2d 316, 654 P.2d 94.

69. See, e.g., Rutter v. Northeastern Beaver County School District, 1981, 496 Pa. 590, 437 A.2d 1198; Campbell v. Nordco Products, 7th Cir. 1980, 629 F.2d 1258 (Ill. law); Zrust v. Spencer Foods, Inc., 8th Cir. 1982, 667 F.2d 760 (Neb. law); Scoggins v. Jude, D.C. App.1980, 419 A.2d 999; Shahrokhfar v. State Farm Mutual Automobile Insurance Co., 1981, ___ Mont. ___, 634 P.2d 653; Antcliff v. Datzman, 1982, ___ Ind.App. ___, 436 N.E.2d 114; cf. Employers Casualty Co. v. Hagendorfer, Ala.1981, 393 So.2d 999.

70. Aldes v. St. Paul Baseball Club, 1958, 251 Minn. 440, 88 N.W.2d 94; Freedman v. Hurwitz, 1933, 116 Conn. 283, 164 A. 647; Everton Silica Sand Co. v. Hicks, 1939, 197 Ark. 980, 125 S.W.2d 793. See Rutter v. Northeastern Beaver County School District, 1981, 496 Pa. 590, 437 A.2d 1198 (16-year-old high school football player).

In Greene v. Watts, 1962, 21 Cal.App.2d 103, 26 Cal. Rptr. 334, it was held that a child aged 3½ was incapable of assumption of risk, as well as contributory negligence.

71. Dee v. Parish, 1959, 160 Tex. 171, 327 S.W.2d 449, on remand, 1960, 332 S.W.2d 764; Hanley v. California Bridge & Construction Co., 1899, 127 Cal. 232, 59 P. 577.

72. See Garcia v. City of South Tucson, App.1981, 131 Ariz. 315, 640 P.2d 1117; Halepeska v. Callihan Interests, Inc., Tex.1963, 371 S.W.2d 368, on remand, 376 S.W.2d 932; Dana v. Bursey, Fla.App.1964, 169 So.2d 845.

73. Sometimes he will instead admit that he knew of the risk, and consequently be out of court. See Moran v. Raymond Corp., 7th Cir. 1973, 484 F.2d 1008, certiorari denied 1974, 415 U.S. 932, 94 S.Ct. 1445, 39 L.Ed.2d 490; cf. Rickey v. Boden, 1980, ___ R.I. ___, 421 A.2d 539; Kaplan v. Missouri-Pacific Railroad Co., La.App.1981, 409 So.2d 298 (teenagers testified that they discussed risks of train approaching before they crossed railroad trestle).

that he is not to be believed, so that in effect something of an objective element enters the case, and the standard applied in fact does not always differ greatly from that of the reasonable person.[74] Thus, the plaintiff will not be heard to say that he did not comprehend a risk which must have been quite clear and obvious to him.[75] There are some things, as for example the risk of injury if one is hit by a baseball driven on a line,[76] which are so far a matter of common knowledge in the community, that in the absence of some satisfactory explanation a denial of such knowledge simply is not to be believed.[77]

As in the case of negligence itself,[78] there are certain risks which anyone of adult age must be taken to appreciate: the danger of slipping on ice,[79] of falling through unguarded openings,[80] of lifting heavy objects,[81] of being squeezed in a narrow space,[82] of inflammable liquids,[83] of driving an automobile whose brakes will not operate,[84] of unguarded circular saws or similar dangerous machinery,[85] and doubtless many others.[86] Furthermore, a plaintiff who has confronted a dangerous situation over a substantial length of time will be taken to have discovered it and to understand the normal, ordinary risks involved in that situation, such as the danger of trains in motion in a railroad yard,[87] or the risk of slipping on a dangerous stairway used every day.[88] Once the plaintiff fully understands the risk, the fact that

---

74. See Campbell v. Nordco Products, 7th Cir. 1980, 629 F.2d 1258 (dead men do not talk; circumstantial evidence showed knowledge of danger). But cf. Dorry v. LaFleur, La.1981, 399 So.2d 559 (rejecting "should have known" objective standard).

75. See, e.g., Harlow v. Connelly, Ky.App.1977, 548 S.W.2d 143 (riding with obviously drunk driver); Wise v. Roger Givens, Inc., Okl.App.1980, 618 P.2d 951 (tripping over can of paint); Benjamin v. Deffet Rentals, Inc., 1981, 66 Ohio St.2d 86, 419 N.E.2d 883 (slipping on wet diving board).

76. Crane v. Kansas City Baseball Co., 1913, 168 Mo.App. 301, 153 S.W. 1076; Brown v. San Francisco Ball Club, 1950, 99 Cal.App.2d 484, 222 P.2d 19.

As to the effect of community knowledge of the risk of attending ice hockey games, compare Modec v. City of Eveleth, 1947, 224 Minn. 556, 29 N.W.2d 453, with Morris v. Cleveland Hockey Club, 1952, 157 Ohio St. 225, 105 N.E.2d 419.

77. Even a minor may be taken to appreciate those risks with which one of his age, experience and intelligence must be familiar. Ciriack v. Merchants' Woolen Co., 1890, 151 Mass. 152, 23 N.E. 829; Benjamin v. Deffet Rentals, Inc., 1981, 66 Ohio St.2d 86, 419 N.E.2d 883; Kirby v. Hylton, 1982, 51 Md.App. 365, 443 A.2d 640 (9-year-old assumed risk). But cf. supra, note 70.

78. See supra, § 32.

79. Shea v. Kansas City, Fort Scott & Memphis Railroad Co., 1898, 76 Mo.App. 29; cf. Benjamin v. Deffet Rentals, Inc., 1981, 66 Ohio St.2d 86, 419 N.E.2d 883 (diving board slippery when wet); Moss v. Atlanta Housing Authority, 1981, 160 Ga.App. 555, 287 S.E.2d 619 (muddy sidewalk at night); Pound v. Augusta National, Inc., 1981, 158 Ga.App. 166, 279 S.E.2d 342 (wet gravel parking lot).

80. Moulton v. Gage, 1885, 138 Mass. 390; Schwartz v. Cornell, 1891, 59 Hun 623, 13 N.Y.S. 355.

81. Ferguson v. Phoenix Cotton Mills, 1901, 106 Tenn. 236, 61 S.W. 53. Cf. Gibson v. Beaver, 1967, 245 Md. 418, 226 A.2d 273; Kirby v. Hylton, 1982, 51 Md.App. 365, 443 A.2d 640 (rolling heavy pipe up slope).

82. Toledo, St. Louis & Western Railroad Co. v. Allen, 1928, 276 U.S. 165, 48 S.Ct. 215, 72 L.Ed. 513, conformed 12 S.W.2d 1116; Mellott v. Louisville & Nashville Railroad Co., 1897, 101 Ky. 212, 40 S.W. 696.

83. Johnson v. Webster Manufacturing Co., 1909, 139 Wis. 181, 120 N.W. 832.

84. Gallegos v. Nash, 1955, 137 Cal.App.2d 14, 289 P.2d 835.

85. Hanson v. Ludlow Manufacturing Co., 1894, 162 Mass. 187, 38 N.E. 363; Ruchinsky v. French, 1897, 168 Mass. 68, 46 N.E. 417 (cogwheels); Dillenberger v. Weingartner, 1900, 64 N.J.L. 292, 45 A. 638 (fan). But see Lawrence v. Grant Parish School Board, La.App. 1982, 409 So.2d 1316 (14-year-old student did not assume risks of power saw used for first time in welding class).

86. See, e.g., Walker v. Hamby, Tenn.1973, 503 S.W.2d 118 (risk to passenger of flying out of dune buggy); Wise v. Roger Givens, Inc., Okla.App.1980, 618 P.2d 951 (tripping over can of paint); McLeod v. Whitten, Miss.1982, 413 So.2d 1020 (pickup truck wheels fell into washout when hunters driving through soybean field); Calhoun v. Royal Globe Insurance Co., La.App.1981, 398 So.2d 1166 (tripping in darkened dance hall); Guidry v. Cheramie, La.App.1981, 397 So. 2d 872 (slipping on dance floor).

87. Wolfe v. Atlantic Coast Line Railroad Co., 1930, 199 N.C. 613, 155 S.E. 459; Chesapeake & Ohio Railway Co. v. Nixon, 1926, 271 U.S. 218, 46 S.Ct. 495, 70 L.Ed. 914, reargument denied 261 N.Y. 620, 185 N.E. 764.

88. Rickey v. Boden, 1980, __ R.I. __, 421 A.2d 539; cf. Smith v. Louisiana Cement Co., La.App.1981, 405 So.2d 687 (muddy wash-down area for trucks, where driver had been over one hundred times).

he has momentarily forgotten it may not protect him.[89] In the usual case, his knowledge and appreciation of the danger will be a question for the jury;[90] but where it is clear that any person in his position must have understood the danger, the issue may be decided by the court.[91]

Even where there is knowledge and appreciation of a risk, the plaintiff may not be barred from recovery where the situation changes to introduce a new element, such as several balls in the air at one time in a baseball park.[92] The fact that the plaintiff is fully aware of one risk, as for example that of the speed at which a car is being driven, does not mean that he assumes another of which he is unaware, such as the failure of the driver to watch the road.[93] And his knowledge of the negligence of one person does not mean that he assumes the risk of negligence of another, of which he does not know.[94]

Since the notion of assumption of the risk rests more fundamentally upon the plaintiff's consent than upon his knowledge, it is quite possible for the plaintiff to assume risks of whose specific existence he is not aware, provided that his intent to do so is made clear. He may, in other words, consent to take his chances as to unknown conditions. He may certainly do so expressly; and there are a few cases in which the assumption has been found by implication. Thus a guest who accepts a gratuitous ride in an automobile has been taken to assume the risk of defects in the car unknown to the driver,[95] just as the same has been said of a licensee who enters another's premises.[96] Workmen used to be said to assume risks of employment of which they had at least equal means or opportunities of knowledge or discovery with the employer, even though they were unaware of what they were.[97] But if the plaintiff has consented only to a vague

89. Jacobs v. Southern Railway Co., 1916, 241 U.S. 229, 36 S.Ct. 588, 60 L.Ed. 970; New York, Chicago & St. Louis Railroad Co. v. McDougall, 6th Cir. 1926, 15 F.2d 283.

90. See, e.g., Kitchens v. Winter Co. Builders, Inc., 1982, 161 Ga.App. 701, 289 S.E.2d 807, 809; Antcliff v. Datzman, 1982, ___ Ind.App. ___, 436 N.E.2d 114; Duffy v. Midlothian Country Club, 1980, 92 Ill.App.3d 193, 47 Ill.Dec. 786, 415 N.E.2d 1099.

91. Benjamin v. Deffet Rentals, Inc., 1981, 66 Ohio St.2d 86, 419 N.E.2d 883 (summary judgment); Myers v. Lennox Co-op Association, S.D.1981, 307 N.W.2d 863 (same); Wise v. Roger Givens, Inc., Okl.App.1980, 618 P.2d 951 (same); Rickey v. Boden, 1980, ___ R.I. ___, 421 A.2d 539 (j.n.o.v.); Kirby v. Hylton, 1982, 51 Md. App. 365, 443 A.2d 640 (directed verdict).

Conversely, where there is no evidence of knowledge, the issue should be resolved in favor of the plaintiff by the court. See Clements v. Stephens, 1975, ___ W.Va. ___, 211 S.E.2d 110; Maxey v. Freightliner Corp., 5th Cir. 1982, 665 F.2d 1367 (Tex. law); Garcia v. City of South Tucson, App.1981, 131 Ariz. 315, 640 P.2d 1117.

92. Cincinnati Baseball Club v. Eno, 1925, 112 Ohio St. 175, 147 N.E. 86.

93. Jewell v. Schmidt, 1957, 1 Wis.2d 241, 83 N.W.2d 487. Cf. Cassidy v. Quisenberry, Ky.1961, 346 S.W.2d 304 (speed of car and roller-coaster road, inexperience of driver); Haugen v. Wittkopf, 1943, 242 Wis. 276, 7 N.W.2d 886 (frosted windshield, inattention of driver); Fred Harvey Corp. v. Mateas, 9th Cir. 1948, 170 F.2d 612 (inexperienced and untrained mule at Grand Canyon); Lee v. National League Baseball Club of Milwaukee, 1958, 4 Wis.2d 168, 89 N.W.2d 811 (negligent supervision in scramble for foul ball); Vierra v. Fifth Avenue Rental Service, 1963, 60 Cal.2d 266, 32 Cal.Rptr. 193, 383 P.2d 777 (known danger of flying particles of concrete, unknown as to flying metal fragments broken off of tool); Fahringer v. Rinehimer, 1980, 283 Pa.Super. 93, 432 A.2d 731 (worker removing block from wheel of truck may have assumed risk of truck rolling backward, but not lurching forward); Holman v. Reliance Insurance Companies, La.App. 1982, 414 So.2d 1298; Dorry v. LaFleur, La.1981, 399 So.2d 559; Wolf v. Graber, S.D.1981, 303 N.W.2d 364 (knowledge of dangers at one entrance to store, but not at other).

94. Host driver and other colliding driver: Smith v. Castle, La.App.1978, 361 So.2d 303, writ denied 362 So. 2d 795; Giemza v. Allied American Mutual Fire Insurance Co., 1960, 10 Wis.2d 555, 103 N.W.2d 538; Miller v. Treat, 1960, 57 Wn.2d 524, 358 P.2d 143. Contra, Baltimore County v. State, Use of Keenan, 1963, 232 Md. 350, 193 A.2d 30. Employer and third person: Wright v. Concrete Co., 1962, 107 Ga.App. 190, 129 S.E.2d 351.

95. Higgins v. Mason, 1930, 255 N.Y. 104, 174 N.E. 77; Gagnon v. Dana, 1897, 69 N.H. 264, 39 A. 982. A line of cases so holding, headed by O'Shea v. Lavoy, 1921, 175 Wis. 456, 185 N.W. 525, was overruled in McConville v. State Farm Mutual Automobile Insurance Co., 1962, 15 Wis.2d 374, 113 N.W.2d 14.

96. See supra, § 60.

97. Miller v. Moran Brothers Co., 1905, 39 Wash. 631, 81 P. 1089; Peterson v. American Ice Co., 1912, 83 N.J.L. 579, 83 A. 872; Dube v. Gay, 1899, 69 N.H. 670, 46 A. 1049. See 4 Labatt, Master and Servant, 2d Ed. 1913, §§ 1327, 1328. It is still said that workers as-

and general hazard, and he is unaware of the presence or nature of the specific risk that injures him, his knowledge may be insufficient for the defense to be established.[98]

Voluntary Assumption

The second important aspect of the defense of assumption of risk is that the plaintiff is barred from recovery only if his choice is a free and voluntary one. As a preliminary matter, this means that there must be some manifestation of consent to relieve the defendant of the obligation of reasonable conduct. It is not every deliberate encountering of a known danger which is reasonably to be interpreted as evidence of such consent. The jaywalker who dashes into the street in the middle of the block, in the path of a stream of cars driven in excess of the speed limit, certainly does not manifest consent that they shall thereafter use no care and run him down. On the contrary, he is insisting that once they see him they shall take reasonable precautions for his safety; and while this may certainly be contributory negligence, it is not necessarily assumption of risk.[99]

But even though his conduct may appear to indicate consent, the risk will not be taken to be assumed if it appears from his words, or from the facts of the situation, that he does not in fact consent to relieve the defendant of the obligation to protect him.[1] Nevertheless, if the plaintiff proceeds to enter voluntarily into a situation which exposes him to the risk, notwithstanding any protests, his conduct will normally indicate that he does not stand on his objection, and has consented, however reluctantly, to accept the risk and look out for himself.[2] If, however, he surrenders his better judgment upon an assurance that the situation is safe, or that it will be remedied, or a promise of protection, he does not assume the risk,[3] unless the danger is so obvious and so extreme that there can be no reasonable reliance upon the assurance.[4] The rule that earlier evolved in employment cases was that a worker does not assume the risk of defects or dangerous conditions which the employer has promised to remedy,[5] until so long a time has elapsed without action that he can no longer continue work in reasonable reliance upon the promise.[6]

Even where the plaintiff does not protest, the risk is not assumed where the conduct of the defendant has left him no reasonable alternative. Where the defendant puts him to a choice of evils, there is a species of duress, which destroys the idea of freedom of elec-

---

sume the ordinary and obvious risks of the job. Baxter v. Grobmyer Brothers Construction Co., 1982, 275 Ark. 400, 631 S.W.2d 265, 267.

98. See supra, note 68.

99. See Story v. Howes, 1973, 41 A.D.2d 925, 344 N.Y.S.2d 10 (merely riding bike on Broadway is not to assume risk of being hit by car); Second Restatement of Torts § 496C, Comment *h*; Rutter v. Northeastern Beaver County School District, 1981, 496 Pa. 590, 437 A.2d 1198, 1203; cf. Hendricks v. Broderick, Iowa 1979, 284 N.W.2d 209 (turkey hunter, going into dark and deep forest, does not assume risk of negligently being shot by other hunters); Parker v. Roszell, Mo. App.1981, 617 S.W.2d 597 (hunter shot). "[A]lthough one may assume the risk of the negligence of another if he is fully informed of such negligence, one is not, under the doctrine of assumption of risk, bound to anticipate the negligent conduct of others." Garcia v. City of South Tucson, App.1981, 131 Ariz. 315, 640 P.2d 1117, 1121 (one policeman shot by another when house was stormed). See supra, note 46 and text.

1. See Antcliff v. Datzman, 1982, ___ Ind.App. ___, 436 N.E.2d 114 (passenger protested driver's speed). In Boyce v. Black, 1941, 123 W.Va. 234, 15 S.E.2d 588, it was held that when one automobile guest protests against the negligence of the driver, others are not necessarily required to protest. And the failure to protest, remonstrate or ask to leave the car may be nothing more than simple negligence. Harrington v. Collins, 1979, 298 N.C. 535, 259 S.E.2d 275.

2. Talbot v. Sims, 1905, 213 Pa. 1, 62 A. 107; Loynes v. Loring B. Hall Co., 1907, 194 Mass. 221, 80 N.E. 472.

3. Oltmanns v. Driver, 1961, 252 Iowa 1066, 109 N.W.2d 446; Manks v. Moore, 1909, 108 Minn. 284, 122 N.W. 5.

4. Burke v. Davis, 1906, 191 Mass. 20, 76 N.E. 1039; Blume v. Ballis, 1940, 207 Minn. 393, 291 N.W. 906.

5. Clarke v. Holmes, 1862, 7 H. & N. 937, 158 Eng. Rep. 751; Deshazer v. Tompkins, 1965, 89 Idaho 347, 404 P.2d 604; Schumaker v. King, Fla.App.1962, 141 So.2d 807. Cf. Ferraro v. Ford Motor Co., 1966, 423 Pa. 324, 223 A.2d 746.

6. Gunning System v. Lapointe, 1904, 212 Ill. 274, 72 N.E. 393; Heathcock v. Milwaukee Platteville Lead & Zinc Mining Co., 1906, 128 Wis. 46, 107 N.W. 463.

tion. Thus a shipper does not assume the risk of a defective car supplied him by a carrier where the only alternative to shipment in it is to let his cabbages rot in the field,[7] and a tenant does not assume the risk of the landlord's negligence in maintaining a common passageway when it is the only exit to the street.[8] In general, the plaintiff is not required to surrender a valuable legal right, such as the use of his own property as he sees fit, merely because the defendant's conduct has threatened him with harm if the right is exercised.[9] He is not, for example, required to forego pasturing his cattle in a field because the defendant has failed in its duty to fence its adjoining railway track.[10] By placing him in the dilemma, the defendant has deprived him of his freedom of choice, and so cannot be heard to say that he has voluntarily assumed the risk. Those who dash in to save their own property,[11] or the lives [12] or property [13] of others, from a peril created by the defendant's negligence, do not assume the risk where the alternative is to allow the threatened harm to occur. In all of these cases, of course, the danger may be out of all proportion to the value of any benefits involved, and so the plaintiff may be charged with contributory negligence for unreasonably choosing to confront the risk.[14] And where there is a reasonably safe alternative open, the plaintiff's choice of the dangerous way is a free one, and may amount to assumption of risk, negligence or both.[15]

The economic pressure which rests upon workers under threat of loss of employment received considerable recognition under the common law of England.[16] Notwithstanding violent denunciation at the hands of every writer who has dealt with the subject,[17] the American law was very slow to keep pace; and in the absence of a statute the greater number of courts for a long time held that a risk was assumed even when a workman acted under a direct command carrying an express or implied threat of discharge for disobedience.[18] Some vestiges of this old law no doubt still remain in fragments here and there; but it has been largely supersed-

---

7. Missouri, Kansas & Texas Railway Co. of Texas v. McLean, 1909, 55 Tex.Civ.App. 130, 118 S.W. 161, error refused.

8. Dollard v. Roberts, 1891, 130 N.Y. 269, 29 N.E. 104; Conroy v. Briley, Fla.App.1966, 191 So.2d 601; Brandt v. Thompson, Mo.1952, 252 S.W.2d 339. See also Mizenis v. Sands Motel, Inc., 1975, 50 Ohio App.2d 226, 362 N.E.2d 661 (motel); Scoggins v. Jude, D.C. App.1980, 419 A.2d 999 (defective ceiling in apartment).

9. See Marshall v. Ranne, Tex.1974, 511 S.W.2d 255 (plaintiff, bitten by neighbor's boar on way to car, did not have to remain prisoner in his own house); cf. Rutter v. Northeastern Beaver County School District, 1981, 496 Pa. 590, 437 A.2d 1198 (high school football player felt compelled to play summer "jungle football" so as not to diminish chances of making team in fall); Note, 1982, 95 Harv.L.Rev. 872, 890 (products liability).

10. Taulbee v. Campbell, 1931, 241 Ky. 410, 44 S.W.2d 275; North Bend Lumber Co. v. City of Seattle, 1921, 116 Wash. 500, 199 P. 988.

But if the danger is more imminent, as where a fire already set on the defendant's land is spreading to plaintiff's property, there may be negligence in failure to avoid the damage. Pribonic v. Fulton, 1922, 178 Wis. 393, 190 N.W. 190; Hall v. Meister, 1932, 42 Ohio App. 425, 182 N.E. 350.

11. Illinois Central Railroad Co. v. Siler, 1907, 229 Ill. 390, 82 N.E. 362; Glanz v. Chicago, Milwaukee & St. Paul Railway Co., 1903, 119 Iowa 611, 93 N.W. 575; Owen v. Cook, 1899, 9 N.D. 134, 81 N.W. 285.

12. Eckert v. Long Island Railroad Co., 1871, 43 N.Y. 502; Cote v. Palmer, 1940, 127 Conn. 321, 16 A.2d 595. See Goodhart, Rescue and Voluntary Assumption of Risk, 1934, 5 Camb.L.J. 192.

13. Henshaw v. Belyea, 1934, 220 Cal. 458, 31 P.2d 348. "Undoubtedly more risks may be taken to protect life than to protect property without involving imputation of negligence, but the rule is that a reasonable effort may be made even in the latter case." Andrews, J., in Wardrop v. Santi Moving & Express Co., 1922, 233 N.Y. 227, 135 N.E. 272.

14. Harding v. Philadelphia Rapid Transit Co., 1907, 217 Pa. 69, 66 A. 151; Devine v. Pfaelzer, 1917, 277 Ill. 255, 115 N.E. 126.

15. Rickey v. Boden, 1980, ___ R.I. ___, 421 A.2d 539, 544 (plaintiff "had several options reasonably available to her"); Myers v. Lennox Co-op Association, S.D.1981, 307 N.W.2d 863.

16. Yarmouth v. France, 1887, 19 Q.B.D. 647; Smith v. Baker & Sons, [1891] A.C. 325; Thrussell v. Handyside & Co., 1888, 20 Q.B.D. 359.

17. See for example Labatt, Volenti Non Fit Injuria as a Defense to Actions by Injured Servants, 1898, 32 Am.L.Rev. 57, 66; 3 Labatt, Master and Servant, 2d Ed. 1913, §§ 960–964.

18. Dougherty v. West Superior Iron & Steel Co., 1894, 88 Wis. 343, 60 N.W. 274; Hallstein v. Pennsylvania Railroad Co., 6th Cir. 1929, 30 F.2d 594; Nashville, Chattanooga & St. Louis Railway Co. v. Cleaver, 1938, 274 Ky. 410, 118 S.W.2d 748.

ed by the workers' compensation acts,[19] and even where these acts do not apply the defense of assumption of risk has been limited or removed, in many instances, by statute,[20] or by decision in those areas where no statute applies.[21] In the products liability context, where an injured worker's claim is against the manufacturer of an industrial machine, a number of courts have refused to allow the assumption of risk defense on similar reasoning,[22] although the defense has been allowed in this context by other courts.[23]

The defendant may be under a legal duty, which he is not free to refuse to perform, to exercise reasonable care for the plaintiff's safety, so that the plaintiff has a corresponding legal right to insist on that care. In such a case it is commonly said that the plaintiff does not assume the risk when he proceeds to make use of the defendant's services or facilities, notwithstanding his knowledge of the danger. This is undoubtedly true where the plaintiff acts reasonably, and the defendant has left him with no reasonable alternative, other than to forego the right entirely. Thus a common carrier,[24] or other public utility,[25] which has negligently provided a dangerously defective set of steps to its waiting room, cannot set up assumption of risk against a patron who makes use of the steps as the only convenient means of access. The same is true of a city maintaining a public highway or sidewalk,[26] or other public place which the plaintiff has a right to use,[27] and of premises upon which the plaintiff has a contractual right to enter.[28]

Violation of Statute

Where the defendant's negligence consists of the violation of a statute, the general view has been that the plaintiff may still assume the risk.[29] Thus a guest who accepts a night ride in an automobile without lights has been held to consent to relieve the defendant of the duty of conforming to the standard established by the statute for his

19. See Gow, The Defense of Volenti Non Fit Injuria, 1949, 61 Jurid.Rev. 37.

20. See infra, § 80.

21. See Kitchens v. Winter Co. Builders, Inc., 1982, 161 Ga.App. 701, 289 S.E.2d 807, 809 ("his course of conduct was restricted by the circumstances and the coercion of his employment"); Hobbs v. Armco, Fla. App.1982, 413 So.2d 118 (Mo. law); Haworth v. State, 1979, 60 Hawaii 557, 592 P.2d 820 (no assumption of risk by prisoners at forced labor); Hurd v. Hurd, Me. 1981, 423 A.2d 960 (awareness of obvious workplace hazard should go only to reduce, not bar, recovery under comparative negligence). But see Carroll v. Getty Oil Co., D.Del.1980, 498 F.Supp. 409 (independent contractor's employee); Rickey v. Boden, 1980, ___ R.I. ___, 421 A.2d 539 (landlord's employee); Baxter v. Grobmyer Brothers Construction Co., 1982, 275 Ark. 400, 631 S.W.2d 265; Riley v. Davison Construction Co., 1980, 381 Mass. 432, 409 N.E.2d 1279.

22. "It is illogical to prevent the employer from raising the defense of assumption of risk on the ground that the employee lacks freedom of choice, * * * while simultaneously allowing the manufacturer of the product used in the workplace to escape liability on the ground that the employee voluntarily assumed the risks." Note, 1982, 95 Harv.L.Rev. 872, 889–90 n. 68. See Johnson v. Clark Equipment Co., 1976, 274 Or. 403, 547 P.2d 132; Rhoads v. Service Machine Co., E.D.Ark.1971, 329 F.Supp. 367, 381 ("The 'voluntariness' with which a worker assigned to a dangerous machine in a factory 'assumes the risk of injury' from the machine is illusory.").

23. See, e.g., Alley v. Praschak Machine Co., Miss. 1979, 366 So.2d 661; Vargus v. Pittman Manufacturing Co., E.D.Pa.1981, 510 F.Supp. 116, affirmed 673 F.2d 1301, rehearing denied 675 F.2d 73; Carroll v. Getty Oil Co., D.Del.1980, 498 F.Supp. 409; Campbell v. Nordco Products, 7th Cir. 1980, 629 F.2d 1258 (Ill. law).

24. Letang v. Ottawa Electric R. Co. [1926] A.C. 725; Toroian v. Parkview Amusement Co., 1932, 331 Mo. 700, 56 S.W.2d 134; Dierks v. Alaska Air Transport, 1953, 14 Alaska 159, 109 F.Supp. 695.

25. Williamson v. Derry Electric Co., 1938, 89 N.H. 216, 196 A. 265.

26. Ahern v. City of Des Moines, 1943, 234 Iowa 113, 12 N.W.2d 296; Campion v. City of Rochester, 1938, 202 Minn. 136, 277 N.W. 422; Dougherty v. Chas. H. Tompkins Co., 1957, 99 U.S.App.D.C. 348, 240 F.2d 34. But see Moss v. Atlanta Housing Authority, 1981, 160 Ga.App. 555, 287 S.E.2d 619.

27. Orrison v. City of Rapid City, 1956, 76 S.D. 145, 74 N.W.2d 489 (municipal swimming pool); City of Madisonville v. Poole, Ky.1952, 249 S.W.2d 133 (city clubhouse).

28. Seelbach, Inc. v. Mellman, 1943, 293 Ky. 790, 170 S.W.2d 18 (employee of tenant in office building). In accord, as to the tenant himself. Rush v. Commercial Realty Co., 1929, 7 N.J.Misc. 337, 145 A. 476; Roman v. King, 1921, 289 Mo. 641, 233 S.W. 161.

29. See Carroll v. Getty Oil Co., D.Del.1980, 498 F.Supp. 409; Seim v. Garavalia, Minn.1981, 306 N.W.2d 806.

protection, and cannot be heard to complain when he is injured as a result.[30]

There have been certain statutes, however, which clearly are intended to protect the plaintiff against his own inability to protect himself, including his own lack of judgment or inability to resist various pressures. Such, for example, are the child labor acts,[31] and various safety statutes for the benefit of employees,[32] as to which the courts have recognized the economic inequality in bargaining power which induced the passage of the legislation. Since the fundamental purpose of such statutes would be defeated if the plaintiff were permitted to assume the risk, it is generally held that he cannot do so, either expressly or by implication.[33] Courts in a couple of states have held that a plaintiff may not assume the risk of the violation of any safety statute enacted for the protection of the public, sometimes reasoning that the obligation and the right so created are public ones, which it is not within the power of any private individual to waive.[34] This amounts to saying that the protective policy of the statutes simply must be held to override any such private agreements or understandings.

Abolition of the Defense

Assumption of risk has been a defense cordially disliked by the friends of the plaintiff, because of its long history of barring recovery in cases of genuine hardship.[35] There has been a strong movement among some legal writers to abrogate the defense as such in all but the cases of express agreement; to refuse to admit that in other cases it has any valid, or even factual separate existence; and to distribute it between the concepts of duty and contributory negligence.[36] The argument is that assumption of risk serves no purpose which is not fully taken care of by the other doctrines; that it adds only duplication leading to confusion; and that it results in denial of recovery in some cases where it should not be denied.

This attack has had its effect. In addition to the cases of violation of statute, to which reference has been made, a few courts have been led to abolish the defense completely in certain specific areas, such as the liability of an employer to his employee,[37] or that of an automobile driver to his guest.[38] In 1959 New Jersey took the lead in abolishing the defense of implied assumption of risk completely in all cases,[39] and this has now been

---

30. White v. Cochrane, 1933, 189 Minn. 300, 249 N.W. 328; Rittenberry v. Robert E. McKee, Inc., Tex. Civ.App.1960, 337 S.W.2d 197.

31. Lenahan v. Pittston Coal Mining Co., 1907, 218 Pa. 311, 67 A. 642; Dusha v. Virginia & Rainy Lake Co., 1920, 145 Minn. 171, 176 N.W. 482; Clark v. Arkansas Democrat Co., 1967, 242 Ark. 133, 413 S.W.2d 629.

32. Thomas v. Carroll Construction Co., 1957, 14 Ill. App.2d 205, 144 N.E.2d 461; Martin v. George Hyman Construction Co., D.C.App.1978, 395 A.2d 63; Evans v. NAB Construction Corp., 1981, 80 A.D.2d 841, 436 N.Y.S.2d 774. But see Carroll v. Getty Oil Co., D.Del. 1980, 498 F.Supp. 409; Larabee v. Triangle Steel, Inc., 1982, 86 A.D.2d 289, 451 N.Y.S.2d 258.

33. See also Scoggins v. Jude, D.C.App.1980, 419 A.2d 999 (tenant could not assume risks of dangerously defective apartment that violated housing safety regulations).

34. See Casey v. Atwater, 1960, 22 Conn.Sup. 225, 167 A.2d 250; Mulder v. Casho, 1964, 61 Cal.2d 633, 39 Cal.Rptr. 705, 394 P.2d 545. But cf. Baker v. Superior Court, 1982, 129 Cal.App.3d 710, 181 Cal.Rptr. 311, 318.

35. Particularly in cases of injury to employees. See infra, § 80.

36. See 2 Harper and James, Law of Torts, 1956, 1162–1192; Bohlen, Voluntary Assumption of Risk, 1906, 20 Harv.L.Rev. 14, 91; Rice, The Automobile Guest and the Rationale of Assumption of Risk, 1943, 27 Minn.L.Rev. 33; Payne, Assumption of Risk and Negligence, 1957, 35 Can.Bar Rev. 350; Wade, The Place of Assumption of Risk in the Law of Negligence, 1961, 22 La.L.Rev. 5; James, Assumption of Risk: Unhappy Reincarnation, 1968, 78 Yale L.J. 185. See also infra, note 54.

37. Siragusa v. Swedish Hospital, 1962, 60 Wn.2d 310, 373 P.2d 767; Ritter v. Beals, 1961, 225 Or. 504, 358 P.2d 1080; Hines v. Continental Baking Co., Mo. App.1960, 334 S.W.2d 140.

38. McConville v. State Farm Mutual Automobile Insurance Co., 1962, 15 Wis.2d 374, 113 N.W.2d 14; Zumwalt v. Lindland, 1964, 239 Or. 26, 396 P.2d 205; Leavitt v. Gillaspie, Alaska 1968, 443 P.2d 61. See Note, 1963, 38 Wash.L.Rev. 349.

39. In Meistrich v. Casino Arena Attractions Inc., 1959, 31 N.J. 44, 155 A.2d 90, the court urged the elimination of the term; and when this had no effect, McGrath v. American Cyanamid Co., 1963, 41 N.J. 272, 196 A.2d 238, declared that assumption of risk would no longer be recognized as a distinct doctrine.

followed in a number of other states.⁴⁰ The arguments in favor of the abolition have been as follows:

Where the plaintiff acts reasonably in making his choice of conduct, it is insisted that the only effect of assumption of risk is to deny the defendant's duty of care, and hence his negligence. This is certainly true. But it is further said that it follows that, just as there can be no duty when there is assumption of risk, there can be no assumption of risk when there is a duty owed to the plaintiff. This ignores entirely the procedure of a lawsuit, and in particular the burden of pleading and proof. If the question is only one of duty, then the burden of proof of the duty and its breach must normally fall upon the plaintiff; ⁴¹ and in any case where the plaintiff is dead, or otherwise unable to produce evidence that he did not consent, or where the evidence is no more than evenly balanced, he must usually lose. On the other hand, assumption of risk is an affirmative defense, which the defendant is required to plead and prove; ⁴² and if he does not, the plaintiff will recover. If, for example, there is a crash of a private airplane in which everyone is killed, including a passenger, and it appears that the plane was defective and the pilot knew it, treating disclosure to the passenger and his consent as a matter of duty means that he will lose; but if it is a matter of assumption of risk he will recover.⁴³ The shift of ground to "duty" can thus be a disservice to the plaintiff, imposing upon him a real procedural disadvantage, with no corresponding gain. Furthermore, duty is traditionally an issue for the court, whereas assumption of risk is a jury question in all but the clearest cases.⁴⁴

This becomes most readily apparent in the cases where there has been a time sequence. In the ordinary case the plaintiff makes out a prima facie case of a duty owed to him by proving the existence of some relation, such as that of invitor and invitee,⁴⁵ which imposes the full obligation of reasonable care for his protection. This duty does not coincide with those risks which the plaintiff does not in fact assume; rather it is based upon what the defendant can reasonably expect of him. Thus the obligation of the owner of a baseball park is to provide screened seats only for the number of patrons who may reasonably be expected to want them.⁴⁶ If he fails to do so he has, on the face of it, failed in his duty toward anyone seeking a screened seat, and he is liable when such an individual is hit by a ball. But it is still possible for such a person, after entering the park, to change his mind and decide to sit in an unscreened seat, or, on discovering a hole

---

40. Early cases included Bolduc v. Crain, 1962, 104 N.H. 163, 181 A.2d 641; Bulatao v. Kauai Motors, Limited, 1965, 49 Hawaii 1, 406 P.2d 887, rehearing denied 49 Hawaii 42, 408 P.2d 396; Parker v. Redden, Ky. 1967, 421 S.W.2d 586. Most lately is Rutter v. Northeastern Beaver County School District, 1981, 496 Pa. 590, 437 A.2d 1198, 1209 (except for express assumption of risk and strict tort products liability), where the court noted 19 other jurisdictions that have abolished or "seriously modified" the defense, concluding that "the difficulties of using the term 'assumption of risk' outweigh the benefits." See infra, note 56.

41. Cf. Berger v. Shapiro, 1959, 30 N.J. 89, 152 A.2d 20; Hannon v. Hayes-Bickford Lunch System, 1957, 336 Mass. 268, 145 N.E.2d 191.

42. E.g., Campbell v. Nordco Products, 7th Cir. 1980, 629 F.2d 1258 (Ill. law); Frederick v. Goff, 1960, 251 Iowa 290, 100 N.W.2d 624.

43. Suggested by Bruce v. O'Neal Flying Service, 1949, 231 N.C. 181, 56 S.E.2d 560.

44. Pona v. Boulevard Arena, 1955, 35 N.J.Super. 148, 113 A.2d 529.

45. See supra, § 61. Where the plaintiff proves only that he is a licensee, there is only a limited duty to him—for example, to warn him against latent dangers of which he does not know. See supra, § 60. It is quite often said that he "assumes the risk" of other dangers. This has been a fertile source of confusion in the law review articles. Much of it apparently has been due to the different meanings assigned to "duty." See Keeton, Assumption of Risk in Products Liability Cases, 1961, 22 La.L.Rev. 122, 160–164.

46. Brown v. San Francisco Baseball Club, 1950, 99 Cal.App.2d 484, 222 P.2d 19; Brisson v. Minneapolis Baseball & Athletic Association, 1932, 185 Minn. 508, 240 N.W. 903; Anderson v. Kansas City Baseball Club, Mo.1950, 231 S.W.2d 170; Keys v. Alamo City Baseball Co., Tex.Civ.App.1941, 150 S.W.2d 368; Ingersoll v. Onondaga Hockey Club, 1935, 245 App.Div. 137, 281 N.Y.S. 505 (ice hockey); cf. Lang v. Amateur Softball Association of America, Okla.1974, 520 P.2d 659 (10 foot bullpen fence high enough for soft ball pitching warm-up).

in the screen in front of him, to refuse to move—in each case, without any negligence of his own.⁴⁷ What, in such a case, changes "duty" to "no duty;" and if it is not to be called assumption of risk, what better name can be found? And should not the burden be upon the defendant to establish the change in the situation?

It has been proposed that, when the matter is dealt with in terms of duty, the burden of proof as to "no duty" be placed upon the defendant.⁴⁸ It is difficult to see how this amounts to anything more than a change of terminology, or how it offers any advantage, other than the elimination of a phrase which is so cordially disliked by some writers and courts as to amount almost to a phobia. If the consent of the plaintiff to the defendant's negligence is to negative a duty which would clearly otherwise exist, and the burden of proof on the issue is upon the defendant, why not continue to call it assumption of risk, which is the term the courts have always used?

Where the plaintiff acts unreasonably in making his choice, it is said that there is merely one form of contributory negligence, which is in large part true; and from that it is argued that there is, or should be, no distinction between the two defenses, and that there is only useless and confusing duplication. But this is a distinctive kind of contributory negligence, in which the plaintiff knows the risk and voluntarily accepts it; and it has been thought sufficiently different in nature from contributory negligence, in which the plaintiff may merely fail to discover the danger, to support a number of important doctrinal distinctions between the two defenses. Thus, assumption of risk is governed by the subjective standard of the plaintiff himself, whereas contributory negligence is measured by the objective standard of the reasonable man.⁴⁹ Assumption of risk, whether or not it is called contributory negligence, may bar recovery in an action founded on strict liability,⁵⁰ where the plaintiff's ordinary negligence will not. The plaintiff may assume the risk where the conduct of the defendant is willful, wanton or reckless,⁵¹ where his ordinary negligence is no defense; and while there will certainly be many cases in which the encountering of a known high degree of danger will itself be willful, wanton and reckless, and so a bar under either theory,⁵² there will be others where it is not. It also appears that assumption of risk may be a good defense where the defendant has the last clear chance.⁵³

Effect of Comparative Negligence on Assumption of Risk

The rise of comparative negligence has forced the courts and commentators to consider afresh the proper role for the assumption of risk defense.⁵⁴ Indeed, several comparative negligence statutes by their terms

---

47. Kavafian v. Seattle Baseball Club Association, 1919, 105 Wash. 215, 177 P. 776, reversed in 105 Wash. 215, 181 P. 679; Hudson v. Kansas City Baseball Club, 1942, 349 Mo. 1215, 164 S.W.2d 318; Hunt v. Portland Baseball Club, 1956, 207 Or. 337, 296 P.2d 495; Shaw v. Boston American League Baseball Co., 1950, 325 Mass. 419, 90 N.E.2d 840; Chickasha Cotton Oil Co. v. Holloway, Tex.Civ.App.1964, 378 S.W.2d 695, refused, no reversible error. See cases collected in Notes, [1951] Wash.U.L.Q. 434; 1960, 46 Corn.L.Q. 140.

48. James, Assumption of Risk: Unhappy Reincarnation, 1968, 78 Yale L.J. 185; Meistrich v. Casino Arena Attractions, 1959, 31 N.J. 44, 155 A.2d 90.

49. See supra, note 69.

50. See Lipson v. Superior Court, 1982, 31 Cal.3d 362, 182 Cal.Rptr. 629, 644 P.2d 822, 830–31; Armstrong v. Mailand, Minn.1979, 284 N.W.2d 343; Note, 1982, 95 Harv.L.Rev. 872; infra, chapters 13 & 17.

51. Waltanen v. Wiitala, 1960, 361 Mich. 504, 105 N.W.2d 400; Evans v. Holsinger, 1951, 242 Iowa 990, 48 N.W.2d 250; Pierce v. Clemens, 1943, 113 Ind.App. 65, 46 N.E.2d 836; Gill v. Arthur, 1941, 69 Ohio App. 386, 43 N.E.2d 894; Schubring v. Weggen, 1940, 234 Wis. 517, 291 N.W. 788; Vargus v. Pitman Manufacturing Co., E.D.Pa.1981, 510 F.Supp. 116, affirmed 673 F.2d 1301, rehearing denied 675 F.2d 73.

52. See Brown v. Barber, 1943, 26 Tenn.App. 534, 174 S.W.2d 298; Second Restatement of Torts, § 503.

53. Boyles v. Hamilton, 1965, 235 Cal.App.2d 492, 45 Cal.Rptr. 399; cf. Gover v. Central Vermont Railway Co., 1922, 96 Vt. 208, 118 A. 874.

54. See generally Schwartz, Comparative Negligence, 1974, ch. 9; Woods, The Negligence Case—Comparative Fault, 1978, ch. 6; Notes, 1977, 6 U.C.L.A.-Alas.L.Rev. 244; 1978, 39 Ohio St.L.J. 364; 1971, 56

abolish assumption of risk, in addition to contributory negligence, as defenses that will bar liability altogether.[55] Most of the statutes, however, are silent on assumption of risk, and so the matter has been thrown over to the courts.

Like some of the legislatures, some of the courts have held broadly that the defense of assumption of risk should be "abolished" or "merged" into the system of comparative negligence.[56] Although many of the cases have spoken of assumption of risk as if it were a single doctrine, thus "merging," "abolishing" or retaining "it" in all forms in which it has been used, it is important to distinguish again among the various kinds of assumption of risk to understand the proper impact of comparative negligence in this area of the law. Although there are a variety of logical classification schemes, the division followed here will be into "express" assumption of risk, and the various forms of "implied" assumption of risk: "primary," "unreasonable," and "reasonable" assumption of risk.[57]

Express Assumption of Risk. Because express assumption of risk involves an affirmatively demonstrated, and presumably bargained upon, choice by the plaintiff to relieve the defendant of his legal duty toward the plaintiff, this voluntary shifting of legal responsibility between contracting parties would seem by its nature to be outside of the "fault" or negligence allocation debate. Thus, absent policy reasons for prohibiting contractual disclaimers of this type in certain contexts,[58] an express assumption of risk by the plaintiff should continue to serve as a total bar in comparative negligence cases.[59]

Primary Assumption of Risk. On somewhat similar reasoning, but without the additional ceremonial and evidentiary weight of an express agreement, "primary" implied assumption of risk should also logically continue to be an absolute bar after the adoption of comparative fault,[60] even perhaps where a comparative negligence statute broadly abolishes or merges "assumption of risk" into the damages apportionment system.[61] This is because assumption of risk in this form is really a principle of no duty, or no negligence, and so denies the existence of any underlying cause of action. Without a breach of duty by the defendant, there is thus logically nothing to compare with any

---

Minn.L.Rev. 47; 1975, 46 U.Colo.L.Rev. 509; Annot., 1982, 16 A.L.R.4th 700.

55. See Meese v. Brigham Young University, Utah 1981, 639 P.2d 720; Blair v. Mt. Hood Meadows Development Corp., 1981, 291 Or. 293, 630 P.2d 827, rehearing denied and opinion modified 291 Or. 703, 634 P.2d 241; Franco v. Zingarelli, 1980, 72 A.D.2d 211, 424 N.Y.S.2d 185; also, F.E.L.A., and the statutes of Connecticut, Massachusetts and Oklahoma. See Schwartz, supra note 54, § 9.2.

56. See, e.g., Blackburn v. Dorta, Fla.1977, 348 So. 2d 287, on remand 350 So.2d 25; Abernathy v. Eline Oil Field Services, Inc., 1982, ___ Mont. ___, 650 P.2d 772 (except for strict liability; but see infra, note 64); Brittain v. Booth, Wyo.1979, 601 P.2d 532; Lyons v. Redding Construction Co., 1973, 83 Wn.2d 86, 515 P.2d 821; Rutter v. Northeastern Beaver County School District, 1981, 496 Pa. 590, 437 A.2d 1198, 1209 n. 5 (3-1-3) (listing decisions from 19 other states that "have either seriously modified or abolished the assumption of risk doctrine": Alaska, Cal., Del., Hawaii, Idaho, Iowa, Ky., Mich., Minn., N.H., N.J., N.M., N.C., Or., Tex., Wash., Wis., Wyo.); cf. Lipson v. Superior Ct., 1982, 31 Cal.3d 362, 182 Cal.Rptr. 629, 644 P.2d 822; South v. A.B. Chance Co., 1981, 96 Wn.2d 439, 635 P.2d 728 (strict products liability).

57. See Blackburn v. Dorta, Fla.1977, 348 So.2d 287, on remand 350 So.2d 25.

58. See supra, pp. 482–484.

59. See generally Blackburn v. Dorta, Fla.1977, 348 So.2d 287, on remand 350 So.2d 25; Keegan v. Anchor Inns, Inc., 3d Cir. 1979, 606 F.2d 35; Colson v. Rule, 1962, 15 Wis.2d 387, 113 N.W.2d 21; Rutter v. Northeastern Beaver County School District, 1981, 496 Pa. 590, 437 A.2d 1198; Farley v. M M Cattle Co., Tex. 1975, 529 S.W.2d 751, appeal after remand 549 S.W.2d 453, error refused no reversible error; Li v. Yellow Cab Co., 1975, 13 Cal.3d 804, 119 Cal.Rptr. 858, 532 P.2d 1226; Polsky v. Levine, 1976, 73 Wis.2d 547, 243 N.W.2d 503; Thompson v. Weaver, 1977, 277 Or. 299, 560 P.2d 620; Lyons v. Redding Construction Co., 1973, 83 Wn.2d 86, 515 P.2d 821; Brittain v. Booth, Wyo. 1979, 601 P.2d 532.

60. Cf. Strickland v. Roberts, Fla.App.1980, 382 So. 2d 1338; Iepson v. Noren, Minn.1981, 308 N.W.2d 812 (but case did not present it in primary form); see infra, note 62.

61. See Akins v. Glens Falls City School District, 1981, 53 N.Y.2d 325, 441 N.Y.S.2d 644, 424 N.E.2d 531.

misconduct of the plaintiff. Although there has been little judicial authority squarely on this point, most courts have been so inclined to retain this form of assumption of risk as a total bar,[62] while a couple of others have taken the mysterious position that the defense somehow should be factored in to the damages apportionment scheme even in its primary form.[63]

Unreasonable Assumption of Risk. When a plaintiff's implied assumption of risk is unreasonable, it looks most closely like contributory negligence. The defense is therefore most amenable to "merger" into a comparative negligence system when it appears in its "unreasonable" form. The plaintiff by hypothesis has been negligent in choosing to encounter the risk, and so many courts have held that the contributory negligence form of assumption of risk—probably the most common form in which the doctrine appears—should be absorbed into the mainstream of comparative fault, thus serving only to reduce the plaintiff's damages, not to bar them altogether.[64] Other courts, however, have held that the doctrine of assumption of risk continues to serve as an absolute bar in all its traditional splendor,[65] and thus at least by implication that even in its overlap with contributory negligence it may continue to be a total bar to recovery. The reasoning behind this latter approach would seem to be a belief that the plaintiff's deliberate choice to encounter the preexisting risk is more than merely an aggravation of his fault, and that it fairly serves to shift the consequences completely to the plaintiff who has made the final, deliberate, and unreasonable choice to take control of the situation and place himself at risk.

Reasonable Assumption of Risk. Arguments similar to those that support treating unreasonable assumption of risk as a total bar continue when the plaintiff's deliberate choice is instead completely reasonable. Yet where the defendant's negligence has forced the plaintiff into a situation where he must reasonably choose to undergo the risk, there seems to be a fundamental flaw in reasoning that the plaintiff should thereby be held to have forfeited any right to charge the defendant for his resulting injuries. It would thus appear quite odd if the plaintiff's reasonable assumption of the risk to which he was exposed by the negligence of the defendant were treated as an absolute bar. Nor logically should it even factor in to reduce the plaintiff's damages, since his con-

---

62. See Akins v. Glens Falls City School Dist., 1980, 53 N.Y.2d 325, 441 N.Y.S.2d 531, 424 N.E.2d 531 (4–3); Armstrong v. Mailand, Minn.1979, 284 N.W.2d 343; Vargus v. Pitman Manufacturing Co., E.D.Pa.1981, 510 F.Supp. 116, affirmed 673 F.2d 1301, rehearing denied 673 F.2d 73 (obvious danger rule barred recovery by crane operator who hit high-tension line); Baker v. Superior Court, 1982, 129 Cal.App.3d 710, 181 Cal.Rptr. 311, 317 (fireman's rule—"'true' assumption of risk—a negation of the duty to exercise reasonable care"); Lipson v. Superior Court, 1982, 31 Cal.3d 362, 182 Cal. Rptr. 629, 644 P.2d 822 (same); cf. Strickland v. Roberts, Fla.App.1980, 382 So.2d 1338; Iepson v. Noren, Minn.1981, 308 N.W.2d 812 (but case did not present it in primary form); Sunday v. Stratton Corp., 1978, 136 Vt. 293, 390 A.2d 398; Jacobsen Construction Co. v. Structo-Lite Engineering, Inc., Utah 1980, 619 P.2d 306; Keegan v. Anchor Inns, Inc., 3d Cir. 1979, 606 F.2d 35 (V.I. law).

63. See Blair v. Mt. Hood Meadows Development Corp., 1981, 291 Or. 293, 630 P.2d 827, rehearing denied and opinion modified 291 Or. 703, 634 P.2d 241; cf. Parker v. Highland Park, Inc., Tex.1978, 565 S.W.2d 512 (obvious danger no-duty rule toward invitees abolished for land occupiers); Bennett v. Span Industries, Inc., Tex.App.1981, 628 S.W.2d 470, 473, error refused no reversible error; Parks v. Allis-Chalmers Corp., Minn.1979, 289 N.W.2d 456 (same; products liability).

64. See, e.g., Jones v. M.T.D. Products, Inc., M.D. Pa.1980, 507 F.Supp. 8, affirmed without opinion, 3d Cir. 1981, 649 F.2d 859; Paula v. Gagnon, 1978, 81 Cal. 3d 680, 146 Cal.Rptr. 702; Lipson v. Superior Court, 1982, 31 Cal.3d 362, 182 Cal.Rptr. 629, 644 P.2d 822; Jacobsen Construction Co. v. Structo-Lite Engineering, Inc., Utah 1980, 619 P.2d 306. See also Zahrte v. Sturm, Ruger & Co., Inc., 1983, ___ Mont. ___, 661 P.2d 17 (strict liability).

65. See, e.g., Riley v. Davison Construction Co., 1980, 381 Mass. 432, 409 N.E.2d 1279 (prior to enactment of merger statute); Sandberg v. Hoogensen, 1978, 201 Neb. 190, 266 N.W.2d 745; Kirkland v. General Motors Corp., Okl.1974, 521 P.2d 1353; Singleton v. Wiley, Miss.1979, 372 So.2d 272; Capps v. McCarley & Co., 1976, 260 Ark. 839, 544 S.W.2d 850; Rickey v. Boden, 1980, ___ R.I. ___, 421 A.2d 539; Kirby v. Hylton, 1982, 51 Md.App. 365, 443 A.2d 640; Moss v. Atlanta Housing Authority, 1981, 160 Ga.App. 555, 287 S.E.2d 619.

duct has by definition been free from blame. Moreover, as some have noted, there would be a strange anomaly if a plaintiff who negligently assumed the risk recovered part of his damages, but the plaintiff who reasonably did so recovered none.[66]

Jury Instructions on Assumption of Risk After Comparative Fault. Once a legislature or court has determined to "merge" assumption of risk into the comparative fault system, the courts are forced to decide whether to provide the jury with a separate instruction on assumption of risk, in addition to any normal instructions on comparative fault. On this question the courts have so far split, some holding that separate instructions may [67] be given, and others holding that the trial court may properly refuse,[68] or must refuse,[69] to so instruct the jury.

WESTLAW REFERENCES

di assumption of risk
di volenti non fit injuria

Express Agreement
assumption +3 risk /p express** /7 agree!

Implied Acceptance of Risk
implied /s assumption +3 risk

Knowledge and Appreciation of Risk
digest(assumption +3 risk /p kn*w* /s appreciat! /s risk*)

Voluntary Assumption
assumption +3 risk /p voluntar! /8 assum! /8 risk*

Violation of Statute
opinion(assumption +s risk & defendant /s violat! break*** /s statute* law* act*)

Abolition of the Defense
assumption +3 risk /s abolish! limit*** circumscrib! /s defense*

Effect of Comparative Negligence on Assumption of Risk
assumption +3 risk /s "comparative negligence"

Express Assumption of Risk
express** /9 assum! /9 risk*

Primary Assumption of Risk
primary /s assumption +3 risk*

Unreasonable Assumption of Risk
unreasonable /s assumption +3 risk*

Reasonable Assumption of Risk
reasonable /10 assumption +3 risk*

Jury Instructions on Assumption of Risk After Comparative Fault
jury /5 instruction* charg! /s assumption +3 risk*

---

66. See, e.g., Blackburn v. Dorta, Fla.1977, 348 So. 2d 287, on remand 350 So.2d 25; cf. Bolduc v. Crain, 1962, 104 N.H. 163, 181 A.2d 641. But cf. Braswell v. Economy Supply Co., Miss.1973, 281 So.2d 669; Keegan v. Anchor Inns, Inc., 3d Cir. 1979, 606 F.2d 35 (V.I. law); Scoggins v. Jude, D.C.App.1980, 419 A.2d 999 (merging unreasonable assumption of risk into contributory negligence, and leaving reasonable assumption of risk as separate defense).

67. See Singleton v. Wiley, Miss.1979, 372 So.2d 272.

68. See Moore v. Burton Lumber & Hardware Co., Utah 1981, 631 P.2d 865.

69. See Blair v. Mt. Hood Meadows Development Corp., 1981, 291 Or. 293, 630 P.2d 827, rehearing denied and opinion modified 291 Or. 703, 634 P.2d 241; Franco v. Zingarelli, 1980, 72 A.D.2d 211, 424 N.Y.S.2d 185; Wegscheider v. Plastics, Inc., Minn.1980, 289 N.W.2d 167; Polsky v. Levine, 1976, 73 Wis.2d 547, 243 N.W.2d 503; see Sunday v. Stratton Corp., 1978, 136 Vt. 293, 390 A.2d 398; Meese v. Brigham Young University, Utah 1981, 639 P.2d 720.

Chapter 12

IMPUTED NEGLIGENCE

Table of Sections

Sec.
69. Vicarious Liability.
70. Servants.
71. Independent Contractors.
72. Joint Enterprise.
73. Automobile Owners and Others.
74. Imputed Contributory Negligence.

§ 69. Vicarious Liability

A is negligent, B is not. "Imputed negligence" means that, by reason of some relation existing between A and B, the negligence of A is to be charged against B, although B has played no part in it, has done nothing whatever to aid or encourage it, or indeed has done all that he possibly can to prevent it. The result may be that B, in an action against C for his own injuries, is barred from recovery because of A's negligence, to the same extent as if he had been negligent himself. This is commonly called "imputed contributory negligence." [1] Or the result may be that B, in C's action against him, becomes liable as a defendant for C's injuries, on the basis of A's negligence. This is sometimes called imputed negligence. More often it is called vicarious liability, or the principle is given the Latin name of *respondeat superior*.

Since B himself has been free from all fault, when he is held liable to C it is in one sense a form of strict liability. In another it is not.[2] The foundation of the action is still negligence, or other fault, on the part of A; and all that the law has done is to broaden the liability for that fault by imposing it upon an additional, albeit innocent, defendant. It is still an action for negligence, and the ordinary rules of negligence liability are still applied to it.[3] The most familiar illustration,

§ 69

1. See infra, § 74.

2. See Williams, Vicarious Liability: Tort of the Master or of the Servant? 1956, 72 L.Q.Rev. 522; Note, 1957, 20 Mod.L.Rev. 655.

3. Thus the defenses of contributory negligence and assumption of risk are open to B as well as A. And a judgment for A in an action brought against him by C is res judicata as to B's vicarious liability to C.

See, e.g., Medearis v. Miller, N.D.1981, 306 N.W.2d 200; Health & Hospital Corp. of Marion v. Gaither, 1979, ___ Ind. ___, 397 N.E.2d 589; Morehouse v. Wanzo, 1968, 266 Cal.App.2d 846, 72 Cal.Rptr. 607.

One important distinction is that some courts refuse to hold B liable for punitive damages unless B ordered, participated in, or ratified A's misconduct; but other courts apply the normal principles of vicarious liability. See Owen, Punitive Damages in Products Liability Litigation, 1976, 74 Mich.L.Rev. 1257, 1299–1308. Another

of course, is the liability of a master for the torts of his servant in the course of his employment.

The idea of vicarious liability was common enough in primitive law. Not only the torts of servants and slaves, or even wives, but those of inanimate objects, were charged against their owner. The movement of the earlier English law was away from such strict responsibility, until by the sixteenth century it was considered that the master should not be liable for his servant's torts unless he had commanded the particular act.[4] But soon after 1700 this rule was found to be far too narrow to fit the expanding complications of commerce and industry, and the courts began to revert to something like the earlier rule, at first under the fiction of a command to the servant "implied" from the employment itself,[5] and at last, by slow degrees, by minimizing and finally abandoning the fiction of command.

A multitude of very ingenious reasons have been offered for the vicarious liability of a master:[6] he has a more or less fictitious "control" over the behavior of the servant; he has "set the whole thing in motion," and is therefore responsible for what has happened; he has selected the servant and trusted him, and so should suffer for his wrongs, rather than an innocent stranger who has had no opportunity to protect himself; it is a great concession that any man should be permitted to employ another at all, and there should be a corresponding responsibility as the price to be paid for it—or, more frankly and cynically, "In hard fact, the reason for the employers' liability is the damages are taken from a deep pocket."[7] None of these reasons is so self-sufficient as to carry conviction, although they are all in accord with the general common law notion that one who is in a position to exercise some general control over the situation must exercise it or bear the loss. All of them go beyond that notion in holding the defendant liable even though he has done his best. Most courts have made little or no effort to explain the result, and have taken refuge in rather empty phrases, such as "he who does a thing through another does it himself," or the endlessly repeated formula of "respondeat superior," which in itself means nothing more than "look to the man higher up."

What has emerged as the modern justification[8] for vicarious liability is a rule of policy, a deliberate allocation of a risk. The losses caused by the torts of employees, which as a practical matter are sure to occur in the conduct of the employer's enterprise, are placed upon that enterprise itself, as a required cost of doing business. They are placed upon the employer because, having engaged in an enterprise, which will on the basis of all past experience involve harm to others through the torts of employees, and sought to profit by it, it is just that he, rather than the innocent injured plaintiff, should bear them; and because he is better able to absorb them, and to distribute them,

---

distinction is that B may not necessarily have the benefit of immunity from suit, as where A is a husband and the plaintiff is his wife. See infra, § 122; Hamburger v. Henry Ford Hospital, 1979, 91 Mich.App. 580, 284 N.W.2d 155 (hospital not entitled to immunity of employees). But see Hulsman v. Hemmeter Development Corp., 1982, ___ Hawaii ___, 647 P.2d 713 (employer gets benefit of public employee's immunity from suit).

4. Wigmore, Responsibility for Tortious Acts: Its History, 1894, 7 Harv.L.Rev. 315, 383, 441; Holdsworth, History of Engligh Law, 4th ed. 1935, vol. 3, 382–387, vol. 8, 472–482; Baty, Vicarious Liability, 1916, ch. 1.

5. 1 Bl.Comm. 429; Hern v. Nichols, 1708, 1 Salk. 289, 91 Eng.Rep. 256; Brucker v. Fromont, 1796, 6 Term Rep. 659, 101 Eng.Rep. 758.

6. See Baty, Vicarious Liability, 1916, ch. 8; Baty, The Basis of Responsibility, 1920, 32 Jurid.Rev. 159; Smith, Frolic and Detour, 1923, 23 Col.L.Rev. 444, 454; James, Vicarious Liability, 1954, 28 Tulane L.Rev. 161.

7. Baty, Vicarious Liability, 1916, 154.

8. See Seavey, Speculations as to "Respondeat Superior," Harvard Legal Essays, 1934, 433; Laski, The Basis of Vicarious Liability, 1916, 26 Yale L.J. 105; Smith, Frolic and Detour, 1923, 23 Col.L.Rev. 444, 456; Douglas, Vicarious Liability and Administration of Risk, 1929, 38 Yale L.J. 584, 720; Miller, The Master-Servant Concept and Judge-Made Law, 1941, 1 Loyola L.Rev. 25; Neuner, Respondeat Superior in the Light of Comparative Law, 1941, 4 La.L.Rev. 1; Ferson, Bases for Master's Liability and for Principal's Liability to Third Persons, 1951, 4 Vand.L.Rev. 260; Ehrenzweig, Negligence Without Fault, 1966, 54 Calif.L.Rev. 1422.

through prices, rates or liability insurance, to the public, and so to shift them to society, to the community at large.⁹ Added to this is the makeweight argument that an employer who is held strictly liable is under the greatest incentive to be careful in the selection, instruction and supervision of his servants, and to take every precaution to see that the enterprise is conducted safely. Notwithstanding the occasional condemnation of the entire doctrine which used to appear in the past,¹⁰ the tendency is clearly to justify it on such grounds, and gradually to extend it.¹¹

WESTLAW REFERENCES

"imputed negligence" "vicarious liability" "respondeat superior" /p topic(225 148a)
di respondeat superior
vicarious** /s liable liability /s allocat! /s risk* loss**
"deep pocket" & topic(negligence torts "product* liability")

§ 70. Servants

The traditional definition of a servant is that he is a person employed to perform services in the affairs of another, whose physical conduct in the performance of the service is controlled, or is subject to a right of control, by the other.¹

This is, however, a great over-simplification of a complex matter. In determining the existence of "control" or the right to it, many factors are to be taken into account and balanced against one another—the extent to which, by agreement, the employer may determine the details of the work; the kind of occupation and the customs of the community as to whether the work usually is supervised by the employer; whether the one employed is engaged in a distinct business or occupation, and the skill required of him; who supplies the place and instrumentalities of the work; the length of time the employment is to last; the method of payment, and many others.² Consideration of the extensive and detailed ramification of all this must be left to other texts; but it is probably no very inaccurate summary of the whole matter to say that the person employed is a servant when, in the eyes of the community, he would be regarded as a part of the employer's own working staff, and not otherwise.

Once it is determined that the man at work is a servant, the master becomes subject to vicarious liability for his torts. He

---

9. As to proposals to extend this "enterprise liability" to other defendants, see infra, § 85.

10. See Holmes, Agency, 1891, 5 Harv.L.Rev. 14; Baty, Vicarious Liability, 1916, ch. 8; Baty, Basis of Responsibility, 1920, 32 Jurid.Rev. 159. Cf. the testimony of Bramwell before the parliamentary committee of 1876, 1887, Cd. 285, p. 46.

11. Seavey, Speculations as to "Respondeat Superior," Harvard Legal Essays, 1934, 433, 451.

§ 70

1. Second Restatement of Agency, § 220(1); see Peeples v. Kawasaki Heavy Industries, Limited, 1979, 288 Or. 143, 603 P.2d 765; Hale v. Peabody Coal Co., 1976, 168 Ind.App. 336, 343 N.E.2d 316; Gifford-Hill & Co. v. Moore, Tex.Civ.App.1972, 479 S.W.2d 711; Soderbach v. Townsend, 1982, 57 Or.App. 366, 644 P.2d 640 (employment arrangement is examined); Baird v. Sickler, 1982, 69 Ohio St.2d 652, 433 N.E.2d 593 (chief surgeon liable for negligence of nurse-anesthetist); cf. Hodges v. Doctors Hospital, 1977, 141 Ga.App. 649, 234 S.E.2d 116 (doctor-hospital; for jury).

2. See Second Restatement of Agency, § 220(2); Smith v. California Department of Employment, 1976, 62 Cal.App.3d 206, 132 Cal.Rptr. 874; Grant v. Director of Benefit Payments, 1977, 71 Cal.App.3d 647, 139 Cal. Rptr. 533; Atlanta Commercial Builders, Inc. v. Polinsky, 1978, 148 Ga.App. 181, 250 S.E.2d 781; Jones v. Atteberry, 1979, 77 Ill.App.3d 463, 33 Ill.Dec. 28, 396 N.E.2d 104; Truck Insurance Exchange v. Yardley, Utah 1976, 556 P.2d 494; Massey v. Tube Art Display, Inc., 1976, 15 Wn.App. 782, 551 P.2d 1387; Naccash v. Burger, 1982, 223 Va. 406, 290 S.E.2d 825.

As to the "borrowed servant," lent by one employer to another, see Societa per Azioni de Navigazione Italia v. City of Los Angeles, 1982, 31 Cal.3d 446, 183 Cal. Rptr. 51, 645 P.2d 102, certiorari denied, ___ U.S. ___, 103 S.Ct. 346, 74 L.Ed.2d 386; Maynard v. Kenova Chemical Co., 4th Cir. 1980, 626 F.2d 359; Six Flags Over Georgia, Inc. v. Hill, 1981, 247 Ga. 375, 276 S.E.2d 572, affirmed 158 Ga.App. 658, 282 S.E.2d 224; Thate v. Texas & Pacific Railway Co., Tex.Civ.App.1980, 595 S.W.2d 591; LeJeune v. Allstate Insurance Co., La. 1978, 365 So.2d 471, on remand 373 So.2d 212 (hearse driver); Second Restatement of Agency, § 227.

Closely analogous issues are involved in the workers' compensation context. See infra, § 80.

may, of course, be liable on the basis of any negligence of his own in selecting or dealing with the servant, or for the latter's acts which he has authorized or ratified, upon familiar principles of negligence and agency law.[3] But his vicarious liability, for conduct which is in no way his own, extends to any and all tortious conduct of the servant which is within the "scope of the employment." [4] This highly indefinite phrase, which sometimes is varied with "in the course of the employment," is so devoid of meaning in itself that its very vagueness has been of value in permitting a desirable degree of flexibility in decisions. It is obviously no more than a bare formula to cover the unordered and unauthorized acts of the servant for which it is found to be expedient to charge the master with liability, as well as to exclude other acts for which it is not. It refers to those acts which are so closely connected with what the servant is employed to do, and so fairly and reasonably incidental to it, that they may be regarded as methods, even though quite improper ones, of carrying out the objectives of the employment.

As in the case of the existence of the relation itself, many factors enter into the question:[5] the time, place and purpose of the act, and its similarity to what is authorized; whether it is one commonly done by such servants; the extent of departure from normal methods; the previous relations between the parties; whether the master had reason to expect that such an act would be done; and many other considerations, as to which the reader must be referred to texts dealing with the subject at length.[6] It has been said that in general the servant's conduct is within the scope of his employment if it is of the kind which he is employed to perform, occurs substantially within the authorized limits of time and space, and is actuated, at least in part, by a purpose to serve the master.[7]

The fact that the servant's act is expressly forbidden by the master, or is done in a manner which he has prohibited, is to be considered in determining what the servant has been hired to do,[8] but it is usually not conclusive, and does not in itself prevent the act from being within the scope of employment. A master cannot escape liability merely by ordering his servant to act carefully. If he could, no doubt few employers would ever be held liable. Thus, instructions to a sales

---

3. Second Restatement of Agency, §§ 212–218. See Easley v. Apollo Detective Agency, Inc., 1979, 69 Ill.App.3d 920, 26 Ill.Dec. 313, 387 N.E.2d 1241 (negligent hiring); Shore v. Town of Stonington, 1982, 187 Conn. 147, 444 A.2d 1379 (same); International Distributing Corp. v. American District Telephone Co., D.C. Cir.1977, 569 F.2d 136 (negligent supervision); Spahn v. Guild Industries Corp., 1979, 94 Cal.App.3d 143, 156 Cal.Rptr. 375 (ratification). But see Strauss v. Hotel Continental Co., Inc., Mo.App.1980, 610 S.W.2d 109 (no reason to know employee was dangerous). Other important recent cases on negligent hiring or retention include Ponticas v. K.M.S. Investments, Minn.1983, 331 N.W.2d 907; Lockett v. Bi-State Transit Authority, 1983, 94 Ill.2d 66, 67 Ill.Dec. 830, 445 N.E.2d 310 (willful and wanton retention of bus drivers with poor driving record); DiCosala v. Kay, 1982, 91 N.J. 159, 450 A.2d 508.

4. See Smith, Scope of the Business: The Borrowed Servant Problem, 1940, 38 Mich.L.Rev. 1222; Notes, 1936, 21 Corn.L.Q. 294; 1957, 24 Tenn.L.Rev. 241.

The fellow servant rule was a major exception to this principle in former times, and is still so to some extent today. See Thornton v. Thornton, 1980, 45 N.C.App. 25, 262 S.E.2d 326. Contra, abolishing rule, Buckley v. City of New York, 1982, 56 N.Y.2d 300, 452 N.Y.S.2d 331, 437 N.E.2d 1088. See infra, § 80.

5. Second Restatement of Agency, § 229; see Ferrell v. Martin, 1980, 276 Pa.Super. 175, 419 A.2d 152; Scott v. Min-Aqua Bats Water Ski Club, Inc., 1977, 79 Wis.2d 316, 255 N.W.2d 536 (water ski clown negligently fired shotgun in preparation for act).

6. See 6 Labatt, Master and Servant, 1913, ch. 92–105; 2 Mechem Agency, 1952. On the vicarious liability of private franchisors, see Annot., 1977, 81 A.L.R.3d 764.

7. Second Restatement of Agency, § 228; Stanfield v. Laccoarce, 1978, 284 Or. 651, 588 P.2d 1271; Barnes v. Towlson, Del.1979, 405 A.2d 137 (although commuting to and from work is personal, driving own car to meet employer for business purposes is within scope).

8. Thus in Gurley v. Southern Power Co., 1916, 172 N.C. 690, 90 S.E. 943, a custodian of a private swimming pool was instructed not to admit unauthorized swimmers. He did so, and rented them suits. It was held that the orders were conclusive that this was beyond the scope of his employment. See also Moore v. Leaseway Transportation Corp., 1980, 42 N.Y.2d 720, 426 N.Y.S.2d 259, 402 N.E.2d 1160 (vehicle owner not liable for injuries to passenger riding with employee against rules).

clerk never to load a gun while exhibiting it will not prevent liability when the clerk does so, in an effort to sell the gun.[9] If the other factors involved indicate that the forbidden conduct is merely the servant's own way of accomplishing an authorized purpose, the master cannot escape responsibility no matter how specific, detailed and emphatic his orders may have been to the contrary.[10] This has been clear since the leading English case [11] in which an omnibus company was held liable notwithstanding definite orders to its driver not to obstruct other vehicles. It is still the master's enterprise, and the policy which places the risk of the servant's misconduct upon him requires that he shall not be permitted to avoid it by such instructions.

Frolic and Detour

In 1834 Baron Parke [12] uttered the classic phrase, that a master is not liable for the torts of his servant who is not at all on his master's business, but is "going on a frolic of his own." If the servant steps outside of his employment to do some act for himself, not connected with the master's business, there is no more responsibility for what he does than for the acts of any stranger.[13] If he has no intention, not even in part, to perform any service for the employer, but intends only to further a personal end, his act is not within the scope of the employment.[14] This is true, for example, where he borrows the owner's car to go for a ride for his own amusement,[15] or lends it to a friend for the same purpose.[16] But so long as there is an intent, even though it be a subordinate one, to serve the master's purpose, the master may be liable if what is done is otherwise within the service.[17]

Certain activities for the personal benefit of the employee, such as going to the toi-

9. Garretzen v. Duenckel, 1872, 50 Mo. 104. Accord: Mautino v. Piercedale Supply Co., 1940, 338 Pa. 435, 13 A.2d 51 (selling cartridges to minor); cf. Riviello v. Waldron, 1979, 47 N.Y.2d 297, 418 N.Y.S.2d 300, 391 N.E.2d 1278 (bar and grill employee poked out plaintiff's eye while demonstrating art of self-defense with pen knife).

10. Marbury Management, Inc. v. Kohn, 2d Cir. 1980, 629 F.2d 705, certiorari denied 449 U.S. 1011, 101 S.Ct. 566, 66 L.Ed.2d 469 (stock brokerage trainee misrepresented self as broker and portfolio manager); Thompson v. United States, D.S.C.1980, 504 F.Supp. 1087 (employee practicing prohibited fast draw technique with gun); Ohio Farmers Insurance Co. v. Norman, App.1979, 122 Ariz. 330, 594 P.2d 1026 (burning trash); Dickerson v. Reeves, Tex.Civ.App.1979, 588 S.W.2d 854, refused no reversible error (no smoking); Second Restatement of Agency, § 230.

11. Limpus v. London General Omnibus Co., 1862, 1 H. & C. 526, 158 Eng.Rep. 993.

12. In Joel v. Morrison, 1834, 6 C. & P. 501, 172 Eng.Rep. 1338.

13. E.g., Miller v. Reiman-Wuerth Co., Wyo.1979, 598 P.2d 20 (accident while returning to work from bank after depositing paycheck); Beard v. Brown, Wyo.1980, 616 P.2d 726 (3–2) (commuting home from work); Davies v. United States, 9th Cir. 1976, 542 F.2d 1361 (driving back to work to pick up work to take home); Ellis v. Jordan, Ky.App.1978, 571 S.W.2d 635 (false arrest and false imprisonment by off-duty policeman outside of jurisdiction); Molino v. Asher, 1980, 96 Nev. 814, 618 P.2d 878 (parking at work; not on special errand for employer); Roth v. First National Bank of New Jersey, 1979, 169 N.J.Super. 280, 404 A.2d 1182 (bank teller tipped off persons who robbed depositor); Ambrosio v. Price, D.Neb.1980, 495 F.Supp. 381 (off-duty priest driving to see friends); Calhoun v. Hill, Tex.Civ.App.1980, 607 S.W.2d 951 (foreman started race, lost by plaintiff's son who was scrunched beneath hydraulic gate).

14. Salomone v. Yellow Taxi Corp., 1926, 242 N.Y. 251, 151 N.E. 442, reargument denied 242 N.Y. 602, 152 N.E. 445; Herr v. Simplex Paper Box Corp., 1938, 330 Pa. 129, 198 A. 309; Pratt v. Duck, 1945, 28 Tenn.App. 502, 191 S.W.2d 562; Second Restatement of Agency, § 235.

15. May v. Phillips, 1981, 157 Ga.App. 630, 278 S.E.2d 172; Chavez v. Ronquillo, App.1980, 94 N.M. 442, 612 P.2d 234; Beckendorf v. Simmons, Tenn.1976, 539 S.W.2d 31.

16. Robinson v. McNeil, 1897, 18 Wash. 163, 51 P. 355. On the other hand, permitting a friend to drive while the employee remains in the vehicle on the employer's business, is not beyond the scope of employment. Meagher v. Garvin, 1964, 80 Nev. 211, 391 P.2d 507.

17. See Best Steel Buildings, Inc. v. Hardin, Tex.Civ.App.1979, 553 S.W.2d 122, refused no reversible error (trip out of town); Simpson v. United States, W.D.Pa.1980, 484 F.Supp. 387 (Marine recruiter on double date was cultivating "contacts" in the community as per instructions); Combined Insurance Co. of America v. Sinclair, Wyo.1978, 584 P.2d 1034; cf. Gilborges v. Wallace, 1978, 78 N.J. 342, 396 A.2d 338 (whether truck driver's drive to and from home served dual purpose, including one advancing employer's business, for jury); Second Restatement of Agency, § 236.

let,[18] or lighting a fire to keep warm,[19] are quite generally recognized as so necessary, usual, and closely tied in with the work, that they are held not to constitute deviations from the employment. There has been some disagreement over smoking.[20] Most of the older cases held that it is solely for the amusement of the servant, so that it is in itself outside of the scope of employment,[21] although in conjunction with authorized acts, such as pouring gasoline, it may amount to an unauthorized way of doing something which is within it.[22] More recently, however, smoking on the job has quite generally been held to be within the scope of employment.[23]

Questions of fact of unusual difficulty arise in determining whether the servant's conduct is an entire departure from the master's business, or only a roundabout way of doing it—and likewise, the point at which the departure is terminated, and the servant said to have reentered the employment. This is particularly true in the "detour" cases,[24] where the servant deviates from his route on a personal errand, and later returns to it. Various tests have been proposed.

One approach makes the question turn exclusively on the servant's purpose in the deviation, holding to the strict rule that he is outside of his employment while he is off on his own concerns,[25] but that he is still within it while he intends in part to serve his master by or during the departure,[26] or as soon as he starts to return to his route.[27]

This approach in some jurisdictions has been losing ground in recent years, and some courts have shifted their focus more to the foreseeability of the deviation,[28] thereby holding the employer liable for torts occurring in a "zone of risk" within which the servant might reasonably be expected to deviate, even for purposes entirely his own.[29] Time and distance thus become controlling, and the servant who intends to return to his master's business does not resume it at least until he is reasonably near the authorized activity in time and space.[30] It seems to be more or less generally agreed that the master will be liable at least for those slight departures from the performance of the work which might reasonably be expected on the part of servants similarly employed, and

---

18. J. C. Penney Co. v. McLaughlin, 1939, 137 Fla. 594, 188 So. 785.

19. Brown v. Anzalone, 3d Cir. 1962, 300 F.2d 177.

20. See Note, 1950, 4 Ark.L.Rev. 217; Annot., 1968, 20 A.L.R.3d 893.

21. Williams v. Jones, 1865, 3 H. & C. 602, 159 Eng. Rep. 668; Kelly v. Louisiana Oil Refining Co., 1934, 167 Tenn. 101, 66 S.W.2d 997; Shuck v. Carney, 1938, 22 Tenn.App. 125, 118 S.W.2d 896; Herr v. Simplex Paper Box Co., 1938, 330 Pa. 129, 198 A. 309; Tomlinson v. Sharpe, 1946, 226 N.C. 177, 37 S.E.2d 498.

22. Mack v. Hugger Brothers Construction Co., 1929, 10 Tenn.App. 402 (laying explosive floor mixture); Wood v. Saunders, 1930, 228 App.Div. 69, 238 N.Y.S. 571; Jefferson v. Derbyshire Farmers, Limited [1921] 2 K.B. 281; George v. Bekins Van & Storage Co., 1949, 33 Cal.2d 834, 205 P.2d 1037.

23. George v. Bekins Van & Storage Co., 1949, 33 Cal.2d 834, 205 P.2d 1037; Edgewater Motels, Inc. v. Gatzke, Minn.1979, 277 N.W.2d 11; Dickerson v. Reeves, Tex.Civ.App.1979, 588 S.W.2d 854, refused no reversible error; Virginia Surety Co. v. Schlegel, 1967, 200 Kan. 64, 434 P.2d 772.

24. See Smith, Frolic and Detour, 1923, 23 Col.L. Rev. 444, 716; Rouse, Deviation and Departure by Servant, 1929, 17 Ky.L.J. 123; Douglas, Vicarious Liability and Administration of Risk, 1929, 38 Yale L.J. 584; James, Vicarious Liability, 1954, 28 Tulane L.Rev. 161.

25. Skapura v. Cleveland Electric Illuminating Co., 1950, 89 Ohio App. 403, 100 N.E.2d 700; McCauley v. Steward, 1945, 63 Ariz. 524, 164 P.2d 465, Lemarier v. A. Towle Co., 1947, 94 N.H. 246, 51 A.2d 42; Note, 1952, 21 U.Cin.L.Rev. 156.

26. Westberg v. Willde, 1939, 14 Cal.2d 360, 94 P.2d 590; Clawson v. Pierce-Arrow Motor Co., 1921, 231 N.Y. 273, 131 N.E. 914, reargument denied, 231 N.Y. 640, 132 N.E. 921.

27. Sleath v. Wilson, 1839, 9 C. & P. 607, 173 Eng. Rep. 976; see infra, note 41.

28. Smith, Frolic and Detour, 1923, 23 Col.L.Rev. 444, 716.

29. See O'Boyle v. Avis Rent-A-Car System, 1981, 78 A.D.2d 431, 435 N.Y.S.2d 296 (underage gas attendant at car rental agency took car to lunch); cf. Penn Central Transportation Co. v. Reddick, D.C.App.1979, 398 A.2d 27.

30. See Shuman Estate v. Weber, 1980, 276 Pa. Super. 209, 419 A.2d 169 (too far away in time and space); Kelly v. Trans Globe Travel Bureau, Inc., 1976, 60 Cal.App.3d 195, 131 Cal.Rptr. 488; Prince v. Atchison, Topeka & Santa Fe Railway Co., 1979, 76 Ill.App. 3d 898, 32 Ill.Dec. 362, 395 N.E.2d 592 (intent not shown); Manchester Insurance & Indemnity Co. v. Ring, Mo.App.1979, 589 S.W.2d 350 (employee had returned to authorized route); Second Restatement of Agency, §§ 234, 237.

that the foreseeability of such deviations is an important factor in determining the "scope of employment." [31] The tendency has been to recognize a number of factors as affecting the result, which vary with the circumstances.[32] Essentially the question is one of major and minor departures, having always in mind that the employer is to be held liable for those things which are fairly to be regarded as risks of his business.[33]

It has been suggested that such questions ought to be determined by the convenience with which the employer may obtain liability insurance to cover the risk,[34] but as a matter of realistic actuarial practice it appears that this may be unworkable.[35]

Intentional Torts

Early decisions, adhering to the fiction of an "implied command" of the master, refused to hold him liable for intentional or "willful" wrongdoing on the part of the servant, on the ground that it could not be implied that such conduct was ever authorized.[36] Under modern theories of allocation of the risk of the servant's misbehavior, however, it has been recognized that even intentional torts may be so reasonably connected with the employment as to be within its "scope," and the present tendency is to extend the employer's responsibility for such conduct.[37] Here again space does not permit any extended discussion of the subject.[38] It may be said, in general, that the master is held liable for any intentional tort committed by the servant where its purpose, however misguided, is wholly or in part to further the master's business.

Thus he will be held liable where his bus driver crowds a competitor's bus into a ditch,[39] or assaults a trespasser to eject him from the bus,[40] or a salesman makes fraudulent statements about the products he is selling,[41] or defames a competitor [42] or dispar-

31. Compare: Not within scope, Summerville v. Gillespie, 1947, 181 Or. 144, 179 P.2d 719; McCauley v. Steward, 1945, 63 Ariz. 524, 164 P.2d 465; Gordoy v. Flaherty, 1937, 9 Cal.2d 524, 164 P.2d 465. Within scope: Loper v. Morrison, 1944, 23 Cal.2d 600, 145 P.2d 1; Edwards v. Benedict, 1946, 79 Ohio App. 134, 70 N.E.2d 471.

32. Osipoff v. City of New York, 1941, 286 N.Y. 422, 36 N.E.2d 646; Glass v. Davison, 1964, 276 Ala. 328, 161 So.2d 811; Second Restatement of Agency, §§ 229–237.

33. See Ryan v. Western Pacific Insurance Co., 1965, 224 Or. 84, 408 P.2d 84; McCarthy v. Timmins, 1901, 178 Mass. 378, 59 N.E. 1038. But quite extreme deviations have been held not to take the servant out of employment, where the automobile is involved. Cf. Carroll v. Beard-Laney, Inc., 1945, 207 S.C. 339, 35 S.E.2d 425 (25 mile trip, 15 miles off route); M. K. Hall Co. v. Caballero, Tex.Civ.App.1962, 358 S.W.2d 179 (off route, drunk, picked up girl, stopped on highway to allow her to relieve herself, passed out on seat).

34. Douglas, Vicarious Liability and Administration of Risk, 1929, 38 Yale L.J. 584–594; Smith, Frolic and Detour, 1923, 23 Col.L.Rev. 444, 716.

35. Morris, Enterprise Liability and the Actuarial Process—The Insignificance of Foresight, 1961, 70 Yale L.J. 554.

36. McManus v. Crickett, 1800, 1 East 105, 102 Eng. Rep. 43; Wright v. Wilcox, N.Y.1838, 19 Wend. 343; Poulton v. London & S. W. R. Co., 1867, L.R. 2 Q.B. 534; Maille v. Lord, 1868, 39 N.Y. 381.

37. Seavey, Speculations as to "Respondeat Superior," Harvard Legal Essays, 1934, 433, 453; Laski, Basis of Vicarious Liability, 1916, 26 Yale L.J. 105, 118; Notes, 1932, 45 Harv.L.Rev. 348; 1927, 21 Ill.L.Rev. 619. See Limpus v. London General Omnibus Co., 1862, 1 H. & C. 526, 158 Eng.Rep. 993; Cohen v. Dry Dock E. B. & B. R. Co., 1877, 69 N.Y. 170; Howe v. Newmarch, 1866, 94 Mass. (12 Allen) 49; Osipoff v. City of New York, 1941, 286 N.Y. 422, 36 N.E.2d 646; Sage Club v. Hunt, Wyo.1981, 638 P.2d 161.

38. See 2 Mechem, Agency, 2d Ed. 1914, §§ 1916–1927; James, Vicarious Liability, 1954, 28 Tulane L.Rev. 161, 187; Seavey, Studies in Agency, 1949, 249 ff.; Second Restatement of Agency, § 245; Brill, The Liability of an Employer for the Wilful Torts of His Servants, 1968, 45 Chi.Kent L.Rev. 1; Rose, Liability for an Employee's Assaults, 1977, 40 Mod.L.Rev. 420; Annot., 1979, 93 A.L.R.3d 826 (principal's punitive damages liability for false arrest and malicious prosecution).

39. Limpus v. London General Omnibus Co., 1862, 1 H. & C. 526, 158 Eng.Rep. 993.

40. Pelletier v. Bilbiles, 1967, 154 Conn. 544, 227 A.2d 251; Hyde v. Baggett Transportation Co., E.D. Tenn.1964, 236 F.Supp. 194; Tarman v. Southard, 1953, 92 U.S.App.D.C. 297, 205 F.2d 705. Cf. Florida East Coast Railway Co. v. Morgan, Fla.App.1968, 213 So.2d 632 (assault on picket); Faust v. Mendoza, La.App. 1982, 415 So.2d 371 (battery by private policeman hired by ice cream parlor to maintain order). See Note, 1967, 9 Ariz.L.Rev. 110.

41. Rutherford v. Rideout Bank, 1938, 11 Cal.2d 479, 80 P.2d 978; Downey v. Finucane, 1912, 205 N.Y. 251, 98 N.E. 391. See Second Restatement of Agency, §§ 249, 257–264.

ages his product,[43] or where the servant resorts to false imprisonment,[44] or malicious prosecution[45] for a like purpose. Thus a railway ticket agent who assaults, arrests or slanders a passenger, in the belief that he has been given a counterfeit bill for a ticket, is within the scope of his employment,[46] although the employer has not authorized such conduct, or has even expressly prohibited it. But if he acts from purely personal motives, because of a quarrel over his wife which is in no way connected with the employer's interests, he is considered in the ordinary case to have departed from his employment, and the master is not liable.[47] Where the conduct of the servant is unprovoked, highly unusual, and quite outrageous, there has been something of a tendency to find that this in itself is sufficient to indicate that the motive was a purely personal one,[48] but it seems clear that this cannot hold true in all cases.[49]

Even where the servant's ends are entirely personal, the master may be under such a duty to the plaintiff that responsibility for the servant's acts may not be delegated to him.[50] This is true in particular in those cases where the master, by contract or otherwise, has entered into some relation requiring him to be responsible for the protection of the plaintiff.[51] The employees of a carrier, for example, would be under a duty to a passenger to exercise reasonable care to protect him against assaults on the part of third persons;[52] and they are no less under a duty to protect him against their own assaults, from whatever motivation, which is

---

42. Hooper-Holmes Bureau v. Bunn, 5th Cir. 1947, 161 F.2d 102; cf. Pettengill v. Booth Newspapers, Inc., 1979, 88 Mich.App. 587, 278 N.W.2d 682 (paper subject to liability for libel for scurrilous comments in classified ad inserted by unknown employee); Cooper v. Alabama Farm Bureau, Ala.1980, 385 So.2d 630 (insurer's employee defamed insured). But see Sires v. Luke, S.D.Ga.1982, 544 F.Supp. 1155.

43. Rosenberg v. J. C. Penney Co., 1939, 30 Cal. App.2d 609, 623, 86 P.2d 696, 704; Second Restatement of Agency, §§ 247, 248.

44. Gearity v. Strasbourger, 1909, 133 App.Div. 701, 118 N.Y.S. 257; Nash v. Sears, Roebuck & Co., 1968, 12 Mich.App. 553, 163 N.W.2d 471 reversed 383 Mich. 136, 174 N.W.2d 818; see Annot., 1979, 93 A.L.R.3d 826 (punitive damages).

45. O'Donnell v. Chase Hotel, Inc., Mo.App.1965, 388 S.W.2d 489; Eastman v. Leiser Co., 1921, 148 Minn. 96, 181 N.W. 109; see Annot., 1979, 93 A.L.R.3d 826 (punitive damages).

46. Palmeri v. Manhattan Railway Co., 1892, 133 N.Y. 261, 30 N.E. 1001. Accord: Bergman v. Hendrickson, 1900, 106 Wis. 434, 82 N.W. 304 (barkeeper attacking customer who refused to pay); Johnson v. Monson, 1920, 183 Cal. 149, 190 P. 635 (same as to drunken and noisy customer); Rice v. Marler, 1940, 107 Colo. 57, 108 P.2d 868 (taxicab driver assaulting passenger in argument over attempt to collect fare); Freeman v. Lee & Leon Oil Co., La.App.1982, 409 So.2d 408 (employee struck customer over gasoline payment dispute); cf. Davis v. DelRosso, 1977, 371 Mass. 768, 359 N.E.2d 313 (overenthusiastic bouncer battered patron).

47. Cary v. Hotel Rueger, 1954, 195 Va. 980, 81 S.E.2d 421; Sauter v. New York Tribune, 1953, 305 N.Y. 442, 113 N.E.2d 790.

48. See Fitzgerald v. McCutcheon, 1979, 270 Pa. Super. 102, 410 A.2d 1270 (off-duty policeman shot neighbor 6 times); Penn Central Transportation Co. v. Reddick, D.C.App.1979, 398 A.2d 27 (railroad brakeman assaulted cab driver); Nye v. Seymour, Fla.App.1981, 392 So.2d 326 (employee forced neighbor's child riding bike off road, and then attacked him, after child called him obscene name and spit at him); Bozarth v. Harper Creek Board of Education, 1979, 94 Mich.App. 351, 288 N.W.2d 424 (homosexual assault by employee, teacher, on student); Rabon v. Guardsmark, Inc., 4th Cir. 1978, 571 F.2d 1277, certiorari denied 439 U.S. 866, 99 S.Ct. 191, 58 L.Ed.2d 176 (security company not liable for guard's rape of worker in protected building); Baugher v. A. Hattersley & Sons, Inc., 1982, __ Ind.App. __, 436 N.E.2d 126, rehearing denied (rape); cf. Western Railway of Alabama v. Milligan, 1902, 135 Ala. 205, 33 So. 438 (tickling fellow employee).

49. See, e.g., Jamison v. Howard, 1980, 275 S.C. 344, 271 S.E.2d 116 (4–1) (liquor store manager ordered associate to shoot patron who would not repay debt); Johnson v. Weinberg, D.C.App.1981, 434 A.2d 404 (laundromat employee shot patron; for jury).

50. Second Restatement of Agency, § 214; Notes, 1932, 45 Harv.L.Rev. 342, 1927, 21 Ill.L.Rev. 619.

51. See Allen v. Seacoast Products, Inc., 5th Cir. 1980, 623 F.2d 355 (ship captain); Eversole v. Wasson, 1980, 80 Ill.App.3d 94, 35 Ill.Dec. 296, 398 N.E.2d 1246 (school teacher hit student); Truhitte v. French Hospital, 1982, 128 Cal.App.3d 332, 180 Cal.Rptr. 152 (surgeon's duty to remove sponges); cf. Roberts v. Gonzalez, D.V.I.1980, 495 F.Supp. 1310 (airline carrier crash); Alaska Airlines, Inc. v. Sweat, Alaska 1977, 568 P.2d 916, appeal after remand 584 P.2d 544 (same). But see Rabon v. Guardsmark, Inc., 4th Cir. 1978, 571 F.2d 1277 (2–1), certiorari denied 439 U.S. 866, 99 S.Ct. 191, 58 L.Ed.2d 176.

52. See supra, § 56.

the duty of the master as well.[53] The same is true of innkeepers.[54]

The most difficult questions arise where the servant, for strictly personal reasons and not in furtherance of his employment, loses his temper and attacks the plaintiff in a quarrel which arises out of the employment—as where, for example, a truck driver collides with the plaintiff, and an altercation follows. Here, unless some non-delegable duty can be found, the older rule denied recovery, and this is still the holding in some jurisdictions.[55] There has been a tendency in many of the later cases, however, to allow recovery on the ground that the employment has provided a peculiar opportunity and even incentive for such loss of temper.[56]

Dangerous Instrumentalities

In a small group of older cases a master who entrusted his servant with an instrumentality highly dangerous in itself, or capable of being misused in some way involving a high degree of risk to others, was held liable when the servant misused it for a purpose entirely his own.[57] Thus the rule was applied in the case of steam locomotives,[58] torpedoes,[59] and poisons.[60] The cases indicate that the master will be held liable only while the servant is engaged in his employment, and while so engaged has custody of the instrumentality.[61] The doctrine has been rejected by a number of courts.[62] It is not very difficult to find a justification for it in the case of things such as dynamite or vicious animals, which are so extremely dangerous in themselves that strict liability may properly be imposed upon the enterprise which makes use of them, and the employer would be liable even if they were entrusted to an independent contractor.[63] The courts which have extended it beyond such instru-

---

53. Co-op Cab Co. v. Singleton, 1942, 66 Ga.App. 874, 19 S.E.2d 541; Berger v. Southern Pacific Co., 1956, 144 Cal.App.2d 1, 300 P.2d 170; Commodore Cruise Line, Limited v. Kormendi, Fla.App.1977, 344 So.2d 896.

54. See Altamuro v. Milner Hotel, Inc., E.D. Pa.1982, 540 F.Supp. 870; Danile v. Oak Park Arms Hotel, Inc., 1965, 55 Ill.App.2d 2, 203 N.E.2d 706; cf. Vannah v. Hart Private Hospital, 1917, 228 Mass. 132, 117 N.E. 328 (hospital). But see Moritz v. Pines Hotel, Inc., 1976, 52 A.D.2d 1020, 383 N.Y.S.2d 704 (hotel porter struck guest—employer not liable); Cornell v. State, 1979, 46 N.Y.2d 1032, 416 N.Y.S.2d 542, 389 N.E.2d 1064 (mental hospital not liable for homosexual rape).

55. See, e.g., Kuehn v. White, 1979, 24 Wn.App. 274, 600 P.2d 679 (near collision); Sandman v. Hagan, 1967, 261 Iowa 560, 154 N.W.2d 113; Sheffield v. Central Freightlines, Inc., Tex.Civ.App.1968, 435 S.W.2d 954; Sauter v. New York Tribune, 1953, 305 N.Y. 442, 113 N.E.2d 790.

56. See generally Johnson v. Weinberg, D.C.App. 1981, 434 A.2d 404; Sage Club v. Hunt, Wyo.1981, 638 P.2d 161 (bartender lost temper and injured patron); Scott v. Commercial Union Insurance Co., La.App.1982, 415 So.2d 327 (no liability for employee's battery during work, arising out of discussion of personal matter consented to by employer); Prell Hotel Corp. v. Antonacci, 1970, 86 Nev. 390, 469 P.2d 399 (casino employee, provoked by namecalling, struck patron); Kent v. Bradley, Tex.Civ.App.1972, 480 S.W.2d 55 (lemonade dispute); Caldwell v. Farley, 1955, 134 Cal.App.2d 84, 285 P.2d 294.

57. See Horack, The Dangerous Instrument Doctrine, 1917, 26 Yale L.J. 224.

58. Alsever v. Minneapolis & St. Louis Railroad Co., 1902, 115 Iowa 338, 88 N.W. 841; (blowing off steam to frighten child); Toledo, Wabash & Western Railway Co. v. Harmon, 1868, 47 Ill. 298 (similar facts); Stewart v. Cary Lumber Co., 1907, 146 N.C. 47, 59 S.E. 545 (blowing whistle to "make the mule dance").

In Southern Cotton Oil Co. v. Anderson, 1920, 80 Fla. 441, 86 So. 629, this rule was applied to an automobile; and this has continued to be the Florida doctrine. See infra § 73, note 13. All other courts have rejected such an application. See for example Terrett v. Wray, 1937, 171 Tenn. 448, 105 S.W.2d 93.

59. Harriman v. Pittsburgh, Cincinnati & St. Louis Railway Co., 1887, 45 Ohio St. 11, 12 N.E. 451; Euting v. Chicago & North Western Railroad Co., 1902, 116 Wis. 13, 92 N.W. 358.

60. Smith's Administratrix v. Middleton, 1902, 112 Ky. 588, 66 S.W. 388.

61. Obertoni v. Boston & Maine Railroad Co., 1904, 186 Mass. 481, 71 N.E. 980; Johnson v. Chicago, Rock Island & Pacific Railway Co., 1913, 157 Iowa 738, 141 N.W. 430. See Horack, The Dangerous Instrument Doctrine, 1917, 26 Yale L.J. 224.

62. American Railway Express Co. v. Davis, 1922, 152 Ark. 258, 238 S.W. 50, 1063 (pistol); Galveston, H. & S. A. R. Co. v. Currie, 1906, 100 Tex. 136, 96 S.W. 1073 (compressed air); Vadyak v. Lehigh & New England Railroad Co., 1935, 318 Pa. 580, 179 A. 435 (steam locomotive); Thomas-Kincannon-Elkin Drug Co. v. Hendrix, 1936, 175 Miss. 767, 168 So. 287 (powerful laxative); Second Restatement of Agency, § 238, Comment d.

63. See infra, § 71.

mentalities are pursuing a policy of holding the enterprise responsible for the danger, which goes beyond the limitations usually imposed upon strict liability at the present time. The justification for it must lie in the especial opportunity and temptation afforded to the servant to misuse the instrumentality under the conditions likely to arise in the employment—or in other words, again, the foreseeability and indeed especial likelihood of the tort.

Agents Other Than Servants

Since an agent who is not a servant is not subject to any right of control by his employer over the details of his physical conduct, the responsibility ordinarily rests upon the agent alone, and the principal is not liable for the torts which he may commit.[64] There are, however, a number of situations in which such liability may exist. These include cases in which a tort may be based upon the apparent authority of the agent to act for his principal,[65] or in which a tort such as deceit occurs in the course of a consensual transaction between the agent and the injured person.[66] Thus a client may be made liable for the improper institution of legal proceedings by his attorney,[67] and a seller of land or goods may, in most states, be subject to an action of deceit for the fraud of his agent committed in the course of the sale.[68] In such cases liability is based wholly upon the relation of principal and agent, but it is subject, in general, to the same limitations as those placed upon the liability of a master for the tort of a servant.[69] Thus it must appear either that the representations made were within the actual or apparent authority of the agent,[70] or of a kind reasonably to be expected by the employer in connection with the transaction,[71] or that the agent has been placed by the principal in a position which enables him to commit the fraud, while apparently acting within his authority.[72]

The field of vicarious liability is a very large one, and any full discussion of it must be left to texts on the law of master and servant, agency, partnership and the like. The space here available permits only the briefest review of some of the more common problems which have arisen in tort cases.

WESTLAW REFERENCES

digest(servant /s control /s service*)

Frolic and Detour
employee servant /p frolic /s detour

---

64. Second Restatement of Agency, § 250; Scoggins v. Smith, La.1977, 342 So.2d 1130; Halpin v. Prudential Insurance Co. of America, 1979, 48 N.Y.2d 906, 425 N.Y.S.2d 48, 401 N.E.2d 171; Stein v. Beta Rho Alumni Association, Inc., 1980, 49 Or.App. 965, 621 P.2d 632; cf. Vieths v. Ripley, Minn.1980, 295 N.W.2d 659.

65. Second Restatement of Agency, § 265; see Posin v. ABC Motor Court Hotel, 1976, 45 Ohio St.2d 271, 344 N.E.2d 334; Taylor v. Costa Lines, Inc., E.D. Pa.1977, 441 F.Supp. 783; Drummond v. Hilton Hotel Corp., E.D.Pa.1980, 501 F.Supp. 29; cf. Adamski v. Tacoma General Hospital, 1978, 20 Wn.App. 98, 579 P.2d 970. But cf. B. P. Oil Corp. v. Mabe, 1977, 279 Md. 632, 370 A.2d 554 (no reliance).

66. Second Restatement of Agency, §§ 256–261. See Celucci v. Sun Oil Co., 1974, 23 Mass.App. 722, 320 N.E.2d 919, affirmed 1975, 368 Mass. 811, 331 N.E.2d 813. But see Friedman v. Mutual Broadcasting System, Inc., Fla.App.1980, 380 So.2d 1313 (2–1) (intent to serve principals not established); Shane v. Hoffmann, 1974, 227 Pa.Super. 176, 324 A.2d 532 (principal's scienter essential element, contra to general rule).

67. Otto v. Levy, 1935, 244 App.Div. 349, 279 N.Y.S. 462; Second Restatement of Agency, § 253. But see Porter v. Stormont-Vail Hospital, 1980, 228 Kan. 641, 621 P.2d 411. See generally Annot., 1979, 93 A.L.R.2d 826 (punitive damages).

68. See, e.g., Clark Equipment Co. v. Wheat, 1979, 92 Cal.3d 503, 154 Cal.Rptr. 874; Slotkin v. Citizens Casualty Co. of New York, 2d Cir. 1979, 614 F.2d 301, certiorari denied 1980, 449 U.S. 981, 101 S.Ct. 395, 66 L.Ed.2d 243, on remand 530 F.Supp. 789; Keck v. Wacker, E.D.Ky.1976, 413 F.Supp. 1377 (horse sale); cf. Alhino v. Starr, 1980, 112 Cal.3d 158, 169 Cal.Rptr. 136.

69. Second Restatement of Agency, §§ 251–262.

70. Second Restatement of Agency, § 257.

71. Second Restatement of Agency, § 258.

72. Second Restatement of Agency, § 261. See American Lease Plans v. Silver Sand Co., 5th Cir. 1981, 637 F.2d 311; New England Acceptance Corp. v. American Manufacturers Mutual Insurance Co., 1976, 4 Mass.App. 172, 344 N.E.2d 208 adopted 373 Mass. 594, 368 N.E.2d 1385; Dudley v. Estate Life Insurance Co. of America, 1979, 220 Va. 343, 257 S.E.2d 871.

Intentional Torts
intentional /s tort* /p employer master

Dangerous Instrumentalities
dangerous /s instrument! /p master servant

Agents Other Than Servants
digest("apparent authority" deceit /p liab! responsib! /p agent principal)
di apparent authority

§ 71. Independent Contractors

For the torts of an independent contractor, as distinguished from a servant,[1] it has long been said to be the general rule that there is no vicarious liability upon the employer.[2] This doctrine developed, both in English[3] and in American[4] law at a time when such liability for the torts of a servant was well established, and it seems to have been, in its inception, something of a retreat from the rigors of that rule. Various reasons have been advanced for it, but the one most commonly accepted[5] is that, since the employer has no right of control over the manner in which the work is to be done,[6] it is to be regarded as the contractor's own enterprise, and he, rather than the employer, is the proper party to be charged with the responsibility for preventing the risk, and administering and distributing it.

Against this argument, it has been contended[7] that the enterprise is still the employer's, since he remains the person primarily to be benefited by it; that he selects the contractor, and is free to insist upon one who is financially responsible, and to demand indemnity from him, and that the insurance necessary to distribute the risk is properly a cost of his business. Upon this basis, the prediction has been made[8] that ultimately the "general rule" will be that the employer is liable for the negligence of an independent contractor, and that he will be excused only in a limited group of cases where he is not in a position to select a responsible contractor or where the risk of any harm to others from the enterprise is clearly slight. The courts,[9] however, have not gone

§ 71

1. See supra, § 70.

2. Washington Metropolitan Area Transit Authority v. L'Enfant Plaza Properties, Inc., D.C.App.1982, 448 A.2d 864; Soderback v. Townsend, 1982, 57 Or.App. 366, 644 P.2d 640; Fisherman's Paradise, Inc. v. Greenfield, Fla.App.1982, 417 So.2d 306; McCain Manufacturing Corp. v. Rockwell International Corp., D.S.C. 1981, 528 F.Supp. 524, vacated 4th Cir. 1982, 695 F.2d 803; St. Paul Companies v. Capitol Office Supply Co., 1981, 158 Ga.App. 748, 282 S.E.2d 205; Lumpkin v. Streifel, N.D.1981, 308 N.W.2d 878; Second Restatement of Torts, § 409. On independent contractors generally, see Second Restatement of Torts, §§ 409–29.

3. In Bush v. Steinman, 1799, 1 Bos. & P. 404, 121 Eng.Rep. 978, the employer was held liable, despite "great difficulty in stating with accuracy the grounds for liability." But in Laugher v. Pointer, 1826, 5 B. & C. 547, 108 Eng.Rep. 204, the employer was held not liable for the negligence of a hired driver, and this decision was followed in subsequent cases. Quarman v. Burnett, 1840, 6 M. & W. 499, 151 Eng.Rep. 509; Milligan v. Wedge, 1840, 12 Ad. & El. 737, 113 Eng.Rep. 993; Reedie v. London & N. W. R. Co., 1849, 4 Ex. 244, 154 Eng.Rep. 1201.

4. Early cases held the employer liable. Lowell v. Boston & L. R. Corp., 1839, 40 Mass. (23 Pick.) 24; Stone v. Cheshire Railroad Corp., 1839, 19 N.H. 427. Later decisions to the contrary apparently were influenced by the English cases. Blake v. Ferris, 1851, 5 N.Y. 48; Hilliard v. Richardson, 1855, 69 Mass. (3 Gray) 349; Painter v. City of Pittsburgh, 1863, 46 Pa. 213. See Note, 1902, 2 Col.L.Rev. 112.

5. See Harper, The Basis of the Immunity of an Employer of an Independent Contractor, 1935, 10 Ind. L.J. 494; Morris, the Torts of an Independent Contractor, 1935, 29 Ill.L.Rev. 339; Douglas, Vicarious Liability and Administration of Risk, 1929, 38 Yale L.J. 584, 594; Steffen, Independent Contractor and the Good Life, 1935, 2 U.Chi.L.Rev. 501; Brown, Liability for the Torts of an Independent Contractor in West Virginia, 1953, 55 W.Va.L.Rev. 216; Ferson, Liability of Employers for Misrepresentations Made by Independent Contractors, 1949, 3 Vand.L.Rev. 1; James, Vicarious Liability, 1954, 28 Tulane L.Rev. 161; Teh, Liability for Independent Contractors—The Unifying Theme, 1980, 9 Anglo-Am.L.Rev. 216; Notes, 1980, 51 U.Colo.L.Rev. 275; 1973, 40 U.Chi.L.Rev. 661.

6. See Fisherman's Paradise, Inc. v. Greenfield, Fla. App.1982, 417 So.2d 306; Stewart v. Sam Wallace Industrial Co., La.App.1981, 409 So.2d 335; Chesapeake & Potomac Telephone Co. of Maryland v. Chesapeake Utilities Corp., Del.1981, 436 A.2d 314.

7. See the articles cited supra, note 5.

8. Morris, The Torts of an Independent Contractor, 1935, 29 Ill.L.Rev. 339. But see, to the contrary, Steffen, Independent Contractor and the Good Life, 1935, 2 U.Chi.L.Rev. 501, pointing out the difficulties involved.

9. Decisions in at least Colorado and California, however, have so far widened the inherently dangerous and peculiar risk exceptions as almost to swallow the general nonliability rule. See Western Stock Center,

so far, and have continued to repeat the "general rule" of nonliability with exceptions, whose very number may be sufficient to cast doubt upon the validity of the rule.[10]

These exceptions making the employer liable overlap and shade into one another; and cases are infrequent in which at least two of them do not appear. The courts quite typically state and rely upon two or more, as alternative or cumulative grounds. The various types of situations can be roughly grouped together as follows:

Negligence of the Employer

In the first place, quite apart from any question of vicarious responsibility, the employer may be liable for any negligence of his own in connection with the work to be done.[11] Where there is a foreseeable risk of harm to others unless precautions are taken, it is his duty to exercise reasonable care to select a competent, experienced, and careful contractor[12] with the proper equipment,[13] and to provide, in the contract or otherwise, for such precautions as reasonably appear to be called for.[14] So far as he in fact gives directions for the work,[15] furnishes equipment for it,[16] or retains control over any part of it,[17] he is required to exercise reasonable care for the protection of others; and he must likewise interfere to put a stop to any unnecessarily dangerous practices of which he becomes informed,[18] and make a reasonable inspection of the work after it is completed, to be sure that it is safe.[19] If the work is done on the employer's own land, he will be

---

Inc. v. Sevit, Inc., 1978, 195 Colo. 372, 578 P.2d 1045, noted 1980, 51 U.Colo.L.Rev. 275; infra, note 60.

10. See Note, 1930, 39 Yale L.J. 861. "Indeed it would be proper to say that the rule is now primarily important as a preamble to the catalog of its exceptions." Pacific Fire Ins. Co. v. Kenny Boiler & Manufacturing Co., 1937, 201 Minn. 500, 503, 277 N.W. 226, 228. Accord, LaCount v. Hensel Phelps Construction Co., 1978, 79 Cal.App.3d 754, 145 Cal.Rptr. 244 (so many exceptions that general rule of nonliability applied only where no good reason can be found for departing from it).

11. United States v. Arez, 1981, 248 Ga. 19, 280 S.E.2d 345.

12. See, e.g., Hixon v. Sherwin-Williams Co., 7th Cir. 1982, 671 F.2d 1005; Deitz v. Jackson, 1982, 57 N.C.App. 275, 291 S.E.2d 282; Western Stock Center, Inc. v. Sevit, Inc., 1978, 195 Colo. 372, 578 P.2d 1045 (sufficient inquiries must be made before hiring); Becker v. Interstate Properties, 3d Cir.1977, 569 F.2d 1203, certiorari denied 1978, 436 U.S. 906, 98 S.Ct. 2237, 56 L.Ed.2d 404 (contractor financially irresponsible); noted 1978, 31 Vand.L.Rev. 414; Matanuska Electric Association, Inc. v. Johnson, Alaska 1963, 386 P.2d 698 (contra). See generally Second Restatement of Torts, § 411; Annot., 19—, 78 A.L.R.3d 910.

In Arizona, Arkansas and Colorado, an employer's previous successful experience with a particular contractor precludes an action for negligent selection. See Wright v. Newman, D.Ark.1982, 539 F.Supp. 1331. See also Cooper v. Metropolitan Government of Nashville & Davidson County, Tenn.App.1981, 628 S.W.2d 30 (20 years prior successful experience).

13. Risley v. Lenwell, 1954, 129 Cal.App.2d 608, 277 P.2d 897; Kuhn v. P. J. Carlin Construction Co., 1935, 154 Misc. 892, 278 N.Y.S. 635; L. B. Foster & Co. v. Hurnblad, 9th Cir. 1969, 418 P.2d 727.

14. See Lopez v. A/S D/S Svenborg, 2d Cir. 1978, 581 F.2d 319; Aretz v. United States, S.D.Ga.1977, 503 F.Supp. 260, affirmed 5th Cir. 1979, 604 F.2d 417, on rehearing 635 F.2d 485, certified question answered 248 Ga. 19, 280 S.E.2d 345, affirmed and remanded 660 F.2d 531; Mountain States Telephone & Telegraph Co. v. Kelton, 1955, 79 Ariz. 126, 285 P.2d 168 (failure to warn against underground cable); cf. Hardy v. Monsanto Enviro-Chem Systems, Inc., 1982, 414 Mich. 29, 323 N.W.2d 270.

15. See Ellis v. Sheffield Gas Co., 1853, 2 El. & Bl. 767, 118 Eng.Rep. 955; Gonzalez v. United States Steel Corp., 1979, 484 Pa. 277, 398 A.2d 1378; White v. C F, Industries, Inc., La.App.1982, 411 So.2d 511 (employer specified dangerous method for work); Second Restatement of Torts, § 410.

16. Johnson v. J. I. Case Threshing Machine Co., 1916, 193 Mo.App. 198, 182 S.W. 1089; Brady v. Jay, 1904, 111 La. 1071, 36 So. 132; Willis v. San Bernardino Lumber & Box Co., 1927, 82 Cal.App. 751, 256 P. 224.

17. See Everette v. Alyeska Pipeline Service Co., Alaska 1980, 614 P.2d 1341; Dowell v. General Telephone Co. of Michigan, 1978, 85 Mich.App. 84, 270 N.W.2d 711; Franklin v. Puget Sound Tug & Barge Co., 1978, 21 Wash.App. 517, 586 P.2d 489; cf. Sterud v. Chugach Electric Association, Alaska 1982, 640 P.2d 823. But this must be more than the mere general supervisory right to object to something unsatisfactory, which is retained by nearly every employer. Moloso v. State, Alaska 1982, 644 P.2d 205; Snider v. Northern States Power Co., 1977, 81 Wis. 224, 260 N.W.2d 260; Cummings v. Hoosier Marine Properties, Inc., 1977, 173 Ind.App. 372, 363 N.E.2d 1266.

18. See Kojic v. City of New York, 1980, 76 A.D.2d 828, 428 N.Y.S.2d 305; Emelwon, Inc. v. United States, 5th Cir. 1968, 391 F.2d 9, certiorari denied 1968, 393 U.S. 841, 89 S.Ct. 119, 21 L.Ed.2d 111.

19. McGuire v. Hartford Buick Co., 1944, 131 Conn. 417, 40 A.2d 269; Pulaski Housing Authority v. Smith, 1955, 39 Tenn.App. 213, 282 S.W.2d 213; Rumetsch v.

required to exercise reasonable care to prevent activities or conditions which are dangerous to those outside of it,[20] or to those who enter it as invitees.[21] In all of these cases, he is liable for his personal negligence, rather than that of the contractor.

Non-Delegable Duty

A different approach, manifested in several of the exceptions to the general rule of nonliability, has been to hold that the employer's enterprise, and his relation to the plaintiff, are such as to impose upon him a duty which cannot be delegated to the contractor. It has been mentioned earlier [22] that there are numerous situations in which it may be negligence to rely upon another person, and the defendant is not thereby relieved of the obligation of taking reasonable precautions himself. But the cases of "non-delegable duty" go further, and hold the employer liable for the negligence of the contractor, although he has himself done everything that could reasonably be required of him. They are thus cases of vicarious liability.

Such a duty may be imposed by statute,[23] by contract,[24] by franchise or charter,[25] or by the common law.[26] The catalogue is a long one: the duty of a carrier to transport its passengers in safety,[27] of a railroad to fence its tracks properly [28] or to maintain safe crossings,[29] and of a municipality to keep its streets in repair; [30] the duty to afford lateral support to adjoining land,[31] to refrain from obstructing or endangering the public highway,[32] to keep premises reasonably safe for

John Wanamaker, New York, Inc., 1915, 216 N.Y. 379, 110 N.E. 760. But cf. Borden v. Phillips Petroleum Co., Mo.App.1976, 541 S.W.2d 53 (failure to inspect work not negligent).

20. Kraus v. Alamo National Bank of San Antonio, Tex.Civ.App.1979, 586 S.W.2d 202, affirmed 1981, 616 S.W.2d 908 (wall collapse); Wright v. Tudor City Twelfth Unit, 1938, 276 N.Y. 303, 12 N.E.2d 307; Lamb v. South Unit Jehovah's Witnesses, 1950, 232 Minn. 259, 45 N.W.2d 403.

21. Lineaweaver v. John Wanamaker Philadelphia, 1930, 299 Pa. 45, 149 A. 91; Ruhs v. Pacific Power & Light, 10th Cir. 1982, 671 F.2d 1268 (contractor's employee).

22. See supra, § 33.

23. Celestine v. City of New York, 1982, 86 A.D.2d 592, 446 N.Y.S.2d 131 (labor law); Horning v. Gore, 1982, 87 A.D.2d 34, 451 N.Y.S.2d 848 (duty to provide protective devices for workers—employer can then recover over against contractor); Jones v. City of Logansport, 1982, ___ Ind.App. ___, 436 N.E.2d 1138, rehearing denied ___ Ind.App. ___, 439 N.E.2d 666 (workplace safety); Golden v. Conway, 1976, 55 Cal.App.3d 948, 128 Cal.Rptr. 69; Gardenvillage Realty Corp. v. Russo, Spec.App.1976, 34 Md.App. 25, 366 A.2d 101 (city building code); see Annot., 1981, 51 A.L.R.Fed. 285 (vicarious liability of superior under 42 U.S.C. § 1983).

24. See Jones v. City of Logansport, 1982, ___ Ind. App. ___, 436 N.E.2d 1138, rehearing denied ___ Ind. App. ___, 439 N.E.2d 666; Fisherman's Paradise, Inc. v. Greenfield, Fla.App.1982, 417 So.2d 306; Kelley v. Howard S. Wright Construction Co., 1978, 90 Wn.2d 323, 582 P.2d 500.

25. See Murray v. Lehigh Valley Railroad Co., 1895, 66 Conn. 512, 34 A. 506; Sanford v. Pawtucket Street Railway Co., 1896, 19 R.I. 537, 35 A. 67; Tauscher v. Puget Sound Power & Light Co., 1981, 96 Wn.2d 274,

635 P.2d 426; cf. Kreider Truck Service, Inc. v. Augustine, 1979, 76 Ill.2d 535, 31 Ill.Dec. 802, 394 N.E.2d 1179. See also Note, 1930, 79 U.Pa.L.Rev. 90; Louis v. Youngren, 1956, 12 Ill.App.2d 198, 138 N.E.2d 696.

26. Woodman v. Metropolitan Railroad Co., 1889, 149 Mass. 335, 21 N.E. 482; Corrigan v. Elsinger, 1900, 81 Minn. 42, 83 N.W. 492. See Note, 1965, 44 N.C.L. Rev. 242.

27. Dixie Stage Lines v. Anderson, 1931, 222 Ala. 673, 134 So. 23. Or freight. Eli v. Murphy, 1952, 39 Cal.2d 598, 248 P.2d 756.

28. Rockford, Rhode Island & St. Louis Railroad Co. v. Heflin, 1872, 65 Ill. 366; Chicago, Kansas & Western Railroad Co. v. Hutchinson, 1891, 45 Kan. 186, 25 P. 576.

29. Boucher v. New York, New Haven & Hartford Railroad Co., 1907, 196 Mass. 355, 82 N.E. 15; Choctaw, Oklahoma & Western Railway Co. v. Wilker, 1906, 16 Okl. 384, 84 P. 1086.

30. Westby v. Itasca County, Minn.1980, 290 N.W. 2d 437; Storrs v. City of Utica, 1858, 17 N.Y. 104; Prowell v. City of Waterloo, 1909, 144 Iowa 689, 123 N.W. 346; Saari v. State, 1953, 203 Misc. 859, 119 N.Y.S.2d 507, affirmed 1953, 282 App.Div. 526, 125 N.Y.S.2d 507.

31. Wharam v. Investment Underwriters, 1943, 58 Cal.App.2d 346, 136 P.2d 363; Kolodkin v. Griffin, 1953, 87 Ga.App. 725, 75 S.E.2d 197; Levi v. Schwartz, 1953, 201 Md. 575, 95 A.2d 322; Law v. Phillips, 1952, 136 W.Va. 761, 68 S.E.2d 452; see Budagher v. Amrep Corp., 1981, 97 N.M. 116, 637 P.2d 547 (surface waters).

32. Globe Indemnity Co. v. Schmitt, 1944, 142 Ohio St. 595, 53 N.E.2d 790; Brown Hotel Co. v. Sizemore, 1946, 303 Ky. 431, 197 S.W.2d 911; May v. Hrinko, 1948, 137 N.J.L. 324, 59 A.2d 823.

business visitors,[33] to provide employees with a safe place to work;[34] the duty of a landlord to maintain common areas,[35] to make repairs according to covenant,[36] or to use proper care in making them,[37] and no doubt others.[38] The owner of land or a building who entrusts repairs or other work on it to a contractor remains liable for any negligence injuring those on or outside the land, while he retains possession during the progress of the work,[39] or resumes it after completion,[40] but not while he has vacated the premises during the work.[41]

It is difficult to suggest any criterion by which the non-delegable character of such duties may be determined, other than the conclusion of the courts that the responsibility is so important to the community that the employer should not be permitted to transfer it to another.

"Inherently Dangerous" Activities

The leading English case of Bower v. Peate,[42] in which the foundation of the plaintiff's building was undermined by an excavation, adopted still another approach. The court there held that the employer would be liable for the negligence of the contractor if, in the course of the work, injurious consequences might be expected to result "unless means are taken to prevent them." This gave rise to an exceptional category of work likely to be peculiarly dangerous "unless special precautions are taken." [43] American courts on the whole have preferred to adopt the language of Judge Dillon [44] as to work which is "inherently dangerous." [45] Neither phrase has ever yet been very well defined by anyone, and they are apparently intended to mean very much the same thing. They have been used more or less interchangeably

---

33. Daly v. Bergstedt, 1964, 267 Minn. 244, 126 N.W.2d 242; see Ramirez v. Redevelopment Agency of City and County of San Francisco, 1970, 4 Cal.App.3d 397, 84 Cal.Rptr. 356 (maintenance of elevators); Misiulis v. Milbrand Maintenance Corp., 1974, 52 Mich.App. 494, 218 N.W.2d 68 (lessor of shopping center), noted, 1975, 21 N.Y.L.For. 121; Annot., 1979, 96 A.L.R.3d 1213.

34. Stepanek v. Kober Construction, Mont.1981, 625 P.2d 51 (contract); Celestine v. City of New York, 1982, 86 A.D.2d 592, 446 N.Y.S.2d 131 (statute); Jones v. City of Logansport, 1982, ___ Ind.App. ___ 436 N.E.2d 1138, rehearing denied ___ Ind.App. ___, 439 N.E.2d 666; Kelley v. Howard S. Wright Construction Co., 1978, 90 Wn.2d 323, 582 P.2d 500 (contract). Cf. Van Arsdale v. Hollinger, 1968, 68 Cal.2d 245, 66 Cal. Rptr. 20, 437 P.2d 508 (marking lines on busy street).

35. Brown v. George Pepperdine Foundation, 1943, 23 Cal.2d 256, 143 P.2d 929; see Cappaert v. Junker, Miss.1982, 413 So.2d 378; Hill v. McDonald, D.C.App. 1982, 442 A.2d 133.

36. Peerless Manufacturing Co. v. Bagley, 1901, 126 Mich. 225, 85 N.W. 568; Vitale v. Duerbeck, 1933, 332 Mo. 1184, 62 S.W.2d 559; Paltey v. Egan, 1910, 200 N.Y. 83, 93 N.E. 267.

37. See Damron v. C. R. Anthony Co., Tex.Civ.App. 1979, 586 S.W.2d 907; Strayer v. Lindeman, 1981, 68 Ohio St.2d 32, 427 N.E.2d 781; Second Restatement of Torts, § 419.

38. California has applied this to the statutory duty to have automobile brakes in good operating condition. Maloney v. Rath, 1968, 69 Cal.2d 442, 71 Cal.Rptr. 897, 445 P.2d 513; Dutcher v. Weber, 1969, 275 Cal.App.2d 961, 80 Cal.Rptr. 378. See Note, 1969, 14 Vill.L.Rev. 560; Annot., 1981, 8 A.L.R.4th 265 (car owner's liability for negligence of garage).

39. E. R. Harding Co. v. Paducah Street-Railway Co., 1926, 208 Ky. 728, 271 S.W. 1046; Lineaweaver v. John Wanamaker Philadelphia, 1930, 299 Pa. 45, 149 A. 91.

40. Connolly v. Des Moines Investment Co., 1905, 130 Iowa 633, 105 N.W. 400; Cork v. Blossom, 1894, 162 Mass. 330, 38 N.E. 495; Wilkinson v. Detroit Steel & Spring Works, 1888, 73 Mich. 405, 41 N.W. 490.

41. Csaranko v. Robilt, Inc., 1967, 93 N.J.Super. 428, 226 A.2d 43; Boswell v. Laird, 1857, 8 Cal. 469; Thrasher v. Gerken, Iowa 1981, 309 N.W.2d 488; cf. Stewart v. Sam Wallace Industrial Co., La.App.1981, 409 So.2d 335.

42. 1876, 1 Q.B. 321.

43. Second Restatement of Torts, § 416. See generally Conover v. Northern States Power Co., Minn. 1981, 313 N.W.2d 397; Perry v. Northern Indiana Public Service Co., 1982, ___ Ind.App. ___, 433 N.E.2d 44.

44. Dillon, Municipal Corporations, 1st Ed. 1872, § 792. See Note, 1950, 38 Ky.L.J. 282; Second Restatement of Torts, § 427. "Inherent danger" converges not only with "special precautions," but also with "non-delegable duty." The courts not infrequently state all three. Cf. Besner v. Central Trust Co. of New York, 1921, 230 N.Y. 357, 130 N.E. 577.

45. See generally Good Fund, Limited—1972 v. Church, D.Colo.1982, 540 F.Supp. 519; Western Stock Center, Inc. v. Sevit, Inc. 1978, 195 Colo. 372, 578 P.2d 1045. Some courts interchangeably use the phrase "intrinsically dangerous." E.g., Cooper v. Metropolitan Government of Nashville & Davidson County, Tenn. App.1981, 628 S.W.2d 30.

by the courts, which usually state and rely upon both as the basis of an exceptional rule.[46] If there is a distinction, it is that the "special precautions" exception is more commonly applied where the employer should anticipate the need for some one specific precaution, such as a railing around an excavation in the sidewalk, while the "inherent danger" phrase is used more often where the work calls for a whole set of precautions, against a number of hazards, as in the case of painting carried on upon a scaffold above a highway.

Plainly included within either concept are activities, such as the construction of reservoirs,[47] the use or keeping of vicious animals,[48] high tension electric wires,[49] blasting,[50] the exhibition of fireworks,[51] and perhaps crop dusting,[52] which will be dangerous in spite of all reasonable care, so that strict liability might be imposed upon the employer if he should carry them out himself.

But liability on either basis has been extended beyond this, to work which, in its nature, will create some peculiar risk of injury to others unless special precautions are taken—as, for example, excavations in or near a public highway,[53] or construction or repair work on buildings adjoining it [54] or likely to obstruct it,[55] and other activities,[56] such as the clearing of land by fire,[57] tearing down

---

46. See infra, note 66. See also Perry v. Northern Indiana Public Service Co., 1982, ___ Ind.App. ___, 433 N.E.2d 44.

47. Rylands v. Fletcher, 1868, L.R. 3 H.L. 330, was itself a case involving an independent contractor. See also the dam cases in note 59, infra.

48. Stapleton v. Butensky, 1919, 188 App.Div. 237, 177 N.Y.S. 18; Austin v. Bridges, 1912, 3 Tenn.Civ.App. 151; Yazoo & Mississippi Valley Railroad Co. v. Gordon, 1939, 184 Miss. 885, 186 So. 631.

49. Christy v. Florida Power Corp., Fla.App.1970, 232 So.2d 744; Orr v. United States, 5th Cir. 1973, 486 F.2d 270.

50. Gorton v. Phoenix Insurance Co., D.Mass.1972, 339 F.Supp. 241; Anderson v. Chancellor Western Oil Development Corp., 1975, 53 Cal.3d 235, 125 Cal.Rptr. 640; cf. Bramer v. United States, C.D.Cal.1976, 412 F.Supp. 569, affirmed 9th Cir. 1979, 595 F.2d 1141 (radiation leak in atomic laboratory).

51. Blue Grass Fair Association v. Bunnell, 1924, 206 Ky. 462, 267 S.W. 237; see Note, 1927, 37 Yale L.J. 113; Ramsey v. Marutamaya Ogatsu Fireworks Co., 1977, 72 Cal.App.3d 516, 140 Cal.Rptr. 247; Rill v. Chiarella, Sup.1966, 50 Misc.2d 105, 269 N.Y.S.2d 736, modified 30 A.D.2d 852, 293 N.Y.S.2d 1, motion denied 25 N.Y.2d 929, 305 N.Y.S.2d 147, 252 N.E.2d 628, affirmed 25 N.Y.2d 702, 306 N.Y.2d 955, 255 N.E.2d 183.

52. S. A. Gerrard Co. v. Fricker, 1933, 42 Ariz. 503, 27 P.2d 678; Alexander v. Seaboard Air Line Railway Co., 1952, 221 S.C. 477, 71 S.E.2d 299; Pendergrass v. Lovelace, 1953, 57 N.M. 661, 262 P.2d 231; Miles v. A. Arena & Co., 1938, 23 Cal.App.2d 680, 73 P.2d 1260; Southwestern Bell Telephone Co. v. Smith, 1952, 220 Ark. 223, 247 S.W.2d 16; cf. Boroughs v. Joiner, Ala. 1976, 337 So.2d 340 (pesticide application on crops killed neighbor's fish). Contra, Emelwon, Inc. v. United States, 5th Cir. 1968, 391 F.2d 9, certiorari denied 1968, 393 U.S. 841, 89 S.Ct. 119, 21 L.Ed.2d 111; Little v. McGraw, 1971, 250 Ark. 766, 467 S.W.2d 163, appeal after remand 253 Ark. 686, 488 S.W.2d 34. See Annot., 1971, 37 A.L.R.3d 833.

53. Thomas v. Harrington, 1902, 72 N.H. 45, 54 A. 285; Campus v. McElligott, 1936, 122 Conn. 14, 187 A. 29; Evans v. Elliott, 1941, 220 N.C. 253; 17 S.E.2d 125; Washington Metropolitan Area Transit Authority v. L'Enfant Plaza Properties, Inc., D.C.App.1982, 448 A.2d 864.

54. Rohlfs v. Weil, 1936, 271 N.Y. 444, 3 N.E.2d 588; Richman Bros. Co. v. Miller, 1936, 131 Ohio St. 424, 3 N.E.2d 360 (both painting over sidewalk); Whalen v. Shivek, 1950, 326 Mass. 142, 93 N.E.2d 393.

55. Girdzus v. Van Etten, 1918, 211 Ill.App. 524 (piled building materials); Boylhart v. Di Marco & Reimann, 1936, 270 N.Y. 217, 200 N.E. 793 (same); Wright v. Tudor City Twelfth Unit, 1938, 276 N.Y. 303, 12 N.E.2d 307 (washing mats on sidewalk).

56. Besner v. Central Trust Co. of New York, 1921, 230 N.Y. 357, 130 N.E. 577 (installing safety doors on elevator while in use); Watkins v. Gabriel Steel Co., 1932, 260 Mich. 692, 245 N.W. 801 (installing joists on steel building frame); Nashua Gummed & Coated Paper Co. v. Noyes Buick Co., 1945, 93 N.H. 348, 41 A.2d 920 (use of acetylene torch near inflammable materials); Fegles Construction Co. v. McLaughlin Construction Co., 9th Cir. 1953, 205 F.2d 637 (red hot rivets dropped into work below); Deitz v. Jackson, 1982, 57 N.C.App. 275, 291 S.E.2d 282 (ramset nail gun); LaCount v. Hensel Phelps Construction Co., 1978, 79 Cal.App.3d 754, 145 Cal.Rptr. 244 (lifting 100 ton concrete girders with crane); Atlantic Coast Development Corp. v. Napoleon Steel Contractors, Inc., Fla.App. 1980, 385 So.2d 676 (crane).

57. St. Louis & San Francisco Railroad Co. v. Madden, 1908, 77 Kan. 80, 93 P. 586; Cameron v. Oberlin, 1897, 19 Ind.App. 142, 48 N.E. 386.

high walls or chimneys,[58] the construction of a dam,[59] and many other kinds of work.[60]

The principle seems to be limited to work in which there is a high degree of risk in relation to the particular surroundings,[61] or some rather specific risk or set of risks to those in the vicinity, recognizable in advance as calling for definite precautions. The emphasis is often upon the "peculiar" character of the risk,[62] and the need for special, unusual care. One who hires a trucker to transport his goods must, as a reasonable person, always realize that if the truck is driven at an excessive speed, or with defective brakes, some collision or other harm to persons on the highway is likely to occur.[63] But this is not "inherent danger," as the courts have used the term; and for such more or less usual negligence the employer will not be liable.[64] When the trucker is to transport over the highway giant logs which require special care to fasten them securely,[65] there is obviously a special danger, and

---

58. Bonczkiewicz v. Merberg Wrecking Corp., 1961, 148 Conn. 573, 172 A.2d 917; Covington & Cincinnati Bridge Co. v. Steinbrock, 1899, 61 Ohio St. 215, 55 N.E. 618; Hanley v. Central Savings Bank, 1938, 255 App. Div. 542, 8 N.Y.S.2d 371, affirmed 1939, 280 N.Y. 734, 21 N.E.2d 513; Hevel v. Stangier, 1964, 238 Or. 44, 393 P.2d 201; Aceves v. Regal Pale Brewing Co., 1979, 24 Cal.3d 502, 156 Cal.Rptr. 41, 595 P.2d 619 (building demolition); Gonzales v. R. J. Novick Construction Co., Inc., 1978, 20 Cal.3d 798, 144 Cal.Rptr. 408, 575 P.2d 1190.

59. Trump v. Bluefield Waterworks & Improvement Co., 1925, 99 W.Va. 425, 129 S.E. 309; Budagher v. Amrep Corp., 1981, 97 N.M. 116, 637 P.2d 547; Thorne v. United States, 9th Cir. 1973, 479 F.2d 804.

60. Medley v. Trenton Investment Co., 1931, 205 Wis. 30, 236 N.W. 713 (exterminating bedbugs); Alabama Power Co. v. McIntosh, 1929, 219 Ala. 546, 122 So. 677 (cleaning floors with gasoline); Beauchamp v. B. & L. Motor Freight, Inc., 1958, 106 Ohio App. 530, 152 N.E.2d 334 (brakes on heavy tractor-trailer); T. E. Ritter Corp. v. Rose, 1959, 200 Va. 736, 107 S.E.2d 479 (crossing railroad with heavy equipment); Nechodomu v. Lindstrom, 1955, 269 Wis. 455, 69 N.W.2d 608 (mixer machine attracting child); Smith v. Inter-County Telephone Co., Mo.1977, 559 S.W.2d 518 (trenching).

Some of the California decisions have stretched the peculiar risk doctrine so far as to leave little room for the operation of the general rule of nonliability. See, e.g., Griesee v. Dart Industries, Inc., 1979, 23 Cal.3d 578, 153 Cal.Rptr. 213, 591 P.2d 503 (trenching work—collapsed on employee); Castro v. State, 1981, 114 Cal. App.3d 503, 170 Cal.Rptr. 734 (vehicular accident at work site). See also Western Stock Center, Inc. v. Sevit, Inc., 1978, 195 Colo. 372, 578 P.2d 1045 ("inherently dangerous" exception expanded to include any "foreseeable and significant risk").

61. See Evans v. Elliott, 1941, 220 N.C. 253, 17 S.E.2d 125. Thus the employer has been held not liable for blasting in an uninhabited area. Holt v. Texas New Mexico Pipeline Co., 5th Cir. 1945, 145 F.2d 862, certiorari denied 325 U.S. 879, 65 S.Ct. 1570, 89 L.Ed. 1996.

62. Emphasized in some states more than others. See generally Salinero v. Pon, 1981, 124 Cal.App.3d 120, 177 Cal.Rptr. 204; Clausen v. R. W. Gilbert Construction Co., Iowa 1981, 309 N.W.2d 462 ("peculiar risk" exception); Stark v. Weeks Real Estate, 1979, 94 Cal.App.3d 965, 156 Cal.Rptr. 701 (thorough discussion of peculiar risk doctrine); Second Restatement of Torts, §§ 413, 416.

63. There is disagreement over whether the doctrine protects third parties only or includes as well the contractor's employees. *Employees not protected*: Scofi v. McKeon Construction Co., 5th Cir. 1982, 644 F.2d 170 (Fla. law); Cooper v. Metropolitan Government of Nashville and Davidson County, Tenn.App. 1981, 628 S.W.2d 30; Conover v. Northern States Power Co., Minn.1981, 313 N.W.2d 397; Tauscher v. Puget Sound Power & Light Co., 1981, 96 Wn.2d 274, 635 P.2d 426; Peneschi v. National Steel Corp., 1982, ___ W.Va. ___, 295 S.E.2d 1. *Protected*: Warren v. McLough Steel Corp., 1981, 111 Mich.App. 496, 314 N.W.2d 666; Chesapeake & Potomac Telephone Co. of Maryland v. Chesapeake Utilities Corp., Del.1981, 436 A.2d 314 (Md. law).

Compare LaCount v. Hensel Phelps Construction Co., 1978, 79 Cal.App.3d 754, 145 Cal.Rptr. 244 (peculiar risk doctrine strictly interpreted when plaintiff is employee); Nelson v. United States, 9th Cir. 1981, 639 F.2d 469 (noting split).

64. See, e.g., Thrasher v. Gerken, Iowa 1981, 309 N.W.2d 488 (worker fell through uncovered opening in roof of building under construction); Peterson v. City of Golden Valley, N.D.1981, 308 N.W.2d 550 (sewer trench caved in); City of Cordele v. Turton's, 1982, 163 Ga.App. 327, 293 S.E.2d 560 (laying sewer pipe—gas explosion); Hixon v. Sherwin-Williams Co., 7th Cir. 1982, 671 F.2d 1005 (subcontractor laying linoleum floor misused glue); Perry v. Northern Indiana Public Service Co., 1982, ___ Ind.App. ___, 433 N.E.2d 44; Jennings v. United States, D.D.C.1981, 530 F.Supp. 40 (scaffolding work); St. Paul Companies v. Capitol Office Supply Co., Inc., 1981, 158 Ga.App. 748, 282 S.E.2d 205 (damage to adjacent owner from demolition of warehouse by wrecking company); Stark v. Weeks Real Estate, 1979, 94 Cal.App.3d 965, 156 Cal.Rptr. 701 (power saw); Cummings v. Hoosier Marine Properties, Inc., 1977, 173 Ind.App. 372, 363 N.E.2d 1266 (trenching).

65. Risley v. Lenwell, 1954, 129 Cal.App.2d 608, 277 P.2d 897. Cf. Van Arsdale v. Hollinger, 1968, 68 Cal. 2d 245, 66 Cal.Rptr. 20, 437 P.2d 508 (marking lines on busy street, special precautions to detour traffic).

the exception applies.⁶⁶ On the other hand, it is certainly not at all essential that the risk be an unavoidable one, necessarily involved in the work itself.⁶⁷ It is enough that the usual or contemplated ⁶⁸ methods of doing the work are likely to lead to such a special risk, as where, for example, a contractor laying pavement in the street may be expected to follow the usual practice of piling the gravel in the street, and so to create a special hazard for travelers.⁶⁹

"Collateral" Negligence

Another principle holds that the employer is liable only for risks inherent in the work itself, and not for "collateral" or "casual" negligence on the part of the contractor.⁷⁰ This doctrine, apparently originated in some dicta in an English case where, in violation of statutory provisions, the construction of a bridge was permitted to delay traffic on a river for more than three days.⁷¹ It is very closely related to the exception as to "inherent danger," and seems in reality to represent little more than a negative statement of it, describing the type of situation in which the special danger is not necessarily involved in the work to be done, and not contemplated in connection with the way it is expected to be done.⁷²

In some of the cases, the courts seem to regard "collateral" or "casual" negligence as referring to negligence in the operative details of the work, easily controlled by the contractor, and not ordinarily considered or contemplated by the employer,⁷³ as distinguished from its general objective or plan, which must necessarily be so contemplated. This distinction, however, has not always been borne out by the decisions themselves. Thus, it has been held to be "collateral" negligence for the servant of an independent contractor to splash mortar from a mortar box on the ground into the eye of a man passing on the sidewalk, but not to splash mortar from a wall in the course of construction over the plaintiff's windows, and the clothes hanging in her yard; ⁷⁴ to drop a paint bucket out of a window while the workman is painting an inside storeroom,

---

66. "The difficulty * * * lies in making the not altogether obvious distinction between work done by an independent contractor which is intrinsically dangerous in that harm will likely result if precautions are not taken, and work which is not intrinsically dangerous in that it is merely the sort of work which could produce injury if carelessly performed." Deitz v. Jackson, 1982, 57 N.C.App. 275, 291 S.E.2d 282.

67. In this the First Restatement of Torts, § 416, appears definitely to have been in error, and the position is reversed in the Second Restatement, § 416, Comment e.

68. Where the acts of the contractor were neither usual nor contemplated, it is held that the employer is not liable. Oklahoma City v. Caple, 1940, 187 Okl. 600, 105 P.2d 209 (failure to repair leak in other sewer line discovered in course of excavation); Swearsky v. Stanley Dry Goods Co., 1936, 122 Conn. 7, 186 A. 556 (washing windows, water allowed to flow onto sidewalk); Von Longerke v. City of New York, 1912, 150 App.Div. 98, 134 N.Y.S. 832, affirmed 211 N.Y. 558, 105 N.E. 1101 (contractor changed course of tunnel, broke a water main); Kunan v. De Matteo, 1941, 308 Mass. 427, 32 N.E.2d 613 (gasoline shovel used in resurfacing sidewalk broke meter box set in walk); Barrabee v. Crescenta Mutual Water Co., 1948, 88 Cal.App.2d 192, 198 P.2d 558 (contractor drilling a well allowed water to flow into highway).

69. Pine Bluff Natural Gas Co. v. Senyard, 1913, 108 Ark. 229, 158 S.W. 1091.

70. Second Restatement of Torts, § 426. See the excellent discussion in Talbot Smith, Collateral Negligence, 1941, 25 Minn.L.Rev. 399. The leading American case making the distinction is Robbins v. City of Chicago, Illinois 1866, 71 U.S. (4 Wall.) 657, 18 L.Ed. 427.

71. Hole v. Sittingbourne R. Co., 1861, 6 H. & N. 488, 158 Eng.Rep. 201.

72. See Deitz v. Jackson, 1982, 57 N.C.App. 275, 291 S.E.2d 282; Gessell v. Traweek, Tex.App.1982, 628 S.W.2d 479; Stark v. Weeks Real Estate, 1979, 94 Cal. App.3d 965, 156 Cal.Rptr. 701.

73. See for example Hyman v. Barrett, 1918, 224 N.Y. 436, 121 N.E. 271 (dropping board while doing repair work); Long v. Moon, 1891, 107 Mo. 334, 17 S.W. 810 (plank allowed to remain against elevator); Wilton v. City of Spokane, 1913, 73 Wash. 619, 132 P. 404 (leaving stick of dynamite under improved street); Pickett v. Waldorf System, 1922, 241 Mass. 569, 136 N.E. 64 (allowing water to flow onto sidewalk in washing windows); O'Hara v. Laclede Gaslight Co., 1912, 244 Mo. 395, 148 S.W. 884 (pipes carelessly loaded); Salinero v. Pon, 1981, 124 Cal.App.3d 120, 177 Cal.Rptr. 204 (window washer mistakenly moved weights from his partner's ladder rather than his own).

74. Compare Strauss v. City of Louisville, 1900, 108 Ky. 155, 55 S.W. 1075, with Pye v. Faxon, 1892, 156 Mass. 471, 31 N.E. 640.

but not to drop a paint bucket while he is painting a sign over a sidewalk;[75] to dislodge a board from a windowsill while working on a building on private land, but not a stone from a bridge over a public highway;[76] to blast negligently when the contract does not contemplate blasting, but not when it does;[77] to allow water to run onto the sidewalk when the employer has no reason to expect it, but not where he has reason.[78]

The essence of "collateral" negligence, therefore, appears to be, not its character as a minor incident or operative detail of the work to be done, but rather its disassociation from any inherent or contemplated special risk which may be expected to be created by the work. The employer is not liable because the negligence is "collateral" to the risk created—which is to say, that the performance of the work contracted for in the normal manner contemplated by the contract would involve no reasonable expectation of such a risk of harm to the plaintiff, and it is the abnormal departure from usual or contemplated methods by the servants of the contractor which has created the danger.[79] Where the peculiar risk inheres in the work to be done itself, however, as where a sign is to be painted over the sidewalk,[80] the fact that the risk which was to be expected materializes through the incidental negligence of the servant in dropping the bucket will not relieve the employer of liability. But where the employer reasonably expects that windows will be painted in place on the building, and the contractor decides to remove them and in the process drops one five floors,[81] the negligence is collateral to the risk.[82]

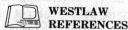

WESTLAW REFERENCES

digest(independent /5 contractor* /p employer* /p liab!)

Negligence of the Employer
aretz & 280 +s 345 & date(after 6/1/83)
restatement /5 torts /5 416

Non-delegable Duty
digest(nondelegable /p employer*)

"Inherently Dangerous" Activities
bower /2 peate & 1 /2 321
digest("inherent! dangerous!" /p employer*)

§ 72. Joint Enterprise

The doctrine of vicarious responsibility in connection with joint enterprises rests upon an analogy to the law of partnership. In a partnership, there is a more or less permanent business arrangement, creating a mutual agency between the partners for the purpose of carrying on some general business, so that the acts of one are to be charged against another. A "joint enter-

---

75. Compare Drennan Co. v. Jordan, 1913, 181 Ala. 570, 61 So. 938, with Richman Brothers Co. v. Miller, 1936, 131 Ohio St. 424, 3 N.E.2d 360; Rohlfs v. Weil, 1936, 271 N.Y. 444, 3 N.E.2d 588. And see Lockowitz v. Melnyk, 1956, 1 A.D.2d 138, 148 N.Y.S.2d 232, where the precise distinction is made.

76. Compare Hyman v. Barrett, 1918, 224 N.Y. 436, 121 N.E. 271, with Philadelphia Baltimore & Washington Railroad Co. v. Mitchell, 1908, 107 Md. 600, 69 A. 422.

77. Compare McNamee v. Hunt, 4th Cir. 1898, 87 F. 298, with Giem v. Williams, 1949, 215 Ark. 705, 222 S.W.2d 800.

78. Compare Pickett v. Waldorf System, 1922, 241 Mass. 569, 136 N.E. 64, with Wright v. Tudor City Twelfth Unit, 1938, 276 N.Y. 303, 12 N.E.2d 307.

79. Cf. Gessell v. Traweek, Tex.App.1982, 628 S.W.2d 479 (son-in-law charged with care of house shot person mistaken for burglar); Salinero v. Pon, 1981, 124 Cal.App.3d 120, 177 Cal.Rptr. 204 (window washer mistakenly removed weights from his partner's ladder rather than his own).

80. Rohlfs v. Weil, 1936, 271 N.Y. 444, 3 N.E.2d 588. Cf. Olah v. Katz, 1926, 234 Mich. 112, 207 N.W. 892 (installing plumbing through street to building, hole in street left unguarded); Watkins v. Gabriel Steel Co., 1932, 260 Mich. 692, 245 N.W. 801 (erecting steel building, failure to secure joists); Hammond Ranch Corp. v. Dodson, 1940, 199 Ark. 846, 136 S.W.2d 484 (spraying field, failure to cut off spray over plaintiff's land); Westby v. Itasca County, Minn.1980, 290 N.W.2d 437 (slippery mud on road from dynamiting beaver dam).

81. Davis v. John L. Whiting & Son Co., 1909, 201 Mass. 91, 87 N.E. 199.

82. See also Smith v. Lucky Stores, Inc., 1976, 61 Cal.App.3d 826, 132 Cal.Rptr. 628 (gust of wind blew sign onto pedestrian after it had been lowered to ground and rested against truck).

prise" is something like a partnership,[1] for a more limited period of time, and a more limited purpose. It is an undertaking to carry out a small number of acts or objectives, which is entered into by associates under such circumstances that all have an equal voice in directing the conduct of the enterprise. The law then considers that each is the agent or servant of the others, and that the act of any one within the scope of the enterprise is to be charged vicariously against the rest.[2] Whether such a relation exists between the parties is normally a question for the jury, under proper instructions from the court.[3] Nearly all courts have accepted the principle of vicarious tort responsibility in such a case, but there is no complete agreement upon any one criterion by which the relation is to be determined.

Where the enterprise is for some commercial or business purpose, and particularly where the parties have agreed to share profits and losses, it usually is called a joint venture.[4] It is then governed, as to tort liability, by the law applicable to partnerships, which is beyond the limited scope of this text.[5] The extension of "joint enterprise" beyond such business ventures is almost entirely a creature of the American courts.[6]

Except in comparatively rare instances,[7] its non-business application has been in the field of automobile law, where it has meant that the negligence of the driver of the vehicle is to be imputed to a passenger riding in it. In relatively few cases, the passenger has been charged with liability as a defendant to a third person injured by the driver's negligence.[8] It is not altogether clear why this has not occurred more frequently, unless it is that, with a financially responsible defendant available in the negligent driver, the plaintiff has not thought it desirable to

§ 72

1. "The rule is founded on the theory of partnership or a relation akin to partnership." Kokesh v. Price, 1917, 136 Minn. 304, 309, 161 N.W. 715, 717; see Connellee v. Nees, Tex.Com.App.1924, 266 S.W. 502.

2. One of the best statements of this is in Howard v. Zimmerman, 1926, 120 Kan. 77, 242 P. 131, 132. See Hamilton v. Slover, Mo.1969, 440 S.W.2d 947; Florida Rock & Sand Co. v. Cox, Fla.App.1977, 344 So.2d 1296; Second Restatement of Torts, § 491, Comment b.

3. Fuller v. Flanagan, Tex.Civ.App. 1971, 468 S.W.2d 171, refused no reversible error; Smalich v. Westfall, 1970, 440 Pa. 409, 269 A.2d 476; Mukasey v. Aaron, 1968, 20 Utah 2d 383, 438 P.2d 702; Florida Rock & Sand Co. v. Cox, Fla.Dist.App.1977, 344 So.2d 1296.

4. See Central of Georgia Railway v. Walker Truck Contractors, 1978, 270 S.C. 533, 243 S.E.2d 923; Swindell v. J.A. Tobin Construction Co., Mo.App.1981, 629 S.W.2d 536; Mechem, The Law of Joint Adventures, 1931, 15 Minn.L.Rev. 644. The terms "joint enterprise" and "joint adventure" have been used more or less interchangeably. See DeSuza v. Andersack, 1976, 63 Cal.App.3d 694, 133 Cal.Rptr. 920.

5. See, e.g., Miller, Cowherd & Kerver, Inc. v. De Montejo, Fla.Dist.App.1981, 406 So.2d 1196; Beck v. Indiana Surveying Co., 1981, ___ Ind.App. ___, 429 N.E.2d 264; Stone v. First Wyoming Bank N. A., Lusk, 10th Cir. 1980, 625 F.2d 332.

6. There is at least one English case, Brooke v. Bool, [1928] 2 K.B. 578, and one Canadian case, Grand Trunk R. Co. v. Dixon, [1920] 51 Dom.L.Rep. 576.

7. One such case is Cullinan v. Tetrault, 1923, 123 Me. 302, 122 A. 770, where the negligence of one boy purchasing liquor for a drinking party was imputed to his companion. See also O'Neil v. Sea Bee Club, 1954, 118 N.E.2d 175, 69 O.L.A. 442 (club members); Ruth v. Hutchinson Gas Co., 1941, 209 Minn. 248, 296 N.W. 136 (hunting party); Eagle Star Insurance Co. v. Bean, 9th Cir. 1943, 134 F.2d 755 (dismantling a sawmill); Shell Oil Co. v. Prestidge, 9th Cir. 1957, 249 F.2d 413 (prospecting for oil).

But compare the refusal to apply the doctrine to pedestrians walking together in Barnes v. Town of Marcus, 1896, 96 Iowa 675, 65 N.W. 984; Bailey v. City of Centerville, 1901, 115 Iowa 271, 88 N.W. 379; Brigham Young University v. Lillywhite, 10 Cir. 1941, 118 F.2d 836, certiorari denied 314 U.S. 638, 62 S.Ct. 73, 86 L.Ed. 512 (chemistry students working in laboratory); cf. Lambert v. Pittsburgh Bridge & Iron Works, 1975, 463 Pa. 237, 344 A.2d 810 (employer's negligence not imputed to employee in action against third party).

With a few exceptions such as these, the "joint enterprise" cases have all involved business ventures or vehicles.

8. Stock v. Fife, 1982, 13 Mass.App.Ct. 75, 430 N.E.2d 845 (passenger drinking companion not engaged in joint enterprise with driver); Cecil v. Hardin, Tenn.1978, 575 S.W.2d 268 (drinking and cavorting; no joint enterprise); Easter v. McNabb, 1975, 97 Idaho 180, 451 P.2d 604 (fishing companions; no joint enterprise); Buford v. Horne, Miss.1974, 300 So.2d 913 (no joint enterprise); Mims v. Coleman, 1966, 248 S.C. 235, 149 S.E.2d 623 (same); DeSuza v. Andersack, 1976, 63 Cal.App.3d 694, 133 Cal.Rptr. 920 (same); Fugate v. Galvin, 1980, 84 Ill.App.3d 573, 40 Ill.Dec. 318, 406 N.E.2d 19 (same); Manley v. Horton, Mo.1967, 414 S.W.2d 254.

complicate matters by joining one who is personally innocent. In by far the greater number of cases, the question has been one of contributory negligence, and the driver's misconduct has been imputed to the passenger to bar his own recovery.[9] "Joint enterprise" is thus of importance chiefly as a defendant's doctrine, imputing the negligence of another to the plaintiff; and as such, it has not been slow to draw the wrath of the plaintiff's partisans.

Considerable confusion still surrounds the doctrine,[10] which no one has succeeded in reducing to any very exact formula or definition. A statement frequently quoted from an opinion of the Supreme Court of Washington [11] attempts the following:

"Briefly stated, a joint adventure arises out of, and must have its origin in, a contract, express or implied, in which the parties thereto agree to enter into an undertaking in the performance of which they have a community of interest, and further, a contract in which each of the parties has an equal right of control over the agencies used in the performance. Thus we note (1) a contract, (2) a common purpose, (3) a community of interest, (4) equal right to a voice, accompanied by an equal right of control."

Common Purpose

One group of older cases, now definitely very much in the minority and almost passing out of the picture, have found a joint enterprise in the mere association of the driver and the passenger in the use of the vehicle for any purpose in which they have a common interest of any kind. Thus friends on a pleasure trip together,[12] members of the same family on the way to church,[13] a group proceeding together to witness a prize fight,[14] a prospective purchaser riding with a salesman,[15] and fellow servants riding together in the course of their employment,[16] have in the past been found to be engaged in a joint enterprise, by reason of that association alone, with the mutual right of control conjured up from the community of interest without more. Such decisions were condemned [17] as effectively restoring in passenger cases the discredited doctrine of imputed contributory negligence,[18] since it is seldom that some element of common purpose cannot be found when two persons are travelling together in a private vehicle. So many

---

9. "Any one of several persons engaged in a joint enterprise, such as to make each member of the group responsible for physical harm to other persons caused by the negligence of any member, is barred from recovery against such other persons by the negligence of any member of the group." Second Restatement of Torts, § 491(1). Cf. Florida Rock & Sand Co. v. Cox, Fla.Dist.App.1977, 344 So.2d 1296 (comparative fault—damages would be reduced, not barred, if joint venture found).

But cf. Pierson v. Edstrom, 1970, 286 Minn. 164, 174 N.W.2d 712, where the court prospectively abolished the imputation of contributory negligence in joint enterprise cases, leaving only the imputation of negligence to the defendant. See also Fuller v. Flanagan, Tex.Civ.App.1971, 468 S.W.2d 171 (driver's negligence not imputable to minor).

10. See generally, Weintraub, The Joint Enterprise Doctrine in Automobile Law, 1931, 16 Corn.L.Q. 320; Rollison, The "Joint Enterprise" in the Law of Imputed Negligence, 1931, 6 Notre Dame Lawyer 172; Keeton, Imputed Contributory Negligence, 1935, 13 Tex.L.Rev. 161; James, Vicarious Liability, 1954, 28 Tulane L.Rev. 161, 210; Notes, 1924, 12 Cal.L.Rev. 238; 1926, 12 Va. L.Rev. 341; 1929, 38 Yale L.J. 810; 1929, 77 U.Pa.L. Rev. 676; 1974, 58 Minn.L.Rev. 978 (joint venturers' negligence combined under comparative fault act).

11. Carboneau v. Peterson, 1939, 1 Wn.2d 347, 95 P.2d 1043.

12. E.g., Washington & Old Dominion Railway Co. v. Zell's Administratrix, 1916, 118 Va. 755, 88 S.E. 309; Wentworth v. Town of Waterbury, 1916, 90 Vt. 60, 96 A. 334.

13. Hurley v. Spokane, 1923, 126 Wash. 213, 217 P. 1004; Delaware & Hudson Co. v. Boyden, 3d Cir. 1921, 269 F. 881 (fishing excursion); Caliando v. Huck, D.Fla.1949, 84 F.Supp. 598 (trip to Florida); Stam v. Cannon, Iowa 1970, 176 N.W.2d 794 (to different jobs).

14. Jensen v. Chicago, Milwaukee & St. Paul Railway Co., 1925, 133 Wash. 208, 233 P. 635.

15. Lawrence v. Denver & Rio Grande Railroad Co., 1918, 52 Utah 414, 174 P. 817.

16. Martin v. Puget Sound Electric Railway Co., 1926, 136 Wash. 663, 241 P. 360; Otis v. Kolsky, 1929, 94 Pa.Super. 548. Cf. Campagna v. Lyles, 1929, 298 Pa. 352, 148 A. 527 (servant riding with employer on employer's business).

17. Pope v. Halpern, 1924, 193 Cal. 168, 223 P. 470; Coleman v. Bent, 1924, 100 Conn. 527, 124 A. 224. See Weintraub, The Joint Enterprise Doctrine in Automobile Law, 1931, 16 Corn.L.Q. 320, 332.

18. See infra, § 74.

of the jurisdictions in which these decisions appear have repudiated them, or departed from them in later cases,[19] that they are now almost entirely discredited; and it is now agreed that something more is required for a joint enterprise than the mere showing of a contract or agreement to travel together to a destination for a common purpose.[20] Something in the nature of a common business, financial or pecuniary interest in the objective of the journey is now generally held to be essential. Recent decisions have thus refused to find a joint enterprise where the parties are casually together for pleasure[21] or for independent ends.[22]

Mutual Right of Control

The prevailing view is that a joint enterprise requires something, beyond the mere association of the parties for a common end, to show a mutual "right of control" over the operation of the vehicle—or in other words, an equal right in the passenger to be heard as to the manner in which it is driven.[23] It is not the fact that he does[24] or does not[25] give directions which is important in itself, but rather the understanding between the parties that he has the right to have his wishes respected, to the same extent as the driver. In the absence of circumstances indicating such an understanding, it has been held that companions on a pleasure trip,[26] members of the same family,[27] parties engaged in a com-

---

19. See for example Director General of Railroads v. Pence's Administratrix, 1923, 135 Va. 329, 116 S.E. 351; Landry v. Hubert, 1927, 100 Vt. 268, 137 A. 97; Rosenstrom v. North Bend Stage Line, 1929, 154 Wash. 57, 280 P. 932; Kocher v. Creston Transfer Co., 3d Cir. 1948, 166 F.2d 680; Alperdt v. Paige, 1928, 292 Pa. 1, 140 A. 555.

20. See, e.g., Coffman v. Kennedy, 1977, 74 Cal.App.3d 28, 141 Cal.Rptr. 267; DeSuza v. Andersack, 1976, 63 Cal.App.3d 694, 133 Cal.Rptr. 920; Scott v. McGaugh, 1973, 211 Kan. 323, 506 P.2d 1155; Fugate v. Galvin, 1980, 84 Ill.App.3d 573, 40 Ill.Dec. 318, 406 N.E.2d 19.

21. Hall v. Blackham, 1966, 18 Utah 2d 164, 417 P.2d 664 (duck hunting); Young v. Bynum, Tex.Civ.App.1953, 260 S.W.2d 696; Edlebeck v. Hooten, 1963, 20 Wis.2d 83, 121 N.W.2d 240 (deer hunting); Stock v. Fife, 1982, 13 Mass.App. 75, 430 N.E.2d 845 (drinking and cavorting); DeSuza v. Andersack, 1976, 63 Cal.App.3d 694, 133 Cal.Rptr. 920 (friends, for pleasure and errands); Cecil v. Hardin, Tenn.1978, 575 S.W.2d 268 (social purposes only); Adams v. Treat, 1970, 256 Or. 239, 472 P.2d 270 (usual family activities); Dimond v. Kling, N.D.1974, 221 N.W.2d 86 (riding double on bicycle to store for popsicles); Huff v. Rosenberg, Ky.1973, 496 S.W.2d 352 (family pleasure trip); Easter v. McNabb, 1975, 97 Idaho 180, 541 P.2d 604 (fishing trip).

22. Kepler v. Chicago, St. Paul, Minneapolis & Omaha Railway Co., 1923, 111 Neb. 273, 196 N.W. 161, certiorari denied 265 U.S. 589, 44 S.Ct. 635, 68 L.Ed. 1194 (passenger driven as accommodation to mail letters); Hilton v. Blose, 1929, 297 Pa. 458, 147 A. 100 (on way to bowl on different teams in different games); Kuser v. Barengo, 1953, 70 Nev. 66, 254 P.2d 447 (delegates to convention); Mims v. Coleman, 1966, 248 S.C. 235, 149 S.E.2d 623 (picking up tools); DeSuza v. Andersack, 1976, 63 Cal.App.3d 694, 133 Cal.Rptr. 920 (friends, for pleasure and errands); Shoemaker v. Estate of Whistler, Tex.1974, 513 S.W.2d 10 (airplane search mission).

The doctrine thus does not apply to car pools. Connor v. Southland Corp., Fla.App.1970, 240 So.2d 822; Southard v. Lira, 1973, 212 Kan. 763, 512 P.2d 409; Husser v. Bogalusa Coca Cola Bottling Co., La.App. 1968, 215 So.2d 921; cf. Campanella v. Zajic, 1978, 62 Ill.App.3d 886, 20 Ill.Dec. 33, 379 N.E.2d 866 (husband and wife commuting to work); Stam v. Cannon, Iowa 1970, 176 N.W.2d 794 (same).

23. Scott v. McGaugh, 1973, 211 Kan. 323, 506 P.2d 1155; Shoemaker v. Estate of Whistler, Tex.1974, 513 S.W.2d 10; Easter v. McNabb, 1975, 97 Idaho 180, 541 P.2d 604; Adams v. Treat, 1970, 256 Or. 239, 472 P.2d 270 (no evidence of actual control by wife over husband); Cecil v. Hardin, Tenn.1978, 575 S.W.2d 268; Helton v. Missouri Pacific Railway Co., 1976, 260 Ark. 342, 538 S.W.2d 569 (motorcycle passenger did not have equal control); Lollar v. Dewitt, 1971, 255 S.C. 452, 179 S.E.2d 607 (mule-drawn wagon); cf. Freeman v. United States, 6th Cir. 1975, 509 F.2d 626 (parachutists could not control pilot).

The control requirement is met, of course, if both paties are in fact physically sharing the control. Flager v. Associated Truck Lines, Inc., 1974, 52 Mich.App. 280, 216 N.W.2d 922 (motor scooter; one operating throttle and steering, the other operating brakes). But cf. Massey v. Scripter, 1977, 401 Mich. 385, 258 N.W.2d 44 (tandem bicycle).

24. Webb v. Huffman, Tex.Civ.App.1959, 320 S.W.2d 893, refused no reversible error; Quave v. Ray, S.D.Miss.1974, 377 F.Supp. 125.

25. Crescent Motor Co. v. Stone, 1924, 211 Ala. 516, 101 So. 49; Howard v. Zimmerman, 1926, 120 Kan. 77, 242 P. 131.

26. Hulse v. Driver, 1974, 11 Wn.App. 509, 524 P.2d 255; Easter v. McNabb, 1975, 97 Idaho 180, 541 P.2d 604 (fishing trip); Fugate v. Galvin, 1980, 84 Ill.App.3d 573, 40 Ill.Dec. 318, 406 N.E.2d 19.

27. Huff v. Rosenberg, Ky.1973, 496 S.W.2d 352 (child driver, parent passenger); Schmitt v. Jenkins

mercial transaction,[28] servants riding with the employer,[29] or fellow servants in the course of their employment,[30] although they may have a common purpose in the ride, are not engaged in a joint enterprise. Nor, of course, is the fact that the passenger has requested the driver to make the trip for his benefit sufficient to establish such a right of control.[31]

If the purpose of the journey is a business or financial one, in which the parties have a common interest, the mutual right to direct the operation of the car is much more readily found.[32] Some courts [33] have gone farther, and said that the mutual right of control does not exist, and a joint enterprise does not exist, in the absence of such a common pecuniary interest in the use of the car for the trip. The justification for this position may be that such a financial venture involves a closer analogy to the law of partnership, and affords more reason for regarding the risk as properly to be charged against all those engaged in it. This is certainly the direction toward which the courts are tending to move.

In the past, the theoretical right to an equal voice in the operation of the car was quite often found when the driver and the passenger had a common property interest in the vehicle—as where they owned it in common,[34] or joined in hiring [35] or borrowing [36] it. This not infrequently has meant that an entirely innocent plaintiff is barred from all recovery by the negligence of one with whom he happens to be a joint owner; and since the right to an equal voice in the operation is sometimes, and particularly in the case of husband and wife,[37] more theoretical than real, there has been quite a pronounced reaction against such decisions. The present tendency is to hold that joint ownership, while it may be a fact to be considered, does not of itself necessarily estab-

---

Truck Lines, Inc., Iowa 1969, 170 N.W.2d 632; Adams v. Treat, 1970, 256 Or. 239, 472 P.2d 270 (spouses in car).

28. Spradley v. Houser, 1966, 247 S.C. 208, 146 S.E.2d 621; Bloom v. Leech, 1929, 120 Ohio St. 239, 166 N.E. 137; Churchill v. Briggs, 1938, 225 Iowa 1187, 282 N.W. 280.

29. Flynn v. Wallace, 1959, 173 Cal.App.2d 592, 343 P.2d 767 (employee driving); Laird v. State Farm Insurance Co., La.App.1974, 290 So.2d 343, writ denied 293 So.2d 184 (same).

30. Scott v. McGaugh, 1973, 211 Kan. 323, 506 P.2d 1155; Bach v. Liberty Mutual Fire Insurance Co., 1967, 36 Wis.2d 72, 152 N.W.2d 911; Mims v. Coleman, 1966, 248 S.C. 235, 149 S.E.2d 623; Laird v. State Farm Insurance Co., La.App.1974, 290 So.2d 343, writ denied 293 So.2d 184.

31. Webb v. Huffman, Tex.Civ.App.1959, 320 S.W.2d 893, refused no reversible error; Sandrock v. Taylor, 1970, 185 Neb. 106, 174 N.W.2d 186; Buford v. Horne, Miss.1974, 300 So.2d 913; Fugate v. Galvin, 1980, 84 Ill.App.3d 573, 40 Ill.Dec. 318, 406 N.E.2d 19 (taking passenger home).

32. See Chaney v. Tingley, 1977, 174 Ind.App. 191, 366 N.E.2d 707; Vanderbloemen v. Suchosky, 1959, 7 Wis.2d 367, 97 N.W.2d 183; cf. Wilkinson v. Stevison, Tex.1974, 514 S.W.2d 895 (husband and wife); Allegheny Airlines Inc. v. United States, 7th Cir. 1974, 504 F.2d 104, certiorari denied 1975, 421 U.S. 978, 95 S.Ct. 1979, 44 L.Ed.2d 470, on remand 420 F.Supp. 1339, affirmed in part, reversed in part 7th Cir., 586 F.2d 53 (aircraft and flying school owner, student pilot), noted, 1975, 41 J.Air.L. & Com. 511.

33. Fugate v. Galvin, 1980, 84 Ill.App.3d 573, 40 Ill. Dec. 318, 406 N.E.2d 19; Cecil v. Hardin, Tenn.1978, 575 S.W.2d 268; Shoemaker v. Estate of Whistler, Tex. 1974, 513 S.W.2d 10, noted, 1975, 6 Tex.Tech.L.Rev. 1193; Campanella v. Zajic, 1978, 62 Ill.App.3d 886, 20 Ill.Dec. 33, 379 N.E.2d 866 (husband and wife commuting to work; no joint enterprise); DeSuza v. Andersack, 1976, 63 Cal.App.3d 694, 133 Cal.Rptr. 920; Leuck v. Goetz, 1972, 151 Ind.App. 528, 280 N.E.2d 847; Sumner v. Amacher, 1968, 150 Mont. 544, 437 P.2d 630; Bach v. Liberty Mutual Fire Insurance Co., 1967, 36 Wis.2d 72, 152 N.W.2d 911; Easter v. McNabb, 1975, 97 Idaho 180, 541 P.2d 604. Compare Bray v. Chicago, Rock Island & Pacific Railway Co., Minn.1975, 232 N.W.2d 97 (gratuitously helping friend in his business; no joint enterprise).

34. Moore v. Skiles, 1954, 130 Colo. 191, 274 P.2d 311; Roddy v. Francis, Mo.App.1961, 349 S.W.2d 488; Shoe v. Hood, 1960, 251 N.C. 719, 112 S.E.2d 543; Caliando v. Huck, N.D.Fla.1949, 84 F.Supp. 598.

35. Christopherson v. Minneapolis, St. Paul & Sault Ste. Marie Railway Co., 1914, 28 N.D. 128, 147 N.W. 791; Wosika v. St. Paul City Railway Co., 1900, 80 Minn. 364, 83 N.W. 386.

36. Curran v. Lehigh Valley Railroad Co., 1930, 299 Pa. 584, 149 A. 885; Union Bus Co. v. Smith, 1932, 104 Fla. 569, 140 So. 631.

37. Clemens v. O'Brien, 1964, 85 N.J.Super. 404, 204 A.2d 895; Workman v. City of San Diego, 1968, 267 Cal.App.2d 36, 72 Cal.Rptr. 509.

lish the "right of control" required for a joint enterprise.[38]

Beyond this, there are other factors which tend to establish such a mutual right of control, but which usually are not regarded as conclusive. An agreement to share the expenses of the trip is some evidence of such a right in the passenger,[39] as is the fact that he determines the route to be taken,[40] or alternates in the driving,[41] but none of these is necessarily inconsistent with his status as a mere paying passenger, or a guest, who will not be responsible for the driver's misconduct. The essential question is whether the parties can be found by implication to have agreed to an equal voice in the management of the vehicle,[42] which in the normal and usual case is merely an issue of fact for the jury.

Passenger v. Driver

Some early courts, entirely mistaking the nature of the vicarious liability in the joint enterprise cases, held that the negligence of the driver is to be imputed to the passenger to bar recovery even when he brings his action against the negligent driver himself.[43] There seems to be no possible justification for such a result.[44] It is well settled that the vicarious liability which is designed for the protection of third persons against the risks of the enterprise does not extend to any action between the parties themselves, and that a negligent servant will be liable to his master,[45] or one member of a partnership to another.[46] Most of the courts which have considered the question have recognized this, and have held that the driver's negligence, which is itself the cause of action, will not bar the passenger's recovery.[47] It has been held, however, that as between two passengers in a joint enterprise, neither may recover from the other for the negligence of the driver,[48] upon analogy to the agency rule that where two principals employ the same agent to deal with their common interests,

---

38. E.g., Stover v. Patrick, Mo.1970, 459 S.W.2d 393 (overruling earlier cases); Pavlos v. Albuquerque National Bank, App.1971, 82 N.M. 756, 487 P.2d 187; Koroluck v. Giordano's Service Center, Inc., 1970, 34 A.D.2d 1013, 312 N.Y.S.2d 804; Kennedy v. Kennedy, Tex.Civ.App.1974, 505 S.W.2d 393.

39. Pence v. Berry, 1942, 13 Wn.2d 564, 125 P.2d 645; Hopkins v. Golden, 1937, 281 Mich. 389, 275 N.W. 184; cf. Annot., 1971, 39 A.L.R.3d 1224 (expense sharing as affecting guest status under auto guest statutes).

But the jury may still find that the management of the car was left entirely to the driver. Eg., Buford v. Horne, Miss.1974, 300 So.2d 913 ($2 worth of gas); cf. Conino v. Landry, La.App.1969, 222 So.2d 525, application denied 254 La. 767, 226 So.2d 524 (offer to pay motor bike operator 25 cents for ride insufficient); Babington v. Bogdanovic, 1972, 7 Ill.App.3d 593, 288 N.E.2d 40, 44 ("mere sharing of picayune and paltry minimal expenses will [not] satisfy the fundamental 'business' factor required"); Connor v. Southland Corp., Fla.App.1970, 240 So.2d 822 (car pool).

40. Dick v. Carey, 7th Cir. 1969, 408 F.2d 555; Quave v. Ray, S.D.Miss.1974, 377 F.Supp. 125; cf. Huff v. Rosenburg, Ky.1973, 496 S.W.2d 352 (minor driver would have followed father's directions); Webb v. Huffman, Tex.Civ.App.1959, 320 S.W.2d 893, refused no reversable error. The "normal and usual courtesies, deferring to one another's wishes on the trip," do not show any mutual right of control. Virginia Transit Co. v. Simmons, 1956, 198 Va. 122, 92 S.E.2d 291.

41. Isaacson v. Boston, Worchester & New York Street Railway Co., 1932, 278 Mass. 378, 180 N.E. 118; Carroll v. Hutchinson, 1938, 172 Va. 43, 200 S.E. 644; Webb v. Huffman, Tex.Civ.App.1959, 320 S.W.2d 893, refused no reversable error. The jury may still find that control was left entirely to the driver of the moment. MacGregor v. Bradshaw, 1952, 193 Va. 787, 71 S.E.2d 361; Sumner v. Amacher, 1968, 150 Mont. 544, 437 P.2d 630.

42. See Stock v. Fife, 1982, 13 Mass.App. 75, 430 N.E.2d 845; Adams v. Treat, 1970, 256 Or. 239, 472 P.2d 270; Scott v. McGaugh, 1973, 211 Kan. 323, 506 P.2d 1155.

43. Frisorger v. Shepse, 1930, 251 Mich. 121, 230 N.W. 926; Barnett v. Levy, 1919, 213 Ill.App. 129; see Jacobs v. Jacobs, 1917, 141 La. 272, 286, 74 So. 992, 997.

44. See Notes, 1932, 20 Cal.L.Rev. 458; 1936, 20 Minn.L.Rev. 401, 410; Weintraub, The Joint Enterprise Doctrine in Automobile Law, 1934, 16 Corn.L.Q. 320, 324.

45. Mechem, Agency, 2d ed. 1914, § 1275.

46. Second Restatement of Agency, § 14A, Comment *a*.

47. Williams v. Knapp, 1968, 248 Md. 506, 237 A.2d 450; Dosher v. Hunt, 1955, 243 N.C. 247, 90 S.E.2d 374; Le Sage v. Pryor, 1941, 137 Tex. 455, 154 S.W.2d 446; Sackett v. Haeckel, 1957, 249 Minn. 290, 81 N.W.2d 833; Brown v. Sohn, Ky.1970, 449 S.W.2d 920; Sommermeyer v. Price, 1979, 198 Colo. 548, 603 P.2d 135; Galloway v. Korzokwa, N.D.Miss.1972, 346 F.Supp. 1086; Second Restatement of Torts, § 491(2).

48. Murphy v. Keating, 1939, 204 Minn. 269, 283 N.W. 389; Hume v. Crane, Mo.1962, 352 S.W.2d 610;

one cannot charge the other with the misconduct of their mutual agent, unless the other is personally at fault.[49]

Criticism

One must seriously doubt the logic and fairness of imposing vicarious responsibility, whether as plaintiff or as defendant, upon the passenger who is engaged in a "joint enterprise," for the negligence of his driver.[50] The contractual agreement by which he is said to enter into such an arrangement is all too obviously a fiction in situations where the parties have merely gotten together for the ride; and upon this there is erected a second fiction, that the passenger shares a "right of control" of the operation of the vehicle; and on this is erected in turn a third fiction, that the driver is his agent or servant. This topheavy structure tends to fall of its own weight. In the usual case the passenger has no physical ability to control the operation of the car, and no opportunity to interfere with it; and any attempt on his part to do so in fact would be a dangerously distracting piece of backseat driving which might very well amount to negligence in itself.

Unless the limitation to business ventures of a character really approaching a partnership is to be accepted, the doctrine will most often be applied to enterprises which are not commercial and are matters of friendly cooperation and accommodation, where there is not at all the same reason for placing all risks upon the enterprise itself. Normally it is the driver, and not the passenger, who might be expected to carry insurance. It has been said that the courts do not regard the doctrine with favor.[51] The courts should be expected to continue to narrow the scope of the doctrine in order to ameliorate its rigors.

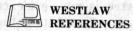
WESTLAW REFERENCES

"joint enterprise" /p vicarious! /s responsib!
di joint enterprise

Common Purpose
common /s purpose /p "joint enterprise"

Mutual Right of Control
"right of control" /p joint /s enterprise

Passenger v. Driver
"joint enterprise" /p passenger /p driver

---

§ 73. Automobile Owners and Others

As in the case of the doctrine of joint enterprise,[1] the advent of the automobile has been responsible for a number of other extensions of the principle of vicarious liability. The enormous annual traffic accident toll,[2] together with the frequent financial irresponsibility of the individual driving the car,[3] has led to a search for some basis for imposing liability upon the owner of the vehicle, even though he is free from negligence himself. Bluntly put, it is felt that, since automobiles are expensive, the owner is more likely to be able to pay any damages than the driver, who may be entirely impecunious; and that the owner is the obvious person to carry the necessary insurance to cover the risk, and so to distribute any losses among motorists as a class.[4] Beyond this, also, is

---

O'Neil v. Sea Bee Club, 1954, 118 N.E.2d 175, 69 O.L.A. 442; Stearns v. Lindow, 1934, 63 U.S.App.D.C. 134, 136, 70 F.2d 738, 740; Zeigler v. Ryan, 1937, 65 S.D. 110, 271 N.W. 767. See Note, 1939, 23 Minn.L.Rev. 666; Second Restatement of Torts, § 491(2).

49. Cf. Brown v. Wisconsin Natural Gas Co., 1973, 59 Wis.2d 334, 208 N.W.2d 769; Roschmann v. Sanborn, 1934, 315 Pa. 188, 172 A. 657; Koogler v. Koogler, 1933, 127 Ohio St. 57, 186 N.E. 725.

50. See Weintraub, The Joint Enterprise Doctrine in Automobile Law, 1931, 16 Corn.L.Q. 320, 334; James, Vicarious Liability, 1954, 28 Tulane L.Rev. 161, 214.

51. See Gilmore v. Grass, 10th Cir. 1933, 68 F.2d 150, 153; Dooley, Modern Tort Law, 1977, vol. 1, at 111: "It never served a purpose * * * other than to create problems [and] ought to be nullified, even as a theory."

§ 73

1. Supra, § 72.
2. See infra, § 84.
3. See infra, ch. 14.
4. "The justification for imputing negligence to an innocent party is the social necessity to provide injured plaintiffs with financially responsible defendants." Nowak v. Nowak, 1978, 175 Conn. 112, 394 A.2d 716, 723.

the feeling that one who originates such a danger by setting the car upon the highway in the first instance should be held responsible for the negligence of the person to whom he entrusts it; and also the idea that the assumption of such responsibility is a fair price for the owner to pay for the privilege of having the car operated, at the cost of the taxpayers, over the expensive highways of the state.

This quest for a financially responsible defendant has led, in the automobile cases, to a variety of measures. Where the owner of the car entrusts it to an unsuitable driver,[5] he is held liable for the negligence of the driver, upon the basis of his own negligence in not preventing it. But even where the owner has exercised all due care of his own, vicarious responsibility has been imposed. When the owner is present as a passenger in his own car, a number of courts have held that he retains such a "right of control" over the operation of the vehicle that the driver is to be regarded as his agent or servant. In many of these cases, it is not clear that anything more is meant than that the owner has failed, when he had the opportunity, to interfere with the negligent driving, and so has been negligent himself.[6] In others, special circumstances have indicated that the owner in fact retained the authority to give directions as to the operation of the car.[7] But some courts clearly have gone further, and have held that the right of control, sufficient to impose responsibility, is established by the mere presence of the owner in the car.[8] Most jurisdictions have rejected such an arbitrary rule, and have held that the owner may surrender his right to give directions, and become a guest in his own car.[9] It is generally agreed that the plaintiff may be aided by a presumption that the driver is an agent or servant,[10] but the owner may prove the contrary.

If the owner is not present in the car, but has entrusted it to a driver who is not his servant, there is merely a bailment, and there is usually no basis for imputing the

---

5. See, e.g., Mathis v. Stacy, Tenn.App.1980, 606 S.W.2d 290; Allen v. Toledo, 1980, 109 Cal.App.3d 415, 167 Cal.Rptr. 270; Chiniche v. Smith, Ala.1979, 374 So. 2d 872; Bohnen v. Wingereid, 1979, 80 Ill.App.3d 232, 35 Ill.Dec. 254, 398 N.E.2d 1204; Worth v. Dortman, 1979, 94 Mich.App. 103, 288 N.W.2d 603 (independent from owner consent statute). See generally Annot., 1968, 19 A.L.R.3d 1175 (intoxicated driver).

Compare the "special circumstances" rule applied in some states holding the owner liable, for negligently leaving the keys in the car, to third persons injured by a thief who foreseeably steals the car. See, e.g., Hosking v. Robles, 1979, 98 Cal.App.3d 98, 159 Cal.Rptr. 369; Illinois Farmers Insurance Co. v. Tapemark, Co., Minn.1978, 273 N.W.2d 630.

6. Cf. Dofflemyer v. Gilley, La.1980, 384 So.2d 435 on remand 395 So.2d 403; Bauer v. Johnson, 1980, 79 Ill.3d 324, 38 Ill.Dec. 149, 403 N.E.2d 237.

7. Archambault v. Holmes, 1939, 125 Conn. 167, 4 A.2d 420 (prospective purchaser); Kelley v. Thibodeau, 1921, 120 Me. 402, 115 A. 162 (inexperienced driver); Chambers v. Hawkins, 1930, 233 Ky. 211, 25 S.W.2d 363 (driving at owner's request); Smith v. Spirek, 1923, 196 Iowa 1328, 195 N.W. 736 (driving under actual directions); see Ritter v. Taucher, 1978, 65 Ill.App.3d 464, 22 Ill.Dec. 23, 382 N.E.2d 343 (jury could find mother should have warned son about taking car on snowy day).

8. See, e.g., Boker v. Luebbe, 1977, 198 Neb. 282, 252 N.W.2d 297; Hover v. Clamp, 1978, 40 Colo.App. 410, 579 P.2d 1181 (noting that rule has been "criticized severely"); cf. Parrish v. Walsh, 1982, 69 Ohio St.2d 11, 429 N.E.2d 1176 (retaining rule in actions involving third parties, but abandoning it when owner-passenger sues driver).

Such "control" used to be found quite frequently when one spouse was driving the other's car. Gochee v. Wagner, 1931, 257 N.Y. 344, 178 N.E. 553; Fisch v. Waters, 1948, 136 N.J.L. 651, 57 A.2d 471. "If the law supposes that," said Mr. Bumble, "the law is a ass."

9. Davis v. Spindler, 1952, 156 Neb. 276, 56 N.W.2d 107; Sackett v. Haeckel, 1957, 249 Minn. 290, 81 N.W.2d 833; Reiter v. Grober, 1921, 173 Wis. 493, 181 N.W. 739. His presence is merely "an important element in showing agency or control by inference." Neese v. Toms, 1941, 196 S.C. 67, 12 S.E.2d 859; Grinter v. Haag, 1976, 168 Ind.App. 595, 344 N.E.2d 320.

See also Kalechman v. Drew Auto Rental, Inc., 1973, 33 N.Y.2d 397, 353 N.Y.S.2d 414, 308 N.E.2d 886 (abolishing doctrine imputing driver's contributory negligence to owner-passenger in action against third party); Parrish v. Walsh, 1982, 69 Ohio St.2d 11, 429 N.E.2d 1176 (same, except limiting abolition to actions by owner-passenger against his own driver); Note, 1974, 6 St. Mary's L.J. 526.

10. Ritter v. Taucher, 1978, 65 Ill.App.3d 464, 22 Ill. Dec. 23, 382 N.E.2d 343; Rhoads v. Bryant, 1982, 56 N.C.App. 635, 289 S.E.2d 637 (imputed contributory negligence).

driver's negligence to the owner.[11] It is here that the owner's liability to the injured plaintiff stops at common law.[12] Only the courts of Florida have gone the length of saying that an automobile is a "dangerous instrumentality," [13] for which the owner remains responsible when it is negligently driven by another. Courts in other states have refused to accept this simple but sweeping approach,[14] and have instead struggled hard to find some foundation for vicarious liability in the circumstances of the particular case.

Family Purpose Doctrine

One such device used in some jurisdictions [15] is the "family car," or "family purpose" doctrine.[16] Under this doctrine, the owner of an automobile who permits members of his household to drive it for their own pleasure or convenience is regarded as making such a family purpose his "business," so that the driver is treated as his servant.[17] Sometimes it is said that the owner would be liable for the negligence of a chauffeur whom he hires to drive his family, and therefore should be liable when he entrusts the same task to a member of his family instead.[18] There is obviously an element of unblushing fiction in this manufactured agency; and it has quite often been recognized, without apology, that the doctrine is an instrument of policy, a transparent device intended to place the liability upon the party most easily held responsible.[19]

To come within the application of the doctrine, the defendant must own the automobile,[20] or be in control of its use,[21] or at least

---

11. E.g., Moyer Car Rental, Inc. v. Halliburton Co., Okl.1980, 610 P.2d 232 (rental car); Siverson v. Martori, App.1978, 119 Ariz. 440, 581 P.2d 285 (motorcycle); Great Central Insurance Co. v. Harris, 1977, 46 Ill.App.3d 542, 4 Ill.Dec. 776, 360 N.E.2d 1151 (no liability for damage caused by garage operator bailee's employees); Woods v. Nichols, Miss.1982, 416 So.2d 659 (car); cf. Littles v. Avis Rent-A-Car System, 1969, 433 Pa. 72, 248 A.2d 837 (rental truck); Forrester v. Kuck, Mont.1978, 579 P.2d 756 (same); Strickland v. King, 1977, 293 N.C. 731, 239 S.E.2d 243 (co-owner with driver).

12. "We know of no statutory or jurisprudential rule that would make a non-negligent automobile owner liable for the torts commited by a friend while operating the owner's car." Rhodes v. Fromenthal, La. App.1980, 385 So.2d 415, 416 (owner not liable for accident caused by his live-in girlfriend on way to beauty parlor).

13. See, e.g., Langston v. Personal Service Insurance Co., Fla.App.1977, 377 So.2d 993; Slitkin v. Avis Rent A Car System, Inc., Fla.App.1980, 382 So. 883 (plaintiff has burden of proof to show owner's knowledge and consent); Fort Myers Airways, Inc. v. American States Insurance Co., Fla.Dist.App.1982, 411 So.2d 883 (airplane is dangerous instrumentality); Atlantic Coast Development Corp. v. Napoleon Steel Contractors, Inc., Fla.Dist.App.1980, 385 So.2d 676 (crane).

14. See, e.g., Hunter v. First State Bank of Morrilton, 1930, 181 Ark. 907, 28 S.W.2d 712; Leonard v. North Dakota Co-op Wool Marketing Association, 1942, 72 N.D. 310, 6 N.W.2d 576; Elliott v. Harding, 1923, 107 Ohio St. 501, 140 N.E. 338. Cf. Boyd v. White, 1954, 128 Cal.App.2d 641, 276 P.2d 92 (airplane).

15. The doctrine prevails in about a dozen states, including Ariz., Colo., Conn., Ga., Neb., N.M., N.C., N.D., Or., S.C., Wash., and W.Va.

16. The doctrine is at least as old as Lashbrook v. Patten, 1864, 62 Ky. (1 Duv.) 316, where "the son must be regarded as in the father's employment, discharging a duty usually performed by a slave."

See generally Kidd, Vicarious Liability and the "Family Car," 1971, 121 New L.J. 529; Fridman, The Doctrine of the "Family Car:" A Study in Contrasts, 1976, 8 Tex.Tech.L.Rev. 323; Lattin, Vicarious Liability and the Family Automobile, 1928, 26 Mich.L.Rev. 846; Notes, 1950, 38 Ky.L.J. 156; 1952, 22 Tenn.L.Rev. 535; 1966, 18 S.C.L.Rev. 638; 1967, 55 Ky.L.J. 502; 1978, 14 Wake For.L.Rev. 699 (motorcycles on private property); Annot., 1966, 8 A.L.R.3d 1191.

17. See State Farm Mutual Automobile Insurance Co. v. Duran, App.1979, 93 N.M. 489, 601 P.2d 722; Williams v. Wachovia Bank & Trust Co., 1977, 292 N.C. 416, 233 S.E.2d 589.

18. Davis v. Littlefield, 1914, 97 S.C. 171, 81 S.E. 487; Griffin v. Russell, 1915, 144 Ga. 275, 87 S.E. 10.

19. "The Family Purpose Doctrine is a humanitarian one designed for the protection of the public generally, and resulted from recognition of the fact that in the vast majority of instances an infant has not sufficient property in his own right to indemnify one who may suffer from his negligent act." Turner v. Hall's Administratrix, Ky.1952, 252 S.W.2d 30, 32. See also Heenan v. Perkins, 1977, 278 Or. 583, 564 P.2d 1354; Bartz v. Wheat, 1982, ___ W.Va. ___, 285 S.E.2d 894.

20. South v. Martin, 1978, 147 Ga.App. 198, 248 S.E.2d 230; McNamara v. Prather, 1939, 277 Ky. 754, 127 S.W.2d 160; Stevens v. Van Deusen, 1952, 56 N.M. 128, 241 P.2d 331. See Fisher v. Pippin, 1979, 40 Or. App. 421, 595 P.2d 513.

21. See Durso v. A.D. Cozzolino, Inc., 1941, 128 Conn. 24, 20 A.2d 392; Gray v. Golden, 1946, 301 Ky. 477, 192 S.W.2d 371; cf. Herman v. Magnuson, N.D. 1979, 277 N.W.2d 445.

have some recognized property interest in it [22] or supply it,[23] and he must have made it available for family use, rather than for use in his business.[24] It has been held that the car must be made available for general use, and not merely to take out on a particular occasion,[25] although whatever policy may underlie this odd business would appear to apply no less to the special permission. The owner need not, however, be the head of the family.[26] The driver must be a member of the defendant's immediate household,[27] as distinguished from a more distant or collateral relative such as a brother-in-law.[28] The fact that the driver is an adult son or daughter usually is held not to prevent the agency relation where he or she is still a member of the household.[29]

The car must be found to have been driven at the time with the permission or acquiescence of the defendant,[30] although his consent may be inferred from a failure to protest at frequent violations of his orders not to use the car.[31] His liability does not

22. In Emanuelson v. Johnson, 1921, 148 Minn. 417, 182 N.W. 521, the doctrine was applied to a bailee of an automobile who permitted his daughter to use it. Cf. Mann v. Cook, Tex.Civ.App.1929, 23 S.W.2d 860 (servant-bailee). In Smith v. Doyle, 1938, 68 App.D.C. 60, 98 F.2d 341, nominal ownership of a car bought by members of the family for their own use was held not to be enough.

23. See Herman v. Magnuson, N.D.1979, 277 N.W. 2d 445; cf. Dillard v. Clements, 1978, 144 Ga.App. 512, 241 S.E.2d 838.

In Gray v. Golden, 1945, 301 Ky. 477, 192 S.W.2d 371, a defendant who bought a car for family use and put legal title in another member of the family was held to fall within the rule.

24. Hanford v. Goehry, 1946, 24 Wn.2d 859, 167 P.2d 678; Lambert v. Polen, 1943, 346 Pa. 352, 30 A.2d 115; Cook v. Hall, 1948, 308 Ky. 500, 214 S.W.2d 1017; Hawes v. Haynes, 1941, 219 N.C. 535, 14 S.E.2d 503. See also Jones v. Adamson's, Inc., 1978, 147 Ga.App. 282, 248 S.E.2d 514. But see Heenan v. Perkins, 1977, 278 Or. 583, 564 P.2d 1354 (truck used in family farming business).

25. See, e.g., Costanzo v. Sturgill, 1958, 145 Conn. 92, 139 A.2d 51; Studdard v. Turner, 1954, 91 Ga.App. 318, 85 S.E.2d 537; Greenwood v. Kier, 1952, 125 Colo. 333, 243 P.2d 417.

26. Hill v. Smith, 1949, 32 Tenn.App. 172, 222 S.W.2d 207 (mother); Perfetto v. Wesson, 1952, 138 Conn. 506, 86 A.2d 565 (same); Turner v. Gackle, 1926, 168 Minn. 514, 209 N.W. 626 (child). See Note, 1950, 3 Vand.L.Rev. 644. Contra, Ramsay v. Rimpley, 1976, 196 Neb. 516, 244 N.W.2d 78.

It has been held that a corporation cannot have a "family" or "household" within the doctrine. Keller v. Federal Bob Brannon Truck Co., 1924, 151 Tenn. 427, 269 S.W. 914. But in Durso v. A.D. Cozzolino, Inc., 1941, 128 Conn. 24, 20 A.2d 392, it was applied to a family corporation where the car was used for family purposes.

27. Heenan v. Perkins, 1977, 278 Or. 583, 564 P.2d 1354 (step-son); Rutherford v. Smith, 1940, 284 Ky. 592, 145 S.W.2d 533 (grandson). In Smart v. Bissonette, 1927, 106 Conn. 447, 138 A. 365, the doctrine was applied to the use of a car by the housekeeper of a Catholic priest. But cf. Scott v. Greene, 1926, 242 Ill. App. 405, 413. In Rutherford v. Smith, 1940, 284 Ky. 592, 145 S.W.2d 533, a grandson was held to be included.

28. Bryant v. Keen, 1931, 43 Ga.App. 251, 158 S.E. 445; Scott v. Greene, 1926, 242 Ill.App. 405; McBroom v. Wolsleger, 1966, 180 Neb. 622, 144 N.W.2d 199 (brother); Johnston v. Hare, 1926, 30 Ariz. 253, 246 P. 546 (second cousin); Chambers v. Scarboro, 1979, 49 Ga.App. 172, 253 S.E.2d 798 (divorced spouse); cf. State Farm Mutual Automobile Insurance Co. v. Duran, App.1979, 93 N.M. 489, 601 P.2d 722 (brother, who lived off and on with owner).

29. Burkhart v. Corn, 1955, 59 N.M. 343, 284 P.2d 226; Garska v. Harris, 1961, 172 Neb. 339, 109 N.W.2d 529 (need not be permanent member of household). Cf. Robinson v. Hartley, 1958, 98 Ga.App. 765, 106 S.E.2d 861 (nephew); LeDoux v. Southern Farm Bureau Casualty Insurance Co., La.App.1976, 339 So.2d 966, application denied 341 So.2d 1130 (17-year-old son who had moved out a few months earlier but still used mother's car to get to work). Contra: Adkins v. Nanney, 1935, 169 Tenn. 67, 82 S.W.2d 867; Bradley v. Schmidt, 1928, 223 Ky. 784, 4 S.W.2d 703.

An adult child living apart is not included. Bell v. West, 1981, ___ W.Va. ___, 284 S.E.2d 885; Clemons v. Busby, 1977, 144 Ga.App. 207, 240 S.E.2d 764; Herman v. Magnuson, N.D.1979, 277 N.W.2d 445 (son rented trailer owned by father); cf. Farmer v. Stidham, Ky. 1969, 439 S.W.2d 71 (military service; doctrine does not normally apply to adult children, even if they are living at home). But see Dunn v. Caylor, 1962, 218 Ga. 256, 127 S.E.2d 367 (military service).

30. See Todd v. Hargis, 1945, 299 Ky. 841, 187 S.W.2d 739 (negligently leaving car unlocked not enough).

It is not required, however, that the car actually be driven by the person to whom the permission was given, if that person is present in the car. Dibble v. Wolff, 1949, 135 Conn. 428, 65 A.2d 479; Turner v. Hall's Administratrix, Ky.1952, 252 S.W.2d 30; Dixon v. Phillips, 1976, 236 Ga. 271, 223 S.E.2d 678; cf. Rucker v. Frye, 1979, 151 Ga.App. 415, 260 S.E.2d 373 (child not in car, doctrine inapplicable).

31. Watson v. Burley, 1928, 105 W.Va. 416, 143 S.E. 95. Cf. Grier v. Woodside, 1931, 200 N.C. 759, 158 S.E. 491 (habitual use).

extend to any use beyond the "family purpose," [32] which, however, will include all normal family activities, including mere driving for the pleasure of an individual.[33] Questions of deviation from the precise scope of the consent given often have been dealt with much as in the case of a servant's deviation from the scope of his employment.[34] A few older cases held that there could be a family purpose only when two or more members of the family are in the car; [35] but other courts have rejected this requirement [36] which appears to have generally withered away.

The courts have split on whether to apply the family car doctrine to impute the contributory negligence of the driver to the owner suing for damage to the car or to his own person. Logically, if there is an agency, it should apply both ways; and it has been so held.[37] But since the whole purpose of the device has been to protect plaintiffs against financial irresponsibility, rather than to cut down their recoveries, there are a few courts which of late have declared that the policy involved does not require the imputation of the contributory negligence.[38]

The family car doctrine has been rejected entirely in most jurisdictions [39] as a fictitious agency without any basis in fact.[40] It is of course entirely contrary to the accepted rule that the head of a household is not liable when, without negligence, he entrusts other chattels, such as shotguns or golf clubs, to members of his family for similar purposes.[41] It fails to distinguish between mere permissive use for the driver's own ends and a use subject to the control of the owner as master and connected with his affairs.[42] Its connection with the peculiar dangers and financial responsibilities of the automobile is indicated by decisions in some jurisdictions holding that it has no application to motor-

32. Johnson v. Brant, 1955, 93 Ga.App. 44, 90 S.E.2d 587 (lending car to a friend); McCray v. Hunter, 1981, 157 Ga.App. 509, 277 S.E.2d 795 (mother loaned car to son while his was being repaired). But the purpose for which the car is used by the child may not have to be the same as intended by the parent. See Granley v. Crandall, 1970, 288 Minn. 310, 180 N.W.2d 190.

33. Harmon v. Haas, 1932, 61 N.D. 772, 241 N.W. 70; Hanson v. Eilers, 1931, 164 Wash. 185, 2 P.2d 719.

34. See for example McDowell v. Hurner, 1933, 142 Or. 611, 20 P.2d 395; Vaughn v. Booker, 1940, 217 N.C. 479, 8 S.E.2d 603. See supra, § 70.

If the use is within the general scope of the consent given, liability is not defeated by the fact that the car is being used at a place or in a manner which the owner has forbidden. Richardson v. True, Ky.1953, 259 S.W.2d 70; Turner v. Hall's Administratrix, Ky.1952, 252 S.W.2d 30; Jones v. Cook, 1924, 96 W.Va. 60, 123 S.E. 407.

In Driver v. Smith, 1959, 47 Tenn.App. 505, 339 S.W. 2d 135, a daughter turned the car over to her boyfriend to drive, and was injured, while enthusiastically kissing him, when he lost control of the car. The father was held liable for her negligent failure to supervise the driver.

35. See Doran v. Thomsen, 1908, 76 N.J.L. 754, 71 A. 296; Stumpf v. Montgomery, 1924, 101 Okl. 257, 226 P. 65.

36. Crittenden v. Murphy, 1918, 36 Cal.App. 803, 173 P. 595; Davis v. Littlefield, 1913, 97 S.C. 171, 81 S.E. 487.

An automobile guest act does not protect the owner of the car liable under the family car doctrine. Lopez v. Barreras, 1966, 77 N.M. 52, 419 P.2d 251.

37. Prendergast v. Allen, 1922, 44 R.I. 379, 117 A. 539; Pearson v. Northland Transportation Co., 1931, 184 Minn. 560, 239 N.W. 602; Russell v. Hamlett, 1964, 261 N.C. 603, 135 S.E.2d 547.

38. Michaelsohn v. Smith, N.D.1962, 113 N.W.2d 571; White v. Yup, 1969, 85 Nev. 527, 458 P.2d 617; Bartz v. Wheat, 1982, ___ W.Va. ___, 285 S.E.2d 894; Mertz v. Weibe, N.D.1970, 180 N.W.2d 664. By statute in Connecticut. Conn.Gen.Stat. § 52–572i.

39. The doctrine does not apply in roughly three-quarters of the states. See supra, note 15.

40. See Grimes v. Labreck, 1967, 108 N.H. 26, 226 A.2d 787; Hackley v. Robey, 1938, 170 Va. 55, 195 S.E. 689 (overruling prior cases); Johnson v. Peterson, 1974, 38 Cal.App.3d 619, 113 Cal.Rptr. 445; Grinter v. Haag, 1976, 168 Ind.App. 595, 344 N.E.2d 320.

A finding of actual agency will still render the parent liable. Smith v. Jordan, 1912, 211 Mass. 269, 97 N.E. 761 (father instructed son to drive mother); Zeidler v. Goelzer, 1926, 191 Wis. 378, 211 N.W. 140 (implied request to operate car for father's benefit).

41. Fleming v. Kravitz, 1918, 260 Pa. 428, 103 A. 831. See Van Blaricom v. Dodgson, 1917, 220 N.Y. 111, 115 N.E. 443; Piquet v. Wazelle, 1927, 288 Pa. 463, 136 A. 787; Wilbanks v. Brazil, Ala.1983, 425 So. 2d 1123 (golf clubs).

42. See Doran v. Thomsen, 1908, 76 N.J.L. 754, 71 A. 296; Lattin, Vicarious Liability and the Family Automobile, 1928, 26 Mich.L.Rev. 846, 860.

boats or motorcycles.[43] It clearly is to be regarded as a fictitious device, resorted to as a partial step in the direction of an ultimate rule which would hold the owner of the car liable in all cases for the negligence of the driver to whom he entrusts it. When such a rule is adopted by statute, the doctrine will have served its purpose, and might reasonably be discarded.[44]

Automobile Consent Statutes

About a dozen states have accomplished this result outright by legislation.[45] The first such "automobile consent" statute was adopted in Michigan in 1909, and four years later was held constitutional.[46] Such statutes make the owner of the automobile liable for injuries to third persons caused by the negligence of any person, whether a member of the family or not,[47] who is operating the car on the public highway with the owner's consent.[48] In effect, an arbitrary statutory agency is created, which results in vicarious liability.[49]

The term "owner" has been construed to exclude persons, such as conditional sellers, who have legal title without power to control the use of the vehicle.[50] The liability is limit-

---

43. Felcyn v. Gamble, 1932, 185 Minn. 357, 241 N.W. 37; Meinhardt v. Vaughn, 1929, 159 Tenn. 272, 17 S.W.2d 5. Cf. Pflugmacher v. Thomas, 1949, 34 Wn.2d 687, 209 P.2d 443 (bicycle); Maddox v. Queen, 1979, 150 Ga.App. 408, 257 S.E.2d 918 (riding lawnmower). See Note, 1932, 16 Minn.L.Rev. 970.

Contra, Stewart v. Stephens, 1969, 225 Ga. 185, 166 S.E.2d 890, conformed to 119 Ga.App. 629, 168 S.E.2d 325; Williams v. Wachovia Bank & Trust Co., 1977, 292 N.C. 416, 233 S.E.2d 589 (motorcycle); Quattlebaum v. Wallace, 1980, 156 Ga.App. 518, 275 S.E.2d 104 (motorboat); Kimbell v. DuBose, 1976, 139 Ga.App. 224, 228 S.E.2d 205 (aircraft).

44. McMartin v. Saemisch, 1962, 254 Iowa 45, 116 N.W.2d 491. But cf. Quattlebaum v. Wallace, 1980, 156 Ga.App. 518, 275 S.E.2d 104.

45. See Conn.Gen.Stat.Ann. § 52–182 (family members); Mich.C.L.A. § 257.401; R.I.G.L. § 31–33–6; Minn.Stat.Ann. § 65B.41–.71; N.Y.Veh. & Traf.L., Art. 11, § 388; West's Ann.Cal.Veh.Code § 388; Iowa Code Ann. § 321.493; Idaho Code § 49–1404; Nev.Rev.Stat. § 41.440 (family members).

At least Georgia has a special motorboat owner consent statute. See Wallace v. Lessard, 1981, 158 Ga.App. 772, 282 S.E.2d 153, affirmed 248 Ga. 575, 285 S.E.2d 14. At least Nebraska has a leased truck owner consent statute. Neb.Rev.Stat. § 39–6,193. At least Minnesota has an aircraft owner consent statute. See Ewers v. Thunderbird Aviation, Inc., Minn.1979, 289 N.W.2d 94. At least North Carolina has codified its family purpose doctrine. N.C.Gen.Stat. § 75A–10.1.

Some states have statutes imputing the negligence of minor drivers to the parent or other person who signed the minor's permit or license application. See Otto v. Leany, Utah 1981, 635 P.2d 410; Annot., 1952 26 A.L.R.2d 1320.

See generally Brodsky, Motor Vehicle Owners' Statutory Vicarious Liability in Rhode Island, 1939, 19 Boston U.L.Rev. 448; Hilliker, Vicarious Liability for Aircraft Owners Under State Laws, 1977, 60 Marq.L.Rev. 1031.

46. In Daugherty v. Thomas, 1913, 174 Mich. 371, 140 N.W. 615. Accord: Young v. Masci, 1933, 289 U.S. 253, 53 S.Ct. 599, 77 L.Ed. 1158; Holmes v. Lilygren Motor Co., 1937, 201 Minn. 44, 275 N.W. 416; Robinson v. Bruce Rent-A-Ford Co., 1927, 205 Iowa 261, 215 N.W. 724; Stapleton v. Independent Brewing Co., 1917, 198 Mich. 170, 164 N.W. 520.

47. The statutes in Nevada and Florida are limited to the family. See Molino v. Asher, 1980, 96 Nev. 814, 618 P.2d 878, 880 n. 3; Conn.Gen.Stat.Ann. § 52–182.

48. Consent may be presumed. Aetna Casualty & Surety Co. v. Brice, 1979, 72 A.D.2d 927, 422 N.Y.S.2d 203, affirmed mem., 1980, 50 N.Y.2d 958, 431 N.Y.S.2d 528, 409 N.E.2d 1000.

Without consent, express or implied, there is no liability. See Hosking v. Robles, 1979, 98 Cal.App.3d 98, 159 Cal.Rptr. 369 (theft); Colborn v. Freeman, 1977, 98 Idaho 427, 566 P.2d 376 ("purchase" of car from dealer with bad checks; permission vitiated by fraud); Fout v. Dietz, 1977, 75 Mich.App. 128, 254 N.W.2d 813, affirmed 401 Mich. 403, 258 N.W.2d 53 (house guest sneaked into owner's room and removed keys from dresser); Shelby Mutual Insurance Co. v. Kleman, Minn.1977, 255 N.W.2d 231 (son sneaked out with car).

49. The statutes are liberally construed to effect their objectives. See Shelby Mutual Insurance Co. v. Kleman, Minn.1977, 255 N.W.2d 231, 233 ("We have consistently expanded liability in the past."); cf. Sexton v. Ryder Truck Rental, Inc., 1982, 413 Mich. 406, 320 N.W.2d 843; Kelso v. State, Nev.1979, 95 Nev. 37, 588 P.2d 1035, certiorari denied 442 U.S. 921, 99 S.Ct. 2846, 61 L.Ed.2d 289.

The owner and operator may be considered joint tortfeasors who are jointly and severally liable for the judgment. Burton v. Gardner Motors, Inc., 1981, 117 Cal.App.3d 426, 172 Cal.Rptr. 647.

An owner consent statute is overriden by a specific statute exempting car dealers from liability for accidents involving "loaner" vehicles. Flanagan v. Pierce Chevrolet, Inc., 1980, ___ R.I. ___, 410 A.2d 428.

50. See Campbell v. Security Pacific National Bank, 1976, 62 Cal.App.3d 379, 133 Cal.Rptr. 77 (bank with security interest; statute applicable only to registered owner); Smith v. Simpson, 1963, 260 N.C. 601, 133 S.E.2d 474 (father nominal owner of son's car). But cf. Rutherford v. Gray Line, Inc., 2d Cir. 1980, 615 F.2d 944 (parties with ownership interests in leased tractor

ed to the scope of the consent given, and the owner is not liable where the car is being used at a time [51] or a place [52] or for a purpose [53] which is clearly beyond the scope of the permission. This limitation is, however, very similar to, although of course not identical with, the "scope of employment" where the driver is a servant; [54] and a minor deviation from the permitted use, [55] or a violation of specific instructions as to the manner in which the car is to be operated, [56] will not absolve the owner. If the person to whom the consent is given turns the car over to another without permission to do so, the owner's liability may terminate.[57]

As to the effect of the automobile consent statutes in imputing the contributory negligence of the driver to the owner who sues for damage to the car or to his own person, agreement has not been reached. Decisions have been affected to some extent by the language of the particular act. A few courts have interpreted the statute to impute the driver's negligence both ways, so that the owner's action is barred.[58] The courts in recent years have looked increasingly to the purpose of the statute—which clearly is to protect injured plaintiffs against the financial irresponsibility of drivers, not to diminish any recovery which would otherwise be allowed—and have held that the driver's negligence is not to be imputed to the owner.[59]

Other Imputed Fault Statutes

Apart from the law of automobiles, there are occasional instances of other statutes creating vicarious liability.[60] One quite interesting group of statutes are the "lynching" acts, making municipalities liable for

---

trailer could be held as owners). See generally Annot., 1976, 74 A.L.R.3d 739.

51. Union Trust Co. v. American Commercial Car Co., 1922, 219 Mich. 557, 189 N.W. 23; Truman v. United Products Corp., 1944, 217 Minn. 155, 14 N.W.2d 120; di Rebaylio v. Herndon, 1935, 6 Cal.App.2d 567, 44 P.2d 581.

52. Henrietta v. Evans, 1938, 10 Cal.2d 526, 75 P.2d 1051; Chaika v. Vandenberg, 1929, 252 N.Y. 101, 169 N.E. 103; Robinson v. Shell Petroleum Corp., 1933, 217 Iowa 1252, 251 N.W. 613 (time and place).

53. Heavilin v. Wendell, 1932, 214 Iowa 844, 241 N.W. 654; Krausnick v. Haegg Roofing Co., 1945, 236 Iowa 985, 20 N.W.2d 432; Muma v. Brown, 1967, 378 Mich. 637, 148 N.W.2d 760.

54. See Flaugh v. Egan Chevrolet, Inc., 1938, 202 Minn. 615, 279 N.W. 582; Chaika v. Vandenberg, 1929, 252 N.Y. 101, 106, 169 N.E. 103, 104; Notes, 1929, 24 Minn.L.Rev. 271; 1964, 31 U.Chi.L.Rev. 355. The differences are made clear in Moore v. Palmer, 1957, 350 Mich. 363, 86 N.W.2d 585, where the owner consented to an employee driving the car.

Proof that defendant owned a car which was operated on the highway by another in lawful possession of it makes out a prima facie case of consent. Schultz v. Swift & Co., 1941, 210 Minn. 533, 299 N.W. 7; Houseman v. Walt Neal, Inc., 1962, 368 Mich. 631, 118 N.W.2d 964.

55. Kieszkowski v. Odlewany, 1937, 280 Mich. 388, 273 N.W. 741; Senator Cab Co. v. Rothberg, Mun.App. D.C.1945, 42 A.2d 245; cf. Hardeman v. Mendon Leasing Corp., 1982, 87 A.D.2d 232, 450 N.Y.S.2d 808.

56. Sweeney v. Hartman, 1941, 296 Mich. 343, 296 N.W. 282; Herbert v. Cassinelli, 1943, 61 Cal.App.2d 661, 143 P.2d 752; Grant v. Knepper, 1927, 245 N.Y. 158, 156 N.E. 650; cf. Arcara v. Moresse, 1932, 258 N.Y. 211, 179 N.E. 389, affirmed 233 App.Div. 799, 250 N.Y.S. 946.

57. Fischer v. McBride, 1941, 296 Mich. 671, 296 N.W. 834; Wallace v. Lessard, 1981, 158 Ga.App. 772, 282 S.E.2d 153, affirmed 248 Ga. 575, 285 S.E.2d 14 (motorboat); cf. Guercio v. Hertz Corp., 1976, 40 N.Y.2d 680, 389 N.Y.S.2d 568, 358 N.E.2d 261.

Contra, Shuck v. Means, Minn.1974, 302 Minn. 93, 226 N.W.2d 285; Lange v. Potter, 1965, 270 Minn. 173, 132 N.W.2d 734; Delaney v. Burnett, 1975, 63 Mich. App. 639, 234 N.W.2d 741 (contrary to rental contract provision); Souza v. Corti, 1937, 22 Cal.2d 454, 139 P.2d 645; Arcara v. Moresse, 1932, 258 N.Y. 211, 179 N.E. 389, affirmed 233 App.Div. 799, 250 N.Y.S. 946; Webb v. Moreno, 8th Cir. 1966, 363 F.2d 97.

58. McCants v. Chenault, 1954, 98 Ohio App. 529, 130 N.E.2d 382; National Trucking & Storage Co. v. Driscoll, Mun.App.D.C.1949, 64 A.2d 304; Birnbaum v. Blunt, 1957, 152 Cal.App.2d 371, 313 P.2d 86; Davis Pontiac Co. v. Sirois, 1954, 82 R.I. 32, 105 A.2d 792; cf. Di Leo v. Du Montier, La.App.1940, 195 So. 74.

59. Wick v. Widdell, 1967, 276 Minn. 51, 149 N.W.2d 20; Houlahan v. Brockmeier, 1966, 258 Iowa 1197, 141 N.W.2d 545 supplemented 258 Iowa 1197, 141 N.W.2d 924; Bush v. Oliver, 1963, 86 Idaho 380, 386 P.2d 967; York v. Day's, Inc., 1958, 153 Me. 441, 140 A.2d 730; DeGrove v. Sanborn, 1976, 70 Mich.App. 568, 246 N.W.2d 157; Kalechman v. Drew Auto Rental, Inc., 1973, 33 N.Y.2d 397, 353 N.Y.S.2d 414, 308 N.E.2d 886. See Note, 1956, 31 Notre Dame L. 724. In Mason v. Russell, 1958, 158 Cal.App.2d 391, 322 P.2d 486, it was held that the statute was inapplicable to an action by the owner against the negligent driver. See generally Annot., 1983, 21 A.L.R. 4th 459.

60. See Note, 1931, 45 Harv.L.Rev. 171.

damages within their corporate limits which result from mob violence.⁶¹ Another group of statutes are the parental liability acts, which typically hold the parent liable for the child's malicious damage, usually up to a modest maximum amount.⁶²

WESTLAW REFERENCES

automobile* car cars vehicle* /p vicarious** /s liability

Family Purpose Doctrine

"family car" "family purpose" /p owner /p negligen** liab!

Automobile Consent Statutes

court(mi) & 257.401

§ 74. Imputed Contributory Negligence

Ordinarily the plaintiff's action for his damages will not be barred by the negligence of any third person who may have contributed to them. He may treat the defendant and the stranger as joint tort feasors, so far as each is a legal cause of the harm, and recover from either.¹ But if the plaintiff and the third person stand in such a relation to one another—as for example that of master and servant ²—that the plaintiff will be charged with that person's negligence as a defendant, it will ordinarily follow that he will likewise be charged with it as a plaintiff.³ Normally the responsibility is applied "both ways." As we have seen in the car owner context, however,⁴ there may be special reasons of policy in particular cases which will lead to the imputation of the negligence to a defendant, but not to a plaintiff.⁵

There are additional complications, which are now largely a matter of purely historical interest. "Imputed contributory negligence" has had a very bad name of its own, because of a group of quite unreasonable and rather senseless rules which were at one time applied to defeat the recovery of the injured plaintiff by imputing to him the negligence of another, even though he would not have been at all liable for that negligence as a defendant. This was done where the plaintiff and the third person stood within a

---

61. One of the early ones was in Clark v. Inhabitants of the Hundred of Blything, 1823, 2 B. & C. 254, 107 Eng.Rep. 378, which involved a Riot Act making the hundred liable. See generally Annot., 1969, 26 A.L.R.3d 1142.

62. See, e.g., Bryan v. Kitamura, D.Hawaii 1982, 529 F.Supp. 394 (liable for any tortious act of child; no limit to liability; constitutional); Turner v. Bucher, La. 1975, 308 So.2d 270; Motorists Mutual Insurance Co. v. Bill, 1978, 56 Ohio St.2d 258, 383 N.E.2d 880; Board of Education of Piscataway Township v. Caffiero, 1981, 86 N.J. 308, 431 A.2d 799, dismissed 454 U.S. 1025, 102 S.Ct. 560, 70 L.Ed.2d 470 (damage to school property; statute construed to cover only "willful or malicious acts"; no limit to liability; constitutional); Vanthournout v. Burge, 1979, 69 Ill.App.3d 193, 25 Ill.Dec. 685, 387 N.E.2d 341 (constitutional). Georgia's statute is the only one to have been held unconstitutional. Corley v. Lewless, 1971, 277 Ga. 745, 182 S.E.2d 766. See generally infra, § 123; Freer, Parental Liability for Torts of Children, 1965, 53 Ky.L.J. 254; Frankel, Parental Liability for a Child's Tortious Acts, 1977, 81 Dick.L.Rev. 755; Annots., 1973, 54 A.L.R.3d 974 (intentional acts); 1966, 8 A.L.R.3d 612 (torts generally). For the parent's criminal responsibility for acts of a child, see Annot., 1982, 12 A.L.R.4th 673.

§ 74

1. See supra, § 47. Although joint liability has been abolished in several comparative negligence states. See supra, § 67.

2. See Notes, 1967, 51 Minn.L.Rev. 377; 1966, 45 Tex.L.Rev. 364; Annot., 1973, 53 A.L.R.3d 664.

3. As to master and servant, see for example Louisville & Nashville Railroad Co. v. Tomlinson, Ky.1963, 373 S.W.2d 601; Weckerly v. Abear, Minn.1977, 256 N.W.2d 79.

4. See, e.g., Kalechman v. Drew Auto Rental, Inc., 1973, 33 N.Y.2d 397, 353 N.Y.S.2d 414, 308 N.E.2d 886 (driver's contributory negligence would not be imputed to owner-passenger); Cole v. Woods, Tenn.1977, 548 S.W.2d 640 (same); Note, 1974, 6 St. Mary's L.Rev. 526; supra, § 73.

5. In Weber v. Stokely-Van Camp, Inc., 1966, 274 Minn. 482, 144 N.W.2d 540, the court overthrew the "both ways" rule in the master-servant automobile context and held that the contributory negligence of the servant would not be imputed. The case was rejected in Wilson v. Great Northern Railway Co., 1968, 83 S.D. 207, 157 N.W.2d 19. Compare Cole v. Woods, Tenn. 1977, 548 S.W.2d 640, 650 ("henceforth, in automobile cases, only a master-servant relationship or a finding of joint enterprise will justify an imputation of contributory negligence"); Smalich v. Westfall, 1970, 440 Pa. 409, 269 A.2d 476 (same; Roberts, J., dissenting, approving of *Weber*).

limited group of special relations to one another, on the basis of which fictitious agencies were created to accomplish the result. There was much denunciation of these fictions and their consequences,[6] as a result of which they steadily lost ground. Except for vestigial remnants which are at most moribund historical survivals, "imputed contributory negligence" in its own right has now disappeared. The result at which the courts have arrived is that the plaintiff will never be barred from recovery by the negligence of a third person unless the relation between them is such that the plaintiff would be vicariously liable as a defendant to another who might be injured.[7]

The various relations [8] in which contributory negligence was formerly imputed may be considered briefly, as follows:

Driver and Passenger

In 1849 an unfortunate English decision imputed the negligence of the driver of an omnibus to his passenger, who was injured through the negligent operation of another vehicle.[9] The reason given was that there was an agency relation, since the plaintiff must be taken to be in "control" of the driver, for the reason that he had selected the means of conveyance. This resulted in imputing the contributory negligence of every driver to his passenger. This nonsensical fiction was overruled in England some forty years later,[10] but in the meantime it had been taken up in the United States. The American cases which accepted it now have been overruled everywhere.[11] The last state to abandon the idea was Michigan,[12] in 1946. It is now held that the driver's negligence will not be imputed to the passenger, whether the transportation be in a common carrier,[13] a hired vehicle,[14] or a gratuitous conveyance,[15] unless the relation between them is such that the passenger would be vicariously liable as a defendant.[16]

Such vicariously imputed negligence must be distinguished from the contributory negligence of the passenger himself. He is required to exercise reasonable care for his own safety, and will be barred from recovery, or have his damages reduced, if he voluntarily rides with a driver whom he knows to be intoxicated, reckless or incompetent, or unreasonably fails to warn the driver of a danger which he discovers, or to make use

---

6. See Gilmore, Imputed Negligence, 1921, 1 Wis.L. Rev. 193, 237; Keeton, Imputed Contributory Negligence, 1936, 13 Tex.L.Rev. 161; Gregory, Vicarious Responsibility and Contributory Negligence, 1932, 41 Yale L.J. 831; Lessler, The Proposed Discard of the Doctrine of Imputed Contributory Negligence, 1951, 20 Ford L.Rev. 156; James, Imputed Contributory Negligence, 1954, 14 La.L.Rev. 340; Notes, 19 Bos.U.L.Rev. 90; 1959, 26 Tenn.L.Rev. 531; 1975, 28 Okla.L.Rev. 941 (imputed comparative negligence); 1974, 34 Md.L.Rev. 155 (landlord liability for lead poisoning); 1982, 5 U.Ark.L.R.L.Rev. 289; Annot., 1968, 21 A.L.R.3d 469 (spouse or child).

7. Second Restatement of Torts, § 485.

8. For developments in the car owner-passenger context, see supra, § 73.

9. Thorogood v. Bryan, 1849, 8 C.B. 115, 137 Eng. Rep. 452.

10. Mills v. Armstrong (The Bernina), 1888, L.R. 13 A.C. 1.

11. Ashworth v. Baker, 1956, 197 Va. 582, 90 S.E.2d 860; Reiter v. Grober, 1921, 173 Wis. 493, 181 N.W. 739; Bessey v. Salemme, 1939, 302 Mass. 188, 19 N.E.2d 75; Koplitz v. City of St. Paul, 1902, 86 Minn. 373, 90 N.W. 794; Fechley v. Springfield Traction Co., 1906, 119 Mo.App. 358, 96 S.W. 421.

12. Bricker v. Green, 1946, 313 Mich. 218, 21 N.W.2d 105.

13. Bennett v. New Jersey Railroad & Transportation Co., 1873, 36 N.J.L. 225; Sullivan v. United States, N.D.Ala.1968, 299 F.Supp. 621, affirmed 5th Cir. 1969, 411 F.2d 794.

14. Little v. Hackett, 1886, 116 U.S. 366, 6 S.Ct. 391, 29 L.Ed. 652; Isom v. Schettino, 1973, 129 Ga.App. 73, 199 S.E.2d 89 (taxi); Kleinman v. Frank, 1970, 34 A.D.2d 121, 309 N.Y.S.2d 651, affirmed 1971, 28 N.Y.2d 603, 319 N.Y.S.2d 852, 268 N.E.2d 648 (subleased vehicle).

15. See, e.g., Dinda v. Sirois, 1974, 166 Conn. 68, 347 A.2d 75; Ruiz v. Cold Storage & Insulation Contractors, Inc., Fla.App.1975, 306 So.2d 153; Wilson v. Don LaCost, Inc., 1974, 20 Ill.App.3d 624, 314 N.E.2d 27; Smalich v. Westfall, 1970, 440 Pa. 409, 269 A.2d 476.

16. As where the passenger is the master of the driver or the owner of the vehicle. See supra, §§ 70–73.

of any ability to control the negligence which he may possess.[17]

Domestic Relations

Another old rule imputed the contributory negligence of one spouse to another, by reason of the marital relation alone. The origin of this lay in the legal identity of the wife with her husband at common law,[18] which meant that each was to be charged with the negligence of the other, and any recovery by one inured to the benefit of the other. The Married Women's Acts have long since terminated this legal identity in all states, for better or worse, and permit the wife to maintain an action for a personal tort in her own name, without joining her husband.[19] As a result, the wife is now regarded, in the eyes of the law, as a separate individual, whose negligence is no more to be attributed to the husband, or his to her, than in the case of any other person; and imputed contributory negligence on the basis of the marriage alone has vanished from the law of most jurisdictions.[20] One exception is found in the case of several jurisdictions which, under the influence of the civil law, treat the damages recoverable by either spouse as community property, and therefore continue to impute the negligence of one to the other in order to prevent the negligent party from profiting as community owner by his own wrong.[21]

Another old rule, of a particularly hideous character, imputed the contributory negligence of a parent to his child. Here there was never any legal identity; but in 1829, in one of those bleak decisions which have here and there marred the face of our law, it was held in New York that a child two years old who was injured by the negligence of the defendant in running him down with a sleigh was barred from recovery by the negligence of his father, who was supposed to be looking after him at the time.[22] The mistake was repeated, but subsequently overruled, in England.[23] This barbarous rule, which denied to the innocent victim of the negligence of two parties any recovery against either, and visited the sins of the fathers upon the children,[24] was accepted in several American States until it was at one time very nearly the prevailing rule; but it now is abrogated,

17. See, e.g., Bauer v. Johnson, 1980, 79 Ill.2d 324, 38 Ill.Dec. 149, 403 N.E.2d 237 (no imputed negligence; owner-passenger not personally negligent on the facts); Nowak v. Nowak, 1978, 175 Conn. 112, 394 A.2d 716, 723 (same; driving instructor: "general trend is away from imputing contributory negligence"); Cole v. Woods, Tenn.1977, 548 S.W.2d 640 (no imputed negligence; possible contributory negligence of passenger personally on facts); Kirby v. Larson, 1977, 400 Mich. 585, 256 N.W.2d 400. See generally supra, ch. 11.

18. See infra, § 122.

19. Id.

20. See, e.g., Dashiell v. Keauhou-Kona Co., 9th Cir. 1973, 487 F.2d 957 (Hawaii law); Glidden v. Butler, 1972, 112 N.H. 68, 288 A.2d 695; Sumner v. Amacher, 1968, 150 Mont. 544, 437 P.2d 630; Dickey v. Nations, Mo.App.1972, 479 S.W.2d 208.

21. See, e.g., DeLozier v. Smith, 1974, 22 Ariz.App. 136, 524 P.2d 970; Brown v. Spokane County Fire Protection District No. 1, 1978, 21 Wn.App. 886, 586 P.2d 1207; Graham v. Franco, Tex.1972, 488 S.W.2d 390; Maturin v. Dronet, La.App.1974, 288 So.2d 690; cf. Ellis v. K-Lan Co., Inc., 5th Cir. 1983, 695 F.2d 157 (Tex. law) (child's medical expenses).

But the act must be in the course of managing the community property or for its benefit. E.g., Farman v. Farman, 1980, 25 Wn.App. 896, 611 P.2d 1314 (new wife making harassing telephone calls to old wife).

As to the tangled California history, see Brunn, California Personal Injury Damage Awards to Married Persons, 1966, 13 UCLA L.Rev. 587. Effective January 1, 1970, the legislature restored the community property status of the action, but abolished the imputed negligence.

There are one or two states in which the negligence of one spouse is still imputed to the other to bar an action for wrongful death of a child. See, e.g., Stull v. Ragsdale, 1981, 273 Ark. 277, 620 S.W.2d 264, 269 (damages reduced under comparative fault) (Purtle, J., dissenting: "The majority has marched full speed ahead into the Nineteenth Century * * *."), noted, 1982, 5 U.Ark.L.R.L.Rev. 289. Contra, Singletary v. National Railroad Passenger Corp., Fla.App.1979, 376 So.2d 1191. See generally infra, chapters 23 & 24.

22. Hartfield v. Roper, N.Y.1829, 21 Wend. 615. As this developed, it was limited to cases where both parent and child were negligent, and the parent's negligence consisted in failure properly to look after the child. See Cadman v. White, 1936, 296 Mass. 117, 5 N.E.2d 19; Kupchinsky v. Vacuum Oil Co., 1933, 263 N.Y. 128, 188 N.E. 278; Notes, 1934, 47 Harv.L.Rev. 874; 1934, 34 Col.L.Rev. 575.

23. Waite v. North Eastern R. Co., 1858, 1 El.Bl. & El. 719, 120 Eng.Rep. 679, overruled by Oliver v. Birmingham & Midland Omnibus Co., [1933] 1 K.B. 35.

24. See the denunciation in Neff v. City of Cameron, 1908, 213 Mo. 350, 111 S.W. 1139.

by statute [25] or by decision [26] everywhere except in Maine,[27] where it should be hoped that it will not long survive. The "agency" of the parent to look after the child is of course the sheerest nonsense, and the fear that the parent may profit by his own negligence should be diminished by the power of the court to put the proceeds in trust for the child.[28]

Imputed negligence in domestic relations also appears in connection with actions for expenses, loss of services and wrongful death, which are more conveniently considered at a later point.[29]

Bailments

Until the year 1897, nearly all courts imputed the contributory negligence of a bailee to his bailor, in an action by the latter for damage to the chattel inflicted by the defendant.[30] The basis for the rule was obscure; but it appears to have rested upon the fact that the bailor had selected the bailee, that either might sue the tortfeasor and recover, and therefore it was assumed that there was an identity of their interests, and so the rule in the two suits should be the same.[31] With modern acceptance of the interests of the bailor and the bailee as quite separate and distinct, the earlier decisions have now been overruled in every jurisdiction.[32] It is now held that in the absence of statute the bailment is not sufficient in itself to impute the contributory negligence of the bailee, and that the bailor will be charged with such negligence only where there are additional factors which would make him liable to a third person as a defendant.[33] And even where the bailor would be liable as a defendant, as under an owner consent statute, the more modern view is also to refuse to impute the bailee's contributory negligence to the bailor.[34]

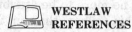

WESTLAW REFERENCES

imputed /2 contributory /2 negligence

Driver and Passenger

court(mi) & thorogood /2 bryan & 8 /5 115

---

25. See Novak v. State, 1950, 199 Misc. 588, 99 N.Y.S.2d 962; Gill v. Jakstas, 1950, 325 Mass. 309, 90 N.E.2d 527; Zaccari v. United States, D.Md.1956, 144 F.Supp. 860; Whittle v. Johnston, 1971, 124 Ga.App. 785, 186 S.E.2d 129.

26. See, e.g., Sheley v. Guy, 1975, 29 Ill.App.3d 361, 330 N.E.2d 567, affirmed 63 Ill.2d 544, 348 N.E.2d 835; Rogers v. Toro Manufacturing Co., Mo.App.1975, 522 S.W.2d 632; Alabama Power Co. v. Taylor, 1975, 293 Ala. 484, 306 So.2d 236; Collazo v. Manhattan & Bronx Surface Transit Operating Authority, Sup.1972, 72 Misc.2d 946, 339 N.Y.S.2d 809; Price v. Seaboard Air Line Railway Co., 1968, 274 N.C. 32, 161 S.E.2d 590; Shelton v. Mullins, 1966, 207 Va. 17, 147 S.E.2d 754; McKeon v. Goldstein, 1960, 53 Del. (3 Storey) 24, 164 A.2d 260; Lucas v. Ambridge Yellow Cab Co., 1958, 185 Pa.Super. 350, 137 A.2d 819; Botelho v. Curtis, 1970, 28 Conn.Sup. 493, 267 A.2d 675; Note, 1974, 34 Md.L.Rev. 155; Second Restatement of Torts, § 488(1).

27. Gravel v. Le Blanc, 1932, 131 Me. 325, 162 A. 789; Wood v. Balzano, 1940, 137 Me. 87, 15 A.2d 188; Orr v. First National Stores, Inc., Me.1971, 280 A.2d 785 (comparative negligence).

28. See Note, 1932, 80 U.Pa.L.Rev. 1123, 1131.

29. See infra, chapters 23 & 24.

30. Forks Township v. King, 1877, 84 Pa. 230; Texas & Pacific Railway Co. v. Tanskersley, 1885, 63 Tex. 57; Illinois Central Railroad Co., v. Sims, 1899, 77 Miss. 325, 27 So. 527; Welty v. Indianapolis & Vincennes Railroad Co., 1886, 105 Ind. 55, 4 N.E. 410.

31. Gregory, Vicarious Responsibility and Contributory Negligence, 1932, 41 Yale L.J. 831, 834; Reno, Imputed Contributory Negligence in Automobile Bailments, 1934, 82 U.Pa.L.Rev. 213. It should be recalled that originally the bailor could not maintain the action at all, and all damages had to be recovered by the bailee. See Holmes, The Common Law, 1881, 164 ff.; Bordwell, Property in Chattels, 1916, 29 Harv.L.Rev. 731.

32. The Leading case is New York, Lake Erie & Western Railway Co. v. New Jersey Electric Railway Co., 1897, 60 N.J.L. 338, 38 A. 828, affirmed 61 N.J. Law 287, 41 A. 1116. Texas was the last state to fall into line. Rollins Leasing Corp. v. Barkley, Tex.1976, 531 S.W.2d 603. Accord: Fisher v. Andrews & Pierce, 1950, 76 R.I. 464, 72 A.2d 172; White v. Saunders, 1942, 289 Ky. 268, 158 S.W.2d 393; Robinson v. Warren, 1930, 129 Me. 172, 151 A. 10; Nash v. Lang, 1929, 268 Mass. 407, 167 N.E. 762; Jones v. Taylor, Mo.App. 1966, 401 S.W.2d 183; Second Restatement of Torts, § 480.

33. See, e.g., Crader v. Jamison, Mo.App.1973, 496 S.W.2d 263; Wenisch v. Hoffmeister, 1976, 168 Ind. App. 247, 342 N.E.2d 665; Rumbolz v. Wipf, 1966, 82 S.D. 327, 145 N.W.2d 520; Sprague v. Bartlett, 1968, 109 N.H. 137, 244 A.2d 202; Howle v. McDaniel, 1957, 232 S.C. 125, 101 S.E.2d 255; Eggerding v. Bicknell, 1955, 20 N.J. 106, 118 A.2d 820.

34. See, e.g., Continental Auto Lease Corp. v. Campbell, 1967, 19 N.Y.2d 350, 280 N.Y.S.2d 123, 227 N.E.2d 28. See supra, § 73.

Domestic Relations

imputed /s contributory /s negligence /p spouse husband wife

imputed /s contributory /s negligence /p parent /s child

Bailments

contributory /s negligence /p bailee bailor

Chapter 13

STRICT LIABILITY FOR PHYSICAL HARM TO PERSONS AND TANGIBLE THINGS FROM ACCIDENTAL INVASIONS

Table of Sections

Sec.
75. Basis of Liability.
76. Animals.
77. Fire.
78. Abnormally Dangerous Things and Activities.
79. Extent of Liability.
80. Employers' Liability.
81. Other Applications.

§ 75. Basis of Liability

"Strict liability," as that term is used in this chapter, and as that term is commonly used by modern courts, means liability that is imposed on an actor apart from either (1) an intent to interfere with a legally protected interest without a legal justification for doing so, or (2) a breach of a duty to exercise reasonable care, i.e., actionable negligence. This is often referred to as liability without fault. That reference can be misleading, since much of the liability imposed for intentionally and negligently interfering with legally protected interests is liability without moral fault.

As we have seen,[1] the early law of torts was not concerned primarily with the moral responsibility, or "fault" of the wrongdoer. It occupied itself chiefly with keeping the peace between individuals, by providing a remedy which would be accepted in lieu of private vengeance.[2] While it is probable that even from the beginning the idea of moral guilt never was entirely absent from the minds of the judges,[3] it was not the most important consideration. Originally the person who hurt another by pure accident,[4] or in self-defense,[5] was required to make good the damage inflicted. "In all civil acts," it was said, "the law doth not so much regard

---

§ 75

1. Supra, ch. 1, § 6.
2. Holmes, The Common Law, 1881, 2, 3.
3. Winfield, The Myth of Absolute Liability, 1926, 42 L.Q.Rev. 37.

4. See supra, § 29.
5. 1319, Y.B. 12 ed. II, 381.

the intent of the actor, as the loss and damage of the party suffering." [6] There was, in other words, a rule, undoubtedly supported by the general feeling in the community, that "he who breaks must pay."

Until about the close of the nineteenth century, the history of the law of torts was that of a slow, and somewhat unsteady,[7] progress toward the recognition of "fault" or moral responsibility as the basis of the remedy.[8] With a growing moral consciousness in the community, there was a general movement in the direction of identifying legal liability with conduct which would not be expected of a good citizen.[9] This tendency was so marked that efforts were made by noted writers to construct a consistent theory of tort law upon the basic principle that there should be no liability without fault.[10]

But "fault," in this sense, never has become quite synonymous with moral blame. Not only is a great deal of morally reprehensible conduct vested with complete legal immunity—as where the expert swimmer who sees another drowning before his eyes is permitted to stand on the dock and watch him drown—[11] but at the same time the law finds "fault" in much that is morally innocent. "Fault" is a failure to live up to an ideal of conduct to which no one conforms always and which may be beyond the capacity of the individual. It may consist of sheer ignorance,[12] lack of intelligence,[13] or an honest mistake.[14] It may consist even in acts which are the normal and usual thing in the community.[15] Even the infant and the lunatic [16] who cannot help what they do are held liable for their torts.

So much can be collected in the way of cases imposing liability without any vestige of moral blame that a number of writers [17] have maintained that negligence is rapidly losing, if it has not entirely lost, its character as a branch of "fault" liability, so that those who are entirely innocent are now required to pay for the damage they do, and that negligence should therefore largely be jettisoned. This perhaps begs the question, by asigning to "fault" a criminal law connotation of moral blame which it seldom has been given in the law of torts. There is a broader sense in which "fault" means nothing more than a departure from a standard of conduct required of a person by society for the protection of his neighbors; [18] and if the departure is an innocent one, and the de-

---

6. Lambert v. Bessey, 1681, T.Ray. 421, 83 Eng. Rep. 220. As late as 1783, "Erskine said in his argument in the celebrated case of The Dean of St. Asaph [21 St.Tr. 1022] (and he said it by way of a familiar illustration of the difference between civil and criminal liability) that 'if a man rising in his sleep walks into a china shop and breaks everything about him, his being asleep is a complete answer to an *indictment* for trespass, but he must answer in an *action* for everything he has broken.'" Pollock, Law of Torts, 13th ed. 1929, 146.

7. Isaacs, Fault and Liability, 1918, 31 Harv.L.Rev. 954, 966, contends that the law has moved in cycles, alternating periods of strict liability with liability based on fault.

8. Wigmore, Responsibility for Tortious Acts: Its History, 1894, 7 Harv.L.Rev. 315, 383, 441.

9. Ames, Law and Morals, 1908, 22 Harv.L.Rev. 97.

10. Holmes, The Common Law, 1881, 144–163; Salmond, Law of Torts, 7th ed. 1924, 11–12; Smith, Tort and Absolute Liability, 1917, 30 Harv.L.Rev. 241, 319, 409.

11. Yania v. Bigan, 1959, 397 Pa. 316, 155 A.2d 343; Osterlind v. Hill, 1928, 263 Mass. 73, 160 N.E. 301. See supra, § 56.

12. Michigan City v. Rudolph, 1938, 104 Ind.App. 643, 12 N.E.2d 970; Note, 1939, 23 Minn.L.Rev. 628. See supra, § 32.

13. Worthington v. Mencer, 1892, 96 Ala. 310, 11 So. 72. See supra, § 32.

14. The Germanic, 1905, 196 U.S. 589, 25 S.Ct. 317, 49 L.Ed. 610.

15. Ault v. Hall, 1928, 119 Ohio St. 422, 164 N.E. 518; Marsh Wood Products Co. v. Babcock & Wilcox Co., 1932, 207 Wis. 209, 240 N.W. 392; Grant v. Graham Chero-Cola Bottling Co., 1918, 176 N.C. 256, 97 S.E. 27.

16. See infra, §§ 134, 135.

17. Ehrenzweig, Negligence Without Fault, 1951; Leflar, Negligence in Name Only, 1952, 27 N.Y.U.L. Rev. 564; McNiece and Thornton, Is the Law of Negligence Obsolete, 1952, 26 St. Johns L.Rev. 255; James Accident Proneness and Accident Law, 1950, 63 Harv. L.Rev. 769.

18. "In fact, legal fault upon which liability is based has little connection with personal morality or with justice to the individual; it is always tinctured with a supposed expediency in shifting the loss from one harmed to one who has caused the harm by acting below the standard imposed by the courts or legislators." Sea-

fendant cannot help it, it is none the less a departure, and a social wrong. The distinction still remains between the person who has deviated from the standard, and the person who has not. The defendant may not be to blame for being out of line with what society requires of him, but he is none the less out of line.

In this broader sense there is "fault" in much innocent conduct. Tort liability never has been inconsistent with the ignorance which is bliss, or the good intentions with which hell is said to be paved. A trespasser is not excused by the honest, reasonable belief that the land is his own;[19] a bona fide purchaser of stolen goods is held liable for conversion;[20] the publisher of a libel commits a tort, although he has no means of knowing the defamatory nature of his words.[21] There are many situations in which a careful person is held liable for an entirely reasonable mistake.[22] In all this there is nothing new. Socially, and legally, these defendants are at fault; whether they are individually so, in spite of the fact that they are blameless, appears to be entirely a matter of definition, rather than substance, and the argument leads only to a pointless dispute over the meaning of a word.[23]

Strict Liability

But even beyond all this, the last hundred years have witnessed the overthrow of the doctrine of "never any liability without fault," even in the legal sense of a departure from reasonable standards of conduct. It has seen a general acceptance of the principle that in some cases the defendant may be held liable, although he is not only charged with no moral wrongdoing, but has not even departed in any way from a reasonable standard of intent or care. In some instances, as where liability is imposed upon the keepers of animals,[24] new reasons of social policy have been found for the continuance of an older rule of strict liability. In others, involving abnormally dangerous conditions or activities,[25] the courts have in effect recognized a new doctrine, that the defendant's enterprise, while it will be tolerated by the law, must pay its way.[26] There is "a strong and growing tendency, where there is blame on neither side, to ask, in view of the exigencies of social justice, who can best bear the loss and hence to shift the loss by creating liability where there has been no fault."[27]

vey, Speculations as to "Respondeat Superior," Harvard Legal Essays, 1934, 433, 442.

19. Loewenberg v. Rosenthal, 1899, 18 Or. 178, 22 P. 601; Hazelton v. Week, 1880, 49 Wis. 661, 6 N.W. 309; Perry v. Jefferies, 1901, 61 S.C. 292, 39 S.E. 515.

20. Stephens v. Elwall, 1815, 4 M. & S. 259, 105 Eng.Rep. 830; Hyde v. Noble, 1843, 13 N.H. 494. See supra, § 15.

21. Hulton & Co. v. Jones, [1909] 2 K.B. 444, [1910] A.C. 20; Taylor v. Hearst, 1895, 107 Cal. 262, 40 P. 392; Washington Post Co. v. Kennedy, 1924, 55 App.D.C. 162, 3 F.2d 207. See, however, changes brought about by the Supreme Court of the United States in creating the constitutional privilege to defame. Section 113.

22. Gill v. Selling, 1928, 125 Or. 587, 267 P. 812, affirmed 126 Or. 584, 270 P. 411; Holmes v. Blyler, 1890, 80 Iowa 365, 45 N.W. 756. See supra, § 17.

23. "To be of any service as a test of liability, fault must be used in its actual, its subjective meaning of some conduct repugnant to accepted moral or ethical ideals or some act or omission falling below the standard of conduct required of society of its members. It is possible to state all liabilities in terms of fault, to say that one is legally, if not morally or socially, in fault, wherever the law holds him liable."

"Compare Jaco v. Baker, 1944, 174 Or. 191, 148 P.2d 938, where the intentional creation of the risk involved in keeping a vicious dog was held to be sufficient "malice" to prevent a discharge under the Bankruptcy Act. But this is reasoning in a vicious circle. It involves as the premise, the assumption of the very point in dispute, that legal liability cannot exist without fault. The reasoning is this, there can be no legal liability without fault, the defendant is liable, therefore he is at fault, if not actually at least legally. Not only is such reasoning vicious as reasoning, but, by confounding liability and fault, it destroys all value of fault as an element determinative of liability." Bohlen, The Rule in Rylands v. Fletcher, 1911, 59 U.Pa.L.Rev. 298, 313.

24. See infra, § 76.

25. See infra, § 78.

26. The theory is developed at length in Ehrenzweig, Negligence Without Fault, 1951.

27. See Pound, The End of Law as Developed in Legal Rules and Doctrines, 1914, 27 Harv.L.Rev. 195, 233; Bohlen, The Rule in Rylands v. Fletcher, 1911, 59 U.Pa.L.Rev. 298; Harris, Liability Without Fault, 1932, 6 Tulane L.Rev. 337; Carpenter, The Doctrine of Green v. General Petroleum Corporation, 1932, 5 So.Cal.L.Rev. 263; Stallybrass, Dangerous Things and the Non-Natu-

An entire field of legislation, illustrated by the workers' compensation acts,[28] has been based upon the same principle.

This new policy frequently has found expression where the defendant's activity is unusual and abnormal in the community, and the danger which it threatens to others is unduly great—and particularly where the danger will be great even though the enterprise is conducted with every possible precaution. The basis of the liability is the defendant's intentional behavior in exposing those in his vicinity to such a risk. The conduct which is dealt with here occupies something of a middle ground. It is conduct which does not so far depart from social standards as to fall within the traditional boundaries of negligence—usually because the advantages which it offers to the defendant and to the community outweigh even the abnormal risk; but which is still so far socially unreasonable that the defendant is not allowed to carry it on without making good any actual harm which it does to his neighbors.

The courts have tended to lay stress upon the fact that the defendant is acting for his own purposes, and is seeking a benefit or a profit from such activities, and that he is in a better position to administer the unusual risk by passing it on to the public than is the innocent victim. The problem is dealt with as one of allocating a more or less inevitable loss to be charged against a complex and dangerous civilization, and liability is imposed upon the party best able to shoulder it. The defendant is held liable merely because, as a matter of social adjustment, the conclusion is that the responsibility should be so placed. This modern attitude, which is largely a thing of the last four decades, is of course a far cry from the individualistic viewpoint of the common law courts.

While such strict liability often is said to be imposed "without fault," it can scarcely be said that there is less of a moral point of view involved in the rule that one who innocently causes harm should make it good. The traditional analysis regards such a result as something of an exception to more or less well established rules, and says that the defendant is not at "fault" because he has only done a reasonable thing in a reasonable way, and that he is liable notwithstanding.[29] But it may be questioned whether "fault," with its popular connotation of personal guilt and moral blame, and its more or less arbitrary legal meaning, which will vary with the requirements of social conduct imposed by the law,[30] is of any real assistance in dealing with such questions, except perhaps as a descriptive term. It might be quite as easy to say that one who conducts blasting operations which may injure a neighbor is at "fault" in conducting them at all,[31] and is privileged to do so only in so far as he insures that no harm shall result, as to say that he is not at fault, but is liable nev-

---

ral Use of Land, 1929, 3 Camb.L.J. 376; Feezer, Capacity to Bear Loss as a Factor in the Decision of Certain Types of Tort Cases, 1930, 78 U.Pa.L.Rev. 805, 1931, 79 U.Pa.L.Rev. 742; James, Some Reflections on the Bases of Strict Liability, 1958, 18 La.L.Rev. 293; Ognall, Some Facets of Strict Tortious Liability in the United States and Their Implications, 1958, 33 Notre Dame L. 239. As to similar developments on the continent, see Takayanagi, Liability Without Fault in the Modern Civil and Common Law, 1921–1923, 16 Ill.L.Rev. 163, 268; 17 Ill.L.Rev. 185, 416.

28. Smith, Sequel to Workmen's Compensation Acts, 1914, 27 Harv.L.Rev. 235; Bohlen, The Drafting of Workmen's Compensation Acts, 1912, 25 Harv.L. Rev. 544. See infra, § 80.

29. Smith, Tort and Absolute Liability, 1917, 30 Harv.L.Rev. 241, 319, 409; Harper, Law of Torts, 1933, §§ 155, 203.

30. Seavey, Speculations as to "Respondeat Superior," Harvard Legal Essays, 1934, 433, 435–442.

31. See Smith, Liability for Substantial Physical Damage to Land by Blasting, 1920, 33 Harv.L.Rev. 542, 549. Compare the view that liability for the keeping of vicious animals is based on negligence, 2 Cooley, Torts, 3d ed. 1906, ch. XI; also the view that Rylands v. Fletcher, 1868, L.R. 3 H.L. 330, could have been decided upon grounds of negligence. 1 Street, Foundations of Legal Liability, 1906, 62, 63; Smith, Tort and Absolute Liability, 1917, 30 Harv.L.Rev. 409, 414, n. 23; Bishop, Non-Contract Law, 1889, § 839; see Thayer, Liability Without Fault, 1916, 29 Harv.L.Rev. 801. See also the conclusion in Salmond, Law of Torts 8th Ed. 1934, 596–599, that there is no sufficient reason for any line of demarcation between strict liability and negligence; also the editorial comment in [1928] 4 Dom.L.Rep.No. 3, and the ensuing controversy be-

ertheless. If he is not "at fault" because the social desirability of the blasting justifies the risk,[32] his conduct is still so far socially questionable that it does not justify immunity. The basis of his liability in either case is the creation of an undue risk of harm to other members of the community.[33] It has been said [34] that there is "conditional fault," meaning that the defendant is not to be regarded as at fault unless or until his conduct causes some harm to others, but he is then at fault, and to be held responsible. If this analysis helps anyone, it is certainly as permissible as another.[35]

Once the legal concept of "fault" is divorced, as it has been, from the personal standard of moral wrongdoing, there is a sense in which liability with or without "fault" must beg its own conclusion. The term requires such extensive definition, that it seems better not to make use of it at all, and to refer instead to strict liability, apart from either wrongful intent or negligence.

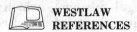 **WESTLAW REFERENCES**

di strict liability
"strict liability" /4 means defined definition term

Strict Liability
digest("strict liability" /s fault)

---

tween A.L. MacDonald and V.C. MacDonald in 1929, 7 Can.Bar.Rev. 140, 208, 330.

32. Harper, Law of Torts, 1933, 203.

33 Harper, The Foreseeability Factor in the Law of Torts, 1932, 7 Notre Dame Lawyer 468.

34. Keeton, Conditional Fault in the Law of Torts, 1959, 72 Harv.L.Rev. 401.

35. It has often been said that strict liability arises from conduct which is so far legitimate that it will not be enjoined, but it will make the defendant liable when it causes damage. The writer has been unable to trace the origin of this notion; but since there appears to be nothing whatever to support it, it may have come from a law professor. Decisions are not lacking in which conduct has been enjoined on the ground that it would entail strict liability. See for example Attorney-General v. Cory Bros., [1921] 1 A.C. 521; Attorney-General v. Corke, [1933] Ch. 89; Gas Light & Coke Co. v. Vestry of St. Mary Abbott's, 1885, 15 Q.B.D. 1; Jones v. Llanrwst Urban District Council, [1911] 1 Ch. 393; Snow v. Whitehead, 1884, 27 Ch. Div. 588; Mallett v. Taylor, 1915, 78 Or. 208, 152 P. 873. And as to denying injunction even where there is clear fault, see Mc-

§ 76. Animals

Primitive law tended to hold the owner of property strictly liable for the harm it did. The owner of a slave, an animal, or even an inanimate thing, was so far identified with his chattel that he was liable, without any fault of his own, for the damage it might inflict on his neighbors.[1] It is characteristic of certain stages of development in all legal systems of which we have knowledge, that he might escape liability by surrendering the harmful agent itself, either to the injured party or to the crown.[2] The present state of the common law may be said to begin with the disappearance of this "noxal surrender" and the rule of strict liability for harm done by harmless things. So far as the responsibility of keepers of animals is concerned, the survival of the primitive notion of strict liability has been due in part to modern views of policy. Certain kinds of animals involve an obvious danger to the community, even if they are carefully kept; everyone knows the propensity of cattle and horses to escape and roam and do mischief,[3] and a bear or an elephant [4] can never be regarded as safe. Those who keep such animals for their own purposes are required to protect the community, at their peril, against the risk involved.

Clintock, Discretion to Deny Injunction Against Trespass and Nuisance, 1928, 12 Minn.L.Rev. 565; Walsh, Equity, 1930, 284–298.

§ 76

1. There is a controversy as to whether this was the earliest rule, or a somewhat later development. See Williams, Liability for Animals, 1939; Holmes, The Common Law, 1881, 15–24; Wigmore, Responsibility for Tortious Acts: Its History, 1894, 7 Harv.L.Rev. 315, 352 et seq.; 2 Pollock and Maitland, History of English Law, 2d ed. 1911, 472 et seq.

2. 1 Street, Foundations of Legal Liability, 1906, 50; 2 Pollock and Maitland, History of English Law, 2d ed. 1911, 473. As late as 1842, in Regina v. Eastern Counties R. Co., 10 M. & W. 58, 152 Eng.Rep. 380, a railway engine which had run over a man was forfeited as a deodand.

3. Page v. Hollingsworth, 1855, 7 Ind. 317; Gresham v. Taylor, 1874, 51 Ala. 505.

4. Crunk v. Glover, 1959, 167 Neb. 816, 95 N.W.2d 135; Filburn v. People's Palace & Aquarium Co., 1890, L.R. 25 Q.B.D. 258.

The strict liability is, in general, co-extensive with the obvious risk.

Trespassing Livestock

It was said in an earlier case [5] that "where my beasts of their own wrong without my will and knowledge break another's close I shall be punished, for I am the trespasser with my beasts * * * for I am held by the law to keep my beasts without their doing wrong to anyone." The action was in trespass rather than case,[6] but the liability was similar to that of a defendant who had trespassed in person.[7] While this primitive idea of the identity of the owner with the animal has vanished, it remains the common law in most jurisdictions that the keeper of animals of a kind likely to roam and do damage is strictly liable for their trespasses. This has been true in the case of cattle,[8] horses,[9] sheep,[10] hogs,[11] and such wandering fowls as turkeys, chickens and pigeons;[12] and also, no doubt, to any kept wild animals of a kind likely to escape, tresspass and do damage.[13] On the other hand, in the case of such domestic favorites as dogs [14] and cats,[15] nearly all courts have refused to impose strict liability for the trespass, although such liability may be rested upon knowledge on the part of the owner of any mischievous propensity.[16] This is perhaps to be traced to the old rule, long since discarded, that the owner could have no property right in such "base" animals;[17] but the justification now given is, together with the community custom to allow such animals to wander, that their trespasses are likely to be trivial and to do no serious harm, so that there is no necessity for protection against anything more than negligence.[18] This justification has been criticized [19] as unlikely to appeal to adjoining owners of flower beds and poultry; and statutes in many states have imposed strict liability for all damages done by dogs.[20]

---

5. 12 Hen. VII, Keilwey 3b, 72 Eng.Rep. 156. This was repeated in substance in Wells v. Howell, N.Y. 1822, 19 Johns 385. In Tonawanda Railroad Co. v. Munger, N.Y.1848, 5 Denio 255, affirmed, 1850, 4 N.Y. 349, it was added that there is absolute liability for the trespass of cattle even though the defendant has exercised all ordinary care and prudence in taking care of them.

6. See 27 Lib.Assis. pl. 56.

7. See supra, § 13.

8. McKee v. Trisler, 1924, 311 Ill. 536, 143 N.E. 69; Page v. Hollingsworth, 1855, 7 Ind. 317; Angus v. Radin, 1820, 5 N.J.L. 815; Stackpole v. Healy, 1819, 16 Mass. 33.

9. Decker v. Gammon, 1857, 44 Me. 322; Morgan v. Hudnell, 1895, 52 Ohio St. 552, 40 N.E. 716; Ellis v. Loftus Iron Co., 1874, L.R. 10 C.P. 10.

10. Theyer v. Purnell, [1918] 2 K.B. 333; see Marsh v. Hand, 1890, 120 N.Y. 315, 24 N.E. 463.

11. Gresham v. Taylor, 1874, 51 Ala. 505. See, as to trespassing animals generally, Notes 1919, 32 Harv. L.Rev. 420; 1949, 34 Iowa L.Rev. 318.

12. McPherson v. James, 1896, 69 Ill.App. 337; Lapp v. Stanton, 1911, 116 Md. 197, 81 A. 675; Adams Brothers v. Clark, 1920, 189 Ky. 279, 224 S.W. 1046; Taylor v. Granger, 1896, 19 R.I. 410, 34 A. 153, 37 A. 13; see Tate v. Ogg, 1938, 170 Va. 95, 195 S.E. 496. But see contra, repudiating the common law rule as not applicable to the customs of the state: Kimple v. Schafer, 1913, 161 Iowa 659, 143 N.W. 505; Evans v. McLalin, 1915, 189 Mo.App. 310, 175 S.W. 294. See Notes, 1924, 9 Va.L.Reg.,N.S., 481; 1921, 19 Mich.L. Rev. 422.

13. King v. Blue Mountain Forest Association, 1956, 100 N.H. 212, 123 A.2d 151 (wild boar).

14. Sanders v. Teape & Swan, 1884, 51 L.T. 263; Van Etten v. Noyes, 1908, 128 App.Div. 406, 112 N.Y.S. 888; Blair v. Forehand, 1838, 100 Mass. 136; McDonald v. Castle, 1925, 116 Okl. 46, 243 P. 215; Olson v. Pederson, 1939, 206 Minn. 415, 288 N.W. 856. Otherwise where the owner is himself responsible for the trespass, as in the case of fox hunting. Pegg v. Gray, 1954, 240 N.C. 548, 82 S.E.2d 757; Baker v. Howard County Hunt, 1936, 171 Md. 159, 188 A. 223, (negligence). See Note, 1954, 33 N.C.L.Rev. 134.

15. Buckle v. Holmes, [1926] 2 K.B. 125; McDonald v. Jodry, 1890, 8 Pa.Co.Ct. 142; see Bischoff v. Cheney, 1914, 89 Conn. 1, 92 A. 660. See Alderman, Legal Status of the Cat, 1917, 20 Law Notes 204; Hibschman, The Cat and the Law, 1937, 12 Temple L.Q. 89; Note, 1928, 13 Corn.L.Q. 150.

16. See infra, p. 542.

17. Mason v. Keeling, 1691, 12 Mod. 332, 1 Ld. Raym. 606, 88 Eng.Rep. 1359.

18. Buckle v. Holmes, [1926] 2 K.B. 125; McDonald v. Castle, 1925, 116 Okl. 46, 243 P. 215.

19. See Note, 1928, 13 Corn.L.Q. 150.

20. See for example Granniss v. Weber, 1928, 107 Conn. 622, 141 A. 877. Three courts have reached the same result, as to trespassing dogs, at common law. Chunot v. Larson, 1868, 43 Wis. 536; Doyle v. Vance, 1880, 6 Vict.L.Rep. 87; McClain v. Lewiston Interstate

In earlier days in the United States, many courts rejected entirely the rule of strict liability for animal trespasses, as contrary to established local custom, particularly in western country where cattle were allowed to graze at large on the range.[21] This view still prevails in some parts of our western states. But as the country has become more closely settled, the tendency has been to restore the common law rule, either by statute or by decision.[22] The matter is now very largely governed by statutory provisions. The first legislation to be adopted consisted of "fencing out" statutes, which provided that if the plaintiff properly fenced his land there was strict liability when the animals broke through the fence, but otherwise there was liability only when the owner was at fault.[23] As the country became more settled, the conflict between the grazing and the agricultural interests resulted in many states in "fencing in" statutes, which required the owner of the animals to fence or otherwise restrain them, and made him strictly liable if he did not do so.[24] Sometimes the final step was taken, by legislation restoring the common law rule. In a good many states individual counties are permitted to choose the rule that they wish to apply, so that the law varies in different parts of the state. It is of course generally agreed that there is liability for any negligence leading to the animal trespass.[25]

One exception to the common law rule which the courts were compelled to recognize early[26] was the case of animals straying from a highway on which they were being driven lawfully.[27] While the owner would be liable for any negligence in failing to control them, or to pursue them promptly and bring them back,[28] the privilege to make use of the highway to move them from one place to another[29] involves, as a more or less inevitable incident, immunity as to any casual trespass on adjoining lands by the way.[30] But the privilege extends only to property immediately abutting on the highway, and not to any lands removed from it, upon which the cattle may trespass once they have strayed from the road.[31] On the highway itself, even an escaped animal is not a

Fair & Racing Association, 1909, 17 Idaho 63, 104 P. 1015.

21. Delaney v. Errickson, 1880, 10 Neb. 492, 6 N.W. 600, reversed on other grounds, 1881, 11 Neb. 533, 10 N.W. 451; Wagner v. Bissell, 1856, 3 Iowa 396; Beinhorn v. Griswold, 1902, 27 Mont. 79, 69 P. 557; Overbey v. Poteat, 1960, 206 Tenn. 146, 332 S.W.2d 197.

22. Phillips v. Bynum, 1906, 145 Ala. 549, 39 So. 911; Bulpit v. Matthews, 1893, 145 Ill. 345, 34 N.E. 525; Puckett v. Young, 1901, 112 Ga. 578, 37 S.E. 880; Gumm v. Jones, 1906, 115 Mo.App. 597, 92 S.W. 169; Nelson v. Tanner, 1948, 113 Utah 293, 194 P.2d 468.

23. See for example Buford v. Houtz, 1890, 133 U.S. 320, 10 S.Ct. 305, 33 L.Ed. 618; Garcia v. Sumrall, 1942, 58 Ariz. 526, 121 P.2d 640; Osborne v. Osmer, 1927, 82 Colo. 80, 256 P. 1092; Johnston v. Mack Manufacturing Co., 1909, 65 W.Va. 544, 64 S.E. 841. In Robinson v. Kerr, 1960, 144 Colo. 48, 355 P.2d 117, it was held that such a statute applied only to damage to land, and not to personal injuries inflicted by a trespassing horse.

See also, at common law, Johnson v. Robinson, 1968, 11 Mich.App. 707, 162 N.W.2d 161.

24. See for example Arizona Code Ann., 1949, § 50–606.

25. Howland v. Cressy, 1948, 95 N.H. 205, 60 A.2d 128; Lyons v. Merrick, 1870, 105 Mass. 71; Grimes v. Eddy, 1894, 126 Mo. 168, 28 S.W. 756.

26. Harvy v. Gulson, 1604, Noy 107, 74 Eng.Rep. 1072.

27. The rule has no application when cattle are at large unlawfully upon the highway. Stackpole v. Healy, 1819, 16 Mass. 33; Avery v. Maxwell, 1827, 4 N.H. 36; Harrison v. Brown, 1856, 5 Wis. 27.

28. Goodwyn v. Cheveley, 1859, 4 H. & N. 631, 157 Eng.Rep. 989; Erdman v. Gottshall, 1899, 9 Pa.Super. 295; Wood v. Snider, 1907, 187 N.Y. 28, 79 N.E. 858. Cf. Bender v. Welsh, 1942, 344 Pa. 392, 25 A.2d 182.

29. Including, at common law, the privilege to drive them through city streets. Tillett v. Ward, 1882, L.R. 10 Q.B. 17 (no liability to shop owner). It may be suggested that, even if not forbidden by ordinance, this might now be negligence in large cities.

30. Goodwyn v. Cheveley, 1859, 4 H. & N. 631, 157 Eng.Rep. 989; Rightmire v. Shepard, 1891, 36 St.R. 768, 59 Hun 620, 12 N.Y.S. 800; Cool v. Crommet, 1836, 13 Me. 250; Hartford v. Brady, 1874, 114 Mass. 466; Boutwell v. Champlain Realty Co., 1915, 89 Vt. 80, 94 A. 108.

31. Wood v. Snider, 1907, 187 N.Y. 28, 79 N.E. 858; McDonnell v. Pittsfield & North Adams Railroad Corp., 1874, 115 Mass. 564.

trespasser, and there is no strict liability for any harm which it may do upon that basis.³²

The foundation of the strict liability is commonly said to be possession and the power of control of the animals. Thus one whose lands are crossed, without one's consent, by the cattle of another before they enter the plaintiff's land, is not liable for the trespass.³³ But a bailee to whom they are delivered becomes strictly responsible for their escape.³⁴ Whether the owner is also liable in such a case is a matter on which the courts have not agreed. There is authority that his duty of keeping the animals safe is so absolute that he cannot delegate it to another.³⁵ Such a view may be appropriate to the ownership of such a dangerous beast as a tiger,³⁶ but it is scarcely called for in the case of animals so relatively harmless and so easily restrained as cattle. It seems the better conclusion that the owner is relieved of responsibility by the bailment.³⁷

The consequences of the trespass for which the defendant will be held liable are more appropriately considered at a later point.³⁸

Liability Apart from Trespassing Livestock

Strict liability for damage done by dangerous animals, apart from any trespass on land, is of very ancient origin, but finds its first modern statement in 1846, in the English case of May v. Burdett,³⁹ where the plaintiff was bitten by the defendant's monkey. It has been thought ⁴⁰ to rest on the basis of negligence in keeping the animal at all; but this does not coincide with the modern analysis of negligence as conduct which is unreasonable in view of the risk, since it may not be an unreasonable thing to keep even a tiger in a zoo. It is rather an instance of the strict responsibility placed upon those who, even with proper care, expose the community to the risk of a very dangerous thing. While two or three jurisdictions insist that there is no liability without some negligence in keeping the animal,⁴¹ by far the greater number impose strict liability.

The kind of "dangerous animal" that will subject the keeper to strict liability requires identification. In general, it can be said that the animal must pose some kind of an abnormal risk to the particular community where the animal is kept; hence, the keeper is en-

32. Gardner v. Black, 1940, 217 N.C. 573, 9 S.E.2d 10; Eddy v. Union Railroad Co., 1903, 25 R.I. 451, 56 A. 677; Bombard v. Newton, 1920, 94 Vt. 354, 111 A. 510. There may, however, be liability for negligence in looking after the animal. Deen v. Davies, [1935] 2 K.B. 282; Shaw v. Joyce, 1959, 249 N.C. 415, 106 S.E.2d 459; Traill v. Ostermeir, 1941, 140 Neb. 432, 300 N.W. 375. Or strict liability on the basis of scienter as to dangerous traits. See infra, this section on Liability Apart from Trespassing Livestock.

33. Lawrence v. Combs, 1858, 37 N.H. 331; Hanson v. Northern Pacific Railway Co., 1916, 90 Wash. 516, 156 P. 553; Little v. McGuire, 1876, 43 Iowa 447.

34. Moulton v. Moore, 1884, 56 Vt. 700; Tewksbury v. Bucklin, 1835, 7 N.H. 518; Van Slyck v. Snell, N.Y. 1872, 6 Lans. 299.

35. 1638, 2 Rolle Abr. 526(b) 1; Sheridan v. Bean, 1844, 49 Mass. (8 Metc.) 284; Blaisdell v. Stone, 1881, 60 N.H. 507; Weymouth v. Gile, 1882, 72 Me. 446; see Marsh v. Hand, 1890, 120 N.Y. 315, 24 N.E. 463.

36. See infra, this section on Liability Apart from Trespassing Livestock.

37. Rossell v. Cottom, 1858, 31 Pa. 525; Reddick v. Newburn, 1882, 76 Mo. 423; Ward v. Brown, 1872, 64 Ill. 307; Mott v. Scott, 1905, 35 Colo. 68, 83 P. 779; Restatement of Torts, § 504, Comment *f*. Cf. Reuter v. Swarthout, 1924, 182 Wis. 453, 196 N.W. 847.

38. See infra, § 79.

39. 1846, 9 Q.B. 101, 115 Eng.Rep. 1213.

40. See Williams, Liability for Animals, 1939, 327; 3 Bl.Comm. 211; 2 Cooley, Torts, 3d ed. 1906, ch. XI.

41. Vaughan v. Miller Brothers "101" Ranch Wild West Show, 1931, 109 W.Va. 170, 153 S.E. 289; Panorama Resort v. Nichols, 1935, 165 Va. 289, 182 S.E. 235; Hansen v. Brogan, 1965, 145 Mont. 224, 400 P.2d 265. See Note, 1931, 25 Ill.L.Rev. 962. In all of these cases the plaintiff was injured while on the defendant's premises, and the statements made as to the state of the authorities are misleading, to say the least. An attempt was made to add Louisiana in Briley v. Mitchell, La.App.1959, 110 So.2d 169, but this was overruled, and the strict liability reinstated, in Briley v. Mitchell, 1959, 238 La. 551, 115 So.2d 851, on remand 1960, 119 So.2d 668.

See the excellent analysis in McNeely, A Footnote on Dangerous Animals, 1939, 37 Mich.L.Rev. 1181, concluding that the decisions might be harmonized on the basis of strict liability outside of the keeper's land, but liability only for negligence for harm occurring upon it, because of assumption of risk.

gaged in an activity that subjects those in the vicinity, including those who come onto his property, to an abnormal risk. It is the exposing of others to an abnormal risk that is regarded as justifying strict liability. Since the abnormality of the risk is the basis for the imposition of strict liability, courts have generally and for many years distinguished between wild animals and domestic animals. The Restatement of Torts differentiates between these two classes of animals by defining a domestic animal to be an animal that is customarily devoted to the service of mankind at the time and in the place where it is kept. This appears to describe accurately the result of the cases.

The possessor of a wild animal is strictly liable for physical harm done to the person of another or to another's animal if that harm results from a dangerous propensity that is characteristic of wild animals of that class. Thus, strict liability has been imposed on keepers of lions and tigers,[42] bears,[43] elephants,[44] wolves,[45] monkeys,[46] and other similar animals.[47] No member of such a species, however domesticated, can ever be regarded as safe, and liability does not rest upon any experience with the particular animal.[48]

A possessor of a domestic animal is not subject to liability for harm simply and solely because it resulted from a dangerous propensity of the domestic animal. To be strictly liable, the possessor must have known or had reason to know of a dangerous propensity or trait that was not characteristic of a domestic animal of like kind. Thus, cattle, sheep, horses, dogs, and cats are regarded as domestic animals virtually everywhere, and as to these, therefore, strict liability requires a showing that the defendant knew, or had reason to know, of an abnormal propensity. There are certain classes of domestic animals, including bulls,[49] stallions,[50] bees,[51] mules,[52] and rams, in which dangerous propensities are normal, and as to these, the keeper is not subject to strict liability.

42. Stamp v. Eighty-Sixth Street Amusement Co., 1916, 95 Misc. 599, 159 N.Y.S. 683 (lion); see Opelt v. Al. G. Barnes Co., 1919, 41 Cal.App. 776, 183 P. 241 (leopard).

43. Crunk v. Glover, 1959, 167 Neb. 816, 95 N.W.2d 135; City of Tonkawa v. Danielson, 1933, 166 Okl. 241, 27 P.2d 348; Vredenburg v. Behan, 1881, 33 La.Ann. 627; City of Mangum v. Brownlee, 1938, 181 Okl. 515, 75 P.2d 174; see Bottcher v. Buck, 1928, 265 Mass. 4, 163 N.E. 182; Malloy v. Starin, 1908, 191 N.Y. 21, 83 N.E. 588.

44. Filburn v. People's Palace & Aquarium Co., 1890, 25 Q.B.D. 258; Behrens v. Bertram Mills Circus, Ltd., [1957] 2 Q.B. 1; see Scribner v. Kelley, N.Y.1862, 38 Barb. 14.

45. Hayes v. Miller, 1907, 150 Ala. 621, 43 So. 818; Collins v. Otto, 1962, 149 Colo. 489, 369 P.2d 564 (coyote); Temple v. Elvery, Sask., [1926] 3 W.W.R. 652 (cross between Great Dane and coyote).

46. May v. Burdett, 1846, 9 Q.B. 101, 115 Eng.Rep. 1213; Copley v. Wills, Tex.Civ.App.1913, 152 S.W. 830; Phillips v. Garner, 1914, 106 Miss. 828, 64 So. 735; Garelli v. Sterling-Alaska Fur & Game Farms, Inc., 1960, 25 Misc.2d 1032, 206 N.Y.S.2d 130; cf. Candler v. Smith, 1935, 50 Ga.App. 667, 179 S.E. 395 (baboon). But in Abrevaya v. Palace Theatre & Realty Co., 1960, 25 Misc.2d 600, 197 N.Y.S.2d 27, it was held that a domesticated rhesus monkey was not a matter for strict liability in the absence of scienter.

47. Marlor v. Ball, 1900, 16 T.L.R. 239 (zebras); Smith v. Jalbert, 1966, 351 Mass. 432, 221 N.E.2d 744 (same). A humorous extension of the idea is York, In re Wrestlers, 1941, 13 Rocky Mt. L.Rev. 171.

48. Filburn v. People's Palace & Aquarium Co., 1890, 25 Q.B.D. 258, 59 L.J.Q.B. 471; Hayes v. Miller, 1907, 150 Ala. 621, 43 So. 818; Copley v. Wills, Tex.Civ. App.1913, 152 S.W. 830.

49. Banks v. Maxwell, 1933, 205 N.C. 233, 171 S.E. 70; Mann v. Stanley, 1956, 141 Cal.App.2d 438, 296 P.2d 921. Cf. Yazoo & Mississippi Valley Railroad Co. v. Gordon, 1939, 184 Miss. 885, 186 So. 631 (steer); Young v. Blaum, La.App.1933, 146 So. 168 (male goat); Oakes v. Spaulding, 1867, 40 Vt. 347 (the battering ram). As to this last, see Browne, The Sign of the Ram, 1889, 1 Green Bag 328.

50. Hammond v. Melton, 1891, 42 Ill.App. 186.

51. Earl v. Van Alstyne, N.Y.1850, 8 Barb. 630; Parsons v. Manser, 1903, 119 Iowa 88, 93 N.W. 86; Ammons v. Kellogg, 1925, 137 Miss. 551, 102 So. 562.

Thus it has been said that the keeper of such animals is not liable for acts normal to the kind, in the absence of some notice of a special propensity in the individual, or some negligence. Clinton v. Lyons & Co., [1912] 3 K.B. 198; Manton v. Brocklebank, [1923] 2 K.B. 212; Buckle v. Holmes, [1926] 2 K.B. 125; Goodwin v. E.B. Nelson Grocery Co., 1921, 239 Mass. 232, 132 N.E. 51.

52. Rector v. Southern Coal Co., 1926, 192 N.C. 804, 136 S.E. 113; Robidoux v. Busch, Mo.App.1966, 400 S.W.2d 631. See the justly noted remarks of Lamm, J., on the Missouri mule in Lyman v. Dale, 1914, 262 Mo. 353, 360, 171 S.W. 352, 354.

In deciding whether or not an animal is a wild or domestic animal, undoubtedly the customs of the community and the social utility of keeping the animal in the particular locality have entered into a determination of its classification. An elephant is regarded as a safe animal in Burma,[53] but an unsafe animal in England.[54]

The emphasis is placed upon the abnormal nature of the animal in the particular community; hence, the abnormal character of the risk to which the defendant exposes others is the justification for creating the strict liability. The characteristically dangerous types of animal that are customarily kept, domesticated, and devoted to the service of mankind are sanctioned by common usage to such an extent as to make inapplicable the doctrine of strict liability.

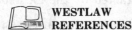

WESTLAW REFERENCES

strict! absolut! /1 liab! /s animal* livestock /p trespass!

Trespassing Livestock

strict! absolut! /1 liab! /p dog* cat*
fenc! /s statute* law* act* /p animal* herd* livestock* cattle
animal* livestock* cattle /p bail! trespass! damag!

Liability Apart from Trespassing Livestock

may /5 burdett /5 9 /5 101

---

53. Maung Kyan Dun v. Ma Kyian, 1900, 2 Upper Burma Rulings, Civ. 570.

54. Behrens v. Bertram Mills Circus, Ltd., [1957] 2 Q.B. 1. Similarly, the Indian buffalo is regarded as "cattle" in India. Madho v. Akaji, 1912, 17 Ind.Cas. 899. But not in Ceylon, where it is said not to be so domesticated as to be "harmless." Anonymous, 1851, Austin's Rep., Ceylon, 153.

Camels, which are now domesticated virtually everywhere they are found, were held not to be "wild" animals in McQuacker v. Goddard, [1940] 1 K.B. 687, and Nada Shah v. Sleeman, 1917, 19 West.Aust.L.Rep. 119; but the contrary was held in Gooding v. Chutes Co., 1909, 155 Cal. 620, 102 P. 819.

§ 77

1. See Beaulieu v. Fingham, 1401, Y.B. 2 Hen. 4, 18, pl. 61; Tubervil v. Stamp, 1697, variously reported in 1 Salk. 13, 1 Ld.Raym. 264, Carthew 425, 91 Eng.Rep. 1072. The allegation was for "negligently" keeping the fire; but it seems clear that this meant less than the modern significance of negligence, and the only uncertainty is as to how much less. See Wigmore, Re-

restatement /5 torts /p wild domestic! /s animal* synopsis,digest(liab! /p wild domestic! /2 animal*) 28k69

---

§ 77. Fire

The dangerous potentialities of fire seem to have been recognized very early. Something approaching strict liability for fire apparently was imposed upon landholders by the early common law, although it is a matter of dispute just what its limitations may have been.[1] Certainly some excuses were recognized, such as the intervention of an act of God, or the act of a stranger.[2] But whatever the early rule may have been, it was altered by a statute passed in 1707, and amended in 1774,[3] which provided that no action should be maintained against one in whose building or estate a fire accidentally began. Under this statute, the English courts have held that the landholder ordinarily is not liable,[4] unless the fire originates or spreads through his negligence,[5] or is intentionally set.[6] But where the fire has its origin in the course of an activity which is regarded as abnormally dangerous, even on the defendant's land, they have reverted to their present understanding of the earlier rule, and have held him to strict responsibili-

---

sponsibility for Tortious Acts: Its History, 1893, 7 Harv.L.Rev. 315, 448; Winfield, The Myth of Absolute Liability, 1926, 42 L.Q.Rev. 37, 46.

2. Tubervil v. Stamp, 1697, 1 Salk. 13, 1 Ld.Raym. 264, 91 Eng.Rep. 1072. Cf. Rayonier, Inc. v. United States, 9th Cir. 1955, 225 F.2d 642, vacated on other grounds 352 U.S. 315, 77 S.Ct. 374, 1 L.Ed.2d 354 (fire from other land sweeping across defendant's).

3. 6 Anne, c. 31, § 6, made permanent by 10 Anne, c. 14, § 1, later amended by 14 Geo. 3, c. 78, § 86.

4. Job Edwards, Ltd. v. Birmingham Navigations, [1924] 1 K.B. 341; Collingwood v. Home and Colonial Stores, [1936] 3 All Eng.Rep. 200.

5. Vaughan v. Menlove, 1837, 3 Bing. 468, 132 Eng. Rep. 490; Maclenan v. Segar, [1917] 2 K.B. 325; Sochacki v. Sas, [1947] 1 All Eng.Rep. 344; Vaughan v. Taff Vale R. Co., 1860, 5 H. & N. 679, 157 Eng.Rep. 1357; Howard v. Furness Houlder Argentine Lines, [1936] 2 All Eng.Rep. 781, 41 Com Cas. 290.

6. In Filliter v. Phippard, 1847, 11 Q.B. 347, 116 Eng.Rep. 506, the statute was held inapplicable to a fire intentionally kindled, as not of "accidental" origin.

ty.[7] Thus the owner of a steam engine, driven along the highway, has been held liable without negligence for sparks setting fire to a haystack.[8]

The American courts, influenced by the English statutes as a part of the common law taken over in this country,[9] have consistently rejected the older rule, and have held, in the absence of legislation, that there is no liability for the escape of fire where the defendant was not negligent.[10] It is recognized, of course, that fire is a dangerous thing, and a great amount of care is required in dealing with it.[11] There may be liability for negligence in starting a fire,[12] or in failing to take precautions against its occurrence, as where combustible materials are left unprotected,[13] or in failing to control it after it is started,[14] or neglecting to have the means to extinguish it at hand.[15] But its utility is so great, and it is so clearly sanctioned by universal use, that strict liability, even on the part of industrial enterprises, is not considered convenient or desirable.[16]

Statutes, however, in many states, have restored the rule of strict liability in certain very dangerous situations—as where a fire is set during a specified dry season,[17] or a prairie fire is started intentionally.[18] A very common type of statute makes railroad companies strictly liable, without negligence, for fires set by their locomotives,[19] or provides that the fire shall be "conclusive" as to negligence,[20] which of course amounts to the same thing. Such statutes have been held constitutional, as reasonable measures for the protection of property and the adjustment of an inevitable risk.[21] The only question in such a case is one of whether the fire was in fact started by the locomotive, which

---

7. See Bankes, L.J., in Musgrove v. Pandelis, [1919] 2 K.B. 43.

8. Mansell v. Webb, 1919, 88 L.J.K.B. 323; Powell v. Fall, 1880, 3 Q.B.D. 597; cf. Musgrove v. Pandelis, [1919] 2 K.B. 43. The same rule was applied to railway locomotives, Jones v. Festiniog R. Co., 1868, L.R. 3 Q.B. 733, except where they were run under statutory privilege. Vaughan v. Taff Vale R. Co., 1860, 5 H. & N. 678, 157 Eng.Rep. 1351; Canadian Pac. R. Co. v. Roy, [1902] A.C. 220. The liability of railways is now governed by special statute. See Attorney General v. Great Western R. Co., [1924] 2 K.B. 1.

9. Lansing v. Stone, N.Y.1862, 37 Barb. 15, 14 Abb. Prac. 199; Bachelder v. Heagan, 1840, 18 Me. 32.

10. B.W. King, Inc. v. Town of West New York, 1967, 49 N.J. 318, 230 A.2d 133; Clark v. Foot, N.Y. 1811, 8 Johns. 421; Fahn v. Reichart, 1859, 8 Wis. 255; Mitchell v. Reitchick, 1923, 123 Me. 30, 121 A. 91; Wallace v. New York, New Haven & Hartford Railroad Co., 1911, 208 Mass. 16, 94 N.E. 306.

11. Piraccini v. Director General of Railroads, 1920, 95 N.J.L. 114, 112 A. 311; Cobb v. Twitchell, 1926, 91 Fla. 539, 108 So. 186. In McNally v. Colwell, 1892, 91 Mich. 527, 52 N.W. 70, it is suggested that greater care is required as to an industrial fire than as to one in the home.

12. Burlington & Missouri River Railroad Co. v. Westover, 1876, 4 Neb. 268; Brummit v. Furness, 1891, 1 Ind.App. 401, 27 N.E. 656; Piraccini v. Director General of Railroads, 1920, 95 N.J.L. 114, 112 A. 311.

13. Eisenkramer v. Eck, 1924, 162 Ark. 501, 258 S.W. 368; Collins v. George, 1904, 102 Va. 509, 46 S.E. 684; Keyser Canning Co. v. Klots Throwing Co., 1923, 94 W.Va. 346, 118 S.E. 521; Phillips Petroleum Co. v. Berry, 1933, 188 Ark. 431, 65 S.W.2d 533; cf. Riley v. Standard Oil Co., 1934, 214 Wis. 15, 252 N.W. 183.

14. Cobb v. Twitchell, 1926, 91 Fla. 539, 108 So. 186; Farrell v. Minneapolis & Rainy River Railway Co., 1913, 121 Minn. 357, 141 N.W. 491; Sandberg v. Cavanaugh Timber Co., 1917, 95 Wash. 556, 164 P. 200.

15. McNally v. Colwell, 1892, 91 Mich. 527, 52 N.W. 70; Keyser Canning Co. v. Klots Throwing Co., 1923, 94 W.Va. 346, 118 S.E. 521.

16. O'Day v. Shouvlin, 1922, 104 Ohio St. 519, 136 N.E. 289.

17. See Seckerson v. Sinclair, 1913, 24 N.D. 625, 140 N.W. 239; Thorburn v. Campbell, 1890, 80 Iowa 338, 45 N.W. 769.

18. See Interstate Galloway Cattle Co. v. Kline, 1893, 51 Kan. 23, 32 P. 628; State v. Phillips, 1929, 176 Minn. 472, 233 N.W. 912.

19. Peck Iron & Metal Co. v. Seaboard Air Line Railway Co., 1959, 200 Va. 698, 107 S.E.2d 421; Baltimore & Ohio Railroad Co. v. Kreager, 1899, 61 Ohio St. 312, 56 N.E. 203; Hooksett v. Concord Railroad Co., 1859, 38 N.H. 242; Fleming v. Southern Railway Co., 1922, 120 S.C. 242, 113 S.E. 73; Carr v. Davis, 1924, 159 Minn. 485, 199 N.W. 237. A striking case is Dickelman Manufacturing Co. v. Pennsylvania Railroad Co., N.D.Ohio 1929, 34 F.2d 70, where the railroad was held liable for a fire resulting from a train wreck, caused by an undiscoverable defect in a car which it was required by law to accept and transport.

20. See Schaff v. Coyle, 1926, 121 Okl. 228, 249 P. 947; and cf. Martin v. New York & New England Railroad Co., 1892, 62 Conn. 331, 25 A. 239 (presumption).

21. St. Louis & San Francisco Railroad Co. v. Mathews, 1896, 165 U.S. 1, 17 S.Ct. 243, 41 L.Ed. 611; Union Pacific Railroad Co. v. De Busk, 1886, 12 Colo. 294, 20 P. 752; Grissell v. Housatonic Railroad Co., 1886, 54 Conn. 447, 9 A. 137.

is frequently one of circumstantial evidence.²² Presumptions have been created in many jurisdictions to aid the plaintiff in his proof, based on the passage of an engine shortly before the fire begins, or proof of the emission of sparks, or similar facts.²³

Again the question of the extent of the liability created by such statutes is more conveniently left to a later section.²⁴

 WESTLAW REFERENCES
topic(320) /p fire*

§ 78. Abnormally Dangerous Things and Activities

English Cases

The doctrine of strict liability for abnormally dangerous conditions and activities ¹ is a comparatively recent one in the law. The leading case from which it has developed is Rylands v. Fletcher,² decided in England in 1868. The defendants, mill owners in Lancashire, constructed a reservoir upon their land. The water broke through into the disused and filled-up shaft of an abandoned coal mine, and flooded along connecting passages into the adjoining mine of the plaintiff. The actual work was done by independent contractors, who were probably negligent,³ but the arbitrator who stated the case found that the defendants themselves were ignorant of the existence of the old coal workings, and free from all personal blame. No trespass could be found, since the flooding was not direct or immediate; nor any nuisance, as the term was then understood, since there was nothing offensive to the senses and the damage was not continuous or recurring. But it was held, upon the analogy of the strict liability for trespassing cattle, dangerous animals and "absolute" nuisance, which was extended to cover the facts in question, that the plaintiff might recover.

Justice Blackburn, in the Exchequer Chamber, used language which has been much quoted since, and is often erroneously said to be the "rule" of the case: "We think that the true rule of law is that the person who for his own purposes brings on his land and collects and keeps there anything likely to do mischief if it escapes, must keep it at his peril, and if he does not do so is prima facie answerable for all the damage which is the natural consequence of its escape." ⁴

In the House of Lords this broad statement was sharply limited, and placed upon a different footing. Lord Cairns said that the principle applied only to a "non-natural" use of the defendant's land, as distinguished from "any purpose for which it might in the ordinary course of the enjoyment of land be used." ⁵ The emphasis was thus shifted to the abnormal and inappropriate character of

---

22. See Harper and Harper, Establishing Railroad Liability for Fires, 1929, 77 U.Pa.L.Rev. 629; Note, 1937, 31 Ill.L.Rev. 549. The plaintiff has the burden of proof on the issue. State v. Pennsylvania Railroad Co., 1956, 101 Ohio App. 521, 136 N.E.2d 738.

23. Gibbons v. Wisconsin Valley Railroad Co., 1886, 66 Wis. 161, 28 N.W. 170; Nelson v. Chicago, Burlington & Quincy Railroad Co., 1924, 47 S.D. 228, 197 N.W. 288; Missoula Trust & Savings Bank v. Northern Pacific Railway Co., 1926, 76 Mont. 201, 245 P. 949; Stockdale v. Midland Valley Railroad Co., 1923, 113 Kan. 635, 215 P. 1021.

24. See infra, § 79.

§ 78

1. See, generally, Bohlen, The Rule in Rylands v. Fletcher, 1911, 59 U.Pa.L.Rev. 298; Pollock, Duties of Insuring Safety: The Rule in Rylands v. Fletcher, 1886, 2 L.Q.Rev. 52; Thayer, Liability Without Fault, 1916, 29 Harv.L.Rev. 801; Carpenter, The Doctrine of Green v. General Petroleum Corporation, 1932, 5 So. Cal.L.Rev. 263; Morris, Hazardous Enterprises and Risk Bearing Capacity, 1952, 61 Yale L.J. 1172; Stallybrass, Dangerous Things and the Non-Natural User of Land, 1929, 3 Camb.L.J. 376; Prosser, The Principle of Rylands v. Fletcher, in Prosser, Selected Topics in the Law of Torts, 1954, 134.

2. Fletcher v. Rylands, 1865, 3 H. & C. 774, 159 Eng.Rep. 737, reversed in Fletcher v. Rylands, 1866, L.R. 1 Ex. 265, affirmed in Rylands v. Fletcher, 1868, L.R. 3 H.L. 330.

3. The case arose eleven years before it was first held, in Bower v. Peate, 1876, 1 Q.B.D. 321, that an employer might be liable for the negligence of an independent contractor.

4. Fletcher v. Rylands, 1866, L.R. 1 Ex. 265, 279–80.

5. Rylands v. Fletcher, 1868, L.R. 3 H.L. 330, 338. The attempt of Newark, Non-Natural User and Rylands v. Fletcher, 1961, 24 Mod.L.Rev. 21, to explain

the defendant's reservoir in coal mining country, rather than the mere tendency of all water to escape.

More than a hundred subsequent decisions in British jurisdictions have fully borne out this interpretation of the case. The strict liability has been said many times to be confined to things or activities which are "extraordinary," [6] or "exceptional," [7] or "abnormal," [8] and not to apply to the "usual and normal." [9] There must be "some special use bringing with it increased danger to others, and must not merely be the ordinary use of land or such a use as is proper for the general benefit of the community." [10]

In determining what is a "non-natural use" the English courts have looked not only to the character of the thing or activity in question, but also to the place and manner in which it is maintained and its relation to its surroundings.[11] Water collected in large quantity in hydraulic power mains [12] a cellar,[13] or a plant for washing film,[14] all in dangerous proximity to the plaintiff's land, is a "non-natural use" for which there is strict liability. But water in a cistern,[15] in household pipes,[16] or in a barnyard tank supplying cattle,[17] is a natural use for which the defendant will not be liable in the absence of negligence. Gas [18] or electricity [19] in household pipes or wires is a natural use; gas in quantity [20] or high-powered electricity [21] under the street is another matter entirely. Fire in a fireplace [22] or in an authorized railway engine [23] is a normal thing, and so is a steam boiler on a ship;[24] but fire in an unlicensed

---

"natural" as meaning arising in the course of nature, appears to run counter to the language of the opinion, the cases cited, and certainly all the subsequent English interpretation of the case.

6. Kekewich, J., in National Tel. Co. v. Baker, [1893] 2 Ch. 186; Farwell, L.J., in West v. Bristol Tramways, [1908] 2 K.B. 14; Wright, J., in Noble v. Harrison, [1926] 2 K.B. 332.

7. Lord Buckmaster, in Rainham Chemical Works v. Belvedere Fish Guano Co., [1921] 2 A.C. 465, 471.

8. Farwell, L.J., in Barker v. Herbert, [1911] 2 K.B. 633, 645.

9. Wright, J., in Noble v. Harrison, [1926] 2 K.B. 332, 342; Fletcher Moulton, L.J., in Barker v. Herbert, [1911] 2 K.B. 633. Cf. Sutton and Ash v. Card, [1886] W.N. 120 ("ordinary way of using a man's own property").

10. Lord Moulton, in Rickards v. Lothian, [1913] A.C. 263, 280; Lord Wright, in Sedleigh-Denfield v. O'Callaghan, [1940] A.C. 880, 888; Scott, L.J., in Read v. J. Lyons & Co., 1944, 61 T.L.R. 149, 153; Bramwell, B., in Nichols v. Marsland, 1875, L.R. 10 Ex. 255, 259; Wright, J., in Blake v. Woolf, [1898] 2 Q.B. 426, 427.

11. Stallybrass, Dangerous Things and the Non-Natural User of Land, (1929) 3 Camb.L.J. 376, 387, comes to the conclusion that it is all a matter of relativity, and that "just as there is nothing which is at all times and in all circumstances dangerous, so it seems that there is scarcely anything which is in all circumstances safe." See also Fleming, Torts, 3d ed. 1965, 302–303.

12. Charing Cross Elec. Supply Co. v. Hydraulic Power Co., [1914] 3 K.B. 772.

13. Snow v. Whitehead, 1884, 27 Ch.Div. 588. Cf. Ballard v. Tomlinson, 1885, 29 Ch.Div. 115 (pollution of well by percolation).

14. Western Engraving Co. v. Film Laboratories, Ltd., [1936] 1 All Eng.Rep. 106.

15. Blake v. Land and House Property Corp., Q.B. 1887, 3 T.L.R. 667.

16. Rickards v. Lothian, [1913] A.C. 263; A. Prosser & Son, Ltd. v. Levy, [1955] 1 W.L.R. 1224; Tilley v. Stevenson, [1939] 4 All Eng.Rep. 207; Torette House v. Berkman, 1940, 62 Comm.L.Rep., Aust., 637. Cf. Ross v. Fedden, 1872, L.R. 7 Q.B. 661 (water closet); Peters v. Prince of Wales Theatre, [1943] K.B. 73 (sprinkler system).

17. Bartlett v. Tottenham, [1932] 1 Ch. 114.

18. Miller v. Robert Addie & Son's Collieries, [1934] S.C. 150.

19. Collingwood v. Home & Colonial Stores, [1936] 1 All Eng.Rep. 74; Spicer v. Smee, [1946] 1 All Eng. Rep. 489.

20. Northwestern Utilities v. London Guarantee & Accident Co., [1936] A.C. 108; Hanson v. Wearmouth Coal Co., [1939] 3 All Eng.Rep. 47; Batcheller v. Tunbridge Wells Gas Co., 1901, 84 T.L.R. 765.

21. National Tel. Co. v. Baker, [1893] 2 Ch. 186; Eastern & South African Tel. Co. v. Cape Town Tramways Co., [1902] A.C. 381; Midwood & Co. v. Manchester Corp., [1905] 2 K.B. 597.

22. Sochacki v. Sas, [1947] 1 All Eng.Rep. 344; Hazlewood v. Webber, 1934, 52 Comm.L.Rep., Aust., 268 (household cooking).

23. Vaughan v. Taff Vale R. Co., 1860, 5 H. & N. 679, 157 Eng.Rep. 1351.

24. Howard v. Furness Houlder Argentine Lines, [1936] 2 All Eng.Rep. 781, 41 Com.Cas. 290. Accord, Wise Bros. Pty. v. Commissioner for Railways, 1947, 75 Comm.L.Rep., Aust., 59 (in flour mill for manufacturing).

locomotive [25] or in a steam engine travelling on the highway and shooting out sparks [26] is not normal, and is a proper matter for strict liability. The automobile, dangerous and fatal to thousands as it undoubtedly is, is today a usual, customary phenomenon on the street, for which there is no strict liability,[27] but a ten ton traction engine [28] or a steam roller [29] which crushes conduits under the street is definitely extraordinary. The storage in quantity of explosives [30] or inflammable liquids,[31] or blasting,[32] or the accumulation of sewage,[33] or the emission of creosote fumes,[34] or pile driving which sets up excessive vibration,[35] all have the same element of the unusual, excessive and bizarre, and have been considered "non-natural" uses, leading to strict liability when they result in harm to another.

The place where all this occurs, the customs of the community, and the natural fitness or adaptation of the premises for the purpose, all are highly important in determining whether the rule applies. In Burma an elephant is not a non-natural creature, but a domestic animal, no more a subject for strict liability than a horse;[36] but the same elephant, transported to England in a circus, becomes an abnormal danger to that community.[37] Just so coal mining,[38] gravel pits,[39] and the removal of shingle from the seashore,[40] are regarded as natural uses of the particular land, since that is what such land is for; and it is only when the methods adopted are unusual or abnormal, as in the case of letting in a river [41] or pumping water to a level from which it will flow onto the plaintiff's land,[42] that the strict liability is held to apply.

In short, what emerges from the English decisions as the "rule" of Rylands v. Fletcher is that the defendant will be liable when he damages another by a thing or activity unduly dangerous and inappropriate to the

25. Jones v. Festiniog R. Co., 1868, L.R. 3 Q.B. 733.

26. Powell v. Fall, 1880, 5 Q.B.D. 597; Mansel v. Webb, 1918.

27. Wing v. London General Omnibus Co., [1909] 2 K.B. 652; Phillips v. Britannia Hygienic Laundry Co., [1923] 1 K.B. 539.

28. Chichester Corp. v. Foster, [1906] 1 K.B. 167.

29. Gas Light & Coke Co. v. Vestry of St. Mary Abbott's, 1885, 15 Q.B.D. 1.

30. Rainham Chemical Works v. Belvedere Fish Guano Co., [1921] 2 A.C. 465; J.P. Porter v. Bell, [1955] 1 Dom.L.Rep. 62.

31. Mulholland & Tedd, Ltd. v. Baker, [1939] 3 All Eng.Rep. 253; Smith v. Great Western R. Co., 1926, 135 L.T. 112; Ekstrom v. Deagon & Montgomery, [1946] 1 Dom.L.Rep. 208.

32. Miles v. Forest Rock Granite Co., 1918, 34 T.L.R. 500.

33. Humphries v. Cousins, 1877, 2 C.P.Div. 239; Jones v. Llanrwst Urban District Council, [1911] 1 Ch. 393.

34. West v. Bristol Tramways, [1908] 2 K.B. 14. Accord, Halsey v. Esso Petroleum Co., [1961] 1 W.L.R. 683. See Note, [1961] Camb.L.J. 168.

35. Hoare & Co. v. McAlpine, [1923] 1 Ch. 167. Compare the following:

"Natural" uses: Wilkins v. Leighton, [1932] 2 Ch. 106 (ordinary building); Noble v. Harrison, [1926] 2 K.B. 332 (ordinary tree); Ilford Urban District Council v. Beal and Judd, [1925] 1 K.B. 671 (retaining wall); Barker v. Herbert, [1911] 2 K.B. 633 (area protected by a railing); Haseldine v. C.A. Dow & Son, Ltd., [1941] 3 K.B. 343 (elevator in apartment building).

"Non-natural" uses: Attorney-General v. Cory Bros. & Co., [1921] 1 A.C. 521 (pile of sliding coal mine refuse); Hurdman v. North Eastern R. Co., 1878, 3 C.P. Div. 168 (artificial mound shedding water); Cheater v. Cater, [1918] 1 K.B. 247 (poisonous tree); Hale v. Jennings Bros., [1938] 1 All Eng.Rep. 579 (centrifugal amusement device whirling chairs at a giddy angle); Shiffman v. Order of St. John, [1936] 1 All Eng.Rep. 557 (unsafe flagpole in the wrong place).

36. Maung Hyan Dun v. Ma Kyian, 1900, 2 Upper Burma Rulings (Civ.) 570.

37. Behrens v. Bertram Mills Circus, [1957] 2 Q.B. 1.

38. Smith v. Kenrick, 1849, 7 C.B. 515, 137 Eng. Rep. 205; Wilson v. Waddell, 1876, 2 A.C. 95; Westhoughton Coal & Cannel Co. v. Wigan Coal Corp., [1939] Ch. 800.

39. Rouse v. Gravelworks, Ltd., [1940] 1 K.B. 489.

40. Attorney-General v. Tomline, 1879, 12 Ch.Div. 214.

41. Compton v. Lea, 1874, 19 Eq. 115.

42. Baird v. Williamson, 1863, 15 C.B., N.S., 376, 143 Eng.Rep. 531; Westminster Brymbo Coal & Coke Co. v. Clayton, 1867, 36 L.J.Ch. 476; Hodgkinson v. Ennor, 1863, 4 B. & S. 229, 122 Eng.Rep. 446 (discharging pollution into stream); West Cumberland Iron & Steel Co. v. Kenyon, 1877 L.R. 6 Ch.Div. 773 ("any means not in the ordinary and proper course of working his mine").

place where it is maintained, in the light of the character of that place and its surroundings.[43]

In 1947 the House of Lords abruptly put a stop to the expansion of the doctrine of Rylands v. Fletcher, in a case [44] in which a government inspector was injured by an explosion in the defendant's munitions plant. On its face the case looks like one in which the plaintiff might have been held to have assumed the risk;[45] but the court elected instead to limit the principle of strict liability to cases in which there has been an "escape" of a dangerous substance from land under the control of the defendant. Two of the judges [46] thought that it was not applicable at all to cases of personal injury. The decision appears definitely out of line with other English cases;[47] and if it is to be followed, which is not yet entirely certain as to either point,[48] it is at least a sudden, and rather unexplained, reversal of what had before appeared to be a definite trend in the English law.

American Cases—Prosser's Interpretation in the 1971 Edition

In the United States Rylands v. Fletcher was promptly accepted by the courts of Massachusetts and Minnesota.[49] Almost immediately afterward the whole doctrine was received with a triple bath of ice water, and entirely repudiated, by decisions in New Hampshire,[50] New York,[51] and New Jersey.[52] Two of these cases involved the explosion of ordinary steam boilers, and the third a runaway horse on the highway. They were obviously cases of customary, natural uses, to which the English courts would never have applied the rule.[53] In all three cases the attack was directed at Blackburn's broad statement in the intermediate court, and the final decision of the House of Lords was ignored. Rylands v. Fletcher was treated as holding that the defendant is absolutely liable in all cases whenever anything under his control escapes and does damage. In other words, the law of the case was misstated, and as misstated rejected, on facts to which it had no proper application in the first place.

On the heels of these decisions, the doctrine was condemned by legal writers [54] as an unjustifiable extension of liability to unavoidable accidents, in a field where the law of negligence, aided by the principle of res ipsa loquitur, would be adequate to cover the cases where recovery should be allowed.

---

43. Cf. Sutherland, J., in Village of Euclid v. Ambler Realty Co., 1926, 272 U.S. 365, 388, 47 S.Ct. 114, 118, 71 L.Ed. 303, speaking of nuisance: " * * * merely the right thing in the wrong place—like a pig in the parlor instead of the barnyard." See Prosser, The Principle of Rylands v. Fletcher, in Prosser, Selected Topics on the Law of Torts, 1954, 134–149.

44. Read v. J. Lyons & Co., Ltd., [1947] A.C. 156.

45. Cf. E.I. Du Pont De Nemours & Co. v. Cudd, 10th Cir. 1949, 176 F.2d 855, as to an employee.

46. Per Lord Macmillan, at p. 173, and Lord Uthwatt, at 186.

47. Cf. Hoare & Co. v. McAlpine, [1923] 1 Ch. 167 (vibration); Midwood v. Mayor of Manchester, [1905] 2 K.B. 597 (fusing of defendant's electric cable under the public highway); Powell v. Fall, 1880, 5 Q.B.D. 597 (engine emitting sparks on the highway); Mansel v. Webb, 1918, 88 L.J.K.B. 323 (same); Rainham Chemical Works v. Belvedere Fish Guano Co., [1921] 2 A.C. 465. As to personal injuries, see Miles v. Forest Rock Granite Co., 1918, 34 T.L.R. 500; Shiffman v. Order of St. John, [1936] 1 All Eng.Rep. 557; Hale v. Jennings Bros., [1938] 1 All Eng.Rep. 579; Schubert v. Sterling Trust Co., [1943] 4 Dom.L.Rep. 584.

48. As to "escape," the case was followed in Barrette v. Franki Compressed Pile Co., [1955] 2 Dom.L. Rep. 665, in holding that vibration is not a matter for strict liability. As to personal injuries, it was disregarded in Aldridge v. Van Patter, [1952] 4 Dom.L.Rep. 93, and in Perry v. Kendrick's Transp., [1956] 1 W.L.R. 85, 92.

49. Ball v. Nye, 1868, 99 Mass. 582 (percolation of filthy water); Cahill v. Eastman, 1871, 18 Minn. 324 (underground water tunnel broke through into plaintiff's property).

50. Brown v. Collins, 1873, 53 N.H. 442.

51. Losee v. Buchanan, 1873, 51 N.Y. 476.

52. Marshall v. Welwood, 1876, 38 N.J.L. 339.

53. Cf. Howard v. Furness Houlder Argentine Lines, [1936] 2 All Eng.Rep. 781, 41 Com.Cas. 290; Huff v. Austin, 1889, 46 Ohio St. 386, 21 N.E. 864.

54. Holmes, The Theory of Torts, 1873, 7 Am.L. Rev. 652; Thayer, Liability Without Fault, 1916, 29 Harv.L.Rev. 801; Smith, Tort and Absolute Liability, 1917, 30 Harv.L.Rev. 241, 319, 408. Cf. Pollock, Duties of Insuring Safety: The Rule in Rylands v. Fletcher, 1886, 2 L.Q.Rev. 52.

One important reason often given for the rejection of the strict liability was that it was not adapted to an expanding civilization. Dangerous enterprises, involving a high degree of risk to others, were clearly indispensable to the industrial and commercial development of a new country and it was considered that the interests of those in the vicinity of such enterprises must give way to them, and that too great a burden must not be placed upon them.[55] With the disappearance of the frontier, and the development of the country's resources, it was to be expected that the force of this objection would be weakened, and that it would be replaced in time by the view that the hazardous enterprise, even though it be socially valuable, must pay its way, and make good the damage inflicted. After a long period during which Rylands v. Fletcher was rejected by the large majority of the American courts which considered it,[56] the pendulum has swung to acceptance of the case and its doctrine in the United States.

At this writing, Rylands v. Fletcher still is rejected by name in seven American jurisdictions: Maine,[57] New Hampshire,[58] New York,[59] Oklahoma,[60] Rhode Island,[61] Texas,[62] and probably Wyoming.[63] It has been approved by name, or a statement of principle clearly derived from it has been accepted, in some thirty jurisdictions, with the number expanding at the rate of about one a year.[64]

The conditions and activities to which the rule has been applied have followed the English pattern. They include water collected in quantity in a dangerous place,[65] or allowed to percolate;[66] explosives[67] or inflammable liquids[68] stored in quantity in the

---

55. On this basis, it had been held, in earlier cases, that the owners of mill dams in the natural bed of streams were not liable, in the absence of negligence, for the escape of the water. Shrewsbury v. Smith, 1853, 66 Mass. (12 Cush.) 177; Livingston v. Adams, N.Y.1828, 8 Cow. 175; Everett v. Hydraulic Flume Tunnel Co., 1863, 23 Cal. 225. Again, surely, a "natural use."

56. It is still commonly, and erroneously, said that Rylands v. Fletcher is rejected by the great majority of the American courts. The writer pleads guilty. Prosser, Torts, 1st ed. 1941, 452.

57. Reynolds v. W.H. Hinman Co., 1950, 145 Me. 343, 75 A.2d 802.

58. Brown v. Collins, 1873, 53 N.H. 442; Garland v. Towne, 1874, 55 N.H. 55.

59. Losee v. Buchanan, 1873, 51 N.Y. 476; cf. Cosulich v. Standard Oil Co., 1890, 122 N.Y. 118, 25 N.E. 259.

60. Gulf Pipe Line Co. v. Sims, 1934, 168 Okl. 209, 32 P.2d 902; Sinclair Prairie Oil Co. v. Stell, 1942, 190 Okl. 344, 124 P.2d 255. See Foster and Keeton, Liability Without Fault in Oklahoma, 1950, 3 Okl.L.Rev. 1, 172.

61. Rose v. Socony-Vacuum Corp., 1934, 54 R.I. 411, 173 A. 627.

62. Gulf, Colorado & Santa Fe Railway Co. v. Oakes, 1900, 94 Tex. 155, 58 S.W. 999; Turner v. Big Lake Oil Co., 1936, 128 Tex. 155, 96 S.W.2d 221. See Prosser, Nuisance Without Fault, 1942, 20 Tex.L.Rev. 399.

63. Jacoby v. Town of City of Gillette, 1947, 62 Wyo. 487, 174 P.2d 505.

64. See for example Healey v. Citizens Gas & Electric Co., 1924, 199 Iowa 82, 201 N.W. 118; Central Exploration Co. v. Gray, 1954, 219 Miss. 757, 70 So.2d 33; Thigpen v. Skousen & Hise, 1958, 64 N.M. 290, 327 P.2d 802; Berg v. Reaction Motors Division, Thiokol Chemical Corp., 1962, 37 N.J. 396, 181 A.2d 487; Loe v. Lenhardt, 1961, 227 Or. 242, 362 P.2d 312; Enos Coal Mining Co. v. Schuchart, 1962, 243 Ind. 692, 188 N.E.2d 406; Wallace v. A.H. Guion & Co., 1960, 237 S.C. 349, 117 S.E.2d 359.

65. Wilson v. City of New Bedford, 1871, 108 Mass. 261; Defiance Water Co. v. Olinger, 1896, 54 Ohio St. 532, 44 N.E. 238; Bridgeman-Russell Co. v. City of Duluth, 1924, 158 Minn. 509, 197 N.W. 971; Weaver Mercantile Co. v. Thurmond, 1911, 68 W.Va. 530, 70 S.E. 126; Smith v. Board of County Road Commissioners of Chippewa County, 1966, 5 Mich.App. 370, 146 N.W.2d 702, affirmed 381 Mich. 363, 161 N.W.2d 561. Cf. Kennecott Copper Corp. v. McDowell, 1966, 100 Ariz. 276, 413 P.2d 749 (water in stream diverted against bridge).

66. Ball v. Nye, 1868, 99 Mass. 582; Kall v. Carruthers, 1922, 59 Cal.App. 555, 211 P. 43; Healey v. Citizens Gas & Electric Co., 1924, 199 Iowa 82, 201 N.W. 118; Norfolk & Western Railway Co. v. Amicon Fruit Co., 4th Cir. 1920, 269 F. 559.

67. Exner v. Sherman Power Construction Co., 2d Cir. 1931, 54 F.2d 510; Bradford Glycerine Co. v. St. Mary's Woolen Manufacturing Co., 1899, 60 Ohio St. 560, 54 N.E. 528; French v. Center Creek Powder Manufacturing Co., 1913, 173 Mo.App. 220, 158 S.W. 723; cf. Koster & Wythe v. Massey, 9th Cir. 1961, 293 F.2d 922, certiorari denied 368 U.S. 927, 82 S.Ct. 362, 7 L.Ed. 2d 191 (incendiary bomb). See Notes, 1932, 17 Corn. L.Q. 703; 1966, 39 U.Colo.L.Rev. 161.

68. Brennan Construction Co. v. Cumberland, 1907, 29 U.S.App.D.C. 554; Berger v. Minneapolis Gaslight Co., 1895, 60 Minn. 296, 62 N.W. 336; Yommer v. McKenzie, 1969, 255 Md. 220, 257 A.2d 138. Cf. MacKen-

midst of a city; blasting;[69] pile driving;[70] crop dusting;[71] the fumigation of part of a building with cyanide gas;[72] drilling oil wells or operating refineries in thickly settled communities;[73] an excavation letting in the sea;[74] factories emitting smoke, dust or noxious gases in the midst of a town;[75] roofs so constructed as to shed snow into a highway;[76] and a dangerous party wall.[77]

On the other hand the conditions and activities to which the American courts have refused to apply Rylands v. Fletcher, whether they purport to accept or to reject the case in principle, have been with few exceptions what the English courts would regard as a "natural" use of land, and not within the rule at all. They include water in household pipes,[78] the tank of a humidity system,[79] or authorized utility mains;[80] gas in a meter,[81] electric wiring in a machine shop,[82] and gasoline in a filling station;[83] a dam in the natural bed of a stream;[84] ordinary steam boilers;[85] an ordinary fire in a factory;[86] an automobile;[87] Bermuda grass on a

---

zie v. Fitchburg Paper Co., 1966, 351 Mass. 292, 218 N.E.2d 579 (dumping inflammable ink at city dump).

69. Caporale v. C.W. Blakeslee & Sons, Inc., 1961, 149 Conn. 79, 175 A.2d 561; Sachs v. Chiat, 1968, 281 Minn. 540, 162 N.W.2d 243.

70. Colton v. Onderdonk, 1886, 69 Cal. 155, 10 P. 395; Britton v. Harrison Construction Co., S.D.W.Va. 1948, 87 F.Supp. 405; Central Exploration Co. v. Gray, 1954, 219 Miss. 757, 70 So.2d 33; Brown v. L.S. Lunder Construction Co., 1942, 240 Wis. 122, 2 N.W.2d 859; Davis v. L. & W. Construction Co., Iowa 1970, 176 N.W.2d 223; see McNeal, Use of Explosives and Liability Questions Involved, 1956, 23 Ins.Counsel J. 125.

71. Young v. Darter, Okl.1961, 363 P.2d 829; Loe v. Lenhardt, 1961, 227 Or. 242, 362 P.2d 312; Gotreaux v. Gary, La.App., 1957, 232 La. 373, 94 So.2d 293, appeal transferred 80 So.2d 578.

Contra: S.A. Gerrard Co. v. Fricker, 1933, 42 Ariz. 503, 27 P.2d 678; Miles v. A. Arena & Co., 1937, 23 Cal. App.2d 680, 73 P.2d 1260; Lawler v. Skelton, 1961, 241 Miss. 274, 130 So.2d 565. See Notes, 1968, 19 Hast.L.J. 476; 1962, 40 Tex.L.Rev. 527; 1963, 49 Iowa L.Rev. 135.

72. Luthringer v. Moore, 1948, 31 Cal.2d 489, 190 P.2d 1.

73. Green v. General Petroleum Corp., 1928, 205 Cal. 328, 270 P. 952; Niagara Oil Co. v. Jackson, 1910, 48 Ind.App. 238, 91 N.E. 825; Helms v. Eastern Kansas Oil Co., 1917, 102 Kan. 164, 169 P. 208; Berry v. Shell Petroleum Co., 1934, 140 Kan. 94, 33 P.2d 953, rehearing denied, 1935, 141 Kan. 6, 40 P.2d 359. Cf. State Highway Commission v. Empire Oil & Refining Co., 1935, 141 Kan. 161, 40 P.2d 355. See Green, Hazardous Oil and Gas Operations: Tort Liability, 1955, 33 Tex.L.Rev. 574.

74. Mears v. Dole, 1883, 135 Mass. 508.

75. Susquehanna Fertilizer Co. v. Malone, 1890, 73 Md. 268, 20 A. 900; Frost v. Berkeley Phosphate Co., 1894, 42 S.C. 402, 20 S.E. 280; Holman v. Athens Empire Laundry Co., 1919, 149 Ga. 345, 100 S.E. 207.

76. Shipley v. Fifty Associates, 1869, 101 Mass. 251, affirmed 1870, 106 Mass. 194; Hannem v. Pence, 1889, 40 Minn. 127, 41 N.W. 657.

77. Gorham v. Gross, 1878, 125 Mass. 232.

78. McCord Rubber Co. v. St. Joseph Water Co., 1904, 181 Mo. 678, 81 S.W. 189; Stevens-Salt Lake City, Inc. v. Wong, 1953, 123 Utah 309, 259 P.2d 586; Shanander v. Western Loan & Building Co., 1951, 103 Cal.App.2d 507, 229 P.2d 864.

79. Fibre Leather Manufacturing Corp. v. Ramsay Mills, Inc., 1952, 329 Mass. 575, 109 N.E.2d 910.

80. Midwest Oil Co. v. City of Aberdeen, 1943, 69 S.D. 343, 10 N.W.2d 701; Interstate Sash & Door Co. v. City of Cleveland, 1947, 148 Ohio St. 325, 74 N.E.2d 239; Grace & Co. v. City of Los Angeles, S.D.Cal.1958, 168 F.Supp. 344, affirmed 9th Cir.1960, 278 F.2d 771. But a city which deliberately adopted a policy of burying cast iron pipe six feet underground and leaving it there until leaks developed, was held to strict liability in Lubin v. Iowa City, 1964, 257 Iowa 383, 131 N.W.2d 765.

81. Triple-State Natural Gas & Oil Co. v. Wellman, 1902, 114 Ky. 79, 70 S.W. 49. Cf. St. Mary's Gas Co. v. Brodbeck, 1926, 114 Ohio St. 423, 151 N.E. 323.

82. Mangan's Administrator v. Louisville Electric Light Co., 1906, 122 Ky. 476, 91 S.W. 703. Cf. McKenzie v. Pacific Gas & Electric Co., 1962, 200 Cal.App.2d 731, 19 Cal.Rptr. 628 (power line).

83. Greene v. Spinning, Mo.App.1932, 48 S.W.2d 51. Cf. Collins v. Liquid Transporters, Inc., Ky.1953, 262 S.W.2d 382 (tank trucks on highway).

84. City Water Power Co. v. City of Fergus Falls, 1910, 113 Minn. 33, 128 N.W. 817; Barnum v. Handschiegel, 1919, 103 Neb. 594, 173 N.W. 593; McHenry v. Ford Motor Co., E.D.Mich.1956, 146 F.Supp. 896, affirmed, 6th Cir.1959, 261 F.2d 833, rehearing 269 F.2d 18; New Brantner Extension Ditch Co. v. Ferguson, 1957, 134 Colo. 502, 307 P.2d 479. Cf. Esson v. Wattier, 1893, 25 Or. 7, 34 P. 756; Clark v. United States, D.Or.1952, 109 F.Supp. 213, affirmed 9th Cir.1955, 218 F.2d 446.

85. Huff v. Austin, 1889, 46 Ohio St. 386, 21 N.E. 864; Losee v. Buchanan, 1873, 51 N.Y. 476; Marshall v. Welwood, 1876, 38 N.J.L. 339. Cf. Fritz v. E. I. Du Pont De Nemours & Co., 1950, 45 Del. (6 Terry) 427, 75 A.2d 256 (chlorine gas in industrial plant where specific use not shown).

86, 87. See notes 86 and 87 on page 551.

railroad right of way;[88] a small quantity of dynamite kept for sale in a Texas hardware store;[89] barnyard spray in a farmhouse;[90] a division fence;[91] the wall of a house left standing after a fire;[92] coal mining operations regarded as usual and normal;[93] vibrations from ordinary building construction;[94] earth moving operations in grading a hillside;[95] the construction of a railroad tunnel;[96] and even a runaway horse.[97] There remain a few cases, including such things as water reservoirs or irrigation ditches in dry country,[98] or properly conducted[99] oil wells in Texas[1] or Oklahoma,[2] which are undoubtedly best explained upon the basis of a different community view which makes such things "natural" to the particular locality. The conclusion is, in short, that the American decisions, like the English ones, have applied the principle of Rylands v. Fletcher only to the thing out of place, the abnormally dangerous condition or activity which is not a "natural" one where it is.[3]

The Restatement of Torts[4] has accepted the principle of Rylands v. Fletcher, but has limited it to an "ultrahazardous activity" of the defendant, defined as one which "necessarily involves a risk of serious harm to the person, land or chattels of others which cannot be eliminated by the exercise of the utmost care," and "is not a matter of common usage." This goes beyond the English rule in ignoring the relation of the activity to its surroundings, and falls short of it in the insistence on extreme danger and the impossibility of eliminating it with all possible care. The shift of emphasis is not at all reflected in the American cases, which have laid quite as much stress as the English ones upon the place where the thing is done.[5]

---

86. O'Day v. Shouvlin, 1922, 17 Ohio App. 62, affirmed 104 Ohio St. 519, 136 N.E. 289.

87. Steffen v. McNaughton, 1910, 142 Wis. 49, 124 N.W. 1016.

88. Gulf, Colorado & Santa Fe Railway Co. v. Oakes, 1900, 94 Tex. 155, 58 S.W. 999.

89. Barnes v. Zettlemoyer, 1901, 25 Tex.Civ.App. 468, 62 S.W. 111. Cf. Henn v. Universal Atlas Cement Co., Ohio Com.Pl.1957, 144 N.E.2d 917 (blasting in a rural area, causing vibration).

90. Branstetter v. Robbins, 1955, 178 Kan. 8, 283 P.2d 455.

91. Quinn v. Crimmings, 1898, 171 Mass. 255, 50 N.E. 624.

92. Ainsworth v. Lakin, 1902, 180 Mass. 397, 62 N.E. 746.

93. Pennsylvania Coal Co. v. Sanderson, 1886, 113 Pa. 126, 6 A. 453; Kentucky Block Fuel Co. v. Roberts, 1925, 207 Ky. 137, 268 S.W. 802; Venzel v. Valley Camp Coal Co., 1931, 304 Pa. 583, 156 A. 240; Jones v. Robertson, 1886, 116 Ill. 543, 6 N.E. 890.

94. Gallin v. Poulou, 1956, 140 Cal.App.2d 638, 295 P.2d 958.

95. Beck v. Bel Air Properties, 1955, 134 Cal.App.2d 834, 286 P.2d 503.

96. Marin Municipal Water District v. Northwestern Pacific Railroad Co., 1967, 253 Cal.App.2d 83, 61 Cal.Rptr. 520.

97. Brown v. Collins, 1873, 53 N.H. 442.

98. Turner v. Big Lake Oil Co., 1936, 128 Tex. 155, 96 S.W.2d 221; Anderson v. Rucker Brothers, 1919, 107 Wash. 595, 183 P. 70, affirmed 107 Wash. 595, 186 P. 293; Clark v. Di Prima, 1966, 241 Cal.App.2d 823, 51 Cal.Rptr. 49; Jacoby v. Town of City of Gillette, 1947, 62 Wyo. 487, 174 P.2d 505, rehearing denied 62 Wyo. 487, 177 P.2d 204. Contra, Union Pacific Railroad Co. v. Vale, Oregon Irrigation District, D.Or.1966, 253 F.Supp. 251; see Note, 1967, 46 Or.L.Rev. 239.

99. Otherwise where the operation is abnormal. Teel v. Rio Bravo Oil Co., 1907, 47 Tex.Civ.App. 153, 104 S.W. 420.

1. Turner v. Big Lake Oil Co., 1936, 128 Tex. 155, 96 S.W.2d 221; Cosden Oil Co. v. Sides, Tex.Civ.App. 1931, 35 S.W.2d 815; cf. East Texas Oil Refining Co. v. Mabee Consolidated Corp., Tex.Civ.App.1937, 103 S.W.2d 795, appeal dismissed 1939, 133 Tex. 300, 127 S.W.2d 445 (pipe line). See Green, Hazardous Oil and Gas Operations: Tort Liability, 1955, 33 Tex.L.Rev. 574.

2. Tidal Oil Co. v. Pease, 1931, 153 Okl. 137, 5 P.2d 389; Gulf Pipe Line Co. v. Alred, 1938, 182 Okl. 400, 77 P.2d 1155; Sinclair Prairie Oil Co. v. Stell, 1942, 190 Okl. 344, 124 P.2d 255. Cf. United Fuel Gas Co. v. Sawyers, Ky.1953, 259 S.W.2d 466. See Note, 1967, 20 Okl.L.Rev. 86.

3. See Prosser, The Principle of Rylands v. Fletcher, in Selected Topics on the Law of Torts, 1953, 135.

4. Sections 519, 520.

5. Tentative Draft No. 10 of the Second Restatement of Torts, § 520, tentatively approved by the American Law Institute, has eliminated "ultrahazardous" in favor of "abnormally dangerous," and has stated six factors to be considered, one of which is "whether the activity is inappropriate to the place where it is carried on." This was accepted and applied in Yommer v. McKenzie, 1969, 255 Md. 220, 257 A.2d 138, where gasoline was stored in a rural community, in dangerous proximity to the plaintiff's well. See also McLane v. Northwest Natural Gas Co., 1969, 255 Or. 324, 467 P.2d 635.

Actually even the jurisdictions which reject Rylands v. Fletcher by name have accepted and applied the principle of the case under the cloak of various other theories.[6] Most frequently, in all of the American courts, the same strict liability is imposed upon defendants under the name of nuisance.

The "absolute nuisances"[7] for which strict liability is found without intent to do harm or negligence fall into categories already familiar. They include water collected in quantity in the wrong place,[8] or allowed to percolate;[9] explosives[10] or inflammable liquids[11] stored in quantity in thickly settled communities or in dangerous proximity to valuable property; blasting;[12] fireworks set off in the public streets;[13] oil wells[14] or abnormal mining operations;[15] the accumulation of sewage;[16] concussion or vibration from a rock crusher;[17] and in addition such things as smoke, dust, bad odors, noxious gases and the like from industrial enterprises,[18] all obviously closely related to the cases following Rylands v. Fletcher. There has been general recognition in these nuisance cases that the relation of the activity to its surroundings is the controlling factor; and a magazine of explosives or a huge tank full of gasoline in the midst of a populous city may be an absolute nuisance, where the

---

6. See Prosser, The Principle of Rylands v. Fletcher, in Prosser, Selected Topics on the Law of Torts, 1954, 135, 159–177.

7. See infra, § 88C. In England there has been little confusion, because it is recognized that the application of Rylands v. Fletcher is one basis for finding a nuisance. See Miles v. Forest Rock Granite Co., 1918, 34 T.L.R. 500; Hoare & Co. v. McAlpine, [1923] 1 Ch. 167, 92 L.J.Ch. 81; National Tel. Co. v. Baker, [1893] 2 Ch. 186, 62 L.J.Ch. 699. See Winfield, Nuisance as a Tort, 1931, 4 Camb.L.J. 189. Also Newark, The Boundaries of Nusiance, 1949, 65 L.Q.Rev. 480, 488, contending that Rylands v. Fletcher is but a branch of a broader principle of nuisance, differing only in that it permits recovery for an isolated incident.

8. Filtrol Corp. v. Hughes, 1945, 199 Miss. 10, 23 So.2d 891; Pruitt v. Bethell, 1917, 174 N.C. 454, 93 S.E. 945; De Vaughn v. Minor, 1887, 77 Ga. 809, 1 S.E. 433; Alabama Western Railroad Co. v. Wilson, 1911, 1 Ala. App. 306, 55 So. 932; Smith v. Board of County Road Commissioners, 1966, 5 Mich.App. 370, 146 N.W.2d 702, affirmed 381 Mich. 363, 161 N.W.2d 561.

9. Pixley v. Clark, 1866, 35 N.Y. 520; Goodyear Tire & Rubber Co. v. Gadsden Sand & Gravel Co., 1946, 248 Ala. 273, 27 So.2d 578; International & Great Northern Railroad Co. v. Slusher, 1906, 42 Tex.Civ. App. 631, 95 S.W. 717; City of Barberton v. Miksch, 1934, 128 Ohio St. 169, 190 N.E. 387.

10. Heeg v. Licht, 1880, 80 N.Y. 579; McAndrews v. Collerd, 1880, 42 N.J.L. 189; Comminge v. Stevenson, 1890, 76 Tex. 642, 13 S.W. 556; Forster v. Rogers, 1915, 247 Pa. 54, 93 A. 26; Cumberland Torpedo Co. v. Gaines, 1923, 201 Ky. 88, 255 S.W. 1046; St. Joseph Lead Co. v. Prather, 8th Cir. 1956, 238 F.2d 301.

11. Whittemore v. Baxter Laundry Co., 1914, 181 Mich. 564, 148 N.W. 437; Great Northern Refining Co. v. Lutes, 1921, 190 Ky. 451, 227 S.W. 795; McGuffey v. Pierce-Fordyce Oil Association, Tex.Civ.App.1919, 211 S.W. 335; O'Hara v. Nelson, 1906, 71 N.J.Eq. 161, 63 A. 836.

12. Gossett v. Southern Railway Co., 1905, 115 Tenn. 376, 89 S.W. 737; Blackford v. Heman Construction Co., 1908, 132 Mo.App. 157, 112 S.W. 287; Dixon v. New York Trap Rock Corp., 1944, 293 N.Y. 509, 58 N.E.2d 517, motion denied, 1945, 294 N.Y. 654, 60 N.E.2d 385; Fontenot v. Magnolia Petroleum Co, 1955, 227 La. 866, 80 So.2d 845; Opal v. Material Service Corp., 1956, 9 Ill.App.2d 433, 133 N.E.2d 733.

13. Landau v. City of New York, 1904, 180 N.Y. 48, 72 N.E. 631; Harris v. City of Findlay, 1938, 59 Ohio App. 375, 18 N.E.2d 413; Moore v. City of Bloomington, 1911, 51 Ind.App. 145, 95 N.E. 374.

14. Teel v. Rio Bravo Oil Co., 1907, 47 Tex.Civ.App. 153, 104 S.W.2d 420 (abnormal discharge of salt water); Niagara Oil Co. v. Ogle, 1912, 177 Ind. 292, 98 N.E. 60; McGregor v. Camden, 1899, 47 W.Va. 193, 34 S.E. 936. See Keeton and Jones, Tort Liability and the Oil and Gas Industry, 1956, 35 Tex.L.Rev. 1.

15. Jones v. Robertson, 1886, 116 Ill. 543, 6 N.E. 890; Beach v. Sterling Iron & Zinc Co., 1895, 54 N.J. Eq. 65, 33 A. 286, affirmed 55 N.J.Eq. 824, 41 A. 1117; Pennsylvania Railroad Co. v. Sagamore Coal Co., 1924, 281 Pa. 233, 126 A. 386, certiorari denied 267 U.S. 592, 45 S.Ct. 228, 69 L.Ed. 803; H. B. Bowling Coal Co. v. Ruffner, 1907, 117 Tenn. 180, 100 S.W. 116.

16. Jutte v. Hughes, 1876, 67 N.Y. 267; In re Haugh's Appeal, 1883, 102 Pa. 42; Ryan v. City of Emmetsburg, 1942, 232 Iowa 600, 4 N.W.2d 435.

17. Gilbert v. Davidson Construction Co., 1922, 110 Kan. 298, 203 P. 1113; Dilucehio v. Shaw, 1922, 31 Del. 509, 115 A. 771.

18. See for example Dutton v. Rocky Mountain Phosphates, 1968, 151 Mont. 54, 438 P.2d 674; Bartel v. Ridgefield Lumber Co., 1924, 131 Wash. 183, 229 P. 306; Susquehanna Fertilizer Co. v. Malone, 1890, 73 Md. 268, 20 A. 900; King v. Columbian Carbon Co., 5th Cir. 1945, 152 F.2d 636; Columbian Carbon Co. v. Tholen, Tex.Civ.App.1947, 199 S.W.2d 825, error refused.

same explosive [19] or inflammable liquid [20] in the wilderness or under less highly and obviously dangerous conditions is not. The "non-natural use" becomes an "unreasonable use." [21]

There is in fact probably no case applying Rylands v. Fletcher which is not duplicated in all essential respects by some American decision which proceeds on the theory of nuisance; [22] and it is quite evident that under that name the principle is in reality universally accepted.[23]

Blasting, which has been so commonly given as an illustration of an activity which falls clearly within Rylands v. Fletcher that it has come to typify all such activities, actually has run the gamut of all possible theories of liability.[24] The first cases to arise were those in which rocks were thrown upon the plaintiff's premises, and it was possible to impose strict liability upon the ground that there was a trespass to land.[25] The courts are still virtually unanimous in holding that there is such liability when this occurs,[26] or where some flying object strikes a person.[27] Where the damage is the result merely of concussion or vibration, some five or six continue to adhere to the ancient distinction between trespass and case,[28] and regard the injury as an "indirect" one, for which there can be no recovery except on the basis of negligence.[29] This distinction, which has often been denounced [30] as a marriage of procedural technicality with scientific ignorance, is rejected by the great majority of the courts, which hold the defendant

---

19. Tuckachinsky v. Lehigh & Wilkesbarre Coal Co., 1901, 199 Pa. 515, 49 A. 308; Kleebauer v. Western Fuse & Explosives Co., 1903, 138 Cal. 497, 71 P. 617; Henderson v. Sullivan, 6th Cir. 1908, 159 F. 46; Whaley v. Sloss-Sheffield Steel & Iron Co., 1909, 164 Ala. 216, 51 So. 419.

20. Thomas v. Jacobs, 1916, 254 Pa. 255, 98 A. 863; Adams Co. v. Buchanan, 1920, 42 S.D. 548, 176 N.W. 512; Shell Petroleum Co. v. Wilson, 1936, 178 Okl. 355, 65 P.2d 173; State ex rel. Stewart v. Cozad, 1923, 113 Kan. 200, 213 P. 654.

21. See infra, § 88.

22. Even Attorney-General v. Corke, [1933] Ch. 89, where the defendant's harboring of disreputable gypsies was held to come within Rylands v. Fletcher, finds a close parallel in the tenement full of Mexican peons in Harty v. Guerra, Tex.Civ.App.1925, 269 S.W. 1064, and the workhouse in District of Columbia v. Totten, D.C.Cir.1925, 5 F.2d 374. Compare also Shipley v. Fifty Associates, 1869, 101 Mass. 251, affirmed 1870, 106 Mass. 194 (roof shedding snow), with Davis v. Niagara Falls Tower Co., 1902, 171 N.Y. 336, 64 N.E. 4 (tower shedding ice).

23. See Prosser, Nuisance Without Fault, 1942, 20 Tex.L.Rev. 399; Notes, 1934, 29 Ill.L.Rev. 372; 1947, 95 U.Pa.L.Rev. 781.

24. See McNeal, Use of Explosives and Liability Questions Involved, 1956, 23 Ins.Counsel J. 125; Smith, Liability for Substantial Physical Damage to Land by Blasting, 1920, 33 Harv.L.Rev. 542, 667; Gregory, Trespass to Negligence to Absolute Liability, 1951, 37 Va.L.Rev. 359; Notes, 1910, 10 Col.L.Rev. 465; 1935, 19 Minn.L.Rev. 322; 1937, 16 Tex.L.Rev. 426; 1962, 40 N.C.L.Rev. 640.

25. See supra, § 13.

26. Hay v. Cohoes Co., 1849, 2 N.Y. 159; Mulchanock v. Whitehall Cement Manufacturing Co., 1916, 253 Pa. 262, 98 A. 554; Adams & Sullivan v. Sengel, 1917, 177 Ky. 535, 197 S.W. 974; Central Iron & Coal Co. v. Vanderheurk, 1906, 147 Ala. 546, 41 So. 145; Asheville Construction Co. v. Southern Railway Co., 4th Cir. 1927, 19 F.2d 32.

27. Sullivan v. Dunham, 1900, 161 N.Y. 290, 55 N.E. 923; Wells v. Knight, 1911, 32 R.I. 432, 80 A. 16; Louisville & Nashville Railroad Co. v. Smith's Administrator, 1923, 203 Ky. 513, 263 S.W. 29.

28. See supra, § 7.

29. Coalite, Inc. v. Aldridge, 1969, 285 Ala. 137, 229 So.2d 539, on remand 45 Ala.App. 721, 229 So.2d 541; Wadleigh v. City of Manchester, 1956, 100 N.H. 277, 123 A.2d 831; Albison v. Robbins & White, Inc., 1955, 151 Me. 114, 116 A.2d 608.

Kentucky and Vermont have recently abandoned this position. Lynn Mining Co. v. Kelly, Ky.1965, 394 S.W. 2d 755; Malloy v. Lane Construction Co., 1963, 123 Vt. 500, 194 A.2d 398. It has very probably received its death blow when New York joined them, in Spano v. Perini Corp., 1969, 25 N.Y.2d 11, 302 N.Y.S.2d 527, 250 N.E.2d 31, on remand 33 A.D.2d 516, 304 N.Y.S.2d 15.

30. Smith, Liability for Substantial Physical Damage to Land by Blasting, 1920, 33 Harv.L.Rev. 542, 667; Salmond, Law of Torts, 7th ed. 1928, 231; Notes, 1910, 10 Col.L.Rev. 465; 1935, 19 Minn.L.Rev. 322; 1937, 16 Tex.L.Rev. 426; 1967, 31 Alb.L.J. 370. It is, however, defended by Fleming, Torts, 3d ed. 1965, 40 on the basis that a nuisance action allows for reasonable use and abnormal sensitivity, while trespass does not. This may be valid as to the form of action, but scarcely as to the substance of strict liability.

There is excellent discussion in Louden v. City of Cincinnati, 1914, 90 Ohio St. 144, 106 N.E. 970; and in Watson v. Mississippi River Power Co., 1916, 174 Iowa 23, 156 N.W. 188.

strictly liable for concussion damage.[31] Many of the later cases [32] have come to the conclusion, which might be drawn with fair success from the facts of the entire group of blasting cases,[33] that the strict liability is entirely a question of the relation of the activity to its surroundings; and that the use of explosives on an uninhabited mountainside is a matter of negligence only, while any one who blasts in the center of a large city does so at his peril, and must bear the responsibility for the damage he does, despite all proper care.

Recent Developments and Reviser's Comments

The failure to make a careful distinction between intentional and accidental invasions of all kinds of interests has led to much confusion about strict liability, liability for trespass to land, and liability for a private nuisance. The "Trespass" [34] and "Private Nuisance" [35] chapters have been substantially revised for this reason. In some of the cases involving the so-called "escape of dangerous things," the courts have regarded the problem with which it was confronted as one relating to strict liability simply because defendant was exercising utmost care to avoid interference or harm in the way in which the condition was being maintained or the activity was being conducted although he knew to a substantial certainty that an invasion or harm of some kind would result.[36] When one knows that seismographic explosions on one's land will result in vibrations penetrating the land of another on, above, or beneath the surface, he intends those intrusions. The question then is what liability should result from intentionally causing such intrusions and thereby exposing the adjoining landowner to a risk of harm from such vibrations. The question may be similar to that when an unintended explosion causes vibrations, but it is not the same. The tort liability for harm arising from intentional intrusions on the land of another is dealt with in the chapter on "Private Nuisance." Such liability as is imposed is not regarded as strict liability because it is liability for harm arising out of intentional intrusions onto the land of another and often the risk of loss should be on the enterpriser who brings about such an intrusion, however reasonable the conduct may be. This is clearly so, if the defendant also knows that the intrusions intended will result either in physical harm or in some other kind of substantial interference with the use and enjoyment of adjoining land.

Strict liability as used in this edition refers to liability that is imposed apart from any recovery on a theory that defendant knowingly or purposely interfered with a legally protected interest or was negligent. Prosser concluded that the American decisions, like the English ones, have applied the principle of Rylands v. Fletcher only to the thing out of place, the abnormally dangerous condition or activity which is not a "natural" one where it is.[37] If, therefore, according to this idea the defendant was making a so-called

---

31. Western Geophysical Co. of America v. Mason, 1966, 240 Ark. 767, 402 S.W.2d 657; Enos Coal Mining Co. v. Schuchart, 1963, 243 Ind. 692, 188 N.E.2d 406; Wallace v. A. H. Guion & Co., 1960, 237 S.C. 349, 117 S.E.2d 359; Thigpen v. Skousen & Hise, 1958, 64 N.M. 290, 327 P.2d 802; Whitney v. Ralph Myers Contracting Corp., 1961, 146 W.Va. 130, 118 S.E.2d 622.

32. Robison v. Robison, 1964, 16 Utah 2d 2, 394 P.2d 876; Boonville Collieries Corp. v. Reynolds, 1960, 130 Ind.App. 331, 163 N.E.2d 627; Alonso v. Hills, 1950, 95 Cal.App.2d 778, 214 P.2d 50; Cashin v. Northern Pacific Railway Co., 1934, 96 Mont. 92, 28 P.2d 862; Carson v. Blodgett Construction Co., 1915, 189 Mo.App. 120, 174 S.W. 447.

33. Thus compare McKenna v. Pacific Electric Railway Co., 1930, 104 Cal.App. 538, 286 P. 445, with Houghton v. Loma Prieta Lumber Co., 1907, 152 Cal. 500, 93 P. 82; also Klepsch v. Donald, 1892, 4 Wash. 436, 30 P. 991, with Patrick v. Smith, 1913, 75 Wash. 407, 134 P. 1076; also Freebury v. Chicago, Milwaukee & Puget Sound Railroad Co., 1914, 77 Wash. 464, 137 P. 1044, with Kendall v. Johnson, 1909, 51 Wash. 477, 99 P. 310.

34. See ch. 3.

35. See ch. 15.

36. See Private Nuisance, ch. 15.

37. See the subsection, supra, in this section entitled "American Cases—Prosser's Interpretation in the 1971 Edition."

"natural" or "ordinary" use of the property, however abnormal the use might be in terms of whether the usage is one that is customarily carried on by people in the same area, then strict liability would be applicable to harm resulting from a risk that made that activity somewhat dangerous.

The First Restatement of Torts, attempting to describe the best view, accepted the general idea of some kind of strict liability for engaging in a dangerous activity but chose to accept the concept "ultra hazardous." An ultra-hazardous activity was defined as one which (1) necessarily involves a risk of serious harm to the person, land, or chattels of others which cannot be eliminated by the exercise of utmost care, and (2) is not a matter of common usage.[38] Thus, the idea was to visit strict liability on all those actors, almost altogether enterprisers, who elected to engage in an activity, however socially desirable, that introduced into the community an abnormal risk of a serious nature. The policy position is that such an enterprise should bear the costs of accidents attributable to highly dangerous activities that are both highly dangerous and unusual.

The Second Restatement of Torts, without any substantial change in judicial decisions, attempted a third statement of the best view of the result of case authority. It is an attempt to combine Prosser's original ideas as to "non-natural" or "extraordinary uses" with the ideas accepted in the First Restatement and the result is unsatisfactory. It employs the term "abnormally dangerous activities" and then lists six factors that are to be considered.[39] These six factors are an attempt to include the ideas of (a) unnatural or extraordinary uses, (b) serious nature of the harm threatened, and (c) the extent to which the activity is not commonly carried on. The factors to be considered are as follows: (a) the existence of a high degree of risk of some harm to the person, land, or chattels of others; (b) the likelihood that the harm that results from it will be great; (c) inability to eliminate the risk by the exercise of reasonable care; (d) extent to which the activity is not a matter of common usage; (e) inappropriateness of the activity to the place where it is carried on, and (f) extent to which its value to the community is outweighed by its dangerous attributes. Thus, there is no requirement that the magnitude of the danger be great; the seriousness of the harm threatened is only one of the factors. There is no requirement that the activity be of the kind that is not commonly engaged in; that is only one of the factors. The fact that an activity is appropriate to its surroundings is a factor of importance, however dangerous the activity; but however important such a factor might be on the issue of negligence, it is of doubtful importance on the question of whether one should be strictly liable when engaging in a highly dangerous activity.[39a] Finally, it is said that the extent to which an activity's value to the community is outweighed by its dangerousness is important. That is, of course, quite relevant on whether or not conduct is unreasonable and therefore the basis for liability on either (a) a negligence theory or (b) a nuisance theory if there is an intentional or knowing interference and injunctive relief is sought; it is irrelevant on whether or not a risk should be allocated to the defendant because of the dangerousness, as such, of the activity. When a court applies all of the factors suggested in the Second Restatement it is doing virtually the same thing as is done with the negligence concept, except for the fact that it is the function of the court to apply the abnormally dangerous concept to the facts as found by the jury.

It is submitted that the First Restatement set forth the best way of articulating and describing the requirements that ought to be met for applying strict liability to dangerous activities. The choice between the labels "ultra hazardous" and "abnormally danger-

---

38. See First Restatement of Torts, § 520.

39. See Second Restatement of Torts, § 520. See Comments e and f particularly.

39a. Yukon Equipment, Inc. v. Fireman's Fund Insurance Co., Alaska 1978, 585 P.2d 1206.

ous" is not too important, but there should be some rather well-understood requirements to be satisfied so that there can be some degree of predictability about when strict liability will be applicable. This will prevent unnecessary litigation. If an enterpriser deliberately and consciously engages in an activity that is highly dangerous even when reasonable care is exercised and if the activity is one that is not the kind commonly engaged in such as automobile driving, then such intentional exposure of another to great danger, however socially desirable the activity, can generally be regarded as a sound basis on which to allocate the risk of loss to the person or entity engaging in that ultra-hazardous and abnormally dangerous activity. This seems to best describe the result of most recent cases. An activity can be ultra-hazardous for two reasons: first, because although harm from a mishap may not be very serious, and the social utility of the conduct may outweigh the danger, a mishap resulting in some harm to the plaintiff is very likely to occur;[40] second, because the activity involves an appreciable chance of causing serious injury.[41] The point is that certain conditions and activities may be so hazardous to another or to the public generally and of such relative infrequent occurrence to justify allocating the risk of loss to the enterpriser engaging in such conduct as a cost of doing business.

The Restatement of Torts accepts the position that this rule of strict liability for ultra-hazardous and abnormally dangerous activities does not apply if the activity is one that is carried on in pursuance of a public duty or as a common carrier.[42] However, a federal district court held a railroad company strictly liable for harm resulting from an explosion occurring in the course of transporting 18 bomb-loaded box cars pursuant to a contract with the federal government.[43]

Aircraft, Rockets, and Nuclear Energy

Ground damage from aviation has been a matter of controversy, not yet entirely determined.[44] Flying was of course regarded at first as a questionable and highly dangerous enterprise, the province exclusively of venturesome fools, and so properly subject to strict liability for any harm to persons and property beneath, and this was encouraged by the fact that the first cases[45] arose in New York, where there was strict liability for any physical invasion of land.[46] Notwithstanding vigorous agitation on the part of the developing industry,[47] the First Restatement of Torts[48] in 1939 took the posi-

40. Mowrer v. Ashland Oil & Refining Co., Inc., 7th Cir. 1975, 518 F.2d 659; Clark-Aiken Co. v. Cromwell-Wright Co., Inc., 1975, 367 Mass. 70, 323 N.E.2d 876; Bringle v. Lloyd, 1975, 13 Wn.App. 844, 537 P.2d 1060 (dynamite set off 200 feet from plaintiff's machine shed).

41. Siegler v. Kuhlman, 1972, 81 Wn.2d 448, 502 P.2d 1181, certiorari denied 411 U.S. 983, 93 S.Ct. 2275, 36 L.Ed.2d 959 (gasoline truck and trailer unit; gasoline spilled everywhere when trailer disengaged; explosion and fire resulted); Chavez v. Southern Pacific Transportation Co., E.D.Cal.1976, 413 F.Supp. 1203 (18 bomb-loaded box cars exploded).

42. Second Restatement of Torts, § 521 (1977).

43. Chavez v. Southern Pacific Transportation Co., E.D.Cal.1976, 413 F.Supp. 1203 (18 bomb-loaded box cars exploded. The contract to transport was with the Department of Navy).

44. See Orr, Is Aviation Ultra-Hazardous?, 1954, 21 Ins.Counsel J. 48; Vold, Strict Liability for Airplane Crashes, 1953, 5 Hastings L.J. 1; Eubank, Land Damage Liability in Aircraft Cases, 1953, 57 Dick.L.Rev. 155; Orr, Airplane Tort Law, 1952, 19 Ins.Counsel J. 67; Vold, Aircraft Operator's Liability for Ground Damage and Passenger Injury, 1935, 13 Neb.L.Rev. 373; Notes, 1955, 31 Ind.L.J. 63; 1957, 19 U.Pitt.L.Rev. 154; 1955, 43 Cal.L.Rev. 309.

45. Guille v. Swan, N.Y.1822, 19 Johns. 381; Rochester Gas & Electric Corp. v. Dunlop, 1933, 148 Misc. 849, 266 N.Y.S. 469. See Baldwin, Liability for Accidents in Aerial Navigation, 1910, 9 Mich.L.Rev. 20.

46. See ch. 3.

47. See, criticizing strict liability as putting its advocates in the "ranks of those passed on, but not forgotten, solons who required a man with a red lantern to precede a railroad train," 1931, 2 J.Air Law 549; Cooper, Aircraft Liability to Persons and Property on Ground, 1931, 17 A.B.A.J. 435; Ewing, The Ground Rule of Torts by Aircraft at the American Law Institute, 1934, 5 Air L.Rev. 323; Report of American Bar Ass'n Standing Committee on Aeronautical Law, 1931.

48. § 520, Comment b. See, upholding this position, Vold, Strict Liability for Aircraft Crashes and Forced Landings, 1953, 5 Hastings L.J. 1; Bohlen, Aviation Under the Common Law, 1934, 45 Harv.L.Rev. 216.

tion that aviation had not reached such a stage of safety as to justify treating it by analogy to the railroads, and classified it as an "ultrahazardous activity" upon which strict liability for ground damage was to be imposed. This position was also incorporated in Section 5 of the Uniform Aeronautics Act,[49] promulgated by the Commissioners on Uniform State Laws in 1922.

With the further development of the industry, and an improved safety record,[50] later years have witnessed a considerable amount of hesitancy over the strict liability, efforts to avoid passing upon it whenever possible, and at last a definite reversal of the trend. In 1943 the Uniform Act was withdrawn by the Commissioners for further study, and it has not been reissued.[51] Several of the states which have adopted it have eliminated, repealed or modified the section providing for strict liability for ground damage.[52]

Notwithstanding these steps away from strict liability, the Second Restatement of Torts, published in 1977, adopted the position that aviation had not "yet reached the stage of development where the risks of physical harm to persons or to land or chattels on the ground is properly to be borne by those who suffer the harm rather than by the industry itself."[53] It is reasonable to argue that physical harm accidentally caused by airplane crashes should be a cost borne by those engaged in that kind of undertaking since it is not as yet an activity in which people are generally engaged.

In spite of all the discussion, cases dealing with the liability at common law have been astonishingly few. The cases arising in New York first adhered to the rule of that state as to strict liability for any land trespass,[54] but they are now apparently in process of being overruled,[55] in common with other accidental trespass cases. There have been two or three decisions from other jurisdictions which, without a statute, have imposed strict liability for ground damage,[56] in line with the Uniform Act. About as many others[57] have rejected such a rule, and have

49. See 9 Uniform Laws Ann. 17; Note, [1948] Wis. L.Rev. 356. The Act was applied in United States v. Praylou, 4th Cir. 1953, 208 F.2d 291, certiorari denied 347 U.S. 934, 74 S.Ct. 628, 98 L.Ed. 1085. (South Carolina law); United States v. Pendergrast, 4th Cir. 1957, 241 F.2d 687 (same); Prentiss v. National Airlines, D.N.J.1953, 112 F.Supp. 306 (New Jersey; held constitutional); Adler's Quality Bakery, Inc. v. Gaseteria, Inc., 1960, 32 N.J. 55, 159 A.2d 97.

Cf. D'Anna v. United States, 4th Cir. 1950, 181 F.2d 335 (presumption of negligence under Maryland statute).

50. See Orr, Is Aviation Ultra-Hazardous?, 1954, 21 Ins.Counsel J. 48; Sweeney, Is Special Aviation Liability Legislation Essential?, 1952, 19 J.Air Law 166, 311. Report of Civil Aeronautics Board, Bureau of Safety, Feb. 25, 1965.

51. See 9 Uniform Laws Ann. xvi.

52. The statutes are summarized up to 1953, in Eubank, Land Damage Liability in Aircraft Cases, 1953, 57 Dick.L.Rev. 188, 193. As of the end of 1967, the state of the statutory law was as follows:

Nine jurisdictions had strict liability provisions: Delaware, Hawaii, Minnesota, Montana, New Jersey, North Dakota, South Carolina, Tennessee, Wyoming; Five provided for a presumption of negligence, rebuttable by proof of due care: Georgia, Maryland, Nevada, Rhode Island, Wisconsin; Eight had provisions apparently rejecting strict liability, and stating that the "ordinary rules of law" shall govern: Arizona, Arkansas, California, Idaho, Missouri, Pennsylvania, South Dakota, Vermont; Five had repealed strict liability provisions, and were without legislation: Connecticut, Indiana, Michigan, North Carolina, Utah. The rest never have had any legislation.

53. Section 520A, Comment c.

54. Rochester Gas & Electric Corp. v. Dunlop, 1933, 148 Misc. 849, 266 N.Y.S. 469; Margosian v. United States Airlines, E.D.N.Y.1955, 127 F.Supp. 464; Hahn v. United States Airlines, E.D.N.Y.1954, 127 F.Supp. 950.

55. Wood v. United Air Lines, Inc., 1961, 32 Misc.2d 955, 223 N.Y.S.2d 692, affirmed mem. 16 A.D.2d 659, 226 N.Y.S.2d 1022, appeal dismissed 11 N.Y.2d 1053, 230 N.Y.S.2d 207, 184 N.E.2d 180; Crist v. Civil Air Patrol, 1967, 53 Misc.2d 289, 278 N.Y.S.2d 430.

56. Parcell v. United States, S.D.W.Va.1951, 104 F.Supp. 110 (collision of two military planes); Gaidys v. United States, D.Colo., [1951] U.S.Av.Rep. 352 (military aircraft crashed while flying low after take-off); D'Anna v. United States, 4th Cir. 1950, 181 F.2d 335 (fall of auxiliary gas tank from military plane); cf. Long v. United States, W.D.S.C.1965, 241 F.Supp. 286 (under South Carolina statute). See Notes, 1951, 4 Vand.L.Rev. 867; 1953, 38 Corn.L.Q. 570; 1963, 15 Syr. L.Rev. 1.

57. Johnson v. Dew, 1964, 204 Pa.Super. 526, 205 A.2d 880; Southern California Edison Co. v. Coleman, 1957, 150 Cal.App.2d Supp. 829, 310 P.2d 504; In re Kinsey's Estate, 1949, 152 Neb. 95, 40 N.W.2d 526, 531;

insisted that the liability must rest upon proof of negligence. Most of the decisions have gone off upon proof of specific negligence,[58] or have resorted to res ipsa loquitur,[59] which by inference, at least, would indicate a rejection of strict liability. The question cannot be said to be finally determined; and since nearly half of the jurisdictions now have statutes bearing on the matter, its ultimate solution appears very likely to be in the form of legislation.

One possible suggestion as to the ultimate outcome is that strict liability might be retained as to what may be called "abnormal" aviation including all such things as stunt flying,[60] crop dusting,[61] experimental aircraft and military planes not designed primarily for safety,[62] and "sonic booms,"[63] while "normal" aviation, including all common commercial flights, might require proof of negligence. Rapid technological changes would, however, make such a classification extremely difficult to maintain.

Rockets[64] and nuclear energy have now made their appearance in the field of strict liability. However, the federal government is heavily involved in these matters and the federal government cannot be held strictly liable under the Federal Tort Claims Act.[65]

It is quite clear that those who produce, package for shipping, transport and use nuclear materials are engaged in abnormally dangerous activities in the sense that there is an appreciable chance of serious harm (in fact a calamity) even when utmost care is exercised and the activity is not one that is commonly engaged in by people generally. In fact, such activities are mentioned in the commentary to the Second Restatement. The federal government originally reserved to itself an absolute monopoly on the development of atomic power but private enterprise now operates in the field pursuant to the Atomic Energy Act of 1954 as amended.[66] In general, this Act leaves the issue of civil liability of private enterprise to be determined by each state in the absence of an extraordinary nuclear occurrence so that the applicable law for harm resulting from a nuclear mishap would be the appro-

State to Use of Birckhead v. Sammon, 1936, 171 Md. 178, 189 A. 265.

See also the following, where the action was against the owner of the plane, and the court rejected the contention that he was liable because the activity was "ultrahazardous," "inherently dangerous," and the like: Fosbroke-Hobbes v. Airwork, Ltd., [1936] 1 All Eng. Rep. 108; D'Aquilla v. Pryor, S.D.N.Y.1954, 122 F.Supp. 346; Johnson v. Central Aviation Corp., 1951, 103 Cal.App.2d 102, 229 P.2d 114; Spartan Aircraft Co. v. Jamison, 1938, 181 Okl. 645, 75 P.2d 1096; Herrick & Olson v. Curtiss, Sup.Ct. Nassau County, N.Y., [1932] U.S.Av.Rep. 110.

58. San Diego Gas & Electric Co. v. United States, 9th Cir. 1949, 173 F.2d 92 (low flying); Bright v. United States, E.D.Ill.1956, 149 F.Supp. 620 (flying into storm); Evans v. United States, W.D.La.1951, 100 F.Supp. 5 (inexperienced pilot); Leisy v. United States, D.Minn.1954, 102 F.Supp. 789 (low flying); Maitland v. Twin City Aviation Corp., 1949, 254 Wis. 541, 37 N.W.2d 74 (same); Murphy v. Neely, 1935, 319 Pa. 437, 179 A. 439 (bad operation).

59. United States v. Kesinger, 10th Cir. 1951, 190 F.2d 529; Northwestern National Insurance Co. v. United States, N.D.Ill.1949, [1949] U.S.Av.Rep. 316; Kadylak v. O'Brien, W.D.Pa.1941, 32 F.Supp. 281; Goodwin v. United States, E.D.N.C.1956, 141 F.Supp. 445; Sollak v. State, N.Y.Ct.Cl.1927, [1929] U.S.Av. Rep. 42. See also the following, which refused to apply res ipsa loquitur, and denied recovery: Williams v. United States, 5th Cir. 1955, 218 F.2d 473 (jet bomber exploded, flaming fuel fell on plaintiff's house—a horrible case); Deojay v. Lyford, 1942, 139 Me. 234, 29 A.2d 111 (bad landing); Prokop v. Becker, 1942, 345 Pa. 607, 29 A.2d 23 (same).

60. Johnson v. Curtiss Northwest Airplane Co., D. Ramsey County, Minn.1923, [1928] U.S.Av.Rep. 42 (enjoined at any altitude).

61. See supra, this section on American Cases.

62. Cf. Canney v. Rochester Agricultural & Mechanical Association, 1911, 76 N.H. 60, 79 A. 517 (balloon).

63. See Note, 1958, 31 So.Cal.L.Rev. 259.

64. Berg v. Reaction Motors Division, Thiokol Chemical Corp., 1962, 37 N.J. 396, 181 A.2d 487; Smith v. Lockheed Propulsion Co., 1967, 247 Cal.App.2d 774, 56 Cal.Rptr. 128.

65. Laird v. Nelms, 1972, 406 U.S. 797, 92 S.Ct. 1899, 32 L.Ed.2d 499, rehearing denied 409 U.S. 902, 93 S.Ct. 95, 34 L.Ed.2d 165 (sonic boom generated by aircraft); H. L. Properties, Inc. v. Aerojet-General Corp., S.D.Fla.1971, 331 F.Supp. 1006, affirmed, 5th Cir. 1972, 468 F.2d 1397 (per curiam) (as employer of corporation testing rocket engine, but court imposed a non-delegable duty to see that work done safely).

66. 1970, 42 U.S.C. § 2210.

priate state's law.[67] Numerous commentators have unanimously concluded that the federal Atomic Energy Act left the issue of liability determinations to state law.[68]

Most private enterprisers who are engaged in the production, transportation, and handling of nuclear materials and energy are either operating under a license procured under the federal government and are often either public utilities or of a similar type and not the ordinary private enterprises operating in a competitive environment. This being so the question can be raised as to whether or not the enterpriser is the type upon which liability without fault should be visited.[69] This is briefly discussed hereafter. The Atomic Energy Act takes no position but it does limit liability for a nuclear disaster to 560 million dollars. The constitutionality of this limitation has been established.[70]

WESTLAW REFERENCES

rylands /5 fletcher

American Cases—Prosser's Interpretation in 1971 Edition

restatement /5 torts /10 519 520
synopsis,digest(blast! /p strict! absolut! /5 liab!)
164k12

Recent Developments and Revisor's Comments

ultrahazardous extrahazardous abnormal! hazard! /p strict! absolut! /5 liab! & date(after 1971)

Aircraft, Rockets and Nuclear Energy

rocket* nuclear* /p ultrahazardous hazard! abnormal! /p strict! absolut! /5 liab!
title(silkwood & kerr-mcgee)
sh 667 f.2d 908
silkwood /10 kerr-mcgee
ic 667 f2d 908

---

67. Silkwood v. Kerr-McGee Corp., W.D.Okl.1979, 485 F.Supp. 566, affirmed in part, reversed in part, 10th Cir.1982, 667 F.2d 908.

68. See Moore, Radiation and Preconception Injuries: Some Interesting Problems in Tort Law, 1974, 28 Sw.L.J. 414, 427; Green, Nuclear Power: Risk, Liability, and Indemnity, 1973, 71 Mich.L.Rev. 479, 496.

69. See infra, § 79 under "Privilege."

70. Duke Power Co. v. Carolina Environmental Study Group, Inc., 1978, 438 U.S. 59, 98 S.Ct. 2620, 57 L.Ed.2d 595. See Note, The "Extraordinary Nuclear Occurrence" Threshold and Uncompensated Injury Under the Price-Anderson Act, 1974, 6 Rutgers-Camden L.J. 360.

42 /10 2210

§ 79. Extent of Liability

In dealing with the extent of strict liability, and the limitations upon it, it is convenient to group together all of the areas in which it is applied, since, with some occasional exceptions, reasonably consistent rules have developed which are common to all of them. It is clear, first of all, that unless a statute requires it, strict liability will never be found unless the defendant is aware of the abnormally dangerous condition or activity, and has voluntarily engaged in or permitted it.[1] Mere negligent failure to discover or prevent it is not enough, although it may, of course, be an independent basis of liability.

Once the responsibility is established, it frequently is stated, in cases of strict liability, that the defendant acts "at his peril," [2] and is an insurer against the consequences of his conduct. What is meant is that he is liable although (1) he did not intend an invasion on the basis of which liability could be imposed and (2) he was not negligent in proximately causing harm. But there are not lacking indications that the liability itself is thought to be an extensive one. Baron Bramwell[3] once carried this to the length of saying that if a person kept a tiger and lightning broke its chain, he might be liable for all the mischief the tiger might do.

But such extended responsibility may undoubtedly impose too heavy a burden upon the defendant. It is one thing to say that a

§ 79

1. Zampos v. United States Smelting, Refining & Mining Co., 10th Cir. 1953, 206 F.2d 171; The Nitroglycerine Case (Parrott v. Wells, Fargo & Co.), 1872, 82 U.S. (15 Wall.) 524, 21 L.Ed. 206; Hunt v. Hazen, 1953, 197 Or. 637, 254 P.2d 210; Dickson v. Graham-Jones Paper Co., Fla.1956, 84 So.2d 309.

2. Rylands v. Fletcher, 1868, L.R. 3 H.L. 330, 37 L.J.Ex. 161; Exner v. Sherman Power Construction Co., 2d Cir. 1931, 54 F.2d 510.

3. In Nichols v. Marsland, 1875, L.R. 10 Ex. 255.

dangerous enterprise must pay its way within reasonable limits, and quite another to say that it must bear responsibility for every extreme of harm that it may cause. The same practical necessity for the restriction of liability within some reasonable bounds, which arises in connection with problems of "proximate cause" in negligence cases,[4] demands here that some limit be set. It might be expected that this limit would be a narrower one where no initial departure from a social standard is to be found. In general, this has been true. Just as liability for negligence has tended to be restricted within narrower boundaries than when intentional misconduct is involved,[5] there is a visible tendency to restrict it still further when there is not even negligence. The intentional wrongdoer is commonly held liable for consequences extending beyond the scope of the foreseeable risk created,[6] and many courts have carried negligence liability beyond the risk to some extent.[7] But where there is neither intentional harm nor negligence, the line is generally drawn at the limits of the risk,[8] or even within it. This limitation has been expressed by saying that the defendant's duty to insure safety extends only to certain consequences.[9] More commonly, it is said that the defendant's conduct is not the "proximate cause" of the damage.[10] But ordinarily in such cases no question of causation is involved, and the limitation is one of the policy underlying liability.

Nature of Risk and Type of Harm Threatened

The nature of the risk and the type of damage threatened by the conduct which entails strict liability is well defined. The keeping of vicious animals involves the risk that human beings or other animals will be attacked; the risk of abnormally dangerous things and activities, such as high tension electricity or blasting, is sufficiently obvious. In general, strict liability has been confined to consequences which lie within the extraordinary risk whose existence calls for such special responsibility.

Thus, the owner of trespassing animals has been held strictly liable for consequences of the trespass which were reasonably to be expected from an invasion by animals of the particular kind—including, of course, damage to crops, attacks upon other animals,[11] infecting them with disease,[12] or the misalliance of a scrub bull with a pedigreed heifer.[13] The same has been true of personal injuries suffered by the owner in an attempt to put the animal out, which has been regarded as foreseeable, reasonably likely to occur, and to provoke resistance.[14] On the other hand, there are several cases[15] denying recovery for injuries from quite un-

---

4. See supra, § 42; Carpenter, Proximate Cause, 1942, 15 So.Cal.L.Rev. 188, 195–198.

5. See supra, § 43.

6. Cf. Wyant v. Crouse, 1901, 127 Mich. 158, 86 N.W. 527; Isham v. Dow's Estate, 1898, 70 Vt. 588, 41 A. 585; Derosier v. New England Telephone & Telegraph Co., 1925, 81 N.H. 451, 130 A. 145.

7. See supra, § 43.

8. See Harper, Liability Without Fault and Proximate Cause, 1932, 30 Mich.L.Rev. 1001.

9. See Pollock, Duties of Insuring Safety: The Rule in Rylands v. Fletcher, 1886, 2 L.Q.Rev. 52.

10. See Harper, Liability Without Fault and Proximate Cause, 1932, 30 Mich.L.Rev. 1001.

11. Dolph v. Ferris, 1844, 7 Watts & S. 367 (bull); McKee v. Trisler, 1924, 311 Ill. 536, 143 N.E. 69 (bull); Morgan v. Hudnell, 1893, 52 Ohio St. 552, 40 N.E. 716 (horse); Ellis v. Loftus Iron Co., 1874, L.R. 10 C.P. 10 (horse); Hilton v. Overly, 1918, 69 Pa.Super. 348 (boar hog). Cf. Houska v. Hrabe, 1915, 35 S.D. 269, 151 N.W. 1021 (playful horse).

12. Anderton v. Buckton, 1718, 11 Mod. 304, 88 Eng.Rep. 1054; Theyer v. Purnell [1918] 2 K.B. 333; Lee v. Burk, 1884, 15 Ill.App. 651.

13. Crawford v. Williams, 1878, 48 Iowa 247; McLean v. Brett, 1919, 15 Alta.L.Rep. 43, 49 Dom.L.Rep. 162; Cousins v. Greaves, 1920, 13 Sask.L.Rep. 443, 54 Dom.L.Rep. 630. See, among the classics of legal humor on this subject, Kopplin v. Quade, 1911, 145 Wis. 454, 130 N.W. 511.

14. Troth v. Wills, 1897, 8 Pa.Super. 1; Nixon v. Harris, 1968, 15 Ohio St.2d 105, 238 N.E.2d 785; Walker v. Nickerson, 1935, 291 Mass. 522, 197 N.E. 451; Robinson v. Kerr, 1960, 144 Colo. 48, 355 P.2d 117; Harris Park Lakeshore, Inc. v. Church, 1963, 152 Colo. 278, 381 P.2d 459.

15. Leipske v. Guenther, 1959, 7 Wis.2d 86, 95 N.W.2d 774, rehearing denied 7 Wis.2d 86, 96 N.W.2d 821 (horse reached over high fence and bit schoolgirl in

provoked attacks, on the ground that they could not reasonably be expected to follow from the trespass; and it has also been denied for more indirect and unlikely results, as where a trespassing cow breaks through a rotten floor, and the plaintiff, in the dark, later falls into the hole.[16] In general, the cases support the view that the defendant will be liable only for normal consequences of the trespass, lying within the risk,[17] which will vary with the type of animal involved,[18] and may often be a jury question.

If no trespass can be established, the question becomes one of strict liability for keeping the animal at all.[19] Here again the same conclusion is to be drawn. Thus the keeper of a wild animal, such as a bear or an elephant, has been held not liable for the fright of a horse at the mere sight of the animal on the highway, on the ground that the foreseeable risk of keeping the animal did not extend to such an event;[20] but strict liability has been imposed for the fright of a person whom such an animal attempts to attack.[21] Recovery has been denied where a dog known to attack other animals but never human beings unexpectedly attacked a man;[22] where animals which escape onto the highway attack people[23] or interfere with vehicles,[24] or while trespassing cause unexpected personal injuries of a kind not to be anticipated from such an animal.[25] The statutory strict liability for the escape of fire has been held not to extend to cattle frightened into a stampede,[26] on the ground that this was not the risk at which the statute was directed. The doctrine of Rylands v. Fletcher has been held not to apply where dangerous electric current caused electrical interference with telegraph communications,[27] or the heat from the defendant's mill damaged a very delicate type of paper which

the ear); Harvey v. Buchanan, 1904, 121 Ga. 384, 49 S.E. 281 (mule killing kid); Klenberg v. Russell, 1890, 125 Ind. 531, 25 N.E. 596 (unprovoked attack on plaintiff by cow); Street v. Craig, 1920, 48 Ont.L.Rep. 324, 56 Dom.L.Rep. 105, (same); Bradley v. Wallace's Ltd., [1913] 3 K.B. 629 (horse killed a man).

16. Hollenbeck v. Johnson, 1894, 79 Hun 499, 29 N.Y.S. 945. Cf. Durham v. Goodwin, 1870, 54 Ill. 469, where defendant's horses broke down a fence, and let in the horses of a third party, which did the damage.

17. See Troth v. Wills, 1898, 8 Pa.Super. 1; Theyer v. Purnell, [1918] 2 K.B. 333; Street v. Craig, 1920, 48 Ont.L.Rep. 324, 56 Dom.L.Rep. 105; Note, 1919, 32 Harv.L.Rev. 420; and compare Fox v. Koehnig, 1926, 190 Wis. 528, 209 N.W. 708. This seems to amount to saying that knowledge of the propensity of the animal to inflict such injuries is necessary, but that in certain cases the owner will not be heard to deny it.

18. See the dissenting opinion in Troth v. Wills, 1898, 8 Pa.Super. 1, putting the case of injury to a child by a trespassing pet lamb or hen.

19. Manton v. Brocklebank, [1923] 2 K.B. 212; Dufer v. Cully, 1871, 3 Or. 377; Van Leuven v. Lyke, 1848, 1 N.Y. 515. Thus in Peterson v. Conlan, 1909, 18 N.D. 205, 119 N.W. 367, a mere licensee on the land was not allowed to recover on the basis of trespass. See, however, Troth v. Wills, 1898, 8 Pa.Super. 1, allowing recovery by a member of the household of the landholder.

20. Scribner v. Kelley, N.Y.1862, 38 Barb. 14; Bostock-Ferari Amusement Co. v. Brocksmith, 1895, 34 Ind.App. 566, 73 N.E. 281.

21. Candler v. Smith, 1935, 50 Ga.App. 667, 179 S.E. 395 (baboon); cf. Netusil v. Novak, 1931, 120 Neb. 751, 235 N.W. 335.

22. Keightlinger v. Egan, 1872, 65 Ill. 235; Ewing v. Prince, Ky.1968, 425 S.W.2d 732 (mare); Glanville v. Sutton, [1928] 1 K.B. 571. Accord, Koetting v. Conroy, 1936, 223 Wis. 550, 270 N.W. 625, rehearing denied 223 Wis. 550, 271 N.W. 369 (vicious dog, instead of attacking plaintiff, accidentally ran into him).

23. Cox v. Burbidge, 1863, 13 C.B.,N.S., 430, 143 Eng.Rep. 171; Klenberg v. Russell, 1890, 125 Ind. 531, 25 N.E. 596; Brady v. Straub, 1917, 177 Ky. 468, 197 S.W. 938. But compare the view that a kick from a horse is not beyond the risk involved in allowing the horse to be free on the street. Healey v. P. Ballentine & Sons, 1901, 66 N.J.L. 339, 49 A. 511. Liability may of course be based on negligence in allowing the animal to be at large. Cf. Dickson v. McCoy, 1868, 39 N.Y. 400; Netusil v. Novak, 1931, 120 Neb. 751, 235 N.W. 335.

24. Hadwell v. Righton, [1907] 2 K.B. 345 (fowl flying into wheel of bicycle); Marsh v. Koons, 1908, 78 Ohio St. 68, 84 N.E. 599 (cow frightening horse); Zumstein v. Shrumm, [1895] 22 Ont.App. 262 (turkey frightening horse); Fox v. Koehnig, 1926, 190 Wis. 528, 209 N.W. 708 (automobile colliding with horse); Dyer v. Mudgett, 1919, 118 Me. 267, 107 A. 831 (same). Liability may, however, be predicated on negligence in allowing the animal to be at large. Drew v. Gross, 1925, 112 Ohio St. 485, 147 N.E. 757; Wedel v. Johnson, 1936, 196 Minn. 170, 264 N.W. 689; Roberts v. Griffith Co., 1929, 100 Cal.App. 456, 280 P. 199.

25. See supra, § 76.

26. Chicago, Burlington & Quincy Railroad Co. v. Gelvin, 8th Cir. 1916, 238 F. 14.

27. Eastern & South African Tel. Co. v. Cape Town Tramways Co., [1902] A.C. 381, 71 L.J.P.C. 122; Lake Shore & Michigan Southern Railway Co. v. Chicago,

the plaintiff was keeping for sale on his premises.[28]

Class of Persons Protected

In much the same manner, the class of persons who are threatened by the abnormal danger, and the kind of damage they may be expected to incur, usually are well marked out. Strict liability probably is limited to such plaintiffs and such damages. Thus, it has been held that where the defendant's blasting hurls a rock to such a distance that no experience would have recognized the danger,[29] or causes frightened mink to kill their young,[30] the plaintiff cannot recover without a finding of negligence.

Injuries occurring on the premises of the defendant involve primarily questions of the nature or kind of negligence required as a basis for liability.[31] Although there are one or two cases[32] in which, apparently on the ground of unforeseeability, trespassers were denied recovery for abnormally dangerous conditions, most of the cases have involved vicious dogs. It seems clear that the owner may not intentionally keep such a dog for the purpose of attacking mere trespassers,[33] where he would not be privileged to inflict serious injury if he were present in person.[34] But even where there is no such intent, the danger has been considered so extreme, and the situation so unreasonable, that even a trespasser is entitled to protection against it, and can recover when the necessary scienter is established.[35] In all of these cases, however, harm to the trespasser was considered foreseeable, and within the risk. It has been contended that unanticipated trespassers are not within the class of persons entitled to protection, and that liability to trespassers, as well as to others entering the owner's premises, should rest upon ordinary principles of negligence.[36]

Licensees and invitees are apparently denied recovery under the doctrine of Rylands v. Fletcher, by the last English decision.[37]

Lake Shore & South Bend Railway Co., 1911, 48 Ind. App. 584, 92 N.E. 989; Postal Telegraph-Cable Co. v. Pacific Gas & Electric Co., 1927, 202 Cal. 382, 260 P. 1101; Amphitheatres, Inc. v. Portland Meadows, 1948, 184 Or. 336, 198 P.2d 847. See, 1928, 12 Minn.L.Rev. 414; 1928, 16 Cal.L.Rev. 331.

28. Robinson v. Kilvert, 1889, 41 Ch.Div. 88.

29. Klepsch v. Donald, 1892, 4 Wash. 436, 30 P. 991; cf. Houghton v. Loma Prieta Lumber Co., 1907, 152 Cal. 500, 93 P. 82.

30. Madsen v. East Jordan Irrigation Co., 1942, 101 Utah 552, 125 P.2d 794; Foster v. Preston Mill Co., 1954, 44 Wn.2d 440, 268 P.2d 645; Gronn v. Rogers Construction, Inc., 1960, 221 Or. 226, 350 P.2d 1086. But there may be liability for negligence if the defendant, knowing the risk, is found to act unreasonably. Summit View, Inc. v. W. W. Clyde & Co., 1965, 17 Utah 2d 26, 403 P.2d 919; MacGibbon v. Robinson, [1952] 4 Dom.L.Rep. 142.

31. See § 6.

32. McGehee v. Norfolk & Southern Railway Co., 1908, 147 N.C. 142, 60 S.E. 912 (stored dynamite, trespasser shot at the building). Similar, and in accord, is St. Joseph Lead Co. v. Prather, 8th Cir. 1956, 238 F.2d 301, where, however, recovery was allowed on other grounds.

33. Loomis v. Terry, N.Y.1837, 17 Wend. 496; Brewer v. Furtwangler, 1933, 171 Wash. 617, 18 P.2d 837; Conway v. Grant, 1891, 88 Ga. 40, 13 S.E. 803. Otherwise if the dog is safely confined, and kept only for warning. Woodbridge v. Marks, 1897, 17 App.Div. 139, 45 N.Y.S. 156.

34. Thus, keeping the dog may be privileged against a felonious intruder, or where the owner would be privileged to set him on in person. See Woolf v. Chalker, 1862, 31 Conn. 121; cf. Ryan v. Marren, 1914, 216 Mass. 556, 104 N.E. 353.

35. Marble v. Ross, 1878, 124 Mass. 44; Eberling v. Mutillod, 1917, 90 N.J.L. 478, 101 A. 519; Woolf v. Chalker, 1862, 31 Conn. 121; Brewer v. Furtwangler, 1933, 171 Wash. 617, 18 P.2d 837; Darby v. Clare Food & Relish Co., 1934, 111 Pa.Super. 537, 170 A. 387; Radoff v. Hunter, 1958, 158 Cal.App.2d 770, 323 P.2d 202. Cf. Glidden v. Moore, 1883, 14 Neb. 84, 15 N.W. 326 (vicious bull).

36. McNeely, A Footnote on Dangerous Animals, 1939, 37 Mich.L.Rev. 1181; Williams, Liability for Animals, 1939, 349–352; Winfield, Torts, 5th Ed. 1950, 541. Thus the Restatement of Torts, §§ 511, 512, takes the position that there is liability to trespassers only where the land is subject to constant intrusion and the owner fails to give such warning. See Broke v. Copeland, 1794, 1 Esp. 202, 170 Eng.Rep. 328; Sarch v. Blackburn, 1830, 4 C. & P. 297, 172 Eng.Rep. 712. Compare, as to anticipated trespassers, Meibus v. Dodge, 1875, 38 Wis. 300.

37. Read v. J. Lyons & Co., [1947] A.C. 156. In E. I. Du Pont de Nemours & Co. v. Cudd, 10th Cir. 1949, 176 F.2d 855, a similar case, recovery was denied on the basis of assumption of risk.

§ 79 EXTENT OF LIABILITY

The American rule appears to be definitely to the contrary,[38] particularly as to abnormally dangerous animals. It has been held often enough that the strict liability, both as to vicious dogs[39] and as to wild animals,[40] applies in favor of both licensees and invitees upon the premises. However, other decisions[41] hold that there is no liability to those who come on the premises, including invitees as well as licensees, except on a negligence theory and on the same basis as the occupier is liable for ordinary dangerous conditions maintained on the property.

While strict liability for engaging in dangerous activities may well extend to some licensees and invitees on land and chattels, if such a person voluntarily encounters the risk that makes the activity ultra-hazardous or abnormally dangerous with awareness of that danger in order to utilize the service of that activity, then the risk of harm will probably be allocated to such person.[42] Thus, those passengers who utilize the services of the commercial airline will not be able to recover except for negligence.

Manner of Occurrence

Forces of nature and actions of third persons and animals, often rare and unusual and in that sense not reasonably foreseeable, frequently contribute to the bringing about of damaging events from abnormally dangerous and ultra-hazardous activities just as they do from negligent conduct. Both the First and Second Restatements of Tort have taken the position that a defendant should not be excused or relieved of entire responsibility simply because it would not have happened but for the unexcusable action of a human being, an animal, or by a force of nature. So long as the accident resulted from a risk that made the activity ultra-hazardous there is liability. This is a kind of absolute liability. The strong current of authority is to the contrary.[43] In Siegler v. Kuhlman,[44] the Supreme Court of Washington concluded to apply strict liability against a transporter of gasoline for harm resulting from an explosion following a disengagement of a tank trailer from a tank truck. But in the opinion of one of the concurring judges, the observation was made that the owner of the vehicle should be held liable only for damages caused "when the flammable or explosive substance is allowed to escape without the apparent intervention of any outside force beyond the control of the manufacturer, the owner, or the operator of the vehicle hauling it."[45] Thus in the leading case of Rylands v. Fletcher,[46] where the defendant's reservoir broke through into the plaintiff's mine, it was suggested that the defendant might be excused by showing that the event was caused by an

---

38. McLane v. Northwest Natural Gas Co., 1969, 255 Or. 324, 467 P.2d 635, specifically rejecting the English case.

39. Invitees: Zarek v. Fredericks, 3d Cir. 1943, 138 F.2d 689; Frederickson v. Kepner, 1947, 82 Cal.App.2d 905, 187 P.2d 800; Burke v. Fischer, 1944, 298 Ky. 157, 182 S.W.2d 638; Flynn v. Lindenfield, 1967, 6 Ariz.App. 459, 433 P.2d 639; Gerulis v. Lunecki, 1936, 284 Ill. App. 44, 1 N.E.2d 440.

Licensees: Thompson v. Wold, 1955, 47 Wn.2d 782, 289 P.2d 712; Carrow v. Haney, 1920, 203 Mo.App. 485, 219 S.W. 710.

40. Opelt v. Al. G. Barnes Co., 1919, 41 Cal.App. 776, 183 P. 241; Copley v. Wills, Tex.Civ.App.1913, 152 S.W. 830; Crunk v. Glover, 1959, 167 Neb. 816, 95 N.W.2d 135; City of Tonkawa v. Danielson, 1933, 166 Okl. 241, 27 P.2d 348; Bottcher v. Buck, 1928, 265 Mass. 4, 163 N.E. 182. See, however, McNeely, A Footnote on Dangerous Animals, 1939, 37 Mich.L.Rev. 1181, 1192, pointing out that in nearly all such cases liability might have been rested on negligence.

41. Panorama Resort v. Nichols, 1935, 165 Va. 289, 182 S.E. 235; Vaughan v. Miller Brothers "101" Ranch Wild West Show, 1930, 109 W.Va. 170, 153 S.E. 289; Hansen v. Brogan, 1965, 145 Mont. 224, 400 P.2d 265; Parker v. Cushman, 8th Cir. 1912, 195 F. 715; Marquet v. La Duke, 1893, 96 Mich. 596, 55 N.W. 1006.

42. O'Leary v. Coenen, N.D.1977, 251 N.W.2d 746 (there was no discussion of strict liability); Richmond v. Knowles, Del.Super.1970, 265 A.2d 53 (a statute was involved).

43. Harper, Liability Without Fault and Proximate Cause, 1932, 30 Mich.L.Rev. 1001, 1009.

44. 1973, 81 Wn.2d 448, 502 P.2d 1181, certiorari denied 411 U.S. 983, 93 S.Ct. 2275, 36 L.Ed.2d 959.

45. 502 P.2d 1181, 1188.

46. 1868, L.R. 3 H.L. 330. Compare the dictum in Tubervil v. Stamp, 1601, 1 Salk. 13, 1 Ld.Raym. 264, Carthew 425, 91 Eng.Rep. 13, that liability for the escape of fire might be avoided "if a sudden storm had arisen, which he could not stop."

act of God—meaning, obviously, an unforeseeable intervening force of nature. In a later case,[47] where the defendant's dam was carried away by an unprecedented cloudburst, the "act of God" exception was applied, and the defendant was excused from liability. Subsequent decisions have applied the same rule to extraordinary rainfall,[48] a rat gnawing a hole in a receptacle for the storage of water,[49] and even the operation of frost in causing leakage from a pond.[50]

In the same manner, the defendant has been relieved from liability by the independent act of a third person, which he could not have foreseen or prevented. In still another reservoir case,[51] where the escape of the water was caused by a discharge from a reservoir upstream, it was held that the defendant's responsibility did not extend to the wrongful act of a stranger. The decision has been followed in cases involving the escape of water from the upper floor of a building,[52] and oil from a truck,[53] through the meddling of a stranger; and a very similar rule has been applied where the escape of fire from a locomotive was caused by the release of gasoline vapor by the plaintiff's employees.[54] On the same basis, where the defendant's cattle strayed onto the highway and were driven onto the plaintiff's land by an intermeddling stranger, it was held that the defendant was not responsible.[55] On the other hand, in two cases where the attack of an abnormally dangerous animal was brought about by the deliberate interference of a third person,[56] it was held that the defendant was strictly liable, without any

---

47. Nichols v. Marsland, 1876, L.R. 2 Ex.Div. 1.

48. Bratton v. Rudnick, 1933, 283 Mass. 556, 186 N.E. 669; Golden v. Amory, 1952, 329 Mass. 484, 109 N.E.2d 131; Barnum v. Handschiegel, 1919, 103 Neb. 594, 173 N.W. 593; Smith v. Board of County Road Commissioners, 1966, 5 Mich.App. 370, 146 N.W.2d 702, affirmed 381 Mich. 363, 161 N.W.2d 561; McDougall v. Snider, [1913] 15 Dom.L.Rev. 111.

See also Jacoby v. City of Gillette, 1947, 62 Wyo. 487, 174 P.2d 505, rehearing denied 62 Wyo. 487, 177 P.2d 204; Sutliff v. Sweetwater Water Co., 1920, 182 Cal. 34, 186 P. 766; Charlesworth, Law of Negligence, 1938, 220–233; MacDonald, The Rule of Rylands v. Fletcher and Its Limitations, 1923, 1 Can.Bar Rev. 140, 145.

49. Carstairs v. Taylor, 1871, L.R. 6 Ex. 217.

50. Murphy v. Gillum, 1898, 73 Mo.App. 487. Cf. Tuckachinsky v. Lehigh & Wilkes-Barre Coal Co., 1901, 199 Pa. 515, 49 A. 308 (magazine of explosives destroyed by lightning).

51. Box v. Jubb, 1879, L.R. 4 Ex.Div. 76. A fortiori where the escape is caused by the act of the plaintiff himself. Rozewski v. Simpson, 1937, 9 Cal.2d 515, 71 P.2d 72.

52. Rickards v. Lothian, [1913] A.C. 263, 82 L.J.P.C. 42.

53. Smith v. Great Western R. Co., 1926, 42 T.L.R. 391. Accord: Perry v. Kendricks Transport, Ltd., [1956] 1 W.L.R. 85; Kaufman v. Boston Dye House, 1932, 280 Mass. 161, 182 N.E. 297; Langabaugh v. Anderson, 1903, 68 Ohio St. 131, 67 N.E. 286; Cohen v. Brockton Savings Bank, 1947, 320 Mass. 690, 71 N.E.2d 109. Compare, as to the result, Kleebauer v. Western Fuse & Explosives Co., 1903, 138 Cal. 497, 71 P. 617; McGehee v. Norfolk & Southern Railway Co., 1908, 147 N.C. 142, 60 S.E. 912.

54. Davis v. Atlas Assurance Co., 1925, 112 Ohio St. 543, 147 N.E. 913. But cf. Spokane International Railway Co. v. United States, 10th Cir. 1934, 72 F.2d 440, giving the statute a broader interpretation.

55. Hartford v. Brady, 1874, 114 Mass. 466. Accord, M'Gibbon v. M'Curry, 1909, 43 Ir.L.T. 132 (stranger left gate open). But apparently contra is Noyes v. Colby, 1855, 30 N.H. 143, where the defendant's cow was released from confinement by the act of a third party.

56. In Vredenburg v. Behan, 1881, 33 La.Ann. 627, a bear chained to the corner of defendant's clubhouse was teased by a boy setting a dog on him, escaped his collar, and injured the plaintiff. It would seem that the defendant was negligent in keeping the bear without a cage; but in any case, in view of the public place, such interference would appear to be clearly within the risk. The same is true of the very similar case of Kinmouth v. McDougall, 1892, 64 Hun 636, 19 N.Y.S. 771, affirmed 1893, 139 N.Y. 612, 35 N.E. 204.

In Baker v. Snell, [1908] 2 K.B. 352, 825, a vicious dog was entrusted to a servant to be taken for a run. The servant released the dog, and incited it to attack the plaintiff. The actual decision of the case ordered a new trial on the issue of whether the servant was acting in the course of his employment; but two of the three final judges, in quite unclear opinions, apparently thought that the owner should be liable even if he were not. In any case, since the servant was entrusted with the dog, the decision is scarcely authority as to the acts of complete strangers. It was followed, under compulsion, in Behrens v. Bertram Mills Circus, [1957] 2 Q.B. 1, where the negligence of a third party allowed a dog to frighten an elephant. Contra is the Scottish case of Fleeming v. Orr, 1857, 2 Macq. 14; also, apparently, Strubing v. Mahar, 1899, 46 App.Div. 409, 61 N.Y.S. 799.

English writers have, on the whole, disagreed with Baker v. Snell. See Pollock, The Dog and the Potman, or "Go It, Bob," 1909, 25 L.Q.Rev. 317; Beven, The Responsibility at Common Law for the keeping of Ani-

question of negligence on his part. These decisions appear to be out of line. If they are to be justified, it may be upon the ground that the extraordinary risk of keeping such abnormal animals includes the likelihood that strangers will interfere with them, since it is so easily done; and hence that the defendant's strict responsibility extends to the prevention of such an occurrence.[57]

Plaintiff's Conduct

It frequently is said that the contributory negligence of the plaintiff is not a defense in cases of strict liability.[58] This involves the seemingly illogical position that the fault of the plaintiff will relieve the defendant of liability when he is negligent, but not when he is innocent. The explanation must lie in part in the element of wilful creation of an unreasonable risk to others by abnormal conduct which is inherent in most of the strict liability cases; and in part in the policy which places the absolute responsibility for preventing the harm upon the defendant, whether his conduct is regarded as fundamentally anti-social, or he is considered merely to be in a better position to transfer the loss to the community.[59] The statutory policy of the workmen's compensation acts,[60] which places all risk upon the defendant, finds a parallel in strict liability at common law.

Thus, a plaintiff who is injured by the defendant's dangerous animal is not barred from recovery by his own lack of ordinary care in failing to discover its presence,[61] or in inadvertently coming in contact with it.[62] Likewise the plaintiff's negligent failure to maintain fences on his own land will not prevent strict liability for the trespass of the defendant's horse.[63] Nor is contributory negligence in failing to take precautions a defense to the statutory liability for the escape of fire.[64] And in cases where the defendant is carrying on an abnormally dangerous activity, such as blasting, contributory negligence which merely fails to discover the peril and avoid it will not prevent the plaintiff's action.[65]

At the same time, contributory negligence by way of knowingly and unreasonably subjecting oneself to a risk of harm from an abnormally dangerous animal will constitute a defense. This must be carefully distin-

---

mals, 1909, 22 Harv.L.Rev. 317; Williams, Liability for Animals, 1939, 334–335; Salmond, Law of Torts, 13th ed.1961, 616–617; Winfield, Law of Tort, 6th ed.1954, 647. Defending it are Goodhart, The Third Man, 1951, 4 Curr.Leg.Prob. 184–187; Fleming, Law of Torts, 2d ed.1961, 317.

57. Compare City of Mangum v. Brownlee, 1938, 181 Okl. 515, 75 P.2d 174, where the act of a stranger in leading an escaped bear back to the zoo was held to be clearly within the risk. Also Andrew v. Kilgour, [1910] 19 Man.L.Rep. 545, as to the act of a third person in fighting off an attack from a raccoon, and dumping it out in the yard. Cf. Clinkenbeard v. Reinert, 1921, 284 Mo. 569, 225 S.W. 667, discussed in Note, 1921, 34 Harv.L.Rev. 771, holding that it is within the risk that a vicious dog will go mad.

58. "As negligence, in the ordinary sense, is not the ground of liability, so contributory negligence, in its ordinary meaning, is not a defense." Muller v. McKesson, 1878, 73 N.Y. 195.
Cf. Osinger v. Christian, 1963, 43 Ill.App.2d 480, 193 N.E.2d 872 (not a defense in action under Dramshop Act); and see Note, 1942, 37 Ill.L.Rev. 57.

59. Lowndes, Contributory Negligence, 1934, 22 Georgetown L.J. 674, 689–697.

60. See infra, § 80.

61. Muller v. McKesson, 1878, 73 N.Y. 195; Sandy v. Bushey, 1925, 124 Me. 320, 128 A. 513; Burke v. Fischer, 1944, 298 Ky. 157, 182 S.W.2d 638. Accord, under dog statutes: Wojewoda v. Rybarczyk, 1929, 246 Mich. 641, 225 N.W. 555; Siegfried v. Everhart, 1936, 55 Ohio App. 351, 9 N.E.2d 891.
Compare the cases of nuisance, infra, Ch. 15.

62. Fake v. Addicks, 1890, 45 Minn. 37, 47 N.W. 450 (stepping on dog); Wojewoda v. Rybarczyk, 1929, 246 Mich. 641, 225 N.W. 555 (same); Klatz v. Pfeffer, 1928, 333 Ill. 90, 164 N.E. 224; Tubbs v. Shears, 1916, 55 Okl. 610, 155 P. 549; Johnston v. Ohls, 1969, 76 Wn.2d 398, 457 P.2d 194.

63. Holgate v. Bleazard, [1917] 1 K.B. 443; Stackpole v. Healy, 1819, 16 Mass. 33; cf. Mozingo v. Cooley, 1930, 157 Miss. 636, 128 So. 771.

64. Evins v. St. Louis & San Francisco Railroad Co., 1912, 104 Ark. 79, 147 S.W. 452; Matthews v. Missouri Pacific Railway Co., 1897, 142 Mo. 645, 44 S.W. 802; Fraser-Patterson Lumber Co. v. Southern Railway Co., W.D.S.C.1948, 79 F.Supp. 424.

65. See, as to "absolute" nuisances, Bowman v. Humphrey, 1906, 132 Iowa 234, 109 N.W. 714; Niagara Oil Co. v. Ogle, 1912, 177 Ind. 292, 98 N.E. 60; Wilks v. New York Telephone Co., 1924, 208 App Div 542, 203 N.Y.S. 665; Hoffman v. City of Bristol, 1931, 113 Conn. 386, 393, 155 A. 499, 502. See Note, 1934, 29 Ill. L.Rev. 372.

guished from what is usually meant by assumption of the risk which is not a fault defense but it is commonly used to mean a type of defense based upon a consent doctrine. Thus, a plaintiff who voluntarily and unreasonably comes within reach of an animal which he knows to be dangerous, [66] or intentionally irritates or provokes it, [67] has no cause of action when it attacks him. The same is true when he rashly rushes into the path of the defendant's fire.[68] And where the defendant's activity is a dangerous one imposing strict liability, such as blasting, a plaintiff who has discovered the danger will have recovered barred or diminished by his own "wanton, wilful or reckless misconduct" which materially increases the probabilities of injury[69] or what amounts to "invitation to injury, or at least indifference to consequences."[70]

The question of when a person's conscious decision to encounter an appreciated risk of harm should deprive him of recovery has commonly been considered as a problem relating to a defense referred to as voluntary assumption of the risk. Its application to particular situations has been the source of much confusion. The question here is whether or not the risk related to an abnormally dangerous activity should be allocated to the plaintiff if he knowingly chooses to expose himself to it. This depends upon the relationship between the plaintiff and the defendant at the time the risk was encountered. The mere fact that one outside the defendant's premises does not choose to move away from the area of the defendant's activity will not affect his recovery if defendant's activity is found to be abnormally dangerous or ultra-hazardous. On the other hand, if the plaintiff without a privilege by law to do so encounters the risk pursuant to a contract with the defendant or pursuant to any kind of consensual arrangement, then it is quite possible that as between the parties it was impliedly if not expressly understood that there would be no liability in the absence of negligence. Risks should be allocated in the way parties would normally expect those risks to be allocated in the absence of coercion or an expression to the contrary. So, there are many consensual arrangements in which the plaintiff should be allowed to proceed on the assumption that the defendant will protect him against a risk, as when an invitee is on the premises of a zoo or to attend a circus. But generally, one who utilizes the services of a defendant engaged in an abnormally dangerous activity will be regarded as assuming the risk that is universally known to exist. Thus, a passenger in an airline will assume the risk that is normally associated with air travel even though the use of airplanes may be regarded as abnormally dangerous. The liability is to those on the ground who did not voluntarily encounter the danger by utilizing the service. Likewise, if plaintiff agrees to work with dangerous animals, he assumes the risk, and cannot recover when they injure him.[71] And where the defendant's activity is carried on in part for the plaintiff's

---

66. Opelt v. Al. G. Barnes Co., 1918, 41 Cal.App. 776, 183 P. 241 (crawling under rope near leopard's cage); Hosmer v. Carney, 1920, 228 N.Y. 73, 126 N.E. 650 (going behind vicious horse); Swerdfeger v. Krueger, 1960, 145 Colo. 180, 358 P.2d 479 (going within reach of vicious dog); Hughey v. Fergus County, 1934, 98 Mont. 98, 37 P.2d 1035 (entering field with bull); Heidemann v. Wheaton, 1948, 72 S.D. 375, 34 N.W.2d 492 (going within reach of bear).

67. Lehnhard v. Robertson's Administratrix, 1917, 176 Ky. 322, 195 S.W. 441 (prodding bear); Wolff v. Lamann, 1900, 108 Ky. 343, 56 S.W. 408 (teasing dog); Donahue v. Frank E. Scott Transfer Co., 1908, 141 Ill. App. 174 (irritating jackass). Cf. Dorman v. Carlson, 1927, 106 Conn. 200, 137 A. 749 (under dog statute).

68. Bowen v. Boston & Albany Railroad Co., 1901, 179 Mass. 524, 61 N.E. 141. But an adjoining landowner does not assume the risk of fire by failing to take precautions against it, where the defendant forces an unreasonable alternative upon him. Leroy Fibre Co. v. Chicago, Milwaukee & St. Paul Railway Co., 1914, 232 U.S. 340, 34 S.Ct. 415, 58 L.Ed. 631.

69. Worth v. Dunn, 1922, 98 Conn. 51, 62, 118 A. 467, 471; Wells v. Knight, 1911, 32 R.I. 432, 80 A. 16; Robinson v. Robinson, 1964, 16 Utah 2d 2, 394 P.2d 876.

70. See McFarlane v. City of Niagara Falls, 1928, 247 N.Y. 340, 160 N.E. 391; Muller v. McKesson, 1878, 73 N.Y. 195.

71. Cooper v. Robert Portner Brewing Co., 1900, 112 Ga. 894, 38 S.E. 91, rehearing and motion to modified judgment denied 113 Ga. 1, 38 S.E. 347; Armington v. Providence Ice Co., 1912, 33 R.I. 484, 82 A. 263; Bowles v. Indiana Railway Co., 1901, 27 Ind.App. 672,

benefit, as where water[72] or gas[73] pipes are maintained for his use, his willingness to encounter the risk is found by implication from his acceptance of the situation.

Privilege

There are certain conditions under which conduct which would otherwise result in strict liability may be privileged. The most obvious one is that of a sanction given by statutory authority, or by well defined local law.[74] Within the limitations of the constitution,[75] the legislature may authorize acts which involve a high degree of risk to others, and such authority amounts at least to a declaration that the acts are not antisocial, but desirable for the benefit of the community. In the absence of a provision expressly preserving the defendant's liability for any resulting damage,[76] the courts have on occasion interpreted the statute as condoning the consequences in advance, and have refused to hold the defendant liable for doing what was authorized. Thus where gas,[77] water,[78] or electric[79] conduits are laid in the street under legislative sanction, it has been held that there is no liability for the damage they may do, in the absence of some negligence.[80] Likewise a contractor, doing work involving blasting for the state, has been held not subject to strict liability.[81] The tendency in the later cases has been to avoid such a conclusion, by strict construction of the authorizing statute,[82] or by finding an implied condition that there shall be liability,[83] or that the manner of doing the work, or the resulting damage itself, are not authorized or necessary consequences of the sanctioned work.[84]

Even without a statutory exemption from strict liability, express or implied, the defendant may be regarded as so engaged in the rendition of such an essential public service as to justify an exception to the general rule of strict liability. It is generally held that the rules of strict liability do not apply if the activity is carried on in pursuance of a public duty.[85] The custodians of a public zo-

---

62 N.E. 94; Gomes v. Byrne, 1959, 51 Cal.2d 418, 333 P.2d 754; Brown v. Barber, 1943, 26 Tenn.App. 534, 174 S.W.2d 298.

72. Carstairs v. Taylor, 1871, L.R. 6 Ex. 217; Rickards v. Lothian, [1913] A.C. 263; Blake v. Woolf, [1898] 2 Q.B. 426.

73. Cf. Hess v. Greenway, Ont.1919, 48 Dom.L.Rep. 630; E. I. Du Pont de Nemours & Co. v. Cudd, 10th Cir. 1949, 176 F.2d 855 (plaintiff participating in activity).

74. See Linden, Strict Liability—Nuisance and Legislative Authorization, 1966, 4 Osgoode Hall L.Rev. 196. Also Madras R. Co. v. Zemindar of Carvatenagarum, 1874, L.R. 1 Ind.App. 364, 30 L.T. 770; Notes, 1960, 12 Stan.L.Rev. 691; 1938, 13 Notre Dame L. 229.

75. See generally Bacon v. City of Boston, 1891, 154 Mass. 100, 28 N.E. 9; Cohen v. Mayor of New York, 1889, 113 N.Y. 532, 21 N.E. 700; Rose v. State, 1942, 19 Cal.2d 713, 123 P.2d 505; Chick Springs Water, Inc. v. State Highway Department, 1931, 159 S.C. 481, 157 S.E. 842.

76. In such a case there is liability without negligence. Midwood & Co. v. Mayor of Manchester, [1905] 2 K.B. 597; Charing Cross Elec. Supply Co. v. Hydraulic Power Co., [1914] 3 K.B. 772.

77. Gould v. Winona Gas Co., 1907, 100 Minn. 258, 261, 111 N.W. 254, 255; Schmeer v. Gas Light Co., 1895, 147 N.Y. 529, 42 N.E. 202, 205; Price v. South Metropolitan Gas Co., 1895, 65 L.J.Q.B. 126.

78. Green v. Chelsea Waterworks Co., 1894, 70 L.T. 547.

79. National Tel. Co. v. Baker, [1893] 2 Ch. 186; Dumphy v. Montreal Light Co., [1907] A.C. 455. Compare the rule that a railway run under statutory authority is not liable for the escape of fire. Vaughan v. Taff Vale R. Co., 1860, 5 H. & N. 678, 157 Eng.Rep. 1351; Canadian Pac. R. Co. v. Roy, [1902] A.C. 220.

80. The statute does not relieve the defendant from liability for negligence. Northwestern Utilities v. London Guar. & Acc. Co., [1936] A.C. 105.

81. Pumphrey v. J. A. Jones Construction Co., 1959, 250 Iowa 559, 94 N.W.2d 737; Nelson v. McKenzie-Hague Co., 1934, 192 Minn. 180, 256 N.W. 96; V. N. Green & Co. v. Thomas, 1965, 205 Va. 903, 140 S.E.2d 635. Accord: Benner v. Atlantic Dredging Co., 1892, 134 N.Y. 156, 31 N.E. 328; Fitzgibbon v. Western Dredging Co., 1908, 141 Iowa 328, 117 N.W. 878. See Notes, 1934, 19 Minn.L.Rev. 129; 1966, 23 Wash. & Lee L.Rev. 118.

82. Cogswell v. New York, New Haven & Hartford Railroad Co., 1886, 103 N.Y. 10, 8 N.E. 537; Messer v. City of Dickinson, 1942, 71 N.D. 568, 3 N.W.2d 241, 245. Cf. McLane v. Northwest Natural Gas Co., 1969, 255 Or. 324, 467 P.2d 635.

83. Smith v. Aldridge, Mo.App.1962, 356 S.W.2d 532; Ferriter v. Herlihy, 1934, 287 Mass. 138, 191 N.E. 352, 354.

84. Whitney v. Ralph Myers Contracting Co., 1961, 146 W.Va. 130, 118 S.E.2d 622; Webster Co. v. Steelman, 1939, 172 Va. 342, 1 S.E.2d 305; Hakkila v. Old Colony Broken Stone & Concrete Co., 1928, 264 Mass. 447, 162 N.E. 895. Cf. Monroe v. Razor Construction Co., 1961, 252 Iowa 1249, 110 N.W.2d 250 (negligence).

85. Second Restatement of Torts, § 521. Boxes, Ltd. v. British Waterways Bd., 1970, 2 Lloyd's L.R. 434 (Q.B.).

ological garden are not subject to strict liability for harm done by the animals kept,[86] and a carrier which is required to accept dangerous animals,[87] or explosives[88] for transportation has been held liable only for negligence. The public utility that is engaged in generating and distributing electricity, no doubt an abnormally dangerous activity, is often intensively regulated as to rates and manner of rendition of the service. That being so, such an activity, authorized, sanctioned, and regulated in such a manner, may not be regarded as the kind that should be subjected to strict liability. This could depend in large part upon whether ratepayers for the service rendered should be required to absorb the costs of unavoidable accidents.

WESTLAW REFERENCES
synopsis,digest(damages /p limit! extend extent! /p strict! absolut! /s liab!)

Nature of Risk and Type of Harm Threatened
synopsis,digest(dog* cattle animal! livestock! horse* cow*) & strict! absolut! /s liab! & foresee! unforesee! reason! normal /s consequence! risk! harm*
28k70

Class of Persons Protected
synopsis,digest(dog* /p trespasser*)
28k68 /p trespasser* invitee* licensee*
wild vicious /s dog* animal* /p strict! absolut! /s liab!

Manner of Occurrence
siegler /5 kulhman
synopsis,digest(contributory /p strict! absolut! /s liab!) % topic(313a)
synopsis,digest(assumption assume* /s risk* /p strict! absolut! /s liab!) % topic(313a)

Privilege
zoo zoological /p strict! absolut! /s liab!

---

§ 80. Employers' Liability

The outstanding statutory application of the principle of strict liability is in the workers' compensation acts, which have very largely preempted the whole field of the liability of employers for injuries to their employees. Basically they do not rest upon any theory of tort liability, but upon one of social insurance.

The background of these statutes lay in the very limited tort liability of the master to his servant at common law. The extent of the employer's responsibility, although it was said to rest upon the understanding of the parties, undoubtedly was fixed by the courts upon the basis of old industrial conditions, and a social philosophy and an attitude toward labor, which are long since outmoded. The cornerstone of the common law edifice was the economic theory that there was complete mobility of labor, that the supply of work was unlimited, and that the worker was an entirely free agent, under no compulsion to enter into the employment. He was expected therefore to accept and take upon himself all of the usual risks of the trade, together with any unusual risks of which he had knowledge, and to relieve the employer of any duty to protect him. The economic compulsion which left him no choice except starvation, or equally dangerous employment elsewhere, was entirely disregarded. The employer's responsibility

---

86. Jackson v. Baker, 1904, 24 App.D.C. 100; Guzzi v. New York Zoological Society, 1920, 192 App.Div. 263, 182 N.Y.S. 257, affirmed 1922, 233 N.Y. 511, 135 N.E. 897.
The city itself is not liable where it has legislative authority. McKinney v. City and County of San Francisco, 1952, 109 Cal.App.2d 844, 241 P.2d 1060; Hibbard v. City of Wichita, 1916, 98 Kan. 498, 159 P. 399. It is, however, strictly liable where it has no authority. City of Mangum v. Brownlee, 1938, 181 Okl. 515, 75 P.2d 174; Collentine v. City of New York, 1938, 279 N.Y. 119, 124, 17 N.E.2d 792, 795; Hyde v. City of Utica, 1940, 259 App.Div. 477, 20 N.Y.S.2d 335.

87. Malloy v. Starin, 1908, 191 N.Y. 21, 83 N.E. 588. The Restatement of Torts, § 517, takes the position that if the carrier is not required to accept the shipment it may be strictly liable. But see, to the effect that it is sufficient that it is authorized to accept it as a carrier, Stamp v. Eighty-Sixth Street Amusement Co., 1916, 95 Misc. 599, 159 N.Y.S. 683; cf. Pope v. Edward M. Rude Carrier Corp., 1953, 138 W.Va. 218, 75 S.E.2d 584 (dynamite).

88. Actiesselskabet Ingrid v. Central Railroad Co. of New Jersey, 2d Cir. 1914, 216 F. 72, rehearing denied 216 F. 991, certiorari denied 238 U.S. 615, 35 S.Ct. 284, 59 L.Ed. 1490; Pope v. Edward M. Rude Carrier Corp., 1953, 138 W.Va. 218, 75 S.E.2d 584.

was limited to certain rather specific minimum obligations, which it was felt that any worker had the right to demand. Even as to these obligations, the employer was not an insurer of safety, and was liable only for a failure to exercise reasonable care,[1] and in addition, the employer was not responsible for the negligence of fellow-servants of the injured worker, as distinguished from the employer's own misconduct.[2] The result was that for the great majority of industrial accidents there was no recovery, either because no lack of proper care could be charged against the employer, or because the worker was taken to have assumed the risk.

The specific common law duties of the master for the protection of his servants were commonly classified as follows:

1. The duty to provide a safe place to work.[3]

2. The duty to provide safe appliances, tools, and equipment for the work.[4]

3. The duty to give warning of dangers of which the employee might reasonably be expected to remain in ignorance.[5]

4. The duty to provide a sufficient number of suitable fellow servants.[6]

5. The duty to promulgate and enforce rules for the conduct of employees which would make the work safe.[7]

The possibility of the injured worker's recovery, which was limited at the outset to cases where the employer had failed to exercise proper care in the foregoing specific respects, was restricted further by the "unholy trinity" of common law defenses—contributory negligence, assumption of risk, and the fellow servant rule. The effect of these defenses was to relieve the employer of responsibility even though he, or his other servants, had failed in respect of the specific obligations for the protection of the servant listed above. The second and third in particular offered formidable obstacles to any recovery for the usual industrial accident.

The workers were required to exercise reasonable care for their own safety, and their recovery was barred by their contributory negligence.[8] The defense was of course subject to all of the rules usually applicable to it, and the servant might recover

§ 80

1. Cf. Armour v. Hahn, 1884, 111 U.S. 313, 4 S.Ct. 433, 28 L.Ed. 440; Wonder v. Baltimore & Ohio Railroad Co., 1870, 32 Md. 411; Curley v. Hoff, 1899, 62 N.J.L. 758, 42 A. 731.

2. See infra this section.

3. Armour v. Golkowska, 1903, 202 Ill. 144, 66 N.E. 1037; Burns v. Delaware & Atlantic Telegraph & Telephone Co., 1904, 70 N.J.L. 745, 59 A. 220, 592; McGuire v. Bell Telephone Co. of Buffalo, 1901, 167 N.Y. 208, 60 N.E. 433; Butterman v. McClintic-Marshall Construction Co., 1903, 206 Pa. 82, 55 A. 839.

The duty was not only to protect against dangers of which the employer knew, but also to exercise reasonable care to make inspections to discover conditions of which he did not. White v. Consolidated Freight Lines, 1937, 192 Wash. 146, 73 P.2d 358; Chicago & Eastern Illinois Railroad Co. v. Kneirim, 1894, 152 Ill. 458, 39 N.E. 324; Simone v. Kirk, 1902, 173 N.Y. 7, 65 N.E. 739; Smith v. Erie Railroad Co., 1902, 67 N.J.L. 636, 52 A. 634.

4. Petrol Corp. v. Curtis, 1948, 190 Md. 652, 59 A.2d 329; Toy v. United States Cartridge Co., 1893, 159 Mass. 313, 34 N.E. 461; Chicago Union Traction Co. v. Sawusch, 1905, 218 Ill. 130, 75 N.E. 797; Byrne v. Eastmans Co., 1900, 163 N.Y. 461, 57 N.E. 738; Daniels v. Luechtefeld, Mo.App.1941, 155 S.W.2d 307.

5. Engelking v. City of Spokane, 1910, 59 Wash. 446, 110 P. 25; Baumgartner v. Pennsylvania Railroad Co., 1928, 292 Pa. 106, 140 A. 622; Brennan v. Gordon, 1890, 118 N.Y. 489, 23 N.E. 810; Moore v. Morse & Malloy Shoe Co., 1938, 89 N.H. 332, 197 A. 707; Bassett v. New York, Chicago & St. Louis Railroad Co., 3d Cir. 1956, 235 F.2d 900 (obstructions in area where employee was to travel by motor car).

6. Filke v. Boston & Albany Railroad Co., 1873, 53 N.Y. 549; Johnson v. Ashland Water Co., 1888, 71 Wis. 553, 37 N.W. 823; Peterson v. American Grass Twine Co., 1903, 90 Minn. 343, 96 N.W. 913; Di Bari v. J. W. Bishop Co., 1908, 199 Mass. 254, 85 N.E. 89; Wyman v. Lehigh Valley Railroad Co., 2d Cir. 1908, 158 F. 957.

7. Tremblay v. J. Rudnick & Sons, 1940, 91 N.H. 24, 13 A.2d 153; Lake Shore & Michigan Southern Railway Co. v. Lavalley, 1880, 36 Ohio St. 221; Cooper v. Central Railroad of Iowa, 1876, 44 Iowa 134; Doing v. New York, Ontario & Western Railway Co., 1897, 151 N.Y. 579, 45 N.E. 1028; Southern Package Corp. v. Mitchell, 5th Cir. 1940, 109 F.2d 609.

8. Schlemmer v. Buffalo, Rochester & Pittsburgh Railway Co., 1911, 220 U.S. 590, 31 S.Ct. 561, 55 L.Ed. 596; Meunier v. Chemical Paper Co., 1901, 180 Mass. 109, 61 N.E. 810; Limberg v. Glenwood Lumber Co., 1900, 127 Cal. 598, 60 P. 176; Narramore v. Cleveland, Cincinnati, Chicago & St. Louis Railway Co., 6th Cir. 1899, 96 F.2d 298, certiorari denied 175 U.S. 724, 20 S.Ct. 1021, 44 L.Ed. 337.

if it could be found that the master had the last clear chance,[9] or that his conduct was wilful or wanton.[10] But it frequently meant that a momentary lapse of caution on the part of the worker was penalized by casting the entire burden of his injury upon him, in the face of continued and greater negligence of the employer.

The risks which did not lie within the scope of the specific obligations of the master were considered to be accepted by the servant as an incident of his employment, and the employer was under no duty to protect him against them. He was said to have bargained away his right to hold the employer responsible,[11] or to have assumed the risk of hazards normally incident to his employment.[12] But even where the master had clearly violated his duty in the first instance, as to appliances,[13] the place to work,[14] or his rules and methods,[15] the worker might be denied recovery on the ground that he had assumed the risk, and consented[16] to relieve the employer of his obligation. If he remained at work voluntarily[17] after he knew[18] and appreciated[19] the danger, he was found to accept the situation, and to undertake to look out for himself, notwithstanding the employer's breach of his obligation. Even though he continued his work under protest,[20] or under a direct order carrying a threat of discharge,[21] he still was

---

9. Small v. Boston & Maine Railroad Co., 1934, 87 N.H. 25, 173 A. 381; Raines v. Southern Railway Co., 1915, 169 N.C. 189, 85 S.E. 294; see Louisville & Nashville Railroad Co. v. Young, 1910, 168 Ala. 551, 53 So. 213.

10. Louisville & Nashville Railroad Co. v. York, 1901, 128 Ala. 305, 30 So. 676; see Arkley v. Niblack, 1916, 272 Ill. 356, 112 N.E. 67.

11. Lang v. United States Reduction Co., 7th Cir. 1940, 110 F.2d 441, 442; Ehrenberger v. Chicago, Rock Island & Pacific Railway Co., 1918, 182 Iowa 1339, 1342, 166 N.W. 735, 736.

12. Cooper v. Mayes, 1959, 234 S.C. 491, 495, 109 S.E.2d 12, 13; Jones v. Adams, 1952, 56 N.M. 510, 245 P.2d 843; Walsh v. West Coast Mines, Inc., 1948, 31 Wn.2d 396, 406, 197 P.2d 233, 238; Conboy v. Crofoot, 1964, 194 Kan. 46, 397 P.2d 326.

13. Errico v. Washburn Williams Co., M.D.Pa.1909, 170 F. 852; Crown v. Orr, 1893, 140 N.Y. 450, 35 N.E. 648; Painter v. Nichols, 1954, 118 Vt. 306, 108 A.2d 384; Abercrombie v. Ivey, 1938, 59 Ga.App. 296, 200 S.E. 551; see Bartlett v. Gregg, 1958, 77 S.D. 406, 92 N.W.2d 654.

14. Eiban v. Widsteen, 1948, 31 Wn.2d 655, 198 P.2d 667; Kline v. Abraham, 1904, 178 N.Y. 377, 70 N.E. 923; Gutierrez v. Valley Irrigation & Livestock Co., 1960, 68 N.M. 6, 357 P.2d 664, 666; Richter v. Razore, 1960, 56 Wn.2d 580, 354 P.2d 706; Morris & Co. v. Alvis, 1921, 130 Va. 434, 107 S.E. 664.

15. Abbot v. McCadden, 1892, 81 Wis. 563, 51 N.W. 1079; Schultz v. Chicago & Northwestern Railway Co., 1887, 67 Wis. 616, 31 N.W. 321.

The usual form of statement was that the employee "assumes (1) such dangers as are ordinarily and normally incident to the work, and a workman of mature years is presumed to know them whether he does or not; (2) such extraordinary and abnormal risks as he (a) knows and appreciates and faces without complaint or (b) are obvious and apparent." Boatman v. Miles, 1921, 27 Wyo. 481, 487, 199 P. 933, 935.

16. See Note, 1961, 47 Va.L.Rev. 1444. Assumption of risk was sometimes said to be a matter of the contract of employment, as in Conway v. Furst, 1895, 57 N.J.L. 645, 32 A. 380; B. Shoninger Co. v. Mann, 1905, 219 Ill. 242, 76 N.E. 354. It is generally recognized, however, that it rests merely on consent, and that the risk may be assumed after the workman has been employed. O'Maley v. South Boston Gas Light Co., 1893, 158 Mass. 135, 32 N.E. 1119; Rase v. Minneapolis, St. Paul & Sault Ste. Marie Railway Co., 1909, 107 Minn. 260, 120 N.W. 360; Knisley v. Pratt, 1896, 148 N.Y. 372, 42 N.E. 986, reargument denied 149 N.Y. 582, 43 N.E. 988.

As to the distinction between assumption of risk and contributory negligence, see supra, § 68.

17. Thus the defense does not apply to one who is not free to leave the employment. Chattahoochee Brick Co. v. Braswell, 1893, 92 Ga. 631, 18 S.E. 1015; Sloss-Sheffield Steel & Iron Co. v. Long, 1910, 169 Ala. 337, 53 So. 910 (convicts); Lafourche Packet Co. v. Henderson, 5th Cir. 1899, 94 F. 871 (seaman). Cf. Olney v. Boston & Maine Railroad, 1902, 71 N.H. 427, 52 A. 1097 (engineer would endanger others by leaving engine).

18. See supra, § 68; Uhlrig v. Shortt, 1964, 194 Kan. 68, 397 P.2d 321.

19. Heinlen v. Martin Miller Orchards, 1952, 40 Wn. 2d 356, 242 P.2d 1054; McDaniel v. Chicago, Rock Island & Pacific Railway Co., 1936, 338 Mo. 481, 92 S.W.2d 118; Choctaw, Oklahoma & Gulf Railroad Co. v. Jones, 1906, 77 Ark. 367, 92 S.W. 244; Davidson v. Cornell, 1892, 132 N.Y. 228, 30 N.E. 573.

20. Atchison, Topeka & Santa Fe Railway Co. v. Schroeder, 1891, 47 Kan. 315, 27 P. 965; Galveston, Harrisburg & San Antonio Railway Co. v. Drew, 1883, 59 Tex. 10; Talbot v. Sims, 1905, 213 Pa. 1, 62 A. 107; Loynes v. Loring B. Hall Co., 1907, 194 Mass. 221, 80 N.E. 472.

21. Burke v. Davis, 1906, 191 Mass. 20, 76 N.E. 1039; Hallstein v. Pennsylvania Railroad Co., 6th Cir. 1929, 30 F.2d 594; Clairmont v. Cilley, 1931, 85 N.H. 1, 153 A. 465; Nashville, Chattanooga & St. Louis Railway Co. v. Cleaver, 1938, 274 Ky. 410, 118 S.W.2d 748. Contra: New York, New Haven & Hartford Railroad Co. v. Vizvari, 2d Cir. 1913, 210 F. 118; Goss v. Kurn, 1940, 187 Miss. 679, 193 So. 783.

found to have consented, however reluctantly, to assume the risk. The fact that the alternative was the loss of his means of subsistence and that it was "his poverty and not his will which consented," [22] although it was recognized to some extent in England,[23] was almost entirely ignored by the American courts. It was only where the peril was not imminent,[24] and the master gave an assurance of safety [25] or a promise to remedy the defect,[26] that the worker was held not to assume the risk by remaining in his employment, and then only until such time as it became apparent that the assurance was not to be relied on.[27]

The rule that the employer was not liable for injuries caused solely by the negligence of a fellow servant first appeared in England in 1837,[28] and almost immediately afterward in the United States,[29] where it was stated elaborately in a well known opinion of Chief Justice Shaw of Massachusetts in Farwell v. Boston & Worcester Railway.[30] Although it has been assailed as a direct departure from the established rule of vicarious liability for the torts of servants within the scope of their employment, it probably should be regarded as an inherent limitation upon that rule itself, which seems to have been conceived as an obligation of the head of the household to those who were not his servants.[31] The reasons usually assigned [32] for it, however, were that the plaintiff upon entering the employment assumed the risk of negligence on the part of his fellow servants,[33] and the master did not undertake to protect him against it; that he was as likely to know of their deficiencies and to be in a position to guard against them as his employer; and that it would promote the safety of the public and of all servants to make each one watchful of the conduct of others for his own protection. While these reasons might perhaps have been appropriate to small enterprises and shops, where the workers had close contact and acquaintance with one another, they had little validity in the case of large industries, where the plaintiff might be injured by the negligence of a fellow servant whom he had never seen. The explanation of the rule probably lay in the highly individualistic viewpoint of the common law courts, and their desire to en-

22. Hawkins, J., in Thrussell v. Handyside & Co., 1888, 20 Q.B.D. 359.

23. Yarmouth v. France, 1887, 19 Q.B.D. 647; Smith v. Baker & Sons, [1891] A.C. 325; Bowalter v. Rowley Regis Corp., [1944] 1 K.B. 476. Accord, Groner v. Hedrick, 1961, 403 Pa. 148, 169 A.2d 302. See Gow, The Defense of Volenti Non Fit Injuria, 1949, 61 Jurid.Rev. 37.

24. Greene v. Minneapolis & St. Louis Railroad Co., 1883, 31 Minn. 248, 17 N.W. 378; Dowd v. Erie Railroad Co., 1904, 70 N.J.L. 451, 57 A. 248; Curran v. A. H. Stange Co., 1898, 98 Wis. 598, 74 N.W. 377. Cf. Burke v. Davis, 1906, 191 Mass. 20, 76 N.E. 1039; Rohrabacher v. Woodward, 1900, 124 Mich. 125, 82 N.W. 797 (imminent danger).

25. Brown B. Lennane, 1908, 155 Mich. 686, 118 N.W. 581; McKee v. Tourtellotte, 1896, 167 Mass. 69, 44 N.E. 1071; Manks v. Moore, 1909, 108 Minn. 284, 122 N.W. 5.

26. Hough v. Texas & Pacific Railway Co., 1879, 100 U.S. 213, 25 L.Ed. 612; Rice v. Eureka Paper Co., 1903, 174 N.Y. 385, 66 N.E. 979; Dowd v. Erie Railroad Co., 1904, 70 N.J.L. 451, 57 A. 248; Cheek v. Eyth, 1939, 149 Kan. 586, 89 P.2d 11. But a promise by an unauthorized agent, or other third person is not sufficient. Liptak v. Karsner, 1940, 208 Minn. 168, 293 N.W. 612.

27. Faulkner v. Big Rock Stone & Material Co., 1940, 201 Ark. 124, 143 S.W.2d 883; Gunning System v. Lapointe, 1904, 212 Ill. 274, 72 N.E. 393; Andrecsik v. New Jersey Tube Co., 1906, 73 N.J.L. 664, 63 A. 719; Heathcock v. Milwaukee Platteville Lead & Zinc Mining Co., 1906, 128 Wis. 46, 107 N.W. 463.

28. Priestley v. Fowler, 1837, 3 M. & W. 1, 150 Eng. Rep. 1030.

29. Murray v. South Carolina R. Co., 1938, 1 McMul. L., S.C., 385.

30. 1849, 45 Mass. (4 Metc.) 49.

31. Holmes, Agency, 1891, 4 Harv.L.Rev. 345.

32. 2 Labatt, Master and Servant, 1904, §§ 472, 473; Powell, Some Phases of the Law of Master and Servant, 1910, 10 Col.L.Rev. 1, 30; Mechem, Employer's Liability, 1910, 44 Am.L.Rev. 221; Burdick, Is Law the Expression of Class Selfishness?, 1912, 25 Harv.L. Rev. 349, 357–381; Farwell v. Boston & Worcester Railway Co., 1849, 45 Mass. (4 Metc.) 49; Coon v. Syracuse & Utica Railroad Co., N.Y.1849, 6 Barb. 231, affirmed 1851, 5 N.Y. 492; Ryan v. Cumberland Valley Railroad Co., 1854, 23 Pa. 384.

33. Thus it was held that a convict entering employment under compulsion and a minor too inexperienced to appreciate the danger, were not subject to the fellow servant rule. Buckalew v. Tennessee Coal Iron & Railroad Co., 1895, 112 Ala. 146, 20 So. 606; Kendrick v. Ideal Holding Co., 1939, 137 Fla. 600, 188 So. 778.

courage industrial undertakings by making the burden upon them as light as possible.[34]

The general rule thus declared was later restricted in a number of respects, as its hardship upon labor became apparent.

The most important restriction was that generally accepted in the United States,[35] that the fellow servant rule did not apply to the negligence of a "vice-principal." By this was meant a servant who represented the employer in his responsibility to the plaintiff. In some decisions, it was held that a vice-principal must be a superior servant, such as a foreman, in a position of direct authority over the plaintiff.[36] Most courts rejected this requirement, and defined a vice-principal to include any servant, of whatever rank, who was charged by the master with the performance of his common law duties toward the plaintiff, such as the maintenance of a safe place to work[37] or safe appliances,[38] the employment of competent workmen,[39] or the giving of warning or instruction.[40] These duties were said to be non-delegable, in the sense that the employer could not escape responsibility for them by entrusting them to another, whether he be a servant or an independent contractor.[41]

Consequently he remained liable for the negligence of a fellow servant who represented him in that capacity. The vice-principal rule was, however, subject to the qualification that it did not apply to incidental dangers arising in the operative details of the fellow servant's work,[42] against which the master had no duty to take precautions, as distinct from a specific responsibility for the performance of a duty placed upon the servant.

Some slow progress toward the imposition of liability upon the employer may be traced through the common law cases, but the tendency in this direction was in large part superseded by the passage of the workers' compensation acts.

Statutory Changes

Under the common law system, by far the greater proportion[43] of industrial accidents remained uncompensated, and the burden fell upon the worker, who was least able to support it. Furthermore, the litigation which usually was necessary to any recovery meant delay, pressure upon the injured person to settle his claim in order to live, and heavy attorneys' fees and other expenses which frequently left him only a

---

34. Dodd, Administration of Workmen's Compensation, 1936, 7.

35. Rejected in England, in Wilson v. Merry, 1868, L.R. 1 H.L.Sc.App.Cas. 326.

36. Berea Stone Co. v. Kraft, 1877, 31 Ohio St. 287; Lamb v. Littman, 1903, 132 N.C. 978, 44 S.E. 646; Chap-Tan Drilling Co. v. Myers, 1950, 203 Okl. 642, 225 P.2d 373; cf. May v. Sharp, 1936, 191 Ark. 1142, 89 S.W.2d 735; McDonald v. Louisville & Nashville Railroad Co., 1930, 232 Ky. 734, 24 S.W.2d 585.

37. Smith v. Erie Railroad Co., 1902, 67 N.J.L. (38 Vroom) 636, 52 A. 634; Nuckolls v. Great Atlantic & Pacific Tea Co., 1939, 192 S.C. 156, 5 S.E.2d 862; Boettger v. Mauran, 1940, 64 R.I. 340, 12 A.2d 285; Cadden v. American Steel Barge Co., 1894, 88 Wis. 409, 60 N.W. 800.

38. Union Pacific Railroad Co. v. Daniels, 1894, 152 U.S. 684, 14 S.Ct. 756, 38 L.Ed. 597; Green River Light & Water Co. v. Beeler, 1923, 197 Ky. 818, 248 S.W. 201; Nuckolls v. Great Atlantic & Pacific Tea Co., 1939, 192 S.C. 156, 5 S.E.2d 862; Herdler v. Bucks Stove & Range Co., 1896, 136 Mo. 3, 37 S.W. 115; cf. Plemmons v. Antles, 1958, 52 Wn.2d 269, 324 P.2d 823 (truck driver with exclusive control).

39. Flike v. Boston & Albany Railroad Co., 1873, 53 N.Y. 549; Gilman v. Eastern Railway Co., 1866, 95 Mass. (13 Allen) 433.

40. Tedford v. Los Angeles Electric Co., 1901, 134 Cal. 76, 66 P. 76; Brennan v. Gordon, 1890, 118 N.Y. 489, 23 N.E. 810; Moore v. Morse & Malloy Shoe Co., 1938, 89 N.H. 332, 197 A. 707; Carey Reed Co. v. McDavid, 5th Cir. 1941, 120 F.2d 843.

41. Pullman's Palace Car Co. v. Laack, 1892, 143 Ill. 242, 32 N.E. 285; Moran v. Corliss Steam Engine Co., 1899, 21 R.I. 386, 43 A. 874.

42. Armour v. Hahn, 1884, 111 U.S. 313, 4 S.Ct. 433, 28 L.Ed. 440; James Stewart & Co. v. Newby, 4th Cir. 1920, 266 F. 287; Citrone v. O'Rourke Engineering Construction Co., 1907, 188 N.Y. 339, 80 N.E. 1092; Curley v. Hoff, 1899, 62 N.J.L. 758, 42 A. 731; Manning v. Genesee River & Lake Ontario Steamboat Co., 1901, 66 App.Div. 314, 72 N.Y.S. 677.

43. Variously estimated as follows: 70 per cent, 1 Schneider, Workmen's Compensation, 2d ed. 1932, 1; 80 per cent, Lumbermen's Reciprocal Association v. Behnken, Tex.Civ.App.1920, 226 S.W. 154, affirmed 112 Tex. 103, 246 S.W. 72; 83 per cent, Downey, History of Work Accident Indemnity in Iowa, 1912, 71; 87 per cent, First Report of New York Employers' Liability Comm., 1910, Vol. 1, p. 25; 94 per cent, Report of Ohio Employers' Liability Comm., 1911, part 1, xxxv–xliv.

small part of the money finally paid.[44] Coupled with this were working conditions of an extreme inhumanity in many industries, which the employer was under no particular incentive to improve. Early legislative attempts to regulate these conditions sometimes were nullified by decisions holding that the worker assumed the risk of the employer's violation of the statute.[45] The reluctance of the courts to face the problem and modify the common law rules made it clear that any change must come through some general legislation, and led to a movement for the passage of workers' compensation acts, modeled upon the statute already in existence in Germany.[46] Increasing agitation at last brought about the first statutes, in England in 1897, and in the United States, for government employees, in 1908. This was followed by the first state statute in New York in 1910. By 1921 all but a few of the American states had enacted such legislation. It is now in effect in all of the states, with Hawaii the last to fall into line in 1963. It has been said that no subject of labor legislation ever has made such progress or received such general acceptance of its principles in so brief a period.[47]

The theory underlying the workers' compensation acts never has been stated better than in the old campaign slogan,[48] "the cost of the product should bear the blood of the workman."[49] The human accident losses of modern industry are to be treated as a cost of production, like the breakage of tools or machinery. The financial burden is lifted from the shoulders of the employee, and placed upon the employer, who is expected to add it to his costs, and so transfer it to the consumer. In this he is aided and controlled by a system of compulsory liability insurance, which equalizes the burden over the entire industry. Through such insurance both the master and the servant are protected at the expense of the ultimate consumer.

Workers' compensation is thus a form of strict liability. The employer is charged with the injuries arising out of his business, without regard to any question of his negligence, or that of the injured employee. He is liable for injuries caused by pure unavoidable accident, or by the negligence of the worker. The three wicked sisters of the common law—contributory negligence, assumption of risk, and the fellow servant rule—are abolished as defenses.[50] The only questions remaining to be litigated are, first, were the worker and his injury within the act, and second, what shall be the compensation paid.[51] Since in most cases the compensation is fixed by the statute itself,[52] "the result has been most satisfactory in that injured employees receive immediate relief, a fruitful source of friction between employer and employee has been eliminated,

---

44. First Report of New York Employers' Liability Comm., 1910, Vol. 1, p. 31; Report of Michigan Employers' Liability Comm., 1911, p. 16; Wisconsin Bureau of Labor Statistics, 13th Bien.Rep., 1907–1908, 13.

45. St. Louis Cordage Co. v. Miller, 8th Cir. 1903, 126 F. 495; Knisley v. Pratt, 1896, 148 N.Y. 372, 42 N.E. 986; Cleveland & Eastern Railway Co. v. Somers, 1902, 14 Ohio Cir.Ct.Rep. 67, reversed on other grounds, 1906, 74 Ohio St. 477, 78 N.E. 1122.

46. Passed in 1884, amended from time to time, and finally codified in an act of July 6th, 1911.

47. U. S. Bureau of Labor Statistics, Bull. No. 126, 1913, p. 9.

48. The writer has heard this attributed to Lloyd George, but has been unable to trace its origin.

49. Bohlen, A Problem in the Drafting of Workmen's Compensation Acts, 1912, 25 Harv.L.Rev. 328, 401, 517; Wambaugh, Workmen's Compensation Acts, 1911, 25 Harv.L.Rev. 129; Walton, Workmen's Compensation and the Theory of Professional Risk, 1911, 11 Col.L.Rev. 36; Stertz v. Industrial Insurance Commission of Washington, 1916, 91 Wash. 588, 158 P. 256; In re Petrie, 1915, 215 N.Y. 335, 109 N.E. 549; Wangler Boiler & Sheet Metal Works v. Industrial Commission, 1919, 287 Ill. 118, 122 N.E. 366; Bundy v. State of Vermont Highway Department, 1929, 102 Vt. 84, 146 A. 68.

50. Borgnis v. Falk Co., 1911, 147 Wis. 327, 133 N.W. 209; Imperial Brass Manufacturing Co. v. Industrial Commission, 1922, 306 Ill. 11, 137 N.E. 411; American Ice Co. v. Fitzhugh, 1916, 128 Md. 382, 97 A. 999; see Grand Trunk Railway Co. of Canada v. Knapp, 6th Cir. 1916, 233 F. 950.

51. First Report of New York Employers' Liability Comm., 1910, Vol. 1, p. 56.

52. The statutes contain elaborate and detailed schedules of compensation for particular injuries. Thus: "For the loss of a thumb, sixty-six and two-thirds per centum of the daily wage at the time of injury during sixty-five weeks." Minn.Stat.Ann., § 176.101.

* * * a tremendous amount of burden and expensive litigation has been eliminated, and a more harmonious relation between the employers and employees exists than was possible under the old system." [53]

The law of workers' compensation lies outside of the scope of this text.[54] When an injury to a servant is found to be covered by a workers' compensation act, it is uniformly held that the statutory compensation is the sole remedy, and that any recovery against the employer at common law is barred.[55] It is recognized that this remedy is in the nature of a compromise, by which the worker is to accept a limited compensation, usually less than the estimate which a jury might place upon his damages, in return for an extended liability of the employer, and an assurance that he will be paid. Accordingly, even though his damages are partly of a nature not compensated under the act, he has no cause of action based on the negligence of his employer.[56]

There are, however, many injuries to servants which still are not covered by the workers' compensation acts. There are important groups, such as farm laborers,[57] domestic servants,[58] railway workers,[59] corporate officers and working partners,[60] and those employed by enterprises having less than a minimum number of employees,[61] who are excluded from most of the statutes. In most instances such exclusions have been the result of political compromise at the time of the adoption of the act. One important group, of "casual" employees, or those "not in the usual course of trade or business of the employer," has been excluded largely because of the difficulty of obtaining insurance coverage for such occasional work.[62]

In addition, many of the acts, because of early doubts as to constitutionality, were made elective and remain so, so that the ser-

---

53. 1 Schneider, Workmen's Compensation, 2d ed., 1932, 6.

54. See Schneider, Workmen's Compensation, 3d ed. 16 vols., 1939–53; Larson, Workmen's Compensation Law, 2 vols., 1952; Somers and Somers, Workmen's Compensation, 1954; Kossoris et al., Workmen's Compensation in the United States, 1953, 76 Monthly Lab. Rev. 359, 480, 602, 709, 826, 1063, 1179, 1289; Bureau of Labor Statistics Bull. No. 1149, 1954; Riesenfeld, Study of the Workmen's Compensation Law in Hawaii, 1963, Hawaii Leg.Ref.Bureau Rep. No. 1; Dittmar, State Workmen's Compensation Laws, 1959; Cheit, Injury and Recovery in the Course of Employment, 1961; Larson, The Nature and Origins of Workmen's Compensation, 1952, 37 Corn.L.Q. 206; Riesenfeld, Forty Years of American Workmen's Compensation, 1951, 35 Minn.L.Rev. 525; Riesenfeld, Basic Problems in the Administration of Workmen's Compensation, 1952, 36 Minn.L.Rev. 119; Somers et al., Current Status of Workmen's Compensation, 1953, 7 Industrial & Lab. Rel.Rev. 31.

An excellent brief review of the comparatively recent state of the law is Riesenfeld, Contemporary Trends in Compensation for Industrial Accidents Here and Abroad, 1954, 42 Cal.L.Rev. 531.

55. See Note, 1936, 14 North Car.L.Rev. 199.

56. Hyett v. Northwestern Hospital for Women and Children, 1920, 147 Minn. 413, 180 N.W. 552; Gregutis v. Waclark Wire Works, 1914, 86 N.J.L. 610, 38 N.J. L.J. 11, 92 A. 354; Smith v. Baker, 1932, 157 Okl. 155, 11 P.2d 132; Freese v. John Morrell & Co., 1931, 58 S.D. 634, 237 N.W. 886; Shanahan v. Monarch Engineering Co., 1916, 219 N.Y. 469, 114 N.E. 795. See Page, The Exclusivity of the Workmen's Compensation Remedy, 1963, 4 B.C.Ind. & Com.L.Rev. 555.

57. See for example Anderson v. Last Chance Ranch Co., 1924, 63 Utah 551, 228 P. 184; Greischar v. St. Mary's College, 1928, 176 Minn. 100, 222 N.W. 525; In re Roby, 1939, 54 Wyo. 439, 93 P.2d 940; Taylor v. Hostetler, 1960, 186 Kan. 788, 352 P.2d 1042; Pestlin v. Haxton Canning Co., 1949, 299 N.Y. 477, 87 N.E.2d 522.

58. See for example Anderson v. Ueland, 1936, 197 Minn. 518, 267 N.W. 517, rehearing denied 197 Minn. 518, 267 N.W. 927; cf. Congressional Country Club v. Baltimore & Ohio Railroad Co., 1950, 194 Md. 533, 71 A.2d 696; Barres v. Watterson Hotel Co., 1922, 196 Ky. 100, 244 S.W. 308. See Note, 1937, 21 Minn.L.Rev. 227.

59. See infra, this section.

60. See Grossman v. Industrial Commission, 1941, 376 Ill. 198, 33 N.E.2d 444; Carville v. A. F. Bornot & Co., 1927, 288 Pa. 104, 135 A. 652; Benson v. Hygienic Artificial Ice Co., 1936, 198 Minn. 250, 269 N.W. 460; Rasmussen v. Trico Feed Mills, 1947, 148 Neb. 855, 29 N.W.2d 641; Pederson v. Pederson, 1949, 229 Minn. 460, 39 N.W.2d 893.

61. Ranging from two in Nevada and Oklahoma to fifteen in South Carolina. See Bureau of Labor Standards, Bulletin No. 125, 1950.

62. See Bohlen, Casual Employment and Employment Outside of Business, 1923, 11 Cal.L.Rev. 221; Note, 1926, 10 Minn.L.Rev. 626; Billmayer v. Sanford, 1929, 177 Minn. 465, 225 N.W. 426; Moore v. Clarke, 1936, 171 Md. 39, 187 A. 887; Cochrane v. William Penn Hotel, 1940, 339 Pa. 549, 16 A.2d 43; Ludwig v. Kirby, 1951, 13 N.J.Super. 116, 80 A.2d 239.

vant may be deprived of coverage, either by his own choice or that of the employer.[63] Some of the statutes do not cover all industries, but apply only to "hazardous" employments.[64] Nearly all of the acts are limited to injuries arising "by accident"; and while there has been considerable expansion of the definition,[65] it may still in some states exclude damage caused gradually over a period of time,[66] or resulting merely from the usual work under the usual conditions.[67] Occupational diseases have not been fully covered in all states.[68] Most of the statutes are limited to injuries "arising out of and in the course of employment," and it may still be found that damage caused by the negligence of the employer lies outside of the scope of this restriction.[69] In all such cases, the statute is held to have no application, and the worker is left to the tort remedy at common law.[70] There is thus a substantial, and still important, area of labor litigation in which the older law still has significance and vitality. The whole trend is toward cutting it down, making further inroads upon it by bringing as much as possible within the compensation acts; and its ultimate extinction appears to be only a question of time—which, however, may not mean anything immediate.

As in the past, the common law action is founded on a theory of negligence, and must be based upon proof of a violation of some specific duty of care resting upon the employer. In the absence of legislation it is still subject to the old trio of defenses,[71] assumption of risk,[72] contributory negligence,[73] and the fellow servant rule.[74] This last has

63. See Bureau of Labor Standards, Bulletin No. 125, 1950.
64. Cf. Illinois Publishing & Printing Co. v. Industrial Commission, 1921, 299 Ill. 189, 132 N.E. 511; Morris v. Department of Labor and Industries, 1934, 179 Wash. 423, 38 P.2d 395; Mattes v. City of Baltimore, 1942, 180 Md. 579, 26 A.2d 390.
65. See for example Caddy v. R. Maturi & Co., 1944, 217 Minn. 207, 14 N.W.2d 393; Winkelman v. Boeing Airplane Co., 1949, 166 Kan. 503, 203 P.2d 171; Atlas Coal Corp. v. Scales, 1947, 198 Okl. 658, 185 P.2d 177; Benjamin F. Shaw Co. v. Musgrave, 1949, 189 Tenn. 1, 222 S.W.2d 22; Hardin's Bakeries v. Ranager, 1953, 217 Miss. 463, 65 So.2d 461. See Riesenfeld, Forty Years of Amercian Workmen's Compensation, 1951, 35 Minn.L.Rev. 524.
66. See for example Aistrop v. Blue Diamond Coal Co., 1943, 181 Va. 287, 24 S.E.2d 546; Kress & Co. v. Burkes, 1944, 153 Fla. 868, 16 So.2d 106; Di Maria v. Curtiss-Wright Corp., 1947, 135 N.J.L. 470, 52 A.2d 698; Wilson & Co. v. McGee, 1933, 163 Okl. 99, 21 P.2d 25; Industrial Commission v. Lambert, 1933, 126 Ohio St. 501, 186 N.E. 89.
67. See for example Hartford Accident & Indemnity Co. v. Industrial Commission, 1947, 66 Ariz. 259, 186 P.2d 959; Muff v. Brainard, 1949, 150 Neb. 650, 35 N.W.2d 597; Rathmell v. Wesleyville Borough, 1944, 351 Pa. 14, 40 A.2d 28; Schlange v. Briggs Manufacturing Co., 1950, 326 Mich. 552, 40 N.W.2d 454; Masse v. James H. Robinson Co., 1950, 301 N.Y. 34, 92 N.E.2d 56. See Sears and Groves, Worker Protection Under Occupational Disease Disability Statutes, 1959, 31 Rocky Mt.L.Rev. 462.
68. See Bureau of Labor Standards, Bull. No. 125, 1950
69. Thus the worker may be injured by negligence of his employer not connected with the employment, or while he is out of the course of his employment. National Biscuit Co. v. Litzky, 6th Cir. 1927, 22 F.2d 939;

Collins v. Troy Laundry Co., 1931, 135 Or. 580, 297 P. 334; Conrad v. Youghiogheny & Ohio Coal Co., 1923, 107 Ohio St. 387, 140 N.E. 482; Norwood v. Tellico River Lumber Co., 1922, 146 Tenn. 682, 244 S.W. 490. See Note, 1936, 14 North Car.L.Rev. 199.
See Malone, The Compensable Risk, 1959, 31 Rocky Mt.L.Rev. 397; Larson, The Legal Aspects of Causation in Workmen's Compensation, 1954, 8 Rutgers L.Rev. 423.
70. See for example Billo v. Allegheny Steel Co., 1937, 328 Pa. 97, 195 A. 110; Triff v. National Bronze & Aluminum Foundry Co., 1939, 135 Ohio St. 191, 20 N.E.2d 232; Echord v. Rush, 1927, 124 Kan. 521, 261 P. 820; Jellico Coal Co. v. Adkins, 1923, 197 Ky. 684, 247 S.W. 972; Jones v. Rinehart & Dennis Co., 1933, 113 W.Va. 414, 168 S.E. 482.
Contra, as to a schedule of occupational diseases: Thomas v. Parker Rust Proof Co., 1938, 284 Mich. 260, 279 N.W. 504; Murphy v. American Enka Corp., 1938, 213 N.C. 218, 195 S.E. 538.
71. All of which may be involved in a single case. See Rawlins v. Nelson, 1951, 38 Wn.2d 570, 231 P.2d 281; McDonald v. Louisville & Nashville Railroad Co., 1930, 232 Ky. 734, 24 S.W.2d 585.
72. Jones v. Adams, 1952, 56 N.M. 510, 245 P.2d 843; Taylor v. Hostetler, 1960, 186 Kan. 788, 352 P.2d 1042; Syverson v. Nelson, 1955, 245 Minn. 63, 70 N.W.2d 880; Heinlen v. Martin Miller Orchards, 1952, 40 Wn.2d 356, 242 P.2d 1054; Painter v. Nichols, 1954, 118 Vt. 306, 108 A.2d 384. See Note, 1961, 47 Va.L. Rev. 1444.
73. Frei v. Frei, 1953, 263 Wis. 430, 57 N.W.2d 731; Price v. New Castle Refractories Co., 1939, 332 Pa. 507, 3 A.2d 418; Steiner v. Spencer, 1940, 24 Tenn.App. 389, 145 S.W.2d 547; Kolenko v. Certain-Teed Products Corp., W.D.N.Y.1937, 20 F.Supp. 920.
74. May v. Sharp, 1936, 191 Ark. 1142, 89 S.W.2d 735; Parker v. Nelson Grain & Milling Co., 1932, 330 Mo. 95, 48 S.W.2d 906; Richardson v. American Cotton

been said to have "practically disappeared with workers' compensation," [75] and not to be at all popular with the courts, which will apply it only where it is unavoidable.[76] Some courts have concluded not to recognize the defense in the future.[77]

Legislation has not, however, stopped with the workers' compensation acts. There are a good many scattered statutes regulating working conditions, which have been construed to place full responsibility upon the employer, so that he is under strict liability when an injury results from their violation, even though he has exercised all possible care.[78] There are other statutes which have abrogated the fellow servant rule,[79] and the defenses of assumption of risk [80] or contributory negligence; [81] and the last named defense frequently is limited to a reduction of the plaintiff's damages on a comparative negligence basis.[82] Such legislation usually has been limited in its scope to particular industries or particular hazards; and while it has done a great deal to palliate the rigors of the common law, and the courts have been eager to seize almost any excuse to do the same, the uncompensated industrial injury remains one of the chief reproaches to the law, and a field in which further remedies are still badly needed.

Exceptions to Exclusivity

Workers' Compensation statutes usually provide for a remedy to employees who are "accidentally" injured in the course of employment. Sometimes the statute will specifically preserve a common law right to sue for an injury intentionally inflicted by the employer. But the language of the statute is not always the same and not always precise. So claims have often been filed for the purpose of expanding the area within which the exclusivity provision does not apply. This leaves some room for judicial interpretation. The vast majority of courts have held that conduct that falls short of an intent to injure will not permit an employee to overcome the exclusivity provision.[83] How-

---

Mills, 1925, 189 N.C. 653, 127 S.E. 834; Mariani v. Nanni, 1962, 95 R.I. 153, 185 A.2d 119. Cf. Taylor v. Hostetler, 1960, 186 Kan. 788, 352 P.2d 1042 (on basis of assumption of risk). See Note, 1948, 13 Mo.L.Rev. 327.

75. Reboni v. Case Brothers, Inc., 1951, 137 Conn. 501, 78 A.2d 887.

A number of states have deprived the employer of all three defenses where the tort liability survives because of the employer's election of non-coverage by workers' compensation. See for example Fitch v. Mayer, Ky. 1953, 258 S.W.2d 923; Kansas City Stockyards Co. v. Anderson, 8th Cir. 1952, 199 F.2d 91 (Missouri); Muldrow v. Weinstein, 1951, 234 N.C. 587, 68 S.E.2d 249; Baldassarre v. West Oregon Lumber Co., 1952, 193 Or. 556, 239 P.2d 839.

Nearly all of the acts contain such a provision in the event of failure to obtain insurance. See for example Haralson v. Rhea, 1953, 76 Ariz. 74, 259 P.2d 246; McCoy v. Cornish, 1954, 220 Miss. 577, 71 So.2d 304; Evans v. Phipps, 1953, 152 Tex. 487, 259 S.W.2d 723.

76. Buss v. Wachsmith, 1937, 190 Wash. 673, 70 P.2d 417, adhered to 193 Wash. 600, 74 P.2d 999.

77. Crenshaw Brothers Produce Co. v. Harper, 1940, 142 Fla. 27, 194 So. 353; Ritter v. Beals, 1961, 225 Or. 504, 358 P.2d 1080; Siragusa v. Swedish Hospital, 1962, 60 Wn.2d 310, 373 P.2d 767.

78. Koenig v. Patrick Construction Corp., 1948, 298 N.Y. 313, 83 N.E.2d 133; Lu May v. Van Drisse Motors, 1929, 199 Wis. 310, 226 N.W. 301; Johnson v. Weborg, 1942, 142 Neb. 516, 7 N.W.2d 65; Grasty v. Sabin, 1927, 32 Ariz. 463, 259 P. 1049; O'Donnell v. Elgin, Joliet & Eastern Railway Co., 1949, 338 U.S. 384, 70 S.Ct. 200, 94 L.Ed. 187, rehearing denied 338 U.S. 945, 70 S.Ct. 427, 94 L.Ed. 583 (Federal Safety Appliance Act).

79. See Ferguson v. Ringsby Truck Line, 10th Cir. 1949, 174 F.2d 744 (Colorado Employers' Liability Act); Pitzer v. M. D. Tomkies & Sons, 1951, 136 W.Va. 268, 67 S.E.2d 437 (child labor); Phillips Petroleum Co. v. Jenkins, 1936, 297 U.S. 629, 56 S.Ct. 611, 80 L.Ed. 943, rehearing denied 298 U.S. 691, 56 S.Ct. 745, 80 L.Ed. 1409 (employees of corporations in Arkansas); Union Oil Co. of California v. Hunt, 9th Cir. 1940, 111 F.2d 269 (hazardous industries in Oregon).

80. Osborne v. Salvation Army, 2d Cir. 1939, 107 F.2d 929; Union Oil Co. of California v. Hunt, 9th Cir. 1940, 111 F.2d 269 (Oregon law); Brown v. Hames, 1944, 207 Ark. 196, 179 S.W.2d 689; N. O. Nelson Manufacturing Corp. v. Dickson, 1944, 114 Ind.App. 668, 53 N.E.2d 640; Price v. New Castle Refractories Co., 1939, 332 Pa. 507, 3 A.2d 418. The same result has been achieved by judicial decision. See supra, note 77.

81. Osborne v. Salvation Army, 2d Cir. 1939, 107 F.2d 929; Koenig v. Patrick Construction Corp., 1948, 298 N.Y. 313, 83 N.E.2d 133; Brown v. Hames, 1944, 207 Ark. 196, 179 S.W.2d 689; N. O. Nelson Manufacturing Corp. v. Dickson, 1944, 114 Ind.App. 668, 53 N.E.2d 640; Maurizi v. Western Coal & Mining Co., 1928, 321 Mo. 378, 11 S.W.2d 268.

82. See for example Price v. McNeill, 1946, 237 Iowa 1120, 24 N.W.2d 464; Edwards v. Hollywood Canteen, 1945, 27 Cal.2d 802, 167 P.2d 729; McKee v. New Idea, Inc., Ohio App.1942, 44 N.E.2d 697; Tampa Electric Co. v. Bryant, 1931, 101 Fla. 204, 133 So. 887.

83. See, Birnbaum and Wrubel, Workers' Compensation and the Employer's Immunity Shield: Recent

ever, some courts have recently departed from this narrow interpretation.[84] So gross negligence, fraudulent nondisclosure of serious risks, and the like, may be regarded as such intentional misconduct as to justify a recovery against the employer on a tort theory. This would appear to be a very doubtful interpretation of most statutes.

There is a doctrine espoused at least by the Supreme Court of California pursuant to which an employer can be regarded as acting in a dual capacity with respect to an employee.[85] Under the dual capacity doctrine, an employer could be a manufacturer-supplier of a product to the employee and subject to liability as such and also an employer subject to liability as such under Workers' Compensation. In Bell v. Industrial Vangas, Inc.,[86] plaintiff was employed as a route salesman. He was severely injured in a fire which occurred when he delivered flammable gas to the premises of a customer. Since the defendant was engaged in the business of manufacturing and selling flammable gas, a defect in the product that was being delivered by the plaintiff was held to subject the defendant to liability as a manufacturer. This holding has not been followed.[87] As has been noted, the exclusive remedy is part of the *"quid pro quo* in which the sacrifices and gains of employees and employers are to some extent put in balance, for, while the employer assumes a new liability without fault, he is relieved of the prospect of large damage verdicts."[88]

Carrier Employees

The most important single group of employees not covered by the workers' compensation acts are those of railroads. Legislation with respect to railway employees antedated workers' compensation in the United States. In 1906 Congress enacted a Federal Employers' Liability Act, covering all employees of common carriers by rail when the carrier was engaged in interstate or foreign commerce. This act was held unconstitutional as exceeding the power of Congress, in that it applied to employees who were themselves engaged in intrastate commerce at the time of injury.[89] A second Act,[90] passed in 1908, and limited to employees who were themselves in interstate or foreign commerce, was held constitutional,[91] and is now in effect. Since the application of the statute thus depended upon the type of commerce in which the worker was engaged when he was hurt, the courts were faced with the difficult problem of separating out the duties of employees or interstate railways into categories, and classifying them as interstate or intrastate, with some rather refined splitting of hairs in the process. This difficulty was removed to a considerable extent by an amendment to the Act in 1939, which broadened its terms to include all activities which further interstate commerce, or which directly or closely and substantially affect it.[92] Thus, if the task performed by the worker at the time of his injury is to be regarded as a part of inter-

Exceptions to Exclusivity, 1982, 5 J. of Products Liability 119; Keating v. Shell Chemical Co., 5th Cir. 1980, 610 F.2d 328; Great Western Sugar Co. v. District Court, Mont.1980, 610 P.2d 717; Kittell v. Vermont Weatherboard, Inc., 1980, 138 Vt. 439, 417 A.2d 926.

84. Johns-Manville Products Corp. v. Contra Costa Superior Court, 1980, 27 Cal.3d 465, 165 Cal.Rptr. 858, 612 P.2d 948; Blankenship v. Cincinnati Milacron Chemicals, Inc., 1982, 69 Ohio St.2d 608, 433 N.E.2d 572.

85. Duprey v. Shane, 1952, 39 Cal.2d 781, 249 P.2d 8.

86. Bell v. Industrial Vangas, Inc., 1981, 30 Cal.3d 268, 179 Cal.Rptr. 30, 637 P.2d 266.

87. Billy v. Consolidated Machine Tool Corp., 1980, 51 N.Y.2d 152, 432 N.Y.S.2d 879, 412 N.E.2d 934, 939; Latendresse v. Preskey, N.D.1980, 290 N.W.2d 267.

88. 2A. A. Larson, The Law of Workmen's Compensation, 1976, and Supplement, 1982, § 65.11 at 12–2 to 12–6; see also, Birnbaum and Wrubel, supra, note 83, at p. 135 of that article.

89. Employers' Liability Cases, 1908, 207 U.S. 463, 28 S.Ct. 141, 52 L.Ed. 297.

90. Federal Employers' Liability Act, 45 U.S.C.A. § 51 et seq. See Symposium, 1953, 18 Law & Contemp.Prob. 110–431; Richter and Forer, Federal Employers' Liability Act, 1952, 12 F.R.D. 13; Richter and Forer, Federal Employers' Liability Act—A Real Compensatory Law for Railroad Workers, 1951, 36 Corn. L.Q. 203.

91. Second Employers' Liability Cases, 1912, 223 U.S. 1, 32 S.Ct. 169, 56 L.Ed. 327.

92. See Reed v. Pennsylvania Railroad Co., 1956, 351 U.S. 502, 76 S.Ct. 958, 100 L.Ed. 1366; Southern Pacific Co. v. Gileo, 1956, 351 U.S. 493, 76 S.Ct. 952,

state commerce, or as directly, or closely and substantially, affecting it, the Federal Act applies, and since Congress has occupied the field, it operates to the exclusion of all state remedies.[93] On the other hand, as to injuries during activities which are strictly intrastate,[94] or as to employees of carriers other than by rail,[95] the states are not deprived of the power to legislate. Many of them have enacted special railway labor acts, modeled upon the federal statute.[96]

The Federal Employers' Liability Act, and the state acts patterned after it, included the modifications of the common law which had won popular favor up to the year 1908, and were regarded as important steps forward when they were enacted. Liability must still be based on negligence, the breach of some duty found to rest upon the employer,[97] and to this extent the statutes do no more than to preserve the common law remedy. The fellow servant rule, however, is abolished.[98] Assumption of risk was left untouched by the original Federal Act, except as to the employer's violation of statutes enacted for the safety of employees.[99] The amendments of 1939 specifically changed the Act to provide that the employee shall not be held to have assumed the risks of his employment in any case where injury results in whole or in part from the negligence of the carrier or its servants.[1] Contributory negligence is not allowed to bar recovery, but goes only to reduce it by an apportionment of damages according to fault. For a long time this provision was to some extent defeated by a rather unaccountable series of decisions of the Supreme Court beginning in 1916,[2] which drew a distinction between the mere negligence of the plaintiff contributing to his injury, and his violation of a "primary duty," which was the "sole proximate cause" of his injury. In 1943 the Court quite as unexpectedly declared[3] that the "primary duty" rule had been in reality a form of assumption of risk, and that it had been eliminated by the amendments of 1939.

The history of the Federal Employers' Liability Act since that year has been one of gradual but persistent liberalization[4] in the

---

100 L.Ed. 1357; Lillie v. Thompson, 1947, 332 U.S. 459, 68 S.Ct. 140, 92 L.Ed. 73; Bailey v. Central Vermont Railway Co., 1943, 319 U.S. 350, 63 S.Ct. 1062, 87 L.Ed. 1444, conformed to 113 Vt. 433, 35 A.2d 365.

93. New York Central Railroad Co. v. Winfield, 1917, 244 U.S. 147, 37 S.Ct. 546, 61 L.Ed. 1045.

As to coverage of employees, see Miller, F.E.L.A. Revisited, 1956, 6 Catholic U.L.Rev. 158.

94. Boston & Maine Railroad Co. v. Armburg, 1932, 285 U.S. 234, 52 S.Ct. 336, 76 L.Ed. 729.

95. State ex rel. Washington Motor Coach Co. v. Kelly, 1937, 192 Wash. 394, 74 P.2d 16; Hall v. Industrial Commission of Ohio, 1936, 131 Ohio St. 416, 3 N.E.2d 367; Ben Wolf Truck Lines v. Bailey, 1936, 102 Ind.App. 208, 1 N.E.2d 660. In these cases employees of motor carriers were engaged in interstate commerce.

96. See for example Louisville & Nashville Railroad Co. v. Chapman's Administratrix, 1945, 300 Ky. 835, 190 S.W.2d 542; Boyleston v. Southern Railway Co., 1947, 211 S.C. 232, 44 S.E.2d 537.

97. Herdman v. Pennsylvania Railroad Co., 1957, 352 U.S. 518, 77 S.Ct. 455, 1 L.Ed.2d 508. See, generally, Smith, The Federal Employers' Liability Act, 1926, 12 A.B.A.J. 486; Funkhouser, What is a Safe Place to Work Under the F.E.L.A.?, 1956, 17 Ohio St.L.J. 367.

The negligence may, however, be proved by circumstantial evidence, including res ipsa loquitur. Jesionowski v. Boston & Maine Railroad Co., 1947, 329 U.S. 452, 67 S.Ct. 401, 91 L.Ed. 416. Or negligence per se may be found where a statute permitting no excuse is violated. Myers v. Reading Co., 1947, 331 U.S. 477, 67 S.Ct. 1334, 91 L.Ed. 1615 (Safety Appliance Act).

98. The Act makes the carrier liable for the negligence of its officers, agents and employees. In Sinkler v. Missouri Pacific Railway Co., 1958, 356 U.S. 326, 78 S.Ct. 758, 2 L.Ed.2d 799, rehearing denied 356 U.S. 978, 78 S.Ct. 1133, 2 L.Ed.2d 1152, this was held to include an independent contractor "engaged in furthering the operational activities" of the railroad by conducting switching operations.

See Metzenbaum and Schwartz, Defenses Under the F.E.L.A., 1956, 17 Ohio St.L.J. 416.

99. Seaboard Air Line Railway Co. v. Horton, 1914, 233 U.S. 492, 34 S.Ct. 635, 58 L.Ed. 1062.

1. 45 U.S.C.A. § 54; Tiller v. Atlantic Coast Line Railroad Co., 1943, 318 U.S. 54, 63 S.Ct. 444, 87 L.Ed. 610; Blair v. Baltimore & Ohio Railroad Co., 1945, 323 U.S. 600, 65 S.Ct. 545, 89 L.Ed. 490. See Metzenbaum and Schwartz, Defenses Under the F.E.L.A., 1956, 17 Ohio St.L.J. 416.

2. Great Northern Railway Co. v. Wiles, 1916, 240 U.S. 444, 36 S.Ct. 406, 60 L.Ed. 732.

3. In Tiller v. Atlantic Coast Line Railroad Co., 1943, 318 U.S. 54, 63–64, 63 S.Ct. 444, 449, 87 L.Ed. 610. See Keith v. Wheeling & Lake Erie Railroad Co., 6th Cir. 1947, 160 F.2d 654, certiorari denied 332 U.S. 763, 68 S.Ct. 67, 92 L.Ed. 348; Rogers v. Missouri Pacific Railway Co., 1957, 352 U.S. 500, 77 S.Ct. 443, 1 L.Ed.2d 493.

4. The initial stages of this are reviewed, without enthusiam, in Alderman, The New Supreme Court and

direction of allowing the plaintiff to recover whenever he is injured in the course of his employment, as under a compensation act. Following a series of decisions in which the question of the railroad's negligence went to the jury although the evidence bearing upon it was circumstantial, sketchy, or the omission or departure from ordinary care was very slight,[5] the Supreme Court finally declared [6] that "Under this statute the text of a jury case is simply whether the proofs justify with reason the conclusion that employer negligence played *any part, even the slightest*,[7] in producing the injury or death for which damages are sought." This has been said to reduce the extent of the negligence required, as well as the quantum of proof necessary to establish it, to the "vanishing point." [8] While it is still undoubtedly true that there must be some shreds of proof both of negligence and of causation,[9] and that "speculation, conjecture and possibilities" will not be enough,[10] there appears to be little doubt that under the statute jury verdicts for the plaintiff can be sustained upon evidence which would not be sufficient in the ordinary negligence action.[11]

The Federal Employers' Liability Act has been, and is still a subject of much controversy. It undoubtedly has resulted in considerable extension of liability to the employee.[12] But it probably has resulted, on the whole, in increasing rather than diminishing litigation; and whether it has brought a sufficient advantage to the railway worker is a matter of dispute.[13] It has been said that "a law inspired by laudable motives at a time when remedial state legislation was in its infancy has outlived its usefulness and has become an obstacle to the fulfillment of its own purposes." [14] For more than forty years there has been discussion of some system similar to the workers' compensation

the Old Law of Negligence, 1953, 18 Law & Con.Prob. 111. A different view is taken in Griffith, The Vindication of a National Public Policy Under the Federal Employers' Liability Act, 1953, 18 Law & Con.Prob. 160.

5. Tennant v. Peoria & Pekin Union Railway Co., 1944, 321 U.S. 29, 64 S.Ct. 409, 88 L.Ed. 520, rehearing denied 321 U.S. 802, 64 S.Ct. 610, 88 L.Ed. 1089; Bailey v. Central Vermont Railway, Inc., 1943, 319 U.S. 350, 63 S.Ct. 1062, 87 L.Ed. 1444, conformed to 113 Vt. 433, 35 A.2d 365; Hayes v. Wabash Railroad Co., 1950, 360 Mo. 1223, 233 S.W.2d 12; Williams v. New York Central Railroad Co., 1949, 402 Ill. 494, 84 N.E.2d 399; Sadowski v. Long Island Railroad Co., 1944, 292 N.Y. 448, 55 N.E.2d 497. The last of these is Gallick v. Baltimore & Ohio Railroad Co., 1963, 372 U.S. 108, 83 S.Ct. 659, 9 L.Ed.2d 618, reversing the Supreme Court of Ohio, 1961, 172 Ohio St. 488, 178 N.E.2d 597.

6. In Rogers v. Missouri Pacific Railway Co., 1957, 352 U.S. 500, 77 S.Ct. 443, 1 L.Ed.2d 493, rehearing denied 353 U.S. 943, 77 S.Ct. 808, 1 L.Ed.2d 764, and 352 U.S. 521, 77 S.Ct. 459, 1 L.Ed.2d 515.

7. Italics supplied.

8. Atlantic Coast Line Railroad Co. v. Barrett, Fla. 1958, 101 So.2d 37; see Corso, How FELA Became Liability Without Fault, 1966, 15 Cleve.Marsh.L.Rev. 344.

9. New York, New Haven & Hartford Railroad Co. v. Henagan, 1960, 364 U.S. 441, 81 S.Ct. 198, 5 L.Ed.2d 183; Herdman v. Pennsylvania Railroad Co., 1957, 352 U.S. 518, 77 S.Ct. 455, 1 L.Ed.2d 508; Dessi v. Pennsylvania Railroad Co., 3d Cir. 1958, 251 F.2d 149, 151, certiorari denied 356 U.S. 967, 78 S.Ct. 1006, 2 L.Ed.2d 1073; Callihan v. Great Northern Railway Co., 1960, 137 Mont. 93, 350 P.2d 369; Inman v. Baltimore & Ohio Railroad Co., 1959, 361 U.S. 138, 80 S.Ct. 242, 4 L.Ed.2d 198. As to causation, see Notes, 1966, 18 Stan.L.Rev. 829; 1966, 35 U.Cin.L.Rev. 140.

10. Memorandum of Mr. Justice Frankfurter, denying certiorari in Elgin, Joliet & Eastern Railway Co. v. Gibson, 1957, 355 U.S. 897, 78 S.Ct. 270, 2 L.Ed.2d 193.

11. Cf. Gibson v. Thompson, 1957, 355 U.S. 18, 78 S.Ct. 2, 2 L.Ed.2d 1, rehearing denied 335 U.S. 900, 78 S.Ct. 258, 2 L.Ed.2d 197 (engineer on way from roundhouse to engine slipped and fell on loose gravel); Stinson v. Atlantic Coast Line Railroad Co., 1957, 355 U.S. 62, 78 S.Ct. 136, 2 L.Ed.2d 93, rehearing denied 355 U.S. 910, 78 S.Ct. 338, 2 L.Ed.2d 281, mandate conformed to, 1958, 267 Ala. 537, 103 So.2d 183 (nude body of engineer found on track under mysterious circumstances); Ringhiser v. Chesapeake & Ohio Railway Co., 1957, 354 U.S. 901, 77 S.Ct. 1093, 1 L.Ed.2d 268 (worker injured while answering call of nature in a gondola car). See McCoid, The Federal Railroad Safety Acts and the F.E.L.A.: A Comparison, 1956, 17 Ohio St.L.J. 494.

12. See Delisi, Federal Employers' Liability Act—Scope and Recent Developments, 1947, 18 Miss.L.J. 206; Richter and Forer, The Federal Employers' Liability Act, 1952, 12 F.R.D. 13; De Parcq, The Ten Most Important Cases Under the Federal Employers' Liability Act, 1967, 44 N.D.L.Rev. 7.

13. Dodd, Administration of Workmen's Compensation, 1936, 773–780. Not the least of the reasons for this, as in the case of other federal acts, is the uncertainty as to which of the various industrial accident statutes is to apply. See Edises, Multiplicity of Remedies in the Field of Industrial Accident Law, 1933, 21 Cal.L.Rev. 430.

14. Schoene and Watson, Workmen's Compensation on Interstate Railways, 1934, 47 Harv.L.Rev. 389, 424. See also Miller, The Quest for a Federal Workmen's Compensation Law for Railroad Employees, 1953, 18 Law & Con.Prob. 188; Parker, Federal Employers' Lia-

acts to cover injuries in the course of railway labor.¹⁵ The same kind of agitation led to the passage in 1927 of a federal compensation act for longshoremen and harbor workers.¹⁶ In the case of seamen, however, the Jones Act of 1915 and the Merchant Marine Act of 1920 have placed them on the same basis as railway employees under the Federal Employers' Liability Act.¹⁷ On the whole the railway and maritime unions have been satisfied with the present statutes, and it is their opposition which has operated chiefly to prevent any change.¹⁸

 WESTLAW REFERENCES

farwell /5 worcester
topic(413) & vice-principal

Statutory Changes

di workmen's!
"cost of the product should bear the blood of the workman"
413k1530
topic(413) /p "assumption of risk" "assumption of the risk" "contributory negligen!" "comparative negligen!" "fellow servant rule*"
413k2112
413k772

Exceptions to Exclusivity

"dual capacity" /s doctrine rationale term*

bility Act or Uniform Compensation for All Workers, 1953, 18 Law & Con.Prob. 208.

15. See Schoene and Watson, Workmen's Compensation on Interstate Railways, 1934, 47 Harv.L.Rev. 389; Gellhorn, Federal Workmen's Compensation for Transportation Employees, 1934, 43 Yale L.J. 906; Miller, Workmen's Compensation for Railroad Employees, 1944, 2 Loyola L.Rev. 138; Miller, The Quest for a Federal Workmen's Compensation Law for Railroad Employees, 1953, 18 Law & Contemp.Prob. 188; Parker, FELA or Uniform Compensation for All Workers, 1953, 18 Law & Contemp.Prob. 208; Pollack, The Crisis in Work Injury Compensation On and Off the Railroads, 1953, 18 Law & Contemp.Prob. 296.

16. See Alaska Packers' Association v. Industrial Accident Commission of California, 1928, 276 U.S. 467, 48 S.Ct. 346, 72 L.Ed. 656; Athearn, The Longshoremen's Act and the Courts, 1935, 23 Cal.L.Rev. 129; Stumberg, Harbor Workers and Workmen's Compensation, 1929, 7 Tex.L.Rev. 197.

17. See Panama Railroad Co. v. Johnson, 1924, 264 U.S. 375, 44 S.Ct. 391, 68 L.Ed. 748; Stumberg, The Jones Act: Remedies of Seamen, 1956, 17 Ohio St.L.J. 416; Gardner, Remedies for Personal Injuries to Seamen, Railroadmen and Longshoremen, 1938, 71 Harv.L.Rev. 438.

bell /5 vangas

Carrier Employees

synopsis,digest("federal employers' liability act" /p railroad* railway*)

§ 81. Other Applications

Writing in 1914, Jeremiah Smith¹ foresaw with trepidation the extension of the principle of strict liability into many new fields, either by statute or by modification of the common law, until the ultimate result would be the extinction of the requirement of legal fault for all tort liability. On the continent of Europe there has been considerable realization of this prediction, as to automobile accidents.² In this country, however, the expansion of strict liability, although it has occurred, still falls far short of this sweeping prediction.

A policy somewhat similar to that of the workers' compensation acts is found in such statutes as the Federal Safety Appliance Act,³ which requires railroads engaged in interstate commerce to equip their trains with certain safety devices, and makes them responsible without negligence for any defi-

18. See Richter and Forer, Federal Employers' Liability Act—A Real Compensatory Law for Railroad Workers, 1951, 36 Corn.L.Q. 203; Kossoris and Zisman, Workmen's Compensation for Seamen, 1946, 62 Monthly Lab.Rev. 851. See, however, suggesting improvements from the plaintiff's point of view, Richter and Forer, Proposed Changes in the Laws Governing Injuries in Interstate Transportation, 1954, 67 Harv.L.Rev. 1003.

§ 81

1. Smith, Sequel to Workmen's Compensation Acts, 1914, 27 Harv.L.Rev. 235, 344. This has been referred to as a latter-day "Lamentations of Jeremiah." Malone, Damage Suits and the Contagious Principle of Workmen's Compensation, 1952, 12 La.L.Rev. 231.

2. See Malone, Damage Suits and the Contagious Principle of Workmen's Compensation, 1952, 12 La.L. Rev. 231; Esmein, Liability in French Law for Damages Caused by Motor Vehicle Accidents, 1953, 2 J.Am. Comp.Law 156; Ussing, The Scandinavian Law of Torts, 1952, 1 J.Am.Comp.Law 359; Deák, Automobile Accidents: A Comparative Study of the Laws of Liability in Europe, 1931, 79 U.Pa.L.Rev. 271.

3. 45 U.S.C.A. § 1 et seq.

ciency which injures employees,[4] or others likely to suffer harm.[5] Child labor statutes,[6] by reason of the obvious social policy underlying them, generally have been construed to provide strict liability for injuries to the child, although the employer has exercised proper care and did not know the child's age. The same has been true of a number of factory acts, scaffold acts, and the like intended for the protection of employees.[7] The sale of goods involving a considerable risk to the public has been dealt with in much the same manner. Prior to the judicial revolution that brought about strict liability under the common law, many of the pure food acts [8] made the seller of defective food liable to the injured consumer, even though the seller had used all reasonable care. "Dram Shop" or Civil Liability Acts [9] in some states impose strict liability, without negligence, upon the seller of intoxicating liquors, when the sale results [10] in harm to the interests of a third person because of the intoxication of the buyer. These statutes, which have been held constitutional,[11] and are liberally construed,[12] protect the third party not only against injuries resulting directly from affirmative acts of the intoxicated person, such as assault and battery,[13] but also against the loss of family support due to injuries to the intoxicated person,[14] including those inflicted upon him in self-defense by those whom he has attacked.[15] There are numerous other strict liability statutes applicable to particular situations, such as ground damage from airplane crashes,[16] or, for example, the Pennsylvania act making pipe lines strictly liable when oil escapes and pollutes a well.[17]

4. O'Donnell v. Elgin, Joliet & Eastern Railway Co., 1949, 338 U.S. 384, 70 S.Ct. 200, 94 L.Ed. 187, rehearing denied 338 U.S. 945, 70 S.Ct. 427, 94 L.Ed. 583.

5. Fairport, Painesville & Eastern Railroad Co. v. Meredith, 1934, 292 U.S. 589, 54 S.Ct. 826, 78 L.Ed. 1446 (highway traveler). See Note, 1938, 23 Minn.L. Rev. 103.

6. Beauchamp v. Sturges & Burn Manufacturing Co., 1911, 250 Ill. 303, 95 N.E. 204, affirmed 1914, 231 U.S. 320, 34 S.Ct. 60, 58 L.Ed. 245; Krutlies v. Bulls Head Coal Co., 1915, 249 Pa. 162, 94 A. 459; Blanton v. Kellioka Coal Co., 1921, 192 Ky. 220, 232 S.W. 614; Second Restatement of Torts, § 286, Comment f; Note, 1930, 39 Yale L.J. 908.

7. See supra, § 18.

8. Meshbesher v. Channellene Oil & Manufacturing Co., 1909, 107 Minn. 104, 119 N.W. 428; Culbertson v. Coca-Cola Bottling Co., 1930, 157 S.C. 352, 154 S.E. 424; Donaldson v. Great Atlantic & Pacific Tea Co., 1938, 186 Ga. 870, 199 S.E. 213, conformed to 59 Ga. App. 79, 200 S.E. 498; Great Atlantic & Pacific Tea Co. v. Hughes, 1936, 131 Ohio St. 501, 3 N.E.2d 415. Cf. Pine Grove Poultry Farm v. Newtown By-Products Manufacturing Co., 1928, 248 N.Y. 293, 162 N.E. 84, reversed 222 App.Div. 834, 226 N.Y.S. 886 (animal food); McAleavy v. Lowe, 1951, 259 Wis. 463, 49 N.W.2d 487 (same). Contra; Howson v. Foster Beef Co., 1935, 87 N.H. 200, 177 A. 656; Cheli v. Cudahy Brothers Co., 1934, 267 Mich. 690, 255 N.W. 414. See Melick, The Sale of Food and Drink, 1936, 284; Note, 1939, 26 Va.L.Rev. 100.

9. See Appleman, Civil Liability Under the Illinois Dramshop Act, 1939, 34 Ill.L.Rev. 30; Ogilvie, History and Appraisal of the Illinois Dramshop Act, [1958] U.Ill.Law Forum 175; Note, 1959, 4 Villanova L.Rev. 575.

10. Pierce v. Albanese, 1957, 144 Conn. 241, 129 A.2d 606, appeal dismissed 355 U.S. 15, 78 S.Ct. 36, 2 L.Ed.2d 21; Galvin v. Jennings, 3d Cir. 1961, 289 F.2d 15; Kvanli v. Village of Watson, 1965, 272 Minn. 481, 139 N.W.2d 275.

11. Pierce v. Albanese, 1957, 144 Conn. 241, 129 A.2d 606, appeal dismissed 355 U.S. 15, 78 S.Ct. 36, 2 L.Ed.2d 21; Huckaba v. Cox, 1958, 14 Ill.2d 126, 150 N.E.2d 832.

12. Iszler v. Jorda, N.D.1957, 80 N.W.2d 665; Pierce v. Albanese, 1957, 144 Conn. 241, 129 A.2d 606, appeal dismissed 355 U.S. 15, 78 S.Ct. 36, 2 L.Ed.2d 21; Hahn v. City of Ortonville, 1953, 238 Minn. 428, 57 N.W.2d 254; Danhof v. Osborne, 1956, 10 Ill.App.2d 529, 135 N.E.2d 492.

13. Fernandez v. Chamberlain, Fla.App.1967, 201 So.2d 781; Geocaris v. Bangs, 1968, 91 Ill.App.2d 81, 234 N.E.2d 17 (battery); Wendelin v. Russell, 1966, 259 Iowa 1152, 147 N.W.2d 188 (drunken driving); St. Clair v. Douvas, 1959, 21 Ill.App.2d 444, 158 N.E.2d 642 (wife recovered for loss of support due to killing son); Manning v. Yokas, 1957, 389 Pa. 136, 132 A.2d 198 (negligent driving).

14. Bistline v. Ney Brothers, 1907, 134 Iowa 172, 111 N.W. 422 (shooting himself); Bejnarowicz v. Bakos, 1947, 332 Ill.App. 151, 74 N.E.2d 614 (collision due to reckless driving); Sworski v. Coleman, 1940, 208 Minn. 43, 293 N.W. 297 (death from drinking). Cf. Iszler v. Jorda, N.D.1957, 80 N.W.2d 665 (funeral expenses). The intoxicated person himself usually is held not to be covered. Nolan v. Morelli, 1967, 154 Conn. 432, 226 A.2d 383.

15. Kiriluk v. Cohn, 1958, 16 Ill.App.2d 385, 148 N.E.2d 607; Currier v. McKee, 1904, 99 Me. 364, 59 A. 442.

16. See supra, § 79.

17. Jackson v. United States Pipe Line, 1937, 325 Pa. 436, 191 A. 165.

While the common law has not altogether kept pace with these statutory developments, it has shown in recent years a very marked tendency to extend strict liability into new fields. Sellers of goods have generally been held liable for defects which cause harm to the purchaser, under the guise of an "implied warranty" which becomes a term of the contract, and permits recovery without any proof of negligence.[18] First in food cases, and later as to all other products, the considerable majority of the American jurisdictions have extended the strict liability to the ultimate consumer even in the absence of privity of contract, either upon the theory of an implied warranty to the consumer by implication of law, or, more lately, on the basis of outright strict liability in tort.[19] In particular the tort liability has been found at the common law in the "Dramshop" situation, where the defendant sells liquor to an intoxicated person, and a third person suffers injury.[20] Strict liability has also been extended into the field of misrepresentation, to cover innocent statements made without negligence, for which some courts permit recovery in an action of deceit,[21] and, in the case of harm to third persons without privity of contract, recovery has been based upon an express "warranty" of truth.[22]

There are some survivals of older rules, as to which the fundamental policy of the law as to the administration of the risk involved is now advanced as a justification. The liability of a carrier[23] or an innkeeper[24] for goods entrusted to his care is one such instance. Prior to the decisions of the Supreme Court of the United States relating to a constitutional privilege to defame under the First Amendment, defamatory statements[25] were subject to a similar strict rule, which is perhaps primarily an historical anomaly, but has been supported as an instrument of policy. Vicarious liability[26] is now quite generally recognized as a form of strict liability, designed to administer the risk. Still another instance is the common law rule, now often modified by statute, which makes a defendant strictly liable, despite all due care, if he removes naturally necessary lateral or subjacent support for the plaintiff's land.[27] On the other hand, there are other such rules that are now losing favor, particularly that as to trespass to land,[28] as it is realized that there is no longer any social necessity or justification for them.

Frequently, when the courts have been unwilling to say outright that the defendant is liable without negligence, something approaching this result has been accomplished by the creation of presumptions. Thus, it has been held that upon proof of an injury at the hands of a carrier, a passenger is entitled to a presumption of the carrier's negligence, which the carrier must meet by producing affirmative evidence, or suffer a directed verdict for the plaintiff.[29] In some cases, at whose number one may only guess, where there has in fact been no negligence but the defendant is unable to prove it, this will arrive at the same result as strict liabili-

18. See infra, § 95.
19. See infra, §§ 97, 98.
20. See infra, § 104.
21. See infra, § 107.
22. See infra, § 97.
23. Thomas v. Boston & Providence Railroad Corp., 1845, 51 Mass. (10 Metc.) 472; see Dobie, Bailments and Carriers, 1914, 324, 325; Hutchinson, Law of Carriers, 3d ed.1906, § 4.
24. Hulett v. Swift, 1865, 33 N.Y. 571; Fisher v. Bonneville Hotel Co., 1920, 55 Utah 588, 188 P. 856, 12 A.L.R. 255; Featherstone v. Dessert, 1933, 173 Wash. 264, 22 P.2d 1050. The common law rule has been altered by statutes in many states and rejected by decisions in others. See Brown, Personal Property, 1936, § 102; Notes, 1929, 13 Minn.L.Rev. 615; 1942, 22 Or.L. Rev. 95.

25. See infra, § 113.
26. See supra, § 69.
27. See 5 Powell, Real Property, 1962, ch. 63; Note, 1941, 50 Yale L.J. 1125; Obert v. Dunn, 1897, 140 Mo. 476, 41 S.W. 901; Schaefer v. Hoffman, 1929, 198 Wis. 233, 223 N.W. 847; Hemsworth v. Cushing, 1897, 115 Mich. 92, 72 N.W. 1108; Walker v. Strosnider, 1910, 67 W.Va. 39, 67 S.E. 1087; Chesapeake & Ohio Railway Co. v. May, 1914, 157 Ky. 708, 163 S.W. 1112.
28. See supra, § 13.
29. Southern Pacific Co. v. Cavin, 9th Cir. 1906, 144 F. 348; Steele v. Southern Railway Co., 1899, 55 S.C. 389, 33 S.E. 509; Williams v. Spokane Falls & Northern Railway Co., 1905, 39 Wash. 77, 80 P. 1100, reversed 42 Wash. 597, 84 P. 1129. See Prosser, Res Ipsa Loquitur: Collisions of Carriers with Other Vehicles, 1936, 30 Ill.L.Rev. 980.

ty.³⁰ The difference between the two, however, lies in the fact that the door is not closed to whatever proof of proper care the defendant may be able to offer; and since he can often offer such proof, it is a difference of importance. A similar presumption of negligence has been created where goods are lost or damaged in the hands of a bailee.³¹ Subject to constitutional limitations, such presumptions have been created by some statutes.³² The courts which give the doctrine of res ipsa loquitur ³³ more than its normal procedural effect as circumstantial evidence regard it as an instrument of policy, requiring the defendant to prove that due care was exercised, or be regarded as negligent.

The last few years have witnessed the renewed and more vigorous advocacy of strict liability on an even broader scale, in which liability insurance is to play the key and dominating role. Discussion of these proposals is best deferred to a later chapter.³⁴

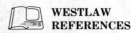

313ak5
topic("implied warrant!")

---

30. As to the policy underlying such presumptions, see Bohlen, The Effect of Rebuttable Presumptions of Law Upon the Burden of Proof, 1920, 68 U.Pa.L.Rev. 307; Morgan, Some Observations Concerning Presumptions, 1931, 44 Harv.L.Rev. 906.

31. Rustad v. Great Northern Railway Co., 1913, 122 Minn. 453, 142 N.W. 727; Schaefer v. Washington Safety Deposit Co., 1917, 281 Ill. 43, 117 N.E. 781. See Brown, Personal Property, 1936, § 87.

32. See Brosman, The Statutory Presumption, 1930, 5 Tulane L.Rev. 17; Morgan, Federal Constitutional Limitations Upon Presumptions Created by State Legislation, Harvard Legal Essays, 1934, 323.

33. See supra, § 40.

34. See infra, ch. 14.

Chapter 14

COMPENSATION SYSTEMS

Table of Sections

Sec.
82. Liability Insurance and Its Impact on Tort Law.
83. Deficiencies of the Tort and Liability Insurance System.
84. Enacted and Proposed Remedies.
85. Principles of Compensation in American Legal Systems.

§ 82. Liability Insurance and Its Impact on Tort Law

The Nature of Liability Insurance

The last half century has brought forth a deluge of legal writing concerning the relation between liability insurance and the law of torts. There are hundreds of law review articles on the subject, as well as dozens of books.[1]

The first step to understanding the controversy that spawned this extensive writing is to understand liability insurance. Liability insurance contracts customarily provide that the insurer agrees to pay on behalf of the insureds all sums the insureds shall become legally obligated to pay as damages because of harms or injuries within the scope of the coverage. Thus, insurance payments come due by reason of an insured's becoming legally liable to a third person. This is a mat-

---

§ 82

1. Here are listed a few landmarks: Columbia University Council for Research in the Social Sciences, Report by the Committee to Study Compensation for Automobile Accidents, 1932; James, Accident Liability Reconsidered: The Impact of Liability Insurance, 1948, 57 Yale L.J. 549; James and Thornton, The Impact of Insurance on the Law of Torts, 1950, 15 Law & Con. Prob. 431; Friedmann, Social Insurance and the Principles of Tort Liability, 1950, 63 Harv.L.Rev. 241; Grad, Recent Developments in Automobile Accident Compensation, 1950, 50 Col.L.Rev. 300; Ehrenzweig, Negligence Without Fault, 1951; Morris, Hazardous Enterprises and Risk-Bearing Capacity, 1952, 61 Yale L.J. 1172; McNiece and Thornton, Is the Law of Negligence Obsolete? 1952, 26 St.Johns L.Rev. 255; McNiece and Thornton, Automobile Accident Prevention and Compensation, 1952, 27 N.Y.U.L.Rev. 585; Green, The Individual's Protection Under Negligence Law: Risk Sharing, 1953, 47 Nw.U.L.Rev. 751; Ehrenzweig, "Full Aid" Insurance for the Traffic Victim—A Voluntary Compensation Plan, 1954, also published, 1955, at 43 Calif.L. Rev. 1; Green, Traffic Victims: Tort Law and Insurance, 1958; James, The Columbia Study of Compensation Law for Automobile Accidents: An Unanswered Challenge, 1959, 59 Col.L.Rev. 408; Morris & Paul, The Financial Impact of Automobile Accidents, 1962, 110 U.Pa.L.Rev. 913; O'Connell, Taming the Automobile, 1963, 58 Nw.U.L.Rev. 299; Conard, Morgan, Pratt, Voltz & Bombaugh, 1964, Automobile Accident Costs and Payments—Studies in the Economics of Injury Reparation. See also infra, §§ 83, 84, in relation to "no-fault" automobile insurance proposals and developments in the 1960's and thereafter.

ter of a contract, the insurance policy, between the insurer and the insured, to which in the first instance the third person is not a party (unless treated in law as a "third-party beneficiary"). Liability insurance is thus to be distinguished from accident insurance, in which the obligation is directly to the injured person. Unless there is statutory or administrative regulation, as there frequently may be, the insurer's undertaking is entirely a matter of the terms of the particular policy, in which there may be, and in fact is, a good deal of variation.

Provisions indemnifying against liability appeared in early insurance policies, as for example those of marine insurance, by which the insurer undertook, among other risks, that of liability for damages inflicted on other ships through collision.[2] In its modern form, the separate liability policy began to appear in England not long after 1880, and developed first as a means of protecting employers against the increased litigation and liability resulting from employers' liability and workers' compensation acts. As the experience with this proved satisfactory, new demands were made for protection against other risks, and the protection was expanded into other fields in a rather unplanned and haphazard manner.[3] In addition to the employer's liability, common subjects of insurance today are the risks resulting from the use of premises, whether open to the public or privately used; from faulty products which injure consumers; from the use of vehicles in all forms of transportation; and those arising out of the practice of professions, such as surgery, medicine, law, accounting, and trusteeship. There are even policies available for protection against relatively unusual risks, such as that of liability of a publisher for defamation. By far the greatest amount of liability insurance today, however, covers the risks arising from automobile accidents. This has become a business of enormous proportions.

Almost from the beginning, the liability insurer began to undertake more than the indemnification for the loss or liability itself. One of the primary purposes of the policy always has been to protect the insured against the expense and inconvenience of litigation. The investigation of the third person's claim, negotiation with the claimant, the posting of a bond when it is required, or even providing bail where there is an arrest, the defense of the action brought against the insured and the payment of attorney's fees and all other expenses which it may involve—all these have become recognized as the responsibility of the insurer.

For a time in the beginning, there was considerable uncertainty as to whether any contract by which one was to be protected against the consequences of one's own negligence or other fault was contrary to public policy. Liability insurance was attacked as a form of maintenance, by which professional litigants were provided to replace the true defendants, and as an encouragement to antisocial conduct and a relaxation of viligance toward the rights of others, by relieving the actual wrongdoer of liability.[4] That the latter objection had at least some substance is illustrated by one case in which, a moment before the crash, the defendant replied to the plaintiff's protest against his reckless

---

2. See Delanoy v. Robson, 1814, 5 Taunt. 605, 606, 128 Eng.Rep. 827, mentioning "societies of persons, who insured each other's vessels not only against sea risks, but against all sums which the owner might be obliged to pay for damages done by their vessels." The marine insurance policy, which has not been changed substantially since it was first put into use in 1613, is set out in R. Keeton, Insurance Law Basic Text, 1971, Appendix C.

3. "Like a New England Farmhouse, with unplanned additions stuck on as occasion demanded." McNeely, Illegality as a Factor in Liability Insurance, 1941, 41 Col.L.Rev. 26, 28. See, as a full description of one type, Arnold, Products Liability Insurance, [1957] Wis.L.Rev. 429.

4. See Coffman v. Louisville & Nashville Railroad Co., 1913, 184 Ala. 474, 63 So. 527; Employers' Liability Assurance Corp. Limited v. Kelly-Atkinson Construction Co., 1913, 182 Ill.App. 372; Aetna Life Insurance Co. v. Weck, 1915, 163 Ky. 37, 173 S.W. 317; Standard Life & Accident Insurance Co. v. Bambrick Brothers Construction Co., 1912, 163 Mo.App. 504, 143 S.W. 845; In re Aldrich, 1913, 86 Vt. 531, 86 A. 801.

driving, "Don't worry, I carry insurance." [5] With the passage of time, when it became apparent that no dire consequences in fact resulted,[6] these objections passed out of the picture, and the validity of a liability insurance contract as such is no longer questioned.

Following two leading cases in which the insurance contract was sustained where an employer had hired the injured employee in violation of a statute setting an age limit,[7] and the insured's car was being operated, against the law, by a person under age,[8] it is now generally agreed that violations of criminal statutes such as driving without a license,[9] speeding,[10] and the like,[11] will not invalidate the insurance, or deprive the violator of its protection. There will almost certainly be cases in which the misconduct is so flagrant and extreme that it will be considered entirely against public policy to indemnify against it;[12] but it seems equally clear that it is only in the plainest and most outrageous cases that this will be true.[13] Of course, policy provisions may exclude liability for some kinds of illegal conduct as to which the law does not forbid coverage. Thus, absent a statutory mandate to the contrary, an insurance policy may deny coverage for injuries resulting from assault and battery or other intentional infliction of harm, or the operation of a car by an unlicensed minor, or by a drunken driver.[14]

Since, in its inception, liability insurance was intended solely for the benefit and protection of the insured, which is to say the tortfeasor, it followed that the injured plaintiff, who was not a party to the contract, had at common law no direct remedy against the insurance company.[15] In order to make this quite certain, and so far as possible to delay or avoid the liability which they had been paid to assume, insurance companies inserted in the policy "no action" clauses, which required payment of a judgment by the insured before they became obligated to him.[16] This meant that insolvency of the insured, settlement and release of the insurer,

---

5. Herschensohn v. Weisman, 1923, 80 N.H. 557, 119 A. 705.

6. See the references to empirical data indicating that the number of accidents did not increase with the growth of liability insurance, in Merchants' Mutual Automobile Liability Insurance Co. v. Smart, 1925, 267 U.S. 126, 45 S.Ct. 320, 69 L.Ed. 538; In re Opinion of the Justices, 1925, 251 Mass. 569, 147 N.E. 681.

7. Edward Stern & Co. v. Liberty Mutual Insurance Co., 1921, 269 Pa. 559, 112 A. 865.

8. Messersmith v. American Fidelity Co., 1921, 232 N.Y. 161, 133 N.E. 432. Accord, Davis v. Highway Motor Underwriters, 1931, 120 Neb. 734, 235 N.W. 325.

9. McMahon v. Pearlman, 1922, 242 Mass. 367, 136 N.E. 154; Odden v. Union Indemnity Co., 1930, 156 Wash. 10, 286 P. 59; Neat v. Miller, 1932, 170 Wash. 625, 17 P.2d 32; Sills v. Schneider, 1939, 197 Wash. 659, 86 P.2d 203 (taxicab).

10. Miller v. United States Fidelity & Casualty Co., 1935, 291 Mass. 445, 197 N.E. 75; Firemen's Fund Insurance Co. v. Haley, 1922, 129 Miss. 525, 92 So. 635; Rothman v. Metropolitan Casualty Insurance Co., 1938, 134 Ohio St. 241, 16 N.E.2d 417 (plus improper driving).

11. Security Underwriters v. Rousch Motor Co., 1928, 88 Ind.App. 112, 161 N.E. 569 (cable across highway); Lopez v. Townsend, 1933, 37 N.M. 574, 25 P.2d 809 (carrier violating operating rules); Bowman v. Preferred Risk Mutual Insurance Co., 1957, 348 Mich. 531, 83 N.W.2d 434 (moving another's car illegally); Wolff v. General Casualty Co. of America, 1963, 68 N.M. 292, 361 P.2d 330 (assault and battery). See Note, 1967, 12 S.D.L.Rev. 373.

12. See for example Acme Finance Co. v. National Insurance Co., 1948, 118 Colo. 445, 195 P.2d 728, refusing to enforce a liability policy because the accident occurred while the insured was engaged in robbery and murder. See R. Keeton, Insurance Law Basic Text, 1971, § 5.3(f).

13. See, allowing recovery where there was drunken driving, Neat v. Miller, 1932, 170 Wash. 625, 17 P.2d 32; Tinline v. White Cross Ins. Ass'n, [1921] 3 K.B. 327; James v. British Gen. Ins. Co. [1927] 2 K.B. 311. Contra, where the car was being operated at very high speed. O'Hearn v. Yorkshire Ins. Co., 1921, 67 Ont.L. Rep. 735.

14. See McNeely, Illegality as a Factor in Liability Insurance, 1941, 41 Col.L.Rev. 26.

15. Bain v. Atkins, 1902, 181 Mass. 240, 63 N.E. 414; Kinnan v. Fidelity & Casualty Co., 1903, 107 Ill. App. 406; Smith Stage Co. v. Eckert, 1919, 21 Ariz. 28, 184 P. 1001; Fidelity & Casualty Co. v. Martin, 1915, 163 Ky. 12, 173 S.W. 307. A noted diatribe in condemnation of this is Laube, The Social Vice of Accident Indemnity, 1931, 80 U.Pa.L.Rev. 189.

16. "No action shall lie against the company to recover for any loss or expense under this policy, unless it shall be brought by the assured for loss or expense actually sustained and paid in money by him after trial of the issue." Quoted in Patterson v. Adan, 1912, 119 Minn. 308, 309–311, 138 N.W. 281, 282. See also Good-

death or removal from the jurisdiction, or merely the fact that the insured was judgment-proof, would defeat all recovery in favor of anyone.[17] Unscrupulous companies were even known to put the insured through bankruptcy, as a cheap way of paying off the policy.[18] Various theories which were resorted to in order to obtain a direct action against the insurer, such as subrogation,[19] garnishment,[20] and the like,[21] were strikingly unsuccessful. The two which succeeded to some limited extent were the device by which a cooperative insured paid off the judgment with a note,[22] and an estoppel precluding the insurer from setting up the clause where it had assumed control of the lawsuit and defended it.[23]

All of this is now extensively modified by legislation.[24] Statutes, variously worded, have prevented the insurer from conditioning its duty to pay upon prior payment by the insured, and provide that the injured person holding an unsatisfied judgment against the insured may proceed against the insurer,[25] or that the insolvency or bankruptcy of the insured shall not release the company.[26] The policy forms now in general use provide specifically that bankruptcy or insolvency of the insured or of his estate shall not relieve the company of any of its obligations under the policy. Wisconsin and Louisiana[27] have gone farthest of all, and have provided a direct action in every case against the liability insurer.

Clauses in the policy almost invariably limit the liability of the insurer to much less than the insured may possibly incur. Most obvious and important, of course, is the limitation in amount, which is graduated according to the premium paid. In addition, var-

man v. Georgia Life Insurance Co., 1914, 189 Ala. 130, 66 So. 649; Ohio Casualty Insurance Co. v. Beckwith, 5th Cir. 1934, 74 F.2d 75.

17. Hollings v. Brown, 1922, 202 Ala. 504, 80 So. 792; Shea v. United States Fidelity & Casualty Co., 1923, 98 Conn. 447, 120 A. 286; Cushman v. Carbondale Fuel Co., 1904, 122 Iowa 656, 98 N.W. 509; Transylvania Casualty Insurance Co. v. Williams, 1925, 209 Ky. 626, 273 S.W. 536.

18. See Roth v. National Automobile Mutual Casualty Co., 1922, 202 App.Div. 667, 669, 195 N.Y.S. 865, 867, dismissed 1923, 235 N.Y. 605, 139 N.E. 752.

19. Pfeiler v. Penn Allen Portland Cement Co., 1913, 240 Pa. 468, 87 A. 623; Allen v. Aetna Life Insurance Co., 3d Cir. 1906, 145 F. 881.

20. Shea v. United States Fidelity & Casualty Co., 1923, 98 Conn. 447, 120 A. 286; Combs v. Hunt, 1924, 140 Va. 627, 125 S.E. 661; Hollings v. Brown, 1919, 202 Ala. 504, 80 So. 792; Fidelity & Casualty Co. v. Martin, 1915, 163 Ky. 12, 173 S.W. 307; Ford v. Aetna Life Insurance Co., 1912, 70 Wash. 29, 126 P. 69.

Where the policy is construed to insure against liability, before payment, the injured party, after judgment against the insured establishes the liability, may garnish the insurer. Fentress v. Rutledge, 1924, 140 Va. 685, 125 S.E. 668; Wehrhahn v. Fort Dearborn Casualty Underwriters, 1928, 221 Mo.App. 230, 1 S.W.2d 242.

21. Luger v. Windell, 1921, 116 Wash. 375, 199 P. 760 (assignment of the policy); Connolly v. Bolster, 1905, 187 Mass. 266, 72 N.E. 981 (resort to equity).

22. Herbo-Phosa Co. v. Philadelphia Casualty Co., 1912, 34 R.I. 567, 84 A. 1093; Taxicab Motor Co. v. Pacific Coast Casualty Co., 1913, 73 Wash. 631, 132 P. 393; Standard Printing Co. v. Fidelity & Deposit Co., 1917, 138 Minn. 304, 164 N.W. 1022; Hoagland Wagon Co. v. London Guarantee & Accident Co., 1919, 201 Mo. App. 490, 212 S.W. 393. Even this failed in Wisconsin as a "mere subterfuge." Stenbohm v. Brown-Corliss Engine Co., 1909, 137 Wis. 564, 119 N.W. 308.

23. Patterson v. Adan, 1912, 119 Minn. 308, 138 N.W. 281; American Indemnity Co. v. Felbaum, 1924, 114 Tex. 127, 263 S.W. 908; Sanders v. Frankfort Marine, Accident & Plate Glass Insurance Co., 1904, 72 N.H. 485, 57 A. 655; Elliott v. Aetna Life Insurance Co., 1917, 100 Neb. 833, 161 N.W. 579; Elliott v. Belt Automobile Association, 1924, 87 Fla. 545, 100 So. 797; Maryland Casualty Co. v. Peppard, 1915, 53 Okl. 515, 157 P. 106. Apart from statute, however, this was definitely a minority position. See Vance, Insurance, 3d Ed. 1951, 803.

24. See Dodge, An Injured Party's Rights Under an Automobile Liability Policy, 1952, 38 Iowa L.Rev. 116; Lassiter, Direct Actions Against the Insurer, [1949] Ins.L.J. 411; Leigh, Direct Actions Against Liability Insurer, [1949] Ins.L.J. 633; Rudser, Direct Actions Against Insurance Companies, 1969, 45 N.D.L.Rev. 483; Notes, 1933, 46 Harv.L.Rev. 1325; 1952, 27 N.Y. U.L.Rev. 817; 1970, 23 Vand.L.Rev. 631.

25. See Guerin v. Indemnity Insurance Co., 1928, 107 Conn. 649, 142 A. 268; Stacey v. Fidelity & Casualty Co., 1926, 114 Ohio St. 633, 151 N.E. 718; Riding v. Travelers Insurance Co., 1927, 48 R.I. 433, 138 A. 186.

26. Merchants' Mutual Automobile Liability Insurance Co. v. Smart, 1925, 267 U.S. 126, 45 S.Ct. 320, 69 L.Ed. 538; Coleman v. New Amsterdam Casualty Co., 1927, 247 N.Y. 271, 160 N.E. 367, affirmed 220 App. Div. 748, 222 N.Y.S. 788; Indemnity Insurance Co. of North America v. Davis' Administrator, 1928, 150 Va. 778, 143 S.E. 328.

27. See Notes [1953] Wis.L.Rev. 688; 1937, 11 Tulane L.Rev. 443.

ious plaintiffs, such as members of the insured's own family, are quite commonly excluded. The automobile guest statutes,[28] which are largely the work of insurance companies in the legislatures, have tended to cut down on liability to guests.

As in the case of other contracts of insurance, that of liability insurance may be defeated by misrepresentation of material facts on the part of the insured at the time of applying for the policy.[29] In addition, practically all policies provide that the insured must give the insurer immediate notice, or notice as soon as practicable, of any accident which may result in a claim. Legislation requiring insurance, or giving the injured person direct rights against the insurer, has been held, except in a few states,[30] not to do away with this requirement of notice.[31] There has, however, been a tendency in some of the cases to hold that the insurer is not relieved of liability where it is not prejudiced by the delay.[32]

Another standard provision of liability insurance policies requires the insured to "cooperate with" and assist the insurer in the defense of any action covered by the policy. This means first of all that the insured must give the company full and accurate information as to the facts of the accident.[33] It requires also that the insured attend the trial, and take part in it,[34] and do nothing to aid the injured person against the insurer, as for example by giving a collusive statement admitting liability.[35] On the other hand, mere truthful statements, or expressions of sympathy, or of a desire that the injured person recover, normally are held not to amount to a violation of the cooperation clause;[36] and most courts have held that the insurer is not released in any case unless it has been in some way prejudiced by the failure to cooperate.[37]

---

28. See supra, § 34.

29. See R. Keeton, Insurance Law Basic Text, 1971, §§ 5.6–5.8, 6.1–6.7.

30. Edwards v. Fidelity & Casualty Co. of New York, 1929, 11 La.App. 176, 123 So. 162; West v. Monroe Bakery, 1950, 217 La. 189, 46 So.2d 122; National Indemnity Co. v. Simmons, 1962, 230 Md. 234, 186 A.2d 595.

31. Lorando v. Gethro, 1917, 228 Mass. 181, 117 N.E. 185; Hynding v. Home Accident Insurance Co., 1932, 214 Cal. 743, 7 P.2d 999; Coleman v. New Amsterdam Casualty Co., 1928, 247 N.Y. 271, 160 N.E. 367, affirmed 220 App.Div. 748, 222 N.Y.S. 788; Stacey v. Fidelity & Casualty Co., 1926, 114 Ohio St. 633, 151 N.E. 718.

32. Gibson v. Colonial Insurance Co., 1949, 92 Cal. App.2d 33, 206 P.2d 387; Kennedy v. Dashner, 1947, 319 Mich. 491, 30 N.W.2d 46; Massachusetts Bonding & Insurance Co. v. Arizona Concrete Co., 1936, 47 Ariz. 420, 56 P.2d 188; Brookville Electric Co. v. Utilities Insurance Co., Mo.App.1940, 142 S.W.2d 803; Frank v. Nash, 1950, 166 Pa.Super. 470, 71 A.2d 835; Johnson Controls, Inc. v. Bowes, 381 Mass. 278, 409 N.E.2d 185 (1980). See Note, 1952, 51 Mich.L.Rev. 275; R. Keeton, Insurance Law Basic Text, 1971, § 7.1.

33. Coleman v. New Amsterdam Casualty Co., 1927, 247 N.Y. 271, 160 N.E. 367, affirmed 220 App. Div. 748, 222 N.Y.S. 788; Ohio Casualty Co. of Hamilton, Ohio v. Swan, 8th Cir. 1937, 89 F.2d 219; Hilliard v. United Pacific Casualty Co., 1938, 195 Wash. 478, 81 P.2d 513; Standard Accident Insurance Co. of Detroit, Michigan v. Winget, 9th Cir. 1952, 197 F.2d 97.

34. Indemnity Insurance Co. of North America v. Smith, 1951, 197 Md. 160, 78 A.2d 461; Roberts v. Commercial Standard Insurance Co., D.Ark.1956, 138 F.Supp. 363; Curran v. Connecticut Indemnity Co., 1941, 127 Conn. 692, 20 A.2d 87; Hynding v. Home Accident Insurance Co., 1932, 214 Cal. 743, 7 P.2d 999.

35. Kindervater v. Motorists Casualty Insurance Co., 1938, 120 N.J.L. 373, 199 A. 606. Compare, as to other instances of "collusion," Bassi v. Bassi, 1925, 165 Minn. 100, 205 N.W. 947; Collins' Executors v. Standard Accident Insurance Co., 1916, 170 Ky. 27, 185 S.W. 112; Conroy v. Commercial Casualty Insurance Co., 1928, 292 Pa. 219, 140 A. 905; State Farm Mutual Automobile Insurance Co. v. Bonacci, 8th Cir. 1940, 111 F.2d 412.

36. Maryland Casualty Co. v. Lamarre, 1928, 83 N.H. 206, 140 A. 174; Johnson v. Johnson, 1939, 228 Minn. 282, 37 N.W.2d 1. See R. Keeton, Insurance Law Basic Text, 1971, § 7.5.

37. State Farm Mutual Automobile Insurance Co. v. Koval, 10th Cir. 1944, 146 F.2d 118; MacClure v. Accident & Casualty Insurance Co., 1948, 229 N.E. 305, 49 S.E.2d 742; MFA Mutual Insurance Co. v. Sailors, 1966, 180 Neb. 201, 141 N.W.2d 846; Marcum v. State Automobile Mutual Insurance Co., 1950, 134 W.Va. 144, 59 S.E.2d 433; Billington v. Interinsurance Exchange of Southern California, 1969, 71 Cal.2d 728, 79 Cal.Rptr. 326, 456 P.2d 982. See R. Keeton, Insurance Law Basic Text, 1971, § 7.5.

Conflicting Inferences about the Impact of Liability Insurance

Dedicated advocates of sweeping change, in which liability insurance was to play a predominant part, in some instances sought to buttress their arguments by the contention that such insurance already had revolutionized the law of torts; that it had rendered obsolete the rules of negligence, making them a mere set of formulae to which the courts afford lip service, while in fact looking to the insurance; that the change, already half made, therefore should be completed.[38]

Although liability insurance undoubtedly has had its effect, a dispassionate observer, if one is to be found in this area, might quite as readily conclude that the impact of insurance upon the law of torts has been amazingly slight; that most of the changes that have been pointed out are due to other causes; and that it is in truth astonishing that a system by which the defendants can and do obtain relief from all liability upon payment of a relatively small premium has received so little mention and visible recognition in the tort decisions.

The difference between the two points of view will turn upon the extent to which one is willing to assume, without proof, that the changes in tort law going on for most of this century, and which have resulted in increased protection for the plaintiff in nearly all areas, are due more to this one factor than to a number of others. An illustration is instructive. In 1915 it was held in Nebraska,[39] as a matter of law, that the failure of a surgeon dealing with a bone fracture to take X-ray photographs was not negligence, or evidence from which the jury could find negligence. In 1947, in California,[40] the court took judicial notice of the fact that good surgical practice always requires that such photographs be taken, and held that the failure to do so was in itself enough to support a finding of negligence. In the meantime, insurance against liability for medical malpractice, which was available but not prevalent in 1915, had expanded into an enormous business. It would be easy to attribute the change in the law to this alone, and no doubt some observers would do so. But this is to ignore the greatly advanced standards of medicine and surgery, the superior medical education, the increased familiarity of all medical practitioners with X-rays, the improvement in the equipment, its lower cost, and its availability in nearly all communities; and, above all, the demands which the public now makes, and reasonably makes, upon the profession. It would be quite as reasonable to say that the spread of the malpractice insurance itself is a consequence of the expanded liability, which is rather the result of a multitude of such other factors.[41]

---

38. The pioneer piece of writing of this kind was Feezer, Capacity to Bear Loss as a Factor in the Decision of Certain Types of Tort Cases, 1930, 78 U.Pa.L. Rev. 805. Next, and fuller was James, Accident Liability Reconsidered: The Impact of Liability Insurance, 1948, 57 Yale L.J. 549. This was followed by the booklet by Ehrenzweig, Negligence Without Fault, 1951, which is the outstanding work along these lines. See also James and Thornton, The Impact of Insurance on the Law of Torts, 1950, 15 Law & Con.Prob. 431; Friedmann, Social Insurance and the Principles of Tort Liability, 1950, 63 Harv.L.Rev. 241; Leflar, Negligence in Name Only, 1952, 27 N.Y.U.L.Rev. 564; McNiece and Thornton, Is the Law of Negligence Obsolete? 1952, 26 St. Johns L.Rev. 255; Atkins, The Impact of the Growth of Enterprise Liability on the Theory of Damages in Accident Cases, 1959, 20 La.L.Rev. 50.

39. In Van Boskirk v. Pinto, 1915, 99 Neb. 164, 155 N.W. 889.

40. In Agnew v. City of Los Angeles, 1947, 82 Cal. App.2d 616, 186 P.2d 450.

41. "It is often argued that 'liberal' legal policies in respect of tort liability, i.e., those which seem to broaden the base of what is compensable and raise the price of the penalty of carelessness, are moving in this direction [of compensation of every casualty without regard to predictability or fault]. The fact is that a century or more ago, the failure to guard against dangers that ought to be foreseen was treated in the same spirit as now; what has changed in the accelerated pace and the enhanced mechanism utilized by society is merely the range and scope of the danger to be guarded against. The law of tort is more 'liberal' precisely because experience shows more predictable casualties. Compare the failure to tie up the horse which ran away and injured the plaintiff, considered by the Court of Common Pleas in 1854 (McCahill v. Kipp, 2 E.D.Smith 413) with the failure of a responsible third party to warn a work-

"Invisible" Effects

Two of the effects upon the law claimed for liability insurance have been so-called "invisible" ones, which are not reflected by or in any way apparent from the opinions of appellate courts. One of these is the settlement of cases. The insurance companies, engaged in the business for profit, and managed by unsentimental individuals interested in financial results, customarily settle a substantial portion of their claims without regard to the existence of any liability. In other words, many claims are paid in which it is clear that the defendant was not at fault, or that the plaintiff was; and the result is compensation not based on fault at all, but on the existence of insurance. This is good business, since it retains the good will of both the plaintiff and the defendant, who may buy more insurance, and it helps the reputation of the company as a liberal payer of claims. It is also the cheapest way out in any case in which the "nuisance value" of the suit, which means the probable cost of investigation, preparation and trial, together with the off chance that the plaintiff might after all be able to prove a case, exceeds the amount paid. For obvious reasons, the claims so settled are almost invariably the smaller ones.

All this is certainly true; but its impact may not be distinctive to tort law. Contract claims are customarily settled on the same basis; the return of goods to a store by an unsatisfied customer is a familiar example. Habitual defendants, such as railroad companies, always have settled claims on this basis, and so does the ordinary individual who uses common sense.

The other "invisible" effect is upon the verdict of the jury. It is more or less notorious among lawyers [42] that juries, in general, tend to return verdicts, or larger verdicts, against defendants who have liability insurance, for the simple reason that they are aware that the defendant will not have to pay the judgment, and that the company has been paid a premium for undertaking the liability. In most jurisdictions the jury are not supposed to be told in so many words that there is insurance in the case,[43] unless the evidence is somehow relevant as bearing upon some other issue.[44] Plaintiff's attorneys have, however, become very adroit in managing to convey the information. One method is to ask jurors, upon voir dire, about their possible interest in or employment by a liability insurance company.[45] By way of emphasis of the idea, a question asked of a witness may produce an "unexpected" and unresponsive mention of insurance,[46] which, whether it is uttered in good faith or not, is virtually impossible to prevent or control. Even where no such information can be conveyed, jurors are quite

---

man engaged to thaw out a line of electricity of the presence of methane gas, an explosive which injured him, considered in 1949 in Appier v. Million, 299 N.Y. 715, 87 N.E.2d 125." Bergan, J., in McPartland v. State, 1950, 277 App.Div. 103, 98 N.Y.S.2d 665, 668, reargument and appeal denied In re Sage's Estate, 1951, 277 App.Div. 1063, 100 N.Y.S.2d 958.

42. The tendency may not be so great as is commonly supposed, now that most jurors drive cars and have liability insurance of their own. See Kalven, The Jury, the Law, and the Personal Injury Damage Award, 1958, 19 Ohio St.L.J. 158, 170–171, reporting on the University of Chicago jury study.

43. See McCormick, Evidence, 1954, 355–358; James Stewart & Co. v. Newby, 4th Cir. 1920, 266 F. 287; Fielding v. Publix Cars, Inc., 1936, 130 Neb. 576, 265 N.W. 726, 105 A.L.R. 1306; Watson v. Adams, 1914, 187 Ala. 490, 65 So. 528; Roche v. Llewellyn Ironworks Co., 1903, 140 Cal. 563, 74 P. 147. See Note, 1966, 51 Iowa L.Rev. 726.

44. See early discussions of this issue in Rapoport, Proper Disclosure During Trial that Defendant is Insured, 1940, 26 Corn.L.Q. 137; Aguilera v. Reynolds Well Service, Inc., Tex.Civ.App.1950, 234 S.W.2d 282 error refused.

45. See Kiernan v. Van Schaik, 3d Cir. 1965, 347 F.2d 775; mathena v. Burchett, 1962, 189 Kan. 350, 369 P.2d 487; White v. Teague, 1944, 353 Mo. 247, 182 S.W.2d 288; Santee v. Haggart Construction Co., 1938, 202 Minn. 361, 278 N.W. 520; Wheeler v. Rudek, 1947, 397 Ill. 438, 74 N.E.2d 601. See Notes, 1948, 43 Ill.L. Rev. 650; 1966, 51 Iowa L.Rev. 726.

In some jurisdictions this is not permitted. For comment, see Green, Blindfolding the Jury, 1954, 33 Tex.L. Rev. 137; Gay, "Blindfolding" the Jury; Another View, 1956, 34 Tex.L.Rev. 368; Green, A Rebuttal, 1956, 34 Tex.L.Rev. 382.

46. See for example Pillsbury Flour Mills v. Miller, 8th Cir. 1941, 121 F.2d 297; Williams v. Consumers' Co., 1933, 352 Ill. 51, 185 N.E. 217; Cain v. Kohlman,

likely to assume that any defendant who owns an automobile and is worth suing is probably insured—which in no way operates to the benefit of a defendant who in fact has no insurance. With financial responsibility laws in many states making insurance compulsory or practically so for every driver, the whole question of disclosure of insurance is no longer the burning issue that it formerly was; and courts in increasing numbers have asserted that the jurors assume anyway that the defendant is insured.[47]

The result of all this is said, and no doubt quite correctly, to be a substantial increase in the proportion of recoveries in some types of cases, as well as larger recoveries, by plaintiffs as a class. This in turn, of course, has had its effect upon liability insurance rates, which undoubtedly have increased at a pace not entirely to be accounted for by inflation and the increase in the accident rate itself.

For many years before liability insurance became prevalent, of course, railroad companies, public utilities, municipalities, industrial enterprises, and large corporations in general, who among them made up the majority of all negligence defendants, were subjected to this treatment at the hands of juries, and against them, too, the recoveries ran, and still run, quite high. All that the insurance has done is to provide, in lieu of many private individuals such as automobile drivers, a large new source of payment in the form of an additional group against whom the jury may give expression to their natural human desire to see compensation made to an injured human being, at the expense of another who, they feel, should be able to pay it without comparable hardship. From the social point of view such a development of course has considerable significance, even if it takes place entirely within the framework of the existing law.

Jury Issues

Over the last century there has been a great decrease in the proportion of directed verdicts. Issues are now commonly left to the jury which a hundred, or even fifty years ago, would have been decided for the defendant by the court. Since juries are well known to favor the injured plaintiff when they are permitted to do so, this works to the plaintiff's advantage. This too has been ascribed to the presence, or availability, of insurance, either as the sole explanation or as a decisive factor.

Again there is nothing in the opinions to indicate it, but those who are inclined to think that courts always act for unexpressed reasons which they are unwilling to admit can readily assert that this is the only explanation. It is an assertion impossible to prove or to disprove. There are, however, other factors to be accounted for.

The tendency of the courts to submit more issues to jury determination has not been confined to cases in which there is insurance, or any likelihood of it. It has not been confined to tort cases, but has been general across the law. The tendency certainly has not been discouraged by the election of judges, who become reluctant to make unpopular decisions, and by the active resentment of the bar against interference from the court. The same judicial retreat has been apparent in the issuance of injunctions, in punishments for contempt, and in the refusal of the judge, in most American jurisdictions, to comment on the evidence even when permitted to do so.

The most likely explanation may be simply the same general shift in popular opinion, and in judicial response to it in favor of the

---

1941, 344 Pa. 63, 22 A.2d 667; Sheldon v. River Lines, 1949, 91 Cal.App.2d 478, 205 P.2d 37.

47. "He [the juror] doesn't require a brick house to fall on him to give him an idea." Bliss, C. J., in Connelly v. Nolte, 1946, 237 Iowa 114, 21 N.W.2d 311, 320. Accord: Brown v. Walter, 2d Cir. 1933, 62 F.2d 798;

Takoma Park Bank v. Abbott, 1941, 179 Md. 249, 19 A.2d 169, certiorari denied 314 U.S. 672, 62 S.Ct. 134, 86 L.Ed. 538; Odegard v. Connolly, 1941, 211 Minn. 342, 1 N.W.2d 137. Cf. Waid v. Bergschneider, 1963, 94 Ariz. 21, 381 P.2d 568 (mention not prejudicial).

plaintiff, which has been going on in all tort law, and which leads the judge quite reasonably to refuse to deprive the injured person of a chance of recovery in any case in which a doubtful question can fairly be presented. The tendency has been most marked as to the defenses of contributory negligence and assumption of risk, as to both of which directed verdicts have largely disappeared from the scene. Both defenses have been under attack for many years;[48] and the same reasons which have induced the courts to say that they are disfavored, and to develop such halfway measures as the last clear chance, and which have led to the adoption of comparative negligence acts, are in themselves quite adequate explanation. It can scarcely be supposed that insurance has not been something of a factor, but there is no satisfactory indication that it is the whole story or even the primary influence.

Shift of Emphasis in Negligence

Some writers have made a great deal of a supposed change in the character of negligence itself. Beginning, along with the criminal law, with a purpose only of "admonition" of the defendant and deterrence of others, and hence with an insistence upon moral blame as essential to liability, it is said to have altered in the direction of a primary concern with compensation of the victim, and so to have become negligence "without fault," of "in name only." Thus one who is only stupid, ignorant, excitable or congenitally clumsy, or otherwise lacking in the capacity to behave as a normal individual, is held liable for negligence[49] even though in no way to blame for it. The psychologists have come up with the classification of the "accident prone,"[50] who are predisposed to catastrophe and unable to protect themselves or others against it; and whether this is, as might be suspected, merely a matter of innate stupidity, slow reaction time, poor training and bad habits, or, as some of the psychologists would have it, of a "guilt complex" and a "death wish" subconsciously seeking punishment for past misdeeds,[51] it is undoubtedly true that there are such individuals who have a history of repetition, and that, whether they can help it or not, they are held liable. Professor Ehrenzweig[52] even provided us with a "psychoanalysis of negligence," to explain our social attitude toward those who cannot help committing torts.

It may be suggested that much of this, at least, is setting up a straw man to knock him down. The dual purpose of tort law goes back to very ancient times, and moral blame never has been a requisite of legal liability. As long ago as 1616, it was said[53] that a lunatic is liable for his torts, although not for his crimes. At least since tort law finally split away from crime, it has been primarily concerned with compensation. The very first case in which the objective standard of the reasonable person first emerged was Vaughan v. Menlove[54] in 1837, one of a stupid mistake of an ignorant man who honestly used his own bad judgment. These are developments of earlier centuries, and not of the present day. Nor is liability without moral blame the same thing as liability without fault. There is still legal fault, which is a departure from a standard of conduct required by the community. The defendant may not be to blame for being out of line with it, but is none the less liable when out of line.

48. See supra, ch. 11.

49. See supra, § 32.

50. See James and Dickinson, Accident Proneness and Accident Law, 1950, 63 Harv.L.Rev. 869; Maloney and Risk, The Accident-Prone Driver: The Automotive Age's Biggest Unsolved Problem, 1962, 14 U.Fla.L. Rev. 364.

51. See McLean, Accident Proneness—A Clinical Approach to Injury-Liability, 1955, 24 Indus.Med. & Surg. 121; Jenkins, The Accident-Prone Personality, Personnel, July, 1956, 29; Tillman & Hobbs, Accident-Prone Automobile Drivers; Study of Psychiatric and Social Background, 1949, 106 Am.J. Psychiatry 321.

52. Ehrenzweig, A Psychoanalysis of Negligence, 1953, 47 Northwestern U.L.Rev. 855.

53. In Weaver v. Ward, 1616, Hob. 134, 80 Eng. Rep. 284.

54. 1837, 3 Bing.N.C. 467, 132 Eng.Rep. 490.

As has been stated above,[55] the principle of res ipsa loquitur has been used to permit recovery in cases where there is no direct proof of negligence or of its absence, and it may very possibly not have existed in fact. This also has been hailed as a part of the advancing front of strict liability,[56] and, by some, attributed to the existence of insurance, although the decisions never mention it.

This, at least, has almost certainly been overstated. In the ordinary case, res ipsa loquitur amounts to nothing more than recognition of a reasonable inference that there has been negligence, which the jury are entitled to draw on the basis of probabilities. The door is open to the defendant to refute it by proof; and so long as this is true, there is no liability without fault. One might as well say that conviction of an innocent person of crime upon circumstantial evidence amounts to a law of guilt without crime. In the relatively few situations[57] in which procedural disadvantages have been imposed upon defendants against whom no such inference was to be drawn, there has invariably been a special relation between the plaintiff and the defendants, or between two or more defendants, which justifies the special responsibility imposed.

Vicarious Liability

The principle of respondeat superior,[58] originating in cases of master and servant, has been extended to impose vicarious liability in other situations. One who is free from all moral blame or legal fault is held liable for the tort of another, and this may be described as a form of liability without fault. Some of these developments have been statutory; but others, as in the case of the family car doctrine and the employers of independent contractors,[59] have been a matter of common law.

The changes are undoubtedly there, although to attribute them to insurance may require some stretch of the imagination, where no court has said anything about it. They represent an obvious effort to find a financially responsible defendant who can be charged with the liability of another who, in general, cannot be relied on to pay a judgment. Two limitations are, however, to be pointed out. The basis of liability is still the negligence or other fault of the one actually at fault; and without such fault no one is liable at all. And the defendant who is to be charged always stands in such a relation to the wrongdoer as to properly be held responsible for the wrongdoer's conduct; and in the absence of such a relation there is again no liability. What has been done, in other words, is not to institute a system of liability without fault, but to broaden the fault liability to include those who may properly be held responsible for the fault that occurred.

Nevertheless, this is so far a matter of judge-made policy, deliberately adopted to the end of insuring compensation of the injured, that it may serve as an analogy for holding other "enterprises" liable for the more or less inevitable harm which they inflict upon others.[60]

Specific Mention of Insurance

Until recent decades, there was, in the opinions in tort cases, astonishingly little mention of insurance as a reason for holding the defendant liable. This is all the more remarkable when one considers the number of cases in which the court has been scrabbling hard for any reason or argument to support a change in the law. The failure even to mention insurance under such conditions suggests rather a determination *not* to take it into account than an important and influential, but unstated, reason. On the other hand, it has been said often enough that liability insurance does not create liability, but

---

55. Supra, § 40.

56. This goes back to Thayer, Liability Without Fault, 1916, 29 Harv.L.Rev. 801.

57. See supra, § 40.

58. Supra, § 73.

59. See supra, §§ 71, 73.

60. As to the proposals made, see infra, § 84.

only provides a means of indemnity against it once it has arisen; and that it is not to be considered in determining whether anyone is liable in the first instance.

There were, however, a few cases, out of many thousand, in which insurance received specific mention as a factor. As long ago as Ryan v. New York Central Railroad Co.,[61] in 1866, the prevalence of fire insurance among urban property owners was mentioned as one reason for applying a narrower rule of "proximate cause" in fire cases; and this finds a parallel in some of the decisions denying recovery for private fire losses against a water company which has contracted to supply water to a city.[62]

There was a striking Wisconsin decision [63] of the 1960s in which the prevalence of liability insurance was given as one reason for a change in the rule that a host is not liable to an automobile guest for defects in the car of which the host does not know. There was also a passage from a concurring opinion of Mr. Justice Traynor of California [64] which has been much quoted, in which the possibility that the manufacturer of a product can insure against liability, and so distribute the risk, is mentioned as one reason, among others, for holding the manufacturer strictly liable to the injured consumer. The liability for defective products is a field which was undergoing rapid and spectacular change in the 1950s and 1960s,[65] with many courts writing long opinions mustering all available reasons for holding manufacturers and sellers liable without negligence; and dissenting opinions, as well as challenges from other sources, put them upon their mettle and under considerable pressure to ignore no possible justification. In view of this, it appears quite astonishing that, out of a few thousand opinions dealing with products liability, this was for a long time the *only* one in which there was any mention whatever of insurance. On any conceivable basis, it is not easy to account for the fact; but it is at least some indication that the courts responsible for the changes in this area of the law did not consider the prevalence of liability in-

61. 1866, 35 N.Y. 210.

62. See Reimann v. Monmouth Consolidated Water Co., 1952, 9 N.J. 134, 87 A.2d 325; William Burford & Co. v. Glasgow Water Co., 1928, 223 Ky. 54, 2 S.W.2d 1027; Ancrum v. Camden Water Co., 1908, 82 S.C. 284, 64 S.E. 151.

63. "Liability insurance is widely prevalent today. In few cases will the new rule shift the burden of loss from the injured guest to the negligent host personally. In the great majority of cases it will shift part or all the burden of loss from the injured individual to the motoring public. The policy concept that it is unfair to shift the burden from the injured person to his host where the injured person knowingly and voluntarily exposed himself to dangers created by the host is no longer applicable." McConville v. State Farm Mutual Automobile Insurance Co., 1962, 15 Wis.2d 374, 113 N.W.2d 14, 19.

Cf. Siragusa v. Swedish Hospital, 1962, 60 Wn.2d 310, 373 P.2d 767, mentioning the prevalence of "social insurance" covering employees as a reason for abrogating the defense of assumption of risk in cases of injury to them.

64. "Traynor, J. I concur in the judgment, but I believe the manufacturer's negligence should no longer be singled out as the basis of a plaintiff's right to recover in cases like the present one. In my opinion it should now be recognized that a manufacturer incurs an absolute liability when an article that he has placed on the market, knowing that it is to be used without inspection, proves to have a defect that causes injury to human beings. * * *

"Even if there is no negligence, however public policy demands that responsibility be fixed wherever it will most effectively reduce the hazards to life and health inherent in defective products that reach the market. It is evident that the manufacturer can anticipate some hazards and guard against the recurrence of others, as the public cannot. Those who suffer injury from defective products are unprepared to meet its consequences. The cost of an injury and the loss of time or health may be an overwhelming misfortune to the person injured, and a needless one, *for the risk of injury can be insured by the manufacturer and distributed among the public as a cost of doing business.* [Italics supplied]. It is to the public interest to discourage the marketing of products having defects that are a menace to the public. If such products nevertheless find their way into the market it is to the public interest to place the responsibility for whatever injury they may cause upon the manufacturer, who even if he is not negligent in the manufacture of the product, is responsible for its reaching the market. However, intermittently such injuries may occur and however haphazardly they may strike, the risk of their occurrence is a constant risk and a general one. Against such a risk there should be general and constant protection, and the manufacturer is best situated to afford such protection." Escola v. Coca Cola Bottling Co., 1944, 24 Cal.2d 453, 461–462, 150 P.2d 436, 440–441.

65. See infra, ch. 17.

surance as a valid reason for imposing strict liability on those who have insurance, or could easily have it.

The chief visible effect of liability insurance on tort law has occurred in a context not involving a change from negligence to strict liability. Rather, the change has been in connection with the abrogation of various immunities from liability. All of these have been under attack for many years,[66] as outmoded vestiges of antique law arising out of historical origins that long since have passed away and been forgotten, and as without practical or moral justification. The presence, or availability, of liability insurance has provided an additional argument, since it means that, having paid an insurance premium, a defendant who suffers an adverse judgment in a tort action will not have to pay it. In some instances this added factor has been enough to tip the scale. For example, there have been decisions [67] eliminating the "family" immunity of parents toward their children for injuries sustained in the course of business activities of the parents which were covered by liability insurance. There were, however, other cases in which the business activities alone, without the insurance, were held to be sufficient reason for abrogating immunity; [68] and a great many more in which the "family" immunity between husband and wife was abrogated,[69] or numerous other exceptions developed to that between parent and child,[70] in which insurance was not a visible factor at all. Where the question arose, the overwhelming majority of the decisions for a long time declared that liability insurance does not create liability, but only provides indemnity against it when it has arisen; that it is not in itself a sufficient reason for any change in the rule, and any such change must be for the legislature; and that the presence of insurance in the particular case makes no difference.[71] There were even several decisions which gave the insurance as a reason for *not* abrogating the immunity, because of the opportunity for fraud and collusion against the insurance company.[72]

Finally, however, when the modern wave of decisions [73] began to engulf the family immunities, the existence or the possibility of liability insurance began to be stated in nearly all of the overruling cases, as one of the primary reasons for the change.[74]

The immunity of charities has had much the same history. Since 1942 it has been in full retreat, and it appears only a question of time before it is to disappear from American law.[75] The visible part which insurance has played in the change has been quite meagre. In some states, by statute or decision, the immunity was not recognized when the charity in fact had the insurance, on the ground that liability would not deplete trust funds or discourage donors.[76]

---

66. See infra, §§ 122, 131–133.

67. Dunlap v. Dunlap, 1930, 84 N.H. 352, 150 A. 905; Lusk v. Lusk, 1932, 113 W.Va. 17, 166 S.E. 538; Worrell v. Worrell, 1939, 174 Va. 11, 4 S.E.2d 343 (under compulsory insurance statute); Edwards v. Royal Indemnity Co., 1935, 182 La. 171, 161 So. 191 (under statute providing for direct action of injured person against insurer).

68. Signs v. Signs, 1952, 156 Ohio St. 566, 103 N.E.2d 743; Borst v. Borst, 1952, 41 Wn.2d 642, 251 P.2d 149.

69. See infra, § 122.

70. See infra, § 122.

71. Levesque v. Levesque, 1954, 99 N.H. 147, 106 A.2d 563; Harralson v. Thomas, Ky.1954, 269 S.W.2d 276; Parker v. Parker, 1956, 230 S.C. 28, 94 S.E.2d 12; Prince v. Prince, 1959, 205 Tenn. 451, 326 S.W.2d 908; Fehr v. General Accident, Fire & Life Assurance Corp., 1944, 246 Wis. 228, 16 N.W.2d 787.

72. Hastings v. Hastings, 1960, 33 N.J. 247, 163 A.2d 147; Villaret v. Villaret, 1948, 83 App.D.C. 311, 169 F.2d 677; Luster v. Luster, 1938, 299 Mass. 480, 13 N.E.2d 438; Parks v. Parks, 1957, 390 Pa. 287, 135 A.2d 65; Turner v. Carter, 1935, 169 Tenn. 553, 89 S.W.2d 751.

73. See infra, § 122.

74. See for example Gelbman v. Gelbman, 1969, 23 N.Y.2d 434, 297 N.Y.S.2d 529, 245 N.E.2d 192; Balts v. Balts, 1966, 273 Minn. 419, 142 N.W.2d 66; Tamashiro v. DeGama, 1969, 51 Haw. 74, 450 P.2d 998; Immer v. Risko, 1970, 56 N.J. 482, 267 A.2d 481; France v. A.P.A. Transport Corp., 1970, 56 N.J. 500, 267 A.2d 490.

75. See infra, § 133.

76. Michael v. St. Paul Mercury Indemnity Co., W.D.Ark.1950, 92 F.Supp. 140 (Arkansas statute); Michard v. Myron Stratton Home, 1960, 144 Colo. 251, 355 P.2d 1078 (no immunity, but judgment can be satis-

There have been a few opinions [77] in which the availability of insurance has been stated to be one reason, among others, for the termination of the immunity; but most of the courts which have abrogated it entirely have made no mention of any such reason. And on the other hand, there are a very large number of cases in which it has been declared specifically that the presence or availability of insurance is not a factor to be considered at all in deciding whether any change shall be made in the law.[78] Governmental immunity, which is also under heavy fire,[79] has undergone little specific change that can be traced to insurance.[80] There are a few decisions [81] holding that statutory authorization to take out the insurance constitutes a "waiver" of the immunity, which makes the government liable; but the large majority of the cases have held that such authorization is not a waiver, and the immunity is not affected by the insurance.[82]

The list is far from being an impressive testimonial to the importance of liability insurance as a factor in the development of the law of torts up to the present day. The conclusions which seem to emerge are that having liability insurance is not alone treated as a sufficient basis for imposing tort liability and that the availability of liability insurance (as distinguished from defendant's having insurance applicable to the case at hand) is ordinarily considered relevant, if at all, only as an indication of capacity to bear and spread risk. Thus, its open recognition as a factor in tort law is subject to all the controversy surrounding risk bearing and spreading generally.[83]

WESTLAW REFERENCES

The Nature of Liability Insurance
"no action clause*"

topic(217) /p misrepresent! misstate! /s appl! /s policy /s void! defeat**

topic(217) /p cooperat! assist /s defense

Conflicting Inferences about the Impact of Liability Insurance
agnew & 186 /5 450

"Invisible" Effects
jury /s inform! /s insurance

Jury Issues
"last clear chance" /s defin! application

Shift of Emphasis in Negligence
moral! /4 blame /p tort* negligen!

Vicarious Liability
"liability insurance" /p "respondeat superior" "vicarious! liab!"

Specific Mention of Insurance
mcconville & 113 +s 14 19

sh 150 p2d 436

family parental interspousal /1 immunity /p insurance

---

fied only out of funds not held in trust); Cox v. De Jarnette, 1961, 104 Ga.App. 664, 123 S.E.2d 16; Howard v. South Baltimore General Hospital, 1948, 191 Md. 617, 62 A.2d 574 (statute); O'Quin v. Baptist Memorial Hospital, 1947, 184 Tenn. 570, 201 S.W.2d 694.

77. President and Directors of Georgetown University v. Hughes, D.C.Cir.1942, 130 F.2d 810, 823–824; Avellone v. St. Johns Hospital, 1956, 165 Ohio St. 467, 135 N.E.2d 410.

78. Cristini v. Griffin Hospital, 1948, 134 Conn. 282, 57 A.2d 262; Haynes v. Presbyterian Hospital Association, 1950, 241 Iowa 1269, 45 N.W.2d 151; Kreuger v. Schmiechen, 1954, 364 Mo. 568, 264 S.W.2d 311; Muller v. Nebraska Methodist Hospital, 1955, 160 Neb. 279, 70 N.W.2d 86; Pierce v. Yakima Valley Memorial Hospital Association, 1953, 43 Wn.2d 162, 260 P.2d 765.

79. See infra, § 131.

80. Molitor v. Kaneland Community Unit District No. 302, 1959, 18 Ill.2d 11, 163 N.E.2d 89, certiorari denied 362 U.S. 968, 80 S.Ct. 955, 4 L.Ed.2d 900, declared that insurance was immaterial. Most decisions (see infra, § 131) abrogating governmental immunity have not mentioned it at all.

81. City of Knoxville v. Bailey, 6th Cir. 1954, 222 F.2d 520; Lynwood v. Decatur Park District, 1960, 26 Ill.App.2d 431, 168 N.E.2d 185; Rogers v. Butler, 1936, 170 Tenn. 125, 92 S.W.2d 414; Taylor v. Knox County Board of Education, 1942, 292 Ky. 767, 167 S.W.2d 700. Cf. Christie v. Board of Regents of University of Michigan, 1961, 364 Mich. 202, 111 N.W.2d 30.

82. Maffei v. Incorporated Town of Kemmerer, 1959, 80 Wyo. 33, 338 P.2d 808, rehearing denied 80 Wyo. 33, 340 P.2d 759; Hummer v. School City of Hartford City, 1953, 124 Ind.App. 30, 112 N.E.2d 891; Rittmiller v. School District No. 84, D.Minn.1952, 104 F.Supp. 187; Jones v. Scofield Brothers, D.Md.1947, 73 F.Supp. 395. See Gibbons, Liability Insurance and the Tort Immunity of State and Local Governments, [1959] Duke L.J. 588; Notes, 1956, 54 Mich.L.Rev. 404; 1949, 33 Minn.L.Rev. 634.

83. See supra, § 4.

§ 83. Deficiencies of the Tort and Liability Insurance System

The deficiencies of our present system for compensating personal injuries are manifold, and have been pointed out many times. Because the problem is most acute in relation to automobile accidents, most of the discussion has centered about them. The first comprehensive study is a rather remarkable Report of a Committee to Study Compensation for Automobile Accidents, for the Columbia University Council for Research in the Social Sciences,[1] which was published in 1932. It called forth a deluge of discussion,[2] which has continued until the present day.

No one needs to be told of the number of automobile accidents, and the gravity of the problem they present. In December, 1951, the millionth person was killed by an automobile in the United States. In 1968 there were 55,700 deaths, an annual number which had considerably more than tripled since 1921. In that same year there were 14 million automobile accidents in the United States, and over 2 million personal injuries. Somewhere in this country there was an automobile death every thirteen minutes, and an automobile injury every twenty-three seconds. The losses totaled at least eleven billion dollars, which is a good round sum.[3] Under a variety of influences the trend of annual increases in numbers of deaths leveled off in the 1970s, but injuries and dollars of damage have continued to increase.

Thus far liability insurance has been quite inadequate to provide and assure compensation to those who suffer such injuries. It had its inception solely as a device for the protection and benefit of the insured who paid for it, and not as any part of a scheme for social betterment; and it has largely retained that original character. The remaining evils may be reviewed briefly, as follows:

Uncompensated Plaintiffs

Unless required by statute to carry insurance, a defendant is under no incentive to do so, except for whatever impact the fear of liability may have. Even in fields where liability insurance is most prevalent, there are still many defendants who do not have it.

Moreover, the uninsured are, as a group, those who are least responsible financially, and so unlikely to be able to pay a judgment. The Columbia Report estimated, in 1932, that *some* payment was made in over 85 per cent of all cases in which the defendant was insured, but that against an uninsured driver the injured plaintiff had only about one chance in four of collecting anything at all.[4] It is also undoubtedly true that uninsured drivers on the highway are those who tend on the whole to be driving unsafe vehicles, to be the most slipshod, law-violating and reckless, and to cause a disproportionately large percentage of the accidents. It is, in short, those who are unable to pay for the harm they do, who are most likely to do harm.[5]

---

§ 83

1. Discussed, and to some extent summarized, in Smith, Lilly and Dowling, Compensation for Automobile Accidents: A Symposium, 1932, 32 Col.L.Rev. 785.

2. Kline and Pearson, The Problem of the Uninsured Motorist, 1951; Marx, Compulsory Compensation Insurance, 1925, 25 Col.L.Rev. 164; Corstvet, The Uncompensated Accident and Its Consequences, 1936, 3 Law & Con.Prob. 467; Lewis, The Merits of the Automobile Accident Compensation Plan, 1936, 3 Law & Con.Prob. 583; Marx, Compensation Insurance for Automobile Accident Victims: The Case for Compulsory Automobile Insurance, 1954, 15 Ohio St.L.J. 134; Netherton, Highway Safety Under Different Types of Liability Legislation, 1954, 15 Ohio St.L.J. 110; James, The Columbia Study of Compensation Law for Automobile Accidents: An Unanswered Challenge, 1959, 59 Col.L.Rev. 408. A good summary in a nutshell appears in Ehrenzweig, "Full Aid" Insurance for the Traffic Victim, 1954, 1–8.

3. National Safety Council, Accident Facts, 1969, 5.40; Statistical Abstract of the United States, 1969, 547–52.

4. Committee to Study Compensation for Automobile Accidents, Report to the Columbia University Council for Research in the Social Sciences, 1932, 75, 77, 86, 87, 203–04, 261–66, 269–73.

5. Kline and Pearson, The Problem of the Uninsured Motorist, 1951.

Inadequate Coverage

Even where there is insurance, it is very often inadequate in amount. Coverage varies according to the premium paid, and poverty, economy and optimism tend to keep it down. A substantial percentage of the automobile liability policies are still written for ten-and-twenty, which is to say with a limit of $10,000 upon liability to any one person, and of $20,000 for the total liability arising out of any one accident. With present-day verdicts for really serious personal injuries running well in excess of $100,000, and in a few cases over $1,000,000, it is obvious that such insurance does not meet the risk. The injured plaintiff may still collect what can be collected, in excess of the policy, on the judgment against the tortfeasor. To the extent that an injured person does so, the policy fails to protect the insured. To the extent that the injured person fails to collect more, liability insurance fails to meet the need of compensating for the tort.

Even if the amount is adequate, the coverage may still fail. For example, the plaintiff may be excepted from the terms of the policy, or an automobile guest act may prevent recovery, or the person driving may have been one excluded from the policy coverage. Misrepresentation or concealment on the part of the insured, failure to give notice of the accident, or failure to "cooperate" with the insurance company, may still defeat the recovery;[6] and in any jurisdiction where there is no direct remedy against the insurer, anything which will prevent suit against the insured may do the same.[7]

Liability Only for Fault

By its terms liability insurance does not purport to provide compensation for injuries, but only to protect the insured against legal liability. In the present state of our law, except in the case of products liability, abnormally dangerous animals, conditions or activities, and a few other instances, such liability is incurred only when the defendant has been at fault, which in the usual case means negligence. There are many types of enterprises and activities, of which the automobile is the common example, which are not classified as abnormally dangerous, and yet produce their inevitable quota of accidents and injuries, a substantial part of which occur without any negligence or other fault on the part of anyone.

Even where there is fault in fact, it must be proved before liability is established; and there are many cases in which the injured person, struck and knocked unconscious by something that he never saw, is quite unable to offer such proof. To some extent the injured person is aided by the doctrine of res ipsa loquitur;[8] but there are still many cases, such as those of collisions of moving vehicles, to which it does not apply. And even when the plaintiff succeeds in offering proof of the defendant's negligence, it can still be denied and refuted; and even when it is beyond dispute, the defenses of contributory negligence and assumption of risk can still be interposed to defeat or reduce the recovery.

The result is a substantial number of cases, known to exist by all trial lawyers, but impossible to number with any accuracy, in which legal fault either does not exist, or if it exists cannot be proved, or if proved can still be defeated. In all such cases the insurance, even if carried with full coverage, affords no protection to the victim.

Litigation

The process by which the question of legal fault, and hence of liability, is determined in our courts is a cumbersome, time-consuming, expensive, and almost ridiculously inaccurate one. The evidence given in personal injury cases usually consists of highly contradictory statements from the two sides, estimating such factors as time, speed, distance and visibility, offered months after the

---

6. See supra, § 82.

7. See supra, § 82.

8. See supra, § 39.

event by witnesses who were never very sure just what happened when they saw it, and whose faulty memories are undermined by lapse of time, by bias, by conversations with others, and by the subtle influence of counsel. Upon such evidence, a jury of twelve inexperienced citizens, called away from their other business if they have any, are invited to retire and make the best guess they can as to whether the defendant, the plaintiff, or both were "negligent," which is itself a wobbly and uncertain standard based upon the supposed mental processes of a hypothetical and non-existent reasonable person. European lawyers view the whole thing with utter amazement; and the extent to which it has damaged the courts and the legal profession by bringing the law and its administration into public disrepute can only be guessed.

Delay

The process inundates our courts with tort cases, and particularly those involving automobile accidents. In many areas calendars are congested and are years behind,[9] which means that the injured person must wait that long before the case can even be heard, to say nothing of the further delay that may result from various motions and an appeal. Since in the meantime the injured person has to live, is unable to work if seriously injured, and has hospital bills and other expenses to meet, the most extreme economic pressure exists to settle the claim on any terms available.[10] Since a hungry plaintiff cannot afford to litigate, it is still true, as it always has been, that in a personal injury case delay usually helps the defendant; and in the poker game of negotiation for settlement, that ace is up the defendant's sleeve.

Attorneys and Fees

To combat all this, lawyers who specialize in personal injury cases abound. By and large they are reputable persons, but there are those who definitely are not, and fake claim rackets are a problem.[11] The attorneys interview the injured, investigate the facts, produce witnesses, prepare the case, settle it if they can, and end by trying it if they cannot. As a group they have developed to an extreme the fine art of showmanship in the courtroom, and of extracting the last possible dime from sympathetic and impressionable juries; and some of the verdicts they have obtained run to staggering figures.

For these services they charge fees upon a contingent basis, which means that they are paid only if they win the case or succeed in obtaining a settlement. Since the successes must pay for the failures, these fees are high. Normally, they run to a third of the amount recovered; but in difficult cases, or those of protracted litigation, they may be as much as a half. Thus the plaintiff who finally recovers a verdict and judgment of $90,000 may find that $30,000 of it goes for the lawyer's fee, and an additional $10,000 for repayment of expenses.

Summary

The whole picture is one of a fumbling and uncertain process of awarding a judgment upon the basis of unreliable evidence, fraught with ruinous delay, which fails entirely when proof of fault fails, leaves the entire remedy worthless against many defendants who are not financially responsible, and diverts a large share of the money to attorney fees even when it can be collected. The Columbia Report found in 1932 that in

---

9. See Rosenberg and Sovern, Delay and the Dynamics of Personal Injury Litigation, 1959, 59 Col.L.Rev. 1116; Burger, The Courts on Trial: A Call for Action Against Delay, 1958, 44 A.B.A.J. 738; James and Law, Compensation for Auto Accident Victims: A Story of Too Little and Too Late, 1952, 26 Conn.Bar J. 70; Steinbrink and Lockwood, Facts, Figures and Recommendations re Trial Calendars of the Supreme Court, Kings County, 1932 to 1952, 1952; 1952, 19 Rep.N.Y. Judicial Council 32; Note, 1951, 51 Col.L.Rev. 1037.

10. Corstvet, The Uncompensated Accident and Its Consequences, 1936, 3 Law & Con.Prob. 466; Hogan and Stubbs, The Sociological and Legal Problem of the Uncompensated Motor Victim, 1938, 11 Rocky Mt.L.Rev. 12.

11. See Monaghan, The Liability Claim Racket, 1936, 3 Law & Con.Prob. 491.

ten states in which studies were made, 47% of the temporary injuries, 56% of the permanent injuries, and 55% of those that were fatal, resulted in actual receipt of less than the medical and other expenses of the accident, without any compensation for other damage such as disability and loss of earnings. Since 1932 improvements in insurance, and in financial responsibility laws in most of the states, have brought about improvement in these figures, the extent of which is in controversy. Later studies have indicated, however, that the fundamental picture of how the tort and liability insurance system works in automobile accident cases is unchanged.[12]

WESTLAW REFERENCES

Uncompensated Plaintiffs
di uninsured motorist coverage

Inadequate Coverage
fail! /2 cooperate "give notice" /p insur!

Attorneys and Fees
percent! proportion portion fraction /s "contingent fee" & "personal injury"

§ 84. Enacted and Proposed Remedies

In two minor respects the insurance companies themselves endeavored in the 1940s and 1950s to meet the automobile accident compensation problem with extended policy provisions. One of these agrees to pay, without regard to any question of fault, first medical expenses of the injured person, or, for a higher premium, all such expenses incurred within a year after the accident.[1] The other provides, along with coverage of any liability of the insured, casualty protection against his inability to collect a valid claim or judgment against an uninsured motorist.[2] Both of these are of course voluntary schemes, and their weakness is that they must rely upon the common sense, good will or liberality of the insured.

Most of the other proposals call for legislation that is in some ways analogous to the worker compensation acts,[3] which, while they are admittedly far from perfect, are generally conceded to constitute a great advance upon the common law system of litigation based on fault which preceded them. The system of worker compensation involves five basic elements:

(1) strict liability of employers for injuries to workers arising out of and in the course of employment;

(2) compulsory insurance against the liability, with resulting distribution of the losses over an entire industry through the premiums paid;

(3) a schedule of compensation limiting the worker's recovery considerably short of

---

12. See Brown, Automobile Accident Litigation in Wisconsin: A Factual Study, 1935, 10 Wis.L.Rev. 170; Survey Analysis of Studied Cases of Victims: Report of the Joint Legislative Committee to Investigate Automobile Insurance, 1938, N.Y.Leg.Doc. No. 91; Temple University Bureau of Economic and Business Research, Economic-Financial Consequences of Personal Injuries Sustained in 1953 Philadelphia Auto Accidents, 1955, 7 J.Econ. & Bus., Bull.No. 3; James, Compensation for Auto Accident Victims: A Study of Too Little and Too Late, 1952, 26 Conn.Bar J. 70; Marx, "Motorism," Not "Pedestrianism": Compensation for Automobile Victims, 1956, 42 Am.Bar Assn.J. 421; Morris and Paul, The Financial Impact of Automobile Accidents, 1962, 110 U.Pa.L.Rev. 913; Calabresi, The Cost of Accidents (1970); Conard et al., Automobile Accident Costs and Payments: Studies in the Economics of Injury Reparation (1964); Conard, The Economic Treatment of Automobile Injuries, 1964, 63 Mich.L.Rev. 279; Keeton & O'Connell, Basic Protection for the Traffic Victim, 1965; Henderson, No-Fault Insurance for Automobile Accidents, 1977, 56 Oregon Law Rev. 287; Standards for No-Fault Motor Vehicle Accident Benefit Act, Senate Committee on Commerce, Science, and Transportation, S.Rep. No. 95–975, 1978.

§ 84

1. See Liability Revisions, 1947, 48 Best's Ins.Rep. No. 2, p. 45; Sawyer, Frontiers of Liability Insurance, 1938, 39 Best's 439, 440; Melendes and Craig, Medical Payments Provisions of the Automobile Insurance Policy, 1969, 52 Marq.L.Rev. 445.

2. See Widiss, A Guide to Uninsured Motorist Coverage (1969); Caverly, New Provisions for Protection from Injuries Inflicted by an Uninsured Automobile, [1956] Ins.L.J. 19; Morgenbesser, Some Legal Aspects of the New York Uninsured Motorists' Coverage, [1956] Ins.L.J. 241; Graham, The Uninsured Motorist Endorsement: Its Terms and Developing Case Law, 1968, 19 Fed.Ins.Couns. I. 85; Panel Discussion, Uninsured Motorist Coverage, 1970, 20 Fed.Ins.Couns. I. 56; Note, 1964, 15 West.Res.L.Rev. 386.

3. See supra, § 80.

the damages recoverable in a tort action for negligence;

(4) a commission or other administrative body to hear claims and award compensation without a jury, in lieu of the courts;

(5) limitation of attorney's fees.

Nearly all of the proposals made for legislation dealing with automobile accidents have involved the first two of these elements. A few have involved all five.

Financial Responsibility Laws

Among the earliest proposals affecting automobiles, and the first steps actually taken, were "financial responsibility" laws.[4] The first of these was enacted in Connecticut in 1925.[5] In their original form they required any motorist who had failed to satisfy a judgment against him for an accident to furnish proof that he was capable of satisfying future judgments up to a specified amount. This was under penalty of revocation of his license to drive, or of the registration of his automobile. The easy form of proof of such financial responsibility is obviously a certificate that the driver has taken out liability insurance; and the practical effect of the legislation is to require it of those who default on judgments.

The weaknesses of such statutes are obvious. They leave the first person injured with no assurance of collecting a judgment, and no aid in doing so except the threat that a report to the authorities will compel insurance for the future, which is by no means a dire threat. In this respect they have been described as "locking the barn door after the horse is stolen," and as examples of a philosophy analogous to the old myth that "every dog is entitled to one bite."[6] Even as to future injuries, they fail to have any effect upon even the negligent driver who, because known to be judgment proof, is not worth suing, and so escapes a judgment; and even when there is an unpaid judgment, the administration of the acts has been at the mercy of some method of following it up. There are, in addition, many such drivers who fail to surrender registration or license cards, or who continue to drive without them.

For such reasons the original statutes were replaced, in about half of the states, by "security-responsibility laws,"[7] the first of which[8] was adopted in New Hampshire in 1937. Their constitutionality was upheld,[9] with rare exception.[10] They require any driver involved in an accident, under the same penalties, to furnish proof of capability of paying a judgment for that accident, or to deposit security for such payment, up to the

4. See Braun, The Financial Responsibility Law, 1936, 3 Law & Con.Prob. 505; Feinsinger, Operation of Financial Responsibility Laws, 1936, 3 Law & Con. Prob. 519; Feinsinger, Financial Responsibility Laws and Compulsory Insurance—The Problem in Wisconsin, 1935, 10 Wis.L.Rev. 192; Aberg, Effects of and Problems Arising from Financial Responsibility Laws, 1943–44 A.B.A.Proc. 45; Stoeckel, Administrative Problems of Financial Responsibility Laws, 1936, 3 Law & Con.Prob. 531; Burtis, Operation of the Kansas Financial Responsibility Law, 1941, 9 Kan.Bar A.J. 367; Wagner, Safety Responsibility Laws—A Review of Recent Developments, 1946, 9 Ga.Bar J. 160; Notes, 1943, 20 N.C.L.Rev. 198; 1938, 16 N.Y.U.L.Q.Rev. 126; 1936, 24 Ky.L.J. 495; 1941, 41 Col.L.Rev. 1461; 1949, 1 Stan. L.Rev. 263.

5. Conn.Pub.Acts, 1925, c. 183. An early analysis of such statutes was Heyting, Automobiles and Compulsory Liability Insurance, 1930, 16 A.B.A.J. 362.

6. See supra, § 76.

7. See Johnson, The Modern Trend in Financial Responsibility Legislation, 1944 A.B.A.Proc. 67, 69; Wagner, Safety Responsibility Laws—A Review of Recent Developments, 1946, 9 Ga.Bar J. 160; Braun, The Need for Revision of Financial Responsibility Legislation, 1945, 40 Ill.L.Rev. 237; Netherton, Highway Safety Under Different Types of Liability Legislation, 1954, 15 Ohio St.L.J. 110; Vorys, A Short Survey of Laws Designed to Exclude the Financially Irresponsible Driver from the Highway, 1954, 15 Ohio St.L.J. 101; Johnson, The Modern Trend in Financial Responsibility Legislation, 1944 A.B.A.Ins. Section 67.

8. N.H.Rev.Laws, 1942, c. 122.

9. Hadden v. Aitken, 1952, 156 Neb. 215, 55 N.W.2d 620; Escobedo v. State Department of Motor Vehicles, 1950, 35 Cal.2d 870, 222 P.2d 1; Doyle v. Kahl, 1951, 242 Iowa 153, 46 N.W.2d 52; Ballow v. Reeves, Ky. 1951, 238 S.W.2d 141; Gillaspie v. Department of Public Safety, 1953, 152 Tex. 459, 259 S.W.2d 177, certiorari denied 347 U.S. 933, 74 S.Ct. 625, 98 L.Ed. 1084; State v. Stehlek, 1953, 262 Wis. 642, 56 N.W.2d 514.

10. People v. Nothaus, 1962, 147 Colo. 210, 363 P.2d 180.

specified amounts. This clearly is better; but the amounts specified have been grossly inadequate. The system may still fail to affect the driver who is willing to settle, is not sued, and so does not come before the court, or the obstinate individual who would rather forego the privilege of driving than provide such proof or security.

There appears to be very little doubt that such "security" legislation has encouraged voluntary liability insurance.[11]

Compulsory Liability Insurance

As to common carriers, and many commercial vehicles, virtually all states have gone beyond the financial responsibility laws, and have required the owner of the vehicle, as a condition of obtaining permission in the first instance to operate it on the public highway, to carry liability insurance.[12]

In 1927, following an affirmative advisory opinion as to constitutionality,[13] Massachusetts enacted a statute requiring all automobile drivers to carry insurance against liability up to specified amounts.[14] In part, at least, because of the opposition of the insurance companies themselves,[15] no other state followed this lead until New York, in 1956, adopted a statute requiring advance proof of financial responsibility on the part of all drivers of motor vehicles, and North Carolina followed suit the next year.[16] Compulsory insurance has been common enough on the continent of Europe,[17] and similar bills were introduced without success into a number of American legislatures in the 1950s.[18] As in the case of some of the financial responsibility laws [19] the problem of the motorist who is so bad a risk as not to be wanted by any insurance company is dealt with by "assigned risk" provisions, under which state authorities allocate the coverage of such individuals among the companies doing business in the state; and this, as much as any other single element, aroused the opposition of the insurers. There was a long experience under the Massachusetts act;[20] and

11. See Wagner, Safety Responsibility Laws—A Review of Recent Developments, 1946, 9 Ga.Bar J. 160, 166, stating the following increases in the percentages of insured cars: New Hampshire, 36% before enactment of security law, about 85% after enactment; New York, 30% before, about 75% after; Indiana, 33% before, about 74% after; Maine, 36% before, 60% after. In Minnesota about 80% of the cars were insured eight months after a security law was enacted.

12. See Brownfield, Compulsory Liability Insurance for Commercial Motor Vehicles, 1936, 3 Law & Con. Prob. 571.

13. Opinion of the Justices, 1925, 251 Mass. 569, 147 N.E. 681. After the statute was adopted, its constitutionality was carried to the Supreme Court of the United States, which, in a brief per curiam opinion, affirmed a dismissal for lack of a federal question.

14. Mass.Ann.Laws 1932, c. 175, §§ 113A–113D. Now considerably modified, as of January 1, 1971, by the Massachusetts Personal Injury Protection Act, Mass.Laws 1970, chs. 670, 744. See infra, this section.

15. See McVay, The Case Against Compulsory Automobile Insurance, 1954, 15 Ohio St.L.J. 150; Virginia Assn. of Insurance Agents, The Uninsured Motorist, 1957; Kline and Pearson, The Problem of the Uninsured Motorist (State of New York Insurance Dept. 1951); Casualty Insurance Companies Serving Massachusetts, The First Thirty Years: A Commentary on the Operation of the Massachusetts Compulsory Liability Insurance Act, 1957.

16. N.Y.Vehicle & Traffic Laws, Art. 6, §§ 310–321.

17. See Ehrenzweig, Assurance Obligé—A Comparative Study, 1950, 15 Law & Con.Prob. 445; Deák, Liability and Compensation for Automobile Accidents, 1937, 21 Minn.L.Rev. 123; Deák, Automobile Accidents: A Comparative Study of the Law of Liability in Europe, 1931, 79 U.Pa.L.Rev. 271; Bolgár, Motor Vehicle Accident Compensation: Types and Trends, 1953, 2 Am.J.Comp.Law 515.

18. See California Legislature, Assembly Interim Committee on Finance and Insurance, Semifinal Report, Sec. 3, 1953; Missouri State Chamber of Commerce, Motor Vehicle Financial Responsibility, [1952] Ins.L.J. 722; New Jersey Legislature, Report of Joint Committee on Improvements of the Motor Vehicle Financial Responsibility Law, 1952; North Dakota Legislature, Report on Automobile Liability Insurance, 1950; Wisconsin Report of Legislative Council Committee on Motor Vehicle Accidents, 1953; Kline and Pearson, The Problem of the Uninsured Motorist, State of New York Insurance Dept., 1951; Marx, The Case for Compulsory Automobile Compensation Insurance, 1954, 15 Ohio St.L.J. 134; McVay, The Case Against Compulsory Automobile Insurance, 1954, 15 Ohio St.L.J. 150.

19. See for example California State Automobile Association Inter-Insurance Bureau v. Maloney, 1951, 341 U.S. 105, 71 S.Ct. 601, 95 L.Ed. 788.

20. See Report of Mass. Senate Special Commission to Study Compulsory Motor Vehicle Liability Insurance and Related Matters, 1930, 15 Mass.L.Q. 8–288; Blanchard, Compulsory Motor Vehicle Liability Insurance in Massachusetts, 1936, 3 Law & Con.Prob. 537; Carpenter, Compulsory Motor Vehicle Insurance and

while every other attempt to duplicate it was defeated under heavy fire,[21] it nevertheless received high praise in its time.[22]

Compulsory liability insurance obviously affords protection to more plaintiffs than the financial responsibility acts; but it has two definite inadequacies. One is that the amounts of insurance coverage required by the statutes are necessarily low, since they must be geared to fit the purse of the impecunious driver; and since the specified limits tend to set a standard, and such legislation apparently generates some hostility on the part of the motoring public, a state having such a law tends also to have a lower percentage of policies above its compulsory limits.[23] The other is that even the compulsory insurance covers only liability upon the basis of fault. It fails when proof of fault fails, or is defeated; and it does relatively little to meet the unsatisfactory situation of the delays in litigation and the attorney's fee.

As will be explained more fully later in this section, compulsory liability insurance is one feature of many of the "no-fault" statutes enacted in the 1970s. Other features of the "no-fault" statutes have been aimed at deficiencies of compulsory liability insurance alone.

Unsatisfied Judgment Funds

Several states,[24] as well as most of the Canadian provinces, have set up state funds for the purpose of paying unsatisfied automobile liability judgments up to specified limits. These are financed by additional taxation, either upon all motorists, upon those who do not have insurance, or upon liability insurance companies doing business in the jurisdiction. These measures, too, undoubtedly have been of some aid in relieving the lack of available compensation for valid tort claims.

The criticism of all of these steps is that they take only one bite at the cherry. They do not affect liability beyond the particular limits specified, which are low. These usually are set at not more than $10,000 for any one plaintiff, and $20,000 for any one accident. They do not affect any accident in which there is no fault, or in which it cannot be proved, or in which contributory negligence and assumption of risk will defeat recovery. Nor do they, obviously, affect materially the delay of litigation, with its inevitable pressure for cheap settlement, or the share going into attorney's fees. It is for this reason that other proposals have gone back to the analogy of the worker compensation acts.

The Columbia Plan

Even before 1932 there had been several writers [25] who had advocated the extension of the worker compensation principle to automobile accidents. In that year appeared

Court Congestion in Massachusetts, 1936, 3 Law & Con.Prob. 554.

21. Wilkie, The Recurring Question of Compulsory Automobile Insurance, 1940, 30 Rep.Wis.Bar Assn. 77.

22. Grad, Recent Developments in Automobile Accident Compensation, 1950, 50 Col.L.Rev. 300, 315–316.

23. See Netherton, Highway Safety Under Differing Types of Liability Legislation, 1954, 15 Ohio St.L.J. 110, 125. See also Virginia Assn. of Insurance Agents, The Uninsured Motorist, 1957, 3, reporting that only 38% of Massachusetts motorists carry insurance in excess of the $5,000/$10,000 statutory requirement, while 75 to 90% of those in Wisconsin, for example, buy higher limits. Also only 38% of Massachusetts drivers buy medical payments protection while the national average outside of Massachusetts is 61%.

24. New Jersey Laws 1952, ch. 174. See New Jersey's Uninsured Motorist Law, J.Am.Ins., March 1959, p. 8. Bambrick, A Look at the New Jersey Unsatisfied Claim and Judgment Fund, [1956] Ins.L.J. 825; Note, 1966, 65 Mich.L.Rev. 180. The act was applied in Dietz v. Meyer, 1963, 79 N.J.Super. 194, 191 A.2d 182. See also Bergeson, The North Dakota Unsatisfied Judgment Plan, 1953, 3 Fed. of Ins. Counsel Q. 35; Denny, Uninsured Motorist Coverage in Virginia, 1961, 47 Va.L.Rev. 145; Court, Virginia's Experience with the "Uninsured Motorist" Act, 1962, 3 Wm. & Mary L.Rev. 237. As to South Carolina, see Note, 1963, 15 S.C.L.Rev. 739.

25. See Chamberlin, Make the Automobile Liable for the Injury, National Underwriter, May 2, 1898, summarized in Bowers, Compulsory Automobile Compensation, 1929, at 282; Rollins, A Proposal to Extend the Compensation Principle to Accidents in the Streets, 1919, 4 Mass.L.Q. 392; Carman, Is a Motor Vehicle Accident Compensation Act Advisable? 1919, 4 Minn.L.Rev. 1; Marx, Compulsory Compensation Insurance, 1925, 25 Col.L.Rev. 164; Elsbree and Roberts, Compul-

the Columbia Report,[26] which was the work of a distinguished committee made up of Arthur A. Ballantine as chairman, Shippen Lewis, Dean Charles E. Clark, Walter F. Dodd, William Draper Lewis, Robert S. Marx, Horace Stern, and Ogden L. Mills. It proposed to take over the worker compensation system for all automobile accidents. Strict liability was to be imposed upon the owner of the vehicle who was to be required to carry liability insurance to cover it. A schedule of compensation was to be set up, substantially identical with that of the worker compensation law at the time. Claims were to be heard and awards to be made by a special board following worker compensation procedure, which was to have power to limit attorney's fees.

This plan never was adopted anywhere, although it received serious consideration in the legislatures of New York, Connecticut, Virginia, North Dakota, and Wisconsin, among others. But the proposal set off a torrent of discussion;[27] and the Columbia Report was the basis, or at least the point of departure, for a large number of suggestions, proposals, and even bills in the legislatures.

The Saskatchewan Plan

Until 1970, the one English-speaking jurisdiction which had adopted a compensation plan for automobile accidents was the Canadian province of Saskatchewan.

The Saskatchewan Automobile Accident Insurance Act was adopted in 1946.[28] It sets up a state insurance fund for the compensation of all victims of automobile accidents, without regard to fault. Such accidents include every injury to the person as a result of driving in, riding in, colliding with, or being run down by a motor vehicle in Saskatchewan, whether or not another vehicle is involved. The fund is financed by annual assessment of all drivers and car owners, at the time of their registration. Essentially the plan is one of accident insurance. The terms of the insurance are contained in the statute, and the only "policy" issued is the registration certificate or the driver's license. The coverage expires with it, but the person injured by an unlicensed driver is still compensated, and the state is subrogated to his rights against the driver. The payment of claims is administered by the Government Insurance Office, and the claimant ordinarily has no need of an attorney. A schedule of compensation is set up, somewhat lower than the benefits under the New York worker compensation law.[29]

The unique feature of the Saskatchewan plan is that it does not supersede tort liability, and leaves the plaintiff the possibility of an action in the courts to recover additional compensation on the basis of fault. In that event the defendant is covered by state liability insurance, in the amounts of $10,000 and $20,000. As to this insurance, the Government Insurance Office plays much the same part in litigation and settlement as private insurance companies elsewhere. Obviously the plaintiff is likely to resort to court only when there is a reasonable chance of

sory Insurance Against Motor Vehicle Accidents, 1928, 76 U.Pa.L.Rev. 690.

26. Report of Committee to Study Compensation for Automobile Accidents, for Columbia University Council for Research in the Social Sciences, 1932.

27. This is well reviewed in James, The Columbia Study of Compensation for Automobile Accidents: An Unanswered Challenge, 1959, 59 Col.L.Rev. 408. See also Ballantine, Compensation for Automobile Accidents, 1932, 18 A.B.A.J. 221; Smith, Lilly and Dowling, Compensation for Automobile Accidents, 1932, 32 Col. L.Rev. 785; Lewis, The Merits of the Automobile Compensation Plan, 1936, 3 Law & Con.Prob. 513; Malone, Damage Suits and the Contagious Principle of Workmen's Compensation, 1952, 12 La.L.Rev. 231.

28. It was re-enacted in its entirety in 1952. Sask. Rev.Stats. c. 409 (1965).

29. For a fuller summary, and discussion of many of the details of the plan, see Green, The Automobile Accident Insurance Act of Saskatchewan, 1949, 31 J.Comp.Leg. & Int.Law 39. See also Green, the Automobile Accident Insurance Act of Saskatchewan, 1952, 2 Chitty's L.J. 38; Fines, The Saskatchewan Plan, 1953, 3 Fed. of Ins.Counsel Q. 51; Shumiatcher, State Compulsory Insurance Act—An Appraisal, 1961, 39 Can. Bar Rev. 107; Grad, Recent Developments in Automobile Accident Compensation, 1950, 50 Col.L.Rev. 300.

establishing the defendant's fault, and damages exceed the state compensation by an amount sufficient to justify the litigation and attorney's fees. Remarkably enough, the experience has been that few such suits are filed.

The reports from Saskatchewan, with some occasional dissent, are that the plan has worked as well as worker compensation, which is to say, that although it may leave a good deal to be desired as an ultimate solution of the problem, it is regarded there as a considerable advance over what had gone before.[30] It served as a point of departure for several proposals in American legislatures, and for a book by Dean Leon Green,[31] who advocated what was essentially the Saskatchewan plan, with the elimination of the schedule of compensation, and the substitution of common law damages other than pain and suffering. It also led to a report of a Committee of the Ontario Parliament in 1963,[32] and to a similar committee proposal in California[33] in 1965.

Academic Suggestions

Professor Ehrenzweig, in a booklet[34] proposed an alternative of his own. It involved an extension of the "first aid" clauses commonly written into liability insurance policies, by which the insurer obligates itself to compensate for the first medical expenses of the accident—or, for an additional premium, for all such expenses within a year—without regard to fault or legal liability of the insured. The proposal was that such clauses be expanded to include benefits, of the kind found in accident insurance policies, which would be sufficient to afford a minimum of compensation to anyone injured in an automobile accident by the insured, without any question of fault or liability. Any owner or operator of an automobile who carries such "full aid" insurance in statutory minimum amounts, would be relieved of his common law liability for ordinary negligence, as distinguished from aggravated negligence such as drunken driving. In addition, anyone injured by a car not so insured, other than a member of the driver's family, would be entitled to recover the same "full aid" benefits from an uncompensated-injury fund, financed either by "tort fines" collected from those who are criminally negligent, or from tax sources deemed to correspond to the savings in relief payments, and to the taxpayer's fair share of automobile losses as a non-motorized user of the highways.

In the 1960s proposals proliferated, without much agreement. Among others may be mentioned the rather elaborate "social insurance" plan, with vocational rehabilitation of the victims and provision for their subsistence, offered by Professor Conard and his associates;[35] the general proposal of Professor Franklin[36] for compensation for all accidents, without limitation to automobiles; and the social welfare approach of Professors Blum and Kalven,[37] contending that the way out is not to impose the burden upon the automobile driver, but to broaden the scope of social security and put the burden

30. See articles cited in the preceding note, particularly Grad, Recent Developments in Automobile Accident Compensation, 1950, 50 Col.L.Rev. 300, 320–325.

31. Green, Traffic Victims—Tort Law and Insurance, 1958.

32. Ontario Select Committee on Automobile Insurance, Final Report (1963); Linden, The Report of the Osgoode Hall Study on Compensation for Victims of Automobile Accidents (1965); Linden, Automobile Accident Compensation in Ontario, 1967, 15 Am.J.Comp.L. 301.

33. Cal.State Bar., Report of Committee on Personal Injury Claims, 1965, 40 J.St.B.Cal. 148, 216.

34. Ehrenzweig, "Full Aid" Insurance for the Traffic Victim, 1954. Also covered in 1955, 43 Cal.L.Rev. 1.

35. Conard et al., Automobile Accident Costs and Payments: Studies in the Economics of Insuring Reparation (1964); Conard, The Economic Treatment of Automobile Injuries, 1964, 63 Mich.L.Rev. 279; Conard and Jacobs, New Hope for Consensus in Automobile Injury Impasse, 1966, 52 A.B.A.J. 533.

36. Franklin, Replacing the Negligence Lottery: Compensation and Selective Reimbursement, 1967, 53 Va.L.Rev. 774.

37. Blum and Kalven, Public Law Perspectives on a Private Law Problem, 1965, 83–85; Blum and Kalven, A Stopgap Plan for Compensating Auto Accident Victims, [1968] Ins.L.J. 661; Blum and Kalven, Public Law Perspectives on a Private Law Problem, 1964, 31 U.Chi.L.Rev. 641. This led to a lively exchange of polite brickbats in Calabresi, Fault, Accidents, and the

on the state. There were various other proposals emanating from insurance companies,[38] and others,[39] which for the most part broadened the basis of recovery beyond fault, while limiting the amount of the damages.

The Keeton-O'Connell Plan

In 1965, Professors Robert E. Keeton and Jeffrey O'Connell proposed a plan of "Basic Protection" for the traffic victim.[40] The plan was accompanied by a proposed statute, which became the basis for bills introduced before many state legislatures. A great deal of discussion and debate immediately followed,[41] during which plans generally based on the Keeton-O'Connell proposal came to be known as "No-Fault Plans."

Rather than traditional liability insurance with its three-party claims procedure, the Keeton-O'Connell plan relied primarily on loss insurance, analogous to medical payments coverage, under which the victim ordinarily claims directly against the insurance company covering the insured's own car, or, if a guest, the host's car, or, if a pedestrian, the car striking the pedestrian. The coverage applies regardless of fault.

The plan calls for compulsory insurance providing "basic protection" for bodily injuries up to $10,000 for reasonable expenses incurred and loss of income from work, less a small deductible amount, and less any losses covered by benefits from other sources.

The most distinctive feature of the Keeton-O'Connell Plan is its partial tort exemption. Under this provision, unless damages for pain and suffering exceed $5,000, or other personal damages exceed $10,000, the basic protection coverage replaces any tort action for damages. If the damages do exceed these figures, the negligence action is preserved but recovery is reduced by these amounts.

The First American Statutes

The first American statute actually adopted was in the Commonwealth of Puerto Rico in 1968, to take effect the following year.[42] It established an Automobile Accident Compensation Administration providing medical and rehabilitation services for traffic victims, paying death and disability benefits according to a schedule like worker compensation, and paying weekly compensation for 50% of wage loss for two years with a weekly maximum of $50 for the first year and $25 for the second year. Benefits from collateral sources are deducted. The Administration is financed by an initial appropriation of $1,000,000, and a tax on the registration of automobiles. A tort action remains open to the victim, subject to deductions. The

---

Wonderful World of Blum and Kalven, 1966, 75 Yale L.J. 216; Blum and Kalven, The Empty Cabinet of Dr. Calabresi, 1967, 34 U.Chi.L.Rev. 239. See also Calabresi, Some Thoughts on Risk Distribution and the Law of Torts, 1961, 70 Yale L.J. 499; Note, 1949, 63 Harv.L.Rev. 330.

38. Collected in King, The Insurance Industry and Compensation Plans, 1968, 43 N.Y.U.L.Rev. 1137; Davies, The Minnesota No-Fault Auto Insurance, 1970, 54 Minn.L.Rev. 921; Logan, Insure the Driver, [1968] Ins. L.J. 682.

39. New York Insurance Dept., Automobile Insurance. * * * For Whose Benefit? (1970); Ghiardi & Kircher, Automobile Insurance: The Rockefeller-Stewart Plan, 1970, 37 Ins.Couns.J. 324; Conn.Ins.Dept., A Program for Automobile Insurance and Accident Benefit Reform (1969).

40. Keeton and O'Connell, Basic Protection for the Traffic Victim: A Blueprint for Reforming Automobile Insurance, 1965.

See Keeton and O'Connell. Basic Protection—A Proposal for Improving Automobile Claims Systems, 1965, 78 Harv.L.Rev. 329; O'Connell, Basic Protection—Relief for the Ills of Automobile Insurance Cases, 1967, 27 La.L.Rev. 647.

41. Inst.Cont.Leg.Ed., Protection for the Traffic Victim: The Keeton-O'Connell Plan and Its Critics (1967); Am.Ins.Assn., Report of Special Committee to Study and Evaluate the Keeton-O'Connell Basic Protection Plan (1968); Marryott, The Tort System and Automobile Claims, 1966, 52 A.B.A.J. 639; Symposia, 1967, 3 Trial 10–54; [1967] U.Ill.L.F. 361–633; (1968), 1 Conn. L.Rev. 1; Keeton and O'Connell, Basic Protection: A Rebuttal to Its Critics, 1967, 53 A.B.A.J. 633.

42. P.R.Laws Ann. (Supp.1968) tit. 9, §§ 2051–65. See Aponte and Denenberg, The Automobile Problem in Puerto Rico: Dimensions and Proposed Solution [1968] Ins.L.J. 884.

whole program bears a great many similarities to that of Saskatchewan.[43]

The first state to adopt an automobile accident reparations statute was Massachusetts in 1970, to become effective January 1, 1971. The Massachusetts Compulsory Personal Injuries Protection Act took many of its features from the Keeton-O'Connell Plan,[44] which had passed one house of the legislature a few years before; but it is obviously an independent piece of legislation.[45]

The Massachusetts statute is based on the existing compulsory bodily injury liability insurance provisions (the limits of $5,000 per person and $10,000 per accident being retained). Strict liability is required as a part of the liability insurance policy, in favor of the named insured, members of the household, any authorized operator or passenger of the vehicle, or any pedestrian it strikes. There is also coverage for the insured and members of the household if they are hit by an uninsured motorist.

The benefits run up to $2000. Within a period of two years after the accident they cover reasonable medical and hospital expenses; net loss of wages, or for unemployed persons, net loss of earning power, up to 75%; costs of substitute services, such as hiring individuals for family services which would have been rendered by the injured person. Some collateral benefits are not deducted, but others are, such as wages paid under a wage continuation program.

Although the Massachusetts statute adopted the distinctive feature of the partial tort exemption, the form of that exemption differs substantially from that proposed by Keeton and O'Connell. Under this act, the benefits are in lieu of tort damages; and any person covered by the compulsory insurance is exempted from liability to the extent of the coverage. An injured person can recover in tort for pain and suffering only if reasonable medical expenses exceed $500, or the injury results in death, loss of a body member or sight or hearing, a fracture, or "permanent and serious disfigurement." Property damage is not covered, and is left to the common law. The policy may provide for exclusion of benefits to a person injured while driving under the influence of alcohol or drugs, committing a felony, or intending to cause injury to himself or others.

During the 1970's, sixteen states [46] enacted statutes that are "no-fault" legislation in the sense of providing for a partial tort exemption from claims for bodily injury arising out of the operation of a motor vehicle. Eight additional states [47] enacted statutes that, though not providing for any tort exemption, are nevertheless sometimes referred to as "no-fault" statutes. Critics of the type of legislation enacted in these eight states have referred to such a statute as an "add-on" statute—one that simply adds no-fault coverage without the trade-off of a partial tort exemption.[48]

With the enactment of no-fault laws, controversy over needs for reform was transformed into controversy over performance, together with continued debate over validity

43. See supra, this section.

44. See supra, this section.

45. There were successive statutes. The first, Mass.Laws 1970, ch. 670 contained provisions as to a 15% reduction in premiums, and forbidding cancellation or refusal to renew a policy. This was very unpalatable to the insurance companies, some of which threatened to withdraw from the state. A second Act, Mass. Laws 1970, ch. 744, authorized a refusal to renew under restricted conditions.

The two acts amended provisions found in various chapters of the Massachusetts General Laws, and are hence distributed. See Mass.Ann.Laws, Cum.Supp. 1970, ch. 90, §§ 34A, 34D, 34M, 34N; ch. 231, § 6D; ch. 175, §§ 22E, 22F, 22G, 22H, 113B, 113C.

46. Colorado, Connecticut, Florida, Georgia, Hawaii, Kansas, Kentucky, Massachusetts, Michigan, Minnesota, Nevada (repealed, effective in 1980), New Jersey, New York, North Dakota, Pennsylvania, and Utah. A no-fault bill was enacted in the District of Columbia in 1982. Much amending legislation has been enacted; a current status report appears in the CCH Automobile Insurance Service.

47. Arkansas, Delaware, Maryland, Oregon, South Carolina, South Dakota, Texas, and Virginia.

48. An analysis of the types of enacted statutes appears in Henderson, No-Fault Plans for Automobile Accidents, 1977, 56 Ore.L.Rev. 287.

of the claims of deficiencies in the tort and liability insurance system.[49] The controversy remains unresolved.

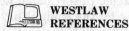
WESTLAW REFERENCES

elements /4 "work! compensation"

Financial Responsibility Laws
requir! /4 "financial responsibility law*" "security responsibility law*"

Compulsory Liability Insurance
compulsory /4 "liability insurance"

Unsatisfied Judgment Funds
fund* /4 "unsatisfied judgment*"

Academic Suggestions
ehrenzweig /p "full aid" & court(nj)

The Keeton-O'Connell Plan
keeton /4 o'connell

First American Statutes
court(ma) & no-fault /s benefits & date(after 1970)

§ 85. Principles of Compensation in American Legal Systems

Any legal system tends to develop within itself not one but many compensation systems—many bodies of doctrine and practice applying rather different arrangements for compensation responsive to different needs. For example, worker injuries may be treated differently from highway injuries, and injuries from foods and drugs may be treated in yet another way, all within the legal system operating in a given time and place. Nevertheless, a few key principles of compensation tend to appear somewhere in most, if not all, legal systems.

Three key ideas stand out as basic explanations for rules and practices about awarding and denying compensation. For convenience, they are referred to here as the fault principle,[1] the strict accountability principle,[2] and the welfare principle.

The Fault Principle

Intended harms are ordinarily compensable unless caused by conduct aimed at serving some interest that the legal system values above the harms done. The basic reason is the fault principle. Unless other interests served outweigh intended harms and are treated as justification,[3] conduct causing intended harms is blameworthy. When blameworthy conduct causes harms to others, the blameworthy actor ought, in general, to compensate for those harms. Similarly, unintended harms are ordinarily compensable if caused by conduct that involves undue risks[4]—risks that, along with other costs, outweigh the usefulness of the conduct causing the harms. Conduct of this kind is socially undesirable and deserves to be classified as blameworthy. The fault principle applies.

As stated in the preceding paragraph, the fault principle applies only to conduct that is antisocial in the sense that its costs (including harms) outweigh its benefits. In Anglo-American law this weighing of benefits against costs (including harms) is accomplished, in relation to intended harms, through theories of justification,[5] such as defense of person, defense of property, and public necessity. In relation to unintended harms, the weighing occurs in determining whether the conduct was negligent.[6] In both instances, the conduct is determined not to be blameworthy when benefits outweigh costs.

In any comparison of costs and benefits, the outcome of the calculus depends heavily on the values assigned to the various inter-

---

49. The principal arguments for and against no-fault legislation are summarized, and references to the large body of published writings of 1967–77, when the debate was most active, are collected in Keeton and Keeton, Cases and Materials on the Law of Torts, 2d ed. 1977, 775–828.

§ 85

1. See supra, § 4.

2. See supra, ch. 13.

3. See supra, ch. 4.

4. See supra, ch. 5.

5. See supra, ch. 4.

6. See supra, ch. 5.

ests at stake on both sides of the comparison. Thus, quite different outcomes may be reached in different legal systems because of different valuations of interests at stake, even though the different systems are alike in adhering to a principle of fault that compares benefits and costs.

Probably the best justification that can be offered for the fault principle is the assertion that most people believe it is fair. In short, the justification is an assertion of commonly shared values—an appeal to others to agree that, in their experience, the values implicit in the fault principle deserve recognition.

The Strict Accountability Principle

When fault is not found—when conduct is found to be more socially beneficial than harmful and is therefore to be encouraged in the overall interest of society—the conduct may nevertheless cause harms. Should these harms be compensated? If the answer is yes, we must also face a second question. By whom?

If the answer to these two questions is that compensation should be paid by an actor whose conduct caused (or, more precisely, was one of the causes of) the harms, the key idea is within the scope of the principle referred to here as the principle of strict accountability.

In Anglo-American law, some instances of liability without fault have been the product of case-by-case judicial development (examples are liability of keepers of wild animals,[7] liability of landowners under the doctrine of Rylands v. Fletcher,[8] and strict products liability[9]). Other instances of liability without fault have been the product of statute. Examples include "pure foods" statutes that long preceded a general doctrine of strict products liability.[10] One way of viewing these varied judicial and statutory developments is to see them as independent of each other and to see in Anglo-American law no coherent principle of strict liability but instead an accumulation of rather independent doctrines of strict liability. To suggest a principle of strict accountability is to suggest, instead, that in these developments can be found some common theme beyond the mere fact that they are instances of liability imposed upon an actor who is not at fault. This point and counterpoint are reminiscent of the controversy of an earlier time among scholars about whether the English legal system developed a law of tort or instead only a law of torts,[11] not responsive to any single set of guiding principles. Here, as there, probably the more general perspective discloses only part of the whole truth, but a part well worth attention.

The phrase "strict accountability" is an abbreviated reference to an idea that may also be described in a somewhat longer and more suggestive phrase as "strict accountability for harms within the scope of risks distinctive to an actor's conduct or activity." The principle proposed as the key idea underlying most strict liabilities is that an actor, even though not at fault, should be liable for harms and risks distinctive to the actor's conduct or activity.

The outcomes of application of this principle will depend heavily on decisions assigning responsibility to one or another activity for risks that result when both activities are pursued. The range of cases in which the principle is likely to be useful as a guide to decision will depend heavily on consensus, or at least the potentiality of developing a consensus, on the allocation of particular kinds of risks to particular kinds of activities.

Within the scope of consensus that certain risks are distinctive to certain activities, what reasons can be advanced for strict accountability?

7. See supra, § 76.
8. See supra, § 78.
9. See infra, ch. 17.
10. See infra, § 99.
11. See supra, § 1.

One response to this basic question is a notion that the benefits derived from conduct produce an "enrichment" that is "unjust" unless the actor pays for the harms done.[12] As one reflects on this idea, it becomes readily apparent that the principle of strict accountability is broader in scope than the common law rules associated with the phrase "unjust enrichment." Under this broader principle of strict accountability, the costs of conduct, including the costs of compensating for harms it causes, should be borne by the actor, who in turn will be able to pass those costs along to others who benefit from the actor's conduct. The net effect is that costs may be borne by those who benefit and, ideally, in proportion to their respective shares of the benefits.

Allocating in this way the burden of compensating for harms done has inherent appeal to one's sense of fairness—an appeal reflected in the phrase "unjust enrichment." It has appeal, also, from a point of view concerned with social cost accounting and economic efficiency. Strict accountability for harms caused by conduct (or by an enterprise) assigns to the conduct (or to the enterprise) the costs of the harms it causes and tends to cause those costs to be included in the price of any product of that conduct (or enterprise). If the conduct is socially useful (its benefits outweighing costs) it will survive in the marketplace even at the higher price that includes the cost of compensating for harms done. If the added cost prices the products of the conduct out of the market, this outcome demonstrates that the conduct was not socially useful. Its costs outweighed its benefits, and society will be best served by discouraging such conduct. Thus, strict accountability serves to provide deserved compensation, to deter antisocial conduct, and to assist the community in arriving at rational and well informed choices about what conduct is socially desirable and what conduct is not.

As one illustration of the application of this principle, consider the case of a mining operation that, when conducted with the greatest of care, nevertheless causes harm to nearby property and to persons upon it. Also assume that even after the costs of compensating for these harms is taken into account, the mining operation is socially beneficial in the sense that its benefits outweigh its costs. The fault principle does not support compensation in this case, but the principle of strict accountability does.

At least after the mining operation has been underway long enough for its impact on surrounding property to be known, many of the harmful consequences caused by continuing the operation may be classified as intended.[13] Even so, they would not be within the scope of the fault principle as it has been stated above because on net balance the conduct of continuing the operation, with due care in the method of operation, produces benefits outweighing its costs. The illustration is one of intended harms that would be justified if the fault principle alone were applied to the case. The strict accountability principle, though not condemning the activity and not supporting an order prohibiting it, does support compensation.

As a second illustration of the strict accountability principle, consider an instance of harm that is both not intended and not caused by fault. For example, carefully transporting gasoline by tank truck on public highways is socially desirable conduct, not classified as fault. Yet some American courts have held, and more may be expected to hold, that this is an "abnormally dangerous activity" that gives rise to strict liability for harms resulting from explosion of the cargo.[14] Harms from nonnegligent collision of the truck and another vehicle would not be within the scope of the risk distinctive to this abnormally dangerous activity and would not be covered by the strict liability.[15] Since, by hypothesis, the conduct causing

---

12. See supra, § 4.

13. See supra, § 8.

14. See supra, § 78.

15. Cf. supra, § 42.

the collision was not faulty, those harms would go uncompensated. Only harms from the distinctive explosion risk are within the scope of the principle of strict accountability.

Compulsory no-fault automobile insurance [16] is a third area in which the strict accountability principle is, in part, a basis for the legal outcomes prescribed by the system. Even though prudent operation of motor vehicles is socially beneficial and therefore not classified as blameworthy, it nevertheless causes harms. Compulsory no-fault automobile insurance statutes impose upon each motorist a responsibility for a share of the cost of compensating for harms sustained by motoring victims. Most American no-fault statutes, providing only a partial rather than a total exemption from liability based on fault,[17] are founded partly on the fault principle as well as partly on the strict accountability principle. But partial dependence on the latter principle is nevertheless clear, since even the driver who is not careless, either in causing the particular injury that is the subject of a current claim or in causing previous injuries, is subject to the legal obligation to contribute to meeting the burdens of the system by carrying the compulsory no-fault insurance.

Different applications of the principle of strict accountability may be treated very differently in legal doctrine. Of the three illustrations just given, American legal writings generally treat the first (harm from the prudently conducted mining operation) under the law of nuisance,[18] the second (harm from the explosion risk in transporting gasoline) under the law of strict liability for abnormally dangerous activities,[19] and the third under statutory no-fault law.[20] Strict products liability [21] is a fourth illustration. The suggestion presented here is that, despite the quite different doctrinal explanations, these four bodies of law are fundamentally alike in their dependence, in part at least, on one principle—the principle of strict accountability.

Probably there is more variation among different legal systems in the scope of application of this principle than in the scope of application of the fault principle. Also, the scope of its application has grown markedly in the 20th century. One of the most dramatic examples in American law is the rapid spread of strict products liability throughout American states in the 1960's and 1970's. The theory has been applied, for example, to power machinery of all types (including cars), to foods and drugs, and in a few cases to construction of buildings.[22] The requirement that the product be "defective" may be seen as a way of limiting the scope of the liability to harms caused by risks distinctive to the product. In contrast are risks related as much or more to other circumstances—for example, to abnormal and unexpectable use of the product, or to other activities associated with the harmful event.

Strict products liability and no-fault automobile insurance, though both depending on the principle of strict accountability, illustrate quite different mechanisms of enforcing the principle. Strict products liability does so by declaring tort liability and depending either on liability insurance or "self-insurance" of very large enterprises to guarantee payments and spread costs among the purchasers of the products. No-fault automobile insurance, on the other hand, enforces the principle of strict accountability through compulsory loss insurance (rather than liability insurance), which also serves to spread the costs among motorists generally. These very different mechanisms of administration may tend to obscure but they do not alter the similarity of these two bodies of law as applications of the principle of strict accountability.

16. See supra, § 84.
17. See supra, § 84.
18. See infra, ch. 15.
19. See supra, § 78.
20. See supra, § 84.
21. See infra, ch. 17.
22. See infra, ch. 17.

Another difference between strict products liability and no-fault automobile insurance concerns the measure of recovery. The law of strict products liability, spawned primarily in courts, adopts the traditional tort measure of damages, including compensation for pain and suffering. No-fault automobile compensation systems, spawned in legislatures, adopt a more limited measure of recovery that commonly excludes compensation for pain and suffering unless the injury is serious enough to be beyond a defined threshold of severity.

These illustrations make the point that details of two compensation systems within a single legal system may vary considerably even though both are founded in whole or in part on the same basic principle of compensation. The differences are likely to be even greater when one or both also reflect the influence of another basic principle as well—as in the case of a no-fault system founded on both the principle of fault and the principle of strict accountability.

The Welfare Principle

Consider again a pair of questions stated in discussion of the strict accountability principle. When fault is not found—when conduct is more socially beneficial than harmful and is therefore to be encouraged in the overall interest of society—but the conduct nevertheless causes harms, should the harms be compensated? If so, by whom?

If the answer to these two questions is that compensation should be paid not by the actor whose socially beneficial conduct caused the harm but instead by society, through one of its representative governmental entities, the key idea is within the scope of the welfare principle.

The welfare principle, however, is both broader and narrower than this answer to the two stated questions. It is broader because it applies to illness and other misfortunes as well as to accidental harms. It is narrower in that, as usually embraced, it aims at providing only a certain minimum of economic welfare for every member of society, and not compensation to the full extent of the need. Another characteristic of the welfare principle is that it supports compensation of persons not because they are victims of a particular kind of accident or illness or other misfortune but instead because they are needy, whatever the cause of the need may be.

When the welfare principle alone serves as the foundation for a compensation system, the obligation to provide compensation is an obligation of the society and not distinctively of some individual or other legal entity in the society. In this setting, the most appropriate source of compensation is a governmental entity, a portion of whose general tax revenues may be applied to this purpose. When instead the responsibility for compensation is placed upon an entity that draws the revenues used for this purpose from a particular segment of society, the compensation system is drawing in part upon an accountability principle—either the fault principle or the strict accountability principle—even though it uses a governmental rather than private enterprise entity as the channel of accountability.

Roles of Causal Concepts

In its purest form the welfare principle, as noted above, depends on a criterion of need that applies without regard to the source of the need. No concept of cause is required for its application.

In contrast, both the principle of fault and the principle of strict accountability depend upon some concept of causation as well as some other criterion, such as fault or distinctive risk. Inherently, the principles of fault and distinctive risk imply that some among all the antecedents of a harm for which compensation is claimed will be separated out and treated as legally relevant causes. Other antecedents are legally irrelevant; they are treated as not being among the legal causes of the harm for which compensation is claimed.

The breadth or narrowness of the concepts of cause associated with particular applications of a principle—either the fault principle or the principle of strict accountability may have great influence upon the number of persons compensated and the amounts of compensation.

Concepts of legal cause [23] may also dilute the practical contrast—the practical difference in outcomes—under fault and strict accountability principles. This point is illustrated in the early history of Anglo-American law. Reliance on some form of fault principle as an important element in decisions to award or deny compensation probably has an origin as ancient as law itself. This point is not disproved by the observation of Anglo-American legal historians that the early common law declared that one is liable for harms caused by one's acts. Even the earliest recorded decisions suggest a limitation of liability with respect to which events among all subsequent events are conceived to be "caused" by one's acts and which are not. An outside observer of the system may see in these conceptions of legal cause a set of ideas that, from another perspective, might be described as notions of fault. Holdsworth, for example, remarked that the conception of negligence is latent in the limitation of liability to proximate consequences of one's acts, even though this latent conception goes unrecognized in early periods of development.[24]

Arguments for Negative Application of Each Basic Principle

Each of the three key principles of compensation has been stated above as a principle to be applied affirmatively. That is, it is a principle supporting liability when its conditions are met. Thus the fault principle supports liability when fault is found, and, as noted before, probably the most persuasive justification is the assertion that most people believe that application of the fault principle in this affirmative way is fair.

Is there similar consensus about what the outcome should be when fault is not found? It happens, of course, that human conduct that is socially desirable may nevertheless be substantially risky. That is, even though conduct is more socially beneficial than harmful, and is therefore to be encouraged in the overall interest of society, it may nevertheless cause harm to some persons or to their property. Should those harms be compensated? Does the fault principle speak to this question?

When in a particular context the answer is given that harms caused by socially beneficial conduct should not be compensated, one might think of the answer as a negative application of the fault principle. That is, one might advance the fault principle both as a reason for awarding compensation (when fault is found) and as a reason for denying compensation (when fault is not found). In the United States, arguments for this kind of dual application of the fault principle have often been used in opposition to the statutory adoption of "no-fault" automobile insurance laws and to the judicial development of strict liability (both in products cases and in other areas of the law).

In some contexts, however, as illustrated in the discussion of the principle of strict accountability, conclusions have been reached that affirmative application of another principle justifies compensation even when fault is not found. This is at least a rejection, for these instances, of the notion that the fault principle should be applied negatively (denying compensation when no fault is found) as well as affirmatively. One might argue that a negative application occurs in those other instances—of which there are surely some in every legal system—in which harms caused by risky, nonfaulty conduct are not compensated. Another way of viewing the matter, however, is that those are simply instances in which neither the fault principle nor any other principle of compensation applies af-

23. See supra, § 42.
24. See 3 Holdsworth, A History of English Law, 5th ed. 1942, 378–80; 8 id., 2d ed. 1937, 446–47.

firmatively and the outcome of denial of compensation is based on the absence of an affirmative case for compensation rather than the strength of an argument that compensation should be denied because the conduct causing harm was socially desirable. From this perspective, the fault principle is not in conflict with the two other principles of compensation, each of which may support compensation in the absence of fault. Rather, the three principles are independent bases for compensation. Though they may overlap and provide two or even three bases for compensation in particular fact situations, any one of the three is alone enough to support compensation when it applies affirmatively. None of the three, from this perspective, should be understood as a dual principle that opposes compensation when its stated conditions are not satisfied as well as supporting compensation when its conditions are satisfied.

Probably the opposing position—the argument that compensation should not be awarded because the sole person against whom the claim is made was not at fault in causing it—is most often advanced, and with most effect in two types of contexts. They are, first, situations in which plainly neither of the other two principles of compensation applies and the claimant's main hope for compensation is to claim fault and, second, situations in which the argument that an actor not at fault should not be held accountable for compensation is being used as an attack against the principle of strict accountability. In each of these types of situations it would seem that the force of the argument does not depend squarely on a premise that the fault principle applies negatively as well as affirmatively. Instead, one may view the defensive argument as having two elements, one of which is that the fault principle does not apply affirmatively to support compensation and the other of which is that neither of the other two principles

should be applied in this context, though each admittedly applies elsewhere in the legal system.

The Contest for Dominance

A contest among principles remains even if the three key principles of compensation are viewed as compatible—even if each is treated as providing an independent basis for compensation and not as having a negative application that opposes compensation when its conditions are not met but the conditions of one or both of the other two principles are met. At the least, the three principles compete for dominance in the sense that in any legal system one of the three will account for more compensation, and more decisions about compensation, than either of the other two, and will thus set the central theme of compensation systems in that legal system.

Surely it is also true that they tend to compete in another sense. Psychological fidelity to one principle may impede readiness to embrace another principle and extend its application. For example, consider some common arguments of "subsidy" and "lottery." [25] Measured by the fault principle, both strict liability and liability to taxes in support of welfare compensation may be seen as unjustified exactions—as enforced "subsidies"—from persons whose activities are socially beneficial. Conversely, however, measured by the welfare principle, both negligence law and strict liability are "lotteries"—"lotteries" among victims to the extent that compensation depends on factors other than need and "lotteries" among those against whom claims are made to the extent that assigned obligations depend on factors apart from economic welfare. Each of these arguments of "subsidy" and "lottery" is, of course, only as valid as the criterion of evaluation on which it is based. The basic controversy concerns the validity of the criterion of evaluation. It concerns substantive

---

25. See Ison, The Forensic Lottery, 1967; Franklin, Replacing the Negligence Lottery: Compensation and Selective Reimbursement, 1967, 53 Va.L.Rev. 774.

differences over the desirability or undesirability of applying the welfare principle, or the strict accountability principle, or the fault principle, in a particular context.

In Anglo-American law, whatever the mix of influence of these different principles may have been in earlier periods of history, the fault principle was clearly dominant between the mid-nineteenth and mid-twentieth centuries. By the end of that hundred-year period, however, a number of different developments foretold increased influence of the strict accountability principle. In the first half of the twentieth century, the system for compensating worker injuries shifted from a basis in fault to a basis in strict accountability. In the years since 1950, a second major shift has occurred—an almost universal acceptance of strict products liability—and application of the fault principle to highway injuries has been eroded in some states by no-fault legislation. The time may be near, if it has not already arrived, in which more compensation is paid on the basis of strict accountability than on the basis of fault.

 WESTLAW REFERENCES

The Fault Principle
di fault

The Strict Accountability Principle
rylands /5 fletcher
"abnormally dangerous activit!"
di product liability
recover! /s "pain and suffering" /s no-fault

Roles of Causal Concepts
di legal cause

Arguments for Negative Application of Each Basic Principle
fault /p strict /p welfare & court(il)

Chapter 15

NUISANCE

Table of Sections

Sec.
86. Meaning of Nuisance—Historical Origins.
87. Private Nuisance: The Tort Action for Damages.
88. Substantial and Unreasonable Interference.
88A. Unreasonable Conduct and Injunctive Relief.
88B. Conduct of Others and the Plaintiff as Factors of Importance.
88C. "Absolute" Nuisance.
89. Remedies.
90. Public Nuisance: Remedies Available to the State.
91. Interference With Use and Enjoyment of Private Property—Negligence and Strict Liability.

§ 86. Meaning of Nuisance—Historical Origins

There is perhaps no more impenetrable jungle in the entire law than that which surrounds the word "nuisance." It has meant all things to all people,[1] and has been applied indiscriminately to everything from an alarming advertisement[2] to a cockroach baked in a pie.[3] There is general agreement that it is incapable of any exact or comprehensive definition.[4] Few terms have afforded so excellent an illustration of the familiar tendency of the courts to seize upon a

§ 86

1. "* * * many wrongs are indifferently termed nuisance or something else, at the convenience or whim of the writer. Thus, injuries to ways, to private lands, various injuries through negligence, wrongs harmful to the physical health, disturbances of the peace, and numberless other things are often or commonly spoken of as nuisances while equally they are called by the other name, and the other name may include other things also which are not nuisances." Bishop, Non-Contract Law, 1889, § 411, note 1. See Smith, Torts Without Particular Names, 1921, 69 U.Pa.L.Rev. 91, 110–112.

As to the difficulties which the English courts and writers have had with the term, see Newark, The Boundaries of Nuisance, 1949, 65 L.Q.Rev. 480; Winfield, Nuisance as a Tort, 1931, 4 Camb.L.J. 189; Paton, Liability for Nuisance, 1942, 37 Ill.L.Rev. 1.

2. Commonwealth v. Cassidy, Pa.1865, 6 Phila. 82.

3. Carroll v. New York Pie Baking Co., 1926, 215 App.Div. 240, 213 N.Y.S. 553.

4. It is indeed impossible, having regard to the wide range of subject-matter embraced under the term nuisance, to frame any general definition. * * *" Garrett and Garrett, Law of Nuisances, 3d Ed. 1908, 4; Winfield, Law of Tort, 1937, 462; Cooley, Torts, 2d ed. 1888, 672; Terry, Leading Principles of Anglo-American Law, 1884, § 434.

catchword as a substitute for any analysis of a problem; the defendant's interference with the plaintiff's interests is characterized as a "nuisance," and there is nothing more to be said. With this reluctance of the opinions to assign any particular meaning to the word, or to get to the bottom of it, there has been a rather astonishing lack of any full consideration of "nuisance" on the part of legal writers.[5] It was not until the publication of the First Restatement of Torts[6] in 1939 that there was any really significant attempt to determine some definite limits to the types of tort liability which are associated with the name.

History

Most of this vagueness, uncertainty, and confusion has been due to the fact that the word "nuisance," which in itself means no more than hurt, annoyance or inconvenience,[7] has come by a series of historical accidents to cover the invasion of different kinds of interests, and of necessity to refer to various kinds of conduct on the part of the defendant. The word first emerges in English law to describe interferences with servitudes or other rights to the free use of land. It became fixed in the law as early as the thirteenth century with the development of the assize of nuisance, which was a criminal writ affording incidental civil relief, designed to cover invasions of the plaintiff's land due to conduct wholly on the land of the defendant. This was superseded in time by the more convenient action on the case for nuisance, which became the sole common law action.[8] The remedy was limited strictly to interference with the use or enjoyment of land,[9] and thus was the parent of the law of private nuisance as it stands today.

Parallel with this civil remedy protecting rights in land, there developed an entirely separate principle, that an infringement of the rights of the crown, or of the general public, was a crime. The earliest cases appear to have involved purprestures, which were encroachments upon the royal domain or the public highway, and might be redressed by a suit by the crown.[10] There was enough of a superficial resemblance between the blocking of a private right of way and the blocking of a public highway to keep men contented with calling the latter a nuisance as well; and "thus was born the public nuisance, that wide term which came to include obstructed highways, lotteries, unlicensed stage-plays, common scolds, and a host of other rag ends of the law."[11] By the time of Edward III, the principle had been extended to such things as interference with a market, smoke from a lime-pit, and diversion of water from a mill, and by analogy the word "nuisance," which still had acquired no very definite meaning, was carried over and applied rather loosely to these mat-

---

5. Both Wood, Law of Nuisances, 3d ed. 1893, and Garrett and Garrett, Law of Nuisances, 3d ed. 1908, are of dubious value. Of the scanty literature on the subject, the following are helpful as general discussion: Winfield, Nuisance as a Tort, 1931, 4 Camb.L.J. 189; Winfield, Law of Tort, 5th ed. 1950, ch. 18; Smith, Reasonable Use as Justification for Damage to Neighbor, 1917, 17 Col.L.Rev. 383; Paton, Liability for Nuisance, 1942, 37 Ill.L.Rev. 1.

See also, as to the law of particular states, Kenworthy, The Private Nuisance Concept in Pennsylvania, 1949, 54 Dick.L.Rev. 109; Leesman, Private Nuisances in Illinois, 1930, 24 Ill.L.Rev. 876; Notes, 1934, 29 Ill.L.Rev. 372; 1947, 95 U.Pa.L.Rev. 781; 1941, 13 Miss.L.Rev. 224.

6. First Restatement of Torts, §§ 822–840.

7. The word is distantly derived from the Latin *nocumentum,* by way of the French *nuisance.* Thus in the Statute of Bridges, 22 Hen. VIII, ch. 5, the word used is "annoyance."

8. The history is traced in Winfield, Nuisance as a Tort, 1931, 4 Camb.L.J. 189; Winfield, Law of Tort, 5th ed. 1950, ch. 18; 1 Street, The Foundations of Legal Liability, 1906, 213; Newark, The Boundaries of Nuisance, 1949, 65 L.Q.Rev. 480; McRae, Development of Nuisance in the Early Common Law, 1948, 1 U.Fla.L. Rev. 27.

9. Thus the action on the case for nuisance was always local in character. Warren v. Webb, 1808, 1 Taunt. 379, 127 Eng.Rep. 880.

10. Garrett and Garrett, Law of Nuisances, 3d ed. 1908, 1. Modern examples of purprestures are Adams v. Commissioners of Town of Trappe, 1954, 204 Md. 165, 102 A.2d 830; Long v. New York Central Railroad Co., 1929, 248 Mich. 437, 227 N.W. 739; Sloan v. City of Greenville, 1959, 235 S.C. 277, 111 S.E.2d 573.

11. Newark, The Boundaries of Nuisance, 1949, 65 L.Q.Rev. 480, 482.

ters too.[12] By degrees the class of offenses recognized as "common nuisances" was greatly enlarged, until it came to include any "act not warranted by law, or omission to discharge a legal duty, which inconveniences the public in the exercise of rights common to all Her Majesty's subjects."[13] The remedy remained exclusively a criminal one until the sixteenth century, when it was recognized that a private individual who had suffered special damage might have a civil action in tort for the invasion of the public right.[14]

Public and Private Nuisance

These two lines of development, the one narrowly restricted to the invasion of interests in the use or enjoyment of land, and the other extending to virtually any form of annoyance or inconvenience interfering with common public rights, have led to the prevailing uncertainty as to what a nuisance is. A private nuisance is a civil wrong, based on a disturbance of rights in land.[15] The remedy for it lies in the hands of the individual whose rights have been disturbed. A public or common nuisance, on the other hand, is a species of catch-all criminal offense, consisting of an interference with the rights of the community at large,[16] which may include anything from the obstruction of a highway to a public gaming-house or indecent exposure.[17] As in the case of other crimes, the normal remedy is in the hands of the state. The two have almost nothing in common, except that each causes inconvenience to someone,[18] and it would have been fortunate if they had been called from the beginning by different names. Add to this the fact that a public nuisance may also be a private one, when it interferes with the enjoyment of land,[19] and that even apart from this there are circumstances in which a private individual may have a tort action for the public offense itself,[20] and it is not difficult to explain the existing confusion.

If "nuisance" is to have any meaning at all, it is necessary to dismiss a considerable number of cases [21] which have applied the term to matters not connected either with land or with any public right, as mere aberration, adding to the vagueness of an al-

---

12. Garrett and Garrett, Law of Nuisances, 3d ed. 1908, 2; Jeudwine, Tort, Crime, and Police in Mediaeval Britain, 1917, 218.

13. Stephen, General View of the Criminal Law of England, 1890, 105.

14. 8 Holdsworth, History of English Law, 2d ed. 1937, 424–425; 1535, Y.B. 27 Hen. VIII, Mich., pl. 10; Williams's Case, 1595, 5 Co.Rep. 73a, 77 Eng.Rep. 164; Fineux v. Hovenden, 1598, Cro.Eliz. 664, 78 Eng.Rep. 902; Fowler v. Sanders, Cro.Jac. 446, 79 Eng.Rep. 382.

15. See infra, § 87.

16. Salmond, Law of Torts, 8th ed. 1934, 233. "Public nuisances may be considered as offenses against the public by either doing a thing which tends to the annoyance of all the King's subjects, or by neglecting to do a thing which the common good requires." Russell, Crimes and Misdemeanors, 8th ed. 1923, 1691.

17. A very good case on the distinction between the two is Mandell v. Pivnick, 1956, 20 Conn.Sup. 99, 125 A.2d 175, which found neither. Plaintiff was injured by a defectively installed awning on defendant's building. It was held that no private nuisance was pleaded, because there was no allegation of any interference with rights in land; and no public nuisance, because there was no allegation that the awning interfered with the public highway, or with plaintiff's rights as a member of the general public.

In accord is Radigan v. W.J. Halloran Co., 1963, 97 R.I. 122, 196 A.2d 160 (personal injury from negligent operation of a crane).

18. "Public and private nuisances are not in reality two species of the same genus at all. There is no generic concept which includes the crime of keeping a common gaming-house and the tort of allowing one's trees to overhang the land of a neighbor." Salmond, Law of Torts, 8th ed. 1934, 233.

"What generic conception, it has been asked, connects public nuisances like the woman who is a common scold, or the boy who fires a squib, with private nuisances like blocking up the ancient lights of a building or excessive playing on the piano? The only link which we can suggest is inconvenience, and loose as this term is, it is probably the best that can be offered. At any rate, be the ground of the distinction what it may, the distinction itself cannot be cast aside without departing from settled legal terminology, and ignoring not only the fact that a public nuisance may become a private one but also the very practical consequence of the distinction which is that a public nuisance is a crime while a private nuisance is a tort." Winfield, Law of Tort, 1937, 466.

19. See infra, § 90.

20. See infra, § 90.

21. For example, Carroll v. New York Pie Baking Co., 1926, 215 App.Div. 240, 213 N.Y.S. 553.

ready uncertain word. Unless the facts can be brought within one of the two categories mentioned, there is not, with any accurate use of the term, a nuisance.[22]

 WESTLAW REFERENCES

di nuisance

History

histor! /p defin! mean! /s nuisance* & court(ny)

Public and Private Nuisance

public common /3 nuisance* /s private /s nuisance*

§ 87. Private Nuisance: The Tort Action for Damages

The Interest Protected

The essence of a private nuisance is an interference with the use and enjoyment of land.[1] The ownership or rightful possession of land necessarily involves the right not only to the unimpaired condition of the property itself, but also to some reasonable comfort and convenience in its occupation. Thus, many interferences with personal comfort, such as a dog next door which makes night hideous with his howls,[2] which at first glance would appear to be wrongs purely personal to the landholder, are treated as nuisances because they interfere with that right to the undisturbed enjoyment of the premises which is inseparable from ownership of the property.[3]

The different ways and combinations of ways in which the interest in the use or enjoyment of land may be invaded are infinitely variable. A private nuisance may consist of an interference with the physical condition of the land itself, as by vibration[4] or blasting[5] which damages a house, the destruction of crops,[6] flooding,[7] raising the water table,[8] or the pollution of a stream[9] or of an underground water supply.[10] It may consist of a disturbance of the comfort or convenience of the occupant, as by unpleasant odors,[11] smoke or dust or gas,[12] loud

---

22. Mandell v. Pivnick, 1956, 20 Conn.Sup. 99, 125 A.2d 175; Dahlstrom v. Roosevelt Mills, Inc., 1967, 27 Conn.Sup. 355, 238 A.2d 431.

§ 87

1. And without it, the fact of personal injury, or of interference with some purely personal right, is not enough for such a nuisance. Cox v. Ray M. Lee Co., 1959, 100 Ga.App. 333, 111 S.E.2d 246; Stanley v. City of Macon, 1957, 95 Ga.App. 108, 97 S.E.2d 330; Lederman v. Cunningham, Tex.Civ.App.1955, 283 S.W.2d 108; Mandell v. Pivnick, 1956, 20 Conn.Sup. 99, 125 A.2d 175.

2. Brill v. Flagler, N.Y.1840, 23 Wend. 354; Hubbard v. Preston, 1892, 90 Mich. 221, 51 N.W. 209; Adams v. Hamilton Carhartt Overall Co., 1943, 293 Ky. 443, 169 S.W.2d 294.

3. 1 Street, Foundations of Legal Liability, 1906, 211, 212; Restatement of Torts, § 822, Comment c. It is not necessary that the condition endanger the health of the occupant, if it is offensive to the senses and renders enjoyment of life and property uncomfortable. Miller v. Coleman, 1957, 213 Ga. 125, 97 S.E.2d 313 (dog kennel).

4. Hoare & Co. v. McAlpin & Sons, [1928] 1 Ch. 167, 92 L.J.Ch. 81; Sam Warren & Son Stone Co. v. Gruesser, 1948, 307 Ky. 98, 209 S.W.2d 817; Transcontinental Gas Pipe Line Co. v. Gault, 4th Cir. 1952, 198 F.2d 196.

5. Beecher v. Dull, 1928, 294 Pa. 17, 143 A. 498. Cf. Heeg v. Licht, 1880, 80 N.Y. 579; Laflin & Rand Powder Co. v. Tearney, 1890, 131 Ill. 322, 23 N.E. 389; Davis v. Niagara Falls Tower Co., 1902, 171 N.Y. 336, 64 N.E. 4 (ice falling on roof). See Notes, 1929, 77 U.Pa.L.Rev. 550; 1930, 19 Cal.L.Rev. 94.

6. United Verde Extension Mining Co. v. Ralston, 1931, 37 Ariz. 554, 296 P. 262; Andrews v. Andrews, 1955, 242 N.C. 382, 88 S.E.2d 88; Campbell v. Seaman, 1876, 63 N.Y. 568 (trees and plants); Stevens v. Moon, 1921, 54 Cal.App. 737, 202 P. 961 (trees).

7. Mueller v. Fruen, 1886, 36 Minn. 273, 30 N.W. 886; Rindge v. Sargent, 1886, 64 N.H. 294, 9 A. 723; William Tackaberry Co. v. Sioux City Service Co., 1911, 154 Iowa 358, 132 N.W. 945, rehearing denied 154 Iowa 358, 134 N.W. 1064. Cf. Spaulding v. Cameron, 1952, 38 Cal.2d 265, 239 P.2d 625 (mud).

8. Cason v. Florida Power Co., 1917, 74 Fla. 1, 76 So. 535; Shields v. Wondries, 1957, 154 Cal.App.2d 249, 316 P.2d 9.

9. Beach v. Sterling Iron & Zinc Co., 1895, 54 N.J.Eq. 65, 33 A. 286, affirmed 55 N.J.Eq. 824, 41 A. 1117; Johnson v. City of Fairmont, 1933, 188 Minn. 451, 247 N.W. 572; Farley v. Crystal Coal & Coke Co., 1920, 85 W.Va. 595, 102 S.E. 265; Rose v. Standard Oil Co. of New York, 1936, 56 R.I. 272, 185 A. 251, reargument denied 56 R.I. 472, 188 A. 71.

10. Cities Service Co. v. Merritt, Okl.1958, 332 P.2d 677; Burr v. Adam Eidemiller, Inc., 1956, 386 Pa. 416, 126 A.2d 403.

11. Aldred's Case, 1611, 9 Co.Rep. 57, 77 Eng.Rep. 816; Sarraillon v. Stevenson, 1950, 153 Neb. 182, 43

noises,[13] excessive light or high temperatures,[14] or even repeated telephone calls;[15] or of his health, as by a pond full of malarial mosquitoes.[16] Likewise, it may disturb merely his peace of mind, as in the case of a bawdy house,[17] the depressing effect of an undertaking establishment,[18] or the unfounded fear of contagion from a tuberculosis hospital.[19] A threat of future injury may be a present menace and interference with enjoyment, as in the case of stored explosives,[20] inflammable buildings or materials,[21] or a vicious dog;[22] and even though no use is being made of the plaintiff's land at the time, the depreciation in the use value of the property because of such conditions or activities is sufficient present damage upon which an action may be based.[23] Many nuisances involve an assortment of interferences: a factory may cause vibration, smoke and dust, loud noises, pollution of a stream, and a fire hazard.[24] So long as the interference is substantial and unreasonable,[25] and such as would be offensive or inconvenient to the normal person,[26] virtually any disturbance of the enjoyment of the property may amount to a nuisance.

N.W.2d 509; Hedrick v. Tubbs, 1950, 120 Ind.App. 326, 92 N.E.2d 561; Johnson v. Drysdale, 1939, 66 S.D. 436, 285 N.W. 301; Higgins v. Decorah Produce Co., 1932, 214 Iowa 276, 242 N.W. 109.

12. Alster v. Allen, 1935, 141 Kan. 661, 42 P.2d 969; Riblet v. Spokane-Portland Cement Co., 1952, 41 Wn.2d 249, 248 P.2d 380; Dill v. Dance Freight Lines, 1966, 247 S.C. 159, 146 S.E.2d 574; Menolascino v. Superior Felt & Bedding Co., 1942, 313 Ill.App. 557, 40 N.E.2d 813; cf. Waters v. McNearney, 1959, 8 A.D.2d 13, 185 N.Y.S.2d 29, affirmed 1960, 8 N.Y.2d 808, 202 N.Y.S.2d 24, 168 N.E.2d 255 (blown sand).

13. Guarina v. Bogart, 1962, 407 Pa. 307, 180 A.2d 557; Hooks v. International Speedways, Inc., 1965, 263 N.C. 686, 140 S.E.2d 387; Gorman v. Sabo, 1956, 210 Md. 155, 122 A.2d 475; Borsvold v. United Dairies, 1957, 347 Mich. 672, 81 N.W.2d 378; Jenner v. Collins, 1951, 211 Miss. 770, 52 So.2d 638; cf. Herbert v. Smyth, 1967, 155 Conn. 78, 230 A.2d 235, appeal after remand 158 Conn. 615, 259 A.2d 646 (barking dogs). See Lloyd, Noise as a Nuisance, 1933, 82 U.Pa.L.Rev. 567; Spater, Noise and the Law, 1965, 63 Mich.L.Rev. 1373.

14. Light: The Shelburne, Inc. v. Crossan Corp., 1923, 95 N.J.Eq. 188, 122 A. 749; Hansen v. Independent School District, 1940, 61 Idaho 109, 98 P.2d 959. See Notes, 1949, 2 Okl.L.Rev. 259; 1948, 1 Ala.L.Rev. 67.

Temperature: Sanders-Clark v. Grosvenor Mansions Co., [1900] 2 Ch. 373; Grady v. Wolsner, 1871, 46 Ala. 381.

15. Brillhardt v. Ben Tipp, Inc., 1956, 48 Wn.2d 722, 297 P.2d 232; Wiggins v. Moskins Credit Clothing Store, E.D.S.C.1956, 137 F.Supp. 764; see Roland v. Slesinger, 1959, 16 Misc.2d 1087, 185 N.Y.S.2d 303. See Note, 1956, 55 Mich.L.Rev. 310.

16. Yaffe v. City of Fort Smith, 1928, 178 Ark. 406, 10 S.W.2d 886; Mills v. Hall & Richards, N.Y.1832, 9 Wend. 315; Towaliga Falls Power Co. v. Sims, 1909, 6 Ga.App. 749, 65 S.E. 844.

17. Crawford v. Tyrrell, 1891, 128 N.Y. 341, 28 N.E. 514; Tedescki v. Berger, 1907, 150 Ala. 649, 43 So. 960; cf. Reid v. Brodsky, 1959, 397 Pa. 463, 156 A.2d 334 (taproom frequented by disorderly characters).

18. Howard v. Etchieson, 1958, 228 Ark. 809, 310 S.W.2d 473; Tureman v. Ketterlin, 1924, 304 Mo. 221, 263 S.W. 202; Williams v. Montgomery, 1939, 184 Miss. 547, 186 So. 302; Kundinger v. Bagnasco, 1941, 298 Mich. 15, 298 N.W. 386. Cf. Lowe v. Prospect Hill Cemetery Association, 1898, 58 Neb. 94, 78 N.W. 488 (cemetery); Jones v. Trawick, Fla.1954, 75 So.2d 785 (same); see Notes, 1938, 16 Tex.L.Rev. 278; 1934, 18 Minn.L.Rev. 482.

19. Everett v. Paschall, 1910, 61 Wash. 47, 111 P. 879; City of Baltimore v. Fairfield Improvement Co., 1898, 87 Md. 352, 39 A. 1081; Cherry v. Williams, 1908, 147 N.C. 452, 61 S.E. 267; Stotler v. Rochelle, 1910, 83 Kan. 86, 109 P. 788.

20. Cumberland Torpedo Co. v. Gaines, 1923, 201 Ky. 88, 255 S.W. 1046; Whittemore v. Baxter Laundry Co., 1914, 181 Mich. 564, 148 N.W. 437. Cf. Hogle v. H.H. Franklin Manufacturing Co., 1910, 199 N.Y. 388, 92 N.E. 794 (throwing junk from windows).

21. Richardson v. Murphy, 1953, 198 Or. 640, 259 P.2d 116; Griswold & Day v. Brega & Roster, 1895, 57 Ill.App. 554, affirmed 160 Ill. 490, 43 N.E. 864; Fields v. Stokley, 1882, 99 Pa. 306.

22. Rider v. Clarkson, 1910, 77 N.J.Eq. 469, 78 A. 676.

23. Wilson v. Townend, 1860, 1 Drew & Sm. 324, 62 Eng.Rep. 403; Busch v. New York, Lackawanna & Western Railway Co., 1890, 34 N.Y.St.Rep. 7, 12 N.Y.S. 85; Bowden v. Edison Electric Illuminating Co., 1899, 29 Misc. 171, 60 N.Y.S. 835; Romano v. Birmingham Railway, Light & Power Co., 1913, 182 Ala. 335, 62 So. 677.

24. See for example McClung v. Louisville & Nashville Railroad Co., 1951, 255 Ala. 302, 51 So.2d 371; Kosich v. Poultrymen's Service Corp., 1945, 136 N.J. Eq. 571, 43 A.2d 15; Gus Blass Dry Goods Co. v. Reinman & Wolfort, 1912, 102 Ark. 287, 143 S.W. 1087; Vowinckel v. N. Clark & Sons, 1932, 216 Cal. 156, 13 P.2d 733; Hoadley v. M. Seward & Son Co., 1899, 71 Conn. 649, 42 A. 997.

25. See infra, § 88.

26. See infra, § 88.

Property Rights Protected

The original character of private nuisance as an invasion of interests in land has been preserved. Apparently any interest sufficient to be dignified as a property right will support the action. Thus it will lie in favor of a tenant for a term,[27] or from week to week,[28] or a mortgagor in possession after foreclosure,[29] or even one in adverse possession without title.[30] Likewise it may be maintained by the holder of an easement, such as a right of way[31] or a right to passage, light and air.[32] But in each case the protection is limited to the interest of the plaintiff. Thus a tenant may recover damages for the depreciation in market value of his term,[33] but not for that of the reversion, in which he has no interest;[34] and a reversioner may recover for permanent harm to the property or loss of its rental value,[35] but not for harm which goes merely to the present enjoyment of the man in possession.[36] Once the invasion of the property interest is established, however, consequential damages to the possessor which result from it, such as injuries to his own health,[37] or loss of services of his family,[38] may be recovered.

On the other hand, it is generally agreed that anyone who has no interest in the property affected, such as a licensee,[39] an employee[40] or a lodger[41] on the premises, cannot maintain an action based on a private nuisance. But although there is authority to the contrary,[42] the greater number of cases

---

27. McClosky v. Martin, Fla.1951, 56 So.2d 916; Bly v. Edison Electric Illuminating Co., 1902, 172 N.Y. 1, 64 N.E. 745; Green v. T.A. Shoemaker & Co., 1909, 111 Md. 69, 73 A. 688; American Electronics, Inc. v. Christe Poules & Co., 1964, 43 Misc.2d 302, 250 N.Y.S.2d 738 (one tenant liable to another). A fortiori a life tenant. Price v. Grose, 1921, 78 Ind.App. 62, 133 N.E. 30.

28. See Jones v. Chappell, 1875, L.R. 20 Eq. 539; Bowden v. Edison Electric Illuminating Co., 1899, 29 Misc. 171, 60 N.Y.S. 835 (tenant from month to month); Towaliga Falls Power Co. v. Sims, 1909, 6 Ga.App. 749, 65 S.E. 844 (tenant at will).

29. Lurssen v. Lloyd, 1892, 76 Md. 360, 25 A. 294.

30. Brink v. Moeschl Edwards Corrugating Co., 1911, 142 Ky. 88, 133 S.W. 1147; cf. Denner v. Chicago, Milwaukee & St. Paul Railway Co., 1883, 57 Wis. 218, 15 N.W. 158.

31. Lane v. Capsey, [1891] 3 Ch. 411; Herman v. Roberts, 1890, 119 N.Y. 37, 23 N.E. 442.

32. Webber v. Wright, 1924, 124 Me. 190, 126 A. 737.

33. Bowden v. Edison Electric Illuminating Co., 1899, 29 Misc. 171, 60 N.Y.S. 835; Klassen v. Central Kansas Cooperative Creamery Association, 1946, 160 Kan. 697, 165 P.2d 601. He may maintain the action even against the landlord for interference with his present use. Jubb v. Maslanka, 1961, 22 Conn.Sup. 373, 173 A.2d 604.

34. Klassen v. Central Kansas Cooperative Creamery Association, 1946, 160 Kan. 697, 165 P.2d 601. Cf. National Glue Co. v. Thrash, 1921, 76 Ind.App. 381, 132 N.E. 311; Yoos v. City of Rochester, 1895, 92 Hun 481, 36 N.Y.S. 1072, appeal dismissed 159 N.Y. 541, 53 N.E. 1134.

35. Jeffer v. Gifford, 1767, 4 Burr. 2141, 98 Eng. Rep. 116; Kidgill v. Moor, 1850, 9 C.B. 364, 137 Eng. Rep. 934. Cf. Smith v. Morse, 1889, 148 Mass. 407, 19 N.E. 393.

36. Gotwals v. City of Wessington Springs, 1932, 60 S.D. 428, 244 N.W. 649; Miller v. Edison Electric Illuminating Co., 1906, 184 N.Y. 17, 76 N.E. 734; McDonnell v. Cambridge Railroad Co., 1890, 151 Mass. 159, 23 N.E. 841.

The interests of vendor and vendee are similarly divided before the conveyance. Missouri Pacific Railway Co. v. Davis, 1932, 186 Ark. 401, 53 S.W.2d 851; Irvine v. City of Oelwein, 1915, 170 Iowa 653, 150 N.W. 674.

37. Vann v. Bowie Sewerage Co., 1936, 127 Tex. 97, 90 S.W.2d 561; O'Connor v. Aluminum Ore Co., 1922, 224 Ill.App. 613; Millett v. Minnesota Crushed Stone Co., 1920, 145 Minn. 475, 177 N.W. 641, reargument denied 145 Minn. 475, 179 N.W. 682; Dixon v. New York Trap Rock Corp., 1944, 293 N.Y. 509, 58 N.E.2d 517, motion denied 1945, 294 N.Y. 654, 60 N.E.2d 385. City of Evansville v. Rinehart, 1968, 142 Ind.App. 164, 233 N.E.2d 495.

38. United States Smelting Co. v. Sisam, 8th Cir. 1911, 191 F. 293; Towaliga Falls Power Co. v. Sims, 1909, 6 Ga.App. 749, 65 S.E. 844; Millett v. Minnesota Crushed Stone Co., 1920, 145 Minn. 475, 177 N.W. 641, reargument denied 145 Minn. 475, 179 N.W. 682.

39. Malone v. Laskey, [1907] 2 K.B. 141; Elliott v. Mason, 1911, 76 N.H. 229, 81 A. 701; Owen v. Henman, Pa.1841, 1 Watts & S. 548.

40. Page v. Niagara Chemical Division, Fla.1953, 68 So.2d 382; Broderick v. City of Waterbury, 1944, 130 Conn. 601, 36 A.2d 585; Kilts v. Supervisors of Kent County, 1910, 162 Mich. 646, 127 N.W. 821; Daurizio v. Merchants' Despatch Transportation Co., 1934, 152 Misc. 716, 274 N.Y.S. 174.

41. Reber v. Illinois Central Railroad Co., 1932, 161 Miss. 885, 138 So. 574. Cf. Miller v. Edison Electric Illuminating Co., 1906, 184 N.Y. 17, 76 N.E. 734.

42. Cunard and Wife v. Antifyre, Ltd., [1933] 1 K.B. 551, Ellis v. Kansas City, St. Joseph & Council Bluff's Railroad Co., 1876, 63 Mo. 131, 21 Am.Rep. 436; Hughes v. City of Auburn, 1899, 161 N.Y. 96, 55 N.E. 389; Millett v. Minnesota Crushed Stone Co., 1920, 145

have regarded members of the family of the possessor as sharing the possession with him, and hence as entitled to recover damages which they have sustained, on the basis of nuisance.[43] The existence of a nuisance to the land does not of course preclude an independent tort action for ordinary negligence resulting in interference with the bodily security of the individual.[44]

Distinguished from Trespass

The distinction between trespass and nuisance was originally that between the old action of trespass and the action on the case.[45] If there was a direct physical invasion of the plaintiff's land, as by casting water on it, it was a trespass; if the invasion was indirect, as where the defendant constructed a spout from which the water ultimately flowed upon the land, it was a nuisance.[46] Coupled with this was the fact that the old strict liability, which persisted as to trespass to land, was modified relatively early in nuisance cases—hence the anomalous rule, still followed in one or two jurisdictions,[47] that the defendant was strictly liable if his blasting operations cast rocks upon the plaintiff's premises, but not if they shook down his house.

With the abandonment of the old procedural forms, direct and indirect invasions have lost their significance, and the line between trespass and nuisance has become wavering and uncertain. The distinction which is now accepted [48] is that trespass is an invasion of the plaintiff's interest in the exclusive possession of his land, while nuisance is an interference with his use and enjoyment of it. The difference is that between walking across his lawn and establishing a bawdy house next door; between felling a tree across his boundary line and keeping him awake at night with the noise of a rolling mill.

The Requirements for Recovery on a Private Nuisance Theory

Private nuisance is a tort that protects the interest of those who own or occupy land from conduct committed with the intention of interfering with a particular interest—the interest in use and enjoyment. It is, therefore, like trespass, a tort arising from the intentional interference of an interest in land that is deemed worthy of legal protection.

As the term "private nuisance" is used in this edition, the tort is committed only if, and in the absence of an intrusion on land amounting to an intentional entry and a trespass, the following requirements are satisfied:

(1) The defendant acted with the intent of interfering with the use and enjoyment of the land by those entitled to that use;

(2) There was some interference with the use and enjoyment of the land of the kind intended, although the amount and extent of that interference may not have been anticipated or intended;

(3) The interference that resulted and the physical harm, if any, from that interference proved to be substantial. It is this requirement and the next that is most important in distinguishing between trespassory-type in-

---

Minn. 475, 177 N.W. 641, reargument denied 145 Minn. 475, 179 N.W. 682; Kavanagh v. Barber, 1892, 131 N.Y. 211, 30 N.E. 235.

43. Fort Worth & Rio Grande Railway Co. v. Glenn, 1904, 97 Tex. 586, 80 S.W. 992; Hosmer v. Republic Iron & Steel Co., 1913, 179 Ala. 415, 60 So. 801; Hodges v. Town of Drew, 1935, 172 Miss. 668, 159 So. 298; Pere Marquette Railroad Co. v. Chadwick, 1917, 65 Ind. App. 95, 115 N.E. 678.

44. See Kilts v. Supervisors of Kent County, 1910, 162 Mich. 646, 127 N.W. 821; Daurizio v. Merchants' Despatch Transportation Co., 1934, 158 Misc. 716, 274 N.Y.S. 174; Malone v. Laskey, [1907] 2 K.B. 141; Cunard and Wife v. Antifyre, [1933] 1 K.B. 551.

45. See supra, § 7.

46. Reynolds v. Clarke, 1725, 1 Strange 634, 93 Eng.Rep. 747. This distinction is repeated in such modern cases as Pan American Petroleum Co. v. Byars, 1934, 228 Ala. 372, 153 So. 616; Wright v. Syracuse, Binghamton & New York Railroad Co., 1888, 49 Hun 445, 3 N.Y.S. 480, affirmed 1891, 124 N.Y. 668, 27 N.E. 854; Central of Georgia R. Co. v. Americus Construction Co., 1909, 133 Ga. 392, 65 S.E. 855.

47. See supra, ch. 13, § 78.

48. Second Restatement of Torts, Introductory Note to ch. 40. See Ryan v. City of Emmetsburg, 1942, 232 Iowa 600, 4 N.W.2d 435.

vasions from those that are actionable on a nuisance theory. Any intentional and unprivileged entry on land is a trespass without a showing of damage, since those who own land have an exclusive right to its use; but an act that interferes with use but is not in itself a use is not actionable without damage. The substantial interference requirement is to satisfy the need for a showing that the land is reduced in value because of the defendant's conduct;[49]

(4) The interference that came about under such circumstances was of such a nature, duration or amount as to constitute unreasonable interference with the use and enjoyment of the land.[50] This does not mean that the defendant's conduct must be unreasonable. It only means that the interference must be unreasonable and this requires elaboration.

The above are the four requirements for the recovery of damages. When these requirements are satisfied, it can be said that (1) the defendant has acted with the intention of interfering with plaintiff's use and enjoyment, and (2) his conduct has caused measurable harm in the sense of detriment in fact. Ofttimes, the occupier or owner of the land will prefer to have conduct that is a private nuisance or is a threatened private nuisance enjoined. The fact that the conduct is tortious or is likely to be so does not necessarily mean that court will give the plaintiff equitable relief by way of an injunction. Courts have consistently required the plaintiff to resort to the remedy of damages, either by way of requiring a separate action for damages or by way of conditioning a denial of injunctive relief on the payment of damages. In such cases, the courts are treating the interference as being unreasonable although the conduct is regarded as reasonable and socially desirable. The two concepts—unreasonable interference and unreasonable conduct—are not at all identical. The failure to make this clear distinction between the requirements for injunctive relief and the requirements for damages has been a fertile source of confusion.[51]

Another source of confusion as regards the tort of private nuisance has resulted from the use of the term "nuisance" to describe all nontrespassory but actionable interferences with the use and enjoyment of land. Just as different interests of personality, such as bodily integrity and privacy, are protected in different ways and with a different set of rules and principles, so also is this true as regards interests in property. Tangible physical damage to land is protected from negligent conduct[52] and from abnormally dangerous activities[53] and perhaps, occasionally, from other kinds of conduct, such as conduct that undermines lateral support,[54] or alters the flow of surface water;[55] but the utilization of the same label to describe all these types of actionable conduct brings about much confusion regarding when the conduct is actionable and what the defenses to such conduct should be.

49. Second Restatement of Torts, § 821F, Comment c.

50. See infra, § 88.

51. See infra, § 88A.

52. See supra, § 57. See Long v. Magnolia Hotel Co., 1956, 227 Miss. 625, 86 So.2d 493.

53. See supra, § 78. Hutchinson v. Capeletti Brothers, Inc., Fla.App.1981, 397 So.2d 952; Puckett v. Sullivan, 1961, 190 Cal.App.2d 489, 12 Cal.Rptr. 55, 87 A.L.R.2d 704; Levi v. Schwartz, 1953, 201 Md. 575, 95 A.2d 322, 36 A.L.R.2d 1241. Second Restatement of Torts, § 817.

54. Second Restatement of Torts, § 78. Puckett v. Sullivan, 1961, 190 Cal.App.2d 489, 12 Cal.Rptr. 55, 87 A.L.R.2d 704; Levi v. Schwartz, 1953, 201 Md. 575, 95 A.2d 322, 36 A.L.R.2d 1241.

55. There are conflicting rules about the rights of adjoining landowners as regards surface waters. One group held in what came to be regarded as the common enemy doctrine that each landowner was entitled to do as he pleased, on his own land, to dispose of surface water without liability for adverse consequences. Another group followed the rule of the civil law that adjoining landowners were entitled to have the normal course of natural drainage maintained. See Annot., 59 A.L.R.2d 421, 423, Sec. 1.

Physical Harm and Mental or Physical Discomfort Distinguished

The policy considerations that dictate that there should be liability for physical harm to land, either by way of an airplane crash or by way of noxious gases on the basis of certain legal doctrines do not necessarily apply when the only "injury" is a temporary discomfort due to fear or some other disagreeable mental or emotional disturbance. In nearly all of the cases in which it has been found that so-called unintentional or accidental interference was actionable, physical damage or harm to land, water or improvements was the consequence of the conduct. Typical cases are those involving soil and water pollution.[56]

In the cases and literature dealing with the issues related to the tort liability of those who allow harmful liquids to escape and pollute soil and water, both underground and surface, there are at least five distinct theories upon the basis of which liability has been imposed, several of which have been adopted in a particular jurisdiction. These five theories are (1) trespass,[57] (2) nuisance,[58] (3) negligence,[59] (4) strict liability under some version of the Rylands v. Fletcher doctrine[60] or the Restatement's Abnormally Dangerous Activity doctrine,[61] and (5) a "natural right" to water or riparian right theory in its natural purity and with no consideration being given to the quality of the defendant's conduct or the nature of his activity.[62] The theories should be carefully distinguished. Trespass has been discussed in an earlier chapter.

The Intentional Interference Requirement

Early cases of "private nuisance" seem to have assumed that the defendant was strictly liable, and to have made no inquiry as to the nature of his conduct. These were usually cases involving physical harm due to the escape of noxious substances. As late as 1705, in a case where sewage from the defendant's privy percolated into the cellar of the plaintiff's adjoining house, Chief Justice Holt considered it sufficient that it was defendant's wall and the defendant's filth because "he was bound of common right to keep his wall so his filth would not damnify his neighbor."[63] Over a period of many years, the general modifications of the theory of tort liability to which reference has been made heretofore[64] have included private nuisance and other theories upon which interests in the use and enjoyment of property are protected. Courts have resorted to various theories of recovery other than trespass (intentional entry) including nuisance, negligence, and strict liability of one kind or another. As a result of these changes, it seems highly desirable to limit nuisance to intentional interferences if confusion is to be avoided.

Occasionally, the defendant may act from a malicious desire to so harm for its own sake[65]; but more often the situation involving a private nuisance is one where the inva-

---

56. City of Barberton v. Miksch, 1934, 128 Ohio St. 169, 190 N.E. 387; Healey v. Citizens' Gas & Electric Co., 1924, 199 Iowa 82, 201 N.W. 118; Keeton, Tort Liability and the Oil and Gas Industry II, 1961, 39 Tex.L. Rev. 253.

57. See supra, § 13.

58. See infra, §§ 88, 88A, 88B, 88C, 89, and this section.

59. Primarily considered, supra, under § 57.

60. See supra, § 78.

61. See Second Restatement of Torts, ch. 21.

62. See, infra, § 88C on "Absolute" Nuisance.

63. Tenant v. Goldwin, 1705, 1 Salk. 360, 91 Eng. Rep. 314, adding, "and that it was a trespass [the action was on the case] on his neighbor, as if his beasts should escape, or one should make a great heap upon his ground, and it should tumble and fall down upon his neighbor's." See also Sutton v. Clarke, 1815, 6 Taunt. 29, 44, 128 Eng.Rep. 943; Humphries v. Cousins, 1877, 2 C.P.D. 239, 46 L.J.C.P. 438.

64. Supra, ch. 1. See 8 Holdsworth, History of English Law, 2d Ed. 1937, 446–459.

65. See for example the spite fence cases of Welsh v. Todd, 1963, 260 N.C. 527, 133 S.E.2d 171, and Larkin v. Tsavaris, Fla.1956, 85 So.2d 731. Also Medford v. Levy, 1888, 31 W.Va. 649, 8 S.E. 302; Smith v. Morse, 1889, 148 Mass. 407, 19 N.E. 393; Christie v. Davey, [1893] 1 Ch. 316; Hollywood Silver Fox Farm v. Emmett, [1936] 2 K.B. 468; Collier v. Ernst, Pa.1941, 31 Del. 49. See Friedmann, Motive in the English Law of Nuisance, 1954, 40 Va.L.Rev. 583.

sion is intentional merely in the sense that the defendant has created or continued the condition causing the interference with full knowledge that the harm to the plaintiff's interests are occurring or are substantially certain to follow.[66] Thus, a defendant who continues to spray chemicals into the air after he is notified that they are blown onto the plaintiff's land is to be regarded as intending that result,[67] and the same is true when he knows that he is contaminating the plaintiff's water supply with his slag refuse,[68] or that blown sand from the land he is improving is ruining the paint on the plaintiff's house.[69] If the interference is unreasonable,[70] it is tortious and subjects him to liability.

It is apparent from what has been said hereafter that the conduct may often result in substantial interference, as when a cement factory locates next to a small farmer, without such conduct being unreasonable, and even when defendant is exercising utmost care while utilizing all the technical know-how available. It has often been observed that liability, if imposed in such a case, is liability without fault.[71] But this is a mistake. The harm is intentional. Private property cannot be physically harmed or its value impaired in this way, however socially desirable the conduct, without payment being made for the harm done, if the interference that is the consequence of the activity is substantial and considered to be unreasonable. This, of course, does not mean that the activity will be enjoined. When the defendant engages in an activity with knowledge that this activity is interfering with the plaintiff in the use and enjoyment of his property, and the interference is substantial and unreasonable in extent, the defendant is liable, and the monetary recovery is simply a cost of engaging in the kind of activity in which the defendant is engaged.[72] This is so whether the conduct is committed in the air (as by low-flying airplanes), on the highways, or on private property. Occasionally, a court that is generally opposed to the imposition of liability without fault will not impose liability except when the conduct is found to be unreasonable, or there is negligence in the manner in which the activity was being carried on. Such a court is not making any distinction between intentional interference and accidental interference. In Wales Trucking Co. v. Stallcup,[73] the plaintiffs, homeowners adjoining an unpaved highway, brought suit against the defendant trucking company for rust damage sustained by them as a result of the defendant's activity in hauling eight loads of pipe on the highway during a period of several months. The court said: "We do not, however, regard the facts in this case before us as warranting a holding of liability without fault, or nuisance without fault * * * where the activity is of a temporary nature and simply involves the lawful use of a public road to deliver pipe for a public water supply project." [74] With deference to the court, it should be said that the importance of the project and the desirability of the conduct does not alter the fact that the harm was in-

66. See supra, § 8.

67. Vaughn v. Missouri Power & Light Co., Mo. App.1935, 89 S.W.2d 699; Smith v. Staso Milling Co., 2d Cir. 1927, 18 F.2d 736; Jost v. Dairyland Power Cooperative, 1969, 45 Wis.2d 164, 172 N.W.2d 647. Cf. Morgan v. High Penn Oil Co., 1953, 238 N.C. 185, 77 S.E.2d 682; E. Rauh & Sons Fertilizer Co. v. Shreffler, 6th Cir. 1943, 139 F.2d 38. See Note, 1955, 8 Vand.L. Rev. 921.

68. Burr v. Adam Eidemiller, Inc., 1956, 386 Pa. 416, 126 A.2d 403.

69. Waters v. McNearney, 1959, 8 A.D.2d 13, 185 N.Y.S.2d 29, affirmed 1960, 8 N.Y.2d 808, 202 N.Y.S.2d 24, 168 N.E.2d 255.

70. See infra, § 88.

71. 1 Harper & James, Torts, 1956, Sec. 1.24 at 69; Prosser, Nuisance Without Fault, 1942, 20 Tex.L.Rev. 399, 419–20.

72. Morgan v. High Penn Oil Co., 1953, 238 N.C. 185, 77 S.E.2d 682; Bartel v. Ridgefield Lumber Co., 1924, 131 Wash. 183, 229 P. 306; Dixon v. New York Trap Rock Corp., 1944, 293 N.Y. 509, 58 N.E.2d 517. Keeton, Trespass, Nuisance, and Strict Liability, 1959, 59 Colum.L.Rev. 457. See, also, Second Restatement of Torts, § 822.

73. Tex.1971, 474 S.W.2d 184.

74. Id. at 189.

tentionally inflicted. Therefore, if liability is imposed, it is not liability without fault.

 WESTLAW REFERENCES

The Interest Protected
nuisance* /s howl! bark! /s dog*
private /4 nuisance* & hazard! toxic poison! chemical /s waste wastes

Property Rights Protected
private /4 nuisance* /p "property right*"

Distinguished from Trespass
private /4 nuisance* /p trespass!

The Requirements for Recovery on a Private Nuisance Theory
private /4 nuisance* /p interfer! /p intent!

Physical Harm and Mental or Physical Discomfort Distinguished
nuisance* /p fear /p explod! explosion*

The Intentional Interference Requirement
nuisance* /s continu! /s know! aware! % "attractive nuisance*"

§ 88. Substantial and Unreasonable Interference

The law does not concern itself with trifles, or seek to remedy all the petty annoyances and disturbances of everyday life in a civilized community even from conduct committed with knowledge that annoyance and inconvenience will result.[1] Acting with the intention of causing mental distress is, therefore, not a tort and acting with the intention of annoying someone in the use and enjoyment of his property is not in and of itself a tort. The interference must be substantial and unreasonable.[2] Thus, it has been held that there is no nuisance arising from the mere unsightliness of the defendant's premises,[3] from the temporary muddying of a well,[4] or from an occasional unpleasant odor[5] or whiff of smoke.[6] But all of these types of interferences can under certain circumstances be actionable. The interference must be substantial and unreasonable. Substantial simply means a significant harm to the plaintiff and unreasonably means that it would not be reasonable to permit the defendant to cause such an amount of harm intentionally without compensating for it. It is not necessarily a justification on the issue of damages that the social value or utility of the defendant's conduct outweighs the gravity of the harm that is being done.

§ 88

1. Thus even the legislature may not constitutionally declare a thing a nuisance when it does not interfere substantially with public or private interests. Yates v. City of Milwaukee, 1870, 77 U.S. (10 Wall.) 497, 19 L.Ed. 984; Boyd v. Board of Councilmen of Frankfort, 1903, 117 Ky. 199, 77 S.W. 669; Prior v. White, 1938, 132 Fla. 1, 180 So. 347; City of San Antonio v. Salvation Army, Tex.Civ.App.1910, 127 S.W. 860, error refused.

2. Theil v. Cernin, 1955, 224 Ark. 854, 276 S.W.2d 677; McCann v. Chasm Power Co., 1914, 211 N.Y. 301, 105 N.E. 416; City of Richmond v. House, 1917, 177 Ky. 814, 198 S.W. 218; Cook v. City of Fall River, 1921, 239 Mass. 90, 131 N.E. 346; Gainey v. Folkman, D.Ariz.1954, 114 F.Supp. 231.

3. State Road Commission v. Oakes, 1966, 150 W.Va. 709, 149 S.E.2d 293; Livingston v. Davis, 1951, 243 Iowa 21, 50 N.W.2d 592; Feldstein v. Kammauf, 1956, 209 Md. 479, 121 A.2d 716; Crabtree v. City Auto Salvage Co., 1960, 47 Tenn.App. 616, 340 S.W.2d 940; Vermont Salvage Corp. v. Village of St. Johnsbury, 1943, 113 Vt. 341, 34 A.2d 188.

In Mathewson v. Primeau, 1964, 64 Wn.2d 929, 395 P.2d 183, it was said that there was a trend toward the protection of aesthetic values, but it was by legislation and not by injunction.

Aesthetic considerations may, however, play an important part in determining reasonable use. See Parkersburg Builders Material Co. v. Barrack, 1937, 118 W.Va. 608, 191 S.E. 368, 192 S.E. 291; Noel, Unaesthetic Sights as Nuisance, 1939, 25 Corn.L.Q. 1; Note, 1937, 44 W.Va.L.Q. 58.

4. Taylor v. Bennett, 1836, 7 C. & P. 329, 173 Eng. Rep. 146.

5. Jones v. Adler, 1913, 183 Ala. 435, 62 So. 777; Francisco v. Department of Institutions and Agencies, 1935, 13 N.J.Misc. 663, 180 A. 843; Thiel v. Cernin, 1955, 224 Ark. 854, 276 S.W.2d 677; cf. Wade v. Miller, 1905, 188 Mass. 6, 73 N.E. 849.

6. Holman v. Athens Empire Laundry Co., 1919, 149 Ga. 345, 100 S.E. 207. This may have been carried too far in Reynolds v. Community Fuel Co., 1949, 309 Ky. 716, 218 S.W.2d 950, where there appears to have been substantial noise and dust disturbing plaintiff's dwelling, but recovery was denied because most of the witnesses said that they would not have objected to it.

Physical Harm to Land or Tangible Property

When the invasion affects the physical condition of the plaintiff's land,[7] the substantial or significant character of the interference is not in doubt. It is generally true also that it is regarded as unreasonable not to compensate the plaintiff for the significant harm thus caused.[8] In Jost v. Dairyland Power Cooperative,[9] the fact that defendant's coal burning electric generating plant caused some physical damage and loss of value to plaintiff's alfalfa crops and, therefore, a diminution in market value of the land was enough to constitute substantial damage as a matter of law. It would seem reasonably clear that almost any measurable economic loss suffered as a consequence of physical damage intentionally caused will be regarded as substantial. Moreover, if it appears to be fairer and more feasible, technologically and economically, to internalize this as a cost of carrying on the defendant's industrial or business enterprise, the interference will be regarded as unreasonable.[10] Thus, if it is found that the defendant has knowingly polluted soil, surface, or underground water and this pollution has affected to any measurable extent the rental or market value of the plaintiff's land, there normally would be both substantial and unreasonable interference.[11] Moreover, soil and water pollution are especially likely to result in the granting of injunctive relief, without a showing of any existing reduction in rental or market value. This would be due in part to the enormous weight that is given to the preservation of our natural resources and the protection of the environment from physical impairment. It is also attributable to the fact that injunctive relief is ofttimes available when a tort is merely threatened, if the threat is of the kind that could result in irreparable harm.[12] The rule that injunctive relief will not be available until there is a reasonable likelihood of substantial harm resulting therefrom[13] is not as likely to be applied in this type of situation.[14]

Physical Discomfort and Mental Annoyance

When defendant's conduct involves mere physical discomfort or mental annoyance, there is somewhat more difficulty in deciding when the interference is substantial and unreasonable justifying a recovery for damages. Probably a good working rule would be that the annoyance cannot amount to unreasonable interference until it results in a depreciation in the market or rental value of the land. It has been said that the standard for the determination of significant and unreasonable is the standard of normal persons in the particular locality. If normal

---

7. Hoare & Co. v. McAlpin & Sons, [1928] 1 Ch. 167, 92 L.J.Ch. 81; Sam Warren & Son Stone Co. v. Gruesser, 1948, 397 Ky. 98, 209 S.W.2d 817; Transcontinental Gas Pipe Line Co. v. Gault, 4th Cir. 1952, 198 F.2d 196.

8. Weinstein v. Lake Pearl Park, Inc., 1964, 347 Mass. 91, 196 N.E.2d 638. Cf. Lind v. City of San Luis Obispo, 1895, 109 Cal. 340, 42 P. 437 (depositing sewage); Hark v. Mountain Fork Lumber Co., 1945, 127 W.Va. 586, 34 S.E.2d 348 (laying tramway tracks). See also, Millet v. Minnesota Crushed Stone Co., 1920, 145 Minn. 475, 177 N.W. 641, reargument denied 145 Minn. 475, 179 N.W. 682; Dixon v. New York Trap Rock Corp., 1944, 293 N.Y. 509, 58 N.E.2d 517.

9. 1970, 45 Wis.2d 164, 172 N.W.2d 647.

10. See, Boomer v. Atlantic Cement Co., 1970, 26 N.Y.2d 219, 309 N.Y.S.2d 312, 257 N.E.2d 870, on remand 72 Misc.2d 834, 340 N.Y.S.2d 97, affirmed 42 A.D.2d 496, 349 N.Y.S.2d 199.

11. On one theory or another, courts have normally imposed liability. Conner v. Woodfill, 1890, 126 Ind. 85, 25 N.E. 876; Rinzler v. Folsom, 1953, 209 Ga. 549, 74 S.E.2d 661; Ciconte v. Shockley, 1950, 31 Del.Ch. 376, 75 A.2d 242. Annot., 48 A.L.R. 1248. See Keeton, Tort Liability and the Oil and Gas Industry II, 1961, 39 Tex.L.Rev. 253.

12. Swaine v. Great Northern Railway Co., 1864, 4 De G.J. & S. 211, 46 Eng.Rep. 899; Rhodes v. Dunbar, 1868, 57 Pa. 274; Purcell v. Davis, 1935, 100 Mont. 480, 50 P.2d 255.

13. Hannum v. Oak Lane Shopping Center, 1956, 383 Pa. 618, 119 A.2d 213; Wilcher v. Sharpe, 1952, 236 N.C. 308, 72 S.E.2d 662; Kimmons v. Benson, 1952, 220 Ark. 299, 247 S.W.2d 468; Foster v. County of Genesee, 1951, 329 Mich. 665, 46 N.W.2d 426; Turner v. City of Spokane, 1951, 39 Wn.2d 332, 235 P.2d 300.

14. See, Nicholson v. Connecticut Half-Way House, Inc., 1966, 153 Conn. 507, 218 A.2d 383, 21 A.L.R.3d 1051.

persons living in the area or community would regard the invasion in question as definitely offensive, seriously annoying, or intolerable, then the invasion is both significant and unreasonable.[15]

As has been stated, the conduct must affect "the ordinary comfort of human existence as understood by the American people in their present state of enlightenment."[16] It is not a nuisance to ring a church bell, merely because it throws a hypersensitive individual into convulsions,[17] to blow a whistle,[18] or play croquet[19] or even baseball[20] where the noise affects the health of a nervous invalid, or to run a factory where the smoke aggravates the plaintiff's bronchitis,[21] or the vibration shakes down a rickety house.[22] In some of these instances, the harm may very well be significant to the plaintiff but the interference cannot be regarded as the kind for which the defendant should be liable in damages. Business enterprise should not be required to bear the costs of suffering of those who are hypersensitive.

The plaintiff cannot, by devoting his own land to an unusually sensitive use, such as a drive-in motion picture theatre easily affected by light,[23] make a nuisance out of conduct of the adjoining defendant which would not involve significant annoyance or harm to one making a normal use. By the same token, the fact that there are people who are hardened to the discomfort will not prevent the existence of a nuisance affecting a normal

---

15. See Second Restatement of Torts, § 821F, Comment d.

16. Joyce, Nuisances, 1906, § 20; Everett v. Paschall, 1910, 61 Wash. 47, 111 P. 879. The customs of the community are to be taken into account. In a small Massachusetts town in 1905, poultry odors and noises were held not to be offensive to the ordinary citizen. Wade v. Miller, 1905, 188 Mass. 6, 73 N.E. 849.

17. Rogers v. Elliott, 1888, 146 Mass. 349, 15 N.E. 768. Accord: Dorsett v. Nunis, 1941, 191 Ga. 559, 13 S.E.2d 371 (church); Lord v. DeWitt, C.C.N.Y.1902, 116 F. 713 (blasting; plaintiff had a weak heart); Gunther v. E.I. Du Pont de Nemours & Co., N.D.W.Va.1957, 157 F.Supp. 25, appeal dismissed 4th Cir., 1958, 255 F.2d 710 (blasting; nervous woman frightened by noise); Myer v. Minard, La.App.1945, 21 So.2d 72 (crowing rooster).

"Exceptionally nervous persons, or those whose refinement exceeds the standards of the 'American people in their present state of enlightenment,' as the Washington court put it, must seek refuge in sound proof rooms, if they can afford them, or take their chances of the padded cell." Lloyd, Noise as a Nuisance, 1934, 82 U.Pa.L.Rev. 567, 582.

18. Meeks v. Wood, 1918, 66 Ind.App. 594, 118 N.E. 591. The disturbing effect of a continued noise which is not unduly loud may, however, be enough to make it a nuisance. Kentucky & West Virginia Power Co. v. Anderson, 1941, 288 Ky. 501, 156 S.W.2d 857; Stodder v. Rosen Talking Machine Co., 1922, 241 Mass. 245, 135 N.E. 251.

19. Akers v. Marsh, 1901, 19 App.D.C. 28. Accord: Wade v. Miller, 1905, 188 Mass. 6, 73 N.E. 849 (odor and noise from henhouse); Columbus Gaslight & Coke Co. v. Freeland, 1861, 12 Ohio St. 392 (factory odors); Meyer v. Kemper Ice Co., 1935, 180 La. 1037, 158 So. 378 (factory noise).

20. Warren Co. v. Dickson, 1938, 185 Ga. 481, 195 S.E. 568; Beckman v. Marshall, Fla.1956, 85 So.2d 552; Lieberman v. Township of Saddle River, 1955, 37 N.J. Super. 62, 116 A.2d 809.

21. Ladd v. Granite State Brick Co., 1894, 68 N.H. 185, 37 A. 1041. Accord: Aldridge v. Saxey, 1965, 242 Or. 238, 409 P.2d 184 (German shepherd dogs not a nuisance because plaintiff suffered from emphysema and was home all day); Erickson v. Hudson, 1952, 70 Wyo. 317, 249 P.2d 523 (allergy to creosote). Cf. Salvin v. North Brancepeth Coal Co., 1874 L.R. 9 Ch. 705 ("the damage must be such as can be shewn by a plain witness to a plain common juryman").

22. Cremidas v. Fenton, 1916, 223 Mass. 249, 111 N.E. 855. Accord: Henn v. Universal Atlas Cement Co., Ohio C.P.1957, 144 N.E.2d 917 (blasting in farm area, causing non-damaging earth tremors). Cf. Hoare & Co. v. McAlpin & Sons, [1923] 1 Ch. 167, 92 L.J.Ch. 81.

23. Amphitheatres, Inc. v. Portland Meadows, 1948, 184 Or. 336, 198 P.2d 847; Sheridan Drive-In Theatre v. State, Wyo.1963, 384 P.2d 597; Belmar Drive-In Theatre Co. v. Illinois State Toll Highway Commission, 1966, 34 Ill.2d 544, 216 N.E.2d 788.

Accord, as to electrical interference: Eastern & South African Tel. Co. v. Cape Town Tramways Co., [1902] A.C. 381; Lake Shore & Michigan Southern Railway Co. v. Chicago, Lake Shore & South Bend Railway Co., 1911, 48 Ind.App. 584, 92 N.E. 989, rehearing denied 48 Ind.App. 584, 95 N.E. 596; Postal Telegraph-Cable Co. v. Pacific Gas & Electric Co., 1927, 202 Cal. 382, 260 P. 1101. Cf. Robinson v. Kilvert, 1889, 41 Ch. Div. 88 (sensitive photographic equipment).

The possibility should be noted, however, that if the defendant is aware of plaintiff's extra-sensitive use he may be liable for negligence, although not for nuisance. Bell v. Gray-Robinson Construction Co., 1954, 265 Wis. 652, 62 N.W.2d 390 (mink frightened by noisy machinery); Lahar v. Barnes, 1958, 353 Mich. 408, 91 N.W.2d 261 (same).

person.[24] Fears and feelings common to most of the community are to be considered; and the dread of contagion from a pesthouse, common to ordinary citizens, may make it a nuisance, although there is no foundation in scientific fact.[25]

Unreasonable Interference

The interference with the protected interest must not only be substantial, but it must also be unreasonable. "Life in organized society, and especially in populous communities, involves an unavoidable clash of individual interests. Practically all human activities, unless carried on in a wilderness, interfere to some extent with others or involve some risk of interference, and these interferences range from mere trifling annoyances to serious harms. It is an obvious truth that each individual in a community must put up with a certain amount of annoyance, inconvenience and interference, and must take a certain amount of risk in order that all may get on together. The very existence of organized society depends upon the principle of 'give and take, live and let live,' and therefore the law of torts does not attempt to impose liability or shift the loss in every case where one person's conduct has some detrimental effect on another. Liability is imposed only in those cases where the harm or risk to one is greater than he ought to be required to bear under the circumstances, at least without compensation." [26]

Confusion has resulted from the fact that the intentional interference with the plaintiff's use of his property can be unreasonable even when the defendant's conduct is reasonable. This is simply because a reasonable person could conclude that the plaintiff's loss resulting from the intentional interference ought to be allocated to the defendant. The ultimate decision as to the unreasonableness of the interference is for the jury in a suit for damages, except when the circumstances are such as to indicate no basis for a reasonable difference of opinion.[27] Courts have often found the existence of a nuisance on the basis of unreasonable use when what was meant is that the interference was unreasonable, i.e., it was unreasonable for the defendant to act as he did without paying for the harm that was knowingly inflicted on the plaintiff. Thus, an industrial enterprise who properly locates a cement plant or a coal-burning electric generator, who exercises utmost care in the utilization of known scientific techniques for minimizing the harm from the emission of noxious smoke, dust and gas and who is serving society well by engaging in the activity may yet be required to pay for the inevitable harm caused to neighbors.[28] This is simply a decision that the harm thus intentionally inflicted should be regarded as a cost of doing the kind of business in which the defendant is engaged.

This has led to the fallacious notion that nuisance liability is a type of liability with-

---

24. Powell v. Bentley & Gerwig Furniture Co., 1891, 34 W.Va. 804, 12 S.E. 1085; Cunningham v. Miller, 1922, 178 Wis. 220, 189 N.W. 531; Cumberland Corp. v. Metropoulos, 1922, 241 Mass. 491, 135 N.E. 693; Wheat Culvert Co. v. Jenkins, 1932, 246 Ky. 319, 55 S.W.2d 4; Board of Health of Lyndhurst Township v. United Cork Companies, 1934, 116 N.J.Eq. 4, 172 A. 347, affirmed 1935, 117 N.J.Eq. 437, 176 A. 142.

25. Everett v. Paschall, 1910, 61 Wash. 47, 111 P. 879; City of Baltimore v. Fairfield Improvement Co., 1898, 87 Md. 352, 39 A. 1081; Cherry v. Williams, 1908, 147 N.C. 452, 61 S.E. 267; Stotler v. Rochelle, 1910, 83 Kan. 86, 109 P. 788; cf. Benton v. Pittard, 1944, 197 Ga. 843, 31 S.E.2d 6 (venereal disease clinic). See, however, Nicholson v. Connecticut Half-way House, Inc., 1966, 153 Conn. 507, 218 A.2d 383 (mere unfounded apprehension not enough in itself).

26. Second Restatement of Torts, § 822, Comment j.

27. The jury decides what constitutes an "unreasonable interference" with the use and enjoyment of property for purposes of the legal action for damages resulting from a nuisance. Patterson v. Peabody Coal Co., 1954, 3 Ill.App.2d 311, 122 N.E.2d 48; Fuchs v. Curran Carbonizing & Engineering Co., Mo.App.1955, 279 S.W.2d 211.

28. Wheat v. Freeman Coal Mining Corp., 1974, 23 Ill.App.3d 14, 319 N.E.2d 290; Jost v. Dairyland Power Cooperative, 1970, 45 Wis.2d 164, 172 N.W.2d 647; Boomer v. Atlantic Cement Co., 1970, 26 N.Y.2d 219, 309 N.Y.S.2d 312, 257 N.E.2d 870, on remand 72 Misc. 2d 834, 340 N.Y.S.2d 97, affirmed 42 A.D.2d 496, 349 N.Y.S.2d 199.

out fault. But this is not so since the harm or loss results from an intentional rather than an accidental invasion.

Whether or not the plaintiff or the defendant should be required to bear the loss of substantial interference to plaintiff from defendant's reasonable conduct depends upon a number of factors. Some of these would be the following: (1) the amount of the harm resulting from the interference; (2) the relative capacity of the plaintiff and the defendant to bear the loss by way of shifting the loss to the consuming public at large as a cost of doing business or by other means such as some type of insurance; (3) the nature of the plaintiff's use of his property; (4) the nature of the defendant's use of his property; (5) the nature of the locality; (6) priority in time as to the respective activities of the plaintiff and the defendant in the area.

If both plaintiff and defendant are enterprisers and in a position to bear the costs and neither is making a particularly sensitive use of his property, plaintiff may very well be required to absorb the loss as one of the necessary consequences of living and working in a complex, industrialized society.[29] If, on the other hand, plaintiff is a farmer, it is likely that the destruction of the value of his farm by a giant corporate enterprise will not be tolerated, however unreasonable the conduct.[30] If the plaintiff's use of his property is highly sensitive, the risk of loss from such a usage would normally be borne by the plaintiff unless it could be shown that defendant's conduct was unreasonable under the circumstances.[31] Those who build residences in a rural area, and beyond the limits of a city and zoning regulations and the protection thus afforded, do so for many reasons, but they may justly and fairly be required to accept certain hazards of so doing.[32] Moreover, if an industrial enterpriser first arrived in an area and plaintiff at a modest price purchased a tract for residential use, the fact that his use and enjoyment for such a purpose is substantially affected is not, generally speaking, a sufficient justification for relief.

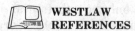

WESTLAW REFERENCES

private /4 nuisance* /s substantial /s unreasonable

Physical Harm to Land or Tangible Property

nuisance* /p recover! damages award! /s reduc! loss diminution /s value* price*

Physical Discomfort and Mental Annoyance

nuisance* /s hypersensitiv! sensitiv!

Unreasonable Interference

nuisance* /s unreasonabl! /s interfer!

---

§ 88A. Unreasonable Conduct and Injunctive Relief

As stated earlier, practically all human activities interfere to some extent with others in the use and enjoyment of land. Those who engage in such activities, therefore, are knowingly and thus intentionally interfering with the use and enjoyment of land. Such conduct is unreasonable only if the gravity of the harm caused outweighs the utility of the conduct. This would be so if a reasonable person would conclude that the amount of the harm done outweighs the benefits served by the conduct. It is also true even if the benefits outweigh the harm, if a reasonable person would conclude that there was a feasible way, economically and scien-

---

29. Morris on Torts, 2nd ed. 1980, Ch. 10 on Private Nuisance, Sec. 8 on Nuisance Litigation Between Commercial or Industrial Neighbors.

30. Madison v. Ducktown Sulphur, Copper & Iron Co., 1904, 113 Tenn. 331, 83 S.W. 658; Jost v. Dairyland Power Cooperative, 1970, 45 Wis.2d 164, 172 N.W.2d 647. See, Morris on Torts, 2nd ed. 1980, supra, note 29 at p. 267.

31. Amphitheaters, Inc. v. Portland Meadows, 1948, 184 Or. 336, 198 P.2d 847; Lynn Open Air Theatre, Inc.

v. Sea Crest Cadillac-Pontiac, Inc., 1973, 1 Mass.App. Ct. 186, 294 N.E.2d 473.

32. Oak Haven Trailer Court, Inc. v. Western Wayne County Conservation Association, 1966, 3 Mich. App. 83, 141 N.W.2d 645, affirmed 380 Mich. 526, 158 N.W.2d 463; Mercer v. Brown, Fla.App.1966, 190 So.2d 610.

tifically, to avoid a substantial amount of the harm without material impairment to the benefits.

When the plaintiff wishes to have an activity enjoined on the theory of a nuisance, it is necessary to show that defendant's conduct in carrying on the activity at the place and at the time the injunction is sought is unreasonable.[1] Thus, the issue is quite different from that as to entitlement of damages. There has ofttimes been a failure to perceive this fundamental distinction between entitlement to damages and entitlement to abatement of the nuisance. A court which arms the plaintiff with an injunction when the defendant's conduct is reasonable may stifle or oppress a reasonable enterprise at the location where it is being carried out rather than require it to carry its just and fair costs. The line must be drawn between enterprises and activities of such social value that they should be continued on the condition that those injured may be made whole, and those of insufficient value justifying a footing of the bill for the harms which they do.[2]

It is, therefore, clear that when defendant acts knowing, and therefore intending, that his conduct will or does interfere with plaintiff in the use and enjoyment of his property, a court may arrive at one of three conclusions: (1) the social interest is best served by requiring the plaintiff to bear the burden of the type of hardship suffered; (2) the social interest is best served by concluding that the defendant's activity is a socially desirable one under the circumstances and should not be altered or abated, but a cost of carrying on that activity should be borne by the defendant; therefore, the activity is a nuisance, justifying a tort action for damages; or (3) the social interest is best served by permitting the plaintiff, if he wishes, to enjoin the activity on the theory that the conduct at the time and place is unreasonable in the sense that the gravity of the harm outweighs the utility of the conduct.

The denial of injunctive relief for conduct that has been regarded as a nuisance justifying a damage recovery has generally in the past been based on a doctrine commonly referred to as "balancing the equities."[3] The approach to enjoining a nuisance is much like the approach to enjoining encroachment of a building—the relative equities of the parties and the interests of the public and an injunction issued or denied as the balance seems to indicate. The weighing of hardships and interests on the issue of injunctive relief has generally been regarded as an issue of law in large part because of the fact that issues related to equitable relief have not historically been tried to a jury.[4]

There is an older tradition that once a nuisance is established and it is shown that

---

§ 88A

1. Boomer v. Atlantic Cement Co., 1970, 26 N.Y.2d 219, 309 N.Y.S.2d 312, 257 N.E.2d 870, on remand 72 Misc.2d 834, 340 N.Y.S.2d 97, affirmed 42 A.D.2d 496, 349 N.Y.S.2d 199; Keeton, Trespass, Nuisance and Strict Liability, 1959, 59 Colum.L.Rev. 457, 458–59.

2. Keeton & Morris, Notes on Balancing the Equities, 1940, 18 Texas Law Review 412, 418; for interesting cases raising the problem, see Salem Iron Co. v. Hyland, 1906, 74 Ohio St. 160, 77 N.E. 751; Berkey v. Berwind-White Coal Mining Co., 1908, 220 Pa. 65, 69 A. 329, 16 L.R.A. 851; Whiles v. Grand Junction Mining and Fuel Co., 1929, 86 Colo. 418, 282 P. 260; Madison v. Ducktown Sulphur, Copper & Iron Co., 1904, 113 Tenn. 331, 83 S.W. 658.

3. Haack v. Lindsay Light & Chemical Co., 1946, 393 Ill. 367, 66 N.E.2d 391 (essential war work); Storey v. Central Hide & Rendering Co., 1950, 148 Tex. 509, 226 S.W.2d 615 (only plant in county); Antonik v. Chamberlain, 1947, 81 Ohio App. 465, 78 N.E.2d 752 ("life and death of a legitimate and necessary business"); Koseris v. J.R. Simplot Co., 1960, 82 Idaho 263, 352 P.2d 235 (over 1,000 employees).

As to the balancing of several factors, see Elliott Nursery Co. v. Du Quesne Light Co., 1924, 281 Pa. 166, 126 A. 345; Edwards v. Allouez Mining Co., 1878, 38 Mich. 46; Bliss v. Washoe Copper Co., 9th Cir. 1911, 186 F. 789, certiorari dismissed 231 U.S. 764, 34 S.Ct. 327, 58 L.Ed. 471; McCarthy v. Bunker Hill & Sullivan Mining & Coal Co., 9th Cir. 1908, 164 F. 927, certiorari denied 212 U.S. 583, 29 S.Ct. 692, 53 L.Ed. 660.

See McClintock, Equity, 1936, §§ 140, 141; McClintock, Discretion to Deny Injunction Against Trespass and Nuisance, 1926, 12 Minn.L.Rev. 565; Morris and Keeton, Notes on "Balancing the Equities," 1940, 18 Tex.L.Rev. 412; Notes, 1927, 37 Yale L.J. 96; 1922, 36 Harv.L.Rev. 211; 1933, 40 W.Va.L.Q. 59.

4. See Dobbs, Remedies, 1973, Sec. 2.6 on Law and Equity Today—The Effects of Merger.

damages do not furnish an adequate remedy, an injunction must issue.[5] There are certainly cases following this extreme view as, for example, the New York case in which the court in 1913 shut down a pulp mill representing an investment of over a million dollars because of its stream pollution.[6] But in 1970, New York rejected its older cases and accepted the notion that some balancing was necessary. As a result, the Court of Appeals denied an injunction that would have closed a 45 million dollar cement plant and granted permanent damages instead.[7] It has been observed that this decision may well draw into the majority camp any remaining holdouts against the balancing doctrine.[8] The old view was calculated to lead to two different kinds of questionable results: sometimes a court would be reluctant to conclude that a nuisance did exist when the enterprise ought to have been required to bear the cost; at other times, it led to the granting of injunctive relief when the plaintiff should have been limited to a recovery of damages. In any event, the modern and best approach is to grant the equitable remedy of injunctive relief when the gravity of the harm from the activity exceeds the utility of the conduct.

The fundamental difference between the right to damages and the right to equitable relief as regards activities that constitute alleged nuisances is well illustrated by a fairly recent case.

In Baldwin v. McClendon,[9] plaintiff's home had for some fifteen years been a forty-seven acre farm located in a rural area. The defendant commenced hog production on a large commercial scale adjoining the plaintiff's home. The court concluded in the first place that the odors and gases which came from the hog product in operations were of such volume and intensity as to cause substantial interference justifying a recovery of damages. On the other hand, the court also held that if the plaintiffs were compensated for the depreciation in the market value of the land then the activity would not be enjoined. Even in this type of case, if the activity is of the kind that is likely to be continued indefinitely, most modern courts are likely to order the nuisance abated unless a lump sum amount for the depreciation in market value is paid. Thus, the plaintiff is not burdened with the problem of either bringing successive actions for damages or of collecting an unsecured judgment for permanent damages.

Legislative Authority

Just as the legislature, within its constitutional limitations [10] may declare particular conduct to be a public nuisance and punishable and enjoinable as such by the proper governmental unit, or tortious as a private nuisance, it may authorize that which would otherwise be either a public nuisance or a private nuisance. In England where parliamentary authority is not limited, such action is final, and it is a complete defense that nothing has been done except that which has been authorized.[11] In America, the power of a legislative body, i.e., the Congress, the state legislature, or a city council, is, of course, subject to constitutional restraints, discussion of which is beyond the scope of this text. In general, the state cannot take or authorize the taking of private property, even for a public purpose, without compensating the owner therefor.[12] So authorizing someone to commit a private nuisance can

---

5. See Annot. 61 A.L.R. 924.

6. Whalen v. Union Bag & Paper Co., 1913, 208 N.Y. 1, 101 N.E. 805.

7. Boomer v. Atlantic Cement Co., 1970, 26 N.Y.2d 219, 309 N.Y.S.2d 312, 257 N.E.2d 870, on remand 72 Misc.2d 834, 340 N.Y.S.2d 97, affirmed 42 A.D.2d 496, 349 N.Y.S.2d 199.

8. Dobbs, Remedies, 1973, Sec. 5.7, p. 358.

9. 1974, 292 Ala. 43, 288 So.2d 761.

10. See Yates v. City of Milwaukee, 1870, 77 U.S. (10 Wall.) 497, 19 L.Ed. 984; City of Evansville v. Miller, 1897, 146 Ind. 613, 45 N.E. 1054; Boyd v. Board of Councilmen of Frankfort, 1903, 117 Ky. 199, 77 S.W. 669; Prior v. White, 1938, 132 Fla. 1, 180 So. 347.

11. Hammersmith R. Co. v. Brand, 1869, L.R. 4 H.L. 171; Quebec R. Co. v. Vandry, [1920] A.C. 662, 89 L.J.P.C. 99; Salmond, Law of Torts, 8th ed. 1934, 47.

12. See Richards v. Washington Terminal Co., 1914, 233 U.S. 546, 34 S.Ct. 654, 58 L.Ed. 1088; Sawyer v.

be an authorization to take property unconstitutionally.

In a good many instances, the activity of the defendant, from which the plaintiff seeks either injunctive or damage relief, is the kind of activity permitted by a zoning ordinance or license or special statute. This does not mean that the enacting body intended to immunize a defendant (even if it could do so) who made this kind of use at any location within the area of permissible use and under all circumstances. The fact that the activity is of the general kind permitted is relevant as indicating something about the present and probable future character of the neighborhood. Most courts hold that zoning ordinances do not protect the defendant from a claim by a particular plaintiff that the defendant's use is an unreasonable interference with the use and enjoyment by the plaintiff of his property and, therefore, a private nuisance, justifying under some circumstances abatement and under other circumstances only damages.[13] Generally, however, compliance with a zoning ordinance will preclude a finding of a public nuisance.[14]

There would seem to be a fundamental difference between a general zoning ordinance that authorizes many different kinds of uses within broad classifications and an authorization of a specific use such as the authorization of a site for an airport or the authorization of an airport extension. When a legislative body authorizes a specific use, that would seem to be a declaration that it is in the public interest for the activity to be conducted at that particular place. So long, therefore, as reasonable care is exercised to minimize the extent of the interference with others, the activity would probably not be enjoinable as a private nuisance.[15] If, on the other hand, the market value of private property were substantially depreciated as a consequence of the activity, a court could conclude that there was such an unreasonable interference as to constitute a private nuisance or an unconstitutional taking of private property.

 WESTLAW REFERENCES

sh 288 so2d 761

Legislative Authority
zon! /p private /4 nuisance

§ 88B. Conduct of Others and the Plaintiff as Factors of Importance

Conduct of Others

The extent to which others in the vicinity are causing a similar interference with the plaintiff's convenience is a factor to be considered in determining whether the defendant's conduct is reasonable. If a locality is given over predominantly to manufacturing, the plaintiff will have less right to complain of factory noise or smoke than if it is of a residential character.[1] What is a nuisance in Palm Springs is not necessarily one in Pittsburgh. But where such other activities fall short of devoting the locality to a particular use,[2] or where the defendant's conduct is found to be unreasonable even in such a

---

Davis, 1884, 136 Mass. 239; Bacon v. City of Boston, 1891, 154 Mass. 100, 28 N.E. 9; Sadlier v. City of New York, 1903, 40 Misc. 78, 81 N.Y.S. 308, reversed on other grounds 1905, 104 App.Div. 82, 93 N.Y.S. 579, affirmed 1906, 185 N.Y. 408, 78 N.E. 272.

13. Maykut v. Plasko, 1976, 170 Conn. 310, 365 A.2d 1114; DeNucci v. Pezza, 1974, 114 R.I. 123, 329 A.2d 807; Hobbs v. Smith, 1972, 177 Colo. 299, 493 P.2d 1352; Desruisseau v. Isley, 1976, 27 Ariz.App. 257, 553 P.2d 1242; Ebel v. County Road Commissioners of Saginaw, 1972, 386 Mich. 598, 194 N.W.2d 365.

14. See § 90 on Public Nuisance.

15. See Hub Theatres, Inc. v. Massachusetts Port Authority, 1976, 370 Mass. 153, 346 N.E.2d 371, appeal dismissed, certiorari denied 429 U.S. 891, 97 S.Ct. 249, 50 L.Ed.2d 174.

§ 88B

1. Thus activities of others which are in themselves no defense are to be considered in determining the nature of the locality. Hobson v. Walker, La.App.1949, 41 So.2d 789; Waier v. Peerless Oil Co., 1933, 265 Mich. 398, 251 N.W. 552. See supra, § 88.

2. Cleveland v. Citizens' Gaslight Co., 1869, 20 N.J. Eq. 201.

place,³ the fact that others are polluting a stream,⁴ diverting water from it,⁵ flooding the plaintiff's land,⁶ or filling the air with noise⁷ or smells and smoke,⁸ will not be a defense to an action based on the defendant's nuisance. A dozen nuisances do not each obtain immunity because they all interfere with the plaintiff's use of his land. Where the damage done is incapable of any practical division, as where a river polluted with oil burns a barn,⁹ or poisons cattle,¹⁰ each will be liable for the entire loss. But in the usual case the interference with the plaintiff's enjoyment, by noise, smoke, odors, pollution or flooding, is regarded by the courts as capable of some rough apportionment according to the extent to which each defendant has contributed, and it is held that each will be liable only for his proportionate share of the harm.¹¹

There are occasional cases in which the conduct of each of two or more defendants, taken alone, would cause no unreasonable interference, but all together amount to a nuisance. One may pollute a stream to some extent without any harm, but if several do the same thing the plaintiff's use of the stream may be destroyed. It has been held consistently in these cases that each defendant is liable.¹² The explanation given is that mentioned earlier,¹³ that the conduct of each, however reasonable it would be in itself, becomes unreasonable in view of what the others are doing. It may not be a nuisance to obstruct a small part of a highway and leave room for passage, but it becomes one when some one else obstructs the rest of the street.¹⁴

Coming to a Nuisance—Conduct of Plaintiff

Courts have quite frequently given consideration to the problem of "coming to a nuisance." Priority in time as to the respective uses by plaintiff and defendant is an important consideration, both as to the existence of a nuisance giving rise to a right to re-

---

3. Waier v. Peerless Oil Co., 1933, 265 Mich. 398, 251 N.W. 552; Ross v. Butler, 1868, 19 N.J.Eq. 294.

4. Beach v. Sterling Iron & Zinc Co., 1895, 54 N.J.Eq. 65, 33 A. 286, affirmed 55 N.J.Eq. 824, 41 A. 1117; Parker v. American Woolen Co., 1913, 215 Mass. 176, 102 N.E. 360; Weston Paper Co. v. Pope, 1900, 155 Ind. 394, 57 N.E. 719; Thomas v. Ohio Coal Co., 1916, 199 Ill.App. 50.

5. Gould v. Stafford, 1888, 77 Cal. 66, 18 P. 879; Elkhart Paper Co. v. Fulkerson, 1905, 36 Ind.App. 219, 75 N.E. 283.

6. Coleman v. Bennett, 1902, 111 Tenn. 705, 69 S.W. 734; Verheyen v. Dewey, 1915, 27 Idaho 1, 146 P. 1116; Birch v. Boston & Maine Railroad, 1927, 259 Mass. 528, 156 N.E. 859.

7. Fox v. Ewers, 1949, 195 Md. 650, 75 A.2d 357; Robinson v. Baugh, 1875, 31 Mich. 290.

8. Bollinger v. American Asphalt Roof Co., 1929, 224 Mo.App. 98, 19 S.W.2d 544; Richards v. Daugherty, 1902, 133 Ala. 569, 31 So. 934; Waier v. Peerless Oil Co., 1933, 265 Mich. 398, 251 N.W. 552; Jordan v. United Verde Copper Co., D.Ariz.1925, 9 F.2d 144, affirmed 14 F.2d 299, affirmed 14 F.2d 304, certiorari denied 273 U.S. 734, 47 S.Ct. 243, 71 L.Ed. 865.

Custom is not necessarily a defense. Iverson v. Vint, 1952, 243 Iowa 949, 54 N.W.2d 494.

9. Northup v. Eakes, 1918, 72 Okl. 66, 178 P. 266; Phillips Petroleum Co. v. Vandergriff, 1942, 190 Okl. 280, 122 P.2d 1020. Cf. Slater v. Mersereau, 1878, 64 N.Y. 138; Folsom v. Apple River Log-Driving Co., 1877, 41 Wis. 602. See supra, § 52.

10. Tidal Oil Co. v. Pease, 1931, 153 Okl. 137, 5 P.2d 389; see Orton v. Virginia Carolina Chemical Co., 1918, 142 La. 790, 77 So. 632.

11. See supra, § 52. As to the burden of proof on the issue of apportionment, see supra, same section.

The distinction made in West Muncie Strawboard Co. v. Slack, 1904, 164 Ind. 21, 72 N.E. 879, between a public and a private nuisance in this respect has nothing to recommend it, and was rejected in City of Mansfield v. Brister, 1907, 76 Ohio St. 270, 81 N.E. 631, and Mitchell Realty Co. v. City of West Allis, 1924, 184 Wis. 352, 199 N.W. 390.

12. Woodyear v. Schaefer, 1881, 57 Md. 1 (pollution); Woodland v. Portneuf-Marsh Valley Irrigation Co., 1915, 26 Idaho 789, 146 P. 1106 (flooding); Sloggy v. Dilworth, 1888, 38 Minn. 179, 36 N.W. 451 (flooding); Harley v. Merrill Brick Co., 1891, 83 Iowa 73, 48 N.W. 1000 (smoke); Warren v. Parkhurst, 1904, 45 Misc. 466, 92 N.Y.S. 725, affirmed 105 App.Div. 239, 93 N.Y.S. 1009, affirmed 186 N.Y. 45, 78 N.E. 579.

13. Supra, § 52.

14. See Sadler v. Great Western R. Co., [1895] L.R. 2 Q.B. 688; Woodyear v. Schaefer, 1881, 57 Md. 1; Lambton v. Mellish, [1894] 2 Ch. 163. Cf. Parker v. American Woolen Co., 1907, 195 Mass. 591, 81 N.E. 468; Weidman Silk Dyeing Co. v. East Jersey Water Co., N.J.Super.1914, 91 A. 338, reversed 88 N.J.L. 400, 96 A. 1103.

cover damages and also as to the issue of whether plaintiff is entitled to injunctive relief of some kind.[15] The matter of "coming to the nuisance" is simply one factor on the issue of whether or not the defendant's use is an unreasonable interference. The Supreme Court of Michigan stated that plaintiff who "came" to a village dump to operate a mink ranch could recover damages even though the plaintiff's operation was of the sensitive type. It was said that "while coming to the nuisance may properly be entertained while weighing the equities in an abatement action, it is irrelevant in a damage suit."[16]

Such a general proposition would seem to be questionable. The result reached in the case can be justified because of other circumstances including especially the fact that the noxious operations at the village dump were greatly expanded after the plaintiff began using his property as a mink farm.

If a plaintiff comes to a "nuisance" in the sense that he comes to an area where the defendant has already been making a particular kind of use of his property, such as for a feed lot, and then is allowed successfully to maintain a suit either for damages or for abatement of the nuisance, the court could quite frequently be in the position of giving the plaintiff a windfall capital gain to which he is not entitled, and at the expense of the defendant. Plaintiff would be in the position of having purchased at a depressed price because of the presence of the feed lot and then at substantial expense to the defendant brought about an abatement, thereby increasing to a substantial extent the market value of the land. The Supreme Court of Arizona, utilizing the flexible equitable powers available to it in the granting or withholding of equitable relief, concluded to enjoin the operation of a feed lot at the behest of a real estate developer who "came to" the feed lot, and thereby changed the area to a residential one. The feed lot as a consequence was regarded as both a public nuisance and a private nuisance to nearby residents who purchased homes from the developer. However, the court held that the developer should be required to indemnify the feed lot operator for the costs of removing his operations.[17] Thus, a new device was utilized. The abatement of the undesirable use was withheld unless the plaintiff was willing to indemnify the defendant who was engaging in the undesirable use.

The prevailing rule is that in the absence of a prescriptive right,[18] the defendant cannot condemn the surrounding premises to endure his operation, and that the purchaser is entitled to a reasonable use and enjoyment of his land to the same extent as any other owner,[19] so long as he buys in good faith and not for the sole purpose of a vexatious lawsuit.[20] There are cases, however, which have held that the plaintiff is barred by his voluntary choice of a place to live,[21] particularly where the defendant's activity is

---

15. McCarty v. Natural Carbonic Gas Co., 1907, 189 N.Y. 40, 81 N.E. 549; Peck v. Newburgh Light, Heat & Power Co., 1909, 132 App.Div. 82, 116 N.Y.S. 433; Staton v. Atlantic Coast Line Railroad, 1908, 147 N.C. 428, 61 S.E. 455, 17 LRA (N.S.) 949 (injunction was denied against a railroad because of its heavy investment and because of plaintiff moving to it, but damages were approved); Dill v. Excel Packing Co., 1958, 183 Kan. 513, 331 P.2d 539 (cattle feed lot).

16. Kellogg v. Viola, 1975, 67 Wis.2d 345, 227 N.W. 55.

17. Spur Industries, Inc. v. Dell E. Webb Development Co., 1972, 108 Ariz. 178, 494 P.2d 700.

18. There is no prescriptive right until the nuisance has done actual damage for the required period. Campbell v. Seaman, 1876, 63 N.Y. 568; United Verde Copper Co. v. Ralston, 9th Cir. 1931, 46 F.2d 1. In Anneberg v. Kurtz, 1944, 197 Ga. 188, 28 S.E.2d 769, pollution of a stream for twenty years was held sufficient.

19. Campbell v. Seaman, 1876, 63 N.Y. 568; Ensign v. Walls, 1948, 323 Mich. 49, 34 N.W.2d 549; Lawrence v. Eastern Air Lines, Fla.1955, 81 So.2d 632; Forbes v. City of Durant, 1950, 209 Miss. 246, 46 So.2d 551; Mahone v. Autry, 1951, 55 N.M. 111, 227 P.2d 623.

20. Thus in Edwards v. Allouez Mining Co., 1879, 38 Mich. 46, an injunction was denied for this reason. Cf. Abdella v. Smith, 1967, 34 Wis.2d 393, 149 N.W.2d 537.

21. McClung v. Louisville & Nashville Railroad Co., 1951, 255 Ala. 302, 51 So.2d 371; Oetjen v. Goff Kirby Co., Ohio App.1942, 49 N.E.2d 95, appeal dismissed 140 Ohio St. 544, 45 N.E.2d 607. See Notes, 1943, 17 Temp.L.Q. 449; 1953, 41 Cal.L.Rev. 148; 1953, 32 Or.L. Rev. 264; 1952, 4 Baylor L.Rev. 382.

one in which the public has a major interest.²²

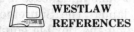
WESTLAW REFERENCES

Conduct of Others

nuisance* /p conduct! standard* condition* nature location character! /4 local! vicinity community neighborhood surround* % obscen!

Coming to a Nuisance—Conduct of Plaintiff

coming came come* /s nuisance % "attractive nuisance"

"absolute nuisance*"

§ 88C. "Absolute" Nuisance

The term "absolute nuisance" has been used in the cases with several meanings and these different meanings should be understood.

In some types of cases, the conclusion that the nuisance is "absolute" rests upon the view of some courts that certain property rights and privileges, such as that of a riparian owner to the use of a stream in its "natural" condition,¹ or that of a landowner to make use of percolating or subterranean waters,² or particularly that of disposing of surface water³ are fixed and invariable rather than relative. These cases are based on the notion that "any" intentional pollution or any intentional interference with this "natural" property right is actionable just as any intentional entry onto land is an actionable trespass. When the interests of landowners come into conflict, these courts seek some rule which will give one complete protection to recover damages at the expense of the other, as by holding that the lower riparian owner is entitled to the "natural flow" of the stream, and that any diversion which substantially interferes with it is a nuisance.⁴ The question here is whether or not some of the interests in natural attributes of land, especially fresh water, are of such importance to society and are of such a fundamental value to future generations as to justify the kind of protection that eliminates any effort at balancing the interests. Most courts have found it necessary to retreat from such a position.⁵ Except in the case of surface waters,⁶ the prevailing view is that such property rights and privileges are not absolute, but relative. And that the rules related to the right to damages and injunctive relief are the same as for other interferences with use, such as pollution of the air with smoke and odors.⁷

A second meaning of "absolute nuisance" is that it is a condition or an activity which

---

22. East St. Johns Shingle Co. v. City of Portland, 1952, 195 Or. 505, 246 P.2d 554; Powell v. Superior Portland Cement, 1942, 15 Wn.2d 14, 129 P.2d 536.

§ 88C

1. See Kinyon, What Can a Riparian Proprietor Do, 1937, 21 Minn.L.Rev. 512.

2. See Clayberg, The Law of Percolating Waters, 1915, 14 Mich.L.Rev. 119; Huffcut, Percolating Waters: The Rule of Reasonable User, 1904, 13 Yale L.J. 222; MacArtor v. Graylyn Crest III Swim Club, Del. Ch.1963, 187 A.2d 417.

3. See Kinyon and McClure, Surface Waters, 1940, 24 Minn.L.Rev. 891; Note, 1962, 50 Ky.L.J. 254.

4. See for example Robertson v. Arnold, 1936, 182 Ga. 664, 186 S.E. 806; Roberts v. Martin, 1913, 72 W.Va. 92, 77 S.E. 535; Clark v. Pennsylvania Railroad Co., 1891, 145 Pa. 438, 22 A. 989; Exton v. Glen Gardner Water Co., 1925, 3 N.J.Misc. 613, 129 A. 255; Harvey Realty Co. v. Borough of Wallingford, 1930, 111 Conn. 352, 150 A. 60. See Kinyon, What Can a Riparian Proprietor Do, 1937, 21 Minn.L.Rev. 512, 517–522. There is a good review of all this in Harris v. Brooks, 1955, 225 Ark. 436, 283 S.W.2d 129.

5. See for example Southern Cal. Investment Co. v. Wilshire, 1904, 144 Cal. 68, 77 P. 767; Nesalhous v. Walker, 1907, 45 Wash. 621, 88 P. 1032; Pennsylvania Railroad Co. v. Miller, 1886, 112 Pa. 34, 3 A. 780; Watkins Land Co. v. Clements, 1905, 98 Tex. 578, 86 S.W. 733; Helfrich v. Cantonsville Water Co., 1891, 74 Md. 269, 22 A. 72.

6. As to surface waters, most of the states still adhere to either the civil law rule that the natural flow of surface water may not be interfered with (see Nininger v. Norwood, 1882, 72 Ala. 277), or the common law or "common enemy" rule, that a landowner may deal with surface water as he sees fit, regardless of the effect upon adjoining land (see Bowlsby v. Speer, 1865, 31 N.J.L. 351. An increasing minority of the jurisdictions have adopted the "reasonable use" doctrine expressly (see supra, § 88), while others have accepted it in effect. See for example Keys v. Romley, 1966, 64 Cal.2d 396, 50 Cal.Rptr. 273, 412 P.2d 529. See Kinyon and McClure, Surface Waters, 1940, 24 Minn.L.Rev. 891; Note, 1962, 50 Ky.L.J. 254.

7. See, supra, § 88 on Substantial and Unreasonable Interference.

will inevitably result in the kind of interference with the use and enjoyment of property of others as to amount to unreasonable interference and a nuisance at all times and under any circumstances.[8] Hardly anything except a use declared to be unlawful at the place where the defendant is operating would be an absolute nuisance in this sense, and such a notion is hardly of any practical importance except insofar as a court chooses to adopt the principle that the violation of a legislative rule enacted for the purpose of guarding against the interference with the use and enjoyment of property is a nuisance per se as to all those for whose benefit the legislative rule was passed. The problem usually arises in connection with zoning restrictions. Zoning restrictions are normally enforced by the city either because the ordinance provides for such a remedy or on the theory that the violation constitutes a public nuisance. Most courts have not permitted a private plaintiff to recover without a showing of "special damages," meaning without a showing that the conduct constituted an unreasonable interference in fact with the use and enjoyment of his property.[9] Since it can be said that virtually all zoning ordinances are passed to protect those within the restricted zone in the use and enjoyment of this property, it is reasonable to conclude that unreasonable interference should be deemed to exist as a matter of law, and that the violation of such a zoning ordinance is an absolute nuisance giving each resident in the restricted area a right to enjoin the operation in the absence of some such defense as waiver or estoppel. But proof that the conduct amounts to a common law nuisance is ordinarily required. Thus in Padjen v. Shipley,[10] the court held that it was error to treat the violation of an ordinance requiring the defendant to keep his dogs 40 feet away from the plaintiff's house as a nuisance per se even though the dogs were kept within 18 feet.

A third meaning is that a nuisance is absolute if the defendant is engaging in an activity at a place where the interference that results is unreasonable, even though reasonable care is exercised to minimize the harm.[11]

Finally, it is often said that the conduct is an "absolute nuisance" if defendant is held liable without fault for harm resulting from accidental invasions, such as from abnormally dangerous conduct or from conduct that results in water pollution, a "natural right." But the use of the term "nuisance" to describe the tort liability that sometimes results from accidental invasions produces too much confusion. This problem is discussed in this chapter under the section on strict liability.[12]

§ 89. Remedies

Once the existence of a nuisance is established, the plaintiff normally has three possible remedies: an action for damages which he has suffered, equitable relief by injunction, and abatement by self-help.

Damages

As to the remedy of damages, the following quotation from another book [1] by one of the contributing editors of this book has been adopted:

"Once a nuisance is established under substantive law, damages are similar to those in many trespass cases. Indeed, many cases analyzed in terms of nuisance seem indistinguishable from trespass or negligence cases, except perhaps on grounds that are insignificant under modern law.[2] If the nuisance, whatever it is, whether in the form of noxious gases, or

---

8. Essick v. Shillam, 1943, 347 Pa. 373, 32 A.2d 416; Bluemer v. Saginaw Central Oil & Gas Service, Inc., 1959, 356 Mich. 399, 97 N.W.2d 90 (1959); Wilcher v. Sharpe, 1952, 236 N.C. 308, 72 S.E.2d 662.

9. See, supra, § 88A.

10. Utah 1976, 553 P.2d 938.

11. See the discussion, supra, § 88.

12. See, infra, § 91.

§ 89

1. See Dobbs, Remedies, 1973, 332–335.

2. Courts tend to classify indirect physical entries on the land as "nuisance," rather than trespasses, perhaps because they lack the direct application of force

noise, or water pollutants, is permanent, the same measure of damages as in cases of permanent damages by trespass is normally used—that is, the depreciation in the market value of the realty by reason of the nuisance.³ As a rule this will mean a nuisance that is, in the physical nature of things, unlikely to abate or to be avoided by any reasonable expenditure of money, though some states may define permanent nuisances more narrowly.⁴ Where a permanent nuisance is involved and for reasons of policy courts will not abate it by injunction, the tortfeasor acquires what amounts to an easement to commit the nuisance, on payment of the depreciation in market value. Some courts, apparently on the theory that the 'easement' is not acquired until the tortfeasor pays the depreciation, have allowed the plaintiff in permanent nuisance cases to recover not only the diminution in his land value by reason of the nuisance, but also any special damages, such as loss of crops, which he suffered before trial.⁵

"Where the nuisance, or the injury arising from it, is not permanent and has been or can be abated, damages are usually measured differently. The plaintiff usually recovers the depreciation in the rental or use value of his property during the period in which the nuisance exists, plus any special damages.⁶ Rental value and use value are not necessarily the same thing, and some courts allow a plaintiff who actually occupies the premises to recover the 'use value,' or special value to him, but limit the recovery of the owner who does not occupy the premises to the more objective measure of rental value.⁷ Discomfort or inconvenience in the use of the property is, of course, relevant both to establish special damage⁸ and as evidence bearing on the loss of rental or use

---

required for the common law writ of trespass. See, e.g., Aldworth v. City of Lynn, 153 Mass. 53, 26 N.E. 229, 10 L.R.A. 210, 25 Am.St.Rep. 608 (1891) (percolation of water a nuisance). Love Petroleum Co. v. Jones, 205 So.2d 274 (Miss.1967). Likewise, trespass is associated with *possession,* and where the plaintiff's rights in the land are not possessory or not exclusive, courts tend to avoid trespass terminology, for example in cases of easements. E.g., Hancock v. Moriarity, 215 Ga. 274, 110 S.E.2d 403 (1959) (defendant blocked alley in which plaintiff had a right to travel, "nuisance"). In a good many situations, the plaintiff may proceed on either theory or on both. E.g., City of Holdenville v. Griggs, 411 P.2d 521 (Okl.1966). [Footnote numbered 5 in original source.]

3. E.g., Spaulding v. Cameron, 38 Cal.2d 265, 239 P.2d 625 (1952); Robertson v. Cincinnati, New Orleans & Tex.Pac.Ry., 207 Tenn. 272, 339 S.W.2d 6 (1960) (Chattanooga Choo-choo noise). [Footnote numbered 6 in original source.]

4. In Akers v. Ashland Oil & Refining Co., 139 W.Va. 682, 80 S.E.2d 884 (1954) defendant accumulated oil in a pond, which, due to an unusual flood, was washed out of the pond and onto plaintiff's farm land. Evidence was that this would affect the land for many years, though not forever. Permanent damages were allowed based on diminished value of the land. Apparently this was because the damage was not readily repairable (see § 5.1, supra). However, the court also discussed the rules about permanent *sources* of nuisance or trespass, so that it is difficult to be sure what the basis of the decision is. [Footnote numbered 7 in original source referred reader to footnote 2, p. 335, of original source.]

5. Lassiter v. Norfolk & Carolina R.R., 126 N.C. 509, 36 S.E. 48 (1900). [Footnote numbered 8 in original source.]

6. Ledbetter Bros., Inc. v. Holcomb, 108 Ga.App. 282, 132 S.E.2d 805 (1963); Bates v. Quality Ready-Mix Co., 261 Iowa 696, 154 N.W.2d 852 (1968); Love Petroleum Co. v. Jones, 205 So.2d 274 (Miss.1967).

Occasionally cases allow the diminution measure for a continuing abatable nuisance. See, e.g., City of Phoenix v. Johnson, 51 Ariz. 115, 75 P.2d 30 (1938).

As in other cases, use value or rental value may be arrived at, if necessary, by first calculating the capital value of the property in question and then using current interest rates on that value as evidence of rental value, since interest is the "rental value of money." In Wilson v. Farmers Chemical Ass'n, 444 S.W.2d 185 (Tenn.App.1969) a temporary nuisance diminished the land value by a total of $73,000. The court upheld an award of interest based on this sum. [Footnote numbered 9 in original source.]

7. Nitram Chemicals v. Parker, 200 So.2d 220 (Fla. App.1967); Adams Const. Co. v. Bentley, 335 S.W.2d 912 (Ky.1960). In the latter case the court said: "Hence it is possible for property which is not rentable to have some use value to the occupant, though it might well be measured by what rent he would have to pay for something comparable." 335 S.W.2d at 914. And in the converse situation, one who has leased out his property and who continues to receive the agreed-upon rent from the tenant has no loss of "rental" resulting from the nuisance; unless he is given a purely theoretical loss in "rental *value*" recovery will be denied for temporary, though not for permanent, nuisances. See Attwood v. City of Bangor, 83 Me. 582, 22 A. 466 (1891); Widmer v. Fretti, 95 Ohio App. 7, 116 N.E.2d 728 (1952). [Footnote numbered 10 in original source.]

8. See Annot., 142 A.L.R. 1307 (1943) and discussion below. [Footnote numbered 11 in original source.]

value.⁹ Damages for temporary nuisances are not necessarily limited to depreciated rental values or use values, however. Where the nuisance is the kind that does more or less tangible harm to the premises, the cost of repair or restoration may be the appropriate measure of damages, just as it is the appropriate measure where similar harm is done in trespass cases.¹⁰ Whether the nuisance is temporary or permanent, the land occupant may recover special damages in addition to the depreciation in the market or use value. This commonly includes damages for personal discomfort or illness resulting from the nuisance,¹¹ though theoretically this might result in overpayment, since the depreciation in the rental value is itself a result of the discomfort or potential discomfort of the occupant.¹² A problem arises where the nuisance causes illness in a member of the landowner's family rather than in the landowner himself. Since private nuisance is usually associated with protection of use and enjoyment of land, it is usually also associated with ownership of an interest in land, and it is sometimes said that an occupant of land who has no interest in it cannot recover on a theory of nuisance.¹³ This would suggest that a husband who owned the premises affected by a nuisance could recover for discomfort or illness resulting but that his wife could not. One solution to this problem is to allow the owner to recover only for his own discomfort, with the recognition, however, that his discomfort is increased where his family is also made uncomfortable,¹⁴ or to allow a head of a household to recover for his spouse's separate illness.¹⁵ Another approach is to minimize the significance of legal title, either by discarding it altogether as a limit on nuisance recoveries,¹⁶ or by recognizing, as courts usually do, that an occupant or possessor as well as a legal interest owner, has a nuisance claim where he in fact has spe-

9. E.g., Town of Braggs v. Slape, 207 Okl. 420, 250 P.2d 214 (1952). [Footnote numbered 12 in original source.]

10. Burk v. High Point Homes, Inc., 22 Misc.2d 492, 197 N.Y.S.2d 969 (Sup.Ct.1960); Shearing v. City of Rochester, 51 Misc.2d 436, 273 N.Y.S.2d 464 (Sup.Ct. 1966); Riblet v. Spokane-Portland Cement Co., 45 Wash.2d 346, 274 P.2d 574 (1954). As in trespass cases, courts sometimes insist that the measure is the diminution in market value of which the cost of repairs is only *evidence*. Where repairs would put property in a better condition than it was in before the nuisance, difficult calculations may be avoided by using the diminution in market value rule. See Medford Housing Authority v. Marinucci Bros. & Co., 354 Mass. 699, 241 N.E.2d 834 (1968). As to the same problem in trespass cases see § 5.1 supra. [Footnote numbered 13 in original source.]

11. E.g., Nitram Chemicals v. Parker, 200 So.2d 220 (Fla.App.1967); Frey v. Queen City Paper Co., 79 Ohio App. 64, 66 N.E.2d 252 (1946). Oklahoma City v. West, 155 Okl. 63, 7 P.2d 888 (1931); Vestal v. Gulf Oil Corp., 149 Tex. 487, 235 S.W.2d 440 (1951); Riblet v. Spokane-Portland Cement Co., 45 Wash.2d 346, 274 P.2d 574 (1954). Annot., 142 A.L.R. 1307 (1943). Very little guide can be furnished for determining this kind of damage, of course, and the amount of such damages is peculiarly a jury question. Flanigan v. City of Springfield, 360 S.W.2d 700 (Mo.1962). [Footnote numbered 14 in original source.]

12. Swift v. Broyles, 115 Ga. 885, 42 S.E. 277, 58 L.R.A. 390 (1902) held it error to submit to the jury both the discomfort element and the loss of rental value element as a visitation of double damages. Later decisions from Georgia cast doubt on the authority of that case. See Towaliga Falls Power Co. v. Sims, 6 Ga.App. 749, 65 S.E. 844 (1909). Arkansas relied on the Swift case to deny damages for discomfort in addition to loss of rental value, quoting Swift to the effect that the occupant had elected "to be at once his own landlord and tenant, to get an amount of enjoyment out of it equal to the sum he would be obliged to pay as rent for premises of a like rental value belonging to another." The Arkansas case may be explained on narrower grounds—uncertainty of the damage—and it is by no means clear authority. Kentucky, according to a decision of the 6th Circuit has abandoned its earlier rule against allowing recovery for both personal discomfort and loss of rental value. See Kentucky West Virginia Gas Co. v. Lafferty, 174 F.2d 848, 10 A.L.R.2d 661 (6th Cir. 1949). It is at least true that Kentucky does not always deny recovery for both elements. See Mahan v. Doggett, 27 Ky.L.Rep. 103, 84 S.W. 525 (1905) (dictum that plaintiff could recover both); Gay v. Perry, 205 Ky. 38, 265 S.W. 437 (1924) (stating that in some cases plaintiff can recover both diminution in value of the use and for discomfort, but not where the loss in the value of the use was due to the discomfort or sickness); Price v. Dickson, 317 S.W.2d 156 (Ky. 1958) (discomfort an element in determining diminution of use value). [Footnote numbered 15 in original source.]

13. See Neuber v. Royalty Realty Co., 86 Cal.App. 2d 596, 195 P.2d 501 (1948); Second Restatement of Torts, Chapter 40, Introductory Note. [Footnote numbered 16 in original source.]

14. Millett v. Minnesota Crushed Stone Co., 145 Minn. 475, 177 N.W. 641 (1920). [Footnote numbered 17 in original source.]

15. See Gorman v. Sabo, 210 Md. 155, 122 A.2d 475 (1956). [Footnote numbered 18 in original source.]

16. See Towaliga Falls Power Co. v. Sims, 6 Ga. App. 749, 65 S.E. 844 (1883) (dictum, plaintiff was actually a tenant on the land). [Footnote numbered 19 in original source.]

cial damages.[17] An occupant who is not an owner may recover if the nuisance is a public one and he has special damages,[18] and even if this is not the case he may have an ordinary action for personal injury based on negligence or ultrahazardous activity.[19] Also, in addition to the depreciation measure of damages, the plaintiff in a nuisance case may recover the reasonable cost of his own efforts to abate the nuisance or prevent future injury. For example, where a sewer line backed up and overflowed into the plaintiff's theater, the plaintiff hired a contractor to re-lay lateral sewer lines to avoid the problem in the future, and the contractor's charges being reasonable, the plaintiff was allowed to recover them.[20] Such decisions seem correct, though it should also be noted that to the extent the plaintiff is in fact able to abate the nuisance by his own efforts, or to the extent it is abatable by injunction, permanent damages are not assessed.[21]"

Injunctive Protection From Nuisances

The power of a court of equity, in a proper case, to enjoin a nuisance is of long standing, and apparently never has been questioned since the earlier part of the eighteenth century.[22] As in other cases of equity jurisdiction, it must appear that the recovery of damages at law will not be an adequate remedy;[23] but since equity regards every tract of land as unique, it considers that damages are not adequate where its usefulness is seriously impaired.[24] The possibility that the defendant's act, if continued, may ripen into prescription has been regarded by some courts as enough to make the injury irreparable, and justify relief by injunction.[25]

One distinguishing feature of equitable relief is that it may be granted upon the threat of harm which has not yet occurred. The defendant may be restrained from entering upon an activity where it is highly probable [26] that it will lead to a nuisance, although

---

17. E.g., Kentucky West Virginia Gas Co. v. Lafferty, 174 F.2d 848 (6th Cir. 1949). This case applies the shorter personal injury statute to the personal discomfort and illness claims, however. See Gorman v. Sabo, 210 Md. 155, 122 A.2d 475 (1956). [Footnote numbered 20 in original source.]

18. Hampton v. North Carolina Pulp Co., 223 N.C. 535, 27 S.E.2d 538 (1943). See Prosser, Private Action for Public Nuisance, 52 Va.L.Rev. 997 (1966). [Footnote numbered 21 in original source.]

19. Page v. Niagara Chemical Division of Food Machinery & Chem. Corp., 68 So.2d 382 (Fla.1953) is a good illustration. Plaintiffs in that case were employees of a railroad. Seniority rights gave them the right to work in a particular yard, a place regarded as particularly suitable. Defendant's insecticide plant was adjacent and the yard workers claimed it a nuisance. Injunction against the nuisance was denied because the employees had no estate in the land. But the court pointed out that the employees might have personal injury actions based on negligence, and implied that damages might be granted, at least if a public nuisance plus special damages could be established. [Footnote numbered 22 in original source.]

20. Stratford Theater v. Town of Stratford, 140 Conn. 422, 101 A.2d 279, 41 A.L.R.2d 1060 (1953); Piedmont Cotton Mills, Inc. v. General Warehouse No. Two, Inc., 222 Ga. 164, 149 S.E.2d 72 (1966); Nally & Gibson v. Mulholland, 399 S.W.2d 293 (Ky.1966) (provision of new water supply for stock when nuisance drove stock away from old pond, a proper "factor" to consider in determining the diminution in the value of the use); Annot., 41 A.L.R.2d 1064 (1955). [Footnote numbered 23 in original source.]

21. Spaulding v. Cameron, 38 Cal.2d 265, 239 P.2d 625 (1952); Bates v. Quality Ready-Mix Co., 261 Iowa 696, 154 N.W.2d 852 (1968). [Footnote numbered 24 in original source.]

22. See Baines v. Baker, 1752, 1 Amb. 158, 27 Eng. Rep. 105; Crowder v. Tinkler, 1816, 19 Ves. 617, 34 Eng.Rep. 645; 3 Bl.Comm.Ch. 11; Wilmont Homes, Inc. v. Weiler, 1964, 42 Del.Ch. 8, 202 A.2d 576; De Funiak, Equitable Relief Against Nuisances, 1950, 38 Ky.L.J. 223; Walsh, Equitable Relief Against Nuisance, 1930, 7 N.Y.U.L.Rev. 352; Note, 1965, 78 Harv. L.Rev. 997 ff.

23. Swaine v. Great Northern R. Co., 1864, 4 De G.J. & S. 211, 46 Eng.Rep. 899; Rhodes v. Dunbar, 1868, 57 Pa. 274; Purcell v. Davis, 1935, 100 Mont. 480, 50 P.2d 255.

24. Shipley v. Ritter, 1855, 7 Md. 408; Wilson v. City of Mineral Point, 1875, 39 Wis. 160; McIntosh v. Brimmer, 1924, 68 Cal.App. 770, 230 P. 203; Krocker v. Westmoreland Planing Mill Co., 1922, 274 Pa. 143, 117 A. 669. See McClintock, Equity, 1936, § 132.

25. Lindsay-Strathmore Irrigation District v. Superior Court of Tulare County, 1920, 182 Cal. 315, 187 P. 1056; Amsterdam Knitting Co. v. Dean, 1900, 162 N.Y. 278, 56 N.E. 757; Murphy v. Lincoln, 1891, 63 Vt. 278, 22 A. 418.

26. Hamilton Corp. v. Julian, 1917, 130 Md. 597, 101 A. 558; De Give v. Seltzer, 1879, 64 Ga. 423; Edmunds v. Duff, 1924, 280 Pa. 355, 124 A. 489; Mullins v. Morgan, 1940, 176 Va. 201, 10 S.E.2d 593. Absolute certainty is not required. Nelson v. Swedish Evangelical Lutheran Cemetery Association, 1910, 111 Minn. 149, 126 N.W. 723, 127 N.W. 626.

if the possibility is merely uncertain or contingent he may be left to his remedy of damages until after the nuisance has occurred.[27] Furthermore, even where there is an existing nuisance and present harm, the equity court may in its discretion deny the injunction where the balance of the equities involved is in favor of the defendant. It may take into consideration the relative economic hardship which will result to the parties from the granting or denial of the injunction,[28] the good faith or intentional misconduct of each,[29] and the interest of the general public in the continuation of the defendant's enterprise.[30] Where liability for damages is concerned, the defendant's conduct may be found to be so unreasonable that he should pay for the harm that his factory is causing, but where an injunction is in question, it may be found to be still so far reasonable that he should be allowed to continue it if payment is made.[31] For these reasons denial of relief by way of injunction is not always a precedent for denial of relief by way of damages, and this fact has added no little to the confusion surrounding the law of nuisance.

Abatement

The privilege of abatement of a nuisance by self-help is of ancient origin, and existed at a time when early common law actions afforded a legal means of compelling the nuisance to be discontinued.[32] It is closely related to the privilege of using reasonable force to protect the exclusive possession of land against trespass,[33] and may be justified on the same basis, that injuries, "which obstruct or annoy such things as are of daily convenience and use, require an immediate remedy, and cannot wait for the slow process of the ordinary forms of justice." [34] Consequently the privilege must be exercised within a reasonable time after knowledge of the nuisance is acquired or should have been acquired by the person entitled to abate; if there has been sufficient delay to allow a resort to legal process, the reason for the privilege fails, and the privilege with it.[35]

Summary abatement of a private nuisance by self-help is open only to those whose interests in the enjoyment of land are interfered with, or in other words, to those to

---

27. Hannum v. Oak Lane Shopping Center, 1956, 383 Pa. 618, 119 A.2d 213; Wilcher v. Sharpe, 1952, 236 N.C. 308, 72 S.E.2d 662; Kimmons v. Benson, 1952, 220 Ark. 299, 247 S.W.2d 468; Foster v. County of Genesee, 1951, 329 Mich. 665, 46 N.W.2d 426; Turner v. City of Spokane, 1951, 39 Wn.2d 332, 235 P.2d 300.

28. City of Harrisonville v. W.S. Dickey Clay Manufacturing Co., 1933, 289 U.S. 334, 53 S.Ct. 602, 77 L.Ed. 1208; Canfield v. Quayle, 1939, 170 Misc. 621, 10 N.Y.S.2d 781; Dundalk Holding Co. v. Easter, 1958, 215 Md. 549, 137 A.2d 667, certiorari denied 358 U.S. 821, 79 S.Ct. 34, 3 L.Ed.2d 62, rehearing denied 358 U.S. 901, 79 S.Ct. 219, 3 L.Ed.2d 151; Koseris v. J.R. Simplot Co., 1960, 82 Idaho 263, 352 P.2d 235; Akers v. Mathieson Alkali Works, 1928, 151 Va. 1, 144 S.E. 492. But the factor of disproportionate expense is not always controlling in itself. Metropoulos v. Macpherson, 1922, 241 Mass. 491, 135 N.E. 693.

29. Jack v. Torrant, 1950, 136 Conn. 414, 71 A.2d 705.

30. Haack v. Lindsay Light & Chemical Co., 1946, 393 Ill. 367, 66 N.E.2d 391 (essential war work); Storey v. Central Hide & Rendering Co., 1950, 148 Tex. 509, 226 S.W.2d 615 (only plant in county); Antonik v. Chamberlain, 1947, 81 Ohio App. 465, 78 N.E.2d 752 ("life and death of a legitimate and necessary business"); Koseris v. J.R. Simplot Co., 1960, 82 Idaho 263, 352 P.2d 235 (over 1,000 employees).

As to the balancing of several factors, see Elliott Nursery Co. v. Du Quesne Light Co., 1924, 281 Pa. 166, 126 A. 345; Edwards v. Allouez Mining Co., 1878, 38 Mich. 46; Bliss v. Washoe Copper Co., 9th Cir. 1911, 186 F. 789, certiorari dismissed 231 U.S. 764, 34 S.Ct. 327, 58 L.Ed. 471; McCarthy v. Bunker Hill & Sullivan Mining & Coal Co., 9th Cir. 1908, 164 F. 927, certiorari denied 212 U.S. 583, 29 S.Ct. 692, 53 L.Ed. 660.

See McClintock, Equity, 1936, §§ 140, 141; McClintock, Discretion to Deny Injunction Against Trespass and Nuisance, 1926, 12 Minn.L.Rev. 565; Morris and Keeton, Notes on "Balancing the Equities," 1940, 18 Tex.L.Rev. 412; Notes, 1927, 37 Yale L.J. 96; 1922, 36 Harv.L.Rev. 211; 1933, 40 W.Va.L.Q. 59.

31. Second Restatement of Torts, Introductory Note to chapter 40, preceding § 821A.

32. See, 1322, Y.B. 14 Edw. II, f. 422, pl. 3; 1469, Y.B. 8 Edw. IV, f. 5, pl. 14.

33. See supra, § 21.

34. 3 Bl.Com. 6.

35. Moffett v. Brewer, Iowa 1848, 1 G.Greene 348; Hentz v. Long Island Railroad Co., N.Y.1852, 13 Barb. 646.

whom it is a nuisance.[36] It is often said that the privilege is available only to one who might have an action for damages,[37] but such a statement is perhaps too broad, since there must be situations of imminent danger which will justify action before any harm has occurred.[38] Likewise, a public nuisance may be abated by a private individual only when it causes or threatens special damage to himself apart from that to the general public,[39] and then only to the extent necessary to protect his own interests. Thus a traveller on a highway may remove only so much of an obstruction as is required to permit him to proceed on his journey.[40] Again, because nuisances so often involve debatable questions of reasonable conduct, the privilege of abating conditions outside of the land affected differs from that of defending possession from a trespass,[41] in that it depends upon the actual existence of a nuisance. The actor who adopts such a summary remedy rather than resort to the law must take his chances that he is justified, and an honest belief that he is right will not protect him from criminal prosecution[42] or civil liability.[43]

The privilege of abatement extends to entry upon the land of another,[44] and to the use of all reasonable force in a reasonable manner which is necessary to terminate the nuisance, even to the destruction of valuable property,[45] where the damage done is not greatly disproportionate to the threatened harm. But it does not extend to unnecessary or unreasonable damage, and there will be liability for any excess.[46] It may not be justifiable, for instance, to destroy a house merely because it is used for prostitution.[47] What is reasonable is of course to be determined in the light of all the circumstances of the case, including the gravity of the nuisance and the necessity for prompt action, and the existence of any reasonable alternative method.[48] It is quite generally agreed,

36. Lincoln v. Chadbourne, 1868, 56 Me. 197; Gates v. Blincoe, 1833, 32 Ky. (2 Dana) 158; see Hummel v. State, 1940, 69 Okl.Cr. 38, 99 P.2d 913.

37. Adams v. Barney, 1853, 25 Vt. 225, 231; 2 Wood, Law of Nuisances, 3d Ed.1893, § 825. Cf. Priewe v. Fitzsimons & Connell Co., 1903, 117 Wis. 497, 94 N.W. 317; Toledo, St. Louis & Kansas City Railroad Co. v. Loop, 1894, 139 Ind. 542, 39 N.E. 306.

38. See Lipnik v. Ehalt, 1921, 76 Ind.App. 390, 132 N.E. 410; and cf. Second Restatement of Torts, § 203, Comment b.

39. Brown v. Perkins, 1858, 78 Mass. (12 Gray) 89, 101; Corthell v. Holmes, 1896, 87 Me. 24, 32 A. 715; Harrower v. Ritson, N.Y.1861, 37 Barb. 301; Nation v. District of Columbia, 1910, 34 App.D.C. 453. Earlier cases were to the contrary. Burnham v. Hotchkiss, 1841, 14 Conn. 311, 318; Day v. Day, 1853, 4 Md. 262, 270.

A private individual may, however, be privileged to act under public necessity to avert a public disaster. See supra, § 24. Cf. Seavey v. Preble, 1874, 64 Me. 120; Meeker v. Van Rensselaer, N.Y.1836, 15 Wend. 397 (abating nuisance to prevent spread of disease).

40. Harrower v. Ritson, N.Y.1861, 37 Barb. 301; James v. Hayward, 1631, Cro.Car. 184, 79 Eng.Rep. 761; Johnson v. Maxwell, 1891, 2 Wash. 482, 27 P. 1071.

41. Supra, § 21.

42. State v. Moffett, Iowa 1848, 1 G.Greene 247.

43. Graves v. Shattuck, 1847, 35 N.H. 257; Grant v. Allen, 1874, 41 Conn. 156; Humphreys Oil Co. v. Liles, Tex.Civ.App.1924, 262 S.W. 1058, affirmed Tex.Com. App.1925, 277 S.W. 100; Tissot v. Great Southern Telephone & Telegraph Co., 1887, 39 La.Ann. 996, 3 So. 261 (public nuisance).

44. Jones v. Williams, 1843, 11 M. & W. 176, 152 Eng.Rep. 764.

45. Amoskeag Manufacturing Co. v. Goodale, 1865, 46 N.H. 53 (dam); Maryland Telephone & Telegraph Co. v. Ruth, 1907, 106 Md. 644, 68 A. 358 (telephone pole); McKeesport Sawmill Co. v. Pennsylvania Co., C.C.Pa.1903, 122 F. 184 (barge); Hubbard v. Preston, 1892, 90 Mich. 221, 51 N.W. 209 (dog).

46. Gates v. Blincoe, 1833, 32 Ky. (2 Dana) 158; Finley v. Hershey, 1875, 41 Iowa 389; Ely v. Niagara County Supervisors, 1867, 36 N.Y. 297. Thus the defendant may be privileged to cut off branches of overhanging trees, but not to enter his neighbor's land and cut down the trees. Fick v. Nilson, 1950, 98 Cal.App. 2d 683, 220 P.2d 752. Or to move a car from a place where it is illegally parked, but not negligently to release the brakes and let it roll down hill to destruction. Russell v. Aragon, 1961, 146 Colo. 332, 361 P.2d 346.

47. Moody v. Board of Supervisors of Niagara County, N.Y.1866, 46 Barb. 659, affirmed 36 N.Y. 297. Accord: Ohio Valley Electric Railway Co. v. Scott, 1916, 172 Ky. 183, 189 S.W. 7; Morrison v. Marquardt, 1867, 24 Iowa 35; Brightman v. Bristol, 1876, 65 Me. 426.

48. Great Falls Co. v. Worster, 1844, 15 N.H. 412; Maryland Telephone & Telegraph Co. v. Ruth, 1907, 106 Md. 644, 68 A. 358; McKeesport Sawmill Co. v. Pennsylvania Co., C.C.Pa.1903, 122 F. 184; Ohio Valley Electric Railway Co. v. Scott, 1916, 172 Ky. 183, 189 S.W. 7.

however, that the abatement of a nuisance does not justify the infliction of personal injury,[49] or conduct which amounts to a breach of the peace.[50] Most courts have held that before one is privileged to abate a nuisance he must notify the wrongdoer of its existence and demand its removal;[51] but obviously this will not be required in an emergency where there is no time for it,[52] or where it is apparent that he is already aware of the nuisance and that such a demand would be futile.[53]

 WESTLAW REFERENCES

Damages
damages /p "private nuisance*"

Injunctive Protection From Nuisances
279k80

Abatement
summar! /s abate! /s nuisance*
abate! /s "private nuisance*"

§ 90. Public Nuisance: Remedies Available to the State

This is not the place to discuss in any detail the remedies available to the state and other governmental units to protect the general welfare from conduct regarded as so inimical to so many people as to constitute a public nuisance. The remedies usually available are those of criminal prosecution and abatement by way of an injunctive decree or order. Equity followed the law generally speaking in adopting a broad definition of what would constitute a public nuisance. The equitable remedy of injunction to enjoin a public nuisance developed early in the history of the development of equity jurisprudence, and this remedy is available to the state or the appropriate governmental entity even though the conduct may not be a crime.[1]

It is an entirely different concept from that of a private nuisance. It is a much broader term and encompasses much conduct other than the type that interferes with the use and enjoyment of private property.

No better definition of a public nuisance has been suggested than that of an act or omission "which obstructs or causes inconvenience or damage to the public in the exercise of rights common to all Her Majesty's subjects." [2] The term comprehends a miscellaneous and diversified group of minor criminal offenses, based on some interference with the interests of the community, or the comfort or convenience of the general public. It includes interferences with the public health, as in the case of a hogpen,[3] the keeping of diseased animals,[4] or a mala-

---

49. See Rex v. Rosewell, 1699, 2 Salk. 459, 91 Eng. Rep. 396; Stiles & Davis v. Laird, 1855, 5 Cal. 120; Walker v. Davis, 1917, 139 Tenn. 475, 202 S.W. 78.

50. Day v. Day, 1853, 4 Md. 262; Earp v. Lee, 1873, 71 Ill. 193; People v. Severance, 1901, 125 Mich. 556, 84 N.W. 1089.

51. State v. Brown, 1926, 191 N.C. 419, 132 S.E. 5; Martin v. Martin, Tex.Civ.App.1952, 246 S.W.2d 718; Hickey v. Michigan Central Railroad Co., 1893, 96 Mich. 498, 55 N.W. 989; Maryland Telephone & Telegraph Co. v. Ruth, 1907, 106 Md. 644, 68 A. 358.

52. Childers v. New York Power & Light Corp., 1949, 275 App.Div. 133, 89 N.Y.S.2d 11. See Jones v. Williams, 1843, 11 M. & W. 176, 152 Eng.Rep. 764; Buck v. McIntosh, 1908, 140 Ill.App. 9.

53. See Jones v. Williams, 1843, 11 M. & W. 176, 152 Eng.Rep. 764; Hickey v. Michigan Central Railroad Co., 1893, 96 Mich. 498, 55 N W 989.

§ 90

1. Attorney General v. Utica Ins. Co., N.Y.1817, 2 John Ch. 371; Attorney General v. Jamaica Pond Aqueduct Corp., 1882, 133 Mass. 361; Commonwealth v. McGovern, 1903, 116 Ky. 212, 75 S.W. 261, 66 L.R.A. 280.

2. Stephen, General View of the Criminal Law of England, 1890, 105; Salmond, Law of Torts, 8th Ed. 1934, 233; Mayor and Council of Alpine v. Brewster, 1951, 7 N.J. 42, 80 A.2d 297.

"A common or public nuisance is the doing of or the failure to do something that injuriously affects the safety, health or morals of the public, or works some substantial annoyance, inconvenience or injury to the public." Commonwealth v. South Covington & Cincinnati Street Railway Co., 1918, 181 Ky. 459, 463, 205 S.W. 581, 583, 6 A.L.R. 118; cf. City of Selma v. Jones, 1918, 202 Ala. 82, 83, 79 So. 476, 477.

3. Seigle v. Bromley, 1912, 22 Colo.App. 189, 124 P. 191; Gay v. State, 1891, 90 Tenn. 645, 18 S.W. 260.

4. Durand v. Dyson, 1915, 271 Ill. 382, 111 N.E. 143; Fevold v. Board of Supervisors of Webster County, 1926, 202 Iowa 1019, 210 N.W. 139. Cf. Rex v. Vantandillo, 1815, 4 M. & S. 73, 105 Eng.Rep. 762 (carrying child with smallpox along the highway).

rial pond;[5] with the public safety, as in the case of the storage of explosives,[6] the shooting of fireworks in the streets,[7] harboring a vicious dog,[8] or the practice of medicine by one not qualified;[9] with public morals, as in the case of houses of prostitution,[10] illegal liquor establishments,[11] gambling houses,[12] indecent exhibitions,[13] bullfights,[14] unlicensed prize fights,[15] or public profanity;[16] with the public peace, as by loud and disturbing noises,[17] or an opera performance which threatens to cause a riot;[18] with the public comfort, as in the case of bad odors, smoke, dust and vibration;[19] with public convenience, as by obstructing a highway[20] or a navigable stream,[21] or creating a condition which makes travel unsafe[22] or highly disa-

5. Mills v. Hall & Richards, N.Y.1832, 9 Wend. 315. Cf. Ajamian v. Township of North Bergen, 1968, 103 N.J.Super. 61, 246 A.2d 521, affirmed 107 N.J.Super. 175, 257 A.2d 726, certiorari denied 398 U.S. 952, 90 S.Ct. 1873, 26 L.Ed.2d 292 (unsanitary conditions in tenement house).

6. State v. Excelsior Powder Manufacturing Co., 1914, 259 Mo. 254, 169 S.W. 267; McAndrews v. Collerd, 1880, 42 N.J.L. 189.

7. Jenne v. Sutton, 1881, 43 N.J.L. 257; Landau v. City of New York, 1904, 180 N.Y. 48, 72 N.E. 631. Accord, Parker v. City of Fort Worth, Tex.Civ.App.1955, 281 S.W.2d 721 (keeping and selling).

8. King v. Kline, 1847, 6 Pa. 318; Browning v. Belue, 1928, 22 Ala.App. 437, 116 So. 509; Patterson v. Rosenwald, 1928, 222 Mo.App. 973, 6 S.W.2d 664.

9. State v. Scopel, Mo.1958, 316 S.W.2d 515; State ex rel. Marron v. Compere, 1940, 44 N.M. 414, 103 P.2d 273.

10. Black v. Circuit Court of Eighth Judicial District, 1960, 78 S.D. 302, 101 N.W.2d 520; State v. Navy, 1941, 123 W.Va. 722, 17 S.E.2d 626; Tedeschi v. Berger, 1907, 150 Ala. 649, 43 So. 960; People ex rel. Dyer v. Clark, 1915, 268 Ill. 156, 108 N.E. 994; State ex rel. Wilcox v. Ryder, 1914, 126 Minn. 95, 147 N.W. 953.

11. Brown v. Perkins, 1858, 78 Mass. (12 Gray) 89; State v. Bertheol, Ind.1843, 6 Blackf. 474.

12. State ex rel. Williams v. Karston, 1945, 208 Ark. 703, 187 S.W.2d 327; State ex rel. Johnson v. Hash, 1944, 144 Neb. 495, 13 N.W.2d 716; State ex rel. Leahy v. O'Rourke, 1944, 115 Mont. 502, 146 P.2d 168; State ex rel. Trampe v. Multerer, 1940, 234 Wis. 50, 289 N.W. 600. Compare, as to lotteries, State ex rel. Regez v. Blumer, 1940, 236 Wis. 129, 294 N.W. 491; State ex rel. Cowie v. La Crosse Theaters Co., 1939, 232 Wis. 153, 286 N.W. 707; Engle v. State, 1939, 53 Ariz. 458, 90 P.2d 988.

13. Weis v. Superior Court of San Diego County, 1916, 30 Cal.App. 730, 159 P. 464; Truet v. State, 1912, 3 Ala.App. 114, 57 So. 512. Cf. City of Chicago v. Shaynin, 1913, 258 Ill. 69, 101 N.E. 224; Adams v. Commonwealth, 1915, 162 Ky. 76, 171 S.W. 1006.

14. State v. Canty, 1907, 207 Mo. 439, 105 S.W. 1078.

15. Commonwealth v. McGovern, 1903, 116 Ky. 212, 75 S.W. 261.

16. State v. Chrisp, 1881, 85 N.C. 528; Wilson v. Parent, 1961, 228 Or. 354, 365 P.2d 72.

17. Rex v. Smith, 1725, 2 Stra. 704, 93 Eng.Rep. 795; People v. Rubenfeld, 1930, 254 N.Y. 245, 172 N.E. 485; Town of Davis v. Davis, 1895, 40 W.Va. 464, 21 S.E. 906. Cf. State v. Turner, 1942, 198 S.C. 487, 18 S.E.2d 372; McMillan v. Kuehnle, 1909, 76 N.J.Eq. 256, 73 A. 1054, reversed on other grounds 1911, 78 N.J.Eq. 251, 78 A. 185 (Sunday baseball); Town of Preble v. Song Mountain, Inc., 1970, 62 Misc.2d 353, 308 N.Y.S.2d 1001 ("rock festival").

See Lloyd, Noise as a Nuisance, 1933, 82 U.Pa.L.Rev. 567.

18. Star Opera Co. v. Hylan, 1919, 109 Misc. 132, 178 N.Y.S. 179.

19. Transcontinental Gas Pipe Line Corp. v. Gault, 4th Cir. 1952, 198 F.2d 196; State v. Primeau, 1966, 70 Wn.2d 109, 422 P.2d 302; Potashnick Truck Service v. City of Sikeston, 1943, 351 Mo. 505, 173 S.W.2d 96, transferred 157 S.W.2d 808; Soap Corp. of America v. Reynolds, 5th Cir. 1950, 178 F.2d 503; Board of Health of Lyndhurst Township v. United Cork Companies, 1934, 116 N.J.Eq. 4, 172 A. 347, affirmed 117 N.J.Eq. 437, 176 A. 142.

20. James v. Hayward, 1631, Cro.Car. 184, 79 Eng. Rep. 761; Harrower v. Ritson, N.Y.1861, 37 Barb. 301; Pilgrim Plywood Corp. v. Melendy, 1938, 110 Vt. 112, 1 A.2d 700. Cf. Adams v. Commissioners of Town of Trappe, 1954, 204 Md. 165, 102 A.2d 830 (encroachment); Sloan v. City of Greenville, 1959, 235 S.C. 277, 11 S.E.2d 573 (enclosure by construction of an overhanging building); Salsbury v. United Parcel Service, 1953, 203 Misc. 1008, 120 N.Y.S.2d 33 (double parking).

21. Willard v. City of Cambridge, 1862, 85 Mass. (3 Allen) 574; Piscataqua Navigation Co. v. New York, New Haven & Hartford Railroad Co., D.Mass.1898, 89 F. 362; Carver v. San Pedro, Los Angeles & Salt Lake Railroad Co., C.C.Cal.1906, 151 F. 334; Swain & Son v. Chicago, Burlington & Quincy Railroad Co., 1912, 252 Ill. 622, 97 N.E. 247. See Waite, Public Rights to Use and Have Access to Navigable Waters, [1958] Wis.L. Rev. 335.

22. Lamereaux v. Tula, 1942, 312 Mass. 359, 44 N.E.2d 789 (ice on sidewalk); State ex rel. Detienne v. City of Vandalia, 1906, 119 Mo.App. 406, 94 S.W. 1009 (noise frightening horse); Town of Newcastle v. Grubbs, 1908, 171 Ind. 482, 86 N.E. 757 (excavation); McFarlane v. City of Niagara Falls, 1928, 247 N.Y. 340, 160 N.E. 391 (defective sidewalk). It must, however, be travel on the public highway. Mandell v. Pivnick, 1956, 20 Conn.Sup. 99, 125 A.2d 175.

greeable,[23] or the collection of an inconvenient crowd;[24] and in addition, such unclassified offenses as eavesdropping on a jury,[25] or being a common scold.[26]

To be considered public, the nuisance must affect an interest common to the general public, rather than peculiar to one individual,[27] or several.[28] Thus the pollution of a stream which merely inconveniences a number of riparian owners is a private nuisance only,[29] but it may become a public one if it kills the fish.[30] It is not necessary, however, that the entire community be affected, so long as the nuisance will interfere with those who come in contact with it in the exercise of a public right.[31] The most obvious illustration, of course, is the obstruction of a public highway, which inconveniences only those who are travelling upon it. It is, furthermore, rather obvious that any condition or activity which substantially interferes with the private interests of any considerable number of individuals in a community is very likely to interfere also with some public right, such as the comfortable use of the highway;[32] and for this reason the question of the number of persons affected has seldom arisen.

At common law, a public nuisance was always a crime, and punishable as such.[33] In

---

23. Town of Mount Pleasant v. Van Tassell, 1957, 7 Misc.2d 643, 166 N.Y.S.2d 458, affirmed 1958, 6 A.D.2d 880, 177 N.Y.S.2d 1010 (bad odors, rats and flies from piggery).

24. Lyons Sons & Co. v. Gulliver, [1914] 1 Ch. 631, Ann.Cas.1916B, 959; Shamhart v. Morrison Cafeteria, 1947, 159 Fla. 629, 32 So.2d 727, 2 A.L.R.2d 429; Tushbant v. Greenfield's, 1944, 308 Mich. 626, 14 N.W.2d 520; Shaw's Jewelry Shop v. New York Herald Co., 1915, 170 App.Div. 504, 156 N.Y.S. 651, affirmed 1919, 224 N.Y. 731, 121 N.E. 890. See Notes, 1948, 26 Chicago-Kent L.Rev. 355; 1948, 1 Ala.L.Rev. 67.

In Rex v. Carlisle, 1834, 6 C. & P. 636, 172 Eng.Rep. 1397, there is reference in a note to the daughter of a Mr. Very, a confectioner in Regent Street, who was so wondrous fair that her presence in the shop caused three or four hundred people to assemble every day in the street before the window to look at her, so that her father was forced to send her out of town. Counsel was led to inquire whether she might not have been indicted as a public nuisance.

25. State v. Pennington, 1859, 40 Tenn. (3 Head) 299.

26. Commonwealth v. Mohn, 1866, 52 Pa. 243. Cf. State ex rel. Goff v. O'Neil, 1939, 205 Minn. 366, 286 N.W. 316 (loan shark); State v. Hooker, N.D.1957, 87 N.W.2d 337 (same). See Note, 1939, 38 Mich.L.Rev. 273.

27. City of Phoenix v. Johnson, 1938, 51 Ariz. 115, 75 P.2d 30; Pennsylvania Coal Co. v. Mahon, 1922, 260 U.S. 393, 43 S.Ct. 158, 67 L.Ed. 322. Cf. Attorney-General ex rel. Muskegon Booming Co. v. Evart Booming Co., 1876, 34 Mich. 462. Thus in Miller v. Morse, 1959, 9 A.D.2d 188, 192 N.Y.S.2d 571, appeal denied, 10 A.D.2d 598, 195 N.Y.S.2d 398, it was held that a defect in the floor of a two-family house, not intended for public use, did not make it a public nuisance.

28. Rex v. Lloyd, 1802, 4 Esp. 200, 170 Eng.Rep. 691; Higgins v. Connecticut Light & Power Co., 1943, 129 Conn. 606, 30 A.2d 388; People v. Brooklyn & Queens Transit Corp., 1939, 258 App.Div. 753, 15 N.Y.S.2d 295, affirmed 1940, 283 N.Y. 484, 28 N.E.2d 925.

There are, however, statutes in two or three states which define a public nuisance to include interference with any "considerable number of persons;" and under these no public right, as such, need be involved. See Boudinot v. State, Okl.1959, 340 P.2d 268; People v. Rubenfeld, 1930, 254 N.Y. 245, 172 N.E. 485; Ballenger v. City of Grand Saline, Tex.Civ.App.1955, 276 S.W.2d 874.

29. Smith v. City of Sedalia, 1899, 152 Mo. 283, 53 S.W. 907. Accord: Hartung v. County of Milwaukee, 1958, 2 Wis.2d 269, 86 N.W.2d 475, rehearing denied 2 Wis.2d 269, 87 N.W.2d 799 (quarry); Biggs v. Griffith, Mo.App.1950, 231 S.W.2d 875 (outdoor public address system); Soap Corp. of America v. Reynolds, 5th Cir. 1950, 178 F.2d 503; District of Columbia v. Totten, 1925, 55 U.S.App.D.C. 312, 5 F.2d 374, certiorari denied 269 U.S. 562, 46 S.Ct. 21, 70 L.Ed. 412; State v. Wright Hepburn Webster Gallory Limited, Sup.Ct.1970, 64 Misc.2d 423, 314 N.Y.S.2d 661, affirmed 37 A.D.2d 698, 323 N.Y.S.2d 389.

30. State ex rel. Wear v. Springfield Gas & Electric Co., Mo.App.1918, 204 S.W. 942.

31. State v. Hooker, N.D.1957, 87 N.W.2d 337; State v. Turner, 1942, 198 S.C. 487, 18 S.E.2d 372; Parker v. City of Fort Worth, Tex.Civ.App.1955, 281 S.W.2d 721; Dean v. State, 1921, 151 Ga. 371, 106 S.E. 792; Finkelstein v. City of Sapulpa, 1925, 106 Okl. 297, 234 P. 187.

32. See for example Town of Mount Pleasant v. Van Tassell, 1957, 7 Misc.2d 643, 166 N.Y.S.2d 458, affirmed 1958, 6 A.D.2d 880, 177 N.Y.S.2d 1010 (odors, rats and flies from piggery).

33. 2 Russell, Crimes, 8th ed. 1923, 1692; Mayor and Council of Alpine v. Brewster, 1951, 7 N.J. 42, 80 A.2d 297.

No case has been found of tort liability for a public nuisance which was not a crime. Cases of the liability of municipal corporations, infra, § 131, are of course not in point—one might as well say that murder is not a crime because a lunatic or an infant cannot be convicted of it.

the United States, all jurisdictions have enacted broad criminal statutes covering such nuisances without attempting to define them, or with at most a very general and rather meaningless definition. Such statutes commonly are construed to include anything which would have been a public nuisance at common law.[34] In addition there are in every state a multitude of specific provisions declaring that certain things, such as bawdy houses, black currant plants, buildings where narcotics are sold, mosquito breeding waters, or unhealthy multiple dwellings,[35] are public nuisances. Apparently the question has not arisen whether, in a state which has no common law crimes, there may be liability in tort for a common law public nuisance which is not covered by any general or specific statute. But since tort liability has been imposed upon municipal corporations, which are not criminally responsible but may be held liable for the creation or maintenance of a nuisance,[36] one might hazard the guess that if the question should arise common law principles would be held to control in such a case.

The Tort Action—General Case Approach

Tort liability for public nuisance originated in an anonymous case [37] in 1536, which is one of the two instances since the days of the old action of trespass in which a crime has become per se a tort.[38] In that case it was first held that the action would lie if the plaintiff could show that he had suffered damage particular to him, and not shared in common by the rest of the public. This qualification has persisted, and it is uniformly held that a private individual has no action for the invasion of the purely public right, unless his damage is in some way to be distinguished from that sustained by other members of the general public.[39] It is not enough that he suffers the same inconvenience or is exposed to the same threatened injury as everyone else.[40] Redress of the wrong to the community must be left to its appointed representatives. The best reason that has been given for the rule is that it relieves the defendant of the multiplicity of actions which might follow if everyone were free to sue for the common harm.[41]

34. People v. Lim, 1943, 18 Cal.2d 872, 118 P.2d 472; Engle v. State, 1939, 53 Ariz. 458, 90 P.2d 988; People v. Clark, 1915, 268 Ill. 156, 108 N.E. 994; First Avenue Coal & Lumber Co. v. Johnson, 1911, 171 Ala. 470, 54 So. 598.

35. See New York Consol.Laws, Cahill 1930, ch. 46, §§ 343a, 409a, 434; ch. 10, § 57a; New York Sess. Laws 1937, ch. 353, § 2. As to the constitutionality of statutes declaring nuisances, see Noel, Retroactive Zoning and Nuisances, 1941, 41 Col.L.Rev. 457. See also Smith v. Costello, 1955, 77 Idaho 205, 290 P.2d 742, holding unconstitutional a statute as to dogs running at large in territory inhabited by deer.

36. Dubois v. City of Kingston, 1888, 102 N.Y. 219, 6 N.E. 273; Cohen v. Mayor of New York, 1889, 113 N.Y. 532, 21 N.E. 700; White, Negligence of Municipal Corporations, 1920, ch. VII; Note, 1923, 23 Col.L.Rev. 56.

37. Y.B. 27 Hen. VIII, Mich., pl. 10. See Holdsworth, History of English Law, 2d ed. 1937, 424.

38. The other instance, of course, is libel. See infra, § 112.

39. Alexander v. Wilkes-Barre Anthracite Coal Co., 1916, 254 Pa. 1, 98 A. 794 (coal mining); Dozier v. Troy Drive–In Theatres, Inc., 1956, 265 Ala. 93, 89 So.2d 537 (gaming); Taylor v. Barnes, 1946, 303 Ky. 562, 198 S.W.2d 297 (obstruction of highway); Painter v. Gunderson, 1913, 123 Minn. 323, 143 N.W. 910 (access to lake cut off); Bouquet v. Hackensack Water Co., 1916, 90 N.J.L. 203, 101 A. 379 (pollution of public waters); Missouri Veterinary Medical Association v. Glisan, Mo. App.1950, 230 S.W.2d 169 (unlicensed professional activity).

But the rule does not preclude an ordinary negligence action for the particular damage, not founded in the invasion of the public right. Kneece v. City of Columbia, 1924, 128 S.C. 375, 123 S.E. 100.

40. Schroder v. City of Lincoln, 1952, 155 Neb. 599, 52 N.W.2d 808; Schlirf v. Loosen, 1951, 204 Okl. 651, 232 P.2d 928; Christy v. Chicago, Burlington & Quincy Railroad Co., 1948, 240 Mo.App. 632, 212 S.W.2d 476; Poulos v. Dover Boiler & Plate Fabricators, 1950, 5 N.J. 580, 76 A.2d 808.

41. 4 Bl.Comm. 166; Winfield, Law of Tort, 1st ed. 1937, 466; 5 Pomeroy, Equity Jurisprudence, 2d ed. 1919, § 1892. See, however, Smith, Private Action for Obstruction to Public Right of Passage, 1915, 15 Col.L. Rev. 1, 2–9, contending that actual, substantial damage is necessary, and that those who suffer it will be few, so that no undue burden will result from allowing them to recover.

Recent ferment in the field of environmental law has led to some agitation for abolition of the rule. See for example Davis, the Liberalized Law of Standing, 1970, 37 U.Chi.L.Rev. 450; Hanks and Hanks, an Environmental Bill of Rights: The Citizen Suit and the National Environmental Policy Act of 1969, 1970, 24 Rut.L.

Once this rule is accepted, however, the courts have not always found it at all easy to determine what is sufficient "particular damage" to support the private action, and some rather fine lines have been drawn in the decisions.[42] There is general agreement on the requirement that the plaintiff's damage be different in kind, rather than in degree, from that shared by the general public;[43] and that, for example, the fact that the plaintiff has occasion to use a highway[44] or a navigable stream[45] five times as often as anyone else gives him no private right of action when it is obstructed. One good reason for such a conclusion is the extreme difficulty of fixing any lines of demarcation in terms of "degree" of public damage, since anyone who uses the highway or the stream at all will obviously suffer greater inconvenience than one who does not use it.

There have been writers[46] who have contended that, while the plaintiff should of course have no cause of action for the infringement of a purely theoretical right common to the public, he should not be denied relief in any case where that infringement causes him substantial harm, even though he shares it with others. This has not been borne out at all by the decisions; and when a whole community has been commercially affected by the closing of a drawbridge or a river,[47] or the destruction of fish in a lake,[48] a plaintiff who has suffered greater pecuniary loss than anyone else has not been allowed to recover for it.

Degree cannot, however, be left entirely out of account in determining difference in kind. Normally there may be no difference in the kind of interference with one who travels a road once a week and with one who

Rev. 230; Jaffe, Standing to Sue in Conservation Suits, in Law and Environment, 1970, 123.

Reliance has been placed by these writers on decisions under such statutes as the Federal Power Act and the Rivers and Harbors Act, which give a person "aggrieved" by the action of a Federal administrative agency the right to maintain a proceeding challenging the action of the agency. In such cases as Scenic Hudson Preservation Conference v. Federal Power Commission, 2d Cir. 1965, 354 F.2d 608, certiorari denied 384 U.S. 941, 86 S.Ct. 1462, 16 L.Ed.2d 540, and Citizens Committee for the Hudson Valley v. Volpe, 2d Cir. 1970, 425 F.2d 97, certiorari denied 400 U.S. 949, 91 S.Ct. 237, 27 L.Ed.2d 256, this was held to authorized suits by groups interested in the protection of scenic values.

There are also statutes in a few states that provide for suit by individual citizens in the public interest to abate a public nuisance. For example Fla.Stat.1969, 60.05; Mich.Pub.Acts 1970, No. 127, Mich.Stat.Ann. 14.528; Wis.Stat.1958, 280.02. See Note, 1970, 16 Wayne L.Rev. 1085, 1127.

In the absence of such statutory authorization, no case has been found in which a private individual has been held to have standing to sue for a public nuisance in the absence of particular damage to him. The remedy was denied to a wildlife society in National Audubon Society v. Johnson, S.D.Tex.1970, 317 F.Supp. 1330.

42. See Smith, Private Action for Obstruction to Public Right of Passage, 1915, 15 Col.L.Rev. 1, 149; Prosser, Private Action for Public Nuisance, 1966, 52 Va.L.Rev. 997; Note, 1918, 2 Minn.L.Rev. 210.

Interesting questions of "proximate cause" were raised in the second Wagon Mound decision, Overseas Tankship (U.K.) Ltd. v. Morts Dock & Eng. Co., Ltd., [1961] A.C. 388. See Dias, Trouble on Oiled Waters: Problems of The Wagon Mound (No. 2), [1967] Camb. L.J. 62; Green, The Wagon Mound No. 2—Foreseeability Revisted, [1967] Utah L.Rev. 197.

43. Page v. Niagara Chemical Division of Food Machinery & Chemical Corp., Fla.1953, 68 So.2d 382; Smedberg v. Moxie Dam Co., 1952, 148 Me. 302, 92 A.2d 606; Willard v. City of Cambridge, 1862, 85 Mass. (3 Allen) 574; Bouquet v. Hackensack Water Co., 1916, 90 N.J.L. 203, 101 A. 379; Livingston v. Cunningham, 1920, 188 Iowa 254, 175 N.W. 980.

44. Poulos v. Dover Boiler & Plate Fabricators 1950, 5 N.J. 580, 76 A.2d 808; Borton v. Mangus, 1915, 93 Kan. 719, 145 P. 835; Painter v. Gunderson, 1913, 123 Minn. 342, 143 N.W. 911; Christy v. Chicago, Burlington & Quincy Railroad Co., 1948, 240 Mo.App. 632, 212 S.W.2d 476; Zettel v. City of West Bend, 1891, 79 Wis. 316, 48 N.W. 379.

45. Whitmore v. Brown, 1906, 102 Me. 47, 65 A. 516; Swanson v. Mississippi & Rum River Boom Co., 1890, 42 Minn. 532, 44 N.W. 986.

46. Smith, Private Action for Obstruction of Public Right of Passage, 1915, 15 Col.L.Rev. 1, 15–23; Fleming, Torts, 3d ed. 1965, 367–369.

47. Willard v. City of Cambridge, 1862, 85 Mass. (3 Allen) 574; Swanson v. Mississippi & Rum River Boom Co., 1890, 42 Minn. 532, 44 N.W. 986. Cf. Hohmann v. City of Chicago, 1892, 140 Ill. 226, 29 N.E. 671; Prosser v. City of Ottumwa, 1876, 42 Iowa 509; Walls v. C.D. Smith & Co., 1910, 167 Ala. 138, 52 So. 320.

48. Smedberg v. Moxie Dam Co., 1952, 148 Me. 302, 92 A.2d 606. Cf. Anthony Wilkinson Live Stock Co. v. McIlquam, 1905, 14 Wyo. 209, 83 P. 364 (interference with grazing rights); Livingston v. Cunningham, 1920, 188 Iowa 254, 175 N.W. 980.

travels it once a day. But if he traverses it a dozen times a day,[49] he always has some special reason to do so, which will almost invariably be based upon some special interest of his own not common to the community. Substantial interference with that interest must be particular damage. Deprivation of immediate access to land, which is quite clearly a special kind of damage, shades off by imperceptible stages into the remote obstruction of a highway, which is just as clearly not.[50] It follows that the degree can never be ignored when it bears legitimately upon the issue of kind.[51]

Where the plaintiff suffers personal injury,[52] or harm to his health,[53] or even mental distress,[54] there is no difficulty in finding a different kind of damage. The same is true as to physical harm to his chattels,[55] or interference with the physical condition of land, as by flooding it;[56] or silting up irrigation ditches.[57] It is likewise true where there is any substantial interference with the plaintiff's use and enjoyment of his own land,[58] as where a bawdy house, which disturbs the public morals, also makes life disagreeable in the house next door.[59] This makes the nuisance a private as well as a public one; and since the plaintiff does not lose his rights as a landowner merely because others suffer damage of the same kind or even of the same degree, there is general agreement that he may proceed upon either theory, or upon both.[60] Where this is the case, the action founded on the public nuisance may sometimes be preferable, because it is well settled that prescriptive rights, laches and the statute of limitations do not run against it.[61]

---

49. Wiggins v. Boddington, 1828, 3 Car. & P. 544, 172 Eng.Rep. 539 (hauling carts full of sand).

50. See infra, p. 649.

51. "Where to draw the line between cases where the injury is more general or more equally distributed, and cases where it is not, where, by reason of local situation, the damage is comparatively much greater to the special few, is often a difficult task. In spite of all the refinements and distinctions which have been made, it is often a mere matter of degree, and the courts have to draw the line between the more immediate obstruction or peculiar interference, which is ground for special damage, and the more remote obstruction or interference, which is not." Kaje v. Chicago, St. Paul, Minneapolis & Omaha Railway Co., 1894, 57 Minn. 422, 424, 59 N.W. 493.

52. Downes v. Silva, 1937, 57 R.I. 343, 190 A. 42; Flaherty v. Great Northern R. Co., 1944, 218 Minn. 488, 16 N.W.2d 553; White v. Suncook Mills, 1940, 91 N.H. 92, 13 A.2d 729; Delaney v. Philhern Realty Holding Corp., 1939, 280 N.Y. 461, 21 N.E.2d 507; Beckwith v. Town of Stratford, 1942, 129 Conn. 506, 29 A.2d 775.

53. Sullivan v. American Manufacturing Co. of Massachusetts, 4th Cir. 1929, 33 F.2d 690; Hunnicutt v. Eaton, 1937, 184 Ga. 485, 191 S.E. 919; Savannah, Florida & Western Railway Co. v. Parish, 1903, 117 Ga. 893, 45 S.E. 280; De Vaughn v. Minor, 1887, 77 Ga. 809, 1 S.E. 433; Code v. Jones, 1923, 54 Ont.L.Rep. 425.

54. Wilson v. Parent, 1961, 228 Or. 354, 365 P.2d 72 (public profanity addressed to plaintiff).

55. Lynn v. Hooper, 1899, 93 Me. 46, 44 A. 127; Larson v. New England Telephone & Telegraph Co., 1945, 141 Me. 326, 44 A.2d 1; Dygert v. Schenck, N.Y. 1840, 23 Wend. 446. Even where this is consequential, as where corn is spoiled when it cannot be moved over a blocked highway. Maynell v. Saltmarsh, 1665, 1 Keb. 847, 83 Eng.Rep. 1278; Cottman v. Lochner, 1929, 40 Wyo. 378, 278 P. 71.

56. Weinstein v. Lake Pearl Park, Inc., 1964, 347 Mass. 91, 196 N.E.2d 638. Cf. Lind v. City of San Luis Obispo, 1895, 109 Cal. 340, 42 P. 437 (depositing sewage); Hark v. Mountain Fork Lumber Co., 1945, 127 W.Va. 586, 34 S.E.2d 348 (laying tramway tracks).

57. Ravndal v. Northfork Placers, 1939, 60 Idaho 305, 91 P.2d 368.

58. Karpisek v. Cather & Sons Construction, Inc., 1962, 174 Neb. 234, 117 N.W.2d 322 (dust from asphalt plant); Buckmaster v. Bourbon County Fair Association, 1953, 174 Kan. 515, 256 P.2d 878 (noise and disturbance from automobile races); Weinstein v. Lake Pearl Park, Inc., 1964, 347 Mass. 91, 196 N.E.2d 638 (riparian land made wetter); Morris v. Borough of Haledon, 1952, 24 N.J.Super. 171, 93 A.2d 781 (noises and smoke); Morse v. Liquor Control Commission, 1947, 319 Mich. 52, 29 N.W.2d 316 (illegal sale of liquor interfering with church).

59. Crawford v. Tyrrell, 1891, 128 N.Y. 341, 28 N.E. 514; Tedescki v. Berger, 1907, 150 Ala. 649, 43 So. 960.

60. Adams v. City of Toledo, 1939, 163 Or. 185, 96 P.2d 1078; Tedescki v. Berger, 1907, 150 Ala. 649, 43 So. 960; Bishop Processing Co. v. Davis, 1957, 213 Md. 465, 132 A.2d 445; District of Columbia v. Totten, 1925, 55 U.S.App.D.C. 312, 5 F.2d 374, certiorari denied 269 U.S. 562, 46 S.Ct. 21, 70 L.Ed. 412; McManus v. Southern Railway Co., 1909, 150 N.C. 655, 64 S.E. 766.

61. Wade v. Campbell, 1962, 200 Cal.App.2d 54, 19 Cal.Rptr. 173; Elves v. King County, 1956, 49 Wn.2d 201, 299 P.2d 206; City of Meridian v. Tingle, 1956, 226 Miss. 317, 84 So.2d 388; Hazen v. Perkins, 1918, 92 Vt. 414, 105 A. 249; Long v. New York Central Railroad Co., 1929, 248 Mich. 437, 227 N.W. 739. The contention that this is true only when the private damages are of

There is more difficulty where the obstruction of a highway interferes with the landowner's access to his property, which is itself a property right. Where immediate ingress and egress are completely cut off, there is no doubt that there is particular damage, for which the private action will lie.[62] But there need not be complete deprivation; and it is enough that one entrance is closed, although there is another available,[63] or that the obstruction makes use of the passage unreasonably burdensome or inconvenient,[64] or unsafe.[65] It is only when the obstruction is so minor or partial that it is not regarded as a substantial interference with access[66] that the remedy is denied.

More distant obstructions of the highway, preventing entry by a particular route, offer more of a problem. Where access is completely cut off by blocking the only road in, and the plaintiff is "marooned far up on the mountain side,"[67] there is no doubt that there is particular damage. But where other routes are open, and it is only one that is blocked, the line must somehow be drawn between deprivation of access to land, which is a property right, and mere deprivation of the public right of passage, which is not.[68] This is essentially a matter of degree. In general,[69] when the obstruction is close to the land, as for example two hundred feet away in the same block,[70] so that the plaintiff must detour to travel in one direction, it has been treated as interference with access, while more remote obstructions, permitting the plaintiff to make a substantial start on his journey before he is forced to detour, have been regarded as nothing more than interference with the public right of travel.[71]

Pecuniary loss to the plaintiff has been regarded as different in kind when the defendant's obstruction has prevented the plaintiff from performing a particular contract, as for example to transport goods over the

---

the same nature as the public invasion was effectively refuted in Weeks-Thorn Paper Co. v. Glenside Woolen Mills, 1909, 64 Misc. 205, 118 N.Y.S. 1027, affirmed 140 App.Div. 878, 124 N.Y.S. 2, affirmed 204 N.Y. 563, 97 N.E. 1118, reargument denied 204 N.Y. 639, 98 N.E. 1136.

62. Cushing-Wetmore Co. v. Gray, 1907, 152 Cal. 118, 92 P. 70; Owens v. Elliott, 1962, 257 N.C. 250, 125 S.E.2d 589; Lindauer v. Hill, Okl.1953, 262 P.2d 697; Stephens v. Hubbard, 1930, 234 Ky. 115, 27 S.W.2d 665; Mayo v. Schumer, Mo.App.1923, 256 S.W. 549.

63. Brown v. Hendricks, 1947, 211 S.C. 395, 45 S.E.2d 603; Fassion v. Landrey, 1890, 123 Ind. 136, 24 N.E. 96; Hindi v. Smith, 1963, 73 N.M. 335, 388 P.2d 60; Purvis v. Busey, 1954, 260 Ala. 373, 71 So.2d 18; White Mountain Freezer Co. v. Levesque, 1954, 99 N.H. 15, 104 A.2d 525.

64. Graceland Corp. v. Consolidated Laundries Corp., 1958, 7 A.D.2d 89, 180 N.Y.S.2d 644, affirmed 1959, 6 N.Y.2d 900, 190 N.Y.S.2d 708, 160 N.E.2d 926; Michelsen v. Dwyer, 1954, 158 Neb. 427, 63 N.W.2d 513; Fugate v. Carter, 1928, 151 Va. 108, 144 S.E. 483; Regester v. Lincoln Oil Refining Co., 1933, 95 Ind.App. 425, 183 N.E. 693.

65. Baldocchi v. Four Fifty Sutter Corp., 1933, 129 Cal.App. 383, 18 P.2d 682.

66. Wynn v. Hale, 1957, 227 Ark. 765, 301 S.W.2d 466 (forced to open and close gates); Holland v. Grant County, 1956, 208 Or. 50, 298 P.2d 832 (minor detour); Ayers v. Stidham, 1954, 260 Ala. 390, 71 So.2d 95 (seldom used route); Schroder v. City of Lincoln, 1952, 155 Neb. 599, 52 N.W.2d 808 (bank teller window at curb); Magee v. Omansky, 1948, 187 Va. 422, 46 S.E.2d 443 (encroachment of eighteen inches); Richard v. Gulf Theatres, 1945, 155 Fla. 626, 21 So.2d 715 (15 feet of street obstructed, leaving 60 feet clear).

67. Colvin v. Tallassee Power Co., 1930, 199 N.C. 353, 360, 154 S.E. 678, 682; Pilgrim Plywood Corp. v. Melendy, 1938, 110 Vt. 112, 1 A.2d 700; Smart v. Aroostook Lumber Co., 1907, 103 Me. 37, 68 A. 527; Miller v. Schenck, 1889, 78 Iowa 372, 43 N.W. 225; Stricker v. Hillis, 1909, 15 Idaho 709, 99 P. 831.

68. See State ex rel. Anderson v. Preston, 1963, 2 Ohio App.2d 244, 207 N.E.2d 664, saying that otherwise "a bridge in Louisiana would logically subject that state to claims by all owners on the Mississippi and its many tributaries."

69. Missouri has adopted an arbitrary rule that unless access is completely cut off there must be an interference with entry to land at the point of the obstruction, and no detour is enough. Arcadia Realty Co. v. City of St. Louis, 1930, 326 Mo. 273, 30 S.W.2d 995; Christy v. Chicago, Burlington & Quincy Railroad Co., 1948, 240 Mo.App. 632, 212 S.W.2d 476.

70. O'Brien v. Central Iron & Steel Co., 1902, 158 Ind. 218, 63 N.E. 302. Accord: Young v. Rothrock, 1903, 121 Iowa 588, 96 N.W. 1105; Purvis v. Busey, 1954, 260 Ala. 373, 71 So.2d 18; Bennett v. Nations, 1945, 49 N.M. 389, 164 P.2d 1019; Yates v. Tiffany, 1927, 126 Me. 128, 136 A. 668. The greatest distance found is two blocks, in Sloss-Sheffield Steel & Iron Co. v. Johnson, 1906, 147 Ala. 384, 41 So. 907.

71. Ayers v. Stidham, 1954, 260 Ala. 390, 71 So.2d 95; Magee v. Omansky, 1948, 187 Va. 422, 46 S.E.2d 443; McKay v. Enid, 1910, 26 Okl. 275, 109 P. 520; Guttery v. Glenn, 1903, 201 Ill. 275, 66 N.E. 305; Zettel v. City of West Bend, 1891, 79 Wis. 316, 48 N.W. 379.

highway in question,⁷² or when it has put him to additional expense, or expensive delay, in performing it.⁷³ It has also been considered sufficient where the plaintiff has an established business⁷⁴ making a commercial use of the public right with which the defendant interferes, as where a river is blocked and plaintiff operates a steamboat line⁷⁵ or rafts logs,⁷⁶ or collects tolls for passage.⁷⁷ There are several cases in which commercial fisheries making a localized use of public waters have been allowed to recover for pollution,⁷⁸ where the ordinary citizen deprived of his occasional piscatorial Sunday pleasure could not do so. Even where the business is not itself founded on the exercise of the public right, there may still be recovery for loss of customers,⁷⁹ or interference with transportation which prevents it from obtaining materials or labor,⁸⁰ or from shipping its goods to market.⁸¹ Where, however, the pecuniary loss is common to the whole community, or a large part of it, as where a whole area of a town is cut off by a viaduct,⁸² or the draining of a good fishing lake affects all the fishing camps in the vicinity,⁸³ it has been regarded as no different in kind from the common misfortune and the private action cannot be maintained.

The Tort Action—A Recommended Approach

It is suggested that a better description of the results of cases would show that a private individual cannot complain of public nuisance either by way of maintaining a tort

---

72. Gulf States Steel Co. v. Beveridge, 1923, 209 Ala. 473, 96 So. 587 (taxi unable to deliver passenger); Brewer v. Missouri Pacific Railway Co., 1923, 161 Ark. 525, 257 S.W. 53 (contract to do work on flooded road).

73. Tuell v. Marion, 1913, 110 Me. 460, 86 A. 980; Commissioners of Anne Arundel County v. Watts, 1910, 112 Md. 353, 76 A. 82; Sholin v. Skamania Boom Co., 1909, 56 Wash. 303, 105 P. 632; Knowles v. Pennsylvania Railroad Co., 1896, 175 Pa. 623, 34 A. 974; cf. Campbell v. Mayor of Paddington, [1911] 1 K.B. 869.

The mere delay and inconvenience of a detour around a highway obstruction, common to all who pass that way, is not enough in the way of particular damage, in the absence of some showing of special pecuniary loss. Winterbottom v. Lord Derby, 1867, L.R. 2 Ex. 316; Ayers v. Stidham, 1954, 260 Ala. 390, 71 So.2d 95; Magee v. Omansky, 1948, 187 Va. 422, 46 S.E.2d 443; McKay v. Enid, 1910, 26 Okl. 275, 109 P. 520; Guttery v. Glenn, 1903, 201 Ill. 275, 66 N.E. 305.

74. It is not enough that the plaintiff contemplates commercial transactions, since anyone might do so. Clark v. Chicago & Northwestern Railway Co., 1888, 70 Wis. 593, 36 N.W. 326; President & Fellows of Harvard College v. Stearns, 1860, 81 Mass. (15 Gray) 1.

75. Carver v. San Pedro, Los Angeles & Salt Lake Railroad Co., S.D.Cal.1906, 151 F. 334; Piscataqua Navigation Co. v. New York, New Haven & Hartford Railroad Co., D.Mass.1898, 89 F. 362; Viebahn v. Board of Crow Wing Commissioners, 1906, 96 Minn. 276, 104 N.W. 1089; City of Philadelphia v. Gilmartin, 1872, 71 Pa. 140.

76. Wakeman v. Wilbur, 1895, 147 N.Y. 657, 42 N.E. 341; Page v. Mille Lacs Lumber Co., 1893, 53 Minn. 492, 55 N.W. 608, vacated on other grounds 53 Minn. 492, 55 N.W. 1119; Gates v. Northern Pacific Railway Co., 1885, 64 Wis. 64, 24 N.W. 494, error dismissed Northern Pacific Railway Co. v. Gates, 131 U.S. 442, 9 S.Ct. 801, 33 L.Ed. 218.

77. Wisconsin River Improvement Co. v. Lyons, 1872, 30 Wis. 61.

78. Hampton v. North Carolina Pulp Co., 1943, 223 N.C. 535, 27 S.E.2d 538; Columbia River Fishermen's Protective Union v. City of St. Helens, 1939, 160 Or. 654, 87 P.2d 195; Strandholm v. Barbey, 1933, 145 Or. 427, 26 P.2d 46; Morris v. Graham, 1897, 16 Wash. 343, 47 P. 752; Carson v. Hercules Powder Co., 1966, 240 Ark. 887, 402 S.W.2d 640. See Note, 1967, 20 Ark.L. Rev. 407.

79. East Cairo Ferry Co. v. Brown, 1930, 233 Ky. 299, 25 S.W.2d 730; Johnson v. Town of Oakland, 1925, 148 Md. 432, 129 A. 648; Duy v. Alabama Western Railroad Co., 1912, 175 Ala. 162, 57 So. 724; Aldrich v. City of Minneapolis, 1893, 52 Minn. 164, 53 N.W. 1072; Flynn v. Taylor, 1891, 127 N.Y. 596, 28 N.E. 418.

80. Farmers' Co-operative Manufacturing Co. v. Albemarle & Raleigh Railroad Co., 1895, 117 N.C. 579, 23 S.E. 43; Williams v. Tripp, 1878, 11 R.I. 447. A good case is Pedrick v. Raleigh & Pamlico Sound Railroad Co., 1906, 143 N.C. 485, 55 S.E. 877, in which the owner of a sawmill on the river was permitted to maintain the action, while citizens keeping sailboats on the water for pleasure were not.

81. E.A. Chatfield Co. v. City of New Haven, D.Conn.1901, 110 F. 788; Carl v. West Aberdeen Land & Improvement Co., 1896, 13 Wash. 616, 43 P. 890; Mehrhof Brothers Brick Manufacturing Co. v. Delaware, Lackawanna & Western Railroad Co., 1888, 51 N.J.L. 56, 16 A. 12; Little Rock, Mississippi River & Texas Railway Co. v. Brooks, 1882, 39 Ark. 403.

82. Hohman v. City of Chicago, 1892, 140 Ill. 226, 29 N.E. 671 (construction of viaduct); Willard v. City of Cambridge, 1862, 85 Mass. (3 Allen) 574 (closing drawbridge); Swanson v. Mississippi & Rum River Boom Co., 1890, 42 Minn. 532, 44 N.W. 986 (blocking river); Prosser v. City of Ottumwa, 1876, 42 Iowa 509 (business of ferry).

83. Smedberg v. Moxie Dam Co., 1952, 148 Me. 302, 92 A.2d 606. Cf. Anthony Wilkinson Live Stock Co. v. McIlquam, 1905, 14 Wyo. 209, 83 P. 364 (public grazing rights).

action for damages or by way of obtaining an abatement of the so-called nuisance unless the conduct has resulted in the commission of an independent tort to the plaintiff. In order to answer this question properly, one must consider the nature of the interest that the public nuisance is designed to protect. The social interest to be protected is necessarily one that is designed to foster some individual interest of people in society. So, the issue is whether or not specific individuals whose interest is or may be adversely affected should have a remedy in addition to the remedy available to the governmental entity that is established to further such interest. In order to answer this question, a classification of public nuisances must be made on the basis of the individual interest affected by the nuisance.

One of the most frequent examples of a public nuisance is the purpresture or obstruction that is created upon or placed upon governmentally owned or occupied property, such as the highway or sidewalk.[84] This is the unlawful trespassory intrusion on public property that interferes with the freedom to travel. Those who intentionally intrude upon private property as trespassers are often liable without another kind of fault for harm to the occupier resulting therefrom, however unforeseeable that harm might be.[85] But this does not necessarily mean that there would be liability to third persons for any kind of unforeseeable loss. It is clear that courts have held that there is no liability for mere annoyance and inconvenience to those whose "right" to travel has been interfered with. It would appear that some courts would allow recovery for physical harm on the theory that the trespasser on the highway should be legally accountable without reference to the usual rules regarding liability for negligently causing physical injury.[86] It would also appear that the creator of the nuisance is liable for economic loss, if the plaintiff's restriction to travel has been affected in a special way, as when egress or ingress to his property is obstructed.[87] Some obstruction to the highway or sidewalk may have been accidental, as when a wall collapses or a tree falls, in which event it is highly unlikely that the defendant should ever be liable for "injury" resulting therefrom unless the injury is the kind that is generally protected through the rules pertaining to negligence. The fact that this accidental intrusion resulted in an obstruction of a public highway is no more significant than if the intrusion resulted in the obstruction of a private alley or road.

Another general type of "public nuisance" is one that is regarded as such because of its impact on the environment, and therefore the use and enjoyment of private property, now and in the future. Here, the answer is rather simple. The air pollution, the soil pollution, the noise pollution or the water pollution must affect the plaintiff in a substantial way and for that reason constitute a private nuisance.[88] It is not irrelevant that others are affected and that so many others are affected as to constitute a public nuisance. This would mean that the conduct is unreasonable and enjoinable. It would be enjoinable, it would seem, by anyone affected in a substantial way because it would then be a private nuisance, *i.e.*, the interference would be unreasonable as to all those affected in a substantial way, such as if the market value of the land was affected.[89]

Then, there are those activities that are a "public nuisance" because the defendant is

---

84. See, supra, this section at p. 649.

85. See, supra, § 13.

86. See for a discussion of this problem Deane v. Johnston, Fla.1958, 104 So.2d 3; McFarlane v. City of Niagara Falls, 1928, 247 N.Y. 340, 160 N.E. 391, 57 A.L.R. 1; Delahunta v. City of Waterbury, 1948, 134 Conn. 630, 59 A.2d 800, 7 A.L.R.2d 218.

87. Colvin v. Tallassee Power Co., 1930, 199 N.C. 353, 360, 154 S.E. 678, 682; Pilgrim Plywood Corp. v. Melendy, 1938, 110 Vt. 112, 1 A.2d 700; Smart v. Aroostook Lumber Co., 1907, 103 Me. 37, 68 A. 527; Miller v. Schenck, 1889, 78 Iowa 372, 43 N.W. 225; Stricker v. Hillis, 1909, 15 Idaho 709, 99 P. 831.

88. See, supra, § 88.

89. See, supra, § 88.

engaged in a continuing course of conduct that is calculated to result in physical harm or economic loss to so many persons as to become a matter of serious concern. Such activities as practicing law or medicine without a license would be included in this category. It would appear that this conduct is negligent as a matter of law to each and every person whom the defendant attempts to serve. The fact that the conduct is enjoinable by the state as a public nuisance is not, however, helpful in deciding the issue of liability to an individual for personal injuries. Moreover, it is probably that the conduct is not enjoinable by an individual.[90]

Then there are the public nuisances that are said to be such because of their possible effect on the morals of the people, such as houses of prostitution, obscene movies, and massage parlors. It is possible that the location of such an establishment can be a common law private nuisance, especially if there is a zoning restriction violated, simply because its presence interferes with the use and enjoyment of private property, but it cannot be a tort to a person simply because that person was induced to engage in immoral or sinful conduct. The law of torts does not attempt to give redress to those who have been led into sin by watching obscene pictures or using massage parlors. This much has been said by way of attempting to show that if the individual interest that the public nuisance is designed to protect is the type protected under tort law, then the conduct that is regarded as a public nuisance will quite often be regarded also as either a private nuisance or some other tort to those who are adversely affected.

WESTLAW REFERENCES

synopsis("public nuisance")

The Tort Action—General Case Approach
private /s right action /s "public nuisance*"

The Tort Action—A Recommended Approach
di purpresture*

---

90. See, supra, § 89 on Remedies.

purpresture*
practic! /s law legal medic! dental dentis! optomet! chiroprac! profession! /s unlicensed licens! unauthorized authori! /p nuisance*

§ 91. Interference With Use and Enjoyment of Private Property—Negligence and Strict Liability

In the Second Restatement of Torts,[1] it is said that one is subject to liability for a private nuisance by way of interfering with another's private interest in the use and enjoyment of his land not only when the interference is intentional and proves to be unreasonable, but also when the interference is accidental and otherwise actionable under rules controlling liability either for negligent, reckless, or abnormally dangerous conduct. This was simply a statement designed to label all actionable conduct interfering with the use and enjoyment of land as a nuisance. This has produced much confusion and some erroneous results. In the first place, the so-called interest in the use and enjoyment of property is not a single type of interest. There are several distinct individual interests that can be included under the general label of "use and enjoyment." There are four distinctly different kinds of losses involved: (a) physical harm to land and tangible things on the land, such as crops, soil, and water; (b) physical harm to those who are using and occupying land; (c) mental annoyance and physical discomfort, this being a type of harm not normally protected from conduct other than conduct committed with the intention of causing it; and (d) economic loss. These different interests of individuals and other legal entities are not protected in the same way from all kinds of conduct, and the effort to include all kinds of interferences with interests in land as either trespass or nuisance has not been helpful. Trespass and nuisance are terms that should describe intentional torts, *i.e.*, torts arising out of intentional invasions.

§ 91

1. Second Restatement of Torts, § 822.

A source of much confusion has resulted from the notion that if liability is imposed on those who act reasonably in intentionally interfering with others, then such liability is a kind of liability without fault. It is not; rather, it is liability for harm caused by an intentional invasion; and it may be no justification for not paying for the harm caused that the defendant inflicted the harm reasonably in his own interest or that of the general public.[2]

Another fallacy results from the notion that if one's conduct is a nuisance only to the extent that there was a failure to exercise reasonable care to avoid some of the interference, such as dust from a factory, or smoke from an electric generating plant or the like, then this is liability for negligence when in fact the defendant realized what was happening. Negligence as a theory of recovery applies when harm results from an event unintentionally caused and from conduct that exposed the plaintiff to an unreasonable risk of harm. Strict liability as a theory of recovery is based on the idea that defendant was engaged in some kind of activity exposing others to a risk of harm from an accidental invasion under circumstances that justify allocating certain losses from such risk to the defendant, even though the defendant acted with reasonable care.

Physical Harm to Persons and Tangible Things

The law related to liability for physical harm to persons and tangible things from accidental invasions is considered in other chapters in this book. If defendant through a simple act or a continuous course of conduct allows noxious substances to escape without knowing that such is occurring, then liability may be imposed either because of negligence, or because he was engaged in an abnormally dangerous activity or because of some property rights doctrine of "natural rights." Thus, it could be found that one who uses explosives is subject to liability without fault for physical damage to water wells, or homes from vibrations, simply because the conduct was abnormally dangerous and for the very reason that it was likely to result in physical harm to property from vibrations. This does not include the notion that there should be liability for a temporary emotional disturbance. Of course, some courts may conclude that any water pollution is actionable on the theory of a "right" to the water in its natural purity, but the solution to the problem cannot be aided by referring to the result as a nuisance.

Mental Annoyance and Physical Discomfort

When the defendant's conduct accidentally causes only mental disturbance, without accompanying physical injury or physical consequences or any other independent basis for tort liability, there is general agreement that in the ordinary case there can be no recovery.[3] It is seldom that a simple act of negligence or other kind of conduct without causing physical harm will cause enough mental discomfort to constitute a substantial interference of the kind that would affect the market value of the land prior to the time that the defendant realizes that it is happening. But a single act of negligence can have a protracted effect. In Macca v. General Telephone Co. of Northwest, Inc.,[4] an action was brought for emotional distress resulting from plaintiff's repeated reception of telephone calls for the after-hours number of a floral shop because of the negligence of the telephone company in listing the wrong number. The court called this a nuisance because there was an interference with the use and enjoyment of property. This is a case involving the negligent rendition of a public utility service. Whether or not a public utility should be liable and rate payers should be requested to bear the cost for all kinds of mental annoyance and physical discomfort resulting from single acts of

2. See, supra, § 88.
3. See, supra, § 54.

4. 1972, 262 Or. 414, 495 P.2d 1193.

negligence is an issue about which there can be much disagreement. If there is to be liability, it should probably be contractual in its nature. Interruptions in the delivery of electricity, gas, water, and the like to residential users may often be attributable to negligence, but rate payers cannot reasonably be expected to pay for noneconomic losses attributable to mental annoyance and discomfort.

If and when negligent conduct results in accidental invasions over a protracted period of time causing mental disturbance (without physical harm) of such a nature as to affect the market value of the property for a substantial period of time perhaps mental disturbance of this kind can justifiably be differentiated from that generally caused by negligent conduct. This would be a rare situation.

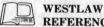
WESTLAW REFERENCES

negligen! /s intend! intentional /s nuisance*

Physical Harm to Persons and Tangible Things
explosives /p liab! /p fault negligen! duty %
 topic(313a)

Mental Annoyance and Physical Discomfort
emotional mental /s annoy! disturb! distress! discomfort
 /p nuisance

Chapter 16

TORT AND CONTRACT

Table of Sections

Sec.
92. Tort and Contract Obligations as Between Parties to a Contract.
93. Liability of a Party to a Contract to Third Parties.
94. Election to Sue for Restitution.

§ 92. Tort and Contract Obligations as Between Parties to a Contract

The distinction between tort and contract liability, as between parties to a contract, has become an increasingly difficult distinction to make. It would not be possible to reconcile the results of all cases. The availability of both kinds of liability for precisely the same kind of harm has brought about confusion and unnecessary complexity. It is to be hoped that eventually the availability of both theories—tort and contract—for the same kind of loss with different requirements both for the claimant's *prima facie* case and the defendant's affirmative defenses will be reduced in order to simplify the law and reduce the costs of litigation.

Tort obligations are in general obligations that are imposed by law—apart from and independent of promises made and therefore apart from the manifested intention of the parties—to avoid injury to others. By injury here is meant simply the interference with the individual's interest or an interest of some other legal entity that is deemed worthy of legal protection. The variety of interests that are protected through tort law in one way or another are divisible into three general categories: (1) interests of personality; (2) interests in tangible things, real and personal; and (3) a large body of intangible interests, both economic and relational. There are three considerations of utmost importance in deciding about duties, i.e., tort obligations, apart from manifested intentions through promises made.

These considerations are: (1) the nature of the defendant's activity such as a builder or a manufacturer-seller of a product; (2) the relationship between the parties, such as occupier of land and business guest; and (3) the type of injury or harm threatened. The obligations which give rise to tort actions and which are imposed on the basis of the three factors just mentioned are created primarily on the basis of policy reasons of one kind or another apart from enforcing a commitment of an intention to do or not to do something in the future. These obligations, commonly referred to as duties, are often owed to all those within the range of harm or at least to some considerable class of people that can include parties to a contract.

The type of injury or harm threatened under modern law has much to do with whether or not an obligation to avoid such harm can be regarded as either contractual or tortious or both. Losses resulting from the sale by merchants and manufacturers of defective products can be categorized into four areas. These are personal injuries, intangible economic losses attributable neither to personal injuries nor to physical damage to the product itself or other property, physical damage to property other than the defective product itself, and physical damage to the defective product itself.

Contract obligations are created to enforce promises which are manifestations not only of a present intention to do or not to do something, but also of a commitment to the future. They are, therefore, obligations based on the manifested intention of the parties to a bargaining transaction. Generally speaking, there is a fundamental distinction between a representation and a promise. A representation is a statement by the representer as to his existing state of mind regarding the existence of a past or present fact. Therefore, such liability as is imposed on a representer for stating something that proves to be false must be based on a tort theory. But it is a mistake to assume that a statement in the form of a representation cannot also be an implied promise to give some kind of satisfaction if the representation proves to be false. Therefore, warranty-representations or representations made under circumstances when the representee can reasonably regard the statements as manifestations of an intention to guarantee are the basis for contractual obligations and contract claims. Thus, a merchant-seller, in the absence of stipulations in the contract of sale clearly indicating the contrary, impliedly represents that the product he sells is merchantable and therefore reasonably fit for its primary purposes, and that he will give satisfaction of some kind if it is not.

It is suggested that the results of most cases will support the following seven generalizations and that these generalizations, if followed, would be helpful in resolving some of the existing complexities:

1. *Obligations imposed by law are tort obligations.* Tort obligations are in general obligations that are imposed by law on policy considerations to avoid some kind of loss to others. They are obligations imposed apart from and independent of promises made and therefore apart from any manifested intention of parties to a contract or other bargaining transaction. Therefore, if the alleged obligation to do or not to do something that was breached could not have existed but for a manifested intent, then contract law should be the *only* theory upon which liability would be imposed.

2. *Tort obligations may not be disclaimable.* It has often been assumed that as between the parties to a contract or bargaining transaction, tort as well as contract obligations can be disclaimed if this is clearly and unmistakably done so that the intent of both parties is clearly manifested. But to accept this is simply to approve the notion that the manifested intent of the parties, as ascertained through appropriate rules of construction, controls the obligations of the parties. But since tort obligations are based on policy considerations apart from manifested intent, the extent to which such obligations can be impaired by contract depends a great deal on the relationship between the parties, the nature of the bargaining transaction, and the type of loss for which liability is disclaimed. This is especially true as regards disclaimers by those who make and sell products.[1]

3. *Misfeasance or negligent affirmative conduct in the performance of a promise generally subjects an actor to tort liability as well as contract liability for physical harm to persons and tangible things.* Gen-

§ 92

1. Supra, Chapter 11, § 68, on Express Assumption of the Risk.

erally speaking, there is a duty to exercise reasonable care in how one acts to avoid physical harm to persons and tangible things.[2] Entering into a contract with another pursuant to which one party promises to do something does not alter the fact that there was a preexisting obligation or duty to avoid harm when one acts. Thus, when a patient contracts with a physician for medical treatment and the physician is guilty of negligence in diagnosis or treatment, there is liability on a tort theory as well as on a contract theory for failure to render the service with reasonable skill and care.[3] There is both a breach of an implied promise and a breach of a duty imposed by law.

4. *Recovery of intangible economic losses is normally determined by contract law.* Generally speaking, there is no general duty to exercise reasonable care to avoid intangible economic loss or losses to others that do not arise from tangible physical harm to persons and tangible things.[4] This being so, the manifested intent of the parties should ordinarily control the nature and extent of the obligations of the parties to a contract of sale, either of real or personal property or a contract of service. This is not to say that this should always be so. The position of the consumer in the market place may be such as to justify certain obligations on those who supply goods and render service apart from promises made and intentions manifested. No doubt there are some consumer transactions where courts or legislatures do conclude that certain obligations cannot be disclaimed and when freedom of contract is restricted and regulated. But if this be so and if freedom to negotiate is restricted in such a way that even without a defect in the negotiation process there is liability notwithstanding a disclaimer, the liability would appear to be tortious in nature and ought to be regarded as such.

5. *There is no tort liability for nonfeasance, i.e., for failing to do what one has promised to do in the absence of a duty to act apart from the promise made.* In most situations, where a party to a bargaining transaction renders a service or sells a product, there would have been no duty to render that service or sell a product except for the voluntary undertaking to do so. That being so, the contract or bargaining transaction normally defines the scope of the obligation that the service provides or the product supplier undertakes. There is a fundamental difference between doing something that causes physical harm and failing to do something that would have prevented harm or if one prefers a fundamental difference between lack of performance of something that would have prevented harm and defective performance that caused harm either from a dangerous force or a dangerous condition of something.

6. *Duties of affirmative action are often imposed by law apart from promises made.* Duties of affirmative action, especially to avoid physical harm to persons and tangible things, are often imposed by law on the basis of certain factors and especially the relationship between two parties. A contract or bargaining transaction brings into existence a relationship of one kind or another at or after the contract or bargaining transaction is made.[5] When one undertakes custodial care of another such as when a common carrier undertakes to transport a passenger or when a hotel provides a room for a patron, the relationship thus created by the bargaining transaction results in the creation of duties of affirmative action such as protection from the misconduct of third persons that is separate and apart from the

---

2. Supra, § 53.

3. Du Bois v. Decker, 1891, 130 N.Y. 325, 29 N.E. 313; McNevins v. Lowe, 1866, 40 Ill. 209; Napier v. Greenzweig, 2d Cir. 1919, 256 F. 196.

4. Chrysler Corp. v. Taylor, 1977, 141 Ga.App. 671, 234 S.E.2d 123 ("lemon" automobile); Inglis v. American Motors Corp., 1965, 3 Ohio St.2d 132, 209 N.E.2d 583 (car that squeaked and rattled); Clark v. International Harvester Co., 1978, 99 Idaho 326, 581 P.2d 784 (no recovery for "down-time" due to repairs). Supra, Chapter 25 on Economic Relations.

5. Supra, § 56.

promises made and intentions manifested.[6] Therefore, the breach of these affirmative duties imposed by law may coincide with an implied promise giving rise to a contract action for breach of the promissory obligation. This may be a duty that cannot be disclaimed. Relationships created through bargaining transactions are of many kinds and varieties, such as landlord and tenant, tenants in common of real property, bailor and bailee, owner of land and independent contractor. The obligations as between parties to such contracts are not always obligations based entirely on the manifested intent of the parties.

7. *Damage for a loss suffered by a promisee in reliance on a promisor to carry out a promise may be recoverable on a tort negligence theory.* When one makes a promise—a commitment as to what he will do or will not do in the future—this generally induces reasonable reliance thereon, and reliance damage apart from benefit of the bargain damage is likely to result. Some courts are likely to hold that there is a duty to exercise reasonable care, even if the promise is not enforceable as such under contract law, to prevent foreseeable harm to the promisee (as well as to third parties) from reasonable reliance on the promisor to carry out the promise as made. This is not a duty to perform but rather a duty to prevent reliance damage. Since the loss suffered is the result of reliance on a manifested intention, it might be preferable to regard the recovery when justified as a type of contractual recovery, especially when the claim is by a promisee and not by a third party. But contractual liability can be regarded as limited to the type of case where promises are found to be enforceable, and the damage results from the breach of an enforceable promise.

Early History—The Distinction Between Misfeasance and Nonfeasance

The earliest cases arising in the borderland were those of negligence in the rendition of services on the part of those engaged in a public trade or calling, as where a ferryman overloaded his boat and drowned the plaintiff's horses,[7] or a smith lamed a horse while shoeing it.[8] The action was on the case, and the underlying theory seems to have been at first one in tort for breach of a duty imposed by law to render the service and in rendering the service to do so with some degree of skill and care. In the course of time, the defendant's "assumpsit" or undertaking or implied promise to render the service with reasonable skill and care came to be regarded as the real foundation for the action;[9] and with the development of the action of assumpsit and the idea of consideration,[10] the obligation of the contract became recognized as itself a basis of liability. The tort remedy survived, however, in the situations where it had already existed; and the more or less inevitable efforts of lawyers [11] to turn every breach of contract into a tort forced the English courts to find some line of demarcation. There is a general rule of tort law to the effect that one who acts is under a duty to exercise reasonable care to avoid physical harm to persons and tangible property of others and this general duty or obligation would extend to parties in bargaining transactions such as sales and service transactions as well as to those who are not parties to bargaining transactions. Entering into a bargaining transaction, pursuant to which one party promises to do something, does not alter the fact that if he did

6. Supra, § 56.

7. 1348, Y.B. 22 Lib.Ass. 94, pl. 41.

8. 1372, Y.B. 46 Edw. III, f. 19, pl. 19. See Fifoot, History and Sources of the Common Law, Tort and Contract, 1949, c. 2, 4, 6, 9; Kiraffy, The Action on the Case, 1951, 137–150.

9. 3 Street, Foundations of Legal Liability, 1906, 173.

10. Ames, The History of Assumpsit, 1888, 2 Harv. L.Rev. 1.

11. See for example Courtenay v. Earle, 1850, 10 C.B. 73, 138 Eng.Rep. 30, where the attempt was made to turn the non-payment of a bill of exchange into a tort.

choose to do something that he promised, there was a preexisting obligation to act with reasonable care to avoid physical harm to persons and tangible things in the vicinity of his conduct. But in general there is no duty or obligation imposed by law and apart from promises or guarantees made in bargaining transactions to use reasonable care to prevent economic loss by interfering with contractual and business relations. Such torts as have been recognized are based on fraud or coercion in inducing bargaining transactions [12] or intentional interference without a justifiable reason of contractual or business relations.[13] This is not to say that in some situations when one undertakes to act he may be doing so under circumstances where, apart from the contract that he makes, there should be a duty to exercise reasonable care to others whose economic interests are likely to be affected by the way the conduct is performed. This is especially true of representations made to a client by a lawyer or an accountant that are made with the knowledge that they are to be communicated to and relied upon by others.[14] In addition to the duty that is owed to the promisor under the contract, there may be the additional obligation imposed by law (which cannot be altered by the contract of the parties) that is tortious in nature and should be regarded as such. It is suggested that to the extent that the duty a party to a contract owes to another party or a third party beneficiary is to be determined upon the basis of the first party's manifested intention, the obligation is contractual and entirely contractual. This would normally be so when the claim is for economic loss. Such a claim should not be translatable into a tort action in order to escape some roadblock to recovery on a contract theory. If the obligation is one that cannot be disclaimed by one engaged in the type of transaction involved and is imposed without reference to manifested intent, then the obligation should be regarded as tortious in character. Thus, a builder or a contractor would normally be subject to liability on a contract theory only, to the promisee and a third-party beneficiary for delays in construction or defects in construction that do not result in physical harm to persons and tangible things, other than the thing itself that is being constructed or repaired.[15] On the other hand, it is quite possible that lawyers or accountants may be subject to tort liability as well as contract liability for economic loss suffered as a consequence of reliance by third parties on negligent misrepresentations made in the course of rendering a service pursuant to a contract.[16]

The line of division which developed quite early [17] was that between "nonfeasance,"

12. See, infra, Chapter 18 on Misrepresentation.

13. See, infra, Chapter 24 on Economic Relations.

14. See, infra, Chapter 18 on Misrepresentation.

15. It is generally said that a contractor's liability for economic loss is fixed by the terms of his contract. Hall v. MacLeod, 1950, 191 Va. 665, 62 S.E.2d 42; Leavell & Co. v. Vilbig Bros., Inc., Tex.1960, 335 S.W.2d 211. Tort liability is in general limited to situations where the conduct of the builder causes an accident out of which physical harm occurs to some person or tangible thing other than the building itself that is under construction. See Annotation, 62 A.L.R.2d 1052. Flintkote Co. v. Dravo Corp., 11th Cir. 1982, 678 F.2d 942 (applying Georgia law); McClain v. Harveston, 1979, 152 Ga.App. 422, 263 S.E.2d 228; Album Graphics, Inc. v. Beatrice Foods Co., 1980, 87 Ill.App.3d 238, 42 Ill.Dec. 332, 408 N.E.2d 1041 ("Plaintiff has suffered only economic losses. Plaintiff should have his remedy for breach of contract but he should not be allowed to recover under tort law that which he may or may not be entitled to recover under the contract or contract law." Id. at p. 1050.); Altevogt v. Brinkoetter, 1981, 81 Ill.App.3d 711, 37 Ill.Dec. 209, 401 N.E.2d 1302; Foxcroft Townhome Owners Association v. Hoffman Rosner Corp., 1982, 105 Ill.App.3d 951, 61 Ill.Dec. 721, 435 N.E.2d 210; Redarowicz v. Ohlendorf, 1981, 95 Ill.App.3d 444, 50 Ill.Dec. 892, 420 N.E.2d 209.

16. See, infra, Chapter 18 on Misrepresentation.

17. The distinction appears to have originated in Watton v. Brinth, 1400, Y.B. 2 Hen. IV, f. 3, pl. 9, where it was pleaded that the defendant had undertaken to rebuild houses within a certain time and had failed to do so. Lord Holt approved the case in Coggs v. Bernard, 1703, 2 Ld.Raym. 909, 92 Eng.Rep. 107; and when the identical situation was repeated in Elsee v. Gatward, 1793, 5 Term Rep. 143, 101 Eng.Rep. 82, it was held that a tort action would lie only on a second count pleading that the defendant had in fact repaired the house with the wrong materials.

which meant not doing the thing at all, and "misfeasance," which meant doing it improperly. Much scorn has been poured on the distinction, but it does draw a valid line between the complete non-performance of a promise, which in the ordinary case is a breach of contract only, and a defective performance, which may also be a matter of tort. In general, the courts have adhered to the line thus drawn; and a failure even to begin or attempt performance of an agreement to lend money,[18] to employ the plaintiff, to furnish transportation, to deliver goods ordered,[19] to furnish light for a room,[20] to obtain the dissolution of an injunction and permit the plaintiff to proceed with the construction of a road,[21] or to attend as a physician,[22] all are held to amount to mere breaches of contract, for which no tort action will lie.

Misfeasance

Where the defendant has done something more than remain inactive, and is to be charged with "misfeasance," the possibility of recovery in tort is considerably increased. The older liability has carried over, and a carrier remains liable in tort, as well as on the contract, for negligent injury to a passenger [23] or for carrying him past his station,[24] for negligent loss or damage to goods shipped,[25] or for delay in their delivery.[26] Here again the duty is an incident of the relation rather than the contract, and the carrier would be liable if the passenger were carried free.[27]

Beyond this, the American courts [28] have extended the tort liability for misfeasance to virtually every type of contract where defective performance may injure the promisee. An attorney [29] or an abstractor [30] examining

---

18. Farabee-Treadwell Co. v. Union & Planters Bank & Trust Co., 1916, 135 Tenn. 208, 186 S.W. 92; John Deere Co. of St. Louis v. Short, Mo.1964, 378 S.W.2d 496.

19. Dawson Cotton Oil Co. v. Kenan, McKay & Speir, 1918, 21 Ga.App. 688, 94 S.E. 1037. Cf. Mulvey v. Staab, 1887, 4 N.M. 50, 12 P. 699 (to supply goods if plaintiff opened a store); Ketcham v. Miller, 1922, 104 Ohio St. 372, 136 N.E. 145 (refusal to turn over premises under lease).

20. Stone v. Johnson, 1938, 89 N.H. 329, 197 A. 713, affirmed in 1939, 90 N.H. 311, 8 A.2d 743.

21. Chase v. Clinton County, 1928, 241 Mich. 478, 217 N.W. 565.

22. Randolph's Administrator v. Snyder, 1910, 139 Ky. 159, 129 S.W. 562. See, generally, Note, 1932, 45 Harv.L.Rev. 164.

23. Kelly v. Metropolitan St. R. Co., [1895] 1 Q.B. 944; Williamson v. Pacific Greyhound Lines, 1945, 67 Cal.App.2d 250, 153 P.2d 990; Webber v. Herkimer & Mohawk Street Railroad Co., 1888, 109 N.Y. 311, 16 N.E. 358; Herron v. Miller, 1923, 96 Okl. 59, 220 P. 36; Baltimore City Passenger Railway Co. v. Kemp, 1883, 61 Md. 619. See Feldman, Actions in Contract Resulting from Aircraft Crashes, 1963, 12 Cleve.Marsh.L. Rev. 472.

24. Seals v. Augusta Southern Railroad Co., 1898, 102 Ga. 817, 29 S.E. 116; McKeon v. Chicago, Milwaukee & St. Paul Railway Co., 1896, 94 Wis. 477, 69 N.W. 175. Or for putting him off at the wrong station. Wilkes v. Chicago, Rock Island & Pacific Railway Co., 1924, 197 Iowa 832, 198 N.W. 44, 36 A.L.R. 1012; Forrester v. Southern Pacific Co., 1913, 36 Nev. 247, 134 P. 753, rehearing denied 1913, 36 Nev. 245, 136 P. 705. Or letting him down at an improper and dangerous place. Vines v. Crescent Transit Co., 1955, 264 Ala. 114, 85 So.2d 436.

25. Turner v. Stallibrass, [1898] 1 Q.B. 56; Sumsion v. Streator-Smith, Inc., 1943, 103 Utah 44, 132 P.2d 680; Ellis v. Taylor, 1931, 172 Ga. 830, 159 S.E. 266; Quaker Worsted Mills Corp. v. Howard Trucking Corp., 1938, 131 Pa.Super. 1, 198 A. 691.

26. Virginia-Carolina Peanut Co. v. Atlantic Coast Line Railroad Co., 1911, 155 N.C. 148, 71 S.E. 71; Owens Brothers v. Chicago, Rock Island & Pacific Railway Co., 1908, 139 Iowa 538, 117 N.W. 762; Texas & Pacific Railway Co. v. Bufkin, Tex.Civ.App.1932, 46 S.W.2d 714.

27. Flint & Pere Marquette Railway Co. v. Weir, 1877, 37 Mich. 111; Littlejohn v. Fitchburg Railroad Co., 1889, 148 Mass. 478, 20 N.E. 103; Pittsburgh, Cincinnati, Chicago & St. Louis Railway Co. v. Higgs, 1905, 165 Ind. 694, 76 N.E. 299.

28. The later English decisions have been much more reluctant to find tort liability. See Groom v. Crocker, [1939] 1 K.B. 194 (attorney); Steljes v. Ingram, 1903, 19 T.L.R. 534 (architect); Jarvis v. Moy, Davies, Smith, Vanderwell & Co., [1936] 1 K.B. 399. But an injured servant has been permitted to sue the master in contract. Matthews v. Kuwait Bechtel Corp., [1959] 2 Q.B. 57.

29. Trimboli v. Kinkel, 1919, 226 N.Y. 147, 123 N.E. 205 (title search); Sullivan v. Stout, 1938, 120 N.J.L. 304, 199 A. 1 (same); Ramage v. Cohn, 1937, 124 Pa. Super. 525, 189 A. 496 (surrender of check); O'Neill v. Gray, 2d Cir. 1929, 30 F.2d 776, certiorari denied 279 U.S. 865, 49 S.Ct. 480, 73 L.Ed. 1003 (delay in suit). See Coggin, Attorney Negligence—A Suit Within a Suit, 1958, 60 W.Va.L.Rev. 225; Note, 1951, 37 Va.L. Rev. 429.

30. See note 30 on page 661.

a title, a physician treating a patient,[31] a surveyor,[32] an agent collecting a note[33] or lending money[34] or settling a claim,[35] or a liability insurer defending a suit,[36] all have been held liable in tort for their negligence. The same is true of contractors employed to build a structure,[37] to transport people or goods,[38] to install a windmill[39] or a lightning rod,[40] or to shoot an oil well,[41] or a beauty shop giving a permanent wave,[42] of suppliers of chattels,[43] and of many others.[44] The principle which seems to have emerged from the decisions in the United States is that there will be liability in tort for misperformance of a contract whenever there would be liability for gratuitous performance without the contract—[45] which is to say, whenever such misperformance involves a foreseeable, unreasonable risk of harm to the interests of the plaintiff.

There has been little consideration of the problem of just where inaction ceases and "misfeasance" begins. It is clear that it is not always a question of action or inaction as to the particular act or omission which has caused the damage. Failure to blow a whistle[46] or to shut off steam[47] is readily treated as negligent operation of a train, and the omission to repair a gas pipe is regarded as negligent distribution of gas.[48] On the other hand, the affirmative act of discharging an employee is uniformly considered to be no more than non-performance of the

---

30. Dorr v. Massachusetts Title Insurance Co., 1921, 238 Mass. 490, 131 N.E. 191; Ehmer v. Title Guarantee & Trust Co., 1898, 156 N.Y. 10, 50 N.E. 420.

31. Huysman v. Kirsch, 1936, 6 Cal.2d 302, 57 P.2d 908; McDonald v. Camas Prairie Railroad Co., 1935, 180 Wash. 555, 38 P.2d 515; Cochran v. Laton, 1918, 78 N.H. 562, 103 A. 658; Gillette v. Tucker, 1902, 67 Ohio St. 106, 65 N.E. 865.

32. Ferrie v. Sperry, 1912, 85 Conn. 337, 82 A. 577. Cf. Gagne v. Bertran, 1954, 43 Cal.2d 481, 275 P.2d 15 (test hole driller).

33. Robinson v. Threadgill, 1851, 35 N.C. 39. Cf. Adams v. Robinson, 1880, 65 Ala. 586 (renting premises to an insolvent).

34. Shipherd v. Field, 1873, 70 Ill. 438.

35. Thuringer v. Bonner, 1924, 74 Colo. 539, 222 P. 1118.

36. Attleboro Manufacturing Co. v. Frankfort Marine Accident & Plate Glass Insurance Co., 1st Cir. 1909, 171 F. 495, affirmed 1 Cir. 1917, 240 F. 573; Wynnewood Lumber Co. v. Travelers Insurance Co., 1917, 173 N.C. 269, 91 S.E. 946. See Note, 1959, 34 N.Y.U.L.Rev. 783.

37. Lord Electric Co. v. Barber Asphalt Paving Co., 1919, 226 N.Y. 427, 123 N.E. 756; E. & M. Construction Co. v. Bob, 1967, 115 Ga.App. 127, 153 S.E.2d 641 (repair). Cf. Pinnix v. Toomey, 1955, 242 N.C. 358, 87 S.E.2d 893.

38. McClure v. Johnson, 1937, 50 Ariz. 76, 69 P.2d 573. Cf. Compton v. Evans, 1939, 200 Wash. 125, 93 P.2d 341 (employer).

39. Flint & Walling Manufacturing Co. v. Beckett, 1906, 167 Ind. 491, 79 N.E. 503. Cf. Olesen v. Beckanstin, 1919, 93 Conn. 614, 107 A. 514 (hot water system).

40. Holmes v. Schnoebelen, 1935, 87 N.H. 272, 178 A. 258; Whittle v. Miller Lightning Rod Co., 1918, 110 S.C. 557, 96 S.E. 907.

41. Jackson v. Central Torpedo Co., 1926, 117 Okl. 245, 246 P. 426.

42. Banfield v. Addington, 1932, 104 Fla. 661, 140 So. 893.

43. See infra, Chapter 17.

44. See for example Winchester v. O'Brien, 1929, 266 Mass. 33, 164 N.E. 807 (breach of landlord's covenant of quiet enjoyment by making noise); Smith v. Weber, 1944, 70 S.D. 232, 16 N.W.2d 537 (landlord burning rubbish and turning off lights); De Mirjian v. Ideal Heating Corp., 1949, 91 Cal.App.2d 905, 206 P.2d 20 (tenant damaging premises); Eads v. Marks, 1952, 39 Cal.2d 807, 249 P.2d 257 (negligence in leaving milk bottle); Mauldin v. Sheffer, 1966, 113 Ga.App. 874, 150 S.E.2d 150 (negligence of engineer in furnishing plans).

45. "If a defendant may be held liable for the neglect of a duty imposed on him, independently of any contract, by operation of law, a fortiori ought he to be liable when he has come under an obligation to use care as the result of an undertaking founded on a consideration. Where the duty has its roots in contract, the undertaking to observe due care may be implied from the relationship, and should it be the fact that a breach of the agreement also constitutes such a failure to exercise care as amounts to a tort, the plaintiff may elect, as the common-law authorities have it, to sue in case or in assumpsit." Flint & Walling Manufacturing Co. v. Beckett, 1906, 167 Ind. 491, 498, 79 N.E. 503, 505.

Cf. Coss v. Spaulding, 1912, 41 Utah 447, 126 P. 468, where defendant was a physician hired by a motorist who had run over a boy, to give him medical treatment.

46. Southern Railway Co. v. Grizzle, 1906, 124 Ga. 735, 53 S.E. 244.

47. Kelly v. Metropolitan R. Co. [1895] 1 Q.B. 944.

48. Consolidated Gas Co. v. Connor, 1911, 114 Md. 140, 78 A. 725. Cf. Osborne v. Morgan, 1881, 130 Mass. 102; Horner v. Lawrence, 1874, 37 N.J.L. 46; Lottman v. Barnett, 1876, 62 Mo. 159.

agreement to continue employment,[49] and the same conclusion has been reached as to the revocation of a theatre ticket and the expulsion of the patron.[50] The question appears to be rather whether the defendant's performance, as distinct from his promise or his preparation, has gone so far that it has begun to affect the interests of the plaintiff beyond the expected benefits of the contract itself,[51] and is to be regarded, by analogy to the cases of gratuitous undertaking,[52] as a positive act assuming the obligation.

Public Utility Services and Other Services Required by Law

There are, however, a few situations in which failure to perform a contract may amount to a tort. One notable instance is the survival of the old tort duty to serve all comers which arose as to common callings before the idea of contract had developed.[53] Under modern law this duty to serve exists only as to public officers,[54] common carriers,[55] innkeepers,[56] public warehousemen,[57] and public utilities,[58] who become liable in tort for nonperformance of their contracts, or even for refusal to enter into a contract at all. No such obligation rests today upon ordinary citizens engaged in other activities; and in the absence of legislation a physician,[59] a restaurant[60] or a racetrack[61] will not be liable for turning people away, for any reason or none. This is subject to the qualification that civil rights statutes, prohibiting under criminal penalty discrimination against any person on the ground of race or color, are commonly interpreted as intended to provide a tort action as a remedy.[62]

49. Addis v. Gramophone Co., Ltd. [1909] A.C. 488; May v. Tidewater Power Co., 1939, 216 N.C. 439, 5 S.E.2d 308; W. B. Davis & Son v. Ruple, 1930, 222 Ala. 52, 130 So. 772; Manley v. Exposition Cotton Mills, 1933, 47 Ga.App. 496, 170 S.E. 711; United Protective Workers v. Ford Motor Co., 7th Cir. 1955, 223 F.2d 49. Cf. Hart v. Ludwig, 1956, 347 Mich. 559, 79 N.W.2d 895, where discontinuance of work on a contract for care and maintenance of an orchard was held to be no more than failure to complete a contract.

On the other hand a physician who starts in to treat a patient and abandons him has been held liable in tort. Mehigan v. Sheehan, 1947, 94 N.H. 274, 51 A.2d 632.

50. Marrone v. Washington Jockey Club, 1913, 227 U.S. 633, 33 S.Ct. 401, 57 L.Ed. 679; Horney v. Nixon, 1905, 213 Pa. 20, 61 A. 1088; Shubert v. Nixon Amusement Co., 1912, 83 N.J.L. 101, 83 A. 369; Boswell v. Barnum & Bailey, 1916, 135 Tenn. 35, 185 S.W. 692.

51. See the language of Cardozo, C. J., in H. R. Moch Co. v. Rensselaer Water Co., 1928, 247 N.Y. 160, 159 N.E. 896, 898.

52. See supra, § 56.

53. See Arterburn, The Origin and First Test of Public Callings, 1927, 75 U.Pa.L.Rev. 411; Burdick, The Origin of the Peculiar Duties of Public Service Companies, 1911, 11 Col.L.Rev. 514.

54. Horner v. Terpin, 1934, 63 S.D. 309, 258 N.W. 140; Moffitt v. Davis, 1934, 205 N.C. 565, 172 S.E. 317; Hupe v. Sommer, 1913, 88 Kan. 561, 129 P. 136.

55. Beck & Gregg Hardware Co. v. Associated Transport, Inc., 1954, 210 Ga. 545, 81 S.E.2d 515 (refusal to receive goods); Pittsburgh, Cincinnati & St. Louis Railway Co. v. Morton, 1878, 61 Ind. 539 (failure to furnish cars); Williams v. Carolina & Northwestern Railroad Co., 1907, 144 N.C. 498, 57 S.E. 216 (failure to stop train); Nevin v. Pullman Palace Car Co., 1883, 106 Ill. 222 (failure to provide Pullman berth); Zabron v. Cunard Steamship Co., 1911, 151 Iowa 345, 131 N.W. 18 (failure to deliver ticket).

56. Jackson v. Virginia Hot Springs Co., 4th Cir. 1914, 213 F. 969; Atwater v. Sawyer, 1884, 76 Me. 539; Odom v. East Ave. Corp., 1942, 178 Misc. 363, 34 N.Y.S.2d 312, affirmed 1942, 264 App.Div. 985, 37 N.Y.S.2d 491.

57. Nash v. Page & Co., 1882, 80 Ky. 539; Gray v. Central Warehouse Co., 1921, 181 N.C. 166, 106 S.E. 657.

58. Oklahoma Natural Gas Co. v. Graham, 1941, 188 Okl. 521, 111 P.2d 173 (gas); Ashelford v. Illinois Northern Utilities Co., 1936, 284 Ill.App. 655, 4 N.E.2d 397 (electricity); Alabama Water Co. v. Knowles, 1929, 220 Ala. 61, 124 So. 96 (water); Masterson v. Chesapeake & Potomac Telephone Co., 1923, 52 U.S.App.D.C. 23, 299 F. 890 (telephone).

But even the public utility is liable only for breach of its public duty. Thus a telephone company, while it may be liable for failure to complete a call, is not required to deliver a message. Mentzer v. New England Telephone & Telegraph Co., 1931, 276 Mass. 478, 177 N.E. 549; Bess v. Citizens Telephone Co., 1926, 315 Mo. 1056, 287 S.W. 466.

59. Hurley v. Eddingfield, 1901, 156 Ind. 416, 59 N.E. 1058; see Randolph's Administrator v. Snyder, 1910, 139 Ky. 159, 129 S.W. 562.

60. Nance v. Mayflower Tavern, 1933, 106 Utah 517, 150 P.2d 773.

61. Madden v. Queens County Jockey Club, 1947, 296 N.Y. 249, 72 N.E.2d 697; Garifine v. Monmouth Park Jockey Club, 1959, 29 N.J. 47, 148 A.2d 1.

62. Crawford v. Kent, 1960, 341 Mass. 125, 167 N.E.2d 620 (dancing school); Odom v. East Ave. Corp.,

Most public utilities are now rather intensely regulated both as to rates and manner of service. The rates established must be or should be directly related to the nature and extent of liability imposed for interruptions of service or defective performance of service. The consequential damages from a blackout that could be attributable to negligence can be enormous and most regulatory agencies take this into account in establishing limitations on liability. Therefore, the duty and responsibilities of the regulated industries should be and are largely determined, by and large, by the regulatory agencies.[63] In dealing with the civil liability of a public utility for damages, primary attention has been given to the nature of the loss for which recovery is sought. Intangible consequential damages for interruptions of service and defective performance will normally be allocated to the customer under tariff provisions approved by regulatory agencies. Substantial losses of this kind are normally incurred by industrial and commercial customers who can insure against losses. Utility ratepayers should not ordinarily be assuming these losses. Damages for personal injuries and physical harm to electrical equipment would normally be recoverable against the distributor of electricity. In the light of this regulatory process, the civil liability is neither tortious nor contractual but is rather *sui generis*.

Relationships Created by Contract and Duties of Affirmative Action

Another type of exception arises where the contract results in or accompanies some relation between the parties which the law recognizes as giving rise to a duty of affirmative care. The typical case is that of a bailment, where the bare fact that the defendant has possession of the plaintiff's property is enough to create the duty,[64] and it would exist if there were no contract at all and the goods were found on the highway.[65] The tort liability is limited to the scope of the recognized tort duty. A bailee may be liable in tort for failure to take ordinary precautions against the destruction of the goods by fire,[66] but the breach of an agreement to keep a horse in a separate stall [67] or to store butter at a definite temperature [68] is a matter of contract only. Likewise an employer may be liable in tort for a failure to furnish a safe place to work [69] or proper tools,[70] but an agreement to provide special facilities [71] or medical attention [72] must be enforced by a contract action. Mention al-

1942, 178 Misc. 363, 34 N.Y.S.2d 312, affirmed 264 App. Div. 985, 37 N.Y.S.2d 491 (restaurant); Bolden v. Grand Rapids Operating Corp., 1927, 239 Mich. 318, 214 N.W. 241; Anderson v. Pantages Theatre Co., 1921, 114 Wn.2d 24, 194 P. 813 (theatre); Orloff v. Los Angeles Turf Club, 1947, 30 Cal.2d 110, 180 P.2d 321 (race track).

63. Devers v. Long Island Lighting Co., 1974, 79 Misc.2d 165, 359 N.Y.S.2d 940; Shubitz v. Consolidated Edison of New York, 1969, 59 Misc.2d 782, 301 N.Y.S.2d 926; see Comment, Rates Follow Service: The Power of the Public Utility Commission to Regulate Quality of Service, 1976, 28 Baylor L.Rev. 1137; Western Union Telegraph Co. v. Esteve Brothers, 1921, 256 U.S. 566, 571, 41 S.Ct. 584, 586, 65 L.Ed. 1094; Warner v. Southwestern Bell Telephone Co., Mo.1968, 428 S.W.2d 596.

64. Turner v. Stallibrass, [1898] L.R. 1 Q.B. 56; Springfield Crystallized Egg Co. v. Springfield Ice & Refrigeration Co., 1914, 259 Mo. 664, 168 S.W. 772.

65. Ryan v. Chown, 1910, 160 Mich. 204, 125 N.W. 46. Cf. Weeg v. Iowa Mutual Insurance Co., 1966, 82 S.D. 104, 141 N.W.2d 913 (contract to maintain fence in safe condition).

66. Aircraft Sales & Service, Inc. v. Bramlett, 1950, 254 Ala. 588, 49 So.2d 144. Cf. Pinnix v. Toomey, 1955, 242 N.C. 358, 87 S.E.2d 893, holding that an owner of a building who brought a tort action against a plumbing contractor for negligently damaging his building could rely only on the common law standard of care, and contract provisions calling for a higher standard were not applicable.

67. Legge v. Tucker, 1856, 1 H. & N. 500, 156 Eng. Rep. 1298.

68. Kings Laboratories v. Yucaipa Valley Fruit Co., 1936, 18 Cal.2d 47, 62 P.2d 1054. Cf. Jacobs, Malcolm & Burtt v. Northern Pacific Railway Co., 1925, 71 Cal. App. 42, 234 P. 328 (ventilation of car).

69. Denning v. State, 1899, 123 Cal. 316, 55 P. 1000; Kinnare v. City of Chicago, 1897, 70 Ill.App. 106, affirmed 171 Ill. 332, 49 N.E. 536.

70. Obanhein v. Arbuckle, 1905, 80 App.Div. 465, 81 N.Y.S. 133.

71. Stone v. Johnson, 1938, 89 N.H. 329, 197 A. 713, affirmed 1939, 90 N.H. 311, 8 A.2d 743.

72. Willey v. Alaska Packers' Association, 9th Cir. 1926, 9 F.2d 937, affirmed 18 F.2d 8; Galveston, Har-

ready has been made [73] of the controversy as to whether a landlord's covenant to repair sets up a relation which is the basis of a tort duty to the tenant.

Another important exception to the nonliability for nonfeasance is the holding that a promise made without intent to perform it may be fraud for which a tort action in deceit will lie.[74]

Election and Gravamen

Where on the facts either an action in contract or one in tort is open to the plaintiff, his choice may have important consequences. Some considerations may lead the plaintiff to prefer action on the contract. A contract may lead to strict liability for failure to perform, as in the case of a physician's undertaking to cure his patient,[75] where the tort action would require proof of negligence or some other wrongful conduct. A shorter statute of limitations may bar the tort action,[76] or it may not survive the death of one of the parties.[77] Some immunities, such as those of municipal corporations [78] or charities [79] may prevent recovery in tort, but not in contract. The damages recoverable on the contract may sometimes be greater, to the extent that they give the plaintiff the benefit of the bargain made, rather than compensation for a loss.[80] A contract claim may be assignable where a tort claim is not,[81] or an inferior court may have jurisdiction over it,[82] or the venue may offer more latitude,[83] or the contract suit may open the way to remedies such as attachment [84] or summary judgment,[85] or be available as a set-off [86] or counterclaim,[87] where the other

---

risburg & San Antonio Railway Co. v. Hennigan, 1903, 33 Tex.Civ.App. 314, 76 S.W. 452. But in Mueller v. Winston Brothers Co., 1931, 165 Wash. 130, 4 P.2d 854, the duty to provide a qualified physician was held to arise as a matter of the relation, and the tort action was sustained.

73. See supra, § 63.

74. See infra, § 107.

75. Frankel v. Wolper, 1918, 181 App.Div. 485, 169 N.Y.S. 15, affirmed 1919, 228 N.Y. 582, 127 N.E. 913; Schuster v. Sutherland, 1916, 92 Wash. 135, 158 P. 730; Robins v. Finestone, 1955, 308 N.Y. 543, 127 N.E.2d 330. Cf. Noel v. Proud, 1961, 189 Kan. 6, 367 P.2d 61 (plaintiff's condition to be made no worse); Johnston v. Rodis, D.C.Cir. 1958, 251 F. 917 (treatment perfectly safe); Camposano v. Claiborn, 1963, 2 Conn.Cir. 135, 196 A.2d 129 (warranty against scars). See Miller, The Contractual Liability of Physicians and Surgeons, [1953] Wash.U.L.Q. 413.

76. Whitaker v. Poston, 1907, 120 Tenn. 207, 110 S.W. 1019; Lipman, Wolfe & Co. v. Phoenix Assurance Co., 9 Cir. 1919, 258 F. 544; Manning v. 1234 Corp., 1940, 174 Misc. 36, 20 N.Y.S.2d 121, affirmed 1941, 260 App.Div. 914, 24 N.Y.S.2d 302, appeal denied 1941, 261 App.Div. 804, 25 N.Y.S.2d 780; McCoy v. Wesley Hospital & Nurse Training School, 1961, 188 Kan. 325, 362 P.2d 841; Stanley v. Chastek, 1962, 34 Ill.App.2d 220, 180 N.E.2d 512.

77. See infra, § 126.

78. Harlan County v. Cole, 1927, 218 Ky. 819, 292 S.W. 501; City of Hazard v. Eversole, 1931, 237 Ky. 242, 35 S.W.2d 313; Schilling v. Carl Township, 1931, 60 N.D. 480, 235 N.W. 126; Kerns v. Couch, 1932, 141 Or. 147, 12 P.2d 1011, adhered to 141 Or. 147, 17 P.2d 323. See Note, 1932, 31 Mich.L.Rev. 864.

79. Ward v. St. Vincent's Hospital, 1899, 39 App. Div. 624, 57 N.Y.S. 784.

80. Particularly in cases of fraud, in jurisdictions which adopt the out-of-pocket measure of damages for deceit. See infra, § 110.

Even in quasi-contract the unjust enrichment of the defendant may exceed the damages which the plaintiff has suffered. Gilmore v. Wilbur, 1831, 29 Mass. (12 Pick.) 120; cf. Galvin v. Mac Mining & Milling Co., 1894, 14 Mont. 508, 37 P. 366.

81. Vogel v. Cobb, 1943, 193 Okl. 64, 141 P.2d 276. Likewise a contract action may carry interest, where a tort action does not. Miller v. Foltis Fisher, Inc., 1934, 152 Misc. 24, 272 N.Y.S. 712.

82. White v. Eley, 1907, 145 N.C. 36, 58 S.E. 437; Chudnovski v. Eckels, 1908, 232 Ill. 312, 83 N.E. 846; Busch v. Interborough Rapid Transit Co., 1907, 110 App.Div. 705, 96 N.Y.S. 747, affirmed 1907, 187 N.Y. 388, 80 N.E. 197.

83. Bufkin v. Grisham, 1930, 157 Miss. 746, 128 So. 563; Wright v. Southern Railway Co., 1910, 7 Ga.App. 542, 67 S.E. 272.

84. Thuringer v. Bonner, 1924, 74 Colo. 539, 222 P. 1118; De Mirjian v. Ideal Heating Corp., 1949, 91 Cal. App.2d 905, 206 P.2d 20; First National Bank of Nashua v. Van Voohris, 1895, 6 S.D. 548, 62 N.W. 378.

85. Garfunkel v. Pennsylvania Railroad Co., 1932, 148 Misc. 810, 266 N.Y.S. 35; Bishop v. Specter, 1932, 150 Misc. 360, 269 N.Y.S. 76.

86. John A. Eck Co. v. Pennsylvania Railroad Co., 1931, 261 Ill.App. 43; Ellis v. Taylor, 1931, 172 Ga. 830, 159 S.E. 266.

87. Manhattan Egg Co. v. Seaboard Terminal & Refrigeration Co., 1930, 137 Misc. 14, 242 N.Y.S. 189; Farmers & Merchants' National Bank v. Huckaby, 1923, 89 Okl. 214, 215 P. 429; Casner v. Hoskins, 1913, 64 Or. 254, 128 P. 841, affirmed on rehearing 64 Or. 254, 130 P. 55.

remedy would not. Finally, the plaintiff may, by his own conduct so far, have accepted and affirmed the contract as to be bound by it, to the exclusion of tort remedies he might otherwise have had.[88]

Generally speaking, the tort remedy is likely to be more advantageous to the injured party in the greater number of cases, if only because it will so often permit the recovery of greater damages. Under the rule of Hadley v. Baxendale,[89] the damages recoverable for breach of contract are limited to those within the contemplation of the defendant at the time the contract was made,[90] and in some jurisdictions, at least, to those for which the defendant has tacitly agreed to assume responsibility.[91] They may be further limited by the contract itself,[92] where a tort action might avoid the limitation.[93] In contract actions, other than those for breach of promise to marry, punitive damages are not allowed,[94] and there can ordinarily be no recovery for mental suffering.[95] In the tort action the only limitations are those of "proximate cause," [96] and the policy which denies recovery to certain types of interests themselves.[97]

The tort action may offer other advantages. It may permit recovery for wrongful death,[98] for which a contract action normally will not lie. It may be open where the contract fails for lack of proof,[99] for uncertainty,[1] for illegality,[2] for want of consideration,[3] or because of the statute of frauds [4] or the

88. Cf. Schmidt v. Mesmer, 1897, 116 Cal. 267, 48 P. 54; Timmerman v. Gurnsey, 1928, 206 Iowa 35, 217 N.W. 879; Simon v. Goodyear Metallic Rubber Shoe Co., 6th Cir., 1900, 105 F. 573; cf. Pohl v. Johnson, 1930, 179 Minn. 398, 229 N.W. 555 (delay in cashing a bad check).

89. 1854, 9 Ex. 341, 156 Eng.Rep. 145. See McCormick, Damages, 1935, ch. 22; Bauer, Consequential Damages in Contract, 1932, 80 U.Pa.L.Rev. 687.

90. Dice's Administrator v. Zweigart's Administrator, 1914, 161 Ky. 646, 171 S.W. 195; Timmons v. Williams Wood Products Corp., 1932, 164 S.C. 361, 162 S.E. 329; Korach v. Loeffel, 1912, 168 Mo.App. 414, 151 S.W. 790. In Trammell v. Eastern Air Lines, W.D.S.C.1955, 136 F.Supp. 75, the contract measure was applied where an air line refused to allow plaintiff to board a plane for which he had a ticket. Cf. Edd v. Western Union Telegraph Co., 1928, 127 Or. 500, 272 P. 895 (telegraph transmission of money).

91. Globe Refining Co. v. Landa Cotton Oil Co., 1903, 190 U.S. 540, 23 S.Ct. 764, 47 L.Ed. 1171; Armstrong Rubber Co. v. Griffith, 2d Cir. 1930, 43 F.2d 689; Givens v. North Augusta Electric & Improvement Co., 1912, 91 S.C. 417, 74 S.E. 1067. Contra, McKibbin v. Pierce, Tex.Civ.App.1917, 190 S.W. 1149.

92. Hart v. Pennsylvania Railroad Co., 1884, 112 U.S. 331, 5 S.Ct. 151, 28 L.Ed. 717; Libby v. St. Louis, Iron Mountain & Southern Railroad Co., 1909, 137 Mo.App. 276, 117 S.W. 659; Merchants' & Miners' Transportation Co. v. Moore & Co., 1905, 124 Ga. 482, 52 S.E. 802.

93. Cf. Woodruff & Sons v. Brown, 5th Cir. 1958, 256 F.2d 391; Danann Realty Corp. v. Harris, 1959, 5 N.Y.2d 317, 184 N.Y.S.2d 599, 157 N.E.2d 597. See Note, 1959, 59 Col.L.Rev. 525.

94. McCormick, Damages, 1935, 289, 290. Thus it has been held that punitive damages cannot be awarded where the action is on the contract, although the defendant's conduct constituted a tort. Trout v. Watkins Livery & Undertaking Co., 1910, 148 Mo.App. 621, 130 S.W. 136; Ketcham v. Miller, 1922, 104 Ohio St. 372, 136 N.E. 145; Southwestern Telegraph & Telephone Co. v. Luckett, 1910, 60 Tex.Civ.App. 117, 127 S.W. 856. Contra, Williams v. Carolina & Northwestern Railway Co., 1907, 144 N.C. 498, 57 S.E. 216.

95. Western Union Telegraph Co. v. Speight, 1920, 254 U.S. 17, 41 S.Ct. 11, 65 L.Ed. 104; Morton v. Western Union Telegraph Co., 1895, 53 Ohio St. 431, 41 N.E. 689; Western Union Telegraph Co. v. Choteau, 1911, 28 Okl. 664, 115 P. 879. In Stewart v. Rudner, 1957, 349 Mich. 459, 84 N.W.2d 816, where there was a contract action for a surgeon's failure to perform a Caesarian operation, the court broke away from the rule, and allowed the damages.

96. See supra, ch. 7.

97. For example, negligent interference with contract relations, infra, § 129. Or mental suffering at injury or peril to a third person, supra, § 54.

98. Keiper v. Anderson, 1917, 138 Minn. 392, 165 N.W. 237; Greco v. S. S. Kresge Co., 1938, 277 N.Y. 26, 12 N.E.2d 557; Gosling v. Nichols, 1943, 59 Cal.App.2d 442, 139 P.2d 86; Rodwell v. Camel City Coach Co., 1933, 205 N.C. 292, 171 S.E. 100.

99. Pittsburgh, Cincinnati, Chicago & St. Louis Railway Co. v. Higgs, 1905, 165 Ind. 694, 76 N.E. 299; Corry v. Pennsylvania Railroad Co., 1900, 194 Pa. 516, 45 A. 341; Jacksonville Street Railway Co. v. Chappell, 1886, 22 Fla. 616, 1 So. 10.

1. Richey & Gilbert Co. v. Northern Pacific Railway Co., 1910, 110 Minn. 347, 125 N.W. 897.

2. Costello v. Ten Eyck, 1891, 86 Mich. 348, 49 N.W. 152.

3. Daniel v. Daniel, 1921, 190 Ky. 210, 226 S.W. 1070; Pease & Elliman v. Wegeman, 1928, 223 App.Div. 682, 229 N.Y.S. 398.

4. Burgdorfer v. Thielemann, 1936, 153 Or. 354, 55 P.2d 1122; Kinkaid v. Rossa, 1913, 31 S.D. 559, 141 N.W. 969; McNaughton v. Smith, 1904, 136 Mich. 368, 99 N.W. 382.

parol evidence rule.[5] It may sometimes avoid some defenses, such as infancy [6] or a discharge in bankruptcy; [7] and it may avoid some counterclaims.[8] It may avoid the necessity of joining several defendants,[9] or permit successive actions for multiple breaches of a single contract,[10] or the application of a favorable rule under the conflict of laws.[11]

Frequently, where either tort or contract will lie and inconsistent rules of law apply to the two actions, the question arises whether the plaintiff may elect freely which he will bring, or whether the court must itself decide that on the facts pleaded and proved the "gist" or "gravamen" of his cause of action is one or the other. As to this the decisions are in considerable confusion,[12] and it is difficult to generalize.

Where the particular point at issue is one of adjective law only, affecting the suit or its procedure, but not the merits of the cause of action, the courts have tended to be quite liberal in giving the plaintiff his freedom of choice, and have upheld his action of tort or contract as he has seen fit to bring it.[13] Likewise where the point is one affecting substantive rights, but the claim is one for damages to property or to pecuniary interests only, the tendency has been, with some occasional dissent,[14] to allow the election.[15] But when the claim is one for personal injury, the decision usually [16] has been that the gravamen of the action is the mis-

---

5. New England Foundation Co. v. Elliott A. Watrous, Inc., 1940, 306 Mass. 177, 27 N.E.2d 756; Duholm v. Chicago, Milwaukee & St. Paul Railway Co., 1920, 146 Minn. 1, 177 N.W. 72; McNeill v. Wabash Railroad Co., 1921, 207 Mo.App. 161, 231 S.W. 649.

6. Vermont Acceptance Corp. v. Wiltshire, 1931, 103 Vt. 219, 153 A. 199; Wisconsin Loan & Finance Corp. v. Goodnough, 1931, 201 Wis. 101, 228 N.W. 484; Patterson v. Kasper, 1914, 182 Mich. 281, 148 N.W. 690.

7. The National Bankruptcy Act, 11 U.S.C.A. § 33, excepts from discharge liabilities for obtaining money by false pretenses or false representations, and for wilful and malicious injuries to the person or property of another. See Joslin, Torts and Bankruptcy—A Synthesis, 1960, 1 Bos.Coll.Ind. & Comm.L.Rev. 185; Gleick, Tort Liabilities: To What Extent Are They Dischargeable by Bankruptcy, 1964, 19 Bus.L.Rev. 339; Note, 1939, 23 Minn.L.Rev. 958.

8. Zapfe v. Werner, 1923, 120 Misc. 326, 199 N.Y.S. 293; Sattler v. Neiderkorn, 1926, 190 Wis. 464, 209 N.W. 607.

9. See Clark, Code Pleading, 1928, 257, 260; Keller v. Blasdel, 1865, 1 Nev. 491 (contract); Elliott v. Hayden, 1870, 104 Mass. 180 (tort). It has been held that an action in quasi-contract, the tort being "waived," is several. City National Bank v. National Park Bank, 1884, 32 Hun, N.Y., 105.

10. Lloyd v. Farmers Coop. Store, 1936, 197 Minn. 387, 267 N.W. 204.

11. Quaker Worsted Mills Corp. v. Howard Trucking Corp., 1938, 131 Pa.Super. 1, 198 A. 691; Schmitt v. Postal Telegraph Co., 1914, 164 Iowa 654, 146 N.W. 467; Pittsburgh, Cincinnati, Chicago & St. Louis Ry. Co. v. Grom, 1911, 142 Ky. 51, 133 S.W. 977.

12. See Prosser, The Borderland of Tort and Contract, in Prosser, Selected Topics on the Law of Torts, 1954, 380, 429–450; Thornton, The Elastic Concept of Tort and Contract as Applied by the Courts of New York, 1948, 14 Brook.L.Rev. 196.

13. Busch v. International Rapid Transit Co., 1907, 187 N.Y. 388, 80 N.E. 197 (jurisdiction of court); Bufkin v. Grisham, 1930, 157 Miss. 746, 128 So. 563 (venue); Atlantic & Pacific Railway Co. v. Laird, 1896, 164 U.S. 393 (joinder of parties); Felder v. Reeth, 8th Cir. 1929, 34 F.2d 744 (counterclaim); Oil Well Core Drilling Co. v. Barnhart, 1937, 20 Cal.App.2d 677, 67 P.2d 696 (attachment).

14. See for example Jackson v. Central Torpedo Co., 1926, 117 Okl. 245, 246 P. 426 (statute of limitations); Cassidy v. Kraft-Phenix Cheese Co., 1938, 285 Mich. 426, 280 N.W. 814 (statute of frauds); Better Food Markets v. American District Telegraph Co., 1953, 40 Cal.2d 179, 253 P.2d 10 (liquidated damages clause in contract to install burglar alarm).

15. Micheletti v. Moidel, 1934, 94 Colo. 587, 32 P.2d 266 (survival); Southern Pacific Railroad Co. of Mexico v. Gonzales, 1936, 48 Ariz. 260, 61 P.2d 377 (statute of limitations); Schleifer v. Worcester North Sav. Inst., 1940, 306 Mass. 226, 27 N.E.2d 992 (statute of frauds); Burgdorfer v. Thielemann, 1936, 153 Or. 354, 55 P.2d 1122 (same); Mid-West Chevrolet Corp. v. Noah, 1935, 173 Okl. 198, 48 P.2d 283 (parol evidence).

16. Again there has been occasional disagreement, as in Forrester v. Southern Pacific Railway Co., 1913, 36 Nev. 247, 134 P. 753, rehearing denied 1913, 36 Nev. 247, 136 P. 705 (survival). Particularly as to the election of the contract action to avoid a short tort statute of limitations. Doughty v. Maine Central Transportation Co., 1944, 141 Me. 124, 39 A.2d 758; Williams v. Illinois Central Railroad Co., 1950, 360 Mo. 501, 229 S.W.2d 1; Stanley v. Chastek, 1962, 34 Ill.App.2d 220, 180 N.E.2d 512; Stitt v. Gold, 1962, 33 Misc.2d 273, 225 N.Y.S.2d 536, affirmed 1962, 17 App.Div. 642, 230 N.Y.S.2d 677. See Lillich, The Malpractice Statute of Limitations in New York, 1962, 47 Corn.L.Q. 339.

Compare, where plaintiff sues as a third party beneficiary of the contract: Thompson v. Harry C. Erb Co., 3d Cir. 1957, 240 F.2d 452; Keefer v. Lombardi, 1954, 376 Pa. 367, 102 A.2d 695, certiorari denied 347 U.S. 1016, 74 S.Ct. 871, 98 L.Ed. 1138.

conduct and the damage, and that it is essentially one of tort, which the plaintiff cannot alter by his pleading.[17] This has the odd result that the negligence of an attorney will survive the death of his client,[18] while that of a physician is oft interred with his patient's bones.[19] Actually, the courts appear to have preserved a great deal of flexibility, and to have been influenced in their decisions by their attitude toward the rule of law in question.

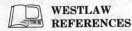

WESTLAW REFERENCES

synopsis,digest(physician* doctor* surgeon* & malpractice tort* negligen! & contract* contractual warranty warranties)

Early History—The Distinction Between Misfeasance and Nonfeasance

di misfeasance
di nonfeasance

Misfeasance

moch /5 rensselaer

Public Utility Services and Other Services Required by Law

"duty to serve" /p utilit!
synopsis,digest(bailee /p care precaution*)

Election and Gravamen

hadley /5 baxendale
synopsis,digest(tort! /p contract* contractual /p gravamen gist elect!)
topic(143) /p contract contractual /p tort!

§ 93. Liability of a Party to a Contract to Third Parties

The responsibility of a contracting party to a third person with whom he has made no contract for physical injuries and physical harm to tangible things resulting from dangerous conditions of things supplied, repaired, or constructed has a long history, and has presented problems of similar difficulty to those surrounding the relations of the immediate parties to the contract. There is no problem about tort liability to third parties for the mismanagement of things such as driving a car or flying an airplane. The mere fact that the defendant may be engaged in performing a service pursuant to a contract and transaction is completely irrelevant on his duty toward those in the vicinity of danger of his activity. Moreover, it is clear that parties to a contract cannot alter or modify any preexisting duty owed to third parties as regards the management of dangerous forces. But when defendant was acting, pursuant to a contract, in building, supplying or repairing things, it was not perceived at first that there could be a duty other than to the person with whom he was dealing. The first obstacle which arises is the fact that there has been no direct transaction between the plaintiff and the defendant, which usually is expressed by saying that they are not in "privity" of contract. There is thus no logical basis upon which the one may be required to perform the contract for the other, unless the contract has been made expressly for the benefit of the plaintiff, or it has been assigned to him.[1]

In other words, the absence of "privity" between the parties makes it difficult to impose any duty to the plaintiff upon the contract itself. But by entering into a contract with A, the defendant may place himself in such a relation toward B that the law will

---

17. McClure v. Johnson, 1937, 50 Ariz. 76, 69 P.2d 573 (survival; good discussion); Kozan v. Comstock, 5th Cir. 1959, 270 F.2d 839 (statute of limitations); Oklahoma Natural Gas Co. v. Pack, 1939, 186 Okl. 330, 97 P.2d 768 (measure of damages); Rubino v. Utah Canning Co., 1954, 123 Cal.App.2d 18, 266 P.2d 163 (warranty).

18. Knights v. Quarles, 1820, 2 Brod. & B. 102, 129 Eng.Rep. 896; Stimpson v. Sprague, 1830, 6 Me. 470. Or permit a longer statute of limitations. Schirmer v. Nethercutt, 1930, 157 Wash. 172, 288 P. 265.

19. Huysman v. Kirsch, 1936, 6 Cal.2d 302, 57 P.2d 908; Cochran v. Laton, 1918, 78 N.H. 562, 103 A. 658; Mullane v. Crump, 1947, 272 App.Div. 922, 71 N.Y.S.2d 40, appeal denied 272 App.Div. 934, 72 N.Y.S.2d 417. Or be barred by the tort statute of limitations. Wilder v. Haworth, 1949, 187 Or. 688, 213 P.2d 797; Trimming v. Howard, 1932, 52 Idaho 412, 15 P.2d 661; Howard v. Middlesborough Hospital, 1932, 242 Ky. 602, 47 S.W.2d 77.

§ 93

1. Two of the classic statements of this proposition are found in Winterbottom v. Wright, 1842, 10 M. & W. 109, 152 Eng.Rep. 402, and National Savings Bank v. Ward, 1879, 100 U.S. 195, 25 L.Ed. 621.

impose upon him an obligation, sounding in tort and not in contract, to act in such a way that B will not be injured. The incidental fact of the existence of the contract with A does not negative the responsibility of the actor when he enters upon a course of affirmative conduct which may be expected to affect the interests of another person.[2]

This idea was slow to find recognition in the courts. In 1842, in Winterbottom v. Wright,[3] the Court of Exchequer held that the breach of a contract to keep a mailcoach in repair after it was sold could give no cause of action to a passenger in the coach who was injured when it collapsed. The decision held only that no action could be maintained on the contract itself; but certain dicta of the judges, and particularly the words of Lord Abinger, who foresaw "the most absurd and outrageous consequences, to which I can see no limit,"[4] "unless we confine the operation of such contracts as this to the parties who entered into them," were taken to mean that there could be no action even in tort, and that this was true of any misperformance of a contract, including even the sale of a defective coach in the first instance.[5] The error of this interpretation of the case has been exposed long since;[6] But from it there developed a general rule, which prevailed into the twentieth century, that there was no liability of a contracting party to one with whom he was not in "privity."[7]

The development of the law away from this position in the case of the seller of products has been spectacular in the extreme, and remains to be considered at a later point.[8] As to other contracting parties, such as those who undertake to furnish labor or services, the development has on the whole not kept pace with that as to the seller. Strict liability has gained almost no foothold at all, except as the contract itself may be extended to cover a restricted group of third party beneficiaries;[9] and as to negligence, the law has tended to lag some twenty or thirty years behind. The requirement of privity of contract has been abandoned as a basis for recovery by third parties for physical harm to themselves and tangible things against those who negligently supply, repair, or construct things so as to leave them in an unreasonably dangerous condition.[10] Moreover, strict liability in tort has been extended to those who sell or lease houses with defects of a kind that subject users and others to an unreasonable risk of harm. Such strict liability has not, however, been extended generally against contractors who build houses on land owned by others and who repair products or buildings pursuant to contracts made with the owner or possessor of things.[11]

Nonfeasance and Intangible Economic Loss

The refusal to find any liability to third persons has been most definite where (1) the only wrong of the defendant consisted in the failure to perform a promise made as to be distinguished from defective performance, and (2) the loss suffered was economic in character. Such "nonfeasance" ordinarily

---

2. "The question is: Has the defendant broken a duty apart from the contract? If he has merely broken his contract, none can sue him but a party to it, but if he has violated a duty to others, he is liable to them." Peters v. Johnson, 1902, 50 W.Va. 644, 41 S.E. 190.

3. 1842, 10 M. & W. 109, 152 Eng.Rep. 402. See also Langridge v. Levy, 1842, 2 M. & W. 519, 150 Eng. Rep. 863.

4. The source of a most amusing bit, "The Most Outrageous Consequences," in James Reid Parker, Attorneys at Law, 1941, 87–96.

5. See for example Huset v. J. I. Case Threshing Machine Co., 8th Cir. 1903, 120 F. 865; Earl v. Lubbock, [1905] 1 K.B. 253.

6. Bohlen, The Basis of Affirmative Obligations in the Law of Tort, 1905, 44 Am.L.Reg.,N.S., 209, 280–285, 289–310; and see Lord Atkin, in Donoghue v. Stevenson, [1932] A.C. 562, 588–589.

7. Bohlen, Fifty Years of Torts, 1937, 50 Harv.L. Rev. 1225, 1232.

8. See infra, ch. 17.

9. See 2 Williston, Contracts, Rev.Ed.1936, ch. 14.

10. See, infra, Chapter 17 on Products Liability; also, see, Second Restatement of Torts, §§ 385 and 404.

11. See, infra, Chapter 17, § 104A.

leads to no tort liability even to the promisee, whose remedy must be on the contract itself;[12] and it follows that a third person—who is not a party to the contract—has no chance of recovery in tort or any theory.[13] Thus, it is quite generally agreed that if the defendant contracts to accept employment with A, in work which will affect the safety of B, and then entirely fails to appear for work and never enters upon the employment, he may be liable to A for breach of his contract, but he will have no liability in contract or in tort to B.[14] In fact, there would ordinarily be no liability for economic loss as a consequence of misfeasance or defective performance unless there was some kind of special relationship between the defendant and the third party apart from the contract on the basis of which liability for negligence in tort could be imposed beyond that imposed to the promisee on the basis of a manifested intent.

Tort Liability for Physical Harm to Persons and Tangible Things Resulting from Failure to Repair or Inspect

There can be no doubt but what some courts have held even quite recently that the failure to perform a promise to repair or inspect will not subject the promisor to tort liability to third persons.[15]

In some of the situations involving this problem, the defendant has been regarded as having the kind of interest and control over the property that was the subject of the contract to repair to justify the imposition of a duty to third parties to perform the promise as made. Mention has already been made of the cases holding that a landlord's covenant with his tenant to repair the premises violates a relationship of "control" which makes him responsible to third persons entering in the right of the tenant.[16] There are a few other situations in which such a relationship has been found. Where an agent or a servant has accepted the control of property under contract with his principal, and under circumstances where there is an obvious risk of harm to outsiders if he does not use reasonable care, the affirmative conduct has been imposed upon him.[17] While there are cases to the contrary,[18] the prevailing view now recognizes the same responsibility where the agent or servant has in fact entered upon his employment, and undertaken to be responsible for the performance of a duty [19] which the employer owes to others, as where, for example, a construction superintendent is hired to in-

12. See supra, § 56.

13. See for example Olsness v. State, 1929, 58 N.D. 20, 224 N.W. 913 (bank negligently forwarding checks to drawee not liable to surety); Gardner v. Hines, Ohio 1946, 68 N.E.2d 397 (contract to support mother; not liable to son-in-law); Mears v. Crocker First National Bank of San Francisco, 1950, 97 Cal.App.2d 482, 218 P.2d 91 (stock transfer agent not liable to owner for delay); Standard Iron Works v. Southern Bell Telephone Co., W.D.S.C.1917, 256 F. 548 (nonsubscriber using telephone); Baca v. Britt, 1963, 73 N.M. 1, 385 P.2d 61 (failure to repair traffic light).

14. See Waters v. Anthony, 1949, 252 Ala. 244, 40 So.2d 316; Franklin v. May Department Stores, E.D. Miss.1938, 25 F.Supp. 735; Landreth v. Phillips Petroleum Co., W.D.Mo.1947, 74 F.Supp. 801; Sloss-Sheffield Steel & Iron Co. v. Wilkes, 1936, 231 Ala. 511, 165 So. 764; Osborne v. Morgan, 1881, 130 Mass. 102.

See also Hanson v. Blackwell Motor Co., 1927, 143 Wash. 547, 255 P 939, where defendant did not perform its promise to repair an automobile. The misrepresentation, however, should have led to a different conclusion, as in Moody v. Martin Motor Co., 1948, 76 Ga.App. 456, 46 S.E.2d 197.

15. Baca v. Britt, 1963, 78 N.M. 1, 385 P.2d 61 (failure to repair traffic light pursuant to contract with governmental entity); Hanson v. Blackwell Motor Co., 1927, 143 Wash. 547, 255 P. 939 (failure to perform a promise to repair an automobile).

16. See, supra, Chapter 10, § 63.

17. The obvious case is that of a manager or superintendent taking over the care of a building. Lough v. John Davis & Co., 1902, 30 Wash. 204, 70 P. 491; Tippecanoe Land & Trust Co. v. Jester, 1913, 180 Ind. 357, 101 N.E. 915; Lambert v. Jones, 1936, 339 Mo. 677, 98 S.W.2d 752; Restatement of Agency, Second, § 355.

18. Scott v. Huffman, 10th Cir. 1956, 237 F.2d 396; Davis v. St. Louis & San Francisco Railroad Co., N.D. Okl.1934, 8 F.Supp. 519; Knight v. Atlantic Coast Line Railroad Co., 5th Cir. 1934, 73 F.2d 76; Kelly v. Robinson, E.D.Mo.1920, 262 F. 695; Norwood v. Carolina Power & Light Co., E.D.S.C.1947, 74 F.Supp. 483.

19. Otherwise where the work he is employed to do does not involve such a duty. Miller v. Muscarelle, 1961, 67 N.J.Super. 305, 170 A.2d 437; cf. Southeastern Greyhound Lines v. Callahan, 1943, 244 Ala. 449, 13 So. 2d 660.

spect scaffolding to be used by employees,[20] or a track walker to inspect poles adjoining a highway.[21]

In virtually any case when the defendant contracts with an owner or possessor to repair or inspect property, real or personal, he does or ought to foresee the likelihood of physical harm to third persons as a result of reasonable reliance by the owner on him to discover or repair dangerous conditions. Therefore, it is reasonable to argue that there should be a duty imposed by law to third persons to exercise reasonable care to prevent harm from reasonable reliance by the owner on his promise to do so. Therefore, any negligence either in failing to perform or to notify of inability to perform would be the basis for liability. This is not only true of those who promise to inspect or repair. This is also true of other kinds of promises to render other types of services as well.

Reliance or Misfeasance or Both

It has often been held that a company which enters upon a contract to inspect or maintain or repair a boiler,[22] or an elevator[23] may become liable when the employer relies upon its performance, and as a result a third person is injured. The duty may be limited by the contract,[24] but does not depend upon it, and it may arise even where the undertaking is a gratuitous one.[25] In most of these cases on which liability has been found, there has been something in the nature of entering upon performance, such as partial inspection,[26] or making an initial one,[27] and it can be said that there is something in the nature of "misfeasance" rather than "nonfeasance";[28] but this would not appear to be a sound explanation for the results since there was nothing defective about what was done and no harm resulted from what was done. The harm was a consequence of what was not done. The sounder explanation would appear to be that defendant has a duty imposed by law to avoid foreseeable harm to third persons as a consequence of reasonable reliance by the owner or employer on his promise or manifested intent to repair or inspect. It is time to dispense with the distinction between misfeasance and nonfeasance when foreseeable harm has resulted from reasonable reliance on a promisor to do what was promised.

20. Mayer v. Thompson-Hutchison Building Co., 1894, 104 Ala. 611, 16 So. 670. Accord: Sloss-Sheffield Steel & Iron Co. v. Wilkes, 1936, 231 Ala. 511, 165 So. 764; West Kentucky Coal Co. v. Hazel's Administratrix, 1939, 279 Ky. 5, 129 S.W.2d 1000; Stanolind Oil & Gas Co. v. Bunce, 1936, 51 Wyo. 1, 62 P.2d 1297; Devine v. Kroger Grocery & Baking Co., 1942, 349 Mo. 621, 162 S.W.2d 813.

21. Murray v. Cowherd, 1932, 148 Ky. 591, 147 S.W. 6. Cf. Hill v. James Walker Memorial Hospital, 4th Cir. 1969, 407 F.2d 1036 (contract with hospital to exterminate rats).

22. Van Winkle v. American Steam Boiler Insurance Co., 1899, 52 N.J.L. 240, 19 A. 472, American Mutual Liability Insurance Co. v. St. Paul Fire & Marine Insurance Co., 1970, 48 Wisc.2d 305, 179 N.W.2d 864. Cf. Gimino v. Sears, Roebuck & Co., 1944, 308 Mich. 666, 14 N.W.2d 536 (kerosene stove).

23. Durham v. Warner Elevator Manufacturing Co., 1956, 166 Ohio St. 31, 139 N.E.2d 10; Dickerson v. Shepard Warner Elevator Co., 6th Cir. 1961, 287 F.2d 255; Otis Elevator Co. v. Robinson, 5th Cir. 1961, 287 F.2d 62; Evans v. Otis Elevator Co., 1961, 403 Pa. 13, 168 A.2d 573; Wroblewski v. Otis Elevator Co., 1959, 9 A.D.2d 294, 193 N.Y.S.2d 855.

24. Wolfmeyer v. Otis Elevator Co., Mo.1953, 262 S.W.2d 18 (maintaining elevator involves no duty as to structural plan); Otis Elevator Co. v. Embert to Use of South St. Corp., 1951, 198 Md. 585, 84 A.2d 876 (maintenance involves no duty as to operation); Ulwelling v. Crown Coach Corp., 1962, 206 Cal.App.2d 96, 23 Cal. Rptr. 631, 651 (inspection for insurance purposes only).

25. Hill v. United States Fidelity & Guaranty Co., 5th Cir. 1970, 428 F.2d 112, certiorari denied 400 U.S. 1008, 91 S.Ct. 564, 27 L.Ed. 621; Sheridan v. Aetna Casualty & Surety Co., 1940, 3 W.2d 423, 100 P.2d 1024; Fabricius v. Montgomery Elevator Co., 1963, 254 Iowa 319, 121 N.W.2d 361; Smith v. American Employer's Insurance Co., 1960, 102 N.H. 530, 163 A.2d 564; Bollin v. Elevator Construction & Repair Co., 1949, 361 Pa. 7, 63 A.2d 19. Cf. Cain v. Meade County, 1929, 54 S.D. 540, 223 N.W. 734 (county agreeing with state to maintain highway).

26. For example Hoppendietzel v. Wade, 1941, 66 Ga.App. 132, 17 S.E.2d 239.

27. Pilinko v. Merlau, 1958, 10 Misc.2d 63, 171 N.Y.S.2d 718, reversed on other grounds 7 App.Div. 617, 179 N.Y.S.2d 136 (liable "once it enters upon its contractual obligations with the owner"); Evans v. Otis Elevator Co., 1961, 403 Pa. 13, 168 A.2d 573 (contract for periodic inspections, complete failure to make one).

28. See supra, § 92.

Water, Gas, and Electricity

The "nonfeasance" line has been drawn most sharply in a large number of cases holding that a company which contracts with a city to supply water to the public is not liable to a private citizen when the service fails at a critical moment and his house is destroyed by fire as a result,[29] although if contaminated water is supplied, there is no difficulty in finding liability for misfeasance.[30] The usual explanation of the fire cases has been that the defendant, by entering upon the supplying of the water for other purposes, has not begun an undertaking to extinguish fires.[31] But a more satisfactory explanation is that liability should not be extended to failing to prevent fire damage attributable to other accidental and often negligent causes since these losses are commonly covered by fire insurance, and little is accomplished by providing insurers a windfall in the way of subrogation claims.[32]

Similar non-liability rules have been applied to physical injuries and physical harm to tangible things resulting from the interruptions of gas or electricity. But the imposition of tort liability on those who must render continuous service of this kind to all who apply for it under all kinds of circumstances could be ruinous and the expense of litigating and settling claims over the issue of whether or not there was negligence could be a greater burden to the rate payer than can be socially justified. This is the more important question. The harm is just as foreseeable from complete non-performance as it is from partial performance and an interruption of service thereafter. But some interruptions will occur without negligence and this being so, those who bargain for this service should take precautions to guard against injuries to patrons, employees, and patients in hospitals who are dependent on a continuous supply of electrical energy for life and survival. This does not answer all questions. It is simply to say that the distinction between misfeasance and nonfeasance is not a good basis for establishing limits to liability to third parties resulting from reasonable reliance by the promisee on the promisor to render the service promised.

A few courts have permitted recovery against a water company.[33]

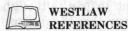
WESTLAW REFERENCES

Nonfeasance and Intangible Economic Loss
nonfeasance /p third /1 part*** person*

Tort Liability for Physical Harm to Persons and Tangible Things Resulting from Failure to Repair or Inspect
topic(233) /p third /1 part*** person /p repair!

Reliance or Misfeasance or Both
synopsis,digest(elevator* /p inspect! maintain! repair! /p third /1 part*** person*)

Water Gas and Electricity
synopsis,digest(water /5 furnish! provi! supply supplied /p fire /p negligen** tort*)
405k206

---

29. H. R. Moch Co. v. Rensselaer Water Co., 1928, 247 N.Y. 160, 159 N.E. 896; Reimann v. Monmouth Consolidated Water Co., 1952, 9 N.J. 134, 87 A.2d 325; Earl E. Roher Transfer & Storage Co. v. Hutchinson Water Co., 1958, 182 Kan. 546, 322 P.2d 810; Cole v. Arizona Edison Co., 1939, 53 Ariz. 141, 86 P.2d 946; Consolidated Biscuit Co. v. Illinois Power Co., 1939, 303 Ill.App. 80, 24 N.E.2d 582. See Note, 1952, 26 Temp. L.Q. 214.

30. Hayes v. Torrington Water Co., 1914, 88 Conn. 609, 92 A. 406.

31. An interesting comparison is McClendon v. T. L. James & Co., 5th Cir. 1956, 231 F.2d 802, where a contractor which had begun work under a contract to repair a highway was held to have no responsibility to post a warning of a bad condition six miles further on.

32. Such decisions as Town of Ukiah City v. Ukiah Water & Implement Co., 1904, 142 Cal. 173, 75 P. 773, and Inhabitants of Milford v. Bangor Railway & Electric Co., 1909, 106 Me. 316, 76 A. 696, denying recovery where the property destroyed by fire was that of the city which had the contract, indicate that the basis of the rule is the type of loss, and not lack of privity of contract.

33. Mugge v. Tampa Water Works Co., 1906, 52 Fla. 371, 42 So. 81; Woodbury v. Tampa Water Works Co., 1909, 57 Fla. 243, 49 So. 556; Harlan Water Co. v. Carter, 1927, 220 Ky. 493, 295 S.W. 426; Tobin v. Frankfort Water Co., 1914, 158 Ky. 348, 164 S.W. 956; Fisher v. Greensboro Water Supply Co., 1901, 128 N.C. 375, 38 S.E. 912; Potter v. Carolina Water Co., 1960, 253 N.C. 112, 116 S.E.2d 374; Doyle v. South Pittsburgh Water Co., 1964, 414 Pa. 199, 199 A.2d 875.

§ 94. Election to Sue for Restitution

The interrelation of tort and contract was further complicated when the common law courts, late in the seventeenth century, began to take over into the law some of the principles and remedies of equity. The judges, becoming conscious of their shortcomings and jealous of the expanding powers of the chancery courts, sought to broaden their own jurisdiction into equity fields, and found a means ready to their hand in the action of assumpsit.[1] By a series of ingenious fictions it was held first, that assumpsit would lie where a debt existed and a promise to pay it could be inferred, as a fact, from the circumstances of the case; then that the promise would be "implied" by the law from the mere existence of a debt which the defendant ought to pay, although there was nothing to show that the promise was really made; and finally, that the law would "imply" both the debt and the promise whenever one had received or used something for which "natural justice"[2] would require that he compensate another.

The assumpsit action was held to lie at first where the defendant had received the emoluments of a public office to which the plaintiff was entitled;[3] and then where he had converted and sold the plaintiff's goods.[4] It was soon held to include the case where money or property was obtained by misrepresentation,[5] and the plaintiff was permitted to rescind the transaction of his own motion and recover the value of what he had parted with. In later cases the principle was even extended to allow the plaintiff to rescind and maintain a property action of replevin[6] or conversion[7] for specific goods which he had surrendered to the defendant. The assumpsit action avoided so many of the technical difficulties of pleading which surrounded the older tort actions[8] that it became a popular substitute for them; and its survival and greatly increased use undoubtedly has been due to the genuine advantages which a contract action sometimes offers today.[9] With the disappearance of the form of action of assumpsit, the unblushing fiction of the implied promise has generally been discarded, and the remedy has acquired the name of quasi-contract, or restitution.

Out of this common law procedure there has developed the doctrine that where the commission of a tort results in the unjust enrichment of the defendant at the plaintiff's expense, the plaintiff may disregard, or "waive"[10] the tort action, and sue instead on a theoretical and fictitious contract of restitution of the benefits which the defendant

---

§ 94

1. See Winfield, Province of the Law of Tort, 1931, ch. vii; Restatement of Restitution, Introductory Note to Part I.

2. Mansfield, L. J., in Moses v. Macferlan, 1760, 2 Burr. 1005, 97 Eng.Rep. 676.

3. Woodward v. Ashton, 1676, 2 Mod.Rep. 95, 86 Eng.Rep. 961.

4. Lamine v. Dorrell, 1705, 2 Ld.Raym, 1216, 92 Eng.Rep. 303. See Ames, History of Assumpsit, 1888, 2 Harv.L.Rev. 1, 53, 67.

5. Hill v. Perrott, 1810, 3 Taunt. 274, 128 Eng.Rep. 109; Roth v. Palmer, N.Y.1858, 27 Barb. 652; Crown Cycle Co. v. Brown, 1901, 39 Or. 285, 64 P. 451; Dashaway Association v. Rogers, 1889, 79 Cal. 211, 21 P. 742; Western Assurance Co. v. Towle, 1886, 65 Wis. 247, 26 N.W. 104.

6. John V. Farwell Co. v. Hilton, D.C.Wis.1897, 84 F. 293; Furber v. Stephens, D.C.Mo.1888, 35 F. 17; Pearson v. Wallace, 1919, 204 Mich. 643, 171 N.W. 402.

7. Thurston v. Blanchard, 1839, 39 Mass. (22 Pick.) 18; Holland v. Bishop, 1895, 60 Minn. 23, 61 N.W. 681; Yeager v. Wallace, 1868, 57 Pa. 365; Baird v. Howard, 1894, 51 Ohio St. 57, 36 N.E. 732. See supra, § 15.

8. Winfield, Province of the Law of Tort, 1931, 141–146.

9. See supra, § 92 on Election and Gravamen, p. 664. Also House, Unjust Enrichment: The Applicable Statute of Limitations, 1950, 35 Corn.L.Q. 797; Note, 1950, 25 N.Y.U.L.Rev. 655.

10. "Thoughts much too deep for tears subdue the court

When I assumpsit bring, and god-like waive a tort."—Adolphus, The Circuiteers, an Eclogue, 1885, 1 L.Q.Rev. 232.

There seems to be some unwritten rule that this must be quoted by anyone who discusses this remedy. The writer is not one to depart from the tradition, although he must confess that the peculiar merit of the jingle escapes him.

has so received.[11] "Waiver" of the tort is an unfortunate term, since the quasi-contract action itself is still based on the tort, and there is merely an election between alternative, co-existing remedies,[12] and the unsuccessful pursuit of the "implied" contract will not bar a later action for the tort itself.[13]

The ordinary delictual action for a tort usually is not concerned with restitution, since it seems to compensate the injured person for his loss, irrespective of the receipt of anything by the defendant. Even those tort actions which demand the return of specific property, such as replevin or ejectment, are in theory, at least, seeking to restore the plaintiff to his prior position, although they may often have the incidental effect of giving him the benefit of the increased value of the property. Restitution in quasi-contract, on the other hand, looks to what the defendant has received which in good conscience should belong to the plaintiff; and this may be either more or less[14] than the amount of the plaintiff's actual loss.

The election to sue for restitution is by no means allowed in all tort cases. It is not permitted where the defendant has merely damaged the plaintiff, negligently[15] or otherwise,[16] without benefit to himself; and the plaintiff may not, merely by declaring that he "waives" the tort, create any implied promise to pay in such a case.[17] Restitution is restricted to those cases in which the common counts in the old action of general assumpsit could be used—that is to say, those in which the wrongdoer has been unjustly enriched by his tort, and "is under an obligation from the ties of natural justice to refund," so that "the law implies a debt and gives this action, founded in the equity of the plaintiff's case, as it were upon a contract."[18]

Thus where the defendant has appropriated the plaintiff's money,[19] or has taken his property and sold it,[20] a quasi-contract count will lie for money had and received to the plaintiff's use, through the fiction of an implied promise to repay. If the property has not been sold, but the defendant has retained it, the courts are not in agreement as to whether the owner may sue on an implied contract of sale to the wrongdoer. Some decisions, restricting the doctrine to its original form, where the assumpsit count used was that for money had and received to the defendant's use, have held that it does not ap-

---

11. See Corbin, Waiver of Tort and Suit in Assumpsit, 1910, 19 Yale L.J. 221; Keener, Waiver of Tort, 1893, 6 Harv.L.Rev. 223, 269; Teller, Restitution as an Alternative Remedy, 1956, 2 N.Y.Law Forum 40; Note, 1927, 11 Minn.L.Rev. 532.

12. Keener, Quasi-Contracts, 1893, 159, 160.

13. Gibbs v. Jones, 1868, 46 Ill. 319; Bains v. Price, 1922, 207 Ala. 337, 92 So. 447; Kirkman v. Philips' Heirs, 1871, 54 Tenn. (7 Heisk) 222. But cf. Terry v. Munger, 1890, 121 N.Y. 161, 24 N.E. 272.

14. Felder v. Reeth, 8th Cir. 1929, 34 F.2d 744; Heinze v. McKinnon, 2d Cir. 1913, 123 C.C.A. 492, 205 F. 366; In re Baker, 1932, 5 W.W.Harr., Del., 198, 162 A. 356; Galvin v. Mac Mining & Milling Co., 1894, 14 Mont. 508, 37 P. 366; Huganir v. Cotter, 1899, 102 Wis. 323, 78 N.W. 423.

15. Altepeter v. Virgil State Bank, 1952, 345 Ill. App. 585, 104 N.E.2d 334; New York Central Railroad Co. v. State, 1936, 242 App.Div. 421, 287 N.Y.S. 850; Kyle v. Chester, 1911, 42 Mont. 522, 113 P. 749.

16. Erickson v. Borchardt, 1929, 177 Minn. 381, 225 N.W. 145 (fraud); Howard v. Swift & Co., 1934, 356 Ill. 80, 190 N.E. 102 (directors buying stock for corporation); Burleson v. Langdon, 1928, 174 Minn. 264, 219 N.W. 155 (conversion); Soderlin v. Marquette National Bank, 1943, 214 Minn. 408, 8 N.W.2d 331 (bank paying check on forgery).

17. Patterson v. Prior, 1862, 18 Ind. 440; Tightmeyer v. Mongold, 1878, 20 Kan. 90; Minor v. Baldridge, 1898, 123 Cal. 187, 55 P. 783; Patterson v. Kasper, 1914, 182 Mich. 281, 148 N.W. 690; Parkersburg & Marietta Sand Co. v. Smith, 1915, 76 W.Va. 246, 85 S.E. 516.

18. Lord Mansfield, in Moses v. Macferlan, 1760, 2 Burr. 1005, 1008, 97 Eng.Rep. 676. See Corbin, Waiver of Tort and Suit in Assumpsit, 1910, 19 Yale L.J. 221; Note, 1927, 11 Minn.L.Rev. 532.

19. Billig v. Goodrich, 1917, 199 Mich. 423, 165 N.W. 647; Craig v. Craig's Estate, 1914, 167 Iowa 340, 149 N.W. 454; Burgoyne v. McKillip, 8th Cir. 1910, 182 F. 452; Humbird v. Davis, 1904, 210 Pa. 311, 59 A. 1082; Guernsey v. Davis, 1903, 67 Kan. 378, 73 P. 101.

20. McDonald v. First National Bank of McKeesport, 1945, 353 Pa. 29, 44 A.2d 265; Taylor Motor Car Co. v. Hansen, 1929, 75 Utah 80, 282 P. 1040; Dallas v. H. J. Koehler Sporting Goods Co., 1914, 86 N.J.L. 651, 92 A. 356; Heinze v. McKinnon, 2d Cir. 1913, 205 F. 366; Smith Lumber Co. v. Scott County Garbage Reducing & Fuel Co., 1910, 149 Iowa 272, 128 N.W. 389.

ply where the goods have not been exchanged for money.[21] The better reasoning, now followed by the great majority of the courts, is that restitution will be allowed because so long as the entire doctrine is based on a fiction created by the law, there is no reason to draw any distinction between unjust enrichment through the proceeds of a sale of goods and through the goods themselves.[22] On the same basis, it has been held that one who has converted goods and used them, and subsequently has returned them to the owner, may be liable in quasi-contract, on the fiction of a hiring and an obligation to pay value for it.[23] The principle also has been extended to cases where the defendant has tortiously obtained labor or services from the plaintiff,[24] or has wrongfully manufactured and sold the plaintiff's invention.[25]

The wrongful use and occupation of real property, by one who is not a tenant, was not considered by the earlier cases[26] to be sufficient ground to invoke the quasi-contract action. The explanation lay in the historical reason that the assumpsit count for use and occupation of land would lie only where there was a tenancy,[27] and perhaps in a number of cases in which the defendant was claiming some rights in the land, and the court was unwilling to litigate the title indirectly.[28] This is perhaps still the prevailing rule. Again, however, in the realm of fiction, there is no visible reason to distinguish between unjust enrichment derived from real and that from personal property.[29] The later tendency has been to allow the action in quasi-contract, where, for example, a corporation having the power of eminent domain has taken possession of land without complying with the statutory procedure;[30] where a valuable part of the soil has been

---

21. Janiszewski v. Behrmann, 1956, 345 Mich. 8, 75 N.W.2d 77; Anderson Equipment Co. v. Findley, 1944, 350 Pa. 399, 39 A.2d 520; Cox v. Awtry, 1924, 211 Ala. 356, 100 So. 337; Lyon v. Clark, 1902, 129 Mich. 381, 88 N.W. 1046; Woodruff v. Zaban & Son, 1909, 133 Ga. 24, 65 S.E. 123.

See Corbin, Waiver of Tort and Suit in Assumpsit, 1910, 19 Yale L.J. 221, 229; Teller, Restitution as an Alternative Remedy, 1956, 2 N.Y.Law Forum 40; Notes, 1927, 11 Minn.L.Rev. 532, 538; 1948, 20 Rocky Mt.L.Rev. 300.

Some of these courts rather inconsistently allow suit in quasi-contract where the property was acquired rightfully, as under a bailment, and later converted by the defendant, though he did not sell it. Ford & Co. v. Atlantic Compress Co., 1912, 138 Ga. 496, 75 S.E. 609; Brown v. Foster, 1904, 137 Mich. 35, 100 N.W. 167. "For the reason that the relation of the parties, out of which the duty violated grew, had its inception in contract." Tuttle v. Campbell, 1889, 74 Mich. 652, 42 N.W. 384.

22. Downs v. Finnegan, 1894, 58 Minn. 112, 59 N.W. 981; Daniels v. Foster & Kleiser, 1920, 95 Or. 502, 187 P. 627; Garrity v. State Board of Administration of Educational Institutions, 1917, 99 Kan. 695, 162 P. 1167; School Board of Lipps District No. 4 v. Saxon Lime & Lumber Co., 1917, 121 Va. 594, 93 S.E. 579; Heber v. Heber's Estate, 1909, 139 Wis. 472, 121 N.W. 328.

23. Olwell v. Nye & Nissen Co., 1947, 26 Wn.2d 282, 173 P.2d 652; Fanson v. Linsley, 1878, 20 Kan. 235; Stockett v. Watkins' Administrators, 1830, 2 Gill & J. 326; Jones v. Randall, 1774, 1 Cowp. 37, 98 Eng.Rep. 954. Cf. Paar v. City of Prescott, 1942, 59 Ariz. 497, 130 P.2d 40 (using water system).

24. Patterson v. Prior, 1862, 18 Ind. 440; Abbot v. Town of Fremont, 1857, 34 N.H. 432; Boardman v. Ward, 1889, 40 Minn. 399, 42 N.W. 202. Contra, Thompson v. Bronk, 1901, 126 Mich. 455, 85 N.W. 1084.

Accord, as to plaintiff's child, Smith v. Gilbert, 1906, 80 Ark. 525, 98 S.W. 115; Illinois Central Railroad Co. v. Sanders, 1913, 104 Miss. 257, 61 So. 309.

25. Eckert v. Braun, 7th Cir. 1946, 155 F.2d 517. Cf. Caskie v. Philadelphia Rapid Transit Co., 1936, 321 Pa. 157, 184 A. 17 (interference with contract).

26. Rogers v. Libbey, 1853, 35 Me. 200; Lloyd v. Hough, 1843, 42 U.S. (1 How.) 153, 11 L.Ed. 83; Hurley v. Lameraux, 1882, 29 Minn. 138, 12 N.W. 447; Ackerman v. Lyman, 1866, 20 Wis. 454; National Oil Refining Co. v. Bush, 1879, 88 Pa. 335.

27. See Ames, Assumpsit for Use or Occupation, 1889, 2 Harv.L.Rev. 377; Note, 1932, 30 Mich.L.Rev. 1087; Atlanta, Knoxville & Northern Railway Co. v. McHan, 1900, 110 Ga. 543, 35 S.E. 634; Hurley v. Lameraux, 1882, 29 Minn. 138, 12 N.W. 447 (" * * * a trespasser cannot be converted into a tenant without his consent.")

28. See Halleck v. Mixer, 1860, 16 Cal. 574; Parks v. Morris, Layfield & Co., 1907, 63 W.Va. 51, 59 S.E. 753; City of Boston v. Binney, 1831, 28 Mass. (11 Pick.) 1.

29. "The trespasser is unjustly enriched, and the plaintiff has as much need of a remedy in assumpsit as in the case of any other tort enriching the tort feasor." Corbin, Waiver of Tort and Suit in Assumpsit, 1910, 19 Yale L.J. 221, 232; Note, 1932, 30 Mich.L.Rev. 1087.

30. Snowden v. Fort Lyon Canal Co., 8th Cir. 1916, 238 F. 495; Wayne County v. Elk Spring Valley Turnpike Co., 1930, 233 Ky. 741, 26 S.W.2d 1049; Efird v.

removed;[31] where cattle have been grazed upon the land, irrespective of any damage done to it;[32] and even, in a few cases, where there has been outright occupation and use by a trespasser.[33]

The quasi-contract action is particularly applicable to those torts in which money or property is obtained by fraudulent misrepresentation,[34] as where the defendant induces a sale of goods by misrepresenting his intention to pay or the state of his credit. In such a case the plaintiff may have a choice of a number of remedies, which are considered in a later chapter.[35]

The common law courts recognized that they were invading the province of equity,[36] and the relief which they granted by way of restitution has continued to be subject to equitable rules. Unless he is excused by special circumstances, the plaintiff must restore what he has himself received,[37] and his right to restitution is lost by any conduct affirming the transaction,[38] or even by inaction for an unreasonable length of time after discovery of the facts.[39] The measure of his recovery is determined on the equitable basis of the unjust enrichment of the defendant,[40] rather than the tort basis of the plaintiff's loss. Thus, a purchaser defrauded in the sale of a horse who seeks a remedy by way of restitution ordinarily must return the horse, and may recover the price he has paid, regardless of the extent of his loss on the transaction. The recovery may be defeated by a subsequent change in the defendant's position which destroys his unjust enrichment.[41]

City of Winston-Salem, 1930, 199 N.C. 33, 153 S.E. 632; Mayer v. Studer & Manion Co., 1935, 66 N.D. 190, 262 N.W. 925; cf. Kerns v. Couch, 1932, 141 Or. 147, 12 P.2d 1011, 17 P.2d 323.

31. Shell Petroleum Corp. v. Scully, 5th Cir. 1934, 71 F.2d 772; West v. McClure, 1904, 85 Miss. 296, 37 So. 752; Franks v. Lockwood, 1959, 146 Conn. 273, 150 A.2d 215; Frankfort Land Co. v. Hughett, 1917, 137 Tenn. 32, 191 S.W. 530; Hudson v. Iguano Land & Min. Co., 1912, 71 W.Va. 402, 76 S.E. 797.

32. Norden v. Jones, 1873, 33 Wis. 600; Lazarus v. Phelps, 1894, 152 U.S. 81, 14 S.Ct. 477, 38 L.Ed. 363; Tsuboi v. Cohn, 1924, 40 Idaho 102, 231 P. 708; Simmonds v. Richards, 1906, 74 Kan. 311, 86 P. 452; Baldwin v. Bohl, 1909, 23 S.D. 395, 122 N.W. 247.

33. Raven Red Ash Coal Co. v. Ball, 1946, 185 Va. 534, 39 S.E.2d 231; West St. Auto Service, Inc. v. Schmidt, 1966, 26 A.D.2d 662, 272 N.Y.S.2d 615; Edwards v. Lee's Administrator, 1936, 265 Ky. 418, 96 S.W.2d 1028; Taggart v. Shepherd, 1932, 122 Cal.App. 755, 10 P.2d 808; Parkinson v. Shew, 1899, 12 S.D. 171, 80 N.W. 189.

34. Tabor v. Universal Exploration Co., 8th Cir. 1931, 48 F.2d 1047; Philpott v. Superior Court, 1934, 1 Cal.2d 512, 36 P.2d 635; Wallace v. Perry, 1953, 74 Idaho 86, 257 P.2d 231; Heilbronn v. Herzog, 1900, 165 N.Y. 98, 58 N.E. 759. Cf. Chandler v. Sanger, 1874, 114 Mass. 364 (duress).

35. See infra, ch. 18.

36. Moses v. Macferlan, 1760, 2 Burr. 1005, 97 Eng. Rep. 676 ("founded in the equity of the plaintiff's case"); Clarke v. Shee, 1774, 1 Cowp. 197, 98 Eng.Rep. 1041 ("liberal action in the nature of a bill in equity"); Straton v. Rastall, 1788, 2 Term Rep 366, 100 Eng.Rep. 197 ("Must shew that he has equity and conscience on his side, and that he could recover it in a court of equity"); Mason v. Madson, 1931, 90 Mont. 489, 4 P.2d 475. But see Hanbury, The Recovery of Money, 1924, 40 L.Q.Rev. 31, stressing the legal nature of the action, and the vagueness of the "equity" involved.

37. Byard v. Holmes, 1868, 33 N.J.L. 119; Houghton v. Nash, 1874, 64 Me. 477; Adam, Meldrum & Anderson Co. v. Stewart, 1901, 157 Ind. 678, 61 N.E. 1002; James Music Co. v. Bridge, 1908, 134 Wis. 510, 114 N.W. 1108. See Note, 1929, 29 Col.L.Rev. 791.

38. Brennan v. National Equitable Investment Co., 1928, 247 N.Y. 486, 160 N.E. 924, rehearing denied 248 N.Y. 560, 162 N.E. 524; Samples v. Guyer, 1898, 120 Ala. 611, 24 So. 942; Sherwood v. Walker, 1887, 66 Mich. 568, 33 N.W. 919; Bayer v. Winton Motor Car Co., 1916, 194 Mich. 222, 160 N.W. 642. Cf. Maki v. St. Luke's Hospital Association, 1913, 122 Minn. 444, 142 N.W. 705.

39. Wilbur v. Flood, 1867, 16 Mich. 40; Grant v. Lovekin, 1926, 285 Pa. 257, 132 A. 342; Long v. International Vending Machine Co., 1911, 158 Mo.App. 662, 139 S.W. 819; Everson v. J. L. Owens Manufacturing Co., 1920, 145 Minn. 199, 176 N.W. 505.

40. Seneca Wire & Manufacturing Co. v. A. B. Leach & Co., 1928, 247 N.Y. 1, 159 N.E. 700; Note, 1934, 32 Mich.L.Rev. 968. Cf. Houser & Haines Manufacturing Co. v. McKay, 1909, 53 Wash. 337, 101 P. 894; Pfeiffer v. Independent Plumbing & Heating Supply Co., Mo.App.1934, 72 S.W.2d 138 (rescission for breach of warranty); and see Rogge, Damages upon Rescission for Breach of Warranty, 1929, 28 Mich.L. Rev. 26.

The relief granted on this theory is of course capable of considerable variation. Thus a defrauded seller ordinarily does not restore anything, or recover what he has given, but recovers the reasonable value of what he has sold, subject to deduction of any payment already received.

41. See Cohen, Change of Position in Quasi-Contracts, 1932, 45 Harv.L.Rev. 1333; Langmaid, Quasi-Contract—Change of Position by Receipt of Money in

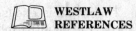
WESTLAW REFERENCES

tort* /p contract* /p remed! restitution damages /s elect! % electric

moses /5 macferlan

Satisfaction of a Preexisting Obligation, 1933, 21 Cal.L. Rev. 311; Woodward, Quasi-Contracts, 1913, §§ 25, 27; Keener, Quasi-Contracts, 1893, 61–67.

Chapter 17

PRODUCTS LIABILITY

Table of Sections

Sec.
95. Theories of Recovery and Types of Losses.
95A. Warranty and Intangible Economic Losses.
96. Negligence and Liability for Physical Harm to Persons and Tangible Things.
97. Strict Liability in Warranty for Physical Harm to Persons and Tangible Things.
98. Strict Liability in Tort for Physical Harm to Persons and Tangible Things.
99. Meaning of Dangerously Defective or Unsafe Products.
100. Parties.
101. Summary—Interests Protected and Theories of Recovery.
102. Contributory Negligence, Misuse, and Other Intervening Misconduct.
103. Proof.
104. Other Suppliers.
104A. Real Estate Transactions.

§ 95. Theories of Recovery and Types of Losses

Products liability is the name currently given to the area of the law involving the liability of those who supply goods or products for the use of others to purchasers, users, and bystanders for losses of various kinds resulting from so-called defects in those products.

At the very outset, it is important to make a distinction between two types of product conditions that can result in some kind of loss either to the purchaser or a third person. One is a dangerous condition of the product or, if one prefers, a product hazard;[1] the other is the inferior condition or

§ 95

1. A recent government estimate placed the number of consumer product injuries (both in and out of the home) at 36 million for 1977. See Prod.Saf. & Liab. Rep. (BNA), June 29, 1979, 511. The total cost of such injuries to the nation has been estimated at $20 billion or more per year. Owen, Punitive Damages in Products Liability Litigation, 1976, 74 Mich.L.Rev. 1258–59 n. 2.

677

the type of condition that may disappoint the purchaser's expectations as to its efficacy or fitness for the purposes intended.[2] The first is calculated to result in damaging events such as traffic accidents, airplane crashes, medical mishaps, industrial accidents, and the like, and the second is likely to cause only intangible economic losses.

These different types of conditions can lead to at least five different kinds of losses that can result either to a purchaser or others.[3] The kind of loss for which a claimant seeks recovery has much to do with the theory—contract or tort—on which a claimant may and ought to be able to recover. An understanding of the various issues involved in dealing with product liability claims justifies a breakdown of losses and therefore claims into five categories. These are: (1) personal injuries, (2) physical harm to tangible things, other than the assembled product such as an automobile, a helicopter, or an industrial machine of some kind, (3) physical harm to or destruction of the assembled product purchased by the first purchaser for use, (4) physical harm to or destruction of a product that was constructed with or repaired with the use of the target seller's component part, and (5) direct economic loss resulting from the purchase of an inferior product, and indirect consequential loss, such as loss of profits, resulting from the unfitness of the product adequately to serve the purchaser's purposes, such as when a plastic pipe purchased for an irrigation system on a golf course is unsatisfactory and requires replacement.[4]

Currently those who suffer these different kinds of losses can be classified into three general groups as: (1) purchasers, (2) users who are not purchasers, and (3) nonusers who are commonly referred to as bystanders when physical injuries are suffered.

Four possible theories of recovery are available under the complexities of modern products liability law. These are: (1) strict liability in contract for breach of a warranty, express or implied,[5] (2) negligence liability in contract for breach of an express or implied warranty that the product was designed and constructed in a workmanlike manner,[6] (3) negligence liability in tort largely for physical harm to persons and tangible things,[7] and (4) strict liability in tort largely for physical harm to persons and tangible things.[8]

The nature or kind of loss suffered by a claimant has had and should have much to do with the resolution of a variety of issues

2. See, generally, Ribstein, Guidelines for Deciding Product Economic Loss Cases, 1978, 29 Mercer L.Rev. 493; Edmeades, The Citadel Stands: The Recovery of Economic Loss in American Products Liability, 1977, 27 Case W.Res.L.Rev. 647; Wade, Is section 402A of the Second Restatement of Torts Preempted by the UCC and Therefore Unconstitutional?, 1974, 42 Tenn.L.Rev. 123.

3. See, Keeton, Annual Survey of Texas Law of Torts, 1979, 33 Sw.L.J. 1, commenting on two decisions by the Texas Supreme Court of Mid Continent Aircraft Corp. v. Curry County Spraying Service, Inc., Tex.1978, 572 S.W.2d 308, and Signal Oil and Gas Co. v. Universal Oil Products, Tex.1978, 572 S.W.2d 320.

4. Travelers Indemnity Co. v. Evans Pipe Co., 6th Cir. 1970, 432 F.2d 211; see Reitz and Seabolt, Warranties and Product Liability: Who Can Sue and Where?, 1973, 46 Temp.L.Q. 527; Comment, Strict Products Liability to the Bystander: A Study in Common Law Determinism, 1971, 38 U.Chi.L.Rev. 625; Comment, The Bystander's Liberation Front—U.C.C. § 2–318 or Strict Liability?, 1971, 19 Kan.L.Rev. 251; Uniform Commercial Code, Sec. 2–318; Keeton, Annual Survey of Texas Law of Torts, 1978, 32 Sw.L.J. 1.

5. White and Summers, Handbook of the Law Under the Uniform Commercial Code, 1972, 286–95; Nordstrom, Handbook of the Law of Sales, 1970, 235–36.

6. This theory not applicable against supplier of a product under the Uniform Commercial Code but is held to be applicable against a housing merchant. See, generally, Roberts, The Case of the Unwary Home Buyer: The Housing Merchant Did It, 1967, 52 Cor. L.Q. 835; see, also, Schipper v. Levitt & Sons, Inc., 1965, 44 N.J. 70, 207 A.2d 314; Humber v. Morton, Tex.1968, 426 S.W.2d 554.

7. MacPherson v. Buick Motor Co., 1916, 217 N.Y. 382, 111 N.E. 1050; Pike v. Frank G. Hough Co., 1970, 2 Cal.3d 466, 85 Cal.Rptr. 629, 467 P.2d 229; Katz, Negligence in Design: A Current Look, 1965 Ins.L.J. 5; Noel, Manufacturer's Negligence of Design or Directions for Use of a Product, 1962, 71 Yale L.J. 816.

8. Greenman v. Yuba Power Products, Inc., 1962, 59 Cal.2d 57, 27 Cal.Rptr. 697, 377 P.2d 897; Phipps v. General Motors Corp., 1976, 278 Md. 337, 363 A.2d 955; Keeton, Products Liability—Some Observations About Allocation of Risks, 1966, 64 Mich.L.Rev. 1329.

and the proper theory or theories of recovery for the resolution of such a claim. Some of the major issues to be resolved in product liability claims are the following: (1) Will fault in the sense of negligence be a necessary basis for recovery? (2) To what extent will a supplier be subject to strict liability? (3) If product defect rather than negligence is the basis or a basis on which liability can be imposed, when is a product to be regarded as defective or unfit in the kind of way that will subject a supplier to liability for the kind of loss suffered? (4) When will a provision to limit liability in some way in the contract of sale or other bargaining transaction be effective as to reduce a seller's or other supplier's liability that would otherwise have been imposed? (5) When, if at all, can the first purchaser for use, normally the so-called consumer purchaser, bring an action against a seller in the marketing chain other than his immediate seller? (6) Under what circumstances can a person other than a purchaser bring suit against a seller or other supplier of a defective product? (7) What kind of conduct or misconduct on the part of a purchaser, a user, or a victim will constitute either a defense or a cause of a kind that will be regarded as a superseding cause severing the chain of legal causation? (8) What will be the appropriate statute of limitations applicable to the cause of action and when will the cause of action be regarded as coming into existence? (9) What will be the appropriate conflict of laws rule to apply as between the law of two or more states? (10) What effect, if any, will the failure to give prompt notification to a seller or other supplier of a defect in a product after it was discovered or should have been discovered in the exercise of ordinary care have on recovery?

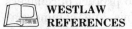

WESTLAW REFERENCES

Theories of Recovery and Types of Losses
di product liability
citation(279 +5 443) & court(il)

Warranty and Intangible Economic Losses
topic("product* liability") & caveat emptor"
topic(313a) & express /5 warrant!
topic(313a) & implied /5 warrant!

§ 95A. Warranty and Intangible Economic Losses

The courts in early America adopted the notion of *caveat emptor* so that there was initially no liability of a seller of a product on any theory—tort or contract—on behalf of anyone including a purchaser against his immediate seller in the absence of fraud, i.e., intentional deception, or an express manifestation of an intention to guarantee some specific characteristic or quality of the product that was the subject matter of a sale.[1] This notion came from the celebrated English case of Chandelor v. Lopus.[2] But considerable pressure developed for the protection of the intangible economic interest of those making bargaining transactions. This resulted in the development of the warranty theory of recovery. It came to be recognized that (1) express warranties could result from express statements made amounting to representations or affirmations of fact about the characteristics of goods sold,[3] and (2) implied warranties could result simply as a consequence of the act of selling when the sale was by a merchant.[4] This law that recognized the existence of express warranties flowing from express representa-

§ 95A

1. Prosser, The Implied Warranty of Merchantable Quality, 1943, 27 Minn.L.Rev. 117; Horowitz, The Transformation of American Law, 1780–1860, 1977, 167, 180, 330, n. 113.

2. 1603, 79 Eng Rep 3

3. 1 Williston, Sales, Rev.ed.1948, §§ 195, 196. "Any affirmation of fact or any promise by the seller relating to the goods is an express warranty if the natural tendency of such affirmation or promise is to induce the buyer to purchase the goods, and if the buyer purchases the goods relying thereon." Uniform Sales Act, § 12.

4. Lambert v. Sistrunk, Fla.1952, 58 So.2d 434; Southern Iron & Equipment Co. v. Bamberg, Ehrhardt & Walterboro Railway Co., 1929, 151 S.C. 506, 149 S.E. 271, 278; Lane v. Trenholm Building Co., 1976, 267 S.C. 497, 229 S.E.2d 728, 730.

tions of fact and implied warranties from the act of selling by a merchant developed from a felt need to protect purchasers from intangible economic and commercial losses suffered as a consequence of the frustration of their expectations about the worth, efficacy, or desirability of the product to serve their needs. It was not from a desire to provide security from dangerous conduct. While it is said in the Uniform Commercial Code which has been adopted in all of the states of the United States that a specific intent to guarantee is not a requirement for a finding of an existence of an express warranty,[5] it would appear that there is normally an objective manifestation of an intent to guarantee, i.e., an objective implied promise to be responsible in some way if the product does not conform to the express or implied representations that are made.[6] Therefore, the obligation should quite clearly be contractual in its nature as to be distinguished from tort obligations that are imposed by law on policy grounds and independent of any promise to do or not to do something. Some courts and writers have taken the position that the warranty obligation is in its nature tortious rather than contractual and that it is an obligation imposed by law on policy grounds and without respect to any manifestation of an intent to guarantee.[7] But insofar as liability for economic losses are concerned, it would appear that the obligations of warranty law have been obligations imposed on the basis of express or implied promises or express or implied representations by the seller, and these representations are made under circumstances manifesting an intent to guarantee. If this has not been so, it should be in so in order to make an intelligible distinction between contractual obligations and tortious obligations.

Early in the Nineteenth Century,[8] the slow growth of business practice by which reputable sellers stood behind their goods,[9] and a changing viewpoint toward the seller's responsibility [10] led to the development of "implied" warranties of quality, which were attached by law to certain types of sales, and which in effect made the seller an insurer of the fitness of his goods for their ordinary purposes and for the particular purpose of the purchaser in those instances when the purchaser was relying on the seller to the seller's knowledge. Detailed consideration of these warranties must be left to texts on the law of sales.[11] So far as the remedy between buyer and seller is concerned, the law, as it stands today, is very largely statutory, with the developments of the common law crystallized, first in the provisions of the Uniform Sales Act,[12] and later in those of the Uniform Commercial Code.[13] The Uniform Commercial Code is generally regarded as the *exclusive source* for ascertaining when a seller is subject to liability for damages if the claim is based on intangible economic loss not attributable to physical injury to person or harm to a tangible thing other than the defective product itself. Those

---

5. U.C.C., Sec. 2–313(2). Under this subdivision, it is not necessary that the seller use formal words such as "warrant" or "guarantee" or that he have a specific intention to make a warranty.

6. This is quite clearly the English view. See Miller and Lovell, Product Liability, 1977, 36–41.

7. See Bekkevold v. Potts, 1927, 173 Minn. 87, 216 N.W. 790; Hoe v. Sanborn, 1860, 21 N.Y. 552, 564; Lee v. Cohrt, 1930, 57 S.D. 387, 232 N.W. 900; 1 Williston, Sales, 2d ed. 1924, § 197. Williston, Liability for Honest Misrepresentations, 1911, 24 Harv.L.Rev. 415, 420; Smith, Surviving Fictions, 1917, 27 Yale L.J. 147, 317, 326.

See Note, 1955, 43 Cal.L.Rev. 381.

8. The development is traced in Prosser, The Implied Warranty of Merchantable Quality, 1943, 27 Minn.L.Rev. 117.

9. See Bogert and Fink, Business Practices Regarding Warranties in the Sale of Goods, 1931, 21 Ill.L.Rev. 400, 415.

10. See Llewellyn, Of Warranty of Quality and Society, 1936, 36 Col.L.Rev. 699, 1937, 37 Col.L.Rev. 404.

11. See 1 Williston, Sales, Rev. ed.1948, ch. 9; Vold, Sales, 2d ed.1959, §§ 84–95. Also Frumer and Friedman, Products Liability, 1961, §§ 19–19.08.

12. §§ 12 (express warranty); 14 (sale by description); 15 (implied warranties of quality). See 1 and 1A Uniform Laws Ann.

13. §§ 2–313 (express warranty); 2–314 (implied warranty of merchantability); 2–315 (implied warranty of fitness for a particular purpose). See Cudahy, Limitations of Warranty Under the Uniform Commercial Code, 1963, 47 Marq.L.Rev. 127; Note, 1963, 38 Ind. L.J. 648.

who drafted the Uniform Commercial Code were without doubt thinking primarily about the intangible economic interest of those who purchase products.

The implied warranties of quality are reduced to two: a warranty that the goods are fit for the particular purpose of the buyer, when that purpose is made known to the seller and the latter knows that the buyer is relying upon his skill and judgment to select and furnish suitable goods;[14] and a warranty that the goods are of merchantable quality when they are bought from one who deals in goods of that description.[15] Goods to be merchantable must be reasonably fit for the ordinary purposes for which such goods are used.

There were two fundamental doctrines pertaining to the liability of a seller for claims based on the interference with intangible economic interests. These were that (1) privity of contract was normally a prerequisite to recovery leading to the conclusion that only a purchaser or one standing in the shoes of a purchaser as a third party beneficiary could sue for breach of a warranty and then only against his immediate seller[16] and (2) disclaimers and other contract provisions which negate warranties, express or implied, or limit the remedy for breach of a warranty—if fairly negotiated and bargained about—were valid and enforceable.[17] There was and is nothing novel or unsound about these propositions so long as liability is based on a representational theory, and on the theory that the parties should be permitted by contract to allocate the risk of losses as they choose.

§ 96. Negligence and Liability for Physical Harm to Persons and Tangible Things

The law of products liability with respect to liability for physical harm to persons and tangible things began with the case of Winterbottom v. Wright[1] decided in 1842 and which has been described as a fishbone in the throat of the law. That case, with the broad language of Lord Abinger, was taken to mean that there could be no action, even in tort, for the misperformance of a contract of sale of a chattel in the first instance.[2] It was not until 1905 that the error of this interpretation of the case was pointed out in a noted article by Professor Bohlen;[3] and in the meantime the nineteenth century had firmly established the general rule that the original seller of goods was not liable for damages caused by their defects to anyone except his immediate buyer, or one in privity with him.[4]

Various reasons were given in support of this rule.[5] One was that the seller's misconduct was not the cause of the damage to the consumer in a legal sense, because no such harm was to be anticipated from any defects in the goods, and there was an intervening resale by a responsible party, which "insulated" the negligence of the manufacturer.

---

14. See Corman, Implied Sales Warranty of Fitness for Particular Purpose, [1958] Wis.L.Rev. 219.

15. See Prosser, The Implied Warranty of Merchantable Quality, 1943, 27 Minn.L.Rev. 117; Notes, 1956, 5 De Paul L.Rev. 273; 1962, 48 Va.L.Rev. 152.

16. Annot., 1967, 16 A.L.R.3d 683 (privity requirement in economic loss cases); Ribstein, Guidelines for Deciding Product Economic Loss Cases, 1978, 29 Mercer L.Rev. 493; Edmeades, The Citadel Stands: The Recovery of Economic Loss in American Products Liability, 1977, 27 Case W.Res.L.Rev. 647.

17. Franklin, When Worlds Collide: Liability Theories and Disclaimers in Defective-Product Cases, 1966, 18 Stan.L.Rev. 974.

§ 96

1. 1842, 10 M & W 109, 152 Eng.Rep. 402.

2. See for example Huset v. J. I. Case Threshing Machine Co., 8th Cir. 1903, 57 C.C.A. 237, 120 F. 865; Earl v. Lubbock, [1905] 1 K.B. 253.

3. Bohlen, The Basis of Affirmative Obligations in the Law of Tort, 1905, 44 Am.L.Reg.,N.S., 209, 280–285, 289–310. See also Lord Atkin, in Donoghue v. Stevenson, [1932] A.C. 562, 588–589.

4. Hasbrouck v. Armour & Co., 1909, 139 Wis. 357, 121 N.W. 157; Lebourdais v. Vitrified Wheel Co., 1907, 194 Mass. 341, 80 N.E. 482; Burkett v. Studebaker Brothers Manufacturing Co., 1912, 126 Tenn. 467, 150 S.W. 421; Stone v. Van Noy Railroad News Co., 1913, 153 Ky. 240, 154 S.W. 1092; Liggett & Myers Tobacco Co. v. Cannon, 1915, 132 Tenn. 419, 178 S.W. 1009.

5. Particularly in Huset v. J.I. Case Threshing Machine Co., 8th Cir. 1903, 57 C.C.A. 237, 120 F. 865.

This argument of course has been exploded long since: if goods are sold to a dealer, nothing is more foreseeable than that they will be resold to a consumer, or, if they are dangerously defective, that he will be injured by them; and the case falls well within the limits of legal causation. A second reason, which was typical of the social viewpoint of the nineteenth century, was that it would place too heavy a burden upon manufacturers and sellers to hold them responsible to hundreds of persons at a distance whose identity they could not even know, and that it was better to let the consumer suffer. As to this, at least, there has been a definite change in our social philosophy. It is now generally recognized that a manufacturer or even a dealer has a responsibility to the ultimate consumer, based upon nothing more than the sufficient fact that he has so dealt with the goods that they are likely to come into the hands of another, and to do harm if they are defective.[6] The existence of a contract with the buyer of course does not prevent the existence of a tort duty to a third person who will be affected by the seller's conduct.[7] The battle over liability for negligence has been fought and won by the plaintiff, both in England[8] and in the United States,[9] and the scene of combat shifted in the 1960's to the field of strict liability.[10]

The courts began by the usual process of recognizing several exceptions, which whittled down the general rule derived from the supposed holding of Winterbottom v. Wright. These are now largely of purely historical interest. The most important of them held the seller liable to a third person for negligence in the preparation or sale of an article "imminently" or "inherently" dangerous to human safety.[11] This originated in a New York case [12] in 1852; and for more than half a century the category remained vague and imperfectly defined. There was much rather pointless dispute, for example, as to how such products as soap,[13] chewing tobacco,[14] or the container of a beverage [15] were to be classified.

Finally, in 1916 in the famous case of MacPherson v. Buick Motor Co.,[16] the problem fell into the hands of Judge Cardozo, in connection with the liability of a manufacturer of an automobile with a defective wheel, bought from a dealer by an ultimate purchaser, who was injured by its collapse. Cardozo's opinion struck through the fog of the "general rule" and its various exceptions, and held the maker liable for negligence. On its face the decision purported merely to extend the class of "inherently dangerous" articles to include anything which would be dangerous if negligently

6. See Bohlen, Liability of Manufacturers to Persons Other than Their Immediate Vendees, 1929, 45 L.Q.Rev. 343; Feezer, Tort Liability of Manufacturers and Vendors, 1925, 10 Minn.L.Rev. 1; Feezer, Tort Liability of Manufacturers, 1935, 19 Minn.L.Rev. 752; Russell, Manufacturers' Liability to the Ultimate Consumer, 1933, 21 Ky.L.J. 388; Jeanblanc, Manufacturers' Liability to Persons Other than Their Immediate Vendees, 1937, 24 Va.L.Rev. 134.

7. Labatt, Negligence in Relation to Privity of Contract, 1900, 16 L.Q.Rev. 168; Bohlen, The Basis of Affirmative Obligations in the Law of Tort, 1905, 44 Am. L.Reg.,N.S., 209, 280–285, 289–310.

8. Donoghue v. Stevenson, [1932] A.C. 562; Grant v. Australian Knitting Mills, [1936] A.C. 85. See Fleming, Law of Torts, 2d ed.1961, ch. 21.

9. See Wilson, Products Liability, 1955, 43 Cal.L. Rev. 614, 809; James, Products Liability, 1955, 34 Tex. L.Rev. 192; Noel, Products Liability of a Manufacturer in Tennessee, 1953, 22 Tenn.L.Rev. 985. Also Gillam, Products Liability in a Nutshell, 1958, 37 Or.L.Rev. 119, 128–30, listing more than two solid pages of books and articles.

10. See infra, §§ 97, 98.

11. Or, as it was put in Huset v. J.I. Case Threshing Machine Co., 8th Cir. 1903, 57 C.C.A. 237, 120 F. 865, "intended to preserve, destroy, or affect human life."

12. Thomas v. Winchester, 1852, 6 N.Y. 397.

13. Compare Armstrong Packing Co. v. Clem, Tex. Civ.App.1912, 151 S.W. 576, with Hasbrouck v. Armour & Co., 1909, 139 Wis. 357, 121 N.W. 157.

14. Liggett & Myers Tobacco Co. v. Cannon, 1915, 132 Tenn. 419, 178 S.W. 1009 (no); Pillars v. R.J. Reynolds Tobacco Co., 1918, 117 Miss. 490, 78 So. 365 (yes).

15. Stone v. Van Noy Railroad News Co., 1913, 153 Ky. 240, 154 S.W. 1092 (no); Coca Cola Bottling Works v. Shelton, 1926, 214 Ky. 118, 282 S.W. 778 (yes).

16. 1916, 217 N.Y. 382, 111 N.E. 1050. The story of the case is told, with sidelights, in Peck, Decision at Law, 1961, 38–69.

made.[17] But its effect was to make the exception swallow up the rule; and its reasoning and its fundamental philosophy were clearly that the manufacturer, by placing the car upon the market, assumed a responsibility to the consumer, resting not upon the contract but upon the relation arising from his purchase, together with the foreseeability of harm if proper care were not used. Legal writers [18] were quick to supply the justification that the manufacturer derives an economic benefit from the sale and the subsequent use of the chattel, and his duty is therefore analogous to that of a possessor of land toward his business visitor; and there has been added some notion of a representation of safety in the mere act of offering the goods for sale, which, because of the original buyer's reliance upon it, deprives the consumer of possible protection at his hands. Such rationalization adds little, however, to the conclusion that the duty is one imposed by the law because of the defendant's affirmative conduct, which he must know to be likely to affect the interests of another.

This decision found immediate acceptance,[19] and at the end of some forty years is universal law in the United States, with Mississippi the last state to fall into line [20] in 1966. Massachusetts, which was one of the later jurisdictions to capitulate, has said that "The MacPherson case caused the exception to swallow the asserted general rule of nonliability, leaving nothing upon which that rule could operate." [21] Some of the courts continued for a time to speak the language of "inherent danger," [22] but it now seems clear that this means nothing more than that substantial harm is to be anticipated if the chattel should be defective.[23] The rule was presently extended to include physical harm to property,[24] and even to negligence in the sale of goods, such as animal food, which involve no recognizable risk of personal injury, and are foreseeably dangerous only to property.[25] The rule that has finally emerged is that the seller is liable for negligence in the manufacture or sale of any product which may reasonably be expected to be capable of inflicting substantial harm if it is defective.[26]

17. "If the nature of a thing is such that it is reasonably certain to place life and limb in peril when negligently made, it is then a thing of danger. Its nature gives warning of the consequences to be expected. If to the element of danger there is added knowledge that the thing will be used by persons other than the purchaser and used without new tests, then, irrespective of contract, the manufacturer of this thing of danger is under a duty to make it carefully. That is as far as we are required to go for the decision of this case." MacPherson v. Buick Motor Co., 1916, 217 N.Y. 382, 389, 111 N.E. 1050.

18. Particularly Bohlen, Liability of Manufacturers to Persons Other than Their Immediate Vendees, 1929, 45 L.Q.Rev. 343.

19. Johnson v. Cadillac Motor Car Co., 2d Cir. 1919, 261 F. 878, reversing 2d Cir. 1915, 221 F. 801.

20. Actually the Mississippi court never has expressly accepted the MacPherson decision, but leaped over it to strict liability in State Stove Manufacturing Co. v. Hodges, Miss.1966, 189 So.2d 113, certiorari denied 386 U.S. 912, 87 S.Ct. 860, 17 L.Ed.2d 784. Federal courts, purporting to apply Mississippi law, have concluded that the case has been accepted. Necaise v. Chrysler Corp., 5th Cir. 1964, 335 F.2d 562; Grey v. Hayes-Sammons Chemical Co., 5th Cir. 1962, 310 F.2d 291.

21. Carter v. Yardley & Co., 1946, 319 Mass. 92, 64 N.E.2d 693, 700. See Peairs, The God in the Machine, 1949, 29 Boston U.L.Rev. 37.

22. See for example Kalash v. Los Angeles Ladder Co., 1934, 1 Cal.2d 229, 34 P.2d 481; Crane Co. v. Sears, 1934, 168 Okl. 603, 35 P.2d 916. New York, in particular, took a very narrow view as to what is to be considered "dangerous if negligently made," and denied liability for such things as a bed, Field v. Empire Case Goods Co., 1917, 179 App.Div. 253, 166 N.Y.S. 509, or a can with a key, in Boyd v. American Can Co., 1936, 249 App.Div. 644, 291 N.Y.S. 205, affirmed 274 N.Y. 526, 10 N.E.2d 532. See Davis, a Reexamination of the Doctrine of MacPherson v. Buick, 1955, 24 Ford. L.Rev. 204; Note, 1948, 14 Brook.L.Rev. 126.

23. Restatement of Torts, § 395.

24. See infra, § 101.

25. Cohan v. Associated Fur Farms, 1952, 261 Wis. 584, 53 N.W.2d 788; Dunn v. Ralston Purina Co., 1954, 38 Tenn.App. 229, 272 S.W.2d 479; Brown v. Bigelow, 1949, 325 Mass. 4, 88 N.E.2d 542; Ellis v. Lindmark, 1929, 177 Minn. 390, 225 N.W. 395; Pine Grove Poultry Farm v. Newtown By-Products Manufacturing Co., 1928, 248 N.Y. 293, 162 N.E. 84, reversed 222 App.Div. 834, 226 N.Y.S. 886.

26. See Pitts v. Basile, 1965, 55 Ill.App.2d 37, 204 N.E.2d 43, reversed on other grounds, 1966, 35 Ill.2d 49, 219 N.E.2d 472 (child's dart); Sheward v. Virtue, 1942, 20 Cal.2d 410, 126 P.2d 345 (chair); Smith v. S.S.

Since the liability is to be based on negligence, the defendant is required to exercise the care of a reasonable person under the circumstances.[27] His negligence may be found over an area quite as broad as his whole activity in preparing and selling the product.[28] He may, for example, be negligent in failing to inspect or test his materials, or the work itself,[29] or the finished product,[30] to discover possible defects, or dangerous propensities;[31] and in doing so he is held to the standard of an expert in the field.[32] At the other extreme, he must use reasonable care in his methods of advertising and sale, to avoid misrepresentation of the product,[33] and to disclose defects and dangers of which he knows.[34] In between lies the entire process of manufacture and sale.

Prior to 1960, a person who was physically harmed or whose property was physically harmed seldom recovered on a contract-warranty theory because of two obstacles. In the first place, parties were free to contract out all liability resulting from objective manifestations of intent to guarantee against defects because of prevailing notions about freedom of contract.[35] The second obstacle to recovery, which could be even more profound for those victimized by products that were defective in the kind of way that made them unreasonably dangerous, was that under contract law only those who were privy to the contract of purchase and sale could recover for breach of warranty.[36] The first purchaser for use was generally not in privity with the manufacturer, and marketing or vertical privity was considered to be a prerequisite to recovery. Moreover, those who were not purchasers and were injured in person or in property were seldom third party beneficiaries of the manufacturer's warranties in the conventional sense.[37] There was no so-called horizontal privity.

Kresge Co., 8th Cir. 1935, 79 F.2d 361 (hair combs); Carter v. Yardley & Co., 1946, 319 Mass. 92, 64 N.E.2d 693 (perfume); Simmons Co. v. Hardin, 1947, 75 Ga. App. 420, 43 S.E.2d 553 (sofa bed).

27. Considered in the light of the probability of defects, the magnitude of the possible harm, the cost of effective inspection, and the customs of the business. Marsh Wood Products Co. v. Babcock & Wilcox Co., 1932, 207 Wis. 209, 240 N.W. 392; Kalash v. Los Angeles Ladder Co., 1934, 1 Cal.2d 229, 34 P.2d 481; Smith v. Peerless Glass Co., 1932, 259 N.Y. 292, 181 N.E. 576, motion denied 259 N.Y. 664, 182 N.E. 225; Grant v. Graham Chero-Cola Bottling Co., 1918, 176 N.C. 256, 97 S.E. 27. Hence ordinarily a question for the jury.

28. See Noel, Manufacturers' Liability for Negligence, 1966, 33 Tenn.L.Rev. 444; Noel, Products Liability of a Manufacturer in Tennessee, 1953, 22 Tenn.L. Rev. 985; James, Products Liability, 1955, 34 Tex.L. Rev. 192; Wilson, Products Liability: The Protection of the Injured Person, 1955, 43 Cal.L.Rev. 614.

29. Trowbridge v. Abrasive Co., 3d Cir. 1951, 190 F.2d 825; Pierce v. Ford Motor Co., 4th Cir. 1951, 190 F.2d 910, certiorari denied, 1951, 342 U.S. 887, 72 S.Ct. 178, 96 L.Ed. 666; Willey v. Fyrogas Co., 1952, 363 Mo. 406, 251 S.W.2d 635; Ford Motor Co. v. Zahn, 8th Cir. 1959, 265 F.2d 729; Sitta v. American Steel & Wire Division, 6 Cir. 1958, 254 F.2d 12.

30. Kross v. Kelsey Hayes Co., 1968, 29 A.D.2d 901, 287 N.Y.S.2d 926.

31. Walton v. Sherwin-Williams Co., 8th Cir. 1951, 191 F.2d 277; Chapman Chemical Co. v. Taylor, 1949, 215 Ark. 630, 222 S.W.2d 820; Ebers v. General Chemical Co., 1945, 310 Mich. 261, 17 N.W.2d 176; Zesch v. Abrasive Co. of Philadelphia, 1944, 353 Mo. 558, 183 S.W.2d 140. See Dillard and Hart, Product Liability: Directions for Use and Duty to Warn, 1955, 41 Va.L. Rev. 145, 159; Note, 1950, 3 Vand.L.Rev. 341.

32. Seward v. Natural Gas Co., 1950, 11 N.J.Super. 144, 78 A.2d 129, reversed on other grounds, 1951, 8 N.J. 45, 83 A.2d 716; Cornbrooks v. Terminal Barber Shops, 1940, 282 N.Y. 217, 26 N.E.2d 25, conformed to 259 App.Div. 375, 19 N.Y.S.2d 390; Trowbridge v. Abrasive Co., 3d Cir. 1951, 190 F.2d 825.

33. Hoskins v. Jackson Grain Co., Fla.1953, 63 So. 2d 514; La Plant v. E.I. Dupont de Nemours & Co., Mo.App.1961, 346 S.W.2d 231; Peterson v. Standard Oil Co., 1910, 55 Or. 511, 106 P. 337; Wise v. Hayes, 1961, 58 Wn.2d 106, 361 P.2d 171; Waters-Pierce Oil Co. v. Deselms, 1909, 212 U.S. 159, 29 S.Ct. 270, 53 L.Ed. 453.

34. Schubert v. J.R. Clark Co., 1892, 49 Minn. 331, 51 N.W. 1103; Lewis v. Terry, 1896, 111 Cal. 39, 43 P. 398; Huset v. J.I. Case Threshing Machine Co., 8th Cir. 1903, 57 C.C.A. 237, 120 F. 865; Sterchi Bros. Stores v. Castleberry, 1938, 236 Ala. 349, 182 So. 474. See, as to warning and directions, infra p. 685.

35. See, supra, note 17, this Section.

36. See, supra, note 16, this Section.

37. Jeanblanc, Manufacturers' Liability to Persons Other than Their Immediate Vendees, 1937, 24 Va.L. Rev. 134; Feezer, Manufacturer's Liability for Injuries Caused by his Product, 1938, 37 Mich.L.Rev. 1; Spruill, Privity of Contract as a Requisite for Recovery on a Warranty, 1941, 19 N.C.L.Rev. 551; James, Products Liability, 1955, 34 Tex.L.Rev. 192; Wilson, Products Liability, 1955, 43 Cal.L.Rev. 614, 809; Noel, Manufacturers of Products—The Drift Toward Strict Liability,

The manufacturer-seller could, however, be negligent in one of several possible ways:

1. *Negligence in creating or failing to discover a flaw.* A manufacturer or other seller in the marketing chain is subject to liability for negligence in selling a product with a flaw in the product.[38] A flaw in a product is a condition of the product that is different from what it was intended to be. A manufacturer who fails to exercise reasonable care to avoid and discover unintended dangers occurring in the construction process is subject to liability. Others in the marketing chain, including resellers and retainers, can be negligent in creating or failing to discover flaws. Normally, a retail dealer would not be negligent, as a matter of law, in selling a flawed or defectively designed product of a reputable manufacturer. The existence of a flaw in a product does not necessarily bespeak negligence and proof of negligence is a difficult matter except when a court is willing to apply *res ipsa loquitur* against a particular seller,[39] which is not often.

2. *Negligence in failing to warn or failing adequately to warn.* A manufacturer or other seller is subject to liability for failing either to warn or adequately to warn about a risk or hazard inherent in the way a product is designed that is related to the intended uses as well as the reasonably foreseeable uses that may be made of the products it sells.[40] There can be no negligence in failing to warn about a risk in the absence of evidence that would justify a finding that a manufacturer or other seller knew or in the exercise of ordinary care should have known about it.[41] Moreover, it is the state of the art in the sense of the scientific knowledge and technological information regarding danger that was available to a seller at the time such seller surrendered possession that is relevant and admissible as regards what he should have known.[42] The information which a manufacturer should have known would include information that would be obtainable from a reasonable inquiry of experts and a reasonable research of scientific literature.

There are two separate goals to be achieved by adequate warnings. These are risk reduction and the protection of individual autonomy in decision-making.[43] In any event, the defendant can be negligent because: (1) no warning at all was given as to a particular risk or hazard related to the use of a product;[44] (2) a warning was given but it was inadequate in that it was not as specific as it could have been;[45] (3) a warning was given that was adequate if found and read, but the means used were inadequate to reach all those to whom harm was reasona-

---

1957, 24 Tenn.L.Rev. 963; Prosser, The Assault Upon the Citadel, 1960, 69 Yale L.J. 1099.

Opposed were Peairs, The God in the Machine, 1949, 29 Bos.U.L.Rev. 37; Plant, Strict Liability of Manufacturers for Injuries Caused by Defects in Products—An Opposing View, 1957, 24 Tenn.L.Rev. 938; Freedman, The Three-Pronged Sword of Damocles, Defense Research Institute, 1961.

38. MacPherson v. Buick Motor Co., 1916, 217 N.Y. 382, 111 N.E. 1050; Jenkins v. General Motors Corp., 5th Cir. 1971, 446 F.2d 377, certiorari denied 405 U.S. 922, 92 S.Ct. 959, 30 L.Ed.2d 793; Ford Motor Co. v. Zahn, 8th Cir. 1959, 265 F.2d 729.

39. See Section 103 on Proof.

40. Boyl v. California Chemical Co., D.C.Or.1963, 221 F.Supp. 669; Wright v. Carter Products, Inc., 2d Cir. 1957, 244 F.2d 53; Moran v. Faberge, Inc., 1975, 273 Md. 538, 332 A.2d 11.

41. Comment, Foreseeability in Product Design and Duty to Warn Cases—Distinctions and Misconceptions, 1968 Wis.L.Rev. 228.

42. Thornhill v. Carpenter-Morton Co., 1915, 220 Mass. 593, 108 N.E. 474; Stahlheber v. American Cyanamid Co., Mo.1970, 451 S.W.2d 48, 61; First National Bank in Albuquerque v. Nor-Am Agricultural Products, 1975, 88 N.M. 74, 537 P.2d 682, 690.

43. Keeton, Owen & Montgomery, Products Liability and Safety, 1980, Ch. 3, Sec. 3, p. 294; Twerski, Weinstein, Donaher, Piehler, The Use and Abuse of Warnings in Product Liability—Design Defect Litigation Comes of Age, 1976, 61 Corn.L.Rev. 495.

44. Moran v. Faberge, Inc., supra, note 40; Shuput v. Heublein, Inc., 10th Cir. 1975, 511 F.2d 1104.

45. Boyl v. California Chemical Co., supra, note 40; Burch v. Amsterdam Corp., D.C.App.1976, 366 A.2d 1079; Michael v. Warner/Chilcott, App.1978, 91 N.M. 651, 579 P.2d 183.

bly foreseeable.⁴⁶ With many products, there may be several possible methods of alerting users to product hazards, and there may be a variety of foreseeable ways to misuse products. Thus, this ground of negligence is probably the most difficult one for the manufacturer to manage on a satisfactory basis. Those who argue for warning as the judicial solution to latent design defects labor under a naive belief that one can warn against all significant risks. Too much detail can be counterproductive. A warning to be effective must be read and understood.

The feasibility of conveying a warning directly to those affected by the product in an understandable way is always important. It has been held that a helmet manufacturer was justifiably found to be negligent in failing to warn that a football helmet would not protect against a blood clot resulting from a violent head-to-head clash,⁴⁷ but it can reasonably be argued that the responsibility for explaining to players the hazards of football and the extent to which protective equipment can guard against those hazards should be the responsibility of coaches so long as coaches are adequately informed. Some courts have held that warning an industrial purchaser of a risk or hazard related to the use of a product satisfies seller's responsibility to the purchaser's employees;⁴⁸ others have held that it is, at least, a jury question under certain circumstances.⁴⁹

(a) **Obvious dangers and unforeseeable misuse.** Two areas of some difficulty relate to the need for warning about (a) obvious dangers and (b) misuse. It is often said that there is no duty to warn of obvious dangers.⁵⁰ It is clear that there should be no liability for failing to warn someone of a risk or hazard which he appreciated to the same extent as a warning would have provided.⁵¹ This could easily be explained on the ground that the failure was not a cause of any harm to the plaintiff or on the ground that there was no breach of duty to the claimant under the circumstances. But courts have usually meant by "obvious danger" a condition that would ordinarily be seen and the danger of which would ordinarily be appreciated by

---

46. Berkebile v. Brantly Helicopter Corp., 1976, 225 Pa.Super. 349, 311 A.2d 140, affirmed 462 Pa. 83, 337 A.2d 893 (manufacturer of helicopter warned of emergency procedures to be followed in case of engine failure both in flight manual and cockpit placard; jury question as to adequacy); West v. Broderick & Bascom Rope Co., Iowa 1972, 197 N.W.2d 202 [strength limits of metal cable set forth in literature provided to retailer. Held, that jury could find negligence in failing to have a metal tag).

47. Rawlings Sporting Goods Co. v. Daniels, Tex. Civ.App.1981, 619 S.W.2d 435, error refused n.r.e.

48. Wilhelm v. Globe Solvent Co., Del.Super.1977, 373 A.2d 218; Schmeiser v. Trus Joist Corp., 1975, 273 Or. 120, 540 P.2d 998.

49. West v. Broderick & Bascom Rope Co., Iowa 1972, 197 N.W.2d 202, 210–11; Borel v. Fibreboard Paper Products Corp., 5th Cir. 1973, 493 F.2d 1076, 1092–1094, certiorari denied, 1974, 419 U.S. 869, 95 S.Ct. 127, 42 L.Ed.2d 107.

50. Jamieson v. Woodward & Lothrop, 1957, 101 U.S.App.D.C. 32, 247 F.2d 23, certiorari denied 355 U.S. 855, 78 S.Ct. 84, 2 L.Ed.2d 63 (exerciser rope slipped off of foot); Kientz v. Carlton, 1957, 245 N.C. 236, 96 S.E.2d 14 (obvious lack of safety features in power mower); Murphy v. Cory Pump & Supply Co., 1964, 47 Ill.App.2d 382, 197 N.E.2d 849 (same); Harrist v. Spencer-Harris Tool Co., 1962, 244 Miss. 84, 140 So.2d 558 (defect in oil rig); Morris v. Toy Box, 1962, 204 Cal. App.2d 468, 22 Cal.Rptr. 572.

One case much criticized in this connection is Campo v. Scofield, 1950, 301 N.Y. 468, 95 N.E.2d 802, where the defendant sold an onion-topping machine without a guard. Cf. Yaun v. Allis-Chalmers Manufacturing Co., 1948, 253 Wis. 558, 34 N.W.2d 853. In each case there was clear foreseeability that the employee using the machine might momentarily forget the absence of the guard.

Gibson v. Torbert, 1901, 115 Iowa 163, 88 N.W. 443 (inflammable nature of phosphorus); Dempsey v. Virginia Dare Stores, 1945, 239 Mo.App. 355, 186 S.W.2d 217 (same as to fuzzy lounging robe); Sawyer v. Pine Oil Sales Co., 5th Cir. 1946, 155 F.2d 855 (splashing cleaning fluid into eye); Katz v. Arundel-Brooks Concrete Co., 1959, 220 Md. 200, 151 A.2d 731 (bringing hands in contact with ready-mix concrete); Simmons v. Rhodes & Jamieson, 1956, 46 Cal.2d 190, 293 P.2d 26 (same).

51. Martinez v. Dixie Carriers, Inc., 5th Cir. 1976, 529 F.2d 457; Garrett v. Nissen Corp., 1972, 84 N.M. 16, 498 P.2d 1359, 1364; McIntyre v. Everest & Jennings, Inc., 8th Cir. 1978, 575 F.2d 155, certiorari denied 439 U.S. 864, 99 S.Ct. 187, 58 L.Ed.2d 173; Bradco Oil & Gas Co. v. Youngstown Sheet & Tube Co., 5th Cir. 1976, 532 F.2d 501, rehearing denied 540 F.2d 1084, certiorari denied 429 U.S. 1095, 97 S.Ct. 111, 51 L.Ed.2d 542; May v. Allied Chlorine and Chemical Products, Inc., Fla.App.1964, 168 So.2d 784.

those who would be expected to use the product.[52] This objective approach to the issue of *warning* about obvious dangers may be regarded as reasonable, if the court is willing to find obvious dangers defective when there is a feasible way to make the *design* safer. The practical difficulties of litigating about whether an obvious danger was actually appreciated by a particular claimant justifies either an objective test of an obvious danger (thereby ruling out failure to warn as a basis for recovery) or simply regarding the obvious nature of a danger as a factor that is relevant on the issue of negligence.

It is often said that there is no duty to guard against unforeseeable misuse.[53] This probably means nothing more than concluding that a misuse may be so rare and unusual that a manufacturer must be regarded as not negligent as a matter of law in failing to warn against a damaging event produced in this manner. As stated earlier, warnings can be counterproductive and a long list of the rare and unusual ways in which people can possibly misuse hazardous products may not be helpful, if the hazard itself is either obvious or identified. Generally, the misuse would be of a kind or character the danger of which was obvious to those who would likely be influenced by the kind of warning that would be feasible. Thus, in one case, a 5-year-old child sprinkled himself with highly flammable fingernail polish which had no warning.[54] The child was burned to death when the polish ignited while he was playing with the polish. It was held that there was no duty to warn against this kind of misuse. But the real reason would appear to be that a warning against this kind of rare use would probably have served no purpose in most instances since those who read or could read would already know of the existence of the likely flammability of the product.

(b) **Toxic and allergic reactions.** There has been a substantial amount of litigation related to liability for failure to warn as regards toxic or allergic reactions to products intended for intimate bodily use, especially (a) over-the-counter drugs and cosmetics, and (b) prescription drugs and vaccines.

Over-the-counter drugs and cosmetics. Over-the-counter drugs and cosmetics are products that do not ordinarily involve a risk of serious injury or death. They are products that bring about toxic, allergic, or idiosyncratic reactions to some persons, at least on some occasions.[55] Some courts have held that there is no breach of duty to warn users of the risk of an adverse reaction—toxic, allergic, or idiosyncratic—unless the plaintiff establishes that (1) the product contained an ingredient to which an appreciable number of persons would get an adverse reaction, (2) the defendant knew or should have known in the exercise of ordinary care that this was so, and (3) that plaintiff's abnormal adverse reaction was due to the fact that he was in the abnormal group.[56] This is based on the notion that there should be no duty to warn except on a showing that there was a risk or hazard of sufficient magnitude to involve adverse effects to an appreciable number of persons. This kind of quantitative no-duty rule avoids very difficult decision points about negligence and causation when the danger is not a serious one and the effectiveness of a warning would be doubtful. But other courts have chosen to reject any simple quantitative standard, and have held that

---

52. See, supra, note 50.

53. Sawyer v. Pine Oil Sales Co., 5th Cir. 1946, 155 F.2d 855; Hentschel v. Baby Bathinette Corp., 2d Cir. 1954, 215 F.2d 102, certiorari denied 349 U.S. 923, 75 S.Ct. 663, 99 L.Ed. 1254; McCready v. United Iron and Steel Co., 10th Cir. 1959, 272 F.2d 700.

54. Lawson v. Benjamin Ansehl Co., Mo.App.1944, 180 S.W.2d 751.

55. Panel Discussion, Medico-Legal Aspects of Allergies, 1957, 24 Tenn.L.Rev. 840–842; Whitmore, Allergies and Other Reactions Due to Drugs and Cosmetics, 1965, 19 Sw.L.J. 76.

56. Kaempfe v. Lehn & Fink Products Corp., 1964, 21 A.D.2d 197, 249 N.Y.S.2d 840, affirmed 1967, 20 N.Y.2d 818, 284 N.Y.S.2d 708, 231 N.E.2d 294; Robbins v. Alberto-Culver Co., 1972, 210 Kan. 147, 499 P.2d 1080; Alberto-Culver Co. v. Morgan, Tex.Civ.App.1969, 444 S.W.2d 770, refused n.r.e.

each case involves an *ad hoc* inquiry into whether or not there was negligence which requires a weighing of the amount of the danger to be avoided by a warning against the burden of guarding against the harm without unduly discouraging beneficial use.[57] Even under such an approach, it is always theoretically possible for a trial judge or an appellate court to conclude that there was no evidence to support a finding of negligence.

Prescription drugs and vaccines. The marketing situation as regards prescription drugs and vaccines is a unique one. The ultimate purchaser for use and the person for whose benefit the drug or vaccine is utilized is not the person who selects and orders the drug.

This is the prescribing physician who is an expert. There is another unique feature or circumstance and this is the role of the federal government through the Federal Drug Administration. In the process, other agencies have been given the responsibility of establishing standards for a general class of products of like kind, but here the drug approval process involves a complex and often *ad hoc* balancing of imponderable and incommensurate factors related to danger and utility of marketing a specific new drug. This is because of the substantial risk of serious harm or death from the use of prescription drugs for the prevention and treatment of diseases. Virtually all courts have agreed that there can be no breach of duty to warn on any theory—negligence or strict liability for breach of warranty or in tort—until such time as a producer or other seller knew or should have known in the exercise of ordinary care of the risk or hazard not warned about.[58] The producer's basic responsibility in this area is to provide adequate warnings to physicians. It is the physician who is in the best position to decide when to use and how and when to inform his patient regarding risks and benefits pertaining to drug therapy. Occasionally, however, as would be true with a mass innoculation project or as would be true with many clinical innoculations, a producer will have knowledge that persons will be innoculated without the supervision of physicians. In such instances, it has been held that the producer must utilize a warning system that will likely reach the person or his guardian directly so that an informed choice can be made and individual autonomy in decision-making can be guaranteed.[59]

In any event, the producer will be required to disclose a risk of serious injury, however rare and infrequent its occurrence may be, especially to a physician.[60] That will give the physician the knowledge needed to make an informed decision as to when to prescribe its use and what to disclose to the patient, if anything. This absolute duty to warn of a slight chance of serious injury has been regarded as a kind of strict liability but it can also be regarded as a negligence per se rule since there can be no liability for failure to warn unless the producer knew or should have known about the risk or hazard which he failed to warn about.

3. *Negligence in the sale of a defectively designed product.* A manufacturer or other seller can be negligent in marketing a product because of the way it was designed. In short, even if a seller had done all that he could reasonably have done to warn about a risk or hazard related to the way a product was designed, it could be that a reasonable person would conclude that the magnitude of the reasonably foreseeable harm as designed outweighed the utility of the product

---

57. Wright v. Carter Products, Inc., 2d Cir. 1957, 244 F.2d 53; Braun v. Roux Distributing Co., Mo.1958, 312 S.W.2d 758.

58. Sterling Drug Co. v. Yarrow, 8th Cir. 1969, 408 F.2d 978; Davis v. Wyeth Laboratories, Inc., 9th Cir. 1968, 399 F.2d 121; Reyes v. Wyeth Laboratories, 5th Cir. 1974, 498 F.2d 1264, certiorari denied 419 U.S. 1096, 95 S.Ct. 687, 42 L.Ed.2d 688.

59. Davis v. Wyeth Laboratories, Inc., 9th Cir. 1968, 399 F.2d 121; Reyes v. Wyeth Laboratories, 5th Cir. 1974, 498 F.2d 1264, certiorari denied 419 U.S. 1096, 95 S.Ct. 687, 42 L.Ed.2d 688.

60. Supra, note 59.

as so designed. If so, such conduct would be negligence unless some no-duty rule is interposed to prevent liability on this basis.[61] Prior to the development of strict liability in tort based on the sale of a product that was defective in the kind of way that made it unreasonably dangerous—a development that has come about largely since 1960—there were only a few scattered cases involving any evaluation by the courts of the way products were designed.[62] This was because of the notion that the manufacturer could satisfy any duty of care with respect to design hazards by taking proper precautions to keep purchasers for use informed about the risks or hazards related to the inherent dangers of products.[63] One central idea is that competition and the market place is the best means for giving the kind of optimal safety that is needed.[64] The manufacturer's duty was to see to it that purchasers were informed purchasers and were not deceived as to the dangerousness of products. There are many today, especially economists who would urge that judges and juries should not be attempting to evaluate how safely farm machinery, industrial tools and motor vehicles should be designed so long as (a) those who purchase for use know the dangers involved in the use of what they are buying, and (b) no safety regulation adopted by the political or legislative branch has been violated. At any rate, it was the law that the duty of care could be satisfied by giving adequate warning as to those risks and hazards that were knowable in the exercise of ordinary care. It was the responsibility of the purchasers for use to avoid accidents. So, it was generally held prior to 1960 that there was no duty to warn about or design out obvious dangers and any duty of care regarding latent risks or hazards could be satisfied by an adequate warning. The development of strict liability for selling a defective product was accompanied by an acceptance of the notion that a product can be defective as designed.[65] This has been regarded by some courts as nothing more than a recognition of the fact that a manufacturer may depart from proper and reasonable standards of care in designing products so that liability is essentially a matter of negligence.[66] But a product can be defective as designed without a manufacturer being in a position to perceive this to be the case, if one adopts a proper test as to what constitutes a bad product.[67] Therefore, one can be either negligent or without negligence in designing a bad product; this will be discussed hereafter under strict liability in tort.

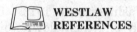

WESTLAW REFERENCES

winterbottom /15 152 /5 402
topic(313a) /p imminent! inherent! /3 danger!
topic(313a) /p negligen** /p fail! adequate** /p warn!
topic(313a) & obvious /2 danger*
topic(313a) /p misuse*
313ak27

---

61. Nader and Page, Automobile Design and the Judicial Process, 1967, 55 Calif.L.Rev. 645; Katz, Negligence in Design: A Current Look, 1965 Ins.L.J. 5; Noel, Manufacturer's Negligence of Design or Directions for Use of a Product, 1962, 71 Yale L.J. 816. Annot., 1961, 76 A.L.R.2d 91.

62. Keeton, Owen & Montgomery, Cases and Materials on Products Liability and Safety, 1980, 76.

63. Keeton, Products Liability—Inadequacy of Information, 1970, 48 Tex.L.Rev. 398.

64. Calabresi, Transaction Costs, Resource Allocation and Liability Rules—A Comment, 1968, 11 J.Law & Eco. 67; Coase, The Problem of Social Cost, 1960, 3 J.Law & Eco. 1.

65. See, supra note 61.

66. Balido v. Improved Machinery, Inc., 1973, 29 Cal.App.3d 633, 105 Cal.Rptr. 890, 895 (The court noted: "[s]ince the issue is whether [the defendant] designed and put into circulation a product unreasonably dangerous for use and since the unreasonableness of the danger must be determined by the potential available to the designer at the time of the design, it is apparent that the strict liability and negligence claims merge.") See, Birnbaum, Unmasking the Test for Design Defect: From Negligence [to Warranty] to Strict Liability to Negligence, 1980, 33 Vand.L.Rev. 593, and footnote 52.

67. See, Keeton, Product Liability and the Meaning of Defect, 1973, 5 St. Mary's L.J. 30; Wade, On Product "Design Defects" and Their Actionability, 1980, 33 Vand.L.Rev. 551; Birnbaum, Unmasking the Test for Design Defect: From Negligence [to Warranty] to Strict Liability to Negligence, 1980, 33 Vand.L.Rev. 593.

manufactur! producer* /5 drug* vaccine* /p warn! /p risk* danger*

product* /p design** /p risk* danger* hazard* /p warn! & date(after 1959)

§ 97. Strict Liability in Warranty for Physical Harm to Persons and Tangible Things

Some legal history. With the liability of the seller of chattels to the ultimate consumer once established on the basis of negligence, it was to be expected that some attempt would be made to carry his responsibility even further, and to find some ground of strict liability which would make the seller in effect an insurer of the safety of the product, even though he had exercised all reasonable care and even when there was no privity of contract between the victim and the target defendant. The first case—on the heels of a prolonged agitation over food and drink—which discarded the requirement of privity of contract was Mazetti v. Armour & Co.[1] in Washington in 1913. It was followed, rapidly and then slowly, over almost half a century, by other courts which found strict liability as to defective food and drink,[2] until by 1960 the majority of American courts had made it an established rule.[3] The movement ran considerably ahead of any legal justification to support it.

Beyond Food

The extension of the implied warranty beyond food and drink for human consumption began with animal food,[4] and what might be called products for intimate bodily use, such as cosmetics.[5] A partial extension to other products came in 1958, with Spence v. Three Rivers Builders & Masonry Supply, Inc.,[6] where the Michigan court found a warranty, without privity and without negligence, of cinder building blocks when the user's home collapsed. The decision was followed in half a dozen other jurisdictions, until in 1960 there came, in New Jersey, what is now commonly regarded as the leading case, Henningsen v. Bloomfield Motors, Inc.[7] It held both the manufacturer of an automobile and the dealer who sold it to the purchaser's wife (who was driving the car) liable on an implied warranty of safety carried over from the food cases.

What followed was the most rapid and altogether spectacular overturn of an established rule in the entire history of the law of torts. There was a deluge of cases in other jurisdictions following the lead of New Jersey, and finding an implied warranty of safety as to a wide assortment of products.[8] It is quite clear that the "citadel of privity" has fallen.

The earlier cases in this avalanche proceeded on the basis of an "implied warranty" made directly to the user or consumer. Even in the food cases, however, it had al-

---

§ 97

1. Wash.1913, 135 P. 633.

2. Narrated in Regier, The Struggle for Federal Food and Drugs Legislation, 1933, 1 Law & Con.Prob. 3.

3. See, supra, note 37, Section 96.

4. McAfee v. Cargill, Inc., S.D.Cal.1954, 121 F.Supp. 5; Midwest Game Co. v. M.F.A. Milling Co., Mo.1959, 320 S.W.2d 547.

5. Graham v. Bottenfield's Inc., 1954, 176 Kan. 68, 269 P.2d 413 (hair dye); Rogers v. Toni Home Permanent Co., 1958, 167 Ohio St. 244, 147 N.E.2d 612 (permanent wave solution); Worley v. Procter & Gamble Manufacturing Co., 1952, 241 Mo.App. 1114, 253 S.W. 2d 532.

6. 1958, 353 Mich. 120, 90 N.W.2d 873. This was, appropriately enough, from the point of view of the defendants, an opinion of Justice Voelker, author of the popular best seller, Anatomy of a Murder, which became a motion picture.

7. 1960, 32 N.J. 358, 161 A.2d 69. The development is narrated in Prosser, The Fall of the Citadel, 1966, 50 Minn.L.Rev. 791.

8. Picker X-Ray Corp. v. General Motors Corp., Mun.App.D.C.1962, 185 A.2d 919 (automobile); B.F. Goodrich Co. v. Hammond, 10th Cir. 1959, 269 F.2d 501 (tire); Goldberg v. Kollsman Instrument Corp., 1963, 12 N.Y.2d 432, 240 N.Y.S.2d 592, 191 N.E.2d 81 (airplane); Simpson v. Powered Products of Michigan, Inc., 1963, 24 Conn.Supp. 409, 192 A.2d 555 (power golf cart); Deveny v. Rheem Manufacturing Co., 2d Cir. 1963, 319 F.2d 124 (water heater, Vermont law); McQuaide v. Bridgeport Brass Co., D.Conn.1960, 190 F:Supp. 252 (insecticide, Pennsylvania law).

ready become apparent that "warranty" was attended by numerous difficulties. The term had become so closely identified with contract in the minds of most courts and lawyers that contract rules were assumed necessarily to apply to it; and this presented a serious problem where there was no contract. Traditionally "warranty" required that the plaintiff should act in reliance upon some express or implied representation or assurance, or some promise or undertaking, on the part of the defendant; and this was sometimes impossible to make out, as where, for example, the consumer did not even know the name of the maker. Warranties on the sale of goods were governed in most states by the Uniform Sales Act, and then by its successor, the Uniform Commercial Code; and neither of these statutes had been drawn with anything in mind but a contract between a "seller" and his immediate "buyer."[9]

Two problems in particular gave considerable trouble. Both the Sales Act and the Commercial Code contain provisions which prevent the buyer from recovering on a warranty unless he gives notice to the seller within a reasonable time after he knows or should know of the breach.[10] As between the immediate parties to the sale, this is a sound commercial rule, designed to protect the seller against unduly delayed claims for damages. As applied to personal injuries, and notice to a remote seller, it becomes a booby-trap for the unwary. The injured consumer is seldom "steeped in the business practice which justifies the rule,"[11] and at least until he has legal advice it will not occur to him to give notice to one with whom he has had no dealings. In order to circumvent the statute, the courts were forced to resort to rather transparent devices, holding that a long delay is "reasonable,"[12] or that the provision was not intended to apply to personal injuries.[13] A few took the obvious way out by holding that it was entirely inapplicable as between parties who had not dealt with one another.[14]

The other provision of the statutes is that of sanctioning disclaimers by the seller, which will defeat the warranty.[15] This means that he is free to insert in his contract of sale an effective agreement that he does not warrant at all, or that he warrants only against certain consequences or defects, or that his liability shall be limited to particular remedies, such as replacement, repair, or return of the purchase price.[16] Commercially this may not be at all an unreasonable thing, particularly where the seller does not know the quality of what he is selling, and the buyer is really willing to take his chances. Commercial buyers usually are quite able to protect themselves. It is another thing entirely to say that the consumer who buys at retail is to be bound by a disclaimer which he has never seen, and to which he would certainly not have agreed if he had known of it, but which defeats a duty imposed by the law for his protection. And if the opportuni-

---

9. As to the various difficulties arising in connection with "warranty," see Prosser, The Assault Upon the Citadel, 1960, 69 Yale L.J. 1099, 1127–1133.

10. Uniform Sales Act, § 49, carried over into U.C.C. § 2–607(3).

11. James, Products Liability, 1955, 34 Tex.L.Rev. 44, 192, 197.

12. Bonker v. Ingersoll Products Co., D.C.Mass. 1955, 132 F.Supp. 5; Whitfield v. Jessup, 1948, 31 Cal. 2d 826, 193 P.2d 1; Brown v. Chapman, 9th Cir. 1962, 304 F.2d 149; Pritchard v. Liggett & Myers Tobacco Co., 3d Cir. 1961, 295 F.2d 292; Hampton v. Gebhardt's Chili Powder Co., 9th Cir. 1961, 294 F.2d 172.

13. Silverstein v. R.H. Macy & Co., 1943, 266 App. Div. 5, 40 N.Y.S.2d 916; Wright Bachman, Inc. v. Hodnett, 1956, 235 Ind. 307, 133 N.E.2d 713.

14. La Hue v. Coca Cola Bottling, Inc., 1957, 50 Wn. 2d 645, 314 P.2d 421; Ruderman v. Warner-Lambert Pharmaceutical Co., 1962, 23 Conn. 416, 184 A.2d 63; Hampton v. Gebhardt's Chili Powder Co., 9th Cir. 1961, 294 F.2d 172.

15. Uniform Sales Act, 71, considerably modified in U.C.C. § 2–316.

16. See Notes, 1961, 109 U.Pa.L.Rev. 453; 1963, 11 Kan.L.Rev. 574; 1963, 51 Cal.L.Rev. 586; James, Products Liability, 1955, 34 Tex.L.Rev. 44, 192, 210–212; Wilson, Products Liability, 1955, 43 Cal.L.Rev. 614, 809, 835–840; Prosser, The Implied Warranty of Merchantable Quality, 1943, 27 Minn.L.Rev. 117, 157–167; Keeton, Assumption of Risk in Products Liability Cases, 1961, 22 La.L.Rev. 122.

ty is to remain open to the seller to frustrate that policy completely by the mere addition to the label on the package of such words as "Not Warranted in Any Way," it may be assumed that there will be those who will avail themselves of it. The courts have displayed no very favorable attitude toward disclaimers, construing them away, or finding that they were not adequately brought home to the plaintiff.[17] There are now a good many of the strict liability cases [18] which have held disclaimers to the consumer to be entirely invalid, either as adhesion contracts with no equality of bargaining position, or outright as unconscionable and contrary to the policy of the law.

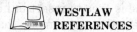

WESTLAW REFERENCES

privity /2 contract p/ strict /s liability
313ak20

Beyond Food

court(mi) & title(spence & rivers & builders & masonry)
sh 90nw2d873

§ 98. Strict Liability in Tort for Physical Harm to Persons and Tangible Things

It gradually became apparent that strict liability on "warranty" concepts based on implied misrepresentation or promise involving an objective manifestation of an intent to guarantee carries far too much luggage in the way of undesirable complications, and is more trouble than it is worth. The policy reasons that courts and writers were giving around 1960 to justify the imposition of strict liability on manufacturers and other merchant sellers for physical harm to persons and tangible things went far beyond any liability based on conventional contractual notions. The liability that was being imposed was liability based on the fact that defendant ought to have an obligation to pay for the costs attributable to damaging events caused by defects of a kind that made the product more dangerous than it would otherwise be. Often, there was no clear notion about the "meaning of defect," especially in the design context, and it was apparent that a movement was in progress to impose a kind of strict liability (1) without proof of negligence, (2) without manifestation of intent to guarantee, (3) without the requirement of privity of contract as a prerequisite to recovery, and (4) without recognizing the validity of contractual disclaimers of liability. Frustration of consumer or user expectations continued to be regarded as an important factor justifying such a kind of strict liability [1] but there were other and perhaps more important policy justifications for a type of liability that went far beyond concepts about promissory or contractual obligations.[2] Those which have proved convincing to the courts which have accepted strict liability in tort can be condensed into about three ideas:

(1) The costs of damaging events due to defectively dangerous products can best be borne by the enterprisers who make and sell

---

17. Cases are collected in Prosser, The Assault Upon the Citadel, 1960, 69 Yale L.J. 1099, 1132. See also Note, 1963, 77 Harv.L.Rev. 318; De Chaine, Products Liability and the Disclaimer, 1967, 4 Willam.L.Rev. 364.

18. In Henningsen v. Bloomfield Motors, Inc., 1960, 32 N.J. 358, 161 A.2d 69, the court threw out a "standard automobile warranty," in reality a disclaimer of almost all liability of consequences. See in accord State Farm Mutual Automobile Insurance Co. v. Anderson-Weber, Inc., 1961, 252 Iowa 1289, 110 N.W.2d 449; Ford Motor Co. v. Tritt, 1968, 244 Ark. 883, 430 S.W.2d 778; Crown v. Cecil Holland Ford, Inc., Fla. App.1968, 207 So.2d 67; Walsh v. Ford Motor Co., 1969, 59 Misc.2d 241, 298 N.Y.S.2d 538; Vandermark v. Ford Motor Co., 1963, 61 Cal.2d 256, 37 Cal.Rptr. 896, 391 P.2d 168.

§ 98

1. See, Shapo, A Representational Theory of Consumer Protection: Doctrine, Function, and Legal Liability for Product Disappointment, 1974, 60 Va.L.Rev. 1109; Fischer, Products Liability—The Meaning of Defect, 1974, 39 Mo.L.Rev. 339, 348; Vincer v. Ester Williams All-Aluminum Swimming Pool Co., 1975, 69 Wis. 2d 326, 230 N.W.2d 794; Bellotte v. Zayre Corp., 1976, 116 N.H. 52, 352 A.2d 723; Heaton v. Ford Motor Co., 1967, 248 Or. 467, 435 P.2d 806.

2. Wade, Strict Tort Liability of Manufacturers, 1965, 19 Sw.L.J. 5; Keeton, Products Liability—The Nature and Extent of Strict Liability, 1964, U. of Ill. L.F. 693; Keeton, Products Liability—Some Observations About Allocation of Risks, 1966, 64 Mich.L.Rev. 1329.

these products.³ Those who are merchants and especially those engaged in the manufacturing enterprise have the capacity to distribute the losses of the few among the many who purchase the products. It is not a "deep pocket" theory but rather a "risk-bearing economic" theory. The assumption is that the manufacturer can shift the costs of accidents to purchasers for use by charging higher prices for the costs of products. This can be regarded as a fairness and justice reason of policy. The costs of accidents attributable to defective products are internalized and passed on in a rough sort of way, although some may be unable to survive a disastrous experience with a particular product.

(2) The cause of accident prevention can be promoted by the adoption of strict liability and the elimination of the necessity for proving negligence.⁴ There are those who would argue that strict liability, as it is applied, may not induce any greater care than liability based on negligence. Moreover, it can be argued that strict liability may indeed not only eliminate negligence but will tend to inhibit the development of new products.

(3) It has been said that even if fault or negligence were regarded as the primary justification for the imposition of liability on a manufacturer or other seller for the costs of accidents attributable to defective products, it is often present but difficult to prove, and for institutional reasons and because of the costs of litigation, proof of the existence of fault or negligence in the sale of a defective product should no longer be required, especially if product defect is properly defined and limited.⁵

These policy reasons led to the adoption by the American Law Institute of Section 402A of the Second Restatement of Torts.⁶ This section accepts the principle of strict liability in tort as a more realistic theory of recovery than that of contract-warranty when a person or other legal entity incurs a loss due to physical harm to tangible things or physical harm to persons arising out of damaging events caused by defectively dangerous products.

A tort theory based on the dangerousness of conduct is more adaptable to dealing with physical harm to persons and things than that of a contract theory based on the breach of an implied promise and can be applied without so many of the nuances and complexities related to obvious defects and contractual disclaimers that are applicable to claims for damages based on commercial losses and other types of intangible economic losses. Unfortunately, those who drafted the Uniform Commercial Code did so at a point in time when a tort theory was not openly recognized as such; therefore, three provisions were adopted in the Code to make certain that recovery for physical harm would be available on a warranty theory to purchasers and third party beneficiaries. These were: (1) a provision stating that "injury to person or property proximately resulting from any breach of warranty" is a type of consequential damage that is recoverable;⁷ (2) a provision adopting three alternatives from which the states were to select

---

3. See, Traynor in Escola v. Coca-Cola Bottling Co. of Fresno, 1944, 24 Cal.2d 453, 150 P.2d 436; Greenman v. Yuba Power Products, Inc., 1962, 59 Cal.2d 57, 27 Cal.Rptr. 697, 377 P.2d 897; Goldberg v. Kollsman Instrument Corp., 1963, 12 N.Y.2d 432, 240 N.Y.S.2d 592, 191 N.E.2d 81; Helene Curtis Industries, Inc. v. Pruitt, 5th Cir. 1967, 385 F.2d 841, 862, certiorari denied 391 U.S. 913, 88 S.Ct. 1806, 20 L.Ed.2d 652, citing Wilson, Products Liability, 1955, 43 Calif.L.Rev. 809.

4. Phillips v. Kimwood Machine Co., 1974, 269 Or. 485, 525 P.2d 1033, 1041–1042; First National Bank of Albuquerque v. Nor-Am Agricultural Products, Inc., 1975, 88 N.M. 74, 537 P.2d 682, certiorari denied 88 N.M. 29, 536 P.2d 1085. Some have argued that strict liability will not generally be an effective deterrent. See, Raleigh, The "State of the Art" in Product Liability: A New Look at an Old "Defense," 1977, 4 Ohio N.L.Rev. 249; Plant, Strict Liability of Manufacturers for Injuries Caused by Defects in Products—An Opposing View, 1957, 24 Tenn.L.Rev. 938.

5. Phipps v. General Motors Corp., 1976, 278 Md. 337, 363 A.2d 955. The conventional justifications for strict liability are critically examined by Owen, Rethinking the Policies of Strict Liability, 1980, 33 Vand. L.Rev. 681.

6. See Comment c, p. 349.

7. U.C.C., Sec. 2–715(2)(b).

one, for identifying those non-purchasers who could recover for breach of a warranty, especially when suffering physical injury;[8] and (3) a provision declaring that a "limitation of consequential damages for injury to the person in the case of consumer goods is prima facie unconscionable * * *."[9]

The first case to apply a tort theory of strict liability generally was Greenman v. Yuba Power Products, Inc.,[10] in California in 1963. That decision and the final acceptance of Section 402A of the Second Restatement of Torts by the American Law Institute in 1964 were immediately relied upon for the adoption of strict liability in tort throughout the country. Section 402A liability in tort swept the country, just as the expansion of warranty liability under *Henningsen*[11] had done until at the present writing nearly all states have adopted some version of it.

Three alternative theories. This now means that a claimant seeking damages against a merchant seller has three alternative theories available, all of which are often utilized in the same case. These are: (a) negligence in tort, (b) strict liability for breach of a warranty, express or implied, and (c) strict liability in tort.

A partial solution to the inordinate complexities attributable to the availability of both tort theories and contractual-warranty theories (especially to those who cannot be regarded as either parties to a contract or third-party beneficiaries in a conventional contractual sense) is for the state legislatures to amend the three pertinent provisions of the Code so as to limit recovery of consequential damages for breach of a warranty in the sale of a product to intangible financial losses and physical harm to the product itself or tangible things that are made or repaired with the product.

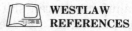
WESTLAW REFERENCES

402a /s strict /2 liability

§ 99. Meaning of Dangerously Defective or Unsafe Products

There is today no doubt at all that the seller's liability for negligence extends to and includes any kind of product that is sold.[1] Likewise, since the break through the barrier beyond food, there is no question that the strict liability, whether it is called warranty or declared outright in tort, extends to any kind of product which is recognizably dangerous to those who may come in contact with it. The decisions range from automobiles[2] and airplanes[3] to cinder building blocks,[4] glass doors,[5] and paper cups.[6] The tide of decisions has swept away the highly metaphysical distinction between the product and the container in which it is sold, which used to perplex some courts in the food cases.[7] The two are sold as an integrated whole, and it is inconceivable that anyone would buy one without the other. When a bottle of beer explodes and puts out the eye of the man about to drink it, surely nothing should be less material than wheth-

---

8. U.C.C., Sec. 2–318.

9. U.C.C., Sec. 2–719(3).

10. 1963, 59 Cal.2d 57, 27 Cal.Rptr. 697, 377 P.2d 897.

11. Supra, § 97.

§ 99

1. See supra, § 96.

2. Henningsen v. Bloomfield Motors, Inc., 1960, 32 N.J. 358, 161 A.2d 69; State Farm Mutual Automobile Insurance Co. v. Anderson-Weber, Inc., 1961, 252 Iowa 1289, 110 N.W.2d 449; Vandermark v. Ford Motor Co., 1964, 61 Cal.2d 256, 37 Cal.Rptr. 896, 391 P.2d 168.

3. Goldberg v. Kollsman Instrument Corp., 1963, 12 N.Y.2d 432, 240 N.Y.S.2d 592, 191 N.E.2d 81.

4. Spence v. Three Rivers Builders & Masonry Supply, Inc., 1958, 353 Mich. 120, 90 N.W.2d 873.

5. Gutierrez v. Superior Court, 1966, 243 Cal.App.2d 710, 52 Cal.Rptr. 592.

6. Bernstein v. Lily-Tulip Cup Corp., Fla.1966, 181 So.2d 641.

7. See for example McIntyre v. Kansas City Coca-Cola Bottling Co., W.D.Mo.1949, 85 F.Supp. 708; Soter v. Griesedieck Brewery Co., 1948, 200 Okl. 302, 193 P.2d 575.

er the explosion is due to a flaw in the glass of the bottle or to overcharged contents.[8]

In strict liability, the plaintiff is not required to impugn the conduct of the maker or other seller but he is required to impugn the product. Under Section 402A, it is said that the product must be in "a defective condition unreasonably dangerous." This simply means that the product must be defective in the kind of way that subjects persons or tangible property to an unreasonable risk of harm. The difference between this liability and negligence liability can only be ascertained by further elaboration of when a product is unreasonably dangerous.

A product is defective as marketed in the kind of way that makes it unreasonably dangerous for any of the following reasons: (1) a flaw in the product that was present in the product at the time the defendant sold it; (2) a failure by the producer or assembler of a product adequately to warn of a risk or hazard related to the way the product was designed; or (3) a defective design.

(1) *The flaw in the product.* As stated heretofore in the section on negligence, a flaw in a product is defined as an abnormality or a condition that was unintended, and makes the product more dangerous than it would have been as intended.[9] A flaw that is created in the construction or marketing processes makes the product unreasonably dangerous as a matter of law since it causes the product to be more dangerous than it was designed to be.[10] A target defendant, manufacturer, reseller, or retail dealer who sells a product with a construction flaw or a flaw developed in the course of marketing sells a defective product and is subject to liability for so doing. This is a far cry from negligence liability since the target defendant is liable without proof that there was any negligence on the part of the target defendant in creating or failing to discover the flaw. In the celebrated case of Henningsen v. Bloomfield Motors, Inc.,[11] the only evidence required for recovery against the manufacturer of the new car that swerved off the road was the testimony of the driver, the victim, that "she heard a loud noise" from the bottom of the hood; it felt as if "something cracked," and that the steering wheel "spun in her hands" and the automobile went out of control. This was regarded as sufficient evidence from which to infer that a "flaw" was present and attributable to a miscarriage in the construction process, albeit it was regarded as insufficient to infer negligence. The point is that even if there were negligence somewhere in the construction or marketing processes, the principal problem with respect to proof of negligence is the inability or impossibility in most instances of discovering direct or even circumstantial evidence of a specific act or omission on the part of anyone related to these processes that could then be evaluated and found to be negligence. The doctrine of *res ipsa loquitur* was seldom applied against a manufacturer[12] because of the necessity for indulging two or more inferences, such as:

---

8. Kroger Co. v. Bowman, Ky.1967, 411 S.W.2d 339; Vallis v. Canada Dry Ginger Ale, Inc., 1960, 190 Cal. App.2d 35, 11 Cal.Rptr. 823; Renninger, Inc. v. Foremost Dairies, Inc., Fla.App.1965, 171 So.2d 602; Addeo v. Metropolitan Bottling Co., 1963, 39 Misc.2d 474, 241 N.Y.S.2d 120, affirmed 20 App.Div.2d 967, 251 N.Y.S.2d 412; Nichols v. Nold, 1953, 174 Kan. 613, 258 P.2d 317.

9. MacPherson v. Buick Motors, 1916, 217 N.Y. 382, 111 N.E. 1050 (rotten wheel); McLean v. Goodyear Tire and Rubber Co., 5th Cir. 1936, 85 F.2d 150, certiorari denied 299 U.S. 600, 57 S.Ct. 193, 81 L.Ed. 442 (bubble in a tire); Coca-Cola Bottling Works v. Lyons, 1927, 145 Miss. 876, 111 So. 305 (broken glass in a bottle of Coca-Cola); Chandler v. Anchor Serum Co., 1967, 198 Kan. 571, 426 P.2d 82.

10. See, generally, Keeton, Product Liablity and the Meaning of Defect, 1973, 5 St. Mary's L.J. 30; Owen, Rethinking the Policies of Strict Products Liability, 1980, 33 Vand.L.Rev. 681; Wade, Strict Tort Liability of Manufacturers, 1965, 19 Sw.L.J. 5.

11. 1960, 32 N.J. 358, 161 A.2d 69.

12. See Keeton, Products Liability—Proof of the Manufacturer's Negligence, 1963, 49 Va.L.Rev. 675; Keeton, Products Liability—Problems Pertaining to Proof of Negligence, 1965, 19 Sw.L.J. 26; Keeton, Products Liability—Inadequacy of Information, 1970, 48 Tex.L.Rev. 398; Emroch, Pleading and Proof in a Strict Products Liability Case [1966] Ins.L.J. 581; Notes, 1966, 45 Neb.L.Rev. 189; 1969, 21 Stan.L.Rev. 1777; 1969, 22 Me.L.Rev. 189. See also, Lynch v. International Harvester Co., 10th Cir. 1932, 60 F.2d 223;

(a) an inference of a flaw as a cause of the event; (b) an inference of the flaw's presence at the time the target defendant sold, and (c) an inference that there was negligence in creating or failing to discover the flaw. There can be no doubt about the fact that the elimination of the necessity for proving negligence has greatly improved a claimant's chances for recovery in a particular case against one or more of the sellers in the marketing chain since it has removed the necessity for showing circumstances justifying an inference of negligence.[13]

The problems of proof can best be understood by dividing the cases into three evidentiary types for treatment and for evaluation of the sufficiency of the circumstantial evidence. The first is when evidence is introduced, usually of an expert, of an identifiable flaw that could have caused the damaging event. Ofttimes, the "flaw" will be the kind that by its very nature is such as in all probability would have occurred in the construction process, as a defective weld of an engine to the wing of an airplane. At other times, the "flaw" could have occurred in the marketing or using processes or it could have been caused by the accident rather than the accident causing the flaw.[14] Three kinds of evidence are helpful in tracing the flaw to a target defendant: (1) the testimony of experts as to the "probable causes" for such a flaw; (2) the life history of the product for the purpose of showing that misuse was unlikely; and (3) evidence by the user and others to negate misuse, poor maintenance, and overuse as a cause for the flaw.[15]

The second general type of evidentiary situation exists when the user or someone present testifies that a component part malfunctions, but for some reason, either because the accident destroys the evidence or the product disappears, there is no evidence as to an identifiable flaw that could have caused the accident.[16] This was the situation in Henningsen to which reference was previously made. The court permitted the inference to be drawn of some kind of a flaw in the steering mechanism. The older the product, the less likely it is that evidence of malfunctioning will suffice as an inference of a construction flaw, although some courts would permit plaintiff to negative misuse and overuse in such a case.

The third situation is when plaintiff is relying primarily on the nature of the accident as circumstantial evidence of a construction or marketing flaw. The accident itself indicates product failure. Thus, if a new tire blows out, some courts have permitted an inference to be drawn that the tire was flawed in the construction process.[17] Even negligence has been inferred, pursuant to *res ipsa loquitur*, in certain rare types of accidents such as injuries from bottle breakages or so-called bottle explosions.[18] The point is that without any evidence other than evi-

---

Solomon v. White Motor Co., W.D.Pa.1957, 153 F.Supp. 917; Patrol Valve Co. v. Farrell, Tex.Civ.App.1958, 316 S.W.2d 92, 96.

13. The facts in *Henningsen* present a classical example.

14. Holloway v. General Motors Corp., 1978, 403 Mich. 614, 271 N.W.2d 777 (break in ball joint assembly); Jenkins v. General Motors Corp., 5th Cir. 1977, 446 F.2d 377, certiorari denied 405 U.S. 922, 92 S.Ct. 959, 30 L.Ed.2d 793; Lewis v. United States Rubber Co., 1964, 414 Pa. 626, 202 A.2d 20; Darryl v. Ford Motor Co., Tex.1969, 440 S.W.2d 630.

15. Annots., 1973, 51 A.L.R.3d 8 (proof of defect generally); 1974, 54 A.L.R.3d 1079 (proof that defect was present when product left defendant's hands).

16. Scanlon v. General Motors Corp., 1974, 65 N.J. 582, 326 A.2d 673; Moraca v. Ford Motor Co., 1975, 66 N.J. 454, 332 A.2d 599. See Annots., supra, note 15.

17. Lindsay v. McDonnell Douglas Aircraft Co., 8th Cir. 1972, 460 F.2d 631, on remand D.C. 352 F.Supp. 633, affirmed 8th Cir. 485 F.2d 1288 (new Navy jet airplane caught on fire and crashed into sea. Court held that the fire was evidence of a malfunction which in turn would indicate some defect); Lee v. Crookston Coca-Cola Bottling Co., 1971, 290 Minn. 321, 188 N.W.2d 426 (bottle explosion). The res ipsa doctrine is frequently utilized in litigation involving exploding bottles and bottles containing foreign objects. See, Keeton, Owen & Montgomery, Cases and Materials on Products Liability and Safety, 1980, p. 843.

18. Hewitt v. General Tire & Rubber Co., 1955, 3 Utah 2d 354, 284 P.2d 471; McCann v. Atlas Supply Co., W.D.Pa.1971, 325 F.Supp. 701. But cf. Goodyear Tire & Rubber Co. v. Hughes Supply, Inc., Fla.1978, 358 So.2d 1339.

dence of an eyewitness as to the nature of the accident, the more likely reason for a damaging event may be a construction flaw in the product. Moreover, some courts would hold that proof that the damaging event is the kind that would not ordinarily happen but for a product flaw can be established by expert evidence as to probable causes for such an accident.[19]

In any event, the availability of a recovery in tort without proof of negligence as a cause of a damaging event has vastly improved a victim's opportunity for recovery against a manufacturer or other supplier of a product that was involved in such an event. Moreover, the nature and quality of the circumstantial and other evidence that a court regards as sufficient to justify a finding that a flaw that was traceable to a product when possession was surrendered by a target defendant is of primary importance when the basis for recovery is a flaw in the product. Once it is established that a target defendant sold a product that was flawed in the kind of way that made it more dangerous than it would otherwise have been, the plaintiff has established the kind of defect that makes the product "unreasonably dangerous" as a matter of law.

(2) *The failure to warn.* It is commonly said that a product can be defective in the kind of way that makes it unreasonably dangerous by failing to warn or failing adequately to warn about a risk or hazard related to the way a product is designed. But notwithstanding what a few courts have said, a claimant who seeks recovery on this basis must, according to the generally accepted view, prove that the manufacturer-designer was negligent.[20] There will be no liability without a showing that the defendant designer knew or should have known in the exercise of ordinary care of the risk or hazard about which he failed to warn. Moreover, there will be no liability unless manufacturer failed to take the precautions that a reasonable person would take in presenting the product to the public. Although this ground of recovery is sometimes referred to as strict liability, it is really nothing more than a ground of negligence liability described as the sale of a product in a defective condition, subject, however, only to the defenses and other limitations on liability applicable to strict liability rather than negligence.

There is one aspect of this so-called strict liability in addition to the matter of defenses and limitations on liability that distinguish it from negligence liability. When a manufacturer or assembler markets without adequate warnings, a reseller is subject to liability without negligence in reselling the product without adequate warning. Thus, all those in the marketing chain subsequent to a sale by the manufacturer are liable without negligence for the negligence of the manufacturer in failing to warn or adequately to warn.

It must be said that a few courts have held that strict liability for failure to warn of a risk will be imposed on a manufacturer if, had he known of the danger, he would have been negligent in failing to warn of such risk.[21] While the knowability of a risk or hazard should be irrelevant on the issue

---

19. Supra, note 15.

20. Parke-Davis and Co. v. Stromsodt, 8th Cir. 1969, 411 F.2d 1390; Sterling Drug, Inc. v. Yarrow, 8th Cir. 1969, 408 F.2d 978; Tinnerholm v. Parke-Davis & Co., S.D.N.Y.1968, 285 F.Supp. 432, affirmed 411 F.2d 48; Rumsey v. Freeway Manor Minimax, Tex.Civ.App. 1968, 423 S.W.2d 387; Davis v. Wyeth Laboratories, Inc., 9th Cir. 1968, 399 F.2d 121 (regarded as strict liability but said no duty to warn of unknowable risks); Borel v. Fibreboard Paper Products Corp., 5th Cir. 1973, 493 F.2d 1076, certiorari denied 419 U.S. 869, 95 S.Ct. 127, 42 L.Ed.2d 107.

21. Phillips v. Kimwood Machine Co., 1974, 269 Or. 485, 525 P.2d 1033; Little v. PPG Industries, Inc., Wash.1978, 19 Wn.App. 812, 579 P.2d 940, 946–47, modified 92 Wn.2d 118, 594 P.2d 911; Jackson v. Coast Paint and Lacquer Co., 9th Cir. 1974, 499 F.2d 809; Freund v. Cellofilm Properties, Inc., 1981, 87 N.J. 229 432 A.2d 925. In *Freund*, the court cited an article by Page Keeton in support of its position that the knowability of the risk should be unimportant on the issue of whether or not the product was defectively marketed because of inadequacy of warning. The article cited was Keeton, Product Liability—Inadequacy of Information, 1970, 48 Tex.L.Rev. 398, 404. The posi-

of whether or not a product is defectively designed as will be discussed below, it would seem to be extending strict liability too far to require a manufacturer to bear the costs of accidents to a few who were victimized by an unknowable risk of a good product that was a boon to humanity—such as when penicillin was first marketed.

(3) *The design defect.* Much of the difficulty related to products liability litigation centers around the meaning of defect in the kind of way that makes a product unreasonably dangerous in relation to design hazards. There are essentially two different approaches that have been utilized in evaluating design hazards—a consumer-purchaser or consumer-user contemplation test and a risk-utility test.[22]

The consumer-contemplation test. Under the consumer-contemplation test, as so stated in Section 402A of the Second Restatement of Torts, a product is defectively dangerous if it is dangerous to an extent beyond that which would be contemplated by the ordinary consumer who purchased it with the ordinary knowledge common to the community as to the product's characteristics.[23] In an effort to expand the scope of liability and protection to non-purchasers, many courts have substituted "ordinary user" or "foreseeable user" for "ordinary purchaser" thereby making it possible for victims to recover if the hazard was of a kind that would not have been contemplated by reasonably foreseeable users even though it was one that would have been contemplated by the ordinary purchaser-consumer.[24] This test reflects the origins of strict liability rooted as they were in contract law that was designed to deal with commercial losses.[25] The consumer-purchaser or its alternative, the user-purchaser contemplation test, is generally inadequate as a test for evaluating the dangerousness of the designs of products for at least three reasons:

(1) Under this test, a victim could never recover for harm suffered as a result of a design hazard that was open or obvious or one with respect to which the purchaser was adequately informed. So, the test can result in finding products to be not defective that could easily have been designed safer without great expense or effect on the benefits or functions to be served by the product;[26]

(2) This test can result in the identification of products as being defectively dangerous that are clearly not,[27] as when a new drug is a great boon to humanity but a few

---

tion taken does indeed support the holding but Page Keeton has changed his position. See, Keeton, The Meaning of Defect in Products Liability Law—A Review of Basic Principles, 1980, 45 Mo.L.Rev. 579, 586–87. See also, Beshada v. Johns-Manville Products Corp., 1982, 90 N.J. 191, 447 A.2d 539.

22. For a general discussion of this area, see the following: Carsey, What Constitutes a Design Defect in Product Liability Cases, 1970, 21 Fed.Ins.Counsel Q. 107; Keeton, Manufacturer's Liability: The Meaning of "Defect" in the Manufacture and Design of Products, 1969, 20 Syracuse L.Rev. 559; Keeton, Product Liability and the Meaning of Defect, 1973, 5 St. Mary's L.J. 30; Wade, On the Nature of Strict Tort Liability for Products, 1973, 44 Miss.L.J. 825, 830; Keeton, Products Liability—Design Hazards and the Meaning of Defect, 1979, 10 Cum.L.Rev. 293; Wade, On Product "Design Defects" and Their Actionability, 1980, 33 Vand.L.Rev. 551; Henderson, Design Defect Litigation Revisited, 1976, 61 Corn.L.Rev. 541; Montgomery & Owen, Reflections on the Theory and Administration of Strict Tort Liability for Defective Products, 1976, 27 S.C.L.Rev. 803.

23. Second Restatement of Torts, § 402A, Comment i.

24. This can be important as regards injuries to children, employees who use industrial tools, and patients who use prescription drugs. See, Bellotte v. Zayre Corp., 1976, 116 N.H. 52, 352 A.2d 723 (a child); Mueller & Co. v. Corley, Tex.Civ.App.1978, 570 S.W.2d 140 (patient of doctor); Rourke v. Garza, Tex.1976, 530 S.W.2d 794 (employee using scaffold without cleats on boards).

25. The comments to Section 402A recognize the development of strict liability out of the law of warranty. See, also, Fischer, Products Liability—The Meaning of Defect, 1974, 39 Mo.L.Rev. 339, 348; Shapo, A Representational Theory of Consumer Protection: Doctrine, Function and Legal Liability for Product Disappointment, 1974, 60 Va.L.Rev. 1109.

26. This was a criticism of this test as the sole test for a design defect by the Supreme Court of California in Barker v. Lull Engineering Co., Inc., 1978, 20 Cal.3d 413, 143 Cal.Rptr. 225, 573 P.2d 443.

27. See General Motors Corp. v. Simmons, Tex.Civ. App.1977, 545 S.W.2d 502, reversed on other grounds, Tex.1977, 558 S.W.2d 855.

are victimized by a side effect or adverse reaction that was an unknowable risk;

(3) The meaning is ambiguous and the test is very difficult of application to discrete problems.[28] What does the reasonable purchaser contemplate? In one sense, he does not "expect" to be adversely affected by a risk or hazard unknown to him. In another sense, he does contemplate the "possibility" of unknown "side effects." In a sense the ordinary purchaser cannot reasonably expect anything more than that reasonable care in the exercise of the skill and knowledge available to design engineers has been exercised. The test can be utilized to explain most any result that a court or jury chooses to reach. The application of such a vague concept in many situations does not provide much guidance for a jury. In one Texas case decided in 1976 on the basis of this test, which does not represent current law in Texas, the plaintiff lost his eyesight when the side window of his automobile was shattered, and small, dull particles of glass became lodged in his eye. The side window of the car involved in the collision was made of tempered glass, as were virtually all side windows of automobiles. This kind of glass shatters, but unlike plate glass, it shatters into small, dull particles. The trial judge charged the jury pursuant to the consumer-contemplation test, and the jury found for the plaintiff. It was concluded on appeal that the jury was justified in believing that this kind of a risk or hazard related to the side windows would not have been contemplated by the ordinary consumer simply because the risk was "unknown."[29] But two factors were not considered—(a) the impairment of benefits resulting from the use of laminated glass that would make access to those trapped inside difficult, and (b) the extra costs involved in guarding against "freak" accidents.

The danger-utility test. Under this approach, a product is defective as designed if, but only if, the magnitude of the danger outweighs the utility of the product.[30] The theory underlying this approach is that virtually all products have both risks and benefits and that there is no way to go about evaluating design hazards intelligently without weighing danger against utility. There have been somewhat different ways of articulating this ultimate standard or test. But in essence, the danger-utility test directs attention of attorneys, trial judges, and juries to the necessity for weighing the danger-in-fact of a particular feature of a product against its utility. Under this test, a product can be said to be defective in the kind of way that makes it "unreasonably dangerous" if a reasonable person would conclude that the danger-in-fact, whether foreseeable or not, outweighs the utility of the product. There are three primary reasons for so concluding: (1) the harmful consequences in fact from intended and reasonably foreseeable uses resulting from the way the product was designed and marketed up to the time of plaintiff's injury outweighed the benefits in terms of wants, desires, and human needs served by the product; (2) although the harmful consequences in fact did not exceed the benefits, alternative products were available to serve the same needs or desires with less risk of harm; (3) although the harmful consequences did not outweigh the benefits, there was a feasible way to design the product with less harmful consequences.[31] Most

28. Hubbard, Reasonable *Human* Expectations: A Normative Model for Imposing Strict Liability for Defective Products, 1978, 29 Mercer L.Rev. 465; Rheingold, What Are the Consumer's "Reasonable Expectations"?, 1967, 22 Bus.Law 589; Montgomery and Owen, Reflections on the Theory and Administration of Strict Tort Liability for Defective Products, 1976, 27 S.C.L.Rev. 803, 823.

29. General Motors Corp. v. Simmons, Tex.Civ.App. 1977, 545 S.W.2d 502, reversed on other grounds 558 S.W.2d 855.

30. Turner v. General Motors Corp., Tex.1979, 584 S.W.2d 844, 850–851; Azzarello v. Black Brothers Co., 1978, 480 Pa. 547, 391 A.2d 1020, 1026–1027; Raney v. Honeywell, Inc., 8th Cir. 1976, 540 F.2d 932, 935; see articles by Keeton and Wade, supra, note 22.

31. This method of setting forth three reasons for concluding that a product as designed can be unreasonably dangerous was set forth by Page Keeton in a recent survey article commenting on *Turner-General Motors Corp.*, supra, note 30. The survey article is

of the products liability litigation related to design hazards has been concerned with the feasibility of a safer alternative design.

An alternative design that was not utilized is to be considered as feasible when a reasonable person would conclude that the (1) magnitude of the danger-in-fact that could have been avoided by such alternative design in the (2) utilization of the scientific technological know-how reasonably available to the defendant outweighed the (1) financial costs of guarding against such avoidable danger, (2) the impairment of the benefits, and (3) any new danger-in-fact that would have been created by the alternative design.

State of the art and discoverability of danger. Some courts have concluded that the use of a danger-utility balancing test constitutes a resort to a negligence standard, and that strict liability as to design hazards pursuant to such a test becomes a myth.[32] But this is not so if (a) the danger that is to be considered and weighed in the formula is danger-in-fact as to be distinguished from foreseeable danger, and (b) the benefits are those that are actually found to flow from the use of the product as designed rather than as perceived at the time the product was designed and marketed.[33] The fact that a risk or hazard related to the use of a product was not discoverable under existing technology and in the exercise of utmost care or the fact that the benefits were overevaluated are both irrelevant if the product itself and not defendant's conduct is being evaluated.

Even so, it has often been asserted that if a machine, drug, or other product was designed or constructed by a producer or maker in conformity with the "state of the art" at the time possession was surrendered, then either (1) the product should not be regarded as defective in such a manner as to be unreasonably dangerous; or (2) if defective, an affirmative defense or excuse should be recognized. The 1960's witnessed a series of cases over the risk of contracting lung cancer from smoking cigarettes, and one of the several issues involved was the scientific undiscoverability of the risk or danger of contracting lung cancer from smoking. Only two or three appellate decisions were based on this issue and they are in conflict.[34] If inability to discover a risk or hazard related to product design is regarded as a defense, then it is true that the only practical difference between strict liability for design hazards using a danger-utility test and negligence is a change in the burden of proof. The defendant under so-called strict liability is required to prove both that reasonable or utmost care was exercised and that the risk was undiscoverable.

The scientific inability to avoid occasional flaws in products due to miscarriages in the construction process has never altered the fact that an impure or flawed product is defective if the product proves to be more dangerous than it was intended to be. Therefore, the scientific inability to discover in advance that the harmful side effects of a drug outweigh all its benefits does not alter the fact that, if it proves to do so, it was a bad and defective product. A court may

Keeton, Torts, Annual Survey of Texas Law, 1981, 35 Sw.L.J. 1, 9.

32. Jones v. Hutchinson Manufacturing, Inc., Ky. 1973, 502 S.W.2d 66, 69–70; Balido v. Improved Machinery, Inc., 1973, 29 Cal.App.3d 633, 105 Cal.Rptr. 890, 895.

33. See, Newman v. Utility Trailer and Equipment Co., 1977, 278 Or. 395, 564 P.2d 674, 675–676.

34. See Green v. American Tobacco Co., 5th Cir. 1969, 409 F.2d 1166, certiorari denied 397 U.S. 911, 90 S.Ct. 912, 25 L.Ed.2d 93 (testimony on scientific knowledge was admissible); Ross v. Phillip Morris & Co., 8th Cir. 1964, 328 F.2d 3 (scientific unknowability is a defense); Lartigue v. R.J. Reynolds Tobacco Co., 5th Cir. 1963, 317 F.2d 19, certiorari denied 375 U.S. 865, 84 S.Ct. 137, 11 L.Ed.2d 92 (scientific unknowability regarded as a defense under Louisiana law); Pritchard v. Liggett & Myers Tobacco Co., 3d Cir. 1961, 295 F.2d 292 (scientific unknowability is not a defense if the risk or hazard in the product constituted a breach of warranty); Green v. American Tobacco Co., Fla.1963, 154 So.2d 169, conformed to 325 F.2d 673, certiorari denied 377 U.S. 943, 84 S.Ct. 1349, 12 L.Ed.2d 306 and 377 U.S. 943, 84 S.Ct. 1351, 12 L.Ed.2d 306 (scientific unknowability of the risk of lung cancer is irrelevant). See generally Wegman, Cigarettes and Health—A Legal Analysis, 51 Cornell L.Q. 678 (1966).

conclude that as a matter of policy in one or the other or both such circumstances scientific inability to detect the risk or hazard justifies excusing the manufacturer. If so, this is simply a recognition of the notion that fault in the sense of negligence should be a prerequisite to recovery. It is generally agreed, however, that inability to prevent flaws from occurring will not excuse,[35] but there is considerable diversity of opinion about inability to discover or appreciate hazards related to the way products are designed and composed.[36] It has been suggested that there should be a difference between prescription drugs and other products, especially mechanical products, the thought being that scientific inability to discover a risk or hazard related to the use of a product should not ordinarily be an excuse but that prescription drugs should be treated differently.[37]

State of the art and designing out danger. It is generally agreed that a product cannot be regarded as defectively designed when sold simply because after the sale and prior to the time of trial or to the time of a claimant's injury, there was a technological breakthrough of some kind making it possible to eliminate a risk of harm altogether or reduce the magnitude of the danger from a risk. The courts have almost universally held that the feasibility of designing a safer product must be determined as of the time the product was designed.[38] So, even if no consideration is given to the impossibility or impracticability of discovering danger, the same consideration is given to the impossibility or impracticability of designing out danger as would be given to that matter on the issue of negligence.

Some other tests. Some courts have approved what is in effect a danger-utility test for design conditions by adopting a hindsight negligence test. Under such a test, as proposed by the New Jersey Supreme Court in 1978 in Cepeda v. Cumberland Engineering Co.,[39] a product is unreasonably dangerous and therefore defective if it is so likely to be harmful to persons or property that a reasonably prudent manufacturer who had actual knowledge of its harmful character would not have [placed it on the market] [marketed it as he did]. The bracketed material is for the purpose of indicating that the test can be articulated somewhat differently. There are some substantive problems with the precise manner of describing the standard. It can be carried so far as to impose liability on a manufacturer for failing to warn of an unknowable risk, if, had the manufacturer known of it, there would have been negligence in selling it without warning.[40] This is a minority view and can reasonably be regarded as an extreme position.

---

35. See, Barker v. Lull Engineering Co., 1978, 20 Cal.3d 413, 143 Cal.Rptr. 225, 573 P.2d 443; Cepeda v. Cumberland Engineering Co., 1978, 76 N.J. 152, 386 A.2d 816; Keeton, Product Liability and the Meaning of Defect, 1973, 5 St. Mary's L.J. 30; Wade, Strict Tort Liability of Manufacturers, 1971, 32 Ala.Law. 455. A clear distinction is made in these cases and these articles between design hazards and construction flaws or abnormalities. This is not to say that some tolerance standard for "flaws" or "unintended" abnormalities that are natural incidents of food products or basic metallic materials is permissible. Provision must be made for allowing some natural abnormalities that cannot be completely eliminated in any satisfactory manner in the construction process. Therefore, they must be dealt with as design defects.

36. See, generally, Willig, The Comment k Character: A Conceptual Barrier to Strict Liability, 1978, 29 Mercer L.Rev. 545; James, The Untoward Effects of Cigarettes and Drugs: Some Reflections on Enterprise Liability, 1966, 54 Calif.L.Rev. 1550; Connolly, The Liability of a Manufacturer for Unknowable Hazards Inherent in His Product, 1965, 32 Ins.Coun.J. 303; Rheingold, Products Liability—The Ethical Drug Manufacturer's Liability, 1964, 18 Rutgers L.Rev. 947. Annot., 1961, 80 A.L.R.2d 681.

37. Lewis v. Baker, 1966, 243 Or. 317, 413 P.2d 400; Incolligno v. Ewing, 1971, 444 Pa. 263, 282 A.2d 206; Leibowitz v. Ortho Pharmaceutical Corp., 1973, 224 Pa. Super. 418, 307 A.2d 449; McDaniel v. McNeil Laboratories, Inc., 1976, 196 Neb. 190, 241 N.W.2d 822.

38. Caterpillar Tractor v. Beck, Alaska 1979, 593 P.2d 871; Anderson v. Heron Engineering Co., 1979, 198 Colo. 391, 604 P.2d 674; Olson v. A.W. Chesterton Co., N.D.1977, 256 N.W.2d 530; Note, Product Feasibility Reform Proposals: The State of the Art Defense, 1979, 43 Alb.L.Rev. 941, 950.

39. 1978, 76 N.J. 152, 386 A.2d 816. The test approved was later modified in Suter v. San Angelo Foundry & Machine Co., 1979, 81 N.J. 150, 406 A.2d 140.

40. Phillips v. Kimwood Machine Co., 1974, 269 Or. 485, 525 P.2d 1033; Jackson v. Coast Paint & Lacquer Co., 9th Cir. 1974, 499 F.2d 809; Freund v. Cellofilm

It can be regarded as meaning that a product cannot be regarded as defective in the way in which it is designed unless a reasonable person would not market the product even with an adequate warning as to the risk.[41] This can reasonably be regarded as too restrictive, since the danger may well outweigh the utility of the product during the period of time when no warning was given due to scientific unknowability. It is for these reasons that it would seem preferable to articulate the test in terms of weighing danger-in-fact as it is found to be at the trial with utility.

At least two courts have seen fit to give the claimant an option of proving defect through either (1) a consumer-contemplation test or (2) a risk-utility test.[42] This was first adopted by the Supreme Court of California in Barker v. Lull Engineering Co.[43] There the court said that a product is defectively designed in a particular aspect if either (1) the plaintiff proves that the product fails to perform as safely as the ordinary consumer would expect when used in an intended or reasonably foreseeable manner, or (2) the plaintiff proves that the product's design proximately caused the injury and the *defendant fails to prove*, in the light of relevant factors, that on balance, the benefits of the challenged design outweigh the risk or danger inherent in such design.[44] With this test, the court convincingly demonstrates that the consumer-contemplation test is inadequate as a basis for impugning the design of products with obvious dangers but fails to recognize that it *can* impugn the design of products with latent and unknowable risks where the benefits already outweigh the danger-in-fact. Another important aspect of the bifurcated test as adopted in California and approved elsewhere is that the only burden of proof on claimant as regards the risk-utility prong of this bifurcated test is to prove a product as designed in a particular way was a proximate cause of the damaging event out of which the plaintiff's injury arose.[45] It is then a matter of defense for the defendant to prove that the utility of the product outweighs the danger. This, of course, is an irrational presumption of a defect just because a design hazard caused a damaging event and such a presumption can be justified only on the policy position that, in fairness, the defendant is in the better position to explain why a safer product could not have been designed.

The courts that have adopted the California bifurcated test, accompanied by a shifting of the burden of proof to the defendant to show that utility outweighs danger, have been concerned about one of the underlying policy reasons for the adoption of strict liability—the difficulty of discovering evidence necessary to show that danger outweighs benefits. It would seem that this could be accomplished in a less drastic manner. There is no reason for not accompanying the danger-utility test with a presumption that danger outweighs utility if the product fails under circumstances when the ordinary purchaser or user would not have so expected. This effects a combination of the two ideas in a way that does not do violence to logic or fairness and to the disposition of cases on the basis of the truth.

WESTLAW REFERENCES

digest,synopsis(402a & ordinary foreseeable /p user purchaser consumer)

court(ca) & citation(573 +s 443)

sh 573p2d443

Properties, Inc., 1981, 87 N.J. 229, 432 A.2d 925. Supra, note 21.

41. See, Crocker v. Winthrop Laboratories, Tex. 1974, 514 S.W.2d 429.

42. Barker v. Lull Engineering Co., 1978, 20 Cal.3d 413, 143 Cal.Rptr. 225, 573 P.2d 443; Caterpillar Tractor Co. v. Beck, Alaska 1979, 593 P.2d 871.

43. 1978, 20 Cal.3d 413, 143 Cal.Rptr. 225, 573 P.2d 443. This test had been proposed in Montgomery & Owen, Reflections on the Theory and Administration of Strict Tort Liability for Defective Products, 1976, 27 S.C.L.Rev. 803.

44. Id., 143 Cal.Rptr. at p. 234, 573 P.2d at p. 452.

45. Id. 143 Cal.Rptr. at p. 237, 573 P.2d at p. 455.

§ 100. Parties

Plaintiffs

The MacPherson decision [1] did not carry the liability of the seller for negligence beyond the ultimate purchaser himself. It was, however, soon expanded to other users and consumers of the product, and then to those who were "in the vicinity of the chattel's probable use," [2] or, as it is now put by the Second Restatement, [3] "those whom he should expect to be endangered by its probable use." There is no longer any doubt that the negligence liability extends to any lawful [4] user of the thing supplied, as well as to a mere bystander, [5] or a pedestrian in the path of a car. [6] For negligence, in other words, there is liability to any foreseeable plaintiff.

Perhaps because the early decisions were grounded on a theory of warranty, the strict liability of the seller was at first limited to "users" or "consumers" of the product. Both terms were, however, applied in a very broad sense. Passengers in automobiles [7] and airplanes [8] were held to be users; and so was a customer in a beauty shop whose hair was treated with the defendant's dye, [9] a shopper in a self-service store who had not yet bought, [10] a wife preparing rabbits for her husband's dinner; [11] a filling station mechanic doing work on a car, [12] and even one who tried to walk through an invisible glass door. [13] But one who was making no use at all of the product except to be injured by it, as in the case of a pedestrian hit by an automobile, [14] or a bystander injured by the explosion of a beer bottle, [15] were denied recovery in the absence of negligence, on the ground that they were not within the class of persons whom the seller had been seeking to reach in marketing the product, and they

§ 100

1. Supra, p. 682.
2. First Restatement of Torts, § 395.
3. Second Restatement of Torts, § 395.
4. An evenly divided appellate court (3–3) failed to reverse a trial court's denial of recovery to a thief-user in the only decision found on "unlawful users." Pegg v. General Motors Corp., 1978, 258 Pa. Super. 59, 391 A.2d 1074.
5. Gall v. Union Ice Co., 1951, 108 Cal.App.2d 303, 239 P.2d 48; McLeod v. Linde Air Products Co., 1927, 318 Mo. 397, 1 S.W.2d 122; Hopper v. Charles Cooper & Co., 1927, 104 N.J.L. 93, 139 A. 19; Benton v. Sloss, 1952, 38 Cal.2d 399, 240 P.2d 575 (passenger in colliding car).
6. Gaidry Motors v. Brannon, Ky.1954, 268 S.W.2d 627; Flies v. Fox Brothers Buick Co., 1928, 196 Wis. 196, 218 N.W. 855; cf. Ford Motor Co. v. Zahn, 8th Cir. 1959, 265 F.2d 729; Carpini v. Pittsburgh & Weirton Bus Co., 3d Cir. 1954, 216 F.2d 404 (passenger in bus); Greyhound Corp. v. Brown, 1959, 269 Ala. 520, 113 So. 2d 916 (same).
7. Thompson v. Reedman, E.D.Pa.1961, 199 F.Supp. 120; Hacker v. Rector, D.C.Mo.1966, 250 F.Supp. 300.
8. Hinton v. Republic Aviation Corp., S.D.N.Y.1959, 180 F.Supp. 31; Ewing v. Lockheed Aircraft Corp., D.Minn.1962, 202 F.Supp. 216; King v. Douglas Aircraft Co., Fla.App.1963, 159 So.2d 108; Goldberg v. Kollsman Instrument Corp., 1963, 12 N.Y.2d 432, 240 N.Y.S.2d 592, 191 N.E.2d 81.
9. Graham v. Bottenfield's Inc., 1954, 176 Kan. 68, 269 P.2d 413; Garthwait v. Burgio, 1965, 153 Conn. 284, 216 A.2d 189.
10. Rogers v. Karem, Ky.1966, 405 S.W.2d 741; Faucette v. Lucky Stores, Inc., 1963, 219 Cal.App.2d 196, 33 Cal.Rptr. 215. Cf. Delaney v. Towmotor Corp., 2d Cir. 1964, 339 F.2d 4 (trying out product); Matthews v. Lawnlite Co., Fla.1956, 88 So.2d 299 (same).
11. Haut v. Kleene, 1943, 320 Ill.App. 273, 50 N.E.2d 855.
12. Connolly v. Hagi, 1963, 24 Conn.Sup. 198, 188 A.2d 884. Cf. Keener v. Dayton Electric Manufacturing Co., Mo.1969, 445 S.W.2d 362 (lifting sump pump in aiding friend to clear water from basement); Cottom v. McGuire Funeral Service, Inc., D.C.App.1970, 262 A.2d 807, appeal after remand 284 A.2d 50 (pallbearer carrying casket). In Guarino v. Mine Safety Appliance Co., 1969, 25 N.Y.2d 460, 306 N.Y.S.2d 942, 255 N.E.2d 173, the court found strict liability to a rescuer of a user of a safety mask for miners.
13. Gutierrez v. Superior Court, 1966, 243 Cal.App.2d 710, 52 Cal.Rptr. 592.
14. Mull v. Ford Motor Co., 2d Cir. 1967, 368 F.2d 713; Hahn v. Ford Motor Co., 1964, 256 Iowa 27, 126 N.W.2d 350 (driver of colliding car); Berzon v. Don Allen Motors, Inc., 1965, 23 App.Div.2d 530, 256 N.Y.S.2d 643 (passenger in colliding car); Davidson v. Leadingham, E.D.Ky.1968, 294 F.Supp. 155 (occupants of colliding car); Schneider v. Chrysler Motors Corp., 8th Cir. 1968, 401 F.2d 549.
15. Kasey v. Suburban Gas Heat, Inc., 1962, 60 Wn.2d 468, 374 P.2d 549 (cafe wrecked by explosion of propane gas). Cf. Torpey v. Red Owl Stores, 8th Cir. 1955, 228 F.2d 117 (guest opening glass jar); Rodriguez v. Shell's City, Inc., Fla.App.1962, 141 So.2d 590 (bystander injured by disintegration of sanding kit); and see Alexander Funeral Homes, Inc. v. Pride, 1964, 261 N.C. 723, 136 S.E.2d 120 (building run into by car).

had not relied in any way upon his implied representation of safety. Their only qualification for recovery was that they were there when the accident happened, which is a thing not uncommon in plaintiffs.

The break away from these decisions came in Michigan [16] in 1965, when a bystander was injured by the explosion of a shotgun. The case was followed by a few other courts.[17] The first real discussion of the basis of liability was in Elmore v. American Motors Corp.,[18] in California in 1969, when an automobile veered across the center line of the highway and collided head-on with the plaintiff. Justice Peters said that the purpose of the strict liability in tort was to make the industry responsible for all of the foreseeable harm done by its defective products, with the expectation that the losses would be distributed to the public through liability insurance added to the cost; and that the bystander was as much entitled to protection as the consumer, and more in need of it. Other jurisdictions have agreed with this decision,[19] until it is by now generally followed. Its effect is obviously to put the strict liability on the same footing as negligence, as to all foreseeable injuries.

Defendants

(1) *Negligence.* So far as liability for negligence is concerned, there is no longer any doubt that it attaches to any seller of a product, including the maker of a component part of the final product,[20] and an assembler of parts supplied by others,[21] or even a mere processor under contract with the maker.[22] It applies to dealers, whether at wholesale or retail,[23] and to a second-hand dealer who reconditions automobiles for sale.[24] It is obvious that less in the way of care may be required of some of these sellers than of others; [25] but if reasonable care has not been exercised, there may be liability.

In a number of cases it has been held that one who labels a product with his own name, or otherwise represents it to be his own,[26] is to be treated on the same basis as if he had

---

16. Piercefield v. Remington Arms Co., 1965, 375 Mich. 85, 133 N.W.2d 129.

17. Trojan Boat Co. v. Lutz, 5th Cir. 1966, 358 F.2d 299 (cabin cruiser blew up and set fire to other boats in the vicinity); Mitchell v. Miller, 1965, 26 Conn.Sup. 142, 214 A.2d 694 (driver of colliding car); Webb v. Zern, 1966, 422 Pa. 424, 220 A.2d 853 (bystander injured by explosion of beer keg); Toombs v. Fort Pierce Gas Co., Fla.1968, 208 So.2d 615 (bystander injured by explosion of tank of propane gas). See also Ford Motor Co. v. Cockrell, Miss.1968, 211 So.2d 833.

18. 1969, 70 Cal.2d 578, 75 Cal.Rptr. 652, 451 P.2d 84. Followed in Johnson v. Standard Brands Paint Co., 1969, 274 Cal.App.2d 369, 79 Cal.Rptr. 194; Preissman v. D'Ornellas, 1969, 1 Cal.App.3d 841, 82 Cal.Rptr. 108.

19. Darryl v. Ford Motor Co., Tex.1969, 440 S.W.2d 630 (driver of colliding car); Caruth v. Mariani, 1970, 11 Ariz.App. 188, 463 P.2d 83 (same); Sills v. Massey-Ferguson, Inc., N.D.Ind.1969, 296 F.Supp. 776 (bystander hit by object thrown 150 feet by power mower); Wasik v. Borg, 2d Cir. 1970, 423 F.2d 44 (Vermont law); Pike v. Frank O. Hough Co., 1970, 85 Cal.Rptr. 629, 467 P.2d 229.

See, King and Neville, The Bystander's Right Under Strict Liability Does Exist: A Call for Reform of the Restatement, 1981, 25 Saint Louis L.J. 543.

20. Smith v. Peerless Glass Co., 1932, 259 N.Y. 292, 181 N.E. 576, motion denied 259 N.Y. 664, 182 N.E. 225; Spencer v. Madsen, 10th Cir. 1944, 142 F.2d 820; State for Use of Woodzell v. Garzell Plastics Industries, E.D.Mich.1957, 152 F.Supp. 483; Fredericks v. American Export Lines, 2d Cir. 1955, 227 F.2d 450, certiorari denied 350 U.S. 989, 76 S.Ct. 475, 100 L.Ed. 855; Willey v. Fyrogas Co., 1952, 363 Mo. 406, 251 S.W.2d 635.

21. Sheward v. Virtue, 1942, 20 Cal.2d 410, 126 P.2d 345; Rauch v. American Radiator & Standard Sanitary Corp., 1960, 252 Iowa 1, 104 N.W.2d 607; Alexander v. Nash-Kelvinator Corp., 2d Cir. 1958, 261 F.2d 187; Spencer v. Madsen, 10th Cir. 1944, 142 F.2d 820; Comstock v. General Motors Corp., 1959, 358 Mich. 163, 99 N.W.2d 627.

22. Block v. Urban, E.D.Mich.1958, 166 F.Supp. 19.

23. Jones v. Burgermeister Brewing Corp., 1961, 198 Cal.App. 198, 18 Cal.Rptr. 311; Ellis v. Lindmark, 1929, 177 Minn. 390, 225 N.W. 395; Egan Chevrolet Co. v. Bruner, 8th Cir. 1939, 102 F.2d 373; Stout v. Madden, 1956, 208 Or. 294, 300 P.2d 461; Gall v. Union Ice Co., 1951, 108 Cal.App.2d 303, 239 P.2d 48.

24. Flies v. Fox Brothers Buick Co., 1928, 196 Wis. 196, 218 N.W. 855; Gaidry Motors v. Brannon, Ky. 1952, 268 S.W.2d 327; Bock v. Truck & Tractor, Inc., 1943, 18 Wash.2d 458, 139 P.2d 706; Jones v. Raney Chevrolet Co., 1940, 217 N.C. 693, 9 S.E.2d 395.

25. See, as to the dealer, Shroder v. Barron-Dady Motor Co., Mo.1937, 111 S.W.2d 66; Zesch v. Abrasive Co. of Philadelphia, 1944, 353 Mo. 558, 183 S.W.2d 140.

26. Where the goods are merely labeled with the seller's name as distributor, it is held that he is not responsible for the maker's negligence. Degouveia v. H.D. Lee Merc. Co., 1937, 231 Mo.App. 447, 100 S.W.2d

manufactured it, and so is liable for any negligence on the part of the actual maker.[27] The courts have talked occasionally of an "estoppel" on the part of the seller to deny that the negligence is his own; but this is quite difficult to make out where, as is often enough the case, the injured plaintiff never heard of either seller. The basis of liability appears to be nothing more than the fact that the defendant has vouched for the product, and so made the responsibility his own.

(2) *Strict liability and merchant sellers.* Only a seller who can be regarded as a merchant or one engaged in the business of supplying goods of the kind involved in the case is subject to strict liability, either on warranty or in tort.[28] When a housewife, on one occasion, sells a jar of jam to her neighbor, or a private owner of an automobile trades it to a dealer,[29] there would be no liability except for negligence in the sale of a product when the seller knew or had reason to know of a dangerous condition. This is because in such a case (a) there would be no implied representation of fitness which is the basis for implied warranty of merchantability, and (b) the policy considerations that are the basis for enterprise liability in tort are not applicable.[30]

(3) *Strict liability and component part sellers.* Strict liability originated with actions against assembler-manufacturers.[31] So all states would accept the proposition that strict liability extends to such a defendant, as well as to one who vouches for the manufacturer-assembler by selling a product assembled by another as his own.[32] But there has been some reluctance to impose strict liability in tort on the maker of a component part who sells that part to an assembler.[33] But if the "defect" is with the component part itself and not with the manner of its use by the assembler-manufacturer, it would seem that the component part maker should be directly responsible to one physically harmed by an event proximately caused by such defect.[34] Thus, care must be exercised in ascertaining the reason for the failure of the component part to serve the manner of use made of it. If the failure was due to a flaw in the component part, then the component part is itself defective and

---

336; Fleetwood v. Swift & Co., 1921, 27 Ga.App. 502, 108 S.E. 909; Second Restatement of Torts, § 400, Comment d.

27. Smith v. Regina Manufacturing Corp., 4th Cir. 1968, 396 F.2d 826; Penn v. Inferno Manufacturing Corp., La.App.1967, 199 So.2d 210, writ refused 251 La. 27, 202 So.2d 649; Standard Motor Co. v. Blood, Tex. Civ.App.1964, 380 S.W.2d 651; Swift & Co. v. Blackwell, 4th Cir. 1936, 84 F.2d 130; Sears, Roebuck & Co. v. Morris, 1961, 273 Ala. 218, 136 So.2d 883.

28. A warranty that the goods shall be merchantable is implied when the sale is by a merchant seller. U.C.C., Section 2.314. Strict liability in tort under Section 402A only applies when the seller is engaged in the business of selling the kind of product that proved to be defective when sold. Section 402A(1)(a) and comment f. It does not apply to the occasional seller.

29. In Thrash v. U-Drive-It Co., 1953, 158 Ohio St. 465, 110 N.E.2d 419, an owner trading a car "as is" to a second-hand dealer was held not even to be under a duty of reasonable care. See also Wagner v. Coronet Hotel, 1969, 10 Ariz.App. 296, 458 P.2d 390; Magrine v. Krasnica, 1967, 94 N.J.Super. 228, 227 A.2d 539, affirmed 53 N.J. 259, 250 A.2d 129, affirmed in Magrine v. Spector, 1967, 100 N.J.Super. 223, 241 A.2d 637 affirmed 53 N.J. 259, 250 A.2d 129; Southwest Forest Industries, Inc. v. Westinghouse Electric Corp., 9 Cir. 1970, 422 F.2d 1013, certiorari denied 400 U.S. 902, 91 S.Ct. 138, 27 L.Ed.2d 138; Freitas v. Twin City Fishermen's Co-operative Association, Tex.Civ.App.1970, 452 S.W.2d 931, refused n.r.e., appeal after remand 452 S.W.2d 931, refused n.r.e.

30. Sections 97 and 98.

31. Putman v. Erie City Manufacturing Co., 5 Cir. 1964, 338 F.2d 911; Ford Motor Co. v. Mathis, 5th Cir. 1963, 322 F.2d 267; King v. Douglas Aircraft Co., Fla. App.1963, 159 So.2d 108; Courtois v. General Motors Corp., 1962, 37 N.J. 525, 182 A.2d 545; Holman v. Ford Motor Co., Fla.App.1970, 239 So.2d 40, appeal after remand 254 So.2d 812.

32. Schwartz v. Macrose Lumber & Trim Co., 1966, 50 Misc.2d 547, 270 N.Y.S.2d 875, motion denied 50 Misc.2d 1055, 272 N.Y.S.2d 227, reversed on other grounds, 29 App.Div.2d 781, 287 N.Y.S.2d 706, affirmed 24 N.Y.2d 856, 301 N.Y.S.2d 91, 248 N.E.2d 920.

33. See, Goldberg v. Kollsman Instrument Corp., 1963, 12 N.Y.2d 432, 240 N.Y.S.2d 592, 191 N.E.2d 81; Union Supply Co. v. Pust, 1978, 196 Colo. 162, 583 P.2d 276; Parker v. Warren, Tenn.App.1974, 503 S.W.2d 938.

34. City of Franklin v. Badger Ford Truck Sales, Inc., 1973, 58 Wis.2d 641, 207 N.W.2d 866; d'Hedouville v. Pioneer Hotel Co., 9th Cir. 1977, 552 F.2d 886; Union Supply Co. v. Pust, 1978, 196 Colo. 162, 583 P.2d 276; Taylor v. Paul O. Abbe, Inc., 3d Cir. 1975, 516 F.2d 145.

the cause for the assembled product being defective.[35] If the failure was due to the fact that the assembled product was unreasonably dangerous because the component part, such as an altimeter for an airplane, was unfit for its ordinary purposes, then quite clearly the component part itself was defective as designed.[36] If, on the other hand, the assembled product was unreasonably dangerous because the component part was unfit for the particular use that the assembler was making of it, then arguably the defect is in the design of the assembled product rather than in the design of the component part. If the maker of the component part, such as a steel rod, knows or has reason to know that the part will be used in a way that will make the assembled product unreasonably dangerous then such a seller may well be subjected to liability on a warranty of fitness theory if the purchaser was relying on the seller,[37] or a negligent entrustment theory [38] or perhaps strict liability in tort without regard to reliance.[39] It has, for example, been held that knowledge on the part of the seller of a component part that a purchaser intends to use it in a way that is found to be unreasonably dangerous subjects the supplier of the component part to strict liability in tort as well as the assembler.[40]

(4) *Strict liability and dealers.* It has been urged that the only argument in favor of a general rule of retailer liability for defects in products that he sells is that it affords an alternative remedy when the manufacturer is insolvent, out of business, or cannot be reached, the latter of which is seldom the case today since most states have statutes making it possible to get jurisdiction of a defendant who sells the kind of product that he contemplates will be resold to the first purchaser for use in the state where the suit is filed.[41] But both strict liability for breach of the implied warranty of merchantability and strict liability in tort have generally been applied against dealers and wholesalers.[42] Moreover, in considering issues about the liability of resellers, one must take account of (a) the diverse methods for the production and distribution of products in our private enterprise system, and (b) the fact that flaws in products can be created in the marketing process as well as in the construction process and therefore a flaw that is present when the product is sold by a dealer may not be one that was present when sold by the manufacturer. Therefore, various policy arguments can be advanced to support strict liability of resellers.

The retailer is in a more favorable position to bear the costs of accidents due to the defectively dangerous products he sells than is the first purchaser for use. If the defect is one that is traceable to the manufacturer, the retailer may be more likely to get acceptance of financial responsibility without litigation than is the consumer purchaser. If the manufacturer is insolvent or is a corporation that has been dissolved, or if the de-

---

35. See, Clark v. Bendix Corp., 1973, 42 A.D.2d 727, 345 N.Y.S.2d 662.

36. Goldberg v. Kollsman Instrument Corp., 1963, 12 N.Y.2d 432, 240 N.Y.S.2d 592, 191 N.E.2d 81.

37. Gellenbeck v. Sears, Roebuck & Co., 1975, 59 Mich.App. 339, 229 N.W.2d 443 (warranties of merchantability and fitness for a particular purpose attached to sale of chains for swing set).

38. Suchomajcz v. Hummel Chemical Co., 3d Cir. 1975, 524 F.2d 19.

39. Rourke v. Garza, Tex.1976, 530 S.W.2d 794.

40. Id.

41. Waite, Retail Responsibility and Judicial Law-Making, 1936, 34 Mich.L.Rev. 494, 518; Waite, Retail Responsibility—A Reply, 1939, 23 Minn.L.Rev. 612, 614.

42. Mead v. Warner Pruyn Division, 1977, 57 A.D. 2d 340, 394 N.Y.S.2d 483 (tort); Casrell v. Altec Industries, Inc., Ala.1976, 335 So.2d 128; Hiigel v. General Motors Corp., 1976, 190 Colo. 57, 544 P.2d 983 (tort); Second Restatement of Torts, 402A, Comment *f*; Pierce v. Liberty Furniture Co., 1977, 141 Ga.App. 175, 233 S.E.2d 33 (warranty); Dougall v. Brown Bay Boat Works & Sales, 1970, 287 Minn. 290, 178 N.W.2d 217; Vlases v. Montgomery Ward & Co., 3d Cir. 1967, 377 F.2d 846.

There are some decisions, however, that do not impose strict tort or warranty liability on the retailer. Shainberg Co. of Jackson v. Barlow, Miss. 1972, 258 So. 2d 242 (latent defect created by manufacturer); Batiste v. American Home Products Corp., N.C.App.1977, 32 N.C.App. 1, 231 S.E.2d 269 (prescription drug sold by pharmacist).

fect is one that is not traceable to the manufacturer, the loss is one that can best be borne by the retailer as a cost of doing business.

The goal of accident prevention is best served by the imposition of strict liability on the retailer. Such liability will induce care in the selection of manufacturers who are responsible both in (a) designing and constructing safe products, and (b) in providing financial security for those victimized by dangerously defective products. Finally, victims of dangerously defective products will be relieved of the difficult burden of proving when, in the marketing chain, a defect originated.

(5) *Endorsers, licensors of trademarks, and licensors of patents.* It can be said that all those who participate in the process of making products available to users for profit or financial gain are subject to liability on a negligence theory. This would include endorsers,[43] licensors of trademarks, and franchisers, and perhaps also those who license another to manufacture and sell a patented invention.

The more difficult inquiry relates to strict liability either on a theory of breach of warranty or strict liability in tort. Franchising, for example, has become a common means of marketing products and services but the courts have not yet arrived at settled principles for determining the liability of franchisers for injuries sustained by the customers of franchisees. The states that have passed on the question have treated the franchiser as if he were the seller, at least in those cases where many members of the general public would believe that the franchiser was either the owner-seller or at least exercising substantial control over the franchisee's processes.[44]

The licensor of a patent is often in a somewhat different position. The licensor's contract is generally nothing more than a contract authorizing the use of an alleged patent, i.e., an invention. The product sold by the licensee is generally not sold under the trade name of the licensor of the patent. The general public is not in most instances relying on the licensor. This is not to say that the licensor may not participate to such an extent in the construction and sale of products made pursuant to a patent to justify the imposition of strict liability.

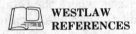 **WESTLAW REFERENCES**

Plaintiffs
elmore & american & piercefield & remington

§ 101. Summary—Interests Protected and Theories of Recovery

At the beginning of the chapter,[1] losses related to product liability claims were classified into five categories. These are: (a) personal injuries, (b) physical harm to tangible things other than the assembled product, (c) physical harm to or destruction of an assembled product purchased by the first purchaser for use, (d) physical harm to or destruction of a product that was constructed or repaired with the use of the target seller's component part, and (e) intangible direct and consequential economic loss resulting from the inferior quality or unfitness of the prod-

---

43. Hanberry v. Hearst Corp., 1969, 276 Cal.App.2d 680, 81 Cal.Rptr. 519 (endorser of a product); Hempstead v. General Fire Extinguisher Corp., D.C.Del.1967, 269 F.Supp. 109. On the liability of the certifiers of product safety, see, generally, Carlin, Liability of the Product Endorser—Developing a New Perspective, 1969, 15 N.Y.L.F. 835; Jensvold, A Modern Approach Among Tortfeasors in Products Liability Cases, 1974, 58 Minn.L.Rev. 723; Notes, 1970, 74 Dick.L.Rev. 792; 1974, 58 Minn.L.Rev. 723; 1970, 11 Wm. & Mary L.Rev. 771; Annot., 1971, 39 A.L.R.3d 181.

44. Kosters v. The Seven-Up Co., 6th Cir. 1979, 595 F.2d 347; City of Hartford v. Associated Construction Co., 1978, 34 Conn.Sup. 204, 384 A.2d 390; Kasel v. Remington Arms Co., Inc., 1972, 24 Cal.App.3d 711, 101 Cal.Rptr. 314; Carter v. Joseph Bancroft & Sons Co., E.D.Pa.1973, 360 F.Supp. 1103. On trademark licensors, see generally, Goldstein, Products Liability and the Trademark Owner—"When a Trademark is a Warranty," 1977, 32 Bus.Law 957; Note, Tort Liability of Trademark Licensors, 1970, 55 Iowa L.Rev. 693.

§ 101

1. Section 95.

uct adequately to serve the purchaser's purposes. For convenience in treatment, the last category will be discussed first.

(1) *Intangible economic and commercial losses.* Where products do not have defects that endanger others, it can reasonably be argued that they cannot be so poor in quality as to be unworthy of sale if the price is right. Therefore, the immediate contract between the retailer and the user-purchaser, as well as the contract between the manufacturer and its market-purchaser is of utmost importance with regard to whether the user-purchaser should be permitted to recover directly against the manufacturer. Notwithstanding the obvious difficulty in ascertaining and interpreting the terms of immediate contracts in cases where the retailer is not a party to a suit for damages against a manufacturer, much can be said for disregarding marketing privity, especially when the user-purchaser is an ordinary consumer rather than an industrial or commercial enterpriser. Therefore, even though marketing privity can justifiably be disregarded, the manifested intent of each seller would usually be controlling as regards the scope of any guarantees related to the condition of the goods sold. Historically, therefore, the only tort action available to a disappointed purchaser suffering intangible commercial loss has been the tort action of deceit for fraud and the only contract action has been for breach of a warranty, express or implied.[2] This remains the generally accepted view. A few courts in recent years have permitted either a tort action for negligence [3] or one in strict liability.[4] Usually, the reason for so doing has been to escape the requirement of privity of contract as a prerequisite to recovery on a warranty theory.[5] But the elimination of this requirement for recovery on a contract-warranty theory would seem to constitute the more satisfactory technique.

(2) *Physical harm to persons and tangible things, other than the defective product itself.* The generally accepted view today would be that recovery for this kind of loss is available under three separate theories: negligence in tort,[6] strict liability for breach of warranty,[7] and strict liability in tort.[8] Strict liability for breach of warranty is available primarily as a consequence of the recognition that personal injuries and physical harm to tangible things proximately resulting from a breach of warranty constitute consequential damages.[9] This came about as heretofore related prior to the development of strict liability in tort.[10] This brings about unnecessary complexity and since this kind of liability based as it is on policy considerations—and not on a manifested intent to guarantee—ought not to be disclaimable by contract, even as between parties to the contract, the commercial codes in the states should be amended so as to eliminate this type of consequential damages from recovery for breach of a warranty. The duty to avoid this kind of harm is an obligation imposed by law without regard to manifested intent and may be properly regarded as inescapable.

(3) *Physical damage to the defective product itself.* It has been held that if a dangerously defective product causes an ac-

---

2. See Keeton, Rights of Disappointed Purchasers, 1953, 32 Tex.L.Rev. 1; Superwood Corp. v. Siempelkamp Corp., Minn.1981, 311 N.W.2d 159; Moorman Manufacturing Co. v. National Tank Co., Ill.1982, 92 Ill.App.3d 136, 47 Ill.Dec. 186, 435 N.E.2d 443; Purvis v. Consolidated Energy Products Co., 4th Cir. 1982, 674 F.2d 217.

3. Berg v. General Motors Corp., 1976, 87 Wn.2d 584, 555 P.2d 818; Nobility Homes v. Shivers, Tex. 1977, 557 S.W.2d 77. Contra: Chrysler Corp. v. Taylor, 1977, 141 Ga.App. 671, 234 S.E.2d 123; Inglis v. American Motors Corp., 1965, 3 Ohio St.2d 132, 209 N.E.2d 583; Clark v. International Harvester Co., 1978, 99 Idaho 326, 581 P.2d 784.

4. Santor v. A & M Karagheusian, Inc., 1965, 44 N.J. 52, 207 A.2d 305; Lang v. General Motors Corp., N.D.1965, 136 N.W.2d 805.

5. Supra, note 3.

6. Section 96.

7. Section 97.

8. Section 98.

9. U.C.C., Section 2–715(2)(b).

10. See Section 97.

cident, then any loss resulting from that accident, including damage to the product itself, should be recoverable on a theory of strict liability in tort.[11] Although this is a reasonable position, the risk of harm to the product itself due to the condition of the product would seem to be a type of risk that the parties to a purchase and sale contract should be allowed to allocate pursuant to the terms of the contract.[12] This is especially so as regards transactions involving commercial or industrial products. Therefore, contract law and the rules pertaining to contract restrictions on warranty liability should control rather than the rules and principles of tort law. There are certain provisions in the Uniform Commercial Code to guard against surprise and lack of negotiation about adhesion-type disclaimers of warranties and limitations of remedies for breach of warranties.[13] Moreover, the Magnuson-Moss Warranty Act substantially restricts the freedom of the parties as regards the implied warranty of merchantability with respect to consumer transactions.[14] The policy considerations dictating strict liability in tort for dangerously defective products are not subverted so long as the seller is held strictly accountable for physical harm to persons and tangible things other than the defective product itself.

Making liability depend upon whether or not the loss results from an "accident" creates a difficult issue and arguably an irrelevant issue with respect to the validity of contract provisions allocating the risk of loss for harm to the defective product itself to the purchaser. Distinguishing "accidental" damage to the product from mere economic loss is difficult in many cases, such as a defect in a component of a television set that burns out the tubes, or an electric connection to the engine of a refrigerator that destroys the engine.

Notwithstanding these arguments, most courts have permitted plaintiff to recover for damage to the defective product itself on a strict tort theory, but have at the same time permitted disclaimer of such liability when such disclaimer is negotiated about and is set forth clearly and unambiguously.[15] So losses resulting from physical damage to property is treated differently from those resulting from personal injuries.

(4) *Physical harm to or destruction of a product that was constructed or repaired with the use of a target seller's component part.* Often, paint or other products and materials are purchased for use in the construction or repair of products that are to be assembled or are already assembled.[16] The use of the target seller's component part may cause substantial economic loss simply because it was not suitable for the use that was made of it. Even if this causes damage to the assembled product and other consequential damages, such liability as is imposed on the immediate or remote seller to the purchaser has ordinarily been based on warranty theories. The risk that a component part of the product is not suitable for use in the repair or assembly of another product is a risk that sophisticated parties (enterprisers) should be free to allocate by contract. If it is a risk that the parties should not be free to allocate, then the liability should be treated as tort liability.

11. Trans World Airlines v. Curtiss-Wright Corp., 1955, 1 Misc.2d 477, 148 N.Y.S.2d 284; Cloud v. Kit Manufacturing Co., Alaska 1977, 563 P.2d 248, 251.

12. See, Keeton, Annual Survey of Texas Law of Torts, 1979, 33 Sw.L.J. 1, 7–8, discussing Mid Continent Aircraft Corp. v. Curry County Spraying Service, Inc., Tex.1978, 572 S.W.2d 308.

13. U.C.C. Section 2–316.

14. 15 U.S.C.A. § 2308; Rothschild, The Magnuson-Moss Warranty Act: Does it Balance Warrantor and Consumer Interests?, 1976, 44 Geo.Wash.L.Rev. 335.

15. Seely v. White Motor Co., 1965, 63 Cal.2d 9, 45 Cal.Rptr. 17, 403 P.2d 145, 152; Russell v. Ford Motor Co., 1978, 281 Or. 587, 575 P.2d 1383 (if the product was defective in the kind of way that caused it to be dangerous to the person); Delta Airlines, Inc. v. McDonnell Douglas Corp., 5th Cir. 1974, 503 F.2d 239; Keystone Aeronautics Corp. v. R.J. Enstrom Corp., 3d Cir. 1974, 499 F.2d 146.

Contra: Mid Continent Aircraft Corp. v. Curry County Spraying Service, Inc., Tex.1978, 572 S.W.2d 308.

16. Catania v. Brown, 1967, 4 Conn.Cir. 344, 231 A.2d 668.

Dangerously Defective Products and Qualitatively Defective Products Distinguished

It is possible to draw a simple distinction between dangerously defective products and qualitatively defective products, and then to hold that the right to recover on tort theories of negligence and strict liability will apply to all kinds of losses suffered as a proximate consequence of the sale of a dangerously defective product. This would mean that if a dangerous defect was discovered before an accident occurs and is repaired by the purchaser, this economic loss would be recoverable on a strict liability in tort theory. There does not seem to be any support for this position.

WESTLAW REFERENCES

title(superwood & siempelkamp) & court(mn)

Physical Harm to or Destruction of a Product That Was Constructed or Repaired With The Use of a Target Seller's Component Part

component /p warrant! /p damage*

§ 102. Contributory Negligence, Misuse, and Other Intervening Misconduct

Often, negligent conduct or misuse of some kind or character of either an intermediate seller, a claimant, or a third person is, in combination with a product defect, a producing cause of a damaging event, such as a drug mishap, traffic accident, airline crash, or a workplace accident. If this conduct is that of a claimant or chargeable to a claimant, then it may constitute a defense that will either diminish or bar recovery.[1]

It is also generally agreed that just as negligence of a user must be a proximate cause of claimant's injury, so also product defect under strict liability must be a proximate cause of claimant's injury.[2] Therefore, virtually all courts have seemingly agreed that the conduct or misconduct of another, including an intermediate seller, the claimant, or anyone else, may be of such a nature or kind as to constitute a superseding cause.

It is quite helpful in understanding the law and predicting results to classify intervening conduct that can likely affect recovery of a claimant into four general categories.

The first is misconduct related to the use or maintenance of the defective product by the purchaser-user and those to whom the product is entrusted. This can be further broken down into four types: (a) negligent maintenance, including negligence in failing to follow instructions; (b) failure to discover a defect or to guard against the existence of a defect; (c) unreasonable or negligent use with knowledge of the condition that constitutes unreasonable danger and with appreciation of that danger to the extent necessary to indicate its unreasonableness; (d) misuse of the product, including negligent use, abnormal use in the sense of a use different in kind from what was intended, and unforeseeable misuse in the sense of a use that could not reasonably have been anticipated by the manufacturer.

The second is misconduct of an intermediate seller or supplier in the marketing chain. This can also be broken down into three kinds: (a) negligence in failing to inspect, discover and either correct or warn about a defect as can often be true in the sale of a motor vehicle by a dealer; (b) failure to follow instructions regarding the installation of a safety device that would have prevented

---

§ 102

1. For some general discussions of product liability defenses based on the claimant's misconduct, see Vargo, The Defenses to Strict Liability in Tort: A New Vocabulary With an Old Meaning, 1978, 29 Mercer L.Rev. 447; Noel, Defective Products: Abnormal Use, Contributory Negligence, and Assumption of the Risk, 1972, 25 Vand.L.Rev. 93; Epstein, Products Liability: Defenses Based on Plaintiff's Conduct, 1968 Utah L.Rev. 267; Twerski, The Use and Abuse of Compara- tive Negligence in Products Liability, 1977, 10 Ind.L.Rev. 797; Walkowiak, Reconsidering Plaintiff's Fault in Product Liability Litigation: The Proposed Conscious Design Choice Exception, 1981, 33 Vand.L.Rev. 651.

2. Winnett v. Winnett, 1974, 57 Ill.2d 7, 310 N.E.2d 1; LaGorga v. Kroger Co., W.D.Pa.1967, 275 F.Supp. 373, affirmed 3d Cir., 407 F.2d 671; Comstock v. General Motors Corp., 1959, 358 Mich. 163, 99 N.W.2d 627.

the defect in the product from causing the accident; and (c) failure to correct a defect upon request from the defendant seller as when a purchaser or dealer negligently fails to comply with a request of seller in a recall letter.

The third has to do with alteration of a product, either by (a) someone in the marketing chain, (b) the consumer-purchaser, or (c) a third person.

The fourth is misconduct unrelated to the defective product, such as when a truck driver negligently runs into a car not properly designed to guard against aggravation of injuries from accidents caused by others.

Proximate Cause and Strict Liability in Tort

There has always been considerable doubt and uncertainty about when intervening misconduct will constitute a superseding cause in any kind of a negligence case and the same is true with products liability. There is a tendency for courts to hold that intervening conduct or misconduct of a kind that is rare and unusual, and in that sense not reasonably foreseeable, will sever the chain of causation.[3] This is a debatable position unless the intervening conduct changes entirely the nature of the occurrence from the kind that one would reasonably anticipate from the nature of the defect that was proved. However, the majority American position seems to be that an unforeseeable misuse of a product that is a proximate cause of an accident (thereby concurring with product defect to cause it) is a superseding cause.[4] Sometimes in so holding, the court simply means by "unforeseeable" that which is "rare" and "unusual." But more often this is said to mean that the use must be one that a maker could not be expected to guard against in the designing of his product. So if the product was defective as designed for its ordinary and reasonably foreseeable uses or if defective because of a flaw in it, but a use was made of the product that the maker could not be expected to guard against, then the accident was not proximately caused by the product defect. Thus, the manufacturer of a power mower was held not liable when a seven-year-old boy was using the mower as a toy and a plaything even though the mower might have been defectively designed.[5] Likewise, any substantial alteration of a product that was not contemplated by the manufacturer is likely to sever the chain of causation.[6] Generally, when there has been an unforeseeable or uncontemplated alteration in a product or an unforeseeable misuse of a product, it is difficult to determine (1) whether there was ever a defect in the product when sold and (2) if so, whether the defect contributed to the damaging event. Thus, intervening conduct can be of such a nature as to foreclose the use of the litigation process for ascertaining product defect as a proximate cause of an occurrence.

Conduct of Claimant and Strict Liability in Tort

Strict liability in tort preceded the accelerated movement beginning about 1965 to eliminate contributory negligence as a complete bar to recovery on a negligence theory. The notion that contributory negligence of any kind or character should bar recovery

---

3. Wenzell v. MTD Products, Inc., 1978, 32 Ill.App. 3d 279, 336 N.E.2d 125 (4-year-old boy playing with a power mower); Eshbach v. W.T. Grant's & Co., 3d Cir. 1973, 481 F.2d 940.

4. Shell Oil Co. v. Gutierrez, App.1978, 119 Ariz. 426, 581 P.2d 271; Noonan v. Buick Co., Fla.App.1968, 211 So.2d 54; Drayton v. Jiffee Chemical Corp., N.D. Ohio, 1975, 395 F.Supp. 1081, motion denied 413 F.Supp. 834.

5. Wenzell v. MTD Products, Inc., 1978, 32 Ill.App. 3d 279, 336 N.E.2d 125 (4-year-old boy playing with a power mower).

6. Temple v. Wean United, Inc., 1977, 50 Ohio St. 317, 364 N.E.2d 267; Hanlon v. Cyril Bath Co., 3d Cir. 1975, 541 F.2d 343. Comment, Substantial Change: Alteration of a Product as a Ban to a Manufacturer's Strict Liability, 1976, 80 Dick.L.Rev. 245; Annot., 1972, 41 A.L.R.3d 1251. Second Restatement of Torts, § 402.A(1)(b), provides for liability only if the product "is expected to and does reach the user or consumer without substantial change in the condition in which it is sold."

against a manufacturer selling a defectively dangerous product was anathema to the judiciary creating this new and revolutionary tort action, and so both contributory negligence and voluntary assumption of the risk were abolished as defenses by most courts.[7] Perhaps if comparative negligence had preceded the development of strict liability, contributory negligence would have been recognized as a defense that would diminish recovery in proportion to the percentage of the plaintiff's fault. But courts were operating on the all-or-nothing doctrines of the common law. In most of those states that have not adopted a comprehensive comparative fault statute, in which the sale of a defective product is defined as fault, two very narrow defenses that bar recovery have been recognized. These are: (1) misuse that is of the kind that is not reasonably foreseeable,[8] and (2) voluntary and unreasonable (negligent) use with knowledge of the defective condition and appreciation of its danger.[9] Both are examples of what would be negligence of a special kind and indeed such intervening conduct as would perhaps constitute a superseding cause.[10]

In some states, defenses to claims for personal injuries and tangible property based on negligence or strict liability are the same.[11] This is gaining acceptance by way of adoption either by legislation or judicial decision of a comprehensive comparative fault system.[12] Such a comparative fault system has the following characteristics: fault is defined so as to include not only negligence but also the sale of a defectively dangerous product; second, voluntary assumption of the risk is abolished as a defense; third, contributory negligence is recognized as a defense that only diminishes recovery. This is not the place to discuss the nuances of the different issues that can be raised under such a system. It is enough to say here that some kind of a comparative fault system is likely to be regarded as the best and fairest way to allocate the costs of accidents between multiple parties whose tortious acts contribute to bringing about a damaging event.

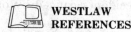
WESTLAW REFERENCES

313ak56

---

§ 103. Proof

Procedural rules relating to pleading and burden of proof as between litigants are rules that have the effect of allocating risks of losses between claimants and defendants just as surely as do rules of substantive law. The nature and quality of the evidence needed as proof by the plaintiff to recover against a target defendant for an injury or an illness attributable to a defectively dangerous condition of a product are therefore of considerable significance. In general and on the basis of what has been said heretofore, the plaintiff, in order to recover against a target defendant, has the burden of introducing some evidence which, if be-

---

7. McCown v. International Harvester Co., 1975, 463 Pa. 13, 342 A.2d 381; Cepeda v. Cumberland Engineering Co., 1978, 76 N.J. 152, 386 A.2d 816; Findlay v. Copeland Lumber Co., 1973, 265 Or. 300, 509 P.2d 28; Annot., 1972, 46 A.L.R.3d 240.

8. Singer v. Walker, 1972, 39 A.D.2d 90, 331 N.Y.S.2d 823, affirmed 32 N.Y.2d 786, 345 N.Y.S.2d 542, 298 N.E.2d 681; McDevitt v. Standard Oil Co., 5th Cir. 1968, 391 F.2d 364.

9. Johnson v. Clark Equipment Co., 1976, 274 Or. 403, 547 P.2d 132; Messick v. General Motors Corp., 5th Cir. 1972, 460 F.2d 485 (an erroneous prediction of Texas law); see Comment n to § 402A, Second Restatement of Torts.

10. See comments on Proximate Cause, this section, supra.

11. See Casrell v. Altec Industries, Inc., Ala.1976, 335 So.2d 128, 134; Annot., 46 A.L.R.3d 240.

12. Daly v. General Motors Corp., 1978, 20 Cal.3d 725, 144 Cal.Rptr. 380, 575 P.2d 1162; Busch v. Busch Construction, Inc., Minn.1977, 262 N.W.2d 377; Twerski, The Use and Abuse of Comparative Negligence in Products Liablity, 1977, 10 Ind.L.Rev. 797, 819–823; Fischer, Products Liability—Applicability of Comparative Negligence, 1978, 43 Mo.L.Rev. 431; Wade, Products Liability and Plaintiff's Fault—The Uniform Comparative Fault Act, 1978, 29 Mercer L.Rev. 373; Schwartz, Strict Liability and Comparative Negligence, 1974, 42 Tenn.L.Rev. 171.

lieved, would justify a reasonable person in concluding that it was more likely than not that: (1) claimant's injury or illness was attributable to a dangerous condition of a product identified as being one that was supplied by the target defendant, either as a manufacturer or some other seller or supplier in the marketing chain; (2) the product was defectively dangerous at the time of the damaging event out of which the claimant's injury or illness arose; (3) the defective condition was a cause of the damaging event; (4) the defective condition was in existence at the time possession was surrendered by the defendant; and (5) the defective condition was a proximate or legal cause of the damaging event.

It is quite important to note that the claimant is relieved of the necessity for proving that the target defendant was negligent in selling the product in a defective and unreasonably dangerous condition. It is enough that the product was defective in the kind of way that constitutes either a breach of a warranty or makes the product "unreasonably dangerous" pursuant to the theory of strict liability in tort.

Identification of the Defendant as a Supplier of the Defective Product

It is quite clear that an essential element of the plaintiff's case has been the identification of the named defendant as the manufacturer or supplier of the defective product.[1] Most of the cases on this point have involved beverage manufacturers.[2] In recent years, some courts have held that policy considerations as to who should bear the risk of loss when the precise manufacturer cannot be identified justifies allocating the risk of loss to two or more or even a large group of manufacturers, anyone of whom could have been the manufacturer, as when each one of a group of manufacturers makes and sells an identical type product, such as a generic drug.[3] The problem was catapulted into prominence as a consequence of a large number of claims in two separate and distinct general situations: (1) claims based on the notion that a drug commonly referred to as DES has caused a type of cervical or vaginal cancer in the daughters of mothers who were treated with the drug to prevent miscarriages,[4] and (2) claims that have been made nationwide during the last decade by insulation workers who acquired fatal lung cancer and other lung disorders against defendants who made and sold insulation products containing varying amounts of asbestos.[5]

An alternative liability theory has been applied in a few product liability cases, other than the DES and asbestos cases.[6] These have been cases where the product was identified and plaintiff could show a type of accident attributable either to negligent use or product defect, but could not identify the responsible tortious actor. Probably the most notable is the New Jersey case of Anderson v. Somberg[7] where the plaintiff suffered injury in the course of a back operation when a surgical instrument broke off and lodged

§ 103

1. Drayton v. Jiffee Chemical Corp., N.D.Ohio, 1975, 395 F.Supp. 1081, motion denied 413 F.Supp. 834.

2. Baker v. Coca-Cola Bottling Works, 1961, 132 Ind.App. 390, 177 N.E.2d 759; Smith v. Ariens Co., 1978, 375 Mass. 620, 377 N.E.2d 954. See generally, Annot., 1973, 51 A.L.R.3d 1344.

3. Sindell v. Abbott Laboratories, 1980, 26 Cal.3d 588, 163 Cal.Rptr. 132, 607 P.2d 924, certiorari denied, 449 U.S. 912, 101 S.Ct. 286, 66 L.Ed.2d 140.

4. Greenwald, Barlow, Nesca & Burnett, Vaginal Cancer After Maternal Treatment With Synthetic Estrogen, 1971, 285 New Eng.J.Med. 390; Comment, DES and a Proposed Theory of Enterprise Liability, 1978, 46 Fordham L.Rev. 963.

5. See, Note, Compensating Victims of Occupational Disease, 1980, 93 Harv.L.Rev. 916.

6. Snider v. Bob Thibedeau Ford, Inc., 1972, 42 Mich.App. 708, 202 N.W.2d 727; Anderson v. Somberg, 1973, 134 N.J.Super. 1, 338 A.2d 35, affirmed, 1975, 67 N.J. 291, 338 A.2d 1, certiorari denied 423 U.S. 929, 96 S.Ct. 279, 46 L.Ed.2d 258, appeal after remand 158 N.J. Super. 384, 386 A.2d 413; Nichols v. Nold, 1953, 174 Kan. 613, 258 P.2d 317; Loch v. Confair, 1953, 372 Pa. 212, 93 A.2d 451.

7. 1975, 67 N.J. 291, 338 A.2d 1, certiorari denied 423 U.S. 929, 96 S.Ct. 279, 46 L.Ed.2d 258, appeal after remand 158 N.J.Super. 384, 386 A.2d 413.

in her spine. Several defendants were held liable. The court held that a surgeon who used the needle, the hospital that supplied the needle after several previous uses, and the manufacturer of the needle could each be held liable for the entire amount of damages, *in the absence of exculpatory evidence by a particular defendant*.[8] Under the alternative liability theory, the burden of proof is shifted to each defendant to show either the responsible source or that he was not a legally responsible source of the damaging event. But the alternative liability theory has only been successfully used against those in the marketing chain or users who have had some identification with a specific product that was identified; and the defendant who was responsible for the defect was not identified.

The case that has attracted the most attention and which adopted a slight variation of the alternative liability doctrine is Sindell v. Abbott Laboratories.[9] The Supreme Court of California adopted what has been commonly referred to as *enterprise and market share liability*. The court imposed liability on each of eleven drug makers of DES that were joined in the lawsuit for a proportionate share of a particular victim's damage for cancer attributable to DES. The requirements for market-share liability seem to be: (1) injury or illness occasioned by a fungible product (identical-type product) made by all of the defendants joined in the lawsuit; (2) injury or illness due to a design hazard, with each having been found to have sold the same type product in a manner that made it unreasonably dangerous; (3) inability to identify the specific manufacturer of the product or products that brought about the plaintiff's injury or illness; and (4) joinder of enough of the manufacturers of the fungible or identical product to represent a substantial share of the market.

There are several important points to make about market-share liability. First, while there is some ambiguity about the *Sindell* opinion, it can be implied that the court did not intend to provide for joint and several liability, but each defendant is liable for the proportion of plaintiff's damage equal to the defendant's proportionate market share; second, the application of the principle depends upon the joinder of enough defendants to represent a substantial share of the market; third, the substantial share requirement exists so that more likely than not the culpable party is one of the defendants and will not escape all responsibility, and, therefore, substantial share ought to mean more than 50% of the market; fourth, there are difficulties in defining and ascertaining appropriate market as to time, purpose, and geography; fifth, applying such a doctrine usually means applying it to cases long after the "injury-causing or illness-causing" exposure and this means that there is no way to ascertain if the cause for the "illness or injury" was attributable to a flaw or to a design and the court simply assumes that since the product is the kind that is intended to be identical, all units of all makers will be identical; sixth, it can reasonably be argued that it would not be appropriate to apply this fungible product concept to asbestos-containing products because they are by no means identical since they contain widely varying amounts of asbestos.

Proof That Defendant Sold a Defective Product and That the Defect Caused the Damaging Event

The development of strict liability and the removal of certain restrictions to recovery on a warranty theory substantially eased the plaintiff's burden of proof. The problems related to proving that the defendant sold a product that was defective because of the evidence of a flaw is discussed heretofore in Section 99. The problems related to the proof of design defects differ considerably from those relating to construction flaws

---

8. Id. at 4.

9. Sindell v. Abbott Laboratories, 1980, 26 Cal.3d 588, 163 Cal.Rptr. 132, 607 P.2d 924, certiorari denied, 449 U.S. 912, 101 S.Ct. 286, 66 L.Ed.2d 140.

and can be affected by the standard or standards utilized for ascertaining when a hazard related to the way a product is designed justifies a finding that the product is defectively dangerous and the basis for strict liability, either in tort or for breach of warranty. Types of proof that have been utilized in proving that the danger-in-fact outweighs the utility, as that standard has been explained in Section 99, include the following: (a) post-accident changes in design; [10] (b) similar accidents due to like failures of products designed in like manner; [11] (c) recall letters, or letters to purchasers urging purchasers to bring in product for the purpose of altering the design; [12] (d) trade and industrial association design and warning safety standards violated; [13] (e) governmental design and warning safety standards, state or federal, violated; [14] (f) expert evidence, especially opinion evidence, relating to (1) the cause for an occurrence, and (2) the technological possibility and feasibility of an alternative way to design the product without so much danger.[15]

The rules regarding the effect and admissibility of different types of evidence can be quite different in a state court and that of a federal court sitting in the same state. Moreover, the rules can vary appreciably from state to state. This is an important subject which must be left for detailed treatment elsewhere. But it must be observed that expert testimony as regards design matters is often of crucial importance and sometimes is absolutely necessary. Courts traditionally prohibited experts, as well as other witnesses, from usurping the function of the jury by giving opinions on the ultimate fact at issue, which, in this case, would be the unreasonably dangerous condition of a product. For various reasons, in recent years the rule has been breaking down, and under one of the federal rules of evidence testimony of an expert in the form of an opinion or inference otherwise admissible is not necessarily objectionable because it embraces an ultimate issue.[16]

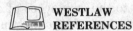
WESTLAW REFERENCES

des /p vaginal cervical /p cancer
sindell /2 abbott & 607 +s 924

§ 104. Other Suppliers

Bailors

As to defendants other than sellers, who supply chattels under contract, there has been much the same development in the law of negligence as in the case of sellers. The lessor of an automobile, or any other bailor for hire, is liable to a guest in the vehicle, or a person run down by it on the highway, not only if he knows that the car is dangerously defective at the time he turns it over,[1] or

---

10. Ault v. International Harvester Co., 1974, 13 Cal.3d 113, 117 Cal.Rptr. 812, 528 P.2d 1148; Chart v. General Motors Corp., Wis.1977, 80 Wis.2d 91, 258 N.W.2d 680; Good v. A.B. Chance Co., 1977, 39 Colo. App. 70, 565 P.2d 217. Contra: Phillips v. J.L. Hudson Co., 1977, 79 Mich.App. 425, 263 N.W.2d 3; Haysom v. Coleman Lantern Co., Inc., 1978, 89 Wn.2d 474, 573 P.2d 785, 791; Ortho Pharmaceutical Corp. v. Chapman, 1979, 180 Ind.App. 33, 388 N.E.2d 541, 562.

11. Warshaw v. Rockresorts, Inc., 1977, 57 Hawaii 645, 562 P.2d 428; Ginnis v. Mapes Hotel Corp., 1970, 86 Nev. 408, 470 P.2d 135.

12. See, generally, Ramp, The Impact of Recall Campaigns on Products Liability, 1977, 44 Ins.C.J. 83; Annot., 1978, 84 A.L.R.3d 1220.

13. Nordstrom v. White Metal Rolling & Stamping Corp., 1969, 75 Wn.2d 629, 453 P.2d 619; McComish v. DeSoi, 1964, 42 N.J. 274, 200 A.2d 116; Annot., 1974, 58 A.L.R.3d 148.

14. Pyatt v. Engel Equipment, Inc., 1974, 17 Ill. App.3d 1070, 309 N.E.2d 225.

15. Philo and Atkinson, Products Liability: The Expert Witness, Nov., 1978, 14 Trial 11, p. 36.

16. Fed.R.Evid. 704; Opinion on Ultimate Issue: "Testimony in the form of an opinion or inference otherwise admissible is not objectionable because it embraces an ultimate issue to be decided by the trier of fact."

§ 104

1. Broome v. Budget Rent-A-Car of Jax, Inc., Fla. App.1966, 182 So.2d 26; Lynch v. Richardson, 1895, 163 Mass. 160, 39 N.E. 801; Trusty v. Patterson, 1930, 299 Pa. 469, 149 A. 717; Ferraro v. Taylor, 1936, 197 Minn. 5, 265 N.W. 829. Cf. Bryson v. Hines, 4th Cir. 1920, 268 F. 290.

that the person entrusted with it is incompetent to handle it,² but also if he merely fails to make reasonable inspection to discover possible defects before turning it over.³ The same responsibility has been imposed upon a caterer serving food to the plaintiff under contract with another,⁴ and upon a shipper of goods where a servant of the carrier or the consignee is injured while unloading a defective vehicle which the shipper has furnished for transportation.⁵ Although there are old cases to the contrary,⁶ the modern view is definitely that the obligation of a railway company to make reasonable inspection and repair of its cars before supplying them extends to the employees of a shipper,⁷ of a consignee,⁸ and of a connecting carrier.⁹ In such a case, however, it has been held that the responsibility does not extend beyond the use of the car in accordance with the original contract, and that a reconsignment by a connecting carrier terminates the liability.¹⁰ A similar duty of reasonable care has been imposed upon owners of premises ¹¹ and contractors ¹² who supply chattels for use by employees of others in connection with work to be done under a contract. The conclusion seems to be that any person furnishing a chattel for a use in which he has a business interest may be liable for his negligence to anyone who may reasonably be expected to be in the vicinity of its probable use.¹³

Occasionally in such cases it has been held that the duty of the person supplied to inspect the chattel himself relieves the supplier of liability, because there is "superseding negligence." ¹⁴ But as in the case of a seller, most courts have held that his failure to make such inspection is within the foreseeable risk, and does not excuse the supplier.¹⁵ When the defect is disclosed to the one sup-

2. See infra, p. 717.

3. Hinson v. Phoenix Pie Co., 1966, 3 Ariz.App. 523, 416 P.2d 202; Ikeda v. Okada Trucking Co., 1964, 47 Haw. 588, 393 P.2d 171; Austin v. Austin, 1960, 252 N.C. 283, 113 S.E.2d 553; Scharf v. Gardner Cartage Co., 1953, 95 Ohio App. 153, 113 N.E.2d 717; Mitchell v. Lonergan, 1934, 285 Mass. 266, 189 N.E. 39.

4. Bishop v. Weber, 1885, 139 Mass. 411, 1 N.E. 154. Cf. Hayes v. Torrington Water Co., 1914, 88 Conn. 609, 92 A. 406 (water supplied under contract with city).

5. Elliott v. Hall, 1885, 15 Q.B.D. 315; Standard Oil Co. v. Wakefield's Administrator, 1904, 102 Va. 824, 47 S.E. 830; Gaston v. Wabash Railroad Co., Mo.1959, 322 S.W.2d 865; Fouraker v. Hill & Morton, 1958, 162 Cal. App.2d 668, 328 P.2d 527; Yandell v. National Fireproofing Corp., 1953, 239 N.C. 1, 79 S.E.2d 223. See Note, 1966, 54 Geo.L.J. 1439.

6. Roddy v. Missouri Pacific Railway Co., 1891, 104 Mo. 234, 15 S.W. 1112; Missouri, Kansas & Texas Railway Co. v. Merrill, 1902, 65 Kan. 436, 70 P. 358; Glynn v. Central Railroad Co. of New Jersey, 1900, 175 Mass. 510, 56 N.E. 698.

7. Chicago, Rock Island & Pacific Railway Co. v. Williams, 8th Cir. 1957, 245 F.2d 397, certiorari denied 355 U.S. 855, 78 S.Ct. 83, 2 L.Ed.2d 63; Bierzynski v. New York Central Railroad Co., 1969, 31 App.Div.2d 294, 297 N.Y.S.2d 457, on remand 59 Misc.2d 315, 298 N.Y.S.2d 584; Missouri Pacific Railway Co. v. Burks, 1939, 199 Ark. 189, 133 S.W.2d 9; Peneff v. Duluth, Missabe & Northern Railway Co., 1925, 164 Minn. 6, 204 N.W. 524; Chicago, Indianapolis & Louisville Railway v. Pritchard, 1906, 168 Ind. 398, 81 N.E. 78.

8. D'Almeida v. Boston & Maine Railroad Co., 1911, 209 Mass. 81, 95 N.E. 398; Wabash Railroad Co. v. Hartog, 8th Cir. 1958, 257 F.2d 401; Brehmer v. Chicago & Northwestern Railway Co., 1955, 269 Wis. 383, 69 N.W.2d 565; Erie Railroad Co. v. Murphy, 6th Cir. 1940, 108 F.2d 817, 126 A.L.R. 1093; Chicago, Rock Island & Pacific Railway Co. v. Sampson, 1940, 200 Ark. 906, 142 S.W.2d 221.

9. Moon v. Northern Pacific Railway Co., 1891, 46 Minn. 106, 48 N.W. 679; Pennsylvania Railroad Co. v. Snyder, 1896, 55 Ohio St. 342, 45 N.E. 559.

10. Sawyer v. Minneapolis & St. Louis Railroad Co., 1888, 38 Minn. 103, 35 N.W. 671; Demers v. Illinois Central Railroad Co., 1959, 339 Mass. 247, 158 N.E.2d 672; cf. Caledonian R. Co. v. Mulholland, [1898] A.C. 216.

11. Heaven v. Pender, 1883, 11 Q.B.D. 503; Coughtry v. Globe Woolen Co., 1874, 56 N.Y. 124; Johnson v. Spear, 1889, 76 Mich. 139, 42 N.W. 1092; The Student, 4th Cir. 1917, 156 C.C.A. 319, 243 F. 807, certiorari denied 245 U.S. 658, 38 S.Ct. 14, 62 L.Ed. 534.

12. See infra, p. 722.

13. Second Restatement of Torts, § 392. See for example Perfection Paint & Color Co. v. Kouduris, 1970, 147 Ind.App. 106, 258 N.E.2d 681.

14. Risque's Administrator v. Chesapeake & Ohio Railway Co., 1905, 104 Va. 476, 51 S.E. 730; Louisville & Nashville Railroad Co. v. Weldon, 1915, 165 Ky. 654, 177 S.W. 459; Missouri, Kansas & Texas Railway Co. v. Merrill, 1902, 65 Kan. 436, 70 P. 358.

15. Gaston v. Wabash Railroad Co., Mo.1959, 322 S.W.2d 865; Yandell v. National Fireproofing Corp., 1953, 239 N.C. 1, 79 S.E.2d 223; D'Almeida v. Boston & Maine Railroad Co., 1911, 209 Mass. 81, 95 N.E. 398; Chicago, Indianapolis & Louisville Railway Co. v. Pritchard, 1906, 168 Ind. 398, 81 N.E. 78; Peneff v. Du-

plied, or is in fact discovered by him, the supplier usually is relieved of responsibility;[16] but in a few cases of extreme danger, as where an automobile unfit to be driven on the highway is delivered to one who may be expected to use it nevertheless, the supplier has been held liable to a third person notwithstanding such discovery.[17]

The cases which have dealt with gratuitous lenders and bailors have held that there is no greater obligation toward a third person than to the immediate bailee. The bailor is therefore under no duty to inspect the chattel before delivering it,[18] and the bailee assumes the full responsibility for its condition. There is liability only for a failure to disclose defects of which the bailor has knowledge which may render it dangerous to others.[19] In all such cases, however, the bailor may be liable if he entrusts the chattel to a person whom he knows or should know[20] to be incompetent to use it safely. Thus even a gratuitous lender of an automobile may be liable to one who is struck on the highway through the negligence of an inexperienced,[21] unlicensed,[22] immature,[23] intoxicated[24] or habitually careless[25] driver, if

luth, Missabe & Northern Railway Co., 1925, 164 Minn. 6, 204 N.W. 524; Second Restatement of Torts, § 393.

16. American Mutual Liability Insurance Co. of Boston v. Chain Belt Co., 1937, 224 Wis. 155, 271 N.W. 828; McCallion v. Missouri Pacific Railway Co., 1906, 74 Kan. 785, 88 P. 50; Dominices v. Monongahela Connecting Railroad Co., 1937, 328 Pa. 203, 195 A. 747; Moore v. Ellis, Tex.Civ.App.1964, 385 S.W.2d 261, reversed 401 S.W.2d 789.

17. Trusty v. Patterson, 1930, 299 Pa. 469, 149 A. 717; Ferraro v. Taylor, 1936, 197 Minn. 5, 265 N.W. 829; Mitchell v. Lonergan, 1934, 285 Mass. 266, 189 N.E. 39.

18. Johnson v. H.M. Bullard Co., 1920, 95 Conn. 251, 111 A. 70; Hill v. Lyons Plumbing & Heating Co., Ky.1970, 457 S.W.2d 503; Davis v. Sanderman, 1938, 225 Iowa 1001, 282 N.W. 717; Ruth v. Hutchinson Gas Co., 1941, 209 Minn. 248, 296 N.W. 136; Nelson v. Fruehauf Trailer Co., 1952, 20 N.J.Super. 445, 89 A.2d 445, affirmed 1953, 11 N.J. 413, 94 A.2d 655.

Since the bailee may reasonably assume in many cases that the chattel is in good condition, this may leave the plaintiff with no remedy. Where the bailor knows that an automobile will be driven without inspection, it seems reasonable to impose the duty. See Kaplan v. Stein, 1951, 198 Md. 414, 84 A.2d 81; Marsh, The Liability of the Gratuitous Transferor; A Comparative Study, 1950, 66 L.Q.Rev. 39; Note, 1944, 48 Dick. L.Rev. 103.

19. See cases cited in note 55. Also Russell Construction Co. v. Ponder, 1945, 143 Tex. 412, 186 S.W.2d 233; Sturtevant v. Pagel, 1939, 134 Tex. 46, 130 S.W.2d 1017; Clancy v. R. O'Brien & Co., 1963, 345 Mass. 772, 187 N.E.2d 865; Pereza v. Mark, 2d Cir. 1970, 423 F.2d 149, and cf. Pease v. Sinclair Refining Co., 2d Cir. 1939, 104 F.2d 183.

There is, however, no duty to warn the bailee of an obvious condition. Villanueva v. Nowlin, 1966, 77 N.M. 174, 420 P.2d 764.

20. See Saunders Drive-It-Yourself Co. v. Walker, 1926, 215 Ky. 267, 284 S.W. 1088; White v. Holmes, 1925, 89 Fla. 251, 103 So. 623; Neubrand v. Kraft, 1915, 169 Iowa 444, 151 N.W. 455; Restatement of Torts, § 390; see Note, 1927, 13 Va.L.Rev. 564. Cf. Green v. Hatcher, 1958, 236 Miss. 830, 105 So.2d 624 (garage for repairs).

21. Lorts v. McDonald, 1958, 17 Ill.App.2d 278, 149 N.E.2d 768; Harris v. Smith, 1969, 119 Ga.App. 306, 167 S.E.2d 198; Rounds v. Phillips, 1933, 166 Md. 151, 170 A. 532, second appeal 1935, 168 Md. 120, 177 A. 174; Hopkins v. Droppers, 1924, 184 Wis. 400, 198 N.W. 738; Elliott v. Harding, 1923, 107 Ohio St. 501, 140 N.E. 338. See Woods, Negligent Entrustment, 1966, 20 Ark.L.Rev. 101; Notes, 1963, 30 Tenn.L.Rev. 658; 1967, 19 Bay.L.Rev. 75.

Cf. Syah v. Johnson, 1966, 247 Cal.App.2d 534, 55 Cal.Rptr. 741 (epileptic).

22. This was held conclusive as to incompetence in Gordon v. Bedard, 1929, 265 Mass. 408, 164 N.E. 374; Roark v. Stone, 1930, 224 Mo.App. 554, 30 S.W.2d 647; Wery v. Seff, 1940, 136 Ohio St. 307, 25 N.E.2d 692. In Canzoneri v. Hickert, 1936, 223 Wis. 25, 269 N.W. 716, it was held merely to create a presumption. Cf. Toole v. Morris-Webb Motor Co., La.App.1938, 180 So. 431 (entrusting license plates).

23. La Faso v. La Faso, 1966, 126 Vt. 90, 223 A.2d 814; McBerry v. Ivie, 1967, 116 Ga.App. 808, 159 S.E.2d 108; Miles v. Harrison, 1967, 115 Ga.App. 143, 154 S.E.2d 377, reversed on other grounds 223 Ga. 352, 155 S.E.2d 6, conformed to 115 Ga.App. 821, 155 S.E.2d 864.

24. Deck v. Sherlock, 1956, 162 Neb. 86, 75 N.W.2d 99; Harrison v. Carroll, 4th Cir. 1943, 139 F.2d 427; Pennington v. Davis-Child Motor Co., 1936, 143 Kan. 753, 57 P.2d 428; Owensboro Undertaking & Livery Association v. Henderson, 1938, 273 Ky. 112, 115 S.W.2d 563; Alspach v. McLaughlin, 1969, 144 Ind. App. 592, 247 N.E.2d 840.

Or one who may reasonably be expected to become intoxicated. Powell v. Langford, 1941, 58 Ariz. 281, 119 P.2d 230 (dipsomaniac); State of Maryland for Use of Weaver v. O'Brien, D.C.Md.1956, 140 F.Supp. 306 (history of drinking); Mitchell v. Churches, 1922, 119 Wash. 547, 206 P. 6 (declared intention); Crowell v. Duncan, 1926, 145 Va. 489, 134 S.E. 576.

25. Frasier v. Pierce, Tex.Civ.App.1965, 398 S.W.2d 955, refused n.r.e.; Fogo v. Steele, 1956, 180 Kan. 326, 304 P.2d 451; Dinkins v. Booe, 1960, 252 N.C. 731, 114

such characteristics were apparent when the car was turned over.

There are cases,[26] such as the one in Kentucky [27] in which a fond mother gave an automobile to her son knowing that he was an alcoholic and a drug addict, which have held that the donor in such a case is not liable to an injured third person, on the ground that the passage of title makes all the difference. Such decisions have been severely criticized,[28] and look definitely wrong. Even a seller who delivers a dangerous thing to one whom he should know to be unfit to handle it has been held liable for the harm which results to others—as where, for example, a gun is sold to a child,[29] or an automobile to a known incompetent driver.[30] There are by now a good many cases of so-called "common law dramshop" liability, in which a seller has been held liable to third parties for the sale of intoxicating liquor to a minor,[31] or to an intoxicated person.[32] It is the negligent entrusting which creates the unreasonable risk; and this is none the less when the goods are conveyed. There are decisions the other way, which appear to be preferred.[33]

The primary difference between a conventional sale and a conventional bailment is that in the case of a sale the seller transmits the product to the purchaser for the purchaser's use and enjoyment without retaining a reversionary interest and with no expectation of return except for failure to pay, whereas in a bailment the possessor of the product is transmitted to the bailee for the bailee's use and enjoyment and for some fraction of its useful life, but with the expectation of receiving it back.[34] The courts often refer to the bailment transaction as a lease or rental contract. Those who are in the business of renting products, such as automobiles, trucks, and the like, are often in an even more critical position than a retailer for affecting in a substantial way the incidence of harm from damaging events due to defectively dangerous defects in products rental. The policy arguments in support of strict liability—accidental prevention, enterprise risk-shifting capacity and difficulties of proving negligence—have especial relevance to the rental agency. It is not surprising that New Jersey in 1965 in the case of Cintrone v. Hertz Truck Leasing & Rental Service [35] subjected the truck rental agency defendant to strict liability for physical harm to an employee of the bailee for hire. This was the first case, and while warranty lan-

---

S.E.2d 672; Chaney v. Duncan, 1937, 194 Ark. 1076, 110 S.W.2d 21; Tyree v. Tudor, 1922, 183 N.C. 340, 111 S.E. 714. Cf. Roberts v. Williams, N.D.Miss.1969, 302 F.Supp. 972, affirmed in part, remanded in part 5th Cir., 456 F.2d 819, certiorari denied 404 U.S. 866, 92 S.Ct. 83, 30 L.Ed.2d 110 (shotgun entrusted to prisoner known to be violent).

26. Brown v. Harkleroad, 1955, 39 Tenn.App. 657, 287 S.W.2d 92 (gift of car to son known to be reckless, incompetent and drinking driver); Shipp v. Davis, 1932, 25 Ala.App. 104, 141 So. 366 (drinking). Cf. Rush v. Smitherman, Tex.Civ.App.1956, 294 S.W.2d 873, error refused (sale of car to unlicensed driver); Smith's Administrator v. Corder, Ky.1956, 286 S.W.2d 512 (gun entrusted to known heavy drinker with violent disposition).

27. Estes v. Gibson, Ky.1953, 257 S.W.2d 604 (4–3 decision).

28. See Notes, 1954, 32 Chicago-Kent L.Rev. 479; 1954, 43 Ky.L.J. 178; 1954, 2 Kan.L.Rev. 311; 1953, 33 Bos.U.L.Rev. 538; 1954, 29 N.Y.U.L.Rev. 530.

29. Anderson v. Settergren, 1907, 100 Minn. 294, 111 N.W. 279; Semeniuk v. Chentis, 1954, 1 Ill.App.2d 508, 117 N.E.2d 883. Cf. Neff Lumber Co. v. First National Bank, 1930, 122 Ohio St. 302, 171 N.E. 327; Stone v. Shaw Supply Co., 1934, 148 Or. 416, 36 P.2d 606; Bosserman v. Smith, 1920, 205 Mo.App. 657, 226 S.W. 608.

30. Johnson v. Casetta, 1961, 197 Cal.App.2d 272, 17 Cal.Rptr. 81.

31. Elder v. Fisher, 1966, 247 Ind. 598, 217 N.E.2d 847; Rappaport v. Nichols, 1959, 31 N.J. 188, 156 A.2d 1.

32. Jardine v. Upper Darby Lodge Co. 1964, 413 Pa. 626, 198 A.2d 550; Galvin v. Jennings, 3d Cir. 1961, 289 F.2d 15; Berkeley v. Park, 1965, 47 Misc.2d 381, 262 N.Y.S.2d 290; Adamian v. Three Sons, Inc., 1968, 353 Mass. 498, 233 N.E.2d 18; Colligan v. Cousar, 1963, 38 Ill.App.2d 392, 187 N.E.2d 292. See Cahn, New Common Law Dramshop Rule, 1960, 9 Cleve.Marsh.L.Rev. 302; Note, 1966, 18 West.Res.L.Rev. 251.

33. Liability was found in Golembe v. Blumberg, 1941, 262 App.Div. 759, 27 N.Y.S.2d 692, where a father bought a car for his epileptic son. Also in Bugle v. McMahon, Sup.Ct.1942, 35 N.Y.S.2d 193, reversed 265 App.Div. 830, 37 N.Y.S.2d 540 (alcoholic).

34. On bailments, generally, see Annot. 1973, 48 A.L.R.3d 668.

35. 1965, 45 N.J. 434, 212 A.2d 769.

guage was used, it appears that the court meant to regard the liability as strict liability in tort. This would be the generally accepted view today because there is no visible reason for any distinction between those engaged in the business of renting and those engaged in the business of selling. Indeed, in one respect, some courts, including New Jersey, may conclude to apply a more exacting type of strict liability. In *Cintrone*, it was held that the rental agency would be subject to liability for physical harm arising out of any damaging event proximately caused by a defect coming into existence at any time during the lease period, if such defect was the result of ordinary wear and tear.[36] This is much more questionable, especially if the bailment term is a long-term one and the bailee agrees to maintain the bailed property. The longer the bailment, the more questionable is this holding.

Often, a seller who is primarily in the business of selling a type of product will, at least on some occasions, utilize the technique of renting a container or some other type of facility to the purchaser in order to sell and deliver the product. Thus, an oil company may supply a tank truck to an airline for refueling airplanes.[37] In such a case, the defendant is not in the business of renting a product; rather, the defendant is in the business of selling products and sometimes rents a product as an incident to the sale of the product. The volume of such rental transactions is not likely to be large and costs incurred as a result cannot be shifted simply to those making this type of purchasing transaction. However, this argument is not likely to be persuasive to most courts,[38] and the defect in the incidental container that is supplied as a necessary incident to the sale and delivery of a product will be treated in the same way as a defect in the product, such as bottled beverage, canned food, and the like.

License to Use

The bailment or rental transactions should not be identified with transactions involving a license to use something. There is a fundamental difference between a license to use something and a bailment. But there are different kinds of license to use transactions, even by those engaged in business. Some enterprisers are engaged in the very business of licensing the use of property on their premises and charging for that use. Such a transaction is very similar to that of a rental transaction. This would be the operator of a laundromat.[39] A quite different transaction is that which is involved when a customer is using a shopping cart as a convenience in a grocery store.[40] There is little, if any, difference between using a defective shopping cart and using a slippery floor. It may be that some time in the foreseeable future all enterprisers will be subject to strict liability for harm resulting from unreasonably dangerous conditions of things utilized by such enterprisers. Until such time, it would seem that strict liability should not be extended to one who licenses others to use something on his premises unless the defendant is in the business of providing the product to the public for such use.

Services

It is no longer in dispute that one who renders services to another is under a duty to exercise reasonable care in doing so, and that he is liable for any negligence to anyone who may foreseeably be expected to be injured as a result.[41] This applies in particu-

---

36. Id. at pp. 778–779.

37. Price v. Shell Oil Co., 1970, 2 Cal.3d 245, 466 P.2d 722.

38. Id. See, however, Freitas v. Twin City Fisherman's Cooperative Association, Tex.Civ.App.1970, 452 S.W.2d 931, refused n.r.e.

39. Garcia v. Halsett, 1970, 3 Cal.App.3d 319, 82 Cal.Rptr. 420.

40. Keen v. Dominick's Finer Foods, Inc., 1977, 49 Ill.App.3d 480, 7 Ill.Dec. 341, 364 N.E.2d 502; compare, Wagner v. Coronet Hotel, App.1969, 10 Ariz. 296, 458 P.2d 390 (plaintiff slipped on allegedly defective rubber shower mat supplied to hotel guest by defendant hotel).

41. See for example Kalinowski v. Truck Equipment Co., 1933, 237 App.Div. 472, 261 N.Y.S. 657; Zierer v. Daniels, 1956, 40 N.J.Super. 130, 122 A.2d 377;

lar to the testing of products, by those who do not supply them.[42]

Efforts to induce the courts to apply strict liability in tort to those engaged in rendering services have not entirely failed and the law is in a state of considerable uncertainty. Much of the difficulty relates to the fact that the typical activity of many enterprisers is one involving a sales-service hybrid transaction. There are three primary factors that courts have utilized in deciding whether or not to impose strict liability on the defendant who causes harm in the course of using a defective product. These are: (1) the nature of the defendant's activity; (2) whether the defective product was transmitted by the defendant in the course of rendering a service or only used; (3) whether the service of the defendant or the product transmitted was the principal thing bargained for.

Hospitals, medical doctors, and other professionals who provide health care services have not generally been held strictly liable even when, in the course of rendering health care services, defective products are transmitted.[43] They are not regarded as the kind of enterprisers, akin to the producer of mass products, that can conveniently bear the costs of accidents attributable to defective things used and transmitted. Moreover, the principal thing bargained for is not the product transmitted but the professional services of the defendant. It should be said that drawing the line between professional and nonprofessional services is not always easy and perhaps in the final analysis the real question is whether or not the service provider is the kind of enterpriser who ought in the public interest to be strictly accountable for harm resulting from the defects in things transmitted in the course of rendering services.

Those who are engaged in the business of repairing products generally have not been held subject to strict liability for harm resulting from defects attributable either to the repairing process or to defects in component parts used in the repair of products.[44] It should be observed that an injured party will often have extreme difficulty in proving whether or not product failure following a repair job was attributable to defect in a component part supplied or defect attributable to the repair process. For this reason, negligence will be difficult to prove against the repairman and this is a strong argument to support strict liability.

Again, the courts have not agreed about whether strict liability principles should be applied to installers.[45] An installer may be the seller who, as a part of the bargaining transaction, agrees to install the product sold, such as a water heater, stove, or heating system. On the other hand, an installer may be an independent contractor such as a plumber. A seller who also installs should, it would seem, be subject to strict liability for defects attributable to inadequate installation as well as defects in the product installed. But this means that those who buy products and have them installed by independent contractors, such as plumbers, elec-

---

Central & Southern Truck Lines v. Westfall G.M.C. Truck, Inc., Mo.App.1958, 317 S.W.2d 841.

42. Hanberry v. Hearst Corp., 1969, 276 Cal.App.2d 820, 81 Cal.Rptr. 519 (Good Housekeeping certification as to shoes); Hempstead v. General Fire Extinguisher Corp., D.C.Del.1967, 269 F.Supp. 109 (testing and prescribing standards for fire extinguishers); Buszta v. Souther, 1967, 102 R.I. 609, 232 A.2d 396 (motor vehicle inspection station).

43. Magrine v. Krasnica, 1967, 94 N.J.Super. 228, 227 A.2d 539, affirmed 53 N.J. 259, 250 A.2d 129, affirmed sub nominee, Magrine v. Spector, 1968, 100 N.J.Super. 223, 241 A.2d 637, affirmed 1969, 53 N.J. 259, 250 A.2d 129; Barbee v. Rogers, Tex.1968, 425 S.W.2d 342, noted in, 1969, 23 Sw.L.J. 1, 6–9.

44. Hoffman v. Simplot Aviation, Inc., 1975, 97 Idaho 32, 539 P.2d 584; Lemley v. J & B Tire Co., W.D.Pa. 1977, 426 F.Supp. 1378 ("Even in those hybrid sale-service transactions in which the seller is held subject to 402A that liability is limited to defects in the product supplied and does not include non-negligent mistakes in the service.").

45. Strict liability was adopted for installation defects in the O'Laughlin v. Minnesota Natural Gas Co., Minn.1977, 253 N.W.2d 826; Air Heaters, Inc. v. Johnson Electric, Inc., N.D.1977, 258 N.W.2d 649. Strict liability was not applied to installation defects in the following cases: Hoover v. Montgomery Ward & Co., 1974, 270 Or. 498, 528 P.2d 76; Samuelson v. Chutich, 1974, 187 Colo. 155, 529 P.2d 631.

tricians, and the like, are not getting the protection they would have if purchases were made from those who were also installing the products.

WESTLAW REFERENCES

common /3 law /p dramshop /p minor* drunk intoxicat!

§ 104A. Real Estate Transactions

Vendors

The liability for negligence of vendors and lessors of buildings and other real property has already been considered. Strict liability was late in making its appearance as to either, in large part because of the presence of a written deed or lease, which was considered to embody the entire agreement of the parties, and to exclude parol obligations. But in the case of the builder-vendor who sold his own product, the analogy of the manufacturer of chattels [1] finally began to prevail.[2]

Colorado led off [3] in 1964 with Carpenter v. Donohoe,[4] holding that the builder of a new house who sold it to an initial buyer was liable to him on implied warranties that the dwelling conformed to statutory requirements, and was built in a workmanlike manner and fit for habitation. This small beginning led to a sudden flood of decisions [5] finding similar warranties. While there are still courts that have held back,[6] the acceptance of the strict liability has been so rapid and extensive that it now appears that it is destined soon to become the prevailing rule. California has even applied it to the financer of the construction.[7] There is, however, as yet no case applying the strict liability to any vendor who has not constructed the building; and it appears unlikely that there will be one, for the reason that he is not engaged in the business of selling.

There is now a growing body of authority for applying strict liability in tort for physical harm to persons and tangible things to the sale of new homes by the housing merchant, especially those constructed by mass production developers, as was true in the landmark decision of Schipper v. Levitt & Sons, Inc.[8] There is more doubt about the custom builder who works on only two or three houses at a time. Such an enterpriser is not substantially different from the typical building contractor as regards capacity to shift costs of accidents due to defects in buildings. The mass producer is likely to be treated in like manner as the mass producer of automobiles, washing machines, and other products, and thus subject to liability for defectively dangerous conditions of structures attributable to flaws, design hazards, and dangerous conditions of installed products and materials.

§ 104A

1. See supra, § 97.

2. See Dunham, Vendor's Obligation as to Fitness of Land for a Particular Purpose, 1953, 37 Minn.L.Rev. 108; Haskell, Case for an Implied Warranty of Quality in Sales of Real Property, 1965, 53 Geo.L.J. 633; Bearman, Caveat Emptor in Sales of Realty, 1961, 14 Vand.L.Rev. 541; Notes, 1965, 26 U.Pitt.L.Rev. 862; 1967, 28 Ohio St.L.J. 343; 1967, 18 West.Res.L.Rev. 706; 1969, 48 Or.L.Rev. 411; 1969, 47 N.C.L.Rev. 989.

3. There had been prior decisions in Louisiana, based on a statute borrowed from the French Civil Code. For example, Foreman v. Jordan, La.App.1961, 131 So.2d 796; Glynn v. Delcuze, La.App.1963, 149 So. 2d 667.

4. 1964, 154 Colo. 78, 388 P.2d 399.

5. Bethlahmy v. Bechtel, 1966, 91 Idaho 55, 415 P.2d 698; Waggoner v. Midwestern Development, Inc., S.D.1967, 154 N.W.2d 803; Humber v. Morton, Tex. 1968, 426 S.W.2d 554; House v. Thornton, 1969, 76 Wn. 2d 428, 457 P.2d 199; Crawley v. Terhune, Ky.1969, 437 S.W.2d 743; Rothberg v. Olenik, 1970, 128 Vt. 295, 262 A.2d 461; Wawak v. Stewart, 1970, 247 Ark. 1093, 449 S.W.2d 922.

6. Mitchem v. Johnson, 1966, 7 Ohio St.2d 66, 218 N.E.2d 594; Dooley v. Berkner, 1966, 113 Ga.App. 162, 147 S.E.2d 685.

7. Connor v. Great Western Savings & Loan Association, 1968, 69 Cal.2d 850, 73 Cal.Rptr. 369, 447 P.2d 609, noted in 1969, 10 W. & M.L.Rev. 1000. Cf. Avner v. Longridge Estates, 1969, 272 Cal.App.2d 607, 77 Cal. Rptr. 633 (manufacturer of lot).

8. 1965, 44 N.J. 70, 207 A.2d 314.

Lessor Liability for Defects in Leased Premises

As stated in an earlier chapter,[9] the rule of caveat emptor, or more precisely "caveat lessee," dominated for centuries the contractual law of real estate lessees. The lease was regarded as primarily a conveyance of an interest in land and any covenants made by the parties were independent of each other. Some of the injustices of this situation was corrected by the general acceptance of the constructive eviction doctrine when leased premises became uninhabitable.[10] The tenant was entitled to vacate the premises and defend against an action for rent.

About twenty years ago, courts began to find a warranty of habitability in leases of *residential premises*.[11]

In many of these cases, relief by way of damages for breach of the warranty has been authorized.[12] There seems to be growing support for the position that the nature of a realty lease, especially a lease of residential premises and, even more especially, a lease of an apartment, is not sufficiently different from that of a personal property bailment to justify different rules of liability. Therefore, all the rules related to negligence, implied warranties, and strict liability in tort are likely to become applicable as against that kind of lessor or landlord who can be regarded as being engaged in the business of renting apartments and other structures as part of his business as a realtor.

The Building Contractor

The liability of building contractors,[13] engaged as they are in the construction of buildings and other structures pursuant to a contract, has tended to follow the general path of development as that related to the supplier of chattels pursuant to bargaining transactions, but to lag behind it by some twenty years. This was a field in which the ghost of Winterbottom v. Wright[14] died very hard. Initially it was held that, while the contractor would be liable for any injury resulting from his negligence before his work was completed,[15] his responsibility was terminated, and he was not liable to any third person once the structure was completed and accepted by the owner.[16]

As in the case of sellers of goods, the change which has occurred began with inroads upon the general rule with a long list of exceptions. The earliest to develop held the contractor liable for "something like fraud" if he turned the work over knowing that it was dangerously defective.[17] Some

---

9. See Chapter 10.

10. See, Love, Landlord's Liability for Defective Premises: Caveat Lessee, Negligence, or Strict Liability?, 1975 Wisc.L.Rev. 19, 34.

11. Pines v. Perssion, 1961, 14 Wis.2d 590, 111 N.W.2d 409; Reste Realty Corp. v. Cooper, 1969, 53 N.J. 444, 251 A.2d 268; see, also, Buckner v. Azulai, 1967, 251 Cal.App.2d Supp. 1013, 59 Cal.Rptr. 806; Lemle v. Breeden, 1969, 51 Hawaii 426, 462 P.2d 470; Javins v. First National Realty Corp., D.C.Cir. 1970, 428 F.2d 1071.

12. Kamarath v. Bennett, Tex.1978, 568 S.W.2d 658; Old Town Development Co. v. Langford, Ind.App.1976, 349 N.E.2d 744, set aside in *per curiam* opinion, Ind. 1977, 369 N.E.2d 404; Boston Housing Authority v. Hemingway, 1973, 363 Mass. 184, 293 N.E.2d 831; Kline v. Burns, 1971, 111 N.H. 87, 276 A.2d 248; Berzito v. Gambino, 1973, 63 N.J. 460, 308 A.2d 17.

13. See Tucker and Kuhn, The Decline of the Privity Rule in Tort Liability, 1950, 11 U.Pitts.L.Rev. 236; Eldredge, The Liability of Manufacturers and Contractors to Persons Not in Privity of Contract With Them, 1934, 6 Pa.Bar A.Q. 154, reprinted in Eldredge, Modern Tort Problems, 1941, 103; Notes, 1938, 22 Minn.L.Rev. 709; 1949, 24 Ind.L.J. 286; 1954, 14 Md.L.Rev. 77; 1956, 44 Geo.L.J. 534; 1957, 42 Corn.L.Q. 441; 1957, 4 St. Louis U.L.Rev. 344; 1958, 19 La.L.Rev. 221.

14. See supra, § 96.

15. Mann v. Leake & Nelson Co., 1945, 132 Conn. 251, 43 A.2d 161; S. Blickman, Inc. v. Chilton, Tex.Civ. App.1938, 114 S.W.2d 646; Bacak v. Hogya, 1950, 4 N.J. 417, 73 A.2d 167; Stiers v. Marshall, 1952, 207 Okl. 218, 248 P.2d 1047.

16. Curtin v. Somerset, 1891, 140 Pa. 70, 21 A. 244; Daugherty v. Herzog, 1896, 145 Ind. 255, 44 N.E. 457; Galbraith v. Illinois Steel Co., 7th Cir. 1904, 133 F. 485, certiorari denied 1906, 201 U.S. 643, 26 S.Ct. 759, 50 L.Ed. 902; Young v. Smith & Kelly Co., 1905, 124 Ga. 475, 52 S.E. 765; Ford v. Sturgis, 1926, 56 App.D.C. 361, 14 F.2d 253, 619.

17. Pennsylvania Steel Co. v. Elmore & Hamilton Contracting Co., D.N.Y.1909, 175 F. 176; O'Brien v. American Bridge Co., 1910, 110 Minn. 364, 125 N.W. 1012; Lechman v. Hooper, 1890, 52 N.J.L. 253, 19 A. 215; Ryan v. St. Louis Transit Co., 1905, 190 Mo. 621,

courts attempted to discover something resembling "privity" of contract in the fact that use by the individual plaintiff was intended or to be anticipated.[18] Still other cases relied on the analogy of the seller of goods, and found a duty to use care where the product of the work could be regarded as "inherently" or "imminently" dangerous.[19] Where there was an interference with the rights of the public,[20] or with the use or enjoyment of adjoining land,[21] the contractor was held liable for creating a nuisance; and where his misconduct could be found to go entirely beyond and outside of the contract, the question was treated as one of ordinary negligence liability.[22]

As in the case of the seller of chattels, the exceptions tended gradually to swallow up the prevailing rule, until the analogy of MacPherson v. Buick Motor Co.[23] was persuasive, and was finally accepted. It is now the almost universal rule that the contractor is liable to all those who may foreseeably be injured by the structure, not only when he fails to disclose dangerous conditions known to him,[24] but also when the work is negligently done.[25] This applies not only to contractors doing original work,[26] but also to those who make repairs,[27] or install parts,[28] as well as supervising architects and engineers.[29] There may be liability for negligent design,[30] as well as for negligent construction.

One important limitation recognized in several cases is that the contractor is not liable if he has merely carried out carefully the plans, specifications and directions given him, since in that case the responsibility is assumed by the employer, at least where the plans are not so obviously defective and dangerous that no reasonable man would follow

89 S.W. 865; Bryson v. Hines, 4th Cir. 1920, 268 F. 290; Bray v. Cross, 1958, 98 Ga.App. 612, 106 S.E.2d 315.

18. Grodstein v. McGivern, 1931, 303 Pa. 555, 154 A. 794; McGuire v. Dalton Co., La.App.1939, 191 So. 168; cf. Barabe v. Duhrkop Oven Co., 1919, 231 Mass. 466, 121 N.E. 415.

19. Holland Furnace Co. v. Nauracaj, 1938, 105 Ind. App. 574, 14 N.E.2d 339; McCloud v. Leavitt Corp., E.D.Ill.1948, 79 F.Supp. 286; Johnston v. Long, 1943, 56 Cal.App.2d 834, 133 P.2d 409; Foley v. Pittsburgh-Des Moines Co., 1949, 363 Pa. 1, 68 A.2d 517; Cox v. Ray M. Lee Co., 1959, 100 Ga.App. 333, 111 S.E.2d 246, followed 1959, 100 Ga.App. 340, 111 S.E.2d 251.

20. Schumacher v. Carl G. Neumann Dredging & Imp. Co., 1931, 206 Wis. 220, 239 N.W. 459; see Delaney v. Supreme Investment Co., 1947, 251 Wis. 374, 29 N.W.2d 754.

21. Thompson v. Gibson, 1841, 7 M. & W. 456, 151 Eng.Rep. 845; Ackerman v. Ellis, 1911, 81 N.J.L. 1, 79 A. 883; cf. Davey v. Turner, 1937, 55 Ga.App. 786, 191 S.E. 382.

22. Konskier v. B. Goodman, Ltd., [1928] 1 K.B. 421 (continuing trespass); Van Alstyne v. Rochester Telephone Corp., 1937, 163 Misc. 258, 296 N.Y.S. 726 (same). Cf. Oestrike v. Neifert, 1934, 267 Mich. 462, 255 N.W. 226; Littell v. Argus Production Co., 10 Cir. 1935, 78 F.2d 955.

23. Supra, § 96.

24. Gasteiger v. Gillenwater, 1966, 57 Tenn.App. 206, 417 S.W.2d 568; Rogers v. Scyphers, 1968, 251 S.C. 128, 161 S.E.2d 81.

25. Kapalczynski v. Globe Construction Co., 1969, 19 Mich.App. 396, 172 N.W.2d 852; Moran v. Pittsburgh-Des Moines Steel Co., 3d Cir. 1948, 166 F.2d 908, certiorari denied 334 U.S. 846, 68 S.Ct. 1516, 92 L.Ed. 1770; Hale v. Depaoli, 1948, 33 Cal.2d 228, 201 P.2d 1; Hunter v. Quality Homes, 1949, 6 Terry (45 Del.) 100, 68 A.2d 620; Wright v. Holland Furnace Co., 1932, 186 Minn. 265, 243 N.W. 387. See Notes, 1949, 24 Ind.L.J. 286; 1958, 19 La.L.Rev. 221; 1945, 62 Harv.L.Rev. 145.

26. Fisher v. Simon, 1961, 15 Wis.2d 207, 112 N.W.2d 705; Cosgriff Neon Co. v. Matthews, 1962, 78 Nev. 281, 371 P.2d 819; Thompson v. Burke Engineering Sales Co., 1960, 252 Iowa 146, 106 N.W.2d 351; Leigh v. Wadsworth, Okl.1961, 361 P.2d 849; Krisovich v. John Booth, 1956, 181 Pa.Super. 5, 121 A.2d 890.

27. Colton v. Foulkes, 1951, 295 Wis. 142, 47 N.W.2d 901; Hanna v. Fletcher, 1956, 97 U.S.App.D.C. 246, 231 F.2d 469, certiorari denied 359 U.S. 912, 79 S.Ct. 590, 3 L.Ed.2d 576.

28. Dow v. Holly Manufacturing Co., 1958, 49 Cal. 2d 720, 321 P.2d 736 (elevator); Banaghan v. Dewey, 1959, 340 Mass. 73, 162 N.E.2d 807 (same); Marine Insurance Co. v. Strecker, 1957, 234 La. 522, 100 So.2d 493 (cabinet).

29. United States for Use and Benefit of Los Angeles Testing Laboratory v. Rogers & Rogers, S.D.Cal. 1958, 161 F.Supp. 132; Paxton v. Alameda County, 1953, 119 Cal.App.2d 393, 259 P.2d 934; Harley v. Blodgett Engineering & Tool Co., 1925, 230 Mich. 510, 202 N.W. 953; McDonnell v. Wasenmiller, 8th Cir. 1934, 74 F.2d 320; Pastorelli v. Associated Engineers, D.C.R.I.1959, 176 F.Supp. 159. See Bell, Professional Negligence of Architects and Engineers, 1959, 12 Vand.L.Rev. 711; Witherspoon, When is an Architect Liable? 1960, 32 Miss.L.J. 40.

30. Cross v. M.C. Carlisle & Co., 1st Cir. 1966, 368 F.2d 947; Hunt v. Star Photo Finishing Co., 1967, 115 Ga.App. 1, 153 S.E.2d 602.

them.[31] Where this is the case, there appears to be no doubt that there will be liability.[32] It seems clear, by analogy to the case of the supplier of chattels, that the owner's failure to discover the danger, even though it may be negligent, will not relieve the contractor of liability to another.[33] If he does discover it,[34] or it is obvious to him,[35] and he fails to remedy it, it has been held that his responsibility supersedes that of the contractor. It would appear, however, that this has no bearing upon the contractor's duty of care, and goes only to the issue of "proximate cause," in the form of a responsibility taken over by the owner.[36]

The building contractor who, pursuant to a construction contract with an owner of land, constructs a hotel, office building, residence or other structure on owner's land, must be carefully distinguished from the real estate promoter or housing merchant who constructs residences and other buildings on his own land and sells or leases such dwellings and other structures to others. The transaction of the building contractor has generally been regarded as a transaction involving the rendition of a service even though the result of the service is to supply a structure or building to the owner. Therefore, the rules relating to strict liability of the housing merchant are inapplicable to the building contractor.

The generally accepted view has not been to impose strict liability, either on a warranty or tort theory, to the building contractor who is regarded as being engaged primarily in the rendition of a service, i.e., the construction of a building on land owned by another pursuant to plans and specifications provided by the owner.[37] Nevertheless, strict liability has been imposed on a building contractor on the theory that in essence the structure, which is completed and transmitted under the contract, is a product and sold within the meaning of a sale as contemplated by the rule for strict liability.[38]

The ultimate answer to the question of strict liability should depend on whether or not the typical or paradigmatic building contractor is a sufficiently different type of enterpriser from the housing merchant to warrant a distinction being made between them as regards the subject of strict liability for defects attributable to (a) construction defects, (b) defects in products incorporated into the building, and (c) design defects of the structure.

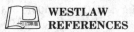

WESTLAW REFERENCES

carpenter /s donohoe & 388 /5 399
sh 388p2d399

Lessor Liability for Defects in Leased Premises
lease! /p residential apartment* /p warranty /3 habitability

---

31. Leininger v. Stearns-Roger Manufacturing Co., 1965, 17 Utah 2d 37, 404 P.2d 33; Johnson v. City of San Leandro, 1960, 179 Cal.App.2d 794, 4 Cal.Rptr. 404; Davis v. Henderlong Lumber Co., N.D.Ind.1963, 221 F.Supp. 129; Person v. Cauldwell-Wingate Co., 2d Cir. 1951, 187 F.2d 832, certiorari denied 341 U.S. 936, 71 S.Ct. 855, 95 L.Ed. 1364; Lydecker v. Board of Chosen Freeholders of Passaic County, 1918, 91 N.J.L. 622, 103 A. 251.

32. See Belk v. Jones Construction Co., 6th Cir. 1959, 272 F.2d 394; Trustees of First Baptist Church v. McElroy, 1955, 223 Miss. 327, 78 So.2d 138; Loesch v. R.P. Farnsworth & Co., La.App.1943, 12 So.2d 222.

33. Foley v. Pittsburgh-Des Moines Co., 1949, 363 Pa. 1, 68 A.2d 517.

34. Leininger v. Stearns-Roger Manufacturing Co., 1965, 17 Utah 2d 37, 404 P.2d 33; Miner v. McNamara, 1909, 81 Conn. 690, 72 A. 138.

35. Inman v. Binghamton Housing Authority, 1957, 3 N.Y.2d 137, 164 N.Y.S.2d 699, 143 N.E.2d 895; Price v. Johnston Cotton Co. of Wendell, 1946, 226 N.C. 758, 40 S.E.2d 344; Howard v. Reinhart & Donovan Co., 1946, 196 Okl. 506, 166 P.2d 101.

36. Strakos v. Gehring, Tex.1962, 360 S.W.2d 787.

37. Wright v. Creative Corp., 1972, 30 Colo.App. 575, 498 P.2d 1179; Chapman v. Lily Cache Builders, Inc., 1977, 48 Ill.App.3d 919, 6 Ill.Dec. 176, 362 N.E.2d 811; Leininger v. Stearns-Roger Manufacturing Co., 1965, 17 Utah 2d 37, 404 P.2d 33; Castaldo v. Pittsburgh-Des Moines Steel Co., Inc., Del.1977, 376 A.2d 88; Ridley Investment Co. v. Croll, Del. 1963, 192 A.2d 925.

38. Worrell v. Barnes, 1971, 87 Nev. 204, 484 P.2d 573.

Chapter 18

MISREPRESENTATION AND NONDISCLOSURE

Table of Sections

Sec.
105. Remedies for Misrepresentation.
106. Representation and Nondisclosure.
107. Basis of Responsibility.
108. Justifiable Reliance—Materiality.
109. —— Opinion and Intention.
110. Damages.

§ 105. Remedies for Misrepresentation

Misrepresentation and nondisclosure runs all through the law of torts, as a method of accomplishing various types of tortious conduct which, for reasons of historical development or as a matter of convenience, usually are grouped under categories of their own. Thus a battery may be committed by feeding the plaintiff poisoned chocolates,[1] or by inducing his consent to a physical contact by misrepresenting its character;[2] false imprisonment may result from a pretense of authority to make an arrest,[3] a trespass to land from fraudulent statements inducing another to enter,[4] or a conversion from obtaining possession of goods by false representations;[5] and a malicious lie may give rise to a cause of action for the intentional infliction of mental suffering.[6] A great many of the common and familiar forms of negligent conduct, resulting in invasions of tangible interests of person or property, are in their essence nothing more than misrepresentation,[7] from a misleading signal by a driver of an automobile about to make a turn, or an assurance that a danger does not exist,[8] to

---

§ 105

1. Commonwealth v. Stratton, 1873, 114 Mass. 303; State v. Monroe, 1897, 121 N.C. 677, 28 S.E. 547.

2. Bartell v. State, 1900, 106 Wis. 342, 82 N.W. 142; De May v. Roberts, 1861, 46 Mich. 160, 9 N.W. 146; Crowell v. Crowell, 1920, 180 N.C. 516, 105 S.E. 206, rehearing denied, 1921, 181 N.C. 66, 106 S.E. 149.

3. Whitman v. Atchison, Topeka & Santa Fe Railway Co., 1911, 85 Kan. 150, 116 P. 234; Hebrew v. Pulis, 1906, 73 N.J.L. 621, 64 A. 121.

4. Donovan v. Consolidated Coal Co., 1900, 187 Ill. 28, 58 N.E. 290; Hendrix v. Black, 1918, 132 Ark. 473,

201 S.W. 283; Murrell v. Goodwill, 1925, 159 La. 1057, 106 So. 564.

5. Holland v. Bishop, 1895, 60 Minn. 23, 61 N.W. 681; Hagar v. Norton, 1905, 188 Mass. 47, 73 N.E. 1073; Baird v. Howard, 1894, 51 Ohio St. 57, 36 N.E. 732.

6. Wilkinson v. Downton, [1897] 2 Q.B. 57, 66 L.J. Q.B. 493; cf. Nickerson v. Hodges, 1920, 146 La. 735, 84 So. 37.

7. See supra, § 33.

8. Skillings v. Allen, 1919, 143 Minn. 323, 173 N.W. 663; Washington & Berkeley Bridge Co. v. Penn-

false statements [9] concerning a chattel sold, or non-disclosure of a latent defect by one who is under a duty to give warning.[10] In addition, misrepresentation may play an important part in the invasion of intangible interests, in such torts as defamation,[11] malicious prosecution,[12] or interference with contractual relations.[13] In all such cases the particular form which the defendant's conduct has taken has become relatively unimportant, and misrepresentation has been merged to such an extent with other kinds of misconduct that neither the courts nor legal writers have found any occasion to regard it as a separate basis of liability.

This chapter is limited and relates to the extent to which tort actions are available to protect intangible economic interests of those who are induced by mistake to enter into bargaining transactions as a consequence of a fraud of misrepresentation of others. The tort action of deceit is sometimes used as the name of the tort for covering all kinds of actions now available for all kinds of so-called actionable misrepresentations or nondisclosure. Sometimes that term is more narrowly used to cover the tort remedy that was available under the common law and prior to recent developments. But the more important question relates to the extent of liability on any theory for misrepresentations and nondisclosures. The reasons for the separate development of this action, and for its peculiar limitations, are in part historical, and in part connected with the fact that in the great majority of the cases which have come before the courts the misrepresentations have been made in the course of a bargaining transaction between the parties.[14] Consequently the action has been colored to a considerable extent by the ethics of bargaining between distrustful adversaries. Its separate recognition has been confined in practice very largely to the invasion of interests of a financial or commercial character, in the course of business dealings. There is no essential reason to prevent a deceit action from being maintained, for intentional misstatements at least, where other types of interests are invaded; and there are a few cases in which it has been held to lie for personal injuries,[15] for tricking the plaintiff into an invalid marriage [16] or marriage with one who is physically unfit,[17] or for inducing the plaintiff to leave a husband,[18] or to incur criminal penalties.[19] In general, however, other theories of action have been sufficient to deal with non-pecuniary damage, and the somewhat narrower theory of deceit is not called into question. The typi-

---

sylvania Steel Co., 4th Cir. 1915, 226 F. 169; Valz v. Goodykoontz, 1911, 112 Va. 853, 72 S.E. 730; Virginia Dare Stores v. Schuman, 1938, 175 Md. 287, 1 A.2d 897.

9. Cunningham v. C.R. Pease House Furnishing Co., 1908, 74 N.H. 435, 69 A. 120; Ahrens v. Moore, 1944, 206 Ark. 1035, 178 S.W.2d 256; Andreotalla v. Gaeta, 1927, 260 Mass. 105, 156 N.E. 731; Dalrymple v. Sinkoe, 1949, 230 N.C. 453, 53 S.E.2d 437.

10. Huset v. J.I. Case Threshing Machine Co., 8th Cir. 1903, 120 F. 865 (seller of chattel and third person); Benson v. Dean, 1921, 232 N.Y. 52, 133 N.E. 125 (surgeon and patient); Cowen v. Sunderland, 1887, 145 Mass. 363, 14 N.E. 117 (landlord and tenant); Campbell v. Boyd, 1883, 88 N.C. 129 (possessor of premises and licensee).

11. See infra, ch. 19.

12. See infra, ch. 21.

13. See infra, § 129.

14. See Second Restatement of Torts, Scope Note to chapter 22, preceding § 525.

15. Benoit v. Perkins, 1918, 79 N.H. 11, 104 A. 254; Langridge v. Levy, 1837, 2 M. & W. 519, 150 Eng.Rep. 863; Kuelling v. Roderick Lean Manufacturing Co., 1905, 183 N.Y. 78, 75 N.E. 1098. Cf. Graham v. John R. Watts & Son, 1931, 238 Ky. 96, 36 S.W.2d 859 (damage to property). "The injury to one's person by the fraud of another is quite as serious as an injury to one's pocketbook." Start, C.J., in Flaherty v. Till, 1912, 119 Minn. 191, 137 N.W. 815.

16. Sham marriage: Jekshewitz v. Groswald, 1929, 265 Mass. 413, 164 N.E. 609; Tuck v. Tuck, 1964, 14 N.Y.2d 341, 251 N.Y.S.2d 653, 200 N.E.2d 554. Bigamy: Morris v. MacNab, 1957, 25 N.J. 271, 135 A.2d 657; Humphreys v. Baird, 1956, 197 Va. 667, 90 S.E.2d 796; Wolf v. Fox, 1922, 178 Wis. 369, 190 N.W. 90.

17. Kujek v. Goldman, 1896, 150 N.Y. 176, 44 N.E. 773; Leventhal v. Liberman, 1933, 262 N.Y. 209, 186 N.E. 675, affirmed 237 App.Div. 808, 260 N.Y.S. 976.

18. Work v. Campbell, 1912, 164 Cal. 343, 128 P. 943.

19. Burrows v. Rhodes, [1899] 1 Q.B. 816. Cf. Stryk v. Mnichowicz, 1918, 167 Wis. 265, 167 N.W. 246, (false statements by parent as to child's age inducing plaintiff to employ child, with resulting tort liability for violation of statute when child was injured).

cal case of deceit is one in which the plaintiff has parted with money, or property of value, in reliance upon the defendant's representations.

The law of misrepresentation is thus considerably broader than the action for deceit. Liability in damages for misrepresentation, in one form or another, falls into the three familiar divisions with which we have dealt throughout this text—it may be based upon intent to deceive, upon negligence, or upon a policy which requires the defendant to be strictly responsible for his statements without either. For the most part, the courts have limited deceit to those cases where there is an intent to mislead, and have left negligence and strict liability to be dealt with in some other type of action.[20] There has been a good deal of overlapping of theories,[21] and no little confusion, which has been increased by the indiscriminate use of the word "fraud," a term so vague that it requires definition in nearly every case. Further difficulty has been added by a failure to distinguish the requisites of the action in tort at law from those of equitable remedies, and to distinguish the different forms of misrepresentation from one another, and misrepresentation itself from mere mistake.[22] Any attempt to bring order out of the resulting chaos must be at best a tentative one, with the qualification that many courts do not agree.

The Cause For a Mistake and Its Importance

The mistake under which a party to a transaction was laboring at the time of the closing of the transaction may, of course, have been induced in a variety of ways. Sometimes the mistake may be common to both parties without either having been responsible for the mistake of the other by way of making a misrepresentation. This is commonly referred to in this area as a situation involving a mutual mistake. Sometimes, however, the mistake is not common to both parties, in which event the mistake of one party although not induced by the misrepresentation of another may or may not be known by the latter. These two types of situations can be conveniently differentiated by referring to one as a unilateral palpable mistake and the other as a unilateral impalpable mistake. In the former type of situation, the problem has usually been treated by the courts as one relating to the extent of the duty of a person to disclose material facts about which he knows another is uninformed. Often, a mistake of a party to a transaction is induced by the misrepresentation of the other party, some agent of the other party, or some stranger to the transaction. In such an event, the misrepresenter may have been either dishonest, honest but negligent, or finally, honest and careful. Therefore, it is necessary in order to decide about relief, if any, to the mistaken party to recognize the following types of situations relative to the manner in which the mistake was induced:

(1) unilateral impalpable mistake;

(2) mutual mistake;

(3) unilateral palpable mistake;

(4) mistake induced by a misrepresentation of the other party to the transaction or his agent;

(5) mistake induced by the misrepresentation of a third person.

The Tort Action for Damages

The tort action for damages, commonly referred to as the action for deceit, is of very ancient origin. There was an old writ of deceit known as early as 1201, which lay only against a person who had misused legal procedure for the purpose of swindling some-

---

20. See infra, § 107.

21. See Green, Deceit, 1930, 16 Va.L.Rev. 749, contending that the resulting flexibility is a desirable thing, and a great advantage to the courts in dealing with varying types of cases.

22. See infra, § 106.

one.²³ At a later period this writ was superseded by an action on the case in the nature of deceit, which became the general common law remedy for fraudulent or even non-fraudulent misrepresentation resulting in actual damage.²⁴ In particular, it was extended to afford a remedy for many wrongs which we should now regard as breaches of contract, such as false warranties in the sale of goods.²⁵ Its use was limited almost entirely to cases of direct transactions between the parties, and it came to be regarded as inseparable from some contractual relation.²⁶ It was not until 1789, in Pasley v. Freeman,²⁷ which is the parent of the modern law of deceit, that the action was held to lie where the plaintiff had had no dealings with the defendant, but had been induced by his misrepresentation to deal with a third person. After that date deceit was recognized as purely a tort action, and not necessarily founded upon a contract. At about the same time,²⁸ the remedy for a breach of warranty was taken over into the action of assumpsit, and it was thus established that it had a contract character. Thereafter the two lines of recovery slowly diverged, although some vestiges of confusion between the two still remain in many courts, particularly as to the measure of damages.²⁹ The distinction was made clear in the English courts by decisions holding that the tort action of deceit requires something in the way of knowledge of the falsity of the statement and an intention to mislead,³⁰ while the contract action on a warranty does not.³¹

The elements of the tort cause of action in deceit which at last emerged from this process of development frequently have been stated ³² as follows:

1. A false representation ³³ made by the defendant. In the ordinary case, this representation must be one of fact.³⁴

2. Knowledge or belief on the part of the defendant that the representation is false— or, what is regarded as equivalent, that he has not a sufficient basis of information to make it. This element often is given the technical name of "scienter." ³⁵

3. An intention to induce the plaintiff to act or to refrain from action in reliance upon the misrepresentation.³⁶

4. Justifiable reliance upon the representation on the part of the plaintiff, in taking action or refraining from it.³⁷

5. Damage to the plaintiff, resulting from such reliance.³⁸

As will be seen, some of these elements have undergone modification or qualification in some jurisdictions. In addition, it must be repeated that such an action of deceit is only one of several possible remedies for various forms of misrepresentation, even where

---

23. 1 Street, Foundations of Legal Liability, 1906, 375; Winfield, History of Conspiracy, 1921, 33.

24. 1 Street, Foundations of Legal Liability, 1906, 376; Winfield, Province of the Law of Tort, 1931, 13–14.

25. 3 Holdsworth, History of English Law, 4th Ed. 1935, 428–434; 1 Street, Foundations of Legal Liability, 1906, 377–382; Ames, History of Assumpsit, 1888, 2 Harv.L.Rev. 1, 8ff.

26. As late as Roswel v. Vaughan, 1607, Cro.Jac. 196, 79 Eng.Rep. 171.

27. 1789, 3 Term Rep. 51, 100 Eng.Rep. 450. "The Court in Pasley v. Freeman were convinced that they were creating a new tort. In fact, it was the novelty of it that frightened Grose, J. (a very conservative judge) into dissent." Winfield, Law of Tort, 1937, 400n.

28. Stuart v. Wilkins, 1778, 1 Dougl. 18, 99 Eng. Rep. 15.

29. See infra, § 110.

30. Derry v. Peek, 1888, 14 A.C. 337. See infra § 107.

31. Williamson v. Allen, 1802, 2 East 446, 102 Eng. Rep. 439.

32. Restatement of Torts, 525; Suburban Properties Management v. Johnson, 1964, 236 Md. 455, 204 A.2d 326; Broberg v. Mann, 1965, 66 Ill.App.2d 134, 213 N.E.2d 89; Traylor Engineering & Manufacturing Co. v. National Container Corp., 1949, 6 Terry, Del. 143, 70 A.2d 9; Safety Investment Corp. v. State Land Office Board, 1944, 308 Mich. 246, 13 N.W.2d 278; McKay v. Anheuser-Busch, Inc., 1942, 199 S.C. 335, 19 S.E.2d 457.

33. See infra, § 106.

34. See infra, § 109.

35. See infra, § 107.

36. See infra, § 107.

37. See infra, § 108.

38. See infra, § 110.

there is only pecuniary loss. Before proceeding to consider the elements of the cause of action in deceit, it is desirable to distinguish other theories upon which relief may be granted, the proximity of which has been a fertile source of the general confusion and uncertainty surrounding the deceit action itself.

The Contract-Warranty Cause of Action for Damages

The divorce of a warranty action from deceit was completed about the beginning of the Nineteenth Century. By that time, the warranty basis for recovery became identified with an unqualified representation of a material fact made by a seller of personal property about the subject matter of the sale to his immediate purchaser, and the notion was that this gave rise to an objective manifestation of an intent by the seller to guarantee the truth of the statement to the purchaser.[39] Warranty-representations are now regarded by many courts as giving rise to recovery by purchaser-consumers and third parties who are permitted to stand in the shoes of the purchaser on the basis of very liberal ideas about third-party beneficiaries, thereby disregarding orthodox ideas about privity of contract as a prerequisite to recovery.[40] Moreover, bailors, housing merchants and some sellers of services will not be regarded by some courts as warranting the truth of unqualified representations of fact related to such transactions.[41] In any event, those who are entitled to recover on a warranty-contract theory do so without proving fault simply because there is an implied obligation to guarantee the truth of the matter asserted.

The Equitable Remedy for Rescission

Misrepresentation and mistake were recognized very early as a basis for jurisdiction of courts of equity because of the inadequacies of the legal remedy of damages to deal with the injuries resulting therefrom. The most common equitable remedies for misrepresentation were rescission or reformation of the contract, deed, lease, or other written transaction or requiring the defendant who had been unjustly enriched as a consequence of performance from the mistaken party to hold the money or property he had received subject to a constructive trust, or an equitable lien. The objective of these remedies was to restore the parties to *status quo* and therefore to prevent the misrepresenter from gaining a benefit from the transaction. It can be said that, in general, when a contract, or other bargaining transaction, such as a conveyance of an interest in land, is induced by a material misrepresentation by one of the parties to the transaction, the other party who is adversely affected may rescind without respect to fault of any kind either dishonesty or negligence.[42] This is said to be because the misrepresenter cannot justify gaining a benefit out of a bargaining transaction which was induced by his material misrepresentation.

Even beyond this, an adversely affected party can rescind a contract or other bargaining transaction if the transaction was induced by a mutual mistake as to a basic assumption on which the contract was made.[43]

---

39. It is quite clear that subjective intent to be bound by the misrepresenter became unnecessary but it has never been clear as to the precise basis for the imposition of strict liability. See, Williston, Representatives and Warranty in Sales—Helibut v. Buckleton, 1913, 27 Harv.L.Rev. 1; Ames, The History of Assumpsit, 1888, 2 Harv.L.Rev. 1; Miller and Lovell, 1977, Product Liability, p. 36.

40. Reid v. Volkswagen of America, Inc., 6th Cir. 1975, 512 F.2d 1294; Hamon v. Digliani, 1961, 148 Conn. 710, 174 A.2d 294; Rogers v. Toni Home Permanent Co., 1958, 167 Ohio St. 244, 147 N.E.2d 612, 75 A.L.R.2d 103.

41. See chapter 17, § 104.

42. Williston, Rescission for Breach of Warranty, 1903, 16 Harv.L.Rev. 465; Keeton, Actionable Misrepresentation: Legal Fault as a Requirement, II. Rescission, 1949, 2 Okla.L.Rev. 56; Seneca Wire & Manufacturing Co. v. A.B. Leach & Co., 1928, 247 N.Y. 1, 159 N.E. 700.

43. Second Restatement of Contracts, 1981, § 152; Beachcomber Coins, Inc. v. Boskett, 1979, 166 N.J. Super. 442, 400 A.2d 78; Aluminum Co. of America v. Essex Group, Inc., W.D.Pa.1980, 499 F.Supp. 53.

Underlying this doctrine is the idea of an imbalance in the exchange. There are even some extreme circumstances when a unilateral impalpable mistake would make enforcement of the contract unconscionable and would justify rescission on behalf of the mistaken party.

Equitable relief, when it was granted, was subject to restrictions peculiar to equity. The plaintiff must himself do equity by restoring whatever he had received,[44] unless excused by special circumstances; and he must do nothing inconsistent with the relief demanded, so that the right to rescind a sale, for example, would be lost by any conduct affirming the transaction,[45] or even by nonaction for an unreasonable length of time after discovery of the facts.[46] These restrictions, of course, had no application to actions at law.

Restitution at Law

The confusion arising from the co-existence of these legal and equitable remedies was not lessened when a considerable part of the relief afforded by equity was taken over into actions at law. Reference has already been made [47] to the process by which the idea of "quasi-contract" became engrafted upon the action of assumpsit, to permit the plaintiff to rescind a transaction of his own motion and recover the value of what he had parted with, without resort to a court of equity.

In granting such relief, the common law courts recognized that they were invading the province of equity, and retained the equity rules. Thus, so far as misrepresentation is concerned, most courts [48] have held that it is unnecessary to establish for restitution the mental element of knowledge commonly required in the tort action of deceit, and it is sufficient to show an honest misrepresentation,[49] or even, in some cases, a mere mistake.[50] Likewise, unless he is excused by special circumstances, the plaintiff must restore what he has himself received,[51] and his action is lost by any conduct affirming the transaction,[52] or even by nonaction for an unreasonable length of time,[53] after discov-

---

44. Hunt v. Silk, 1804, 5 East 449, 102 Eng.Rep. 1142; De Montague v. Bacharach, 1902, 181 Mass. 256, 63 N.E. 435; Fay v. Oliver, 1848, 20 Vt. 118.

45. Parsons v. McKinley, 1894, 56 Minn. 464, 57 N.W. 1134 (affirmance); Day v. Fort Scott Investment & Improvement Co., 1894, 153 Ill. 293, 38 N.E. 567 (affirmance); Bell v. Keepers, 1888, 39 Kan. 105, 17 P. 785 (continued payments); In re Warner's Estate, 1914, 168 Cal. 771, 145 P. 504 (accepting payments); Romanoff Land & Mining Co. v. Cameron, 1902, 137 Ala. 214, 33 So. 864 (use). See Yerkes, Election of Remedies in Cases of Fraudulent Misrepresentation, 1953, 26 So.Cal.L.Rev. 157.

46. Howie v. North Birmingham Land Co., 1891, 95 Ala. 389, 11 So. 15; Litchfield v. Browne, 8th Cir. 1895, 70 F. 141; Clampitt v. Doyle, 1907, 73 N.J.Eq. 678, 70 A. 129; Wilbur v. Flood, 1867, 16 Mich. 40. See Friedman, Delay as a Bar to Rescission, 1941, 26 Corn.L.Q. 426.

47. Supra, § 94.

48. Occasional decisions, such as New York Title & Mortgage Co. v. Hutton, 1934, 63 App.D.C. 266, 71 F.2d 989, and Ebbs v. St. Louis Union Trust Co., 1930, 199 N.C. 242, 153 S.E. 858, have lost sight of history, and required scienter for rescission.

49. Flight v. Booth, 1834, 1 Bing.N.C. 370, 131 Eng. Rep. 1160; Seneca Wire & Manufacturing Co. v. A.B. Leach & Co., 1928, 247 N.Y. 1, 159 N.E. 700; Agricultural Bond & Credit Corp. v. August Brandt Co., 1931, 204 Wis. 48, 234 N.W. 369; Henry v. Kopf, 1925, 104 Conn. 73, 131 A. 412; Joslyn v. Cadillac Automobile Co., 6th Cir. 1910, 177 F. 863. See Keeton, Actionable Misrepresentation: Legal Fault as a Requirement, 1948, 1 Okl.L.Rev. 21, 1949, 2 Okl.L.Rev. 56; Note, 1928, 37 Yale L.J. 1141.

50. Grand Lodge, A.O.U.W. of Minnesota v. Towne, 1917, 136 Minn. 72, 161 N.W. 403; Ketchum v. Catlin, 1849, 21 Vt. 191; Strauss v. Hensey, 1896, 9 App.D.C. 541; De Wolff v. Howe, 1906, 112 App.Div. 104, 98 N.Y.S. 262; Ex parte Richard & Thalheimer, 1913, 180 Ala. 580, 61 So. 819.

51. Byard v. Holmes, 1868, 33 N.J.L. 119; Houghton v. Nash, 1874, 64 Me. 477; Adam, Meldrum & Anderson Co. v. Stewart, 1901, 157 Ind. 678, 61 N.E. 1002; James Music Co. v. Bridge, 1908, 134 Wis. 510, 114 N.W. 1108. See Note, 1929, 29 Col.L.Rev. 791.

52. Brennan v. National Equitable Inv. Co., 1928, 247 N.Y. 486, 160 N.E. 924, reargument denied 248 N.Y. 560, 162 N.E. 524; Samples v. Guyer, 1898, 120 Ala. 611, 24 So. 942; Bayer v. Winton Motor Car Co., 1916, 194 Mich. 222, 160 N.W. 642. Cf. Maki v. St. Luke's Hospital Association, 1913, 122 Minn. 444, 142 N.W. 705. See Deinard v. Deinard, Election of Remedies, 1922, 6 Minn.L.Rev. 341, 480; Yerkes, Election of Remedies in Fraudulent Misrepresentation, 1953, 26 So.Cal.L.Rev. 157; Notes, 1949, 2 U.Fla.L.Rev. 142.

53. Wilbur v. Flood, 1867, 16 Mich. 40; Grant v. Lovekin, 1926, 285 Pa. 257, 132 A. 342; Long v. International Vending Machine Co., 1911, 158 Mo.App. 662, 139 S.W. 819; Everson v. J.L. Owens Manufacturing

ery of the facts. Furthermore, the measure of his recovery is determined on the equitable basis of the unjust enrichment of the defendant,[54] rather than the tort basis of the plaintiff's loss. Thus a purchaser defrauded in the sale of a horse who seeks a remedy by way of restitution ordinarily must return the horse, and may recover the price he has paid, regardless of the extent of his loss on the transaction.

Misrepresentation as a Defense

Further complications arise when there is added the possibility that misrepresentation may be set up as a defense to an action brought by the adverse party, as where one who is sued on a contract claims that he was induced by false statements to enter into it. The common law courts, apparently recognized at a very early date the kind of misrepresentation which went to the existence of the contract itself, as where a man who could not read was induced to sign an instrument, such as a promissory note, which was represented to be of a different character, as a mere receipt. Such misrepresentation, which was called fraud in the factum, or in the essence of the contract, could be shown as a defense under a plea denying that there was a contract at all.[55] But at least in the case of sealed instruments, misrepresentation going merely to the inducement or the consideration of the contract was not available as a defense at law, and the defrauded party was compelled to resort to equity for affirmative relief setting the transaction aside.[56] As the law courts invaded equity fields, the "equitable" defense of fraud in the inducement gradually filtered into the common law actions,[57] although it was held as late as 1854 in England,[58] and still later in the United States,[59] particularly in the federal courts,[60] that it was not available. Modern procedure codes, which have terminated the separate existence of equity courts, and permit equitable defenses to be pleaded in actions at law,[61] have very largely obliterated the distinction; and except as to matters of pleading,[62] the right to a jury trial,[63] and questions arising as to whether the transaction is to be considered as void or merely voidable, the American courts have treated

---

Co., 1920, 145 Minn. 199, 176 N.W. 505. See Friedman, Delay as a Bar to Recission, 1941, 26 Corn.L.Q. 426.

54. Seneca Wire & Manufacturing Co. v. A.B. Leach & Co., 1928, 247 N.Y. 1, 159 N.E. 700; Note, 1934, 32 Mich.L.Rev. 968. Cf. Houser & Haines Manufacturing Co. v. McKay, 1909, 53 Wash. 337, 101 P. 894; Pfeiffer v. Independent Plumbing & Heating Supply Co., Mo.App.1934, 72 S.W.2d 138 (rescission for breach of warranty); and see Rogge, Damages Upon Rescission for Breach of Warranty, 1929, 28 Mich.L. Rev. 26.

55. Thoroughgood's Case, 1584, 2 Co.Rep. 9a, 76 Eng.Rep. 408; Stone v. Compton, 1838, 5 Bing.N.C. 142, 132 Eng.Rep. 1059; see Smith v. Ryan, 1908, 191 N.Y. 452, 84 N.E. 402; Ames, Specialty Contracts and Equitable Defenses, 1895, 9 Harv.L.Rev. 49, 51.

56. 1 Holdsworth, History of English Law, 5th Ed. 1931, 576. The reason being that covenant, upon a sealed instrument, was the only contract action originally available.

57. Fitzherbert v. Mather, 1785, 1 Term Rep. 12, 99 Eng.Rep. 944; Grew v. Beaven, 1822, 3 Stark. 134, 171 Eng.Rep. 798; Raphael v. Goodman, 1838, 8 Ad. & El. 565, 112 Eng.Rep. 952; Hazard v. Irwin, 1836, 35 Mass. (18 Pick.) 95. See Abbot, Fraud as a Defence at Law in the Federal Courts, 1915, 15 Col.L.Rev. 489, 504–505.

58. Mason v. Ditchbourne, 1835, 1 Mood. & Rob. 460, 174 Eng.Rep. 158; Feret v. Hill, 1854, 15 C.B. 207, 139 Eng.Rep. 400. The rule was altered by the Common Law Procedure Act of 1854, permitting the pleading of equitable defenses at law.

59. Dyer v. Day, 1871, 61 Ill. 336; Eaton v. Eaton, 1874, 37 N.J.L. 108; McArthur v. Johnson, 1867, 61 N.C. 317; Richelieu Hotel Co. v. International Military Encampment Co., 1892, 140 Ill. 248, 29 N.E. 1044.

60. Hartshorn v. Day, 1856, 60 (19 How.) U.S. 211, 15 L.Ed. 605; George v. Tate, 1880, 102 U.S. 564, 26 L.Ed. 232. The rule was abandoned as to instruments not under seal, if it ever applied to them. American Sign Co. v. Electro-Lens Sign Co., D.Cal.1913, 211 F. 196. See Abbot, Fraud as a Defence at Law in the Federal Courts, 1915, 15 Col.L.Rev. 489; McBaine, Equitable Defenses to Actions at Law in the Federal Courts, 1929, 17 Cal.L.Rev. 591. It was finally abrogated by a statute in 1915, permitting the pleading of equitable defenses at law, and terminated by the Federal Rules of Civil Procedure, uniting law and equity practice, in 1938.

61. See Clark, Code Pleading, 2d Ed. 1947, § 98; Hinton, Equitable Defenses Under Modern Codes, 1920, 18 Mich.L.Rev. 716; Cook, Equitable Defenses, 1923, 32 Yale L.J. 645; Moreland, Equitable Defenses, 1940, 1 Wash. & Lee L.Rev. 153.

62. Fraud in the factum negatives the existence of the contract, and may be shown under a denial of the obligation. Boxberger v. New York, New Haven &

63. See note 63 on page 732.

the two kinds of "fraud" upon the same footing.

The fusion of law and equity under modern procedure, and the hybrid character of the "equitable" defense where it had been recognized earlier at law, have resulted in a great deal of uncertainty as to its nature. Some courts have regarded it as a form of rescission in equity, permitting the defendant to set up innocent misrepresentation [64] or even mere mistake,[65] requiring him to act promptly and restore what he has received,[66] and holding that the defense is lost by any act affirming the transaction.[67] Others have considered it as something analogous to a tort action of deceit, set up by way of defense to avoid circuity of action,[68] and have required knowledge of the falsity of the statements, or at least conscious ignorance of the truth,[69] and have permitted the defendant to retain what he has received and recoup his damages when he is sued, usually on the theory of a failure of the consideration promised him.[70]

The nature of the defense is seldom discussed and nowhere definitively established, and seems to be poorly comprehended by the courts. The logic of the matter would seem to be, that when the defense takes the form of avoidance of the transaction sued upon, or seeks relief by way of restitution, it is an equitable remedy, and the defendant should be permitted to set up innocent misrepresentation or even mere mutual mistake; he should be required to act promptly and to restore what he has received, and should be held to have lost the defense by any act affirming the transaction, to the same extent as though he were suing for rescission or restitution as a plaintiff. Where the defense is set up by way of recoupment, or by way of affirmative counterclaim, it in no way operates in avoidance of the transaction, but seeks relief analogous to that afforded by a tort action of deceit, and therefore should be governed by the requirements of that action. Most courts have arrived at a result similar to that achieved in the case of breach of warranty in the sale of goods,[71] allowing the defendant the option of rescission and recovery of what he has paid, or affirmance and recoupment of his damages, but without very clearly distinguishing the grounds for

Hartford Railroad Co., 1923, 237 N.Y. 75, 142 N.E. 357; Walton Plow Co. v. Campbell, 1892, 35 Neb. 173, 52 N.W. 883; Christianson v. Chicago, St. Paul, Minneapolis & Omaha Railway Co., 1895, 61 Minn. 249, 63 N.W. 639. Fraud in the inducement must be pleaded specially. Burlington Grocery Co. v. Lines, 1923, 96 Vt. 405, 120 A. 169; Daly v. Proetz, 1874, 20 Minn. 411; cf. Whipple v. Brown Brothers Co., 1919, 225 N.Y. 237, 121 N.E. 748.

63. Thus it has been held that fraud in the factum is a legal defense, to be determined by the jury, while fraud in the inducement is equitable and hence for the court. Pringle v. Storrow, D.Mass.1925, 9 F.2d 464; Hoad v. New York Central Railroad Co., D.N.Y.1934, 6 F.Supp. 565. See Note, 1931, 15 Minn.L.Rev. 805.

64. Evans v. Edmonds, 1853, 13 C.B. 777, 138 Eng. Rep. 1407; Frenzel v. Miller, 1871, 37 Ind. 1; New York Life Insurance Co. v. Marotta, 3d Cir. 1932, 57 F.2d 1038; Taylor v. Burr Printing Co., 2d Cir. 1928, 26 F.2d 331, cert. denied 278 U.S. 641, 49 S.Ct. 36, 73 L.Ed. 556; Standard Manufacturing Co. v. Slot, 1904, 121 Wis. 14, 98 N.W. 923.

65. Crary v. Goodman, 1855, 12 N.Y. 266; Leach v. Leach, 1925, 162 Minn. 159, 202 N.W. 448.

66. Bwlch-Y-Plwn Lead Mining Co. v. Baynes, 1867, L.R. 2 Ex. 324; Clough v. London & N.W.R. Co., 1871, L.R. 7 Ex. 26; Heaton v. Knowlton, 1876, 53 Ind. 357; cf. Harris v. Equitable Life Assurance Society of United States, 1876, 64 N.Y. 196. See 1 Bigelow, Fraud, 1888, 79.

67. Bell v. Baker, 1890, 43 Minn. 86, 44 N.W. 676; Marks v. Stein, 1916, 61 Okl. 59, 160 P. 318.

68. Peck v. Brewer, 1868, 48 Ill. 54; Piper v. Menifee, 1851, 51 (12 B.Mon.) Ky. 465; Gillespie v. Torrance, 1862, 25 N.Y. 306. Cf. Byers v. Lemay Bank & Trust Co., 1955, 365 Mo. 341, 282 S.W.2d 512 ("set-off" of equitable character). A fortiori, a counterclaim for damages under code procedure is clearly the equivalent of a tort action for deceit.

69. Public Motor Service Co. v. Standard Oil Co. of New Jersey, 1938, 69 App.D.C. 89, 99 F.2d 124; Schlossman's, Inc. v. Niewinski, 1951, 12 N.J.Super. 500, 79 A.2d 870; Weintrob v. New York Life Insurance Co., 3 Cir. 1936, 85 F.2d 158; Latta v. Robinson Erection Co., 1952, 363 Mo. 47, 248 S.W.2d 569; Hodgens v. Jennings, 1912, 148 App.Div. 879, 133 N.Y.S. 584.

70. Williston, Contracts, Rev.Ed.1937, § 1524; American Sign Co. v. Electro-Lens Sign Co., D.Cal. 1913, 211 F. 196; Peck v. Brewer, 1868, 48 Ill. 54; Sharp v. Ponce, 1883, 74 Me. 470; Huber Manufacturing Co. v. Hunter, 1903, 99 Mo.App. 46, 72 S.W. 484.

71. See Uniform Sales Act, § 69(1); Uniform Commercial Code, § 2–601; 2 Williston, Sales, Rev.Ed.1948, §§ 604, 605, 605a, 608.

the two. This uncertainty has had its effect in turn upon the affirmative tort action for deceit itself.

Estoppel

Still another form in which misrepresentation may play an important part in the law of torts is that of estoppel. An estoppel is a rule which precludes a party from taking a particular legal position because of some impediment or bar recognized by the law.[72] It was applied originally to prevent a party from challenging the validity of a legal record, or his own deed; but the equity courts developed it later as a general principle, used as a means of preventing him from taking an inequitable advantage of a predicament in which his own conduct had placed his adversary. It was taken over in turn by the common law judges, as a device to enable them to lengthen their arm, and afford a relief which equity had always offered.[73] Such equitable estoppel, or as it is often called, estoppel in pais, has been defined as "an impediment or bar, by which a man is precluded from alleging, or denying, a fact, in consequence of his own previous act, allegation or denial to the contrary." [74]

For obvious reasons, it appears most frequently as a defense to an action brought by the party to be estopped; but, while it never has been recognized as a cause of action in itself, it may serve as an important, or even the sole, aid to the plaintiff.[75] Thus a warehouseman, who represents that he holds goods for another in response to an inquiry by an intending purchaser from that other, [76] or one who informs such a purchaser that his signature forged to a negotiable instrument is genuine,[77] may be estopped to deny the truth of his statement if the purchase is made in reliance upon it; or a corporation which fails to require surrender of an old stock certificate when a new one is issued may find itself estopped as against a holder for value of the old certificate.[78] In such cases the plaintiff prevails, not on the theory that the defendant's misrepresentation is tortious in itself, but because the defendant is not allowed to assert the truth, which would otherwise be a defense to some other action. Estoppel, of course, is not confined to tort cases, and runs throughout the entire field of law.

Such equitable estoppel may be separated into two branches. The first is based upon some definite misrepresentation of fact, made with reason to believe that another will rely upon it, upon which the other does rely in changing his position to his prejudice.[79] Perhaps because of the equity origin of the doctrine, such misrepresenta-

---

72. "'Estoppel' cometh of the French word *estoupe*, from whence the English word *stopped;* and it is called an estoppel, or conclusion, because a man's own act, or acceptance, stoppeth or closeth up his mouth to allege or plead the truth." Co.Litt. 352a. It was at one time regarded as a rule of pleading, or of evidence; but since it goes to the position taken upon the merits, it is clearly a rule of substantive law. Williston, Liability for Honest Misrepresentation, 1911, 24 Harv.L.Rev. 415, 425.

73. Bacon, V.C., in Keate v. Phillips, 1881, 18 Ch. Div. 560, 577. The leading case in which the principle of estoppel is fully recognized at law is Pickard v. Sears, 1837, 6 Ad. & El. 469, 112 Eng.Rep. 179.

74. 2 Jacob, Law Dictionary, 1811, 439; Ewart, Principles of Estoppel, 1900, 4.

75. Second Restatement of Torts, § 872; Williston, Liability for Honest Misrepresentation, 1911, 24 Harv. L.Rev. 415, 425; Weisiger, Basis of Liability for Misrepresentation, 1930, 24 Ill.Rev. 866, 867–869; Harper and McNeely, A Synthesis of the Law of Misrepresentation, 1938, 22 Minn.L.Rev. 938, 971, 972.

76. Commercial National Bank v. Nacogdoches Compress & Warehouse Co., 5th Cir. 1904, 133 F. 501; Tradesmen's National Bank v. Indiana Bicycle Co., 1895, 166 Pa. 554, 31 A. 337. Cf. Burrowes v. Lock, 1805, 10 Ves.Jr. 470, 32 Eng.Rep. 927; Low v. Bouverie, [1891] 3 Ch. 82 (trustee making false statements as to extent of cestui's interest to prospective purchaser).

77. Wolfe v. First National Bank, 1922, 140 Md. 479, 117 A. 898; Corner Stone Bank v. Rhodes, 1904, 5 Indiana Territory 256, 82 S.W. 739; Furst & Thomas v. Smith, 1939, 280 Ky. 601, 133 S.W.2d 941.

78. Joslyn v. St. Paul Distilling Co., 1890, 44 Minn. 183, 46 N.W. 337; Jarvis v. Manhattan Beach Co., 1896, 148 N.Y. 652, 43 N.E. 68. Cf. also Nickerson v. Massachusetts Title Insurance Co., 1901, 178 Mass. 308, 59 N.E. 814 (title company certifying title as unencumbered when it held a mortgage, estopped to assert its lien against purchaser); Fry v. Smellie, [1912] 3 K.B. 282, and many cases of apparent authority of an agent.

79. Second Restatement of Torts, §§ 872, 894(1).

tion has not been identified with that required for the action of deceit, but rather with that necessary for equitable relief. Although there are occasional decisions [80] to the effect that estoppel cannot arise unless the party estopped had knowledge of the falsity of his statement, or was at least negligent in making it, it seems to be quite clearly established that entirely innocent misrepresentation may be sufficient.[81] It is the inequity of seeking to take advantage of another's position resulting from a misleading statement which is the basis of the relief.

The second branch does not depend upon positive misrepresentation, but is based upon a mere failure to take action. It arises where the party "stands by" and allows another to deal with his property, or to incur some liability toward him, without informing the other of his mistake.[82] Thus he may not remain silent when he sees his goods sold to a stranger,[83] or improvements made upon his land,[84] and still enforce his rights against the innocent wrongdoer. The law of estoppel creates a duty to speak, under penalty of loss of the right to assert the truth at a later time. Since in such a case there is no active misleading of the other party, who has misled himself, the courts have insisted upon some fault in connection with the conduct of the one to be estopped. There is no estoppel where he has remained silent reasonably and in good faith; he must be aware of his rights,[85] and must realize that the other is about to act under a mistaken belief.[86] Thus this branch of estoppel requires either an intent to mislead or unreasonable conduct amounting to negligence in failing to act,[87] rather than the strict responsibility imposed in estoppel by misrepresentation.

These two branches of equitable estoppel not only have been confounded with one another, but have added their contribution to the uncertainty in which the whole subject of misrepresentation has at times been lost.

Summary

Let it be supposed that A buys a horse and a cow from B, relying upon B's statement that he owns both animals. A pays one-third of the purchase price at the time of sale, and contracts to pay the balance at a later time. When it develops that the cow is in fact owned by C, A may have the possibility of no less than eight different remedies based upon some form of misrepresentation. These are:

1. A tort action for damages for deceit. In many jurisdictions this requires proof that B knew that his statement was false, or at least was consciously ignorant of the truth. In others, it has been extended to include negligence, or even strict liability.

2. A tort action for damages for negligence, upon proof that B made the state-

---

80. For example Eaton v. Wilkins, 1912, 163 Cal. 742, 127 P. 71; Brian v. Bonvillain, 1902, 111 La. 441, 35 So. 632; Bishop v. Minton, 1893, 112 N.C. 524, 17 S.E. 436.

81. McLearn v. Hill, 1931, 276 Mass. 519, 177 N.E. 617; Kelly v. Richards, 1938, 95 Utah 560, 83 P.2d 731; Dill v. Widman, 1953, 413 Ill. 448, 109 N.E.2d 765; Chambers v. Bookman, 1903, 67 S.C. 432, 46 S.E. 39; Two Rivers Manufacturing Co. v. Day, 1899, 102 Wis. 328, 78 N.W. 440. See Restatement of Torts, § 894, Comment *b*; Williston, Liability for Honest Misrepresentation, 1911, 24 Harv.L.Rev. 415, 423–426; Ewart, Principles of Estoppel, 1900, 83–88.

82. Second Restatement of Torts, § 894(2); Ewart, Principles of Estoppel, 1900, 88–94.

83. Pickard v. Sears, 1837, 6 Ad. & El. 469, 112 Eng.Rep. 179; Milligan v. Miller, 1912, 253 Ill. 511, 97 N.E. 1054; Helwig v. Fogelsong, 1914, 166 Iowa 715, 148 N.W. 990; Craig v. Crossman, 1920, 209 Mich. 462, 177 N.W. 400; McNamara v. Feihe, 1921, 139 Md. 516, 115 A. 753.

84. Logan v. Gardner, 1890, 136 Pa. 588, 20 A. 625; Martin v. Maine Central Railroad Co., 1890, 83 Me. 100, 21 A. 740; Bastrup v. Prendergast, 1899, 179 Ill. 553, 53 N.E. 995; Macomber v. Kinney, 1910, 114 Minn. 146, 130 N.W. 851. See also the forgery cases supra, note 77.

85. Titus v. Morse, 1855, 40 Me. 348; Formby v. Hood, 1898, 119 Ala. 231, 24 So. 359; Starr v. Bartz, 1909, 219 Mo. 47, 117 S.W. 1125; Milburn v. Michel, 1921, 137 Md. 415, 112 A. 581.

86. Beechley v. Beechley, 1906, 134 Iowa 75, 108 N.W. 762; Scharman v. Scharman, 1893, 38 Neb. 39, 56 N.W. 704; Allen v. Shaw, 1881, 61 N.H. 95; Sullivan v. Moore, 1909, 84 S.C. 426, 66 S.E. 561.

87. Restatement of Torts, § 894(2); Terrell Hills Baptist Church v. Pawel, Tex.Civ.App.1956, 286 S.W.2d 204.

ment without reasonable care to learn the truth.

3. A contract action for damages for breach of warranty, which regards the statement as a part of the contract, and therefore requires only proof that it was made and relied on.

4. In some jurisdictions, at least,[88] a suit in equity to rescind the sale, by which A seeks to return both animals and recover the payment made. This also will lie where the statement was an innocent one.

5. A restitution action at law, on the theory that A rescinds the sale of his own motion, is willing to return both animals, and seeks to recover the payment made. This will also lie where the statement was innocent.

6. If B brings an action for the balance of the purchase price, A may set up the misrepresentation as a defense, upon the theory that he rescinds the sale and is willing to return both animals, and defeat all recovery. This remedy is likewise available, in most jurisdictions, for innocent misrepresentation.

7. In B's action for the balance of the price, A may retain the horse and set up the misrepresentation as a defense, claiming recoupment of his damages by reducing the amount of B's recovery to any excess value the horse may have over the amount paid. There is still considerable uncertainty as to whether this remedy is available for innocent misstatements.[89]

8. If C claims the cow from A, A may set up by way of estoppel the fact that C actively misrepresented to him that B was its owner, or that C stood by knowing that A was about to purchase from B, and failed to assert his claim.

One has only to consider the variety of these remedies to understand why the law of misrepresentation has not been clarified by the courts. Considering them by the numbers given 1, 2, 3, 7 and 8 proceed upon the theory of affirmance of the transaction and retention of what has been received; 4, 5 and 6 upon the theory of disaffirmance and rescission. Number 1 is based by some courts upon wrongful intent, by others upon negligence or strict liability; 2 is a matter of negligence; 3, 4, 5 and 6 of strict responsibility; 8 falls into two branches, one based on strict liability, the other on negligence; while 7 has been assigned by various courts to each of the three theories.

Our chief concern is of course with the tort action of deceit. But any discussion of that action obviously would be incomplete without reference to the divergent rules which have developed as to the other remedies, and the disturbing effect which they have had upon the deceit action itself.

 WESTLAW REFERENCES

synopsis,digest(nondisclosure* deceit! /p tort* negligen**)
liab! /s misrepresent! /s damages
restatement /s torts /5 551
18.85.230 & court(wa)

The Cause for a Mistake and its Importance
digest(mistake! mistook /s misrepresent! /s mutual**)
mistake! mistook /s misrepresent! /s unilateral!

The Tort Action for Damages
element* /s deceit /s tort action
restatement /s torts /5 525

The Contract-Warranty Cause of Action for Damages
warranty /s material /s representation* & damage* /s breach*** /s warranty
"ex contractu" /s breach /s warrant!

The Equitable Remedy for Rescission
digest(rescission rescind*** /s misrepresent! /s contract* deed* lease* agreement*)
misrepresent! /s equit! /s relief remed!

---

[88]. As noted in this section on Rescission, supra, p. 715, some courts refuse to allow this remedy, upon the ground that there is an adequate remedy at law, in the form of a restitution action.

[89]. See supra, in this section on Misrepresentation as a Defense. In the case supposed, of course, the statement might amount to a warranty, for which recoupment would be allowed even if it were innocently made. See Uniform Sales Act, § 69(1).

Restitution at Law
restitution /s equit! /s relief remed!
restitution /s misrepresent!

Misrepresentation as a Defense
misrepresent! /10 defense /10 affirmative
fraud +4 factum /s defense*

Estoppel
estopp** /s defense* /s misrepresent!

§ 106. Representation and Nondisclosure

The representation [1] which will serve as a basis for an action of deceit, as well as other forms of relief, usually consists, of course, of oral or written words; but it is not necessarily so limited. The exhibition of a document,[2] turning back the odometer of an automobile offered for sale,[3] drawing a check without funds,[4] or a wide variety of other conduct calculated to convey a misleading impression under the circumstances of the case,[5] may be sufficient. Merely by entering into some transactions at all, the defendant may reasonably be taken to represent that some things are true—as for example, that a bank which receives deposits is solvent,[6] or that a stock certificate sold is a valid one,[7] and he has a permit to sell it.[8] It is trite to say in such cases that "actions may speak louder than words."

The significance to be assigned to such words or conduct will be determined according to the effect they would produce, under the circumstances, upon the ordinary mind.[9] Ambiguous statements, which are reasonably capable of both a true and a false meaning, will amount to misrepresentation if the false meaning is accepted, and is intended [10] or known [11] to be accepted—although if the true meaning is intended and believed to be understood, it would seem that any liability would be in negligence rather than deceit.[12] Likewise, misrepresentation may be found in statements which are literally true, but which create a false impression in the mind

§ 106

1. Mention should be made also of Neibuhr v. Gage, 1906, 99 Minn. 149, 108 N.W. 884, affirmed 99 Minn. 149, 109 N.W. 1; Smith v. Blakesburg Savings Bank, 1917, 182 Iowa 1190, 164 N.W. 762; and Woodham v. Allen, 1900, 130 Cal. 194, 62 P. 398, all of which say that duress provides a basis for an action in tort, on the same basis as misrepresentation. This is scanty authority. It usually is held that the duress merely invalidates the plaintiff's consent, leaving open to him any action, such as conversion, which would have been open to him if it had not been given. Grainger v. Hill, 1838, 4 Bing.N.C. 212, 132 Eng.Rep. 769; General Motors Acceptance Corp. v. Davis, 1931, 151 Okl. 255, 7 P.2d 157; Saunders v. Mullinix, 1950, 195 Md. 235, 72 A.2d 720; Murphy v. Hobbs, 1884, 8 Colo. 17, 5 P. 637, rehearing denied 1886, 8 Colo. 130, 11 P. 55.

2. Baker v. Hallam, 1897, 103 Iowa 43, 72 N.W. 419; Leonard v. Springer, 1902, 197 Ill. 532, 64 N.E. 299; McCall v. Davis, 1867, 56 Pa. 431.

3. Osborn v. Gene Teague Chevrolet Co., 1969, 254 Or. 486, 459 P.2d 988; District Motor Co. v. Rodill, Mun.App.D.C.1952, 88 A.2d 489; Chapman v. Zakzaska, 1956, 273 Wis. 64, 76 N.W.2d 537; Sarwark Motor Sales, Inc. v. Husband, App.1967, 5 Ariz. 304, 426 P.2d 404; Boise Dodge, Inc. v. Clark, 1969, 92 Idaho 902, 453 P.2d 551. Cf. Lindberg Cadillac Co. v. Aron, Mo.App.1963, 371 S.W.2d 651 (trading in car with cracked engine block, painted over).

4. Eastern Trust & Banking Co. v. Cunningham, 1908, 103 Me. 455, 70 A. 17; Sieling v. Clark, 1896, 18 Misc. 464, 41 N.Y.S. 982; cf. City National Bank v. Burns, 1880, 68 Ala. 267.

5. Such as stacking aluminum sheets to conceal corroded ones in the middle. Salzman v. Maldaver, 1946, 315 Mich. 403, 24 N.W.2d 161.

6. Cassidy v. Uhlmann, 1902, 170 N.Y. 505, 63 N.E. 554, reargument denied 171 N.Y. 660, 64 N.E. 1119.

7. Hutchings v. Tipsword, Mo.App.1962, 363 S.W.2d 40; MacDonald v. Reich & Lievre, 1929, 100 Cal.App. 736, 281 P. 106.

8. Pennebaker v. Kimble, 1928, 126 Or. 317, 269 P. 981.

9. Downey v. Finucane, 1912, 205 N.Y. 251, 98 N.E. 391; Windram v. French, 1890, 151 Mass. 547, 24 N.E. 914; Miles v. Stevens, 1846, 3 Pa. 21; Davis v. Louisville Trust Co., 6th Cir. 1910, 181 F. 10.

10. "If they palter with him in a double sense, it may be that they lie like truth; but I think they lie, and it is a fraud. Indeed, as a question of casuistry, I am inclined to think the fraud is aggravated by a shabby attempt to get the benefit of a fraud, without incurring the responsibility." Lord Blackburn, in Smith v. Chadwick, 1884, L.R. 9 A.C. 187.

11. Busch v. Wilcox, 1890, 82 Mich. 315, 46 N.W. 940, affirmed 82 Mich. 336, 47 N.W. 328; Degman v. Mason County, 1874, 15 Ky.L.Abs. 876; Angus v. Clifford, [1891] 2 Ch.Div. 449, 472. See Terry, Intent to Defraud, 1915, 25 Yale L.J. 87, 94.

12. Nash v. Minnesota Title Insurance & Trust Co., 1895, 163 Mass. 574, 40 N.E. 1039; Slater Trust Co. v. Gardiner, 2d Cir. 1910, 183 F. 268; Restatement of Torts, § 528. See Smith v. Chadwick, 1884, L.R. 9 A.C. 187; Angus v. Clifford, [1891] 2 Ch.Div. 449, 472.

of the hearer,[13] as is sometimes the case where a complicated financial statement is issued by a seller of securities. "A fraud may be as effectually perpetrated by telling the truth as a falsehood; by calling things by their right names as by their wrong names." [14]

In addition to such representations by word or conduct, which might be called definite or positive, deceit, as well as other remedies, may be based upon an active concealment of the truth.[15] Any words or acts which create a false impression covering up the truth,[16] or which remove an opportunity that might otherwise have led to the discovery of a material fact—as by floating a ship to conceal the defects in her bottom,[17] sending one who is in search of information in a direction where it cannot be obtained,[18] or even a false denial of knowledge by one in possession of the facts—[19] are classed as misrepresentation, no less than a verbal assurance that the fact is not true.

Nondisclosure

A much more difficult problem arises as to whether mere silence, or a passive failure to disclose facts of which the defendant has knowledge, can serve as the foundation of a deceit action.[20] It has commonly been stated as a general rule,[21] particularly in the older cases, that the action will not lie for such tacit nondisclosure.[22] This rule of course reflected the dubious business ethics of the bargaining transactions with which deceit was at first concerned, together with a touch of the old tort notion that there can be no liability for nonfeasance, or merely doing nothing.[23] It finds proper application in cases where the fact undisclosed is patent,[24] or the plaintiff has equal opportunities for obtaining information which he may be expected to utilize,[25] or the defendant has no reason to think that he is acting under any misapprehension.[26] There are, however, occasional modern cases which have held that so long as one adversary does not actively

---

13. Cahill v. Readon, 1929, 85 Colo. 9, 273 P. 653 (rent values had "become stabilized"—at zero). Cf. Lomerson v. Johnston, 1890, 47 N.J.Eq. 312, 20 A. 675; Downey v. Finucane, 1912, 205 N.Y. 251, 98 N.E. 391; Wolfe v. A.E. Kusterer & Co., 1934, 269 Mich. 424, 257 N.W. 729; Atwood v. Chapman, 1877, 68 Me. 38. See the language of Baron Alderson in Moens v. Heyworth, 1842, 10 M. & W. 147, 152 Eng.Rep. 418.

14. Mulligan v. Bailey, 1859, 28 Ga. 507.

15. See Keeton, Fraud—Concealment and Non-Disclosure, 1936, 15 Tex.L.Rev. 1, 2–5; Wilson, Concealment or Silence as a Form of Fraud, 1895, 5 Counsellor 230.

16. Croyle v. Moses, 1879, 90 Pa. 250 (cribbing horse offered for sale tied up short); Kuelling v. Roderick Lean Manufacturing Co., 1905, 183 N.Y. 78, 75 N.E. 1098 (defects in road roller concealed with putty and paint); Ten-Cate v. First National Bank, Tex. Civ.App.1932, 52 S.W.2d 323 (portion of contract omitted in reading it). Cf. Pickering v. Dowson, 1813, 4 Taunt. 779, 128 Eng.Rep. 537 (defects in house covered with plaster and paint); Weikel v. Sterns, 1911, 142 Ky. 513, 134 S.W. 908.

17. Schneider v. Heath, 1813, 3 Camp. 505, 170 Eng. Rep. 1462.

18. Chisolm v. Gadsden, 1847, 1 Strob., S.C., 220; Stewart v. Wyoming Cattle Ranche Co., 1888, 128 U.S. 383, 9 S.Ct. 101, 32 L.Ed. 439. Cf. Griffiths v. Thrasher, 1953, 95 Mont. 210, 26 P.2d 995 (staffing hotel with confederates).

19. Smith v. Beatty, 1843, 37 N.C. 456, 2 Ired.Eq. 456.

20. See Keeton, Fraud—Concealment and Non-Disclosure, 1936, 15 Tex.L.Rev. 1; Notes, 1942, 22 Bos. U.L.Rev. 607; 1948, 21 Temple L.Q. 368; 1956, 20 So. Cal.L.Rev. 378.

21. Derived originally from the language of Lord Cairns in Peek v. Gurney, 1873, L.R. 6 H.L. 377. See Bower, Actionable Nondisclosure, 1915, 134; and cf. Beachey v. Brown, 1860, El.Bl. & El. 796, 120 Eng.Rep. 706.

22. Keates v. Earl of Cardogan, 1851, 10 C.B. 591, 138 Eng.Rep. 234; Crowell v. Jackson, 1891, 53 N.J.L. 656, 23 A. 426; Boileau v. Records & Breen, 1913, 165 Iowa 134, 144 N.W. 336; Iron City National Bank v. Anderson, Du Puy & Co., 1899, 194 Pa. 205, 44 A. 1066; Windram Manufacturing Co. v. Boston Blacking Co., 1921, 239 Mass. 123, 131 N.E. 454.

23. See supra, § 56.

24. Riley v. White, Mo.App.1950, 231 S.W.2d 291; Schnader v. Brooks, 1926, 150 Md. 52, 132 A. 381; cf. Gibson v. Mendenhall, 1950, 203 Okl. 558, 224 P.2d 251 (generally known); Kapiloff v. Abington Plaza Corp., Mun.App.D.C.1948, 59 A.2d 516 (act of Congress).

25. Phillips v. Homestake Consolidated Placer Mines Co., 1929, 51 Nev. 226, 273 P. 657; Oates v. Taylor, 1948, 31 Wn.2d 898, 199 P.2d 924.

26. Haddad v. Clark, 1945, 132 Conn. 229, 43 A.2d 221; Egan v. Hudson Nut Products, Inc., 1955, 142 Conn. 344, 114 A.2d 213; Industrial Bank of Commerce v. Selling, 1952, 203 Misc. 154, 116 N.Y.S.2d 274; Blair v. National Security Insurance Co., 3d Cir. 1942, 126 F.2d 955. Cf. Lindquist v. Dilkes, 3d Cir. 1942, 127 F.2d 21.

mislead another, he is perfectly free to take advantage, no matter how unfair, of ignorance; and that the owner of a dwelling which he knows to be riddled with termites can unload it with impunity upon a buyer unaware, and go on his way rejoicing.[27] These are surely singularly unappetizing cases.

To this general rule, if such it be, the courts have developed a number of exceptions, some of which are as yet very ill defined, and have no very definite boundaries. The most obvious one is that if the defendant does speak, he must disclose enough to prevent his words from being misleading,[28] and that there is fraud in a statement as to the rental of property which does not mention that it is illegal,[29] or as to the income of an amusement center which does not disclose that there has been a police raid which is likely to affect it,[30] or in the disclosure of the existence of one graveyard on premises without disclosing another.[31] In other words, half of the truth may obviously amount to a lie, if it is understood to be the whole. Again, one who has made a statement, and subsequently acquires new information which makes it untrue or misleading, must disclose such information to anyone whom he knows to be still acting on the basis of the original statement—as, for example, where there is a serious decline in the profits of a business pending its sale.[32]

Another exception is found where the parties stand in some confidential or fiduciary relation to one another, such as that of principal and agent,[33] executor and beneficiary of an estate,[34] bank and investing depositor,[35] majority and minority stockholders,[36] old friends,[37] or numerous others where special trust and confidence is reposed.[38] In addition, certain types of contracts, such as

---

27. Swinton v. Whitinsville Savings Bank, 1942, 311 Mass. 677, 42 N.E.2d 808; Fegeas v. Sherrill, 1958, 218 Md. 472, 147 A.2d 223; Hendrick v. Lynn, 1958, 37 Del. Ch. 402, 144 A.2d 147.

28. Smith v. Pope, 1961, 103 N.H. 555, 176 A.2d 321; Newell v. Randall, 1884, 32 Minn. 171, 19 N.W. 972; Noved Realty Corp. v. A.A.P. Co., 1937, 250 App. Div. 1, 293 N.Y.S. 336; Berry v. Stevens, 1934, 168 Okl. 124, 31 P.2d 950; Dennis v. Thomson, 1931, 240 Ky. 727, 43 S.W.2d 18.

Otherwise where the statement does not purport to tell the whole truth. Potts v. Chapin, 1882, 133 Mass. 276.

29. Palmiter v. Hackett, 1919, 95 Or. 12, 185 P. 1105, modified 95 Or. 12, 186 P. 581; Tucker v. Beazley, Mun.App.D.C.1948, 57 A.2d 191; cf. Kraft v. Lowe, Mun.App.D.C.1950, 77 A.2d 554 (statement that plumbing is all right, without disclosing septic tank). Otherwise where the defendant honestly believes that the rental is legal. Ceferatti v. Boisvert, 1950, 137 Conn. 280, 77 A.2d 82.

30. Dyke v. Zaiser, 1947, 80 Cal.App.2d 639, 182 P.2d 344.

31. Elsey v. Lamkin, 1914, 156 Ky. 836, 162 S.W. 106; Junius Construction Co. v. Cohen, 1931, 257 N.Y. 393, 178 N.E. 672 (streets), affirmed 233 A.D. 684, 249 N.Y.S. 928.

32. With v. O'Flanagan, [1936] 1 Ch. 575; Loewer v. Harris, 2d Cir. 1893, 57 F. 368; Guastella v. Wardell, Miss.1967, 198 So.2d 227; Fischer v. Kletz, S.D.N.Y. 1967, 266 F.Supp. 180; Restatement of Torts, § 551(2). Cf. Equitable Life Insurance Co. of Iowa v. Halsey, Stuart & Co., 1941, 312 U.S. 410, 61 S.Ct. 623, 85 L.Ed. 920; Hush v. Reaugh, E.D.Ill.1938, 23 F.Supp. 646. See Note, 1968, 116 U.Pa.L.Rev. 500.

Cf. Pilmore v. Hood, 1838, 5 Bing.N.C. 97, 132 Eng. Rep. 1042 (statement made without intent that plaintiff should rely on it must be corrected when reliance is discovered).

33. McDonough v. Williams, 1905, 77 Ark. 261, 92 S.W. 783.

34. Foreman v. Henry, 1922, 87 Okl. 272, 210 P. 1026; Murphy v. Cartwright, 5th Cir. 1953, 202 F.2d 71.

35. Brasher v. First National Bank, 1936, 232 Ala. 340, 168 So. 42.

36. Speed v. Transamerica Corp., D.C.Del.1951, 99 F.Supp. 808, supplemented 100 F.Supp. 461, petition denied 100 F.Supp. 463.

37. Feist v. Roesler, Tex.Civ.App.1953, 86 S.W.2d 787. Cf. In re Estate of Enyart, 1916, 100 Neb. 337, 160 N.W. 120, overruled in part Kingsley v. Noble, 1935, 129 Neb. 808, 263 N.W. 222 (affianced).

38. Edward Barron Estate Co. v. Woodruff Co., 1912, 163 Cal. 561, 126 P. 351. "* * * for instance, the relations of trustee and cestui que trust, principal and agent, attorney and client, physician and patient, priest and parishioner, partners, tenants in common, husband and wife, parent and child, guardian and ward, and many others of like character." Farmers State Bank of Newport v. Lamon, 1925, 132 Wash. 369, 231 P. 952, 42 A.L.R. 1072. There is dispute as to the confidential nature of certain relations. Thus tenants in common, Phillips v. Homestake Consolidated Placer Mines Co., 1929, 51 Nev. 226, 273 P. 657; Neill v. Shamburg, 1893, 158 Pa. 263, 27 A. 992, and corporate directors purchasing stock from stockholders. Crowell v. Jackson, 1891, 53 N.J.L. 656, 23 A. 426; Goodwin v. Agassiz, 1933, 283 Mass. 358, 186 N.E. 659, have been held to be under no duty to make disclosure. As to the

those of suretyship or guaranty,[39] insurance,[40] partnership and joint adventure,[41] are recognized as creating something in the nature of a confidential relation, and hence as requiring the utmost good faith, and full and fair disclosure of all material facts.

Beyond, this, there has been a rather amorphous tendency on the part of most courts in recent years to find a duty of disclosure when the circumstances are such that the failure to disclose something would violate a standard requiring conformity to what the ordinary ethical person would have disclosed. The issue has been regarded as one for the court rather than the jury. Some factors of importance are as follows:

(1) The difference in the degree of intelligence of the parties to the transaction. This is simply because the community sense of justice demands it;

(2) The relation that the parties bear to each other;

(3) The manner in which the information is acquired. Information which affects the value of the subject matter of a contract may have been acquired by chance, by effort, or by an illegal act. It makes a difference on the ethical equality of non-disclosure.

(4) The nature of the fact not disclosed. In contracts of sale of real property, if the vendor conceals an intrinsic defect not discoverable by reasonable care, there is a much greater likelihood of the existence of a duty to disclose the non-discoverable and intrinsic defect than there would be to disclose something extrinsic likely to affect market value;

(5) The general class to which the person who is concealing the information belongs. It is much more likely that a seller will be required to disclose information than a purchaser;

(6) The nature of the contract itself. In releases, and contracts of insurance, practically all material facts must be disclosed;

(7) The importance of the fact not disclosed;

(8) Any conduct of the person not disclosing something to prevent discovery.[42] The active concealment of any material fact—anything that might prevent the purchaser from buying at the price agreed on is, and should be, as a matter of law fraudulent.

When the plaintiff seeks relief of an equitable character, as by rescission of the transaction and recovery of what he has parted with, a more liberal rule usually is applied. Mutual mistake as to a material fact ordinarily is sufficient ground for such relief; and when the plaintiff is proceeding under a material mistake, the defendant's position can scarcely be improved if he stands by with knowledge of the error, fails to make disclosure, and takes advantage of the situation.[43] Likewise, as has previously been mentioned,[44] there is one branch of estoppel in pais which is based upon a failure to take action, or to disclose the truth, where a reasonable man would not fail to do so. The

---

latter, see Note, 1930, 14 Minn.L.Rev. 530, and the numerous articles there cited.

39. Cf. Connecticut General Life Insurance Co. v. Chase, 1900, 72 Vt. 176, 47 A. 825; Atlantic Trust & Deposit Co. v. Union Trust & Title Corp., 1909, 110 Va. 286, 67 S.E. 182; Arant, Suretyship, 1931, 77–81.

40. See Vance, Insurance, 2d Ed. 1930, §§ 96–98; Note, 1928, 14 Corn.L.Q. 91.

41. Cf. Noble v. Fox, 1912, 35 Okl. 70, 128 P. 102.

42. Keeton, Fraud—Concealment and Non-Disclosure, 1936, 15 Tex.L.Rev. 1; see, also, Securities and Exchange Commission v. Capital Gains Research Bureau, Inc., 1963, 375 U.S. 180, 84 S.Ct. 275, 11 L.Ed.2d 237 ("Courts have imposed on a fiduciary an affirmative duty of 'utmost good faith, and full and fair disclosure of all material facts.'"); but see, A.B.C. Packard, Inc. v. General Motors Corp., 9th Cir. 1960, 275 F.2d 63 ("No cases are cited by appellant which approve the theory advanced by Mr. Keeton in his law review article. Apparently no court, during the twenty-three years since its (the law review's) publication, has seen fit to adopt his theories.").

43. Hill v. Gray, 1816, 1 Starkie 434, 171 Eng.Rep. 521; Simmons v. Evans, 1927, 185 Tenn. 282, 206 S.W.2d 295; Salmonson v. Horswill, 1917, 39 S.D. 402, 164 N.W. 973; Tyra v. Cheney, 1915, 129 Minn. 428, 152 N.W. 835; Clauser v. Taylor, 1941, 44 Cal.App.2d 453, 112 P.2d 661. See Note, 1918, 27 Yale L.J. 691.

44. Supra, § 105 on Estoppel.

greater liberality found as to such remedies is probably due to the fact that they are primarily concerned with preventing the defendant from obtaining an unfair advantage of his own, while the action of deceit requires him to go further, and compensate the plaintiff for the loss he has sustained.

WESTLAW REFERENCES

misrepresent! /s fals! untrue truth /s meaning* impression* understanding* % topic(110)

Nondisclosure
disclos! nondisclos! /s silence* tacit % topic(110)

§ 107. Basis of Responsibility

Misrepresentation, as has been said before,[1] may be separated into the three familiar tort classifications of intent, negligence, and strict responsibility. The earlier cases made little or no attempt to distinguish the three, no doubt because there had been no occasion to distinguish the possible remedies. The actions for deceit and for breach of warranty, with their common origin in the action on the case, were not yet clearly recognized as separate,[2] and it was assumed, by the text writers at least,[3] that negligent misrepresentation would find a remedy in deceit. It was not until as late as 1889 that the House of Lords, in the leading case of Derry v. Peek,[4] clearly identified the deceit action with intentional misrepresentation, and left negligence and strict responsibility to be dealt with by other remedies.

In that case the defendants, who were directors of a tramway corporation, issued a prospectus to induce the public to subscribe for stock, which contained the unqualified statement that " * * * the company has the right to use steam, or mechanical motive power, instead of horses. * * * " In fact, the company had no such right. The plaintiff, who had purchased stock on the faith of the statement, brought an action of deceit. The court took an extremely charitable view of the evidence, and concluded that the defendants had honestly believed the statement to be true, although they had no reasonable ground for any such belief. It was held that the action could not be maintained, since nothing more than negligence was shown. For deceit there must be proof "that a false representation has been made (1) knowingly, or (2) without belief in its truth, or (3) recklessly, careless whether it be true or false." [5]

This decision, which excluded from the action of deceit any misrepresentation that is innocent, or merely negligent, has been something of a storm center ever since. It has been condemned as a backward step in the law, and in cases where there is a contract between the parties, a substantial minority group of the American courts flatly refuse to follow it.[6] The majority purport to accept it as sound law,[7] but a great many of them have devised various more or less ingenious fictions and formulae [8] which permit them to render lip service to Derry v. Peek, and yet allow recovery in deceit for misrepresentation which falls short of actual intent to deceive. If one looks to the facts of the cases rather than the formulae adopted by the courts, it is by no means clear that Der-

---

§ 107

1. Supra, § 105.

2. See, slowly working out the distinction, Williamson v. Allison, 1802, 2 East 446, 102 Eng.Rep. 439; Vail v. Strong, 1838, 10 Vt. 457; Mahurin v. Harding, 1853, 28 N.H. 128; Pierce v. Carey, 1875, 37 Wis. 232.

3. See Beven, Negligence, 2d Ed., 1474; 1 Bigelow, Fraud, 1st Ed. 1888, 509, 516, 517; 2 Pomeroy, Equity Jurisprudence, 1st ed. 1882, § 884.

4. 1889, 14 A.C. 337.

5. Per Lord Herschell, 14 A.C. 374.

6. See infra, this section on Negligence.

7. Lambert v. Smith, 1964, 235 Md. 284, 201 A.2d 491; Kountze v. Kennedy, 1895, 147 N.Y. 124, 41 N.E. 414; Wishnick v. Frye, 1952, 111 Cal.App.2d 926, 245 P.2d 532; Dundee Land Co. v. Simmons, 1948, 204 Ga. 248, 49 S.E.2d 488; Sledge & Norfleet Co. v. Mann, 1937, 193 Ark. 884, 103 S.W.2d 630.

8. See infra, p. 745. Green, Deceit, 1930, 16 Va.L. Rev. 749, considers the resulting flexibility desirable, since it enables the courts to accomplish substantial justice and still preserve the appearance of a fixed rule. There is, of course, not so much to be said for the resulting unpredictability of decisions.

ry v. Peek is supported by the weight of American authority. The controversy which has raged about the case [9] has been concerned more with the question of the form of action which should be available, rather than with the substantive law of liability. It may be suggested that it is the latter which is of primary importance,[10] and that once it is determined that liability is to be imposed, it is a comparatively easy matter to find an appropriate remedy in deceit, negligence or warranty. The problem may be approached as one of the bases of liability, with only incidental regard for the form of the remedy.

Scienter—Intent to Deceive

The intent which underlies an intentional misrepresentation is a more complex matter than the relatively simple intention in the case of assault and battery.[11] It involves the intent that a representation shall be made, that it shall be directed to a particular person or class of persons,[12] that it shall convey a certain meaning,[13] that it shall be believed, and that it shall be acted upon in a certain way.[14] In the usual case, all of this is present beyond dispute. In addition, there is the intent to accomplish an ultimate purpose, as to benefit the speaker, or to cause harm to the one addressed. It is well settled that, except as to the issue of punitive damages,[15] this last is of no importance. The fact that the defendant was disinterested,[16] that he had the best of motives, and that he thought he was doing the plaintiff a kindness,[17] will not absolve him from liability, so long as he did in fact intend to mislead.

So far as culpability is concerned, none of these intentions is controlling. The intent which becomes important is the intent to deceive, to mislead, to convey a false impression. Obviously this intent, which has been given the name of "scienter" by the courts, must be a matter of belief, or of absence of belief, that the representation is true; and it was this element which was so strongly emphasized in Derry v. Peek. The state of the speaker's mind, notwithstanding its elusiveness as a matter of psychology and its difficulty of proof, must be looked to in determining whether the action of deceit can be maintained.

There is of course no difficulty in finding the required intent to mislead where it appears that the speaker believes his statement to be false.[18] Likewise there is general agreement that it is present when the representation is made without any belief as to its truth,[19] or with reckless disregard

9. See Smith, Liability for Negligent Language, 1909, 14 Harv.L.Rev. 184; Williston, Liability for Honest Misrepresentation, 1911, 24 Harv.L.Rev. 415; Bohlen, Misrepresentation as Deceit, Negligence or Warranty, 1929, 42 Harv.L.Rev. 733; Carpenter, Responsibility for Intentional, Negligent and Innocent Misrepresentation, 1930, 24 Ill.L.Rev. 749; Weisiger, Basis of Liability for Misrepresentation, 1930, 24 Ill.L. Rev. 866; Green, Deceit, 1930, 16 Va.L.Rev. 749, 750–762; Morris, Liability for Innocent Misrepresentation, 1930, 64 U.S.L.Rev. 121; Bohlen, Should Negligent Misrepresentations Be Treated as Negligence or Fraud, 1932, 18 Va.L.Rev. 703; Green, Innocent Misrepresentation, 1933, 19 Va.L.Rev. 742; Keeton, Fraud: The Necessity for an Intent to Deceive, 1958, 5 U.C. L.A.L.Rev. 583; Notes, 1927, 12 Corn.L.Q. 539; 1928, 28 Col.L.Rev. 216; 1928, 37 Yale L.J. 1141; 1931, 26 Ill. L.Rev. 49; 1937, 21 Minn.L.Rev. 434.

10. See Harper and McNeely, A Synthesis of the Law of Misrepresentation, 1939, 22 Minn.L.Rev. 939.

11. See Terry, Intent to Defraud, 1915, 25 Yale L.J. 87.

12. As to this, see infra, this section, p. 742.

13. As to intent or negligence in the case of ambiguous statements, see supra, § 106.

14. As to this, see infra, this section, p. 729.

15. Thompson v. Modern School of Business and Correspondence, 1920, 183 Cal. 112, 190 P. 451; Laughlin v. Hopkinson, 1920, 292 Ill. 80, 126 N.E. 591; Kluge v. Ries, 1917, 66 Ind.App. 610, 117 N.E. 262.

16. Foster v. Charles, 1830, 7 Bing. 105, 131 Eng. Rep. 40; Holloway v. Forsyth, 1917, 226 Mass. 358, 115 N.E. 483; Endsley v. Johns, 1887, 120 Ill. 469, 12 N.E. 247; Wilson v. Jones, Tex.Com.App.1932, 45 S.W.2d 572.

17. Polhill v. Walter, 1832, 3 B. & Ad. 114, 110 Eng. Rep. 43; Boyd's Executors v. Browne, 1847, 6 Pa. 310; Smith v. Chadwick, 1884, L.R. 9 A.C. 187.

18. See for example Howard v. Gould, 1856, 28 Vt. 523.

19. Shackett v. Bickford, 1900, 74 N.H. 57, 65 A. 252; Griswold v. Gebbie, 1889, 126 Pa. 353, 17 A. 673. See Derry v. Peek, 1889, 14 A.C. 337; Second Restatement of Torts, § 526(b).

whether it be true or false.[20] Further than this, it appears that all courts have extended it to include representations made by one who is conscious that he has no sufficient basis of information to justify them.[21] A defendant who asserts a fact as of his own knowledge, or so positively as to imply that he has knowledge,[22] under circumstances where he is aware that he will be so understood [23] when he knows that he does not in fact know whether what he says is true, is found to have the intent to deceive, not so much as to the fact itself, but rather as to the extent of his information. Since the state of his mind may be inferred from the circumstances, and in the absence of satisfactory evidence to the contrary it may sometimes be quite reasonable to infer that he must have known that he did not know,[24] there is a certain amount of leeway in the direction of holding the defendant to something like a reasonable standard of judgment.

Apparently it is at this point that the line is to be drawn between an intent to mislead and mere negligence. An honest belief, however unreasonable, that the representation is true and the speaker has information to justify it, was held in Derry v. Peek [25] to be no sufficient basis for deceit. It is of course clear that the very unreasonableness of such a belief may be strong evidence that it does not in fact exist; and where this conclusion is reached as an inference of fact,[26] or even through a presumption capable of being rebutted,[27] there is nothing inconsistent with a basis of intent. But the courts which go further and adopt arbitrary rules as to when an honest belief does not exist [28] would appear to cross the boundaries of intent, and to impose liability upon another basis.

Thus far, attention has been directed to the action of deceit. Other remedies for misrepresentation are more liberal in their scope; and it has never been disputed that the "scienter" or intent which is a basis for deceit is sufficient to justify relief in equity, restitution at law, the defense of fraud, or estoppel.

---

20. Rosenberg v. Howle, Mun.App.D.C.1948, 56 A.2d 709; Atkinson v. Charlotte Builders, 1950, 232 N.C. 67, 59 S.E.2d 1; Otis & Co. v. Grimes, 1935, 97 Colo. 219, 48 P.2d 788; Richards v. Foss, 1927, 126 Me. 413, 139 A. 231; Zager v. Setzer, 1955, 242 N.C. 493, 88 S.E.2d 94.

21. Hadcock v. Osmer, 1897, 153 N.Y. 604, 47 N.E. 923; Sovereign Pocohontas Co. v. Bond, 1941, 74 U.S. App.D.C. 175, 120 F.2d 39; Fausett & Co. v. Bullard, 1950, 217 Ark. 176, 229 S.W.2d 490; Zager v. Setzer, 1955, 242 N.C. 493, 88 S.E.2d 94; Hollerman v. F.H. Peavey & Co., 1964, 269 Minn. 221, 130 N.W.2d 534.

22. An unqualified assertion of fact is regarded as made as of the speaker's own knowledge. Bullitt v. Farrar, 1889, 42 Minn. 8, 43 N.W. 566; Schlossman's v. Niewinski, 1951, 12 N.J.Super. 500, 79 A.2d 870; Kirkpatrick v. Reeves, 1889, 121 Ind. 280, 22 N.E. 139; First National Bank of Tigerton v. Hackett, 1914, 159 Wis. 113, 149 N.W. 703; Pumphrey v. Quillen, 1956, 165 Ohio St. 343, 135 N.E.2d 328.

As to the distinction between knowledge of falsity and conscious ignorance, see Joseph Greenspon's Son Pipe Corp. v. Hyman-Michaels Co., Mo.App.1939, 133 S.W.2d 426.

23. Thus where the matter is clearly susceptible of knowledge. Wiley v. Simons, 1927, 259 Mass. 159, 156 N.E. 23. Otherwise where it is clear to the plaintiff that it is not, or that the defendant is not asserting knowledge. Harris v. Delco Products Co., 1940, 305 Mass. 362, 25 N.E.2d 740; Smith v. Badlam, 1941, 112 Vt. 143, 22 A.2d 161; cf. Duryea v. Zimmerman, 1907, 121 App.Div. 560, 106 N.Y.S. 237.

24. Coman v. Williams, N.D.1954, 65 N.W.2d 377; Trebelhorn v. Bartlett, 1951, 154 Neb. 113, 47 N.W.2d 374; Clark v. Haggard, 1954, 141 Conn. 668, 109 A.2d 358; Mayfield Motor Co. v. Parker, 1954, 222 Miss. 152, 75 So.2d 435; Pumphrey v. Quillen, 1956, 165 Ohio St. 343, 135 N.E.2d 328. See Keeton, Fraud: The Necessity for an Intent to Deceive, 1958, 5 U.C.L.A.L.Rev. 583.

25. See supra, p. 740. Accord: Boddy v. Henry, 1901, 113 Iowa 462, 85 N.W. 771; Donnelly v. Baltimore Trust & Guarantee Co., 1905, 102 Md. 1, 61 A. 301.

26. Kimber v. Young, 8th Cir. 1905, 137 F. 744; Ultramares Corp. v. Touche, 1931, 255 N.Y. 170, 174 N.E. 441; State Street Trust Co. v. Ernst, 1938, 278 N.Y. 104, 15 N.E.2d 416; see People's National Bank v. Central Trust Co. of Kansas City, 1904, 179 Mo. 648, 78 S.W. 618; Schaffner v. National Supply Co., 1917, 80 W.Va. 111, 92 S.E. 580.

27. See Vincent v. Corbitt, 1908, 94 Miss. 46, 47 So. 641 (defendant made false statement as of his own knowledge, where facts were available to him; presumption that he knew it was false, which he must rebut).

28. See infra, this section on Negligence.

Once the intent to mislead is established, troublesome questions arise as to the persons to whom the representer will be liable.[29]

In the leading English case of Peek v. Gurney,[30] in which the directors of a corporation issued a prospectus for the purpose of inducing the public to purchase stock from the company itself, it was held that there was no liability to an investor who bought his stock on the market from a stockholder. The court limited responsibility to those whom the defendants had desired to influence, in the manner which had occasioned the damage.[31]

The doctrine of transferred intent,[32] which has been applied in the case of personal violence intended for one person which injures another, was thus rejected in the case of misrepresentation, for the obvious reason[33] of policy that the class of persons who may conceivably learn of a misstatement and be influenced by it is so enormous that an impossible burden, likely to be out of all proportion to the fault involved, might be cast upon anyone who makes a false assertion. This decision, which has been accepted by the Restatement of Torts,[34] has been followed by numerous American courts, in cases involving, for example, similar remote investors,[35] an assignee[36] or a subpurchaser[37] from the one originally dealt with, a casual bystander who overhears but is not expected to take action,[38] and others who were not intended to be affected by the representation, with no special reason to expect them to act upon it.[39] The same has been true in cases where the transaction which resulted was of a type different from that originally intended, as where one to whom statements were made in his capacity as agent for another buys for himself.[40]

The limitation thus imposed must, however, be qualified to a considerable extent. The class of persons whom the speaker

---

29. See Keeton, The Ambit of a Fraudulent Representor's Responsibility, 1938, 17 Tex.L.Rev. 1; Prosser, Misrepresentation and Third Persons, 1966, 19 Vand.L.Rev. 231.

30. 1873, L.R. 6 Eng. & Ir.App. 377.

31. Where there is a sale or contract between the parties, and the representation occurs during the preliminary bargaining between them, the desire is conclusively presumed. See Brady v. Finn, 1894, 162 Mass. 260, 38 N.E. 506; Hadley v. Clinton County Importing Co., 1862, 13 Ohio St. 502; Boddy v. Henry, 1904, 126 Iowa 31, 101 N.W. 447.

32. See supra, § 8.

33. See 2 Cooley, Torts, 3d Ed. 1906, 940–942; Keeton, The Ambit of a Fraudulent Representor's Responsibility, 1938, 17 Tex.L.Rev. 1, 7, 8. The latter author, however, suggests that a broader rule would impose no liability upon any honest man, and that the total *amount* of damages would seldom be increased. Also that the true reason for the limitation may be the ease with which reliance upon the representation may be claimed, and the difficulty of disproving it.

34. § 531, as qualified by § 532 (document or other thing) and § 536 (information required by statute).

35. Cheney v. Dickinson, 7th Cir. 1909, 172 F. 109; Greenville National Bank v. National Hardwood Co. 1928, 241 Mich. 524, 217 N.W. 786; Gillespie v. Hunt, 1923, 276 Pa. 119, A. 815, certiorari denied 261 U.S. 622, 43 S.Ct. 519, 67 L.Ed. 832; New York Title & Mortgage Co. v. Hutton, 1934, 63 U.S.App.D.C. 266, 71 F.2d 989, certiorari denied 293 U.S. 605, 55 S.Ct. 122, 79 L.Ed. 696; Wheelwright v. Vanderbilt, 1914, 69 Or. 326, 138 P. 857.

36. Butterfield v. Barber, 1897, 20 R.I. 99, 37 A. 532; Puffer v. Welch, 1911, 144 Wis. 506, 129 N.W. 525; Pamela Amusement Co. v. Scott Jewelry Co., D.Mass.1960, 190 F.Supp. 465; Nearpark Realty Corp. v. City Investing Co., Sup.Ct.1952, 112 N.Y.S.2d 816.

37. Abel v. Paterno, 1935, 245 App.Div. 285, 281 N.Y.S. 58; Cohen v. Citizens National Trust & Savings Bank, 1956, 143 Cal.App.2d 480, 300 P.2d 14; Bechtel v. Bohannon, 1930, 198 N.C. 730, 153 S.E. 316; Ellis v. Hale, 1962, 13 Utah 2d 279, 373 P.2d 382; Nash v. Minnesota Title Insurance & Trust Co., 1893, 159 Mass. 437, 34 N.E. 625.

38. Westcliff Co. v. Wall, 1954, 153 Tex. 271, 267 S.W.2d 544. Otherwise where defendant knows that such a person is interested, and may be expected to act in reliance on the representation. Southern States Fire & Casualty Co. v. Cromartie, 1913, 181 Ala. 295, 61 So. 907.

39. McCracken v. West, 1842, 17 Ohio 16 (letter intended to be shown to A used to induce B to act). Williamson v. Patterson, Tex.Civ.App.1937, 106 S.W.2d 753, error dismissed (statement to A before he became the agent of B); Lembeck v. Gerken, 1916, 88 N.J.L. 329, 96 A. 577.

40. Wells v. Cook, 1865, 16 Ohio St. 67; Walker v. Choate, 1929, 228 Ky. 101, 14 S.W.2d 406; McCane v. Wokoun, 1920, 189 Iowa 1010, 179 N.W. 332; Butterfield v. Barber, 1897, 20 R.I. 99, 37 A. 532. Cf. Wollenberger v. Hoover, 1931, 346 Ill. 511, 179 N.E. 42 (purchase of land instead of bonds).

desires to influence may of course be a very large one, as where he publishes a statement in a newspaper intending to reach a whole class of purchasers or investors,[41] or furnishes information to a credit agency in the expectation that it will be passed on to those with whom he may deal,[42] or where a manufacturer advertises his goods to possible consumers.[43] A statement may be intended to be directed to others in addition to the immediate recipient,[44] as where an auditor's report is prepared to be exhibited to the plaintiff,[45] or information is given to a promoter for the purpose of inducing action by the corporation to be formed.[46]

But apart from such cases, there is a very definite tendency to depart from the old position, and to extend liability to those whom there is no desire to influence, but whose reliance upon the representation there is some special reason to anticipate. This has been almost a matter of necessity where the representation is embodied in a document, such as a negotiable instrument,[47] a bill of lading,[48] a deed,[49] or a stock certificate,[50] or even an article of commerce [51] of a kind customarily relied upon by third persons; and likewise, of course, where a statute enacted for the protection of a particular class of persons [52] requires the information to be published or filed.[53] Beyond this, the same

41. Holloway v. Forsyth, 1917, 226 Mass. 358, 115 N.E. 483; Willcox v. Harriman Securities Corp., S.D.N.Y.1933, 10 F.Supp. 532; cf. Sims v. Tigrett, 1934, 229 Ala. 486, 158 So. 326; Diel v. Kellogg, 1910, 163 Mich. 162, 128 N.W. 420 (letter written to be shown to investors).

42. Tindle v. Birkett, 1902, 171 N.Y. 520, 64 N.E. 210; Hulsey v. M.C. Kiser Co., 1925, 21 Ala.App. 123, 105 So. 913; Reliance Shoe Co. v. Manly, 4th Cir. 1928, 25 F.2d 381; Forbes v. Auerbach, Fla.1952, 56 So.2d 895; Manly v. Ohio Shoe Co., 4th Cir. 1928, 25 F.2d 384.

In Davis v. Louisville Trust Co., 6th Cir. 1910, 181 F. 10, and Jamestown Iron & Metal Co. v. Knofsky, 1927, 291 Pa. 60, 139 A. 611, plaintiffs, who were not even subscribers, were allowed to recover, where there was reason to expect that the information would reach them.

43. Baxter v. Ford Motor Co., 1932, 168 Wash. 456, 12 P.2d 409, 15 P.2d 1118, second appeal in 1934, 179 Wash. 123, 35 P.2d 1090.

44. Henry v. Dennis, 1901, 95 Me. 24, 49 A. 58 (business associate); Iowa Economic Heater Co. v. American Economic Heater Co., C.C.Ill.1887, 32 F. 735; Harold v. Pugh, 1959, 174 Cal.App.2d 603, 345 P.2d 112.

45. American Indemnity Co. v. Ernst & Ernst, Tex. Civ.App.1937, 106 S.W.2d 763 error refused. Accord: Wice v. Schilling, 1954, 124 Cal.App.2d 735, 269 P.2d 231 (exterminator certifying for vendor that premises were free from vermin held liable to purchaser); Reservoir Manor Corp. v. Lumbermen's Mut. Insurance Casualty Co., 1957, 334 Mass. 620, 137 N.E.2d 912 (report of boiler inspection).

46. Scholfield Gear & Pulley Co. v. Scholfield, 1898, 71 Conn. 1, 40 A. 1046. Accord, Crystal Pier Amusement Co. v. Cannon, 1933, 219 Cal. 184, 25 P.2d 839, 91 A.L.R. 1357; E.M. Fleischmann Lumber Corp. v. Resources Corp. International, D.Del.1952, 105 F.Supp. 681.

Cf. Mullen v. Eastern Trust & Savings Bank, 1911, 108 Me. 498, 81 A. 948 (trustee certifying overissue of bonds, to induce the public to buy); Taylor v. Thomas, 1907, 55 Misc. 411, 106 N.Y.S. 538, modified and affirmed 124 App.Div. 53, 108 N.Y.S. 454, affirmed 195 N.Y. 590, 89 N.E. 1113, affirmed 224 U.S. 73, 32 S.Ct. 403, 56 L.Ed. 673 (false report by bank officer).

47. Peoples National Bank v. Dixwell, 1914, 217 Mass. 436, 105 N.E. 435; National Shawmut Bank of Boston v. Johnson, 1945, 317 Mass. 485, 58 N.E.2d 849.

48. National Bank of Savannah v. Kershaw Oil Mill, 4th Cir. 1912, 202 F. 90.

49. Baker v. Hallam, 1897, 103 Iowa 43, 72 N.W. 419. Cf. Leonard v. Springer, 1902, 197 Ill. 532, 64 N.E. 299 (fictitious deed recorded).

50. Merchants' National Bank v. Robison, 1892, 8 Utah 256, 30 P. 985; Bruff v. Mali, 1867, 36 N.Y. 200, 34 How.Prac. 338; Bank of Montreal v. Thayer, C.C. Iowa 1881, 7 F. 622, 2 McCrary 1 (receiver's certificate); Stickel v. Atwood, 1903, 25 R.I. 456, 56 A. 687 (bond).

51. Graham v. John R. Watts & Son, 1931, 238 Ky. 96, 36 S.W.2d 859 (mislabeled sack of seed).

52. Otherwise where the statute is construed to be for the benefit of the state only. Ashuelot Savings Bank v. Albee, 1884, 63 N.H. 152; Hunnewell v. Duxbury, 1891, 154 Mass. 286, 28 N.E. 267; Utley v. Hill, 1900, 155 Mo. 232, 55 S.W. 1091; Hindman v. First National Bank, 6th Cir. 1902, 112 F. 931, cert. denied 186 U.S. 483, 22 S.Ct. 943, 46 L.Ed. 1261.

53. Mason v. Moore, 1906, 73 Ohio St. 275, 76 N.E. 932; Gerner v. Mosher, 1899, 58 Neb. 135, 78 N.W. 384; Warfield v. Clark, 1902, 118 Iowa 69, 91 N.W. 833; Ver Wys v. Vander Mey, 1919, 206 Mich. 499, 173 N.W. 504. See Restatement of Torts, § 536.

Compare the cases where a false statement was made to rent control authorities for the purpose of evicting plaintiff as a tenant. Lyster v. Berberich, 1949, 3 N.J.Super. 78, 65 A.2d 632; Alabiso v. Schuster, 1948, 273 App.Div. 655, 80 N.Y.S.2d 314. See Note, 1949, 33 Minn.L.Rev. 194.

result sometimes has been reached by finding that that was "intended" which was merely specially foreseeable;[54] and in a few cases by holding outright that it is enough that the defendant should have contemplated the plaintiff's reliance.[55] The limitation to a "desire" to influence the plaintiff seems clearly too narrow, and there is much merit in the contention [56] that, while the defendant is not required to investigate or otherwise guard against the possibility that his statements may come into the hands of strangers and affect their conduct, his responsibility should at least extend to those who might reasonably be expected to assume from appearances that the representation was intended to reach them.

Negligence

A representation made with an honest belief in its truth may still be negligent, because of lack of reasonable care in ascertaining the facts,[57] or in the manner of expression,[58] or absence of the skill and competence required by a particular business or profession.[59] As has been repeated above,[60] misrepresentation frequently occurs in ordinary negligence actions for personal injuries or property damage, in the form of misleading words or acts, or non-disclosure of known facts, and the courts have not found it necessary to distinguish it in any way from any other negligence. It is only where intangible economic interests are invaded that they have become alarmed at possible liability of unknown or virtually unlimited extent,[61] and have developed a more restricted rule. This has taken the form of limitation of the group of persons to whom the defendant may be liable, short of the foreseeability of possible harm.[62]

Perhaps, when the law on this subject became crystallized, all that was expected of those engaged in negotiating bargaining transactions was honesty, and, of course, dishonesty in the area of dealer's talk was a much wider privilege than it is at the present time.[63] While the courts have justifiably been somewhat more conservative in the protection of intangible economic and business interests than they have with respect to interests in freedom from physical damage to things and persons, there would seem to be very little justification for not extending liability to all parties and agents to a bargaining transaction for making misrepresentations negligently. Only in a few jurisdic-

54. Cf. New York Title & Mortgage Co. v. Hutton, 1934, 63 App.D.C. 266, 71 F.2d 989; Southern States Fire & Casualty Insurance Co. v. Cromartie, 1913, 181 Ala. 295, 61 So. 907.

55. Davis v. Louisville Trust Co., 6th Cir. 1910, 181 F. 10; Ultramares Corp. v. Touche, Niven & Co., 1931, 255 N.Y. 170, 174 N.E. 441; State Street Trust Co. v. Ernst, 1938, 278 N.Y. 104, 15 N.E.2d 416; Fidelity & Deposit Co. of Maryland v. Atherton, 1944, 47 N.M. 443, 144 P.2d 157.

56. Keeton, The Ambit of a Fraudulent Representor's Responsibility, 1938, 17 Tex.L.Rev. 1, 11; Seavey, Mr. Justice Cardozo and the Law of Torts, 1939, 52 Harv.L.Rev. 372, 404, 48 Yale L.J. 390, 39 Col. L.Rev. 20.

57. International Products Co. v. Erie Railroad Co., 1927, 244 N.Y. 331, 155 N.E. 662, certiorari denied 275 U.S. 527, 48 S.Ct. 20, 72 L.Ed. 408; Houston v. Thornton, 1898, 122 N.C. 365, 29 S.E. 827; Maxwell Ice Co. v. Brackett, Shaw & Lunt Co., 1921, 80 N.H. 236, 116 A. 34.

58. See Nash v. Minnesota Title Insurance & Trust Co., 1895, 163 Mass. 574, 40 N.E. 1039; Slater Trust Co. v. Gardiner, 2d Cir. 1910, 183 F. 268; Angus v. Clifford, 1891, 2 Ch.Div. 449, 472; Restatement of Torts, § 528.

59. Dickel v. Nashville Abstract Co., 1890, 89 Tenn. 431, 14 S.W. 896; Brown v. Sims, 1899, 22 Ind.App. 317, 53 N.E. 779. See Rouse, Legal Liability of the Public Accountant, 1934, 23 Ky.L.J. 3.

60. Supra, § 105.

61. "If liability for negligence exists, a thoughtless slip or blunder, the failure to detect a theft or forgery beneath the cover of deceptive entries, may expose accountants to a liability in an indeterminate amount for an indeterminate time to an indeterminate class. The hazards of a business conducted on these terms are so extreme as to enkindle doubt whether a flaw may not exist in the implication of a duty that exposes to these consequences." Cardozo, C.J., in Ultramares Corp. v. Touche, Niven & Co., 1931, 255 N.Y. 170, 174 N.E. 441. See also Smith, Liability for Negligent Language, 1909, 14 Harv.L.Rev. 184, 195; Seavey, Mr. Justice Cardozo and the Law of Torts, 1939, 52 Harv.L.Rev. 372, 400, 48 Yale L.J. 390, 39 Col.L.Rev. 20; Note, 1934, 8 Temple L.Q. 404.

62. See infra, this section on Negligence.

63. Keeton, Rights of Disappointed Purchasers, 1953, 32 Tex.L.Rev. 1; Pound, The End of the Law as Developed in Legal Rules and Doctrines, 1914, 27 Harv.L.Rev. 195.

tions, including California, New Hampshire, and Oklahoma, have the courts clearly adopted this position.[64] By far the majority have gone from the extreme of requiring dishonesty or moral fault to the other extreme of making the misrepresenter strictly accountable.[65] It must be recognized, however, that where the misrepresenter has based his statement on unreliable information, the fact that a reasonable person would have known better has resulted in a finding of dishonesty by way of a mandatory or permissive inference thereof.[66] Thus, there may not be so very much practical difference in actual results between those jurisdictions where dishonesty is required and those where negligence as well as dishonesty will suffice for recovery.

No doubt virtually all courts today would recognize the existence of some situations where the nature of a representer's activity or a pre-existing relationship between the representer and the representee or the two factors together will constitute the basis for the imposition of a duty to exercise reasonable care to avoid harm from reasonable and expectable reliance on what is said at least about certain matters related to the subject matter of the transaction. Thus, it was held by the House of Lords in 1963 that a banker who undertakes to give financial information about a customer to another will ordinarily be subject to liability for negligence in the absence of a disclaimer of responsibility.[67] Even before that case was decided, a bailor had been subjected to liability for negligence in giving erroneous information to a bailee as to the location of goods as a consequence of which the bailee was unable to recover for insurance when the goods were destroyed by fire,[68] and directors of a corporation were held liable for negligence even in the absence of any statute for issuing bonds containing misstatements of fact upon which a purchaser relied.[69] It can reasonably be expected that courts will recognize other "special relationships" and "activities" that will justify the imposition of a duty to exercise reasonable care to avoid purely intangible economic loss.

A more difficult problem relates to the tort liability, and the extent that tort liability, of lawyers, accountants and other professionals for economic loss suffered as a consequence of reliance by third parties on misrepresentations made in the course of rendering a service pursuant to a contract. The obligation arising out of the implied promise to render the service with reasonable care extends to the promisee and third party beneficiaries, and it is extremely doubtful if courts have carried liability any further than could have been carried through the reasonable application of third party beneficiary ideas. The main point to be made is that liability that has been imposed could have been imposed on a contractual basis. A leading case decided in 1879 stated the general rule that an attorney could not, in the absence of special circumstances, be held liable for the consequences of his professional negligence except to his

---

64. West's Ann.Cal.Civ.Code § 1572; 15 Okla.Stat. Ann. § 58; Gagne v. Bertran, 1954, 43 Cal.2d 481, 275 P.2d 15; Weston v. Brown, 1925, 82 N.H. 157, 131 A. 141.

65. Stein v. Treger, D.C.Cir.1950, 182 F.2d 696, noted, 1951, 49 Mich.L.Rev. 450; Ham v. Hart, 1954, 58 N.M. 550, 273 P.2d 748, noted, 1955, 28 So.Calif.L.Rev. 193; Aldrich v. Scribner, 1908, 154 Mich. 23, 117 N.W. 581; Fidelity Casualty Co. of New York v. Pittman Tractor Co., 1943, 244 Ala. 354, 13 So.2d 669; Pratt v. Thompson, 1925, 133 Wash. 218, 233 P. 637; Russo v. Williams, 1955, 160 Neb. 564, 71 N.W.2d 131; Wilson v. Jones, Tex.Com.App.1932, 45 S.W.2d 572; Moulton v. Norton, 1931, 184 Minn. 343, 238 N.W. 686.

66. Clark v. Haggard, 1954, 141 Conn. 668, 109 A.2d 358; Laney-Payne Farm Loan Co. v. Greenhaw, 1928, 177 Ark. 589, 9 S.W.2d 19; Tott v. Duggan, 1924, 199 Iowa 238, 200 N.W. 411; Chatham Furnace Co. v. Moffatt, 1888, 147 Mass. 403, 18 N.E. 168; Pumphrey v. Quillen, 1956, 165 Ohio St. 343, 135 N.E.2d 328; Solozzi v. Casola, 1952, 345 Ill.App. 409, 103 N.E.2d 164.

67. Hedley Vyrne & Co. v. Heller & Partners, [1964] A.C. 465.

68. International Products Co. v. Erie Railroad Co., 1927, 244 N.Y. 331, 155 N.E. 662, 56 A.L.R. 1377, certiorari denied 275 U.S. 527, 48 S.Ct. 20, 72 L.Ed. 408.

69. Ashby v. Peters, 1935, 128 Neb. 338, 258 N.W. 639, 99 A.L.R. 843.

client.[70] It can be argued that those who negotiate transactions should be encouraged to rely upon counsel of their own choosing employed for the very purpose of serving the interest of the person being represented.[71] Interests of clients and others who may choose to rely on counsel's opinion are generally not identical. Moreover, the possibility of liability to third persons for negligence in the handling of client's affairs can often hamper an attorney's freedom to represent the client vigorously. And finally, the foreseeable class of persons who can be adversely affected by reliance upon a lawyer's or accountant's advice or opinion can be so large as to make liability to third parties a ruinous and catastrophic kind, a burden that cannot reasonably be imposed on the lawyer or the accountant except for fraud or other intentional misconduct.

The first significant case subjecting one who in the course of employment supplies false information pursuant to his contract to tort liability for economic loss was Glanzer v. Shepard[72] in which Judge Cardozo speaking for a majority of the New York Court of Appeals allowed plaintiff, the purchaser of a quantity of beans, to recover on a tort theory from a public weigher who certified an incorrect weight of the beans to the seller. In allowing recovery, the court said, "The bounds of duty are enlarged by knowledge of prospective use." The leading case on this entire subject is a 1931 decision by the New York Court of Appeals in Ultramares Corp. v. Touche.[73]

Recent cases involving the liability of surveyors and abstractors to subsequent purchasers and others relying on the accuracy of the surveys and the abstracts express a rule of liability based on the range of foreseeability of harm,[74] but these are all cases in which the liability is necessarily limited in amount to the value of the property. Thus, in 1974 the Supreme Court of Michigan asserted that the cause of action in tort for negligent misrepresentation arising out of an abstractor's contractural duty runs to those persons *an abstractor could reasonably foresee as relying on the accuracy of the abstract that is put into circulation.*[75] Likewise, a recent Texas case held that an accountant would be liable for negligence in the certification of four audit reports to corporations knowing that these reports would be used by creditors in making loans to corporations.[76] *There is language in the opinion that would indicate that liability would extend to all those within the general class of persons who would likely be dealing with the corporations in reasonable reliance on the erroneous certifications*, but actually under the facts the accountants knew the identity of the plaintiffs whom the client intended to influence with the audit report.

Thus, liability has not in fact been extended much beyond that indicated in the Second Restatement of Torts, if any.[77] This means that foreseeability of harm is not the test. The plaintiff must have been a person for whose use the representation was intended, and it is not enough that the defendant ought reasonably to have foreseen reliance by someone such as the plaintiff. Also, if the plaintiff is not an identifiable person for whose benefit the statement was intended, he must at least have been a member of some very small group of persons for whose guidance the representation was made.[78] It

---

70. National Savings Bank of the District of Columbia v. Ward, 1880, 100 U.S. 195, 25 L.Ed. 621.

71. Keeton, Professional Malpractice, 1978, 17 Washburn L.Rev. 445, 448.

72. 1922, 233 N.Y. 236, 135 N.E. 275.

73. 1931, 255 N.Y. 170, 174 N.E. 441.

74. Anderson v. Spriestersbach, 1912, 69 Wash. 393, 125 P. 166; Dickel v. Nashville Abstract Co., 1890, 89 Tenn. 431, 14 S.W. 896; Western Loan & Savings Co. v. Silver Bow Abstract Co., 1904, 31 Mont. 448, 78 P. 774; Beckovsky v. Burton Abstract & Title Co., 1919, 208 Mich. 224, 178 N.W. 238; see Phoenix Title & Trust Co. v. Continental Oil Co., 1934, 43 Ariz. 219, 29 P.2d 1065.

75. Williams v. Polger, 1974, 391 Mich. 6, 215 N.W.2d 149.

76. Shatterproof Glass Corp. v. James, Tex.Civ.App. 1971, 466 S.W.2d 873, refused no reversible error.

77. Second Restatement of Torts, § 552(2).

78. Second Restatement of Torts, § 552(2)(a).

is difficult, however, to explain the liability of title abstractors to remote purchasers on this *Restatement* principle. Normally the abstractor cannot be said to be performing the service and certifying the state of title to a tract of land for their guidance. But at least the liability is limited by the very nature of the situation since in that type case a test based on foreseeability can only lead to a liability no greater than the amount of value of the land.

Strict Responsibility

While legal fault in the sense of dishonesty or an intent to deceive is commonly required in the paradigmatic bargaining transaction, there is a significant number of cases in which the courts have imposed strict liability.[79] In all but a relatively small percentage of cases, the misrepresenter has been a party to the transaction. As has been frequently observed, if a party to a contract seeks and is given damages against a misrepresenter, who is also a party to the contract, only to the extent necessary to compensate the plaintiff for the fact that he was induced to part with something more valuable than that which he has received, the effect is substantially the same as rescission. The misrepresenter is not being allowed to gain any benefit or enrichment from the transaction and the measure of the plaintiff's recovery or damage is equal to the amount of the defendant's gain.[80] Actually, rescission may often be more of a hardship on the innocent misrepresenter than damages limited to the amount of the gain. Thus, unjust enrichment can be prevented either by way of rescinding the entire transaction or by way of a monetary recovery to the prejudiced party. The *Second Restatement of Torts* has adopted this minority position in the kinds of bargaining transactions to which it can be readily applied.[81] These are sales, rental, and exchange transactions. This is an important development in connection with real estate transactions. Thus, a grantee of a house and lot should not necessarily be given rescission against an innocent grantor if the latter is willing to reimburse the grantee for the fact that he got property worth less than the purchase price due to a defect in the house, if the defect is one that can be easily repaired.[82]

A more difficult question relates to when, if at all, strict liability in tort should be imposed on some misrepresenters, at least for some types of false representations, that would subject the misrepresenter to liability for damages incurred in reliance on the misrepresentation without any limitation of the recovery to the amount of the unjust enrichment or benefit acquired by the misrepresenter. An affirmation of fact made by the seller of goods to a buyer which relates to the goods and becomes part of the basis of the bargain creates an express warranty under the Uniform Commercial Code but this is because the seller has in essence promised to sell goods of the kind described by his representation.[83] There is an objective manifestation of an intention to be bound, even if there was no specific intention to be bound. Warranty representations may be regarded by the courts as being made in other situations such as in the case

---

[79]. Stein v. Treger, D.C.Cir. 1950, 182 F.2d 696, noted, 1951, 49 Mich.L.Rev. 450; Ham v. Hart, 1954, 58 N.M. 550, 273 P.2d 748, noted, 1955, 28 So.Calif.L.Rev. 193; Aldrich v. Scribner, 1908, 154 Mich. 23, 117 N.W. 581; Fidelity Casualty Co. of New York v. Pittman Tractor Co., 1943, 244 Ala. 354, 13 So.2d 669; Pratt v. Thompson, 1925, 133 Wash. 218, 233 P. 637; Russo v. Williams, 1955, 160 Neb. 564, 71 N.W.2d 131; Wilson v. Jones, Tex.Com.App.1932, 45 S.W.2d 572; Moulton v. Norton, 1931, 184 Minn. 343, 238 N.W. 686.

[80]. Keeton, Fraud: The Necessity for an Intent to Deceive, 1958, 5 U.C.L.A.L.Rev. 583, 600.

[81]. Section 552C.

[82]. La Bar v. Lindstrom, 1924, 158 Minn. 453, 197 N.W. 756. See, however, Dubovy v. Woolf, 1928, 127 Me. 269, 143 A. 58, where a contract for the sale of a tenement building was rescinded though the defects could have been repaired for $50. See, note, 1918, 28 Yale L.J. 178.

[83]. See the Official Comment to the Uniform Commercial Code, Section 2–313, which states, "In actual practice affirmations of fact made by the seller about the goods during a bargain are regarded as part of the description of those goods; * * *."

of bailments for hire. But courts have been reluctant to ascribe to representers an objective intent to guarantee except in the sale of goods in the absence of an express statement to that effect. This does not mean that some representers, especially those in the business of selling goods or those who are mass producers of houses should not be strictly accountable in tort for economic losses suffered as a consequence of justifiable reliance on unqualified representations of fact that prove to be false. Imposing a type of enterprise liability on those engaged in the business of selling goods for economic loss resulting from misrepresentations made in advertising, labels, brochures, and the like, similar to that which is imposed on merchant sellers of dangerously defective products for physical harm to persons and tangible things is quite reasonable. Such a proposal was considered for adoption in the *Restatement of Torts* but was not adopted.[84] A few courts have specifically authorized recovery on a tort theory.[85] Others have in similar situations permitted recovery on a warranty theory without regard to privity of contract or the notion that the representation must have been a basis for the bargain.[86] When notions about contract-express warranties extend this far, the distinction between tort and contract liability is blurred. Whatever the theory, strict liability is being imposed without respect to fault or without respect to any objective manifestation of an intent to be bound if the representation proves to be false. It would be easy to dismiss the question of whether the liability was tort or contract were it not for the fact that there are some issues that will be affected by the theory upon which recovery is allowed, such as damages, the proper limitations period, the effect of disclosures of any warranties not incorporated in a written contract finally executed, and defenses of one kind or another.

WESTLAW REFERENCES

liab! /s negligen! /s misrepresent! % topic(insurance)
liab! /s intent! /s misrepresent! % topic(insurance)
liab! /s strict /s misrepresent! % topic(insurance)

Scienter-Intent to Deceive
scienter /s decei! misrepresent!
digest(intent! /s decei! misrepresent! /s element*)
honest /2 belief mistake /s misrepresent! represent!

Negligence
headnote(liab! /s negligen! /s misrepresent!)
negligen! /s misrepresent! /p economic monetary money /s loss**

Strict Responsibility
strict** /p responsib! liab! /p misrepresent!
restatement /5 torts /5 552
2–313 & misrepresent! nondisclos!
implied /s warrant! /p "strict** liab!)

---

§ 108. Justifiable Reliance—Materiality

Reliance

Not only must there be reliance but the reliance must be justifiable under the circumstances.[1] There has been a vast amount of misunderstanding regarding the basis for the requirement of justifiability of reliance, especially when plaintiff is required to prove or at least does prove an intent to deceive and therefore intentional misconduct on the part of the misrepresenter. What is the basis for the requirement of justifiability of reliance if defendant did intend to deceive the plaintiff and was able to accomplish his objective? The principal argument in support of some such requirement as justifiability of

---

84. See tentative draft, Section 552D (Council Draft No. 17, p. 76). This draft paralleled Section 402B which was adopted.

85. Graham v. John R. Watts & Son, 1931, 238 Ky. 96, 36 S.W.2d 859; Ford Motor Co. v. Lonon, 1966, 217 Tenn. 400, 398 S.W.2d 240; Contra: Dimoff v. Ernie Majer, Inc., 1960, 55 Wn.2d 385, 347 P.2d 1056.

86. Gherna v. Ford Motor Co., 1966, 246 Cal.App.2d 639, 55 Cal.Rptr. 94; Klein v. Asgrow Seed Co., 1966, 246 Cal.App.2d 87, 54 Cal.Rptr. 609; Randy Knitwear, Inc. v. American Cyanamid Co., 1962, 11 N.Y.2d 5, 226 N.Y.S.2d 363, 181 N.E.2d 399; Inglis v. American Motors Corp., 1965, 3 Ohio St.2d 132, 209 N.E.2d 583.

§ 108

1. See Second Restatement of Torts, § 537

reliance would seem to be that of providing some objective corroboration to plaintiff's claim that he did rely. If plaintiff can claim reliance on the basis of the kind of statement on which no reasonable person would rely for one reason or another, then it is quite likely that plaintiff did not rely and if his testimony that he did is allowed as sufficient evidence on the basis of which a finder of fact can find reliance, then it will be too easy for a party to a contract to escape the consequences of his own bad judgment in making a bargain of some kind. Therefore, the foolish nature of the plaintiff's conduct if he did rely is relevant primarily because of the likelihood that he did not rely.

Justifiability of the Reliance

The plaintiff's conduct must not be so utterly unreasonable, in the light of the information apparent to him, that the law may properly say that his loss is his own responsibility. In some cases, of course, the unreasonableness of his conduct has been regarded as sufficient evidence that he did not in fact rely upon the representation—he may testify to his reliance,[2] but the court or the jury is not compelled to believe him.[3] But in some cases where the plaintiff's reliance in fact, and his good faith, are unquestioned, it may still be held that his conduct was so foolish as to bar his recovery. If he is a person of normal intelligence, experience and education, he may not put faith in representations which any such normal person would recognize at once as preposterous, as, for example, that glasses, once fitted, will alter shape and adapt themselves to the eye,[4] or which are shown by facts within his observation to be so patently and obviously false that he must have closed his eyes to avoid discovery of the truth,[5] and still compel the defendant to be responsible for his loss.

There have been cases [6] in which it was said that such reliance is contributory negligence, and that the plaintiff must exercise the care of a reasonably prudent person for his own protection. Undoubtedly such language is appropriate if the defendant's misrepresentation itself is merely negligent; [7] but where there is an intent to mislead, it is clearly inconsistent with the general rule [8] that mere negligence of the plaintiff is not a defense to an intentional tort. The better reasoned cases [9] have rejected contributory negligence as a defense applicable to intentional deceit, taking account of the effect which the representation is intended to have upon the plaintiff's mind.[10]

---

2. Pease v. Brown, 1870, 104 Mass. 291; Weaver v. Cone, 1896, 174 Pa. 104, 34 A. 551; Continental Coal, Land & Timber Co. v. Kilpatrick, 1916, 172 App.Div. 541, 158 N.Y.S. 1056.

3. "It may be that the mis-statement is trivial—so trivial as that the Court will be of opinion that it could not have affected the plaintiff's mind at all, or induced him to enter into the contract." Smith v. Chadwick, 1882, 20 Ch.Div. 27, 45. Accord: Bond v. Ramsey, 1878, 89 Ill. 29.

4. H. Hirschberg Optical Co. v. Michaelson, 1901, 1 Neb., Unof., 137, 95 N.W. 461. Accord: Bishop v. Small, 1874, 63 Me. 12; and see that foremost classic of legal humor, the sad but remarkable tale of the Land of Shalam, in Ellis v. Newbrough, 1891, 6 N.M. 181, 27 P. 490.

5. Williams v. Rank & Son Buick, Inc., 1969, 44 Wis.2d 239, 170 N.W.2d 807; Narup v. Benson, 1929, 154 Wash. 646, 283 P. 179; Security Trust Co. v. O'Hair, 1936, 103 Ind.App. 56, 197 N.E. 694, rehearing denied 103 Ind.App. 56, 199 N.E. 602; Kaiser v. Nummerdor, 1904, 120 Wis. 234, 97 N.W. 932; Long v. Warren, 1877, 68 N.Y. 426.

6. For example, Dunn v. White, 1876, 63 Mo. 181; Osborne v. Missouri Pacific Railroad Co., 1904, 71 Neb. 180, 98 N.W. 685.

7. See § 107 on Negligence.

8. See § 65 on Scope of the Defense. As to strict responsibility for innocent misrepresentation cf. Rogers v. Portland & Brunswick Street Railway Co., 1905, 100 Me. 86, 60 A. 713 (estoppel), in accord with the view generally accepted that contributory negligence is no defense to strict liability.

9. Seeger v. Odell, 1941, 18 Cal.2d 409, 115 P.2d 977; Butler v. Olshan, 1966, 280 Ala. 181, 191 So.2d 7; Roda v. Berko, 1948, 401 Ill. 335, 81 N.E.2d 912; Knox v. Anderson, D.Hawaii 1958, 159 F.Supp. 795, supplemented 162 F.Supp. 338, affirmed 297 F.2d 702, certiorari denied 370 U.S. 915, 82 S.Ct. 1555, 8 L.Ed.2d 498; Pelkey v. Norton, 1953, 149 Me. 247, 99 A.2d 918. See Seavey, Caveat Emptor as of 1960, 1960, 38 Tex.L.Rev. 439.

10. "He has a right to retort upon his objector, 'You, at least, who have stated what is untrue, or have concealed the truth, for the purpose of drawing me into a contract, cannot accuse me of want of caution because I relied implicitly upon your fairness and hones-

It is a sufficient indication that the person deceived is not held to the standard of precaution, or of minimum knowledge, or of intelligent judgment, of the hypothetical reasonable man, that people who are exceptionally gullible,[11] superstitious,[12] ignorant, stupid, dim-witted,[13] or illiterate,[14] have been allowed to recover when the defendant knew it, and deliberately took advantage of it. "The design of the law is to protect the weak and credulous from the wiles and stratagems of the artful and cunning, as well as those whose vigilance and security enable them to protect themselves,"[15] and "no rogue should enjoy his ill-gotten plunder for the simple reason that his victim is by chance a fool."[16]

Rather than contributory negligence, the matter seems to turn upon an individual standard of the plaintiff's own capacity and the knowledge which he has, or which may fairly be charged against him from the facts within his observation in the light of his individual case, and so comes closer to the rules which are associated with assumption of risk.[17] "More succinctly stated, the rule is that one cannot be heard to say he relied upon a statement so patently ridiculous as to be unbelievable on its face, unless he happens to be that special object of the affections of a court of Equity, an idiot."[18] The other side of the shield is that one who has special knowledge, experience and competence may not be permitted to rely on statements for which the ordinary man might recover,[19] and that one who has acquired expert knowledge concerning the matter dealt with may be required to form his own judgment, rather than take the word of the defendant.[20]

The last half-century has seen a marked change in the attitude of the courts toward the question of justifiable reliance. Earlier decisions, under the influence of the prevalent doctrine of "caveat emptor," laid great stress upon the plaintiff's "duty" to protect himself and distrust his antagonist, and held that he was not entitled to rely even upon positive assertions of fact made by one with whom he was dealing at arm's length.[21] It was assumed that any one may be expected to overreach another in a bargain if he can, and that only a fool will expect common honesty. Therefore the plaintiff must make a reasonable investigation, and form his own judgment. The recognition of a new standard of business ethics, demanding that statements of fact be at least honestly and

---

ty.'" Lord Chelmsford, in Central R. Co. of Venezuela v. Kisch, 1867, L.R. 2 H.L. 99. Accord: Cottrill v. Crum, 1890, 100 Mo. 397, 13 S.W. 753; Crompton v. Beedle & Thomas, 1910, 83 Vt. 287, 75 A. 331.

Likewise, where strict liability is imposed, the general rule of policy that contributory negligence is not a defense (supra, § 79) has been followed in cases of misrepresentation. Bahlman v. Hudson Motor Car Co., 1939, 290 Mich. 683, 288 N.W. 309; Challis v. Hartloff, 1933, 136 Kan. 823, 18 P.2d 199 (implied warranty).

11. Adan v. Steinbrecher, 1911, 116 Minn. 174, 133 N.W. 477; Sutton v. Greiner, 1916, 177 Iowa 532, 159 N.W. 268.

12. Hyma v. Lee, 1953, 338 Mich. 31, 60 N.W.2d 920 (belief in spiritualism).

13. Teter v. Shultz, 1942, 110 Ind.App. 541, 39 N.E.2d 802; Jenness v. Moses Lake Development Co., 1951, 39 Wn.2d 151, 234 P.2d 865; Kempf v. Ranger, 1916, 132 Minn. 64, 155 N.W. 1059; King v. Livingston Manufacturing Co., 1912, 180 Ala. 118, 60 So. 143; Porter v. United Railways Co. of St. Louis, 1912, 165 Mo.App. 619, 148 S.W. 162.

14. Weatherford v. Home Finance Co., 1954, 225 S.C. 313, 82 S.E.2d 196; Soltan v. Shahboz, 1956, 383 Pa. 485, 119 A.2d 242; Pimpinello v. Swift & Co., 1930, 253 N.Y. 159, 170 N.E. 530.

15. Ingalls v. Miller, 1889, 121 Ind. 188, 191, 22 N.E. 995.

16. Chamberlin v. Fuller, 1887, 59 Vt. 247, 256, 9 A. 832, 836.

17. See Frenzel v. Miller, 1897, 37 Ind. 1; Green, Deceit, 1930, 16 Va.L.Rev. 749, 763.

18. Obiter Dicta, 1956, 25 Ford.L.Rev. 395, 397.

19. Graff v. Geisel, 1951, 39 Wn.2d 131, 234 P.2d 884; Hanson v. Acceptance Finance Corp., Mo.App. 1954, 270 S.W.2d 143; Babb v. Bolyard, 1950, 194 Md. 603, 72 A.2d 13.

20. Puget Sound National Bank v. McMahon, 1958, 53 Wn.2d 51, 330 P.2d 559; Schmidt v. Landfield, 1960, 20 Ill.2d 89, 169 N.E.2d 229; Poe v. Voss, 1955, 196 Va. 821, 86 S.E.2d 47.

21. Sherwood v. Salmon, Conn.1805, 2 Day, 128; Page v. Parker, 1861, 43 N.H. 363; Graffenstein v. E Epstein & Co., 1880, 23 Kan. 443; Schwabacker v. Riddle, 1891, 99 Ill. 343; Mabardy v. McHugh, 1909, 202 Mass. 148, 88 N.E. 894.

carefully made,[22] and in many cases that they be warranted to be true,[23] has led to an almost complete shift in this point of view.[24]

It is now held that assertions of fact as to the quantity[25] or quality[26] of land or goods[27] sold, the financial status of corporations,[28] and similar matters[29] inducing commercial transactions, may justifiably be relied on without investigation, not only where such investigation would be burdensome or difficult, as where land which is sold lies at a distance,[30] but likewise where the falsity of the representation might be discovered with little effort by means easily at hand.[31] The plaintiff is not required, for example, to examine public records to ascertain the true state of the title claimed by the defendant.[32] It is only where, under the circumstances, the facts should be apparent to one of his knowledge and intelligence from a cursory glance,[33] or he has discovered something which should serve as a warning that he is being deceived,[34] that he is required to make an investigation of his own. The compara-

---

22. "And, generally speaking, until there be written into the law some precept or rule to the effect that the heart of a man is as prone to wickedness as is the smoke to go upward, and that every man must deal with his fellow man as if he was a thief and a robber, it ought not to be held that trust cannot be put in a positive assertion of a material fact, known to the speaker and unknown to the hearer, and intended to be relied upon." Lamm, J., in Judd v. Walker, 1908, 215 Mo. 312, 114 S.W. 979.

23. See supra, § 97.

24. See Harper and McNeely, A Synthesis of the Law of Misrepresentation, 1938, 22 Minn.L.Rev. 939, 957–960; Restatement of Torts, §§ 538(3), 540.

25. Lanning v. Sprague, 1951, 71 Idaho 138, 227 P.2d 347; Judd v. Walker, 1908, 215 Mo. 312, 114 S.W. 979; George v. Kurdy, 1916, 92 Wash. 277, 158 P. 965; Antle v. Sexton, 1891, 137 Ill. 410, 27 N.E. 691.

26. Erickson v. Midgarden, 1948, 226 Minn. 55, 31 N.W.2d 918; Ashburn v. Miller, 1958, 161 Cal.App.2d 71, 326 P.2d 229; Blackman v. Howes, 1947, 82 Cal. App.2d 275, 185 P.2d 1019; Warne v. Finseth, 1923, 50 N.D. 347, 195 N.W. 573; McGuffin v. Smith, 1926, 215 Ky. 606, 286 S.W. 884.

27. Lunnie v. Gadapee, 1950, 116 Vt. 261, 73 A.2d 312; Morrow v. Bonebrake, 1911, 84 Kan. 724, 115 P. 585; Graves v. Haynes, Tex.Civ.App.1921, 231 S.W. 383; Stewart v. Stearns, 1884, 63 N.H. 99.

28. Fargo Gas & Coke Co. v. Fargo Gas & Electric Co., 1894, 4 N.D. 219, 59 N.W. 1066; Buckley v. Buckley, 1925, 230 Mich. 504, 202 N.W. 955; Gallon v. Burns, 1917, 92 Conn. 39, 101 A. 504; cf. Hise v. Thomas, 1917, 181 Iowa 700, 165 N.W. 38; Russell v. Industrial Transportation Co., 1923, 113 Tex. 441, 251 S.W. 1034, affirmed 113 Tex. 441, 258 S.W. 462.

29. Bishop v. E.A. Strout Realty Agency, 4th Cir. 1950, 182 F.2d 503 (depth of water); Champneys v. Irwin, 1919, 106 Wash. 438, 180 P. 405 (amount of rental); Werline v. Aldred, 1916, 57 Okl. 391, 157 P. 305 (value and rental); Roda v. Berko, 1948, 401 Ill. 335, 81 N.E.2d 912; Twin State Fruit Corp. v. Kansas, 1932, 104 Vt. 154, 157 A. 831 (buyer representing he was the owner of a business).

30. Haskell v. Starbird, 1890, 152 Mass. 117, 142 N.E. 695; Ladner v. Balsley, 1897, 103 Iowa 674, 72 N.W. 787; Brees v. Anderson, 1922, 154 Minn. 123, 191 N.W. 266; Gridley v. Ross, 1926, 37 Idaho 693, 217 P. 989. Cf. Warne v. Finseth, 1923, 50 N.D. 347, 195 N.W. 573; Christensen v. Jauron, Iowa 1919, 174 N.W. 499.

31. Buckley v. Buckley, 1925, 230 Mich. 504, 202 N. W. 955; Gallon v. Burns, 1917, 92 Conn. 39, 101 A. 504; Currie v. Malloy, 1923, 185 N.C. 206, 116 S.E. 564; King v. Livingston Manufacturing Co., 1912, 180 Ala. 118, 60 So. 143; Board of Public Instruction of Dade County v. Everett W. Martin & Sons, Fla.1957, 97 So. 2d 21. There are still occasional cases to the contrary, such as Taylor v. Arneill, 1954, 129 Colo. 185, 268 P.2d 695. See Seavey, Caveat Emptor as of 1960, 1960, 38 Tex.L.Rev. 439.

32. Citizens Savings & Loan Association v. Fischer, 1966, 67 Ill.App.2d 315, 214 N.E.2d 612; Linch v. Carlson, 1952, 156 Neb. 308, 56 N.W.2d 101; Pattridge v. Youmans, 1941, 107 Colo. 122, 109 P.2d 646; Cowles' Executor v. Johnson, 1944, 297 Ky. 454, 179 S.W.2d 674; Campanelli v. Vescera, 1949, 75 R.I. 71, 63 A.2d 722. See Seavey, Actions for Economic Harm—A Comment, 1957, 32 N.Y.U.L.Rev. 1242.

Constructive notice under recording acts does not apply to misrepresentations. Schoedel v. State Bank of Newburg, 1944, 245 Wis. 74, 13 N.W.2d 534.

33. Duckworth v. Walker, 1854, 46 N.C. 507; Kaiser v. Nummerdor, 1904, 120 Wis. 234, 97 N.W. 932; Dalhoff Construction Co. v. Block, 8th Cir. 1907, 157 F. 227; Security Trust Co. v. O'Hair, 1936, 103 Ind.App. 56, 197 N.E. 694; Id., rehearing denied 103 Ind.App. 56, 199 N.E. 602. Accord: Dunham Lumber Co. v. Holt, 1898, 123 Ala. 336, 26 So. 663 (intelligent person, able to read and not prevented by defendant's conduct, signing document without reading it).

As to the distinction between that which is obvious to the senses and that which requires the effort of investigation, see Frenzel v. Miller, 1871, 37 Ind. 1; Robertson v. Smith, Mo.App.1918, 204 S.W. 413; Gallon v. Burns, 1917, 92 Conn. 39, 101 A. 504.

34. Feak v. Marion Steam Shovel Co., 9th Cir. 1936, 84 F.2d 670, certiorari denied 299 U.S. 604; Carpenter v. Hamilton, 1936, 18 Cal.App.2d 69, 62 P.2d 1397; Dillman v. Nadlehoffer, 1886, 119 Ill. 567, 7 N.E. 88; Godfrey v. Navratil, 1966, 3 Ariz.App. 47, 411 P.2d 470 (written warning of falsity). But the reliance may still be reasonable if the defendant allays the plaintiff's

tive availability of information to the parties may, however, be of considerable importance in determining whether the representation is to be regarded as an assurance of fact, or merely as a statement of opinion.[35]

The requirement of justifiability according to the *Second Restatement of Torts* refers to whether or not the representation relates to a matter about which a reasonable person would attach importance in determining a choice of action.[36] It relates therefore to (a) immaterial misrepresentation, (b) opinions and statements of intention that are commonly regarded as dealer's talk or puffing, and (c) statements about the law. It does not refer to contributory negligence in failing to discover the falsity of a representation about a matter which a reasonable person would regard as of substantial importance.

Materiality

The party deceived must not only be justified in his belief that the representation is true, but he must also be justified in taking action on that basis. This usually is expressed by saying that the fact represented must be a material one. There are misstatements which are so trivial, or so far unrelated to anything of real importance in the transaction, that the plaintiff will not be heard to say that they substantially affected his decision. Necessarily the test must be an objective one,[37] and it cannot be stated in the form of any definite rule, but must depend upon the circumstances of the transaction itself. The most cogent reason for the requirement of materiality is that of promoting stability in commercial transactions. It has been described as "some assurance that the representee is not merely using the misrepresentation as a pretext for escaping a bargain that he is dissatisfied with on other grounds." [38]

Thus, in particular cases, matters entirely collateral to a contract, and apparently of no significance to any reasonable man under the circumstances, have been held to be immaterial: the defendant's social, political and religious associations;[39] his motive or purpose in entering into the bargain;[40] the details of a seller's title, where good title is still conveyed;[41] a false financial statement which still gives an accurate picture;[42] the identity of the party for whom a purchase is made;[43] and many other items of similar nature.[44]

On the other hand facts to which a reasonable man might be expected to attach importance in making his choice of action, such as the identity of an individual[45] or the direc-

suspicions. Forsyth v. Dow, 1914, 81 Wash. 137, 142 P. 490; cf. Moncrief v. Wilkinson, 1890, 93 Ala. 373, 9 So. 159.

35. Harper and McNeely, A Synthesis of the Law of Misrepresentation, 1938, 22 Minn.L.Rev. 939, 960. See infra, § 109.

36. Second Restatement of Torts, § 538(2)(b).

37. Babb v. Bolyard, 1950, 194 Md. 603, 72 A.2d 13; Hall v. Johnson, 1879, 41 Mich. 286, 2 N.W. 55; Davis v. Davis, 1893, 97 Mich. 419, 56 N.W. 774; Bower, Actionable Misrepresentation, 2d Ed. 1927, ch. 11; Note 1951, 29 Tex.L.Rev. 644.

38. Keeton, Actionable Misrepresentation, 1949, 2 Okl.L.Rev. 56, 59.

39. Farnsworth v. Duffner, 1891, 142 U.S. 43, 12 S.Ct. 164, 35 L.Ed. 931.

40. Byrd v. Rautman, 1897, 85 Md. 414, 36 A. 1099; Lucas v. Long, 1915, 125 Md. 420, 94 A. 12.

41. Provident Loan Trust Co. v. McIntosh, 1904, 68 Kan. 452, 75 P. 498; Saxby v. Southern Land Co., 1909, 109 Va. 196, 63 S.E. 423. Cf. Kevorkian v. Bemis, 1927, 258 Mass. 456, 155 N.E. 452 (land owned by other corporation of which defendant held all the shares).

42. Gerner v. Yates, 1900, 61 Neb. 100, 84 N.W. 596.

43. Haverland v. Lane, 1916, 89 Wash. 557, 154 P. 1118; Cowan v. Fairbrother, 1896, 118 N.C. 406, 24 S.E. 212; O'Brien v. Luques, 1888, 81 Me. 46, 16 A. 304. Otherwise where a hostile interest is involved. Wann v. Scullin, 1907, 210 Mo. 429, 109 S.W. 688.

44. Babb v. Bolyard, 1950, 194 Md. 603, 72 A.2d 13 (price at which other dealers are selling cars); Blewett v. McRae, 1894, 88 Wis. 280, 60 N.W. 258 (commission of agent); Kaplan v. Suher, 1926, 254 Mass. 180, 150 N.E. 9 (length of time facts known); Blair v. Buttolph, 1887, 72 Iowa 31, 33 N.W. 349 (funds to build railway beyond certain point); Stufflebean v. Peaveler, Mo. App.1925, 274 S.W. 926 (person from whom seller bought); Greenawalt v. Rogers, 1907, 151 Cal. 630, 91 P. 526 (trivial assets where insolvency represented).

45. Gordon v. Street, [1899] 2 Q.B. 641. Saxton v. Harris, Alaska, 1964, 395 P.2d 71.

tors of a corporation [46] with whom he is dealing, the character of stock sold as treasury stock,[47] the age, horsepower and capacity of an automobile,[48] or the fact that it is a used car,[49] the train service to a suburb,[50] the solvency of purchasers,[51] the limited number of persons whose biographies are to be published in a book,[52] or the number of places where the seller's goods are made,[53] have been held to be material. The question is frequently for the jury [54] whether the statement made might justifiably induce the action taken.

One distinction that seems to have been made, however, is that where the representation is intended to deceive, it will be regarded as material if the maker knows that the recipient is peculiarly disposed to regard it as important, even though the standard reasonable man would not do so.[55] An individual may be known to attach importance to considerations which the normal man would disregard as trivial. He may send his daughter to a school because it has been attended by her former classmates,[56] give money to a college because it is to be named after a certain person,[57] buy pictures because his wife likes them,[58] lay in a stock of goods because another merchant carries them,[59] or do other things for similar personal reasons.[60] One who deliberately practices upon such known idiosyncracies cannot complain if he is held liable when he is successful, and the understanding of the parties themselves makes the statement "material." On the other hand, when the representation is an innocent one and strict responsibility is in question, the courts have tended to adhere rather closely to an objective standard, and to deny relief if the fact is so trivial that only personal peculiarity could regard it as important.[61]

WESTLAW REFERENCES

Reliance
headnote(justif! /s reliance relied /s misrepresent!)

Justifiability of the Reliance
digest(misrepresent! /s "affirmative defense*")

Materiality
headnote(assert! statement* /s material! /s fact* /s misrepresent!) % topic(217)

headnote(misrepresent! /s material! /s element* essential*)

---

46. Hedden v. Griffin, 1884, 136 Mass. 229; Penn Mutual Life Insurance Co. v. Crane, 1883, 134 Mass. 56.

47. Caswell v. Hunton, 1895, 87 Me. 277, 32 A. 899; Stillwell v. Rankin, 1918, 55 Mont. 130, 174 P. 186.

48. Smithpeter v. Mid-State Motor Co., Mo.App. 1934, 74 S.W.2d 47; Fosberg v. Couture, 1923, 126 Wash. 181, 217 P. 1001; Halff Co. v. Jones, Tex.Civ. App.1914, 169 S.W. 906; Angerosa v. White Co., 1936, 248 App.Div. 425, 290 N.Y.S. 204.

49. Friendly Irishman, Inc. v. Ronnow, 1958, 74 Nev. 316, 330 P.2d 497.

50. Holst v. Stewart, 1894, 161 Mass. 516, 37 N.E. 755.

51. Oswego Starch Factory v. Lendrum, 1881, 57 Iowa 573, 10 N.W. 900. Cf. Dezero v. Turner, 1941, 112 Vt. 194, 22 A.2d 173 (buyer represented he has just received money from an estate).

52. Greenleaf v. Gerald, 1900, 94 Me. 91, 46 A. 799.

53. Porter v. Stone, 1883, 62 Iowa 442, 17 N.W. 654.

54. Ochs v. Woods, 1917, 221 N.Y. 335, 117 N.E. 305; Davis v. Davis, 1893, 97 Mich. 419, 56 N.W. 774, reversed 100 Mich. 162, 58 N.W. 651; Montgomery v. Jacob Brothers Co., Del.1931, 5 W.W.Harr. 112, 159 A. 374.

55. Restatement of Torts, § 538(1)(b).

56. Brown v. Search, 1907, 131 Wis. 109, 111 N.W. 210.

57. Collinson v. Jeffries, 1899, 21 Tex.Civ.App. 653, 54 S.W. 28.

58. Washington Post Co. v. Sorrells, 1910, 7 Ga. App. 774, 68 S.E. 337; J.I. Case Threshing Machine Co. v. Webb, Tex.Civ.App.1916, 181 S.W. 853, error refused (automobile).

59. Roebuck v. Wick, 1906, 98 Minn. 130, 107 N.W. 1054; National Novelty Import Co. v. Reed, 1921, 105 Neb. 697, 181 N.W. 654.

60. See Stuart v. Lester, 1888, 49 Hun 58, 17 St.R. 248, 1 N.Y.S. 699; Valton v. National Fund Life Assurance Co., 1859, 20 N.Y. 32, 37; Cooper v. Fort Smith & Western Railroad Co., 1909, 23 Okl. 139, 99 P. 785, 790; Hester v. Shuster, Tex.Civ.App.1921, 234 S.W. 713 error dismissed. Similarly, the transaction itself may show that a fact which normally would be material is regarded as immaterial. Nounnan v. Sutter County Land Co., 1889, 81 Cal. 1, 22 P. 515.

61. See Restatement of Restitution, § 9, Comment b.

§ 109. Justifiable Reliance—Opinion and Intention

A statement of opinion is one which either indicates some doubt as to the speaker's belief in the existence of a state of facts, as where he says, "I think this is true, but I am not sure," or merely expresses his judgment on some matter of judgment connected with the facts, such as quality, value, authenticity and the like, as where he says, "This is a very fine picture." [1] It is not, however, the form of the statement which is important or controlling, but the sense in which it is reasonably understood. Statements very positive in form, asserting facts without qualification, may be held to be only those of opinion, where the recipient is aware that the speaker has no sufficient information or knowledge as to what he asserts; [2] and, as will be seen, [3] there are numerous circumstances in which statements which are in form only of opinion will be held to convey the assertion of accompanying facts.

It is stated very often as a fundamental rule in connection with all of the various remedies for misrepresentation, that they will not lie for misstatements of opinion, as distinguished from those of fact. The usual explanation is that an opinion is merely an assertion of one man's belief as to a fact, of which another should not be heard to complain, since opinions are a matter "of which many men will be of many minds, and which is often governed by whim and caprice. Judgment and opinion, in such case, implies no knowledge." [4]

But this explanation is scarcely adequate, since an expression of opinion is itself always a statement of at least one fact—the fact of the belief, the existing state of mind, of the one who asserts it. The true reason lies rather in the highly individualistic attitude of the common law toward the bargaining transactions with which the law of deceit has developed. The parties are expected to deal at arm's length and to beware of one another, and each is supposed to be competent to look after his own interests, and to draw his own conclusions. So long as he has not been misled by positive statements of fact, he has no right to rely upon the judgment of his opponent. Justifiable reliance, of course, is essential to any form of relief for misrepresentation.[5] It is more correct to say, therefore, that a statement of opinion is a representation of a fact, but of an immaterial fact, on which the law will not permit the opposing party to rely.[6] When, for any reason, such reliance is regarded as reasonable and permissible, a misstatement of opinion may be a sufficient basis for relief.[7]

In the absence, then of special circumstances affording some reason to the contrary, a representation which purports to be one of opinion only is not a sufficient foundation for the action of deceit.[8] There can be no recovery, for example, for a statement that the plaintiff is being offered an exceptionally good bargain,[9] that he would be foolish not to take advantage of the offer,[10] that

§ 109

1. See Keeton, Fraud—Misrepresentations of Opinion, 1937, 21 Minn.L.Rev. 643.

2. Batchelder v. Birchard Motors, 1958, 120 Vt. 429, 144 A.2d 298 (statements by seller of car assembled to order for plaintiff); Harris v. Delco Products, 1940, 305 Mass. 362, 25 N.E.2d 740 (well dug on land would find water); Saxby v. Southern Land Co., 1909, 109 Va. 196, 63 S.E. 423 (acres of land in timber).

3. See infra, this section.

4. Buller, J., in Pasley v. Freeman, 1789, 3 Term Rep. 51, 57.

5. See supra, § 108.

6. Keeton, Fraud—Misrepresentations of Opinion, 1937, 21 Minn.L.Rev. 643, 644, 650–651; Keeler v. Fred T. Ley & Co., 1st Cir. 1933, 65 F.2d 499; Ouilette v. Theobald, 1918, 78 N.H. 547, 103 A. 306.

7. See infra, this section.

8. Saxby v. Southern Land Co., 1909, 109 Va. 196, 63 S.E. 423; Wilson v. Mason, N.M.App.1970, 78 N.M. 27, 426 P.2d 789; Sorrells v. Clifford, 1922, 23 Ariz. 448, 204 P. 1013; Penney v. Pederson, 1927, 146 Wash. 31, 261 P. 636; Welch Veterinary Supply Co. v. Martin, Tex.Civ.App.1958, 313 S.W.2d 111, refused n.r.e.

9. Henning v. Kyle, 1949, 190 Va. 247, 56 S.E.2d 67.

10. Tampa Union Terminal Co. v. Richards, 1933, 108 Fla. 516, 146 So. 591.

his present holdings are a poor investment,[11] that there is water under land,[12] or that a building will withstand earthquakes,[13] where it is clear that these are no more than expressions of opinion. The same rule is carried over into other forms of relief. Thus statements of opinion are not regarded as warranties in contracts for the sale of goods,[14] nor do they afford a basis for estoppel.[15] When the plaintiff seeks equitable relief, as by rescission of a transaction, the equity courts usually have been willing to follow the law in saying that the plaintiff must form his own opinions, and is not entitled to rely upon those of his adversary.[16] But, since equity is concerned primarily with the unjust enrichment of the defendant, they have shown some tendency to be more liberal as to what is a "material" representation,[17] and more willingness to find some reason for holding reliance on an opinion to be justified, particularly where the statement of the opinion itself is an intentional lie.[18] Also, of course, rescission is allowed for a mutual mistake which is basic to the transaction; and such a mistake frequently can be found where the defendant has stated, and the plaintiff has relied upon, an entirely honest opinion.[19]

An opinion may take the form of a statement of quality, of more or less indefinite content. One common application of the opinion rule is in the case of loose general statements made by sellers in commending their wares. No action lies against a dealer who describes the automobile he is selling as a "dandy," a "bearcat," a "good little car," and a "sweet job;"[20] or as the "pride of our line" and the "best in the American market;"[21] or who merely makes use of broad, and vague, commendatory language compar-

11. Blakeslee v. Wallace, 6th Cir. 1930, 45 F.2d 347.

12. Harris v. Delco Products, 1940, 305 Mass. 362, 25 N.E.2d 740.

13. Finch v. McKee, 1936, 18 Cal.App.2d 90, 62 P.2d 1380. Cf. Han v. Horwitz, 1965, 2 Ariz.App. 245, 407 P.2d 786.

14. Mantle Lamp Co. v. Rucker, 1924, 202 Ky. 777, 261 S.W. 263; Seitz v. Brewer's Refrigerating Machine Co., 1891, 141 U.S. 510, 12 S.Ct. 46, 35 L.Ed. 837; Van Horn v. Stautz, 1921, 297 Ill. 530, 131 N.E. 153; Boston Consolidated Gas Co. v. Folsom, 1921, 237 Mass. 565, 130 N.E. 197. "No affirmation of the value of the goods, nor any statement purporting to be a statement of the seller's opinion only shall be construed as a warranty." Uniform Sales Act, § 12.

15. The Belle of the Sea, 1874, 87 U.S. (20 Wall.) 421, 22 L.Ed. 362; Intermountain Building & Loan Association v. Casper Mutual Building & Loan Association, 1934, 46 Wyo. 394, 28 P.2d 103; Hammerslough v. Kansas City Building, Loan & Savings Association, 1883, 79 Mo. 80; Aunt Jemima Mills Co. v. Rigney & Co., 2d Cir. 1917, 247 F. 407, certiorari denied 1918, 245 U.S. 672, 38 S.Ct. 222, 62 L.Ed. 540.

16. Southern Development Co. v. Silva, 1888, 125 U.S. 247, 8 S.Ct. 881, 31 L.Ed. 678; Culton v. Asher, 1912, 149 Ky. 659, 149 S.W. 946; Hart v. Marbury, 1921, 82 Fla. 317, 90 So. 173; Vian v. Hilberg, 1923, 111 Neb. 232, 196 N.W. 153; Seymour v. Chicago & Northwestern Railway Co., 1917, 181 Iowa 218, 164 N.W. 352.

17. See supra, § 108.

18. "There is a growing unwillingness on the part of the courts to allow statements to be made without liability, which are calculated to induce, and do induce, action on the part of the hearer. Where a statement is made with fraudulent intent, there is still more reason for regarding it as a ground of liability, even though couched in the form of an opinion, or though it relates to a matter as to which certainty is impossible." Schmitt v. Ornes Esswein & Co., 1921, 149 Minn. 370, 183 N.W. 840. Cf. Restatement of Contracts, § 474; Restatement of Restitution, § 8, Comment d.

19. Cf. Daniel v. Mitchell, C.C.Me.1840, Fed.Cas.No. 3,562, 1 Story 172; Thwing v. Hall & Ducey Lumber Co., 1889, 40 Minn. 184, 41 N.W. 815.

20. Bertram v. Reed Automobile Co., Tex.Civ.App. 1932, 49 S.W.2d 517, error refused: "Common experience and observation causes one to marvel at the moderation of the selling expert in making his trade talk to appellant. * * * These are relative terms, they may mean anything the orator or the listener wants, and neither may be penalized if the one exaggerates or the other is disappointed. There may be something more definite in the representations that the car had been well taken care of, had good rubber on it, had been driven but 19,000 miles, had not been mistreated, that mechanics had found it in perfect condition."

Cf. Buckingham v. Thompson, Tex.Civ.App.1911, 135 S.W. 652, where a Texas realtor let himself go; and see the fun with the case in Obiter Dicta, 1957, 25 Ford.L. Rev. 395. Also Keating v. De Arment, Fla.App.1967, 193 So.2d 694 ("This vessel is in perfect shape, and she is my pride and joy").

21. Prince v. Brackett, Shaw & Lunt Co., 1925, 125 Me. 31, 130 A. 509. Accord: Nichols v. Lane, 1919, 93 Vt. 87, 106 A. 592 ("no better land in Vermont"); Gleason v. McPherson, 1917, 175 Cal. 594, 166 P. 332 ("gilt-edge" bonds); Thorpe v. Cooley, 1917, 138 Minn. 431, 165 N.W. 265 (bonds "as good as gold").

ing his goods favorably with others,[22] or praising them as "good," "proper," "sufficient," and the like.[23]

Such sales talk, or puffing, as it is commonly called, is considered to be offered and understood as an expression of the seller's opinion only, which is to be discounted as such by the buyer, and on which no reasonable man would rely. "A statement that a cigarette is made from the purest tobaccos grown, that an automobile is the most economical car on the market, that a stock is the safest investment in the world, that a machine is 100 per cent efficient, that a household device is absolutely perfect, that a real estate investment will insure a handsome profit, that an article is the greatest bargain ever offered, and similar claims are intended and understood to be merely emphatic methods of urging a sale. * * * These things, then, the buyer must disregard in forming a sober judgment as to his conduct in the transaction. If he succumbs to such persistent solicitation, he must take the risk of any loss attributable to a disparity between the exaggerated opinion of the purchaser and a reasonable or accurate judgment of the value of the article."[24] "The law recognizes the fact that men will naturally overstate the value and qualities of the articles which they have to sell. All men know this, and a buyer has no right to rely upon such statements,"[25] whether the remedy sought be deceit, warranty,[26] or rescission.[27] Although the question seldom has arisen, the same probably is true of the disparaging words of a buyer seeking to obtain a favorable price.[28]

The "puffing" rule amounts to a seller's privilege to lie his head off, so long as he says nothing specific, on the theory that no reasonable man would believe him, or that no reasonable man would be influenced by such talk. It is not surprising, therefore, that the rule has not been a favored one; and that whenever it can be found under the circumstances that the buyer reasonably understood that he was receiving something in the way of assurance as to specific facts, the question of actionable misrepresentation has been left to the jury.[29]

---

22. McHargue v. Fayette Coal & Feed Co., Ky.1955, 283 S.W.2d 170; Thomas v. Mississippi Valley Gas Co., 1959, 237 Miss. 100, 113 So.2d 535; Hayes Construction Co. v. Silverthorn, 1955, 343 Mich. 421, 72 N.W.2d 190.

23. Poley v. Bender, 1959, 87 Ariz. 35, 347 P.2d 696; cf. John A. Frye Shoe Co. v. Williams, 1942, 312 Mass. 656, 46 N.E.2d 1.

24. Harper and McNeely, A Synthesis of the Law of Misrepresentation, 1938, 22 Minn.L.Rev. 939, 1004. Accord: Nichols v. Lane, 1919, 93 Vt. 87, 106 A. 592 ("no better land in Vermont"); Miller v. Protrka, 1951, 193 Or. 585, 238 P.2d 753 ("hardly ever a vacancy" in motel); Lambert v. Sistrunk, Fla.1952, 58 So.2d 434 (stepladder "strong; will last a lifetime and never break"); American Laundry Machinery Co. v. Skinner, 1945, 225 N.C. 285, 34 S.E.2d 190 (machine "will do better work, cheaper and with less labor" than one buyer has); James Spear Stove & Heating Co. v. General Electric Co., D.C.Pa.1934, 12 F.Supp. 977 (prospectus advertising).

25. Kimball v. Bangs, 1887, 144 Mass. 321, 11 N.E. 113. "There are some kinds of talk which no sensible man takes seriously, and if he does he suffers from his credulity. If we were all scrupulously honest, it would not be so; but, as it is, neither party usually believes what the seller says about his own opinions and each knows it. Such statements, like the claims of campaign managers before election, are rather designed to allay the suspicion which would attend their absence than to be understood as having any relation to objective truth." Learned Hand, J., in Vulcan Metals Co. v. Simmons Manufacturing Co., 2d Cir. 1918, 248 F. 853.

"The rule of law is hardly to be regretted, when it is considered how easily and insensibly words of hope or expectation are converted by an interested memory into statements of quality or value when the expectation has been disappointed." Holmes, J., in Deming v. Darling, 1889, 148 Mass. 504, 20 N.E. 107.

26. Ireland v. Louis K. Liggett Co., 1922, 243 Mass. 243, 137 N.E. 371; Rowe Manufacturing Co. v. Curtis-Straub Co., 1937, 223 Iowa 858, 273 N.W. 895; Michelin Tire Co. v. Schulz, 1929, 295 Pa. 140, 145 A. 67; Keenan v. Cherry & Webb, 1924, 47 R.I. 125, 131 A. 309.

27. Black v. Irvin, 1915, 76 Or. 561, 149 P. 540; Hunter v. McLaughlin, 1873, 43 Ind. 38; French v. Griffin, 1867, 18 N.J.Eq. 279; Rendell v. Scott, 1886, 70 Cal. 514, 11 P. 779.

28. Fisher v. Budlong, 1873, 10 R.I. 525; Smith v. Boothe, 1918, 90 Or. 360, 176 P. 793; Mathews v. Hogueland, 1916, 98 Kan. 341, 157 P. 1179. "It is naught, it is naught, saith the buyer; but when he is gone his way, then he boasteth." Prov. 20:14.

29. Maxwell Ice Co. v. Brackett, Shaw & Lunt Co., 1921, 80 N.H. 236, 116 A. 34 (capacity of machine); Holland Furnace Co. v. Korth, 1953, 43 Wn.2d 618, 262 P.2d 772, 1166 (capacity of furnace); Herzog v. Capital Co., 1945, 27 Cal.2d 349, 164 P.2d 8 (house "in perfect

Statements of value, in general, as well as predictions as to profits to be made from the thing sold,[30] fall into the same class of statements not to be relied on. The value, or financial worth, of property is regarded as a matter of opinion, on which each party must form his own judgment, without trusting to his adversary, and as to which "puffing" and exaggeration are normally to be expected.[31] Very little, however, is required to transform a statement of opinion as to value into one of fact. Thus a representation as to the price paid for the property by the defendant himself is regarded as one of fact,[32] as is also a statement as to the price at which similar property is selling,[33] the amount of an offer made by a third person,[34] the state of the market,[35] or even the lowest price at which a purchase can be made from another.[36] There is a very noticeable tendency to find such additional elements wherever possible, and to give relief by treating statements of value as covering something more than mere opinion.

Misrepresentations of Law

Statements of law likewise are commonly said to be mere assertions of opinion, which are insufficient as a basis for deceit,[37] estoppel,[38] or equitable relief.[39] There may ordinarily be no recovery, for example, for a statement that a divorce will be valid,[40] that a writing will have the legal effect of a

---

condition"); Glock v. Carpenter, E.D.Ky.1960, 184 F.Supp. 829, affirmed in 6th Cir. 1961, 286 F.2d 431, certiorari denied 366 U.S. 930, 81 S.Ct. 1651, 6 L.Ed.2d 389 ("pure, sweet, premium gas"); Traylor Engineering & Manufacturing Co. v. National Container Corp., 1949, 45 Del. (6 Terry) 143, 70 A.2d 9 (capacity and qualities of machine).

30. Kulesza v. Wyhowski, 1921, 213 Mich. 189, 182 N.W. 53; Jewell v. Shell Oil Co., 1933, 172 Wash. 603, 21 P.2d 243; Penfield v. Bennett Film Laboratories, 1935, 4 Cal.App.2d 306, 40 P.2d 587; Lloyd v. Junkin, Tex.Civ.App.1934, 75 S.W.2d 712; Law v. Sidney, 1936, 47 Ariz. 1, 53 P.2d 64.

31. Tetreault v. Campbell, 1948, 115 Vt. 369, 61 A.2d 591; Byers v. Federal Land Co., 8th Cir. 1924, 3 F.2d 9; Sacramento Suburban Fruit Lands Co. v. Melin, 9th Cir. 1929, 36 F.2d 907, followed 36 F.2d 923; Reeder v. Guaranteed Foods, Inc., 1965, 194 Kan. 386, 399 P.2d 822; Rothermel v. Phillips, 1928, 292 Pa. 371, 141 A. 241. See Note, 1953, 7 Ark.L.Rev. 154.

32. Fairchild v. McMahon, 1893, 139 N.Y. 290, 34 N.E. 779; Dorr v. Cory, 1899, 108 Iowa 725, 78 N.W. 682; Kohl v. Taylor, 1911, 62 Wash. 678, 114 P. 874; Knopfler v. Flynn, 1917, 135 Minn. 333, 160 N.W. 860; Stoney Creek Woolen Co. v. Smalley, 1896, 111 Mich. 321, 69 N.W. 722. A few cases have held that the fact is immaterial and the reliance unreasonable. Bishop v. Small, 1874, 63 Me. 12; Cooper v. Lovering, 1870, 106 Mass. 77.

33. Gray v. Wikstrom Motors, 1942, 14 Wn.2d 448, 128 P.2d 490; Brody v. Foster, 1916, 134 Minn. 91, 158 N.W. 824; Weaver v. Cone, 1896, 174 Pa. 104, 34 A. 551; Conlan v. Roemer, 1889, 52 N.J.L. 53, 18 A. 858. Contra, Babb v. Bolyard, 1950, 194 Md. 603, 72 A.2d 13.

34. Kabatchnick v. Hanover-Elm Building Corp., 1952, 328 Mass. 341, 103 N.E.2d 692; Baloyan v. Furniture Exhibition Building Co., 1932, 258 Mich. 244, 241 N.W. 886; Seaman v. Becar, 1896, 15 Misc. 616, 38 N.Y.S. 69; Strickland v. Graybill, 1899, 97 Va. 602, 34 S.E. 475; Smith, Kline & French Co. v. Smith, 1895, 166 Pa. 563, 31 A. 343. See Notes, 1953, 2 De Paul L.Rev. 107; [1952] Wash.U.L.Q. 593; 1953, 7 Ala.L.Rev. 163.

35. Zimmern v. Blount, 5th Cir. 1917, 238 F. 740; Stoll v. Wellborn, N.J.Eq.1903, 56 A. 894; American Hardwood Lumber Co. v. Dent, 1907, 121 Mo.App. 108, 98 S.W. 814; McDonald v. Lastinger, Tex.Civ.App.1919, 214 S.W. 829.

36. As by a broker to a prospective customer. Hokanson v. Oatman, 1911, 165 Mich. 512, 131 N.W. 111; Estes v. Crosby, 1920, 171 Wis. 73, 175 N.W. 933, amendment of mandate denied 171 Wis. 73, 177 N.W. 512. Contra: Bradley v. Oviatt, 1912, 86 Conn. 63, 84 A. 321; Ripy v. Cronan, 1909, 131 Ky. 631, 115 S.W. 791. In Duvall v. Walton, 1932, 107 Fla. 60, 144 So. 318, the principal was held not liable, on the ground that he would not have been liable if he had made such a representation himself.

37. Gormely v. Gymnastic Association, 1882, 55 Wis. 350, 13 N.W. 242; Metzger v. Baker, 1933, 93 Colo. 165, 24 P.2d 748; Meacham v. Halley, 5th Cir. 1939, 103 F.2d 967; Unckles v. Hentz, 1896, 18 Misc. 644, 43 N.Y.S. 749; Yappel v. Mozina, 1929, 33 Ohio App. 371, 169 N.E. 315. It is possible to warrant the law expressly, Municipal Metallic Bed Manufacturing Corp. v. Dobbs, 1930, 253 N.Y. 313, 171 N.E. 75, but certainly the intent to warrant must be made clear.

38. Sturm v. Boker, 1893, 150 U.S. 312, 14 S.Ct. 99, 37 L.Ed. 1093; Aunt Jemima Mills Co. v. Rigney & Co., 2d Cir. 1917, 247 F. 407, certiorari denied 245 U.S. 672, 38 S.Ct. 222, 62 L.Ed. 540; Shapley v. Abbott, 1870, 42 N.Y. 443.

39. Adkins v. Hoskins, 1928, 176 Ark. 565, 3 S.W.2d 322; Dillman v. Nadlehoffer, 1886, 119 Ill. 567, 7 N.E. 88; Champion v. Woods, 1889, 79 Cal. 17, 21 P. 534; Abbott v. Treat, 1886, 78 Me. 121, 3 A. 44. Cf. Jaggar v. Winslow, 1883, 30 Minn. 263, 15 N.W. 242 (defense of fraud); McFarland v. Hueners, 1920, 96 Or. 579, 190 P. 584 (same).

40. Christopher v. Whitmire, 1945, 199 Ga. 280, 34 S.E.2d 100.

guaranty,[41] that particular conduct will or will not lead to legal liability,[42] or that the plaintiff will have the legal right to sell liquor.[43] In explanation, two reasons have been repeated, sometimes in the same decision: first, that every man is presumed to know the law, and hence the plaintiff cannot be heard to say that he reasonably believed the statement made to him;[44] and second, that no man, at least without special training, can be expected to know the law, and so the plaintiff must have understood that the defendant was giving him nothing more than an opinion.[45] The contradiction is sufficiently obvious; and both reasons are challenged in turn by the contrast of the generally accepted holding that statements as to the law of a foreign state are to be regarded as representations of fact, on which the plaintiff may reasonably rely.[46] The general rule seems to have arisen rather out of a deliberate policy requiring the parties to a bargain to deal at arm's length with respect to the law, and not to rely upon one another.

The present tendency is strongly in favor of eliminating the distinction between law and fact as "useless duffle of an older and more arbitrary day,"[47] and recognizing that a statement as to the law, like a statement as to anything else, may be intended and understood either as one of fact or one of opinion only, according to the circumstances of the case.[48] Most courts still render lip service to the older rule, but they have been inclined whenever possible to find statements of fact "implied" in representations as to the law. Thus an assertion that a company has the legal right to do business in a state carries an assurance that it has, as a matter of fact, been duly qualified;[49] a representation that certain lands may be obtained by patent free from mineral reservations amounts to saying that the government does not classify them as mineral lands;[50] and statements as to the title to land,[51] the priority of a particular lien,[52] or the validity of a note,[53] as well as many similar legal conclusions,[54] have been held to convey similar implica-

41. Ackerman v. Bramwell Investment Co., 1932, 80 Utah 52, 12 P.2d 623.

42. Williams v. Dougherty County, 1960, 101 Ga. App. 193, 113 S.E.2d 168; Goodspeed v. MacNaughton, Greenawalt & Co., 1939, 288 Mich. 1, 284 N.W. 621.

43. Ad. Dernehl & Sons Co. v. Detert, 1925, 186 Wis. 113, 202 N.W. 207. Cf. Metzger v. Baker, 1933, 93 Colo. 165, 24 P.2d 748 (zoning ordinance will prevent another drug store); McDonald v. Goodman, Ky.1951, 239 S.W.2d 97 (law requires an autopsy); Vokal v. United States, 9th Cir. 1949, 177 F.2d 619 (plaintiffs subject to renegotiation statute).

44. See Beall v. McGehee, 1876, 57 Ala. 438; Abbott v. Treat, 1886, 78 Me. 121, 3 A. 44; Burt v. Bowles, 1879, 69 Ind. 1. It has, of course, been pointed out many times that there is never a "presumption" that any man knows the law. The proper statement is that, in many situations, ignorance of the law is no excuse—a very different thing. See Broom's Legal Maxims, 9th Ed. 1924, 178–188.

Abbott, C.J.: "No attorney is bound to know all the law. God forbid that it should be imagined that an attorney, or a counsel, or even a judge, is bound to know all the law." Montriou v. Jeffries, 1825, 2 C. & P. 116, 172 Eng.Rep. 51.

45. See Champion v. Woods, 1889, 79 Cal. 17, 21 P. 534; Thompson v. Phoenix Insurance Co., 1883, 72 Me. 55; Fish v. Cleland, 1864, 33 Ill. 238.

46. Wood v. Roeder, 1897, 50 Neb. 476, 70 N.W. 21; Schneider v. Schneider, 1904, 125 Iowa 1, 98 N.W. 159; Hembry v. Parreco, Mun.App.D.C.1951, 81 A.2d 77.

This has been explained on the basis of a supposed analogy to the rule that courts will not take judicial notice of foreign law, which must be proved as a fact. Bethell v. Bethell, 1883, 92 Ind. 318; Epp v. Hinton, 1914, 91 Kan. 513, 138 P. 576. The explanation seems a highly artificial one, where the real question is one of reasonable reliance.

47. Peterson v. First National Bank, 1925, 162 Minn. 369, 375, 203 N.W. 53.

48. Fainardi v. Pausata, R.I.1924, 126 A. 865; Restatement of Restitution, § 55(a), and cases cited in the Supplement, Reporters' Notes to § 55; Restatement of Torts, § 545; Keeton, Fraud—Misrepresentations of Law, 1937, 15 Tex.L.Rev. 409; Notes, 1943, 22 Tex.L. Rev. 102; 1932, 32 Col.L.Rev. 1018; 1925, 73 U.Pa.L. Rev. 307; 1929, 14 Iowa L.Rev. 453.

49. Miller v. Osterlund, 1923, 154 Minn. 495, 191 N.W. 919. Accord: Myers v. Lowery, 1920, 46 Cal. App. 682, 189 P. 793 (accredited hospital); Harris-Emery Co. v. Pitcairn, 1904, 122 Iowa 595, 98 N.W. 476 (powers of insurance company); Kerr v. Shurtluff, 1914, 218 Mass. 167, 105 N.E. 871 (power of college to grant medical degree).

50. Pieh v. Flitton, 1927, 170 Minn. 29, 211 N.W. 964; Moreland v. Atchison, 1857, 19 Tex. 303.

51. Motherway v. Wall, 1897, 168 Mass. 333, 47 N.E. 135; Barnett v. Kunkle, 8th Cir. 1919, 256 F. 644, appeal dismissed Harjo v. Kunkle, 1921, 254 U.S. 620,

52–54. See notes 52–54 on page 760.

tions of fact. Since it is obvious that representations of law almost never are made in such a vacuum that supporting facts are not to be "implied,"[55] it would seem that very little can be left of the "general rule" in the face of a series of such decisions.

Justifiable Reliance on Opinion

The courts have developed numerous exceptions to the rule that misrepresentations of opinion are not a basis for relief. Apparently all of these may be summed up by saying that they involve situations where special circumstances make it very reasonable or probable that the plaintiff should accept the defendant's opinion and act upon it, and so justify a relaxation of the distrust which is considered admirable between bargaining opponents.[56] Thus where the parties stand in a relation of trust and confidence, as in the case of members of the same family,[57] partners,[58] attorney and client,[59] executor and beneficiary of an estate,[60] principal and agent,[61] insurer and insured,[62] close friendship,[63] and the like,[64] it is held that reliance upon an opinion, whether it be as to a fact or a matter of law, is justifiable, and relief is granted.

Further than this, it has been recognized very often that the expression of an opinion may carry with it an implied assertion, not only that the speaker knows no facts which would preclude such an opinion,[65] but that he does know facts which justify it.[66] There is quite general agreement that such an assertion is to be implied where the defendant holds himself out[67] or is understood as having special knowledge of the matter which is

41 S.Ct. 319, 65 L.Ed. 442; Baldock v. Johnson, 1887, 14 Or. 542, 13 P. 434. See Note, 1942, 30 Cal.L.Rev. 197.

52. Kehl v. Abram, 1904, 210 Ill. 218, 71 N.E. 347; Faust v. Hosford, 1903, 119 Iowa 97, 93 N.W. 58.

53. Brown v. Rice's Administrator, 1875, 67 Va. (26 Grat.) 467.

54. Westervelt v. Demarest, 1884, 46 N.J.L. 37 (liability of directors); Commercial Savings Bank v. Kietges, 1928, 206 Iowa 90, 219 N.W. 44 (same); Kathan v. Comstock, 1909, 140 Wis. 427, 122 N.W. 1044 (legal effect of tax deeds); Unger v. Eagle Fish Co., 1945, 185 Misc. 134, 56 N.Y.S.2d 265, affirmed 269 App. Div. 950, 58 N.Y.S.2d 332 (no price ceiling on frozen fish); Sorenson v. Gardner, 1959, 215 Or. 255, 334 P.2d 471 (compliance of house with state building code).

55. See Eaglesfield v. Marquis of Londonderry, 1877, L.R. 4 Ch. 693; West London Commercial Bank v. Kitson, 1884, 13 Q.B.D. 360. See also the discussion as to what is "law" in the Note, 1932, 32 Col.L.Rev. 1018, 1028–1030.

56. See Keeton, Fraud—Misrepresentations of Opinion, 1937, 21 Minn.L.Rev. 643; Notes, 1948, 28 Bos.U.L.Rev. 352; 1928, 13 Corn.L.Q. 140; 1932, 32 Col.L.Rev. 1018; 1929, 14 Iowa L.Rev. 453; 1938, 38 Col.L.Rev. 1110.

57. Sims v. Ferrill, 1872, 45 Ga. 585; Baldock v. Johnson, 1887, 14 Or. 542, 13 P. 434; Collins v. Lindsay, Mo.1930, 25 S.W.2d 84; cf. Jekshewitz v. Groswald, 1929, 265 Mass. 413, 164 N.E. 609 (affianced).

58. Teachout v. Van Hoesen, 1878, 76 Iowa 113, 40 N.W. 96.

59. Ward v. Arnold, 1958, 52 Wn.2d 581, 328 P.2d 164 (law); Rice v. Press, 1953, 117 Vt. 442, 94 A.2d 397 (legal right to fee); Benson v. Bunting, 1900, 127 Cal. 532, 59 P. 991; Allen v. Frawley, 1900, 106 Wis. 638, 82 N.W. 593; Hicks v. Deemer, 1899, 87 Ill.App. 384, reversed 187 Ill. 164, 58 N.E. 252. Cf. Squyres v. Christan, Tex.Civ.App.1951, 242 S.W.2d 786, error dismissed (accountant).

60. Stephens v. Collison, 1911, 249 Ill. 225, 94 N.W. 664; Schuttler v. Brandfass, 1895, 41 W.Va. 201, 23 S.E. 808; Tompkins v. Hollister, 1886, 60 Mich. 470, 27 N.W. 651.

61. Rogers v. Brummet, 1923, 92 Okl. 216, 220 P. 362; Cheney v. Gleason, 1873, 125 Mass. 166.

62. Colby v. Life Indemnity & Investment Co., 1894, 57 Minn. 510, 59 N.W. 539; Knox v. Anderson, D.C.Hawaii 1958, 159 F.Supp. 795, supplemented 162 F.Supp. 338; Stark v. Equitable Life Assurance Society, 1939, 205 Minn. 138, 285 N.W. 466.

63. Erickson v. Frazier, 1926, 169 Minn. 118, 210 N.W. 868; Spiess v. Brandt, 1950, 230 Minn. 246, 41 N.W.2d 561; Casper v. Bankers' Life Insurance Co. of Lincoln, 1927, 238 Mich. 300, 212 N.W. 970.

64. Rowe v. Phillips, 1919, 214 Ill.App. 582 (banker and investor); Hassman v. First State Bank, 1931, 183 Minn. 453, 236 N.W. 921 (confidence reposed for ten years); Pulliam v. Gentry, 1925, 206 Ky. 763, 268 S.W. 557 (past business association); Dombrowski v. Tomasino, 1965, 27 Wis.2d 378, 134 N.W.2d 420 (past reliance); Emily v. Bayne, Mo.App.1963, 371 S.W.2d 663 (law).

65. Zingale v. Mills Novelty Co., 1943, 244 Wis. 144, 11 N.W.2d 644.

66. Shepherd v. Kendrick, 1938, 236 Ala. 289, 181 So. 782. Cf. Ward v. Jenson, 1918, 87 Or. 314, 170 P. 538, where the opinion was "so blended with statements of fact supporting it" as to carry an inference that it was itself a statement of fact.

67. Lambach v. Lundberg, 1934, 177 Wash. 568, 33 P.2d 105 (express assertion); Eno Brick Corp. v. Barber-Greene Co., 1968, 109 N.H. 156, 245 A.2d 545.

not available to the plaintiff, so that his opinion becomes in effect an assertion summarizing his knowledge. Thus the ordinary man is free to deal in reliance upon the opinion of an expert jeweler as to the value of a diamond,[68] of an attorney upon a point of law,[69] of a physician upon a matter of health,[70] of a banker upon the validity of a signature,[71] or the owner of land at a distance as to its worth,[72] even though the opinion is that of his antagonist in a bargaining transaction. On the same basis it has been held that statements by a seller as to the capacity of the thing sold,[73] or the condition of land,[74] or other matters,[75] which on the part of one without special knowledge would be regarded as mere opinion, may be relied on as statements of fact.

Notwithstanding the finding of an implied assertion of fact, the true reason for these holdings appears to be that when the parties do not purport to be dealing on an equal footing as to available information, the basis for the individualistic approach of the common law is destroyed.[76] This is borne out by the fact that the plaintiff is allowed to recover when the disparity of knowledge arises, not from any special information on the part of the defendant, but from the ignorance or illiteracy of the plaintiff.[77] Consistent with this is the further exception which allows recovery where the defendant, after expressing his opinion, makes use of artifice or trickery to prevent further investigation, and so deprives the plaintiff of other sources

68. Picard v. McCormick, 1862, 11 Mich. 68. Accord: Carruth v. Harris, 1894, 41 Neb. 789, 60 N.W. 106 (corporate officer to purchaser of stock); Fourth National Bank in Wichita v. Webb, 1930, 131 Kan. 167, 290 P. 1 (bank dealing in oil stock to inexperienced farmers); Haserot v. Keller, 1924, 67 Cal.App. 659, 228 P. 383 (inventor to co-owner of patent); Warwick v. Corbett, 1919, 106 Wash. 554, 180 P. 928 (owner of business representing profits to be made).

69. Sainsbury v. Pennsylvania Greyhound Lines, 3d Cir. 1950, 183 F.2d 548; Security Savings Bank v. Kellams, 1928, 321 Mo. 1, 9 S.W.2d 967; Rosenberg v. Cyrowski, 1924, 227 Mich. 508, 198 N.W. 905; Bowman v. Payne, 1921, 55 Cal.App. 789, 204 P. 406; Regus v. Schartkoff, 1957, 156 Cal.App.2d 382, 319 P.2d 721.

70. Hedin v. Minneapolis Medical & Surgical Institute, 1895, 62 Minn. 146, 64 N.W. 158; St. Louis & San Francisco Railroad Co. v. Reed, 1913, 37 Okl. 350, 132 P. 355; Brown v. Ocean Accident & Guarantee Corp., 1913, 153 Wis. 196, 140 N.W. 1112. Accord: Rodee v. Seaman, 1914, 33 S.D. 184, 145 N.W. 441 (real estate expert); Board of Water Commissioners v. Robbins & Potter, 1910, 82 Conn. 623, 74 A. 938 (engineer); Vilett v. Moler, 1900, 82 Minn. 12, 84 N.W. 452 (expert barber school); Powell v. Fletcher, N.Y.C.P.1892, 18 N.Y.S. 451 (violin expert); McDonald v. Lastinger, Tex.Civ.App.1919, 214 S.W. 829 (stockbroker selling bonds).

71. Wilson v. Jones, Tex.Com.App.1932, 45 S.W.2d 572. Accord, Sparks v. Guaranty State Bank, 1956, 179 Kan. 236, 293 P.2d 1017 (credit of drawer of a check).

72. Scott v. Burnight, 1906, 131 Iowa 507, 107 N.W. 422; Heal v. Stoll, 1922, 176 Wis. 137, 185 N.W. 242; Bonnarjee v. Pike, 1919, 43 Cal.App. 502, 185 P. 479; Long v. Freeman, 1934, 228 Mo.App. 1002, 69 S.W.2d 973. Cf. Smith v. Land & House Prop. Corp., 1884, L.R. 28 Ch.Div. 7 (statement by landlord as to his tenant).

73. F.B. Connelly Co. v. Schleuter Brothers, 1923, 69 Mont. 65, 220 P. 103; Schmitt v. Ornes Esswein & Co., 1921, 149 Minn. 370, 183 N.W. 840; Burroughs Adding Machine Co. v. Scandinavian-American Bank, 9th Cir. 1917, 239 F. 179; Pitney Bowes, Inc. v. Sirkle, Ky.1952, 248 S.W.2d 920.

74. Doran v. Milland Development Co., 1958, 159 Cal.App.2d 322, 323 P.2d 792.

75. Aldrich v. Worley, 1925, 200 Iowa 1009, 205 N.W. 851 (suitability of land for raising rice); F.H. Smith Co. v. Low, 1927, 57 App.D.C. 167, 18 F.2d 817 (value of property sold); Coleman v. Night Commander Lighting Co., 1928, 218 Ala. 196, 118 So. 377 (expected carbide consumption of lighting plant); Mears v. Accomac Banking Co., 1933, 160 Va. 311, 168 S.E. 740 (bonds as good investment); Bankers Bond Co. v. Cox, 1936, 263 Ky. 481, 92 S.W.2d 790 (seller's bonds better than buyer's); Sluss v. Brown-Crummer Investment Co., 1936, 143 Kan. 14, 53 P.2d 900 (bonds "gilt edge," "safe and sound").

76. Shepherd v. Woodson, Mo.1959, 328 S.W.2d 1; Gugel v. Neitzel, 1929, 248 Mich. 312, 226 N.W. 869; cf. Gable v. Niles Holding Co., 1941, 209 Minn. 445, 296 N.W. 525.

Compare Powell v. Fletcher, 1892, 45 N.Y. 294, 18 N.Y.S. 451 (violin expert to layman) and Plimpton v. Friedberg, 1933, 110 N.J.L. 427, 166 A. 295 (art expert to layman), with Banner v. Lyon & Healy Co., 1937, 249 App.Div. 569, 293 N.Y.S. 236, affirmed 1938, 277 N.Y. 570, 13 N.E.2d 774 (violin expert to experienced violinist); Smith v. Zimbalist, 1934, 2 Cal.App.2d 324, 38 P.2d 170 (same).

77. Benedict v. Heirs of Dickens, 1935, 119 Conn. 541, 177 A. 715; Crofford v. Bowden, Tex.Civ.App. 1958, 311 S.W.2d 954, error refused; Ellis v. Gordon, 1930, 202 Wis. 134, 231 N.W. 585; Hoptowit v. Brown, 1921, 115 Wash. 661, 198 P. 370; Kraus v. National Bank of Commerce, 1918, 140 Minn. 108, 167 N.W. 353.

of information.[78] And for the same reason, where the opinion is that of one who purports to be a disinterested person, not involved in any dealing with the plaintiff, it is generally agreed that there may be reasonable reliance upon it.[79]

Prediction and Intention

Ordinarily a prediction as to events to occur in the future is to be regarded as a statement of opinion only, on which the adverse party has no right to rely.[80] It was said very early that "one cannot warrant a thing which will happen in the future,"[81] and where the statement is that prices will remain unchanged,[82] that taxes will be reduced,[83] that cattle will reach a given weight within a specified time,[84] that the plaintiff will be able to obtain a position,[85] or that he will have profitable building lots next to a highway,[86] the law has required him to form his own conclusions. Such prophecy does, however, always carry an implied representation that the speaker knows of no facts which will prevent it from being accomplished;[87] and as in the case of any other opinion, it has been held that there may be reasonable reliance upon the assertion where the speaker purports to have special knowledge of facts which would justify the expectations he is raising.[88]

On the other hand, statements of intention, whether of the speaker himself or of another,[89] usually are regarded as statements of fact.[90] "The state of a man's mind," said Lord Bowen[91] in 1882, "is as much a fact as the state of his digestion;" and this catch phrase has been repeated ever since in explanation of the distinction between prediction and intention. But any statement of an opinion is at least as much an assertion of the fact of a present state of

---

78. Adan v. Steinbrecher, 1911, 116 Minn. 174, 133 N.W. 477; Crompton v. Beedle, 1910, 83 Vt. 287, 75 A. 331; Owens v. Norwood-White Coal Co., 1919, 188 Iowa 1092, 174 N.W. 851. Cf. Mattauch v. Walsh Brothers & Miller, 1907, 136 Iowa 225, 113 N.W. 818; Scheele v. Union Loan & Finance Co., 1937, 200 Minn. 554, 274 N.W. 673.

79. Medbury v. Watson, 1843, 47 Mass. (6 Metc.) 246; Batchelder v. Stephenson, 1921, 150 Minn. 215, 184 N.W. 852; Melgreen v. McGuire, 1958, 214 Or. 128, 327 P.2d 1114; Kenner v. Harding, 1877, 85 Ill. 264; Samp v. Long, 1926, 50 S.D. 492, 210 N.W. 733.

80. Sawyer v. Prickett, 1875, 86 U.S. (19 Wall.) 146, 22 L.Ed. 105; McElrath v. Electric Investment Co., 1911, 114 Minn. 358, 131 N.W. 380; Farwell v. Colonial Trust Co., 8th Cir. 1906, 147 F. 480; Henry v. Continental Building & Loan Association, 1909, 156 Cal. 667, 105 P. 960; Davis v. Reynolds, 1910, 107 Me. 61, 77 A. 409.

81. Choke, J., in Y.B. 11 Edw. IV, 6.

82. Coe v. Ware, 1930, 271 Mass. 570, 171 N.E. 732; Hilgendorf v. Shuman, 1939, 232 Wis. 625, 288 N.W. 184.

83. 3700 S. Kedzie Building Corp. v. Chicago Steel Foundry Co., 1959, 20 Ill.App.2d 483, 156 N.E.2d 618.

84. Wright v. Couch, Tex.Civ.App.1932, 54 S.W.2d 207. Cf. Kennedy v. Flo-Tronics, Inc., 1966, 274 Minn. 327, 143 N.W.2d 827 (stock would triple in value within a year); Ashalter v. Peterson, 1927, 240 Mich. 64, 214 N.W. 964 (black foxes to be born in particular year).

85. Schwitters v. Des Moines Commercial College, 1925, 199 Iowa 1058, 203 N.W. 265. Cf. Moser v. New York Life Insurance Co., 9th Cir. 1945, 151 F.2d 396 (future earnings).

86. Campbell County v. Braun, 1943, 295 Ky. 96, 174 S.W.2d 1. Cf. Leece v. Griffin, 1962, 150 Colo. 132, 371 P.2d 264 (predicted income); Alropa Corp. v. Flatley, 1938, 226 Wis. 561, 277 N.W. 108 (canal to be constructed).

87. Hill v. Stewart, 1956, 93 Ga.App. 792, 92 S.E.2d 829; Patterson v. Correll, 1955, 92 Ga.App. 214, 88 S.E.2d 327, appeal transferred 211 Ga. 372, 86 S.E.2d 113; Rochester Civic Theater, Inc. v. Ramsey, 8th Cir. 1966, 368 F.2d 748.

88. Claus v. Farmers & Stockgrowers State Bank, 1936, 51 Wyo. 45, 63 P.2d 781; Eastern States Petroleum Co. v. Universal Oil Products Co., 1939, 24 Del.Ch. 11, 3 A.2d 768; Potter v. Crawford, 1934, 106 Vt. 517, 175 A. 229; Freggens v. Clark, 1927, 100 N.J.Eq. 389, 135 A. 681; Russell v. Industrial Transportation Co., 1924, 113 Tex. 441, 251 S.W. 1034, affirmed 113 Tex. 441, 258 S.W. 462.

89. Cofield v. Griffin, 1953, 238 N.C. 377, 78 S.E.2d 131; McElrath v. Electric Investment Co., 1911, 114 Minn. 358, 131 N.W. 380; Jeck v. O'Meara, 1938, 341 Mo. 419, 107 S.W.2d 782; City Deposit Bank v. Green, 1908, 138 Iowa 156, 115 N.W. 893; Shaffer v. Rhyne, Tex.Civ.App.1934, 75 S.W.2d 133. See Note, 1942, 20 Tex.L.Rev. 625.

90. Keeton, Fraud—Statements of Intention, 1937, 15 Tex.L.Rev. 185; Restatement of Torts, § 544; Notes, 1938, 38 Col.L.Rev. 1461; 1945, 24 N.C.L.Rev. 49; 1949, 2 Okl.L.Rev. 365.

91. In Edgington v. Fitzmaurice, 1882, L.R. 29 Chi. Div. 359.

mind; and the justification of the distinction must be that the intention is regarded as a material fact, by which the adverse party may reasonably be expected to govern his conduct.[92] A promise, which carries an implied representation that there is a present intention to carry it out,[93] is recognized everywhere as a proper basis for reliance; and assertions of intention which are not promissory in form may be, although they are not always,[94] quite as material and persuasive.[95] All but a few courts [96] regard a mistatement of a present intention as a misrepresentation of a material fact;[97] and a promise made without the intent to perform it [98] is held to be a sufficient basis for an action of deceit,[99] or for restitution or other equitable relief.[1] A very common illustration is the purchase of goods with a preconceived intention not to pay for them.[2] The door is thus opened to a tort remedy which may offer important advantages over any action on the contract itself,[3] including the possibility of the recovery of specific goods surrendered in the course of the transaction.[4] The question frequently arises, whether the action for misrepresentation can be maintained when the promise itself cannot be enforced—as where it is without consideration,[5] is illegal,[6] is barred by the statute of

92. See Keeton, Fraud—Statements of Intention, 1937, 15 Tex.L.Rev. 185; Restatement of Torts, § 544.

93. Church v. Swetland, 2d Cir. 1917, 243 F. 289, appeal dismissed 249 U.S. 579, 39 S.Ct. 256, 63 L.Ed. 785; Feldman v. Witmark, 1926, 254 Mass. 480, 150 N.E. 329; Hobaica v. Byrne, 1924, 123 Misc. 107, 205 N.Y.S. 7; Foster v. Dwire, 1924, 51 N.D. 581, 199 N.W. 1017; Maguire v. Maguire, 1927, 171 Minn. 492, 214 N.W. 666.

94. Assertions of a collateral intention, not reasonably understood as a binding obligation, obviously offer less justification for reliance, and occasionally are held not to be enough for an action founded on misrepresentation. Marlin v. Drury, 1951, 124 Mont. 576, 228 P.2d 803; Adams v. Gillig, 1910, 199 N.Y. 314, 92 N.E. 670; Reed v. Cooke, 1932, 331 Mo. 507, 55 S.W.2d 275, See Restatement of Contracts, § 473.

95. Edgington v. Fitzmaurice, 1882, L.R. 29 Ch.Div. 459; Rorer Iron Co. v. Trout, 1887, 83 Va. 397, 2 S.E. 713; Bedell v. Daugherty, 1951, 362 Mo. 598, 242 S.W.2d 572. And a prediction may be made in such terms as to imply an intention to bring it about. McElrath v. Electric Investment Co., 1911, 114 Minn. 358, 131 N.W. 380.

96. Illinois and Indiana flatly reject the doctrine. Brodsky v. Frank, 1930, 342 Ill. 110, 173 N.E. 775; Sachs v. Blewett, 1933, 206 Ind. 151, 185 N.E. 856. Missouri makes a rather incomprehensible distinction between the intention contained in a promise, which is not actionable in tort, and a collateral intention, for which the action will lie. Younger v. Hoge, 1908, 211 Mo. 444, 111 S.W. 20; Metropolitan Paving Co. v. Brown-Crummer Investment Co., 1925, 309 Mo. 638, 274 S.W. 815; Ashton v. Buchholz, 1949, 359 Mo. 296, 221 S.W.2d 496. Apparently the same distinction is made in Vermont. Compare, Woods v. Scott, 1935, 107 Vt. 249, 178 A. 886, with Comstock v. Shannon, 1950, 116 Vt. 245, 73 A.2d 111.

See, applying Illinois and Missouri law, Gass v. National Container Corp., S.D.Ill.1959, 171 F.Supp. 441, appeal dismissed 271 F.2d 231.

97. See Sallies v. Johnson, 1911, 85 Conn. 77, 81 A. 974; Adams v. Gillig, 1910, 199 N.Y. 314, 92 N.E. 670; Feldman v. Witmark, 1926, 254 Mass. 480, 150 N.E. 329. See Burdick, Deceit by False Statement of Intent, 1918, 3 So.L.Q. 118; Keeton, Fraud—Statements of Intention, 1937, 15 Tex.L.Rev. 185; Note, 1938, 38 Col.L. Rev. 1461.

98. In Elk Refining Co. v. Daniel, 4th Cir. 1952, 199 F.2d 479, under West Virginia Law, it was held that the mere absence of an intent to perform is enough, and that a positive intent not to perform is not required.

The same is true when the defendant knows that the promise cannot be carried out. Taylor v. Cowit, 1962, 20 A.D.2d 699, 246 N.Y.S.2d 962.

99. Sweet v. Kimball, 1896, 166 Mass. 332, 44 N.E. 243; Sabo v. Delman, 1957, 3 N.Y.2d 155, 164 N.Y.S.2d 714, 143 N.E.2d 906; Hunt v. Goodimate Co., 1947, 94 N.H. 421, 55 A.2d 75; Page v. Pilot Life Ins. Co., 1939, 197 S.C. 88, 14 S.E.2d 625; Kauffman v. Bobo & Wood, 1950, 99 Cal.App.2d 322, 221 P.2d 750.

1. Morgan v. Morgan, 1946, 94 N.H. 116, 47 A.2d 569; Waddell v. White, 1940, 56 Ariz. 420, 108 P.2d 565, rehearing denied 56 Ariz. 525, 109 P.2d 843; Brittingham v. Huyler's, 1935, 118 N.J.Eq. 352, 179 A. 275, affirmed 120 N.J.Eq. 198, 184 A. 529; Daniel v. Daniel, 1921, 190 Ky. 210, 226 S.W. 1070; Nelson v. Berkner, 1918, 139 Minn. 301, 166 N.W. 347.

2. Swift v. Rounds, 1896, 19 R.I. 527, 35 A. 45; Burrill v. Stevens, 1882, 73 Me. 395; Donovan v. Clifford, 1917, 225 Mass. 435, 114 N.E. 681; Syracuse Knitting Co. v. Blanchard, 1898, 69 N.H. 447, 43 A. 637.

3. See supra, § 92.

4. See Dow v. Sanborn, 1861, 85 Mass. (3 Allen) 181; Hotchkin v. Third National Bank, 1891, 127 N.Y. 329, 27 N.E. 1050.

5. Maintainable: Lampesis v. Comolli, 1958, 101 N.H. 279, 140 A.2d 561; Daniel v. Daniel, 1921, 190 Ky. 210, 226 S.W. 1070; Pease & Elliman v. Wegeman, 1928, 223 App.Div. 682, 229 N.Y.S. 398. Contra: Rankin v. Burnham, 1929, 150 Wash. 615, 274 P. 98; First Restatement of Contracts, § 473, Comment d.

6. See Keeton, Fraud—Statements of Intention, 1937, 15 Tex.L.Rev. 185, 213–216, concluding that "the

frauds,[7] or the statute of limitations,[8] or falls within the parol evidence rule,[9] or a disclaimer of representations.[10]

One group of cases, undoubtedly in the minority, have held that it cannot, arguing that to allow the action would be to permit an evasion of the particular rule of law which makes the promise unenforceable, or that the promisee must be deemed to know the law, and must be held not to have been deceived by such a promise. The prevailing view, however, permits the action to be maintained, considering that the policy which invalidates the promise is not directed at cases of dishonesty in making it, and that it may still reasonably be relied on even where it cannot be enforced. Obviously the conclusion will depend upon the favor with which the particular rule of law is regarded by the court under the circumstances of the case; but the tendency is clearly to treat the misrepresentation action as a separate matter from the contract.

Unless the present state of mind is misstated, there is of course no misrepresentation. When a promise is made in good faith, with the expectation of carrying it out, the fact that it subsequently is broken gives rise to no cause of action, either for deceit,[11] or for equitable relief.[12] Otherwise any breach of contract would call for such a remedy.[13] The mere breach of a promise is never enough in itself to establish the fraudulent intent.[14] It may, however, be inferred from

---

parties are never in pari delicto where the promisor does not intend to perform his bargain from the time he made it, and a tort action in deceit should lie, although it is admitted that the opposite conclusion could be supported by a strong argument."

As to infancy of the promisor, see § 134.

7. Maintainable: Burgdorfer v. Thielemann, 1936, 153 Or. 354, 55 P.2d 1122; Channel Master Corp. v. Aluminum Limited Sales, Inc., 1958, 4 N.Y.2d 403, 176 N.Y.S.2d 259, 151 N.E.2d 833; Pao Chen Lee v. Gregoriou, 1958, 50 Cal.2d 502, 326 P.2d 135; Charpentier v. Socony-Vacuum Oil Co., 1940, 91 N.H. 38, 13 A.2d 141; Kinkaid v. Rossa, 1913, 31 S.D. 559, 141 N.W. 969.

Contra: Cassidy v. Kraft-Phenix Cheese Corp., 1938, 285 Mich. 426, 280 N.W. 814; Dawe v. Morris, 1889, 149 Mass. 188, 21 N.E. 313; Sachs v. Blewett, 1933, 206 Ind. 151, 185 N.E. 856, rehearing denied, 1934, 206 Ind. 151, 188 N.E. 674. See General Corp. v. General Motors Corp., D.C.Minn.1960, 184 F.Supp. 231, saying that there should be no bar only where tort damages are claimed. See Note, 1958, 7 Buffalo L.Rev. 332.

8. Maintainable: Redgrave v. Hurd, 1881, L.R. 20 Ch.Div. 1; Fidelity-Philadelphia Trust Co. v. Simpson, 1928, 293 Pa. 577, 143 A. 202. Contra: Brick v. Cohn-Hall-Marx, 1937, 276 N.Y. 259, 11 N.E.2d 902.

9. Maintainable: Gifford v. Wichita Falls & Southern Railroad Co., 5th Cir. 1954, 211 F.2d 494; Thomas & Howard Co. v. Fowler, 1954, 225 S.C. 354, 82 S.E.2d 454; Sharkey v. Burlingame Co., 1929, 131 Or. 185, 282 P. 546; Palmetto Bank & Trust Co. v. Grimsley, 1926, 134 S.C. 493, 133 S.E. 437; Kett v. Graeser, 1966, 241 Cal.App.2d 571, 50 Cal.Rptr. 727.

Contra: Beers v. Atlas Assurance Co., 1934, 215 Wis. 165, 253 N.W. 584; McCreight v. Davey Tree Expert Co., 1934, 191 Minn. 489, 254 N.W. 623. See Sweet, Promissory Fraud and the Parol Evidence Rule, 1961, 49 Cal.L.Rev. 877.

10. Maintainable ("fraud vitiates everything it touches"): Nyquist v. Foster, 1954, 44 Wn.2d 465, 268 P.2d 442; Miller v. Troy Laundry Machinery Co., 1936, 178 Okl. 313, 62 P.2d 975; S. Pearson & Son v. Lord Mayor of Dublin, [1907] A.C. 351; Katz v. Dunn, 1934, 285 Mass. 340, 189 N.E. 54.

Contra: Abbot v. Stevens, 1955, 133 Cal.App.2d 242, 284 P.2d 159; Danann Realty Corp. v. Harris, 1959, 5 N.Y.2d 317, 184 N.Y.S.2d 599, 157 N.E.2d 597; cf. Billington v. Vest, Tex.Civ.App.1954, 268 S.W.2d 705.

11. Ford v. C. E. Wilson & Co., 2d Cir. 1942, 129 F.2d 614; Kirk v. Vaccaro, 1955, 344 Mich. 226, 73 N.W.2d 871; Sparks v. Rudy Fick, Inc., Mo.App.1958, 309 S.W.2d 687; Beach v. Fleming, 1958, 214 Ga. 303, 104 S.E.2d 427; Hills Transportation Co. v. Southwest Forest Industries, 1968, 266 Cal.App.2d 702, 72 Cal. Rptr. 441. And when the defendant has an option to do one of two things, an intent not to do one is not enough. Blake v. Paramount Pictures, S.D.Cal.1938, 22 F.Supp. 249.

12. Bigelow v. Barnes, 1913, 121 Minn. 148, 140 N.W. 1032; Stewart v. Larkin, 1913, 74 Wash. 681, 134 P. 186; Farwell v. Colonial Trust Co., 8th Cir. 1906, 147 F. 480.

13. See Brooks v. Pitts, 1919, 24 Ga.App. 386, 100 S.E. 776. As to a broken promise as a possible basis for action in tort, see supra, § 92.

14. Justheim Petroleum Co. v. Hammond, 10th Cir. 1955, 227 F.2d 629; Galotti v. United States Trust Co., 1957, 335 Mass. 496, 140 N.E.2d 449; Conzelmann v. Northwest Poultry & Dairy Products Co., 1950, 190 Or. 332, 225 P.2d 757; Fanger v. Leeder, 1951, 327 Mass. 501, 99 N.E.2d 533; Janssen v. Carolina Lumber Co., 1952, 137 W.Va. 561, 73 S.E.2d 12.

Cf. Pybus v. Grasso, 1945, 317 Mass. 716, 59 N.E.2d 289 (promise to convey land which defendant did not own, but might still acquire); Lowe v. Kohn, 1941, 128 Conn. 45, 20 A.2d 407 ("promise" that third party would guarantee plaintiff against loss).

the circumstances, such as the defendant's insolvency [15] or other reason to know that he cannot pay,[16] or his repudiation of the promise soon after it is made, with no intervening change in the situation,[17] or his failure even to attempt any performance,[18] or his continued assurances after it is clear that he will not do so.[19]

So far as estoppel is concerned, the courts have gone to considerable lengths to avoid the injustice which may result from reliance on a broken promise, by developing a doctrine of "promissory estoppel," [20] whose chief function has been to provide a substitute for consideration in enforcing contract liability. Discussion of that doctrine is necessarily beyond the scope of this text.

WESTLAW REFERENCES

justif! /s reliance relied /s opinion* /p misrepresent!
misrepresent! /s quality & topic(272 313a 379)
misrepresent! /s puff!

Misrepresentations of Law
headnote(misrepresent! /s law /s statement*)

Justifiable Reliance on Opinion
restatement /s torts /5 525

Predictions and Intention
misrepresent! /s future* prediction* intention* /s rely relied reliance
misrepresent! /s "state of mind" % topic(110)
fraud! deceit decepti! /s "state of mind"

§ 110. Damages

Since the modern action of deceit is a descendant of the older action on the case, it carries over the requirement that the plaintiff must have suffered substantial damage before the cause of action can arise.[1] Nominal damages are not awarded in deceit,[2] and there can be no recovery if the plaintiff is none the worse off for the misrepresentation, however flagrant it may have been, as where for example he receives all the value that he has been promised and has paid for,[3] or is induced to do only what his legal duty would require him to do in any event.[4] The same is undoubtedly true of any negligence action for misrepresentation.[5]

When restitution is sought, either in equity or at law,[6] a much more liberal policy has been adopted.[7] Since the purpose is not to compensate the plaintiff's loss, but to re-

---

15. City of Southport v. Williams, E.D.N.C.1923, 290 F. 488, affirmed, 4th Cir.1924, 298 F. 1023; Gillespie v. J. C. Piles, 8th Cir.1910, 178 F. 886; In re Barnet Manufacturing Co., D.Mass.1926, 11 F.2d 873. See Note, 1950, 11 U.Pitts.L.Rev. 666.

16. Evola Realty Co. v. Westerfield, Ky.1952, 251 S. W.2d 298; California Conserving Co. v. D'Avanzo, 2d Cir.1933, 62 F.2d 528; Watson v. Silsby, 1896, 166 Mass. 57, 43 N.E. 1117; In re Whitewater Lumber Co., D.Ala.1925, 7 F.2d 410.

17. Guy T. Bisbee Co. v. Granite City Investment Co., 1924, 159 Minn. 238, 199 N.W. 14; Dowd v. Tucker, 1874, 41 Conn. 197.

18. Law v. Sidney, 1936, 47 Ariz. 1, 53 P.2d 64; Foster v. Dwire, 1924, 51 N.D. 581, 199 N.W. 1017; Chicago, Texas & Mexican Central Railway Co. v. Titterington, 1892, 84 Tex. 218, 19 S.W. 472.

19. Charpentier v. Socony-Vacuum Oil Co., 1940, 91 N.H. 38, 13 A.2d 141.

20. See 1 Williston, Contracts, Rev.ed.1936, §§ 139, 140; Restatement of Contracts, § 90; Boyer, Promissory Estoppel: Requirements and Limitations of the Doctrine, 1950, 98 U.Pa.L.Rev. 459; Fuller and Perdue, The Reliance Interest in Contract Damages, 1937, 46 Yale L.J. 52, 373; Snyder, Promissory Estoppel as Tort, 1949, 35 Iowa L.Rev. 28; Notes, 1938, 22 Minn.L. Rev. 843; 1939, 48 Yale L.J. 1036.

§ 110

1. Casey v. Welch, Fla.1951, 50 So.2d 124; Tsang v. Kan, 1947, 78 Cal.App.2d 275, 177 P.2d 630; Castleman v. Stryker, 1923, 107 Or. 48, 213 P. 436; Benson v. Garrett Investment Co., 1955, 135 Cal.App.2d 853, 287 P.2d 405; Dilworth v. Lauritzen, 1967, 18 Utah 386, 424 P.2d 136.

2. Alden v. Wright, 1891, 47 Minn. 225, 49 N.W. 767; Bailey v. Oatis, 1911, 85 Kan. 339, 116 P. 830; Castelli v. Abramo, Mun.Ct.N.Y.1956, 12 Misc.2d 145, 176 N.Y.S.2d 525; and cases cited immediately above in note 15. They may, however, be awarded where there is proof that actual damage has occurred, but no proof as to the amount. Oates v. Glover, 1934, 228 Ala. 656, 154 So. 786.

3. See infra, this section.

4. Musconetcong Iron Works v. Delaware, Lackawanna & Western Railroad Co., 1909, 78 N.J.L. 717, 76 A. 971; Story v. Conger, 1867, 36 N.Y. 673.

5. See supra, § 107. Cf. Heyer v. Flaig, 1969, 70 Cal.2d 223, 74 Cal.Rptr. 225, 449 P.2d 161.

6. Seneca Wire & Manufacturing Co. v. A. B. Leach & Co., 1928, 247 N.Y. 1, 159 N.E. 700.

7. McCleary, Damage as Requisite to Rescission for Misrepresentation, 1937, 36 Mich.L.Rev. 1, 227; Notes, 1935, 48 Harv.L.Rev. 480; 1934, 32 Mich.L.Rev. 968.

store what the defendant has received, the courts look to the inequity of allowing him to retain it, rather than to the damage which the plaintiff has sustained. It is often repeated that damage must be shown for rescission, and recovery has been denied on that basis;[8] but the assertion is so far honored in the breach that it has little or no validity.[9] The plaintiff will not be permitted to rescind where he has received substantially what he bargained for,[10] or where subsequent events have made the representation good.[11] But sufficient "damage" has been found, or dispensed with, where the plaintiff has received property of a different character or condition than he was promised, although of equal value,[12] where the transaction proves to be less advantageous than as represented, although there is no actual loss;[13] and where the false statement was important to the plaintiff for reasons personal to himself, not affecting any financial value or profit.[14] It seems correct to say rather that damage is not essential to rescission, but that it is merely one factor to be considered in determining whether it is equitable to allow the transaction to stand.[15]

Where misrepresentation is set up as a defense to an action brought by the adverse party, the prevailing confusion as to the character of the defense has obscured the distinction between legal and equitable relief. It is obvious that damage, proximately caused, is necessary where the claim is one of recoupment of a loss by reduction of the amount due;[16] but if the defense takes the form of rescission of the bargain, with restoration of what has been received, no more damage should be required than in any other case of rescission.[17]

Measure of Damages in Tort Actions

Where, as is commonly the case, the defendant's actionable misrepresentation or non-disclosure induces a transaction that involves the transfer of something of value, courts normally resort to a general measure of damages often referred to as direct damages, and, in addition thereto, will allow such other damages as special or consequential damages as the plaintiff can prove.[18]

When the defendant's fraudulent conduct does not involve the transfer of property,

---

8. Jakway v. Proudfit, 1906, 76 Neb. 62, 106 N.W. 1039, 109 N.W. 388; Russell v. Industrial Transportation Co., 1923, 113 Tex. 441, 251 S.W. 1034, affirmed, 1924, 258 S.W. 462; Ziegler v. Stinson, 1924, 111 Or. 243, 224 P. 641; Hewlett v. Saratoga Carlsbad Spring Co., 1895, 84 Hun 248, 32 N.Y.S. 697.

9. First Restatement of Contracts, § 476, Comment c; McCleary, Damage as Requisite to Rescission for Misrepresentation, 1937, 36 Mich.L.Rev. 1, 227; Note, 1935, 48 Harv.L.Rev. 480.

10. Mason v. Madson, 1931, 90 Mont. 489, 4 P.2d 475; Bomar v. Rosser, 1901, 131 Ala. 215, 31 So. 430; Struve v. Tatge, 1918, 285 Ill. 103, 120 N.E. 549; Aultman, Miller & Co. v. Nilson, 1900, 112 Iowa 634, 84 N.W. 692; Hays v. Hays, 1897, 179 Pa. 277, 36 A. 311. It frequently is held in such cases that the representation is "immaterial," and could not justifiably have induced reliance. See Ziegler v. Stinson, 1924, 111 Or. 243, 224 P. 641; Ryals v. Livingston, 1932, 45 Ga.App. 43, 163 S.E. 286; American Building & Loan Association v. Bear, 1896, 48 Neb. 455, 67 N.W. 500; McCleary, Damage as Requisite to Rescission for Misrepresentation, 1937, 36 Mich.L.Rev. 1, 254.

11. Billingsley v. Benefield, 1908, 87 Ark. 128, 112 S.W. 188; Farwell v. Colonial Trust Co., 8th Cir.1906, 147 F. 480; National Leather Co. v. Roberts, 6th Cir. 1915, 221 F. 922; Smith v. Johns, 1925, 113 Or. 351, 232 P. 786.

12. Tonkovich v. South Florida Citrus Industries, Inc., Fla.App.1966, 185 So.2d 710, cause remanded 196 So.2d 438, on remand 202 So.2d 579; Mosely v. Johnson, 1954, 90 Ga.App. 165, 82 S.E.2d 163; Nance v. McClellan, 1936, 126 Tex. 580, 89 S.W.2d 774; Dimond v. Peace River Land & Development Co., 1918, 182 Iowa 400, 165 N.W. 1032; Hirschman v. Healy, 1925, 162 Minn. 328, 202 N.W. 734.

13. In jurisdictions which adopt the out-of-pocket measure of damages (infra, note 47): King v. Lamborn, 9th Cir.1911, 186 F. 21; Ludowese v. Amidon, 1914, 124 Minn. 288, 144 N.W. 965; Stillwell v. Rankin, 1918, 55 Mont. 130, 174 P. 186.

14. Brett v. Cooney, 1902, 75 Conn. 338, 53 A. 729, 1124; Williams v. Kerr, 1893, 152 Pa. 560, 25 A. 618; Rice v. Gilbreath, 1898, 119 Ala. 424, 24 So. 421; Thompson v. Barry, 1903, 184 Mass. 429, 68 N.E. 674.

15. Cf. La Bar v. Lindstrom, 1924, 158 Minn. 453, 197 N.W. 756; Baker v. Combs, 1930, 232 Ky. 73, 22 S.W.2d 442; Murphy v. Sheftel, 1932, 121 Cal.App. 533, 9 P.2d 568.

16. Hammatt v. Emerson, 1847, 27 Me. 308.

17. Stuart v. Lester, 1888, 49 Hun 58, 1 N.Y.S. 699, 17 N.Y.St.Rep. 248; Metropolitan Life Insurance Co. v. James, 1935, 231 Ala. 295, 164 So. 377.

18. Dobbs, Remedies, 1973, Sec. 9.2.

the plaintiff necessarily proves his claim by proving special or consequential damages if he can do so.

Consequential damages must be established with reasonable certainty, and must not be speculative or contingent,[19] although a loss reasonably certain to occur in the future, such as an established liability to a third person, may be compensated.[20] Furthermore, the consequential or special damages must have been proximately caused by the fraudulent conduct. In general and with only a few exceptions,[21] the courts have restricted recovery to those losses which might be expected to follow from the fraud and from events that are reasonably foreseeable.[22] Thus, if the plaintiff stores his goods in a warehouse represented by him to be fireproof and they are destroyed when it burns down, he can recover,[23] and likewise, when he invests in an automobile agency, after false assurance of profits made by similar agencies, and the agency goes bankrupt.[24] But if false statements are made in connection with the sale of corporate stock, losses due to a subsequent decline in the market, or insolvency of the corporation brought about by business conditions or other factors in no way relate to the representations will not afford any basis for recovery.[25] It is only where the fact misstated was of a nature calculated to bring about such a result that damages for it can be recovered.[26] Sometimes this has been expressed by saying that the representation in such a loss is "immaterial" to the result; but the conclusion is reached even though the plaintiff has in fact relied, and justifiably so, upon what he has been told.

The availability of other forms of relief for actionable misrepresentations, especially breach of warranty against sellers of goods, has been reflected in the conflicting rules which have been adopted as to the normal measure of general or direct damages where there was a transfer of something of value.

The American courts are divided over two standards of measurement. One of these, the so-called "out of pocket" rule, looks to the loss which the plaintiff has suffered in the transaction, and gives him the difference between the value of what he has parted with and the value of what he has received. If what he received was worth what he paid for it, he has not been damaged, and there can be no recovery.[27] This rule is followed in deceit actions by the English courts,[28] and by a minority of perhaps a dozen American

---

19. Ansley v. Bank of Piedmont, 1896, 113 Ala. 467, 21 So. 59; Fitzsimmons v. Chapman, 1877, 37 Mich. 139, 26 Am.Rep. 508 (speculative); Freeman v. Venner, 1876, 120 Mass. 424; Dunn & McCarthy v. Bishop, R.I. 1914, 90 A. 1073 (contingent).

20. Hoffman v. Toft, 1914, 70 Or. 488, 142 P. 365; Ely v. Stannard, 1878, 46 Conn. 124; Luetzke v. Roberts, 1906, 130 Wis. 97, 109 N.W. 949. Cf. Briggs v. Brushaber, 1880, 43 Mich. 330, 5 N.W. 383 (loan on poor security); Currier v. Poor, 1898, 155 N.Y. 344, 49 N.E. 937.

21. Fottler v. Moseley, 1901, 170 Mass. 295, 60 N.E. 788; affirmed, 1904, 185 Mass. 563, 70 N.E. 1040. Accord: David v. Belmont, 1935, 291 Mass. 450, 197 N.E. 83.

22. See Note, 1955, 43 Cal.L.Rev. 356.

23. Rosenblatt v. John F. Ivory Storage Co., 1933, 262 Mich. 513, 247 N.W. 733. See also Mortimer v. Otto, 1912, 206 N.Y. 89, 99 N.E. 189; The Normannia, S.D.N.Y.1894, 62 F. 469.

24. Hanson v. Ford Motor Co., 8th Cir.1960, 278 F.2d 586. A particularly good opinion.

25. Waddell v. White, 1940, 56 Ariz. 420, 108 P.2d 565, rehearing denied 56 Ariz. 525, 109 P.2d 843; Morrell v. Wiley, 1935, 119 Conn. 578, 178 A. 121; Boatmen's National Co. v. M. W. Elkins & Co., 8th Cir.1933, 63 F.2d 214; Beare v. Wright, 1905, 14 N.D. 26, 103 N.W. 632; Morgan v. Hodge, 1911, 145 Wis. 143, 129 N.W. 1083.

Cf. Ward Cook, Inc. v. Davenport, 1966, 243 Or. 301, 413 P.2d 387 (embezzlement).

26. Haentze v. Loehr, 1940, 233 Wis. 583, 290 N.W. 163. In Hotaling v. A. B. Leach Co., 1928, 247 N.Y. 84, 159 N.E. 870, where bonds were bought for investment and "weakness inherent in the investment" was covered by the misrepresentations, recovery was allowed for a collapse during a subsequent financial crisis. But in People v. S. W. Straus & Co., 1935, 156 Misc. 642, 282 N.Y.S. 972, it was denied where the loss was found to be due entirely to external economic conditions. See also, Lowrey v. Dingmann, 1957, 251 Minn. 124, 86 N.W.2d 499; Dobbs, Remedies, Sec. 9.2 (1973).

27. Urtz v. New York Central & Hudson River Railroad Co., 1911, 202 N.Y. 170, 95 N.E. 711; Alden v. Wright, 1891, 47 Minn. 225, 49 N.W. 767; Doyle v. Union Bank & Trust Co., 1936, 102 Mont. 563, 59 P.2d 1171.

28. Peek v. Derry, 1887, L.R. 37 Ch.Div. 541.

jurisdictions.[29] It is always adopted as to a defense in the nature of recoupment,[30] and is of course the practical result reached by rescission, where each party is restored to his original position. The other measurement, called the "loss-of-bargain" rule, gives the plaintiff the benefit of what he was promised, and allows recovery of the difference between the actual value of what he has received and the value that it would have had if it had been as represented. This, of course, is the rule applied in contract actions for breach of warranty,[31] and it is consistent with the result in cases of estoppel. It has been adopted by some two-thirds of the courts which have considered the question in actions of deceit.[32] There is the same conflict where the recovery is based on negligent misrepresentation.[33]

As a matter of the strict logic of the form of action, the first of these two rules is more consistent with the purpose of tort remedies, which is to compensate the plaintiff for a loss sustained, rather than to give him the benefit of any contract bargain.[34] Also, it must of necessity be adopted where the defendant is a third party who has made no contract with the plaintiff,[35] and it has been contended that the presence of a contract should not change the damages where the action is not on the contract itself.[36] On the other hand, it is urged in support of the majority rule that the form of the action should be of little importance, that in an action in the form of tort for breach of warranty the plaintiff is given the benefit of his bargain and the addition of an allegation of intent to deceive should certainly not decrease his recovery, and that in many cases the out-of-pocket measure will permit the fraudulent defendant to escape all liability and have a chance to profit by the transaction if he can get away with it.[37]

Few courts have followed either rule with entire consistency,[38] and various proposals have been made to introduce some flexibility into the measure of damages. Thus it has been suggested that the loss-of-bargain rule should be applied in cases of intentional misrepresentation, the out-of-pocket rule where it is innocent;[39] that the plaintiff be given

---

29. Beardmore v. T. D. Burgess Co., 1967, 245 Md. 387, 226 A.2d 329; Reno v. Bull, 1919, 226 N.Y. 546, 124 N.E. 144, reargument denied 227 N.Y. 591, 125 N.E. 924; Heidegger v. Burg, 1917, 137 Minn. 53, 162 N.W. 889; Browning v. Rodman, 1920, 268 Pa. 575, 111 A. 877.

This was formerly the rule of the federal courts. Smith v. Bolles, 1889, 132 U.S. 125, 10 S.Ct. 39, 33 L.Ed. 279.

30. This is true even in warranty cases. Impervious Products Co. v. Gray, 1915, 127 Md. 64, 96 A. 1; Hunter v. Finnerty, 1922, 119 Misc. 724, 197 N.Y.S. 215; Hirschl v. Richards, 1927, 28 Ohio App. 38, 162 N.E. 616.

31. Cf. Uniform Sales Act, § 69(7).

32. Dempsey v. Marshall, Ky.1961, 344 S.W.2d 606; Polley v. Boehck Equipment Co., 1956, 273 Wis. 432, 78 N.W.2d 737; Nelson v. Leo's Auto Sales, Inc., 1962, 158 Me. 368, 185 A.2d 121; Yoder v. Nu-Enamel Corp., 8th Cir.1944, 145 F.2d 420 (Nebraska law); Brown v. Ohman, Miss.1949, 42 So.2d 209, suggestion of error overruled, 1950, 43 So.2d 727.

Where this measure is adopted, it has been held to preclude allowance for loss of plaintiff's time, or other out-of-pocket losses. Salter v. Heiser, 1951, 39 Wn.2d 826, 239 P.2d 327.

33. See Morin v. Divide County Abstract Co., 1921, 48 N.D. 214, 183 N.W. 1006 (out of pocket); Williams v. Spazier, Cal.App.1933, 21 P.2d 470 (same), vacated 134 Cal.App. 340, 25 P.2d 851; Long v. Douthitt, 1911, 142 Ky. 427, 134 S.W. 453 (loss of bargain); Spreckels v. Gorrill, 1907, 152 Cal. 383, 92 P. 1011 (same); Hartwell Corp. v. Bumb, 9th Cir.1965, 345 F.2d 453, certiorari denied 382 U.S. 891, 86 S.Ct. 182, 15 L.Ed.2d 148 (same).

34. See Second Restatement of Torts, § 549; 2 Sedgwick, Measure of Damages, 9th ed.1912, §§ 780, 781.

35. Macdonald v. Roeth, 1918, 179 Cal. 194, 176 P. 38; Sorensen v. Gardner, 1959, 215 Or. 255, 334 P.2d 471. Cf. Morin v. Divide County Abstract Co., 1921, 48 N.D. 214, 183 N.W. 1006.

36. See 2 Sedgwick, Measure of Damages, 9th ed. 1912, 1628. But see Harper and McNeely, A Synthesis of the Law of Misrepresentation, 1938, 22 Minn.L.Rev. 939, 964, 990, 1000, supporting a different rule in the two types of cases.

37. 5 Williston, Contracts, Rev.ed.1936, §§ 1391, 1392; Hannigan, The Measure of Damages in Tort for Deceit, 1938, 18 Bos.U.L.Rev. 681.

38. See cases collected in the annotation, 1940, 124 A.L.R. 37; Note, 1930, 34 Dick.L.Rev. 181. As to the New York history, see Note, 1942, 55 Harv.L.Rev. 1019.

39. See McCormick, Damages, 1935, 453, 454, pointing out that the possibility of punitive damages may be a sufficient differentiation as to intentional fraud.

the option of either rule,[40] or that the court should adopt the rule which best fits the certainty of the damages proved, and so avoid the possibility that a plaintiff who has suffered a real damage may be denied recovery because he is unable to prove values.[41] A leading Oregon decision,[42] which seems to have given more careful consideration to the problem than any other and now has been followed in a few other jurisdictions,[43] reduces the matter to four rules, as follows:

1. If the defrauded party is content with the recovery of only the amount he has actually lost, his damages will always be measured under that rule.

2. If the fraudulent transaction also amounted to a warranty, he may recover for loss of the bargain, because a fraud accompanied by a broken promise should cost the wrongdoer as much as the breach of promise alone.

3. Where the circumstances disclosed by the proof are so vague as to cast virtually no light upon the value of the property had it conformed to the representations, damages will be awarded equal to the loss sustained, and

4. Where the damages under the benefit-of-bargain rule are proved with reasonable certainty, that rule will be employed.

In addition to such a normal measure of damages under whatever rule the court may adopt, the plaintiff may recover for consequential damages, such as personal injuries,[44] damage to other property,[45] or expenses to which he has been put,[46] provided that they are regarded as "proximate" results of the misrepresentation.[47] If the deception is found to have been deliberate or wanton, punitive damages may be recovered, as in the case of other torts of similar character.[48]

Any act amounting to affirmance of the transaction after the plaintiff has discovered the fraud will preclude the remedy of rescis-

The distinction was made, however, in Williams v. Spazier, Cal.App.1933, 21 P.2d 470, vacated 134 Cal. App. 340, 25 P.2d 851.

40. See Harper and McNeely, A Synthesis of the Law of Misrepresentation, 1938, 22 Minn.L.Rev. 939, 964, 990, 1000.

41. McCormick, Damages, 1935, 454. This seems in effect to be the result reached by a number of courts. Hines v. Brode, 1914, 168 Cal. 507, 143 P. 729; Jammie v. Robinson, 1921, 114 Wash. 275, 195 P. 6; Monsanto Chemical Works v. American Zinc, Lead & Smelting Co., Mo.1923, 253 S.W. 1006. In the case of the sale of corporate securities, a similar flexibility has been achieved in some cases by looking to the value of the securities at a time after the purchase. See Hotaling v. A. B. Leach & Co., 1928, 247 N.Y. 84, 159 N.E. 870; David v. Belmont, 1935, 291 Mass. 450, 197 N.E. 83; Cartwright v. Hughes, 1933, 226 Ala. 464, 147 So. 399. As to the provisions of the Federal Securities Act, see Shulman, Civil Liability and the Securities Act, 1933, 43 Yale L.J. 227, 244–248.

42. Selman v. Shirley, 1938, 161 Or. 582, 85 P.2d 384, adhered to 161 Or. 582, 91 P.2d 312.

43. Weitzel v. Jukich, 1942, 73 Idaho 301, 251 P.2d 542; Zeliff v. Sabatino, 1954, 15 N.J. 70, 104 A.2d 54; United States v. Ben Grunstein & Sons Co., D.N.J.1955, 137 F.Supp. 197; Rice v. Price, 1960, 340 Mass. 502, 164 N.E.2d 891; Salter v. Heiser, 1951, 39 Wn.2d 826, 239 P.2d 327.

44. Vezina v. Souliere, 1931, 103 Vt. 190, 152 A. 798.

45. Sampson v. Penney, 1922, 151 Minn. 411, 187 N.W. 135; Economy Hog & Cattle Powder Co. v. Compton, 1922, 192 Ind. 222, 135 N.E. 1.

46. Edward Barron Estate v. Woodruff Co., 1912, 163 Cal. 561, 126 P. 351; Snyder v. Markham, 1912, 172 Mich. 693, 138 N.W. 234; Commonwealth Fuel Co. v. McNeil, 1925, 103 Conn. 390, 130 A. 794; Garrett v. Perry, 1959, 53 Cal.2d 178, 346 P.2d 758; Cole v. Gerhart, 1967, 5 Ariz.App. 24, 423 P.2d 100; cf. Lowrey v. Dingmann, 1957, 251 Minn. 124, 86 N.W.2d 499 (loss of other sales, harm to reputation as dealer).

47. Cf. Foster v. De Paolo, 1923, 236 N.Y. 132, 140 N.E. 220.

48. See generally, Dobbs, Remedies, 1973, Secs. 3.9 & 9.2; Owen, Punitive Damages in Products Liability Litigation, 1976, 74 Mich.L.Rev. 1257, 1329. A number of state and federal statutes authorize punitive or multiple damages for misrepresentation or related conduct, notably, the unfair or deceptive trade practices acts in some states, and RICO—prohibiting certain mail, wire, securities law, and other fraud—at the federal level. See generally, Maxwell, Public and Private Rights and Remedies Under the Deceptive Trade Practices—Consumer Protection Act, 1977, 8 St. Mary's L.J. 617; Lovett, State Deceptive Trade Practice Legislation, 1972, 46 Tulane L.Rev. 758; Patton, Civil RICO: Statutory and Implied Elements of the Treble Damages Remedy, 1983, 14 Tex.Tech.L.Rev. 377; Blakey & Gettings, Racketeer Influenced and Corrupt Organizations (RICO): Basic Concepts—Criminal and Civil Remedies, 1980, 53 Temp.L.Q. 1009; Notes, 1982, 95 Harv.L.Rev. 1101; 24 Wm. & Mary L.Rev. 429.

sion.⁴⁹ But, since the tort action for damages is based on an acceptance of the contract, it is not barred by mere acts of affirmance.⁵⁰ If, however, the plaintiff discovers the truth while the contract is still entirely executory,⁵¹ or almost entirely so,⁵² and then performs his part of it, he has been denied recovery for the resulting damages upon the ground that they are self-inflicted, without reliance upon the representation. If he has executed a substantial part of his performance before discovery, it is generally recognized that it is too late to require him to rescind, and that his continued performance is merely affirmance, and not a waiver of his action for damages.⁵³ He must, however, deal at arm's length and comply with the terms of the contract, asking no modifications,⁵⁴ favors or concessions,⁵⁵ or he will be held to have surrendered his claim in return for what is in effect a new agreement, replacing the old one.

WESTLAW REFERENCES

nominal /5 damages /s misrepresent! deceit
damage* /s rescission rescind! /s misrepresent!
headnote(misrepresent! /s "affirmative defense")

Measure of Damages in Tort Actions
headnote(measure! /s damages /s misrepresent! fraud! deceit deceptive)
consequential /5 damages /s deceit misrepresent!
pocket /s damage* /s misrepresent!

---

49. Maki v. St. Luke's Hospital Association, 1913, 122 Minn. 444, 142 N.W. 705; Marks v. Stein, 1916, 61 Okl. 59, 160 P. 318 (defense).

50. Van Vliet Fletcher Automobile Co. v. Crowell, 1914, 171 Iowa 64, 149 N.W. 861; Engen v. Merchants' & Manufacturers State Bank, 1925, 164 Minn. 293, 204 N.W. 963.

51. Thompson v. Libby, 1886, 36 Minn. 287, 31 N.W. 52; McDonough v. Williams, 1905, 77 Ark. 261, 92 S.W. 783; Minnesota Thresher Manufacturing Co. v. Gruben, 1897, 6 Kan.App. 665, 50 P. 67. See Notes, 1936, 34 Mich.L.Rev. 384; 1930, 14 Minn.L.Rev. 299.

52. Thus where the performance before discovery has been so slight as to be negligible. Simon v. Goodyear Metallic Rubber Shoe Co., 6th Cir.1900, 105 F. 573; Kingman & Co. v. Stoddard, 7th Cir.1898, 85 F. 740; Ponder v. Altura Farms Co., 1914, 57 Colo. 519, 143 P. 570.

53. Elson v. Harris, 1959, 356 Mich. 175, 96 N.W.2d 767; Forsberg v. Baker, 1941, 211 Minn. 59, 300 N.W. 371; Weckert v. Wentworth & Irwin, 1920, 129 Or. 342, 277 P. 815; Pryor v. Foster, 1891, 130 N.Y. 171, 29 N.E. 123; Van Natta v. Snyder, 1916, 98 Kan. 102, 157 P. 432.

54. Fryar v. Forrest, Tex.Civ.App.1941, 155 S.W.2d 679; Timmerman v. Gurnsey, 1928, 205 Iowa 35, 217 N.W. 879; Burne v. Lee, 1909, 156 Cal. 221, 104 P. 438; Kintz v. Galvin, 1922, 219 Mich. 48, 188 N.W. 408; Franklin Motor Car Co. v. Hilkert, 1925, 82 Ind.App. 513, 146 N.E. 825.

55. Schmidt v. Mesmer, 1897, 116 Cal. 267, 48 P. 54; Schagun v. Scott Manufacturing Co., 8th Cir.1908, 162 F. 209; Tuttle v. Stovall, 1910, 134 Ga. 325, 67 S.E. 806; Humphrey v. Sievers, 1917, 137 Minn. 373, 163 N.W. 737. See Note, 1930, 14 Minn.L.Rev. 299.

Chapter 19

DEFAMATION

Table of Sections

Sec.
111. Defamation.
112. Libel and Slander.
113. Basis of Liability.
113A. Defamatory Opinion.
114. Absolute Privilege.
115. Qualified Privilege.
116. Truth and Other Defenses.
116A. Damages and Matters in Mitigation.

§ 111. Defamation

Defamation is made up of the twin torts of libel and slander—the one being, in general, written while the other in general is oral, with somewhat different rules applicable to each, as will be explained later. In either form, defamation is an invasion of the interest in reputation and good name. This is a "relational" interest,[1] since it involves the opinion which others in the community may have, or tend to have, of the plaintiff. Consequently defamation requires that something be communicated to a third person that may affect that opinion. Derogatory words and insults directed to the plaintiff himself may afford ground for an action for the intentional infliction of mental suffering,[2] but unless they are communicated to another the action cannot be one for defamation,[3] no matter how harrowing they may be to the feelings. Defamation is not concerned with the plaintiff's own humiliation, wrath or sorrow, except as an element of "parasitic" damages attached to an independent cause of action.[4]

It must be confessed at the beginning that there is a great deal of the law of defamation which makes no sense. It contains anomalies and absurdities for which no legal writer ever has had a kind word,[5] and it is a curious compound of a strict liability imposed upon innocent defendants, as rigid and

---

§ 111

1. Green, Relational Interests, 1936, 31 Ill.L.Rev. 35.
2. See supra, § 12.
3. See infra, § 113.
4. See infra, § 112.

5. "No branch of the law has been more fertile of litigation than this (whether plaintiffs be more moved by a keen sense of honour, or by the delight of carrying on personal controversies under the protection and with the solemnities of civil justice), nor has any been more perplexed with minute and barren distinctions. * * * The law went wrong from the beginning in making the damage and not the insult the cause of ac-

extreme as anything found in the law, with a blind and almost perverse refusal to compensate the plaintiff for real and very serious harm. The explanation is in part one of historical accident and survival, in part one of the conflict of opposing ideas of policy in which our traditional notions of freedom of expression have collided violently with sympathy for the victim traduced and indignation at the maligning tongue.

The actions for defamation developed according to no particular aim or plan.[6] Originally the common law courts took no jurisdiction, leaving defamatory utterances to be dealt with by the local seigniorial courts. When these began to fall into decay, the ecclesiastical courts stepped in, regarding defamation as a sin, and punishing it with penance. As these courts in turn lost their power, there was in the sixteenth century a slow infiltration of tort actions for slander into the common law courts. For a considerable length of time there were conflicts over jurisdiction between the two sets of tribunals, which led the common law courts to hold that unless "temporal" damage could be proved, defamation was a "spiritual" matter which should be left to the Church.[7] When the common law jurisdiction was once established, an unexpected flood of actions was let loose upon the judges, who seem to have been annoyed and dismayed by it, and so proceeded to hedge the remedy about with rigid restrictions, some of which still survive.[8]

Later, about the beginning of the seventeenth century, the Court of Star Chamber, of infamous memory, began quite independently to punish the crime of political libel, in order to suppress the seditious publications which had come with the spread of printing. Originating strictly as a crime, and a form of sedition, this was later extended to non-political libels. Later still, tort damages were awarded to the person defamed, probably in order to provide a legal substitute for the duel when it was forbidden. With the abolition of the Star Chamber, jurisdiction over libel in turn passed to the common law courts. They continued, however, to recognize the difference between libel, which was criminal as well as tortious, and the earlier action for slander, which was not.

One heritage of this haphazard development is the present distinction between libel and slander, to be considered below.[9] Another is the set of arbitrary and illogical rules which surround both, but particularly the latter. Still further difficulties arose when the law of defamation encountered the rising tide of sentiment in favor of freedom of speech and of the press, which, together with hatred of the memory of the Star Chamber, made the action an unpopular one, and the courts somewhat timid in dealing with it.[10] It is to this that we owe the gener-

tion." Pollock, Law of Torts, 13th ed. 1929, 243, 249. See also 1 Street, Foundations of Legal Liability, 1906, 273 ("marred in the making"); Winfield, Law of Tort, 5th ed. 1950, 244; Veeder, History and Theory of the Law of Defamation, 1904, 4 Col.L.Rev. 33; Carr, The English Law of Defamation, 1902, 18 L.Q.Rev. 255, 388; Courtney, Absurdities of the Law of Slander and Libel, 1902, 36 Am.L.Rev. 552.

6. See Veeder, History and Theory of the Law of Defamation, 1903, 3 Col.L.Rev. 546, 1904, 4 Col.L.Rev. 33; Donnelly, History of Defamation, [1949] Wis.L.Rev. 99; Holdsworth, Defamation in the Sixteenth and Seventeenth Centuries, 1924, 40 L.Q.Rev. 302, 397, 1925, 41 L.Q.Rev. 13; Green, Slander and Libel, 1872, 6 Am.L.Rev. 592; Carr, The English Law of Defamation, 1902, 18 L.Q.Rev. 255, 388; 1 Street, Foundations of Legal Liability, 1906, c. XIX; Kelly, Criminal Libel and Free Speech, 1958, 6 Kan.L.Rev. 295. Second Restatement of Torts, § 568, Comment b.

7. See Ogden v. Turner, 1703, 6 Mod.Rep. 104, 87 Eng.Rep. 862; Regina v. Read, 1708, Fortescue 98, 92 Eng.Rep. 777. The common law courts required proof of "temporal" damage. Palmer v. Thorpe, 1883, 4 Co. Rep. 20a, 76 Eng.Rep. 909; Davies v. Gardiner, 1593, Popham 36, 79 Eng.Rep. 1155; Matthew v. Crass, 1614, Cro.Jac. 323, 79 Eng.Rep. 276.

8. See Lovell, The Reception of Defamation by the Common Law, 1962, 15 Vand.L.Rev. 1051.

9. See infra, § 112.

10. See Pound, Equitable Relief Against Defamation and Injuries to Personality, 1916, 29 Harv.L.Rev. 640; Shientag, From Seditious Libel to Freedom of the Press, 1942, 11 Brook.L.Rev. 125; Leflar, Legal Liability for the Exercise of Free Speech, 1956, 10 Ark.L.Rev. 155; Leflar, The Free-ness of Free Speech, 1962, 15 Vand.L.Rev. 1073; Sedler, Injunctive Relief and Personal Integrity, 1964, 9 St.L.L.Rev. 147.

al rule that defamation will not be enjoined,[11] unless it is incident to some other tort,[12] and more indirectly the holding of the Supreme Court of the United States that a statute authorizing injunctions against defamatory publications is an unconstitutional denial of the guaranty of freedom of the press.[13] The late nineteenth century found something of a swing of the pendulum back in the direction of no disfavor for defamation,[14] as the courts became more tender of reputations injured by the modern newspaper; but in recent years, if one were to hazard a guess, it would be that the trend is again toward a more restricted liability.[15] No very comprehensive attempt ever has been made to overhaul and untangle this entire field of law,[16] and, unhappily, there seems to be none in prospect.

Definition

While the general idea of defamation is sufficiently well understood, the courts have not been altogether in harmony in dealing with it, so that very often a particular rule or holding is peculiar to a small number of jurisdictions. A defamatory communication usually has been defined as one which tends to hold the plaintiff up to hatred, contempt or ridicule, or to cause him to be shunned or avoided.[17] This definition is certainly too narrow, since an imputation of insanity,[18] or poverty,[19] or an assertion that a woman has been raped,[20] which would be likely to arouse only pity or sympathy in the minds of all decent people, have been held to be defamatory. Defamation is rather that which tends to injure "reputation" in the popular sense; to diminish the esteem, respect, goodwill or confidence in which the plaintiff is held,[21] or to excite adverse, derogatory or unpleasant feelings or opinions against him.[22] It necessarily, however, involves the idea of disgrace; and while a statement that a person is a Republican may very possibly arouse adverse feelings against him in the minds of many Democrats, and even diminish him in their esteem, it cannot be found in itself to be defamatory, since no reasonable

11. Kwass v. Kersey, 1954, 139 W.Va. 497, 81 S.E.2d 237; Krebiozen Research Foundation v. Beacon Press, 1956, 334 Mass. 86, 134 N.E.2d 1, certiorari denied, 1956, 352 U.S. 848, 77 S.Ct. 65, 1 L.Ed.2d 58; Montgomery Ward & Co. v. United Retail, Wholesale & Department Store Employees, 1948, 400 Ill. 38, 79 N.E.2d 46; Kuhn v. Warner Brothers Pictures, S.D. N.Y.1939, 29 F.Supp. 800; Howell v. Bee Publishing Co., 1916, 100 Neb. 39, 158 N.W. 358. See Note, 1954, 33 Tex.L.Rev. 265; Leflar, Legal Remedies for Defamation, 1952, 6 Ark.L.Rev. 423.

12. Cf. Gompers v. Buck's Stove & Range Co., 1911, 221 U.S. 418, 31 S.Ct. 492, 55 L.Ed. 797; Lawrence Trust Co. v. Sun-America Publishing Co., 1923, 245 Mass. 262, 139 N.E. 655; American Malting Co. v. Keitel, D.N.Y.1914, 217 F. 672. See McClintock, Equity, 2d ed. 1948, §§ 151, 154.

13. Near v. Minnesota ex rel. Olson, 1931, 283 U.S. 697, 51 S.Ct. 625, 75 L.Ed. 1357.

14. See the instructions to the jury, approved in Lewis v. Williams, 1916, 105 S.C. 165, 89 S.E. 647, that slander suits are proper, are frequent in civilized countries, and are better than taking the law into one's own hands.

15. See Wettach, Recent Developments in Newspaper Libel, 1928, 13 Minn.L.Rev. 21.

16. See, however, the reforms made by the English Defamation Act of 1952, noted in 1953, 16 Mod.L.Rev. 198; 1953, 66 Harv.L.Rev. 476; and see Paton, Reform and the English Law of Defamation, 1939, 33 Ill.L.Rev. 669.

17. "Words which tend to expose one to public hatred, shame, obloquy, contumely, odium, contempt, ridicule, aversion, ostracism, degradation or disgrace, or to induce an evil opinion of one in the minds of right-thinking persons, and to deprive one of their confidence and friendly intercourse in society." Kimmerle v. New York Evening Journal, 1933, 262 N.Y. 99, 186 N.E. 217. The definition appears to have originated with Baron Parke in Parmiter v. Coupland, 1840, 6 M. & W. 105, 151 Eng.Rep. 340.

18. Kenney v. Hatfield, 1958, 351 Mich. 498, 88 N.W.2d 535; Cowper v. Vannier, 1959, 20 Ill.App.2d 499, 156 N.E.2d 761; Seip v. Deshler, 1895, 170 Pa. 334, 32 A. 1032; Totten v. Sun Printing & Publishing Ass'n, 2d Cir.1901, 109 F. 289; Moore v. Francis, 1890, 121 N.Y. 199, 23 N.E. 1127. Cf. Miles v. Record Publishing Co., 1926, 134 S.C. 462, 133 S.E. 99 (typhoid carrier).

19. Katapodis v. Brooklyn Spectator, 1941, 287 N.Y. 17, 38 N.E.2d 112. See Notes, 1942, 27 Iowa L.Rev. 656; 1942, 26 Minn.L.Rev. 563.

20. Youssoupoff v. Metro-Goldwyn-Mayer Pictures, 1934, 50 T.L.R. 581, 51 L.Q.Rev. 281.

21. Bower, Actionable Defamation, 2d ed. 1923, 4; Second Restatement of Torts, § 559.

22. Salmond, Law of Torts, 8th ed. 1934, 398.

person could consider that it reflects upon his character.[23]

Perhaps the best statement is that found in the *Second Restatement of Torts*, where it is said that a communication is defamatory if it tends so to harm the reputation of another as to lower him in the estimation of the community or to deter third persons from associating or dealing with him. In the application of this idea it is enough that the communication would tend to prejudice the plaintiff in the eyes of a substantial and respectable minority, but in such a case it must be shown that the communication did reach one or more persons of that minority group. This would normally be presumed, if the communication was a public one which was made in the newspaper or over radio or television.[24]

The question of whether or not the meaning of a particular communication is defamatory is one for the court, and courts have quite obviously disagreed about particular or specific imputations. But perhaps a brief description of a variety of results will be somewhat helpful.

In the absence of special circumstances which add another meaning to the words, it is not defamatory to say that a person is dead,[25] that he is overly cautious with money,[26] that he has refused to abate his fees [27] or made a charge for cashing poor relief checks,[28] that he has refused to make concessions to a union,[29] that he has led an eventful life,[30] that he has no known permanent address; [31] that he has no export license,[32] that he is not entitled to communion in a particular church,[33] that he is a labor agitator,[34] that he left his employment during a strike,[35] that he has taken advantage of his legal rights,[36] that construction work he is performing is unduly delayed,[37] that itinerant solicitors have sold space in his newspaper at higher cost than he sold it himself,[38] that he has possession of the goods of another and owes him money,[39] or that he "figured quite prominently in some of the squatter riots." [40] Such language, if it is false and malicious, may afford a basis for anoth-

---

23. Cf. Frinzi v. Hanson, 1966, 30 Wis.2d 271, 140 N.W.2d 259; Steinman v. Di Roberts, 1965, 23 A.D.2d 693, 257 N.Y.S.2d 695, affirmed 17 N.Y.2d 512, 267 N.Y.S.2d 512, 214 N.E.2d 789 ("liberal"); Haas v. Evening Democrat Co., 1961, 252 Iowa 517, 107 N.W.2d 444 (conservative).

Similarly, a charge of a single act of negligence does not reflect on the plaintiff's character. Cowan v. Time, Inc., 1963, 41 Misc.2d 198, 245 N.Y.S.2d 723.

24. See § 559, Comment *e*.

25. Cohen v. New York Times Co., 1912, 153 App. Div. 242, 138 N.Y.S. 206; Lemmer v. The Tribune, 1915, 50 Mont. 559, 148 P. 338; O'Neil v. Edmonds, E.D.Va.1958, 157 F.Supp. 649; Cardiff v. Brooklyn Eagle, 1947, 190 Misc. 730, 75 N.Y.S.2d 222.

26. Kelly v. Partington, 1833, 5 B. & Ad. 645, 110 Eng.Rep. 929.

27. De Pasquale v. Westchester Newspapers, 1938, 170 Misc. 268, 8 N.Y.S.2d 829; Gang v. Hughes, 9th Cir.1954, 218 F.2d 432.

28. Lynch v. Lyons, 1939, 303 Mass. 116, 20 N.E.2d 953.

29. Montgomery Ward & Co. v. McGraw-Hill Publishing Co., 7th Cir.1944, 146 F.2d 171.

30. Harriman v. New Nonpareil Co., 1906, 132 Iowa 616, 110 N.W. 33. Cf. Kimmerle v. New York Evening Journal, 1933, 262 N.Y. 99, 186 N.E. 217 (woman "courted by a murderer"); Pogany v. Chambers, 1954, 206 Misc. 933, 134 N.Y.S.2d 691, appeal denied 285 App.Div. 934, 139 N.Y.S.2d 887 (brother of a Communist).

31. Kamsler v. Chicago American Publishing Co., 1967, 82 Ill.App.2d 86, 225 N.E.2d 434.

32. Frawley Chemical Corp. v. A. P. Larson Co., 1949, 274 App.Div. 643, 86 N.Y.S.2d 710.

33. Cf. Carter v. Papineau, 1916, 222 Mass. 464, 111 N.E. 358. In Nichols v. Item Publishers, 1956, 309 N.Y. 596, 132 N.E.2d 860, a statement that a pastor had been removed from his office in a church by a meeting which was deemed illegal by a jury was held, by a vote of 4 to 2, not to be defamatory.

34. Vallen v. Fanjo Taxi Corp., Sup.Ct.1947, 73 N.Y.S.2d 23; Wabash Railroad Co. v. Young, 1904, 162 Ind. 102, 69 N.E. 1003; Chicago, Rock Island & Pacific Railroad Co. v. Medley, 1916, 55 Okl. 145, 155 P. 211.

35. Kansas City, Memphis & Birmingham Railroad Co. v. Delaney, 1899, 102 Tenn. 289, 52 S.W. 151.

36. Hollenbeck v. Hall, 1897, 103 Iowa 214, 72 N.W. 518; Fey v. King, 1922, 194 Iowa 835, 190 N.W. 519; Homer v. Engelhardt, 1875, 117 Mass. 539; Foot v. Pitt, 1903, 83 App.Div. 76, 82 N.Y.S. 464.

37. Grande & Son v. Chace, 1955, 333 Mass. 166, 129 N.E.2d 898.

38. Digest Publishing Co. v. Perry Publishing Co., Ky.1955, 284 S.W.2d 832.

39. Sim v. Stretch, [1936] 2 All Eng.Rep. 1237.

40. Clarke v. Fitch, 1871, 41 Cal. 472.

er type of tort action for any special damage resulting,[41] but it lacks the element of personal disgrace necessary for defamation; and the fact that the plaintiff finds it unpleasant and offensive is not enough.[42]

On the other hand it is defamatory upon its face to say that the plaintiff has attempted suicide,[43] that he refuses to pay his just debts,[44] that he is immoral or unchaste,[45] or "queer," [46] or has made improper advances to women,[47] or is having "wife trouble," and is about to be divorced;[48] that he is a coward,[49] a drunkard,[50] a hypocrite,[51] a liar,[52] a scoundrel,[53] a crook,[54] a scandalmonger,[55] an anarchist,[56] a skunk,[57] a bastard,[58] a eunuch,[59] or a "rotten egg";[60] that he is "unfair" to labor,[61] or that he has done a thing which is oppressive or dishonorable,[62] or heartless,[63] because all of these things obviously tend to affect the esteem in which he is held by his neighbors.

41. See supra, § 12.
42. Gang v. Hughes, S.D.Cal.1953, 111 F.Supp. 27, affirmed 9th Cir.1954, 218 F.2d 432.
43. Wandt v. Hearst's Chicago American, 1900, 129 Wis. 419, 109 N.W. 70. Cf. Quinn v. Sun Printing & Publishing Co., 1907, 55 Misc. 572, 105 N.Y.S. 1092, affirmed 1908, 125 App.Div. 900, 109 N.Y.S. 1143 (found dead under disgraceful circumstances).
44. Neaton v. Lewis Apparel Stores, 1944, 267 App. Div. 728, 48 N.Y.S.2d 492, appeal granted 1944, 268 App.Div. 834, 50 N.Y.S.2d 463; Sheppard v. Dun & Bradstreet, S.D.N.Y.1947, 71 F.Supp. 942; Thompson v. Adelberg & Berman, 1918, 181 Ky. 487, 205 S.W. 558; Turner v. Brien, 1918, 184 Iowa 320, 167 N.W. 584; Muetze v. Tuteur, 1890, 77 Wis. 236, 46 N.W. 123.

But not to say merely that one has debts, or is unable to pay them, unless he is engaged in business (see infra, p. 790). Hollenbeck v. Hall, 1897, 103 Iowa 214, 72 N.W. 518; Harrison v. Burger, 1925, 212 Ala. 670, 103 So. 842.

45. Hall v. Hall, 1920, 179 N.C. 571, 103 S.E. 136; More v. Bennett, 1872, 48 N.Y. 472; Flues v. New Nonpareil Co., 1912, 155 Iowa 290, 135 N.W. 1083; Collins v. Dispatch Publishing Co., 1893, 152 Pa. 187, 25 A. 546. Cf. Sydney v. McFadden Newspaper Publishing Corp., 1926, 242 N.Y. 208, 151 N.E. 209 (married woman the "lady love" of a man); Martin v. Johnson Publishing Co., Sup.Ct.1956, 157 N.Y.S.2d 409 ("man hungry" woman); White v. Birmingham Post Co., 1937, 233 Ala. 547, 172 So. 649 (Arab sheik wanted to buy American girl for his harem).
46. Buck v. Savage, Tex.Civ.App.1959, 323 S.W.2d 363, ref. n.r.e.
47. Jamison v. Rebenson, 1959, 21 Ill.App.2d 364, 158 N.E.2d 82.
48. Gersten v. Newark Morning Ledger Co., 1958, 52 N.J.Super. 152, 145 A.2d 56; Lyman v. New England Newspaper Publishing Co., 1934, 286 Mass. 258, 190 N.E. 542.
49. Price v. Whitley, 1872, 50 Mo. 439; Byrne v. Funk, 1905, 38 Wash. 506, 80 P. 772.
50. Buck v. Hersey, 1850, 31 Me. 558; Hay v. Reid, 1891, 85 Mich. 296, 48 N.W. 507; Holmes v. Jones, 1895, 147 N.Y. 59, 41 N.E. 409; Dawkins v. Billingsley, 1918, 69 Okl. 259, 172 P. 69.
51. Knox v. Meehan, 1896, 64 Minn. 280, 66 N.W. 1149; Newby v. Times-Mirror Co., 1916, 173 Cal. 387, 160 P. 233; Overstreet v. New Nonpareil Co., 1918, 184 Iowa 485, 167 N.W. 669.
52. Prewitt v. Wilson, 1905, 128 Iowa 198, 103 N.W. 365; Smith v. Lyons, 1918, 142 La. 975, 77 So. 896; Paxton v. Woodward, 1904, 31 Mont. 195, 78 P. 215; Colvard v. Black, 1900, 110 Ga. 642, 36 S.E. 80; Murphy v. Harty, 1964, 238 Or. 228, 393 P.2d 206.
53. Upton v. Hume, 1893, 24 Or. 420, 33 P. 810; Crocker v. Hadley, 1885, 102 Ind. 416, 1 N.E. 734 ("hoary-headed filcher"); Candrian v. Miller, 1898, 98 Wis. 164, 73 N.W. 1004 ("smooth swindler"); Bell v. Stone, 1798, 1 Bos. & P. 331, 126 Eng.Rep. 933 ("villain").
54. Pandolfo v. Bank of Benson, 9th Cir.1921, 273 F. 48. Accord: Stevens v. Snow, 1923, 191 Cal. 58, 214 P. 968 ("crooked methods"); Peterson v. Western Union Telegraph Co., 1896, 65 Minn. 18, 67 N.W. 646; Thompson v. Upton, 1958, 218 Md. 433, 146 A.2d 880 (engaged in a "racket").
55. Patton v. Cruce, 1904, 72 Ark. 421, 81 S.W. 380.
56. Cerveny v. Chicago Daily News Co., 1891, 139 Ill. 345, 28 N.E. 692; Lewis v. Daily News Co., 1895, 81 Md. 466, 32 A. 246 ("would be an anarchist if he thought it would pay").
57. Massuere v. Dickens, 1887, 70 Wis. 83, 35 N.W. 349; Solverson v. Peterson, 1885, 64 Wis. 198, 25 N.W. 14 ("swine").
58. Shelby v. Sun Printing & Publishing Association, 1886, 38 Hun, N.Y., 474; Harris v. Nashville Trust Co., 1914, 128 Tenn. 573, 162 S.W. 584.
59. Eckert v. Van Pelt, 1904, 69 Kan. 357, 76 P. 909.
60. Pfitzinger v. Dubs, 7th Cir.1894, 64 F. 696.
61. Paducah Newspapers v. Wise, Ky.App.1951, 247 S.W.2d 989, certiorari denied 1952, 343 U.S. 942, 72 S.Ct. 1035, 96 L.Ed. 1347. This may, however, be privileged. See infra, § 115.
62. Clement v. Chivis, 1829, 9 B. & C. 172, 109 Eng. Rep. 64; Snyder v. Fulton, 1871, 34 Md. 128.
63. MacRae v. Afro-American Co., E.D.Pa.1959, 172 F.Supp. 184, affirmed 3d Cir.1960, 274 F.2d 287 (mother responsible for daughter's suicide); Brown v. Du Frey, 1956, 1 N.Y.2d 190, 151 N.Y.S.2d 649, 134 N.E.2d 469 (husband had neglected wife, treated her with indifference, failed to support her).

The defamatory character of the statement may arise from and affect a particular characteristic or activity of the plaintiff, as where a kosher meat dealer is accused of selling bacon,[64] an amateur golfer is called a professional,[65] an actor of standing is said to have stooped below his class of entertainment,[66] a physician is reported to have advertised,[67] or the incumbent of a public office for which only citizens are eligible is said not to be a citizen.[68] The form of the statement is not important, so long as the defamatory meaning is conveyed; and it may be merely a report of "rumors and whispers," [69] or even conditional, so long as the condition is known to the hearer to be satisfied.[70]

The courts have, however, attempted to make something like the distinction found in the law of misrepresentation,[71] between assertions of fact and those of opinion, and have held [72] that mere words of abuse, indicating that the defendant dislikes the plaintiff and has a low opinion of him, but without suggesting any specific charge against him, are not to be treated as defamatory. A certain amount of vulgar name-calling is tolerated, on the theory that it will necessarily be understood to amount to nothing more. It may be significant that most of the cases have involved slander, which would not have been actionable in any event without proof of special damage,[73] but there are occasional decisions in which what would otherwise be clearly defamatory has been dismissed as only hasty, ill-tempered abuse.[74] There has been, however, more willingness than in the case of misrepresentation to find that an opinion carries with it assertions of fact; [75] and even when the facts are fully known to the hearer, an unprivileged [76] comment or opinion has often been regarded as sufficiently defamatory in itself.[77] But the mere fact that an opinion is defamatory does not

---

64. Braun v. Armour & Co., 1939, 254 N.Y. 514, 173 N.E. 845.

65. Tolley v. J. S. Fry & Sons, Ltd., [1931] A.C. 333.

66. Lahr v. Adell Chemical Co., 1st Cir.1962, 300 F.2d 256; Louka v. Park Entertainments, 1936, 294 Mass. 268, 1 N.E.2d 41. Cf. Clevenger v. Baker Voorhis & Co., 1960, 8 N.Y.2d 187, 203 N.Y.S.2d 812, 168 N.E.2d 643 (book revised by plaintiff said to be full of errors).

67. Gershwin v. Ethical Publishing Co., 1937, 166 Misc. 39, 1 N.Y.S.2d 904.

68. MacInnis v. National Herald Printing Co., 1918, 140 Minn. 171, 167 N.W. 550.

69. MacRae v. Afro-American Co., E.D.Pa.1959, 172 F.Supp. 184, affirmed 3d Cir.1960, 274 F.2d 287.

70. Clarke v. Zettick, 1891, 153 Mass. 1, 26 N.E. 234; Ruble v. Bunting, 1903, 31 Ind.App. 654, 68 N.E. 1041; American Life Insurance Co. v. Shell, 1956, 265 Ala. 306, 90 So.2d 719.

71. See supra, § 109.

72. The distinction is an old one. See Penfold v. Westcote, 1806, 2 Bos. & P. N. R. 335, 127 Eng.Rep. 636; Barnett v. Allen, 3 H. & N. 376, 157 Eng.Rep. 516; Rice v. Simmons, 1841, 2 Har., Del. 309, 417; Robbins v. Treadway, Ky.1829, 2 J.J.Marsh. 540. All on the ground that the words must have been understood as mere bad temper.

73. Crozman v. Callahan, W.D.Okl.1955, 136 F.Supp. 466 (obscene language from military official to enlisted man); Durr v. Smith, La.App.1956, 90 So.2d 147 ("invective epithet which deleteriously reflected upon the validity of his parentage"); Notarmuzzi v. Shevack, Sup.Ct.1951, 108 N.Y.S.2d 172 ("You are a bleached blond bastard, a God damn son of a bitch and a bum and a tramp; get the hell out of here"); Halliday v. Cienkowski, 1939, 333 Pa. 123, 3 A.2d 372; Mann v. Roosevelt Shop, Fla.1949, 41 So.2d 894.

But in White v. Valenta, 1965, 234 Cal.App.2d 243, 44 Cal.Rptr. 241, "son of a bitch" was held under the circumstances to impute unfair business dealing.

74. Tomakian v. Fritz, 1949, 75 R.I. 496, 67 A.2d 834 ("drunken driver"); Curtis Publishing Co. v. Birdsong, 5 Cir.1966, 360 F.2d 344 ("bastards"); Cowan v. Time, Inc., 1963, 41 Misc.2d 198, 245 N.Y.S.2d 723 ("idiot"); Morrissette v. Beatte, 1941, 66 R.I. 73, 17 A.2d 464 (sodomy); Hansen v. Dethridge, N.Y.1946, 67 N.Y.S.2d 168.

In extreme cases abuse may be actionable as the intentional infliction of mental disturbance. See supra, § 12.

75. Cf. Cole v. Millspaugh, 1910, 111 Minn. 159, 126 N.W. 626 ("I would not touch him with a ten foot pole"); Eikhoff v. Gilbert, 1900, 124 Mich. 353, 83 N.W. 110; Davis & Sons v. Shepstone, 1886, 11 App.Cas. 187.

76. Statements of opinion may be privileged in some cases where statements of fact are not. See infra, § 115.

77. Thomas v. Bradbury, Agnew & Co., [1906] 2 K.B. 627; Woolston v. Montana Free Press, 1931, 90 Mont. 299, 2 P.2d 1020; Professional & B. M. Life Insurance Co. v. Bankers Life Co., D.Mont.1958, 163 F.Supp. 274; Goldwater v. Ginzburg, S.D.N.Y.1966, 261 F.Supp. 784.

mean that it is actionable in like manner as a defamatory statement of fact.[77a]

It has been said that a common form of defamation is ridicule, and it has been so held in a number of cases.[78] In some of these cases, the courts seem to hold that the publication is defamatory, even if it asserts nothing false whatsoever about the plaintiff. The basis for the result is simply the notion that the publication was the kind that would subject the plaintiff to ridicule. These cases were decided prior to holdings permitting recovery for intentional interference with peace of mind, and prior to the greater protection accorded to speech under the first amendment of the United States Constitution. It is doubtful that an article or publication subjecting a person to ridicule because of the happening of a true occurrence should be regarded as actionable, and, if actionable, on the basis of defamation. Defamation should be limited to imputations about the plaintiff that prove to be false and discreditable.

The question of the standard by which defamation is to be determined has given rise to some difficulty.[79] It has been held in England[80] that the communication must tend to defame the plaintiff in the eyes of the community in general, or at least of a reasonable person,[81] rather than in the opinion of any particular group or class. The American courts have taken a more realistic view, recognizing that the plaintiff may suffer real damage if he is lowered in the esteem of any substantial and respectable group,[82] even though it may be quite a small minority.[83] It has sometimes been said that these must be "right-thinking people"; but this seems clearly wrong, since the court cannot be called upon to make a definitive pronouncement upon whether the views of different segments of the community are right or wrong, sound, or morally justifiable.[84] Thus, without regard to whether such opinions are "right-thinking," the publication of the plaintiff's picture in connection with a whiskey advertisement,[85] the statement that he is about to be divorced,[86] the insinuation that a white person is a Negro,[87] that a business person is a price-

77a. Sec. 113A.

78. Eldredge, The Law of Defamation, 1978, Sec. 7, p. 31. Megarry v. Norton, 1955, 137 Cal.App.2d 581, 290 P.2d 571 (sign, "Nuts to You—You Old Witch"); Powers v. Durgin-Snow Pub. Co., 1958, 154 Me. 108, 144 A.2d 294 (making own funeral casket, will next dig his own hole for it); Burton v. Crowell Pub. Co., 2d Cir. 1936, 82 F.2d 154; see Naughton and Gilbertson, Libelous Ridicule by Journalists, 1969, 18 Cleve.Marsh. L.Rev. 450.

79. See Notes, 1939, 24 Corn.L.Q. 258; 1949, 58 Yale L.J. 1387.

80. Clay v. Roberts, 1863, 8 L.T. 397; Miller v. David, 1874, L.R. 9 C.P. 118; Myroft v. Sleight [1921] 90 L.J.K.B. 853.

81. See Tolley v. J. S. Fry & Sons, [1930] 1 K.B. 467, [1931] A.C. 333 (holding it libel to call an amateur golfer a professional).

82. Second Restatement of Torts, § 559 Comment e. Accord: Munden v. Harris, 1910, 153 Mo.App. 652, 134 S.W. 1076 (infant defamed only in eyes of infants); Foster-Milburn Co. v. Chinn, 1909, 134 Ky. 424, 120 S.W. 364; Morley v. Post Printing & Publishing Co., 1928, 84 Colo. 41, 268 P. 540; Reiman v. Pacific Development Society, 1930, 132 Or. 82, 284 P. 575; Brauer v. Globe Newspaper Co., 1966, 351 Mass. 53, 217 N.E.2d 736. See Note, 1970, 34 Alb.L.Rev. 634.

83. Thus in Ben-Oliel v. Press Publishing Co., 1929, 251 N.Y. 250, 167 N.E. 432, it was held that plaintiff was defamed by attributing to him the authorship of a bad book on the culture of Palestine, although only a few experts in that field would recognize that it was a bad one.

84. Grant v. Reader's Digest Association, 2d Cir. 1945, 151 F.2d 733, certiorari denied 326 U.S. 797, 66 S.Ct. 492, 90 L.Ed. 485; Herrmann v. Newark Morning Ledger Co., 1958, 49 N.J.Super. 551, 140 A.2d 529; Ingalls v. Hastings & Sons Publishing Co., 1939, 304 Mass. 31, 22 N.E.2d 657.

85. Peck v. Tribune Co., 1909, 214 U.S. 185, 29 S.Ct. 554, 53 L.Ed. 960 (Holmes, J.: "Liability is not a question of majority vote").

86. Gersten v. Newark Morning Ledger Co., 1958, 52 N.J.Super. 152, 145 A.2d 56. Cf. Geriepy v. Pearson, 1953, 92 U.S.App.D.C. 337, 207 F.2d 15 (alienation of plaintiff's affections); Brown v. Du Frey, 1956, 1 N.Y.2d 190, 151 N.Y.S.2d 649, 134 N.E.2d 469 (marital discord). See Note, 1956, 23 Brook.L.Rev. 156.

87. Natchez Times Publishing Co. v. Dunigan, 1954, 221 Miss. 320, 72 So.2d 681; Bowen v. Independent Publishing Co., 1957, 230 S.C. 509, 96 S.E.2d 564; Jones v. R. L. Polk & Co., 1915, 190 Ala. 243, 67 So. 577; Spencer v. Looney, 1914, 116 Va. 767, 82 S.E. 745; Upton v. Times-Democrat Publishing Co., 1900, 104 La. 141, 28 So. 970.

cutter [88] or a kosher meat dealer sells bacon,[89] that the plaintiff is anti-Semitic,[90] or the daughter of a murderer,[91] may be defamatory even though it be assumed that all adverse opinions are wrong, and that the majority of the community will think none the worse. The line is drawn, however, when the group who will be unfavorably impressed becomes so small as to be negligible,[92] or one whose standards are so clearly anti-social that the court may not properly consider them.[93] The state of mind of the particular community must of course be taken into account,[94] as well as its fluctuations over a period of time; and the accusation of membership in the Communist party, or of Communist affiliation or sympathy,[95] which has led to varying conclusions over the last several decades,[96] is at present all but universally regarded as clearly defamatory.[97]

Who May be Defamed

Any living person may be defamed. The civil action is personal to the plaintiff, and cannot be founded on the defamation of another;[98] but it is of course possible that two persons may stand in such a relation that defamation of one will be found to reflect upon the reputation of the other—as where, for example, it is said that the plaintiff's mother was not married to his father; and where such is the case, the plaintiff may have an action in his own right.[99] Likewise, no civil action will lie for the defamation of one who is dead,[1] unless there is a reflection upon those still living, who are themselves

---

88. Meyerson v. Hurlbut, 1938, 68 App.D.C. 360, 98 F.2d 232, certiorari denied 1938, 305 U.S. 610, 59 S.Ct. 69, 83 L.Ed. 388.

89. Braun v. Armour & Co., 1930, 254 N.Y. 514, 173 N.E. 845.

90. Sweeney v. Schenectady Union Publishing Co., 2d Cir.1941, 122 F.2d 288, affirmed 316 U.S. 642, 62 S.Ct. 1031, 86 L.Ed. 1727, rehearing denied 316 U.S. 710, 62 S.Ct. 1266, 86 L.Ed. 1776.

91. Van Wiginton v. Pulitzer Publishing Co., 8th Cir.1914, 218 F. 795.

92. Second Restatement of Torts, § 559, Comment e. Cf. Galveston Tribune v. Guisti, Tex.Civ.App.1911, 134 S.W. 239, reversed 105 Tex. 497, 150 S.W. 874, rehearing denied 105 Tex. 497, 152 S.W. 167.

93. Thus the criminal's dislike of informers. Mawe v. Piggott, 1869, Ir.Rep. 4 C.L. 54; Connelly v. McKay, 1941, 176 Misc. 685, 28 N.Y.S.2d 327; Rose v. Borenstein, City Ct.N.Y.1953, 119 N.Y.S.2d 288. See also, the classic opinion of Minturn, J., In the Matter of Kirk, 1925, 101 N.J.L. 450, 130 A. 569, dealing with popular esteem of the bootlegger.

94. Oles v. Pittsburg Times, 1896, 2 Pa.Super. 130 ("witch" in community believing in witchcraft); Larean v. La. Compagnie d'Imprimerie de la Minerve, Quebec 1883, 27 L.C.J. 336 ("freemason" in Catholic community).

95. Grant v. Reader's Digest Association, 2d Cir. 1945, 151 F.2d 733, certiorari denied 326 U.S. 797, 66 S.Ct. 492, 90 L.Ed. 485; Utah State Farm Bureau Federation v. National Farmers Union Service Corp., 10th Cir.1952, 198 F.2d 20; Mosler v. Whelen, 1958, 48 N.J. Super. 491, 138 A.2d 559, reversed as question of fact 1959, 28 N.J. 397, 147 A.2d 7; MacLeod v. Tribune Publishing Co., 1959, 52 Cal.2d 536, 343 P.2d 36.

96. Toomey v. Jones, 1926, 124 Okl. 167, 254 P. 736 ("red;" defamatory); Garriga v. Richfield, 1940, 174 Misc. 315, 20 N.Y.S.2d 544 (not defamatory); Levy v. Gelber, 1941, 175 Misc. 746, 25 N.Y.S.2d 148 (Russia allied with Germany; defamatory); Mencher v. Chesley, 1946, 270 App.Div. 1040, 63 N.Y.S.2d 108, reversed 297 N.Y. 94, 75 N.E.2d 257 (Russia allied with United States; defamatory only in relation to business or office); McAndrew v. Scranton Republican Publishing Co., 1950, 364 Pa. 504, 72 A.2d 780 (not defamatory).

See Notes, 1947, 45 Mich.L.Rev. 518; 1950, 50 Col.L. Rev. 526; 1953, 29 N.D.L.Rev. 296; 1954, 19 Mo.L.Rev. 91; [1953] Wash.U.L.Q. 331.

97. Spanel v. Pegler, 2d Cir.1947, 160 F.2d 619; Toomey v. Farley, 1956, 2 N.Y.2d 71, 156 N.Y.S.2d 840, 138 N.E.2d 221; Ward v. League for Justice, Ohio App. 1950, 93 N.E.2d 723, appeal dismissed 154 Ohio St. 367, 95 N.E.2d 769; Joopanenko v. Gavagan, Fla.1953, 67 So.2d 434; Herrmann v. Newark Morning Ledger Co., 1958, 48 N.J.Super. 420, 138 A.2d 61, second appeal 49 N.J.Super. 551, 140 A.2d 529.

As to whether the accusation is slander per se, see infra, § 112.

98. Ryan v. Hearst Publications, 1940, 3 Wn.2d 128, 100 P.2d 24 (family); Alfone v. Newark Umbrella Frame Co., 1951, 13 N.J.Super. 526, 80 A.2d 589 (wife); Security Sales Agency v. A. S. Abell Co., D.Md.1913, 205 F. 941; Child v. Emerson, 1894, 102 Mich. 38, 60 N.W. 292; Pogany v. Chambers, 1954, 206 Misc. 933, 134 N.Y.S.2d 691, affirmed 1955, 285 App.Div. 866, 137 N.Y.S.2d 828, appeal denied 1955, 285 App.Div. 934, 139 N.Y.S.2d 887 (brother of a Communist).

99. Merrill v. Post Publishing Co., 1908, 197 Mass. 185, 83 N.E. 419. Accord: Vicars v. Worth, 1722, 1 Stra. 471, 93 Eng.Rep. 641; Hodgkins v. Corbett, 1723, 1 Stra. 545, 93 Eng.Rep. 690; Ryalls v. Leader, 1866, L.R. 1 Ex. 296; Huckle v. Reynolds, 1859, 7 C.B., N.S., 114; Second Restatement of Torts, § 564, Comment e.

1. Gruschus v. Curtis Publishing Co., 10th Cir.1965, 342 F.2d 775; Bello v. Random House, Inc., Mo.1968, 422 S.W.2d 339; Mahaffey v. Official Detective Stories,

defamed.² Statutes in several states have made defamation of the dead a crime, but they have been construed as intended only to protect the public interest and the memory of the deceased, and so to afford no civil action to the surviving relatives.³

A corporation is regarded as having no reputation in any personal sense, so that it cannot be defamed by words, such as those imputing unchastity, which would affect the purely, personal repute of an individual.⁴ But it has prestige and standing in the business in which it is engaged, and language which casts an aspersion upon its honesty,⁵ credit,⁶ efficiency or other business character may be actionable.⁷ The same is true of a partnership,⁸ or an unincorporated association.⁹ Non-trading organizations, such as those formed for benevolent or charitable purposes, may still be dependent upon the donations or support of the public, and so may still be defamed by attacks which would tend to decrease contributions.¹⁰ An organization is not defamed by words directed at its officers, stockholders or employees,¹¹ nor are they defamed by words directed at it,¹² unless the words are such, in the light of the connection between them, as to defame

Inc., W.D.La.1962, 210 F.Supp. 251, affirmed 5th Cir. 1968, 389 F.2d 525; Kelly v. Johnson Publishing Co., 1958, 160 Cal.App.2d 718, 325 P.2d 659; Insull v. New York World Telegram Corp., N.D.Ill.1959, 172 F.Supp. 615, affirmed 1960, 273 F.2d 166, certiorari denied 362 U.S. 942, 80 S.Ct. 807, 4 L.Ed.2d 770.

See Notes, 1940, 26 Corn.L.Q. 372; 1940, 40 Col.L. Rev. 1267; 1941, 10 Ford.L.Rev. 319.

2. See Eagles v. Liberty Weekly, 1930, 137 Misc. 575, 244 N.Y.S. 430; Walton, Libel upon the Dead and The Bath Club Case, 1927, 9 J.Comp.Leg. & Int.Law 1; Restatement of Torts, § 560. But cf. Rose v. Daily Mirror, 1940, 284 N.Y. 335, 31 N.E.2d 182, reargument denied 285 N.Y. 616, 33 N.E.2d 548.

3. Saucer v. Giroux, 1921, 54 Cal.App. 732, 202 P. 887; Renfro Drug Co. v. Lawson, 1942, 138 Tex. 434, 160 S.W.2d 246. See Armstrong, Nothing But Good of the Dead, 1932, 18 A.B.A.J. 5229.

4. Reporters' Association of America v. Sun Printing & Publishing Association, 1906, 186 N.Y. 437, 79 N.E. 710; People's United States Bank v. Goodwin, 1912, 167 Mo.App. 211, 149 S.W. 1148; Adirondack Record v. Lawrence, 1922, 202 App.Div. 251, 195 N.Y.S. 627; see Axton-Fisher Tobacco Co. v. Evening Post Co., 1916, 169 Ky. 64, 183 S.W. 269.

5. Den Norske Ameriekalinje Actiesselskabet v. Sun Printing & Publishing Association, 1919, 226 N.Y. 1, 122 N.E. 463; Pullman Standard Car Manufacturing Co. v. Local Union No. 2928, 7th Cir.1945, 152 F.2d 493.

6. Aetna Life Insurance Co. v. Mutual Benefit Health & Accident Association, 8th Cir.1936, 82 F.2d 115; Maytag Co. v. Meadows Manufacturing Co., 7th Cir.1930, 45 F.2d 299, certiorari denied, 283 U.S. 843, 51 S.Ct. 489, 75 L.Ed. 1452; Wayne Works v. Hicks Body Co., 1944, 115 Ind.App. 10, 55 N.E.2d 382; Brayton v. Crowell-Collier Publishing Co., 2d Cir.1953, 205 F.2d 644.

7. Axton-Fisher Tobacco Co. v. Evening Post Co., 1916, 169 Ky. 64, 183 S.W. 269; Cross Coal Co. v. Rose, 1905, 126 Wis. 24, 105 N.W. 225; Di Giorgio Fruit Corp. v. American Federation of Labor, etc., 1963, 215 Cal.App.2d 560, 30 Cal.Rptr. 350; Utah State Farm Bureau Federation v. National Farmers Union Service Corp., 10th Cir.1952, 198 F.2d 20; R. H. Bouligny, Inc. v. United Steelworkers of America, 1967, 270 N.C. 160, 154 S.E.2d 344.

8. Both the partnership and individual partners may be defamed. Vogel v. Bushnell, 1920, 203 Mo.App. 623, 221 S.W. 819; Constitution Publishing Co. v. Way, 1894, 94 Ga. 120, 21 S.E. 139; Donaghue v. Gaffey, 1885, 53 Conn. 43, 2 A. 397; Stone v. Textile Examiners & Shrinkers Employers' Association, 1910, 137 App. Div. 655, 122 N.Y.S. 460.

9. Kirkman v. Westchester Newspapers, 1942, 287 N.Y. 373, 39 N.E.2d 919; Daniels v. Sanitarium Association, 1963, 59 Cal.2d 602, 30 Cal.Rptr. 828, 381 P.2d 652; Di Giorgio Fruit Co. v. American Federation of Labor, 1963, 215 Cal.App.2d 560, 30 Cal.Rptr. 350; Calore v. Powell-Savory Corp., 1964, 21 A.D.2d 877, 251 N.Y.S.2d 732.

10. New York Society for Suppression of Vice v. McFadden Publications, 1927, 129 Misc. 408, 221 N.Y.S. 563, affirmed 1928, 222 App.Div. 739, 226 N.Y.S. 870; Finnish Temperance Society Sovittaja v. Finnish Socialistic Publishing Co., 1921, 238 Mass. 345, 130 N.E. 845; Aetna Life Insurance Co. v. Mutual Benefit Health & Accident Association, 8th Cir.1936, 82 F.2d 115; Boston Nutrition Society Inc. v. Stare, 1961, 342 Mass. 439, 173 N.E.2d 812; Americans for Democratic Action v. Meade, 1950, 72 Pa.D. & C. 306.

11. Life Printing & Publishing Co. v. Field, 1946, 327 Ill.App. 486, 64 N.E.2d 383; Hapgoods v. Crawford, 1908, 125 App.Div. 856, 110 N.Y.S. 122; People's United States Bank v. Goodwin, 1912, 167 Mo.App. 211, 149 S.W. 1148; Brayton v. Cleveland Special Police Co., 1900, 63 Ohio St. 83, 57 N.E. 1085; Novick v. Hearst Corp., D.Md.1968, 278 F.Supp. 277.

Cf. Gilbert v. Crystal Fountain Lodge, 1887, 80 Ga. 284, 4 S.E. 905 (Bleckley, C. J.: "The venereal disease was not a partnership malady. That was individual property.")

12. Gilbert Shoe Co. v. Rumpf Publishing Co., D.Mass.1953, 112 F.Supp. 228 (president); McBride v. Crowell-Collier Publishing Co., 5th Cir.1952, 196 F.2d 187 (stockholder).

both.[13] It has been held in some cases[14] that a municipal corporation cannot maintain an action for defamation; but the decisions have turned upon the particular facts and questions of privilege, and have been criticized.[15]

Interpretation: Inducement, Innuendo, and Colloquium

In order that the defendant's words may be defamatory, they must be understood in a defamatory sense. It is not necessary that anyone believe them to be true,[16] since the fact that such words are in circulation at all concerning the plaintiff must be to some extent injurious to his reputation—although obviously the absence of belief will bear upon the amount of the damages. There must be, however, a defamatory meaning conveyed. Thus it is always open to the defendant to show that the words were not understood at all,[17] that they were taken entirely in jest,[18] or that some meaning other than the obvious one was attached by all who heard or read.[19] The form of the language used is not controlling, and there may be defamation by means of a question,[20] an indirect insinuation,[21] an expression of belief or opinion,[22] or sarcasm or irony.[23] The imputation may be carried quite indirectly, as where the plaintiff's name is signed as author to a false[24] or very bad[25] piece of writing, or the plaintiff is made to appear willing to publish a love affair to the world.[26]

The reluctance with which the common law courts at first entertained actions for defamation led them to hold that words must be interpreted in the best possible

---

13. Brayton v. Crowell-Collier Publishing Co., 2d Cir.1953, 205 F.2d 644 (individual identified with corporation); De Mankowski v. Ship Channel Development Co., Tex.Civ.App.1927, 300 S.W. 118 (officers "a bunch of crooks"); Neiman-Marcus Co. v. Lait, S.D.N.Y.1952, 107 F.Supp. 96 (employees); Axton-Fisher Tobacco Co. v. Evening Post Co., 1916, 169 Ky. 64, 183 S.W. 269. See Note 1953, 51 Mich.L.Rev. 611.

14. Mayor of Manchester v. Williams, [1891] 1 Q.B. 94, 63 L.T. 805; City of Chicago v. Chicago Tribune Co., 1923, 307 Ill. 595, 139 N.E. 86; City of Albany v. Meyer, 1929, 99 Cal.App. 651, 279 P. 213.

15. Bower, Actionable Defamation, 2d ed. 1923, 245; 1924, 9 Corn.L.Q. 211. The Restatement of Torts, § 561, Caveat, expresses no opinion.

16. Knight v. Gibbs, 1834, 1 Ad. & El. 43, 110 Eng. Rep. 1124; Gillett v. Bullivant, 1846, 7 L.T., O.S., 490; Marble v. Chapin, 1882, 132 Mass. 225; see Modisette & Adams v. Lorenze, 1927, 163 La. 505, 112 So. 397; Dall v. Time, Inc., 1937, 252 App.Div. 636, 300 N.Y.S. 680, affirmed 1938, 278 N.Y. 635, 16 N.E.2d 297, reargument denied 1938, 278 N.Y. 718, 17 N.E.2d 138.

17. Thus in the case of words spoken in a foreign language. Price v. Jenkins, 1601, Cro.Eliz. 805, 78 Eng.Rep. 1091; Rich v. Scalio, 1904, 115 Ill.App. 166; Mielenz v. Quasdorf, 1886, 68 Iowa 726, 28 N.W. 41; Economopoulos v. A. G. Pollard Co., 1914, 218 Mass. 294, 105 N.E. 896.

18. See the comments in this Section under Definition.

19. Ayers v. Grider, 1853, 15 Ill. 37; Fawsett v. Clark, 1878, 48 Md. 494; Brown v. Myers, 1883, 40 Ohio St. 99; Line v. Spies, 1905, 139 Mich. 484, 102 N.W. 993; Insurance Research Service v. Associates Finance Co., M.D.Tenn.1955, 134 F.Supp. 54. But where the words are open only to one defamatory meaning under the circumstances, a witness will not be permitted to testify that he understood them in a different sense. Smith v. Smith, 1940, 194 S.C. 247, 9 S.E.2d 584.

20. State v. Norton, 1896, 89 Me. 290, 36 A. 394; Goodrich v. Davis, 1846, 52 Mass. (11 Metc.) 473; Meaney v. Loew's Hotels, Inc., 1968, 29 A.D.2d 850, 288 N.Y.S.2d 217.

21. Merrill v. Post Publishing Co., 1908, 197 Mass. 185, 83 N.E. 419; Gendron v. St. Pierre, 1905, 73 N.H. 419, 62 A. 966; Palmerlee v. Nottage, 1912, 119 Minn. 351, 138 N.W. 312; Sherin v. Eastwood, 1922, 46 S.D. 24, 190 N.W. 320.

See Spiegel, Defamation by Implication—In the Confidential Manner, 1956, 29 So.Cal.L.Rev. 306.

22. Nye v. Otis, 1811, 8 Mass. 122; Gendron v. St. Pierre, 1905, 73 N.H. 419, 62 A. 966; Prewitt v. Wilson, 1905, 128 Iowa 198, 103 N.W. 365.

23. Boydell v. Jones, 1838, 4 M. & W. 36, 150 Eng. Rep. 1333; Diener v. Star-Chronicle Publishing Co., 1910, 230 Mo. 613, 132 S.W. 1143; Buckstaff v. Viall, 1893, 84 Wis. 129, 54 N.W. 111.

24. Locke v. Benton & Bowles, 1937, 165 Misc. 631, 1 N.Y.S.2d 240, reversed 253 A.D. 369, 2 N.Y.S.2d 150; Ben-Oliel v. Press Publishing Co., 1929, 251 N.Y. 250, 167 N.E. 432.

25. D'Altomonte v. New York Herald Co., 1913, 154 App.Div. 453, 139 N.Y.S. 200, affirmed 208 N.Y. 596, 102 N.E. 1101; Sperry Rand Corp. v. Hill, 1st Cir.1966, 356 F.2d 181, certiorari denied 384 U.S. 973, 86 S.Ct. 1859, 16 L.Ed.2d 683. Cf. Carroll v. Paramount Pictures, S.D.N.Y.1943, 3 F.R.D. 47 (bad motion picture); Gardella v. Log Cabin Products Co., 2d Cir.1937, 89 F.2d 891 (impersonation and inferior performance).

26. Karjavainean v. MacFadden Publications, 1940, 305 Mass. 573, 26 N.E.2d 538.

sense, and that the plaintiff must entirely negative any possible nondefamatory meaning. The result was a set of artificial and absurd rules of pleading and proof, by which "Thou art as arrant a thief any is in England" was not actionable until it was pleaded that there were thieves in England,[27] and "Thou art a murderer, for thou art the fellow that didst kill Mr. Sydnam's man" required an averment that any man of Mr. Sydnam's had in fact been murdered.[28] This triumph of technicality, some traces of which still remain,[29] has long since largely been buried in the past, and it is now held that words are to be taken in the sense in which they are reasonably understood under the circumstances, and are to be presumed to have the meaning ordinarily attached to them by those familiar with the language used.[30] Thus Horace Greeley's well-known words concerning James Fenimore Cooper, "He will not bring the action in New York, for we are known here, nor in Otsego, for he is known there" were held to carry the imputation of bad repute in Otsego.[31] On the other hand, no artificial and unreasonable construction placed upon innocent words by the evil-minded can add a defamatory meaning not fairly to be found in the light of the circumstances.[32] If there are listeners who reasonably understand the words in a defamatory sense, the fact that most of those who hear them will give them an innocent meaning will not prevent defamation.[33]

It is for the court in the first instance to determine whether the words are reasonably capable of a particular interpretation, or whether they are necessarily so;[34] it is then for the jury to say whether they were in fact so understood.[35] If the language used is open to two meanings, as in the case of the French word "cocotte," which, according to one court, signifies either a prostitute or a poached egg, it is for the jury to determine whether the defamatory sense was the one conveyed.[36] One obvious rule of limitation is

---

27. Foster v. Browning, 1625, Cro.Jac. 688, 79 Eng. Rep. 596.

28. Barrons v. Ball, 1614, Cro.Jac. 331, 79 Eng.Rep. 282; cf. Lacy v. Reynolds, 1591, Cro.Eliz. 215, 78 Eng. Rep. 471; Holt v. Astgrigg, 1611, Cro.Jac. 184, 79 Eng. Rep. 161; Ball v. Roane, 1593, Cro.Eliz. 308, 78 Eng. Rep. 559.

29. See for example Davis v. Niederhof, 1965, 246 S.C. 192, 143 S.E.2d 367.

30. World Publishing Co. v. Mullen, 1894, 43 Neb. 126, 61 N.W. 108; Boyer v. Pitt Publishing Co., 1936, 324 Pa. 154, 188 A. 203; Lorentz v. R. K. O. Radio Pictures, 9th Cir.1946, 155 F.2d 84, certiorari denied 329 U.S. 727; Budd v. J. Y. Gooch Co., 1948, 157 Fla. 716, 27 So.2d 172; MacRae v. Afro-American Co., E.D.Pa. 1959, 172 F.Supp. 184, affirmed, 3d Cir.1960, 274 F.2d 287; Second Restatement of Torts, § 563. California abandoned the old position in MacLeod v. Tribune Publishing Co., 1959, 52 Cal.2d 536, 343 P.2d 36.

31. Cooper v. Greeley, N.Y.1845, 1 Denio 347.

32. Phillips v. Union Indemnity Co., 4th Cir.1928, 28 F.2d 701; Marshall v. National Police Gazette Corp., 8th Cir.1952, 195 F.2d 993; Lorentz v. R. K. O. Radio Pictures, 9th Cir.1946, 155 F.2d 84, certiorari denied 329 U.S. 727, 67 S.Ct. 81, 91 L.Ed. 629; Campbell v. Post Publishing Co., 1933, 94 Mont. 12, 20 P.2d 1063; Kluender v. Semann, 1927, 203 Iowa 68, 212 N.W. 326.

33. Ervin v. Record Publishing Co., 1908, 154 Cal. 79, 97 P. 21; cf. Wandt v. Hearst's Chicago American, 1906, 129 Wis. 419, 109 N.W. 70; Van Wiginton v. Pulitzer Publishing Co., 8th Cir.1914, 218 F. 795; Fetler v. Houghton Mifflin Co., 2d Cir.1966, 364 F.2d 650.

34. Hays v. American Defense Society, 1929, 252 N.Y. 266, 169 N.E. 380; Davis v. R. K. O. Radio Pictures, 8th Cir.1951, 191 F.2d 901; Lane v. Washington Daily News, 1936, 66 App.D.C. 245, 85 F.2d 822; Smith v. Smith, 1940, 194 S.C. 247, 9 S.E.2d 584; Morrissette v. Beattie, 1941, 66 R.I. 73, 17 A.2d 464.

Constitutional and statutory provisions in many states, modeled after Fox's Libel Act, 1792, 32 Geo. III, ch. 60, that the jury shall determine the law in libel cases, have been construed to mean merely that the jury shall apply the law as instructed by the court. State v. Heacock, 1898, 106 Iowa 191, 76 N.W. 654 (court may instruct); People v. McDowell, 1886, 71 Cal. 194, 11 P. 868 (jury may not disregard existing law); Paxton v. Woodward, 1904, 31 Mont. 195, 78 P. 215 (erroneous instruction). But it has been held that the court can not set aside a verdict once rendered. Harrington v. Butte Miner Co., 1914, 48 Mont. 550, 139 P. 451; State v. Zimmerman, 1883, 31 Kan. 85, 1 P. 257. See Note, 1927, 11 Minn.L.Rev. 472.

35. Washington Post Co. v. Chaloner, 1919, 250 U.S. 290; Gariepy v. Pearson, D.C.Cir.1953, 207 F.2d 15, certiorari denied 346 U.S. 909, 74 S.Ct. 241, 98 L.Ed. 407; Linehan v. Nelson, 1910, 197 N.Y. 482, 90 N.E. 1114; Alderson v. Kahle, 1914, 73 W.Va. 690, 80 S.E. 1109; Clark v. Pearson, D.D.C.1965, 248 F.Supp. 188; Restatement of Torts, § 614.

36. Rovira v. Boget, 1925, 240 N.Y. 314, 148 N.E. 534. Accord, Clark v. Pearson, D.D.C.1965, 248 F.Supp. 188; Eadie v. Pole, 1966, 91 N.J.Super. 504, 221 A.2d 547; MacDonough v. A. S. Beck Shoe Corp., Del.1939, 1 Terry 318, 10 A.2d 510 (man "intimate"

that an entire writing, conversation or motion picture,[37] must be construed as a whole. The plaintiff may not lift words out of their context, and the defamation contained in one line may be negatived or explained away by what appears elsewhere.[38] It is clear, however, that an undue emphasis may be given a part of the publication, as in the case of headlines, which may convey a meaning which the remainder does not remedy.[39]

A publication may be defamatory upon its face; or it may carry a defamatory meaning only by reason of extrinsic circumstances. The distinction is not the same as that between defamation which is actionable of itself and that which requires proof of special damage, which is considered below.[40] There has been no little confusion as to this, sometimes with unfortunate results.[41] If the defamatory meaning arises only from facts not apparent upon the face of the publication, the plaintiff has the burden of pleading and proving such facts, by way of what is called "inducement."[42] Likewise, he must establish the defamatory sense of the publication with reference to such facts, or the "innuen-

do."[43] Thus a statement that the plaintiff has burned his own barn is not defamatory on its face, since he was free to do so; but when it is pleaded as inducement that he had insured his barn, and as innuendo that the words were understood to mean that he was defrauding the insurance company, a charge of the crime of arson is made out, which is defamatory.[44] Or, in the case of words spoken in a foreign language, or in an unusual sense, the inducement would consist of the fact that there were those present who had reason to understand them to have a defamatory meaning, and the innuendo of the meaning itself.[45] The technical rules of common law pleading in such cases became so artificial and intricate that justice was often "smothered in her own robes,"[46] but somewhat less technicality is required under the codes.[47]

The function of the innuendo is merely to explain the words in the light of the facts. No mere claim of the plaintiff can add a defamatory meaning where none is apparent from the publication itself in the light of the inducement;[48] and it remains a question for

with girl employees); Nettles v. MacMillan Petroleum Corp., 1947, 210 S.C. 200, 42 S.E.2d 57.

37. Houston v. Interstate Circuit, Tex.Civ.App.1939, 132 S.W.2d 903.

38. Ledger-Enquirer Co. v. Grimes, 1958, 214 Ga. 422, 105 S.E.2d 229; Helton v. Joplin, Ky.1955, 281 S.W.2d 917; Yakavicke v. Valentukevicius, 1911, 84 Conn. 350, 80 A. 94; Macurda v. Lewiston Journal Co., 1912, 109 Me. 53, 82 A. 438; First National Bank of Waverly v. Winters, 1918, 225 N.Y. 47, 121 N.E. 459. See Note, 1946, 95 U.Pa.L.Rev. 98.

39. Brown v. Ledger-Enquirer Co., 1958, 97 Ga.App. 595, 105 S.E.2d 616, reversed as matter of interpretation 1958, 214 Ga. 422, 105 S.E.2d 229; Shubert v. Variety, Inc., 1926, 128 Misc. 428, 219 N.Y.S. 233, affirmed 1927, 221 App.Div. 856, 224 N.Y.S. 913. Cf. Landon v. Watkins, 1895, 61 Minn. 137, 63 N.W. 615; Gustin v. Evening Press Co., 1912, 172 Mich. 311, 137 N.W. 674. See Note, 1942, 7 Mo.Rev. 80.

40. See infra, § 112.

41. See infra, § 112. The distinction is illustrated by Bowie v. Evening News, 1925, 148 Md. 569, 129 A. 797; Woolston v. Montana Free Press, 1931, 90 Mont. 299, 2 P.2d 1020. As the terms "defamation per se" and "defamation per quod" are used indiscriminately in both senses, they are avoided throughout the text.

42. McLaughlin v. Fisher, 1890, 136 Ill. 111, 24 N.E. 60; McNamara v. Goldan, 1909, 194 N.Y. 315, 87 N.E.

440; Penry v. Dozier, 1909, 161 Ala. 292, 49 So. 909; Kee v. Armstrong, Byrd & Co., 1919, 75 Okl. 84, 182 P. 494; Ten Broeck v. Journal Printing Co., 1926, 166 Minn. 173, 207 N.W. 497.

43. Pfeifly v. Henry, 1921, 269 Pa. 533, 112 A. 768; Kee v. Armstrong, Byrd & Co., 1919, 75 Okl. 84, 182 P. 494; Penry v. Dozier, 1909, 161 Ala. 292, 49 So. 909. No innuendo need be pleaded, however, where the publication is clearly defamatory in the light of the inducement. Sharpe v. Larson, 1897, 70 Minn. 209, 72 N.W. 961.

44. Bloss v. Tobey, 1824, 19 Mass. (2 Pick.) 320. Cf. Arne v. Johnson, 1712, 10 Mod. 111, 88 Eng.Rep. 651 ("You are a soldier," when it was the practice for tradesmen to protect themselves against their creditors by counterfeit enlistment); Cassidy v. Daily Mirror Newspapers, [1929] 2 K.B. 331, 69 A.L.R. 720; Traynor v. Seiloff, 1895, 62 Minn. 420, 64 N.W. 915.

45. Cf. Price v. Jenkings, 1601, Cro.Eliz. 805, 78 Eng.Rep. 1091; Pelzer v. Benish, 1886, 67 Wis. 291, 30 N.W. 366; Acker v. McCullough, 1875, 50 Ind. 447; Wimer v. Allbaugh, 1889, 78 Iowa 79, 42 N.W. 587.

46. Harris v. Zanone, 1892, 93 Cal. 59, 28 P. 845.

47. Clark, Code Pleading, 2d ed. 1947, 315.

48. Grice v. Holk, 1959, 268 Ala. 500, 108 So.2d 359; Sarkees v. Warner-West Corp., 1944, 349 Pa. 365, 37 A.2d 544; Marshall v. National Police Gazette Corp., 8th Cir.1952, 195 F.2d 993; Lorentz v. R. K. O. Radio

the court whether the meaning claimed might reasonably be conveyed,[49] and for the jury whether it was so understood.[50] But where the alleged defamatory matter is published publicly and therefore to a large number of recipients, it can be presumed that if the publication was ambiguous on its face and could be construed with two reasonable meanings, some recipients would give it a defamatory construction. This is not to say that testimony would not be admissible from some witnesses for the purpose of showing the magnitude of the damages resulting from the publication and the extent of the harm done to the plaintiff's reputation. Such testimony would not seem to be necessary as a prerequisite to recovery. If the statement published was not susceptible of a meaning that could be regarded as defamatory on its face, then, of course, there would have to be proof of extrinsic facts at least known to some that would give rise to a reasonable interpretation that would be regarded as defamatory. It might be necessary in some cases of this kind to have evidence of some witnesses to the effect that they construed the statement to have a meaning which would be regarded by the court as defamatory in order for the jury to find that there had been a defamatory communication.

Reference to Plaintiff and Defamation of a Group, Including Plaintiff

It is necessary that some recipient of a defamatory communication believe that it refers to the plaintiff, because it is a prerequisite to recovery that there be a publication of a defamatory communication of and concerning the plaintiff. If the defendant did intend to refer to the plaintiff, and a recipient of the communication did regard the communication as referring to the plaintiff, then this requirement is satisfied, however extraordinary it may have been to regard the statement as referring to the plaintiff.[51]

A publication may clearly be defamatory as to somebody, and yet on its face make no reference to the individual plaintiff. In such a case the plaintiff must sustain the burden of pleading and proof, by way of "colloquium," that the defamatory meaning attached to him. If he fails to do so, he has not made out his case.[52] He need not, of course, be named, and the reference may be an indirect one, with the identification depending upon circumstances known to the hearers,[53] and it is not necessary that every listener understand it, so long as there are some who reasonably do;[54] but the understanding that the plaintiff is meant must be a reasonable one,[55] and if it arises from extrinsic facts, it must be shown that these were known to those who heard.[56]

Pictures, 9th Cir.1946, 155 F.2d 84, certiorari denied 329 U.S. 727; Carey v. Evening Call Publishing Co., 1948, 74 R.I. 473, 62 A.2d 327.

49. Cleary v. Webster, 1927, 170 Minn. 420, 212 N.W. 898; Herrick v. Tribune Co., 1903, 108 Ill.App. 244; Naulty v. Bulletin Co., 1903, 206 Pa. 128, 55 A. 862; Kilgour v. Evening Star Newspaper Co., 1902, 96 Md. 16, 53 A. 716; Davis v. R. K. O. Radio Pictures, 8th Cir.1951, 191 F.2d 901.

50. Linehan v. Nelson, 1910, 197 N.Y. 482, 90 N.E. 1114; Holmes v. Clisby, 1904, 121 Ga. 241, 48 S.E. 934; Cassidy v. Gannett Co., 1940, 173 Misc. 634, 18 N.Y.S.2d 729.

51. Second Restatement of Torts, § 564, Comment a.

52. Gnapinsky v. Goldyn, 1957, 23 N.J. 243, 128 A.2d 697; Brodsky v. Journal Publishing Co., 1950, 73 S.D. 343, 42 N.W.2d 855; Helmicks v. Stevlingson, 1933, 212 Wis. 614, 250 N.W. 402; Weidman v. Ketcham, 1938, 278 N.Y. 129, 15 N.E.2d 426; Ryan v. Hearst Publications, 1940, 3 Wn.2d 128, 100 P.2d 24. See Yankwich, Certainty in the Law of Defamation, 1954, 1 U.C.L.A.L.Rev. 163; Note, 1947, 12 Mo.L.Rev. 365.

53. Mothersill v. Voliva, 1910, 158 Ill.App. 16; Overstreet v. New Nonpareil Co., 1918, 184 Iowa 485, 167 N.W. 669; Brown v. Journal Newspaper Co., 1914, 219 Mass. 486, 107 N.E. 358; Connell v. A. C. L. Haase & Sons Fish Co., 1923, 302 Mo. 48, 257 S.W. 760; Cosgrove Studio & Camera Shop, Inc. v. Pane, 1962, 408 Pa. 314, 182 A.2d 751.

54. Colvard v. Black, 1900, 110 Ga. 642, 36 S.E. 80; Fitzpatrick v. Age-Herald Publishing Co., 1913, 184 Ala. 510, 63 So. 980; Youssoupoff v. Metro-Goldwyn-Mayer Pictures, 1934, 50 T.L.R. 581, 99 A.L.R. 864.

55. Davis v. R. K. O. Pictures, 8th Cir.1951, 191 F.2d 901.

56. Gnapinsky v. Goldyn, 1957, 23 N.J. 243, 128 A.2d 697.

Group Defamation

Ordinarily, no action lies for the publication of a general condemnation concerning a large group or class of persons, simply because such a general condemnation could not reasonably be regarded as referring to each individual or any particular individual within the group; nor is it calculated to induce the reasonable belief of enough likelihood of its applicability to a particular person to impair or injure such person's reputation. But the size of the class, the nature or generality of the charge, and the extravagance of the accusation are all factors that can have a considerable bearing on whether or not the statement can be said to relate to the plaintiff to the extent of casting enough suspicion on the plaintiff to cause others to believe reasonably that the statement is probably applicable to the plaintiff.

It has been observed that there are in reality at least three separate types of derogatory or defamatory statements about groups.[57]

There is in the first place the general statement—such as the derogatory statement that all lawyers are liars, or a disparaging statement about an entire minority racial group. Such statements are held not to be actionable by individual members of the group or class in the absence of evidence of special circumstances at the time of publication which reasonably give rise to the conclusion that there is particular reference to a particular member.[58] But if the plaintiff is the only lawyer present, or for some other reason, the words are reasonably understood by the hearers or readers to be directed individually at him, the personal application may be made to appear.

Then there is the more specific statement of derogatory conduct about a rather definite number of persons. Here, there is much more likelihood that the statement can reasonably be believed to refer or probably refer to the plaintiff.[59] Some courts seem to require that the statement be susceptible of the reasonable construction of applicability to each member of the group, or at least to the particular plaintiff. Others, and it would seem the preferable view, would be satisfied if a reasonable person would conclude that statement is probably applicable to the plaintiff. The 1962 decision by the Supreme Court of Oklahoma in Fawcett Publications, Inc. v. Morris[60] may, as Eldredge has indicated, become a landmark in American law. There the plaintiff was a fullback on the alternate squad of a football team (composed of 60 or 70 players) that was allegedly using an amphetamine drug to "hop up" football players. A judgment on a verdict for the plaintiff was upheld.

The third type of statement is the kind where only some members of a relatively small group—such as engineers of a particular company or 25 members of the staff—have been accused of specific or discreditable conduct. At one point in time, the statement was made that a right of action was uniformly denied because the statement could not reasonably be regarded as referring to each member of the group, and therefore the person or persons to whom it referred[61] could not be identified. But most courts today would probably take into consideration the circumstances and decide each case on the basis of the magnitude of the suspicion cast on each person in the group.[62] If plaintiff's standing with others could rea-

---

57. Eldredge, The Law of Defamation, 1978, 54.

58. See Second Restatement of Torts, § 564A.

59. Foler v. Curtis Publishing Co., D.C.Cir. 1950, 182 F.2d 377 (60 cab drivers employed by one company—no recovery); Louisville Times v. Stivers, 1934, 252 Ky. 843, 68 S.W.2d 411 ("Stivers clan"—no recovery); Bornmann v. Star Co., 1903, 174 N.Y. 212, 66 N.E. 723 (12 doctors at a hospital—recovery).

60. Okl.1962, 377 P.2d 42, appeal dismissed, certiorari denied 376 U.S. 513, 84 S.Ct. 964, 11 L.Ed.2d 968,

rehearing denied 377 U.S. 925, 84 S.Ct. 1218, 12 L.Ed. 2d 217.

61. Note, Liability for Defamation of a Group, 1934, 34 Colum.L.Rev. 1322, 1327.

62. Hardy v. Williamson, 1891, 86 Ga. 551, 12 S.E. 874 ("some" of 11 engineers employed by one company); Neiman-Marcus Co. v. Lait, S.D.N.Y.1952, 13 F.R.D. 311 (25 salesmen; "most of the sales staff are fairies"); American Broadcasting-Paramount Theatres,

sonably be affected—a jury question—by the likelihood of the applicability of the defamatory conduct to the plaintiff, then it is actionable.

Nonactionable group defamation has been a fertile and dangerous weapon of attack on various racial, religious, and political minorities,[63] and has led to the enactment of criminal statutes in a number of states.[64] Thus far, any civil remedy for such broadside defamation has been lacking.

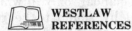
WESTLAW REFERENCES

di defamation
topic(defamation)
defamation /5 means defin! term restatement /s torts /5 558
defamation /s history commonlaw england
defam! /s injunction enjoin!
headnote(defam! /s "first amendment")
headnote(defam! /s free! /s speech)

Definition
restatement /s torts /5 559
defam! libel! slander! /s coward drunkard hypocrite liar scoundrel crook anarchist skunk bastard eunuch "rotten egg" heartless
headnote(defam! libel! slander! /s hatred contempt ridicule)
defam! libel! slander! /s namecalling
defam! libel! slander! /p standard* /s conduct behavior

Who May Be Defamed
defam! libel! slander! /s cause action! /s dead deceased living alive
topic(237) /p abatement survival /p death deceased died

Interpretation: Inducement, Innuendo and Colloquium
headnote(defam! slander! libel! /s innuendo)
defam! slander! libel! /p jest fun irony sarcasm satir! allusion

Inc. v. Simpson, 1962, 106 Ga.App. 230, 126 S.E.2d 873 (one of two).

63. See Riesman, Democracy and Defamation: Control of Group Libel, 1942, 42 Col.L.Rev. 727; Tanenhaus, Group Libel, 1950, 35 Corn.L.Q. 261.

64. See Scott, Criminal Sanctions for Group Libel: Feasibility and Constitutionality, 1951, 1 Duke B.J. 218; Beth, Group Libel and Free Speech, 1955, 39 Minn.L. Rev. 167; Notes, 1947, 42 Col.L.Rev. 727; 1952, 32 Bos. U.L.Rev. 414; 1952, 61 Yale L.J. 252; 1953, 33 Or.L. Rev. 360.

§ 112

1. See supra, § 111.

headnote(defam! slander! libel! /p implication implied**)

Reference to Plaintiff and Defamation of a Group, Including Plaintiff
defam! slander! libel! /p technical! /s pleading* proof prov!

Group Defamation
restatement /s torts /5 564a

§ 112. Libel and Slander

The erratic and anomalous historical development of the law of defamation[1] has led to the survival until the present day of two forms of action for defamatory publications. One is libel, which originally concerned written or printed words; the other slander, which might be, and usually was, of an oral character. Libel was criminal in its origin, and it has remained a common law crime;[2] while slander was never criminal in itself, and could become so only when the words amounted to some other offense, such as sedition, blasphemy, or a breach of the peace.[3] When the two at last met in the common law courts, they tended to become separate rather than united; and since libel was already established as the greater wrong, greater responsibility continued to be attached to it.[4] There is some reason to believe that this was in part at least a conscious effort to rescue a portion of the law of defamation from the morass into which the law of slander had fallen;[5] and no doubt it was encouraged by the reverence of an illiterate nation for the printed word, and its correspondingly greater potentialities for harm. It was accordingly held that some kinds of defamatory words might be actionable without proof

2. See Kelly, Criminal Libel and Free Speech, 1958, 6 Kan.L.Rev. 295; Leflar, The Social Utility of the Criminal Law of Defamation, 1956, 34 Tex.L.Rev. 984.

3. 1 Russell, Crimes, 8th ed. 1923, 983. Some slanderous words, such as those imputing unchastity to a woman, are now made criminal by special statutes in various jurisdictions.

4. Holdsworth, Defamation in the Sixteenth and Seventeenth Centuries, 1925, 41 L.Q.Rev. 13, 16; Kelly, Criminal Libel and Free Speech, 1958, 6 Kan.L.Rev. 295; Note, 1955, 25 U.Chi.L.Rev. 132.

5. 1 Street, Foundations of Legal Liability, 1906, 292.

of any actual damage to the plaintiff if they were written, where such damage must be proved if they were spoken.[6] This remains the chief importance of the distinction. As early as 1812 [7] Sir James Mansfield condemned it as indefensible in principle, but held it to be too well established to be repudiated.

Distinction

The distinction itself between libel and slander is not free from difficulty and uncertainty. As it took form in the seventeenth century, it was one between written and oral words. But later on libel was extended to include pictures,[8] signs,[9] statues,[10] motion pictures,[11] and even conduct carrying a defamatory imputation, such as hanging the plaintiff in effigy,[12] erecting a gallows before his door,[13] dishonoring his valid check drawn upon the defendant's bank,[14] or even, in one Wisconsin case, following him over a considerable period in a conspicuous manner.[15] From this it has been concluded that libel is that which is communicated by the sense of sight, or perhaps also by touch or smell,[16] while slander is that which is conveyed by the sense of hearing. But this certainly does not fit all of the cases, since it seems to be agreed that defamatory gestures or the signals of a deaf-mute are to be regarded as slander only,[17] while matter communicated by sound to be reduced to writing afterwards, as in the case of a telegraph message,[18] or dictation to a stenographer,[19] or even an interview given to a reporter,[20] is considered libel. Furthermore, it is generally held that it is a publication of a libel to read a defamatory writing aloud.[21] This might suggest that the distinction is

6. King v. Lake, 1670, Hardres 470, 145 Eng.Rep. 552; Austin v. Culpepper, 1633, 2 Show.K.B. 313, 89 Eng.Rep. 960; Cillers v. Monsley, 1799, 2 Wils.K.B. 403, 95 Eng.Rep. 886.

7. Thorley v. Lord Kerry, 1812, 4 Taunt. 355, 128 Eng.Rep. 367.

8. Du Bost v. Beresford, 1810, 2 Camp. 511, 170 Eng.Rep. 1235; Francis Mazzera's Case, 1817, 2 N.Y. City Hall Recorder 113; Thayer v. Worcester Post Co., 1933, 284 Mass. 160, 187 N.E. 292; Burton v. Crowell Publishing Co., 2d Cir. 1936, 82 F.2d 154; Dunlop v. Dunlop Rubber Co., [1920] 1 Ir.Rep. 280. See Note, 1938, 33 Ill.L.Rev. 87.

9. See Tarpley v. Blabey, 1836, 2 Bing.N.C. 437, 132 Eng.Rep. 171; Haylock v. Sparke, 1853, 1 El. & Bl. 471, 118 Eng.Rep. 512.

10. Monson v. Tussauds, [1894] 1 Q.B. 671.

11. Merle v. Sociological Research Film Corp., 1915, 166 App.Div. 376, 152 N.Y.S. 829.

12. Eyre v. Garlick, 1878, 42 J.P. 68; Johnson v. Commonwealth, Pa.1888, 14 A. 425, 22 Wkly.Notes Cas. 68.

13. De Libellis Famosis, 1605, 5 Co.Rep. 125a, 77 Eng.Rep. 250; cf. Jefferies v. Duncombe, 1809, 11 East 226, 103 Eng.Rep. 991 (lantern indicating bawdy house); Thompson v. Adelberg & Berman, 1918, 181 Ky. 487, 205 S.W. 558 (collector has called).

14. Svendsen v. State Bank of Duluth, 1896, 64 Minn. 40, 65 N.W. 1086; Cox v. National Loan & Exchange Bank, 1927, 138 S.C. 381, 136 S.E. 637; Gatley, Libel and Slander, 2d ed. 1929, 19. See, 1930, 9 North Car.L.Rev. 94.

15. Schultz v. Frankfort Marine, Accident & Plate Glass Insurance Co., 1913, 151 Wis. 537, 139 N.W. 386. See Note, 1920, 5 Corn.L.Q. 340. Accord, Varner v. Morton, 1919, 53 Nova Scotia 180, 10 B.R.C. 218 (charivari). Contra, under statute, Collins v. Oklahoma State Hospital, 1919, 76 Okl. 229, 184 P. 946 (placing white person in colored ward). Cf. Molt v. Public Indemnity Co., 1940, 10 N.J.Misc. 879, 161 A. 346 (insurance investigation held to be "continuing slander").

16. As in the case of a blind person reading Braille, or feeling a defamatory statue? Or one spraying the plaintiff with a malodorous liquid, with a defamatory imputation?

17. Bennett v. Norban, 1959, 396 Pa. 94, 151 A.2d 476 (searching pockets on the street); Lonardo v. Quaranta, 1964, 99 R.I. 70, 205 A.2d 837 (omitting name of daughter from obituary notice). See Lord Abinger, in Gustole v. Mathers, 1836, 1 M. & W. 495, 501, 150 Eng.Rep. 530; Lord Ellenborough, in Cook v. Cox, 1814, 3 M. & S. 110, 114, 105 Eng.Rep. 552; Bower, Actionable Defamation, 2d ed. 1923, 20–21; Restatement of Torts, § 568, Comment *d*.

18. Peterson v. Western Union Telegraph Co., 1896, 65 Minn. 18, 67 N.W. 646; Peterson v. Western Union Telegraph Co., 1898, 72 Minn. 41, 74 N.W. 1022; 1899, 75 Minn. 368, 77 N.W. 985. See Smith, Liability of a Telegraph Company for Transmitting a Defamatory Message, 1920, 20 Col.L.Rev. 30, 44–46.

19. See infra, Section 113 on Publication.

20. Valentine v. Gonzalez, 1920, 190 App.Div. 490, 179 N.Y.S. 711.

21. Bander v. Metropolitan Life Insurance Co., 1943, 313 Mass. 337, 47 N.E.2d 595; Ohio Public Service Co. v. Myers, 1934, 54 Ohio App. 40, 6 N.E.2d 29; Miller v. Donovan, 1896, 16 Misc. 453, 39 N.Y.S. 820; McCoombs v. Tuttle, Ind.1840, 5 Blackf. 431; Adams v. Lawson, 1867, 58 Va. (17 Grat.) 250. Cf. Hartmann v. Winchell, 1947, 296 N.Y. 296, 73 N.E.2d 30.

one of embodiment in some more or less permanent physical form, and frequently it is so stated. There has been semihumorous speculation as to a phonograph record, or words taught to a parrot,[22] but the cases have not arisen.

The unexpected advent of new methods of communication has left the courts struggling with the distinction. They have found no difficulty in holding that the sound in a "talking" picture is libel, since it accompanies and is identified with the film itself.[23] Defamation by radio and television is, however, still a subject of violent debate.[24] It has been considered by comparatively few courts, and held by some to be libel,[25] by one slander,[26] by others to be libel if the broadcaster reads from a script,[27] but slander if he does not; while still others apparently have regarded it as having special characteristics half way between the two,[28] and one court has even coined a barbarous new word, "defamacast," to avoid calling it either.[29]

Television obviously will follow radio,[30] wherever radio may be going, rather than an analogy to motion pictures.

In the Second Restatement, it is said that libel consists in the publication of defamatory matters by (1) written or printed words, (2) its embodiment in physical form, or (3) any other form of communication which has the potentially harmful qualities characteristic of written or printed words. It is then said that (1) the area of dissemination, (2) the deliberate and premeditated character of its publication, and (3) the persistence of the defamatory conduct are factors to be considered on whether or not the form of communication has the potentially harmful qualities characteristic of written or printed words. The position is also taken by a special section that broadcasting of defamatory matter by means of radio or television is libel, whether or not it is read from a manuscript, for the reason that such defamacast has the potentially harmful qualities characteristic

---

22. 1935, 51 L.Q.Rev. 281–283, 573, 574; Winfield, Law of Tort, 1937, 259. See A.P. Herbert, Uncommon Law, 1936, 43–48 ("the law is clear"—but owing to the sudden demise of Lord Goat, it is not clear in what direction it is clear).

23. Youssoupoff v. Metro-Goldwyn-Mayer Pictures, 1934, 50 T.L.R. 581, 51 L.Q.Rev. 281; Brown v. Paramount Publix Corp., 1934, 240 App.Div. 520, 270 N.Y.S. 544; Kelly v. Loew's, Inc., D.Mass.1948, 76 F.Supp. 473.

24. See Donnelly, Defamation by Radio: A Reconsideration, 1948, 34 Iowa L.Rev. 12; Yankwich, Trends in the Law Affecting Media of Communication, 1954, 15 F.R.D. 291; Notes, 1935, 51 L.Q.Rev. 573; 1938, 23 Wash.U.L.Q. 262; 1938, 26 Geo.L.J. 475; 1941, 39 Mich.L.Rev. 1002; 1942, 25 Chicago-Kent L.Rev. 142; 1947, 33 Va.L.Rev. 612; 1957, 43 Corn.L.Q. 320; 1961, 33 Miss.L.J. 33; 1964, 2 Houst.L.Rev. 238; 1964, 15 Mercer L.Rev. 450.

25. Sorensen v. Wood, 1932, 123 Neb. 348, 243 N.W. 82, appeal dismissed 290 U.S. 599, 54 S.Ct. 209, 78 L.Ed. 527; Coffey v. Midland Broadcasting Co., D.Mo. 1934, 8 F.Supp. 889; Wanamaker v. Lewis, D.D.C.1959, 173 F.Supp. 126; Shor v. Billingsley, Sup.1956, 4 Misc. 2d 857, 158 N.Y.S.2d 476, affirmed without opinion 1957, 4 A.D.2d 1017, 169 N.Y.S.2d 416. The English Defamation Act of 1952, 15 & 16 Geo. 6 & 1 Eliz. 2, ch. 66, cl. 1–2, makes such defamation libel.

26. Meldrum v. Australian Broadcasting Co., [1932] Vict.L.Rep. 425, [1932] Aust.L.Rep. 452.

27. Hartmann v. Winchell, 1947, 296 N.Y. 296, 73 N.E.2d 30; Hryhorijiv v. Winchell, 1943, 180 Misc. 574,

45 N.Y.S.2d 31, affirmed 1944, 267 App.Div. 817, 47 N.Y.S.2d 102; Gibler v. Houston Post Co., Tex.Civ.App. 1958, 310 S.W.2d 377, refused n.r.e.; Charles Parker Co. v. Silver City Crystal Co., 1955, 142 Conn. 605, 116 A.2d 440. Cf. Weglein v. Golder, 1935, 317 Pa. 437, 177 A. 47 (script sent to newspapers).

The distinction makes no great amount of sense, when the listener does not know whether there is a script. See the vigorous concurring opinion of Fuld, J., in Hartmann v. Winchell, supra. What if the defendant falsely says "I am reading you a letter," etc.?

28. Summit Hotel Co. v. National Broadcasting Co., 1939, 336 Pa. 182, 8 A.2d 302; Kelly v. Hoffman, 1948, 137 N.J.L. 695, 61 A.2d 143; Irwin v. Ashurst, 1938, 158 Or. 61, 74 P.2d 1127. See Newhouse, Defamation by Radio: A New Tort, 1938, 17 Or.L.Rev. 314; Note, 1933, 12 Or.L.Rev. 149.

Other courts have avoided the issue, as in Lynch v. Lyons, 1939, 303 Mass. 116, 20 N.E.2d 953; Miles v. Louis Wasmer, Inc., 172 Wash. 466, 20 P.2d 847; Singler v. Journal Co., 1935, 218 Wis. 263, 260 N.W. 431.

29. American Broadcasting-Paramount Theatres, Inc. v. Simpson, 1962, 106 Ga.App. 230, 126 S.E.2d 873. The defendant was held liable, however, as if there were libel.

30. Remington v. Bentley, S.D.N.Y.1949, 88 F.Supp. 166 (held to be slander in the absence of a script); Landau v. Columbia Broadcasting System, 1954, 205 Misc. 357, 128 N.Y.S.2d 254, affirmed 1 A.D.2d 660, 147 N.Y.S.2d 687 (libel with a script).

of the written or printed word which has historically been regarded as libel.[31]

In England, the Defamation Act of 1952 provides that the broadcasting of words by means of wireless telegraphy shall be treated as publication in permanent form or libel.[32] Several states have enacted statutes on this subject in the United States. They vary greatly. There has not been much activity in this area in recent years.

Slander Actionable Without Proof of Damage

The reluctance with which the common law courts at first received the action of slander, and their fear of invading the province of ecclesiastical law, led them to hold that the action would not lie without proof of "temporal" damage. From this there developed the rule that slander, in general, is not actionable unless actual damage is proved. To this the courts very early established certain specific exceptions: the imputation of crime, of a loathsome disease, and those affecting the plaintiff in his business, trade, profession, office or calling—which required no proof of damage. The exact origin of these exceptions is in some doubt, but probably it was nothing more unusual than a recognition that by their nature such words were especially likely to cause pecuniary, or "temporal," rather than "spiritual" loss.[33] Modern statutes and decisions have added a fourth category, the imputation of unchastity to a woman. For these four kinds of slander, no proof of any actual harm to reputation or any other damage is required for the recovery of either nominal[34] or substantial[35] damages. Otherwise stated, proof of the defamation itself is considered to establish the existence of some damages, and the jury is permitted, without other evidence, to estimate their amount.

1. *Crime.* The original basis of the exception as to words imputing crime seems to have been that the plaintiff was thereby placed in danger of criminal prosecution.[36] Hence the rule that accusations of the mere intent to commit a crime are not sufficient,[37] and that crimes not recognized by the law, as in the case of larceny of land,[38] are not included. With the passage of time, the emphasis shifted to the social ostracism involved, and it was held that the action lay without proof of damage although the words made it clear that the plaintiff had been punished[39] or pardoned,[40] or could not be punished,[41] or that prosecution was barred by the statute of limitations.[42]

---

31. Second Restatement of Torts, § 568A.

32. 1952, 15 & 16 Geo. 6 & 1 Eliz. 2, C. 66, Sec. 16(3).

33. Holdsworth, Defamation in the Sixteenth and Seventeenth Centuries, 1924, 40 L.Q.Rev. 302, 397, 398–401. Thus as late as 1851 the Exchequer was still talking of "spiritual" damage, and denying recovery for slander of a clergyman on the ground that no "temporal" damage was proved. Gallwey v. Marshall, 1851, 9 Ex. 294, 156 Eng.Rep. 126.

34. Mayo v. Goldman, 1909, 57 Tex.Civ.App. 475, 122 S.W. 499; Wilson v. Sun Publishing Co., 1915, 85 Wash. 503, 148 P. 774.

35. Taylor v. Gumpert, 1910, 96 Ark. 354, 131 S.W. 968; Ventresca v. Kissner, 1927, 105 Conn. 533, 136 A. 90. Even evidence that no actual damage was suffered goes only to mitigate the damages recovered. First National Bank of Forrest City v. N.R. McFall & Co., 1920, 144 Ark. 149, 222 S.W. 40.

36. Heming v. Power, 1842, 10 M. & W. 564, 569, 152 Eng.Rep. 595; 1 Street, Foundations of Legal Liability, 1906, 279.

37. Fanning v. Chace, 1891, 17 R.I. 388, 22 A. 275. Cf. Stees v. Kemble, 1858, 27 Pa. 112; Stokes v. Arey, 1860, 53 N.C. (8 Jones) 66.

38. Ogden v. Riley, 1833, 14 N.J.L. 186; Jackson v. Adams, 1835, 2 Bing.N.C. 402, 132 Eng.Rep. 158; Lemon v. Simmons, 1888, 57 L.J.Q.B. 260; Barnes v. Crawford, 1894, 115 N.C. 76, 20 S.E. 386. This although the speaker intends to charge the commission of a crime, and is understood to do so. Such a statement, if in writing, may be libel. Dooley v. Press Publishing Co., 1915, 170 App.Div. 492, 156 N.Y.S. 381, affirmed 1954, 224 N.Y. 640, 121 N.E. 865; Note, 1916, 29 Harv. L.Rev. 857.

39. Fowler v. Dowdney, 1838, 2 Moo. & Rob. 119, 174 Eng.Rep. 234; Krebs v. Oliver, 1858, 78 Mass. (12 Gray) 239; Wiley v. Campbell, 1827, 5 T.B.Mon., 21 Ky. 396; Smith v. Stewart, 1847, 5 Pa. 372.

40. Shipp v. McCraw, 1819, 7 N.C. 463.

41. Thus as to infancy, Stewart v. Howe, 1855, 17 Ill. 71; Chambers v. White, 1855, 47 N.C. (2 Jones) 383.

42. Van Ankin v. Westfall, N.Y.1817, 14 Johns. 233; Brightman v. Davies, 1925, 3 N.J.Misc. 113, 127 A. 327. Cf. French v. Creath, 1820, 1 Ill. 31 (statute creating

With the extension of criminal punishment to many minor offenses, it was obviously necessary to make some distinction as to the character of the crime, since a charge of a traffic violation, for example, would not exclude a person from society, and today would do little, if any, harm to his reputation at all. The English courts arrived at the rule that the crime must be one subject to corporal punishment, which in practice now means death or imprisonment.[43] The American jurisdictions, in general, began by adding the requirement that it must be subject to indictment, either at common law or by statute.[44] This is obviously a poor test, since it makes the decision turn upon the eccentricities of the criminal procedure provided by the legislature; and with the general modern tendency to substitute the information for the indictment, it has now very largely passed from the picture. Other courts, following an early New York case,[45] have required that, even though indictable, the offense must be one that involves an "infamous" or "disgraceful" punishment.[46] The vagaries of criminal punishments have made this too unreliable. The formula upon which most courts are now agreed is that the crime must be one which involves "moral turpitude."[47] A number of courts require this alone, without the possibility of an indictment or infamous punishment;[48] the greater number, however, state it as an alternative to one or the other.[49] Neither infamous punishment nor moral turpitude has received more than the vaguest definition; the former seems to mean death or imprisonment,[50] while the latter is said to refer to "inherent baseness or vileness of principle in the human heart."[51] It seems clear that it is not always the crime, but rather the character of the act charged, which will be determinative. It is not every trivial assault or battery which involves "moral turpitude," but an accusation that the plaintiff beat his mother necessarily does so.[52]

The idea toward which the courts obviously have been struggling is that the imputation is to be actionable without proof of damages only if it involves a major social disgrace, which might very well be the ultimate test. On this basis, it has been held that the character of the crime is to be determined by the law of the place where the defamatory statement is heard, rather than where the crime is alleged to have been committed.[53]

---

offense repealed); Tenney v. Clement, 1838, 10 N.H. 52 (person asserted to have been murdered alive).

43. Hellwig v. Mitchell, [1910] 1 K.B. 609.

44. Brooker v. Coffin, N.Y.1809, 5 Johns. 188; Birch v. Benton, 1858, 26 Mo. 153; Tharp v. Nolan, 1905, 119 Ky. 870, 84 S.W. 1168; Herzog v. Campbell, 1896, 47 Neb. 370, 66 N.W. 424; Cullen v. Stough, 1917, 258 Pa. 196, 101 A. 937.

45. Brooker v. Coffin, N.Y.1809, 5 Johns. 188.

46. Blake v. Smith, 1896, 19 R.I. 476, 34 A. 995; Deese v. Collins, 1926, 191 N.C. 749, 133 S.E. 92; McKee v. Wilson, 1882, 87 N.C. 300; Stevens v. Wilber, 1931, 136 Or. 599, 300 P. 329.

47. Wooten v. Martin, 1910, 140 Ky. 781, 131 S.W. 783; Morris v. Evans, 1918, 22 Ga.App. 11, 95 S.E. 385; Ranger v. Goodrich, 1863, 17 Wis. 78; Murray v. McAllister, 1856, 38 Vt. 167; Walker v. Tucker, 1927, 220 Ky. 363, 295 S.W. 138, 53 A.L.R. 547.

48. Larson v. R.B. Wrigley Co., 1931, 183 Minn. 28, 235 N.W. 393; Brown v. Nickerson, 1855, 71 Mass. (5 Gray) 1; Halley v. Gregg, 1888, 74 Iowa 563, 38 N.W. 416; Kelly v. Flaherty, 1888, 16 R.I. 234, 14 A. 876.

49. Amick v. Montross, 1928, 206 Iowa 51, 220 N.W. 51; Woodville v. Pizatti, 1919, 119 Miss. 85, 80 So. 491; Shaw v. Killingsworth, 1925, 213 Ala. 655, 106 So. 138; Barnett v. Phelps, 1920, 97 Or. 242, 191 P. 502; Cline v. Holdredge, 1931, 122 Neb. 151, 239 N.W. 639.

50. See Earley v. Winn, 1906, 129 Wis. 291, 109 N.W. 633; Mackin v. United States, 1886, 117 U.S. 348, 6 S.Ct. 777, 29 L.Ed. 909; Geary v. Bennett, 1881, 53 Wis. 444, 10 N.W. 602; Note, 1922, 8 Corn.L.Q. 50.

51. Hughey v. Bradrick, 1931, 39 Ohio App. 486, 177 N.E. 911; Sipp v. Coleman, D.N.J.1910, 179 F. 997; Amick v. Montross, 1928, 206 Iowa 51, 220 N.W. 51; In re Henry, 1909, 15 Idaho 755, 99 P. 1054; In re Hopkins, 1909, 54 Wash. 569, 103 P. 805; Note, 1928, 12 Minn.L.Rev. 172.

As to particular crimes, see Hughey v. Bradrick, 1931, 39 Ohio App. 486, 177 N.E. 911 (theft); Pett-Morgan v. Kennedy, 1895, 62 Minn. 348, 64 N.W. 912 (habitual drunkenness); Le Moine v. Spicer, 1941, 146 Fla. 758, 1 So.2d 730 (same); Stevens v. Wilber, 1931, 136 Or. 599, 300 P. 329 ("bootlegger"); but cf. Bartos v. United States District Court, 8th Cir. 1927, 19 F.2d 722 (violation of National Prohibition Act).

52. Sipp v. Coleman, D.N.J.1910, 179 F. 997.

53. Klumph v. Dunn, 1870, 66 Pa. 141; Shipp v. McCraw, 1819, 7 N.C. 463. Contra: Dufresne v. Weise,

If these requirements are met, no particular form of language is necessary to liability. Technical precision as to the particular crime is not called for,[54] and "thief" is enough,[55] as are slang synonyms, such as "pimp"[56] or "bootlegger."[57] It is not even necessary that the commission of any particular crime be charged at all, so long as it is said that the defendant has done something which meets the test; and a "deed without a name," such as "I know enough to put him in jail"[58] will be sufficient.

2. *Loathsome disease.* The basis of the exception as to the imputation of a loathsome disease seems originally to have been the exclusion from society which would result.[59] From the beginning it was limited to cases of venereal disease,[60] with a few instances of leprosy,[61] and it was not applied to more contagious and equally repugnant disorders such as smallpox.[62] The basis of the distinction was in all probability the fact that syphilis and leprosy were regarded originally as permanent, lingering and incurable, while from smallpox one either recovered or died in short order. The advance of medical science tended to keep the exception within its original limits; and today accusations of insanity[63] or of tuberculosis[64] or other communicable diseases[65] are not included. Furthermore, since there would not be the same social avoidance of one who had recovered, it is well established that the imputation that the plaintiff has had even a venereal disease in the past is not sufficient without proof of damage.[66]

3. *Business, trade, profession or office.* "The law has always been very tender of the reputation of tradesmen, and therefore words spoken of them in the way of their trade will bear an action that will not be ac-

---

1879, 46 Wis. 290, 1 N.W. 59; Kinney v. Hosea, Del. 1839, 3 Harr. 77.

54. Bihler v. Gockley, 1886, 18 Ill.App. 496; Garrett v. Dickerson, 1863, 19 Md. 418; Seller v. Jenkins, 1884, 97 Ind. 430; Payne v. Tancil, 1900, 98 Va. 262, 35 S.E. 725.

55. O'Cana v. Espinosa, 1960, 141 Colo. 371, 347 P.2d 1118; Robins v. Franks, 1601, Cro.Eliz. 857, 78 Eng.Rep. 1083; cf. Tennyson v. Werthman, 1958, 167 Neb. 208, 92 N.W.2d 559 ("kidnaper").

56. Lander v. Wald, 1926, 218 App.Div. 514, 219 N.Y.S. 57, affirmed 1927, 245 N.Y. 590, 157 N.E. 870. Cf. Toal v. Zito, 1958, 11 Misc.2d 260, 171 N.Y.S.2d 393 ("confidence man").

57. Kammerer v. Sachs, 1928, 131 Misc. 640, 227 N.Y.S. 641; Stevens v. Wilber, 1931, 136 Or. 599, 300 P. 329.

58. Webb v. Beaven, 1883, 11 Q.B.D. 699; Johnson v. Shields, 1855, 25 N.J.L. 116. Accord (and doubtful): Munafo v. Helfand, S.D.N.Y.1956, 140 F.Supp. 234 ("a known criminal"). Cf. Lorillard v. Field Enterprises, Inc., 1965, 65 Ill.App.2d 65, 213 N.E.2d 1 (suit against plaintiff for bigamy).

On the other hand, "You should be jailed" was held insufficient in Tex Smith, The Harmonica Man v. Godfrey, 1951, 198 Misc. 1006, 102 N.Y.S.2d 251. And "You have a criminal record" was obviously insufficient in Riley v. Baddour, Sup.1947, 73 N.Y.S.2d 140.

59. See Crittal v. Horner, 1619, Hob. 219, 80 Eng. Rep. 366; Taylor v. Hall, 1743, 2 Stra. 1189, 93 Eng. Rep. 1118; Carlslake v. Mapledoram, 1788, 2 Term Rep. 473, 100 Eng.Rep. 255.

60. Crittal v. Horner, 1619, Hob. 219, 80 Eng.Rep. 366; Smith v. Hobson, 1647, Style 112, 82 Eng.Rep. 571; Kaucher v. Blinn, 1875, 29 Ohio St. 62; McDonald v. Nugent, 1904, 122 Iowa 651, 98 N.W. 506; Sally v. Brown, 1927, 220 Ky. 576, 295 S.W. 890.

61. Taylor v. Perkins, 1607, Cro.Jac. 144, 79 Eng. Rep. 126; Lewis v. Hayes, 1913, 165 Cal. 527, 132 P. 1022; Simpson v. Press Publishing Co., 1900, 33 Misc. 228, 67 N.Y.S. 401. There is occasional mention in the decisions of the plague, but no case seems to have been reported.

62. James v. Rutledge, 1599, Moore 573, 4 Co.Rep. 17a, 76 Eng.Rep. 900.

63. Count Joannes v. Burt, 1863, 88 Mass. (6 Allen) 236. As to the history of that extraordinary litigant, the "Count" Joannes, see Browne, Count Johannes, 1896, 8 Green Bag 435. Cf. Barry v. Baugh, 1965, 111 Ga.App. 813, 143 S.E.2d 489 ("crazy").

64. Rade v. Press Publishing Co., 1902, 37 Misc. 254, 75 N.Y.S. 298; Kassowitz v. Sentinel Co., 1938, 226 Wis. 468, 277 N.W. 177. Contra, under statute, Brown v. McCann, 1927, 36 Ga.App. 812, 138 S.E. 247; and cf. Kirby v. Smith, 1929, 54 S.D. 608, 224 N.W. 230 (affecting employment).

65. Lowe v. De Hoog, Mo.App.1917, 193 S.W. 969 ("a bad" communicable disease). Cf. Cobb v. Tinsley, 1922, 195 Ky. 781, 243 S.W. 1009 (bed wetting). In Miles v. Record Publishing Co., 1926, 134 S.C. 462, 133 S.E. 99, a statement that plaintiff was a typhoid carrier was held to be libel per se; but this was in part on the basis of interference with plaintiff's business.

66. Smith's Case, 1604, Noy 151, 74 Eng.Rep. 1112; Taylor v. Hall, 1743, 2 Stra. 1189, 93 Eng.Rep. 1118; Bruce v. Soule, 1879, 69 Me. 562; Nichols v. Guy, 1850, 2 Ind. 82; Halls v. Mitchell, [1927] 1 Dom.L.Rep. 163.

tionable in the case of another person." [67] The likelihood of "temporal" damage in such a case is sufficiently obvious; and the rule was soon extended to cover anyone engaged in a business [68] or profession, or holding a public [69] or even a private office.[70] Any calling is included, "be it ever so base," [71] but it must be a legal one, entitled to such a sanction.[72] Furthermore, since the object of the exception is to protect the plaintiff in his office or calling, it was decided quite early that it must appear that he held or was engaged in it, or at least about to be so engaged, when the words complained of were published.[73]

For the same reason, the exception was limited to defamation of a kind incompatible with the proper conduct of the business, trade, profession or office itself. The statement must be made with reference to a matter of significance and importance for that purpose, rather than a more general reflection upon the plaintiff's character or qualities, where such special significance is lacking.[74] Thus it is actionable without proof of damage to say of a physician that he is a butcher and the speaker would not have him for a dog,[75] of an attorney that he is a shyster,[76] of a school teacher that he has been guilty of improper conduct as to his pupils,[77] of a clergyman that he is the subject of scandalous rumors,[78] of a chauffeur that he is habitually drinking,[79] of a merchant that his credit is bad [80] or that he sells adulterated goods,[81] of a public officer that he has accepted a bribe or has used his office for cor-

---

67. Harman v. Delany, 1731, 2 Strange 898, 93 Eng. Rep. 925. See, generally, Lawson, The Slander of a Person in His Calling, 1881, 15 Am.L.Rev. 573.

68. In Carter v. Sterling Finance Co., Fla.App.1961, 132 So.2d 430, an allegation of interference with "business relations" was held to be sufficient, without specifying the business.

69. Foley v. Hoffman, 1947, 188 Md. 273, 52 A.2d 476; Correia v. Santos, 1961, 191 Cal.App.2d 844, 13 Cal.Rptr. 132. See Note, 1942, 51 Yale L.J. 693.

70. It has been held in England that the mere imputation of lack of ability in connection with an honorary office, as distinguished from one of profit, is not actionable without proof of damage. Alexander v. Jenkins, [1892] 1 Q.B. 797. Otherwise as to misconduct in office. Booth v. Arnold, [1895] 1 Q.B. 571. The American cases apparently have not distinguished in any way between offices of honor and of profit. Doherty v. Lynett, C.C.Pa.1907, 155 F. 681; Fitzgerald v. Piette, 1923, 180 Wis. 625, 193 N.W. 86; Maidman v. Jewish Publications, Inc., 1960, 54 Cal.2d 643, 7 Cal.Rptr. 617, 355 P.2d 265; Correia v. Santos, 1961, 191 Cal.App.2d 844, 13 Cal.Rptr. 132; Dietrich v. Hauser, 1965, 45 Misc.2d 805, 257 N.Y.S.2d 716.

71. Terry v. Hooper, 1663, 1 Lev. 115, 83 Eng.Rep. 325. Accord: Fitzgerald v. Redfield, N.Y.1868, 51 Barb. 484 (mason); Burtch v. Nickerson, N.Y.1819, 17 Johns. 217 (blacksmith); Lloyd v. Harris, 1923, 156 Minn. 85, 194 N.W. 101 (tenant farmer); cf. Hoeppner v. Dunkirk Printing Co., 1930, 254 N.Y. 95, 172 N.E. 139 (football coach).

72. Hunt v. Bell, 1822, 1 Bing. 1, 130 Eng.Rep.1; Hargan v. Purdy, 1892, 93 Ky. 424, 20 S.W. 432; Williams v. New York Herald Co., 1914, 165 App.Div. 529, 150 N.Y.S. 838, dismissed 1916, 218 N.Y. 625, 112 N.E. 1079; Weltmer v. Bishop, 1902, 171 Mo. 110, 71 S.W. 167, dismissed 191 U.S. 560, 24 S.Ct. 848, 48 L.Ed. 302.

73. Collis v. Malin, 1632, Cro.Car. 282, 79 Eng.Rep. 847; Gallwey v. Marshall, 1851, 9 Ex. 294, 156 Eng. Rep. 126; Forward v. Adams, N.Y.1831, 7 Wend. 204.

74. See Second Restatement of Torts, § 573; Ireland v. McGarvish, N.Y.1847, 3 Super. (1 Sandf.) 155. Thus in Bruno v. Schukart, 1958, 12 Misc.2d 383, 177 N.Y.S.2d 51, "liar" and "no-good crook" were held not to meet the test, in the absence of some showing that they would affect the plaintiff's business.

75. Cruikshank v. Gorden, 1890, 118 N.Y. 178, 23 N.E. 457. Accord: Crane v. Darling, 1899, 71 Vt. 295, 44 A. 359; Depew v. Robinson, 1883, 95 Ind. 109; Elmergreen v. Horn, 1902, 115 Wis. 385, 91 N.W. 973.

76. Rush v. Cavenaugh, 1845, 2 Pa. 187; Nolan v. Standard Publishing Co., 1923, 67 Mont. 212, 216 P. 571; Kraushaar v. LeVin, 1943, 181 Misc. 508, 42 N.Y.S.2d 857 ("unethical"). Accord: Mains v. Whiting, 1891, 87 Mich. 172, 49 N.W. 559; Patangall v. Mooers, 1915, 113 Me. 412, 94 A. 561.

77. Thompson v. Bridges, 1925, 209 Ky. 710, 273 S.W. 529. Accord: Bray v. Callihan, 1900, 155 Mo. 43, 55 S.W. 865; Wertz v. Lawrence, 1919, 66 Colo. 55, 179 P. 813; Cavarnos v. Kokkinak, 1959, 338 Mass. 355, 155 N.E.2d 185 (introducing Communist literature into school).

78. Cobbs v. Chicago Defender, 1941, 308 Ill.App. 55, 31 N.E.2d 323.

79. Louisville Taxicab & Transfer Co. v. Ingle, 1929, 229 Ky. 518, 17 S.W.2d 709.

80. Jones v. Littler, 1841, 7 M. & W. 423, 151 Eng. Rep. 831; Fred v. Traylor, 1903, 115 Ky. 94, 72 S.W. 768; Phillips v. Hoefer, 1845, 1 Pa. 62; Walter v. Duncan, Sup.1956, 153 N.Y.S.2d 916 ("You never pay your bills"); Meyerson v. Hurlbut, 1938, 68 App.D.C. 360, 98 F.2d 232, certiorari denied 305 U.S. 610, 59 S.Ct. 69, 83 L.Ed. 388.

81. Mowry v. Raabe, 1891, 89 Cal. 606, 27 P. 157; Blumhardt v. Rohr, 1889, 70 Md. 328, 17 A. 266; Singer

rupt purposes,[82] or that he is a Communist,[83] or of any of these that he is dishonest,[84] incompetent,[85] or insane [86]—since these things obviously discredit him in his chosen calling.

On the other hand it has been held not to be actionable without proof of damage to say of a gas company clerk that he has been consorting with prostitutes,[87] since he might still be a satisfactory clerk; or of a stenographer that she does not pay her bills,[88] since she might still be a good stenographer; or of a physician that he has committed adultery,[89] of a dancing teacher that he has been drunk,[90] of an attorney that he has lost thousands,[91] or of an engineer that he is a Communist,[92] or of a Congressman and that he is anti-Semitic.[93] Sometimes this has been carried to ridiculous lengths, as in the case of the decision [94] that an attorney is not defamed in his profession by being called a "bum in a gin mill." The effect of a charge that the plaintiff is insolvent, illiterate, a coward or has been seen drunk, may depend upon whether he is a merchant, a professor, a solider, or a clergyman.[95] An accusation of a single act of misconduct may not be sufficient, since one mistake does not amount to incompetence,[96] but if it fairly imputes either habitual conduct or a lack of qualities which the public has a right to expect of the plaintiff in his calling, it may be actionable.[97]

4. *Unchastity.* An accusation of unchastity was at first regarded as purely a "spiritual matter"—that is, a sin—and so was not

v. Bender, 1885, 64 Wis. 169, 24 N.W. 903. As to the distinction between defamation of the person and disparagement of the goods, see Wham, Disparagement of Property, 1926, 21 Ill.L.Rev. 26; Hibschman, Defamation or Disparagement, 1940, 24 Minn.L.Rev. 625; infra, § 108.

82. Earle v. Johnson, 1900, 81 Minn. 472, 84 N.W. 332; Heller v. Duff, 1898, 62 N.J.L. 101, 40 A. 691; Gottbehuet v. Hubachek, 1875, 36 Wis. 515; Reilly v. Curtiss, 1912, 83 N.J.L. 77, 84 A. 199; Jarman v. Rea, 1902, 137 Cal. 339, 70 P. 216.

83. Remington v. Bentley, S.D.N.Y.1949, 88 F.Supp. 166.

84. Correia v. Santos, 1961, 191 Cal.App.2d 844, 13 Cal.Rptr. 132 (private office); Lendino v. Fiorenza, 1952, 203 Misc. 115, 115 N.Y.S.2d 160 (attorney); Badame v. Lampke, 1955, 242 N.C. 755, 89 S.E.2d 466 (business person); Fitzgerald v. Piette, 1923, 180 Wis. 625, 193 N.W. 86 (trustee of church); Wallace v. Jameson, 1897, 179 Pa. 98, 36 A. 142; Noeninger v. Vogt, 1886, 88 Mo. 589.

85. Stevens v. Morse, 1925, 185 Wis. 500, 201 N.W. 815 (farm labor organizer said to be utterly ignorant of farming); MacInnis v. National Herald Printing Co., 1918, 140 Minn. 171, 167 N.W. 550 (office holder said not to be a citizen, where this necessary to eligibility); Foley v. Hoffman, 1947, 188 Md. 273, 52 A.2d 476 (incapacity for office held); Fitzgerald v. Redfield, N.Y. 1868, 51 Barb. 484; Hellstern v. Katzer, 1899, 103 Wis. 391, 79 N.W. 429.

86. Fitzgerald v. Young, 1911, 89 Neb. 693, 132 N.W. 127; Wertz v. Lawrence, 1919, 66 Colo. 55, 179 P. 813; Clifford v. Cochrane, 1882, 10 Ill.App. 570; Lynott v. Pearson, 1910, 138 App.Div. 306, 122 N.Y.S. 986.

87. Lumby v. Allday, 1831, 1 C. & J. 301, 148 Eng. Rep. 1434. See also Buck v. Savage, Tex.Civ.App.1959, 323 S.W.2d 363, refused n.r.e. (homosexuality attributed to druggist).

88. Liebel v. Montgomery Ward & Co., 1936, 103 Mont. 370, 62 P.2d 667.

89. Ayre v. Craven, 1834, 2 Ad. & El. 2, 111 Eng. Rep. 1. Accord: Jones v. Jones, [1916] 2 A.C. 481. Cf. Ireland v. McGarvish, N.Y.1847, 3 Super. (1 Sandf.) 155; Redway v. Gray, 1859, 31 Vt. 292; Dallavo v. Snider, 1906, 143 Mich. 542, 107 N.W. 271; Vinson v. O'Malley, 1923, 25 Ariz. 552, 220 P. 393.

90. Buck v. Hersey, 1850, 31 Me. 558.

91. Dauncey v. Holloway, [1901] 2 K.B. 441. Cf. Doyley v. Roberts, 1837, 3 Bing.N.C. 835, 132 Eng.Rep. 632 (defrauded his creditors and was horsewhipped off the course at Doncaster).

92. Gurtler v. Union Parts Manufacturing Co., 1955, 285 App.Div. 643, 140 N.Y.S.2d 254, motion dismissed 286 App.Div. 832, 143 N.Y.S.2d 627, affirmed 1956, 1 N.Y.2d 5, 150 N.Y.S.2d 4, 132 N.E.2d 889.

93. Sweeney v. Philadelphia Record Co., 3d Cir. 1942, 126 F.2d 53; Sweeney v. Patterson, D.C.Cir. 1942, 128 F.2d 457, certiorari denied 317 U.S. 678, 63 S.Ct. 160, 87 L.Ed. 544.

94. Weidberg v. La Guardia, 1939, 170 Misc. 374, 10 N.Y.S.2d 445.

95. Cf. Winsette v. Hunt, 1899, 53 S.W. 522, 21 Ky. Law Rep. 922; Darling v. Clement, 1897, 69 Vt. 292, 37 A. 779; Hayner v. Cowden, 1875, 27 Ohio St. 292; Boling v. Clinton Cotton Mills, 1932, 163 S.C. 13, 161 S.E. 195; Cobbs v. Chicago Defender, 1941, 308 Ill.App. 55, 31 N.E.2d 323.

96. Camp v. Martin, 1854, 23 Conn. 86; Foot v. Brown, N.Y.1811, 8 Johns. 64.

97. Secor v. Harris, N.Y.1854, 18 Barb. 425; Sumner v. Utley, 1829, 7 Conn. 257; Amick v. Montross, 1928, 206 Iowa 51, 220 N.W. 51. Charges of repeated misconduct nearly always have been held sufficient, as in High v. Supreme Lodge of the World, 1943, 214 Minn. 164, 7 N.W.2d 675; Dickey v. Brannon, 1968, 118 Ga.App. 33, 162 S.E.2d 827.

actionable without proof of "temporal" damage such as the loss of a particular marriage.[98] This remained the law of England until 1891, when it was remedied, as to the female sex, by the Slander of Women Act.[99] Similar statutory changes of the common law rule have been made in a number of American states,[1] and several courts have accomplished much the same result by holding that an imputation of unchastity to either sex is equivalent to a charge of the crime of adultery or fornication, which involves an infamous punishment or moral turpitude.[2] In some jurisdictions cases following the older rule have not yet been overruled,[3] although it does not appear very likely that they will be followed today. Most courts, however, have now rebelled at the reproach to the law involved in such a result, and have held that an oral imputation of unchastity to a woman is actionable without proof of damage without regard to whether it charges a crime.[4] Such a rule never has been applied to a man. Even so, the American Law Institute chose to expand the rule to make actionable an oral imputation of serious sexual misconduct to anyone[5]—without proof of special harm—in part on the notion that constitutional requirements as to equality of treatment between the sexes might be held to require it. There have been some indications that imputation of deviate sexual behavior would be actionable on the part of either a man or a woman.

Special Damage

All other slanderous words, no matter how grossly defamatory or insulting they may be, which cannot be fitted into the arbitrary categories listed above, are actionable only upon proof of "special" damage—special in the sense that it must be supported by specific proof, as distinct from the damage assumed to follow in the case of libel or the kinds of slander already considered.[6] This is true, for example, of the accusation that the plaintiff is a bastard,[7] or the related imputation of canine ancestry,[8] or that he is a crook,[9] a damn liar,[10] or a Communist[11] where none of the exceptional rules is appli-

---

98. Davies v. Gardiner, 1593, Popham 36, 79 Eng. Rep. 1155; Oxford v. Cross, 1599, 4 Co.Rep. 18, 76 Eng.Rep. 902; Matthew v. Crass, 1614, Cro.Jac. 323, 79 Eng.Rep. 276.

99. 1891, 54 & 55 Vict. ch. 51.

1. See Richter v. Stolze, 1909, 158 Mich. 594, 123 N.W. 13; Vanloon v. Vanloon, 1911, 159 Mo.App. 255, 140 S.W. 631; Pink v. Catanich, 1876, 51 Cal. 420; Smith v. Gaffard, 1857, 31 Ala. 45.

2. Davis v. Sladden, 1889, 17 Or. 259, 21 P. 140; Kelly v. Flaherty, 1888, 16 R.I. 234, 14 A. 876; Zeliff v. Jennings, 1884, 61 Tex. 458; Reitan v. Goebel, 1885, 33 Minn. 151, 22 N.W. 291.

3. Pollard v. Lyon, 1875, 91 U.S. 225, 23 L.Ed. 308; Barnett v. Phelps, 1920, 97 Or. 242, 191 P. 502; Ledlie v. Wallen, 1895, 17 Mont. 150, 42 P. 289; Douglas v. Douglas, 1895, 4 Idaho 293, 38 P. 934.

4. Biggerstaff v. Zimmerman, 1941, 108 Colo. 194, 114 P.2d 1098; Hollman v. Brady, 1956, 16 Alaska 308, 233 F.2d 877 (Alaska law); Gnapinsky v. Goldyn, 1952, 23 N.J. 243, 128 A.2d 697; Crellin v. Thomas, 1952, 122 Utah 122, 247 P.2d 264; Cooper v. Seaverns, 1909, 81 Kan. 267, 105 P. 509.

5. Second Restatement of Torts, § 574, and Comment c.

6. McCormick, Damages, 1935, 442.

7. Walker v. Tucker, 1927, 220 Ky. 363, 295 S.W. 138; Hoar v. Ward, 1875, 47 Vt. 657; Paysse v. Paysse, 1915, 84 Wash. 351, 146 P. 840; Mishkin v. Roreck, 1952, 202 Misc. 653, 115 N.Y.S.2d 269.

8. Ringgold v. Land, 1937, 212 N.C. 369, 193 S.E. 267; Martin v. Sutter, 1922, 60 Cal.App. 8, 212 P. 60; Torres v. Huner, 1912, 150 App.Div. 798, 135 N.Y.S. 332. Cf. Dalton v. Woodward, 1938, 134 Neb. 915, 280 N.W. 215.

9. Nelson v. Rosenberg, 1938, 135 Neb. 34, 280 N.W. 229; Mishkin v. Roreck, 1952, 202 Misc. 653, 115 N.Y.S.2d 269; Hofstadter v. Bienstock, 1925, 213 App. Div. 807, 208 N.Y.S. 453; Eggleston v. Whitlock, 1927, 242 Ill.App. 379; Gaare v. Melbostad, 1932, 186 Minn. 96, 242 N.W. 466 ("If Joe had not been a crooked son-of-a-bitch that bank would never have gone broke").

10. Shipe v. Schenk, App.D.C.1960, 158 A.2d 910.

11. Johnson v. Nielsen, N.D.1958, 92 N.W.2d 66; Gurtler v. Union Parts Manufacturing Co., 1956, 1 N.Y.2d 5, 150 N.Y.S.2d 4, 132 N.E.2d 889; Ward v. Forest Preserve District, 1957, 13 Ill.App.2d 257, 141 N.E.2d 753; Pecyk v. Semoncheck, Ohio App.1952, 105 N.E.2d 61. See Booker, The Accusation of Communism as Slander Per Se, 1954, 4 Duke Bar J. 1.

cable,[12] or that he does not pay his debts,[13] or is dirty,[14] or wets the bed.[15]

This was in all conscience bad enough; but since "temporal" damage was necessary, the courts made matters worse by requiring that the special damage be pecuniary in its nature. Thus, while the loss of customers or business,[16] or a particular contract [17] or employment,[18] or of an advantageous marriage,[19] will be sufficient to make the slander actionable, it is not enough that the plaintiff has lost the society of his friends and associates,[20] unless their hospitality or assistance was such that it could be considered a pecuniary benefit;[21] or that he has suffered acute mental distress and serious physical illness as a result of the defamation,[22] or has been put to expense to refute it.[23]

On the other hand, once the cause of action is established, either by the character of the defamation itself or by the proof of pecuniary loss, the bars are lowered, and "general" damages may be recovered for the injury to the plaintiff's reputation,[24] his wounded feelings and humiliation,[25] and resulting physical illness and pain,[26] as well as estimated future damages of the same kind.[27] In other words, such damages are insufficient in themselves to make the slander actionable, but once the cause of action

---

12. In some jurisdictions the accusation has been held to charge a crime. Grein v. La Poma, 1959, 54 Wn.2d 844, 340 P.2d 766; Joopanenko v. Gavagan, Fla. 1953, 67 So.2d 434; Lightfoot v. Jennings, 1953, 363 Mo. 878, 254 S.W.2d 596; Solosko v. Paxton, 1956, 383 Pa. 419, 119 A.2d 230. See Note, 1959, 33 So.Cal.L. Rev. 104.

13. Urban v. Hartford Gas Co., 1952, 139 Conn. 301, 93 A.2d 292; Patton v. Jacobs, 1948, 118 Ind.App. 358, 78 N.E.2d 789; Hudson v. Pioneer Service Co., 1959, 218 Or. 561, 346 P.2d 123; cf. Shipe v. Schenk, Mun. App.D.C.1960, 158 A.2d 910 ("deadbeat"); Loyd v. Pearse, 1618, Cro.Jac. 424, 79 Eng.Rep. 362 ("bankrupt rogue").

14. Larson v. R.B. Wrigley Co., 1931, 183 Minn. 28, 235 N.W. 393. Cf. Newman v. Ligo Operating Co., 1955, 142 N.Y.S.2d 821 ("bum").

15. Cobb v. Tinsley, 1922, 195 Ky. 781, 243 S.W. 1009.

16. Evans v. Harries, 1856, 1 H. & N. 251, 156 Eng. Rep. 1197; Brooks v. Harison, 1883, 91 N.Y. 83; Ross v. Fitch, 1882, 58 Tex. 148; Schoen v. Washington Post, D.C.Cir. 1957, 246 F.2d 670; Morasse v. Brochu, 1890, 151 Mass. 567, 25 N.E. 74. It was formerly the rule, and still is in some states that these must be pleaded and proved "with particularity." Life Printing & Publishing Co. v. Field, 1944, 324 Ill.App. 254, 58 N.E.2d 307. The prevailing rule today is that a general allegation, with proof of a general decline in business and the elimination of other causes, is sufficient where it is impossible to be more specific. Ellsworth v. Martindale-Hubbell Law Directory, 1938, 68 N.D. 425, 280 N.W. 879. See infra, § 128.

17. Storey v. Challands, 1837, 8 C. & P. 234, 173 Eng.Rep. 475. Cf. Prettyman v. Shockley, 1890, 4 Har. Del., 112 (loss of credit).

18. Dixon v. Smith, 1860, 5 H. & N. 450, 157 Eng. Rep. 1257; Hartley v. Herring, 1799, 8 Term Rep. 130, 101 Eng.Rep. 1305; Wilson v. Cotterman, 1886, 65 Md. 190, 3 A. 890; Lombard v. Lennox, 1891, 155 Mass. 70, 28 N.E. 1125.

19. Matthew v. Crass, 1614, Cro.Jac. 323, 79 Eng. Rep. 276; Moody v. Baker, N.Y.1826, 5 Cow. 351.

20. Allsop v. Allsop, 1860, 5 H. & N. 534, 157 Eng. Rep. 431; Roberts v. Roberts, 1864, 5 B. & S. 384, 122 Eng.Rep. 874; Beach v. Ranney, N.Y.1842, 2 Hill 309; Williams v. Riddle, 1911, 145 Ky. 459, 140 S.W. 661; Clark v. Morrison, 1916, 80 Or. 240, 156 P. 429.

21. Moore v. Meagher, 1807, 1 Taunt. 39, 127 Eng. Rep. 745; Davies v. Solomon, 1871, 7 Q.B. 112, 115 Eng.Rep. 431; Corcoran v. Corcoran, 1857, 7 Ir.C.L. Rep. 272; Pettibone v. Simpson, N.Y.1873, 66 Barb. 492.

22. Allsop v. Allsop, 1860, 5 H. & N. 534, 157 Eng. Rep. 1292; Terwilliger v. Wands, 1858, 17 N.Y. 54; Harrison v. Burger, 1925, 212 Ala. 670, 103 So. 842; Clark v. Morrison, 1916, 80 Or. 240, 156 P. 429; Scott v. Harrison, 1939, 215 N.C. 427, 2 S.E.2d 1. See Day, Mental Suffering as an Element of Damages in Defamation Cases, 1966, 15 Cleve.Marsh.L.Rev. 26.

23. Bigelow v. Brumley, 1941, 138 Ohio St. 574, 37 N.E.2d 584.

24. Craney v. Donovan, 1917, 92 Conn. 236, 102 A. 640.

25. Pion v. Caron, 1921, 237 Mass. 107, 129 N.E. 369; Viss v. Calligan, 1916, 91 Wash. 673, 158 P. 1012; Baker v. Winslow, 1922, 184 N.C. 1, 113 S.E. 570; Finger v. Pollack, 1905, 188 Mass. 208, 74 N.E. 317; Poleski v. Polish-American Publishing Co., 1931, 254 Mich. 15, 235 N.W. 841. See Day, Mental Suffering as an Element of Damages in Defamation Cases, 1966, 15 Cleve.Marsh.L.Rev. 26.

It usually is held, however, that "reflex" mental suffering caused by the mental distress of the plaintiff's family over the defamation is not recoverable. Bishop v. New York Times Co., 1922, 233 N.Y. 446, 135 N.E. 845; Dennison v. Daily News Pub. Co., 1903, 82 Neb. 675, 118 N.W. 568. See Note, 1922, 8 Corn.L.Q. 65.

26. Sweet v. Post Publishing Co., 1913, 215 Mass. 450, 102 N.E. 660; Garrison v. Sun Printing & Publishing Association, 1912, 207 N.Y. 1, 100 N.E. 430. Contra, holding it "too remote," Butler v. Hoboken Printing & Publishing Co., 1905, 73 N.J.L. 45, 62 A. 272.

27. Craney v. Donovan, 1917, 92 Conn. 236, 102 A. 640; Elms v. Crane, 1919, 118 Me. 261, 107 A. 852.

is made out without them, they may be tacked on as "parasitic" to it.[28] The tendency has been to leave the amount to be awarded, within very wide limits, to the jury; and there has been a wide range of variation, running from six cents to $1,000,000 in compensatory damages with an additional $1,250,000 in punitive damages.[29]

So far as "proximate cause" is concerned, recovery has been limited very definitely to those damages which are regarded as reasonably foreseeable or normal consequences of the defamation.[30] Formerly it was held that the original defamer was liable only for the damages caused by his own publication, and was not reponsible for repetition by others, on the theory that the "last human wrongdoer" must be responsible, and there is still some authority to this effect;[31] but there has been the same broadening of "proximate cause" as in other fields of liability, and the prevailing view now appears to be that there is liability for damages due to such a repetition when it was authorized or intended, or when the circumstances were such that it might reasonably have been anticipated.[32]

Libel and the Necessity for Proving Harm of Some Kind

Any defamatory imputation may, of course, be conveyed in libelous form. By the beginning of the nineteenth century, it was well-established that any libel, as distinct from the same imputation in the form of slander, was actionable per se, meaning that it was actionable without the necessity of pleading and proving that the plaintiff had suffered any impairment of his reputation or other harm as a result.[33] In other words, the existence of damage was conclusively presumed or assumed from the publication of the libel itself, without any evidence to show actual harm of any kind. The practical result of that approach was to allow the jury to award not only nominal damages,[34] but also substantial sums in compensation of the supposed harm to the plaintiff's reputation[35] without proof of harm. In fact, a nominal damage award is inconsistent with the notion of assumed damage. At least it is the accepted rule in England that a recovery is allowed on proof of the unprivileged publication of a libel.

The great majority of American courts adopted the same position prior to recent de-

---

28. Compare supra, § 54.

29. In Faulk v. Aware, Inc., 1962, 35 Misc.2d 302, 231 N.Y.S.2d 270, reversed 19 A.D.2d 464, 244 N.Y.S.2d 259, motion denied 14 N.Y.S.2d 719, 250 N.Y.S.2d 64, 199 N.E.2d 163, affirmed 14 N.Y.2d 899, 252 N.Y.S.2d 95, 200 N.E.2d 778, amended 14 N.Y.2d 954, 253 N.Y.S.2d 990, 202 N.E.2d 372 (accusation of communism, causing plaintiff to be blacklisted). See McCormick, Damages, 1935, 444–445, listing various cases with amounts. Also Gregory and Kalven, Cases and Materials on Torts, 1959, 925–926.

30. Lynch v. Knight, 1861, 9 H.L.C. 577, 11 Eng. Rep. 854; Anonymous, 1875, 60 N.Y. 262; Georgia v. Kepford, 1876, 45 Iowa 48; Field v. Colson, 1892, 93 Ky. 347, 20 S.W. 264.

31. Vicars v. Wilcocks, 1806, 8 East 1, 103 Eng.Rep. 244; Lehner v. Kelley, 1934, 215 Wis. 265, 254 N.W. 634; Hastings v. Stetson, 1879, 126 Mass. 329; Maytag v. Cummins, 8th Cir. 1919, 260 F. 74; Age-Herald Publishing Co. v. Waterman, 1914, 188 Ala. 272, 66 So. 16.

32. Zier v. Hofflin, 1885, 33 Minn. 66, 21 N.W. 862; Sawyer v. Gilmers, Inc., 1925, 189 N.C. 7, 126 S.E. 183; Southwestern Telephone & Telegraph Co. v. Long, Tex. Civ.App.1915, 183 S.W. 421; Elms v. Crane, 1919, 118 Me. 261, 107 A. 852; Fitzgerald v. Young, 1911, 89 Neb. 693, 132 N.W. 127. See Restatement of Torts, § 576. Apparently damage due to repetition alone is sufficient to make slander actionable. Cf. Gillett v. Bullivant, 1846, 7 L.T.,O.S., 490; Derry v. Handley, 1867, 16 L.T.,N.S., 263; cf. Weaver v. Beneficial Finance Co., 1957, 199 Va. 196, 98 S.E.2d 687.

There is, however, still no liability for a republication which could not reasonably have been anticipated. Waite v. Stockgrowers' Credit Corp., 1933, 63 N.D. 763, 249 N.W. 910.

33. Thorley v. Lord Kerry, 1812, 4 Taunt. 355, 128 Eng.Rep. 367.

34. Jones v. Register & Leader Co., 1916, 177 Iowa 144, 158 N.W. 571; Godin v. Niebuhr, 1920, 236 Mass. 350, 128 N.E. 406.

35. Youssoupoff v. Metro-Goldwyn-Mayer Pictures, 1934, 50 T.L.R. 581, 99 A.L.R. 864 (£25,000); Lewis v. Hayes, 1918, 177 Cal. 587, 171 P. 293; Oklahoma Publishing Co. v. Givens, 10th Cir. 1933, 67 F.2d 62; Starks v. Comer, 1914, 190 Ala. 245, 67 So. 440. Even positive evidence that there was in fact no damage to the plaintiff's reputation does not go to defeat the action, but only to mitigate damages. First National Bank v. N.R. McFall & Co., 1920, 144 Ark. 149, 222 S.W. 40.

cisions of the Supreme Court on the first amendment and defamation and held that at least as to the publication of matter which was defamatory on its face and unambiguous, the publication was actionable per se, and harm would be presumed. Where there has been a publication of defamatory matter to the general public, it is rational to presume or assume that there has been some harm to reputation, and the jury should be allowed to decide what that harm is with such evidence as may be made available on the matter. But it is not so obvious that any impairment to reputation—or whether or not it will be substantial—will inevitably result from the publication of a libel privately to one or more persons who may in fact not believe the statement to be true, and so testify. In such a case, it will probably be possible to show that the recipient or recipients did not believe the statement to be true, and thereby to show no damage and prevent a recovery. This is aside from the decisions of the Supreme Court and the first amendment related to this subject.

Prior to the decision of the Supreme Court in Gertz v. Robert Welch, Inc.,[36] a substantial disagreement developed among the American courts about the necessity for proving special damage in two types of cases.[36a] These were when (1) the publication was innocent on its face and became defamatory only to those who were aware of defamatory facts "extrinsic" to the matter published, commonly referred to as libel "per quod," [37] and (2) the statement published was susceptible of more than one reasonable meaning, one of which was innocuous. Perhaps, the principal justification for the notion that special damage should be a prerequisite to recovery is that the type of defamation in such a case is more like slander than the typical publication of libel in a newspaper, journal, book, or the like. It becomes defamatory only to the few who know the extrinsic facts or to the few who give the statement the defamatory meaning. But another argument frequently given and warmly debated at the American Law Institute was the notion that strict liability should not be extended to such length since defamation was a kind of strict liability with respect to truth or falsity in the absence of a recognized privilege.

In any event, the presumed damage rule must be regarded as almost abrogated, if not entirely so, when a publication is made through the use of a public medium and honestly. In *Gertz*, it was held by the Supreme Court that the first amendment of the United States Constitution does not permit recovery of presumed or punitive damages—at least against the press or broadcasting media and those who utilize these means—unless the plaintiff establishes clearly and convincingly that the defendant had knowledge of the falsity or acted in reckless disregard of the truth of the defamatory matter published. As the court said, "In short, the private defamation plaintiff who establishes liability under a less demanding standard than that stated by *New York Times* may recover only such damages as are sufficient to compensate him for actual injury." [38]

It is not at all clear that the constitutional privilege to defame others that has been extended to the media is a privilege that extends to all persons and legal entities and for all kinds of defamatory communica-

---

36. 1974, 418 U.S. 323, 94 S.Ct. 2997, 41 L.Ed.2d 789.

36a. See Prosser, Libel Per Quod, 1960, 46 Va.L. Rev. 839; Eldredge, The Spurious Rule of Libel Per Quod, 1966, 79 Harv.L.Rev. 733; Henn, Libel-By-Extrinsic-Fact, 1961, 47 Corn.L.Q. 14; Hinsdale v. Orange Co. Publications, Inc., 1966, 17 N.Y.2d 284, 270 N.Y.S. 2d 592, 217 N.E.2d 650; MacLeod v. Tribune Publishing Co., Inc., 1959, 52 Cal.2d 536, 343 P.2d 36.

37. This was the phrase formerly used to precede the portion of the declaration alleging special damage, in the old common law pleading. Black's Law Dictionary, 4th Ed. 1951, 1293. See, as to the distinction between libel per se and per quod, Thompson v. Upton, 1958, 218 Md. 433, 146 A.2d 880. The classic case of libel per quod is Morrison v. Ritchie & Co. [1902] 4 Fraser, Sess.Cas., 645, 39 Scot.L.Rep. 432, where defendant's newspaper published a report that the plaintiff had given birth to twins. There were readers who knew that she had been married only one month.

38. 1974, 418 U.S. 323, at 350, 94 S.Ct. 2997, at 3012.

tions.³⁹ But the American Law Institute has accepted the idea that a prerequisite to recovery in any action for defamation is proof of harm to reputation and such harm will not be presumed in the absence of proof that the defendant published the defamatory matter with knowledge of its falsity or in reckless disregard of its truth or falsity.⁴⁰

When there has been a publication of defamatory matter to the general public, it is rational to permit the jury to assume that there has been some harm to reputation, and substantial compensatory damages should be awarded as vindication of the plaintiff's good name. But it is not so obvious that any impairment to reputation will inevitably result from the publication of libel privately to one or more persons who may or may not believe the statement to be true.

In any event, the presumed damage rule cannot be said to be generally applicable today. The constitutional privilege of freedom of the press demands proof of some harm from the publication of the defamatory matter in the absence of proof of actual malice when suit is brought against a public medium or someone who utilizes the public medium. But this does not mean special damage. It does not even mean impairment of reputation. It can be established by proof that plaintiff suffered mental anguish or humiliation.⁴¹

It would seem, however, that courts should require as a minimum for recovery in every case either evidence from which harm to reputation could reasonably be inferred or direct evidence of harm to reputation.

WESTLAW REFERENCES

libel /s distinction difference distinguish /s slander

39. Infra, § 113.
40. Second Restatement of Torts, § 621.
41. Infra, § 116a. In Time, Inc. v. Firestone, 1976, 424 U.S. 448, 96 S.Ct. 958, 47 L.Ed.2d 154, on remand 332 So.2d 68, the Supreme Court rejected the argument that claims of injury must be based on active harm to reputation. Proof of emotional stress and anxiety as a consequence of a defamatory report was found to be sufficient.

Slander Actionable Without Proof of Damage
opinion(requir! necessity necessary unnecessary /s proof proving proved prove /s damages /p libel! slander! defam!)

Crime
slander! /p imput! /5 crime criminal
"slander per se" /p imput! /5 crime criminal

Loathsome Disease
"slander per se" /p loathsome /5 disease

Business, Trade, Profession or Office
slander! defam! /p business trade profession office /s reputation*
slander! defam! /p business trade profession office /p dishonest! incompetent! insan!
slander! defam! & business trade profession office /p illiterate coward drunk lush
237k7(16)

Special Damage
headnote(slander! defam! libel! /s "special damage*")
opinion(slander! defam! libel! /s "special damage*" /s proof prove proving proved)

Libel and the Necessity for Proving Harm of Some Kind
libel! /s requir! mandat! need necessity necessary /s proof prove proving proved /s damage* injury
gertz /s 418 +5 323 /p damage* /s 10 presumption presumed

§ 113. Basis of Liability

Publication

Since the interest protected is that of reputation, it is essential to tort liability for either libel or slander that the defamation be communicated to some one other than the person defamed.¹ This element of communication is given the technical name of "publication," but this does not mean that it must be printed or written; it may be oral, or conveyed by means of gestures, or the exhibition of a picture or statue.² Where there is no communication to any one but the plain-

§ 113

1. Thus failure of the complaint to allege when, where and to whom the defamation was published is a fatal omission on demurrer. McGuire v. Adkins, 1969, 284 Ala. 602, 226 So.2d 659.

2. Cf. Hird v. Wood, 1894, 38 Sol.J. 234 (pointing at sign); Schultz v. Frankfort Marine, Accident & Plate Glass Insurance Co., 1913, 151 Wis. 537, 139 N.W. 386 (shadowing); Louka v. Park Entertainments, 1936, 294

tiff there may be criminal responsibility,³ or a possible action for the intentional infliction of mental suffering,⁴ but no tort action can be maintained upon the theory of defamation.⁵ It is not enough that the words are uttered in the presence of others unless they are in fact overheard; ⁶ nor, although there is some authority to the contrary,⁷ is it usually regarded as sufficient that they were sent through the mail on a postcard,⁸ or in an unsealed letter,⁹ unless it is proved that a third person read them. Furthermore, since it is the defamatory meaning which must be communicated, it must be shown that the utterance was understood in that sense.¹⁰

Thus words spoken in a foreign tongue are not actionable unless they are heard by one who understands the language.¹¹ In the case of publication in a newspaper, however, even in a foreign language, it is presumed that there are readers familiar with the ordinary meaning of the words.¹²

There may be publication to any third person. It may be made to a member of the plaintiff's family, including his wife,¹³ or to the plaintiff's agent or employee.¹⁴ It may be made to the defendant's own agent, employee or officer, even where the defendant is a corporation.¹⁵ The dictation of defamatory matter to a stenographer generally is

---

Mass. 268, 1 N.E.2d 41 (picture); Monson v. Tussauds, [1894] 1 Q.B. 671 (statue).

3. Since it tends to a breach of the peace. Regina v. Brooke, 1857, 7 Cox C.C. 251; Regina v. Adams, 1886, 22 Q.B.D. 66. In Jacobs v. Transcontinental & Western Air, Mo.App.1947, 205 S.W.2d 887, a criminal statute was held to support a civil action. This was criticized in Notes, 1948, 13 Mo.L.Rev. 235; 1948, 32 Minn.L.Rev. 841, and reversed on other grounds in 1948, 358 Mo. 674, 216 S.W.2d 523. The court refused to follow it in Insurance Research Service v. Associates Finance Corp., M.D.Tenn.1955, 134 F.Supp. 54.

4. See supra, § 12.

5. Yousling v. Dare, 1904, 122 Iowa 539, 98 N.W. 371; Fry v. McCord Brothers, 1895, 95 Tenn. 678, 33 S.W. 568; Busby v. First Christian Church, 1923, 153 La. 377, 95 So. 869; Insurance Research Service v. Associates Finance Corp., M.D.Tenn.1955, 134 F.Supp. 54; Almy v. Kvamme, 1963, 63 Wash.2d 326, 387 P.2d 372 (over telephone).

6. Tocker v. Great Atlantic & Pacific Tea Co., D.C. Cir. 1963, 190 A.2d 822; Sheffill v. Van Deusen, 1859, 79 Mass. (13 Gray) 304; Gelhaus v. Eastern Air Lines, 5th Cir. 1952, 194 F.2d 774; Davidson v. Walter, 1958, 214 Ga. 187, 104 S.E.2d 113, conformed to 97 Ga.App. 728, 104 S.E.2d 337.

This may, however, be proved by circumstantial evidence, that there were those nearby who probably heard. Gaudette v. Carter, 1965, 100 R.I. 259, 214 A.2d 197.

7. Ostro v. Safir, 1937, 165 Misc. 647, 1 N.Y.S.2d 377. See Robinson v. Jones, 1879, 4 L.R.Ir. 391; Huth v. Huth, [1915] 3 K.B. 32; Logan v. Hodges, 1907, 146 N.C. 38, 59 S.E. 349.

8. McKeel v. Latham, 1932, 202 N.C. 318, 162 S.E. 747; Steele v. Edwards, 1897, 15 Ohio Cir.Ct. 52, 8 Ohio Dec. 161. Cf. Continental National Bank v. Bowdre, 1893, 92 Tenn. 723, 23 S.W. 131. See Note, 1916, 64 U.Pa.L.Rev. 193.

9. Huth v. Huth, [1915] 3 K.B. 32. Cf. Renfro Drug Co. v. Lawson, 1942, 138 Tex. 434, 160 S.W.2d 246 (exhibition of magazine for sale not enough without proof that it was sold or read). Cf. Neeley v. Winn-Dixie Greenville, Inc., 1971, 255 S.C. 301, 178 S.E.2d 662.

10. See supra, § 111. See for example Geraghty v. Suburban Trust Co., 1965, 238 Md. 197, 208 A.2d 606.

11. Mielenz v. Quasdorf, 1886, 68 Iowa 726, 28 N.W. 41; Economopoulos v. A.G. Pollard Co., 1914, 218 Mass. 294, 105 N.E. 896; Pouchan v. Godeau, 1914, 167 Cal. 692, 140 P. 952; Rich v. Scalio, 1904, 115 Ill.App. 166. Cf. Sullivan v. Sullivan, 1892, 48 Ill.App. 435 (too young).

12. Steketee v. Kimm, 1882, 48 Mich. 322, 12 N.W. 177.

13. Wenman v. Ash, 1853, 13 C.B. 836, 138 Eng. Rep. 1432; Theaker v. Richardson, [1962] 1 All Eng. 229; Schenck v. Schenck, 1843, 20 N.J.L. 208; Luick v. Driscoll, 1895, 13 Ind.App. 279, 41 N.E. 463; Bonkowski v. Arlan's Department Store, 1970, 383 Mich. 90, 174 N.W.2d 765.

As to publication by one spouse to the other, see infra, § 115.

14. Duke of Brunswick v. Harmer, 1849, 14 Q.B.D. 185, 53 L.J.Q.B. 20; Brown v. Elm City Lumber Co., 1914, 167 N.C. 9, 82 S.E. 961. There have been occasional cases which, apparently confusing publication with privilege, have held the contrary, as in Patrick v. Thomas, Okl.1962, 376 P.2d 250.

15. Fulton v. Atlantic Coast Line Railroad Co., 1951, 220 S.C. 287, 67 S.E.2d 425; Bacon v. Michigan Central Railroad Co., 1884, 55 Mich. 224, 21 N.W. 324; Kennedy v. James Butler, Inc., 1927, 245 N.Y. 204, 156 N.E. 666; Cochran v. Sears, Roebuck & Co., 1945, 72 Ga.App. 458, 34 S.E.2d 296.

There is some authority to the contrary, apparently as a result of confusing publication with privilege. Prins v. Holland-North America Mortgage Co., 1919, 107 Wash. 206, 181 P. 680; Chalkley v. Atlantic Coast Line Railroad Co., 1928, 150 Va. 301, 143 S.E. 631; Burney v. Southern Railway Co., 1964, 276 Ala. 637, 165 So.2d 726. In Walter v. Davidson, 1958, 214 Ga. 187, 104 S.E.2d 113, conformed to 97 Ga.App. 728, 104 S.E.2d 337, this was carried to the length of holding

regarded as sufficient publication,[16] although it may be privileged.[17] A few courts, with a tendency to confuse the question of publication with that of privilege, have held that it is not, regarding dictation as an indispensable method in modern business transactions, and therefore merely equivalent to the defendant's own writing.[18]

Every repetition of the defamation is a publication in itself,[19] even though the repeater states the source,[20] or resorts to the customary newspaper evasion "it is alleged,"[21] or makes it clear that he does not himself believe the imputation.[22] The courts have said many times that the last utterance may do no less harm than the first, and that the wrong of another cannot serve as an excuse to the defendant.[23] Likewise every one who takes part in the publication, as in the case of the owner,[24] editor,[25] printer,[26] vendor,[27] or even carrier[28] of a newspaper is charged with publication, although so far as strict liability is concerned the responsibility

that there was no publication in a communication between two members of a college faculty.

See Note, 1952, 38 Va.L.Rev. 400.

16. Pullman v. Walter Hill & Co., [1891] 1 Q.B. 524, 60 L.J.Q.B. 209; Rickbeil v. Grafton Deaconess Hospital, 1946, 74 N.D. 525, 23 N.W.2d 247, 166 A.L.R. 99; Ostrowe v. Lee, 1931, 256 N.Y. 36, 175 N.E. 505; Arvey Corp. v. Peterson, E.D.Pa.1959, 178 F.Supp. 132; Gambrill v. Schooley, 1901, 93 Md. 48, 48 A. 730; Berry v. City of New York Insurance Co., 1923, 210 Ala. 369, 98 So. 290. See Notes, 1954, 27 So.Cal.L.Rev. 229; 1954, 27 Temple L.Q. 127; 1950, 2 S.Car.L.Q. 290; 1964, 17 Ala.L.Rev. 176.

Some of these courts have held that there is publication only by the individual dictating, and not by the corporation employing both. Mims v. Metropolitan Life Insurance Co., 5th Cir. 1952, 200 F.2d 800, certiorari denied 345 U.S. 940, 73 S.Ct. 831, 97 L.Ed. 1366; Owen v. Ogilvie Publishing Co., 1898, 32 App.Div. 465, 53 N.Y.S. 1033; Prins v. Holland-North America Mortgage Co., 1919, 107 Wash. 206, 181 P. 680.

17. See infra, § 115 on Abuse of Qualified Privilege. This seems to be much the better position. Suppose the defendant seizes the occasion to dictate to the stenographer an unprivileged letter to her fiancé, which defames him? Is there no publication?

18. Watson v. Wannamaker, 1950, 216 S.C. 295, 57 S.E.2d 477; Cartwright-Caps Co. v. Fischel & Kaufman, 1917, 113 Miss. 359, 74 So. 278; Satterfield v. McLellan Stores Co., 1939, 215 N.C. 582, 2 S.E.2d 709; Insurance Research Service v. Associates Finance Corp., M.D.Tenn.1955, 134 F.Supp. 54.

19. Nance v. Flaugh, 1952, 221 Ark. 352, 253 S.W.2d 207; Lubore v. Pittsburgh Courier Publishing Co., D.D.C.1951, 101 F.Supp. 234, affirmed D.C.Cir. 1952, 200 F.2d 355; Folwell v. Providence Journal Co., 1896, 19 R.I. 551, 37 A. 6. See Painter, Republication Problems in the Law of Defamation, 1961, 47 Va.L. Rev. 1131; Notes, 1958, 26 Ford L.Rev. 713; 1957, 43 Va.L.Rev. 1132. In Weaver v. Beneficial Finance Co., 1957, 199 Va. 196, 98 S.E.2d 687, a foreseeable republication by third person after the lapse of a year was held to afford a new cause of action against the original publisher, which started a new limitations period running.

20. McPherson v. Daniels, 1829, 10 B. & C. 263, 109 Eng.Rep. 448; Haines v. Campbell, 1891, 74 Md. 158,

21 A. 702; Vanover v. Wells, 1936, 264 Ky. 461, 94 S.W.2d 999; Times Publishing Co. v. Carlisle, 8th Cir. 1899, 94 F. 762; Lorillard v. Field Enterprises, Inc., 1965, 65 Ill.App.2d 65, 213 N.E.2d 1.

In MacFadden v. Anthony, Sup.1952, 117 N.Y.S.2d 520, a mere reference to the existence of an article, without repeating its contents, was held not to be a publication.

21. Lundin v. Post Publishing Co., 1914, 217 Mass. 213, 104 N.E. 480; Lancour v. Herald & Globe Association, 1941, 111 Vt. 371, 17 A.2d 253; Maloof v. Post Publishing Co., 1940, 306 Mass. 279, 28 N.E.2d 458; Cobbs v. Chicago Defender, 1941, 308 Ill.App. 55, 31 N.E.2d 323 (it is rumored).

22. Branstetter v. Dorrough, 1882, 81 Ind. 527; Morse v. Times-Republican Printing Co., 1904, 124 Iowa 707, 100 N.W. 867; Cobbs v. Chicago Defender, 1941, 308 Ill.App. 55, 31 N.E.2d 323; Bishop v. Journal Newspaper Co., 1897, 168 Mass. 327, 47 N.E. 119.

23. "Talebearers are as bad as talemakers." Cavalier v. Original Club Forest, La.App.1952, 59 So.2d 489.

24. Crane v. Bennett, 1904, 177 N.Y. 106, 69 N.E. 274; Davis v. Hearst, 1911, 160 Cal. 143, 116 P. 530; Wahlheimer v. Hardenbergh, 1914, 160 App.Div. 190, 145 N.Y.S. 161, reversed on other grounds 1916, 217 N.Y. 264, 111 N.E. 826.

25. Smith v. Utley, 1896, 92 Wis. 133, 65 N.W. 744; World Publishing Co. v. Minahan, 1918, 70 Okl. 107, 173 P. 815.

26. Baldwin v. Elphinstone, 1775, W.Bl. 1037; cf. Youmans v. Smith, 1897, 153 N.Y. 214, 219, 47 N.E. 265, 266. In Rex v. Clerk, 1728, 1 Barn. 304, 94 Eng. Rep. 207, a servant of the printer "whose business was only to clap down the press" was convicted of criminal libel.

27. Staub v. Van Benthuysen, 1884, 36 La.Ann. 467; Vizetelly v. Mudie's Select Library, [1900] 2 K.B. 170, 69 L.J.Q.B. 654; see Bigelow v. Sprague, 1886, 140 Mass. 425, 5 N.E. 144.

28. Cf. Arnold v. Ingram, 1912, 151 Wis. 438, 138 N.W. 111; Paton v. Great Northwestern Telegraph Co. of Canada, 1919, 141 Minn. 430, 170 N.W. 511 (telegraph company).

of some of these has been somewhat relaxed.[29]

The English rule[30] has been that every sale or delivery of each single copy of a newspaper is a distinct publication, and a separate basis for a cause of action. This rule had received the unqualified acceptance of the First Restatement of Torts,[31] and there are American jurisdictions in which it is still the last word of the courts.[32] The majority of the American courts, however, have developed, in cases involving venue[33] or the statute of limitations,[34] a "single publication rule," [35] under which an entire edition[36] of a newspaper, magazine or book[37] is treated as only one publication, and the plaintiff is permitted to plead and prove merely a general distribution of the libel[38] and show the extent of the circulation as evidence bearing on the damages.[39] Under this rule the publication has been treated as complete when "the finished product was released by the publisher for sale in accord with trade practice." [40] This rule has been adopted by the Commissioners on Uniform State Laws in the Uniform Single Publication Act.[41] It has been accepted in the Second Restatement of Torts.[42] It was formerly held by several courts[43] that the single publication rule could not cross a state line, so that there must be at least as many separate causes of action as there were states in-

---

29. See infra, this section on Fault Issues in Defamation Law.

30. Duke of Brunswick v. Harmer, 1849, 14 Q.B. 185, 117 Eng.Rep. 75.

31. § 578, Comment *b*. The context makes it clear, however, that the language is directed at the liability of those who repeat defamation, and that no thought was given to the problem of separate sales or communications by the same defendant.

32. Staub v. Van Benthuysen, 1848, 36 La.Ann. 467; Renfro Drug Co. v. Lawson, 1942, 138 Tex. 434, 160 S.W.2d 246; Louisville Press Co. v. Tennelly, 1899, 105 Ky. 365, 49 S.W. 15; Holden v. American News Co., E.D.Wash.1943, 52 F.Supp. 24, dismissed 3d Cir. 144 F.2d 249; Hartmann v. American News Co., W.D.Wis. 1947, 69 F.Supp. 736, affirmed 7th Cir. 1948, 171 F.2d 581. Georgia abandoned this position in Rives v. Atlanta Newspapers, Inc., 1964, 110 Ga.App. 184, 138 S.E.2d 100, reversed 220 Ga. 485, 139 S.E.2d 395, conformed to 111 Ga.App. 6, 140 S.E.2d 304.

33. Julian v. Kansas City Star Co., 1908, 209 Mo. 35, 107 S.W. 496, error dismissed 215 U.S. 589, 30 S.Ct. 406, 54 L.Ed. 340; Age-Herald Publishing Co. v. Huddleston, 1921, 207 Ala. 40, 92 So. 193; O'Malley v. Statesman Printing Co., 1939, 60 Idaho 326, 91 P.2d 357; Forman v. Mississippi Publishers Corp., 1943, 195 Miss. 90, 14 So.2d 344. See, however, Firstamerica Development Corp. v. Daytona Beach News-Journal Corp., Fla.1967, 196 So.2d 97.

34. The subsequent mailing of late copies, or sales from stock, is regarded as a part of the original publication, and will not extend the statute. Stephenson v. Triangle Publications, S.D.Tex.1952, 104 F.Supp. 215; McGlue v. Weekly Publications, Inc., D.Mass.1946, 63 F.Supp. 744; Winrod v. Time, Inc., 1948, 334 Ill.App. 59, 78 N.E.2d 708; Gregoire v. G.P. Putnam's Sons, 1948, 298 N.Y. 119, 81 N.E.2d 45, motion denied 298 N.Y. 753, 83 N.E.2d 152; Wolfson v. Syracuse Newspapers, 1938, 254 App.Div. 211, 4 N.Y.S.2d 640, affirmed 1939, 279 N.Y. 716, 18 N.E.2d 676, reargument denied 280 N.Y. 572, 20 N.E.2d 21 (reading in defendant's files).

35. See Prosser, Interstate Publication, 1953, 51 Mich.L.Rev. 959, reprinted in Prosser, Selected Topics on the Law of Torts, 1954, 70; Leflar, The Single Publication Rule, 1953, 25 Rocky Mt.L.Rev. 263; notes, 1949, 62 Harv.L.Rev. 1041; 1957, 19 U.Pitt.L.Rev. 98; 1962, 56 Northwestern U.L.Rev. 823; 1956, 32 N.D.L. Rev. 120; 1957, 35 N.C.L.Rev. 535.

36. Each edition is a separate publication. Wheeler v. Dell Publishing Co., 7th Cir. 1962, 300 F.2d 372; Fisher v. New Yorker Staats-Zeitung, 1906, 114 App. Div. 824, 100 N.Y.S. 185; Gordon v. Journal Publishing Co., 1908, 81 Vt. 237, 69 A. 742; Backus v. Look, Inc., S.D.N.Y.1941, 39 F.Supp. 662.

37. Gregoire v. G.P. Putnam's Sons, 1948, 298 N.Y. 119, 81 N.E.2d 45, motion denied 298 N.Y. 753, 83 N.E.2d 152; Ogden v. Association of the United States Army, D.D.C.1959, 177 F.Supp. 498.

38. Bigelow v. Sprague, 1886, 140 Mass. 425, 5 N.E. 144; Palmer v. Mahin, 8th Cir. 1903, 120 F. 737; Brian v. Harper, 1919, 144 La. 585, 80 So. 885; Fried, Mendelson & Co. v. Edmund Halstead, Limited, 1922, 203 App. Div. 113, 196 N.Y.S. 285.

39. Fry v. Bennet, 1863, 28 N.Y. 324; Bigelow v. Sprague, 1886, 140 Mass. 425, 5 N.E. 144; Palmer v. Mahin, 8th Cir. 1903, 120 F. 737.

40. Cassius v. Mortimer, S.D.N.Y.1957, 161 F.Supp. 74. Accord: Osmers v. Parade Publications, Inc., S.D. N.Y.1964, 234 F.Supp. 924; Zuck v. Interstate Publishing Corp., 2d Cir. 1963, 317 F.2d 727; Sorge v. Parade Publications, Inc., 1964, 20 A.D.2d 338, 247 N.Y.S.2d 317; Brush-Moore Newspapers v. Pollitt, 1959, 220 Md. 132, 151 A.2d 530.

41. See Leflar, The Single Publication Rule, 1953, 25 Rocky Mt.L.Rev. 263; Notes, 1958, 15 Wash. & Lee L.Rev. 321; 1956, 44 Cal.L.Rev. 146.

42. Section 577A.

43. O'Reilly v. Curtis Publishing Co., D.Mass.1940, 31 F.Supp. 364; Hartmann v. American News Co., W.D.Wis.1947, 69 F.Supp. 736; Sheldon-Claire Co. v. Judson Roberts Co., S.D.N.Y.1949, 88 F.Supp. 120; Sidis v. F–R Publishing Co., 2d Cir. 1940, 113 F.2d 806,

volved. The later cases[44] have held that it can do so; but the resulting problems of the conflict of laws,[45] which lie beyond the scope of this book, become extremely complex and difficult.

There may be responsibility for publication by another, as in the case of defamation published by an agent within the scope of his authority,[46] or an express or implied authorization to publish, as where a statement is made to a newspaper reporter.[47] It has even been held, in a few cases,[48] that there may be an affirmative duty to remove a publication made by another, where for example the defendant's bulletin board is used for the purpose.

The probate of defamatory wills has presented a good many problems.[49] Since the executor is under a duty to probate the will, any defamation can scarcely be charged against him,[50] and since the publication has occurred after the death of the testator, there are logical difficulties in the way of holding his estate, including the generally accepted rule that liability for defamation dies with the defamer.[51] For such reasons three American decisions have refused to find any liability at all.[52] Three others have held the estate liable, more or less frankly recognizing that the recovery, whether or not it fits very well into common law principles, is necessary as a matter of policy for the protection of those who would otherwise be helpless against the malice of the dead.[53] One possible solution may be for the probate

certiorari denied 311 U.S. 711, 61 S.Ct. 393, 85 L.Ed. 462; Donahue v. Warner Brothers Pictures, 10th Cir. 1952, 194 F.2d 6.

44. Hartmann v. Time, Inc., 3d Cir. 1948, 166 F.2d 127, certiorari denied 334 U.S. 838, 68 S.Ct. 1495, 92 L.Ed. 1763; Kilian v. Stackpole Sons, Inc., M.D.Pa. 1951, 98 F.Supp. 500; Insull v. New York World-Telegram Corp., N.D.Ill.1959, 172 F.Supp. 615, affirmed 7th Cir., 273 F.2d 166, certiorari denied 362 U.S. 942, 80 S.Ct. 807, 4 L.Ed.2d 770; Palmisano v. News Syndicate Co., S.D.N.Y.1955, 130 F.Supp. 17; Anderson v. Hearst Publishing Co., Inc., S.D.Cal.1954, 120 F.Supp. 850.

45. See Prosser, Interstate Publication, 1953, 51 Mich.L.Rev. 959, reprinted in Prosser, Selected Topics on the Law of Torts, 1954, 70; Notes, 1957, 35 N.C.L. Rev. 535; 1956, 32 N.D.L.Rev. 120; 1962, 56 Northwestern U.L.Rev. 823; 1957, 19 U.Pitt.L.Rev. 98; 1949, 35 Va.L.Rev. 627; 1953, 28 N.Y.U.L.Rev. 1006; 1953, 14 Ohio St.L.J. 96; 1963, 32 U.Cin.L.Rev. 520; 1964, 77 Harv.L.Rev. 1463.

46. Draper v. Hellman Commercial Trust & Savings Bank, 1928, 203 Cal. 26, 263 P. 240; Aetna Life Insurance Co. v. Brewer, 1926, 56 App.D.C. 283, 12 F.2d 818; Manion v. Jewel Tea Co., 1916, 135 Minn. 250, 160 N.W. 767. See Note, 1936, 20 Minn.L.Rev. 805.

47. Bond v. Douglas, 1836, 7 C. & P. 626, 173 Eng. Rep. 275; Valentine v. Gonzalez, 1929, 190 App.Div. 490, 179 N.Y.S. 711; Taylor v. Kinston Free Press Co., 1953, 237 N.C. 551, 75 S.E.2d 528; Storch v. Gordon, 1960, 23 Misc.2d 477, 197 N.Y.S.2d 309, reargument 23 Misc.2d 477, 202 N.Y.S.2d 43; Commonwealth v. Pratt, 1911, 208 Mass. 553, 95 N.E 105. Otherwise if no authorization can be found, Schoepflin v. Coffey, 1900, 162 N.Y. 12, 56 N.E. 502, reargument denied 162 N.Y. 663, 57 N.E. 1123; Henry v. Pittsburgh & Lake Erie Railroad Co., 1891, 139 Pa. 289, 21 A. 157.

48. Byrne v. Dean, [1937] 1 K.B. 818. Accord: Fogg v. Boston & Lowell Railroad Co., 1889, 148 Mass.

513, 20 N.E. 109; Woodling v. Knickerbocker, 1883, 31 Minn. 268, 17 N.W. 387; Tidmore v. Mills, 1947, 33 Ala. App. 243, 32 So.2d 769, certiorari denied 249 Ala. 648, 32 So.2d 782; Hellar v. Bianco, 1952, 111 Cal.App.2d 424, 244 P.2d 757. Contra, Scott v. Hull, 1970, 22 Ohio App.2d 141, 259 N.E.2d 160. See Notes, 1952, 40 Cal. L.Rev. 625; 1952, 31 N.C.L.Rev. 130; 1953, 5 Stan.L. Rev. 363.

49. See Freifield, Libel by Will, 1933, 19 A.B.A.J. 301; Di Falco, Libel in Wills, 1962, 8 N.Y.Law Forum 405; Notes, 1955, 24 Ford.L.Rev. 417; 1955, 12 Wash. & Lee L.Rev. 288; 1949, 6 Wash. & Lee L.Rev. 247; 1954, 1 U.C.L.A.L.Rev. 575; [1950] Wash.U.L.Rev. 122; 1949, 48 Mich.L.Rev. 220; 1945, 32 Va.L.Rev. 189; 1954, 33 N.C.L.Rev. 146; 1937, 21 Minn.L.Rev. 870.

50. Brown v. Mack, 1945, 185 Misc. 368, 56 N.Y.S. 2d 910; See Harris v. Nashville Trust Co., 1913, 128 Tenn. 573, 162 S.W. 584; Carver v. Morrow, 1948, 213 S.C. 199, 48 S.E.2d 814.

51. See infra, § 126.

52. Carver v. Morrow, 1948, 213 S.C. 199, 48 S.E.2d 814; Citizens & Southern National Bank v. Hendricks, 1933, 176 Ga. 692, 168 S.E. 313, conformed to 46 Ga. App. 670, 168 S.E. 925; Binder v. Oregon Bank, 1978, 284 Or. 89, 585 P.2d 655 overruling Kleinschmidt v. Matthieu, 1954, 201 Or. 406, 266 P.2d 686.

In Nagle v. Nagle, 1934, 316 Pa. 507, 175 A. 487, the will was held to be privileged, by analogy to pleadings filed in an action. The case does not make it clear whether the privilege is absolute or qualified.

53. Harris v. Nashville Trust Co., 1913, 128 Tenn. 573, 162 S.W. 584; Brown v. Mack, 1945, 185 Misc. 368, 56 N.Y.S.2d 910; In re Gallagher's Estate, Pa.1901, 10 Dist. 733; Brown v. Du Frey, 1956, 1 N.Y.2d 190, 151 N.Y.S.2d 649, 134 N.E.2d 469.

court to strike the defamatory matter from the copy of the will admitted to probate.[54]

Ordinarily the defendant is not liable for any publication made to others by the plaintiff himself, even though it was to be expected that he might publish it.[55] There are, however, a few cases in which, because of the plaintiff's blindness or immaturity,[56] or because of some necessity he was under to communicate the matter to others,[57] it was reasonably to be anticipated that he would do so, and the writer has been held to be responsible.

Fault Issues in Defamation Law

As a prerequisite to recovery, it has always been necessary for the plaintiff to prove as a part of his prima facie case that the defendant (1) published a statement that was (2) defamatory (3) of and concerning the plaintiff. In the typical case of defamation, the publisher (1) realized that the statement made was defamatory, (2) intended to refer to the plaintiff, and (3) intended to communicate it to a third person or persons. Thus, the publisher clearly acted with the intent to discredit another. There were then two critical issues—the truth or falsity of the statement and that of deciding which party should bear the risk of harm from falsehood. But the question of whether liability shall be imposed with or without fault arises in a variety of ways in connection with this tort, and the problems are quite different from those involved in the question of whether tort liability shall be imposed without respect to fault when the defendant's conduct has resulted in physical injury to persons or damage to tangible things. In many situations, the defendant's intent or state of mind may differ significantly from that present in the typical case just assumed.

First, the defendant may not have intended to communicate the statement to anyone, or at least to anyone other than the person disparaged, but due to some mishap, foreseeable or otherwise, publication to others occurred. Must there be fault with respect to publication?

In the second place, the defendant may not have intended a defamatory meaning and thus may have lacked the intent to communicate a defamatory statement.

In the third place, the defendant may have made a statement that was innocuous on its face, but by virtue of extrinsic facts unknown to the publisher, the statement actually carries a defamatory meaning to those who have knowledge of the extrinsic facts.

In the fourth place, the publisher might not intend to make any statement at all about the plaintiff. It might have been a statement about what was intended as a fictional character or someone else without knowledge of extrinsic facts that tie the statement to the particular plaintiff.

Finally, and most importantly, the publisher might have reasonably believed an unambiguous statement that was false and defamatory on its face to be true.

---

54. In re Estate of White, Eng. 1914, 30 T.L.R. 215, 83 L.J.P. 67; In re Draske's Will, 1936, 160 Misc. 587, 290 N.Y.S. 581. See Notes, 1937, 21 Minn.L.Rev. 870; 1945, 32 Va.L.Rev. 189. The solution is not a complete one, since defamatory words which are an inseparable part of dispositive clauses obviously cannot be expunged.

55. Lyle v. Waddle, 1945, 144 Tex. 90, 188 S.W.2d 770; Wilcox v. Moon, 1892, 64 Vt. 450, 24 A. 244; Lyon v. Lash, 1906, 74 Kan. 745, 88 P. 262; Konkle v. Haven, 1905, 140 Mich. 472, 103 N.W. 850; cf. Olson v. Molland, 1930, 181 Minn. 364, 232 N.W. 625 (negligence of plaintiff).

56. Lane v. Schilling, 1929, 130 Or. 119, 279 P. 267; Hedgpeth v. Coleman, 1922, 183 N.C. 309, 111 S.E. 517; Davis v. Askin's Retail Stores, 1937, 211 N.C. 551, 191 S.E. 33. Cf. Stevens v. Haering's Grocetorium, 1923, 125 Wash. 404, 216 P. 870 (hysterical Plaintiff).

But in Riley v. Askin & Marine Co., 1926, 134 S.C. 198, 132 S.E. 584, a more mature minor was held not to be expected to make the publication.

57. Colonial Stores v. Barrett, 1946, 73 Ga.App. 839, 38 S.E.2d 306 (wartime certificate of availability which plaintiff was required to exhibit); Grist v. Upjohn Co., 1969, 16 Mich.App. 452, 168 N.W.2d 389 (inquiry of prospective employer); Bretz v. Mayer, 1963, 1 Ohio Misc. 59, 203 N.E.2d 665 (letter to pastor containing very real threat to existence of church).

Fault and the Publication Requirement

Courts have never imposed strict liability on the defendant for accidental and non-negligent publication of defamatory matter. There is in fact no liability for publication which the defendant did not intend and could not reasonably anticipate, as in the case of words spoken with no reason to suppose that anyone but the plaintiff would overhear them,[58] or a sealed letter sent to the plaintiff himself which is unexpectedly opened and read by another.[59]

As stated heretofore, there may be several publishers of defamatory matter contained in a book or magazine, or broadcast over radio or television.[60] The author of a book is a publisher of the contents; so is the book publisher. The columnist whose daily column is printed in a newspaper is a publisher; so is the newspaper. Likewise, the person who utters a defamatory statement over television is a publisher, but so is the television station, even though the person who utters the statement is not an authorized agent of the television station. Those who are in the business of making their facilities available to disseminate the writings composed, the speeches made, and the information gathered by others may also be regarded as participating to such an extent in making the books, newspapers, magazines, and information available to others as to be regarded as publishers. They are intentionally making the contents available to others, sometimes without knowing all of the contents—including the defamatory content—and sometimes without any opportunity to ascertain, in advance, that any defamatory matter was to be included in the matter published. The question is to what extent should one who is in the business of making available to the general public what another writes or says be subject to liability for the defamatory matter that was published. In this connection, it is necessary to classify participants into three categories: primary publishers, secondary publishers or disseminators, and those who are suppliers of equipment and facilities and are not publishers at all.

The category into which a participant belongs depends upon the extent to which he participates with an author or a composer of the defamatory statement in its publication. Those who publish books by way of approving the printing of them and those who print and sell newspapers, magazines, journals, and the like are subject to liability as primary publishers. Those who play a secondary role in delivering and transmitting the possession of a physical embodiment of the defamatory matter, including selling and renting, are secondary publishers or disseminators. This would include libraries,[61] news vendors,[62] distributors,[63] or perhaps even carriers, according to some courts.[64]

---

58. See Hall v. Balkind, [1918] N.Z.L.Rep. 740; McNichol v. Grandy, [1931] Can.S.C.Rep. 696. Cf. Weir v. Hoss, 1844, 6 Ala. 881 (document copied and published without consent of defendant).

59. Yousling v. Dare, 1904, 122 Iowa 539, 98 N.W. 371; Riley v. Askin & Marine Co., 1926, 134 S.C. 198, 132 S.E. 584; Fordson Coal Co. v. Carter, 1937, 269 Ky. 805, 108 S.W.2d 1007; Olson v. Molland, 1930, 181 Minn. 364, 232 N.W. 625; Weidman v. Ketcham, 1938, 278 N.Y. 129, 15 N.E.2d 426.

The mere fact that defendant thought it possible that some third person might open the letter was held not sufficient for publication, where he had no special reason to expect it. Barnes v. Clayton House Motel, Tex. Civ.App.1968, 435 S.W.2d 616.

60. Supra, this section on Publication

61. Martin v. British Museum Trustees, 1894, 10 T.L.R. 338; Vizetelly v. Mudie's Select Library, [1900] 2 Q.B. 170.

62. Balabanoff v. Fossani, 1948, 192 Misc. 615, 81 N.Y.S.2d 732; Emmons v. Pottle, 1885, 16 Q.B.D. 354; Weldon v. Times Book Co., 1911, 28 T.L.R. 143.

63. Bottomley v. F.W. Woolworth & Co., Ct.App. 1932, 48 T.L.R. 521; Sexton v. American News Co., N.D.Fla.1955, 133 F.Supp. 591. See Hartmann v. American News Co., W.D.Wis.1947, 69 F.Supp. 736; Hartmann v. American News Co., 7th Cir. 1949, 171 F.2d 581, certiorari denied 337 U.S. 907, 69 S.Ct. 1049, 93 L.Ed. 1719.

64. Day v. Bream, 1837, 2 Moo. & R. 54, 174 Eng. Rep. 212 (porter distributing handbills). Accord: Layton v. Harris, Del.1842, 3 Har. 406; see Arnold v. Ingram, 1912, 151 Wis. 438, 138 N.W. 111. Cf. McLeod v. St. Aubyn, [1899] A.C. 549 (private lending of newspaper).

Those who supply equipment to others who use the equipment so supplied for the publication of defamatory matter are not publishers. This has been held to apply to a telephone company, whether the telephone is in a pay station or a private home.[65] In all such cases, the primary publisher as well as the disseminator publisher can be said to intend to publish all statements made by the author. But there are other fault questions to be considered. Those who assist the author in transmitting the defamatory matter may not be aware of the statement or have an opportunity to become aware of the statement, as when the statement is made in a speech in a television or radio broadcast. They may become aware of the statement, as is usually the case with a newspaper that prints the statements of a columnist or a publisher of a book that prints and sells the book containing defamatory statements.

This fault issue will be considered later.[66]

Fault With Respect to Truth or Falsity

Historically, the individual's interest in the enjoyment and maintenance of a good reputation has been regarded as so socially significant that both English and American law have protected the reputational interest by holding one who intentionally published defamatory material to a standard of strict liability or liability without consideration of fault. The intentional publisher of defamatory matter published at his peril in assessing the truth or falsity of the matter published. Moreover, the burden of proving the truth of the matter rested on the defendant-publisher. As a countervailing consideration, however, both England and America have recognized that if a free society is to function effectively, the people must have access to all relevant information about all kinds of activities carried on in society.

That being so, the courts have always entertained the view that the failure to make any allowances for "mistakes" in reporting about what is believed to be true would unduly hinder important speech and would discourage many from publishing the disparaging truth for fear of being unable to prove it. The established common law attempted to accommodate these competing values by the general notion that the defendant published at his peril unless he could prove that the statement was either true or that it was made on a privileged occasion.[67] It was through the development of a complex structure of privileges that the courts protected the societal interest in the free flow of ideas. This complex structure has not been eliminated, although the need therefor has been somewhat diminished as a consequence of the decisions of the Supreme Court of the United States with respect to the constitutional guarantees of freedom of the press and speech and could be easily diminished further by the adoption of Section 580 of the Second Restatement of Torts.

The numerous decision points and technicalities that have resulted from the efforts to strike a proper balance between the inconsistent and competing values of protecting speech on the one hand and reputation of people on the other have been the subject of severe criticisms by some English judges in recent years.[68] But a report of a committee in 1975 appointed by the Lord High Chancellor suggests that most of these complexities stem from the need to maintain a proper balance between the individual's right to his reputation and the public interest to preserve free speech.

Substantial changes have been wrought in the tort law of defamation since 1964 on the issue of fault as a prerequisite to recovery

---

65. Second Restatement of Torts, § 581, Comment b.

66. Infra, this section on Publishers and Disseminators.

67. Owens v. Scott Publishing Co., 1955, 46 Wn.2d 666, 284 P.2d 296; certiorari denied 1956, 350 U.S. 968, 76 S.Ct. 437, 100 L.Ed. 840; Hulton v. Jones, 1910 A.C. 20; Peck v. Tribune Co., 1909, 214 U.S. 185, 29 S.Ct. 554, 53 L.Ed. 960.

68. See Keeton, Defamation and Freedom of the Press, 1976, 54 Tex.L.Rev. 1221 at 1224; see also, Slim v. Daily Tel. Ltd., [1968] 2 Q.B. 157, 179 (C.A.) (Diplock. L.J.).

with respect to the truth or falsity of a defamatory statement intentionally published. Beginning in that year with New York Times v. Sullivan,[69] the Supreme Court of the United States has created, then expanded,[70] but now seemingly halted,[71] any further expansion of a constitutional privilege based on the First Amendment privileges of freedom of the press and speech that defeats a defamation recovery against those utilizing the mass media for disseminating information to the general public. The precise boundaries of the constitutional privilege have not as yet been determined, and they may not be for many years. Meanwhile, the states must conform the common law to the perceived requirements of the first amendment and consider other changes that ought to be made as a consequence.

In marking out the constitutional dimensions of the privilege to defame, the Supreme Court has directed attention to at least four considerations: (1) the important role of the press and the electronic media in the dissemination of facts and ideas about people and their activities, and the danger of self-censorship inherent in the common law rule of publishing at peril; (2) the nature of a defamed person's opportunity to gain access to a public medium to answer a defamatory imputation and to protect his reputation by a process of self-defense; (3) the extent to which a person should be expected to assume the risk of false and defamatory statements being made about himself or herself as a consequence of assuming a role of importance in the resolution of issues of general public concern; and (4) the difference between communications that are made primarily to protect and advance interests or that relate to matters of general public concern, and those that relate to private matters. The precise extent of the change in the law that has been made or that will be the consequences of the constitutional change in a particular state cannot be predicted. But the changes have affected a number of issues, especially the issue as to the nature of the fault, if any, required as a prerequisite to liability in a particular situation.

Defamation of Public Officials and Public Figures

The constitutional privilege, as it has been described, has abolished the common law principle that a public medium—such as (a) publisher of a book, magazine, or newspaper, and (b) television or radio broadcaster—publishes at its peril and substitutes therefor the requirement that in every case fault is a prerequisite to liability.[72] The common law rule subjecting the media to liability except when there was either a qualified or absolute privilege to publish or proof by the defendant-publisher of the truth of all discreditable statements does not afford adequate protection to the First Amendment guarantee of freedom of the press.

The constitutional privilege extended to the press and to any public medium requires a differentiation between private individuals on the one hand and public officials and public figures on the other. Statements made about public officials and public figures, especially when made by a public medium, generally relate to matters of general public interest and are made about people that have substantial influence and impact on the lives of other people. Moreover, "public officials" and "public figures" generally have some access to a public medium for answering disparaging falsehood, whereas private individuals do not have ready access to a medium reaching the recipients of private defamatory communications.

---

69. 1964, 376 U.S. 254, 84 S.Ct. 710, 11 L.Ed.2d 686, motion denied 376 U.S. 967, 84 S.Ct. 1130, 12 L.Ed.2d 83.

70. Rosenbloom v. Metromedia, Inc., 1971, 403 U.S. 29, 91 S.Ct. 1811, 29 L.Ed.2d 296.

71. Gertz v. Robert Welch, Inc., 1974, 418 U.S. 323, 94 S.Ct. 2997, 41 L.Ed.2d 789.

72. New York Times v. Sullivan, 1964, 376 U.S. 254, 84 S.Ct. 710, 11 L.Ed.2d 686, motion denied 376 U.S. 967, 84 S.Ct. 1130, 12 L.Ed.2d 83; Gertz v. Robert Welch, Inc., 1974, 418 U.S. 323, 94 S.Ct. 2997, 41 L.Ed.2d 789; Time, Inc. v. Firestone, 1976, 424 U.S. 448, 96 S.Ct. 958, 47 L.Ed.2d 154, on remand Fla., 332 So.2d 68.

The category of public officials includes not only those who are commonly classified as public officers but also public employees who exercise any substantial governmental power.[73] In this connection, it is well to observe that police officials, even the patrolman on the beat, have uniformly been treated as public officials within the meaning of the *New York Times* rule. This is because a wholesome respect for the law by those who are enforcing the law is considered to be of great importance in a society that is dedicated to the preservation of individual human dignity.[74]

In Gertz v. Robert Welch, Inc., the Supreme Court in 1974 made it clear that the public figure status is one that should only be applied to a person who has assumed a role of importance in the resolution of public affairs or affairs of general importance or concern to the people generally. Two types of public figures were envisioned: (1) those who are public figures for all purposes because they have achieved such a significant role in the resolution of issues of importance as to make most true and discreditable conduct and characteristic matters of legitimate public interest, relating as such information does to credibility, trustworthiness, and integrity; (2) those who are public figures only because they have voluntarily injected themselves into the resolution of particular controversies or issues of importance to the general public. Thus, as Justice Powell observed: "It is preferable to reduce the public-figure question to a more meaningful context by looking to the nature and extent of an individual's participation in the particular controversy giving rise to the defamation." [75]

Subsequent cases seem to stress three matters about the constitutional privilege in relation to the limited public figure principle:

(1) the plaintiff must have voluntarily injected himself into the resolution of an issue or controversy; (2) the issue or controversy must have been one the resolution of which can affect the general public or some substantial segment of it in an appreciable way and is, therefore, a public controversy; and (3) the defamation must have grown out of or be related to such an issue. Thus, the socialite wife of a wealthy industrialist was not a public figure merely because she was socially prominent and her divorce suit was highly publicized.[76] Nor was a mental health researcher a public figure simply because his research had been made a public issue by a senator who chose to disparage his research and the use of public funds for such purpose by way of bestowing on him a "Golden Fleece Award." The defendant projected the plaintiff into the controversy.[77]

The constitutional privilege which requires that a public official or a public figure establish with clear and convincing clarity that the defamatory falsehood was published with knowledge of its falsity or recklessly is inapplicable if the defamatory matter relates to aspects of the person's life that does not relate to a legitimate public interest. It is quite possible that some defamatory imputations about high ranking public officials—or public figures for all purposes—will not be considered of enough legitimate concern to the general public to be concerned about self-censorship. Certainly this would seem to be true of many public officials.

The question of whether the plaintiff is a public official or a public figure subject to the rules set forth above is one of federal law for the judge to resolve. Probably, the burden of proof will be on the defendant to show such facts as necessary to establish the favored category.

---

73. Rosenblatt v. Baer, 1966, 383 U.S. 75, 86 S.Ct. 669, 15 L.Ed.2d 597.

74. Gray v. Udevitz, 10th Cir. 1981, 656 F.2d 588 and the cases therein cited.

75. Gertz v. Robert Welch, Inc., 1974, 418 U.S. 323, 352, 94 S.Ct. 2997, 3013, 41 L.Ed.2d 789, 812.

76. Time, Inc. v. Firestone, 1976, 424 U.S. 448, 96 S.Ct. 958, 47 L.Ed.2d 154, on remand Fla., 332 So.2d 68.

77. See also Wolston v. Reader's Digest Association, Inc., 1979, 443 U.S. 157, 99 S.Ct. 2701, 61 L.Ed.2d 450.

There remains some doubt as to whether a non-media individual defendant who utilizes a public medium for the publication of defamatory matter will be accorded the same privilege as the public medium. The New York Times privilege was based in large part on the notion that the framers of the constitution believed the success of self-government and the prevention of tyranny depended to a considerable extent upon an unencumbered flow of information to the citizenry from a free press.[78] Chief Justice Burger observed in Hutchinson v. Proxmire that the Supreme Court had not yet decided whether the *New York Times* standard can apply to an individual defendant as well as to a media defendant.[79] It appears that a good many courts have simply assumed that the privilege which has been extended to the media applies also to those who use the media.[80]

A further question relates to whether the constitutional privilege available to the media and those who use the media should or does extend to all persons and entities with respect to private communication or communications to a narrow audience about public officials and public figures. Courts have usually said that defamatory communications about public officials and public figures made privately or to small groups are protected in the same manner and to the same extent, at least if the matter communicated is related to a matter of genuine public concern.[81] Thus, a disparaging statement made about a law school dean in an accreditation report by a member of the American Bar Association's accreditation team was held to be constitutionally privileged under *New York Times*, even though made to a narrow audience. The law school accreditation process was regarded as a public controversy—an issue of public concern—into which the dean had voluntarily injected himself.[82]

The American Law Institute has taken the position that in principle, and even though the constitutional protections of freedom of speech do not demand it, a public figure or a public official should not be allowed to recover against anyone for defamatory communications relating to such a person's conduct, fitness, or role in such capacity without proof that the communication was made with knowledge of the falsity or in reckless disregard of it.[83]

Defamation Regarding Private Matters About Public Officials and Public Figures and Defamation of Private Persons

In Gertz v. Robert Welch, Inc.,[84] the Supreme Court specifically held that the First Amendment does not permit the imposition of liability without fault on the public medium that publishes a defamatory statement even about private individuals and private matters. This holding has been construed to mean that the medium must have published with either knowledge of the falsity of the statement or recklessly or negligently with respect to the truth or falsity of the statement in any case. And as regards defamation of public officials and public figures, this constitutional privilege will no doubt be regarded as extending to those who utilize a medium as well as the medium itself. The assumption behind the holding in *Gertz* is that normally information about matters that are communicated publicly through the media are of some legitimate interest and

---

78. Whitney v. California, 1927, 274 U.S. 357, 375–376, 47 S.Ct. 641, 71 L.Ed. 1095, rehearing granted 269 U.S. 538, 46 S.Ct. 120, 70 L.Ed. 400.

79. 1979, 443 U.S. 111, 133, fn. 16, 99 S.Ct. 2675, 2687, fn. 16, 61 L.Ed.2d 411, 430, fn. 16.

80. See Woy v. Turner, W.D.Ga.1981, 533 F.Supp. 102 (defamatory remarks made in a telecast).

81. Davis v. Schuchat, D.C.Cir. 1975, 510 F.2d 731; Avins v. White, 3d Cir. 1980, 627 F.2d 637, certiorari denied 449 U.S. 982, 101 S.Ct. 398, 66 L.Ed.2d 244.

82. Avins v. White, supra, note 81.

83. Second Restatement of Torts, § 580A, Comment *h*. Recklessness requires evidence sufficient to permit the conclusion that the defendant entertained serious doubts. St. Amant v. Thompson, 1968, 390 U.S. 727, 88 S.Ct. 1323, 20 L.Ed.2d 262.

84. 1974, 418 U.S. 323, 94 S.Ct. 2997, 41 L.Ed.2d 789.

importance to the general public; therefore, no decision should be made that something is not newsworthy unless, if true, its publication would constitute such an outrageous example of offensive conduct as to constitute an invasion of privacy. It is quite obvious that non-negligent mistakes can be made in reporting about newsworthy events involving private persons. There is much to be said for allowing the news media the privilege of publishing whatever is reasonably regarded as true and newsworthy.

It does not follow that this constitutional privilege, which is extended to the public medium and those who use it to publish whatever is deemed to be newsworthy and true so long as the publisher has reasonable grounds to believe in the truth of the matter published, will be extended to those who communicate privately about private persons regarding matters that do not involve public officials or public figures. The Supreme Court has sought to avoid "self-censorship" of those who publish about matters involving the public interest. It may be that the qualified and absolute privileges structure that has been developed under the common law is more than adequate to protect speech about private interests generally.[85] However, the American Law Institute has predicted that state law will require as a prerequisite to recovery in any case of defamation a showing of at least negligence with respect to truth or falsity and that such should be the law.[86] Private interests have been protected under the common law through the recognition of a variety of conditionally privileged occasions discussed later. This has resulted in a great deal of complexity. Much could be accomplished by way of simplifying the law and adequately protecting speech in the private area by way of requiring fault with respect to truth or falsity of the matter published in all situations. Most qualified privileges could then be abolished. Unfortunately, the American Law Institute chose to retain the conditional privilege structure by way of requiring dishonesty or malice as a requirement for recovery.

Other Fault Issues

As indicated heretofore, a defendant in a defamation case may have published what proved to be a defamatory statement that (1) was innocuous on its face, or (2) could reasonably be construed to have been innocuous on its face or defamatory on its face, or (3) was not intended by the defendant to refer to the plaintiff. As to all three of these matters, the common law rule was that the defendant was strictly liable and published at his peril.

In 1910, in the celebrated case of Hulton & Co. v. Jones,[87] the English courts carried this to its logical conclusion. The defendants published in their newspaper a story from their Paris correspondent to the effect that one Artemus Jones, a person whom they intended and believed to be entirely fictitious, had been seen at Dieppe with a woman not his wife. Out of the wilds of North Wales appeared a real Artemus Jones—incidentally a lawyer—claiming that the story had been understood by his neighbors to refer to him. The House of Lords affirmed a decision in his favor, holding, to the extent of £1,750 in damages, that the defendant's innocence did not excuse him from liability.

Following the rule laid down by the English decisions, the defendant has been held liable, without regard to any question of negligence, in a series of cases where he did not intend to make the particular statement at all, as where a typographical error has changed "cultured gentleman" into "colored gentleman;"[88] where he did not intend to

---

85. See, Robertson, Defamation and the First Amendment, 1976, 54 Tex.L.Rev. 199, 217.

86. See § 580B and Comment f.

87. [1909] 2 K.B. 44, affirmed, [1910] A.C. 20. See Holdsworth, A Chapter of Accidents in the Law of Libel, 1941, 57 L.Q.Rev. 74; Smith, Jones v. Hulton: Three Conflicting Views as to Defamation, 1912, 60 U.Pa.L.Rev. 364, 461.

88. Upton v. Times-Democrat Publishing Co., 1900, 104 La. 141, 28 So. 970; Taylor v. Hearst, 1896, 107 Cal. 262, 40 P. 392; Id., 1897, 118 Cal. 366, 50 P. 541. Cf. Burton v. Crowell Publishing Co., 2d Cir. 1936, 82 F.2d 154 (obscene optical illusion in photograph).

refer to the plaintiff or was ignorant of his existence,[89] as in the case of a mistake as to the name, photograph or address,[90] or the use of a name believed to be fictitious,[91] or where the statement was true of one of two persons of the same name but not as to the other;[92] where he did not expect the words to be understood in any defamatory sense,[93] or the meaning was attached solely by extrinsic facts of which he was quite unaware—as in the Scottish case[94] in which the plaintiff who was stated to have given birth to twins had been married only one month; where the defendant honestly and reasonably believed his statement to be true, and was repeating it on good authority;[95] where he intended to praise the plaintiff rather than to defame him;[96] where he believed in good faith that he was exercising a privilege which did not exist;[97] and where he was drunk at the time and did not know what he was saying.[98]

The only limitation placed upon the liability is that the defamatory meaning and the reference to the plaintiff must be reasonably conveyed to and understood by others;[99] and in the case of the use of a name for an obviously fictitious character in a book, it has been held that there is no liability where no sensible person would understand that it is intended to depict the plaintiff.[1]

The effect of this strict liability is to place the printed, written, or spoken word in the same class with the use of explosives or the keeping of dangerous animals. If a defamatory meaning, which is false, is reasonably understood, the defendant publishes at his peril, and there is no possible defense except the rather narrow one of privilege. The rule has not gone without criticism.[2] In the interest of our traditional freedom of expres-

89. Switzer v. Anthony, 1922, 71 Colo. 291, 206 P. 391.

90. Laudati v. Stea, 1922, 44 R.I. 303, 117 A. 422 ("The question is not who was aimed at, but who was hit"); Walker v. Bee-News Publishing Co., 1932, 122 Neb. 511, 240 N.W. 579; Hatfield v. Gazette Printing Co., 1918, 103 Kan. 513, 175 P. 382; Whitcomb v. Hearst Corp., 1952, 329 Mass. 193, 107 N.E.2d 295; Petransky v. Repository Printing Co., 1935, 51 Ohio App. 306, 200 N.E. 647.

91. Hulton & Co. v. Jones, [1909] 2 K.B. 44, affirmed [1910] A.C. 20; Corrigan v. Bobbs-Merrill Co., 1920, 228 N.Y. 58, 126 N.E. 260.

92. Washington Post Co. v. Kennedy, 1925, 55 App. D.C. 162, 3 F.2d 207; Newstead v. London Express Newspapers, [1940] 1 K.B. 377; Lee v. Wilson and MacKinnon, 1934, 51 Comm.L.Rep., Aust., 276. See Notes, 1935, 51 L.Q.Rev. 572; 1941, 89 U.Pa.L.Rev. 676.

Otherwise where there are accompanying words indicating the other person. Carter Publications v. Fleming, 1937, 129 Tex. 667, 106 S.W.2d 672 ("father of the accused").

93. Hankinson v. Bilby, 1847, 16 M. & W. 442, 153 Eng.Rep. 1262; Barr v. Birkner, 1895, 44 Neb. 197, 62 N.W. 494; Nash v. Fisher, 1917, 24 Wyo. 535, 162 P. 933; Ladwig v. Heyer, 1907, 136 Iowa 196, 113 N.W. 767; Milam v. Railway Express Agency, 1937, 185 S.C. 194, 193 S.E. 324.

94. Morrison v. Ritchie & Co., 1904, 4 Fraser, Sess. Cas., 645, 39 Scot.L.Rep. 432. Accord: Cassidy v. Daily Mirror Newspapers, [1929] 2 K.B. 331.

95. Bromage v. Prosser, 1825, 4 B. & C. 247, 107 Eng.Rep. 1051; Barnes v. Campbell, 1879, 59 N.H. 128;

Oklahoma Publishing Co. v. Givens, 10th Cir. 1933, 67 F.2d 62; Szalay v. New York American, 1938, 254 App. Div. 249, 4 N.Y.S.2d 620; Kelly v. Independent Publishing Co., 1912, 45 Mont. 127, 122 P. 735.

96. Martin v. The Picayune, 1906, 115 La. 979, 40 So. 376. Cf. Triggs v. Sun Printing & Publishing Association, 1904, 179 N.Y. 144, 71 N.E. 739 (jest); Dall v. Time, Inc., 1937, 252 App.Div. 636, 300 N.Y.S. 680, affirmed, 1938, 278 N.Y. 635, 16 N.E.2d 297, reargument denied 278 N.Y. 718, 17 N.E.2d 138 (intended as fiction).

97. See Stuart v. Bell, [1891] 2 Q.B. 341; Hebditch v. MacIlwaine, [1894] 2 Q.B. 54. The defendant's good faith belief, however, may bear upon the existence of the privilege itself. See infra, § 115.

98. Reed v. Harper, 1868, 25 Iowa 87.

99. Macfadden's Publications, Inc. v. Turner, Tex. Civ.App.1936, 95 S.W.2d 1027.

1. Clare v. Farrell, D.Minn.1947, 70 F.Supp. 276. Accord: Nebb v. Bell Syndicate, D.N.Y.1941, 41 F.Supp. 929 (comic strip character); Landau v. Columbia Broadcasting System, 1954, 205 Misc. 357, 128 N.Y.S.2d 254, affirmed 1 A.D.2d 660, 147 N.Y.S.2d 687 (name on door in television broadcast); Newton v. Grubbs, 1913, 155 Ky. 479, 159 S.W. 994 (rumor identifying woman not named by defendant).

2. See Notes, 1941, 25 Minn.L.Rev. 495; 1947, 25 Cal.L.Rev. 462; 1909, 25 L.Q.Rev. 341; 1912, 32 Can. L.T. 621, 1916, 29 Harv.L.Rev. 533; 1925, 38 Harv.L. Rev. 1100; 1925, 10 Corn.L.Q. 527. The rule is defended, however, by Smith, Jones v. Hulton: Three Conflicting Views as to a Question of Defamation, 1912, 60

sion, it is not clear that the losses due to innocently inflicted harm to reputation should be borne by the publishing industry, or a fortiori by the individual speaker—particularly if libel, and some forms of slander, are to be actionable without proof that harm has occurred. The opportunity for extortionate suits is great, and it is an open secret that plaintiffs frequently take advantage of it; and while the law of libel provides a useful restraint upon irresponsible journalism, it is achieved at the expense of a heavy burden upon innocent and careful publishers. It is not at all certain that liability for negligence, coupled with a high standard of care and a presumption that defamatory publications are made negligently, would not provide all the protection that is really desirable.[3] There has been something of an undercurrent of rebellion against the strict liability rule, and a tendency to hold that at least negligence is essential to the cause of action.[4]

It cannot be said that the constitutional privilege of free speech necessarily relates to these questions. The decisions related to the constitutional privilege have been concerned about the danger of self-censorship resulting from the likelihood that what one believes to be true may sometimes prove to be false. However, strict liability with respect to these collateral issues is a substantial burden placed on freedom of expression, and it is not likely that such liability as to these matters will survive the revolution that has occurred in the law of defamation.

Fault in the sense of either negligence or recklessness is quite likely to be a prerequisite to recovery on all such matters as regards all publications of defamation that relate to the public interest.

Publishers and Disseminators

Those who manufacture books by way of printing and selling them, and those who print and sell newspapers, magazines, journals, and the like, are subject to liability as primary publishers because they have the opportunity to know the content of the material being published and should therefore be subject to the same liability rules as are the author and originator of the written material. This does not mean that such a primary publisher is vicariously liable for the author's tortious conduct.[5] It only means that the publisher is subject to liability for publishing with actual malice or negligence, depending upon the plaintiff's status.

Prior to *New York Times* and its progeny, the primary publisher was strictly liable in the same way as the author. Today, the primary publisher as a public medium will not be subject to liability except on proof of fault of an authorized agent.

It would appear quite clearly that those who perform a secondary role in disseminating defamatory matter authored and published by others in the form of books, magazines, and the like—as in the case of libraries,[6] news vendors,[7] distributors,[8] and

U.Pa.L.Rev. 365, 461; Morris, Inadvertent Newspaper Libel and Retraction, 1937, 32 Ill.L.Rev. 36.

3. It should be noted that many of the cases cited above, involving typographical errors, mistakes as to the identity of the person, or the interpretation of the words used, might have reached the same conclusion on the basis of negligence. Other examples of careless reporting: Thorson v. Albert Lea Publishing Co., 1933, 190 Minn. 200, 251 N.W. 177, 90 A.L.R. 1169; Park v. Detroit Free Press Co., 1888, 72 Mich. 560, 40 N.W 731; Coffman v. Spokane Chronicle Publishing Co., 1911, 65 Wash. 1, 117 P. 596; Turton v. New York Recorder Co., 1894, 144 N.Y. 144, 38 N.E. 1009; Turner v. Hearst, 1896, 115 Cal. 394, 47 P. 129.

4. Hanson v. Globe Newspaper Co., 1893, 159 Mass. 293, 34 N.E. 462 (mistake in name; discredited, however-

er, in Sweet v. Post Publishing Co., 1913, 215 Mass. 450, 102 N.E. 660); Jones v. R.L. Polk & Co., 1915, 190 Ala. 243, 67 So. 577 (typographical error); Memphis Commercial Appeal v. Johnson, 6th Cir. 1938, 96 F.2d 672 (identity of person). Cf. Layne v. Tribune Co., 1933, 108 Fla. 177, 146 So. 234 (honest and reasonable republication); Summit Hotel Co. v. National Broadcasting Co., 1939, 336 Pa. 182, 8 A.2d 302 (interpolation in radio broadcast).

5. See, Washington Post Co. v. Keogh, D.C.Cir 1966, 365 F.2d 965, certiorari denied 385 U.S. 1011, 87 S.Ct. 708, 17 L.Ed.2d 548.

6. Martin v. British Museum Trustees, 1894, 10 T.L.R. 338; Vizetelly v. Mudie's Select Library, [1900] 2 Q.B. 170.

carriers[9]—would not be subject to liability to anyone in the absence of proof that they knew or had reason to know of the existence of defamatory matter contained in matter published. But this would not be the extent of the protection that should be accorded most of those who have commonly been regarded as disseminators or transmitters of defamatory matter who simply assist primary publishers in distributing information. Indeed, it is at least arguable that some, if not all, of those engaged in transmitting information of primary publishers, especially those who have an obligation or duty to transmit matters that the primary publisher appears to be privileged to publish by the method used, should have some kind of special privilege to transmit defamatory matter known to be false. It would be rather ridiculous, under most circumstances, to expect a bookseller or a library to withhold distribution of a good book because of a belief that a derogatory statement contained in the book was both false and defamatory of the plaintiff. Under the *Second Restatement of Torts*, a special privilege is recognized on behalf of a disseminator, but it is not an absolute privilege. It applies despite awareness on the part of the disseminator that the communication is both false and defamatory and is therefore a much broader privilege than the constitutional or qualified privilege of the primary publisher. It is a privilege to disseminate or transmit a statement known to be both defamatory and false, if either (a) the originator had a privilege or (b) the disseminator reasonably believed that the originator had a privilege. But it is said that the privilege—albeit, a special one since it is a privilege to publish defamatory matter known to be false—is not an absolute one and can be abused, as when one publishes solely for the purpose of doing harm.[10] This is a doubtful resolution of the problem. It is at least arguable that transmitters or disseminators should not be subjected to litigation over the issue of whether or not they disseminated with an improper motive. A particular transmitter's privilege should be either absolute or the privilege should be limited to the type of case where he did not know or have reason to know of the falsity of the defamatory matter being transmitted. This could easily depend upon the type of transmitter and the transmitter's relationship to the originating publisher. At any rate, the privilege has been explained as a privilege to make it possible for the primary publisher to utilize effectively his privilege, constitutional or otherwise.

The telegraph company presents a somewhat special problem.

In 1940, a federal court questioned whether a telegraph company, required as it is to serve all and without discrimination, "is ever to be held liable for the routine transmission of a defamatory message" and, if so, whether it should "only be in the necessarily rare cases where the transmitting agent of the telegraph company happened to know that the message was spurious or that the sender was acting, not in the protection of any legitimate interest, but in bad faith and for the purpose of traducing another." [11] Ten years later, it was held that a telegraph company would be liable if an agent knew or had reason to know that the sender was not privileged to send the defamatory message.[12]

7. Balabanoff v. Fossani, 1948, 192 Misc. 615, 81 N.Y.S.2d 732; Emmons v. Pottle, 1885, 16 Q.B.D. 354; Weldon v. Times Book Co., 1911, 28 T.L.R. 143.

8. Bottomley v. F.W. Woolworth & Co., Ct.App. 1932, 48 T.L.R. 521; Sexton v. American News Co., N.D.Fla.1955, 133 F.Supp. 591. See Hartmann v. American News Co., W.D.Wis.1947, 69 F.Supp. 736; Hartmann v. American News Co., 7th Cir. 1949, 171 F.2d 581, certiorari denied 337 U.S. 907, 69 S.Ct. 1049, 93 L.Ed. 1719.

9. Day v. Bream, 1837, 2 Moo. & R. 54, 174 Eng. Rep. 212 (porter distributing handbills). Accord: Layton v. Harris, Del.1842, 3 Har. 406; see Arnold v. Ingram, 1912, 151 Wis. 438, 138 N.W. 111. Cf. McLeod v. St. Aubyn, [1899] A.C. 549 (private lending of newspaper).

10. Second Restatement of Torts, § 612, Comment e.

11. O'Brien v. Western Union Telegraph Co., 1st Cir. 1940, 113 F.2d 539, 543.

12. Western Union Telegraph Co. v. Lesesne, 4th Cir. 1950, 182 F.2d 135.

That case seemed to subject the telegraph company to liability for sending a message defamatory on its face, if, but only if, it knew or had reason to know that the sender was not privileged to send the message. Thus, the privilege is much more likely to protect the telegraph company, since it can assume that the sender of a defamatory message is privileged unless it has some information to believe the contrary.[13]

Defamacast

There has been a lively dispute over defamation by television or radio, which has turned chiefly on whether broadcasting companies are to be held primarily responsible, like a newspaper, for their cooperation in publishing defamation originating with others[14] or only secondarily so, by analogy to the telegraph company and the news vendors.[15] Six decisions have dealt with the question, prior to *New York Times*, and three of them held the station strictly liable,[16] while the other three held that it was not liable[17] in the absence of intent or negligence. Statutes in a number of states, urged by the National Broadcasting Association, have adopted the latter position.[18] On the other hand, the English Defamation Act of 1952 imposed strict liability.[19] This all happened when strict liability was imposed on a primary publisher of defamation. But the situation is now quite different. Even if a broadcasting defendant is held to be accountable as a primary publisher of the defamatory utterances of one who is not an agent, such a media defendant will not be liable in the absence of some kind of fault in permitting a false and defamatory statement to be published. Moreover, if the broadcasting station is considered a primary publisher, as it probably should be, it will probably not be subject to vicarious liability of the originator. This is so even when the station deprives itself of the opportunity to become aware of the defamatory statement before its broadcast by its failure to use an electronic delay system for ascertaining defamatory statements before they are transmitted.[20] Moreover, it has been assumed in at least two cases of this nature that if the plaintiff is a public official or a public figure, the kind of fault required on the part of the broadcasting station—in depriving itself of the opportunity to evaluate the truth or falsity of a statement made by an anonymous telephone caller as a part of a talk show—must be recklessness with respect to the truth or falsity of defamatory statements that might be made.[21]

13. Second Restatement of Torts, § 612, Comment g.

14. See Vold, The Basis of Liability for Defamation by Radio, 1935, 19 Minn.L.Rev. 611; Vold, Defamation by Radio, 1932, 2 J.Radio Law 673; Vold, Defamatory Interpolations in Radio Broadcasts, 1940, 88 U.Pa.L. Rev. 249; Donnelly, Defamation by Radio: A Reconsideration, 1948, 34 Iowa L.Rev. 212; Remmers, Recent Trends in Defamation by Radio, 1951, 64 Harv.L.Rev. 727; Leflar, Radio and TV Defamation: Fault or Strict Liability? 1954, 15 Ohio St.L.J. 252; Notes, 1933, 11 Neb.L.B. 325; 1932, 81 U.Pa.L.Rev. 249; 1941, 39 Mich.L.Rev. 1002; 1964, 2 Houst.L.Rev. 238; 1964, 15 Mercer L.Rev. 450.

15. See Bohlen, Fifty Years of Torts, 1937, 50 Harv. L.Rev. 725, 729–31; Sprague, Freedom of the Air, 1937, 8 Air L.Rev. 30; Sprague, More Freedom of the Air, 1940, 11 Air L.Rev. 17; Farnham, Defamation by Radio and the American Law Institute, 1936, 16 Bos. U.L.Rev. 1; Haley, The Law on Radio Programs, 1937, 5 Geo.Wash.L.Rev. 157; Guider, Liability for Defamation in Political Broadcasts, 1932, 2 J.Radio Law 728; Seitz, Responsibility of Radio Stations for Extemporaneous Defamation, 1940, 24 Marq.L.Rev. 117.

16. Sorenson v. Wood, 1932, 123 Neb. 348, 243 N.W. 82; Miles v. Louis Wasmer, Inc., 1933, 172 Wash. 466, 20 P.2d 847; Coffey v. Midland Broadcasting Co., D.Mo.1934, 8 F.Supp. 889. See also Irwin v. Ashurst, 1938, 158 Or. 61, 67, 74 P.2d 1127, 1130.

17. Summit Hotel Co. v. National Broadcasting Co., 1939, 336 Pa. 182, 8 A.2d 302; Kelly v. Hoffman, 1948, 137 N.J.L. 695, 61 A.2d 143; Josephson v. Knickerbocker Broadcasting Co., 1942, 179 Misc. 787, 38 N.Y.S.2d 985.

18. See Remmers, Recent Legislative Trends in Defamation by Radio, 1951, 64 Harv.L.Rev. 727; Leflar, Radio and TV Defamation: Fault or Strict Liability, 1954, 15 Ohio St.L.J. 252; Note, 1956, 9 Okla.L.Rev. 103.

19. See Williams, Committee on the Law of Defamation: The Porter Report, 1949, 12 Mod.L.Rev. 217; Todd, The Defamation Act, 1952, 1953, 16 Mod.L.Rev. 476; Note, 1953, 66 Harv.L.Rev. 476.

20. Adams v. Frontier Broadcasting Co., Wyo.1976, 555 P.2d 556.

21. Adams v. Frontier Broadcasting Co., Wyo.1976, 555 P.2d 556; Snowden v. Pearl River Broadcasting

§ 113A DEFAMATORY OPINION 813

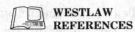

WESTLAW REFERENCES

Publication

publication* publish! /s element* /s defam! libel! slander!

publication* publish! /s libel! slander! defam! /s family spouse wife husband

publication* publish! /s libel! slander! defam! /s repeat! repetition* republish republication*

defam! libel! /s probat*** /s will testament

Fault Issues in Defamation Law

opinion(libel! slander! defam! & fault /s publish! publication*)

Fault With Respect to Truth or Falsity

libel! slander! defam! /p liab! fault /s truth untrue fals!

libel! slander! defam! /p constitutional /5 privilege*

Defamation of Public Officials and Public Figures

defam! libel! slander! /s public /5 offic! figure*

defam! libel! slander! /p public /5 offic! figure* /p "constitutional privilege*"

gertz /s 418 +5 323 /p public +4 offic! figure*

Defamation Regarding Private Matters About Public Officials and Public Figures and Defamation of Private Persons

defam! libel! slander! /p knowledge /5 falsity /p reckless** /5 disregard!

restatement /s torts /5 580a

defam! libel! slander! /p innocuous innocent /s liable liability fault

defam! libel! slander! /s "strict liability"

Publishers and Disseminators

slander! libel! defam! /p vicarious** /5 liable liability

slander! defam! libel! /p telegraph

Defamacast

di defamacast

defam! slander! libel! /p radio television broadcast! /p liable liability fault /s primar! secondar! strict**

§ 113A. Defamatory Opinion

The English-American law of defamation has always distinguished between the publication of defamatory statements of fact and derogatory or defamatory expression of opinions about others.¹ The distinction is a necessary and important one. In the first place, truth served as a defense for one who published defamation. If truth constituted a defense when defendant published a defamatory statement of fact, then it must have been a defense when one published a defamatory opinion. But the ascertainment of what is truth when one publishes an opinion poses a quite different question from that which is presented when one publishes a statement of fact about another. In the second place and aside from the defense of truth, everyone had under the common law a qualified privilege of "fair comment" on matters of public interest.² In the third place, the First Amendment constitutional privileges are likely to encompass all *pure* opinions, even those that have heretofore been regarded as false and actionable, that would make the expression of pure opinions non-actionable.

Kinds of Defamatory Opinions

At least three separate and distinct kinds of derogatory opinions can be identified: deductive opinions only, evaluation opinions only, and opinions (deductive or evaluative) that imply information that would reasonably support such opinions.

A deductive opinion only is published if the publisher implies or deduces misconduct to the plaintiff or some other disparaging fact about plaintiff, such as being a part of a conspiracy or murdering his partner, on the

---

Corp., La.App.1971, 251 So.2d 405, application denied 259 La. 887, 253 So.2d 217.

§ 113A

1. Restatement of Torts §§ 566, 606 (1938); 1 F. Harper & F. James, Law of Torts, § 5.28; W. Prosser, supra note 6, § 115, at 792. Gatley states: "It is comment to say that a certain act which a man has done is disgraceful or dishonourable; it is an allegation of fact to say that he did the act so criticised." C. Gatley on Libel and Slander, supra note 3, at ¶ 705.

2. Triggs v. Sun Printing & Publishing Association, 1904, 179 N.Y. 144, 154, 71 N.E. 739, 742; Broadway Approvals Ltd. v. Odhams Press, [1965] 1 W.L.R. 805 (C.A.); Restatement of Torts § 606 (1938); C. Gatley on Libel and Slander, supra note 3, at ¶ 701; see Comment, Privilege of Fair Comment, 62 Harv.L.Rev. 41 (1930); Comment, Libel and Slander—Fair Comment—Statements of Opinion, 16 Texas L.Rev. 87 (1938); Comment, Fair Comment, 8 Texas L.Rev. 41 (1930).

basis of true information supplied to the public or considered to be available to the public. This has probably been regarded in the past as a false imputation of fact by most courts if the deduction of misconduct proved to be false.

The evaluation opinion only is published when the publisher makes a value judgment about another or another's conduct—e.g., that it was discreditable, dishonorable, or corrupt—on the basis of true informational background either supplied to, assumed to be known by, or available to those receiving the communication. The value judgment opinion does not charge or impute a false fact unless "goodness" or "badness" are to be treated as facts rather than concepts; the deductive opinion by contrast actually charges the plaintiff with a false fact. The evaluation opinion has often been regarded as false if either the defendant did not entertain the opinion expressed and was misstating his own state of mind or if a reasonable and fair-minded person could not have entertained the derogatory opinion on the basis of the information upon which he relied.

The informational opinion is published when the publisher can reasonably be regarded as conveying information even though the statement made about the plaintiff is in the form of an opinion. It is present when the expression of the publisher's opinion gives rise to an inference that there are undisclosed facts that justify the opinion expressed.[3] If the undisclosed facts do not justify the conclusion drawn, the statement made is to be regarded as a misstatement of the undisclosed facts.

Non-Actionable Opinions

The Second Restatement of Torts provides that a defamatory communication in the form of an opinion is not actionable unless it implies the allegation of undisclosed defamatory facts as the basis for the opinion.[4] Thus, the position is taken that the publication of a derogatory opinion that is a pure opinion of either the deductive or evaluative variety is no longer actionable, however dishonest the publisher might be in expressing that opinion. This position is based on the notion that the constitutional privilege of freedom of the press and speech have now rendered actions for defamation based on pure opinions as unconstitutional. As the Supreme Court said in Gertz v. Robert Welch, Inc.: "Under the First Amendment there is no such thing as a false idea. However pernicious an opinion may seem, we depend for its correction not on the conscience of judges and juries, but on the competition of other ideas. But there is no constitutional value in false statements of fact.[5] And in a companion case to *Gertz*, it was said a defendant does not possess knowledge of falsity unless the statement contains a falsehood, and if the statement is not one of fact, it cannot contain a falsehood.[6] But in answer to this, it can be said that the state of a person's mind is a fact and if a publisher misrepresents his state of mind, he misrepresents a fact even though it is only an opinion. However, it would not seem to be practical or in the interests of free speech to make the kind of inquiries that are necessary to ascertain the precise meaning, especially of evaluative-type opinions, in order to ascertain falsity and dishonesty in the expression of the opinion. In Avins v. White,[7] a Federal Court of Appeals held that some disparaging statements made by a member of an American Bar Association accrediting team in his accreditation report were pure opinion and non-actionable on the ground that the state court would probably follow the Restatement. It can reasonably be argued that a distinction should be made

---

3. See Second Restatement of Torts, § 566, Comment *a;* see also, illustration 3: "A writes to B about his neighbor C: 'I think he must be an alcoholic.'"

4. Section 566, Second Restatement of Torts.

5. 1974, 418 U.S. 323, 340, 94 S.Ct. 2997, 3007, 41 L.Ed.2d 789, 805.

6. Old Dominion Branch No. 496, Letter Carriers v. Austin, 1974, 418 U.S. 264, 94 S.Ct. 2770, 41 L.Ed.2d 745.

7. 3d Cir. 1980, 627 F.2d 637, certiorari denied 449 U.S. 982, 101 S.Ct. 398, 66 L.Ed.2d 244.

between an evaluative-type opinion and the deductive type. In the latter type, the publisher does impute a fact that can be proved to be false as when the publisher concludes from facts stated that the plaintiff murdered his partner. Such an imputation can be regarded as an imputation of a fact even though the facts to support the deduction are set forth. If in such a case the facts do not reasonably support such a conclusion, and the statement was made about a private person, the position might well be taken that there was no constitutional or common law privilege to publish the statement.

If pure opinions of all types are held to be non-actionable either because of a constitutional privilege or because a state court may choose as a matter of policy to adopt this position, then the qualified privilege that has historically been recognized to comment on matters of public interest would no longer serve any purpose and would in effect be abrogated in favor of a much broader absolute privilege. But the contours of the common law privilege of fair comment will be discussed in Section 115 because of the likelihood that the constitutional privilege will not necessarily prevent defamatory actions by private persons against those who make private publications of some pure defamatory opinions, especially of the deductive variety.

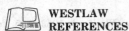
WESTLAW REFERENCES

restatement /s torts /5 566 606
digest(defam! slander! libel! /7 impli! imput! deduc!)

Kinds of Defamatory Opinions
actionable /s defamatory /s impli! insinuat!
opinion* /s defamatory /s fact*

§ 114
1. See, supra, § 113.
2. Many courts and writers have limited "privilege" to the *occasion* on which the defendant may speak with immunity, as distinguished from questions of the "fairness" of comment or criticism. See for example Wagner v. Retail Credit Co., 7th Cir. 1964, 338 F.2d 598; infra, § 115. As no difference in principle is apparent, the term is used in the text to include both. Cf. First Restatement of Torts, § 606.

Non-Actionable Opinion
nonactionable /s opinion* /p defam! slander! libel!

§ 114. Absolute Privilege

Privilege

Prior to New York Times v. Sullivan and later decisions related to the constitutional privilege to publish false and defamatory matter about others,[1] it was recognized under the common law that the failure to make any allowance for "mistakes" in reporting what one believed to be true in a variety of situations would unduly hinder important speech, and would discourage many from publishing the disparaging truth about others for fear of being unable to prove it. The courts developed a complex structure of privileges to protect and advance the societal and individual interests in the free flow of ideas and information. Much of the structure would have been unnecessary and much of the complexity resulting from the development of qualified privileges discussed hereafter could have been obviated if negligence, or something worse, with respect to truth or falsity of the matter published had been a prerequisite to recovery in any case.

The defense of privilege,[2] or immunity,[3] in cases of defamation does not differ essentially from the privileges, such as those of self-defense, protection of property, or legal authority, available as to assault and battery.[4] It rests upon the same idea, that conduct which otherwise would be actionable is to escape liability because the defendant is acting in furtherance of some interest of social importance, which is entitled to protection even at the expense of uncompensated harm to the plaintiff's reputation.[5] The in-

3. Certainly the more accurate term, although the courts have not adopted it. See Bower, Actionable Defamation, 2d ed. 1923, Appendix VIII; Green, Relational Interests, 1935, 30 Ill.L.Rev. 314; Green, The Right to Communicate, 1960, 35 N.Y.U.L.Rev. 903; Evans, Legal Immunity for Defamation, 1940, 24 Minn.L. Rev. 607, 613.

4. See supra, § 16.

5. See Note, 1954, 15 Ohio St.L.J. 330; Holmes Privilege, Malice and Intent, 1894, 8 Harv.L.Rev. 1;

terest thus favored may be one of the defendant himself, of a third person, or of the general public. If it is one of paramount importance, considerations of policy may require that the defendant's immunity for false statements be absolute, without regard to his purpose or motive, or the reasonableness of his conduct. If it has relatively less weight from a social point of view, the immunity may be qualified,[6] and conditioned upon good motives and reasonable behavior. The defendant's belief in the truth of what he says, the purpose for which he says it, and the manner of publication, all of which were immaterial under the common law when no question of privilege is involved,[7] may determine the issue when he enters the defense of such a conditional privilege.

Absolute immunity has been confined to a very few situations where there is an obvious policy in favor of permitting complete freedom of expression, without any inquiry as to the defendant's motives. By general agreement, it is limited to the following situations:

Absolute Immunity

1. *Judicial proceedings.* The judge on the bench must be free to administer the law under the protection of the law, independently and freely, without fear of consequences. No such independence could exist if he were in daily apprehension of having an action brought against him, and his administration of justice submitted to the opinion of a jury.[8] As in the case of other acts in his judicial capacity,[9] therefore, the judge is absolutely privileged as to any defamation he may utter, even though he knows it to be false and is motivated by personal ill will toward the plaintiff.[10] The privilege extends to the official publication of his judicial opinions.[11] For the same reason, a similar absolute immunity is conferred upon grand[12] and petit[13] jurors in the performance of their functions. It likewise has been conferred upon witness-

---

Harper, Privileged Defamation, 1936, 22 Va.L.Rev. 642; Veeder, Absolute Immunity in Defamation, 1909, 9 Col. L.Rev. 463; Veeder, Freedom of Public Discussion, 1910, 23 Harv.L.Rev. 413.

6. Bower, Actionable Defamation, 2d ed. 1923, Appendix VIII, prefers to call it a "defeasible" immunity.

7. See supra, § 113.

8. Scott v. Stansfield, 1868, L.R. 3 Ex. 220; Veeder, Absolute Immunity in Defamation, 1909, 9 Col.L.Rev. 463, 474. Otherwise "no man but a beggar or a fool would be a judge." Lord Stair, in Miller v. Hope, 1824, 2 Shaw, Sc.App.Cas., 125.

Louisiana, operating under a civil law heritage, rejects the absolute privilege in judicial proceedings entirely. There is a qualified privilege only. Oakes v. Alexander, La.App.1961, 135 So.2d 513.

9. See infra, § 132.

10. Scott v. Stansfield, 1868, L.R. 3 Ex. 220; Irwin v. Ashurst, 1938, 158 Or. 61, 74 P.2d 1127; Ginger v. Bowles, 1963, 369 Mich. 680, 120 N.W.2d 842, certiorari denied 375 U.S. 856, 84 S.Ct. 116, 11 L.Ed.2d 82, rehearing denied 375 U.S. 982, 84 S.Ct. 492, 11 L.Ed.2d 429; Mundy v. McDonald, 1921, 216 Mich. 444, 185 N.W. 877; Karelas v. Baldwin, 1932, 237 App.Div. 265, 261 N.Y.S. 518 (justice of the peace).

11. Hanft v. Heller, Sup.1970, 64 Misc.2d 947, 316 N.Y.S.2d 255 (both judge and publisher). The only remedy is to strike the defamatory opinion from the record. Nadeau v. Texas Co., 1937, 104 Mont. 558, 69 P.2d 586.

In Murray v. Brancato, 1943, 290 N.Y. 52, 48 N.E.2d 257 it was held that there was only a qualified privilege to publish unofficially in the New York Law Journal and the New York Supplement Reports. See Note, 1943, 12 Ford.L.Rev. 193. But in Garfield v. Palmieri, S.D.N.Y.1961, 193 F.Supp. 137, affirmed 2d Cir., 297 F.2d 526, certiorari denied 369 U.S. 871, 82 S.Ct. 1139, 8 L.Ed.2d 275 publication in the Federal Supplement was held to be absolutely privileged, where there was no official published report, and no other way of letting the bar know of the opinion.

12. Hayslip v. Wellford, 1953, 195 Tenn. 621, 263 S.W.2d 136, certiorari denied 346 U.S. 911, 74 S.Ct. 243, 98 L.Ed. 408; Ryon v. Shaw, Fla.1955, 77 So.2d 455; O'Regan v. Schermerhorn, 1946, 25 N.J.Misc. 1, 50 A.2d 10; Griffith v. Slinkard, 1896, 146 Ind. 117, 44 N.E. 1001; Engelke v. Chouteau, 1889, 98 Mo. 629, 12 S.W. 358. See Notes, 1937, 31 Minn.L.Rev. 500; 1955, 8 U.Fla.L.Rev. 342.

A report not followed by indictment was held to go outside of the grand jury's functions, and to be only qualifiedly privileged, in Bennett v. Stockwell, 1916, 197 Mich. 50, 163 N.W. 482; Rich v. Eason, Tex.Civ.App.1915, 180 S.W. 303; Rector v. Smith, 1860, 11 Iowa 302. Contra, Greenfield v. Courier-Journal & Louisville Times Co., Ky.1955, 283 S.W.2d 839.

13. Dunham v. Powers, 1868, 42 Vt. 1; Irwin v. Murphy, 1933, 129 Cal.App. 713, 19 P.2d 292; see Hoosac Tunnel Dock & Elevator Co. v. O'Brien, 1874, 137 Mass. 424.

es,[14] whether they testify voluntarily[15] or not, and even though their testimony is by affidavit or deposition.[16] The resulting lack of any really effective civil remedy against perjurers[17] is simply part of the price that is paid for witnesses who are free from intimidation by the possibility of civil liability for what they say. Likewise the privilege extends to counsel in the conduct of the case;[18] and, since there is an obvious public interest in affording to everyone the utmost freedom of access to the courts, it extends also to the parties[19] to private litigation,[20] as well as to defendants and instigators of prosecution in criminal cases.[21] The privilege covers anything that may be said in relation to the matter at issue, whether it be in the pleadings,[22] in affidavits,[23] or in open court.[24]

It is the rule in England that the immunity exists as to any utterance arising out of the judicial proceeding and having any reasonable relation to it, although it is quite irrelevant to any issue involved.[25] Nearly all of the American courts, alarmed at the idea that a court of justice might become a place where extraneous defamation may be published with complete freedom, have said that there is no immunity unless the particular statement is in some way "relevant" or "pertinent" to some issue in the case.[26] On this

---

14. Seaman v. Nethercliff, 1876, L.R. 2 C.P. 53, 46 L.J.C.P. 128; Massey v. Jones, 1944, 182 Va. 200, 28 S.E.2d 623; Veazey v. Blair, 1952, 86 Ga.App. 721, 72 S.E.2d 481; Johnson v. Dover, 1940, 201 Ark. 175, 143 S.W.2d 1112; Taplin-Rice-Clerkin Co. v. Hower, 1931, 124 Ohio St. 123, 177 N.E. 203. Even where the testimony is perjured and malicious. Felts v. Paradise, 1942, 178 Tenn. 421, 158 S.W.2d 727; Kinter v. Kinter, 1949, 84 Ohio App. 399, 87 N.E.2d 379; Buchanan v. Miami Herald Publishing Co., Fla.App.1968, 206 So.2d 465.

15. Beggs v. McCrea, 1901, 62 App.Div. 39, 70 N.Y.S. 864; Buschbaum v. Heriot, 1909, 5 Ga.App. 521, 63 S.E. 645; Ginsburg v. Halpern, 1955, 383 Pa. 178, 118 A.2d 201. Cf. Weil v. Lynds, 1919, 105 Kan. 440, 185 P. 51 (volunteered statement in court).

16. Dunbar v. Greenlaw, 1956, 152 Me. 270, 128 A.2d 218; Dyer v. Dyer, 1941, 178 Tenn. 234, 156 S.W.2d 445; Mezullo v. Maletz, 1954, 331 Mass. 233, 118 N.E.2d 356; Jarman v. Offutt, 1954, 239 N.C. 468, 80 S.E.2d 248. Cf. Thornton v. Rhoden, 1966, 245 Cal. App.2d 80, 53 Cal.Rptr. 706, (making transcript). This does not, however, extend to one who improperly procures the affidavit to be made. Bailey v. McGill, 1957, 247 N.C. 286, 100 S.E.2d 860. See Note, 1958, 36 N.C.L.Rev. 552.

As to other documents filed in the proceeding, cf. Soter v. Christoforacos, 1964, 53 Ill.App.2d 133, 202 N.E.2d 846.

17. See Note, 1960, 2 Osgoode Hall L.J. 154; McClintock, What Happens to Perjurors, 1940, 24 Minn.L. Rev. 747; Ginsburg v. Halpern, 1955, 383 Pa. 178, 118 A.2d 201. See Note, 1966, 19 Ark.L.Rev. 386.

18. Munster v. Lamb, 1883, 11 Q.B.D. 588; Irwin v. Ashurst, 1938, 158 Or. 61, 74 P.2d 1127; Ginsburg v. Black, 7th Cir. 1951, 192 F.2d 823, certiorari denied 343 U.S. 934, 72 S.Ct. 770, 96 L.Ed. 1342, rehearing denied 343 U.S. 958, 72 S.Ct. 1050, 96 L.Ed. 1358; Carpenter v. Ashley, 1906, 148 Cal. 422, 83 P. 444; McDavitt v. Boyer, 1897, 169 Ill. 475, 48 N.E. 317. See Note, 1957, 35 N.C.L.Rev. 541.

19. In Laun v. Union Electric Co. of Missouri, 1943, 350 Mo. 572, 166 S.W.2d 1065, the privilege was held not to extend to one not a party or counsel in the case who inserted defamatory matter in a pleading.

20. Lann v. Third National Bank in Nashville, 1955, 198 Tenn. 70, 277 S.W.2d 439.

21. Boulton v. Clapham, 1640, W. Jones 431, 82 Eng.Rep. 227; Trotman v. Dunn, 1915, 4 Camp. 211, 66 Eng.Rep. 297; Second Restatement of Torts, § 587.

22. Di Blasio v. Kolodner, 1964, 233 Md. 512, 197 A.2d 245; Taliaferro v. Sims, 5th Cir. 1951, 187 F.2d 6; Fletcher v. Maupin, 4th Cir. 1943, 138 F.2d 742, certiorari denied 322 U.S. 750, 64 S.Ct. 1153, 88 L.Ed. 1581; McClure v. Stretch, 1944, 20 Wn.2d 460, 147 P.2d 935; Greenberg v. Aetna Insurance Co., 1967, 427 Pa. 511, 235 A.2d 576, certiorari denied 392 U.S. 907, 88 S.Ct. 2063, 20 L.Ed.2d 1366 (answer).

23. Sacks v. Stecker, 2d Cir. 1932, 60 F.2d 73; Hager v. Major, 1945, 353 Mo. 1166, 186 S.W.2d 564; Stone v. Hutchinson Daily News, 1928, 125 Kan. 715, 266 P. 78; Keeley v. Great Northern Railway Co., 1914, 156 Wis. 181, 145 N.W. 664; Tonkonogy v. Jaffin, 1963, 41 Misc.2d 155, 244 N.Y.S.2d 840, appeal dismissed 21 A.D.2d 264, 249 N.Y.S.2d 934. Cf. Richeson v. Kessler, 1953, 73 Idaho 548, 255 P.2d 707 (counsel's letter to judge on substitution of attorneys).

24. Wells v. Carter, 1932, 164 Tenn. 400, 50 S.W.2d 228; Nissen v. Cramer, 1889, 104 N.C. 574, 10 S.E. 676; Clemmons v. Danforth, 1895, 67 Vt. 617, 32 A. 626; McDavitt v. Boyer, 1897, 169 Ill. 475, 48 N.E. 317.

25. Munster v. Lamb, 1883, 11 Q.B.D. 588, 52 L.J. Q.B. 726; Seaman v. Nethercliff, 1876, L.R. 2 C.P. 53, 46 L.J.C.P. 128; Bower, Actionable Defamation, 2d ed. 1923, 91, 92.

26. Adams v. Alabama Lime & Stone Corp., 1932, 225 Ala. 174, 142 So. 424; La Porta v. Leonard, 1916, 88 N.J.L. 663, 97 A. 251; Magelo v. Roundup Coal Mining Co., 1939, 109 Mont. 293, 96 P.2d 932; Penick v. Ratcliffe, 1927, 149 Va. 618, 140 S.E. 664; Laing v. Mitten, 1904, 185 Mass. 233, 70 N.E. 128. In Stahl v. Kincade, 1963, 135 Ind.App. 699, 192 N.E.2d 493, it was held that a counterclaim entirely irrelevant and in no way pertinent to the complaint was not absolutely privileged.

basis defendants have been held liable, for example, for entirely foreign and irrelevant defamation of a person in no way involved in the suit.[27] But it is generally agreed that "relevancy" does not mean that the statement must come within the technical rules of evidence,[28] since a witness should not be required to determine at his peril whether his testimony may safely be given, or deterred by fear of suit from what he believes to be proper,[29] and if he is asked a question, he may reasonably be expected to reply with anything reasonably responsive to it.[30] Most of our courts have adopted what appears to be a standard of good faith,[31] requiring only that the statement have some reasonable relation or reference to the subject of inquiry,[32] or be one that "may possibly be pertinent,[33] with all doubts resolved in favor of the defendant—a conclusion which seems in effect to adopt the English rule.[34]

The "judicial proceeding" to which the immunity attaches has not been defined very exactly. It includes any hearing before a tribunal which performs a judicial function,[35] ex parte[36] or otherwise, and whether the hearing is public or not.[37] It includes, for example, lunacy,[38] bankruptcy,[39] or naturalization[40] proceedings, and an election contest.[41] It extends also to the proceedings of many administrative officers, such as boards

27. Anonymous v. Trenkman, 2d Cir. 1931, 48 F.2d 571; Wels v. Rubin, 1939, 280 N.Y. 233, 20 N.E.2d 737. Cf. Dayton v. Drumheller, 1919, 32 Idaho 283, 182 P. 102 (old evidence on motion for new trial); Harshaw v. Harshaw, 1941, 220 N.C. 145, 16 S.E.2d 666 (evidence whose falsity defendant was estopped to deny); McLaughlin v. Cowley, 1879, 127 Mass. 316 (extraneous allegation of murder and adultery in pleading); Dodge v. Gilman, 1913, 122 Minn. 177, 142 N.W. 147; Barnett v. Loud, 1917, 226 Mass. 447, 115 N.E. 767.

28. Taliaferro v. Sims, 5th Cir. 1951, 187 F.2d 6; Brown v. Shimabukuro, 1940, 73 U.S.App.D.C. 194, 118 F.2d 17; Johnston v. Schlarb, 1941, 7 Wn.2d 528, 110 P.2d 190.

29. See Veeder, Absolute Immunity in Defamation, 1909, 9 Col.L.Rev. 463, 600, 608; Bussewitz v. Wisconsin Teachers' Association, 1925, 188 Wis. 121, 205 N.W. 808.

30. Greenberg v. Ackerman, 1956, 41 N.J.Super. 146, 124 A.2d 313; Aborn v. Lipson, 1970, 357 Mass. 71, 256 N.E.2d 442.

31. Johnson v. Dover, 1940, 201 Ark. 175, 143 S.W.2d 1112 (an honest belief that the statement is pertinent is enough). Tonkonogy v. Jaffin, 1963, 41 Misc. 2d 155, 244 N.Y.S.2d 840, appeal dismissed 21 A.D.2d 264, 249 N.Y.S.2d 934 (enough that defendant "believed that the language would have a tendency to move the court's discretion.").

32. Ginsburg v. Black, 7th Cir. 1951, 192 F.2d 823 certiorari denied 343 U.S. 934, 72 S.Ct. 770, 96 L.Ed. 1342, rehearing denied 343 U.S. 958, 72 S.Ct. 1050, 96 L.Ed. 1358; Johnston v. Schlarb, 1941, 7 Wn.2d 528, 110 P.2d 190; Matthis v. Kennedy, 1954, 243 Minn. 219, 67 N.W.2d 413.

33. Bleecker v. Drury, 2d Cir. 1945, 149 F.2d 770; Andrews v. Gardiner, 1918, 224 N.Y. 440, 121 N.E.2d 341; McKinney v. Cooper, 1940, 163 Or. 512, 98 P.2d 711; Young v. Young, 1927, 57 App.D.C. 157, 18 F.2d 807; Seltzer v. Fields, 1963, 20 A.D.2d 60, 244 N.Y.S.2d 792, affirmed 14 N.Y.2d 624, 249 N.Y.S.2d 174, 198 N.E.2d 368.

The fact that the language used is unduly extreme will not defeat the privilege. Parker v. Kirkland, 1939, 298 Ill.App. 340, 18 N.E.2d 709; Irwin v. Ashurst, 1938, 158 Or. 61, 74 P.2d 1127.

A litigant may be allowed more latitude than his counsel. Compare, as to interjections in court, Wells v. Carter, 1932, 164 Tenn. 400, 50 S.W.2d 228 with Breeding v. Napier, 1929, 230 Ky. 85, 18 S.W.2d 872.

34. Kemper v. Fort, 1907, 219 Pa. 85, 67 A. 991; Myers v. Hodges, 1907, 53 Fla. 197, 44 So. 357; Harlow v. Carroll, 1895, 6 App.D.C. 128; Greenberg v. Aetna Insurance Co., 1967, 427 Pa. 511, 235 A.2d 576.

35. See Note, 1948, 13 Mo.L.Rev. 320.

36. Gunter v. Reeves, 1945, 198 Miss. 31, 21 So.2d 468 (search warrant); Stone v. Hutchinson Daily News, 1928, 125 Kan. 715, 266 P. 78 (same); Beiser v. Scripps-McRae Publishing Co., 1902, 113 Ky. 383, 68 S.W. 457.

37. Schultz v. Strauss, 1906, 127 Wis. 325, 106 N.W. 1066 (grand jury); Sands v. Robison, 1849, 20 Miss. (12 Smedes & M.) 704 (same); Taafe v. Downes, 1812, 3 Moo.P.C. 36 (in chambers).

38. Corcoran v. Jerrel, 1919, 185 Iowa 532, 170 N.W. 776; Dunbar v. Greenlaw, 1956, 152 Me. 270, 128 A.2d 218; Mezullo v. Maletz, 1954, 331 Mass. 233, 118 N.E.2d 356; Jarman v. Offutt, 1954, 239 N.C. 468, 80 S.E.2d 248; Dyer v. Dyer, 1941, 178 Tenn. 234, 156 S.W.2d 445.

39. Rogers v. Thompson, 1916, 89 N.J.L. 639, 99 A. 389; Abrams v. Crompton-Richmond Co., 1957, 7 Misc. 2d 461, 164 N.Y.S.2d 124, affirmed 1958, 5 A.D.2d 811, 170 N.Y.S.2d 981.

40. Nickovich v. Mollart, 1929, 51 Nev. 306, 274 P. 809.

41. Penick v. Ratcliffe, 1927, 149 Va. 618, 140 S.E. 664. See also Youmans v. Smith, 1893, 153 N.Y. 214, 47 N.E. 265 (disbarment); Note, 1938, 23 Iowa L.Rev. 83 (same); Talley v. Alton Box Board Co., 1962, 37 Ill. App.2d 137, 185 N.E.2d 349 (proceeding to recover attorney's fees); Jenson v. Olson, 1966, 273 Minn. 390, 141 N.W.2d 488 (civil service hearing).

and commissions,[42] so far as they have powers of discretion in applying the law to the facts which are regarded as judicial, or "quasi-judicial," in character. Thus the ordinary administrative proceeding to revoke a license[43] is held to lie within the privilege. On the other hand, of course, the mere fact that an officer must make a decision or determine the existence of a fact does not make his function a judicial one,[44] and the powers and procedure of such agencies vary so greatly that no very definite classifications can be made.[45] There are frequent dicta to the effect that the tribunal must have jurisdiction, or power to act in the situation presented;[46] but this would compel everyone concerned to decide the question of jurisdiction at his peril, and it seems clear that the correct rule is that a mere color of jurisdiction, in fact assumed, is sufficient.[47]

The immunity extends to every step in the proceeding[48] until final disposition,[49] although it does not cover publications made before commencement[50] or after termination.[51] Conversations preliminary to the proceeding have given some difficulty. Although there is some authority to the contrary,[52] the better view seems to be that an informal complaint to a prosecuting attorney or a magistrate is to be regarded as an initial step in a judicial proceeding, and so entitled to an absolute, rather than a quali-

---

42. Bleecker v. Drury, 2d Cir. 1945, 149 F.2d 770 (industrial board); Parker v. Kirkland, 1939, 298 Ill.App. 340, 18 N.E.2d 709 (tax board of appeals); White v. United Mills Co., 1948, 240 Mo.App. 443, 208 S.W.2d 803 (state labor commissioners, separation notice); Reagan v. Guardian Life Insurance Co., 1942, 140 Tex. 105, 166 S.W.2d 909 (insurance commission); Loudin v. Mohawk Airlines, Inc., 1964, 44 Misc.2d 926, 255 N.Y.S.2d 302 modified on other grounds, 24 A.D.2d 447, 260 N.Y.S.2d 899 (Civil Aeronautics Board).

43. Lininger v. Knight, 1951, 123 Colo. 213, 226 P.2d 809 (liquor); Rainier's Dairies v. Raitan Valley Farms, 1955, 19 N.J. 552, 117 A.2d 889 (dairymen); Robertson v. Industrial Insurance Co., Fla.1954, 75 So. 2d 198, 45 A.L.R.2d 1292 (insurance agent).

Compare, as to complaints to grievance committee of integrated state bar association, Ramstead v. Morgan, 1959, 219 Or. 383, 347 P.2d 594; Wiener v. Weintraub, 1968, 22 N.Y.2d 330, 292 N.Y.S.2d 667, 239 N.E.2d 540; McAfee v. Feller, Tex.Civ.App.1970, 452 S.W.2d 56.

44. Fedderwitz v. Lamb, 1943, 195 Ga. 691, 25 S.E.2d 414 (state revenue commission); Johnson v. Independent Life & Accident Insurance Co., E.D.S.C. 1951, 94 F.Supp. 959 (insurance commission); Longo v. Tauriello, 1951, 201 Misc. 35, 107 N.Y.S.2d 361 (state housing rent commission); Blakeslee v. Carroll, 1894, 64 Conn. 223, 29 A. 473 (investigating committee of aldermen); Elder v. Holland, 1967, 208 Va. 15, 155 S.E.2d 369 (departmental hearing before police superintendent).

45. See Meyer v. Parr, 1941, 69 Ohio App. 344, 37 N.E.2d 637 (board of embalmers and funeral directors); Grubb v. Johnson, 1955, 205 Or. 624, 289 P.2d 1067 (revocation of insurance license); Ellish v. Goldman, Sup.1952, 117 N.Y.S.2d 867 (zoning board of appeals).

46. See Johnson v. Brown, 1878, 13 W.Va. 71; Jones v. Brownlee, 1901, 161 Mo. 258, 61 S.W. 795; Ball v. Rawles, 1892, 93 Cal. 222, 28 P. 937.

47. Lake v. King, 1680, 2 Keb. 832, 84 Eng.Rep. 526; Allen v. Crofoot, N.Y.1829, 2 Wend. 515, 20 Am. Dec. 647. In the case of the immunity of the judge, however, it would seem that he must at least have sufficient color of jurisdiction so that it can be said that he is acting as a court.

As to the general privilege of officers acting without jurisdiction, see infra, § 132.

48. McKinney v. Cooper, 1940, 163 Or. 512, 98 P.2d 711 (objection to final account); Glasson v. Bowen, 1928, 84 Colo. 57, 267 P. 1066 (change of venue); Stone v. Hutchinson Daily News, 1928, 125 Kan. 715, 266 P. 78 (application for search warrant); Simon v. Stim, 1958, 11 Misc.2d 653, 176 N.Y.S.2d 475, affirmed 1959, 10 A.D.2d 647, 199 N.Y.S.2d 405 (pleading, and letter to judge concerning it); Spoehr v. Mittelstadt, 1967, 34 Wis.2d 653, 150 N.W.2d 502 (pre-trial conference).

49. Jones v. Trice, 1962, 210 Tenn. 535, 360 S.W.2d 48 (motion for new trial); Hager v. Major, 1945, 350 Mo. 1166, 186 S.W.2d 564 (same); Brown v. Shimabukuro, 1941, 73 App.D.C. 194, 118 F.2d 17 (motion for rehearing); Hammett v. Hunter, 1941, 189 Okl. 455, 117 P.2d 511 (modification of decree); Petty v. General Accident, Fire & Life Assurance Corp., 3d Cir. 1966, 365 F.2d 419 (settlement in open court, entered in the record).

50. Gould v. Hulme, 1829, 3 C. & P. 625, 172 Eng. Rep. 574; Koehler v. Dubose, Tex.Civ.App.1918, 200 S.W. 238, error refused; Timmis v. Bennett, 1958, 352 Mich. 355, 89 N.W.2d 748 (attorney writing letter concerning contemplated lawsuit); Johnston v. Cartwright, 8th Cir. 1966, 355 F.2d 32.

51. Burlingame v. Burlingame, N.Y.1828, 8 Cow. 141; Paris v. Levy, 1860, 9 C.B.,N.S., 342, 142 Eng. Rep. 135. Cf. Bigner v. Hodges, 1903, 82 Miss. 215, 33 So. 980 (statement to person not concerned in case).

52. Magness v. Pledger, Okl.1959, 334 P.2d 792; Pecue v. West, 1921, 233 N.Y. 316, 135 N.E. 515; Marshall v. Gunter, S.C.1853, 6 Mich. 419; Miller v. Nuckolls, 1905, 77 Ark. 64, 91 S.W. 759; Hathaway v. Bruggink, 1919, 168 Wis. 390, 170 N.W. 244.

fied immunity.⁵³ On the other hand preliminary communications between an interested party and his own attorney⁵⁴ usually have been regarded as something apart from the proceeding itself, and so at best conditionally privileged, although an interview of the attorney with a prospective witness⁵⁵ has been considered a necessary step in taking legal action, and the immunity has been held to be absolute. It is clear, however, that statements given to the newspapers concerning the case are no part of a judicial proceeding, and are not absolutely privileged.⁵⁶

2. *Legislative proceedings.* A long struggle between crown and parliament⁵⁷ established by the time of the English revolution the immunity, indispensable in any system of free democratic government, of members of legislative bodies for acts in the performance of their duties. An absolute immunity was recognized at common law as to defamatory statements made by legislators in the course of any of their functions as such,⁵⁸ whether it be in debate, voting, reports, or work in committee.⁵⁹ The common law immunity was subject to the limitation that the defamation must have some relation to the business of the legislature;⁶⁰ but in this country federal⁶¹ and state⁶² constitutional provisions generally have extended it to anything whatever that is said in the course of legislative proceedings themselves. The privilege includes the official publication of what is said, as for example in the Congressional Record;⁶³ but it has been held that no absolute immunity is attached to republication, as by unofficial distribution of reprints from the Record, outside of the legislature.⁶⁴

Witnesses in legislative hearings are given the same protection as in judicial proceedings,⁶⁵ and there is some rather doubtful authority⁶⁶ that petitions addressed to legislatures, under the constitutional guaranty, enjoy an absolute immunity. There has been disagreement over whether the abso-

53. Vogel v. Gruaz, 1884, 110 U.S. 311, 4 S.Ct. 12, 28 L.Ed. 158; Gabriel v. McMullin, 1905, 127 Iowa 426, 103 N.W. 355; Hott v. Yarbrough, 1922, 112 Tex. 179, 245 S.W. 676; Wells v. Toogood, 1911, 165 Mich. 677, 131 N.W. 124; Schultz v. Strauss, 1906, 127 Wis. 325, 106 N.W. 1066.

54. Lapetina v. Santangelo, 1908, 124 App.Div. 519, 108 N.Y.S. 975; Kruse v. Rabe, 1910, 80 N.J.L. 378, 79 A. 316. Contra, More v. Weaver, [1928] 2 K.B. 520.

55. Watson v. M'Ewan, [1905] A.C. 480, 74 L.J.P.C. 151; Beresford v. White, 1914, 30 T.L.R. 591; Youmans v. Smith, 1897, 153 N.Y. 214, 47 N.E. 265; Beggs v. McCrea, 1901, 62 App.Div. 39, 70 N.Y.S. 864.

Contra, Robinson v. Home Fire & Marine Insurance Co., 1953, 244 Iowa 1084, 59 N.W.2d 776 (qualified privilege only).

56. Kennedy v. Cannon, 1962, 229 Md. 92, 182 A.2d 54.

57. Veeder, Absolute Immunity in Defamation, 1910, 10 Col.L.Rev. 130–134; Yankwich, The Immunity of Congressional Speech—Its Origin, Meaning and Scope, 1951, 99 U.Pa.L.Rev. 960; Field, The Constitutional Privilege of Legislators, 1925, 9 Minn.L.Rev. 442. See also Hynes, Defamation During Congressional Investigations: A Proposed Statute, 1966, 39 U.Colo.L. Rev. 48; Note, 1949, 16 U.Chi.L.Rev. 544.

58. Ex parte Wason, 1869, L.R. 4 Q.B. 73; Dillon v. Balfour, 1887, 20 L.R.Ir. 600; see Coffin v. Coffin, 1808, 4 Mass. 1.

59. See Coffin v. Coffin, 1808, 4 Mass. 1.

60. Id.

61. See Cochran v. Couzens, 1930, 59 App.D.C. 374, 42 F.2d 783, certiorari denied 282 U.S. 874, 51 S.Ct. 79, 75 L.Ed. 772; Kilbourn v. Thompson, 1880, 103 U.S. 168, 26 L.Ed. 377.

62. See Cole v. Richards, 1932, 108 N.J.L. 356, 158 A. 466; Field, The Constitutional Privileges of Legislators, 1925, 9 Minn.L.Rev. 442.

63. Methodist Federation for Social Action v. Eastland, D.D.C.1956, 141 F.Supp. 729.

64. Rex v. Abingdon, 1795, 1 Esp. 226, 170 Eng. Rep. 337; Rex v. Creevy, 1813, 1 M. & S. 273, 105 Eng. Rep. 102; Cole v. Richards, 1932, 108 N.J.L. 356, 158 A. 466; Long v. Ansell, 1934, 293 U.S. 76, 55 S.Ct. 21, 79 L.Ed. 208; McGovern v. Martz, D.D.C.1960, 182 F.Supp. 343.

65. Kelly v. Daro, 1941, 47 Cal.App.2d 418, 118 P.2d 37; Logan's Super Markets, Inc. v. McCalla, 1961, 208 Tenn. 68, 343 S.W.2d 892; Wright v. Lathrop, 1889, 149 Mass. 385, 21 N.E. 963; Sheppard v. Bryant, 1906, 191 Mass. 591, 78 N.E. 394; Terry v. Fellows, 1869, 21 La. Ann. 375; see Notes, 1962, 29 Tenn.L.Rev. 314; 1942, 15 So.Cal.L.Rev. 276. In Fiore v. Rogero, Fla.App. 1962, 144 So.2d 99, it was held that volunteered testimony was only qualifiedly privileged.

66. Lake v. King, 1680, 1 Lev. 240, 83 Eng.Rep. 387; Harris v. Huntington, Vt.1802, 2 Tyler 129; see Cook v. Hill, N.Y.1849, 5 Super. (3 Sandf.) 341; Veeder, Absolute Immunity in Defamation, 1910, 10 Col.L.Rev. 131, 138.

In Bigelow v. Brumley, 1941, 138 Ohio St. 574, 37 N.E.2d 584, a statement to the electorate in connection

lute privilege extends to the proceedings of subordinate bodies performing a legislative function, such as municipal councils. A substantial number of cases have held that it does.[67] A scant majority have held that such proceedings are not within the policy underlying the immunity, and that the members of such bodies are sufficiently protected by a qualified privilege in the exercise of good faith.[68] Some statutes extend an absolute privilege to such proceedings.[69]

3. *Executive communications.* Under the same policy, the protection of absolute immunity also is extended to certain executive officers, at least, of the government in the discharge of their duties.[70]

The doctrine originated in 1895, with two decisions in England[71] and the Supreme Court of the United States,[72] both of which involved members of the cabinet, and held that the immunity was essential in order that the administration of government should not be hampered by the fear of lawsuits against such officers. In England the rule has been quite strictly limited to those on the highest level, whose conduct constitutes an "act of state."[73] In this country it was extended to other superior officers of the executive departments and branches of the federal,[74] and in a few cases, of the state[75] governments. Originally the line was drawn at such superior officers.[76] Over several years, however, a series of decisions in the lower federal courts[77] extended the immunity to lower federal officers and employees as to communications which they are re-

with an initiative proposal for a constitutional amendment was held to be part of the legislative process.

67. Wachsmuth v. Merchants' National Bank, 1893, 96 Mich. 426, 56 N.W. 9; Trebilcock v. Anderson, 1898, 117 Mich. 39, 75 N.W. 129; Tanner v. Gault, 1925, 20 Ohio App. 243, 153 N.E. 124; McNayr v. Kelly, Fla. 1966, 184 So.2d 428, conformed to 185 So.2d 194; Larson v. Doner, 1961, 32 Ill.App.2d 471, 178 N.E.2d 399; Cornett v. Fetzer, Tenn.App.1980, 604 S.W.2d 62.

68. Cowman v. LaVine, Iowa 1975, 234 N.W.2d 114; Richards v. Gruen, 1974, 62 Wis.2d 99, 214 N.W.2d 309; Cohen v. Bowdoin, Me.1972, 288 A.2d 106; McClendon v. Coverdale, Del.Super.1964, 7 Storey 568, 203 A.2d 815; Mills v. Denny, 1954, 245 Iowa 584, 63 N.W.2d 222. Accord, Gardner v. Hollifield, 1976, 97 Idaho 607, 549 P.2d 266 (school board); Jones v. Monico, 1967, 276 Minn. 371, 150 N.W.2d 213 (board of county commissioners); Royal Aquarium v. Parkinson, 1892, 1 Q.B. 431 (county court).

Accord, as to town meetings: Smith v. Higgins, 1860, 82 Mass. (16 Gray) 251; Bradford v. Clark, 1897, 90 Me. 298, 38 A. 229.

69. West's Ann.Cal.Civ.Code § 47, applied Harnish v. Smith, 1956, 138 Cal.App.2d 307, 291 P.2d 532; Utah Code Ann. 1953, 45–2–3, applied Carter v. Jackson, 1960, 10 Utah 2d 284, 351 P.2d 957; Ky.Rev.Stat. 84.050(5), applied Jacobs v. Underwood, Ky.1972, 484 S.W.2d 855, as amended by Ky.Rev.Stat. 83A.060(15).

70. Handler and Klein, The Defense of Privilege in Defamation Suits Against Government Executive Officials, 1960, 74 Harv.L.Rev. 44; Becht, The Absolute Privilege of the Executive in Defamation, 1962, 15 Vand.L.Rev. 1127; Gray, Private Wrongs of Public Servants, 1959, 47 Cal.L.Rev. 303; Notes, 1960, 44 Minn.L.Rev. 547; 1960, 55 Northwestern U.L.Rev. 228; 1954, 7 Okl.L.Rev. 105; 1954, 32 N.C.L.Rev. 564; 1953, 20 U.Chi.L.Rev. 677; 1953, 37 Minn.L.Rev. 141; 1952, 38 Iowa L.Rev. 186; 1942, 40 Mich.L.Rev. 919.

71. Chatterton v. Secretary of State for India, [1895] 2 Q.B. 189.

72. Spalding v. Vilas, 1896, 161 U.S. 483, 16 S.Ct. 631, 40 L.Ed. 780 (Postmaster General).

73. Szalatnay-Stacho v. Fink, [1947] 1 K.B. 1; Gibbons v. Duffell, 1932, 47 Comm.L.Rep., Aust., 520, 530; Jackson v. McGrath, 1947, 75 Comm.L.Rep., Aust., 293, 306.

74. Standard Nut Margarine Co. v. Mellon, 1934, 63 U.S.App.D.C. 339, 72 F.2d 557, certiorari denied 293 U.S. 605, 55 S.Ct. 124, 79 L.Ed. 696 (Secretary and Assistant Secretary of Treasury); Adams v. Home Owners' Loan Corp., 8th Cir. 1939, 107 F.2d 139 (officers of Home Owners Loan Corporation); Pearson v. Wright, D.D.C.1957, 156 F.Supp. 136 (Chairman of Federal Commission on Government Service); Short v. News-Journal Co., Del.1965, 212 A.2d 718 (Director of Internal Revenue).

75. Ryan v. Wilson, 1941, 231 Iowa 33, 300 N.W. 707 (governor); Matson v. Margiotti, 1952, 371 Pa. 188, 88 A.2d 892 (attorney general); Gold Seal Chinchillas, Inc. v. State, 1966, 69 Wn.2d 828, 420 P.2d 698 (same); Hackworth v. Larson, 1969, 83 S.D. 674, 165 N.W.2d 705 (Secretary of State); Hughes v. Bizzell, 1941, 189 Okl. 472, 117 P.2d 763 (president of state university).

76. Maurice v. Worden, 1880, 54 Md. 233; Hemmens v. Nelson, 1893, 138 N.Y. 517, 34 N.E. 342; Peterson v. Steenerson, 1910, 113 Minn. 87, 129 N.W. 147.

77. See for example Miles v. McGrath, D.Md.1933, 4 F.Supp. 603 (naval officer); Taylor v. Glotfelty, 6th Cir. 1952, 201 F.2d 51 (psychiatrist at medical center); United States to Use of Parravicino v. Brunswick, 1934, 63 U.S.App.D.C. 65, 69 F.2d 383 (consul); Lang v. Wood, 1937, 67 U.S.App.D.C. 287, 92 F.2d 211, certiorari denied 302 U.S. 686, 58 S.Ct. 48, 82 L.Ed. 530 (warden of a prison); Harwood v. McMurtry, D.Ky.1938, 22 F.Supp. 572 (internal revenue agent).

quired or authorized to make in connection with the performance of their duties.

In Barr v. Matteo,[78] the Supreme Court not only confirmed the extension to all such federal personnel, but held that it included all publications within the "outer perimeter" of their "line of duty," such as defamatory press releases explaining their actions to the public.[79] While there are a few state court decisions which appear to reach the same conclusion as to subordinate state officers,[80] such courts in general have refused to accept the extension, and have recognized no absolute privilege on the part of such officers as superintendents of schools,[81] mayors and aldermen,[82] prosecuting attorneys and policemen,[83] state investigators,[84] and the like. Unless such an executive officer can claim immunity on the basis of a quasi-judicial or legislative function,[85] he is held to be subject to a qualified privilege only. It seems to be generally agreed, also, that petitions or complaints of private citizens to executive officers concerning public affairs are likewise only qualifiedly privileged.[86]

Immunity for defamation is only part of a larger problem, of the limits to the responsibility of public officers for torts against private citizens.[87] The argument in favor of Barr v. Matteo is that a qualified privilege would not be adequate protection for the public officer, since it would necessitate calling him as a witness to deny malice, and so subject him to cross-examination upon his official conduct in a private suit, and would end by submitting it to the eccentric and unreliable judgment of a jury; and that in the public interest no good and worthy public servant should be deterred from accepting office or acting by the fear of such a proceeding. It does not appear, however, that anyone has been deterred in those states where only the qualified privilege is recognized; and the decision has been attacked with vigor[88] as affording a golden opportunity for utterly unscrupulous politicians to

---

78. 1959, 360 U.S. 564, 79 S.Ct. 1335, 3 L.Ed.2d 1434, rehearing denied 361 U.S. 855, 80 S.Ct. 41, 4 L.Ed.2d 93 (Acting Director of Office of Rent Stabilization). This was a 5–4 decision, with Mr. Justice Black concurring specially. See also Preble v. Johnson, 10th Cir. 1960, 275 F.2d 275 (civil service employees and naval enlisted man).

79. Accord, as to press releases: Glass v. Ickes, 1940, 73 U.S.App.D.C. 3, 117 F.2d 273, certiorari denied 311 U.S. 718, 61 S.Ct. 441, 85 L.Ed. 468 (Secretary of the Interior); Ryan v. Wilson, 1941, 231 Iowa 33, 300 N.W. 707 (governor); Matson v. Margiotti, 1952, 371 Pa. 188, 88 A.2d 892 (attorney general); Short v. News-Journal Co., Del.1965, 212 A.2d 718 (Director of Internal Revenue).

80. Sheridan v. Crisona, 1964, 14 N.Y.2d 108, 249 N.Y.S.2d 161, 198 N.E.2d 359 (borough president); McNayr v. Kelly, Fla.1966, 184 So.2d 428, conformed to 185 So.2d 194 (county manager); Long v. Mertz, 1965, 2 Ariz.App. 215, 407 P.2d 404 (highway department engineer); Montgomery v. City of Philadelphia, 1958, 392 Pa. 178, 140 A.2d 100 (city commissioner of public property and city architect); Schlinkert v. Henderson, 1951, 331 Mich. 284, 49 N.W.2d 180 (liquor control commissioner).

81. Barry v. McCollom, 1908, 81 Conn. 293, 70 A. 1035; Tanner v. Stevenson, 1910, 138 Ky. 578, 128 S.W. 878; Hemmens v. Nelson, 1893, 138 N.Y. 517, 34 N.E. 342 (principal of state institution for deaf mutes); Collins v. Oklahoma State Hospital, 1916, 76 Okl. 229, 184 p. 946 (superintendent of state asylum); Ranous v. Hughes, 1966, 30 Wis.2d 452, 141 N.W.2d 251 (board of education).

82. Mayo v. Sample, 1865, 18 Iowa 306; Weber v. Lane, 1903, 99 Mo.App. 69, 71 S.W. 1099; Ranous v. Hughes, 1966, 30 Wis.2d 452, 141 N.W.2d 251 (county manager). See Note, 1967, 21 U.Miami L.Rev. 498.

83. Earl v. Winne, 1953, 14 N.J. 119, 101 A.2d 535; Carr v. Watkins, 1962, 227 Md. 578, 177 A.2d 841 (particularly good on difference between federal and state law).

84. Peeples v. State, 1942, 179 Misc. 272, 38 N.Y.S.2d 690 (state examiner of accounts); In re Investigating Commission, 1887, 16 R.I. 751, 11 A. 429 (governor's investigating commission). Cf. Pearce v. Brower, 1884, 72 Ga. 243 (road commissioners).

85. Cf. Larkin v. Noonan, 1865, 19 Wis. 82; McAlister & Co. v. Jenkins, 1926, 214 Ky. 802, 284 S.W. 88; Trebilcock v. Anderson, 1898, 117 Mich. 39, 75 N.W. 129.

86. Licciardi v. Molnar, 1945, 23 N.J.Misc. 361, 44 A.2d 653; Bingham v. Gaynor, 1911, 203 N.Y. 27, 96 N.E. 84; Maurice v. Worden, 1880, 54 Md. 233; Andrews v. Gardiner, 1918, 224 N.Y. 440, 121 N.E. 341.

87. See infra, § 132.

88. See Handler and Klein, The Defense of Privilege in Defamation Suits Against Government Executive Officials, 1960, 74 Harv.L.Rev. 44; Becht, The Absolute Privilege of the Executive in Defamation, 1962, 15 Vand.L.Rev. 1127; Gray, Private Wrongs of Public Servants, 1959, 47 Cal.L.Rev. 303; Note, 1962, 48 Corn. L.Q. 199.

abuse their position by inflicting outrageous injury upon the helpless and innocent, for the worst kind of motives, and with no redress. It can scarcely be said that our governments, state or federal, have always been so free of scoundrels as to inspire confidence in such a rule.[89]

One limiting factor, of obvious importance, lies in the general agreement that the publication must at least be found to lie within the defendant's authorized functions. It is no part of the duties of a janitor, or a United States marshal,[90] to issue a press release concerning what he sees and hears, of school district trustees to issue such statements concerning the superintendent or pupils,[91] of a state conservation commissioner to make dinner speeches attacking other officials,[92] or of a mayor to act as an unofficial censor of art.[93]

4. *Consent of the plaintiff.* The general social policy of denying recovery for conduct to which the plaintiff has given his consent[94] finds expression in an absolute immunity in cases where consent is given to defamation.[95] One who has himself invited or instigated the publication of defamatory words cannot be heard to complain of the resulting damage to his reputation,[96] and this is true although the publication was procured for the very purpose of decoying the defendant into a lawsuit.[97] At the same time, of course, it is not every request to speak which manifests consent to slander,[98] and an honest inquiry as to what is meant,[99] or an investigation in good faith to find out what the defendant has been saying[1] will not bar the action, even though it is made for the ultimate purpose of vindication at law. As in other cases of consent, the privilege is limited by the scope of the assent apparently given, and consent to one form of publication does not confer a license to publish to other persons, or in a different manner.[2]

---

89. One rather startling, and perhaps alarming, decision is Heine v. Raus, D.Md.1966, 261 F.Supp. 570 on remand 305 F.Supp. 816, affirmed 4th Cir., 432 F.2d 1007, holding that an employee of CIA was absolutely privileged in reports he made to third persons. See Note, 1967, 67 Col.L.Rev. 752.

90. Colpoys v. Gates, 1940, 73 U.S.App.D.C. 193, 118 F.2d 16. Cf. Jacobs v. Herlands, Sup.1940, 17 N.Y.S.2d 711, affirmed 259 App.Div. 823, 19 N.Y.S.2d 770 (investigator of crime).

91. Lipman v. Brisbane Elementary School District, 1961, 55 Cal.2d 224, 11 Cal.Rptr. 97, 359 P.2d 465; Elder v. Anderson, 1962, 205 Cal.App.2d 326, 23 Cal.Rptr. 48. Cf. Tanner v. Stevenson, 1910, 138 Ky. 578, 128 S.W. 878 (matters outside of county).

92. Cheatum v. Wehle, 1959, 5 N.Y.2d 585, 186 N.Y.S.2d 606, 159 N.E.2d 166.

93. Walker v. D'Alesandro, 1957, 212 Md. 163, 129 A.2d 148.

94. See supra, § 18.

95. Where the plaintiff is uncertain as to just what will be said, but consents to publication which he has reason to believe may be defamatory, the defense would seem properly to be one of assumption of risk. Cf. Chapman v. Ellesmere, [1932] 2 K.B. 431.

96. Shinglemeyer v. Wright, 1900, 124 Mich. 230, 82 N.W. 887; Christopher v. Akin, 1913, 214 Mass. 332, 101 N.E. 971; Burdett v. Hines, 1921, 125 Miss. 66, 87 So. 470; Taylor v. McDaniels, 1929, 139 Okl. 262, 281 P. 967. Cf. Mick v. American Dental Association, 1958, 49 N.J.Super. 262, 139 A.2d 570 (request for opinion); Patrick v. Thomas, Okl.1962, 376 P.2d 250 (plaintiff's agent entered into correspondence).

In Mims v. Metropolitan Life Insurance Co., 5th Cir. 1952, 200 F.2d 800, certiorari denied 345 U.S. 940, 73 S.Ct. 831, 97 L.Ed. 1366, and National Disabled Soldiers' League v. Haan, 1925, 55 App.D.C. 243, 4 F.2d 436, the inquiry of a United States Senator instigated by the plaintiff was held to show consent.

97. Richardson v. Gunby, 1912, 88 Kan. 47, 127 P. 533; Howland v. George F. Blake Manufacturing Co., 1892, 156 Mass. 543, 31 N.E. 656; Melcher v. Beeler, 1910, 48 Colo. 233, 110 P. 181; Gordon v. Spencer, Ind. 1829, 2 Blackf. 286; Hellesen v. Knaus Truck Lines, Inc., Mo.1963, 370 S.W.2d 341.

98. Nelson v. Whitten, D.N.Y.1921, 272 F. 135 (request for recommendation); Arvey Corp. v. Peterson, E.D.Pa.1959, 178 F.Supp. 132 (request for payment of wages).

99. Smith v. Dunlop Tire & Rubber Co., 1938, 186 S.C. 456, 196 S.E. 174.

1. Thorn v. Moser, N.Y.1845, 1 Denio 488; Griffiths v. Lewis, 1846, 7 Q.B. 61, 115 Eng.Rep. 411; Wharton v. Chunn, 1909, 53 Tex.Civ.App. 124, 115 S.W. 887.

2. See Cook v. Ward, 1830, 6 Bing. 409, 130 Eng. Rep. 1338; Luzenberg v. O'Malley, 1906, 116 La. 699, 41 So. 41; Hope v. L'Anson, 1901, 18 T.L.R. 201. But in Sharman v. C. Schmidt & Sons, Inc., E.D.Pa.1963, 216 F.Supp. 401, consent to the use of plaintiff's picture in advertising was held to include beer advertising.

5. *Husband and wife.* The few cases which have considered the question[3] have dealt with communications between husband and wife upon the basis that there is no publication, retaining the venerable fiction that man and wife are but one person, and no one can publish to himself. Since this hoary absurdity has long since been discarded elsewhere,[4] and since a third person may publish defamation concerning one spouse to the other,[5] the better explanation is that there is an absolute immunity as to what is said between husband and wife, based upon the very confidential character of the relation.[6]

6. *Political broadcasts.* The provision of the Federal Communications Act[7] that radio stations shall afford equal opportunities to all political candidates,[8] and that the station shall have no power of censorship over their speeches, has meant that the station may be unable to refuse time on the air, yet powerless to exert any control over what is said. This at first gave rise to a dispute, with a few opinions of lower courts divided,[9] as to whether the statute necessarily carried the implication of absolute immunity on the part of the broadcaster. In 1959 the controversy was finally settled by the Supreme Court of the United States, which held that the publication is absolutely privileged.[10] In all probability the same conclusion would be reached as to any other publication required by law, as in the case of a newspaper required to publish a legal notice.[11]

WESTLAW REFERENCES

Privilege
defense* /s privilege* /s slander! defam! libel!
defense* /s privilege* /s slander! defam! libel! /p constitution! unconstitution!

Judicial Proceedings
libel! slander! defam! /p "absolute immunity" /p judge* prosecutor* "public defender*" "judicial proceeding*"

Legislative Proceedings
libel! slander! defam! /p "absolute immunity" /s legislat! congress!
237k37

Executive Communications
libel! slander! defam! /p absolute** /s immun! /s executive

Consent of the Plaintiff
libel! slander! defam! /p absolute** /s immun! privilege* /s consen!

Husband and Wife
opinion(libel! slander! defam! /p absolut** /s immun! privilege* spous** husband* wife)

Political Broadcasts
372k435 & court(ca5)

§ 115. Qualified Privilege

It was recognized under the common law and prior to the development of the constitutional privilege to defame pursuant to the First Amendment that there are a variety of

---

3. Wennhak v. Morgan, 1880, 20 Q.B.D. 635, 57 L.J.Q.B. 241; Dyer v. MacDougall, E.D.N.Y.1950, 93 F.Supp. 484; Lawler v. Merritt, 1944, 182 Misc. 648, 48 N.Y.S.2d 843, affirmed 1945, 269 App.Div. 662, 53 N.Y.S.2d 465; Springer v. Swift, 1931, 59 S.D. 208, 239 N.W. 171; Conrad v. Roberts, 1915, 95 Kan. 180, 147 P. 795.

4. See infra, § 122.

5. Wenman v. Ash, 1853, 13 C.B. 836, 138 Eng.Rep. 1432; Schenck v. Schenck, 1843, 20 N.J.L. 208; Luick v. Driscoll, 1895, 13 Ind.App. 279, 41 N.E. 463; Bonkowski v. Arlan's Department Store, 1970, 383 Mich. 90, 174 N.W.2d 765.

6. Restatement of Torts, § 592; see Campbell v. Bannister, 1886, 79 Ky. 205, 2 Ky.Law Rep. 72.

7. Federal Communications Act of 1934, 47 U.S.C.A. § 315.

8. Held in Felix v. Westinghouse Radio Stations, 3d Cir. 1950, 106 F.2d 1, certiorari denied 341 U.S. 909, 71 S.Ct. 622, 95 L.Ed. 1347 not to apply to supporters of candidates.

9. See Snyder, Liability of Station Owners for Defamatory Statements by Political Candidates, 1953, 37 Va.L.Rev. 303; Berry and Goodrich, Political Defamation: Radio's Dilemma, 1948, 1 U.Fla.L.Rev. 343; Notes, 1956, 25 Ford.L.Rev. 385; 1958, 32 So.Cal.L.Rev. 71; 1959, 8 Buff.L.Rev. 275; 1958, 107 U.Pa.L.Rev. 280.

10. Farmers Educational and Co-op. Union of America, North Dakota Division v. WDAY, Inc., 1959, 360 U.S. 525, 79 S.Ct. 1302, 3 L.Ed.2d 1407.

11. Cf. Becker v. Philco Corp., 4th Cir. 1967, 372 F.2d 771, certiorari denied 389 U.S. 979, 88 S.Ct. 408, 19 L.Ed.2d 473 (employer required by defense contract to report any loss or compromise of classified information).

situations in which the interest which the defendant is seeking to vindicate or further is regarded as being sufficiently important to justify some latitude for making mistakes, so that publication of defamation should be conditionally or qualifiedly privileged.[1] It is difficult to reduce these cases to any single statement, and perhaps no better formula can be offered than that of Baron Parke,[2] that the publication is privileged when it is "fairly made by a person in the discharge of some public or private duty, whether legal or moral, or in the conduct of his own affairs, in matters where his interest is concerned." It might have been better, as stated before, to have required negligence with respect to truth or falsity as a prerequisite to recovery in any case than to have adopted a policy of publishing at peril with a large number of qualifications. At least, much complexity could have been avoided. The qualified privilege structure has not been automatically abrogated as a consequence of the constitutional privilege for two reasons. First, the common law rules related to how and when a qualified privilege can be abused in a way that will subject the publisher to liability are not the same as those related to the constitutional privilege. Second, the constitutional privilege has not been held to extend to many situations where a qualified privilege would be recognized. This would be especially so with respect to private publications of defamatory statements about private individuals to further and vindicate private interests. The complex qualified privilege structure pertains primarily to this type of defamatory publication. The position has been taken in the *Second Restatement of Torts* that negligence or something worse as to truth or falsity should be a prerequisite to recovery in all cases. If a state court should see fit to adopt this as a policy position, even though not required to do so as a constitutional matter, then it would seem that most qualified privileges could be abrogated. Most private interests would be adequately protected without the necessity for a recognition of a qualified privilege requiring knowledge of falsity or recklessness with respect to the truth or falsity of the defamatory matter published.

Aside from a constitutional privilege, the types of interests which are protected by a qualified privilege may be classified as follows:

1. *Interest of publisher.* Roughly similar to the privileges of self-defense or the defense of property [3] is the privilege which attaches to the publication of defamatory matter for the protection or advancement of the defendant's own legitimate interests. Thus he may publish, in an appropriate manner, anything which reasonably appears to be necessary to defend his own reputation against the defamation of another [4] including, of course, the allegation that his accuser is an unmitigated liar and the truth is not in him. He will, however, be liable if he adds anything irrelevant and unconnected with the charges made against him, as where he attempts to refute an accusation of immorality by saying that the plaintiff has stolen a horse.[5] A similar privilege extends to the protection of his other interests of any im-

§ 115

1. See generally First Restatement of Torts, §§ 593-612; Bower, Actionable Defamaton, 2d ed. 1923, Appendix VIII; Harper, Privileged Defamation, 1936, 22 Va.L.Rev. 642; Evans, Legal Immunity for Defamation, 1940, 24 Minn.L.Rev. 607; Jones, Interest and Duty in Relation to Qualified Privilege, 1924, 22 Mich.L.Rev. 437; Smith, Conditional Privilege for Mercantile Agencies, 1914, 14 Col.L.Rev. 187, 296; Note, 1963, 30 Tenn.L.Rev. 569.

2. In Toogood v. Spyring, 1834, 1 C. M. & R. 181, 149 Eng.Rep. 1044.

3. See supra, §§ 19, 21.

Prosser & Keeton Torts 5th Ed. HB—19

4. Haycox v. Dunn, 1958, 200 Va. 212, 104 S.E.2d 800; Shenkman v. O'Malley, 1956, 2 A.D.2d 567, 157 N.Y.S.2d 290; Preston v. Hobbs, 1914, 161 App.Div. 363, 146 N.Y.S. 419; Duncan v. Record Publishing Co., 1927, 145 S.C. 196, 143 S.E. 31; Craig v. Wright, 1938, 182 Okl. 68, 76 P.2d 248. See Note, 1969, 34 Alb.L.J. 95.

5. Brewer v. Chase, 1899, 121 Mich. 526, 80 N.W. 575; Fish v. St. Louis County Printing & Publishing Co., 1903, 102 Mo.App. 6, 74 S.W. 641; Sternberg Manufacturing Co. v. Miller, Du Brul & Peters Manufacturing Co., 8th Cir. 1909, 170 F. 298; Ivie v. King, 1914, 167 N.C. 174, 83 S.E. 339, rehearing denied 1915, 169 N.C. 261, 85 S.E. 413; cf. Conroy v. Fall River Herald

portance. He may make a reasonable effort to recover stolen property [6] or to that end to discover and prosecute the thief,[7] to collect money due him,[8] or to prevent others from collecting it,[9] to warn his servants against the conduct of the plaintiff, or others of questionable character,[10] to consult an attorney for legal advice,[11] to protest against the mismanagement of a concern in which he has an interest,[12] or to protect his business against unethical competition.[13] In all of these cases the privilege is lost if he says more than reasonably appears to be necessary,[14] or if the publication is made to a person who apparently [15] is in no position to give legitimate assistance, as where complaint is made to an employer that his employee will not pay the defendant a debt.[16]

2. *Interest of others.* The privilege to use force to protect the safety of another [17] finds a general parallel in the privilege to publish defamation for the protection of the interests of persons other than the publisher. The publication may be made to the individual who is thus protected, as in the case of a warning to a woman not to marry a supposed ex-convict, or it may be made to a third person, as where the warning is given to her father. As in the case of the use of force, the defendant must have reason to believe that the publication is necessary for the purpose, and that the other is unable to protect himself. Thus there is no privilege to refute a libel on behalf of one who is quite able to publish his own denial,[18] although the privilege may exist if he is precluded by army orders from speaking.[19]

The extent of this privilege has been a matter of considerable discussion,[20] and because the fact situations are of infinite varie-

News Co., 1940, 306 Mass. 488, 28 N.E.2d 729. As to mitigation of damages because of provocation, see infra, § 116A. Louisiana denies recovery in cases of "mutual vituperation." Bloom v. Crescioni, 1903, 109 La. 667, 33 So. 724; Pelliffigue v. Judice, 1923, 154 La. 782, 98 So. 244.

6. Padmore v. Lawrence, 1840, 11 Ad. & El. 380, 113 Eng.Rep. 460; Brow v. Hathaway, 1866, 95 Mass. (13 Allen) 239; Faber v. Byrle, 1951, 171 Kan. 38, 229 P.2d 718; Bavington v. Robinson, 1914, 124 Md. 85, 91 A. 777.

Cf. Ripps v. Herrington, 1941, 241 Ala. 209, 1 So.2d 899 (claim to fidelity insurance company).

7. Ram v. Lamley, 1633, Hut. 113, 123 Eng.Rep. 1139; Klinck v. Colby, 1871, 46 N.Y. 427; Flanagan v. McLane, 1913, 87 Conn. 220, 87 A. 727, 88 A. 96; cf. Ginsberg v. Union Surety & Guaranty Co., 1902, 68 App.Div. 141, 74 N.Y.S. 561.

8. Dickinson v. Hathaway, 1909, 122 La. 644, 48 So. 136. In Miller v. Howe, 1932, 245 Ky. 568, 53 S.W.2d 938, a mere collecting agent was held to have no interest justifying a privilege.

9. Blackham v. Pugh, 1846, 2 C.B. 611, 135 Eng. Rep. 1086; Gassett v. Gilbert, 1856, 72 Mass. (6 Gray) 94; Hatch v. Lane, 1870, 105 Mass. 394; cf. Holmes v. Royal Fraternal Union, 1909, 222 Mo. 556, 121 S.W. 100; Tierney v. Ruppert, 1912, 150 App.Div. 863, 135 N.Y.S. 365 (warning against purchase of mortgaged property).

10. Somerville v. Hawkins, 1851, 10 C.B. 583, 138 Eng.Rep. 231; Nichols v. J. J. Newberry Co., 9th Cir. 1945, 150 F.2d 15; Lawler v. Earle, 1862, 87 Mass. (5 Allen) 22; Hunt v. Great Northern R. Co., [1891] 1 Q.B. 601.

Cf. Conner v. Taylor, 1930, 233 Ky. 706, 26 S.W.2d 561 (effort to keep diseased employee away so that others would work).

11. Lapetina v. Santangelo, 1908, 124 App.Div. 519, 108 N.Y.S. 975; see Kruse v. Rabe, 1910, 80 N.J.L. 378, 79 A. 316.

12. McDougall v. Claridge, 1808, 1 Camp. 267, 170 Eng.Rep. 953.

13. Powell v. Young, 1928, 151 Va. 985, 144 S.E. 624, 145 S.E. 731; cf. John W. Lovell Co. v. Houghton, 1889, 116 N.Y. 520, 22 N.E. 1066; Hovey v. Rubber Tip Pencil Co., 1874, 57 N.Y. 119.

14. Holmes v. Clisby, 1904, 121 Ga. 241, 48 S.E. 934. See infra this section on Abuse of Qualified Privilege.

15. As to the effect of reasonable belief in the existence of the privilege, see infra, this section on Abuse of Qualified Privilege.

16. Over v. Schiffling, 1885, 102 Ind. 191, 26 N.E. 91; Vail v. Pennsylvania Railroad Co., 1927, 103 N.J.L. 213, 136 A. 425; cf. Hollenbeck v. Ristine, 1901, 114 Iowa 358, 86 N.W. 377; Brown v. Vanneman, 1893, 85 Wis. 451, 55 N.W. 183; Preston v. Frey, 1891, 91 Cal. 107, 27 P. 533.

17. See supra, § 20.

18. Ritschy v. Garrels, 1916, 195 Mo.App. 670, 187 S.W. 1120.

19. Adam v. Ward, [1917] A.C. 309. Cf. Israel v. Portland News Publishing Co., 1936, 152 Or. 225, 53 P.2d 529 (deceased husband). See Notes, 1936, 20 Minn.L.Rev. 438; 1936, 49 Harv.L.Rev. 839. In Smith v. Levitt, 9th Cir. 1955, 227 F.2d 855, a combination of this privilege and that of fair comment was held to jus-

20. See note 20 on page 827.

ty, it is not possible to reduce them to any formula, other than the general one that the publication must be justified by the importance of the interest served, and it must be called for by a legal or moral "duty," or by generally accepted standards of decent conduct.[21] The privilege is clearest when some definite legal relation exists between the defendant and the person on whose behalf he intervenes. Thus a man may advise a member of his family not to marry one believed to be a scoundrel,[22] or protest to school authorities against the students with whom his daughter is brought in contact,[23] or a physician may speak to protect the interest of his patient,[24] an attorney that of his client,[25] or an agent or employee that of his principal or employer.[26]

Beyond this, the courts have recognized in many instances a moral justification, where under ordinary social standards a reasonable man would feel called upon to speak. It is permissible to warn a present[27] or prospective[28] employer of the misconduct or bad character of an employee, to notify an insurance company that it is being swindled by the insured,[29] to inform a landlord that his tenant is undesirable,[30] a creditor that his debtor is insolvent,[31] or one who appears likely to deal with the plaintiff that his credit or character is bad.[32]

A point is reached at which the line must be drawn against officious intermeddling, where a reasonable person would conclude that the matter is none of his affair, and that he would do better to remain silent. Particularly in the case of interference with personal or family matters, such as a word

tify defense of a United States Senator by his political friends and supporters.

20. See Jones, Interest and Duty in Relation to Qualified Privilege, 1924, 22 Mich.L.Rev. 437; Smith, Conditional Privilege for Mercantile Agencies, 1914, 14 Col.L.Rev. 187, 296; Harper, Privileged Defamation, 1936, 22 Va.L.Rev. 642; Evans, Legal Immunity for Defamation, 1940, 24 Minn.L.Rev. 607.

21. See Second Restatement of Torts, § 595.

22. Todd v. Hawkins, 1837, 8 C. & P. 88, 173 Eng. Rep. 411; cf. McBride v. Ledoux, 1904, 111 La. 398, 35 So. 615; Kimble v. Kimble, 1896, 14 Wash. 369, 44 P. 866; Harriott v. Plimpton, 1896, 166 Mass. 585, 44 N.E. 992.

23. Hansen v. Hansen, 1914, 126 Minn. 426, 148 N.W. 457. Cf. Kenney v. Gurley, 1923, 208 Ala. 623, 95 So. 34 (school to parent); Coopersmith v. Williams, 1970, 171 Colo. 511, 468 P.2d 739.

24. Cameron v. Cockran, Del.1895, 2 Marv. 166, 42 A. 454; Cash Drug Store v. Cannon, Tex.Civ.App.1932, 47 S.W.2d 861. Cf. Thornburg v. Long, 1919, 178 N.C. 589, 101 S.E. 99 (one physician to another).

25. Kruse v. Rabe, 1910, 80 N.J.L. 378, 79 A. 316.

26. Scarll v. Dixon, 1864, 4 F. & F. 250, 176 Eng. Rep. 552; Lewis v. Chapman, 1857, 16 N.Y. 369; Ritchie v. Arnold, 1898, 79 Ill.App. 406. Accord, as to reporting theft: Bell v. Bank of Abbeville, 1947, 211 S.C. 167, 44 S.E.2d 328; Lee v. Cannon Mills, 4th Cir. 1939, 107 F.2d 109; Snyder v. Fatherly, 1930, 153 Va. 762, 151 S.E. 149.

Accord, as to hired investigators: Combes v. Montgomery Ward & Co., 1951, 119 Utah 407, 228 P.2d 272; Roscoe v. Schoolitz, 1970, 105 Ariz. 310, 464 P.2d 333; Campbell v. Willmark Service System, 3d Cir. 1941, 123 F.2d 204.

27. Coxhead v. Richards, 1846, 2 C.B. 569, 135 Eng. Rep. 1069; Doyle v. Clauss, 1920, 190 App.Div. 838, 180 N.Y.S. 671. Cf. Simonsen v. Swenson, 1920, 104 Neb. 224, 177 N.W. 831 (physician informing hotel owner his employee had syphilis); Leonard v. Wilson, 1942, 150 Fla. 503, 8 So.2d 12 (physician reporting on fitness for work); Cochran v. Sears, Roebuck & Co., 1945, 72 Ga.App. 458, 34 S.E.2d 296 (nurse reporting disease).

28. Fresh v. Cutter, 1890, 73 Md. 87, 20 A. 774; Doane v. Grew, 1915, 220 Mass. 171, 107 N.E. 620; Hoff v. Pure Oil Co., 1920, 147 Minn. 195, 179 N.W. 891; Carroll v. Owen, 1914, 178 Mich. 551, 146 N.W. 168; Zeinfeld v. Hayes Freight Lines, Inc., 1969, 41 Ill. 2d 345, 243 N.E.2d 217. In Williams v. Kansas City Transit, Inc., Mo.1960, 339 S.W.2d 792, a discharging employer, required by statute to give the employee a letter stating the cause for his leaving the service, was held to be conditionally privileged. Accord, Henthorn v. Western Maryland Railroad Co., 1961, 226 Md. 499, 174 A.2d 175 (hearing required under collective bargaining provisions of Railway Labor Act).

29. Noonan v. Orton, 1873, 32 Wis. 106; Hubbard v. Rutledge, 1879, 57 Miss. 7.

30. Morton v. Knipe, 1908, 128 App.Div. 94, 112 N.Y.S. 451; Rose v. Tholborn, 1910, 153 Mo.App. 408, 134 S.W. 1093.

31. See Ormsby v. Douglass, 1867, 37 N.Y. 477; Lewis v. Chapman, 1857, 16 N.Y. 369; Ritchie v. Arnold, 1898, 79 Ill.App. 406.

32. Melcher v. Beeler, 1910, 48 Colo. 233, 110 P. 181; Richardson v. Gunby, 1912, 88 Kan. 47, 127 P. 533; Fahr v Hayes, 1888, 50 N.J.L. 275, 13 A. 261; Froslee v. Lund's State Bank, 1915, 131 Minn. 435, 155 N.W. 619; Browne v. Prudden-Winslow Co., 1921, 195 App.Div. 419, 186 N.Y.S. 350 (warning customers against salesman discharged for dishonesty).

to a husband about the conduct of his wife,[33] or to a woman concerning her prospective husband,[34] the courts have been inclined to say that the tale-bearing "friend" who stirs up domestic discord has no privilege, and must take the chance that his information is wrong. It has proved, however, unusually difficult to draw any definite line as to what is improper. In all such cases, the fact that the defendant has been requested to give information, or to obtain it,[35] becomes quite important, although not conclusive. Such a request on the part of one who has no other apparent interest than that of idle curiosity will not of course create a privilege in itself;[36] but it does indicate that the recipient regards the matter as important to his interests, and if those interests are otherwise apparent it will ordinarily make it reasonable to speak.[37] It has been said that volunteered information is never privileged,[38] and that it is privileged to the same extent as though it has been requested.[39] It seems clear that neither statement is correct, and that while more in the way of good reason to speak may be required of a volunteer, the absence of a request is merely one factor to be considered, along with the importance of the interest to be protected [40] and other elements, in determining the propriety of the defendant's conduct.[41] The same is no doubt true of the fact that the statement is made to a third person, rather than directly to the one for whose protection it is intended.[42]

3. *Common interest.* A conditional privilege is recognized in many cases where the publisher and the recipient have a common interest, and the communication is of a kind reasonably calculated to protect or further it. Frequently in such cases there is a legal, as well as a moral obligation to speak. This is most obvious, of course, in the case of those who have entered upon or are considering business dealings with one another,[43] or where the parties are members of a group [44] with a common pecuniary interest, as where officers, agents or employees of a business organization communicate with

33. Watt v. Longsdon, [1930] 1 K.B. 130; Burton v. Mattson, 1917, 50 Utah 133, 166 P. 979.

34. Krebs v. Oliver, 1858, 78 Mass. (12 Gray) 239; Joannes v. Bennett, 1862, 87 Mass. (5 Allen) 169.

35. Rude v. Nass, 1891, 79 Wis. 321, 48 N.W. 555.

36. Swift & Co. v. Gray, 9th Cir. 1939, 101 F.2d 976 (customers of discharged truck driver); Byam v. Collins, 1888, 111 N.Y. 143, 19 N.E. 75; Carpenter v. Willey, 1892, 65 Vt. 168, 26 A. 488; Ritchie v. Widdemer, 1896, 59 N.J.L. 290, 35 A. 825.

37. Restatement of Torts, § 595, Comment *i;* Rude v. Nass, 1891, 79 Wis. 321, 48 N.W. 555; Posnett v. Marble, 1889, 62 Vt. 481, 20 A. 813; Rosenbaum v. Roche, 1907, 46 Tex.Civ.App. 237, 101 S.W.2d 1164; Zeinfeld v. Hayes Freight Lines, Inc., 1969, 41 Ill.2d 345, 243 N.E.2d 217. Cf. Stevenson v. Baltimore Baseball Club, 1968, 250 Md. 482, 243 A.2d 533.

38. Draper v. Hellman Commercial Trust & Savings Bank, 1928, 203 Cal. 26, 263 P. 240; cf. Rosenbaum v. Roche, 1907, 46 Tex.Civ.App. 237, 101 S.W. 1164.

39. See Pattison v. Jones, 1828, 8 B. & C. 578, 108 Eng.Rep. 1157; Fresh v. Cutter, 1890, 73 Md. 87, 20 A. 774.

40. See Samples v. Carnahan, 1898, 21 Ind.App. 55, 51 N.E. 425; Second Restatement of Torts, § 595, Comment *j*.

41. Thus volunteered information to protect interests of importance was held privileged in Hubbard v. Rutledge, 1879, 57 Miss. 7; Morton v. Knipe, 1908, 128 App.Div. 94, 112 N.Y.S. 451; Rose v. Tholborn, 1910, 153 Mo.App. 408, 134 S.W. 1093; Fahr v. Hayes, 1888, 50 N.J.L. 275, 13 A. 261; Fresh v. Cutter, 1890, 73 Md. 87, 20 A. 774.

42. This may be entirely reasonable, as in Hansen v. Hansen, 1914, 126 Minn. 426, 148 N.W. 457, where a father protested to school authorities against students with whom his daughter ws brought in contact. Or it may be found to be totally unnecessary and unjustified, as in Krebs v. Oliver, 1858, 78 Mass. (12 Gray) 239. In Berry v. Moench, 1958, 8 Utah 2d 191, 331 P.2d 814, where a psychiatrist passed on the word that plaintiff was a psychopathic personality to the family doctor of a woman contemplating marriage with him, the question was left to the jury.

43. Johns v. Associated Aviation Underwriters, 5th Cir. 1953, 203 F.2d 208, certiorari denied 346 U.S. 834, 74 S.Ct. 38, 98 L.Ed. 356 (insurers to insured); Cook v. Gust, 1914, 155 Wis. 594, 145 N.W. 225 (promoter to prospective investor); Hales v. Commercial Bank of Spanish Fork, 1948, 114 Utah 186, 197 P.2d 910 (bank to payee of forged check); Flowers v. Smith, Tex.Civ. App.1934, 80 S.W.2d 392 (employee of electric company to housewife); West v. People's Banking & Trust Co., 1967, 14 Ohio App.2d 69, 236 N.E.2d 679 (bank and commercial borrower).

44. See Evans, Legal Immunity for Defamation, 1940, 24 Minn.L.Rev. 607, regarding the privilege as attached to the group relation.

stockholders,[45] or with other employees or branch offices[46] about the affairs of the organization itself, or taxpayers discuss the management of public funds,[47] or an association of property owners the desirability of a prospective purchaser,[48] or creditors the affairs of a common debtor.[49]

Mutual credit organizations for protection against bad credit risks or delinquent debtors usually are given the privilege,[50] so long as it is exercised in good faith and not as a mere cloak for coercion of payment.[51] Mercantile credit rating agencies were for a considerable time a subject of considerable disagreement. They were denied any privilege in England,[52] on the ground that they were mere business ventures trading for profit in the characters of other people. Although there are American courts which have agreed with this,[53] the great majority of them have recognized that such agencies perform a useful business service for the benefit of those who have a legitimate interest in obtaining the information, and who request the agency to obtain it for them. Such agencies are therefore held to have a qualified privilege,[54] where their inquiries are honestly made and the information is furnished to subscribers in good faith.[55] There is general agreement, however, that the privilege is limited by the extent to which the particular subscriber to whom the publication is made has an apparent, present interest in the report; and that in so far as there is general publication to those without such an interest, the risk of false information is one to be borne by the business.[56]

---

45. Philadelphia Wilmington & Baltimore Railroad Co. v. Quigley, 1858, 62 U.S. (21 How.) 202, 16 L.Ed. 73; Montgomery v. Knox, 1887, 23 Fla. 595, 3 So. 211; Garey v. Jackson, 1917, 197 Mo.App. 217, 193 S.W. 920.

Accord, as to communications between stockholders: Chambers v. Leiser, 1906, 43 Wash. 285, 86 P. 627; Ashcroft v. Hammond, 1910, 197 N.Y. 488, 90 N.E. 1117; Baker v. Clark, 1920, 186 Ky. 816, 218 S.W. 280. Cf. Loewinthan v. Levine, 1946, 270 App.Div. 512, 60 N.Y.S.2d 433 (hospital trustees to trustees).

46. Bander v. Metropolitan Life Insurance Co., 1943, 313 Mass. 337, 47 N.E.2d 595; Miley v. Foster, 1956, 229 Miss. 106, 90 So.2d 172; Peoples Life Insurance Co. of Washington v. Talley, 1936, 166 Va. 464, 186 S.E. 42; Louisiana Oil Corp. v. Renno, 1934, 173 Miss. 609, 157 So. 705; Johnson v. Rudolph Wurlitzer Co., 1928, 197 Wis. 432, 222 N.W. 451.

47. Spencer v. Amerton, 1835, 1 Moo. & Rob. 470, 174 Eng.Rep. 162; Smith v. Higgins, 1860, 82 Mass. (16 Gray) 251.

48. Bufalino v. Maxon Brothers, 1962, 368 Mich. 140, 117 N.W.2d 150.

49. Smith Brothers & Co. v. W. C. Agee & Co., 1912, 178 Ala. 627, 59 So. 647. Cf. Edwards v. Kevil, 1909, 133 Ky. 392, 118 S.W. 273 (owners of buildings destroyed by fire); Spielberg v. A. Kuhn & Bro., 1911, 39 Utah 276, 116 P. 1027 (defendants in lawsuits brought by plaintiff); cf. Rodgers v. Wise, 1940, 193 S.C. 5, 7 S.E.2d 517 (attorneys engaged in same suit).

50. Putnal v. Inman, 1918, 76 Fla. 553, 80 So. 316; Woodhouse v. Powles, 1906, 43 Wash. 617, 86 P. 1063; McDonald v. Lee, 1914, 246 Pa. 253, 92 A. 135; Ideal Motor Co. v. Warfield, 1925, 211 Ky. 576, 277 S.W. 862; Pavlovsky v. Board of Trade of San Francisco, 1959, 171 Cal.App.2d 110, 340 P.2d 63.

51. Traynor v. Seiloff, 1895, 62 Minn. 420, 64 N.W. 915; Hartnett v. Goddard, 1900, 176 Mass. 326, 57 N.E. 677; Muetze v. Tuteur, 1890, 77 Wis. 236, 46 N.W. 123.

52. MacIntosh v. Dunn, [1908] A.C. 300.

53. Johnson v. Bradstreet Co., 1886, 77 Ga. 172; Pacific Packing Co. v. Bradstreet Co., 1914, 25 Idaho 696, 139 P. 1007.

54. Altoona Clay Products, Inc. v. Dun & Bradstreet, Inc., W.D.Pa.1968, 286 F.Supp. 899, vacated on other grounds 308 F.Supp. 1068; Retail Credit Co. v. Garraway, 1961, 240 Miss. 230, 126 So.2d 271; A.B.C. Needlecraft Co. v. Dun & Bradstreet, 2d Cir. 1957, 245 F.2d 775; Petition of Retailers Commercial Agency, 1961, 342 Mass. 515, 174 N.E.2d 376; Barker v. Retail Credit Co., 1960, 8 Wis.2d 664, 100 N.W.2d 391.

See Smith, Conditional Privilege for Mercantile Agencies, 1941, 14 Col.L.Rev. 187, 296; Notes, 1953, 2 De Paul L.Rev. 69; 1957, 31 Temple L.Q. 50; 1960, 36 N.Dak.L.Rev. 201.

55. The privilege is lost when the agency acts with conscious indifference and reckless disregard of the plaintiff's rights. Dun & Bradstreet v. Robinson, 1961, 233 Ark. 168, 345 S.W.2d 34. Mere negligence, however, is not enough to defeat the privilege. H.R. Crawford Co. v. Dun & Bradstreet, 4th Cir. 1957, 241 F.2d 387; A.B.C. Needlecraft Co. v. Dun & Bradstreet, 2d Cir. 1957, 245 F.2d 775; Dun and Bradstreet, Inc. v. O'Neil, Tex.1970, 456 S.W.2d 896.

56. King v. Patterson, 1887, 49 N.J.L. 417, 9 A. 705; Pollasky v. Minchener, 1890, 81 Mich. 280, 46 N.W. 5; Sunderlin v. Bradstreet, 1871, 46 N.Y. 188. Mitchell v. Bradstreet Co., 1893, 116 Mo. 226, 22 S.W. 358, 724, motion for rehearing overruled 116 Mo. 226, 22 S.W. 724; Hanschke v. Merchants' Credit Bureau, 1931, 256 Mich. 272, 239 N.W. 318.

The agency is not, however, liable for unauthorized republication by its customers to third parties. Pea-

The privilege has also been extended to the members of groups with a common interest of a non-pecuniary character, such as religious [57] or professional [58] societies, fraternal,[59] social [60] or educational [61] organizations, families,[62] or labor unions,[63] if the matter communicated is pertinent to the interest of the group. In all such cases, however, the privilege is lost if the defamation goes beyond the group interest,[64] or if publication is made to persons who have no reason to receive the information.[65]

4. *Communications to one who may act in the public interest.* The interest of the general public, as distinguished from that of any individual, has given rise to two qualified privileges, which often have been confused. One is broad as to what may be said, but narrow as to those to whom it may be communicated; the other is more restricted as to content, but broader as to publication. The first, sometimes called the "public interest" privilege, involves communications made to those who may be expected to take official action of some kind for the protection of some interest of the public. It is on this basis that communications from one public officer to another, in an effort to discharge official duty, are held to be at least qualifiedly privileged,[66] even where no absolute privilege [67] is found. But private citizens likewise are privileged to give information to proper [68] authorities for the prevention or detection of crime,[69] or to complain to them about the conduct of public officials and seek their removal from office.[70]

---

cock v. Retail Credit Co., N.D.Ga.1969, 302 F.Supp. 418.

57. Jarvis v. Hatheway, N.Y.1808, 3 Johns. 180; Slocinski v. Radwan, 1929, 83 N.H. 501, 144 A. 787; Creswell v. Pruitt, Tex.Civ.App.1951, 239 S.W.2d 165; Pinn v. Lawson, 1934, 63 U.S.App.D.C. 370, 72 F.2d 742; Stewart v. Ging, 1958, 64 N.M. 270, 327 P.2d 333.

In Warren v. Pulitzer Publishing Co., 1934, 336 Mo. 184, 78 S.W.2d 404, a hearing before a church tribunal was held to be absolutely privileged. In Van Vliet v. Vander Naald, 1939, 290 Mich. 365, 287 N.W. 564, and Browning v. Gomez, Tex.Civ.App.1960, 332 S.W.2d 588, it was held that there was only a qualified privilege.

58. Barrows v. Bell, 1856, 73 Mass. (7 Gray) 301; McKnight v. Hasbrouck, 1890, 17 R.I. 70, 20 A. 95; Mick v. American Dental Association, 1958, 49 N.J. Super. 262, 139 A.2d 570; Judge v. Rockford Memorial Hospital, 1958, 17 Ill.App.2d 365, 150 N.E.2d 202; Willenbucher v. McCormick, D.Colo.1964, 229 F.Supp. 659 (association of retired army officers).

59. Reininger v. Prickett, 1943, 192 Okl. 486, 137 P.2d 595; Peterson v. Cleaver, 1920, 105 Neb. 438, 181 N.W. 187; Cadle v. McIntosh, 1912, 51 Ind.App. 365, 99 N.E. 779; Bayliss v. Grand Lodge of State of Louisiana, 1912, 131 La. 579, 59 So. 996.

60. Hayden v. Hasbrouck, 1912, 34 R.I. 556, 84 A. 1087; cf. Kersting v. White, 1904, 107 Mo.App. 265, 80 S.W. 730.

61. Gattis v. Kilgo, 1905, 140 N.C. 106, 52 S.E. 249; cf. Clark v. McBaine, 1923, 299 Mo. 77, 252 S.W. 428.

62. Zanley v. Hyde, 1919, 208 Mich. 96, 175 N.W. 261; Brown v. Radebaugh, 1901, 84 Minn. 347, 87 N.W. 937.

63. Bereman v. Power Publishing Co., 1933, 93 Colo. 581, 27 P.2d 749; Ward v. Painters' Local Union No. 300, 1953, 41 Wn.2d 859, 252 P.2d 253; Sheehan v. Tobin, 1950, 326 Mass. 185, 93 N.E.2d 524; Wise v. Brotherhood of Locomotive Firemen and Enginemen, 8th Cir. 1918, 252 F. 961; De Mott v. Amalgamated Meat Cutters & Butchers, 1958, 157 Cal.App.2d 13, 320 P.2d 50; Manbeck v. Ostrowski, 1967, 128 U.S.App. D.C. 1, 384 F.2d 970, certiorari denied 390 U.S. 966.

64. Cf. Smith v. Smith, 1940, 194 S.C. 247, 9 S.E.2d 584; Hocks v. Sprangers, 1901, 113 Wis. 123, 87 N.W. 1101, 89 N.W. 113; Carpenter v. Willey, 1893, 65 Vt. 68, 26 A. 488; York v. Johnson, 1875, 116 Mass. 482; Lovejoy v. Whitcomb, 1899, 174 Mass. 586, 55 N.E. 322.

65. See infra, this section on Abuse of Qualified Privilege.

66. Peterson v. Steenerson, 1910, 113 Minn. 87, 129 N.W. 147; Hemmens v. Nelson, 1893, 138 N.Y. 517, 34 N.E. 342; Greenwood v. Cobbey, 1889, 26 Neb. 449, 42 N.W. 413; Barry v. McCollom, 1908, 81 Conn. 293, 70 A. 1035; Tanner v. Stevenson, 1910, 138 Ky. 578, 128 S.W. 878.

67. See supra, § 114.

68. As to the effect of a reasonable belief that the authority is the proper one, see infra, this section on Abuse of Qualified Privilege.

69. Foltz v. Moore McCormack Lines, 2 Cir. 1951, 189 F.2d 537, certiorari denied 342 U.S. 871; Robinson v. Van Auken, 1906, 190 Mass. 161, 76 N.E. 601; Joseph v. Baars, 1910, 142 Wis. 390, 125 N.W. 913; Taylor v. Chambers, 1907, 2 Ga.App. 178, 58 S.E. 369; Hutchinson v. New England Telephone & Telegraph Co., 1966, 350 Mass. 188, 214 N.E.2d 57 (bomb threat). See Notes, 1951, 51 Col.L.Rev. 244; 1952, 30 Tex.L. Rev. 875. In Otten v. Schutt, 1962, 15 Wis.2d 497, 113 N.W.2d 152, a communication to a police officer accusing the plaintiff of crime was held not to be privileged where it was not made for the bona fide purpose of investigation or prosecution.

70. Nuyen v. Slater, 1964, 372 Mich. 654, 127 N.W.2d 369; Sowder v. Nolan, D.C.Mun.App.1956, 125 A.2d 52; Ponder v. Cobb, 1962, 257 N.C. 281, 126 S.E.2d 67; Dempsky v. Double, 1956, 386 Pa. 542, 126

Thus, for example, complaints made by members of the public to school boards about the character, competence or conduct of their teachers are subject to a qualified privilege.[71] The privilege includes false statements of fact concerning the plaintiff made in good faith; but, although it is not impossible that communications to other non-official interested persons will be protected,[72] publication to the world at large in a newspaper is not.[73]

5. *Fair comment on matters of public concern.* Defamatory opinions that do not imply the allegation of undisclosed defamatory facts are probably no longer actionable, even though they are expressed about matters that do not involve a public interest. This has been discussed in Section 113A. However, as stated in that section, this may not be universally accepted, and the demands of the constitutional privilege may not extend to the unreasonable or dishonest deduction of a false fact, as therein set forth. Therefore, the common law privilege of fair comment on matters of public concern may still have some viability.

The common law privilege of "fair comment" in public discussion was not limited to officers and candidates, but extended to other matters of public concern, such as work to be paid for out of public funds,[74] the admission or disbarment of attorneys,[75] and the management of institutions, such as schools,[76] charities,[77] and churches,[78] in which the public has a legitimate interest. Likewise any private enterprise,[79] to the extent that it begins to affect the general interests of the community, as by the distribution of food,[80] the pollution of the water supply,[81] quack medical services,[82] the

A.2d 915; Hancock v. Mitchell, 1919, 83 W.Va. 156, 98 S.E. 65.

Cf. Lee v. W.E. Fuetterer Battery & Supplies Co., 1929, 323 Mo. 1204, 23 S.W.2d 45 (complaint to bar association about attorney); Licciardi v. Molnar, 1945, 23 N.J.Misc. 361, 44 A.2d 653 (memorial to officers about conduct of other officers).

71. Bodwell v. Osgood, 1825, 20 Mass. (3 Pick.) 379; Wieman v. Mabee, 1881, 45 Mich. 484, 8 N.W. 71; Wakefield v. Smithwick, 1857, 49 N.C. (4 Jones) 327; Johnson v. Langley, 1933, 247 Ky. 387, 57 S.W.2d 21; Segall v. Piazza, 1965, 46 Misc.2d 700, 260 N.Y.S.2d 543.

72. Thus in Dempsky v. Double, 1956, 386 Pa. 542, 126 A.2d 915, a copy sent to the League of Women Voters was held to be privileged, on the ground that it was a reputable organization which might cooperate in requesting an investigation.

73. Bingham v. Gaynor, 1911, 203 N.Y. 27, 96 N.E. 84.

74. Bailey v. Charleston Mail Association, 1943, 126 W.Va. 292, 27 S.E.2d 837; Holway v. World Publishing Co., 1935, 171 Okl. 306, 44 P.2d 881; Yancey v. Gillespie, 1955, 242 N.C. 227, 87 S.E.2d 210; Grell v. Hoard, 1931, 206 Wis. 187, 239 N.W. 428; Bishop v. Wometco Enterprises, Inc., Fla.App.1970, 235 So.2d 759 (preferential tax treatment).

75. Kennedy v. Item Co., 1941, 197 La. 1050, 3 So. 2d 175; Spriggs v. Cheyenne Newspapers, 1947, 63 Wyo. 416, 182 P.2d 801.

76. O'Connor v. Sill, 1886, 60 Mich. 175, 27 N.W. 13, rehearing denied 60 Mich. 175, 28 N.W. 162; Clark v. McBaine, 1923, 299 Mo. 77, 252 S.W. 428; Hoeppner v. Dunkirk Printing Co., 1930, 254 N.Y. 95, 172 N.E. 139.

77. Cox v. Feeney, 1863, 4 F. & F. 13, 176 Eng.Rep. 552; Campbell v. Spottiswoode, 1863, 3 B. & S. 769, 122 Eng.Rep. 288.

78. Klos v. Zahorik, 1901, 113 Iowa 161, 84 N.W. 1046; Shurtleff v. Stevens, 1879, 51 Vt. 501; Kelly v. Tinling, 1865, L.R. 1 Q.B. 699.

79. The fact that the business deals with the public was not enough in itself to make it a matter of public concern. Atkinson v. Detroit Free Press Co., 1881, 46 Mich. 341, 9 N.W. 501 (lawyer); Tryon v. Evening News Association, 1878, 39 Mich. 636 (reporter); Baker v. State, 1940, 199 Ark. 1005, 137 S.W.2d 938, certiorari denied 311 U.S. 666, 61 S.Ct. 25, 85 L.Ed.2d 428 (privately owned hospital); Wilson v. Fitch, 1871, 41 Cal. 363.

80. Hubbard v. Allyn, 1908, 200 Mass. 166, 86 N.E. 356; Schwarz Brothers Co. v. Evening News Publishing Co., 1913, 84 N.J.L. 486, 87 A. 148. Accord: Hahnemannian Life Insurance Co. v. Beebe, 1868, 48 Ill. 87 (insurance); Duffy v. New York Evening Post Co., 1905, 109 App.Div. 471, 96 N.Y.S. 629 (political leader); Flanagan v. Nicholson Publishing Co., 1915, 137 La. 588, 68 So. 964 (transfer of exhibition to another city); South Hetton Coal Co. v. North-Eastern News Association, [1894] 1 Q.B. 133 (sanitary conditions in which two thousand people were housed).

81. Williams v. Standard-Examiner Publishing Co., 1933, 83 Utah 31, 27 P.2d 1. Cf. Mick v. American Dental Association, 1958, 49 N.J.Super. 262, 139 A.2d 570 (fluoridation).

82. Brinkley v. Fishbein, 5th Cir. 1940, 110 F.2d 62, certiorari denied 311 U.S. 672, 61 S.Ct. 34, 85 L.Ed. 432. Cf. Blanchard v. Claremont Eagle, 1949, 95 N.H. 375, 62 A.2d 791 (inability to get medical treatment).

promotion of race hatred,[83] the employment of a large number of people,[84] or the operation of a railroad,[85] was held to be a proper subject for such privileged comment.

Picked up and clearly included in the process[86] was the privilege, recognized at common law, of "fair comment" upon anything submitted to the public for its approval, as in the case of books,[87] articles,[88] advertisements,[89] radio and television programs,[90] exhibitions of art,[91] music,[92] acting and similar entertainments,[93] or sports,[94] scientific discoveries,[95] or projects appealing for support.[96]

Abuse of Qualified Privilege Regarding Private Publications of Private Matters

The condition attached to all such qualified privileges is that they must be exercised in a reasonable manner and for a proper purpose. The immunity is forfeited if the defendant steps outside of the scope of the privilege, or abuses the occasion.[97] Thus, qualified privilege does not extend, in any of the above cases, to the publication of irrelevant defamatory matter with no bearing upon the public or private interest which is entitled to protection;[98] nor does it include publication to any person other than those whose hearing of it is reasonably believed to be necessary or useful for the furtherance of that interest.[99] The owner of property is not privileged to accuse the plaintiff of theft of it in the presence of a third person who has no legitimate interest in the matter.[1] There is authority in England[2] to the effect that a publication made in the mistaken belief that the recipient is a proper person to

---

83. Beauharnais v. Pittsburgh Courier Publishing Co., 7th Cir. 1957, 243 F.2d 705.

84. Charles Parker Co. v. Silver City Crystal Co., 1955, 142 Conn. 605, 116 A.2d 440.

85. Crane v. Waters, C.C.Mass.1882, 10 F. 619.

86. Cepeda v. Cowles Magazine & Broadcasting Co., 9th Cir. 1968, 392 F.2d 417, certiorari denied 393 U.S. 840, 89 S.Ct. 117, 21 L.Ed.2d 110; Paulsen v. Personality Posters, Inc., 1968, 59 Misc.2d 444, 299 N.Y.S.2d 501.

87. Carr v. Hodd, 1808, 1 Camp. 355, 170 Eng.Rep. 983; Dowling v. Livingstone, 1896, 108 Mich. 321, 66 N.W. 225.

88. Potts v. Die, D.C.Cir.1942, 132 F.2d 734, certiorari denied 319 U.S. 762, 63 S.Ct. 1316, 87 L.Ed. 1713, rehearing denied 320 U.S. 808, 64 S.Ct. 28, 88 L.Ed. 488; Thompson v. Matthiasen, 1912, 150 App.Div. 739, 135 N.Y.S. 796.

89. Paris v. Levy, 1860, 9 C.B., N.S., 342, 142 Eng. Rep. 135; Willis v. O'Connell, D.Ala.1916, 231 F. 1004; cf. Press Co. v. Stewart, 1888, 119 Pa. 584, 14 A. 51.

90. Lyon v. Daily Telegraph, [1943] 1 K.B. 746; McCarthy v. Cincinnati Enquirer, 1956, 101 Ohio App. 297, 136 N.E.2d 393; Rutherford v. Dougherty, 3d Cir. 1937, 91 F.2d 707. Cf. Julian v. American Business Consultants, 1956, 2 N.Y.2d 1, 155 N.Y.S.2d 1, 137 N.E.2d 1 (Communist infiltration of industry).

91. Thompson v. Shackell, 1828, Moo. & Mal. 187, 173 Eng.Rep. 1126; Battersby v. Collier, 1898, 34 App. Div. 347, 54 N.Y.S. 363; Outcault v. New York Herald Co., 1907, 117 App.Div. 534, 102 N.Y.S. 685 (cartoonist); Soane v. Knight, 1827, Moo. & Mal. 74, 173 Eng.Rep. 1086 (architecture).

92. McQuire v. Western Morning News Co., [1903] 2 K.B. 100; cf. Brown v. New York Evening Journal, 1932, 143 Misc. 199, 255 N.Y.S. 403, affirmed 235 App. Div. 840, 257 N.Y.S. 903; Man v. Warner Brothers, Inc., S.D.N.Y.1970, 317 F.Supp. 50.

93. Cherry v. Des Moines Leader, 1901, 114 Iowa 298, 86 N.W. 323; Cleveland Leader Printing Co. v. Nethersole, 1911, 84 Ohio St. 118, 95 N.E. 735. Cf. Gott v. Pulsifer, 1877, 122 Mass. 235 (the "Cardiff Giant").

94. Cohen v. Cowles Publishing Co., 1954, 45 Wn.2d 262, 273 P.2d 893 (horse racing); Lloyds v. United Press International, Inc., 1970, 63 Misc.2d 421, 311 N.Y.S.2d 373 (same); Hoeppner v. Dunkirk Printing Co., 1930, 254 N.Y. 95, 172 N.E. 139 (football).

95. Hunter v. Sharpe, 1866, 4 F. & F. 983, 176 Eng. Rep. 875; Dakhyl v. Labouchere, [1908] 2 K.B. 325; cf. Brinkley v. Fishbein, 5th Cir. 1940, 110 F.2d 62, certiorari denied 311 U.S. 672, 61 S.Ct. 34, 85 L.Ed. 432.

96. Henwood v. Harrison, 1872, 7 C.P. 606; Kulesza v. Chicago Daily News, 1941, 311 Ill.App. 117, 35 N.E.2d 517.

97. See, generally, Hallen, Excessive Publication in Defamation, 1932, 16 Minn.L.Rev. 160; Hallen, Character of Belief Necessary for the Conditional Privilege in Defamation, 1931, 25 Ill.L.Rev. 865.

98. Huntley v. Ward, 1859, 6 C.B.,N.S., 514, 141 Eng.Rep. 557; Hines v. Shumaker, 1910, 97 Miss. 669, 52 So. 705; Sullivan v. Strahorn-Hutton-Evans Comm. Co., 1899, 152 Mo. 268, 53 S.W. 912; Lathrop v. Sundberg, 1909, 55 Wash. 144, 104 P. 176.

99. Vail v. Pennsylvania R. Co., 1927, 103 N.J.L. 213, 136 A. 425; Over v. Schiffling, 1885, 102 Ind. 191, 26 N.E. 91; Pollasky v. Minchener, 1890, 81 Mich. 280, 46 N.W. 5; Sheftall v. Central of Georgia R. Co., 1905, 123 Ga. 589, 51 S.E. 646; Ramsdell v. Pennsylvania R. Co., 1910, 79 N.J.L. 379, 75 A. 444.

1.–2. See notes 1–2 on page 833.

hear it is not privileged; but the few American cases [3] which have considered the question tend to adopt what seems clearly to be the more desirable rule, that while a misguided notion as to the defendant's moral obligation or justification to make the statement will not exonerate him,[4] he is privileged to publish it to any person who reasonably appears to have a duty, interest or authority in connection with the matter.

Any reasonable and appropriate method of publication may be adopted which fits the purpose of protecting the particular interest. The dictation of a business letter to a stenographer,[5] or the use of the telegraph where time is important [6], may be privileged on a proper occasion.

In all such cases, the fact that the communication is incidentally read or overheard by a person to whom there is no privilege to publish it will not result in liability, if the method adopted is a reasonable and appropriate one under the circumstances.[7] But the fact that there will be such incidental publication to improper persons is itself important in determining whether the method is a reasonable one; and the defendant may be liable if he unnecessarily sends a defamatory message on a postcard [8] or uses the telegraph [9] or speaks so that he will be overheard,[10] instead of resorting to some adequate but less public alternative.

Furthermore, the qualified privilege will be lost if the defendant publishes the defamation in the wrong state of mind. The word "malice," which has plagued the law of defamation from the beginning, has been much used in this connection, and it frequently is said that the privilege is forfeited if the publication is "malicious." It is clear that this means something more than the fictitious "legal malice" which is "implied" as a disguise for strict liability in any case of un-

1. Sias v. General Motors Corp., 1964, 372 Mich. 542, 127 N.W.2d 357; Southwest Drug Stores of Miss., Inc. v. Garner, Miss.1967, 195 So.2d 837; Williams v. Kroger Grocery & Baking Co., 1940, 337 Pa. 17, 10 A.2d 8; Galvin v. New York, N. H. & H. R. Co., 1960, 341 Mass. 293, 168 N.E.2d 262; Washington Annapolis Hotel Co. v. Riddle, 1948, 83 U.S.App.D.C. 288, 171 F.2d 732.

2. Hebditch v. MacIlwaine, [1894] 2 Q.B. 54.

3. See McKee v. Hughes, 1916, 133 Tenn. 455, 181 S.W. 930; Joseph v. Baars, 1910, 142 Wis. 390, 125 N.W. 913; Popke v. Hoffman, 1926, 21 Ohio App. 454, 153 N.E. 248; Berot v. Porte, 1919, 144 La. 805, 81 So. 323; Finkelstein v. Geismar, 1918, 92 N.J.L. 251, 106 A. 209; Harper, Privileged Defamation, 1936, 22 Va.L. Rev. 642, 651–654.

4. See Whiteley v. Adams, 1863, 15 C.B.,N.S., 392, 412, 143 Eng.Rep. 838; Stuart v. Bell, [1891] 2 Q.B. 341.

5. Ostrowe v. Lee, 1931, 256 N.Y. 36, 175 N.E. 505; Globe Furniture Co. v. Wright, 1920, 49 App.D.C. 315, 265 F. 873; Montgomery Ward & Co. v. Nance, 1935, 165 Va. 363, 182 S.E. 264; Domchick v. Greenbelt Consumer Services, 1952, 200 Md. 36, 87 A.2d 831; Mick v. American Dental Assn., 1958, 49 N.J.Super. 262, 139 A.2d 570. Apparently contra is Rickbeil v. Grafton Deaconess Hospital, 1946, 74 N.D. 525, 23 N.W.2d 247. See Smith, Liability of a Telegraph Company for Transmitting a Defamatory Message, 1920, 20 Col.L.Rev. 30, 35–46; Notes, 1921, 6 Corn.L.Q. 430, 1930, 16 Corn.L. Q. 103; 1930, 28 Mich.L.Rev. 348.

Some courts have accomplished the same result by holding that there is no publication, which seems erroneous. See supra, § 113.

6. Edmondson v. Birch & Co., [1907] 1 K.B. 371; Ashcroft v. Hammond, 1910, 197 N.Y. 488, 90 N.E. 1117; Western Union Tel. Co. v. Brown, 8 Cir. 1923, 294 F. 167; Nye v. Western Union Tel. Co., C.C.Minn. 1900, 104 F. 628.

7. Montgomery Ward & Co. v. Watson, 4 Cir. 1932, 55 F.2d 184; Shoemaker v. Friedberg, 1947, 80 Cal. App.2d 911, 183 P.2d 318; McKenzie v. Wm. J. Burns International Detective Agency, 1921, 149 Minn. 311, 183 N.W. 516; New York & Porto Rico S.S. Co. v. Garcia, 1 Cir. 1926, 16 F.2d 734; Hoover v. Jordan, 1915, 27 Colo.App. 515, 150 P. 333.

Allowance must be made for the exigencies of the occasion. Kroger Grocery & Baking Co. v. Yount, 8 Cir. 1933, 66 F.2d 200; Gust v. Montgomery Ward & Co., 1935, 229 Mo.App. 371, 80 S.W.2d 286.

8. Logan v. Hodges, 1907, 146 N.C. 38, 59 S.E. 349.

9. Williamson v. Freer, 1874, L.R. 9 C.P. 393, 43 L.J.C.P. 161; Monson v. Lathrop, 1897, 96 Wis. 386, 71 N.W. 596; Williams v. Equitable Credit Co., 1925, 33 Ga.App. 441, 126 S.E. 855.

10. Montgomery Ward & Co. v. Nance, 1935, 165 Va. 363, 182 S.E. 264; Perry Bros. Variety Stores v. Layton, 1930, 119 Tex. 130, 25 S.W.2d 310, conformed to, 1930, 32 S.W.2d 863; Williams v. Kroger Grocery & Baking Co., 1940, 337 Pa. 17, 10 A.2d 8; Fields v. Bynum, 1911, 156 N.C. 413, 72 S.E. 449; Kruse v. Rabe, 1911, 80 N.J.L. 378, 79 A. 316.

privileged defamation.[11] On the other hand, it may mean something less than spite, ill will, or a desire to do harm for its own sake;[12] and, while there is authority to the contrary,[13] it is the better and perhaps more generally accepted view that the mere existence of such ill will does not necessarily defeat the privilege. If the privilege is otherwise established by the occasion and a proper purpose, the addition of the fact that the defendant feels indignation and resentment toward the plaintiff and enjoys defaming him will not always forfeit it.[14] Perhaps the statement which best fits the decided cases is that the court will look to the primary motive or purpose by which the defendant apparently is inspired. Discarding "malice" as a meaningless and quite unsatisfactory term, it appears that the privilege is lost if the publication is not made primarily for the purpose of furthering the interest which is entitled to protection.[15] If the defendant acts chiefly from motives of ill will,[16] he will certainly be liable; and the vehemence of his language may be evidence against him in this respect.[17] But he will likewise be liable if he publishes his statement to accomplish a distinct objective, which may be legitimate enough in itself but is not within the privilege—as, for example, to retain a servant in his employment,[18] to obtain assistance in collecting a debt,[19] or to increase the circulation of a newspaper.[20]

Finally, since there is no social advantage in the publication of a deliberate lie, the privilege is lost if the defendant does not believe what he says.[21] Many courts have gone further, and have said that it is lost if the defamer does not have reasonable grounds, or "probable cause" to believe it to be true,[22] while others have insisted that good faith, no matter how unreasonable the basis, is all

---

11. See supra, § 113. As to the distinction, see Cherry v. Des Moines Leader, 1901, 114 Iowa 298, 86 N.W. 323; Kirkpatrick v. Eagle Lodge No. Thirty-Two, 1881, 26 Kan. 384; Gattis v. Kilgo, 1905, 140 N.C. 106, 52 S.E. 249; Iverson v. Frandsen, 10 Cir. 1956, 237 F.2d 898; Jolly v. Valley Pub. Co., 1964, 63 Wash.2d 537, 388 P.2d 139.

12. See Hooper v. Truscott, 1836, 3 Bing.N.C. 457, 132 Eng.Rep. 486; Fahr v. Hayes, 1888, 50 N.J.L. 275, 13 A. 261; Iden v. Evans Model Laundry, 1931, 121 Neb. 184, 236 N.W. 444; Stevens v. Morse, 1925, 185 Wis. 500, 201 N.W. 815; Kennedy v. Mid-Continent Telecasting Co., Inc., 1964, 193 Kan. 544, 394 P.2d 400.

13. Phillips v. Bradshaw, 1910, 167 Ala. 199, 52 So. 662; Gerlach v. Gruett, 1921, 175 Wis. 354, 185 N.W. 195; Tanner v. Stevenson, 1910, 138 Ky. 578, 128 S.W. 878; Hemmens v. Nelson, 1893, 138 N.Y. 517, 34 N.E. 342.

14. Fahr v. Hayes, 1888, 50 N.J.L. 275, 13 A. 261; Craig v. Wright, 1938, 182 Okl. 68, 76 P.2d 248; Doane v. Grew, 1915, 220 Mass. 171, 107 N.E. 620; New York & Porto Rico S. S. Co. v. Garcia, 1 Cir. 1926, 16 F.2d 734; Second Restatement of Torts, § 603. See Purrington, Malice as an Essential Element of Responsibility for Defamation Uttered on a Privileged Occasion, 1898, 57 Albany L.J. 134, 149; Evans, Legal Immunity for Defamation, 1940, 24 Minn.L.Rev. 607, 610.

15. Second Restatement of Torts, § 603.

16. Brewer v. Second Baptist Church of Los Angeles, 1948, 32 Cal.2d 791, 197 P.2d 713; Mullen v. Lewiston Evening Journal, 1952, 147 Me. 286, 86 A.2d 164; Rosenberg v. Mason, 1931, 157 Va. 215, 160 S.E. 190; Joseph v. Baars, 1910, 142 Wis. 390, 125 N.W. 913.

17. Newark Trust Co. v. Bruwer, 1958, 51 Del. (1 Storey) 188, 141 A.2d 615.

Malice may be inferred from republication after suit. O'Donnell v. Philadelphia Record Co., 1947, 356 Pa. 307, 51 A.2d 775. Or from a refusal to retract, after notice of falsity. Morgan v. Dun & Bradstreet, Inc., 5 Cir. 1970, 421 F.2d 1241.

18. Jackson v. Hopperton, 1864, 16 C.B.,N.S., 829, 143 Eng.Rep. 1352.

19. Hollenbeck v. Ristine, 1901, 114 Iowa 358, 86 N.W. 377; Over v. Schiffling, 1885, 102 Ind. 191, 26 N.E. 91. Cf. Stevens v. Sampson, 1879, 5 Ex.Div. 53, where an attorney in a case sent a report of it to newspapers, with the objective of doing harm to the opposition.

20. Cf. McNally v. Burleigh, 1897, 91 Me. 22, 39 A. 285; Maclean v. Scripps, 1883, 52 Mich. 214, 17 N.W. 815, 18 N.W. 209; Ramsey v. Cheek, 1891, 109 N.C. 270, 13 S.E. 775; Lowry v. Vedder, 1889, 40 Minn. 475, 42 N.W. 542; Doane v. Grew, 1915, 220 Mass. 171, 107 N.E. 620.

21. Russell v. Geis, 1967, 251 Cal.App.2d 560, 50 Cal.Rptr. 569; Caldwell v. Personal Finance Co. of St. Petersburg, Fla.1950, 46 So.2d 726; Froslee v. Lund's State Bank, 1915, 131 Minn. 435, 155 N.W. 619; Lawless v. Muller, 1923, 99 N.J.L. 9, 123 A. 104; Phillips v. Bradshaw, 1910, 167 Ala. 199, 52 So. 662. Cf. Vigil v. Rice, 1964, 74 N.M. 693, 397 P.2d 719 (failure to correct medical report discovered to be false).

22. Ranous v. Hughes, 1966, 30 Wis.2d 452, 141 N.W.2d 251; Altoona Clay Products, Inc. v. Dun & Bradstreet, Inc., 3 Cir. 1966, 367 F.2d 625; Stationers Corp. v. Dun & Bradstreet, Inc., 1965, 62 Cal.2d 412, 42 Cal.Rptr. 449, 398 P.2d 785; Mulderig v. Wilkes-Barre Times Co., 1906, 215 Pa. 470, 64 A. 636.

that is required.[23] Neither position seems tenable in all cases. Certainly no reasons of policy can be found for conferring immunity upon the foolish and reckless defamer who blasts an innocent reputation without making any attempt to verify his statements; but on the other hand there are occasions on which it may be entirely proper to give information of a rumor or a mere suspicion, as such, without any belief or any reason to believe that it represents the truth.[24] Probably the best statement of the rule is that the defendant is required to act as a reasonable person under the circumstances, with due regard to the strength of his belief, the grounds that he has to support it, and the importance of conveying the information.[25] However, the Second Restatement of Torts has taken the position that either dishonesty or negligence is a prerequisite to recovery for all actions of defamation. This being so, negligence is no longer regarded as sufficient to amount to an abuse of a qualified privilege.[26]

Burden of Proof—Court and Jury

The burden is upon the defendant in the first instance to establish the existence of a privileged occasion for the publication, by proof of a recognized public or private interest which would justify the utterance of the words.[27] Whether the occasion was a privileged one [28] is a question to be determined by the court as an issue of law, unless of course the facts are in dispute, in which case the jury will be instructed as to the proper rules to apply.[29] Once the existence of the privilege is established, the burden is upon the plaintiff to prove that it has been abused by excessive publication, by use of the occasion for an improper purpose, or by lack of belief or grounds for belief in the truth of what is said.[30] Unless only one conclusion can be drawn from the evidence, the determination of the question whether the privilege has been abused is for the jury.[31] Undoubtedly the very vagueness of the rules as to the public or private interest which will be protected, the "fairness" of comment or criticism, and the "malice" in cases where the privilege is abused, has been of considerable

---

23. Clark v. Molyneux, 1877, 3 Q.B.Div. 237; Joseph v. Baars, 1910, 142 Wis. 390, 125 N.W. 913; International & G. N. R. Co. v. Edmundson, Tex.Comm.App. 1920, 222 S.W. 181; H. E. Crawford Co. v. Dun & Bradstreet, 4 Cir. 1957, 241 F.2d 387; A. B. C. Needlecraft Co. v. Dun & Bradstreet, 2 Cir. 1957, 245 F.2d 775.

In several cases the influence of the Supreme Court decisions on constitutional privilege has had its effect, and it has been held that there is "malice" only if the publication is known to be false, or is in reckless disregard of the truth. Phifer v. Foe, Wyo.1968, 443 P.2d 870; Roemer v. Retail Credit Co., 1970, 3 Cal.App.3d 368, 83 Cal.Rptr. 540; Petition of Retailers Commercial Agency, Inc., 1961, 342 Mass. 515, 174 N.E.2d 376; Dun & Bradstreet, Inc. v. O'Neil, Tex.1970, 456 S.W.2d 896. Cf. Hogan v. New York Times Co., 2 Cir. 1963, 313 F.2d 354.

24. See Doane v. Grew, 1915, 220 Mass. 171, 107 N.E. 620; Pecue v. West, 1922, 233 N.Y. 316, 135 N.E. 515; British Ry. Traffic Co. v. C. R. C. Co., [1922] 2 K.B. 260; Billings v. Fairbanks, 1885, 139 Mass. 66, 29 N.E. 544.

25. See Hallen, Character of Belief Necessary for the Conditional Privilege in Defamation, 1931, 25 Ill.L. Rev. 865; Restatement of Torts, §§ 600–602.

26. Second Restatement of Torts, Sec. 600.

27. Hebditch v. MacIlwaine, [1894] 2 Q.B. 54, 63 L.J.Q.B. 587; Howland v. George F. Blake Mfg. Co., 1892, 156 Mass. 543, 31 N.E. 656; Salinger v. Cowles, 1922, 195 Iowa 873, 191 N.W. 167; Savage v. Stover, 1914, 86 N.J.L. 478, 92 A. 284; Peterson v. Rasmussen, 1920, 47 Cal.App. 694, 191 P. 30.

28. Hebditch v. MacIlwaine, [1894] 2 Q.B. 54, 63 L.J.Q.B. 587; Israel v. Portland News Pub. Co., 1936, 152 Or. 225, 53 P.2d 529; Kenney v. Gurley, 1923, 208 Ala. 623, 95 So. 34; Byam v. Collins, 1888, 111 N.Y. 143, 19 N.E. 75; Nichols v. Eaton, 1900, 110 Iowa 509, 81 N.W. 792.

29. Brinsfield v. Howeth, 1908, 107 Md. 278, 68 A. 566; Switzer v. American Ry. Exp. Co., 1922, 119 S.C. 237, 112 S.E. 110; Warner v. Press Pub. Co., 1892, 132 N.Y. 181, 30 N.E. 393; Carpenter v. Ashley, 1906, 148 Cal. 422, 83 P. 444.

30. Cook v. Pulitzer Pub. Co., 1912, 241 Mo. 326, 145 S.W. 480; Hayden v. Hasbrouck, 1912, 34 R.I. 556, 84 A. 1087; Williams Print. Co. v. Saunders, 1912, 113 Va. 156, 73 S.E. 472; Gattis v. Kilgo, 1905, 128 N.C. 402, 38 S.E. 931; Wetherby v. Retail Credit Co., 1964, 235 Md. 237, 201 A.2d 344.

31. Thomas v. Bradbury, Agnew & Co., [1906] 2 K.B. 627; Hamilton v. Eno, 1880, 81 N.Y. 116; Conrad v. Allis-Chalmers Mfg. Co., 1934, 228 Mo.App. 817, 73 S.W.2d 438; Stevenson v. Northington, 1933, 204 N.C. 690, 169 S.E. 622; Williams v. Standard-Examiner Pub. Co., 1933, 83 Utah 31, 27 P.2d 1.

aid to the courts in achieving a degree of flexibility which permits the particular issue to be determined by the court or passed over to the jury, as the particular case seems to demand.[32]

Report of Public Proceedings—A Special Type of Privilege

The common law privilege. Prior to the recognition of any constitutional privilege to defame, it was clearly recognized to be in the public interest that information be made available as to what takes place in certain kinds of judicial, legislative, and other public proceedings. Therefore, a qualified privilege of a special kind was recognized under which a newspaper or anyone else [33] might make such a report to the public.[34] The privilege rests upon the idea that any member of the public, if he were present, might see and hear for himself, so that the reporter is merely a substitute for the public eye—this, together with the obvious public interest in having public affairs made known to all. The privilege of reporting extends to all legislative proceedings,[35] including the investigations of committees [36] and the deliberations of municipal councils,[37] and to the acts of executive or administrative officials of the national, state or municipal governments, including their official reports and communications.[38]

There are cases [39] in a few jurisdictions which have extended it further, to include meetings open to the public, at which matters of public concern were discussed. It is clear, however, that there was no common law privilege to report the proceedings of any private group, such as the stockholders of a corporation,[40] unless the meeting is open to the public, and what is said there itself bears upon the public interest, as "fair comment" or otherwise.[41] There is also no privilege to report the unofficial talk of such officials as policemen,[42] as distinct from their official utterances or acts, such as an

---

32. See Green, Relational Interests, 1936, 30 Ill.L. Rev. 314, 1936, 31 Ill.L.Rev. 35.

33. First Restatement of Torts, § 686, Comment *f.* See Poulos v. Poulos, 1967, 351 Mass. 603, 222 N.E.2d 887.

34. Ratcliffe v. Walker, 1915, 117 Va. 569, 85 S.E. 575; Glass v. Bennett, 1891, 89 Tenn. 478, 14 S.W. 1085; Smith v. Smith, 1916, 192 Mich. 566, 159 N.W. 349; Baird v. Carle, 1914, 157 Wis. 565, 147 N.W. 834; Wohlfort v. Wohlfort, 1928, 125 Kan. 234, 263 P. 1062.

35. Wason v. Walter, 1868, L.R. 4 Q.B. 573; Garby v. Bennett, 1901, 166 N.Y. 392, 59 N.E. 1117. See Bryan Publication of Record Libel, 1918, 5 Va.L.Rev. 513.

36. Cresson v. Louisville Courier Journal, 6th Cir. 1924, 299 F. 487 (report of majority of Congressional committee); Terry v. Fellows, 1869, 21 La.Ann. 375. Accord, Coleman v. Newark Morning Ledger Co., 1959, 29 N.J. 357, 149 A.2d 193 (senator's press conference); Bray v. Providence Journal Co., 1966, 101 R.I. 111, 220 A.2d 531 (public meeting of school committee). See Notes, 1959, 59 Col.L.Rev. 521; 1959, 13 Rutgers L.Rev. 723.

37. Swede v. Passaic Daily News, 1959, 30 N.J. 320, 153 A.2d 36; Meteye v. Times-Democrat Publishing Co., 1895, 47 La.Ann. 824, 17 So. 314; Leininger v. New Orleans Item Publishing Co., 1924, 156 La. 1044, 101 So. 411. See Note, 1924, 23 Mich.L.Rev. 420.

38. Brandon v. Gazette Publishing Co., 1961, 234 Ark. 332, 352 S.W.2d 92 (report to governor of official investigation); Sciandra v. Lynett, 1963, 409 Pa. 595, 187 A.2d 586 (same); Painter v. E.W. Scripps Co., 1957, 104 Ohio App. 237, 148 N.E.2d 503 (order of county coroner); Begley v. Louisville Times Co., 1938, 272 Ky. 805, 115 S.W.2d 345 (adjutant general); Briarcliff Lodge Hotel v. Citizen-Sentinel Publishing Co., 1932, 260 N.Y. 106, 183 N.E. 193, reargument denied 261 N.Y. 537, 185 N.E. 728 (water board).

39. Jackson v. Record Publishing Co., 1935, 175 S.C. 211, 178 S.E. 833 (report of words of a candidate at a political rally); Phoenix Newspapers v. Choisser, 1957, 82 Ariz. 271, 312 P.2d 150 (same at Chamber of Commerce "forum"); Pulvermann v. A.S. Abell Co., 4th Cir. 1956, 228 F.2d 797 (report of speech of candidate for President); Borg v. Boas, 9th Cir. 1956, 231 F.2d 788 (report of mass meeting held to urge calling grand jury to investigate local law enforcement); see Hartzog v. United Press Associations, 4th Cir. 1953, 202 F.2d 81 (ejection of member at meeting of Republican Executive Committee); Abram v. Odham, Fla.1956, 89 So.2d 334 (speech of candidate for office).

40. Kimball v. Post Publishing Co., 1908, 199 Mass. 248, 85 N.E. 103. Cf. Lewis v. Hayes, 1913, 165 Cal. 527, 132 P. 1022 (casual conversation at social banquet).

41. Barrows v. Bell, 1856, 7 Gray, Mass. 301; cf. Lothrop v. Adams, 1882, 133 Mass. 471; Shurtleff v. Stevens, 1879, 51 Vt. 501; Rabb v. Trevelyan, 1908, 122 La. 174, 47 So. 455.

42. Kelley v. Hearst Corp., 1956, 2 App.Div.2d 480, 157 N.Y.S.2d 498, amended 1957, 3 App.Div.2d 610, 158 N.Y.S.2d 781, reargument and appeal denied 3 App. Div.2d 963, 163 N.Y.S.2d 937; Hornby v. Hunter, Tex. Civ.App.1964, 385 S.W.2d 473; Sorge v. Parade Publications, 1964, 20 App.Div.2d 338, 247 N.Y.S.2d 317.

arrest.[43] An important field for the privilege is the reporting of any judicial proceeding,[44] no matter how inferior the tribunal,[45] and regardless of its jurisdiction over the particular matter.[46] The proceeding may be an ex parte one,[47] so long as some official action is taken, even though it is only the holding of a hearing; but a mere contemplated lawsuit not yet begun is clearly not enough.[48] Because of the opportunity afforded for malicious public defamation and even extortion,[49] through suits begun and promptly discontinued, most courts are agreed that some official action is essential to the privilege. Thus it is the prevailing view, with some few courts to the contrary,[50] that a pleading [51] or a deposition [52] filed in a case but not yet acted upon may not be reported under the claim of privilege. Likewise, sealed records and documents withheld from the public eye under court order [53] may not be so reported.

It is of course essential to the privilege that it covers defamation of those who are not themselves involved in the proceeding in any way.[54] But it has always been held that the report must be a fair and accurate one, and the privilege did not cover false statements of fact as to what has occurred,[55] or mistakes in the names of parties,[56] or the interpolation of defamatory matter, or a one-

43. Francois v. Capital City Press, La.App.1964, 166 So.2d 84; Piracci v. Hearst Corp., D.Md.1966, 263 F.Supp. 511, affirmed memorandum 4th Cir. 1966, 371 F.2d 1016; cf. Lotrich v. Life Printing & Publishing Co., 1969, 117 Ill.App.2d 15, 253 N.E.2d 899.

44. Alexandria Gazette Corp. v. West, 1956, 198 Va. 154, 93 S.E.2d 274 (proceeding to disqualify judge); Rhodes v. Star Herald Printing Co., 1962, 173 Neb. 496, 113 N.W.2d 658 (posting bonds); Greenfield v. Courier Journal & Louisville Times Co., Ky.1955, 283 S.W.2d 839 (grand jury report); Grossman v. Globe-Democrat Publishing Co., 1941, 347 Mo. 869, 149 S.W.2d 362; Irwin v. Ashurst, 1938, 158 Or. 61, 74 P.2d 1127.

45. Hahn v. Holum, 1917, 165 Wis. 425, 162 N.W. 432 (justice court); McBee v. Fulton, 1878, 47 Md. 403 (same); Flues v. New Nonpareil Co., 1912, 155 Iowa 290, 135 N.W. 1083 (police court); Parsons v. Age-Herald Co., 1913, 181 Ala. 439, 61 So. 345 (grand jury); Williams v. Journal Co., 1933, 211 Wis. 362, 247 N.W. 435 (same).

46. Lee v. Brooklyn Union Publishing Co., 1913, 209 N.Y. 245, 103 N.E. 155; Hahn v. Holum, 1917, 165 Wis. 425, 162 N.W. 432; Usill v. Hales, 1878, 3 C.P.D. 319. But cf. Trebby v. Transcript Publishing Co., 1898, 74 Minn. 84, 76 N.W. 961 (city council exceeding its powers).

47. Fitch v. Daily News Publishing Co., 1928, 116 Neb. 474, 217 N.W. 947; American Publishing Co. v. Gamble, 1906, 115 Tenn. 663, 90 S.W. 1005; Beiser v. Scripps-McRae Publishing Co., 1902, 113 Ky. 383, 68 S.W. 457; Metcalf v. Times Publishing Co., 1898, 20 R.I. 674, 40 A. 864.

48. Gariepy v. Pearson, 1953, 92 U.S.App.D.C. 337, 207 F.2d 15, certiorari denied 346 U.S. 909, 74 S.Ct. 241, 98 L.Ed. 407.

49. See Nadelmann, The Newspaper Privilege and Extortion by Abuse of Legal Process, 1954, 54 Col.L. Rev. 359.

Cf. Williams v. Williams, 1969, 23 N.Y.2d 592, 298 N.Y.S.2d 473, 246 N.E.2d 333, where defendant filed a pleading and then circulated it himself.

50. Langford v. Vanderbilt University, 1956, 199 Tenn. 389, 287 S.W.2d 32; Campbell v. New York Evening Post, 1927, 245 N.Y. 320, 157 N.E. 153; Lybrand v. State Co., 1936, 179 S.C. 208, 184 S.E. 580; Johnson v. Johnson Publishing Co., D.C.App.1970, 271 A.2d 696; American District Telegraph Co. v. Brink's Inc., 7th Cir. 1967, 380 F.2d 131.

51. Sanford v. Boston Herald-Traveler Corp., 1945, 318 Mass. 156, 61 N.E.2d 5; Byers v. Meridian Printing Co., 1911, 84 Ohio St. 408, 95 N.E. 917; Nixon v. Dispatch Printing Co., 1907, 101 Minn. 309, 112 N.W. 258; Meeker v. Post Printing & Publishing Co., 1913, 55 Colo. 355, 135 P. 457; Park v. Detroit Free Press Co., 1888, 72 Mich. 560, 40 N.W. 731. See Note, 1946, 44 Mich.L.Rev. 675.

As to the privilege of legal commentators, see Note, 1933, 31 Mich.L.Rev. 255.

52. Mannix v. Portland Telegram, 1933, 144 Or. 172, 23 P.2d 138.

53. Danziger v. Hearst Corp., 1952, 304 N.Y. 244, 107 N.E.2d 62, modifying 1951, 279 App.Div. 560, 107 N.Y.S.2d 423, appeal granted 1951, 279 App.Div. 644, 107 N.Y.S.2d 1007. Cf. McCurdy v. Hughes, 1933, 63 N.D. 435, 248 N.W. 512 (preliminary inquiry into disbarment).

54. Sherwood v. Evening News Association, 1931, 256 Mich. 318, 239 N.W. 305; Lehner v. Berlin Publishing Co., 1932, 209 Wis. 536, 245 N.W. 685; Mortensen v. Los Angeles Examiner, 1931, 112 Cal.App. 194, 296 P. 297; Schaffran v. Press Publishing Co., 1932, 258 N.Y. 207, 179 N.E. 387.

55. Brush-Moore Newspapers v. Pollitt, 1959, 220 Md. 132, 151 A.2d 530; Carey v. Hearst Publications, 1943, 19 Wn.2d 655, 143 P.2d 857; Bowerman v. Detroit Free Press, 1939, 287 Mich. 443, 283 N.W. 642; Hartzog v. United Press Association, 4th Cir. 1953, 202 F.2d 81; Atlanta Journal Co. v. Doyal, 1950, 82 Ga. App 321, 60 S.E.2d 802.

56. Whitcomb v. Hearst Corp., 1952, 329 Mass. 193, 107 N.E.2d 295; Switzer v. Anthony, 1922, 71 Colo. 291, 206 P. 391. But an immaterial mistake, such as an

sided account.[57] Neither did it include garbled[58] or partial[59] reports, although it was obviously not essential that the proceedings be set forth verbatim, and a summary of substantial accuracy was enough.[60]

As stated, the common law privilege was to report fairly and accurately. The publisher did so at his peril in the sense that he was subject to strict liability for any inaccuracies as to what was said or what transpired during the proceeding reported about. Moreover, it was generally assumed that the publisher could be liable if he published solely for an improper purpose or motive.[61] But as a practical matter, if the publisher was accurate and fair in reporting about what was said and done, he had in effect an immunity to report, even though he may not have believed the truth of a defamatory statement made in the proceeding and included in the report. In the *Second Restatement of Torts*, the position has been taken that malice in the sense of an improper motive or purpose in publishing a fair and accurate report of public proceedings containing a defamatory statement about the plaintiff will not constitute an abuse of the privilege or constitute the kind of fault that will justify the imposition of liability on the defendant, even when the publisher believed the defamatory statement made about the plaintiff to be false.[62] But there is substantial judicial authority to the contrary, and the result does not appear to be constitutionally mandated.

The Constitutional Privilege

In Time, Inc. v. Firestone, the defendant urged upon the court the position that in publishing inaccurately about the basis upon which a divorce was granted to the plaintiff's husband, it was making a report of a judicial proceeding, and, therefore, the subject matter deserved the protection of the dishonesty standard even if the report was inaccurate. But the court held that as to inaccurate reports "we think *Gertz* provides an adequate safeguard for the constitutionally protected interests of the press and affords it a tolerable margin for error by requiring some kind of fault." [63] While the issue addressed here is much broader than the narrow one in that case, which involved the misconstruction of a divorce decree, it would seem that the mass media and those who report publicly about what transpires in public proceedings—and perhaps those who publish privately—have a constitutional privilege to make a mistake in reporting about many kinds of public proceedings. This does not mean that anything more than negligence would be required. So if the defendant was found to have been negligent in the making of an inaccurate report, *he would not gain the benefit of any additional protection* by virtue of the fact that he was attempting to republish accurately what someone else said or did in a public proceed-

---

error in stating the age of a victim of forcible rape, does not make the defendant liable. Torski v. Mansfield Journal Co., 1956, 100 Ohio App. 538, 137 N.E.2d 679.

57. Robinson v. Johnson, 8th Cir. 1917, 239 F. 671. Cf. Brown v. Providence Telegram Publishing Co., 1903, 25 R.I. 117, 54 A. 1061; Jones v. Pulitzer Publishing Co., 1912, 240 Mo. 200, 144 S.W. 441; Atlanta News Publishing Co. v. Medlock, 1905, 123 Ga. 714, 51 S.E. 756. Cf. Purcell v. Westinghouse Broadcasting Co., 1963, 411 Pa. 167, 191 A.2d 662 (embellishment of account of judicial proceeding with extra-judicial "investigation").

58. Arnold v. Sayings Co., 1898, 76 Mo.App. 159; Thomas v. Croswell, 1810, 7 Johns., N.Y., 264. Cf. Pape v. Time, Inc., 7th Cir. 1963, 318 F.2d 652 (what official document merely stated to be "alleged," newspaper stated as fact); Hogan v. New York Times Co., 2d Cir. 1963, 313 F.2d 354 ("reckless disregard of the truth.")

59. Metcalf v. Times Publishing Co., 1898, 20 R.I. 674, 40 A. 864; Saunders v. Mills, 1829, 6 Bing. 213, 130 Eng.Rep. 1262; Brown v. Publishers: George Knapp & Co., 1908, 213 Mo. 655, 112 S.W. 474.

60. Milissich v. Lloyd's, 1877, 13 Cox C.C. 575, 46 L.J.C.P. 404; Salisbury v. Union & Advertiser Co., 1887, 45 Hun, N.Y. 120, 9 N.Y.St.Rep. 465; Boogher v. Knapp, 1889, 97 Mo. 122, 11 S.W. 45; Lehner v. Berlin Publishing Co., 1932, 209 Wis. 536, 245 N.W. 685.

61. See Second Restatement of Torts, § 611. Eldredge, Law of Defamation, 1978, Sec. 79, p. 421.

62. Section 611.

63. 1976, 424 U.S. 448, 458, 96 S.Ct. 958, 967, 47 L.Ed.2d 154, 165, on remand, Fla., 332 So.2d 68.

ing. The mere fact that the publication was not privileged because it was inaccurately and negligently made does not mean of course that under present law the plaintiff would recover. The plaintiff, as a public official, or public figure, or private person, would have to establish the kind of fault on the part of the defendant with respect to the truth or falsity of the alleged defamatory imputation made about the plaintiff in the proceeding as is constitutionally required.

 WESTLAW REFERENCES

digest(qualified /5 privilege* immunity /s defam! slander! libel!)

qualified /5 privilege* immunity /p defam! slander! libel! /p constitution! unconstitution!

Interest of Publisher

topic(237) /p selfdefense selfprotection
237k46

Interest of Others

restatement /s torts +5 603

libel! slander! defam! /p limited qualified /5 privilege /s profession**

restatement /s torts /5 595 596

Common Interest

digest(defam! libel! slander! /p "common interest*")
237k51(4)

Communications of One Who May Act in the Public Interest

libel! slander! defam! /p "public interest" /s qualified /s immunity privilege

237k51(5)

digest(libel! slander! defam! /p public /p "fair comment")

Abuse of Qualified Privilege Regarding Private Publication of Private Matters

opinion(abus! misus! /s qualified conditional /s privilege immunity)

"private defamation"

Burden of Proof—Court and Jury

digest(defam! slander! libel! /p "burden of proof")

defam! slander! libel! /p burden /4 proof proving /s defense privilege* immunity

Report of Public Proceedings—A Special Type of Privilege

defam! slander! libel! /p public legislative executive council committee /7 proceeding* meeting* /s report!

fair** accurate** correct** /s report! /s public legislative executive council committee /s proceeding* meeting* /p libel! slander! defam!

The Constitution Privilege

negligen! /s publish! publication! /p defam! libel! slander! /p constitution! unconstitution!

§ 116. Truth and Other Defenses

Truth or Justification

To create liability for defamation, there must be publication of matter that is both defamatory and false.[1] The well-settled common law rule prior to decisions by the United States Supreme Court related to the constitutional privilege to defame was that truth is an affirmative defense which the defendant must plead and prove. Thus, under the common law rule, the defamatory statement is regarded as false unless the defendant proves truth. It has been said that meeting the constitutional requirements regarding the necessity for proof of at least negligence with respect to the truth or falsity of a defamatory statement makes it necessary for the plaintiff to allege and prove the falsity of the communication.[2] The basis for this position is that the Supreme Court of the United States, in holding that the plaintiff must establish some kind of fault with respect to the issue of truth or falsity, has by implication allocated the issue of falsity to the plaintiff. But there can be two answers to this. In the first place, the constitutional privilege to defame may not extend to defamatory utterances privately made about private persons.[3] In the second place, there is no inconsistency in assuming falsity until defendant publisher proves otherwise and requiring the plaintiff to prove negligence or recklessness with respect to the truth or falsity of the imputation. There is, in other words, nothing inconsistent about requiring the defendant to prove truth if absolute protection is to be provided for a

§ 116

1. Second Restatement of Torts, § 581A, Comment a.

2. See, Second Restatement of Torts, § 613, Comment j; Eldredge, The Law of Defamation, 1978, Sec. 63; Morris on Torts, Second edition, 1980, p. 350.

3. See § 113.

defamatory imputation while at the same time requiring the plaintiff to prove that the defendant acted negligently or recklessly in publishing the statement on the basis of the information that was available to him. The situation is very much the same as that which has existed historically under the common law when the defendant publishes a defamatory statement about the plaintiff on a privileged occasion. If he wished to escape altogether, he could prove truth. He could also plead a privilege, and if he established circumstances giving rise to a privilege, then the plaintiff would find it necessary to show some kind of fault as a prerequisite to recovery. So, if the defendant publishes a defamatory statement on a constitutionally privileged occasion, he can either prove truth or require the plaintiff to prove fault. The mere fact that it may be difficult to establish recklessness or negligence without some evidence of falsity does not mean that fault in reporting something to be true cannot be found in the absence of an affirmative finding that the statement was true.

Truth

The defense that the defamatory statement is true has been given the technical name of justification. Under the common law, justification was not a recognized defense in prosecutions for criminal libel. That crime, which was originated to suppress sedition, and later extended to prevent breaches of the peace, took no account of any freedom to publish the truth with immunity,[4] since neither sedition nor the provocation to a duel was at all lessened because the defamation was true.[5] Hence the criminal courts declared that "the greater the truth the greater the libel."[6] This rule, which later was changed by statute in England,[7] was taken over by the early American decisions[8] along with the rest of the common law of defamation; but it was so obviously incompatible with all public policy in favor of free dissemination of the truth that it has been altered by statute in nearly every state,[9] usually to make truth a complete defense, provided that it is published with good motives and for justifiable ends.

The criminal law rule seems never to have been applied in civil actions.[10] Whether the reason was that the delinquent plaintiff was precluded from any standing in court by reason of his own bad character,[11] or that the defendant was considered to have rendered a public service in exposing him,[12] or merely that public policy demands that the truth shall not be fettered by fear of damage suits,[13] truth was a defense to any civil action for either libel or slander, and it remains so in the great majority of jurisdictions. It is immaterial that the defendant published the facts for no good reason or for the worst possible motives,[14] or even that he did not believe at the time that they were

---

4. De Libellis Famosis, 1605, 5 Co.Rep. 125, 77 Eng. Rep. 250; Franklin's Case, 1731, 9 Hargrave St. Trials 255, 269. See Ray, Truth: A Defense to Libel, 1931, 16 Minn.L.Rev. 43; Harnett and Thornton, The Truth Hurts: A Critique of a Defense to Defamation, 1949, 35 Va.L.Rev. 425.

5. Bl.Com. 151; Trial of Jutchin, 1704, 5 Hargrave St. Trials 527, 532.

6. This maxim usually is attributed to Lord Mansfield. Thus:

"Dost know that old Mansfield
Who writes like the Bible,
Says the more 'tis a truth, sir,
The more 'tis a libel?"

—Burns, "The Reproof."

7. By Lord Campbell's Act, 1843, 6 & 7 Vict., ch. 96, § 6.

8. People v. Croswell, N.Y.1804, 3 Johns. 337; Commonwealth v. Morris, 1811, 1 Va.Cas. 176; see Commonwealth v. Snelling, 1834, 32 Mass. (15 Pick.) 337; State v. Lehre, S.C.1811, 2 Brev. 446.

9. The statutes are collected in Angoff, Handbook of Libel, 1946, passim.

10. Johns v. Gittings, 1590, Cro.Eliz. 230, 78 Eng. Rep. 495; Hilsdon v. Saunders, 1624, Cro.Jac. 677, 79 Eng.Rep. 586; Holdsworth, Defamation in the Sixteenth and Seventeenth Centuries, 1925, 41 L.Q.Rev. 13, 28.

11. Starkie, Slander and Libel, Folkard's Am. ed. 1858, 692.

12. 3 Bl.Com. 125.

13. See Ray, Truth: A Defense to Libel, 1931, 16 Minn.L.Rev. 43, 56–58; Harnett and Thornton, The

14. See note 14 on page 841.

true.[15] The rule has been attacked [16] on the ground that it affords immunity for morally indefensible malevolence and needlessly kicking a man when he is down. There is some indication of a tendency to depart from it. Some ten states have statutory provisions,[17] requiring that the publication must have been made for good motives or for justifiable ends, and New Hampshire [18] has reached the same conclusion without a statute. In 1969, an Illinois decision [19] held that a statute of this type was unconstitutional as a violation of the freedom of the press provision of the First Amendment. The recognition by nearly all courts of the right of privacy [20] has afforded a remedy in many cases apart from that of defamation, and may perhaps explain failure to modify the rule.

Out of a tender regard for reputations, the law presumes in the first instance that all defamation is false, and the defendant has the burden of pleading and proving its truth.[21] His justification must be as broad, and as narrow, as the defamatory imputation itself. He may not avoid liability by proving that the imputation was true in part,[22] or, if the charge is one of persistent misconduct, by showing that it was true in a single instance.[23] If the defendant repeats the defamation as reported by another, it will not be enough to prove the fact of the report, without proving the truth of the imputation reported.[24] Specific charges cannot be justified by showing the plaintiff's general bad character;[25] and if the accusation is one of particular misconduct, such as stealing a watch from A, it is not enough to show a different offense, even though it be a more serious one, such as stealing a clock from A,[26] or six watches from B.[27] The courts never have looked with any great favor upon

---

Truth Hurts: A Critique of a Defense to Defamation, 1949, 35 Va.L.Rev. 425, 434–437.

14. Cochrane v. Wittbold, 1960, 359 Mich. 402, 102 N.W.2d 459; McCuddin v. Dickinson, 1941, 230 Iowa 1141, 300 N.W. 308; Herald Publishing Co. v. Feltner, 1914, 158 Ky. 35, 164 S.W. 370; Craig v. Wright, 1938, 182 Okl. 68, 76 P.2d 248; Lancaster v. Hamburger, 1904, 70 Ohio St. 156, 71 N.E. 289; Restatement of Torts, § 582, Comment a.

15. Foss v. Hildreth, 1865, 92 Mass. (10 Allen) 76; First Restatement of Torts, § 582, Comment g.

16. Ray, Truth: A Defense to Libel, 1931, 16 Minn. L.Rev. 43; Harnett and Thornton, The Truth Hurts: A Critique of a Defense to Defamation, 1949, 35 Va.L. Rev. 425.

17. See, for example, Perry v. Hearst Corp., 1st Cir. 1964, 334 F.2d 800 (freedom from actual malice); Stanley v. Prince, 1919, 118 Me. 360, 108 A. 328 (good motive); Briggs v. Brown, 1908, 55 Fla. 417, 46 So. 325 (same); Ogren v. Rockford Star Printing Co., 1919, 288 Ill. 405, 123 N.E. 587 (good motive and justifiable ends); Burkhart v. North American Co., 1906, 214 Pa. 39, 63 A. 410 (freedom from malice or negligence, and a proper purpose). See Angoff, Handbook of Libel, 1946, Passim; Note, 1961, 56 Northwestern U.L.Rev. 547.

18. Hutchins v. Page, 1909, 75 N.H. 215, 72 A. 689 (good faith, proper occasion, and justifiable purpose).

19. Farnsworth v. Tribune Co., 1969, 43 Ill.2d 286, 253 N.E.2d 408. See Franklin, The Origins and Constitutionality of Limitations on Truth as a Defense in Tort Law, 1964, 16 Stan.L.Rev. 789.

20. See infra, § 117.

21. Atwater v. Morning News Co., 1896, 67 Conn. 504, 34 A. 865; Langton v. Hagerty, 1874, 35 Wis. 150; Bingham v. Gaynor, 1911, 203 N.Y. 27, 96 N.E. 84.

22. Weaver v. Lloyd, 1824, 2 B. & C. 678, 107 Eng. Rep. 535; Shepard v. Merrill, N.Y.1816, 13 Johns. 475; Register Newspaper Co. v. Stone, 1907, 31 Ky.L.Rep. 458, 102 S.W. 800; White v. White, 1921, 129 Va. 621, 106 S.E. 350. Cf. Stewart v. Enterprise Co., Tex.Civ. App.1965, 393 S.W.2d 372, refused n.r.e., appeal after remand 439 S.W.2d 674, refused n.r.e.

If the publication imputes to the plaintiff willingness to publish the defamatory truth, the proof must extend to that. Karjavainean v. MacFadden Publications, 1940, 305 Mass. 573, 26 N.E.2d 538. An assertion of personal observation is not supported by proof that others saw it. Kilian v. Doubleday & Co., 1951, 367 Pa. 117, 79 A.2d 657.

23. Rutherford v. Paddock, 1902, 180 Mass. 289, 62 N.E. 381 ("dirty old whore" not supported by proof of adultery); Crellin v. Thomas, 1952, 122 Utah 122, 247 P.2d 264 ("whore" not supported by career as dance hall girl); Wakley v. Cooke, 1849, 4 Exch. 511, 154 Eng.Rep. 1316.

24. Watkin v. Hall, 1868, L.R. 3 Q.B. 396, 37 L.J. Q.B. 125; Fountain v. West, 1867, 23 Iowa 9; Dement v. Houston Printing Co., 1896, 14 Tex.Civ.App. 391, 37 S.W. 985.

25. Dowie v. Priddle, 1905, 216 Ill. 553, 75 N.E. 243. Cf. Crane v. New York World Telegram Corp., 1955, 308 N.Y. 470, 126 N.E.2d 753 ("under indictment" not justified by "indictment" in a moral sense because plaintiff accused of crime by various people).

26. Hilsden v. Mercer, 1624, Cro.Jac. 677, 79 Eng. Rep. 586; Eastland v. Caldwell, 1810, 5 Ky. (2 Bibb) 21;

27. See note 27 on page 842.

the defense of truth, and formerly these rules were carried to ridiculous extremes,[28] but it is now generally agreed that it is not necessary to prove the literal truth of the accusation in every detail, and that it is sufficient to show that the imputation is substantially true,[29] or, as it is often put, to justify the "gist," the "sting," or the "substantial truth" of the defamation.[30] Thus an accusation that the mayor of a town has wasted $80,000 of the taxpayers' money has been held to be justified by proof that he wasted $17,500, since there is no more opprobrium attached to the greater amount.[31] If, however, the defendant adds to the facts stated an opinion or comment of his own, the comment must be justified as a proper one in the light of the facts proved.[32]

The defense of truth frequently is a hazardous venture for the defendant, since if he fails to sustain it the jury may be permitted to find that he has reiterated the defamation, and to consider the fact in aggravation of the damages.[33] The modern cases, however, have tended quite properly to recognize that the defendant is entitled to present an honest defense without being penalized, and have limited such aggravation to cases where it appears that the defense was entered in bad faith, without evidence to support it.[34]

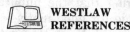

WESTLAW REFERENCES

Truth or Justification
digest(defam! libel! slander! /s truth /s defense)
defam! libel! slander! /p commonlaw /p burden /5 proof proving

Truth
justification /s libel! slander! defam!
truth /s justification /s libel! slander! defam!

§ 116A. Damages and Matters in Mitigation

Damages which may be recovered in an action for defamation are: (1) compensatory or actual, which may be either (a) general or (b) special; (2) punitive or exemplary; and (3) nominal.[1]

Downs v. Hawley, 1873, 112 Mass. 237; Sun Printing & Publishing Association v. Schenck, 2d Cir. 1900, 98 F. 925; Kilian v. Doubleday & Co., 1951, 367 Pa. 117, 79 A.2d 657.

27. Gardner v. Self, 1852, 15 Mo. 480; Buckner v. Spaulding, 1891, 127 Ind. 229, 26 N.E. 792; Pallet v. Sargent, 1858, 36 N.H. 496; Haddock v. Naughton, 1893, 74 Hun 390, 26 N.Y.S. 455. Cf. Stewart v. Enterprise Co., Tex.Civ.App.1965, 393 S.W.2d 372, refused n.r.e., appeal after remand 439 S.W.2d 674, refused n.r.e. (two accusations, truth of only one proved).

28. See for example Swann v. Rary, Ind.1833, 3 Blackf. 298 (two hogs and one); Sharpe v. Stephenson, 1851, 34 N.C. (12 Ired.) 348 (time and place); cf. Coffin v. Brown, 1901, 94 Md. 190, 50 A. 567 (time and place). See Courtney, Absurdities of the Law of Slander and Libel, 1902, 36 Am.L.Rev. 552, 561–564.

29. Alexander v. North Eastern R. Co., 1865, 6 B. & S. 340, 122 Eng.Rep. 1221; Zoll v. Allen, S.D.N.Y.1950, 93 F.Supp. 95; Florida Publishing Co. v. Lee, 1918, 76 Fla. 405, 80 So. 245; McGuire v. Vaughan, 1896, 106 Mich. 280, 64 N.W. 44; Skrocki v. Stahl, 1910, 14 Cal. App. 1, 110 P. 957.

30. Edwards v. Bell, 1824, 1 Bing. 403, 130 Eng. Rep. 162; Bell Publishing Co. v. Garrett Engineering Co., Tex.Civ.App.1941, 154 S.W.2d 885, affirmed 141 Tex. 51, 170 S.W.2d 197.

31. Fort Worth Press Co. v. Davis, Tex.Civ.App. 1936, 96 S.W.2d 416. Cf. Smith v. Byrd, 1955, 225 Miss. 331, 83 So.2d 172 (statement that sheriff shot a man justified by proof that sheriff was acting in concert with deputy who shot him).

32. Cooper v. Lawson, 1838, 8 Ad. & El. 746, 112 Eng.Rep. 1020; Commercial Publishing Co. v. Smith, 6th Cir. 1907, 149 F. 704; cf. Morrison v. Harmer, 1837, 3 Bing.N.C. 759, 132 Eng.Rep. 603.

33. Will v. Press Publishing Co., 1932, 309 Pa. 539, 164 A. 621; Coffin v. Brown, 1901, 94 Md. 190, 50 A. 567; Krulic v. Petcoff, 1913, 122 Minn. 517, 142 N.W. 897; Hall v. Edwards, 1942, 138 Me. 231, 23 A.2d 889 (with other evidence of malice). See Note, 1958, 56 Mich.L.Rev. 659.

In Domchick v. Greenbelt Consumer Services, 1952, 200 Md. 36, 87 A.2d 831, it was held that pleading truth makes a prima facie case as to malice. In Shumate v. Johnson Publishing Co., 1956, 139 Cal.App.2d 121, 293 P.2d 531, a publisher who verified a pleading of truth was held subject to punitive damages, although he was out of the state and took no other part.

34. Webb v. Gray, 1913, 181 Ala. 408, 62 So. 194; Fodor v. Fuchs, 1910, 79 N.J.L. 529, 76 A. 1081; Willard v. Press Publishing Co., 1900, 52 App.Div. 448, 65 N.Y.S. 73; Las Vegas Sun, Inc. v. Franklin, 1958, 74 Nev. 282, 329 P.2d 867; Snyder v. Fatherly, 1930, 153 Va. 762, 151 S.E. 149.

§ 116A

1. See, Stidham v. Wachtel, Del.1941, 2 Terry 327, 21 A.2d 282; Dobbs, Remedies, 1973, Sec. 7.2, pp. 513–523.

General Damages—Impairment of Reputation

General damages, as that term is used in defamation actions, refer to losses sustained which are normal and usual and are to be anticipated when a person's reputation is impaired.[2] When one's reputation is impaired, this affects one's relations with others, including business, social, religious, and family. The impairment of one's relations does interfere in a variety of unpredictable and unknowable ways with the enjoyment of life. Under the English and American common law, as heretofore explained,[3] harm to reputation was presumed from the publication of a libel or slander per se. Therefore, actual damages were normally assessable by the jury without proof by the plaintiff that there had been any impairment of reputation. Thus, general damages at common law were an estimate, however rough, of the probable extent of actual loss a person had suffered and would suffer in the future, even though the loss could not be identified in terms of advantageous relationships lost, either from a monetary or enjoyment-of-life standpoint.[4] Since some of the interests served by way of protecting a good reputation are of a peace-of-mind and dignitary nature rather than economic in character, such losses are not readily measurable in monetary terms. However, it is often not necessary for the jury to believe that the plaintiff has suffered or will suffer pecuniary or economic loss,[5] even though some types of defamatory imputations are by their very nature calculated to result in economic loss, and can be presumed to have caused such.[6]

In Gertz v. Robert Welch, Inc.,[7] the Supreme Court held the common law rule that harm to reputation from the publication of a libel was presumed to be incompatible with the First Amendment—at least in suits against the mass media and those who used the media—unless the plaintiff proves that the defamatory publication was made with knowledge of its falsity, or recklessly with regard to the truth or falsity of the statement. The purpose of this limitation was to prevent the giving of awards by the jury greatly in excess of what would be reasonable. So it would appear that there is now a constitutional limitation to the common law rule that harm to reputation can be presumed from the publication of a libel or slander per se. This does not mean that items of losses must be established with specificity. But it may be necessary for the plaintiff to introduce evidence to show that the defamatory publication did have the effect of impairing the plaintiff's reputation if damages for impairment of reputation are to be obtainable in actions to which the constitutional privilege applies. The position has been taken in the Second Restatement of Torts that even if the constitutional privilege does not extend to defamation made privately about private matters, the common law rule as to presumed damage by way of a presumption of impairment of reputation should be abrogated, except when there has been proof that the publication of the defamatory matter was made with knowledge of its falsity, or recklessly.[8] It would seem, however, that in the absence of rebuttal testimony to show that the only recipients to whom the defamatory matter was published did not believe it, the presumption should continue to be applied, at least to libel which is published publicly. Normally, the publication of false and defamatory matter about the plaintiff is circumstantial evidence in and of itself that there was some impairment to reputation.

---

2. Second Restatement of Torts, § 904.

3. Supra, § 112.

4. Dalton v. Meister, 1971, 52 Wis.2d 173, 188 N.W.2d 494, certiorari denied 405 U.S. 934, 92 S.Ct. 947, 30 L.Ed.2d 810.

5. Supra, § 112.

6. Supra, § 112.

7. 1974, 418 U.S. 323, 349–50, 94 S.Ct. 2997, 3011–12, 41 L.Ed.2d 789.

8. Second Restatement of Torts, § 621.

Special Damages

Special damages may be proven to enhance general damages.[9] Special damages are damages that do not so frequently result from the publication as to be recoverable as general damages; moreover, if the defamation is not the kind that is actionable per se—i.e., libel or slander per se—then special damage means also pecuniary or material loss.[10] The defamatory publication by the defendant must have been a proximate cause of the special damage for the special damage to be recoverable.[11]

So far as "proximate cause" is concerned, recovery has been limited very definitely to those damages which are regarded as reasonably foreseeable or normal consequences of the defamation.[12] Formerly, it was held that the original defamer was liable only for the damages caused by his own publication, and was not responsible for repetition by others, on the theory that the "last human wrongdoer" must be responsible, and there is still some authority to this effect;[13] but there has been the same broadening of "proximate cause" as in other fields of liability, and the prevailing view now appears to be that there is liability for damages due to such a repetition when it was authorized or intended, or when the circumstances were such that it might reasonably have been anticipated.[14]

Mental Anguish

The law of defamation has been developed primarily for the protection of the reputational interest. This being so, it would appear to be somewhat anomalous to permit a plaintiff to recover actual damages without a filing of actual harm to his reputation, based either on a presumption or proof of such harm. Yet, this very result was countenanced by the Supreme Court in Time, Inc. v. Firestone.[15] In this case, the plaintiff withdrew any claim for damages to reputation on the eve of trial, and sought to recover mental anguish damages based on the false report that her husband's divorce was granted on the ground of adultery. The jury decided that mental "injuries" should be compensated, and an award of $100,000 was upheld. This holding seems to emasculate—by and large—the holding in *Gertz* that harm to reputation should not be presumed as a technique to avoid excessive awards.[16] Unless the plaintiff's reputation can be regarded realistically as having been impaired, there would seem to be little, if any, justification for a recovery of actual damages. Any recovery of damages for mental anxiety should be for anxiety which comes about as a consequence of impairment or probable impairment of reputation. Unless the defamation was published under circumstances and in a way likely to impair reputation, a recovery is difficult to justify, unless at least the publication of the defamatory matter was

---

9. Snowden v. Pearl River Broadcasting Corp., La. App.1971, 251 So.2d 405, application denied 259 La. 887, 253 So.2d 217; Dobbs, Remedies, 1973, Sec. 7.2, p. 520.

10. See, supra, § 112.

11. Second Restatement of Torts, § 622.

12. Lynch v. Knight, 1861, 9 H.L.C. 577, 11 Eng. Rep. 854; Anonymous, 1875, 60 N.Y. 262; Georgia v. Kepford, 1876, 45 Iowa 48; Field v. Colson, 1892, 93 Ky. 347, 20 S.W. 264.

13. Vicars v. Wilcocks, 1806, 8 East 1, 103 Eng.Rep. 244; Lehner v. Kelley, 1934, 215 Wis. 265, 254 N.W. 634; Hastings v. Stetson, 1879, 126 Mass. 329; Maytag v. Cummins, 8th Cir. 1919, 260 F. 74; Age-Herald Publishing Co. v. Waterman, 1914, 188 Ala. 272, 66 So. 16.

14. Zier v. Hoflin, 1885, 33 Minn. 66, 21 N.W. 862; Sawyer v. Gilmers, Inc., 1925, 189 N.C. 7, 126 S.E. 183;

Southwestern Telephone & Telegraph Co. v. Long, Tex. Civ.App.1915, 183 S.W. 421; Elms v. Crane, 1919, 118 Me. 261, 107 A. 852; Fitzgerald v. Young, 1911, 89 Neb. 693, 132 N.W. 127. See Restatement of Torts, § 576. Apparently damage due to repetition alone is sufficient to make slander actionable. Cf. Gillett v. Bullivant, 1846, 7 L.T.,O.S., 490; Derry v. Handley, 1867, 16 L.T.,N.S., 263; cf. Weaver v. Beneficial Finance Co., 1957, 199 Va. 196, 98 S.E.2d 687.

There is, however, still no liability for a republication which could not reasonably have been anticipated. Waite v. Stockgrowers' Credit Corp., 1933, 63 N.D. 763, 249 N.W. 910.

15. 1976, 424 U.S. 448, 96 S.Ct. 958, 47 L.Ed.2d 154, on remand Fla., 332 So.2d 68.

16. Supra, this section on General Damages.

made with knowledge of the falsity, or recklessly. In that case, a better basis for recovery would seem to be a claim based on the tort of intentional interference with peace of mind, rather than on defamation.[17]

Punitive Damages

Punitive damages have been awarded in actions for defamation when the defendant publishes maliciously, either in the sense of with (a) an improper motive, or (b) knowledge of the falsity of the statement, or recklessly with respect to truth or falsity.[18] But it is quite clear that the constitutional privilege as set forth by the Supreme Court of the United States has abrogated any right to the recovery of punitive damages against the press or broadcasting media on the basis simply of an improper motive.[19] Moreover, there is considerable doubt about whether or not an improper motive will be constitutionally permitted as a basis for the recovery of punitive damages against one who publishes privately.[20]

Nominal Damages

A nominal damage award can be justified in a tort action only if there is some reason for awarding a judgment in favor of a claimant who has not proved or does not claim a compensable loss with sufficient certainty to justify a recovery of compensatory or actual damages. There may be such a reason in an action for defamation, since a nominal damage award serves the purpose of vindicating the plaintiff's character by a verdict of the jury that establishes the falsity of the defamatory matter. It has generally been held that when the plaintiff proves the publication of matter which is actionable per se—libel or slander per se—an award of nominal damages should be made.[21] But if the jury believes that no substantial harm has been done to reputation, perhaps the action should be regarded as trivial in nature, and, therefore, the plaintiff should not be rewarded with a judgment and costs of court assessed against the defendant, especially if the defendant published in good faith. It is possible that the constitutional privilege will be regarded as requiring proof of actual harm to reputation, or at least actual harm of some nature justifying a recovery of actual damages, as a prerequisite to a judgment in favor of the plaintiff in those cases to which the constitutional privilege is applicable.

Mitigation of Damages and Retraction

In addition to the complete defenses of privilege and truth already considered, there are partial defenses open to the defendant, which will not avoid his liability, but will go to reduce the damages recovered by the plaintiff. Perhaps the most important of these is a retraction of the defamatory statement. At common law a retraction does not exonerate the defamer, unless it is made immediately after the defamation, and is so clearly connected with it that in effect it negatives the utterance itself.[22] If it follows so far behind that the words have had time to make an impression and be spread further, the courts refuse to hold that it has en-

---

17. Supra, § 12.

18. Conard v. Dillingham, 1922, 23 Ariz. 596, 206 P. 166; Fields v. Bynum, 1911, 156 N.C. 413, 72 S.E. 449; Childers v. San Jose Mercury Printing & Publishing Co., 1894, 105 Cal. 284, 38 P. 903; Cotton v. Fisheries Products Co., 1921, 181 N.C. 151, 106 S.E. 487; Corrigan v. Bobbs-Merrill Co., 1920, 228 N.Y. 58, 126 N.E. 260.

19. Gertz v. Robert Welch, Inc., 1974, 418 U.S. 323, 94 S.Ct. 2997, 41 L.Ed.2d 789; Davis v. Schuchat, D.C. Cir 1975, 510 F.2d 731, 737–38; Buckley v. Littell, 2d Cir. 1976, 539 F.2d 882, 897, certiorari denied 429 U.S. 1062, 97 S.Ct. 785, 50 L.Ed.2d 777; Appleyard v. Transamerican Press, Inc., 4th Cir. 1976, 539 F.2d 1026, 1029–30, certiorari denied 429 U.S. 1041, 97 S.Ct. 740, 50 L.Ed.2d 753; Carson v. Allied News Co., 7th Cir. 1976, 529 F.2d 206, 214. See, also, Eldredge, Law of Defamation, 1978, Sec. 95, pp. 541–42.

20. See, however, Calero v. Del Chemical Corp., 1975, 68 Wis.2d 487, 228 N.W.2d 737; Stuempges v. Parke, Davis & Co., Minn.1980, 297 N.W.2d 252.

21. Second Restatement of Torts, § 620; 1978, Eldredge, Law of Defamation, Sec. 95, p. 939. See also, Conard v. Dillingham, 1922, 23 Ariz. 596, 206 P. 166; Wilson v. Sun Publishing Co., 1915, 85 Wash. 503, 148 P. 774.

22. Trabue v. Mays, 1835, 33 Ky. (3 Dana) 138; Linney v. Maton, 1855, 13 Tex. 449.

tirely repaired the damage.²³ Evidence of a retraction may, however, be admissible for three purposes.²⁴ It may go to show that the plaintiff has suffered less than he claims in the way of actual damage to his reputation.²⁵ It may tend to negative the "malice" or outrageous conduct which is a basis for punitive damages.²⁶ Finally, where privilege is in question, it would seem that it may be evidence of the defendant's good intentions and worthy motives, from which the jury may conclude that the privilege has not been abused.²⁷ By the same token, of course, a refusal to retract when a request has been made may be evidence in favor of the plaintiff, tending to show malevolence or an improper purpose in the original publication.²⁸

When the defendant's motives are in issue, any evidence tending to show that he is in a different state of mind about the publication may be admissible. A retraction, as such, however, can be effective only if it is a full²⁹ and unequivocal one, which does not contain lurking insinuations, hypothetical or hesitant withdrawals, or new calumnies in disguise. It must, in short, be an honest endeavor to repair all of the wrong done by the defamatory imputation, or it will merely aggravate the original offense.³⁰ A statement that the plaintiff has not the manners of a hog is not corrected by an assertion that he has the manners of a hog.³¹ The retraction must, in general, be given the same publicity and prominence as the defamation.³² An offer to make a public apology or retraction which is refused will go to mitigate damages,³³ but a mere offer to publish any statement the plaintiff himself cares to make is not an offer to retract.³⁴ In a number of states, the matter of retraction is covered by statutes, which usually limit the damages recoverable in cases where a proper retraction is made, or is not demanded.³⁵ Some of these statutes have been declared unconsti-

---

23. Lehrer v. Elmore, 1896, 100 Ky. 56, 37 S.W. 292; Dixie Fire Insurance Co. v. Betty, 1912, 101 Miss. 880, 58 So. 705; De Severinus v. Press Publishing Co., 1911, 147 App.Div. 161, 132 N.Y.S. 80; Taylor v. Hearst, 1895, 107 Cal. 262, 40 P. 392.

24. See Note, 1922, 35 Harv.L.Rev. 867. Also the excellent discussion of mitigation of damages and the proper instruction to the jury in Morris, Inadvertent Newspaper Libel and Retraction, 1937, 32 Ill.L.Rev. 36. Also Leflar, Legal Remedies for Defamation, 1952, 6 Ark.L.Rev. 423.

25. Webb v. Call Publishing Co., 1920, 173 Wis. 45, 180 N.W. 263; Turner v. Hearst, 1896, 115 Cal. 394, 47 P. 129; Meyerle v. Pioneer Publishing Co., 1920, 45 N.D. 568, 178 N.W. 792; White v. Sun Publishing Co., 1905, 164 Ind. 426, 73 N.E. 890; O'Connor v. Field, 1943, 266 App.Div. 121, 41 N.Y.S.2d 492.

Contra, Kehoe v. New York Tribune Co., 1930, 229 App.Div. 220, 241 N.Y.S. 676.

26. Fessinger v. El Paso Times Co., Tex.Civ.App. 1913, 154 S.W. 1171, error refused; Meyerle v. Pioneer Publishing Co., 1920, 45 N.D. 568, 178 N.W. 792; O'Connor v. Field, 1943, 266 App.Div. 121, 41 N.Y.S.2d 492.

27. See Note, 1922, 35 Harv.L.Rev. 867.

28. Brown v. Fawcett Publications, Inc., Fla.App. 1967, 196 So.2d 465; Vigil v. Rice, 1964, 74 N.M. 693, 397 P.2d 719; Crane v. Bennett, 1904, 177 N.Y. 106, 69 N.E. 274; Reid v. Nichols, 1915, 166 Ky. 423, 179 S.W. 440; Morgan v. Dun & Bradstreet, Inc., 5th Cir. 1970, 421 F.2d 1241. See Note, 1922, 35 Harv.L.Rev. 867.

29. Luna v. Seattle Times Co., 1936, 186 Wash. 618, 59 P.2d 753; Monaghan v. Globe Newspaper Co., 1906, 190 Mass. 394, 77 N.E. 476; Goolsby v. Forum Printing Co., 1913, 23 N.D. 30, 135 N.W. 661; Gray v. Times Newspaper Co., 1898, 74 Minn. 452, 77 N.W. 204.

30. Hotchkiss v. Oliphant, N.Y.1842, 2 Hill 510; Lehrer v. Elmore, 1896, 100 Ky. 56, 37 S.W. 292; Palmer v. Mahin, 8th Cir. 1903, 120 F. 737.

31. Winfield, Law of Tort, 1937, 323.

32. Storey v. Wallace, 1871, 60 Ill. 51; Kent v. Bonzey, 1854, 38 Me. 435; Lafone v. Smith, 1858, 3 H. & N. 735, 157 Eng.Rep. 664.

33. Dinkenspiel v. New York Evening Journal Publishing Co., 1903, 42 Misc. 74, 85 N.Y.S. 570, modified 91 App.Div. 96, 86 N.Y.S. 375; Dalziel v. Press Publishing Co., 1906, 52 Misc. 207, 102 N.Y.S. 909; Emery v. Cooper & Sons, 1909, 19 Pa.Dist. 509.

34. Coffman v. Spokane Chronicle Publishing Co., 1911, 65 Wash. 1, 117 P. 596; Constitution Publishing Co. v. Way, 1894, 94 Ga. 120, 21 S.E. 139; cf. Williams v. Hicks Printing Co., 1914, 159 Wis. 90, 150 N.W. 183.

35. See Miami Herald Publishing Co. v. Brown, Fla. 1953, 66 So.2d 679; White v. Sun Publishing Co., 1905, 164 Ind. 426, 73 N.E. 890; Gray v. Times Newspaper Co., 1898, 74 Minn. 452, 77 N.W. 204; Osborn v. Leach, 1904, 135 N.C. 628, 47 S.E. 811; Comer v. Age Herald Publishing Co., 1907, 151 Ala. 613, 44 So. 673. As to the "mangling" of these statutes by judicial interpretation, see Morris, Inadvertent Newspaper Libel and Retraction, 1937, 32 Ill.L.Rev. 36.

The California statute, which is unique in that it includes intentional, malicious libel, has been held not to apply to publication in magazines, because of a requirement of retraction within three weeks of demand. Morris v. National Federation of the Blind, 1961, 192

tutional,[36] while others have been sustained.[37] They usually have been held to call for a specific retraction of the original publication, with reference to it, rather than a mere second explanatory article stating the true facts.[38] Nevada and Mississippi [39] go further, and provide a "right of reply," under which the plaintiff may publish his own version of the matter with the defendant's facilities. This is a common remedy among European countries, and has had numerous advocates in the United States.

Mitigation of Damages and Evidence of Bad Reputation

It is well settled that the defendant may offer evidence of the plaintiff's general bad reputation or bad character.[40]

Moreover, the defendant may introduce evidence that the plaintiff's general reputation is bad with respect to that aspect of character pertaining to the defendant's defamation.[41] Since the plaintiff seeks to recover in nearly all cases for harm to his reputation, evidence that his reputation is already bad insofar as it relates to that aspect of the claimant's character about which the defamatory matter refers is admissible in mitigation of damages. It should be noted, therefore, that the primary reason that a claimant would have for waiving any claim for harm to reputation and seeking a recovery for mental anguish only is to prevent the admission of this evidence of bad character. In Rogers v. Doubleday & Co.,[42] plaintiff who had been appointed to the state optometry board was erroneously charged with having been indicted three times for practicing without a license. The plaintiff brought suit for punitive damages only, waiving any claim for actual damages, and recovered $2,500,000, which was upheld. It was found that the statement was false and recklessly published. Serious questions can be raised about the wisdom of permitting a plaintiff to recover a large amount in windfall punitive damages against a newspaper, however reckless the newspaper may have been, unless the plaintiff can prove that he had a reputation which was harmed by the false statement.

It usually is held that evidence of a rumor or report that the plaintiff has committed the particular act charged is not sufficient,[43]

Cal.App.2d 162, 13 Cal.Rptr. 336. The New Jersey statute, notwithstanding language limiting recovery to "actual damages proved," has been held to prevent only the recovery of punitive damages. Gersten v. Newark Morning Ledger Co., 1958, 52 N.J.Super. 152, 145 A.2d 56; Bock v. Plainfield Courier-News, 1957, 45 N.J. Super. 302, 132 A.2d 523.

36. Hanson v. Krehbiel, 1889, 68 Kan. 670, 75 P. 1041; Park v. Detroit Free Press Co., 1888, 72 Mich. 560, 40 N.W. 731; Byers v. Meridian Printing Co., 1911, 84 Ohio St. 408, 95 N.E. 917; Holden v. Pioneer Broadcasting Co., 1961, 228 Or. 405, 365 P.2d 845, appeal dismissed and certiorari denied 370 U.S. 157, 82 S.Ct. 1253, 8 L.Ed.2d 402. See Note, 1956, 36 Or.L. Rev. 70.

37. Allen v. Pioneer Press Co., 1889, 40 Minn. 117, 41 N.W. 936; Osborn v. Leach, 1904, 135 N.C. 628, 47 S.E. 811; Werner v. Southern California Associated Newspapers, 1950, 35 Cal.2d 121, 216 P.2d 825; Meyerle v. Pioneer Publishing Co., 1920, 45 N.D. 568, 178 N.W. 792. See Note, 1950, 38 Cal.L.Rev. 951.

38. Roth v. Greensboro News Co., 1940, 217 N.C. 13, 6 S.E.2d 882; Brogan v. Passaic Daily News, 1956, 22 N.J. 139, 123 A.2d 473. Cf. Kirby v. Pittsburgh Courier Publishing Co., 2d Cir. 1945, 150 F.2d 480.

39. Nev.Comp. Laws, Hillyer, 1929, § 10506; Miss. Code Ann.1942, § 3175. See Manasco v. Walley, 1953, 216 Miss. 614, 63 So.2d 91; Donnelly, The Right of Reply: An Alternative to an Action for Libel, 1948, 34 Va. L.Rev. 867; Leflar, Legal Remedies for Defamation, 1952, 6 Ark.L.Rev. 423.

40. Small v. Chronicle & Gazette Publishing Co., 1950, 96 N.H. 265, 74 A.2d 544; Hopkins v. Tate, 1916, 255 Pa. 56, 99 A. 210; Bausewine v. Norristown Herald, Inc., 1945, 351 Pa. 634, 41 A.2d 736, certiorari denied 326 U.S. 724, 66 S.Ct. 29, 90 L.Ed. 429; Eldredge, The Law of Defamation, 1978, Sec. 97, p. 564.

41. Sclar v. Resnick, 1921, 192 Iowa 669, 185 N.W. 273; Sickra v. Small, 1895, 87 Me. 493, 33 A. 9; Towle v. St. Albans Publishing Co., 1960, 122 Vt. 134, 165 A.2d 363.

42. Tex.Civ.App.1982, 644 S.W.2d 833. This comment is based on a slip opinion dated October 21, 1982, and may never be published.

43. Utah State Farm Bureau Federation v. National Farmers Union Service Corp., 10th Cir. 1952, 198 F.2d 20; Abell v. Cornwall Industrial Corp., 1925, 241 N.Y. 327, 150 N.E. 132; Mahoney v. Belford, 1882, 132 Mass. 393; Pease v. Shippen, 1876, 80 Pa. 513. See Note, 1953, 32 Neb.L.Rev. 121. Nor is evidence of other misconduct of the plaintiff admissible, since it shows "not that the plaintiff's reputation is bad, but that it ought to be bad." Sun Printing & Publishing Association v. Schenck, 2d Cir. 1900, 98 F. 925, 929; Berg-

unless it is shown to have been so widely diffused as to affect his general reputation.⁴⁴ Proof that the defendant was merely repeating what others had said is, however, held by most courts to be admissible,⁴⁵ along with any other facts tending to show a reasonable belief that his statement was true,⁴⁶ for the purpose of proving good faith and absence of "malice." Provocation by the plaintiff, indicating that the defendant uttered the words in the heat of passion or the excitement of the moment caused by the plaintiff's improper conduct, may be admitted for the same purpose.⁴⁷ The greater number of courts have held that such evidence to negative "malice" may be considered by the jury only as bearing upon the punitive damages recoverable where the defendant has been motivated by ill will.⁴⁸ There is a more realistic minority view that since the humiliation or mental suffering of the plaintiff may be enhanced by the defendant's ill will and outrageous conduct, proof of his good faith is to be considered in reduction of this element of compensatory damages.⁴⁹

WESTLAW REFERENCES

General Damages—Impairment of Reputation
digest(slander! libel! defam! /s damages /7 general)

Special Damages
libel! slander! defam! /s special +5 damages

Mental Anguish
libel! slander! defam! /s damages /s mental emotional /s anguish distress

Punitive Damages
digest(libel! slander! defam! /s damages /5 punitive)

Nominal Damages
libel! slander! defam! /s "nominal damages"

Mitigation of Damages and Retraction
defam! libel! slander! /p mitigat! /s damages
defam! libel! slander! /s retract!
237k104(1)

Mitigation of Damages & Evidence of Bad Reputation
libel! slander! defam! /p bad /5 reputation character

---

strom v. Ridgway Co., 1910, 138 App.Div. 178, 123 N.Y.S. 29.

44. Blickenstaff v. Perrin, 1867, 27 Ind. 527; Wetherbee v. Marsh, 1847, 20 N.H. 561; Stuart v. News Publishing Co., 1902, 67 N.J.L. 317, 51 A. 709.

45. Broadfoot v. Bird, 1926, 217 App.Div. 325, 216 N.Y.S. 670; Darling v. Mansfield, 1923, 222 Mich. 278, 192 N.W. 595; Pfister v. Milwaukee Free Press Co., 1909, 139 Wis. 627, 121 N.W. 938; Gill v. Ruggles, 1913, 95 S.C. 90, 78 S.E. 536. Contra, Preston v. Frey, 1891, 91 Cal. 107, 27 P. 533.

46. Massee v. Williams, 6th Cir. 1913, 207 F. 222; Scripps v. Foster, 1879, 41 Mich. 742, 3 N.W. 216; Davis v. Hearst, 1911, 160 Cal. 143, 116 P. 530; Gressman v. Morning Journal Association, 1910, 197 N.Y. 474, 90 N.E. 1131. Where truth was not pleaded, and so not admissible as an absolute defense, it has been held that the defendant could still show it on the issue of malice. Schlaf v. State Farm Mutual Automobile Insurance Co., 1957, 15 Ill.App.2d 194, 145 N.E.2d 791.

47. McLeod v. American Publishing Co., 1923, 126 S.C. 363, 120 S.E. 70; Schockey v. McCauley, 1905, 101 Md. 461, 61 A. 583; Ivie v. King, 1914, 167 N.C. 174, 83 S.E. 339, rehearing denied 169 N.C. 261, 85 S.E. 413. But the mere fact that the words are spoken in the heat of a quarrel is not sufficient, unless it is shown that plaintiff brought on the quarrel. Rohr v. Riedel, 1922, 112 Kan. 130, 210 P. 644.

48. Farrell v. Kramer, 1963, 159 Me. 387, 193 A.2d 560; Palmer v. Mahin, 8th Cir. 1903, 120 F. 737; Callahan v. Ingram, 1894, 122 Mo. 355, 26 S.W. 1020; Garrison v. Robinson, 1911, 81 N.J.L. 497, 79 A. 278.

49. Craney v. Donovan, 1917, 92 Conn. 236, 102 A. 640; Massee v. Williams, 6th Cir. 1913, 207 F. 222; Faxon v. Jones, 1900, 176 Mass. 206, 57 N.E. 359; Conroy v. Fall River Herald News Co., 1940, 306 Mass. 488, 28 N.E.2d 729. It may be suggested that the distinction is almost entirely academic, and that once the evidence is admitted the jury will use it for any purpose they see fit.

Chapter 20

PRIVACY

Table of Sections

Sec.
117. Right of Privacy.

§ 117. Right of Privacy

The recognition and development of the so-called "right of privacy," [1] is perhaps the outstanding illustration of the influence of legal periodicals upon the courts. Prior to the year 1890, no English or American court ever had granted relief expressly based upon the invasion of such a right, although there were cases [2] which in retrospect seem to have been groping in that direction, and Judge Cooley [3] had coined the phrase, "the right to be let alone." In 1890 there appeared in the Harvard Law Review a famous article,[4] by Samuel D. Warren and Louis D. Brandeis, which reviewed a number of cases in which relief had been afforded on the basis of defamation, invasion of some property right,[5] or breach of confidence or an implied contract,[6] and concluded that they were in reality based upon a broader principle which was entitled to separate recognition. In support of their argument they contended [7] that the growing excesses of the press made

---

§ 117

1. This term has been difficult of definition. See Davis, What Do We Mean By "Right to Privacy," 1959, 4 S.Dak.L.Rev. 1. It frequently has been misused, by those politically inclined, as a means of begging the question whether an individual may refuse to give information demanded of him by legal authorities. See for example Note, 1962, 40 N.C.L.Rev. 788. In the tort sense, at least, it has no such significance.

2. For example De May v. Roberts, 1881, 46 Mich. 160, 9 N.W. 146 (intrusion upon childbirth); Lord Byron v. Johnston, 1816, 2 Mer. 29, 35 Eng.Rep. 851 (authorship of spurious poem attributed).

3. Cooley, Torts, 2d ed. 1888, 29.

4. Warren and Brandeis, The Right to Privacy, 1890, 4 Harv.L.Rev. 193.

5. Woolsey v. Judd, N.Y.1855, 4 Duer 379, 11 How. Pr. 49 (publication of private letters); Gee v. Pritchard, 1819, 2 Swans. 402, 36 Eng.Rep. 670 (same); Prince Albert v. Strange, 1849, 1 Mach. & G. 25, 41 Eng.Rep. 1171, affirmed 1849, 2 De. G. & Sm. 652, 64 Eng.Rep. 293 (exhibition of private etchings and publication of catalogue).

6. Yovatt v. Winyard, 1820, 1 Jac. & W. 394, 37 Eng.Rep. 425 (publication of recipes obtained surreptitiously by employee); Abernathy v. Hutchinson, 1825, 3 L.J.Ch. 209 (publication of lectures delivered to class of which defendant was a member); Pollard v. Photographic Co., 1888, 40 Ch.Div. 345 (publication of plaintiff's picture made by defendant).

7. "The press is overstepping in every direction the obvious bounds of propriety and of decency. Gossip is no longer the resource of the idle and of the vicious, but has become a trade, which is pursued with industry as well as effrontery. To satisfy a prurient taste the details of sexual relations are spread broadcast in the columns of the daily papers. To occupy the indolent, column upon column is filled with idle gossip, which can only be procured by intrusion upon the domestic circle. The intensity and complexity of life, attendant upon advancing civilization, have rendered necessary some retreat from the world, and man, under the refining influence of culture, has become more sensitive to

a remedy upon such a distinct ground essential to the protection of private individuals against the unjustifiable infliction of mental pain and distress. Although there was at first some hesitation,[8] a host of other legal writers have taken up the theme,[9] and no other tort has received such an outpouring of comment in advocacy of its bare existence.

The first state really to come to grips with the doctrine thus advanced was New York. After cases in its lower courts [10] had accepted the existence of the right of privacy proposed by Warren and Brandeis, it fell into the hostile hands of the Court of Appeals in Roberson v. Rochester Folding-Box Co.,[11] where the defendant made use of the picture of a pulchritudinous young lady to advertise its flour without her consent. In a four-to-three decision, with a vigorous dissent, the court flatly denied the existence of any right to protection against such conduct, because of the lack of precedent, the purely mental character of the injury, the "vast amount of litigation" which might be expected to follow, the difficulty of drawing a distinction between public and private characters, and the fear of undue restriction of liberty of speech and freedom of the press.

The immediate result of the Roberson decision was a storm of public disapproval, which led one of the concurring judges to take the unprecedented step of publishing a law review article in defense of the decision.[12] In consequence the next New York legislature enacted a statute [13] making it both a misdemeanor and a tort to make use of the name, portrait or picture of any per-

---

publicity, so that solitude and privacy have become more essential to the individual; but modern enterprise and invention have, through invasions upon his privacy, subjected him to mental pain and distress, far greater than could be inflicted by mere bodily injury." Warren and Brandeis, The Right to Privacy, 1890, 4 Harv.L. Rev. 193, 196.

8. See O'Brien, The Right of Privacy, 1902, 2 Col.L. Rev. 437; Notes, 1902, 2 Col.L.Rev. 486; 1902, 64 Albany L.J. 428. Later dissenting voices are Lisle, The Right of Privacy (A Contra View), 1931, 19 Ky.L.J. 137; Kalven, Privacy in Tort Law—Were Warren and Brandeis Wrong? 1966, 31 Law & Con.Prob. 326; Notes, 1925, 29 Law Notes 64; 1929, 43 Harv.L.Rev. 297; 1931, 26 Ill.L.Rev. 63.

9. Among others Larremore, The Law of Privacy, 1912, 12 Col.L.Rev. 693; Ragland, The Right of Privacy, 1929, 17 Ky.L.J. 101; Winfield, Privacy, 1931, 47 L.Q.Rev. 23; Green, The Right of Privacy, 1932, 27 Ill. L.Rev. 237; Kacedan, The Right of Privacy, 1932, 12 Bos.U.L.Rev. 353, 600; Dickler, The Right of Privacy, 1936, 70 U.S.L.Rev. 435; Harper and McNeely, A Reexamination of the Basis of Liability for Emotional Distress, [1938] Wis.L.Rev. 436; Nizer, The Right of Privacy, 1941, 39 Mich.L.Rev. 526; Feinberg, Recent Developments in the Law of Privacy, 1948, 48 Col.L.Rev. 713; Ludwig, "Peace of Mind" in 48 Pieces vs. Uniform Right of Privacy, 1948, 32 Minn.L.Rev. 734; Yankwich, The Right of Privacy, 1952, 27 Notre Dame L. 429; Prosser, Privacy, 1960, 48 Cal.L.Rev. 383; Brittan, The Right of Privacy in England and The United States, 1963, 37 Tul.L.Rev. 235; Symposium, 1966, 31 Law & Con.Prob. 251 ff.

Also Notes in 1929, 43 Harv.L.Rev. 297; 1929, 7 N.C.L.Rev. 435; 1931, 26 Ill.L.Rev. 63; 1933, 81 U.Pa. L.Rev. 324; 1938, 33 Ill.L.Rev. 87; 1939, 13 So.Cal.L. Rev. 81; 1941, 15 Temple L.Q. 148; 1941, 25 Minn.L. Rev. 619; 1945, 30 Corn.L.Q. 398; 1948, 48 Col.L.Rev. 713; 1948, 15 U.Chi.L.Rev. 926; 1952, 6 Ark.L.Rev. 459; 1952, 38 Va.L.Rev. 117; 1953, 28 Ind.L.J. 179; 1958, 44 Va.L.Rev. 1303; 1960, 31 Miss.L.J. 191.

The foreign law is discussed in Gutteridge, The Comparative Law of the Right to Privacy, 1931, 47 L.Q. Rev. 203; Walton, The Comparative Law of the Right to Privacy, 1931, 47 L.Q.Rev. 219.

10. The first case to allow recovery on the independent basis of the right of privacy was an unreported decision of a New York trial judge, where an actress very scandalously appeared on the stage in tights, and the defendant snapped her picture from a box, and was enjoined from publishing it. Manola v. Stevens, N.Y. Sup.Ct.1890, in N.Y. Times, June 15, 18, 21, 1890. This was followed by decisions in New York, and in a Massachusetts federal court, in which the courts appeared to be quite willing to accept the principle. McKenzie v. Soden Mineral Springs Co., 1891, 27 Abb.N.C. 402, 18 N.Y.S. 240; Marks v. Jaffa, 1893, 6 Misc. 290, 26 N.Y.S. 908; Schuyler v. Curtis, 1895, 147 N.Y. 434, 42 N.E. 22, reargument denied 148 N.Y. 738, 42 N.E. 726; Corliss v. E. W. Walker Co., D.Mass.1894, 64 F. 280. Michigan, however, flatly rejected the whole idea, in Atkinson v. John E. Doherty & Co., 1899, 121 Mich. 372, 80 N.W. 285, where a brand of cigars was named after a deceased public figure.

11. 1902, 171 N.Y. 538, 64 N.E. 442. See the account of the case in Peck, Decision at Law, 1961, 70–96.

12. O'Brien, The Right of Privacy, 1902, 2 Col.L. Rev. 437.

13. N.Y.Sess.Laws 1903, ch. 132, §§ 1–2. Now, as amended in 1921, N.Y.—McKinney's Civil Rights Law, §§ 50–51. Held constitutional in Rhodes v. Sperry & Hutchinson Co., 1908, 193 N.Y. 223, 85 N.E. 1097, affirmed 1911, 220 U.S. 502, 31 S.Ct. 490, 55 L.Ed.2d 561. See, generally, Hofstadter, The Development of the Right of Privacy in New York, 1954.

son for "advertising purposes or for the purposes of trade" without his written consent. This act remains the law of New York, where there have been upwards of a hundred decisions dealing with it. Except as the statute itself limits the extent of the right, the New York decisions are quite consistent with the common law as it has been worked out in other states, and they are customarily cited in privacy cases throughout the country. Three years later the supreme court of Georgia had essentially the same question presented in Pavesich v. New England Life Insurance Co.,[14] where the defendant's insurance advertising made use of the plaintiff's name and picture, as well as a spurious testimonial from him. With the example of New York before it, George in turn rejected the Roberson case, accepted the views of Warren and Brandeis, and recognized the existence of a distinct right of privacy. This became the leading case.

For a time authority was divided, but along in the thirties, with the benediction of the First Restatement of Torts,[15] the tide set in strongly in favor of recognition, and the rejecting decisions began to be overruled. In one form or another the rights of privacy are recognized in virtually all jurisdictions.[16] It is recognized only in a limited form and by statute in some states, including New York, Oklahoma, Utah, Virginia, Wisconsin, and Nebraska.[17] And it has even been said that the only state not recognizing a right of privacy in some form or to some extent as of 1980 was Rhode Island.[18]

The early cases in all jurisdictions were understandably preoccupied with the question whether the right of privacy existed at all, and gave little or no consideration to what it would amount to if it did. Today, with several hundred cases in the books, some rather definite conclusions are possible. What has emerged is no very simple matter. As it has appeared in the cases thus far decided, it is not one tort, but a complex of four. To date the law of privacy comprises four distinct kinds of invasion of four different interests of the plaintiff, which are tied together by the common name, but otherwise have almost nothing in common except that each represents an interference with the right of the plaintiff "to be let alone." Whether there may be invasions of other interests which are properly to be included under the same generic term of "privacy" is a matter to be considered later,[19] after the existing four have been dealt with.

Appropriation

The first form of invasion of privacy to be recognized by the courts consists of the appropriation, for the defendant's benefit or advantages, of the plaintiff's name or likeness.[20] By reason of its early appearance in

---

14. 1905, 122 Ga. 190, 50 S.E. 68.

15. § 867, approving a cause of action for "unreasonable and serious" interference with privacy.

16. Comparatively recent decisions adding new jurisdictions to the list include Carr v. Watkins, 1962, 227 Md. 578, 177 A.2d 841; Truxes v. Kenco Enterprises, Inc., 1963, 80 S.D. 104, 119 N.W.2d 914; Olan Mills, Inc. of Texas v. Dodd, 1962, 234 Ark. 495, 353 S.W.2d 22; Barbieri v. News-Journal Co., Del.1963, 189 A.2d 773; Korn v. Rennison, 1959, 21 Conn.Sup. 400, 156 A.2d 476; Fergerstrom v. Hawaiian Ocean View Estates, 1968, 50 Hawaii 374, 441 P.2d 141. See also Billings v. Atkinson, Tex.1973, 489 S.W.2d 858.

17. N.Y.—McKinney's Civ. Rights Law Secs. 50–51; Okla.Stat.Ann., tit. 21 Secs. 839.1 to .3; Utah Code Ann.1953, 76–9–401 to 76–9–406; Va.Code 1950, §§ 2.1–377 to 2.1–386; Wis.Stat.Ann. 895.50; Neb.Rev. Stat. §§ 20–201 to 211, 25–804.01.

18. See Note, Tort Recovery for Invasion of Privacy, 1980, 59 Neb.L.Rev. 808.

19. See infra, this section on Constitutionl Expansion.

20. See Gordon, Right of Property in Name, Likeness, Personality and History, 1961, 55 Northwestern U.L.Rev. 553; Note, 1953, 26 So.Cal.L.Rev. 311. It is not impossible that, in the absence of a limiting statute, there might be invasion of privacy by appropriation of the plaintiff's identity, as by impersonation, without the use of either his name or his likeness. In Carlisle v. Fawcett Publications, Inc., 1962, 201 Cal.App.2d 733, 20 Cal.Rptr. 405, the name "John," with accompanying description sufficient to identify the plaintiff, was held to be enough.

On the other hand, in Lahr v. Adell Chemical Co., 1st Cir. 1962, 300 F.2d 256, it was held that the New York

the Roberson case,[21] and the resulting New York statute, this form of invasion has bulked rather large in the law of privacy. Thus in New York, as well as in many other states, there are a great many decisions in which the plaintiff has recovered when his name [22] or picture,[23] or other likeness,[24] has been used without his consent to advertise the defendant's product, or to accompany an article sold,[25] to add luster to the name of a corporation,[26] or for other business purposes.[27] The statute in New York and the others patterned after it are limited by their terms to uses for advertising or for "purposes of trade," and the common law of other states may therefore be somewhat broader in its scope;[28] but in general, there has been no very significant difference in the cases.

It is the plaintiff's name as a symbol of his identity that is involved here, and not as a mere name. Unless there is some tortious use made of it, there is no such thing as an exclusive right to the use of a name; and any one can be given or assume any name he likes.[29] It is only when he makes use of the name to pirate the plaintiff's identity for some advantage of his own, as by impersonation to obtain credit or secret information,[30] or by posing as the plaintiff's wife,[31] or providing a father for a child on a birth certificate,[32] that he becomes liable. It is in this sense that "appropriation" must be understood. It is therefore not enough that a

---

statute as to name or likeness did not include appropriation of the plaintiff's distinctive voice.

21. Supra, this section, n. 11.

22. Brociner v. Radio Wire Television, Inc., 1959, 15 Misc.2d 843, 183 N.Y.S.2d 743; Birmingham Broadcasting Co. v. Bell, 1953, 259 Ala. 656, 68 So.2d 314, later appeal, 1957, 266 Ala. 266, 96 So.2d 263; Kerby v. Hal Roach Studios, 1942, 53 Cal.App.2d 207, 127 P.2d 577; Fairfield v. American Photocopy Equipment Co., 1955, 138 Cal.App.2d 82, 291 P.2d 194; Manger v. Kree Institute of Electrolysis, Inc., 2d Cir. 1956, 233 F.2d 5.

It has been held that the New York statute does not protect a stage or other assumed name. Geisel v. Poynter Products, Inc., S.D.N.Y.1968, 295 F.Supp. 331: On its face this looks foolish; it means that Samuel L. Clemens would have a cause of action, but Mark Twain would not.

23. Flores v. Mosler Safe Co., 1959, 7 N.Y.2d 276, 196 N.Y.S.2d 975, 164 N.E.2d 853; Olan Mills, Inc., of Texas v. Dodd, 1962, 234 Ark. 495, 353 S.W.2d 22; Colgate-Palmolive Co. v. Tullos, 5th Cir. 1955, 219 F.2d 617 (Georgia law); Eick v. Perk Dog Food Co., 1952, 347 Ill.App. 293, 106 N.E.2d 742; Flake v. Greensboro News Co., 1938, 212 N.C. 780, 195 S.E. 55.

24. Young v. Greneker Studios, 1941, 175 Misc. 1027, 26 N.Y.S.2d 357 (manikin). See Note, 1964, 9 Vill.L.Rev. 274.

25. Lane v. F.W. Woolworth Co., 1939, 171 Misc. 66, 11 N.Y.S.2d 199, affirmed, 256 App.Div. 1065, 12 N.Y.S.2d 352; Jansen v. Hilo Packing Co., 1952, 202 Misc. 900, 118 N.Y.S.2d 162, affirmed, 282 App.Div. 935, 125 N.Y.S.2d 648; Miller v. Madison Square Garden Corp., 1941, 176 Misc. 714, 28 N.Y.S.2d 811; Selsman v. Universal Photo Books, Inc., 1963, 18 A.D.2d 151, 238 N.Y.S.2d 686.

26. Von Thodorovich v. Franz Josef Beneficial Association, E.D.Pa.1907, 154 F. 911; Edison v. Edison Polyform Manufacturing Co., 1907, 73 N.J.Eq. 136, 67 A. 392.

27. Binns v. Vitagraph Co. of America, 1913, 210 N.Y. 51, 103 N.E. 1108 (motion picture); Stryker v. Republic Pictures Corp., 1951, 108 Cal.App.2d 191, 238 P.2d 670 (same); Almind v. Sea Beach Co., 1912, 157 App.Div. 230, 141 N.Y.S. 842 (picture of plaintiff entering and leaving street car used to teach other passengers how to do it); Selsman v. Universal Photo Books, Inc., 1963, 18 A.D.2d 151, 238 N.Y.S.2d 686 (motion picture star's photograph used in camera manual).

28. See, as illustrations of possible differences: Cardy v. Maxwell, 1957, 9 Misc.2d 329, 169 N.Y.S.2d 547 (use of name to extort money not commercial use within statute); Hamilton v. Lumbermen's Mutual Casualty Co., La.App.1955, 82 So.2d 61, appeal transferred, 226 La. 644, 76 So.2d 916 (advertising in name of plaintiff for witnesses of accident); State ex rel. La Follette v. Hinkle, 1924, 131 Wash. 86, 229 P. 317 (use of name as candidate for office by political party); Burns v. Stevens, 1926, 236 Mich. 443, 210 N.W. 482 (posing as plaintiff's wife); Vanderbilt v. Mitchell, 1907, 72 N.J.Eq. 910, 67 A. 97 (providing father for child on birth certificate).

29. Du Boulay v. Du Boulay, 1869, L.R. 2 P.C. 430; Cowley v. Cowley, [1901] A.C. 450; Brown Chemical Co. v. Meyer, 1891, 139 U.S. 540, 11 S.Ct. 625, 35 L.Ed. 247; Smith v. United States Casualty Co., 1910, 197 N.Y. 420, 90 N.E. 947; Baumann v. Baumann, 1929, 250 N.Y. 382, 165 N.E. 819, reargument denied, 250 N.Y. 612, 166 N.E. 344; Bartholomew v. Workman, 1946, 197 Okl. 267, 169 P.2d 1012.

30. Goodyear Tire & Rubber Co. v. Vandergriff, 1936, 52 Ga.App. 662, 184 S.E. 452. The decision had been predicted in Green, The Right of Privacy, 1932, 27 Ill.L.Rev. 237, 243–44.

31. Burns v. Stevens, 1926, 236 Mich. 443, 210 N.W. 482.

32. Vanderbilt v. Mitchell, 1907, 72 N.J.Eq. 910, 67 A. 97.

name which is the same as the plaintiff's is used in a novel,[33] or the title of a corporation,[34] unless the context or the circumstances [35] indicate that the name is that of the plaintiff. On the other hand, there is no liability for the publication of a picture of his hand, leg or foot,[36] or of his house, his automobile, or his dog,[37] with nothing to indicate whose they are. Nor is there any liability when the plaintiff's character, occupation, and the general outline of his career, with many real incidents in his life, are used as the basis for a figure in a novel who is still clearly a fictional one.[38]

Once the plaintiff is identified, there is the further question whether the defendant has appropriated the name or likeness for his own advantage. Under the statutes the advantage must be a pecuniary one; but the common law is almost certainly not limited in this manner.[39] The New York courts were faced very early with the obvious fact that newspapers and magazines, to say nothing of radio, television and motion pictures, are by no means philanthropic institutions, but are operated for profit. As against the contention that everything published by these agencies must necessarily be "for purposes of trade," they were compelled to hold that there must be some closer and more direct connection, beyond the mere fact that the newspaper itself is sold; and that the presence of advertising matter in adjacent columns,[40] or even the duplication of a news item for the purpose of advertising the publication itself,[41] does not make any difference. Any other conclusion would in all probability have been an unconstitutional interference with the freedom of the press.[42] Accordingly, it has been held that the mere incidental mention of the plaintiff's name in

33. Harrison v. Smith, 1869, 20 T.L.R.,N.S., 713; Swacker v. Wright, 1935, 154 Misc. 822, 277 N.Y.S. 296; People on Complaint of Maggio v. Charles Scribner's Sons, 1954, 205 Misc. 818, 130 N.Y.S.2d 514. Cf. Nebb v. Bell Syndicate, S.D.N.Y.1941, 41 F.Supp. 929 (comic strip).

34. Pfaudler v. Pfaudler Co., 1920, 114 Misc. 477, 186 N.Y.S. 725.

35. See for example Uproar Co. v. National Broadcasting Co., D.Mass.1934, 8 F.Supp. 358, affirmed as modified, 1st Cir. 1936, 81 F.2d 373, certiorari denied 298 U.S. 670, 56 S.Ct. 835, 80 L.Ed. 1393; Kerby v. Hal Roach Studios, 1942, 53 Cal.App.2d 207, 127 P.2d 577; Krieger v. Popular Publications, 1938, 167 Misc. 5, 3 N.Y.S.2d 480.

The addition of other elements may make out the reference. McKenzie v. Soden Mineral Springs Co., 1891, 27 Abb.N.C. 402, 18 N.Y.S. 240 (signature); Orsini v. Eastern Wine Corp., 1947, 190 Misc. 235, 73 N.Y.S.2d 426, affirmed, 1948, 273 App.Div. 947, 78 N.Y.S.2d 224, appeal denied, 273 App.Div. 996, 79 N.Y.S.2d 870 (coat of arms).

36. Brewer v. Hearst Publishing Co., 1950, 185 F.2d 846. Compare, as to pictures of unidentifiable dead bodies, Sellers v. Henry, Ky.1959, 329 S.W.2d 214; Waters v. Fleetwood, 1956, 212 Ga. 161, 91 S.E.2d 344.

37. Rozhon v. Triangle Publications, 7th Cir. 1956, 230 F.2d 359 (house); Branson v. Fawcett Publications, E.D.Ill.1954, 124 F.Supp. 429 (car); Lawrence v. Ylla, 1945, 184 Misc. 807, 55 N.Y.S.2d 343 (dog).

38. Toscani v. Hersey, 1946, 271 App.Div. 445, 65 N.Y.S.2d 814. Cf. Bernstein v. National Broadcasting Co., D.D.C.1955, 129 F.Supp. 817, affirmed D.C.Cir. 1956, 98 U.S.App.D.C. 112, 232 F.2d 369, certiorari denied 352 U.S. 945, 77 S.Ct. 267, 1 L.Ed.2d 239; Miller v. National Broadcasting Co., D.Del.1957, 157 F.Supp. 240; Levey v. Warner Bros. Pictures, S.D.N.Y.1944, 57 F.Supp. 40; see also Motschenbacher v. R.J. Reynolds Tobacco Co., 9th Cir. 1974, 498 F.2d 821; Rosemont Enterprises, Inc., v. Irving, 1964, 49 A.D.2d 445, 375 N.Y.S.2d 864, dismissed 41 N.Y.2d 829, 393 N.Y.S.2d 399, 361 N.E.2d 1047.

39. See for example State ex rel. La Follette v. Hinkle, 1924, 131 Wash. 86, 229 P. 317 (use of name as candidate by political party); Hinish v. Meier & Frank Co., 1941, 166 Or. 482, 113 P.2d 438 (name signed to telegram urging governor to veto a bill); Schwartz v. Edrington, 1913, 133 La. 235, 62 So. 660 (name signed to petition); Hamilton v. Lumbermen's Mut. Cas. Co., La.App.1955, 82 So.2d 61, appeal transferred, 1955, 226 La. 644, 76 So.2d 916 (advertising in name of plaintiff for witnesses of accident); Burns v. Stevens, 1926, 236 Mich. 443, 210 N.W. 482 (posing as plaintiff's common law wife); Vanderbilt v. Mitchell, 1907, 72 N.J.Eq. 910, 67 A. 97 (birth certificate naming plaintiff as father).

40. Colyer v. Richard K. Fox Publishing Co., 1914, 162 App.Div. 297, 146 N.Y.S. 999.

41. Booth v. Curtis Publishing Co., 1962, 15 A.D.2d 343, 223 N.Y.S.2d 737, affirmed 11 N.Y.2d 907, 228 N.Y.S.2d 468, 182 N.E.2d 812. See Note, 1962, 31 Ford.L.Rev. 394; cf. Rand v. Hearst Corp., 1969, 31 App.Div.2d 406, 298 N.Y.S.2d 405, affirmed 26 N.Y.2d 806, 309 N.Y.S.2d 348, 257 N.E.2d 895. But in Hill v. Hayes, 1963, 18 A.D.2d 485, 240 N.Y.S.2d 286, where the revival of past events involving the plaintiff was found to be primarily for the purpose of increasing circulation and advertising a play, plaintiff was allowed to recover.

42. See Donahue v. Warner Brothers Picture Distributing Corp., 1954, 2 Utah 2d 256, 272 P.2d 177.

a book or a motion picture [43] is not an invasion of his privacy; nor is the publication of a photograph [44] or a newsreel [45] in which he incidentally appears.

Although the element of protection of the plaintiff's personal feelings is obviously not to be ignored in such a case,[46] the effect of the appropriation decisions is to recognize or create an exclusive right in the individual plaintiff to a species of trade name, his own, and a kind of trade mark in his likeness. It seems quite pointless to dispute over whether such a right is to be classified as "property;"[47] it is at least clearly proprietary in its nature. Once protected by the law, it is a right of value upon which the plaintiff can capitalize by selling licenses. It has been held in the Second Circuit [48] that an exclusive licensee has what has been called a "right of publicity,"[49] which entitles him to enjoin the use of the name or likewise by a third person.

Unreasonable Intrusion

An obviously different form of invasion consists of an unreasonable and highly offensive intrusion upon the seclusion of another. This is said to consist of intentional interference with another's interest in solitude or seclusion, either as to his person or to his private affairs or concerns.[50] One form of invasion consists of intrusion upon the plaintiff's physical solitude or seclusion,[51] as by invading his home [52] or other quarters,[53] or an illegal search of his shopping bag in a store.[54] The principle has, however, been carried beyond such physical intrusion, and extended to eavesdroppping upon private conversations by means of wiretapping [55] and microphones; [56] and there

---

43. University of Notre Dame Du Lac v. Twentieth Century-Fox Film Corp., 1965, 22 A.D.2d 452, 256 N.Y.S.2d 301, affirmed 15 N.Y.2d 940, 259 N.Y.S.2d 832, 207 N.E.2d 508; Shubert v. Columbia Pictures Corp., 1947, 189 Misc. 734, 72 N.Y.S.2d 851, affirmed 274 App.Div. 751, 80 N.Y.S.2d 724, appeal denied 274 App.Div. 80, 83 N.Y.S.2d 233. Compare, as to a commentary on news which is part of an advertisement, Wallach v. Bacharach, 1948, 192 Misc. 979, 80 N.Y.S.2d 37, affirmed 274 App.Div. 919, 84 N.Y.S.2d 894; and see O'Brien v. Pabst Sales Co., 5th Cir. 1941, 124 F.2d 167, certiorari denied 315 U.S. 823, 62 S.Ct. 917, 86 L.Ed 1220.

44. Dallessandro v. Henry Holt & Co., 1957, 4 A.D.2d 470, 166 N.Y.S.2d 805, appeal dismissed 7 N.Y. 2d 735, 193 N.Y.S.2d 635, 162 N.E.2d 726. Cf. Moglen v. Varsity Pajamas, Inc., 1961, 13 A.D.2d 114, 213 N.Y.S.2d 999.

45. Humiston v. Universal Film Manufacturing Co., 1919, 189 App.Div. 467, 178 N.Y.S. 752; Merle v. Sociological Research Film Corp., 1915, 166 App.Div. 376, 152 N.Y.S. 829.

46. Foster-Milburn Co. v. Chinn, 1909, 134 Ky. 424, 120 S.W. 364.

47. See Rhodes v. Sperry & Hutchinson Co., 1908, 193 N.Y. 223, 85 N.E. 1097, affirmed, 1911, 220 U.S. 502, 31 S.Ct. 490, 55 L.Ed. 561; Gautier v. Pro-Football, Inc., 1952, 304 N.Y. 354, 107 N.E.2d 485; Mau v. Rio Grande Oil, Inc., N.D.Cal.1939, 28 F.Supp. 845; Hull v. Curtis Publishing Co., 1956, 182 Pa.Super. 86, 125 A.2d 644; Metter v. Los Angeles Examiner, 1939, 35 Cal. App.2d 304, 95 P.2d 491. See Gordon, Right of Property in Name, Likeness, Personality and History, 1961, 55 Nw.L.Rev. 553; Ludwig, "Peace of Mind" in 48 Pieces v. Uniform Right of Privacy, 1948, 32 Minn.L. Rev. 734.

48. Haelan Laboratories v. Topps Chewing Gum, Inc., 2d Cir. 1953, 202 F.2d 866, certiorari denied 346 U.S. 816, 74 S.Ct. 26, 98 L.Ed. 343.

49. Nimmer, The Right of Publicity, 1954, 19 Law & Con.Prob. 203; Notes, 1953, 62 Yale L.J. 1123; 1953, 41 Geo.L.J. 583. But see contra, Strickler v. National Broadcasting Co., S.D.Cal.1958, 167 F.Supp. 68.

50. Second Restatement of Torts, § 652B, Comment a.

51. See Ezer, Intrusion on Solitude, 1961, 21 Law in Transition 63.

52. Dietemann v. Time, Inc., D.C.Cal.1968, 284 F.Supp. 925; Young v. Western & A.R. Co., 1929, 39 Ga.App. 761, 148 S.E. 414 (search without warrant); Thompson v. City of Jacksonville, Fla.App.1961, 130 So. 2d 105 (same); Walker v. Whittle, 1951, 83 Ga.App. 445, 64 S.E.2d 87 (entry without legal authority to arrest husband); Welsh v. Pritchard, 1952, 125 Mont. 517, 241 P.2d 816 (landlord moving in on tenant). Cf. De May v. Roberts, 1881, 46 Mich. 160, 9 N.W. 146 (intruding on childbirth). In Ford Motor Co. v. Williams, 1963, 108 Ga.App. 21, 132 S.E.2d 206, reversed 219 Ga. 505, 134 S.E.2d 32, conformed to 108 Ga.App. 723, 134 S.E.2d 483, entry into plaintiff's home was held to be an invasion of his privacy, even though he was not there at the time.

53. Newcomb Hotel Co. v. Corbett, 1921, 27 Ga. App. 365, 108 S.E. 309 (hotel room); Byfield v. Candler, 1924, 33 Ga.App. 275, 125 S.E. 905 (woman's stateroom on steamboat).

54. Sutherland v. Kroger Co., 1959, 144 W.Va. 673, 110 S.E.2d 716.

55. Rhodes v. Graham, 1931, 238 Ky. 225, 37 S.W. 2d 46; La Crone v. Ohio Bell Telephone Co., 1961, 114 Ohio App. 299, 182 N.E.2d 15. Even though no one listens, as in Hamberger v. Eastman, 1964, 106 N.H. 107,

56. See note 56 on page 855.

are decisions indicating that it is to be applied to peering into the windows of a home,[57] as well as persistent and unwanted telephone calls.[58] The tort has been found in the case of unauthorized prying into the plaintiff's bank account,[59] and the same principle has been used to invalidate a blanket subpoena duces tecum requiring the production of all his books and documents,[60] and an illegal compulsory blood test.[61]

It is clear, however, that there must be something in the nature of prying or intrusion, and that mere noises which disturb a church congregation,[62] or bad manners, harsh names, and insulting gestures in public,[63] are not enough. It is clear also that the intrusion must be something which would be offensive or objectionable to a reasonable person, and that there is no tort when the landlord stops by on Sunday morning to ask for the rent.[64] It is clear also that the thing into which there is intrusion or prying must be, and be entitled to be, private. The plaintiff has no right to complain when his pretrial testimony is recorded,[65] or when the police, acting within their powers, take his photograph, fingerprints or measurements,[66] or when there is inspection and public disclosure of corporate records which he is required by law to keep and make available.[67] On the public street, or in any other public place, the plaintiff has no legal right to be alone; and it is no invasion of his privacy to do no more than follow him about and watch him there.[68] Neither is it such an

---

206 A.2d 239; or the information obtained is not disclosed to others. Fowler v. Southern Bell Telephone & Telegraph Co., 5th Cir. 1965, 343 F.2d 150. See Sullivan, Wiretapping and Eavesdropping: A Review of the Current Law, 1966, 18 Hast.L.J. 59; Notes, 1965, 2 Houst.L.Rev. 285; 1967, 52 Corn.L.Q. 975; 1969, 36 Tenn.L.Rev. 362; see also, Marks v. Bell Telephone Co. of Pennsylvania, 1975, 460 Pa. 73, 331 A.2d 424 (no action allowed merely because of the use of a recording system since there was no evidence that it was replayed to an unauthorized person).

56. McDaniel v. Atlanta Coca-Cola Bottling Co., 1939, 60 Ga.App. 92, 2 S.E.2d 810; Roach v. Harper, 1958, 143 W.Va. 869, 105 S.E.2d 564. Elson v. Bowen, 1967, 83 Nev. 515, 436 P.2d 12. See Note, 1969, 20 Syr. L.Rev. 601.

57. Souder v. Pendleton Detectives, Inc., La.App. 1956, 88 So.2d 716; Moore v. New York Elevated Railroad Co., 1892, 130 N.Y. 523, 29 N.E. 997; Pritchett v. Board of Commissioners of Knox County, 1908, 42 Ind. App. 3, 85 N.E. 32; cf. Pinkerton National Detective Agency, Inc. v. Stevens, 1963, 108 Ga.App. 159, 132 S.E.2d 119.

This topic gave rise to a possible nomination for the all-time prize law review title, in the Note, Crimination of Peeping Toms and Other Men of Vision, 1951, 5 Ark. L.Rev. 388.

58. Housh v. Peth, 1956, 165 Ohio St. 35, 133 N.E. 2d 340, affirming 1955, 99 Ohio App. 485, 135 N.E.2d 440; Harms v. Miami Daily News, Inc., Fla.1961, 127 So.2d 715; Carey v. Statewide Finance Co., 1966, 3 Conn.Cir. 716, 223 A.2d 405.

59. Brex v. Smith, 1929, 104 N.J.Eq. 386, 146 A. 34; Zimmermann v. Wilson, 3d Cir. 1936, 81 F.2d 847.

60. Frey v. Dixon, 1848, 141 N.J.Eq. 481, 58 A.2d 86; State ex rel. Clemons v. Witthaus, 1950, 360 Mo. 274, 228 S.W.2d 4 (court order).

61. Bednarik v. Bednarik, 1940, 18 N.J.Misc. 633, 16 A.2d 80. See Notes, 1967, 14 UCLA L.Rev. 680; 1967,

19 Ala.L.Rev. 174; 1967, 45 N.C.L.Rev. 174; 1967, 28 Ohio St.L.J. 185.

62. Owen v. Henman, Pa.1841, 1 Watts & S. 548.

63. Lisowski v. Jaskiewicz, Pa.1950, 76 D. & C. 79; Christie v. Greenleaf, Pa.1951, 78 D. & C. 191.

64. Horstman v. Newman, Ky.1956, 291 S.W.2d 567. Accord, Harms v. Miami Daily News, Inc., Fla. 1961, 127 So.2d 715 (for the jury whether telephone calls objectionable to a reasonable person).

65. Gotthelf v. Hillcrest Lumber Co., 1952, 280 App. Div. 668, 116 N.Y.S.2d 873.

66. Voelker v. Tyndall, 1947, 226 Ind. 43, 75 N.E.2d 548; McGovern v. Van Riper, 1947, 140 N.J.Eq. 341, 54 A.2d 469; Norman v. City of Las Vegas, 1947, 64 Nev. 38, 177 P.2d 442; Mabry v. Kettering, 1909, 89 Ark. 551, 117 S.W. 746, second appeal, 1909, 92 Ark. 81, 122 S.W. 115; Hodgeman v. Olsen, 1915, 86 Wash. 615, 150 P. 1122; Walker v. Lamb, Del.Ch.1969, 254 A.2d 265, affirmed 259 A.2d 663. Cf. Herschel v. Dyra, 7th Cir. 1966, 365 F.2d 17, cert. denied 385 U.S. 973, 87 S.Ct. 513, 17 L.Ed.2d 436 (retaining record of arrest); Kolb v. O'Connor, 1957, 14 Ill.App.2d 81, 142 N.E.2d 818 (same); Anthony v. Anthony, 1950, 9 N.J.Super. 411, 74 A.2d 919 (compulsory blood test in paternity suit).

67. Bowles v. Misle, D.Neb.1946, 64 F.Supp. 835; United States v. Alabama Highway Express Co., D.Ala. 1942, 46 F.Supp. 450; Alabama State Federation of Labor v. McAdory, 1944, 246 Ala. 1, 18 So.2d 810, certiorari dismissed 325 U.S. 450, 65 S.Ct. 1384, 89 L.Ed. 1725.

68. Chappell v. Stewart, 1896, 82 Md. 323, 33 A. 542; Forster v. Manchester, 1963, 410 Pa. 192, 189 A.2d 147; see Pinkerton National Detective Agency, Inc. v. Stevens, 1963, 108 Ga.App. 159, 132 S.E.2d 119. Cf. McKinzie v. Huckaby, W.D.Okl.1953, 112 F.Supp. 642, where defendant, calling at plaintiff's home, brought along a policeman, who remained outside in the car. But in Pinkerton National Detective Agency, Inc. v. Stevens, 1963, 108 Ga.App. 159, 132 S.E.2d 119,

invasion to take his photograph in such a place,[69] since this amounts to nothing more than making a record, not differing essentially from a full written description, of a public sight which anyone would be free to see. On the other hand, when the plaintiff is confined to a hospital bed,[70] and when he is merely in the seclusion of his home,[71] the making of a photograph is an invasion of a private right, of which he is entitled to complain. And even in a public place, there can be some things which are still private, so that a woman who is photographed with her dress unexpectedly blown up in a "fun house" has a right of action.[72]

The most recent cases on this tort seem to indicate the existence of two factors of primary importance in determining whether or not an intrusion which effects access to private information is actionable. The first is the means used. If the means used is abnormal in character for gaining access to private information, then the intrusion is likely to be actionable regardless of the purpose. Thus, wiretapping, and the use of electronic devices would generally be actionable regardless of the purpose.[73] The second is the defendant's purpose for obtaining the information. Keeping the plaintiff under surveillance by shadowing techniques through the use of private detectives would be actionable when such a method is used for some purposes but not others.[74]

Public Disclosure of Private Facts

Another group of cases have found a cause of action in publicity, of a highly objectionable kind, given to private information about the plaintiff, even though it is true and no action would lie for defamation. Two important questions relate to this type of unreasonable invasion of the right of privacy. They are: (1) the requirements for recovery under the common law, and (2) the extent to which restrictions have been created on the common law recovery by decisions protecting freedom of speech and the press under the First Amendment to the Constitution.

The common law. There has been some difference of opinion among writers about controlling principles in this area, and substantial differences have developed among courts in the precise handling of this tort. Prosser was of the view that three requirements had to be satisfied for recovery. These were that (1) the disclosure of the private facts must be a public disclosure and not a private one;[75] (2) the facts disclosed to the public must be private facts, and not public ones; and (3) the matter made public must be one which would be highly offensive and objectionable to a reasonable per-

ostentatious shadowing on the street, which drew public attention, was held to be an invasion of privacy.

69. Forster v. Manchester, 1963, 410 Pa. 192, 189 A.2d 147; Gill v. Hearst Publishing Co., 1953, 40 Cal.2d 224, 253 P.2d 441; Berg v. Minneapolis Star & Tribune Co., D.Minn.1948, 79 F.Supp. 957 (courtroom); Lyles v. State, Okl.Cr.1958, 330 P.2d 734 (television in court). Cf. Gautier v. Pro-Football, Inc., 1953, 304 N.Y. 354, 107 N.E.2d 485. In United States v. Gugel, E.D.Ky. 1954, 119 F.Supp. 897, the right to take such pictures was said to be protected by the Constitution of the United States. See Fitzpatrick, Unauthorized Photographs, 1932, 20 Geo.L.J. 134; Note, 1938, 33 Ill.L.Rev. 87.

70. Barber v. Time, Inc., 1942, 348 Mo. 1199, 159 S.W.2d 291. Cf. Clayman v. Bernstein, 1940, 38 Pa.D. & C. 543 (picture of semi-conscious patient taken by physician). Without the intrusion, publication of matters of public interest was held to be privileged in Pearson v. Dodd, 1969, 133 U.S.App.D.C. 279, 410 F.2d 701, certiorari denied 395 U.S. 947, 89 S.Ct. 2021, 23 L.Ed.2d 465. See, Froelich v. Werbin, 1976, 219 Kan. 461, 548 P.2d 482 (no invasion of privacy when hair sample was taken from a brush lying on a dresser).

71. Dietemann v. Time, Inc., C.D.Cal.1968, 284 F.Supp. 925.

72. Daily Times Democrat v. Graham, 1964, 276 Ala. 380, 162 So.2d 474. See, however, Neff v. Time, Inc., W.D.Pa.1976, 406 F.Supp. 858 (photograph taken at a public event. Plaintiff's picture showed zipper of his trousers was open. No action).

73. Nader v. General Motors Corp., 1970, 25 N.Y.2d 560, 307 N.Y.S.2d 647, 255 N.E.2d 765.

74. McLain v. Boise Cascade Corp., 1975, 271 Or. 549, 533 P.2d 343.

75. Santiesteban v. Goodyear Tire & Rubber Co., 5th Cir. 1962, 306 F.2d 9.

son of ordinary sensibilities.[76] In the Second Restatement of Torts, it is said, in addition to those three requirements, that the public must not have a legitimate interest in having the information made available.[77] Alfred Hill has, on the other hand, suggested that the controlling basis, in the final analysis, is the single principle of the shocking character of the disclosure, such as when there is a disclosure of the name of a rape victim long after the crime; therefore, the nature of the publication, the extent of the public interest in the matter disclosed, and other circumstances would simply be factors in arriving at the final decision which should be made by the court and not the jury.[78] There is much to be said for Hill's approach, especially because of the difficulties of distinguishing between public and private facts, and matters that are of *no* public concern and those that are of *some* public concern.

All are in agreement that the matter made public must be one which would be highly offensive and objectionable to a reasonable person of ordinary sensibilities.[79]

The law is not for the protection of the hypersensitive, and all of us must, to some reasonable extent, lead lives exposed to the public gaze. Anyone who is not a hermit must expect the more or less casual observation of his neighbors and the passing public as to what he is and does, and some reporting of his daily activities. The ordinary reasonable person does not take offense at mention in a newspaper of the fact that he has returned home from a visit, or gone camping in the woods, or given a party at his house for his friends. It is quite a different matter when the details of sexual relations are spread before the public eye,[80] or there is highly personal portrayal of his intimate private characteristics or conduct.[81] The outstanding decision in this area is Sidis v. F-R Publishing Corp.,[82] where a magazine revived the history of a former infant mathematical prodigy, and described his present whereabouts and activities, and it was held that there was nothing in this which would be objectionable to any normal person. The case, when compared with Melvin v. Reid,[83] with its revelation of the past of a prostitute and a murder defendant, suggests something in the nature of a "mores" test,[84] under which there will be liability only for publicity given to those things which the customs and ordinary views of the community would regard as highly objectionable.

There is considerable doubt about the necessity for a public disclosure. Public disclosure by a creditor of indebtedness of a claimant as a self-help way of collecting a debt has been regarded as an invasion of privacy,[85] whereas a private disclosure to an employer or some other person with a legiti-

---

76. Reed v. Real Detective Publishing Co., 1945, 63 Ariz. 294, 162 P.2d 133; Davis v. General Finance & Thrift Corp., 1950, 80 Ga.App. 708, 57 S.E.2d 225; Gill v. Hearst Publishing Co., 1953, 40 Cal.2d 224, 253 P.2d 441; Samuel v. Curtis Publishing Co., N.D.Cal.1954, 122 F.Supp. 327; Meetze v. Associated Press, 1956, 230 S.C. 330, 95 S.E.2d 606. Cf. Hamilton v. Crown Life Ins. Co., 1967, 246 Or. 1, 423 P.2d 771.

77. See Comment *d* of § 652D; also see, Virgil v. Time, Inc., 9th Cir. 1975, 527 F.2d 1122, certiorari denied 425 U.S. 998, 96 S.Ct. 2215, 48 L.Ed.2d 823, on remand 424 F.Supp. 1286.

78. See, Hill, Defamation and Privacy Under the First Amendment, 1976, 76 Colum.L.Rev. 1205, 1258–62.

79. See supra, footnote 76. See, Johnson v. Harcourt, Brace, Jovanovich, Inc., 1974, 43 Cal.App.3d 880, 118 Cal.Rptr. 370; Taylor v. K.T.V.B., Inc., 1974, 96 Idaho 202, 525 P.2d 984; Roshto v. Hebert, La.App. 1982, 413 So.2d 927 (local newspaper printed "page from the past").

80. Garner v. Triangle Publications, S.D.N.Y.1951, 97 F.Supp. 546. Cf. Myers v. United States Camera Publishing Corp., 1957, 9 Misc.2d 765, 167 N.Y.S.2d 771; Feeney v. Young, 1920, 191 App.Div. 501, 181 N.Y.S. 481; Banks v. King Features Syndicate, S.D. N.Y.1939, 30 F.Supp. 352.

81. Cason v. Baskin, 1944, 155 Fla. 198, 20 So.2d 243; second appeal, 1947, 159 Fla. 31, 30 So.2d 635. Cf. Stryker v. Republic Pictures Corp., 1951, 108 Cal. App.2d 191, 238 P.2d 670.

82. 2d Cir. 1940, 113 F.2d 806, affirming S.D.N.Y. 1938, 34 F.Supp. 19.

83. 1931, 112 Cal.App. 285, 297 P. 91.

84. Suggested by the lower court in Sidis v. F-R Publishing Corp., S.D.N.Y.1938, 34 F.Supp. 19, affirmed 2d Cir. 1940, 113 F.2d 806, certiorari denied, 311 U.S. 711, 61 S.Ct. 393, 85 L.Ed. 462.

85. Brents v. Morgan, 1927, 221 Ky. 765, 299 S.W. 967. "Dr. W.R. Morgan owes an account here of $49.67. And if promises would pay an account this ac-

mate interest in the matter has generally been regarded as permissible.[86] And it has been said that any disclosure to be actionable must be a public disclosure.[87] But such a general requirement ought not to be a prerequisite to recovery in any kind of a disclosure case. Thus, it has been held to be an invasion of the plaintiff's right of privacy to communicate a private fact to a newspaper,[88] military agency,[89] neighbor,[90] or disinterested employer.[91]

Warren and Brandeis[92] thought that the publication would have to be written or printed unless some special damage could be shown and there have been decisions[93] that the action will not lie for oral publicity; but the development of radio alone has been enough to make this obsolete,[94] and there now can be little doubt that a writing is not required.

It has recently been said that the purpose of the tort is to protect an individual against unwarranted publication of private facts.[95] In the last edition, it was said:

> "The facts disclosed to the public must be private facts, and not public ones. The plaintiff cannot complain when an occupation in which he publicly engages is called to public attention [96] or when publicity is given to matters such as the date of his birth or marriage,[97] or his military service record,[98] which are a matter of public record, and open

count would have been settled long ago. This account will be advertised as long as it remains unpaid."; 1931, 112 Cal.App. 285, 297 P. 91. See also, under statute, Nappier v. Jefferson Standard Life Insurance Co., 4th Cir. 1963, 322 F.2d 502 (name of victim of rape); Trammell v. Citizens News Co., 1941, 285 Ky. 529, 148 S.W.2d 708; Biederman's of Springfield, Inc. v. Wright, Mo.1959, 322 S.W.2d 892; Tollefson v. Price, 1967, 247 Or. 398, 430 P.2d 990; cf. Bennett v. Norban, 1959, 396 Pa. 94, 151 A.2d 476. A rather spectacular case is Santiesteban v. Goodyear Tire & Rubber Co., 5th Cir. 1962, 306 F.2d 9, where a creditor stripped the tires off the debtor's car in public, and it was held to be a "demonstrative publication" of the debt. See Note, 1963, 49 Iowa L.Rev. 208.

86. Vogel v. W.T. Grant Co., 1974, 458 Pa. 124, 327 A.2d 133; Voneye v. Turner, Ky.Ct.App.1951, 240 S.W.2d 588; Hendry v. Conner, 1975, 303 Minn. 317, 226 N.W.2d 921.

87. Santiesteban v. Goodyear Tire & Rubber Co., 5th Cir. 1962, 306 F.2d 9; Schwartz v. Thiele, 1966, 242 Cal.App.2d 799, 51 Cal.Rptr. 767; French v. Safeway Stores, Inc., 1967, 247 Or. 554, 430 P.2d 1021.

88. Trammell v. Citizens News Co., 1941, 285 Ky. 529, 148 S.W.2d 708.

89. Beaumont v. Brown, 1977, 401 Mich. 80, 257 N.W.2d 522.

90. Bowden v. Spiegel, Inc., 1950, 96 Cal.App.2d 793, 216 P.2d 571.

91. Carr v. Watkins, App.1962, 227 Md. 578, 177 A.2d 841. On the other hand, it is generally agreed that employers have an interest that will allow creditors to contact them about an employee's debts. See also, Household Finance Corp. v. Bridge, 1969, 252 Md. 531, 250 A.2d 878; Timperley v. Chase Collection Service, 1969, 272 Cal.App.2d 697, 77 Cal.Rptr. 782; Harrison v. Humble Oil & Refining Co., D.C.S.C.1967, 264 F.Supp. 89; Yoder v. Smith, 1962, 253 Iowa 505, 112 N.W.2d 862; Berrier v. Beneficial Finance, Inc., N.D. Ind.1964, 234 F.Supp. 204. Contra is Pack v. Wise, La. App.1964, 155 So.2d 909, writ refused 245 La. 84, 157 So.2d 231; but the case was limited, in Passman v. Commercial Credit Plan of Hammond, Inc., La.App. 1969, 220 So.2d 758, application denied 254 La. 287, 223 So.2d 410, to some attempt at coercion. See Note, 1969, 36 Brook.L.Rev. 95.

92. Warren and Brandeis, The Right to Privacy, 1890, 4 Harv.L.Rev. 193, 217.

93. Martin v. F.I.Y. Theatre Co., 1838, 1 Ohio Supp. 19, 10 O.O. 338; Gregory v. Bryan-Hunt Co., 1943, 295 Ky. 345, 174 S.W.2d 510; Pangallo v. Murphy, Ky.1951, 243 S.W.2d 496; Lewis v. Physicians & Dentists Credit Bureau, 1947, 27 Wash.2d 267, 177 P.2d 896; Grimes v. Carter, 1966, 241 Cal.App.2d 694, 50 Cal.Rptr. 808.

94. Mau v. Rio Grande Oil, Inc., N.D.Cal.1939, 28 F.Supp. 845; Strickler v. National Broadcasting Co., S.D.Cal.1958, 167 F.Supp. 68; Binns v. Vitagraph Co. of America, 1913, 210 N.Y. 51, 103 N.E. 1108 (motion picture); Donahue v. Warner Bros. Pictures, 10th Cir. 1952, 194 F.2d 6 (same); Ettore v. Philco Television Broadcasting Co., 3d Cir. 1956, 229 F.2d 481, certiorari denied 351 U.S. 926, 76 S.Ct. 783, 100 L.Ed. 1456 (motion picture film on television).

95. Rawlins v. Hutchinson Publishing Co., 1975, 218 Kan. 295, 543 P.2d 988.

[96.] Reed v. Orleans Parish Schoolboard, La.App. 1945, 21 So.2d 895 (compulsory disclosure of war work and other outside activities on part of schoolteacher).

[97.] Meetze v. Associated Press, 1956, 230 S.C. 330, 95 S.E.2d 606.

[98.] Stryker v. Republic Pictures Corp., 1951, 108 Cal.App.2d 191, 238 P.2d 670; Continental Optical Co. v. Reed, 1949, 119 Ind.App. 643, 86 N.E.2d 306, rehearing denied 119 Ind.App. 643, 88 N.E.2d 55. Accord: Thompson v. Curtis Publishing Co., 3d Cir. 1952, 193 F.2d 953 (patent obtained by plaintiff); Langford v. Vanderbilt University, 1956, 199 Tenn. 389, 287 S.W.2d 32 (pleading filed in lawsuit); Johnson v. Scripps Publishing Co., Com.Pl.1940, 6 Ohio Supp. 13 (signature on nominating petition).

to public inspection.[99] It seems to be generally agreed that anything visible in a public place can be recorded and given circulation by means of a photograph, to the same extent as by a written description, since this amounts to nothing more than giving publicity to what is already public and what anyone present would be free to see.[1] The contention [2] that when an individual is thus singled out from the public scene and undue attention is focused upon him, there is an invasion of his private rights, has not been borne out by the decisions.[3] On the other hand, it is clear that when a picture is taken without the plaintiff's consent in a private place,[4] or one already made is stolen,[5] or obtained by bribery or other inducement of breach of trust,[6] the plaintiff's appearance which is thus made public is still a private thing, and there is an invasion of a private right, for which an action will lie."

But merely because a fact is one that occurred at a public place and in the view of the general public, which may have been only a few persons or merely because it can be found in a public record, does not mean that it should receive widespread publicity if it does not involve a matter of public concern. There can be such a thing as highly offensive publicity to something that happened long ago even though it occurred in a public place.[7]

The press, public figures, and news. There was a general recognition, at common law, of two closely related propositions, both of which were founded upon the basic idea of freedom of the press.[8] One was the privilege of giving further publicity to existing public figures; the other that of giving publicity to news, and other matters of public interest. The one primarily concerned the person to whom publicity was given; the other the event, fact or subject matter in which he was involved. They were, however, obviously only different phases of the same thing, and in practice frequently became so merged as to be inseparable.[9]

A public figure has been defined as a person who, by his accomplishments, fame, or

---

[99.] Hubbard v. Journal Publishing Co., 1962, 69 N.M. 473, 368 P.2d 147 (court record); Bell v. Courier-Journal & Louisville Times Co., Ky.1966, 402 S.W.2d 84 (tax delinquency); cf. Rome Sentinel Co. v. Boustedt, 1964, 43 Misc.2d 598, 252 N.Y.S.2d 10 (death certificate); Lamont v. Commissioner of Motor Vehicles, S.D. N.Y.1967, 269 F.Supp. 880, affirmed 386 F.2d 449, certiorari denied 391 U.S. 915, 88 S.Ct. 1811, 20 L.Ed.2d 654 (motor vehicle registration records).

Otherwise where the record is not an open one. Maysville Transit Co. v. Ort, 1944, 296 Ky. 524, 177 S.W.2d 369 (income tax returns); Munzer v. Blaisdell, 1944, 183 Misc. 777, 49 N.Y.S.2d 919, affirmed 1945, 269 App.Div. 970, 58 N.Y.S.2d 360 (records of mental institution); Patterson v. Tribune Co., Fla.App.1962, 146 So.2d 623 (progress records of narcotic addict). Cf. Sellers v. Henry, Ky.1959, 329 S.W.2d 214 (police photograph).

[1.] Gill v. Hearst Publishing Co., 1953, 40 Cal.2d 224, 253 P.2d 441 (plaintiff embracing his wife in market place); Humiston v. Universal Film Mfg. Co., 1919, 189 A.D. 467, 178 N.Y.S. 752 (street); Berg v. Minneapolis Star & Tribune Co., D.Minn.1948, 79 F.Supp. 957 (courtroom); Gautier v. Pro-Football, Inc., 1952, 304 N.Y. 354, 107 N.E.2d 485 (football game); Jacova v. Southern Radio & Television Co., Fla.1955, 83 So.2d 34 (cigar store raid). The parent case is Sports & General Press Agency v. "Our Dogs" Publishing Co., [1916] 2 K.B. 880.

[2.] See Note, 1958, 44 Va.L.Rev. 1303.

[3.] There is one decision to that effect, Blumenthal v. Picture Classics, 1932, 235 App.Div. 570, 257 N.Y.S. 800, affirmed 1933, 261 N.Y. 504, 185 N.E. 713. It was, however, later explained upon the basis of the introduction of an element of fiction into the accompanying narrative. Sarat Lahiri v. Daily Mirror, 1937, 162 Misc. 776, 295 N.Y.S. 382.

[4.] Barber v. Time, Inc., 1942, 348 Mo. 1199, 159 S.W.2d 291 (hospital bed); cf. Clayman v. Bernstein, Pa.1940, 38 D. & C. 543 (picture of semi-conscious patient taken by physician).

[5.] Peed v. Washington Times, D.C.1927, 55 Wash. L.Rep. 182. This was conceded in Metter v. Los Angeles Examiner, 1939, 35 Cal.App.2d 304, 95 P.2d 491, but the court refused to permit the obvious conclusion from the evidence.

[6.] Bazemore v. Savannah Hospital, 1930, 171 Ga. 257, 155 S.E. 194; Douglas v. Stokes, 1912, 149 Ky. 506, 149 S.W. 849.

7. See Street v. National Broadcasting Co., 6th Cir. 1981, 645 F.2d 1227, certiorari dismissed 454 U.S. 1095, 102 S.Ct. 667, 70 L.Ed.2d 636 (plaintiff was a prosecuting witness in a celebrated rape case some 30 years before the defendant presented a historical drama. Court held no liability).

8. See Note, 1953, 28 Ind.L.J. 180.

9. See for example Elmhurst v. Pearson, 1946, 80 U.S.App.D.C. 372, 153 F.2d 467; Martin v. Dorton, 1951, 210 Miss. 668, 50 So.2d 391; Stryker v. Republic Pictures Corp., 1951, 108 Cal.App.2d 191, 238 P.2d 670; Molony v. Boy Comics Publishers, 1950, 277 App.Div. 166, 98 N.Y.S.2d 119.

mode of living, or by adopting a profession or calling which gives the public a legitimate interest in his doings, his affairs, and his character, has become a "public personage."[10] He is, in other words, a celebrity. Obviously to be included in this category are those who have achieved some degree of reputation by appearing before the public, as in the case of an actor,[11] a professional baseball player,[12] a pugilist,[13] or any other entertainer.[14] The list is, however, broader than this. It includes public officers,[15] famous inventors[16] and explorers,[17] war heroes[18] and even ordinary soldiers,[19] an infant prodigy,[20] and no less a personage than the Grand Exalted Ruler of a lodge.[21] It includes, in short, anyone who has arrived at a position where public attention is focused upon him as a person.

Such public figures were held to have lost, to some extent at least, their right of privacy. Three reasons were given, more or less indiscriminately, in the decisions: that they had sought publicity and consented to it, and so could not complain when they received it; that their personalities and their affairs had already become public, and could no longer be regarded as their own private business; and that the press had a privilege, under the Constitution, to inform the public about those who have become legitimate matters of public interest. On one or another of these grounds, and sometimes all, it was held that there was no liability when they were given additional publicity, as to matters legitimately within the scope of the public interest they had aroused.

The privilege of giving publicity to news, and other matters of public interest, was held to arise out of the desire and the right of the public to know what is going on in the world, and the freedom of the press and other agencies of information to tell it. "News" includes all events and items of information which are out of the ordinary humdrum routine, and which have "that indefinable quality of information which arouses public attention."[22] To a very great extent the press, with its experience or instinct as to what its readers will want, has succeeded in making its own definition of news, as a glance at any morning newspaper will sufficiently indicate. It includes homicide[23] and other crimes,[24] arrests[25] and po-

---

10. Cason v. Baskin, 1947, 159 Fla. 31, 30 So.2d 635, 638.

11. Paramount Pictures v. Leader Press, W.D.Okl. 1938, 24 F.Supp. 1004, reversed on other grounds, 10th Cir. 1939, 106 F.2d 229; Chaplin v. National Broadcasting Co., S.D.N.Y.1953, 15 F.R.D. 134.

12. Ruth v. Educational Films, 1920, 194 App.Div. 893, 184 N.Y.S. 948. Cf. O'Brien v. Pabst Sales Co., 5th Cir. 1941, 124 F.2d 167, certiorari denied 315 U.S. 823, 62 S.Ct. 917, 86 L.Ed. 1220.

13. Jeffries v. New York Evening Journal Publishing Co., 1910, 67 Misc. 570, 124 N.Y.S. 780; Cohen v. Marx, 1950, 94 Cal.App.2d 704, 211 P.2d 320; Oma v. Hillman Periodicals, 1953, 281 App.Div. 240, 118 N.Y.S.2d 720.

14. Colyer v. Richard K. Fox Publishing Co., 1914, 162 App.Div. 297, 146 N.Y.S. 999 (high diver); Koussevitzky v. Allen, Towne & Heath, 1947, 188 Misc. 479, 68 N.Y.S.2d 779, affirmed 1947, 272 App.Div. 759, 69 N.Y.S.2d 432, appeal denied 272 App.Div. 794, 71 N.Y.S.2d 712 (symphony conductor); Gavrilov v. Duell, Sloan & Pearce, 1948, 84 N.Y.S.2d 320, affirmed 1950, 276 App.Div. 826, 93 N.Y.S.2d 715 (dancer); Redmond v. Columbia Pictures Corp., 1938, 277 N.Y. 707, 14 N.E.2d 636 (trick shot golfer).

15. Martin v. Dorton, 1951, 210 Miss. 668, 50 So.2d 391 (sheriff); Hull v. Curtis Publishing Co., 1956, 182 Pa.Super. 86, 125 A.2d 644 (arrest by policeman).

16. Corliss v. E.W. Walker Co., D.Mass.1894, 64 F. 280.

17. Smith v. Suratt, 1926, 7 Alaska 416.

18. Stryker v. Republic Pictures Corp., 1951, 108 Cal.App.2d 191, 238 P.2d 670; cf. Molony v. Boy Comics Publishers, 1950, 277 App.Div. 166, 98 N.Y.S.2d 119 (heroic rescuer).

19. See Continental Optical Co. v. Reed, 1949, 119 Ind.App. 643, 86 N.E.2d 306, rehearing denied 119 Ind. App. 643, 88 N.E.2d 55.

20. Sidis v. F-R Publishing Corp., 2d Cir. 1940, 113 F.2d 806, certiorari denied 311 U.S. 711, 61 S.Ct. 393, 85 L.Ed. 462.

21. Wilson v. Brown, 1947, 189 Misc. 79, 73 N.Y.S. 2d 587.

22. Sweenek v. Pathe News, E.D.N.Y.1936, 16 F.Supp. 746, 747. See Note, 1963, 30 U.Chi.L.Rev. 722.

23. Jones v. Herald Post Co., 1929, 230 Ky. 227, 18 S.W.2d 972; Bremmer v. Journal-Tribune Co., 1956, 247 Iowa 817, 76 N.W.2d 762; Waters v. Fleetwood, 1956, 212 Ga. 161, 91 S.E.2d 344; Jenkins v. Dell Pub-

24 & 25. See notes 24 and 25 on page 861.

lice raids,[26] suicides,[27] marriages[28] and divorces,[29] accidents,[30] a death from the use of narcotics,[31] a woman with a rare disease,[32] the birth of a child to a twelve year old girl,[33] the reappearance of one supposed to have been murdered years ago,[34] and undoubtedly many other similar matters of genuine, if more or less deplorable, popular appeal.[35]

The privilege of enlightening the public was not, however, limited to the dissemination of news in the sense of current events. It extended also to information or education, or even entertainment and amusement,[36] by books, articles, pictures, films and broadcasts concerning interesting phases of human activity in general,[37] as well as the reproduction of the public scene in newsreels and travelogues.[38] In determining where to draw the line, the courts were invited to exercise a species of censorship over what the public may be permitted to read; and they were understandably liberal in allowing the benefit of the doubt.

Caught up and entangled in this web of news and public interest were a great many people who had not sought publicity, but indeed, as in the case of any accused criminal, had tried assiduously to avoid it. They had nevertheless lost some part of their right of privacy. The misfortunes of the frantic victim of sexual assault,[39] the woman whose husband was murdered before her eyes,[40] or the innocent bystander who was caught in a raid on a cigar store and mistaken by the police for the proprietor,[41] could be broadcast to the world, and they had no remedy. Such individuals became public figures for a sea-

---

lishing Co., W.D.Pa.1956, 143 F.Supp. 952, affirmed 3d Cir. 1958, 251 F.2d 447, certiorari denied 357 U.S. 921, 78 S.Ct. 1362, 2 L.Ed.2d 1365; Bernstein v. National Broadcasting Co., D.D.C.1935, 129 F.Supp. 817, affirmed 1956, 98 U.S.App.D.C. 112, 232 F.2d 369, certiorari denied 352 U.S. 945, 77 S.Ct. 267, 1 L.Ed.2d 239.

24. Elmhurst v. Pearson, 1946, 80 U.S.App.D.C. 372, 153 F.2d 467 (sedition); Miller v. National Broadcasting Co., D.Del.1956, 157 F.Supp. 240 (robbery); Hillman v. Star Publishing Co., 1911, 64 Wash. 691, 117 P. 594 (mail fraud).

25. Frith v. Associated Press, E.D.S.C.1959, 176 F.Supp. 671; Coverstone v. Davies, 1952, 38 Cal.2d 315, 239 P.2d 876, certiorari dismissed Mock v. Davies, 344 U.S. 840, 73 S.Ct. 50, 97 L.Ed. 653; Hull v. Curtis Publishing Co., 1956, 182 Pa.Super. 86, 125 A.2d 644.

26. Jacova v. Southern Radio & Television Co., Fla. 1955, 83 So.2d 34; cf. Schnabel v. Meredith, 1956, 378 Pa. 609, 107 A.2d 860.

27. Metter v. Los Angeles Examiner, 1939, 35 Cal. App.2d 304, 95 P.2d 491; Samuel v. Curtis Publishing Co., N.D.Cal.1954, 122 F.Supp. 327 (attempted).

28. Aquino v. Bulletin Co., 1959, 190 Pa.Super. 528, 154 A.2d 422.

29. Berg v. Minneapolis Star & Tribune Co., D.Minn.1948, 79 F.Supp. 957; Aquino v. Bulletin Co., 1959, 190 Pa.Super. 528, 154 A.2d 422.

30. Kelley v. Post Publishing Co., 1951, 327 Mass. 275, 98 N.E.2d 286; cf. Strickler v. National Broadcasting Co., S.D.Cal.1958, 167 F.Supp. 68.

31. Rozhon v. Triangle Publications, 7th Cir. 1956, 230 F.2d 359. Cf. Abernethy v. Thornton, 1955, 263 Ala. 496, 83 So.2d 235 (death of criminal paroled for federal offense).

32. See Barber v. Time, Inc., 1942, 348 Mo. 1199, 159 S.W.2d 291.

33. Meetze v. Associated Press, 1956, 230 S.C. 330, 95 S.E.2d 606.

34. Smith v. Doss, 1948, 251 Ala. 250, 37 So.2d 118.

35. Smith v. National Broadcasting Co., 1956, 138 Cal.App.2d 807, 292 P.2d 600 (report to police concerning escape of black panther); Themo v. New England Newspaper Publishing Co., 1940, 306 Mass. 54, 27 N.E.2d 753 (unspecified).

36. Ruth v. Educational Films, 1920, 194 App.Div. 893, 184 N.Y.S. 948 (baseball); Sweenek v. Pathe News, E.D.N.Y.1936, 16 F.Supp. 746 (group of fat women reducing with novel and comical apparatus) and see Jenkins v. Dell Publishing Co., W.D.Pa.1956, 143 F.Supp. 952, affirmed 3d Cir. 1958, 251 F.2d 447, certiorari denied 357 U.S. 921, 78 S.Ct. 1362, 2 L.Ed.2d 1365.

37. Kline v. Robert M. McBride & Co., 1939, 170 Misc. 974, 11 N.Y.S.2d 674 (strike-breaking); Samuel v. Curtis Publishing Co., N.D.Cal.1954, 122 F.Supp. 327 (suicide); Hogan v. A.S. Barnes Co., Pa.C.P.1957, 114 U.S.P.Q. 314 (golf); Oma v. Hillman Periodicals, 1953, 281 App.Div. 240, 118 N.Y.S.2d 720 (boxing); Delinger v. American News Co., 1958, 6 A.D.2d 1027, 178 N.Y.S.2d 231 (muscular development and virility).

38. Humiston v. Universal Film Manufacturing Co., 1919, 189 App.Div. 467, 178 N.Y.S. 752. Accord: Gill v. Hearst Publishing Co., 1953, 40 Cal.2d 224, 253 P.2d 441; Berg v. Minneapolis Star & Tribune Co., D.Minn. 1948, 79 F.Supp. 957; Lyles v. State, Okl.Cr.1958, 330 P.2d 734.

39. Hubbard v. Journal Publishing Co., 1962, 69 N.M. 473, 368 P.2d 147.

40. Jones v. Herald Post Co., 1929, 230 Ky. 227, 18 S.W.2d 972.

41. Jacova v. Southern Radio & Television Co., Fla. 1955, 83 So.2d 34. Cf. Frith v. Associated Press, E.D. S.C.1959, 176 F.Supp. 671.

son; and "until they have reverted to the lawful and unexciting life led by the great bulk of the community, they are subject to the privileges which publishers have to satisfy the curiosity of the public as to their leaders, heroes, villains, and victims." [42] The privilege extended even to identification and some reasonable depiction of the individual's family,[43] although there must certainly be some limits as to their own private lives into which the publisher could not go.[44]

What was called for was some logical connection between the plaintiff and the matter of public interest. Perhaps the most extreme cases of the privilege were those in which the likeness of an individual were used to illustrate a book or an article on some general topic, rather than any specific event. Where this was appropriate and pertinent, as where the picture of a strikebreaker was used to illustrate a book on strike-breaking,[45] or that of a Hindu illusionist was employed to illustrate an article on the Indian rope trick,[46] it is held that there was no liability, since the public interest justified any invasion of privacy. On the other hand, where the illustration was not pertinent, and a connection was suggested which did not exist, as where the picture of a decent model appeared in connection with an article on "man hungry" women,[47] the plaintiff was placed in a false light, and might recover on that basis.[48]

The public figure concept as developed in these decisions on the right of privacy must not be confused with the later public figure concept developed by the Supreme Court as a basis for dealing with the constitutional privilege to publish false and defamatory speech. The courts were simply developing the notion that there was some room, but very little room, for the imposition of liability on the press for the publication of the truth; the point being that if the press thought there was enough justification for publication of the truth as news then it always would be in the public interest not to subject the press to harassing lawsuits about the appropriateness of a discrete publication.

The constitutional restrictions. The Supreme Court in Time, Inc. v. Hill [49] in 1967 recognized the possibility of tort liability for

42. First Restatement of Torts, § 867, Comment *f.*

43. Smith v. Doss, 1948, 251 Ala. 250, 37 So.2d 118 (family of man who disappeared, was believed murdered, and his body was brought home); Coverstone v. Davies, 1952, 38 Cal.2d 315, 239 P.2d 876, certiorari denied Mock v. Davies, 344 U.S. 840, 73 S.Ct. 50, 97 L.Ed. 653 (father of boy arrested for "hot-rod" racing); Kelley v. Post Publishing Co., 1951, 327 Mass. 275, 98 N.E.2d 286 (parents of girl killed in accident); Aquino v. Bulletin Co., 1959, 190 Pa.Super. 528, 154 A.2d 422 (parents of girl secretly married and then divorced); Jenkins v. Dell Publishing Co., W.D.Pa.1956, 143 F.Supp. 952, affirmed 3d Cir. 1958, 251 F.2d 447, certiorari denied 357 U.S. 921, 78 S.Ct. 1362, 2 L.Ed.2d 1365 (family of boy kicked to death by hoodlums).

44. This is indicated in Martin v. New Metropolitan Fiction, 1931, 139 Misc. 290, 248 N.Y.S. 359, affirmed 234 App.Div. 904, 254 N.Y.S. 1015 and Shiles v. News Syndicate Co., 1970, 27 N.Y.2d 9, 313 N.Y.S.2d 104, 261 N.E.2d 251, certiorari denied 400 U.S. 999, 91 S.Ct. 454, 27 L.Ed.2d 450.

45. People on Complaint of Stern v. Robert R. McBride & Co., 1936, 159 Misc. 5, 288 N.Y.S. 501; Kline v. Robert M. McBride & Co., 1939, 170 Misc. 974, 11 N.Y.S.2d 674. Cf. Klein v. McGraw-Hill, Inc., D.C.D.C. 1966, 263 F.Supp. 919 (picture of high school student who had made important contribution used in radio textbook); LaForge v. Fairchild Publications, 1965, 23 A.D.2d 636, 257 N.Y.S.2d 127 (picture of dressy individual used to illustrate article on current fashions).

46. Sarat Lahiri v. Daily Mirror, 1937, 162 Misc. 776, 295 N.Y.S. 382. Accord: Delinger v. American News Co., 1958, 6 A.D.2d 1027, 178 N.Y.S.2d 231 (physical training instructor, article on relation between muscular development and virility); Dallessandro v. Henry Holt & Co., 1957, 4 A.D.2d 470, 166 N.Y.S.2d 805, appeal dismissed 7 N.Y.2d 735, 193 N.Y.S.2d 635, 162 N.E.2d 726 (picture of plaintiff conversing with priest who was subject of the book); Oma v. Hillman Periodicals, 1953, 281 App.Div. 240, 118 N.Y.S.2d 720 (boxer, article on boxing); Gavrilov v. Duell, Sloan & Pearce, Sup.1948, 84 N.Y.S.2d 320, affirmed 276 App. Div. 826, 93 N.Y.S.2d 715 (dancer, book on dancing).

47. Martin v. Johnson Publishing Co., Sup.1956, 157 N.Y.S.2d 409. Accord, Peay v. Curtis Publishing Co., D.D.C.1948, 78 F.Supp. 305 (cheating taxi drivers).

48. Cf. Samuel v. Curtis Publishing Co., N.D.Cal. 1954, 122 F.Supp. 327 (picture of plaintiff arguing with a would-be suicide on a bridge properly used to illustrate article on suicide), with Metzger v. Dell Publishing Co., 1955, 207 Misc. 182, 136 N.Y.S.2d 888 (picture of boy in slums improperly used to illustrate article on juvenile delinquency).

49. 1967, 385 U.S. 374, 87 S.Ct. 534, 17 L.Ed.2d 456.

unwarranted publicity of the truth. In a footnote in which the Court cited Sidis v. F-R Publishing Corp.,[50] it was stated that "revelations may be so intimate and so unwarranted in view of the victim's position as to outrage the community's notion of decency."[51] However, the prospects of a privacy recovery, even within the limits of the *Sidis* principle of outrageous publicity, have been sharply curtailed in consequence of Cox Broadcasting Corp. v. Cohn decided by the Supreme Court in 1975.[52] There the Court said: "The First and Fourteenth Amendments command nothing less than that states may not impose sanctions for the publication of truthful information contained in official records open to public inspection."[53] As to disclosures of facts not a matter of public record—public or private—the opinion of the Court in Cox Broadcasting Corporation indicates receptivity to possible liability.[54]

False Light in the Public Eye

The third form of invasion of privacy consists of publicity which places the plaintiff in a false light in the public eye.[55] It seems to have made its first appearance in 1816, when Lord Byron succeeded in enjoining the circulation of a bad poem which had been attributed to his pen.[56] Over a good many years the principle made a rather nebulous appearance in a line of decisions[57] in which falsity or fiction was held to defeat the privilege of reporting news or other matters of public interest. It is only in late years that it has begun to receive independent recognition of its own.

One form in which it occasionally appears, as in Byron's case, is that of publicly attributing to the plaintiff some opinion or utterance, such as spurious books or articles,[58] or the unauthorized use of his name on a petition,[59] or as a candidate for office,[60] or to advertise for witnesses to an accident,[61] or the entry of an actor, without his consent, in a popularity contest of an embarrassing

50. 2d Cir. 1940, 113 F.2d 806, certiorari denied 311 U.S. 711, 61 S.Ct. 393, 85 L.Ed. 462.

51. 1967, 385 U.S. 374, 383 n. 7, 87 S.Ct. 534, 539 n. 7, 17 L.Ed.2d 456.

52. 1975, 420 U.S. 469, 95 S.Ct. 1029, 43 L.Ed.2d 328, on remand 234 Ga. 67, 214 S.E.2d 530.

53. 1975, 420 U.S. 469, 495, 95 S.Ct. 1029, 1046, 43 L.Ed.2d 328, on remand 234 Ga. 67, 214 S.E.2d 530.

54. 1975, 420 U.S. 469, 491, 95 S.Ct. 1029, 1044, 43 L.Ed.2d 328, on remand 234 Ga. 67, 214 S.E.2d 530. See, Hill, Defamation and Privacy Under the First Amendment, 1976, 76 Colum.L.Rev. 1205, 1268.

55. See, generally, Wade, Defamation and the Right of Privacy, 1962, 15 Vand.L.Rev. 1093; Note, 1962, 50 Cal.L.Rev. 357.

56. Lord Byron v. Johnston, 1816, 2 Mer. 29, 35 Eng.Rep. 851.

57. See the following cases: Martin v. Johnson Publishing Co., Sup.1956, 157 N.Y.S.2d 409; Peay v. Curtis Publishing Co., D.D.C.1948, 78 F.Supp. 305 (cheating taxi drivers); Samuel v. Curtis Publishing Co., N.D.Cal. 1954, 122 F.Supp. 327 (picture of plaintiff arguing with a would-be suicide on a bridge properly used to illustrate article on suicide); Metzger v. Dell Publishing Co., 1955, 207 Misc. 182, 136 N.Y.S.2d 888 (picture of boy in slums improperly used to illustrate article on juvenile delinquency).

58. D'Altomonte v. New York Herald Co., 1913, 154 App.Div. 453, 139 N.Y.S. 200, modified, as not within the New York statute in 1913, 208 N.Y. 596, 102 N.E. 1101; Goldberg v. Ideal Publishing Corp., Sup.1960, 210 N.Y.S.2d 928; Hogan v. A.S. Barnes & Co., Pa.C.P. 1957, 114 U.S.P.Q. 314; cf. Kerby v. Hal Roach Studios, 1942, 53 Cal.App.2d 207, 127 P.2d 577. See Wigmore, The Right Against False Attribution of Belief or Utterance, 1916, 4 Ky.L.J. No. 8, p. 3.

Compare, as to the use of fictitious testimonials in advertising, Pavesich v. New England Life Insurance Co., 1905, 122 Ga. 190, 50 S.E. 68; Manger v. Kree Institute of Electrolysis, Inc., 2d Cir. 1956, 233 F.2d 5; Foster-Milburn Co. v. Chinn, 1909, 134 Ky. 424, 120 S.W. 364; Fairfield v. American Photocopy Equipment Co., 1955, 138 Cal.App.2d 82, 291 P.2d 194.

59. Schwartz v. Edrington, 1913, 133 La. 235, 62 So. 660. Accord, Hinish v. Meier & Frank Co., 1941, 166 Or. 482, 113 P.2d 438 (telegram to governor urging him to veto a bill).

60. State ex rel. La Follette v. Hinkle, 1924, 131 Wash. 86, 229 P. 317; Battaglia v. Adams, Fla.1964, 164 So.2d 195.

61. Hamilton v. Lumbermen's Mutual Casualty Co., La.App.1955, 82 So.2d 61, appeal transferred 226 La. 644, 76 So.2d 916.

kind,[62] or filing suit in the plaintiff's name without authorization.[63]

Another form in which it frequently appears is the use of the plaintiff's picture to illustrate a book or an article with which he has no reasonable connection, with the implication that such a connection exists—as where, for example, the face of an honest taxi driver is used to ornament a story about the cheating propensities of taxi drivers in the city.[64] Still another is the inclusion of the plaintiff's name, photograph or fingerprints in a public "rogue's gallery" of convicted criminals, when he has not in fact been convicted of any crime.[65]

The false light need not necessarily be a defamatory one,[66] although it very often is,[67] so that a defamation action will also lie. It seems clear, however, that it must be something that would be objectionable to the ordinary reasonable person under the circumstances, and that, as in the case of disclosure,[68] the hypersensitive individual will not be protected.[69] Thus minor and unimportant errors in an otherwise accurate biography, as to dates and places, and incidents of no significance, do not entitle the subject of the book to recover,[70] nor does the erroneous description of the plaintiff as a cigarette girl when an inquiring photographer interviews her on the street.[71] Again, in all probability, something of a "mores" test must be applied.

The action for defamation and the action for invasion of privacy should be carefully distinguished. The former is to protect a person's interest in a good reputation, and recovery is to be made available on the basis of legal concepts set forth in Chapter 19. The latter is to protect a person's interest in being let alone and is available when there has been publicity of a kind that is highly offensive.

It is suggested that virtually all actionable invasions of privacy have been intentional invasions or invasions of a kind that defendant

62. Marks v. Jaffa, 1893, 6 Misc. 290, 26 N.Y.S. 908.

63. Steding v. Battistoni, 1964, 3 Conn.Cir. 76, 208 A.2d 559.

64. Peay v. Curtis Publishing Co., D.D.C.1948, 78 F.Supp. 305. Accord: Valerni v. Hearst Magazines, Sup.1949, 99 N.Y.S.2d 866 (similar as to waiters); Leverton v. Curtis Publishing Co., 3d Cir. 1951, 192 F.2d 974 (negligence of children); Gill v. Curtis Publishing Co., 1952, 38 Cal.2d 273, 239 P.2d 630 (profane love); Martin v. Johnson Publishing Co., Sup.1956, 157 N.Y.S.2d 409 ("man hungry" women); Metzger v. Dell Publishing Co., 1955, 207 Misc. 182, 136 N.Y.S.2d 888 (juvenile delinquents).

65. Itzkovitch v. Whitaker, 1950, 115 La. 479, 39 So. 499; see Downs v. Swann, 1909, 111 Md. 53, 73 A. 653; State ex rel. Mavity v. Tyndall, 1946, 224 Ind. 364, 66 N.E.2d 755; Norman v. City of Las Vegas, 1947, 64 Nev. 38, 177 P.2d 442.

Distinguish the use of the picture for identification before trial, or after conviction. Hodgeman v. Olsen, 1915, 86 Wash. 615, 150 P. 1122; Bartletta v. McFeeley, 1930, 107 N.J.Eq. 141, 152 A. 17, affirmed 1931, 109 N.J.Eq. 241, 156 A. 658; cf. McGovern v. Van Riper, 1945, 137 N.J.Eq. 24, 43 A.2d 514, affirmed 1946, 137 N.J.Eq. 548, 45 A.2d 842 (fingerprints).

66. See Zolich, Laudatory Invasion of Privacy, 1967, 16 Clev.Marsh.L.Rev. 540.

67. Bennett v. Norban, 1959, 396 Pa. 94, 151 A.2d 476 (public accusation of theft); Linehan v. Linehan, 1955, 134 Cal.App.2d 250, 285 P.2d 326 (public statement plaintiff not a lawful wife); D'Altomonte v. New York Herald Co., 1913, 154 App.Div. 453, 139 N.Y.S. 200, modified 208 N.Y. 596, 102 N.E. 1101 (imputing authorship of absurd story); Martin v. Johnson Publishing Co., Sup.1956, 157 N.Y.S.2d 409 ("man hungry" women); Russell v. Marboro Books, 1959, 18 Misc.2d 166, 183 N.Y.S.2d 8 (picture used in bawdy advertisement).

68. See, supra, this section on Public Disclosure of Private Facts.

69. Carlisle v. Fawcett Publications, Inc., 1962, 201 Cal.App.2d 733, 20 Cal.Rptr. 405. In Strickler v. National Broadcasting Co., S.D.Cal.1958, 167 F.Supp. 68, it was left to the jury whether fictitious details of plaintiff's conduct in an airplane crisis, as portrayed in a broadcast, would be objectionable to a reasonable person.

70. Koussevitzky v. Allen, Towne & Heath, 1947, 188 Misc. 479, 68 N.Y.S.2d 779, affirmed 272 App.Div. 759, 69 N.Y.S.2d 432, appeal denied 272 App.Div. 794, 71 N.Y.S.2d 712. Cf. Carlisle v. Fawcett Publications, Inc., 1962, 201 Cal.App.2d 733, 20 Cal.Rptr. 405.

71. Middleton v. News Syndicate Co., 1937, 162 Misc. 516, 295 N.Y.S. 120. Accord: Molony v. Boy Comics Publishers, 1950, 277 App.Div. 166, 98 N.Y.S.2d 119; Reardon v. News-Journal Co., Del.1960, 3 Storey 29, 164 A.2d 263; Werner v. Times-Mirror Co., 1961, 193 Cal.App.2d 111, 14 Cal.Rptr. 208. It would appear, however, that this was carried entirely too far in Jones v. Herald Post Co., 1929, 230 Ky. 227, 18 S.W.2d 972, where in an account of the murder of plaintiff's husband false and sensational statements were attributed to her, that she had fought with the criminals, and would have killed them if she could.

knew or had reason to know would not only be offensive but highly so and are therefore examples of outrageous conduct that was committed with knowledge or with reason to know that it would cause severe mental stress. Recovery for an invasion of privacy on the ground that the plaintiff was depicted in a false light makes sense only when the account, if true, would not have been actionable as an invasion of privacy. In other words, the outrageous character of the publicity comes about in part by virtue of the fact that some part of the matter reported was false and deliberately so. Most people are offended by fictionalized accounts of events in which they were involved as involuntary or even voluntary participants. Whether or not an action for defamation will lie is not really relevant. It is possible that one or more of the false statements made in a fictionalized report is defamatory. If so, it is quite possible that an action for defamation is available. But a false statement may be defamatory and yet may make publicity about an event or matter actionable as an invasion of privacy; more importantly, it may not be defamatory and it may still make the publicity actionable as an invasion of privacy. This is the position that has been adopted in the *Second Restatement of Torts*. It is there said that the publicity must be the kind that would be highly offensive to a reasonable person.[72] This position of the *Restatement* is well illustrated by two of the cases that have reached the Supreme Court on the constitutional issue of freedom of the press under the First Amendment.

The constitutional privilege and false light claims. In 1967, in Time, Inc. v. Hill,[73] the Supreme Court extended the constitutional privilege of freedom of the press to include this type of invasion of privacy.[74] The plaintiff's home had been invaded in 1952 by three escaped convicts, and he and his family had been held prisoners for nineteen hours. In 1953, a writer published a novel about the incident, in which he resorted to several elements of pure fiction; and later, the novel was made into a play, which contained the same elements of fiction.[75] In 1955, *Life* magazine published an article about the play, with the pictures from it, which portrayed the play as a reenactment of the actual experience of the Hill family, who were named. In an action under the New York statute, for invasion of privacy, the New York courts held that there was liability because of the false statements of fact.[76] On certiorari, the analogy of defamation was manifest and persuasive; and the Supreme Court applied the rule of New York Times Co. v. Sullivan,[77] holding the publication to be privileged unless it was found that the false statements were made by the defendant with knowledge of falsity or reckless disregard of the truth.

Somewhat similar to the *Times* case was Cantrell v. Forest City Publishing Co.[78] In that case, the Supreme Court sustained a recovery on a false light theory. Recovery was based upon a newspaper report concerning a destitute family of the victim of a bridge disaster. The story was published almost eight months after the disaster itself. So the public had very little interest, as such, in a republication of the matter at such time. In essence, the Court stated that in publishing the false feature story, the defendant made the plaintiffs objects of pity and ridicule and caused them to suffer great mental stress and humiliation. The Court held that the newspaper could constitutional-

---

72. Section 652D and Comment *c.*

73. 1967, 385 U.S. 374, 87 S.Ct. 534, 17 L.Ed.2d 456.

74. Id.

75. Neither the novel nor the play named or in any way identified the Hill family, so that there was no action for invasion of privacy.

76. The last New York decision was Hill v. Hayes, 1965, 15 N.Y.2d 986, 260 N.Y.S.2d 7, 207 N.E.2d 604, amended 16 N.Y.2d 658, 261 N.Y.S.2d 289, 209 N.E.2d 282, set aside Time, Inc. v. Hill, 1967, 385 U.S. 374, 87 S.Ct. 534, 17 L.Ed.2d 456.

77. 1964, 376 U.S. 254, 84 S.Ct. 710, 11 L.Ed.2d 686, motion denied 376 U.S. 967, 84 S.Ct. 1130, 12 L.Ed.2d 83.

78. 1974, 419 U.S. 245, 95 S.Ct. 465, 42 L.Ed.2d 419

ly be held vicariously liable for the conduct of its agents in knowingly placing the plaintiffs in a false light.

Applicability of defamation restrictions. When the false publicity is defamatory, it is at least arguable that limitations of long standing that have been found desirable for the action for defamation should not be successfully evaded by proceeding upon a different theory of later origin.[79] These restrictions may include the requirement that special damage be proved when the publication of the defamatory matter is not actionable per se. It may also include restrictions imposed by retraction statutes. But the restrictions applicable to the defamation action are not necessarily applicable when it is established that the defendant knowingly publicized false and defamatory matter that made the publicity highly offensive as an invasion of the plaintiff's interest in being let alone. It is enough in such a case that the publicity is likely to cause and does cause severe emotional stress and not because of the amount of harm to reputation that is likely to result. This tort is much more likely to be utilized in those cases where the false statement is not defamatory. If the false statement is defamatory, the plaintiff will usually have a better chance of recovery on a defamation theory than on a privacy theory, especially if the plaintiff is a private person because negligence with respect to truth or falsity will satisfy both the constitutional and common law requirements for recovery. This is not likely to be the case as regards this tort. The outrageous nature of the defendant's conduct arises in large part from the fact that the account about the plaintiff was deliberately falsified in order to enhance the sensational character of the story. Usually, the plaintiff will either be a private person who was catapulted into prominence by being involuntarily involved in a tragic or newsworthy event, or a public official or public figure involuntarily involved in a matter that did not affect his fitness or role in his public capacity. All of this being true, it appears likely that a prerequisite to recovery by anyone on this false light basis will be the requirement that the defendant publish the false statements with knowledge of the falsity or recklessly.

Constitutional Expansion

Not long after 1950, the Supreme Court of the United States began, in cases of criminal prosecutions raising questions about improper actions of government officers, to talk of a "constitutional" right of privacy which protected the individual against such acts.[80] These were cases of what might fairly be called "intrusions," [81] but in Griswold v. Connecticut [82] in 1965 the Court held unconstitutional a statute prohibiting the giving of contraceptive information on the ground that it deprived married couples of a "right of privacy" guaranteed by the Constitution.

The "zone of privacy," so to speak, that is now safeguarded by the Constitution when state action is involved has been enlarged in recent years. It embraces not only the interests protected by the common law action, as discussed in this chapter, but it also protects to a considerable extent the autonomy of the individual to make certain important decisions of a very personal nature. This latter interest—the personal autonomy interest—generally relates to matters of mar-

---

79. Second Restatement of Torts, § 652E, Comment e.

80. Although preceded by Wolf v. People of the State of Colorado, 1949, 338 U.S. 25, 69 S.Ct. 1359, 93 L.Ed. 1782, the leading case of this type is Rochin v. California, 1952, 342 U.S. 165, 72 S.Ct. 205, 96 L.Ed. 183 where a stomach pump was used on a protesting individual accused of crime. See also Tehan v. United States ex rel. Shott, 1966, 382 U.S. 406, 86 S.Ct. 459, 15 L.Ed.2d 453, rehearing denied 383 U.S. 931, 86 S.Ct. 925, 15 L.Ed.2d 850; Beaney, The Constitutional Right to Privacy in the Supreme Court, [1962] Sup.Ct.Rev. 212; Long, The Right to Privacy: The Case Against the Government, 1965, 10 St.L.L.Rev. 1.

81. See supra, this section on Intrusion.

82. 1965, 381 U.S. 479, 85 S.Ct. 1678, 14 L.Ed.2d 510. See Beaney, The Griswold Case and the Expanding Right to Privacy, [1966] Wis.L.Rev. 979; Symposium, 1965, 64 Mich.L.Rev. 197 Notes, 1966, 38 U.Colo.L.Rev. 267; [1966] Duke L.J. 562.

riage, procreation, contraception, family relationships, child rearing, and education.[83]

No effort is being made here to discuss the contours of this constitutional right of privacy. It must be recognized, however, that it is now well established that damages by way of tort actions will be available to plaintiffs whose constitutional privacy rights have been violated by public agents, and others where state action is involved, and who cannot successfully defend on the basis of some kind of an immunity.[84]

Defenses

There would seem to be no real affirmative defenses to engaging in highly offensive invasions of privacy. It has been said that chief among the defenses at common law is the plaintiff's consent to the invasion. But there would be no offensive invasion of privacy if the plaintiff consented. So, in fact, plaintiff would have to show that the invasion was without his or her consent. It is reasonably clear that consent to particular conduct will prevent that conduct from constituting an actionable invasion.[85] It may be given expressly or by conduct, such as posing for a picture with knowledge of the purposes for which it is to be used,[86] or industriously seeking publicity of the same kind.[87]

A gratuitous consent can be revoked at any time before the invasion;[88] but if the agreement is a matter of contract, it is normally irrevocable, and there is no liability for any publicity or appropriation within its terms.[89] But if the actual invasion goes beyond the contract, fairly construed, as for example by alteration of the plaintiff's picture,[90] or publicity differing materially in kind or in extent from that contemplated,[91] or exceeding the authorized duration,[92] there

---

83. Whalen v. Roe, 1977, 429 U.S. 589, 599–600, 97 S.Ct. 869, 876, 51 L.Ed.2d 64; Paul v. Davis, 1976, 424 U.S. 693, 713, 96 S.Ct. 1155, 1166, 47 L.Ed.2d 405, rehearing denied 425 U.S. 985, 96 S.Ct. 2194, 48 L.Ed.2d 811; Roe v. Wade, 1973, 410 U.S. 113, 93 S.Ct. 705, 35 L.Ed.2d 147, rehearing denied 410 U.S. 959, 93 S.Ct. 1409, 35 L.Ed.2d 694.

84. Bivens v. Six Unknown Named Agents of Federal Bureau of Narcotics, 1971, 403 U.S. 388, 91 S.Ct. 1999, 29 L.Ed.2d 619; Birnbaum v. United States, E.D.N.Y.1977, 436 F.Supp. 967, affirmed in part, reversed in part 2d Cir., 588 F.2d 319; Doe v. United States Civil Service Commission, S.D.N.Y.1980, 483 F.Supp. 539; see also, Whitman, Constitutional Torts, 1980, 79 Mich. L.Rev. 5. Congress passed a Civil Rights Act in 1871 and that statute is now codified as 42 U.S.C.A. § 1983. The statute authorized civil damage actions against those who "under color of state law" deprived others of constitutional rights. In Price v. Shepard, Minn. 1976, 239 N.W.2d 905, the Supreme Court held that a medical director assuming custody and care of a mentally ill minor pursuant to involuntary commitment would, for future cases, be subject to liability for violating the minor's constitutional right of privacy for utilizing electroshock therapy.

85. Grossman v. Frederick Brothers, Artists Corp., Sup.Ct.1942, 34 N.Y.S.2d 785; Jenkins v. Dell Publishing Co., W.D.Pa.1956, 143 F.Supp. 952, affirmed 3d Cir. 1958, 251 F.2d 447, certiorari denied 357 U.S. 921, 78 S.Ct. 1362, 2 L.Ed.2d 1365; Reitmeister v. Reitmeister, 2d Cir. 1947, 162 F.2d 691; Tanner-Brice Co. v. Sims, 1931, 174 Ga. 13, 161 S.E. 819; Volk v. Auto-Dine Corp., N.D.1970, 177 N.W.2d 525.

86. Gill v. Hearst Publishing Co., 1953, 40 Cal.2d 224, 253 P.2d 441; Thayer v. Worcester Post Co., 1933, 284 Mass. 160, 187 N.E. 292; Wendell v. Conduit Machine Co., 1911, 74 Misc. 201, 133 N.Y.S. 758; Johnson v. Boeing Airplane Co., 1953, 175 Kan. 275, 262 P.2d 808.

87. O'Brien v. Pabst Sales Co., 5th Cir. 1941, 124 F.2d 167, certiorari denied 315 U.S. 823, 62 S.Ct. 917, 86 L.Ed. 1220; Gautier v. Pro-Football, Inc., 1952, 304 N.Y. 354, 107 N.E.2d 485. Cf. Schmieding v. American Farmers Mutual Insurance Co., D.Neb.1955, 138 F.Supp. 167 (failure to object).

88. Garden v. Parfumerie Rigaud, 1933, 151 Misc. 692, 271 N.Y.S. 187; State ex rel. La Follette v. Hinkle, 1924, 131 Wash. 86, 229 P. 317.

89. Lillie v. Warner Brothers Pictures, 1934, 139 Cal.App. 724, 34 P.2d 835; Long v. Decca Records, Sup.1947, 76 N.Y.S.2d 133; Fairbanks v. Winik, 1922, 119 Misc. 809, 198 N.Y.S. 299, reversed on other grounds 1923, 206 App.Div. 449, 201 N.Y.S. 487; Marek v. Zanol Products Co., 1937, 298 Mass. 1, 9 N.E.2d 393; Johnson v. Boeing Airplane Co., 1953, 175 Kan. 275, 262 P.2d 808.

90. Cf. Manger v. Kree Institute of Electrolysis, 2d Cir.1956, 233 F.2d 5 (letter); Myers v. Afro-American Publishing Co., 1938, 168 Misc. 429, 5 N.Y.S.2d 223, affirmed 1938, 255 App.Div. 838, 7 N.Y.S.2d 662.

91. Ettore v. Philco Television Broadcasting Co., 3d Cir. 1956, 229 F.2d 481, certiorari denied 351 U.S. 926, 76 S.Ct. 783, 100 L.Ed. 1456; Sinclair v. Postal Telegraph & Cable Co., Sup.1935, 72 N.Y.S.2d 841; Russell v. Marboro Books, 1959, 18 Misc.2d 166, 183 N.Y.S.2d 8; Smith v. WGN, Inc., 1964, 47 Ill.App.2d 183, 197 N.E.2d 482.

92. Colgate-Palmolive Co. v. Tullos, 5th Cir. 1955, 219 F.2d 617; McAndrews v. Roy, La.App.1961, 131 So. 2d 256. See Note, 1962, 8 Wayne L.Rev. 348.

is liability. The statutes [93] all require that the consent be given in writing. The defendant's honest belief that he has the plaintiff's consent, when he has not, will go to mitigate punitive damages, but otherwise is not a defense.[94]

Other defenses have appeared only infrequently. Warren and Brandeis [95] thought that the action for invasion of privacy must be subject to any privilege which would justify the publication of libel or slander, reasoning that if there is a privilege to publish matter which is both false and defamatory, there must necessarily be the same privilege to publish what is not defamatory, or true. There is still no reason to doubt this conclusion, since the absolute privilege of a witness,[96] or an executive officer in the performance of his duty,[97] as well as the qualified one to report public proceedings,[98] have been recognized. The qualified privilege of the defendant to protect or further his own legitimate interest has appeared in a few cases, as where a telephone company has been permitted to monitor calls,[99] or the defendant was allowed to make use of the plaintiff's name in insuring his life without his consent.[1] Unquestionably reasonable investigations of credit,[2] or of insurance claims [3] are privileged.

It has been held that where uncopyrighted literature is in the public domain, and the defendant is free to publish it, the name of the plaintiff may be used to indicate its authorship,[4] and that when the plaintiff has designed dresses for the defendant, it is no invasion of his privacy to disclose his connection with the product in advertising.[5]

WESTLAW REFERENCES

digest("right of privacy")
brandeis /5 warren /s right +s privacy
roberson /5 rochester /15 171 64 /3 538 442

Appropriation

privacy /p appropriat! exploit! /s name likeness image* photograph*

Unreasonable Intrusion

privacy /p objectionable offensive /s reasonable /s person* man % title(people state)

Public Disclosure of Private Facts

public** /s disclos! /s private /s fact* information & privacy % title(state people)

The Common Law

restatement /5 torts /5 652

---

93. Supra, this section, note 17, p. 851.

94. Fisher v. Murray M. Rosenberg, Inc., 1940, 175 Misc. 370, 23 N.Y.S.2d 677; Barber v. Time, Inc., 1942, 348 Mo. 1199, 159 S.W.2d 291; Wilk v. Andrea Radio Corp., Sup.1960, 200 N.Y.S.2d 522, modified 1961, 13 A.D.2d 745, 216 N.Y.S.2d 662.

95. Warren and Brandeis, The Right to Privacy, 1890, 4 Harv.L.Rev. 193, 216.

96. Application of Tiene, 1955, 19 N.J. 149, 115 A.2d 543.

97. Carr v. Watkins, 1962, 227 Md. 578, 177 A.2d 841; Sellers v. Henry, Ky.1959, 329 S.W.2d 214.

98. Reardon v. News-Journal Co., Del.1960, 3 Storey 29, 164 A.2d 263 (court); cf. Johnson v. Scripps Publishing Co., 1940, 6 Ohio Supp. 13 (filing nominating petition for office); Langford v. Vanderbilt University, 1956, 199 Tenn. 389, 287 S.W.2d 32 (pleadings in civil suit); Lyles v. State, Okl.Cr.1958, 330 P.2d 734 (television in courtroom); Blount v. TD Publishing Co., 1967, 77 N.M. 384, 423 P.2d 421 (news distributor not liable where no knowledge of the invasion).

99. Schmukler v. Ohio-Bell Telephone Co., Ohio C.P. 1953, 116 N.E.2d 819. Accord: Thomas v. General Electric Co., W.D.Ky.1962, 207 F.Supp. 792 (time and motion studies of employees); People v. Appelbaum, 1950, 277 App.Div. 43, 97 N.Y.S.2d 807, affirmed 301 N.Y. 738, 95 N.E.2d 410 (tapping own telephone to protect own interests); Wheeler v. P. Sorenson Manufacturing Co., Ky.1967, 415 S.W.2d 582 (publication of wages and deductions of employees to combat drive by union); City of University Heights v. Conley, 1969, 20 Ohio Misc. 112, 252 N.E.2d 198 (spying on suspected thief).

1. Holloman v. Life Insurance Co. of Va., 1940, 192 S.C. 454, 7 S.E.2d 169.

2. Shorter v. Retail Credit Co., D.C.S.C.1966, 251 F.Supp. 329. See Note, 1969, 57 Geo.L.J. 509.

3. Tucker v. American Employers' Insurance Co., Fla.App.1965, 171 So.2d 437. See Alabama Electric Cooperative, Inc. v. Partridge, 1969, 284 Ala. 442, 225 So. 2d 848; Forster v. Manchester, 1963, 410 Pa. 192, 189 A.2d 147; and cf. Bodrey v. Cape, 1970, 120 Ga.App. 859, 172 S.E.2d 643 (father deprived of custody of child investigating wife). See Note, 1964, 17 Vand.L.Rev. 1342.

4. Ellis v. Hurst, 1910, 70 Misc. 122, 128 N.Y.S. 144, affirmed 1911, 145 App.Div. 918, 130 N.Y.S. 1110; Shostakovitch v. Twentieth-Century Fox Film Corp., 1948, 196 Misc. 67, 80 N.Y.S.2d 575, affirmed 1949, 275 App.Div. 692, 87 N.Y.S.2d 430.

5. Brociner v. Radio Wire Television, Inc., 1959, 15 Misc.2d 843, 183 N.Y.S.2d 743.

privacy /p hypersensitive supersensitive % title(people state)

The Press, Public Figures, and News
"right of privacy" /s public /2 figure* offic!

Constitutional Restrictions
"right of privacy" /s free! /s press
time /5 hill /15 385 /3 374
headnote(constitution! /s privacy) % topic(110) title (people state)

False Light In the Public Eye
privacy /p false /s light /s public /s eye
privacy /s "false light"

The Constitutional Privilege and False Light Claims
privacy /p "false light" /p constitution! % topic(110)

privacy /p reckless /s disregard /s truth
privacy /p knowledge /s falsity
times /5 sullivan /15 376 /3 254 /p privacy

Constitutional Expansion
griswold /5 connecticut /p privacy
"zone of privacy" % topic(110)

Defenses
defense* /s privacy % topic(110)
affirmative /s defense* /s invasion* right /s privacy
synopsis,digest(defense* /p invasion* right /s privacy)

Chapter 21

MISUSE OF LEGAL PROCEDURE

Table of Sections

Sec.
119. Malicious Prosecution.
120. Wrongful Civil Proceedings.
121. Abuse of Process.

§ 119. Malicious Prosecution

The interest in freedom from unjustifiable litigation is protected by actions for malicious prosecution and abuse of process. Since one who is wrongfully prosecuted may suffer both in reputation and by confinement, these actions bear considerable resemblance to claims for defamation and false imprisonment. Since a wrongful prosecution may be pursued under color of state law, the malicious prosecution action also bears at times a strong resemblance to a federal civil rights action. The elements of these several actions, as well as the defenses to them, differ one from another, and for this reason care must be taken to distinguish them.[1]

In malicious prosecution cases themselves, the emphasis is upon the misuse of criminal—and sometimes civil [2]—actions as a means for causing harm. For example, a store guard has plaintiff prosecuted for shoplifting, though there is no reasonable evidence to suggest that the plaintiff was guilty;[3] or a merchant prosecutes plaintiff for fraud simply because the plaintiff's check was dishonored by the bank;[4] or an employer prosecutes the plaintiff in the unjustified belief that plaintiff was stealing the employer's goods.[5] Since prosecuting officials are normally immune from tort liability based on their prosecutions,[6] the defendant in malicious prosecution cases is often the private citizen who made the initial accusation, though occasionally police officers are held liable under state law [7] or in civil rights actions.[8]

§ 119

1. See infra, pp. 885–887.

2. See infra, § 120.

3. Hoene v. Associated Dry Goods Corp., Mo.1972, 487 S.W.2d 479; Tweedy v. J.C. Penney Co., 1976, 216 Va. 596, 221 S.E.2d 152.

4. Shipp v. Autoville Limited, 1975, 23 Md.App. 555, 328 A.2d 349 (stop payment order on disputed bill); Johnston v. Zale Corp., Tenn.1972, 484 S.W.2d 531.

5. Koris v. Norfolk & Western Railway, 1975, 30 Ill. App.3d 1055, 333 N.E. 217; Lampos v. Bazar, 1974, 270 Or. 256, 527 P.2d 376.

6. Infra, § 132.

7. Palermo v. Cottom, Mo.App.1975, 525 S.W.2d 758; see Vander Linden v. Crews, Iowa 1975, 231 N.W.2d 904 (state Pharmacy Board official).

8. See Nesmith v. Alford, 5th Cir. 1963, 318 F.2d 110, rehearing denied 319 F.2d 859, certiorari denied 375 U.S. 975, 84 S.Ct. 489, 11 L.Ed.2d 420.

The law supports the use of litigation as a social means for resolving disputes, and it encourages honest citizens to bring criminals to justice. Consequently the accuser must be given a large degree of freedom to make mistakes and misjudgments without being subjected to liability. On the other hand, no one should be permitted to subject a fellow citizen to prosecution for an improper purpose and without an honest belief that the accused may be found guilty. The individual interest in freedom from unjustifiable litigation and the social interest in supporting resort to law have traditionally been balanced by the requirement that the plaintiff must prove four elements to establish a malicious prosecution action against an accuser:

1. A criminal [9] proceeding instituted or continued by the defendant against the plaintiff.

2. Termination of the proceeding in favor of the accused.

3. Absence of probable cause for the proceeding.

4. "Malice," or a primary purpose other than that of bringing an offender to justice.

Each of these elements in turn has required considerable definition and elaboration and it is necessary to examine each separately.

Institution of Proceeding

Any proceeding of a criminal character [10] will support an action of malicious prosecution. Although there is some authority to the contrary, most courts have held that it makes no difference that the court or magistrate before whom it is brought has no jurisdiction,[11] or that the indictment or complaint upon which the prosecution is based lacks essential particulars,[12] or even that it fails to charge the commission of any offense known to the criminal law.[13] So long as the proceeding is treated by the court as a proper one, the plaintiff's interests have been invaded, the plaintiff's reputation has suffered, and the plaintiff has been put to the expense of defense. The plaintiff is not to be dismissed from court with the consoling assurance that there was never really any prosecution at all; [14] nor is it any the less a prosecution because it is successfully defended on the law rather than the facts.[15]

The proceeding must, however, have been commenced. It is not enough that a mere complaint has been made to the proper authorities for the purpose of setting prosecution in motion, where no official action ever has been taken,[16] or that evidence has been presented to a grand jury which refuses to indict.[17] On the other hand, it usually is held to be sufficient that a warrant has been issued for the plaintiff's arrest, although it never has been served.[18] The initial step is

---

9. As to civil proceedings, see, infra, § 120.

10. Second Restatement of Torts, § 654. As to quasi criminal proceedings, such as bastardy or juvenile delinquency, see infra, pp. 890–891. There must, however, be a judicial proceeding; and a mere investigation by the district attorney is not enough. Losi v. Natalicchio, Sup.1952, 112 N.Y.S.2d 706.

11. Morris v. Scott, N.Y.1839, 21 Wend. 281; Sutor v. Wood, 1890, 76 Tex. 403, 13 S.W. 321.

Contra: Vinson v. Flynn, 1897, 64 Ark. 453, 43 S.W. 146, 46 S.W. 186.

See Byrd, Malicious Prosecution in North Carolina, 1969, 47 N.C.L.Rev. 285, 304 (criticizing the minority rule).

12. Harrington v. Tibbet, 1904, 143 Cal. 78, 76 P. 816; Minneapolis Threshing Machine Co. v. Regier, 1897, 51 Neb. 402, 70 N.W. 934. Contra, Hawkins v. Reynolds, 1952, 236 N.C. 422, 72 S.E.2d 874, 36 A.L.R.2d 782.

13. George v. Williams, 1924, 26 Ariz. 91, 222 P. 410; Finn v. Frink, 1892, 84 Me. 261, 24 A. 851.

Contra: Moser v. Fulk, 1950, 237 N.C. 302, 74 S.E.2d 729.

14. See Shaul v. Brown, 1869, 28 Iowa 37; Dennis v. Ryan, 1875, 65 N.Y. 385; Bell v. Keepers, 1887, 37 Kan. 64, 14 P. 542; Mask v. Rawls, 1879, 57 Miss. 270.

15. Cf. Finn v. Frink, 1892, 84 Me. 261, 24 A. 851.

16. Cooper v. Armour, C.C.N.Y.1893, 42 F. 215; Reach v. Quinn, 1909, 159 Ala. 340, 48 So. 540; Larocque v. Dorsey, 2d Cir. 1924, 299 F. 556.

17. Byne v. Moore, 1813, 5 Taunt. 187, 128 Eng. Rep. 658.

18. Halberstadt v. New York Life Insurance Co., 1909, 194 N.Y. 1, 86 N.E. 801; Coffey v. Myers, 1882, 84 Ind. 105; Haden v. Tinnin, 1915, 170 N.C. 84, 86 S.E. 1017. Contra: Davis v. Sanders, 1901, 133 Ala. 275, 32

of course a matter of the procedure of the particular jurisdiction; and where prosecution is begun by an indictment, or an information filed by the prosecuting attorney, it seems clear that this should be enough,[19] since it constitutes official action and sets the law in motion.

The defendant may be liable either for initiating or for continuing [20] a criminal prosecution without probable cause. But the defendant cannot be held responsible unless the defendant takes some active part in instigating or encouraging the prosecution.[21] The defendant is not liable merely because of approval or silent acquiescence in the acts of another,[22] nor for appearing as a witness against the accused,[23] even though the testimony be perjured, since the necessities of a free trial demand that witnesses are not to be deterred by fear of tort suits, and shall be immune from liability.[24] On the other hand, if the defendant advises or assists another person to begin the proceeding,[25] ratifies it when it is begun in defendant's behalf,[26] or takes any active part in directing or aiding the conduct of the case,[27] the defendant will be responsible.

The question of information laid before prosecuting authorities has arisen in many cases. If the defendant merely states what is believed, leaving the decision to prosecute entirely to the uncontrolled discretion of the officer,[28] or if the officer makes an independent investigation,[29] or prosecutes for an offense other than the one charged by the defendant,[30] the latter is not regarded as

So. 499; Mitchell v. Donanski, 1906, 28 R.I. 94, 65 A. 611.

19. See Second Restatement of Torts, § 654(2)(b).

20. Laney v. Glidden Co., 1940, 239 Ala. 396, 194 So. 849; Killen v. Olson, Fla.1952, 59 So.2d 524.

One who continues active prosecution after learning of exculpatory facts may be liable for continuing the prosecution though he would not be liable for instituting it. See Lampos v. Bazar, Inc., 1974, 270 Or. 256, 527 P.2d 376. But if responsibility has passed on to some other officer, such as a prosecutor, a failure to come forward with exculpatory facts will not necessarily result in liability. Walsh v. Eberlein, App.1977, 114 Ariz. 342, 560 P.2d 1249.

21. Wood v. Palmer Ford, Inc., 1981, 47 Md.App. 692, 425 A.2d 671; Schleicher v. Western State Bank, N.D.1982, 314 N.W.2d 293.

22. McNamara v. Pabst, 1921, 137 Md. 468, 112 A. 812; Dugan v. Midwest Cap Co., 1931, 213 Iowa 751, 239 N.W. 697; Mark v. Merz, 1894, 53 Ill.App. 458; Marks v. Hastings, 1893, 101 Ala. 165, 13 So. 297.

23. McClarty v. Bickel, 1913, 155 Ky. 254, 159 S.W. 783; Yianitsas v. Mercantile National Bank at Dallas, Tex.Civ.App.1967, 410 S.W.2d 848 (under subpoena); King v. Martin, 1928, 150 Va. 122, 142 S.E. 358; Atkinson v. Birmingham, 1922, 44 R.I. 123, 116 A. 205, reargument denied 117 A. 274; Taplin-Rice-Clerkin Co. v. Hower, 1931, 124 Ohio St. 123, 177 N.E. 203. The immunity of the witness does not extend to one who suborns him to commit perjury. Rice v. Coolidge, 1876, 121 Mass. 393.

Evidence that the defendant testified as a witness is, however, admissible with other acts and circumstances to show instigation or active encouragement of the prosecution or an improper motive. Fitzjohn v. Mackinder, 1861, 9 C.B.N.S. 505, 142 Eng.Rep. 199; Stansbury v. Fogle, 1873, 37 Md. 369; Dennis v. Ryan, 1875, 65 N.Y. 385; Hall v. Adams, 1917, 128 Ark. 116, 193 S.W. 520; Angelozzi v. Cossentino, 1931, 160 Md. 678, 155 A. 178; Fusario v. Cavallaro, 1928, 108 Conn. 40, 142 A. 391.

24. See Note, Civil Remedies for Perjury, 1977, 19 Ariz.L.Rev. 349. Some authority permits a malicious prosecution action on the basis of perjured testimony before a grand jury. See Wheeler v. Satilla Rural Electric Membership Corp., 1961, 103 Ga.App. 401, 119 S.E.2d 375. Bribery of a judge may be actionable, if not as some other tort then as a denial of due process and hence a violation of federal civil rights. See Dennis v. Sparks, 1980, 449 U.S. 24, 101 S.Ct. 183, 66 L.Ed. 2d 185.

25. Meraz v. Valencia, 1922, 28 N.M. 174, 210 P. 225; Gilbert v. Emmons, 1866, 42 Ill. 143; Mowry v. Miller, 1832, 30 Va. (3 Leigh.) 561, 24 Am.Dec. 680.

26. See Grimes v. Greenblatt, 1910, 47 Colo. 495, 107 P. 1111; Shannon v. Sims, 1906, 146 Ala. 673, 40 So. 574.

27. Lemke v. Anders, 1952, 261 Wis. 555, 53 N.W.2d 436; Bair v. Shoultz, 1943, 233 Iowa 980, 7 N.W.2d 904.

28. Archer v. Cachat, 1956, 165 Ohio St. 286, 135 N.E.2d 404; Second Restatement of Torts, § 653, Comment g. See Seelig v. Harvard Cooperative Society, 1969, 355 Mass. 532, 246 N.E.2d 642 (dictum). See Dobbs, Belief and Doubt in Malicious Prosecution and Libel, 1979, 21 Ariz.L.Rev. 607 (arguing that citizen-accuser is not an instigator if officer is relied on to make decision to charge, even though officer cannot give legal advice).

29. Cox v. Lauritsen, 1914, 126 Minn. 128, 147 N.W. 1093; Christy v. Rice, 1908, 152 Mich. 563, 116 N.W. 200; Malloy v. Chicago, Milwaukee & St. Paul Railway Co., 1914, 34 S.D. 330, 148 N.W. 598.

30. Bennett v. Black, Ala.1828, 1 Stew. 494; Frankfurter v. Bryan, 1883, 12 Ill.App. 549; Carter v. Sutherland, 1884, 52 Mich. 597, 18 N.W. 375; Hamburg v. Eagleson, 1921, 116 Wash. 616, 200 P. 306.

having instigated the proceeding. In such a case the harm done the wrongly accused plaintiff will often find no remedy, or only an inadequate one, since the prosecuting officials are almost always immune.[31] To the extent that a police officer who lodges the initial charge is exercising prosecutorial judgment, it is conceivable that the absolute immunity would be extended to protect the police officer as well.[32] There are, however, cases in which officers are held responsible for initiating a prosecution without probable cause.[33] On the other hand, the citizen who actively persuades the prosecutor or magistrate to issue a warrant or otherwise to proceed with prosecution,[34] the citizen who gives information with knowledge of its falsity,[35] and the citizen who actively induces prosecution by signing an affidavit for a criminal warrant[36] can all be regarded in proper circumstances as initiators of the prosecution and liable for it.

In some instances an accuser's involvement with the prosecution is second-hand but nevertheless so significant that the accuser is held as an instigator, though no complaint to any official was made at all. It goes without saying that private attorneys are liable if they swear out complaints themselves without probable cause,[37] but it has been held also that they are liable if they assist in a prosecution knowing there is no basis for it,[38] though of course they are entitled to advise their clients as to the law[39] and to represent them in good faith.[40] On occasion a private citizen has been held to be an instigator of the prosecution on the basis of the fact that he has persuaded another private citizen to prosecute, though he himself has refused to file an official complaint.[41] In a unique case, an arsonist-defendant was held liable to the plaintiff who had been charged erroneously with the arsonist's crime.[42] In the absence of serious misbehavior, such as crime or intentional tort, the mere fact that prosecution of the plaintiff is a foreseeable result of the defendant's remarks to other citizens is not enough to justify liability, however, even where those remarks are negligently made.[43]

31. See § 132, supra.

32. Several courts have suggested that an officer might enjoy a special privilege without deciding the issue. Brewer v. Mele, 1972, 267 Md. 437, 298 A.2d 156; Rogers v. Hill, 1978, 281 Or. 491, 576 P.2d 328. Cf. Vander Linden v. Crews, Iowa 1975, 231 N.W.2d 904 ("public officials" not liable without more stringent showing of "malice."). In Butz v. Economou, 1978, 438 U.S. 478, 98 S.Ct. 2894, 57 L.Ed.2d 895, on remand S.D. N.Y., 466 F.Supp. 1351, affirmed 2d Cir., 633 F.2d 203, the Court followed a "functional" analysis and concluded that an administrative law judge whose "function" was like that of judicial judges would partake of the absolute privilege accorded the latter.

33. E.g., Haaf v. Grams, D.Minn.1973, 355 F.Supp. 542 (§ 1983 action, only "good faith and probable cause" as defense); Rogers v. Hill, 1978, 281 Or. 491, 576 P.2d 328. Cf. Dellums v. Powell, D.C.Cir. 1977, 566 F.2d 167 (police chief could be liable for giving misleading information to prosecuting attorney if prosecutor did not make independent judgment).

34. Zenik v. O'Brien, 1951, 137 Conn. 592, 79 A.2d 769. Cf. Creelman v. Svenning, 1966, 67 Wash.2d 882, 410 P.2d 606.

35. Dennis v. Ryan, 1875, 65 N.Y. 385; cf. Wilmerton v. Sample, 1891, 42 Ill.App. 254.

36. Peters v. Hall, 1953, 263 Wis. 450, 57 N.W.2d 723. A sworn affidavit made to induce a warrant or other criminal action is typically assumed to be instigation of prosecution without discussion. E.g., Shipp v. Autoville Limited, 1974, 23 Md.App. 555, 328 A.2d 349. But where defendant merely signs an affidavit or complaint at an officer's direction, it is otherwise. Hughes v. Van Bruggen, 1940, 44 N.M. 534, 105 P.2d 494.

37. Whitney v. New York Casualty Insurance Association, 1898, 27 App.Div. 320, 50 N.Y.S. 227.

38. Burnap v. Marsh, 1852, 13 Ill. 535; Warfield v. Campbell, 1859, 35 Ala. 349; Staley v. Turner, 1886, 21 Mo.App. 244; Anderson v. Canaday, 1913, 37 Okl. 171, 131 P. 697.

39. See Burnap v. Marsh, 1852, 13 Ill. 535.

40. Bicknell v. Dorion, 1835, 33 Mass. (16 Pick.) 478; Peck v. Chouteau, 1887, 91 Mo. 138, 3 S.W. 577; Stockley v. Hornidge, 1837, 8 C. & P. 11, 173 Eng.Rep. 377.

41. Gordon v. McLearn, 1916, 123 Ark. 496, 185 S.W. 803; Centers v. Dollar Markets, 1950, 99 Cal.App. 2d 534, 222 P.2d 136.

42. Seidel v. Greenberg, 1969, 108 N.J.Super. 248, 260 A.2d 863, 40 A.L.R.3d 987.

43. See Bromund v. Holt, 1964, 24 Wis.2d 336, 129 N.W.2d 149 (pathologist who erroneously reported that wife died of blow to skull not liable when husband prosecuted).

Termination in Favor of Accused

In order to maintain his action for malicious prosecution, the plaintiff must show not only that the criminal proceeding has terminated,[44] but also that it has terminated in his favor.[45] Consistent with this, it has been said that the termination must not only be favorable to the accused, but must also reflect the merits and not merely a procedural victory.[46] The requirement of termination is probably a matter of ripeness, a belief that the malicious prosecution action should not be tried at a time when it might tend to chill testimony in the criminal action, when the issues may still be narrowed by the criminal process, and when the civil dispute might still be resolved by compromise or other nonjudicial measures if the criminal trial can but proceed to an end. The requirement that the criminal prosecution terminate in favor of the malicious prosecution plaintiff, however, is primarily important not as an independent element of the malicious prosecution action but only for what it shows about probable cause or guilt-in-fact.[47] Any disposition of the criminal action which does not terminate it but permits it to be renewed, as in the case of the refusal of a grand jury to indict which is not followed by discharge,[48] cannot serve as a foundation for the action.

On the other hand, it will be enough that the proceeding is terminated in such a manner that it cannot be revived, and the prosecutor, if he proceeds further, will be put to a new one.[49] This is true, for example, of an acquittal in court,[50] a discharge by a magistrate[51] or a justice of the peace[52] upon preliminary hearing, or by a governor in extradition proceedings,[53] a failure of a grand jury to indict which results in discharge,[54] the quashing of an indictment,[55] the entry of a nolle prosequi[56] or a dismissal,[57] abandonment of the prosecution by the prosecuting attorney or the complaining witness,[58] or continuance beyond a time limit,[59] where any of these things have the effect of ending the particular proceeding and requiring new process or other official action to commence a new prosecution. It may be said generally,

---

44. "Otherwise he might recover in the action and yet be convicted in the original prosecution." Fisher v. Bristow, 1779, 1 Dougl. 215, 99 Eng.Rep. 140.

The statute of limitations does not begin to run until termination of the criminal action in favor of the accused. Sicola v. First National Bank of Altoona, 1961, 404 Pa. 18, 170 A.2d 584.

45. Nataros v. Superior Court of Maricopa County, 1976, 113 Ariz. 498, 557 P.2d 1055; Foster v. Turner, Miss.1975, 319 So.2d 233.

46. Lackner v. LaCroix, 1979, 25 Cal.3d 747, 159 Cal.Rptr. 693, 602 P.2d 393.

47. See infra, p. 885.

48. Knott v. Sargent, 1878, 125 Mass. 95; Stark v. Bindley, 1899, 152 Ind. 182, 52 N.E. 804. Cf. Komar v. City of New York, 1965, 24 A.D.2d 941, 265 N.Y.S.2d 331 (release on own recognizance); Prentice v. Bertken, 1942, 50 Cal.App.2d 344, 123 P.2d 96 (non-arraignment).

49. See Graves v. Scott, 1905, 104 Va. 372, 51 S.E. 821; Apgar v. Woolston, 1881, 43 N.J.L. 57; Casebeer v. Drahoble, 1885, 13 Neb. 465, 14 N.W. 397; Southern Car & Foundry Co. v. Adams, 1901, 131 Ala. 147, 32 So. 503.

50. Singer Manufacturing Co. v. Bryant, 1906, 105 Va. 403, 54 S.E. 320.

51. See v. Gosselin, 1946, 133 Conn. 158, 48 A.2d 560; Jaffe v. Stone, 1941, 18 Cal.2d 146, 114 P.2d 335.

52. Overson v. Lynch, 1957, 83 Ariz. 158, 317 P.2d 948.

53. Keller v. Butler, 1927, 246 N.Y. 249, 158 N.E. 510. Contra, Cowan v. Gamble, Mo.1952, 247 S.W.2d 779. See Note, 5 Stan.L.Rev. 560.

54. Kearney v. Mallon Suburban Motors, 1945, 23 N.J.Misc. 83, 41 A.2d 274; Zello v. Glover, Tex.Civ.App. 1933, 59 S.W.2d 877; Wells v. Parker, 1905, 76 Ark. 41, 88 S.W. 602; Graves v. Dawson, 1881, 130 Mass. 78; McIver v. Russell, D.Md.1967, 264 F.Supp. 22.

55. Lytton v. Baird, 1884, 95 Ind. 349; Reit v. Meyer, 1914, 160 App.Div. 752, 146 N.Y.S. 75.

56. De La Riva v. Owl Drug Co., 1967, 253 Cal.App.2d 593, 61 Cal.Rptr. 291; Harvey v. Bertaut, La.App. 1974, 303 So.2d 211. Contra, Fogg v. First National Bank, 1929, 268 Mass. 25, 167 N.E. 251.

57. Myhre v. Hessey, 1943, 242 Wis. 638, 9 N.W.2d 106; Green v. Warnock, 1936, 144 Kan. 170, 58 P.2d 1059; Rankin v. Saenger, Tex.Civ.App.1952, 250 S.W.2d 465, refused n.r.e.

58. Glover v. Heyward, 1918, 108 S.C. 486, 94 S.E. 878; Empire Gas & Fuel Co. v. Wainscott, 1923, 91 Okl. 66, 216 P. 141; McRae v. Brant, 1967, 108 N.H. 177, 230 A.2d 753 (appeal).

59. Winkler v. Lenoir & Blowing Rock Lines, 1928, 195 N.C. 673, 143 S.E. 213.

that this is true whenever the charges or the proceeding are withdrawn on the initiative of the prosecution. There is, however, authority that when a proceeding is withdrawn merely in order to substitute immediately another one for the same offense, it is to be regarded as one continuous proceeding, which is not terminated.[60]

On the other hand, where charges are withdrawn or the prosecution is terminated at the instigation of the accused himself,[61] or by reason of a compromise into which he has entered voluntarily,[62] there is no sufficient termination in favor of the accused. Sometimes it is said that this is an admission of probable cause;[63] or that the accused has consented to a termination which leaves open the question of his guilt and possible conviction and so cannot take advantage of it [64] after the prosecutor has foregone the opportunity of proving that there was really guilt.[65] The compromise or consent in these cases is often no more than an agreement by the accused to pay a bad check or other obligation on which the prosecution was based,[66] and there are certainly extreme cases in which the malicious prosecution action has been barred by a termination interpreted as a "compromise." [67] Where the accused's obligation is disputed, courts have, however, sometimes given relief in the form of a holding that the supposed compromise was made under duress of the criminal proceedings themselves, and that one who is forced to choose between prosecution and compromise should not be prevented from maintaining a malicious prosecution suit that is otherwise a good one.[68] But this view of the matter is necessarily applied to a limited range of facts, and the mere fact that the accused is embarrassed by the criminal prosecution and wants to avoid it does not mean that his compromise settlement was given under duress or that he can thereafter bring a malicious prosecution action.[69]

Where the prosecution has terminated by reason of suppression of evidence or other improper conduct on the part of the accused, malicious prosecution will not lie,[70] and the same is true where it was impossible to bring him to trial because he has left the jurisdiction.[71]

60. Second Restatement of Torts, § 660. Accord: Freeman v. Logan, Ky.1972, 475 S.W.2d 636.

61. This does not include a motion to dismiss for lack of prosecution, where the prosecution has abandoned the case. Gumm v. Heider, 1960, 220 Or. 5, 348 P.2d 455.

62. Bristol v. Eckhardt, 1949, 254 Wis. 297, 36 N.W.2d 56; Mondrow v. Selwyn, 1980, 172 N.J.Super. 379, 412 A.2d 447. It has been held that a release of all tort claims given by the accused to induce dismissal of the criminal charge is valid. Hoines v. Barney's Club, Inc., 1980, 28 Cal.3d 603, 170 Cal.Rptr. 42, 620 P.2d 628.

63. Nelson v. National Casualty Co., 1929, 179 Minn. 53, 228 N.W. 437; Saner v. Bowker, 1924, 69 Mont. 463, 222 P. 1056.

64. Second Restatement of Torts, § 660, Comment c.

65. "If this should be allowed, the defendant would be deceived by the consent, as without that he would certainly have gone on with the action, and might have shown a foundation for it." Wilkinson v. Howell, 1830 M. & M. 495, 173 Eng.Rep. 1236.

66. E.g., Freedman v. Crabro Motors, Inc., Fla.App. 1967, 199 So.2d 745; Cimino v. Rosen, 1975, 193 Neb. 162, 225 N.W.2d 567.

67. See Leonard v. George, 4th Cir. 1949, 178 F.2d 312, certiorari denied 339 U.S. 965, 70 S.Ct. 1000, 94 L.Ed. 1374; Tucker v. Duncan, 4th Cir. 1974, 499 F.2d 963.

68. White v. International Text Book Co., 1912, 156 Iowa 210, 136 N.W. 121; Morton v. Young, 1867, 55 Me. 24; Smith v. Markensohn, 1908, 29 R.I. 55, 69 A. 311; Lyons v. Davy-Pocahontas Coal Co., 1915, 75 W.Va. 739, 84 S.E. 744. An analogy may be suggested to the cases of contracts compounding a felony.

69. Hoines v. Barney's Club, Inc., 1980, 28 Cal.3d 603, 170 Cal.Rptr. 42, 620 P.2d 628. But cf. MacDonald v. Musick, 9th Cir. 1970, 425 F.2d 373, certiorari denied 400 U.S. 852, 91 S.Ct. 54, 27 L.Ed.2d 90 (prosecutor's effort to induce accused to stipulate to probable cause as condition of dropping charge regarded as extortionate).

70. See Leyenberger v. Paul, 1890, 40 Ill.App. 516; Halberstadt v. New York Life Insurance Co., 1909, 194 N.Y. 1, 86 N.E. 801; Second Restatement of Torts, § 660(b).

71. Halberstadt v. New York Life Insurance Co., 1909, 194 N.Y. 1, 86 N.E. 801.

Probable Cause

Malicious prosecution is an action which runs counter to obvious policies of the law in favor of encouraging proceedings against those who are apparently guilty, and letting finished litigation remain undisturbed and unchallenged.[72] It has never been regarded with any favor by the courts, and it is hedged with restrictions which make it very difficult to maintain. Chief among these is the requirement that the plaintiff must sustain the burden of proof [73] that the criminal proceeding was initiated or continued by the defendant without "probable cause." This is true even though the defendant is found to have acted with "malice," for an improper purpose,[74] since it is the part of a good citizen to bring about the prosecution of those who are reasonably suspected of crime, and the addition of a personal motive should not result in liability for performing a public obligation. The existence of such "malice" does not create even an inference that probable cause was lacking.[75]

Probable cause is a reasonable ground for belief in the guilt of the party charged.[76] Though the facts need not warrant a belief in guilt beyond a reasonable doubt,[77] they must at least warrant a grave suspicion in the mind of a prudent person.[78] A want of probable cause thus involves unreasonable conduct under the circumstances and in that respect bears some resemblance to the idea of negligence.[79]

Probable cause is judged by appearances [80] to the defendant at the time he initiates prosecution, not by facts discovered later.[81] Later discovered facts will be relevant only to show the entirely different defense based on the accused's guilt in fact. The appearances must be such as to lead a reasonable person to set the criminal process in motion.[82] Unfounded suspicion and conjecture will not do.[83] On the other hand, it is not necessary for the accuser to verify his information where it appears to be reliable.[84] Verification may be required to establish probable cause where the source of the information seems untrustworthy,[85] or where

---

72. See Griswold v. Horne, 1917, 19 Ariz. 56, 165 P. 318; Schubkegel v. Gordino, 1943, 56 Cal.App.2d 667, 133 P.2d 475; Johnson v. Pearce, La.1975, 313 So.2d 812; Green, Judge and Jury, 1930, 338–39.

73. Lind v. Schmid, 1975, 67 N.J. 255, 337 A.2d 365; Bain v. Phillips, 1976, 217 Va. 387, 228 S.E.2d 576.

74. Foshay v. Ferguson, N.Y.1846, 2 Denio 617; Stewart v. Sonneborn, 1878, 98 U.S. 187, 25 L.Ed. 116; Glenn v. Lawrence, 1917, 280 Ill. 581, 117 N.E. 757; Jordan v. Alabama Great Southern Railroad Co., 1886, 81 Ala. 220, 8 So. 191; Smith v. Pierson, Tex.Civ.App. 1912, 151 S.W. 1113. Contra, Curley v. Automobile Finance Co., 1941, 343 Pa. 280, 23 A.2d 48.

75. Page v. Rose, Okl.1975, 546 P.2d 617, appeal after remand 566 P.2d 439; Noell v. Angle, 1977, 217 Va. 656, 231 S.E.2d 330.

76. Slade v. City of Phoenix, 1975, 112 Ariz. 298, 541 P.2d 550; Colegrove v. City of Corning, 1976, 54 A.D.2d 1093, 388 N.Y.S.2d 964.

77. Second Restatement of Torts, § 662, Comment c.

78. Birwood Paper Co. v. Damsky, 1969, 285 Ala. 127, 229 So.2d 514.

79. Green, Judge and Jury, 1930, 342.

80. The fact that the defendant's information was false of course does not prevent his having probable cause. Kennedy v. Burbidge, 1919, 54 Utah 497, 183 P. 325.

81. Smith v. King, 1893, 62 Conn. 515, 26 A. 1059; Galloway v. Stewart, 1874, 49 Ind. 156; Orso v. City and County of Honolulu, 1975, 56 Hawaii 241, 534 P.2d 489.

82. Well stated by Vann, J., in Burt v. Smith, 1905, 181 N.Y. 1, 73 N.E. 495, error dismissed 203 U.S. 129, 27 S.Ct. 37, 51 L.Ed. 121. Accord: Perry v. Hurdle, 1948, 229 N.C. 216, 49 S.E.2d 400; Casavan v. Sage, 1909, 201 Mass. 547, 87 N.E. 893 (a "cautious man"). See Note, 1949, 3 Ark.L.Rev. 445.

83. Hyman v. New York Central Railroad Co., 1925, 240 N.Y. 137, 147 N.E. 613; Graeter v. Williams, 1876, 55 Ind. 461; Krol v. Plodick, 1915, 77 N.H. 557, 94 A. 261; Stone v. Stevens, 1837, 12 Conn. 219.

84. Campbell v. Yellow Cab Co., 3d Cir. 1942, 137 F.2d 918; Brodie v. Huck, 1948, 187 Va. 485, 47 S.E.2d 310; Johnson v. Southern Pacific Co., 1910, 157 Cal. 333, 107 P. 611; Birdsall v. Smith, 1909, 158 Mich. 390, 122 N.W. 626; Kansas & Texas Coal Co. v. Galloway, 1903, 71 Ark. 351, 74 S.W. 521.

85. Blunk v. Atchison, Topeka & Santa Fe Railway Co., C.C.Mo.1889, 38 F. 311; Plassan v. Louisiana Lottery Co., 1882, 34 La.Ann. 246; Chapman v. Dunn, 1885, 56 Mich. 31, 22 N.W. 101. Admissions of the accused may provide probable cause. Rawls v. Bennett, 1942, 221 N.C. 127, 19 S.E.2d 126.

further information about a serious charge would be readily available.[86] The reputation of the accused,[87] his opportunity to offer an explanation[88] and the need for prompt action,[89] if any, are all factors in determining whether unverified information furnishes probable cause.

If the reasonable appearances to the accuser support an inference of guilt, probable cause may be found even though the accuser does not believe conviction to be likely.[90] By the same token, whether the accuser believes the facts in his possession amount to probable cause is unimportant aside from the malice issue, provided the known facts would induce a reasonable person to prosecute.[91]

A number of cases have said, however, that the accuser has no probable cause unless he holds a personal, subjective belief in the guilt of the accused, and that it is not enough to show that the evidence would convince a reasonable person of guilt if it did not in fact convince the accuser.[92] This view has been supported by the Restatement,[93] but it seems inconsistent with the rule that the accuser is entitled to entertain considerable doubt about the matter.[94] It is also inconsistent with the traditional test of probable cause, which focuses on the evidence known to the accuser and the reasonable inferences to be drawn from it rather than on the accuser's personal state of mind. The accuser who has good evidence of guilt but believes in the accused's innocence may be guilty of malice, but he probably has probable cause for prosecution.[95]

Since probable cause is a matter of the appearances presented to the defendant, a mistake of fact as to the conduct of the accused will of course not prevent its existence. Some courts have held[96] that a mistake of law, as to whether such conduct amounts to a criminal offense, or to the particular offense charged, cannot protect the instigator of prosecution—apparently upon the antique and questionable theory that he is required at his peril to know the law. For the most part such cases appear to have involved mistakes of law so extreme that they would be unreasonable even for a layman to make.

The Second Restatement has accordingly taken the view that a mistake of law stands on the same footing as a mistake of fact and

---

86. Lacy v. Mitchell, 1864, 23 Ind. 67; Thompson v. Price, 1894, 100 Mich. 558, 59 N.W. 253; Boyd v. Mendenhall, 1893, 53 Minn. 274, 55 N.W. 45; Lewis v. Williams, Tenn.1981, 618 S.W.2d 299 ("investigator can not close his eyes to the truth of matters within his actual possession"). The difficulty and danger of obtaining information is obviously important on this issue. Fisher v. Hamilton, 1874, 49 Ind. 341.

87. Woodworth v. Mills, 1884, 61 Wis. 44, 20 N.W. 728; Stubbs v. Mulholland, 1902, 168 Mo. 47, 67 S.W. 650; Hirsch v. Feeney, 1876, 83 Ill. 548.

88. Hutchinson v. Wenzel, 1900, 155 Ind. 49, 56 N.E. 845; Norrell v. Vogel, 1888, 39 Minn. 107, 38 N.W. 705; Bechel v. Pacific Express Co., 1902, 65 Neb. 826, 91 N.W. 853; Lacy v. Mitchell, 1864, 23 Ind. 67.

89. Second Restatement of Torts, § 662, Comment j.

90. Michael v. Matson, 1909, 81 Kan. 360, 105 P. 537; Schwartz v. Boswell, 1913, 156 Ky. 103, 160 S.W. 748.

91. Michael v. Matson, 1909, 81 Kan. 360, 105 P. 537; cf. Ricehill v. Brewer, 8th Cir. 1972, 459 F.2d 537.

92. Harkrader v. Moore, 1872, 44 Cal. 144; Watson v. Cain, 1911, 171 Ala. 151, 54 So. 610. See Dobbs, Belief and Doubt in Malicious Prosecution and Libel, 1979, 21 Ariz.L.Rev. 607.

93. Second Restatement of Torts, § 662, Comment c.

94. Bowen v. W.A. Pollard & Co., 1917, 173 N.C. 129, 91 S.E. 711. See Second Restatement of Torts, § 662, Comment c.

95. See Dobbs, Belief and Doubt in Malicious Prosecution and Libel, 1979, 21 Ariz.L.Rev. 607.

"Probable cause is such a state of facts in the mind of the prosecutor as would lead a man of ordinary caution and prudence to believe, or entertain an honest and strong suspicion, that the person arrested is guilty." Shaw, C.J. in Bacon v. Towne, 1849, 58 Mass. (4 Cush.) 217. This focuses on what a person of ordinary caution would believe, not what the accuser did believe. Many states have used some variant on Shaw's language, e.g., Giant of Virginia, Inc. v. Pigg, 1967, 207 Va. 679, 152 S.E.2d 271.

96. Gray v. Bennett, 1959, 250 N.C. 707, 110 S.E.2d 324; Dunn v. Alabama Oil & Gas Co., 1956, 42 Tenn. App. 108, 299 S.W.2d 25; Vasser v. Berry, 1952, 85 Ga. App. 435, 69 S.E.2d 701; Brown v. Kisner, 1942, 192 Miss. 746, 6 So.2d 611; Nehr v. Dobbs, 1896, 47 Neb. 863, 66 N.W. 864. See Note, 1958, 25 Tenn.L.Rev. 316.

that the accuser is protected if he reasonably believes he knows the law.[97] This has the support of about half the cases.[98]

The layman's ignorance of the law has been taken into account in the almost universal[99] holding that probable cause is established where the prosecution was instituted with the advice of counsel.[1] Such advice is properly addressed to the question of probable cause, since it bears upon the defendant's reasonable belief that he has a legal justification for the criminal proceeding; and for this purpose it is effective even though it may be erroneous and not warranted by the facts submitted to counsel.[2] It must, however, be followed,[3] and in good faith, rather than as a mere pretext or cover for the defendant's personal ends.[4] In states where probable cause turns on the accuser's subjective belief in the accused's guilt, an attorney's advice to prosecute furnishes no defense unless the accuser acts on his own belief in that guilt as well as on the attorney's advice.[5] Furthermore, the defendant must have made full and fair disclosure to the attorney of everything within his knowledge and information[6] which a reasonable man would regard as material for the attorney to know[7] in order to give a sound opinion; and the failure to disclose any such information,[8] or false statements to the attorney[9] will prevent any justifiable reliance on the advice given. Some courts have gone further, and have required that the defendant use the diligence of a reasonable man to ascertain anything that he does not know before consulting counsel,[10] but the prevailing view, which seems the better one, is that this is unnecessary where he informs the attorney of the state of his information and is

---

97. Second Restatement of Torts, § 662(c).

98. Whipple v. Gorsuch, 1907, 82 Ark. 252, 101 S.W. 735; Nettleton v. Cook, 1917, 30 Idaho 82, 163 P. 300; Vincioni v. Phelps Dodge Corp., 1930, 35 N.M. 81, 290 P. 319; Kuhnhausen v. Stadelman, 1944, 174 Or. 290, 148 P.2d 239, rehearing denied 174 Or. 290, 149 P.2d 168; Franklin v. Irvine, 1921, 52 Cal.App. 286, 198 P. 647. Cf. Dunlap v. New Zealand Fire & Marine Insurance Co., 1895, 109 Cal. 365, 42 P. 29 (advice of counsel). Accord, as to unconstitutional statutes: Birdsall v. Smith, 1909, 158 Mich. 390, 122 N.W. 626.

Without discussing the point, a number of cases reach the same result. See West v. Baumgartner, 1972, 228 Ga. 671, 187 S.E.2d 665; Lincoln v. Shea, 1972, 361 Mass. 1, 277 N.E.2d 699.

99. See Preston, Advice of Counsel as a Defense, 1941, 28 Va.L.Rev. 26, 34. A small number of courts have held that advice of counsel is not a complete defense, but only to be considered by the jury on the issue of proable cause. Aland v. Pyle, 1919, 263 Pa. 254, 106 A. 349; Gulf, Colorado & Santa Fe Railway Co. v. James, 1889, 73 Tex. 12, 10 S.W. 744; Bassinov v. Finkle, 1964, 261 N.C. 109, 134 S.E.2d 130.

1. Reid v. True, Ky.1957, 302 S.W.2d 846; Thomas v. Hinton, 1955, 76 Idaho 337, 281 P.2d 1050; Kunz v. Johnson, 1953, 74 S.D. 577, 57 N.W.2d 116; Citizens State Bank of Long Beach v. Hoffman, 1941, 44 Cal. App.2d 854, 113 P.2d 221; White v. Pacific Telephone & Telegraph Co., 1939, 162 Or. 270, 90 P.2d 193. See Note, 1937, 21 Minn.L.Rev. 217.

2. Kompass v. Light, 1899, 122 Mich. 86, 80 N.W. 1008; Steed v. Knowles, 1885, 79 Ala. 446; Chapman v. Anderson, 1925, 55 App.D.C. 165, 3 F.2d 336; Brodrib v. Doberstein, 1928, 107 Conn. 294, 140 A. 483.

3. Manning v. Finn, 1888, 23 Neb. 511, 37 N.W. 314.

4. Adkin v. Pillen, 1904, 136 Mich. 682, 100 N.W. 176; McCarthy v. Kitchen, 1877, 59 Ind. 500; Neufeld v. Rodeminski, 1893, 144 Ill. 83, 32 N.E. 913; Hopkinson v. Lehigh Valley Railroad Co., 1928, 249 N.Y. 296, 164 N.E. 104.

5. Burke v. Watts, 1922, 188 Cal. 118, 204 P. 578; Gurden v. Stevens, 1906, 146 Mich. 489, 109 N.W. 856.

6. But not, of course, what he does not know, Elmer v. Chicago & Northwestern Railway, 1952, 260 Wis. 567, 51 N.W.2d 707, and not hearsay or opinion as to reputation, Thomas v. Cisneros, Tex.Civ.App.1980, 596 S.W.2d 313. Full disclosure by a corporate agent who instigates the prosecution is sufficient to establish the defense, even though other agents of the corporation have additional knowledge that is not revealed. Meyer v. Ewald, 1974, 66 Wis.2d 168, 224 N.W.2d 419. Contra: Hogan v. Robert H. Irwin Motors, Inc., 1981, 121 N.H. 737, 433 A.2d 1322.

7. But not minor collateral details. Brooks v. Bolde, 1941, 11 Wn.2d 37, 118 P.2d 193.

8. Southern Farmers Association v. Whitfield, 1964, 238 Ark. 607, 383 S.W.2d 506; Jackson v. Beckham, 1963, 217 Cal.App.2d 264, 31 Cal.Rptr. 739.

But non-disclosure of exculpatory facts has been held an insufficient basis for liability where the authorities already knew of such facts. Walsh v. Eberlein, App.1977, 114 Ariz. 342, 560 P.2d 1249.

9. Drakos v. Jones, 1941, 189 Okl. 593, 118 P.2d 388; Smith v. Hensley, 1941, 107 Colo. 180, 109 P.2d 909.

10. Jones v. Flaherty, 1917, 139 Minn. 97, 165 N.W. 963; Nelson v. Peterman, 1926, 119 Okl. 125, 249 P. 333.

assured that he need not seek to learn anything more.[11]

Some courts appear to feel that once defendant proves a disclosure to counsel it will be taken to be an adequate and fair one unless plaintiff proves otherwise.[12] A number of other courts have said that the burden falls upon the defendant in the first instance to show not only the disclosure itself, but that it was full and fair.[13]

The advice of counsel establishes probable cause only when it is given by an apparently competent attorney, duly admitted to the practice of law within the state where the proceedings are brought,[14] or, if he is admitted to practice elsewhere, apparently qualified to offer a reliable opinion as to the applicable law.[15]

Advice of lay persons, including magistrates and justices of the peace who are not licensed attorneys, is ordinarily insufficient.[16] But there are at least some cases in which a private citizen is reasonable in relying upon a police official's advice, or choice of criminal charge, and in such cases it would be an onerous burden on the citizen, if not a perversion of the law, to make him bear the brunt of the officer's mis-decision.[17] If the citizen's reliance on official advice does not always prove probable cause, it may at least tend to show that he lacked malice, or that he was not an instigator of the prosecution because he relied upon official judgment, or that some other element of the plaintiff's case is missing and that the citizen-accuser cannot be held responsible.[18]

The attorney must advise in his professional capacity, and can give no protection when it is clear that he is not speaking as an attorney;[19] but the fact that he is regularly employed by the defendant does not prevent his giving reliable professional advice.[20] Prosecuting attorneys employed by the state are at least as well qualified to give advice on criminal proceedings as any others, and it is agreed everywhere that their advice is sufficient to establish probable cause.[21]

The attorney must be apparently disinterested, and there cannot be justifiable reli-

11. Johnson v. Miller, 1886, 69 Iowa 562, 29 N.W. 743; Scrivani v. Dondero, 1900, 128 Cal. 31, 60 P. 463; Hess v. Oregon German Baking Co., 1897, 31 Or. 503, 49 P. 803; King v. Apple River Power Co., 1907, 131 Wis. 575, 111 N.W. 668.

12. Dawson v. Mead, 1976, 98 Idaho 1, 557 P.2d 595; Jackson v. Train, Tex.Civ.App.1972, 495 S.W.2d 36.

13. Chipouras v. A.J. & L. Corp., 1982, 223 Va. 511, 290 S.E.2d 859; Watzek v. Walker, 1971, 14 Ariz.App. 545, 485 P.2d 3; Partridge v. Sawyer, Ala.Civ.App. 1980, 383 So.2d 184, certiorari denied Ala., 383 So.2d 187 (semble). See Hogan v. Robert H. Irwin Motors, Inc., 1981, 121 N.H. 737, 433 A.2d 1322 ("the defendant must show that he made a full and fair disclosure to the attorney.")

14. Competence: Clement v. Major, 1896, 8 Colo. App. 86, 44 P. 776; Stubbs v. Mulholland, 1902, 168 Mo. 47, 67 S.W. 650; Roy v. Goings, 1885, 112 Ill. 656. License for practice: Stanton v. Hart, 1873, 27 Mich. 539; Davis v. Baker, 1899, 88 Ill.App. 251; Murphy v. Larson, 1875, 77 Ill. 172; Anderson v. Fletcher, 1923, 228 Ill.App. 372. In the last two cases it was held that one who consulted a person whom he had reason to believe a qualified attorney was not protected. It is at least open to question whether a layman should be required at his peril to know the membership of the bar.

15. Truman v. Fidelity & Casualty Co., 1961, 146 W.Va. 707, 123 S.E.2d 59; Closgard Wardrobe Co. v. Normandy, 1932, 158 Va. 50, 163 S.E. 355.

16. Kable v. Carey, 1918, 135 Ark. 137, 204 S.W. 748; 12 A.L.R. 1227; Brown v. Kisner, 1942, 192 Miss. 746, 6 So.2d 611.

Accord: Mowell v. Von Moschzisker, 1932, 109 N.J.L. 241, 160 A. 680 (handwriting expert); Groda v. American Stores Co., 1934, 315 Pa. 484, 173 A. 419 (state constabulary).

Contra: Monaghan v. Cox, 1892, 155 Mass. 487, 30 N.E. 467; Ball v. Rawles, 1892, 93 Cal. 222, 28 P. 937; Meadows v. Grant, 1971, 15 Ariz.App. 104, 486 P.2d 216.

17. Dobbs, Belief and Doubt in Malicious Prosecution and Libel, 1979, 21 Ariz.L.Rev. 607.

18. Mondrow v. Selwyn, 1980, 172 N.J.Super. 379, 412 A.2d 447.

19. See Marks v. Hastings, 1893, 101 Ala. 165, 174, 13 So. 297, 299; Morin v. Moreau, 1914, 112 Me. 471, 92 A. 527, 528; Mayer v. Goodman, 1923, 94 Okl. 12, 15, 220 P. 656, 659.

20. Truman v. Fidelity & Casualty Co., 1961, 146 W.Va. 707, 123 S.E.2d 59; Miller v. American National Bank in Little Falls, 1943, 216 Minn. 19, 11 N.W.2d 655; Closgard Wardrobe Co. v. Normandy, 1932, 158 Va. 50, 163 S.E. 355; Bell v. Jewel Tea Co., D.Ky.1955, 135 F.Supp. 745; Ashland v. Lapiner Motor Co., 1956, 247 Iowa 596, 75 N.W.2d 357.

21. Schnathorst v. Williams, 1949, 240 Iowa 561, 36 N.W.2d 739, 10 A.L.R.2d 1199; Page v. Rose, Okl.1975, 546 P.2d 617, appeal after remand 566 P.2d 439.

ance upon his opinion where he is known to have an interest of his own to protect by the prosecution,[22] or to be biased or prejudiced against the plaintiff,[23] or where his fees will depend upon the number of prosecutions brought.[24] Although one attorney, as a defendant, may be protected by the advice of another,[25] it is sufficiently obvious that no man can justify his conduct by reliance upon his own opinion as his own counsel.[26] The ordinary interest which any attorney feels in the affairs of his client, however, even though it be inspired by the prospect of a fee, will not disqualify his advice; and the opinion of a retained counsel, who has represented the defendant in other litigation, has been held to be sufficient.[27]

A great many cases have been concerned with the effect of the disposition of the criminal case in proving or disproving the existence of probable cause. In these cases the manner in which the criminal issue is disposed of often becomes important. Much may also depend on whether the criminal case ruling tends to exonerate or tends to incriminate the accused.

The plaintiff may be exonerated in the criminal case by acquittal at trial, by a magistrate's dismissal of the charge (or a grand jury's refusal to indict), or by a nolle prosequi or other abandonment of the prosecution. The courts are agreed that acquittal of the accused at trial is no evidence that probable cause was lacking, since acquittal amounts only to a decision that guilt has not been proved beyond a reasonable doubt.[28] Most courts, however, hold that discharge by the examining magistrate (or refusal to indict by a grand jury) is prima facie evidence that no probable cause existed, because for the magistrate and the grand jury probable cause is the central issue to be determined.[29] In such cases the malicious prosecution defendant is permitted to counter the inference by showing if he can that the magistrate's decision was not based on a probable cause determination at all. For example, the defendant may show that the magistrate's decision was the product of official misconduct,[30] or that it was based upon a supposed want of jurisdiction,[31] or that it turned on the ultimate determination of innocence rather than on probable cause.[32] He may also show that he in fact had probable cause to prosecute, that the magistrate's action, though correct, was a mere technicality,[33] or that in spite of the magistrate's discharge there was a subse-

---

22. White v. Carr, 1880, 71 Me. 555; Union v. United Battery Service Co., 1929, 35 Ohio App. 68, 171 N.E. 608; Vinal v. Core, 1881, 18 W.Va. 1; Adkin v. Pillen, 1904, 136 Mich. 682, 100 N.W. 176. Cf. Smith v. Hensley, 1941, 107 Colo. 180, 109 P.2d 909 (counsel husband).

But the fact that the advice was not given in good faith will not affect the defendant where he had no reason to suspect it. Seabridge v. McAdam, 1897, 119 Cal. 460, 51 P. 691; Shea v. Cloquet Lumber Co., 1904, 92 Minn. 348, 100 N.W. 111.

23. Perrenoud v. Helm, 1902, 65 Neb. 77, 90 N.W. 980; Smith v. Fields, 1910, 139 Ky. 60, 129 S.W. 325.

24. McGarry v. Missouri Pacific Railway Co., 1889, 36 Mo.App. 340.

25. Steadman v. Topham, 1959, 80 Wyo. 63, 338 P.2d 820; Terre Haute & Indianapolis Railroad Co. v. Mason, 1897, 148 Ind. 578, 46 N.E. 332.

26. Epstein v. Berkowsky, 1896, 64 Ill.App. 498; Whipple v. Gorsuch, 1907, 82 Ark. 252, 101 S.W. 735. Cf. Union v. United Battery Service Co., 1929, 35 Ohio App. 68, 171 N.E. 608 (officer and director of defendant corporation); but see contra, Charles City Plow & Manufacturing Co. v. Jones, 1887, 71 Iowa 234, 32 N.W. 280.

27. Miller v. American National Bank in Little Falls, 1943, 216 Minn. 19, 11 N.W.2d 655; Kroger Grocery & Baking Co. v. Hamlin, 1921, 193 Ky. 116, 235 S.W. 4; Steppuhn v. Chicago Great Western Railway Co., 1918, 199 Mo.App. 571, 204 S.W. 579.

28. Norvell v. Safeway Stores Inc., 1957, 212 Md. 14, 128 A.2d 591, 59 A.L.R.2d 1407; Applestein v. Preston, Fla.App.1976, 335 So.2d 604.

29. Tucker v. Bartlett, 1916, 97 Kan. 163, 155 P. 1; Tritchler v. West Virginia Newspaper Publishing Co., Inc., 1972, 156 W.Va. 335, 193 S.E.2d 146.

30. Second Restatement of Torts, § 663.

31. Gastman v. Myer, 1955, 285 App.Div. 611, 139 N.Y.S.2d 602.

32. Harper v. Harper, 1901, 49 W.Va. 661, 39 S.E. 661.

33. Nettleton v. Cook, 1917, 30 Idaho 82, 163 P. 300 (magistrate's dismissal because wrong statute used in charge).

quent indictment.[34] In the absence of some such showing, however, the magistrate's dismissal after a preliminary hearing is said to establish defendant's want of probable cause in prosecuting. It is at least conceivable that there are constitutional objections to this view, since it binds the defendant by judicial action in which he has no participation [35] and since a lack of probable cause at the time of the hearing does not necessarily suggest a lack of probable cause at the time prosecution was initiated.[36] At any rate a number of courts have firmly rejected the rule and refuse to give any effect at all to the magistrate's dismissal or the grand jury's refusal to indict.[37] Occasionally the plaintiff is discharged in the criminal case because his accuser abandons the prosecution or supports a motion for dismissal. It is usually said that this abandonment is no evidence that the accuser lacked probable cause,[38] or that at most it furnishes some evidence on the issue under particular circumstances and along with other evidence,[39] but that it is not, standing alone, prima facie evidence that probable cause is lacking.[40] Abandonment of the prosecution by the public prosecutor's nolle prosequi is treated in much the same way.[41]

There is good agreement that certain rulings unfavorable to the accused in the criminal case furnish evidence or presumptions that the prosecutor had probable cause. The magistrate's commitment [42] and the grand jury's indictment [43] constitute at least some evidence of probable cause. Sometimes it is said that these rulings establish a "prima facie" case of probable cause, but since the plaintiff in malicious prosecution has the burden of proving a want of probable cause in the first place,[44] such statements seem to mean only that the commitment or indictment is important evidence on the issue.[45] However, in a few states the magistrate's ruling is given special significance, and the plaintiff is permitted in such cases to show a want of probable cause only if he can show fraud, corruption or falsification in the magistrate's court.[46] In much the same way, the accused who waives preliminary examination and is thus committed without a hearing runs the risk that his waiver will be treated as an admission of probable cause that bars the later malicious prosecution action.[47] A conviction after tri-

34. Welch v. Bergeron, 1975, 115 N.H. 179, 337 A.2d 341.

35. See Davis v. McMillan, 1905, 142 Mich. 391, 105 N.W. 862 ("an act, not that of the defendant, cannot be evidence to bind him").

36. See Stohr v. Donahue, 1974, 215 Kan. 528, 527 P.2d 983 (inference of no probable cause rebutted because of time difference).

37. Glenn v. Lawrence, 1917, 280 Ill. 581, 117 N.E. 757 (no indictment); Davis v. McMillan, 1905, 142 Mich. 391, 105 N.W. 862 (discharge); Shoemaker v. Shoemaker, 1951, 11 N.J.Super. 471, 78 A.2d 605.

38. Western Union Telegraph Co. v. Thomasson, 4th Cir. 1918, 251 F. 833. See Shoemaker v. Shoemaker, 1951, 11 N.J.Super. 471, 78 A.2d 605.

39. See Norvell v. Safeway Stores, 1957, 212 Md. 14, 128 A.2d 591, 59 A.L.R.2d 1407; DeFusco v. Brophy, 1973, 112 R.I. 461, 311 A.2d 286.

40. Contra, stating a prima facie rule, Schnathorst v. Williams, 1949, 240 Iowa 561, 36 N.W.2d 739. See also Second Restatement of Torts, § 665(1).

41. Exxon Corp. v. Kelly, 1978, 281 Md. 689, 381 A.2d 1146 (evidentiary effect of nolle prosqui depends on circumstances of its entry, since it may not be based on want of probable cause); Nicholson v. Roop, N.D. 1954, 62 N.W.2d 473, 43 A.L.R.2d 1031; Second Restatement of Torts, § 665(2).

42. Newton v. McGowan, 1962, 256 N.C. 421, 124 S.E.2d 142; Lampos v. Bazar, Inc., 1974, 270 Or. 256, 527 P.2d 376.

43. Freides v. Sani-Mode Manufacturing Co., 1965, 33 Ill.2d 291, 211 N.E.2d 286, 28 A.L.R.3d 741; Gladding Chevrolet, Inc. v. Fowler, 1972, 264 Md. 499, 287 A.2d 280.

44. See Huffstutler v. Coates, Mo.1960, 335 S.W.2d 70; Hryciuk v. Robinson, 1958, 213 Or. 542, 326 P.2d 424; Duckwall v. Davis, 1924, 194 Ind. 670, 142 N.E. 113; Conder v. Morrison, 1938, 275 Ky. 360, 121 S.W.2d 930; Randol v. Kline's, Inc., 1932, 330 Mo. 343, 49 S.W.2d 112.

45. See Zalewski v. Gallagher, 1977, 150 N.J.Super. 360, 375 A.2d 1195; Hryciuk v. Robinson, 1958, 213 Or. 542, 326 P.2d 424.

46. Gallucci v. Milavic, Fla.1958, 100 So.2d 375, 68 A.L.R.2d 1164; Trottier v. West, 1976, 54 A.D.2d 1025, 388 N.Y.S.2d 180.

47. Brady v. Stiltner, 1895, 40 W.Va. 289, 21 S.E. 729; Hess v. Oregon German Baking Co., 1897, 31 Or. 503, 49 P. 803; Jones v. Wilmington & Weldon Railroad Co., 1899, 125 N.C. 227, 34 S.E. 398; Ferguson v. Rein-

al, even though it is subsequently reversed,[48] obviously presents strong evidence that there was enough of a case to convince a jury, and it usually is held to be conclusive as to the existence of probable cause,[49] in the absence of a showing that the conviction was obtained by fraud, perjury or other corrupt means.[50] There is a considerable minority view which regards the conviction as creating only a presumption, which may be rebutted by any competent evidence showing that probable cause for the prosecution did not in fact exist.[51] Very possibly, however, the practical effect of the two rules is the same, since proceeding without probable cause will ordinarily involve a fraud upon the court.[52]

The courts have always distrusted malicious prosecution actions, and have retained a strong hand over them. For this reason the existence of probable cause, which involves only the conduct of a reasonable man under the circumstances, and does not differ essentially from the determination of negligence, usually is taken out of the hands of the jury, and held to be a matter for decision by the court.[53] That is to say, the court will determine whether upon the appearances presented to the defendant, a reasonable person would have instituted the proceeding.[54] If there are questions of fact in dispute, as to what appeared to the defendant or what he did or did not do, they are submitted to the jury for a special verdict, or under instructions declaring what state of facts would constitute or not constitute probable cause.[55] The issue in such cases is called a mixed question of law and fact, but this only means that it is for the jury to say what the facts are and for the judge to say whether those facts constituted probable cause.[56] A few jurisdictions have rejected the rule that probable cause is for the court, and have held that where more than one conclusion may be drawn as to the reasonableness of the defendant's conduct, the question is for the jury.[57]

Malice: Improper Purpose

Second in importance to the issue of probable cause is that of "malice," which has given the action its name. The plaintiff has the burden of proving[58] that the defendant instituted the proceeding "maliciously." This unfortunate word, which has so much vexed the kindred law of defamation,[59] requires no less in the way of definition here. It means something more than the fictitious "malice in law" which has been developed in defamation cases as a cloak for strict liability.

hart, 1937, 125 Pa.Super. 154, 190 A. 153 (nolo contendere).

48. If the conviction is unreversed, there is of course no termination in favor of the accused. See supra, p. 874.

49. Brewster v. Woodward & Lothrop, Inc., 1976, 174 U.S.App.D.C. 164, 530 F.2d 1016; Tarantino v. Griebel, 1960, 9 Wis.2d 37, 100 N.W.2d 350, 86 A.L.R. 2d 1084.

50. Wisniski v. Ong, 1963, 94 Ariz. 123, 382 P.2d 233; Taylor v. Nohalty, Ky.1966, 404 S.W.2d 448. Krieg v. Dayton-Hudson Corp., 1981, 104 Wis.2d 455, 311 N.W.2d 641 (conclusory allegation of collateral fraud insufficient).

51. Nesmith v. Alford, 5th Cir. 1963, 318 F.2d 110, rehearing denied 319 F.2d 859, certiorari denied 375 U.S. 975, 84 S.Ct. 489, 11 L.Ed.2d 420 (Alabama law); McRae v. Brant, 1967, 108 N.H. 177, 230 A.2d 753.

52. See McElroy v. Catholic Press Co., 1912, 254 Ill. 290, 98 N.E. 527.

53. Green, Judge and Jury, 1930, 342; Restatement of Torts, § 673(1). It has been said, however, that this is true only as to the question of the reasonableness of the defendant's belief in the guilt of the accused, and that the actual existence of such belief is for the jury. Stewart v. Sonneborn, 1878, 98 U.S. 187, 25 L.Ed. 116.

54. Slade v. City of Phoenix, 1975, 112 Ariz. 298, 541 P.2d 550; Gustafson v. Payless Drug Stores Northwest, Inc., 1974, 269 Or. 354, 525 P.2d 118.

55. Sarwark Motor Sales, Inc. v. Woolridge, 1960, 88 Ariz. 173, 354 P.2d 34. As to the difficulties of writing an instruction see Byrd, Malicious Prosecution in North Carolina, 1969, 47 N.C.L.Rev. 285, 301. See also New York Pattern Jury Instructions PJI 3:50.

56. Treloar v. Harris, 1917, 66 Ind.App. 59, 117 N.E. 975.

57. Edgington v. Glassmeyer, Ohio App.1959, 168 N.E.2d 425, 11 O.O.2d 439; Elletson v. Dixie Home Stores, 1957, 231 S.C. 565, 99 S.E.2d 384.

58. Purcell v. Macnamara, 1808, 9 East 361, 103 Eng.Rep. 610; Gibson v. Chaters, 1800, 2 Bos. & P. 129, 126 Eng.Rep. 1196; Dietz v. Langfitt, 1869, 63 Pa. 234; McKown v. Hunter, 1864, 30 N.Y. 625.

59. See § 128, infra.

There must be "malice in fact."[60] At the same time it does not necessarily mean that the defendant was inspired by hatred, spite or ill will;[61] and there is authority that if his purpose was otherwise a proper one, the addition of the incidental fact that he felt indignation or resentment toward the plaintiff will not make him liable.[62] As in the cases of qualified privilege in defamation,[63] the courts seem to have looked to the primary purpose behind the defendant's action. If he is found to have acted chiefly to give vent to motives of ill will, "malice" is established.[64] But it is found also where his primary purpose was merely something other than the social one of bringing an offender to justice, which alone is recognized as a justification for a criminal proceeding.[65] "Malice" is found when the defendant uses the prosecution for the purpose of obtaining any private advantage,[66] for instance, as a means to extort money,[67] to collect a debt,[68] to recover property[69] to compel performance of a contract,[70] to "tie up the mouths" of witnesses in another action,[71] or as an experiment to discover who might have committed the crime[72]. On the other hand, any purpose legitimate in itself will not be "malice" if it is clearly secondary and incidental to the disinterested one of convicting the guilty.[73]

Unlike probable cause, the question of "malice" is to be determined by the jury,[74] unless only one conclusion may reasonably be drawn from the evidence.[75] The defendant's improper purpose usually is proved by circumstantial evidence.[76] The plaintiff must establish malice in addition to the absence of probable cause.[77] However, some

60. Downing v. Stone, 1910, 152 N.C. 525, 68 S.E. 9; Metropolitan Life Insurance Co. v. Miller, 1903, 114 Ky. 754, 71 S.W. 921; Levy v. Brannan, 1870, 39 Cal. 485; Griswold v. Horne, 1917, 19 Ariz. 56, 165 P. 318 ("malice of the evil motive").

61. Brault v. Town of Milton, 2d Cir. 1975, 527 F.2d 730; Tweedy v. J.C. Penney Co., Inc., 1976, 216 Va. 596, 221 S.E.2d 152.

62. Lalor v. Byrne, 1892, 51 Mo.App. 578; Sharp v. Johnston, 1877, 4 Mo.App. 576; Restatement of Torts, § 668, Comment *f*.

63. See supra, § 115.

64. Smith v. Kidd, Ky.1952, 246 S.W.2d 155; Meyer v. Ewald, 1974, 66 Wis.2d 168, 224 N.W.2d 419; Mondrow v. Selwyn, 1980, 172 N.J.Super. 379, 412 A.2d 447 (grand jury returned no bill, but with recommendation that new complaint for misdemeanor be made out in municipal court, held, the no-bill was not a termination and the municipal proceeding, though on a lesser charge, should be regarded as part of one continuous proceeding.)

65. Nesmith v. Alford, 5th Cir. 1963, 318 F.2d 110, rehearing denied 319 F.2d 859, certiorari denied 375 U.S. 975, 84 S.Ct. 489, 11 L.Ed.2d 420; Glover v. Fleming, 1977, 36 Md.App. 381, 373 A.2d 981.

66. Creelman v. Svenning, 1969, 1 Wn.App. 402, 461 P.2d 557; Restatement of Torts, § 668, Comment *g*.

67. Cf. Krug v. Ward, 1875, 77 Ill. 603.

68. Kitchens v. Barlow, Miss.1964, 250 Miss. 121, 164 So.2d 745; Peters v. Hall, 1953, 263 Wis. 450, 57 N.W.2d 723.

69. Suchey v. Stiles, 1964, 155 Colo. 363, 394 P.2d 739; White v. Apsley Rubber Co., 1907, 194 Mass. 97, 80 N.E. 500; Hall v. American Investment Co., 1928, 241 Mich. 349, 217 N.W 18; Wadkins v. Digman, 1918, 82 W.Va. 623, 96 S.E. 1016.

70. Whiteford v. Henthorn, 1893, 10 Ind.App. 97, 37 N.E. 419. Cf. Munson v. Linnick, 1967, 255 Cal.App.2d 589, 63 Cal.Rptr. 340.

71. Haddrick v. Heslop, 1848, 12 Q.B. 267, 116 Eng. Rep. 869. Cf. Hammond v. Rowley, 1912, 86 Conn. 6, 84 A. 94 (to frighten off other trespassers).

72. Johnson v. Ebberts, C.C.Or.1880, 11 F. 129; Glover v. Fleming, 1977, 36 Md.App. 381, 373 A.2d 981.

73. Thompson v. Beacon Valley Rubber Co., 1888, 56 Conn. 493, 16 A. 554 ("it can hardly be expected that all selfish aims and desires can be eliminated from such prosecutions"); Kelsea v. Swett, 1919, 234 Mass. 79, 125 N.E. 143; Wenger v. Phillips, 1900, 195 Pa. 214, 45 A. 927; Williams v. Kyes, 1896, 9 Colo.App. 220, 47 P. 839.

74. Lambert v. Sears, Roebuck & Co., 1977, 280 Or. 123, 570 P.2d 357; Giant of Virginia, Inc. v. Pigg, 1967, 207 Va. 679, 152 S.E.2d 271.

75. Atkinson v. Birmingham, 1922, 44 R.I. 123, 116 A. 205, reargument denied 117 A. 274; Virginia Electric & Power Co. v. Wynne, 1928, 149 Va. 882, 141 S.E. 829.

76. Severns v. Brainerd, 1895, 61 Minn. 265, 63 N.W. 477; Thurston v. Wright, 1889, 77 Mich. 96, 43 N.W. 860; Pierce v. Thompson, 1828, 23 Mass. (6 Pick.) 193; Holden v. Merritt, 1894, 92 Iowa 707, 61 N.W. 390. It may be inferred from a gross or reckless disregard of the plaintiff's rights. Blunk v. Atchison Topeka & Santa Fe Railway Co., C.C.Mo.1889, 38 F. 311; Stubbs v. Mulholland, 1902, 168 Mo. 47, 67 S.W. 650.

77. Vanderbilt v. Mathis, N.Y.1856, 5 Duer 304; Dietz v. Langfitt, 1869, 63 Pa. 234; Atkinson v. Birmingham, 1922, 44 R.I. 123, 116 A. 205, reargument denied 117 A. 274.

courts have said that there is no legitimate purpose in the prosecution unless the prosecutor has an honest belief in the guilt of the accused.[78] On this theory, it is held that lack of probable cause may give rise to an inference of malice, since if the accuser had almost no basis for belief in guilt, the jury may infer that he did not in fact believe in the accused's guilt and must have acted for an improper purpose.[79] The Restatement limits the inference of malice from want of probable cause to such cases,[80] but courts may at times permit the inference without such a restriction.[81] Perhaps it would be more accurate to say that in certain cases it is not so much malice that is required as a serious abuse of authority.[82]

There is at least a degree of dissatisfaction with the traditional treatment of malice in these cases. For instance, when the prosecutor is a privileged public official, several courts have said or suggested that the malice necessary to the action for malicious prosecution is something more than the malice to be inferred from a lack of probable cause.[83] Apparently this is a recognition that the inference from lack of probable cause is sometimes wholly fictional. Other cases,[84] perhaps recognizing that malicious prosecution is in one sense merely a special case of defamation, have adapted the constitutionally required definition of malice from New York Times v. Sullivan[85] and like cases. Some judges have expressed doubts about the whole doctrine of inferred malice,[86] and at least one case has indicated that malice may not be inferred from a want of probable cause when want of probable cause itself was merely presumed from a magistrate's dismissal of the criminal charge.[87] Whether these are isolated instances or signs of change to come remains to be seen.

In any event there are mitigating rules. The jury is not compelled to draw the inference that the accuser was guilty of malice merely because probable cause was lacking, and it is free to decide that malice has not been proven.[88] The advice of counsel is evidence tending to negative malice by proving honest belief and good faith, and may be accepted as sufficient by the jury.[89] The termination of the prosecution in favor of the accused of course affords no evidence that

78. Harkrader v. Moore, 1872, 44 Cal. 144; Watson v. Cain, 1911, 171 Ala. 151, 54 So. 610.

79. Griswold v. Horne, 1917, 19 Ariz. 56, 165 P. 318; Martin v. City of Albany, 1977, 42 N.Y.2d 13, 396 N.Y.S.2d 612, 364 N.E.2d 1304.

80. Restatement of Torts, § 669.

81. See Haswell v. Liberty Mutual Insurance Co., Mo.1977, 557 S.W.2d 628 (inference permitted without qualification); Martin v. City of Albany, 1977, 42 N.Y.2d 13, 396 N.Y.S.2d 612, 364 N.E.2d 1304 (inference of malice permitted where second officer to scene mistook plaintiff for guilty party); Lambert v. Sears, Roebuck & Co., 1977, 280 Or. 123, 570 P.2d 357.

82. This may be the explanation for Martin v. City of Albany, 1977, 42 N.Y.2d 13, 396 N.Y.S.2d 612, 364 N.E.2d 1304, where an abusive officer, second on the scene of an arrest, wrongly assumed that plaintiff was involved. There seems to have been neither improper purpose nor personal spite, merely arrogance and abuse of power. Malice is also found when the prosecutor is in a position of informal power, as in the case of the store security guard. Where he denies the accused an opportunity to explain himself before prosecuting "malice" may again be found. This may be the explanation for Lambert v. Sears, Roebuck & Co., 1977, 280 Or. 123, 570 P.2d 357.

83. Williams v. Crews, 8th Cir. 1977, 564 F.2d 263; Vander Linden v. Crews, Iowa 1975, 231 N.W.2d 904; Brewer v. Mele, 1972, 267 Md. 437, 298 A.2d 156.

84. Spencer v. Burglass, La.App.1976, 337 So.2d 596, writ denied, La., 340 So.2d 990; Carter v. Catfish Cabin, La.App.1975, 316 So.2d 517.

85. See § 113, supra.

86. See Lambert v. Sears, Roebuck & Co., 1977, 280 Or. 123, 570 P.2d 357 (concurring opinion).

87. Barker v. Waltz, 1952, 40 Wn.2d 866, 246 P.2d 846.

88. Engelgau v. Walter, 1947, 181 Or. 481, 182 P.2d 987; Hanowitz v. Great Northern Railway Co., 1913, 122 Minn. 241, 142 N.W. 196; Reinhardt v. Reitz, 1917, 176 Cal. 209, 167 P. 865; Pierce v. Doolittle, 1906, 130 Iowa 333, 106 N.W. 751; Atkinson v. Birmingham, 1922, 44 R.I. 123, 116 A. 205, reargument denied 117 A.2d 274.

89. Estes v. Hancock County Bank, 1972, 259 Ind. 542, 289 N.E.2d 728; Ramsey v. Arrott, 1885, 64 Tex. 320; El Reno Gas & Electric Co. v. Spurgeon, 1911, 30 Okl. 88, 118 P. 397. It has been held that the advice of a justice of the peace who is not an attorney is evidence to negative malice. Kable v. Carey, 1918, 135 Ark. 137, 204 S.W. 748.

the defendant had an improper purpose in commencing it.[90]

Defenses

Even if the plaintiff in malicious prosecution can show that the defendant acted maliciously and without probable cause in instigating a prosecution, it is always open to the defendant to escape liability by showing in the malicious prosecution suit itself that the plaintiff was in fact guilty of the offense with which he was charged.[91] The defense of guilt in fact is a good one even if the jury in the criminal prosecution had acquitted the accused,[92] since the not guilty verdict does not establish innocence but merely the prosecution's failure to prove guilt beyond a reasonable doubt.[93] The defense is obviously analogous to the truth defense in defamation cases and the burden is upon the defendant[94] in the malicious prosecution action to prove that the plaintiff, if not guilty of the exact offense for which he was prosecuted, was at least guilty of a substantially equivalent one.[95]

One problem not yet resolved is whether the Constitutional limitations imposed by the Supreme Court[96] in libel cases will also apply to malicious prosecution claims.[97] Since malicious prosecution does involve a defamatory communication—the charge of crime—there is more than a little basis for imposing the same limitations that apply in defamation cases.[98] Even if those limitations are applied, however, the impact may produce little substantive change, since the requirement in malicious prosecution cases that the defendant must act without probable cause may well meet the Constitutional requirements that he act recklessly in disregard of the truth. On the damages side, however, application of the Constitutional limitations as set forth in *Gertz*[99] may well operate to prohibit recovery in excess of probable harms.[1]

Related Torts

Malicious prosecution is closely related to a number of claims, both common law and statutory, and in any given case counsel may assert several different theories of liability. Frequently malicious prosecution claims are coupled with claims for false imprisonment, but the two are entirely distinct. So long as

90. Bekkeland v. Lyons, 1903, 96 Tex. 255, 72 S.W. 56; McClafferty v. Philp, 1892, 151 Pa. 86, 24 A. 1042; Malloy v. Chicago, Milwaukee & St. Paul Railway Co., 1914, 34 S.D. 330, 148 N.W. 598. Similarly, commitment by a magistrate is no evidence of lack of malice. Lewton v. Hower, 1895, 35 Fla. 58, 16 So. 616.

91. Clary v. Hale, 1959, 175 Cal.App.2d 880, 1 Cal. Rptr. 91; Shoemaker v. Selnes, 1960, 220 Or. 573, 349 P.2d 473; Restatement of Torts, § 657.

92. Mooney v. Mull, 1939, 216 N.C. 410, 5 S.E.2d 122; Wiggs v. Farmer, 1964, 205 Va. 149, 135 S.E.2d 829.

93. Second Restatement of Torts, § 657.

94. Shelton v. Southern Railway, D.Tenn.1918, 255 F. 182; Levin v. Costello, 1919, 214 Ill.App. 505; Magowan v. Rickey, 1900, 64 N.J.L. 402, 45 A. 804. Courts occasionally put the burden on the plaintiff to prove his actual innocence. Jackson v. Train, Tex.Civ.App.1972, 495 S.W.2d 36; Parker v. Dallas Hunting & Fishing Club, Tex.Civ.App.1971, 463 S.W.2d 496. This may be inadvertent, but it might be justified on analogy the Constitutional rules in defamation cases that now require the plaintiff to prove the defamatory charge is untrue. As to this see ch. 19, supra.

95. This is especially difficult where several charges grow out of the same transaction, where there are lesser included offenses, and where a charge is technically, but not substantially, wrong. Compare Ruff v. Eckerds Drugs, Inc., 1975, 265 S.C. 563, 220 S.E.2d 649 with Cuthrell v. Zayre of Virginia, Inc., 1974, 214 Va. 427, 201 S.E.2d 779; see Patterson v. Brogan, 1973, 261 S.C. 87, 198 S.E.2d 586.

96. See § 113, supra.

97. See Dobbs, Belief and Doubt in Malicious Prosecution and Libel, 1979, 21 Ariz.L.Rev. 607. In Allard v. Church of Scientology of California, 1976, 58 Cal.App. 3d 439, 129 Cal.Rptr. 797, certiorari denied 429 U.S. 1091, 97 S.Ct. 1101, 51 L.Ed.2d 537 the court rejected the constitutional limitations as to damages imposed in libel cases. But in City of Long Beach v. Bozek, 1982, 31 Cal.3d 527, 183 Cal.Rptr. 86, 645 P.2d 137, the court invoked a number of constitutional decisions, including those in libel cases, to deny a city the right to pursue a malicious prosecution claim against a citizen.

98. See Dobbs, Belief and Doubt in Malicious Prosecution and Libel, 1979, 21 Ariz.L.Rev. 607.

99. Gertz v. Robert Welch, Inc., 1974, 418 U.S. 323 94 S.Ct. 2997, 41 L.Ed.2d 789; cf. Carey v. Piphus, 1978, 435 U.S. 247, 97 S.Ct. 1642, 55 L.Ed.2d 252 (forbidding dignitary damages for due process violation). Gertz is discussed supra, § 116A.

1. This argument was rejected in Allard v. Church of Scientology of California, 1976, 58 Cal.App.3d 439, 129 Cal.Rptr. 797.

the plaintiff has been detained by legal process, it cannot be said that he has been falsely imprisoned and the claim, if there is one, must be for malicious prosecution,[2] where malice and a want of probable cause must be shown. If there is no process issued at all and the plaintiff is arrested without a warrant or any other valid basis for an arrest, there is no malicious prosecution but a false arrest.[3] Where an unjustified detention takes place, followed by improper prosecution, the plaintiff may be required to assert both false imprisonment and malicious prosecution to recover all his damages.[4]

Malicious prosecution also resembles the tort of libel since it necessarily involves the written charges of a crime.[5] Though the harm done to the plaintiff may include not only loss of reputation but also actual confinement and out of pocket losses, the real difference between defamation and malicious prosecution, if there is one, lies in the belief that resort to the judicial processes should not be discouraged and in the special protection given to those who use such processes.[6] Because of the substantial similarity if not outright identity between the malicious prosecution action and the defamation suit, the Constitutional rules now applied in defamation may be carried over to malicious prosecution.[7]

A number of statutory claims may accomplish the same purpose as the common law malicious prosecution action on particular facts. Federal civil rights actions under § 1983 [8] have been brought [9] on facts that may also give rise to a state law malicious prosecution claim. To a large extent the state law of tort has been incorporated into such actions [10] and the substantive law difference between the two actions may be very small, though of course the § 1983 action gives the plaintiff a federal forum and a potential for recovery of attorneys' fees as well.[11]

A federal labor statute [12] has been interpreted [13] to permit a claim by union members against their union, based on the union's improper litigation, and the Supreme Court has held [14] that federal antitrust actions may be based upon unjustified litigation aimed at suppressing competition. There is even a

---

2. Nesmith v. Alford, 5th Cir. 1963, 318 F.2d 110, rehearing denied 319 F.2d 859, certiorari denied 375 U.S. 975, 84 S.Ct. 489, 11 L.Ed.2d 420 (Alabama law); Harper, Malicious Prosecution, False Imprisonment and Defamation, 1937, 15 Tex.L.Rev. 157.

3. Broughton v. State, 1975, 37 N.Y.2d 451, 373 N.Y.S.2d 87, 335 N.E.2d 310, certiorari denied 423 U.S. 929, 96 S.Ct. 277, 46 L.Ed.2d 257.

4. See p. 888, infra.

5. See Harper, Malicious Prosecution, False Imprisonment and Defamation, 1937, 15 Tex.L.Rev. 157. The private instigator usually must sign an affidavit, but even if the charges are oral, an expectation that they will be written down would call for their treatment as libel rather than slander if any difference remains in those two torts.

6. This is reflected in the substantial judicial control retained over the malicious prosecution action. See, e.g., supra p. 882. Cf. Sweeney v. Abramovitz, D.Conn.1978, 449 F.Supp. 213 (federal courts will determine whether state law can recognize malicious prosecution of a civil rights claim).

7. See p. 887, infra.

8. 42 U.S.C.A. § 1983.

9. Phillips v. International Association of Bridge, Structural & Ornamental Iron Workers, 9th Cir. 1977, 556 F.2d 939; Tucker v. Duncan, 4th Cir. 1974, 499 F.2d 963; Bryant v. Commonwealth, 6th Cir. 1974, 490 F.2d 1273 (all denying relief on various grounds).

10. Cramer v. Crutchfield, 4th Cir. 1981, 648 F.2d 943 (state statute of limitations governed); Tucker v. Duncan, 4th Cir.1974, 499 F.2d 963 (termination rules applied to bar § 1983 action); Hahn v. Sargent, D.Mass.1975, 388 F.Supp. 445, affirmed 1st Cir., 523 F.2d 461, certiorari denied 1976, 425 U.S. 904, 96 S.Ct. 1495, 47 L.Ed.2d 754 (presumption of probable cause from indictment, perjury rules applied in § 1983 action).

11. 42 U.S.C.A. § 1988 permits recovery of attorneys' fees for the prevailing party. The general American rule in the absence of statute is otherwise. See D. Dobbs, Remedies, § 3.8.

12. 29 U.S.C.A. § 411(a)(4) ("No labor organization shall limit the right of any member thereof to institute an action in any court. * * *")

13. Phillips v. International Association of Bridge, Structural & Ornamental Iron Workers, 9th Cir.1977, 556 F.2d 939.

14. California Motor Transport Co. v. Trucking Unlimited, 1972, 404 U.S. 508, 92 S.Ct. 609, 30 L.Ed.2d 642; Otter Tail Power Co. v. United States, 1973, 410 U.S. 366, 93 S.Ct. 1022, 35 L.Ed.2d 359, rehearing denied 411 U.S. 910, 93 S.Ct. 1523, 36 L.Ed.2d 201, on remand, D.Minn., 360 F.Supp. 451, affirmed 417 U.S. 901, 94 S.Ct. 2594, 41 L.Ed.2d 207.

provision in the UCC[15] that may be used to permit recovery of damages resulting from a prosecution when a bank wrongfully dishonors a check.

As a result of such developments facts giving rise to malicious prosecution claims may also give rise to a number of other actions that may be more or less useful.

Damages

According to one theory, there could be no recovery of damages in tort actions derived from the action on the case unless actual damage was shown.[16] This generalization, however, has not been applied to many of the dignitary torts, where some serious interference with personal rights is involved;[17] and in malicious prosecution cases, as well as in others, damages have been permitted in substantial sums on the theory that there is a serious harm in the violation of the plaintiff's right, quite apart from any out of pocket losses.[18] Thus damages may be awarded for loss of reputation, credit or standing;[19] or for mental suffering or humiliation.[20] It is, of course, open to the plaintiff to offer evidence of such intangible losses if he can do so subject to the rules of evidence,[21] but explicit proof is not traditionally required as a basis for the award.[22] Perhaps this is because a jury is likely to know from the proof of prosecution itself the probable extent of plaintiff's injury to feelings and because such damages are not in any event subject to exact measurement.

Whether the traditional award of "general" damages without proof of loss continues to be permissible is an open question. The Supreme Court of the United States has said it is not in certain defamation cases, where "actual damage" must now be proven to recover at all.[23] The Court has taken a similar view about tortious violations of due process rights.[24] On the other hand, the requirement in the malicious prosecution action that the accuser be guilty of serious fault may serve to distinguish the two kinds of cases.[25] If such a distinction is not accepted, however, the close similarity between malicious prosecution and defamation actions may compel the application of the limits now observed in defamation cases. It is possible that proof of actual damage could be satisfied by a ritual statement of shock and distress, but if so the ritual may still be required.

In any event, there may be recovery of other damages, designated as "special," if there is specific pleading and proof. The plaintiff may recover compensation for any arrest or imprisonment,[26] including damages

---

15. UCC § 4–402.

16. Byne v. Moore, 1813, 5 Taunt. 187, 128 Eng. Rep. 658; Stanford v. A.F. Messick Grocery Co., 1906, 143 N.C. 419, 55 S.E. 815.

17. D. Dobbs, Remedies § 7.3.

18. E.g., Young v. Jack Boring's, Inc., Mo.App. 1976, 540 S.W.2d 887 (mistaken replevin of TV, which was quickly returned; out of pocket, $350, award, $8,000 compensatory, $25,000 punitive); Jefferson v. S.S. Kresge Co., La.App.1977, 344 So.2d 1118 (specials $334, award $2500).

19. Bertero v. National General Corp., 1975, 13 Cal. 3d 43, 118 Cal.Rptr. 184, 529 P.2d 608, 65 A.L.R.3d 878; Young v. Jack Boring's, Inc., Mo.App.1976, 540 S.W.2d 887.

20. Haswell v. Liberty Mutual Insurance Co., Mo. 1977, 557 S.W.2d 628. Cf. Raine v. Drasin, Ky.1981, 621 S.W.2d 895 (based on wrongful civil action against doctors).

21. As in Green v. Meadows, Tex.Civ.App.1975, 527 S.W.2d 496, refused n.r.e. (" * * * he was in a state of shock * * * and unable to work; that he couldn't sleep and couldn't concentrate. He was despondent and depressed * * * generally upset * * * shocked and frightened * * * difference in the way friends treated him. * * *" Award: $20,000 plus specials.)

22. Second Restatement of Torts, § 670; D. Dobbs, Remedies § 7.3.

23. Gertz v. Robert Welch, Inc., 1974, 418 U.S. 323, 94 S.Ct. 2997, 41 L.Ed.2d 789. See § 116A, supra.

24. Carey v. Piphus, 1978, 435 U.S. 247, 98 S.Ct. 1042, 55 L.Ed.2d 252.

25. The requirement of "actual damage" was not imposed in New York Times v. Sullivan, 1964, 376 U.S. 254, 84 S.Ct. 710, 11 L.Ed.2d 686, motion denied 376 U.S. 967, 84 S.Ct. 1130, 12 L.Ed.2d 83 where, perhaps instead, intentional misconduct was involved. By analogy the intentional misconduct in malicious prosecution may relieve the burden of proving "actual damages."

26. Rich v. Rogers, 1925, 250 Mass. 587, 146 N.E. 246; Wilson v. Bowen, 1887, 64 Mich. 133, 31 N.W. 81.

for discomfort or injury to his health,[27] or loss of time [28] and deprivation of the society of his family.[29] He may recover any reasonable expenses to which he has been put in defending the prosecution and establishing his innocence,[30] including attorney's fees in the criminal proceeding,[31] although such fees in the action for malicious prosecution itself are normally not recoverable.[32] In addition, he may recover for any specific financial loss such as the loss of present [33] or prospective [34] employment, or loss of business profits [35] which can be proved with reasonable certainty to have been caused [36] by the prosecution, provided that it is regarded as a foreseeable, or normal consequence of the criminal proceeding.[37] The limitations upon recovery in terms of "proximate cause" are apparently much the same as in cases of defamation.[38] Because of the intentional and outrageous nature of the tort, malicious prosecution is peculiarly adapted to the award of punitive damages, and it is agreed generally that the jury may award them when they find personal ill will or oppressive conduct in the prosecution.[39]

One problem in assessing damages requires a careful distinction between the claim for false imprisonment or arrest and the claim for malicious prosecution. If there is a false arrest claim, damages for that claim cover the time of detention up until issuance of process or arraignment, but not more. From that point on, any damages recoverable must be based on a malicious prosecution claim and on the wrongful use of judicial process rather than detention itself. If the malicious prosecution claim cannot be established the recovery must be limited to the period of imprisonment, and could not,

27. Stoecker v. Nathanson, 1904, 5 Neb. (Unof.) 435, 98 N.W. 1061; Grimes v. Grennblatt, 1910, 47 Colo. 495, 107 P. 1111; Equitable Life Assurance Society v. Lester, Tex.Civ.App.1908, 110 S.W. 499. But see contra, on the ground that bad conditions or bad treatment in the jail are not a normal consequence: Duckwall v. Davis, 1924, 194 Ind. 670, 142 N.E. 113; Seidler v. Burns, 1911, 84 Conn. 111, 79 A. 53; Redman v. Hudson, 1916, 124 Ark. 26, 186 S.W. 312.

28. Helfer v. Hamburg Quarry Co., 1921, 208 Mo.App. 58, 233 S.W. 275; Hunter v. Laurent, 1925, 158 La. 874, 104 So. 747; Jacquemin v. Bunker, 1922, 15 Ohio App. 491; Davis v. Teague, Tex.Civ.App.1923, 256 S.W. 957.

29. Walling v. Fields, 1923, 209 Ala. 389, 96 So. 471; Killebrew v. Carlisle, 1892, 97 Ala. 535, 12 So. 167. Cf. Davis v. Seeley, 1894, 91 Iowa 583, 60 N.W. 183.

30. Seidler v. Burns, 1912, 86 Conn. 249, 85 A. 369; Wheeler v. Hanson, 1894, 161 Mass. 370, 37 N.E. 382; Blazek v. McCartin, 1909, 106 Minn. 461, 119 N.W. 215; Blunk v. Atchison, Topeka & Santa Fe Railway Co., C.C.Mo.1889, 38 F. 311.

31. Tully v. Dasher, 1968, 250 Md. 424, 244 A.2d 207 (recoverable though paid by another); Mercury v. Mustachia, Tex.Civ.App.1976, 540 S.W.2d 339. Fees incurred before the prosecution is initiated may be recoverable if there is a false arrest, but for malicious prosecution, only those incurred after the prosecution is initiated can be recovered. See Broughton v. State, 1975, 37 N.Y.2d 451, 373 N.Y.S.2d 87, 335 N.E.2d 310, certiorari denied 423 U.S. 929, 96 S.Ct. 277, 46 L.Ed.2d 257.

32. Benderach v. Grujicich, 1925, 30 N.M. 331, 233 P. 520; cf. Stewart v. Sonneborn, 1878, 98 U.S. 187, 25 L.Ed. 116; Beckham v. Collins, 1909, 54 Tex.Civ.App. 241, 117 S.W. 431. In Davis v. Tunison, 1957, 153 Ohio Ab. 474, 477, 153 N.E.2d 190, reversed on other grounds, 1959, 168 Ohio St. 471, 155 N.E.2d 904, it was held that there can be recovery where there is "fraud, malice, or willful misconduct."

33. H.S. Leyman Co. v. Short, 1926, 214 Ky. 272, 283 S.W. 96.

34. Stoecker v. Nathanson, 1904, 5 Neb. (Unof.) 435, 98 N.W. 1061; Davis v. McMillian, 1922, 28 Ga.App. 689, 112 S.E. 913, reversed on other grounds, 154 Ga. 803, 115 S.E. 494, cf. Long v. Burley State Bank, 1917, 30 Idaho 392, 165 P. 1119 (profits).

35. Colegrove v. City of Corning, 1976, 54 A.D.2d 1093, 388 N.Y.S.2d 964.

36. Cf. Baer v. Chambers, 1912, 67 Wash. 357, 121 P. 843 (cold caught while in prison).

37. Hanson v. Rhodes-Burford Furniture Co., 1923, 227 Ill.App. 471; Laing v. Mitten, 1904, 185 Mass. 233, 70 N.E. 128; Seidler v. Burns, 1911, 84 Conn. 111, 79 A. 53; Redman v. Hudson, 1916, 124 Ark. 26, 186 S.W. 312; Duckwall v. Davis, 1924, 194 Ind. 670, 142 N.E. 113.

38. Restatement of Torts, § 671, Comment d.

39. Chavez v. Sears, Roebuck & Co., 10th Cir.1975, 525 F.2d 827; Montgomery Ward & Co., Inc. v. Keulemans, 1975, 275 Md. 441, 340 A.2d 705. It has been held that the malice to be inferred from lack of probable cause is not sufficient to support a punitive award, for which there must be actual malice. Sparrow v. Vermont Savings Bank, 1921, 95 Vt. 29, 112 A. 205; Motsinger v. Sink, 1915, 168 N.C. 548, 84 S.E. 847; Park v. Security Bank & Trust Co., Okl.1973, 512 P.2d 113.

Cf. Columbus Finance, Inc. v. Howard, 1975, 42 Ohio St.2d 178, 327 N.E.2d 654 (wrongful execution, but no evidence of actual malice, no punitive damages).

for example, include attorneys' fees incurred in defending the prosecution.[40]

 WESTLAW REFERENCES

di malicious prosecution

headnote(essential /3 element* /s malicious +2 prosecution)

Institution of Proceeding

"malicious prosecution" /s institut! begin! initiat! /s judicial criminal /s proceeding* action

Termination in Favor of Accused

"malicious prosecution" /s terminat! /s favor /s accused

restatement /s torts /s 660 /p "malicious prosecution"

"malicious prosecution" /s compromis!

Probable Cause

"malicious prosecution" /s lack /s "probable cause"

"malicious prosecution" /p "advice of counsel" /s "probable cause"

"nolle prosequi" /p "malicious prosecution"

Malice: Improper Purpose

di malice

"malicious prosecution" /p motive* motivation* /s malice

249k30

"malicious prosecution*" /p malice /s jury /s question

Defenses

"malicious prosecution" /p escap! avoid! /5 liab!

249k40

"malicious prosecution" /9 defense*

Related Torts

168k3

"malicious prosecution" /s distinguish! distinct /s "false imprisonment"

Damages

249k67

249k66

"malicious prosecution" /s special /3 damages

---

40. Superx Drugs of Kentucky, Inc. v. Rice, Ky. App.1977, 554 S.W.2d 903; Broughton v. State, 37 N.Y.2d 451, 373 N.Y.S.2d 87, 335 N.E.2d 310, certiorari denied, 423 U.S.2d 929, 96 S.Ct. 277, 46 L.Ed.2d 257; City of Miami Beach v. Bretagna, Fla.App.1966, 190 So. 2d 364, 21 A.L.R.3d 1064.

§ 120

1. E.g., Peerson v. Ashcraft Cotton Mills, 1917, 201 Ala. 348, 78 So. 204; Kaufman v. A.H. Robins Co., 1969, 223 Tenn. 515, 448 S.W.2d 400; Cisson v. Pickens Savings & Loan Association, 1972, 258 S.C. 37, 186

§ 120. Wrongful Civil Proceedings

The action of malicious prosecution, which began as a remedy for unjustifiable criminal proceedings, has been undergoing a slow process of extension into the field of the wrongful initiation of civil suits. Most American courts now impose liability for malicious civil claims brought without probable cause,[1] but a very large minority protect the malicious litigant only if his victim can show a "special grievance," such as interference with his person or property by reason of the litigation.[2]

Three reasons have been advanced to justify this special grievance rule. One is that the successful party to a civil litigation is awarded costs, which are intended as full compensation, and hence as an exclusive remedy, for any damages that he has suffered. This may perhaps have been true in earlier days, and is still true to some limited extent in England, where the costs awarded include the fees of the party's attorney—although even there other damages, such as harm to his reputation, remain uncompensated. But in the United States, where the costs are set by statute at trivial amounts, and no attorney's fees are allowed, there can be no pretense at compensation even for the expenses of the litigation itself.[3] As a second reason, it is said that honest litigants are to be encouraged to seek justice and not to be deterred by fear of an action in return; and as a third, that litigation must end somewhere, and that if one counter-action may be brought, so may another, and another.

To these reasons the Michigan Court has added a fourth, namely, that lawyers and legal commentators are too prone to prefer a

---

S.E.2d 822. See Annot., 150 ALR 897. See also Second Restatement of Torts, § 674.

2. Taylor v. Greiner, 1981, 247 Ga. 526, 277 S.E.2d 13; Krashes v. White, 1975, 275 Md. 549, 341 A.2d 798; O'Toole v. Franklin, 1977, 279 Or. 513, 569 P.2d 561; Louis v. Blalock, Tex.Civ.App.1976, 543 S.W.2d 715, refused n.r.e.

3. D. Dobbs, 1973, Remedies § 3.8. Where, however, attorneys' fees are awarded under statute, as is often true in civil rights cases, this reason may have become sound although it was spurious when originated.

second suit to remedy the first, but that not all ills can be relieved by more litigation.[4] Courts have differed considerably in their assessment of these reasons. Courts that reject the "special injury" restriction upon recovery in effect insist that vexatious litigation must not be tolerated and that the plaintiff's heavy burden of proof provides sufficient protection to the honest litigant. Other courts, however, emphasize the chilling effect that potential liability may have on the completely honest litigant [5] and justify the requirement of special injury on this ground.[6] These continued and deep differences should be taken, perhaps, to reflect the intractability of the problem itself.

In any event, even the restrictive jurisdictions have recognized liability in a large group of exceptional cases in which special injury or grievance is found to exist.

The most obvious exception is that of civil actions which are recognized as quasi-criminal in character, or which involve an interference with the person, as in the case of proceedings in lunacy,[7] contempt,[8] bastardy,[9] juvenile delinquency,[10] arrest under civil process,[11] or binding over to keep the peace.[12] But the extension of the remedy has gone even further, and has included proceedings in which there has been interference with property or business, or damage differing in kind from the ordinary burden of defending a lawsuit,[13] such as attachment,[14] garnishment,[15] replevin,[16] the search of premises under a warrant,[17] injunctions,[18] proceedings in bankruptcy,[19] or for the dissolution of a part-

4. Friedman v. Dozorc, 1981, 412 Mich. 1, 312 N.W.2d 585. Some of the judges proposed an expansion of the prevailing party's right to recover attorneys' fees in lieu of the malicious prosecution action.

5. Defamation actions may chill free speech and for this reason there are constitutional limitations on such actions. See ch. 19, § 113, supra. Access to courts, also protected by First Amendment considerations, may come under similar protections. See City of Long Beach v. Bozek, 1982, 31 Cal.3d 527, 183 Cal.Rptr. 86, 645 P.2d 137. Whether the special grievance rule erects the appropriate protection is another question.

6. Spencer v. Burglass, La.App.1976, 337 So.2d 596, writ denied, La., 340 So.2d 990 ("chilling effect" on "basic right of a citizen to seek redress in court for what he considers to be a wrong); O'Toole v. Franklin, 1977, 279 Or. 513, 569 P.2d 561 ("The question is not whether a plaintiff should sue only in good faith, but under what circumstances he must be prepared to defend his good faith in a countersuit").

7. Fowle v. Fowle, 1965, 263 N.C. 724, 140 S.E.2d 398; Yelk v. Seefeldt, 1967, 35 Wis.2d 271, 151 N.W.2d 4; Hill v. Carlstrom, 1959, 216 Or. 300, 338 P.2d 645; Lowen v. Hilton, 1960, 142 Colo. 200, 351 P.2d 881; Alexander v. Alexander, 4th Cir.1956, 229 F.2d 111 (Florida law). See Note, 1918, 16 Mich.L.Rev. 457.

8. Sebring v. Van Aken, 1932, 235 App.Div. 420, 257 N.Y.S. 104; Tavenner v. Morehead, 1895, 41 W.Va. 116, 23 S.E. 673.

9. Coffey v. Myers, 1882, 84 Ind. 105.

10. Lueptow v. Schraeder, 1938, 226 Wis. 437, 277 N.W. 124. See Note, 1938, 22 Minn.L.Rev. 1060.

11. Woodley v. Coker, 1903, 119 Ga. 226, 46 S.E. 89; Collins v. Hayte, 1869, 50 Ill. 353; Lauzon v. Charroux, 1894, 18 R.I. 467, 28 A. 975.

12. Oliver v. Haspil, Fla.App.1963, 152 So.2d 758; Lanterman v. Delaware, Lackawanna & Western Railroad Co., D.N.J.1916, 229 F. 770; Hyde v. Greuch, 1884, 62 Md. 577.

13. As to this requirement, see Petrich v. McDonald, 1954, 44 Wn.2d 211, 266 P.2d 1047; Capitol Electric Co. v. Cristaldi, D.Md.1958, 157 F.Supp. 646; Luckett v. Cohen, S.D.N.Y.1956, 169 F.Supp. 808.

14. Leeseberg v. Builders Plumbers Supply Co., 1967, 6 Mich.App. 321, 149 N.W.2d 263; Blankenship v. Staton, Ky.1961, 348 S.W.2d 925; Dangel v. Offset Printing Co., 1961, 342 Mass. 170, 172 N.E.2d 610; Morfessis v. Baum, 1960, 108 U.S.App.D.C. 303, 281 F.2d 938; Martin v. Rexford, 1915, 170 N.C. 540, 87 S.E. 352. Cf. Peebler v. Olds, 1945, 71 Cal.App.2d 382, 162 P.2d 953 (action to quiet title, creating lien on property); Chappelle v. Gross, 1966, 26 A.D.2d 340, 274 N.Y.S.2d 555 (lis pendens filed); Baber v. Fitzgerald, 1949, 311 Ky. 382, 224 S.W.2d 135 (forcible detainer).

15. Gore v. Gorman's, Inc., W.D.Mo.1956, 143 F.Supp. 9; Novick v. Becker, 1958, 4 Wis.2d 432, 90 N.W.2d 620; Atlanta Hub Co. v. Bussey, 1956, 93 Ga.App. 171, 91 S.E.2d 66; King v. Yarbray, 1911, 136 Ga. 212, 71 S.E. 131; Gundermann v. Buschner, 1897, 73 Ill.App. 180.

16. Brounstein v. Sahlein, 1892, 65 Hun 365, 20 N.Y.S. 213.

17. Hollinshed v. Shadrick, 1957, 95 Ga.App. 88, 97 S.E.2d 165, error transferred, 1956, 212 Ga.App. 624, 94 S.E.2d 705; Whitson v. May, 1880, 71 Ind. 269; Shaw v. Moon, 1926, 117 Or. 558, 245 P. 318.

18. Mayflower Industries v. Thor Corp., 1951, 15 N.J.Super. 139, 83 A.2d 246, affirmed 1952, 9 N.J. 605, 89 A.2d 242; Black v. Judelsohn, 1937, 251 App.Div. 559, 296 N.Y.S. 860; Shute v. Shute, 1920, 180 N.C. 386, 104 S.E. 764.

19. Neumann v. Industrial Sound Engineering, Inc., 1966, 31 Wis.2d 471, 143 N.W.2d 543; Hubbard v. Beatty & Hyde, Inc., 1961, 343 Mass. 258, 178 N.E.2d 485;

nership.[20] Even proceedings before an administrative agency [21] have been held to be sufficient, where they result in similar interference, as in the case of one for the suspension of an officer,[22] or for the revocation of a license to do business.[23] Several jurisdictions [24] allow an action of malicious prosecution for any civil suit initiated a second time without ground, where they do not allow it for the first.

It is generally held, however, that damage to reputation that may result when one is sued by a patient or client for professional malpractice is not by itself sufficient special injury.[25] Hence surgeons who have been sued for professional malpractice have lost their own "counterattack" suits based on malicious prosecution.[26] The same rule applies to lawyers [27] and others [28] who may be especially vulnerable to losses from unwarranted attacks on professional competence; in each case, something more than injury to reputation will be required to show special injury.

A slight majority of American courts have taken the position that no special injury or grievance is required to establish a good claim for unjustified civil litigation, provided that the necessary elements are present and material damage results.[29] The authority of some of the cases in this group may be weakened, however, by the fact that special injury was actually shown in some of the cases adopting the more liberal rule.[30] It is also possible that if the plaintiff's only claim is one for loss of reputation resulting from a

---

Balsiger v. American Steel & Supply Co., 1969, 254 Or. 204, 458 P.2d 932; Nassif v. Goodman, 1932, 203 N.C. 451, 166 S.E. 308; Norin v. Scheldt Manufacturing Co., 1921, 297 Ill. 521, 130 N.E. 791.

20. Luby v. Bennett, 1901, 111 Wis. 613, 87 N.W. 804.

21. Kauffman v. A.H. Robbins Co., 1969, 223 Tenn. 515, 448 S.W.2d 400. See Notes, [1962] Wis.L.Rev. 701; 1957, 31 So.Cal.L.Rev. 105; 1955, 24 Ford.L.Rev. 479.

22. Fulton v. Ingalls, 1914, 165 App.Div. 323, 151 N.Y.S. 130, affirmed 214 N.Y. 665, 108 N.E. 1094. Accord, Hardy v. Vial, 1957, 48 Cal.2d 577, 311 P.2d 494 (dismissal of professor at state college).

23. National Surety Co. v. Page, 4th Cir.1932, 58 F.2d 145, 59 F.2d 370, rehearing denied 59 F.2d 370 (insurance agent); Melvin v. Pence, 1942, 76 App.D.C. 154, 130 F.2d 423 (private detective); Dixie Broadcasting Co. v. Rivers, 1952, 209 Ga. 98, 70 S.E.2d 734 (broadcasting station); Carver v. Lykes, 1964, 262 N.C. 345, 137 S.E.2d 139 (real estate broker).

24. Shedd v. Patterson, 1922, 302 Ill. 355, 134 N.E. 705; Soffos v. Eaton, 1945, 80 U.S.App.D.C. 306, 152 F.2d 682; Davis v. Boyle Brothers, Inc., Mun.App.D.C. 1950, 73 A.2d 517; see Perry v. Arsham, 1956, 101 Ohio App. 285, 136 N.E.2d 141; cf. Holt v. Boyle Brothers, Inc., 1954, 95 U.S.App.D.C. 1, 217 F.2d 16 (unfounded appeal); see Note, 1920, 30 Yale L.J. 1310.

Contra: Carnation Lumber Co. v. McKenney, 1960 224 Or. 541, 356 P.2d 932; Myhre v. Hessey, 1943, 242 Wis. 638, 9 N.W.2d 106; Pye v. Cardwell, 1920, 110 Tex. 572, 222 S.W. 153, answers conformed to Civ.App., 224 S.W. 542; Rappaport v. Rappaport, 1964, 44 Misc. 2d 523, 254 N.Y.S.2d 174, affirmed 24 A.D.2d 844, 263 N.Y.S.2d 442.

25. O'Toole v. Franklin, 1977, 279 Or. 513, 569 P.2d 561; Fielder Agency v. Eldan Construction Corp., 1977, 152 N.J.Super. 344, 377 A.2d 1220.

26. Ammerman v. Newman, D.C.App.1978, 384 A.2d 637; Bickel v. Mackie, D.Iowa 1978, 447 F.Supp. 1376, affirmed, 8th Cir., 590 F.2d 341; Friedman v. Dozorc, 1981, 412 Mich. 1, 312 N.W.2d 585; Drago v. Buonagurio, 1978, 46 N.Y.2d 778, 413 N.Y.S.2d 910, 386 N.E.2d 821; O'Toole v. Franklin, 1977, 279 Or. 513, 569 P.2d 561. See Annot., 1978, 84 A.L.R.3d 811.

Even where the special grievance requirement is inapplicable, only a few decisions have so far recognized a potential for liability. See Nelson v. Miller, 1980, 227 Kan. 271, 607 P.2d 438; Raine v. Drasin, Ky.1981, 621 S.W.2d 895; cf. Bull v. McCuskey, 1980, 96 Nev. 706, 615 P.2d 957 (abuse of process theory). There is extensive writing about the problem. See, among many, Birnbaum, Physicians Counterattack: Liability of Lawyers for Instituting Unjustified Medical Malpractice Actions, 1977, 45 Ford.L.Rev. 1003; Note, Liability for Proceeding with Unfounded Litigation, 1980, 33 Vand. L.Rev. 743; Note, Physician Countersuits, 1976, 45 U.Cin.L.Rev. 604; Note, Groundless Litigation and the Malicious Prosecution Debate, 1979, 88 Yale L.J. 1218.

27. Madda v. Reliance Insurance Co., 1977, 53 Ill. App.3d 67, 11 Ill.Dec. 29, 368 N.E.2d 580.

28. Fielder Agency v. Eldan Construction Corp., 1977, 152 N.J.Super. 344, 377 A.2d 1220.

29. Peerson v. Ashcraft Cotton Mills, 1917, 201 Ala. 348, 78 So. 204; Ahring v. White, 1942, 156 Kan. 60, 131 P.2d 669; Rosenblum v. Ginis, 1937, 297 Mass. 493, 9 N.E.2d 525; Shaeffer v. O.K. Tool Co., 1930, 110 Conn. 528, 148 A. 330; Ryerson v. American Surety Co. of New York, 1963, 213 Tenn. 182, 373 S.W.2d 436. See Note, [1941] Wis.L.Rev. 257.

30. E.g., Ackerman v. Kaufman, 1932, 41 Ariz. 110, 15 P.2d 966, sometimes listed as supporting the majority rule, involved an exasperated plaintiff who had been sued six times over the same claims, so that the repeated litigation exception would have covered the case.

malicious civil suit there would be constitutional requirements akin to those in defamation cases.[31] But such constitutional restrictions relating to proof of "actual harm" may not prove to be a problem.[32]

Compared with Malicious Prosecution

Where a cause of action founded upon a civil proceeding is recognized, it usually is called malicious prosecution, although "prosecution" is something of a misnomer. In general, it is governed by the same rules and limitations as the action based upon criminal proceedings; but there are a few significant differences arising out of the type of suit involved.[33]

Ordinarily the plaintiff must prove the termination of the former proceeding in his favor.[34] But there are necessary exceptions where, as in the case of putting a man under bond to keep the peace,[35] the proceeding is an ex parte one and relief is granted without an opportunity for the party against whom it is sought to be heard. This is true also as to proceedings ancillary to a civil suit, such as attachment[36] or arrest under civil process,[37] as to which, if they are themselves unjustified, it is unnecessary to show a favorable termination of the main action. It usually is held, however, with a little authority to the contrary,[38] that if an opportunity has been given to contest the facts,[39] the plaintiff must show a favorable termination of the ancillary proceeding itself.[40] As in the case of criminal proceedings, a termination of the suit by way of compromise and settlement is not sufficient to support the cause of action;[41] but the filing of a bond for the release of property attached is not regarded as such a compromise, since the party acts under compulsion.[42]

The termination requirement operates to preclude a defendant from filing a counterclaim for malicious prosecution; since the main claim has not terminated when the counterclaim is filed, the counterclaim is premature and subject to dismissal,[43] unless it is

---

31. See p. 884 supra. See, recognizing the First Amendment impact in malicious prosecution as similar to that in defamation, City of Long Beach v. Bozek, 1982, 31 Cal.3d 527, 183 Cal.Rptr. 86, 645 P.2d 137 (just as governmental entity may not sue for defamation, it may not sue for malicious prosecution or wrongful civil proceedings).

32. See Gertz v. Robert Welch, Inc., 1974, 418 U.S. 323, 94 S.Ct. 2997, 41 L.Ed.2d 789; Time, Inc. v. Firestone, 1976, 424 U.S. 448, 96 S.Ct. 958, 47 L.Ed.2d 154, on remand, Fla., 332 So.2d 68. See also, ch. 19, § 113.

33. See, Second Restatement of Torts, § 674, Comment e.

34. Nichols v. Severtsen, 1951, 39 Wn.2d 836, 239 P.2d 349; Moffett v. Commerce Trust Co., Mo.1955, 283 S.W.2d 591; Martin v. Cedar Lake Ice Co., 1920, 145 Minn. 452, 177 N.W. 631; Dangel v. Offset Printing, Inc., 1961, 342 Mass. 170, 172 N.E.2d 610; Schwartz v. Schwartz, 1938, 25 Cal.App.2d 303, 77 P.2d 260. Thus a default judgment must be set aside. McMahon v. May Department Stores Co., Mo.1964, 374 S.W.2d 82.

35. Steward v. Gromett, 1859, 7 C.B., N.S., 191, 141 Eng.Rep. 788; Hyde v. Greuch, 1884, 62 Md. 577; Lanterman v. Delaware, Lackawanna & Western Railroad Co., D.N.J.1916, 229 F. 770.

36. Blankenship v. Staton, Ky.1961, 348 S.W.2d 925; McLaughlin v. Davis, 1875, 14 Kan. 168; Zinn v. Rice, 1891, 154 Mass. 1, 27 N.E. 772.

37. Ingram v. Root, 1889, 51 Hun 238, 3 N.Y.S. 858; Hogg v. Pinckney, 1881, 16 S.C. 387.

38. Fortman v. Rottier, 1858, 8 Ohio St. 548. Brand v. Hinchman, 1888, 68 Mich. 590, 36 N.W. 664. The reason advanced is that damage has been caused immediately on issuance and execution of the writ, which was ex parte.

39. Otherwise where there was no opportunity to vacate the attachment. Bump v. Betts, N.Y.1830, 19 Wend. 421. Or where the only method of vacating it does not put in issue the grounds on which it was sued out. Donnell v. Jones, 1848, 13 Ala. 490; Rossiter v. Minnesota Bradner-Smith Paper Co., 1887, 37 Minn. 296, 33 N.W. 855.

40. Dixon v. Smith-Wallace Shoe Co., 1918, 283 Ill. 234, 119 N.E. 265; Pixley v. Reed, 1879, 26 Minn. 80, 1 N.W. 800; Wright v. Harris, 1912, 160 N.C. 542, 76 S.E. 489; Kassel Poultry Co. v. Sheldon Produce Co., 1925, 3 N.J.Misc. 277, 129 A. 424.

41. Nolan v. Allstate Home Equipment Co., Mun. App.D.C.1959, 149 A.2d 426; Fenton Storage Co. v. Feinstein, 1937, 129 Pa.Super. 125, 195 A. 176; Paskle v. Williams, 1931, 214 Cal. 482, 6 P.2d 505; Baird v. Aluminum Seal Co., 3d Cir.1957, 250 F.2d 595; Webb v. Youmans, 1967, 248 Cal.App.2d 851, 57 Cal.Rptr. 11.

42. Rossiter v. Minnesota Bradner-Smith Paper Co., 1887, 37 Minn. 296, 33 N.W. 855; cf. Slater v. Kimbro, 1892, 91 Ga. 217, 18 S.E. 296; Alexander v. Jacoby, 1872, 23 Ohio St. 358.

43. Nataros v. Superior Court of Maricopa County, 1976, 113 Ariz. 498, 557 P.2d 1055; Babb v. Superior Court of Sonoma County, 1971, 3 Cal.3d 841, 92 Cal. Rptr. 179, 479 P.2d 379.

provided otherwise by statute,[44] or the counterclaim is based on some previous litigation rather than on the complaint in the instant action.[45]

The defendant is not liable for proceedings unless he has initiated them. He need not be named as a party or sign the pleadings and it is sufficient if he plays a major role in instigating the action.[46] Nor is it necessary that defendant file the main claim; it has been held that one who asserts a counterclaim has "initiated" proceedings and that he will be held liable if that counterclaim is asserted maliciously and without probable cause.[47] Apparently, however, the mere assertion of an affirmative defense is not initiation of a claim, so long as the defendant does not go further and demand damages or other relief.[48] A bad faith defense, however, may subject the defendant to liability for attorneys' fees even when no statute so provides and this may serve to accomplish most of the purposes of a malicious prosecution action.[49]

The plaintiff must also prove that the proceeding was initiated without probable cause.[50] But obviously less in the way of grounds for belief will be required to justify a reasonable man in bringing a civil rather than a criminal suit. Sometimes this is expressed by saying that want of probable cause must be "very clearly proven," [51] or "very palpable," [52] or that "greater latitude" must be allowed than in a criminal case.[53] Apparently what is meant is merely that the instigator need not have the same degree of certainty as to the facts, or even the same belief in the soundness of his case, and that he is justified in bringing a civil suit when he reasonably believes that he has a good chance of establishing it to the satisfaction of the court or the jury.[54] He may, for example, reasonably submit a doubtful issue of law, where it is uncertain which view the court will take.[55]

It has been argued that a counterclaim should be permitted if the judge in the original suit cannot impose an "internal sanction" by assessing attorneys' fees and costs against the bad faith litigant. See Note, Groundless Litigation and the Malicious Prosecution Debate, 1979, 88 Yale L.J. 1219.

A counterclaim for abuse of process, as distinct from malicious prosecution or wrongful civil proceedings, may be permitted. Brownsell v. Klawitter, 1981, 102 Wis.2d 108, 306 N.W.2d 41. See § 121, below.

44. E.g., West's Fla.Stat.Ann. § 768.56(1), authorizing an award of attorneys' fees to the prevailing party in malpractice actions. As to this and other similar statutes see Spencer & Roth, Closing the Courthouse Door: Florida's Spurious Claims Statute, 1981, 10 Stet. L.Rev. 397; Comment, 1978, 14 Willamette L.J. 401; 1980, 9 Colo.L. 1172. The common law rule also permits an award of fees where the litigation is oppressive or frivolous, and in such cases a motion in the case or a cost bill would reach the issue without the need of a separate action.

45. McGuire v. Armitage, 1979, 184 Mont. 407, 603 P.2d 253; Rasmussen Buick-GMC, Inc. v. Roach, Iowa 1982, 314 N.W.2d 374.

46. Devlin v. Greiner, 1977, 147 N.J.Super. 446, 371 A.2d 380 (detective's intentionally false report that a wife was engaged in adultery would be sufficiently instrumental in causing divorce action).

47. Bertero v. National General Corp., 1974, 13 Cal. 3d 43, 118 Cal.Rptr. 184, 529 P.2d 608, 65 A.L.R.3d 878.

48. See Ritter v. Ritter, 1943, 381 Ill. 549, 46 N.E.2d 41; Annot., 65 A.L.R.3d 901.

49. Oklahoma has said that not only will a bad faith defense justify an attorneys' fee award but also that a bad faith dismissal of the claim will justify it. See Moses v. Hoebel, Okl.1982, 646 P.2d 601.

50. See, giving the term the same meaning as in criminal prosecutions: Stewart v. Sonneborn, 1878, 98 U.S. 187, 25 L.Ed. 116; Le Clear v. Perkins, 1894, 103 Mich. 131, 61 N.W. 357; Hill Co. v. Contractors' Supply Co., 1910, 156 Ill.App. 270, affirmed 249 Ill. 304, 94 N.E. 544; Wilcox v. Gilmore, 1928, 320 Mo. 980, 8 S.W.2d 961.

51. Eickhoff v. Fidelity & Casualty Co., 1898, 74 Minn. 139, 76 N.W. 1030; United States Tire Co. v. Kirk, 1918, 102 Kan. 418, 170 P. 811; see Owens v. Graetzel, 1926, 149 Md. 689, 132 A. 265.

52. Kasal v. Picha, 1923, 156 Minn. 446, 195 N.W. 280; Brown v. Keyes, 1929, 54 S.D. 596, 223 N.W. 819.

53. Virtue v. Creamery Package Manufacturing Co., 1913, 123 Minn. 17, 142 N.W. 930, reargument denied 123 Minn. 17, 142 N.W. 1136.

54. Smith v. Smith, 1944, 296 Ky. 785, 178 S.W.2d 613. See Pangburn v. Bull, N.Y.1828, 1 Wend. 345; Allen v. Codman, 1885, 139 Mass. 136, 29 N.E. 537; Hubbard v. Beatty & Hyde, Inc., 1961, 343 Mass. 258, 178 N.E.2d 485; and cf. Connery v. Manning, 1895, 163 Mass. 44, 39 N.E. 558.

55. Hoffmann v. Kimmel, 1933, 142 Or. 397, 20 P.2d 393. See Bill Dreiling Motor Co. v. Herlein, 1975, Colo. App., 543 P.2d 1283. In Standley v. Western Auto Supply Co., Mo.App.1959, 319 S.W.2d 924, this was car-

Advice of counsel to the effect that there is a reasonable chance that the claim will be found to be valid is enough to establish probable cause.[56]

This, of course, is to be distinguished from the attorney's own malicious actions without probable cause, for which the client may be held liable on agency grounds even though the client himself is innocent.[57] And it goes without saying that the attorney is liable for his own actions in prosecuting a client's claim maliciously and without probable cause,[58] but that he is not liable for the malice or want of probable cause of his client.[59]

It is generally agreed that the termination of the proceeding in favor of the person against whom it is brought is no evidence that probable cause was lacking, since in a civil action there is no preliminary determination of the sufficiency of the evidence to justify the suit.[60] But such a judgment, if it is on the merits of the controversy, is a final adjudication of the matters then in dispute, and the unsuccessful instigator cannot, as in the case of a criminal proceeding, relitigate his claim in the tort action by setting up the defense that he was right upon the facts.[61] A recovery by the plaintiff in the original action usually is regarded as conclusive evidence of the existence of probable cause,[62] even though it is subsequently reversed,[63] unless it can be shown to have been obtained by fraud or other imposition upon the court.[64]

The plaintiff must also prove "malice" in bringing the former action; but here again somewhat more latitude is permitted than in the case of criminal prosecutions, since the plaintiff in a civil suit is always seeking his

---

ried to the length of holding that there was probable cause when suit was brought on an otherwise valid claim known to be discharged in bankruptcy, since the defense might be waived if the debtor chose not to avail himself of it. But see contra, Gore v. Gorman's Inc., W.D.Mo.1956, 143 F.Supp. 9, noted in 1957, 22 Mo. L.Rev. 215.

56. Harter v. Lewis Stores, Ky.1951, 240 S.W.2d 86; Dorr Cattle Co. v. Des Moines National Bank, 1904, 127 Iowa 153, 98 N.W. 918, rehearing denied 1905, 127 Iowa 153, 102 N.W. 836. It has been held that in a proper case expert advice may have the same effect. Allen v. Codman, 1885, 139 Mass. 136, 29 N.E. 537 (fire hazard); Bode v. Schmoldt, 1922, 177 Wis. 8, 187 N.W. 648, 1024 (lunacy). But not, of course, where full disclosure is not made. Alexander v. Alexander, 4th Cir. 1956, 229 F.2d 111.

57. Nyer v. Carter, Me.1977, 367 A.2d 1375; Second Restatement of Agency, § 253.

58. See Second Restatement of Torts, § 674, Comment d. The attorney is entitled to submit to the courts even claims he believes unfounded, so long as his purpose is proper adjudication of his client's claim. He is not required to weigh the evidence or act as judge of his client's case. See Tool Research & Engineering Corp. v. Henigson, 1975, 46 Cal.App.3d 675, 120 Cal.Rptr. 291. But if the claim against the attorney is not barred for some other reason such as the special injury requirement, the attorney may be held liable. In Mahaffey v. McMahon, Ky.1982, 630 S.W.2d 68 the attorney, sued for representing the plaintiff in a medical malpractice action, advised his client to invoke the attorney-client privilege as to all their pre-suit discussions. The court held that, given this claim of privilege, the doctor had made a prima facie case of malicious prosecution against the attorney by his own testimony that the medical treatment was sound.

59. Tool Research & Engineering Corp. v. Henigson, 1975, 46 Cal.App.3d 675, 120 Cal.Rptr. 291.

60. Barton v. Woodward, 1919, 32 Idaho 375, 182 P. 916; O'Malley-Kelley Oil & Auto Supply Co. v. Gates Oil Co., 1923, 73 Colo. 140, 214 P. 398; Milner v. Hare, 1926, 125 Me. 460, 134 A. 628; Reichert v. Neacy, 1914, 158 Wis. 657, 149 N.W. 586; Novick v. Becker, 1958, 4 Wis.2d 432, 90 N.W.2d 620.

There are courts which have said that a voluntary dismissal or discontinuance affords evidence that probable cause was lacking. Kolka v. Jones, 1897, 6 N.D. 461, 71 N.W. 558; Wetmore v. Mellinger, 1884, 64 Iowa 741, 18 N.W. 870. Contra: Asevado v. Orr, 1893, 100 Cal. 293, 34 P. 777; Cohn v. Saidel, 1902, 71 N.H. 558, 53 A. 800; Warner v. Gulf Oil Corp., N.D.N.C.1959, 178 F.Supp. 481.

61. Since the parties are the same and the judgment is res judicata as to such issues. Ackerman v. Kaufman, 1932, 41 Ariz. 110, 15 P.2d 966.

62. Rouse v. Twin Pines Sanitarium, Inc., 1958, 162 Cal.App.2d 639, 328 P.2d 536; Lancaster & Love, Inc. v. Mueller Co., Tex.Civ.App.1958, 310 S.W.2d 659, error refused.

63. Jordan v. Empiregas, Inc. of Belle Mina, Ala. 1976, 337 So.2d 732; Goldstein v. Sabella, Fla.1956, 88 So.2d 910; Laughlin v. St. Louis Union Trust Co., 1932, 330 Mo. 523, 50 S.W.2d 92; Overton v. Combs, 1921, 182 N.C. 4, 108 S.E. 357; McBride v. Alles, 1928, 222 Ky. 725, 2 S.W.2d 391; Goldner-Siegel Corp. v. Kraemer Hosiery Co., 1934, 153 Misc. 159, 274 N.Y.S. 681.

64. Lockett & Williams v. Gress Manufacturing Co., 1911, 8 Ga.App. 772, 70 S.E. 255; see Palmer v. Avery, N.Y.1864, 41 Barb. 290, affirmed 41 N.Y. 619.

own ends. "Malice" may consist of a primary motive of ill will, or a lack of belief in any possible success of the action;[65] but neither is necessary to it. It has been found where the proceeding was begun primarily for a purpose other than the adjudication of the claim in suit, such as preventing an owner from selling his land to another.[66] Some courts have gone further and have found malice where the defendant's conduct is probably only reckless or negligent, but where that conduct is a clear abuse of defendant's position of power or an exploitation of the plaintiff's position of weakness.[67] As in malicious prosecution proper, the jury may infer an improper purpose from the lack of probable cause, although the converse inference may not be drawn.[68]

Finally, damages recoverable in an action founded upon an ordinary civil suit may differ slightly from those in an action founded upon malicious criminal prosecution. Most wrongful civil actions, for example, do not constitute a defamatory charge, and damages for loss of reputation will not be awarded except where, as in the case of a wrongful lunacy or bankruptcy proceeding, reputation is seriously put in issue.[69] Subject to this kind of limitation it may be said that most actual damages proximately resulting from the wrongful suit may be recovered. Damages for detention of the person,[70] seizure of or interference with property,[71] harm to credit[72] and other financial damages may be recovered.[73] Counsel fees incurred in defending against the wrongful civil suit are prominent among items of recovery,[74] though counsel fees incurred in bringing suit for the unjustified prior action are entirely distinct and may not be recovered in the absence of statute.[75] Where the plaintiff can recover some of his losses under a rule or statute that permits recovery of attorneys' fees on motion in the wrongful suit, or can recover a part of his losses as taxable costs, or on a bond given by the defendant who has sought a provisional remedy, the plaintiff apparently must credit the defendant to this extent, so that his recovery for unjustified litigation is limited to losses that exceed recovery gained by other means.[76]

65. Pangburn v. Bull, N.Y.1828, 1 Wend. 345; Wills v. Noyes, 1832, 29 Mass. (12 Pick.) 324; Southwestern Railroad Co. v. Mitchell, 1880, 80 Ga. 438, 5 S.E. 490.

66. Malone v. Belcher, 1913, 216 Mass. 209, 103 N.E. 637; Burhans v. Sanford & Brown, N.Y.1838, 19 Wend. 417; Wills v. Noyes, 1832, 29 Mass. (12 Pick.) 324; Southwestern Railroad Co. v. Mitchell, 1880, 80 Ga. 438, 5 S.E. 490. Cf. Johnson v. Mount Ogden Enterprises, Inc., 1969, 23 Utah 2d 169, 460 P.2d 333 (injunction suit to gain time).

67. See Robinson v. Goudchaux's, La.1975, 307 So. 2d 287 (customer sued after bill had been paid, no spite or improper purpose but malice found to exist); Martin v. City of Albany, 1977, 42 N.Y.2d 13, 396 N.Y.S.2d 612, 364 N.E.2d 1304 (officer negligently assumed plaintiff involved in an arrest).

In Shahrokhfar v. State Farm Mutual Automobile Insurance Co., 1981, ___ Mont. ___, 634 P.2d 653, an insurer brought suit against the wrong person, who refused to defend. As a result the insurer took a default judgment and the defendant lost his driver's license. He then sued the insurer and was allowed to recover on a negligence theory, with a reduction in compensatory damages under the comparative negligence statute.

68. Stewart v. Sonneborn, 1878, 98 U.S. 187, 25 L.Ed. 116; National Surety Co. v. Page, 4th Cir.1932, 58 F.2d 145, 59 F.2d 370; Kryszke v. Kamin, 1910, 163 Mich. 290, 128 N.W. 190; Henderson v. Cape Trading Co., 1926, 316 Mo. 384, 289 S.W. 332; Cole v. Neaf, 8th Cir.1964, 334 F.2d 326.

69. See Second Restatement of Torts, § 681, Comment c.

70. See Closson v. Staples, 1869, 42 Vt. 209.

71. Farrar v. Brackett, 1890, 86 Ga. 463, 12 S.E. 686; Moffatt v. Fisher, 1877, 47 Iowa 473; Boland v. Ballaine, 9th Cir.1920, 266 F. 22.

72. Malone v. Belcher, 1913, 216 Mass. 209, 103 N.E. 637; Bradford v. Lawrence, 1922, 208 Ala. 248, 94 So. 103; Lord v. Guyot, 1902, 30 Colo. 222, 70 P. 683; Sonsee v. Jones & Green, 1923, 157 Ark. 131, 248 S.W. 289.

73. Slater v. Kimbro, 1892, 91 Ga. 217, 18 S.E. 296; Boland v. Ballaine, 9th Cir.1920, 266 F. 22; Magmer v. Renk, 1886, 65 Wis. 364, 27 N.W. 26; Munro Hotel Co. v. Brough, 1915, 26 Ohio Cir.Ct.R., N.S. 185.

74. Haswell v. Liberty Mutual Insurance Co., Mo. 1977, 557 S.W.2d 628; Second Restatement of Torts, § 681, Comment d.

75. Stewart v. Sonneborn, 1878, 98 U.S. 187, 25 L.Ed. 116; cf. Bertero v. National General Corp., 1975, 13 Cal.3d 43, 118 Cal.Rptr. 184, 529 P.2d 608.

76. See McCardle v. McGinley, 1882, 86 Ind. 538; Carbondale Investment Co. v. Burdick, 1903, 67 Kan. 329, 72 P. 781; Lipscomb v. Shofner, 1896, 96 Tenn. 112, 33 S.W. 818.

Intangible, non-pecuniary damages, such as damages to reputation where it can be proven, humiliation or anxiety, emotional distress and the like, can be recovered in addition to the pecuniary losses.[77] Though there may be constitutional limitations on the recovery of damage to reputation unless actual proof of such damage is offered,[78] courts have been willing to allow other intangible damages with little or no proof, apparently in the belief that at least some damages would be suffered by anyone subjected to wrongful litigation.[79]

Punitive damages are also recoverable in a proper case, though it is perhaps not just any degree of malice that will suffice to warrant a punitive recovery.[80]

Compared to Other Remedies

The remedy for unjustified litigation imposes, at least theoretically, a heavy burden on the plaintiff to show malice and a want of probable cause; but there are other grounds for recovery in certain cases that impose no such burden. An attachment or garnishment of property believed to belong to a debtor but in fact belonging to another, may operate as a simple conversion of that property, so that the owner may recover for the attachment without proof of termination, malice or probable cause.[81] In such a case the gist of the tort of conversion is an interference with the property, not a misuse of the legal system, and the restrictions imposed in a malicious prosecution action are withdrawn. The wrongful appointment of a receiver of real property or a business is closely analogous and may operate as a trespass, with similar results.[82] In addition to these tort remedies, the victim of an erroneously issued provisional remedy, such as a preliminary injunction, can recover on the bond that ordinarily must be posted by one who seeks a provisional remedy.[83] Finally, there has been legislation in recent years expanding the right of the prevailing party to recover attorneys' fees in specific situations,[84] and since attorneys' fees constitute a major element of damages in cases of unjustified civil litigation, these statutes may as a practical matter tend to supplant the tort remedy in cases to which they apply.[85]

WESTLAW REFERENCES

digest("malicious prosecution" /s civil /s proceeding*procedure*)
wrongful /3 civil /3 proceeding*

Compared with Malicious Prosecution
wrongful /3 civil /3 proceeding*
wrongful /3 civil /3 proceeding* /p "malicious prosecution"
restatement /s torts /s 674

---

77. See Second Restatement of Torts, § 681.

78. See Gertz v. Robert Welch, Inc., 1974, 418 U.S. 323, 94 S.Ct. 2997, 41 L.Ed.2d 789 (free speech limits recovery in some defamation cases to actual damages); Time, Inc. v. Firestone, 1976, 424 U.S. 448, 96 S.Ct. 958, 47 L.Ed.2d 154, on remand, Fla., 332 So.2d 68. See Chapter 19, section 113.

79. Robinson v. Goudchaux's, La.1975, 307 So.2d 287 ("Damages are * * * to be presumed," $500 recovery for "minimal mental anguish, humiliation and embarassment"); Sonnichsen v. Streeter, 1967, 4 Conn. Cir. 659, 239 A.2d 63.

80. Bertero v. National General Corp., 1975, 13 Cal. 3d 43, 118 Cal.Rptr. 184, 529 P.2d 608; Sonnichsen v. Streeter, 1967, 4 Conn.Cir. 659, 239 A.2d 63; Young v. Jack Boring's, Inc., Mo.App.1976, 540 S.W.2d 887.

81. Lundgren v. Western State Bank of Duluth, 1933, 189 Minn. 476, 250 N.W. 1, 91 A.L.R. 919; Crouter v. United Adjusters, Inc., 1971, 259 Or. 348, 485 P.2d 1208, appeal after remand 266 Or. 6, 510 P.2d 1328.

82. Braun v. Pepper, 1978, 224 Kan. 56, 578 P.2d 695.

83. See, as to recovery on injunction bonds, Dobbs, Should Security Be Required as a Pre-Condition to Provisional Injunctive Relief, 52 N.C.L.Rev. 1091. Recovery is limited to the amount provided in the bond except in half a dozen states, Smith v. Coronado Foothills Estates Homeowners Association, Inc., 1977, 117 Ariz. 171, 571 P.2d 668.

84. E.g., 42 U.S.C. § 1988 (civil rights cases, attorneys' fees to prevailing party); Idaho Code § 12–121 ("any civil case," judge may award fees).

85. It has been argued that an "internal sanction," is preferable to an "external" or separate suit, and that attorneys' fees could be taxed against the bad faith litigant in the original suit, or, alternatively, that the good faith litigant should be permitted to counterclaim in that suit. See Note, Groundless Litigation and the Malicious Prosecution Debate, 1979, 88 Yale L.J. 1219. The increasing use of the attorneys' fee award is clearly a shift in this direction.

Compared to other Remedies
"attorney* fee*" /p unjustif! /5 litigation* suit* action*

§ 121. Abuse of Process

The action for malicious prosecution, whether it be permitted for criminal or civil proceedings, has failed to provide a remedy for a group of cases in which legal procedure has been set in motion in proper form, with probable cause, and even with ultimate success, but nevertheless has been perverted to accomplish an ulterior purpose for which it was not designed. In such cases a tort action has been developed for what is called abuse of process.[1] In the leading English case[2] the defendant had the plaintiff arrested under civil process in order to compel him through duress to surrender the register of a vessel, without which the plaintiff could not go to sea. Although malicious prosecution would not lie because the proceeding had not been terminated, the court refused to permit its process to be misused for such an end, and held the defendant liable. This decision has been widely followed, and the tort is now well established.

Abuse of process differs from malicious prosecution in that the gist of the tort is not commencing an action or causing process to issue without justification, but misusing, or misapplying process justified in itself for an end other than that which it was designed to accomplish.[3] The purpose for which the process is used, once it is issued, is the only thing of importance. Consequently in an action for abuse of process it is unnecessary for the plaintiff to prove that the proceeding has terminated in his favor,[4] or that the process was obtained without probable cause or in the course of a proceeding begun without probable cause.[5] It is often said that proof of "malice" is required;[6] but it seems well settled that, except on the issue of punitive damages,[7] this does not mean spite or ill will, or anything other than the improper purpose itself for which the process is used,[8] and that even a pure spite motive is not sufficient where process is used only to accomplish the result for which it was created.[9] Thus if the defendant prosecutes an inno-

§ 121

1. See Goldoftas, Abuse of Process, 1964, 13 Cleve. Marsh.L.Rev. 163 Notes, 1938, 16 N.C.L.Rev. 277; 1948, 32 Minn.L.Rev. 805; 1937, 7 Brook.L.Rev. 123; Restatement of Torts, § 682. Cf. White v. Scarritt, 1937, 341 Mo. 1004, 111 S.W.2d 18 ("duress").

As to the distinction between malicious prosecution, "malicious use of process" in civil proceedings, and abuse of process, see Baldwin v. Davis, 1939, 188 Ga. 587, 4 S.E.2d 458.

2. Grainger v. Hill, 1838, 4 Bing.N.C. 212, 132 Eng. Rep. 769.

3. Wood v. Graves, 1887, 144 Mass. 365, 11 N.E. 567; Garland v. Wilson, 1927, 289 Pa. 272, 137 A. 266; Abernethy v. Burns, 1936, 210 N.C. 636, 188 S.E. 97; Glidewell v. Murray-Lacy & Co., 1919, 124 Va. 563, 98 S.E. 665; Assets Collecting Co. v. Myers, 1915, 167 App.Div. 133, 152 N.Y.S. 930.

Regularity or irregularity of the process itself makes no difference. Compare Hall v. Field Enterprises, Inc., Mun.App.D.C.1953, 94 A.2d 479, with Hoppe v. Klapperich, 1947, 224 Minn. 224, 28 N.W.2d 780.

4. Lambert v. Breton, 1929, 127 Me. 510, 144 A. 864; Sneeden v. Harris, 1891, 109 N.C. 349, 13 S.E. 920; Brantley v. Rhodes-Haverty Furniture Co., 1908, 131 Ga. 276, 62 S.E. 222; Kool v. Lee, 1913, 43 Utah 394, 134 P. 906; Moore v. Michigan National Bank, 1962, 368 Mich. 71, 117 N.W.2d 105.

Consequently, a counterclaim may be permitted for abuse of process, though such a claim is impermissible when it asserts malicious prosecution or wrongful civil proceedings. Brownsell v. Klawitter, 1981, 102 Wis.2d 108, 306 N.W.2d 41.

5. Mayer v. Walter, 1870, 64 Pa. 283; Brownsell v. Klawitter, 1981, 102 Wis.2d 108, 306 N.W.2d 41.

6. Shaw v. Fulton, 1929, 266 Mass. 189, 165 N.E. 26; Lambert v. Breton, 1929, 127 Me. 510, 144 A. 864.

7. See Blackmon v. Gilmer, 1930, 221 Ala. 554, 130 So. 192; McGann v. Allen, 1926, 105 Conn. 177, 134 A. 810; Sokolowske v. Wilson, 1931, 211 Iowa 1112, 235 N.W. 80; Saliem v. Glovsky, 1934, 132 Me. 402, 172 A. 4; Whelan v. Miller, 1912, 49 Pa.Super. 91, 100.

8. Glidewell v. Murray-Lacy & Co., 1919, 124 Va. 563, 98 S.E. 665; Coplea v. Bybee, 1937, 290 Ill.App. 117, 8 N.E.2d 55; Pittsburg, Johnstown, Ebensburg & Eastern Railroad Co. v. Wakefield Hardware Co., 1906, 143 N.C. 54, 55 S.E. 422; Bourisk v. Derry Lumber Co., 1931, 130 Me. 376, 156 A. 382; Petry v. Childs & Co., 1904, 43 Misc. 108, 88 N.Y.S. 286.

9. Rosemont Enterprises, Inc. v. Random House, Inc., S.D.N.Y.1966, 261 F.Supp. 691; Blackstock v. Tatum, Tex.Civ.App.1965, 396 S.W.2d 463; Bonney v. King, 1903, 201 Ill. 47, 66 N.E. 377; Carpenter, Baggott & Co. v. Hanes, 1914, 167 N.C. 551, 83 S.E. 577; Docter v. Riedel, 1897, 96 Wis. 158, 71 N.W. 119.

cent plaintiff for a crime without reasonable grounds to believe him guilty, it is malicious prosecution; if he prosecutes him with such grounds to extort payment of a debt, it is abuse of process.[10] But the two torts have the common element of an improper purpose in the use of legal process, and there are many cases in which they overlap and either will lie, such as the excessive attachment of property to coerce settlement of a suit,[11] or indeed any unjustified criminal prosecution or civil action in which legal process is used for an end other than that of the proceeding itself.[12]

The essential elements of abuse of process, as the tort has developed, have been stated to be: first, an ulterior purpose, and second, a wilful act in the use of the process not proper in the regular conduct of the proceeding.[13] Some definite act or threat not authorized by the process, or aimed at an objective not legitimate in the use of the process, is required; and there is no liability where the defendant has done nothing more than carry out the process to its authorized conclusion, even though with bad intentions.[14] The improper purpose usually takes the form of coercion to obtain a collateral advantage, not properly involved in the proceeding itself, such as the surrender of property or the payment of money, by the use of the process as a threat or a club. There is, in other words, a form of extortion, and it is what is done in the course of negotiation, rather than the issuance or any formal use of the process itself, which constitutes the tort.

Some of the decisions have said that there must be an improper act, such as an extortion attempt, after the process has issued and that an act committed beforehand is not enough.[15] Most of these cases probably stand only for the narrower proposition that there must be an overt act and that bad purpose alone is insufficient. Thus a demand for collateral advantage that occurs before the issuance of process may be actionable, so long as process does in fact issue at the defendant's behest,[16] and as a part of the attempted extortion.

But it is clear that the judicial process must in some manner be involved.[17] A repairman's notice of a lien and sale, for example, is not an invocation of process and cannot form the basis for an abuse of process action.[18] By the same token, mere threats that process will be invoked, at least in the absence of any demand for special advantage from it, will be insufficient.[19]

---

10. Hotel Supply Co. v. Reid, 1918, 16 Ala.App. 563, 80 So. 137; Moore v. Michigan National Bank, 1962, 368 Mich. 71, 117 N.W.2d 105; Cardy v. Maxwell, 1957, 9 Misc.2d 329, 169 N.Y.S.2d 547; McClenny v. Inverarity, 1909, 80 Kan. 569, 103 P. 82; Marlatte v. Weickgenant, 1907, 147 Mich. 266, 110 N.W. 1061.

11. State for Use of Little v. United States Fidelity & Guaranty Co., 1953, 217 Miss. 576, 64 So.2d 697 (both). Cf. Zinn v. Rice, 1891, 154 Mass. 1, 27 N.E. 772; Harris v. Harter, 1926, 79 Cal.App. 190, 249 P. 39 (malicious prosecution) with Saliem v. Glovsky, 1934, 132 Me. 402, 172 A. 4; Pittsburg, Johnstown, Ebensburg & Eastern Railroad Co. v. Wakefield Hardware Co., 1905, 138 N.C. 175, 50 S.E. 571 (abuse of process).

12. See Bond v. Chapin, 1844, 49 Mass. (8 Metc.) 31; Antcliff v. June, 1890, 81 Mich. 477, 45 N.W. 1019; Coulter v. Coulter, 1923, 73 Colo. 144, 214 P. 400.

13. Huggins v. Winn-Dixie Greenville, Inc., 1967, 249 S.C. 206, 153 S.E.2d 693, 27 A.L.R.3d 1195; Three Lakes Association v. Whiting, 1977, 75 Mich.App. 564, 255 N.W.2d 686.

14. Barnette v. Woody, 1955, 242 N.C. 424, 88 S.E.2d 223; Moffett v. Commerce Trust Co., Mo.1955, 283 S.W.2d 591; Mullins v. Sanders, 1949, 189 Va. 624, 54 S.E.2d 116; Brown v. Robertson, 1950, 120 Ind.App. 434, 92 N.E.2d 856; Elliott v. Warwick Stores, 1952, 329 Mass. 406, 108 N.E.2d 681.

15. Melton v. Rickman, 1945, 225 N.C. 700, 36 S.E.2d 276, 162 A.L.R. 793; Drago v. Buonagurio, 1978, 61 A.D.2d 282, 402 N.Y.S.2d 250 (physician allegedly subjected to malpractice claim purely as a discovery device, no abuse of process), reversed on other grounds, 46 N.Y.2d 778, 413 N.Y.S.2d 910, 386 N.E.2d 821.

16. Huggins v. Winn-Dixie Greenville, Inc., 1967, 249 S.C. 206, 153 S.E.2d 693, 27 A.L.R.3d 1195.

17. Julian J. Studley, Inc., v. Lefrak, 1977, 41 N.Y.2d 881, 393 N.Y.S.2d 980, 362 N.E.2d 611 (affidavit sent to regulatory department requesting appropriate discipline not "process".

18. Amabello v. Colonial Motors, 1977, 117 N.H. 556, 374 A.2d 1182, appeal after remand 120 N.H. 524, 418 A.2d 1279.

19. Larsen v. Credit Bureau, Inc. of Georgia, 1977, 279 Or. 405, 568 P.2d 657.

Many kinds of process have lent themselves to extortion, including attachment,[20] execution,[21] garnishment,[22] sequestration proceedings,[23] arrest of the person[24] and criminal prosecution[25] and even such infrequent cases as the use of a subpoena for the collection of a debt.[26]

The ulterior motive may be shown by showing a direct demand for collateral advantage; or it may be inferred from what is said or done about the process.[27] It may also be inferred in some cases from the way process was carried out, as for example in the case of excessive attachment from which the inference may be drawn that defendant sought extortionate advantage by tying up all the plaintiff's property when attachment of a small amount would provide sufficient security for the debt.[28] Similarly one court has permitted the jury to conclude that a lawyer's unfounded and uninvestigated medical malpractice claim, followed by a low-figure demand for settlement and a trial in which no expert testimony was produced, reflected an attempt to extort a nuisance settlement for which the lawyer would be liable.[29] The case so far stands alone in allowing a recovery on the facts,[30] but even if it is correct to say that motives may be inferred from acts in these cases, the inference is not reversible and it is not possible to infer acts from the existence of an improper motive alone.[31]

Damages in the case of an excessive attachment or garnishment may be measured by the use value of the property detained

---

20. Saliem v. Glovsky, 1934, 132 Me. 402, 172 A. 4 (excessive attachment, appointment of keeper); Malone v. Belcher, 1913, 216 Mass. 209, 103 N.E. 637; Pittsburg, Johnstown, Ebensburg & Eastern Railroad Co. v. Wakefield Hardware Co., 1905, 138 N.C. 174, 50 S.E. 571.

21. Coplea v. Bybee, 1937, 290 Ill.App. 117, 8 N.E.2d 55 (exacting conditions for surrender); Docter v. Riedel, 1897, 96 Wis. 158, 71 N.W. 119; Antcliff v. June, 1890, 81 Mich. 477, 45 N.W. 1019; Little v. Sowers, 1949, 167 Kan. 72, 204 P.2d 605 (execution on void judgment).

22. Buckenhizer v. Times Publishing Co., 1934, 267 Mich. 393, 255 N.W. 213 (assignment of claim to avoid garnishment offset); see Williams v. Adelman, 1930, 41 Ga.App. 424, 153 S.E. 224.

23. Casey v. Hanrick, 1887, 69 Tex. 44, 6 S.W. 405. Cf. Ludwick v. Penny, 1911, 158 N.C. 104, 73 S.E. 228 (claim and delivery).

24. Brantley v. Rhodes-Haverty Furniture Co., 1908, 131 Ga. 276, 62 S.E. 222; Lockhart v. Bear, 1895, 117 N.C. 298, 23 S.E. 484; Ash v. Cohn, 1937, 119 N.J.L. 54, 194 A. 174.

25. Ellis v. Wellons, 1944, 224 N.C. 269, 29 S.E.2d 884; Lader v. Benkowitz, 1946, 188 Misc. 906, 66 N.Y.S.2d 713; Glidewell v. Murray-Lacy & Co., 1919, 124 Va. 563, 98 S.E. 665; Jackson v. American Telephone & Telegraph Co., 1905, 139 N.C. 347, 51 S.E. 1015; Marlatte v. Weickgenant, 1907, 147 Mich. 266, 110 N.W. 1061.

26. Dishaw v. Wadleigh, 1897, 15 App.Div. 205, 44 N.Y.S. 207. Cf. Dean v. Kochendorfer, 1924, 237 N.Y. 384, 143 N.E. 229 (abuse by magistrate issuing process); Bond v. Chapin, 1844, 49 Mass. (8 Metc.) 31 (bringing civil suit in name of another without authority); Cardy v. Maxwell, 1957, 9 Misc.2d 329, 169 N.Y.S.2d 547 (deceit action to force payment of money in order to avoid adverse publicity).

27. Kool v. Lee, 1913, 43 Utah 394, 134 P. 906; Glidewell v. Murray-Lacy & Co., 1919, 124 Va. 563, 98 S.E. 665; Tranchina v. Arcinas, 1947, 78 Cal.App.2d 522, 178 P.2d 65.

Where the defendant's motive is mixed, the primary motive is said to be the test. Nienstedt v. Wetzel, App. 1982, 133 Ariz. 348, 651 P.2d 876. This problem occurs whenever motive is an element of the tort, and solution is not very satisfactory. In some areas of the law the test is not primary purpose but whether the legitimate purpose of the defendant would have been sufficient to induce the same actions. See Behring International, Inc. v. National Labor Relations Board, 3d Cir. 1982, 675 F.2d 81. The primary purpose doctrine is criticized in Dobbs, Tortious Interference with Contractual Relationships, 1981, 34 Ark.L.Rev. 335, 348–50.

28. American Credit Bureau, Inc. v. Bel-Aire Interiors, Inc., 1970, 105 Ariz. 590, 469 P.2d 75, 61 A.L.R.3d 979; Nevada Credit Rating Bureau, Inc. v. Williams, 1972, 88 Nev. 601, 503 P.2d 9, 56 A.L.R.3d 483.

29. Bull v. McCuskey, 1980, 96 Nev. 706, 615 P.2d 957.

30. Most of the physician counterattack cases have proceeded upon a "malicious prosecution" approach. See § 119, supra. Those proceeding on abuse of process have generally fared no better. See Brody v. Ruby, Iowa 1978, 267 N.W.2d 902; Drago v. Buonagurio, 1978, 61 A.D.2d 282, 402 N.Y.S.2d 250, reversed on other grounds, 46 N.Y.2d 778, 413 N.Y.S.2d 910, 386 N.E.2d 821.

31. Jeffery v. Robbins, 1897, 73 Ill.App. 353; Bartlett v. Christhilf, 1888, 69 Md. 219, 14 A. 518; Saliem v. Glovsky, 1934, 132 Me. 402, 172 A. 4.

and any damages to that property.[32] However, a cause of action is also recognized where no property is taken at all and where the attempted extortion was wholly unsuccessful.[33] Although some courts might limit plaintiff's right to recover to cases in which there is some interference with property or person,[34] interference with person has been found in an arrest that may be entirely legitimate in the sense that it may have been made with probable cause.[35] With this liberal definition of interference, the net result appears to be that damages may be awarded to vindicate the right itself and to maintain the integrity of the judicial process. Once the plaintiff's right is established, actual damages proximately caused can be recovered, including indirect losses such as injury to financial standing [36] and intangible losses such as "mental injury." [37] Specific proof of intangible damages apparently has not been required as a prerequisite to an award if it is clear that such damages would accrue to a normal person.[38] Punitive damages may also be recovered in an appropriate case.[39]

Recovery of attorneys' fees incurred in defending against the abuse of process is problematical. It is settled that such fees can be recovered in the case of a levy or attachment that is wholly wrongful, since this amounts to a trespass or conversion of goods, though even in such a case the award may be limited to fees incurred in obtaining a release of the levy rather than in defending the main action.[40] Presumably an analogous rule would apply in abuse of process by excessive attachment. Where the abuse of process leads to arrest or criminal prosecution, authority is sparse on the question of attorneys' fees incurred in the defense of the prosecution. If grounds for malicious prosecution are not shown, the prosecution is, by definition, one that is in some sense justified and the only ground for complaint is not the prosecution as such but the collateral purpose to which it was turned. In such a case it is arguable that there should be no award of attorneys' fees for defending the criminal prosecution and that damages should be limited to items that result from the extortionate purposes behind it.[41]

WESTLAW REFERENCES

digest("abuse of process" /s ulterior)
313k168
"abuse of process" /s defense*
"abuse of process" /10 element*
"abuse of process" /s damage*

---

32. Nevada Credit Rating Bureau, Inc. v. Williams, 1972, 88 Nev. 601, 503 P.2d 9, 56 A.L.R.3d 483.

33. Ledford v. Smith, 1937, 212 N.C. 447, 193 S.E. 722 (plaintiff refused to make additional payment demanded, recovery); Huggins v. Winn-Dixie Greenville, Inc., 1967, 249 S.C. 206, 153 S.E.2d 693, 27 A.L.R.3d 1195 (same).

34. The usual statement is that ulterior motive plus an act to accomplish that motive after process has issued are the only elements of the tort, and the implication is that there is no requirement of interference with person or property. Most of the cases do involve one kind of interference or another, and it may be required in some jurisdictions. See Note, Physician Counterattack, 1976, 45 Clev.-St.L.Rev. 604, 620.

35. Hoppe v. Klapperich, 1947, 224 Minn. 224, 28 N.W.2d 780, 173 A.L.R. 819. In a number of cases damages have been allowed consistent with this approach but without any reference to it. See, e.g., Ledford v. Smith, 1937, 212 N.C. 447, 193 S.E. 722.

36. Saliem v. Glovsky, 1934, 132 Me. 402, 172 A. 4; Malone v. Belcher, 1913, 216 Mass. 209, 103 N.E. 637.

37. McGann v. Allen, 1926, 105 Conn. 177, 134 A. 810; Huggins v. Winn-Dixie Greenville, Inc., 1969, 252 S.C. 353, 166 S.E.2d 297.

38. Huggins v. Winn-Dixie Greenville, Inc., 1969, 252 S.C. 353, 166 S.E.2d 297 so holds. Other cases appear to imply the same thing. See McGann v. Allen, 1926, 105 Conn. 177, 134 A. 810.

39. E.g., Nienstedt v. Wetzel, App.1982, 133 Ariz. 348, 651 P.2d 876.

40. See Annot., 65 A.L.R.2d 1426.

41. See Spellens v. Spellens, 1957, 49 Cal.2d 210, 317 P.2d 613; McGann v. Allen, 1926, 105 Conn. 177, 134 A. 810. But see Hoppe v. Klapperich, 1947, 224 Minn. 224, 28 N.W.2d 780, 173 A.L.R. 819, holding that arrest itself may give rise to damages for abuse of process and hence implying that defense of the prosecution would represent appropriate damages.

Chapter 22

DOMESTIC RELATIONS

Table of Sections

Sec.
122. Torts in the Family.
123. Vicarious Liability for Torts of Family.
124. Interference With Family Relations.
125. Injuries to Members of the Family.

§ 122. Torts in the Family

Causes of action founded upon tortious conduct may be affected by the fact that at least one of the persons involved is a member of a family. The tortfeasor, a stranger to the family relation, may injure one who is a party to the relation; the tortfeasor, a party to the relation, may injure a stranger to the relation; one member of a family may injure another. Few topics in the law of torts have proved to be more difficult. This is true particularly of the third situation named, where the question is as to the civil liability of husband or wife, or of parent or minor child, to one another for acts, which if they were done by one ordinary person to another would be torts. Here there is waged a battle between conflicting conceptions of the family and between ideas of individual and relational rights and duties. Here the last few decades have witnessed a great revival of interest, and a shift in the tendencies of the law in the direction of liability where it did not exist before.[1]

Husband and Wife

The older common law was founded on the idea that upon marriage, the wife's legal identity merged with that of her husband. The effect of this was to place the wife under a number of disabilities.[2] She could not enter contracts; her husband was entitled to the possession and the profits of her property; there were restrictions on her power to litigate. For the same reason, neither spouse could maintain a tort action against the other, for either personal[3] or property

---

§ 122

1. The paragraph is paraphrased from McCurdy, Torts Between Persons in Domestic Relations, 1930, 43 Harv.L.Rev. 1030. See also, generally, as to tort actions within the family, Sanford, Personal Torts Within the Family, 1956, 9 Vand.L.Rev. 823; Note, 1961, 26 Mo.L.Rev. 152.

2. See H. Clark, Domestic Relations 219 (1968); McCurdy, Property Torts Between Spouses, 1957, 2 Villanova L.Rev. 447; McCurdy, Personal Injury Torts Between Spouses, 1959, 4 Villanova L.Rev. 303; Sanford, Personal Torts Within the Family, 1956, 9 Vand.L.Rev. 823; Notes, 1952, 30 Chicago-Kent L.Rev. 343; 1952, 32 Or.L.Rev. 60; 1954, 42 Ky.L.J. 497; 1954, 7 Vand.L. Rev. 717; 1958, 30 So.Cal.L.Rev. 431; 1959, 14 U.Miami L.Rev. 99; 1961, 26 Mo.L.Rev. 152.

3. Thompson v. Thompson, 1910, 218 U.S. 611, 31 S.Ct. 111, 54 L.Ed. 1180; Freethy v. Freethy, N.Y.1865,

torts.⁴ It was often said, perhaps with more accuracy than humor, that at common law the husband and wife were one, and the husband was that one.

About 1844 the states began to pass Married Women's Property Acts, which now exist in some form in all American jurisdictions.⁵ The central aim of these statutes, the details and language of which differ a great deal, is to secure to a married woman a separate legal identity, with her own rights in property and her own capacity to sue and be sued.

Courts generally agreed that these statutes permitted the wife to maintain a tort action against her husband to vindicate her property interests. Thus she could recover for conversion,⁶ fraud,⁷ trespass to land ⁸ and for negligent injury to her property.⁹ Since the statutes destroyed the unity of persons, the husband was held to have similar rights against the wife for torts to his property.¹⁰

But the Married Women's Acts were held not to destroy the spousal immunity when it came to personal torts, and during the remainder of the 19th and most of the 20th century courts refused to permit recovery against a spouse for either negligent ¹¹ or intentional ¹² torts. Though the legal identity of the spouses was destroyed by the statutes, courts found two major new arguments in favor of the immunity. The first was that suits between husband and wife would be fictitious and fraudulent.¹³ The second, inconsistently, was that spousal actions would be all too genuine and would destroy the peace and harmony of the home.¹⁴

Almost no legal writer has had any use for these arguments, and under repeated criticism and reiterated attacks on them in the courts, judicial perception of these arguments has slowly shifted. The danger of fraud has come to seem no greater than in many other cases where suit is allowed, such as the host-guest case or the suit between friends,¹⁵ and in any event it is now thought that the remedy for fraudulent claims is to expose the fraud rather than to discard all

42 Barb. 641; Libby v. Berry, 1883, 74 Me. 286; Peters v. Peters, 1875, 42 Iowa 182; Nickerson v. Nickerson, 1886, 65 Tex. 281.

4. See Kelley v. Kelley, 1931, 51 R.I. 173, 153 A. 314; Plotkin v. Plotkin, Del.1924, 2 W.W.Harr. 455, 125 A. 455; Smith v. Gorman, 1856, 41 Me. 405; Howe v. Blanden, 1849, 21 Vt. 315.

5. H. Clark, 1968, Domestic Relations 222; McCurdy, Property Torts Between Spouses, 1957, 2 Vill.L. Rev. 447, 461.

6. Hamilton v. Hamilton, 1950, 255 Ala. 284, 51 So. 2d 13; Madget v. Madget, 1949, 85 Ohio App. 18, 87 N.E.2d 918; Eddleman v. Eddleman, 1937, 183 Ga. 766, 189 S.E. 833, conformed to 55 Ga.App. 333, 190 S.E. 365; Carpenter v. Carpenter, 1908, 154 Mich. 100, 117 N.W. 598.

7. Langley v. Schumacker, 1956, 46 Cal.2d 601, 297 P.2d 977; Adams v. Adams, 1883, 51 Conn. 135; Whiting v. Whiting, 1916, 114 Me. 382, 96 A. 500; Heckman v. Heckman, 1906, 215 Pa. 203, 64 A. 425; Moreau v. Moreau, 1924, 250 Mass. 110, 145 N.E. 43; see Keen v. Coleman, 1861, 39 Pa. 299; Note, 1956, 4 U.C.L.A. L.Rev. 114. See Note, 1963, 38 Wash.L.Rev. 371.

8. Weldon v. De Bathe, 1884, 14 Q.B.D. 339; Larison v. Larison, 1881, 9 Ill.App. 27.

9. Hubbard v. Ruff, 1958, 97 Ga.App. 251, 103 S.E.2d 134; cf. Vigilant Insurance Co. v. Bennett, 1955, 197 Va. 216, 89 S.E.2d 69.

10. Mason v. Mason, 1892, 66 Hun 386, 21 N.Y.S. 306 (conversion); Shewalter v. Wood, Mo.App.1916, 183 S.W. 1127 (same); Lombard v. Morse, 1891, 155 Mass. 136, 29 N.E 205 (fraud); Hedlund v. Hedlund, 1930, 87 Colo. 607, 290 P. 285 (replevin); Vigilant Insurance Co. v. Bennett, 1955, 197 Va. 216, 89 S.E.2d 69 (negligence).

11. Rubalcava v. Gisseman, 1963, 14 Utah 2d 344, 384 P.2d 389; Campbell v. Campbell, 1960, 145 W.Va. 245, 114 S.E.2d 406.

12. Thompson v. Thompson, 1910, 218 U.S. 611, 31 S.Ct. 111, 54 L.Ed. 1180; Fisher v. Toler, 1965, 194 Kan. 701, 401 P.2d 1012.

13. "* * * and this would add a new method by which estates could be plundered." Abbott v. Abbott, 1877, 67 Me. 304. No wife would want to sue her husband for a negligent tort except as a "raid on an insurance company." Newton v. Weber, 1922, 119 Misc. 240, 196 N.Y.S. 113.

14. Ritter v. Ritter, 1858, 31 Pa. 396: "The flames which litigation would kindle on the domestic hearth would consume in an instant the conjugal bond, and bring on a new era indeed—an era of universal discord, of unchastity, of bastardy, of dissoluteness, of violence, cruelty, and murders."

15. Immer v. Risko, 1970, 56 N.J. 482, 267 A.2d 481.

the honest claims along with the bad ones.[16] Similarly, it has come to seem doubtful that peace and harmony of the home can be preserved or restored by refusing to redress a palpable wrong or to compensate a genuine injury, and there is no reason to believe that personal injury claims are more disruptive than property claims, which are actionable.[17]

As the arguments for immunity have come to seem less weighty, the principle of compensation for tort has acquired a preeminent position in the solution of the problem,[18] and by 1970 about a dozen courts had rejected any universal principle of immunity between spouses.[19] In the decade that followed more than a dozen other courts joined them in abrogating the immunity,[20] including courts in community property states where special problems created practical difficulties in discarding the immunity.[21] The movement to abolish the unqualified immunity has continued,[22] and it now appears that spousal actions will be permitted for personal injuries in a majority of the states, at least in some circumstances, though some courts have indicated that they will scrutinize such actions with care or that immunity might be retained in some class of case,[23] and that there might well be conduct that would be tortious among strangers that is still not actionable between spouses.[24]

This leaves a respectable minority of courts that continue to provide for an absolute immunity between spouses in personal tort actions.[25] In these states the injured spouse may, however, find some comfort in one of the recognized exceptions to immunity. It has been held that a spouse may recover against the other spouse for pre-marital torts.[26] A few courts have permitted recovery for torts during or before the marriage once the marriage is terminated by di-

16. Klein v. Klein, 1962, 58 Cal.2d 692, 26 Cal.Rptr. 102, 376 P.2d 70; Beaudette v. Frana, 1969, 285 Minn. 366, 173 N.W.2d 416.

17. Cramer v. Cramer, Alaska, 1963, 379 P.2d 95; Brooks v. Robinson, 1972, 259 Ind. 16, 284 N.E.2d 794.

18. See Lewis v. Lewis, 1976, 370 Mass. 619, 351 N.E.2d 526; Beaudette v. Frana, 1969, 285 Minn. 366, 173 N.W.2d 416.

19. These decisions reflect a process of slow erosion beginning in the teenaged years of the century and continuing until the landslide of 1970–80. See, e.g., Klein v. Klein, 1962, 58 Cal.2d 692, 26 Cal.Rptr. 102, 376 P.2d 70; Crowell v. Crowell, 1920, 180 N.C. 516, 105 S.E. 206, rehearing denied 181 N.C. 66, 106 S.E. 149.

20. Rogers v. Yellowstone Park Co., 1974, 97 Idaho 14, 539 P.2d 566; Brooks v. Robinson, 1972, 259 Ind. 16, 284 N.E.2d 794; Shook v. Crabb, Iowa 1979, 281 N.W.2d 616; Lewis v. Lewis, 1976, 370 Mass. 619, 351 N.E.2d 526, 92 A.L.R.3d 890; Hosko v. Hosko, 1971, 385 Mich. 39, 187 N.W.2d 236; Imig v. March, 1979, 203 Neb. 537, 279 N.W.2d 382; Merenoff v. Merenoff, 1978, 76 N.J. 535, 388 A.2d 951; Maestas v. Overton, 1975, 87 N.M. 213, 531 P.2d 947; State Farm Mutual Automobile Insurance Co. v. Westlake, 1974, 35 N.Y.2d 587, 364 N.Y.S.2d 482, 324 N.E.2d 137 (considered dictum); Rupert v. Stienne, 1974, 90 Nev. 397, 528 P.2d 1013; Richard v. Richard, 1973, 131 Vt. 98, 300 A.2d 637; Surratt v. Thompson, 1971, 212 Va. 191, 183 S.E.2d 200; Freehe v. Freehe, 1972, 81 Wn.2d 183, 500 P.2d 771; Coffindaffer v. Coffindaffer, 1978, ___ W.Va. ___, 244 S.E.2d 338.

21. The problem is to prevent recovery from going to the "community" when one of the community is a tortfeasor. See Rogers v. Yellowstone Park Co., 1974, 97 Idaho 14, 539 P.2d 566; Maestas v. Overton, 1975, 87 N.M. 213, 531 P.2d 947.

22. Fernandez v. Romo, 1982, 132 Ariz. 447, 646 P.2d 878; MacDonald v. MacDonald, Me.1980, 412 A.2d 71. Hack v. Hack, Pa.1981, 433 A.2d 859.

23. Abrogation of the immunity has often come first in automobile injury cases and at times courts have suggested that the immunity might be otherwise retained. But the implication has been difficult to carry out in practice, and courts suggesting such limits have had occasion since to state a more general principle of abrogation. Compare Lewis v. Lewis, 1976, 370 Mass. 619, 351 N.E.2d 526, 92 A.L.R.3d 890 with Brown v. Brown, 1980, 381 Mass. 231, 409 N.E.2d 717; Immer v. Risko, 1970, 56 N.J. 482, 267 A.2d 481 with Merenoff v. Merenoff, 1978, 76 N.J. 535, 388 A.2d 951.

24. Lewis v. Lewis, 1976, 370 Mass. 619, 351 N.E.2d 526; Beaudette v. Frana, 1969, 285 Minn. 366, 173 N.W.2d 416 ("intimate sharing * * * injurious contact [must be] plainly excessive or a gross abuse of a normal privilege. * * * ").

25. Alfree v. Alfree, Del.1979, 410 A.2d 161, appeal dismissed 446 U.S. 931, 100 S.Ct. 2145, 64 L.Ed.2d 783 (but recommending legislative attention); Raisen v. Raisen, Fla.1979, 379 So.2d 352, certiorari denied 449 U.S. 886, 101 S.Ct. 240, 66 L.Ed.2d 111; Bonkowsky v. Bonkowsky, 1982, 69 Ohio St.2d 152, 431 N.E.2d 998.

26. Moulton v. Moulton, Me.1973, 309 A.2d 224; Childress v. Childress, Tenn.1978, 569 S.W.2d 816 (possibly excluding torts impliedly released by marriage, such as seduction).

vorce,[27] though this is not a favored exception with many courts.[28] Likewise, a few have held that upon the death of one spouse a wrongful death action may be maintained against the other, since the reasons for the immunity no longer exist.[29] Still another exception sometimes recognized is that intentional torts by a spouse are actionable even where negligent torts are not.[30] These exceptions have at least on occasion turned out to be stepping stones toward a complete abolition of the immunity, since once the exception is recognized it does not, on analysis, seem to furnish a logical stopping place.[31] From all this it may be expected that the trend towards spousal liability for torts will continue.

Parent and Child

The common law had no similar conception of unity of legal identity in the case of a parent and his minor child. Although the parent was given custody of the child, the latter remained a separate legal person, entitled to the benefits of his own property and to the enforcement of his own choses in action, including those in tort, and was liable in turn as an individual for his own torts.[32] Consequently there were no such theoretical difficulties, no emancipation acts similar to the Married Women's Acts were necessary, and statutory construction has not entered into the question of tort liability between parent and child.

In matters affecting property, causes of action seem always to have been freely recognized on the part of either the parent [33] or the child.[34] Although there were no old decisions, the speculation on the matter has been that there is no good reason to think that the English law would not permit actions for personal torts as well,[35] subject always to the parent's privilege to enforce reasonable discipline against the child; [36] and there are decisions in Canada [37] and Scotland [38] holding that such an action will lie. But beginning in 1891 with Hewellette v. George,[39] a Mississippi case of false imprisonment which cited no authorities, the American courts adopted a general rule refusing to allow actions between parent and minor child for personal torts, whether they are intentional [40] or negligent [41] in character. For rea-

27. Lorang v. Hays, 1949, 69 Idaho 440, 209 P.2d 733; Goode v. Martinis, 1961, 58 Wn.2d 229, 361 P.2d 941 (tort committed while parties separated, divorce pending and later granted); Burns v. Burns, 1974, 111 Ariz. 178, 526 P.2d 717 (intentional torts); Gaston v. Pittman, Fla.1969, 224 So.2d 326 (recovery after divorce for premarital tort).

28. Ebel v. Ferguson, Mo.1972, 478 S.W.2d 334; Nickerson v. Nickerson, 1886, 65 Tex. 281 (divorce does not create a cause of action where none existed before).

29. Herget National Bank of Pekin v. Berardi, 1976, 64 Ill.2d 467, 356 N.E.2d 529; Annot., 28 A.L.R.2d 662.

30. Lusby v. Lusby, 1978, 283 Md. 334, 390 A.2d 77; Apitz v. Dames, 1955, 205 Or. 242, 287 P.2d 585; Bounds v. Caudle, Tex.1977, 560 S.W.2d 925, appeal after new trial, 611 S.W.2d 685, refused n. r. e.

31. Klein v. Klein, 1962, 58 Cal.2d 692, 26 Cal.Rptr. 102, 376 P.2d 70; Maestas v. Overton, 1975, 87 N.M. 213, 531 P.2d 947.

32. As to the minor's abilities and disabilities see H. Clark, 1968, Domestic Relations § 8.1. Procedural limits, such as guardianship, might be imposed in litigation.

33. Young v. Wiley, 1914, 183 Ind. 449, 107 N.E. 278; McKern v. Beck, 1920, 73 Ind.App. 92, 126 N.E. 641; McCall v. McCall, 1873, 1 Tenn.Ch. 500.

34. During minority: Roberts v. Roberts, 1657, Hard. 96, 145 Eng.Rep. 399; Alston v. Alston, 1859, 34 Ala. 15; Lamb v. Lamb, 1895, 146 N.Y. 317, 41 N.E. 26; Preston v. Preston, 1925, 102 Conn. 96, 128 A. 292. After majority for acts occurring during minority: Thomas v. Thomas, 1855, 2 K. & J. 79, 69 Eng.Rep. 701; McLain v. McLain, 1921, 80 Okl. 113, 194 P. 894.

35. See Reeve, Domestic Relations, 1816, 287; Eversley, Domestic Relations, 3d Ed. 1906, 578; Dunlap v. Dunlap, 1930, 84 N.H. 352, 150 A. 905.

36. See supra, § 27.

37. Deziel v. Deziel, [1953] 1 Dom.L.Rep. 651.

38. Young v. Rankin, [1934] Sess.Cass. 499.

39. 1891, 68 Miss. 703, 9 So. 885.

40. McKelvey v. McKelvey, 1903, 111 Tenn. 388, 77 S.W. 664; Roller v. Roller, 1905, 37 Wash. 242, 79 P. 788; Cook v. Cook, 1939, 232 Mo.App. 994, 124 S.W.2d 675; Miller v. Pelzer, 1924, 159 Minn. 375, 199 N.W. 97 (deceit); Smith v. Smith, 1924, 81 Ind.App. 566, 142 N.E. 128 (action after majority for assault during minority).

41. Villaret v. Villaret, 1948, 83 U.S.App.D.C. 311, 169 F.2d 677 (Maryland law); Stevens v. Murphy, 1966, 69 Wn.2d 939, 421 P.2d 668; Chaffin v. Chaffin, 1964, 239 Or. 374, 397 P.2d 771; Hastings v. Hastings, 1961, 33 N.J. 247, 163 A.2d 147; Ownby v. Kleyhammer, 1952, 194 Tenn. 109, 250 S.W.2d 37.

sons that are not altogether clear, however, and perhaps are to be explained only on the basis of an initial retreat from the general rule,[42] the action nearly always has been permitted against one who is not a parent but merely stands in the place of one, such as a stepfather, or another relative who has custody of the child.[43] And more recently this has been extended to allow a child to claim against the parent himself where a divorce decree has deprived him of general custody.[44]

The courts that deny the action have relied heavily on the analogy of husband and wife, which seems quite inapplicable because of the difference in the common law concept of the relations, and the absence of statutes to be construed.[45] In addition, they have invented much the same variety of unconvincing reasons as in the case of the marital relation.[46] The danger of "fraud" has been stressed, although it is difficult to see why it is any greater as between the parties themselves than in any other tort action involving an infant. The prevalence of liability insurance was once regarded as likely to increase fraudulent or collusive claims between parents and children, but this has been rejected by contemporary decisions as a ground for immunity since fraud is always a danger against which the courts must guard and since there is no more likelihood of fraud between minors and their parents than between adult or emancipated family members, who have always been permitted to sue.[47] Other arguments in favor of the family immunity have mentioned the possibility that the defendant might inherit the amount recovered in case of the plaintiff's death, or that the family exchequer might be depleted at the expense of other children—neither of which reasons seems to outweigh the desirability of compensating the injured one for his damage. But again, as in the case of husband and wife, the chief reason offered is that domestic tranquillity and parental discipline and control would be disturbed by the action—and again on the theory that an uncompensated tort makes for peace in the family and respect for the parent, even though it be rape[48] or a brutal beating,[49] and even though the relation itself has been terminated by death before the suit.[50] But none of these arguments has been held suf-

42. Brown v. Cole, 1939, 198 Ark. 417, 129 S.W.2d 245 (stepfather poisoning stepson); Treschman v. Treschman, 1901, 28 Ind.App. 206, 61 N.E. 961; Clasen v. Pruhs, 1903, 69 Neb. 789, 95 N.W. 640; Steber v. Norris, 1925, 188 Wis. 366, 206 N.W. 173; Dix v. Martin, 1913, 171 Mo.App. 266, 157 S.W. 133. On their reasoning these cases appear to contradict the explanations offered for the rule as to parents.

43. Bricault v. Deveau, 1960, 21 Conn.Sup. 486, 157 A.2d 604 (stepfather); Brown v. Cole, 1939, 198 Ark. 417, 129 S.W.2d 245 (adoptive parent); Wilkins v. Kane, 1962, 74 N.J.Super. 414, 181 A.2d 417 (grandparent); Cwik v. Zylstra, 1959, 58 N.J.Super. 29, 155 A.2d 277 (grandparent). Contra, Wooden v. Hale, Okl.1967, 426 P.2d 679.

The state itself, or its agency, is liable when it takes custody of the child and negligently places the child in a dangerous foster home. E.g., Koepf v. County of York, 1977, 198 Neb. 67, 251 N.W.2d 866. And the foster parent in such a situation may also be held. Andrews v. County of Otsego, Sup.Ct.1982, 112 Misc.2d 37, 446 N.Y.S.2d 169. Schools, which have temporary custody or control of the child, are also held liable for negligence. E.g., Larson v. Independent School District, Minn.1979, 289 N.W.2d 112.

44. Fugate v. Fugate, Mo.1979, 582 S.W.2d 663; Buffalo v. Buffalo, 1982, ___ Ind.App. ___, 441 N.E.2d 711.

45. The height of inconsistency was reached by some courts which permitted action by the wife but denied it to the child. Redding v. Redding, 1952, 235 N.C. 638, 70 S.E.2d 676; Mesite v. Kirchstein, 1929, 109 Conn. 77, 145 A. 753; Wick v. Wick, 1927, 192 Wis. 260, 212 N.W. 787; Rambo v. Rambo, 1938, 195 Ark. 832, 114 S.W.2d 468.

46. Discussed at length in McCurdy, Torts Between Persons in Domestic Relations, 1930, 43 Harv.L.Rev. 1030, 1072–1077; McCurdy, Torts Between Parent and Child, 1960, 5 Vill.L.Rev. 521; Sanford, Personal Torts Within the Family, 1956, 9 Vand.L.Rev. 823; Notes, 1961, 23 Mo.L.Rev. 152; 1963, 48 Iowa L.Rev. 748; 1966, 44 N.C.L.Rev. 1169; 1976, 12 William.L.Rev. 605. The only kind word spoken for the immunity is in Cooperrider, Child v. Parent in Tort: A Case for the Jury, 1958, 43 Minn.L.Rev. 73.

47. See Gelbman v. Gelbman, 1969, 23 N.Y.2d 434, 297 N.Y.S.2d 529, 245 N.E.2d 192; Freehe v. Freehe, 1972, 81 Wn.2d 183, 500 P.2d 771 (husband-wife).

48. Roller v. Roller, 1905, 37 Wash. 242, 79 P. 788.

49. Cook v. Cook, 1939, 232 Mo.App. 994, 124 S.W.2d 675; McKelvey v. McKelvey, 1903, 111 Tenn. 388, 77 S.W. 664; cf. Hewellette v. George, 1891, 68 Miss. 703, 9 So. 885 (imprisonment in insane asylum).

50. Lasecki v. Kabara, 1940, 235 Wis. 645, 294 N.W. 33; Harralson v. Thomas, Ky.1954, 269 S.W.2d 276;

ficient to bar an action by or against an unemancipated minor for a tort against property, although they are all quite obviously equally applicable in such a case. Nor, by common agreement, have they been sufficient to prevent an action for a personal tort between minor brothers and sisters, which uniformly has been allowed.[51]

Although it would appear that no shadow of a difference in principle or policy is to be discovered, the retreat from the common law as to parent and child has lagged behind that as to husband and wife, apparently for no better reason than the absence of statutes such as the Married Women's Acts. It is, however, under way. As in the case of husband and wife, the courts began by recognizing a series of exceptions which have whittled the immunity down. The rule never applied to adult children, and by extension of this idea the action has been allowed where the chid has been "emancipated" by the parent's surrender of the right to his earnings and services, and to parental control.[52] Another exception allows recovery when personal injuries are inflicted intentionally,[53] and several courts have extended this to include "wilful or wanton," or in other words reckless misconduct,[54] sometimes on the manufactured ground that such conduct terminates or "forfeits" the relationship, and steps outside of it.

As in the case of husband and wife, some courts have allowed recovery when the relation has been terminated by the death of either parent or child, and the action is brought under a wrongful death[55] or a survival[56] act. Even this has been extended to permit an action between parent and child for the wrongful death of the other parent[57] or loss of services of another child,[58] on the ground that these are derivative actions, turning primarily upon the possibility of suit by another. Finally, there are half a dozen courts which have allowed recovery where the child is injured in the course of a business, rather than a personal, activity of the parent,[59] or where the child is injured by the

---

Shaker v. Shaker, 1942, 129 Conn. 518, 29 A.2d 765; Damiano v. Damiano, 1928, 6 N.J.Misc. 849, 143 A. 3 (both parent and child dead).

51. Midkiff v. Midkiff, 1960, 201 Va. 829, 113 S.E.2d 875; Herrell v. Haney, 1960, 207 Tenn. 532, 341 S.W.2d 574; Overlock v. Ruedemann, 1960, 147 Conn. 649, 165 A.2d 335; Emery v. Emery, 1955, 45 Cal.2d 421, 289 P.2d 218; Tucker v. Tucker, Okl.1964, 395 P.2d 67. See Notes, 1939, 37 Mich.L.Rev. 658; 1940, 38 Mich.L. Rev. 743; 1939, 23 Minn.L.Rev. 838; 1961, 28 Tenn.L. Rev. 419.

52. Weinberg v. Underwood, 1968, 101 N.J.Super. 448, 244 A.2d 538; Fitzgerald v. Valdez, 1967, 77 N.M. 769, 427 P.2d 655; Carricato v. Carricato, Ky.1964, 384 S.W.2d 85; Tucker v. Tucker, Okl.1964, 395 P.2d 67; Logan v. Reaves, 1962, 209 Tenn. 631, 354 S.W.2d 789. As to what constitutes emancipation, see Gillikin v. Burbage, 1965, 263 N.C. 317, 139 S.E.2d 753.

Cf. Reese v. Reese, 1977, 142 Ga.App. 243, 236 S.E. 2d 20 (adult of limited mental competence "both adult and emancipated").

53. Treschman v. Treschman, 1901, 28 Ind.App. 206, 61 N.E. 961; Gillett v. Gillett, 1959, 168 Cal.App.2d 102, 335 P.2d 736; Brown v. Cole, 1939, 198 Ark. 417, 129 S.W.2d 245; Mahnke v. Moore, 1951, 197 Md. 61, 77 A.2d 923; Felderhoff v. Felderhoff, Tex.1971, 473 S.W.2d 928. See also Brown v. Selby, 1960, 206 Tenn. 71, 332 S.W.2d 166; Meyer v. Ritterbush, 1949, 196 Misc. 551, 92 N.Y.S.2d 595.

54. Attwood v. Estate of Attwood, 1982, 276 Ark. 230, 633 S.W.2d 366; Nudd v. Matsoukas, 1956, 7 Ill.2d 608, 131 N.E.2d 525.

55. Hale v. Hale, 1950, 312 Ky. 867, 230 S.W.2d 610; Morgan v. Leuck, 1952, 137 W.Va. 546, 72 S.E.2d 825; Logan v. Reaves, 1962, 209 Tenn. 631, 354 S.W.2d 789; Harlan National Bank v. Gross, Ky.1961, 346 S.W.2d 482. See Note, 1964, 16 U.Me.L.Rev. 238.

56. Thurman v. Etherton, Ky.1970, 459 S.W.2d 402; Palcsey v. Tepper, 1962, 71 N.J.Super. 294, 176 A.2d 818; Krause v. Home Mutual Insurance Co., 1961, 14 Wis.2d 666, 112 N.W.2d 134; Brinks v. Chesapeake & Ohio Railway Co., W.D.Mich.1969, 295 F.Supp. 1318; Union Bank & Trust Co. of Mt. Holley, New Jersey v. First National Bank & Trust Co. of Waynesboro, Pa., 5th Cir. 1966, 362 F.2d 311, appeal after remand, 396 F.2d 795.

57. Shiver v. Sessions, Fla.1955, 80 So.2d 905; Fowler v. Fowler, 1963, 242 S.C. 252, 130 S.E.2d 568; Johnson v. Ottemeier, 1954, 45 Wn.2d 419, 275 P.2d 723; Brown v. Selby, 1960, 206 Tenn. 71, 332 S.W.2d 166; Minkin v. Minkin, 1939, 336 Pa. 49, 7 A.2d 461.

Accord, as to the death of another child: Munsert v. Farmers Mutual Automobile Insurance Co., 1938, 229 Wis. 581, 281 N.W. 671. Contra: Durham v. Durham, 1956, 227 Miss. 76, 85 So.2d 807; Wright v. Davis, 1949, 132 W.Va. 722, 53 S.E.2d 335.

58. Becker v. Rieck, 1959, 19 Misc.2d 104, 188 N.Y.S.2d 724.

59. Dunlap v. Dunlap, 1930, 84 N.H. 352, 150 A. 905; Lusk v. Lusk, 1932, 113 W.Va. 17, 166 S.E. 538;

parent's violation of a larger duty to the public generally and where the family relationship is only collaterally or fortuitously involved in the tort.[60]

Finally, in 1963, Wisconsin took the lead in declaring that the parent-child immunity was abrogated entirely in that jurisdiction,[61] except as to exercises of parental control and authority, or parental discretion with respect to such matters as food and care. The decision set off something of a long-overdue landslide; and at the present writing more than half the states have now abrogated the absolute immunity, either by case [62] law or by statute.[63] In a few instances courts have, at least as a first step, limited family liabilities to those cases in which insurance exists or is likely,[64] or, what is much the same thing, to motor vehicle cases,[65] but even in such jurisdictions these limits may be discarded when nonmotor vehicle cases arise.[66]

Limited Duties of Family Members

The abrogation of tort immunities among family members has been so far a moderate reform rather than a radical revision. The Wisconsin Court, abolishing the parent-child immunity in 1963, expressly retained the protection for the exercise of "parental authority," and "ordinary parental discretion" in providing "food, clothing, housing, medical and dental services and other care."[67] California stated the standard as that of the "reasonable and prudent *parent*," without explicit protection for discretionary activities, but at the same time recognized that "traditional concepts of negligence cannot be blindly applied" and that parental discretion must be taken into account in determin-

---

Signs v. Signs, 1952, 156 Ohio St. 566, 103 N.E.2d 743; Borst v. Borst, 1952, 41 Wn.2d 642, 251 P.2d 149; Trevarton v. Trevarton, 1963, 151 Colo. 418, 378 P.2d 640; Felderhoff v. Felderhoff, Tex.1971, 473 S.W.2d 928. Cf. Worrell v. Worrell, 1939, 174 Va. 11, 4 S.E.2d 343 (under compulsory insurance statute).

60. Cummings v. Jackson, 1978, 57 Ill.App.3d 68, 14 Ill.Dec. 848, 372 N.E.2d 1127 (parent's failure to trim trees in violation of ordinance obstructed view of driver, who struck child); Schenk v. Schenk, 1968, 100 Ill. App.2d 199, 241 N.E.2d 12 (daughter ran into pedestrian who in fact was father).

61. Goller v. White, 1963, 20 Wis.2d 402, 122 N.W.2d 193. Followed in Ertl v. Ertl, 1966, 30 Wis.2d 372, 141 N.W.2d 208.

62. Hebel v. Hebel, Alaska 1967, 435 P.2d 8; Streenz v. Streenz, 1970, 106 Ariz. 86, 471 P.2d 282, 41 A.L.R.3d 891; Gibson v. Gibson, 1971, 3 Cal.3d 914, 92 Cal.Rptr. 288, 479 P.2d 648; Williams v. Williams, Del. 1976, 369 A.2d 669; Ard v. Ard, Fla.1982, 414 So.2d 1066 (immunity is waived to the extent of the parent's available liability insurance); Peterson v. City and County of Honolulu, 1970, 51 Hawaii 484, 462 P.2d 1007; Turner v. Turner, Iowa 1981, 304 N.W.2d 786 (reserving question whether areas of parental discretion and authority should exist); Nocktonick v. Nocktonick, 1980, 227 Kan. 758, 611 P.2d 135; Rigdon v. Rigdon, Ky.1971, 465 S.W.2d 921; Deshotel v. Travelers Indemnity Co., 1971, 257 La. 567, 243 So.2d 259 (direct action against insurer permitted); Black v. Solmitz, Me.1979, 409 A.2d 634, 6 A.L.R.4th 1054; Sorenson v. Sorenson, 1975, 369 Mass. 350, 339 N.E.2d 907; Plumley v. Klein, 1972, 388 Mich. 1, 199 N.W.2d 169; Silesky v. Kelman, 1968, 281 Minn. 431, 161 N.W.2d 631; Rupert v. Stienne, 1974, 90 Nev. 397, 528 P.2d 1013; Briere v. Briere, 1966, 107 N.H. 432, 224 A.2d 588; France v. A. P. A. Transport Corp., 1976, 56 N.J. 500, 267 A.2d 490; Gelbman v. Gelbman, 1969, 23 N.Y.2d 434, 245 N.E.2d 192; Nuelle v. Wells, N.D.1967, 154 N.W.2d 364; Falco v. Pados, 1971, 444 Pa. 372, 282 A.2d 351; Silva v. Silva, 1982, ___ R.I. ___, 446 A.2d 1013; Elam v. Elam, 1980, 275 S.C. 132, 268 S.E.2d 109; Wood v. Wood, 1977, 135 Vt. 119, 370 A.2d 191; Smith v. Kaufman, 1971, 212 Va. 181, 183 S.E.2d 190; Merrick v. Sutterlin, 1980, 93 Wash.2d 411, 610 P.2d 891; Lee v. Comer, 1976, 159 W.Va. 585, 224 S.E.2d 721; Goller v. White, 1963, 20 Wis.2d 402, 122 N.W.2d 193.

Missouri has adopted what may be a substantial abrogation of the doctrine, apparently contemplating a case by case decision on liability and an evidentiary hearing as to whether liability would disturb family relations. See Kendall v. Sears, Roebuck & Co., Mo. 1982, 634 S.W.2d 176.

63. Conn.Gen.Stat. § 52–572c (motor vehicle cases); N.C.Gen.Stats. § 1–539.21 (child versus parent in motor vehicle operated by parent).

64. See Briere v. Briere, 1966, 107 N.H. 432, 224 A.2d 588; Sorenson v. Sorenson, 1975, 369 Mass. 350, 339 N.E.2d 907. Cf. Deshotel v. Travelers Indemnity Co., 1971, 257 La. 567, 243 So.2d 259 (where father could bring direct action against insurer for son's negligence).

65. Williams v. Williams, Del.1976, 369 A.2d 669; Smith v. Kaufman, 1971, 212 Va. 181, 183 S.E.2d 190.

66. Compare, e.g., Lewis v. Lewis, 1976, 370 Mass. 619, 351 N.E.2d 526, 92 A.L.R.3d 890 with Brown v. Brown, 1980, 381 Mass. 231, 409 N.E.2d 717 and both with Sorenson v. Sorenson, 1975, 369 Mass. 350, 339 N.E.2d 907, reflecting the fact that initial limitations were discarded.

67. Goller v. White, 1963, 20 Wis.2d 402, 122 N.W.2d 193, 198.

ing whether, under all the circumstances, there actually was negligence.[68] New York, emphasizing parental discretion heavily, has at times said that a parent's failure to supervise children at play is a discretionary matter and is not actionable.[69] Regardless which formula is used, however, it is clear that the parent-child relationship remains a special one and that not every act or omission by a parent will be regarded as actionable negligence, even if, as to some other persons, negligence might be found to exist.

The cases have not yet drawn a clear picture of parental liability. New York has taken the most protective view of the parents, holding that there is no liability for negligent supervision of the child, and that a parent who gives a motorcycle to a 16-year-old boy, blind in one eye and with poor vision in the other, is merely supervising the child in a negligent way, so that there is no liability to the child,[70] even though there is liability to a member of the public injured, even indirectly, by the child's use of the motorcycle.[71] Some courts would no doubt differ on these facts,[72] but a number of decisions show a distinct sympathy with the parent who merely fails to instruct or supervise adequately. It is thus held that the parent who fails to instruct a child on the precautions required for crossing streets in safety,[73] or on the use of seat belts in a car,[74] is not liable. Some courts have also held that the parent who fails to keep constant attention necessary for the perfect safety of a small child is also absolved when the child wanders into traffic or other dangers,[75] although much will turn in such cases on the particular facts as well as on the liberality of the court, and some decisions have imposed liability in cases of negligent supervision.[76]

Though it is not possible to state an exact rule as to the scope of "parental discretion," there are patterns in the cases that may be significant. Courts apparently feel that the jury should not be permitted to second-guess the parent as to the exact amount of supervision, training or freedom a child should have, and similarly that household dangers such as the vaporizer,[77] electrical cord[78] or slippery rug[79] are such constant and common risks that negligence should not too readily be inferred when they cause harm. But if the parent engaged in an affirmative activity,[80] as where he drives a tractor,[81] or where he recognizes a danger and tries to guard against it, but does so in a negligent

68. Gibson v. Gibson, 1971, 3 Cal.3d 914, 92 Cal. Rptr. 288, 479 P.2d 648.

69. Holodook v. Spencer, 1974, 36 N.Y.2d 35, 364 N.Y.S.2d 859, 324 N.E.2d 338.

70. Nolechek v. Gesuale, 1978, 46 N.Y.2d 332, 413 N.Y.S.2d 340, 385 N.E.2d 1268.

71. Nolechek v. Gesuale, 1978, 46 N.Y.2d 332, 413 N.Y.S.2d 340, 385 N.E.2d 1268, holding that in the claim by the child or estate against A, A would be entitled to contribution or indemnity against the negligent parent, even though the child himself could not claim against the parent. This was limited to the situation in which the parent, by furnishing a dangerous instrumentality, created a risk to A and other third parties.

72. In Horn v. Horn, Ky.1982, 630 S.W.2d 70 a father permitted a 15-year-old son to ride a motorbike not equipped with lights or turn signals, while the father followed behind to protect him. The boy was seriously injured when he was struck making a left turn. The father was held not immune.

73. Lemmen v. Servais, 1968, 39 Wis.2d 75, 158 N.W.2d 341.

74. Latta v. Siefke, 1978, 60 A.D.2d 991, 401 N.Y.S.2d 937.

75. Sandoval v. Sandoval, 1981, 128 Ariz. 11, 623 P.2d 800 (parent left gate open, child struck when he rode tricycle through it); Foldi v. Jeffries, 1981, 182 N.J.Super. 90, 440 A.2d 58 (small child wandered off, bitten by dog).

76. Anderson v. Stream, Minn.1980, 295 N.W.2d 595 (small child wandered into driveway and was struck); Thoreson v. Milwaukee & Suburban Transport Co., 1972, 56 Wis.2d 231, 201 N.W.2d 745 (small child left alone in house, wandered off and was struck).

77. Hush v. Devilbiss Co., 1977, 77 Mich.App. 639, 259 N.W.2d 170.

78. Cherry v. Cherry, 1972, 295 Minn. 93, 203 N.W.2d 352.

79. Cosmopolitan National Bank of Chicago v. Heap, 1970, 128 Ill.App.2d 165, 262 N.E.2d 826.

80. Romanik v. Toro Co., Minn.1979, 277 N.W.2d 515: "A parent who entrusts a potentially dangerous piece of machinery to a child and negligently instructs him to operate it contrary to the operator's manual cannot characterize his misconduct as negligent supervision. At the very least, it is an affirmative act of negligence. * * *"

81. See note 81 on page 891.

manner,[82] the role of "parental discretion"[83] is much smaller and liability may be imposed. Even to allow a small child near dangerous instrumentalities may be enough to justify liability,[84] and even more clearly is this so where the parent himself maintains a dangerous instrument such as dynamite caps[85] or a vicious dog[86] in the home. It has been argued[87] that, in addition, the parents should be liable for negligent or intentional pre-natal injury to a child, as where the mother ingests drugs that cause a deformity, and one decision has lent some support to this thesis.[88] Finally it may be said that most of the cases involve physical injury and that, though there is no hard and fast rule against recovery for purely dignitary or purely economic harm, it is unlikely that claims for bad parenting[89] or slander or poor education will meet with much enthusiasm in the courts, at least in the absence of genuine ill-will on the part of the parent.[90]

In the case of spousal actions there is room for neither disciplinary authority nor parental discretion, but most courts have recognized that, even with the general abolition of immunity, some areas of the marital relationship will remain untouched by tort law. Not every act that is tortious between strangers will be so regarded when it is committed between spouses because there are many "mutual concessions implied in the marital relationship."[91] Thus consent, both that understood from past conduct or the spouses' way of doing things and that understood from social habits generally, will be an important defense as to some intentional torts. But it should go without saying, however, that a "gross abuse of normal privilege"[92] will receive no protection, and the victim of an outright rape or beating[93] or of systematic infliction of mental distress[94] has not "consented" merely because the spouse's earlier bad conduct has not been reported, and indeed the cases on such unpleasant facts have not even raised the issue of consent. Nevertheless courts appear to feel that there may be some relatively trivial, or at least highly transitory, harms that may be excluded from the protection of tort law.[95] Good candidates for this class of cases would probably be the purely technical battery and the normal hurts of intimate living. Beyond this courts so far have said little except that the abolition of immunity will not result in automatic liability and that the courts will be sure to respect the "subtle ebb and flow of married life."[96] On this basis it

81. Goller v. White, 1963, 20 Wis.2d 402, 122 N.W.2d 193.
82. Cf. Thoreson v. Milwaukee & Suburban Transport Co., 1972, 56 Wis.2d 231, 201 N.W.2d 745 (child known to run for street was left alone, liability).
83. In Horn v. Horn, Ky.1982, 630 S.W.2d 70 the court said: "An exercise of parental authority simply involves acts of disciplining a child while an exercise of discretion in providing for the care and necessities of a child is limited to those provisions which a parent is legally obligated to furnish."
84. Howes v. Hansen, 1972, 56 Wis.2d 247, 201 N.W.2d 825; Cole v. Sears, Roebuck & Co., 1970, 47 Wis.2d 629, 177 N.W.2d 866.
85. Goedkoop v. Ward Pavement, 1976, 51 A.D.2d 542, 378 N.Y.S.2d 417.
86. Dower v. Goldstein, 1976, 143 N.J.Super. 418, 363 A.2d 373 (strict liability).
87. Parental Liability for Prenatal Injury, 1978, 14 Colum.J.L. and Soc.Probs. 47.
88. Grodin v. Grodin, 1981, 102 Mich.App. 396, 301 N.W.2d 869 (prescription drug taken during pregnancy caused child's teeth to be brown, liability if mother was not "reasonable" under all the facts).

89. Burnette v. Wahl, 1978, 284 Or. 705, 588 P.2d 1105 (parental desertion, though damaging, not actionable, vigorous dissents).
90. See Mroczynski v. McGrath, 1966, 34 Ill.2d 451, 216 N.E.2d 137 (divorce causing mental suffering of child, no liability); Zepeda v. Zepeda, 1963, 41 Ill.App. 2d 240, 190 N.E.2d 849, certiorari denied 1964, 379 U.S. 945, 85 S.Ct. 444, 13 L.Ed.2d 545 (child complaining of illegitimate birth, no liability).
91. Lewis v. Lewis, 1976, 370 Mass. 619, 351 N.E.2d 526, 532.
92. Beaudette v. Frana, 1969, 285 Minn. 366, 173 N.W.2d 416.
93. Lusby v. Lusby, 1978, 283 Md. 334, 390 A.2d 77.
94. Davis v. Bostick, 1978, 282 Or. 667, 580 P.2d 544. In Vance v. Vance, 1979, 286 Md. 490, 408 A.2d 728, a putative husband was held liable for emotional distress resulting to the would-be wife when, upon petition for divorce, he revealed they had never been validly married.
95. Merenoff v. Merenoff, 1978, 76 N.J. 535, 388 A.2d 951.
96. Merenoff v. Merenoff, 1978, 76 N.J. 535, 388 A.2d 951.

may be expected that courts will leave some matters to be adjusted by the parties themselves rather than by the courts, especially in areas of strong marital privacy interests and where agreement, consent or planning by the parties is possible.[97] Although there are few decisions, it is probably also a good guess at this point that in the absence of intended harm [98] little protection will be given in the case of purely economic or other intangible loss where the plaintiff-spouse suffers no accompanying physical injury.[99]

Contribution against Family Members

Where immunities are retained, they protect the negligent family member not only against a direct suit by the injured spouse or child, but also against a contribution action brought by a third person and based on a family member's injury.[1] If a wife is injured by the combined negligence of a husband and a third person, she is free to sue the third person, who is then made to bear the whole judgment alone, since he cannot obtain contribution from the negligent husband. With the abolition of the immunities of the family this rule has apparently become obsolete, and contribution claims against negligent spouses or parents now seem destined to succeed in any case in which the spouse or parent would be directly liable.[2]

In a unique case [3] New York has gone further and has held that a parent, immune from suit by a child under the supervision rule applied in New York, may nevertheless be liable for contribution to a joint tortfeasor whose negligence joins with that of the parent in causing injury to the child. This is limited, however, to cases in which the parent has furnished the child a dangerous instrumentality or has otherwise created a risk of harm to the public generally. This case illustrates an important point: The policy reasons relied upon to justify an immunity to tort liability are often inapplicable to prevent contribution.

Liability of Third Parties

In the jurisdictions which deny the action where only members of the family are concerned, further dispute has arisen as to the liability of third parties. Under the Married Women's Acts, there is general agreement that an agent of one spouse may be liable to the other for a tort committed within the scope of his employment,[4] and also that a conspirator or other joint tort-feasor will be

---

97. Cf. Stephen K. v. Roni L., 1980, 105 Cal.App.3d 640, 164 Cal.Rptr. 618 (unmarried sexual partner allegedly represented she was taking birth control pills, she is not liable for fraud, court won't supervise promises of partners in consensual sexual relationship); but cf. Pamela P. v. Frank S., 1981, 110 Misc.2d 978, 443 N.Y.S.2d 343 (similar, father held not primarily liable for child support).

98. In Davis v. Bostick, 1978, 282 Or. 667, 580 P.2d 544 the court said that, had suit been timely brought, a husband's death threats and slanders would have been actionable. Though these did not involve claims to physical injury, they did involve intended harms and in addition were extreme on the facts and hardly part of the "subtle ebb and flow of married life." But even some intended harms, if they cause no physical injury, will probably be insufficient. Cf. Browning v. Browning, Ky.App.1979, 584 S.W.2d 406 (defendant caused spouse mental distress by openly consorting with another).

99. The point is not that physical harm or intent is always required, but that special considerations counsel a reluctance to interfere in intimate relationships. Where no physical harm is done or threatened, the case is likely to involve the "ebb and flow of marital life" that courts should avoid. In Plain v. Plain, 1976, 307 Minn. 399, 240 N.W.2d 330 the wife negligently injured herself and the husband sued for medical expenses he incurred and loss of consortium. Recovery was denied as to both. In Browning v. Browning, Ky.App.1979, 584 S.W.2d 406 a spouse was denied mental distress recovery based on the other spouse's activities with a third party. A similar case with similar result is Weicker v. Weicker, 1968, 22 N.Y.2d 8, 290 N.Y.S.2d 732, 237 N.E.2d 876. Cf. Stephen K. v. Roni L., 1980, 105 Cal.App.3d 640, 164 Cal.Rptr. 618 (sexual partner misrepresented she was taking birth control pills, no liability); but cf. Pamela P. v. Frank S., 1981, 110 Misc. 2d 978, 443 N.Y.S.2d 343 (similar, father held not primarily liable for child support in light of the fraud).

1. See § 50, supra.

2. See Goedkoop v. Ward Pavement, 1976, 51 A.D. 2d 542, 378 N.Y.S.2d 417; Thoreson v. Milwaukee & Suburban Transport Co., 1972, 56 Wis.2d 231, 201 N.W.2d 745.

3. Nolechek v. Gesuale, 1978, 46 N.Y.2d 332, 413 N.Y.S.2d 340, 385 N.E.2d 1268.

4. Pepper v. Morrill, 1st Cir. 1928, 24 F.2d 320; Burns v. Kirkpatrick, 1892, 91 Mich. 364, 51 N.W. 893.

liable for his own tortious conduct notwithstanding the immunity of the spouse who joins with him.[5] But as to liability which is purely vicarious, such as that of an employer of a husband or father for injury to the wife or child, the courts were for a long time divided. The older, but now almost entirely obsolete view denied recovery in such a case,[6] arguing first that since the master's liability is founded on the servant's tort, he should not be liable where the servant is not; and second, that the master's right of indemnity against the servant would circumvent the domestic immunity, and defeat it by throwing the ultimate loss upon the servant. The first argument confuses immunity from suit with lack of responsibility—the servant has committed a tort which by ordinary rules of law should make the master liable, and there is no reason to include the latter within the purely personal immunity of the family. The second misses the point that the master's recovery over against the servant is not based upon any continuation of the original domestic claim, but upon the servant's independent duty of care for the protection of the master's interests;[7] and that if protection of the servant is still the sine qua non, it can always be accomplished merely by denying the indemnity.[8]

Accordingly the majority of the courts now hold that the employer is liable even though the servant is immune from suit.[9] A similar conclusion has been reached as to the vicarious liability of partnerships[10] and associations[11] of which the person immune is a member, and as to that of an automobile owner for the negligence of one whom he allows to operate his car.[12]

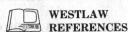

WESTLAW REFERENCES

tort! /s famil! int**famil! +s relation!

Husband and Wife

husband /s wife /s one unity /s commonlaw england english /5 immun!

interspousal /3 immunity

discard! abrogat! lessen /s interspousal /s immun!

---

5. Ewald v. Lane, 1939, 70 U.S.App.D.C. 89, 104 F.2d 222, certiorari denied 308 U.S. 568, 60 S.Ct. 81, 84 L.Ed. 477; Lorang v. Hays, 1949, 69 Idaho 440, 209 P.2d 733; Rogers v. Rogers, 1915, 265 Mo. 200, 177 S.W. 382; Kimatian v. New England Telephone & Telegraph Co., 1928, 49 R.I. 146, 141 A. 331; Smith v. Smith, 1889, 73 Mich. 445, 41 N.W. 499. Contra, Graham v. Miller, 1945, 182 Tenn. 434, 187 S.W.2d 622.

See Notes, 1940, 25 Corn.L.Q. 312; 1940, 38 Mich.L. Rev. 745.

6. Myers v. Tranquility Irrigation District, 1938, 26 Cal.App.2d 385, 79 P.2d 419; Maine v. James Maine & Sons Co., 1924, 198 Iowa 1278, 201 N.W. 20; Sacknoff v. Sacknoff, 1932, 131 Me. 280, 161 A. 669; Emerson v. Western Seed & Irrigation Co., 1927, 116 Neb. 180, 216 N.W. 297. A late example is Pinette v. Pinette, 1965, 106 N.H. 345, 211 A.2d 403 (Maine law).

7. See Jones v. Kinney, W.D.Mo.1953, 113 F.Supp. 923; Hudson v. Gas Consumers' Association, 1939, 123 N.J.L. 252, 8 A.2d 337; Schubert v. August Schubert Wagon Co., 1928, 249 N.Y. 253, 164 N.E. 42; and see Notes, 1928, 23 Ill.L.Rev. 174; 1927, 13 Corn.L.Q. 106; 1928, 6 N.Y.U.L.Rev. 53; 1940, 25 Corn.L.Q. 312.

8. Cf. American Automobile Insurance Co. v. Molling, 1953, 239 Minn. 74, 57 N.W.2d 847; Yellow Cab Co. v. Dreslin, 1950, 86 U.S.App.D.C. 231, 181 F.2d 626.

9. McSwain v. United States, D.Pa.1968, 291 F.Supp. 386 (United States' liability for serviceman's tort to wife); Bradley v. Tenneco Oil Co., 1978, 146 Ga. App. 161, 245 S.E.2d 862 (employer liable for husband's intentional torts to wife); Steward v. Borough of Magnolia, 1975, 134 N.J.Super. 312, 340 A.2d 678; Second Restatement of Agency, § 217, Comment b.

See Annot., 1 A.L.R.3d 677.

10. Eule v. Eule Motor Sales, 1961, 34 N.J. 537, 170 A.2d 241; Cody v. J. A. Dodds & Sons, 1961, 252 Iowa 1394, 110 N.W.2d 255; Wayne-Oakland Bank v. Adams Rib, 1973, 48 Mich.App. 144, 210 N.W.2d 121; cf. Tobin v. Hoffman, 1953, 202 Md. 382, 96 A.2d 597 (other partner sued individually). See also Rosefield v. Rosefield, 1963, 221 Cal.App.2d 431, 34 Cal.Rptr. 479 (third person conniving with parent to abduct child). See Gerdes, Right of a Wife Against Her Husband's Partners for Partnership Torts, 1936, 5 Brook.L.Rev. 174; Notes, 1961, 47 Va.L.Rev. 1450; 1936, 21 Corn.L.Q. 157.

11. Damm v. Elyria Lodge No. 465, 1952, 158 Ohio St. 107, 107 N.E.2d 337; Hary v. Arney, 1957, 128 Ind. App. 174, 145 N.E.2d 575. See Note, 1953, 22 U.Cin.L. Rev. 122.

12. Silverman v. Silverman, 1958, 145 Conn. 663, 145 A.2d 826; May v. Palm Beach Chemical Co., Fla. 1955, 77 So.2d 468; Winnick v. Kupperman Construction Co., 1968, 29 A.D.2d 261, 287 N.Y.S.2d 329; Davis v. Harrod, 1969, 132 U.S.App.D.C. 345, 407 F.2d 1280; Broaddus v. Wilkenson, 1940, 281 Ky. 601, 136 S.W.2d 1052. Cf. Freeland v. Freeland, 1968, 152 W.Va. 332, 162 S.E.2d 922 (family car doctrine).

Contra: Raines v. Mercer, 1932, 165 Tenn. 415, 55 S.W.2d 263; Riser v. Riser, 1927, 240 Mich. 402, 215 N.W. 290; Ownby v. Kleyhammer, 1952, 194 Tenn. 109, 250 S.W.2d 37.

```
absolute**  /s  immun!  /s  spousal interspousal
   husband wife
```
Parent and Child
```
famil! int**famil!  /s  tort!  /s  immun!
parent  /s  child  /s  tort!  /s  immun!
"parental immunity"
```
Limited Duties of Family Members
```
abolish! abrogat!  /s  parent** child  /s  immun!
parent**  /3  discretion!  &  tort negligence
285k11
```
Contribution against Family Members
```
headnote(contribution  /p  int**famil!)
topic(contribution)  /p  spous** interspousal
```
Liability of Third Parties
```
headnote(spouse husband wife  /s  third  /s  tort
   negligen**  /s  recover sue liab!)
```

§ 123. Vicarious Liability for Torts of Family

As one of the incidents of marriage at common law, a husband became liable for the torts of his wife,[1] even though they occurred without his knowledge[2] or consent,[3] and out of his presence,[4] or even while the wife was living separate and apart.[5] Various reasons were given for this liability: the wife was incapable of being sued alone, so that the husband must necessarily be joined with her; he was given control of all her property and earnings, so that a judgment against her would be practically worthless, and it was only fair that he should pay instead; he was supposed to exercise his authority over her to keep her in good behavior and see that she did not commit torts.

Curiously enough, the wife herself was not absolved from responsibility, but remained liable for her own torts, and had to be joined with her husband as a defendant.[6] By analogy to the criminal law, an exception was recognized where she acted in his presence and by his direction, since the law then assumed that she was coerced by fear of him or his authority, and so held that the tort was his alone and not hers.[7] Added to this was the presumption, which might be rebutted,[8] that any act done in his presence was done by his direction, so that in the absence of evidence of the wife's independent conduct the husband only was liable.[9]

These common law rules, which of course make no sense whatever in the light of modern ideas of the social and legal position of married women, are now almost entirely abrogated by statute.[10] In about two-thirds of the states there are specific provisions making the wife fully responsible for her own

---

§ 123

1. Henley v. Wilson, 1902, 137 Cal. 273, 70 P. 21; Missio v. Williams, 1914, 129 Tenn. 504, 167 S.W. 473; Atwood v. Higgins, 1884, 76 Me. 423.

Even though the tort was committed before marriage. Hawk v. Harman, Pa.1812, 5 Bin. 43; Phillips v. Richardson, 1830, 27 Ky. (4 J.J.Marsh.) 212.

2. Roberts v. Lisenbee, 1882, 86 N.C. 136.

3. Baker v. Young, 1867, 44 Ill. 42; Edwards v. Wessinger, 1902, 65 S.C. 161, 43 S.E. 518.

4. Edwards v. Wessinger, 1902, 65 S.C. 161, 43 S.E. 518; Sargeant v. Fedor, 1925, 3 N.J.Misc. 832, 130 A. 207.

5. Head v. Briscoe, 1833, 5 C. & P. 484, 172 Eng. Rep. 1064. See, generally, Miller, Liability of a Husband for Wife's Torts, 1932, 18 Iowa L.Rev. 30; Harbison, Family Responsibility in Tort, 1956, 9 Vand. L.Rev. 809; Notes, 1925, 34 Yale L.J. 543; 1926, 2 Camb.L.J. 250; 1926, 74 U.Pa.L.Rev. 305; 1936, 41 Dick.L.Rev. 55.

6. Smith v. Taylor, 1852, 11 Ga. 20; Baker v. Young, 1867, 44 Ill. 42; Heckle v. Lurvey, 1869, 101 Mass. 344; Crawford v. Doggett, 1891, 82 Tex. 139, 17 S.W. 929; Sargeant v. Fedor, 1925, 3 N.J.Misc. 832, 130 A. 207; see Gill v. State, 1894, 39 W.Va. 479, 20 S.E. 568.

7. McKeown v. Johnson, S.C.1822, 1 McCord, 578; McElroy v. Capron, 1902, 24 R.I. 561, 54 A. 44; Thayer v. Spear, 1886, 58 Vt. 327, 2 A. 161.

8. Miller v. Sweitzer, 1871, 22 Mich. 391; Wagener v. Bill, N.Y.1855, 19 Barb. 321; Smith v. Schoene, 1896, 67 Mo.App. 604; McElroy v. Capron, 1902, 24 R.I. 561, 54 A. 44; Hildreth v. Camp, 1879, 41 N.J.L. 306.

"If the law supposes that," said Mr. Bumble, "the law is a ass—a idiot. If that's the eye of the law, the law is a bachelor; and the worst I wish the law is, that his eye may be opened by experience—by experience." Dickens, Oliver Twist, ch. 51.

9. Brazil v. Moran, 1863, 8 Minn. 236; Marshall v. Oakes, 1864, 51 Me. 308; Kosminski v. Goldberg, 1884, 44 Ark. 401; Emmons v. Stevane, 1906, 73 N.J.L. 349, 64 A. 1014, reversed 77 N.J.L. 570, 73 A. 544. This was rejected in Hux v. Butler, 6th Cir. 1964, 339 F.2d 696.

10. See Harbison, Family Responsibility in Tort, 1956, 9 Vand.L.Rev. 809; Note, 1966, 17 Bay.L.Rev. 177.

torts, and doing away with the husband's liability for them.[11] Nearly all of the remaining jurisdictions have arrived at the same result by construction of the ordinary Married Women's Acts giving the wife capacity to be sued alone, and control over her own property.[12] Even the common law, of course, never went to the length of making the wife liable for the tort of her husband.[13] In all probability the dying gasp of the old rule was a Florida decision[14] in 1949, which was promptly changed by statute;[15] and henceforth the vicarious liability of one spouse, as such,[16] or the torts of the other is to be of purely historical interest.

Since the relation of parent and child involved no such fusion of legal identity as in the case of husband and wife, the common law, unlike that of the civil law countries,[17] never has made the parent vicariously liable as such for the conduct of the child. The infant, as a separate legal individual, has been held liable for his own torts,[18] and the parent has, at common law, no legal responsibility for them.[19] Since the child is usually not financially responsible and the parent is not liable, juvenile torts are mostly uncompensated except where the child is himself covered by a liability policy. This led to the adoption, in virtually all states, of statutes imposing liability upon parents.[20] The provisions vary considerably, but most of these are limited to wilful or wanton torts of the child and limited as to the amount of liability as well, with limits ranging from $300 to several thousand dollars in most instances. Many commentators have attacked these statutes as unfair, unlikely to curb juvenile delinquency, and an unwarranted intrusion into family affairs,[21] and one decision holds the statutes unconstitutional where the parents' liability is unlimited.[22] But the typical limited-liability statute has been upheld repeatedly as against constitutional challenge.[23]

Apart from any basis of the family relation itself, one member of the family may of course be held responsible for the torts of

11. These are collected in the Note, 1950, 3 U.Fla.L. Rev. 206. See Strouse v. Leipf, 1893, 101 Ala. 433, 14 So. 667; Christensen v. Johnston, 1917, 207 Ill.App. 209; Moore v. Doerr, 1918, 199 Mo.App. 428, 203 S.W. 672; McElroy v. Capron, 1902, 24 R.I. 561, 54 A. 44.

12. Hageman v. Vanderdoes, 1914, 15 Ariz. 312, 138 P. 1053; Bourland v. Baker, 1919, 141 Ark. 280, 216 S.W. 707; Curtis v. Ashworth, 1928, 165 Ga. 782, 142 S.E. 111, conformed to 38 Ga.App. 220, 143 S.E. 463; Caplan v. Caplan, 1928, 83 N.H. 318, 142 A. 121; Claxton v. Pool, Mo.1917, 197 S.W. 349. See Notes, 1953, 2 De Paul L.Rev. 345; 1950, 4 U.Miami L.Q. 358.

13. See Vanneman v. Powers, 1874, 56 N.Y. 39; Blake v. Smith, 1896, 19 R.I. 476, 34 A. 995; Scott v. Chambers, 1886, 62 Mich. 532, 29 N.W. 94; Bice v. Brown, 1917, 98 Wash. 416, 167 P. 1097.

14. Rogers v. Newby, Fla.1949, 41 So.2d 451. There are jurisdictions, such as Connecticut and Wyoming, in which statutes do not clearly abrogate the liability, and there are no decisions.

15. West's Fla.Stats.Ann.1961, § 741.23, enacted in 1951.

16. But in community property states the property of the marital community is sometimes subjected to a tort claim, even though the tort was committed only by one of the spouses. See Annot., 10 A.L.R.2d 988. Also if the tort produced benefits, as where one spouse embezzles funds which are invested in a house, such assets can still be reached, though the other spouse would not be personally liable. See D. Dobbs, 1973, Remedies §§ 4.3, 5.16.

17. See Takayanagi, Liability Without Fault in the Modern Civil and Common Law, 1921, 16 Ill.L.Rev. 163, 291; Note, 1934, 19 Corn.L.Q. 643; Toca v. Rojas, 1922, 152 La. 317, 93 So. 108; Hudson v. Von Hamm, 1927, 85 Cal.App. 323, 259 P. 374.

18. See infra, § 134.

19. Parsons v. Smithey, 1973, 109 Ariz. 49, 504 P.2d 1272, 54 A.L.R.3d 964; Anderson v. Butler, 1974, 284 N.C. 723, 202 S.E.2d 585. White v. Seitz, 1931, 342 Ill. 266, 174 N.E. 371.

20. Shong, The Legal Responsibility of Parents for their Children's Delinquency, 1972, 6 Fam.L.Q. 145; Note, The Iowa Parental Responsibility Act, 1970, 55 Iowa L.Rev. 1037 (listing statutes).

21. See Freer, Parental Liability for Torts of Children, 1965, 53 Ky.L.J. 254; Comment, Parental Responsibility Ordinances, 1973, 19 Wayne L.Rev. 1551.

22. Corley v. Lewless, 1971, 227 Ga. 745, 182 S.E.2d 766.

23. General Insurance of America v. Faulkner, 1963, 259 N.C. 317, 130 S.E.2d 645; Mahaney v. Hunter Enterprises, Wyo.1967, 426 P.2d 442; Watson v. Gradzik, 1977, 34 Conn.Com.Pl. 7, 373 A.2d 191; In re Sorrell, 1974, 20 Md.App. 179, 315 A.2d 110; Kelly v. Williams, Tex.Civ.App.1961, 346 S.W.2d 434, refused n. r. e see Rudnay v. Corbett, 1977, 53 Ohio App.2d 311, 374 N.E.2d 171. In Alber v. Nolle, App.1982, 98 N.M. 100, 645 P.2d 456, the court upheld a statute and applied it even where the minor was almost 18 years of age and a constant runaway who was at the time of the tort living with her boyfriend.

another to the same extent as for those of any other person. A parent may be liable for the tortious act of the child if the parent has directed it [24] or encouraged it,[25] or has ratified it by accepting its benefits.[26] Also, of course, a member of the family may act as agent or servant for another member of the family, and to the extent the tort is committed within the scope of the agency,[27] the parent [28] or spouse [29] may be vicariously liable. Because children and many married women are financially unable to respond in damages, some courts have gone to considerable lengths to find an agency in the case of family relations.[30] One notable instance is the "family car" doctrine previously discussed,[31] which proceeds upon the rather unconvincing theory that the owner of an automobile who permits a member of his family to drive it makes the family affairs or pleasure his "business," and the driver his servant. This doctrine, which obviously is little more than a deliberately fictitious instrument of policy, is rejected by about half of the jurisdictions, and has been replaced in some others by automobile "consent" statutes making the owner responsible for the negligence of anyone whom he allows to drive the car.[32]

Finally, of course, liability for the torts of the family may be based upon the negligence of the defendant himself.[33] A parent, for example, like anyone else, may be negligent in entrusting to a child a dangerous instrument such as a gun,[34] or a thing dangerous in the hands of that particular child because of his handicaps or propensity to misuse it, for example, matches [35] or an automobile.[36] Similarly the parent may be negligent in leaving such things where they are accessible to the child where misuse is a risk.[37] But beyond this, the parent has a special power of control over the conduct of the child, which he is under a duty to exercise reasonably for the protection of

---

24. Trahan v. Smith, Tex.Civ.App.1922, 239 S.W. 345; Harrington v. Hall, Del.1906, 6 Pennewill 72, 63 A. 875; Smith v. Jordan, 1912, 211 Mass. 269, 97 S.E. 761.

25. Stewart v. Swartz, 1914, 57 Ind.App. 249, 106 N.E. 719; Condel v. Savo, 1944, 350 Pa. 350, 39 A.2d 51; Ryley v. Lafferty, D.Idaho 1930, 45 F.2d 641; Sharpe v. Williams, 1889, 41 Kan. 56, 20 P. 497; cf. Knott v. Litton, La.App.1955, 81 So.2d 124 (husband inciting wife to attack plaintiff). But cf. Bowen v. Mewborn, 1940, 218 N.C. 423, 11 S.E.2d 372 (encouragement to illicit intercourse does not include rape).

26. Hower v. Ulrich, 1893, 156 Pa. 410, 27 A. 37; Howell v. Norton, 1924, 134 Miss. 616, 99 So. 440.

27. Cf. Hagerty v. Powers, 1885, 66 Cal. 368, 5 P. 622; Smith v. Jordan, 1912, 211 Mass. 269, 97 N.E. 761.

28. Second Restatement of Agency, §§ 224, Comment a; 238, Comment c.

29. Rogers v. Frush, 1970, 257 Md. 233, 262 A.2d 549, 40 A.L.R.3d 847.

30. Cf. Hiroux v. Baum, 1908, 137 Wis. 197, 118 N.W. 533; Zeidler v. Goelzer, 1926, 191 Wis. 378, 211 N.W. 140; Graham v. Page, 1921, 300 Ill. 40, 132 N.E. 817; Smith v. Jordan, 1912, 211 Mass. 269, 97 N.E. 761; McCrossen v. Moorhead, 1922, 202 App.Div. 560, 195 N.Y.S. 164, 1923, 205 App.Div. 497, 200 N.Y.S. 581, appeal dismissed, 1924, 236 N.Y. 614, 142 N.E. 318. See Lattin, Vicarious Liability and the Family Automobile, 1928, 26 Mich.L.Rev. 846.

31. Supra, § 73.

32. See supra, § 73.

33. Second Restatement of Torts, § 316; see Wigmore, Parent's Liability for Child's Torts, 1924, 19 Ill.L. Rev. 202; Jordan, Liability of Parent for Child's Tort, 1926, 11 Va.L.Reg.,N.S., 734; Notes, 1941, 19 N.C.L. Rev. 605; 1944, 22 N.C.L.Rev. 333; 1954, 28 Tul.L.Rev. 503; 1929, 23 Ill.L.Rev. 830; 1967, 19 Ala.L.Rev. 123; 1964, 31 Tenn.L.Rev. 553.

34. Lichtenthal v. Gawoski, 1974, 44 A.D.2d 771, 354 N.Y.S.2d 267; Howell v. Hairston, 1973, 261 S.C. 292, 199 S.E.2d 766; Prater v. Burns, Tenn.App.1975, 525 S.W.2d 846.

35. Thibodeau v. Cleff [1911] 24 Ont.L.Rep. 211; Gudziewski v. Stemplesky, 1928, 263 Mass. 103, 160 N.E. 334; Johnson v. Glidden, 1898, 11 S.D. 237, 76 N.W. 933; Jarboe v. Edwards, 1966, 26 Conn.Sup. 350, 223 A.2d 402. Cf. May v. Goulding, 1961, 365 Mich. 143, 111 N.W.2d 862 (mentally ill child with semi-automatic rifle); Davis v. Gavalas, 1927, 37 Ga.App. 242, 139 S.E. 577 (velocipede); Zuckerberg v. Munzer, 1950, 277 App.Div. 1061, 100 N.Y.S.2d 910 (baseball bat). But the parent must know of the tendency. Lane v. Chatham, 1959, 251 N.C. 400, 111 S.E.2d 598 (mother, who knew, liable; father, who did not, not liable).

36. Thompson v. Havard, 1970, 285 Ala. 718, 235 So.2d 853; Nolechek v. Gesuale, 1978, 46 N.Y.2d 332, 413 N.Y.S.2d 340, 385 N.E.2d 1268.

Cf. Gossett v. Van Egmond, 1945, 176 Or. 134, 155 P.2d 304 (mental defective driving car).

37. Williams v. Davidson, 1966, 241 Ark. 699, 409 S.W.2d 311 (air-gun); Whalen v. Bennett, 1966, 4 Mich. App. 81, 143 N.W.2d 797 (same); Seabrook v. Taylor, Fla.App.1967, 199 So.2d 315.

others.³⁸ He may thus be liable for failure to take the gun from the child when he finds him with it.³⁹ More broadly, the parent who has notice of a child's dangerous tendency or proclivity must exercise reasonable care to control the child for the safety of others,⁴⁰ and the parent who ignores the child's tendency to beat other children⁴¹ or shoot horses⁴² may be held for his or her own negligence in failing to exercise control. Probably, however, the effect of the decided cases is that there is no liability upon the parent unless he has notice of a specific type of harmful conduct, and an opportunity to interfere with it.⁴³ It has been said⁴⁴ that it would be extending the hardships of harassed and exasperated parents too far to hold them liable for general incorrigibility, a bad education and upbringing, or the fact that the child turns out to have a nasty disposition. The parent may, however, be under a duty to warn others of such characteristics⁴⁵ if there is an opportunity,⁴⁶ and it is undoubtedly true that the parent must take these factors into account in what he does once specific dangerous tendencies have been manifested.⁴⁷

WESTLAW REFERENCES

vicarious** /s liab! /p parent** husband /s child wife
vicarious** /s liab! /p husband /s wife

§ 124. Interference with Family Relations

As has been explained above,¹ the law of torts is concerned not only with the protection of interests of personality and of property, tangible or intangible, but also with what may be called "relational" interests,² founded upon the relation in which the plaintiff stands toward one or more third persons. An interference with the continuance of the relation, unimpaired, may be redressed by a tort action; and of this the relations of the family are a conspicuous example.³ In this field the law is "rather ragged in form," with a certain amount of dead timber to be cleared away before it becomes very intelligible.⁴ It developed in the begin-

---

38. See Harper and Kime, The Duty to Control the Conduct of Another, 1934, 43 Yale L.J. 886.

39. Johnson v. Glidden, 1898, 11 S.D. 237, 76 N.W. 933; Gudziewski v. Stemplesky, 1928, 263 Mass. 103, 160 N.E. 334; Kuchlik v. Feuer, 1933, 239 App.Div. 338, 267 N.Y.S. 256, affirmed, 1934, 264 N.Y. 542, 191 N.E. 555; Salisbury v. Crudale, 1918, 41 R.I. 33, 102 A. 731.

40. Caldwell v. Zaher, 1962, 344 Mass. 590, 183 N.E.2d 706; Eldredge v. Kamp Kachess Youth Services, Inc., 1978, 90 Wn.2d 402, 583 P.2d 626 (camp for delinquents owed parents' duty to control dangerous proclivities).

41. Norton v. Payne, 1929, 154 Wash. 241, 281 P. 991; Bieker v. Owens, 1961, 234 Ark. 97, 350 S.W.2d 522; Polk v. Trinity Universal Insurance Co., La.App. 1959, 115 So.2d 399; Bocock v. Rose, 1963, 213 Tenn. 195, 373 S.W.2d 441; Linder v. Bidner, 1966, 50 Misc.2d 320, 270 N.Y.S.2d 427.

42. Hoverson v. Noker, 1884, 60 Wis. 511, 19 N.W. 382.

43. See Parsons v. Smithey, 1973, 109 Ariz. 49, 504 P.2d 1272, 54 A.L.R.3d 964 (threatening behavior and several recommendations for psychiatric help, but parents could not foresee child would attack with a hammer or saw off an ear); DePasquale v. Dello Russo, 1965, 349 Mass. 655, 212 N.E.2d 237 (parent who knew of two instances of fireworks attacks not liable when son lit smoke bombs in plaintiff's pocket causing severe burns).

44. Capps v. Carpenter, 1930, 129 Kan. 462, 283 P. 655; Gissin v. Goodwill, Fla.1955, 80 So.2d 701; Corby v. Foster [1913] 29 Ont.L.Rep. 83; Paul v. Hummel, 1868, 43 Mo. 119.

45. Ellis v. D'Angelo, 1953, 116 Cal.App.2d 310, 253 P.2d 675 (baby sitter); Zuckerberg v. Munzer, 1950, 277 App.Div. 1061, 100 N.Y.S.2d 910.

46. Cooper v. Meyer, 1977, 50 Ill.App.3d 69, 7 Ill. Dec. 916, 365 N.E.2d 201 (no opportunity to warn).

47. See Paul v. Hummel, 1868, 43 Mo. 119; Cluthe v. Svendsen, 1885, 9 Ohio Dec. 458; Salisbury v. Crudale, 1918, 41 R.I. 33, 102 A. 731; Haunert v. Speier, 1926, 214 Ky. 46, 281 S.W. 998. See Note, 1930, 78 U.Pa.L.Rev. 1032.

§ 124

1. Supra, § 111.

2. Green, Relational Interests, 1935, 29 Ill.L.Rev. 460; Foster, Relational Interests of the Family, [1962] U.Ill.L.Forum 493.

3. See Pound, Individual Interests in the Domestic Relations, 1916, 14 Mich.L.Rev. 177; Green, Relational Interests, 1935, 29 Ill.L.Rev. 460; Lippman, The Breakdown of Consortium, 1930, 30 Col.L.Rev. 651.

4. Winfield, Law of Tort, 5th ed. 1950, 231.

ning as an offshoot of the action for enticing away a servant and depriving the master of the quasi-proprietary interest in his services.[5] Since the status of a wife, as well as that of minor children, under the early common law was that of more or less valuable superior servants of the husband and father, that action was extended to include the deprivation of their services;[6] and thus the loss of such services became the gist of the action, and remained indispensable to it until comparatively recent years. There has been a gradual shift of emphasis away from "services" and toward a recognition of more intangible elements in the domestic relations, such as companionship and affection.[7] This has progressed further at some points than at others. But though such intangible values are recognized, they are not afforded the same degree of protection in every case. Where companionship and affection are interfered with indirectly, through physical injury to a family member, the more traditional view affords somewhat less protection than where the interference is directly aimed at the relationship itself, and such indirect interferences are considered separately.[8] Likewise, the relationship between parent and child is accorded somewhat less protection than the relationship between spouses. In recent years the protection afforded even to direct harms to the family relationship has been limited or withdrawn as well, because of an increasing perception that judicial intervention is unwarranted.

Spouses

The husband's interest in his relation with his wife first received recognition as a matter of her services to him as a servant. Over a period of some centuries it took form as something considerably broader than this, which was given the name of "consortium." Consortium was said to be made up of a bundle of legal rights to the alliterative trio of the services, society and sexual intercourse of the wife. To these elements the modern law has added a fourth, that of conjugal affection. The rights of the husband extend to all four; and while it is seldom that the defendant's conduct interferes with only one of them, it now seems clear in nearly all jurisdictions that such interference with any one will be sufficient as a foundation for the action. The loss of services, essential at the beginning, no longer is indispensable,[9] and is now only one element upon which the action may be based.

At common law the wife had no action for interference with her relationship with her husband, since she could not sue in her own name against anyone, and the erring husband, who might otherwise have sued for injury to the wife, was hardly a suitable plaintiff in this kind of case.[10] Even after the Married Women's Acts a few courts refused to recognize an action in the wife, giving reasons that would be recognized as spurious today in every court.[11] The modern law has put all this aside, however, and allows the wife a right of recovery for interference with her spousal relations on the same basis it allows the husband a right.[12]

---

5. See infra, § 129.

6. See Guy v. Livesey, 1619, Cro.Jac. 501, 79 Eng. Rep. 428; Hyde v. Scyssor, 1620, Cro.Jac. 538, 79 Eng. Rep. 462; Galizard v. Rigault, 1702, 2 Salk. 552, 91 Eng.Rep. 467; 8 Holdsworth, History of English Law, 2d ed. 1937, 427–430; 1 Street, Foundations of Legal Liability, 1906, 262, 267; Wigmore, Interference with Social Relations, 1887, 21 Am.L.Rev. 764.

7. See Holbrook, The Change in the Meaning of Consortium, 1923, 22 Mich.L.Rev. 1; Lippman, The Breakdown of Consortium, 1930, 30 Col.L.Rev. 651.

8. § 125, below.

9. See Brown, The Action for Alienation of Affections, 1934, 82 U.Pa.L.Rev. 472; Holbrook, The Change in the Meaning of Consortium, 1923, 22 Mich.L.Rev. 1; Lippman, The Breakdown of Consortium, 1930, 30 Col. L.Rev. 651.

10. An attempt to obviate this difficulty by joining the husband as defendant was unsuccessful. See Lynch v. Knight, 1861, 9 H.L.Cas. 577, 11 Eng.Rep. 854.

11. Duffies v. Duffies, 1890, 76 Wis. 374, 45 N.W. 522; Hodge v. Wetzler, 1903, 69 N.J.L. 490, 55 A. 49; Doe v. Roe, 1890, 82 Me. 503, 20 A. 83.

12. E.g., Emerson v. Fleming, 1972, 127 Ga.App. 296, 193 S.E.2d 249; Wilson v. Hilske, 1974, 132 Vt. 506, 321 A.2d 16. See Second Restatement of Torts, § 683, Comment *d*. But, to avoid discrimination, a

§ 124 INTERFERENCE WITH FAMILY RELATIONS

Types of interference. There was an early writ of "ravishment" which listed the wife with the husband's chattels, and was available to him when she was taken away forcibly or eloped with another.[13] This was later replaced by the action of trespass for depriving him of a servant. It was ultimately recognized that this involved a loss of consortium, and with the development of the rule that the wife as well as the husband had rights to spousal services and society, the courts allowed either spouse to sue for enticement, abduction or harboring of the other spouse.[14] The action lay against anyone who, without justification or privilege, and for the purpose of disrupting the marital relationship, influenced or assisted one spouse to separate or remain apart from the other, and of course against anyone who actually abducted one spouse.[15] In this action the separation itself, with concomitant loss of society and services, is sufficient damage, and it is not necessary to prove that the departed spouse has had sexual intercourse with the defendant or even that the affections were alienated.[16]

A second form of interference with the marital relationship is that of adultery with one of the spouses, which in its tort aspects is usually called criminal conversation.[17] For this, the other spouse might maintain an action. This is obvious enough in the case of rape,[18] but courts also permitted an action even where the adulterous spouse consented to intercourse or even initiated it.[19] The argument for this position is that one spouse cannot give a consent that would prejudice the interests of the other.[20] The idea that one spouse can recover for an act the other spouse has willingly consented to is perhaps better suited to an era that regarded one spouse as the property of another, and at least one court has suggested that in such a case only nominal damages might be allowed[21] and some judges have opposed the action altogether.[22]

Since even an impotent husband has been allowed recovery,[23] it seems clear that the court might equally abolish the husband's right of recovery, which the Maryland court did as to criminal conversation in Kline v. Ansell, 1980, 287 Md. 585, 414 A.2d 929, relying in part on the state's Equal Rights Amendment.

13. 1 Street, Foundations of Legal Liability, 1906, 263; Winfield, Law of Tort, 5th ed. 1950, 234.

14. Boland v. Stanley, 1909, 88 Ark. 562, 115 S.W. 163 (husband's claim); Bradstreet v. Wallace, 1926, 254 Mass. 509, 150 N.E. 405 (wife's claim).

15. Second Restatement of Torts, § 684. According to the Restatement, knowledge that disruption will follow is insufficient if there is no purpose to cause disruption. Thus defendant is free to offer the wife a job in a foreign city knowing the husband cannot join her. Id., Comment *f.*

16. Second Restatement of Torts, § 684, Comment *j.*

17. "Criminal" because it was an ecclesiastical crime; "conversation" in the sense of intercourse. For the history of the tort, see Lippman, The Breakdown of Consortium, 1930, 30 Col.L.Rev. 651, 654–660.

"In its general and comprehensive sense, the term 'criminal conversation,' is synonymous with 'adultery;' but in its more limited and technical signification, in which it is here to be considered, it may be defined as adultery in the aspect of a tort." Turner v. Heavrin, 1918, 182 Ky. 65, 206 S.W. 23.

18. Egbert v. Greenwalt, 1880, 44 Mich. 245, 6 N.W. 654; Bigaouette v. Paulet, 1883, 134 Mass. 123, 45 Am. Rep. 307; Jacobson v. Siddal, 1885, 12 Or. 280, 7 P. 108.

19. Tinker v. Colwell, 1904, 193 U.S. 473, 24 S.Ct. 505, 48 L.Ed. 754; Wales v. Miner, 1883, 89 Ind. 118; Powell v. Strickland, 1913, 163 N.C. 393, 79 S.E. 872; Pierce v. Crisp, 1935, 260 Ky. 519, 86 S.W.2d 293; cf. Hirschy v. Coodley, 1953, 116 Cal.App.2d 102, 253 P.2d 93. "It is but the old cowardly excuse set up by the first man, 'The woman gave me of the tree and I did eat.' It did not save from the penalty the first defendant, and cannot under the law save this one." Seiber v. Pettitt, 1901, 200 Pa. 58, 49 A. 763.

Tennessee has said, however, that there is no liability where the defendant is not the pursuer, and the wife is "not particular as to her partner." Wilson v. Bryant, 1934, 167 Tenn. 107, 67 S.W.2d 133; Archer v. Archer, 1947, 31 Tenn.App. 657, 219 S.W.2d 919.

Defendant's act must be a cause of the tort in any event. See Comte v. Blessing, Mo.1964, 381 S.W.2d 780.

20. 8 Holdsworth, History of English Law, 2d ed. 1937, 430.

21. Felsenthal v. McMillan, Tex.1973, 493 S.W.2d 729 (Chief Justice Greenhill).

22. Several courts have abolished the action judicially. Bearbower v. Merry, Iowa 1978, 266 N.W.2d 128; Kline v. Ansell, 1980, 287 Md. 585, 414 A.2d 929; Fadgen v. Lenkner, 1976, 469 Pa. 272, 365 A.2d 147.

23. Bedan v. Turney, 1893, 99 Cal. 649, 34 P. 442.

real basis of the action for criminal conversation is not any interference with "service" owed, but defilement of the marriage bed or a very special case of the infliction of mental distress.[24] Consequently it has become unnecessary to prove that the aggrieved spouse has been deprived of intercourse or any other services of the participating spouse,[25] or any affection.[26] Recovery has been allowed even though the spouses were separated or contemplating divorce,[27] though this may affect the issue of damages.[28]

A third type of interference, which seems to have been recognized first in New York[29] in 1866 and to have been accepted at one time by the courts of all states except Louisiana,[30] has been given the name of "alienation of affections." It consists merely in depriving one spouse of the affections, which is to say the love, society, companionship and comfort, of the other. Though of course the alienated spouse must manifest a change of attitude by some external conduct or words,[31] it is not necessary to show adultery[32] or that the plaintiff spouse has been deprived of any household services[33] or has suffered any pecuniary loss.[34] Nor is it necessary that the alienated spouse abandon the home[35] or that there be more than a partial loss of affections or attentions.[36] On the other hand, the fact that the spouses are separated already when the tort occurs is no defense, since the possibility of a reconciliation is one of the conjugal rights.[37] The gist of the tort is not sexual intimacy but an interference with the marital relation that changes one spouse's mental attitude toward the other.[38] Though the lover or alleged lov-

24. Bigaouette v. Paulet, 1883, 134 Mass. 123; Stark v. Johnson, 1908, 43 Colo. 243, 95 P. 930; Yundt v. Hartrunft, 1866, 41 Ill. 9; Wood v. Mathews, 1877, 47 Iowa 409; Johnston v. Disbrow, 1881, 47 Mich. 59, 10 N.W. 79.

25. Yundt v. Hartrunft, 1866, 41 Ill. 9; Long v. Booe, 1894, 106 Ala. 570, 17 So. 716; Disch v. Closset, 1926, 118 Or. 111, 244 P. 71; Wood v. Mathews, 1877, 47 Iowa 409; Bigaouette v. Paulet, 1883, 134 Mass. 123.

26. Stark v. Johnson, 1908, 43 Colo. 243, 95 P. 930; Baltrunas v. Baubles, 1926, 23 Ohio App. 104, 154 N.E. 747; Merritt v. Cravens, 1916, 168 Ky. 155, 181 S.W. 970; Watkins v. Lord, 1918, 31 Idaho 352, 171 P. 1133; Rosefield v. Rosefield, 1963, 221 Cal.App.2d 431, 34 Cal.Rptr. 479.

27. Chambers v. Caulfield, 1805, 6 East 244; Browning v. Jones, 1893, 52 Ill.App. 597; Michael v. Dunkle, 1882, 84 Ind. 544; Cross v. Grant, 1883, 62 N.H. 675; Pierce v. Crisp, 1935, 260 Ky. 519, 86 S.W.2d 293.

28. The lack of affection, whether shown by separation or otherwise, clearly bears on damages in the alienation of affection action. Presumably it has some weight in the criminal conversation claim. Cf. Wilson v. Hilske, 1974, 132 Vt. 506, 321 A.2d 16 (alienation of affection action with admission of "intimacy"); Rank v. Kuhn, 1945, 236 Iowa 854, 20 N.W.2d 72 (intimate touchings shown, but no intercourse, unhappy relations of spouses goes to damages).

29. Heermance v. James, N.Y.1866, 47 Barb. 120.

30. Moulin v. Monteleone, 1927, 165 La. 169, 115 So. 447.

Massachusetts, which for a long time held back, now appears to recognize the tort, at least where the husband is deprived of sexual intercourse, or something more than "affection." See Gordon v. Parker, D.Mass. 1949, 83 F.Supp. 45, affirmed in Parker v. Gordon, 1st Cir. 1949, 178 F.2d 888.

31. Carrieri v. Bush, 1966, 69 Wn.2d 536, 419 P.2d 132; Alaimo v. Schwanz, 1972, 56 Wis.2d 198, 201 N.W.2d 604; Second Restatement of Torts, § 683, Comment f.

32. Hardison v. Gregory, 1955, 242 N.C. 324, 88 S.E.2d 96; Georgacopoulos v. Katralis, 1945, 318 Mass. 34, 60 N.E.2d 10; Callis v. Merrieweather, 1903, 98 Md. 361, 57 A. 201; Rinehart v. Bills, 1884, 82 Mo. 534; Ireland v. Ward, 1908, 51 Or. 102, 93 P. 932.

33. Gregg v. Gregg, 1905, 37 Ind.App. 210, 75 N.E. 674; Jenness v. Simpson, 1911, 84 Vt. 127, 78 A. 886.

34. Adams v. Main, 1891, 3 Ind.App. 232, 29 N.E. 792; Woodhouse v. Woodhouse, 1925, 99 Vt. 91, 130 A. 758; Lavigne v. Lavigne, 1923, 80 N.H. 559, 119 A. 869; Woodson v. Bailey, 1924, 210 Ala. 568, 98 So. 809.

35. Foot v. Card, 1889, 58 Conn. 1, 18 A. 1027; Tice v. Mandel, N.D.1956, 76 N.W.2d 124. Alaimo v. Schwanz, 1972, 56 Wis.2d 198, 201 N.W.2d 604.

36. Fratini v. Caslini, 1894, 66 Vt. 273, 29 A. 252.

37. Gibson v. Gibson, 1968, 244 Ark. 327, 424 S.W.2d 871.

38. Wright v. Lester, 1961, 105 Ga.App. 107, 123 S.E.2d 672, affirmed in part, reversed in part, 1962, 218 Ga. 31, 126 S.E.2d 419, on remand 106 Ga.App. 452, 127 S.E.2d 193; Grobart v. Grobart, 1950, 5 N.J. 161, 74 A.2d 294. "There are two primary rights in the case: one is the right of the plaintiff to the body of his wife and the other to her mind, unpolluted." Sullivan v. Valiquette, 1919, 66 Colo. 170, 180 P. 91; Hudima v. Hudyma, 1944, 131 Conn. 281, 39 A.2d 890; Annarina v. Boland, 1920, 136 Md. 365, 111 A. 84; Johnson v. Richards, 1930, 50 Idaho 150, 294 P. 507; Restatement Second of Torts, § 683.

er is often a defendant whether the action is brought by the wife [39] or by the husband,[40] the action may also be brought against in-laws,[41] ministers [42] and others [43] who have attempted to interfere.

For some purposes, enticement, criminal conversation and alienation of affections can be regarded simply as different means by which the marriage relationship is subjected to interference. When the action is for criminal conversation, proof of enticement or alienation of affections is admissible to enhance damages; [44] likewise, where the action is for alienation of affections, proof of criminal conversation or enticement will bear on damages.[45] There is thus a tendency to lump all these together, or even to hold that there is but one tort which may be accomplished by different means.[46] For some purposes, however, a distinction may be maintained, as where a statute of limitations bars a criminal conversation claim but not the alienation action,[47] or where a statute [48] or judicial decision [49] abolishes one kind of claim but not the other. There is also some difference in defenses and privileges according to whether criminal conversation or alienation is claimed.[50]

Basis of liability. To be liable for interference with the marriage relation the defendant must in some way have acted affirmatively. The defendant who remains entirely passive and indifferent cannot be held responsible if the plaintiff's spouse has chosen to fall in love with defendant.[51] But active participation or encouragement by the defendant will be sufficient for liability, even if the initiative comes from the plaintiff's spouse.[52] Thus it is usually held that it is no defense to a criminal conversation claim that the conversing spouse was the aggressor and the seducer.[53] In addition, of course, the defendant's conduct must have been a cause of the harm to the marital rela-

---

39. E.g., Sebastian v. Kluttz, 1969, 6 N.C.App. 201, 170 S.E.2d 104; Wilson v. Hilske, 1974, 132 Vt. 506, 321 A.2d 16.

40. E.g., Vogel v. Sylvester, 1961, 148 Conn. 666, 174 A.2d 122; Giltner v. Stark, Iowa 1974, 219 N.W.2d 700.

41. Boland v. Stanley, 1909, 88 Ark. 562, 115 S.W. 163; Glatstein v. Grund, 1952, 243 Iowa 541, 51 N.W.2d 162, 36 A.L.R.2d 531 (claim against husband's mother, with claim she had sexual relations with her son).

42. Bear v. Reformed Mennonite Church, 1975, 462 Pa. 330, 341 A.2d 105 (bishop ordering wife to shun husband); Carrieri v. Bush, 1966, 69 Wn.2d 536, 419 P.2d 132 (minister alienated wife over period of time, conduct designed to alienate affections is not protected as free exercise of religion). In Radecki v. Schuckardt, 1976, 50 Ohio App.2d 92, 361 N.E.2d 543 the bishop's religious motives were held to preclude an alienation of affections action against him. Relief was denied against the Unification Church on the ground that the cause of action had been abolished by statute. Schuppin v. Unification Church, D.Vt.1977, 435 F.Supp. 603, affirmed 573 F.2d 1295 (daughter).

43. Boland v. Stanley, 1909, 88 Ark. 562, 115 S.W. 163 (stranger assisting plaintiff's in-laws); Vogel v. Sylvester, 1961, 148 Conn. 666, 174 A.2d 122 (mother of man who alienated wife's affections.)

44. Hargraves v. Ballou, 1926, 47 R.I. 186, 131 A. 643; Sullivan v. Valiquette, 1919, 66 Colo. 170, 180 P. 91; Bullock v. Maag, Del.1952, 8 Terry 519, 94 A.2d 382.

45. Barlow v. Barnes, 1916, 172 Cal. 98, 155 P. 457; Watkins v. Lord, 1918, 31 Idaho 352, 171 P. 1133;

Nabors v. Keaton, 1965, 216 Tenn. 637, 393 S.W.2d 382; Joseph v. Naylor, 1917, 257 Pa. 561, 101 A. 846; Hutchinson v. Taylor, 1933, 129 Cal.App. 369, 18 P.2d 722. See Brown, The Action for Alienation of Affections, 1934, 82 U.Pa.L.Rev. 472, 473; Restatement of Torts, § 683, Comment c.

46. Skaggs v. Stanton, Ky.1975, 532 S.W.2d 442 ("the tort is interference with the marriage relation and * * * criminal conversation, enticement and alienation of affections are no more than methods by which this tort may be committed").

47. Gibson v. Gibson, 1966, 240 Ark. 827, 402 S.W.2d 647, appeal after remand 244 Ark. 327, 424 S.W.2d 871.

48. See below p. 929 as to statutory abolition.

49. E.g., Kline v. Ansell, 1980, 287 Md. 585, 414 A.2d 929; Hunt v. Hunt, S.D.1981, 309 N.W.2d 818.

50. See Bearbower v. Merry, Iowa 1978, 266 N.W. 2d 128.

51. McQuarters v. Ducote, Tex.Civ.App.1950, 234 S.W.2d 433, refused n. r. e.; Berger v. Levy, 1935, 5 Cal.App.2d 554, 43 P.2d 610; Curtis v. Miller, 1921, 269 Pa. 509, 112 A. 747; Woodson v. Bailey, 1924, 210 Ala. 568, 98 So. 809; Pederson v. Jirsa, 1963, 267 Minn. 48, 125 N.W.2d 38. Cf. Anderson v. Sturm, 1956, 209 Or. 190, 303 P.2d 509 (at most approval of husband's actions in leaving wife). See Note, 1918, 3 Corn.L.Q. 228.

52. Norris v. Stoneham, Tex.Civ.App.1932, 46 S.W.2d 363.

53. Wilson v. Hilske, 1974, 132 Vt. 506, 321 A.2d 16.

tion; and if the erring spouse acted entirely of his or her own volition,[54] or because of the plaintiff's own fault,[55] there is no liability. As in other cases where causation is in issue, however, it is not necessary that the defendant be the sole cause of the loss of consortium, but merely that he be a substantial factor;[56] or, as some courts put it,[57] a "controlling" or "procuring" cause in bringing it about.

Again, there seems to be general agreement that there is no liability in this type of action[58] unless the defendant has acted for the very purpose of affecting the marital relation.[59] Merely negligent conduct which results in the alienation of affections,[60] or even intentional acts directed at another end which the defendant believes will incidentally have that effect,[61] will not be sufficient. It is not essential that the defendant be motivated by spite or ill will toward the plaintiff,[62] and the "malice" which sometimes is said to be necessary means nothing more than an intent to act without justification or excuse.[63] But the tort must at least be an intentional one, directed at the relation itself; and it has been held that there is no liability for alienation of affections where the defendant was ignorant of the existence of the marriage—although the contrary is true where there has been adultery, since the intercourse cannot be lawful and harmless in itself, so that the defendant must take the risk that the participating partner is married.[64] All this is subject, however, to the obvious qualification that the purpose can be inferred from a course of conduct which would naturally tend toward that result.[65]

---

54. Stefanich v. Kuhns, Ohio App.1950, 96 N.E.2d 318; Curtis v. Miller, 1921, 269 Pa. 509, 112 A. 747; Eklund v. Hackett, 1919, 106 Wash. 287, 179 P. 803. Plaintiff has the burden of pleading and proof that the acts of defendant were "the active controlling cause of the loss of affections." Curry v. Kline, 1960, 187 Kan. 109, 353 P.2d 508.

See Wilson v. Aylward, 1971, 207 Kan. 254, 484 P.2d 1003.

55. Oyler v. Fenner, 1933, 263 Mich. 119, 248 N.W. 567; Annarina v. Boland, 1920, 136 Md. 365, 111 A. 84.

56. Swearingen v. Vik, 1958, 51 Wn.2d 843, 322 P.2d 876; Lisle v. Lunch, Tex.Civ.App.1958, 318 S.W.2d 763, refused n. r. e.; Booth v. Krouse, 1946, 78 Ohio App. 461, 65 N.E.2d 89; Sargent v. Robertson, 1932, 104 Vt. 412, 160 A. 182; Poulos v. Poulos, 1967, 351 Mass. 603, 222 N.E.2d 887. Restatement Second of Torts, § 683, Comment k.

57. Hadley v. Heywood, 1876, 121 Mass. 236; Pugsley v. Smyth, 1921, 98 Or. 448, 194 P. 686; Kleber v. Allin, 1922, 153 Minn. 433, 190 N.W. 786; Maahs v. Schultz, 1932, 207 Wis. 624, 242 N.W. 195; Wilson v. Aylward, 1971, 207 Kan. 254, 484 P.2d 1003.

58. As to loss of consortium through negligent personal injuries to the wife, see infra, § 122.

59. Wilson v. Aylward, 1971, 207 Kan. 254, 484 P.2d 1003; Second Restatement of Torts, § 683, Comment h. But some courts have spoken of inherently wrongful acts importing liability. See Rank v. Kuhn, 1945, 236 Iowa 854, 20 N.W.2d 72; Gibson v. Frowein, Mo.1966, 400 S.W.2d 418.

60. Lilligren v. Burns International Detective Agency, 1916, 135 Minn. 60, 160 N.W. 203 (detective negligently reporting on wife, with the result that husband accused her of unchastity and her affections were alienated); but see, Kelsey-Seybold Clinic v. Maclay, Tex.1971, 466 S.W.2d 716 (partnership might be liable for partner's intentional alienation of affections if partnership negligently failed to protect patients).

61. Anderson v. McGill Club, 1928, 51 Nev. 16, 266 P. 913, certiorari denied 278 U.S. 557, 49 S.Ct. 14, 73 L.Ed. 504 (inducing spouse to spend time and money gambling); Hughes v. Holman, 1924, 110 Or. 415, 223 P. 730 (inviting wife to take part in religious services); Osborn v. Engleman, W.D.Mo.1949, 85 F.Supp. 228 (incidental to employment); Jennings v. Cooper, Mo.App. 1921, 230 S.W. 325 (same); Wilson v. Aylward, 1971, 207 Kan. 254, 484 P.2d 1003; see Radecki v. Schuckardt, 1976, 50 Ohio App.2d 92, 361 N.E.2d 543.

62. Eklund v. Hackett, 1919, 106 Wash. 287, 179 P. 803; Moelleur v. Moelleur, 1918, 55 Mont. 30, 173 P. 419; Hodge v. Brooks, 1922, 153 Ark. 222, 240 S.W. 2; Restatement of Torts, § 683, Comment h.

63. Smithhisler v. Dutter, 1952, 157 Ohio St. 454, 105 N.E.2d 868; Harlow v. Harlow, 1928, 152 Va. 910, 143 S.E. 720, certiorari denied 279 U.S. 869, 49 S.Ct. 483, 73 L.Ed. 1006; Boland v. Stanley, 1909, 88 Ark. 562, 115 S.W. 163; Wallace v. Wallace, 1929, 85 Mont. 492, 279 P. 374. Accord, as to criminal conversation: Tinker v. Colwell, 1903, 193 U.S. 473, 24 S.Ct. 505, 48 L.Ed. 754; Paulson v. Scott, 1951, 260 Wis. 141, 50 N.W.2d 376; Alexander v. Johnson, 1930, 182 Ark. 270, 31 S.W.2d 304.

64. McGrath v. Sullivan, 1939, 303 Mass. 327, 21 N.E.2d 533; see Madison v. Neuberger, 1927, 130 Misc. 650, 224 N.Y.S. 461; Loper v. Askin, 1917, 178 App. Div. 163, 164 N.Y.S. 1036; Second Restatement of Torts, § 683, Comment i, § 685, Comment f.

65. Swearingen v. Vik, 1958, 51 Wn.2d 843, 322 P.2d 876; Boyle v. Clark, 1955, 47 Wn.2d 418, 287 P.2d 1006; Martin v. Ball, 1923, 30 Ga.App. 729, 119 S.E.

Defenses. This type of action is subject to a number of possible defenses. One of the most obvious is that there was no marital relation in existence with which to interfere—or in other words, that there were no "affections" to be alienated. This usually is treated as a matter of defense, on the basis of a presumption that affection always exists between husband and wife.[66] It appears quite logical to hold, as some courts have done,[67] that after a complete and permanent breach of the relation, as by separation, there can be no liability for enticement, harboring or alienation of affections. Other decisions,[68] however, have allowed recovery in such a case for deprivation of whatever chance there might be of reconciliation, and have held that the existing estrangement goes merely to mitigate the damages.[69] The conflict may be more apparent than real, since in the latter group of cases there usually has been reason to believe that a possibility of reconciliation existed,[70] and of course it is not every quarrel or separation that is to be regarded as permanent. As to adultery, however, it is generally agreed that separation or estrangement of the spouses is not a complete defense and bears only on the question of damages,[71] as does the participating spouse's general proclivity to play the field.[72] Consent of the non-participating spouse to the conduct complained of, whether as alienation[73] or criminal conversation,[74] is a total defense; but condonation or forgiveness of the offenses after they have occurred does not bar recovery against the interfering defendant,[75] and is considered only in reduction of damages.[76] The same is true of a divorce[77] or a separation[78] occurring after the tort, even where it is obtained by the alienated spouse.[79]

222; Allen v. Lindeman, Iowa 1969, 164 N.W.2d 346; Gibson v. Frowein, Mo.1966, 400 S.W.2d 418.

66. Donnell v. Donnell, 1967, 220 Tenn. 169, 415 S.W.2d 127; Overton v. Overton, 1926, 121 Okl. 1, 246 P. 1095; Weyer v. Vollbrecht, 1929, 208 Iowa 914, 224 N.W. 568; Buckley v. Francis, 1931, 78 Utah 606, 6 P.2d 188; Squire v. Hill, 1937, 100 Colo. 226, 66 P.2d 822. Contra, Curry v. Kline, 1960, 187 Kan. 109, 353 P.2d 508.

67. Fleming v. Fisk, 1936, 66 App.D.C. 350, 87 F.2d 747; Servis v. Servis, 1902, 172 N.Y. 438, 65 N.E. 270; Smith v. Rice, 1916, 178 Iowa 673, 160 N.W. 6; Cutter v. Cooper, 1924, 234 Mass. 307, 125 N.E. 634.

68. McNelis v. Bruce, 1961, 90 Ariz. 261, 367 P.2d 625 (defendant did not even meet plaintiff's spouse until after formal separation); Gibson v. Gibson, 1968, 244 Ark. 327, 424 S.W.2d 871.

69. Ruble v. Ruble, 1938, 203 Minn. 399, 281 N.W. 529; Scott v. Bontekoe, 1930, 252 Mich. 185, 233 N.W. 215; Hollinghausen v. Ade, 1921, 289 Mo. 362, 233 S.W. 39; Clark v. Orr, 1937, 127 Fla. 411, 173 So. 155; Amellin v. Leone, 1932, 114 Conn. 478, 159 A. 293; Alaimo v. Schwanz, 1972, 56 Wis.2d 198, 201 N.W.2d 604 (separations, divorce suits, violence; "what was in the store before it was burglarized" sets limit on damages).

70. See Brown, The Action for Alienation of Affections, 1934, 82 U.Pa.L.Rev. 472, 488.

71. Pierce v. Crisp, 1935, 260 Ky. 519, 86 S.W.2d 293; Cross v. Grant, 1883, 62 N.H. 675; Michael v. Dunkle, 1882, 84 Ind. 544; Browning v. Jones, 1893, 52 Ill.App. 597; Fennell v. Littlejohn, 1962, 240 S.C. 189, 125 S.E.2d 408; Kremer v. Black, 1978, 201 Neb. 467, 268 N.W.2d 582.

72. White v. Longo, 1973, 190 Neb. 703, 212 N.W.2d 84.

73. Nulsen v. Nulsen, 1934, 3 Cal.App.2d 407, 39 P.2d 509; Kaye v. Newhall, 1969, 356 Mass. 300, 249 N.E.2d 583, appeal after remand 360 Mass. 701, 277 N.E.2d 697; Comte v. Blessing, Mo.1964, 381 S.W.2d 780; Milewski v. Kurtz, 1908, 77 N.J.L. 132, 71 A. 107. "Connivance," operates as a consent and may be found from mere passive sufferance. Nadeau v. Dallaire, 1933, 132 Me. 178, 168 A. 778.

74. Hodges v. Windham, 1791, Peake 53, 170 Eng. Rep. 76; Cook v. Wood, 1858, 30 Ga. 891; Morning v. Long, 1899, 109 Iowa 288, 80 N.W. 390; Kohlhoss v. Mobley, 1905, 102 Md. 199, 62 A. 236; Prettyman v. Williamson, Del.1898, 1 Penn. 224, 39 A. 731.

75. Smith v. Hockenberry, 1904, 138 Mich. 129, 101 N.W. 207; Sikes v. Tippins, 1890, 85 Ga. 231, 11 S.E. 662; Guilbault v. Marcoux, 1921, 121 Me. 568, 115 A. 468; Peak v. Rhyno, 1925, 200 Iowa 864, 205 N.W. 515. Cf. Barker v. Dowdy, 1943, 223 N.C. 151, 25 S.E.2d 404, where the protesting husband continued to live with his wife.

76. Smith v. Hockenberry, 1906, 146 Mich. 7, 109 N.W. 23; Rehling v. Brainard, 1914, 38 Nev. 16, 144 P. 167; Sikes v. Tippins, 1890, 85 Ga. 231, 11 S.E. 662.

77. Vogel v. Sylvester, 1961, 148 Conn. 666, 174 A.2d 122; Sutton v. Sutton, Mo.1979, 567 S.W.2d 147; Sadleir v. Knapton, 1956, 5 Utah 2d 26, 296 P.2d 278.

78. Wilson v. Coulter, 1898, 29 App.Div. 85, 51 N.Y.S. 804; Patterson v. Hill, 1920, 212 Mich. 635, 180 N.W. 352.

79. Vogel v. Sylvester, 1961, 148 Conn. 666, 174 A.2d 122; Dunbier v. Mengedoht, 1930, 119 Neb. 706, 230 N.W. 669; Eklund v. Hackett, 1919, 106 Wash. 287, 179 P. 803; Pollard v. Ward, 1921, 289 Mo. 275, 233 S.W. 14; Philpott v. Kirkpatrick, 1912, 171 Mich. 495, 137 N.W. 232.

The most important defense, however, is that of privilege. The interest of parents in advising and protecting their children, even after marriage, is recognized by a privilege to alienate the affections of a spouse,[80] or to induce one spouse to leave another,[81] where it is done to advance what they reasonably believe to be their child's welfare. The privilege is a qualified or limited one, and it is forfeited when the primary purpose of the parents is something other than the benefit of their child, such as ill will toward the plaintiff [82] or other unworthy motives,[83] or where the interference is reckless, without proper investigation,[84] or "from an ill regulated mind not sufficiently cautious before it occasions the injury." [85] In short the parents, while they are not required to be pleasant to the son- or daughter-in-law,[86] and are aided by a strong inference of proper motives,[87] are privileged to interfere only to the extent that a reasonable person would do so under the circumstances.[88]

The same privilege has been extended to other near relatives, such as brothers and sisters,[89] uncles and aunts,[90] step-parents,[91] guardians,[92] or brothers- and sisters-in-law,[93] with of course similar limitations. A stranger, however, has no such general privilege of interference for the protection of what he believes to be anyone's welfare.[94] He is no doubt justified in giving shelter [95] or advice [96] to a spouse who asks his help, where current standards of decent conduct permit it. In addition, there may be professional, business or social relationships that justify

---

80. Koehler v. Koehler, 1956, 248 Iowa 144, 79 N.W.2d 791; Bishop v. Glazener, 1957, 245 N.C. 592, 96 S.E.2d 870; Beckler v. Yates, 1935, 338 Mo. 208, 89 S.W.2d 650; Bradford v. Bradford, 1940, 165 Or. 297, 107 P.2d 106; Pierson v. Pierson, 1935, 133 Me. 367, 178 A. 617.

81. Hutcheson v. Peck, N.Y.1809, 5 Johns. 196; Beisel v. Gerlach, 1908, 221 Pa. 232, 70 A. 721; Ray v. Parsons, 1915, 183 Ind. 344, 109 N.E. 202; Bourne v. Bourne, 1919, 43 Cal.App. 516, 185 P. 489; Oyler v. Fenner, 1933, 263 Mich. 119, 248 N.W. 567.

82. Multer v. Knibbs, 1907, 193 Mass. 556, 79 N.E. 762; Smith v. Smith, 1916, 192 Mich. 566, 159 N.W. 349; Francis v. Outlaw, 1916, 127 Md. 315, 96 A. 517; Woodhouse v. Woodhouse, 1925, 99 Vt. 91, 130 A. 758; Gross v. Gross, 1912, 70 W.Va. 317, 73 N.E. 961.

Poulos v. Poulos, 1967, 351 Mass. 603, 222 N.E.2d 887 (parent may have "acted with such aggressiveness and vehemence as to constitute an abuse of the privilege.").

83. Rank v. Kuhn, 1945, 236 Iowa 854, 20 N.W.2d 72; Ramsey v. Ramsey, 1931, 34 Del. (4 W.W.Harr.) 576, 156 A. 354; Poulos v. Poulos, 1967, 351 Mass. 603, 222 N.E.2d 887.

84. Brown v. Brown, 1899, 124 N.C. 19, 32 S.E. 320; Biggs v. Biggs, 1926, 78 Colo. 310, 241 P. 539.

85. Birchfield v. Birchfield, 1923, 29 N.M. 19, 217 P. 616; Wallace v. Wallace, 1929, 85 Mont. 492, 279 P. 374; Westlake v. Westlake, 1878, 34 Ohio St. 621; Roberts v. Cohen, 1922, 104 Or. 177, 206 P. 293.

86. Smith v. Smith, 1916, 192 Mich. 566, 159 N.W. 349. Still less to support him or permit him to live with them. Beisel v. Gerlach, 1908, 221 Pa. 232, 70 A. 721. But, while they have the legal privilege to disinherit the child, they may not use the threat of disinheritance as a club to break up the marriage. Wallace v. Wallace, 1929, 85 Mont. 492, 279 P. 374; Woodhouse v. Woodhouse, 1925, 99 Vt. 91, 130 A. 758.

87. Worth v. Worth, 1935, 48 Wyo. 441, 49 P.2d 649; Gregg v. Gregg, 1905, 37 Ind.App. 210, 75 N.E. 674; Cornelius v. Cornelius, 1911, 233 Mo. 1, 135 S.W. 65; McLery v. McLery, 1925, 186 Wis. 137, 202 N.W. 156; Miller v. Levine, 1931, 130 Me. 153, 154 A. 174. The effect of the presumption usually is stated to be to increase the burden of proof upon the plaintiff.

88. Second Restatement of Torts, § 686, Comment f. See Poulos v. Poulos, 1967, 351 Mass. 603, 222 N.E.2d 887.

89. Ratcliffe v. Walker, 1915, 117 Va. 569, 85 S.E. 575; Glass v. Bennett, 1891, 89 Tenn. 478, 14 S.W. 1085; Smith v. Smith, 1916, 192 Mich. 566, 159 N.W. 349; Baird v. Carle, 1914, 157 Wis. 565, 147 N.W. 834; Wohlfort v. Wohlfort, 1928, 125 Kan. 234, 263 P. 1062.

90. Falk v. Falk, 1932, 279 Mass. 530, 181 N.E. 715; Cole v. Johnson, 1922, 103 Or. 319, 205 P. 282.

91. Townsend v. Holderby, 1929, 197 N.C. 550, 149 S.E. 855; Brison v. McKellop, 1914, 41 Okl. 374, 138 P. 154. Accord, as to stepchildren: Strader v. Armstrong, 1922, 192 Iowa 1368, 186 N.W. 407; McGregor v. McGregor, Ky.1909, 115 S.W. 802.

92. Trumbull v. Trumbull, 1904, 71 Neb. 186, 98 N.W. 683.

93. Powell v. Benthall, 1904, 136 N.C. 145, 48 S.E. 598. Accord, Turner v. Estes, 1807, 3 Mass. 317 (son-in-law).

94. See Johnson v. Allen, 1888, 100 N.C. 131, 5 S.E. 666; Hartpence v. Rodgers, 1898, 143 Mo. 623, 45 S.W. 650; Modisett v. McPike, 1881, 74 Mo. 636; Alexander v. Johnson, 1930, 182 Ark. 270, 31 S.W.2d 304.

95. Berthon v. Cartwright, 1796, 2 Esp. 480, 170 Eng.Rep. 426; Johnson v. Allen, 1888, 100 N.C. 131, 5 S.E. 666.

96. Modisett v. McPike, 1881, 74 Mo. 636.

acts tending to disrupt the marriage relation.[97] But if the stranger's conduct is otherwise actionable, the claim against him is not defeated merely because he lacks actual malice.[98]

Religious freedom and perhaps the guarantee of free speech afford a privilege for at least a certain amount of proselytizing, and religious motives in enticing a spouse may protect the clergy in an alienation of affections action.[99] But where the minister has deliberately invaded the marital relation, even religious purposes have been held not to fully protect him.[1]

The marital relation. The only relationship so far protected in these actions has been the legitimized marital relation. A mere engagement to marry does not entitle the parties to the legal protection afforded to spouses,[2] and a marriage that is entirely void is equally ineffective.[3] But a common law marriage[4] or one merely voidable for lack of statutory age of one party,[5] has been held sufficient. In the absence of a marital relationship, there may be, in some jurisdictions, a valid contractual agreement between the parties;[6] conceivably, at least, this might give rise to an action for interference with contract[7] if not one for alienation of affections.

Remedies. The remedy most commonly awarded for any form of interference with marital relations is the damages remedy. Since the loss of marital rights is a species of mental distress, there is no "measuring stick" and considerable leeway is given to the jury in fixing substantial damages,[8] even in the absence of economic loss. Economic loss may be considered as an element of damages, however, as where alienation of affections causes a loss of support not compensated for by alimony or otherwise.[9] Punitive damages may also be awarded in appropriate cases.[10]

Equitable relief[11] by way of injunction against the defendant is not often sought and is probably impractical. Injunctions against interference with the spousal relation have been granted in Alabama[12] and Texas[13] and a New Jersey court once said an injunction could be granted if enforcement became practical.[14] Other courts have

---

97. See Jennings v. Cooper, Mo.App.1921, 230 S.W. 325; Carrieri v. Bush, 1966, 69 Wn.2d 536, 419 P.2d 132 (pastor); Second Restatement of Torts, § 686, Comment d.

98. Grilnberger v. Brotherton, 1933, 173 Wash. 292, 22 P.2d 983; Warren v. Graham, 1916, 174 Iowa 162, 156 N.W. 323.

99. Radecki v. Schuckardt, 1976, 50 Ohio App.2d 92, 361 N.E.2d 543.

1. Bear v. Reformed Mennonite Church, 1975, 462 Pa. 330, 341 A.2d 105; Carrieri v. Bush, 1966, 69 Wn.2d 536, 419 P.2d 132.

2. See Nelson v. Melvin, 1945, 236 Iowa 604, 19 N.W.2d 685; Davis v. Condit, 1914, 124 Minn. 365, 144 N.W. 1089; Homan v. Hall, 1917, 102 Neb. 70, 165 N.W. 881; Conway v. O'Brien, 1929, 269 Mass. 425, 169 N.E. 491; Note, 1926, 10 Corn.L.Q. 259; Restatement Second of Torts, § 698.

3. See Stark v. Johnson, 1908, 43 Colo. 243, 95 P. 930; Jowett v. Wallace, 1914, 112 Me. 389, 92 A. 321; Hutchins v. Kimmell, 1875, 31 Mich. 126; Jacobson v. Siddal, 1885, 12 Or. 280, 7 P. 108.

4. Hollinghausen v. Ade, 1921, 289 Mo. 362, 233 S.W. 39; Butterfield v. Ennis, 1916, 193 Mo.App. 638, 186 S.W. 1173.

5. Luke v. Hill, 1911, 137 Ga. 159, 73 S.E. 345; Holtz v. Dick, 1884, 42 Ohio St. 23.

6. Marvin v. Marvin, 1976, 18 Cal.3d 660, 134 Cal. Rptr. 815, 557 P.2d 106.

7. See below § 129.

8. Vaughn v. Blackburn, Ky.1968, 431 S.W.2d 887; Alaimo v. Schwanz, 1972, 56 Wis.2d 198, 201 N.W.2d 604.

9. See Sebastian v. Kluttz, 1969, 6 N.C.App. 201, 170 S.E.2d 104.

10. Giltner v. Stark, Iowa 1974, 219 N.W.2d 700; Vogel v. Sylvester, 1961, 148 Conn. 666, 174 A.2d 122.

11. See Moreland, Injunctive Control of Family Relations, 1930, 18 Ky.L.J. 207; Pound, Equitable Relief Against Defamation and Injuries to Personality, 1916, 29 Harv.L.Rev. 640, 674; Long, Equitable Jurisdiction to Protect Personal Rights, 1923, 33 Yale L.J. 115, 126; Notes, 1925, 19 Ill.L.Rev. 587; 1933, 27 Ill.L.Rev. 440.

12. Latham v. Karger, 1958, 267 Ala. 433, 103 So.2d 336.

13. Ex parte Warfield, 1899, 40 Tex.Cr.Rep. 413, 50 S.W. 933. Followed in Witte v. Bauderer, Tex.Civ.App. 1923, 255 S.W. 1016; Smith v. Womack, Tex.Civ.App. 1925, 271 S.W. 209, error refused.

14. Devine v. Devine, 1952, 20 N.J.Super. 522, 90 A.2d 126.

generally denied such injunctions, however, as a serious infringement of the personal freedom of the other spouse and beyond the appropriate reach of equity.[15]

Parent

Enticement and abduction. The law has been somewhat more reluctant to protect the relation of parent and child than that of husband and wife. So far as abduction is concerned, there was an old writ giving an action for the taking away of an heir, which apparently was based upon the pecuniary loss to the parent of the heir's marriage prospects, and so did not apply to any other children.[16] When this became obsolete, it was superseded by an action for loss of services of the child, similar to that of any other master.[17] For this some actual loss of services was essential in the beginning, and there could be no recovery when the child was too small to render services,[18] or where they had been contracted away to another.[19] Likewise, while anyone standing in the place of the father might maintain the action,[20] the mother, who had no legal right to the child's services while the father was living with her, could not do so,[21] unless the child was illegitimate,[22] or the father had died or abandoned it.[23]

From this position the law has moved slowly and incompletely toward a recognition of something like the "consortium" found in the relation of husband and wife. While about half of the courts still appear to require a loss of "services" as the foundation for the action,[24] most of them are willing to find a "constructive" loss whenever the plaintiff has the right to services, although none are being rendered,[25] as in the case of the kidnapping of a child four months old.[26] Once loss of services is established, the parent is allowed to recover damages for deprivation of the child's society, expenses to which he has been put in recovering it, and the wound to his own feelings.[27] A few courts, recognizing that the real cause of action is the interference with the relation have adopted the "modern view" [28]

---

15. Snedaker v. King, 1924, 111 Ohio St. 225, 145 N.E. 15; Bank v. Bank, 1942, 180 Md. 254, 23 A.2d 700; White v. Thomson, 1949, 324 Mass. 140, 85 N.E.2d 246; Spitzer v. Spitzer, 1947, 191 Misc. 343, 77 N.Y.S.2d 279, affirmed 1948, 274 App.Div. 806, 81 N.Y.S.2d 155; Lyon v. Izen, 1971, 131 Ill.App.2d 594, 268 N.E.2d 436; Hadley v. Hadley, 1949, 323 Mich. 555, 36 N.W.2d 144; Pearce v. Pearce, 1951, 37 Wn.2d 918, 226 P.2d 895.

16. Barham v. Dennis, 1600, Cro.Eliz. 770, 78 Eng.Rep. 1001.

17. Cf. Fores v. Wilson, 1791, 1 Peake 77, 170 Eng.Rep. 85 (enticing and debauching plaintiff's maid servant). See the historical discussion in Pickle v. Page, 1930, 252 N.Y. 474, 169 N.E. 650; and cf. Meredith v. Buster, 1925, 209 Ky. 623, 273 S.W. 454; Oversmith v. Lake, 1940, 295 Mich. 627, 295 N.W. 339.

18. Hall v. Hollander, 1825, 4 B. & C. 660, 107 Eng.Rep. 1206.

19. Dean v. Peel, 1804, 5 East 45, 102 Eng.Rep. 986; Hodges v. Tagg, 1872, L.R. 7 Ex. 283; cf. Terry v. Hutchinson, 1868, L.R. 3 Q.B. 599 (contract terminated by discharge). Contra Bolton v. Miller, 1855, 6 Ind. 262, on the ground that the parent has the power, if not the right, to break the contract and reclaim the child's services.

20. Moritz v. Garnhart, Pa.1838, 7 Watts, 302; Clark v. Bayer, 1877, 32 Ohio St. 299.

21. Pyle v. Waechter, 1926, 202 Iowa 695, 210 N.W. 926; Soper v. Igo, Walker & Co., 1905, 121 Ky. 550, 89 S.W. 538.

22. Illinois Central Railroad Co. v. Sanders, 1913, 104 Miss. 257, 61 So. 309.

23. Magnuson v. O'Dea, 1913, 75 Wash. 574, 135 P. 640. Cf. Steward v. Gold Medal Shows, 1943, 244 Ala. 583, 14 So.2d 549 (mother entitled to custody); Yost v. Grand Trunk Ry. Co., 1910, 163 Mich. 564, 128 N.W. 784; Horgan v. Pacific Mills, 1893, 158 Mass. 402, 33 N.E. 581.

24. See Magnuson v. O'Dea, 1913, 75 Wash. 574, 135 P. 640; Clark v. Bayer, 1877, 32 Ohio St. 299; Magee v. Holland, 1858, 27 N.J.L. 86; Hare v. Dean, 1897, 90 Me. 308, 38 A. 227.

25. See Magee v. Holland, 1858, 27 N.J.L. 86; Washburn v. Abrams, 1906, 122 Ky. 53, 90 S.W. 997; Hare v. Dean, 1897, 90 Me. 308, 38 A. 227; Moritz v. Garnhart, 1838, Pa. 7 Watts, 302; Clark v. Bayer, 1877, 32 Ohio St. 299.

26. See Magee v. Holland, 1858, 27 N.J.L. 86.

27. Magee v. Holland, 1858, 27 N.J.L. 86; Little v. Holmes, 1921, 181 N.C. 413, 107 S.E. 577; Meredith v. Buster, 1925, 209 Ky. 623, 273 S.W. 454.

28. So called although it is not particularly recent in its origin. Pickle v. Page, 1930, 252 N.Y. 474, 169 N.E. 650; Steward v. Gold Medal Shows, 1943, 244 Ala. 583, 14 So.2d 549; Montgomery v. Crum, 1928, 199 Ind. 660, 161 N.E. 251; Howell v. Howell, 1913, 162 N.C. 283, 78 S.E. 222; Idleman v. Groves, 1921, 89 W.Va. 91, 108 S.E. 485. See Notes, 1929, 14 Corn.L.Q. 496; 1930, 15 Iowa L.Rev. 505; 1931, 25 Ill.L.Rev. 726.

that loss of services is not essential where a child has been taken from its parent, and that such other damages are a sufficient basis for the action.

With these qualifications, the defendant may be liable for abducting the child by force,[29] for enticing it away from its parent,[30] or for "harboring" it in the sense of inducing or encouraging it to remain away from home,[31] or even for providing the means by which the child was carried off in violation of a court order.[32] The consent of the child is of course no defense to the parent's action.[33] As in the case of husband and wife, the interference with the relation must be a deliberate one, although not necessarily motivated by ill will or anything other than kindness or affection toward the child,[34] and there is no liability for harboring or employing a minor unless there is reason to believe that it is without the parent's consent.[35] No special privilege has been recognized in the other parent to interfere with legal custody of the child and there is authority that one parent may be held liable for abducting his own child,[36] as where he refuses to respect court custody orders.[37] At least one state has held, however, that violation of a child custody decree must be remedied solely by contempt proceedings.[38] Presumably even a stranger, and certainly the non-custodial parent, could step in to protect the child from physical violence in excess of the parental privilege of discipline.[39]

Damages in these cases include the traditional award for loss of services and society and the costs of locating and recovering the child,[40] but also punitive damages and an award for emotional distress where the facts warrant.[41] Presumably an injunction will issue in an appropriate case as well, though this remedy may be excluded in federal di-

---

29. Magee v. Holland, 1858, 27 N.J.L. 86; Pickle v. Page, 1930, 252 N.Y. 474, 169 N.E. 650; Howell v. Howell, 1913, 162 N.C. 283, 78 S.E. 222. Cf. Oversmith v. Lake, 1940, 295 Mich. 627, 295 N.W. 339 (false imprisonment and commitment).

30. Evans v. Walton, 1867, L.R. 2 C.P. 615; Armstrong v. McDonald, 1958, 39 Ala.App. 485, 103 So.2d 818; Horowitz v. Sacks, 1928, 89 Cal.App. 336, 265 P. 281; Selman v. Barnett, 1908, 4 Ga.App. 375, 61 S.E. 501; Hare v. Dean, 1897, 90 Me. 308, 38 A. 227.

31. Everett v. Sherfey, 1855, 1 Iowa 356; Washburn v. Abrams, 1906, 122 Ky. 53, 90 S.W. 997; Sargent v. Mathewson, 1859, 38 N.H. 54; Caughey v. Smith, 1872, 47 N.Y. 244.

32. McEvoy v. Helikson, 1977, 277 Or. 781, 562 P.2d 540 (attorney allegedly provided passports to plaintiff's former wife in violation of court order and stipulation).

Cf. Lloyd v. Loeffler, D.Wis.1982, 539 F.Supp. 998 (grandparents liable for hindering father's location of abducted child).

33. Fort Wayne, Cincinnati & Louisville Railway Co. v. Beyerle, 1887, 110 Ind. 100, 11 N.E. 6; Horowitz v. Sacks, 1928, 89 Cal.App. 336, 265 P. 281.

34. See Second Restatement of Torts, § 700, Comment b.

35. Kenney v. Baltimore & Ohio Railroad Co., 1905, 101 Md. 490, 61 A. 581; Arnold v. St. Louis & San Francisco Railroad Co., 1903, 100 Mo.App. 470, 74 S.W. 5; Butterfield v. Ashley, 1850, 60 Mass. (6 Cush.) 249; Caughey v. Smith, 1872, 47 N.Y. 244; see Tavlinsky v. Ringling Brothers Circus Co., 1925, 113 Neb. 632, 204 N.W. 388.

36. Bennett v. Bennett, D.C.Cir. 1982, 682 F.2d 1039; Lloyd v. Loeffler, D.Wis.1982, 539 F.Supp. 998; Kipper v. Vokolek, Mo.App.1977, 546 S.W.2d 521. This appears indirectly where others are held liable for assisting the parent, since in such cases their liability depends on his. See Rosefield v. Rosefield, 1963, 221 Cal. App.2d 431, 34 Cal.Rptr. 479; Brown v. Brown, 1953, 338 Mich. 492, 61 N.W.2d 656, certiorari denied 348 U.S. 816, 75 S.Ct. 27, 99 L.Ed. 644.

37. In Brown v. Brown, 1953, 338 Mich. 492, 61 N.W.2d 656, certiorari denied 348 U.S. 816, 75 S.Ct. 27, 99 L.Ed. 644, there was no actual court decree affecting custody, but the plaintiff-parent had general right to custody upon filing a divorce under a statute and this appeared to be the basis for holding that the defendant-parent's act was tortious. In Coleman v. Shirlen, 1981, 53 N.C.App. 573, 281 S.E.2d 431 the court may have assumed that one parent's abduction in violation of a separation agreement would be sufficient basis for a tort action.

38. McGrady v. Rosenbaum, 1970, 62 Misc.2d 182, 308 N.Y.S.2d 181, affirmed 37 A.D.2d 917, 324 N.Y.S. 2d 876; Friedman v. Friedman, 1974, 79 Misc.2d 646, 361 N.Y.S.2d 108.

39. See Second Restatement of Torts, § 700, Comment e.

40. Second Restatement of Torts, § 700, Comment g.

41. Lloyd v. Loeffler, D.Wis.1982, 539 F.Supp. 998; Brown v. Brown, 1953, 338 Mich. 492, 61 N.W.2d 656, certiorari denied 348 U.S. 816, 75 S.Ct. 27, 99 L.Ed. 644.

versity cases under the "domestic relations" exception to federal jurisdiction.[42]

Seduction. The parents' interests historically received the broadest protection in the action for sexual intercourse with a child, which is roughly analogous to the action for criminal conversation and involves similar injury to feelings. If the action is to be entertained at all in the future [43] there is probably no good reason why it should not lie for intercourse with a male child; [44] but in practice it has been limited to the debauching of daughters. The intercourse may be by forcible rape,[45] or molestation of a small child,[46] but it is more commonly a matter of seduction with the consent of the daughter, which consent will not defeat the parents' action.[47] The common law rule that makes such a consent a bar to any action by a woman for her own seduction [48] led the courts to strain every point to provide a remedy at least for the parent, with the result that the action for seduction, like the tort itself, sometimes is supported by very ingenious fictions.

The action developed as trespass [49] or case [50] for loss of services, which was the most convenient device available. The earliest cases were those in which pregnancy or illness deprived the parent of actual services; and it remains the law in England that loss of services is essential to the cause of action,[51] and that it cannot be maintained where the services of the child have been contracted away to another.[52] The American courts, in general, have said that loss of services is the gist of the action, which must fail without it.[53] But once technical loss of services is established, the action has been recognized as one for interference with other aspects of the relation; and the plaintiff, who sues as a master, has been permitted to recover as a parent,[54] with damages for medical and other expenses of caring for the daughter,[55] for loss of her society and com-

---

42. Bennett v. Bennett, D.C.Cir. 1982, 682 F.2d 1039. But cf. Lloyd v. Loeffler, D.Wis.1982, 539 F.Supp. 998 (punitive damages to increase at the rate of $2,000 per month until child returned, an effect arguably similar to injunction).

43. "[W]e believe that an action for seduction is socially unwise in modern society. * * *" Breece v. Jett, Mo.App.1977, 556 S.W.2d 696.

44. "Nor in my judgment does the remedy depend upon the sex of the servant. The debased woman, who lures to her vile embrace an innocent boy and infects him with loathsome disease, is equally liable to this action, if an injury to his master's right to service follow from her crime." Davis, J., in White v. Nellis, 1856, 31 N.Y. 405. No such case has been found.

45. Kennedy v. Shea, 1872, 110 Mass. 147; Lawrence v. Spence, 1885, 99 N.Y. 669, 2 N.E. 145; Lavery v. Crooke, 1881, 52 Wis. 612, 9 N.W. 599; Silva v. Mills, 1926, 47 R.I. 193, 131 A. 695. Cf. Monahan v. Clemons, 1926, 212 Ky. 504, 279 S.W. 974 (statutory rape).

46. Schurk v. Christensen, 1972, 80 Wn.2d 652, 497 P.2d 937 (parents' mental anguish damages excluded, however).

47. Reutkemeier v. Nolte, 1917, 179 Iowa 342, 161 N.W. 290; Simpson v. Grayson, 1891, 54 Ark. 404, 16 S.W. 4.

48. Welsund v. Schueller, 1906, 98 Minn. 475, 108 N.W. 483; Oberlin v. Upson, 1911, 84 Ohio St. 111, 95 N.E. 511; Overhultz v. Row, 1922, 152 La. 9, 92 So. 716. See supra, § 18. It is to be noted that criminal statutes fixing the age of consent are construed to provide a civil action in nearly all jurisdictions, where the plaintiff is below that age.

49. Tullidge v. Wade, 1769, 3 Wils.K.B. 18, 95 Eng. Rep. 909; MacFadzen v. Olivant, 1805, 6 East 387, 102 Eng.Rep. 1335.

50. Norton v. Jason, 1653, Style 398, 82 Eng.Rep. 809; Grinnell v. Wells, 1844, 7 Man. & G. 1033, 135 Eng.Rep. 419. Apparently the writs were concurrent. See McKinney, J., in Parker v. Meek, 1855, 35 Tenn. (3 Sneed) 29.

51. Grinnell v. Wells, 1844, 7 Man. & G. 1033, 135 Eng.Rep. 419; Eager v. Grimwood, 1847, 1 Exch. 61, 154 Eng.Rep. 26; Whitbourne v. Williams, [1901] 2 K.B. 722.

52. Dean v. Peel, 1804, 5 East 45, 102 Eng.Rep. 986; Hedges v. Tagg, 1872, L.R. 7 Ex. 283. Accord Dain v. Wycoff, 1852, 7 N.Y. 191. Cf. Terry v. Hutchinson, 1868, L.R. 3 Q.B. 599 (discharge before seduction). The American courts, however, have tended to hold that the power of the parent to break the agreement and reclaim the child's services is sufficient. Martin v. Payne, N.Y.1812, 9 Johns, 387; Bolton v. Miller, 1855, 6 Ind. 262.

53. Tittlebaum v. Boehmcke, 1911, 81 N.J.L. 697, 80 A. 323; Blagge v. Ilsley, 1879, 127 Mass. 191; Parker v. Meek, 1855, 35 Tenn. (3 Sneed) 29; Wendt v. Lentz, 1929, 197 Wis. 569, 222 N.W. 798 ("some slight loss of services" necessary).

54. The plaintiff "comes into court as a master; he goes before the jury as a father." Briggs v. Evans, 1844, 27 N.C. (5 Ired.) 16, 20; Simpson v. Grayson, 1891, 54 Ark. 404, 16 S.W. 4.

55. Middleton v. Nichols, 1898, 62 N.J.L. 636, 43 A. 575; Haeissig v. Decker, 1918, 139 Minn. 422, 166 N.W. 1085; Anderson v. Aupperle, 1908, 51 Or. 556, 95 P.

fort,[56] for his wounded feelings [57] and his sense of dishonor to himself and his family,[58] and for the evil example to his other children,[59] with punitive damages superimposed.[60]

The tendency, both in England and in America, has been to reduce to a minimum this element of "services," which obviously is a mere peg on which to hang the real damages. Any services actually rendered, no matter how trivial, such as making a cup of tea for the parent [61] or milking the cows [62] is sufficient. A minor daughter living in her father's home is presumed, without proof, to perform such services,[63] and the fact that she was temporarily absent from home when the seduction occurred will not defeat recovery.[64] From this it has been a comparatively easy step to hold that the right to services is enough, even though none are rendered in fact.[65] A few courts have reached the logical conclusion that the loss of services is an obsolete fiction and is no longer necessary to an action for seduction; [66] and statutes to this effect now have been enacted in some of the states.[67] Still more striking are decisions in several jurisdictions which recognize that the parent's action itself is something in the nature of a fiction, as a makeshift device to permit recovery where the daughter could not sue, and accordingly have held that the action may be maintained by the woman herself as the real party in interest where her consent was invalid [68] or obtained by artifice

---

330. There is no dispute that there may be recovery for the expenses of caring for pregnancy, venereal disease, or other illness resulting directly from the intercourse. White v. Nellis, 1865, 31 N.Y. 405; Manvell v. Thomson, 1826, 2 C. & P. 303, 172 Eng.Rep. 136; Abrahams v. Kidney, 1870, 104 Mass. 222. But there has been considerable reluctance to include illness resulting from fear of exposure or from abandonment by the seducer. Knight v. Wilcox, 1879, 14 N.Y. 413; Boyle v. Brandon, 1845, 13 M. & W. 738, 153 Eng.Rep. 310. Compare the case of demoralization, sexual misconduct and imprisonment in Wendt v. Lentz, 1929, 197 Wis. 569, 222 N.W. 798, and the vigorous attack on the case by Professor Edgerton in 1930, 24 Ill.L.Rev. 232.

56. Bedford v. McKowl, 1800, 3 Esp. 119, 170 Eng. Rep. 560; Milliken v. Long, 1898, 188 Pa. 411, 41 A. 540; Tillotson v. Currin, 1918, 176 N.C. 479, 97 S.E. 395.

57. Andrews v. Askey, 1837, 8 C. & P. 7, 173 Eng. Rep. 376; Dwire v. Stearns, 1919, 44 N.D. 199, 172 N.W. 69; Stevenson v. Belknap, 1858, 6 Iowa 97; Lunt v. Philbrick, 1879, 59 N.H. 59; Barbour v. Stephenson, C.C.Ky.1887, 32 F. 66, affirmed 1891, 140 U.S. 48, 11 S.Ct. 690, 35 L.Ed. 338.

58. Dwire v. Stearns, 1919, 44 N.D. 199, 172 N.W. 69; Riddle v. McGinnis, 1883, 22 W.Va. 253; Mighell v. Stone, 1893, 175 Ill. 261, 51 N.E. 906.

59. Lavery v. Crooke, 1881, 52 Wis. 612, 9 N.W. 599; Stevenson v. Belknap, 1858, 6 Iowa 97; Bedford v. McKowl, 1800, 3 Esp. 119, 170 Eng.Rep. 560.

60. Lawyer v. Fritcher, 1891, 130 N.Y. 239, 29 N.E. 267; Willeford v. Bailey, 1903, 132 N.C. 402, 43 S.E. 928; Berghammer v. Mayer, 1926, 189 Wis. 197, 207 N.W. 289; Anderson v. Aupperle, 1908, 51 Or. 556, 95 P. 330.

61. Carr v. Clarke, 1818, 2 Chit. 260; Manvell v. Thomson, 1826, 2 C. & P. 303, 172 Eng.Rep. 136; Briggs v. Evans, 1844, 27 N.C. (5 Ired.) 16, 20.

62. See Bennett v. Allcott, 1787, 2 Term Rep. 166, 168, 100 Eng.Rep. 90. Accord: Ball v. Bruce, 1859, 21 Ill. 161; Kendrick v. McCrary, 1852, 11 Ga. 603; Badgley v. Decker, N.Y.1865, 44 Barb. 577.

63. Jones v. Brown, 1794, 1 Esp. 217, 170 Eng.Rep. 334; Noice v. Brown, 1877, 39 N.J.L. 569.

64. Lipe v. Eisenlerd, 1865, 32 N.Y. 229; Clark v. Fitch, N.Y.1829, 2 Wend. 459; Ingwaldson v. Skrivseth, 1898, 7 N.D. 388, 75 N.W. 772; Blagge v. Ilsley, 1879, 127 Mass. 191; Hudkins v. Haskins, 1883, 22 W.Va. 645.

65. Bolton v. Miller, 1855, 6 Ind. 262; Martin v. Payne, N.Y.1812, 9 Johns. 387; Emery v. Gowen, 1826, 4 Me. (Greenl.) 33; Kennedy v. Shea, 1872, 110 Mass. 147; Reutkemeier v. Nolte, 1917, 179 Iowa 342, 161 N.W. 290.

66. Simpson v. Grayson, 1891, 54 Ark. 404, 16 S.W. 4; Anthony v. Norton, 1899, 60 Kan. 341, 56 P. 529; Dwire v. Stearns, 1919, 44 N.D. 199, 172 N.W. 69; Snider v. Newell, 1903, 132 N.C. 614, 44 S.E. 354; Breining v. Lippincott, 1916, 125 Ark. 77, 187 S.W. 915.

67. Idaho Code § 5–308; Iowa R. of Court, R. 6; Miss.Code Ann. § 11–709; Montana Rev.Code § 93–2807; Nevada Rev.Stat. § 12–060; S.D.Comp.L. § 21–4–3; Tenn.Code Ann. § 20–107; Utah Code Ann. § 78–11–4; A number of states formerly having some such provision have abolished the seduction action altogether, often along with alienation of affections or criminal conversation actions, as to which see p. 929 infra. Most of the statutes cited allocate the seduction claim to an "unmarried female." Utah and Montana, however, give the action to an unmarried "individual" or "person." Utah and Nevada give the action only to persons under 18 and 20 respectively.

68. Robinson v. Moore, Tex.Civ.App.1966, 408 S.W.2d 582.

Cf. Cotton v. Kambly, 1980, 101 Mich.App. 537, 300 N.W.2d 627 (patient stated good claim against doctor who induced her to consent to sexual relations "as part of her prescribed therapy," analogized to improper administration of drug and not barred by statute abolishing claims for seduction).

or fraud,[69] or where intercourse itself is unlawful.[70] In line with this are statutes in a number of states authorizing the woman's action, and so doing away with the common law defense of consent.[71]

The chief importance of "loss of services" at the present time is that it still is necessary for the parent to show that he is a person who would be entitled to the services of the daughter. If the latter has been emancipated, so that the right to her services is lost, the action cannot be maintained.[72] Furthermore, the action is primarily in the father,[73] and it is only after his death[74] or desertion of the family,[75] that it is in the mother, although any third party who stands in the position of a father may be in a position to sue.[76] If the parents' action has any continued vitality at all such differential treatment of the mother may well be abandoned in the light of current standards of equality. If so, however, some other device may be required to avoid multiple actions with each parent bringing his or her own claim.

It seems to be agreed that the parent's action is not limited to the seduction of minor children, and that it applies to an adult daughter provided that she is rendering actual services to him;[77] but there is a difference of opinion as to whether such services will be presumed from the mere fact of her residence in his house. The prevailing American view seems to be that the presumption does not arise as to an adult.[78] The parent's consent to the intercourse, or conduct inviting it, will of course bar his action.[79]

Alienation of affections. Although a parent may recover for mental anguish and other elements of harm where there is an actual interference with the custody of a child,[80] and, traditionally, where there is a seduction, no similar recovery was permitted for alienation of the child's affections standing alone.[81] There is scant authority permitting the claim,[82] but no discernible trend in its favor and a number of courts have reaffirmed the rule against it, not only where

69. Breece v. Jett, Mo.App.1977, 556 S.W.2d 696 (but suggesting that higher authority should abolish the action); Piggott v. Miller, Mo.App.1977, 557 S.W.2d 692; Hyatt v. McCoy, 1927, 194 N.C. 25, 138 S.E. 405 (held however, not to apply to an infant female in Scarlett v. Norwood, 1894, 115 N.C. 284, 20 S.E. 459); Watson v. Watson, 1883, 49 Mich. 540, 14 N.W. 489; Rabeke v. Baer, 1897, 115 Mich. 328, 73 N.W. 242; Johnson v. Harris, 1940, 187 Okl. 239, 102 P.2d 940. See Note, 1928, 12 Minn.L.Rev. 190. Contra, Kirkpatrick v. Parker, 1939, 136 Fla. 689, 187 So. 620.

70. Slawek v. Stroh, 1974, 62 Wis.2d 295, 215 N.W.2d 9.

71. Collected in 4 Vernier, American Family Laws, 1936, § 252.

72. Roberts v. Connelly, 1848, 14 Ala. 235; White v. Murtland, 1874, 71 Ill. 250. In Collis v. Hoskins, 1948, 306 Ky. 391, 208 S.W.2d 70, the emancipated daughter returned home after the seduction and the father was allowed to recover medical expenses of pregnancy.

73. Mulvehall v. Millward, 1854, 11 N.Y. 343; Scarlett v. Norwood, 1894, 115 N.C. 284, 20 S.E. 459; Peters v. Jones, [1914] 2 K.B. 781; Kaufman v. Clark, 1917, 141 La. 316, 75 So. 65.

74. Furman v. Van Sise, 1874, 56 N.Y. 435; Felkner v. Scarlet, 1867, 29 Ind. 154; Gray v. Durland, 1873, 51 N.Y. 424; Coon v. Moffitt, 1809, 3 N.J.L. 583.

75. Malone v. Topfer, 1915, 125 Md. 157, 93 A. 397; Badgley v. Decker, N.Y.1865, 44 Barb. 577; Abbott v. Hancock, 1898, 123 N.C. 99, 31 S.E. 268. The mother of a bastard may recover for seduction. Bunker v. Mains, 1942, 139 Me. 231, 28 A.2d 734.

76. Ball v. Bruce, 1859, 21 Ill. 161 (brother-in-law); Tittlebaum v. Boehmcke, 1911, 81 N.J.L. 697, 80 A. 323 (stepfather); Manvell v. Thomson, 1826, 2 C. & P. 303, 172 Eng.Rep. 136 (uncle); Anderson v. Aupperle, 1908, 51 Or. 556, 95 P. 330 (grandfather).

77. Bennett v. Allcott, 1787, 2 Term Rep. 166, 100 Eng.Rep. 90; Sutton v. Huffman, 1866, 32 N.J.L. 58; Nickleson v. Stryker, N.Y.1813, 10 Johns. 115; Beaudette v. Gagne, 1895, 87 Me. 534, 33 A. 23; Palmer v. Baum, 1905, 123 Ill.App. 584.

78. Harper v. Luffkin, 1827, 7 B. & C. 387, 108 Eng. Rep. 767; Parker v. Meek, 1855, 35 Tenn. (3 Sneed) 29; Nickleson v. Stryker, N.Y.1813, 10 Johns. 115. But see Sutton v. Huffman, 1866, 32 N.J.L. 58; Lipe v. Eisenlerd, 1865, 32 N.Y. 229; Stevenson v. Belknap, 1858, 6 Iowa 97.

79. Reddie v. Scoolt, 1794, Peake 240, 170 Eng.Rep. 169; Smith v. Masten, N.Y.1836, 15 Wend. 270; Vossel v. Cole, 1847, 10 Mo. 634.

80. Lloyd v. Loeffler, D.Wis.1982, 539 F.Supp. 998; Brown v. Brown, 1953, 338 Mich. 492, 61 N.W.2d 656.

81. Pyle v. Waechter, 1926, 202 Iowa 695, 210 N.W. 926; Miles v. Cuthbert, Sup.Ct.1909, 122 N.Y.S. 703. See Notes, 1927, 40 Harv.L.Rev. 771; 1927, 27 Col.L. Rev. 604; 1927, 11 Minn.L.Rev. 570; 1927, 25 Mich.L. Rev. 682.

82. Strode v. Gleason, 1973, 9 Wn.App. 13, 510 P.2d 250, 60 A.L.R.3d 924.

one family member turns the child against another,[83] but also where church groups or cults convert the child to an alien way of life.[84]

Child

The older common law gave the child no right to the services of a parent—as distinguished from support—and there was no claim analogous to claims by spouses or parents for enticement, criminal conversation or seduction. Since 1923 a number of cases have raised the issue, however, whether a child might recover for the alienation of a parent's affections.[85] The overwhelming response has been that no such action will lie.[86] Two states have held otherwise and have permitted the action,[87] and the indication is that two other states might do so.[88] But these decisions have commanded no following and recent holdings in other states have continued to reject any action by the child for alienation of parental affections.[89] Some of the reasons given for denying a right of action to the child, for example, the absence of precedent, are not persuasive, and it has been contended with obvious reason that the interest of the child in an undisturbed family life is at least of equal importance with that of the parents and entitled to equal or greater protection at the hands of the law.[90] But it is obvious that the child's claim may be used as a surrogate for the claim of a disgruntled parent, who can no longer sue in most states, and courts are no doubt reluctant to allow one parent to use children as pawns, with probable further disruption of family ties. This, together with a growing scepticism in the courts about the usefulness of judicial intervention in family life by way of tort suits makes it unlikely that the child's alienation action will be substantially expanded.

Abolition of Actions

Those actions for interference with domestic relations which carry an accusation of sexual misbehavior—that is to say, criminal conversation, seduction, and to some extent alienation of affections—have been peculiarly susceptible to abuse. Together with the action for breach of promise to marry, it is notorious that they have afforded a fertile field for blackmail and extortion by means of manufactured suits in which the threat of publicity is used to force a settlement. There is good reason to believe that even genuine actions of this type are brought more frequently than not with purely mercenary or vindictive motives; that it is impossible to compensate for such damage with what has derisively been called "heart balm;" that people of any decent instincts do not bring an action which merely adds to the family disgrace; and that no preventive purpose is served, since such torts seldom are committed with deliberate plan.[91] Added

---

83. Bock v. Lindquist, Minn.1979, 278 N.W.2d 326; Ronan v. Briggs, 1966, 351 Mass. 700, 220 N.E.2d 909; McGrady v. Rosenbaum, 1970, 62 Misc.2d 182, 308 N.Y.S.2d 181, affirmed 37 A.D.2d 917, 324 N.Y.S.2d 876.

84. Orlando v. Alamo, 8th Cir. 1981, 646 F.2d 1288 (Arkansas law); Schuppin v. Unification Church, D.Vt. 1977, 435 F.Supp. 603, affirmed 2d Cir., 573 F.2d 1295.

85. Beginning with Coulter v. Coulter, 1923, 73 Colo. 144, 214 P. 400.

86. E.g., Mode v. Barnett, 1962, 235 Ark. 641, 361 S.W.2d 525; Rudley v. Tobias, 1948, 84 Cal.App.2d 454, 190 P.2d 984; Henson v. Thomas, 1949, 231 N.C. 173, 56 S.E.2d 432, 12 A.L.R.2d 1171; Wallace v. Wallace, 1971, 155 W.Va. 569, 184 S.E.2d 327. See Annot., 60 A.L.R.3d 931.

87. Johnson v. Luhman, 1947, 330 Ill.App. 598, 71 N.E.2d 810; Miller v. Monson, 1949, 228 Minn. 400, 37 N.W.2d 543.

88. See Strode v. Gleason, 1973, 9 Wn.App. 13, 510 P.2d 250, 60 A.L.R.3d 924 (permitting action by parent); Russick v. Hicks, D.Mich.1949, 85 F.Supp. 281 (forecasting Michigan law).

89. Hunt v. Chang, 1979, 60 Hawaii 608, 594 P.2d 118; Wheeler v. Luhman, Iowa, 1981, 305 N.W.2d 466; Hale v. Buckner, Mo.App.1981, 615 S.W.2d 97.

90. See Nocca, Should a Child Have a Right of Action Against a Third Person Who Has Enticed One of His Parents Away from the Home, 1956, 2 N.Y.Law Forum 357; Notes, 1951, 39 Cal.L.Rev. 294; 1952, 32 Bos.U.L.Rev. 82; 1953, 6 Vand.L.Rev. 926; 1953, 6 Okl. L.Rev. 500; 1953, 2 St. Louis U.L.J. 305; 1954, 14 La.L. Rev. 713; 1954, 37 Marq.L.Rev. 271; 1956, 8 S.C.L.Q. 477; 1956, 42 Corn.L.Q. 115; 1957, 6 Kan.L.Rev. 95.

91. See, generally, Feinsinger, Legislative Attack on "Heart Balm," 1935, 33 Mich.L.Rev. 979; Feinsinger, Current Legislation Affecting Breach of Promise to Marry, Alienation of Affections and Related

to this is the increasing recognition that each spouse is an autonomous human being,[92] that neither is the property of the other, and that a home so easily broken is not worth maintaining.

The result of all this has been a considerable attack upon the actions named. Since the 1930s half the states [93] have abolished or severely limited the action for alienation of affections or the action for criminal conversation or both. Some of the statutes abolish the actions for seduction and breach of promise to marry as well.[94] At least one state has legislated against most of the normal damage elements in such actions [95] and another has intimated that only nominal damages might be available in some instances.[96] England never recognized a claim for alienation [97] of affections and Louisiana flatly rejected it from the start.[98] Several states have now abolished the criminal conversation action by judicial decision,[99] and others have judicially abolished the alienation of affections claim.[1] The result is that a clear majority of states have now either abolished one or both claims or have narrowed them to insignificance. Although a few courts have said that abolition of the claims is for the legislature, not the judiciary,[2] they have offered no kind words for the actions themselves. Where legislatures have in fact acted to abolish the claims, the statutes have been held constitutional in virtually every case.[3] The trend against such actions has moved slowly, but in the light of increased emphasis in our society on personal choice, the decriminalization of sexual activities in many states,[4] and scepticism about the role of law in protecting feelings and enforcing highly personal morality, it seems doubtful that the trend will be reversed. It is, however, possible to draw distinctions, and to provide relief where the interference with family relations is accomplished by means of some independent tort, such as fraud or defamation, or where the defendant has taken advantage of a person incapable of full consent, such as a child or an incompetent. It may well be that the accommodation of the conflicting ideals of personal freedom on the one hand and stable family life on the other will in the future be accom-

Actions, 1935, 10 Wis.L.Rev. 417; Kane, Heart Balm and Public Policy, 1936, 5 Ford.L.Rev. 62; Kingsley, The Anti-Heart Balm Statute, 1939, 13 So.Cal.L.Rev. 37; Notes, 1935, 22 Va.L.Rev. 205; 1936, 5 Brook.L. Rev. 196; 1972, 48 N.D.Law 426; 1977, 12 Gonzaga L.Rev. 545.

92. See Dobbs, Tortious Interference with Contractual Relationships, 1980, 34 Ark.L.Rev. 335, 358–59; Note, 1981, 23 Ariz.L.Rev. 323.

93. Ala.Code 1975, § 6–5–331; Ariz.Rev.Stats. § 25–341; West's Ann.Cal.Civ.Code § 43.5; Colo.Rev. Stat. 1973, 13–20–202; Conn.Gen.Stat.Ann. § 52–57b; 10 Del.Code § 3924; D.C.Code 1981, § 16–923; West's Fla.Stat.Ann. § 771.01; Official Ga.Code Ann. § 105–1203; West's Ann.Ind.Code 34–4–4–1; 19 Maine Rev.Stat.Ann. § 164; Md.Code, Courts & Jud.Proc., § 5–301 et seq.; Mich.Comp.Laws Ann. § 27A.2901; Minn.Stat.Ann. § 553.01; Mont.Rev.Code 1947, § 17–1201; Nev.Rev.Stat. 41.380; N.J.Stat.Ann. 2A:- 23–1; N.Y.—McKinney's Civ.Rights Law § 80a; Ohio Rev.Code § 2305.29; 76 Okl.Stat.Ann. § 8.1; Or.Rev. Stat. § 30.840; 48 Pa.Code Stat.Ann. § 170; 15 Vt.Stat. Ann. § 1001; Va.Code 1950, § 8.01–220; W.Va.Code 56–3–2a; Wis.Stat.Ann. § 248.01 renumbered by L.1979, c. 32, § 51 and is now § 768.01; Wyo.Stat.1977, § 1–101.

94. E.g., Colo.Rev.Stats. § 41–3–1.

95. Ill.Ann.Stat, c. 68, §§ 34–40.

96. Felsenthal v. McMillan, Tex.1973, 493 S.W.2d 729.

97. See Payne, Tortious Invasion of the Right of Marital Consortium, 1968, 8 J.Fam.L. 41.

98. Moulin v. Monteleone, 1927, 165 La. 169, 115 So. 447.

99. Bearbower v. Merry, Iowa 1978, 266 N.W.2d 128; Kline v. Ansell, 1980, 287 Md. 585, 414 A.2d 929; Fadgen v. Lenkner, 1976, 469 Pa. 272, 365 A.2d 147; Hunt v. Hunt, S.D.1981, 309 N.W.2d 818.

1. Fundermann v. Mickelson, Iowa 1981, 304 N.W. 2d 790; Wyman v. Wallace, 1980, 94 Wn.2d 99, 615 P.2d 452.

2. Gorder v. Sims, 1975, 306 Minn. 275, 237 N.W.2d 67.

3. Hanfgarn v. Mark, 1937, 274 N.Y. 22, 8 N.E.2d 47, second appeal, 1938, 274 N.Y. 570, 10 N.E.2d 556, appeal dismissed, 302 U.S. 641, 58 S.Ct. 57, 82 L.Ed. 498; Magierowski v. Buckley, 1956, 39 N.J.Super. 534, 121 A.2d 749; Chiyoko Ikuta v. Shunji K. Ikuta, 1950, 97 Cal.App.2d 787, 218 P.2d 854; Rotwein v. Gersten, 1948, 160 Fla. 736, 36 So.2d 419; see 56 Nw.L.Rev. 538.

4. See Bearbower v. Merry, Iowa 1978, 266 N.W.2d 128; Fadgen v. Lenkner, 1976, 469 Pa. 272, 365 A.2d 147 both pointing out the anomaly that would exist if a tort were predicated upon legal sexual acts.

§ 125   INJURIES TO MEMBERS OF THE FAMILY   931

plished along these lines rather than by retaining the pure common law actions.

 WESTLAW REFERENCES

interfere*** /s famil! /s relation!

Spouses

wife /s equal /s right standing /s "loss of consortium" /s husband
di consortium
205k209

Types of Interference

"criminal conversation" /p adulter***
"alienation of affection*"
headnote(alienation +4 affection*)
205k341

Basis of Liability

"alienation of affection*" /p defendant* +s intent! /p caus** liab!
"criminal conversation" /p adulter*** /p caus** liab!

Defenses

"criminal conversation" "alienation of affection*" /p defense* /p divorce estrangement privilege separation consent

The Marital Relation

"loss of consortium" /s prior subsequent later /s marriage

Remedies

"criminal conversation" "alienation of affection*" /p remed! damage*

Enticement and Abduction

abduction /p parent father mother /s child! daughter* son*
di abduction
los* +s consortium service* /s child! daughter* son*

Seduction

di seduction
topic(350)
seduction entice! /p minor +s child! daughter* /p los* +s consortium service*

Alienation of Affections

abolish! abrogat! /s "alienation of affection*"

Abolition of Actions

abolish! abrogat! /p "heart balm" seduction abduction

§ 125

1. See Wigmore, Interference with Social Relations, 1887, 21 Am.L.Rev. 764.

2. Hyde v. Scyssor, 1620, Cro.Jac. 538, 79 Eng.Rep. 462; Guy v. Livesey, 1629, Cro.Jac. 501, 79 Eng.Rep. 428.

3. See Wood v. Mobil Chemical Co., 1977, 50 Ill.App. 3d 465, 8 Ill.Dec. 701, 365 N.E.2d 1087; Crowe v. Bumford, 1970, 22 Ohio St.2d 78, 258 N.E.2d 110 (incorporating damages recoverable by wife under Clouston v. Remlinger Oldsmobile Cadillac, Inc., 1970, 22 Ohio St.2d 65, 258 N.E.2d 65); Whittlesey v. Miller, Tex.

abolish! abrogat! /p "criminal conversation"

§ 125. Injuries to Members of the Family

Spouses

From a very early date the common law recognized a right of action in the master when his servant was injured by tort, since, in such a case, the master would suffer a loss of services in addition to whatever loss the servant himself suffered.[1] By 1619 this idea was carried over and applied to marital services and the husband was allowed to recover from the tortfeasor who had injured his wife.[2] Recovery in these cases initially emphasized a loss of "services," but it eventually became clear that the husband's recovery for loss of consortium, as it is called, included damages for loss of sexual attentions, society, and affection,[3] as well as for medical expenditures made on the wife's behalf.[4]

There was, originally, no similar action in favor of the wife when the husband was injured. Since the husband's claim for consortium developed by an expansion of the "services" owed to him by the wife, and since he owed the wife no services at all, it followed that she had no claim when he was injured.[5] Though her support might be provided for, indirectly, by the husband's recovery of his loss of earning capacity, she was without remedy for the loss of household assistance, sexual intercourse, companionship and affection. This blatant discrimination, almost always criticized,[6] was repudiated in 1950 by

1978, 572 S.W.2d 665 (either spouse, "affection, solace, comfort, companionship, society, assistance, and sexual relations * * *").

4. Hughey v. Ausborn, 1967, 249 S.C. 470, 154 S.E.2d 839, 25 A.L.R.3d 1406; Sulkowski v. Schaefer, 1966, 31 Wis.2d 600, 143 N.W.2d 512.

5. "* * * the inferior hath no kind of property in the company, care, or assistance of the superior * * * and therefore can suffer no loss or injury." 3 Bl.Com. 142.

6. Holbrook, The Change in the Meaning of Consortium, 1923, 22 Mich.L.Rev. 1; Lippman, The Break-

the District of Columbia Circuit [7] and in the generation following a strong majority of American courts have followed suit, so that most states today allow the loss of consortium claim to either spouse, as a matter of reform in the common law [8] or as a matter of equal protection under Constitutional or statutory provisions.[9] A small group of courts have achieved equality of the spouses by moving in the opposite direction and denying a recovery for loss of consortium to either spouse.[10]

Courts have repeatedly emphasized that the claim is derived from the marital relationship and the rights attendant upon it. Accordingly they have not shown much disposition to extend a recovery for loss of consortium to unmarried consorts,[11] or even to married consorts when the injury occurred before marriage.[12]

Any tort causing direct physical injury to one spouse will give rise to a claim for loss of consortium by the other. Thus the action has been approved when injuries result from assault and battery,[13] malpractice [14] or other negligence,[15] the sale of habit-forming drugs,[16] and the keeping of dangerous animals.[17] Beyond this, the action will lie when the one spouse is subjected to false imprisonment or malicious prosecution,[18] libel or slander,[19] or intentional infliction of mental distress,[20] provided an actual loss of consortium results to the other spouse. The mere fact that one is libeled,[21] or imprisoned [22] or

---

down of Consortium, 1930, 30 Col.L.Rev. 651; Green, Relational Interests, 1934, 29 Ill.L.Rev. 460, 466; Simeone, The Wife's Action for Loss of Consortium—Progress or No? 1957, 4 St. Louis U.L.Rev. 424; Notes, 1951, 29 N.C.L.Rev. 178; 1951, 20 Ford.L.Rev. 342; 1953, 41 Geo.L.J. 443; 1954, 39 Corn.L.Q. 761; 1957, 14 Wash. & Lee L.Rev. 324; 1958, 31 Temp.L.Q. 284; 1958, 13 U.Miami L.Rev. 92; 1960, 20 La.L.Rev. 731; 1962, 50 Ky.L.J. 263. Contra, Thurman, Recovery by Wife for Loss of Consortium of Husband, 1957, 24 Ins. Counsel J. 224; 1969, 18 Buff.L.Rev. 615; 1969, 47 N.C.L.Rev. 1006; 1965, 10 S.D.L.Rev. 120; 1967, 18 West.Res.L.Rev. 621; 1966, 10 St.L.L.Rev. 276.

7. Hitaffer v. Argonne Co., 1950, 87 U.S.App.D.C. 57, 183 F.2d 811, certiorari denied 340 U.S. 852, 71 S.Ct. 80, 95 L.Ed. 624.

8. Swartz v. United States Steel Corp., 1974, 293 Ala. 439, 304 So.2d 881; Rodriguez v. Bethlehem Steel Corp., 1974, 12 Cal.3d 382, 115 Cal.Rptr. 765, 525 P.2d 669; Millington v. Southeastern Elevator Co., 1968, 22 N.Y.2d 498, 293 N.Y.S.2d 305, 239 N.E.2d 897, 36 A.L.R.3d 891; Nicholson v. Hugh Chatham Memorial Hospital, Inc., 1980, 300 N.C. 295, 266 S.E.2d 818; Whittlesey v. Miller, Tex.1978, 572 S.W.2d 665; Annot., 36 A.L.R.3d 900.

Cf. American Export Lines, Inc. v. Alvez, 1980, 444 U.S. 924, 100 S.Ct. 261, 62 L.Ed.2d 180 (wife-consortium in admiralty).

9. Gates v. Foley, Fla.1971, 247 So.2d 40 (Florida Constitution in part); Hastings v. James River Aerie No. 2337, N.D.1976, 246 N.W.2d 747; Hopkins v. Blanco, 1974, 457 Pa. 90, 320 A.2d 139.

10. Floyd v. Miller, 1950, 190 Va. 303, 57 S.E.2d 114; Taylor v. S. H. Kress & Co., 1932, 136 Kan. 155, 12 P.2d 808.

11. Leonardis v. Morton Chemical Co., 1982, 184 N.J.Super. 10, 445 A.2d 45; see Childers v. Shannon, 1982, 183 N.J.Super. 591, 444 A.2d 1141. Recovery was said to be permissible by unmarried cohabitants in Bulloch v. United States, D.N.J.1980, 487 F.Supp. 1078 as a matter of New Jersey law. The case was disapproved in both the New Jersey decisions cited above.

12. Sawyer v. Bailey, Me.1980, 413 A.2d 165; Trembley v. Carter, Fla.App.1980, 390 So.2d 816.

13. Berger v. Jacobs, 1870, 21 Mich. 215; Baer v. Hepfinger, 1913, 152 Wis. 558, 140 N.W. 345; Klingman v. Holmes, 1873, 54 Mo. 304.

14. Mewhirter v. Hatten, 1875, 42 Iowa 288; Hoard v. Peck, N.Y.1867, 56 Barb. 202.

15. Hopkins v. Atlantic & St. Lawrence Railroad Co., 1857, 36 N.H. 9; Skoglund v. Minneapolis Street Railway Co., 1891, 45 Minn. 330, 47 N.W. 1071; Fuller v. Naugatuck Railroad Co., 1852, 21 Conn. 557; Wilton v. Middlesex Railroad Co., 1878, 125 Mass. 130.

16. Hoard v. Peck, N.Y.1867, 56 Barb. 202; Holleman v. Harward, 1896, 119 N.C. 150, 25 S.E. 972; Tidd v. Skinner, 1919, 225 N.Y. 422, 122 N.E. 247.

17. Durden v. Barnett, 1844, 7 Ala. 169; Karr v. Parks, 1872, 44 Cal. 46.

18. Rogers v. Smith, 1861, 17 Ind. 323. Cf. Hastings v. James River Aerie No. 2337, (N.D.1976), 246 N.W.2d 747 (supplier of intoxicants held liable to wife when intoxicated husband became involved in a shooting and was ultimately convicted of homicide and imprisoned).

19. Garrison v. Sun Printing & Publishing Association, 1912, 207 N.Y. 1, 100 N.E. 430. Cf. Dengate v. Gardiner, 1838, 4 M. & W. 6, 150 Eng.Rep. 1320; Van Vacter v. McKillip, Ind.1845, 7 Blackf. 578.

20. Agis v. Howard Johnson Co., 1976, 371 Mass. 140, 355 N.E.2d 315.

21. See White v. Spence, 1977, 5 Mass.App. 679, 369 N.E.2d 731.

22. See Bly v. Skaggs Drug Centers, Mo.App.1978, 562 S.W.2d 723 (apparently a brief detention.) Loss of services might be inferred in the case of longer imprisonment.

wrongfully discharged,[23] however, does not give rise to a consortium action and there can be no recovery by the other spouse in the absence of a basis for inferring that services or affection were actually lost.

As all this indicates, one of the chief problems in the consortium claim is the concern to avoid duplicative or impermissible damage awards. So far as damages are based on intangible losses of society and affection, there is some risk that a jury hearing the husband's claim will consciously or not, include something in the verdict for the wife's loss as well, and vice versa. To minimize this risk, some courts have required that the main claim and the consortium claim be tried together, at least in the ordinary situation.[24] Difficult problems remain, however. Since the injured husband (for example) is entitled to recover for his own diminished earning capacity,[25] the wife's consortium claim for loss of services must not be allowed to include lost services that are also part of that diminished capacity. The wife who gives up her job to nurse her husband must not be allowed to recover for her loss of wages or the value of her services for the same reason—her husband is entitled to recover the reasonable value of needed services and nursing and to allow both claims is to allow a double recovery.[26] Similarly, the wife has been given no legal interest in her husband's reputation, and if he is libeled, her embarrassment is not itself a ground for recovery if the libel does not in fact incapacitate the husband.[27]

In addition to the claims recoverable by either spouse for loss of services and society, the husband was allowed to recover the cost of the wife's medical treatment.[28] This rule was based on the legal obligations of the husband to provide medical attention for his wife and on the fact that the wife was likely to be dependent upon the husband for such attention. Considerable social change has taken place since this rule was first followed, and the contemporary decisions show no special fondness for it. If the wife has paid the medical bills, or has obligated her credit specifically to do so,[29] or if the injury occurred before marriage,[30] the wife will be permitted to recover her own medical expenses. Some courts have spoken, somewhat generally, about allowing the wife to recover when appropriate,[31] or to recover for future medical, though not past.[32] At least one court has said that equality of treatment requires that the wife always recover her own losses,[33] and statutes in some states have been interpreted to reach the same result.[34] The wife rather than the husband

---

23. See Pstragowski v. Metropolitan Life Insurance, 1st Cir. 1977, 553 F.2d 1 (benefits to wife under husband's employment contract not recoverable by wife, but by husband); Slovensky v. Birmingham News Co., Ala.App.1978, 358 So.2d 474.

24. Ekalo v. Constructive Service Corp. of America, 1965, 46 N.J. 82, 215 A.2d 1; Deems v. Western Maryland Railway Co., 1967, 247 Md. 95, 231 A.2d 514; Moran v. Quality Aluminum Casting Co., 1967, 34 Wis.2d 542, 150 N.W.2d 137; Thill v. Modern Erecting Co., 1969, 284 Minn. 508, 170 N.W.2d 865. Nicholson v. Hugh Chatham Memorial Hospital, Inc., 1980, 300 N.C. 295, 266 S.E.2d 818.

25. See D. Dobbs, Remedies § 8.1.

26. Rodriguez v. Bethlehem Steel Corp., 1974, 12 Cal.3d 382, 115 Cal.Rptr. 765, 525 P.2d 669; Tribble v. Gregory, Miss.1974, 288 So.2d 13, 74 A.L.R.3d 797.

27. See White v. Spence, 1977, 5 Mass.App. 679, 369 N.E.2d 731.

28. Boland v. Morrill, 1967, 275 Minn. 496, 148 N.W.2d 143; Annot., 21 A.L.R.3d 1113.

29. Cook v. Sweatt, 1968, 282 Ala. 177, 209 So.2d 891; Hyland v. Southwell, Del.Super. 1974, 320 A.2d 767.

30. Sulkowski v. Schaefer, 1966, 31 Wis.2d 600, 143 N.W.2d 512.

31. Hyland v. Southwell, Del.Super.1974, 320 A.2d 767; Kelley v. Lee, 1969, 204 Kan. 317, 461 P.2d 806.

32. Cassidy v. Constantine, 1929, 269 Mass. 56, 168 N.E. 169, 66 A.L.R. 1186.

In Busch v. Busch Construction, Inc., Minn.1977, 262 N.W.2d 377 the court held that the wife would be entitled to recover her own debts, whether based on necessities or not, but that since the husband was secondarily liable for future medical expense, he could properly move the trial court to place the funds for future medical care in trust, similar to those held in guardianships.

33. Patusco v. Prince Macaroni, Inc., 1967, 50 N.J. 365, 235 A.2d 465.

34. Woodard v. Des Moines, 1917, 182 Iowa 1102, 165 N.W. 313; Helmstetler v. Duke Power Co., 1945, 224 N.C. 821, 32 S.E.2d 611.

will be entitled in most states to recover punitive damages for her own physical injury.[35]

Parent

Since the father was, under the common law rule, entitled to the services of his child, he was entitled to recover for a loss of services or earning capacity not only when the child was enticed away or seduced,[36] but also when the child was tortiously injured.[37] And since the father was obliged to provide medical attention to the child, he was likewise entitled to recover against the tortfeasor for the child's medical expenses.[38] But the claim for the loss of the child's services did not expand to include intangible losses of consortium as it did when a spouse was injured: where the child was negligently injured the parent had no claim for loss of the child's society and companionship[39] except so far as the claim for loss of services in a modern society is a fictional one.[40]

A partial exception to this rule developed under the wrongful death statutes in some states, where loss of the child's society, companionship or affection may be a recoverable item of damages for surviving parents,[41] since otherwise a tortfeasor causing death might escape all liability.[42] Several states have also enacted statutes carrying this item of damage over into cases involving injury to a child,[43] and in 1975 the Wisconsin Court, overruling precedent, held that both parents of a newborn infant who was allegedly blinded by medical malpractice, stated a cause of action for loss of his society and companionship.[44] Although the decision has had the support of some writers,[45] who have shown that the traditional arguments against recovery for loss of a child's society and affections[46] are not always convincing, there is virtually no support for this kind of action in the courts[47] and it has been rejected wherever it has been considered,[48] partly, no doubt, because recognition of a cause of action would impose higher costs without actually remedying the loss.[49]

As to the parent's action for loss of the child's services or earning capacity, or for the medical expenses incurred on behalf of the child, the rules are generally the same as those applied in the spousal action. For some purposes the parent's action is an independent one, vested in him and not in the child. Thus if both parent and child are injured in a single collision, the parent must include his claim for loss of the child's services and medical expense in the parent's ac-

---

35. Hughey v. Ausborn, 1967, 249 S.C. 470, 154 S.E.2d 839; Annot., 25 A.L.R.3d 1406.

36. See § 124, supra.

37. Jones v. Brown, 1794, 1 Esp. 217, 170 Eng.Rep. 334.

38. Doss v. Sewell, 1962, 257 N.C. 404, 125 S.E.2d 899; Skollingsberg v. Brookover, 1971, 26 Utah 2d 45, 484 P.2d 1177.

39. Second Restatement of Torts § 703, Comment h.

40. See H. Clark, Domestic Relations, 1968, 278.

41. See § 127, infra; D. Dobbs, Remedies § 8.4.

42. See Borer v. American Airlines, Inc., 1977, 19 Cal.3d 441, 138 Cal.Rptr. 302, 563 P.2d 858; D. Dobbs, Remedies § 8.4.

43. See Love, Tortious Interference with the Parent-Child Relationship: Loss of an Injured Person's Society and Companionship, 1976, 51 Ind.L.J. 591, 592.

44. Shockley v. Prier, 1975, 66 Wis.2d 394, 225 N.W.2d 495.

45. Love, Tortious Interference with the Parent-Child Relationship: Loss of an Injured Person's Society and Companionship, 1976, 51 Ind.L.J. 591.

46. These are (1) precedent, (2) historical analogy to master-servant relations, (3) speculative damages, (4) the risk of duplicating damages awards, (5) multiple actions, (6) increased costs. These are summarized and attacked in Love, Tortious Interference with the Parent-Child Relationship: Loss of an Injured Person's Society and Companionship, 1976, 51 Ind.L.J. 591, 595–606. Professor Love also suggests arguments in favor of the cause of action based on equal protection.

47. Several cases, without discussion or seeming adversion to the point, have simply characterized a claim which was upheld as one for "services and society" of the injured child. See Yordon v. Savage, Fla.1973, 279 So.2d 844, which in turn relies on Wilkie v. Roberts, 1926, 91 Fla. 1064, 109 So. 225 and which seems to deal with pecuniary losses only.

48. See Baxter v. Superior Court of Los Angeles, 1977, 19 Cal.3d 461, 138 Cal.Rptr. 315, 563 P.2d 871, based on arguments set out in detail in a companion case on similar facts, Borer v. American Airlines, Inc., 1977, 19 Cal.3d 441, 138 Cal.Rptr. 302, 563 P.2d 858; Annot., 69 A.L.R.3d 553.

49. Borer v. American Airlines, Inc., 1977, 19 Cal.3d 441, 138 Cal.Rptr. 302, 563 P.2d 858.

tion for his own personal injuries, and if he does not do so he cannot later sue for the loss of services.[50] The parent is not, of course, entitled to recover for the child's injury as such except in his formal capacity as next friend or guardian ad litem. He cannot, therefore, recover for the child's own pain and suffering [51] or for any other tort to the child that does harm to the child without impairing the right to services or causing medical expense.[52] Nor may he recover for any loss of services or medical expense expected to occur after the child's majority [53] or his emancipation.[54] The parent's cause of action may be waived and the child allowed to sue for those elements of damage that belong to the parent if the parent participates in the child's action without asserting a claim.[55]

The common law rule gave the right to recover for loss of services and the child's medical expense to the father, and the mother could not recover [56] unless the child was illegitimate or she had become entitled to its services through the death of the father or a decree giving her custody.[57] Allocation of the action to only one parent had the procedural advantage of avoiding a multiplicity of suits and of assuring the defendant that he would not be sued again by a second parent. But as with other gender-based distinctions in this area, the rule is somewhat out of touch with the times and courts have shown considerable willingness in recent years to permit the mother to recover where there was any particular reason for doing so,[58] or even to insist that the parents have an equal right and must be joined when the claim for loss of a child's services is asserted.[59]

Child

The interest of the child in proper parental care and affection, which received only scanty recognition in cases of intentional interference with the parent-child relationship,[60] ran into a stone wall where the defendant was merely negligent in causing an injury to the parent. In such cases the parent is entitled to recover for economic harms, such as lost wages, and the child is thus indirectly protected against loss of support, but there is no protection given for loss of society, guidance and attention that no doubt results in many cases of parental injury. The liability was rejected even in the District of Columbia,[61] which began the recognition of the wife's cause of action for consortium. Up until 1980, virtually all oth-

---

50. Retherford v. Halliburton Co., Okl.1977, 572 P.2d 966.

51. Pattison v. Gulf Bag Co., 1906, 116 La. 963, 41 So. 224; Kirk v. Middlebrook, 1907, 201 Mo. 245, 100 S.W. 450; Durkee v. Central Pacific R. Co., 1880, 56 Cal. 388; Cuming v. Brooklyn City Railroad Co., 1888, 109 N.Y. 95, 16 N.E. 65; Tennessee Central Railway Co. v. Doak, 1905, 115 Tenn. 720, 92 S.W. 853.

52. Sorenson v. Balaban, 1896, 11 App.Div. 164, 42 N.Y.S. 654; Atlanta Journal Co. v. Farmer, 1934, 48 Ga.App. 273, 172 S.E. 647. Boyd v. Blaisdell, 1860, 15 Ind. 73. Cf. Sorrells v. Matthews, 1907, 129 Ga. 319, 58 S.E. 819; Donahoe v. Richards, 1854, 38 Me. 376.

53. Lopez v. Waldrum's Estate, 1970, 249 Ark. 558, 460 S.W. 61; Butler v. State Farm Mutual Automobile Co. (La.App.1967), 195 So.2d 314.

54. See Childs v. Rayburn, 1976, 169 Ind.App. 147, 346 N.E.2d 655; Kennedy v. Kennedy, Tex.Civ.App. 1974, 505 S.W.2d 393.

55. Cabaniss v. Cook (Ala.1977), 353 So.2d 784; Doss v. Sewell, 1962, 257 N.C. 404, 125 S.E.2d 899. Cf. Skollingsberg v. Brookover, 1971, 26 Utah 2d 45, 484 P.2d 1177 (father who participated in mother's action for child's medical estopped, mother could recover).

56. Keller v. City of St. Louis, 1899, 152 Mo. 596, 54 S.W. 438, laying stress on the correlation between the right to services and the duty to support. See Note, 1928, 42 Harv.L.Rev. 112.

57. Marks v. City of New York, 1950, 101 N.Y.S.2d 105; Southwestern Gas & Electric Co. v. Denney, 1935, 190 Ark. 934, 82 S.W.2d 17; McGarr v. National & Providence Worsted Mills, 1902, 24 R.I. 447, 53 A. 320; Briscoe v. Price, 1916, 275 Ill. 63, 113 N.E. 881.

58. Winnick v. Kupperman Construction Co., 1968, 29 A.D.2d 261, 287 N.Y.S.2d 329 (mother has equal duty to support and if she paid medical she can recover); Skollingsberg v. Brookover, 1971, 26 Utah 2d 45, 484 P.2d 1177 (equal duty to support, father will be held estopped to assert the same claim since he participated in mother's action).

59. Yordon v. Savage, Fla.1973, 279 So.2d 844 (parents are equal and both must join).

60. See supra, § 124.

61. Hill v. Sibley Memorial Hospital, D.D.C.1952, 108 F.Supp. 739; Pleasant v. Washington Sand & Gravel Co., 1958, 104 U.S.App.D.C. 374, 262 F.2d 471.

er courts that had considered the matter had rejected it as well,[62] and several major decisions emerged on the point.[63] But, beginning in 1980, Massachusetts,[64] Michigan[65] and Iowa[66] in quick succession declared that a cause of action for the child would exist when the parent was injured, at least if the injury seriously disrupts the parent-child relationship.[67] Though this element of damage is often recognized in wrongful death actions,[68] other courts have continued to follow the traditional view under which the claim is denied,[69] partly because the award of damages does not replace the parents' attention and does impose charges that will tend to cause higher insurance premiums or more uninsured motorists, so that costs may rise[70] without providing a corresponding real benefit to the child, who, in the words of one court, may simply become a wealthy child without parental care rather than an ordinary child without such care.[71] In addition, it has been suggested that awards to seriously injured parents are likely to provide indirectly but effectively for protection of the children and that a separate award for the child is likely to duplicate such recoveries at least in part.[72] But able criticisms have been mounted against the traditional rule,[73] and it must now be recognized that the more liberal view may well gain further adherents. In addition to this it must be said that a number of jurisdictions, including some which deny the child's consortium claim, do recognize a claim for emotional distress or at least psychic injury from such distress when one family member is injured in the presence of another, or a nervous shock to a family member has resulted from substantially contemporaneous observance of an injury or death to another family member.[74]

62. Jeune v. Del E. Webb Construction Co., 1954, 77 Ariz. 226, 269 P.2d 723; Turner v. Atlantic Coast Line Railroad Co., N.D.Ga.1958, 159 F.Supp. 590; Hoffman v. Dautel, 1961, 189 Kan. 165, 368 P.2d 57; Erhardt v. Havens, Inc., 1958, 53 Wn.2d 103, 330 P.2d 1010; see Annot., 69 A.L.R.3d 528.

63. Borer v. American Airlines, Inc., 1977, 19 Cal.3d 441, 138 Cal.Rptr. 302, 563 P.2d 858; Russell v. Salem Transportation Co., 1972, 61 N.J. 502, 295 A.2d 862, 69 A.L.R.3d 522.

64. Ferriter v. Daniel O'Connell's Sons, Inc., 1980, 381 Mass. 507, 413 N.E.2d 690. The court required minority plus a dependence "rooted not only in economic requirements, but also in filial needs for closeness, guidance, and nurture."

65. Berger v. Weber, 1981, 411 Mich. 1, 303 N.W.2d 424.

66. Weitl v. Moes, Iowa 1981, 311 N.W.2d 259. Part of this decision turned on the fact that a parent in Iowa could recover for loss of a child's companionship and society both in injury and death cases. The court required a compulsory joinder of the child's claim with the parent's claim for injury unless joinder was not "feasible."

67. Weitl v. Moes, Iowa 1981, 311 N.W.2d 259.

68. See Love, Tortious Interference with the Parent-Child Relationship: Loss of an Injured Person's Society and Companionship, 1976, 51 Ind.L.J. 591.

69. The most detailed consideration of the issue appears in Judge Linde's opinion in Norwest v. Presbyterian Intercommunity Hospital, 1982, 293 Or. 543, 652 P.2d 318. Other recent decisions rejecting the child's claim include Borer v. American Airlines, Inc., 1977, 19 Cal.3d 441, 138 Cal.Rptr. 302, 563 P.2d 858; Salin v. Kloempken, Minn.1982, 322 N.W.2d 736; Russell v. Salem Transportation Co., 1972, 61 N.J. 502, 295 A.2d 862; DeAngelis v. Lutheran Medical Center, 1981, 84 A.D.2d 17, 445 N.Y.S.2d 188; Mueller v. Hellrung Construction Co., 1982, 107 Ill.App.3d 337, 63 Ill.Dec. 140, 437 N.E.2d 789. See Schmeck v. City of Shawnee, 1982, 231 Kan. 588, 647 P.2d 1263.

70. Russell v. Salem Transportation Co., 1972, 61 N.J. 502, 295 A.2d 862, 69 A.L.R.3d 522; DeAngelis v. Lutheran Medical Center, 1981, 84 A.D.2d 17, 445 N.Y.S.2d 188.

71. Borer v. American Airlines, Inc., 1977, 19 Cal.3d 441, 138 Cal.Rptr. 302, 563 P.2d 858. Although the court rejected liability in Norwest v. Presbyterian Intercommunity Hospital, 1982, 293 Or. 543, 652 P.2d 318, it did not agree with this reason, but insisted instead that "ordinarily negligence as a legal source of liability gives rise only to an obligation to compensate the person immediately injured. * * *"

72. DeAngelis v. Lutheran Medical Center, 1981, 84 A.D.2d 17, 445 N.Y.S.2d 188.

73. Love, Tortious Interference with the Parent-Child Relationship: Loss of an Injured Person's Society and Companionship, 1976, 51 Ind.L.J. 591.

74. One who witnesses injury to another family member may recover for one's own suffering if that one was himself in the zone of danger or feared for himself. A number of jurisdictions have now imposed a greater liability and allowed recovery to one who witnesses injury to a family member, though the witness was not in danger. These cases in turn have been liberalized to permit recovery by those who encounter the injury soon after it takes place and even to cases that involve little or no physical injury at all but only disquieting medical advice. The topic is considered generally in § 54 supra.

Defenses

The right of the spouse or parent to recover will of course depend upon the existence of tortious conduct on the part of the defendant. Normally this means that there must be a tort for which an action might be maintained by the injured spouse or child. Thus a parent may not recover where the child's injury results from the negligence of an independent contractor [75] or a fellow servant [76] for which the defendant is not responsible, or where the defendant owes the child no duty of care,[77] or takes all reasonable precautions.[78]

From this the courts generally have concluded that the recovery of the spouse or parent will be defeated or diminished by defenses which would bar or diminish that of the injured spouse or child. Thus contributory negligence [79] or assumption of risk [80] on the part of the injured person has been held to defeat recovery, or, in comparative negligence states, to reduce it.[81] Likewise if the injured spouse or child is barred by a statute of limitations,[82] or because workers' compensation represents his exclusive remedy,[83] the deprived spouse or parent will be barred. The same has been true under the limitations set up in wrongful death actions,[84] although the contrary conclusion has been reached under other statutes.[85] As would be expected, the same principle would forbid the jury to bring in inconsistent verdicts on the two claims, finding against the wife on the main claim and in favor of the husband's claim for medical expense.[86] In line with these rules, a number of cases have held that once the main claim has gone to judg-

75. Regan v. Superb Theater, 1915, 220 Mass. 259, 107 N.E. 984.

76. Zarba v. Lane, 1947, 322 Mass. 132, 76 N.E.2d 318; Harris v. A. J. Spencer Lumber Co., 1914, 185 Ala. 648, 64 So. 557; King v. Floding, 1916, 18 Ga.App. 280, 89 S.E. 451.

77. Jones v. Schmidt, 1953, 349 Ill.App. 336, 110 N.E.2d 688 (landowner); Shiels v. Audette, 1934, 119 Conn. 75, 174 A. 323 (automobile guest); Arritt v. Fisher, 1938, 286 Mich. 419, 282 N.W. 200 (same); Cavanaugh v. First National Stores, 1952, 329 Mass. 179, 107 N.E.2d 307 (prenatal injury).

Cf. Harrison v. United States, D.Conn.1979, 479 F.Supp. 529, affirmed 2d Cir., 622 F.2d 573, certiorari denied 449 U.S. 828, 101 S.Ct. 93, 66 L.Ed.2d 32 (governmental immunity as to husband's claim under Feres doctrine bars wife's consortium claim.)

78. Gurll v. Massasoit Greyhound Association, 1949, 325 Mass. 76, 89 N.E.2d 12; Neville v. American Barge Line Co., W.D.Pa.1952, 105 F.Supp. 405, affirmed 3d Cir., 218 F.2d 190; Warrior Manufacturing Co. v. Jones, 1908, 155 Ala. 379, 46 So. 456; Savage v. New York, New Haven & Hartford Railroad Co., 2 Cir. 1911, 185 F. 778.

79. Wife: Chicago, Burlington & Quincy Railroad Co. v. Honey, 8 Cir. 1894, 63 F. 39, 26 L.R.A. 42; Jordan v. City of Pittsburgh, 1939, 332 Pa. 230, 3 A.2d 677; Ross v. Cuthbert, 1964, 239 Or. 429, 397 P.2d 529; Cawley v. La Crosse City Railway Co., 1900, 106 Wis. 239, 82 N.W. 197; Pioneer Construction Co. v. Bergeron, 1969, 170 Colo. 474, 462 P.2d 589.

Child: Brown v. Slentz, 1958, 237 Ind. 497, 147 N.E.2d 239; Callies v. Reliance Laundry Co., 1925, 188 Wis. 376, 206 N.W. 198; Boyett v. Airline Lumber Co., Okl.1954, 277 P.2d 676; Barlow v. Lowery, 1948, 143 Me. 214, 59 A.2d 702; Wineman v. Carter, 1942, 212 Minn. 298, 4 N.W.2d 83.

80. McNally v. Addis, 1970, 65 Misc.2d 204, 317 N.Y.S.2d 157. A number of cases of intentional confrontation with a known risk are simply called cases of contributory negligence. See Meyer v. State, Ct.Cl. 1978, 92 Misc.2d 996, 403 N.Y.S.2d 420.

81. Nelson v. Busby, 1969, 246 Ark. 247, 437 S.W.2d 799; Meyer v. State, Ct.Cl.1978, 92 Misc.2d 996, 403 N.Y.S.2d 420; Victorson v. Milwaukee & Suburban Transport Co., 1975, 70 Wis.2d 336, 234 N.W.2d 332.

82. Carter v. Harlan Hospital Association, 1936, 265 Ky. 452, 97 S.W.2d 9; Morgan v. United States, D.N.J. 1956, 143 F.Supp. 580. Cf. Pitrelli v. Cohen, 1938, 169 Misc. 117, 6 N.Y.S.2d 696, reversed 257 App.Div. 845, 12 N.Y.S.2d 71 (parent's action barred although son's not barred). Contra, Corpman v. Boyer, 1960, 171 Ohio St. 233, 169 N.E.2d 14. See Note, 1938, 52 Harv.L.Rev. 169.

83. Williams v. Byrd, 1978, 242 Ga. 80, 247 S.E.2d 874; Coddington v. City of Lewiston, 1974, 96 Idaho 135, 525 P.2d 330; Fritzson v. City of Manhattan, 1974, 215 Kan. 810, 528 P.2d 1193; Lowery v. Wade Hampton Co., 1978, 270 S.C. 194, 241 S.E.2d 556.

84. Lampe v. Lagomarcino-Grupe Co., 1959, 251 Iowa 204, 100 N.W.2d 1; Hoekstra v. Helgeland, 1959, 78 S.D. 82, 98 N.W.2d 669.

85. King v. Viscoloid Co., 1914, 219 Mass. 420, 106 N.E. 988. Some authority formerly so holding, e.g., Roxana Petroleum Co. v. Cope, 1928, 132 Okl. 152, 269 P. 1084, has been overruled by statute, see Okl.Stat. Ann., tit. 85, § 12.

86. Bias v. Ausbury, 1963, 369 Mich. 378, 120 N.W.2d 233; Hennig v. Crocker, 1972, 40 A.D.2d 582, 334 N.Y.S.2d 118.

ment,[87] or has been settled,[88] this will bar the claim for consortium. This is also the result of the rule, followed in a number of states, that the consortium claim must be joined with the personal injury claim or be lost.[89] It is of course obvious that the plaintiff's own contributory negligence or assumption of risk will defeat or reduce his recovery for the resulting injury to a spouse or child.[90]

There are a few cases that obtain different results where the defendant injures a person who cannot well be expected to protect himself, as where he employs a known minor. In such a case he is held liable to the parent for injuries to the minor in spite of the latter's contributory negligence.[91] Similarly one who sells habit forming drugs to a spouse is liable for losses to the other spouse in spite of putative consent.[92] Such cases do not appear to deviate from the general principle which holds that the consortium claim is derived from and rises no higher than the personal injury claim, and in fact liability might with some justice be extended to encompass the personal injury itself on such facts.

Writers, however, have long questioned the derivative liability principle, at least as applied to such matters as contributory negligence.[93] In recent years courts have at times echoed this attitude, holding that the injured person's own fault will not necessarily bar a consortium claim by a family member,[94] or even reduce it under a comparative negligence system, and that a judgment in a personal injury action will not bar a later claim by a family member for consortium.[95] Where these decisions apply, the consortium claim is less "derivative" than it is wholly independent.

Other courts have continued to follow the traditional view that the consortium claim is derivative and stands or falls with the main claim.[96] The conflict that appears to be developing in the cases, however, suggests the need for basic explanations, of which there has been something of a shortage. Courts have commonly said that the consortium ac-

---

87. Sisemore v. Neal, 1963, 236 Ark. 574, 367 S.W.2d 417; Laws v. Fisher, Okl.1973, 513 P.2d 876.

88. Swartz v. United States Steel Corp., 1974, 293 Ala. 439, 304 So.2d 881; Rodriguez v. Bethlehem Steel Corp., 1974, 12 Cal.3d 382, 115 Cal.Rptr. 765, 525 P.2d 669.

89. See supra, p. 932.

90. See Second Restatement of Torts, §§ 694A (negligence of deprived spouse), 704A (negligence of parent).

Negligence of another family member, however, would appear to be irrelevant to the consortium claim as such, though conceivably of importance on other issues, such as contribution or indemnity. See Buckett v. Republic Insurance Co., 1981, 101 Wis.2d 634, 305 N.W.2d 156.

91. Marbury Lumber Co. v. Westbrook, 1898, 121 Ala. 179, 25 So. 914; Hendrickson v. Louisville & Nashville Railroad Co., 1910, 137 Ky. 562, 126 S.W. 117; Seglinski v. Baltimore Copper Smelting & Rolling Co., 1926, 149 Md. 541, 131 A. 774; Haynie v. North Carolina Electric Power Co., 1911, 157 N.C. 503, 73 S.E. 198; Boutotte v. Daigle, 1915, 113 Md. 539, 95 A. 213; Texas & Pacific Railway Co. v. Brick, 1892, 83 Tex. 526, 18 S.W. 947. These cases also hold that the parent's consent to employment in a non-dangerous occupation will not preclude recovery if the employer sets the child to work in a dangerous one, and he is injured as a result.

92. Hoard v. Peck, N.Y.1867, 56 Barb. 202; Holleman v. Harward, 1896, 119 N.C. 150, 25 S.E. 972; Morris v. Owen, 1960, 102 Ga.App. 71, 115 S.E.2d 604; cf. Flandermeyer v. Cooper, 1912, 85 Ohio St. 327, 98 N.E. 102; Moberg v. Scott, 1917, 38 S.D. 422, 161 N.W. 998; Pratt v. Daly, 1940, 55 Ariz. 535, 104 P.2d 147. Compare the parent's action for seduction, supra, pp. 907–08.

93. Gregory, the Contributory Negligence of Plaintiff's Wife or Child in an Action for Loss of Services, 1935, 2 U.Chi.L.Rev. 173; Gregory, Vicarious Responsibility and Contributory Negligence, 1932, 41 Yale L.J. 831; Gilmore, Imputed Negligence, 1921, 1 Wis.L.Rev. 193, 203, 211; James, Imputed Contributory Negligence, 1954, 14 La.L.Rev. 340, 354; Notes, 1926, 21 Mich.L.Rev. 592; 1932, 80 U.Pa.L.Rev. 1128, 1130.

94. Macon v. Seaward Construction Co., 1st Cir. 1977, 555 F.2d 1 (New Hampshire comparative negligence statute); Fuller v. Buhrow, Iowa 1980, 292 N.W.2d 672 (contributory negligence of spouse no bar to consortium claim); Feltch v. General Rental Co., 1981, 383 Mass. 603, 421 N.E.2d 67 (comparative negligence, no reduction); Lantis v. Condon, 1979, 95 Cal. App.3d 152, 157 Cal.Rptr. 22.

95. Scudder v. Seaboard Coast Line Railroad, Fla. 1971, 247 So.2d 46; Reid v. Spadone Machine Co., 1979, 119 N.H. 198, 400 A.2d 54; Sayre v. Davis, 1960, 111 Ohio App. 471, 170 N.E.2d 276.

96. Eggert v. Working, Alaska 1979, 599 P.2d 1389; Nelson v. Busby, 1969, 246 Ark. 247, 437 S.W.2d 799; White v. Lunder, 1975, 66 Wis.2d 563, 225 N.W.2d 442.

tion is derivative and must fall with the main claim, but as they could as well have said that it was independent, this sounds more like a conclusion than a reason, and indeed the courts which hold that the injured person's contributory negligence does not reduce damages in the consortium claim have said exactly that. But it must also be observed that the label "independent action" for the consortium claim is equally a conclusion. One argument given in favor of this more liberal rule is that the consortium claim should be satisfied in spite of fault of the injured person, since otherwise the effect is to impute the negligence of the injured to others in the family.[97] But this argument in turn may be based on the assumption that the consortium claim is in reality independent, which is the very thing the argument is aimed at proving. In the end the reasons for adopting one line of cases or another may turn less on logic than on perceptions of social needs and justice to the parties. In this regard it may be that the cost of supporting not only injury claims but consortium claims which go unreduced by the injured person's fault should be taken into account, as well as the danger of duplicated recoveries.

WESTLAW REFERENCES

Spouses

205k209(3)
205k209(4)

Parent

115k172(2)
117k95(4)
personal +s injur*** /s child! son* daughter* /p "loss of service*"

Child

injur! /p parent* father mother /p child! son* daughter* /s right /s action
"parental consortium"

Defenses

205k326
consortium /p contributory comparative +2 negligence
consortium /p statute +2 limitation*
consortium /s derivative /s personal +3 injur!
work! +s compensation /p exclusive +s remedy /p consortium

---

97. Feltch v. General Rental Co., 1981, 383 Mass. 603, 421 N.E.2d 67.

Chapter 23

SURVIVAL AND WRONGFUL DEATH

Table of Sections

Sec.
125A. Survival and Wrongful Death.
126. Actions Under Survival Statutes.
127. Actions Under Wrongful Death Statutes.

§ 125A. Survival and Wrongful Death

The common law of England enforced three restrictive rules concerning the death of a person in personal injury cases:

1. If the tortfeasor died before the victim recovered for the tort, the victim's right of action died with him.[1]

2. If the victim of a tort himself died (from whatever cause) before he recovered in tort, the victim's right of action also died.[2]

3. If the tortfeasor caused a victim's death, relatives and dependents of the victim who were deprived of financial support or who suffered emotional loss, had no cause of action of their own.[3]

The first two rules were said to be rules about "survival"—the cause of action, though once vested in the tort victim, did not survive either his death or that of the tortfeasor. These rules did not apply to contract actions,[4] or even to all tort actions. Thus actions for damage to or conversion of personalty did survive,[5] and restitution was available to prevent unjust enrichment of a defendant who had received tangible benefits from his tort.[6] But there was no survival of the action after the death of either party in the case of torts against real property, such as trespass,[7] waste,[8] or private nuisance;[9] or those affecting the person, such

---

§ 125A

1. See Smedley, Wrongful Death—Bases of the Common Law Rules, 1960, 13 Vand.L.Rev. 605.

2. Higgins v. Butcher, K.B. 1607, Yelv. 89, 80 Eng. Rep. 61.

3. Baker v. Bolton, N.P. 1808, 1 Camp. 493, 170 Eng.Rep. 1033.

4. See 3 Holdsworth, History of English Law, 3d ed. 1923, 576–585.

5. 4 Edw. III, c. 7; 25 Edw. III, st. 5, c. 5; see Smith v. Colgay, 1595, Cro.Eliz. 384, 78 Eng.Rep. 630; Russell's Case, 1565, 5 Co.Rep. 27a, 77 Eng.Rep. 91.

6. Patton v. Brady, 1902, 184 U.S. 608, 22 S.Ct. 493, 46 L.Ed. 713; Phillips v. Homfray, C.A.1883, 24 Ch.Div. 439; Malone, The Genesis of Wrongful Death, 1965, 17 Stan.L.Rev. 1043, 1046.

7. Sims v. Davis, 1904, 70 S.C. 362, 49 S.E. 872; Reed v. Peoria & Oquawka Railroad Co. 1857, 18 Ill. 403; O'Connor v. Corbitt, 1853, 3 Cal. 370; cf. Johnson v. Elwood, 1880, 82 N.Y. 362 (injunction).

8. Browne v. Blick, 1819, 7 N.C. 511.

9. Grobart v. North Jersey District Water Supply Commission, 1948, 142 N.J.Eq. 60, 58 A.2d 796 (diversion); Holmes v. Moore, 1827, 22 Mass. (5 Pick.) 257 (same); Forist v. Androscoggin River Improvement

as assault and battery,[10] false imprisonment,[11] medical malpractice,[12] or other negligent personal injuries,[13] even though the negligence was a breach of contract.[14] The same was true as to invasions of more intangible interests of personality, such as defamation,[15] malicious prosecution,[16] alienation of affections,[17] seduction[18] or loss of services of a wife or child.[19] Actions for misrepresentation likewise did not survive,[20] but this rule could be avoided by treating them as essentially contractual in nature,[21] or as a deprivation of property,[22] and the same result was sometimes reached as to actions for interference with business relations,[23] or any tort that could be fitted into the desired category.

The third rule was not concerned with the survival of the victim's cause of action. It went much further and denied a cause of action against the tortfeasor to the spouse, child or other dependents of the victim.

Co., 1872, 52 N.H. 477 (flowing); Kennedy v. McAfee's Executrix, 1822, 11 Ky. (1 Litt.) 69 (same).

10. Byrd v. Byrd, 1940, 122 W.Va. 115, 7 S.E.2d 507; Henshaw v. Miller, 1854, 58 U.S. (17 How.) 212, 15 L.Ed. 222; Brown v. Wightman, 1915, 47 Utah 31, 151 P. 366; Hadley v. Bryars' Administrator, 1877, 58 Ala. 185.

11. First National Bank of Portland v. Wall, 1939, 161 Or. 152, 88 P.2d 311; Harker v. Clark, 1881, 57 Cal. 245; Whitten v. Bennett, C.C.Conn.1896, 77 F. 271.

12. Ulvig v. McKennan Hospital, 1930, 56 S.D. 509, 229 N.W. 383; Kuhn v. Brownfield, 1890, 34 W.Va. 252, 12 S.E. 519; Boor v. Lowery, 1885, 103 Ind. 468, 3 N.E. 151; Vittum v. Gilman, 1869, 48 N.H. 416. Actions against attorneys for professional negligence sometimes were held to survive as primarily based on breach of contract. Tichenor v. Hayes, 1879, 41 N.J.L. 193; Miller v. Wilson, 1854, 24 Pa. 114; Stimpson v. Sprague, 1830, 6 Me. 470.

13. Pulling v. Great Eastern R. Co., 1882, L.R. 9 Q.B.D. 110; Herzog v. Stern, 1934, 264 N.Y. 379, 191 N.E. 23, certiorari denied 293 U.S. 597, 55 S.Ct. 112, 79 L.Ed. 690; Brown v. Stephens, 1932, 165 Tenn. 85, 52 S.W.2d 146; Simons v. Kidd, 1949, 73 S.D. 41, 38 N.W.2d 883; Clark v. Goodwin, 1915, 170 Cal. 527, 150 P. 357.

14. The fact that the action is in form one for breach of contract does not affect the result. McClure v. Johnson, 1937, 50 Ariz. 76, 69 P.2d 573 (private transportation); Compton v. Evans, 1939, 200 Wash. 125, 93 P.2d 341 (same); Gosling v. Nichols, 1943, 59 Cal.App.2d 442, 139 P.2d 86 (same); Tuttle v. Short, 1930, 42 Wyo. 1, 288 P. 524 (injury to prisoner action on sheriff's bond); Byrd v. Byrd, 1940, 122 W.Va. 115, 7 S.E.2d 507 (same). See supra, § 92.

15. Begole v. Ferguson, 1941, 299 Mich. 416, 300 N.W. 146; Jones v. Matson, 1940, 4 Wn.2d 659, 104 P.2d 591; Alles v. Interstate Power Co., 1936, 176 Okl. 252, 55 P.2d 751; Miller v. Nuckolls, 1905, 76 Ark. 485, 89 S.W. 88; Blodgett v. Greenfield, 1929, 101 Cal.App. 399, 281 P. 694; Chiagouris v. Jovan, 1963, 43 Ill.App. 2d 220, 193 N.E.2d 205.

16. Meyer v. Peter, 1931, 9 N.J.Misc. 1309, 157 A. 250; Scheirman v. Pemberton, 1932, 180 Okl. 196, 68 P.2d 857; Woodford v. McDaniels, 1914, 73 W.Va. 736, 81 S.E. 544; Lapique v. Dunnigan, 1930, 210 Cal. 281, 291 P. 184; Shedd v. Patterson, 1924, 312 Ill. 371, 144 N.E. 5.

17. Summers v. Boston Safe Deposit Co., 1938, 301 Mass. 167, 16 N.E.2d 670; Howard v. Lunaburg, 1927, 192 Wis. 507, 213 N.W. 301; White v. Safe Deposit & Trust Co. of Baltimore, 1922, 140 Md. 593, 118 A. 77; Gross' Administrator v. Ledford, 1921, 190 Ky. 526, 228 S.W. 24.

18. Brawner v. Sterdevant, 1850, 9 Ga. 69; Shafer v. Grimes, 1867, 23 Iowa 550.

19. State ex rel. National Refining Co. v. Seehorn, 1939, 344 Mo. 547, 127 S.W.2d 418; Gorlitzer v. Wolffberg, 1913, 208 N.Y. 475, 102 N.E. 528; Hey v. Prime, 1908, 197 Mass. 474, 84 N.E. 141; King v. Southern Railway Co., 1906, 126 Ga. 794, 55 S.E. 965. See Note, 1932, 9 N.Y.U.L.Q.Rev. 344.

20. Ahern v. McGlinchy, 1914, 112 Me. 58, 90 A. 709; State ex rel. Baeder v. Blake, 1919, 107 Wash. 294, 181 P. 685; Grabow v. Bergeth, 1930, 59 N.D. 214, 229 N.W. 282; Givens v. Powell, 1921, 239 Mass. 110, 131 N.E. 193; Halsey v. Minnesota-South Carolina Land & Timber Co., E.D.S.C.1932, 54 F.2d 933.

Accord, as to actions of tort or contract for breach of warranty: Harkins v. Provenzo, 1921, 116 Misc. 61, 189 N.Y.S. 258; Bernstein v. Queens County Jockey Club, 1927, 222 App.Div. 191, 225 N.Y.S. 449; Singley v. Bigelow, 1930, 108 Cal.App. 436, 291 P. 899.

Restitution, however, was available where defendant had received tangible benefits. Lufkin v. Cutting, 1917, 225 Mass. 599, 114 N.E. 822.

21. Booth's Administrator v. Northrop, 1858, 27 Conn. 325; Bryant v. Estate of Rich, 1895, 104 Mich. 124, 62 N.W. 146.

22. Vragnizan v. Savings Union Bank & Trust Co., 1916, 31 Cal.App. 709, 161 P. 507; Riedi v. Heinzl, 1942, 240 Wis. 297, 3 N.W.2d 366; Czako v. Orban, 1938, 133 Ohio St. 248, 13 N.E.2d 121; Trust Co. of Norfolk v. Fletcher, 1929, 152 Va. 868, 148 S.E. 785; Zartner v. Holzhauer, 1931, 204 Wis. 18, 234 N.W. 508.

23. Sullivan v. Associated Billposters and Distributors of United States and Canada, 2d Cir. 1925, 6 F.2d 1000, 42 A.L.R. 503; Bethlehem Fabricators v. H. D. Watts Co., 1934, 286 Mass. 556, 190 N.E. 828, 93 A.L.R. 1124. Contra: Caillouet v. American Sugar Refining Co., D.La.1917, 250 F. 639; Jones v. Matson, 1940, 4 Wn.2d 659, 104 P.2d 591.

Thus a child whose parent was negligently killed by the tortfeasor, and who lost his sole means of support and whatever guidance and comfort a parent might provide, had no cause of action at all, with the result that from the defendant's point of view it was cheaper to kill a person than to scratch him.[24]

All three of these rules have now been changed in most American states. The first two rules have been changed by acts known generally as "survival statutes," which permit the cause of action the victim himself owned at the time of tort to survive so that it may be carried on if either the plaintiff or defendant dies. The third rule has been changed by acts generally known as "wrongful death" statutes. The statutes vary in their provisions so that the reader must be referred to the particular acts of each jurisdiction.[25] The sections that follow, therefore, must be limited to very general statements about the nature and operation of the statutes.

WESTLAW REFERENCES

"wrongful death" /s commonlaw /s action cause
cause action /s surviv** /p death /s victim*
  tortfeasor* wrongdoer* /p commonlaw

§ 126. Actions Under Survival Statutes

The historical reasons for the rule that personal tort actions died with the person of either the plaintiff or the defendant are obscure. Probably they derive from a day when little distinction was drawn between tort and crime; death of defendant minimized the capacity of the law to exact punishment, and death of the plaintiff minimized the need to substitute tort damages for vengeance.[1] These grounds have, of course, disappeared with the establishment of tort as a separate branch of law with emphasis on compensation as well as punishment,[2] and by today's standards the defendant's death provides no ground to protect his estate, at least in the case of personal injury torts. It is sometimes argued, however, that if the tort claim is permitted to survive the death of the injured person the heirs get an undeserved windfall, with a concomitant overall cost of liability insurance. Against this it may be said that so far as survival is limited to actual economic loss, the net effect is not to protect the heirs but the creditors.[3] In any event, virtually every state[4] today has some form of survival statute, the exact provisions of which vary but the gist of which is to permit a personal injury action to continue after the death of either the plaintiff or defendant. Federal injury statutes, such as the FELA, make similar provisions.[5]

The survival action, as it is called, is not a new cause of action. It is rather the cause of action held by the decedent immediately before or at death, now transferred to his personal representative.[6] Because the cause of action is not a new one, it is subject to the same defenses that could have been urged

---

24. Most lawyers are familiar with the legend, quite unfounded, that this was the original reason that passengers in Pullman car berths rode with their heads to the front. Also that the fire axes in railroad coaches were provided to enable the conductor to deal efficiently with those were merely injured.

25. See S. Speiser, Recovery for Wrongful Death (2d ed. 1975), Appendix A, listing all statutes.

§ 126

1. See Winfield, Death as Affecting Liability in Tort, 1929, 29 Col.L.Rev. 239; Smedley, Wrongful Death—Bases of the Common Law Rules, 1960, 13 Vand.L.Rev. 605; 3 Holdsworth, History of English Law, 3d ed. 1923, 333–336, 576–585, 676–677; Pollock, Law of Torts, 12th ed. 1923, 66–72; Holdsworth Origin of the Rule in Baker v. Bolton, 1916, 32 L.Q.Rev. 431;

Evans, Survival of Claims For and Against Executors and Administrators, 1931, 19 Ky.L.J. 195; Note, 1929, 18 Cal.L.Rev. 44.

2. There is a good discussion of the history of this matter, and the shift to compensation purposes, in Thompson v. Estate of Petroff, Minn.1982, 319 N.W.2d 400.

3. See Moyer v. Phillips, 1975, 462 Pa. 395, 341 A.2d 441, 77 A.L.R.3d 1339.

4. See S. Speiser, 2d ed. 1975, Recovery for Wrongful Death, App. A, listing all statutes.

5. 45 U.S.C.A. § 59.

6. Barragan v. Superior Court of Pima County, 1970, 12 Ariz.App. 402, 470 P.2d 722; DeHerrera v. Herrera, Wyo.1977, 565 P.2d 479.

against the decedent had he lived and brought the claim.[7] By the same token, unless the statute limits damages, the recovery is the same one the decedent would have been entitled to at death, and thus includes such items as wages lost[8] after injury and before death,[9] medical expenses incurred,[10] and pain and suffering.[11] The pain and suffering recovery on behalf of the estate, however, is clearly a windfall to the heirs and a respectable number of states explicitly exclude such damages in the survival action.[12] Some states also exclude punitive or exemplary damages.[13]

Although some statutes are very general in providing for survival of most tort actions, perhaps the greatest number exclude certain torts, particularly those involving intangible interests in personality, such as defamation.[14] There is, on the other hand, some tendency to extend survival statutes,[15] or to construe them liberally to preserve a cause of action where there is doubt,[16] and some authority has gone further, holding that a survival statute may not arbitrarily retain the common law rule against survival in particular cases, such as those involving libel[17] or intentional torts,[18] and that a statute of this kind is unconstitutional as a violation of equal protection, with the result that such claims survive and provide a basis for recovery in spite of the narrow statute. Under most statutes, the cause of death is not significant and the action will survive whether or not the death was the result of the defendant's tort or entirely independent of it.[19] Under a few statutes, however, if death results from the tort, there is no survival and any claim must be made on behalf of beneficiaries of the wrongful death action.[20] Some courts have also imposed a special limitation to the effect that there is no action to survive at all if death is instantaneous.[21]

7. Carney v. Barnett, D.Pa.1967, 278 F.Supp. 572 (statute of limitations); Wise v. George C. Rothwell, Inc., D.Del.1974, 382 F.Supp. 563 (contributory negligence).

8. Roundtree v. Technical Welding and Fabrication Co., La.App.1978, 364 So.2d 1325, writ denied 367 So.2d 389; Rodgers v. Ferguson, App.1976, 89 N.M. 688, 556 P.2d 844, certiorari denied 90 N.M. 7, 558 P.2d 619.

9. In a few states earnings that would have been income to the decedent but for the death will be recoverable for his life expectancy, with a deduction for living or family expenses. See Haw.Stats. § 663–8; Note, 47 Wash.L.Rev. 690. Since future expected earnings is the fund from which wrongful death proceeds are calculated in part, there is at least some risk of duplicated recovery. See below p. 955.

10. Roundtree v. Technical Welding and Fabrication Co., La.App.1978, 364 So.2d 1325, writ denied 367 So.2d 389; Plank v. Heirigs, 1968, 83 S.D. 173, 156 N.W.2d 193. See Imel v. Travelers Indemnity Co., 1972, 152 Ind.App. 75, 281 N.E.2d 919.

11. Gaudette v. Webb, 1972, 362 Mass. 60, 284 N.E.2d 222; Landreth v. Reed, Tex.Civ.App.1978, 570 S.W.2d 486.

12. E.g., Ariz.Rev.Stats. § 14–477; Wash.Rev.Code Ann. § 4.20.046.

13. E.g., Colo.Rev.Stats. § 153–1–9; Idaho Code Ann. § 5–327.

14. E.g., Ky.Rev.Stats. § 411.140 (slander, libel, criminal conversation,) and parts of malicious prosecution action); N.C.Gen.Stat. § 28–175 (libel, slander, false imprisonment).

15. Ivey v. Wiggins, 1964, 276 Ala. 106, 159 So.2d 618 (wrongful death action survives death of defendant). See Miller, Dead People in Torts, 1972, 22 Cath. U.L.Rev. 73.

16. See Harrison v. Loyal Protective Life Insurance Co., 1979, 379 Mass. 212, 396 N.E.2d 987 (infliction of mental distress is "harm to person" within meaning of survival statute and action thus survives); McDaniel v. Bullard, 1966, 34 Ill.2d 487, 216 N.E.2d 140 (infant's claim for wrongful death of her parents survived infant's death and could be prosecuted by administrator; claim considered "property" within meaning of survival statute); Weller v. Home News Publishing Co., 1970, 112 N.J.Super. 502, 271 A.2d 738 (privacy claim survives under statute authorizing survival of "trespass" claims).

17. Moyer v. Phillips, 1975, 462 Pa. 395, 341 A.2d 441, 77 A.L.R.3d 1339.

18. Thompson v. Estate of Petroff, Minn.1982, 319 N.W.2d 400.

19. Murphy v. Martin Oil Co., 1974, 56 Ill.2d 423, 308 N.E.2d 583 (tortious injury caused death); DeHerrera v. Herrera, Wyo.1977, 565 P.2d 479 (death independent of tortious injury).

20. E.g., Rev.Stat.Mo. § 537.020. See Semler v. Psychiatric Institute of Washington, D.C., D.C.Cir. 1978, 575 F.2d 922, 925 (discussing Virginia law).

21. Benson v. Lynch, D.Del.1975, 404 F.Supp. 8. But consciousness may be inferred and substantial awards made for short periods. E.g., Landreth v. Reed, Tex.Civ.App.1978, 570 S.W.2d 486 (child drowned, conscious pain inferred, $30,000); Haynes v. Monroe Plumbing and Heating Co., 1973, 48 Mich.App.

Substantial development of federal statutory torts in recent years, led by litigation of constitutional and civil rights torts, has generated survival problems peculiar to the federal tort. Some federal statutory torts provide explicitly for survival,[22] and certain civil rights statutes appear to do the same.[23] Other federal statutes seem to make no provision for survival either way,[24] but where the statute, though in some sense protecting against discrimination, is also protecting economic rights, as in the case of job discrimination or interference, the action might be thought to survive as a matter of common law if not as a matter of clear federal policy.[25] A third group of statutes contains no survival provision itself but refers to state law to fill gaps of this kind.[26] Rights asserted under this group of statutes, for instance claims based on interference with constitutional rights of the plaintiff, either survive or not according to whether a similar action would survive under state law, though of course a state law denying survival would not be permitted to conflict with federal statutory purpose.[27] Likewise, a state survival statute that limited damages in a way that failed to protect federally guaranteed rights would presumably give way to the superior federal purposes.[28] In addition to these complexities there is an entirely separate action available against federal officers, not grounded in statute but based directly on the constitution, for violation thereof.[29] Quite arguably such claims would survive the death of either party even if state law would abate similar claims.[30]

The traditional view makes survival of an action the test of its assignability, so that if the claim is the kind that survives, it may be assigned by the injured party to another person, otherwise not.[31] It has also been held that if the claim is known to be assignable, it will also survive.[32] Some courts, however, have rejected this tandem approach, insisting that the policies behind assignability and survival are quite different, and in such

707, 211 N.W.2d 88 ("from the time he was scalded by the steam until the moment he struck the floor. * * * ").

22. As in the Federal Employers' Liability Act, 45 U.S.C.A. § 59. See S. Speiser, 2d ed. 1975, Recovery for Wrongful Death, App. A.

23. 42 U.S.C.A. § 1986 (one having knowledge of conspiracies prohibited by § 1985 and who does nothing, "shall be liable to the party injured, or his legal representatives. * * * ").

24. E.g., 42 U.S.C.A. § 2000e-5(g) (employment discrimination); 42 U.S.C.A. § 3616 (Fair housing). Some general provisions of these statutes might be construed broadly to refer to state survival laws, see 42 U.S.C.A. § 2000e-7 and 42 U.S.C.A. § 3615, but a federal survival policy might be preferable.

25. See Barnes Coal Corp. v. Retail Coal Merchants Association, 4th Cir. 1942, 128 F.2d 645 (antitrust statutes, common law survival); Layne v. International Brotherhood of Electrical Workers, D.S.C.1976, 418 F.Supp. 964 (union member's claim against union under Landrum-Griffin Act, survival).

26. A number of major civil rights statutes are covered by 42 U.S.C.A. § 1988, which provides that state laws are to be used, when consistent with the statutory purposes, to fill the gaps and deficiencies in the federal statutes.

27. Robertson v. Wegmann, 1978, 436 U.S. 584, 98 S.Ct. 1991, 56 L.Ed.2d 554, on remand 5th Cir., 591 F.2d 1208 (fact that particular action abates is not inconsistent with general purpose of federal statutes, state statute abating action applied).

28. See Robertson v. Wegmann, 1978, 436 U.S. 584, 98 S.Ct. 1991, 56 L.Ed.2d 554, on remand 5th Cir., 591 F.2d 1208; Espinoza v. O'Dell, Colo.1981, 633 P.2d 455, case dismissed 456 U.S. 430, 102 S.Ct. 1865, 72 L.Ed.2d 237 (state wrongful death statute's damages inadequate to secure federally guaranteed interests and would not be used as a limit on recovery; survival statute's limits presented no conflict and would be upheld.)

29. Bivens v. Six Unknown Named Agents of Federal Bureau of Narcotics, 1971, 403 U.S. 388, 91 S.Ct. 1999, 29 L.Ed.2d 619. See Dellinger, Of Rights and Remedies: The Constitution as a Sword, 1972, 85 Harv. L.Rev. 1532.

30. See Green v. Carlson, 7th Cir. 1978, 581 F.2d 669, affirmed 446 U.S. 14, 100 S.Ct. 1468, 64 L.Ed.2d 15 (death allegedly resulted from constitutional violation, application of state statute would bar the claim and defeat federal policy, action survives). A federal judge-made law of survival is supported in Barnes Coal Corp. v. Retail Coal Merchants Association, 4th Cir. 1942, 128 F.2d 645 (antitrust).

31. Jolly v. General Accident Group., D.S.C.1974, 382 F.Supp. 265; Davenport v. State Farm Mutual Automobile Insurance Co., 1965, 81 Nev. 361, 404 P.2d 10. See Annot., 40 A.L.R.2d 500.

32. McGill v. Lazzaro, 1978, 62 Ill.App.3d 151, 19 Ill. Dec. 501, 379 N.E.2d 16, appeal after remand 92 Ill. App.3d 393, 48 Ill.Dec. 134, 416 N.E.2d 29.

courts the two questions are independent of one another.³³

 WESTLAW REFERENCES

"survival statute*" /p limit* limitation* exclud** except*** /p recover*** damage* pain suffering
surviv! /s action /s abate! /s death
"survival statute*" /p "wrongful death"
federal +s statut*** tort* /p survivor** /p death /p cause action
117k10
117k31
170bk401
38k24(1)

§ 127. Actions Under Wrongful Death Statutes

The common law not only denied a tort recovery for injury once the tort victim had died,¹ it also refused to recognize any new and independent cause of action in the victim's dependents or heirs for their own loss at his death.² Possibly such an action might once have been maintained,³ but in 1808 Lord Ellenborough, perhaps in line with the understanding of the time,⁴ held that a husband had no action for loss of his wife's services through her death, and declared in broad terms that "in a civil court the death of a human being could not be complained of as an injury." ⁵ The decision was accepted and followed, not without dissent, in England,⁶ and notwithstanding a good start to the contrary,⁷ in the United States.⁸

The result was that it was cheaper for the defendant to kill the plaintiff than to injure him, and that the most grievous of all injuries left the bereaved family of the victim, who frequently were destitute, without a remedy. Since this was intolerable, it was changed in England by the passage of the Fatal Accidents Act ⁹ of 1846, otherwise known as Lord Campbell's Act, which has become a generic name for similar statutes. Every American state now has a statutory remedy for wrongful death.¹⁰ Federal statutes provide for wrongful death recoveries in particular situations,¹¹ and special agree-

---

33. Southern Farm Bureau Casualty v. Wright Oil Co., 1970, 248 Ark. 803, 454 S.W.2d 69; Harleysville Mutual Insurance Co. v. Lea, 1966, 2 Ariz.App. 538, 410 P.2d 495. In the Southern Farm Bureau case, supra, Justice George Rose Smith stated: "[W]henever courts have explored the policy considerations pertinent to the issue, they have held—without exception, we think—that survivability of personal injury claims does not attract assignability in its wake."

§ 127

1. Supra, p. 940.

2. See Holdsworth, The Origin of the Rule in Baker v. Bolton, 1916, 32 L.Q.Rev. 431; 3 Holdsworth, History of English Law, 3d Ed. 1923, 331–336; Malone, The Genesis of Wrongful Death, 1965, 17 Stan.L.Rev. 1043; Winfield, Death as Affecting Liability in Tort, 1929, 29 Col.L.Rev. 239; Hay, Death as a Civil Cause of Action in Massachusetts, 1893, 7 Harv.L.Rev. 170; Smedley, Wrongful Death—Bases of the Common Law Rules, 1960, 13 Vand.L.Rev. 605.

3. Winfield, Death as Affecting Liability in Tort, 1929, 29 Col.L.Rev. 239, 252.

4. See Finkelstein, The Goring Ox: Some Historical Perspectives on Deodands, Forfeitures, Wrongful Death and the Western Notion of Sovereignty, 46 Temp.L.Q. 169 (1973).

5. Baker v. Bolton, 1808, 1 Camp. 493, 170 Eng.Rep. 1033.

6. Osborn v. Gillett, 1873, L.R. 8 Exch. 88; Clark v. London General Omnibus Co., [1906], 2 K.B. 648; Admiralty Comm'rs v. S. S. Amerika, [1917] A.C. 38.

7. Ford v. Monroe, N.Y.1838, 20 Wend. 210; Cross v. Guthery, Conn.1794, 2 Root 90; Shields v. Yonge, 1854, 15 Ga. 349. See Malone, American Fatal Accident Statutes—The Legislative Birth Pains, [1965] Duke L.J. 673; Hay, Death as a Civil Cause of Action in Massachusetts, 1893, 7 Harv.L.Rev. 170; Signor, Action for Death by Wrongful Act at Common Law and Under the New York Statute, 1905, 67 Albany, L.J. 133.

8. Mobile Life Insurance Co. v. Brame, 1877, 95 U.S. 754, 24 L.Ed. 580; Jackson v. Pittsburgh, Cincinnati, Chicago & St. Louis Railway Co., 1894, 140 Ind. 241, 39 N.E. 663; Major v. Burlington Cedar Rapids & Northern Railroad Co., 1902, 115 Iowa 309, 88 N.W. 815; Kennedy v. Davis, 1911, 171 Ala. 609, 55 So. 104; Perham v. Portland General Electric Co., 1898, 33 Or. 451, 53 P. 14, 24, rehearing denied 33 Or. 451, 53 P. 24.

9. 9 & 10 Vict. c. 93. See Laughton-Scott, The Fatal Accidents Act, 1954, 9 Ind.L.Q.Rev. 5.

10. An excellent text is Speiser, Recovery for Wrongful Death (2d ed. 1975).

11. FELA, 45 U.S.C.A. § 51–60 (railroad employees in interstate commerce); Jones Act, 46 U.S.C.A. § 688 (seamen); Death on the High Seas Act, 46 U.S.C.A. §§ 761–768 (any person more than a maritime league from shore). Some federal rights may carry their own death statute, see 42 U.S.C.A. § 1986, or may permit use of state death statutes for vindication, see 42 U.S.

ments govern international air travel deaths.[12] In addition, the United States Supreme Court has created a judge-made cause of action for wrongful death in Admiralty.[13] Most statutes were modeled on Lord Campbell's Act, a "death" action creating a new cause of action in favor of a representative and for the benefit of certain designated persons, usually those most likely to have suffered a loss from the victim's death. Other statutes, a minority,[14] sought to accomplish a similar result by expanding the survival statute to include damages resulting from the victim's death as well as damages accrued at the moment he died. The chief difference between the pure death statute and the expanded survival statute lies in the methods of computing damages and in the distribution of the recovery,[15] but the aim of both kinds of statute is similar. A third kind of statute, now in force only in Alabama, is interpreted to be penal in character, and damages are based on the culpability of the defendant rather than on losses to the estate or to the survivors.[16] Finally, other statutes may supersede tort liability for death, as in the case of workers' compensation statutes for injuries arising out of and in the course of employment,[17] or may supplement tort liability for death, as in the case of social security benefits.[18]

The wrongful death statutes usually provide that the action can be maintained for "any wrongful act, neglect or default" which causes death. They are therefore held to cover intentional, as well as negligent, torts.[19] Recovery for wrongful death has also been allowed on the basis of strict liability, both in cases of abnormally dangerous activities[20] and in cases of defective products,[21] as well as in Admiralty under the unseaworthiness doctrine.[22] The conventional understanding, based on a small number of cases, has been that wrongful death statutes do not authorize recovery for a simple breach of contract, even though that breach causes death.[23] On this basis some courts have held there can be no claim for death resulting from a defective product and based

C.A. § 1988. There is a judge-made right to recover for death in Admiralty under Moragne v. States Marine Lines, Inc., 1970, 398 U.S. 375, 90 S.Ct. 1772, 26 L.Ed. 2d 339, on remand 5th Cir., 446 F.2d 906.

12. The Warsaw Convention, 49 Stat. 3000, originally set limits on damages at about $8,000. Subsequent agreements have raised the limits. See S. Speiser, Recovery for Wrongful Death, 2d ed. 1975, §§ 7.5–7.6.

13. Moragne v. States Marine Lines, Inc., 1970, 398 U.S. 375, 90 S.Ct. 1772, 26 L.Ed.2d 339, on remand 5th Cir., 446 F.2d 906. The basis for and subsequent history of this claim are concisely stated in Maraist, Maritime Wrongful Death—Higginbotham Reverses Trend and Creates New Questions, 1978, 39 La.L.Rev. 81.

14. The statutes are classified in Comment, 1966, 44 N.C.L.Rev. 401. Earlier classifications may be found in Rose, Foreign Enforcement of Actions for Wrongful Death, 1935, 33 Mich.L.Rev. 545; Note, 39 Iowa L.Rev. 494.

15. See pp. 949–951 below.

16. See Louisville & Nashville Railroad v. Bogue, 1912, 177 Ala. 349, 58 So. 392; Eich v. Gulf Shores, 1974, 293 Ala. 95, 300 So.2d 354. Massachusetts used a penal statute until its revision in 1974. See S. Speiser, Recovery for Wrongful Death, 2d ed. 1975, § 3.3.

One result of the punitive theory of wrongful death damages is to complicate the possible recovery in death actions against the United States, which is not liable for punitive damages. The Federal Tort Claims Act now provides a special federal rule of damages for cases which, otherwise, would be governed by Alabama law and under which recovery would be denied. 28 U.S.C.A. § 2674. However, where suit is not under the FTCA but under some other statute, all recovery may be denied, since the only recovery permitted would be punitive. See Painter v. TVA, 5th Cir. 1973, 476 F.2d 943.

17. See A. Larsen, Workmen's Compensation Law § 64.00.

18. 42 U.S.C.A. § 402; H. McCormick, 2d ed. 1978, Social Security Claims and Procedures §§ 351–370.

19. Welch v. Creech, 1915, 88 Wash. 429, 153 P. 355; Tucker v. State, 1899, 89 Md. 471, 43 A. 778, 44 A. 1004; Suell v. Derricott, 1909, 161 Ala. 259, 49 So. 895; Howard's Administrator v. Hunter, 1907, 126 Ky. 685, 104 S.W. 723; Kling v. Torello, 1913, 87 Conn. 301, 87 A. 987.

20. Sullivan v. Dunham, 1900, 161 N.Y. 290, 55 N.E. 923.

21. Often without discussing the question. Pike v. Frank G. Hough, 1970, 2 Cal.3d 465, 85 Cal.Rptr. 629, 467 P.2d 229; Melia v. Ford Motor Co., 8th Cir. 1976, 534 F.2d 795; Keener v. Dayton Electric Manufacturing Co., Mo.1969, 445 S.W.2d 362 (explicit discussion).

22. Landry v. Two R. Drilling Co., 5th Cir. 1975, 517 F.2d 675.

23. Barley's Administratrix v. Clover Splint Coal Co., 1941, 286 Ky. 218, 150 S.W.2d 670; Annot., 86 A.L.R.2d 316.

on a warranty theory.[24] But if a contract is made to assure or enhance personal safety and death results from its breach, there may well be a tort as well as a breach of contract, so that the death action will lie,[25] as indeed it should whether the claim is called tort or contract.[26] The breach of warranty claims, which have been the source of most of the "contract" litigation in contemporary death cases, have taken this direction and there is now a substantial body of authority permitting the death action on warranty grounds as well as on grounds of strict tort liability.[27]

Plaintiff and Beneficiaries

Under survival acts the proper plaintiff is of course the executor or administrator of the plaintiff's estate. Under the death acts the action usually is to be brought by such a representative, or by an administrator appointed by the court for the purpose of bringing it, where there is no other estate;[28] but under many of the statutes some one or more of those who are to benefit by recovery may sue.[29] It is usually held, however, that only one action can be brought and that any claimant not joined or named is barred.[30]

The beneficiaries frequently are designated by the act, in accordance with the purpose of compensating members of the family who might have expected to receive support or assistance from the deceased if he had lived. Lord Campbell's Act, for example, specified that the action was for the benefit of the husband, wife, parent or child, and many of the American acts have limited it to a similar restricted group.[31] Since the wrongful death acts usually designate beneficiaries by class, such as "spouse," "heirs," or "children," they preclude recovery by those who actually suffer loss but who fall outside the named group. A live-in lover, for example, is neither spouse nor heir, and though utterly dependent upon the decedent cannot recover as a member of those classes.[32] In this regard the death statutes stand in sharp contrast to many workers' compensation acts, which often permit recovery by any actual dependent of the decedent.[33] The problem is not limited to live-in lovers, and recovery may be denied to wholly dependent brothers or sisters or even to unadopted step-children, neither of which fit in categories adopted by many statutes.[34] So far as these statutory classifications ex-

24. The precise wording of the wrongful death statute may be critical. See Higginbotham v. Ford Motor Co., 5th Cir. 1976, 540 F.2d 762, rehearing denied 561 F.2d 831 ("criminal or other negligence" in Georgia statute excludes warranty claim); McCullough v. Beech Aircraft Corp., 5th Cir. 1979, 587 F.2d 754 (Mississippi death statute allowed warranty claim on items for human consumption only).

25. Braun v. Riel, Mo.1931, 40 S.W.2d 621, 80 A.L.R. 875; Mueller v. Winston Brothers Co., 1931, 165 Wash. 130, 4 P.2d 854; Pearlman v. Garrod Shoe Co., 1937, 276 N.Y. 172, 11 N.E.2d 718; Thaggard v. Vafes, 1928, 218 Ala. 609, 119 So. 647; Earley v. Pacific Electric Railway Co., 1917, 176 Cal. 79, 167 P. 513.

26. A contract or warranty not involving personal safety, that is, a commercial agreement or an economic one only, would not provide a basis for liability for death any more than it would provide a basis for liability for personal injury. The reason lies in the scope of the obligation, not in the death statute.

27. Greco v. S. S. Kresge Co., 1938, 277 N.Y. 26, 12 N.E.2d 557; Schnabl v. Ford Motor Co., 1972, 54 Wis. 2d 345 195 N.W.2d 602, rehearing denied 54 Wis.2d 345, 198 N.W.2d 161; Notes, 4 Cum.Sam.L.Rev. 658; 22 Bay.L.Rev. 384, 51 Iowa L.Rev. 1010, 29 Mer.L.Rev. 649; 4 St. Mary's L.Rev. 277; 39 Temp.L.Rev. 352.

28. Hartford & New Haven Railroad Co. v. Andrews, 1869, 36 Conn. 213; Reutenik v. Gibson Packing Co., 1934, 132 Wash. 108, 231 P. 773.

29. Nunez v. Nunez, 1976, 25 Ariz.App. 558, 545 P.2d 69 (spouse to bring suit under statute for self and children, but illegitimate children must be permitted to assert their claims as well); Cummins v. Woody, 1941, 177 Tenn. 636, 152 S.W.2d 246.

30. See Helling v. Lew, 1972, 28 Cal.App.3d 434, 104 Cal.Rptr. 789; Muzychuk to Use and Benefit of Burns v. Yellow Cab Co., 1941, 343 Pa. 335, 22 A.2d 670.

31. See S. Speiser, Recovery for Wrongful Death, 2d ed. 1975, §§ 10.1–10.21.

32. Aspinall v. McDonnell Douglas Corp., 9th Cir. 1980, 625 F.2d 325; Cassano v. Durham, 1981, 180 N.J. Super. 620, 436 A.2d 118.

33. See, e.g., Ore-Ida Foods, Inc., v. Indian Head Cattle Co., 1981, 290 Or. 909, 627 P.2d 469 (live-in not married to decedent could recover workers' compensation benefits but could not recover in tort against negligent third party). As to compensation statutes generally see A. Larson, Workmen's Compensation Law § 62.10.

34. Blom v. United Air Lines, Inc., 1963, 152 Colo. 486, 382 P.2d 993 (wholly dependent sister); Klossner

clude illegitimate children solely because of illegitimacy, they have been held unconstitutional as a denial of equal protection.[35] But so far as they exclude legitimate dependents they have been upheld as against constitutional attack.[36] It is thus possible that a relative who had never met the decedent will recover, or that no one will,[37] while a dependent who suffers a serious loss goes uncompensated.

The statutes typically protect the wrongful death award, as distinct from the survival award, from the decedent's creditors,[38] and it follows that if there is no designated beneficiary living at the time of the wrongful death, the action fails since there is no one entitled to compensation.[39]

If the sole beneficiary, or all of the beneficiaries, die after the decease of the person wrongfully killed, but before action is begun, or even after commencement of the action but before judgment,[40] there is authority to the effect that the action does not survive to the beneficiary's estate. Probably the prevailing view is that the cause of action vests in the beneficiary immediately upon the wrongful death, becomes his property, and survives to his representative.[41] Where the statute sets up a primary and secondary class of beneficiaries a similar question arises when the primary beneficiary dies,[42] or is guilty of negligence that would bar his claim,[43] or has no pecuniary loss of the kind required to give him standing to sue.[44] In this situation the courts are again divided,[45] some holding that the action passes to beneficiaries in the secondary class,[46] others holding that the action fails entire-

v. San Juan County, 1980, 93 Wn.2d 42, 605 P.2d 330 (step-children); Aymond v. State Through Department of Highways, La.App.1976, 333 So.2d 380, writ denied 337 So.2d 875 (same). But in Chausse v. Southland Corp., La.App.1981, 400 So.2d 1199, writ denied 404 So.2d 278 recovery was allowed to both the adoptive father and to the natural mother, who had given up custody.

In Crystal v. Hubbard, 1981, 414 Mich. 297, 324 N.W.2d 869 the court held that siblings of the decedent could recover for lost companionship, even though there was a surviving spouse and parents who were the immediate next of kin.

35. Levy v. Louisiana, 1968, 391 U.S. 68, 88 S.Ct. 1509, 20 L.Ed.2d 436, rehearing denied 393 U.S. 898, 89 S.Ct. 65, 21 L.Ed.2d 185, on remand 253 La. 73, 216 So.2d 818; Weber v. Aetna Casualty & Surety Co., 1972, 406 U.S. 164, 92 S.Ct. 1400, 31 L.Ed.2d 768 (workers' compensation). Likewise, a parent must be permitted to sue for death of an illegitimate child, Glona v. American Guarantee & Liability Insurance Co., 1968, 391 U.S. 73, 88 S.Ct. 1515, 20 L.Ed.2d 441, rehearing denied 393 U.S. 898, 89 S.Ct. 66, 21 L.Ed.2d 185, though a state may constitutionally vest the right of action in the mother only and exclude the father from recovery. Parham v. Hughes, 1979, 441 U.S. 347, 99 S.Ct. 1742, 60 L.Ed.2d 269. The illegitimate child's action will probably be permitted for the wrongful death of either the mother or the father. See Jordan v. Delta Drilling Co., Wyo.1975, 541 P.2d 39.

36. Steed v. Imperial Airlines, 1974, 12 Cal.3d 115, 115 Cal.Rptr. 329, 524 P.2d 801, appeal dismissed 420 U.S. 916, 95 S.Ct. 1108, 43 L.Ed.2d 387.

37. If the statute permits recovery only to spouses, heirs and next-of-kin, and decedent is survived by a wholly dependent step-child and a wholly independent brother, the step-child has damages but cannot recover. The brother is in the category for recovery but has no damages. If such a statute is constitutional, the court may allow the brother to recover for the child's loss, or may deny recovery altogether.

38. Sonner v. Cordano, D.Nev.1963, 228 F.Supp. 435; State v. Cambria, 1951, 137 Conn. 604, 80 A.2d 516.

39. Collins v. Becnel, La.App.1974, 297 So.2d 510, writ refused 300 So.2d 842; Pittock v. Gardner, Mo. 1975, 530 S.W.2d 217 (only beneficiary had no pecuniary loss, no action).

40. Danis v. New York Central Railroad Co., 1954, 160 Ohio St. 474, 117 N.E.2d 39, 43 A.L.R.2d 1286; Pedroli v. Missouri Pacific Railway Co., Mo.App.1975, 524 S.W.2d 882.

41. Schneider v. Baisch, N.D.1977, 256 N.W.2d 370; Adams v. Sparacio, 1973, 156 W.Va. 678, 196 S.E.2d 647; Willis v. Duke Power Co., 1979, 42 N.C.App. 582, 257 S.E.2d 471, 13 A.L.R. 4th 1047.

42. See Shipley v. Daly, 1939, 106 Ind.App. 443, 20 N.E.2d 653 (once right accrues to widow it cannot pass on her death to another class of beneficiary).

43. Cote v. Martel, 1960, 103 N.H. 110, 165 A.2d 590 (spouse was primary beneficiary, his negligence barred him, no claim for children, who were secondary beneficiaries).

44. Missouri-Kansas-Texas Railway Co. v. Canada, 1928, 130 Okl. 171, 265 P. 1045 (primary beneficiaries had no pecuniary loss, secondary beneficiary did and could sue).

45. See the detailed coverage of these points in S. Speiser, Recovery for Wrongful Death, 2d ed. 1975, §§ 8.17–8.21.

46. Rushton v. Smith, 1958, 233 S.C. 292, 104 S.E.2d 376; Collins v. Gee, 1978, 82 Wis.2d 376, 263 N.W.2d 158.

ly.⁴⁷ Where the wrongful death action is permitted to survive the death of the beneficiary and is vested in his estate, damages are usually limited to those accrued up to the beneficiary's death.⁴⁸ Florida has refined this further by holding that the beneficiary's mental anguish can furnish no item of damages to his estate.⁴⁹ Where the death action passes from the primary beneficiary to a secondary class of beneficiaries, the damages suffered by the primary beneficiary become irrelevant and the recovery is for damages that are personal to the class which recovers.⁵⁰ On the same basis, the death of a beneficiary of a particular class does not affect the rights of others of the same class, who will claim their own damages.⁵¹

The older rule was that the action for wrongful death did not survive the death of the tortfeasor himself.⁵² This now appears to have been put aside by statute or decision in the great majority of jurisdictions, so that the plaintiff's right is not lost by the tortfeasor's death, provided the tortfeasor outlived the decedent.⁵³ Probably the same result should be reached where the tortfeasor dies first, though the cases of this sort may be regarded as more difficult.⁵⁴

Damages

The damages recoverable for death present a large topic, which lies beyond the scope of this text.⁵⁵ Brief mention may be made of some of its more salient features. The basis of recovery will of course depend upon the theory of the action, as to those who are to benefit by it. Under Lord Campbell's Act and the great majority of the death acts the action proceeds on the theory of compensating the individual beneficiaries for loss of the economic benefit which they might reasonably have expected to receive from the decedent in the form of support, services or contributions during the remainder of his lifetime if he had not been killed.⁵⁶

A handful of states, consistent with the expanded survival type of death action, base

---

47. Ondrey v. Shellmar Products Corp., N.D.Ind. 1955, 131 F.Supp. 542; Chicago, Burlington & Quincy Railroad Co. v. Wells-Dickey Trust Co., 1927, 275 U.S. 161, 48 S.Ct. 73, 72 L.Ed. 216; White v. Atchison, Topeka & Santa Fe Railway Co., 1928, 125 Kan. 537, 265 P. 73; Wilcox v. Warren Construction Co., 1920, 95 Or. 125, 186 P. 13; Hammond v. Lewiston, Augusta & Waterville Street Railway, 1909, 106 Me. 209, 76 A. 672.

48. Adams v. Sparacio, 1973, 156 W.Va. 678, 196 S.E.2d 647; Schneider v. Baisch, N.D.1977, 256 N.W.2d 370.

49. Clarklift, Inc. v. Reutimann, Fla.App.1975, 323 So.2d 640, certiorari denied 336 So.2d 1181, 341 So.2d 293.

50. Jenkins v. Midland Valley Railroad Co., 1918, 134 Ark. 1, 203 S.W. 1; Bagley v. City of St. Louis, 1916, 268 Mo. 259, 186 S.W. 966.

51. Holt v. Stollenwerck, 1911, 174 Ala. 213, 56 So. 912; Fitzgerald v. Edison Electric Illuminating Co., 1903, 207 Pa. 118, 56 A. 350; Heald v. Wallace, 1902, 109 Tenn. 346, 71 S.W. 80; Taylor v. Western Pacific Railway Co., 1873, 45 Cal. 323.

52. Mennemeyer v. Hart, 1949, 359 Mo. 423, 221 S.W.2d 960; Ickes v. Brimhall, 1938, 42 N.M. 412, 79 P.2d 942.

53. Meads v. Dibble, 1960, 10 Utah 2d 229, 350 P.2d 853; Fish v. Liley, 1949, 120 Colo. 156, 208 P.2d 930; Kuhnle v. Swedlund, 1945, 220 Minn. 573, 20 N.W.2d 396; Ivey v. Wiggins, 1964, 276 Ala. 106, 159 So.2d 618; Putnam v. Savage, 1923, 244 Mass. 83, 138 N.E.

808. Some states have special provisions for survival. See Evans, Survival of the Action for Death by Wrongful Act, 1933, 1 U.Chi.L.Rev. 102; Notes, 1950, 22 Rocky Mt.L.Rev. 99; 1929, 13 Minn.L.Rev. 632. Some 38 statutes are listed as supporting recovery in addition to a number of court decisions in S. Speiser, Recovery for Wrongful Death, 2d ed. 1974, § 8.15.

54. See Notes, 48 Harv.L.Rev. 1008; 38 Mich.L. Rev. 907 (arguing that the wrongful act, not the death of plaintiff's decedent, is the basis of liability).

55. See Russel, Measure of Damages Under Missouri Wrongful Death Act, 1950, 15 Mo.L.Rev. 31; Duffey, The Maldistribution of Damages in Wrongful Death, 1958, 19 Ohio St.L.J. 264; Duffey, Life Expectancy and Loss of Earning Capacity, 1958, 19 Ohio St. L.J. 314; Bostwick, Wrongful Death and Rightful Damages, 1967, 2 Land & Water Rev. 405; Notes, 1948, 28 Bos.U.L.Rev. 368; 1963, 48 Iowa L.Rev. 666; 1966, 44 N.C.L.Rev. 402; 1967, 19 S.C.L.Rev. 220.

56. Michigan Central Railroad v. Vreeland, 1912, 227 U.S. 59, 33 S.Ct. 192, 57 L.Ed. 417; Martin v. Mansfeldt, 1950, 100 Cal.App.2d 327, 223 P.2d 501; Thoirs v. Pounsford, 1941, 210 Minn. 462, 299 N.W. 16; Goodyear Yellow Pine Co. v. Anderson, 1934, 171 Miss. 530, 157 So. 700.

It is sometimes said that income from decedent's investments is not to be included, but pension benefits and the like, if lost by reason of death, may be considered. Bryant v. Woodlief, 1960, 252 N.C. 488, 114 S.E.2d 241, 81 A.L.R.2d 939.

damages on the loss to the estate rather than loss to the dependents or survivors.[57] Under this rule, the decedent's expected lifetime earnings,[58] less his living expenses or contributions, or some variation of this formula, becomes the basis for damages, which may then be collected by the estate.[59] This may or may not reflect actual losses and may or may not actually benefit dependents.[60]

A number of states have both death acts and survival acts. There are then two causes of action, and it usually is held that they may be prosecuted concurrently to successful judgment.[61] The usual method of dealing with the two causes of action has been to allocate the pain and suffering, expenses and loss of earnings of the decedent up to the date of his death to the survival action, and hence to the estate,[62] and the loss of benefits of the survivors to the action for wrongful death, and so to the beneficiaries.[63] This has, in the ordinary jurisdiction, the effect of denying all recovery to anyone for the loss of the accumulated savings which the decedent might have been expected to make during the period of his pre-accident life expectancy, or in other words, of the inheritance he might have been expected to leave to his widow and children.[64] A number of federal courts have allowed such damages in death actions under the Federal Employers Liability Act or the Jones Act,[65] and under the Death on the High Seas Act.[66] The same may result under the judge-made law of death in Admiralty.[67] There is also some support for this element of damages in a few states as well,[68] and a handful of jurisdictions have permitted the decedent's estate, under the survival statute, to recover the savings or net earnings he would have had in a normal lifetime.[69]

57. Most lists include Connecticut, Iowa, New Hampshire and Kentucky. In narrow situations some other states use the loss to the estate measure. See Note, 1966, 44 N.C.L.Rev. 402; S. Speiser, Recovery for Wrongful Death, 2d ed. 1975, § 3.2. Other states that once used this measure have changed over in some instances, and statutes must be consulted.

58. Income from pensions and the like may be considered in fixing damages under this accumulations rule. See Pike v. United States, 9th Cir. 1981, 652 F.2d 31.

59. Neal v. United States, 5th Cir. 1977, 562 F.2d 338 (decedent's earning capacity, not necessarily actual wages, Kentucky law); Haumersen v. Ford Motor Co., Iowa 1977, 257 N.W.2d 7.

60. As in Egan v. Naylor, Iowa 1973, 208 N.W.2d 915.

61. Gorman v. Columbus & Southern Ohio Electric Co., 1945, 144 Ohio St. 593, 60 N.E.2d 700; Koehler v. Waukesha Milk Co., 1926, 190 Wis. 52, 208 N.W. 901; Annot., 35 A.L.R.2d 1377.

62. National Bank of Bloomington v. Norfolk & Western Railway, 1978, 73 Ill.2d 160, 23 Ill.Dec. 48, 383 N.E.2d 919 (pain survives distinct from wrongful death); Murphy v. Martin Oil Co., 1974, 56 Ill.2d 423, 308 N.E.2d 583 (wage loss survives up to time of death); Hindmarsh v. Sulpho Saline Bath Co., 1922, 108 Neb. 168, 187 N.W. 806.

63. Biro v. Schombert, 1979, 41 Md.App. 658, 398 A.2d 519, vacated on procedural grounds 285 Md. 290, 402 A.2d 71; Murray v. Templeton, Tex.Civ.App.1978, 576 S.W.2d 138 (battle between beneficiaries).

64. Farrington v. Stoddard, 1st Cir. 1940, 115 F.2d 96; Hindmarsh v. Sulpho Saline Bath Co., 1922, 108 Neb. 168, 187 N.W. 806; Fleming, The Lost Years: A Problem in the Computation and Distribution of Damages, 50 Cal.L.Rev. 598. In loss-to-the-estate jurisdictions, of course, these accumulations are awarded, but to the estate rather than to the dependents.

65. Martin v. Atlantic Coast Line Railroad, 5th Cir. 1959, 268 F.2d 397 (FELA); Daughdrill v. Diamond "M" Drilling Co., D.La.1969, 305 F.Supp. 836 (Jones Act), reversed on other grounds 5th Cir. 1971, 447 F.2d 781, certiorari denied 405 U.S. 997, 92 S.Ct. 1261, 31 L.Ed.2d 466.

66. National Airlines, Inc. v. Stiles, 5th Cir. 1949, 268 F.2d 400, certiorari denied 361 U.S. 885, 80 S.Ct. 157, 4 L.Ed.2d 121, rehearing denied 361 U.S. 926, 80 S.Ct. 291, 4 L.Ed.2d 241 (widow); Solomon v. Warren, 5th Cir. 1976, 540 F.2d 777, rehearing denied 545 F.2d 1298, certiorari dismissed 434 U.S. 801, 98 S.Ct. 28, 54 L.Ed.2d 59 (children).

67. See Rischmiller v. Dahl, 6th Cir. 1974, 505 F.2d 517, certiorari denied 420 U.S. 975, 95 S.Ct. 1399, 43 L.Ed.2d 655 (denying recovery of loss of inheritance to non-dependent collaterals, but apparently approving the principle for appropriate cases).

68. Salinas v. Kahn, 1965, 2 Ariz.App. 181, 407 P.2d 120, modified on other grounds 2 Ariz.App. 348, 409 P.2d 64; Reynolds v. Willis, Del.1965, 209 A.2d 760, following the forecast in O'Toole v. United States, 3d Cir. 1957, 242 F.2d 308; Sternfels v. Metropolitan Street Railway Co., 1902, 73 App.Div. 494, 77 N.Y.S. 309, affirmed 174 N.Y. 512, 66 N.E. 1117; Annot., 91 A.L.R.2d 477. See New York Pattern Jury Instructions PJI 2:320.

69. McClinton v. White, 1982, 497 Pa. 610, 444 A.2d 85; Criscuola v. Andrews, 1973, 82 Wn.2d 68, 507 P.2d

Where the damages recoverable are based upon the loss to the surviving beneficiaries, it is the general rule that only pecuniary loss is to be considered. The death acts obviously are aimed at protection of the relational interest, and bear a close analogy to the action of the spouse or parent for loss of services through injury to the other spouse or child. But the original English act received a very strict construction at the hands of a court alarmed at the difficulty of evaluating the impalpable injuries to sentiments and affections because of death,[70] which has been followed in interpreting most of the American statutes to limit the recovery to loss of pecuniary benefits.[71] Thus except for nominal damages [72] recovery has been repeatedly denied where the beneficiaries in the specified class have suffered no pecuniary loss.[73] This has meant that damages for grief or mental suffering of the survivors are not permitted in most jurisdictions.[74] Punitive damages are likewise denied under most wrongful death statutes.[75] The same fear of excessive verdicts that produced these restrictive rules led some legislatures to set a dollar limit on death recoveries, though this seems to be passing from the picture.[76]

In line with expanding tort liability generally, however, there has been a good deal of change. In the first place, most courts will permit a recovery for the "pecuniary value" of services that the decedent would have contributed,[77] if any.[78] In addition, though recovery for loss of society and comfort is denied under some statutes,[79] it is an item usually recognized and made the basis for

149 (no survivors, estate recovers); Annot., 76 A.L.R.3d 125. Statutes explicitly require this result in some states. West's Fla.Stat.Ann. § 768.21; Haw.Rev. Stat. § 663–8.

70. Blake v. Midland R. Co., 1852, 18 Q.B. 93, 118 Eng.Rep. 42.

71. Karr v. Sixt, 1946, 146 Ohio St. 527, 67 N.E.2d 331; Louisville & Nashville Railroad v. Stephens, 1944, 298 Ky. 328, 182 S.W.2d 447; Gaydos v. Domabyl, 1930, 301 Pa. 523, 152 A. 549; Tufty v. Sioux City Transit Co., 1943, 69 S.D. 368, 10 N.W.2d 767; Lehrer v. Lorenzen, 1951, 124 Colo. 17, 233 P.2d 382. See Green, Relational Interests, 1934, 29 Ill.L.Rev. 460, 473; Miller, Dead Men in Torts; Lord Campbell's Act was Not Enough, 1970, 19 Cath.U.L.Rev. 310; Speiser and Malawer, An American Tragedy: Damages for Mental Anguish of Bereaved Relatives in Wrongful Death Actions, 51 Tul.L.Rev. 1 (1976).

72. Most courts apparently will permit nominal damages in a death action. See Annot., 69 A.L.R.2d 628. In some nominal damages will be allowed only to beneficiaries who have a "presumed" loss. Acton v. Shields, Mo.1965, 386 S.W.2d 363.

73. San Antonio & Aransas Pass Railway Co. v. Long, 1894, 87 Tex. 148, 27 S.W. 113; Courtney v. Apple, 1956, 345 Mich. 223, 76 N.W.2d 80. The poverty, wealth, or physical helplessness of the survivor is immaterial, except as it may bear upon the probability of contributions from the decedent. See Chicago, Peoria & St. Louis Railway v. Woolridge, 1898, 174 Ill. 330, 51 N.E. 701.

74. Herbertson v. Russell, 1962, 150 Colo. 110, 371 P.2d 422; Hepp v. Ader, 1942, 64 Idaho 240, 130 P.2d 859; Tufty v. Sioux Transit Co., 1943, 69 S.D. 368, 10 N.W.2d 767; Ferne v. Chadderton, 1949, 363 Pa. 191, 69 A.2d 104; see Todd v. Weikle, 1977, 36 Md.App. 663, 376 A.2d 104 (reflecting incomplete legislative change).

75. Rubeck v. Huffman, 1978, 54 Ohio St.2d 20, 374 N.E.2d 411. This was held constitutional in In re Paris Air Crash, 9th Cir. 1980, 622 F.2d 1315, certiorari denied 449 U.S. 976, 101 S.Ct. 387, 66 L.Ed.2d 237. There is a careful approach to punitive damages in death actions in R. Keeton, Statutes, Gaps, and Values in Tort Law, 44 J.Air L. 1.

76. See D. Dobbs, Remedies, § 8.5 (1973).

77. Michigan Central Railroad v. Vreeland, 1913, 227 U.S. 59, 33 S.Ct. 192, 57 L.Ed. 417; Lockhart v. Besel, 1967, 71 Wn.2d 112, 426 P.2d 605; McPike v. Scheuerman, Wyo.1965, 398 P.2d 71; Gulf Transport Co. v. Allen, 1950, 209 Miss. 206, 46 So.2d 436; Seaboard Air Line Railway Co. v. Martin, Fla.1952, 56 So. 2d 509; Gardner v. Hobbs, 1949, 69 Idaho 288, 206 P.2d 539.

78. Smith v. United States, 3d Cir. 1978, 587 F.2d 1013 (decedent with history of mental illness could not have provided nurture or services).

79. See Mobil Oil Corp. v. Higginbotham, 1978, 436 U.S. 618, 98 S.Ct. 2010, 56 L.Ed.2d 581, on remand 5th Cir., 578 F.2d 565, rehearing denied 439 U.S. 884, 99 S.Ct. 232, 58 L.Ed.2d 200 (Death on High Seas Act compels rejection of this element though it is compensable under general maritime law); Ivy v. Security Barge Lines, Inc., 5th Cir. 1979, 606 F.2d 524, certiorari denied 1980, 446 U.S. 956, 100 S.Ct. 2927, 64 L.Ed.2d 815, rehearing denied 448 U.S. 912, 101 S.Ct. 27, 65 L.Ed.2d 1173, on remand 89 F.R.D. 322 (Jones Act/FELA do not compensate for this element). Liff v. Schildkrout, 1980, 49 N.Y.2d 622, 427 N.Y.S.2d 746, 404 N.E.2d 1288. As to the possible scope of general maritime law which allows recovery for loss of society, see Maraist, Maritime Wrongful Death—Higginbotham Reversed Trend and Creates New Questions, 1978, 39 La.L.Rev. 81.

an award,[80] at times apparently substantial.[81] These consortium damages clearly include many intangible forms of loss, including love and affection, and the juror may find it quite difficult indeed to distinguish a spouse's loss of love from the forbidden "mental anguish," [82] with the result, probable in many cases, that substantial awards will be made for intangible losses under one name or another. Even jurisdictions that have rejected the loss of society or consortium claim, as such, have permitted one form of it, namely a loss of guidance and advice that the decedent would have provided, at least in the case of deceased parents.[83] Beyond this, some form of mental distress damage is explicitly recognized in a number of states and the list appears to be growing.[84] A similar change seems to be taking place as to punitive damages.[85]

Where pecuniary loss to survivors is still the ostensible standard for recovery, the decedent who is not in the labor market has presented a special problem, since such a person is not making direct money contributions to survivors, and there is certainly no direct pecuniary loss. Yet it has almost always seemed unjust to say that a child,[86] or nonworking wife or mother,[87] or an aged person [88] is worth nothing to the survivors, and juries have at times rendered substantial verdicts in such cases. A leading decision of the Michigan Court [89] many years ago held that the "pecuniary value" of a child must include such intangibles as contributions to family life, and, apparently, that

---

80. Sea-Land Services, Inc. v. Gaudet, 1974, 414 U.S. 573, 94 S.Ct. 806, 39 L.Ed.2d 9, rehearing denied 415 U.S. 986, 94 S.Ct. 1582, 39 L.Ed.2d 883 (general maritime law); Krouse v. Graham, 1977, 19 Cal.3d 59, 137 Cal.Rptr. 863, 562 P.2d 1022; Elliott v. Willis, 1982, 92 Ill.2d 530, 65 Ill.Dec. 852, 442 N.E.2d 163; Caradori v. Fitch, 1978, 200 Neb. 186, 263 N.W.2d 649 (child); Green v. Bittner, 1980, 85 N.J. 1, 424 A.2d 210 (child). Statutes are sometimes explicit in permitting such items, e.g., Ann.L.Mass. c. 229 § 2 ("services, protection, care, assistance, society, companionship, comfort, guidance, counsel and advice").

81. It has been suggested that the loss of society award might be made primarily symbolic rather than substantial, but the issue is not decided at this writing. See Mobil Oil Corp. v. Higginbotham, 1978, 436 U.S. 618, 624 at note 20, 98 S.Ct. 2010, 2014 at note 20.

82. Sea-Land Services, Inc. v. Gaudet, 1974, 414 U.S. 573, 94 S.Ct. 806, 39 L.Ed.2d 9, rehearing denied 415 U.S. 986, 94 S.Ct. 1582, 39 L.Ed.2d 883; Krouse v. Graham, 1977, 19 Cal.3d 59, 137 Cal.Rptr. 863, 562 P.2d 1022; Childs v. Rayburn, 1976, 169 Ind. 147, 346 N.E.2d 655; but see Mobil Oil Corp. v. Higginbotham, 1978, 436 U.S. 618, 98 S.Ct. 2010, 56 L.Ed.2d 581, on remand 5th Cir., 578 F.2d 565, rehearing denied 439 U.S. 884, 99 S.Ct. 232, 58 L.Ed.2d 200 (such awards might be limited to "symbolic" sum).

83. Michigan Central Railroad v. Vreeland, 1912, 227 U.S. 59, 33 S.Ct. 192, 57 L.Ed. 417 (FELA); Kaiserman v. Bright, 1978, 61 Ill.App.3d 67, 18 Ill.Dec. 108, 377 N.E.2d 261.

84. City of Tucson v. Wondergem, 1970, 105 Ariz. 429, 466 P.2d 383; Alizzi v. Employer Insurance of Wausau, La.App.1977, 351 So.2d 258, writ denied 353 So.2d 1037. Recent legislation has liberalized recovery here, but has sometimes left gaps. See Wojcik v. United Services Automobile Association, Fla.App.1977, 347 So.2d 1051; Todd v. Weikle, 1977, 36 Md.App. 663, 376 A.2d 104. The difficulties of one court with this item over many years are recounted in St. Louis Southwestern Railway Co. v. Pennington, 1977, 261 Ark. 650, 553 S.W.2d 436. Recognition of this element of damages may be important in determining substantive rights under the death act. See Moen v. Hanson, 1975, 85 Wn. 2d 597, 537 P.2d 266 (death of unborn child actionable since parents would have mental anguish).

85. Statutory change is reflected in Boies v. Cole, 1965, 99 Ariz. 198, 407 P.2d 917, and in Ann.L.Mass. c. 229, § 2; N.C.Gen.Stats. § 28–18–2; see, summarizing jurisdictions, Note, 54 N.D.L.Rev. 104.

86. Kinney v. Smith, 1973, 95 Idaho 328, 508 P.2d 1234 (11-year old, $35,000); Baird v. Chicago, Burlington & Quincy Railroad Co., 1975, 32 Ill.App.3d 1, 334 N.E.2d 920, affirmed 63 Ill.2d 463, 349 N.E.2d 413 ("presumed" damages to parents); Annot., 49 A.L.R.3d 934. A number of cases are collected in Lane v. Hatfield, 1943, 173 Or. 79, 143 P.2d 230.

87. George v. County of Erie, 1971, 66 Misc.2d 871, 322 N.Y.S.2d 278 (motherly care, $100,000); Hurlburt v. Planters National Bank & Trust Co., Tex.Civ.App. 1976, 539 S.W.2d 97, refused n.r.e. (similar); Annot., 47 A.L.R.3d 971. See also D. Dobbs, 1973, Remedies § 8.4. As to testimony and theories, see Hauserman and Fethke, Valuation of a Homemaker's Services, 22 Tr.Law.Guide 249 (discussing replacement and opportunity costs); Note, 21 Buff.L.Rev. 205.

88. Elsberry v. Lewis, 1976, 140 Ga.App. 324, 231 S.E.2d 789 (75 year old, $60,000); Kardas v. State, 1964, 44 Misc.2d 243, 253 N.Y.S.2d 470, reversed on other ground 24 A.D.2d 789, 263 N.Y.S.2d 727 (permitting consideration of pension or disability payments to decedent if they were cut off at death); Annot., 52 A.L.R.3d 1289.

89. Wycko v. Gnodtke, 1960, 361 Mich. 331, 105 N.W.2d 118. The unhappy tale of Wycko's death and resurrection can be gleaned from Smith v. City of Detroit, 1972, 388 Mich. 637, 202 N.W.2d 300.

there need be no deduction for the cost of rearing the child. Though not all courts have accepted this last point,[90] there is very broad agreement that the recovery should include damages for the loss of society and companionship,[91] which, as already noted, may be substantial. The insistence, however, that such intangibles are in some manner "pecuniary" losses, coupled with the approval of large verdicts for such items, may invite the jury to leave its respect for the administration of justice at the courthouse door. Whether that is true or not, the "pecuniary" standard seems to permit or encourage wildly erratic verdicts because some juries take the term literally while others accept the tacit invitation to make an award for bereavement, and it might be better to drop the pecuniary loss requirement altogether.[92]

The matter of death damages is still very much a matter of rules peculiar to individual statutes, which of course must be consulted; but the decisions and statutes of recent years have moved in the direction of increased support for the recovery of intangible losses and for some degree of protection for the bereavement of survivors.

Perhaps the largest group of death cases, however, involves pecuniary loss to survivors as the main element of damage, and in most jurisdictions this turns on contributions the beneficiary might have expected to receive if death had not intervened,[93] with a reduction of all such future expected losses to present value.[94] This necessarily involves a large element of speculation, turning on such matters as life expectancy,[95] income,[96] habits and health of the deceased,[97] past contributions to his family,[98] the probability of increased earnings and contributions in the future,[99] and, in some jurisdictions, the probability of future inflation.[1] The difficulties of assessing such damages apparently

---

90. Though permitting a recovery for loss of society and companionship, the court in Haumersen v. Ford Motor Co., Iowa 1977, 257 N.W.2d 7, required a deduction for the cost of support that would have been incurred had the child lived.

91. Caradori v. Fitch, 1978, 200 Neb. 186, 263 N.W.2d 649; Anderson v. Lale, 1974, 88 S.D. 111, 216 N.W.2d 152 (good review of Wycko and its acceptance.)

92. As noted in Fussner v. Andert, 1962, 261 Minn. 347, 113 N.W.2d 355, law in this situation may become luck. One study showed that jury awards were more erratic when the pecuniary standard was used and suggested that this worked a discrimination that might raise constitutional questions. Finkelstein, Pickrel & Glasser, The Death of Children: A Nonparametric Statistical Analysis of Compensation for Anguish, 1974, 74 Colum.L.Rev. 884.

93. Hertz v. McDowell, 1948, 358 Mo. 383, 214 S.W.2d 546; American Barge Line Co. v. Leatherman's Administratrix, 1947, 306 Ky. 284, 206 S.W.2d 955; Thompson v. Town of Fort Branch, 1931, 204 Ind. 152, 178 N.E. 440; Blackwell v. American Film Co., 1922, 189 Cal. 689, 209 P. 999; Kansas City Southern Railway Co. v. Leslie, 1916, 125 Ark. 516, 189 S.W. 171.

94. See D. Dobbs, 1973, Remedies § 8.7.

95. Gill v. Baltimore & Ohio Railroad, 1924, 302 Mo. 317, 259 S.W. 93, certiorari denied 265 U.S. 592, 44 S.Ct. 636, 68 L.Ed. 1196; Gaydos v. Domabyl, 1930, 301 Pa. 523, 152 A. 549. The life expectancy of the beneficiary also limits recovery. Ure v. Maggio Brothers Co., 1938, 24 Cal.App.2d 490, 75 P.2d 534; Goodyear Yellow Pine Co. v. Anderson, 1934, 171 Miss. 530, 157 So. 700.

96. Director General of Railroads v. Platt, 1st Cir. 1920, 265 F. 918; Perry v. Ryback, 1931, 302 Pa. 559, 153 A. 770.

97. Louisville & Nashville Railroad v. Scott's Administrator, 1920, 188 Ky. 99, 220 S.W. 1066; Morton v. Southwestern Telegraph & Telephone Co., 1920, 280 Mo. 360, 217 S.W. 831.

98. Rogers v. Hime, 1948, 76 Ga.App. 523, 46 S.E.2d 367; American Barge Line Co. v. Leatherman's Administratrix, 1947, 306 Ky. 284, 206 S.W.2d 955; Director General of Railroads v. Platt, 1st Cir. 1920, 265 F. 918; Austin Gaslight Co. v. Anderson, Tex.Civ.App.1924, 262 S.W. 136, error dismissed.

99. United States v. Furumizo, 9th Cir. 1967, 381 F.2d 965; Zaninovich v. American Airlines, Inc., 1966, 26 A.D.2d 155, 271 N.Y.S.2d 866.

1. Bach v. Penn Central Transportation Co., 6th Cir. 1974, 502 F.2d 1117 (jury may consider inflation but may not hear economic testimony about it); Feldman v. Allegheny Airlines, Inc., D.Conn.1974, 382 F.Supp. 1271, affirmed in relevant part 2d Cir., 524 F.2d 384, on remand 452 F.Supp. 151 (discount rate in reducing present value is reduced to allow for inflation); Kaczkowski v. Bolubasz, 1980, 491 Pa. 561, 421 A.2d 1027 (inflation considered by refusing to discount to present value). See Note, 63 Va.L.Rev. 105. Increased income from merit raises and increased productivity of the industry as a whole raise separate problems. See John Henderson, The Consideration of Increased Productivity and the Discounting of Future Earnings to Present Value, 20 S.D.L.Rev. 49.

were foreseen by the framers of the acts, most of which leave to the jury a wide range of discretion [2] and authorize some resort to conjecture without demanding mathematical precision.[3] Proof of death damages, however, has become increasingly complicated and there are many issues concerning such damages that are beyond the scope of this book.[4]

Defenses

Under the survival type of death statute, which merely continues the decedent's own cause of action beyond his death and enhances it with damages for the death, it is of course clear that any defenses which might have been set up against him if he had lived are still available to the defendant.[5] The contrary might perhaps have been expected of the wrongful death acts, which create a separate and independent cause of action, founded upon the death itself, for the benefit of the designated survivors. The original Lord Campbell's Act, however, contained an express provision limiting the death action to those cases where the deceased might have recovered damages if he had lived;[6] and this provision has been carried over into most of the American acts, or has been read into them by implication where it does not expressly appear.[7] It obviously is intended at least to prevent recovery for death where the decedent could never at any time have maintained an action, as, for example, where there was simply no tortious conduct toward him.[8]

On the same basis, there has been general agreement denying recovery where the defendant's conduct has been tortious toward the decedent and has caused his death, thus causing loss to the innocent survivors, but the defendant would have had a defense available against the decedent himself. This has been true of contributory negligence,[9] assumption of risk,[10] or valid consent to the defendant's conduct [11] which defeat recovery

---

2. See Kansas Pacific Railway Co. v. Cutter, 1877, 19 Kan. 83, 91; Hunt v. Central Vermont Railway Co., 1923, 99 Conn. 657, 122 A. 563; True & True Co. v. Woda, 1902, 104 Ill.App. 15, affirmed 1903, 201 Ill. 315, 66 N.E. 369; Butler v. Townend, 1931, 50 Idaho 542, 298 P. 375.

3. American Motor Car Co. v. Robbins, 1913, 181 Ind. 417, 103 N.E. 641; Bottum v. Kamen, 1921, 43 S.D. 498, 180 N.W. 948; Fisher v. Treser, 1930, 119 Neb. 529, 229 N.W. 901.

4. Among the many specialized problems are the use of economic data; statistical data on life expectancy, which may have a discriminatory impact, see Manhart v. Los Angeles, 1978, 435 U.S. 702, 98 S.Ct. 1370, 55 L.Ed.2d 657, on remand 9th Cir., 577 F.2d 98, appeal after remand 652 F.2d 904; remarriage of a spouse, see D. Dobbs, 1973, Remedies § 8.6; the effect of future income taxes saved, see D. Dobbs, 1973, Remedies, § 8.8; taxability of death or survival awards under inheritance, succession or estate tax schemes, see Notes, 1975, 60 Iowa L.Rev. 1072; 1973 Wash.U.L.Q. 445.

5. Wright v. Davis, 1949, 132 W.Va. 722, 53 S.E.2d 335 (immunity of spouse); Cogswell v. Boston & Maine Railroad, 1917, 78 N.H. 379, 101 A. 145.

6. 9 & 10 Vict., ch. 93: " * * * That whensoever the Death of a Person shall be caused by wrongful Act, Neglect or Default, and the Act, Neglect or Default is such as would (if Death had not ensued) have entitled the Party injured to maintain an Action and recover Damages in respect thereof, then and in every such Case the Person who would have been liable if Death had not ensued shall be liable to an Action for Damages, notwithstanding the Death of the Person injured."

7. Murphy v. Boston & Maine Railroad, 1913, 216 Mass. 178, 103 N.E. 291; State Farm Mutual Automobile Insurance Co. v. Leary, 1975, 168 Mont. 482, 544 P.2d 444; Moen v. Hanson, 1975, 85 Wn.2d 597, 537 P.2d 266. See Nourse, Is Contributory Negligence of Deceased a Defense to a Wrongful Death Action?, 1954, 42 Cal.L.Rev. 310.

8. State to Use of Bond v. Consolidated Gas, Electric, Light & Power Co., 1924, 146 Md. 390, 126 A. 105; Emery v. Rochester Telephone Corp., 1936, 271 N.Y. 306, 3 N.E.2d 434; cf. Callais v. Allstate Insurance Co., La.1976, 334 So.2d 692 (father killed by his own negligence, his insurer not liable).

9. Sullivan v. Davidson, 1958, 183 Kan. 713, 332 P.2d 507; Buckley v. Chadwick, 1955, 45 Cal.2d 183, 288 P.2d 12, rehearing denied 45 Cal.2d 183, 289 P.2d 242; Purdy v. Kerentoff, 1949, 152 Ohio St. 391, 89 N.E.2d 565; Zabawa v. Eshenroeder, 1946, 313 Mich. 555, 21 N.W.2d 852; Indiana Harbor Belt Railroad Co. v. Jones, 1941, 220 Ind. 139, 41 N.E.2d 361. See Note, 1956, 29 So.Cal.L.Rev. 344.

10. Francis v. Southern Pacific Co., 1948, 333 U.S. 445, 68 S.Ct. 611, 92 L.Ed. 798; Marbury Lumber Co. v. Jones, 1922, 206 Ala. 669, 91 So. 623; LaFrenz v. Lake County Fair Board, 1977, 172 Ind.App. 389, 360 N.E.2d 605 (exculpatory agreement in demolition derby).

11. The text statement was originally supported by illegal abortion cases, see Miller v. Bennett, 1949, 190 Va. 162, 56 S.E.2d 217; Szadiwicz v. Cantor, 1926, 257 Mass. 518, 154 N.E. 251. The standing of these cases as to illegality has been changed by Roe v. Wade, 410

for the death, as does the fellow-servant rule, if there is anywhere where it still applies,[12] or justifications such as self-defense[13] or defense of property.[14] Under comparative negligence statutes, contributory fault of the decedent will be given the same effect in the death action as it would have had in a personal injury claim, normally to reduce damages.[15] Most of the courts which have considered the question have given the same effect to the immunity of one member of a family for torts against another,[16] although there is a strong minority view to the contrary, based upon the theory that death destroys the reason for the immunity,[17] which seems very much to be preferred.

Since the injured individual is not merely a conduit for the support of others, he is master of his own claim and he may settle the case or win or lose a judgment on his own injury even though others may be dependent upon him. If he lives after such a settlement, both he and his dependents take the consequences of the settlement, and the majority of courts hold that the same is true if he thereafter dies from the injuries. Under this view, a judgment for [18] or against [19] the decedent in an action for his injuries commenced during his lifetime, or the compromise and release of such an action,[20] will operate as a bar to any subsequent suit founded upon his death. The wrongful death action for the benefit of survivors is, like other actions based on injuries to others,[21] derivative in nature, arising out of and dependent upon the wrong done to the injured person and thus barred when his claim would be barred. The courts undoubtedly have been influenced in so holding by a fear of a double recovery.[22] This is of

U.S. 113, 93 S.Ct. 705, 35 L.Ed.2d 147, rehearing denied 410 U.S. 959, 93 S.Ct. 1409, 35 L.Ed.2d 694, but the principle that a valid consent is a bar would seem to survive to apply to any other set of facts.

12. Senior v. Ward, 1859, 1 El. & El. 385, 120 Eng. Rep. 954; Ohio & Mississippi Railway Co. v. Tindall, 1859, 13 Ind. 366.

13. Burdon v. Wood, 7th Cir., 1944, 142 F.2d 303, certiorari denied 325 U.S. 733, 65 S.Ct. 70, 89 L.Ed. 588; McMurrey Corp. v. Yawn, Tex.Civ.App.1940, 143 S.W.2d 664, error refused; Hunt-Berlin Coal Co. v. Paton, 1918, 139 Tenn. 611, 202 S.W. 935. Cf. Harris v. Embrey, 1939, 70 App.D.C. 232, 105 F.2d 111 (justifiable homicide).

14. Suell v. Derricott, 1909, 161 Ala. 259, 49 So. 895; Foster v. Shepherd, 1913, 258 Ill. 164, 101 N.E. 411; but see Howsley v. Gilliam, Tex.1975, 517 S.W.2d 531 (no summary judgment for doctor who shot boy stealing battery).

15. Anderson v. Gailey, 1976, 97 Idaho 813, 555 P.2d 144; Griffin v. Gehret, 1977, 17 Wn.App. 546, 564 P.2d 332; V. Schwartz, Comparative Negligence § 13.2.

16. State Farm Mutual Automobile Insurance Co. v. Leary, 1975, 168 Mont. 482, 544 P.2d 444; Bounds v. Caudle, Tex.Civ.App.1977, 549 S.W.2d 438, reversed 560 S.W.2d 925 (abolishing immunity).

17. See Hull v. Silver, Utah 1978, 577 P.2d 103; Annots., 28 A.L.R.2d 662, 87 A.L.R.3d 849. As to the abolition of immunities, see § 122 supra.

18. Walrod v Southern Pacific Co., 9th Cir. 1971, 447 F.2d 930; Roberts v. Union Carbide Corp., 3d Cir. 1969, 415 F.2d 474; Perry's Administrator v. Louisville & Nashville Railroad Co., 1923, 199 Ky. 396, 251 S.W. 202; Harris v. Illinois Central Railroad Co., 1916, 111 Miss. 623, 71 So. 878; Edwards v. Interstate Chemical Co., 1916, 170 N.C. 551, 87 S.E. 635; Seaboard Air Line Railway Co. v. Oliver, 5th Cir. 1919, 261 F. 1.

19. Collins v. Hall, 1934, 117 Fla. 282, 157 So. 646; Frescoln v. Puget Sound Traction, Light & Power Co., D.Wash.1915, 225 F. 441; Brammer's Administrator v. Norfolk & Western Railway Co., 1907, 107 Va. 206, 57 S.E. 593. Occasionally this is based upon the doctrine of res judicata, as in Little v. Blue Goose Motor Coach Co., 1927, 244 Ill.App. 427, where the tort-feasor recovered from the decedent.

20. Mellon v. Goodyear, 1927, 277 U.S. 335, 48 S.Ct. 541, 72 L.Ed. 906 (FELA); Schlavick v. Manhattan Brewing Co., D.Ill.1952, 103 F.Supp. 744; Hutton v. Davis, 1976, 26 Ariz.App. 215, 547 P.2d 486; Crockett v. Missouri Pacific Railway Co., 1929, 179 Ark. 527, 16 S.W.2d 989; Warren v. Cohen, Fla.App.1978, 363 So.2d 129; Harris v. Illinois Central Railroad Co., 1916, 111 Miss. 623, 71 So. 878; Haws v. Luethje, Okl.1972, 503 P.2d 871. Cf. Burke v. Burnham, 1952, 97 N.H. 203, 84 A.2d 918 (release of joint tortfeasor; amount received must be credited). See Notes, 1952, 5 Okl.L.Rev. 93; 1963, 16 Okl.L.Rev. 116. California applies this rule to a release of a worker's compensation claim followed by death of the worker. Johnson v. Workmen's Compensation Appeals Board, 1970, 2 Cal.3d 964, 88 Cal.Rptr. 202, 471 P.2d 1002.

21. As in claims for loss of services, society and support where death does not ensue, see § 125, supra. See the comparison in Hasson v. Ford Motor Co., 1977, 19 Cal.3d 530, 138 Cal.Rptr. 705, 564 P.2d 857 and Stickney v. E. R. Squibb & Sons, Inc., Fla.1974, 377 F.Supp. 785.

22. See Schumacher, Rights of Action Under Death and Survival Statutes, 1924, 23 Mich.L.Rev. 114; Fleming, The Lost Years: A Problem in the Computation

course possible in point of law, not only under the survival type of death act,[23] but also in any jurisdiction where the decedent would be allowed to recover for the prospective earnings lost through his diminished life expectancy.[24] In other words the trial or settlement in the decedent's lifetime is intended to cover all damages, including earnings he would have received if he had lived out his normal life and out of which the benefits to the survivors would be expected to come. If the damages were fairly estimated, there has been a full recovery already; if not, there is still no more basis for setting aside a concluded settlement than there is in any other case.[25]

Opposed to this is the counterdanger of an improvident settlement by an optimistic individual, confident that he is not going to die, which takes no account of shortened life expectancy, or of the interests of the survivors. Perhaps because of this there is a minority view that neither a judgment in his action [26] nor his release of his claim [27] will bar the action for wrongful death. The possibility of double compensation either has been ignored, on the ground that legally it could not arise,[28] or has been met by a deduction from the award to the death beneficiaries, of the amount found to have been paid to the decedent covering the permanent destruction of his earning capacity,[29] or the suggestion that the expectancy of the survivors be deducted from the probable earnings in the decedent's own action.[30] Something of the conflict can perhaps be seen in the fact that the Supreme Court has accepted the minority rule permitting two actions, but only in cases involving seamen injured in territorial waters; [31] in other cases, such as those arising under the Federal Employers Liability Act, the same Court has steadfastly applied the majority rule.[32] It should be ob-

and Distribution of Damages, 1962, 50 Cal.L.Rev. 598; Notes, 1928, 13 Minn.L.Rev. 47; 1932, 80 U.Pa.L.Rev. 993; 1963, 16 Okl.L.Rev. 116.

23. As in Kling v. Torello, 1913, 87 Conn. 301, 87 A. 987; Perry v. Philadelphia, Baltimore & Washington Railroad Co., Del.1910, 1 Boyce 399, 77 A. 725; Cogswell v. Boston & Maine Railroad, 1917, 78 N.H. 379, 101 A. 145.

24. As in Prairie Creek Coal Mining Co. v. Kittrell, 1912, 106 Ark. 138, 153 S.W. 89; Louisville Belt & Iron Co. v. Hart, 1905, 122 Ky. 731, 92 S.W. 951; Borcherding v. Eklund, 1952, 156 Neb. 196, 55 N.W.2d 643; Littman v. Bell Telephone Co. of Pennsylvania, 1934, 315 Pa. 370, 172 A. 687.

25. The fact that injury is greater than assumed by the plaintiff when he accepted a settlement is no grounds for setting the settlement aside. See Dobbs, Conclusiveness of Personal Injury Settlements, 41 N.C.L.Rev. 665.

26. Sea-Land Services, Inc. v. Gaudet, 1974, 414 U.S. 573, 94 S.Ct. 806, 39 L.Ed.2d 9, rehearing denied 415 U.S. 986, 94 S.Ct. 1582, 39 L.Ed.2d 883; Alfone v. Sarno, 1981, 87 N.J. 99, 432 A.2d 857; De Hart v. Ohio Fuel Gas Co., 1948, 84 Ohio App. 62, 85 N.E.2d 586; Blackwell v. American Film Co., 1922, 189 Cal. 689, 209 P. 999; Dougherty v. New Orleans Railway & Light Co., 1913, 133 La. 993, 63 So. 493. Accord, as to workmen's compensation claim, Halling v. Industrial Commission, 1927, 71 Utah 112, 263 P. 78.

27. Goodyear v. Davis, 1923, 114 Kan. 557, 220 P. 282, rehearing denied 115 Kan. 20, 220 P. 1049 (Federal Employers' Liability Act); Earley v. Pacific Electric Railway Co., 1917, 176 Cal. 79, 167 P. 513; Phillips v. Community Traction Co., 1933, 46 Ohio App. 483, 189 N.E. 444; Rowe v. Richards, 1915, 35 S.D. 201, 151 N.W. 1001; cf. Ransmeier v. Camp Cody, Inc., 1977, 117 N.H. 736, 378 A.2d 752 (receipt of workers' compensation no bar to death claim). In re Air Crash in Bali, Indonesia, D.Cal.1978, 462 F.Supp. 1114, the court held that the death action was independent and the survivors would not be bound by limited liability agreements of the decedent with air carriers.

28. See De Hart v. Ohio Fuel Gas Co., 1948, 84 Ohio App. 62, 85 N.E.2d 586; Robinette v. May Coal Co., 1929, 31 Ohio App. 113, 166 N.E. 818, affirmed 120 Ohio St. 110, 165 N.E. 576; Rowe v. Richards, 1915, 35 S.D. 201, 151 N.W. 1001.

29. Dougherty v. New Orleans Railway & Light Co., 1913, 133 La. 993, 63 So. 493.

30. Rohlfing v. Moses Akiona, Limited, 1961, 45 Hawaii 373, 443, 369 P.2d 96; see Haw.Rev.Stat. § 663–8.

31. Sea-Land Services, Inc. v. Gaudet, 1974, 414 U.S. 573, 94 S.Ct. 806, 39 L.Ed. 2d 9, rehearing denied 415 U.S. 986, 94 S.Ct. 1582, 39 L.Ed.2d 883. The ruling does not apply where the Death on the High Seas Act covers the case, see Mobil Oil Co. v. Higginbotham, 1978, 436 U.S. 618, 98 S.Ct. 2010, 56 L.Ed.2d 581, on remand 5th Cir., 578 F.2d 565, rehearing denied 439 U.S. 884, 99 S.Ct. 232, 58 L.Ed.2d 200.

32. Mellon v. Goodyear, 1928, 277 U.S. 335, 48 S.Ct. 541, 72 L.Ed. 906; (FELA); see also Flynn v. New York, New Haven & Hartford Railroad, 1931, 283 U.S. 53, 51 S.Ct. 357, 75 L.Ed. 837, (statute of limitations barred claim before death). This rule would apparently survive the contrary rule for seamen in Sea-Land Services, Inc. v. Gaudet, 1974, 414 U.S. 573, 94 S.Ct. 806, 39 L.Ed.2d 9, rehearing denied 415 U.S. 986, 94 S.Ct. 1582, 39 L.Ed.2d 883. See Mobil Oil Co. v. Hig-

vious, as some of the Justices have agreed,[33] that as yet no satisfactory systematic solution to the whole problem has been found.[34]

As to the defense of the statute of limitations, which is distinguishable mainly in that it does not involve the danger of double compensation, the considerable majority of the courts have held that the statute runs against the death action only from the date of death, even though at that time the decedent's own action would have been barred while he was living.[35] Only a few courts hold that it runs from the time of the original injury, and consequently that the death action may be lost before it has ever accrued.[36] The existence of two distinct claims, one for death and one for personal injury or a survival of the injury action, presents such complications that neither rule may be entirely satisfactory.[37] The liberal rules applied in some personal injury actions hold that the cause of action does not accrue and the statute does not begin to run until the injury is actually discovered or should have been discovered by the plaintiff. This rule has produced added complications where the plaintiff suffers a disease from continuous exposure to drugs or industrial pollutants, since in such cases the victim may be well aware that he is suffering without realizing that the condition is permanent or that the defendant is the cause of it. Some decisions in the personal injury field have said that the statute does not begin to run in such cases until the claimant knows or should know of the condition and its cause, and even that the condition is a permanent one.[38] This approach has so far been rejected where the claim is for wrongful death or is asserted in a survival action.[39]

It is usually held that actions may be prosecuted under both death and survival acts, and that an action under one cannot be defended on the ground that recovery or settlement has been received under the other,[40] at least so long as the beneficiaries are dif-

ginbotham, 1978, 436 U.S. 618, 98 S.Ct. 2010, 56 L.Ed. 2d 581, on remand 5th Cir., 578 F.2d 565, rehearing denied 439 U.S. 884, 99 S.Ct. 232, 58 L.Ed.2d 200.

33. Sea-Land Services, Inc. v. Gaudet, 414 U.S. 573, 608, 94 S.Ct. 806, 826, 39 L.Ed.2d 9, rehearing denied 415 U.S. 986, 94 S.Ct. 1582, 39 L.Ed.2d 883 (Powell, J. dissenting, quoting this statement from an earlier edition).

34. "What emerges fairly from the preceding discussion is that this complex situation, like so many others involving multiple party interests, is singularly taxing to a system of law which is primarily geared to the adversary process and the demands for simplicity in loss administration imposed by the limitations inherent in jury trial. Each of the various solutions to the present problem that have been canvassed as conceivable alternatives falls in some respect short of the ideal due to the irritating intrusion of administrative or procedural restraints, but, in the absence of a much more drastic overhaul of our whole system for adjusting accident losses, nothing more ambitious can probably be realized with the relatively crude tools presently at our disposal." Fleming, The Lost Years: A Problem in the Computation and Distribution of Damages, 1962, 50 Cal.L.Rev. 598.

35. Larcher v. Wanless, 1976, 18 Cal.3d 646, 135 Cal.Rptr. 75, 557 P.2d 507; De Hart v. Ohio Fuel Gas Co., 1948, 84 Ohio App. 62, 85 N.E.2d 586 (death after 12 years); Western Union Telegraph Co. v. Preston, 3d Cir. 1918, 254 F. 229, certiorari denied 248 U.S. 585, 39 S.Ct. 182, 63 L.Ed. 433 (death after 10 years); Smith v. McComb Infirmary Association, Miss.1967, 196 So.2d 91; Annot., 97 A.L.R.2d 1151.

36. Crownover v. Gleichman, 1977, 194 Colo. 48, 574 P.2d 497, certiorari denied 435 U.S. 905, 98 S.Ct. 1450, 55 L.Ed.2d 495; Mason v. Gerin Corp., 1982, 231 Kan. 718, 647 P.2d 1340; Lambert v. Village of Summit, 1982, 104 Ill.App.3d 1034, 60 Ill.Dec. 778, 433 N.E.2d 1016.

37. In Caffaro v. Trayna, 1974, 35 N.Y.2d 245, 360 N.Y.S.2d 847, 319 N.E.2d 174, 71 A.L.R.2d 924 decedent sued for injury in 1968, but died in 1969 before the case had gone to trial. In 1972 his personal representative was substituted as plaintiff in the personal injury (survival) claim. In 1973 the personal representative sought to add a claim for wrongful death. The wrongful death statute was two years, and ran from the decedent's death. However, the court permitted the amendment to claim for wrongful death so long as it was asserted in the survival action.

38. See Urie v. Thompson, 1949, 337 U.S. 163, 69 S.Ct. 1018, 93 L.Ed. 1282; Schiele v. Hobart Corp., 1978, 284 Or. 483, 587 P.2d 1010.

39. DeCosse v. Armstrong Cork Co., Minn.1982, 319 N.W.2d 45; Anthony v. Koppers Co., Inc., 1981, 496 Pa. 119, 436 A.2d 181.

40. Pantazis v. Fidelity & Deposit Co. of Maryland, 1952, 369 Pa. 221, 85 A.2d 421; Koehler v. Waukesha Milk Co., 1926, 190 Wis. 52, 208 N.W. 901; Hindmarsh v. Sulpho Saline Bath Co., 1922, 108 Neb. 108, 187 N.W. 806; Puget Sound Traction, Light & Power Co. v. Frescoln, 9th Cir. 1917, 245 F. 301; St. Louis & San Francisco Co. v. Goode, 1914, 42 Okl. 784, 142 P. 1185.

ferent [41] and there is no duplication in the elements of damages.[42] Statutes may require consolidation of the two actions [43] or may provide that only one of the two actions may be brought,[44] however. So long as elements of damages are completely different in the two actions, it seems consistent to permit both claims, even though the decedent's own action in his lifetime will bar the death action. The difference is that the decedent's lifetime claim includes some of the same elements of damages recoverable in the later wrongful death action, so that the danger of duplicated recoveries, or the cost of procedures and testimony to avoid such duplicate recoveries, is quite high. These dangers do not exist, however, where both death and survival actions are brought together.

Defenses available against the beneficiaries themselves offer a still more troublesome problem, on which all courts have not agreed.[45] Where the action is brought under a survival act, it is in theory still on behalf of the decedent, and the contributory negligence of even a sole beneficiary has been held not to prevent recovery.[46] The same conclusion has been reached under wrongful death acts where the damages are recoverable on behalf of the decedent's estate, on the ground that the estate is distinct from the beneficiary.[47] Under the usual death act the recovery is for the beneficiaries, and the contributory negligence [48] or the consent or assumption of risk [49] of a sole beneficiary or of all beneficiaries generally is held to preclude the action, on the same principle that would bar any other plaintiff in interest. Some few statutes have been construed to the contrary.[50]

Where only one of several beneficiaries is contributorily negligent, the better view, and now the prevailing one, is that the action is not barred as to those who were not negligent, but that recovery is diminished to the extent of the damages of the negligent beneficiary, who is denied all share in the proceeds.[51] The same conclusion has been

41. Epps v. Railway Express Agency, Fla.1940, 40 So.2d 131.

42. Fries v. Stieben, D.S.D.1978, 455 F.Supp. 1204.

43. Martin v. United Security Services, Fla.1975, 314 So.2d 765.

44. See Plaza Express Co. v. Galloway, 1955, 365 Mo. 166, 280 S.W.2d 17.

45. See Wettach, Wrongful Death and Contributory Negligence, 1938, 16 N.C.L.Rev. 211; Wigmore, Contributory Negligence of the Beneficiary as a Bar to an Administrator's Action for Death, 1908, 2 Ill.L.Rev. 487; Gilmore, Imputed Negligence, 1921, 1 Wis.L.Rev. 193, 257, 259–273.

46. Lundberg v. Hagen, 1974, 114 N.H. 110, 316 A.2d 177; Mitchell v. Akers, Tex.Civ.App.1966, 401 S.W.2d 907, refused n.r.e.; Stockton v. Baker, 1948, 213 Ark. 918, 213 S.W.2d 896; Koehler v. Waukesha Milk Co., 1926, 190 Wis. 52, 208 N.W. 901; Love v. Detroit, Jackson & Chicago Railroad Co., 1912, 170 Mich. 1, 135 N.W. 963; Nashville Lumber Co. v. Busbee, 1911, 100 Ark. 76, 139 S.W. 301. See Notes, 1967, 4 Houst.L.Rev. 534; 1967, 19 Bay.L.Rev. 153; Annot., 2 A.L.R.2d 785.

47. O'Connor v. Benson Coal Co., 1938, 301 Mass. 145, 16 N.E.2d 636; Davis v. Margolis, 1929, 108 Conn. 645, 144 A. 665; Bloomquist v. City of La Grande, 1926, 120 Or. 19, 251 P. 252; Consolidated Traction Co. v. Hone, 1896, 59 N.J.L. 275, 35 A. 899, reversed 1897, 60 N.J.L. 444, 38 A. 759. See Note, 1955, 29 St.Johns L.Rev. 321.

48. Acres v. Hall's Administrator, Ky.1952, 253 S.W.2d 373; Nichols v. Nashville Housing Authority, 1949, 187 Tenn. 683, 216 S.W.2d 694; Jenson v. Glemaker, 1935, 195 Minn. 556, 263 N.W. 624; Butterfield v. Community Light & Power Co., 1946, 115 Vt. 23, 49 A.2d 415; Womack v. Preach, 1946, 64 Ariz. 61, 165 P.2d 657; Brown v. Spokane County Fire Protection District No. 1, 1978, 21 Wn.App. 886, 586 P.2d 1207 (reduction under comparative negligence).

Under particular statutes, other conduct of a beneficiary may be a complete or partial defense. See for example Matthews v. Hicks, 1955, 197 Va. 112, 87 S.E.2d 629 (adultery of wife). As to immunity of the defendant toward a beneficiary, see supra, p. 955.

49. Lee v. New River & Pocahontas Consolidated Coal Co., 4th Cir. 1913, 203 F. 644; Dickinson v. Stuart Colliery Co., 1912, 71 W.Va. 325, 76 S.E. 654; Missouri, Kansas & Texas Railway Co. of Texas v. Evans, 1897, 16 Tex.Civ.App. 68, 41 S.W. 80; Hodges v. Savannah Kaolin Co., 1923, 155 Ga. 143, 116 S.E. 303, opinion conformed to 30 Ga.App. 294, 117 S.E. 829 (all cases of consent of parent to employment of child in dangerous occupation).

50. McKay v. Syracuse Rapid Transit Railway Co., 1913, 208 N.Y. 359, 101 N.E. 885; Danforth v. Emmons, 1924, 124 Me. 156, 126 A. 821; Bastedo v. Frailey, 1932, 109 N.J.L. 390, 162 A. 621.

51. Richardson v. State Department of Roads, 1978, 200 Neb. 225, 263 N.W.2d 442, supplemented 200 Neb. 781, 265 N.W.2d 457; Bartholomay v. St. Thomas Lumber Co., N.D.1967, 148 N.W.2d 278; City of Louisville

reached as to assumption of risk.⁵² In a comparative negligence state, a beneficiary's contributory negligence presumably would reduce his own recovery, not the recovery as a whole. A few decisions have gone the other way, holding that the entire action was barred⁵³ by the negligence of one beneficiary in a contributory negligence jurisdiction; but since the leading decision to this effect has lately been overruled in Illinois,⁵⁴ it appears unlikely that these will be followed today. About all that remains of the barred action is the antique rule in a small number of states⁵⁵ which "imputes" the negligence of one parent to the other when the action is for the death of a child. Except where it can be justified on the basis that the damages recovered will be community property,⁵⁶ this, too, has generally been rejected as a senseless survival of a discarded concept of marital unity.⁵⁷

Releases given by beneficiaries or by the personal representative claiming on their behalf may or may not operate as a defense. The wrongful death acts are usually construed to provide that there is only one cause of action, even though there may be several beneficiaries.⁵⁸ Where the cause of action is vested in a personal representative or trustee, who must then distribute the recovery to the beneficiaries, his settlement is binding on all.⁵⁹ If the personal representative's interest is adverse to some beneficiaries, they may be permitted to intervene in the death action; ⁶⁰ and if he makes an improper settlement, they have an action

v. Stuckenborg, Ky.1969, 438 S.W.2d 94; Oviatt v. Camarra, 1957, 210 Or. 445, 311 P.2d 746; Lindley v. Sink, 1940, 218 Ind. 1, 30 N.E.2d 456; Walden v. Coleman, 1962, 105 Ga.App. 435, 124 S.E.2d 695.

The same conclusion is reached when the defendant is one of the beneficiaries. Nosser v. Nosser, 1931, 161 Miss. 636, 137 So. 491; Bays v. Cox' Administrator, 1950, 312 Ky. 827, 229 S.W.2d 737. See also, as to statutes of limitations, Cross v. Pacific Gas & Electric Co., 1964, 60 Cal.2d 690, 36 Cal.Rptr. 321, 388 P.2d 353.

52. Kentucky Utilities Co. v. McCarty's Administrator, 1916, 169 Ky. 38, 183 S.W. 237.

53. Hazel v. Hoopeston-Danville Motor Bus Co., 1923, 310 Ill. 38, 141 N.E. 392; Wilson v. Clarendon County, 1927, 139 S.C. 333, 138 S.E. 33; Darbrinsky v. Pennsylvania Co., 1915, 248 Pa. 503, 94 A. 269. At the other extreme were such cases as Herrell v. St. Louis-San Francisco, Railroad Co., 1929, 324 Mo. 38, 23 S.W.2d 102, refusing even to reduce the damages. Cf. Kokesh v. Price, 1917, 136 Minn. 304, 161 N.W. 715 (reduction not demanded).

54. In Nudd v. Matsoukas, 1956, 7 Ill.2d 608, 131 N.E.2d 525. See also Walden v. Coleman, 1962, 217 Ga. 599, 124 S.E.2d 265, declining to follow prior authority.

55. Klepper v. Breslin, Fla.1955, 83 So.2d 587; Shelton v. Williams, 1959, 204 Tenn. 417, 321 S.W.2d 807; Beasley v. United States, D.C.S.C.1948, 81 F.Supp. 518.

56. Cervantes v. Maco Gas Co., 1970, 177 Cal.App. 2d 246, 2 Cal.Rptr. 75; Crevelli v. Chicago, Milwaukee & St. Paul Railway, 1917, 98 Wash. 42, 167 P. 66. Cf. DeLozier v. Smith, 1974, 22 Ariz.App. 136, 524 P.2d 970 (H's negligence imputed to W under community property rules, W as decedent guilty of imputed negligence and all beneficiaries barred). Most community property states have now made provision for separate property in some portions of the tort recovery. This appears to remove the basis for the decisions cited. See Rogers v. Yellowstone Park Co., 1975, 97 Idaho 14, 539 P.2d 566; Freehe v. Freehe, 1972, 81 Wn.2d 183, 500 P.2d 771.

57. Reynolds v. Thompson, Mo.1948, 215 S.W.2d 452; Lindley v. Sink, 1940, 218 Ind. 1, 30 N.E.2d 456; Los Angeles & Salt Lake Railroad Co. v. Umbaugh, 1942, 61 Nev. 214, 123 P.2d 224; Tufty v. Sioux Transit Co., 1945, 70 S.D. 352, 17 N.W.2d 700; Pearson v. National Manufacture & Stores Corp., 1941, 219 N.C. 717, 14 S.E.2d 811.

58. Daubert v. Western Meat Co., 1915, 139 Cal. 480, 69 P. 297, affirmed 139 Cal. 480, 73 P. 244; Gulf & Ship Island Railroad Co. v. Bradley, 1915, 110 Miss. 152, 69 So. 666; Cowan v. Atchison, Topeka & Sante Fe Railway Co., 1917, 66 Okl. 273, 168 P. 1015; Edwards v. Interstate Chemical Co., 1916, 170 N.C. 551, 87 S.E. 635. But see contra: Nelson v. Galveston, Harrisburg & San Antonio Railway Co., 1890, 78 Tex. 621, 14 S.W. 1021; Eichorn v. New Orleans & Carrollton, Railroad, Light & Power Co., 1905, 114 La. 712, 38 So. 526.

59. Williams v. Louisville & Nashville Railroad, 6th Cir. 1967, 371 F.2d 125, certiorari denied 388 U.S. 919, 87 S.Ct. 2138, 18 L.Ed.2d 1364; Campbell v. C & H Transportation Co., Miss.1982, 411 So.2d 1284; Hughes v. White, 1980, 289 Or. 13, 609 P.2d 365. Statutes may require court approval of the settlement itself. See Caputo v. Holt, 1976, 217 Va. 302, 228 S.E.2d 134.

If one procures an appointment as personal representative through forgery, a settlement he makes may not bar beneficiaries, though they may be compelled to credit the defendant for the payment actually made. Kelly v. Peerless Insurance Co., 1981, 121 N.H. 253, 428 A.2d 491.

60. Smith v. Clark Sherwood Oil Field Contractors, 5th Cir. 1972, 457 F.2d 1339, certiorari denied 409 U.S. 980, 93 S.Ct. 308, 34 L.Ed.2d 243; Benoit v. Fireman's Fund Insurance Co., La.1978, 355 So.2d 892, on remand 361 So.2d 1332.

against him, not against the tortfeasor who has settled with the proper person.[61] Even under this rule, however, some courts have been especially solicitous of children and have said that they are not bound by the personal representative's settlement unless there was a guardian appointed to assert their interests, or a court approval of the settlement, or at least notice to them before the settlement was effected.[62] Where the beneficiary settles and gives a release, he bars his own claim, but his release ordinarily will not bar the claims of other beneficiaries or the claim of the personal representative on their behalf.[63] This rule has been followed even where a beneficiary, having settled in his individual capacity, is later appointed as personal representative, in which case he is permitted to pursue the claim for the benefit of other beneficiaries.[64]

The impression gained from a survey of the law of wrongful death and survival is that both the statutes and the decisions sometimes fall short of what is needed to provide compensation and avoid costly windfalls. Much improvement might be made by a comprehensive statute,[65] but recent statutes have not always been logical or neutral, and no doubt the law will continue to need thoughtful and vigorous judicial action to fill the gaps that inevitably exist in all statutes, including, or especially, the wrongful death acts.[66]

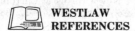 **WESTLAW REFERENCES**

(lord +1 campbell) +4 act

"wrongful death" /p super*ede* override* preclude* /p "work! compensation" "survival statute"
"wrongful death" /p basis theory grounds /s recovery /s "intent! tort*" negligence "strict**liab!"
"wrongful death" /p breach /s warranty contract

Plaintiff and Beneficiaries

headnote(wrongful +1 death /s action* /s bring* brought /s executor* administrator* "personal representative*")
digest("wrongful death" /p behalf /p surviv*** beneficiar***
digest(sole +5 heir* beneficiar*** /s "wrongful death")
"wrongful death" /s creditor*
117k32

Damages

digest("wrongful death" /p compensat*** recover*** /p support service* contribution* benefit* earnings /s decedent*)
headnote("wrongful death" /p "pecuniary loss**")
headnote("wrongful death" /p los*** /s intangible consortium society comfort affection guidance advice love companionship)
117k93
headnote("wrongful death" /p funeral /3 expense* cost*
"wrongful death" /p impair! diminish! lessen! reduc! /s earning* income /s capacity
headnote(damages /p "wrongful death" /p instruction* /s jury jurors)

Defenses

(117k15 & headnote(deceased decedent /p "wrongful death")
opinion(wrongful +1 death /s "contributory negligence" "comparative negligence" consent assumption +2 risk)
"wrongful death" /p marital int**famil! int**spousal +s immunity
"wrongful death" /p judicata "collateral estop!"
digest(wrongful +1 death /p statute* of limitation*)
topic(241) /p "wrongful death"
survival +2 act* action* statute* /p "wrongful death" /p bar* estop! foreclose* limit*** preclude* prevent*

---

61. Williams v. Louisville & Nashville Railroad, 6th Cir. 1967, 371 F.2d 125, certiorari denied 388 U.S. 919, 87 S.Ct. 2138, 18 L.Ed.2d 1364, suggesting an accounting. In re Milliman, 1966, 101 Ariz. 54, 415 P.2d 877 the court suggested that a constructive trust or equitable lien might be appropriate on a proper set of facts.

62. In re Milliman, 1966, 101 Ariz. 54, 415 P.2d 877; Wood v. Dunlop, 1974, 83 Wn.2d 719, 521 P.2d 1177.

Court approval of a settlement by a person who, under the statute, has no authority to settle, of course adds nothing and the settlement is not binding. In re Milliman, supra; Benoit v. Fireman's Fund Insurance Co., La.1978, 355 So.2d 892, on remand 361 So.2d 1332.

63. Kroger Grocery & Baking Co. v. Reddin, 8th Cir. 1942, 128 F.2d 787; McVeigh v. Minneapolis & Rainy River Railroad Co., 1910, 110 Minn. 184, 124 N.W. 971; Pittsburgh, Cincinnati, Chicago & St. Louis Railway Co. v. Moore, 1898, 152 Ind. 345, 53 N.E. 290.

64. Kroger Grocery & Baking Co. v. Reddin, 8th Cir. 1942, 128 F.2d 787; Todd v. Adams, 1974, 23 N.C. App. 104, 208 S.E.2d 237.

65. See Notes, 1935, 48 Harv.L.Rev. 1008; 1931, 44 Harv.L.Rev. 980; Killion, Wrongful Death Actions in California: Some Needed Amendments, 1937, 25 Cal.L. Rev. 170.

66. See R. Keeton, Statutes, Gaps & Values in Tort Law, 1978, 44 J.Air L. 1.

beneficiar*** plaintiff* execut! administrator* /s "comparative negligence" "contributory negligence" consent assumption +2 risk /p survival +2 statute* act* action*

beneficiar*** /s "comparative negligence" "contributory negligence" consent assumption +2 risk /p "wrongful death" /p bar* defense estop! limit*** preclud***

beneficiar*** personal +2 representative /s release* discharge* relinquish* settle! /p "wrongful death"

negligen! /s imput! /s parent /s child & "wrongful death"

"wrongful death" /p windfall*

Chapter 24

ECONOMIC RELATIONS

Table of Sections

Sec.
128. Injurious Falsehood.
129. Interference With Contractual Relations.
130. Interference With Prospective Advantage.

§ 128. Injurious Falsehood

A considerable body of law has grown up about the subject of interference with commercial or economic relations. Included in the field of such relations are of course existing contracts, and agreements and understandings which are contractual in their nature—and particularly contracts of a business or commercial character, or those of employment; and in addition, the expectation of pecuniary or economic advantage from dealings with others, such as the prospect of obtaining future customers, or of future employment. The relation may exist between the plaintiff and one individual only, as in the case of an existing contract, or it may be a general relation with such members of the public as may be expected to deal with the plaintiff.[1]

The recognition that such relations are entitled to protection against unreasonable interference is on the whole a comparatively recent development. In one respect, however, it is very old. Pecuniary loss inflicted by interference with the plaintiff's personal reputation already has been encountered in defamation.[2] Because of its ancient, left-handed association with defamation, the kind of interference by falsehoods which are not personally defamatory, and yet cause pecuniary loss, has for some centuries been regarded as a more or less distinct tort in itself.

The earliest cases,[3] which arose shortly before 1600, involved oral aspersions cast upon the plaintiff's ownership of land, by which he was prevented from leasing or selling it; and from this the tort acquired the name of "slander of title."[4] The plaintiff's

§ 128

1. Green, Relational Interests, 1935, 29 Ill.L.Rev. 1041, 30 Ill.L.Rev. 1.

2. See supra, § 116A.

3. Gerrard v. Dickenson, 1588, Cro.Eliz. 196, 78 Eng.Rep. 452; Pennyman v. Rabanks, 1895, Cro.Eliz. 427, 78 Eng.Rep. 668; see Earl of Northumberland v.

Byrt, 1606, Cro.Jac. 163, 79 Eng.Rep. 143. See the chronological list of English Cases in Bower, Actionable Defamation, 2d ed. 1923, 212 note.

4. Bower, Actionable Defamation, 2d ed. 1923, 210 note, traces this to the use of "slander" as a generic term for injury or depreciation of any kind.

title or property seems to have been regarded as somehow personified, and so defamed.[5] Because of the unfortunate association with "slander," a supposed analogy to defamation has hung over the tort like a fog, and has had great influence upon its development.[6] On the other hand, the action seems to have been recognized from the beginning as only loosely allied to defamation, and to be rather an action on the case for the special damage resulting from the defendant's interference. In the nineteenth century it was enlarged by slow degrees, first to include written aspersions[7] and the title to property other than land,[8] and then to cover disparagement of the quality of the property,[9] rather than its title, and many contemporary cases concern aspersions cast upon a commercial product[10] or even on a business operation itself.[11] The tort is thus called by various names such as "disparagement of property," "slander of goods," "commercial disparagement," and "trade libel."[12] As a matter of fact, subsequent decisions have shown that the tort is broader in its scope than any of these terms would indicate.

The principle has been applied, for example, to statements injurious to the plaintiff's business but casting no reflection upon either his person or his property, such as the assertion that he has died or gone out of business,[13] or defamatory words concerning his employees.[14] It has even been carried over to interference with non-commercial relations, such as the expectancy of a marriage,[15] or the right to remain in the United States rather than be deported,[16] or the case of an employer falsely reporting payments to an employee which subject him to income tax prosecution,[17] or a forged assignment of

---

5. " * * * by a sort of figure of speech, in which the title is personified and made subject to many of the rules applicable to personal slander, when the words themselves are not actionable." Kendall v. Stone, 1851, 5 N.Y. 14. Accord: Coley v. Hecker, 1928, 206 Cal. 22, 272 P. 1045; Carroll v. Warner Brothers Pictures, S.D.N.Y.1937, 20 F.Supp. 405.

6. Thus, for example, the statute of limitations applicable to defamation is commonly held to apply, as in Norton v. Kanouff, 1957, 165 Neb. 435, 86 N.W.2d 72; Woodard v. Pacific Fruit & Produce Co., 1940, 165 Or. 250, 106 P.2d 1043.

Contra, Henry V. Vaccaro Construction Co. v. A. J. DePace, Inc., 1975, 137 N.J.Super. 512, 349 A.2d 570. Other statutes that mention libel or slander but not injurious falsehood may create similar problems of interpretation. See Menefee v. Columbia Broadcasting System, Inc., 1974, 458 Pa. 46, 329 A.2d 216 (survival statute).

7. See Malachy v. Soper, 1836, 3 Bing.N.C. 371, 132 Eng.Rep. 453; Coley v. Hecker, 1928, 206 Cal. 22, 272 P. 1045; Barkhorn v. Adlib Associates, Inc., D.Hawaii 1962, 203 F.Supp. 121.

8. Malachy v. Soper, 1836, 3 Bing.N.C. 371, 132 Eng.Rep. 453.

9. Western Counties Manure Co. v. Lawes Chem. Manure Co., 1874, L.R. 9 Ex. 218.

10. System Operations, Inc. v. Scientific Games Development Corp., 3d Cir. 1977, 555 F.2d 1131; Testing Systems, Inc. v. Magnaflux Corp., D.Pa.1966, 251 F.Supp. 286.

11. Bromage v. Prosser, 1825, 107 Eng.Rep. 1051 (bank closed); Young v. Geiske, 1904, 209 Pa. 515, 58 A. 887 (dividend illegal); Menefee v. Columbia Broadcasting System, Inc., 1974, 458 Pa. 46, 329 A.2d 216, 74 A.L.R.3d 290 (radio performer's rating down).

12. See the excellent Note, 1953, 63 Yale L.J. 65. Also Wood, Disparagement of Title and Quality, 1942, 20 Can.Bar Rev. 296, 430; Notes, 1945, 33 Geo.L.J. 213; 1945, 19 So.Cal.L.Rev. 45; 1943, 28 Corn.L.Q. 226.

13. Ratcliffe v. Evans, [1892] Q.B. 524; Dudley v. Briggs, 1886, 141 Mass. 582, 6 N.E. 717; American Insurance Co. v. France, 1903, 111 Ill.App. 382; Davis v. New England Railway Publishing Co., 1909, 203 Mass. 470, 89 N.E. 565. Cf. Sheppard Publishing Co. v. Press Publishing Co., 1905, 10 Ont.L.Rep. 243; House of Directories v. Lane Directory Co., 1918, 182 Ky. 384, 206 S.W. 475; Jarrahdale Timber Co. v. Temperley & Co., 1894, 11 T.L.R. 119 (statement that plaintiff does not import certain wood); and see Balden v. Shorter, [1933] Ch. 427 (statement that plaintiff was employed by defendant, as a result of which he lost commissions).

14. Riding v. Smith, 1876, 1 Ex. 91, 154 Eng.Rep. 38. Cf. Casey v. Arnott, 1876, 2 C.P.D. 24 (statement that plaintiff's ship was unseaworthy, as a result of which the crew refused to go to sea).

15. Shepherd v. Wakeman, 1662, 1 Sid. 79, 82 Eng. Rep. 982. Cf. Freeman v. Busch Jewelry Co., N.D.Ga. 1951, 98 F.Supp. 963 (marriage).

16. Al Raschid v. News Syndicate Co., 1934, 265 N.Y. 1, 191 N.E. 713. See Note, 1934, 14 Boston U.L. Rev. 856.

17. Gale v. Ryan, 1941, 263 App.Div. 76, 31 N.Y.S. 2d 732; Penn-Ohio Steel Corp. v. Allis-Chalmers Manufacturing Co., 1966, 50 Misc.2d 860, 272 N.Y.S.2d 266, reversed on other grounds 28 A.D.2d 659, 280 N.Y.S.2d 679, affirmed 21 N.Y.2d 916, 289 N.Y.S.2d 753, 237 N.E.2d 73. Cf. Owens v. Mench, Pa.1952, 81 D. & C. 314, 24 Leh.L.J. 522 (physician falsely reporting on injury, necessitating suit for workmen's compensation); Felis v. Greenberg, 1966, 51 Misc.2d 441, 273 N.Y.S.2d 288 (physician falsely reporting to insurer); Cooper v.

commissions resulting in plaintiff's discharge by his employer,[18] or even solicitation of money in the plaintiff's name without sending the tips on the races promised in return.[19] Undoubtedly the best and most inclusive name for the tort is that of "injurious falsehood," coined by Sir John Salmond.[20] The term has now been adopted by the Restatement[21] and has begun to appear in the cases[22] and the professional literature.[23] The term is a useful one by which to distinguish personal defamation claims. Since in every case of injurious falsehood the plaintiff must prove special damage, such as the loss of a present or prospective advantage,[24] it seems clear that the injurious falsehood claim should be regarded merely as one form of intentional interference with economic relations[25] rather than as a branch of the more general harm to reputation involved in libel and slander,[26] even though,

under the impact of Constitutional decisions, the rules governing the two torts may often prove to be much the same.[27]

Although it is important to distinguish between personal defamation of the plaintiff on the one hand and disparagement of his property on the other, it is not always easy to do so.[28] If the statement charges the plaintiff with personal misconduct, or imputes to him reprehensible personal characteristics, it is regarded as libel or slander.[29] This carried with it at common law a right, in a large number of cases, to recover without proof of special damages, and it carries with it today certain Constitutional constraints arising out of the First Amendment's protection of free speech. On the other hand, if the aspersions reflect only upon the quality of what the plaintiff has to sell,[30] or the character of his business as such,[31] it is merely disparagement, and proof

---

Weissblatt, 1935, 154 Misc. 522, 277 N.Y.S. 709 (deceiving church tribunal, forcing plaintiff to defend suit); Morgan v. Graham, 10th Cir. 1956, 228 F.2d 625 (president of liability insurer denying coverage, plaintiff dismissed his action against insured).

18. Bartlett v. Federal Outfitting Co., 1933, 133 Cal. App. 747, 24 P.2d 877.

19. Wise v. Western Union Telegraph Co., Del.1934, 6 W.W.Harr. 155, 172 A. 757. Cf. Kelite Products Inc. v. Binzel, 5th Cir. 1955, 224 F.2d 131 (filing change of address card with post-office, so that plaintiff did not receive business mail).

Cf. Morrison v. National Broadcasting Co., 1965, 24 A.D.2d 284, 266 N.Y.S.2d 406, reversed on other grounds 19 N.Y.2d 453, 280 N.Y.S.2d 641, 227 N.E.2d 572; and see Note, 1966, 35 U.Cin.L.Rev. 523.

20. Salmond, Law of Torts, § 151.

21. Second Restatement of Torts, § 623A.

22. E.g., Diehl & Sons, Inc. v. International Harvester, D.N.Y.1978, 445 F.Supp. 282; Direct Import Buyers Association v. K.S.L., Utah 1975, 538 P.2d 1040, appeal after remand 572 P.2d 692.

23. Lynn, Injurious Falsehood! 1978, 52 Fla.Bar J. 360.

24. See infra, p. 970. Other important differences arise as to the burden of proof. See infra, p. 948.

25. Green, Relational Interest, 1935, 35 Ill.Rev. 1, 37.

26. As to the differences between defamation and disparagement before the constitutional decisions governing defamation, see Smith, Disparagement of Property, 1913, 13 Col.L.Rev. 13, 21.

27. See below p. 970.

28. See Wham, Disparagement of Property, 1926, 21 Ill.L.Rev. 26; Hibschman, Defamation or Disparagement, 1940, 24 Minn.L.Rev. 625; Note, 1953, 63 Yale L.J. 65, 69–74; Note, 1975, 75 Colum.L.Rev. 963.

29. Merle v. Sociological Research Film Corp., 1915, 166 App.Div. 376, 152 N.Y.S. 829 (factory used as place of assignation); Kilpatrick v. Edge, 1913, 85 N.J.L. 7, 88 A. 839 (misconduct in a Turkish bath); Crinkley v. Dow Jones and Co., 1979, 67 Ill.App.3d 869, 24 Ill.Dec. 573, 385 N.E.2d 714.

In Dubourcq v. Brouwer, Sup.1953, 124 N.Y.S.2d 61, affirmed 282 App.Div. 861, 124 N.Y.S.2d 842, affirmed 283 App.Div. 942, 131 N.Y.S.2d 300, it was held that where defamation will lie disparagement is excluded. Contra, Hatchard v. Mége, 1887, 18 Q.B.D. 771 (survival).

30. Drug Research Corp. v. Curtis Publishing Co., 1960, 7 N.Y.2d 435, 199 N.Y.S.2d 33, 166 N.E.2d 319; National Dynamics Corp. v. Petersen Publishing Co., S.D.N.Y.1960, 185 F.Supp. 573; Blens Chemicals v. Wyandotte Chemical Corp., 1950, 197 Misc. 1066, 96 N.Y.S.2d 47; Testing Systems, Inc. v. Magnaflux Corp., E.D.Pa.1966, 251 F.Supp. 286; Berman v. Medical Society of New York, 1965, 23 A.D.2d 98, 258 N.Y.S.2d 497 (medical test developed by doctor is like "product").

31. Fowler v. Curtis Publishing Co., D.C.Cir. 1950, 182 F.2d 377; General Market Co. v. Post-Intelligencer Co., 1917, 96 Wash. 575, 165 P. 482; National Refining Co. v. Benzo Gas Motor Fuel Co., 8th Cir. 1927, 20 F.2d 763, certiorari denied 275 U.S. 570, 48 S.Ct. 157, 72 L.Ed. 431; Dust Sprayer Manufacturing Co. v. Western Fruit Grower, 1907, 126 Mo.App. 139, 103 S.W. 566; Cleveland Leader Printing Co. v. Nethersole, 1911, 84

of damage has always been essential to the cause of action. There is the possibility that the First Amendment will not apply, or not apply in the same way, to this kind of "commercial" speech. The difficulty in the distinction between the personal aspersion and the commercial disparagement lies in the fact that many statements effectuate both harms. It might be possible to imply some accusation of personal inefficiency or incompetence, at least, in nearly every imputation directed against a business or its product.[32] The courts have gone to some lengths, however, in refusing to do so,[33] particularly where the most that can be made out of the words is a charge of ignorance or negligence.[34] Personal defamation is found only where the imputation fairly implied is that the plaintiff is dishonest or lacking in integrity, or that he is deliberately perpetrating a fraud upon the public by selling a product which he knows to be defective.[35] Such, at least, is the theory of the cases; yet it is not always easy to find the purported distinction in the actual facts.[36]

Interests Protected

For the most part the injurious falsehood cases have been concerned with aspersions upon the title to property, or its quality. Any type of legally protected [37] property interest that is capable of being sold may be the subject of disparagement, including land,[38] remainders,[39] leases,[40] mineral

---

Ohio St. 118, 95 N.E. 735; Fairyland Amusement Co. v. Metromedia, Inc., D.Mo.1976, 413 F.Supp. 1290.

32. Cf. Summit Hotel Co. v. National Broadcasting Co., 1939, 336 Pa. 182, 8 A.2d 302 ("rotten hotel" held to reflect on the operators or management).

33. Australian Newspaper Co. v. Bennett, [1894] A.C. 284 ("Ananias"); Nonpareil Cork Manufacturing Co. v. Keasbey & Mattison Co., D.Pa.1901, 108 F. 721 (product a "fraud"); Erick Bowman Remedy Co. v. Jensen Salsbery Laboratories, 8th Cir. 1926, 17 F.2d 255 (Barnum was right); Bosi v. New York Herald Co., 1901, 33 Misc. 622, 68 N.Y.S. 898, affirmed 58 App.Div. 619, 68 N.Y.S. 1134 (hotel a favorite resort of anarchists).

34. Dooling v. Budget Publishing Co., 1887, 144 Mass. 258, 10 N.E. 809 (poor dinner served by caterer); Marlin Fire Arms Co. v. Shields, 1902, 171 N.Y. 384, 64 N.E. 163 (poor quality firearms); Shaw Cleaners & Dyers v. Des Moines Dress Club, 1932, 215 Iowa 1130, 245 N.W. 231 (garments only "half cleaned"); Adolf Philipp Co. v. New Yorker Staats-Zeitung Co., 1914, 165 App.Div. 377, 150 N.Y.S. 1044 (theatre and play); Hopkins Chemical Co. v. Read Drug & Chemical Co., 1941, 124 Md. 210, 92 A. 478.

35. Harwood Pharmacal Co. v. National Broadcasting Co., 1961, 9 N.Y.2d 460, 214 N.Y.S.2d 725, 174 N.E.2d 602 (product containing habit-forming drugs); Rosenberg v. J. C. Penney Co., 1939, 30 Cal.App.2d 609, 86 P.2d 696 (shoddy garments); Vitagraph Co. of America v. Ford, S.D.N.Y.1917, 241 F. 681 (false motives and deceptive advertising); Puget Sound Navigation Co. v. Carter, W.D.Wash.1916, 233 F. 832 (exorbitant rates and ruthless competition); Tobin v. Alfred M. Best Co., 1907, 120 App.Div. 387, 105 N.Y.S. 294 ("fake" insurance policy). See Hibschman, Defamation or Disparagement, 1940, 24 Minn.L.Rev. 625.

36. As where a corporation is permitted to recover without proof of special damages because of an erroneous credit report showing an unpaid judgment against it. See Grove v. Dun & Bradstreet, Inc., 3d Cir. 1971, 438 F.2d 433, certiorari denied 404 U.S. 898, 92 S.Ct. 204, 30 L.Ed.2d 175.

37. Doubtful titles have been denied protection. Millman v. Pratt, 1824, 2 B. & C. 486, 107 Eng.Rep. 465; Thompson v. White, 1886, 70 Cal. 135, 11 P. 564; Stovall v. Texas Co., Tex.Civ.App.1924, 262 S.W. 152, error denied 1926, 114 Tex. 582, 278 S.W. 1115; cf. Welsbach Light Co. v. American Incandescent Lamp Co., C.C.N.Y.1899, 99 F. 501. Also a mere expectancy. Nelson v. Staff, 1618, Cro.Jac. 422, 79 Eng.Rep. 360; Humphreys v. Stanfield, 1638, Cro.Car. 469, 79 Eng.Rep. 1005. Massachusetts has refused to protect an equitable interest, Hurley v. Donovan, 1902, 182 Mass. 64, 64 N.E. 685, and Alabama a debt claim. Pickens v. Hal J. Copeland Grocery Co., 1929, 219 Ala. 697, 123 So. 223. Since both are capable of being sold, the last two decisions seem wrong. On the other hand, in L–M Co. v. Blanchard, La.App.1967, 197 So.2d 178, writ refused 250 La. 908, 199 So.2d 918, mere adverse possession of land was held to be sufficient.

38. Thus the tort frequently arises out of the assertion of a lien or other claim against land, preventing its sale or lease. Cronkhite v. Chaplin, 10th Cir. 1922, 282 F. 579; Greenlake Investment Co. v. Swarthout, Mo.App.1942, 161 S.W.2d 697; Frega v. Northern New Jersey Mortgage Association, 1958, 51 N.J.Super. 331, 143 A.2d 885. Cf. Cawrse v. Signal Oil Co., 1940, 164 Or. 666, 103 P.2d 729; Lehman v. Goldin, 1948, 160 Fla. 710, 36 So.2d 259; Baker v. Kale, 1947, 83 Cal.App.2d 89, 189 P.2d 57. Compare, as to disparagement of quality, Paull v. Halferty, 1869, 63 Pa.St. 46 (iron ore about to run out).

As to claims for abuse of process based on excessive attachment, garnishment or levy, see § 121, supra. Injunctions and receiverships affecting use or vendibility of property may give rise to claims under statutes or bonds. See Braun v. Pepper, 1978, 224 Kan. 56, 578 P.2d 695; Dobbs, Security, Provisional Injunctive Relief, 1974, 52 N.C.L.Rev. 1091.

39 & 40. See notes 39 and 40 on page 966.

rights,[41] chattels,[42] and intangible interests, such as trade marks,[43] copyrights,[44] patents,[45] corporate shares,[46] or literary property,[47] such as motion pictures.[48]

It seems clear, however, that entirely too much emphasis has been placed upon the property element. The gist of the tort is the interference with the prospect of sale or some other advantageous relation; and it is equally possible to disparage the plaintiff's business by reflecting upon its existence [49] or character,[50] the manner in which it is conducted,[51] its employees,[52] or its customers,[53] or its popularity [54] or danger [55] without affecting any property. A common illustration is the assertion that the sale of the plaintiff's product infringes the defendant's patent or copyright,[56] which scarcely can be said to disparage the title or quality of the goods themselves. The disparagement itself may be by implication, as where the statement that one portrait of a President is the first one made of him is understood to mean that another is not.[57] As has been suggest-

39. Vaughn v. Ellis, 1609, Cro.Jac. 213, 79 Eng.Rep. 185.

40. Hopkins v. Drowne, 1898, 21 R.I. 20, 41 A. 567; Fleming v. McDonald, 1911, 230 Pa. 75, 79 A. 226; Brook v. Rawl, 1849, 4 Exch. 521, 154 Eng.Rep. 1320 (assignee of lease).

41. Reynolds v. Villines, 1931, 148 Okl. 191, 298 P. 262.

42. Woodard v. Pacific Fruit & Produce Co., 1940, 165 Or. 250, 106 P.2d 1043 (crop); Miller v. First National Bank of Gladbrook, 1935, 220 Iowa 1266, 264 N.W. 272 (sheep); Youngquist v. American Railway Express Co., 1926, 49 S.D. 373, 206 N.W. 576 (horses). See also the cases of disparagement of quality of goods, supra, p. 964.

43. Hatchard v. Mége, 1887, 18 Q.B.D. 771; Royal Baking Powder Co. v. Wright, 1900, 18 Reg.Pat.Cas. 95; Herbert Products v. Oxy-Dry Sprayer Corp., 1955, 1 Misc.2d 71, 145 N.Y.S.2d 168; Big O Tire Dealers, Inc. v. Goodyear Tire & Rubber Co., 10th Cir. 1977, 561 F.2d 1365, certiorari denied 434 U.S. 1052, 98 S.Ct. 905, 54 L.Ed.2d 805.

44. Dicks v. Brooks, 1880, 15 Ch.Div. 22.

45. Hanson v. Hall Manufacturing Co., 1922, 194 Iowa 1213, 190 N.W. 967; Andrew v. Deshler, 1881, 43 N.J.L. 16; Croft v. Richardson, N.Y.1880, 59 How.Pr. 356.

46. Malachy v. Soper, 1836, 3 Bing.N.C. 371, 132 Eng.Rep. 453; Coronado Development Corp. v. Millikin, 1940, 175 Misc. 1, 22 N.Y.S.2d 670, appeal dismissed 1941, 262 App.Div. 1019, 30 N.Y.S.2d 847.

47. See Hygienic Fleeced Underwear Co. v. Way, 1908, 35 Pa.Super. 229; John W. Lovell Co. v. Houghton, 1889, 116 N.Y. 520, 22 N.E. 1066.

48. Paramount Pictures v. Leader Press, 10th Cir. 1939, 106 F.2d 229; Carroll v. Warner Brothers Pictures, D.N.Y.1937, 20 F.Supp. 405 (title). Cf. Advance Music Corp. v. American Tobacco Co., 1946, 296 N.Y. 79, 70 N.E.2d 401, reversing 1944, 268 App.Div. 707, 53 N.Y.S.2d 337 (song hit); Pendleton v. Time, Inc., 1949, 339 Ill.App. 188, 89 N.E.2d 435 (portrait of President Truman).

49. See cases cited supra, note 13.

Debt, bad credit, and bankruptcy would seem logically to be in the same category. Courts have at times, however, treated these imputations as personal slander or libel and have said that they are actionable without proof of special damages. See Altoona Clay Products, Inc. v. Dun & Bradstreet, Inc., 3d Cir. 1966, 367 F.2d 625, on remand 286 F.Supp. 899, vacated 308 F.Supp. 1068, reversed 438 F.2d 433, certiorari denied 404 U.S. 898, 92 S.Ct. 204, 30 L.Ed.2d 175. But in many such cases special damages probably existed. See Lion Oil Co. v. Sinclair Refining Co., 1929, 252 Ill.App. 92. Many of the cases that speak of libel per se in this context may mean only that the meaning is clear on the face of the statement. See Annot., 49 A.L.R.3d 163.

50. Cf. Le Massena v. Storm, 1901, 62 App.Div. 150, 70 N.Y.S. 882 (suitability of newspaper for advertising); Lyne v. Nicholls, 1906, 23 T.L.R. 86 (circulation of newspaper); Braun v. Armour & Co., 1930, 254 N.Y. 514, 173 N.E. 845 (kosher butcher listed as selling bacon).

51. Shaw Cleaners & Dyers v. Des Moines Dress Club, 1932, 215 Iowa 1130, 245 N.W. 231 (garments only half cleaned); Dooling v. Budget Publishing Co., 1887, 144 Mass. 258, 10 N.E. 809 (poor dinner served by caterer); Australian Newspaper Co. v. Bennett, [1894] A.C. 284 (newspaper "Ananias").

52. Cf. Riding v. Smith, 1876, 1 Exch. 91, 154 Eng. Rep. 38.

53. Cf. Kennedy v. Press Publishing Co., 1886, 41 Hun 422, 3 N.Y.St.Rep. 139; Bosi v. New York Herald Co., 1901, 33 Misc. 622, 68 N.Y.S.2d 898, affirmed 58 App.Div. 619, 68 N.Y.S. 1134; Maglio v. New York Herald Co., 1903, 83 App.Div. 44, 82 N.Y.S. 509; Id., 1904, 93 App.Div. 546, 87 N.Y.S. 927; El Meson Espanol v. NYM Corp., 2d Cir. 1975, 521 F.2d 737 (good place to meet a "connection" for cocaine).

54. Menefee v. Columbia Broadcasting System, Inc., 1974, 458 Pa. 46, 329 A.2d 216 (performer's popularity said to be down).

55. Fairyland Amusement Co. v. Metromedia, Inc., D.Mo.1976, 413 F.Supp. 1290 (report of high rape incidence near amusement park, plaintiff required to prove special damages).

56. See cases cited supra, notes 44, 45.

57. Pendleton v. Time, Inc., 1949, 339 Ill.App. 188, 89 N.E.2d 435. Cf. Advance Music Corp. v. American Tobacco Co., 1946, 296 N.Y. 79, 70 N.E.2d 401, reversing 1944, 268 App.Div. 707, 53 N.Y.S.2d 337 (failure to

ed above,[58] the cause of action probably is as broad as any injurious falsehood which disturbs prospective advantage, and it is not necessarily confined even to commercial relations.

Elements of Cause of Action

Injurious falsehood, or disparagement, then, may consist of the publication of matter derogatory to the plaintiff's title to his property, or its quality, or to his business in general, or even to some element of his personal affairs, of a kind calculated to prevent others from dealing with him, or otherwise to interfere with his relations with others to his disadvantage.[59]

The plaintiff must prove special damages in the form of pecuniary loss,[60] and this necessarily requires that the falsehood be communicated to a third person,[61] since the tort consists of an interference with the relationship. The communication must play a material and substantial part [62] in inducing others not to deal with the plaintiff, with the result that special damage, in the form of the loss of trade or other dealings, is established.[63]

In addition, the plaintiff must carry the burden of proving that the disparaging statement is false, and if he does not do so he has no claim.[64] It has been argued that liability should be imposed even for truthful statements if they are published for the purpose of doing harm,[65] and in some countries the law appears to be even more severe than that; [66] but the American courts, partly out of concern for free speech and partly out of concern for consumer information,[67] have protected truthful publications regardless of motive.

It is not entirely clear whether the requirement of a "false" statement excludes liability for mere opinions that imply no misstatement of objectively verifiable fact.[68] Liability has been denied for many opinion statements in the comparable area of

include song hits in "Hit Parade"); Davis v. New England Railway Publishing Co., 1909, 203 Mass. 470, 89 N.E. 565 (failure to list plaintiff in directory); and cf. National Refining Co. v. Benzo Gas Motor Fuel Co., 8th Cir. 1927, 20 F.2d 763, certiorari denied 275 U.S. 570, 48 S.Ct. 157, 72 L.Ed. 431; Paramount Pictures v. Leader Press, 10th Cir. 1939, 106 F.2d 229.

58. Supra, p. 963.

59. This definition is somewhat broader than that given in Bower, Actionable Defamation, 2d ed. 1923, 210, and the Restatement of Torts, § 629.

As to disparagement under the Uniform Deceptive Practices Act, see Note, 1966, 51 Iowa L.Rev. 1066.

60. Second Restatement of Torts, § 623A.

61. Hill v. Ward, 1848, 13 Ala. 310; Potosi Zinc Co. v. Mahoney, 1913, 36 Nev. 390, 135 P. 1078; Womack v. McDonald, 1929, 219 Ala. 75, 121 So. 57; Rhoades v. Bugg, 1910, 148 Mo.App. 707, 129 S.W. 38; Arnold v. Producer's Oil Co., Tex.Civ.App.1917, 196 S.W. 735.

Filing of liens, mortgages and other encumbrances is a sufficient publication to disparage title. Coffman v. Henderson, 1913, 9 Ala.App. 553, 63 So. 808; Moore v. Rolin, 1892, 89 Va. 107, 15 S.E. 520; New England Oil & Pipe Line Co. v. Rogers, 1932, 154 Okl. 285, 7 P.2d 638; Dwelle v. Home Realty & Investment Co., 1932, 134 Kan. 520, 7 P.2d 522; Kelly v. First State Bank, 1920, 145 Minn. 331, 177 N.W. 347.

62. Fleming v. McDonald, 1911, 230 Pa. 75, 79 A. 226; Neville v. Higbie, 1933, 130 Cal.App. 669, 20 P.2d 348; Farmers' State Bank v. Hintz, 1928, 206 Iowa 911, 221 N.W. 540; Houston Chronicle Publishing Co. v. Martin, Tex.Civ.App.1933, 64 S.W.2d 816, error dismissed; Union Car Advertising Co. v. Collier, 1934, 263 N.Y. 386, 189 N.E. 463.

63. See infra, p. 970.

64. Brinson v. Carter, 1922, 29 Ga.App. 159, 113 S.E. 820; Allis-Chalmers Manufacturing Co. v. Lowry, 1927, 124 Kan. 566, 261 P. 828; Fant v. Sullivan, Tex. Civ.App.1913, 152 S.W. 515, error refused; Long v. Rucker, 1912, 166 Mo.App. 572, 149 S.W. 1051; Felt v. Germania Life Insurance Co., 1912, 149 App.Div. 14, 133 N.Y.S. 519. The matter falsified must cause the damage, and there is no action if it does not. Kirsch v. Barnes, N.D.Cal.1957, 153 F.Supp. 260 (false acknowledgment of genuine contract).

65. See Wolff, Unfair Competition by Truthful Disparagement, 1938, 47 Yale L.J. 1304.

66. See Note, 1978, 53 Tul.L.Rev. 190, 202.

67. See Testing Systems, Inc. v. Magnaflux Corp., D.Pa.1966, 251 F.Supp. 286, 288–89.

68. Because the fact-opinion dichotomy is a difficult one, one writer has suggested that the test should be "verifiable or refutable on the basis of objective evidence." See Note, The Law of Commercial Disparagement: Business Defamation's Impotent Ally, 63 Yale L.J. 65 (1953). The test seems workable, but "fact" and "opinion" will no doubt continue to be used as shorthand. In lieu of "objectively verifiable" or "fact-opinion" tests, it is possible to use the test whether a reasonable person could be expected to take the statements "seriously." See De Beers Abrasive Products, Ltd. v. International General Electric Co. of New York, Ltd. [1975] 2 All.E.R. 599 (Ch.).

fraud,[69] and the First Amendment has been read to exclude liability for the publication of ideas or opinions in defamation cases.[70] It is possible that the Constitution would be read to place the same strictures on the injurious falsehood action.[71] In addition, the consumer interest in views about products might be thought to justify derogatory opinions even though the same interest does not justify factual misstatement.[72] A number of cases [73] have subscribed to the view that opinion statements of competitors are not actionable,[74] at least where the opinions are presented as comparisons. In other words, to say the plaintiff's product is not as good as defendant's is not a tort at all. The rationale—that opinions are not likely to mislead—seems broad enough to exclude liability for any pure statement of opinion,[75] whether it is offered in the comparative mode or not. But the matter cannot be regarded as settled.

The basis of the defendant's liability for the publication has given considerable difficulty.[76] It is very often said that proof of "malice" on the part of the defendant is essential to the cause of action.[77] But in such cases the question almost invariably has arisen as a matter of what must be pleaded, or the defendant has asserted a conditional privilege,[78] and the "malice" required has been merely such an improper motive as would defeat the privilege. On the other hand, in the absence of privilege many courts have said that "malice" will be presumed from the mere fact of the publication,[79] while others have gone to the extreme of saying that it means no more than an intent to publish, with a simple lack of privi-

69. See § 109, supra.

70. "Under the First Amendment there is no such thing as a false idea. However pernicious an opinion may seem, we depend for its correction not on the conscience of judges and juries but on the competition of other ideas." Gertz v. Robert Welch, Inc., 418 U.S. 323, 339–340, 94 S.Ct. 2997, 3006–3007, 41 L.Ed.2d 789 (1974). See § 113A, supra.

71. See Wade, The Communicative Torts and the First Amendment, 48 Miss.L.J. 671, 708 (1977); Second Restatement of Torts, § 623A, Comment c.

72. See Systems Operations, Inc. v. Scientific Games Development Corp., 3d Cir. 1977, 555 F.2d 1131 (free debate on matters of public interest including merits of products); Nonpareil Cork Manufacturing Co. v. Keasbey & Matthison Co., C.C.Pa.1901, 108 F. 721 (correctness of opinion is for determination by customers, not courts); Continental Air Ticketing Agency, Inc. v. Empire International Travel, Inc., 1976, 51 A.D.2d 104, 380 N.Y.S.2d 369 (information to consuming public).

73. White v. Mellin, [1895] A.C. 154 (H.L.); Hubbuck & Sons, Ltd. v. Wilkinson, Heywood & Clark, Ltd., [1899] 1 Q.B. 86; National Refining Co. v. Benzo Gas Motor Fuel Co., 8th Cir. 1927, 20 F.2d 763, certiorari denied 275 U.S. 570, 48 S.Ct. 157, 72 L.Ed. 431; Nonpareil Cork Manufacturing Co. v. Keasbey & Mattison Co., C.C.Pa.1901, 108 F. 721; Testing Systems v. Magnaflux Corp., D.Pa.1966, 251 F.Supp. 286; Union Car Advertising Co. v. Collier, 1934, 263 N.Y. 386, 189 N.E. 463; Johnson v. Hitchcock, N.Y.1818, 15 Johns. 185. Cf. Matheson v. Harris, 1977, 98 Idaho 758, 572 P.2d 861 (unenforceable land contract placed on record is not "false," no slander of title action). See also, denying injunction against opinion statements that fell short of "malevolent distortion," Nann v. Raimist, 1931, 255 N.Y. 307, 174 N.E. 690.

74. The cases seem to say that competitors' comparative puffing or opinion statements are not actionable and that the plaintiff fails to show a case when he shows only such statements. The Second Restatement of Torts, § 646A reaches the same result in terms of a privilege, but none of the cases cited in the preceding note use this term nor do they seem to suggest the defendant has any burden to show "privilege" in this situation.

75. A secondary reason for the rule is that courts do not wish to adjudicate which brand is best. This reason, of course, would not cover non-comparative opinions.

76. See Prosser, Injurious Falsehood: The Basis of Liability, 1959, 59 Col.L.Rev. 425.

77. Jarrett v. Ross, 1942, 139 Tex. 560, 164 S.W.2d 550; International Visible Systems Corp. v. Remington-Rand, 6th Cir. 1933, 65 F.2d 540; Waterhouse v. McPheeters, 1940, 176 Tenn. 666, 145 S.W.2d 766; R. Olsen Oil Co. v. Fidler, 10th Cir. 1952, 199 F.2d 868; Local Federal Savings and Loan Association of Oklahoma City v. Sickles, 1946, 196 Okl. 395, 165 P.2d 328; Matheson v. Harris, 1977, 98 Idaho 758, 572 P.2d 861.

78. See infra, p. 973.

79. Andrew v. Deshler, 1883, 45 N.J.L. 167; Kingkade v. Plummer, 1925, 111 Okl. 197, 239 P. 628; New England Oil & Pipe Line Co. v. Rogers, 1932, 154 Okl. 285, 7 P.2d 638; Ontario Ind. Loan Co. v. Lindsey, 1883, 4 Ont. 473; Continental Development Corp. of Florida v. DuVal Title & Abstract Co., Fla.App.1978, 356 So.2d 925.

lege, which is to say without justification, cause or excuse.[80]

From these statements some of the older authorities concluded [81] that if there was no privilege, then the defendant would be liable without any bad purpose, or even without intent to affect the plaintiff at all—in other words, that the defendant would be strictly liable, without regard for his innocence, good intentions or honest belief. This was of course a continuation of the old unsound analogy to personal defamation,[82] when the proper analogy is rather to cases of interference with contract [83] or to fraud,[84] neither of which involves any strict liability at all and both of which have narrowly restricted any liability even for negligence.

It has been forcefully argued, however, that the cases do not sustain strict liability.[85] There is liability when the defendant knowingly or recklessly speaks a falsehood.[86] There has also been liability in the past [87] when the defendant acts from a spite motive and out of a desire to do harm for its own sake.[88] There has also been liability, however, when the defendant acts to harm the plaintiff's interests without a privilege,[89] in which case malice is said to be presumed or implied.[90] It has not been clear whether such presumed or fictional malice could be rebutted by a showing of good faith,[91] and if rebuttal is not permitted, then a defendant can be held strictly liable whenever he speaks without a privileged occasion. If this

---

80. Western Counties Manure Co. v. Lawes Chem. Manure Co., 1874, L.R. 9 Ex. 218 (Baron Pollock: "Without legal necessity or occasion"); Royal Baking Powder Co. v. Wright, Crossley & Co., 1900, 18 Rep. Pat.Cas. 95 (Lord Davey: "without just cause or excuse"). See also Gudger v. Manton, 1943, 21 Cal.2d 537, 134 P.2d 217 (malice "implied" from lack of privilege); Continental Supply Co. v. Price, 1952, 126 Mont. 363, 251 P.2d 553 (malice "presumed" in absence of privilege); Gates v. Utsey, Fla.App.1965, 177 So.2d 486.

81. Smith, Disparagement of Property, 1913, 13 Colum.L.Rev. 12, 121, the argument of which was adopted in the First Restatement of Torts, § 625. Accord: Neward, Malice in Actions on the Case for Words, 1944, 60 L.Q.Rev. 366; Wood, Disparagement of Title and Quality, 1942, 20 Can.Bar Rev. 296, 430–35. Contra: Salmond, Torts, 15th ed. 1969, 531–32; J. Fleming, 5th ed. 1977, The Law of Torts 697–98.

82. See supra, p. 962.

83. See infra, §§ 129–130.

84. See supra, § 105.

85. Prosser, Injurious Falsehood: The Basis of Liability, 1959, 59 Colum.L.Rev. 425. In British Railway Traffic & Elec. Co. v. C. R. C. Co., [1922] 2 K.B. 260, the conclusion was: "The mere absence of just cause or excuse is not itself malice," and "Malice in its proper and accurate sense is a question of motive, intention, or state of mind." The earliest cases may have required a knowing falsehood. See Gerrard v. Dickenson, 1590, 4 Co.Rep. 18a, 76 Eng.Rep. 903 (defendant knew lease under which she claimed was forged "and yet (against her own knowledge) she affirmed and published" her claim to the plaintiff's property).

86. Sinclair Refining Co. v. Jones Super Service Station, 1934, 188 Ark. 1075, 70 S.W.2d 562; see Ezmirlian v. Otto, 1934, 139 Cal.App. 486, 34 P.2d 774; Bourn v. Beck, 1924, 116 Kan. 231, 226 P. 769; Frega v. Northern New Jersey Mortgage Association, 1958, 51 N.J. Super. 331, 143 A.2d 885; Kingkade v. Plummer, 1925, 111 Okl. 197, 239 P. 628; Hopkins v. Drowne, 1898, 21 R.I. 20, 41 A. 567; cf. Woodard v. Pacific Fruit & Produce Co., 1940, 165 Or. 250, 106 P.2d 1043.

87. Under the Constitutional decisions in personal defamation cases, spite is not sufficient basis for liability and there must be a knowing falsehood, or a negligent one. See Second Restatement of Torts, § 623A. This standard may be carried over into injurious falsehood cases; if so spite would no longer suffice.

88. A. B. Farquhar Co. v. National Harrow Co., 3d Cir. 1900, 102 F. 714; Sinclair Refining Co. v. Jones Super Service Station, 1934, 188 Ark. 1075, 70 S.W.2d 562. Cf. Swan v. Tappan, 1849, 59 Mass. (5 Cush.) 104.

89. Olsen v. Kidman, 1951, 120 Utah 443, 235 P.2d 510; Gudger v. Manton, 1943, 21 Cal.2d 537, 134 P.2d 217; First National Bank v. Moore, Tex.Civ.App.1928, 7 S.W.2d 145, error dismissed; Dowse v. Doris Trust Co., 1949, 116 Utah 106, 208 P.2d 956; Ezmirlian v. Otto, 1934, 139 Cal.App. 486, 34 P.2d 774.

90. E.g., Andrew v. Deshler, 1883, 45 N.J.L. 167; Ontario Ind. Loan and Inv. Co. v. Lindsey, Ch.Div.1883, 4 Ont. 473. In some cases the presumption has been stated even where there would apparently be a privilege, as in Continental Development Corp. of Florida v. DuVal Title & Abstract Co., Fla.App.1978, 356 So.2d 925. Such cases may merely represent shorthand expressions. In many instances the "presumption" of malice seems not to mean anything except that malice in fact can be fairly inferred from the circumstances and that a finding of reckless falsehood can be justified on the evidence. See, e.g., Jumping Rainbow Ranch v. Conklin, 1975, 167 Mont. 367, 538 P.2d 1027.

91. In the pre-Constitutional law of defamation, it was said that malice was required, but was always presumed in the absence of a privilege, and that this presumed or implied malice could not be rebutted even by showing a benevolent spirit. See, e.g., Corrigan v. Bobbs-Merrill Co., 1920, 228 N.Y. 58, 126 N.E. 260, though of course this proof would rebut actual malice. Bromage v. Prosser, 4 B. & C. 247, 107 Eng.Rep. 1051 (1825) appeared to hold the same view as to injurious

is indeed the result, it is probably one reached by inadvertence and not one intended by the courts. The solution may lie in the decisions of the Supreme Court, which, in the personal defamation cases, has required some showing of fault as a matter of Constitutional law.[92] Where the plaintiff is a "public figure," the constitutional protection probably applies whether the tort is considered to be a personal libel or an injurious falsehood;[93] but even where the plaintiff is not a public figure, it has been held that the publisher may not be held liable unless the falsehood was a knowing or reckless one.[94]

The Second Restatement of Torts, following this line of development, has proposed to base liability upon defendant's knowing or reckless falsehood.[95] Under this approach, mere spite, or speech on an unprivileged occasion, which the Restatement covers with a *Caveat*, would no longer suffice to impose liability. Negligence, which has never been sufficient to impose liability where defendant's statement is privileged,[96] would likewise be insufficient if a knowing or reckless falsehood were required. Such an approach has much to commend it: a good deal of confusion would be removed, and liability would be placed squarely on serious fault; the confusing question of presumptions would pass out of the picture entirely and to a large extent the matter of privileges, with their shifting burdens of proof, would likewise be avoided.[97] In all probability the Restatement view will be followed and the tort will be established only if there is a falsehood knowingly or recklessly perpetrated.[98]

Special Damage

It is always agreed that the plaintiff must plead, or at least prove, special damages as an essential part of his cause of action for

---

falsehood (no "instance of a verdict for a defendant on the ground of want of malice."). See also Ontario Ind. Loan & Inv. Co. v. Lindsey, Ch.Div.1883, 4 Ont. 473 (when malice is presumed only truth will defeat the claim). The contemporary decisions appear not to clearly deal with the point.

92. New York Times Co. v. Sullivan, 1964, 376 U.S. 254, 84 S.Ct. 710, 11 L.Ed.2d 686, motion denied 376 U.S. 967, 84 S.Ct. 1130, 12 L.Ed. 83; Gertz v. Robert Welch, Inc., 1974, 418 U.S. 323, 94 S.Ct. 2997, 41 L.Ed. 2d 789. See supra, § 113.

93. Business entities, including corporations, may be "public figures" so that federal constitutional limits require proof of knowing or reckless falsehood. Steaks Unlimited, Inc. v. Deaner, 3d Cir. 1980, 623 F.2d 264; Reliance Insurance Co. v. Barron's, D.N.Y.1977, 442 F.Supp. 1341; Trans World Accounts, Inc. v. Associated Press, D.Cal.1977, 425 F.Supp. 814; Bose Corp. v. Consumers Union of United States, Inc., D.Mass. 1981, 508 F.Supp. 1249, supplemented 529 F.Supp. 357. See Fetzer, The Corporate Defamation Plaintiff as First Amendment "Public Figure": Nailing the Jellyfish, 1982, 68 Iowa L.Rev. 35; Comment, 1982 Ariz.St. L.J. 151.

94. Martin Marietta Corp. v. Evening Star Newspaper Co., D.D.C.1976, 417 F.Supp. 947 (trade libel does not involve "essential dignity" of humans and since only such dignitary values can outweigh free speech, the reckless falsehood standard applies). See F. & J. Enterprises, Inc. v. Columbia Broadcasting Systems, Inc., D.Ohio 1974, 373 F.Supp. 292; Note, 27 Emory L.J. 755, 774. Cf. Southard v. Forbes, Inc., 5th Cir. 1979, 588 F.2d 140, rehearing denied 590 F.2d 333, certiorari denied 444 U.S. 832, 100 S.Ct. 62, 62 L.Ed.2d 41 (constitutional standard requires court to define trade "libel" narrowly); Annbar Associates v. American Express Co., Mo.App.1978, 565 S.W.2d 701 (actual malice in some form required).

95. Second Restatement of Torts, § 623A. See also Reddish, The First Amendment in the Marketplace, 39 Geo.Wash.L.Rev. 429, 468–72; Note, The First Amendment and the Basis of Liability in Actions for Corporate Libel, 27 Emory L.Rev. 755.

96. Balden v. Shorter, [1933] Ch. 427; Advance Music Corp. v. American Tobacco Co., 1944, 183 Misc. 645, 50 N.Y.S.2d 287; same, 1945, 268 App.Div. 707, 53 N.Y.S.2d 337, reversed on other grounds 1946, 296 N.Y. 79, 70 N.E.2d 401; Remick Music Corp. v. American Tobacco Co., S.D.N.Y.1944, 57 F.Supp. 475; Dale System v. General Teleradio, S.D.N.Y.1952, 105 F.Supp. 745; Sacco v. Herald Statesman, Inc., 1961, 32 Misc.2d 739, 223 N.Y.S.2d 329. See also Nagy v. Manitoba Free Press, 1907, 16 Man. 619. The only case found to the contrary is Atkins v. Perrin, 1862, 3 F. & F. 179, 176 Eng.Rep. 81. Under some circumstances one may infer more than mere negligence, as where defendant appears to have all the facts at hand but nonetheless misstates them. See, e.g., New England Oil & Pipe Line Co. v. Rogers, 1931, 154 Okl. 285, 7 P.2d 638 apparently drawing an inference of actual malice.

97. A knowing falsehood would destroy most privileges based on factual misstatement. See below, p. 973. If a knowing (or reckless) falsehood were required as part of the plaintiff's case, the issue of privilege would then not arise.

98. In Pecora v. Szabo, 1981, 94 Ill.App.3d 57, 49 Ill. Dec. 577, 418 N.E.2d 431, the court rejected any "implied" or "presumed" malice test. "[T]he weight of authority holds that a showing of malice requires knowledge by defendant that the disparaging statements were false or reckless disregard of this falsity."

injurious falsehood.[99] The requirement goes to the cause of action itself and not merely to the recovery, with the result that the plaintiff will be denied even nominal or punitive damages if he cannot show special damage, since in such a case no cause of action at all is established.[1] For the same reason he will be denied an injunction against continued falsehood if proof of special damages fails.[2]

The special damage rule requires the plaintiff to establish pecuniary loss that has been realized or liquidated, as in the case of specific lost sales.[3] This means that general, implied or presumed damages of the kind formerly available in cases of personal defamation[4] are not sufficient as a ground for recovery in a disparagement claim.[5] By the same token, such personal elements of damage as mental distress have been strictly excluded from these claims.[6] It would seem sufficiently obvious that the pecuniary loss may consist of the breach by a third person of an existing contract with the plaintiff,[7] notwithstanding the decisions of a majority of the American courts which, rejecting the analogy to interference with contract,[8] have held that the remedy on the contract is sufficient, and the plaintiff is entitled to nothing more,[9] at least where the plaintiff could

---

99. Malachy v. Soper, 1836, 3 Bing.N.C. 371, 132 Eng.Rep. 453; System Operations Inc. v. Scientific Games Development Corp., 3d Cir. 1977, 555 F.2d 1131; Business Equipment Center, Limited v. DeJur-Amsco Corp., D.D.C.1978, 465 F.Supp. 775; Continental Air Ticketing Agency, Inc. v. Empire International Travel, Inc., 1976, 51 A.D.2d 104, 380 N.Y.S.2d 369; Gardner v. West-Col, Inc., 1978, 136 Vt. 381, 392 A.2d 383. But see a unique case of trademark disparagement by "reverse confusion," Big O Tire Dealers, Inc. v. Goodyear Tire & Rubber Co., 10th Cir. 1977, 561 F.2d 1365, certiorari denied 434 U.S. 1052, 98 S.Ct. 905, 54 L.Ed.2d 805.

1. Cates v. Barb, Wyo.1982, 650 P.2d 1159; Continental Development Corp. of Florida v. DuVal Title & Abstract Co., Fla.App.1978, 356 So.2d 925.

2. See below, p. 976.

3. In slander of title cases "impaired vendibility" of the land is sometimes stated as the special damage for which recovery is permitted. The phrase is ambiguous and may mean (1) the plaintiff sold the land at a lower price because of the falsehood; (2) the plaintiff sold the land at greater effort, expense or time because of the falsehood; or (3) the land's value has dropped on the market. The last stated element is not special damages, however, but general. The chief characteristic of special damages is a realized loss. Thus loss of specific contracts to purchase may be required proof. A.H. Belo Corp. v. Sanders, Tex.1982, 632 S.W.2d 145. Even this is problematical in the slander of title case because the plaintiff, though he has lost a sale, still has the land. The most satisfactory proof would show a sale at a reduced price or at greater expense. See generally Annot., 4 A.L.R.4th 532.

4. Gertz v. Robert Welch, Inc., 1974, 418 U.S. 323, 94 S.Ct. 2997, 41 L.Ed.2d 789 requires that the defamation plaintiff now prove "actual" damages, even when the plaintiff is not a public figure. But "actual" does not necessarily mean "pecuniary," and proven emotional distress would be recoverable in a defamation action. It also appears that if the plaintiff proved a knowing falsehood, which meets the proof required of a public figure under New York Times Co. v. Sullivan, 1964, 376 U.S. 254, 84 S.Ct. 710, 1 L.Ed.2d 686, motion denied 376 U.S. 967, 84 S.Ct. 1130, 12 L.Ed.2d 83, the "actual" damages requirement might not apply. It is thus important to distinguish the injurious falsehood claim from the claim of personal libel, even after these constitutional decisions have brought the two claims very close together.

5. Penthouse International, Limited v. Playboy Enterprises, 2d Cir. 1981, 663 F.2d 371. If the falsehood imputes personal dishonor and is thus classed as a libel, the rules of defamation rather than the rules of injurious falsehood apply. See Harwood Pharmacal Co. v. National Broadcasting Co., 1961, 9 N.Y.2d 460, 214 N.Y.S.2d 725, 174 N.E.2d 602.

6. Ward v. Gee, Tex.Civ.App.1933, 61 S.W.2d 555, error dismissed; Ebersole v. Fields, 1913, 181 Ala. 421, 62 So. 73; Collier County Publishing Co., Inc. v. Chapman, Fla.App.1975, 318 So.2d 492. Cf. Fowler v. Curtis Publishing Co., D.C.Cir. 1950, 182 F.2d 377; Eversharp, Inc. v. Pal Blade Co., 2d Cir. 1950, 182 F.2d 779 (good will and business prestige).

7. See Ashford v. Choate, 1870, 20 U.C.C.P. 471; Cardon v. McConnell, 1895, 120 N.C. 461, 27 S.E. 109; Humble Oil & Refining Co. v. McLean, Tex.Civ.App. 1925, 268 S.W. 179, reversed 280 S.W. 557; Bower, Actionable Defamation, 2d Ed. 1923, art. 13(b); Smith, Disparagement of Property, 1913, 13 Col.L.Rev. 13, 125–126; Notes, 1933, 33 Col.L.Rev. 90; 1929, 38 Yale L.J. 400.

8. See infra, § 129. The result appears to be that if the defendant has committed either disparagement or interference with contract, the plaintiff can recover; if both, he cannot.

9. Rucker v. Burke, 1938, 183 Okl. 639, 84 P.2d 20; Burkett v. Griffith, 1891, 90 Cal. 532, 27 P. 527; Dent v. Balch, 1925, 213 Ala. 311, 104 So. 651; Felt v. Germania Life Insurance Co., 1912, 149 App.Div. 14, 133 N.Y.S. 519.

The restriction imposed by this rule has no application where the injurious falsehood not only dissuades a promisor from performing but actually makes it impos-

have specific performance of his contract.[10] It would also appear obvious that special damages include the expenses of legal proceedings necessary to remove a cloud on the plaintiff's title caused by the falsehood, and other expenses,[11] including advertising expense[12] reasonably incurred to counteract the disparagement, though here again a few courts have held to the contrary.[13]

Usually, however, the damages claimed have consisted of loss of prospective contracts with the plaintiff's customers. Here the remedy has been so hedged about with limitations that its usefulness to the plaintiff has been seriously impaired.[14] Formerly it was nearly always held that it was not enough to show a general decline in business following the publication of the falsehood,[15] even when there was evidence eliminating other causes for it, and that it was only the loss of specific sales to identified persons that could be recovered.[16] This has meant, in the usual case, that the plaintiff must identify the particular purchasers who have refrained from dealing with him, and specify the transactions of which he claims to have been deprived.[17] Where there has been wide dissemination of the disparagement to persons unknown, this is obviously impossible.

The whole modern tendency is away from any such arbitrary rule. Starting with a few cases involving goods offered for sale at an auction,[18] and extending to others in which there has been obvious impossibility of any identification of the lost customers,[19] a more liberal rule has been applied, requiring the plaintiff to be particular only where it is reasonable to expect him to do so. It is probably still the law everywhere that he must either offer the names of those who have failed to purchase or explain why it is

sible for him to do so, as in Wilko of Nashua, Inc. v. TAP Realty, Inc., 1977, 117 N.H. 843, 379 A.2d 798.

10. See Stiles v. Kuriloff, 1928, 6 N.J.Misc. 271, 141 A. 314; Felt v. Germania Life Insurance Co., 1912, 149 App.Div. 14, 133 N.Y.S. 519 (where specifically performable there is no special damage or loss). Most of the cases involve real estate where specific performance is the usual remedy.

11. Misco Leasing, Inc. v. Keller, 10th Cir. 1974, 490 F.2d 545; Womack v. McDonald, 1929, 219 Ala. 75, 121 So. 57; Home Investments Fund v. Robertson, 1973, 10 Ill.App.3d 840, 295 N.E.2d 85; Chesebro v. Powers, 1889, 78 Mich. 472, 44 N.W. 290; Dowse v. Doris Trust Co., 1949, 116 Utah 106, 208 P.2d 956.

12. Big O Tire Dealers, Inc. v. Goodyear Tire & Rubber Co., 10th Cir. 1977, 561 F.2d 1365, certiorari denied 434 U.S. 1052, 98 S.Ct. 905, 54 L.Ed.2d 805.

13. Cohen v. Minzesheimer, Sup.1909, 118 N.Y.S. 385; McGuinness v. Hargiss, 1909, 56 Wash. 162, 105 P. 233; Barquin v. Hall Oil Co., 1921, 28 Wyo. 164, 201 P. 352, rehearing denied 1922, 28 Wyo. 164, 202 P. 1107.

14. See Handler, Unfair Competition, 1936, 21 Iowa L.Rev. 175, 198; Notes, 1950, 18 U.Chi.L.Rev. 114; 1947, 41 Ill.L.Rev. 661; 1953, 63 Yale L.J. 65, 90–96.

15. Tobias v. Harland, N.Y.1830, 4 Wend. 537; Shaw Cleaners & Dyers v. Des Moines Dress Club, 1932, 215 Iowa 1130, 245 N.W. 231; Denney v. Northwestern Credit Association, 1909, 55 Wash. 331, 104 P. 769; Ward v. Gee, Tex.Civ.App.1933, 61 S.W.2d 555, error dismissed; Tower v. Crosby, 1925, 214 App.Div. 392, 212 N.Y.S. 219.

16. Hunt Oil Co. v. Berry, 1956, 227 Miss. 234, 86 So.2d 7, corrected 227 Miss. 680, 86 So.2d 854; Alcott v. Miller's Karri & Jarrah Forests, [1904] 21 T.L.R. 30, 91 L.T. 722; Stevenson v. Love, C.C.N.J.1901, 106 F. 466; Denney v. Northwestern Credit Association, 1909, 55 Wash. 331, 104 P. 769.

17. Wilson v. Dubois, 1886, 35 Minn. 471, 29 N.W. 68; Landstrom v. Thorpe, 8th Cir. 1951, 189 F.2d 46, certiorari denied 342 U.S. 819, 72 S.Ct. 37, 96 L.Ed. 620; Del Rico Co. v. New Mexican, Inc., 1952, 56 N.M. 538, 246 P.2d 206; Barquin v. Hall Oil Co., 1921, 28 Wyo. 164, 201 P. 352, rehearing denied 28 Wyo. 164, 202 P. 1107; Stevenson v. Love, C.C.N.J.1901, 106 F. 466; Hubbard v. Scott, 1917, 85 Or. 1, 166 P. 33.

18. Hargrave v. Le Breton, 1769, 4 Burr. 2422, 98 Eng.Rep. 269; Roche v. Meyler, [1896] 2 Ir. 35.

19. Ratcliffe v. Evans, [1892] 2 Q.B. 524; Erick Bowman Remedy Co. v. Jensen Salsbery Laboratories, 8th Cir. 1926, 17 F.2d 255; Houston Chronicle Publishing Co. v. Martin, Tex.Civ.App.1928, 5 S.W.2d 170, modified on second appeal in Tex.Civ.App.1933, 64 S.W.2d 816, error dismissed; Dale System v. Time, Inc., D.Conn.1953, 116 F.Supp. 527; Rochester Brewing Co. v. Certa Bottling Works, 1948, 192 Misc. 629, 80 N.Y.S.2d 925. Cf. Trenton Mutual Life & Fire Insurance Co. v. Perrine, 1852, 23 N.J.L. 402; also Craig v. Proctor, 1918, 229 Mass. 339, 118 N.E. 647 (general allegation upheld, but plaintiff may be required to furnish particulars).

In Pendleton v. Time, Inc., 1949, 339 Ill.App. 188, 89 N.E.2d 435, and Advance Music Corp. v. American Tobacco Co., 1946, 296 N.Y. 79, 70 N.E.2d 401, reversing 1944, 268 App.Div. 707, 53 N.Y.S.2d 337, motions to dismiss the complaint were denied, but there is no indication of what evidence would be required.

impossible for him to do so;[20] but where he cannot, the matter is dealt with by analogy to the proof of lost profits resulting from breach of contract.[21] If the possibility that other factors have caused the loss of the general business is satisfactorily excluded by sufficient evidence, this seems entirely justified by the necessities of the situation.[22] Under the impact of more detailed statistical and expert proof, courts have shown increasing willingness in recent years to award a loss of profit in other kinds of cases,[23] and it may be expected that this will carry over into the injurious falsehood cases where the loss is shown with reasonable certainty. Beyond this, it is difficult to escape the impression that courts have sometimes fallen back on a strict enforcement of the special damages requirement as a device to avoid imposing liability upon an innocent defendant whose only fault was "presumed" malice. If, as may be the case,[24] the courts are now in the process of moving to a requirement of actual fault in the form of intentional or reckless falsehood before liability will be imposed, there will be no occasion to insist upon an unreasonably high proof of special damage to protect the innocent defendant. These changes in the law suggest that a more realistic assessment of special damages is likely in the future.

Where a competitor gains the business customers of the plaintiff by publishing an injurious falsehood, it seems arguable that he should be required to disgorge those gains even where there is no proof of a corresponding special damage to the plaintiff. Such unjust enrichment or "restitutionary" claims have been entertained in some other trade tort cases,[25] but apparently the issue has not arisen in the case of pure injurious falsehood.

Privilege

Privilege, which implies an affirmative defense as to which the defendant shoulders the burden of proof,[26] has been the chief protection for the publisher who was in fact innocent but "presumed" to be malicious, since if the publication was privileged liability would not ordinarily be imposed wholly without fault.[27] A qualified privilege, as distinct from an absolute one, is usually destroyed by proof of actual malice, at least if that is shown by proof that the defendant published a knowing or reckless falsehood; and the defendant in such a case, deprived of his privilege, becomes liable.[28] If this same proof is now to be required as a part of the plaintiff's case under the Constitutional decisions or otherwise,[29] much of the law of privilege becomes superfluous and the tort of injurious falsehood and the tort itself will become much simpler.

Absolute privileges, however, will no doubt remain to protect judicial, legislative and even certain executive proceedings even where there is intended falsehood or other forms of malice.[30] It is also presumably true that an absolute privilege attaches when the plaintiff consents to the disparagement.[31]

---

20. Charlottesville Music Center v. Magnepan, Inc., 4th Cir. 1981, 655 F.2d 38; Continental Nut Co. v. Robert L. Berner Corp., 7th Cir. 1968, 393 F.2d 283, certiorari denied 393 U.S. 923, 89 S.Ct. 254, 21 L.Ed.2d 259.

21. See D. Dobbs, Remedies 802 and 150–157; Comment, 56 N.C.L.Rev. 693 (1978).

22. Cf. Fleming v. McDonald, 1911, 230 Pa. 75, 79 A. 226; Neville v. Higbie, 1933, 130 Cal.App. 669, 20 P.2d 348; Farmers' State Bank v. Hintz, 1928, 206 Iowa 911, 221 N.W. 540; Houston Chronicle Publishing Co. v. Martin, Tex.Civ.App.1933, 64 S.W.2d 816, error dismissed.

23. See Comment, 56 N.C.L.Rev. 693 (1978); cf. Schaefer, Uncertainty and the Law of Damages, 1978, 19 Wm. & M.L.Rev. 719.

24. See supra, p. 970.

25. See generally D. Dobbs, 1973 Remedies, §§ 6.4, 6.5, 6.6 and 10.5; G. Palmer, Law of Restitution § 2.8.

26. Second Restatement of Torts, § 651.

27. See Prosser, Injurious Falsehood, 1959, 59 Colum.L.Rev. 425.

28. Second Restatement of Torts, § 650A.

29. See supra, p. 970.

30. See § 132, infra.

31. See Second Restatement of Torts, § 635, Comment b.

Even the qualified or conditional privileges may remain important if courts continue, notwithstanding the Constitutional decisions in the personal defamation cases, to presume malice where none exists in fact or to define that term to include ill-will without an intended or reckless misstatement of facts. If this is to be the law, the main issue in many cases will turn on privilege. As to this, the Second Restatement of Torts states the traditional view that a qualified privilege to disparage exists whenever it would exist in a case of personal defamation.[32] Such a privilege includes the disinterested protection of third persons or the public in general, as where an attorney in good faith asserts his client's claim,[33] or gives an opinion on an abstract of title.[34] It likewise includes the fair report by a publisher of a judicial proceeding,[35] fair comment on matters of public interest,[36] notice given by a carrier concerning the inspection of diseased cattle,[37] and the attempt by a friend of a decedent to discover his will.[38]

Usually, however, the privilege is asserted by a defendant who is seeking to protect his own interests. A rival claimant to the property disparaged, in his capacity as such,[39] is recognized as privileged to assert a bona fide claim by any appropriate means of publication.[40] The same is true of one who claims in good faith that the plaintiff is infringing his patent, copyright or trade mark rights by the sale of goods.[41] The privilege is uniformly held, however, to be a qualified one, and it is defeated if the defendant's motive is shown to be solely a desire to do harm,[42] or if it is found that he did not honestly believe his statements to be true,[43] or that the publication of the statement was excessive.[44] A few cases have gone further and have said that he must have reasonable grounds for believing his disparaging words to be the truth,[45] but the better view, which

32. Second Restatement of Torts, § 646A.

33. Watson v. Reynolds, 1826, Moody & M. 1, 173 Eng.Rep. 1059. Cf. Kendall v. Stone, 1848, 4 N.Y. Super. (2 Sandf.) 269, reversed in 1851, 5 N.Y. (1 Seld.) 14.

34. Hines v. Lumpkin, 1898, 19 Tex.Civ.App. 556, 47 S.W. 818. Cf. Gilchrest House v. Guaranteed Title & Mortgage Co., 1950, 277 App.Div. 788, 97 N.Y.S.2d 226, affirmed 1951, 302 N.Y. 852, 100 N.E.2d 46 (refusal to insure title).

35. Mack, Miller Candle Co. v. MacMillan Co., 1934, 239 App.Div. 738, 269 N.Y.S. 33, affirmed 266 N.Y. 489, 195 N.E. 167; cf. Artloom Corp. v. National Better Business Bureau, D.N.Y.1931, 48 F.2d 897.

36. Gott v. Pulsifer, 1876, 122 Mass. 235; Browning v. Van Rensselaer, C.C.Pa.1899, 97 F. 531. Cf. Purofied Down Products Corp. v. National Association of Bedding Manufacturers, Sup.1950, 97 N.Y.S.2d 683 (industry policing of products); Fahey v. Shafer, 1917, 98 Wash. 517, 167 P. 1118.

37. Youngquist v. American Railway Express Co., 1926, 49 S.D. 373, 206 N.W. 576.

38. Atkins v. Perrin, 1862, 3 F. & F. 179, 176 Eng. Rep. 81. Cf. Pater v. Baker, 1847, 3 C.B. 831, 136 Eng. Rep. 333 (warning given by public officer).

39. There is no privilege to assert a claim in favor of a third person, where the defendant has no reason to protect the other's interests. Pennyman v. Rabanks, 1595, Cro.Eliz. 428, 78 Eng.Rep. 668.

40. Bogosian v. First National Bank of Millburn, 1943, 133 N.J.Eq. 404, 32 A.2d 585; Conway v. Skelly Oil Co., 10th Cir. 1931, 54 F.2d 11; Allison v. Berry, 1942, 316 Ill.App. 261, 44 N.E.2d 929; Miller v. First National Bank of Gladbrook, 1935, 220 Iowa 1266, 264 N.W. 272; Leslie v. Western Steel Co., S.D.Tex.1962, 202 F.Supp. 27.

41. Kemart Corp. v. Printing Arts Research Laboratories, Inc., 9th Cir. 1959, 269 F.2d 375, certiorari denied 361 U.S. 893, 80 S.Ct. 197, 4 L.Ed.2d 151; McIlhenny Co. v. Gaidry, 5th Cir. 1918, 253 F. 613; Virtue v. Creamery Package Manufacturing Co., 8th Cir. 1910, 179 F. 115, affirmed 227 U.S. 8, 33 S.Ct. 202, 57 L.Ed. 393; Oil Conservation Engineering Co. v. Brooks Engineering Co., 6th Cir. 1931, 52 F.2d 783; Alliance Securities Co. v. De Vilbiss, 6th Cir. 1930, 41 F.2d 668.

42. Swan v. Tappan, 1849, 59 Mass. (5 Cush.) 104; Sinclair Refining Co. v. Jones Super Service Station, 1934, 188 Ark. 1075, 70 S.W.2d 562; A.B. Farquhar Co. v. National Harrow Co., 3d Cir. 1900, 102 F. 714.

Cf. Diapulse Corp. of America v. Birtcher Corp., 2d Cir. 1966, 362 F.2d 736, certiorari dismissed 385 U.S. 801, 87 S.Ct. 9, 17 L.Ed.2d 48.

43. Donovan v. Wilson Sporting Goods Co., 1st Cir. 1961, 285 F.2d 714; Frega v. Northern New Jersey Mortgage Association, 1958, 51 N.J.Super. 331, 143 A.2d 885; Ezmirlian v. Otto, 1934, 139 Cal.App. 486, 34 P.2d 774; Sinclair Refining Co. v. Jones Super Service Station, 1934, 188 Ark. 1075, 70 S.W.2d 562; Woodard v. Pacific Fruit & Produce Co., 1940, 165 Or. 250, 106 P.2d 1043.

44. Donovan v. Wilson Sporting Goods Co., 1st Cir. 1961, 285 F.2d 714.

45. Carpenter v. Bailey, 1873, 53 N.H. 590; Conroy v. Pittsburgh Times, 1891, 139 Pa. 334, 21 A. 154.

is now more generally accepted, is that a genuine belief in their truth is sufficient, however unfounded or unreasonable it may be.[46] The absence of probable cause for the belief may permit the jury to infer that it does not exist, but it is not necessarily conclusive;[47] and the advice of counsel, while it is evidence in favor of good faith, is likewise not determinative in itself.[48] When it appears that a privilege exists, the burden is upon the plaintiff to establish the existence of the "malice" which will defeat it.[49]

The privilege of competition for future business, as distinguished from the protection of an existing interest, has been recognized only to a limited extent. False statements of fact disparaging the quality of a competitor's goods, or the conduct of his business, are regarded as "unfair" methods of competition, and, at least where there is "malice" on the part of the defendant, such misstatements of fact are not privileged.[50] Some courts have apparently taken the view that such statements are actionable even if the defendant genuinely believes them,[51] a view that may now be subject to question under both the Constitution and the common law.[52] Even the traditional common law, however, allowed a considerable amount of leeway to those engaged in competition, in the form of "puffing," boasting or exaggeration as to the excellence of their own products, which finds a close parallel in the very similar freedom as to misrepresentations made to customers.[53]

Accordingly, it is held that mere general statements of comparison, declaring that the defendant's goods are the best on the market, or are better than the plaintiff's, are privileged so long as they contain no specific assertions of unfavorable facts reflecting upon the rival product.[54] The feeling has been that the practice of sellers to make consciously exaggerated claims for their own goods is so well known that purchasers attach little or no importance to such assertions, and they usually can do no serious harm. They are sometimes said to be mere statements of opinion. No doubt there has been some reluctance to give the plaintiff free advertising in the form of a verdict declaring a rival's claim to superiority to be unfounded. The courts quite often have been willing, however, to find disparaging

46. Pitt v. Donovan, 1813, 1 M. & S. 639, 105 Eng. Rep. 238; Barry v. McCollum, 1908, 81 Conn. 293, 70 A. 1035; Bays v. Hunt, 1882, 60 Iowa 251, 14 N.W. 785; Hemmens v. Nelson, 1893, 138 N.Y. 517, 34 N.E. 342. See Second Restatement of Torts, § 647.

47. Pitt v. Donovan, 1813, 1 M. & S. 639, 105 Eng. Rep. 238; Pater v. Baker, 1847, 3 C.B. 831, 136 Eng. Rep. 333; Coffman v. Henderson, 1913, 9 Ala.App. 553, 63 So. 808; May v. Anderson, 1896, 14 Ind.App. 251, 42 N.E. 946; Bourn v. Beck, 1924, 116 Kan. 231, 226 P. 769.

48. Humble Oil & Refining Co. v. Luckel, Tex.Civ.App.1943, 171 S.W.2d 902; Noble v. Johnson, 1937, 180 Okl. 169, 68 P.2d 838; Gent v. Lynch, 1863, 23 Md. 58; Haldeman v. Chambers, 1857, 19 Tex. 1.

49. Long v. Rucker, 1912, 166 Mo.App. 572, 149 S.W. 1051; Briggs v. Coykendall, 1929, 57 N.D. 785, 224 N.W. 202; Fearon v. Fodera, 1915, 169 Cal. 370, 148 P. 200; Henry v. Dufilho, 1839, 14 La. 48; Glieberman v. Fine, 1929, 248 Mich. 8, 226 N.W. 669.

50. Western Counties Manure Co. v. Lawes Chem. Manure Co., 1874, L.R.Ex. 218; Alcott v. Millar's Karri & Jarrah Forests, 1904, 21 T.L.R. 30, 91 L.T. 722; National Refining Co. v. Benzo Gas Motor Fuel Co., 8th Cir. 1927, 20 F.2d 763, certiorari denied 275 U.S. 570, 48 S.Ct. 157, 72 L.Ed. 431. Cf. Shaw Cleaners & Dyers v. Des Moines Dress Club, 1932, 215 Iowa 1130, 245 N.W. 231; Hopkins Chemical Co. v. Read Drug & Chemical Co., 1914, 124 Md. 210, 92 A. 478; George v. Blow, 1899, 20 N.S.W. 395. And see the comparison of the plaintiff's beer with another liquid in Dickes v. Fenne, 1640, March 59, Jones W. 444, 82 Eng.Rep. 233.

51. George v. Blow, 1899, 20 N.S.W. 395. Cf. Mowry v. Raabe, 1891, 89 Cal. 606, 27 P. 157; and see Smith, Disparagement of Property, 1913, 13 Col.L.Rev. 13, 138–140.

52. Supra, p. 970.

53. See supra, § 109.

54. White v. Mellin [1895] A.C. 154; Hubbock & Sons v. Wilkinson, [1899] 1 Q.B. 86; Johnson v. Hitchcock, N.Y.1818, 15 Johns. 185; Nonpareil Cork Manufacturing Co. v. Keasbey & Mattison Co., C.C.Pa.1901, 108 F. 721; National Refining Co. v. Benzo Gas Motor Fuel Co., 8th Cir. 1927, 20 F.2d 763, certiorari denied 275 U.S. 570, 48 S.Ct. 157, 72 L.Ed. 431. In Young v. Macrae, 1862, 3 B. & S. 264, 122 Eng.Rep. 100, it was said that if the defendant merely alleges what is true of the plaintiff's product and lies about the merits of his own, there can be no action for disparagement. This is in line with the decisions holding that misrepresentations concerning the defendant's own goods are a fraud only upon the public, and not actionable by a competitor. See infra, pp. 1018–1019.

statements of fact buried in general assertions, and to permit recovery on that basis.[55]

It bears repeating, however, that all this may be in the process of changing. Even if the Constitution itself does not require a knowing or reckless falsehood which would defeat any privilege and make the law of privileges superfluous, the common law decisions themselves may do so. The leading case on a competitor's disparagement asserts that comparative disparagement—puffing—is not a tort at all.[56] A number of other decisions traditionally cited in support of a privilege do not in fact use the term and may require instead that the plaintiff prove a recklessly false statement of fact or something deemed equivalent of it.[57] Such an approach, whether constitutionally mandated or not, would considerably simplify the law of injurious falsehood.

Remedies

As already indicated,[58] special damages in the form of lost profits, or collateral expense in countering the effects of the falsehood or otherwise, must be shown to establish a cause of action. Once such damages are shown, the trier of fact may consider punitive damages and an award of such damages will be upheld if the proof shows sufficient "malice in fact," [59] which is to say actual improper purpose or knowing falsehood.

Since there is no tort at all unless the plaintiff has special damages, it has been held that even the purveyor of an egregious and knowing falsehood cannot be enjoined from continued publication where no special damage is shown.[60] Whatever the merits or demerits of this rule, the more fundamental question is whether an injunction can issue in any case at all. The rule in equity, no doubt reflecting a concern both for free speech and for jury trial rights, was that a personal libel would not be enjoined,[61] even if the publisher were insolvent and could not pay damages.[62] Some courts have carried this same rule over to injurious falsehood cases, which are often in fact couched in terms of libel, with the result that even an impersonal disparagement of a product could not be halted by injunction.[63] Other courts, however, have considered that disparagement stands on a different footing,[64] or have said that it is merely one form of un-

---

55. Thus the assertion that the defendant's goods are the only genuine ones on the market is held to imply that the plaintiff's are not genuine. George v. Blow, 1899, 20 N.S.W. 395; Jarrahdale Timber Co. v. Temperley & Co., 1894, 11 T.L.R. 119; Cf. Lyne v. Nicholls, 1906, 23 T.L.R. 86 (defendant's newspaper circulation "20 to 1 of any other weekly paper"); Acme Silver Co. v. Stacy Hardware Co., 1891, 21 Ont.Rep. 261; Griffiths v. Benn, 1911, 27 T.L.R. 346; Testing Systems, Inc. v. Magnaflux Corp., E.D.Pa.1966, 251 F.Supp. 286.

56. Hubbock & Sons v. Wilkinson, [1899] 1 Q.B. 86, per Linley, M.R. See Smith, Disparagement of Property, 1913, 13 Col.L.Rev. 13, 133; Bower, Actionable Defamation, 2d ed. 1923, 211.

57. National Refining Co. v. Benzo Gas Motor Fuel Co., 8th Cir. 1927, 20 F.2d 763, certiorari denied 275 U.S. 570, 48 S.Ct. 157, 72 L.Ed. 431; Testing Systems v. Magnaflux Corp., D.Pa.1966, 251 F.Supp. 286 (general unfavorable comparisons not actionable).

58. Supra, p. 970.

59. Diapulse Corp. of America v. Birtcher Corp., 2d Cir. 1966, 362 F.2d 736, certiorari dismissed 385 U.S. 801, 87 S.Ct. 9, 17 L.Ed.2d 48; American National Bank & Trust Co. v. First Wisconsin Mortgage Trust, Tex. Civ.App.1979, 577 S.W.2d 312, refused n.r.e.

60. White v. Mellin, [1895] A.C. 154 (H.L.); Marlin Firearms Co. v. Shields, 1902, 171 N.Y. 384, 64 N.E. 163.

61. D. Dobbs, Remedies § 7.2; Annot., 47 A.L.R.2d 715.

62. "We cannot accept the * * * conclusion that the exercise of the constitutional right to freely express one's opinion should be conditioned upon the economic status of the individual asserting that right." Willing v. Mazzocone, 1978, 482 Pa. 377, 393 A.2d 1155.

63. Boston Diatite Co. v. Florence Manufacturing Co., 1873, 114 Mass. 69; Marlin Firearms Co. v. Shields, 1902, 171 N.Y. 384, 64 N.E. 163; A. Hollander & Son v. Jos. Hollander, Inc., 1935, 117 N.J.Eq. 578, 177 A. 80; McMorries v. Hudson Sales Corp., Tex.Civ. App.1950, 233 S.W.2d 938; Schmoldt v. Oakley, Okl. 1964, 390 P.2d 882.

64. Black & Yates v. Mahogany Association, 3d Cir. 1941, 129 F.2d 227, certiorari denied 317 U.S. 672, 63 S.Ct. 76, 87 L.Ed. 539. Cf. Paramount Pictures v. Leader Press, 10th Cir. 1939, 106 F.2d 229; Saxon Motor Sales v. Torino, 1938, 166 Misc. 863, 2 N.Y.S.2d 885 ("more than a mere libel"); and see Montgomery Ward & Co. v. United Retail, Wholesale & Department Store Employees, 1948, 400 Ill. 38, 49–50, 79 N.E.2d 46, 51–52.

fair competition [65] or interference with business relations,[66] and as a result have granted the injunction to prohibit further disparagement. Although some commentators have favored more liberal use of injunctions against injurious falsehood,[67] a good deal of commercial speech now involves public issues, and in recent years the Supreme Court has held that at least some such speech is entitled to First Amendment protections.[68] The claim to an injunction against speech attacking a business for its social [69] or environmental [70] or other policies [71] thought to injure public interests undoubtedly raises the same free speech concerns involved in other public issues. It seems clear that the injunction will not go against an attack that is merely "overcolored and hectic" or the assertion of debatable conclusions deduced from "meager facts." [72] And beyond this, the Constitution itself may compel the court to refuse injunctive relief even where the statement is false if a prior restraint is involved.[73]

Defamation, interference with contract, injurious falsehood and the broader tort of interference with prospective economic relations, are all different phases of the same general wrong of depriving the plaintiff of beneficial relations with others.[74] In the case of personal defamation the Supreme Court has now required at least some degree of personal fault as a prerequisite to liability.[75] At some future day the common basis of all four torts may lead to a comparison and overhauling of each to achieve consistency, to eliminate strict liability, and to provide a clear statement of the conduct that is deemed wrongful before liability is imposed.

WESTLAW REFERENCES

disparage! slander! /p property chattels goods "title" /p "special damage*"
di slander of title
di injurious falsehood
restatement +s torts /p "injurious falsehood"
restatement +s torts /s 623a

Interests Protected

"title" quality intangible sale* saleable business trade economic /s interest* /s protect! /p defam! aspersion disparage! slander "injurious falsehood"
237k137

---

65. Dehydro, Inc. v. Tretolite Co., N.D.Okl.1931, 53 F.2d 273; Bourjois, Inc. v. Park Drug Co., 8th Cir. 1936, 82 F.2d 468; Schering & Glatz v. American Pharmaceutical Co., 1933, 261 N.Y. 304, 185 N.E. 109. See Nims, Unfair Competition by False Statements of Disparagement, 1934, 19 Corn.L.Q. 63; Wolff, Unfair Competition by Truthful Disparagement, 1938, 47 Yale L.J. 1304; Note, [1950] U.Ill.L.Forum 675.

66. Pure Milk Producers Association v. Bridges, 1937, 146 Kan. 15, 68 P.2d 658; I.P. Frink, Inc. v. Erickson, D.Mass.1923, 16 F.2d 496; Davis v. New England Railway Publishing Co., 1909, 203 Mass. 470, 89 N.E. 565; Carter v. Knapp Motor Co., 1943, 243 Ala. 600, 11 So.2d 383; Maytag Co. v. Meadows Manufacturing Co., 7th Cir. 1929, 35 F.2d 403, certiorari denied 281 U.S. 737, 50 S.Ct. 250, 74 L.Ed. 1151. As to the close relation between injurious falsehood and such interference, see Note, 1933, 33 Col.L.Rev. 90; Birmingham Broadcasting Co. v. Bell, 1953, 259 Ala. 656, 68 So. 2d 314.

67. See Pound, Equitable Relief Against Defamation and Injuries to Personality, 1916, 29 Harv.L.Rev. 640, 668; Notes, 1946, 21 N.Y.U.L.Rev. 518; 1953, 63 Yale L.J. 65, 96–104.

68. Virginia State Board of Pharmacy v. Virginia Citizens Consumer Council, Inc., 1976, 425 U.S. 748, 96 S.Ct. 1817, 48 L.Ed.2d 346. The Court made it clear, however, that false and deceptive speech could be regulated by state power.

69. See Organization for a Better Austin v. Keefe, 1971, 402 U.S. 415, 91 S.Ct. 1575, 29 L.Ed.2d 1 (prior restraint not justified to prevent leaflets against real estate broker's alleged "blockbusting," regardless of truth or falsity).

70. See Martin v. Reynolds Metal Co., D.Or.1962, 224 F.Supp. 978, appeal dismissed 9th Cir., 336 F.2d 876, affirmed 337 F.2d 780 (granting injunction).

71. American Broadcasting Companies, Inc. v. Smith Cabinet Manufacturing Co., Inc., 1974, 160 Ind. App. 367, 312 N.E.2d 85 (assertion that baby bed manufactured by plaintiff was flammable); Stansbury v. Beckstrom, Tex.Civ.App.1973, 491 S.W.2d 947, 62 A.L.R.3d 222 (price protest picketing at doctor's office); Krebiozen Research Foundation v. Beacon Press, 1956, 334 Mass. 86, 134 N.E.2d 1, certiorari denied 352 U.S. 848, 77 S.Ct. 65, 1 L.Ed.2d 58 (attack on supposed cancer cure).

72. Nann v. Raimist, 1931, 255 N.Y. 307, 174 N.E. 690.

73. Organization for a Better Austin v. Keefe, 1971, 402 U.S. 415, 91 S.Ct. 1575, 29 L.Ed.2d 1; American Broadcasting Companies, Inc. v. Smith Cabinet Manufacturing Co., Inc., 1974, 160 Ind.App. 367, 312 N.E.2d 85.

74. See Green, Relational Interests, 1935, 29 Ill.L. Rev. 1041, 30 Ill.L.Rev. 1.

75. See supra, § 950.

Elements of Cause of Action

"slander of title" disparage! aspersion "injurious falsehood" /p distortion* fals! lie* /s communicat! publish*** told

"slander of title" disparage! aspersion "injurious falsehood" /p "bad faith" intent! malic! negligen** spite "strict! liab!" /p excuse* "good faith" justif! privilege*

"slander of title" disparage! aspersion "injurious falsehood" /p truth fals! mislead***

"slander of title" disparage! aspersion "injurious falsehood" /p malice /s imply impli! infer** presum!

237k130
237k131
237k134

Special Damage

"slander of title" disparage! aspersion "injurious falsehood" /p allege* allegation* assert*** claim* complain* plead! /s "special damage*" "pecuniary los***"

"slander of title" disparage! aspersion "injurious falsehood" /p business cost* contract* customer* fees profit* /p "special damage*" "pecuniary los***"

Privilege

"slander of title" disparage! aspersion "injurious falsehood" /p privilege* unprivilege*

237k136
237k139 /p privilege*

Remedies

"slander of title" disparage! aspersion "injurious falsehood" /p injunction* enjoin! "restraining order" stay

"slander of title" disparage! aspersion "injurious falsehood" /p punitive exemplary +1 damage*

§ 129. Interference With Contractual Relations

It is usually said that tort liability may be imposed upon a defendant who intentionally and improperly interferes with the plaintiff's rights under a contract with another person if the interference causes the plaintiff to lose a right under the contract or makes the contract rights more costly or less valuable.[1] By extension of this idea, it may also be tortious to interfere with other rights of economic value, such as those embodied in an injunctive decree.[2] And by further extension, it may be tortious to interfere with the plaintiff's prospects of economic gain even where those prospects have not been reduced to a contract right,[3] though in the case of such mere prospects more latitude is generally allowed for interference.

The law of interference with contract is thus one part of a larger body of tort law aimed at protection of relationships,[4] some economic[5] and some personal.[6] To a large extent, common law protection of relational interests has been accomplished through such torts as libel,[7] slander and injurious falsehood,[8] in all of which one's relations with others are protected from damage by false statements. Protection of relational interests has not been limited to protection from falsehood, however. Liability may be imposed for alienating the affection of a spouse even though no falsehood is used at all, though that particular picture is in the process of some considerable change;[9] and liability may be imposed in the case of interference with either personal or business relations if the means of interference are tortious in themselves, as in the case of

---

§ 129

1. Second Restatement of Torts, § 766. As to different formulations of the rule see pp. 983–984 below. Louisiana has refused to recognize the tort. Moss v. Guarisco, La.App.1981, 409 So.2d 323, affirmed La. 1982, 412 So.2d 540.

2. National Merchandising Corp. v. Leyden, 1976, 370 Mass. 425, 348 N.E.2d 771. One is generally liable for contempt for knowingly aiding and abetting violation of an injunction against a third person. See D. Dobbs, 1973, Remedies 101–103.

3. See infra, § 130.

4. Wigmore, The Boycott as Ground for Damages, 1887, 21 Am.L.Rev. 511; Wigmore, Interference with Social Relations, 1887, 21 Am.L.Rev. 764; Wigmore, A General Analysis of Tort—Relations, 1895, 8 Harv.L. Rev. 377; Green, Relational Interests, 1934, 29 Ill.L. Rev. 460, 1041; 30 Ill.L.Rev. 1, 314; W. Malone, 1979, Injuries to Family, Social and Trade Relations (Nutshell Series).

5. See § 128 (injurious falsehood); § 130) interference with prospective economic advantage); § 125 (injury to family member). Libel and slander may also interfere with ecnomic relations by harming reputation, see §§ 111–116A supra; malicious prosecution or its civil variants, §§ 119–121 supra, may also interfere with economic prospects, and so, occasionally, may invasion of privacy, see § 117.

6. See § 124 (interference with family relations); §§ 111–116A (libel and slander).

7. § 111 supra.

8. § 128 supra.

9. § 124 supra.

abduction of a family member,[10] or, more commonly, as in the case of interference with economic interests through violation of antitrust laws, misuse of trade secrets or confidential information and unfair competition generally.[11]

But neither interference with contract relations nor interference with prospective advantages necessarily involves falsehood; and neither necessarily involves an independent tort. It may be sufficient for liability that the defendant has acted intentionally to interfere with a known contract or prospect, that he has caused harm in so doing, and that he has acted in pursuit of some purpose considered improper. Although this "improper" interference was once described as "malicious,"[12] it is now clear that no actual spite has been required at all, and the term has gradually dropped from the cases,[13] leaving a rather broad and undefined tort in which no specific conduct is proscribed and in which liability turns on the purpose for which the defendant acts, with the indistinct notion that the purposes must be considered improper in some undefined way.

In spite of these uncertainties and a great deal of suspicion about the tort based on its "ominous beginning"[14] as a tool to enforce compulsory labor and its later history as a means of suppressing unions,[15] the courts have more or less continuously expanded the tort, with the effect, perhaps, that the uncertainties in its definition have become more rather than less significant. Although the tort continues to find supporters,[16] it has been subjected to serious criticisms on a wide range of grounds from economics[17] to justice to free speech,[18] with a good deal of emphasis on the idea that an actor should not be held liable for interference with contract unless the interference is accomplished by unlawful means or an independent tort.

All of this leaves open a good many questions about the basis of liability and defense,[19] the types of contract or relationship to be protected,[20] and the kind of interference that will be actionable,[21] each of which requires no little attention before the beginning of an answer can be made.

Development of the Tort

One form of the tort now known as inducing breach of contract or interference with contract[22] can be traced back to very ancient times, when it was not the existence of a contract which was important, but the status, or relation recognized by the law, in which the parties stood toward one another, and with which the defendant interfered. In early Roman law the pater-familias, or head of the household, was permitted to bring an action for violence committed upon his wife, his children, his slaves, or other members of his establishment, or even for insults offered

---

10. § 124 supra.

11. These forms of misconduct are often involved or asserted in claims for interference with contract, see, e.g., Feminist Women's Health Center v. Mohammad, 5th Cir.1978, 586 F.2d 530, certiorari denied 444 U.S. 924, 100 S.Ct. 262, 62 L.Ed.2d 180. Because these fields have developed elaborate rules of their own they have been largely omitted from the Second Restatement of Torts, see Introductory Note to Division Nine, and they are not developed here.

12. See pp. 983–984 below.

13. See pp. 983–984 below.

14. Dependahl v. Falstaff Brewing Corp., 8th Cir. 1981, 653 F.2d 1208, 1216, certiorari denied 454 U.S. 968, 102 S.Ct. 512, 70 L.Ed.2d 384.

15. See Note, Tortious Interference with Contractual Relations in the Nineteenth Century: The Transformation of Property, Contract and Tort, 1980, 93 Harv. L.Rev. 1510.

16. See Note, Tortious Interference with Contract: A Reassertion of Society's Interest in Commercial Stability and Contractual Integrity, 1981, 81 Colum.L.Rev. 1491.

17. Perlman, Interference with Contract and Other Economic Expectancies: A Clash of Tort and Contract Theory, 1982, 49 U.Chi.L.Rev. 61.

18. Dobbs, Tortious Interference with Contractual Relationships, 1980, 34 Ark.L.Rev. 335.

19. See p. 982 and following pages below.

20. See pp. 994–997 below.

21. See pp. 991–995 below.

22. See Sayre, Inducing Breach of Contract, 1923, 36 Harv.L.Rev. 663; Carpenter, Interference with Contract Relations, 1928, 41 Harv.L.Rev. 728, 7 Or.L.Rev. 181, 301; Harper, Interference with Contractual Relations, 1953, 47 N.W.U.L.Rev. 873; Notes, 1953, 32 N.C.L.Rev. 110; 1959, 43 Marq.L.Rev. 231; 1961, 56 N.W.U.L.Rev. 391.

to them, on the theory that they were so far identified with him that the wrong was one to himself.[23] By the thirteenth century this Roman law idea had been taken over by the common law, but had been somewhat altered in the transition, so that it became an action for damages sustained by any master through actual loss of the services of a servant because of violence inflicted upon him.[24] In 1349 an additional remedy was created by statute. The Black Death had left England with a great shortage of labor, and to meet the resulting agricultural crisis the famous Ordinance of Labourers[25] was enacted, by which a system of compulsory labor was introduced. A penalty was provided to keep the laborer from running away, and a remedy was given to the employer against anyone who received and retained him in his service. The statutory action for enticing or harboring the servant which thus developed, as well as the older one for violence against him, was enforced in trespass. In time the two became intermingled and confused, so that they were no longer distinguished, and at last both were absorbed into the action on the case.[26]

In the following centuries a broader principle was foreshadowed, in both England and in the United States.[27] It first appeared in definite form in 1853, in the leading modern case of Lumley v. Gye.[28] Miss Johanna Wagner, an opera singer of some distinction, was under contract to the plaintiff to sing exclusively in his theatre for a definite term. The defendant, "knowing the premises, and maliciously intending to injure plaintiff," "enticed and procured" Miss Wagner to refuse to carry out her agreement. Although it was reasonably clear that an operatic artiste was not to be classed as a "servant" within the meaning of the Statute of Labourers, it was held by a divided court that the principle should extend to her, and that it was a tort to persuade her to break her contract. Considerable stress was laid upon the "malice" with which it was alleged that the defendant was animated.

The doctrine thus announced, that intentional interference with a contract may be an actionable tort, was received at first with hesitation or disapproval,[29] but it was reaffirmed nearly thirty years later in England,[30] and then by degrees was extended, first to cover contracts other than those for personal services,[31] and later to include interferences in which no ill-will was to be found on the part of the defendant.[32] The present English law gives it full acceptance, as to all intentional interferences with any type of contract.[33] The American courts were reluctant to accept the doctrine in the beginning,[34] and a few of them rejected it outright as applied to interference with relations oth-

23. See Sayre, Inducing Breach of Contract, 36 Harv.L.Rev. 663 (1923).

24. Owen, Interference with Trade: The Illegitimate Offspring of an Illegitimate Tort? 1976, 3 Mon. L.Rev. 41.

25. 1349, 23 Edw. III, st. 1, administered under the Statute of Labourers, 1350, 25 Edw. III, st. 1.

26. Hart v. Aldridge, 1774, 1 Cowp. 54, 98 Eng.Rep. 964; Blake v. Lanyon, 1795, 6 Term Rep. 221, 101 Eng. Rep. 521. See Sayre, Inducing Breach of Contract, 1923, 36 Harv.L.Rev. 663; Wigmore, Interference with Social Relations, 1887, 21 Am.L.Rev. 764.

27. See Keeble v. Hickeringill, 1706, 11 Mod.Rep. 14, 130, 3 Salk. 9, 103 Eng.Rep. 1127; Tarleton v. McGawley, 1793, Peake N.P. 205, 170 Eng.Rep. 153; Green v. Button, 1835, 2 Cr.M. & R. 707, 150 Eng.Rep. 299; Aldridge v. Stuyvesant, N.Y.1828, 1 Super. (1 Hall 235) 210; Marsh v. Billings, 1851, 61 Mass. (7 Cush.) 322; Restatement of Torts, § 766, Comment b.

28. 1853, 2 El. & Bl. 216, 118 Eng.Rep. 749. The story of the case is told in Peck, Decision at Law, 1961, 125–144.

29. See Pollock, Law of Torts, 8th ed., 328; Langdell, A Brief Survey of Equity Jurisdiction, 1887, 1 Harv.L.Rev. 55, 57; Schofield, Lumley v. Gye, 1888, 2 Harv.L.Rev. 19.

30. Bowen v. Hall, 1881, 6 Q.B.D. 333, 50 L.J.Q.B. 305.

31. Temperton v. Russell [1893] 1 Q.B. 715, 62 L.J. Q.B. 412.

32. South Wales Miners' Federation v. Glamorgan Coal Co., [1905] A.C. 239.

33. Jasperson v. Dominion Tobacco Co., [1923] A.C. 709; Thomson v. Deakin, [1952] Ch. 646. See Payne, The Tort of Interference With Contract, 1954, 7 Curr. Leg.Prob. 94.

34. The history of the New York decisions is quite typical. The early cases denied any right of action unless the contract was one for personal services.

er than that of master and servant.[35] Such decisions have for the most part been overruled,[36] and the tort is now recognized virtually everywhere[37] as to any contract, regardless of its character.[38]

Lumley v. Gye and the succeeding cases laid emphasis upon the existence of the contract, as something in the nature of a property interest in the plaintiff, or a right in rem good against the world.[39] The subsequent development of the law has extended the principle to interference with advantageous economic relations even where they have not been cemented by contract,[40] and the liability for inducing breach of contract now is regarded as merely one instance of protection against such unjustified interference. The addition of the element of a definite contract has its importance, since the person induced to break it is then under a legal duty, and the plaintiff has furnished a consideration for the expectancy with which the defendant interferes. Existence of a contract, as distinct from a mere prospect of business, may therefore narrow the range of interference that may be considered proper by a defendant in pursuit of his own ends,[41] with the result that liability may be more expansive where there is an actual contract. The contract also fixes the limits of the plaintiff's interests, and hence of his damages. In many respects, however, the two claims are alike in principle and they are considered separately chiefly for convenience. In sum, Lumley v. Gye no longer reflects the limit of liability, which now covers virtually any kind of contract, and even

Ashley v. Dixon, 1872, 48 N.Y. 430; Curran v. Galen, 1897, 152 N.Y. 33, 46 N.E. 297. Later recovery still was denied, but the emphasis was shifted to the defendant's "justification" instead of the plaintiff's failure to state a cause of action. National Protective Association of Steam Fitters & Helpers v. Cumming, 1902, 170 N.Y. 315, 63 N.E. 369; Roseneau v. Empire Circuit Co., 1909, 131 App.Div. 429, 115 N.Y.S. 511, motion to amend decision denied 132 App.Div. 947, 117 N.Y.S. 1146. Still later, the earlier cases were overruled and recovery was permitted. S. C. Posner Co. v. Jackson, 1918, 223 N.Y. 325, 119 N.E. 573; Lamb v. S. Cheney & Sons, 1920, 227 N.Y. 418, 125 N.E. 817; Gonzales v. Kentucky Derby Co., 1921, 197 App.Div. 277, 189 N.Y.S. 783, affirmed 1922, 233 N.Y. 607, 135 N.E. 938. Finally intentional interference with contract, in the absence of a privilege, was declared actionable without reservation. Campbell v. Gates, 1923, 236 N.Y. 457, 141 N.E. 914.

35. Boyson v. Thorn, 1893, 98 Cal. 578, 33 P. 492; Kline v. Eubanks, 1902, 109 La. 241, 33 So. 211; Glencoe Sand & Gravel Co. v. Hudson Brothers Commission Co., 1897, 138 Mo. 439, 40 S.W. 93; Swain v. Johnson, 1909, 151 N.C. 93, 65 S.E. 619; Sleeper v. Baker, 1911, 22 N.D. 386, 134 N.W. 716.

Louisiana continues to hold that inducing breach of a contract is no tort unless means unlawful in themselves are used. Robert Heard Hale, Inc. v. Gaiennie, La.App.1958, 102 So.2d 324; Cust v. Item Co., 1942, 200 La. 515, 8 So.2d 361; Hartman v. Greene, 1939, 193 La. 234, 190 So. 390, certiorari denied 308 U.S. 612, 60 S.Ct. 180, 84 L.Ed. 512.

36. Imperial Ice Co. v. Rossier, 1941, 18 Cal.2d 33, 112 P.2d 631; Downey v. United Weatherproofing Co., 1953, 363 Mo. 852, 253 S.W.2d 976; Bryant v. Barber, 1953, 237 N.C. 480, 75 S.E.2d 410; see Bekken v. Equitable Life Assurance Society of United States, 1940, 70 N.D. 122, 293 N.W. 200. See Note, 1953, 32 N.C.L. Rev. 110.

Kentucky appears now to accept the tort. Carmichael-Lynch-Nolan Advertising Agency, Inc. v. Bennett & Associates, Inc., Ky.App.1977, 561 S.W.2d 99.

37. Louis Kamm, Inc. v. Flink, 1934, 113 N.J.L. 582, 175 A. 62; Keviczky v. Lorber, 1943, 290 N.Y. 297, 49 N.E.2d 146, motion denied 290 N.Y. 855, 50 N.E.2d 242; Knickerbocker Ice Co. v. Gardiner Dairy Co., 1908, 107 Md. 556, 69 A. 405; Sorenson v. Chevrolet Motor Co., 1927, 171 Minn. 260, 214 N.W. 754; Beekman v. Marsters, 1907, 195 Mass. 205, 80 N.E. 817.

38. As examples of the application of the doctrine to unusual situations, see: Globe & Rutgers Fire Insurance Co. v. Firemen's Fund Fire Insurance Co., 1910, 97 Miss. 148, 52 So. 454; Cumberland Glass Manufacturing Co. v. De Witt, 1913, 120 Md. 381, 87 A. 927, affirmed 237 U.S. 447, 35 S.Ct. 636, 59 L.Ed. 1042; Prairie Oil & Gas Co. v. Kinney, 1920, 79 Okl. 206, 192 P. 586; Luke v. Du Pree, 1924, 158 Ga. 590, 124 S.E. 13; R and W Hat Shop v. Sculley, 1922, 98 Conn. 1, 118 A. 55.

39. "It seems to us that where a party has entered into a contract with another to do or not to do a particular act or acts, he has as clear a right to its performance as he has to his property, either real or personal; and that knowingly to induce the other party to violate it is as distinct a wrong as it is to injure or destroy his property." Raymond v. Yarrington, 1903, 96 Tex. 443, 72 S.W. 580, 73 S.W. 800. Accord, S. C. Posner Co. v. Jackson, 1918, 223 N.Y. 325, 119 N.E. 573; cf. Goldman v. Harford Road Building Association, 1926, 150 Md. 677, 133 A. 843; Carolina Overall Corp. v. East Carolina Linen Supply, Inc., 1970, 8 N.C.App. 528, 174 S.E.2d 659.

40. See infra, § 130.

41. See infra, p. 986.

cases where economic gain is likely but there is no actual contract for it.

Basis of Liability—Intent

It is usually said that the basis of liability for interference with contract is intent [42] and that negligent interference is not actionable.[43] The exceptions to this rule,[44] such as they are, have been quite limited and principally involve cases of physical harm rather than pure economic harm. These cases aside, it is clear that liability is to be imposed only if the defendant intends to interfere with the plaintiff's contractual relations, at least in the sense that he acts with knowledge that interference will result,[45] and if, in addition, he acts for an improper purpose.

Intentional interference of course presupposes knowledge of the plaintiff's contract or interest, or at least of facts which would lead a reasonable person to believe that such interest exists.[46] Without such knowledge there can be no intent and no liability,[47] even though the defendant has intentionally injured the other party to the contract, as by killing a policy holder whom the plaintiff has insured,[48] or assaulting one whom he has contracted to care for.[49] Once such knowledge is established, the defendant may be held liable for an interference with the plaintiff's known economic interests if the defendant invades those interests by tortious,[50] illegal,[51] or unconstitutional [52] acts. Bribery of an employee, either plaintiff's or an employee of a third person, is clearly an improper means of interference and liability may be imposed not only under common law rules but under statutes as well.[53] But it is not necessary to show such improper means to establish liability and the defendant may be held even for peaceable persuasion, so long as he knows his persuasion will interfere with the plaintiff's contract and so long

---

42. See Carpenter, Interference with Contractual Relations, 1928, 41 Harv.L.Rev. 728, 7 Or.L.Rev. 181, 301; Green, Relational Interests, 1935, 29 Ill.L.Rev. 1041, 1042, 30 Ill.L.Rev. 1, 2; Harper, Interference with Contractual Relations, 1953, 47 N.W.U.L.Rev. 873, 884; Notes, 1953, 20 U.Chi.L.Rev. 283; 1948, 36 Ky. L.J. 142; 1935, 23 Cal.L.Rev. 420; 1933, 18 Corn.L.Q. 292; 1964, 16 Stan.L.Rev. 664.

43. Second Restatement of Torts, § 766C; see Note, Negligent Interference with Contract, 63 Va.L. Rev. 813 (1977).

It has thus been held that the comparative negligence statute has no application. Carman v. Heber, 1979, 43 Colo.App. 5, 601 P.2d 646.

44. See infra, pp. 996–1002.

45. Second Restatement of Torts, § 766, Comment *j*.

46. See Twitchell v. Nelson, 1914, 126 Minn. 423, 148 N.W. 451; Twitchell v. Glenwood-Inglewood Co., 1915, 131 Minn. 375, 155 N.W. 621; Tenta v. Guraly, 1966, 140 Ind.App. 160, 221 N.E.2d 577.

47. Snowden v. Sorenson, 1956, 246 Minn. 526, 75 N.W.2d 795; Augustine v. Trucco, 1954, 124 Cal.App. 2d 229, 268 P.2d 780; Kenworthy v. Kleinberg, 1935, 182 Wash. 425, 47 P.2d 825; Kerr v. Du Pree, 1926, 35 Ga.App. 122, 132 S.E. 393; Thomason v. Sparkman, Tex.Civ.App.1933, 55 S.W.2d 871. See Kelly v. Central Hanover Bank & Trust Co., S.D.N.Y.1935, 11 F.Supp. 497, 513, remanded for finding inter alia on question of knowledge 2d Cir.1936, 85 F.2d 61; Farley v. Kissel, 1974, 18 Ill.App.3d 139, 310 N.E.2d 385.

48. Mobile Life Insurance Co. v. Brame, 1877, 95 U.S. 754, 24 L.Ed. 580. Accord: Rockingham Mutual Fire Insurance Co. v. Bosher, 1855, 39 Me. 253 (setting fire to insured building); Midland Ins. Co. v. Smith, 1881, L.R. 6 Q.B.D. 561 (same).

49. Anthony v. Slaid, 1846, 52 Mass. (11 Met.) 290. But here again actions for loss of services of a servant are an exception. Woodward v. Washburn, N.Y.1846, 3 Denio 369; Jones v. Brown, 1794, 1 Esp. 217.

50. Violent and tortious activity causing economic harm has been a basis of liability for centuries. See Wigmore, 1887, The Boycott and Kindred Practices as Ground for Damages, 21 Am.L.Rev. 509; Owen, Interference with Trade, 1976, 3 Mon.L.Rev. 41; Green, Relational Interests, 1935, 29 Ill.L.Rev. 1041.

51. E.g., misuse of confidential information, see Nager v. Lad 'n Dad Slacks, 1978, 148 Ga.App. 401, 251 S.E.2d 330; Island Air, Inc. v. LaBar, 1977, 18 Wn.App. 129, 566 P.2d 972.

52. Board of Trustees of Weston County School District No. 1 v. Holso, Wyo.1978, 584 P.2d 1009, rehearing denied 587 P.2d 203 (school superintendent secured teacher's non-retention on constitutionally impermissible ground, liability under 42 U.S.C.A. § 1983).

53. Continental Management, Inc. v. United States, Ct.Cl.1975, 527 F.2d 613; Hunter v. Shell Oil Co., 5th Cir.1952, 198 F.2d 485; Sears, Roebuck & Co. v. American Plumbing & Supply Co., D.Wis.1956, 19 F.R.D. 334; Rangen, Inc. v. Sterling Nelson & Sons, Inc., 9th Cir. 1965, 351 F.2d 851, certiorari denied 383 U.S. 936, 86 S.Ct. 1067, 15 L.Ed.2d 853; D. Dobbs, Remedies §§ 10.4, 10.5.

Cf. Diesel Service Inc. v. Accessory Sales, Inc., 1982, 210 Neb. 797, 317 N.W.2d 719 (inducing plaintiff's employee to breach fiducial duties to plaintiff).

as the interference is regarded as "improper" under the circumstances.[54]

It has always been agreed that a defendant might intentionally interfere with the plaintiff's interests without liability if there were good grounds for the interference, or in other words that some kind of unacceptable purpose was required in addition to the intent. Different formulas to express this idea have been in use at different stages in the development of the tort, the first of which was to say that there was liability for intentional interference that was "malicious."[55] It has long been clear, however, that "malice" in the sense of ill-will or spite is not required for liability.[56] In recognition of this, courts and writers adopted a second formula under which liability was imposed for any intentional interference that resulted in harm. Under this formula, the plaintiff made out a prima facie case upon proof of intended interference plus damages, and it was left to the defendant to shoulder if he could the burden of proving he was justified in his actions,[57] for example, by showing that he acted to protect legitimate and prior property or contract interests of his own.[58] This formula subjected the defendant to liability without first describing to him what was forbidden and what was permitted,[59] and it added to this injury by putting the burden upon him to justify his conduct without specifying in any precise way what would amount to such a justification. The Restatement Second of Torts[60] has adopted a third formula, which may meet a part of this objection. Under this, the defendant is subject to liability for a knowing or purposeful interference with contract only if the defendant's action was "improper," either as to means or purpose. This formula might be read, as some of the cases imply,[61] to put the burden

54. See, e.g., Smith v. Ford Motor Co., 1976, 289 N.C. 71, 221 S.E.2d 282; cf. Feminist Women's Health Center v. Mohammad, 5th Cir.1978, 586 F.2d 530, certiorari denied 444 U.S. 924, 100 S.Ct. 262, 62 L.Ed.2d 180 (advice to younger doctors to avoid plaintiff's controversial clinic could be found by trier to be an actionable "threat"). See Second Restatement of Torts, § 766, Ill. 2–3.

55. Lumley v. Gye, 1853, 2 El. & Bl. 216, 118 Eng. Rep. 749; Bowen v. Hall, 1881, 6 Q.B.D. 333, 50 L.J. Q.B. 305; Temperton v. Russell, [1893] 1 Q.B. 715, 62 L.J.Q.B. 412.

56. "Bearing in mind that malice may or may not be used to denote ill will, and that in legal language, presumptive or implied malice is distinguishable from express malice, it conduces to clearness in discussing such cases as these to drop the word 'malice' altogether, and to substitute for it the meaning which is really intended to be conveyed by it. Its use may be necessary in drawing indictments, but when all that is meant by malice is an intention to commit an unlawful act, without reference to spite or ill-feeling, it is better to drop the word malice, and so avoid all misunderstanding." Lord Lindley, in South Wales Miners' Federation v. Glamorgan Coal Co., [1905] A.C. 239. See also Jaffin, Theorems in Anglo-Amercian Labor Law, 1931, 31 Col.L.Rev. 1104, 1123; Fridman, Malice in the Law of Torts, 1958, 21 Mod.L.Rev. 484; Stoner, The Influence of Social and Economic Ideals in the Law of Malicious Torts, 1910, 8 Mich.L.Rev. 468; Green, Relational Interests, 1935, 29 Ill.L.Rev. 1041; Notes, 1928, 12 Minn. L.Rev. 147; 1927, 12 St. Louis L.Rev. 286; 1923, 9 Corn.L.Q. 78.

57. Mogul S. S. Co. v. McGregor Gow & Co., 1889, L.R. 23 Q.B.D. 598, affirmed [1892] A.C. 25; Aikens v. Wisconsin, 1904, 195 U.S. 194, 25 S.Ct. 3, 49 L.Ed. 154; Berry v. Donovan, 1905, 188 Mass. 353, 74 N.E. 603; Connors v. Connolly, 1913, 86 Conn. 641, 86 A. 600; De Minico v. Craig, 1911, 207 Mass. 593, 94 N.E. 317. The two cases last named held the question to be one of law for the court; but the issue of reasonable conduct frequently has been left to the jury. Order of Railway Conductors v. Jones, 1925, 78 Colo. 80, 239 P. 882; Carnes v. St. Paul Union Stockyards Co., 1925, 164 Minn. 457, 205 N.W. 630, rehearing denied 164 Minn. 457, 206 N.W. 396; Berry v. Donovan, supra.

58. Felsen v. Sol Cafe Manufacturing Corp., 1969, 24 N.Y.2d 682, 301 N.Y.S.2d 610, 249 N.E.2d 459; Ciccarello v. Gottlieb, 1979, 22 Wn.App. 858, 592 P.2d 679, opinion withdrawn on stipulation for dismissal, 597 P.2d 1391.

59. "[A] broad generalization [about tortious interference] could make prima facie torts of otherwise lawful activities designed to persuade others to stop smoking cigarettes or eating certain foods, or using certain pesticides, or doing business in South Africa, or buying grapes or other products, leaving the defense in each case to a showing of privilege." Linde, J. in Top Service Body Shop, Inc. v. Allstate Insurance Co., 1978, 283 Or. 201, 582 P.2d 1365. The lack of definition in this tort is criticized as unjust in Dobbs, Tortious Interference with Contractual Relationships, 1980, 34 Ark.L. Rev. 335, 345–46.

60. Second Restatement of Torts, §§ 766, 767, Comments b and k.

61. Swager v. Couri, 1979, 77 Ill.3d 173, 32 Ill.Dec. 540, 395 N.E.2d 921 (failure to plead "lack of justification," therefore judgment for defendant); Top Service Body Shop, Inc. v. Allstate Ins. Co., 1978, 283 Or. 201, 582 P.2d 1365; Alvord and Swift v. Steward M. Muller Construction Co., 1978, 46 N.Y.2d 276, 413 N.Y.S.2d

on the plaintiff in the first instance to show impropriety, and it is no doubt an improvement when so read. But the Second Restatement refused to take a clear position on the point and other cases have left the burden upon the defendant to justify his conduct.[62]

All this still leaves the unresolved question, whenever the defendant has not simplified the matter by using illegal or tortious means of interference, as to what purpose or state of mind will be found improper or unjustified so as to furnish a basis for liability. On this central issue there is no firm answer, and no doubt a good deal of balancing of interests must take place in rendering any decision.[63] In the absence of firm rules, it is only possible to make a general mention of several particular issues that have arisen.

Since Lumley v. Gye there has been general agreement that a purely "malicious" motive, in the sense of spite and a desire to do harm to the plaintiff for its own sake, will make the defendant liable for interference with a contract.[64] The same is true of mere officious intermeddling for no other reason than a desire to interfere.[65] On the other hand, in the few cases in which the question has arisen, it has been held that where the defendant has a proper purpose in view, the addition of ill will toward the plaintiff will not defeat his privilege.[66] It may be suggested that here, as in the case of mixed motives[67] in the exercise of a privilege in defamation and malicious prosecution,[68] the court may well look to the predominant purpose underlying the defendant's conduct.[69]

309, 385 N.E.2d 1238 (without discussion of the point, Breitel, J. seems to have put burden on plaintiff); Adler, Barish, Daniels, Levin & Creskoff v. Epstein, 1978, 482 Pa. 416, 393 A.2d 1175, appeal dismissed, certiorari denied 442 U.S. 907, 99 S.Ct. 2817, 61 L.Ed.2d 272; Lake Gateway Motor Inn v. Matt's Sunshine Gift Shops, Inc., Fla.App.1978, 361 So.2d 769 (without discussion of the point, court seems to place burden on plaintiff).

62. Alyeska Pipeline Service Co. v. Aurora Air Service Inc., Alaska 1979, 604 P.2d 1090. Many cases reflect difficulties on this point. Statements about burden of proof as to the "privilege" may be casual rather than considered, as in Langeland v. Farmers State Bank of Trimont, Minn.1982, 319 N.W.2d 26, and a court putting the burden on the defendant as to good faith may put the burden on the plaintiff to prove "interference," with interference defined in such a way as to exclude liability for proper interference. This may have happened in United Wild Rice, Inc. v. Nelson, Minn.1982, 313 N.W.2d 628. Similarly in Walt Bennett Ford v. Pulaski County Special School District, 1981, 274 Ark. 208, 624 S.W.2d 426, the court first held for defendants on the ground that there was no bad faith, then on supplemental opinion, reaffirmed its earlier rule that bad faith was no part of the plaintiff's case.

63. The Second Restatement of Torts, § 767 lists seven factors to be considered, among them the defendant's motive, the interests of both the defendant and the plaintiff, considerations of freedom for the defendant and security of contractual interests for the plaintiff, no doubt all appropriate enough but not a list that would inspire one to predict an outcome, or decide one's rights or duties.

64. Employment contracts: Jones v. Leslie, 1910, 61 Wash. 107, 112 P. 81; De Minico v. Craig, 1911, 207 Mass. 593, 94 N.E. 317; Carnes v. St. Paul Union Stockyards Co., 1925, 164 Minn. 457, 205 N.W. 630, rehearing denied 164 Minn. 457, 206 N.W. 396; Wheeler-Stenzel Co. v. American Window Glass Co., 1909, 202 Mass. 471, 89 N.E. 28.

Other contracts: Martens v. Reilly, 1901, 109 Wis. 464, 84 N.W. 840; Wesley v. Native Lumber Co., 1910, 97 Miss. 814, 53 So. 346; Dunshee v. Standard Oil Co., 1911, 152 Iowa 618, 132 N.W. 371; Hutton v. Watters, 1915, 132 Tenn. 527, 179 S.W. 134.

65. Sidney Blumenthal & Co. v. United States, 2d Cir.1929, 30 F.2d 247. Cf. Russell v. Croteau, 1953, 98 N.H. 68, 94 A.2d 376 (no reason apparent on record).

66. Lancaster v. Hamburger, 1904, 70 Ohio St. 156, 71 N.E. 289; Gregory v. Dealers' Equipment Co., 1927, 156 Tenn. 273, 300 S.W. 563; Bentley v. Teton, 1958, 19 Ill.App.2d 284, 153 N.E.2d 495; Diver v. Miller, Del. 1929, 4 W.W.Harr. 207, 148 A. 291; Stevens v. Siegel, 1963, 18 A.D.2d 1109, 239 N.Y.S.2d 827; O'Brien v. Western Union Telegraph Co., 1911, 62 Wash. 598, 114 P. 441.

67. One question which seems nowhere to have been considered is whether anything so intrinsically psychological as a mixed motive is really susceptible of proof. Since in many cases the defendant himself is uncertain as to his own motives, and some element of ill will is seldom absent, there is all the more reason for holding that the addition of "malice" should not defeat the privilege.

68. See supra, §§ 115–119.

69. The dominant motive test was adopted in Alyeska Pipeline Service Co. v. Aurora Air Service, Alaska 1979, 604 P.2d 1090. It is criticized as an effort to obtain proper thought at the cost of unsafe action in Dobbs, Tortious Interference with Contractual Relationships, 1980, 34 Ark.L.Rev. 335, 347–350. The test was used when the defendant was an agent for two entities with conflicting interests in Welch v. Bancorp

In contrast, an impersonal or disinterested motive of a laudable character may protect the defendant in his interference. This is true particularly where he seeks to protect a third person toward whom he stands in a relation of responsibility, as in the case of a mother endeavoring to exclude a diseased person from her child's school,[70] school authorities making regulations for the welfare of their students,[71] an agent protecting the interests of his principal,[72] or an employer those of his employee,[73] provided that the steps taken are not unreasonable in view of the harm threatened.[74] There may also be a privilege to protect the public interest, as by removing a danger to public health or morals,[75] or making complaint of the misconduct of an employee of a public utility,[76] or taxpayers objecting to the expenditure of public money.[77] Beyond this, many cases have said that there is a privilege to give bona fide [78] advice to withdraw from a contractual relation,[79] although so far as appears this may be limited to cases where the advice is requested,[80] or the defendant stands in such a relation as to justify his intervention.[81] The privilege of relatives to induce the breach of a contract to marry sometimes has been placed upon this ground.[82]

Management Advisors, 1982, 57 Or.App. 666, 646 P.2d 57.

70. Legris v. Marcotte, 1906, 129 Ill.App. 67.

71. Cf. Gott v. Berea College, 1913, 156 Ky. 376, 161 S.W. 204; Jones v. Cody, 1902, 132 Mich. 13, 92 N.W. 495; Guethler v. Altman, 1901, 26 Ind.App. 587, 60 N.E. 355; Rowan v. Butler, 1908, 171 Ind. 28, 85 N.E. 714 (soldiers' home); Kuryer Publishing Co. v. Messmer, 1916, 162 Wis. 565, 156 N.W. 948 (church). While these are cases of interference with prospective advantage, their language is equally applicable to existing contracts.

72. Said v. Butt, [1920] 3 K.B. 497. Cf. Caverno v. Fellows, 1938, 300 Mass. 331, 15 N.E.2d 483 (high school supervisor, principal and superintendent reporting on conduct of teacher); Bentley v. Teton, 1958, 19 Ill.App.2d 284, 153 N.E.2d 495 (civil servant reporting misconduct of nurse to his superior); Terry v. Zachry, Tex.Civ.App.1954, 272 S.W.2d 157, refused n.r.e. (chairman of board of corporation inducing it to litigate claim); Garcia Sugars Corp. v. New York Coffee & Sugar Exchange, Sup.1938, 7 N.Y.S.2d 532 (broker obeying orders of exchange).

73. Gregory v. Dealers' Equipment Co., 1927, 156 Tenn. 273, 300 S.W. 563; cf. Heywood v. Tillson, 1883, 75 Me. 225, 46 Am.Rep. 373; Hopper v. Lennen & Mitchell, S.D.Cal.1943, 52 F.Supp. 319, affirmed in part and reversed in part 9th Cir., 146 F.2d 364, 161 A.L.R. 282; Lawless v. Brotherhood of Painters, 1956, 143 Cal.App.2d 474, 300 P.2d 159 (international union and local union).

74. There is no privilege where there is no reasonable belief that any harm is threatened. Hutton v. Watters, 1915, 132 Tenn. 527, 179 S.W. 134.

75. Cf. Brimelow v. Casson, [1924] 1 Ch. 302 (preventing prostitution); Stott v. Gamble, [1916] 2 K.B. 504 (preventing improper public entertainment); Legris v. Marcotte, 1906, 129 Ill.App. 67 (preventing spread of disease). Cf. Porter v. King County Medical Society, 1936, 186 Wash. 410, 58 P.2d 367 (ethical rules of medical association).

Occasionally the interest in increasing employment or improving working conditions is said to be a "public interest." Green v. Samuelson, 1935, 168 Md. 421, 178 A. 109; Radio Station KFH Co. v. Musicians Association Local No. 297, 1950, 169 Kan. 596, 220 P.2d 199; Wholesale Laundry Board of Trade v. Tarrullo, Sup. 1951, 103 N.Y.S.2d 23.

76. Lancaster v. Hamburger, 1904, 70 Ohio St. 156, 71 N.E. 289. Cf. Chicago, Rhode Island & Pacific Railway Co. v. Armstrong, 1911, 30 Okl. 134, 120 P. 952 (railway protecting public).

77. Middlesex Concrete Products & Excavating Corp. v. Carteret Industrial Assocation, 1962, 37 N.J. 507, 181 A.2d 774.

78. Otherwise where the advice is given with a spiteful motive. Morgan v. Andrews, 1895, 107 Mich. 33, 64 N.W. 869.

79. Glamorgan Coal Co. v. South Wales Miners' Federation, [1903] 1 K.B. 118, reversed on other grounds in [1905] A.C. 239; Delaware, Lackawanna & Western Railroad Co. v. Switchmen's Union of North America, C.C.N.Y.1907, 158 F. 541. See Northern Wisconsin Co-operative Tobacco Pool v. Bekkedal, 1923, 182 Wis. 571, 197 N.W. 936; Walker v. Cronin, 1871, 107 Mass. 555; Arnold v. Moffitt, 1910, 30 R.I. 310, 75 A. 502; Coakley v. Degner, 1926, 191 Wis. 170, 210 N.W. 359; Holmes, Privilege, Malice and Intent, 1894, 8 Harv.L.Rev. 1, 6.

80. Second Restatement of Torts, § 772.

81. As where an employee advises his employer to discharge another employee. E.g., Martin v. Platt, 1979, 179 Ind.App. 688, 386 N.E.2d 1026; Nola v. Merollis Chevrolet Kansas City, Inc., Mo.App.1976, 537 S.W.2d 627. This protective rule does not extend to the use of improper means, such as lying. See Straube v. Larson, 1979, 287 Or. 357, 600 P.2d 371 (alleged misstatements of fact), or improper purpose, such as a purpose to compel sexual attentions. Tash v. Houston, 1977, 74 Mich.App. 566, 254 N.W.2d 579.

82. Overhultz v. Row, 1922, 152 La. 9, 92 So. 716; Minsky v. Satenstein, 1928, 6 N.J.Misc. 978, 143 A. 512; Lukas v. Tarpilauskas, 1929, 266 Mass. 498, 165 N.E. 513.

The defendant is also permitted to interfere with another's contractual relations to protect his own present existing economic interests, such as the ownership or condition of property,[83] or a prior contract of his own,[84] or a financial interest in the affairs of the person persuaded.[85] He is not free, under this rule, to induce a contract breach merely to obtain customers [86] or other prospective advantage; but he may do so to protect what he perceives to be existing interests, as where a manufacturer or corporate affiliate induces a dealer or subsidiary to terminate an employee or agent.[87] It seems assumed in the usual case [88] that the defendant may use his business judgment and may protect intangible existing interests, such as good will or good relationships, or the character of his business, as where a hotel interferes with a contract to assure that a concession on its premises operates with standards appropriate to the hotel's clientele,[89] or a lessor vetos a sub-lease or an assignment to a tenant whose business

---

83. Diver v. Miller, Del.1929, 4 W.W.Harr. 207, 148 A. 291; O'Brien v. Western Union Telegraph Co., 1911, 62 Wash. 598, 114 P. 441; Winters v. University District Building & Loan Association, 1932, 268 Ill.App. 147; Meason v. Ralston Purina Co., 1940, 56 Ariz. 291, 107 P.2d 224 (mortgagee); cf. Watch Tower Bible & Tract Society v. Dougherty, 1940, 337 Pa. 286, 11 A.2d 147 (religious publication); Owen v. Williams, 1948, 322 Mass. 356, 77 N.E.2d 318.

84. Tidal Western Oil Corp. v. Shackelford, Tex.Civ. App.1927, 297 S.W. 279, error refused; Williams v. Adams, 1937, 250 App.Div. 603, 295 N.Y.S. 86; Quinlivan v. Brown Oil Co., 1934, 96 Mont. 147, 29 P.2d 374; In re Farrell Publishing Corp., S.D.N.Y.1958, 165 F.Supp. 40, affirmed Hendler v. Cuneo Eastern Press, Inc., 2d Cir., 279 F.2d 181; Millers Mutual Casualty Co. v. Insurance Exchange Building Corp., 1920, 218 Ill.App. 12. The holder of the prior contract may even obtain specific performance at the expense of the later one. White Marble Lime Co. v. Consolidated Lumber Co., 1919, 205 Mich. 634, 172 N.W. 603.

But a purpose of terminating the defendant's own contract is not a legitimate justification from inducing breach of the plaintiff's. A. S. Rampell, Inc. v. Hyster Co., 1955, 1 Misc.2d 788, 148 N.Y.S.2d 102, modified 2 A.D.2d 739, 153 N.Y.S.2d 176, appeal denied 2 N.Y.2d 828, 159 N.Y.S.2d 961, 140 N.E.2d 860, affirmed and reversed 3 N.Y.2d 369, 165 N.Y.S.2d 475, 144 N.E.2d 371.

85. Ford v. C. E. Wilson & Co., 2d Cir. 1942, 129 F.2d 614 (taking security from debtor); Knapp v. Penfield, 1932, 143 Misc. 132, 256 N.Y.S. 41; Aalfo Co. v. Kinney, 1929, 105 N.J.L. 345, 144 A. 715; Petit v. Cuneo, 1937, 290 Ill.App. 16, 7 N.E.2d 774; see Note, 1941, 27 Va.L.Rev. 1102.

Langeland v. Farmers State Bank of Trimont, Minn. 1982, 319 N.W.2d 26. But cf. Smith v. Ford Motor Co., 1976, 289 N.C. 71, 221 S.E.2d 282.

See also, as to the interest of directors and stockholders in the affairs of a corporation, Griswold v. Heat, Inc., 1967, 108 N.H. 119, 229 A.2d 183; Coronet Development Co. v. F. S. W., Inc., 1967, 379 Mich. 302, 150 N.W.2d 809.

But a stockholder may be liable for interference with the contract of a corporation for ulterior purposes of his own, even though there is financial advantage in them. W. P. Iverson v. Dunham Manufacturing Co., 1958, 18 Ill.App.2d 404, 152 N.E.2d 615; Mendelson v. Blatz Brewing Co., 1960, 9 Wis.2d 487, 101 N.W.2d 805; Morgan v. Andrews, 1895, 107 Mich. 33, 64 N.W. 869. Compare, as to a workmen's compensation insurer obtaining the discharge of a workman with an accident record, American Surety Co. v. Schottenbauer, 8th Cir. 1958, 257 F.2d 6; Harris v. Traders' & General Insurance Co., Tex.Civ.App.1935, 82 S.W.2d 750, error refused.

86. Azar v. Lehigh Corp., Fla.App.1978, 364 So.2d 860; cf. Adler, Barish, Daniels, Levin & Creskoff v. Epstein, 1978, 482 Pa. 416, 393 A.2d 1175, appeal dismissed, certiorari denied 442 U.S. 907, 99 S.Ct. 2817, 61 L.Ed.2d 272 (former employee of law firm in violation of Code of Professional Responsibility); Island Air, Inc. v. LaBar, 1977, 18 Wn.App. 129, 566 P.2d 972 (confidential information).

87. Babson Brothers Co. v. Allison, Fla.App.1976, 337 So.2d 848; Felsen v. Sol Cafe Manufacturing Corp., 1969, 24 N.Y.2d 682, 301 N.Y.S.2d 610, 249 N.E.2d 459. But see Smith v. Ford Motor Co., 1976, 289 N.C. 71, 221 S.E.2d 282, 79 A.L.R.3d 651 (manufacturer subject to liability for inducing its dealer to terminate employee because of employee's activities in Dealer Alliance). As to automobile manufacturers the Dealers Day in Court Act, 15 U.S.C.A. § 1221 may provide more demanding rules.

Cf. Paul Hardeman, Inc. v. Bradley, Okl.1971, 486 P.2d 731 (prime contractor had right by contract to require subcontractor to discharge unacceptable employees at the work site, no liability).

88. Smith v. Ford Motor Co., 1976, 289 N.C. 71, 221 S.E.2d 282, 79 A.L.R.3d 651 may be an exception. The Court there professed to see no interest of Ford in whether dealers' employees joined the Ford Dealers Alliance and held Ford subject to liability for inducing a termination of the dealer's employee. Professor Perlman has pointed out that nothing in the legal "doctrine helps a court decide whether the prevention of a dealers' alliance is a legitimate business interest." Perlman, Interference with Contracts and Other Economic Expectancies: A Clash of Tort and Contract Theory, 1982, 49 U.Chi.L.Rev. 61.

89. Lake Gateway Motor Inn v. Matt's Sunshine Gift Shops, Inc., Fla.App.1978, 361 So.2d 769.

would be out of character on the premises,[90] or where the defendant exercises any other legal right in a proper way.[91]

But where the defendant's interest is merely one of prospective advantage, not yet realized, he has no such justification. Thus his interference with an existing contract of another is deemed improper if the interference is solely for the purpose of enticing away the other's employees,[92] and equally if it is for the purpose of inducing the plaintiff's former employees to compete with him in violation of a valid non-competition covenant.[93] It is also improper interference to entice away customers who are bound to the plaintiff by contract,[94] or suppliers who are so obligated,[95] or to disrupt an exclusive agency or dealership,[96] or indeed to pursue any competitive scheme [97] that would enhance the defendant's opportunities at the expense of actual existing contract rights in the plaintiff, in the absence of some justification other than competition for future business.

Where the contract interfered with is terminable at will, however, the privilege of competition has been recognized. In such a case there is no contract right to have the relation continued, but only an expectancy, which is similar to the expectancy of a business that a customer will continue to do business with it. With such an expectancy of future relations, and prospective advantage, there has been no doubt that a competitor has the privilege of interfering to acquire the business for himself.[98] Ac-

---

90. Juhasz v. Quik Shops, Inc., 1977, 55 Ohio App. 2d 51, 379 N.E.2d 235; Serafino v. Palm Terrace Apartments, Fla.App.1976, 343 So.2d 851.

91. Coronado Mining Corp. v. Marathon Oil Co., Utah 1978, 577 P.2d 957. In Standard Fruit & Steamship Co. v. Putname, Miss.1974, 290 So.2d 612 defendant would not permit plaintiff on his premises, with the result that plaintiff lost his job as a truck driver. The court thought the defendant privileged because of his fear that plaintiff, who had once recovered substantial sums from defendant, might sue again.

92. Nager v. Lad'n Dad Slacks, 1978, 148 Ga.App. 401, 251 S.E.2d 330; Felicie, Inc. v. Leibovitz, 1979, 67 A.D.2d 656, 412 N.Y.S.2d 625; International Tailoring Co. of New York v. Lukas, Sup.1946, 64 N.Y.S.2d 879; Walker v. Cronin, 1871, 107 Mass. 555; Prairie Oil & Gas Co. v. Kinney, 1920, 79 Okl. 206, 192 P. 586; S. C. Posner Co. v. Jackson, 1918, 223 N.Y. 325, 119 N.E. 573; Employing Printers' Club v. Doctor Blosser Co., 1905, 122 Ga. 509, 50 S.E. 353.

93. National Merchandising Corp. v. Leyden, 1976, 370 Mass. 425, 348 N.E.2d 771.

Cf. Certified Laboratories of Texas, Inc. v. Rubinson, D.Pa.1969, 303 F.Supp. 1014 (defendant hired to violate non-competition covenant and also to get confidential information).

94. Automobile Insurance Co. of Hartford Connecticut v. Guaranty Securities Corp., D.N.Y.1917, 240 F. 222; Azar v. Lehigh Corp., Fla.App.1978, 364 So.2d 860; cf. Adler, Barish, Daniels, Levin & Creskoff v. Epstein, 1978, 482 Pa. 416, 393 A.2d 1175, appeal dismissed, certiorari denied 442 U.S. 907, 99 S.Ct. 2817, 61 L.Ed.2d 272; Island Air, Inc. v. LaBar, 1977, 18 Wn. App. 129, 566 P.2d 972.

95. Friedberg, Inc. v. McClary, 1917, 173 Ky. 579, 191 S.W. 300; Guard-Life Corp. v. S. Parker Hardware Manufacturing Corp., 1979, 67 A.D.2d 658, 412 N.Y.S.2d 623, judgment modified 50 N.Y.2d 183, 428 N.Y.S.2d 628, 406 N.E.2d 445.

96. Beekman v. Marsters, 1907, 195 Mass. 205, 80 N.E. 817; Sorenson v. Chevrolet Motor Co., 1927, 171 Minn. 260, 214 N.W. 754; Schechter v. Friedman, 1948, 141 N.J.Eq. 318, 57 A.2d 251; E. L. Husting Co. v. Coca Cola Co., 1931, 205 Wis. 356, 237 N.W. 85, rehearing denied 205 Wis. 356, 238 N.W. 626, certiorari denied Wisconsin Coca Cola Bottling Co. v. E. L. Husting Co., 285 U.S. 538, 52 S.Ct. 311, 76 L.Ed. 931.

Accord, as to broker's contracts: Horn v. Seth, 1953, 201 Md. 589, 95 A.2d 312; Louis Schlesinger Co. v. Rice, 1950, 4 N.J. 169, 72 A.2d 197; Johnson v. Gustafson, 1938, 201 Minn. 629, 277 N.W. 252; Franklin v. Brown, Fla.App.1964, 159 So.2d 893; Graff v. Whitehouse, 1966, 71 Ill.App.2d 412, 219 N.E.2d 128.

The addition of a spite motive will of course not improve the defendant's position. S.C. Posner Co. v. Jackson, 1918, 223 N.Y. 325, 119 N.E. 573; Globe & Rutgers Fire Insurance Co. v. Firemen's Fund Fire Insurance Co., 1910, 97 Miss. 148, 52 So. 454; Schonwald v. Ragains, 1912, 32 Okl. 22, 122 P. 203; Sorenson v. Chevrolet Motor Co., 1927, 171 Minn. 260, 214 N.W. 754, 84 A.L.R. 35.

97. Bitterman v. Louisville & Nashville Railroad Co., 1907, 207 U.S. 205, 28 S.Ct. 91, 52 L.Ed. 171; Sperry Hutchinson Co. v. Louis Weber & Co., C.C.Ill.1908, 161 F. 219; Wade v. Culp, 1939, 107 Ind.App. 503, 23 N.E.2d 615 (marketing patented article); Wilkinson v. Powe, 1942, 300 Mich. 275, 1 N.W.2d 539 (milk delivery contracts); Nulty v. Hart-Bradshaw Lumber & Grain Co., 1924, 116 Kan. 446, 227 P. 254 (grain partnership); Republic Gear Co. v. Borg-Warner Corp., 7th Cir.1969, 406 F.2d 57, certiorari denied 394 U.S. 1000, 89 S.Ct. 1596, 22 L.Ed.2d 777 (licensing contract); Northeast Airlines, Inc. v. World Airways, Inc., D.Mass.1966, 262 F.Supp. 316.

98. See infra, p. 1012.

cordingly, the considerable weight of authority holds that there is a privilege of competition which extends to inducing the termination of agreements terminable at will, whether they concern employment [99] or other relations.[1] On the same principle, the defendant may protect its legitimate interests, which are not limited to purely competitive interests,[2] by interference with the plaintiff's mere prospects for business.[3]

Although a defendant is free to protect his own existing interests by interfering with a contract that threatens those interests, he is not equally free to interfere with a contract that itself causes him no harm. He may not, in other words, interfere simply to coerce the plaintiff to comply with his wishes on some collateral matter—as where an employer is induced to discharge a workman in order to compel him to pay the defendant a debt,[4] prevent him from bringing suit,[5] or force him to compromise a claim,[6] or for the purpose of extorting money from him.[7]

Although there may be no liability for interference with contract by a mere truthful statement of fact,[8] liability has been imposed without much question where there is no misstatement of fact at all and the defendant has merely advised or persuaded another to breach his contract with the plaintiff,[9] or where the defendant has merely made the other an offer better than the plaintiff's contract.[10] Since persuasion or an offer of a better contract is necessarily speech,[11] there is a question whether the First Amendment, which has had a very sizeable impact in the defamation cases,[12] might restrict liability to those cases in which some degree of personal fault and some false statements of fact are shown.[13] There are assuredly special cases in which speech is addressed to social

---

99. Triangle Film Corp. v. Artcraft Pictures Corp., 2d Cir.1918, 250 F. 981; McCluer v. Super Maid CookWare Corp., 10th Cir.1932, 62 F.2d 426; Coleman & Morris v. Pisciotta, 1951, 279 App.Div. 656, 107 N.Y.S.2d 715; Diodes, Inc. v. Franzen, 1968, 260 Cal. App.2d 244, 67 Cal.Rptr. 19; Vincent Horwitz Co. v. Cooper, 1945, 352 Pa. 7, 41 A.2d 870.

1. Terry v. Dairymen's League Co-operative Association, 1956, 2 A.D.2d 494, 157 N.Y.S.2d 71; National Oil Co. v. Phillips Petroleum Co., W.D.Wis.1966, 265 F.Supp. 320; Biber Brothers News Co. v. New York Evening Post, 1932, 144 Misc. 405, 258 N.Y.S. 31; DuArt Film Laboratories v. Consolidated Film Industries, S.D.N.Y.1936, 15 F.Supp. 689; Kingsbery v. Phillips Petroleum Co., Tex.Civ.App.1958, 315 S.W.2d 561, refused n.r.e.

See Notes, 1962, 56 Nw.U.L.Rev. 391; 1964, 24 Md. L.Rev. 85; 1958, 25 Brook.L.Rev. 73.

2. E.g., Federal Auto Body Works, Inc. v. Aetna Casualty & Surety Co., 1982, __ R.I. __, 447 A.2d 377 (insurer's interest in cost-efficient car repair warranted interference with repair shop's prospective business).

3. United Wild Rice, Inc. v. Nelson, Minn.1982, 313 N.W.2d 628; Second Restatement of Torts, § 769.

4. Warschauser v. Brooklyn Furniture Co., 1913, 159 App.Div. 81, 144 N.Y.S. 257; Giblan v. National Union, [1903] 2 K.B. 600; cf. Tubular Rivet & Stud Co. v. Exeter Boot & Shoe Co., 1 Cir. 1908, 159 F. 824.

5. Johnson v. Aetna Life Insurance Co., 1914, 158 Wis. 56, 147 N.W. 32. Cf. Mealey v. Bemidji Lumber Co., 1912, 118 Minn. 427, 136 N.W. 1090 (enticing employees to prevent performance of contract with defendant).

6. London Guarantee & Accident Co. v. Horn, 1904, 206 Ill. 493, 69 N.E. 526; United States Fidelity & Guaranty Co. v. Millonas, 1921, 206 Ala. 147, 89 So. 732; cf. Joyce v. Great Northern Railway Co., 1907, 100 Minn. 225, 110 N.W. 975; Palatine Insurance Co. v. Griffin, Tex.Civ.App.1918, 202 S.W. 1014, reversed Com.App.1922, 235 S.W. 202, reversal set aside 238 S.W. 637.

7. Lopes v. Connolly, 1912, 210 Mass. 487, 97 N.E. 80; Hill Groc. Co. v. Carroll, 1931, 223 Ala. 376, 136 So. 789; Doucette v. Sallinger, 1917, 228 Mass. 444, 117 N.E. 897; Scott v. Prudential Outfitting Co., 1915, 92 Misc. 195, 155 N.Y.S. 497; Bowen v. Morris, 1929, 219 Ala. 689, 123 So. 222.

8. Second Restatement of Torts, § 772 and Comment b.

9. Smith v. Ford Motor Co., 1976, 289 N.C. 71, 221 S.E.2d 282, 79 A.L.R.3d 651. The Second Restatement of Torts, § 772 recognizes advice as proper if honest and made in response to a request for advice.

10. See, Second Restatement of Torts, § 766, Ill. 3.

11. In many cases of injurious falsehood or libel the damages claimed involved loss of contract or an interference with prospective advantage. The Supreme Court has not intimated that such claims would receive any different constitutional treatment. See Hutchinson v. Proxmire, 1979, 443 U.S. 111, 99 S.Ct. 2675, 61 L. Ed.2d 411.

12. Supra § 113. There may also be an impact in injurious falsehood cases, supra § 128, or even, conceivably, malicious prosecution cases, see § 119.

13. See Dobbs, Tortious Interference with Contractual Relationships, 1980, 34 Ark.L.Rev. 335, 361–63.

or political issues,[14] or in which speech is a part of the citizen's right to petition government,[15] and in these it may be generally expected that the speech will be given protection in the absence of some improper means,[16] even though it interferes with contract or with prospects of one. At this writing the only "fault" considered sufficient to justify a penalty for speech has been fault in ascertaining or speaking the truth. Conceivably courts may therefore protect speech that interferes with contracts on the ground that it is a representation of the truth or at least is not a falsehood; or even on the ground that however bad the speaker's motive may be, this kind of fault does not touch the issue of truth or falsity. But the question is as yet an open one. Aside from this, however, it is probably safe to assume that occasions privileged under the law of defamation are also occasions in which interference with contract by legal means would be considered justified.[17]

Causation and Manner of Interference

In order to be held liable for interference with a contract, the defendant must be shown to have caused the interference and the loss.[18] Sometimes it is said that the defendant must have played an active and substantial part in the loss.[19] It is not enough that he merely has reaped the advantages of the broken contract after the contracting party has withdrawn from it of his own motion.[20] Thus acceptance of an offered bargain is not in itself inducement of the breach

---

14. National Association for Advancement of Colored People v. Claiborne Hardware Co., Inc., 1982, 458 U.S. 886, 102 S.Ct. 3409, 73 L.Ed.2d 1215 (boycott of white merchants in protest over social and political conditions not actionable); State of Missouri v. National Organization for Women, Inc., 8th Cir. 1980, 620 F.2d 1301, certiorari denied 449 U.S. 842, 101 S.Ct. 122, 66 L.Ed.2d 49 (boycott of state that did not support Equal Rights Amendment); Taylor v. Nashville Banner Publishing Co., Tenn.App.1978, 573 S.W.2d 476, certiorari denied 441 U.S. 923, 99 S.Ct. 2032, 60 L.Ed.2d 396 (candidate for office had to meet "malice" requirement in interference claim). Cf. Gold v. Los Angeles Democratic League, 1975, 49 Cal.App.3d 365, 122 Cal.Rptr. 732 (attributing wrong political affiliation to opponent).

But cf. Searle v. Johnson, Utah 1982, 646 P.2d 682 (secondary boycott not protected by First Amendment, but decided before NAACP v. Claiborne Hardware, supra, and arguably contrary to it).

15. Feminist Women's Health Center v. Mohammad, 5th Cir. 1978, 586 F.2d 530, certiorari denied 444 U.S. 924, 100 S.Ct. 262, 62 L.Ed.2d 180 (complaint to state medical official); Arlington Heights National Bank v. Arlington Heights Federal Savings & Loan Association, 1967, 37 Ill.2d 546, 229 N.E.2d 514 (opposition to city's contract with plaintiff is constitutionally protected); McKee v. Hughes, 1915, 133 Tenn. 455, 181 S.W. 930 (similar).

Cf. National Association for Advancement of Colored People v. Claiborne Hardware Co., 1982, 458 U.S. 886, 102 S.Ct. 3409, 73 L.Ed.2d 1215 (boycott of white merchants); Brody v. Montalbano, 1979, 87 Cal.App.3d 725, 151 Cal.Rptr. 206, certiorari denied 444 U.S. 844, 100 S.Ct. 87, 62 L.Ed.2d 57 (parents' opposition to school's vice principal privileged). Anticompetitive conduct that might otherwise be covered by antitrust laws is similarly protected if the conduct is intended to influence governmental action, unless it is merely a sham or pretense. See Eastern Railroad Presidents Conference v. Noerr Motor Freight, Inc., 1961, 365 U.S. 127, 81 S.Ct. 523, 5 L.Ed.2d 464, rehearing denied 365 U.S. 875, 81 S.Ct. 899, 5 L.Ed.2d 864; United Mine Workers of America v. Pennington, 1965, 381 U.S. 657, 85 S.Ct. 1585, 14 L.Ed.2d 626, on remand D.Tenn., 257 F.Supp. 815, affirmed in part, reversed in part 6th Cir., 400 F.2d 806, certiorari denied 393 U.S. 983, 89 S.Ct. 450, 24 L.Ed.2d 444, rehearing denied 393 U.S. 1045, 89 S.Ct. 616, 21 L.Ed.2d 599, appeal after remand 421 F.2d 1380, certiorari denied 398 U.S. 960, 90 S.Ct. 2177, 26 L.Ed.2d 546; California Motor Transport Co. v. Trucking Unlimited, 1972, 404 U.S. 508, 92 S.Ct. 609, 30 L.Ed.2d 642.

16. In Feminist Women's Health Center v. Mohammad, 5th Cir.1978, 586 F.2d 530, certiorari denied 1979, 444 U.S. 924, 100 S.Ct. 262, 62 L.Ed.2d 180, it was suggested that doctors who were concerned about health care at plaintiff's establishment could be subjected to liability for advising younger doctors not to participate in it, on the ground that this would be threatening and hence an illegal mode of interference.

17. See Arlington Heights National Bank v. Arlington Heights Federal Savings & Loan Association, 1967, 37 Ill.2d 546, 229 N.E.2d 514; Taylor v. Nashville Banner Publishing Co., Tenn.App.1978, 573 S.W.2d 476, certiorari denied 441 U.S. 923, 99 S.Ct. 2032, 60 L.Ed.2d 396.

18. Lingard v. Kiraly, Fla.App.1959, 110 So.2d 715; Wahl v. Strous, 1942, 344 Pa. 402, 25 A.2d 820.

19. Wolf v. Perry, 1959, 65 N.M. 457, 339 P.2d 679; Allen v. Powell, 1967, 248 Cal.App.2d 502, 56 Cal.Rptr. 715, 29 A.L.R.3d 1218 (must "actively induce" breach).

20. B. J. Wolf & Sons v. New Orleans Tailor-Made Pants Co., 1904, 113 La. 388, 37 So. 2; Northern Wisconsin Cooperative Tobacco Pool v. Bekkedal, 1923, 182 Wis. 571, 197 N.W. 936; Minnesota Wheat Growers' Cooperative Marketing Association v. Radke, 1925, 163 Minn. 403, 204 N.W. 314; Emery v. A & B Commerical Finishing Co., Okl.1957, 315 P.2d 950; Fischnaller v. Sumner, 1959, 53 Wash.2d 332, 333 P.2d 636; Monarch

of a prior inconsistent contract,[21] and it is not enough that the defendant has done no more than enter into one with knowledge of the other,[22] although he may be liable if he has taken an active part in holding forth an incentive, such as the offer of a better price or better terms.[23] The defendant's breach of his own contract with the plaintiff is of course not a basis for the tort.[24] For this purpose the defendant's employees acting within the scope of their employment are identified with the defendant himself so that they may ordinarily advise the defendant to breach his own contract without themselves incurring liability in tort.[25]

It seems probable, although the question does not appear to have arisen directly, that the mere statement of existing facts, or assembling of information in such a way that the party persuaded recognizes it as a reason for breaking the contract is not enough, so long as the defendant creates no added reason and exerts no other influence or pressure by his conduct.[26]

Some of the earlier decisions denying liability argued that the defendant's conduct can never be a proximate cause of the breach,[27] since there is an intervening voluntary act of the third party promissor; but where that act is intentionally brought about

---

Industrial Towel and Uniform Rental, Inc., v. Model Coverall Service, Inc., 1978, 178 Ind.App. 235, 381 N.E. 2d 1098; Arabesque Studios, Inc. v. Academy of Fine Arts International, Inc., Tex.Civ.App.1975, 529 S.W.2d 564.

21. Stanton v. Texas Co., 5th Cir.1957, 249 F.2d 344; Sweeney v. Smith, D.Pa.1909, 167 F. 385, affirmed 3d Cir.1910, 171 F. 645, certiorari denied 215 U.S. 600, 30 S.Ct. 400, 54 L.Ed. 343; B. J. Wolf & Sons v. New Orleans Tailor-Made Pants Co., 1904, 113 La. 388, 37 So. 2.

22. Horth v. American Aggregates Corp., Ohio 1940, 35 N.E.2d 592; Lamport v. 4175 Broadway, Inc., S.D.N.Y.1934, 6 F.Supp. 923; Caldwell v. Gem Packing Co., 1942, 52 Cal.App.2d 80, 125 P.2d 901; Wolf v. Perry, 1959, 65 N.M. 457, 339 P.2d 679; Second Restatement of Torts, § 766, Comment *n*. A fortiori where there is no knowledge. Augustine v. Trucco, 1954, 124 Cal.App.2d 229, 268 P.2d 780; Snowden v. Sorensen, 1956, 246 Minn. 526, 75 N.W.2d 795.

Apparently contra are Wade v. Culp, 1939, 107 Ind. App. 503, 23 N.E.2d 615; Howard v. Houck, 1962, 210 Tenn. 549, 360 S.W.2d 55 (under statute).

23. Cumberland Glass Manufacturing Co. v. De Witt, 1913, 120 Md. 381, 87 A. 927, affirmed 237 U.S. 447, 35 S.Ct. 636, 59 L.Ed. 1042; Westinghouse Electric & Manufacturing Co. v. Diamond State Fibre Co., D.Del.1920, 268 F. 121; S. C. Posner Co. v. Jackson, 1918, 223 N.Y. 325, 119 N.E. 573; Pure Milk Association v. Kraft, 1955, 8 Ill.2d 102, 130 N.E.2d 765. See Note, 1956, 27 Miss.L.J. 254. Cf. Local Dairymen's Cooperative Association v. Potvin, 1934, 54 R.I. 430, 173 A. 535 (aiding in breach by furnishing transportation for product hold).

24. DiCesare-Engler Productions, Inc. v. Mainman Limited, D.Pa.1979, 81 F.R.D. 703 (even though breach affects plaintiff's contract rights with third persons); Wilmington Trust Co. v. Clark, 1981, 289 Md. 313, 424 A.2d 744 (suicide by one obliged to make monthly payments to former spouse, no tort action for interference with own contract); Glazer v. Chandler, 1964, 414 Pa. 304, 200 A.2d 416 (same); Kvenild v. Taylor, Wyo.1979, 594 P.2d 972 (tortious interference by breach is "hybrid concept unsupported by any authority").

But a promissor's breach may cause the promisee to suffer the loss of other contracts or prospects, and damages for such losses have sometimes been allowed on a tortious interference theory. Bolz v. Myers, 1982, ___ Mont. ___, 651 P.2d 606; Cherberg v. Peoples National Bank of Washington, 1977, 88 Wn.2d 595, 564 P.2d 1137. The effect of this may be to permit recovery of damages that would not be available if the promissor's actions were regarded solely as a breach of contract.

25. Swager v. Couri, 1979, 77 Ill.2d 173, 395 N.E.2d 921, 32 Ill.Dec. 540; Gram v. Liberty Mutual Insurance Co., 1981, 384 Mass. 659, 429 N.E.2d 21; Wampler v. Palmerton, 1968, 250 Or. 65, 439 P.2d 601 (officer's intent to benefit corporation in advising breach is sufficient to protect him); West v. Troelstrup, Fla.App. 1979, 367 So.2d 253; Martin v. Platt, 1979, 179 Ind. App. 688, 386 N.E.2d 1026; Nola v. Merollis Chevrolet Kansas City, Inc., Mo.App.1976, 537 S.W.2d 627. The rule is not affected merely because employees are characterized as co-conspirators. See Moreno v. Marbil Productions, Inc., 2d Cir.1961, 296 F.2d 543. But cf. McAlpine v. AAMCO Automatic Transmissions, Inc., D.Mich.1978, 461 F.Supp. 1232 (several persons contracting independently with one plaintiff may be held if they produce breach in other parties, but franchisees' rebellion here did not).

The rule does not protect one who procures a discharge of the plaintiff for an improper or illegal purpose. See Tash v. Houston, 1977, 74 Mich.App. 566, 254 N.W.2d 579. See generally, Perlman, Interference with Contract and Other Economic Expectancies: A Clash of Tort and Contract Theory, 1982, 49 U.Chi.L. Rev. 61, 119–123.

26. See Stone, J., dissenting in Sorenson v. Chevrolet Motor Co., 1927, 171 Minn. 260, 214 N.W. 754. Also Jensen v. Lundorff, 1960, 258 Minn. 275, 103 N.W.2d 887 (advice to consult attorney).

27. Chambers v. Baldwin, 1891, 91 Ky. 121, 15 S.W. 57; Glencoe Sand & Gravel Co. v. Hudson Brothers Commission Co., 1897, 138 Mo. 439, 40 S.W. 93; Kline v. Eubanks, 1902, 109 La. 241, 33 So. 211.

by the defendant's inducement, or is even a part of the foreseeable risk which he has created, it seems clear that the result is well within the limits of the "proximate." [28] It is a question of fact, and so normally for the jury, whether the defendant has played a material and substantial part in causing the plaintiff's loss of the benefits of the contract.[29]

Inducement of breach may be accomplished in a variety of ways. A promissor may be induced to breach his contract with the plaintiff by the defendant's offer of a more attractive contract, but the cases often reflect inducement by the defendant's threats,[30] or economic coercion,[31] or by persuasion[32] based on mutual interests;[33] and in any of these cases liability may be imposed if the defendant's actions are improper under all the circumstances. The threat need not be explicit to be actionable,[34] nor need there be any direct request to breach the plaintiff's contract if the intent behind the defendant's conduct is clear.[35]

Beyond this it may be said that actual inducement is not necessarily required at all and that interference with contract may be quite sufficient for liability, provided always that it causes harm and that the interference was unjustified. Thus no actual repudiation of the contract is necessary for liability, and it is enough that the contract performance is partly or wholly prevented,[36] or made less valuable,[37] or more burdensome [38] by the defendant's unjustified conduct. The earliest cases were in fact of this sort, involving as they did an action by a master for the loss of services of a servant injured by the defen-

---

28. Bowen v. Hall, 1881, 6 Q.B.D. 333, 50 L.J.Q.B. 305; Doremus v. Hennessy, 1898, 176 Ill. 608, 52 N.E. 924, rehearing denied 1899, 176 Ill. 608, 54 N.E. 524; Heath v. American Book Co., D.W.Va.1899, 97 F. 533; Tubular Rivet & Stud Co. v. Exeter Boot & Shoe Co., 1st Cir.1908, 159 F. 824.

29. Doremus v. Hennessy, 1898, 176 Ill. 608, 52 N.E. 924; Chipley v. Atkinson, 1877, 23 Fla. 206, 1 So. 934; Kock v. Burgess, 1916, 176 Iowa 493, 156 N.W. 174, rehearing denied 176 Iowa 493, 158 N.W. 534; cf. Johnson v. Aetna Life Insurance Co., 1914, 158 Wis. 56, 147 N.W. 32.

30. International Union United Auto., Aircraft and Agricultural Implement Workers of America v. Russell, 1958, 356 U.S. 634, 78 S.Ct. 932, 2 L.Ed.2d 1030, rehearing denied 357 U.S. 944, 78 S.Ct. 1379, 2 L.Ed.2d 1558 (state may recognize action by worker unable to work because of strike with threats of violence); Mobile Mechanical Contractors Association v. Carlough, 5th Cir.1981, 664 F.2d 481, certiorari denied 456 U.S. 975, 102 S.Ct. 2240, 72 L.Ed.2d 850 (illegal strike, federal cause of action but preemption on facts prevented state cause of action); Sumwalt Ice & Coal Co. v. Knickerbocker Ice Co., 1911, 114 Md. 403, 80 A. 48; Childress v. Abeles, 1954, 240 N.C. 667, 84 S.E.2d 176, rehearing dismissed 242 N.C. 123, 86 S.E.2d 916 (refusal to deal threatened unless contract broken).

31. MacKerron v. Madura, Me.1982, 445 A.2d 680 (police officer would not put in a good word for client as long as plaintiff represented him); Sumwalt Ice & Coal Co. v. Knickerbocker Ice Co., 1911, 114 Md. 403, 80 A. 48 (refusal to deal unless contract broken); Pacific Typesetting Co. v. International Typographical Union, 1923, 125 Wash. 273, 216 P. 358; Yankee Network v. Gibbs, 1936, 295 Mass. 56, 3 N.E.2d 228.

32. Lichter v. Fulcher, 1938, 22 Tenn.App. 670, 125 S.W.2d 501; Twitchell v. Nelson, 1914, 126 Minn. 423, 148 N.W. 451, second appeal 1915, 131 Minn. 375, 155 N.W. 621.

33. See Downey v. United Weatherproofing, Inc., 1953, 363 Mo. 852, 253 S.W.2d 976 (persuasion sufficient, repudiating earlier authority requiring something more); Wilkinson v. Powe, 1942, 300 Mich. 275, 1 N.W.2d 539 (refusal to buy promissor's goods unless shipped on defendant's trucks in effect required promissor to breach shipping contract with plaintiff); Feminist Women's Health Center, Inc. v. Mohammad, 5th Cir.1978, 586 F.2d 530, certiorari denied 1979, 444 U.S. 924, 100 S.Ct. 262, 62 L.Ed.2d 180.

34. Cf. Feminist Women's Health Center v. Mohammad, 5th Cir.1978, 586 F.2d 530, certiorari denied 1979, 444 U.S. 924, 100 S.Ct. 262, 62 L.Ed.2d 180 (advice to younger doctor to avoid plaintiff's clinic could be found coercive); but cf. Powell v. South Central Bell Telephone Co., Ala.1978, 361 So.2d 103 (public relations call from defendant to sponsors of feature column after column was critical of defendant did not coerce sponsors into dropping sponsorship).

35. Alyeska Pipeline Service Co. v. Aurora Air. Service, Inc., Alaska 1979, 604 P.2d 1090.

36. E.g., Pelton v. Markegard, 1978, 179 Mont. 102, 586 P.2d 306; Andrews v. Blakeslee, 1861, 12 Iowa 577.

37. Herman v. Endriss, 1982, 187 Conn. 374, 446 A.2d 9; Reichman v. Drake, 1951, 89 Ohio App. 222, 100 N.E.2d 533 (defendant prevented plaintiff from taking possession of property when due); cf. Carpenter v. Williams, 1930, 41 Ga.App. 685, 154 S.E. 298; Gore v. Condon, 1898, 87 Md. 368, 39 A. 1042.

38. McNary v. Chamberlain, 1867, 34 Conn. 384; Piedmont Cotton Mills v. H. W. Ivey Construction Co., 1964, 109 Ga.App. 876, 137 S.E.2d 528 (damage to T's property causing additional expense to one having contract to build or repair).

dant.[39] Although this particular action is virtually obsolete,[40] it has left its imprint on the law of contract interference in the form of a good many holdings in which the defendant's physical interference with the person of the promissor,[41] or with the property,[42] chattels[43] or person[44] of the plaintiff has resulted in the loss of some or all of the plaintiff's contract rights.

The bulk of the cases involving interference as distinct from inducement involve this physical interference with person or property and also involve the commission of some independent tort, as where the defendant interferes with the plaintiff's rights by converting goods to which the plaintiff was entitled under the contract,[45] or commits an injurious falsehood of the kind sometimes called slander of title.[46] Methods tortious in themselves are of course unjustified[47] and liability is appropriately imposed where the plaintiff's contract rights are invaded by violence, threats and intimidation,[48] defamation,[49] misrepresentation,[50] unfair competition,[51] bribery[52] and the like. Constitutional violations have been put in the same category.[53] Thus in many cases interference with contract is not so much a theory of liability in itself as it is an element of damage resulting from the commission of some other tort,[54] or the breach of some other contract.[55]

---

39. See Owen, Interference with Trade, 1976, 3 Mon.L.Rev. 41 (summarizing Yearbook cases).

40. Most contemporary cases are based on negligent injury of an employee rather than intentional injury. See pp. 997–998 below.

41. Sandlin v. Coyle, 1918, 143 La. 121, 78 So. 261; White v. Massee, 1927, 202 Iowa 1304, 211 N.W. 839 (seemingly).

42. American Transportation Co. v. United States Sanitary Specialties Corp., 1954, 2 Ill.App.2d 144, 118 N.E.2d 793 (interference with plaintiff's leased property); Reichman v. Drake, 1951, 89 Ohio App. 222, 100 N.E.2d 533 (same); Zarrow v. Hughes, Okl.1955, 282 P.2d 215 (pollution of stream interfered with pasturage contract); see Walden v. Conn, 1886, 84 Ky. 312, 1 S.W. 537 (dictum that if defendant had ousted tenant and deprived landlord of rents there would be liability).

43. Sidney Blumenthal & Co. v. United States, 2d Cir.1929, 30 F.2d 247; Carpenter v. Williams, 1930, 41 Ga.App. 685, 154 S.E. 298; Southern Railway Co. v. Chambers, 1906, 126 Ga. 404, 55 S.E. 37; Newark Hardware & Plumbing Supply Co. v. Stove Manufacturers Corp., 1948, 136 N.J.L. 401, 56 A.2d 605, affirmed 137 N.J.L. 612, 61 A.2d 240; G. W. K. Ltd. v. Dunlop Rubber Co., K.B.1926, 42 T.L.R. 376, appeal dismissed 42 T.L.R. 593.

44. Bacon v. St. Paul Union Stockyards Co., 1924, 161 Minn. 522, 201 N.W. 326 (barring plaintiff from semi-public place where contract was to be performed); Fradus Contracting Co. v. Taylor, 1922, 201 App.Div. 298, 194 N.Y.S. 286 (similar).

45. Sidney Blumenthal & Co. v. United States, 2d Cir.1929, 30 F.2d 247 (Defendant misdirected goods to which plaintiff was entitled); Carpenter v. Williams, 1930, 41 Ga.App. 685, 154 S.E. 298; Newark Hardware & Plumbing Supply Co. v. Stove Manufacturers Corp., 1948, 136 N.J.L. 401, 56 A.2d 605, affirmed 137 N.J.L. 612, 61 A.2d 240.

46. Vaught v. Jonathan L. Pettyjohn & Co., 1919, 104 Kan. 174, 178 P. 623; Martin v. Sterkx, 1920, 146 La. 489, 83 So. 776; Gore v. Condon, 1898, 87 Md. 368, 39 A. 1042.

47. See Estes, Expanding Horizons in the Law of Torts—Tortious Interference, 1974, 23 Drake L.Rev. 341, 347.

48. Vegelahn v. Guntner, 1896, 167 Mass. 92, 44 N.E. 1077; Sparks v. McCrary, 1908, 156 Ala. 382, 47 So. 332; Minnesota Stove Co. v. Cavanaugh, 1915, 131 Minn. 458, 155 N.W. 638. Cf. Leek v. Brasfield, 1956, 226 Ark. 316, 290 S.W.2d 632 (threat of lawsuit known by defendant to be unjustified).

49. Mason v. Funderburk, 1969, 247 Ark. 521, 446 S.W.2d 543; Loudin v. Mohawk Airlines, Inc., 1964, 44 Misc.2d 926, 255 N.Y.S.2d 302; Max v. Kahn, 1917, 91 N.J.L. 170, 102 A. 737; Woody v. Brush, 1917, 178 App. Div. 698, 165 N.Y.S. 867; Stebbins v. Edwards, 1924, 101 Okl. 188, 224 P. 714. See Note, 1933, 33 Col.L.Rev. 90.

50. Green v. Button, 1835, 2 Cr.M. & R. 707, 150 Eng.Rep. 299; Skene v. Carayanis, 1926, 103 Conn. 708, 131 A. 497; Johnson v. Gustafson, 1938, 201 Minn. 629, 277 N.W. 252; Diver v. Miller, Del.Super.1929, 4 W.W.Harr. 207, 148 A. 291. Cf. Klauder v. Cregar, 1937, 327 Pa. 1, 192 A. 667; Bartlett v. Federal Outfitting Co., 1933, 133 Cal.App. 747, 24 P.2d 877. See also supra, § 128.

51. George G. Fox Co. v. Hathaway, 1908, 199 Mass. 99, 85 N.E. 417. And see, infra, 1013.

52. Angle v. Chicago, St. Paul, Minneapolis & Omaha Railway Co., 1893, 151 U.S. 1, 14 S.Ct. 240, 38 L.Ed. 55. Commercial bribery is often actionable on completely different theories. See D. Dobbs, Remedies, 1973, § 10.6.

53. Board of Trustees of Weston County School District No. 1 v. Holso, Wyo.1978, 584 P.2d 1009, rehearing denied 587 P.2d 203.

54. Wild v. Rarig, 1975, 302 Minn. 419, 234 N.W.2d 775, appeal dismissed, certiorari denied 424 U.S. 902, 96

---

55. See note 55 on page 993.

An interfering defendant may be liable where he commits no independent tort to the plaintiff himself but does commit such a tort to the person with whom the plaintiff has a contract. If the plaintiff's interests and those of the contracting party are sufficiently close, a tort to the one may be sufficient basis for liability to the other, if harm results. This is the case where plaintiff has promised to build or repair a building for a landowner and defendant deliberately damages the work.[56] If the plaintiff must bear the damage it is appropriate that he have the tort recovery, in much the same way that an insurer of the property would be subrogated to the landowner's tort claim. Somewhat similarly, an economic tort such as fraud against a debtor that deprives him of property with which to pay his debts to the plaintiff may in appropriate cases furnish ground for action by the plaintiff-creditor, who may in effect stand in the debtor's shoes.[57]

It is not always necessary, however, that there be an independent tort to the plaintiff or his promissor, though perhaps most cases fall into this pattern. Where there are three or more persons dealing with several interdependent contracts, an interference by any one of these persons with contracts between the other two may be seen as itself a breach of an implied-in-fact contract to respect the mutual arrangements, even though technical privity may be lacking. Some of the cases have actually been decided on this ground rather than on the theory of tortious interference.[58] In other cases it has been found that one party was an agent for another who did not actually sign the contract, with the result that all parties are mutually bound by the contract and again without resort to tort theory.[59] Still other cases involve claims that resemble third-party beneficiary claims and could be justified on those grounds.[60] With all these cases sifted out, however, there remain a few that support liability among interdependent contractors on the theory that any one's interference with the others' contract is a tort.[61]

One means by which a person may induce another to breach his contract is the refusal to deal. In other words *A* may refuse to give his business to *B* unless *B* breaks his existing contract with *C*. The common law view was that any person could decide for himself to whom he would sell or from whom he would buy, and that he might refuse to deal for any reason or no reason at

---

S.Ct. 1093, 47 L.Ed.2d 307, rehearing denied 425 U.S. 945, 96 S.Ct. 1689, 48 L.Ed.2d 190. Cf. Joslyn v. Manship, La.App.1970, 238 So.2d 20, writ refused 256 La. 883, 239 So.2d 541 (no tort recovery but a claim for "unjust enrichment" in the amount defendant profited).

55. Cf. Johnson v. Schmitt, S.D.1981, 309 N.W.2d 838 (landowner could not sell unless defendant would guarantee to supply water to buyer, defendant agreed, then reneged with resulting loss of a sale).

56. McNary v. Chamberlain, 1867, 34 Conn. 384; Cue v. Breland, 78 Miss. 864, 29 So. 850; Piedmont Cotton Mills v. H. W. Ivey Construction Co., 1964, 109 Ga. App. 876, 137 S.E.2d 528.

57. Keene Lumber Co. v. Leventhal, 1st Cir.1948, 165 F.2d 815; Andrews v. Blakeslee, 1861, 12 Iowa 577. See also Angle v. Chicago, St. Paul, Minneapolis & Omaha Railway Co., 1893, 151 U.S. 1, 14 S.Ct. 240, 38 L.Ed. 55. But the reasoning may not be extended to the case where the defendant commits no tort in interfering with a debtor's contracts: in such a case the creditor has been denied recovery. Worldwide Commerce, Inc. v. Fruehauf Corp., 1978, 84 Cal.App.3d 803, 149 Cal.Rptr. 42.

58. Cavender v. Waddingham, 1876, 2 Mo.App. 551; Atkinson v. Pack, 1894, 114 N.C. 597, 19 S.E. 628; Livermore v. Crane, 1901, 26 Wash. 529, 67 P. 221. In each case a party to a contract to sell and purchase real estate reneged, thus depriving the broker-plaintiff of a commission. In each case the reneging party was not under contract to pay the commission, but his repudiation prevented the broker's collection from the other party. In each case the broker recovered on an implied contract theory.

59. Phez Co. v. Salem Fruit Union, 1922, 103 Or. 514, 201 P. 222 (also recognizing tort theory as alternative).

60. See Andrews v. Blakeslee, 1861, 12 Iowa 577. The court's theory was "fraud," but the plaintiff was in the position of a creditor-beneficiary.

61. Craviolini v. Scholer & Fuller Associated Architects, 1960, 89 Ariz. 24, 357 P.2d 611 (subcontractor alleged architect supervising job committed various harassing acts, arbitrarily refused permission needed to do certain work); Mandal v. Hoffman Construction Co., 270 Or. 248, 527 P.2d 387 (dictum); Phez Co. v. Salem Fruit Union, 1922, 103 Or. 514, 201 P. 222 (alternative holding); cf. Fradus Contracting Co. v. Taylor, 1922, 201 App.Div. 298, 194 N.Y.S. 286 (city's agent enjoined from arbitrarily withholding permission necessary for plaintiff to complete contract with city).

all.[62] But since concerted action by an economically powerful group has more potential for intimidation and for harm, a concerted refusal to deal may be more difficult to justify than an individual refusal, and liability was imposed at common law where the boycott was used to coerce breach without justification.[63] Beyond that, even individuals may be held for a refusal to deal if it is coupled with a threat or demand that a contract be breached,[64] always excepting the case in which there is justification on the facts. In still other situations statutes may require individuals to deal, or may limit grounds for refusing to do so, as in the case of public utilities. This is the case under some civil rights statutes, and, within limits, is also the case under federal legislation protecting auto dealers from improper termination of their dealerships.[65] A refusal to deal where dealing is required by law is obviously a special case and a strong one for liability if the refusal is intended to induce a contract breach. For the most part, however, refusals to deal are inextricably involved with the law of antitrust and the law of labor-management conflict, both of which go quite beyond the common law of tort and both of which must be consulted when refusal to deal is at issue.

Nature of Original Contract

Virtually any type of contract is sufficient as the foundation of an action for procuring its breach. It must of course be valid, in force and effect,[66] and not illegal as in restraint of trade,[67] or otherwise opposed to public policy,[68] so that the law will not aid in upholding it. Thus contracts for exclusive dealing tending to stifle competition in the public utility field have been denied the protection,[69] as has the "yellow dog" contract by which an employee agrees with his employer that he will not join a labor union,[70] which is now made unenforceable by federal and much state legislation. The same is true of any contract which requires the breach of a prior contract; and in such a case it is of course the first of the two agreements which will be protected.[71]

---

62. House of Materials, Inc. v. Simplicity Pattern Co., 2d Cir.1962, 298 F.2d 867; Great Atlantic & Pacific Tea Co. v. Cream of Wheat Co., 2d Cir.1915, 227 F. 46; Tarr v. General Electric Co., D.Pa.1977, 441 F.Supp. 40.

63. Jackson v. Stanfield, 1893, 137 Ind. 592, 36 N.E. 345, rehearing denied 137 Ind. 592, 37 N.E. 14; Martell v. White, 1904, 185 Mass. 255, 69 N.E. 1085; Bankers' Fire & Marine Insurance Co. v. Sloss, 1934, 229 Ala. 26, 155 So. 371; Keviczky v. Lorber, 1943, 290 N.Y. 297, 49 N.E.2d 146, affirmed 263 App.Div. 983, 34 N.Y.S.2d 394, motion denied 290 N.Y. 855, 50 N.E.2d 242; Louis Kamm, Inc. v. Flink, 1934, 113 N.J.L. 582, 175 A. 62.

64. Sumwalt Ice & Coal Co. v. Knickerbocker Ice Co., 1911, 114 Md. 403, 80 A. 48; Wilkinson v. Powe, 1942, 300 Mich. 275, 1 N.W.2d 539; Childress v. Abeles, 1954, 240 N.C. 667, 84 S.E.2d 176, rehearing dismissed 242 N.C. 123, 86 S.E.2d 916. Second Restatement of Torts, § 766, Comment *l*.

65. 15 U.S.C.A. § 1221 et seq. See § 130 below.

66. Said v. Butt, [1920] 3 K.B. 497, 11 B.R.C. 317 (no contract made); Triangle Film Corp. v. Artcraft Pictures Corp., 2d Cir.1918, 250 F. 981 (conditions terminated); Cincinnati Bengals, Inc. v. Bergey, D.Ohio, 1974, 453 F.Supp. 129 (post-contract employment); Southern Idaho Realty of Twin Falls, Inc.–Century 21 v. Larry J. Hellhake and Associates, Inc., 1981, 102 Idaho 613, 636 P.2d 168 (contract "void ab initio" where no meeting of the minds).

67. Ford Motor Co. v. Union Motor Sales Co., 6th Cir.1917, 244 F. 156; Paramount Pad Co. v. Baumrind, 1948, 4 N.Y.2d 393, 175 N.Y.S.2d 809, 151 N.E.2d 609; Consolidated Packaging Machine Corp. v. Kelly, 7th Cir. 1958, 253 F.2d 49, certiorari denied 357 U.S. 906, 78 S.Ct. 1151, 2 L.Ed.2d 1156; Argus Cameras v. Hall of Distributors, 1955, 343 Mich. 54, 72 N.W.2d 152; Sunbeam Corp. v. Hall of Distributors, E.D.Mich.1956, 142 F.Supp. 609.

68. Gunnels v. Atlanta Bar Association, 1940, 191 Ga. 366, 12 S.E.2d 602 (usury); Bailey v. Banister, 10th Cir.1952, 200 F.2d 683 (purchase of restricted Indian land); Ely v. Donoho, S.D.N.Y.1942, 45 F.Supp. 27 (contract to file reorganization plan); Seitz v. Michel, 1921, 148 Minn. 474, 181 N.W. 106 (life employment in control of corporation); Mindenberg v. Carmel Film Productions, 1955, 132 Cal.App.2d 598, 282 P.2d 1024 (corporation's purchase of own stock). See Annot., 96 A.L.R.3d 1294.

69. Citizens Light, Heat & Power Co. v. Montgomery Light & Water Power Co., D.Ala.1909, 171 F. 553; Fairbanks, Morse & Co. v. Texas Electric Service Co., 5th Cir.1933, 63 F.2d 702, certiorari denied 290 U.S. 655, 54 S.Ct. 71, 78 L.Ed. 567.

70. Exchange Bakery & Restaurant Co. v. Rifkin, 1927, 245 N.Y. 260, 157 N.E. 130; Interborough Rapid Transit Co. v. Lavin, 1928, 247 N.Y. 65, 159 N.E. 863; La France Electrical Construction & Supply Co. v. International Brotherhood of Electrical Workers, 1923, 108 Ohio St. 61, 140 N.E. 899.

71. Reiner v. North American Newspaper Alliance, 1932, 259 N.Y. 250, 181 N.E. 561, affirmed 233 App.Div. 736, 250 N.Y.S. 843. Cf. Roberts v. Criss, 2d

The agreement need not, however, be enforceable by the plaintiff as a contract. Even under the old Statute of Labourers, from which the remedy is descended, labor was compulsory, and it was interference with the relation which was the essence of the tort, so that no binding agreement for service was required.[72] The law of course does not object to the voluntary performance of agreements merely because it will not enforce them, and it indulges in the assumption that even unenforceable promises will be carried out if no third person interferes. Accordingly, it has been held that contracts which are voidable by reason of the statute of frauds,[73] formal defects,[74] lack of consideration,[75] lack of mutuality,[76] or even uncertainty of terms,[77] or harsh and unconscionable provisions,[78] or conditions precedent to the existence of the obligation,[79] can still afford a basis for a tort action when the defendant interferes with their performance.

There is some authority to the contrary effect as to contracts which the promissor may terminate at will,[80] on the theory that there is really nothing involved but an option on his part to perform or not.[81] However, eminent legal writers [82] to the contrary notwithstanding, the overwhelming majority of the cases have held that interference with employment [83] or other contracts [84] terminable

---

Cir.1920, 266 F. 296; Rhoades v. Malta Vita Pure Food Co., 1907, 149 Mich. 235, 112 N.W. 940; Hocking Valley Railway Co. v. Barbour, 1920, 190 App.Div. 341, 179 N.Y.S. 810. See Notes, 1913, 27 Harv.L.Rev. 273; 1932, 18 Corn.L.Q. 84; 1933, 17 Minn.L.Rev. 209.

72. Sayre, Inducing Breach of Contract, 1923, 36 Harv.L.Rev. 663, 666.

73. Royal Realty Co. v. Levin, 1955, 244 Minn. 288, 69 N.W.2d 667; Childress v. Abeles, 1954, 240 N.C. 667, 84 S.E.2d 176, rehearing dismissed 1955, 242 N.C. 123, 86 S.E.2d 916; McCue v. Deppert, 1952, 21 N.J. Super. 591, 91 A.2d 503; Friedman v. Jackson, 1968, 266 Cal.App.2d 517, 72 Cal.Rptr. 129; Hill & Co. v. Wallerich, 1965, 67 Wn.2d 409, 407 P.2d 956; Clements v. Withers, Tex.1969, 437 S.W.2d 818.

Contra: Evans v. Mayberry, 1955, 198 Tenn. 187, 278 S.W.2d 691, rehearing denied 198 Tenn. 187, 279 S.W.2d 705; Levy v. Ross, Sup.1948, 81 N.Y.S.2d 472 (contract void).

74. Salter v. Howard, 1871, 43 Ga. 601.

75. Rich v. New York Central & Hudson River Railroad Co., 1882, 87 N.Y. 382. Otherwise with a mere gratuitous promise which does not purport to be a contract. Rosenkoff v. Mariani, 1953, 90 App.D.C. 263, 207 F.2d 449.

76. Aalfo Co. v. Kinney, 1929, 105 N.J.L. 345, 144 A. 715; Philadelphia Record Co. v. Leopold, S.D.N.Y. 1941, 40 F.Supp. 346; Moran v. Dunphy, 1901, 177 Mass. 485, 59 N.E. 125; Jackson v. O'Neill, 1957, 181 Kan. 930, 317 P.2d 440; Union Circulation Co. v. Hardel Publishers Service, 1957, 6 Misc.2d 340, 164 N.Y.S.2d 435.

Contra: Wedgewood Carpet Mills, Inc. v. Color-Set, Inc., 1979, 149 Ga.App. 417, 254 S.E.2d 421.

77. Aalfo Co. v. Kinney, 1929, 105 N.J.L. 345, 144 A. 715. See Note, 1928, 28 Mich.L.Rev. 94. In Grimm v Baumgart, 1951, 121 Ind.App. 626, 96 N.E.2d 915, rehearing denied 121 Ind.App. 626, 97 N.E.2d 871, the combination of uncertainty and lack of mutuality was held to prevent the action. If essential terms are missing and the parties did not intend to be bound, there can be no interference with contract. Malevich v. Hakola, Minn.1979, 278 N.W.2d 541.

78. Union Circulation Co. v. Hardel Publishers Service, 1957, 6 Misc.2d 340, 164 N.Y.S.2d 435.

79. For example, the attorney's contract with his client for a contingent fee. Richette v. Solomon, 1963, 410 Pa. 6, 187 A.2d 910; Herron v. State Farm Mutual Insurance Co., 1961, 56 Cal.2d 202, 14 Cal.Rptr. 294, 363 P.2d 310; Employers Liability Assurance Corp. v. Freeman, 10th Cir.1955, 229 F.2d 547; State Farm Fire Insurance Co. v. Gregory, 4th Cir.1950, 184 F.2d 447; Keels v. Powell, 1945, 207 S.C. 97, 34 S.E.2d 482; Cf. Mitchell v. Aldrich, 1960, 122 Vt. 19, 163 A.2d 833.

80. Harris v. Hirschfield, 1936, 13 Cal.App.2d 204, 56 P.2d 1252; E. R. Squibb & Sons v. Ira J. Shapiro, Inc., Sup.1945, 64 N.Y.S.2d 368; McGuire v. Gerstley, 1905, 26 U.S.App.D.C. 193, affirmed 1907, 204 U.S. 489, 27 S.Ct. 332, 51 L.Ed. 581; Harley & Lund Corp. v. Murray Rubber Co., 2d Cir.1929, 31 F.2d 932, certiorari denied 279 U.S. 872, 49 S.Ct. 513, 73 L.Ed. 1007.

Some other cases frequently cited to the same effect, such as Boston Glass Manufactory v. Binney, 1827, 21 Mass. (4 Pick.) 425, appear in reality to hold not that there is no prima facie liability, but merely that the defendant was privileged to interfere.

81. Cf. Richardson v. Terry, Tex.Civ.App.1919, 212 S.W. 523, error dismissed; Roberts v. Clark, Tex.Civ. App.1907, 103 S.W. 417; Campbell v. Cooper, 1856, 34 N.H. 49.

82. Smith, Crucial Issues in Labor Litigation, 1907, 20 Harv.L.Rev. 253, 261; Sayre, Inducing Breach of Contract, 1923, 36 Harv.L.Rev. 663, 701; Harper, Law of Torts, 1933, 475.

83. Canuel v. Oskolin, D.R.I.1960, 184 F.Supp. 70; American Surety Co. v. Schottenbauer, 8th Cir.1958, 257 F.2d 6; Mendelson v. Blatz Brewing Co., 1960, 9 Wis.2d 487, 101 N.W.2d 805; United States Fidelity & Guaranty Co. v. Millonas, 1921, 206 Ala. 147, 89 So. 732; Mays v. Stratton, Fla.App.1966, 183 So.2d 43; Tash v. Houston, 1977, 74 Mich.App. 566, 254 N.W.2d

84. See note 84 on page 996.

at will is actionable, since until it is terminated the contract is a subsisting relation, of value to the plaintiff, and presumably to continue in effect. The possibility of termination does, however, bear upon the issue of the damages sustained,[85] and it must be taken into account in determining the defendant's privilege to interfere.[86] Thus a contract at will is usually not protected when the defendant's interference with it is based on any legitimate business purpose and no improper means is used, as where one employer hires away employees of another whose contract rights are terminable at will.[87] The principle would logically apply to any agreement that could not be enforced as a contract, since such an agreement can be avoided at will, as where a contract lacks mutuality.[88] In all such cases the plaintiff's interest may be protected, but as a prospective advantage [89] rather than as a contract, with the correspondingly greater freedom of action on the defendant's part.

Contracts to marry have received special treatment, and almost without exception,[90] the courts have refused to hold that it is a tort to induce the parties to break them.[91] The American decisions are traceable to a statement of Judge Cooley's,[92] made at a time when the conception of interference with contract was in its formative stages, but there seems to be no disposition to expand liability.[93] Friends and relatives if no others would no doubt have a privilege to give advice against marriage,[94] so that no liability would attach to them in such cases. This, coupled with the feeling that no marriage should be encouraged if any person involved has decided it is a mistake [95] and with a respect for personal autonomy and right of

579; Smith v. Ford Motor Co., 1976, 289 N.C. 71, 221 S.E.2d 282.

84. Childress v. Abeles, 1954, 240 N.C. 667, 84 S.E.2d 176, rehearing dismissed 1955, 242 N.C. 123, 86 N.E.2d 916; W. P. Iverson Co. v. Dunham Manufacturing Co., 1958, 18 Ill.App.2d 404, 152 N.E.2d 615; General Outdoor Advertising Co. v. Hamilton, 1935, 154 Misc. 871, 278 N.Y.S. 226; Falstaff Brewing Corp. v. Iowa Fruit & Produce Co., 8th Cir.1940, 112 F.2d 101; George Jonas Glass Co. v. Glass Bottle Blowers Association, 1908, 77 N.J.Eq. 219, 79 A. 262; and see cases cited supra, note 80. See Note, 1961, 56 N.W.U.L.Rev. 391.

85. See Berry v. Donovan, 1905, 188 Mass. 353, 74 N.E. 603; Scott v. Prudential Outfitting Co., 1915, 92 Misc. 195, 155 N.Y.S. 497; Evans v. McKay, Tex.Civ. App.1919, 212 S.W. 680, error dismissed (nominal damages); Tye v. Finkelstein, D.Mass.1958, 160 F.Supp. 666; United States Fidelity & Guaranty Co. v. Millonas, 1921, 206 Ala. 147, 89 So. 732.

86. Carpenter, Interference with Contract Relations, 1928, 41 Harv.L.Rev. 728, 754, 7 Or.L.Rev. 181, 301.

See National Oil Co. v. Phillips Petroleum Co., W.D. Wis.1966, 265 F.Supp. 320.

87. Triangle Film Corp. v. Artcraft Pictures Corp., 2d Cir.1918, 250 F. 981, 7 A.L.R. 303 (Learned Hand, J.); TAO, Inc. v. Siebert, 1978, 63 Ill.App.3d 1001, 20 Ill.Dec. 754, 380 N.E.2d 963. Use of improper means or inducing breach of the employee's fiducial obligations is of course a different matter. E.g., Bancroft-Whitney Co. v. Glen, 1966, 64 Cal.2d 327, 49 Cal.Rptr. 825, 411 P.2d 921, 24 A.L.R.3d 795.

88. Guard-Life Corp. v. S. Parker Hardware Manufacturing Corp., 1980, 50 N.Y.2d 183, 428 N.Y.S.2d 628, 406 N.E.2d 445.

89. See § 130 below.

90. In Minsky v. Satenstein, 1928, 6 N.J.Misc. 978, 143 A. 512, and Gunn v. Barr, [1926] 1 Dom.L.Rep. 1855, the possibility of a cause of action was recognized, but a privilege to give advice was found on the facts. See also Dora v. Dora, 1958, 392 Pa. 433, 141 A.2d 587 (property settlement between estranged husband and wife).

91. Brown v. Glickstein, 1952, 347 Ill.App. 486, 107 N.E.2d 267; Nelson v. Melvin, 1945, 236 Iowa 604, 19 N.W.2d 685; Clarahan v. Cosper, 1931, 160 Wash. 642, 296 P. 140; Conway v. O'Brien, 1929, 269 Mass. 425, 169 N.E. 491; Ableman v. Holman, 1926, 190 Wis. 112, 208 N.W. 889. See Notes, 1953, 31 Chicago-Kent L.Rev. 175; 1932, 26 Ill.L.Rev. 454; 1931, 25 Ill.L.Rev. 224; 1929, 77 U.Pa.L.Rev. 515; 1932, 5 So.Cal.L.Rev. 150.

Shepherd v. Wakeman, 1661, 1 Sid. 79, 82 Eng.Rep. 982, allowed the action, but there was intentional falsehood involved. There is dictum in National Phonograph Co. v. Edison-Bell Phonograph Co., [1907] 1 Ch. 335, 350, 96 L.T. 218, 224, to the effect that no such action could be maintained.

92. Cooley, Torts, 1st ed.1878, 236–237. See Note, 1925, 10 Corn.L.Q. 258.

93. The rule against such action is retained in the Second Restatement of Torts, §§ 698 and 766.

94. Cf. Minsky v. Satenstein, 1928, 6 N.J.Misc. 978, 143 A. 512; Overhultz v. Row, 1922, 152 La. 9, 92 So. 716; Lukas v. Tarpilauskas, 1929, 266 Mass. 498, 165 N.E. 513; Homan v. Hall, 1917, 102 Neb. 70, 165 N.W. 881.

95. "Social considerations may warrant this exception to the general rule. Society has a vital interest in having the marriage relation endure and hasty and ill-

Intent and Negligence

Interference with contract, which had its modern inception in "malice," has remained almost entirely an intentional tort; and in general, liability has not been extended to the various forms of negligence by which performance of a contract may be prevented or rendered more burdensome.[96] A building contractor's negligent delay in performing his contract, or an owner's negligence in supervising him, may, for example, cause economic loss to a subcontractor whose own performance is thus rendered more costly, but in the absence of intentional and improper interference with the subcontractor's work there is no tort and no liability.[97] But the rule is not addressed at all to the case in which some independent tort to the plaintiff causes an interference with contract. In such cases the plaintiff may recover damages for the tort, including damages for the interference with contract if it is a proximate result. This is not because negligent interference is actionable, but because the interference is an item of damages resulting from some other tort. The most common example is the case of injury to a person who then loses wages as a result of the injury. Recovery for lost wages is commonly permitted for negligent injury,[98] not on the theory that there was a negligent interference with the worker's performance of his contract, but on the theory that the interference, and the wage loss, resulted from the tort to his person. The same principle permits recovery where the defendant interferes with contract performance by committing a public nuisance, as where he blocks a public road[99] or fouls a waterway[1] with the result that the plaintiff has special harm in the form of lost business opportunities or an increased cost of performing a contract.[2] Damage to the plaintiff's own property, like damage to his person, is an obvious case for recovery of all damages proximately caused, including loss of profits if they are adequately proven.[3] All such cases of an independent physical tort to the plaintiff present grounds for recovery and are not excluded by the rule against recovery for negligent contract interference.

A closer question arises if the defendant commits a tort causing physical harm to A which also results in an interference with B's contract rights without actually causing physical harm to B. The early common law

---

conceived marriages are undesirable. Hence, activities which may retard such marriages and possibly secure more permanent ones are to be encouraged." Carpenter, Interference with Contract Relations, 1928, 41 Harv.L.Rev. 728, 751.

96. See James, Limitations on Liability for Economic Loss Caused by Negligence: A Pragmatic Appraisal, 1972, 25 Vand.L.Rev. 43; Carpenter, Interference with Contractual Relations, 1928, 41 Harv.L.Rev. 728, 7 Or. L.Rev. 181, 301; Green, Relational Interests, 1935, 29 Ill.L.Rev. 1041, 1042, 30 Ill.L.Rev. 1, 2; Harper, Interference with Contactual Relations, 1953, 47 Nw.L.Rev. 873, 884; Notes, 1977, 63 Va.L.Rev. 814; 1953, 20 U.Chi.L.Rev. 283; 1948, 36 Ky.L.J. 142; 1935, 23 Cal.L. Rev. 420; 1933, 18 Corn.L.Q. 292; 1964, 16 Stan.L.Rev. 664.

97. Alvord and Swift v. Stewart M. Muller Construction Co., 1978, 46 N.Y.2d 276, 413 N.Y.S.2d 309, 385 N.E.2d 1238 (owner's alleged failure to supervise); Mandal v. Hoffman Construction Co., 1974, 270 Or. 248, 527 P.2d 387 (one contractor's negligent work allegedly caused economic harm to another contractor, rendering his performance more burdensome). But apparently contra is J'Aire Corp. v. Gregory, 1979, 24 Cal.3d 799, 157 Cal.Rptr. 407, 598 P.2d 60, as to which see p. 1001 below.

98. See D. Dobbs, Remedies § 8.1 (1973).

99. Holcomb Construction Co., Inc. v. Armstrong, 9th Cir.1979, 590 F.2d 811; Brewer v. Missouri Pacific Railway Co., 1924, 161 Ark. 525, 257 S.W. 53.

1. Burgess v. M/V Tamano, D.Me.1973, 370 F.Supp. 247; Restatement Second of Torts § 821C, Ill. 11. In Union Oil Co. v. Oppen, 9th Cir.1974, 501 F.2d 558 the court recognized liability for an oil spill causing harm to commercial fishermen. It alluded to nuisance cases but seemingly grounded its decision on broader grounds. See the criticism in R. Epstein, Nuisance Law: Corrective Justice and Its Utilitarian Constraints, 1979, 8 J.Leg.Stud. 49, 51–53.

2. See Second Restatement of Torts, § 821C, Comment h.

3. SCM (U.K.) Ltd. v. W. J. Whittal & Son, Ltd., C.A.1970, 3 All E.R. 245; Newlin v. New England Telephone & Telegraph Co., 1944, 316 Mass. 234, 54 N.E.2d 929.

rule recognized an action in favor of B in one circumstance like this. If the defendant negligently injured a servant, the master was allowed to recover for loss of his services.[4] This rule may have made special sense in a society without excess labor supply and one in which an apprentice system was used to require the master to support the servant in exchange for his services.[5] A few modern cases have permitted the action by the employer,[6] but later decisions in the same jurisdictions have often tacitly overruled these cases or have severely limited them.[7] There has been a considerable attack[8] on the action and it now seems to be clearly confined within its original limits or abolished altogether. Thus there has been very general refusal to extend it to injuries disabling other persons who are employed by the plaintiff but who are not classified as servants.[9] Recovery has been denied for the employer of soldiers,[10] policemen,[11] civil servants[12] and even executives[13] and professional persons[14] whose loss to the employer may represent harms that cannot be avoided by replacing the injured employee with another person. Probably there will be no liability in any case unless the injured servant is in some sense a member of the plaintiff's household[15] or there is an intentional injury to the employee. Recovery has also been denied for damages other than the value of the services themselves, as for example payments which the employer is compelled by contract to make to his injured employee,[16] or an increased workmen's compensation insurance premium resulting from the injury.[17] Now and then there have been courts which

4. Everard v. Hopkins, 1614, 1 Rolle Rep. 124, 80 Eng.Rep. 1164; Hodsoll v. Stallebrass, 1840, 11 Ad. & El. 301, 113 Eng.Rep. 429; Martinez v. Gerber, 1841, 3 Man. & G. 88, 133 Eng.Rep. 1069; Jones, Per Quod Servitium Amisit, 1958, 74 L.Q.Rev. 39.

5. See Dobbs, Tortious Interference with Contractual Relationships, 1980, 34 Ark.L.Rev. 335, 338–39.

6. Mineral Industries, Inc. v. George, 1965, 44 Misc. 2d 764, 255 N.Y.S.2d 114; Jones v. Waterman Steamship Corp., 3d Cir.1946, 155 F.2d 992; Mankin v. Scala Theodrome Co., [1947] K.B. 257; see Earley v. Pacific Electric Railroad Co., 1917, 176 Cal. 79, 167 P. 513; Interstate Telephone & Telegraph Co. v. Public Service Electric Co., 1914, 86 N.J.L. 26, 90 A. 1062.

7. See Ferguson v. Green Island Contracting Corp., 1975, 36 N.Y.2d 742, 368 N.Y.S.2d 163, 328 N.E.2d 792; Inland Revenue Commissioners v. Hambrook, C.A., [1956] 2 Q.B. 641, 3 Week.L.Rep. 643, 3 All Eng. 338, 57 A.L.R.2d 790. See Fleming, The Collateral Source Rule and Loss Allocation in Tort Law, 54 Cal.L.Rev. 1478, 1490, n. 44, showing some other limits.

8. See Seavey, Liability to Master for Negligent Harm to Servant, [1956] Wash.U.L.Q. 309; Guest, Crown Servants, 1956, 34 Can.Bar Rev. 598; Brett, Consortium and Servitium, 1957, 29 Aust.L.J. 321, 389, 428; Cowen, The Consequences of The Commonwealth v. Quince, 1946, 19 Aust.L.J. 2; Fleming, Action Per Quod Sevitium Amisit, 1954, 26 Aust.L.J. 122.

9. In Taylor v. Neri, 1795, 1 Esp. 386, 170 Eng.Rep. 393, recovery was denied to a theatre manager where defendant assaulted an actor and disabled him. See also Cain v. Vollmer, 1910, 19 Idaho 163, 112 P. 686 (jockey).

10. United States v. Standard Oil Co., 1947, 332 U.S. 301, 67 S.Ct. 1604, 91 L.Ed. 2067; Commonwealth v. Quince, [1944] Aust.L.Rep. 50, 68 Comm.L.Rep. 227. To the contrary was Attorney-General v. Valle-Jones, [1935] 2 K.B. 207, but that is now doubtful authority in the light of later decisions. See Inland Revenue Comnrs. v. Hambrook, C.A., [1956] 2 Q.B. 641, 3 Week. L.Rep. 643, 3 All Eng.Rep. 338, 57 A.L.R.2d 790.

11. Attorney-General for New South Wales v. Perpetual Trustee Co., [1955] A.C. 457; Myers v. Hoffman, 1956, 1 Dom.L.Rep.2d 272. To the contrary were Bradford Corp. v. Webster, [1920] 2 K.B. 135; Attorney-General v. Dublin United Tramways Co., [1939] Ir. Rep. 590.

12. Inland Revenue Commissioners v. Hambrook, [1956] 2 Q.B. 641.

13. Offshore Rental Co. v. Continental Oil Co., 1978, 22 Cal.3d 157, 148 Cal.Rptr. 867, 583 P.2d 721.

14. Hartridge v. State Farm Mut. Auto Insurance Co., 1978, 86 Wis.2d 1, 271 N.W.2d 598; Baughman Surgical Associates, Limited v. Aetna Casualty & Surety Co., La.App.1974, 302 So.2d 316, 74 A.L.R.3d 1124.

15. See Inland Revenue Comnrs. v. Hambrook, C.A., [1956] 2 Q.B. 641, 3 Week.L.Rep. 643, 3 All Eng. Rep. 338, 57 A.L.R.2d 790.

16. The Federal No. 2, 2d Cir.1927, 21 F.2d 313; Chelsea Moving & Trucking Co. v. Ross Towboat Co., 1932, 280 Mass. 282, 182 N.E. 477; Interstate Telephone & Telegraph Co. v. Public Service Electric Co., 1914, 86 N.J.L. 26, 90 A. 1062; City of Philadelphia v. Philadelphia Rapid Transit Co., 1940, 337 Pa. 1, 10 A.2d 434; Houston Belt & Terminal Railroad Co. v. Burmester, Tex.Civ.App.1957, 309 S.W.2d 271, refused n.r.e. Contra, Jones v. Waterman Steamship Corp., 3d Cir.1936, 155 F.2d 992.

17. Northern States Contracting Co. v. Oakes, 1934, 191 Minn. 88, 253 N.W. 371; Decker Construction Co. v. Mathis, 1953, 68 Ohio Abs. 280, 122 N.E.2d 38; Crab Orchard Improvement Co. v. Chesapeake & Ohio Railway Co., 4th Cir.1940, 115 F.2d 277, certiorari denied 1941, 312 U.S. 702, 61 S.Ct. 807, 85 L.Ed. 1135. Contra, on the basis of a duty owed directly to the plain-

have expressed doubt as to whether such an action should be permitted at all.[18] Virtually the only legal support for the employer's recovery is found in the federal Medical Care Recovery Act,[19] which gives the United States a right of recovery for medical care it has provided someone, such as a person in the armed services who is injured by the defendant's negligence. The statute creates some problems for the defendant who wishes to settle claims with federal employees[20] and there seems no general movement to permit the action outside the terms of the statute.

An insurer, or anyone in a similar position who pays the losses suffered by the insured, is often permitted to stand in the shoes of the insured and to pursue any claims he might have had against the person causing the loss.[21] This is subrogation, and where insurers are subrogated to the rights of the insured there is indirect protection of the insurer against negligent acts which make the insurer's contract more burdensome. Such cases usually involve physical injury to person or property and always involve an independent tort to the insured,[22] in the absence of which there can be no rights to which the insurer is subrogated. Since subrogation recoveries involve only one loss, the only question being whether it is the insured or insurer who recovers, there is no potential in such cases for a chain of recoveries of the kind that might be threatened under an interference with contract theory, in which interference with one contract also prejudices the performance of another contract and so on more or less indefinitely. It is not surprising therefore that in the absence of grounds for subrogation, insurance companies have been denied recovery for losses due to negligent injury to persons[23] or property[24] which they have insured, and on the same basis relief has been denied against one who negligently sinks a barge which the plaintiff has contracted to tow,[25] or destroys goods which he has contracted to buy,[26] or breaks the ma-

tiff, Midvale Coal Co. v. Cardox Corp., 1949, 152 Ohio St. 437, 89 N.E.2d 673, second appeal, 1952, 157 Ohio St. 526, 106 N.E.2d 556.

18. Chelsea Moving & Trucking Co. v. Ross Towboat Co., 1932, 280 Mass. 282, 182 N.E. 477; City of Philadelphia v. Philadelphia Rapid Transit Co., 1940, 337 Pa. 1, 10 A.2d 434; United States v. Atlantic Coast Line Railroad Co., D.N.C.1946, 64 F.Supp. 289; Employers' Liability Assurance Corp. v. Daley, 1947, 271 App.Div. 662, 67 N.Y.S.2d 233, 68 N.Y.S.2d 743, affirmed 1947, 297 N.Y. 745, 77 N.E.2d 515. The whole doctrine was rejected in Dotoratos v. Greenidge, 1967, 54 Misc.2d 85, 281 N.Y.S.2d 498.

19. 42 U.S.C.A. § 2651.

20. Some federal courts have said the claim by the United States is not subrogation but is an independent claim, so that even if defendant pays in full to the injured employee he may be compelled to pay again to the United States. See, e.g., United States v. Housing Authority of Bremmerton, 9th Cir.1969, 415 F.2d 239; United States v. Merrigan, 3d Cir.1968, 389 F.2d 21; Annot., 7 A.L.R.Fed. 241.

21. See 4 G. Palmer, 1978 Law of Restitution 345–476; R. Keeton, Insurance Law, 1971, § 3.10; D. Dobbs, Remedies, 1973, 250–252.

22. Subrogation may be based on any form of unjust enrichment, as where A pays B's debt to C and is subrogated to C's claim against B; but cases of this sort seem to bear no analogy to interference with contract claims. See 4 G. Palmer, 1978 Law of Restitution 345–476; D. Dobbs, Remedies, 1973, 250–252.

23. Connecticut Mutual Life Insurance Co. v. New York & N. H. R. Co., 1856, 25 Conn. 265. Cf. Economy Auto Insurance Co. v. Brown, 1948, 334 Ill.App. 579, 79 N.E.2d 854 (liability insurer denied recovery under Illinois Dramshop Act).

24. Peoria Marine & Fire Insurance Co. v. Frost, 1865, 37 Ill. 333; Sinram v. Pennsylvania Railroad Co., 2d Cir.1932, 61 F.2d 767.

25. La Société Anonyme de Remorquage à Hélice v. Bennetts, [1911] 1 K.B. 243. Accord: Robins Dry Dock & Repair Co. v. Flint, 1927, 275 U.S. 303, 48 S.Ct. 134, 72 L.Ed. 290 (charterer); Cattle v. Stockton Waterworks Co., 1875, L.R. 10 Q.B. 453; Petition of S. C. Loveland Co., E.D.Pa.1959, 170 F.Supp. 786. Cf. Forcum-James Co. v. Duke Transportation Co., 1957, 231 La. 953, 93 So.2d 228 (negligent damage to bridge which plaintiff was under contract to repair and maintain); Louisville & Nashville Railroad Co. v. Arrow Transportation Co., N.D.Ala.1959, 170 F.Supp. 597 (bridge which plaintiff has contracted to use).

Charterers of ships have been allowed to recover for negligent injury to the vessel, on the basis of a property interest. Hines v. Sangstad Steamship Co., 1 St. Cir.1902, 266 F. 502; The Aquitania, S.D.N.Y.1920, 270 F. 239; Agwilines, Inc. v. Eagle Oil & Shipping Co., 2d Cir.1946, 153 F.2d 869, certiorari denied 328 U.S. 835, 66 S.Ct. 980, 90 L.Ed. 1611.

26. Dale v. Grant, 1870, 34 N.J.L. 142; Thompson v. Seaboard Air Line Railway Co., 1914, 165 N.C. 377, 81 S.E. 315. Cf. Stromer v. Yuba City, 1964, 225 Cal.App. 2d 286, 37 Cal.Rptr. 240 (commission on sale); Rockaway Boulevard Wrecking & Lumber Co. v. Raylite

chinery of another who is furnishing him with power,[27] or pollutes the stream from which a city is supplying him with water,[28] or kills a person with whom he has a contract for his support,[29] or, as an agent, negligently fails to see that his principal's contract is performed.[30] And when it is the plaintiff himself who suffers personal injury, his loss of contracts may be admitted in evidence only as bearing upon the value of his lost time, or diminished earning capacity.[31]

As all this indicates, the defendant who commits an independent tort to the plaintiff himself, or more rarely a tort to a third person, may be liable for all proximately caused harm, including economic harm, resulting from interference with contract. And where the plaintiff is a third party beneficiary of a contract he can of course sue on the contract itself without resort to any theory of negligence.[32] But these cases aside, there is little authority for any liability for negligent interference alone. In one or two cases where the defendant had knowledge of the contract, but apparently was merely negligent, recovery has been allowed by calling the interference "wilful."[33] Telegraph companies have been held liable, without much discussion of the question, for the negligent transmission of messages resulting in the loss of contract benefits.[34] It seems likely that any negligent misperformance of a contract by a public utility or by one in a public calling, such as a lawyer, may be actionable by the person on whose behalf the contract was made,[35] as where a lawyer negligently drafts a will for A, so that the intended beneficiary takes nothing. But if these are cases for lia-

Electric Corp., 1966, 26 A.D.2d 9, 269 N.Y.S.2d 926 (extra costs in performing demolition contract).

Cf. Weller v. Foot and Mouth Disease Research Institute, Q.B.1965, 3 All E.R. 560 (cattle auctioneers had no claim for loss of commissions against one who killed the cattle before auction).

27. S. C. M. (U.K.) Ltd. v. W. J. Whittal & Son, Ltd., C.A.1970, 3 All E.R. 245; British Celanese, Ltd, v. A. H. Hunt, Ltd., Q.B.1969, 2 All E.R. 1252; Byrd v. English, 1903, 117 Ga. 191, 43 S.E. 419. But see Dunlop Tire & Rubber Corp. v. FMC Corp., 1976, 53 A.D.2d 150, 385 N.Y.S.2d 971 (negligently inflicted economic harm not per se beyond recovery, but loss of profits when power was shut off too speculative). Cf. Stevenson v. East Ohio Gas Co., Ohio App.1946, 73 N.E.2d 200, where the negligence damaged a plant and deprived a worker of employment, recovery denied.

Contrast this narrow position as to purely pecuniary loss with Newlin v. New England Telephone & Telegraph Co., 1944, 316 Mass. 234, 54 N.E.2d 929, where defendant's negligence caused a failure of power, and plaintiff recovered for physical damage to his crop of mushrooms.

28. Pure Oil Co. v. Boyle, Tex.Com.App.1930, 26 S.W.2d 161; Zarrow v. Hughes, Okl.1955, 282 P.2d 215.

29. Brink v. Wabash Railroad Co., 1900, 160 Mo. 87, 60 S.W. 1058; Steffan v. Zernes, Fla.App.1960, 124 So. 2d 495 (court decree). Cf. Anthony v. Slaid, 1846, 52 Mass. (11 Metc.) 290 (assault on pauper whom plaintiff had contracted to support); Fifield Manor v. Finston, 1960, 54 Cal.2d 632, 7 Cal.Rptr. 377, 354 P.2d 1073 (negligent injury to one whom plaintiff had contracted to provide with medical care); Baruch v. Beech Aircraft Corp., 10th Cir.1949, 175 F.2d 1, certiorari denied 338 U.S. 900, 70 S.Ct. 251, 94 L.Ed. 554 (assisting pilot to violate contract by flying plane while intoxicated); Morse v. Piedmont Hotel Co., 1964, 110 Ga.App. 509, 139 S.E.2d 133 (salesman lost job because of theft from him negligently permitted by defendants).

30. Baird v. Chesapeake & Potomac Telephone Co., 1955, 208 Md. 245, 117 A.2d 873. Cf. Donovan Construction Co. v. General Electric Co., D.Minn.1955, 133 F.Supp. 870 (negligence in supplying generators delayed plaintiff's contract with the Government); Costello v. Wells Fargo Bank, 1968, 258 Cal.App.2d 90, 65 Cal.Rptr. 612.

31. Steitz v. Gifford, 1939, 280 N.Y. 15, 19 N.E.2d 661; Halloran v. New York, New Haven & Hartford Railroad Co., 1912, 211 Mass. 132, 97 N.E. 631; Gray v. Boston Elevated Railway Co., 1913, 215 Mass. 143, 102 N.E. 71; Ball v. T. J. Pardy Construction Co., 1928, 108 Conn. 549, 143 A. 855.

32. Just's, Inc. v. Arrington Construction Co., Inc., 1978, 99 Idaho 462, 583 P.2d 997.

Cf. Rodrigues v. Campbell Industries, 1978, 87 Cal. App.3d 494, 151 Cal.Rptr. 90 (warranty claim for economic loss by one not in privity).

33. Cue v. Breland, 1901, 78 Miss. 864, 29 So. 850. Cf. Twitchell v. Glenwood-Inglewood Co., 1915, 131 Minn. 375, 155 N.W. 621.

34. Western Union Telegraph Co. v. Mathis, 1926, 215 Ala. 282, 110 So. 399; McPherson v. Western Union Telegraph Co., 1915, 189 Mich. 471, 155 N.W. 557; Barker v. Western Union Telegraph Co., 1908, 134 Wis. 147, 114 N.W. 439; Trapp v. Western Union Telegraph Co., 1912, 92 S.C. 214, 75 S.E. 210; see Note, 1936, 20 Minn.L.Rev. 837. It will be noted that in these cases liability is extended even to interference with prospective contracts.

35. See Biakanja v. Irving, 1958, 49 Cal.2d 647, 320 P.2d 16 (attorneys' liability for failure to provide formalities required for valid will).

bility, the exception is a quite narrow one, turning on a special relationship or an assumption of responsibility by the negligent promissor,[36] and equally on the presence of a narrow and particular class of potential plaintiffs.[37] There is a little authority to the effect that admiralty would recognize an action on behalf of a seaman who loses employment because his ship is negligently damaged,[38] and it has been suggested[39] that positive outlays for loss might be recoverable in a negligent interference case even if recovery for loss of profits is to be denied. Beyond this there are one or two cases[40] in which the defendant, having gratuitously assumed a duty to make payments for the plaintiff on a contract, has been held liable when his failure to do so has resulted in the loss of the contract. The cases of negligent misrepresentation[41] which causes loss to third parties in business dealings seem to stand upon much the same footing, although the element of justifiable reliance and business custom may perhaps distinguish them. The limitation to specifically foreseeable plaintiffs there imposed may suggest an ultimate solution to the problem.

The policy against recovery based on negligence is rooted at least in part on what Professor James has called the "pragmatic objection,"[42] that while physical harm generally has limited effects, a chain reaction occurs when economic harm is done and may produce an unending sequence of financial effects[43] best dealt with by insurance, or by contract, or by other business planning devices. The courts have generally followed this policy and the rather limited and narrow exceptions have had virtually no impact on the law. There are, however, decisions which, if followed, would impose a major change. In the famous *Kinsman II*[44] decision the Second Circuit took the position that there was no per se rule against recovery for negligent interference with contract, and held that it was all a matter of finding proximate cause or lack of it in each case. This approach would remove the bright line that has traditionally marked negligence claims for economic harm as off limits and substitute a case-by-case adjudication on the issue of proximate cause, an approach that may be unacceptable even to those who wish to expand liability for interference.[45] A more significant, and more abrupt, shift is found in a decision[46] of the California Supreme Court which, though involving a quite narrow factual configuration, would recognize liability for negligent interference even where there

---

36. See Harvey, Economic Losses and Negligence, 1972, 50 Can.B.Rev. 580, 603.

37. See Ross v. Caunters, [1979] Ch. 297, [1979] 3 All E.R. 580, [1979] 3 W.L.R. 605 (Ch.Div.); Schiffahrt und Kohlen v. Chelsea Maritime Ltd., [1982] Q.B. 481, [1982] 1 All E.R. 218, [1982] 2 W.L.R. 422 (Q.B.1981). See James, Tort Liability for Economic Loss, 1972, 25 Vand.L.Rev. 43.

38. Carbone v. Ursich, 9th Cir.1953, 209 F.2d 178. Cf. Rodrigues v. Campbell Industries, 1978, 87 Cal. App.3d 494, 151 Cal.Rptr. 90 (fishermen could recover on showing manufacturer sold defective ship either on admiralty law or warranty theory).

39. Note, Negligent Interference with Contract: Knowledge as a Standard for Recovery, 1977, 63 Va.L. Rev. 813, 821. Outlays were said to be recoverable in In re Lyra Shipping Co., Limited, D.La.1973, 360 F.Supp. 1188, but the *ground* for recovery was not an "outlay" exception. Support for recovery of actual outlays is found in Dominion Tape of Canada, Ltd. v. L. R. McDonald & Sons, Ltd., County Ct. 1971, 3 Ont. 627.

40. Spiegel v. Metropolitan Life Insurance Co., 1959, 6 N.Y.2d 91, 188 N.Y.S.2d 486, 160 N.E.2d 40; Walker Bank & Trust Co. v. First Security Corp., 1959, 9 Utah 2d 215, 341 P.2d 944. See Notes, 1960, 12 Stan. L.Rev. 509; 1953, 20 U.Chi.L.Rev. 283.

41. Supra, § 107.

42. James, Tort Liability for Economic Loss, 1972, 25 Vand.L.Rev. 43, 45. See also, Note, Negligent Interference with Contract: Knowledge as a Standard for Recovery, 1977, 63 Va.L.Rev. 813, 821.

43. Where this danger is not present, as where the lawyer negligently drafts A's will so that B, the intended beneficiary does not take, recovery may be entirely proper on the basis of negligence alone. See Ross v. Caunters, [1979] Ch. 297, [1979] 3 All E.R. 580, [1979] 3 W.L.R. 605 (Ch.Div.); Schiffahrt und Kohlen v. Chelsea Maritime Ltd., [1982] Q.B. 481, [1982] 1 All E.R. 218, [1982] 2 W.L.R. 422 (Q.B.1981).

44. In re Kinsman Transit Co., 2d Cir.1968, 388 F.2d 821.

45. See Note, Negligent Interference with Contract: Knowledge as a Standard for Recovery, 1977, 63 Va.L. Rev. 813.

46. J'Aire Corp. v. Gregory, 1979, 24 Cal.2d 799, 157 Cal.Rptr. 407, 598 P.2d 60. The Court required a balancing of six factors, including the extent to which

is neither physical harm nor tortious activity other than the interference itself. Under this rule the California Court envisions potential liability of a building contractor whose undue delay in construction postpones the operation of a business with which he had no contract. The case is opposed not only by the general rule but by decisions on closely similar facts from other important courts,[47] but the first decisions [48] in other jurisdictions have, on narrow facts,[49] cited it favorably, and it may be too soon to predict whether it will be confined to its facts, or to cases in which a chain reaction of liability is not possible.

Labor Law and Unfair Competition

The law of torts, and especially the law of contract interference, was once of considerable significance in labor-management disputes and in the law of trade regulation as well. A strike, for example, might interfere with the contract rights of a worker who did not wish to observe the strike,[50] and a competitor's honest [51] or dishonest [52] persuasions might detach a customer who was otherwise loyal to the plaintiff's business. On such narrow facts as these the common law of torts may still afford a remedy, and there are also a good many cases involving unfair competition to be considered under other topics of tort law.[53] On the whole, however, it may be said with the Second Restatement of Torts [54] that both labor law and unfair competition have now emerged as separate topics, largely the product of statute law and administrative regulation, and quite beyond any useful treatment confined to the common law of torts. In spite of their historical connection with the law of torts, therefore, those topics are excluded from treatment here except that a brief introduction to the law of unfair competition is afforded in another section.[55]

Remedies

Injunctive relief is available in equity to prevent interference with contract in the future when the ordinary grounds for such relief are established and there is a threat of future repeated harm.[56]

The matter of damages is more difficult and relatively few cases have given that topic any discussion at all. It is generally agreed that proof of some damage is necessary to sustain the action,[57] except where

---

the transaction was intended to affect the plaintiff, foreseeability of harm to him, the closeness of the connection, the moral blame and others.

47. Alvord and Swift v. Stewart M. Muller Construction Co., 1978, 46 N.Y.2d 276, 413 N.Y.S.2d 309, 385 N.E.2d 1238; Mandal v. Hoffman Construction Co., 1974, 270 Or. 248, 527 P.2d 387.

48. Hawthorne v. Kober Construction Co., Inc., 1982, ___ Mont. ___, 640 P.2d 467 (supplier to general contractor who did not meet commitments liable for losses to subcontractor); Keel v. Titan Construction Corp., Okl.1981, 639 P.2d 1228.

49. Hawthorne v. Kober Construction Co., Inc., 1982, ___ Mont. ___, 640 P.2d 467 is in a familiar pattern involving a number of independent workers on a common project. When one fails to perform as planned, others may suffer and often they have been given a claim, on third-party beneficiary grounds, implied-in-fact contract grounds, or on tortious interference theories. E.g., Craviolini v. Scholer & Fuller Associated Architects, 1960, 89 Ariz. 24, 357 P.2d 611. Sometimes one contractor is also regarded as agent for the others. See Phez Co. v. Salem Fruit Union, 1922, 103 Or. 514, 205 P. 970. This was also one of the grounds for relief in Keel v. Titan Construction Corp., Okl.1981, 639 P.2d 1228. That case is similarly narrow, and can be explained on the same ground that explains the liability of the lawyer who negligently drafts a will for A with resulting loss to the intended beneficiary, though it also cites J'Aire with general approval.

50. See International Union United Auto, Aircraft and Agriculture Implement Workers of America v. Russell, 1958, 356 U.S. 634, 78 S.Ct. 932, 2 L.Ed.2d 1030, rehearing denied 357 U.S. 944, 78 S.Ct. 1379, 2 L.Ed.2d 1558.

51. See Second Restatement of Torts, § 766, Illustrations 2 and 3.

52. As to injurious falsehood or "trade libel," see § 128, supra. As to fraud, see § 106 supra.

53. See § 128 supra and § 130 below.

54. Second Restatement of Torts, Introductory Note to Division Nine.

55. § 130 infra.

56. Adler, Barish, Daniels, Levin and Creskoff v. Epstein, 1978, 482 Pa. 416, 393 A.2d 1175, appeal dismissed, certiorari denied 442 U.S. 907, 99 S.Ct. 2817, 61 L.Ed.2d 272; Azar v. Lehigh Corp., Fla.App.1978, 364 So.2d 860.

57. Bigelow, Torts, 8th ed. 1907, 255, 266; Hodge v. Meyer, 2d Cir.1918, 252 F. 479, certiorari denied 248

grounds for restitution are shown;[58] but even with the damages claim, a nominal recovery may be allowed where it is clear that damage has in fact occurred and only its extent is in doubt.[59] Although older cases sometimes held to the contrary,[60] it is now agreed that the fact that there is an available action against the party who breaks the contract[61] is no defense to the one who induces the breach,[62] since the two are joint wrongdoers, and each is liable for the loss. Even a judgment in such an action, returned unsatisfied,[63] is no defense.[64] Where substantial loss has occurred, one line of cases tends to adopt the contract measure of damages, limiting recovery to those damages which were within the contemplation of the parties when the original contract was made.[65] Another,[66] apparently somewhat more uncertain of its ground, has applied a tort measure, but has limited the damages to those which are sufficiently "proximate," with some analogy to the rules as to negligent torts. A third has treated the tort as an intentional one, and has allowed recovery for unforeseen expenses,[67] as well as for mental suffering,[68] damage to reputation,[69]

U.S. 565, 39 S.Ct. 9, 63 L.Ed. 424; Exchange Tel. Co. v. Gregory & Co., [1896] 1 Q.B. 147. Thus when the claim is for loss of commissions on sales by a broker, he must prove that the sales would have been made and the commissions earned. Myers v. Arcadio, Inc., 1962, 73 N.J.Super. 493, 180 A.2d 329.

58. See p. 1004 below.

59. Raymond v. Yarrington, 1903, 96 Tex. 443, 73 S.W. 800; Dannerburg v. Ashley, 1894, 10 Ohio C.C. 558; Max Ams Machine Co. v. International Association of Machinists, Bridgeport Lodge, No. 30, 1917, 92 Conn. 297, 102 A. 706. And doubts about the exact amount of damages may be resolved against the tortfeasor whose own conduct obscured the question of damages. See ABC-Paramount Records, Inc. v. Topps Record Distributing Co., 5th Cir.1967, 374 F.2d 455.

60. Chambers v. Baldwin, 1891, 91 Ky. 121, 15 S.W. 57; Glencoe Sand & Gravel Co. v. Hudson Brothers Commission Co., 1897, 138 Mo. 439, 40 S.W. 93; Swain v. Johnson, 1909, 151 N.C. 93, 65 S.E. 619.

61. In Carmen v. Fox Film Corp., 1923, 204 App. Div. 776, 198 N.Y.S. 766, it was held that the plaintiff owed the tort feasor no duty to minimize his damages by seeking other employment.

In Gentile Brothers Corp. v. Rowena Homes, Inc., 1967, 352 Mass. 584, 227 N.E.2d 338, it was held that the recovery of damages for inducing breach of contract was not inconsistent with obtaining specific performance of the contract.

62. Phillips & Benjamin Co. v. Ratner, 2d Cir.1953, 206 F.2d 372; Horn v. Seth, 1953, 201 Md. 589, 95 A.2d 312; Childress v. Abeles, 1954, 240 N.C. 667, 84 S.E.2d 176, rehearing dismissed 242 N.C. 123, 86 S.E.2d 916; Hornstein v. Podwitz, 1930, 254 N.Y. 443, 173 N.E. 674; Kock v. Burgess, 1914, 167 Iowa 727, 149 N.W. 858. But, again by analogy to the law of joint tort feasors, a release of one may release the other. Fowler v. Nationwide Insurance Co., 1962, 256 N.C. 555, 124 S.E.2d 520.

Judgment in an action on the contract has been held to be res judicata in the other action. Israel v. Wood Dolson Co., 1956, 1 N.Y.2d 116, 151 N.Y.S.2d 1, 134 N.E.2d 97; Moreno v. Marbil Productions, Inc., 2d Cir. 1961, 296 F.2d 543.

63. In Bird v. Randall, 1762, 3 Burr. 1345, 97 Eng. Rep. 866, it was held that a satisfied judgment would bar the action. But in Simon v. Noma Electric Corp., 1944, 293 N.Y. 171, 56 N.E.2d 537, motion denied 1945, 293 N.Y. 860, 59 N.E.2d 447, and McNutt Oil & Refining Co. v. D'Ascoli, 1955, 79 Ariz. 28, 281 P.2d 966, it was held that the amount recovered must be credited, but that it did not preclude recovery of other damages that could be shown in the tort action.

64. Angle v. Chicago, St. Paul, Minneapolis & Omaha Railway Co., 1893, 151 U.S. 1, 14 S.Ct. 240, 38 L.Ed. 55; Meason v. Ralston Purina Co., 1940, 56 Ariz. 291, 107 P.2d 224.

65. Swaney v. Crawley, 1916, 133 Minn. 57, 157 N.W. 910; Kerr v. Du Pree, 1926, 35 Ga.App. 122, 132 S.E. 393; Mahoney v. Roberts, 1908, 86 Ark. 130, 110 S.W. 225; R and W Hat Shop v. Sculley, 1922, 98 Conn. 1, 118 A. 55; McNutt Oil & Refining Co. v. D'Ascoli, 1955, 79 Ariz. 28, 281 P.2d 966; Armendariz v. Mora, Tex.Civ.App.1977, 553 S.W.2d 400, refused n.r.e.

66. Anderson v. Moskovitz, 1927, 260 Mass. 523, 157 N.E. 601; Hooker, Corser & Mitchell Co. v. Hooker, 1915, 89 Vt. 383, 95 A. 649; Day v. Hunnicutt, Tex. Civ.App.1913, 160 S.W. 134; Salter v. Howard, 1871, 43 Ga. 601. Cf. McCormick v. Louis Weber & Co., 1914, 187 Ill.App. 290 (no mental suffering).

67. Vaught v. Jonathan L. Pettyjohn & Co., 1919, 104 Kan. 174, 178 P. 623; Martin v. Sterkx, 1920, 146 La. 489, 83 So. 776; Horchheimer v. Prewitt, 1928, 33 N.M. 411, 268 P. 1026; see Smith v. Goodman, Howell & Co., 1885, 75 Ga. 198. Cf. Blum v. William Goldman Theatres, S.D.Pa.1946, 69 F.Supp. 468, modified 3d Cir., 164 F.2d 192 (counsel fees and expenses of litigation in unsuccessful attempt to enforce the contract).

68. Mooney v. Johnson Cattle Co., Inc., 1981, 290 Or. 709, 634 P.2d 1333 (bases for recovery of mental anguish, especially in commercial contracts discussed in several opinions); Carter v. Oster, 1908, 134 Mo.App. 146, 112 S.W. 995; Doucette v. Sallinger, 1917, 228 Mass. 444, 117 N.E. 897; Gould v. Kramer, 1925, 253 Mass. 433, 149 N.E. 142; United States Fidelity & Guaranty Co. v. Millonas, 1921, 206 Ala. 147, 89 So. 732.

69. See note 69 on page 1004.

and punitive damages,[70] by analogy to the cases of intentional injury to person or property.[71]

There is obviously an anomaly in making the defendant liable for a greater sum than that for which the contracting party himself can be held. Where the contract is an ordinary commercial contract in which it is perfectly proper for the contracting party to "buy out" by paying full damages, or in other words where efficient breach is permitted or encouraged,[72] it seems especially inappropriate to hold the interfering defendant for damages in excess of the ordinary contract measure. On the other hand, where the contract is one that is specifically performable, so that no "buy out" or efficient breach is permitted in any event, or where the contract is of the kind the breach of which would warrant punitive damages, it seems especially appropriate to award the higher tort measure of damages against the interfering defendant. This, at least, may be the explanation of some of the cases.[73]

In some cases the plaintiff may prefer restitution to damages, that is, a recovery based not on the plaintiff's loss, but on the defendant's gain.[74] There is authority permitting the plaintiff to recover the profits defendant made from inducing a breach of contract,[75] and in the case of interference by bribery of the plaintiff's employees there is the added advantage that the plaintiff can recover the amount of the bribe though he himself has lost nothing and has no damages.[76]

WESTLAW REFERENCES
digest(interference /s contractual /s relation!)
digest(interference /s business /s relation!)
interference /s contractual /s relation! /p interest* /s protect!
restatement +s torts /s 766

Development of the Tort
interference /s contractual /s relation! /p commonlaw histor! origin* develop! % developer
lumley +2 gye

Basis of Liability-Intent
interference /s contractual /s relation! /s intent! /s knowledge kn*w* aware!
interference /s contractual /s relation! /p privilege* justif! defense* excus! merit!
interference /s contractual /s relation! /p defam! fraud "injuriou falsehood" intimidat*** "slander of title" violence
interference /s contractual /s relation! /p "bad faith" entic! harm malic! spite
interference /s contractual /s relation! /p advi*e* disinterest** "economic interest*" "good faith" "public interest" "terminable at will"
interference /s contractual /s relation! /p compet!

---

69. Westway Trading Corp. v. River Terminal Corp., Iowa 1982, 314 N.W.2d 398; De Minico v. Craig, 1911, 207 Mass. 593, 94 N.E. 317.

70. Burgess v. Tucker, 1913, 94 S.C. 309, 77 S.E. 1016; Cotton v. Cooper, Tex.Civ.App.1913, 160 S.W. 597, affirmed Tex.Com.App.1919, 209 S.W. 135; Oxner v. Seaboard Air Line Railway Co., 1918, 110 S.C. 366, 96 S.E. 559; United States Fidelity & Guaranty Co. v. Millonas, 1921, 206 Ala. 147, 89 So. 732; McNutt Oil & Refining Co. v. D'Ascoli, 1955, 79 Ariz. 28, 281 P.2d 966.

Punitive damages were denied in Dependahl v. Falstaff Brewing Corp., 8th Cir.1981, 653 F.2d 1208, certiorari denied 102 U.S. 641, 102 S.Ct. 641, 70 L.Ed.2d 619 because the federal statute had preempted the common law claim for interference and no such damages were allowable under the statute.

71. See supra, Chaps. 2–3.

72. "The duty to keep a contract at common law means a prediction that you must pay damages if you do not keep it—and nothing else." Oliver Wendell Holmes, The Path of the Law, in Collected Legal Papers, 167, 175 (1920). The idea of efficient breach is that if the promisor can profit from breach and still make the promisee whole then the promisee has no complaint and the community resources are maximized. See R. Posner, 2d ed.1977, Economic Analysis of Law § 4.9.

73. Duff v. Engleberg, 1965, 237 Cal.App.2d 505, 47 Cal.Rptr. 114, involved a land sale contract which was specifically performable, and the interference involved racial discrimination. No efficient breach would be permitted in such a case or on such grounds and the harsher measure of damages was clearly warranted. The court, however, did not observe the distinction just made.

74. See D. Dobbs, Remedies §§ 4.1, 4.3; 6.4, 10.4 and 10.5.

75. National Merchandising Corp. v. Leyden, 1976, 370 Mass. 425, 348 N.E.2d 771; Federal Sugar Refining Co. v. United States Sugar Equalization Board, D.N.Y.1920, 268 F. 575.

Cf. Angle v. Chicago, St. Paul, Minneapolis & Omaha Railway, 1893, 151 U.S. 1, 14 S.Ct. 240, 38 L.Ed. 55 (lien imposed upon benefits in hands of breach-inducer).

76. Continental Management, Inc. v. United States, Ct.Cl.1975, 527 F.2d 613; D. Dobbs, Remedies §§ 6.4, 10.4 and 10.5.

Causation and Manner of Interference

interference /s contractual /s relation! /p material proximate substantial /s caus! reason

interference /s contractual /s relation! /p defendant* /s coerc*** harass! induc! intimidat*** pressure threat!

interference /s contractual /s relation! /p convert*** conversion fraud misrepresentation* "slander of title" violence

interference /s contractual /s relation! /p antitrust boycott*** conspir! "refus! to deal"

Nature of Original Contract

interference /s contractual /s relation /p cancel! illegal invalid! mutuality "statute of fraud*" unconscionable unenforceable void!

interference /s contractual /s relation! & "terminable at will"

interference /s contractual /s relation! & marry marriage

Intent and Negligence

interference /s contractual /s relation! /p negligen***
255k336
255k337

Labor Law and Unfair Competition

interference /s contractual /s relation! /p labor union strike* "unfair competition"

Remedies

interference /s contractual /s relation! /p injunct! enjoin!

interference /s contractual /s relation! /p exemplary pecuniary +1 damage*

headnote(interference /s contractual /s relation! /p damages)

§ 130. Interference with Prospective Advantage

Tort liability for interference with prospective advantage seems to have developed at a very early date in cases having to do with the use of physical violence, or threats of it, to drive away customers from the plaintiff's market,[1] or those who might make donations to his church;[2] but it seems to have been limited rather definitely to the use of such improper means.[3] During the seventeenth and eighteenth centuries there were decisions involving threats and violence to frighten away prospective workmen or customers,[4] and later there were others which gave an action for spiteful shooting to scare off the plaintiff's game.[5] There was even a case in England in 1844 in which an actor was allowed to recover against a defendant who had succeeded in having him hissed off the stage, as a result of which he was unable to obtain further employment.[6] The real source of the modern law, however, may be said to be the case of Temperton v. Russell,[7] in which the Court of Queen's Bench declared that the principles of liability for interference with contract extended beyond existing contractual relations, and that a similar action would lie for interference with relations which were merely prospective or potential.

Upon this foundation, a rather formidable body of law has been erected, which in general has followed along the lines of interference with contract.[8] It has been said that "in a civilized community which recognizes the right of private property among its institutions, the notion is intolerable that a man should be protected by the law in the enjoy-

§ 130

1. Y.B., 1410, 11 Hen. IV 47. Cf., 1356, Y.B. 29 Edw. III 18; 1368, Y.B. 41 Edw. III 24B. See Holt, J., in Keeble v. Hickeringill, 1707, 11 East 574 note, 11 Mod.Rep. 14, 130, 3 Salk. 9, Holt, 14, 103 Eng.Rep. 1127; Wigmore, The Boycott and Kindred Practices as Ground for Damages, 1887, 21 Am.L.Rev. 509, 515ff. There was an earlier writ giving an action for threatening plaintiff's tenants at will so that they departed. 1494, Y.B. 9 Hen. VII 7; 1443, Y.B. 21 Hen. VI 31.

2. Cf. Anonymous, Bellewe 6 (Action on the Case), Eng.Rep. 3 (1396).

3. Y.B., 1410, 11 Hen. IV 47; 1444, Y.B. 22 Hen. VI 14.

4. Garret v. Taylor, 1621, Cro.Jac. 567, 79 Eng.Rep. 485 (threats of mayhem and vexatious suits against customers and workmen); Tarleton v. McGawley, 1793, Peake N.P. 270, 170 Eng.Rep. 153 (firing upon African natives about to trade with the plaintiff).

5. Keeble v. Hickeringill, 1707, 11 Mod.Rep. 14, 130, 103 Eng.Rep. 1127; Carrington v. Taylor, 1809, 11 East 571, 103 Eng.Rep. 1126; Ibottson v. Peat, 1865, 3 H. & C. 644, 159 Eng.Rep. 684.

6. Gregory v. Duke of Brunswick, 1843, 6 M. & G. 205, 134 Eng.Rep. 866, 1178. In Walker v. Cronin, 1871, 107 Mass. 555, a count for persuading prospective employees to refuse to enter service, without justification, was held to state a cause of action.

7. [1893] 1 Q.B. 715. Cf. Quinn v. Leathem, [1901] A.C. 495.

8. See Sarat Basak, Principles of Liability for Interference with Trade, Profession or Calling, 1911, 27 L.Q. Rev. 290, 399, 1912, 28 L.Q.Rev. 52; Kales, Coercive and Competitive Methods in Trade and Labor Disputes,

ment of property once it is acquired, but left unprotected by the law in his effort to acquire it;"[9] and that since a large part of what is most valuable in modern life depends upon "probable expectancies," as social and industrial life becomes more complex the courts must do more to discover, define and protect them from undue interference.[10]

For the most part the "expectancies" thus protected have been those of future contractual relations, such as the prospect of obtaining employment[11] or employees,[12] or the opportunity of obtaining customers.[13] In such cases there is a background of business experience on the basis of which it is possible to estimate with some fair amount of success both the value of what has been lost and the likelihood that the plaintiff would have received it if the defendant had not interfered. The loss of prospective profits is, for example, a familiar element of damages in cases of breach of contract.[14] When the attempt has been made to carry liability for interference beyond such commercial dealings, and into such areas as exclusion from social organizations,[15] or deprivation of the chance of winning a contest,[16] the courts have been disturbed by a feeling that they were embarking upon uncharted seas, and recovery has been denied; and it is significant that the reason usually given is that there is no sufficient degree of certainty that the plaintiff ever would have received the anticipated benefits.

On this basis the earlier cases held that recovery would be denied for interference with an expected gift or a legacy under a will,[17]

1922, 8 Corn.L.Q. 1, 128; Green, Relational Interests, 1935, 29 Ill.L.Rev. 1041, 30 Ill.L.Rev. 1; Handler, Unfair Competition, 1936, 21 Iowa L.Rev. 175; Notes, 1922, 22 Col.L.Rev. 665; 1923, 9 Corn.L.Q. 78; 1927, 12 Minn.L.Rev. 147, 162; 1932, 27 Ill.L.Rev. 96; 1932, 6 U.Cin.L.Rev. 322; 1938, 37 Mich.L.Rev. 115; 1947, 56 Yale L.J. 885; 1964, 77 Harv.L.Rev. 888.

9. Brennan v. United Hatters of North America, 1906, 73 N.J.L. 729, 65 A. 165.

10. Jersey City Printing Co. v. Cassidy, 1902, 63 N.J.Eq. 759, 53 A. 230.

11. Huskie v. Griffin, 1909, 75 N.H. 345, 74 A. 595; Bacon v. St. Paul Union Stockyards Co., 1925, 161 Minn. 522, 201 N.W. 326; Willner v. Silverman, 1909, 109 Md. 341, 71 A. 962; see Hundley v. Louisville & Nashville Railroad Co., 1903, 105 Ky. 162, 48 S.W. 429.

In Longo v. Reilly, 1955, 35 N.J.Super. 405, 114 A.2d 302, fraudulent conduct resulted in plaintiff's defeat in election to an office. This was treated as wrongful interference with a business or property right.

12. Jersey City Printing Co. v. Cassidy, 1902, 63 N.J.Eq. 759, 53 A. 230; Vegelahn v. Guntner, 1896, 167 Mass. 92, 44 N.E. 1077; Erdman v. Mitchell, 1903, 207 Pa. 79, 56 A. 327.

13. Tuttle v. Buck, 1909, 107 Minn. 145, 119 N.W. 946; Graham v. St. Charles Street Railroad Co., 1895, 47 La.Ann. 214, 16 So. 806; Boggs v. Duncan-Schell Furniture Co., 1913, 163 Iowa 106, 143 N.W. 482.

14. See D. Dobbs, Remedies, 1973, § 3.3; Comment, Lost Profits as Contract Damages, 1978, 56 N.C.L.Rev. 693.

15. Trautwein v. Harbourt, 1956, 40 N.J.Super. 247, 123 A.2d 30.

But even a social organization may not expel a member to punish his exercise of a fundamental right. Zelenka v. Benevolent and Protective Order of Elks of the United States, 1974, 129 N.J.Super. 379, 324 A.2d 35. See p. 1028 below.

Where the private association has economic purposes and impacts, as with certain professional associations, admission may be compelled. See Annot., 89 A.L.R.2d 964. Statutes guarantee rights to labor union membership, and other statutes may guarantee a right to be served in places of public accommodation. See generally, Developments in the Law—Judicial Control of Actions of Private Associations, 1963, 76 Harv.L.Rev. 983.

16. Collatz v. Fox Wisconsin Amusement Corp., 1941, 239 Wis. 156, 300 N.W. 162; Harrison v. Jones, 1936, 52 Ga.App. 852, 184 S.E. 889; Phillips v. Pantages Theatre Co., 1931, 163 Wash. 303, 300 P. 1048. Cf. Western Union Telegraph Co. v. Crall, 1888, 39 Kan. 580, 18 P. 719 (chance of winning horse races); Cain v. Vollmer, 1910, 19 Idaho 163, 112 P. 686 (same as to future races); Smitha v. Gentry, 1898, 20 Ky.L. Rep. 171, 45 S.W. 515 (chance of obtaining reward); Klous v. Hennessey, 1881, 13 R.I. 332 (unsecured creditor's chance of levying upon property fraudulently conveyed). See Notes, 1964, 18 Rut.L.Rev. 875; 1967, 19 Ala.L.Rev. 495.

Cf. Gold v. Los Angeles Democratic League, 1975, 49 Cal.App.3d 365, 122 Cal.Rptr. 732 (election).

Compare the cases in which it has been held that it was insufficiently pleaded or proved that plaintiff would have made a contract without the defendant's interference. Wilson v. Loew's, Inc., 1956, 142 Cal.App. 2d 183, 298 P.2d 152, certiorari dismissed 355 U.S. 597, 78 S.Ct. 526, 2 L.Ed.2d 519; Goldman v. Feinberg, 1944, 130 Conn. 671, 37 A.2d 355; Union Car Advertising Co. v. Collier, 1934, 263 N.Y. 386, 189 N.E. 463, remittitur amended 264 N.Y. 599, 191 N.E. 583; Debnam v. Simonson, 1914, 124 Md. 354, 92 A. 782.

17. Hutchins v. Hutchins, N.Y.1845, 7 Hill 104; Lewis v. Corbin, 1907, 195 Mass. 520, 81 N.E. 248;

even though the defendant's motives were unworthy and he had resorted to fraudulent means, because the testator might have changed his mind. This is not necessarily a reason for refusing to protect such non-commercial expectancies, at least where there is a strong probability that they would have been realized.[18] In cases where this probability has approached something like certainty, as in the case of incompetency of the testator to make a change,[19] or suppression of the will after his death,[20] recovery has commonly been allowed; and there are now a number of cases [21] in which it has been permitted on the basis of other evidence of a high degree of probability that the testator would have made or changed a bequest. Courts of equity have granted relief by imposing a constructive trust in such a situation.[22] There appears to be little doubt that the same principle would apply to the frustration of intestate succession by fraudulently inducing a will,[23] or even to a prospective gift.[24] The problem appears in reality to be one of satisfactory proof that the loss has been suffered, instead of the existence of a ground of tort liability.[25] It is to be noted, however, that all of these cases in which recovery has been permitted, whether in a tort action or under a constructive trust, have involved conduct tortious in itself, such as fraud or defamation or conduct depriving

Cunningham v. Edward, 1936, 52 Ohio App. 61, 3 N.E.2d 58; Hall v. Hall, 1917, 91 Conn. 514, 100 A.2d 441. Accord, Hoeft v. Supreme Lodge, Knights of Honor, 1896, 113 Cal. 91, 45 P. 185 (beneficiary of insurance policy). See Notes, 1935, 48 Harv.L.Rev. 984; 1937, 23 Va.L.Rev. 614; 1937, 4 U.Chi.L.Rev. 509; 1937, 32 Corn.L.Q. 440; 1936, 5 Ford.L.Rev. 514.

18. See Schaefer, Uncertainty and the Law of Damages, 1978, 19 Wm. & M.L.Rev. 719 (arguing for a recovery even when damages are uncertain, with a discount for uncertainty and other adjustments).

Compare the cases awarding damages for loss of the value of a chance attended with a high probability of success: Chaplin v. Hicks, [1911] 2 K.B. 786 (beauty contest); Wachtel v. National Alfalfa Journal, 1920, 190 Iowa 1293, 176 N.W. 801 (prize magazine subscription contest); Kansas City, Mexico & Orient Railway Co. of Texas v. Bell, Tex.Civ.App.1917, 197 S.W. 322 (prize at stock show). But see D. Dobbs, 1973, Remedies 155–56 (distinguishing chances that are bought and sold in the market and which can thus be valued from other hoped-for but uncertain opportunities).

19. Cf. Hall v. Hall, 1917, 91 Conn. 514, 100 A. 441; Murphy v. Mitchell, D.N.Y.1917, 245 F. 219, 246 F. 732, 249 F. 499.

20. Creek v. Laski, 1929, 248 Mich. 425, 227 N.W. 817; Allen v. Lowell's Administratrix 1946, 303 Ky. 238, 197 S.W.2d 424; Dulin v. Bailey, 1916, 172 N.C. 608, 90 S.E. 689; Morton v. Petitt, 1931, 124 Ohio St. 241, 177 N.E. 591. Cf. McGregor v. McGregor, D.Colo. 1951, 101 F.Supp. 848 (probate of prior will).

21. Bohannon v. Wachovia Bank & Trust Co., 1936, 210 N.C. 679, 188 S.E. 390; Second Restatement of Torts, § 912. Cf. Harmon v. Harmon, Me.1979, 404 A.2d 1020 (interference with expected devise by inducing conveyance, recovery though would-be devisor still living).

Accord as to the beneficiary of an insurance policy, Mitchell v. Langley, 1915, 143 Ga. 827, 85 S.E. 1050. Constructive trusts were imposed in Cason v. Owens, 1897, 100 Ga. 142, 28 S.E. 75; Daugherty v. Daugherty, 1913, 152 Ky. 732, 154 S.W. 9; Munroe v. Beggs, 1914, 91 Kan. 701, 139 P. 422.

Where the ancestor has been induced to make gifts that may defeat the plaintiff's inheritance, but the ancestor is still living, the plaintiff has been denied relief and the claim if any belongs to the ancestor. Chambers v. Kane, Del.1981, 437 A.2d 163.

See Evans, Torts to Expectancies in Decedents' Estates, 1944, 93 U.Pa.L.Rev. 187; Notes, 1951, 19 U.Kan.City L.Rev. 78; 1952, 1 De Paul L.Rev. 253.

Compare Shepherd v. Wakeman, 1662, 1 Sid. 79, 83 Eng.Rep. 931 (interference with prospective marriage by false statement); and the interesting case of Deon v. Kirby Lumber Co., 1926, 162 La. 671, 111 So. 55, where loss of prospective social relations, rather than economic ones, was held compensable.

22. Latham v. Father Divine, 1949, 299 N.Y. 22, 85 N.E.2d 168, reargument denied 299 N.Y. 599, 86 N.E. 2d 114; Moneyham v. Hamilton, 1936, 124 Fla. 430, 168 So. 522; Bohannon v. Trotman, 1939, 214 N.C. 706, 200 S.E. 852; Seeds v. Seeds, 1927, 116 Ohio St. 144, 156 N.E. 193; Monach v. Koslowski, 1948, 322 Mass. 466, 78 N.E.2d 4; see D. Dobbs, 1973, Remedies § 6.4.

23. Hegarty v. Hegarty, D.Mass.1943, 52 F.Supp. 296; Seeds v. Seeds, 1927, 116 Ohio St. 144, 156 N.E. 193.

24. The possible existence of the tort was recognized in Ross v. Wright, 1934, 286 Mass. 269, 190 N.E. 514, but it was held that there was no liability in the absence of tortious conduct.

25. Logically the damages recovered should be the value of the *chance* of benefit rather than the full value of the legacy. On this basis, there might be recovery for loss of prospects falling considerably short of absolute certainty. See Schaefer, Uncertainty and the Law of Damages, 1978, 19 Wm. & M.L.Rev. 719; cf. King, Causation, Valuation, and Chance in Personal Injury Torts Involving Preexisting Conditions and Future Consequences, 1981, 90 Yale L.J. 1397.

a testator or other actor of the capacity to act, as where there is duress or undue influence. So far as now appears, there still can be no recovery merely upon the basis of intentional interference, without such otherwise improper conduct.[26]

Basis of Liability

The cause of action has run parallel to that for interference with existing contracts.[27] Again, the tort began with "malice," and it has remained very largely a matter of at least intent to interfere. Cases have been quite infrequent in which even the claim has been advanced that the defendant through his negligence has prevented the plaintiff from obtaining a prospective pecuniary advantage; and the usual statement is that there can be no cause of action in such a case.[28] There are, however, a few situations in which recovery has been permitted, all of them apparently to be justified upon the basis of some special relation between the parties. They include the failure of a telegraph company to deliver a message which would have resulted in the plaintiff's obtaining a contract;[29] the failure of a volunteer to continue the performance of a gratuitous promise to obtain insurance and the like for the plaintiff;[30] delay in acting upon an application for insurance;[31] and cases[32] holding that the negligent preparation of a will results in liability to the intended beneficiaries. In all probability, as in the case of interference with existing contracts,[33] liability for negligence is not impossible, but it must depend upon the existence of some special reason for finding a duty of care. A recent California decision[34] may have gone much further than this, however. That case would apparently permit liability based on negligence in any case where a balancing of such factors as foreseeability, closeness of connection and moral blame seem to the decision-maker to warrant such a result.[35] At

---

26. Marshall v. Dehaven, 1904, 209 Pa. 187, 58 A. 141 (inducing testator not to change will); Lowe Foundation v. Northern Trust Co., 1951, 342 Ill.App. 379, 96 N.E.2d 831 (inducing testator to destroy codicil); Ross v. Wright, 1934, 286 Mass. 269, 190 N.E. 514 (refusal to make transfer in completion of gift, where no duty to do so).

27. See supra, § 129.

28. Rickards v. Sun Oil Co., 1945, 23 N.J.Misc. 89, 41 A.2d 267 (destruction of bridge to island, causing business loss to plaintiff); Wooldridge Manufacturing Co. v. United States, 1956, 98 U.S.App.D.C. 286, 235 F.2d 513, certiorari denied 351 U.S. 989, 76 S.Ct. 1054, 100 L.Ed. 1502 (chief of engineers negligently delayed report, causing plaintiff to lose contract); Parker v. Brown, 1940, 195 S.C. 35, 10 S.E.2d 625 (failure to issue executions causing loss of commissions to tax collector); Liesbosch Dredger v. S. S. Edison, [1933] A.C. 449 (damage from collision, loss through inability to charter other vessel).

29. Western Union Telegraph Co. v. Bowman, 1904, 141 Ala. 175, 37 So. 493; Western Union Telegraph Co. v. McKibben, 1887, 114 Ind. 511, 14 N.E. 894.

But where the undelivered message is a mere inquiry, recovery of substantial damages has been denied. Wilson v. Western Union Telegraph Co., 1905, 124 Ga. 131, 52 S.E. 153; McKenry v. Western Union Telegraph Co., 1927, 81 Cal.App. 258, 253 P. 333; Davies v. Western Union Telegraph Co., 1912, 93 S.C. 318, 76 S.E. 820. See Note, 1936, 20 Minn.L.Rev. 837.

30. Evan L. Reed Manufacturing Co. v. Wurts, 1914, 187 Ill.App. 378; Siegel v. Spear & Co., 1923, 234 N.Y. 479, 138 N.E. 414; Carr v. Maine Central Railroad Co., 1917, 78 N.H. 502, 102 A. 532 (obtaining Interstate Commerce Commission approval of refund); Condon v. Exton-Hall Brokerage & Vessel Agency, 1913, 80 Misc. 369, 142 N.Y.S. 548, reversed on other grounds 83 Misc. 130, 144 N.Y.S. 760 (cancelling insurance); Stockmen's National Bank of Casper v. Richardson, 1933, 45 Wyo. 306, 18 P.2d 635 (recording mortgage); Colonial Savings Association v. Taylor, Tex.1976, 544 S.W.2d 116.

31. See cases cited supra, Sec. 56.

32. Biakanja v. Irving, 1958, 49 Cal.2d 647, 320 P.2d 16 (notary public, not properly attested); Lucas v. Hamm, 1961, 56 Cal.2d 583, 15 Cal.Rptr. 821, 364 P.2d 685, certiorari denied 368 U.S. 987, 82 S.Ct. 603, 7 L.Ed. 2d 525 (attorney, negligent drafting); Ross v. Caunters, 1979, Ch. 297, 3 All.E.R. 580, W.L.R. 605 (Ch.Div.). Accord Ward v. Arnold, 1958, 52 Wn.2d 581, 328 P.2d 164 (negligent advice of attorney that no will was necessary); McAbee v. Edwards, Fla.App.1976, 340 So.2d 1167 (failure to advise change in will necessary upon remarriage).

33. See supra, Sec. 129.

34. J'Aire Corp. v. Gregory, 1979, 24 Cal.3d 799, 157 Cal.Rptr. 407, 598 P.2d 60. But see Goodman v. Kennedy, 1976, 18 Cal.3d 335, 134 Cal.Rptr. 375, 556 P.2d 737.

35. The Court would also consider the extent to which the transaction was "intended" to affect the plaintiff, but this apparently does not require any intent to harm him, only a certainty that he would be affected. Other factors to be considered include certainty of harm and the policy of deterring future conduct. The Court did not discuss damages as such. If the on-

this writing, however, the potential impact of the case cannot be judged.[36]

With intent to interfere as the usual basis of the action, the cases have turned almost entirely upon the defendant's motive or purpose, and the means by which he has sought to accomplish it. As in the cases of interference with contract, any manner of intentional invasion of the plaintiff's interests may be sufficient if the purpose is not a proper one. Apart from this, however, the means adopted may be unlawful in themselves; and violence[37] or intimidation,[38] defamation,[39] injurious falsehood[40] or other fraud,[41] violation of the criminal law,[42] and the institution or threat of groundless civil suits[43] or criminal prosecutions[44] in bad faith, all have been held to result in liability, and there is some authority which limits liability to such cases.[45]

Most of the decisions, however, have turned upon the defendant's motive or purpose. Again, as in the case of interference with contract,[46] the defendant has been held liable if the reason underlying his interference is purely a malevolent one, and a desire to do harm to the plaintiff for its own sake.[47] On the other hand, some element of ill will is seldom absent from intentional interference; and if the defendant has a legitimate inter-

---

ly damages recoverable were for diminished value of the plaintiff's lease, the claim would not be one for interference with prospects at all, but for interference with existing property interests. If the damages are for loss of profits, as the Court seemed to assume, the case is one for interference with mere prospective advantage.

36. Approval was given in Hawthorne v. Kober Construction Co., Inc., 1982, ___ Mont. ___, 640 P.2d 467 and in Keel v. Titan Construction Corp., Okl.1981, 639 P.2d 1228. Both cases can be justified on quite narrow grounds. The first involves facts on which claims have often been allowed on third-party beneficiary grounds, or others. The second, though it involves different facts, can be explained on the same principle as is involved in the will-drafting cases.

37. Garret v. Taylor, 1621, Cro.Jac. 567, 79 Eng. Rep. 485; Tarleton v. McGawley, 1793, Peake N.P. 270, 170 Eng.Rep. 153. Cf. Hughes v. McDonough, 1881, 43 N.J.L. 459 (loosening shoe on horse shod by plaintiff, to deprive him of a customer).

38. Guillory v. Godfrey, 1955, 134 Cal.App.2d 628, 286 P.2d 474; Sparks v. McCrary, 1908, 156 Ala. 382, 47 So. 332; International Ticket Co. v. Wendrich, 1937, 122 N.J.Eq. 222, 193 A. 808, affirmed 123 N.J.Eq. 172, 196 A. 474; Gilly v. Hirsh, 1909, 122 La. 966, 48 So. 422; Evenson v. Spaulding, 9th Cir.1907, 150 F. 517.

39. Godin v. Niebuhr, 1920, 236 Mass. 350, 128 N.E. 406; Standard Oil Co. v. Doyle, 1904, 118 Ky. 662, 82 S.W. 271; Kendall v. Lively, 1934, 94 Colo. 483, 31 P.2d 343; Morrison-Jewell Filtration Co. v. Lingane, 1895, 19 R.I. 316, 33 A. 452. See Nims, Unfair Competition by False Statements or Disparagement, 1933, 19 Corn. L.Q. 63.

40. Really only one form of interference with pecuniary advantage. See supra, p. 966.

41. Thus Wise v. Western Union Telegraph Co., 1934, 36 Del. 155, 172 A. 757 (sending forged telegrams purporting to come from plaintiff). As to misrepresentation to the public in competition, see infra, p. 998.

42. Glover v. Malloska, 1927, 238 Mich. 216, 213 N.W. 107 (lottery).

43. Munson Line v. Green, S.D.N.Y.1946, 6 F.R.D. 14, appeal dismissed, 2d Cir., 165 F.2d 321; Maytag Co. v. Meadows Manufacturing Co., 7th Cir.1929, 35 F.2d 403; Dehydro, Inc. v. Tretolite Co., D.Okl.1931, 53 F.2d 273; Sun-Maid Raisin Growers of Calif. v. Avis, D.Ill. 1928, 25 F.2d 303; see Notes, 1932, 10 N.C.L.Rev. 300; 1947, 56 Yale L.J. 885.

44. American Mercury v. Chase, D.Mass.1926, 13 F.2d 224. Cf. People v. Everest, 1889, 51 Hun 19, 3 N.Y.S. 612 (arrest of engineer to delay train); Pratt Food Co. v. Bird, 1907, 148 Mich. 631, 112 N.W. 701.

45. Nifty Foods Corp. v. Great Atlantic & Pacific Tea Co., 2d Cir.1980, 614 F.2d 832 (interference with advantageous relations under New York law requires both improper motive and unlawful means); Paint Products Co. v. Minwax Co., Inc., D.Conn.1978, 448 F.Supp. 656. Cf. Griese-Taylor Corp. v. First National Bank, Etc., 5th Cir.1978, 572 F.2d 1039 (force, fraud, etc. required in interference with contract claim).

Two commentators have argued that liability for interference with either contract or opportunity should be limited in most instances to cases in which improper means of interference is used. Dobbs, Tortious Interference with Contractual Relationships, 1980, 34 Ark.L. Rev. 335; Perlman, Interference with Contract and Other Economic Expectancies: A Clash of Tort and Contract Doctrine, 1982, 49 U.Chi.L.Rev. 61.

46. See supra, p. 985.

47. Tuttle v. Buck, 1909, 107 Minn. 145, 119 N.W. 946; Memphis Steam Laundry-Cleaners v. Lindsey, 1941, 192 Miss. 224, 5 So.2d 227; Graham v. St. Charles Street Railroad Co., 1895, 47 La.Ann. 214, 16 So. 806; Boggs v. Duncan-Schell Furniture Co., 1913, 163 Iowa 106, 143 N.W. 482; United States Aluminum Siding Corp. v. Dun & Bradstreet, S.D.N.Y.1958, 163 F.Supp. 906. Compare the attempt to coerce a settlement with the "white elephant" car in Carter v. Knapp Motor Co., 1943, 243 Ala. 600, 11 So.2d 383. Also the retaliation in National Association for the Advancement of Colored People v. Overstreet, 1965, 221 Ga. 16, 142 S.E.2d 816, certiorari dismissed 384 U.S. 118, 86 S.Ct. 1306, 16 L.Ed.2d 409, rehearing denied 384 U.S. 981, 86

est to protect, the addition of a spite motive usually is not regarded as sufficient to result in liability.[48]

Proof of the intentional interference and resulting damage [49] establishes what the New York courts have called a "prima facie tort," [50] casting upon the defendant the burden [51] of avoiding liability by showing that his conduct was privileged.[52] In general, it may be said that any purpose sufficient to create a privilege to disturb existing contractual relations,[53] such as the disinterested protection of the interests of third persons,[54] or those of the public,[55] or of the defendant's own property or business interests,[56] or the exercise of the right to bring or to threaten

S.Ct. 1857, 16 L.Ed.2d 692. See Note, 1943, 15 Miss. L.J. 213.

There is some authority for the proposition that where only expectations are involved, there must be an independent tort. See Paint Products Co. v. Minwax Co., D.Conn.1978, 448 F.Supp. 656.

48. Holbrook v. Morrison, 1913, 214 Mass. 209, 100 N.E. 1111 (advertising for Negro purchasers for premises). Accord: Beardsley v. Kilmer, 1922, 200 App.Div. 378, 193 N.Y.S. 285, affirmed, 1923, 236 N.Y. 80, 140 N.E. 203; Katz v. Kapper, 1935, 7 Cal.App.2d 1, 44 P.2d 1060; McMaster v. Ford Motor Co., 1921, 122 S.C. 244, 115 S.E. 244; Lewis v. Huie-Hodge Lumber Co., 1908, 121 La. 658, 46 So. 685; West Virginia Transport Co. v. Standard Oil Co., 1902, 50 W.Va. 611, 40 S.E. 591.

However, in Alyeska Pipeline Service Co., v. Aurora Air Service, Inc., Alaska 1979, 604 P.2d 1090 the Court used a dominant motive test. This has been criticized as allowing liability for acts that are, because of other motives and effects, socially useful. Dobbs, Tortious Interference with Contractual Relationships, 1980, 34 Ark.L.Rev. 335. Professor Perlman has made a similar observation, Perlman, Interference with Contract and other Economic Expectancies: A Clash of Tort and Contract Doctrine, 1982, 49 U.Chi.L.Rev. 61.

49. Damages must be proven. Rager v. McCloskey, 1953, 305 N.Y. 75, 111 N.E.2d 214, motion denied 305 N.Y. 924, 114 N.E.2d 476. And it is not enough that the plaintiff shows a reasonable possibility that he would have obtained some economic benefit in the absence of the defendant's intervention; he must instead show that he *would* have obtained the benefit, or in other words must prove his case by stringent standards. Optivision v. Syracuse Shopping Center, D.N.Y. 1979, 472 F.Supp. 665; Union Car Advertising Co. v. Collier, 1934, 263 N.Y. 386, 189 N.E. 463, remittitur amended 264 N.Y. 599, 191 N.E. 583.

50. See Forkosch, An Analysis of the "Prima Facie Tort" Cause of Action, 1957, 42 Corn.L.Q. 465; Halpern, Intentional Torts and the Restatement, 1957, 7 Buff.L.Rev. 7; Brown, The Rise and Threatened Demise of the Prima Facie Tort Principle, 1959, 54 Nw.L. Rev. 563. An unfriendly view of the prima facie tort theory is advanced in Dobbs, Tortious Interference with Contractual Relationships, 1980, 34 Ark.L.Rev. 335, 345, 363.

51. Thompson v. Allstate Insurance Co., 5th Cir. 1973, 476 F.2d 746; Alyeska Pipeline Service Co. v. Aurora Air Service, Inc., Alaska 1979, 604 P.2d 1090.

52. Although there are almost no cases, it appears that the absolute privileges in defamation will be available as a defense here. Thus in Rainier's Dairies v. Raritan Valley Farms, 1955, 19 N.J. 552, 117 A.2d 889, the absolute privilege of a judicial proceeding was applied. Accord, McLaughlin v. Copeland, D.Del.1978, 455 F.Supp. 749, affirmed 595 F.2d 1213.

53. See supra, p. 985.

54. Gott v. Berea College, 1913, 156 Ky. 376, 161 S.W. 204; Jones v. Cody, 1902, 132 Mich. 13, 92 N.W. 495; Guethler v. Altman, 1901, 26 Ind.App. 587, 60 N.E. 355; Rowan v. Butler, 1908, 171 Ind. 28, 85 N.E. 714; Kuryer Publishing Co. v. Messmer, 1916, 162 Wis. 565, 156 N.W. 948.

55. McCann v. New York Stock Exchange, 2d Cir. 1940, 107 F.2d 908, certiorari denied 309 U.S. 649, 60 S.Ct. 807, 84 L.Ed. 1027, rehearing denied 309 U.S. 684, 60 S.Ct. 807, 84 L.Ed. 1027, rehearing denied 310 U.S. 656, 60 S.Ct. 974, 84 L.Ed. 1420 (driving unscrupulous person out of business as stockbroker); Byars v. Baptist Medical Centers, Inc., Ala.1978, 361 So.2d 350 (hospital's standards for referral to independent nurses); Chicago, Rock Island & Pacific Railroad v. Armstrong, 1911, 30 Okl. 134, 120 P. 952 (protection of public against bad hauling); Harris v. Thomas, Tex.Civ.App. 1920, 217 S.W. 1068 (medical association's standards).

Cf. National Association for the Advancement of Colored People v. Claiborne Hardware Co., Inc., 1982, 458 U.S. 886, 102 S.Ct. 3409, 73 L.Ed.2d 1215, (blacks' boycott of white businesses protected under First Amendment); New Negro Alliance v. Sanitary Grocery Co., 1938, 303 U.S. 552, 58 S.Ct. 703, 82 L.Ed. 1012 (blacks' boycott was a labor dispute protected under Norris-LaGuardia Act).

Contra: People v. Kopezak, 1934, 153 Misc. 187, 274 N.Y.S. 629, affirmed 1934, 266 N.Y. 565, 195 N.E. 202 (picketing in protest against fire-trap conditions); A. S. Beck Shoe Corp. v. Johnson, 1934, 153 Misc. 363, 274 N.Y.S. 946 (in protest against nonemployment of Negroes); National Association for Advancement of Colored People v. Webb's City, Fla.App.1963, 152 So.2d 179, judgment vacated on suggestion of mootness, 376 U.S. 190, 84 S.Ct. 635, 11 L.Ed.2d 602. These cases are probably now superseded by First Amendment decisions. See National Association for the Advancement of Colored People v. Claiborne Hardware Co., Inc., 1982, 458 U.S. 886, 102 S.Ct. 3409, 73 L.Ed.2d 1215.

56. Zoby v. American Fidelity Co., 4th Cir.1957, 242 F.2d 76; National Life & Accident Insurance Co. v. Wallace, 1933, 162 Okl. 174, 21 P.2d 492; Karges Furniture Co. v. Amalgamated Woodworkers' Local Union No. 131, 1905, 165 Ind. 421, 75 N.E. 877; Falloon v. Schilling, 1883, 29 Kan. 292; Passaic Print Works v. Ely & Walker Dry-Goods Co., 8th Cir.1900, 105 F. 163,

a bona fide lawsuit,[57] or to complain or petition to public authorities,[58] will also justify interference with relations which are merely prospective. The chief difference lies in the recognition of more extensive privileges where the claim is merely for the loss of prospective advantage rather than an actual interference with an existing contract. Since the privilege is not well defined, either in the case of interference with contract or the case of interference with other relationships, there has been concern that the law has not adequately described to the citizen what is forbidden.[59]

Under the rules adopted by the Second Restatement of Torts,[60] however, the prima facie tort analysis is discarded in favor of a rule that may put the burden on the plaintiff to prove his case rather than on the defendant to justify his actions. Thus under the Restatement rules, the plaintiff may be required to persuade the trier that defendant's interference is improper. Although this is a reversal of the traditional approach which held the defendant liable unless he could establish justification or privilege, there is obviously merit in requiring the plaintiff to make out a case and a number of decisions have followed this approach,[61] though a few have deliberately retained the older rule[62] which placed the burden squarely on the defendant's shoulders.

In addition to this, it must be said that although courts have traditionally felt free to consider the defendant's subjective motives or purposes and such states of mind as spite or ill-will, decisions of the Supreme Court in other communicative tort cases now raise potential Constitutional objections to this approach. It has been held, for example, that in at least some cases of defamation the defendant is not to be held liable unless he has published a falsehood and is negligent[63] or reckless[64] in failing to state the truth. In these cases malice in the sense of spite or ill-will is not a constitutionally acceptable basis

certiorari denied 181 U.S. 617, 21 S.Ct. 922, 45 L.Ed. 1029. See Note, 1966, 50 Minn.L.Rev. 570.

57. Oil Conservation Engineering Co. v. Brooks Engineering Co., 6th Cir.1931, 52 F.2d 783; Everybody's Tool & Die Works v. Costa, D.N.Y.1934, 9 F.Supp. 440; Virtue v. Creamery Package Manufacturing Co., 8th Cir.1910, 179 F. 115, affirmed 1913, 227 U.S. 8, 33 S.Ct. 202, 57 L.Ed. 393; cf. Flynn & Emrich Co. v. Federal Trade Commission, 4th Cir.1931, 52 F.2d 836; Dr. Herman Heuser v. Federal Trade Commission, 7th Cir. 1925, 4 F.2d 632. See Notes, 1932, 10 N.C.L.Rev. 300; 1935, 23 Geo.L.J. 881.

58. McKee v. Hughes, 1916, 133 Tenn. 455, 181 S.W. 930; Kelly v. Morris County Traction Co., 1924, 2 N.J.Misc.R. 802, 126 A. 24. Otherwise where the petition is in bad faith, and the motive is purely spiteful. Vanarsdale v. Laverty, 1871, 69 Pa. 103.

59. Dobbs, Tortious Interference with Contractual Relationships, 1980, 34 Ark.L.Rev. 335.

60. Second Restatement of Torts, § 766B and Introductory Note to Chapter 37.

61. Swager v. Couri, 1979, 77 Ill.2d 173, 32 Ill.Dec. 540, 395 N.E.2d 921 (failure to plead lack of justification, judgment for defendant); Top Service Body Shop, Inc. v. Allstate Insurance Co., 1978, 283 Or. 201, 582 P.2d 1365. A number of cases appear to place the burden on the plaintiff without discussing the point or without reference to the Restatement's formula. See Alvord and Swift v. Steward M. Muller Construction Co., 1978, 46 N.Y.2d 276, 413 N.Y.S.2d 309, 385 N.E.2d 1238. Adler Barish, Daniels, Levin & Creskoff v. Epstein, 1978, 482 Pa. 416, 393 A.2d 1175, appeal dismissed, certiorari denied 442 U.S. 907, 99 S.Ct. 2817, 61 L.Ed.2d 272; Lake Gateway Motor Inn v. Matt's Sunshine Gift Shops, Inc., Fla.App.1978, 361 So.2d 769.

62. Alyeska Pipeline Service Co. v. Aurora Air Service Inc., Alaska 1979, 604 P.2d 1090. Some cases have spoken in terms of a "privilege, with the implication that the burden is on the defendant, but these statements in recent years have been quite casual, as in Langeland v. Farmers State Bank of Trimont, Minn. 1982, 319 N.W.2d 26. The same court may define the plaintiff's burden to prove "interference" in such a way as to effectively place the entire burden on the plaintiff. See United Wild Rice, Inc. v. Nelson, Minn. 1982, 313 N.W.2d 628. Similarly see the original and supplemental opinions in Walt Bennett Ford v. Pulaski County Special School District, 1981, 274 Ark. 208, 624 S.W.2d 426.

63. Gertz v. Robert Welch, Inc., 1974, 418 U.S. 323, 94 S.Ct. 2997, 41 L.Ed.2d 789 (where plaintiff is not a public figure some degree of fault is required on the issue of falsity).

64. New York Times Co. v. Sullivan, 1964, 376 U.S. 254, 84 S.Ct. 710, 11 L.Ed.2d 686, motion denied 376 U.S. 967, 84 S.Ct. 1130, 12 L.Ed.2d 83 (intentional or reckless falsehood required where plaintiff is public official); Curtis Publishing Co. v. Butts, 1967, 388 U.S. 130, 87 S.Ct. 1975, 18 L.Ed.2d 1994, conformed to Associated Press v. Walker, 418 S.W.2d 379, rehearing denied 389 U.S. 889, 88 S.Ct. 11, 19 L.Ed.2d 197, error refused, certiorari denied 391 U.S. 966, 88 S.Ct. 2036, 20 L.Ed.2d 880 (same as to public figures).

for liability in the light of free speech interests.[65] Whether this reasoning will be carried over to protect honest though spiteful communications that interfere with business prospects remains to be seen, but it must be noted as at least a possibility.[66] This obviously has no application, however, to cases where the defendant's means of interference is not constitutionally protected communication, nor to those where the requirements of some independent tort are satisfied, as for example where the defendant physically drives away plaintiff's prospective customers.

Fair Competition

The policy of the common law has always been in favor of free competition,[67] and it goes almost without saying that it is not "improper" to engage in competition for prospective gain, so long as the means used are not in themselves improper.[68] The older habit was to express this by saying that competition was "privileged," so that the prima facie tort made out when the plaintiff showed interference with his prospects was rebutted by a showing of competition; but the result is the same and there is no liability whichever mode of expression is used. This rule does not protect interference with existing contracts or with property,[69] but where the plaintiff's contractual relations are merely contemplated or potential it is considered to be in the interest of the public that any competitor should be free to divert them to himself by all fair and reasonable means, if for no other reason than that any other rule would tend to establishment of trade monopolies. This has been established since an old case[70] in the year books in which it was held that the owner of an established school could not complain when a new school attracted his prospective pupils; and it was emphatically declared in the leading modern case of Mogul Steamship Co. v. McGregor, Gow & Co.,[71] involving competition between steamship companies for the same trade.

In short, it is no tort to beat a business rival to prospective customers. Thus, in the absence of prohibition by statute,[72] illegitimate means, or some other unlawful ele-

---

65. In New York Times Co. v. Sullivan, 1964, 376 U.S. 254, 84 S.Ct. 710, 11 L.Ed.2d 686, motion denied 376 U.S. 967, 84 S.Ct. 1130, 12 L.Ed.2d 83, "malice" was said necessary to support the action, but it was defined to mean knowing or reckless falsehood. It is now clear that malice in the sense of spite or ill-will is not sufficient in cases controlled by Times/Sullivan. E.g., Greenbelt Cooperative Publishing Association, Inc. v. Bresler, 1970, 398 U.S. 6, 90 S.Ct. 137, 26 L.Ed. 2d 6.

66. So far as defendant's speech is directed toward social or political ends, there is at least some constitutional protection, presumably to at least the same degree given defamatory speech. See National Association for the Advancement of Colored People v. Claiborne Hardware Co., Inc., 1982, 458 U.S. 886, 102 S.Ct. 3409, 73 L.Ed.2d 1215; Missouri v. National Organization for Women, Inc., 8th Cir.1980, 620 F.2d 1301, certiorari denied, 449 U.S. 842, 101 S.Ct. 122, 66 L.Ed. 2d 49; Taylor v. Nashville Banner Publishing Co., Tenn.App.1978, 573 S.W.2d 476, certiorari denied 441 U.S. 923, 99 S.Ct. 2032, 60 L.Ed.2d 396; Commercial speech is also entitled to First Amendment protection. Central Hudson Gas & Electric Corp. v. Public Service Commission, 1980, 447 U.S. 557, 100 S.Ct. 2343, 65 L.Ed.2d 341. Where the defendant interferes with the plaintiff's prospects through falsehood, the constitutional standards have been applied so that the plaintiff must show a knowing or reckless falsehood where the plaintiff is a public figure corporation, and presumably negligence in other cases. Bose Corp. v. Consumers Union of United States, Inc., D.Mass.1981, 508 F.Supp. 1249. This would seemingly force the same result if the plaintiff's statement is not false or is a statement of opinion.

67. See Jones, Historical Development of the Law of Business Competition, 1926, 35 Yale L.J. 905, 36 Yale L.J. 42, 207, 351; Wyman, Competition and the Law, 1902, 15 Harv.L.Rev. 427; Kennedy and Finkelman, The Right to Trade, 1933.

68. See Second Restatement of Torts, § 768.

69. See supra, § 129.

70. 1410, Y.B. 11 Hen. IV, F. 47, pl. 21.

71. 1889, 23 Q.B.D. 598, affirmed [1892] A.C. 25.

72. If a statute is interpreted as intended to protect the plaintiff against the competition, he will be entitled to maintain the action for its violation. Forst v. Corporation Commission of Oklahoma, 1929, 278 U.S. 515, 49 S.Ct. 235, 73 L.Ed. 483; National Bank of Detroit v. Wayne Oakland Bank, 6th Cir.1958, 252 F.2d 537; Commercial State Bank v. Gidney, D.D.C.1959, 174 F.Supp. 770, affirmed 108 U.S.App.D.C. 37, 278 F.2d 871; Burden v. Hoover, 1956, 9 Ill.2d 114, 137 N.E.2d 59; Hobson v. Kentucky Trust Co., 1946, 303 Ky. 493, 197 S.W.2d 454. But not if the statute is not so interpreted. Delaware Optometric Corp. v. Sherwood, 1957, 36 Del. 223, 128 A.2d 812; New Hampshire Board of Registration in Optometry v. Scott Jewelry Co., 1939,

ment, a defendant seeking to increase his own business may cut rates or prices,[73] allow discounts or rebates,[74] enter into secret negotiations behind the plaintiff's back,[75] refuse to deal with him [76] or threaten to discharge employees who do,[77] or even refuse to deal with third parties unless they cease dealing with the plaintiff,[78] all without incurring liability. And, since all the members of a group may be free to do what any one of them may do, the added fact that a number of defendants combine or agree to carry out such policies adds nothing in itself and will not necessarily result in liability under the common law of tort.[79] In such cases of group actions, however, the possibility of unprivileged coercion, intimidation, and especially monopolistic restraint of trade are vastly increased, and defendants may be held for concerted actions such as boycotts both under the common law [80] and under antitrust statutes,[81] which always must be consulted in disputes of this kind.

Unfair Competition

Unfair competition is now a generic name for a number of related torts involving improper interference with business prospects. The topic is now a field in itself, and the subject of many articles [82] and treatises [83] and so

90 N.H. 368, 9 A.2d 513; MacBeth v. Gerber's, Inc., 1946, 72 R.I. 102, 48 A.2d 366; Mosig v. Jersey Chiropodists, 1937, 122 N.J.Eq. 382, 194 A. 248.

73. Mogul S. S. Co. v. McGregor, Gow & Co., 1889, 23 Q.B.D. 598, affirmed [1892] A.C. 25; Package Closure Corp. v. Sealright Co., 2d Cir.1944, 141 F.2d 972; Passaic Print Works v. Ely & Walker Dry-Goods Co., 8th Cir.1900, 105 F. 163, certiorari denied 181 U.S. 617, 21 S.Ct. 922, 45 L.Ed.2d 1029; Katz v. Kapper, 1935, 7 Cal.App.2d 1, 44 P.2d 1060; cf. Fleetway, Inc. v. Public Service Interstate Transportation Co., 3d Cir.1934, 72 F.2d 761, certiorari denied 293 U.S. 626, 55 S.Ct. 347, 79 L.Ed. 713 (under Anti-Trust Act).

74. Mogul S. S. Co. v. McGregor, Gow & Co., 1889, 23 Q.B.D. 598, affirmed [1892] A.C. 25; Munhall v. Pennsylvania Railroad Co., 1879, 92 Pa. 150; Lough v. Outerbridge, 1893, 143 N.Y. 271, 38 N.E. 292 and 145 N.Y. 601, 40 N.E. 164.

75. Goldman v. Harford Road Building Association, 1926, 150 Md. 677, 133 A. 843; Debnam v. Simonson, 1914, 124 Md. 354, 92 A. 782; Hansberry v. Holloway, 1928, 332 Ill. 334, 163 N.E. 662; George F. Hewson Co. v. Hopper, 1943, 130 N.J.L. 525, 33 A.2d 889. Otherwise where fraudulent representations are made. Johnson v. Gustafson, 1938, 201 Minn. 629, 277 N.W. 252; Skene v. Carayanis, 1926, 103 Conn. 708, 131 A. 497. Cf. Krigbaum v. Sbarbaro, 1913, 23 Cal.App. 427, 138 P. 364 (intimidation and molestations); Louis Kamm, Inc. v. Flink, 1934, 113 N.J.L. 582, 175 A. 62 (collusion and disclosure of confidential information).

76. Great Atlantic & Pacific Tea Co. v. Cream of Wheat Co., 2d Cir.1915, 227 F. 46; United States v. Colgate & Co., 1919, 250 U.S. 300, 39 S.Ct. 465, 63 L.Ed. 992; Locker v. American Tobacco Co., 2d Cir.1914, 218 F. 447; Baran v. Goodyear Tire & Rubber Co., D.N.Y. 1919, 256 F. 571. See Brown, The Right to Refuse to Sell, 1916, 25 Yale L.J. 194.

77. Lewis v. Huie-Hodge Lumber Co., 1908, 121 La. 658, 46 So. 685; Robison v. Texas Pine Land Association, Tex.Civ.App.1897, 40 S.W. 843 (compelling employees to trade at defendant's store rather than plaintiff's); cf. Celli & Del Papa v. Galveston Brewing Co., Tex.Com.App.1921, 227 S.W. 941 (tenants).

78. Photographic Importing & Distributing Corp. v. Elgeet Optical Co., 1953, 282 App.Div. 223, 122 N.Y.S.2d 215, affirmed, 1953, 282 App.Div. 836, 124 N.Y.S.2d 341; Staroske v. Pulitzer Publishing Co., 1911 235 Mo. 67, 138 S.W. 36; Journal of Commerce Publishing Co. v. Tribune Co., 7th Cir.1922, 286 F. 111; Andrew Jergens Co. v. Woodbury, Inc., D.Del.1920, 271 F. 43; Dye v. Carmichael Produce Co., 1917, 64 Ind.App. 653, 116 N.E. 425.

79. Bohn Manufacturing Co. v. Hollis, 1893, 54 Minn. 223, 55 N.W. 1119; Macauley v. Tierney, 1895, 19 R.I. 255, 33 A. 1; John D. Park & Sons Co. v. National Wholesale Druggists' Association, 1903, 175 N.Y. 1, 67 N.E. 136; Montgomery Ward & Co. v. South Dakota Retail Merchants' & Hardware Dealers' Association, C.C.S.D.1907, 150 F. 413; Sorrell v. Smith, [1925] A.C. 700.

Thus a conspiracy may show that additional parties are liable, but unless some substantive civil wrong is shown, the conspiracy itself is not actionable. Okun v. Superior Court, 1981, 29 Cal.3d 442, 175 Cal.Rptr. 157, 629 P.2d 1369.

80. Jackson v. Stanfield, 1893, 137 Ind. 592, 36 N.E. 345, rehearing denied 137 Ind. 592, 37 N.E. 14. And see infra, p. 1023.

81. See L. Sullivan, 1977, The Law of Antitrust §§ 83–92.

82. See Handler, Unfair Competition, 1936, 21 Iowa L.Rev. 175; Wright, Tort Responsibility for Destruction of Goodwill, 1929, 14 Corn.L.Q. 298; McLaughlin, Legal Control of Competitive Methods, 1926, 21 Iowa L.Rev. 274; Fathchild, Statutory Unfair Competition, 1936, 1 Mo.L.Rev. 20; Callmann, What is Unfair Competition, 1940, 28 Geo.L.J. 585; Callmann, Copyright and Unfair Competition, 1940, 2 La.L.Rev. 648; Chafee, Unfair Competition, 1940, 53 Harv.L.Rev. 1289; Sadtler, Unfair Competition—Past and Present Trends, 1940, 16 Tenn.L.Rev. 400; Bunn, The National Law of Unfair Competition, 1949, 62 Harv.L.Rev. 987; Treece, Patent Police and Preemption: The Stiffel and Compco Cases, 1964, 32 U.Chi.L.Rev. 80; Derenberg, Product Simulation: A Right or a Wrong?, 1964, 64 Colum.L.

large and specialized that the American Law Institute has concluded that it is a separate field, to be excluded from the Restatement of Torts altogether.[84] Under these circumstances it should be obvious that only a sketch of the common law background can be provided, along with very rough indications of the modern statutory development. It has been a traditional view that if the defendant acts from sufficiently bad motive and to gratify some desire unrelated to competition, liability might be imposed for interference with the plaintiff's business prospects.[85] It has been so held where competition is merely "simulated" and is not bona fide competition at all, as where the defendant sets up a rival barber shop [86] or engages in predatory price cutting,[87] not to make profits for himself but to drive the plaintiff out of business. Though the cases do in fact emphasize bad motive of the defendant, it may be doubted whether bad motive alone would always be sufficient. The motive cases fall into rather limited patterns and often involve a secondary boycott,[88] which is usually considered an improper means in itself,[89] or anti-competitive acts that would tend in the long run to reduce competition,[90] and are thus objectionable on the same grounds that support antitrust laws. Even if bad motive alone is sufficient in some cases,[91] it is not likely to provide a universal basis of liability.

Quite apart from any improper motive, unfair competition, or for that matter other interferences with prospects, can be found when the defendant engages in any conduct that amounts to a recognized tort and when that tort deprives the plaintiff of customers or other prospects. Liability for such losses may be imposed for defamation,[92] disparagement,[93] intimidation or harassment of the plaintiff's customers [94] or employees,[95] obstruction of the means of access to his place

Rev. 1192; Developments in the Law—Competitive Torts, 1964, 77 Harv.L.Rev. 888.

83. R. Callmann, 3d ed. various dates, Unfair Competition, Trademarks and Monopolies; J. McCarthy, 1973, Trademarks and Unfair Competition.

84. Second Restatement of Torts, Introductory Note to Division Nine.

85. International & Great Northern Railroad Co. v. Greenwood, 1893, 2 Tex.Civ.App. 76, 21 S.W. 559; Wesley v. Native Lumber Co., 1910, 97 Miss. 814, 53 So. 346; Graham v. St. Charles Street Railroad Co., 1895, 47 La.Ann. 1656, 18 So. 707; Hanchett v. Chiatovich, 9th Cir.1900, 101 F. 742; Peek v. Northern Pacific Railway Co., 1915, 51 Mont. 295, 152 P. 421.

86. Tuttle v. Buck, 1909, 107 Minn. 145, 119 N.W. 946; Dunshee v. Standard Oil Co., 1911, 152 Iowa 618, 132 N.W. 371.

87. Boggs v. Duncan-Schell Furniture Co., 1913, 163 Iowa 106, 143 N.W. 482; Memphis Steam Laundry-Cleaners v. Lindsey, 1941, 192 Miss. 224, 5 So.2d 227. Cf. Thomsen v. Cayser, 1917, 243 U.S. 66, 37 S.Ct. 353, 61 L.Ed. 597 (under Anti-Trust Act).

It should be noted, however, that price discrimination is now extensively regulated by the federal Robinson-Patman Act, and by many state resale price maintenance statutes, which may afford a basis of tort liability. See for example Elizabeth Arden Sales Corp. v. Gus Blass Co., 8th Cir.1945, 150 F.2d 988; Calvert Distillers Corp. v. Nussbaum Liquor Store, 1938, 166 Misc. 342, 2 N.Y.S.2d 320; Burstein v. Charline's Cut Rate, 1940, 126 N.J.Eq. 560, 10 A.2d 646.

88. All of the cases cited in note 85 supra involve an employer-defendant who induces his employees not to deal with the plaintiff, an independent business person. In each case the employer threatened or impliedly threatened employees with discharge if they bought from the plaintiff with whom the employees had no dispute at all.

89. Thus the secondary boycott is expressly outlawed under the National Labor Management Relations Act in 29 U.S.C.A. §§ 154(b)(4) and 187. Even laudable objectives will not justify such a boycott. AFL-CIO v. Allied International, Inc., 1982, 456 U.S. 212, 102 S.Ct. 1656, 72 L.Ed.2d 21.

90. As where the effort is to drive the plaintiff out of business. See Tuttle v. Buck, 1909, 107 Minn. 145, 119 N.W. 946 (competition for spite to drive plaintiff out); Memphis Steam Laundry-Cleaners v. Lindsey, 1941, 192 Miss. 224, 5 So.2d 227 (price cutting to drive plaintiff out).

91. See p. 1009 supra.

92. Standard Oil Co. v. Doyle, 1904, 118 Ky. 662, 82 S.W. 271; Van Horn v. Van Horn, 1890, 52 N.J.L. 284, 20 A. 485; Landon v. Watkins, 1895, 61 Minn. 137, 63 N.W. 615; Kendall v. Lively, 1934, 94 Colo. 483, 31 P.2d 343. As to the relation between unfair competition, defamation and disparagement, see Green, Relational Interests, 1935, 30 Ill.L.Rev. 1; Nims, Unfair Competition by False Statements or Disparagement, 1933, 19 Corn.L.Q. 63; Note, 1933, 33 Colum.L.Rev. 90.

93. See supra, § 128.

94. Tarleton v. McGawley, 1793, Peake N.P. 270, 170 Eng.Rep. 153; Standard Oil Co. v. Doyle, 1904, 118 Ky. 662, 82 S.W. 271; Sparks v. McCrary, 1908, 156 Ala. 382, 47 So. 332; Evenson v. Spaulding, 9th Cir. 1907, 150 F. 517.

of business,[96] threats of groundless suits,[97] commercial bribery [98] and inducing employees to commit sabotage.[99]

Finally it may be said that certain unfair competition torts appear to involve less a question of tortious activity than a question of property to be protected. Intangible interests, such as those involved in patents, copyrights, trade marks and trade secrets, are often treated as property and given protection even from innocent and unknowing infringement by others.[1] In other words, there are cases in which neither fraudulent intent, bad motive, nor improper means are required to establish liability.

Unfair competition thus does not describe a single course of conduct or a tort with a specific number of elements; it instead describes a general category into which a number of new torts may be placed when recognized by the courts. The category is open-ended, and nameless forms of unfair competition may be recognized at any time for the protection of commercial values.[2] Exploration of these would require a separate treatise, but there are, in addition, a group of well-recognized torts, or fact-patterns in unfair competition, which can be discussed here.

Passing off, trademarks and product simulation. Apart from product disparagement [3] and other forms of interference with advantageous relations, the central tort in unfair competition at common law is known as "palming off," or "passing off." It consists in a false representation tending to induce buyers to believe that the defendant's product is that of the plaintiff, usually but not always because the plaintiff's product is better known or has a better reputation.[4] In other words, the defendant is passing his product off as that of the plaintiff's.[5] This may be accomplished directly, as where a retailer fills orders for Brand X by supplying Brand Y,[6] but it is very commonly done by imitating the plaintiff's trade marks,[7] or

---

95. Evenson v. Spaulding, 9th Cir.1907, 150 F. 517; Standard Oil Co. v. Doyle, 1904, 118 Ky. 662, 82 S.W. 271.

96. Shamhart v. Morrison Cafeteria Co., 1947, 159 Fla. 629, 32 So.2d 727, 2 A.L.R.2d 429; cf. Gilly v. Hirsh, 1909, 122 La. 966, 48 So. 422; Brown-Brand Realty Co. v. Saks & Co., 1926, 126 Misc. 336, 214 N.Y.S. 230, affirmed 218 App.Div. 827, 218 N.Y.S. 706.

97. E.g., Sun-Maid Raisin Growers of California v. Avis, D.Ill.1928, 25 F.2d 303; American Mercury v. Chase, D.Mass.1926, 13 F.2d 224.

98. Rangen, Inc. v. Sterling Nelson & Sons, Inc., 9th Cir.1965, 351 F.2d 851, certiorari denied 383 U.S. 936, 86 S.Ct. 1067, 15 L.Ed.2d 853; D. Dobbs, Remedies, §§ 10.4, 10.5. Cf. Sears, Roebuck & Co. v. American Plumbing & Supply Co., D.Wis.1956, 19 F.R.D. 334; Continental Management, Inc. v. United States, 1975, 208 Ct.Cl. 501, 527 F.2d 613.

99. Cf. King v. Cope, 1719, 1 Stra. 144, 93 Eng.Rep. 438.

1. See J. McCarthy, Trademarks and Unfair Competition § 25.1 (1973).

2. E.g., Clairol, Inc. v. Boston Discount Center of Berkley, Inc., 6th Cir.1979, 608 F.2d 1114 (distributor's sales of professional-use hair dye to home-use market is unfair competition).

3. See § 128 supra.

4. Several courts have now approved the "reverse confusion" claim in which the manufacturer of a little known product is allowed to recover from the manufacturer of a well known product on the ground that the more famous manufacturer has imitated the less famous, and on the further ground that this has somehow caused a loss. Big O Tire Dealers, Inc. v. Goodyear Tire & Rubber Co., 10th Cir.1977, 561 F.2d 1365, certiorari denied 434 U.S. 1052, 98 S.Ct. 905, 54 L.Ed.2d 805; Capital Films Corp. v. Charles Fries Productions, 5th Cir.1980, 628 F.2d 387.

5. See for example Dixi-Cola Laboratories v. Coca-Cola Co., 4th Cir.1941, 117 F.2d 352, certiorari denied 314 U.S. 629, 62 S.Ct. 60, 86 L.Ed. 505; Timken Roller Bearing Co. v. Leterstone Sales Co., N.D.Ill.1939, 27 F.Supp. 736; Standard Brands v. Smidler, 2d Cir.1945, 151 F.2d 34; American Distilling Co. v. Bellows & Co., 1951, 102 Cal.App.2d 8, 226 P.2d 751; Smith v. Dental Products Co., 7th Cir.1944, 140 F.2d 140, certiorari denied 322 U.S. 743, 64 S.Ct. 1146, 88 L.Ed. 1576.

Cf. Gold v. Los Angeles Democratic League, 1975, 49 Cal.App.3d 365, 122 Cal.Rptr. 732 (candidate of one party allegedly passed off as candidate of other).

Liability may be imposed for intentionally inducing another to mislabel or misrepresent the goods. See Inwood Laboratories v. Ives Laboratories, Inc., 1982, 456 U.S. 844, 102 S.Ct. 2182, 72 L.Ed.2d 606. As to the intent required see Germain, The Supreme Court's Opinion in the Inwood Case: Declination of Duty, 1982, 70 Ky.L.J. 731.

6. Pic Design Corp. v. Bearings Specialty Co., 1st Cir.1971, 436 F.2d 804; Developments in the Law—Competitive Torts, 1964, 77 Harv.L.Rev. 888, 907.

7. Coca-Cola Co. v. Chero-Cola Co., 1921, 51 App. D.C. 27, 273 F. 755; Walter M. Steppacher & Brother v. Karr, D.Pa.1916, 236 F. 151; Vogue Co. v. Thomp-

names,[8] wrappers, labels or containers,[9] or his vehicles,[10] employee uniforms[11] or the appearance of his place of business.[12] The same thing may be accomplished by using the plaintiff's name with literal accuracy in connection with the defendant's product but in a way that nevertheless suggests that the product is the plaintiff's or that he had a role in it.[13] The test laid down in such cases has been whether the resemblance is so great as to deceive the ordinary customer acting with the caution usually exercised in such transactions, so that he may mistake one for the other.[14] The older rule was that there must be proof of a fraudulent intent, or conscious deception, before there could be any liability, and this is still occasionally repeated;[15] but the whole trend of the later cases is to hold that it is enough that the defendant's conduct results in a false representation which is likely to cause confusion or deception, even though he has no such intention.[16] This shift in emphasis from wrongdoing to something like a property right in trade symbols of all kinds reflects in fact the general adoption of a common law of trademark protection.

Since customer confusion,[17] or its likelihood, has become the basis for liability, there is no liability at all merely for copying a name or feature of the plaintiff's product if no one is misled about the connection between the product and its source. Thus defendant's adoption of a personal name or one that is merely descriptive of the product is not tortious even if the plaintiff has used

---

son-Hudson Co., 6th Cir.1924, 300 F. 509, rehearing denied Vogue Co. v. Vogue Hat Co., 12 F.2d 991 and certiorari denied Thompson v. Vogue Co., 273 U.S. 706, 47 S.Ct. 98, 71 L.Ed. 850; Manitowoc Malting Co. v. Milwaukee Malting Co., 1903, 119 Wis. 543, 97 N.W. 389; Triangle Publications, Inc. v. Rohrlich, 2d Cir.1948, 167 F.2d 969. See Nims, The Law of Unfair Competition and Trade Marks, 4th Ed. 1947; Derenberg, Trade-Mark Protection and Unfair Trading, 1936; Callman, The Law of Unfair Competition and Trade Marks, 2d Ed. 1950; Handler and Pickett, Trade-Marks, 2d Ed. 1950; Handler and Pickett, Trade-Marks and Trade Names—An Analysis and Synthesis, 1930, 30 Colum.L. Rev. 168, 759; Note, 1955, 68 Harv.L.Rev. 814.

8. Sartor v. Schaden, 1904, 125 Iowa 696, 101 N.W. 511; Reddaway v. Banham, [1896] A.C. 199; J. A. Scriven Co. v. Girard Co., 2d Cir.1906, 148 F. 1019; Barton v. Rex-Oil Co., 3d Cir.1924, 2 F.2d 402, modified in 29 F.2d 474; Standard Paint Co. v. Rubberoid Roofing Co., 7th Cir.1915, 224 F. 695; Mayo Clinic v. Mayo's Drug & Cosmetic, Inc., 1962, 262 Minn. 101, 113 N.W.2d 852.

9. Lever Brothers v. Jay's Chemical Corp., E.D. N.Y.1934, 6 F.Supp. 933; New England Awl & Needle Co. v. Marlboro Awl & Needle Co., 1897, 168 Mass. 154, 46 N.E. 386; Charles E. Hires Co. v. Consumers' Co., 7th Cir.1900, 100 F. 809; L. P. Larson, Jr. Co. v. Lamont, Croliss & Co., 7th Cir.1918, 257 F. 270, certiorari denied 249 U.S. 603, 39 S.Ct. 260, 63 L.Ed. 797; American Chicle Co. v. Topps Chewing Gum, Inc., 2d Cir. 1953, 208 F.2d 560.

10. Mundon v. Taxicab Co., 1926, 151 Md. 449, 135 A. 177; Yellow Cab Co. v. Becker, 1920, 145 Minn. 152, 176 N.W. 345; Seattle Taxicab Co. v. De Jarlais, 1925, 135 Wash. 60, 236 P. 785; Yellow Cab Co. of Rhode Island v. Anastasi, 1924, 46 R.I. 49, 124 A. 735.

11. Dallas Cowboys Cheerleaders, Inc. v. Pussycat Cinema, Limited, 2d Cir.1979, 604 F.2d 200; Marsh v. Billings, 1851, 61 Mass. (7 Cush.) 322.

12. Weinstock, Lubin & Co. v. Marks, 1895, 109 Cal. 529, 42 P. 142; Charles S. Cash v. Steinbook, 1927, 220 App.Div. 569, 222 N.Y.S. 61, affirmed 1928, 247 N.Y. 531, 161 N.E. 170.

13. See Shaw v. Time-Life Records, 1975, 38 N.Y.2d 201, 379 N.Y.S.2d 390, 341 N.E.2d 817.

14. See J. McCarthy, Trademarks and Unfair Competition, 1973, § 25.1; Nims, Law of Unfair Competition and Trade Marks, 4th ed. 1947.

15. See for example Fawcett Publications v. Bronze Publications, 5th Cir.1949, 173 F.2d 778, rehearing denied 174 F.2d 646, certiorari denied 338 U.S. 869, 70 S.Ct. 144, 94 L.Ed. 533; Anheuser-Busch, Inc. v. Du Bois Brewing Co., 3d Cir.1949, 175 F.2d 370, certiorari denied 339 U.S. 934, 70 S.Ct. 664, 94 L.Ed. 1354, rehearing denied 339 U.S. 959, 70 S.Ct. 977, 94 L.Ed. 1369.

16. Fry v. Layne-Western Co., 8th Cir.1960, 282 F.2d 97; Lane Bryant, Inc. v. Maternity Lane, Limited of Calif., 9th Cir.1949, 173 F.2d 559; Elastic Stop Nut Corp. of America v. Greer, N.D.Ill.1945, 62 F.Supp. 363; Telechron, Inc. v. Telicon Corp., 3d Cir.1952, 198 F.2d 903; Howard's Clothes, Inc. v. Howard's Clothes Corp., 1952, 236 Minn. 291, 52 N.W.2d 753; David B. Findlay, Inc. v. Findlay, 1966, 18 N.Y.2d 12, 271 N.Y.S.2d 652, 218 N.E.2d 531. Intent to copy or mislead the public may furnish evidence that the public was in fact misled, or likely to be misled. See, e.g., Clairol, Inc. v. Andrea Dumon, Inc., 1973, 14 Ill.App.3d 641, 303 N.E.2d 177, 86 A.L.R.3d 493.

17. "Reverse confusion," in which customers believe plaintiff's relatively unknown goods are in fact the products of the relatively well-known defendant, has been said to be sufficient. Big O Tire Dealers v. Goodyear Tire & Rubber Co., 10th Cir.1977, 561 F.2d 1365, certiorari denied 434 U.S. 1052, 98 S.Ct. 905, 54 L.Ed.2d 805.

the name first.[18] The same is true where the defendant adopts a geographical designation of its location.[19] Where, however, a particular name or design becomes associated in the public mind primarily with the plaintiff's product or business, it is said that a secondary meaning attaches to that name and identifies as the plaintiff's all products or businesses so named or designated.[20] When this is the case, defendant's use of plaintiff's identifying name, mark or design is similar to a passing off and is actionable in the absence of clarifying identification, even though the name was originally only descriptive. This is true even when the defendant uses his own name, once it is shown that the name has become identified exclusively with the plaintiff's product[21] or service.[22] In contrast, the name or mark that is purely fanciful or arbitrary and is neither descriptive nor suggestive, is given immediate[23] and wide[24] protection even without any secondary meaning, either on the presumption that confusion will be likely[25] or because a mark is treated more or less like property.[26] Either kind of mark may lose its protection, however, if it becomes "generic," and loses its association in the public mind with the plaintiff's business or product and becomes instead a designation for all similar products, as in the case of "cola" in many soft drinks.[27]

When a name or mark is protectible, others may be prohibited from using it even where they are not in fact in competition with the plaintiff and could not draw off his customers, provided there is room for customer misunderstanding that the plaintiff "sponsors" or is otherwise affiliated with the defendant who uses his mark.[28] And, beyond this, some states have passed "anti-dilution" statutes in the belief that a non-competitor's use of a mark at least has the ill effect of weakening its capacity to identify the plaintiff.[29]

18. See Restatement of Torts, 1939, §§ 720–723.

19. Wyoming National Bank v. Security Bank & Trust Co., Wyo.1977, 572 P.2d 1120.

20. E.g., President, Etc. of Colby College v. Colby College-New Hampshire, 1st Cir.1975, 508 F.2d 805; First Wisconsin National Bank of Milwaukee v. Wichman, 1978, 85 Wis.2d 54, 270 N.W.2d 168. See Stern and Hoffman, Public Injury and the Public Interest: Secondary Meaning in the Law of Unfair Competition, 1962, 110 U.Pa.L.Rev. 935; J. McCarthy, Trademarks and Unfair Competition, 1973, § 15.1 et seq.

In addition to a claim based on common law trade name infringement that may occur when a personal name is used by a commercial product and confusion results, there is a possible "privacy" theory based on commercial appropriation. See Hirsch v. S. C. Johnson & Son, Inc., 1979, 90 Wis.2d 379, 280 N.W.2d 129.

21. S. C. Johnson & Son, Inc. v. Johnson, 2d Cir. 1940, 116 F.2d 427; cf. David B. Findlay, Inc. v. Findlay, 1966, 18 N.Y.2d 12, 271 N.Y.S.2d 652, 218 N.E.2d 531, remittitur amended 18 N.Y.2d 676, 273 N.Y.S.2d 422, 219 N.E.2d 872, certiorari denied 385 U.S. 930, 87 S.Ct. 289, 17 L.Ed.2d 212 (art gallery).

22. V. J. Doyle Plumbing Co. v. Doyle, App.1978, 120 Ariz. 130, 584 P.2d 594; Baker Realty Co. v. Baker, 1972, 228 Ga. 766, 187 S.E.2d 850; cf. David B. Findlay, Inc. v. Findlay, 1966, 18 N.Y.2d 12, 271 N.Y.S.2d 652, 218 N.E.2d 531.

23. Blisscraft of Hollywood v. United Plastics Co., 2d Cir.1961, 294 F.2d 694.

24. AMF, Inc. v. Sleekcraft Boats, 9th Cir.1979, 599 F.2d 341.

25. Blisscraft of Hollywood v. United Plastics Co., 2d Cir.1961, 294 F.2d 694, 700.

26. Cf. Stern and Hoffman, Public Injury and the Public Interest: Secondary Meaning in the Law of Unfair Competition, 1962, 110 U.Pa.L.Rev. 935.

27. Anti-Monopoly, Inc. v. General Mills Fun Group, Inc., 9th Cir.1982, 684 F.2d 1316 ("Monopoly" had become generic designation for game, not an identification of its producer); King-Seeley Thermos Co. v. Aladdin Industries, Inc., 2d Cir.1963, 321 F.2d 577 ("Thermos" had become generic); Selchow & Righter Co. v. McGraw-Hill Book Co., 2d Cir.1978, 580 F.2d 25 (injunction against publication of dictionary for word game since this might make trademarked name, "Scrabble," generic).

28. Dallas Cowboys Cheerleaders, Inc. v. Pussycat Cinema, Limited, 2d Cir.1979, 604 F.2d 200; Triangle Publications, Inc. v. Rohrlich, 2d Cir.1948, 167 F.2d 969; First Wisconsin National Bank of Milwaukee v. Wichman, 1978, 85 Wis.2d 54, 270 N.W.2d 168.

29. See Community Federal Savings & Loan Association v. Orondorff, 11th Cir.1982, 678 F.2d 1034 (Florida statute, based on Model State Trademark Act); Allied Maintenance Corp. v. Allied Mechanical Trades, Inc., 1977, 42 N.Y.2d 538, 399 N.Y.S.2d 628, 369 N.E.2d 1162. The mark must still be protectible because it is fanciful or has acquired a secondary meaning, and if it has not, the antidilution statute will not help. Giant Mart Corp. v. Giant Discount Foods, 1981, 247 Ga. 775, 279 S.E.2d 683. Some courts believe that protectible but "weak" marks are already diluted and must be entitled to protection under the confusion standard if any protection is to be given. Community Federal Savings

One form of passing off, known as product simulation, raises distinctive problems. A product's shape or design may form a part of its sales appeal; and if the design is distinctive it may also serve to identify the product as that of the plaintiff. In such cases a "slavish copy" of the product itself might amount to a passing off. Nevertheless, the common law rule was that such copying would be permitted as to any "functional" element in the product's design, provided only that reasonable labeling identified the manufacturer.[30] Non-functional elements, such as merely eye-pleasing designs, could not be copied if the effect, through secondary meaning attached to the design, would be to confuse potential customers about the product's source.[31] The Supreme Court, however, has held[32] that mere copying of a product that was not protected by patent or copyright laws, could not be actionable in itself. The decisions specifically left it open to the states, however, to prevent confusion by requirements of reasonable labeling or otherwise, so long as the copying itself was not prohibited. There are also holdings that these decisions at most preempt the field against state law and that they do not forbid protection under federal trademark laws.[33]

The common law tort of passing off is in effect the common law of trademark protection, and it has retained a good deal of its importance especially insofar as it covers conduct that does not actually infringe a trademark. As to trademarks themselves, however, most states now have registration statutes,[34] and the federal statute, known as the Lanham Act,[35] provides for registration of marks, for federal jurisdiction of marks so registered and for certain federal remedies. The result is that the common law tort most often appears pendent to a federal trademark claim and that the lawyer in such cases must consult the statutory as well as the common law.

False advertising. The competitor who falsely advertised his own goods, but who did not pass them off as those of the plaintiff, and who did not disparage the plaintiff's goods, might be liable to a buyer who was deceived by the false statements; but under the common law he was usually immune to

& Loan Association v. Orondorff, 11th Cir.1982, 678 F.2d 1034. But see Wedgwood Homes, Inc. v. Lund, 1983, 294 Or. 493, 659 P.2d 377 (local secondary meaning sufficient for antidilution protection). The lower court suggested that both plaintiff and defendant might be subject to a claim by a more famous user of "Wedgewood," raising the possibility of a long line of sub-diluters. See 58 Or.App. 240, 648 P.2d 393.

30. Restatement of Torts, § 742; West Point Manufacturing Co. v. Detroit Stamping Co., 6th Cir.1955, 222 F.2d 581, certiorari denied 350 U.S. 840, 76 S.Ct. 80, 100 L.Ed. 749; Rader v. Derby, 1950, 120 Ind.App. 202, 89 N.E.2d 724; Johnson Gas Appliance Co. v. Reliable Gas Products Co., 1943, 233 Iowa 641, 10 N.W.2d 23; Pagliero v. Wallace China Co., 9th Cir.1952, 198 F.2d 339; Sylvania Electric Products Co. v. Dura Electric Lamp Co., D.N.J.1956, 144 F.Supp. 112, affirmed 3d Cir.1957, 247 F.2d 730; Duo-Tint Bulb & Battery Co. v. Moline Supply Co., 1977, 46 Ill.App.3d 145, 4 Ill.Dec. 685, 360 N.E.2d 798. Cf. Dallas Cowboys Cheerleaders, Inc. v. Pussycat Cinema, Limited, 2d Cir.1979, 604 F.2d 200 (cheerleaders' uniform not wholly functional).

31. See Derenberg, Product Simulation: A Right or a Wrong?, 1964, 64 Colum.L.Rev. 1192, 1206.

32. Sears, Roebuck & Co. v. Stiffel Co., 1964, 376 U.S. 225, 84 S.Ct. 784, 11 L.Ed.2d 661, rehearing denied 376 U.S. 973, 84 S.Ct. 1131, 12 L.Ed.2d 87; Compco Corp. v. Day-Brite Lighting, Inc., 1964, 376 U.S. 234, 84 S.Ct. 779, 11 L.Ed.2d 669, rehearing denied 377 U.S. 913, 84 S.Ct. 1162, 12 L.Ed.2d 183. See notes, 1968, 2 U.S.F.L.Rev. 292; 1967, 53 Va.L.Rev. 356; 1965, 40 N.Y.U.L.Rev. 101.

33. Ives Laboratories, Inc. v. Darby Drug Co., Inc., 2d Cir.1979, 601 F.2d 631, on remand 488 F.Supp. 394 reversed 638 F.2d 538, reversed on other grounds 456 U.S. 844, 102 S.Ct. 2182; 72 L.Ed.2d 606; Truck Equipment Service Co. v. Fruehauf Corp., 8th Cir.1976, 536 F.2d 1210, certiorari denied 429 U.S. 861, 97 S.Ct. 164, 50 L.Ed.2d 139. It has also been said that when a product design is non-functional and serves to identify the maker and has a secondary meaning, protection can be accorded. See Ideal Toy Corp. v. Plawner Toy Manufacturing Corp., 3d Cir.1982, 685 F.2d 78. This, however, may conflict with the Supreme Court's statements to the effect that the acts of copying and selling cannot be prohibited merely because the "design is 'nonfunctional'" or because it has a secondary meaning. Compco Corp. v. Day-Brite Lighting, Inc., 1964, 376 U.S. 234, 238, 84 S.Ct. 779, 782, 11 L.Ed.2d 669, rehearing denied 377 U.S. 913, 84 S.Ct. 1162, 12 L.Ed. 2d 183.

34. See J. McCarthy, Trademarks and Unfair Competition, 1973, § 22.1 et seq.

35. 15 U.S.C.A. § 1051 et seq.

the claims of competitors, since the competitors could seldom show any actual losses.[36] If the plaintiff competitor was the single source of the true goods that fit the defendant's false description in his advertising, however, he could recover because in such a case it would be provable that customers were diverted from the plaintiff and not from some other competitor.[37] Presumably the principle was sufficiently broad to permit a recovery in any case where proof was adequate to show actual loss, but if so there were few such cases.[38]

Although it has been argued that there is little or no need to give competitors a claim based on the defendant's false advertising, and that in fact to recognize such a claim will entail losses in efficiency and competition,[39] such claims stand today on a much better footing than under the common law rules, partly as a result of the Lanham Trademark Act of 1946, Section 43(a)[40] of which prohibits any false description or representation and also any false representation of origin. The language is so broad that it has brought within its scope much of the law of unfair competition, so that the state law of that subject is now substantially federalized.[41] Thus actions may be brought under the statute for acts amounting to an infringement of common law trademark or for passing off.[42] This, of course, is in addition to claims for a competitor's false advertising which does not amount to any passing off. As to these, claims are allowed not only where the defendant has misrepresented his own product, as by attributing to it qualities it does not in fact have,[43] but also where defendant uses the plaintiff's work product in his own advertisements, as by showing a photograph of the plaintiff's product instead of his own.[44] It is held, however, that Section 43(a) does not protect against mere disparagement of the plaintiff's product, as distinct from false or misleading representations about that of the defendant.[45] But even here there may be an action if by comparative advertising the defendant in effect falsely represents his own product by an untruthful comparison to the plaintiff's.[46] In addition, states have enacted a large number of statutes, mostly aimed at protecting the

---

36. American Washboard Co. v. Saginaw Manufacturing Co., 6th Cir.1900, 103 F. 281; Borden's Condensed Milk Co. v. Horlick's Malted Milk Co., E.D.Wis. 1913, 206 F. 949; California Apparel Creators v. Wieder of California, 2d Cir.1947, 162 F.2d 893; Hall v. Duart Sales Co., N.D.Ill.1939, 28 F.Supp. 838. See Handler, False and Misleading Advertising, 1929, 39 Yale L.J. 22; Callmann, False Advertising as a Competitive Tort, 1948, 48 Colum.L.Rev. 876; Note, 1951, 64 Harv.L.Rev. 1383.

37. Ely-Norris Safe Co. v. Mosler Safe Co., 2d Cir. 1925, 7 F.2d 603, reversed in Mosler Safe Co. v. Ely-Norris Safe Co., 1927, 273 U.S. 132, 47 S.Ct. 314, 71 L.Ed. 578; Motor Improvements, Inc. v. A. C. Spark Plug Co., 6th Cir.1935, 80 F.2d 385, certiorari denied 298 U.S. 671, 56 S.Ct. 939, 80 L.Ed. 1394; Grand Rapids Furniture Co. v. Grand Rapids Furniture Co., 7th Cir.1942, 127 F.2d 245.

38. See J. McCarthy, Trademarks and Unfair Competition, 1973, § 27.1 et seq.

39. Jordan and Rubin, An Economic Analysis of the Law of False Advertising, 1979, 8 J.Leg.Stud. 527.

40. 15 U.S.C.A. § 1125(a).

41. See Bunn, The National Law of Unfair Competition, 1949, 62 Harv.L.Rev. 987; Germain, Unfair Trade Practices Under Section 43(a) of the Lanham Act: You've Come a Long Way, Baby—Too Far, Maybe?, 1973, 49 Ind.L.J. 84; Lunsford, Protection from False and Misleading Advertising, 1976, 35 Fed.Bar J. 87; Comment, The Present Scope of Recovery for Unfair Competition Violations Under Section 43(a), 1978, 58 Neb.L.Rev. 159.

42. Beech-Nut, Inc. v. Warner-Lambert Co., 2d Cir. 1973, 480 F.2d 801; Markel v. Scovil Manufacturing Co., D.N.Y.1979, 471 F.Supp. 1244, affirmed 2d Cir., 610 F.2d 807. See Comment, The Present Scope of Recovery for Unfair Competition Violations Under Section 43(a), 1978, 58 Neb.L.Rev. 159.

43. American Brands, Inc. v. R. J. Reynolds Tobacco Corp., D.N.Y.1976, 413 F.Supp. 1352; Universal Athletic Sales Co. v. American Gym, Recreational & Athletic Equipment Corp., D.Pa.1975, 397 F.Supp. 1063, vacated on other grounds, 3d Cir., 546 F.2d 530, certiorari denied 430 U.S. 984, 97 S.Ct. 1681, 52 L.Ed.2d 378.

44. L'Aiglon Apparel, Inc. v. Lana Lobell, Inc., 3d Cir.1954, 214 F.2d 649; Truck Equip. Service Co. v. Fruehauf Corp., 8th Cir.1976, 536 F.2d 1210, certiorari denied 429 U.S. 861, 97 S.Ct. 164, 50 L.Ed.2d 139.

45. Fur Information & Fashion Council, Inc. v. E. F. Timme & Son, Inc., 2d Cir.1974, 501 F.2d 1048, certiorari denied 419 U.S. 1022, 95 S.Ct. 498, 42 L.Ed.2d 296; Bernard Food Industries, Inc. v. Dietene Co., 7th Cir. 1969, 415 F.2d 1279. Note, The Law of Comparative Advertising, 1976, 76 Colum.L.Rev. 80.

46. American Home Products Corp. v. Johnson & Johnson, 2d Cir.1978, 577 F.2d 160.

consumer but sometimes offering relief to the competitor who is victimized by false advertising or other unfair competition, and these statutes must obviously be consulted in particular cases.[47]

Misappropriation. One important question, which has been much considered but little resolved, is the extent to which one can claim and enforce a property right in intangible trade values or intellectual property apart from the protection afforded by copyright or patent statutes, or in other words whether it is tortious to copy or imitate ideas, designs, reports or products. In a pre-*Erie* decision decided as a matter of general law, the Supreme Court once held that one news agency could be prohibited from copying and sending to its subscribers the news reports of another agency, in spite of the fact that the reports were not copyrighted.[48] It was said that the defendant was "endeavoring to reap where it has not sown." Read broadly, the case, though technically no longer authoritative after the *Erie* decision, would support the idea that a plaintiff might have a protectible interest in almost any work product of his own and that a defendant would be liable for misappropriation of this work product, even where there was no passing off. There are indeed cases that have enforced such a principle in the case of news,[49] broadcast[50] or literary or musical piracy.[51] Still other decisions may have recognized property interests in the name and likeness of famous persons,[52] or in characterizations they have rendered in playing dramatic parts,[53] and in other uncopyrighted public performances, including a

---

47. State statutes vary. Some seem patterned in part on the Federal Trade Commission Act, 15 U.S.C.A. § 45(a), which provides for government but not private enforcement. See Alfred Dunhill Limited v. Interstate Cigar Co., 2d Cir.1974, 499 F.2d 232. Some states whose acts seem similar in this regard have permitted private actions, at least by consumers. See Sellinger v. Freeway Mobile Home Sales, Inc., 1974, 110 Ariz. 573, 521 P.2d 1119, 62 A.L.R.3d 161, Annot., 62 A.L.R.3d 169. Other state statutes may explicitly allow enforcement by "any person," including competitors. This is so with the Uniform Deceptive Trade Practices Act, 7A Uniform Laws Ann. 35. The remedy in this case, however, seems limited to injunction.

48. International News Service v. Associated Press, 1918, 248 U.S. 215, 39 S.Ct. 68, 63 L.Ed. 211, 2 A.L.R. 293.

49. Associated Press v. KVOS, Inc., 9th Cir.1935, 80 F.2d 575, certiorari granted 298 U.S. 650, 56 S.Ct. 938, 80 L.Ed. 1379; Pottstown Daily News Publishing Co. v. Pottstown Broadcasting Co., 1963, 411 Pa. 383, 192 A.2d 657; Veatch v. Wagner, 1953, 14 Alaska 183, 109 F.Supp. 537; Notes, 1935, 44 Yale L.J. 877; 1966, 35 Ford.L.Rev. 385.

50. Pittsburgh Athletic Club v. KQV Broadcasting Co., W.D.Pa.1938, 24 F.Supp. 490; Metropolitan Opera Association v. Wagner-Nichols Recorder Corp., 1950, 199 Misc. 786, 101 N.Y.S.2d 483, affirmed Sup.Ct.A.D., 107 N.Y.S.2d 795; Uproar Co. v. National Broadcasting Co., 1st Cir.1936, 81 F.2d 373, certiorari denied 298 U.S. 670, 56 S.Ct. 835, 80 L.Ed. 1393; Southwestern Broadcasting Co. v. Oil Center Broadcasting Co., Tex.Civ. App.1947, 210 S.W.2d 230, refused n.r.e.; See Nizer, Proprietary Interest in Radio Programs: Recent Developments, 1938, 38 Colum.L.Rev. 538; Solinger, Unauthorized Uses of Television Broadcasts, 1948, 48 Colum.L.Rev. 848; Notes, 1938, 48 Yale L.J. 288; 1954, 29 Notre Dame L. 456.

51. Waring v. WDAS Broadcasting Station, 1937, 327 Pa. 433, 194 A. 631; Waring v. Dunlea, E.D.N.C. 1939, 26 F.Supp. 338. But cf. RCA Manufacturing Co. v. Whiteman, 2d Cir.1940, 114 F.2d 86, certiorari denied 311 U.S. 712, 61 S.Ct. 393, 85 L.Ed. 463; Columbia Broadcasting System, Inc. v. Melody Record, Inc., 1975, 134 N.J.Super. 368, 341 A.2d 348 (record piracy, now covered by copyright statute).

52. Cf. Memphis Development Foundation v. Factors, Etc., Inc., 6th Cir.1980, 616 F.2d 956, certiorari denied 449 U.S. 953, 101 S.Ct. 358, 66 L.Ed.2d 217 (rights to exploit name and likeness of Elvis Presley not descendible and hence not protected from competing uses after his death); Factors, Etc., Inc. v. Pro Arts, Inc., 2d Cir.1981, 652 F.2d 278, certiorari denied 456 U.S. 927, 102 S.Ct. 1973, 72 L.Ed.2d 442 (similar).

53. See Lugosi v. Universal Pictures, 1979, 160 Cal. 3d 323, 160 Cal.Rptr. 323, 603 P.2d 425 (recognizing right but holding it did not pass by inheritance). Conceivably a performer's characterization in addition to name and costuming could come to be associated exclusively with that performance and could operate as a kind of trademark. This was rejected where there was no use of the performer's likeness or name in Booth v. Colgate-Palmolive Co., D.N.Y.1973, 362 F.Supp. 343. Cf. Annot., 23 A.L.R.2d 244. The descendibility of this right, and its exact scope are discussed in Groucho Marx Productions, Inc. v. Day and Night Co., Inc., 2d Cir.1982, 689 F.2d 317.

performance as a giant chicken [54] and a human cannonball.[55]

Against the protectionist view of the misappropriation doctrine, however, there has been a long common law commitment to competition and free use of ideas. Thus in the absence of fraud or abuse of confidence,[56] the defendant is free to use and develop not only abstract ideas of literature or philosophy, but also general ideas of practical value in business [57] or entertainment [58] or advertising,[59] in spite of the fact that the plaintiff may have originated them.[60]

The same rule has been applied to styles [61] and designs [62] as to which there is no copyright, passing off or deception. In line with this, the Supreme Court has also held that once a patent has expired, the idea which it embodies is in the public domain and may be used freely by all.[63] In addition, the Court has also held that the patent and copyright laws preempt the field so that at least some intellectual property which is not patented or copyrighted may be freely used by others where there is no passing off or consumer confusion, with the result that the defendant may copy and market the plaintiff's product design.[64] Where the product design itself is non-functional and has acquired secondary meaning, these decisions might be read to undermine state, if not federal,[65] trademark law, and certainly they would seem on their face to preclude any general application of the misappropriation doctrine. But the Supreme Court has permitted states to regulate piracy of uncopyrighted recording [66] and to impose liability for a television news re-

---

54. KGB, Inc. v. Giannoulas, 1980, 104 Cal.App.3d 844, 164 Cal.Rptr. 571 (owner of the service mark represented by chicken suit did not own the "act" of the person dressed in that suit).

55. Zacchini v. Scripps-Howard Broadcasting Co., 1977, 433 U.S. 562, 97 S.Ct. 2849, 53 L.Ed.2d 965, on remand 54 Ohio St.2d 286, 376 N.E.2d 582 (circus act of human cannonball shown on TV news).

56. See Dior v. Milton, 1956, 9 Misc.2d 425, 155 N.Y.S.2d 443, affirmed 2 A.D.2d 878, 156 N.Y.S.2d 996 ("In violation of the conditions for entry to the displays * * * and in violation of the agreements, the defendants copied and reproduced surreptitiously, designs and models of plaintiffs. * * *").

57. Lueddecke v. Chevrolet Motor Co., 8th Cir.1934, 70 F.2d 345; Alberts v. Remington Rand, 1940, 175 Misc. 486, 23 N.Y.S.2d 892.

58. Grombach Productions v. Waring, 1944, 293 N.Y. 609, 59 N.E.2d 425, motion denied 294 N.Y. 697, 60 N.E.2d 846.

59. Affiliated Enterprises v. Gruber, 1st Cir.1936, 86 F.2d 958; Westminster Laundry Co. v. Hesse Envelope Co., 1913, 174 Mo.App. 238, 156 S.W. 767; cf. Armstrong Seatag Corp. v. Smith's Island Oyster Co., 4th Cir.1918, 254 F. 821. See Note, 1932, 45 Harv.L.Rev. 542.

60. See Logan, Legal Protection of Ideas, 1939, 4 Mo.L.Rev. 239; Callman, He Who Reaps Where He Has Not Sown, 1942, 55 Harv.L.Rev. 595; Havighurst, The Right to Compensation for an Idea, 1954, 49 N.W. U.L.Rev. 295, Callman, Competition in Ideas and Titles, 1954, 42 Cal.L.Rev. 77; Yankwich, Recent Developments in the Law of Creation, Expression and Communication of Ideas, 1953, 48 Nw.U.L.Rev. 543; Notes, 1946, 31 Corn.L.Q. 382; 1934, 47 Harv.L.Rev. 1419.

61. Montegut v. Hickson, 1917, 178 App.Div. 94, 164 N.Y.S. 858. But cf. Margolis v. National Bellas Hess Co., 1931, 139 Misc. 738, 249 N.Y.S. 175.

62. Cheney Brothers v. Doris Silk Corp., 2d Cir. 1929, 35 F.2d 279, certiorari denied 281 U.S. 728, 50 S.Ct. 245, 74 L.Ed. 1145; Richard J. Cole v. Manhattan Modes Co., Sup.Ct.1956, 159 N.Y.S.2d 709, affirmed 2 A.D.2d 593, 157 N.Y.S.2d 259; Samuel Winston, Inc. v. Charles James Services, Inc., Sup.Ct.1956, 159 N.Y.S.2d 716. See Weikart, Design Piracy, 1944, 19 Ind.L.J. 235; Chafee, Unfair Competition, 1940, 53 Harv.L.Rev. 1289; Wolff, Is Design Piracy Unfair Competition, 1941, 23 J.Pat.Off.Soc. 431; Callman, Style and Design Piracy, 1940, 22 J.Pat.Off.Soc. 557.

63. Kellogg Co. v. National Biscuit Co., 1938, 305 U.S. 111, 59 S.Ct. 109, 83 L.Ed. 73, rehearing denied 305 U.S. 674, 59 S.Ct. 246, 83 L.Ed. 437.

64. Sears, Roebuck & Co. v. Stiffel Co., 1964, 376 U.S. 225, 84 S.Ct. 784, 11 L.Ed.2d 661, rehearing denied 376 U.S. 973, 84 S.Ct. 1131, 12 L.Ed.2d 87; Compco Corp. v. Day-Brite Lighting, Inc., 1964, 376 U.S. 234, 84 S.Ct. 779, 11 L.Ed.2d 669, rehearing denied 377 U.S. 913, 84 S.Ct. 1162, 12 L.Ed.2d 183. See Treece, Patent Policy and Preemption: The Stiffel and Compco Cases, 1964, 32 U.Chi.L.Rev. 80; Derenberg, Product Simulation: A Right or a Wrong?, 1964, 64 Colum.L.Rev. 1192 for divergent views.

65. The argument is that federal preemption of state law is not federal preemption of federal law. See Ives Laboratories, Inc. v. Darby Drug Co., Inc., 2d Cir. 1979, 601 F.2d 631 on remand 488 F.Supp 394, reversed 638 F.2d 538, reversed on other grounds 456 U.S. 844, 102 S.Ct. 2182, 72 L.Ed.2d 606. Truck Equipment Service Co. v. Fruehauf Corp., 8th Cir.1976, 536 F.2d 1210, certiorari denied 429 U.S. 861, 97 S.Ct. 164, 50 L.Ed.2d 139.

66. Goldstein v. California, 1973, 412 U.S. 546, 93 S.Ct. 2303, 37 L.Ed.2d 163.

port of an entire performance at a circus.[67] Under these circumstances it can only be said that the misappropriation doctrine is still alive, if not healthy, and the courts continue to find ways to use it to create legal rights in intellectual efforts.[68]

Trade secrets. A breach of confidence committed or induced in obtaining or using a trade secret has been a frequent ground for relief.[69] The trade secret itself is sometimes regarded as a kind of property,[70] but if it is property it stands on a rather different footing from the commercial intangibles involved in the misappropriation doctrine. In the first place, the trade secret is not in the public domain unless it has been placed there by the defendant's tort;[71] and in the second, the secret is not obtained merely by copying a product available to the public but by breach of confidence[72] or contract[73] or even by industrial espionage[74] or other improper means. The emphasis is thus on improper behavior of the defendant.[75] Partly for this reason federal limitations that may be applied to the misappropriation doctrine[76] have no application in the case of trade secrets, which may be protected by the states against abuse of confidence and other misconduct.[77]

In addition to the requirement of secrecy and improper use, the information itself must be of the kind that qualifies for protection. Many kinds of business knowledge will qualify if the knowledge deals with ongoing operations of the business. This has included formulas, patterns, and even compilations of information.[78] Computer programs are obvious candidates for trade secret protection, and their chief means of protection has in fact been through trade secret law,[79] largely because of the Supreme Court's holdings that neither such programs

---

67. Zacchini v. Scripps-Howard Broadcasting Co., 1977, 433 U.S. 562, 97 S.Ct. 2849, 53 L.Ed.2d 965, on remand 54 Ohio St.2d 286, 376 N.E.2d 582.

68. E.g., Standard & Poor's Corp., Inc. v. Commodity Exchange, Inc., 2d Cir.1982, 683 F.2d 704 (defendant preliminarily enjoined from using plaintiff's calculations or "stock index" in computations in its own trading). Cf. Roy Export Co. Establishment of Vaduz, Liechtenstein v. Columbia Broadcasting System, Inc., 2d Cir.1982, 672 F.2d 1095 (common law copyright attached before 1978 copyright revision statute, no preemption).

69. Riess v. Sanford, 1941, 47 Cal.App.2d 244, 117 P.2d 694; Vulcan Detinning Co. v. American Can Co., 1907, 72 N.J.Eq. 387, 67 A. 339; Stone v. Goss, 1903, 65 N.J.Eq. 756, 55 A. 736; Aronson v. Orlov, 1917, 228 Mass. 1, 116 N.E. 951, certiorari denied 245 U.S. 662, 38 S.Ct. 61, 62 L.Ed. 536; Macbeth-Evans Glass Co. v. Schnelbach, 1913, 239 Pa. 76, 86 A. 688. See Whitlock, The Law as to Trade Secrets, 1912, 74 Cent.L.J. 83; McClain, Injunctive Relief Against Employees Using Confidential Information, 1935, 23 Ky.L.J. 248; Notes, 1919, 19 Col.L.Rev. 233; 1923, 23 Colum.L.Rev. 164; 1928, 42 Harv.L.Rev. 254; 1928, 6 Tex.L.Rev. 502; 1928, 37 Yale L.J. 1154; 1930, 14 Minn.L.Rev. 546.

70. See Milgrim, Trade Secrets § 1.01. Cf. E. I. Du Pont de Nemours Powder Co. v. Masland, 1917, 244 U.S. 100, 37 S.Ct. 575, 61 L.Ed. 1016: "The word 'property' as applied to trademarks and trade secrets is an unanalyzed expression of certain secondary consequences of the primary fact that the law makes some rudimentary requirements of good faith."

71. The secrecy requirement is not met if the information in question is public knowledge. Restatement of Torts, 1939, § 757, Comment *b*.

72. Julius Hyman & Co. v. Velsicol Corp., 1951, 123 Colo. 563, 233 P.2d 977, certiorari denied 342 U.S. 870, 72 S.Ct. 113, 96 L.Ed. 654, rehearing denied 342 U.S. 895, 72 S.Ct. 199, 96 L.Ed. 671 (former employees competing after having obtained trade secret in employment); Heyman v. Ar. Winarick, Inc., 2d Cir.1963, 325 F.2d 584, 9 A.L.R.3d 652 (disclosure alleged in negotiations for sale would be protected, but no disclosure found here).

73. Lear Siegler, Inc. v. Ark-Ell Springs, Inc., 5th Cir.1978, 569 F.2d 286 (permitting a contract to protect not necessarily qualifying as trade secret).

74. E. I. duPont DeNemours & Co. v. Christopher, 5th Cir.1970, 431 F.2d 1012, certiorari denied 400 U.S. 1024, 91 S.Ct. 581, 27 L.Ed.2d 637 rehearing denied 401 U.S. 967, 91 S.Ct. 968, 28 L.Ed.2d 250 (aerial photographs); Cf. USM Corp. v. Marson Fastener Corp., 1979, 379 Mass. 90, 393 N.E.2d 895.

75. Developments in the Law—Competitive Torts, 1964, 77 Harv.L.Rev. 888, 949.

76. Supra, p. 1020.

77. Kewanee Oil Co. v. Bicron Corp., 1974, 416 U.S. 470, 94 S.Ct. 1879, 40 L.Ed.2d 315.

78. Restatement of Torts, 1939, § 757, Comment *b*.

79. Bender, Trade Secret Protection of Software, 1970, 38 Geo.Wash.L.Rev. 909; Gemignani, Legal Protection for Computer Software: The View from '79, 1980, 7 J.Comp., Tech. & L. 269. See Amoco Production Co. v. Lindley, 1980, 609 P.2d 733.

Computer programs were protected on a theory of trover and conversion in National Surety Corp. v. Applied Systems, Inc., Ala.1982, 418 So.2d 847 on proof that probably would equally have justified a trade secret theory.

nor mathematical formulae could be patented.[80] The Supreme Court has now appeared to recognize the possibility of patenting a computer program where it is a part of a larger process which taken as a whole may be patented,[81] but it is far from clear that the law of trade secrets has lost any importance in protecting these expensive works.[82] Not every piece of useful information, experience or skill that an employee might acquire in his job will qualify,[83] nor will every agglomeration of experience that amounts to "know-how." There must at least be sufficient novelty that the process would not be obvious to one knowledgeable in the art.[84] The trade secret need not be patentable,[85] and of course cannot be patented without the loss of essential secrecy,[86] but at least some novelty is required by some courts, and on this basis customer lists are sometimes excluded from protection.[87] As all this indicates, misuse of trade secrets is a form of unfair competition that is a field in itself, with a literature of its own that must be consulted.[88]

Boycott. A distinct basis for restricting the privilege of competition lies in the policy of the common law against monopoly and undue restraint of trade. In this field, the law has been concerned with the preservation of competition rather than the regulation of it. There is a long history of combinations, contracts and practices in restraint of trade discountenanced by the law, which lies outside of the scope of this book. One practice which must be mentioned, however, is the boycott. This immortalizes the name of a pariah English land agent in Ireland whose neighbors would have nothing to do with him.[89]

---

80. Gottschalk v. Benson, 1973, 409 U.S. 63, 93 S.Ct. 253, 34 L.Ed.2d 273; Parker v. Flook, 1978, 437 U.S. 584, 98 S.Ct. 2522, 57 L.Ed.2d 451.

81. Diamond v. Diehr, 1981, 450 U.S. 175, 101 S.Ct. 1048, 67 L.Ed.2d 153.

82. Some commentators have been optimistic that computer software can now be patented. Nimtz, Diamond v. Diehr: A Turning Point, 1981, Rut.Comp. & Tech.L.J. 267. Others have been much more pessimistic. See 1981, 50 U.Cin.L.Rev. 645.

83. Hahn & Clay v. A. O. Smith Corp., 5th Cir.1963, 320 F.2d 166, certiorari denied 375 U.S. 944, 84 S.Ct. 351, 11 L.Ed.2d 274; Official Aviation Guide Co. v. American Aviation Associates, Inc., 7th Cir.1945, 150 F.2d 173, certiorari denied 326 U.S. 776, 66 S.Ct. 267, 90 L.Ed. 469, rehearing denied 326 U.S. 811, 66 S.Ct. 335, 90 L.Ed. 495, certiorari denied 326 U.S. 776, 66 S.Ct. 268, 90 L.Ed. 469; G. T. I. Corp. v. Calhoon, D.Ohio 1969, 309 F.Supp. 762; Van Products Co. v. General Welding and Fabricating Co., 1965, 419 Pa. 248, 213 A.2d 769, 30 A.L.R.3d 612.

84. Hahn & Clay v. A. O. Smith Corp., 5th Cir.1963, 320 F.2d 166, certiorari denied 375 U.S. 944, 84 S.Ct. 351, 11 L.Ed.2d 274; Sarkes Tarzian, Inc. v. Audio Devices, Inc., D.Cal.1958, 166 F.Supp. 250, affirmed 9th Cir.1960, 283 F.2d 695, certiorari denied 1961, 365 U.S. 869, 81 S.Ct. 903, 5 L.Ed.2d 859; Nucor Corp. v. Tennessee Forging Steel Service, D.Ark.1972, 339 F.Supp. 1305, affirmed in part, reversed in part 6th Cir., 476 F.2d 386, appeal after remand 513 F.2d 151.

85. R. Milgrim, Trade Secrets § 2.08.

86. See R. Milgrim, Trade Secrets § 8.02; Annot., 92 A.L.R.3d 138, 162.

87. Wright v. Palmer, 1970, 11 Ariz.App. 292, 464 P.2d 363; Progress Laundry Co. v. Hamilton, 1925, 208 Ky. 348, 270 S.W. 834; Woolley's Laundry v. Silva, 1939, 304 Mass. 383, 23 N.E.2d 899; Abalene Exterminating Co. v. Elges, 1947, 137 N.J.Eq. 1, 43 A.2d 165; Fulton Grand Laundry Co. v. Johnson, 1922, 140 Md. 359, 117 A. 753; Jewel Tea Co. v. Grissom, 1938, 66 S.D. 146, 279 N.W. 544. Contra, Empire Steam Laundry Co. v. Lozier, 1913, 165 Cal. 95, 130 P. 1180. See McClain, Injunctive Relief Against Employees Using Confidential Information, 1935, 23 Ky.L.J. 248; Hannigan, The Implied Obligation of an Employee, 1929, 77 U.Pa.L.Rev. 970; Kramer, Protection of Customer Lists in California, 1935, 23 Cal.L.Rev. 399; Annot., 28 A.L.R.3d 7.

88. Developments in the Law—Competitive Torts, 1964, 77 Harv.L.Rev. 888; R. Milgrim, Trade Secrets; A. Turner, 1962, The Law of Trade Secrets.

89. "Captain Boycott, an Englishman, who was agent of Lord Earne and a farmer of Lough Mask, served notices upon the lord's tenants, and they in turn, with the surrounding population, resolved to have nothing to do with him, and, as far as they could prevent it, not to allow anyone else to have. His life appeared to be in danger, and he had to claim police protection. His servants fled from him, and the awful sentence of excommunication could hardly have rendered him more helplessly alone for a time. No one would work for him, and no one would supply him with food. He and his wife were compelled to work in their own fields with the shadows of armed constabulary ever at their heels; Justin MacCarthy's England under Gladstone." Vouvier's Law Dictionary, summarizing statement in State v. Glidden, 1887, 55 Conn. 46, 8 A. 890. See also Wyman, The Law as to the Boycott, 1903, 15 Green Bag 208.

A boycott is an organized effort to withdraw from business relations with another, or to induce third persons to do the same. It may be primary, where the defendant himself refuses to deal with the other; or secondary, where he seeks to compel third persons not to do so, by refusing to have dealings with them if they do; or even tertiary, when he refuses to deal with a fourth party if he deals with the third.[90] All of these may involve the persuasion or coercion of still other persons to join in the boycott.

Under the common law rule, persons are free to deal or refuse to deal for any reason, or even for no reason at all, so long as they do not induce others to join in boycott activities.[91] Competition in business always has been held to be a sufficient justification for a primary boycott on the part of a single defendant,[92] and likewise for a secondary boycott whose object is the immediate appropriation of the trade or patronage diverted from the other—[93] and this notwithstanding the elements of coercion which usually are present. The individual is regarded as free to acquire business by dealing or refusing to deal with anyone he likes.[94]

When several defendants combine in a boycott, however, a different picture is presented. Unless he has monopolistic power,[95] the individual is limited in the damage he can do by his own capacity for economic pressure or persuasion. A combination has far greater potentialities of coercion,[96] not only of others, but also of its own more reluctant members; and it may so far restrict and control the trade of an entire industry as to ruin the plaintiff or drive him out of business. It undoubtedly is true that in the absence of statute combinations to refuse to deal are not in themselves and without more unlawful,[97] particularly where their purpose is merely to protect their members against evils which threaten their own business.[98]

---

90. See the elaborate analysis in Kales, Coercive and Competitive Methods in Trade and Labor Disputes, 1922, 8 Corn.L.Q. 1, 128. Also Kovarsky, A Social and Legal Analysis of the Secondary Boycott, 1956, 35 Or. L.Rev. 71, 223; Lesnick, The Gravamen of the Secondary Boycott, 1962, 62 Colum.L.Rev. 1363; Notes, 1953, 28 Ind.L.J. 467; 1961, 12 West.Res.L.Rev. 759; 1942, 10 Geo.Wash.L.Rev. 302; 1941 41 Colum.L.Rev. 941.

Tertiary boycotts generally have been held to be illegal. See Carlson v. Carpenter Contractors' Association, 1922, 305 Ill. 331, 137 N.E. 222; Burnham v. Dowd, 1914, 217 Mass. 351 104 N.E. 841; New England Cement Gun Co. v. McGivern, 1914, 218 Mass. 198, 105 N.E. 885. It will be noted that every tertiary boycott includes a secondary boycott of the third party, which is not justified if the third party is not a competitor. Lehigh Structural Steel Co. v. Atlantic Smelting & Refining Works, 1920, 92 N.J.Eq. 131, 111 A. 376.

91. PMP Associates, Inc. v. Globe Newspaper Co., 1975, 366 Mass. 593, 321 N.E.2d 915; Rothermel v. International Paper Co., 1978, 163 N.J.Super. 235, 394 A.2d 860; Second Restatement of Torts, § 766, Comment l.

92. Great Atlantic & Pacific Tea Co. v. Cream of Wheat Co., 2d Cir.1915, 227 F. 46; Barish v. Chrysler Corp., 1942, 141 Neb. 157, 3 N.W.2d 91; Guthrie v. Great American Insurance Co., 4th Cir.1945, 151 F.2d 738; Green v. Victor Talking Machine Co., 2d Cir. 1928, 24 F.2d 378, certiorari denied 278 U.S. 602, 49 S.Ct. 9, 73 L.Ed. 530, and see cases cited supra, p. 992. See Brown, The Right to Refuse to Sell, 1916, 25 Yale L.J. 194; Note, 1951, 45 Ill.L.Rev. 784.

93. Photographic Importing & Distributing Co. v. Elgeet Optical Co., 1953, 282 App.Div. 223, 122 N.Y.S. 2d 215, appeal denied, 1953, 282 App.Div. 836, 124 N.Y.S.2d 341; Staroske v. Pulitzer Publishing Co., 1911, 235 Mo. 67, 138 S.W. 36; Journal of Commerce Publishing Co. v. Tribune Co., 7th Cir.1922, 286 F. 111; Andrew Jergens Co. v. Woodbury, Inc., D.Del.1920, 271 F. 43; Dye v. Carmichael Produce Co., 1917, 64 Ind. App. 653, 116 N.E. 425.

See notes, 1965, 52 Geo.L.J. 392, 406; 1965, 19 Sw. L.J. 567.

94. But compare the cases of spiteful motive or remote advantage, supra, p. 1014.

95. Cf. Eastman Kodak Co. of New York v. Southern Photo Materials Co., 1927, 273 U.S. 359, 47 S.Ct. 400, 71 L.Ed. 684.

96. There is a good statement of this in Boutwell v. Marr, 1899, 71 Vt. 1, 42 A. 607.

97. Bohn Manufacturing Co. v. Hollis, 1893, 54 Minn. 223, 55 N.W. 1119; Macauley v. Tierney, 1895, 19 R.I. 255, 33 A. 1; John D. Park & Sons v. National Wholesale Druggists' Association, 1903, 175 N.Y. 1, 67 N.E. 136; Montgomery Ward & Co. v. South Dakota Retail Merchants' & Hardware Dealers' Association, C.C.S.D. 1907, 150 F. 413; Roseneau v. Empire Circuit Co., 1909, 131 App.Div. 429, 115 N.Y.S. 511, motion to amend decision denied 132 App.Div. 947, 117 N.Y.S. 1146.

98. Sorrell v. Smith [1925] A.C. 700; Wolfenstein v. Fashion Originators' Guild of America, 1935, 244 App. Div. 656, 280 N.Y.S. 361; William Filene's Sons Co. v. Fashion Originators' Guild of America, 1st Cir.1937, 90 F.2d 556; Arnold v. Burgess, 1934, 241 App.Div. 364, 272 N.Y.S. 534, affirmed 269 N.Y. 510, 199 N.E. 511; Edelstein v. Gillmore, 2d Cir.1929, 35 F.2d 723, certiora-

But in many cases the combination has been found to be intended to insure its members a monopoly of the business in their particular line, and the boycott, primary or secondary, has been enjoined as an illegal restraint of trade.[99] While it is probably impossible to harmonize all of the decisions, the courts seem to have looked at the aggressive purpose of obtaining monopolistic control, as distinguished from the more or less defensive one of preserving an existing state of competition. There has been extensive statutory regulation of combinations in restraint of trade, by the Sherman Anti-Trust Act [1] and state acts modeled upon it,[2] as well as other legislation, to which reference must be made in a particular case. The tendency of the Supreme Court to treat concerted boycotts as per se unlawful in some situations [3] makes it imperative to consider the federal law as well as the traditional law of torts.

So far as a boycott involves communication, as for example, an effort to persuade others to join it, the boycott may be legally protected as free speech under the First Amendment.[4] First Amendment values have been said to support the boycott of a single defendant such as a broadcaster who refuses to publish the views of the plaintiff even in paid advertising; [5] and, before federal preemption of labor matters, to support peaceful labor picketing which was an attempt to persuade others to join a boycott.[6] Boycotts pursued for religious [7] or political [8]

---

ri denied 280 U.S. 607, 50 S.Ct. 153, 74 L.Ed. 650; Contra, Millinery Creators' Guild v. Federal Trade Commission, 2d Cir.1940, 109 F.2d 175, affirmed 312 U.S. 469, 61 S.Ct. 708, 85 L.Ed. 955; and cf. Fashion Originators' Guild of America v. Federal Trade Commission, 2d Cir. 1940, 114 F.2d 80, affirmed 312 U.S. 457, 61 S.Ct. 703, 85 L.Ed. 949.

99. Jackson v. Stanfield, 1894, 137 Ind. 592, 36 N.E. 345, rehearing denied 137 Ind. 592, 37 N.E. 14; Grillo v. Board of Realtors of Plainfield Area, 1966, 91 N.J. Super. 202, 219 A.2d 635; Brown v. Jacobs' Pharmacy Co., 1902, 115 Ga. 429, 41 S.E. 553; See Note, 1950, 45 Ill.L.Rev. 784.

1. 15 U.S.C.A. § 1 (contracts, combinations or conspiracies in restraint of trade).

2. Cf. Retail Lumber Dealers' Association v. State, 1910, 95 Miss. 337, 48 So. 1021, affirmed in Grenada Lumber Co. v. Mississippi, 1910, 217 U.S. 433, 30 S.Ct. 535, 54 L.Ed. 826.

3. See Klor's, Inc. v. Broadway-Hale Stores, Inc., 1959, 359 U.S. 207, 79 S.Ct. 705, 3 L.Ed.2d 741. There is a very helpful analysis of the cases, with appropriate qualifications about the per se rule, in L. Sullivan, 1977, Antitrust (Hornbook Series).

4. Note, Constitutional Rights of Noncommercial Boycotters, 1982, 10 Hof.L.Rev. 773; Note, Political Boycott Activity and the First Amendment, 1978, 91 Harv.L.Rev. 659; Comment, The Common-Law and Constitutional Status of Anti-Discrimination Boycotts, 1957, 66 Yale L.J. 397. See Coons, Non-Commercial Purpose as a Sherman Act Defense, 1962, 56 Nw.L. Rev. 705.

5. Columbia Broadcasting System, Inc. v. Democratic National Committee, 1973, 412 U.S. 94, 93 S.Ct. 2080, 36 L.Ed.2d 772 (First Amendment does not require broadcaster to accept paid advertising; a rule otherwise would allow the affluent to monopolize the airwaves and destroy the market place of ideas the First Amendment seeks to protect); cf. Miami Herald Publishing Co. v. Tornillo, 1974, 418 U.S. 241, 94 S.Ct. 2831, 41 L.Ed.2d 730 (state statute requiring newspaper to publish plaintiff's reply to an attack violates First Amendment).

6. Thornhill v. Alabama, 1940, 310 U.S. 88, 60 S.Ct. 736, 84 L.Ed. 1093. See, discussing the labor cases in connection with the First Amendment and the problem of social and political boycotts, Note, Political Boycott Activity and the First Amendment, 1978, 91 Harv.L. Rev. 659.

7. Watch Tower Bible & Tract Society v. Dougherty, 1940, 337 Pa. 286, 11 A.2d 147 (boycott threatened to force plaintiff off radio station); Kuryer Publishing Co. v. Messmer, 1916, 162 Wis. 565, 156 N.W. 948 (church letter condemning newspaper); Radecki v. Schuckardt, 1976, 50 Ohio App.2d 92, 361 N.E.2d 543 (action against church officer who in pursuit of his faith induced wife to leave husband). Where the church boycott interfered with marriage, it was held a cause of action was stated in Bear v. Reformed Mennonite Church, 1975, 462 Pa. 330, 341 A.2d 105. Cf. American Mercury, Inc. v. Chase, D.Mass.1926, 13 F.2d 224 (threats of prosecution against newsdealers if they handled plaintiff's magazine, apparently defendants believed magazine immoral; injunction against defendants' threats issued).

8. State of Missouri v. National Organization for Women, Inc., D.Mo.1979, 620 F.2d 1301 (8th Cir.1980), certiorari denied 449 U.S. 842, 101 S.Ct. 122, 66 L.Ed.2d 49 (boycott of State not supporting ERA); cf. Eastern Railroad Presidents Conference v. Noerr Motor Freight, Inc., 1961, 365 U.S. 127, 81 S.Ct. 523, 5 L.Ed.2d 464, rehearing denied 365 U.S. 875, 81 S.Ct. 899, 5 L.Ed.2d 864; United Mine Workers of America v. Pennington, 1965, 381 U.S. 657, 85 S.Ct. 1585, 14 L.Ed.2d 626, on remand 257 F.Supp. 815, affirmed in part, reversed in part 6th Cir., 400 F.2d 806, certiorari denied 393 U.S. 983, 89 S.Ct. 450, 24 L.Ed.2d 444, rehearing denied 393 U.S. 1045, 89 S.Ct. 616, 21 L.Ed.2d 599, appeal after remand 421 F.2d 1380, certiorari denied 398 U.S. 960, 90 S.Ct. 2177, 26 L.Ed.2d 546; California Motor Transport Co. v. Trucking Unlimited,

reasons, have been afforded protection in some courts, and consumer boycotts to condemn prices or other business practices have been treated the same way,[9] so long as no tortious means are used to carry out the boycott and there is no inducement to breach an actual, existing contract. The same principles no doubt apply to the civil rights boycott. Some older decisions held that boycotts to redress what the defendants perceived as racial injustice were illegal and that a purpose to correct injustice did not justify them.[10] More recently some courts have held that civil rights boycotts were illegal and would be enjoined in their entirety where trespass, violence or coercive picketing were involved.[11] It is more likely today, however, that civil rights boycotts will be protected so far as they involve communication with others, and that while violence or trespass may be forbidden, and time, place and manner restrictions imposed,[12] this will not remove protection from the boycott itself under the First Amendment.[13]

Labor Unions

At an early day many of the common law rules concerning interference with business relations were carried over and applied to labor unions, which were at one time regarded as outlaw organizations whose activities were criminal conspiracies to disrupt the social order.[14] Since a strike was obviously a boycott and an interference with business relations, and since the courts tended to find that labor was competing with management for a larger share of the common fund produced, the law of boycotts and unfair competition was readily invoked to regulate union activity quite intensively.[15] The right to

1972, 404 U.S. 508, 92 S.Ct. 609, 30 L.Ed.2d 642 (activities otherwise in violation of antitrust laws protected if conduct was to influence governmental action).

9. Stansbury v. Beckstrom, Tex.Civ.App.1973, 491 S.W.2d 947, 62 A.L.R.3d 222; cf. Plainview Realty, Inc. v. Board of Managers, 1976, 86 Misc.2d 515, 383 N.Y.S.2d 194 (even a boycott secondary in form if not in substance would not be enjoined). The invitation to join a boycott is not always explicit, but consumer complaints would typically be at least suggestive, as in Concerned Consumers League v. O'Neill, D.Wis.1974, 371 F.Supp. 644 (leaflets reporting complaints against retailer protected). And an injunction may be denied even if the pickets contain libelous falsehoods, Willing v. Mazzacone, 1978, 482 Pa. 377, 393 A.2d 1155; Pittman v. Cohn Communities, Inc., 1977, 240 Ga. 106, 239 S.E.2d 526.

10. A. S. Beck Shoe Corp. v. Johnson, 1934, 153 Misc. 363, 274 N.Y.S. 946; see Coons, Non-Commercial Purpose as a Sherman Act Defense, 1962, 56 Nw.L. Rev. 705, 721.

11. National Association for the Advancement of Colored People v. Webb's City, Inc., Fla.App.1963, 152 So.2d 179, judgment vacated on suggestion of mootness, 376 U.S. 190, 84 S.Ct. 635, 11 L.Ed.2d 602. See also National Association for the Advancement of Colored People v. Overstreet, 1965, 221 Ga. 16, 142 S.E.2d 816, certiorari dismissed 384 U.S. 118, 86 S.Ct. 1306, 16 L.Ed.2d 409, rehearing denied 384 U.S. 981, 86 S.Ct. 1857, 16 L.Ed.2d 692; Note, Political Boycott Activity and the First Amendment, 1978, 91 Harv.L.Rev. 659.

12. Residential picketing is especially troublesome. Political picketing at a residence has been enjoined where alternative sites are available. Walinsky v. Kennedy, 1977, 94 Misc.2d 121, 404 N.Y.S.2d 491 (Gay Activists Alliance picketing home of political opponent.)

See Kamin, Residential Picketing and the First Amendment, 1966, 61 Nw.L.Rev. 177; Comment, 1966, Picketing the Homes of Public Officials, 1966, 34 U.Chi.L. Rev. 106, Annot., 42 A.L.R.3d 1353.

13. This now seems clear under National Association for the Advancement of Colored People v. Claiborne Hardware Co., Inc. 1982, 458 U.S. 886, 102 S.Ct. 3409, 73 L.Ed.2d 1215. See also Henry v. First National Bank of Clarksdale, 5th Cir.1979, 595 F.2d 291, rehearing denied 601 F.2d 586, certiorari denied 444 U.S. 1074, 100 S.Ct. 1020, 62 L.Ed.2d 756; Machesky v. Bizzell, 1st Cir.1969, 414 F.2d 283. But secondary labor boycotts are forbidden by the federal statutes and, anomalously, the First Amendment gives these boycotts no protection even when they are carried out solely to express political or social opinion. International Longshoremen's Association, AFL-CIO v. Allied International Inc., 1982, 456 U.S. 212, 102 S.Ct. 1656, 72 L.Ed.2d 21.

14. See Holdsworth, Industrial Combinations and the Law in the Eighteenth Century, 1936, 20 Minn.L. Rev. 367; Wigmore, Interference with Social Relations, 1887, 21 Am.L.Rev. 764; Morris, History of Labor and Conspiracy, 1937, 52 Pol.Sci.Q. 51; Sayre, Criminal Conspiracy, 1922, 35 Harv.L.Rev. 393; Nelles, The First American Labor Case, 1931, 41 Yale L.J. 165; Burdick, Conspiracy as a Crime and as a Tort, 1907, 7 Colum.L.Rev. 229; Burdick, The Tort of Conspiracy, 1908, 8 Colum.L.Rev. 117.

15. See Kales, Coercive and Competitive Methods in Trade and Labor Disputes, 1922, 8 Corn.L.Q. 1, 128; Smith, Crucial Issues in Labor Litigation, 1907, 20 Harv.L.Rev. 253, 345, 429; Sayre, Labor and the Courts, 1930, 39 Yale L.J. 682; Eskin, The Legality of "Peaceful Coercion" in Labor Disputes, 1937, 85 U.Pa. L.Rev. 456; Warm, A Study of the Judicial Attitude Toward Trade Unions and Labor Legislation, 1939, 23

strike for varied labor goals was developed only over a long period. Beginning in the 1930s there was extensive federal statutory regulation of labor matters,[16] and in 1959 the Supreme Court concluded that the Congress had preempted the field,[17] so that quite limited jurisdiction remained to the state courts. Certain artifacts of the common law of tort remain, for example, in the statutory designations of secondary boycotts as an unfair labor practice[18] and the provision that such practices furnish ground for legal action.[19] The states are also free to deal with violence attendant upon a strike[20] and to prohibit actual interference with existing contracts.[21] Likewise strikes by public employees may be prohibited and such a strike may be actionable if it interferes with rights of private citizens.[22] But the general preemption of the field by the federal government, coupled with allocation of extensive powers of regulation to the National Labor Relations Board have substantially eliminated the traditional role of tort law in dealing with the economic results of labor activity. For these reasons, and because the study of labor law has long been a field of study in itself, the Second Restatement of Torts has now excluded labor relations from its scope.[23] The decision seems a wise one and is followed here.

Economic Retaliation

The general rule at common law recognizes that a person having economic power over others is generally free to use that power in harmful ways, so long as no statute or contract is violated and no tortious means used. In the absence of statutes protecting employees from discriminatory discharge,[24] therefore, it was not tortious to terminate an employee's employment even for reasons of spite or malice.[25] If there was to be liability in such cases it was based on the employment contract and limited by its terms, and there was no liability in tort and none on any theory where the employment was "at will." Some decisions continue to adhere to this viewpoint without acknowleged exception.[26]

It is apparent, however, that the state cannot permit employers to use the power of employment to compel illegal acts by an employee through threats of discharge, and if

Minn.L.Rev. 255; Notes, 1938, 32 Ill.L.Rev. 611, 625; 1924, 34 Harv.L.Rev. 880.

16. The Norris-LaGuardia Act, now 29 U.S.C.A. §§ 101–115; the Wagner Act, now 29 U.S.C.A. §§ 151–166; the Labor-Management Relations Act or Taft-Hartley Act, now 29 U.S.C.A. §§ 141–188; and the Labor Management Reporting and Disclosure Act or Landrum-Griffin Act, 1959, 73 Stat. 519, now found in numerous sections of Title 29, U.S.C.A.

17. San Diego Building Trades Council v. Garmon, 1959, 359 U.S. 236, 79 S.Ct. 773, 3 L.Ed.2d 775.

18. 29 U.S.C.A. § 158(b).

19. 29 U.S.C.A. § 187. This applies even if the boycott is carried out for a political purpose in protest of the activities of a third person. International Longshoremen's Association, AFL-CIO v. Allied International Inc., 1982, 456 U.S. 212, 102 S.Ct. 1656, 72 L.Ed.2d 21.

20. See United Mine Workers of America v. Gibbs, 1966, 383 U.S. 715, 86 S.Ct. 1130, 16 L.Ed.2d 218.

21. International Union United Auto, Aircraft and Agricultural Implement Workers of America v. Russell, 1958, 356 U.S. 634, 78 S.Ct. 932, 2 L.Ed.2d 1030, rehearing denied 357 U.S. 944, 78 S.Ct. 1379, 2 L.Ed.2d 1558.

22. Burns Jackson Miller Summit & Spitzer v. Lindner, Sup.Ct.1981, 108 Misc.2d 458, 437 N.Y.S.2d 895.

See Note, Statutory and Common Law Considerations in Defining the Tort Liability of Public Employee Unions to Private Citizens for Damages Inflicted by Illegal Strikes, 1982, 80 Mich.L.Rev. 1271. A number of states have, however, declined the opportunity to impose liability. E.g., Burke & Thomas, Inc. v. International Organization of Masters, Mates & Pilots, Etc., 1979, 92 Wn.2d 762, 600 P.2d 1282.

23. Second Restatement of Torts, Introductory Note to Division Nine.

24. Many kinds of employment discrimination are now statutory torts under civil rights acts, including discrimination based on race, sex and age. See 42 U.S.C. § 2000e–1 et seq. ("Title VII," employment discrimination generally); 29 U.S.C. § 626 ("Age Act"). Despite the enormous significance of these claims, they are beyond the scope of the present edition.

25. Wild v. Rarig, Minn.1975, 302 Minn. 419, 234 N.W.2d 775, appeal dismissed, certiorari denied 424 U.S. 902, 96 S.Ct. 1093, 47 L.Ed.2d 307, rehearing denied 425 U.S. 945, 96 S.Ct. 1689, 48 L.Ed.2d 190; Geary v. United States Steel Corp., 1974, 456 Pa. 171, 319 A.2d 174; Restatement of Torts, § 762.

26. See Phillips v. Goodyear Tire & Rubber Co., 5th Cir.1981, 651 F.2d 1051, rehearing denied 671 F.2d 860 (assessment of Georgia and Texas law).

the employer is not permitted to compel such acts, he is likewise not permitted to retaliate against the employee who refuses to perform them. The employee discharged for refusing to perjure himself thus has an action even though his contract is "at will." [27] By extension of this idea it would seem that the employer could not use the power of employment to force employees to give up rights meant for their protection, or even to avoid duties imposed upon them by law, and from this it would also seem, as a number of courts have now held, that the employer may not discharge an employee in retaliation for a good faith claim to workers' compensation,[28] or for the employee's refusal to engage in social relations with the employer,[29] or, presumably, for the assertion of any other substantial personal right.[30] The same kind of rule has been followed where the employee is discharged for the performance of some public duty, as where employment is terminated because she has served on a jury[31] or has reported the employer's violations of law to the public authorities.[32] Where, however, the duty is not so specific, and the employee merely has a policy difference with the employer, although it is a difference based on a concern for ethics or public safety, the cases have not yet guaranteed protection to the employee.[33]

Most of the retaliation cases have in fact involved the economic power of the employer, but the principle does not seem so limited and a few cases have applied the idea, or one very much like it, to landlords who seek to evict a tenant for reporting the landlord's housing code violations,[34] or to insurers who cancel a policy because the policyholder has given honest but unfavorable testimony in another suit,[35] or to associations who expel members for the exercise of some legal right.[36] Statutes have been enacted in recent years to provide similar but at times more expansive protection for business franchisees.[37] The federal statute, known as the

27. Petermann v. International Brotherhood of Teamsters, Etc., 1959, 174 Cal.App.2d 184, 344 P.2d 25; cf. L'Orange v. Medical Protective Co., 6th Cir.1968, 394 F.2d 57 (cancellation of malpractice policy when policyholder testified against another professional, compared to intimidation of witness).

28. Kelsay v. Motorola, Inc., 1978, 74 Ill.2d 172, 23 Ill.Dec. 559, 384 N.E.2d 353; Frampton v. Central Indiana Gas Co., 1973, 260 Ind. 249, 297 N.E.2d 425; Raden v. City of Azusa, 1979, 97 Cal.App.3d 336, 158 Cal.Rptr. 689.

Statutes make similar provision in some states. See Note, 1980, 58 N.C.L.Rev. 629. There are also anti-retaliation provisions in some federal statutes conferring rights on employees. See 42 U.S.C.A. § 2000e—3(a) (no retaliation against employee asserting rights or participating in proceedings against employer for job discrimination).

29. Monge v. Beebe Rubber Co., 1974, 114 N.H. 130, 316 A.2d 549 (plaintiff, a woman, refused to go out with superior).

30. Perks v. Firestone Tire & Rubber Co., 3d Cir. 1979, 611 F.2d 1363 (where statute prohibited employers from requiring polygraph test, discharge for failure to submit to test would be actionable); cf. Fortune v. National Cash Register Co., 1977, 373 Mass. 96, 364 N.E.2d 1251.

31. Nees v. Hocks, 1975, 272 Or. 210, 536 P.2d 512; Reuther v. Fowler & Williams, Inc., 1978, 255 Pa. Super. 28, 386 A.2d 119.

32. Harless v. First National Bank in Fairmont, 1978, ___ W.Va. ___, 246 S.E.2d 270. Statutes may also deal with this. E.g., 42 U.S.C.A. § 7622 protects employees reporting employer pollution and requires reinstatement if they are discharged for making such reports.

33. Percival v. General Motors Corp., 8th Cir.1976, 539 F.2d 1126; Pierce v. Ortho Pharmaceutical Corp., 1980, 84 N.J. 58, 417 A.2d 505; Geary v. United States Steel Corp., 1974, 456 Pa. 171, 319 A.2d 174.

34. It was first held that a tenant's report of such violations was insufficient ground for the landlord's retaliatory eviction. Edwards v. Habib, D.C.Cir.1968, 397 F.2d 687, certiorari denied 393 U.S. 1016, 89 S.Ct. 618, 21 L.Ed.2d 560; Annot., 40 A.L.R.3d 753. But there is authority that if the landlord does evict, the tenant has a tort action for damages. Aweeka v. Bonds, 1971, 20 Cal.App.3d 278, 97 Cal.Rptr. 650. The Uniform Residential Landlord and Tenant Act §§ 5.101 and 4.107 make similar provisions. Closely similar provisions appear in other state statutes, e.g., N.Y. Real Property Law § 223–b.

35. L'Orange v. Medical Protective Co., 6th Cir. 1968, 394 F.2d 57.

36. Cf. Van Daele v. Vinci, 1972, 51 Ill.2d 389, 282 N.E.2d 728, certiorari denied 409 U.S. 1007, 93 S.Ct. 438, 34 L.Ed.2d 300; Zelenka v. Benevolent & Protective Order of Elks, 1974, 129 N.J.Super. 379, 324 A.2d 35.

37. See Brown, Franchising—A Fiduciary Relationship, 1971, 49 Tex.L.Rev. 650.

Automobile Dealers' Day in Court Act,[38] protects local auto dealers against termination of their franchises in bad faith. A number of state statutes make similar provisions about dealerships generally,[39] or sometimes about particular kinds of dealerships.[40] The statutes are extremely vague, but are presumably intended to protect against economic retaliation as well as against other misuse of economic power.

Most of the cases so far appear to be grounded in intent rather than in negligence. Some courts have considered the problem in terms of contract rather than tort, finding an implied term in the contract for fair dealing and good faith.[41] But the contract approach is by no means the only one. Claims have been asserted on the basis of antitrust[42] and civil rights[43] laws and under statutes specifically providing for protection,[44] as well as in admiralty[45] and on common law tort grounds.[46] Where a tort theory is made out, the aggrieved plaintiff may recover tort damages, including punitive damages[47] and mental distress damages[48] in appropriate cases.

The exact theory of liability and defense in all of this is unclear, beyond the obvious fact that some acts have been considered to be an abuse of economic power. Some cases have spoken of malice or bad motives.[49] But others have insisted that no action will lie unless the misuse of economic power tends to subvert some more or less identifiable public policy, as where an employee is punished for reporting an employer's violation of statute.[50] Some commentators[51] and oc-

---

38. 15 U.S.C.A. § 1222.

39. N.J.Stat.Ann. 56:10–5, 56:10–6; Wis.Stat.Ann. § 135.03.

40. E.g., Ariz.Rev.Stats, § 44–1554 (petroleum products franchises); § 44–1556 (liquor franchises).

41. Fortune v. National Cash Register Co., 1977, 373 Mass. 96, 364 N.E.2d 1251; cf. L'Orange v. Medical Protective Co., 6th Cir. 1968, 394 F.2d 57. But cf. Rothermel v. International Paper Co., 1978, 163 N.J. Super. 235, 394 A.2d 860 (manufacturer had no obligation to continue using broker and could go to direct sales).

42. Ostrofe v. H.S. Crocker Co., Inc., 9th Cir. 1982, 670 F.2d 1378 (allowing the treble damage claim of an employee allegedly discharged for refusal to participate in anticompetitive activities). Contra, disallowing the treble damage claim, In re Industrial Gas Antitrust Litigation (Bichan v. Chemetron Corp.), 7th Cir. 1982, 681 F.2d 514.

43. See Bush v. Lucas, 5th Cir. 1981, 647 F.2d 573 (no liability where there is civil service protection), certiorari granted 458 U.S. 1104, 102 S.Ct. 3481, 73 L.Ed. 2d 1365.

44. E.g., statutes forbidding discrimination against an employee who has participated in a civil rights claim against the employer, see 42 U.S.C.A. § 2000e–3(a); Pettway v. American Cast Iron Pipe Co., 5th Cir. 1969, 411 F.2d 998, rehearing denied 415 F.2d 1376; and statutes forbidding discrimination against an employee engaging in union activity or giving testimony about unfair labor practices, 29 U.S.C. § 158(a)(3) and (4); Behring International, Inc. v. National Labor Relations Board, 3d Cir. 1982, 675 F.2d 83.

45. Smith v. Atlas Off-Shore Boat Service, 5th Cir. 1981, 653 F.2d 1057.

46. Tameny v. Atlantic Richfield Co., 1980, 27 Cal. 3d 167, 164 Cal.Rptr. 839, 610 P.2d 1330; Palmateer v. International Harvester Co., 1981, 85 Ill.2d 124, 52 Ill. Dec. 13, 421 N.E.2d 876; Cloutier v. Great Atlantic & Pacific Tea Co., Inc., 1981, 121 N.H. 915, 436 A.2d 1141.

47. Tameny v. Atlantic Richfield Co., 1980, 27 Cal. 3d 167, 164 Cal.Rptr. 839, 610 P.2d 1330, 9 A.L.R. 4th 314; Harless v. First National Bank in Fairmont, 1982, ___ W.Va. ___, 289 S.E.2d 692 (but not to be granted automatically). In Smith v. Atlas Off-Shore Boat Service, Inc., 5th Cir. 1981, 653 F.2d 1057 the court permitted damages for emotional distress but held that the threat of punitive damages awards might interfere too much with the employer's operation of its own business and declined to permit them for that reason.

48. Smith v. Atlas Off-Shore Boat Service, Inc., 5th Cir. 1981, 653 F.2d 1057; Harless v. First National Bank in Fairmont, 1982, ___ W.Va. ___, 289 S.E.2d 692.

49. Monge v. Beebe Rubber Co., 1974, 114 N.H. 130, 316 A.2d 549; see Jackson v. Minidoka Irrigation District, 1977, 98 Idaho 330, 563 P.2d 54.

50. Keneally v. Orgain, 1980, 186 Mont. 1, 606 P.2d 127; Geary v. United States Steel Corp., 1974, 456 Pa. 171, 319 A.2d 174; Harless v. First National Bank in Fairmont, 1978, ___ W.Va. ___, 246 S.E.2d 270. Cloutier v. Great Atlantic & Pacific Tea Co., Inc., 1981, 121 N.H. 915, 436 A.2d 1140 used this public policy test but left the existence of the policy to the jury.

51. E.g., Blades, Employment at Will vs. Individual Freedom: On Limiting the Abusive Exercise of Employer Power, 1967, 67 Colum.L.Rev. 1404 (emphasizing importance of jobs, control of which is in another's hands); Note, Protecting At Will Employees Against Wrongful Discharge, 1980, 93 Harv.L.Rev. 1816 (advocating a duty to retain in good faith to avoid financial and emotional harms to employees); Note, Economic Retaliation: A New Point of View, 1981, 23 Ariz.L.Rev. 861 (emphasizing employee hardship and plaintiff's injury, with employer's rights to be balanced). See

casionally some courts [52] have emphasized a much broader theory, which, in one form or another, asserts that given the importance of jobs and the lack of union protection for many at-will employees, the employer should no longer have unlimited power to discharge. This theory has not so far been accepted by most courts, who no doubt wish to avoid reviewing day-to-day management decisions or sitting as a grievance committee, and something more than proof of an arbitrary decision seems to be required. Quite possibly it is not the job itself that receives primary protection but other rights of the employee with which the wrongful discharge interferes. That many of these rights are intangible in nature does not deprive them of legal status, and an intended interference with them through the use of economic power is quite similar to other interferences with advantageous relations, with the result that liability is equally or more justified. Thus one's right as a citizen to participate in the processes of politics and government by reporting illegal conduct or by sitting on a jury may not be undermined by discharge or threat of it any more than one's right to claim workers' compensation may be so undermined. Similarly one's rights of autonomy include a right to refuse social or sexual advances of others, and the employer may not interfere with such rights by requiring the employee to choose between those rights and a wage. But equally, an employee has no right to insist that the employer give up its views and accept hers, and a discharge of an employee who differs from the employer in opinion or outlook remains perfectly legitimate.[53] Seen in this light the economic retaliation cases, at least those involving employers, appear to be a special case of interference with advantageous relations or other rights, though unique in that, necessarily, the recovery is measured by the job rather than by the right interfered with.

WESTLAW REFERENCES

interference /s prospective /s advantage*
interference /s prospective /s advantage* /p customer* employee* employment expectanc***
interference /s prospective expect! /p bequest* gift* inheritance legac***
temperton +2 russell

Basis of Liability

interference /s prospective /s advantage* business relation! /p intent! /s knowledge kn*w* aware!
interference /s prospective /s advantage* business relation! /p privilege* justif! defense* excus! merit!
interference /s prospective /s advantage* business relation! /p "bad faith" entic! harm malic! spite
interference /s prospective /s advantage* business relation! /p defam! fraud "injurious falsehood" intimidat*** "slander of title" violence
interference /s prospective /s advantage* business relation! /p advi*e* disinterest** "economic interest*" "good faith" "public interest"
restatement +s torts /s 766b
interference /s prospective /s advantage* business relation! /p negligen**

Fair Competition

interference /s prospective /s advantage* business relation! & fair legitimate reasonable /s competition
379k19(1) & competition

Unfair Competition

interference /s prospective /s advantage* business relation! & "unfair competition"
interference /s prospective /s advantage* business relation! /p defam! disparage! harass! intimidat*** obstruct*** sabotage
interference /s prospective /s advantage* business relation! /p copyright* patent* trademark*

Passing Off, Trademarks and Product Simulation

palm*** pass*** +s off /p confus! deceive* deception fraud! imitat*** misrepresentation*
palm*** pass*** +s off /p descripti** function! generic geographical secondary
product* /s simulat*** ape* copie* copy*** pirat***
382k404

[Symposium], Individual Rights in the Work Place: The Employment-At-Will Issue, 1983, 16 U.Mich.J. Law Ref. 201–464.

52. In Monge v. Beebe Rubber Co., 1974, 114 N.H. 130, 316 A.2d 549 the court asserted that "the employer's interest in running his business as he sees fit must be balanced against the interest of the employee in maintaining his employment, and the public's interest in maintaining a proper balance between the two." Although this would seem to justify any protection the court might deem fair or just or reasonable, the same court has since withdrawn to the requirement that a specific public policy be violated before an action will be entertained. Cloutier v. Great Atlantic & Pacific Tea Co., 1981, 121 N.H. 915, 436 A.2d 1140.

53. See Pierce v. Ortho Pharmaceutical Corp., 1980, 84 N.J. 58, 417 A.2d 505.

False Advertising
"false advertising" /p compar! compet!

Misappropriation
misappropriation piracy pirating /p broadcast* character* design* idea* music** report*

misappropriation piracy pirating /p free independent unfettered unimpeded /p augment develop! expan! improve! use*

di misappropriation

Trade Secrets
"trade secret*" /p breach** violat*** /p confidence contract employment fiduciary

"trade secret*" /s "customer list*" distinctive novel** patentable

379k10(5)

255k60

di trade secret

Boycott
primary secondary tertiary /s boycott* /p intent! purpose* reason* tort!

boycott* /p coerc*** competit*** illegal*** monopol! restraint

boycott* /p "civil rights" consumer labor political religio**

379k10(4)

di boycott

Labor Unions
federal /s preemption /p labor union* /p interference "public employee*" "secondary boycott*" strike* violence

Economic Retaliation
digest(employe** /s coerc*** discharge* intimidat*** retaliat*** threat** /s duty duties illegal*** jury "work! compensation")

digest(employ** /s cancel! discharge* dismiss** fired laid-off /s "bad faith" malic! "public policy" retaliat*** wrongful**)

255k20

Chapter 25

IMMUNITIES

Table of Sections

Sec.
131. Governmental Immunity.
132. Public Officers.
133. Charities.
134. Infants.
135. Insanity.

§ 131. Governmental Immunity

An immunity is a freedom from suit or liability. The immunities discussed in the present chapter are grounded principally in the special status of the defendant as a governmental entity, or an officer thereof, or a family member. The immunity was traditionally quite broad and protected the defendant even in cases that undoubtedly involved tortious behavior. The idea was that, though the defendant might be a wrongdoer, social values of great importance required that the defendant escape liability. The immunity thus might be thought to differ from a privilege, such as the privilege of self-defense, which may reflect the judgment that the defendant's action is not tortious at all, or if tortious, is morally justified.[1]

The reasons of policy given in support of any particular immunity are apt to be grounded in values and perceptions of the times, and with the change in values and perceptions, the immunity itself is likely to undergo change as well. This in fact seems to describe the legal process concerning immunities in the period since World War II, and as many of the immunities have been constricted, they have come more and more to resemble the case of privilege or justification, so that many cases ostensibly decided on immunity may in fact be cases in which the defendant has not acted tortiously at all, as where a governmental officer is given a "qualified immunity" and is protected for good faith decisions.

As Peter H. Schuck has demonstrated the description of immunities today is largely the description of abandonment of and limitation on the immunities erected in an earlier day.[1a] There remain, however, broad categories of immunity in which certain defendants are simply not liable for certain torts at all.

§ 131

1. Second Restatement of Torts, Introductory Note to Chapter 45A (1979).

1a. Schuck, Suing Government, 1983, Yale University Press.

§ 131 GOVERNMENTAL IMMUNITY 1033

The traditional governmental immunity protects governments at all levels from legal actions.[2] At the level of the state and national governments, this immunity is usually referred to as sovereign immunity, and it is associated with the idea that "the King can do no wrong."[3] Though the modern state gradually replaced the individual sovereign, the idea was carried over, partly on the ground that it seemed illogical to enforce a claim against the very authority that created the claim in the first place.[4] Although this logic no longer seems compelling, it remains true that judicial review of executive action in tort suits or otherwise presents some degree of threat to the independence of the executive and the separation of powers, and for this reason even where governmental immunity is generally abolished, there remain substantial areas of executive action that cannot be supervised in tort litigation.[5] In addition to the immunity of government itself, officers of the government are sometimes given immunity,[6] and, by comity, so also are foreign states and foreign ministers.[7]

The United States

Though the notion of sovereign immunity might seem best suited to a government of royal power, the doctrine was nevertheless accepted by American judges in the early days of the republic,[8] and the law of the United States has ever since been that, except to the extent the government consents to suit, it is immune. Consent to liability on contract claims, to be litigated exclusively in the Court of Claims, was given by the Tucker Act in 1887,[9] but no such general consent to tort suits was given at that time. Instead, relief was granted only if the citizen could show that the government committed, not merely a tort, but a "taking of property" compensable under the Constitution,[10] or if he could bring himself within one of the narrow and particular statutes consenting to suit,[11] or if he could maneuver a private bill through the Congress.[12] This process of pri-

2. See, generally, Borchard, Government Liability in Tort, 1924, 34 Yale L.J. 1, 129, 221, 1926, 36 Yale L.J. 1, 757, 1039, 1928, 28 Col.L.Rev. 577, 734; Borchard, Government Liability in Tort, 1948, 26 Can. Bar Rev. 399; Blachly and Oatman, Approaches to Governmental Liability in Tort: A Comparative Survey, 1942, 9 Law & Con.Prob. 181; Braband, Liability in Tort of the Government and Its Employees: A Comparative Analysis with Emphasis on German Law, 1938, 33 N.Y.U.L.Rev. 18; James, Tort Liability of Government Units and Their Officers, 1955, 22 U.Chi. L.Rev. 610; Davis, Tort Liability of Governmental Units, 1956, 40 Minn.L.Rev. 751; Note, 1953, 47 N.W. U.L.Rev. 914.

3. Borchard, Governmental Responsibility in Tort, 1926, 36 Yale L.J. 1; Parker, The King Does No Wrong—Liability for Misadministration, 1952, 5 Vand. L.Rev. 167.

Professor Pugh nicely demonstrates how the meaning and significance of this has been twisted in Pugh, Historical Approach to the Doctrine of Sovereign Immunity, 1953, 13 La.L.Rev. 476.

4. See R. Watkins, The State as a Party Litigant, 1927, 50; Kawananakoa v. Polyblank, 1907, 205 U.S. 349, 27 S.Ct. 526, 51 L.Ed. 834. This ground is broader than the idea that the king can do no wrong, and bars any suit to which the sovereign has not consented, whether in tort or otherwise.

5. See the discussion of discretionary immunity below at page 1039.

6. See § 132 below.

7. Second Restatement of Foreign Relations Law, § 64; Anonymous v. Anonymous, Fam.Ct.1964, 44 Misc.2d 14, 252 N.Y.S.2d 913 (ambassador immune from paternity suit).

8. Osborn v. Bank of United States, 1824, 22 U.S. (9 Wheat) 738, 6 L.Ed. 204. The most-quoted statement is that of Mr. Justice Holmes in Kawananakoa v. Polyblank, 1907, 205 U.S. 249, 27 S.Ct. 526, 51 L.Ed. 834.

9. 24 Stat. 505. The current provisions of the act may be found in 28 U.S.C.A. §§ 507, 1346, 1402, 1491, 1496, 1497, 1501, 1503, 2071, 2411, 2501 and 2512.

10. U.S. Const.Amend. V. See United States v. Causby, 1956, 328 U.S. 256, 66 S.Ct. 1062, 90 L.Ed.2d 1206. A taking not for public purpose may fall under the present tort claims act, see Hatahley v. United States, 1956, 351 U.S. 173, 76 S.Ct. 745, 100 L.Ed. 1065. If the taking is for public purpose, the claimant may be required to bring it in the Court of Claims. See L. Jayson, Handling Federal Tort Claims, 1972, § 212.05.

11. Consent to be sued was provided under several narrow statutes antedating the Tort Claims Act. Very recently statutes authorizing agencies to sue and be sued have been construed to consent to liability that is independent of the federal tort claims act, with the result, presumably, that liability is independent of the procedures and qualifications set forth in that act. See Baker v. F. & F. Investment, 7th Cir. 1972, 489 F.2d 829 (civil rights acts liability of U.S.).

12. Describing this procedure, and a number of particular remedies available for specific torts is Holtzoff,

vate legislation for tort relief in particular cases became so burdensome to Congress that it finally enacted the Federal Tort Claims Act in 1946.[13] This statute gave a general consent of the government to be sued in tort, though it was a consent subject to several particular restrictions.

Although federal officers may be held individually liable for certain civil rights violations,[14] this ruling has not been extended to the government itself,[15] which is generally[16] liable if at all only under the Federal Tort Claims Act. Under this statute the general directive is that the government is to be held "in the same manner and to the same extent as a private individual under the circumstances."[17] The federal courts are directed to follow, not federal law of civil rights or otherwise, but the tort law of the state in which the tort occurred,[18] including its choice of law rules.[19] Thus state-law doctrines of res ipsa loquitur,[20] negligence per se,[21] proximate cause,[22] contributory negligence[23] and assumed risk[24] govern the question of federal liability. The government's duty as landlord[25] or invitor,[26] and its obligations to make contribution and indemnity,[27] are likewise determined by state law, except only so far as the statute as judicially construed may specifically provide otherwise.[28] Whether a government employee is acting within the scope of his employment when he commits a tort is also a state law issue,[29] though federal law governs the question whether the agency committing the tort is a federal agency at all.[30]

The Handling of Tort Claims Against the Federal Government, 1942, 9 Law & Contemp.Prob. 311. The procedure is still available in cases not provided for by the tort claims act. See L. Jayson, Handling Federal Tort Claims, 1964, § 21.01.

13. 60 Stat. 843. Current provisions are found in 28 U.S.C.A. §§ 1346, 1402, 1504, 2110, 2401, 2402, 2411, 2412, 2671, 2672, 2674, 2675, 2676, 2677, 2678, 2679, 2680. In addition, particular provisions of the original act are absorbed into general provision of the judicial code, for example, appellate review, provided for in 28 U.S.C.A. § 1291.

14. See § 132 below.

15. Dellinger, Of Rights and Remedies: The Constitution as a Sword, 1972, 85 Harv.L.Rev. 1532.

16. The FTCA represents the only general scheme of federal tort liability but there are special waivers of the immunity for particular cases, e.g., employment discrimination by the federal government, 42 U.S.C.A. § 2000e–16 (under Title VII); 29 U.S.C.A. § 633a (age discrimination).

17. 28 U.S.C.A. § 2674.

18. 28 U.S.C.A. § 1346(b).

19. Richards v. United States, 1962, 369 U.S. 1, 82 S.Ct. 585, 7 L.Ed.2d 492. But note the possible exception if the duty of the United States is federally created, see note [10] supra.

20. E.g., White v. United States, 9th Cir. 1952, 193 F.2d 505 (state law procedural effect of res ipsa loquitur).

21. See, e.g., Vance v. United States, D.Alaska 1973, 355 F.Supp. 756 (illegal sale of intoxicants negligence per se under state law). Where a federal statute appears to impose a duty upon a federal agency, the federal government may be liable because state law would use the federal statute as a standard of care. See Griffin v. United States, 3d Cir. 1974, 500 F.2d 1059. However, it is not clear whether state or federal law governs the question of excused violation, see Swoboda v. United States, 5th Cir. 1981, 662 F.2d 326, rehearing denied 668 F.2d 532, or the question whether the duty is one enforceable in tort or covers the class of persons of which the plaintiff is a member, see Zabala Clemente v. United States, 1st Cir. 1978, 567 F.2d 1140, certiorari denied 435 U.S. 1006, 98 S.Ct. 1876, 56 L.Ed.2d 388.

22. E.g., Hernandez v. United States, N.D.Tex.1969, 313 F.Supp. 349 (applying Texas' definition of proximate cause).

23. E.g., Orr v. United States, 5th Cir. 1973, 486 F.2d 270 (Florida comparative negligence rule applied rather than general law of contributory negligence).

24. Jones v. United States, 4th Cir. 1957, 241 F.2d 26 (government housing near railroad, Maryland law of assumed risk barred claim for child-tenant's injury).

25. Pumphrey v. Manor Real Estate & Trust Co., 4th Cir. 1949, 176 F.2d 414.

26. American Exchange Bank of Madison, Wisconsin v. United States, 7th Cir. 1958, 257 F.2d 938.

27. United Air Lines, Inc. v. Wiener, 9th Cir. 1964, 335 F.2d 379, certiorari dismissed 379 U.S. 951, 85 S.Ct. 452, 13 L.Ed.2d 549. Where the government is not liable to the injured person, it is not liable for contribution or indemnity. See Stencel Aero Engineering Corp. v. United States, 1977, 431 U.S. 666, 97 S.Ct. 2054, 52 L.Ed.2d 665.

28. Where the FTCA is construed to withhold consent to suit, there is of course no liability even if state law would impose it on the same facts. See Stencel Aero Engineering Corp. v. United States, 1977, 431 U.S. 666, 97 S.Ct. 2054, 52 L.Ed.2d 665.

29. See Williams v. United States, 1955, 350 U.S. 857, 76 S.Ct. 100, 100 L.Ed. 761.

30. See United States v. Orleans, 1976, 425 U.S. 807, 96 S.Ct. 1971, 48 L.Ed.2d 390 (community action agency whose sole financial support was United States

The obligation of the government is, in any event, a tort obligation, and it is not obliged to purchase no-fault insurance in those states adopting some version of the Keeton-O'Connel Plan. In such states, however, the government would presumably remain liable for negligent operation of vehicles and would not be entitled to the tort exemption.[31]

The tort claims act specifically recognizes that liability may be imposed for omissions as well as for affirmative acts, and for this reason the United States may be held for negligent failure to act as well as for affirmative conduct, provided that applicable state law would impose a duty[32] to act upon a private person similarly situated.[33] By the same token, the government is not liable for non-action unless state law does impose such a duty, for example, in cases where no rescue is undertaken.[34]

The act imposes a number of particular limits, both substantive and procedural. On the procedural side three limitations are especially important. First, jurisdiction is vested exclusively in the Federal district courts, and neither a claim against the United States nor a claim against any federal employee arising out of employment can be maintained in state courts.[35] Second, the consent to suit is limited to provide consent for non-jury trials only, so that all claims of this sort are tried to the judge sitting as trier of fact.[36] Third, within two years after a claim arises,[37] it must be presented in writing to the administrative agency whose conduct is deemed responsible for the damages.[38] If the agency denies the claim, the action must be filed within six months. If

was not United States agency); Slagle v. United States, 9th Cir. 1980, 612 F.2d 1157 (whether informer for Drug Enforcement Administration was federal employee a matter of federal law).

31. Lunter, No-Fault and the FTCA: A Conflict in Philosophies, 1974, 41 Ins.Counsel J. 609; Kuzusko, No-Fault Insurance and the Federal Driver: Collision of Liabilities?, 1973, 27 JAG J. 204, 1973 Ins.L.J. 433.

32. Whether government conduct amounts to undertaking a duty or whether it is mere nonaction for which there is no liability is a matter of substantive law of the state. Schindler v. United States, 6th Cir. 1981, 661 F.2d 552. However, federal statutes and regulations may impose a duty, at least if state law would recognize such statutes as a source of duty. See Griffin v. United States, 3d Cir. 1974, 500 F.2d 1059. Where a federal statute appears to impose a duty upon the federal agency, it is not clear whether state or federal law governs the question as to the scope and extent of the duty or whether it was excused on the particular facts. See Zabala Clemente v. United States, 1st Cir. 1978, 567 F.2d 1140, certiorari denied 435 U.S. 1006, 98 S.Ct. 1876, 56 L.Ed.2d 388; Swoboda v. United States, 5th Cir. 1981, 662 F.2d 326, rehearing denied 668 F.2d 532, certiorari denied 457 U.S. 1134, 102 S.Ct. 2961, 73 L.Ed.2d 1351.

33. The private person analogy is read broadly and it is not necessary to find that private persons carry on the activity in question. Indian Towing Co. v. United States, 1955, 350 U.S. 61, 76 S.Ct. 122, 100 L.Ed.2d 48 (government liable for negligent operation of lighthouse). The fact that, under governing local law, a city would not be liable for the government's activity offers no protection to the federal government, since the analogy is to "private persons," not to municipalities. Indian Towing Co. v. United States, supra; Schindler v. United States, 6th Cir. 1981, 661 F.2d 552.

34. United States v. Sandra & Dennis Fishing Corp., 1st Cir. 1967, 372 F.2d 189, certiorari denied 389 U.S. 836, 88 S.Ct. 52, 19 L.Ed.2d 98 (no obligation to keep rescue equipment on Coast Guard vessel); Foltting v. Kaevando, S.D.Tex.1971, 324 F.Supp. 585 (same); Lacey v. United States, D.Mass.1951, 98 F.Supp. 219 (no obligation to rescue in spite of statutory responsibility of Coast Guard). The same often applies to inspections of instrumentalities under federal control. See In re Silver Bridge Disaster Litigation, D.W.Va.1974, 381 F.Supp. 931 (no duty to inspect bridge in spite of statutory obligations).

35. 28 U.S.C.A. § 1346(b); 28 U.S.C.A. § 2679(d) (removal of suits against government employees).

36. 28 U.S.C.A. § 2402.

37. Accrual of the claim has created the same problem here as elsewhere in tort law. See United States v. Kubrick, 1979, 444 U.S. 111, 100 S.Ct. 352, 62 L.Ed. 2d 259 (medical malpractice action against United States accrues no later than the time injury is manifest, though claimant did not know of government responsibility until later).

38. 28 U.S.C.A. §§ 2401(b), 2675. The statute mentions only the "appropriate agency," but it seems assumed that this means the agency whose conduct is in question. See Driggers v. United States, D.S.C.1970, 309 F.Supp. 1377. The act itself is not well constructed, but the legislative purpose seems to have been to require that the claim be asserted to the agency within two years of accrual *and* that suit be commenced within six months after the agency's denial. See S.Rep.No. 1327, 89th Cong., 2d Sess., 2 U.S.Code, Cong. & Ad. News 1966, 2515. See also, Childers v. United States, 5th Cir. 1971, 442 F.2d 1299, certiorari denied 404 U.S. 857, 92 S.Ct. 104, 30 L.Ed.2d 99.

the agency fails to act on the claim within six months, the claimant may at "any time" thereafter opt to treat this non-action as a denial of the claim and file suit.[39]

On the substantive side, certain limits have been read into the tort claims act by judicial construction. The most important of these deals with the question whether the government can be held strictly liable. One section of the statute provides for liability of the government whenever a private person would be liable in like circumstances,[40] and since private persons are often liable without fault, as in cases involving harm from blasting, this section would seem to impose liability upon the government. However, the jurisdictional section of the statute speaks of a "negligent or wrongful act or omission,"[41] language that might be thought to exclude strict liability. The Supreme Court has indeed taken this view, limiting liability in tort claims cases to cases in which there is fault in the sense of negligence or intent, and refusing to impose liability for blasting or sonic boom damage that results without such fault.[42]

Judicial construction has also narrowed the government's liability to various persons who, because of their pre-existing relationship to the government, may be entitled to some other remedy. Although there is no provision in the statute to this effect, the doctrine of the *Feres* case has it that members of the armed forces injured by governmental negligence in the course of their duties are flatly denied any tort recovery.[43] The arguments for this position are that to permit recovery would subvert military discipline, that it would be undesirable to vary the rights of armed forces personnel according to the varied laws of the states as would necessarily be the case under the tort claims act, and that the in-service benefits provided by other statutes, analogous to workers' compensation, should be considered the exclusive remedy. The result is that a member of the armed services can recover for government negligence only if the injury is *not* incident to service, as where injury occurs after discharge or while the plaintiff is on leave.[44] In line with the exclusive remedy rationale, other government employees are limited by statute to the workers' compensation remedy,[45] and the Court has held that federal prisoners entitled to compensation for prison injuries are likewise barred from tort actions.[46]

Although the reasons given in support of the *Feres* rule might seem applicable at most to members of the armed forces, the rule has been extended to prevent recoveries by third persons indirectly harmed by injury to service personnel. It is thus held that a manufacturer of military equipment, held

---

39. 28 U.S.C.A. § 2675(a). See Locke v. United States, D.Hawaii 1972, 351 F.Supp. 185, where death occurred on July 22, 1967 and a claim was asserted administratively on July 17, 1969. This was never denied by the agency and suit was held timely though it was not commenced until July 21, 1971, nearly four years after the action accrued.

40. 28 U.S.C.A. § 2674.

41. 28 U.S.C.A. § 1346(b).

42. Laird v. Nelms, 1972, 406 U.S. 797, 92 S.Ct. 1899, 32 L.Ed.2d 499, rehearing denied 409 U.S. 902, 93 S.Ct. 95, 34 L.Ed.2d 165 (sonic boom); Dalehite v. United States, 1953, 346 U.S. 15, 73 S.Ct. 956, 97 L.Ed. 1427, rehearing denied 346 U.S. 841, 74 S.Ct. 13, 98 L.Ed. 362, rehearing denied 346 U.S. 880, 74 S.Ct. 117, 98 L.Ed. 386, rehearing denied 347 U.S. 924, 74 S.Ct. 511, 98 L.Ed. 1078 (explosion). See Peck, Laird v. Nelms: A Call for Review and Revision of the Federal Tort Claims Act, 1973, 48 Wash.L.Rev. 391.

43. Feres v. United States, 1950, 340 U.S. 135, 71 S.Ct. 153, 95 L.Ed. 152; Frazier v. United States, M.D. Fla.1973, 372 F.Supp. 208.

44. United States v. Brown, 1954, 348 U.S. 110, 75 S.Ct. 141, 99 L.Ed. 139; Brooks v. United States, 1949, 337 U.S. 49, 69 S.Ct. 918, 93 L.Ed. 1200; Annot., 1969, 1 A.L.R.Fed. 563. Post-discharge negligence in failing to treat or warn of in-service injuries presents a difficult case under this rule. Some courts have made liability turn on finding a new and independent tort after discharge. See cases discussed in Broudy v. United States, 9th Cir. 1981, 661 F.2d 125 (in-service exposure to radiation, failure to warn of effects after discharge, liability possible).

45. 5 U.S.C.A. § 8116 now so provides in explicit language.

46. United States v. Demko, 1966, 385 U.S. 149, 87 S.Ct. 382, 17 L.Ed. 258. Where the prisoner is not covered by a compensation plan, he may recover for torts under the tort claims act. United States v. Muniz, 1963, 374 U.S. 150, 83 S.Ct. 1850, 10 L.Ed.2d 805.

liable to a serviceman for equipment-related injury, cannot claim indemnity from the government even if the real fault lay there.[47] Lower courts have at times gone even further in holding that the rule precludes loss of consortium claims by family members, a rule that might be justified on the traditional view that such claims are "derivative."[48] But others have gone so far as to hold that *Feres* prevents a recovery for genetic damage to a child that results when a parent suffers chromosome damage because of armed forces negligence.[49]

So far at least, none of this is changed because the tort alleged is an intentional one or because it involves violation of a federal constitutional right, and the government avoids liability in such cases as well as in ordinary negligence cases.[50]

The reasons given by the Court for this rule do not always seem to apply equally to all the cases and the Court itself has shifted emphasis on the different rationales from time to time.[51] But the rule itself appears to be as well established as if the statute itself had enunciated it.

Quite apart from judicial construction, the Act itself provides a number of limits on liability which are often held to be not merely affirmative defenses for the government, but limitations on the courts' jurisdiction.[52] Some of these merely exclude from the tort claims act those claims that are provided for under other, more specific, legislation, such as those claims to be brought under the Suits in Admiralty Act.[53] Another group of exceptions provides for continued immunity for certain governmental activities, such as

---

47. Stencel Aero Engineering Corp. v. United States, 1977, 431 U.S. 666, 97 S.Ct. 2054, 52 L.Ed.2d 665.

48. Van Sickel v. United States, 9th Cir. 1960, 285 F.2d 87; Harrison v. United States, D.Conn.1979, 479 F.Supp. 529, affirmed 2d Cir., 622 F.2d 573, certiorari denied 1980, 449 U.S. 828, 101 S.Ct. 93, 66 L.Ed.2d 32.

But it appears that a member of the armed forces may recover for injury to a spouse, though the "military discipline" problem would seem just as great as in other cases. Messer v. United States, D.Fla.1951, 95 F.Supp. 512; cf. Rise v. United States, 5th Cir. 1980, 630 F.2d 1068.

Independent injury to a family member is, however, actionable in the same way that injury to a service person who is off duty is actionable. Kohn v. United States, 2d Cir. 1982, 680 F.2d 922 (parents not barred in claim for distress resulting from service's handling of son's death, though they are barred on death itself). Cf. Broudy v. United States, 9th Cir. 1981, 661 F.2d 125.

49. Lombard v. United States, D.C.Cir. 1982, 690 F.2d 215; Monaco v. United States, 9th Cir. 1981, 661 F.2d 129, certiorari denied 456 U.S. 989, 102 S.Ct. 2269, 73 L.Ed.2d 1284 (radiation injuries to serviceman causing genetic injury to children, no claim allowable on behalf of children); In re Agent Orange Product Liability Litigation, D.N.Y.1980, 506 F.Supp. 762, reargument denied 534 F.Supp. 1046. See Laswell v. Brown, 8th Cir. 1982, 683 F.2d 261. Cf. Harten v. Coons, 10th Cir. 1974, 502 F.2d 1363, certiorari denied 420 U.S. 963, 95 S.Ct. 1354, 43 L.Ed.2d 441 (wife's claim based on negligent vasectomy of serviceman-husband denied). Contra: Hinkie v. United States, D.Pa.1981, 524 F.Supp. 277.

50. Jaffee v. United States, 3d Cir. 1979, 592 F.2d 712, on remand D.C.N.J. 468 F.Supp. 632, certiorari denied 441 U.S. 961, 99 S.Ct. 2406, 60 L.Ed.2d 1066 affirmed 663 F.2d 1226, certiorari denied 456 U.S. 972, 102 S.Ct. 2234, 72 L.Ed.2d 845; Jaffee v. United States, 3d Cir. 1981, 663 F.2d 1226, certiorari denied 972 U.S. 456, 102 S.Ct. 2234, 72 L.Ed.2d 845 (allegation that serviceman was required to stand unprotected from radiation near nuclear explosion, *Feres* bars recovery from government and from officers allegedly responsible); Laswell v. Brown, 8th Cir. 1982, 683 F.2d 261 (similar).

51. United States v. Muniz, 1963, 374 U.S. 150, 83 S.Ct. 1850, 10 L.Ed.2d 805 (prisoner allowed recovery, *Feres* interpreted to be concerned mainly with military discipline); United States v. Demko, 1966, 385 U.S. 149, 87 S.Ct. 382, 17 L.Ed.2d 258 (prisoner denied recovery since there was a prisoner-compensation scheme in effect and it furnished exclusive remedy); Stencel Aero Engineering Corp. v. United States, 1977, 431 U.S. 666, 97 S.Ct. 2054, 62 L.Ed.2d 665, rehearing denied 434 U.S. 882, 98 S.Ct. 250, 54 L.Ed.2d 168 (all three rationales treated as factors to be considered in extending application of *Feres*); Hatzlachh Supply Co., Inc. v. United States, 1980, 444 U.S. 460, 100 S.Ct. 647, 62 L.Ed.2d 614 (exclusive remedy rationale treated as main explanation of Stencel).

52. E.g., Smith v. United States, 10th Cir. 1976, 546 F.2d 872. Contra: Stewart v. United States, 7th Cir. 1952, 199 F.2d 517. The jurisdictional view appears to be the most common and it has been extended to cover the judicially created exceptions as well as the statutory exceptions. Stanley v. Central Intelligence Agency, 5th Cir. 1981, 639 F.2d 1146 (*Feres* exception jurisdictional.) The plaintiff must show that, on the face of it, the exceptions in the statute do not apply. Carlyle v. United States, 6th Cir. 1982, 674 F.2d 554.

53. 28 U.S.C.A. § 2680(d) (Admiralty claims); § 2680(e) (Trading with Enemy Act claims). The same result was reached judicially as to civil rights obligations of the United States in Baker v. F. & F. Investment Co., 7th Cir. 1973, 489 F.2d 829.

combatant activities of the military in wartime and delivery of mail.[54]

Two other groups of exceptions are more important. One group continues the immunity, not on the basis of specific governmental activities, but on the basis of the kind of claim or theory on which the plaintiff's action is based. The immunity is retained for claims arising out of assault, battery, false imprisonment or arrest, malicious prosecution, abuse of process, libel, slander, misrepresentation and interference with contract rights.[55] The 1974 Congress, incensed over official invasions of private homes without a warrant, inserted a proviso to make the government liable even for assault, battery and false arrest if any of those torts is committed by law enforcement officers,[56] though in most[57] other cases the immunity for such torts was continued.

Many of the exemptions may have failed to take into account the civil rights implications involved in such claims as batteries by federal officers, but the more general effect of these provisions is to recognize liability in most cases of serious physical interference, as in the case of negligence[58] and trespass,[59] and to exclude liability in most cases of economic harm unaccompanied by physical injury, as in the case of interference with contract or misrepresentation.

There are, however, problems in interpretation, and in some instances the federal courts have taken a rather protective view of the treasury. At one time a physician's operation on the wrong leg was regarded as a battery,[60] as to which liability was excluded, rather than as negligent malpractice, as to which liability would be imposed, though this view probably would not prevail today.[61] The battery exclusion has also given rise to the problem of the sentry or officer who is privileged to use force in a reasonable degree, but who in fact employs an unreasonable amount of force. In some cases this has been regarded a a battery,[62] while in others it has been regarded as negligence,[63] and liability is imposed or not accordingly.

The exclusion of misrepresentation has been read by the Supreme Court to exclude governmental liability for negligent as well as intentional misrepresentation.[64] Lower courts have sometimes carried this to extremes, protecting the government even when it miscommunicated safety information with the result that the plaintiff was

---

54. 28 U.S.C.A. § 2680(b) (mail delivery); § 2680(c) (tax collections); § 2680(f) (quarantines by the United States); § 2680(i) (Treasury fiscal operations); § 2680(j) (combatant activities in wartime); § 2680(k) (activities in foreign countries); § 2680(*l*) (TVA Operations); § 2680(m) (Panama Canal operations); § 2680(n) (certain federal bank operations).

55. 28 U.S.C.A. § 2680(h).

56. Now embodied in 28 U.S.C.A. § 2680(h). See S.Rep. 93–588, 2 U.S.Cong. & Ad.News, 1974, 2789; Boger, Gitenstein & Verkuil, The Federal Tort Claims Act Intentional Torts Amendment: An Interpretative Analysis, 1976, 54 N.C.L.Rev. 497.

57. Statutes dealing with the Public Health Service incorporate the liabilities of the tort claims act by reference, but provide specifically that the government is liable, even for assaults and batteries of PHS employees, "arising out of negligence." 42 U.S.C.A. § 233(e).

58. E.g., Standefer v. United States, 5th Cir. 1975, 511 F.2d 101 (medical malpractice); Yates v. United States, 10th Cir. 1974, 497 F.2d 878 (negligent air traffic control).

59. E.g., Hatahley v. United States, 1956, 351 U.S. 173, 76 S.Ct. 745, 100 L.Ed. 1065 ("trespasses," conversion of horses); Simons v. United States, 5th Cir. 1969, 413 F.2d 531 (oil production on lands claimed by plaintiffs). Where the remedy sought for trespass is specific—ejectment or injunction—the courts have continued to apply sovereign immunity rules, and even in some damages-for-trespass claims relief has been denied against the government if there is a title dispute. See Steadman, "Forgive U.S. Its Trespasses?": Land Title Disputes with the Sovereign, 1972 Duke L.J. 15.

60. Moos v. United States, D.Minn.1954, 118 F.Supp. 275, affirmed 8th Cir. 1955, 225 F.2d 705.

61. Fontenelle v. United States, S.D.N.Y.1971, 327 F.Supp. 801; Lane v. United States, E.D.Va.1964, 225 F.Supp. 850. See note 57 supra.

62. Alaniz v. United States, 10th Cir. 1958, 257 F.2d 108; Smith v. United States, E.D.Mich.1971, 330 F.Supp. 867 (allegation that guardsman on riot duty negligently shot plaintiff held a battery).

63. Tastor v. United States, N.D.Cal.1954, 124 F.Supp. 548 (sentry fired into the air, scuffled with decedent, accidentally shot him in the scuffle).

64. United States v. Neustadt, 1961, 366 U.S. 696, 81 S.Ct. 1294, 6 L.Ed.2d 614. See The Federal Seal of Approval: Government Liability for Negligent Inspection, 1974, 62 Geo.L.J. 937.

personally injured,[65] though most of the decisions have confined this exclusion to cases of economic harm without physical injury or to cases likely to be excluded on other grounds in any event.[66] The other exceptions in this list, such as those dealing with false imprisonment[67] and defamation,[68] have also given rise to problems in interpretation, and no doubt the 1974 amendments will also do so. The one clear thing about this list of exceptions is that the plaintiff's characterization of his action as one for negligence will not control and that the courts will ignore this label and treat the claim as one within the list of exceptions if the pleaded facts seem to warrant.[69]

The last exception is of a different order from the others and is perhaps the most important. The statute retains the immunity for all governmental conduct that involves "discretionary functions or duties."[70] The main idea here is that certain governmental activities are legislative or executive in nature and that any judicial control of those activities, in tort suits or otherwise, would disrupt the balanced separation of powers of the three branches of government. Indeed, judicial review of major executive policies for "negligence" or wrongfulness might well operate to make the judiciary the final and supreme arbiter in government, not only on a constitutional level, but on all matters on which judgment might differ. The discretionary immunity is retained by the FTCA to avoid this, and the statute itself gives one specific example of the kind of discretion that is protected from tort suit: the government is not to be liable for the execution or administration of a statute or regulation, even if the statute or regulation proves to be invalid.[71] The discretionary immunity is, however, much wider than this, and is often said to include any governmental conduct that involves policy judgment.[72] The leading case is Dalehite v. United States,[73] where the government adopted a plan for export of fertilizer to boost crops in friendly countries. The fertilizer was manufactured from explosive materials, and a large amount of it, on board ship in the harbor of Texas City, exploded, doing great destruction to the whole area. The government was allegedly negligent in controlling the manufacture, in handling, and in shipping the fertilizer. The Supreme Court held that there would be no liability because "[w]here there is room for policy judgment and deci-

65. Vaughn v. United States, D.Miss.1966, 259 F.Supp. 286. Cf. Fitch v. United States, 6th Cir. 1975, 513 F.2d 1013, certiorari denied 423 U.S. 866, 96 S.Ct. 127, 46 L.Ed.2d 95 (no liability for wrongful induction into service since this was ultimately traceable to a "misrepresentation" about the plaintiff's lottery number).

66. Kohn v. United States, 2d Cir. 1982, 680 F.2d 922 (fraud exception generally applicable only to "commercial decisions"). Thus negligence in furnishing flight safety information is not protected by the fraud exception. E.g., Ingham v. Eastern Air Lines, Inc., 2d Cir. 1967, 373 F.2d 227, certiorari denied 389 U.S. 931, 88 S.Ct. 295, 19 L.Ed.2d 292. See Annot., 1976, 30 A.L.R.Fed. 421.

67. Duenges v. United States, D.N.Y.1953, 114 F.Supp. 751 (negligent error prevented timely discharge from service, no action since this is false imprisonment). Cf. Fitch v. United States, 6th Cir. 1975, 513 F.2d 1013, certiorari denied 423 U.S. 866, 96 S.Ct. 127, 46 L.Ed.2d 95 (mistaken lottery number basis for wrongful induction into service is "misrepresentation," no action). The United States has consented to liability for "unjust conviction" under a special statute. 28 U.S.C.A. §§ 1495, 2513.

68. Quinones v. United States, 3d Cir. 1974, 492 F.2d 1269 (negligent maintenance of employee records with resulting derogatory information to others held "negligence" not "defamation").

69. Alaniz v. United States, supra note 62, and Duenges v. United States, supra note 67, are typical. But compare Duenges with Quinones v. United States, supra note 68. In both, the complaints alleged negligent maintenance of employee records. In Duenges this led to detention of the employee; in Quinones it led to derogatory statements about him. In Duenges it was said that this was not really negligence but false imprisonment and liability was denied. In Quinones it was said that the complaint, though it alleged defamation, also separately alleged a good claim in negligence. This last seems atypical.

70. 28 U.S.C.A. § 2680(a).

71. 28 U.S.C.A. § 2680(a).

72. Dalehite v. United States, 1953, 346 U.S. 15, 73 S.Ct. 956, 97 L.Ed. 1427, rehearing denied 347 U.S. 924, 74 S.Ct. 511, 98 L.Ed. 1078.

73. 1953, 346 U.S. 15, 73 S.Ct. 956, 97 L.Ed. 1427, rehearing denied 347 U.S. 924, 74 S.Ct. 511, 98 L.Ed. 1078.

sion there is discretion." [74] The Court also seemed to equate policy judgment with the planning level of government and to imply that the more routine, operational level decisions in government would not be considered to be discretionary.

Dalehite may have applied its own test in an unusually demanding way to avoid governmental liability. Since that decision, however, quite a few cases have held that if the government's conduct is at the planning level it is protected by the immunity, but that once a decision is taken at the planning level, its execution—the "operational level"—is not immune and must be carried out with reasonable care.[75] In some instances this has been an easy distinction to apply. The government is thus not liable for adopting or refusing to adopt administrative regulations[76] even though such regulations might promote safety.[77] By the same token it is not liable for adopting or refusing to adopt[78] public programs of improvement or recreation, or programs of relief, safety or defense. Thus, for example, it is not liable for the adoption of a weapons test,[79] though such a test is dangerous, or the adoption of a flood control program,[80] though it may eventually cause damage. The discretionary immunity does not necessarily end with the adoption of a program; it may protect the government's decision to take those risks implicit in the program itself, as where the government exercises its discretion to build a dam and then decides to release some of the water impounded.[81]

At the same time these rules do not justify the government's failure to warn of risks created by its discretionary decisions,[82] or to supply information that will allow other governmental agents or citizens themselves to proceed with greater safety.[83] And affirmative, specific acts of negligence are often clearly "operational," so that the government is readily held liable for the negligent operation of automobiles,[84] airport control towers,[85] lighthouses[86] and other forms of traffic and traffic control;[87] and equally for negligent performance of medical care,[88] for negligent care of prisoners,[89] and for negligent maintenance of property.[90]

---

74. 346 U.S. at 42, 73 S.Ct. at 971.

75. Indian Towing Co. v. United States, 1955, 350 U.S. 61, 76 S.Ct. 122, 100 L.Ed. 48.

76. Emch v. United States, 7th Cir. 1980, 630 F.2d 523, certiorari denied 1981, 450 U.S. 966, 101 S.Ct. 1482, 67 L.Ed.2d 614 (economic loss resulting from government failure to regulate banking practices).

77. Loge v. United States, 8th Cir. 1981, 662 F.2d 1268, certiorari denied 456 U.S. 944, 102 S.Ct. 2009, 72 L.Ed.2d 466 (failure to regulate polio vaccines for safety); Madison v. United States, 8th Cir. 1982, 679 F.2d 736 (inadequate regulations for contractor's safety procedures discretionary).

78. Bearce v. United States, 7th Cir. 1980, 614 F.2d 556, certiorari denied 449, U.S. 837, 101 S.Ct. 112, 66 L.Ed.2d 44, rehearing denied 449 U.S. 1026, 101 S.Ct. 595, 66 L.Ed. 2d 488.

79. E.g., Bartholomae Corp. v. United States, S.D. Cal.1955, 135 F.Supp. 651, affirmed 9th Cir. 1957, 253 F.2d 716 (bomb).

80. Coates v. United States, 8th Cir. 1950, 181 F.2d 816; Spillway Marina, Inc. v. United States, 10th Cir. 1971, 445 F.2d 876.

81. Spillway Marina, Inc. v. United States, 10th Cir. 1971, 445 F.2d 876.

82. Lindgren v. United States, 9th Cir. 1982, 665 F.2d 978 (warning of flood control project's dangers required). Spillway Marina, Inc. v. United States, 10th Cir. 1971, 445 F.2d 876, may have failed to give adequate attention to the separate warning element. Flooding as a result of a flood control project is protected by a specific immunity under 33 U.S.C.A. § 702c, but flooding was not involved in these cases.

83. Payton v. United States, 5th Cir. 1982, 679 F.2d 475.

84. E.g., Sullivan v. United States, N.D.Ill.1955, 129 F.Supp. 713.

85. Ross v. United States, 5th Cir. 1981, 640 F.2d 511; United States v. Union Trust Co., D.C.Cir. 1955, 221 F.2d 62, affirmed 350 U.S. 907, 76 S.Ct. 192, 100 L.Ed. 799 (per curiam).

86. Indian Towing Co. v. United States, 1955, 350 U.S. 61, 76 S.Ct. 122, 100 L.Ed. 48.

87. Driscoll v. United States, 9th Cir. 1975, 525 F.2d 136, 37 A.L.R.Fed. 530 (government may be liable for decision not to use traffic control devices on air force base).

88. E.g., Supchak v. United States, 3d Cir. 1966, 365 F.2d 844.

89. Brown v. United States, E.D.Ark.1974, 374 F.Supp. 723.

90. Pumphrey v. Manor Real Estate & Trust Co., 4th Cir. 1949, 176 F.2d 414 (U.S. as landlord); Ameri-

The distinction between planning and operational errors does not assist judgment in all cases. If the weather bureau negligently fails to report that floods are on their way and people are killed or property destroyed because of this failure, all but the most cynical would prefer to think that the decision was an operational blunder, not the result of government planning. But courts have held that the weather service's failure is discretionary nonetheless.[91] Or again, negligent design of public improvements in a dangerous manner involves "planning" in the sense that can be contrasted with operational decisions; yet the cases are divided and some treat public improvements as discretionary[92] while others do not.[93]

The distinction between planning and operational decisions, if workable at all, is at best difficult to apply,[94] and in a good many cases it is not seriously discussed or even mentioned.[95] In some cases it may be easier to ask whether there is "room for policy judgment," and to reject the immunity if official judgment is based on something else. Something like this was done in Griffin v. United States,[96] where a government agency approved a lot of polio vaccine in spite of tests showing it to be dangerous. The court regarded the decision to release the vaccine as a professional decision about medical safety, not as a decision of administrative policy, and the government was held liable.

Probably no one test will control the decision on discretionary immunity. Although the fact that the government has omitted to act is not in itself a defense,[97] the discretionary immunity is frequently emphasized in nonfeasance cases.[98] On the other hand, where the government's activity is affirmative, specific, and in violation of a statute, regulation[99] or constitutional provision[1] imposing a duty upon government,[2] courts are often willing to say there is no room for dis-

---

can Exchange Bank of Madison, Wisconsin v. United States, 7th Cir. 1958, 257 F.2d 938 (U.S. as invitor).

91. National Manufacturing Co. v. United States, 8th Cir. 1954, 210 F.2d 263, certiorari denied 347 U.S. 967, 74 S.Ct. 778, 98 L.Ed. 1108; Bartie v. United States, W.D.La.1963, 216 F.Supp. 10, affirmed on other grounds 5th Cir., 326 F.2d 754, certiorari denied 1964, 379 U.S. 852, 85 S.Ct. 98, 13 L.Ed.2d 55. Under 33 U.S. C.A. § 702c the government is immune from flooding claims as a result of flood control projects, but this has been interpreted not to cover flood damages unrelated to flood control purposes. See Pierce v. United States, 9th Cir. 1981, 650 F.2d 202.

92. Wright v. United States, 10th Cir. 1977, 568 F.2d 153, certiorari denied 1978, 439 U.S. 824, 99 S.Ct. 94, 58 L.Ed.2d 117; Thomas v. United States, D.Mo. 1949, 81 F.Supp. 881. In some of these cases specifications, designs and "plans" are apparently confused with "planning level" decisions on the basis of the verbal similarilty between "plans" and "planning."

93. Seaboard Coast Line Railroad Co. v. United States, 5th Cir. 1973, 473 F.2d 714 (drainage ditch designed to permit water to undermine plaintiff's railroad track, recovery). Cf. Moyer v. Martin Marietta Corp., 5th Cir. 1973, 481 F.2d 585 (design of gear in plane not discretionary).

94. See Reynolds, The Discretionary Function Exception of the Federal Tort Claims Act, 1968, 57 Geo. L.J. 81, a useful survey of literature on the subject.

95. E.g., Griffin v. United States, 3d Cir. 1974, 500 F.2d 1059.

96. Griffin v. United States, 3d Cir. 1974, 500 F.2d 1059.

97. See Indian Towing Co. v. United States, 1955, 350 U.S. 61, 76 S.Ct. 122, 100 L.Ed. 48.

98. E.g., failure to give flood warnings, National Manufacturing Co. v. United States, 8th Cir. 1954, 210 F.2d 263, certiorari denied 347 U.S. 967, 74 S.Ct. 778, 98 L.Ed. 1108; failure to send an ambulance when needed, Morton v. United States, D.C.Cir. 1955, 228 F.2d 431, certiorari denied 1956, 350 U.S. 975, 76 S.Ct. 452, 100 L.Ed. 845; or failure to seek out adequate information before granting parole to a prisoner, Payton v. United States, 5th Cir. 1982, 679 F.2d 475.

99. Payton v. United States, 5th Cir. 1982, 679 F.2d 475; Griffin v. United States, 3d Cir. 1974, 500 F.2d 1059; Loge v. United States, 8th Cir. 1981, 662 F.2d 1268, certiorari denied 456 U.S. 944, 102 S.Ct. 2009, 72 L.Ed.2d 466; Myers & Myers v. United States Postal Service, 2d Cir. 1975, 527 F.2d 1252, 35 A.L.R.Fed. 466.

In Madison v. United States, 8th Cir. 1982, 679 F.2d 736, the court held that the government might be found liable for failing to enforce its contractor's compliance with regulations of the Contractor's Safety Manual, which was applicable to the contractor by the terms of the contract.

1. Cf. Butz v. Economou, 1978, 438 U.S. 478, 98 S.Ct. 2894, 57 L.Ed.2d 895, on remand D.N.Y., 466 F.Supp. 1351, affirmed 2d Cir., 633 F.2d 203 (semble, federal officer's discretion limited by constitution); Harlow v. Fitzgerald, 1982, 457 U.S. 800, 102 S.Ct. 2727, 73 L.Ed.2d 396 (similar): see Myers & Myers v. United States Postal Service, 2d Cir. 1975, 527 F.2d 1252, 35 A.L.R.Fed. 466.

2. The statute or regulation may not impose a tort duty, or may not impose it in favor of the class of persons that includes the plaintiff. Zabala Clemente v.

cretion. The presence of a pre-existing safety standard, or any appropriate standard governing the activity in question, will also tend to displace the room that otherwise exists for government discretion and immunity.[3] And the absence of such a standard leads to the conclusion that the activity in question is discretionary.[4] Thus the grant and refusal of permits and licenses is typically a matter committed to administrative judgment which cannot be readily evaluated against any known criterion, and consequently it is often said that licensing matters and the like are discretionary and protected.[5] But if the government violates existing procedural standards in denying a hearing,[6] or violates safety standards in the release of dangerous drugs[7] or dangerous prisoners,[8] the immunity disappears. Similarly, there may be no basis for evaluating an administrative decision that denies a patient admission to a hospital, but there is a safety standard for treatment once he is admitted, with the result that there is immunity in the first case[9] but not the second.[10] There is also a safety standard governing the speed of vehicles, and though the FBI agent may exercise good judgment in the speedy pursuit of the public enemy, the government will be liable if his speed causes a collision, since there is a safety standard on which his conduct can be judged and which will displace the discretion that might otherwise exist.[11]

All this may be a way of saying that courts have confused the issues of duty and negligence on the one hand with the issue of the discretionary immunity on the other. It seems fairly clear in at least some of the cases that courts have decided negligence or duty issues under the guise of "discretion."[12] Perhaps this has not always led to

---

United States, 1st Cir. 1978, 567 F.2d 1140, certiorari denied 435 U.S. 1006, 98 S.Ct. 1876, 56 L.Ed.2d 388 (violation of regulation requiring warnings of chartered plane passengers not actionable); Cf. Swoboda v. United States, 5th Cir. 1981, 662 F.2d 326 (violation excusable).

But cf. Madison v. United States, 8th Cir. 1982, 679 F.2d 736 (government might be liable for failure to enforce safety regulations against an independent contractor if state law imposed such a duty, purporting to distinguish Zabala Clemente v. United States, supra).

3. Otherwise put, there must be a basis for evaluating the administrative decision on grounds other than purely administrative ones. See Driscoll v. United States, 9th Cir. 1975, 525 F.2d 136, citing Jaffe, Suits Against Governments and Officers: Damage Actions, 77 Harv.L.Rev. 209.

4. Barton v. United States, 10th Cir. 1979, 609 F.2d 977 ("There are no fixed standards or guides by which the effect of drought on the range forage can be assessed for the purpose of determining whether grazing should be continued on public lands. It is wholly a matter of judgment * * * and clearly within the discretionary exception of the Federal Tort Claims Act.").

5. E.g., Thompson v. United States, 9th Cir. 1979, 592 F.2d 1104; see Bernitsky v. United States, 3d Cir. 1980, 620 F.2d 948, certiorari denied 449 U.S. 870, 101 S.Ct. 208, 66 L.Ed.2d 90.

6. Myers & Myers v. United States Postal Service, 2d Cir. 1975, 527 F.2d 1252, 35 A.L.R.Fed. 466.

7. Griffin v. United States, 3d Cir. 1974, 500 F.2d 1059. See Schindler v. United States, 6th Cir. 1981, 661 F.2d 552. So far, the implication has been that if regulations had permitted dangerous vaccine, or if the government had failed to adopt regulations, there would be no liability. See Garbarino v. United States, 6th Cir. 1981, 666 F.2d 1061 (failure to adopt regulations discretionary).

8. Payton v. United States, 5th Cir. 1982, 679 F.2d 475.

9. Morton v. United States, D.C.Cir. 1955, 228 F.2d 431, certiorari denied 1956, 350 U.S. 975, 76 S.Ct. 452, 100 L.Ed. 845 (prison authority denied medical attention to prisoner, discretionary); Denny v. United States, 5th Cir. 1942, 171 F.2d 365, certiorari denied 1948, 337 U.S. 919, 69 S.Ct. 1161, 93 L.Ed. 1728 (hospital administratively denied attention to would-be patient, discretionary).

10. Supchak v. United States, 3d Cir. 1966, 365 F.2d 844 (medical negligence not discretionary); Rise v. United States, 5th Cir. 1980, 630 F.2d 1068 (similar).

11. Sullivan v. United States, N.D.Ill.1955, 129 F.Supp. 713.

12. A cost-benefit assessment is typical in deciding the negligence issue and it also appears in many cases on the discretionary immunity. E.g., in Slagle v. United States, 9th Cir. 1980, 612 F.2d 1157, a drug informer, out of touch with his government contact, became involved in a gun fight in which the plaintiff was injured. The plaintiff asserted that the government was negligent in failing to have a better system of communication between government agents and informers. The court thought the government protected by the discretionary immunity because this was a "policy decision." It was a policy decision because it involved weighing of costs and benefits of such a system—the very thing that would be involved in determining negligence. There are many cases that seem to involve decisions on negligence in the guise of the immunity is-

a bad result, but the difference is quite important in many cases. The discretionary immunity issue, often viewed as jurisdictional, is usually resolved on motion to dismiss or on summary judgment motion—in other words, resolved without a full trial on the merits. If this device is in fact used to decide negligence and duty issues, the judge is likely to be acting without adequate factual development.

States

General rule. Based on the idea that the king could do no wrong, the immunity of the modern state is much like that of the federal government: the state and its agencies[13] must pay for property taken for public purposes,[14] but in the absence of consent, the immunity is otherwise a complete protection.[15]

Procedural and jurisdictional immunities. In addition to the substantive immunity from tort actions, the states may enjoy procedural or jurisdictional immunities. A procedural immunity may condition the right to sue the state, whether in tort or otherwise, or may eliminate the right altogether. This immunity is often abolished by statutes providing that state agencies may sue or be sued, but even when statutes so provide, the substantive tort immunity may remain intact as a complete defense.[16] The Eleventh Amendment to the United States Constitution provides a procedural or jurisdictional immunity by forbidding federal court suits against the states.[17] This immunity from federal-court suit, however, does not prevent a suit against the state in the courts of a sister-state,[18] nor does it prevent a suit against

---

sue. E.g., Blitz v. Boog, 2d Cir. 1964, 328 F.2d 596, certiorari denied 379 U.S. 855, 85 S.Ct. 106, 13 L.Ed.2d 58; Fahey v. United States, S.D.N.Y.1957, 153 F.Supp. 878 (adding a discretion argument to the decision based on no negligence and no duty). Compare Lipka v. United States, D.N.Y.1965, 249 F.Supp. 213, affirmed 2d Cir. 1966, 369 F.2d 288, certiorari denied 1967, 387 U.S. 935, 87 S.Ct. 2061, 18 L.Ed.2d 997, rehearing denied 388 U.S. 925, 87 S.Ct. 2129, 18 L.Ed.2d 1381 with Brown v. United States, D.Ark.1974, 374 F.Supp. 723 (contrary if decided on immunity but reconcilable if based on duty of care owed to third persons, which exists in the case of prisoners but not in the case of public generally). Nonliability for weather forecasts is inexplicable as a discretionary immunity, but may be reconcilable with the general rule that publishers are not liable to the public generally, at least for economic harm. Compare National Manufacturing Co. v. United States, 8th Cir. 1954, 210 F.2d 263, certiorari denied 347 U.S. 367, 74 S.Ct. 778, 98 L.Ed. 1108 (weather) with Jaillet v. Cashman, 1923, 235 N.Y. 511, 139 N.E. 714 (publisher of ticker-tape not liable to readers for economic harm). See also Dorset Yacht Co., Ltd. v. Home Office, Ct.App., [1969] W.L.R. 1008, appeal dismissed [1970] A.C. 1004. One of the most articulate expressions is Judge Fuld's opinion in Weiss v. Fote, 1960, 7 N.Y.2d 579, 200 N.Y.S.2d 409, 167 N.E.2d 63.

13. State agencies have the same standing to claim the tort immunity as the state. E.g., Taratino v. Allentown State Hospital, 1974, 16 Pa.Cmwlth. 133, 329 A.2d 291, affirmed 1976, 465 Pa. 580, 351 A.2d 247 (hospital); Texas Department of Corrections v. Herring, Tex. 1974, 513 S.W.2d 6 (department of corrections). The immunity of political subdivisions, such as municipalities, however, has a different origin and scope. See below p. 1029. Likewise the Eleventh Amendment immunity from suit in federal court applies to states and their agencies, but not to political subdivisions. Lake Country Estates, Inc. v. Tahoe Regional Planning Agency, 1979, 440 U.S. 391, 99 S.Ct. 1171, 59 L.Ed.2d 401, on remand D.Cal., 474 F.Supp. 901.

14. This is constitutionally required of the states as well as of the federal government. Chicago, Burlington & Quincy Railroad Co. v. Chicago, 1897, 166 U.S. 226, 17 S.Ct. 581, 41 L.Ed. 979; Boxberger v. State Highway Department, 1952, 126 Colo. 438, 250 P.2d 1007; Thornburg v. Port of Portland, 1962, 233 Or. 178, 376 P.2d 100.

15. Second Restatement of Torts, § 895B (1979).

16. Charles E. Brohawn & Brothers, Inc. v. Board of Trustees of Chesapeake College, 1973, 269 Md. 164, 304 A.2d 819; Elizabeth River Tunnel District v. Beecher, 1961, 202 Va. 452, 117 S.E.2d 685; Note, 1961, 74 Harv.L.Rev. 714. But it is a matter of construing each agency's statute, and the provision of one may be a waiver of tort immunity, see Taylor v. New Jersey Highway Authority, 1956, 22 N.J. 454, 126 A.2d 313, while the provision of another is not, see McCabe v. New Jersey Turnpike Authority, 1961, 35 N.J. 26, 170 A.2d 810.

17. "The judicial power of the United States shall not be construed to extend to any suit in law or equity, commenced or prosecuted against one of the United States by citizens of another state, or by citizens or subjects of any foreign state." U.S. Const.Amend. XI. Hans v. Louisiana, 1890, 134 U.S. 1, 10 S.Ct. 504, 33 L.Ed. 842 is interpreted to extend this language to cover suits against a state by its own citizens. See Florida Department of State v. Treasure Salvors, Inc., 1982, 458 U.S. 670, 102 S.Ct. 3304, 73 L.Ed.2d 1057 (Brennan, J., concurring).

18. Nevada v. Hall, 1979, 440 U.S. 410, 99 S.Ct. 1182, 59 L.Ed.2d 416, rehearing denied 441 U.S. 917, 99 S.Ct. 2018, 60 L.Ed.2d 389. Conceivably a state might

individual state officials,[19] so long as the federal courts do not subject the state's own treasury to judgment.[20] The federal courts may also entertain suits against the state for certain civil rights torts under the Fourteenth Amendment,[21] where Congress has so provided.[22]

Remedial immunities. Remedial immunities must also be distinguished from the substantive tort immunity. A state may be liable, for example, in the sense that it is subject to an injunction and therefore not wholly immune to suit; at the same time, it may be immune to claims for money damages,[23] or to claims for punitive damages,[24] with the result that the immunity merely limits the remedy.

Abolition of immunities. Although one or two states seem to have retained something like a total sovereign immunity,[25] the great majority have now consented to at least some liability for torts, in all cases retaining the immunity at least to the extent of basic policy or discretionary decisions. The extent of the states' immunity has shifted rapidly at times as courts and legislatures have adjusted to each other's reforms, but speaking very generally the states can be grouped roughly as follows.

First, about seven or eight states, though technically retaining immunity from suit in the law courts, have established administrative agencies to hear and determine claims against the state.[26] In most cases it appears to be contemplated that the agency's award will be routinely paid or that appropriations will be made to fund it. Usually the agency is directed either to make awards where a judgment would be given against a private person at law,[27] or to do justice and equity.[28] In most instances nearly complete relief seems possible, subject only to any dollar limit on the state's liability that may be imposed.[29]

Second, a group of nine states have waived the tort immunity in some limited class of cases,[30] typically cases in which the state or its agency has procured liability insurance that will pay any judgment,[31] or cases involving the use of motor vehicles[32] or tangible property.[33] One or two states have injected the distinction much followed in the

---

be required to entertain a federal-law suit against it in its own courts, see Testa v. Katt, 1947, 330 U.S. 386, 67 S.Ct. 810, 91 L.Ed. 967, in which case the Eleventh Amendment would presumably offer no protection. Cf. Ezratty v. Commonwealth of Puerto Rico, 1st Cir. 1981, 648 F.2d 770.

19. See § 132 below.

20. Edelman v. Jordan, 1974, 415 U.S. 651, 94 S.Ct. 1347, 39 L.Ed.2d 662, rehearing denied 416 U.S. 1000, 94 S.Ct. 2414, 40 L.Ed.2d 777, on remand D.Ill., 405 F.Supp. 802, reversed 7th Cir., 551 F.2d 152.

21. Fitzpatrick v. Bitzer, 1976, 427 U.S. 445, 96 S.Ct. 2666, 49 L.Ed.2d 614.

22. Quern v. Jordan, 1979, 440 U.S. 332, 99 S.Ct. 1139, 59 L.Ed.2d 358.

23. Under the Eleventh Amendment an injunction may run against officers of the state, though the effect will be to compel state action; but it may not be used to compel payment of state funds. Edelman v. Jordan, 1974, 415 U.S. 651, 94 S.Ct. 1347, 39 L.Ed.2d 662, rehearing denied 416 U.S. 1000, 94 S.Ct. 2414, 40 L.Ed.2d 777, on remand D.Ill., 405 F.Supp. 802, reversed 7th Cir., 551 F.2d 152.

24. Statutes have been construed to confer an immunity from punitive damages in the case of cities, City of Newport v. Fact Concerts, Inc., 1981, 453 U.S. 247, 101 S.Ct. 2748, 69 L.Ed.2d 616. This parallels the common law rule that public entities are not generally liable for punitive damages. See D. Dobbs, Remedies 217–218 (1973).

25. Maryland and Mississippi appear to have retained the immunity as to the state itself, with very little exception. Liability of officers may moderate this immunity.

26. Alabama, Arkansas, Georgia, Kentucky, North Carolina, Tennessee, West Virginia, Wisconsin. In some instances the state may retain its own immunity but waive the immunity of a political subdivision such as a county.

27. E.g., Tenn.Code Ann., § 9–812.

28. E.g., Code of Ala.1975, § 41–9–68 ("moral obligation"), tit. 55, § 344.

29. Some states in all three groups mentioned here impose dollar limits on recovery, e.g., N.C.Gen.Stat. § 143–291 (Administrative process, $30,000); S.C.Code 1962, § 10–2623 (Abrogation limited to motor vehicles, $20,000); West's Fla.Stat.Ann. § 768.28 ($50,000).

30. Connecticut, Delaware, Kansas, New Hampshire, North Dakota, Oklahoma, South Carolina, South Dakota and Texas.

31. E.g., Kan.Stat.Ann. 74–4707–08.

32. E.g., Maine Rev.Stat.Ann., tit. 14, § 157.

33. Vernon's Ann.Tex.Civ.Stat., art. 6252–19, § 3 (motor vehicles, tangible property).

law of municipal immunity so as to retain the immunity for "governmental" activities, but to abolish it for "proprietary" or commercial activities of the state.[34] The practical effect for most of these states is that there will be tort liability in motor vehicle cases and not much else. In one or two instances the state has provided for insurance and waived immunity only for a few of its agencies or departments.[35] Thus, though this group of states partially waives immunity, the protection afforded here for the injured person may come to appreciably less than the protection afforded in states that retain immunity in name and provide a purely administrative redress.

Third, about 30 states, the largest single group, have abrogated the immunity in a substantial or general way.[36] In this group as well as elsewhere, there may be liability for nonfeasance as well as misfeasance,[37] even though the discretionary immunity is retained,[38] usually along with some specifically enumerated immunities as well.[39] On the whole, however, the liability of states in this group is approximately as broad as, or broader than,[40] the liability of the federal government under the tort claims act.

This picture represents a large expansion of state responsibility for tort since the classic study by Leflar and Kantrowicz in 1954.[41] The expansion of liability will probably continue and a few years may produce a quite different picture. At the same time it must be recognized, however, that the abrogation of immunity in itself does not always import liability. Though many states have waived immunity to the extent that the state purchases liability insurance, this waiver operates only if the purchase actually takes place,[42] and there is no way to be sure from the insurance waiver statutes in themselves whether departments authorized to purchase insurance have actually done so. It is quite possible, then, that in many states the law reform here is more apparent than real.

The states have also imposed special procedural limitations in many instances. The insurance-waiver states probably contemplate ordinary jury trial of these actions, but there is no jury trial where the only relief is administrative, and many of the states that have generally abrogated the immunity have also eliminated jury trial.[43] Usually the claimant must attempt an administrative settlement before he resorts to the courts.[44] There is very commonly a dollar limit imposed on recoveries,[45] and special provisions usually require the claimant against the state to give notice of his claim in a very

---

34. Mich.C.L.A. § 3.996(107). Kansas adopted this distinction by judicial decision in Carroll v. Kittle, 1969, 203 Kan. 841, 457 P.2d 21, but a later statutory scheme appears to make this moot.

35. There seems to be no general insurance-waiver statute in Mississippi, but particular statutes sometimes make provision for a particular agency, e.g., Miss.Code 1972, § 37–29–83 (narcotics bureau may insure, immunity waiver).

36. Alaska, Arizona, California, Colorado, Florida, Hawaii, Idaho, Illinois, Indiana, Iowa, Louisiana, Maine, Massachusetts, Minnesota, Missouri, Montana, Nebraska, Nevada, New Jersey, New Mexico, New York, Ohio, Oregon, Pennsylvania, Rhode Island, Utah, Vermont, Virginia, Washington, Wyoming and the District of Columbia. Michigan, which uses a unique scheme of immunities, probably also belongs in this classification. All the states listed here allow tort liability in a variety of situations, but many of them also retain substantial areas of immunity.

37. See Brown v. MacPherson's, Inc., 1975, 86 Wn. 2d 293, 545 P.2d 13 (state would be liable if it gratuitously undertook to warn of avalanche danger, then failed to do so if that deprived plaintiff of warnings from others).

38. See p. 1039 supra.

39. Statutes often list the same exceptions listed in the Federal Tort Claims Act, e.g., the assault and battery exception. E.g., Vt.Stat.Ann. tit. 12 § 5602.

40. Some of the state decisions constrict the discretionary immunity to its purposes more carefully than many of the federal decisions. See, e.g., King v. City of Seattle, 1974, 84 Wn.2d 239, 525 P.2d 228.

41. Leflar and Kantrowitz, Tort Liability of the States, 1954, 29 N.Y.U.L.Rev. 1363.

42. E.g., Holden v. Bundek, Del.Super.1972, 317 A.2d 29.

43. E.g., Alaska Stats. (Code Civ.Proc.) 09.50.290; Iowa Code Ann., § 25A.4.

44. E.g., Charles Gabus Ford, Inc. v. Iowa State Highway Commission, Iowa 1974, 224 N.W.2d 639.

45. See p. 1044 supra.

short time after the injury.[46] This is often a trap for the unwary citizen and even the attorney. It has been argued that these notice provisions violate the equal protection clause in that they treat the victim of the public tort differently from the victim of the private tort. Although a few courts have agreed with this argument and have struck down the special notice requirements,[47] others have upheld these statutes.[48] Varied technical details of this order require careful attention to the local statute in each case.

Tort immunity for basic policy decisions. Even where the sovereign immunity of the state has been abolished, a legislative and a judicial immunity is retained to protect against liability for legislation and for judicial decisions.[49] Similar protection may be afforded to persons such as prosecutors who are intimately involved in the process of legislation or judicial decision.[50]

By analogy, the state and its agencies[51] are also protected from liability for the decisions of executive-branch employees and officers when those decisions involve the kind of basic policy issues typically involved in legislation. The immunity is recognized everywhere[52] under one name or another,[53] and is essentially the same immunity known in federal law as the discretionary immunity. Like its federal counterpart, the immunity is often extended to cases that do not seem to involve basic policy or discretion at all, for example, to cases of negligently designed public works such as highways, though on this as on many immunity issues the cases are divided.[54]

The chief justifications for this immunity have been that the judiciary should not invade the province of the executive branch of government by supervising its decisions through tort law,[55] and that if liability were imposed for discretionary decisions, effective executive action would be chilled.[56] These reasons obviously counsel use of the immunity only when there is no "predictable

---

46. E.g., N.J.Stat.Ann., 59:8–8 (90 days).

47. Gleason v. City of Davenport, Iowa 1979, 275 N.W.2d 431 (where time of notice differed as among different cities); Reich v. State Highway Department, 1972, 386 Mich. 617, 194 N.W.2d 700.

48. Lunday v. Vogelmann, Iowa 1973, 213 N.W.2d 904. Budahl v. Gordon & David Associates, S.D.1980, 287 N.W.2d 489. See Annot., 59 A.L.R.3d 93.

49. Second Restatement of Torts, § 895B, Comment c.

50. See § 132 below.

51. It is generally recognized that the immunity extends to state agencies as well as to the state collectively, but not every public entity is an agency of the state and not everyone enjoys the immunity. E.g., Ohio Valley Contractors v. Board of Education of Wetzel Co., 1982, ___ W.Va. ___, 293 S.E.2d 437 (state's immunity is constitutionally mandated, but county school board does not share that immunity nor a common law immunity). Municipalities are immune at common law but are not agencies of the state and their immunity is a distinct one.

52. Second Restatement of Torts, § 895B.

53. The specific provisions of many state statutes taken together amount to a recognition of this immunity, although the immunity exists without statute. In a few states this immunity is achieved in substantial part through other terminology, as where a state is protected for "governmental" actions.

54. E.g., Donnelly v. Ives, 1970, 159 Conn. 163, 268 A.2d 406 ("quasi-judicial or legislative capacity in adopting a plan for the improvement or repair" of highways, and "sound principles of government and a respect for the expert judgment of agencies" support immunity); Thomas v. State Highway Department, 1976, 398 Mich. 1, 247 N.W.2d 530. Accord as to individual officers, Smith v. Cooper, 1970, 256 Or. 485, 475 P.2d 78, 45 A.L.R.3d 857. Contra, e.g., Lewis v. State, Iowa 1977, 256 N.W.2d 181. See Annot., 1972, 45 A.L.R.3d 875.

"[T]he failure to upgrade an existing road or intersection, as well as the decision to build a road or roads with a particular alignment, are judgmental, planning-level functions and absolute immunity attaches." Department of Transportation v. Neilson, Fla.1982, 419 So.2d 1071. "[I]f a governmental entity plans a road with a sharp curve which cannot be negotiated by an automobile traveling more than twenty-five miles per hour, the entity cannot be liable * * * because the decision to do so is at the judgmental, planning level. If, however, the entity knows when it builds the road that automobiles cannot negotiate the curve at more than twenty-five miles per hour, then an operational-level duty arises to warn motorists of the hazard." City of St. Petersburg v. Collom, Fla.1982, 419 So.2d 1082.

55. Dunbar v. United Steelworkers of America, 1979, 100 Idaho 523, 602 P.2d 21, certiorari denied 446 U.S. 983, 100 S.Ct. 2963, 64 L.Ed.2d 839; Smith v. Cooper, 1970, 256 Or. 485, 475 P.2d 78, 45 A.L.R.3d 857; King v. City of Seattle, 1974, 84 Wn.2d 239, 525 P.2d 228.

56. Lipman v. Brisbane Elementary School District, 1961, 55 Cal.2d 224, 11 Cal.Rptr. 97, 359 P.2d 465 ("extent to which governmental liability might impair free

standard" for decision making,⁵⁷ where there is room for difference in official judgment, and where in fact some official judgment has been brought to bear on the governmental action that has caused the plaintiff harm. A few courts, recognizing this, have said that only conscious decision making by government is protected under the basic policy immunity and that ill-considered or unconsidered decisions are not.⁵⁸

In practice the calculated risk involved in conscious decision-making often amounts to a case of no negligence because the risk taken, though real enough, is a reasonable one given the balance of advantage and alternative and the wide range of choice our society leaves to the political branches of government.⁵⁹ For this reason analysis of the cases in terms of discretionary or basic policy immunity may obscure rather than reveal the issue. Thus a program in which prisoners are left with minimum security, or placed on work-release, or paroled, is obviously a program fraught with danger to innocent citizens, but it is not necessarily negligent to adopt such a program, and the state protected from liability in such cases on the stated ground that there is an immunity⁶⁰ may in fact be protected on the ground that it is not at fault.

There are a great many other cases, however, in which the state clearly appears to be negligent or in which a trier of fact might so find, and in which the state is nonetheless shielded from all responsibility on the ground that there is general discretion or some particular statutory version of it. Thus a state may be willing to impose liability upon a private psychologist who fails to warn others that he has a potentially violent patient,⁶¹ but may interpose the protection of the basic policy immunity when the state gives a furlough to a known violent criminal who has every prospect of raping and murdering a child and who in fact does so.⁶² As such cases illustrate, the immunity at times protects not only the decision to adopt a program for release of those in custody, but also protects specific negligence in the administration of the program once it is adopted, as where a prisoner or mental patient is intentionally⁶³ released without adequate eval-

exercise of the function); DuBree v. Commonwealth, 1978, 481 Pa. 540, 393 A.2d 293 ("the possibility of litigation may tend to discourage the making of clear choices. It is in the public interest to avoid such a chilling effect," officer's liability).

57. Jarrett v. Wills, 1963, 235 Or. 51, 383 P.2d 995 ("a judgment devoid of any of the standard of weights and measures available"); DuBree v. Commonwealth, 1978, 481 Pa. 540, 393 A.2d 293 (where the judgment cannot "be measured against a predictable standard of care").

58. Johnson v. State, 1968, 69 Cal.2d 782, 73 Cal. Rptr. 240, 447 P.2d 352 ("the state must prove that the employee, in deciding to perform the act that led to plaintiff's injury, consciously exercised discretion in the sense of assuming certain risks in order to gain other policy objectives"); King v. City of Seattle, 1974, 84 Wn.2d 239, 525 P.2d 228 ("state must make a showing that such a policy decision, consciously balancing risks and advantages, took place. The fact that an employee normally engages in 'discretionary activity' is irrelevant if * * * the employee did not render a considered decision.")

59. See Home Office v. Dorset Yacht Co. Ltd., H.L., [1970] A.C. 1004 and the comments of Lord Denning, M.R. in the same case in the Court of Appeal, [1969] W.L.R. 1008.

60. State v. Silva, 1970, 86 Nev. 911, 478 P.2d 591 (selection of inmates for honor camp a discretionary act but supervision is not); Epting v. State, Utah 1976, 546 P.2d 242, [1976] Utah L.Rev. 186; Seavey v. New York, 1964, 21 A.D.2d 445, 250 N.Y.S.2d 877, affirmed 17 N.Y.2d 675, 269 N.Y.S.2d 455, 216 N.E.2d 613 (state placed pyromaniac on plaintiff's farm); Home Office v. Dorset Yacht Co. Ltd., H.L. [1970] A.C. 1004.

61. Tarasoff v. Regents of University of California, 1976, 17 Cal.3d 425, 131 Cal.Rptr. 14, 551 P.2d 334.

62. Thompson v. County of Alameda, 1980, 27 Cal. 3d 741, 167 Cal.Rptr. 70, 614 P.2d 728. The prisoner had threatened to kill if released, but this was thought not to create a duty to warn the neighbors of his release since no specific child was threatened. Where a specific person is threatened the same court has gone the other way. Johnson v. State of California, 1968, 69 Cal.2d 782, 73 Cal.Rptr. 240, 447 P.2d 352.

63. The state may be held liable for the escape of a prisoner who causes subsequent harm if the other elements of a tort cause are present, since negligent supervision ordinarily involves no discretionary act. State v. Silva, 1970, 86 Nev. 911, 478 P.2d 591, 44 A.L.R.3d 891. Even here, however, there may be a discretionary immunity if the negligence charged is the design of a supervisory system or the selection of an inexperienced guard. Christensen v. Epley, 1979, 287 Or. 539, 601 P.2d 1216, appeal after remand 57 Or.App. 330, 644 P.2d 627 (evenly divided court).

uation.[64] This may be carrying the immunity far beyond its apparent purposes, as some other courts have now held.[65]

When those in a state's custody do not create dangers to the public but are themselves in danger, there may be less room for discretion and courts have often shown a sympathetic regard for the safety of prisoners, imposing liability when the state negligently fails to protect one prisoner from another,[66] or when it fails to protect a prisoner or patient from his own suicidal impulses,[67] often without discussing immunities at all, though occasionally a specific statutory immunity will bar such claims.[68] Children in the state's custody have also engendered judicial concern and courts have been ready, with little or no discussion of immunities, to hold the state or other public entity responsible for negligent placement of a foster child or for negligent supervision after he is placed in a home where he might be injured, neglected or even tortured.[69] School ground injuries resulting from negligently maintained[70] or supervised[71] premises or similar causes[72] usually involve no issue of discretion at all and again, where sovereign immunity is abolished, liability is imposed or denied under general negligence principles. But the "educational malpractice" claims, based on a school's failure to teach, test or counsel a pupil adequately, with resulting emotional or intellectual harm, have been denied for reasons sometimes similar to those

---

64. Thompson v. County of Alameda, 1980, 27 Cal. 3d 741, 167 Cal.Rptr. 70, 614 P.2d 728; Whitcombe v. County of Yolo, 1977, 73 Cal.App.3d 698, 141 Cal.Rptr. 189; Lloyd v. State, Iowa 1977, 251 N.W.2d 551, 6 A.L.R.4th 1143; Seavy v. New York, 1964, 21 A.D.2d 445, 250 N.Y.S.2d 877, affirmed 1965, 17 N.Y.2d 675, 269 N.Y.S.2d 455, 216 N.E.2d 613; Reiff v. Commonwealth, 1979, 46 Pa.Cmwlth. 335, 406 A.2d 1176. Cases typically turn on statutory structuring of the immunities which, in most instances, appear to be based on specific applications of the discretionary immunity, though often in an extended form.

65. Grimm v. Arizona Board of Pardons and Paroles, 1977, 115 Ariz. 260, 564 P.2d 1227 (limiting liability to cases of gross negligence or recklessness). Cf. Freach v. Commonwealth, 1977, 471 Pa. 558, 370 A.2d 1163 (mental patient, officers liable for gross negligence); Leverett v. State, 1978, 61 Ohio App.2d 35, 399 N.E.2d 106, 15 O.O.3d 62 (mental patient). Some states may allow recovery on keyhole-narrow facts. See Johnson v. State, 1968, 69 Cal.2d 782, 73 Cal.Rptr. 240, 447 P.2d 352 as interpreted in Thompson v. County of Alameda, 1980, 27 Cal.3d 741, 167 Cal.Rptr. 70, 614 P.2d 728.

66. Breaux v. State, La.1976, 326 So.2d 481; Daniels v. Andersen, 1975, 195 Neb. 95, 237 N.W.2d 397.

67. Falkenstein v. City of Bismarck, N.D.1978, 268 N.W.2d 787; cf. Wilson v. City of Kotzebue, Alaska 1981, 627 P.2d 623 (drunk set fire to cell and suffered injury when frozen pipes prevented firefighting).

68. Sheffield v. Turner, 1968, 21 Utah 2d 314, 445 P.2d 367 (statute specifically excluded suits against prison officials); Allen v. State Department of Mental Health, 1977, 79 Mich.App. 170, 261 N.W.2d 247 (excluding liability for "governmental" activities); but cf. Galli v. Kirkeby, 1976, 398 Mich. 527, 248 N.W.2d 149 (alleged homosexual assaults by school principal on child in school not "governmental function").

69. Vonner v. State, La.1973, 273 So.2d 252; Koepf v. County of York, 1977, 198 Neb. 67, 251 N.W.2d 866; Hanson v. Rowe, 1972, 18 Ariz.App. 131, 500 P.2d 916; Elton v. County of Orange, 1970, 3 Cal.App.3d 1053, 84 Cal.Rptr. 27; Bartels v. County of Westchester, 1980, 76 A.D.2d 517, 429 N.Y.S.2d 906. Cf. Galli v. Kirkeby, 1976, 398 Mich. 527, 248 N.E.2d 149 (allegation that school principal committed numerous homosexual attacks on pupil); Bradford v. Davis, 1981, 290 Or. 855, 626 P.2d 1376 (negligent failure to find child adoptive home not necessarily discretionary). But cf. Smith v. Alameda County Social Services Agency, 1979, 90 Cal. App.3d 929, 153 Cal.Rptr. 712 (no tort cause of action for failure of agency to find plaintiff adoptive home).

As to violation of constitutional rights by child protection workers in acquiring state custody of a child, see Note, 1981, 90 Yale L.J. 681.

70. Miller v. Board of Education, Union Free School District No. 1, 1943, 291 N.Y. 25, 50 N.E.2d 529; Sansonni v. Jefferson Parish School Board, La.App.1977, 344 So.2d 42, certiorari denied 346 So.2d 209.

71. Jesik v. Maricopa County Community College District, 1980, 125 Ariz. 543, 611 P.2d 547 (liability for failure to protect against third-person attack); Connett v. Fremont City School District, Wyo.1978, 581 P.2d 1097 (failure to supervise chemistry lab); Ankers v. District School Board of Pasco County, Fla.App.1981, 406 So.2d 72 (supervision in shop room). Cf. Larson v. Independent School District No. 314, Minn.1979, 289 N.W.2d 112 (principal failed to supervise and plan physical education program, considered dangerous in light of new teacher's inexperience).

72. E.g., Akins v. Glen Falls City School District, 1981, 53 N.Y.2d 325, 441 N.Y.S.2d 644, 424 N.E.2d 531 (non-liability for injury at ball game turned on negligence rules, not immunity). Collins v. Board of Education of Kent County, 1981, 48 Md.App. 213, 426 A.2d 10 (non-liability of school for injury to student in private transportation did not turn on immunity).

involved in the discretionary immunity.[73] It is to be expected that choice of curriculum or teaching materials, or location of schools themselves, would ordinarily be discretionary matters for which there is no liability.[74]

When the state does not have custody either of the person who creates the danger or the person who is threatened by it, there has been a strong inclination to invoke the immunity, especially in cases of non-action.[75] Thus, though the public entity may be held liable for negligent police shootings[76] or automobile collisions,[77] a failure to provide police protection,[78] like the failure to provide fire protection,[79] is usually immune, either on the ground that the decision to deny such protection is a discretionary or basic policy decision[80] or on the ground that the duty to protect is owed to the public at large and not to any particular person who might be injured.[81]

So far as this rule is based on the public duty doctrine its foundations may have been eroded in part by a number of decisions that have rejected, discounted or narrowed the scope of that doctrine.[82] Nevertheless, the

73. D.S.W. v. Fairbanks North Star Borough School District, Alaska 1981, 628 P.2d 554 (administrative remedies for schools' misclassification or failure to provide programs for student, difficulty of judging care or appropriate level of success); Peter W. v. San Francisco Unified School District, 1976, 60 Cal.App.3d 814, 131 Cal.Rptr. 854 (no duty because too difficult to develop standards for adjudication); Hunter v. Board of Education of Montgomery County, 1982, 292 Md. 481, 439 A.2d 582 (to allow claim would make courts "overseers of both the day-to-day operation of our educational process as well as the formulation of its governing policies"); Hoffman v. Board of Education of City of New York, 1979, 49 N.Y.2d 121, 424 N.Y.S.2d 376, 400 N.E.2d 317 (interference with school system). See Elson, A Common Law Remedy for the Educational Harms Caused by Incompetent or Careless Teaching, 1978, 73 Nw.L.Rev. 641; Annot., 1980, 1 A.L.R.4th 1139.

Some educational decisions, such as those refusing special aid for handicapped children, are subject to federal statutes which affect injunctive remedies and possibly even permit damage remedies. Boxall v. Sequoia Union High School District, D.Cal.1979, 464 F.Supp. 1104. Contra, Loughran v. Flanders, D.Conn.1979, 470 F.Supp. 110.

74. Carroll v. Lucas, 1974, 39 Ohio Misc. 5, 313 N.E.2d 864 (assigned book with sexual material); Aubrey v. School District of Philadelphia, 1981, 63 Pa. Cmwlth. 330, 437 A.2d 1306 (sex education curriculum). Cf. Walker v. Board of Education of Olean City School District, 1980, 78 A.D.2d 982, 433 N.Y.S.2d 660 (school closing can be attacked only by administrative review).

75. As to non-action by public entities see generally M. Shapo, 1977, The Duty to Act. Nonfeasance is not typically an admitted ground for exempting the public entity from liability, but there is a strong pattern of immunity in nonfeasance cases.

76. Sanchez v. Rice, 1978, 40 Colo.App. 481, 580 P.2d 1261. Liability is denied in a number of cases, but on the absence of negligence rather than the presence of immunity. E.g., Scott v. City of Opa Locka, Fla. App.1975, 311 So.2d 825, 76 A.L.R.3d 1172 (sudden emergency). See Annot., 1977, 76 A.L.R.3d 1176.

77. Brummett v. County of Sacramento, 1978, 21 Cal.3d 880, 148 Cal.Rptr. 361, 582 P.2d 952, 4 A.L.R.4th 858. See Annot., 1981, 4 A.L.R.4th 865.

78. Massengill v. Yuma County, 1969, 104 Ariz. 518, 456 P.2d 376; Riss v. City of New York, 1968, 22 N.Y.2d 579, 293 N.Y.S.2d 897, 240 N.E.2d 860; Simpson's Food Fair, Inc. v. City of Evansville, 1971, 149 Ind.App. 387, 272 N.E.2d 871, 46 A.L.R.3d 1077. Cf. Crouch v. Hall, 1980, ___ Ind.App. ___, 406 N.E.2d 303 (police investigation failed to lead to apprehension of rapist, who, left at large, raped and murdered plaintiff's decedent, no liability of officers under rules for discretion and public duty). Liability may be imposed if there is a special relationship between the police and the individual plaintiff, as where the plaintiff is an informer who is promised protection. See Schuster v. New York, 1958, 5 N.Y.2d 75, 180 N.Y.S.2d 265, 154 N.E.2d 534. A federal civil rights action might succeed where a state tort-law action would fail. See Note, 1981, 94 Harv.L.Rev. 821, 829.

79. See Motyka v. City of Amsterdam, 1965, 15 N.Y.2d 134, 256 N.Y.S.2d 595, 204 N.E.2d 635.

80. Riss v. City of New York, 1968, 22 N.Y.2d 579, 293 N.Y.S.2d 897, 240 N.E.2d 860 (no duty in tort when decision involves deployment of limited community resources, since this is an executive-legislative kind of decision). The rule stated does not protect the public entity from liability for active negligence, including omissions in the course of some police action. Suarez v. Dosky, 1979, 171 N.J.Super. 1, 407 A.2d 1237 (police at accident scene failed to help stranded children across busy highway, two deaths, liability).

81. The public duty doctrine, which holds that some unspecified duties are owed only to the public and that private individuals have no redress for their violation, appears to have originated in T. Cooley, Liability of Public Officers (1877) and to have been repeated in T. Cooley, Torts through its several editions. Its most dramatic support among contemporary cases was Massengill v. Yuma County, 1969, 104 Ariz. 518, 456 P.2d 376, until that case was overruled in 1982 by Ryan v. State, 1982, 134 Ariz. 327, 656 P.2d 616.

82. Ryan v. State, 1982, 134 Ariz. 327, 656 P.2d 616; Commercial Carrier Corp. v. Indian River County, Fla. 1979, 371 So.2d 1010, on remand Fla.App., 372 So.2d 1182, on remand 372 So.2d 1022, appeal after remand

overwhelming current of decisions continues to reject liability based on a general failure to provide police protection.[83]

Not only is there no liability for failure to provide appropriate police protection, there is no liability under the traditional view when the public entity fails to enforce its own laws intended to provide for public safety, as where it fails to enforce fire-safety[84] rules, or building codes,[85] or where it issues a driver's license to an unsafe driver.[86] But the public entity may be held for failure to follow governing legal rules when it carries out its own operations,[87] and beyond this, a number of recent decisions, mostly involving risks to the public, have held that liability might be imposed, at least in cases of active negligence in the enforcement of safety statutes, including the failure to remedy a discovered building hazard[88] and the issuance of a license to a dangerous driver.[89] It is probably not possible to reconcile all these cases.

Under some of these decisions the negligent grant of a license that permits a dangerous activity or building may result in liability to the public entity. Denial of a license, permit, zoning reclassification or the like, however, is more likely to involve the exercise of discretion; in addition, it often results only in an interference with economic opportunities rather than in physical harm. In line with the general reluctance to impose liability for mere negligence in the economic opportunity cases,[90] and with the discretion usually involved, the refusal or delay in issuance of a license is traditionally no basis for liability.[91] The existence of other remedies, such as mandamus or declaratory judgment, had usually been mentioned in the cases[92]

---

398 So.2d 488; Wilson v. Nepstad, Iowa 1979, 282 N.W.2d 664; Stewart v. Schmieder Enterprises, La. 1980, 386 So.2d 1351; Coffey v. City of Milwaukee, 1976, 74 Wis.2d 526, 247 N.W.2d 132; J. & B. Development Co., Inc. v. King County, 1981, 29 Wn.App. 942, 631 P.2d 1002 ("A duty owed to the public generally is also a duty owed to the individual member of the public.").

83. See Note, 1981, 94 Harv.L.Rev. 821; Annot., 46 A.L.R.3d 1084.

84. Cracraft v. City of St. Louis Park, Minn.1979, 279 N.W.2d 801; National Spring Co., Inc. v. Pierpoint Associates, Inc., 1976, 146 N.J.Super. 63, 368 A.2d 973; Motyka v. City of Amsterdam, 1965, 15 N.Y.2d 134, 256 N.Y.S.2d 595, 204 N.E.2d 635.

85. Rich v. City of Mobile, Ala.1982, 410 So.2d 385; Modlin v. City of Miami Beach, Fla.1967, 201 So.2d 70 (negligent building inspection violated only duty to general public, no liability to victim of building collapse); Hoffert v. Owatonna Inn Towne Motel, Inc., 1972, 293 Minn. 220, 199 N.W.2d 158 (approval of construction in violation of building code, motel guests injured and killed in fire, no liability). Cf. Dunbar v. United Steelworkers of America, 1979, 100 Idaho 523, 602 P.2d 21, certiorari denied 446 U.S. 983, 100 S.Ct. 2963, 64 L.Ed.2d 839 (failure to adopt adequate mine safety programs pursuant to general statutory directive but seemingly not in violation of specific provision, no liability).

86. Ryan v. State, 1980, ___ R.I. ___, 420 A.2d 841; Lifer v. Raymond, 1977, 80 Wis.2d 503, 259 N.W.2d 537. Cf. Hensley v. Seminole County, Fla.App.1972, 268 So.2d 452, 70 A.L.R.3d 1235 (negligent vehicle inspection by public entity). But cf. Buszta v. Souther, 1967, 102 R.I. 609, 232 A.2d 396 (negligent vehicle inspection by state-authorized contractor, duty owed).

87. Compare Lorshbough v. Township of Buzzle, Minn.1977, 258 N.W.2d 96 and Florence v. Goldberg, 1978, 44 N.Y.2d 189, 404 N.Y.S.2d 583, with Cracraft v. City of St Louis Park, Minn.1979, 279 N.W.2d 801 and Motyka v. City of Amsterdam, 1965, 15 N.Y.2d 134, 256 N.Y.S.2d 595, 204 N.E.2d 635.

88. Adams v. State, Alaska 1976, 555 P.2d 235 (fire hazards in hotel actually discovered); Wilson v. Nepstad, Iowa 1979, 282 N.W.2d 664 (actual inspection of apartment house, fire, public duty doctrine rejected); Stewart v. Schmieder, La.1980, 386 So.2d 1351 (failure to check plans as required by ordinance, roof collapse, public duty doctrine rejected); Campbell v. City of Bellevue, 1975, 85 Wn.2d 1, 530 P.2d 234 (electrical inspector actually discovered wire in creek but did not correct); Coffey v. City of Milwaukee, 1976, 74 Wis.2d 526, 247 N.W.2d 132 (tenant in office building suffered fire loss, allegedly resulting from city's improper inspection).

89. Oleszczuk v. State, 1979, 124 Ariz. 373, 604 P.2d 637.

90. See §§ 128–130 supra.

91. Selby Realty Co. v. City of San Buenaventura, 1973, 10 Cal.3d 110, 109 Cal.Rptr. 799, 514 P.2d 111 (under statute incorporating the rule); Lockwood v. Village of Buchanan, Co.Ct.1959, 18 Misc. 862, 182 N.Y.S.2d 754; Annot., 1954, 37 A.L.R.2d 694. Cf. Cougar Business Owners Association v. State, 1982, 97 Wn.2d 466, 647 P.2d 481 (governor's decision to restrict access to town near live volcano and interfering with merchants' business opportunities is discretionary).

92. Selby Realty Co. v. City of San Buenaventura, 1973, 10 Cal.3d 110, 109 Cal.Rptr. 799, 514 P.2d 111; Clinard v. City of Winston-Salem, 1917, 173 N.C. 356, 91 S.E. 1039; Holaway v. City of Pipestone, Minn.1978, 269 N.W.2d 28.

and has undoubtedly influenced the development of this rule. But the rule offers no protection if the denial of a license amounts to a taking of property, since that is compensable under constitutional provisions.[93] And some public entities, notably cities, may be held liable for violations of constitutional rights under federal civil rights laws, so that if it can be established that a license denial violates due process or equal protection, the immunity will offer no protection.[94] Beyond this there is a growing group of cases that have rejected any absolute rule of immunity and have recognized the potential for liability for denial of license, at least where the particular facts were thought to warrant it.[95]

There are, of course, a number of cases in which the public entity is routinely subjected to ordinary negligence law and in which the discretionary immunity is of no significance, for example, the ordinary case of injury from negligent operation of an automobile.[96] With the expansion of government, however, the variety of activity is immense, and it is probably not possible to make a comprehensive and accurate statement of the discretionary immunity, which necessarily turns in any event on the particular act in question, the standards available for judging that act, and the court's own judgment of the appropriate scope of action for the political branch. It should go without saying that where the general sovereign immunity is still retained, or where there is a specific governing statutory provision, protection will be accorded on those terms and the discretionary immunity will not be significant.

Municipal Corporations

The traditional rule was that municipalities held a governmental immunity in tort, but one different both in origin and scope from the "sovereign" or governmental immunity of the state. Since municipalities exhibited a corporate or proprietary face as well as a governmental face, the traditional immunity was narrower than the full range of municipal activities, protecting only the governmental activities and not the proprietary ones.

The municipal immunity originated in 1798 in Russell v. Men of Devon[97] at a time when the municipality was not conceived as a separate entity at all, so that the claim was in effect a claim against the whole population of the county. There was no precedent for such an action, nor was there any county treasury from which to pay any judgment. These reasons were persuasive against any liability on the facts, and consequently the immunity was established. Over the years other reasons were elaborated in the courts; for example it was said that there should be no municipal liability because the municipality makes no profit or because it would divert tax funds from public purposes.[98] It is al-

---

93. Severe regulation of land use under zoning ordinances or otherwise is in effect a denial of a license to use and may amount to an unconstitutional taking of property. See Lake Country Estates, Inc. v. Tahoe Regional Planning Agency, 1979, 440 U.S. 391, 99 S.Ct. 1171, 59 L.Ed.2d 401, on remand D.Cal., 474 F.Supp. 901; San Antonio River Authority v. Garrett Brothers, Tex.Civ.App.1975, 528 S.W.2d 266, refused n.r.e.; T. & M. Homes, Inc. v. Township of Mansfield, 1978, 162 N.J.Super. 497, 393 A.2d 613. There are difficulties in distinguishing permissible regulation from unconstitutional takings. See, e.g., Kmiec, Regulatory Takings: The Supreme Court Runs Out of Gas in San Diego, 1982, 57 Ind.L.J. 45.

94. See T & M Homes, Inc. v. Township of Mansfield, 1978, 162 N.J.Super. 497, 393 A.2d 613.

95. J. & B. Development Co., Inc. v. King County, 1981, 29 Wn.App. 942, 631 P.2d 1002; Urbano v. Meneses, 1981, 288 Pa.Super. 103, 431 A.2d 308 (without discussion of the separate discretionary immunity);

accord, Brennen v. City of Eugene, 1979, 285 Or. 401, 591 P.2d 719 (economic harm from issuance of license); Haslund v. City of Seattle, 1976, 86 Wn.2d 607, 547 P.2d 1221 (economic harm from improper issuance of building permit).

96. Brummett v. County of Sacramento, 1978, 21 Cal.3d 880, 148 Cal.Rptr. 361, 582 P.2d 952, 4 A.L.R. 4th 858 (police chase); Eubanks v. Colbert, Tex.Civ. App.1959, 327 S.W.2d 457, 83 A.L.R.2d 378, refused n.r.e. (application of speed limits to police emergency). Cf. Mann v. State, 1977, 70 Cal.App.3d 773, 139 Cal. Rptr. 82 (police negligence at accident scene); Suarez v. Dosky, 1979, 171 N.J.Super. 1, 407 A.2d 1237 (police failure to assist children across highway after accident).

97. 1798, 2 Term Rep. 667, 100 Eng.Rep. 359.

98. These reasons and several others are listed with references in Borchard, Government Liability in Tort, 1924, 34 Yale L.J. 129, 132–33.

most always agreed that these reasons are not sound.[99] In recognition of this, there has been a large movement to abolish the municipal immunity or to restrict it severely.

Abolition of the immunity. By the 1970s about half the states had abolished the municipal immunity either by direct judicial action[1] or legislation[2] or both,[3] except that the usual immunity for legislative and judicial action and for basic policy decisions was retained[4] and strict liability was not imposed.[5] A number of other states have enacted insurance-waiver provisions, so that municipalities may be held liable to the extent that they are covered by liability insurance.[6] The Supreme Court has also held that in actions for certain federal civil rights torts, cities enjoy none of the good faith immunity that protects most individual officers.[7] The change from the traditional immunity has been so profound that the American Law Institute now recognizes the rule to be that municipalities have no general immunity at all.[8] However, where immunity is abolished by a general statute, a tort claims act is usually enacted and particular exceptions are created that vary from state to state.[9]

Basic policy immunity. In both the states that have generally abolished immunity and the states that generally retain it subject to exceptions, it is agreed that the discretionary function or basic policy immunity remains as a shield against municipal liability. In these cases the courts have followed the rules and directions already discussed,[10] so that there is no liability if the city council suspends safety ordinances and someone is injured,[11] or if the city's allocation of limited police resources leaves the plaintiff unprotected,[12] or if the city's selection of a site for a public gathering creates safety problems.[13] So far as these decisions involve the dilemma of policy intended to be resolved by the legislative or executive branches, the courts will refuse to review them in tort actions, and this is so whether the immunity has been generally abolished or not. As in other cases, courts have sometimes extended this immunity beyond its purposes. For exam-

---

99. See, e.g., Borchard, supra note 13 at 134; Borchard, Governmental Responsibility in Tort, 1928, 28 Colum.L.Rev. 577, 594; Gibson, J., concurring in Hack v. City of Salem, 1963, 174 Ohio St. 383, 189 N.E.2d 857.

1. E.g., Hargrove v. Town of Cocoa Beach, Fla. 1957, 96 So.2d 130; Veach v. City of Phoenix, 1967, 102 Ariz. 195, 427 P.2d 335: Merrill v. City of Manchester, 1974, 114 N.H. 722, 332 A.2d 378.

2. E.g., Vernon's Ann.Tex.Civ.Stat., art. 6252–19.

3. E.g., see Muskopf v. Corning Hospital District, 1961, 55 Cal.2d 211, 359 P.2d 457, and West's Ann. Cal. Govt. Code, §§ 810 et seq.

4. E.g., Hargrove v. Town of Cocoa Beach, supra note 1; see Second Restatement of Torts, § 895C(2).

5. Merrill v. City of Manchester, 1974, 114 N.H. 722, 332 A.2d 378.

6. E.g., N.C.Gen.Stat., § 160A–485; Ga.Code, § 56–2437.

7. Owen v. City of Independence, 1980, 445 U.S. 622, 100 S.Ct. 1398, 63 L.Ed.2d 673, on remand 8th Cir., 623 F.2d 550, rehearing denied 446 U.S. 993, 100 S.Ct. 2979, 64 L.Ed.2d 850 (under 42 U.S.C.A. § 1983). The Eleventh Amendment does not protect municipalities from federal actions and they are now subject to damage claims for civil rights torts when a municipality's policy, custom, regulation or "decision officially adopted" violates the Constitution, and perhaps if it violates other federal law. Monell v. Department of Social Services, 1978, 436 U.S. 658, 98 S.Ct. 2018, 56 L.Ed.2d 611. Conceivably a policy or custom requires something close to intentional misconduct, but if so this would often seem to conflict with the rule in Owen, supra, that good faith is no defense. The net result may be that a great weight of analysis will fall on "policy, custom or decision," and that requirement may supply something similar to the good faith defense rejected in Owen. Thus the strict liability imposed in Owen may not always work. Where the suit is directly under the 14th amendment rather than under a statute, intent is required to establish the claim. See General Building Contractors Association, Inc. v. Pennsylvania, U.S. 1982, 102 S.Ct. 3141, 73 L.Ed.2d 835. For an account by the lawyer who represented the city in Owen, see Carlisle, Owen v. City of Independence, 1980, 12 Urb. Law. 292.

8. Second Restatement of Torts, § 895C.

9. E.g., West's Ann.Ind.Code 34–4–16.5–3; New Jersey Stat.Ann., 59:2–1 et seq.

10. See pp. 1039–1043, supra.

11. Hill v. City of Charlotte, 1875, 72 N.C. 55, 21 Am.Rep. 451.

12. See Riss v. City of New York, 1968, 22 N.Y.2d 579, 293 N.Y.S.2d 897, 240 N.E.2d 860.

13. Baker v. State Board of Higher Education, 1974, 20 Or.App. 277, 531 P.2d 716, appeal after remand 28 Or.App. 53, 558 P.2d 1247, appeal after remand 37 Or.App. 87, 586 P.2d 114.

ple, courts have immunized negligently made street plans and designs on the ground that this involved "planning," [14] though it seems reasonably certain that the "planning" to be protected under the basic policy immunity refers, not to architecture or engineering, but to governmental policy planning.[15]

Retention of the immunity. A number of states still retain the municipal immunity and usually apply it not only to pure municipal corporations such as cities and towns but also to other local entities such as school districts and counties.[16] Where the state thus retains the immunity, the municipality usually has no authority to waive it,[17] and where it is retained it is a fertile source of litigation.

Governmental-proprietary distinction. The prime basis of liability in such states is the rule that the municipality is liable for torts committed in its proprietary, as distinguished from its governmental, capacity.[18] For example, activities of police or firefighters, though tortious, are usually considered governmental in the sense that they involve the kind of power expected of government, even if its exercise in the specific case is wrongful.[19] The city is immune as to such activities for this reason. On the other hand, if the city operates a local electric or water company for which fees are charged, this looks very much like private enterprise and is usually considered proprietary.[20] For torts committed in these operations, then, the city is usually held liable.

But though the governmental-proprietary test works rather clearly when such extreme cases are considered, its application is uncertain in many other areas until precedent comes to govern particular conduct. For example, a public park does not readily fit the model of police activities, but neither does it fit the model of the municipally owned electric company. It is no surprise, then, that judicial reaction to torts committed in the operation of a park has reflected much conflict.[21]

Or again, the charge of a fee for services rendered, for example in garbage collection, hospitals, or municipal housing, is often taken as some evidence that the activity in question is proprietary and not immune.[22] But the fact that a municipality does not charge a fee for a given service or the fact that it makes no net operating profit from that service is not in itself conclusive proof that the service is "governmental" and im-

14. See e.g., Raven v. Coates, Fla.App.1961, 125 So. 2d 770 (city failed to replace collapsed stop sign, held discretionary function and city is immune).

15. See the discussion in Baran v. City of Chicago Heights, 1968, 99 Ill.App.2d 221, 240 N.E.2d 381 (planning immunity refers to something more than "specifications" for project), affirmed 43 Ill.2d 177, 251 N.E.2d 227.

16. See E. McQuillin, Municipal Corporations 3d ed. Rev. 1963, §§ 53.05b–.05c.

17. Thus purchase of liability insurance, even when authorized by statute, may not operate to waive immunity unless the statute itself so provides. See Boice v. Board of Education of Rock District, 1931, 111 W.Va. 95, 160 S.E. 566 (school board may not "step down from its pedestal of immunity"); McGrath Building Co. v. City of Bettendorf, 1957, 248 Iowa 1386, 85 N.W.2d 616, 68 A.L.R.2d 1429.

18. See generally C. Antieau, Municipal Corporation Law, 1974, § 11.26; E. McQuillin, Municipal Corporations, 3d ed. Rev. 1963, §§ 53.23–.59.

19. Gardner v. McDowell, 1969, 202 Kan. 705, 451 P.2d 501 (70 year old woman in confused mental state apprehended by officers who opened fire with revolvers piercing her body eleven times, governmental immunity protects); Moffitt v. Asheville, 1889, 103 N.C. 237, 9 S.E. 695, 14 Am.St.Rep. 810 (illness of person jailed because of exposure, immunity); Canade, Inc. v. Town of Blue Grass, Iowa 1972, 195 N.W.2d 734 (fire department not liable).

20. E.g., Ranells v. City of Cleveland, 1975, 41 Ohio St.2d 1, 321 N.E.2d 885 (city water department proprietary, city liable for escape of chlorine gas); Rice v. Lumberton, 1952, 235 N.C. 227, 69 S.E.2d 543 (city electric department).

21. See Jones v. City of Birmingham, 1969, 284 Ala. 276, 224 So.2d 632 (park is governmental, city is not liable for injury on park walk, even though, outside the park the street and sidewalk exception, below note, would make city liable); Murphy v. City of Carlsbad, 1960, 66 N.M. 376, 348 P.2d 492 (park is proprietary, recognizing a trend to so treat it).

22. Town of Douglas v. York, Wyo.1968, 445 P.2d 760 (garbage, fee, proprietary); Greenhalgh v. Payson City, Utah 1975, 530 P.2d 799 (hospital, same); Carter v. City of Greensboro, 1959, 249 N.C. 328, 106 S.E.2d 564 (housing, same).

mune. Thus, though the cases are divided,[23] a number now treat a municipal swimming pool as proprietary, not only when a fee is charged, but also when no fee is charged and when the pool operates at a net loss.[24]

The difficult distinction between governmental and proprietary functions is even more troubling where the city's conduct combines both kinds of function at once.[25] For example, operation of a sanitary sewer may be deemed governmental, but operation of a storm sewer may be deemed proprietary. When a single sewer is operated both for sanitation and drainage, a new problem in classification arises. The same problem occurs where the city operates a local electric plant that is proprietary, but delivers some of the electricity to its police station, which of course is governmental. When injury results from such dual operations at least two kinds of approaches can be seen in the decisions. One approach is to attempt to isolate the particular part of the activity that caused the plaintiff's injury and to erect or dissolve the immunity according to whether that part of the activity is deemed proprietary.[26] The other approach is to treat such dual functions as entirely proprietary or entirely governmental, especially where the conduct in question is not readily divisible.[27] Probably no rational solution to such questions is possible because the distinction itself is basically unworkable, and perhaps it was for this reason that the Supreme Court of the United States long ago refused to accept the distinction in federal law.[28]

Public streets and ways. Most jurisdictions do, however, agree that the construction and maintainence of streets and public ways is not within the immunity, either because for wholly inexplicable reasons this is considered "proprietary," or because, for equally inexplicable reasons, it is considered an independent exception to the immunity.[29] This liability is usually limited to injuries arising out of conditions on the streets, sidewalks and other public ways and is not extended to active operations on or around the streets. On this basis it may be held that if a collision occurs because of a hole or obstruction negligently left in the street, the injured citizen may recover.[30] On the other hand, if the collision occurs because negligently maintained traffic lights above the street gave the right-of-way to all traffic at once, the injured citizen is usually denied recovery.[31]

Nuisance, trespass and taking. Another exception to the immunity is that the municipality is held liable in most states for the commission of a nuisance, and sometimes for a trespass even though the tort is committed in the exercise of a governmental function.[32] The origin of this exception is found in the fact that a nuisance is often equivalent to a taking of land, or at least an easement, and that the municipality would be liable to pay compensation for a "tak-

23. See Annot., 1957, 55 A.L.R.2d 1434.

24. See Weeks v. City of Newark, 1960, 62 N.J. Super. 166, 162 A.2d 312, affirmed 1961, 34 N.J. 250, 168 A.2d 11 (per curiam).

25. See E. McQuillin, Municipal Corporations, 3d ed. Rev. 1963, § 53.32.

26. See Baker v. Lumberton, 1954, 293 N.C. 401, 79 S.E.2d 886 (electrocution by wire feeding "governmental" street lights, though charge in the wire resulted from fact that it crossed a wire feeding "proprietary" household current).

27. Pontarelli Trust v. City of McAllen, Tex.Civ.App.1971, 465 S.W.2d 804 (combination storm and sanitary sewer held governmental, though court recognizes that liability may be imposed in other dual capacity cases); Taylor v. Newport News, 1973, 214 Va. 9, 197 S.E.2d 209 (when two functions coincide, the activity is treated as governmental).

28. Indian Towing Co. v. United States, 1955, 350 U.S. 61, 76 S.Ct. 122, 100 L.Ed.2d 48.

29. Doht v. Village of Walthill, 1980, 207 Neb. 377, 299 N.W.2d 177; Bunch v. Edenton, 1884, 90 N.C. 431 (street liability as a nuisance); Taylor v. City of Newport News, 1973, 214 Va. 9, 197 S.E.2d 209 (street maintenance is proprietary function).

30. E.g., City of Florence v. Stack, 1963, 275 Ala. 367, 155 So.2d 324, 1 A.L.R.3d 490.

31. Town of Fort Oglethorpe v. Phillips, 1968, 224 Ga. 834, 165 S.E.2d 141, 34 A.L.R.3d 1002. Only a few courts have reached the opposite result. See Annot., 1970, 34 A.L.R.3d 1008.

32. E.g., New Mexico Water Quality Control Commission v. City of Hobbs, 1974, 86 N.M. 444, 525 P.2d 371; Morash & Sons, Inc. v. Commonwealth, 1973, 363 Mass. 612, 296 N.E.2d 461 (extending liability for nuisance to state as well as municipality).

ing."[33] But the nuisance exception has been extended to cover public nuisances that involve no taking of property.[34] Some of these involve nothing more than ordinary negligence, and it seems clear that resort to the nuisance exception in such cases is merely one method by which courts have constricted the immunity.

Mob action. Still another exception to the immunity is the peculiar liability imposed upon municipalities by statute in some states for failure to control riots or mob action.[35] Liability under these statutes is sometimes imposed quite without fault on the part of the municipality,[36] but the circumstances that give rise to this liability are very limited. These statutes have led to litigation of very narrow issues about the number of persons and the kinds of motives required to constitute a mob for whose destructive acts liability is imposed.[37]

Procedural conditions on suit. Suits against municipalities, like suits against states, usually involve special procedures, the most common of which is a requirement that the plaintiff notify the city of the claim within a short period after the injury or at least some period before suit is filed. The effect of these provisions is to shorten the statute of limitations in some instances and to lay a trap for the injured person in others, so that special care must be exercised to follow the particular rules of the state or municipality in question. In some instances, however, the trap created by the notice statute has been avoided by a declaration that the statute either violates due process or equal protection or both.[38]

Issues in Abrogating the Immunities

The most striking feature of the tort law of governmental entities today is that the immunities, once almost total, have been largely abolished or severely restricted at almost all levels, often through a complex process in which scholars and commentators,[39] judges[40] and legislators[41] all played an important role. The shift from immunity has prompted a number of debates, in which the principal issues have been whether the immunity should be abolished, and if so whether by courts or legislatures;[42] whether, if abolished by courts, it should be prospectively or retrospectively abolished;[43] and wheth-

---

33. See Harno, Tort Immunity of Municipal Corporations, 1921, 4 Ill.L.Q. 28, 37. Possibly also early decisions involved intended acts by the decision-making body, see Cooperrider, The Court, the Legislature, and Governmental Tort Liability in Michigan, 1973, 72 Mich.L.Rev. 187, 238.

34. See Fankhauser v. City of Mansfield, 1969, 19 Ohio St.2d 102, 249 N.E.2d 789 (traffic signal improperly operated a nuisance, liability for injury); Annot., 1957, 56 A.L.R.2d 1415.

35. See Note, 1968, 81 Harv.L.Rev. 653.

36. See A. & B. Auto Stores of Jones Street, Inc. v. City of Newark, 1971, 59 N.J. 5, 279 A.2d 693.

37. Slaton v. City of Chicago, 1955, 8 Ill.App.2d 47, 130 N.E.2d 205; Landesman v. Board of County Commissioners, 1967, 9 Ohio App.2d 319, 224 N.E.2d 532, 38 O.O.2d 389, 26 A.L.R.2d 1132.

38. Turner v. Staggs, 1973, 89 Nev. 230, 510 P.2d 879, 59 A.L.R.3d 81, certiorari denied 414 U.S. 1079, 94 S.Ct. 598, 38 L.Ed.2d 486.

39. See Borchard, Governmental Responsibility in Tort, 1926, 36 Yale L.J. 1.

40. Many of the initial shifts from immunity were carried out by judicial decision, as in e.g., Stone v. Arizona Highway Commission, 1963, 93 Ariz. 384, 381 P.2d 107 and Mayle v. Pennsylvania Department of Highways, 1978, 479 Pa. 384, 388 A.2d 709. Legislative modification has often followed.

41. See, e.g., Cal.Gov't Code §§ 810–996.6, enacted after the decision in Muskopf v. Corning Hospital District, 1961, 55 Cal.2d 211, 11 Cal.Rptr. 89, 359 P.2d 457; Colo.Rev.Stat.1973, §§ 24–10–101—24–10–117, enacted after the decision in Evans v. Board of Commissioners, 1971, 174 Colo. 197, 482 P.2d 968; New Jersey Stat. Ann., 59:1–1, enacted after the decision in Willis v. Department of Conservation, 1970, 55 N.J. 534, 264 A.2d 34.

42. See e.g., Jivelekas v. City of Worland, Wyo. 1976, 546 P.2d 419; Comment, Judicial Abrogation of Governmental and Sovereign Immunity: A National Trend with a Pennsylvania Perspective, 1973, 78 Dick. L.Rev. 365.

43. Nieting v. Blondell, 1975, 306 Minn. 122, 235 N.W.2d 597; Willis v. Department of Conservation and Economic Development, 1970, 55 N.J. 534, 264 A.2d 34; Note, 1972, 6 U.Rich.L.Rev. 397.

One solution is prospective abrogation except for the plaintiff in the abrogating case, for whom there is immediate abrogation. But this means that other persons injured on the same day or even later will still be barred by the immunity if their injuries occurred before the abrogating date. This was held not to violate

er the reform in immunity law can be achieved within a stable framework of law.⁴⁴ To a large extent it appears that the change will continue, and the day may be at hand when the immunity as traditionally known no longer represents the first line of defense for governmental units.

 WESTLAW REFERENCES

di immunity
di governmental immunity
di sovereign immunity
"king can do no wrong"

The United States
28 +s 2674
"tort claims act" /p "strict! liab!"
393k78(16)
28 +s 2680(h)
"tort claims act" /p "third party" /s indemni!
"tort claims act" /p "law enforcement officer*" police! /s inten! batter!
"tort claims act" /s "discretionary function*"

States
immun! /s state /s enjoin! injunct! restrain!
immun! /s state /s "liability insurance"
immun! /s state /s proprietary % "privileges and immunities"
legislative judicial /1 immunit!
immun! /s state /p nonfeasance nonaction omission*

Municipal Corporations
russell +s "men of devon"
county municipal! city town! village /s park* pool* hospital* cemetar*** zoo* "golf course*" /p proprietary /p immun!
county municipal! city town! village /s street road! avenue parkway sidewalk alley /p proprietary governmental /p immun!
nuisance* trespass! /s county municipal! city town! village /s liab! taking* /s immun!

equal protection of the law in Spearman v. University City Public School District, Mo.1981, 617 S.W.2d 68.

44. See R. Keeton, Creative Continuity in the Law of Torts, 1962, 75 Harv.L.Rev. 463.

§ 132

1. See Second Restatement of Torts, § 895D; L. Jaffe, Judicial Control of Administrative Action 237 (1965); Jennings, Tort Liability of Administrative Officers, 1937, 21 Minn.L.Rev. 263.

2. Bermann, Integrating Governmental and Officer Tort Liability, 1977, 77 Colum.L.Rev. 1174; Cass, Damage Suits against Public Officers, 1981, 129 U.Pa.L. Rev. 1110; Davis, Legal Control of the Police, 1974, 52 Tex.L.Rev. 703; R. Epstein, Private-Law Models for Official Immunity, 1978, 42 L. & Contemp. Problems

Issues in Abrogating the Immunities
immun! /p abolish /p retrospective** prospective** /p judicial legislative

§ 132. Public Officers

It was once said that as a general rule governmental officers and employees were personally liable for their torts, more or less without exception, even where the governmental unit itself was protected by an immunity.¹ This is still true in many cases, and the plaintiff injured by the policeman's negligent driving or imprisoned by an unprivileged arrest may have a claim against the policeman as an individual even though the government that has employed him shields itself with an immunity. However, in many other cases the officer or employee of a governmental entity is immune from liability for acts within the scope of his official duties. The division between those tortious acts that import immunity and those that import liability has been a very difficult one to mark as a body of commentary seems to show.² Much depends on the facts and advocacy in particular cases, but the general lines of development can be marked out somewhat as follows.

Absolute immunity of legislative and judicial officers

It is always agreed that an immunity protects both judges³ and legislators,⁴ so long

53; Mashaw, Civil Liability of Government Officers: Property Rights and Official Accountability, 1978, 42 L. & Contemp. Probs. 8; Shepsle, Official Errors and Official Liability, 1978, 42 L. & Contemp. Probs. 34; Jaffe, 1965, Judicial Control of Administrative Action.

3. E.g., Pierson v. Ray, 1967, 386 U.S. 547, 87 S.Ct. 1213, 18 L.Ed.2d 288; Holland v. Lutz, 1965, 194 Kan. 712, 401 P.2d 1015.

4. E.g., Tenney v. Brandhove, 1951, 341 U.S. 367, 71 S.Ct. 783, 95 L.Ed.1019, rehearing denied 342 U.S. 843, 72 S.Ct. 20, 96 L.Ed. 637 (state legislator on Un-American Activities Committee, Federal Civil Rights Act did not eliminate traditional immunity); Kilbourn v. Thompson, 1881, 103 U.S. 168, 26 L.Ed. 377 (Congressmen immune even though they exceeded powers of Congress in imposing imprisonment for contempt).

as their acts are "judicial"[5] or legislative[6] in nature and within the very general scope of their jurisdiction. It applies in civil rights cases as well as in other tort claims,[7] and it may protect local and inferior court judges[8] and state[9] and municipal[10] legislators as well as others, though some courts have qualified this in the case of purely local legislators[11] and the immunity has sometimes been ignored in the case of magistrates or justices of the peace.[12] The immunity stands even if the official acts in bad faith, or with malice or corrupt motives.[13]

The judicial immunity is not granted wholesale to officials of the executive departments, who normally enjoy only a qualified immunity if any at all. Nevertheless the dominant approach seems to follow the "functional analysis," and the absolute immunity is granted or denied according to whether the officer's functions are judicial in nature.[14] The immunity is thus extended to protect hearing officers or administrative law judges[15] and members of boards or commissions actually engaged in judicial determinations,[16] even though such officers are

5. Stump v. Sparkman, 1978, 435 U.S. 349, 98 S.Ct. 1099, 55 L.Ed.2d 331, rehearing denied 436 U.S. 951, 98 S.Ct. 2862, 56 L.Ed.2d 795, on remand 7th Cir., 601 F.2d 261 (judge did not give teenager a hearing before he ordered her sterilized, his order nevertheless "judicial act" and protected by absolute immunity); Rankin v. Howard, 9th Cir. 1980, 633 F.2d 844, certiorari denied 451 U.S. 939, 101 S.Ct. 2020, 68 L.Ed.2d 326 (judge's agreement in advance to sign a guardianship papers frustrates party's expectation of impartiality and is not a judicial function). Harris v. Harvey, 7th Cir. 1979, 605 F.2d 330, certiorari denied 445 U.S. 938, 100 S.Ct. 1331, 63 L.Ed.2d 772 (judge's racially motivated attacks on plaintiff, made to press, not a judicial act, no immunity); Zarcone v. Perry, 2d Cir. 1978, 572 F.2d 52 (judge brought coffee vendor before him in irons for selling bad coffee, no immunity, punitive damages). The immunity is reduced to qualified immunity when the judge is carrying out a function appropriate to the office but which is non-judicial in character, for example in discharging employees. Lynch v. Johnson, 6th Cir. 1970, 420 F.2d 818.

6. See Hutchinson v. Proxmire, 1979, 443 U.S. 111, 99 S.Ct. 2675, 61 L.Ed.2d 411 (Senator's publication not a legislative function though it was about government, hence no Constitutional immunity under Speech or Debate clause).

7. Pierson v. Ray, 1967, 386 U.S. 547, 87 S.Ct. 1213, 18 L.Ed.2d 288; Stump v. Sparkman, 1978, 435 U.S. 349, 98 S.Ct. 1099, 55 L.Ed.2d 331, rehearing denied 436 U.S. 951, 98 S.Ct. 2862, 56 L.Ed.2d 795, on remand 7th Cir., 601 F.2d 261 (judges); Tenney v. Brandhove, 1951, 341 U.S. 367, 71 S.Ct. 783, 95 L.Ed. 1019, rehearing denied 342 U.S. 843, 72 S.Ct. 20, 96 L.Ed. 637; Supreme Court of Virginia v. Consumers Union of United States, Inc., 1980, 446 U.S. 719, 100 S.Ct. 1967, 64 L.Ed. 2d 641, on remand D.Va., 505 F.Supp. 822, appeal dismissed 451 U.S. 1012, 101 S.Ct. 2998, 69 L.Ed.2d 384 (legislators and judges acting in legislative capacity).

8. Pierson v. Ray, 1967, 386 U.S. 547, 87 S.Ct. 1213, 18 L.Ed.2d 288; Huendling v. Jensen, Iowa 1969, 168 N.W.2d 745 (corrupt justice of peace using his powers to collect civil debts for a commission is immune).

9. Abercrombie v. McClung, 1974, 55 Hawaii 595, 525 P.2d 594 (legislator's comments to newspaper on speech he had made on floor of house). See Penthouse, Inc. v. Saba, Fla.App.1981, 399 So.2d 456. Cf. Sweeney v. Tucker, 1976, 473 Pa. 493, 375 A.2d 698 (procedures in ousting member must meet due process, but otherwise unreviewable).

10. Shellburne, Inc. v. Roberts, 1967, 43 Del.Ch. 485, 238 A.2d 331; Scott v. McDonnell Douglas Corp., 1974, 37 Cal.App.3d 277, 112 Cal.Rptr. 609.

11. Cohen v. Bowdoin, Me.1972, 288 A.2d 106 (alleged defamation in meeting of Board of Selectmen of Town); Jones v. Monico, 1967, 276 Minn. 371, 150 N.W. 2d 213 (similar).

12. Richardson v. Edgeworth, Miss.1968, 214 So.2d 579. Since a justice of the peace or magistrate or the like is usually an "inferior" judge of limited jurisdiction it is presumably easier to show that such a judge has gone beyond his or her jurisdiction. This is made explicit in some cases. E.g., Osbekoff v. Mallory, Iowa 1971, 188 N.W.2d 294. In its modern form, the immunity was originally limited to courts of record. See Block, 1980, Stump v. Sparkman and the History of Judicial Immunity, 1980 Duke L.J. 879, 885 FF.

13. Pierson v. Ray, supra note 3; Second Restatement of Torts, § 895D, Comment c.

14. Established in Butz v. Economou, 1978, 438 U.S. 478, 98 S.Ct. 2894, 57 L.Ed.2d 895, on remand D.N.Y., 466 F.Supp. 1351, affirmed 2d Cir., 633 F.2d 203, and apparently historically justified. See Block, Stump v. Sparkman and the History of Judicial Immunity, 1980 Duke L.J. 879, 887–892.

15. Butz v. Economou, 1978, 438 U.S. 478, 98 S.Ct. 2894, 57 L.Ed.2d 895, on remand D.N.Y., 466 F.Supp. 1351, affirmed 2d Cir., 633 F.2d 203.

16. Butz v. Economou, 1978, 438 U.S. 478, 98 S.Ct. 2894, 57 L.Ed.2d 895, on remand D.N.Y., 466 F.Supp. 1351, affirmed 2d Cir., 633 F.2d 203; Mazzucco v. North Carolina Board of Medical Examiners, 1976, 31 N.C.App. 47, 228 S.E.2d 529, certiorari denied 291 N.C. 323, 230 S.E.2d 676 (defamation). Centennial Land & Development v. Township of Medford, 1979, 165 N.J. Super. 220, 397 A.2d 1136. The privilege may be only a qualified one if the board or hearing officer is not acting on a quasi-judicial matter. Compare Wood v. Strickland, 1975, 420 U.S. 308, 95 S.Ct. 992, 43 L.Ed.2d 214, rehearing denied 421 U.S. 921, 95 S.Ct. 1589, 43 L.Ed.2d 790, with Butz v. Economou, supra.

technically members of the executive branch. Beyond this, the judicial immunity has been extended to prosecuting attorneys,[17] grand juries[18] and a number of other adjuncts of the judicial process.[19] A notable exception to this extension of the immunity is the public defender, who is seen as a lawyer with a primary duty to a client rather than as a public official, and who is thus denied the immunity altogether.[20] It is perhaps reassuring to know also that the judge's immunity does not go so far as to protect the litigant who bribes the judge.[21]

If the executive's function in a judicial role will warrant an absolute immunity, a judge's function in an administrative role will warrant a reduction of the immunity.

Thus the judge is performing a function of office in discharging employees, but it is not a judicial function and the absolute immunity does not apply.[22] The same rule has been applied to other adjuncts of the judicial system, so that a prosecutor enjoys the immunity when making prosecutorial decisions but not when aiding a police investigation.[23]

The immunity, when it exists, covers all decisions within the general ambit of the judge's authority, even if the decision is clearly wrong on the merits. The judge is liable if the conduct does not constitute a "judicial act," [24] or if there is a "clear absence" of jurisdiction, but there is no liability for merely "exceeding jurisdiction" in the

17. Imbler v. Pachtman, 1976, 424 U.S. 409, 96 S.Ct. 984, 47 L.Ed.2d 128 (under Civil Rights Act); Watts v. Gerking, 1924, 111 Or. 1, 222 P. 318, 111 Or. 641, 228 P. 135, 34 A.L.R. 1489; Blake v. Rupe, Wyo.1982, 651 P.2d 1096.

18. Turpen v. Booth, 1880, 56 Cal. 65; Hunter v. Mathis, 1872, 40 Ind. 356.

19. Johnson v. Granholm, 6th Cir. 1981, 662 F.2d 449 (friend of the court); Dineen v. Daughan, Me.1978, 381 A.2d 663 (attorney's pleadings absolutely privileged in libel action); McGranahan v. Dahar, 1979, 119 N.H. 758, 408 A.2d 121 (witness' defamatory statements about third party immune).

20. Ferri v. Ackerman, 1979, 444 U.S. 193, 100 S.Ct. 402, 62 L.Ed.2d 355, on remand 488 Pa. 113, 411 A.2d 213 (federal law provides no immunity to federally appointed defense counsel in suit by client); Reese v. Danforth, 1979, 486 Pa. 479, 406 A.2d 735, 6 A.L.R.4th 758. But cf. Polk County v. Dodson, 1981, 454 U.S. 312, 102 S.Ct. 445, 70 L.Ed.2d 509 (public defender does not act under color of state law). See Annots., 6 A.L.R.4th 774; 36 A.L.R.Fed. 594 (under § 1983).

21. Dennis v. Sparks, 1980, 449 U.S. 24, 101 S.Ct. 183, 66 L.Ed.2d 185.

22. Lynch v. Johnson, 6th Cir. 1970, 420 F.2d 818 (judge also presiding officer of county fiscal body is like judge chairing a PTA meeting, no immunity); Shore v. Howard, D.Tex.1976, 414 F.Supp. 379 (hiring and firing, no immunity).

Cf. Supreme Court of Virginia v. Consumers Union of United States, Inc., 1980, 446 U.S. 719, 100 S.Ct. 1967, 64 L.Ed.2d 641, on remand D.Va., 505 F.Supp. 822, appeal dismissed 451 U.S. 1012, 101 S.Ct. 2998, 69 L.Ed.2d 384 (judge acting in enforcement capacity, analogous to prosecutory, is, like prosecutor, subject to injunction even if immune from damages action).

23. Briggs v. Goodwin, D.C.Cir. 1977, 569 F.2d 10 (prosecutor, investigative activity, no immunity); Forsyth v. Kleindienst, 3d Cir. 1979, 599 F.2d 1203, certiorari denied 453 U.S. 913, 101 S.Ct. 3147, 69 L.Ed.2d 997, rehearing denied 453 U.S. 928, 102 S.Ct. 892, 69 L.Ed.2d 1025; Drake v. City of Rochester, 1978, 96 Misc.2d 86, 408 N.Y.S.2d 847, affirmed 74 A.D.2d 996, 429 N.Y.S.2d 394 (prosecutor's misuse of grand jury subpoena, not judicial and not absolutely immune).

In Blake v. Rupe, Wyo.1982, 651 P.2d 1096, a prosecutor apparently decided to order an investigation and then acted on the basis of that investigation. She was held immune in language that might be broad enough to cover detailed participation by the prosecutor herself.

24. "Judicial act" has been defined by the Supreme Court as one normally performed by a judge and consistent with parties' expectations. Stump v. Sparkman, 1978, 435 U.S. 349, 98 S.Ct. 1099, 55 L.Ed.2d 331, rehearing denied 436 U.S. 951, 98 S.Ct. 2862, 56 L.Ed.2d 795. This definition has been criticized as inadequate, see Block, Stump v. Sparkman and the History of Judicial Immunity, 1980, 1980 Duke L.J. 879 and it is probably inconsistent with the "functional analysis" under which, following the implications of Butz v. Economou, 1978, 438 U.S. 478, 98 S.Ct. 2894, 57 L.Ed.2d 895, on remand D.N.Y., 466 F.Supp. 1351, affirmed 2d Cir., 633 F.2d 203, courts have held that some acts of judges are not "judicial," e.g., Lynch v. Johnson, 6th Cir. 1970, 420 F.2d 818. It seems probable that this definition will require some adjustment. Rankin v. Howard, 9th Cir. 1980, 633 F.2d 844, 847, n. 8, certiorari denied 451 U.S. 939, 101 S.Ct. 2020, 68 L.Ed.2d 326, for instance, refused to accept the definition as complete. In any event, the judicial act rule remains separate from the jurisdictional rule. See Block, supra at 887–892.

sense of going too far.[25] Comparable rules apply to the legislative immunity.[26]

One purpose of this immunity is to encourage independence and freedom of judges and legislators.[27] It is thought unlikely that those officers will often commit abuses, because their acts are constantly submitted to public scrutiny and because the political process in the one case and the review process in the other are likely to prevent more serious torts.[28] In the relatively small number of abuses that may take place, it is thought better that these go unredressed than that judges and legislators be deterred from acting rightly out of fear that they will be charged with malice and subjected to the uncertainties of a jury's verdict and the expense of trial.

Some commentators have attacked judicial immunities in their absolute form, and it has been argued that at least some kinds of judicial behavior should be subjected to liability, as where the judge intentionally deprives a plaintiff of constitutional rights,[29] or where a judge takes improper action that is in its nature final and not subject to the controls of appellate review.[30] So far, however, there is little sign that the judges will be receptive to this form of self-regulation.

Immunities of Executive Officers

State-law claims against state officers. As already indicated, certain executive officers performing as adjuncts to the judiciary[31] and certain others performing judicial tasks are given the absolute immunity of judges.[32] These cases aside, only a few states give protection to the malicious official;[33] in most, officials and employees enjoy no immunity at all for ministerial acts and only a qualified immunity on matters calling for the officer's discretion.[34] The qualified immunity is usually destroyed by

---

25. Bradley v. Fisher, 1872, 80 U.S. (13 Wall.) 335, 20 L.Ed. 646; Stump v. Sparkman, 1978, 435 U.S. 349, 98 S.Ct. 1099, 55 L.Ed.2d 331, rehearing denied 436 U.S. 951, 98 S.Ct. 2862, 56 L.Ed.2d 795, on remand 7th Cir., 601 F.2d 261; Holland v. Lutz, 1965, 194 Kan. 712, 401 P.2d 1015 (applying this rule to furnish immunity to judge of a court of limited jurisdiction). As to the distinction between error and want of jurisdiction see Dobbs, 1965, Trial Court Error as an Excess of Jurisdiction, 43 Tex.L.Rev. 854.

26. See Kilbourn v. Thompson, 1881, 103 U.S. 168, 26 L.Ed. 377 (Congressman who exceeded powers of Congress immune, but perhaps Congress would not be immune for execution of the President of other act clearly outside its powers).

27. See Jennings, Tort Liability of Administrative Officers, 1937, 21 Minn.L.Rev. 263, 271; Second Restatement of Torts, § 895D, Comment c.

28. See Handler and Klein, The Defense of Privilege in Defamation Suits Against Government Executive Officials, 1969, 74 Harv.L.Rev. 44, 53–56.

29. Kates, Immunity of State Judges under the Federal Civil Rights Acts: Pierson v. Ray Reconsidered, 1970, 65 N.W.L.Rev. 615.

30. Stump v. Sparkman and the History of Judicial Immunity, 1980, 1980 Duke L.J. 879, 923–25. The basis of this argument is that, historically, the immunity doctrine's function was to eliminate collateral attack and make possible a system of judicial review. Thus where no review is possible, as where the judge orders sterilization which in fact takes place, liability would be appropriate.

31. Imbler v. Pachtman, 1976, 424 U.S. 409, 96 S.Ct. 984, 47 L.Ed.2d 128 (prosecutor); Johnson v. Granholm, 6th Cir. 1981, 662 F.2d 449 (friend of court).

32. Butz v. Economou, 1978, 438 U.S. 478, 98 S.Ct. 2894, 57 L.Ed.2d 895, on remand D.N.Y., 466 F.Supp. 1351, affirmed 2d Cir., 633 F.2d 203; Sweeney v. Young, 1925, 82 N.H. 159, 131 A. 155 (school board dismissal of student after notice and hearing); Richards v. Ellis, Me.1967, 233 A.2d 37 (license denied).

33. Notably California in Hardy v. Vial, 1957, 48 Cal.2d 577, 311 P.2d 494, 66 A.L.R.2d 739. This case was severely limited in Sullivan v. County of Los Angeles, 1974, 12 Cal.3d 710, 117 Cal.Rptr. 241, 527 P.2d 865 (jailer liable when prisoner kept beyond release date). Some states appear to furnish absolute immunity to some officers, or in some torts, but not as to others. In some states the immunity is usually stated without qualification to the effect that the officer is not liable for acts within the scope of his official authority. Where this formulation is used the absolute immunity that seems promised is seldom forthcoming, however, because the courts either construe the scope of authority to narrow the sphere of immunity or find that the conduct in question was merely ministerial, as to which the immunity affords no protection at all. See Pavlik v. Kinsey, 1977, 81 Wis.2d 42, 259 N.W.2d 709.

34. E.g., Shellburne, Inc. v. Roberts, 1967, 43 Del. Ch. 485, 238 A.2d 331; Medeiros v. Kondo, 1974, 55 Hawaii 499, 522 P.2d 1269 (no immunity if plaintiff can prove malice by "clear and convincing proof"); Towse v. State, 1982, 64 Hawaii 624, 647 P.2d 696 (malice includes improper purpose); Bone v. Andrus, 1974, 96 Idaho 291, 527 P.2d 783; Robinson v. Board of County Commissioners, 1971, 262 Md. 342, 278 A.2d 71; Sustin v. Fee, 1982, 69 Ohio St.2d 143, 431 N.E.2d 992; Utah

"malice," bad faith or improper purpose, or in some instances by objectively unreasonable conduct.[35] The burden in any event is upon the officer to prove entitlement to the immunity.[36]

The qualified immunity is not always available. It is usually said that the immunity protects acts within the scope of the officer's duty only if the acts are "discretionary."[37] This means, more or less, that the acts involve some fairly high level of policymaking. Acts that do not qualify as "discretionary" acts are usually called "ministerial," and for purely ministerial acts of executive officers or employees there is no immunity.[38] Acts that create direct personal risks to others and acts involving ordinary considerations of physical safety are usually in this category where there are no serious governmental concerns.[39]

Though there is no immunity for purely ministerial acts, not all ministerial conduct is actionable, since some is not tortious at all, or if tortious, is privileged under the circumstances.[40] There is no liability in any of these cases, but the distinction between immunity and the absence of a tort is nevertheless important, since if there is no tort at all, the officer's malice or bad faith will not import liability.[41]

State-law claims against federal officers. Though most states afford only a qualified immunity or privilege to executive officers engaged in discretionary functions, the federal courts originally took a more protective view when federal officers were sued under state law, holding that in such cases the federal officers held an absolute immunity for acts within the scope of their discretion.[42] This protected the officer not merely for debatable actions, but even for malicious actions if those actions were deemed to be within the "outer perimeter" of the federal duty. There are now indications that the Court might read the scope of a federal officer's duty more narrowly and that some wrongdoing will be so extreme as to be outside that duty.[43]

Federal-law claims against federal officers. Beginning in the 1970s the federal courts have entertained actions against federal officers directly under the federal Con-

---

State University v. Sutro & Co., Utah 1982, 646 P.2d 715. Gray, Private Wrongs of Public Servants, 1959, 47 Cal.L.Rev. 303, 342.

35. Bad faith or improper purpose is ordinarily sufficient to destroy a privilege or immunity. See Second Restatement of Torts, § 895D, Comment e (distinguishing several situations). When a federal constitutional tort is involved, the objective, reasonable person standard seems to have been adopted, so that the immunity is lost if there is a constitutional violation and a reasonable person would have recognized this. See Harlow v. Fitzgerald, 1982, 457 U.S. 800, 102 S.Ct. 2727, 73 L.Ed.2d 396.

36. Gomez v. Toledo, 1980, 446 U.S. 635, 100 S.Ct. 1920, 64 L.Ed.2d 572.

37. E.g., Bone v. Andrus, 1974, 96 Idaho 291, 527 P.2d 783 (governor's alleged improper appointment of another to office); Lawhorne v. Harlan, 1973, 214 Va. 405, 200 S.E.2d 569 (intern at state hospital).

38. E.g., State v. Stanley, Alaska, 1973, 506 P.2d 1284, rehearing denied 509 P.2d 279 (officer who seized fishing boat for alleged violations negligently failed to protect it from sinking, no immunity); Morash & Sons, Inc. v. Commonwealth, 1973, 363 Mass. 612, 296 N.E.2d 461 (rule affirmed). Pavlik v. Kinsey, 1977, 81 Wis.2d 42, 259 N.W.2d 709.

39. E.g., Baird v. Hosmer, 1976, 46 Ohio St.2d 273, 347 N.E.2d 533 (alleged negligence of gym teacher, injury to student); Herron v. Silbaugh, 1970, 436 Pa. 339, 260 A.2d 755 (police chase, speed limits do not apply but officer is liable for recklessness). Specific statutory provisions may yield a different result. Seymour National Bank v. State, 1981, ___ Ind. ___, 422 N.E.2d 1223 (police chase immunized by statute).

40. See Massengill v. Yuma County, 1969, 104 Ariz. 518, 456 P.2d 376, 41 A.L.R.3d 692 (officer owed no duty to stop speeding car, not liable to injured person even though there are no immunities); Beauregard v. Wingard, 9th Cir. 1966, 362 F.2d 901.

41. See, e.g., Beauregard v. Wingard, 9th Cir. 1966, 362 F.2d 901 (officer's malice irrelevant where he had probable cause for arrest).

42. See Barr v. Matteo, 1959, 360 U.S. 564, 79 S.Ct. 1335, 3 L.Ed.2d 1434, rehearing denied 361 U.S. 855, 80 S.Ct. 41, 4 L.Ed.2d 93 (defamation); Gregoire v. Biddle, 2d Cir. 1949, 177 F.2d 579, certiorari denied 339 U.S. 949, 70 S.Ct. 803, 94 L.Ed. 1363 (most quoted case).

43. See Doe v. McMillan, 1973, 412 U.S. 306, 93 S.Ct. 2018, 36 L.Ed.2d 912, motion denied 419 U.S. 1043, 95 S.Ct. 614, 42 L.Ed.2d 637; Butz v. Economou, 1978, 438 U.S. 478, 98 S.Ct. 2894, 57 L.Ed.2d 895, on remand D.N.Y., 466 F.Supp. 1351, affirmed 2d Cir., 633 F.2d 203 (perhaps suggesting a narrower notion of scope of duty even where constitutional violations are not involved).

stitution.[44] In these cases the Court has said that violation of a federal constitutional right, at least on some occasions, will in itself show that the non-judicial officer was outside the scope of his duty and in such cases the absolute immunity will afford no protection.[45] Instead, following the same rule used when state officers are sued for violation of federal rights, the Court has provided only a qualified immunity, except as to the President, who remains absolutely immune even for violation of Constitutional rights.[46] The good faith in this qualified immunity is not judged subjectively, but objectively and the officer loses the privilege if he violates a constitutional or statutory right of which a reasonable person would have known.[47]

Federal-law claims against state officers. Civil rights statutes creating claims for violation of federal rights under color of state law have been the source of much litigation against state officers as well as others.[48] The Supreme Court has read the common law immunities, or something very close to them, into the civil rights statutes. Thus state legislators[49] and judges[50] are absolutely immune, but other state officers enjoy only the qualified immunity. This immunity originally had a subjective component,[51] necessitating jury trials to resolve any dispute over the officer's state of mind. It now appears, however, that "bare allegations of malice should not suffice," and that, so far as civil rights claims go, the plaintiff will be required to establish a violation of constitutional rights of which a reasonable person would have known."[52] Since cities do not enjoy a good faith immunity in cases brought under the major federal statutes,[53] the preference in many instances is to sue the city instead of the officer, or at least to join the city as a defendant. In some instances the same result may be achieved on the ground that though the individual officer is a named defendant, the suit in substance is one against the municipality and the good faith immunity has no application so far as it would reach the city's assets rather than the officer's.[54]

The absolute immunity, occasionally recognized in the states and in cases of state-law suits against federal officers, is supported by the idea that some such protection

---

44. Bivens v. Six Unknown Named Agents of Federal Bureau of Narcotics, 1971, 403 U.S. 388, 91 S.Ct. 1999, 29 L.Ed.2d 619, on remand 2d Cir., 456 F.2d 1339.

45. Butz v. Economou, 1978, 438 U.S. 478, 98 S.Ct. 2894, 57 L.Ed.2d 895, on remand D.N.Y., 466 F.Supp. 1351, affirmed 2d Cir., 633 F.2d 203; Harlow v. Fitzgerald, 1982, 457 U.S. 800, 102 S.Ct. 2727, 73 L.Ed.2d 396.

46. Nixon v. Fitzgerald, 1982, 457 U.S. 731, 102 S.Ct. 2690, 73 L.Ed.2d 349.

47. Harlow v. Fitzgerald, 1982, 457 U.S. 800, 102 S.Ct. 2727, 73 L.Ed.2d 396. This formulation of the immunity reflects the civil rights context in which it has been litigated and it may be that the formula will be modified slightly when and if liability is extended to other kinds of cases or to other forms of misconduct.

48. 42 U.S.C.A. § 1983 has been the main source of litigation. See, e.g., Scheuer v. Rhodes, 1974, 416 U.S. 232, 94 S.Ct. 1683, 40 L.Ed.2d 90. Litigation may proceed in state court under this federal statute. E.g., Williams v. Horvath, 1976, 16 Cal.3d 834, 129 Cal.Rptr. 453, 548 P.2d 1125.

49. Tenney v. Brandhove, 1951, 341 U.S. 367, 71 S.Ct. 783, 95 L.Ed. 1019, rehearing denied 342 U.S. 843, 72 S.Ct. 20, 96 L.Ed. 637.

50. Pierson v. Ray, 1967, 386 U.S. 547, 87 S.Ct. 1213, 18 L.Ed.2d 288.

51. Wood v. Strickland, 1975, 420 U.S. 308, 95 S.Ct. 992, 43 L.Ed.2d 214, rehearing denied 421 U.S. 921, 95 S.Ct. 1589, 43 L.Ed.2d 790. O'Connor v. Donaldson, 1975, 422 U.S. 563, 95 S.Ct. 2486, 45 L.Ed.2d 396, on remand 5th Cir., 519 F.2d 59. See Harlow v. Fitzgerald, 1982, ___ U.S. ___, 102 S.Ct. 2727, 73 L.Ed.2d 396 (involving federal officers, as to whom the privileges now appear to be similar).

52. Harlow v. Fitzgerald, 1982, 457 U.S. 800, 102 S.Ct. 2727, 73 L.Ed.2d 396 (federal officials). The Supreme Court has treated the immunities of federal and state officials alike in recent years when the complaint alleges a civil rights violation.

53. Owen v. City of Independence, 1980, 445 U.S. 622, 100 S.Ct. 1398, 63 L.Ed.2d 673, on remand 8th Cir., 623 F.2d 550, rehearing denied 446 U.S. 993, 100 S.Ct. 2979, 64 L.Ed.2d 850; see § 131, supra.

54. Kincaid v. Rusk, 7th Cir. 1982, 670 F.2d 737 (suit against sheriff in official capacity is only another way of suing the public entity, hence no good faith immunity); Williams v. Alioto, 9th Cir. 1980, 625 F.2d 845, certiorari denied 450 U.S. 1012, 101 S.Ct. 1723, 68 L.Ed.2d 213; see Monell v. Department of Social Services, 1978, 436 U.S. 658, 690, 98 S.Ct. 2018, 2035, 56 L.Ed.2d 611.

is required to assure fearless administration, since even honest and competent officials might act too timidly if they could be accused of malice and subjected to personal liability. To avoid this they might avoid rigorous action, for fear that a jury might find malice[55] and that the expense of defending themselves would be ruinous.

The qualified immunity is favored by those who believe that quite sufficient leeway is provided most officials if the plaintiff must show, in addition to any other elements of the tort alleged, that the officer is guilty of malice or improper purpose, and that no official who is in fact guilty of bad faith should escape accountability on the off chance that some other official might act too timorously. This view emphasizes the judge's capacity to direct a verdict or grant summary judgment if the evidence is insufficient. Supporters of the qualified immunity have suggested also that in a free society with a limited government the concept of a wholly fearless official, elevated above the law by his immunity, is unacceptable in any event.[56] The current federal retreat from absolute immunity in its most stringent form, though so far limited to the civil rights cases, appears to be more in accord with this latter view.

Application of the Discretionary—ministerial Dichotomy.

Since most states afford a qualified, malice-destructible immunity for discretionary acts, but no immunity at all for "ministerial" acts, the distinction between the two is critical in any case where the plaintiff cannot show malice. Where there is an absolute immunity for discretionary acts, the distinction is critical in all cases. It is not, however, a distinction that judicial, academic or practicing lawyers have been able to define. Actually, the conclusion that the officer's acts were "discretionary" is probably only a shorthand notation for a more complex policy decision, or in some cases, a decision that there is really no tortious act at all. Following the lead of Professor Jaffe,[57] the Restatement[58] and some courts[59] have now said that it is all a matter of assessing various factors, such as the nature of the plaintiff's injury, the availability of alternative remedies, the ability of the courts to judge fault without unduly invading the executive's function, and the importance of protecting particular kinds of official acts. Although a statement of such factors falls far short of resolving particular cases, it is true that factors of this sort do seem important in many cases.

Nature of the plaintiff's claim. It seems clear that the plaintiff's best chance of imposing liability arises where he has suffered physical injury to or restraint of person or property as an immediate result of official action. In the absence of statute, the officer or employee is not immune from liability for negligence in driving a motor vehicle,[60] negligent medical treatment[61] for tortious restraint of person,[62] for injury to a person in custody,[63] or for loss of or damage to prop-

55. See Gregoire v. Biddle, 2d Cir. 1949, 177 F.2d 579, certiorari denied 339 U.S. 949, 70 S.Ct. 803, 94 L.Ed. 1363.

56. This last argument is stated concisely in Becht, The Absolute Privilege of the Executive in Defamation, 1962, 15 Vand.L.Rev. 1127, 1168–69.

57. L. Jaffe, Judicial Control of Administrative Action, 241 (1965).

58. Second Restatement of Torts, § 895D, Comment *f.*

59. Smith v. Cooper, 1970, 256 Or. 485, 475 P.2d 78. The same point has been made with regard to the immunity of public entities. See § 131, supra.

60. See Baselski v. City of Chicago, 1972, 9 Ill.App. 3d 516, 292 N.E.2d 475; Herron v. Silbaugh, 1970, 436 Pa. 339, 260 A.2d 755 (under statute ordinary speed limitations did not apply to officer in pursuit, but officer was liable for reckless conduct).

61. James v. Jane, 1980, 221 Va. 43, 282 S.E.2d 864; Watson v. St. Annes Hospital, 1979, 68 Ill.App.3d 1048, 25 Ill.Dec. 411, 386 N.E.2d 885.

62. Sullivan v. County of Los Angeles, 1974, 12 Cal. 3d 710, 117 Cal.Rptr. 241, 527 P.2d 865 (failure to release prisoner on time, no immunity); Thurston v. Leno, 1964, 124 Vt. 298, 204 A.2d 106 (delay in taking arrested person to magistrate was unlawful restraint).

63. Irwin v. Arrendale, 1967, 117 Ga.App. 1, 159 S.E.2d 719 (forced x-ray actionable in absence of privilege to prevent contagious diseases); State ex rel. Wil-

erty in custody.⁶⁴ Similarly, officers are liable for arrests⁶⁵ or seizures of property⁶⁶ except so far as they may enjoy a privilege such as that provided by a warrant.⁶⁷

Where officials do not take direct physical action themselves but nevertheless create risks of physical harm to the plaintiff, the results are somewhat mixed. Jailers and other custodians owe a duty to provide reasonable protection to prisoners⁶⁸ and patients and others⁶⁹ in custody, including reasonable protection from others in custody, and are held liable for failure to do so even though they themselves may take no direct action in causing the harm. On the other hand, once the special duty to those in custody is out of the picture, officials often escape liability for physical harm when their fault if any does not involve direct action on their part. For example the official who assigns an inexperienced guard may escape liability for harm done by the escaping prisoner.⁷⁰ Similarly, the tendency is to protect decisions to release dangerous persons from custody,⁷¹ though there are now a few dissents from this position where the official is wanton or grossly negligent.⁷²

In contrast to these cases of physical harm where direct action tends to remove the immunity, indirect action leaves somewhat mixed results and the courts have been noticeably more reluctant to impose liability for many kinds of purely economic loss which is unaccompanied by physical harm. Thus, for example, denial or revocation of a license or building permit or zoning request may be wrongful and cause business losses, but the official's decision in these cases is usually discretionary and protected⁷³ by the good faith immunity. The same is true with other forms of interference with contract or economic prospects, so long, at least, as the officer acts in good faith and not with malicious motive.⁷⁴ Similarly, most actions by employees over discharge, promotion or pay involve economic harm only and succeed on-

liams v. Adams, 1975, 288 N.C. 501, 219 S.E.2d 198 (failure to provide medical aid to prisoner).

64. Garren v. Butigan, 1975, 96 Idaho 906, 539 P.2d 259 (loss of property levied on by sheriff); Williams v. Walley, Miss.1974, 295 So.2d 286 (trespass by sheriff); Harris v. Dobson-Tankard Co., 1957, 41 Tenn.App. 642, 298 S.W.2d 28 (sheriff liable for negligence in leaving evicted tenant's property unprotected in the rain).

65. Barr v. County of Albany, 1980, 50 N.Y.2d 247, 428 N.Y.S.2d 665, 406 N.E.2d 481; Wallner v. Fidelity & Deposit Co. of Maryland, 1948, 253 Wis. 66, 33 N.W.2d 215, 10 A.L.R.2d 745. The issue in such cases then turns on the scope of the privilege and whether it was exceeded.

66. Seguin v. Eide, 9th Cir. 1981, 645 F.2d 804 (failure to refer case for forfeiture proceedings after car was confiscated); Dickens v. DeBolt, 1979, 288 Or. 3, 602 P.2d 246 (if officer ate fish after confiscating it, no immunity).

67. See Second Restatement of Torts § 895D, Comment e.

68. Daniels v. Andersen, 1975, 195 Neb. 95, 237 N.W.2d 397; see Annot., 41 A.L.R.3d 1021.

69. As to children in official custody placed in unsafe environs, see Koepf v. County of York, 1977, 198 Neb. 67, 251 N.W.2d 866. In cases of this sort where the public entity is liable, see § 131 supra, the implication is usually clear that the officer would likewise be held.

70. Christensen v. Epley, 1979, 287 Or. 539, 601 P.2d 1216, appeal after remand 57 Or.App. 330, 644 P.2d 627; (divided court) cf. Maynard v. City of Madison, 1981, 101 Wis.2d 273, 304 N.W.2d 163 (police officers negligently revealed identity of informer, presumably subjecting her to some risk of physical harm).

71. Martinez v. State, 1978, 85 Cal.App.3d 430, 149 Cal.Rptr. 519, affirmed 1980, 444 U.S. 277, 100 S.Ct. 553, 62 L.Ed.2d 481, rehearing denied 445 U.S. 920, 100 S.Ct. 1285, 63 L.Ed.2d 606. This position is taken repeatedly in cases involving suits against the public entity, as to which see § 131, supra. Cf. Eide v. Timberlake, D.Kan.1980, 497 F.Supp. 1272 (assignment of prisoner to outside work is discretionary if not done on mechanical basis and if conscious judgment is brought to bear).

72. Grimm v. Arizona Board of Pardons and Paroles, 1977, 115 Ariz. 260, 564 P.2d 1227; Neal v. Donahue, Okl.1980, 611 P.2d 1125 (doctor liable for release of dangerous juvenile, superintendent not).

73. Gorman Towers, Inc. v. Bogoslavsky, 8th Cir. 1980, 626 F.2d 607 (absolute immunity of city council enacting re-zoning); Rottkamp v. Young, 1964, 21 A.D.2d 373, 249 N.Y.S.2d 330, affirmed 1965, 15 N.Y.2d 831, 257 N.Y.S.2d 944, 205 N.E.2d 866 (building permit delayed until zoning ordinance could be amended to prevent diner); Verrill v. Dewey, 1972, 130 Vt. 627, 299 A.2d 182 (revocation of liquor license).

74. Princeton Community Phone Book, Inc. v. Bate, 3d Cir. 1978, 582 F.2d 706, certiorari denied 439 U.S. 966, 99 S.Ct. 454, 58 L.Ed.2d 424 (rule against lawyer advertising), Idlehour Development Co. v. City of St. Charles, 1980, 88 Ill.App.3d 47, 42 Ill.Dec. 929, 409 N.E.2d 544 (liable for malicious interference with lease).

ly if the officer has acted in bad faith[75] or outside the scope or in abuse of authority.[76]

The immunity may also vary according to the kind of tort asserted. Though courts discuss the immunity in general terms, there is some reason to believe that the immunity as applied to defamation cases, for example, might not be identical to the immunity as applied to false imprisonment cases. New York courts have at times made broad pronouncements abut the immunity for official acts and have in some cases made this immunity absolute.[77] But where the tort was a denial of plaintiff's right to appear on a ballot, the immunity was held to be only conditional.[78] California somewhat similarly granted an absolute immunity in a malicious prosecution case,[79] but seems to have denied any immunity at all in a false imprisonment case.[80] And as has already been mentioned, the federal courts have in some instances narrowed the immunity otherwise available when constitutional or civil rights tort claims are asserted.

The nature of the plaintiff's claim is also important where it is based on unjust enrichment rather than on tort. If the action is to force disgorgement of gains to the officer, there is no immunity, since none of the reasons for it are present in such a case.[81] Somewhat similarly, where officers violate a public obligation or fiduciary duty in handling public funds, they may be strictly liable to restore any lost funds, even though they themselves derive no gains.[82]

Alternative remedies. Where administrative action that causes harm can be reviewed judicially, or where there are remedies other than tort damages, the tendency is often to grant the officer immunity, even though the alternative remedy may not be perfect. For example, if an employee is discharged from public employment, the fact that he has an opportunity for judicial review is very likely to preclude a tort action against the officer who fired him.[83] In other cases the plaintiff's rights will be deemed adequately protected by permitting an injunction, but not damages, against officials.[84]

75. Skehan v. Board of Trustees of Bloomsburg St. College, 3d Cir. 1976, 538 F.2d 53, certiorari denied 429 U.S. 977, 97 S.Ct. 490, 50 L.Ed.2d 588, on remand D.Pa., 431 F.Supp. 1379, affirmed and remanded 3d Cir., 590 F.2d 470, certiorari denied 444 U.S. 832, 100 S.Ct. 61, 62 L.Ed.2d 41, on remand 501 F.Supp. 1360; Atcherson v. Siebenmann, 8th Cir. 1979, 605 F.2d 1058; Nicoletta v. North Jersey District Water Supply Commission, 1978, 77 N.J. 145, 390 A.2d 90.

76. Murphy v. City of Topeka-Shawnee County Department of Labor Services, 1981, 6 Kan.App.2d 489, 630 P.2d 186 (retaliatory discharge).

77. See Sheridan v. Crisona, 1964, 14 N.Y.2d 108, 249 N.Y.S.2d 161, 198 N.E.2d 359 (defamation).

78. Schwartz v. Heffernan, 1952, 304 N.Y. 474, 109 N.E.2d 68.

79. Hardy v. Vial, 1957, 48 Cal.2d 577, 311 P.2d 494, 66 A.L.R.2d 739.

80. Sullivan v. County of Los Angeles, 1974, 12 Cal. 3d 710, 117 Cal.Rptr. 241, 527 P.2d 865.

81. See Russell v. Tate, 1890, 52 Ark. 541, 13 S.W. 130, 7 L.R.A. 180, 20 Am.St.Rep. 193.

82. Bird v. McGoldrick, 1938, 277 N.Y. 492, 14 N.E.2d 805, 116 A.L.R. 1059. The exact responsibility of an officer for funds he himself does not receive or control depends on the structure of local law.

83. See Donahue v. Bowers, 1974, 19 Or.App. 50, 526 P.2d 616. Cf. Parratt v. Taylor, 1980, 451 U.S. 527, 101 S.Ct. 1908, 68 L.Ed.2d 420 (state's negligent loss of plaintiff's property not a "taking" where other state remedies available); Gorman Towers, Inc. v. Bogoslavsky, 8th Cir. 1980, 626 F.2d 607 (since rezoning aimed at depriving plaintiff of benefit of property could be reviewed judicially, absolute immunity of city council would bar tort action); Compare Gorman Towers, supra, with International Oceanic Enterprises, Inc. v. Menton, 5th Cir. 1980, 614 F.2d 502 (injunction granted against discriminatory zoning).

84. See Price v. Sheppard, 1976, 307 Minn. 205, 239 N.W.2d 905 (no action on behalf of inmate of mental hospital for unconsented to electroshock treatments, but for the future Court requires procedures for consent); Long v. Seabrook, 1973, 260 S.C. 562, 197 S.E.2d 659 (no tort damages for denial of access of public records, but injunction may issue later); Wilkinson v. Skinner, 1974, 34 N.Y.2d 53, 356 N.Y.S.2d 15, 312 N.E.2d 158 ("Injunctive relief should be granted more readily" in prisoners' claims against prison based on practices and conditions.) See Whitman, Constitutional Torts, 1980, 79 Mich.L.Rev. 5, 42–71, arguing that equitable remedies should often be preferred in cases of constitutional torts as being less disruptive. But cf. Love, Damages: A Remedy for the Violation of Constitutional Rights, 1979, 67 Calif.L.Rev. 1242; Yudof, Liability for Constitutional Torts and the Risk-Averse Public School Official, 1976, 49 S.Cal.L.Rev. 1322, 1371ff.

Interference with a coordinate branch of government. Perhaps the single most significant factor in the discretionary immunity is the long tradition that establishes the legislative, judicial and executive branches of government as coordinate and independent. Courts wish to avoid second-guessing the executive department through the means of torts suits. It is partly for this reason that courts will not hold administrators liable for many plans or decisions, especially where there must be a weighing of governmental objectives and an allocation of governmental resources. In such cases, courts respect the constitutional assignment of power to the executive by refusing to pass judgment on executive decisions, that is, by describing as discretionary a decision for which there is immunity. This outlook has had major impact in several areas, especially those involving allocation of public resources and a failure to provide governmental services or action. In particular, courts have been most unwilling to impose liability for failure to prevent crime or otherwise to enforce the law.[85] On the other hand, where the governmental decision has little or no purely governmental content but instead resembles decisions or activities carried on by people generally, there is an objective standard for judgment by the courts, who can withhold the immunity in such cases and impose liability without undue interference with the executive.[86] Thus, the tendency is to provide immunity for officers who have made advertent policy decisions or plans of a larger sort, even though in retrospect those plans seem dangerous or unreasonable;[87] equally, the tendency is to withhold the immunity from officers where governmental concerns are minimally involved and ordinary standards of safety can be applied.[88] The issue cannot be resolved mechanically, and some judgment is required in each case as to how important the policy is on the particular facts.

Special protection for certain official acts. Some official conduct is more vulnerable to attack than other conduct. Some official conduct especially needs a free range of choice that is not hampered by concerns over potential personal liability. Other official conduct is neither especially vulnerable to complaint nor in need of especially unhampered decision-making. One who repairs the street can do a good job without provoking a citizen suit; the prosecuting attorney cannot do a good job without provoking anger and, sooner or later, a citizen suit. Good operation of the prosecutor's office does adversely affect people (usually criminals, but, unavoidably, others as well); good operation of the street repair department does not harm people, but on the contrary makes their travel safer. Both kinds of work are socially desirable, but one kind, since it is intended to adversely affect others and does so, is more likely to generate claims than the other.[89] The range of free choice needed in the two kinds of work is also quite different. The importance of the officer's freedom of decision and the likelihood of unjust suit for honest decision-making are factors to be considered in deciding whether official conduct is "discretionary" and immune or "ministerial" and unprotected.[90]

Since the main policy involved in assessing this factor is to protect the officer's free

---

85. See Note, Police Liability for Failure to Prevent Crime, 1980, 94 Harv.L.Rev. 821. The cases, most of which involve suits against public entities, are discussed in more detail in § 131, supra.

86. See § 131, supra.

87. Smith v. Cooper, 1970, 256 Or. 485, 475 P.2d 78, 45 A.L.R.3d 857 (highway design); Torres v. Owens, Tex.Civ.App. 1964, 380 S.W.2d 30, refused n.r.e. (dredging without engineer present).

88. Thus the decision to seize a ship may be discretionary, but failure to take ordinary care to prevent its sinking later is simple negligence for which the officer is liable. State v. Stanley, Alaska 1973, 506 P.2d 1284, rehearing denied 509 P.2d 279. The automobile negligence cases furnish another example. Professional negligence furnishes another, see Voss v. Bridwell, 1961, 188 Kan. 643, 364 P.2d 955.

89. See Cass, Damage Suits against Public Officers, 1981, 129 U.Pa.L.Rev. 1110, 1153ff. Professor Cass develops many details to this point.

90. See Second Restatement of Torts, § 895D, Comment *f*.

range of decision-making, it has no application where a specific duty is imposed and the officer clearly violates it. Where the duty is highly specific, the officer may be liable even for relatively remote economic losses flowing from the breach of duty. In this group belong cases of sheriffs who make false returns of process,[91] clerks who improperly register deeds[92] and notaries who improperly acknowledge a signature.[93]

Discretionary Immunity and Negligence

A number of decisions involving the liability of officials as well as a number involving liability of public entities[94] purport to turn on immunity but in fact seem more readily explicable as cases in which no tort was established in the first place. The apparent conflict between decisions as to liability of state-employed physicians, who are sometimes immune[95] and sometimes not[96] is perhaps best explained by recognizing that in some instances liability has been denied not because of immunity but because negligence was not shown. The distinction, in any event, is an important one. If the issue in any given case is properly seen to be negligence, the plaintiff will have the burden of proof to show the elements of the claim and in all likelihood will be entitled to a trial, or at least a judicial analysis of the evidence on unreasonable risk. If, on the other hand, the issue is seen to be one of immunity, the burden of proof at least in some cases will be on the defendant to show good faith,[97] but there remains a tendency for judges to decide the immunity issues themselves, while at the same time sidestepping the negligence analysis that would determine whether a case of tortious conduct has been proven. As a result, it bears repeating that the distinction between the two issues requires the lawyer's attention in every case.

Immunity and Privilege

In addition to whatever immunity is or is not available to the officer simply because of official status, there is a privilege to obey the command of judicial process fair on its face as well as the command of a valid statute. If the officer follows a writ which there is no reason to question, there is an immunity even in the face of personal malice,[98] since regardless of mental state the officer is only complying with a legal duty. The problem in cases of this sort has often turned on the question whether the officer is privileged when he relies on a judicial order issued without jurisdiction or a statute that is unconstitutional. As indicated in an earlier section,[99] the older cases tended to hold the officer liable for technical defects in the command under which he justified his action, while the more recent ones tend to excuse him unless there was reason to doubt the validity of the order of statute.

---

91. Marsh v. Hawkins, 1968, 7 Ariz.App. 226, 437 P.2d 978, 31 A.L.R.3d 1383 (liability for fraud, or negligence rejecting strict liability); Glidden v. Wills, 1955, 136 Cal.App.2d 596, 289 P.2d 55 (failure to file inventory of levy); Crowder v. Jenkins, 1971, 11 N.C.App. 57, 180 S.E.2d 482 (false return).

92. Hoffman v. Schroeder, 1962, 38 Ill.App.2d 20, 186 N.E.2d 381 (forged signatures, statutory liability); Charco, Inc. v. Cohn, 1966, 242 Or. 566, 411 P.2d 264 (clerk's delay in entering judgment).

93. Meyers v. Meyers, 1972, 81 Wn.2d 533, 503 P.2d 59 (forgery). Contra, Nelson v. Comer, 1974, 21 N.C. App. 636, 205 S.E.2d 537 (notary's act "judicial" and privileged, possibly a case of no negligence).

94. See § 131, supra.

95. Estate of Burks v. Ross, 6th Cir. 1971, 438 F.2d 230 (absolute immunity of psychiatric personnel); Anderberg v. Newman, 1972, 5 Ill.App.3d 736, 283 N.E.2d 904 (abstract only); Baker v. Straumfjord, 1972, 10 Or.App. 414, 500 P.2d 496.

96. Henderson v. Bluemink, D.C.Cir. 1974, 511 F.2d 399 ("medical rather than governmental" discretion, in suit against government doctor, no immunity); Voss v. Bridwell, 1961, 188 Kan. 643, 364 P.2d 955; Watson v. St. Annes Hospital, 1979, 68 Ill.App.3d 1048, 25 Ill.Dec. 411, 386 N.E.2d 885, cf. Pettis v. State Department of Hospitals, La:App.1973, 281 So.2d 881, appeal after remand 336 So.2d 521, writ denied 337 So.2d 527, writ denied in part 339 So.2d 851, set aside in part 339 So.2d 855, on remand 340 So.2d 1108; Irwin v. Arrendale, 1967, 117 Ga.App. 1, 159 S.E.2d 719 (prisoner did not consent to x-ray).

97. Gomez v. Toledo, 1980, 446 U.S. 635, 100 S.Ct. 1920, 64 L.Ed.2d 572.

98. Beauregard v. Wingard, 9th Cir. 1966, 362 F.2d 901.

99. § 25, supra.

The privilege to follow the mandate of a judicial order or a statute is not a privilege to follow the impermissible order of a superior executive officer. If the police commissioner orders a general search of inhabitants, the officer who carries out the search is liable for battery and cannot defend on the ground that he simply followed orders. In such a case the police commissioner himself would have no immunity for a search, and his order gives none to the inferior officers.[1] But it is also true that though the superior's command is not a warrant, the junior officer who implements that command shares the senior's immunity if he does in fact have one. If the police commissioner gives a press interview, he is probably acting within his discretion, and if he orders a junior officer to give it instead, the commissioner's discretionary immunity will fall upon the junior.[2]

It is important to notice a matter entirely distinct from either privilege or immunity. Though superior orders may not immunize an officer, information received from superiors and fellow officers may ordinarily be trusted and such information may well furnish a ground for defense on the merits, as where a description furnished the officer gives probable cause for arrest and thus affords a defense to a malicious prosecution action.[3]

Indemnity and Other Protections for the Officer

No statement of the officer's personal immunity is complete without a recognition that protection may be afforded by a specific statute,[4] or by rules or procedures that are entirely independent of the immunity. Some protective rules, such as the privilege to obey a warrant or writ, have already been noted.[5] Another protective rule is that an officer is ordinarily[6] not liable on the basis of *respondeat superior* for the acts of his subordinates,[7] though he may be liable for his own negligence in permitting those acts or otherwise.[8]

In recent years other protections have been added by statutes. There are two important protective provisions of the Federal Tort Claims Act. The "judgment" provision is that a citizen's judgment against the United States under the Act will operate to bar any claim against the employee whose act gave rise to the claim.[9] Since the Act now

---

1. Mason v. Wrightson, 1954, 205 Md. 481, 109 A.2d 128 (general order to search); cf. Forsyth v. Kleindienst, 3d Cir. 1979, 599 F.2d 1203, certiorari denied 453 U.S. 913, 101 S.Ct. 3147, 69 L.Ed.2d 997, rehearing denied 453 U.S. 928, 102 S.Ct. 892, 69 L.Ed.2d 1025 (following orders no defense but may bear on officer's good faith); Chicago Park District v. R.E. Herczel & Co., 1940, 373 Ill. 325, 26 N.E.2d 119 (suit by governmental entity to recover illegally paid funds, no defense that superior had ordered payment).

2. Berndtson v. Lewis, 4th Cir. 1972, 465 F.2d 706 ("Had the Secretary of the Navy uttered the alleged libel, he would be clothed with absolute immunity, and we think this immunity extends to the conduct of Captain Berndtson in compliance with the Secretary's instruction.")

3. E.g., Wilson v. Gutschenritter, 1970, 185 Neb. 311, 175 N.W.2d 282 (mistaken identity arrest based on many accurate circumstantial details communicated by sergeant to officer, probable cause was shown, no false arrest), Johnson v. Reddy, 1955, 163 Ohio St. 347, 128 N.E.2d 911 (information and request for arrest from Pennsylvania to Ohio officers furnished, on the facts, sufficient reasonable ground to justify Ohio arrest).

Cf. Forsyth v. Kleindienst, 3d Cir. 1979, 599 F.2d 1203, certiorari denied 453 U.S. 913, 101 S.Ct. 3147, 69 L.Ed.2d 997, rehearing denied 453 U.S. 928, 102 S.Ct. 892, 69 L.Ed.2d 1025 (following orders no defense but may bear on good faith).

4. E.g., 38 U.S.C.A. § 4116 (medical persons in Veterans Administration department).

5. Supra, note 99.

6. Sheriff under non-delegable or statutory duty to care for safety of prisoner: Davis v. Moore, 1939, 215 N.C. 449, 2 S.E.2d 366; Magenheimer v. State ex rel. Dalton, 1950, 120 Ind.App. 128, 90 N.E.2d 813; Sheriff may be liable for illegal acts of deputies: Mendez v. Blackburn, Fla.1969, 226 So.2d 340.

7. Robertson v. Sichel, 1888, 127 U.S. 507, 8 S.Ct. 1286, 32 L.Ed. 203; Kelly v. Ogilvie, 1966, 35 Ill.2d 297, 220 N.E.2d 174; Alves v. Hayes, 1980, 381 Mass. 57, 406 N.E.2d 1028.

8. Liber v. Flor, 1966, 160 Colo. 7, 415 P.2d 332, 35 A.L.R.3d 1165; see Smith v. Miller, 1950, 241 Iowa 625, 40 N.W.2d 597, 14 A.L.R.2d 345 (sheriff failed to have custodian on hand, prisoner under medication died).

9. 28 U.S.C.A. § 2676.

covers a number of intentional torts,[10] even the officer who commits serious constitutional invasions may be protected in fact if not in theory, since the plaintiff will ordinarily prefer to sue the United States on a deeper pocket theory and since a recovery against the United States will automatically protect the officer. The second or "exclusive remedy" provision is quite different. In the first place it applies only to specific injuries such as motor vehicle injuries caused by government employees.[11] In the second place there is not even a theoretical option to sue the employee as an individual; injuries arising out of motor vehicle injuries must be redressed exclusively by action against the government itself. The effect of this is to place the government driver in much the same position as the private employer's driver who will ordinarily be covered by the employer's liability policy. There are proposals in the Congress, accompanied by much active support, to expand the exclusive remedy principle to cover all torts.[12]

A number of states have taken a different approach. They protect the officer by providing a defense to the suit against him or indemnity or payment of the judgment in the event he is held liable.[13] This is a complete reversal of the traditional rule that the employer, if held vicariously liable because of the employee's tort, is entitled to claim indemnity over against the employee. The state's obligation to protect the employee by indemnity is usually limited to cases that do not involve conscious wrongdoing,[14] though some statutes call for virtually unlimited indemnification[15] where they apply at all. All statutes offer this protection only for acts committed within the scope of official duties.

Still another contemporary protective device now in use by many states does not change the legal relations involved at all. It simply provides liability insurance on the officer's behalf, financed by the state or the governmental entity in question.[16] This device seems to be used at present mainly for the protection of professionals, such as state-employed physicians or attorneys, but is probably capable of considerable expansion to protect other officers.

Although some writers have concluded that tort liability fails to deter official misconduct,[17] others have emphasized the potential for "overdeterrence," in which officials avoid needed action to avoid the risk of claims. To prevent this overdeterrence effect, some writers have proposed that the public entities themselves accept exclusive responsibility for the torts of the individual officers,[18] and at this writing bills have been

10. See 28 U.S.C.A. § 2680.

11. 28 U.S.C.A. § 2679. Several scattered sections make a similar provision for certain cases of medical malpractice. E.g., 10 U.S.C.A. § 1089.

12. See Casto, Government Liability for Constitutional Torts: Proposals to Amend the Federal Tort Claims Act, 1982, 49 Tenn.L.Rev. 201.

13. See Bermann, Integrating Governmental and Officer Tort Liability, 1977, 77 Colum.L.Rev. 1175, 1190ff.

14. West's Ann.Cal.Govt.Code, §§ 825–825.6; N.Y.—McKinney's Pub. Officers Law, § 17; N.C.Gen. Stat., § 143–300.6; Or.Rev.Stat., 30.285; Vernon's Ann.Tex.Civ.Stats., art. 6252–26 (certain departments).

15. Ill.Rev.Ann., Ch. 85, § 2–302 (local public entities, duty to defend, indemnify or both).

16. Nat. Assn. of Attorneys General, Sovereign Immunity Update (1975) reflects a survey showing at least half the states carry liability insurance to protect drivers of motor vehicles and another large group carries malpractice insurance for some or all of its professionals.

17. Littlejohn, Civil Liability and the Police Officer: The Need for New Deterrents to Police Misconduct, 1981, 58 U.Det.J.Urb.L. 365; Project, Suing the Police in Federal Court, 1979, 88 Yale L.J. 781.

18. Cass, Damage Suits against Public Officers, 1981, 129 U.Pa.L.Rev. 1110; Casto, Government Liability for Constitutional Torts: Proposals to Amend the Federal Tort Claims Act, 1982, 49 Tenn.L.Rev. 201; Davis, Legal Control of the Police, 1974, 52 Tex.L.Rev. 703. A number of other writers have expressed doubts that imposition of liability upon the officer personally will effectively impose a regime of accountability. See Mashaw, 1978, 42 L. & Contemp. Prob. 8; Shepsle, Official Errors and Official Liability, 1978, 42 L. & Contemp. Prob. 35. Exclusive liability may also approach strict liability in the case of local public entities violating constitutional rights, see Owen v. City of Independence, 1980, 445 U.S. 622, discussed supra, § 131. Some have advocated strict liability as well as exclu-

introduced in Congress to this effect.[19] This kind of rule would avoid the overdeterrence effect and leave the officer free to act without constraint. At the same time, however, it would permit governmental units to invade constitutional rights at any time they are prepared to pay for the privilege. And, as in the case of insurance or indemnity for the officer, the overdeterrence may be eliminated by also eliminating beneficial deterrence.[20] In addition, even a small chance of recovery of a large sum against a strictly liable public entity which can pay the judgment, may tempt large numbers of persons to file doubtful and unmeritorious claims,[21] adding further to an already costly process. Given these difficulties in devising a system of official accountability it will not be surprising if there continues to be a certain amount of shifting, groping and muddling through in this area.

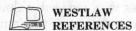

WESTLAW REFERENCES

government state county municipal! city town! village /3 officer* official* employee* worker* /s personal personally /4 liab!

Absolute Immunity of Legislative and Judicial Officers

judicial absolute /5 immun! /p judge* witness** "justice of the peace" "hearing officer*" "grand jur***" "administrative law judge" prosecut! % prosecution

legislative absolute /5 immun! /p legislator* senator* congress! assembly! representat! % representation

Immunities of Executive Officers

administrative executive official /s immun! /s misfeasance "bad faith" malic! dishonesty

government** federal +s officer* official* executive* employee* /s immun! /p statutory constitutional +s right*

283k114

immun! /s civil +1 right* /s state* county* city cities municipal! town! village*

Application of the Discretionary-Ministerial Dichotomy

liab! immun! /s discretion*** /s ministerial

constitution** +s "separation of power*" /p discretion*** ministerial

Discretionary Immunity and Negligence

negligen** /p qualified absolute administrative official executive /s immun!

Immunity and Privilege

officer* official* executive* employee* /s immun! /p legal judicial statut! /s privilege

Indemnity and Other Protections for the Officer

"respondeat superior" /s county municipal! city town! village /s officer* official* employee* executive*

28 +s 2676

28 +s 2679 /p car cars auto* automobile* van* vehicle* truck*

indemni! /p state county municipal! city town! village /s officer* official* executive* employee* /p liab! /s act* actions activit! conduct

§ 133. Charities

On the basis of an English decision of 1846,[1] American courts established a general doctrine that charities were immune from tort liability. The English case was soon repudiated,[2] but American courts continued to

---

8, 23. Professor Whitman's preference for equitable over damages relief in cases of constitutional torts, Whitman, Constitutional Torts, 1980, 79 Mich.L.Rev. 5, 42–71, would probably minimize the problem of overdeterrence and might have the effect of restoring some beneficial deterrence, but this seems effective only as to intended actions at best and is unlikely to be accepted as to completed physical injuries. In addition, pressures generated by litigation costs tend to force heavy reliance on the damages remedy.

21. See Cass, Damage Suits against Public Officers, 1981, 129 U.Pa.L.Rev. 1110, 1179.

§ 133

1. Feoffees of Heriot's Hospital v. Ross, 1846, 12 C. & F. 507, 8 Eng.Rep. 1508.

2. Mersey Docks Trustees v. Gibbs, 1866, 11 H.L. Cas. 686, 11 Eng.Rep. 1500.

---

sive liability in particular situations. Note, Holding Governments Strictly Liable for the Release of Dangerous Parolees, 1980, 55 N.Y.U.L.Rev. 907.

19. See Casto, Government Liability for Constitutional Torts: Proposals to Amend the Federal Tort Claims Act, 1982, 49 Tenn.L.Rev. 201 listing and summarizing.

20. See Cass, Damage Suits against Public Officers, 1981, 129 U.Pa.L.Rev. 1110, 1162. One way to put beneficial deterrence back into effect would be to leave it to the executive branch to discipline officials who commit torts, or to permit the government to seek indemnity from them. See Bermann, Integrating Governmental and Officer Tort Liability, 1977, 77 Colum.L. Rev. 1174. But there are many reasons to doubt that the bureaucracies would in fact successfully supervise or discipline tortious officials. See Mashaw, Civil Liability of Government Officers: Property Rights and Official Accountability, 1978, 42 L. & Contemp. Probs.

apply the immunity for many years on the ground that to impose liability would be to divert trust funds for purposes outside the donor's intent,[3] that respondeat superior should not apply to impose liability upon non-profit charities,[4] that a beneficiary of a charity assumes the risk of the charitable negligence,[5] or that donations to charities would be discouraged if the charities were held liable.[6]

None of these reasons has proved convincing to most contemporary courts, and virtually all states with decisions on the subject at all have rejected the complete immunity of charities, often by judicial decision[7] but at times by statute.[8] This sweeping change is now reflected in the Second Restatement, which provides flatly that charitable and other benevolent enterprises obtain no immunity merely because of their charitable nature.[9]

Only two or three states in recent years have insisted on retaining the full immunity in the absence of legislation to the contrary.[10] Even in some of these states, however, the immunity is only formally complete, since statutes provide a method for reaching any liability insurance funds covering the charity.[11]

A handful of states have attempted to modify the immunity so that it is retained in some cases but not in others. For example, some states permit a recovery against a charity's non-trust fund assets—usually insurance—but not otherwise.[12] This and other exceptions sometimes applied to allow recovery[13] tend to promote litigation over the immunity itself as distinct from the issue of fault. In addition to that disadvantage, the injured person in these states gets the protection of ordinary negligence rules only fortuitously, while the charity gets the protection of the immunity only haphazardly. For these reasons, it seems likely that the trend toward abrogation of the immunity will continue until it has swept along this last group of states. On the other hand, some charities, such as hospitals, may be given other forms of special assistance, as has been done in many states with medical malpractice legislation.[14] In some states the immunity has been retained or reinstituted by statute, but only for certain particular cases.[15] Since states have sometimes held unconstitutional those statutes, like the auto guest statute,

---

3. McDonald v. Massachusetts General Hospital, 1876, 120 Mass. 432; Perry v. House of Refuge, 1885, 63 Md. 20.

4. Evans v. Lawrence & Memorial Associated Hospitals, 1946, 133 Conn. 311, 50 A.2d 433; Bachman v. Young Women's Christian Association, 1922, 179 Wis. 178, 191 N.W. 751; Emery v. Jewish Hospital Association, 1921, 193 Ky. 400, 236 S.W. 577; Thornton v. Franklin Square House, 1909, 200 Mass. 465, 86 N.E. 909; Fire Insurance Patrol v. Boyd, 1888, 120 Pa. 624, 15 A. 553.

5. Powers v. Massachusetts Homeopathic Hospital, 1st Cir. 1901, 109 F. 294, certiorari denied 183 U.S. 695, 22 S.Ct. 932, 46 L.Ed. 394; Wilcox v. Idaho Falls Latter Day Saints Hospital, 1938, 59 Idaho 350, 82 P.2d 849; Forrest v.Red Cross Hospital, Ky.1954, 265 S.W.2d 80; St. Vincent's Hospital v. Stine, 1924, 195 Ind. 350, 144 N.E. 537; Duncan v. Nebraska Sanitarium & Benevolent Association, 1912, 92 Neb. 162, 137 N.W. 1120.

6. Vermillion v. Woman's College of Due West, 1916, 104 S.C. 197, 88 S.E. 649; Jensen v. Maine Eye & Ear Infirmary, 1910, 107 Me. 408, 78 A. 898.

7. E.g., Colby v. Carney Hospital, 1969, 356 Mass. 527, 254 N.E.2d 407; Howle v. Camp Amon Carter, Tex.1971, 470 S.W.2d 629; see Annot., 25 A.L.R.2d 29 (1952).

8. E.g., N.C.Gen.Stat. § 1–539.9; R.I.G.L. 1956, § 9–1–26 (hospitals).

9. Second Restatement of Torts, § 895E.

10. Williams v. Jefferson Hospital Association, 1969, 246 Ark. 1231, 442 S.W.2d 243; Rhoda v. Aroostook General Hospital, Me.1967, 226 A.2d 530.

11. Ark.Stat. § 66–3240 (direct action against insurer authorized where charity would be immune); Me.Rev.Stat.Ann. tit. 14, § 158 (immunity waived to extent of insurance coverage).

12. Morehouse College v. Russell, 1964, 219 Ga. 717, 135 S.E.2d 432, conformed to 109 Ga.App. 301, 136 S.E.2d 179; O'Quin v. Baptist Memorial Hospital, 1947, 184 Tenn. 570, 201 S.W.2d 694.

13. E.g., Jeffcoat v. Caine, 1973, 261 S.C. 75, 198 S.E.2d 258 (intentional tort). Charities have also been held liable for torts arising out of their commercial activities, torts to strangers to the charity who did not assume the risk, and torts by higher "administrative" employees.

14. See Comment, An Analysis of State Legislative Responses to the Medical Malpractice Crisis, 1975, Duke L.J. 1417.

15. N.J.S.A. 2A:53A–7 provides that "religious, charitable, educational or hospital" organizations re-

which give special privileges to one class of persons,[16] a partial immunity statute may be subject to constitutional attack.

 WESTLAW REFERENCES

di "charitable immunity"
"charitable immun!" /p liab! /p legislative** judicial** statutor!

§ 134. Infants

The general rule is that an infant has no tort immunity based solely on the fact of infancy. On the contrary, infants are usually liable for both their negligent[1] and their intentional torts.[2]

Two qualifications must be mentioned. The first is that infants may escape liability for certain intentional torts, not because of immunity in itself but because they lack the mental capacity to commit a tort in the first place. For example, intent to cause bodily contact is an element of battery, and a child who causes such contact is not liable if, because of his limited experience or intelligence, he never had the requisite intent.[3] Somewhat similarly, a child's age and experience is taken into account in determining whether given conduct was negligent.[4] Here again, there is no immunity as such, but age and experience are relevant in determining whether conduct was tortious.[5] Where the invariable rule of law is that children under seven are incapable of negligence or other tort, however, the practical effect is immunity for such children.[6]

The second qualification involves injuries resulting from performance of a minor's contract, as where one agrees to transport the plaintiff but does so negligently. Since minors are usually not liable in contract under the rule that they may disaffirm most contracts if they do so in a proper way,[7] the injured plaintiff cannot recover in such a case on a contract theory. Nor will courts permit the plaintiff to label the claim as one in tort so as to enforce the contract by indirection.[8] To succeed in such a case the plaintiff must establish that the minor violated an obligation imposed by law independent of obligations imposed by the contract itself.

The independent obligation test is difficult to apply. It is easy to confuse duties imposed by law because of relations created by contract with duties imposed directly by the contract itself. For instance, it is now held that a minor is liable in tort for negligent driving, even though the injured plaintiff

---

tain the immunity as to those who are beneficiaries of the charitable work. See Kasten v. Young Mens Christian Association, 1980, 173 N.J.Super. 1, 412 A.2d 1346.

16. As to guest statutes, see § 34, supra. Similarly, South Carolina has held that abolition of the parent-child immunity for automobile cases only was unconstitutional. Elam v. Elam, 1980, 275 S.C. 132, 268 S.E.2d 109.

§ 134

1. Nicosia v. Guillory, La.1975, 322 So.2d 129; Kuhns v. Brugger, 1957, 390 Pa. 331, 135 A.2d 395.

2. E.g., Ellis v. D'Angelo, 1953, 116 Cal.App.2d 310, 253 P.2d 675 (battery); Cleveland Park Club v. Perry, D.C.Mun.App.1960, 165 A.2d 485 (trespass to land). Contra, Hatch v. O'Neill, 1973; 231 Ga. 446, 202 S.E.2d 44, Note, 1974, 26 Mercer L.Rev. 367.

3. See Ellis v. D'Angelo, supra note 2 (child could form requisite intent to touch, since intent to harm not required); Cleveland Park Club v. Perry, supra note 2 (similar as to land trespass).

4. Supra, § 32.

5. E.g., Camerlinck v. Thomas, 1981, 209 Neb. 843, 312 N.W.2d 260; Restatement Second of Torts § 283A. Older infants pursuing "adult activities" or "inherently dangerous" activities may be held liable on an adult standard and this would seem to discount the limited age and experience of the particular child. E.g., Robinson v. Lindsay, 1979, 92 Wn.2d 410, 598 P.2d 392.

6. DeLuca v. Bowden, 1975, 42 Ohio St.2d 392, 329 N.E.2d 109 (under seven no liability for either negligence or intentional tort).

Although the immunity for children under seven is a minority rule, the majority of states would immunize very young children on the ground that they are incapable of negligence. See Gray, The Standard of Care for Children Revisited, 1980, 45 Mo.L.Rev. 597.

7. See H. Clark, Jr., Law of Domestic Relations, 1968 § 8.2 (time for disaffirmance); D. Dobbs, 1973, Remedies § 13.4 (restoring benefits received).

8. See Prosser, The Borderland of Tort and Contract, in 1953, W. Prosser, Selected Topics in the Law of Torts 380, 447.

had contracted for a safe ride,[9] but courts once held that there was only a contract duty in such cases and that it could be avoided by disaffirmance.[10] Similarly, agency is created by contract and courts have usually held that an infant cannot be vicariously liable because of this contractual element.[11] Or again, a minor may escape liability for trivial or negligent misuse of bailed property on the ground that his duties were created by contract,[12] but where the misuse is a serious one courts regarded it as a violation of duties imposed by law for which he is liable in tort.[13]

Another problem in applying the independent obligation test occurs when the infant fraudulently induces another to enter a contract, usually by representing that he is an adult and can make a binding contract. A few cases hold that the minor is not liable even for such a fraud, because the fraud is inseparably connected with contract.[14] Most, however, impose liability in tort for fraudulent misrepresentations,[15] unless the representation is construed to be a mere warranty that can be disaffirmed.[16] A few courts go further and hold that the infant's fraud works an estoppel so that he is liable on the contract itself and not merely in tort.[17]

Probably the independent obligation test is workable only if it is applied with an understanding that the contract immunity is intended to provide a shield against bad bargains, not a sword for the commission of torts.

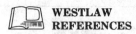

WESTLAW REFERENCES

211k59

§ 135. Insanity

Mentally disabled persons usually have been classed with infants, and held liable for their torts.[1] The rule seems to have originated in a dictum in a case[2] decided in 1616, at a time when the action of trespass still rested upon the older basis of strict liability without regard to the fault of the individual. When the modern law developed to the point of holding the defendant liable only for wrongful intent or negligence, the dictum was still repeated, and there have been numerous decisions in accord with it. Thus an insane person has been held liable in a tort action for assault and battery,[3] false imprisonment,[4] trespass on land,[5] destruction

---

9. See Pokriefka v. Mazur, 1967, 379 Mich. 348, 151 N.W.2d 806; Friedhoff v. Engberg, 1967, 82 S.D. 522, 149 N.W.2d 759.

10. See Brown v. Wood, 1940, 293 Mich. 148, 291 N.W. 255, 127 A.L.R. 1436, overruled in Pokriefka v. Mazur, 1967, 379 Mich. 348, 151 N.W.2d 806.

11. Government Employees Insurance Co. v. Edelman, Tex.Civ.App.1975, 524 S.W.2d 546, refused n.r.e. (joint venture). But see State Farm Mutual Automobile Insurance Co. v. Fields, D.Mo.1970, 325 F.Supp. 1135 (liability insurance procured by father as agent for minor is valid), affirmed 8th Cir. 1971, 441 F.2d 659; 1972, 37 Mo.L.Rev. 150; G.(A.) v. G.(T.), [1970] 2 Q.B. 643, [1970] 3 All.Eng.Rep. 546.

12. Eaton v. Hill, 1870, 50 N.H. 235. Young v. Muhling, 1900, 48 App.Div. 617, 63 N.Y.S. 181.

13. Smith v. Moschetti, 1948, 213 Ark. 968, 214 S.W.2d 73; Vermont Acceptance Corp. v. Wiltshire, 1931, 103 Vt. 219, 153 A. 199.

14. Raymond v. General Motorcycle Co., 1918, 230 Mass. 54, 119 N.E. 359; Greensboro Morris Plan Co. v. Palmer, 1923, 185 N.C. 109, 116 S.E. 261.

15. Doenges-Long Motors, Inc. v. Gillen, 1958, 138 Colo. 31, 328 P.2d 1077; Royal Finance Co. v. Schaefer, Mo.App., 1959, 330 S.W.2d 129.

16. Collins v. Gifford, 1911, 203 N.Y. 465, 96 N.E. 721.

17. Nichols v. English, 1967, 223 Ga. 227, 154 S.E.2d 239, 29 A.L.R.3d 1265 (estopped to repudiate conveyance).

§ 135

1. Second Restatement of Torts, § 283B.

2. Weaver v. Ward, 1616, Hob. 134, 80 Eng.Rep. 284.

3. Mullen v. Bruce, 1959, 168 Cal.App.2d 494, 335 P.2d 945; Kaczer v. Marrero, Fla.App. 1976, 324 So.2d 717; McGuire v. Almy, 1937, 297 Mass. 323, 8 N.E.2d 760; Barylski v. Paul, 1972, 38 Mich.App. 614, 196 N.W.2d 868.

Cf. Vosnos v. Perry, 1976, 43 Ill.App.3d 834, 2 Ill. Dec. 447, 357 N.E.2d 614 (shooting resulting in death).

4. Krom v. Schoonmaker, N.Y.1848, 3 Barb. 647.

5. Cathcart v. Matthews, 1916, 105 S.C. 329, 89 S.E. 1021; Amick v. O'Hara, Ind.1843, 6 Blackf. 258.

of property,[6] conversion,[7] wrongfully suing out an injunction,[8] alienation of affections,[9] infringement of a patent,[10] and injuries caused by the defective condition of his property.[11]

A number of different explanations have been given for the liability of the mentally disabled, none of which has gone unchallenged.[12] It has been said that "where one of two innocent persons must suffer a loss, it should be borne by the one who occasioned it."[13] So far as this is anything more than an historical survival, it represents a conclusion that it is better that the estate of the lunatic should be taken to give compensation for the damage he has done than that it should remain to be administered by guardians for his own incompetent benefit.[14] It has been said also that if he is held liable, his custodians and those interested in his estate will be stimulated to keep him in order;[15] and that since insanity is easily feigned, there would be too much temptation to pretend it.[16] Coupled with this is perhaps an unexpressed fear of introducing into the law of torts the confusion and unsatisfactory tests attending proof of insanity in criminal cases.[17]

Against the liability of mentally disabled it has been said that the rule of liability is a product of an era when confinement of the mentally limited was the accepted social goal, as it no longer is,[18] that it is unjust to impose responsibility without fault upon the disabled when fault is the standard of liability for others,[19] and that at the very least the incompetent should be relieved of any duty of reasonable care toward those who know of his disability and can protect themselves from it.[20]

6. Morse v. Crawford, 1893, 17 Vt. 499 (killing an ox); Cross v. Kent, 1870, 32 Md. 581; Mutual Fire Insurance Co. v. Showalter, 1897, 3 Pa.Super. 452; In re Guardianship of Meyer, 1935, 218 Wis. 381, 261 N.W. 211.

7. Morse v. Crawford, 1893, 17 Vt. 499.

8. Behrens v. McKenzie, 1867, 23 Iowa 333.

9. Shedrick v. Lathrop, 1934, 106 Vt. 311, 172 A. 630; Sweeney v. Carter, 1939, 24 Tenn.App. 6, 137 S.W.2d 892.

10. Avery v. Wilson, W.D.N.C.1884, 20 F. 856.

11. Filip v. Gagne, 1962, 104 N.H. 14, 177 A.2d 509; Morain v. Devlin, 1882, 132 Mass. 87; Campbell v. Bradbury, 1918, 179 Cal. 364, 176 P. 685. Contra, Ward v. Rogers, 1906, 51 Misc. 299, 100 N.Y.S. 1058.

12. See Ellis, Tort Responsibility of Mentally Disabled Persons, 1981 A.B.Found.Res.J. 1081; Seidelson, Reasonable Expectations and Subjective Standards in Negligence Law, 1981, 50 G.W.L.Rev. 17; Curran, Tort Liability of the Mentally Ill and Mentally Deficient, 1960, 21 Ohio St.L.J. 52; Sadoff, 1967, Tortious Liability of the Insane, 39 Pa.Bar.Q. 73; Ague, The Liability of Insane Persons in Tort Actions, 1956, 60 Dick.L.Rev. 211; Bohlen, Liability in Tort of Infants and Insane Persons, 1924, 23 Mich.L.Rev. 9; Hornblower, Insanity and the Law of Negligence, 1905, 5 Colum.L.Rev. 278; Comment, The Tort Liability of Insane Persons for Negligence, 1972, 39 Tenn.L.Rev. 705.

13. See Kaczer v. Marrero, Fla.App.1976, 324 So.2d 717; Seals v. Snow, 1927, 123 Kan. 88, 90, 254 P. 348, 349; Williams v. Hays, 1894, 143 N.Y. 442, 447, 38 N.E. 449, 450; Karow v. Continental Insurance Co., 1883, 57 Wis. 56, 64, 15 N.W. 27, 30.

14. See McGuire v. Almy, 1937, 297 Mass. 323, 8 N.E.2d 760; Bohlen, Liability in Tort of Infants and Insane Persons, 1924, 23 Mich.L.Rev. 9, 17–18.

15. See McGuire v. Almy, 1937, 297 Mass. 323, 8 N.E.2d 760; McIntyre v. Sholty, 1887, 121 Ill. 660, 13 N.E. 239; Seals v. Snow, 1927, 123 Kan. 88, 254 P. 348; Williams v. Hays, 1894, 143 N.Y. 442, 38 N.E. 449.

16. See Young v. Young, 1910, 141 Ky. 76, 132 S.W. 155, and cases cited in the preceding footnote.

17. See Bohlen, Liability in Tort of Infants and Insane Persons, 1924, 23 Mich.L.Rev. 9; Note, 1938, 22 Minn.L.Rev. 853, 862.

18. Ellis, Tort Responsibility of Mentally Disabled Persons, 1981 A.B.Found.Res.J. 1079.

19. Seidelson, Reasonable Expectations and Subjective Standards in Negligence Law: The Minor, the Mentally Impaired, and the Mentally Incompetent, 1981, 50 G.W.L.Rev. 17.

20. Seidelson, Reasonable Expectations and Subjective Standards in Negligence Law: The Minor, the Mentally Impaired, and the Mentally Incompetent, 1981, 50 G.W.L.Rev. 17. Quite apart from insane persons, it would seem that the duty owed toward a person of limited capacity depends on whether the actor knew or should have known of that capacity. See Bexiga v. Havir Manufacturing Corp., 1972, 60 N.J. 402, 290 A.2d 281; Rue v. State Department of Highways, La.1979, 372 So.2d 1197, on remand 376 So.2d 525; Warner v. Kiowa County Hospital Authority, Okl.App. 1976, 551 P.2d 1179. Similarly if an injured person knows he is dealing with a person of limited capacity, the duty of the mentally disabled person may be reduced accordingly. This may be accomplished through the doctrine of contributory negligence, but only fortuitously, because of the difference in burden of proof on "no duty" and contributory negligence and because of

The traditional view, however, has emphasized the fact that a mentally limited person may be capable of having an intent to bring about a specific result, even though the intent is induced by a delusion; and in that respect his acts are to be distinguished from those of an epileptic or a person seized with temporary unconsciousness, which are regarded as involuntary and accidental.[21] If tort liability without fault is to be imposed upon sane persons who make reasonable mistakes,[22] an incompetent who acts under a perpetual mistake, unreasonable in the eyes of the community, may very well be held liable for his intentional torts. It has been recognized, however, that his insanity may be such that he is incapable of entertaining the specific intent necessary for a particular tort, such as deceit,[23] malicious prosecution,[24] defamation,[25] or even battery,[26] and so he should not be liable simply because he has not committed the tort. This, however, has not always been carried through very effectively. As to defamation, there has been almost a complete failure to distinguish between the "legal malice" implied as a fiction from the intent to publish the defamatory words, and the "malice in fact" which will defeat a qualified privilege.[27] It would appear that the insane person may properly be charged with the former, but not the latter.[28] It seems well settled that insanity may be shown to disprove evil intent and mitigate actual damages,[29] and that where the insanity is notorious, it may disprove special damage because no one believes what is said.[30] Since the lunatic is regarded as incapable of the necessary guilty mind, and admonition to him is obviously futile, punitive damages are not recoverable against him,[31] at least unless it can be shown that in spite of his mental incapacity he entertained a mental outlook that makes punitive damages appropriate.[32]

So far as negligence is concerned, the common law cases have usually said that an insane person is liable for failure to conform to the standard of conduct of the reasonable person,[33] with the civil law in Louisiana going the other way.[34] But there has been judicial[35] as well as scholarly criticism of the common law rule, and Wisconsin has taken the view,[36] supported by a Canadian deci-

the widespread adoption of comparative negligence, which would have no effect on a limited duty rationale.

21. See supra, § 29.

22. See supra, § 17.

23. Becker v. Becker, 1954, 207 Misc. 17, 138 N.Y.S.2d 397.

24. Beaubeauf v. Reid, 1926, 4 La.App. 344. But cf. Behrens v. McKenzie, 1867, 23 Iowa 333.

25. Irvine v. Gibson, 1904, 117 Ky. 306, 77 S.W. 1106; Bryant v. Jackson, 1845, 25 Tenn. (6 Humph.) 199; Horner v. Marshall's Administratrix, 1817, 19 Va. (5 Munf.) 466.

26. See Mullen v. Bruce, 1959, 168 Cal.App.2d 494, 335 P.2d 945; also Morriss v. Marsden, [1952] 1 All Eng.Rep. 925, followed in Beal v. Hayward, [1960] N.Z.L.Rep. 131, and Phillips v. Soloway, [1956] 6 Dom. L.Rep.2d 570.

27. See Notes, 1938, 22 Minn.L.Rev. 853, 859–860; 1934, 34 Col.L.Rev. 185.

28. See Gatley, Libel and Slander, 2d ed. 1929, 430, 437; Ullrich v. New York Press Co., 1898, 23 Misc. 168, 50 N.Y.S. 788.

29. See Yeates v. Reed, Ind.1838, 4 Blackf. 463; Gates v. Meredith, 1856, 7 Ind. 440; Dickinson v. Barber, 1812, 9 Mass. 225. Cf. Warner v. Lockerby, 1884, 31 Minn. 421, 18 N.W. 145, rehearing denied 31 Minn. 421, 18 N.W.2d 821 (heat of passion); Alderson v. Kahle, 1914, 73 W.Va. 690, 80 S.E. 1109.

30. Wilson v. Walt, 1933, 138 Kan. 205, 25 P.2d 343; see Dickinson v. Barber, 1812, 9 Mass. 225.

31. Jewell v. Colby, 1890, 66 N.H. 399, 24 A. 902; see Moore v. Horne, 1910, 153 N.C. 413, 69 S.E. 409.

32. Schumann v. Crofoot, 1979, 43 Or.App. 53, 602 P.2d 298.

33. Williams v. Hays, 1894, 143 N.Y. 442, 38 N.E. 449, qualified in 1899, 157 N.Y. 541, 52 N.E. 589; Sforza v. Green Bus Lines, 1934, 150 Misc. 180, 268 N.Y.S. 446; Shapiro v. Tchernowitz, 1956, 3 Misc.2d 617, 155 N.Y.S.2d 1011; Johnson v. Lambotte, 1961, 147 Colo. 203, 363 P.2d 165; Ellis v. Fixico, 1935, 174 Okl. 116, 50 P.2d 162 (statute); Kuhn v. Zabotsky, 1967, 9 Ohio St. 2d 129, 224 N.E.2d 137, 38 O.O.2d 302; Turner v. Caldwell, 1980, 36 Conn.Sup. 350, 421 A.2d 876; Annot., 49 A.L.R.3d 189.

34. See Turner v. Bucher, La.1975, 308 So.2d 270, 273–74 (nondiscerning persons not morally guilty and not liable but their curators are liable).

35. Fitzgerald v. Lawhorn, 1972, 29 Conn.Sup. 511, 294 A.2d 338.

36. Breunig v. American Family Insurance Co., 1970, 45 Wis.2d 536, 173 N.W.2d 619, 49 A.L.R.3d 179.

sion,[37] that where insanity occurs suddenly and without warning, it is to be treated like a heart attack, so that the insane defendant is not held to the reasonable man standard under those circumstances. Judicial doubts about the rule are also expressed in the contributory negligence cases, where the mentally disturbed or defective person is usually held only to the standards he can personally meet.[38]

In the light of these cases, the permanent direction of the law may be in doubt even now. Proposals have been made to compensate the injured through payments by the state and at the same time to relieve the insane defendant.[39] This would avoid the harshness of liability for the insane and at the same time protect the injured. Since similar proposals have received some support elsewhere in tort law, this may represent the course of future development.[40]

WESTLAW REFERENCES

liab! /s insan! sane sanity "mental** ill!" /s negligen** intent!
257Ak411
257Ak412

---

37. Buckley & Toronto Transp. Comm'n v. Smith Transport, Ltd., [1946] Ont.L.Rep. 798, [1946] 4 Dom.L. Rep. 721.

See Picher, The Tortious Liability of the Insane in Canada, 1975, 13 Osgoode Hall L.J. 193.

38. E.g., Mochen v. State, 1974, 43 A.D.2d 484, 352 N.Y.S.2d 290; Comment, 1972, 39 Tenn.L.Rev. 705. The Second Restatement of Torts, § 464 expressly refused to take a position on this.

39. Sadoff, 1967, Tortious Liability of the Insane, 39 Pa.Bar.Q. 73.

40. Crime Victims' Compensation Acts operate on a similar principle. See, e.g., Rothstein, How the Uniform Crime Victims Reparations Act Works, 1974, 60 A.B.A.J. 1531. A number of states reach a similar result where state officials are sued by indemnifying them. See supra, § 132.

Appendix A

WESTLAW REFERENCES

Analysis

The WESTLAW System	1077
Improving Legal Research with WESTLAW	1078
Query Formulation: (a) What a WESTLAW Query Is	1078
Query Formulation: (b) Proximity Connectors	1079
Query Formulation: (c) The TRAC Method	1081
Query Formulation: (d) General Principles of Query Formulation	1082
Search Techniques: (a) Field Searching	1083
Search Techniques: (b) Date Restriction	1084
Search Techniques: (c) Digest Topic and Key Number Searching	1084
Using WESTLAW as a Citator	1084
Shepard's ® Citations on WESTLAW	1086
West's INSTA-CITE ™	1086
Black's Law Dictionary	1086
WESTLAW Case Law Databases	1086
WESTLAW Hornbook Queries: (a) Query Format	1087
WESTLAW Hornbook Queries: (b) Textual Illustrations	1088
Ranking Documents Retrieved on WESTLAW: Age and Terms Options	1089
Conclusion	1090

The WESTLAW System

WESTLAW is a computer-assisted legal research service of West Publishing Company. WESTLAW is accessible through several alternative public communications networks. The materials available from WESTLAW are contained in databases stored at a central computer in St. Paul, Minnesota.

The WESTLAW user sends a query, or message, to the computer where it is processed and documents are identified that satisfy the search request. The text of the retrieved documents is then stored on magnetic disks and transmitted to the user. The data moves through a telecommunication network. The user sees the documents on a video display terminal. When the documents appear on the terminal the user can decide whether or not further research is desired. If another search is necessary, the query may be recalled for editing, or an entirely new query may be sent to the computer. Documents displayed on the terminal may be printed out or, on some terminals, the text may be stored in its own magnetic disks.

In addition to the extensive state and federal case law library to which the preformulated queries in this hornbook are addressed, WESTLAW provides access to many specialized libraries. For example, WESTLAW contains separate topical databases for areas of the law such as federal tax, patents and copyrights, bankruptcy, communications, labor, securities, antitrust and business regulation, military justice, admiralty, and government contracts. WESTLAW also contains the text of the U.S. Code and the Code of Federal Regulations, West's INSTA–CITE™, Shepard's® Citations, *Black's Law Dictionary*, and many other legal sources.

Improving Legal Research with WESTLAW

Traditional legal research begins with the examination of texts, treatises, case digests, encyclopedias, citators, annotated law reports, looseleaf services, and periodicals. These secondary sources of the law provide compilations and summaries of authoritative material contained in primary legal sources. The goal of legal research is to analyze and interpret these primary sources.

In their familiar printed form, such primary sources appear in the state and regional reporters, federal reporters, and in statutory codes and administrative materials. In WESTLAW, these documents are extensively represented in electronic databases, or libraries.

WESTLAW permits access to the many cases that do not get indexed or digested into manual systems of secondary legal sources. With WESTLAW it is possible to index any significant term or combination of terms in an almost unlimited variety of grammatical relationships with other terms by formulating a query composed of those terms.

WESTLAW queries may be made as broad or as specific as desired, depending upon the context of the legal issue to be researched.

WESTLAW queries add a dynamic aspect to the text of this hornbook. Since new cases are continuously being added to the WESTLAW databases as they are decided by the courts, the addition of queries provides a type of self-contained updating service to the publication. Since a query may be addressed to the entire range of cases contained in the database designated for a search—from the earliest decisions to the most recent—the search results obtained from WESTLAW reflect the most current law available on any given issue.

In addition, WESTLAW queries augment the customary role of footnotes to the hornbook text by directing the user to a wider range of supporting authorities. Readers may use the preformulated queries supplied in this edition, as is, or formulate their own queries in order to retrieve cases relevant to the points of law discussed in the text.

Query Formulation: (a) What a WESTLAW Query Is

The query is a message to WESTLAW. It instructs the computer to retrieve documents containing terms in the grammatical relationships specified by the query. The terms in a query are made up of words and/or numbers that pinpoint the legal issue to be researched.

An example of the kind of preformulated queries that appear in this publication is reproduced below. The queries corresponding to each section of the text are listed at the end of the section.

contributory /s negligence /p bailee bailor

The query is taken from chapter 12, section 74, subsection *Bailments*. The query, or question, that is directed to WESTLAW appears at the end of the section of the text. This query is asking WESTLAW to find documents containing the term CONTRIBUTORY within the same sentence as the term NEGLIGENCE and both within the same paragraph as either the term BAILEE or the term BAILOR.

This query illustrates what a standard request to WESTLAW looks like—words or numbers describing an issue, tied together by connectors. These connectors tell WESTLAW in what relationships the terms must appear. WESTLAW will retrieve all documents from the database that contain the terms appearing in those relationships.

The material that follows explains the methods by which WESTLAW queries are formulated, and shows how users of Prosser and Keeton's *Law of Torts* can employ the preformulated queries in this publication in their research of tort law. In addition, there are instructions that will enable readers to modify their queries to fit the particular needs of their research.

Query Formulation: (b) Proximity Connectors

Proximity connectors allow search terms to be ordered so that relevant documents will be retrieved from WESTLAW. The connectors and their meanings appear below.

Space (or). A space between search terms means "or." Leaving a space between the query terms CHILD and MINOR

child minor

instructs the computer to retrieve documents that contain either the word CHILD or the word MINOR (or both).

& (and) or (ampersand). The & symbol means "and." Placing the & between two terms instructs the computer to retrieve documents that contain both of the terms. The terms on either side may be in reverse order. For example, if the & is inserted between the terms PHYSICIAN and MALPRACTICE

physician & malpractice

the computer will retrieve documents containing both the word PHYSICIAN and the word MALPRACTICE in the same document. In any such retrieved document, the word PHYSICIAN may either precede or follow the word MALPRACTICE. The & may be placed between groups of alternative terms. For example, placing the & between PHYSICIAN or DOCTOR and MALPRACTICE or NEGLIGENCE

physician doctor & malpractice negligence

instructs the computer to retrieve documents in which the terms PHYSICIAN or DOCTOR (or both) and MALPRACTICE or NEGLIGENCE (or both) appear in the same document.

/p (same paragraph). The /p symbol means "within the same paragraph." It requires that terms to the left of the /p appear within the same paragraph as terms to the right of the connector. For example, placing a /p between the terms PHYSICIAN and MALPRACTICE

physician /p malpractice

will instruct the computer to retrieve documents in which PHYSICIAN and MALPRACTICE occur in the same paragraph. The terms on each side of the /p may appear in the document in any order within the paragraph. As with &, the /p connector may be placed between groups of alternative terms. Thus, the query

physician doctor /p malpractice negligence

will command the retrieval of all documents in which the words PHYSICIAN or DOCTOR (or both) occur in the same paragraph as the words MALPRACTICE or NEGLIGENCE (or both).

/s (same sentence). The /s symbol requires that one or more search terms on each side of the /s appear in the same sentence. If a /s is placed between the words PHYSICIAN and MALPRACTICE

physician /s malpractice

the computer is instructed to retrieve documents that have the word PHYSICIAN and the word MALPRACTICE in the same sentence, without regard to which of these words occur first in the sentence.

The /s may be placed between groups of alternative terms. Inserting a /s between the terms PHYSICIAN or DOCTOR and MALPRACTICE or NEGLIGENCE

physician doctor /s malpractice negligence

instructs the computer to retrieve documents with either the words PHYSICIAN or DOCTOR (or both) within the same sentence as the words MALPRACTICE or NEGLIGENCE (or both), regardless of which terms appear first.

+s (precedes within sentence). The +s symbol requires that one or more terms to the left of the +s precede one or more terms to the right of the +s within the same sentence. The query

physician +s malpractice

instructs the computer to retrieve all documents in which the word PHYSICIAN precedes the word MALPRACTICE in the same sentence. The +s connector, like the other connectors, may be used between groups of alternative terms. Thus, the query

physician doctor +s malpractice negligence

instructs the computer to retrieve all documents in which the words PHYSICIAN or DOCTOR (or both) precede the words MALPRACTICE or NEGLIGENCE (or both) in the same sentence.

/n (numerical proximity—within n words). The /n symbol means "within n words," where n represents any whole number between 1 and 255, inclusive. It requires that terms to the left of the /n appear within the designated number of words as terms to the right of the connector. For example, placing a /5 between the terms PHYSICIAN and MALPRACTICE

physician /5 malpractice

instructs the computer to retrieve all documents in which the term PHYSICIAN occurs within five words of the term MALPRACTICE. Numerical proximities may also be used between groups of alternative search terms. In addition, the + symbol may be used to require that terms to the left of the numerical proximity symbol precede the terms to the right of the symbol. Thus, placing the +5 symbol between the words PHYSICIAN or DOCTOR and MALPRACTICE or NEGLIGENCE

physician doctor +5 malpractice negligence

instructs the computer to retrieve cases in which either the word PHYSICIAN or the word DOCTOR (or both) occur within five words preceding the word MALPRACTICE or the word NEGLIGENCE (or both).

"_____" (quotation marks/phrase). The "_____" (quotation marks/phrase) symbol can be thought of as the most restrictive grammatical connector. Placing terms within quotation marks instructs the computer to retrieve all documents in which the terms appear in the precise proximity (i.e., contiguousness) and order that they have within the quotation marks. For example, placing the following terms within quotation marks

"caveat emptor"

instructs the computer to retrieve all documents in which the term CAVEAT appears adjacent to, and precedes, the term EMPTOR. Phrases that are constructed with quotation marks may be used as alternatives by leaving a space between them. Thus, the query

"caveat emptor" "buyer beware"

instructs the computer to retrieve all documents in which the phrase CAVEAT EMPTOR or BUYER BEWARE (or both) occur.

This technique of query formulation is effective when used to search legal terms of art, legal concepts, or legal entities that occur together as multiple terms. Some examples are: "res ipsa loquitur", "last clear chance" and "respondeat superior."

Phrase searching should be limited to those instances in which it is certain that the terms will always appear adjacent to each other and in the same order. For example, it would not be advisable to use the following query:

"shifting the burden of proof" /p negligence

Despite the entrenchment into legal jargon of the phrase "shifting the burden of proof", these terms may occur in a different order and not be adjacent to each other. For example, they might appear in the language of relevant case law as ". . . the burden of proof shifts . . .."

Therefore, a better query to use in searching for these terms would be:

burden /3 proof /3 shift*** /p negligence

% (exclusion). The % symbol means "but not." It instructs the computer to exclude documents that contain terms appearing after the % symbol. For example, to retrieve documents containing the terms WITNESS** and TESTIMONY within the same sentence, but not the term EXPERT within the same sentence as TESTIMONY, the following query would be used:

witness** /s testimony % expert /s testimony

Query Formulation: (c) The TRAC Method

The acronym "TRAC" is a convenient mnemonic device for a systematic approach to query formulation on WESTLAW. "TRAC" stands for Terms, Roots, Alternatives, and Connectors. This step-by-step method is explained below.

T *Terms.* After determining the legal issue that is to be researched, the first step in query formulation is to select the key terms from the issue that will be used as search terms in the query. Words, numbers, and various other symbols may be used as search terms.

The goal in choosing search terms is to select the most unique terms for the issue. In selecting such terms it is frequently helpful to imagine how the terms might appear in the language of the documents that will be searched by the query. Moreover, it is necessary to consider the grammatical and editorial structure of the document. This involves a consideration of how the writer of the document (i.e., judge or headnote and synopsis writer) has worded both the factual and legal components of the issues involved in the case.

Although traditional book research generally starts with a consideration of the general legal concepts under which particular problems are subsumed, WESTLAW research starts with a consideration of specific terms that are likely to appear in documents that have addressed those problems. This is so because documents are retrieved from WESTLAW on the basis of the terms they contain. Accordingly, the more precisely terms that will single out the desired documents can be identified, the more relevant the search results will be.

R *Root Expansion (!) and Universal Character (*).* When constructing queries it is necessary to consider various forms of the search terms that are selected. Plurals, possessives, and derivative forms of words should be anticipated due to the variety of ways in which the language in a document may be worded. Various tenses of verbs should also be considered. There are two devices available on WESTLAW for automatically generating alternative forms of search terms in a query. One device is an unlimited root expansion. Placement of the ! symbol at the end of the root term generates other forms containing the root. For example, attaching the ! symbol to the root term INDEMN in the following query:

indemn! /p tortfeasor

instructs the computer to generate the words INDEMNITY, INDEMNIFY, INDEMNIFIED, INDEMNIFYING, and INDEMNIFICATION as search terms for the query. This saves time and space that would otherwise be consumed in typing each of the alternative words in the query.

The other device permits the generation of all possible characters from a designated part of a term. This is done by placing one or more * symbols at the location in the term where universal character generation is desired. For example, placing two * symbols on the term NEGLIGEN in the following query

```
negligen** /p mechanic
```

instructs the computer to generate all forms of the root term NEGLIGEN with up to two additional characters. Thus, the words NEGLIGENT and NEGLIGENCE would be generated by this query. The * symbol may also be embedded inside of a term as in the following query:

```
wom*n /p harrassment /p sexual
```

This will generate the alternative terms WOMAN and WOMEN.

A *Alternative Terms.* Once the initial search terms have been selected for a query, it is important to consider alternative terms, synonyms, and antonyms for those terms. The nature of the legal issue will determine which terms are desirable.

As an illustration, in formulating a query to research the issue of whether a defamation may be enjoined the researcher might first choose as search terms (with their appropriate root expansions) the following:

```
enjoin!    defam!
```

Clearly, the term INJUNCTION* would be a good alternative for ENJOIN!. Similarly, the terms LIBEL! and SLANDER! could be added as synonyms for DEFAM!. Adding these alternatives to the initial search terms produces the following terms:

```
enjoin! injunction*    defam! libel! slander!
```

Note that a space, which means "or" in WESTLAW, should be left between search terms and their alternatives.

C *Connectors.* The next step in query formulation is to consider the appropriate grammatical context in which the search terms will appear. Using the example provided in the preceding section, a grammatical connector will now be placed between the two groups of alternative search terms to obtain the following query:

```
enjoin injunction*  /p  defam! libel! slander!
```

This query would instruct the computer to retrieve documents in which ENJOIN! or INJUNCTION* appear in the same paragraph as DEFAM! or LIBEL! or SLANDER!.

Query Formulation: (d) General Principles of Query Formulation

The art of query formulation is the heart of WESTLAW research. Although the researcher can gain technical skills by using the terminal, there is no strictly mechanical procedure for formulating queries. One must first comprehend the meaning of the legal issue to be researched before beginning a search on WESTLAW. Then the user will need to supply imagination, insight, and legal comprehension with knowledge of the capabilities of WESTLAW to formulate a useful query. Effective query formulation requires an alternative way of thinking about the legal research process.

Using WESTLAW is a constant balancing between generating too many documents and missing important documents. In general, it is better to look through a reasonable number of irrelevant documents than it is to be too restrictive and miss important material. The researcher should take into consideration at the initial query formulation stage what he or she will do if too many, or not enough documents are retrieved. Thought should be given as to how the query might be narrowed or the search broadened, and what can be done if the initial search retrieves zero documents.

Some issues by their very nature will require more lengthy queries than others; however, it is best to strive for efficiency in structuring the query. Look for unique search terms that will eliminate the need for a lengthy query. Keep in mind that WESTLAW is literal. Consider all possible alternative terms. Remember that searching is done by syntactic structure and not by legal concepts.

Always keep in mind the parameters of the system as to date and database content. Especially consider inherent limitations of the computer. It doesn't think, create, or make analogies. The researcher must do that for the computer. All that the computer does is look for the terms in the documents in relationships specified in the query.

The researcher should know what he or she is looking for, at least to the extent of knowing how the terms are likely to show up in relevant documents.

The *WESTLAW Reference Manual* should be consulted for more information on query formulation and WESTLAW commands. The *Reference Manual* is updated periodically to reflect new enhancements of WESTLAW. It provides detailed and comprehensive instructions on all aspects of the WESTLAW system and offers numerous illustrative examples on the proper format for various types of queries. Material contained in the *Reference Manual* enables the user to benefit from all of the system's capabilities in an effective and efficient manner.

Search Techniques: (a) Field Searching

Documents in WESTLAW are divided into separate sections called fields. The computer can be instructed to search for terms within designated fields. This technique is known as field searching. Moreover, in reviewing the documents that have been retrieved in a search, the user may instruct the computer to display specified fields. The fields available for WESTLAW case law databases are described below.

Title Field. The title field contains the title of the case (e.g., *Henningsen v. Bloomfield Motors, Inc.*).

Citation Field. The citation field contains the citation of the case (e.g., 161 A.2d 69).

Court Field. The court field contains abbreviations that allow searches for case law to be restricted to particular states, districts, or courts.

Judge Field. The judge field contains the names of judges or justices who wrote either an individual or a majority opinion.

Synopsis Field. The synopsis field contains the synopsis of the case, prepared by West editors.

Topic Field. The topic field contains the West Digest Topic name and number, the Key Number, and the text of the Key line for each digest paragraph.

Digest Field. The digest field contains digest paragraphs prepared by West editors. It includes headnotes, corresponding Digest Topics and Key Numbers, the title and citation of the case, court, and year of decision.

Headnote Field. The headnote field contains the language of the headnotes, exclusive of the Digest Topic and Key Number lines and case identification information.

Opinion Field. The opinion field contains the text of the case, court and docket numbers, names of attorneys appearing in the case, and judges participating in the decision.

The format for a query that will instruct the computer to search for terms only within specified fields consists of the field name followed by a set of parentheses containing the search terms and grammatical connectors, if any. For example, to retrieve the case appearing at 161 A.2d 69, the citation field, followed by a set of parentheses containing the volume and page numbers of the citation separated by the +3 connector may be used:
citation(161 +3 69)

or

cite(161 +3 69)

Correspondingly, to retrieve the case entitled *Henningsen v. Bloomfield Motors, Inc.*, the title field, followed by a set of parentheses containing the names of the title separated by the & connector may be used:
title(henningsen & bloomfield)

Combination Field Searching

Fields may be combined in a query. For example, terms may be searched for in the digest field and, at the same time the query may limit the search to the courts of a particular state. The following query illustrates this technique:
digest(dramshop /3 act*) & court(mn)

This query instructs the computer to retrieve documents containing the words DRAMSHOP and ACT within the designated proximities in the digest field, and that were issued from Minnesota courts, as designated with the court field restriction. Any number of different fields may be combined with this method.

Moreover, terms may be searched in clusters of fields by joining any number of field names by commas. One application of this technique is to search for terms in the combined synopsis and digest fields. This technique is illustrated below:

synopsis,digest(bailee /p care precaution*)

In this example the terms BAILEE, CARE, and PRECAUTION* are searched in the synopsis and digest fields simultaneously.

The *WESTLAW Reference Manual* should be consulted for further instruction on how to perform searches using the field restrictions.

Search Techniques: (b) Date Restriction

Queries may be restricted to retrieve documents appearing before, after, or on a specified date, or within a range of dates. The date restriction format consists of the word DATE followed by the appropriate restriction(s) within parentheses. The words BEFORE and AFTER may be used to designate the desired date relationships. Alternatively, the symbols < and > may be used. Moreover, the month and day and year may be spelled out (e.g., January 1, 1984) or they may be abbreviated as follows: 1-1-84 or 1/1/84. The date restriction is joined to the rest of the query by the & symbol. For example, to retrieve documents decided or issued after December 31, 1982 that discuss the spousal privilege for marital communications, any of the following formats could be used:

spous** marital husband* wi*e* /3 privilege & date(after 12/31/82)

spous** marital husband* wi*e* /3 privilege & date(>december 31, 1982)

spous** marital husband* wi*e* /3 privilege & date(>12-31-82)

To retrieve documents decided after December 31, 1980 and before March 15, 1983, the following format could be used:

spous** marital husband wi*e* /3 privilege & date(after 12/31/80 and before 3/15/83)

Search Techniques: (c) Digest Topic and Key Number Searching

Searches may be performed using West Digest Topic and Key Numbers as search terms. When this strategy is used, the search term consists of a West Digest Topic Number followed by the letter k, followed by a Key Number classified as a subheading under the Digest Topic. The computer will retrieve all cases that contain a headnote classified with the designated Digest Topic and Key Number. For example, to retrieve cases that contain the Digest Topic classification for Torts (Digest Topic Number 379) and the Key Number for Joint and Several Liability (Key Number 22), the following query would be used:

379k22

A related search technique employs Digest Topic classification numbers in conjunction with other search terms. Since the Digest Topic Numbers appear in the topic and digest fields of the cases, the numbers should be searched for only in these fields by using the field restriction method. For example, to retrieve cases classified under the Digest Topic for Negligence (Digest Topic Number 272) that deal with the accidents sustained on floor, steps or stairs, the following queries would be appropriate:

topic(272) /p floor* step* stair!
digest(272 /p floor* step* stair!)

A complete list of Digest Topics and their numerical equivalents appears in the *WESTLAW Reference Manual*.

Using WESTLAW as a Citator

Research in tort law frequently entails finding decisions that apply to specific sections of state statutes, to federal tort statutes (such as the Federal Tort Claims Act), or to other court decisions. WESTLAW can be used to retrieve documents that contain citations or reference to such authority. Because citation styles are not always uniform, special care must be taken to identify variant forms of citations.

Retrieving Cases that Cite State Codes and Statute Sections

Court decisions that cite to sections of state codes or to sections of state statutes are retrievable by including the section number in the query. For example, to retrieve cases that cite section 4399.01 of the Ohio Statutes, the following query could be used:

4399.01 & court(oh)

Since the section number is a unique term, it is unnecessary to use additional search terms in the query. The appearance of 4399.01 in Ohio case law is not likely to be anything other than a citation to that particular section. Using the number 4399.01 as in the above query will retrieve all subsections of section 4399.01 automatically.

Specific subsections of statutes and codes are retrievable by including the subsection number in the query as follows:

768.31(5)

Retrieving Cases that Cite Federal Torts Statutes

Cases in WESTLAW are derived from West Reporters which routinely include headnotes containing citations to statutes in a standard style. An illustration of a headnote containing a citation to Title 28 U.S.C.A. 1346(b), appears below.

R 1 OF 3 P 3 OF 11 CTA11 P
704 F.2d 587
(2)
393k78(14)
UNITED STATES
k. Place of injury and law governing.
C.A.Ala. 1983.
Clear mandate of Swine Flu Act and Federal Tort Claims Act requires courts to look to law of state where act or omission occurred in determining liability of United States. Public Health Service Act, ss 317, 317(j), 42 U.S.C. (1976 Ed.) ss 247b. 247(j); **28 U.S.C.A. ss 1346(b).** 2671 et seq.

Accordingly, to retrieve cases that contain citations to federal statutes, the following format is recommended:

headnote(28 +5 1346(b))

Retrieving Cases that Cite Other Court Decisions

WESTLAW can be used as a citator of other court decisions if the title of the decision, its citation, or both, are known. When only the title of the case is known, use the following format:

henningson /5 bloomfield

This query instructs the computer to retrieve all documents that have cited the case of *Henningsen v. Bloomfield Motors, Inc.*. The /5 numerical connector requires that the word HENNINGSEN occur within the five words of BLOOMFIELD.

If the citation of the case is known, a query may be constructed that will retrieve documents that have cited the case. This is done by using the numbers of the citation as search terms in the query. For example, to retrieve cases that have cited to *Henningsen* by its citation, 161 A.2d 69, use the following format:

161 /3 69

If both the citation and the case title are known, the following formats may be used:

henningsen /5 bloomfield /15 161 /3 69
henningsen /15 161 /3 69

In the example (1) above the computer is instructed to retrieve all documents that contain the terms HENNINGSEN, BLOOMFIELD, 161, and 69 within the number of words designated by the numerical proximity connectors separating each term. This query would retrieve all documents that contain the full citation: *Henningsen v. Bloomfield Motors, Inc.*, 161 A.2d 69. The query in example (2) above could be used if the name of only one party was known.

The date restriction may be utilized to retrieve documents that cite cases within a given year, range of years, or before or after a given date. For example, to retrieve all documents that have cited *Henningsen v. Bloomfield Motors, Inc.* after the year 1982, this query could be used:

henningsen /5 bloomfield & date(after 12/31/82)

Shepard's® Citations on WESTLAW

From any point in WESTLAW, case citations may be entered to retrieve Shepard's listings for those citations. To enter a citation to be Shepardized, the following format is used:

sh 161 u.s. 483

or

sh 161 us 483

or

sh161us483

When the citation is entered, Shepard's listings for the citation will be displayed. To shepardize a citation it is not necessary to be in the same database as that of the citation. For example, a Supreme Court citation may be entered from the Pacific Reporter database.

West's INSTA–CITE™

INSTA–CITE, West Publishing Company's case history system, allows users to quickly verify the accuracy of case citations and the validity of decisions. It contains prior and subsequent case histories in chronological listings, parallel citations and precedential treatment.

Some examples of the kind of direct case history provided by INSTA–CITE are: "affirmed", "certiorari denied", "decision reversed and remanded", and "judgement vacated." A complete list of INSTA–CITE case history and precedential treatment notations appears in the *WESTLAW Reference Manual*.

An example of an INSTA–CITE reference from this hornbook appears below. The format for instaciting a case citation consists of the letters IC followed by the citation, with or without spaces and periods:

ic 433 u.s. 72

or

ic 433 us 72

or

ic 433us72

Black's Law Dictionary

WESTLAW contains an on-line version of *Black's Law Dictionary*. The dictionary incorporates definitions of terms and phrases of English and American law.

Along with the preformulated queries in this publication appear references to *Black's Law Dictionary* for many important terms in tort law. The format of such commands is as follows:

di negligence

The command consists of letters DI followed by the term to be defined. To see the definition of a phrase, enter the letters DI followed by the phrase (without quotation marks):

di proximate cause

If the precise spelling of a term to be defined is not known, or a list of dictionary terms is desired, a truncated form of the word may be entered with the root expansion symbol (!) attached to it:

di res!

or

di res ipsa

The first example will produce a list of all dictionary terms that begin with RES. The second example will produce a list of dictionary terms, the first of which is RES IPSA LOQUITUR. From the list of terms a number corresponding to the desired terms can be entered to obtain the appropriate definitions.

WESTLAW Case Law Databases

This section discusses the WESTLAW Case Law databases, in which the preformulated queries in this publication have been designed to be used. The case law databases consist of cases from the National Reporter System.

Cases in WESTLAW are in "full text plus." That is, they include the court's decision enhanced by a synopsis of the decision and headnotes stating the legal propositions for which the decision stands. The headnotes are classified to West's Key Number classification system.

WESTLAW contains many databases not discussed here. For example, there are databases that contain the entire United States Code, Code of Federal Regulations, and topical databases covering such areas as bankruptcy, patents and copyrights, federal tax, government contracts, communications, securities, labor, antitrust and business regulation, admiralty, and military justice.

The case law databases are divided into two kinds: multistate databases and federal databases. The multistate databases contain state appellate cases compiled from reporters for geographical regions. These regional reporters (with their corresponding database identifiers indicated in parentheses) are: Atlantic (ATL), Northeastern (NE), Northwestern (NW), Pacific (PAC), Southeastern (SE), Southern (SO), and Southwestern (SW).

In addition, WESTLAW has individual state databases containing decisions from specific states. The database identifier for an individual state database consists of the state's postal abbreviation followed by a hyphen followed by the letters CS (e.g., MN–CS for Minnesota cases).

The federal databases in which the queries in this publication will provide the most useful searches are: Supreme Court Reporter (SCT), U.S. Courts of Appeals (CTA) and U.S. District Courts (DCT).

WESTLAW also contains individual U.S. Courts of Appeals databases. The database identifier for an individual court of appeals database consists of the letters CTA followed by the number of the federal circuit (e.g., CTA8 for the Eighth Circuit Court of Appeals.)

Some issues to which the preformulated queries correspond will only retrieve relevant cases from the state databases, whereas other issues will work satisfactorily only in the federal databases. However, some issues are sufficiently broad or have been so widely litigated that cases may be found with the queries in either the state or federal databases. Finally, some issues may have been litigated only in particular states and not in others, so that a given query may retrieve cases in one state but not in another.

In some instances, the query itself indicates which database it is to be used in. If a query contains a court restriction to a particular state or to a particular federal circuit, then that query should only be used in the database that contains that state or district. For example, the following query contains a court restriction for Oregon cases:

30.260 & court(or)

and therefore should be used in the Pacific Reporter (PAC) database, since that is the database in which Oregon cases appear. Alternatively, the query should be used in the OR–CS database, without the court field restriction. Similarly, the following query contains a court restriction for cases from the Federal Courts of Appeals for the second circuit:

tort* /p foreign! /s countr! sovereign & court(ca2)

and, accordingly, should be used in the CTA database, since that is the only database which contains all of the cases from the Federal Circuit Courts of Appeals. Alternatively, the query could be used in the CTA2 database.

WESTLAW Hornbook Queries: (a) Query Format

The queries that appear in this publication are intended to be illustrative. They are approximately as general as the material in the hornbook text to which they correspond.

Although all of the queries in this publication reflect proper format for use with WESTLAW, there is seldom only one "correct" way to formulate a query for a particular problem. This is so even though some techniques are clearly better than others. Therefore, the queries reflect a wide range of alternative ways that queries may be structured for effective research. Such variances in query style simply reflect the great flexibility that the WESTLAW system affords its users in formulating search strategies.

For some research problems, it may be necessary to make a series of refinements to the queries, such as the addition of search terms or the substitution of different grammatical connectors, to adequately fit the particular needs of the individual researcher's problem. The responsibility remains with the researcher to "fine tune" the WESTLAW queries in accordance with his or her own research requirements. The primary usefulness of the preformulated queries in this hornbook is in providing users with a foundation upon which further query construction can be built.

Individual queries in this hornbook may retrieve from one to over a hundred cases, depending on which database they are addressed to. If a query does not retrieve any cases in a given database, it is because there are no decisions in that reporter which satisfy the grammatical proximity requirements of the query. In this situation, to search another database with the same query, enter the letter S followed by the initials DB, followed by the new database identifier. Thus, if a query was initially addressed to the NE (Northeastern Reporter) database, but retrieved no documents, the user could then search the PAC (Pacific Reporter) database with same query by entering the following command:

s db pac

This command instructs WESTLAW to search the Pacific Reporter database with the same query that was previously used in the Northeastern Reporter database.

The maximum number of cases retrieved by a query in any given database will vary, depending on a variety of factors, including the relative generality of the search terms and grammatical connectors, the frequency of litigation or discussion of the issue in the courts, and the number of documents comprising the database.

WESTLAW Hornbook Queries: Textual Illustrations

This section explains how the queries provided in this hornbook may be used in researching actual tort problems that a student or practitioner might encounter. Examples from the text of this edition have been selected to illustrate how the queries can be expanded, restricted, or altered to meet the specific needs of the reader's research.

A segment of the text from Chapter 13, section 76, of Prosser and Keeton's *Law of Torts* appears below:

§ 76. Animals

Primitive law tended to hold the owner of property strictly liable for the harm it did. The owner of a slave, an animal, or even an inanimate thing, was so far identified with his chattel that he was liable, without any fault of his own, for the damage it might inflict on his neighbors.[1] It is characteristic of certain stages of development in all legal systems of which we have knowledge, that he might escape liability by surrendering the harmful agent itself either to the injured party or to the crown.[2] The present state of the common law may be said to begin with the disappearance of this "noxal surrender" and the rule of strict liability for harm done by harmless things. So far as the responsibility of keepers of animals is concerned, the survival of the primitive notion of strict liability has been due in part to modern views of policy. Certain kinds of animals involve an obvious danger to the community, even if they are carefully kept; everyone knows the propensity of cattle and horses to escape and roam and do mischief,[3] and bear or an elephant[4] can never be regarded as safe. Those who keep such animals for their own purposes are required to protect the community, at their peril, against the risk involved. The strict liability is, in general, co-extensive with the obvious risk.

The text of this section discusses strict liability for damages caused by animals. In order to retrieve cases discussing strict liability for trespassing animals or livestock, the following query:

strict! absolut! /1 liab! /s animal* livestock /p trespass!

is given as a suggested search strategy on WESTLAW.

A headnote of a case that was retrieved from the PAC (Pacific Reporter) database appears below:

```
   R 5 OF 12    P 3 OF 9    PAC  T
627 P.2d 750
28k90
ANIMALS
k. Duties of owners.
Colo. 1981.
Common law held the owner of trespassing livestock
strictly liable for their trespasses on the lands of others.
C.R.S.1973, 35–46–101, 35–46–102.
SaBell's Inc. v. Flens
```

An illustration of a relevant portion of the text of the opinion of this case (*SaBell's, Inc. v. Flens,* 627 P.2d 750, Colo., 1981) appears below:

```
   R 5 OF 12    P 7 OF 9    PAC   T
627 P.2d 750
(1)(2)
The Colorado Fence Law, section 35–46–102, C.R.S.1973,
originally enacted in the latter part of the 19th century,
makes the maintenance of a "lawful fence," as defined in
section 35–46–101, C.R.S. 1973, a condition precedent to
recovery of damages caused by trespassing livestock.
Schaefer v. Mills, 72 Colo. 82, 209 P. 643 (1922). The
statute modified the common law doctrine which held the
owner to trespassing livestock strictly liable for their
trespasses on the lands of others. See Morris v. Fraker, 5
Colo. 425 (1880); Am.Jur.2d Animals s 49 (1962); see
also W. Prosser, Torts s 76, at 496–498 (4th ed. 1971).
"The policy of the (fence) law is to favor stock owners,
and to permit them to range their stock at large. The duty
of protecting crops is placed upon the farmer."
Schaefer v. Mills, supra, 72 Colo. at 84, 209 P. at 644.
```

The query can be altered to meet the need of individual researchers. For example, a student or practitioner may wish to find cases involving strict liability for damage caused by a particular type of animal, say, a zebra. In this situation, the preformulated query shown above can be modified to retrieve documents relevant to the new issue as follows:

strict! absolut! /1 liab! /p zebra

The search term ZEBRA is added as a replacement term for the words ANIMAL* and LIVESTOCK because it is a specific term corresponding to the new issue. The first page (synopsis) of a case that was retrieved by this query from the NE (Northeast Reporter) database appears below:

```
Citation       Rank(R)    Page(P)      Database  Mode
221 N.E.2d 744  R 1 OF 1   P 1 OF 18    NE        T

            Edna SMITH
                 v.
Ervine JALBERT et al. (and three companion cases).
    Supreme Judicial Court of Massachusetts, Hampden.
               Argued Nov. 1, 1966.
               Decided Dec. 2, 1966.
Actions for personal injuries and property damage caused
by escaped zebra. The Superior Court, Hampton County,
Tomasello, J., entered judgements for plaintiffs and
defendants appealed. The Supreme Judicial Court,
Spalding, J., held, inter alia, that evidence, including
defendant's answers to interrogatories admitting it was
owner of a zebra which was kept at certain location and
that zebra which caused damage complained of was seen
running loose about one half mile from the location,
supported finding that zebra which caused damage was
owned by defendant.
    Exception overruled.
```

Ranking Documents Retrieved on WESTLAW: Age and Term Options

Documents retrieved by a query can be ordered in either of two ways. One way is to order retrieved documents by their dates, with the most recent documents displayed first. This is ranking by AGE. Using the AGE option is suggested when the user's highest priority is to retrieve the most recent decisions from a search.

Alternatively, documents can be ranked by the frequency of appearance of query terms. This is as ranking by TERMS. When a search is performed with the TERMS option, the cases containing the greatest number of different search terms will be displayed first.

When a database is accessed by entering a database identifier, WESTLAW displays a message indicating the ranking options available. Once the user selects which type of ranking, AGE or TERMS, is desired, WESTLAW responds with a screen requesting that the query be entered.

The queries offered in this hornbook were formulated and tested for relevancy with use of the TERMS option. Accordingly, in certain instances use of the AGE option with the preformulated queries may display less relevant, yet more recent cases, first.

Conclusion

This appendix has reviewed methods that can be used to obtain the most effective legal research in tort law possible. Prosser and Keeton's *Law of Torts* combines the familiar hornbook publication with a powerful and easily accessed computerized law library. The WESTLAW references at the end of each section of the hornbook text provide a basic framework upon which the law student or lawyer can structure additional research on WESTLAW. The queries may be used as provided or they may be tailored to meet the needs of the researcher's specific problems. The power and flexibility of WESTLAW affords users of this publication a unique opportunity to greatly enhance their access to and understanding of the law of torts.

Table of Cases

References are to Pages

A

A. & B. Auto Stores of Jones Street, Inc. v. City of Newark, 1055
A.B.C. Needlecraft Co. v. Dun & Bradstreet, 829, 835
A.B.C. Packard, Inc. v. General Motors Corp., 739
Aalfo Co. v. Kinney, 986, 995
Aaron v. Ward, 58
Abalene Exterminating Co. v. Elges, 1023
Abalos v. Oil Development Co. of Texas, 464
Abb v. Northern Pacific Railroad Co., 333
Abbot v. McCadden, 570
Abbot v. Stevens, 764
Abbot v. Town of Fremont, 674
Abbott v. Abbott, 77
Abbott v. Hancock, 928
Abbott v. New York Public Library, 423
Abbott, State v., 127
Abbott v. Treat, 758
Abbott v. United States Lines, Inc., 376
Abbott v. Western National Indemnity Co., 13
ABC Builders, Inc. v. Phillips, 164, 447
ABC-Paramount Records, Inc. v. Topps Record Distributing Co., 1003
Abdella v. Smith, 635
Abdin v. Fischer, 416
Abel v. M.H. Pickering Co., 139
Abel v. Paterno, 743
Abell v. Cornwall Industrial Corp., 848
Abercrombie v. Ivey, 570
Abercrombie v. McClung, 1057
Aberdeen Construction Co. v. City of Aberdeen, 342
Abernathy v. Eline Oil Field Services, Inc., 496
Abernathy v. Hutchinson, 849
Abernethy v. Burns, 897
Abernethy v. Thornton, 861
Abingdon, Rex v., 820
Ableman v. Holman, 996
Aborn v. Lipson, 818
Abraham Used Car Co. v. Silva, 62
Abrahams v. Kidney, 927
Abrahamson v. Brown, 331
Abram v. Odham, 836
Abrams v. Crompton-Richmond Co., 818
Abresch v. Northwestern Bell Telephone Co., 380
Abrevaya v. Palace Theatre & Realty Co., 542
Acadia, California, Limited v. Herbert, 60
Aceves v. Regal Pale Brewing Co., 477, 514
Acheson v. Miller, 337

Acker v. McCullough, 782
Ackerberg v. Muskegon Osteopathic Hospital, 427
Ackerman v. Bramwell Investment Co., 759
Ackerman v. Ellis, 723
Ackerman v. Kaufman, 891, 894
Ackerman v. Lyman, 674
Ackerman v. Port of Seattle, 81
Ackers v. Chicago, Saint Paul, Minneapolis & Omaha Railway Co., 222
Acme Finance Co. v. National Insurance Co., 586
Acme Silver Co. v. Stacy Hardware Co., 976
Acres v. Hall's Administrator, 958
Actiesselskabet Ingrid v. Central Railroad Co. of New Jersey, 568
Acton v. Shields, 951
Adair v. Williams, 156
Adam v. Los Angeles Transit Lines, 245
Adam v. Ward, 826
Adam, Meldrum & Anderson Co. v. Stewart, 675, 730
Adamian v. Three Sons, Inc., 718
Adams v. Adams, 902
Adams v. Alabama Lime & Stone Corp., 817
Adams v. American Enka Corp., 422
Adams v. Barney, 642
Adams v. Boyd, 465
Adams v. Brookwood Country Club, 403
Adams v. Broughton, 90
Adams Co. v. Buchanan, 553
Adams v. Chicago Great Western Ry. Co., 134
Adams v. City of Toledo, 648
Adams v. Commissioners of Town of Trappe, 617, 644
Adams v. Commonwealth, 644
Adams v. Dantin, 309
Adams v. Frontier Broadcasting Co., 812
Adams v. Gillig, 763
Adams v. Greer, 186
Adams v. Hamilton Carhartt Overall Co., 619
Adams v. Home Owners' Loan Corp., 821
Adams v. Lawson, 786
Adams v. Leidholdt, 204
Adams v. Main, 918
Adams v. Parrish, 306, 352
Adams, Regina v., 798
Adams v. Rivers, 151
Adams v. Robinson, 661
Adams v. Sparacio, 948, 949
Adams v. State, 150, 381, 1050
Adams v. Treat, 519, 520, 521
Adams v. United States, 423

TABLE OF CASES

Adams v. White Bus Line, 337
Adams, State ex rel. Williams v., 1062
Adams & Frederick Co. v. South Omaha National Bank, 104
Adams & Sullivan v. Sengel, 68, 553
Adams Brothers v. Clark, 539
Adams Const. Co. v. Bentley, 638
Adams Express Co. v. Beckwith, 335
Adams Express Co. v. Mellichamp, 483
Adamski v. Talcoma General Hospital, 508
Adamson v. Hand, 428
Adamson v. Jarvis, 337
Adan v. Steinbrecher, 751, 762
Addair v. Bryant, 240, 451
Addeo v. Metropolitan Bottling Co., 695
Addie & Sons, Robert v. Dumbreck, 393
Addis v. Gramophone Co., Limited, 374, 662
Ader v. Blau, 326, 327, 329
Adirondack Record v. Lawrence, 779
Adkin v. Pillen, 878, 880
Adkins v. Hoskins, 758
Adkins v. Nanney, 525
Adler, Barish, Daniels, Levin & Creskoff v. Epstein, 984, 986, 987, 1002, 1011
Adler's Quality Bakery, Inc. v. Gaseteria, Inc., 557
Admiralty Comm'rs v. S.S. Amerika, 945
Advance Loan Service v. Mandik, 62
Advance Music Corp. v. American Tobacco Co., 966, 970, 972
Aetna Casualty & Surety Co. v. Brice, 527
Aetna Insurance Co. v. Blumenthal, 150
Aetna Life Insurance Co. v. Brewer, 801
Aetna Life Insurance Co. v. Mutual Benefit Health & Accident Association, 779
Aetna Life Insurance Co. v. Weck, 585
Affiliated Enterprises v. Gruber, 1021
AFL–CIO v. Allied International, Inc., 1014, 1027
Age-Herald Publishing Co. v. Waterman, 795, 800, 844
Agent Orange Product Liability Litigation, In re, 1037
Agis v. Howard Johnson Co., 932
Agnew v. City of Los Angeles, 589
Agricultural Bond & Credit Corp. v. August Brandt Co., 730
Aguilar v. Riverdale Cooperative Creamery Association, 413
Aguilera v. Reynolds Well Service, Inc., 590
Agwilines, Inc. v. Eagle Oil & Shipping Co., 999
Ahern v. City of Des Moines, 492
Ahern v. McGlinchy, 941
Ahrens v. Moore, 726
Ahring v. White, 891
Ahsford v. Choate, 971
Aiken v. Holyoke Street Railway Co., 397
Aikens v. Wisconsin, 983
Ainsworth v. Berg, 340
Ainsworth v. Lakin, 551
Air Crash in Bali, Indonesia, In re, 956
Air Heaters, Inc. v. Johnson Electric, Inc., 720
Aircraft Sales & Service, Inc. v. Bramlett, 663
Aistrop v. Blue Diamond Coal Co., 575

Aitchison v. Reter, 456
Ajamian v. Township of North Bergen, 644
Akermanis v. SeaLand Service, Inc., 479
Akers v. Ashland Oil & Refining Co., 638
Akers v. Marsh, 628
Akers v. Mathieson Alkali Works, 641
Akins v. Glens Falls City School District, 238, 484, 485, 496, 497, 1048
Alabama Electric Co-operative, Inc. v. Partridge, 868
Alabama Fuel & Iron Co. v. Baladoni, 56, 63, 360
Alabama Great Southern Railroad Co. v. Broach, 75
Alabama Great Southern Railroad Co. v. Chapman, 292
Alabama Great Southern Railroad Co. v. Evans, 218
Alabama Great Southern Railroad Co. v. Quarles & Couturie, 315
Alabama Highway Express Co., United States v., 855
Alabama Power Co. v. McIntosh, 514
Alabama Power Co. v. Taylor, 532
Alabama State Federation of Labor v. McAdory, 855
Alabama Water Co. v. Knowles, 662
Alabama Western Railroad Co. v. Wilson, 552
Alabiso v. Schuster, 744
Alaimo v. Schwanz, 918, 921, 923
Alamo National Bank v. Kraus, 387
Aland v. Pyle, 878
Alaniz v. United States, 1038, 1039
Alaska Airlines, Inc. v. Sweat, 506
Alaska Packers' Association v. Industrial Accident Commission of California, 580
Albala v. City of New York, 369
Albany, City of v. Meyer, 780
Albaugh v. Cooley, 219
Alber v. Nolle, 913
Albers v. Ottenbacher, 228
Albert v. State, 437
Alberto-Culver Co. v. Morgan, 687
Alberts v. Giebink, 207
Alberts v. Remington Rand, 1021
Albert's Shoes, Inc. v. Crabtree Construction Co., 334
Albertson v. Volkswagenwerk, A.G., 476, 478
Albison v. Robbins & White, Inc., 553
Albrecht v. Groat, 209
Albrecht v. St. Hedwig's Roman Catholic Benevolent Society, 327, 329, 345, 348
Albritton v. Bossier City Hospital Commission, 186
Albritton v. Hill, 452
Album Graphics, Inc. v. Beatrice Foods Co., 659
Alcorn v. Mitchell, 41
Alcott v. Miller's Karri & Jarrah Forests, 972, 975
Alden v. Wright, 765, 767
Alderman v. Ford, 63
Alderson v. Gulf, Colorado & Santa Fe Railway Co., 91
Alderson v. Kahle, 781, 1074
Aldes v. St. Paul Baseball Club, 487
Aldred's Case, 619
Aldrich, In re, 585
Aldrich v. Charles Beauregard & Sons, Inc., 335
Aldrich v. City of Minneapolis, 650
Aldrich v. Scribner, 746, 748
Aldrich v. Worley, 761

TABLE OF CASES

Aldrich v. Wright, 137
Aldridge v. Saxey, 628
Aldridge v. Stuyvesant, 980
Aldridge v. Van Patter, 548
Aldworth v. City of Lynn, 638
Alegria v. Payonk, 174
Ales v. Ryan, 250
Alexander v. Alexander, 890, 894
Alexander v. Delgado, 164
Alexander v. Jacoby, 892
Alexander v. Jenkins, 791
Alexander v. Johnson, 920, 922
Alexander v. Knight, 291
Alexander v. Nash-Kelvinator Corp., 704
Alexander v. North Eastern R. Co., 842
Alexander v. Pacholek, 44
Alexander v. Seaboard Air Line Railway Co., 513
Alexander v. Southey, 100
Alexander v. Swackhamer, 94
Alexander v. Town of New Castle, 201, 264, 317
Alexander v. Wilkes-Barre Anthracite Coal Co., 646
Alexander v. Wrenn, 486
Alexander Funeral Homes, Inc. v. Pride, 703
Alexandria-Gazette Corp. v. West, 837
Alfone v. Newark Umbrella Frame Co., 778
Alfone v. Sarno, 956
Alford, State v., 157
Alford v. Summerlin, 166
Alfree v. Alfree, 903
Alhino v. Starr, 165, 498, 508
Alizzi v. Employer Insurance of Wausau, 952
Allaire v. St. Luke's Hospital, 367, 368
Allard v. Church of Scientology of California, 885
Allegheny Airlines Inc. v. United States, 520
Allegheny Airlines v. Village of Cedarhurst, 81, 82
Allen v. Aetna Life Insurance Co., 587
Allen v. Camp, 146, 147
Allen v. Codman, 893, 894
Allen v. Crofoot, 819
Allen v. Dhuse, 230, 232, 454
Allen v. Equity & Investors Management Corp., 435, 440, 442
Allen v. Frawley, 760
Allen v. Fromme, 47, 48
Allen v. Gornto, 303
Allen v. Hannaford, 46, 57
Allen v. Hixson, 375, 376
Allen v. Jones, 362
Allen v. Keily, 144
Allen v. Lindeman, 920
Allen v. Lowell's Administratrix, 1007
Allen v. Pioneer Press Co., 847
Allen v. Powell, 989
Allen v. Roark, 192
Allen v. Rossi, 15
Allen v. Seacoast Products, Inc., 506
Allen v. Shaw, 734
Allen v. State, 127
Allen, State v., 44
Allen v. State Department of Mental Health, 1048

Allen v. Toledo, 200, 523
Allen v. Trester, 327, 346
Allen v. Yazoo & Mississippi Valley Railroad Co., 389
Alles v. Interstate Power Co., 941
Alley v. Chicago, Rock Island & Pacific Railway Co., 237
Alley v. Praschak Machine Co., 492
Alley v. Siepman, 162
Allgauer v. Le Bastille, Inc., 419, 424, 426, 427
Alliance Securities Co. v. De Vilbiss, 974
Allied Building Credits v. Grogan Builders Supply Co., 91
Allied Maintenance Corp. v. Allied Mechanical Trades, 1017
Allied Mutual Casualty Co. v. Long, 339
Allied Mutual Casualty Corp. v. General Motors Corp. 342
Allied Van Lines, Inc. v. Bratton, 484
Alling v. Northwestern Bell Telephone Co., 269, 306
Allis-Chalmers Manufacturing Co. v. Lowry, 967
Allison v. Berry, 974
Allison v. Fiscus, 135
Allison v. Hodo, 143
Allman v. Bird, 10
Allred v. Bekins Wide World Service, Inc., 167
Allred v. Hinkley, 92
Allsop v. Allsop, 794
Allstate Amusement Co. of Illinois v. Pasinato, 378, 381
Almind v. Sea Beach Co., 852
Almy v. Kvamme, 798
Alonso v. Hills, 554
Alperdt v. Paige, 519
Alropa Corp. v. Flatley, 762
Alsaker v. De Graff Lumber Co., 224
Alsever v. Minneapolis & St. Louis Railroad Co., 507
Alspach v. McLaughlin, 717
Alsteen v. Gehl, 64
Alster v. Allen, 620
Alston v. Alston, 904
Alston v. Baltimore & Ohio Railroad Co., 408
Alt v. Konkle, 309
Altamuro v. Milner Hotel, Inc., 454, 507
Altepeter v. Virgil State Bank, 673
Altevogt v. Brinkoetter, 659
Altoona Clay Products, Inc. v. Dun & Bradstreet, Inc., 829, 966
Altrichter v. Shell Oil Co., 269
Aluma Kraft Manufacturing Co. v. Elmer Fox & Co., 186
Aluminum Co. of America v. Essex Group, Inc., 729
Aluminum Co. of America v. Walden, 422
Alverts v. Giebink, 166
Alves v. Hayes, 1067
Alviar v. Garza, 222
Alvis v. Ribar, 464, 469, 471, 477
Alvord and Swift v. Steward M. Muller Construction Co., 983, 997, 1001, 1011
Alyeska Pipeline Service Co. v. Aurora Air Service Inc., 984, 991, 1010, 1011
Amabello v. Colonial Motors, 898

Amann v. Faidy, 368
Amaya v. Home Ice, Fuel & Supply Co., 24, 366
Ambrosio v. Price, 481, 486, 503
Amellin v. Leone, 921
Amend v. Bell, 474
American Automobile Insurance Co. v. Molling, 911
American Bank & Trust Co. v. Federal Reserve Bank, 28
American Barge Line Co. v. Leatherman's Administratrix, 953
American Brands, Inc. v. R.J. Reynolds Tobacco Corp., 1019
American Broadcasting Companies, Inc. v. Smith Cabinet Manufacturing Co., 977
American Broadcasting-Paramount Theatres, Inc. v. Simpson, 785, 787
American Building & Loan Association v. Bear, 766
American Casualty Co. v. Billingsley, 337
American Chicle Co. v. Topps Chewing Gum, Inc., 1016
American Credit Bureau, Inc. v. Bel-Aire Interiors, Inc., 899
American Distilling Co. v. Bellows & Co., 1015
American District Telegraph Co. v. Brink's Inc., 837
American Electronics, Inc. v. Christe Poules & Co., 621
American Exchange Bank of Madison, Wisconsin v. United States, 1034, 1040
American Export Lines, Inc. v. Alvez, 932
American Express Co. v. Mullins, 97
American Express Co. v. Risley, 304
American Family Mutual Insurance Co. v. Dobrzynski, 245
American Finance & Loan Corp. v. Coots, 61
American Fire & Casualty Co. v. Jackson, 441
American Hardwood Lumber Co. v. Dent, 758
American Home Products Corp. v. Johnson & Johnson, 1019
American Ice Co. v. Fitzhugh, 573
American Indemnity Co. v. Ernst & Ernst, 744
American Indemnity Co. v. Felbaum, 587
American Insurance Co. v. France, 963
American Laundry Machinery Co. v. Skinner, 757
American Lease Plans v. Silver Sand Co., 508
American Legion, Department of Georgia v. Simonton, 423
American Life Insurance Co. v. Shell, 776
American Malting Co. v. Keitel, 773
American Manufacturers Mutual Insurance Co. v. The United States, 147
American Mercury v. Chase, 1009, 1015, 1025
American Motor Car Co. v. Robbins, 954
American Motorcycle Association v. Superior Court, 344, 475, 476
American Mutual Liability Insurance Co. v. St. Paul Fire & Marine Insurance Co., 670
American Mutual Liability Insurance Co. of Boston v. Chain Belt Co., 717
American National Bank v. Wolfe, 421
American National Bank & Trust Co. v. First Wisconsin Mortgage Trust, 976
American Oil Co. v. Colonial Oil Co., 11

American Print Works v. Lawrence, 146
American Publishing Co. v. Gamble, 837
American Railway Express Co. v. Davis, 507
American Railway Express Co. v. Judd, 458
American Railway Express Co. v. Summers, 154
American Security Co. v. Cook, 60, 61, 77
American Sign Co. v. Electro-Lens Sign Co., 731, 732
American Southern Insurance Co. v. Dime Taxi Service, 341
American Surety Co. v. Schottenbauer, 986, 995
American Surety Co. of New York v. Gold, 13
American Transportation Co. v. United States Sanitary Specialties Corp., 992
American Union Telegraph Co. v. Middleton, 93
American Village Corp. v. Springfield Lumber & Building Supply, 242, 261
American Washboard Co. v. Saginaw Manufacturing Co., 1019
Americans for Democratic Action v. Meade, 779
Ames v. Strain, 51
AMF, Inc. v. Sleekcraft Boats, 1017
Amick v. Montross, 789, 792
Amick v. O'Hara, 1072
Ammerman v. Newman, 891
Ammons v. Kellogg, 542
Amoco Pipeline Co. v. Montgomery, 478
Amos v. Prom, Inc., 47
Amoskeag Manufacturing Co. v. Goodale, 642
Amphitheatres, Inc. v. Portland Meadows, 71, 562, 628, 630
Amrine v. Murray, 486
Ams Machine Co., Max v. International Association of Machinists, Bridgeport Lodge, No. 30, p. 1003
Amsden v. Grinnell Mutual Reinsurance Co., 11, 60, 62, 63
Amsterdam Knitting Co. v. Dean, 640
Ancrum v. Camden Water Co., 594
Anderberg v. Newman, 1066
Andersen v. Bingham & Garfield Railway Co., 468
Anderson v. Anderson, 310
Anderson v. Arnold's Executor, 30, 38
Anderson v. Atchison, Topeka & Santa Fe Railroad Co., 376
Anderson v. Aupperle, 926, 927, 928
Anderson v. B.F. Goodrich Co., 406
Anderson v. Baltimore & Ohio Railroad Co., 304
Anderson v. Bushong Pontiac Co., 314
Anderson v. Butler, 913
Anderson v. Canaday, 873
Anderson v. Chancellor Western Oil Development Corp., 513
Anderson v. Cinnamon, 430
Anderson v. Cooper, 421
Anderson v. Cosmopolitan National Bank of Chicago, 449
Anderson v. Dalton, 9
Anderson v. Esposito, 323
Anderson v. Fletcher, 879
Anderson v. Foster, 152
Anderson v. Gailey, 955

TABLE OF CASES

Anderson v. Gouldberg, 103
Anderson v. Green Bay & Western Railroad, 164, 387, 391, 394, 395, 398
Anderson v. Halverson, 348, 350
Anderson v. Hearst Publishing Co., Inc., 801
Anderson v. Heron Engineering Co., 701
Anderson v. Jenkins, 133, 134
Anderson v. Jones, 306
Anderson v. Kansas City Baseball Club, 494
Anderson v. Knox, 64
Anderson v. Lale, 953
Anderson v. Last Chance Ranch Co., 574
Anderson v. McGill Club, 920
Anderson v. Mills, 145
Anderson v. Minneapolis, St. Paul & Sault Ste. Marie Railway Co., 267, 278, 347
Anderson v. Moskovitz, 1003
Anderson v. Neal, 167
Anderson v. Pantages Theatre Co., 663
Anderson v. Payne, 467
Anderson v. Radcliffe, 78
Anderson v. Reeder, 441
Anderson v. Reith-Riley Construction Co., 403
Anderson v. Rucker Brothers, 551
Anderson v. Sears, Roebuck & Co., 55
Anderson v. Settergren, 303, 718
Anderson v. Smith, 137
Anderson v. Somberg, 253, 713
Anderson v. Souza, 81
Anderson v. Speer, 389
Anderson v. Spriesterbach, 747
Anderson v. State, 139
Anderson v. Stream, 908
Anderson v. Sturm, 919
Anderson v. Theisen, 313
Anderson v. Ueland, 574
Anderson v. United States, 75
Anderson, United States v., 40
Anderson v. Wagner, 167, 168
Anderson, State ex rel. v. Preston, 649
Anderson & Nelson Distilling Co. v. Hair, 429
Anderson Equipment Co. v. Findley, 674
Anderton v. Buckton, 560
Anderton v. Mongomery, 162, 164
Andrecsik v. New Jersey Tube Co., 571
Andreen v. Escondido Citrus Union, 226
Andreotala v. Gaeta, 206
Andreozzi v. Rubano, 158
Andreu v. Wellman, 285
Andrew v. Deshler, 966, 968, 969
Andrew v. Kilgour, 565
Andrews v. Andrews, 390, 619
Andrews v. Askey, 927
Andrews v. Blakeslee, 991, 993
Andrews v. County of Otsego, 905
Andrews v. Davis, 309
Andrews v. Gardiner, 818, 822
Andrews v. Goetz, 420
Andrews v. Shattuck, 102
Androws v. Coulter, 123

Angelozzi v. Cossentino, 872
Angerosa v. White Co., 754
Angle v. Chicago, St. Paul, Minneapolis & Omaha Railway Co., 992, 993, 1003, 1004
Angus v. Clifford, 736, 745
Angus v. Radin, 539
Anheuser-Busch, Inc. v. Du Bois Brewing Co., 1016
Anjou v. Boston Elevated Railway Co., 243
Ankeny v. Moffett, 337
Ankers v. District School Board of Pasco County, 1048
Annarina v. Boland, 918, 920
Annbar Associates v. American Express Co., 970
Anneker v. Quinn-Robbins Co., 403
Annenberg v. Kurtz, 635
Anonymous v. Anonymous, 1033
Anonymous v. Trenkman, 795, 818
Ansin v. Thurston, 408
Ansley v. Bank of Piedmont, 767
Ansteth v. Buffalo Railway Co., 45, 134
Antcliff v. Datzman, 453, 455, 460, 462, 480, 487, 489, 490
Antcliff v. June, 898, 899
Anthony v. Anthony, 855
Anthony v. Haney, 140
Anthony v. Koppers Co., 165, 957
Anthony v. Norton, 57, 927
Anthony v. Slaid, 39, 982, 1000
Anthony Co., C.R. v. Williams, 423
Anti-Monopoly, Inc. v. General Mills Fun Group, Inc., 1017
Antle v. Sexton, 752
Anton v. Greyhound Van Lines, Inc., 483, 484
Anton v. Lehpamer, 430
Antoniewicz v. Reszcynski, 397, 433
Antonik v. Chamberlin, 81, 631, 641
Apgar v. Woolston, 874
Apitz v. Dames, 904
Appalachian Insurance Co. v. Knutson, 254
Appalachian Power Co. v. Wilson, 267
Appel v. Muller, 444
Appelbaum, People v., 868
Appier v. Million, 579
Applestein v. Preston, 880
Appleyard v. Transmerican Press, Inc., 845
Application of (see name of party)
Appling v. Jones, 311
Appling v. Stuck, 398
Aquino v. Bulletin Co., 861, 862
Aquitania, The, 999
Arabesque Studios, Inc. v. Academy of Fine Arts International, Inc., 990
Aranda, People v., 37
Arcadia Realty Co. v. City of St. Louis, 649
Arcara v. Moresse, 528
Archambault v. Holmes, 523
Archer v. Archer, 917
Archer v. Cachat, 872
Arden Sales Corp., Elizabeth v. Gus Blass Co., 1014
Ardis v. Griffin, 462
Areal v. Home Owners Loan Corp., 439

Aretz v. United States, 510
Arez, United States v., 510
Argo v. Goodstein, 175
Argus v. Michler, 421
Argus Cameras v. Hall of Distributors, 994
Arkansas Power & Light Co. v. Butterworth, 249
Arkansas Short Line v. Bellars, 414
Arkley v. Niblack, 570
Arko v. Shenango Furnace Co., 304
Arlington Heights National Bank v. Arlington Heights Federal Savings & Loan Association, 989
Arlowski v. Foglio, 132, 140
Armagast v. Medici Gallery & Coffee House, 182
Armendariz v. Mora, 1003
Armfield v. Nash, 458
Armiger v. United States, 381
Armington v. Providence Ice Co., 566
Armored Car Service v. First National Bank of Miami, 92
Armory v. Delamirie, 103
Armour v. Golkowska, 569
Armour v. Hahn, 569, 572
Armstead v. Holbert, 206
Armstead v. Lounsberry, 232, 275
Armstrong v. Bergeron, 310
Armstrong v. Industrial Electric & Equipment Service, 238, 475
Armstrong v. McDonald, 925
Armstrong v. Mailand, 230, 430, 495, 497
Armstrong v. Mongomery Street Railway Co., 291
Armstrong v. New Orleans Public Service, 245
Armstrong v. Warner Brothers Theatres, 176
Armstrong County v. Clarion County, 337
Armstrong Packing Co. v. Clem, 682
Armstrong Rubber Co. v. Griffith, 665
Armstrong Seatag Corp. v. Smith's Island Oyster Co., 1021
Arne v. Johnson, 782
Arneil v. Peterson, 325
Arneson v. City of Fargo, 164
Arnett v. Missouri Pacific Railroad Co., 335
Arnett v. Yeago, 200, 201
Arnold v. Burgess, 1024
Arnold v. Frigid Feed Express Co., 10
Arnold v. Ingram, 799, 803, 811
Arnold v. Laird, 183
Arnold v. Moffitt, 985
Arnold v. Owens, 467
Arnold v. Producer's Oil Co., 967
Arnold v. St. Louis & San Francisco Railroad Co., 925
Arnold v. Sayings Co., 838
Arnold v. Walters, 441
Arnold v. Wiley, 126
Arnst v. Estes, 327, 347
Aronson v. Orlov, 1022
Arp v. State, 129
Arredondo v. Duckwall Stores, Inc., 479
Arrington, Estate of v. Fields, 203
Arritt v. Fisher, 937
Arsnow v. Red Top Cab Co., 311

Artigue v. South Central Bell Telephone Co., 182
Artloom Corp. v. National Better Business Bureau, 974
Arvey Corp. v. Peterson, 799, 823
Arvidson v. Reynolds Metals Co., 70, 71
Aschermann v. Philip Best Brewing Co., 100
Asevado v. Orr, 894
Ash v. Cohn, 899
Ashalter v. Peterson, 762
Ashburn v. Miller, 752
Ashby v. Peters, 746
Ashby v. White, 3, 56
Ashcraft v. Tucker, 98
Ashcroft v. Hammond, 829, 833
Asheim v. Gahey, 445
Ashelford v. Illinois Northern Utilities Co., 662
Asher v. City of Independence, 303
Asheville Construction Co. v. Southern Railway Co., 68, 553
Ashland v. Lapiner Motor Co., 879
Ashland Dry Goods Co. v. Wages, 50
Ashley v. Dixon, 981
Ashley v. United States, 423
Ashton v. Allen, 94
Ashton v. Buchholz, 763
Ashuelot Savings Bank v. Albee, 744
Ashworth v. Baker, 530
Ashworth v. City of Clarksburg, 423
Askew v. State, 128
Aspinall v. McDonnell Douglas Corp., 947
Assets Collecting Co. v. Myers, 897
Associated Press v. KVOS, 1020
Associated Press v. Walker, 1011
Associates Discount Corp. v. Gillineau, 105
Astin v. Chicago, Milwaukee & St. Paul Railway Co., 211
Atcherson v. Siebenmann, 1064
Atchison v. Texas & Pacific Railway Co., 278
Atchison, Topeka & Santa Fe Railroad Co. v. Lan Franco, 344
Atchison, Topeka & Santa Fe Railroad Co. v. Paxton, 461
Atchison, Topeka & Santa Fe Railway Co. v. Calhoun, 309
Atchison, Topeka & Santa Fe Railway Co. v. Hamilton Brothers, 269
Atchison, Topeka & Santa Fe Railway Co. v. Henry, 210
Atchison, Topeka & Santa Fe Railway Co. v. Hinsdell, 152
Atchison, Topeka & Santa Fe Railway Co. v. McGinnis, 46
Atchison, Topeka & Santa Fe Railway Co. v. Morgan, 470
Atchison, Topeka & Santa Fe Railway Co. v. Parry, 198, 319
Atchison, Topeka & Santa Fe Railway Co. v. Schroeder, 570
Atchison, Topeka & Santa Fe Railway Co. v. Stanford, 282, 288, 292
Atchison & Northwest Railroad Co. v. Bailey, 195
Atherton v. Goodwin, 289

Atkins v. Johnson, 337
Atkins v. Perrin, 970, 974
Atkinson v. Bernard, Inc., 81
Atkinson v. Bibb Manufacturing Co., 59
Atkinson v. Birmingham, 872, 883, 884
Atkinson v. Charlotte Builders, 742
Atkinson v. Detroit Free Press Co., 831
Atkinson v. Dixie Grayhound Lines, 49
Atkinson v. John E. Doherty & Co., 850
Atkinson v. Pack, 993
Atlanta, City of v. Chattanooga Foundry & Pipeworks, 328
Atlanta, Knoxville & Northern Railway Co. v. McHan, 674
Atlanta & Charlotte Air-Line Railway Co. v. Leach, 309
Atlanta Coca-Cola Bottling Co. v. Burke, 262
Atlanta Commercial Builders, Inc. v. Polinsky, 501
Atlanta Funtown, Inc. v. Crouch, 398
Atlanta Gas Light Co. v. Brown, 650
Atlanta Hub Co. v. Bussey, 890
Atlanta Hub Co. v. Jones, 60
Atlanta Journal Co. v. Doyal, 837
Atlanta Journal Co. v. Farmer, 935
Atlanta News Publishing Co. v. Medlock, 838
Atlantic & Pacific Railway Co. v. Laird, 666
Atlantic Coast Development Corp. v. Napoleon Steel Contractors, Inc., 513, 524
Atlantic Coast Line Railroad Co. v. Barrett, 579
Atlantic Coast Line Railroad Co. v. Boone, 332, 334
Atlantic Coast Line Railroad Co. v. Coxwell, 463
Atlantic Coast Line Railroad Co., United States v., 999
Atlantic Finance Corp. v. Galvam, 93
Atlantic Gas Light Co. v. Brown, 181
Atlantic Greyhound Corp. v. Austin, 13
Atlantic Greyhound Lines v. Skinner, 482
Atlantic Trust & Deposit Co. v. Union Trust & Title Corp., 739
Atlas Coal Corp. v. Scales, 575
Attleboro Manufacturing Co. v. Frankfort Marine Accident & Plate Glass Insurance Co., 661
Attorney-General v. Corke, 538, 553
Attorney-General v. Cory Bros., 538, 547
Attorney-General v. Dublin United Tramways Co., 998
Attorney General v. Great Western R. Co., 544
Attorney General v. Jamaica Pond Aqueduct Corp., 643
Attorney-General v. Tomline, 547
Attorney General v. Utica Ins. Co., 643
Attorney-General v. Valle-Jones, 998
Attorney-General ex rel. Muskegon Booming Co. v. Evart Booming Co., 645
Attorney-General for New South Wales v. Perpetual Trustee Co., 998
Attwood v. City of Bangor, 638
Attwood v. Estate of Attwood, 906
Atwater v. Morning News Co., 841
Atwater v. Sawyer, 662
Atwood v. Chapman, 737
Atwood v. Higgins, 912
Aubrey v. School District of Philadelphia, 1049
Auburn v. Amoco Oil Co., 435

Augspurger v. Western Auto Supply Co., 260
Augusta Bank & Trust v. Broomfield, 11
Augustin v. General Accident Fire & Life Assurance Corp., 340
Augustine v. Trucco, 982, 990
Auld v. Globe Indemnity Co., 340
Ault v. Hall, 535
Ault v. International Harvester Co., 715
Ault v. Kuiper, 310
Aultman, Miller & Co. v. Nelson, 766
Aune v. Oregon Trunk Railway, 313
Aunt Jemima Mills Co. v. Rigney & Co., 756, 758
Ausmer v. Sliman, 401
Austen v. Willward, 323, 325, 329
Austin v. Austin, 716
Austin v. Beuttner, 423, 439
Austin v. Bridges, 513
Austin v. Carswell, 8
Austin v. Culpepper, 786
Austin v. Metropolitan Life Insurance Co., 131
Austin Gaslight Co. v. Anderson, 953
Australian Newspaper Co. v. Bennett, 965, 966
Automobile Insurance Co. of Hartford Connecticut v. Guaranty Securities Corp., 987
Avellone v. St. Johns Hospital, 596
Avery v. Maxwell, 540
Avery v. Palmer, 207
Avery v. Wilson, 1073
Avins v. White, 807, 814
Avner v. Longridge Estates, 721
Aweeka v. Bonds, 1028
Axton-Fisher Tobacco Co. v. Evening Post Co., 779, 780
Ayer v. Bartlett, 104
Ayers v. French, 90
Ayers v. Grider, 780
Ayers v. Stidham, 649, 650
Aymond v. State Through Department of Highways, 948
Ayre v. Craven, 792
Ayres & Co., L.S. v. Hicks, 376, 377
Azar v. Lehigh Corp., 987, 1002
Azura v. City of Billings, 376
Azzarello v. Black Brothers Co., 699

B

B & B Insulation, Inc. v. Occupational Safety and Health Review Commission, 175
B.P. Oil Corp. v. Mabe, 508
Babb v. Bolyard, 751, 753, 758
Babb v. Carson, 155
Babb v. Superior Court of Sonoma County, 892
Babcock v. Chesapeake & Ohio Railway Co., 196
Baber v. Fitzgerald, 890
Babin v. Zurich Ins. Co., 180
Babington v. Bogdanovic, 521
Babington v. Yellow Taxi Corp., 173
Babson Brothers Co. v. Allison, 986
Baca v. Britt, 669
Bacak v. Hogya, 722

Bach v. Liberty Mutual Fire Insurance Co., 520
Bach v. Penn Central Transportation Co., 953
Bachelder v. Heagan, 544
Bachman v. Young Women's Christian Association, 1070
Bacich v. Northland Transportation Co., 331
Backer v. Pizza Inn, Inc., 419, 425, 427
Backus v. Ames, 382
Backus v. Look, Inc., 800
Backus v. West, 143
Bacon v. City of Boston, 567, 633
Bacon v. Michigan Central Railroad Co., 798
Bacon v. St. Paul Union Stockyards Co., 992, 1006
Bacon v. Sheppard, 78
Bacon v. Towne, 877
Bacsick v. Barnes, 389
Badame v. Lampke, 792
Badgley v. Decker, 927, 928
Baeder, State ex rel. v. Blake, 941
Baer v. Chambers, 888
Baer v. Hepfinger, 932
Baer v. Slater, 97
Bagby v. Kansas City, 395, 403
Baggett v. McCormack, 105
Bagley v. City of St. Louis, 949
Bagre v. Daggett Chocolate Co., 232, 262, 457
Bahlman v. Hudson Motor Car Co., 751
Bahm v. Pittsburgh & Lake Erie Railroad Co., 456
Bail v. Pennsylvania R. Co., 141
Bailey v. Banister, 994
Bailey v. Blacker, 390
Bailey v. Bussing, 337
Bailey v. Central Vermont Railway Co., 578, 579
Bailey v. Charleston Mail Association, 831
Bailey v. City of Centerville, 517
Bailey v. J.L. Roebuck Co., 458
Bailey v. McGill, 817
Bailey v. Morris, 479
Bailey v. Oatis, 765
Bailey v. Warner, 48
Bailey v. Zlotnick, 446
Baily v. State, 454
Bain v. Atkins, 586
Bain v. Phillips, 876
Baines v. Baker, 640
Bains v. Dank, 445
Bains v. Price, 673
Bains v. Western Pacific Railway Co., 214
Bair v. Shoultz, 872
Baird v. Aluminum Seal Co., 892
Baird v. Carle, 836, 922
Baird v. Chesapeake & Potomac Telephone Co., 1000
Baird v. Chicago, Burlington & Quincy Railroad Co., 952
Baird v. Hosmer, 1060
Baird v. Howard, 93, 672, 725
Baird v. Sickler, 501
Baird v. Williamson, 547
Baker, In re, 673
Baker v. B.F. Goodrich Co., 247
Baker v. Beers, 102

Baker v. Bolton, 940, 945
Baker v. Clark, 829
Baker v. Coca-Cola Bottling Works, 713
Baker v. Combs, 766
Baker v. Commonwealth, 128
Baker v. F. & F. Investment, 1033, 1037
Baker v. Hallam, 736, 744
Baker v. Howard County Hunt, 539
Baker v. Kale, 965
Baker v. Lumberton, 1054
Baker v. Snell, 564
Baker v. State, 374, 831
Baker, State v., 44, 46
Baker v. State Board of Higher Education, 1052
Baker v. Story, 187
Baker v. Straumfjord, 1066
Baker v. Superior Court, 493, 497
Baker v. Superior Court for County of Orange, 430, 431
Baker v. Thompson-Hayward Chemical Co., 245
Baker v. Troy Compress Co., 103
Baker v. Winslow, 794
Baker v. Young, 912
Baker Realty Co. v. Baker, 1017
Bakersfield Religious Congregational Society v. Baker, 77
Bakker v. Welsh, 115
Bakunas v. Life Pack, Inc., 183
Balabanoff v. Fossani, 803, 811
Balcom v. City of Independence, 175
Baldassarre v. West Oregon Lumber Co., 576
Balden v. Shorter, 963, 970
Baldinger v. Banks, 36, 41
Baldocchi v. Four Fifty Sutter Corp., 649
Baldock v. Johnson, 760
Baldwin v. Bohl, 675
Baldwin v. Cole, 99
Baldwin v. Davis, 897
Baldwin v. Elphinstone, 799
Baldwin v. Greenwoods Turnpike Co., 317
Baldwin v. Hayden, 139
Baldwin v. McClendon, 632
Baldwin v. McEldowney, 442
Baldwin v. Zoradi, 202
Balfe v. Kramer, 264, 306
Balido v. Improved Machinery Inc., 205, 689, 700
Ball v. Bruce, 927, 928
Ball v. Liney, 100
Ball v. Nye, 548, 549
Ball v. Rawles, 819, 879
Ball v. Roane, 781
Ball v. T.J. Pardy Construction Co., 1000
Ball & Brother Lumber Co. v. Simms Lumber Co., 75
Ballard v. Anderson, 115
Ballard v. North British R. Co., 224
Ballard v. Tomlinson, 546
Ballenger v. City of Grand Saline, 645
Ballenger v. Crowell, 166
Ballenger v. Liberty National Life Insurance Co., 91
Ballew v. Alexander, 8
Ballow v. Reeves, 601

TABLE OF CASES

Balmain New Ferry Co. v. Robertson, 52
Baloyan v. Furniture Exhibition Building Co., 758
Balsiger v. American Steel & Supply Co., 891
Baltimore, City of v. Fairfield Improvement Co., 620, 629
Baltimore & Ohio Railroad Co. v. Cain, 153
Baltimore & Ohio Railroad Co. v. Kreager, 544
Baltimore & Ohio Railroad Co. v. O'Donnell, 106
Baltimore & Ohio Railroad Co. v. State to Use of Woodward, 382
Baltimore & Ohio Railroad Co. v. Sulphur Spring Independent School District, 266
Baltimore & Ohio Railway v. Goodman, 218, 237
Baltimore & Potomac Railroad Co. v. Landrigan, 240
Baltimore City Passenger Railway Co. v. Kemp, 292, 660
Baltimore County v. State, Use of Keenan, 489
Baltrunas v. Baubles, 918
Balts v. Balts, 595
Bamert v. Central General Hospital, 186
Banaghan v. Dewey, 723
Bancroft v. Godwin, 445
Bancroft-Whitney Co. v. Glen, 996
Bander v. Metropolitan Life Insurance Co., 786, 829
Banfield v. Addington, 661
Bang v. Charles T. Miller Hospital, 120
Bangert v. Hubbard, 14
Bank v. Bank, 924
Bank of America v. McNeil, 99
Bank of Montreal v. Thayer, 744
Bankers Bond Co. v. Cox, 761
Bankers' Fire & Marine Insurance Co. v. Sloss, 994
Banks v. Dalbey, 166
Banks v. King Features Syndicate, 857
Banks v. Maxwell, 542
Bankston v. Dumont, 85, 87, 90
Banner v. Lyon & Healy Co., 761
Bannister v. Mitchell, 10, 38
Banque de France v. Equitable Trust Co., 100
Barabe v. Dunkrkop Oven Co., 723
Baran v. City of Chicago Heights, 1053
Baran v. Goodyear Tire & Rubber Co., 1013
Baran v. Silverman, 30
Baratta, State v., 128
Barb v. Farmers Insurance Exchange, 340, 441
Barbee v. Rogers, 720
Barber v. Hohl, 14
Barber v. Time, Inc., 856, 859, 861, 868
Barberton, City of v. Miksch, 72, 552, 624
Barbieri v. Jennings, 199
Barbieri v. News-Journal Co., 851
Barbknecht v. Great Northern Railway Co., 58
Barbour v. Stephenson, 927
Barbre v. Indianapolis Water Co., 393, 394, 407, 409
Barcia v. Estate of Keil, 242, 246
Barclay v. Burlington Northern, Inc., 218
Bard v. Yohn, 325
Barfield v. South Highland Infirmary, 113
Barfoot v. Reynolds, 130
Barham v. Baca, 445

Barham v. Dennis, 924
Barham v. Standridge, 139
Barish v. Chrysler Corp., 1024
Barker v. Brown, 391
Barker v. City of Philadelphia, 289
Barker v. Dinsmore, 94
Barker v. Dowdy, 921
Barker v. Furlong, 95
Barker v. Herbert, 546, 547
Barker v. Lull Engineering Co., 698, 701, 702
Barker v. Miller, 103
Barker v. Retail Credit Co., 829
Barker v. Waltz, 884
Barker v. Washburn, 48
Barker v. Western Union Telegraph Co., 1000
Barker v. Withers, 248
Barkhorn v. Adlib Associates, Inc., 963
Barley's Administratrix v. Clover Splint Coal Co., 946
Barlow v. Barnes, 919
Barlow v. Lowery, 937
Barlye v. Martin, 325
Barnard Co., Geo. D. v. Lane, 286
Barnes v. Campbell, 809
Barnes v. Clayton House Motel, 803
Barnes v. Crawford, 788
Barnes v. Martin, 140
Barnes v. Masterson, 348
Barnes v. Towlson, 502
Barnes v. Town of Marcus, 517
Barnes v. Zettlemoyer, 551
Barnes Coal Corp. v. Retail Coal Merchants Association, 944
Barnet v. New York Central & Hudson River Railroad Co., 316
Barnet Manufacturing Co., In re, 765
Barnett v. Allen, 776
Barnett v. Atlantic City Electric Co., 413
Barnett v. Bachrach, 117, 119
Barnett v. Collection Service Co., 61, 64
Barnett v. Des Moines Electric Co., 308
Barnett v. Kunkle, 759
Barnett v. Levy, 521
Barnett v. Loud, 818
Barnett v. Phelps, 789, 793
Barnette v. Woody, 898
Barnhill v. Davis, 366
Barnhizer v. Paradise Valley Unified School District, 400, 407, 409
Barnum v. Handschiegel, 550, 564
Barquin v. Hall Oil Co., 972
Barr v. Birkner, 809
Barr v. County of Albany, 1063
Barr v. Matteo, 822, 1060
Barr v. Post, 138
Barrabee v. Crescenta Mutual Water Co., 515
Barragan v. Superior Court of Pima County, 942
Barroe v. Watterson Hotel Co., 574
Barrett v. Lake Ontario Beach Improvement Co., 438
Barrett v. Stoneburg, 437
Barrett v. White, 151

Barrette v. Franki Compressed Pile Co., 548
Barringer v. Arnold, 266
Barron v. Liedloff, 444
Barron Estate Co., Edward v. Woodruff Co., 738, 754
Barrons v. Ball, 781
Barrow v. Georgia Lightweight Aggregate Co., 77
Barrows v. Bell, 830, 836
Barrus v. Wilkinson, 341
Barry v. Baugh, 790
Barry v. McCollom, 822, 830, 975
Barry v. New York Central & Hudson River Railroad Co., 413
Barry v. Southern Pacific Railway Co., 465
Barry, State v., 44
Barry v. Third Avenue Railroad Co., 54
Barstow v. Sprague, 77
Bartak v. Bell-Galyardt & Wells, Inc., 240
Bartel v. Ridgefield Lumber, Co., 552, 625
Bartell v. State, 120, 725
Bartels v. City of Williston, 476
Bartels v. Continental Oil Co., 430
Bartels v. Westchester County, 383, 1048
Barth v. Stewart, 126
Bartholomae Corp. v. United States, 1040
Bartholomay v. St. Thomas Lumber Co., 958
Bartholomew v. Workman, 852
Bartie v. United States, 1041
Bartleson v. Glen Alden Coal Co., 404
Bartlett v. Christhilf, 899
Bartlett v. Federal Outfitting Co., 964, 992
Bartlett v. Grasselli Chemical Co., 70
Bartlett v. Gregg, 570
Bartlett v. MacRae, 186, 453
Bartlett, State v., 127
Bartlett v. Taylor, 382
Bartlett v. Tottenham, 546
Bartletta v. McFeeley, 864
Bartoletti v. Kushner, 180
Barton v. Barton, 329, 349
Barton v. Bee Line, 123
Barton v. Rex-Oil Co., 1016
Barton v. United States, 1042
Barton v. Woodward, 894
Bartos v. United States District Court, 789
Bartosh v. Banning, 129
Bartow v. Smith, 61
Bartz v. Wheat, 524, 526
Baruch v. Beech Aircraft Corp., 1000
Barwick v. Barwick, 103
Barylski v. Paul, 1072
Bascho v. Pennsylvania Railroad Co., 378
Bascom v. Dempsey, 78
Bascom v. Hoffman, 126
Baselski v. City of Chicago, 1062
Basely v. Clarkson, 9, 24
Basko v. Sterling Drug Co., 267
Bass v. Aetna Insurance Co., 162
Bass v. Hunt, 425
Bass v. Nooney Co., 364
Bass v. Seaboard Airline Railway Co., 461

Bass v. State, 152
Bassett v. New York, Chicago & St. Louis Railroad Co., 569
Bassi v. Bassi, 588
Bassinov v. Finkle, 878
Basso v. Miller, 433
Bastedo v. Frailey, 958
Bastrup v. Prendergast, 734
Batchelder v. Birchard Motors, 755
Batchelder v. Stephenson, 762
Batcheller v. Tunbridge Wells Gas Co., 546
Bateman v. Ursich, 216
Bates v. Clark, 159
Bates v. Quality Ready-Mix Co., 638, 640
Batiste v. American Home Products Corp., 706
Batiste v. Boh Brothers Construction Co., 403
Batson, State v., 37
Battaglia v. Adams, 863
Battersby v. Collier, 832
Battilla v. Allis Chalmers Manufacturing Co., 168
Battle v. Kilcrease, 9
Battle v. Morris, 331
Batts v. Faggart, 312
Batts v. Home Telephone & Telegraph Co., 418
Bauer v. Harn, 412
Bauer v. Johnson, 523, 531
Bauer v. 141-149 Cedar Lane Holding Co., 382, 445
Baugher v. A. Hattersley & Sons, Inc., 506
Baughman Surgical Associates, Limited v. Aetna Casualty & Surety Co., 998
Baumann v. Baumann, 852
Baumgartner v. Pennsylvania Railroad Co., 569
Baumgartner v. State Farm Insurance Co., 464
Bausewine v. Norristown Herald, Inc., 847
Bavington v. Robinson, 826
Baxley v. Williams Construction Co., 429
Baxter v. Ford Motor Co., 744
Baxter v. Grobmyer Brothers Construction Co., 490, 492
Baxter v. State, 127, 128
Baxter v. Superior Court of Los Angeles, 934
Baxter v. Woodward, 102
Bay Area Rapid Transit District v. Superior Court, 430, 431
Bayer v. Winton Motor Car Co., 675, 730
Bayliss v. Grand Lodge of State of Louisiana, 830
Baynes v. Brewster, 154
Bays v. Cox' Administrator, 959
Bays v. Hunt, 975
Bazemore v. Savannah Hospital, 859
Bazos v. Chouinard, 402, 406, 407
Bazydlo v. Placid Marcy Co., 456
Beach v. Fleming, 764
Beach v. Hancock, 9, 46
Beach v. Ranney, 794
Beach v. Sterling Iron & Zinc Co., 552, 619, 634
Beach v. Trudgain, 146
Beachcomber Coins, Inc. v. Boskett, 729
Beachey v. Brown, 737
Beakley v. Houston Oil & Minerals Corp., 251
Beal v. Hayward, 1074

Beall v. Lo-Vaca Gathering Co., 447
Beall v. McGehee, 759
Beals v. Hayward, 163
Beals v. Walker, 195, 220, 231, 238
Beaman v. Grooms, 438
Bear v. Harriss, 151
Bear v. Reformed Mennonite Church, 919, 923, 1025
Bearbower v. Merry, 917, 919, 930
Bearce v. United States, 1040
Beard v. Brown, 219, 503
Beardlsey v. Wierdsma, 372
Beardmore v. T.D. Burgess Co., 768
Beardsley v. Kilmer, 1010
Beare v. Wright, 767
Beasley v. Baltimore & Potomac Railroad Co., 100
Beasley v. Grand Trunk Western Railway Co., 218
Beasley v. United States, 959
Beatty v. Central Iowa Railway Co., 172
Beatty v. Gilbanks, 318
Beaubeauf v. Reid, 1074
Beauchamp v. B. & L. Motor Freight, Inc., 514
Beauchamp v. Los Gatos Golf Course, 182
Beauchamp v. Saginaw Mining Co., 291, 310
Beauchamp v. Sturges & Burn Manufacturing Co., 581
Beauchene v. Synanon Foundation, Inc., 164, 165
Beaudette v. Frana, 903, 909
Beaudette v. Gagne, 928
Beaudoin v. Watertown Memorial Hospital, 253
Beauharnais v. Pittsburgh Courier Publishing Co., 832
Beaulieu v. Fingham, 543
Beaumaster v. Crandall, 175
Beaumont v. Brown, 858
Beauregard v. Wingard, 1060, 1066
Beavers v. Bowen, 126
Beavers v. Calloway, 130
Beccue v. Rockford Park District, 255
Bechel v. Pacific Express Co., 877
Becher v. Great Eastern Railroad Co., 103
Bechtel v. Bohannon, 743
Beck v. Bel Air Properties, 551
Beck & Gregg Hardware Co. v. Associated Transport, Inc., 662
Beck v. Indiana Surveying Co., 517
Beck v. Minneapolis Union Railway Co., 125
Beck v. Stanley Co. of America, 172
Beck v. The German Klinik, 384
Beck Shoe Corp., A.S. v. Johnson, 1010, 1026
Beckendorf v. Simmons, 503
Becker v. American Airlines, Inc., 253
Becker v. Becker, 1074
Becker v. Eisenstodt, 256
Becker v. Hidalgo, 187
Becker v. Interstate Properties, 510
Becker v. Philco Corp., 824
Becker v. Rieck, 906
Becker v. Schwartz, 371
Beckham v. Collins, 888
Beckham, State v., 135, 155
Beckler v. Yates, 922
Beckman v. Marshall, 628

Beckovsky v. Burton Abstract & Tile Co., 747
Beckwith v. Bean, 48, 53
Beckwith v. Independent Transfer & Storage Co., 95, 98
Beckwith v. Philby, 110, 153
Beckwith v. Somerset Theatres, 389
Beckwith v. State Farm Fire & Casualty Co., 184, 417, 460
Beckwith v. Town of Stratford, 648
Bedan v. Turney, 917
Beddall v. Maitland, 144
Bedell v. Daugherty, 763
Bedell v. Reagan, 337, 339
Bedford v. McKowl, 927
Bednarik v. Bednarik, 855
Beecher v. Dull, 619
Beechley v. Beechley, 734
Beechley v. Mulville, 324
Beech-Nut, Inc. v. Warner-Lambert Co., 1019
Beede v. Nides Finance Corp., 87
Beedle v. Carolan, 335
Beekman v. Marsters, 981, 987
Beers v. Atlas Assurance Co., 764
Beers v. McGinnis, 73
Beggs v. McCrea, 817, 820
Beggs v. Wilson, 180
Begin v. Liederbach Bus Co., 328
Begley v. Louisville Times Co., 836
Begole v. Ferguson, 941
Behrens v. Bertram Mills Circus, Ltd., 542, 543, 547, 564
Behrens v. McKenzie, 1073, 1074
Behring International, Inc. v. National Labor Relations Board, 899, 1029
Behymer v. Milgram Food Stores, 14
Beinhorn v. Griswold, 540
Beisel v. Gerlach, 922
Beiser v. Scripps-McRae Publishing Co., 818, 837
Bejnarowicz v. Bakos, 581
Bekkeland v. Lyons, 885
Bekken v. Equitable Life Assurance Society of United States, 981
Bekkevold v. Potts, 680
Belcher v. Carter, 121
Belcher v. City & County of San Francisco, 182
Belk v. Boyce, 226
Belk v. Jones Construction Co., 724
Bell v. Baker, 732
Bell v. Bank of Abbeville, 827
Bell v. Courier-Journal & Louisville Times Co., 859
Bell v. Gray-Robinson Construction Co., 628
Bell v. Great Northern Railway, 364
Bell v. Horton, 415, 418
Bell v. Industrial Vangas, Inc., 577
Bell v. Jewel Tea Co., 879
Bell v. Keepers, 730, 871
Bell v. Stone, 775
Bell v. West, 525
Dell Finance Co. v. Gefter, 104
Bell Lumber Co. v. Bayfield Transfer Railway Co., 303
Bell Publishing Co. v. Garrett Engineering Co., 842
Bellacome v. Bailey, 172

Belle of the Sea, The, 756
Bellere v. Madsen, 251
Bellflower v. Pennise, 404, 405, 411
Belli v. Forsyth, 105
Bellino v. Columbus Construction Co., 312
Bello v. Random House, Inc., 778
Bellotte v. Zayre Corp., 692, 698
Bellows v. Worcester Storage Co., 312, 313
Belmar Drive-In Theatre Co. v. Illinois State Toll Highway Commission, 628
Belo Corp., A.H. v. Sanders, 971
Belshaw v. Bush, 330
Bence v. Crawford Savings & Loan Association, 383
Bence v. Teddy's Taxi, 465
Bender v. Weber, 438
Bender v. Welsh, 540
Benderach v. Grujicich, 888
Benedict v. Heirs of Dickens, 761
Benedict v. Podwats, 414
Benedict Pineapple Co. v. Atlantic Coast Line Railroad Co., 304
Benevides v. Lucio, 145
Benjamin v. American Telephone & Telegraph Co., 73
Benjamin v. Deffet Rentals, Inc., 488, 489
Benjamin F. Shaw Co. v. Musgrave, 575
Bennan v. Parsonnet, 119
Benner v. Atlantic Dredging Co., 567
Benner v. Philadelphia & Reading Railway Co., 218
Bennett v. Allcott, 927, 928
Bennett v. Austro-Americana Steamship Co., 51
Bennett v. Bennett, 925, 926
Bennett v. Black, 872
Bennett v. Fifield, 326
Bennett v. Geblein, 199
Bennett v. Gitzen, 179
Bennett v. Hymers, 368, 369
Bennett v. Illinois Power & Light Corp., 171
Bennett v. McIntire, 45, 112
Bennett v. Nations, 649
Bennett v. New Jersey Railroad & Transportation Co., 530
Bennett v. Norban, 786, 858, 864
Bennett v. Southern Railway Co., 172, 306
Bennett v. Span Industries, Inc., 236, 358, 497
Bennett v. Stockwell, 816
Bennett Ford, Walt v. Pulaski County Special School District, 984, 1011
Benoit v. Fireman's Fund Insurance Co., 959, 960
Benoit v. Perkins, 726
Ben-Oliel v. Press Publishing Co., 777, 780
Benson v. Baltimore Traction Co., 413
Benson v. Brady, 471
Benson v. Bunting, 760
Benson v. Dean, 207, 726
Benson v. Garrett Investment Co., 765
Benson v. Hygienic Artificial Ice Co., 574
Benson v. Lynch, 943
Benson v. Ross, 271
Benson, State v., 133
Bentley v. Fischer Lumber & Manufacturing Co., 312

Bentley v. Teton, 985
Bentley, Murray & Co. v. La Salle St. Trust & Savings Bank, 91
Benton v. Kernan, 437
Benton v. Pittard, 629
Benton v. Sloss, 703
Berea Stone Co. v. Kraft, 572
Bereman v. Power Publishing Co., 830
Beresford v. White, 820
Berg v. General Motors Corp., 708
Berg v. Great Northern Railway Co., 308
Berg v. Minneapolis Star & Tribune Co., 856, 859, 861
Berg v. Reaction Motors Division, Thiokol Chemical Corp., 549, 558
Berger v. Jacobs, 932
Berger v. Levy, 919
Berger v. Minneapolis Gaslight Co., 549
Berger v. Podolsky Brothers, 328
Berger v. Shapiro, 417, 418, 494
Berger v. Southern Pacific Co., 507
Berger v. Weber, 359, 935
Bergeron v. Illinois Central Gulf Railroad Co., 218
Berghammer v. Mayer, 927
Bergman v. Hendrickson, 506
Bergmann v. United States, 384
Bergstreser v. Mitchell, 369
Bergstrom v. Ridgway Co., 848
Berjian, D.O., Inc., Richard A. v. Ohio Bell Telephone Co., 482
Berkebile v. Brantley Helicopter Corp., 233, 686
Berkeley v. Park, 718
Berkey v. Berwind-White Coal Mining Co., 631
Berko v. Freda, 430
Berkovitz v. American River Gravel Co., 294
Berkowitz v. Winston, 443
Berkson v. Kansas City Cable Railway Co., 327
Berman v. Allan, 371
Berman v. Medical Society of New York, 964
Bermudez v. Jenkins, 197
Bernard v. Russell, 176
Bernard Food Industries, Inc. v. Dietene Co., 1019
Berndtson v. Lewis, 1067
Bernesak v. Catholic Bishop of Chicago, 213
Bernethy v. Walt Failor's, Inc., 199
Bernhardt, United States v., 406
Bernier v. Boston Edison Co., 389
Bernitsky v. United States, 1042
Bernstein v. Lily-Tulip Cup Corp., 694
Bernstein v. National Broadcasting Co., 853, 861
Bernstein v. Queens County Jockey Club, 941
Berot v. Porte, 833
Berrier v. Beneficial Finance, Inc., 62, 858
Berroyer v. Hertz, 190
Berry v. Borough of Sugar Notch, 316, 457
Berry v. Carle, 136
Berry v. City of New York Insurance Co., 799
Berry v. Donovan, 983, 996
Berry v. Empire Indemnity Insurance Co., 475
Berry v. Moench, 828
Berry v. Pullman Co., 335

Berry v. Shell Petroleum Co., 550
Berry v. Stevens, 738
Berry v. Sugar Notch Borough, 264, 306
Berry v. Visser, 305
Berryhill v. Nichols, 265
Berry's Sons Co., James B. v. Presnall, 458
Bertero v. National General Corp., 887, 893, 895, 896
Bertheol, State v., 644
Berthon v. Cartwright, 922
Bertie v. Beaumont, 77
Bertone v. Turco Products, Inc., 340
Bertram v. Reed Automobile Co., 756
Bertsch v. Brewer, 455
Berwald v. Kasal, 186
Berzito v. Gambino, 722
Berzon v. Don Allen Motors, Inc., 703
Besette v. Enderlin School District No. 22, pp. 193, 195
Beshada v. Johns-Manville Products Corp., 698
Besner v. Central Trust Co. of New York, 512, 513
Bess v. Citizens Telephone Co., 662
Bessey v. Salemme, 530
Best v. District of Columbia, 401
Best v. Yerkes, 337, 338
Best Steel Buildings, Inc. v. Hardin, 503
Bethay v. Philadelphia Housing Authority, 240, 398, 404, 409, 411
Bethell v. Bethell, 759
Bethlahmy v. Bechtel, 721
Bethlehem Fabricators v. H.D. Watts Co., 941
Bethlehem Shipbuilding Corp. v. Joseph Gutradt Co., 342
Better Food Markets v. American District Telegraph Co., 666
Bettolo v. Safeway Stores, Inc., 141
Betts v. Gibbins, 337
Betzold v. Erickson, 181
Beverly Bank v. Penn Central Co., 398
Beverly Beach Club v. Marron, 419
Bexiga v. Havir Manufacturing Corp., 1073
Beyer v. Birmingham Railway Light & Power Co., 127
Biakanja v. Irving, 1000
Bias v. Ausbury, 937
Bias v. Montgomery Elevator Co. of Kansas, Inc., 253
Bibb Broom Corn Co. v. Atchison, Topeka & Santa Fe Railway Co., 315
Biber Brothers News Co. v. New York Evening Post, 988
Bice v. Brown, 913
Bichan v. Chemetron Corp., 1029
Bickel v. Mackie, 891
Bickford v. Nolen, 210
Bicknell v. Dorion, 873
Biddle v. Bond, 100
Biederman's of Springfield, Inc. v. Wright, 858
Bieker v. Owens, 915
Biel, Inc. v. Kirsch, 328
Bielitski v. Obadiak, 61, 64
Bielski v. Schulze, 341, 478
Bierkamp v. Rogers, 217
Bierczynski v. Rogers, 323

Bierzynski v. New York Central Railroad Co., 716
Big O Tire Dealers, Inc. v. Goodyear Tire & Rubber Co., 966, 971, 972, 1015, 1016
Bigaouette v. Paulet, 917, 918
Bigbee v. Pacific Telephone & Telegraph Co., 358
Bigelow v. Barnes, 764
Bigelow v. Brumley, 794, 820
Bigelow v. Johnson, 456
Bigelow v. Sprague, 799, 800
Biggers v. Continental Bus System, 299
Biggerstaff v. Zimmerman, 793
Biggs v. Biggs, 922
Biggs v. Griffith, 645
Biggs v. McCarty, 368
Biggs v. Seufferlein, 139
Bigner v. Hodges, 819
Bihler v. Gockley, 790
Bihm v. Hirsch, 75
Bilams v. Metropolitan Transit Authority, 200
Billig v. Goodrich, 673
Billings v. Atkinson, 851
Billings v. Fairbanks, 835
Billingsley v. Benefield, 766
Billington v. Interinsurance Exchange of Southern California, 588
Billington v. Vest, 764
Billmayer v. Sanford, 574
Billo v. Allegheny Steel Co., 575
Billups Petroleum Co. v. Entrekin, 317
Billy v. Consolidated Machine Tool Corp., 577
Bilyeu v. Standard Freight Lines, 308
Bimberg v. Northern Pacific Railway Co., 195
Binder v. General Motors Acceptance Corp., 138
Bingham v. Gaynor, 822, 831, 841
Binns v. Vitagraph Co. of America, 852, 858
Birch v. Benton, 789
Birch v. Boston & Maine Railroad, 634
Birchfield v. Birchfield, 922
Birckhead v. Mayor and City Council of Baltimore, 285
Birckhead v. Sammon, 558
Bird v. Holbrook, 135
Bird v. Jones, 47
Bird v. Lynn, 323
Bird v. McGoldrick, 1064
Bird v. Randall, 1003
Bird v. Richardson, 198
Bird v. St. Paul Fire & Marine Insurance Co., 282
Birdsall v. Duluth-Superior Transit Co., 252
Birdsall v. Lewis, 51
Birdsall v. Smith, 876, 878
Birdsong v. City of Chattanooga, 418
Birmingham Broadcasting Co. v. Bell, 852, 977
Birmingham Railway Light & Power Co. v. Glenn, 58
Birmingham Waterworks Co. v. Brooks, 9
Birnbaum v. Blunt, 528
Birnbuam v. United States, 867
Biro v. Schombert, 950
Birwood Paper Co. v. Damsky, 876
Bisbee Co., Guy T. v. Granite City Investment Co., 765
Bischoff v. Cheney, 539

Bisgaard v. Duvall, 52, 155
Bishop v. Byrne, 18
Bishop v. City of Chicago, 374
Bishop v. E.A. Strout Realty Agency, 752
Bishop v. Glazener, 922
Bishop v. Hamad, 200, 419
Bishop v. Journal Newspaper Co., 799
Bishop v. Liston, 123
Bishop v. Mayor, etc., of Macon, 146
Bishop v. Minton, 734
Bishop v. New York Times Co., 794
Bishop v. Ranney, 43
Bishop v. St. Paul City Railway Co., 283, 291
Bishop v. Shurly, 115
Bishop v. Small, 750, 758
Bishop v. Specter, 664
Bishop v. Weber, 716
Bishop v. Wometco Enterprises, Inc., 831
Bishop Processing Co. v. Davis, 648
Bistline v. Ney Brothers, 581
Bitterman v. Louisville & Nashville Railroad Co., 987
Bittner v. Little, 333
Bivens v. Six Unknown Named Agents of Federal Bureau of Narcotics, 867, 944, 1061
Bixby v. Dunlap, 9
Bixby v. Thurber, 318, 450
Bixenman v. Hall, 181
Bjornquist v. Boston & Albany Railroad Co., 134
Black v. Bringhurst, 330
Black v. Circuit Court of Eighth Judicial District, 644
Black v. City of Cordele, 386
Black v. Davidson, 219
Black v. Irvin, 757
Black v. Judelsohn, 890
Black v. Martin, 335
Black v. Nelson, 442
Black v. New York, New Haven & Hartford Railroad Co., 198
Black v. Partridge, 250
Black v. Solmitz, 907
Black v. State, 153
Black, State v., 159
Black v. Stith, 222
Black & Yates v. Mahogany Association, 976
Blacka v. James, 270
Blackburn v. Boise School Bus Co., 245
Blackburn v. Colvin, 415
Blackburn v. Consolidated Rock Products, 425
Blackburn v. Dorta, 479, 495, 496, 498
Blackford v. Heman Construction Co., 552
Blackford v. Neaves, 139, 140
Blackham v. Pugh, 826
Blackinton v. Pillsbury, 95
Blackman v. Coffin, 8
Blackman v. Crowe, 414
Blackman v. Honer, 15
Blackman v. Howes, 752
Blackmon v. Gilmer, 897
Blackstock v. Tatum, 897
Blackwelder, State v., 153

Blackwell v. Alabama Power Co., 395
Blackwell v. American Film Co., 953, 956
Blades v. Higgs, 87, 139
Blagg v. Fred Hunt Co., 448
Blagge v. Ilsley, 926, 927
Blair v. Baltimore & Ohio Railroad Co., 578
Blair v. Berlo Vending Corp., 439
Blair v. Buttolph, 753
Blair v. Cleveland Twist Drill Co., 342
Blair v. Deakin, 354
Blair v. Eblen, 188
Blair v. Forehand, 539
Blair v. Mt. Hood Meadows Development Corp., 480, 495, 497, 498
Blair v. National Security Insurance Co., 737
Blaisdell v. Stephens, 326
Blaisdell v. Stone, 541
Blake v. Dunn Farms, Inc., 390
Blake v. Ferris, 509
Blake v. Land and House Property Corp., 546
Blake v. Lanyon, 980
Blake v. Paramount Pictures, 764
Blake v. Rupe, 1058
Blake v. Smith, 789, 913
Blake v. Woolf, 546, 567
Blake, State ex rel., Baeder v., 941
Blakeley v. Shortal's Estate, 64
Blakeslee v. Carroll, 819
Blakeslee v. Wallace, 756
Blamey v. Brown, 199
Blanchard v. Brawley, 362
Blanchard v. Claremont Eagle, 831
Blanchard v. Reliable Transfer Co., 286
Blanchard v. Wilt, 340
Bland v. Warwickshire Corp., 333
Blankenship v. Cincinnati Milacron Chemicals, Inc., 577
Blankenship v. Kansas Explorations, 84
Blankenship v. Staton, 890, 892
Blanks v. Saenger Theaters, 317
Blanton v. Kellioka Coal Co., 581
Blanton v. Sisters of Charity, 347
Blarjeske v. Thompson's Restaurant Co., 269
Blass Dry Goods Co., Gus v. Reinman & Wolfort, 620
Blatt v. McBarron, 75
Blauvelt v. Village of Nyack, 340
Blaylock v. Malernee, 397
Blazek v. McCartin, 888
Bleecker v. Colorado & Southern Railway Co., 57, 58
Bleecker v. Drury, 818, 819
Blens Chemicals v. Wyandotte Chemical Corp., 964
Blewett v. McRae, 753
Blickenstaff v. Perrin, 848
Blickman, Inc., S. v. Chilton, 722
Blin v. Campbell, 30
Bliss v. Washoe Copper Co., 631, 641
Blisscraft of Hollywood v. United Plastics Co., 1017
Blitz v. Boog, 1043
Blizzard v. Fitzsimmons, 269, 376
Block v. Pascucci, 364
Block v. Talge, 96

Block v. Urban, 704
Blocker v. Clark, 150
Blodgett v. Greenfield, 941
Blom v. United Air Lines, Inc., 947
Bloom v. Crescioni, 826
Bloom v. Fry's Food Stores, Inc., 426
Bloom v. Leech, 520
Bloomquist v. City of La Grande, 958
Bloss v. Tobey, 782
Blossom v. Barrett, 120
Blount v. TD Publishing Co., 868
Blue Grass Fair Association v. Bunnell, 513
Bluener v. Saginaw Central Oil & Gas Service, 439, 637
Blum v. William Goldman Theatres, 1003
Blume v. Ballis, 490
Blumenfeld v. Harris, 50, 121
Blumenthal v. Picture Classics, 859
Blumenthal & Co., Sidney v. United States, 984
Blumer, State ex rel. Regez v., 644
Blumhardt v. Rohr, 791
Blunk v. Atchison, Topeka & Santa Fe Railway Co., 876, 883, 888
Blunt v. Brown, 339, 340
Blunt v. Spears, 317
Bly v. Edison Electric Illuminating Co., 621
Bly v. Skaggs Drug Centers, 932
Blystone v. Kiesel, 416
Blyth v. Birmingham Waterworks Co., 170, 174, 304, 311
Blyth v. Topham, 394
Board of Commissioners of Monroe County v. Hatton, 220, 225, 230
Board of County Commissioners v. Ridenour, 473
Board of Education of Piscataway Township v. Caffiero, 529
Board of Health of Lyndhurst Township v. United Cork Companies, 629, 644
Board of Public Instruction of Dade County v. Everett W. Martin & Sons, 752
Board of Trustees of Weston County School District No. 1 v. Holso, 982, 992
Board of Water Commissioners v. Robbins & Potter, 761
Boardman v. Gore, 8
Boardman v. McNeff, 416
Boardman v. Sill, 100
Boardman v. Ward, 674
Boatman v. Miles, 570
Boatmen's National Co. v. M.W. Elkins & Co., 767
Bobb v. Bosworth, 138
Bobich v. Dackow, 346
Bobo v. Young, 72
Bock v. Lindquist, 929
Bock v. Plainfield Courier-News, 847
Bock v. Truck & Tractor, Inc., 704
Bock Leung Chew, People v., 153
Bocock v. Rose, 015
Boddy v. Henry, 742, 743
Bode v. Schmoldt, 894
Bodrey v. Cape, 868

Bodwell v. Osgood, 831
Boehringer v. Montalto, 82
Boesch v. Kick, 54
Boese v. Love, 305
Boettger v. Mauran, 572
Boggs v. Duncan-Schell Furniture Co., 27, 1006, 1009, 1014
Bogosian v. First National Bank of Millburn, 974
Bohannon v. Trotman, 1007
Bohannon v. Wachovia Bank & Trust Co., 1007
Bohm v. Chicago, Milwaukee & St. Paul Railway Co., 306
Bohn Manufacturing Co. v. Hollis, 27, 1013, 1024
Bohnen v. Wingereid, 523
Bohnsack v. Driftmier, 484
Bohri v. Barnett, 149
Boice v. Board of Education of Rock District, 1053
Boies v. Cole, 952
Boies v. Raynor, 48, 50
Boileau v. Records & Breen, 737
Boise Dodge, Inc. v. Clark, 736
Boiseau v. Morrisette, 100
Boker v. Luebbe, 523
Boland v. Ballaine, 895
Boland v. Morrill, 933
Boland v. Stanley, 917, 919, 920
Bolander v. Northern Pacific Railway Co., 260
Bolch v. Smith, 417
Bolden v. Grand Rapids Operating Corp., 663
Bolduc v. Crain, 494, 498
Boles v. La Quinta Motor Inns, 426
Bolick v. American Barmag Corp., 168
Bolick v. Gallagher, 347
Boling v. Clinton Cotton Mills, 792
Bollin v. Elevator Construction & Repair Co., 670
Bolling v. Kirby, 92, 100
Bollinger v. American Asphalt Roof Co., 634
Bolton v. Miller, 924, 926, 927
Bolton v. Stewart, 93, 114
Bolton v. Vellines, 49, 53
Bolton v. Ziegler, 334, 336
Bolus v. Martin L. Adams & Son, 465
Bolz v. Myers, 990
Bomar v. Rosser, 766
Bombard v. Newton, 541
Bonczkiewicz v. Merberg Wrecking Corp., 514
Bond v. Baltimore & Ohio Railroad Co., 284, 288, 307, 454
Bond v. Chapin, 898, 899
Bond v. Douglas, 801
Bond v. Otis Elevator Co., 250, 342
Bond v. Ramsey, 750
Bond v. St. Louis-San Francisco Railway Co., 259
Bond v. Toriello, 133
Bondar v. Ar Jay Paint Co., 251
Bondurant v. Holland, Mastin & Sales Co., 299
Bone v. Andrus, 1059, 1060
Boneau v. Swift & Co., 432
Bonfield v. Blackmore, 439
Bonhiver v. Graff, 186

TABLE OF CASES

Bonker v. Ingersoll Products Co., 691
Bonkowski v. Arlan's Department Store, 142, 798, 824
Bonkowsky v. Bonkowsky, 903
Bonnarjee v. Pike, 761
Bonner v. McDonald, 98
Bonner v. Moran, 115
Bonney v. King, 897
Bonrest v. Kotz, 368
Boogher v. Knapp, 838
Booker v. Kansas City Gas Co., 335
Boomer v. Atlantic Cement Co., 627, 629, 630, 632
Boomer v. Southern California Edison Co., 78
Boone v. Mullendore, 206, 372
Boonville Collieries Corp. v. Reynolds, 554
Boor v. Lowery, 941
Booth v. Arnold, 791
Booth v. Colgate-Palmolive Co., 1020
Booth v. Curtis Publishing Co., 853
Booth v. Krouse, 920
Booth & Brother v. Burgess, 108
Boothby v. Town of Yreka City, 439
Booth's Administrator v. Northrop, 941
Boott Mills v. Boston & Maine Railroad Co., 9
Booty v. American Finance Corp. of Shreveport, 62
Borcherding v. Eklund, 956
Borden v. Falk Co., 184
Borden v. Phillips Petroleum Co., 511
Borden's Condensed Milk Co. v. Horlick's Malted Milk Co., 1019
Borderland Hardware Co. v. Saenz, 121
Borders v. Roseberry, 435
Bordynoski v. Bergner, 238
Borel v. Fibreboard Paper Products Corp., 686, 697
Borer v. American Airlines, Inc., 359, 934, 935
Borg v. Boas, 836
Borg & Powers Furniture Co. v. Reiling, 96
Borghese v. Bartley, 256
Borgia v. City of New York, 166
Borgnis v. Falk Co., 573
Borkenstein v. Schrack, 12
Bornmann v. Star Co., 784
Boronkay v. Robinson & Carpenter, 266
Boroughs v. Joiner, 513
Borst v. Borst, 595, 907
Borsvold v. United Dairies, 620
Borton v. Mangus, 647
Borus v. Yellow Cab Co., 176, 376
Borwick, State v., 128, 130
Bose Corp. v. Consumers Union of United States, Inc., 970, 1012
Bosi v. New York Herald Co., 965, 966
Bosiljevac v. Ready Mixed Concrete Co., 396
Bosley v. Andrews, 363
Bosserman v. Smith, 718
Bost v. Metcalfe, 326
Bostian v. Jewell, 441
Bostock-Ferari Amusement Co. v. Brocksmith, 561
Boston v. Chesapeake & Ohio Railway Co., 364
Boston v. Muncy, 126, 127
Boston, City of v. Binney, 674

Boston, City of v. Simmons, 324
Boston & Maine Railroad Co. v. Armburg, 578
Boston & Maine Railroad Co. v. Small, 152
Boston Diatite Co. v. Florence Manufacturing Co., 976
Boston Glass Manufactory v. Binney, 995
Boston Housing Authority v. Hemingway, 20, 722
Boston Nutrition Society Inc. v. Stare, 779
Boswell v. Barnum & Bailey, 59, 662
Boswell v. Laird, 512
Bosworth v. Inhabitants of Swansey, 232, 457
Botelho v. Curtis, 532
Both v. Harband, 244, 250, 437
Botkin, People v., 283
Bott v. McCoy & Johnson, 94
Bottcher v. Buck, 542, 563
Bottomley v. F.W. Woolworth & Co., 803, 811
Bottum v. Kamen, 954
Bottum's Administrator v. Hawks, 400
Boucher v. New York, New Haven & Hartford Railroad Co., 511
Boucher v. Thomsen, 334
Boudinot v. State, 645
Bouillon v. Laclede Gaslight Co., 60, 77
Bouldin v. Sategna, 225
Boulfrois v. United Traction Co., 458
Boulger v. Northern Pacific Railway Co., 349
Bouligny, Inc., R.H. v. United Steelworkers of America, 779
Boulton v. Clapham, 817
Boults v. Mitchell, 73
Bounds v. Caudle, 904, 955
Bouquet v. Hackensack Water Co., 646, 647
Bourisk v. Derry Lumber Co., 897
Bourjois, Inc. v. Park Drug Co., 977
Bourland v. Baker, 913
Bourlier v. Macauley, 27
Bourn v. Beck, 969, 975
Bourne v. Bourne, 922
Bourne v. Pratt & Whitney Aircraft Corp., 10
Bourne v. Whitman, 226
Bourque v. Duplechin, 485
Boutelje v. Tarzian, 389
Boutlier v. City of Malden, 412
Boutotte v. Daigle, 938
Boutte v. Pennsylvania Millers Mutual Insurance Co., 184
Boutwell v. Champlain Realty Co., 147, 540
Boutwell v. Marr, 1024
Bovino v. Metropolitan Dade County, 393, 399
Bowalter v. Rowley Regis Corp., 571
Boward v. Leftwich, 214
Bowden v. Edison Electric Illuminating Co., 620, 621
Bowden v. Spiegel, Inc., 62, 858
Bowditch v. Boston, 146
Bowen v. Boston & Albany Railroad Co., 461, 566
Bowen v. Chemi-Cote Perlite Co., 82
Bowen v. Hall, 970, 983, 991
Bowen v. Independent Publishing Co., 777
Bowen v. Mewborn, 914
Bowen v. Morris, 988

TABLE OF CASES

Bowen v. State, 127
Bowen v. W.A. Pollard & Co., 877
Bower v. Peate, 545
Bowerman v. Detroit Free Press, 837
Bowers v. Cherokee Bob, 145
Bowers v. Schenley Distillers, Inc., 429
Bowers, State v., 128
Bowie v. Evening News, 782
Bowie, City of v. Hill, 392
Bowlan v. Lunsford, 123
Bowler v. Pacific Mills, 422
Bowles v. Indiana Railway Co., 566
Bowles v. Lindley, 352
Bowles v. Mahoney, 435
Bowles v. May, 44
Bowles v. Misle, 855
Bowling Coal Co., H.B. v. Ruffner, 552
Bowlsby v. Speer, 636
Bowman v. Brown, 139
Bowman v. Columbia Telephone Co., 304
Bowman v. Davis, 335
Bowman v. Home Life Insurance Co., 120
Bowman v. Humphrey, 323, 349, 350, 459, 565
Bowman v. Payne, 761
Bowman v. Preferred Risk Mutual Insurance Co., 586
Bowman Remedy Co., Erick v. Jensen Salsbery Laboratories, 965, 972
Bowyer v. Te-Co., Inc., 310
Box v. Jubb, 564
Boxall v. Sequoia Union High School District, 1049
Boxberger v. New York, New Haven & Harford Railroad Co., 731
Boxberger v. State Highway Department, 1043
Boxes, Ltd. v. British Waterways Bd., 567
Boyce v. Black, 490
Boyce v. Greeley Square Hotel Co., 58
Boyd v. American Can Co., 683
Boyd v. Blaisdell, 935
Boyd v. Board of Councilmen of Frankfort, 626, 632
Boyd v. Boyd, 60
Boyd v. City of Duluth, 284
Boyd v. Marion Coca Cola Bottling Co., 247
Boyd v. Mendenhall, 877
Boyd v. Racine Currency Exchange, Inc., 383
Boyd v. State, 158
Boyd v. White, 69, 524
Boydell v. Jones, 780
Boyd's Executors v. Browne, 741
Boyer v. Guidicy Marble, Terrazzo & Tile Co., 410
Boyer v. Iowa High School Athletic Association, 244
Boyer v. Pitt Publishing Co., 781
Boyett v. Airline Lumber Co., 937
Boyette v. Atlantic Coast Line Railroad Co., 407
Boyl v. California Chemical Co., 685
Boyle v. Brandon, 927
Boyle v. Chandler, 62, 63, 64
Boyle v. Clark, 920
Boyle v. Pennsylvania Railroad Co., 437
Boyles v. Hamilton, 461, 495
Boyles v. Knight, 331

Boyles v. Oklahoma Natural Gas Co., 220
Boyleston v. Southern R. Co., 471, 578
Boylhart v. Di Marco & Reimann, 513
Boyson v. Thorn, 27, 981
Bozarth v. Harper Creek Board of Education, 506
Brabazon v. Joannes Bros. Co., 76
Brackett v. Bellows Falls Hydro-Electric Corp., 76, 289
Bradco Oil & Gas Co. v. Youngstown Sheet & Tube Co., 686
Bradford v. Bradford, 922
Bradford v. Brock, 346
Bradford v. Carson, 330
Bradford v. Clark, 821
Bradford v. Davis, 1048
Bradford v. Harding, 149
Bradford v. Lawrence, 895
Bradford Corp. v. Webster, 998
Bradford Glycerin Co. v. St. Mary's Woolen Manufacturing Co., 549
Bradley v. Appalachian Power Co., 456, 471, 472, 474
Bradley v. Boston & Maine Railroad Co., 194
Bradley v. Davis, 85
Bradley v. Fisher, 1059
Bradley v. Oviatt, 758
Bradley v. Roe, 100
Bradley v. Schmidt, 525
Bradley v. Tenneco Oil Co., 911
Bradley v. Wallace's Ltd., 561
Bradley Center, Inc. v. Wessner, 201, 203, 384
Bradshaw v. Commonwealth, 134
Bradshaw v. Frazier, 134, 144, 147
Bradshaw v. Minter, 416
Bradstreet v. Wallace, 917
Brady v. Chicago & Northwestern Railway Co., 288
Brady v. Finn, 743
Brady v. Jay, 510
Brady v. Oregon Lumber Co., 307
Brady v. Schatzel, 44
Brady v. Skinner, 399, 407
Brady v. Stiltner, 881
Brady v. Straub, 561
Brady v. Warren, 390
Bragg v. Central New England Railroad Co., 399
Bragg v. Laraway, 75
Braggs, Town of v. Slape, 639
Brahatcek v. Millard School District, 383
Braitman v. Overlook Terrace Corp., 443
Brame v. Clark, 67
Bramer v. United States, 513
Brammer's Administrator v. Norfolk & Western Railway Co., 955
Branan v. Wimsatt, 414
Branch v. Bekins Van & Storage Co., 97
Brandenburg v. Northwestern Jobbers Credit Bureau, 96, 102
Brandert v. Scottsbluff National Bank & Trust Co., 428
Brandes v. Mitterling, 81
Brandon v. Gazette Publishing Co., 836
Brandstein v. Ironbound Transportation Co., 336
Brandt v. Thompson, 491

Brannan v. Lankenau Hospital, 187
Brannon v. Wood, 257
Branson v. Fawcett Publications, 853
Branstetter v. Dorrough, 799
Branstetter v. Robbins, 551
Brant v. Matlin, 414, 424
Brantley v. Rhodes-Haverty Furniture Co., 897, 899
Brantley v. Stewart Building & Hardware Supplies, Inc., 239, 254, 455
Brasher v. First National Bank, 738
Brasseaux v. Girouard, 127
Braswell v. Economy Supply Co., 498
Bratton v. Rudnick, 564
Brauer v. Globe Newspaper Co., 777
Brault v. Town of Milton, 883
Braun v. Armour & Co., 776, 778, 966
Braun v. Craven, 55, 62
Braun v. Heidrich, 123
Braun v. Pepper, 896, 965
Braun v. Riel, 947
Braun v. Roux Distributing Co., 688
Braun v. Vallade, 420
Brauner v. Leutz, 417
Brawn v. Lyford, 379
Brawner v. Sterdevant, 941
Bray v. Callihan, 791
Bray v. Chicago, Rock Island & Pacific Railway Co., 520
Bray v. Cross, 723
Bray v. Providence Journal Co., 836
Bray-Robinson Clothing Co. v. Higgins, 8
Brayton v. Cleveland Special Police Co., 779
Brayton v. Crowell-Collier Publishing Co., 779, 780
Brazel v. McMurray, 458
Brazil v. Moran, 912
Breault v. Merrill & Ring Lumber Co., 104
Breaux v. State, 383, 1048
Brechtel v. Lopez, 304
Breece v. Jett, 926, 928
Breeding v. Napier, 818
Breen v. Peck, 334
Brees v. Anderson, 752
Brehm v. Lorenz, 251
Brehmer v. Chicago & Northwestern Railway Co., 716
Breining v. Lippincott, 927
Breitenbach v. Trowbridge, 114
Bremer v. Lake Erie & Western Railroad Co., 213, 397
Bremmer v. Journal-Tribune Co., 860
Brendlin v. Beers, 131
Brennan v. Cockrell Investments, Inc., 446
Brennan v. Gordon, 569, 572
Brennan v. National Equitable Investment Co., 675, 730
Brennan v. Public Service Railway Co., 464
Brennan v. United Hatters of North America, 1006
Brennan Construction Co. v. Cumberland, 549
Brenneis v. Marley, 339
Brennen v. City of Eugene, 358, 374, 1051
Brenner v. Haley, 77
Brent v. Kimbell, 137
Brents v. Morgan, 60, 857
Bressler v. New York Rapid Transit Corp., 245

Brett v. Cooney, 766
Bretz v. Mayer, 802
Breunig v. American Family Insurance Co., 178, 1074
Brewer v. Bankord, 445
Brewer v. Chase, 825
Brewer v. Furtwangler, 136, 562
Brewer v. Hearst Publishing Co., 853
Brewer v. Home-Stake Production Co., 9
Brewer v. Mele, 873, 884
Brewer v. Missouri Pacific Railway Co., 650, 997
Brewer v. Second Baptist Church of Los Angeles, 834
Brewer v. State, 129
Brewster v. Woodward & Lothrop, Inc., 882
Brex v. Smith, 855
Brian v. Bonvillain, 734
Brian v. Harper, 800
Briarcliff Lodge Hotel v. Citizen-Sentinel Publishing Co., 836
Bricault v. Deveau, 905
Brick v. Cohn-Hall-Marx, 764
Bricker v. Green, 530
Bridgeman-Russell Co. v. City of Duluth, 549
Bridges v. Arkansas-Missouri Power Co., 181
Bridges v. Kentucky Stone Co., 201
Briere v. Briere, 907
Briere v. Lathrop Co., 378
Briganti v. Connecticut Co., 261
Briggs v. Brown, 841
Briggs v. Brushaber, 767
Briggs v. Coykendall, 975
Briggs v. Evans, 926, 927
Briggs v. Goodwin, 1058
Briggs v. John Yeon Co., 421
Brigham Young University v. Lillywhite, 517
Bright v. United States, 558
Brightman v. Bristol, 642
Brightman v. Davies, 788
Briglia v. City of St. Paul, 311
Brigman v. Fiske-Carter Construction Co., 423
Briley v. Mitchell, 541
Brill v. Flagler, 137, 619
Brillhardt v. Ben Tipp, Inc., 620
Brimelow v. Casson, 985
Brimer v. Scheibel, 331
Bringle v. Lloyd, 462, 556
Brinilson v. Chicago & North Western Railroad Co., 414
Brink v. Moeschl Edwards Corrugating Co., 621
Brink v. Wabash Railroad Co., 1000
Brinkley v. Fishbein, 831, 832
Brinkmeyer v. United Iron & Metal Co., 413
Brinks v. Chesapeake & Ohio Railway Co., 906
Brinsfield v. Howeth, 835
Brinsmead v. Harrison, 325, 330
Brinson v. Carter, 967
Brisboise v. Kansas City Public Service Co., 363
Briscoe v. Price, 935
Briske v. Burnham, 278
Brison v. McKellop, 922
Brisson v. Minneapolis Baseball & Athletic Association, 485, 494

Bristol v. Burt, 99
Bristol v. Eckhardt, 875
Britain v. Cubbon, 405
British Celanese, Ltd. v. A.H. Hunt, Ltd., 1000
British Columbia Elec. R. Co. v. Loach, 468
British Railway Traffic & Elec. Co. v. C.R.C. Co., 835, 969
British Railways Board v. Herrington, 400
Britt v. Allen County Community Junior College, 213, 214, 413, 415, 416, 422, 433, 479
Britt v. Mangum, 308
Brittain v. Atlantic Refining Co., 439
Brittain v. Booth, 495, 496
Brittain v. McKay, 85, 90
Britten v. City of Eau Claire, 406
Brittingham v. Huyler's, 763
Britton v. Doehring, 214
Britton v. Harrison Construction Co., 550
Britz v. LeBase, 184
Broaddus v. Wilkenson, 911
Broadfoot v. Bird, 848
Broadway Approvals Ltd. v. Odhams Press, 813
Broberg v. Mann, 728
Brociner v. Radio Wire Television, Inc., 852, 868
Brock v. Peabody Cooperative Equity Exchange, 307, 454
Brock v. Rogers & Babler, Inc., 447
Brockett v. Kitchen Boyd Motor Co., 199
Broderick v. City of Waterbury, 621
Brodie v. Huck, 876
Brodrib v. Doberstein, 878
Brodsky v. Frank, 763
Brodsky v. Journal Publishing Co., 783
Brodsky v. Rieser, 40
Brody v. Foster, 758
Brody v. Montalbano, 989
Brody v. Ruby, 899
Brogan v. City of Philadelphia, 392
Brogan v. Passaic Daily News, 847
Brogan Cadillac-Oldsmobile Corp. v. Central Jersey Bank & Trust Co., 201
Brohawn & Brothers, Inc., Charles E. v. Board of Trustees of Chesapeake College, 1043
Broke v. Copeland, 562
Bromage v. Prosser, 809, 969
Bromund v. Holt, 873
Brook v. Rawl, 966
Brooke v. Bool, 384, 517
Brooke, Regina v., 798
Brooker v. Coffin, 789
Brooker v. Silverthorne, 45, 56, 59
Brookins v. The Round Table, Inc., 227, 229, 238
Brooklyn & Queens Transit Corp., People v., 645
Brooklyn Hospital, Matter of v. Torres, 115
Brooks v. Bolde, 875
Brooks v. Douglas, 487
Brooks v. E.J. Willig Truck Transportation Co., 377
Brooks v. Francis, 442
Brooks v. Harison, 794
Brooks v. Logan, 389

Brooks v. Mangan, 149
Brooks v. Olmstead, 86
Brooks v. Pitts, 764
Brooks v. Robinson, 903
Brooks v. United States, 1036
Brooks v. Wootton, 10
Brooks' Estate, In re, 116
Brookside-Pratt Mining Co. v. Booth, 131
Brookville Electric Co. v. Utilities Insurance Co., 588
Broome v. Budget Rent-A-Car of Jax, Inc., 715
Broome v. Truluck, 168
Brosnan v. Koufman, 413
Brothers v. Morris, 27
Brotherton v. Day & Night Fuel Co., 228
Brotman v. McNamara, 338
Broudy v. United States, 1036, 1037
Broughton v. State, 886, 888, 889
Broustein v. Sahlein, 890
Brouster v. Fox, 130
Brow v. Hathaway, 826
Browers, State v., 130
Brown v. Anzalone, 504
Brown v. Barber, 495, 567
Brown v. Bigelow, 683
Brown v. Bleiberg, 166
Brown v. Brown, 157, 903, 907, 922, 925, 928
Brown v. Chapman, 54, 691
Brown v. Chicago, Burlington & Quincy Railroad Co., 349
Brown v. Chicago, Milwaukee & St. Paul Railway Co., 291
Brown v. City of Minneapolis, 406
Brown v. Cleveland Baseball Co., 444
Brown v. Cole, 905, 906
Brown v. Collins, 69, 548, 549, 551
Brown v. Crawford, 43
Brown v. Dellinger, 75
Brown v. Dorney Park Coaster Co., 426
Brown v. Du Frey, 775, 777, 801
Brown v. Duke Power Co., 184
Brown v. Elm City Lumber Co., 798
Brown v. Fawcett Publications, Inc., 846
Brown v. Foster, 674
Brown v. Fowler, 448
Brown v. George, 463, 465
Brown v. George Pepperdine Foundation, 445, 512
Brown v. Glickstein, 996
Brown v. Hames, 576
Brown v. Harkleroad, 718
Brown v. Hendricks, 649
Brown v. Howard, 159
Brown v. Jacobs' Pharmacy Co., 1025
Brown v. Journal Newspaper Co., 783
Brown v. Keill, 475, 476
Brown v. Kelly, 223
Brown v. Kendall, 163
Brown v. Keyes, 893
Brown v. Kisner, 877, 879
Brown v. L.S. Lunder Construction Co., 550
Brown v. Ledger-Enquirer Co., 782

Brown v. MacPherson's Inc., 208, 381, 1045
Brown v. McBride, 11
Brown v. McCann, 790
Brown v. Mack, 801
Brown v. Martinez, 38, 133
Brown v. Meier & Frank Co., 152
Brown v. Merlo, 216
Brown v. Murdy, 347
Brown v. Myers, 780
Brown v. Nebraska Public Power District, 387
Brown v. New York Evening Journal, 832
Brown v. New York State Training School for Girls, 309
Brown v. Nickerson, 789
Brown v. Ocean Accident & Guarantee Corp., 761
Brown v. Oestman, 128
Brown v. Ohman, 768
Brown v. Paramount Publix Corp., 787
Brown, People v., 209
Brown v. Perkins, 323, 642, 644
Brown v. Providence Telegram Publishing Co., 838
Brown v. Publishers, 838
Brown v. Radebaugh, 830
Brown v. Reorganization Investment Co., 438
Brown v. Rhoades, 419
Brown v. Rice's Administrator, 760
Brown v. Robertson, 898
Brown v. Rockwell City Canning Co., 406
Brown v. Ross, 289, 308, 454
Brown v. San Francisco Ball Club, 488, 494
Brown v. Sandwood Development Corp., 167
Brown v. Schriver, 219
Brown v. Search, 754
Brown v. Selby, 906
Brown v. Shimabukuro, 818, 819
Brown v. Shyne, 226
Brown v. Sims, 745
Brown v. Slentz, 937
Brown v. Smith, 456
Brown v. Sohn, 521
Brown v. South Broward Hospital District, 220, 231, 420
Brown v. Spokane County Fire Protection District No. 1, pp. 531, 958
Brown, State v., 643
Brown v. Stephens, 941
Brown v. Travelers' Indemnity Co., 294
Brown v. Union Pacific Railroad Co., 240
Brown v. United States, 127, 1040, 1043
Brown, United States v. 1036
Brown v. Vanneman, 826
Brown v. Vinson, 198
Brown v. Walter, 591
Brown v. Wightman, 941
Brown v. Wisconsin Natural Gas Co., 522
Brown v. Wood, 1072
Brown v. Wootton, 325, 330
Brown Chemical Co. v. Meyer, 852
Brown Hotel Co. v. Sizemore, 511
Brown-Brand Realty Co. v. Saks & Co., 1015
Browne v. Blick, 940
Browne v. Dawson, 145

Browne v. Prudden-Winslow Co., 827
Browning v. Belue, 644
Browning v. Browning, 910
Browning v. Eichelman, 404
Browning v. Gomez, 830
Browning v. Jones, 918, 921
Browning v. Rodman, 768
Browning v. Skillman, 87
Browning v. Van Rensselaer, 974
Brownlee v. Pratt, 63
Brownsell v. Klawitter, 893, 897
Bruce v. Housing Authority of City of Pittsburgh, 405
Bruce v. O'Neal Flying Service, 494
Bruce v. Soule, 790
Bruch v. Carter, 27, 85, 90
Brucker v. Fromont, 500
Bruen v. Roe, 93
Bruff, v. Mali, 744
Bruggeman v. York, 284
Brugh v. Bigelow, 289, 308
Bruister v. Haney, 136
Brumfield v. Wofford, 377
Brumm v. Goodall, 269
Brummett v. County of Sacramento, 1049, 1051
Brummit v. Furness, 544
Brune v. Belinkoff, 188
Brunner v. John, 176
Bruno v. Schukart, 791
Brunsden v. Humphrey, 322
Brush v. Lindsay, 51
Brush-Moore Newspapers v. Pollitt, 800, 837
Brushaber v. Stegemann, 47, 49
Bryan v. Comstock, 150
Bryan v. Creaves, 332
Bryan v. Kitamura, 529
Bryant v. Barber, 981
Bryant v. Commonwealth, 886
Bryant v. Estate of Rich, 941
Bryant v. Jackson, 1074
Bryant v. Keen, 525
Bryant v. Northern Pacific Co., 464
Bryant v. State, 128
Bryant, State v., 156
Bryant v. Wardell, 101
Bryant v. Woodlief, 949
Bryant, Inc., Lane v. Maternity Lane, Limited of Calif., 1016
Bryson v. Hines, 715, 723
Bryson, State v., 125
Buch v. Amory Manufacturing Co., 375, 398
Buchanan v. Miami Herald Publishing Co., 817
Buchanan v. Prickett & Son, Inc., 430, 431
Buchanan v. Western Union Telegraph Co., 58
Bucher v. Krause, 10
Buck v. Colbath, 150
Buck v. Hersey, 775, 792
Buck v. McIntosh, 643
Buck v. Miller, 445
Buck v. Savage, 775, 792
Buckalew v. Tennessee Coal Iron & Railroad Co., 571

Buckel v. Maison Blanche Corp., 208
Buckelew v. Grossbard, 239, 241, 247, 254, 256, 257, 258
Buckenhizer v. Times Publishing Co., 899
Buckett v. Republic Insurance Co., 938
Buckeye Cotton Oil Co. v. Horton, 400
Buckeye Pipeline Co. v. Congel-Hazard, Inc., 86
Bucki v. Cone, 78
Buckingham v. Thompson, 756
Buckle v. Holmes, 539, 542
Buckley v. Basford, 340
Buckley v. Buckley, 752
Buckley v. Chadwick, 954
Buckley v. City of New York, 502
Buckley v. Francis, 921
Buckley v. Littell, 845
Buckley & Toronto Transp. Comm'n v. Smith Transport, Ltd., 178, 1075
Buckmaster v. Bourbon County Fair Association, 648
Bucknam v. Great Northern Railway Co., 66
Buckner v. Azulai, 722
Buckner v. Foster, 338
Buckner v. GAF Corp., 168
Buckner v. Spaulding, 842
Buckstaff v. Viall, 780
Budagher v. Amrep Corp., 501, 514
Budahl v. Gordon & David Associates, 1046
Budd v. J.Y. Gooch Co., 781
Budkiewicz v. Elgin, Joliet & Eastern Railway Co., 225
Bufalino v. Maxon Brothers, 829
Buffalo v. Buffalo, 905
Buffington v. Clarke, 99, 100
Bufkin v. Grisham, 664, 666
Buford v. Horne, 517, 520, 521
Buford v. Houtz, 540
Buford v. Jitney Jungle Stores of America, Inc., 427
Bugh v. Webb, 481, 486
Bugle v. McMahon, 718
Buice v. Campbell, 101
Bukowski v. Juranek, 324
Bulatao v. Kauai Motors, Limited, 494
Bull v. McCuskey, 10, 891, 899
Bullard v. Central Vermont Railway, Inc., 363
Bullard v. Harrison, 146
Bullitt v. Farrar, 742
Bulloch v. United States, 932
Bullock v. Maag, 919
Bullock v. Safeway Stores, 425
Bullock v. Tamiami Trail Tours, Inc., 383
Bulpit v. Matthews, 540
Bumgart v. Bailey, 40
Bump v. Betts, 892
Bunch v. Edenton, 1054
Bunda v. Hardwick, 306
Bundt v Embro, 331
Bundy v. City of New York, 340
Bundy v. Maginess, 8
Bundy v. State of Vermont Highway Department, 573
Bunker v. Mains, 928
Bunker Hill & Sullivan Mining & Concentrating Co. v. Polak, 346

Bunnell v. Waterbury Hospital, 422, 439
Bunten v. Davis, 131, 132
Bunting v. Hogsett, 292, 299
Bunyan v. Jordan, 66
Burch v. Amsterdam Corp., 685
Burckhalter v. Mitchell, 94
Burden v. Hoover, 1012
Burdett v. Hines, 823
Burditt v. Hunt, 95
Burdon v. Wood, 955
Buren v. Midwest Industries, Inc., 430
Burford & Co., William v. Glasgow Water Co., 594
Burgdorfer v. Thielemann, 665, 666, 764
Burge v. Forbes, 46
Burgess v. Commonwealth, 46
Burgess v. Graffam, 96
Burgess v. M/V Tamano, 997
Burgess v. State, 157
Burgess v. Tucker, 1004
Burgoyne v. McKillip, 673
Burk v. Creamery Package Manufacturing Co., 304
Burk v. High Point Homes, Inc., 639
Burk v. Walsh, 427
Burk Royalty Co. v. Pace, 400, 401, 405, 411
Burk Royalty Co. v. Walls, 212
Burke v. Burnham, 334, 336, 955
Burke v. Davis, 490, 570, 571
Burke v Fischer, 563, 565
Burke v. O'Neil, 443
Burke v. Pearson, 204
Burke v. Robinson, 48
Burke v. Washington Hospital Center, 204
Burke v. Watts, 878
Burke & Thomas, Inc. v. International Organization of Masters, Mates & Pilots, Etc., 1027
Burkett v. Griffith, 971
Burkett v. Johnston, 255
Burkett v. Studebaker Brothers Manufacturing Co., 681
Burkhart v. Corn, 525
Burkhart v. North American Co., 841
Burkowske v. Church Hospital Corp., 421, 426
Burks v. Madyun, 424, 428
Burks, Estate of v. Ross, 1066
Burleson v. Langdon, 673
Burlie v. Stephens, 306
Burlingame v. Burlingame, 819
Burlington & M.R. Co. v. Westover, 294, 301, 544
Burlington Grocery Co. v. Lines, 732
Burlington Transportation Co. v. Josephson, 52
Burmah Oil Co. v. Lord Advocate, 146
Burmeister v. Youngstrom, 339
Burnaman v. J.C. Penney Co., 141
Burnap v. Marsh, 873
Burne v. Lee, 770
Burnett v. Amalgamated Phosphate Co., 184
Burnett v. Conner, 308
Burnette v. Wahl, 909
Burney v. Southern Railway Co., 798
Burnham v. Beverly Airways, 79
Burnham v. Dowd, 1024

Burnham v. Hotchkiss, 642
Burnham v. Yellow Checker Cab, Inc., 466
Burnight v. Industrial Accident Commission, 311
Burns v. Bradley, 425
Burns v. Burns, 904
Burns v. Commonwealth Trailer Sales, 94
Burns v. Delaware & Atlantic Telegraph & Telephone Co., 569
Burns v. Erben, 154
Burns v. Johnston, 52
Burns v. Kirkpatrick, 910
Burns v. Lamb, 351
Burns v. North Chicago Rolling Mill Co., 380
Burns v. Stevens, 852, 853
Burns Jackson Miller Summit & Spitzer v. Lindner, 1027
Burr v. Adam Eidemiller, Inc., 72, 619, 625
Burrill v. Stevens, 763
Burroughs v. Ben's Auto Park, 439
Burroughs v. Crichton, 115
Burroughs v. Jordan, 365
Burroughs Adding Machine Co. v. Scandinavian-American Bank, 761
Burrow v. Jones, 232
Burrowes v. Lock, 733
Burrows v. Jacobsen, 242
Burrows v. Rhodes, 337
Burstein v. Charline's Cut Rate, 1014
Burt v. Bowles, 759
Burt v. Smith, 876
Burtch v. Nickerson, 791
Burton v. Crowell Publishing Co., 777, 786, 809
Burton v. Fulton, 148
Burton v. Gardner Motors, Inc., 527
Burton v. Mattson, 828
Burton v. Roberson, 52
Burton v. Waller, 128
Burton v. Western & Atlantic Railroad Co., 418
Busby v. First Christian Church, 798
Busch v. Busch Construction, Inc., 712, 933
Busch v. Interborough Rapid Transit Co., 664
Busch v. International Rapid Transit Co., 666
Busch v. Lilly, 456
Busch v. New York, Lackawanna & Western Railway Co., 620
Busch v. Wilcox, 736
Busch & Latta Paint Co. v. Woermann Construction Co., 342
Buschbaum v. Heriot, 817
Bush v. Commonwealth, 310
Bush v. Lucas, 1029
Bush v. Oliver, 528
Bush, People v., 127
Bush v. Steinman, 509
Bushnell v. Telluride Power Co., 312
Business Equipment Center, Limited v. DeJur-Amsco Corp., 971
Buss v. Wachsmith, 576
Bussewitz v. Wisconsin Teachers' Association, 818
Bustamante v. Carborundum Co., 250
Buszta v. Souther, 720, 1050

Butala v. Union Electric Co., 69
Butcher v. Adams, 48
Butigan v. Yellow Cab Co., 163, 164
Butler v. Acme Markets, Inc., 174, 202, 383, 424, 428
Butler v. Frontier Telephone Co., 78
Butler v. Hoboken Printing & Publishing Co., 794
Butler v. Olshan, 750
Butler v. Pardue, 361
Butler v. Rockland, Thomaston & Camden St. Railway Co., 466
Butler v. State Farm Mutual Automobile Co., 935
Butler v. Townend, 954
Butler v. Western Union Telegraph Co., 58
Butner v. Spease, 312
Butrick v. Snyder, 305
Butterfield v. Ashley, 925
Butterfield v. Barber, 743
Butterfield v. Community Light & Power Co., 958
Butterfield v. Ennis, 923
Butterfield v. Forrester, 451
Butterman v. McClintic-Marshall Construction, 569
Button, People v., 127
Butts v. Anthis, 298
Butts v. Ward, 305, 348
Butts v. Watts, 256
Butz v. Economou, 873, 1041, 1057, 1058, 1059, 1060, 1061
Bwlch-Y-Plwn Lead Mining Co. v. Baynes, 732
Byam v. Collins, 828, 835
Byard v. Holmes, 675, 730
Byars v. Baptist Medical Centers, Inc., 1010
Byers v. Federal Land Co., 758
Byers v. Lemay Bank & Trust Co., 732
Byers v. Meridian Printing Co., 837, 847
Byfield v. Candler, 854
Byne v. Moore, 871, 887
Byrd v. Byrd, 941
Byrd v. Commonwealth, 153, 154
Byrd v. Crowder, 334
Byrd v. English, 1000
Byrd v. Hawkins, 466, 468
Byrd v. Melton, 403
Byrd v. Rautman, 753
Byrd, State v., 150
Byrne v. Boadle, 243
Byrne v. City & County of San Francisco, 228, 230, 232
Byrne v. Dean, 801
Byrne v. Eastmans Co., 569
Byrne v. Funk, 775
Byrnes v. Stephens, 299, 300
Byrns v. St. Louis County, 198

C

C.I.T. Corp. v. Brewer, 85
C.I.T. Corp. v. Reeves, 140
C.I.T. Corp. v. Short, 141
Cabaniss v. Cook, 935
Cachick v. United States, 304
Cadden v. American Steel Barge Co., 572

Caddy v. R. Maturi & Co., 575
Cadillac Motor Car Division v. Brown, 363
Cadle v. McIntosh, 830
Cadman v. White, 531
Cadwell v. Farrell, 112
Caffaro v. Trayna, 957
Caffini v. Hermann, 154
Cage Bros. v. Whiteman, 91
Cahill v. Eastman, 548
Cahill v. Readon, 737
Caiazzo v. Volkswagenwerk, 352
Caillouet v. American Sugar Refining Co., 941
Cain v. Friend, 424
Cain v. Houston General Insurance Co., 179
Cain v. Kohlman, 590
Cain v. Meade County, 670
Cain v. Skillin, 125
Cain v. Southern Massachusetts Telephone Co., 245
Cain v. State Farm Mutual Automobile Insurance Co., 167
Cain v. Vollmer, 998, 1006
Cairl v. Minnesota, 384
Calabretta v. National Airlines, Inc., 247
Calahan v. Wood, 485
Caldwell v. Bechtel, Inc., 174
Caldwell v. Farley, 507
Caldwell v. Ford Motor Co., 172
Caldwell v. Gem Packing Co., 990
Caldwell v. Personal Finance Co. of St. Petersburg, 834
Caldwell v. Village of Island Park, 423
Caldwell v. Zaher, 915
Caledonian R. Co. v. Mulholland, 716
Calero v. Del Chemical Corp., 845
Calhoun v. Hill, 503
Calhoun v. Royal Globe Insurance Co., 488
Calhoun v. Universal Credit Co., 10
Caliando v. Huck, 518, 520
California Apparel Creators v. Wieder of California, 1019
California Conserving Co. v. D'Avanzo, 765
California Motor Transport Co. v. Trucking Unlimited, 886, 989
California State Automobile Association Inter-Insurance Bureau v. Maloney, 602
Calkins v. Albi, 318
Callahan v. Dearborn Developments, 404, 411
Callahan v. Ingram, 848
Callahan v. Searles, 48
Callahan Construction Co., State ex rel. W.E. v. Hughes, 405
Callais v. Allstate Insurance Co., 954
Callais v. Furniture Showrooms, Inc., 171
Callies v. Reliance Laundry Co., 937
Callihan v. Great Northern Railway Co., 579
Callihan Interests, Inc. v. Duffield, 338
Callis v. Merrieweather, 918
Calore v. Domnitch, 404
Calore v. Powell-Savory Corp., 779
Caltex, Inc., United States v., 146, 147
Calvert Distillers Corp. v. Nussbaum Liquor Store, 1014

Calway v. Williamson, 158
Camaras v. Moran, 164
Cambell v. Seaman, 635
Cambern v. Sioux Tools, Inc., 473
Cambria, State v., 948
Cambridge Mutual Fire Insurance Co. v. State Farm Fire & Casualty Co., 183
Camerlinck v. Thomas, 1071
Cameron v. Abatiell, 432
Cameron v. Bissonette, 292
Cameron v. Cockran, 827
Cameron v. Kenyon-Connell Commercial Co., 430
Cameron v. Oberlin, 513
Cameron v. Stewart, 229
Camp v. Martin, 792
Camp v. Wood, 438
Campagna v. Lyles, 518
Campanella v. Zajic, 519, 520
Campanelli v. Vescera, 752
Campbell v. Animal Quarantine Station, 364
Campbell v. Arnold, 78
Campbell v. Boyd, 207, 417
Campbell v. Bradbury, 1073
Campbell v. C & H Transportation Co., 959
Campbell v. Campbell, 902
Campbell v. Carpenter, 199
Campbell v. City of Bellevue, 1050
Campbell, Commonwealth v., 38
Campbell v. Consolidated Traction Co., 252
Campbell v. Cooper, 995
Campbell v. Elsie S. Holding Co., 439
Campbell v. Eubanks, 414
Campbell v. Fiorot, 247
Campbell v. First National Bank, 246
Campbell v. Gates, 981
Campbell v. Hagen-Burger, 436
Campbell v. Harrison, 442
Campbell v. Hoffman, 425
Campbell v. Kansas City, Ft. Scott & Memphis Railroad Co., 399
Campbell v. Mayor of Paddington, 650
Campbell v. New York Evening Post, 837
Campbell v. Nordco Products, 486, 487, 488, 492, 494
Campbell v. Northern Signal Co., 399
Campbell v. Portland Sugar Co., 437
Campbell v. Post Publishing Co., 781
Campbell v. Preston, 343
Campbell v. Race, 146
Campbell v. Seaman, 619, 635
Campbell v. Security Pacific National Bank, 527
Campbell v. Sherman, 149
Campbell v. Spottiswoode, 831
Campbell v. Weathers, 421
Campbell v. Willmark Service System, 827
Campbell v. Yellow Cab Co., 876
Campbell County v. Braun, 762
Campion v. City of Rochester, 492
Campo v. Scofield, 686
Campopiano v. Rhode Island Co., 58
Camposano v. Claiborn, 664

Campus v. McElligott, 513
Canade, Inc. v. Town of Blue Grass, 1053
Canadian Bank of Commerce v. McCrea, 91
Canadian Indemnity Co. v. United States Fidelity & Guaranty Co., 341
Canadian Pac. R. Co. v. Roy, 544, 567
Canadian Pacific Railway Co. v. Slayton, 218
Canales v. Dominick's Finer Foods, Inc., 427
Candler v. Smith, 542, 561
Candrian v. Miller, 775
Canfield v. Quayle, 641
Canney v. Rochester Agricultural & Mechanical Association, 558
Cannon v. Pearson, 334
Cannon v. Sears Roebuck & Co., 165, 167
Canterbury v. Spence, 190, 191
Cantor v. Anderson, 199
Cantrell v. Amarillo Hardware Co., 10
Cantrell v. Forest City Publishing Co., 865
Cantwell v. Cermins, 231
Canty, State v., 644
Canty v. Terrebonne Parish Police Jury, 174
Canuel v. Oskolin, 995
Canzoneri v. Hickert, 717
Capaci, State v., 129
Caparco v. Lambert, 180
Capezzaro v. Winfrey, 210
Capital Films Corp. v. Charles Fries Productions, 1015
Capital Transit Co. v. Jackson, 252
Capital Transport Co. v. McDuff, 328
Capitol Airways v. Indianapolis Power & Light Co., 80
Capitol Electric Co. v. Cristaldi, 890
Capitula v. New York Central Railroad Co., 396
Caplan v. Caplan, 336, 913
Caporale v. C.W. Blakeslee & Sons, Inc., 550
Cappaert v. Junker, 512
Capps v. Carpenter, 915
Capps v. McCarley & Co., 497
Capps v. Vasey Brothers, 91
Caputo v. Holt, 959
Caputzal v. Lindsay Co., 365
Caradori v. Fitch, 179, 181, 952, 953
Carbondale Investment Co. v. Burdick, 895
Carbone v. Ursich, 1001
Carboneau v. Peterson, 518
Cardiff v. Brooklyn Eagle, 774
Cardon v. McConnell, 971
Cardwell v. Golden, 456
Cardy v. Maxwell, 852, 898, 899
Carey v. Bilby, 334
Carey v. Davis, 376
Carey v. Evening Call Publishing Co., 783
Carey v. Hearst Publications, 837
Carey v. Lima, Salmon & Tully Mortuary, 362
Carey v. Malley, 441
Carey v. Piphus, 885, 887
Carey v. Pure Distributing Corp., 299
Carey v. Statewide Finance Co., 855
Carey Reed Co. v. McDavid, 572
Cargill, Inc. v. Zimmer, 408

Caribbean Produce Exchange, Inc. v. Sea Land Service, Inc., 482, 483
Carl v. West Aberdeen Land & Improvement Co., 650
Carlinville National Bank v. Rhoads, 365
Carlisle v. Fawcett Publications, Inc., 851, 864
Carlisle, Rex v., 645
Carlisle, Owen v. City of Independence, 1052
Carlock v. Westchester Lighting Co., 231
Carlslake v. Mapledoram, 790
Carlson v. Carpenter Contractors' Association, 1024
Carlson v. Hampl, 447
Carlson v. Tucson Racquet & Swim Club, Inc., 409
Carlton v. Boudar, 327, 347
Carlyle v. United States, 1037
Carman v. Heber, 478, 981, 982
Carmen v. Fox Film Corp., 1003
Carmichael v. Lexington-Fayette Urban County Government, 183, 220, 232
Carmichael v. Silvert, 168
Carmichael-Lynch-Nolan Advertising Agency, Inc. v. Bennett & Associates, Inc., 981
Carnation Lumber Co. v. McKenney, 891
Carnes v. St. Paul Union Stockyards Co., 983, 984
Carnes v. Thompson, 38
Carney v. Barnett, 943
Carney v. Buyea, 289
Carney v. Goodman, 267
Carney v. Rease, 102
Caroff v. Liberty Lumber Co., 432
Carolina, Clinchfield & Ohio Railway Co. v. Hill, 329
Carolina Overall Corp. v. East Carolina Linen Supply, Inc., 981
Caron Enterprises, E.J. v. State Operating Co., 101
Carpenter v. American Building & Loan Association, 106
Carpenter v. Ashley, 817, 835
Carpenter v. Bailey, 974
Carpenter v. Carpenter, 902
Carpenter v. Donohoe, 721
Carpenter v. Hamilton, 752
Carpenter v. W.H. McElwain Co., 332
Carpenter v. Willey, 828, 830
Carpenter v. Williams, 991, 992
Carpenter, Baggott & Co. v. Hanes, 897
Carpini v. Pittsburgh & Weirton Bus Co., 326, 329, 703
Carr v. Clarke, 927
Carr v. Davis, 544
Carr v. Hodd, 832
Carr v. Hoy, 103
Carr v. Maine Central Railroad Co., 379, 1008
Carr v. Minneapolis, St. Paul & Sault Ste. Marie Railway Co., 291
Carr v. State, 154
Carr v. Watkins, 822, 851, 858, 868
Carradine v. City of New York, 406
Carratt v. Morley, 54
Carricato v. Carricato, 906
Carrieri v. Bush, 918, 919, 923
Carrigan v. Henderson, 62, 64
Carrington v. Taylor, 1005

Carroll v. Beard-Laney, Inc., 505
Carroll v. Central Counties Gas Co., 317
Carroll v. Getty Oil Co., 460, 492, 493
Carroll v. Hutchinson, 521
Carroll v. Kerrigen, 331
Carroll v. Kittle, 1045
Carroll v. Lucas, 1049
Carroll v. M. & J. Finance Corp., 102
Carroll v. New York Pie Baking Co., 616, 618
Carroll v. Owen, 827
Carroll v. Paramount Pictures, 780
Carroll v. Spencer, 398
Carroll v. United States, 154
Carroll v. Warner Brothers Pictures, 963, 966
Carroll Towing Co., United States v., 173, 296
Carrow v. Haney, 563
Carroway v. Johnson, 13
Carruth v. Harris, 761
Carson v. Allied News Co., 845
Carson v. Blodgett Construction Co., 554
Carson v. Boston Elevated Railway Co., 209
Carson v. Hercules Powder Co., 650
Carson v. Maurer, 168
Carson, Pirie Scott & Co. v. Chicago Railways Co., 464
Carstairs v. Taylor, 564, 567
Carsten v. Northern Pacific Railway Co., 290
Carstesen v. Town of Stratford, 326
Cartan v. Cruz Construction Co., 118, 151
Carter v. Catfish Cabin, 884
Carter v. City of Greensboro, 1053
Carter v. Franklin, 204
Carter v. Harlan Hospital Association, 937
Carter v. Jackson, 821
Carter v. Joseph Bancroft & Sons Co., 707
Carter v. Knapp Motor Co., 977, 1009
Carter v. Liberty Equipment Co., 245
Carter v. Oster, 1003
Carter v. Papineau, 774
Carter v. Redmond, 231
Carter v. Seaboard Air Line Railway Co., 396
Carter v. State, 128
Carter v. Sterling Finance Co., 791
Carter v. Sutherland, 138, 872
Carter v. Taylor Diving & Salvage Co., 430
Carter v. Thurston, 68, 140, 147
Carter v. Towne, 318
Carter v. United Novelty & Premium Co., 441
Carter v. William Sommerville & Son, Inc., 225
Carter v. Yardley & Co., 683, 684
Carter Publications v. Flemming, 809
Carterville, Village of v. Cook, 317
Cartlidge v. Sloan, 102
Cartwright v. Harris, 466
Cartwright v. Hughes, 769
Cartwright-Caps Co. v. Fischel & Kaufman, 799
Caruso, People v., 154
Caruth v. Mariani, 704
Carver v. Lykes, 891
Carver v. Morrow, 801

Carver v. San Pedro, Los Angeles & Salt Lake Railroad Co., 644, 650
Carville v. A.F. Bornot & Co., 574
Cary v. Hotel Rueger, 506
Casas v. Maulhardt Buick, Inc., 180
Casavan v. Sage, 876
Case v. Arrow Trucking Co., 486
Case Co., J.I. v. Borak, 221
Case Threshing Machine Co., J.I. v. Webb, 754
Casebeer v. Drahoble, 874
Casey v. Arnott, 963
Casey v. Atwater, 493
Casey v. Hanrick, 899
Casey v. Kitchens, 144
Casey v. Phillips Pipeline Co., 270
Casey v. Welch, 765
Cash, Charles S. v. Steinbook, 1016
Cash Drug Store v. Cannon, 827
Cashin v. Northern Pacific Railway Co., 554
Cashman v. Soulia, 104
Caskie v. Philadelphia Rapid Transit Co., 674
Casner v. Hoskins, 664
Cason v. Baskin, 857, 860
Cason v. Florida Power Co., 619
Cason v. Owens, 1007
Casper v. Bankers' Life Insurance Co. of Lincoln, 760
Casrell v. Altec Industries, Inc., 706, 712
Cass v. Higenbotam, 98
Cassano v. Durham, 947
Casserly v. Wheeler, 53
Cassidy v. Airborne Freight Corp., 483
Cassidy, Commonwealth v., 616
Cassidy v. Constantine, 933
Cassidy v. Daily Mirror Newspapers, 782, 809
Cassidy v. Gannett Co., 783
Cassidy v. Kraft-Phenix Cheese Co., 666, 764
Cassidy v. Quisenberry, 489
Cassidy v. Uhlmann, 736
Cassisi v. Maytag Co., 255
Cassity v. Brady, 326
Cassius v. Mortimer, 800
Castaldo v. Pittsburgh-Des Moines Steel Co., 724
Castelli v. Abramo, 765
Castile v. O'Keefe, 394, 466
Castillo v. United States, 229, 231
Castle v. St. Augustine's Links, 392
Castleberry v. Mack, 73
Castleman v. Stryker, 765
Castonguay v. Acme Knitting Machine & Needle Co., 399
Castro v. State, 514
Castro v. United States, 147
Castronovo v. Murawsky, 123
Caswell v. Hunton, 754
Catania v. Brown, 709
Caterpillar Tractor Co. v. Beck, 478, 701, 702
Cates v. Barb, 971
Cates v. Beauregard Electric Coop., Inc., 409, 433
Cathcart v. Matthews, 1072
Catheline v. Seaboard Coast Line Railroad Co., 213, 214

TABLE OF CASES

Catteris v. Cowper, 77
Cattle v. Stockton Waterworks Co., 999
Caudill v. Gibson Fuel Co., 443
Caughey v. Smith, 925
Causby, United States v., 81, 1033
Cauverian v. De Metz, 293, 311
Cavalier v. Pope, 444
Cavanaugh v. First National Stores, 937
Cavanuagh v. Pappas, 449
Cavarnos v. Kokkinak, 791
Cavender v. Waddingham, 993
Caverno v. Fellows, 985
Caviote v. Shea, 233
Cawley v. La Crosse City Railway Co., 937
Cawrse v. Signal Oil Co., 965
Caylor v. B.C. Motor Transportation, 306
CeBuzz, Inc. v. Sniderman, 183
Cecil v. Hardin, 517, 519, 520
Ceco Corp. v. Coleman, 363
Ceferatti v. Boisvert, 738
Celebrity Studios, Inc. v. Civetta Excavating, Inc., 72
Celestine v. City of New York, 511, 512
Celiz & Sanchez' Estates v. Public Utility District No. 1, p. 208
Celli & Del Papa v. Galveston Brewing Co., 1013
Celucci v. Sun Oil Co., 508
Centennial Land & Development v. Township of Medford, 1057
Centers v. Dollar Markets, 873
Central & Southern Truck Lines, v. Westfall G. M. C. Truck, Inc., 720
Central Alarm of Tucson v. Ganem, 203
Central Exploration Co. v. Gray, 549, 550
Central Hudson Gas & Electric Corp. v. Public Service Commission, 1012
Central Iron & Coal Co. v. Vanderheurk, 553
Central Motor Co. v. Roberson, 52
Central Mutual Insurance Co. v. Whetstone, 241
Central of Georgia R. Co. v. Americus Construction Co., 622
Central of Georgia Railway Co. v. Price, 306
Central of Georgia Railway v. Walker Truck Contractors, 517
Central R. Co. of Venezuela v. Kisch, 751
Central Transport, Inc. v. Great Dane Trailers, Inc., 174, 209
Central Wisconsin Trust Co. v. Chicago & Northwestern Railway Co., 309
Centrello v. Basky, 481
Century Display Manufacturing Corp. v. D.R. Wager Construction Co., 449
Cepeda v. Cowles Magazine & Broadcasting Co., 832
Cepeda v. Cumberland Engineering Co., 204, 701, 712
Cernahan v. Chrisler, 106
Cerny v. Domer, 219
Certified Laboratories of Texas, Inc. v. Rubinson, 987
Cervantes v. Maco Gas Co., 959
Cerveny v. Chicago Daily News Co., 775
Cessna v. Coffeyville Racing Association, 387
Cessna, State v., 132

Chacey v. City of Fargo, 317
Chadwick v. Barba Lou, Inc., 419, 424, 426, 428
Chadwick v. City of New York, 465
Chaffin v. Chaffin, 904
Chaika v. Vandenberg, 528
Chalfen v. Kraft, 440
Chalkley v. Atlantic Coast Line Railroad Co., 798
Challis v. Hartloff, 751
Chamberlain v. Chandler, 57
Chamberlain v. McCleary, 339, 344
Chamberlain v. West, 103, 105
Chamberlain v. White and Goodwin, 325
Chambers v. Baldwin, 990, 1003
Chambers v. Bedell, 140
Chambers v. Bookman, 734
Chambers v. Caulfield, 918
Chambers v. Hawkins, 523
Chambers v. Kane, 1007
Chambers v. Leiser, 829
Chambers v. Nottebaum, 119
Chambers v. Scarboro, 525
Chambers v. Whelen, 391
Chambers v. White, 788
Chamberlin v. Fuller, 750
Chamness v. Odum, 186
Champion v. Woods, 759
Champlin v. Walker, 394
Champlin Refining Co. v. Thomas, 291
Champneys v. Irwin, 752
Chandelor v. Lopus, 19
Chandler v. Anchor Serum Co., 695
Chandler v. Forsyth Royal Crown Bottling Co., 377
Chandler v. Sanger, 675
Chaney v. Duncan, 718
Chaney v. Tingley, 520
Channel Master Corp. v. Aluminum Limited Sales, Inc., 764
Chapell v. Schmidt, 132
Chapleyn of Greye's Inn v. ——, 124, 125
Chaplin v. Hicks, 1007
Chaplin v. National Broadcasting Co., 860
Chapman v. Anderson, 878
Chapman v. Dunn, 876
Chapman v. Edgerton, 188
Chapman v. Ellesmere, 823
Chapman v. Fritzche, 411
Chapman v. Hargrove, 125
Chapman v. Lily Cache Builders, Inc., 724
Chapman v. Parking, Inc., 403
Chapman v. State, 9, 179, 181
Chapman v. Thumblethorpe, 140
Chapman Chemical Co. v. Taylor, 684
Chappell v. Dwyer, 417
Chappell v. Stewart, 855
Chappelle v. Gross, 890
Chappetta v. Bowman Transportation, Inc., 364
Chap-Tan Drilling Co. v. Myers, 572
Charbonneau v. MacRury, 179
Charco, Inc. v. Cohn, 1066

Charing Cross Elec. Supply Co. v. Hydraulic Power Co., 546, 567
Charles v. Texas Co., 15
Charles City Plow & Manufacturing Co. v. Jones, 880
Charley v. Cameron, 113
Charlottesville, City of v. Jones, 182
Charlottesville Music Center v. Magnepan, Inc., 973
Charpentier v. Socony-Vacuum Oil Co., 764, 765
Chart v. General Motors Corp., 715
Chartiers Block Coal Co. v. Mellon, 82
Chartrand v. State of New York, 74
Chase v. Clinton County, 660
Chase v. Luce, 411
Chase v. Tingdale Bros., 228
Chase v. Washington Water Power Co., 283, 299, 317
Chastain v. Fuqua Industries, Inc., 375, 377
Chatfield Co., E. A. v. City of New Haven, 650
Chatham Furnace Co. v. Moffatt, 746
Chatkin v. Talarski, 419
Chattahoochee Brick Co. v. Braswell, 570
Chattanooga Railway & Light Co. v. Bettis, 232
Chatterton v. Secretary of State for India, 821
Chausse v. Southland Corp., 179, 948
Chavers v. A.R. Blossman, Inc., 292
Chavez v. Ronquillo, 503
Chavez v. Sears, Roebuck & Co., 888
Chavez v. Southern Pacific Transportation Co., 556
Chavez v. Tolleson Elementary School District, 202
Chavira v. Carnahan, 270
Cheater v. Cater, 547
Cheatum v. Wehle, 823
Cheek v. Eyth, 571
Cheli v. Cudahy Brothers Co., 227, 581
Chelini v. Nieri, 362
Chelsea Moving & Trucking Co. v. Ross Towboat Co., 998, 999
Cheney v. Dickinson, 743
Cheney v. Gleason, 760
Cheney Brothers v. Doris Silk Corp., 1021
Cherberg v. Peoples National Bank of Washington, 990
Cherry v. Cherry, 908
Cherry v. Des Moines Leader, 832, 834
Cherry v. Lake Drummond Canal & Water Co., 78, 84
Cherry, People v., 156
Cherry v. Williams, 620, 629
Cherry-Burrell Co. v. Thatcher, 10
Chesapeake & Ohio Railroad Co. v. Conley's Administratrix, 468
Chesapeake & Ohio Railway Co. v. J. Wix & Sons, 303
Chesapeake & Ohio Railway Co. v. May, 582
Chesapeake & Ohio Railway Co. v. Nixon, 488
Chesapeake & Ohio Railway Co. v. Robinett, 365
Chesapeake & Ohio Railway Co. v. Ryan, 134
Chesapeake & Ohio Railway Co. v. Welch, 153
Chesapeake & Ohio Railroad Co. v. Williams' Administratrix, 328
Chesapeake & Ohio Railroad Co. v. Wills, 452
Chesapeake & Potomac Telephone Co. of Maryland v. Chesapeake Utilities Corp., 420, 509, 514
Chesebro v. Powers, 972

Cheshire Railroad Co. v. Foster, 101
Cheskov v. Port of Seattle, 81, 82
Cheslock v. Pittsburgh Railways Co., 396
Chess v. Kelly, 140
Chester v. Montgomery Ward & Co., 182
Chew v. Gilliland, 131
Chew v. Louchheim, 91
Chew v. Paramount-Richards Theatres, 426
Chiagouris v. Jovan, 941
Chicago & Alton Railroad Co. v. Mayer, 146
Chicago & Eastern Illinois Railroad Co. v. Kneirim, 569
Chicago & Northwestern Railway Co. v. Hunerberg, 289
Chicago, Burlington & Quincy Railroad Co. v. Chicago, 1043
Chicago, Burlington & Quincy Railroad Co. v. Gelvin, 55, 561
Chicago, Burlington & Quincy Railroad Co. v. Honey, 937
Chicago, Burlington & Quincy Railroad Co. v. Johnson, 210
Chicago, Burlington & Quincy Railroad Co. v. Krayenbuhl, 172, 412
Chicago, Burlington & Quincy Railroad Co. v. Murray, 286
Chicago, Burlington & Quincy Railroad Co. v. Payne, 470
Chicago, Burlington & Quincy Railroad Co. v. Wells-Dickey Trust Co., 949
Chicago, City of v. Chicago Tribune Co., 780
Chicago, City of v. Shaynin, 644
Chicago, City of v. Troy Laundry Machinery Co., 82
Chicago, Indianapolis & Louisville Railway v. Pritchard, 716
Chicago, Kansas & Western Railroad Co. v. Hutchinson, 511
Chicago, Peoria & St. Louis Railway v. Woolridge, 951
Chicago, Rock Island & Pacific Railroad Co. v. Medley, 774
Chicago, Rock Island & Pacific Railroad Co., United States v., 343
Chicago, Rock Island & Pacific Railway Co. v. Armstrong, 985, 1010
Chicago, Rock Island & Pacific Railway Co. v. Brown, 385
Chicago, Rock Island & Pacific Railway Co. v. Goodson, 294
Chicago, Rock Island & Pacific Railway Co. v. Hamler, 210
Chicago, Rock Island & Pacific Railway Co. v. Sampson, 716
Chicago, Rock Island & Pacific Railway Co. v. Williams, 716
Chicago, Texas & Mexican Central Railway Co. v. Titterington, 765
Chicago City Railway Co. v. Barker, 251
Chicago Great Western Railway Co. v. Casura, 343
Chicago Park District v. R.E. Herczel & Co., 1067
Chicago South Shore & South Bend Railroad v. Brown, 202

TABLE OF CASES

Chicago Terminal Transfer Railroad Co. v. Kotoski, 399
Chicago Union Traction Co. v. Giese, 245
Chicago Union Traction Co. v. Newmiller, 245
Chicago Union Traction Co. v. Sawusch, 569
Chichester Corp. v. Foster, 547
Chick Springs Water, Inc. v. State Highway Department, 567
Chickasha Cotton Oil Co. v. Holloway, 495
Chickering v. Thompson, 389
Child v. Emerson, 778
Childers v. Gas Lines, Inc., 244
Childers v. New York Power & Light Corp., 643
Childers v. San Jose Mercury Printing & Publishing Co., 845
Childers v. Shannon, 932
Childers, State v., 135, 136
Childers v. United States, 1035
Childress v. Abeles, 991, 994, 996, 1003
Childress v. Childress, 903
Childs v. Rayburn, 935, 952
Chiles v. Drake, 9
Chiles v. Rohl, 268
Chiniche v. Smith, 523
Chipley v. Atkinson, 991
Chipman v. Palmer, 349
Chipouras v. A. J. & L. Corp., 879
Chisolm v. Gadsden, 737
Chisum v. Behrens, 362
Chittick v. Philadelphia Rapid Transit Co., 55, 360
Chiuccariello v. Campbell, 245
Chiuchiolo v. New England Wholesale Tailors, 56, 360
Chiyoko Ikuta v. Shunji K. Ikuta, 930
Chloupek v. Perotka, 77
Chmielewski v. Marich, 328
Chmurka v. Southern Farm Bureau Insurance Co., 363
Choate v. Carter, 417, 418
Choctaw, Oklahoma & Gulf Railroad Co. v. Jones, 484, 570
Choctaw, Oklahoma & Western Railway Co. v. Wilker, 511
Chrestman v. State, 50
Chretien v. F.W. Woolworth Co., 142
Chrisafogeorgis v. Brandenberg, 370
Chrischilles v. Griswold, 166
Chrisp, State v., 644
Christensen v. Epley, 1047, 1063
Christensen v. Jauron, 752
Christensen v. Johnston, 913
Christensen v. Murphy, 430, 431
Christensen v. Northern States Power Co., 269
Christensen v. Pugh, 93
Christensen v. Swedish Hospital, 61
Christensen v. Thornby, 372
Christians v. Homestake Enterprises, Limited, 400, 402, 403, 404, 405, 409
Christiansen v. Weston, 155
Christianson v. Chicago, St. Paul, Minneapolis & Omaha Railway Co., 291, 732
Christie v. Board of Regents of University of Michigan, 596

Christie v. Callahan, 378
Christie v. Davey, 624
Christie v. Greenleaf, 855
Christie v. Griggs, 243, 252
Christini v. Griffin Hospital, 596
Christopher v. Akin, 823
Christopher v. Whitmire, 758
Christopherson v. Bare, 112
Christopherson v. Minneapolis, St. Paul & Sault Ste. Marie Railway Co., 520
Christou v. Arlington Park-Washington Park Race Tracks Corp., 226, 233
Christy v. Chicago, Burlington & Quincy Railroad Co., 646, 647, 649
Christy v. Florida Power Corp., 513
Christy v. Rice, 872
Christy Brothers Circus v. Turnage, 364
Chronopoulos v. Gil Wyner Co., 422
Chrudinsky v. Evans, 329
Chrysler Corp. v. Taylor, 657, 708
Chudnovski v. Eckels, 664
Chumbler v. McClure, 187
Chunot v. Larson, 539
Church v. Meeker, 77
Church, State v., 43, 44, 45
Church v. Swetland, 763
Churchill v. Briggs, 520
Churchill v. Hulbert, 140
Churchill v. Norfolk & Western Railway Co., 206
Ciaglo v. Ciaglo, 414
Ciccarello v. Gottlieb, 983
Ciconte v. Shockley, 627
Cieplinski v. Severn, 47, 49, 51, 307
Cillers v. Monsley, 786
Cincinnati & Hammond Spring Co. v. Brown, 406
Cincinnati, New Orleans & Texas Pacific Railway Co. v. Cundiff, 154
Cincinnati, New Orleans & Texas Pacific Railway Co. v. Marrs' Administratrix, 378
Cincinnati, New Orleans & Texas Pacific Railway Co. v. Thompson, 487
Cincinnati Baseball Club v. Eno, 489
Cincinnati Bengals, Inc. v. Bergey, 994
Cintrone v. Hertz Truck Leasing & Rental Service, 719
Ciriack v. Merchants' Woolen Co., 488
Cirillo v. City of Milwaukee, 474
Cisson v. Pickens Savings & Loan Association, 889
Cities Service Co. v. Merritt, 619
Citizens & Southern National Bank v. Hendricks, 801
Citizens' Bank of Madison v. Shaw, 91
Citizens' Bank of St. Louis v. Tiger Tail Mill & Land Co., 104
Citizens Committee for the Hudson Valley v. Volpe, 647
Citizens Industrial Bank of Austin v. Oppenheim, 100
Citizens Light, Heat & Power Co. v. Montgomery Light & Water Power Co., 994
Citizens Savings & Loan Association v. Fischer, 752
Citizens State Bank v. Martin, 201
Citizens State Bank of Long Beach v. Hoffman, 878
Citrola v. Eastern Air Lines, 260

Citrone v. O'Rourke Engineering Construction Co., 572
City & County of San Francisco v. Ho Sing, 342
City Deposit Bank v. Green, 762
City National Bank v. Burns, 736
City National Bank v. National Park Bank, 666
City of (see name of city)
City Water Power Co. v. City of Fergus Falls, 550
Clafin v. Wilcox, 30
Clarimont v. Cilley, 570
Clairol, Inc. v. Andrea Dumon, Inc., 1016
Clairol, Inc. v. Boton Discount Center of Berkley, Inc., 1015
Clampitt v. Doyle, 730
Clancy v. R. O'Brien & Co., 717
Clapham v. Yanga, 189
Clarahan v. Cosper, 996
Clare v. Farrell, 809
Clark v. Arkansas Democrat Co., 493
Clark v. Associated Retail Credit Men, 62, 63
Clark v. Bayer, 924
Clark v. Bendix Corp., 706
Clark v. Chambers, 307
Clark v. Chase Hotel Co., 438
Clark v. Chicago & Northwestern Railway Co., 650
Clark v. Choctawhatchee Electric Cooperative, 363
Clark v. City of St. Joseph, 219
Clark v. Corby, 430
Clark v. Di Prima, 551
Clark v. Downing, 40
Clark v. E.I. Du Pont de Nemours Powder Co., 318
Clark v. Edging, 204
Clark v. Foot, 544
Clark v. Gay, 39
Clark v. Gibbons, 271
Clark v. Goodwin, 941
Clark v. Haggard, 742, 746
Clark v. Inhabitants of the Hundred of Blything, 529
Clark v. International Harvester Co., 657, 708
Clark v. Keliher, 137
Clark v. London General Omnibus Co., 945
Clark v. Longview Public Service Co., 396
Clark v. McBaine, 830, 831
Clark v. McClurg, 14
Clark v. Maloney, 103
Clark v. Molyneux, 835
Clark v. Morrison, 794
Clark v. Newsam, 323
Clark v. Orr, 921
Clark v. Otis Engineering Corp., 384
Clark v. Pearson, 781
Clark v. Pennsylvania Railroad Co., 636
Clark, People v., 646
Clark v. Rideout, 100, 105
Clark v. Service Auto Co., 143
Clark v. Sheriff, 11
Clark v. Smith, 362
Clark, State v., 127
Clark v. Tilton, 152
Clark v. United States, 550
Clark, United States v., 159

Clark v. Wiles, 78
Clark v. Wilmington & Weldon Railroad Co., 465
Clark v. Winn, 150
Clark, People ex rel. Dyer v., 644
Clark, State ex rel. v. Osborne, 158
Clark-Aiken Co. v. Cromwell-Wright Co., 556
Clark Equipment Co. v. Wheat, 508
Clarke v. City of Greer, 12
Clarke v. Fitch, 774
Clarke v. Holmes, 490
Clarke v. Mylkes, 144
Clarke v. O'Connor, 446
Clarke v. Shee, 675
Clarke v. Zettick, 776
Clarklift, Inc. v. Reutimann, 949
Clark's Administrator v. Kentucky Utilities Co., 171, 304
Clary v. Hale, 885
Clasen v. Pruhs, 157, 158, 159, 905
Claus v. Farmers & Stockgrowers State Bank, 762
Clausen v. R.W. Gilbert Construction Co., 514
Clauser v. Taylor, 739
Clawson v. Pierce-Arrow Motor Co., 504
Claxton v. Pool, 913
Clay v. Roberts, 777
Clayman v. Bernstein, 856, 859
Claypool v. United States, 423
Clayton v. New Dreamland Roller Skating Rink, 37, 42
Clayton v. Penn Central Transportation Co., 403, 404, 408
Cleary v. Booth, 158
Cleary v. Webster, 783
Cleaver v. Dresser Industries, 219
Clegg v. Boston Storage Warehouse Co., 97
Clemens v. O'Brien, 520
Clemens, State ex rel. v. Witthaus, 855
Clement v. Chivis, 775
Clement v. Crosby & Co., 319
Clement v. Major, 879
Clemente v. United States, 374
Clements v. Stephens, 486, 487, 489
Clements v. Withers, 995
Clemm v. Atchison, Topeka & Santa Fe Railroad Co., 362
Clemmons v. Danforth, 817
Clemmons v. King, 339
Clemmons v. Life Insurance Co. of Georgia, 13
Clemons v. Busby, 525
Clerk, Rex v., 799
Cleveland v. American Motorists Insurance Co., 206
Cleveland v. Citizens' Gaslight Co., 633
Cleveland v. City of Bangor, 330
Cleveland & Eastern Railway Co. v. Somers, 573
Cleveland, Cincinnati, Chicago & St. Louis Railway Co. v. Hilligoss, 332, 335
Cleveland, Cincinnati, Chicago & St. Louis Railway Co. v. Kloo, 350, 464
Cleveland, Cincinnati, Chicago & St. Louis Railway Co. v. Stewart, 555
Cleveland-Cliffs Iron Co. v. Metzner, 398

Cleveland Electric Illuminating Co. v. Van Benshoten, 394
Cleveland Leader Printing Co. v. Nethersole, 832, 964
Cleveland Park Club v. Perry, 73, 75, 76, 1071
Clevenger v. Baker Voorhis & Co., 776
Clewell v. Plummer, 182
Clifford v. Cochrane, 792
Clinard v. City of Winston-Salem, 1050
Cline v. Holdredge, 789
Cline v. Tait, 152
Clinkenbeard v. Reinert, 565
Clinkscales v. Carver, 222
Clinton v. Lyons & Co., 542
Clinton v. Myers, 27
Clise v. Prunty, 486
Closgard Wardrobe Co. v. Normandy, 879
Closson v. Staples, 895
Clott v. Greyhound Lines, Inc., 210
Cloud v. Kit Manufacturing Co., 709
Clough v. London & N. W. R. Co., 732
Clouston v. Remlinger Oldsmobile Cadillac, Inc., 931
Cloutier v. Great Atlantic & Pacific Tea Co., 1029, 1030
Clover Fork Coal Co. v. Daniels, 404
Cluff v. Farmers Insurance Exchange, 62
Cluthe v. Svendsen, 915
Clutter v. Johns-Manville Sales Corp., 167
Clyde v. Southern Public Utilities Co., 464
Coakley v. Degner, 985
Coalite, Inc. v. Aldridge, 553
Coates v. Chinn, 390
Coates v. Dewoskin, 294
Coates v. United States, 1040
Coath v. Jones, 383
Coatney v. Southwest Tennessee Electric Membership Corp., 299
Coats v. State, 127, 128
Cobb v. Atlantic Coast Line Railroad Co., 10
Cobb v. Chubeck, 252
Cobb v. Cumberland County Power & Light Co., 232
Cobb, State v., 74
Cobb v. Tinsley, 790, 794
Cobb v. Twitchell, 265, 544
Cobbs v. Chicago Defender, 791, 792, 799
Cobbs v. Grant, 190, 191
Coble v. Lacey, 339
Coburn v. Lenox Homes, Inc., 193, 195
Coburn v. Village of Swanton, 421
Coca Cola Bottling Co. v. Davidson, 262
Coca Cola Bottling Works v. Lyons, 695
Coca Cola Bottling Works v. Shelton, 247, 682
Coca Cola Bottling Works, Inc. v. Crow, 249
Coca-Cola Co. v. Chero-Cola Co., 1015
Cochran v. Abercrombie, 414
Cochran v. Couzens, 820
Cochran v. International Harvester Co., 204
Cochran v. Laton, 661, 667
Cochran v. Sears, Roebuck & Co., 798, 827
Cochran v. Thompson, 398
Cochrane v. William Penn Hotel, 574
Cochrane v. Wittbold, 841

Cocke v. Jenner, 332
Cockrum v. Baumgartner, 372
Coddington v. City of Lewiston, 937
Code v. Jones, 648
Cody v. J.A. Dodds & Sons, 911
Coe v. Ware, 762
Coeur d'Alene Lumber Co. v. Thompson, 404
Coffee v. McDonnell-Douglas Corp., 381
Coffelt, State ex rel. v. Hartford Accident & Indemnity Co., 13
Coffey v. City of Milwaukee, 1050
Coffey v. Midland Broadcasting Co., 787, 812
Coffey v. Myers, 871, 890
Coffin v. Brown, 10, 842
Coffin v. Coffin, 820
Coffindaffer v. Coffindaffer, 903
Coffman v. Henderson, 967, 975
Coffman v. Kennedy, 519
Coffman v. Louisville & Nashville Railroad Co., 585
Coffman v. Spokane Chronicle Publishing Co., 810, 846
Cofield v. Griffin, 762
Coggs v. Bernard, 210, 659
Cogliati v. Ecco High Frequency Corp., 448, 449
Cogswell v. Boston & Maine Railroad, 954, 956
Cogswell v. Murphy, 326
Cogswell v. New York, New Haven & Hartford Railroad Co., 567
Cohan v. Associated Fur Farms, 683
Cohen v. Bowdoin, 821, 1057
Cohen v. Brockton Savings Bank, 564
Cohen v. Citizens National Trust & Savings Bank, 743
Cohen v. Cowles Publishing Co., 832
Cohen v. Davies, 442
Cohen v. Dry Dock E.B. & B.R. Co., 505
Cohen v. Koster, 97
Cohen v. Lit Brothers, 141
Cohen v. Marx, 860
Cohen v. Mayor of New York, 567, 646
Cohen v. Minzesheimer, 972
Cohen v. New York Times Co., 774
Cohn v. Saidel, 894
Coke v. Gutkese, 207
Colborn v. Freeman, 527
Colby v. Carney Hospital, 1070
Colby v. Life Indemnity & Investment Co., 760
Colby v. Porter, 101
Colby v. Schwartz, 378
Colby v. Walker, 332
Colditz v. Eastern Airlines, Inc., 246
Cole v. Arizona Edison Co., 671
Cole v. Atlanta & West Point Railroad Co., 57
Cole v. Drew, 151
Cole v. Fisher, 85
Cole v. Gerhart, 769
Cole v. German Savings & Loan Society, 318
Cole v. Housing Authority of La Salle County, 405, 411, 412
Cole v. Johnson, 922
Cole v. Lippitt, 326
Cole v. Millspaugh, 776

Cole v. Neaf, 895
Cole v. Richards, 820
Cole v. Rowen, 131
Cole v. Schweer, 85, 87
Cole v. Sears, Roebuck & Co., 909
Cole v. Shell Petroleum Corp., 266
Cole v. Turner, 39, 41, 42
Cole v. Woods, 529, 531
Cole, Richard J. v. Manhattan Modes Co., 1021
Colegrove v. City of Corning, 876, 888
Coleman v. Associated Pipeline Contractors, Inc., 397
Coleman v. Bennett, 327, 634
Coleman v. Bent, 518
Coleman v. Francis, 97
Coleman v. Garrison, 371
Coleman v. New Amsterdam Casualty Co., 587, 588
Coleman v. New York & New Haven Railroad Co., 133
Coleman v. Newark Morning Ledger Co., 836
Coleman v. Night Commander Lighting Co., 761
Coleman v. Shirlen, 925
Coleman v. Steinberg, 440
Coleman & Morris v. Pisciotta, 988
Coleman Vitrified Brick Co. v. Smith, 352
Coles v. McNamara, 155
Coley v. Hecker, 963
Colgate-Palmolive Co. v. Tullos, 852, 867
Collatz v. Fox Wisconsin Amusement Corp., 1006
Collazo v. Manhattan & Bronx Surface Transit Operating Authority, 532
Collentine v. City of New York, 568
Collette v. Boston & Maine Railroad Co., 196
Collier v. Citizens Coach Co., 295
Collier v. Ernst, 624
Collier County Publishing Co. v. Chapman, 971
Colligan v. Cousar, 718
Colligen v. Philadelphia Electric Co., 411
Collingwood v. Home and Colonial Stores, 543, 546
Collins v. Altamaha Electric Membership Corp., 174
Collins v. B.F. Goodrich Co., 184
Collins v. Becnel, 948
Collins v. Bennett, 101
Collins v. Board of Education of Kent County, 1048
Collins v. City National Bank & Trust Co., 305
Collins v. City National Bank & Trust Co. of Danbury, 53
Collins v. Cronin, 324
Collins v. Dispatch Publishing Co., 775
Collins v. Gee, 948
Collins v. George, 544
Collins v. Gifford, 1072
Collins v. Hall, 955
Collins v. Hayte, 890
Collins v. Lindsay, 760
Collins v. Liquid Transporters, Inc., 550
Collins v. Malin, 791
Collins v. Oklahoma State Hospital, 786, 822
Collins v. Otto, 542
Collins v. Renison, 132
Collins v. State, 199
Collins v. Troy Laundry Co., 575

Collins v. Virginia Power & Electric Co., 482
Collins v. West Jersey Express Co., 304
Collins Baking Co. v. Savage, 262
Collins' Executors v. Standard Accident Insurance Co., 588
Collinson v. Jeffries, 754
Collis v. Ashe, 254
Collis v. Hoskins, 928
Collyer v. S.H. Kress & Co., 141
Colonial Insurance Co. v. Industrial Accident Commission, 351
Colonial Natural Gas Co. v. Sayers, 422, 440, 441, 487
Colonial Savings Association v. Taylor, 1008
Colonial Stores v. Barrett, 802
Colorado & Southern Railway Co. v. Western Light & Power Co., 343
Colorado Flying Academy, Inc. v. United States, 454
Colorado Mortgage & Investment Co. v. Giacomini, 437, 438
Colpoys v. Gates, 823
Colson v. Rule, 496
Colter v. Lower, 53, 54
Colton v. Foulkes, 723
Colton v. Onderdonk, 550
Columbia, City of v. Wilks, 423
Columbia Broadcasting System, Inc. v. Democratic National Committee, 1025
Columbia Broadcasting System, Inc. v. Melody Record, Inc., 1020
Columbia River Fishermen's Protective Union v. City of St. Helens, 650
Columbian Carbon Co. v. Tholen, 552
Columbus Finance, Inc. v. Howard, 888
Columbus Gaslight & Coke Co. v. Freeland, 628
Columbus Mining Co. v. Napier's Administrator, 397
Colvard v. Black, 775, 783
Colvin v. Tallassee Power Co., 649, 651
Colyer v. Richard K. Fox Publishing Co., 853, 860
Coman v. Williams, 742
Comba v. Town of Ridgefield, 391
Combes v. Montgomery Ward & Co., 827
Combined Insurance Co. of America v. Sinclair, 212, 503
Combow v. Kansas City Ground Investment Co., 447
Combs v. Hunt, 587
Comeau v. Harrington, 223
Comer v. Age Herald Publishing Co., 847
Comer v. Gregory, 478
Comfort v. McCorkle, 379
Comfort v. Penner, 222
Commercial Carrier Corp. v. Indian River County, 1049
Commercial Credit Co. v. Eisenhour, 91
Commercial Credit Co. v. Spence, 141
Commercial National Bank v. Nacogdoches Compress & Warehouse Co., 733
Commercial Publishing Co. v. Smith, 842
Commercial Savings Bank v. Kietges, 760
Commercial State Bank v. Gidney, 1012
Commercial Union Assurance Co. v. Pacific Gas & Electric Co., 148

Commercial Union Fire Insurance Co. v. Blocker, 403, 404
Commercial Union Insurance Co. of New York v. Reichard, 13
Comminge v. Stevenson, 552
Commissioners of Anne Arundel County v. Watts, 650
Commodore Cruise Line, Limited v. Kormendi, 507
Commonwealth v. (see opposing party)
Commonwealth Fuel Co. v. McNeil, 769
Community Federal Savings & Loan Association v. Orondorff, 1017
Campco Corp. v. Day-Brite Lighting, Inc., 1018, 1021
Compere, State ex rel. Marron v., 644
Compton v. Daniels, 239
Compton v. Evans, 661, 941
Compton v. Lea, 547
Comstock v. General Motors Corp., 319, 704, 710
Comstock v. Shannon, 763
Comstock v. Wilson, 364
Comte v. Blessing, 917, 921
Conard v. Dillingham, 845
Conboy v. Crofoot, 570
Concanan v. Boynton, 75
Concerned Consumers League v. O'Neill, 1026
Concordia Fire Insurance Co. v. Simmons Co., 382
Condel v. Savo, 914
Conder v. Morrison, 881
Condict v. Hewitt, 122
Condon v. Exton-Hall Brokerage & Vessel Agency, 1008
Cone v. Inter County Telephone & Telegraph Co., 281, 309
Conery v. Tackmaier, 197
Congressional Country Club v. Baltimore & Ohio Railroad Co., 574
Congrove v. Holmes, 190
Conino v. Landry, 521
Conkright v. Ballantyne of Omaha, Inc., 476
Conlan v. Roemer, 758
Connecticut v. Pennsylvania Railroad Co., 394
Connecticut General Life Insurance Co. v. Chase, 739
Connecticut Mutual Life Insurance Co. v. New York & N.H.R. Co., 999
Connell v. A.C.L. Haasa & Sons Fish Co., 783
Connellan v. Coffey, 268
Connellee v. Nees, 517
Connelly v. Kaufmann & Baer Co., 376
Connelly v. McKay, 778
Connelly v. Nolte, 591
Connelly v. Southern Railway Co., 218
Connelly v. United States Steel Co., 333
Connelly v. Western Union Telegraph Co., 362
Connelly Co., F. B. v. Schleuter Brothers, 761
Conner v. Farmers & Merchants Bank, 382, 445
Conner v. Mangum, 477
Conner v. Mertz, 476
Conner v. Taylor, 826
Conner v. Winton, 184
Conner v. Woodfill, 78, 627
Connery v. Manning, 893
Connett v. Fremont City School District, 1048

Connolly v. Bolster, 587
Connolly v. Des Moines Investment Co., 512
Connolly v. Hagi, 703
Connolly v. Nicollet Hotel, 384, 392
Connor v. Great Western Savings & Loan Association, 721
Connor v. Greenberg, 75
Connor v. Grosso, 349
Connor v. Southland Corp., 519, 521
Connors v. Connolly, 983
Conover v. Northern States Power Co., 420, 512, 514
Conrad v. Allis-Chalmers Mfg. Co., 835
Conrad v. Roberts, 824
Conrad v. Springfield Consolidated Railway Co., 229, 480
Conrad v. Youghiogheny & Ohio Coal Co., 575
Conradi v. Helvogt, 444
Conroy v. Allston Storage Warehouse Co., 422
Conroy v. Briley, 491
Conroy v. Commercial Casualty Insurance Co., 588
Conroy v. Fall River Herald News Co., 825, 848
Conroy v. Pittsburgh Times, 974
Conroy v. 10 Brewster Ave. Corp., 442
Consolidated Biscuit Co. v. Illinois Power Co., 671
Consolidated Coach Corp. v. Burge, 338, 339
Consolidated Gas Co. v. Connor, 374, 661
Consolidated Gas Co. v. Folsom, 756
Consolidated Packaging Machine Corp. v. Kelly, 994
Consolidated Traction Co. v. Hone, 958
Constantino v. Watson Contracting Co., 413
Constantino v. Wolverine Insurance Co., 181
Constitution Publishing Co. v. Way, 779, 846
Continental Air Ticketing Agency, Inc. v. Empire International Travel, Inc., 968, 971
Continental Auto Lease Corp. v. Campbell, 532
Continental Casualty Co. v. Garrett, 60, 62
Continental Coal, Land & Timber Co. v. Kilpatrick, 750
Continental Development Corp. of Florida v. DuVal Title & Abstract Co., 968, 969, 971
Continental Management, Inc. v. United States, 982, 1004, 1015
Continental National Bank v. Bowdre, 798
Continental Nut Co. v. Robert L. Berner Corp., 973
Continental Oil Co. v. Simpson, 220, 226
Continental Optical Co. v. Reed, 858, 860
Continental Paper Bag Co. v. Maine Central Railroad Co., 316
Continental Supply Co. v. Price, 969
Contreras v. St. Luke's Hospital, 257
Convey-all Corp. v. Pacific Intermountain Express Co., 209
Conway v. Furst, 570
Conway v. Grant, 136, 562
Conway v. O'Brien, 173, 923, 996
Conway v. Reed, 30
Conway v. Skelly Oil Co., 974
Conwell v. Emire, 146, 148
Conzelmann v. Northwest Poultry & Dairy Products Co., 764
Cook v. City of Fall River, 626

TABLE OF CASES

Cook v. City of Winston-Salem, 175
Cook v. Cook, 904, 905
Cook v. Cox, 786
Cook v. Demetrakas, 430
Cook v. Export Leaf Tobacco Co., 454
Cook v. Gust, 828
Cook v. Hall, 525
Cook v. Harris, 163
Cook v. Hastings, 52
Cook v. Hill, 820
Cook v. Johnston, 307
Cook v. Kinzua Pine Mills Co., 36, 41
Cook v. Lewis, 271
Cook v. Minneapolis, St. Paul & Sault St. Marie Railway Co., 267, 353
Cook v. Patterson, 103
Cook, People v., 130
Cook v. Pulitzer Pub. Co., 835
Cook v. Seidenverg, 226
Cook, State v., 130, 476
Cook v. Sweatt, 933
Cook v. Thomas, 196, 197
Cook v. Ward, 823
Cook v. Wood, 921
Cool v. Crommet, 540
Cooley v. Public Service Co., 172
Coon v. Moffitt, 928
Coon v. Syracuse & Utica Railroad Co., 571
Co-op Cab Co. v. Singleton, 507
Cooper v. Alabama Farm Bureau, 506
Cooper v. Armour, 871
Cooper v. Central Railroad of Iowa, 569
Cooper v. Chitty, 89
Cooper v. City of Philadelphia, 441
Cooper v. Driggers, 465
Cooper v. Fort Smith & Western Railroad Co., 754
Cooper v. Greeley, 781
Cooper v. Hall, 75
Cooper v. Hoeglund, 223
Cooper v. Lawson, 842
Cooper v. Lovering, 758
Cooper v. Mayes, 570
Cooper v. Metropolitan Government of Nashville & Davidson County, 510, 512, 514
Cooper v. Meyer, 915
Cooper v. Philadelphia Dairy Products Co., 340
Cooper v. Richland County, 307
Cooper v. Robert Portner Brewing Co., 566
Cooper v. Roose, 445
Cooper v. Seaverns, 793
Cooper v. Shepherd, 330
Cooper v. Weissblatt, 963
Coopersmith v. Williams, 827
Cope v. Sharpe, 148
Copeland v. Baltimore & Ohio Railroad Co., 214
Coplea v. Bybee, 897, 899
Copley v. Balle, 438
Copley v. Putter, 271
Copley v. Wills, 542, 563
Corbett v. Clarke, 310, 345, 348

Corbett v. Curtis, 486
Corbett v. Scott, 233
Corbitt v. Ringley-Crockett, Inc., 201
Corby v. Foster, 915
Corby v. Hill, 417
Corby v. Ramsdell, 450
Corcoran v. Banner Super Market, 250
Corcoran v. Corcoran, 794
Corcoran v. Jerrel, 818
Corcoran v. Postal Telegraph Cable Co., 362
Corcoran v. Village of Libertyville, 406, 407, 408, 409
Cordas v. Peerless Transportation Co., 196
Cordele, City of v. Turton's, 514
Cordell v. Standard Oil Co., 50, 120
Cordingley v. Allied Van Lines, Inc., 484
Cordula v. Dietrich, 414
Corey v. Havener, 266
Corinti v. Wittkopp, 313
Cork v. Blossom, 512
Corley v. Lewless, 529, 913
Corliss v. E.W. Walker Co., 850, 860
Corn v. French, 119, 189
Corn v. Sheppard, 65
Cornbrooks v. Terminal Barber Shops, 269, 684
Cornelius v. Cornelius, 922
Cornell v. Mahoney, 97
Cornell v. State, 507
Cornell Steamboat Cor. v. Scholl, 105
Corner Stone Bank v. Rhodes, 733
Cornett v. Agee, 391
Cornett v. Fetzer, 821
Cornman v. Eastern Counties R. Co., 170
Cornpropst v. Sloan, 385
Cornutt v. Bolin, 414, 426
Coronado Development Corp. v. Millikin, 966
Coronado Mining Corp. v. Marathon Oil Co., 987
Coronet Development Co. v. F.S.W., Inc., 986
Corpman v. Boyer, 937
Corporation of City of Glasgow v. Taylor, 403
Correia v. Santos, 791, 792
Correll v. Werner, 456
Corrigal v. Ball & Dodd Funeral Home, Inc., 362
Corrigan v. Antupit, 439, 440
Corrigan v. Bobbs-Merrill Co., 10, 809, 845, 969
Corrigan v. Elsinger, 511
Corrigan v. Janney, 446
Corrington v. Kalicak, 68
Corry v. Pennsylvania Railroad Co., 665
Corso v. Merrill, 366
Cort v. Ash, 221
Cortes v. Baltimore Insular Line, 376
Cortez Roofing, Inc. v. Barolo, 244
Corthell v. Holmes, 642
Corwine v. Maracaibo Oil Exploration Corp., 11
Cory v. Physical Culture Hotel, 79
Cory v. Shierloh, 200
Cosden Oil Co. v. Sides, 551
Cosgriff Neon Co. v. Matthews, 723
Cosgrove v. Shusterman, 457
Cosgrove Studio & Camera Shop, Inc. v. Pane, 783

Cosmopolitan National Bank of Chicago v. Heap, 908
Coss v. Spaulding, 661
Costanzo v. Sturgill, 525
Costello v. Ten Eyck, 665
Costello v. Wells Fargo Bank, 1000
Costigan v. Pennsylvania Railroad Co., 82
Costigan's Case, 336
Coston v. Skyland Hotel, 420, 421
Coston v. State, 37
Cosulich v. Standard Oil Co., 549
Cote v. Litawa, 286, 365
Cote v. Martel, 948
Cote v. Palmer, 491
Cottle v. Johnson, 10
Cottman v. Lochner, 648
Cottom v. McGuire Funeral Service, Inc., 703
Cotton v. Cooper, 14
Cotton v. Fisheries Products Co., 845
Cotton v. Kambly, 186, 927
Cottrill v. Crum, 751
Cougar Business Owners Association v. State, 1050
Coughlin v. United States Tool Co., 410
Coughtry v. Globe Woolen Co., 716
Couillard v. Charles T. Miller Hospital, 334, 335
Coulter v. Coulter, 898, 929
Country Club Apartments, Inc. v. Scott, 435
County of (see name of county)
Courtell v. McEachen, 408
Courtenay v. Earle, 658
Courtney v. Apple, 951
Courtney v. Kneib, 42
Courtois v. General Motors Corp., 705
Courtright v. Southern Compress & Warehouse Co., 407, 410
Courvoisier v. Raymond, 110, 125
Cousins v. Greaves, 560
Covell v. Laming, 85
Coverstone v. Davies, 154, 861, 862
Covington, City of v. Keal, 309
Covington & Cincinnati Bridge Co. v. Steinbrock, 514
Cowan v. Atchison, Topeka & Sante Fe Railway Co., 959
Cowan v. Faribrother, 753
Cowan v. Gamble, 874
Cowan v. Laughridge Construction Co., 220, 231, 420
Cowan v. National Coal Board, 311
Cowan v. One Hour Valet, Inc., 429
Cowan v. Time, Inc., 774, 776
Coward v. Baddeley, 42, 114
Coward v. Borden Foods, Inc., 227
Cowart v. Meeks, 413
Cowden v. Bear Country, Inc., 208, 209
Cowen v. Pressprich, 97
Cowen v. Sunderland, 207, 726
Cowie, State ex rel. v. La Crosse Theaters Co., 644
Cowles' Executor v. Johnson, 752
Cowley v. Cowley, 852
Cowman v. LaVine, 821
Cowper v. Vannier, 773
Cox v. Awtry, 674

Cox v. Burbidge, 561
Cox v. Cameron Lumber Co., 342
Cox v. Cunningham, 145
Cox v. De Jarnette, 596
Cox v. Feeney, 831
Cox v. Klein, 139
Cox v. Lauritsen, 872
Cox v. National Loan & Exchange Bank, 786
Cox v. Northern Airlines, Inc., 255
Cox v. Northwest Airlines, Inc., 247
Cox v. Pearl Investment Co., 333, 334
Cox v. Ray M. Lee Co., 619
Cox v. Rhodes Ave. Hospital, 142
Cox v. Smith, 331
Cox, State v., 127
Cox v. Stolworthy, 10, 11
Cox v. Vernieuw, 162, 164
Cox v. Wagner, 378
Cox v. Wilson, 254
Cox, State ex rel. v. Maryland Electric Railway Co., 335
Cox Broadcasting Corp. v. Cohn, 863
Coxhead v. Richards, 827
Coyne v. Cirilli, 187
Coyne v. Porter-Hayden Co., 167
Cozad, State ex rel. Stewart v., 553
Cozine v. Shuff, 414, 424
Crab Orchard Improvement Co. v. Chesapeake & Ohio Railway Co., 998
Crabtree v. City Auto Salvage Co., 626
Crabtree v. Dawson, 110, 125
Cracraft v. City of St. Louis Park, 1050
Crader v. Jamison, 532
Cragg v. Los Angeles Trust Co., 226
Crago v. Lurie, 220, 223, 231
Craig v. Craig's Estate, 673
Craig v. Crossman, 734
Craig v. Proctor, 972
Craig v. Wright, 825, 834, 841
Craighead v. Sellers, 467
Crain v. Allison, 188, 190, 191, 192
Craker v. Chicago v. Northwestern Railway Co., 37, 42, 55
Cramer v. Cramer, 903
Cramer v. Crutchfield, 886
Cramer v. Tarr, 457
Crane v. Banner, 465
Crane v. Bennett, 799, 846
Crane v. Darling, 791
Crane v. Kansas City Baseball & Exhibition Co., 419, 488
Crane and Hill v. Hummerstone, 323, 325, 329
Crane Co. v. Sears, 683
Crane Lumber Co. v. Bellows, 101
Craney v. Donovan, 794, 848
Crary v. Goodman, 732
Craven v. Wright, 91
Craviolini v. Scholer & Fuller Associated Architects, 993, 1002

Crawford v. Bergen, 42
Crawford v. Brown, 155
Crawford v. Commonwealth, 155
Crawford v. Consumers Power Co., 416
Crawford v. Doggett, 912
Crawford v. Johnson, 237
Crawford v. Kent, 662
Crawford v. Morris, 329, 330
Crawford v. Pacific Western Mobile Estate, Inc., 402, 404, 408, 411
Crawford v. State, 127
Crawford v. Tyrrell, 620, 648
Crawford v. Williams, 560
Crawford Co., H. E. v. Dun & Bradstreet, 835
Crawford Co., H. R. v. Dun & Bradstreet, 829
Crawley v. Terhune, 721
Creasey v. Hogan, 187
Creek v. Laski, 1007
Creelman v. Svenning, 873, 883
Creevy, Rex v., 820
Creighton v. Commonwealth, 127, 128
Crellin v. Thomas, 793, 841
Cremidas v. Fenton, 628
Crenshaw v. O'Connell, 63
Crenshaw Brothers Produce Co. v. Harper, 576
Crescent Motor Co. v. Stone, 519
Cresson v. Louisville Courier Journal, 836
Creswell v. Pruitt, 830
Creswell v. Temple Milling Co., 261
Crevelli v. Chicago, Milwaukee & St. Paul Railway, 959
Crigger v. Coca Cola Bottling Co., 262
Crinkley v. Dow Jones and Co., 964
Crippen v. Pulliam, 119
Criscuola v. Andrews, 950
Crist v. Civil Air Patrol, 557
Criterion Theatre Corp. v. Starns, 426
Crittal v. Horner, 790
Crittenden v. Murphy, 526
Croasdale v. Butell, 78
Crocker v. Carson, 140
Crocker v. Gullifer, 96
Crocker v. Hadley, 775
Crocker v. Winthrop Laboratories, 702
Crockett v. Missouri Pacific Railway Co., 955
Crofford v. Bowden, 761
Croft v. Richardson, 966
Crompton v. Beedle & Thomas, 751, 762
Cronin v. Brownlee, 441
Cronin v. Columbian Manufacturing Co., 177
Cronkhite v. Chaplin, 965
Cropanese v. Martinez, 416
Crosby v. Leng, 8
Cross v. Grant, 918, 921
Cross v. Guthery, 8, 945
Cross v. Huttenlocher, 187, 188, 189
Cross v. Kent, 1073
Cross v. M. C. Carlisle & Co., 723
Cross v. Pacific Gas & Electric Co., 959
Cross v. Trapp, 191
Cross v. Wells Fargo Alarm Services, 380, 381

Crossett v. Campbell, 47
Crosslin v. Alsup, 177
Crossman v. Thurlow, 40
Crosswhite v. Barnes, 41, 150
Croswell, People v., 840
Crotty, Commonwealth v., 149
Crouch v. Hall, 1049
Crouse v. Wilbur-Ellis Co., 342
Crouter v. United Adjusters, Inc., 896
Crow v. Colson, 307, 387
Crow, State v., 45
Crowder v. Jenkins, 1066
Crowder v. Tinkler, 640
Crowe v. Bumford, 931
Crowe v. Domestic Loans, Inc., 347
Crowell v. Crowell, 120, 725, 903
Crowell v. Duncan, 717
Crowell v. Jackson, 737, 738
Crowell v. McCaffrey, 435, 442
Crowhurst v. Amersham Burial Board, 390
Crowley v. Barto, 212
Crown v. Cecil Holland Ford, Inc., 692
Crown v. Orr, 570
Crown Cork & Seal Co. v. Kane, 425
Crown Cycle Co. v. Brown, 672
Crownover v. Gleichman, 957
Croyle v. Moses, 737
Crozman v. Callahan, 776
Cruden v. Fentham, 480
Cruikshank v. Gorden, 791
Crull v. Gleb, 13
Crunk v. Glover, 538, 542, 563
Crutcher v. Cleveland, Cincinnati, Chicago & St. Louis Railway Co., 58
Crutchfield v. Adams, 406
Cruz v. Drezek, 440, 442
Crystal v. Hubbard, 948
Crystal Coca Cola Bottling Co. v. Cathey, 262
Crystal Dome Oil & Gas Co. v. Savic, 14
Crystal Pier Amusement Co. v. Cannon, 744
Csaranko v. Robilt, Inc., 512
Cubit v. O'Dett, 27
Cucinotti v. Ortmann, 44, 45
Cudney v. Braniff Airways, Inc., 247
Cue v. Breland, 993, 1000
Cuellar v. Garcia, 248
Culbert v. Sampson's Supermarkets, Inc., 365, 366
Culbertson v. Coca-Cola Bottling Co., 581
Cullen v. BMW of North America, Inc., 384
Cullen v. City of Minneapolis, 330
Cullen v. Dickinson, 3, 41, 47
Cullen v. Stough, 789
Cullinan v. Tetrault, 517
Cullmann v. Mumper, 416
Culmer v. Wilson, 342
Culp v. Signal Van & Storage Co., 94
Culton v. Asher, 756
Cumberland Corp. v. Metropoulos, 629
Cumberland Glass Manufacturing Co. v. De Witt, 971, 990

Cumberland Telegraph & Telephone Co. v. Martin's Administrator, 413
Cumberland Telephone & Telegraph Co. v. Barnes, 78
Cumberland Torpedo Co. v. Gaines, 552, 620
Cuming v. Brooklyn City Railroad Co., 935
Cummings v. Hoosier Marine Properties, Inc., 510, 514
Cummings v. Jackson, 907
Cummings v. Kendall, 271
Cummings v. Prater, 436
Cummins v. Halliburton Oil Well Cementing Co., 480
Cummins v. Woody, 947
Cunard and Wife v. Antifyre, Ltd., 621, 622
Cunis v. Brennan, 170
Cunningham v. Baltimore & Ohio Railroad Co., 238
Cunningham v. C.R. Pease House Furnishing Co., 206, 726
Cunningham v. Edward, 1007
Cunningham v. Miller, 629
Cunningham v. Reagan, 126
Cunningham v. Rogers, 439
Cunningham v. Yeomans, 140
Cuppy v. Bunch, 385
Curlee v. Scales, 138
Curlender v. Bio-Science Laboratories, 371
Curley v. Automobile Finance Co., 876
Curley v. Hoff, 569, 572
Curnett v. Wolf, 62, 64
Curran v. A.H. Stange Co., 571
Curran v. Connecticut Indemnity Co., 588
Curran v. Galen, 981
Curran v. Lehigh Valley Railroad Co., 520
Currie v. Malloy, 752
Currie v. Silvernale, 147
Currier v. McKee, 581
Currier v. Poor, 767
Curry v. Commonwealth, 154
Curry v. Fruin-Colnon Contracting Co., 179
Curry v. Journal Publishing Co., 286
Curry v. Kline, 920, 921
Curry & Co., Charles F. v. Hedrick, 100
Curtin v. Somerset, 722
Curtis v. Ashworth, 913
Curtis v. Fruin-Colnon Contracting Co., 76
Curtis v. Miller, 919, 920
Curtis v. Perry, 233
Curtis v. Siebrand Brothers Circus & Carnival Co., 12
Curtis v. Traders National Bank, 486
Curtis Bay Towing Co. v. The M/V Maryland Clipper, 471
Curtis Publishing Co. v. Birdsong, 776
Curtis Publishing Co. v. Butts, 1011
Curtiss, People v., 159
Curwen v. Appleton Manufacturing Co., 276
Cushing-Wetmore Co. v. Gray, 649
Cushman v. Carbondale Fuel Co., 587
Cust v. Item Co., 981
Custer v. Kroeger, 126
Custodio v. Bauer, 18, 372
Cuthrell v. Zayre of Virginia, Inc., 885
Cutlip v. Lucky Stores, Inc., 186

Cutter v. Cooper, 921
Cutter v. Hamlen, 436
Cuykendalls' Estate, In re, 43
Cwik v. Zylstra, 905
Czako v. Orban, 941

D

D.S.W. v. Fairbanks North Star Borough School District, 1049
Da Rin v. Casualty Co. of America, 308
Dageforde v. Potomac Edison Co., 366
Daggett v. Davis, 98
Daggett v. Keshner, 288, 314
Daggs v. St. Louis-San Francisco Railway Co., 125
Daggy v. Miller, 323
Dague v. Piper Aircraft Corp., 168
Dahl v. Turner, 379
Dahl v. Valley Dredging Co., 312
Dahlstrom v. Roosevelt Mills, Inc., 619
Dahlstrom v. Shrum, 286, 287, 300
Dahydro, Inc. v. Tretolite Co., 1009
Daigle v. Twin City Ready Mix Concrete Co., 456
Dailey v. City of Birmingham, 380
Daily v. Somberg, 334
Daily Times Democrat v. Graham, 856
Dain v. Wycoff, 926
Daingerfield v. Thompson, 38, 323
Daisey v. Colonial Parking, Inc., 422
Daisey v. Hudson, 78
Dakhyl v. Labouchere, 832
Dakin v. Allis, 333
Dale v. Grant, 999
Dale System v. General Teleradio, 970
Dale System v. Time, Inc., 972
Dalehite v. United States, 1036, 1038
Dalhoff Construction Co. v. Block, 752
Dalkowitz Brothers v. Schreiner, 445
Dall v. Time, Inc., 780, 809
Dallas v. H. J. Koehler Sporting Goods Co., 673
Dallas, City of v. Jackson, 385
Dallas Cowboys Cheerleaders, Inc. v. Pussycat Cinema, Limited, 1016, 1017, 1018
Dallas Railway & Terminal Co. v. Ector, 350
Dallavo v. Snider, 792
Dallessandro v. Henry Holt & Co., 854, 862
D'Almeida v. Boston & Maine Railroad Co., 716
Dalrymple v. Sinkoe, 726
D'Altomonte v. New York Herald Co., 780, 863, 864
Dalton v. Great Atlantic & Pacific Tea Co., 317
Dalton v. Meister, 843
Dalton v. Woodward, 793
Dalton, City of v. Anderson, 444
Daluiso v. Boone, 132, 144
Daly v Bergstedt, 343, 512
Daly v. General Motors Corp., 478, 712
Daly v. Proetz, 732
Daly City v. Holbrook, 7
Dalziel v. Press Publishing Co., 846
Damasiewicz v. Gorsuch, 368

D'Ambra v. United States, 366
D'Ambrosio v. City of Philadelphia, 229
Damiano v. Damiano, 906
D'Amico v. Moriarty Meat Co., 343
D'Amicol v. Alvarez Shipping Co., 366
Damilitis v. Kerjas Lunch Corp., 54
Damm v. Elyria Lodge No. 465, p. 911
Damron v. C. R. Anthony Co., 511
Damron v. Hagy, 164
Damron v. Roach, 76
Dana v. Bursey, 487
Danann Realty Corp. v. Harris, 665, 764
Danculovich v. Brown, 214, 477, 478
Dand v. Sexton, 85
Danforth v. Briggs, 77
Danforth v. Emmons, 958
Dangel v. Offset Printing Co., 890, 892
Danhof v. Osborne, 581
Daniel v. Daniel, 665, 763
Daniel v. Mitchell, 756
Daniel v. Phillips Petroleum Co., 51
Daniel, State v., 44, 46, 56
Danielenko v. Kinney Rent A Car, Inc., 202
Daniels v. Adkins Protective Service, Inc., 362
Daniels v. Andersen, 1048, 1063
Daniels v. Anderson, 203
Daniels v. Celeste, 334
Daniels v. Evans, 181
Daniels v. Florida Central & Peninsular Railroad Co., 58
Daniels v. Foster & Kleiser, 674
Daniels v. Luechtefeld, 569
Daniels v. New York, New Haven & Hartford Railroad Co., 311
Daniels v. Parker, 327
Daniels v. Sanitarium Association, 779
Danielson v. Roche, 119
Danile v. Oak Park Arms Hotel, Inc., 507
Danis v. New York Central Railroad Co., 948
Danley-Evers Furniture Co. v. Cauley, 85
D'Anna v. United States, 557
Danner v. Arnsberg, 299, 307
Dannerburg v. Ashley, 1003
Danos v. St. Pierre, 370
Danziger v. Hearst Corp., 837
Dapkunas v. Cagle, 446
D'Aquilla v. Pryor, 558
Darbrinsky v. Pennsylvania Co., 959
Darby v. Clare Food & Relish Co., 562
Darden v. McMillian, 73
Darling v. Clement, 792
Darling v. Mansfield, 848
Darragh v. County of Nassau, 166
Darryl v. Ford Motor Co., 696, 704
Dart v. Pure Oil Co., 221, 461
Dashaway Association v. Rogers, 672
Dashiell v. Keauhou-Kona Co., 531
Daubert v. Western Meat Co., 959
Daughdrill v. Diamond "M" Drilling Co., 950
Daugherty v. Daugherty, 1007
Daugherty v. Hershberger, 335

Daugherty v. Herzog, 722
Daugherty v. Reveal, 102
Daugherty v. Thomas, 527
Daun v. Truax, 229
Dauncey v. Holloway, 792
Daurizio v. Merchants' Dispatch Transportation Co., 621, 622
Davenport v. State Farm Mutual Automobile Insurance Co., 944
Davey v. Harrow Corp., 391
Davey v. Turner, 723
David v. Belmont, 767, 769
David v. Larochelle, 149
David v. Missouri Pacific Railway Co., 383
Davids v. State, 154
Davidson v. Cornell, 570
Davidson v. Leadingham, 703
Davidson v. Otter Tail Power Co., 303
Davidson v. Walter, 798
Davidson's, Inc. v. Scott, 248
Davies v. Bennison, 79
Davies v. Butler, 178, 478
Davies v. Delaware, Lackawanna & Western Railroad Co., 283, 387, 394
Davies v. Gardiner, 772, 793
Davies v. Land O'Lakes Racing Association, 408
Davies v. Mann, 463
Davies v. Solomon, 794
Davies v. United States, 503
Davies v. Western Union Telegraph Co., 1008
Davila v. Sanders, 196
DaVinci Creations, Inc. v. Nu-Frame Co., 246
Davis v. Askin's Retail Stores, 802
Davis v. Atlas Assurance Co., 564
Davis v. Bostick, 909, 910
Davis v. Boyle Brothers, Inc., 891
Davis v. Broad Street Garage, 337
Davis v. Bushnell, 181
Davis v. Central Congregational Society, 422
Davis v. Collins, 38
Davis v. Commonwealth, 153
Davis v. Condit, 923
Davis v. Cox, 215, 217
Davis v. Davis, 753, 754
Davis v. DelRosso, 506
Davis v. Donohoe-Kelly Banking Co., 97
Davis v. Garden Services, Inc., 423
Davis v. Garrett, 315
Davis v. Gavalas, 914
Davis v. General Finance & Thrift Corp., 857
Davis v. Georgia-Pacific Corp., 70
Davis v. Goodrich, 407
Davis v. Guarnieri, 452
Davis v. Harrod, 911
Davis v. Hearst, 799, 848
Davis v. Henderlong Lumber Co., 724
Davis v. Highway Motor Underwriters, 586
Davis v. Jackson, 255, 417
Davis v. John L. Whiting & Son Co., 516
Davis v. Johnson, 54

Davis v. L. & W. Construction Co., 550
Davis v. Littlefield, 524, 526
Davis v. Louisville Trust Co., 736, 744, 745
Davis v. McKey, 38
Davis v. McMillan, 881, 888
Davis v. Marathon Oil Co., 220
Davis v. Margolis, 958
Davis v. Moore, 1067
Davis v. Nash, 78
Davis v. New England Railway Publishing Co., 963, 967, 977
Davis v. Niagara Falls Tower Co., 553, 619
Davis v. Niederhof, 781
Davis v. Potter, 384
Davis v. R.K.O. Radio Pictures, 781, 783
Davis v. Reynolds, 762
Davis v. Richardson, 45
Davis v. St. Louis & San Francisco Railroad Co., 669
Davis v. Sanderman, 717
Davis v. Sanders, 871
Davis v. Schmitt Brothers, 439
Davis v. Schuchat, 807, 845
Davis v. Seeley, 888
Davis v. Shiappacossee, 300
Davis v. Silverwood, 424
Davis v. Sladden, 793
Davis v. Sobik's Sandwich Shops, Inc., 251, 252
Davis v. Spindler, 523
Davis v. State, 126
Davis, State v., 40, 43, 44, 128
Davis v. Stone, 73
Davis v. Tacoma Railway & Power Co., 58
Davis v. Teague, 888
Davis v. Thornton, 224, 300, 304
Davis v. Tirrell, 187
Davis v. Tunison, 888
Davis v. United States, 154
Davis v. Waterman, 181
Davis v. Wyeth Laboratories, Inc., 688, 697
Davis, Town of v. Davis, 644
Davis' Administrator v. Ohio Valley Banking & Trust Co., 398
Davis & Alcott Co. v. Boozer, 47
Davis & Son, W. B. v. Ruple, 662
Davis & Sons v. Shepstone, 776
Davis Pontiac Co. v. Sirois, 528
Davison v. Snohomish County, 172
Davoust v. City of Alameda, 412
Davy v. Greenlaw, 224
Dawe v. Morris, 764
Dawkins v. Billingsley, 775
Dawson v. Eli Lilly & Co., 167
Dawson v. Kitch, 439
Dawson v. Mead, 879
Dawson Cotton Oil Co. v. Kenan, McKay & Speir, 660
Day v. Bream, 803, 811
Day v. Castilow, 443
Day v. Day, 642, 643
Day v. Edwards, 30
Day v. Fort Scott Investment & Improvement Co., 730

Day v. Great Eastern Casualty Co., 310
Day v. Hunnicutt, 1003
Day v. Pauly, 229
Day v. Porter, 330
Day v. Trans World Airlines, Inc., 220
Day v. Walton, 324
Dayton v. Drumheller, 818
Dayton v. Palmer, 228
De Ark v. Nashville Stone Setting Corp., 388
De Bardelaben v. Stallings, 326, 329
De Beers Abrasive Products, Ltd. v. International General Electric Co. of New York, Ltd., 967
De Castro v. Boylan, 225
De Celles v. Casey, 106
De Clara v. Barber S. S. Lines, 444
De Corsey v. Purex Corp., 351
De Give v. Seltzer, 640
De Groodt v. Skrbina, 400
De Haen v. Rockwood Sprinkler Co., 226
De Hart v. Ohio Fuel Gas Co., 956, 957
De Jesus v. Liberty Mutual Insurance Co., 381
De Kallands v. Washtenaw Home Telephone Co., 484
De La Riva v. Owl Drug Co., 874
De Libellis Famosis, 786, 840
De Luca v. Manchester Laundry & Dry Cleaning Co., 199
De Mankowski v. Ship Channel Development Co., 780
De Marais v. Beckman, 247
De Marasse v. Wolf, 10
De Marentille v. Oliver, 87
De Martini v. Alexander Sanitarium, 178
De May v. Roberts, 60, 725, 849, 854
De Mello v. St. Thomas the Apostle Church Corp., 423
De Minico v. Craig, 983, 984, 1004
De Mirjian v. Ideal Heating Corp., 661, 664
De Montague v. Bacharach, 730
De Mott v. Amalgamated Meat Cutters & Butchers, 830
De Motte v. Arkell, 439
De Nike v. Mowery, 333
De Nucci v. Pezza, 633
De Pasquale v. Westchester Newspapers, 774
De Rosa v. Fordham University, 392
De Ryss v. New York Central Railway Co., 384, 392
De Severinus v. Press Publishing Co., 846
De Shetler v. Kordt, 214
De Soto Auto Hotel v. McDonough, 421
De Vall v. Strunk, 120
De Vaughn v. Minor, 552, 648
De Wald v. Quarnstrom, 212
De Witt v. Gerard, 345, 350
De Wolff v. Howe, 730
Deach v. Woolner Distilling Co., 421
Deacy v. McDonnell, 182
Deal v. Sexton, 368
Dean v. Hershowitz, 445
Dean v. Kochendorfer, 899
Dean v. Martz, 487
Dean v. Peel, 924, 926
Dean v. State, 158, 645
Deane v. Johnston, 651

DeAngelis v. Lutheran Medical Center, 359, 936
Dearbourn v. Union National Bank, 92, 99
Deatley's Administrator v. Phillips, 331
Deaton v. State, 9
DeBerry v. City of La Grange, 413
Debnam v. Simonson, 1006, 1013
Decatur & Macon County Hospital Association v. Erie City Iron Works, 250
Deck v. Sherlock, 717
Decker v. Gammon, 539
Decker v. Gibson Products Co. of Albany, Inc., 201
Decker Construction Co. v. Mathis, 998
DeCosse v. Armstrong Cork Co., 957
Dee v. Parish, 487
DeElena v. Southern Pacific Co., 213, 214
Deems v. Western Maryland Railway Co., 933
Deen v. Davies, 541
Deere Co. of St. Louis, John v. Short, 660
Deese v. Collins, 789
Deevy v. Tassi, 41, 139
Deffland v. Spokane Portland Cement Co., 405
Defiance Water Co. v. Olinger, 549
DeFusco v. Brophy, 881
Degenhardt v. Heller, 46
Degman v. Mason County, 736
Degouveia v. H. D. Lee Merc. Co., 704
DeGrove v. Sanborn, 528
DeHerrera v. Herrera, 942, 943
Dehm v. Hinman, 152
Dehn v. S. Brand Coal & Oil Co, 404
Dehydro, Inc. v. Tretolite Co., 977
Deinard v. Deinard, 730
Deitz v. Cincinnati, New Orleans & Texas Pacific Railway Co., 396
Deitz v. Jackson, 510, 513, 515
Deitz, State v. 154
deJesus v. Seaboard Coast Line R. Co., 231
Del Rico Co. v. New Mexican, Inc., 972
Del Vecchio v. Lund, 164
Delahunt v. Finton, 117, 119
Delahunta v. City of Waterbury, 651
Delair v. McAdoo, 184
Delaney v. Burnett, 528
Delaney v. Erickson, 540
Delaney v. Philhern Realty Holding Corp., 648
Delaney v. Supreme Investment Co., 723
Delaney v. Towmotor Corp., 703
Delanoy v. Robson, 585
Delaware, Lackawanna & Western Railroad Co. v. Switchmen's Union of North America, 985
Delaware & Hudson Co. v. Boyden, 518
Delaware Optometric Corp. v. Sherwood, 1012
Delesdenier, State v., 7
Delinger v. American News Co., 861, 862
Delk v. Sellers, 415
Dellums v. Powell, 873
Dellwo v. Pearson, 181, 291, 292, 294, 297
Delmarva Power & Light Co. v. Burrows, 374
DeLoach v. Mayer Electric Supply Co., 200
DeLong v. County of Erie, 380

DeLozier v. Smith, 531, 959
Delta Air Corp. v. Kersey, 79, 81
Delta Airlines, Inc. v. McDonnell Douglas Corp., 709
Delta Finance Co. v. Ganakas, 63, 64
DeLuca v. Bowden, 179, 180, 1071
Delz v. Winfree, 324
Demarest v. Palisades Realty & Amusement Co., 423
Demato v. People, 155
Dement v. Houston Printing Co., 841
Dement v. Olin-Mathieson Chemical Corp., 253
Demers v. Gerety, 114
Demers v. Illinois Central Railroad Co., 716
Deming v. Darling, 757
Demko, United States v., 1036, 1037
Dempsey v. Marshall, 768
Dempsey v. Virginia Dare Stores, 686
Dempsky v. Double, 830, 831
Den Norske Ameriekalinje Actiesselskabet v. Sun Printing & Publishing Association, 779
Dench v. Walker, 100
Dengate v. Gardiner, 932
Denman v. Denman, 251
Denman v. Johnston, 353
Denman v. Spain, 251
Denneler v. Aubel Ditching Service, 337
Denner v. Chicago, Milwaukee & St. Paul Railway Co., 621
Denney v. Northwestern Credit Association, 972
Denning v. State, 663
Dennis v. Carolina Pines Bowling Center, 246
Dennis v. Ryan, 871, 872, 873
Dennis v. Sparks, 872, 1058
Dennis v. Thomson, 738
Dennison v. Daily News Pub. Co., 794
Dennison Manufacturing Co. v. Wright, 149
Denny v. New York Central Railroad Co., 316
Denny v. United States, 1042
Denson v. McDonald Brothers, 457
Dent v. Balch, 971
Dent v. Bellows Falls & Saxons River Street Railway Co., 468
Denton v. L. W. Vail Co., 396
Denver & Rio Grande Western Railroad Co. v. Clint, 397
Denver Tramway Co. v. Garcia, 406
Denver Union Terminal Railway Co. v. Cullinan, 483
Deojay v. Lyford, 558
Deon v. Kirby Lumber Co., 1007
Department of Transportation v. Neilson, 1046
DePasquale v. Dello Russo, 915
Dependahl v. Falstaff Brewing Corp., 979, 1004
Depew v. Robinson, 791
Depue v. Flatau, 134, 147
Derby v. Prewitt, 335
Derby v. Public Service Co., 448
Dernehl & Sons Co. v. Detert, 759
Derosier v. New England Telephone & Telegraph Co., 37, 209, 213, 287, 293, 560
Derry v. Handley, 795, 844
Derry v. Peek, 728, 740, 741, 742
Dersookian v. Helmick, 314

Dervin v. Frenier, 223, 275
Des Jardins v. Thunder Bay River Boom Co., 78
Des Moines, City of v. Barnes, 342
Desforge v. American-Bristol Home Building Association, 325
Desforge v. City of West St. Paul, 12
Deshazer v. Tompkins, 490
Deshotel v. Travelers Indemnity Co., 907
Deskin v. Brewer, 164
Desrosiers v. Cloutier, 212
Desruisseau v. Isley, 633
Dessi v. Pennsylvania Railroad Co., 579
DeSuza v. Andersack, 517, 519, 520
Detienne, State ex rel. v. City of Vandalia, 644
Deutsch v. Connecticut Co., 350
Deutsch v. Shein, 363
Deveny v. Rheem Manufacturing Co., 690
Devers v. Long Island Lighting Co., 663
DeVinci Creations, Inc. v. Nu-Frame Co., 248
Devine v. Devine, 923
Devine v. Kroger Grocery & Baking Co., 670
Devine v. Pfaelzer, 491
Devlin v. Greiner, 893
Devlin v. Safeway Stores, 378
Devlin v. Snellenburg, 78, 88
DeVoin v. Michigan Lumber Co., 102
Devost v. Twin State Gas & Electric Co., 401
Dewes v. Indian Health Service, 192
Dewire v. Boston & Maine Railroad Co., 457
DeWitt v. Brown, 188
DeWolf v. Ford, 58
Dexter v. Cole, 86, 111
Deyo v. New York Central Railroad Co., 313
Dezero v. Turner, 754
Deziel v. Deziel, 904
d'Hedouville v. Pioneer Hotel Co., 202, 705
Di Bari v. J. W. Bishop Co., 569
Di Blasio v. Kolodner, 817
Di Giorgio Fruit Corp. v. American Federation of Labor, etc., 779
Di Leo v. Du Montier, 528
Di Maria v. Curtiss-Wright Corp., 575
di Rebaylio v. Herndon, 528
Diamond v. Diehr, 1023
Diamond v. Weyerhaeuser, 251
Diamond State Telephone Co. v. Atlantic Refining Co., 286
Diapulse Corp. of America v. Birtcher Corp., 10, 974, 976
Dibble v. Wolff, 525
DiCaprio v. New York Central Railroad Co., 231
Dicenzo v. Berg, 113, 119
Dice's Administrator v. Zweigart's Administrator, 665
DiCesare-Engler Productions, Inc. v. Mainman Limited, 990
Dick v. Carey, 521
Dickau v. Rafala, 425
Dickel v. Nashville Abstract Co., 745, 747
Dickelman Manufacturing Co. v. Pennsylvania Railroad Co., 544

Dickens v. DeBolt, 1063
Dickens, State v., 137
Dickens v. United States, 207
Dickenson v. Watson, 163
Dickerson v. Connecticut Co., 210
Dickerson v. Reeves, 503, 504
Dickerson v. Shepard Warner Elevator Co., 670
Dickerson v. Western Union Telegraph Co., 483
Dickes v. Fenne, 975
Dickeson v. Baltimore & Ohio Chicago Terminal Railroad Co., 408, 410
Dickey v. Brannon, 792
Dickey v. Hochschild, Kohn & Co., 420
Dickey v. Nations, 531
Dickinson v. Barber, 1074
Dickinson v. Hathaway, 826
Dickinson v. Stuart Colliery Co., 958
Dicks v. Brooks, 966
Dickson v. Graham-Jones Paper Co., 559
Dickson v. Hollister, 310
Dickson v. McCoy, 561
Dickson v. Yates, 348
DiCosala v. Kay, 203, 502
Diehl v. A. P. Green Fire Brick Co., 318
Diehl v. Fidelity Philadelphia Trust Co., 318
Diehl & Sons, Inc. v. International Harvester, 964
Diel v. Kellogg, 744
Diener v. Star-Chronicle Publishing Co., 780
Dierberger, State v., 156
Dierkes v. Hauxhurst Land Co., 134
Dierks v. Alaska Air Transport, 492
Dierks Lumber & Coal Co. v. Noles, 471
Diesel Service Inc. v. Accessory Sales, Inc., 982
Dietemann v. Time, Inc., 854
Dietrich v. Hauser, 791
Dietrich v. Inhabitants of Northampton, 367
Dietrichs v. Schaw, 154
Dietz v. Langfitt, 882, 883
Dietz v. Meyer, 603
Dietzman v. Ralston Purina Co., 102
Digest Publishing Co. v. Perry Publishing Co., 774
Digsby v. Carroll Baking Co., 62
Dill v. Dance Freight Lines, 620
Dill v. Excel Packing Co., 635
Dill v. State, 155
Dill v. Widman, 734
Dillard v. Clements, 525
Dillenberger v. Weingartner, 488
Dillman v. Nadlehoffer, 752, 758
Dillon v. Balfour, 820
Dillon v. Legg, 366
Dillon v. Sears-Roebuck, Inc., 49
Dillon v. Twin State Gas & Electric Co., 272, 353
Dilucehio v. Shaw, 552
Dilworth v. Lauritzen, 765
Dimoff v. Ernie Majer, Inc., 749
Dimond v. Kling, 519
Dimond v. Peace River Land & Development Co., 766
DiNatale v. Lieberman, 371
Dincher v. Marlin Firearms Co., 166

TABLE OF CASES

Dinda v. Sirois, 530
Dineen v. Daughan, 1058
Dinkenspiel v. New York Evening Journal Publishing Co., 846
Dinkins v. Booe, 717
Dinwiddie, State ex rel. McClure v. 338
Diodes, Inc. v. Franzen, 988
Dior v. Milton, 1021
Dippold v. Cathlamet Timber Co., 458
Direct Import Buyers Association v. K. S. L., 964
Director General of Railroads v. Pence's Administratrix, 519
Director General of Railroads v. Platt, 953
DiSalvatore v. United States, 454
Disbrow v. Tenbroeck, 102
Disch v. Closset, 918
Dishaw v. Wadleigh, 899
Dishington v. A. W. Kuettel & Sons, 412
Distad v. Cubin, 220, 222, 231
Distefano v. Lamborn, 338
District Motor Co. v. Rodill, 736
District of Columbia v. Cooper, 242
District of Columbia v. Texaco, Inc., 388
District of Columbia v. Totten, 553, 645, 648
District of Columbia v. White, 220, 223, 225, 240
Diver v. Miller, 984, 986, 992
Dix v. Martin, 905
Dix v. Spampinato, 206
Dixi-Cola Laboratories v. Coca-Cola Co., 1015
Dixie Broadcasting Co. v. Rivers, 891
Dixie Fire Insurance Co. v. Betty, 846
Dixie Stage Lines v. Anderson, 511
Dixon v. Bell, 303, 328
Dixon v. Clow, 75
Dixon v. Gaso Pump & Burner Manufacturing Co., 242
Dixon v. Harrison Naval Stores, 138
Dixon v. Hotel Tutwiler Operating Co., 58
Dixon v. Kentucky Utilities Co., 281, 294
Dixon v. New York Trap Rock Corp., 552, 621, 625, 627
Dixon v. Phillips, 525
Dixon v. Smartino, 122
Dixon v. Smith, 794
Dixon v. Smith-Wallace Shoe Co., 892
Dizco, Inc. v. Kenton, 238
Doane v. Grew, 827, 834, 835
Docter v. Riedel, 897, 898
Doctors Hospital, Inc. v. Kovats, 203
Dodd v. Wilson, 467
Dodge v. Gilman, 818
Dodge v. McArthur, 291
Dodson v. Culp, 77
Dodson v. Economy Equipment Co., 95, 98
Dodson v. Maddox, 289, 308
Dodson v. Mock, 29
Dodwell v. Burford, 40
Dodwell v. Missouri Pacific Railroad Co., 146
Doe v. McMillan, 1060
Doe v. New York City Department of Social Services, 213
Doe v. Roe, 916

Doe v. United States Civil Service Commission, 867
Doeg v. Cook, 326, 347
Doenges-Long Motors, Inc. v. Gillen, 1072
Dofflemyer v. Gilley, 523
Doggett v. Welborn, 460
Doherty v. Lynett, 791
Doherty v Shea, 51
Dohm v. R. N. Cardozo & Bro., 232, 233
Dohmann v. Richard, 458
Doht v Village of Walthill, 1054
Doing v. New York, Ontario & Western Railway Co., 569
Dole v. Dow Chemical Co., 344, 476, 477
Dole v. Erskine, 126
Dole v. Hardinger, 348
Dolitsky v. Dollar Bank, 97
Dollard v. Roberts, 491
Dolph v. Ferris, 560
Dombeck v. Chicago, Milwaukee, St. Paul & Pacific Railroad Co., 264
Dombrowski v. Tomasino, 760
Domchick v. Greenbelt Consumer Services, 833, 842
Domenico v. Kaherl, 363
Dominices v. Monongahela Connecting Railroad Co., 717
Dominick v. Rea, 141
Dominion Tape of Canada, Ltd. v. L. R. McDonald & Sons, Ltd., 1001
Donahoe v. Richards, 935
Donahue v. Bowers, 1064
Donahue, Commonwealth v., 137, 138
Donahue v. Frank E. Scott Transfer Co., 566
Donahue v. Gaffey, 779
Donahue v. Rolando, 467
Donahue v. Shippee, 95
Donahue v. Warner Brothers Picture Distributing Corp., 801, 853, 858
Donaldson v. Great Atlantic & Pacific Tea Co., 581
Donehy v. Commonwealth, 156
Donivan v. Manhattan Railway Co., 12
Donnell v. Canadian Pacific Railway Co., 92, 99
Donnell v. Donnell, 921
Donnell v Great Atlantic & Pacific Tea Co., 137
Donnell v. Jones, 892
Donnelly v. Baltimore Trust & Guarantee Co., 742
Donnelly v. Ives, 1046
Donner v. Graap, 30
Donoghue v. Stevenson, 358, 681, 682
Donovan v. Barkhausen Oil Co., 101
Donovan v. Bender, 199
Donovan v. Clifford, 763
Donovan v. Consolidated Coal Co., 73, 725
Donovan v. Hannibal & St. Joseph Railroad Co., 460
Donovan v. Wilson Sporting Goods Co., 974
Donovan Construction Co. v. General Electric Co., 1000
Donta v. Harper, 238
Dooley v. Berkner, 721
Dooley v. Borough of Charleroi, 313, 319
Dooley v. Press Publishing Co., 788
Dooley v. Seventeen Thousand Five Hundred Head of Sheep, 348

Dooley, State v., 138
Dooling v. Budget Publishing Co., 965, 966
Doolittle v. Shaw, 102
Dora v. Dora, 996
Dorais v Paquin, 179, 181
Doran v. Chicago, St. Paul, Minneapolis & Omaha Railway Co., 328
Doran v. Milland Development Co., 761
Doremus v. Hennessy, 991
Dorman v. Carlson, 566
Dorn v. Wilmarth, 10
Dornak v. Lafayette General Hospital, 381
Dorr v. Cory, 758
Dorr v. Massachusetts Title Insurance Co., 661
Dorr Cattle Co. v. Des Moines National Bank, 894
Dorrin v. Union Electric Co., 179, 181
Dorry v. LaFleur, 488, 489
Dorset Yacht Co., Ltd. v. Home Office, 1043
Dorsett v. Nunis, 628
Dorsey v. Chautauqua Institution, 422
Dorsey v. Honda Motor, 213
Dorsey v. Material Service Corp., 326
Dosher v. Hunt, 521
Doss v. Sewell, 934, 935
Doss v. Town of Big Stone Gap, 264, 306, 312
Dotoratos v. Greenidge, 999
Dotson v. Haddock, 414
Doucette v. Sallinger, 988, 1003
Doud, People v., 133
Dougall v. Brown Bay Boat Works & Sales, 706
Dougherty v. Chas. H. Tompkins Co., 492
Dougherty v. New Orleans Railway & Light Co., 956
Dougherty v. Stepp, 75, 78
Dougherty v. West Superior Iron & Steel Co., 491
Doughty v. Maine Central Transportation Co., 666
Doughty v. Turner Mfg. Co., Ltd., 296
Douglas v. Converse, 486
Douglas v. Douglas, 793
Douglas v. Great Atlantic & Pacific Tea Co., 246
Douglas v. Stokes, 859
Douglas, Burt & Buchanan Co. v. Texas & Pacific Railway Co., 353
Douglas, Town of v. York, 1053
Douglas Motor Sales v. Cy Owens, Inc., 93
Douglass v. Hart, 101
Douglass v. Hartford Insurance Co., 200
Douthitt v. United States, 190
Dove v. Lowden, 376
Dow v. Holly Manufacturing Co., 723
Dow v. Sanborn, 763
Dowd v. Erie Railroad Co., 571
Dowd v. Tucker, 765
Dowell v. General Steam Nav. Co., 463
Dowell v. General Telephone Co. of Michigan, 510
Dower v. Goldstein, 909
Dowie v. Priddle, 841
Dowling v. Livingstone, 832
Downer, State v., 150
Downes v. Dilva, 648
Downes v. Elmira Bridge Co., 417

Downes v. Silva, 388
Downey v. Finucane, 505, 736, 737
Downey v. United Weatherproofing Co., 981, 991
Downing v. Dillard, 340
Downing v. Stone, 883
Downs v. Cammarano, 183
Downs v. Finnegan, 674
Downs v. Hawley, 842
Downs v. Jackson, 130
Downs v. Swann, 864
Dowse v. Doris Trust Co., 972
Doyel v. Thompson, 218
Doyle v. Clauss, 827
Doyle v. Kahl, 601
Doyle v. South Pittsburgh Water Co., 671
Doyle v. Union Bank & Trust Co., 767
Doyle v. Vance, 539
Doyle Plumbing Co., V. J. v. Doyle, 1017
Doyley v. Roberts, 792
Dozier v. Pillot, 99
Dozier v. Troy Drive-In Theatres, Inc., 646
Drabek v. Sabley, 126
Dragna v White, 152
Drago v. Buonagurio, 891, 898, 899
Dragotis v. Kennedy, 198
Drake v. City of Rochester, 1058
Drake v. Keeling, 323
Drake v. Reddington, 104
Drake v. State, 392
Drake v. Thomas, 158
Drakos v. Jones, 878
Draper v. Baker, 41, 55, 57
Draper v. Hellman Commercial Trust & Savings Bank, 801, 828
Draper v. Switous, 416
Draper Mortuary v. Superior Court, 202
Draske's Will, In re, 802
Drayton v. Jiffee Chemical Corp., 205, 711, 713
Drazen v. Otis Elevator Co., 319
Dreier v. McDermott, 451
Dreiling Motor Co., Bill v. Herlein, 893
Drennan Co. v. Jordan, 516
Dresser Industries, Inc. v. Foss Launch & Tug Co., 210
Drew v. Gross, 561
Drews v. Mason, 424
Dreyfus & Co. v. Wooters, 309
Driggers v. United States, 1035
Driscoll v. Gaffey, 364
Driscoll v. United States, 1040, 1042
Driver v. Commonwealth, 141
Driver v. Hinnant, 178
Driver v. Smith, 526
Drobner v. Peters, 367
Drown v. New England Telephone & Telegraph Co., 348
Drown v. Northern Ohio Traction Co., 276
Drowse v. Doris Trust Co., 969
Drug Research Corp. v. Curtis Publishing Co., 964
Drum v. Miller, 159
Drummond v. Hilton Hotel Corp., 508
Drury v. Hervey, 141

TABLE OF CASES

Druse v. Wheeler, 84
Dryden v. Contienntal Baking Co., 245, 250
Du-Art Film Laboratories v. Consolidated Film Industries, 988
Du Bois v. Decker, 378, 657
Du Bost v. Beresford, 103, 786
Du Boulay v. Du Boulay, 852
Duarte v. City of San Jose, 384
Duarte v. State, 205, 443
Dube v. Gay, 489
Dubois v. City of Kingston, 646
Dubois v. Roby, 12
Dubourcq v. Brouwer, 964
Dubovy v. Woolf, 748
DuBree v. Commonwealth, 1047
Duck v. Mayeu, 332
Duckwall v. Davis, 881, 888
Duckworth v. Walker, 752
Dudley v. Briggs, 963
Dudley v. Estate Life Insurance Co. of America, 508
Dudley, Regina v., 129, 148
Dudley v. Victor Lynn Lines, 380
Duel v. Mansfield Plumbing Co., 413
Duenges v. United States, 1039
Dufer v. Cully, 561
Duff v. Bonner Building Supply, Inc., 479
Duff v. Engleberg, 1004
Duffies v. Duffies, 916
Duffy v. Midlothian County Club, 419, 426, 428, 486, 489
Duffy v. New York Evening Post Co., 831
Duffy v. Stratton, 425
Dufrene v. Dixie Auto Insurance Co., 200
Dufresne v. Weise, 789
Dugan v. Midwest Cap. Co., 872
Dugan v. Pennsylvania Railroad Co., 411
Dugan v. St. Paul & Duluth Railroad Co., 171, 387
Dugas v. Coca-Cola Bottling Co., 254
Duggan v. Baltimore & Ohio Railroad Co., 48
Duggan v. Esposito, 399, 404
Duhl v. Nash Realty Inc., 455
Duholm v. Chicago, Milwaukee & St. Paul Railway Co., 666
Duke v. Feldman, 324
Duke of Brunswick v. Harmer, 798, 800
Duke of Buccleuch v. Cowan, 354, 355
Duke Power Co. v. Carolina Environmental Study Group, Inc., 559
Dukes v. Barkdoll, 415
Dulieu v. White, 292, 363
Dulin v. Bailey, 1007
Duluth, Missabe & Northern Railroad Co. v. McCarthy, 339
Dumas v. Erie Railroad Co., 152
Dumer v. St. Michael's Hospital, 371
Dumphy v. Montreal Light Co., 567
Dun & Bradstreet v. Robinson, 829
Dun and Bradstreet, Inc. v. O'Neil, 829, 835
Dunahm v. Village of Canisteo, 267
Dunahoo v. Bess, 362
Dunaway v. Maroun, 252

Dunaway v. People, 37
Dunbar v. Greenlaw, 817, 818
Dunbar v. United Steelworkers of America, 1046, 1050
Dunbier v. Mengedoht, 921
Duncan v. Donnell, 62, 65
Duncan v. Lumbermen's Mutual Casualty Co., 283
Duncan v. Nebraska Sanitarium & Benevolent Association, 1070
Duncan v. Record Publishing Co., 825
Dundalk Holding Co. v. Easter, 641
Dundee Land Co. v. Simmons, 740
Dunham v. Powers, 816
Dunham v. Village of Canisteo, 269, 376
Dunham Lumber Co. v. Holt, 752
Dunhill Limited, Alfred v. Interstate Cigar Co., 1020
Dunlap v. Dunlap, 595, 904, 906
Dunlap v. Howard, 438
Dunlap v. Hunting, 99
Dunlap v. New Zealand Fire & Marine Insurance Co., 878
Dunleavy v. Constant, 421
Dunlevy v. Wolferman, 137
Dunlop v. Dunlop Rubber Co., 786
Dunlop Tire & Rubber Corp. v. FMC Corp., 1000
Dunn v. Alabama Oil & Gas Co., 877
Dunn v. Brimer, 225
Dunn v. Brown County Agricultural Society, 419
Dunn v. Caylor, 525
Dunn v. Ralston Purina Co., 683
Dunn v. Rose Way, Inc., 370
Dunn v. State, 127
Dunn v. Teti, 180, 181
Dunn v. Trans World Airlines, Inc., 239
Dunn v. Vogel Chevrolet Co., 248
Dunn v. Western Union Telegraph Co., 58
Dunn v. White, 750
Dunn, State ex rel. Harbin v., 156
Dunn & McCarthy v. Bishop, 767
Dunnigan v. Kirkorian, 445
Dunning v. Kentucky Utilities Co., 262
Dunning, State v., 156
Dunnivant v. Nafe, 312
Dunshee v. Standard Oil Co., 984, 1014
Dunson v. Friedlander, 443
Dunston v. Paterson, 150
Duo-Tint Bulb & Battery Co. v. Moline Supply Co., 1018
Duprey v. Shane, 577
Durand v. Dyson, 643
Durant v. Stuckey, 464
Durden v. Barnett, 932
Durgin v. Gage, 99
Durgin v. Cohen, 49, 51
Durham v. City of Los Angeles, 211, 393
Durham v. Durham, 906
Durham v. Goodwin, 561
Durham v. State, 156
Durham v. Warner Elevator Manufacturing Co., 670
Durkee v. Central Pacific R. Co., 935
Durning v. Hyman, 419
Durr v. Smith, 776

Durso v. A. D. Cozzolino, Inc., 524, 525
Durst v. Wareham, 68
Duryea v. Zimmerman, 742
Dusckiewicz v. Carter, 486
Dusha v. Virginia & Rainy Lake Co., 461, 493
Dust Sprayer Manufacturing Co. v. Western Fruit Grower, 964
Dustin v. Cowdry, 143
Dutcher v. Weber, 512
Duteny v. Pennichuck Water Co., 303
Dutton v. Rocky Mountain Phosphates, 552
Duty v. General Finance Co., 62, 64
Duvall v. Walton, 758
Duy v. Alabama Western Railroad Co., 650
Dwelle v. Home Realty & Investment Co., 967
Dwire v. Stearns, 927
Dwy v. Connecticut Co., 335
Dye v. Carmichael Produce Co., 1013, 1024
Dye v. Rule, 413
Dyer v. Day, 731
Dyer v. Dyer, 155, 817, 818
Dyer v. MacDougall, 824
Dyer v. Mudgett, 561
Dyer, State v., 128
Dyer, People ex rel. v. Clark, 644
Dygert v. Schenck, 648
Dyk v. De Young, 40, 138
Dyke v. Zaiser, 738
Dym v. Merit Oil Corp., 421
Dyrcz v. Missouri Pacific Railway Co., 466
Dziedzic v. St. John's Cleaners & Shirt Launderers, Inc., 459
Dziokonski v. Babineau, 366

E

E. I. du Pont DeNemours & Co. v. Christopher, 1022
E. I. du Pont De Nemours & Co. v. Cudd, 548, 562
E. I. du Pont de Nemours & Co. v. Edgerton, 409
E. I. du Pont de Nemours Powder Co. v. Masland, 1022
E. T. & H. K. Ide v. Boston & Maine Railroad Co., 292, 294, 302
E. & M. Construction Co. v. Bob, 661
Eaddy v. Greensboro-Fayetteville Bus Lines, 13
Eadie v. Pole, 781
Eads v. Marks, 661
Eager v. Grimwood, 926
Eagle Star Insurance Co. v. Bean, 517
Eagles v. Liberty Weekly, 779
Eaglesfield v. Marquis of Londonderry, 760
Earl v. Lubbock, 668, 681
Earl v. Van Alstyne, 542
Earl v. Winne, 822
Earl of Northumberland v. Byrt, 962
Earle v. Johnson, 792
Earley v. Pacific Electric Railway Co., 947, 998
Earley v. Winn, 789
Early Settlers Insurance Co. v. Schweid, 340
Earnest v. Regent Pool, Inc., 396, 397
Earp v. Nobmann, 358

Easley v. Apollo Detective Agency, Inc., 203, 502
East Cairo Ferry Co. v. Brown, 650
East St. Johns Shingle Co. v. City of Portland, 636
East Tennessee, Virginia & Georgia Railway Co. v. Kelly, 315
East Texas Oil Refining Co. v. Mabee Consolidated Corp., 551
Eastburn v. Levin, 406
Easter v. District of Columbia, 178
Easter v. McNabb, 517, 519, 520
Eastern & South African Tel. Co. v. Cape Town Tramways Co., 546, 561, 628
Eastern Counties R. Co., Regina v., 538
Eastern Railroad Presidents Conference v. Noerr Motor Freight, Inc., 989, 1025
Eastern States Petroleum Co. v. Universal Oil Products Co., 762
Eastern Trust & Banking Co. v. Cunningham, 736
Eastland v. Caldwell, 842
Eastman v. Leiser Co., 506
Eastman Kodak Co. of New York v. Southern Photo Materials Co., 1024
Easton v. United Trade School Contracting Co., 363
Eatley v. Mayer, 10
Eaton v. Hill, 1072
Eaton v. R. B. George Investments, 408
Eaton v. Schild, 105
Eaton v. Wilkins, 734
Ebbs v. St. Louis Union Trust Co., 730
Ebel v. County Road Commissioner of Saginaw, 633
Ebel v. Ferguson, 904
Eberhardt v. Glasco Mutual Telephone Association, 312
Eberling v. Mutillod, 562
Ebers v. General Chemical Co., 684
Ebersole v. Fields, 970, 971
Eblin v. Miller's Executors, 445
Echord v. Rush, 575
Eck Co., John A. v. Pennsylvania Railroad Co., 664
Eckenrode v. Life of America Insurance Co., 11, 60, 62, 63
Eckerd v. Weve, 46
Eckert v Braun, 674
Eckert v. Long Island Railroad Co., 171, 288, 491
Eckert v. Van Pelt, 775
Eckleberry v. Kaiser Foundation Northern Hospital, 328
Eckley v. Seese, 269
Eckman v. Lehigh & Wilkes-Barre Coal Co., 350
Eclipse Lumber Co. v. Davis, 382
Economopoulos v. A. G. Pollard Co., 780, 798
Economy Auto Insurance Co. v. Brown, 999
Economy Hog & Cattle Powder Co. v. Compton, 769
Economy Light & Power Co. v. Hiller, 347
Edd v. Western Union Telegraph Co., 665
Eddleman v. Eddleman, 902
Eddy v. Syracuse University, 238
Eddy v. Union Railroad Co., 541
Edelman v. Jordan, 1044
Edelstein v. Gillmore, 1024
Eden v. Conrail, 454
Edgar v. Omaha Public Power District, 52

TABLE OF CASES

Edgar v. Walker, 437
Edgarton v. H. P. Welch Co., 68, 389
Edgecomb v. Great Atlantic & Pacific Tea Co., 267
Edgerton v. New York & Hartford Railroad Co., 245
Edgewater Motels, Inc. v. Gatzke, 504
Edgeworth, State ex rel. Richardson, v., 311
Edgington v. Fitzmaurice, 762
Edgington v. Glassmeyer, 882
Edinburg v. Allen Squire Co., 98
Edison v. Edison Polyform Manufacturing Co., 852
Edlebeck v. Hooten, 519
Edmands v. Olson, 30
Edmondson v. Burch & Co., 833
Edmondson v. Hancock, 309
Edmunds v Duff, 640
Edwards v. Allouez Mining Co., 631, 635, 641
Edwards v. Bell, 842
Edwards v. Benedict, 505
Edwards v. Edwards, 88
Edwards v. Fidelity & Casualty Co. of New York, 588
Edwards v. Gulf Oil Corp., 423
Edwards v. Habib, 1028
Edwards v. Hollywood Canteen, 576
Edwards v. Interstate Chemical Co., 955, 959
Edwards v. Kansas City, 395
Edwards v. Kevil, 829
Edwards v. Lamb, 206
Edwards v. Lee, 82
Edwards v. Lee's Administrator, 82, 675
Edwards v. Max Thieme Chevrolet Co., 98
Edwards v. New York & Harlem Railroad Co., 440
Edwards v. Nulsen, 14, 15
Edwards v. Royal Indemnity Co., 595
Edwards v. Sims, 82
Edwards v. Wessinger, 912
Edwards, Ltd., Job v. Birmingham Navigations, 543
Efird v. City of Winston-Salem, 674
Egan v. Hudson Nut Products, Inc., 737
Egan v. Naylor, 950
Egan Chevrolet Co. v. Bruner, 704
Egbert v. Greenwalt, 917
Egede–Nissen v. Crystal Mountain, Inc., 433
Egge v. West Dependable Stores, 96
Eggen v. Hickman, 303
Eggerding v. Bicknell, 532
Eggert v Working, 938
Eggleston v. Whitlock, 793
Ehmer v. Title Guarantee & Trust Co., 661
Ehrenberger v. Chicago, Rock Island & Pacific Railway Co., 570
Ehret v. Village of Scarsdale, 395
Eiban v. Widsteen, 570
Eich v. Gulf Shores, 946
Eichorn v. New Orleans & Carrollton, Railroad, Light & Power Co., 959
Eichstadt v. Underwood, 310
Eick v. Perk Dog Food Co., 852
Eickhoff v. Fidelity & Casualty Co., 893
Eide v. Timberlake, 1063
Eikhoff v. Gilbert, 776

Eisbrenner v. Stanley, 371
Eisen v. Sportogs, Inc., 413
Eisenkramer v. Eck, 544
Eisentraut v. Madden, 126
Eisiminger v. Dinwiddie, 97
Ekalo v. Constructive Service Corp. of America, 933
Ekberg v. Greene, 202
Ekdahl v. Minnesota Utilities Co., 404
Eklund v. Hackett, 920, 921
Ekstrom v. Deagon & Montgomery, 547
El Meson Espanol v. NYM Corp., 966
El Reno Gas & Electric Co. v. Spurgeon, 884
Elam v. Elam, 907, 1071
Elam v. Ethical Prescription Pharmacy, Inc., 461
Elastic Stop Nut Corp. of America v. Greer, 1016
Elbert v. City of Saginaw, 408
Elder v. Anderson, 823
Elder v. Fisher, 718
Elder v. Holland, 819
Elder v. Lykens Valley Coal Co., 349
Eldred v. Burns, 133
Eldred v. Oconto Co., 111
Eldredge v. Kamp Kachess Youth Services, Inc., 915
Electric Power Co. v. Mayor of New York, 96
Elgin, Joliet & Eastern Railway Co. v. Gibson, 579
Eli v. Murphy, 511
Eli Witt Cigar & Tobacco Co. v. Matatics, 310
Elizabeth River Tunnel District v. Beecher, 1043
Elk, John Bad v. United States, 154
Elk Refining Co. v. Daniel, 763
Elkhart Paper Co. v. Fulkerson, 634
Ellenwood v. Marietta Chair Co., 93
Ellerbe, State v., 127
Ellerman Lines v. Grayson, 453
Elletson v. Dixie Home Stores, 882
Elliot, State v., 138
Elliott v. Aetna Life Insurance Co., 587
Elliott v. Belt Automobile Association, 587
Elliott v. Brown, 126, 371
Elliott v. Ditursi, 226
Elliott v. Hall, 716
Elliott v. Harding, 524, 717
Elliott v. Hayden, 666
Elliott v. Mallory Electric Corp., 203
Elliott v. Mason, 621
Elliott v. Warwick Stores, 898
Elliott v. Willis, 952
Elliott Nursery Co. v. Du Quesne Light Co., 631, 641
Ellis v. Chicago & North Western Railroad Co., 337
Ellis v. Cleveland, 66, 112
Ellis v. D'Angelo, 915, 1071
Ellis v. Essau, 332, 335
Ellis v. Fixico, 1074
Ellis v. Gordon, 761
Ellis v. H.S. Finke, Inc., 265
Ellis v. Hale, 743
Ellis v. Howard, 325
Ellis v. Hurst, 868
Ellis v. Jordan, 503
Ellis v. K-Lan Co., 531

Ellis v. Kansas City, St. Joseph & Council Bluffs Railroad Co., 621
Ellis v. Lindmark, 683, 704
Ellis v. Loftus Iron Co., 79, 539, 560
Ellis v. Louisville & Northwest Railroad Co., 194
Ellis v. McCaskill, 182
Ellis v. Moore & Wardlaw, 487
Ellis v. Newbrough, 750
Ellis v. Sheffield Gas Co., 510
Ellis v. Snell, 103
Ellis v. Stenning, 330
Ellis v. Taylor, 660, 664
Ellis v. Trowen Frozen Products, Inc., 200
Ellis v. Wellons, 899
Ellis Motor Co. v. Hancock, 104
Ellish v. Goldman, 819
Ellmaker v. Goodyear Tire & Rubber Co., 308
Ellsworth v. Martindale-Hubbell Law Directory, 794
Ellsworth v. Massacar, 65
Ellsworth v. Metheney, 418
Elmer v. Chicago & Northwestern Railway, 878
Elmergreen v. Horn, 791
Elmhurst v. Pearson, 859, 861
Elmore v. American Motors Corp., 704
Elmore v Atlantic Coast Line Railroad Co., 27, 374
Elmore v. Des Moines City Railway Co., 196
Elms v. Crane, 794, 795, 844
Elpers v. Kimbel, 347
Elsberry v. Lewis, 952
Elsee v. Gatward, 659
Elsey v. Lamkin, 738
Elson v. Bowen, 855
Elson v. Harris, 770
Elton v. County of Orange, 1048
Elves v. King County, 648
Elvin & Powell, Limited v. Plummer Roddie, Limited, 97
Ely, Commissioner v., 148
Ely v. Donoho, 994
Ely v. Niagara County Supervisors, 642
Ely v. Stannard, 767
Ely-Norris Safe Co. v. Mosler Safe Co., 1019
Emanuelson v. Johnson, 525
Emch v. United States, 1040
Emden v. Vitz, 62
Emelwon, Inc. v. United States, 510, 513
Emerick v. Raleigh Hills Hospital—Newport Beach, 244, 254, 255, 479
Emerson v. Bailey, 219
Emerson v. Fleming, 916
Emerson v. Western Seed & Irrigation Co., 911
Emery v. A & B Commercial Finishing Co., 989
Emery v. Cooper & Sons, 846
Emery v. Emery, 906
Emery v. Gowen, 927
Emery v. Jewish Hospital Association, 1070
Emery v. Rochester Telephone Corp., 954
Emery v. Tilo Roofing Co., 270
Emhardt v. Perry Stadium, 480
Emily v. Bayne, 760
Emmert v. United Bank & Trust Co., 92

Emmke v. De Silva, 12, 58
Emmons, Commonwealth v., 133
Emmons v. Pottle, 803, 811
Emmons v. Quade, 132
Emmons v. Stevane, 912
Emory University v. Lee, 178
Empire Gas & Fuel Co. v. Wainscott, 874
Empire Steam Laundry Co. v. Lozier, 1023
Employers Casualty Co. v. Hagendorfer, 487
Employers' Fire Insurance Co. v. Cotten, 94
Employers' Liability Assurance Corp. v. Daley, 999
Employers' Liability Assurance Corp. v. Freeman, 995
Employers' Liability Assurance Corp. Limited v. Kelly-Atkinson Construction Co., 585
Employers Mutual Casualty Co. v. Chicago, St. Paul, Minneapolis & Ohio Railroad Co., 340
Employing Printers' Club v. Doctor Blosser Co., 987
Emry v. Roanoke Navigation & Water Power Co., 73
Endresz v. Friedberg, 370
Endsley v. Johns, 741
Engelgau v. Walter, 884
Engelke v. Chouteau, 816
Engelking v. City of Spokane, 569
Engelman v. Bird, 86
Engen v. Merchants' & Manufacturers State Bank, 770
England v. Central Pocahontas Coal Co., 63
Engle v. Director General of Railroads, 281
Engle v. Simmons, 60, 77
Engle v. State, 644, 646
Englehart v. Sage, 92
English Whipple Sailyard, Limited v. Yawl Ardent, 210
Ennis v Brawley, 14
Ennis v. Dupree, 197
Eno Brick Corp. v. Barber-Greene Co., 760
Enos Coal Mining Co. v. Schuchart, 549, 554
Enright v. Gibson, 154
Enright v. People, 125
Ensign v. Walls, 635
Enyart, In re Estate of, 738
Enyart v. Blacketor, 222, 229
Epp v. Hinton, 759
Epple v. Western Auto Supply, 467
Epps v. Railway Express Agency, 958
Epstein v. Berkowsky, 880
Epting v. State, 1047
Equitable Life Assurance Society v. Lester, 888
Equitable Life Insurance Co. of Iowa v. Halsey, Stuart & Co., 738
Eramdjian v. Interstate Bakery Corp., 271
Ercanbrack v. Clark, 151
Erckman v. Northern Illinois Gas Co., 260
Erdman v. Gottshall, 540
Erdman v. Mitchell, 1006
Erhardt v. Havens, Inc., 936
Erickson v. Borchardt, 673
Erickson v. Frazier, 760
Erickson v. Hudson, 628
Erickson v. Kongsli, 224
Erickson v. Midgarden, 752
Erickson v. United States, 188

Erie County United Bank v. Berk, 268
Erie Railroad Co. v. Murphy, 716
Ernen v. Crofwell, 207
Ernst v. Sparacino, 164
Errico v. Washburn Williams Co., 487, 570
Ertl v. Ertl, 904
Ervin v. Rocord Publishing Co., 781
Escobar v. Brent General Hospital, 443
Escobedo v. State Department of Motor Vehicles, 601
Escola v. Coca-Cola Bottling Co. of Fresno, 25, 250, 583, 594, 693
Eshbach v. W.T. Grant's & Co., 711
Eshelman v. Rawalt, 10
Espinoza v. O'Dell, 944
Espionosa v. Beverly Hospital, 361
Esposito v. Christopher, 307
Esposito, People v., 153
Esquibel v. City and County of Denver, 406
Esrey v. Southern Pacific Co., 465
Essick v. Shillam, 637
Esson v. Wattier, 550
Estate of (see name of party)
Estes v. Brewster Cigar Co., 138, 141
Estes v. Crosby, 758
Estes v. Gibson, 718
Estes v. Hancock County Bank, 884
Eten v. Luyster, 76
Etheridge v. Norfolk Southern Railway Co., 452
Ethridge v. Nicholson, 348
Ettl v. Land & Loan Co., 391
Ettore v. Philco Television Broadcasting Co., 858, 867
Eubanks v. Colbert, 1051
Euclid, Village of v. Ambler Realty Co., 548
Eule v. Eule Motor Sales, 911
Eureka Coal Co. v. Louisville & Nashville Railroad Co., 343
Euting v. Chicago & North Western Railroad Co., 507
Evans v. Edmonds, 732
Evans v. Elliott, 513, 514
Evans v. Farmer, 306
Evans v. Harries, 794
Evans v. Holsinger, 495
Evans v. Johns Hopkins University, 481
Evans v. Lawrence & Memorial Associated Hospitals, 1070
Evans v. McKay, 996
Evans v. McLalin, 539
Evans v. Mason, 92
Evans v. Mayberry, 995
Evans v. NAB Construction Co., 479, 493
Evans v. Otis Elevator Co., 670
Evans v. Phipps, 576
Evans v. Phoenix Insurance Co., 463
Evans v. Reading Co., 218, 219
Evans v. Roberts, 189
Evans v. S.J. Groves & Sons Co., 353
Evans v. Southern Holding Corp., 388
Evans v. United States, 558
Evans v. Van Kleek, 436
Evans v. Waite, 122

Evans v. Walker, 156
Evans v. Walton, 925
Evansville, City of v. Miller, 632
Evansville, City of v. Rinehart, 621
Eveleth, City of v. Ruble, 186
Evenson v. Spaulding, 1009, 1014, 1015
Ever-Sharp, Inc. v. Pal Blade Co., 971
Everard v. Hopkins, 998
Everest, People v., 1009
Everet v. Williams, 336
Everett v. Bucky Warren, Inc., 185
Everett v. Great Northern Railway Co., 224
Everett v. Hydraulic Flume Tunnel Co., 549
Everett v. Paschall, 620, 628, 629
Everett v. Sherfey, 925
Everett v. White, 407
Everette v. Alyeska Pipeline Service Co., 510
Everette v. City of New Kensington, 175
Evers-Jordan Furniture Co. v. Hartzog, 141
Eversole v. Wasson, 506
Everson v. J.L. Owens Manufacturing Co., 662, 730
Everton Silica Sand Co. v. Hicks, 487
Evertson v. Sutton, 77
Everybody's Tool & Die Works v. Costa, 1011
Evins v. St. Louis & San Francisco Railroad Co., 565
Evola Realty Co. v. Westerfield, 347, 765
Ewald v. Lane, 911
Ewers v. Thunderbird Aviation, Inc., 527
Ewing v. Biddle, 181
Ewing v. Duncan, 309
Ewing v. Lockheed Aircraft Corp., 703
Ewing v. Prince, 561
Ex parte (see name of party)
Excelsior Powder Manufacturing Co., State v., 644
Exchange Bakery & Restaurant Co. v. Rifkin, 994
Exchange Tel. Co. v. Gregory & Co., 1003
Exner v. Sherman Power Construction Co., 549, 559
Exner Sand & Gravel Corp. v. Petterson Lighterage & Towing Corp., 309
Export Co. Establishment of Vaduz, Liechtenstein v. Columbia Broadcasting System, Inc., 1022
Exton v. Glen Gardner Water Co., 636
Exum v. Atlantic Coast Line Railroad Co., 452
Exxon Corp. v. Brecheen, 311
Exxon Corp. v. Kelly, 881
Eyak River Packing Co. v. Huglen, 327
Eyre, Commonwealth v., 45
Eyre v. Garlick, 786
Ezmirlian v. Otto, 969, 974
Ezratty v. Commonwealth of Puerto Rico, 1044

F

F. & J. Enterprises, Inc. v. Columbia Broadcasting Systems, Inc., 970
Fabbri v. Regis Forcier, Inc., 390
Faber v. Byrle, 826
Faber v. Creswick, 443
Fabian v. State, 158
Fabricius v. Montgomery Elevator Co., 670

Faby v. Air France, 254
Factors, Etc., Inc. v. Pro Arts, Inc., 1020
Fadgen v. Lenkner, 917, 930
Fagan v. Atlantic Coast Line Railroad Co., 199
Fagerburg v. Phoenix Flour Mills Co., 334
Fagg's Administrator v. Louisville & Nashville Railroad Co., 378
Fahey v. Shafer, 974
Fahey v. United States, 1043
Fahn v. Reichart, 544
Fahr v. Hayes, 827, 828, 834
Fahringer v. Rinehimer, 453, 458, 489
Fain v. Standard Oil Co., 407
Fainardi v. Pausata, 759
Fairbanks v. Winik, 867
Fairbanks, Morse & Co. v. Texas Electric Service Co., 994
Fairbrother v. Wiley's, Inc., 304
Fairchild v. McMahon, 758
Fairfield v. American Photocopy Equipment Co., 852, 863
Fairmont Creamery Co. v. Thompson, 311
Fairport, Painesville & Eastern Railroad Co. v. Meredith, 468, 581
Fairyland Amusement Co. v. Metromedia, Inc., 965, 966
Fake v. Addicks, 565
Falco v. Pados, 907
Falejczyk v. Meo, 77
Falk v. Falk, 922
Falk v. Finkelman, 275, 284
Falkenstein v. City of Bismarck, 1048
Falloon v. Schilling, 1010
Falstaff Brewing Corp. v. Iowa Fruit & Produce Co., 996
Falvey v. Hamelburg, 223
Fancher v. Southwest Missouri Truck Center, 174, 195
Fanger v. Leeder, 764
Fankhauser v. City of Mansfield, 1055
Fanning v. Chace, 788
Fanson v. Linsley, 674
Fant v. Sullivan, 967
Fantini v. Alexander, 186
Farabee-Treadwell Co. v. Union & Planters Bank & Trust Co., 660
Fargo Gas & Coke Co. v. Fargo Gas & Electric Co., 752
Faribault Woolen Mill Co. v. Chicago Rock Island & Pacific Railway Co., 240
Faris v. Hoberg, 413
Faris v. State, 150
Farkas v. Powell, 102
Farley v. Crystal Coal & Coke Co., 322, 326, 346, 349, 619
Farley v. Edward E. Tower & Co., 304, 319
Farley v. Kissel, 982
Farley v. M M Cattle Co., 183, 198, 496
Farley v. Southeastern Pennsylvania Transportation Authority, 206
Farm Bureau Mutual Auto Insurance Co. v. Hammer, 40
Farman v. Farman, 531

Farmer v. State, 376
Farmer v. Stidham, 525
Farmers & Merchants' National Bank v. Huckaby, 664
Farmers' Co-operative Manufacturing Co. v. Albemarle & Raleigh Railroad Co., 650
Farmers Educational and Co-op Union of America, North Dakota Division v. WDAY, Inc., 824
Farmers Home Mutual Insurance Co. v. Grand Forks Implement Co., 269
Farmers Mutual Auto Insurance Co. v. Milwaukee Automobile Insurance Co., 339
Farmers' State Bank v. Hintz, 967, 973
Farmers' State Bank v. Jeske, 327
Farmers State Bank of Newport v. Lamon, 738
Farmers Union Warehouse Co. v. Barnett, 97
Farmhand, Inc. v. Brandies, 182
Farming Corp. v. Bridgeport Bank, 100
Farney v. Hauser, 342
Farnsworth v. Duffner, 753
Farnsworth v. Tribune Co., 841
Farquhar Co., A.B. v. National Harrow Co., 969, 974
Farr v. Armstrong Rubber Co., 342
Farr v. State Bank of Phillips, 106
Farragher v. City of New York, 447, 448
Farrar v. Brackett, 895
Farrar v. Rollins, 92, 99
Farrell v. Hidish, 172
Farrell v. Kramer, 848
Farrell v. Minneapolis & Rainy River Railway Co., 544
Farrell Publishing Corp., In re, 986
Farrier v. Levin, 421
Farrington v. Stoddard, 950
Farrior v. Payton, 399
Farvour v. Geltis, 12
Farwell v. Colonial Trust Co., 762, 764, 766
Farwell v. Boston & Worcester Railway, 571
Farwell v. Keaton, 377, 382
Farwell Co., John V. v. Hilton, 672
Fashion Originators' Guild of America v. Federal Trade Commission, 1025
Fassion v. Landrey, 649
Faucette v. Lucky Stores, Inc., 703
Faulk v. Aware, Inc., 795
Faulkner v. Big Rock Stone & Material Co., 571
Fausett & Co. v. Bullard, 742
Faust v. Hosford, 760
Faust v. Mendoza, 505
Fauver v. Wilkoske, 14
Fawcett Publications v. Bronze Publications, 1016
Fawcett Publications, Inc. v. Morris, 784
Fawsett v. Clark, 780
Faxon v. Jones, 848
Fay v. Kroblin Refrigerated Xpress, Inc., 238
Fay v. Oliver, 730
Fay v. Parker, 11
Feak v. Marion Steam Shovel Co., 752
Fearon v. Fodera, 975
Featherstone v. Dessert, 582
Fechley v. Springfield Traction Co., 530
Fedderwitz v. Lamb, 819

Federal Auto Body Works, Inc. v. Aetna Casualty & Surety Co., 988
Federal Insurance Co. v. Public Service Co. of Colorado, 208
Federal No. 2, The, 998
Federal Sugar Refining Co. v. United States Sugar Equalization Board, 1004
Feeney v. New York Waist House, 388
Feeney v. Young, 857
Fegeas v. Sherrill, 738
Feger v. Concrete Materials & Construction Co., 327
Fegles Construction Co. v. McLaughlin Construction Co., 513
Fehr v. General Accident, Fire & Life Assurance Corp., 595
Feiges v. Racine Dry Goods Co., 134
Feist v. Roesler, 738
Felcher v. McMillan, 99, 100
Felcyn v. Gamble, 527
Felder v. Butler, 199
Felder v. Reeth, 666, 673
Felderhoff v. Felderhoff, 906, 907
Feldman v. Allegheny Airlines, Inc., 953
Feldman v. Howard, 177, 178
Feldman v. Witmark, 763
Feldstein v. Kammauf, 626
Felger v. Duquesne Light Co., 409
Felicie, Inc. v. Leibovitz, 987
Felis v. Greenberg, 963
Felix v. Westinghouse Radio Stations, 824
Felkner v. Scarlet, 928
Felsen v. Sol Cafe Manufacturing Corp., 983, 986
Felsenthal v. McMillan, 917, 930
Felt v. Germania Life Insurance Co., 967, 971, 972
Feltch v. General Rental Co., 938, 939
Felter v. Delaware & Hudson Railroad Corp., 353, 382
Felton v. Horner, 176
Felts v. Paradise, 817
Felty v. Lawton, 203
Feminist Women's Health Center v. Mohammad, 979, 983, 989, 991
Feneff v. Boston & Maine Railroad Co., 327
Fennell v. Littlejohn, 921
Fennell v. Miller, 237
Fent v. Toledo, Peoria & Western Railway Co., 293
Fenton v. Aleshire, 164
Fenton Storage Co. v. Feinstein, 892
Fentress v. Rutledge, 587
Feoffees of Heriot's Hospital v. Ross, 1069
Ferber v. Orange Blossom Center, Inc., 443
Feres v. United States, 1036, 1037
Feret v. Hill, 731
Fergerson v. Utilities Elkhorn Coal Co., 75
Fergerstrom v. Hawaiian Ocean View Estates, 851
Ferguson v. Bretton, 415
Ferguson v. Green Island Contracting Corp., 998
Ferguson v. Phoenix Cotton Mills, 488
Ferguson v. Reinhart, 881
Ferguson v. Ringsby Truck Line, 576
Fernandes v. Medeiros, 441

Fernandez v. Chamberlain, 581
Fernandez v. Consolidated Fisheries, 398
Fernandez v. Romo, 903
Ferne v. Chadderton, 951
Ferrara v. Galluchio, 363, 364
Ferraro v. Demetrakis, 430, 431
Ferraro v. Ford Motor Co., 490
Ferraro v. Taylor, 319, 717
Ferrell v. Martin, 502
Ferrer v. Harris, 197
Ferri v. Ackerman, 1058
Ferrie v. D'Arc, 182
Ferrie v. Sperry, 661
Ferrill v. Southern Railway, 388
Ferris v. Board of Education, 387
Ferris v. Patch, 456
Ferriter v. Daniel O'Connell's Sons, Inc., 359, 936
Ferriter v. Herlihy, 567
Ferroggiaro v. Bowline, 300
Fertich v. Michener, 158
Fessinger v. El Paso Times Co., 846
Fetler v. Houghton Mifflin Co., 781
Fetzer v. Aberdeen Clinic, 199
Fevold v. Board of Supervisors of Webster County, 643
Fey v. King, 774
Fibre Leather Manufacturing Corp. v. Ramsay Mill, Inc., 550
Fick v. Nilson, 642
Fidelity & Casualty Co. v. Martin, 586, 587
Fidelity & Casualty Co., State ex rel. Verdis v., 154
Fidelity & Casualty Co. of New York v. Chapman, 337
Fidelity Casualty Co. of New York v. Pittman Tractor Co., 746, 748
Fidelity & Deposit Co. v. Grand National Bank, 8
Fidelity & Deposit Co. of Maryland v. Atherton, 745
Fidelity Leasing Corp. v. Dun & Bradstreet, Inc., 212
Fidelity-Philadelphia Trust Co. v. Simpson, 764
Fidelity Storage Co. v. Kingsbury, 483
Fiedler v. Fiedler, 157
Field v. City of Des Moines, 146
Field v. Colson, 795, 844
Field v. Empire Case Goods Co., 683
Fielder, State v., 128
Fielder Agency v. Eldan Construction Corp., 891
Fielding v. Publix Cars, Inc., 590
Fields v. Bynum, 10, 833, 845
Fields v. Morgan, 245
Fields v. Stokley, 620
Fifield v. Maine Central Railroad Co., 99
Fifield Manor v. Finston, 1000
Filburn v. People's Palace & Aquarium Co., 538, 542
Filene's Sons Co., William v. Fashion Originators' Guild of America, 1024
Filip v. Gagne, 1073
Filke v. Boston & Albany Railroad Co., 569
Filler v. Stenvick, 486
Fillis v. Wahlig, 486
Filliter v. Phippard, 543
Filtrol Corp. v. Hughes, 552
Finch v. McKee, 270

TABLE OF CASES

Finch v. State, 156
Finch v. W.R. Roach Co., 424
Findlay v. Copeland Lumber Co., 712
Findlay, Inc., David B. v. Findlay, 1016, 1017
Fineux v. Hovenden, 618
Finger v. Pollack, 794
Fink v. Thomas, 130
Finkelstein v. City of Sapulpa, 645
Finkelstein v. Geismar, 833
Finley v. Atlantic Transport Co., 63
Finley v. Hershey, 84, 642
Finn v. Frink, 871
Finnegan v. Royal Realty Co., 351
Finney v. Lockhart, 15
Finnish Temperance Society Sovittaja v. Finnish Socialistic Publishing Co., 779
Fiore v. Rogero, 820
Fire Insurance Patrol v. Boyd, 1070
Fireman's Fund American Insurance Co. v. Coleman, 454
Fireman's Fund American Insurance Companies v. Knobbe, 251
Firemen's Fund Insurance Co. v. Haley, 586
Firestone v. Rice, 154
Firestone Tire & Rubber Co. v. Lippincott, 170
Firman v. Sacia, 283
First Avenue Coal & Lumber Co. v. Johnson, 646
First City National Bank of Houston v. Japhet, 74
First National Bank v. Moore, 969
First National Bank v. N.R. McFall & Co., 795
First National Bank v. Union Railway Co., 104
First National Bank & Trust Co. of Muskogee v. Winter, 139
First National Bank of Albuquerque v. Nor-Am Agricultural Products, Inc., 685, 693
First National Bank of Bay Shore v. Stamper, 104
First National Bank of Birmingham v. Lowery, 421
First National Bank of Blairstown v. Goldberg, 98
First National Bank of Forrest City v. N. R. McFall & Co., 788
First National Bank of Girard v. Bankers Dispatch Corp., 482
First National Bank of Montgomery v. Montgomery Cotton Manufacturing Co., 91
First National Bank of Nashua v. Van Voohris, 664
First National Bank of Pipestone v. Siman, 95, 98
First National Bank of Portland v. Wall, 941
First National Bank of Tigerton v. Hackett, 742
First National Bank of Waverly v. Winters, 782
First Wisconsin National Bank of Milwaukee v. Wichman, 1017
Firstamerica Development Corp. v. Daytona Beach News-Journal Corp., 800
Firth v. Marhoefer, 441
Fisch v. Waters, 523
Fischer v. Kletz, 738
Fischer v. McBride, 528
Fischer, State v., 159
Fischer, United States v., 153
Fischnaller v. Sumner, 989

Fish v. Cleland, 759
Fish v. Liley, 949
Fish v. St. Louis County Printing & Publishing Co., 825
Fishang v. Eyerman Contracting Co., 424
Fishel v. Givens, 181
Fisher v. Andrews & Pierce, 532
Fisher v. Badger, 137
Fisher v. Bonneville Hotel Co., 582
Fisher v. Bristow, 874
Fisher v. Budlong, 757
Fisher v. Carrousel Motor Hotel, Inc., 40
Fisher v. City of Miami, 12
Fisher v. Greensboro Water Supply Co., 671
Fisher v. Hamilton, 877
Fisher v. Murray M. Rosenberg, Inc., 868
Fisher v. Mutimer, 312
Fisher v. New Yorker Staats-Zeitung, 800
Fisher v. Pippin, 524
Fisher v. Prince, 106
Fisher v. Rumler, 57
Fisher v. Simon, 723
Fisher, State v., 129
Fisher v. Toler, 902
Fisher v. Treser, 954
Fisher v. United States, 185
Fisherman's Paradise, Inc. v. Greenfield, 509, 511
Fiske v. Soland, 188
Fitch v. Adler, 231, 417, 418
Fitch v. Daily News Publishing Co., 837
Fitch v. Mayer, 576
Fitch v. Selwyn Village, 403
Fitch v. United States, 1039
Fitch Co., F. W., State v., 7
Fitchett v. Buchanan, 204, 438
Fitscher v. Rollman & Sons Co., 50, 141
Fitzgerald v. Campbell, 330, 331
Fitzgerald v. Cavin, 118
Fitzgerald v. Chesapeake & Ohio Railway Co., 378, 382
Fitzgerald v. Edison Electric Illuminating Co., 949
Fitzgerald v. Lawhorn, 177, 1074
Fitzgerald v. McCutcheon, 506
Fitzgerald v. Montgomery County Board of Education, 397
Fitzgerald v. Oregon-Washington Railroad & Navigation Co., 471
Fitzgerald v. Piette, 791, 792
Fitzgerald v. Redfield, 791, 792
Fitzgerald v. Union Stock Yards Co., 334, 335
Fitzgerald v. Valdez, 906
Fitzgerald v. Young, 792, 795, 844
Fitzgibbon v. Western Dredging Co., 567
Fitzherbert v. Mather, 731
Fitzjohn v. Mackinder, 872
Fitzpatrick v. Age-Herald Publishing Co., 783
Fitzpatrick v. Bitzer, 1044
Fitzpatrick v. Penfield, 395
Fitzsimmons v. Chapman, 767
Fitzwater v. Sunset Empire, Inc., 223
509 Sixth Avenue Corp. v. New York City Transit Authority, 83

TABLE OF CASES

530 East 89 Corp. v. Unger, 188
Fixico v. State, 125
Fjellman v. Weller, 444
Flager v. Associated Truck Lines, Inc., 519
Flaherty v. Ginsberg, 141
Flaherty v. Great Northern R. Co., 648
Flaherty v. Till, 726
Flake v. Greensboro News Co., 852
Flamm v. Van Nierop, 61
Flanagan v. McLane, 826
Flanagan v. Mount Eden General Hospital, 166
Flanagan v. Nicholson Publishing Co., 831
Flanagan, People v., 131
Flanagan v. Pierce Chevrolet, Inc., 527
Flanagan v. Sanders, 224
Flandermeyer v. Cooper, 938
Flanigan v. City of Springfield, 639
Flannery v. Brewer, 99, 100
Flannery v. Harley, 95, 98
Flatley v. Acme Garage, 413
Flaugh v. Egan Chevrolet, Inc., 528
Fleck v. Nickerson, 417
Fleeming v. Orr, 564
Fleetway, Inc. v. Public Service Interstate Transportation Co., 1013
Fleetwood v. Swift & Co., 705
Fleischer v. Ensminger, 53
Fleischmann Lumber Corp., E.M. v. Resources Corp. v. International, 744
Fleming v. Arkansas Fuel Co., 326
Fleming v. Dane, 324
Fleming v. Fisk, 921
Fleming v. Kravitz, 526
Fleming v. Lockwood, 29
Fleming v. McDonald, 966, 967, 973
Fleming v. Southern Railway Co., 544
Fletcher v. Baltimore & Potomac Railroad Co., 384, 392
Fletcher v. City of Aberdeen, 176
Fletcher v. Fletcher, 155
Fletcher v. Howard, 75
Fletcher v. Kemp, 480
Fletcher v. Maupin, 817
Fletcher v. Perry, 105
Fletcher v. Pump Creek Gas & Oil Syndicate, 99
Fletcher v. Rylands, 545
Fletcher v. Western National Life Insurance Co., 11, 60, 63
Flies v. Fox Brothers Buick Co., 206, 703, 704
Flight v. Booth, 730
Flike v. Boston & Albany Railroad Co., 572
Flint v. Connecticut Hassam Paving Co., 309
Flint & Pere Marquette Railway Co. v. Weir, 660
Flint & Walling Manufacturing Co. v. Beckett, 661
Flintkote Co. v. Dravo Corp., 659
Flom v. Flom, 174
Flood v. Moore, 100
Flood v. Pabst Brewing Co., 443, 444
Flood v. Smith, 291
Flora's Card Shop, Inc. v. Paul Krantz & Co., 166
Florence v. Goldberg, 1050

Florence, City of v. Stack, 1054
Flores v. Mosler Safe Co., 852
Florida Department of State v. Treasure Salvors, Inc., 1043
Florida East Coast Railway Co. v. Morgan, 505
Florida Freight Terminals, Inc. v. Cabanas, 221
Florida Publishing Co. v. Lee, 842
Florida Rock & Sand Co. v. Cox, 517, 518
Florig v. Sears, Roebuck & Co., 269
Flowers v. K-Mart Corp., 427, 428
Flowers v. Price, 58
Flowers v. Smith, 828
Floyd v. Miller, 932
Floyd v. Nash, 184
Flues v. New Nonpareil Co., 775, 837
Flynn v. Gordon, 286
Flynn v. Lindenfield, 563
Flynn v. New York, New Haven & Hartford Railroad, 956
Flynn v. Taylor, 650
Flynn v. Wallace, 520
Flynn & Emrich Co. v. Federal Trade Commission, 1011
Fodor v. Fuchs, 842
Fogden v. Wade, 45
Fogg v. Boston & Lowell Railroad Co., 801
Fogg v. First National Bank, 874
Foggin v. General Guaranty Insurance Co., 415
Fogo v. Steele, 717
Foil v. Ballinger, 166
Folda v. City of Bozeman, 178
Foldi v. Jeffries, 908
Foler v. Curtis Publishing Co., 784
Foley v. H. F. Farnham Co., 389
Foley v. Hoffman, 791, 792
Foley v. Pittsburgh-Des Moines Co., 269, 723, 724
Foley v. Ulrich, 378
Folkman v. Lauer, 430, 438
Folsom v. Apple River Log-Driving Co., 323, 348, 355, 634
Foltting v. Kaevando, 1035
Foltz v. Moore McCormack Lines, 830
Folwell v. Providence Journal Co., 799
Fonseca v. Marlin Marine Corp., 487
Fontainbleau Hotel Corp. v. Postol, 342
Fontanne v. Federal Paper Board Co., 230, 454, 455
Fontenelle v. United States, 1038
Fontenot v. Magnolia Petroleum Co., 552
Fontin v. Katapodis, 128
Food Pageant, Inc. v. Consolidated Edison Co., 211, 237
Foot v. Brown, 792
Foot v. Card, 918
Foot v. Pitt, 775
Forbes v. Auerbach, 744
Forbes v. City of Durant, 635
Forbrick v. General Electric Co., 413
Force v. Gregory, 187
Forcier v. Grand Union Stores, Inc., 426
Forcum-James Co. v. Duke Transportation Co., 999
Ford v. Aetna Life Insurance Co., 587
Ford v. Blythe Brothers Co., 408

Ford v. C. E. Wilson & Co., 764, 986
Ford v. Ford, 112
Ford v. Ja-Sin, 224
Ford v. Monroe, 945
Ford v. State, 127
Ford v. Sturgis, 722
Ford v. Trident Fisheries Co., 265
Ford v. United States, 412, 417
Ford & Co. v. Atlantic Compress Co., 674
Ford Motor Co. v. Atcher, 318
Ford Motor Co. v. Cockrell, 704
Ford Motor Co. v. Lonon, 749
Ford Motor Co. v. Mathis, 705
Ford Motor Co. v. Tritt, 692
Ford Motor Co. v. Union Motor Sales Co., 994
Ford Motor Co. v. Wagoner, 313, 318
Ford Motor Co. v. Williams, 854
Ford Motor Co. v. Zahn, 684, 685, 703
Forde v. Skinner, 41
Fordson Coal Co. v. Carter, 803
Forehand v. Jones, 92, 98
Foreman v. Henry, 738
Foreman v. Jordan, 721
Foreman v. Texas & New Orleans Railroad Co., 285
Fores v. Wilson, 924
Forest City Cotton Co. v. Miller, 75
Forist v. Androscoggin River Improvement Co., 940
Forks Township v. King, 532
Forman v. Mississippi Publishers Corp., 800
Formby v. Hood, 734
Forrest v. Red Cross Hospital, 1070
Forrest City Machine Works, Inc. v. Aderhold, 195
Forrester v. Kuck, 524
Forrester v. Southern Pacific Co., 660
Forrester v. Southern Pacific Railway Co., 666
Forsberg v. Baker, 770
Forsdick v. Collins, 96
Forslund v. Swenson, 329
Forst v. Corporation Commission of Oklahoma, 1012
Forster v. Juniata Bridge Co., 101
Forster v. Manchester, 855, 856, 868
Forster v. Rogers, 552
Forsyth v. Dow, 753
Forsyth v. Kleindienst, 1058, 1067
Forsythe v. Ivey, 155
Fort Myers Airways, Inc. v. American States Insurance Co., 524
Fort Oglethorpe, Town of v. Phillips, 1054
Fort Scott, City of v. Pen Lubric Oil Co., 342
Fort Wayne, Cincinnati & Louisville Railway Co. v. Beyerle, 925
Fort Wayne & Northern Indiana Traction Co. v. Ridenour, 41
Fort Wayne & Northern Indiana Traction Co. v. Stark, 406
Fort Wayne Cooperage Co. v. Page, 387
Fort Wayne Drug Co. v. Flemion, 206
Fort Worth, City of v. Lee, 388
Fort Worth & New Orleans Railway Co. v. Enos, 329
Fort Worth & Rio Grande Railway Co. v. Bryant, 58

Fort Worth & Rio Grande Railway Co. v. Glenn, 622
Fort Worth Press Co. v. Davis, 842
Forte, People v., 130
Fortinberry v. Holmes, 157
Fortman v. Rottier, 892
Fortmeyer v. National Biscuit Co., 327
Fortner v. Koch, 353
Fortney v. Hotel Rancroft, 383
Fortune v. National Cash Register Co., 1028, 1029
Forward v. Adams, 751
Forward v. Pittard, 315
Fosberg v. Couture, 754
Fosbroke-Hobbes v. Airwork, Ltd., 558
Foshay v. Ferguson, 876
Foss v. Chicago, Burlington & Quincy Railroad Co., 299
Foss v. Hildreth, 841
Foster v. Alabama Power Co., 401, 402, 404, 409, 410
Foster v. Barker, 126
Foster v. Browning, 781
Foster v. Charles, 741
Foster v. Commonwealth, 8
Foster v. County of Genesee, 627, 641
Foster v. De Paolo, 769
Foster v. Dwire, 763, 765
Foster v. Emery, 133
Foster v. Floyd, 15
Foster v. Ford Motor Co., 318
Foster v. LaPlante, 308
Foster v. Lusk, 404
Foster v. Preston Mill Co., 562
Foster v. Shepherd, 131, 955
Foster v. Turner, 874
Foster v. Winston Salem Joint Venture, 202, 419, 424, 425, 428
Foster & Co., L. B. v. Hurnblad, 510
Foster-Milburn Co. v. Chinn, 777, 854, 863
Fotheringham v. Adams Express Co., 47
Fottler v. Moseley, 767
Fouche v. Masters, 240
Fouldes v. Willoughby, 90, 92, 96
Foulke v. New York Consolidated Railroad Co., 50
Fountain v. West, 841
Fouraker v. Hill & Morton, 716
Fouraker v. Mullis, 410
Fournell v. Usher Pest Control Co., 364, 365
Fournier v. New York, New Haven & Hartford Railroad Co., 421
Fourth National Bank in Wichita v. Webb, 761
Foust v. Kinney, 75
Fout v. Dietz, 527
Fowle v. Fowle, 890
Fowler v. Curtis Publishing Co., 964, 971
Fowler v. Dowdney, 788
Fowler v. Fowler, 906
Fowler v. Kragel, 94
Fowler v. Lanning, 68, 163
Fowler v. Nationwide Insurance Co., 1003
Fowler v. Sanders, 618
Fowler v. Seaton, 246
Fowler v. Southern Bell Telephone & Telegraph Co., 855

TABLE OF CASES

Fowlks v. Southern Railway Co., 307
Fox v. Boston & Maine Railroad Co., 304, 347
Fox v. Buffalo Park, 438
Fox v. Cohen, 256
Fox v. Ewers, 634
Fox v. Gaunt, 154
Fox v. Illinois Central Railroad Co., 225
Fox v. Koehnig, 561
Fox v. McCurnin, 48
Fox v. Passaic General Hospital, 166
Fox Co., George G. v. Hathaway, 992
Foxcroft Townhome Owners Association v. Hoffman Rosner Corp., 659
Fradus Contracting Co. v. Taylor, 992, 993
Frady v. Smith, 474
Frampton v. Central Indiana Gas Co., 1028
Franc v. Pennsylvania Railroad Co., 396
France v. A. P. A. Transport Corp., 595, 907
Francis v. Outlaw, 922
Francis v. Pic, 446
Francis v. Southern Pacific Co., 954
Francis v. Sun Oil Co., 118, 151
Francisco v. Circle Tours Sightseeing Co., 262
Francisco v. Department of Institutions and Agencies, 626
Franco v. Zingarelli, 496, 498
Francois v. Capital City Press, 837
Frank v. Nash, 588
Frank v. Orleans Parish School Board, 158
Frankel v. Antman, 415, 422
Frankel v. Wolper, 664
Frankfort Land Co. v. Hughett, 675
Frankfurter v. Bryan, 872
Franklin v. Albert, 166
Franklin v. Brown, 987
Franklin v. Irvine, 878
Franklin v. May Department Stores, 669
Franklin v. Puget Sound Tug & Barge Co., 510
Franklin, City of v. Badger Ford Truck Sales, Inc., 705
Franklin Drug Stores v. Gur-Sil Corp., 440
Franklin Motor Car Co. v. Hilkert, 770
Franklin's Case, 840
Franklyn v. Peabody, 119
Frankovitch v. Burton, 419, 424, 426
Franks v. Lockwood, 675
Franks v. Smith, 159
Fraser v. Flanders, 452
Fraser-Patterson Lumber Co. v. Southern Railway Co., 565
Frasier v. Pierce, 717
Fraters v. Keeling, 423
Fratini v. Caslini, 918
Frawley Chemical Corp. v. A. P. Larson Co., 774
Frazier v. Turner, 150
Frazier v. United States, 1036
Frazor v. Osborne, 166
Freach v. Commonwealth, 1048
Frechette v. Welch, 162
Fred v. Traylor, 791
Frederick v. City of Detroit, 209

Frederick v. Goff, 304, 494
Frederick v. Philadelphia Rapid Transit Co., 397, 398
Frederick v. Reed, 418
Fredericks v. American Export Lines, 704
Fredericksen v. Singer Manufacturing Co., 139
Frederickson v. Kepner, 563
Freebury v. Chicago, Milwaukee & Puget Sound Railroad Co., 554
Freedman v. Crabro Motors, Inc., 875
Freedman v. Eastern Mass. Street Railway Co., 364
Freedman v. Hurwitz, 487
Freehe v. Freehe, 903, 905, 959
Freeland v. Freeland, 911
Freeman v. Busch Jewelry Co., 963
Freeman v. Kelly, 392
Freeman v. Lee & Leon Oil Co., 506
Freeman v. Logan, 875
Freeman, State v., 150
Freeman v. United States, 82, 205, 226, 519
Freeman v. Venner, 767
Freese v. John Morrell & Co., 574
Freese v. Lemmon, 207, 231
Freethy v. Freethy, 901
Freezer Storage, Inc. v. Armstrong Cork Co., 168
Frega v. Northern New Jersey Mortgage Association, 965, 969, 974
Freggens v. Clark, 762
Frei v. Frei, 575
Freides v. Sani-Mode Manufacturing Co., 881
Freitas v. Twin City Fishermen's Co-operative Association, 705, 719
French v. Center Creek Powder Manufacturing Co., 549
French v. Creath, 788
French v. Griffin, 757
French v. Grigsby, 477
French v. Mozzali, 466
French v. Safeway Stores, Inc., 858
French Drug Co. v. Jones, 185
Frenzel v. Miller, 732, 751, 752
Frerichs v. Eastern Nebraska Public Power District, 312
Frescoln v. Puget Sound Traction, Light & Power Co., 955
Fresh v. Cutter, 827, 828
Freshwater v. Bulmer Rayon Co., 330, 332, 352
Freund v. Cellofilm Properties, Inc., 697, 701
Freund v. DeBuse, 228
Frew v. Teagarden, 130
Frewen v. Page, 57, 58
Frey v. Dixon, 855
Frey v. Queen City Paper Co., 639
Friday v. United States, 332
Fried, Mendelson & Co. v. Edmund Halstead, Limited, 800
Friedberg, Inc. v. McClary, 987
Friedhoff v. Engberg, 1072
Friedman v. Dozorc, 890, 891
Friedman v. Friedman, 925
Friedman v. Jackson, 995
Friedman v. Lockheed Aircraft Corp., 484

Friedman v. Mutual Broadcasting System, Inc., 508
Friedman v. Richman, 438
Friendly Irishman, Inc. v. Ronnow, 754
Friendship Tel. Co. v. Russom, 317
Fries v. Boisselet, 165
Fries v. Stieben, 958
Friese v. Gulbrandson, 211
Frink, Inc., I. P. v. Erickson, 977
Frinzi v. Hanson, 774
Frisbee v. Town of Marshall, 77
Frisbie v. Morris, 54
Frishett v. State Farm Mutual Automobile Insurance Co., 62
Frisorger v. Shepse, 521
Frith v. Associated Press, 861
Fritscher v. Billiot, 177
Fritz v. E. I. Du Pont De Nemours & Co., 550
Fritzson v. City of Manhattan, 937
Frizzelle, State v., 128
Froelich v. Werbin, 856
Frome v. Dennis, 95, 101
Froslee v. Lund's State Bank, 827, 834
Frost v. Berkeley Phosphate Co., 550
Frost v. Eastern Railroad Co., 400
Frothingham v. Maxim, 150
Frulong v. German-American Press Association, 47
Fry v. Bennet, 800
Fry v. Dubuque & Southwestern Railway Co., 55
Fry v. Layne-Western Co., 1016
Fry v. McCord Brothers, 798
Fry v. Smellie, 733
Fryar v. Forrest, 770
Frye v. City of Detroit, 352
Frye Shoe Co., John A. v. Williams, 757
Fryer v. Cooper, 102
Fuchs v. Curran Carbonizing & Engineering Co., 629
Fuchs v. Mapes, 424
Fuentes v. Gentry, 457
Fugate v. Carter, 649
Fugate v. Fugate, 905
Fugate v. Galvin, 517, 519, 520
Fulgham v. State, 157
Fullam v. Stearns, 151
Fuller v. Buhrow, 938
Fuller v. Chamberlain, 325
Fuller v. Flanagan, 517, 518
Fuller v. Naugatuck Railroad Co., 932
Fuller v. Starnes, 191
Fuller v. State, 44
Fuller Co., George A. v. Otis Elevator Co., 342
Fuller Construction Co., George A. v. Elliott, 289, 308
Fulton v. Atlantic Coast Line Railroad Co., 798
Fulton v. Ingalls, 891
Fulton v. Kalbach, 306
Fulton Grand Laundry Co. v. Johnson, 1023
Fults v. Munro, 143
Fundermann v. Mickelson, 930
Fur Information & Fashion Council, Inc. v. E. F. Timme & Son, Inc., 1019
Furber v. Stephens, 672

Furlong v. Bartlett, 85
Furman v. Van Sise, 928
Furr v. McGrath, 261
Furr v. Spring Grove State Hospital, 384
Furr's Inc. v. Patterson, 424, 426, 427
Furst & Thomas v. Smith, 733
Furukawa v. Yoshio Ogawa, 458
Furumizo, United States v., 953
Fusario v. Cavallaro, 872
Fussner v. Andert, 953

G

G.(A.) v. G.(T.), 1072
G. T. I. Corp. v. Calhoon, 1023
G. W. K., Ltd. v. Dunlop Rubber Co., 85, 101, 992
Gaare v. Melbostad, 793
Gabaldon v. Sanchez, 391
Gabbert v. Wood, 417
Gable v. Niles Holding Co., 761
Gabriel v. McMullin, 820
Gabrielson v. City of Seattle, 388
Gabus Ford, Inc., Charles v. Iowa State Highway Commission, 1045
Gadde v. Michigan Consolidated Gas Co., 251
Gadsden General Hospital v. Hamilton, 57, 141
Gafford v. Trans-Texas Airways, 247
Gage v. Ford Motor Co., 413, 419
Gagne v. Bertran, 661, 746
Gagnon v. Dana, 489
Gagosian v. Burdick's Television & Appliances, 258
Gahagan v. State Farm Mutual Auto Insurance Co., 342
Gaidry Motors v. Brannon, 703, 704
Gaidys v. United States, 557
Gaines v. Briggs, 106
Gaines v. Wolcott, 123
Gainey v. Folkman, 626
Gaither v. Meacham, 123
Gaither v. Meyers, 304
Galbraith v. Busch, 255
Galbraith v. Fleming, 122
Galbraith v. Illinois Steel Co., 722
Galbraith v. Levin, 313
Gale v. Ryan, 963
Galena & Chicago Union Railroad Co. v. Jacobs, 210, 470
Galiano v. Pacific Gas & Electric Co., 388
Galizard v. Rigault, 916
Gall v. Union Ice Co., 703, 704
Gallagher v. Montpelier & Wells River Railroad Co., 171
Gallagher's Estate, In re, 801
Galland v. New Orleans Public Service, Inc., 241
Gallegos v. Nash, 488
Galleher v. City of Wichita, 408
Galli v. Kirkeby, 1048
Galliard v. Laxton, 150
Gallick v. Baltimore & Ohio Railroad Co., 579
Galligan v. Arovitch, 484
Gallin v. Poulou, 69, 551
Gallmon, People v., 147

Gallon v. Bruns, 752
Galloway v. Korzekwa, 521
Galloway v. Lawrence, 335
Galloway v Stewart, 876
Galloway v. United Railroads of San Francisco, 239
Gallucci v. Milavic, 881
Gallwey v. Marshall, 788, 791
Galotti v. United States Trust Co., 764
Galveston, H. & S. A. R. Co. v. Currie, 507
Galveston, H. & S. A. R. Co. v. Hennigan, 379
Galveston, Harrisburg & San Antonio Railway Co. v. Drew, 570
Galveston, Harrisburg & San Antonio Railway Co. v. Hennigan, 664
Galveston, Harrisburg & San Antonio Railroad Co. v. Nass, 347
Galveston Tribune v. Guisti, 778
Galvin v. Bacon, 111
Galvin v. Jennings, 581
Galvin v. Mac Mining & Milling Co., 664, 673
Galvin v. New York, N. H. & H. R. Co., 833
Gambill v. Stroud, 188
Gamble v. Keyes, 10
Gambrill v. Schooley, 799
Gammon v. Edwardsville Community Unit School District No. 7, p. 214
Gandara v. Wilson, 188
Gang v. Hughes, 774, 775
Gann v. Keith, 231
Gantt v. Sissell, 266
Garbarino v. United States, 1042
Garbe v. Halloran, 306
Garbo v. Walker, 313
Garbutt v. Schechter, 176
Garby v. Bennett, 836
Garceau v. Engel, 203
Garcia v. Burlington Northern, Inc., 466
Garcia v. City of South Tucson, 431, 487, 489, 490
Garcia v. Halsett, 719
Garcia v. Presbyterian Hospital Center, 166
Garcia v. Soogian, 406
Garcia v. Sumrall, 540
Garcia Sugars Corp. v. New York Coffee & Sugar Exchange, 985
Gardella v. Log Cabin Products Co., 780
Garden v. Parfumerie Rigaud, 867
Gardenvillage Realty Corp. v. Russo, 511
Gardner v. Allegheny County, 81
Gardner v. Black, 541
Gardner v. Campbell, 151
Gardner v. Hines, 669
Gardner v. Hobbs, 951
Gardner v. Hollifield, 821
Gardner v. Jonathan Club, 483
Gardner v. McDowell, 1053
Gardner v. Murphy, 476
Gardner v. National Bulk Carriers, Inc., 376
Gardner v. Self, 842
Gardner, State v., 127
Gardner v. West-Col, Inc., 971

Garelli v. Sterling-Alaska Fur & Game Farms, Inc., 542
Garey v. Jackson, 829
Garfield v. Palmieri, 816
Garfunkel v. Pennsylvania Railroad Co., 664
Gargotto v. Isenberg, 126
Gariepy v. Pearson, 781, 837
Gariety v. Fleming, 48
Garifine v. Monmouth Park Jockey Club, 662
Garland v. Boston & Maine Railroad Co., 286
Garland v. Nelson, 458
Garland v. Towne, 549
Garland v. Wilson, 897
Garland, City of v. White, 76
Garlock v. Multiple Parking Services, Inc., 241
Garner v. Crawford, 176
Garner v. Mears, 49
Garner v. Triangle Publications, 857
Garnier v. Squires, 53, 154
Garr v. Union Carbide Corp., 198
Garratt v. Dailey, 35, 40
Garren v. Butigan, 1063
Garret v. Taylor, 1005, 1009
Garrett v. Arkansas Power & Light Co., 409
Garrett v. Dickerson, 790
Garrett v. Garrett, 323, 346
Garrett v. McKie, 75
Garrett v. Nissen Corp., 686
Garrett v. Perry, 769
Garrett v. Raytheon Co., 167
Garrett v. Sewell, 76
Garrett v. State, 9
Garretzen v. Duenckel, 503
Garriga v. Richfield, 778
Garrison v. City of Cartersville, 413
Garrison v. Everett, 328
Garrison v. Pacific Northwest Bell, 212, 214
Garrison v. Robinson, 848
Garrison v. Sun Printing & Publishing Association, 794, 932
Garrity v. State Board of Administration of Educational Institutions, 674
Garska v. Harris, 525
Garthe v. Ruppert, 195
Garthwait v. Burgio, 703
Garvin v. Muir, 53
Garzilli v. Howard Johnson's Motor Lodges, Inc., 383
Gas City Transfer Co. v. Miller, 105
Gas Light & Coke Co. v. Vestry of St. Mary Abbott's, 538, 547
Gass v. National Container Corp., 763
Gassett v. Gilbert, 826
Gasteiger v. Gillenwater, 448, 723
Gastkowski v. Roman Catholic Church of Sacred Hearts of Jesus and Mary, 63
Gastman v. Myer, 880
Gaston v. Pittman, 904
Gaston v. Wabash Railroad Co., 716
Gates v. Blincoe, 642
Gates v. Boston & Maine Railroad Co., 269, 270
Gates v. Fleischer, 292, 350

Gates v. Foley, 932
Gates v. Jensen, 189, 219
Gates v. Meredith, 1074
Gates v. Northern Pacific Railway Co., 650
Gates v. St. James Operating Co., 12
Gates v. State, 42
Gates v. Utsey, 969
Gator Marine Service Towing, Inc. v. J. Ray McDermott & Co., 471
Gattis v. Chavez, 167
Gattis v. Kilgo, 830, 834, 835
Gaudette v. Carter, 798
Gaudette v. Webb, 20, 943
Gaupin v. Murphy, 280, 305, 311
Gautier v. Pro-Football, Inc., 854, 856, 859, 867
Gautret v. Egerton, 208, 375, 409
Gavagan, United States v., 381
Gavrilov v. Duell, Sloan & Pearce, 860, 862
Gay v. Perry, 639
Gay v. State, 643
Gaydos v. Domabyl, 951, 953
Gayer v. J.C. Penney Co., 425
Gayler & Pope, Limited v. Davies & Son, Limited, 68, 86
Gaylord Container Corp. v. Miley, 389, 398
Gear v. General Casualty Insurance Co., 406
Gearity v. Strasbourger, 506
Geary v. Bennett, 789
Geary v. United States Steel Corp., 1027, 1028, 1029
Geddes v. Daughters of Charity of St. Vincent De Paul, Inc., 51
Gedeon v. East Ohio Gas Co., 307
Gee v. Pritchard, 849
Gefter v. Rosenthal Caterers, 59
Geise v. Lee, 427
Geisel v. Poynter Products, Inc., 852
Geisking v. Sheimo, 222, 231
Geisler v. David Stevenson Brewing Co., 96
Geissler v. Geissler, 139
Gelbman v. Gelbman, 595, 905, 907
Gelhaus v. Eastern Air Lines, 45, 798
Gellenbeck v. Sears, Roebuck & Co., 706
Gendron v. St. Pierre, 780
General Building Contractors Association, Inc. v. Pennsylvania, 1052
General Casualty Co. of America v. Woodby, 13
General Corp. v. General Motors Corp., 764
General Exchange Insurance Corp. v. Sherby, 8
General Finance Corp. of Jacksonville v. Sexton, 102
General Insurance of America v. Faulkner, 913
General Market Co. v. Post-Intelligencer Co., 964
General Motors Acceptance Corp. v. Davis, 121, 736
General Motors Acceptance Corp. v. Froelich, 12
General Motors Acceptance Corp. v. Hicks, 141
General Motors Corp. v. Grizzle, 366
General Motors Corp. v. Hopkins, 478
General Motors Corp. v. Simmons, 698, 699
General Outdoor Advertising Co. v. Hamilton, 996
Genito v. Rabinowitz, 54
Genner v. Sparkes, 50, 51
Genovese v. New Orleans Public Service Co., 405

Gent v. Lynch, 975
Gentile Brothers Corp. v. Rowena Homes, Inc., 1003
Gentry v. Taylor, 438
Georcaris v. Bangs, 581
Georgacopoulos v. Katralis, 918
Georgakis v. Eastern Air Lines, Inc., 484
George v. Bekins Van & Storage Co., 483, 504
George v. Blow, 975, 976
George v. County of Erie, 952
George v. Guerette, 164, 475
George v. Kurdy, 752
George v. Tate, 731
George v. Williams, 871
George and Richard, The, 368
Georgia v. Kepford, 795, 844
Georgia Power Co. v. Banning Cotton Mills Co., 342
Georgia Railway & Electric Co. v. Baker, 58
Georgia Southern & Florida Railway Co. v. Odom, 465, 466
Geraghty v. Suburban Trust Co., 798
Geraty v. Stern, 39
Gerber v. McCall, 312
Gerchberg v. Loney, 400, 402, 408
Geriepy v. Pearson, 777
Gerkin v. Santa Clara Valley Water District, 225
Gerlach v. Gruett, 834
German-Bey v. National Railroad Passenger Corp., 202
Germanic, The, 535
Germolus v. Sausser, 126
Gerner v. Mosher, 744
Gerner v. Yates, 753
Gerrard v. Dickenson, 962, 969
Gerrard Co., S. A. v. Fricker, 513
Gershwin v. Ethical Publishing Co., 776
Gersten v. Newark Morning Ledger Co., 775, 777, 847
Gertz v. Robert Welch, Inc., 796, 805, 806, 807, 814, 843, 845, 885, 887, 892, 896, 968, 970, 971, 1011
Gerulis v. Lunecki, 136, 563
Gesford v. Star Van & Storage Co., 483
Gessell v. Traweek, 515, 516
Gherna v. Ford Motor Co., 749
Giacomelos v. Bank of America National Trust & Savings Association, 100
Giacona v. Tapley, 410
Giancario v. Karabanowski, 228
Giannini v. Campodonico, 406
Giant Foods, Inc. v. Washington Coca-Cola Bottling Co., 250, 253
Giant Mart Corp. v. Giant Discount Foods, 1017
Giant of Virginia, Inc. v. Pigg, 877, 883
Gibbons v. Duffell, 821
Gibbons v. Pepper, 74, 162
Gibbons v. Wisconsin Valley Railroad Co., 545
Gibbs v. Jones, 673
Gibeline v. Smith, 114
Giblan v. National Union, 988
Gibler v. Houston Post Co., 787
Gibson v. Beaver, 488
Gibson v. Bodley, 352
Gibson v. Chaters, 882

Gibson v. Colonial Insurance Co., 588
Gibson v. Frowein, 920
Gibson v. Garcia, 317
Gibson v. Gibson, 907, 908, 918, 919, 921
Gibson v. Holmes, 152
Gibson v. Hoppman, 442
Gibson v. Johnson, 389
Gibson v. Leonard, 224
Gibson v. Mendenhall, 737
Gibson v. Shelby County Fair Association, 438
Gibson v. Thompson, 579
Gibson v. Torbert, 686
Gibson Circuit Court, State ex rel. Green v., 77
Giddings v. Rogalewski, 75
Giddings v. Superior Oil Co., 405, 407
Giem v. Williams, 516
Giemza v. Allied American Mutual Fire Insurance Co., 489
Gifford v. Wichita Falls & Southern Railroad Co., 764
Gifford v. Wiggins, 52
Gifford-Hill & Co. v. Moore, 501
Gigliotti v. New York, Chicago & St. Louis Railroad Co., 233
Gilbert v. City of Los Angeles, 487
Gilbert v. Crystal Fountain Lodge, 779
Gilbert v. Davidson Construction Co., 552
Gilbert v. Emmons, 872
Gilbert v. Kennedy, 78
Gilbert v. Korvette, Inc., 243, 245, 250, 251, 253, 258
Gilbert v. Mayor & Council of City of Athens, 458
Gilbert v. Peck, 143
Gilbert v. Sabin, 200, 402, 405
Gilbert & Miller v. Peck, 106
Gilbert Shoe Co. v. Rumpf Publishing Co., 779
Gilborges v. Wallace, 503
Gilchrest House v. Guaranteed Title & Mortgage Co., 974
Giles v. Walker, 390
Gill v. Arthur, 495
Gill v. Baltimore & Ohio Railroad, 953
Gill v. Chicago Park District, 170, 385
Gill v. Curtis Publishing Co., 864
Gill v. Hearst Publishing Co., 856, 857, 859, 861, 867
Gill v. Jakstas, 532
Gill v. Middleton, 445
Gill, Rex v., 305
Gill v. Ruggles, 848
Gill v. Selling, 9, 119, 536
Gill v. State, 912
Gillaspie v. Department of Public Safety, 601
Gillespie v. Brooklyn Heights Railroad Co., 58
Gillespie v. Hunt, 743
Gillespie v. J. C. Piles, 765
Gillespie v. Torrance, 732
Gillet v. Roberts, 94
Gillett v. Bullivant, 780, 795, 844
Gillett v. Gillett, 006
Gillette v. Tucker, 661
Gilligan v. Blakesley, 439
Gillikin v. Burbage, 906

Gilliland v. Bondurant, 421
Gillis v. Pennsylvania Railroad Co., 413
Gillot v. Washington Metropolitan Area Transit Authority, 201
Gilly v. Hirsh, 1009, 1015
Gilman v. Central Vermont Railway Co., 277, 452
Gilman v. Eastern Railway Co., 572
Gilman v. Noyes, 198, 266, 304, 321
Gilman, United States v., 342
Gilmore v. Fuller, 122
Gilmore v. Grass, 522
Gilmore v. Wilbur, 664
Giltner v. Stark, 919, 923
Gimino v. Sears, Roebuck & Co., 670
Gimmestad v. Rose Bros. Co., 406
Gimson v. Woodfull, 8
Ginger v. Bowles, 816
Ginnis v. Mapes Hotel Corp., 715
Ginsberg v. Union Surety & Guaranty Co., 826
Ginsberg v. Wineman, 445
Ginsburg v. Black, 817, 818
Ginsburg v. Halpern, 817
Giorgi v. Pacific Gas & Electric Co., 430
Gipson v. Memphis Street Railway Co., 269
Girard v. Anderson, 139, 141
Girdner v. Union Oil Co., 276
Girdzus v. Van Etten, 513
Gissendanner v. Temples, 126
Gissin v. Goodwill, 915
Giuliano Construction Co. v. Simmons, 91
Givens v. North Augusta Electric & Improvement Co., 665
Givens v. Powell, 941
Gladding Chevrolet, Inc. v. Fowler, 881
Glamorgan Coal Co. v. South Wales Miners' Federation, 985
Glanville v. Sutton, 561
Glanz v. Chicago, Milwaukee & St. Paul Railway Co., 307, 491
Glanzer v. Shepard, 747
Glasgow Realty Co. v. Metcalfe, 388
Glass v. Bennett, 836, 922
Glass v. Davison, 505
Glass v. Ickes, 822
Glasscock v. First National Bank, 313
Glassey v. Worcester Consolidated Street Railway Co., 201, 312
Glasson v. Bowen, 819
Glastris v. Union Electric Co., 401, 404, 405, 410
Glatstein v. Grund, 919
Glazener v. Safety Transit Lines, 268
Glazer v. Chandler, 990
Gleason v. City of Davenport, 1046
Gleason v. Hillcrest Golf Course, 392
Gleason v. Jack Alan Enterprises, Inc., 245
Gleason v. McPherson, 756
Gleaton v. Southern Railway Co., 218
Gleitman v. Cosgrove, 370, 371
Glencoe Sand & Gravel Co. v. Hudson Brothers Commission Co., 981, 990, 982, 1003

Glendola, The, 289
Glenn v. Brown, 453
Glenn v. Lawrence, 876, 881
Glick v. Ballentine Produce, Inc., 266
Glickstein v. Setzer, 40
Glidden v. Butler, 531
Glidden v. Moore, 562
Glidden, State v., 1023
Glidden v. Szybiak, 86
Glidden v. Wills, 1066
Glidewell v. Murray-Lacey & Co., 897, 899
Glieberman v. Fine, 975
Glines v. Main Central Railroad Co., 308
Globe & Rutgers Fire Insurance Co. v. Firemen's Fund Fire Insurance Co., 28, 981, 987
Globe Furniture Co. v. Wright, 833
Globe Indemnity Co. v. Schmitt, 511
Globe Malleable Iron & Steel Co. v. New York Central & Hudson River Railroad Co., 382
Globe Refining Co. v. Landa Cotton Oil Co., 665
Glock v. Carpenter, 758
Glona v. American Guarantee & Liability Insurance Co., 948
Glorioso v. Chandler, 387
Glover v. Callahan, 123
Glover v. Fleming, 883
Glover v. Heyward, 874
Glover v. Malloska, 1009
Glynn v. Central Railroad Co. of New Jersey, 716
Glynn v. Delcuze, 721
Gmerek v. Rachlin, 225
Gnapinsky v. Goldyn, 783, 793
Gnatz, People v., 157
Goar v. Village of Stephen, 204, 205, 319
Gobin v. Avenue Food Mart, 253
Gobrecht v. Beckwith, 185, 455
Gochee v. Wagner, 523
Goddard v. Boston & Maine Railroad Co., 243
Goddard v. Grand Trunk Railway Co., 13, 26, 58
Goddard v. Watters, 66
Godfrey v. Navratil, 752
Godfrey v. Tidewater Power Co., 340
Godfrey Pontiac, Inc., Bob v. Roloff, 221, 222
Godin v. Niebuhr, 795, 1009
Godwin v. Collins, 125
Godwin v. Olshan, 442
Goebel v. Clark, 104
Goede v. Rondorf, 319
Goedkoop v. Ward Pavement, 909, 910
Goetzman v. Wichern, 471
Goff, State ex rel. v. O'Neil, 645
Gogue v. MacDonald, 52
Goines v. Pennsylvania Railroad Co., 328
Gold v. Campbell, 48
Gold v. Los Angeles Democratic League, 989, 1005, 1015
Gold & White, Inc. v. Long, 426
Gold Seal Chinchillas, Inc. v. State, 821
Goldberg v. Ideal Publishing Corp., 863

Goldberg v. Kollsman Instrument Corp., 690, 693, 694, 703, 705, 706
Goldberg v. Markowitz, 149
Golden v. Amory, 564
Golden v. Conway, 511
Golden v. Lerch Brothers, 268, 352
Golden v. McCurry, 470
Goldman v. Feinberg, 1006
Goldman v. Harford Road Building Association, 981, 1013
Goldman v. Mitchell-Fletcher Co., 337
Goldner-Siegel Corp. v. Kraemer Hosiery Co., 894
Goldsmith v. Cody, 421
Goldstein v. California, 1021
Goldstein v. Gilbert, 333
Goldstein v. Levy, 262
Goldstein v. Sabella, 894
Goldstein v. Webster, 144
Goldwater v. Ginzburg, 776
Golembe v. Blumberg, 718
Goller v. White, 907, 909
Goman v. Benedik, 456
Gomes v. Byrne, 567
Gomes v. Peter Scalamandre & Sons, Inc., 457
Gomez v. Toledo, 1060, 1066
Gompers v. Buck's Stove & Range Co., 773
Goneau v. Minneapolis, St. Paul & Sault St. Marie Railway Co., 306
Gonzales v. Baltimore & Ohio Railroad Co., 482
Gonzales v. Kentucky Derby Co., 981
Gonzales v. R.J. Novick Construction Co., 514
Gonzalez v. Derrington, 314
Gonzalez v. Sacramento Mem. Lawn, 362
Gonzalez v. United States Steel Corp., 510
Gooch v. Wachowiak, 52
Good v. A.B. Chance Co., 715
Good v. Von Hemert, 445
Good Fund, Limited—1972 v. Church, 512
Goode v. Martinis, 904
Goode, State v., 133
Goodell v. Tower, 47, 48
Goodfellow v. Coggburn, 181
Gooding v. Chutes Co., 543
Goodlander Mill Co. v. Standard Oil Co., 284
Goodman v. Georgia Life Insurance Co., 587
Goodman v. Harris, 438, 439
Goodman v. Kennedy, 1008
Goodrich v. Davis, 780
Goodrich Co., B.F. v. Hammond, 690
Goodspeed v. MacNaughton, Greenawalt & Co., 759
Goodwin v. Agassiz, 738
Goodwin v. E.B. Nelson Grocery Co., 542
Goodwin v. Misticos, 269
Goodwin v. United States, 244, 558
Goodwyn v. Cheveley, 540
Goodyear v. Davis, 956
Goodyear Tire & Rubber Co. v. Gadsden Sand & Gravel Co., 552
Goodyear Tire & Rubber Co. v. Hughes Supply, Inc., 246, 696

Goodyear Tire & Rubber Co. v. Vandergriff, 852
Goodyear Yellow Pine Co. v. Anderson, 949, 953
Goolsby v. Forum Printing Co., 846
Gorder v. Sims, 930
Gordon v. Aztec Brewing Co., 249
Gordon v. Bedard, 717
Gordon v. C.H.C. Corp., 183
Gordon v. Harper, 104, 105
Gordon v. Harris, 411
Gordon v. Hurtado, 228
Gordon v. Journal Publishing Co., 800
Gordon v. McLearn, 873
Gordon v. Niagara Machine & Tool Works, 204
Gordon v. Parker, 918
Gordon v. Spencer, 823
Gordon, State v., 128
Gordon v. Street, 753
Gordoy v. Flaherty, 505
Gordy v. State, 156
Gore v. Condon, 991, 992
Gore v. Gorman's, Inc., 890, 894
Gorger v. New Jersey, 116
Gorham v. Gross, 550
Gorham v. Massillon Iron & Steel Co., 106
Gorlitzer v. Wolffberg, 941
Gorman v. Budlong, 367
Gorman v. Columbus & Southern Ohio Electric Co., 950
Gorman, Commonwealth v., 153
Gorman v. Sabo, 620, 639, 640
Gorman v. State, 157
Gorman Towers, Inc. v. Bogoslavsky, 1063, 1064
Gormely v. Gymnastic Association, 758
Gorris v. Scott, 225, 284
Gorton v. Phoenix Insurance Co., 513
Goshen v. People, 143
Gosling v. Nichols, 941
Goss v. Allen, 181
Goss v. Ellison, 334
Goss v. Kurn, 570
Goss v. Shawnee Post No. 3204, V.F.W., 407
Gosselin v. Silver, 133
Gossett v. Southern Railway Co., 552
Gossett v. Van Egmond, 914
Gostkowski v. Roman Catholic Church, 9, 62
Gotreaux v. Gary, 550
Gott v. Berea College, 985, 1010
Gott v. Pulsifer, 832, 974
Gottbehuet v. Hubachek, 792
Gottesfeld v. Mechanics & Traders Insurance Co., 93
Gotthelf v. Hillcrest Lumber Co., 855
Gottschalk v. Benson, 1023
Gottscho, Inc., Adolph v. American Marking Corp., 334
Gotwals v. City of Wessington Springs, 621
Goudy v. State, 278
Gough, State v., 127
Gould v. De Beve, 408
Gould v. Hulme, 819
Gould v. Kramer, 1003
Gould v. McKenna, 350, 459
Gould v. Stafford, 634

Gould v. Winona Gas Co., 567
Gouna v. O'Neill, 280
Gover v. Central Vermont Railway Co., 495
Government Employees Insurance Co. v. Edelman, 1072
Government Employees Insurance Co. v. Thompson, 206
Gowen, United States v., 154
Gower v. Lamb, 313
Gower v. Waters, 143, 144
Gowin v. Heider, 102
Gowins v. Pennsylvania Railroad Co., 461
Goyette v. Sousa, 421
Grable v. Varela, 430
Grabow v. Bergeth, 941
Grace & Co. v. City of Los Angeles, 550
Graceland Corp. v. Consolidated Laundries Corp., 649
Grady v. Wolsner, 620
Graeber v. Anderson, 442
Graeter v. Williams, 876
Graf v. Taggert, 370
Graf v. Tracy, 259
Graff v. Geisel, 751
Graff v. Whitehouse, 987
Graffenstein v. E. Epstein & Co., 751
Graft v. Crooker, 457
Graham v. Bottenfield's Inc., 690, 703
Graham v. Franco, 531
Graham v. John R. Watts & Son, 726, 744, 749
Graham v. Miller, 911
Graham v. Page, 914
Graham v. Peat, 77
Graham v. Rolandson, 163, 164
Graham v. Smith, 90
Graham v. St. Charles Street Railroad Co., 1006, 1009, 1014
Graham v. United States, 447
Grainger v. Hill, 121, 736, 897
Gram v. Liberty Mutual Insurance Co., 990
Gramlich v. Wurst, 394
Grand Lodge, A.O.U.W. of Minnesota v. Towne, 730
Grand Rapids Furniture Co. v. Grand Rapids Furniture Co., 1019
Grand Trunk R. Co. v. Dixon, 517
Grand Trunk Railway Co. v. Ives, 233
Grand Trunk Railway Co. of Canada v. Knapp, 573
Grande & Son v. Chace, 774
Granier v. Chagnon, 137
Granley v. Crandall, 526
Granniss v. Weber, 539
Grant v. Allen, 146, 642
Grant v. Australian Knitting Mills, 682
Grant v. Director of Benefit Payments, 501
Grant v. Graham Chero-Colo Bottling, Co., 195, 535, 684
Grant v. Knepper, 528
Grant v. Lovekin, 675
Grant v. Reader's Digest Association, 777, 778
Grant Co., W.T. v. Owens, 49, 121, 142
Grasser v. Fleming, 213
Grasty v. Sabin, 576
Graton & Knight Manufacturing Co. v. Redelsheimer, 91

Grau v. Forge, 110, 152
Gravel v. Le Blanc, 532
Gravel v. Roberge, 197
Graver Tank & Manufacturing Co. v. Industrial Commission, 311
Graves v. Dawson, 874
Graves v. Haynes, 752
Graves v. Johnson, 318
Graves v. North Shore Gas Co., 238
Graves v. Scott, 874
Graves v. Severens, 87
Graves v. Shattuck, 642
Gravis v. Physicians and Surgeons Hospital of Alice, 114
Gray v. Bennett, 877
Gray v. Boston Elevated Railway Co., 1000
Gray v. Central Warehouse Co., 662
Gray v. Combs, 135
Gray v. Durland, 928
Gray v. Frazier, 99
Gray v. Golden, 524, 525
Gray v. Grunnagle, 120
Gray v. Times Newspaper Co., 846, 847
Gray v. Udevitz, 806
Gray v. Wikstrom Motors, 758
Gray & Bell v. Scott, 457
Grayson v. Ellerman Lines, 453
Grayson v. St. Louis Transit Co., 56
Great Atlantic & Pacific Tea Co. v. Billups, 47, 49
Great Atlantic & Pacific Tea Co. v. Cream of Wheat Co., 994, 1024
Great Atlantic & Pacific Tea Co. v. Hughes, 581
Great Atlantic & Pacific Tea Co. v. Roch, 61
Great Atlantic & Pacific Tea Co. v. Smith, 48, 141
Great Atlantic & Pacific Tea Co. v. Wilson, 393, 447
Great Atlantic & Pacific Tea Co. v. Yanofsky, 443
Great Central Insurance Co. v. Harris, 524
Great Falls Co. v. Worster, 642
Great Northern Railway Co. v. Wiles, 578
Great Northern Refining Co. v. Lutes, 552
Great Southern Life Insurance Co. v. Dolan, 327
Great Western Sugar Co. v. District Court, 577
Greco v. Bucciconi Engineering Co., 255
Greco v. S.S. Kresge Co., 665, 947
Greear v. Noland Co., 466
Greeley v. Baltimore Transit Co., 246
Greeley v. Spratt, 143
Green v. American Tobacco Co., 700
Green v. Atlanta Charlotte Air Line Railway Co., 202
Green v. Bittner, 952
Green v. Britton, 289, 308
Green v. Button, 970, 992
Green v. Carlson, 944
Green v. Chelsea Waterworks Co., 567
Green v. City of Livermore, 201
Green v. General Petroleum Corp., 550
Green v. Hatcher, 717
Green v. Meadows, 887
Green v. Millsboro Fire Co., 467
Green v. Orion Shipping & Trading Co., 310
Green, People v., 158
Green v. Samuelson, 985
Green v. State through Department of Institutions, 314
Green v. T.A. Shoemaker & Co., 56, 608, 621
Green v. United States, 187
Green v. Victor Talking Machine Co., 1024
Green v. Warnock, 874
Green v. Wellons, Inc., 419, 426, 453
Green, State ex rel. v. Gibson Circuit Court, 77
Green & Co., V.N. v. Thomas, 567
Green River Light & Water Co. v. Beeler, 572
Green-Wheeler Shoe Co. v. Chicago Rock Island & Pacific Railway Co., 315
Greenawalt v. Rogers, 753
Greenbelt Cooperative Publishing Association, Inc. v. Bresler, 1012
Greenberg v. Ackerman, 818
Greenberg v. Aetna Insurance Co., 817, 818
Greenberg v. McCabe, 178
Greenberg v. Michael Reese Hospital, 186
Greenberg v. Stanley, 365
Greenberg v. United Airlines, Inc., 209
Greene v. De Fazio, 411
Greene v. Greene, 166
Greene v. Minneapolis & St. Louis Railroad Co., 571
Greene v. Sibley, Lindsay & Curr Co., 170
Greene v. Spinning, 550
Greene v. Waters, 332
Greene v. Watts, 487
Greenfield v. Courier-Journal & Louisville Times Co., 816, 837
Greenfield v. Freedman, 426
Greenhalch v. Shell Oil Co., 335
Greenhalgh v. Payson City, 1053
Greenlake Investment Co. v. Swarthout, 965
Greenland v. Chaplin, 281
Greenleaf v. Gerald, 754
Greenman v. Smith, 46
Greenman v. Yuba Power Products, Inc., 678, 693, 694
Greensboro Morris Plan Co. v. Palmer, 1072
Greenspon's Son Pipe Corp., Joseph v. Hyman-Michaels Co., 742
Greenville National Bank v. National Hardwood Co., 743
Greenwade v. Drake, 219, 238
Greenwood v. Cobbey, 830
Greenwood v. Kier, 525
Greenwood v. Lyles & Buckner, Inc., 319
Gregg v. Delhi-Taylor Oil Corp., 71
Gregg v. Gregg, 918, 922
Gregoire v. Biddle, 1060, 1062
Gregoire v. G.P. Putnam's Sons, 800
Gregory v. Bryan-Hunt Co., 858
Gregory, Commonwealth v., 120
Gregory v. Dealers' Equipment Co., 984, 985
Gregory v. Duke of Brunswick, 324, 1005
Gregory v. Johnson, 394, 400, 402, 408, 411
Gregutis v. Waclark Wire Works, 574
Grein v. La Poma, 794
Greinke v. Chicago City Railroad Co., 252

Greischar v. St. Mary's College, 574
Grell v. Hoard, 831
Grella v. Lewis Wharf Co., 239
Grenada Lumber Co. v. Mississippi, 1025
Gresham v. Stouffer Corp., 250
Gresham v. Taylor, 538, 539
Gresser v. Taylor, 249
Gressman v. Morning Journal Association, 848
Greve v. Wood-Harmon Co., 78
Grew v. Beaven, 731
Grey v. Hayes-Sammons Chemical Co., 683
Greyhound Corp. v. Brown, 246, 252, 703
Greyhound Corp. v. Townsend, 10
Grice v. Holk, 782
Gridley v. Ross, 752
Grier v. Woodside, 525
Grierson, State v., 128
Griese-Taylor Corp. v. First National Bank, 1009
Griesee v. Dart Industries, Inc., 514
Griffen v. Manice, 244
Griffin v. Clark, 50
Griffin v. Gehret, 955
Griffin v. Hustis, 307
Griffin v. Russell, 524
Griffin v. United States, 1034, 1035, 1041, 1042
Griffith v. Kerrigan, 346
Griffith v. Slinkard, 816
Griffiths v. Benn, 976
Griffiths v. Henry Broderick, Inc., 482
Griffiths v. Lewis, 823
Griffiths v. Lovelette Transfer Co., 431
Griffiths v. Thrasher, 737
Griffiths & Son Co. v. National Fireproofing Co., 342
Griggs v. County of Allegheny, 82
Griggs v. Day, 91
Griggs v. Fleckenstein, 198
Griggs, State v., 128
Grignoli v. Chicago & G.E.R. Co., 259
Grill v. General Iron Screw Collier Co., 210
Grillo v. Board of Realtors of Plainfield Area, 1025
Grilnberger v. Brotherton, 923
Grimes v. Carter, 858
Grimes v. Eddy, 540
Grimes v. Greenblatt, 872
Grimes v. Grennblatt, 888
Grimes v. Hettinger, 377, 402, 409
Grimes v. Labreck, 526
Grimm v. Arizona Board of Pardons and Paroles, 384, 1048, 1063
Grimm v. Baumgart, 995
Grimshaw v. Ford Motor Co., 213, 214
Grinnell v. Wells, 926
Grinter v. Haag, 523, 526
Grisom v. Logan, 128
Grissell v. Housatonic Railroad Co., 544
Grist v. Upjohn Co., 802
Griswold v. Boston & Maine Railroad Co., 877
Griswold v. Connecticut, 866
Griswold v. Gebbie, 741
Griswold v. Heat, Inc., 986

Griswold v. Sedgwick, 150
Griswold & Day v. Brega & Roster, 620
Grobart v. Grobart, 918
Grobart v. North Jersey District Water Supply Commission, 940
Groda v. American Stores, Co., 879
Grodin v. Grodin, 368, 909
Grodstein v. McGivern, 723
Grogan v. O'Keefe's, Inc., 421
Groh v. Hasencamp, 223, 226
Grombach Productions v. Waring, 1021
Groner v. Hedrick, 571
Gronn v. Rogers Construction, Inc., 562
Gronquist v. Olson, 334, 335
Groom v. Crocker, 660
Gross v. Gross, 922
Gross v. Nashville Gas Co., 183, 470
Gross' Administrator v. Ledford, 941
Gross Coal Co. v. Rose, 779
Grossman v. Frederick Brothers, Artists Corp., 867
Grossman v. Globe-Democrat Publishing Co., 837
Grossman v. Industrial Commission, 574
Group Health Association, Inc. v. Blumenthal, 368
Grove v. Dun & Bradstreet, Inc., 965
Grove v. Van Duyn, 149
Groves v. Webster City, 467
Grubb v. Johnson, 819
Gruenberg v. Aetna Insurance Co., 11, 62
Grumon v. Raymond, 149
Grunstein & Sons Co., Ben, United States v., 769
Gruntal v. United States Fidelity & Guaranty Co., 98
Gruschus v. Curtis Publishing Co., 778
Gryc v. Dayton-Hudson Corp., 195, 233
Grzybowski v. Connecticut Co., 351, 352
Guanzon v. Kalamau, 164
Guardian Casualty Co., In re, 289, 300
Guard-Life Corp. v. S. Parker Hardware Manufacturing Corp., 987, 996
Guarina v. Bogart, 620
Guarino v. Mine Safety Appliance Co., 703
Gude Co., O.J. v. Farley, 96
Gudfelder v. Pittsburgh, Cincinnati, Chicago & St. Louis Railway Co., 292
Gudger v. Manton, 969
Gudziewski v. Stemplesky, 914, 915
Guercio v. Hertz Corp., 528
Guerin v. Indemnity Insurance Co., 587
Guernsey v. Davis, 673
Guerrero v. Copper Queen Hospital, 381
Guerrieri v. Tyson, 158
Guethler v. Altman, 985, 1010
Gugel v. Neitzel, 761
Gugel, United States v., 856
Guibault v. Marcoux, 921
Guidry v. Cheramie, 488
Guile v. Greenberg, 457, 459
Guilford v. Yale University, 423
Guille v. Swan, 307, 308, 328, 556
Guillory v. Godfrey, 62, 1009
Guinn v. Delaware & Atlantic Telephone Co., 394

Guith v. Consumers Power Co., 80
Gulczynski, State v., 153
Gulf, Colorado & Santa Fe Railway Co. v. Hayter, 360
Gulf, Colorado & Santa Fe Railway Co. v. James, 878
Gulf, Colorado & Santa Fe Railway Co. v. Oakes, 549, 551
Gulf, Colorado & Sante Fe Railway Co. v. Russell, 396
Gulf, Colorado & Santa Fe Railway Co. v. Wortham, 96
Gulf & Ship Island Railroad Co. v. Bradley, 959
Gulf & Ship Island Railroad v. Sullivan, 115
Gulf & Ship Island Railroad Co. v. Williamson, 397
Gulf Pipe Line Co. v. Alred, 551
Gulf Pipe Line Co. v. Sims, 549
Gulf Production Co. v. Gibson, 147
Gulf Refining Co. v. Myrick, 328
Gulf Refining Co. v. Williams, 171
Gulf Reston, Inc. v. Rogers, 201
Gulf States Steel Co. v. Beveridge, 650
Gulf Transport Co. v. Allen, 951
Gum, State v., 156
Gumbleton v. Grafton, 89
Gumm v. Heider, 875
Gumm v. Jones, 540
Gunder v. Tibbitts, 327, 329
Gundermann v. Buschner, 890
Gunn v. Barr, 996
Gunn v. Parsons, 75
Gunnells v. Dethrage, 181
Gunnels v. Atlanta Bar Association, 994
Gunnels v. Roach, 266
Gunning System v. Lapointe, 490, 571
Gunsolus v. Lormer, 78
Gunter v. Reeves, 818
Gunther v. E.I. Du Pont de Nemours & Co., 628
Gunther v. Lee, 332, 333
Gunther v. Morey Larue Laundry Co., 90
Gunzburger v. Rosenthal, 103
Gurden v. Stevens, 878
Gurley v. Armstead, 95
Gurley v. Southern Power Co., 502
Gurll v. Massasoit Greyhound Association, 937
Gurtler v. Union Parts Manufacturing Co., 792, 793
Gust v. Montgomery Ward & Co., 833
Gustafson v. Gate City Co-op. Creamery, 262
Gustafson v. Payless Drug Stores Northwest, Inc., 882
Gustella v. Wardell, 738
Gustin v. Evening Press Co., 782
Gustole v. Mathers, 786
Guthrie v. Great American Insurance Co., 1024
Guthrie v. Powell, 245
Guthrie v. Reliance Construction Co., 427
Gutierrez v. Public Service Interstate Transportation Co., 242
Gutierrez v. Superior Court, 694, 703
Gutierrez v. Valley Irrigation & Livestock Co., 570
Guttery v. Glenn, 649, 650
Guttner v. Pacific Steam Whaling Co., 85
Gutzman v. Clancy, 126
Guy v. Liederbach, 359
Guy v. Livesey, 916, 931

Guzzi v. New York Zoological Society, 568
Gypsy Oil Co. v. McNair, 376
Gyre v. Culver, 138

H

H.L. Properties, Inc. v. Aerojet-General Corp., 558
Haack v. Linsay Light & Chemical Co., 631, 641
Haack v. Rodenbour, 184
Haaf v. Grams, 873
Haas v. Evening Democrat Co., 774
Haas v. Firestone Tire & Rubber Co., 388
Haas v. Lavin, 391
Haas v. Metz, 62
Haase v. Employers Mutual Liability Insurance Co., 334
Haasman v. Pacific Alaska Air Express, 247
Haber v. County of Nassau, 178
Hack v. Hack, 903
Hackbart v. Cincinnati Bengals, 114, 213, 485
Hackenberger v. Travelers Mutual Casualty Co., 30, 36, 41
Hacker v. Rector, 703
Hackett v. Perron, 204
Hackley v. Robey, 526
Hackworth v. Davis, 347
Hackworth v. Larson, 821
Hadcock v. Osmer, 742
Haddad v. Clark, 737
Haddad v. First National Stores, 400
Hadden v. Aitken, 601
Haddock v. Naughton, 842
Haddrick v. Heslop, 883
Haden v. Hockenberger & Chambers Co., 409
Haden v. Tinnin, 871
Hadley v. Bryars' Administrator, 941
Hadley v. Clinton County Importing Co., 743
Hadley v. Hadley, 924
Hadley v. Heywood, 920
Hadwell v. Righton, 561
Haeg v. Sprague, Warner & Co., 469
Haeissig v. Decker, 57, 926
Haelan Laboratories v. Topps Chewing Gum, Inc., 854
Haentze v. Lehr, 767
Haeussler v. De Loretto, 124
Hafey v. Dwight Manufacturing Co., 413
Haffey v. Lemieux, 417
Hagar v. Norton, 93, 725
Hageman v. Vanderdoes, 913
Hager v. Major, 817, 819
Hagerty v. Powers, 914
Hagglund v. St. Hilaire Lumber Co., 276
Hahn v. City of Ortonville, 581
Hahn v. Ford Motor Co., 703
Hahn v. Holum, 837
Hahn v. Sargent, 886
Hahn v. United States Airlines, 557
Hahn & Clay v. A.O. Smith Corp., 1023
Hahnemannian Life Insurance Co. v. Beebe, 831
Haidri v. Egolf, 242, 251
Haile v. New Orleans Railway & Light Co., 58

TABLE OF CASES

Haines v. Campbell, 799
Haines v. Schultz, 12
Haire v. Brooks, 266
Hake v. George Wiedemann Brewing Co., 243, 244
Hakensen v. Ennis, 247
Hakkila v. Old Colony Broken Stone & Concrete Co., 68, 567
Halberstadt v. New York Life Insurance Co., 871, 875
Haldeman v. Chambers, 975
Hale v. Buckner, 929
Hale v. Clark, 151
Hale v. Depaoli, 723
Hale v. Hale, 906
Hale v. Jennings Bros., 547, 548
Hale v. Peabody Coal Co., 501
Hale, Inc., Robert Heard v. Gaiennie, 981
Halepeska v. Callihan Interests, Inc., 487
Hales v. Commercial Bank of Spanish Fork, 828
Hales v. McCrory-McLellan Corp., 49
Haley v. Colcord, 146
Halff Co. v. Jones, 754
Halio v. Lurie, 61
Hall v. Adams, 872
Hall v. American Investment Co., 883
Hall v. Balkind, 803
Hall v. Blackham, 519
Hall v. Boston & Worcester Railroad Corp., 97
Hall v. Browning, 79
Hall v. Coble Dairies, 311
Hall v. Consolidated Edison Corp., 374
Hall v. Cornett, 165
Hall v. De Weld Mica Corp., 71
Hall v. Duart Sales Co., 1019
Hall v. Edlefson, 408
Hall v. Edwards, 842
Hall v. Field Enterprises, Inc., 897
Hall v. Frankel, 349
Hall v. Hall, 775, 1007
Hall v. Hancock, 368
Hall v. Hollander, 924
Hall v. Holton, 430
Hall v. Industrial Commission of Ohio, 578
Hall v. Johnson, 753
Hall v. MacLeod, 659
Hall v. McClure, 329
Hall v. Macco Corp., 307
Hall v. Meister, 491
Hall v. Merchants' State Bank, 102
Hall v. National Supply Co., 260
Hall v. Pickard, 88
Hall v. Rice, 53
Hall v. Safeco Insurance Co., 198
Hall v. State, 423
Hall v. State ex rel. Freeman, 51
Hall v. Warren, 220, 230, 435, 446
Hall, Inc., George R. v. Superior Trucking Co., 483
Hall Co., M K v. Caballero, 505
Hall Oil Co. v. Barquin, 15
Halldin v. Peterson, 188
Halleck v. Mixer, 674

Hallett v. Stone, 173
Halley v. Gregg, 789
Halliburton-Abbott Co. v. Hodge, 49
Halliday v. Cienkowski, 59, 776
Halling v. Industrial Commission, 956
Hallman v. Cushman, 377
Halloran v. Belt Railway of Chicago, 403
Halls v. Mitchell, 790
Hallstein v. Pennsylvania Railroad Co., 491, 570
Halpin v. Prudential Insurance Co. of America, 508
Halsey v. Esso Petroleum Co., 547
Halsey v. Minnesota-South Carolina Land & Timber Co., 941
Halsey v. Woodruff, 325, 329
Ham v. Greensboro Ice & Fuel Co., 266
Ham v. Hart, 746, 748
Ham v. Maine-New Hampshire Interstate Bridge Authority, 76
Hamakawa v. Crescent Wharf & Warehouse Co., 395
Hamberger v. Eastman, 854
Hambrook v. Stokes Brothers, 365
Hamburg v. Eagleson, 872
Hamburger v. Henry Ford Hospital, 500
Hamet v. Letcher, 94
Hamil v. Bashline, 242
Hamilan Corp. v. O'Neill, 363
Hamill v. Smith, 228
Hamilton v. Arnold, 137
Hamilton v. Barker, 138
Hamilton v. Boyd, 459
Hamilton v. Brown, 413
Hamilton v. Calder, 140
Hamilton v. Crown Life Ins. Co., 857
Hamilton v. Eno, 835
Hamilton v. Green, 170, 225
Hamilton v. Hamilton, 902
Hamilton v. Howard, 132, 133
Hamilton v. Kinsey, 178, 486
Hamilton v. Lumbermen's Mutual Casualty Co., 852, 853, 863
Hamilton v. Slover, 517
Hamilton v. Vare, 294
Hamilton v. Windolf, 27
Hamilton Corp. v. Julian, 640
Hamm v. Thompson, 333
Hammatt v. Emerson, 766
Hammel v. Madison Square Garden Corp., 486
Hammerslough v. Kansas City Building, Loan & Savings Association, 756
Hammersmith R. Co. v. Brand, 632
Hammett, Ex parte, 59
Hammett v. Hunter, 819
Hammond v. Allegretti, 427
Hammond v. Lewiston, Augusta & Waterville Street Railway, 949
Hammond v. Melton, 542
Hammond v. Rowley, 883
Hammond v. Scot Lad Foods, Inc., 258
Hammond v. Vestry of St. Pancras, 228
Hammond Ranch Corp. v. Dodson, 516

Hammonds v. Haven, 454
Hamon v. Digliani, 729
Hampton v. Gebhardt's Chili Powder Co., 691
Hampton v. North Carolina Pulp Co., 640, 650
Hampton, State v., 45
Hampton v. Westover, 8
Han v. Horwitz, 756
Hanaman v. New York Telephone Co., 247
Hanback v. Seaboard Coastline Railroad, 202
Hanberry v. Hearst Corp., 207, 707, 720
Hanchett v. Chiatovich, 1014
Hancock v. Aiken Mills, 407
Hancock v. Mitchell, 831
Hancock v. Moriarity, 638
Handcock v. Baker, 153, 156
Handiboe v. McCarthy, 375
Handley v. Home Insurance Co. of New York, 91
Handy v. Johnson, 46
Haney v. Cheatham, 333
Haney v. General Host Corp., 427
Hanfgarn v. Mark, 930
Hanford v. Goehry, 525
Hanft v. Heller, 816
Hanft v. Southern Bell Telephone & Telegraph Co., 211
Hankins v. Harvey, 174
Hankinson v. Bilby, 809
Hanks v. Drs. Ranson, Swan & Burcj, Ltd., 192
Hanks v. Great Northern Railway Co., 394
Hanley v. California Bridge & Construction Co., 487
Hanley v. Central Savings Bank, 514
Hanlon v. Cyril Bath Co., 711
Hanlon Drydock & Shipbuilding Co. v. Southern Pacific Co., 382
Hanna v. Fletcher, 723
Hanna v. Phelps, 100
Hannabalson v. Sessions, 79
Hannabass v. Florida Home Insurance Co., 479
Hannah v. Jensen, 430
Hannem v. Pence, 550
Hannon v. Hayes-Bickford Lunch System, 494
Hannum v. Oak Lane Shopping Center, 627, 641
Hanowitz v. Great Northern Railway Co., 884
Hans v. Louisiana, 1043
Hansberry v. Holloway, 1013
Hanschke v. Merchants' Credit Bureau, 829
Hansen v. Brogan, 541, 563
Hansen v. Cohen, 425
Hansen v. Collett, 335
Hansen v. Dethridge, 776
Hansen v. Hansen, 827, 828
Hansen v. Independent School District, 620
Hansen v. Lowe, 149
Hansen v. Village of Ralston, 100
Hansen v. Washington Natural Gas Co., 230
Hanson v. Acceptance Finance Corp., 751
Hanson v. Bailey, 396
Hanson v. Blackwell Motor Co., 669
Hanson v. Duluth Missabe & Northern Railway Co., 218
Hanson v. Eilers, 526
Hanson v. Ford Motor Co., 767

Hanson v. Globe Newspaper Co., 810
Hanson v. Hall Manufacturing Co., 966
Hanson v. Krehbiel, 847
Hanson v. Ludlow Manufacturing Co., 488
Hanson v. New Hampshire Pre-Mix Concrete, Inc., 466
Hanson v. Northern Pacific Railway Co., 541
Hanson v. Rhodes-Burford Furniture Co., 888
Hanson v. Rowe, 1048
Hanson v. Town & County Shopping Center, Inc., 427
Hanson v. Wearmouth Coal Co., 546
Hanzlik v. Paustian, 256
Hapgoods v. Crawford, 779
Happy Coal Co. v. Smith, 68
Haralson v. Jones Truck Lines, 378
Haralson v. Rhea, 576
Harber v. Gledhill, 318
Harbeson v. Parke-Davis, Inc., 371
Harbin, State ex rel. v. Dunn, 156
Hardaway v. Consolidated Paper Co., 230
Hardcastle v. South Yorkshire R. & R.D. Co., 389
Hardeman v. Mendon Leasing Corp., 528
Hardeman, Inc., Paul v. Bradley, 986
Harden v. Cummings Truck Lease, Inc., 183
Hardin v. Farris, 166
Hardin v. New York Central Railroad Co., 335
Harding v. Kimwood Corp., 172
Harding v. Philadelphia Rapid Transit Co., 461, 491
Harding Co., E.R. v. Paducah Street-Railway Co., 512
Hardin's Bakeries v. Ranager, 575
Hardison v. Gregory, 918
Hardware Mutual Insurance Co. v. Lukken, 281
Hardwick, People v., 156
Hardy v. Brooks, 377
Hardy v. Dahl, 226
Hardy v. Monsanto Enviro-Chem Systems, Inc., 510
Hardy v. Smith, 180
Hardy v. United States, 33, 36
Hardy v. Vial, 891, 1059, 1064
Hardy v. Williamson, 784
Hare v. Dean, 924, 925
Hargan v. Purdy, 791
Harger v. Caputo, 339
Hargis v. Knoxville Power Co., 55
Hargrave v. Le Breton, 972
Hargraves v. Ballou, 919
Hargrove v. Town of Cocoa Beach, 1052
Harjo v. Kunkle, 759
Hark v. Mountain Fork Lumber Co., 627, 648
Harker v. Clark, 941
Harkins v. Provenzo, 941
Harkrader v. Moore, 877, 884
Harlan County v. Cole, 664
Harlan National Bank v. Gross, 906
Harlan Water Co. v. Carter, 671
Harless v. First National Bank in Fairmont, 1028, 1029
Harley v. Blodgett Engineering & Tool Co., 723
Harley v. Merrill Brick Co., 634
Harley & Lund Corp. v. Murray Rubber Co., 995
Harleysville Mutual Insurance Co. v. Lea, 945
Harllee v. City of Gulfport, 336

TABLE OF CASES

Harlow v. Carroll, 818
Harlow v. Connelly, 178, 238, 486, 488
Harlow v. Fitzgerald, 1041, 1060, 1061
Harlow v. Harlow, 920
Harlow v. Standard Improvement Co., 246
Harman v. Delany, 791
Harmon v. Givens, 336
Harmon v. Haas, 526
Harmon v. Harmon, 1007
Harmon v. Richardson, 269
Harmony Ditch Co. v. Sweeney, 75
Harms v. Miami Daily News, Inc., 855
Harned v. E-Z Finance Co., 64
Harness v. Steele, 152
Harnik v. Levine, 50
Harnish v. Smith, 821
Harnish, United States v., 153
Harold v. Pugh, 744
Harold's Club v. Sanchez, 376
Harpell v. Public Service Coordinated Transport, 383
Harper v. Blasi, 8
Harper v. Brown & Root, Inc., 239
Harper v. Harper, 880
Harper v. Industrial Commission, 311
Harper v. Luffkin, 928
Harper, State v., 130
Harper, Estate of v. Orlando Funeral Home, 362
Harralson v. Thomas, 595, 905
Harrigan v. Rosich, 41
Harrill v. Sinclair Refining Co., 436
Harriman v. New Nonpareil Co., 774
Harriman v. Pittsburgh, Cincinnati & St. Louis Railway Co., 507
Harrington v. Border City Manufacturing Co., 392
Harrington v. Butte Miner Co., 781
Harrington v. City of Huron, 82
Harrington v. Collins, 490
Harrington v. Hall, 914
Harrington v. Tibbet, 871
Harriott v. Plimpton, 349, 827
Harris v. A.J. Spencer Lumber Co., 937
Harris v. Brian, 309
Harris v. Brooks, 636
Harris v. Buckeye Irrigation Co., 408
Harris v. Central Power Co., 78
Harris v. City of Findlay, 552
Harris v. City of Roanoke, 331
Harris v. Clinton, 461
Harris v. Cool, 419, 425
Harris v. Delco Products Co., 742, 755, 756
Harris v. Dobson-Tankard Co., 1063
Harris v. Embrey, 955
Harris v. Equitable Life Assurance Society of United States, 732
Harris v. Grizzle, 188, 256
Harris v. Harter, 898
Harris v. Harvey, 1057
Harris v. Hindman, 40
Harris v. Hirschfield, 995
Harris v. Huntington, 820

Harris v. Illinois Central Railroad Co., 955
Harris v. Indiana General Service Co., 179, 406
Harris v. Jones, 61
Harris v. Lewistown Trust Co., 286
Harris v. McReynolds, 150
Harris v. Moriconi, 180
Harris v. Nashville Trust Co., 775, 801
Harris v. Roberson, 406
Harris v. Seaboard Air Line Railway Co., 104
Harris v. Smith, 717
Harris v. Thomas, 1010
Harris v. Thompson, 390
Harris v. Traders' & General Insurance Co., 986
Harris v. Zanone, 782
Harris & Co., A. v. Caldwell, 142
Harris-Emery Co. v. Pitcairn, 759
Harris Park Lakeshore, Inc. v. Church, 560
Harrison v. Brown, 540
Harrison v. Burger, 775, 794
Harrison v. Carroll, 717
Harrison v. Humble Oil & Refining Co., 858
Harrison v. Jones, 1006
Harrison v. Loyal Protective Life Insurance Co., 943
Harrison v. Middlesex Water Co., 416
Harrison v. Smith, 853
Harrison v. United States, 937, 1037
Harrison v. Wisdom, 146, 147
Harrisonville, City of v. W.S. Dickey Clay Manufacturing Co., 641
Harrist v. Spencer-Harris Tool Co., 686
Harrower v. Ritson, 642, 644
Harshaw v. Harshaw, 818
Hart v. Aldridge, 980
Hart v. Brown, 116
Hart v. Cole, 441
Hart v. Geysel, 122
Hart v. Herzig, 50
Hart v. Ludwig, 662
Hart v. Marbury, 756
Hart v. Pennsylvania Railroad Co., 665
Hart v. Skinner, 106
Hart v. Windsor, 447
Hart, Township of v. Noret, 343
Harten v. Coons, 1037
Hartenbach v. Johnson, 230, 238, 456
Harter v. Lewis Stores, 894
Hartfield v. Roper, 531
Hartford v. Brady, 540, 564
Hartford, City of v. Associated Construction Co., 707
Hartford Accident & Indemnity Co. v. Abdullah, 199
Hartford Accident & Indemnity Co. v. Industrial Commission, 575
Hartford Accident & Indemnity Co., State ex rel. Coffelt v., 13
Hartford & New Haven Railroad Co. v. Andrews, 947
Hartford Fire Insurance Co. v. Chicago, Milwaukee & St. Paul Railway Co., 482
Hartigan v. Dickson, 335
Hartke v. McKelway, 191
Hartley v. Herring, 794

Hartley v. McKelway, 373
Hartley v. Moxham, 85
Hartman v. Brady, 231
Hartman v. Di Lello, 421
Hartman v. Greene, 981
Hartman v. Miller, 423
Hartmann v. American News Co., 800, 803, 811
Hartmann v. Time, Inc., 801
Hartmann v. Winchell, 786, 787
Hartnett v. Goddard, 829
Hartnett v. May Department Stores Co., 259
Hartpence v. Rodgers, 922
Hartridge v. State Farm Mut. Auto Insurance Co., 998
Hartshorn v. Day, 731
Hartung v. County of Milwaukee, 645
Hartwell Corp. v. Bumb, 768
Harty v. Guerra, 553
Hartzog v. United Press Associations, 836, 837
Harvell v. City of Wilmington, 388
Harvey v. Bertaut, 874
Harvey v. Board of Commissioners of Wabash County, 223
Harvey v. Buchanan, 561
Harvey v. Chesapeake & Potomac Telephone Co., 266
Harvey v. City of Bonner Springs, 155
Harvey v. Fridley Medical Center, 188
Harvey v. Machtig, 449
Harvey v. Travelers Insurance Co., 336
Harvey v. Van Aelstyn, 428
Harvey Corp., Fred v. Mateas, 489
Harvey Realty Co. v. Borough of Wallingford, 636
Harvill v. Swift & Co., 419
Harville v. Anchor-Wate Co., 184, 478
Harvy v. Gulson, 540
Harwood v. McMurtry, 821
Harwood v. Siphers, 149
Harwood Pharmacal Co. v. National Broadcasting Co., 965, 971
Hary v. Arney, 911
Hasbrouck v. Armour & Co., 681, 682
Haseldine v. C.A. Dow & Son, Ltd., 547
Haserot v. Keller, 761
Hash, State ex rel. Johnson v., 644
Hashim v. Chimiklis, 425
Hashtani v. Duke Power Co., 410
Haskell v. Starbird, 752
Haskins v. Grybko, 398
Haskins v. Young, 51
Haslund v. City of Seattle, 1051
Hass v. Chicago & Northwestern Railway Co., 387
Hassett v. Palmer, 284
Hassman v. First State Bank, 760
Hasson v. Ford Motor Co., 955
Hastings v. F.W. Woolworth Co., 303
Hastings v. Hastings, 595, 904
Hastings v. James River Aerie No. 2337, p. 932
Hastings v. Stetson, 795, 844
Haswell v. Liberty Mutual Insurance Co., 884, 887, 895
Hatahley v. United States, 1033, 1038
Hatch v. Ford, 226

Hatch v. Globe Laundry Co., 288, 307, 314
Hatch v. Lane, 826
Hatch v. O'Neill, 1071
Hatch v. Smail, 278, 308
Hatchard v. Mege, 964, 966
Hatcher, Battersey's Case, 336
Hatchett v. Blacketer, 42
Hathaway v. Bruggink, 819
Hattiesburg Auto Sales Co. v. Morrison, 98
Hatton v. Chem-Haulers, Inc., 451
Hatzlachh Supply Co. v. United States, 1037
Haugen v. Ford Motor Co., 484
Haugen v. Wittkopf, 489
Haugh's Appeal, In re, 552
Haumersen v. Ford Motor Co., 950, 953
Haunert v. Speier, 915
Haupt v. Swenson, 44
Haut v. Kleene, 703
Hauth v. Sambo, 461
Havas v. Victory Paper Stock Co., 237
Haverland v. Lane, 753
Haverly v. State Line & Sullivan Railroad Co., 301, 303, 318, 347, 455
Hawber v. Raley, 332
Hawes v. Haynes, 525
Hawk v. Harman, 912
Hawke v. Maus, 69
Hawkes v. Goll, 345
Hawkeye-Security Insurance Co. v. Lowe Construction Co., 337, 339
Hawkins v. Commonwealth, 156
Hawkins v. Front Street Cable Railway Co., 353
Hawkins v. Hoffman, 99
Hawkins v. Reynolds, 871
Hawkins v. Roby, 78
Hawks v. De Hart, 165
Haworth v. Elliott, 133
Haworth v. State, 492
Haws v. Luethje, 955
Hawthorne v. Kober Construction Co., 1001, 1009
Hay v. Cohoes County, 68, 553
Hay v. Norwalk Lodge, 391
Hay v. Reid, 775
Haycox v. Dunn, 825
Hayden v. Hasbrouck, 830, 835
Hayden v. Second National Bank of Allentown, 438
Hayes v. Criterion Corp., 407, 411
Hayes v. Hutchinson & Shields, 48
Hayes v. Hyde Park, 277
Hayes v. Malkan, 389
Hayes v. Massachusetts Mutual Life Insurance Co., 91
Hayes v. Michigan Central Railroad Co., 265
Hayes v. Miller, 542
Hayes v. Richfield Oil Corp., 439
Hayes v. Southern Power Co., 411
Hayes v. Torrington Water Co., 671, 716
Hayes v. Wabash Railroad Co., 579
Hayes Construction Co. v. Silverthorn, 757
Hayes Freight Lines v. Wilson, 278
Haylock v. Sparke, 786

Hayner v. Cowden, 792
Haynes v. Monroe Plumbing and Heating Co., 943
Haynes v. Presbyterian Hospital Association, 596
Haynie v. North Carolina Electric Power Co., 938
Hays v. American Defense Society, 781
Hays v. Creary, 150
Hays v. Hays, 766
Hayslip v. Wellford, 816
Haysom v. Coleman Lantern Co., 715
Hazard v. Irwin, 731
Hazard, City of v. Eversole, 664
Hazel v. Hoopeston-Danville Motor Bus Co., 959
Hazelton v. Week, 22, 110, 536
Hazelwood v. Hodge, 310
Hazelwood v. Webber, 546
Hazen v. Creller, 150
Hazen v. Perkins, 648
Heacock, State v., 781
Head v. Briscoe, 912
Heal v. Stoll, 761
Heald v. Carey, 92
Heald v. Wallace, 949
Healey v. Citizens Gas & Electric Co., 72, 549, 624
Healey v. P. Ballentine & Sons, 561
Healing v. Security Steel Equipment Corp., 404
Health & Hospital Corp. of Marion v. Gaither, 499
Healy v. Hoy, 291, 321
Heath v. American Book Co., 991
Heath v. Halfhill, 150
Heath v. Randall, 140
Heath v. Sears, Roebuck & Co., 168
Heath v. Swift Wings, Inc., 186
Heathcock v. Milwaukee Platteville Lead & Zinc Mining Co., 490, 571
Heaton v. Ford Motor Co., 692
Heaton v. Knowlton, 732
Heaven v. Pender, 358
Heavilin v. Wendell, 528
Hebditch v. MacIlwaine, 809, 833, 835
Hebel v. Hebel, 907
Heber v. Heber's Estate, 674
Hebrew v. Pulis, 50, 51, 121
Heckaman v. Northern Pacific Railway Co., 75
Heckle v. Lurvey, 912
Heckman v. Heckman, 902
Hedden v. Griffin, 754
Hedgepath v. City of Durham, 405
Hedges v. Tagg, 926
Hedglin v. Church of St. Paul of Sauk Centre, 425
Hedgpeth v. Coleman, 802
Hedin v. Minneapolis Medical & Surgical Institute, 761
Hedley Vyrne & Co. v. Heller & Partners, 746
Hedlund v. Hedlund, 902
Hedrick v. Tubbs, 620
Heeg v. Licht, 552, 619
Heenan v. Perkins, 524, 525
Heermance v. James, 918
Hefferon v. Reeves, 175
Heffter v. Northern States Power Co., 260
Hegarty v. Hegarty, 1007

Heidbreder v. Northampton Township Trustees, 196, 197
Heidegger v. Burg, 768
Heidemann v. Wheaton, 566
Heil v. Glanding, 470
Heil v. Zink, 126
Heil Co. v. Grant, 487
Heilbronn v. Herzog, 675
Heimke v. Munoz, 456
Hein v. Marcante, 102
Heine v. Raus, 823
Heinlen v. Martin Miller Orchards, 570, 575
Heinold v. Muntz T.V., Inc., 52
Heinrich v. Goodyear Tire & Rubber Co., 381
Heinze v. McKinnon, 673
Heinze v. Murphy, 11, 41, 49
Heisler v. Heisler, 324, 349
Heiting v. Chicago, Rock Island & Pacific Railway Co., 265
Helene Curtis Industries, Inc. v. Pruitt, 693
Helfer v. Hamburg Quarry Co., 888
Helfrich v. Cantonsville Water Co., 636
Helguera v. Cirone, 409
Heliczer, United States v., 128
Hellar v. Bianco, 801
Heller v. Clarke, 149
Heller v. Duff, 792
Hellesen v. Knaus Truck Lines, Inc., 823
Helling v. Carey, 171, 189, 219
Helling v. Lew, 947
Hellstern v. Katzer, 792
Hellwig v. Mitchell, 789
Helmicks v. Stevlingson, 783
Helms v. Eastern Kansas Oil Co., 550
Helmstetler v. Duke Power Co., 933
Helsel v. Fletcher, 137
Helson v. McKenzies, 97
Helton v. Joplin, 782
Helton v. Missouri Pacific Railway Co., 519
Helton v. Montgomery, 404, 410
Helwig v. Fogelsong, 734
Hembry v. Parreco, 759
Heming v. Power, 788
Heminway v. Heminway, 139
Hemmings v. Stoke Poges Golf Club, 144
Hemphill, State v., 42
Hempstead v. Cargill, 75
Hempstead v. General Fire Extinguisher Corp., 207, 707, 720
Hemsworth v. Cushing, 582
Henderson v. Beggs, 98
Henderson v. Bluemink, 1066
Henderson v. Cape Trading Co., 895
Henderson v. Milobsky, 192
Henderson v. Sevey, 342
Henderson v. Sullivan, 553
Henderson v. United States, 353
Hendler v. Coffey, 251
Hendler v. Cuneo Eastern Press, Inc., 986
Hendler Creamery Co. v. Miller, 458

Hendrick v. Lynn, 738
Hendricks v. Broderick, 490
Hendricks v. Pyramid Motor Freight Corp., 199, 312
Hendrickson v. Hodkin, 384
Hendrickson v. Louisville & Nashville Railroad Co., 938
Hendrickson v. Minnesota Power & Light Co., 343
Hendrix v. Black, 73, 725
Hendry v. Conner, 858
Henjum v. Bok, 289, 308
Henke v. McCord, 149
Henley v. Wilson, 912
Henn v. Universal Atlas Cement Co., 551, 628
Hennessey v. Hennessey, 417
Hennig v. Crocker, 937
Henning v. Kyle, 755
Henning v. Parsons, 188, 191
Henningsen v. Bloomfield Motors, Inc., 690, 692, 694, 695, 696
Henningsen v. Markowitz, 224, 318
Henrie v. Griffith, 123
Henrietta v. Evans, 528
Henrioulle v. Marin Ventures, Inc., 435
Henry, In re, 789
Henry v. City of Philadelphia, 321
Henry v. Continental Building & Loan Association, 762
Henry v. Dennis, 309, 744
Henry v. Dufilho, 975
Henry v. First National Bank of Clarksdale, 1026
Henry v. Kopf, 730
Henry v. Pittsburgh & Lake Erie Railroad Co., 801
Henry v. St. Louis, Kansas City & N. Railway Co., 276
Henry v. Vaccaro Construction Co. v. A.J. DePace, Inc., 963
Henshaw v. Belyea, 308, 491
Henshaw v. Miller, 941
Hensley v. Heavrin, 206
Hensley v. Montgomery County, 391
Hensley v. Seminole County, 1050
Henson, Commonwealth v., 46
Henson v. Thomas, 929
Henthorn v. Oklahoma City, 82
Henthorn v. Western Maryland Railroad Co., 827
Henthorne v. Hopwood, 232, 266
Hentschel v. Baby Bathinette Corp., 687
Hentz v. Long Island Railroad Co., 641
Henwood v. Harrison, 832
Hepburn v. Sewell, 90
Hepp v. Ader, 951
Heppner v. Atchison, Topeka & Santa Fe Railway Co., 285, 291, 292
Herald Publishing Co. v. Feltner, 841
Herberger v. Anderson Motor Service Co., 336
Herbert v. Cassinelli, 528
Herbert v. Smyth, 620
Herbert Products v. Oxy-Dry Sprayer Corp., 966
Hebertson v. Cohen, 100
Herbertson v. Russell, 951
Herbo-Phosa Co. v. Philadelphia Casualty Co., 587
Herbrick v. Samardick & Co., 142
Herd v. Weardale Steel, Coal & Coke Co., 52

Herdler v. Bucks Stove & Range Co., 572
Herdman v. Pennsylvania Railroad Co., 578, 579
Hergenrether v. East, 314
Herget National Bank of Pekin v. Berardi, 904
Heritage v. Dodge, 158
Herlihy v. Donohue, 159
Herman v. Endriss, 991
Herman v. Magnuson, 524, 525
Herman v. Roberts, 621
Herman v. Sladofsky, 228
Herman v. Turner, 123
Herman v. United Air Lines, Inc., 247
Hern v. Nichols, 500
Hernandez v. Southern California Gas. Co., 248
Hernandez v. United States, 1034
Herndon v. Arco Petroleum Co., 388
Herndon v. St. Louis & San Francisco Railway, 368
Herr v. Simplex Paper Box Corp., 503, 504
Herrell v. Haney, 906
Herrell v. St. Louis-San Francisco, Railroad Co., 959
Herrero v. Atkinson, 342
Herrick v. Humphrey Hardware Co., 91
Herrick v. Tribune Co., 783
Herrick v. Wixom, 397, 398
Herrick & Olson v. Curtiss, 558
Herries v. Bell, 105
Herrin v. Sutherland, 79
Herring v. Boyle, 48
Herring v. Creech, 97
Herring v. R.L. Mathis Certified Dairy Co., 183
Herrmann v. Newark Morning Ledger Co., 777, 778
Herro v. Board of County Road Commissioners, 78
Herron v. Miller, 660
Herron v. Silbaugh, 1060, 1062
Herron v. State Farm Mutual Insurance Co., 995
Hersch v. Anderson Acres, 437
Herschel v. Dyra, 855
Herschensohn v. Weisman, 586
Hersey v. Chapin, 78
Hersh v. Hendley, 187
Hersh v. Miller, 313
Hershey v. O'Neill, 50
Hershey v. Peake, 118
Herskovits v. Group Health Cooperative of Puget Sound, 272
Hertz v. McDowell, 953
Hertz Driv-Ur-Self System v. Hendrickson, 226
Herzig v. Herzig, 379
Herzog v. Campbell, 789
Herzog v. Capital Co., 757
Herzog v. Stern, 941
Hess v. Greenway, 567
Hess v. Oregon German Baking Co., 879, 881
Hess v. Philadelphia Transportation Co., 363
Hester v. Shuster, 754
Hester v. Watson, 467
Hetfield v. Baum, 147
Hetrick v. Marion-Reserve Power Co., 285
Hett v. Boston & Maine Railroad Co., 100
Heuser, Dr. Herman v. Federal Trade Commission, 1011

Hevel v. Stangier, 514
Hewellette v. George, 48, 904, 905
Hewett v. First National Bank of Atlanta, 420, 428
Hewitt v. General Tire & Rubber Co., 696
Hewlett v. Saratoga Carlsbad Spring Co., 766
Hewson Co., George F. v. Hopper, 1013
Hey v. Prime, 941
Heyer v. Flaig, 765
Heyman v. Ar. Winarick, Inc., 1022
Heywood v. Tillson, 985
Hiatt, State v., 127
Hibbard v. City of Wichita, 568
Hickey v. Michigan Central Railroad Co., 643
Hickey v. Nulty, 405
Hicklin v. Anders, 334
Hickman v. Myers, 372
Hicks v. Deemer, 760
Hicks v. Donoho, 182
Hicks v. Dorn, 146
Hicks v. McCandlish, 10
Hicks Rubber Distributors v. Stacy, 96
Hiell v. Golco Oil Co., 248, 255
Higdon v. Carlebach, 256
Higgenbottom v. Noreen, 447
Higginbotham v. Ford Motor Co., 947
Higginbotham v. Mobil Oil Corp., 246
Higgins v. Butcher, 940
Higgins v. Connecticut Light & Power Co., 645
Higgins v. Decorah Produce Co., 620
Higgins v. Mason, 489
Higgins v. Minagham, 125, 126
Higgins v. New York, Lake Erie & Western Railway Co., 148
Higgins v. Rosso, 342
Higginson v. York, 110
High v. Supreme Lodge of the World, 792
Highland v. Wilsonian Investment Co., 288
Hightower v. Bekins Van Lines Co., 209
Highwayman's Case, 336
Hiigel v. General Motors Corp., 706
Hilbert v. Roth, 331
Hildreth v. Camp, 912
Hilgendorf v. Shuman, 762
Hill v. Associated Transport, Inc., 307
Hill v. Carlstrom, 890
Hill v. Chappel Bros. of Montana, 348, 350
Hill v. City of Charlotte, 1052
Hill v. City of Glenwood, 176
Hill v. Clarke, 166
Hill v. Edmonds, 268, 348
Hill v. General Motors Corp., 204
Hill v. Goodchild, 323, 329
Hill v. Gray, 739
Hill v. Hayes, 98, 853, 865
Hill v. Hill, 260
Hill v. Hospital Authority of Clarke County, 204
Hill v. Husky Briquetting, Inc., 233
Hill v. James Walker Memorial Hospital, 670
Hill v. Kimball, 65, 364
Hill v. Lyons Plumbing & Heating Co., 717

Hill v. McDonald, 445, 512
Hill v. Merrick, 428
Hill v. Peres, 306, 352
Hill v. Perrott, 672
Hill v. Sibley Memorial Hospital, 935
Hill v. Smith, 354, 525
Hill v. Stewart, 762
Hill v. Taylor, 51
Hill v. Thompson, 245
Hill v. Travelers Insurance Co., 63
Hill v. United States Fidelity & Guaranty Co., 670
Hill v. Ward, 967
Hill v. Winsor, 299
Hill v. Yaskin, 203
Hill & Co. v. Wallerich, 995
Hill Co. v. Contractors' Supply Co., 893
Hill Groc. Co. v. Carroll, 988
Hill Hardware Corp. v. Hesson, 340
Hilleary v. Earle Restaurant, 439
Hillen v. I.C.I., 337
Hiller v. Harsh, 423, 440, 441, 442
Hillhouse v. Wolf, 101
Hilliard v. Richardson, 509
Hilliard v. United Pacific Casualty Co., 588
Hillman v. Newington, 354
Hillman v. Star Publishing Co., 861
Hills v. McGillvrey, 228
Hills v. Snell, 112
Hills Transportation Co. v. Southwest Forest Industries, 764
Hilmes v. Stroebel, 323
Hilsden v. Mercer, 842
Hilsdon v. Saunders, 840
Hilton v. Blose, 519
Hilton v. Overly, 560
Himmler v. United States, 207
Hinckley v. Penobscot, 231, 457
Hindi v. Smith, 649
Hindman v. First National Bank, 744
Hindmarsh v. Sulpho Saline Bath Co., 950, 957
Hiner v. Hubbard, 246
Hines v. Brode, 769
Hines v. Continental Baking Co., 493
Hines v. Garrett, 305
Hines v. Lumpkin, 974
Hines v. Morrow, 299, 300, 309
Hines v. St. Paul Fire & Marine Insurance Co., 188
Hines v. Sangstad Steamship Co., 999
Hines v. Shumaker, 832
Hinish v. Meier & Frank Co., 853, 863
Hinkie v. United States, 1037
Hinkle v. Minneapolis, Anoka & Cayuna Range Railway Co., 276
Hinkle, State ex rel. La Follette v., 852, 853, 863, 867
Hinman v. Pacific Air Transport, 79
Hinsdale v. Orange Co. Publications, Inc., 796
Hinson v. Phoenix Pie Co., 716
Hinton v. Republic Aviation Corp., 703
Hintz v. Roberts, 10
Hiort v. Bott, 92, 97

Hird v. Wood, 797
Hires Co., Charles E. v. Consumers' Co., 1016
Hirn v. Edgewater Hospital, 188, 189
Hiroux v. Baum, 914
Hirsch v. Feeney, 877
Hirsch v. S.C. Johnson & Son, Inc., 1017
Hirschberg v. State, 188
Hirschberg Optical Co., H. v. Michaelson, 750
Hirschfield Sons Co., H. v. Colt Industries Operating Corp., 165
Hirschl v. Richards, 768
Hirschman v. Healy, 766
Hirschy v. Coodley, 917
Hise v. City of North Ben, 423
Hise v. Thomas, 752
Hitaffer v. Argonne Co., 932
Hively v. Higgs, 40, 116, 119
Hixon v. Sherwin-Williams Co., 510, 514
Hixson v. Slocum, 45, 56
Hoad v. New York Central Railroad Co., 732
Hoadley v. International Paper Co., 223, 232
Hoadley v. M. Seward & Son Co., 620
Hoag v. Lake Shore & Michigan Southern Railway Co., 292
Hoag v. Pierce, 145
Hoag & Alger v. Lake Shore & Michigan Southern Railway Co., 275, 301
Hoagland v. Forest Park Highlands Amusement Co., 14, 131
Hoagland Wagon Co. v. London Guarantee & Accident Co., 587
Hoar v. Ward, 793
Hoard v. Peck, 932, 938
Hoare & Co. v. McAlpin & Sons, 619, 627, 628
Hoare & Co. v. McAlpine, 547, 548, 552
Hobaica v. Byrne, 763
Hobart v. Hagget, 86
Hobbs v. Armco, 492
Hobbs v. Kizer, 120
Hobbs v. Smith, 633
Hobson v. Kentucky Trust Co., 1012
Hobson v. Walker, 633
Hocking Valley Railway Co. v. Barbour, 995
Hocks v. Sprangers, 830
Hodge v. Borden, 212
Hodge v. Brooks, 920
Hodge v. Meyer, 1002
Hodge v. Piedmont & Northern Railway Co., 150
Hodge v. Wetzler, 916
Hodgeden v. Hubbard, 138, 139
Hodgeman v. Olsen, 855, 864
Hodgens v. Jennings, 732
Hodges v. Doctors Hospital, 501
Hodges v. Hall, 14
Hodges v. Hilton, 444
Hodges v. Savannah Kaolin Co., 958
Hodges v. Tagg, 924
Hodges v. Town of Drew, 622
Hodges v. Windham, 921
Hodgkins v. Corbett, 778

Hodgkins v. Price, 145
Hodgkinson v. Ennor, 547
Hodgson v. St. Paul Plow Co., 98
Hodsoll v. Stallebrass, 998
Hoe v. Sanborn, 680
Hoeft v. Supreme Lodge, Knights of Honor, 1007
Hoekstra v. Helgeland, 937
Hoene v. Associated Dry Goods Corp., 870
Hoeppner v. Dunkirk Printing Co., 791, 831, 832
Hofer v. Meyer, 403, 404, 408
Hoff v. Natural Refining Products Co., 406, 408, 410
Hoff v. Public Service R. Co., 313, 385
Hoff v. Pure Oil Co., 827
Hofferman v. Simmons, 103
Hoffert v. Owatonna Inn Towne Motel, Inc., 1050
Hoffman v. Alpern, 94
Hoffman v. Board of Education of City of New York, 1049
Hoffman v. Carow, 111
Hoffman v. City of Bristol, 565
Hoffman v. Clinic Hospital, 49
Hoffman v. Dautel, 936
Hoffman v. Eppers, 42
Hoffman v. Jones, 471
Hoffman v. King, 282
Hoffman v. Planters Gin Co., 415, 416, 421, 425
Hoffman v. Schroeder, 1066
Hoffman v. Simplot Aviation, Inc., 720
Hoffman v. Southern Pacific Co., 218
Hoffman v. Toft, 767
Hoffmann v. Kimmel, 893
Hofschulte v. Panhandle Hardware Co., 106
Hofstadter v. Bienstock, 793
Hogan v. A.S. Barnes Co., 861, 863
Hogan v. Bragg, 308
Hogan v. New York Times Co., 835, 838
Hogan v. Robert H. Irwin Motors, Inc., 878, 879
Hogan Transfer & Storage Corp. v. Waymire, 483
Hogg v. Pinckney, 892
Hogle v. H.H. Franklin Manufacturing Co., 384, 392, 620
Hohman v. City of Chicago, 647, 650
Hoines v. Barney's Club, Inc., 875
Hokanson v. Oatman, 758
Holaway v. City of Pipestone, 1050
Holbrook v. Morrison, 1010
Holbrook v. Wight, 100
Holcomb v. Meeds, 457
Holcomb Construction Co. v. Armstrong, 997
Holcombe v. Buckland, 415
Holcombe v. Harris, 388
Holden v. American News Co., 800
Holden v. Bundek, 1045
Holden v. Merritt, 883
Holden v. Pioneer Broadcasting Co., 847
Holdenville, City of v. Griggs, 638
Holdorf v. Holdorf, 43, 57
Hole v. Sittingbourne R. Co., 515
Holgate v. Bleazard, 565
Holiday Inns, Inc. v. Drew, 413, 422

Holland v. Baltimore & Ohio Railroad Co., 394, 397, 407, 409, 433
Holland v. Bishop, 93, 672, 725
Holland v. Grant County, 649
Holland v. Lutz, 1056, 1059
Holland v. St. Paul Mercury Insurance Co., 377
Holland v. Southern Pacific Utilities Co., 336
Holland Builders, Inc. v. Leck, 406
Holland Furnace Co. v. Korth, 757
Holland Furnace Co. v. Nauracaj, 723
Hollander & Son, A. v. Jos. Hollander, Inc., 976
Holle v. Lake, 461
Holleman v. Harward, 932, 938
Hollenbeck v. Hall, 774, 775
Hollenbeck v. Johnson, 561
Hollenbeck v. Ristine, 826, 834
Hollerman v. F.H. Peavey & Co., 742
Hollerud v. Malamis, 114
Hollett v. Dundee, Inc., 395
Holley v. Kelley, 133
Holley v. Mix, 110, 152
Holliday v. Peden, 253
Hollidge v. Duncan, 284
Hollinbeck v. Downey, 377
Hollinghausen v. Ade, 921, 923
Hollings v. Brown, 587
Hollingsworth v. Thomas, 163
Hollins v. Fowler, 92, 93, 95
Hollinshed v. Shadrick, 890
Hollman v. Brady, 793
Holloman v. Life Insurance Co. of Va., 868
Holloran v. New York, New Haven & Hartford Railroad Co., 1000
Holloway v. Forsyth, 741, 744
Holloway v. General Motors Corp., 696
Hollywood Shop, Inc. v. Pennsylvania Gas & Water Co., 245
Hollywood Silver Fox Farm v. Emmett, 624
Holm v. Sponco Manufacturing, Inc., 219
Holman v. Athens Empire Laundry Co., 550, 626
Holman v. Chicago, Rock Island & Pacific Railway Co., 224, 265
Holman v. Ford Motor Co., 705
Holman v. Ketchum, 88
Holman v. Reliance Insurance Companies, 254, 489
Holmes v. Blyler, 53, 150, 538
Holmes v. Clisby, 783, 826
Holmes v. Drew, 414
Holmes v. Gamble, 241, 256, 259
Holmes v. Harden, 241
Holmes v. Jones, 775
Holmes v. Lilygren Motor Co., 527
Holmes v. Moore, 940
Holmes v. Royal Fraternal Union, 826
Holmes v. Schnoebelen, 661
Holmes, United States v., 129, 150
Holmes v. Wilson, 75
Holmes v. Worthey, 448
Holmquist v. Volkswagen of America, Inc., 363
Holodook v. Spencer, 908

Holst v. Stewart, 754
Holt v. Astgrigg, 781
Holt v. Boyle Brothers, 891
Holt v. Fuller Cotton Oil Co., 406
Holt v. Kolker, 207
Holt v. Stollenwerck, 949
Holt v. Texas New Mexico Pipeline Co., 514
Holter Hardware Co. v. Western Mortgage & Warranty Title Co., 304, 321, 347
Holtz v. Dick, 923
Holtz v. Holder, 351
Holway v. World Publishing Co., 831
Homac Corp. v. Sun Oil Co., 283
Homan v. Hall, 923, 996
Homans v. Boston Elevated Railway Co., 291, 363
Home Investments Fund v. Robertson, 972
Home Office v. Dorset Yacht Co., Ltd., 1047
Home Public Market v. Newrock, 426
Home Telephone Co. v. Fields, 336
Homer v. Engelhardt, 774
Honea v. Coca Cola Bottling Co., 194, 249
Honeycutt v. Bess, 465
Honeycutt v. Louis Pizitz Dry Goods Co., 30
Hoock v. S. S. Kresge Co., 52
Hooker v. Farmers' Irrigation District, 75
Hooker, State v., 645
Hooker, Corser & Mitchell Co. v. Hooker, 1003
Hooks v. International Speedways, Inc., 620
Hooks v. Southern California Permanente Medical Group, 238
Hooksett v. Concord Railroad Co., 544
Hooper, The T. J., 194, 195
Hooper v. Trustcott, 834
Hooper-Holmes Bureau v. Bunn, 506
Hoosac Tunnel & W. R. Co. v. New England Power Co., 172
Hoosac Tunnel Dock & Elevator Co. v. O'Brien, 816
Hoosier Stone Co. v. McCain, 327
Hooten v. State to Use of Cross County, 91
Hoover v. Gray, 461
Hoover v. Jordan, 833
Hoover v. Montgomery Ward & Co., 720
Hope v. L'Anson, 823
Hopkins, In re, 789
Hopkins v. Atlantic & St. Lawrence Railroad Co., 932
Hopkins v. Blanco, 932
Hopkins v. Colonial Stores, 105
Hopkins v. Droppers, 222, 717
Hopkins v. Drowne, 966, 969
Hopkins v. F.W. Woolworth Co., 424
Hopkins v. Golden, 521
Hopkins v. Hersey, 325
Hopkins v. Tate, 847
Hopkins Chemical Co. v. Read Drug & Chemical Co., 965, 975
Hopkinson v. Lehigh Valley Railroad Co., 878
Hoppe v. Klapperich, 897, 900
Hoppendietzel v. Wade, 670
Hopper v. Charles Cooper & Co., 703
Hopper v. Lennen & Mitchell, 985

Prosser & Keeton Torts 5th Ed. HB—26

Hopper v. Reeve, 40, 85
Hopson v. Goolsby, 229
Hoptowit v. Brown, 761
Horbach's Administrators v. Elder, 337
Horchheimer v. Prewitt, 1003
Hordes v. Kessner, 427
Horgan v. Pacific Mills, 924
Horn v. Horn, 908, 909
Horn v. Seth, 987, 1003
Hornby v. Hunter, 836
Horne v. Trivette, 454
Horner v. Battyn, 51
Horner v. Lawrence, 661
Horner v. Marshall's Administratrix, 1074
Horner v. Northern Pacific Beneficial Association Hospitals, Inc., 253, 256
Horner v. Terpin, 662
Horney v. Nixon, 375, 662
Horning v. Gore, 511
Hornstein v. Podwitz, 1003
Horowitz v. Kevah Konner, Inc., 245, 258
Horowitz v. Sacks, 925
Horrabin v. City of Des Moines, 341, 342
Horstman v. Newman, 855
Horth v. American Aggregates Corp., 990
Horwitz Co., Vincent v. Cooper, 988
Hosein v. Checker Taxi Co., 222, 385
Hosey v. Mobil Oil Corp., 454
Hosking v. Robles, 523, 527
Hoskins v. Jackson Grain Co., 684
Hosko v. Hosko, 903
Hosmer v. Carney, 566
Hosmer v. Republic Iron & Steel Co., 622
Hostetter, State ex rel. United Factories v., 13
Hostettler v. Carter, 53
Hostick v. Hall, 421
Hotaling v. A.B. Leach Co., 767, 769
Hotchkin v. Erdrich, 481
Hotchkin v. Third National Bank, 763
Hotchkiss v. Oliphant, 846
Hotel Riviera, Inc. v. Short, 11
Hotel Supply Co. v. Reid, 898
Hotels Statler Co. v. Safier, 483
Hott v. Yarbrough, 820
Hough v. Iderhoff, 42
Hough v. Texas & Pacific Railway Co., 571
Houghton v. Loma Prieta Lumber Co., 554, 562
Houghton v. Nash, 675, 730
Houlahan v. Brockmeier, 528
Hounchell, Commonwealth v., 130
Houren v. Chicago, Milwaukee & St. Paul Railway Co., 270
House v. European Health Spa, 182
House v. Thornton, 721
House of Directories v. Lane Directory Co., 963
House of Materials, Inc. v. Simplicity Pattern Co., 994
Household Finance Corp. v. Bridge, 858
Housel v. Pacific Electric Railway Co., 252
Houseman v. Walt Neal, Inc., 528

Houser & Haines Manufacturing Co. v. McKay, 675, 731
Housh v. Peth, 62, 855
Housing Authority of Bremmerton, United States v., 999
Houska v. Hrabe, 560
Houston v. Brush, 387
Houston v. Interstate Circuit, 782
Houston v. Strickland, 305
Houston v. Thornton, 745
Houston Belt & Terminal Rail Co. v. O'Leary, 430
Houston Belt & Terminal Railroad Co. v. Burmester, 998
Houston Chronicle Publishing Co. v. Martin, 967, 972, 973
Houston Milling Co. v. Carlock, 379
Houston Water Works Co. v. Kennedy, 83
Hover v. Barkhoof, 174
Hover v. Clamp, 523
Hovermale v. Berkeley Springs Moose Lodge, 419, 425, 426
Hoverson v. Noker, 915
Hovey v. Rubber Tip Pencil Co., 826
Hovland v. Farmers Union Elevator Co., 94
Howard v. Bloodworth, 363
Howard v. Burns, 104
Howard v. Burton, 52
Howard v. Deschambeault, 96
Howard v. Etchieson, 620
Howard v. Furness Houlder Argentine Lines, 543, 546, 548
Howard v. Gould, 741
Howard v. Houck, 990
Howard v. Howard, 162, 451
Howard v. Lunaburg, 941
Howard v. Middlesborough Hospital, 667
Howard v. Redden, 275
Howard v. Reinhart & Donovan Co., 724
Howard v. South Baltimore General Hospital, 596
Howard v. Swift & Co., 673
Howard v. Zimmerman, 517, 519
Howard's Administrator v. Hunter, 946
Howard's Clothes, Inc. v. Howard's Clothes Corp., 1016
Howe v. Blanden, 902
Howe v. Bradstreet Co., 349
Howe v. Jameson, 439
Howe v. Ohmart, 423
Howe, Regina v., 128
Howell v. Bee Publishing Co., 773
Howell v. Hairston, 200, 914
Howell v. Howell, 924, 925
Howell v. Norton, 914
Howell v. Winters, 43
Hower v. Ulrich, 914
Howes v. Hansen, 909
Howie v. North Birmingham Land Co., 730
Howk v. Anderson, 306
Howk v. Minnick, 8
Howland v. Cressy, 540

Howland v. George F. Blake Manufacturing Co., 823, 835
Howland v. Sears, Roebuck, & Co., 180
Howland, Inc., Fred v. Morris, 429
Howle v. Camp Amon Carter, 1070
Howle v. McDaniel, 532
Howlett v. Dorchester Trust Co., 419
Howley v. Scott, 223
Howsley v. Gilliam, 955
Howson v. Foster Beef Co., 227, 581
Hoye v. Great Northern Railroad Co., 347
Hoyem v. Manhattan Beach City School District, 474
Hoyt v. Gelston & Schenck, 87
Hoyt v. Independent Asphalt Paving Co., 309
Hoyt v. Jeffers, 292
Hoyt v. Stuart, 91
Hrabik v. Gottsch, 237
Hrnicek v. Chicago, Milwaukee & St. Paul Railway Co., 43
Hryciuk v. Robinson, 881
Hryhorijiv v. Winchell, 787
Hub Theatres, Inc. v. Massachusetts Port Authority, 633
Hubbard v. Allyn, 831
Hubbard v. Beatty & Hyde, Inc., 890, 893
Hubbard v. Boelt, 224, 430
Hubbard v. Calvin, 187
Hubbard v. Commonwealth, 73
Hubbard v. Journal Publishing Co., 859, 861
Hubbard v. Murray, 277
Hubbard v. Preston, 619, 642
Hubbard v. Ruff, 902
Hubbard v. Rutledge, 827, 828
Hubbard v. Scott, 972
Hubbock & Sons v. Wilkinson, 975, 976
Hubble v. Brown, 216
Hubbuck & Sons, Ltd. v. Wilkinson, Heywood & Clark, Ltd., 968
Huber Manufacturing Co. v. Hunter, 732
Huckaba v. Cox, 581
Huckabee v. Nash, 60
Huckle v. Reynolds, 778
Hudgens v. Chamberlain, 324
Hudgens v. State, 133
Hudgins v. Jones, 339
Hudima v. Hudyma, 918
Hudkins v. Haskins, 927
Hudmon v. Du Bose, 98
Hudson v. Craft, 122
Hudson v. Gas Consumers' Association, 911
Hudson v. Iguano Land & Min. Co., 675
Hudson v. Kansas City Baseball Club, 485, 495
Hudson v. Lehigh Valley Railroad Co., 284
Hudson v. Pioneer Service Co., 794
Hudson v. Von Hamm, 913
Hudson Transit Corp. v. Antonucci, 105, 106
Huendling v. Jensen, 1057
Huey v. Barton, 443
Huey v. Milligan, 268, 456
Huff v. Austin, 548, 550

Huff v. Rosenberg, 519, 521
Huffman v. Southern Railway Co., 58
Huffstutler v. Coates, 881
Huganir v. Cotter, 673
Huggins v. Aetna Casualty & Surety Co., 381
Huggins v. Graves, 337, 339
Huggins v. John Morrell & Co., 249
Huggins v. Winn-Dixie Greenville, Inc., 898, 899, 900
Hughes v. Atlantic City & Shore Railroad Co., 245
Hughes v. Babcock, 132
Hughes v. Bizzell, 821
Hughes v. City of Auburn, 621
Hughes v. Great American Indemnity Co., 345, 350, 352
Hughes v. Holman, 920
Hughes v. Jolliffe, 249, 254
Hughes v. Lord Advocate, 296, 317
Hughes v. McDonough, 1009
Hughes v. Star Homes, 397, 401, 407
Hughes v. State, 125, 156
Hughes, State v., 448
Hughes v. Van Bruggen, 873
Hughes v. Warman Steel Casting Co., 482
Hughes v. White, 959
Hughes, State ex rel. W. E. Callahan Construction Co. v., 405
Hughey v. Ausborn, 931, 934
Hughey v. Bradrick, 789
Hughey v. Fergus County, 566
Hughlett, State v., 153
Hughson v. St. Francis Hospital, 368
Hulett v. Central Illinois Light Co., 456
Hulett v. Swift, 582
Huling v. Henderson, 11
Hull v. Bartlett, 41
Hull v. Curtis Publishing Co., 854, 860, 861
Hull v. Scruggs, 137
Hull v. Silver, 955
Hullander v. McIntyre, 228
Hulse v. Driver, 519
Hulse v. Tollman, 45, 126
Hulsey v. M.C. Kiser Co., 744
Hulsman v Hemmeter Development Corp., 500
Hulton & Co. v. Jones, 536, 804, 808, 809
Hum Quock, State v., 153
Humber v. Morton, 678, 721
Humbird v. Davis, 673
Humble Oil & Refining Co. v. Luckel, 975
Humble Oil & Refining Co. v. McLean, 971
Humble Oil & Refining Co. v. Martin, 344
Humble Pipe Line Co. v. Anderson, 72
Hume v. Crane, 521
Hume v. Hart, 394
Hume v. Oldacre, 328
Humes v. State, 211
Humiston v. Universal Film Manufacturing Co., 854, 859, 861
Hummel v. State, 642
Hummer v. School City of Hartford City, 596
Humphrey v. Michigan United Railways Co., 58
Humphrey v. Sievers, 770

Humphrey v. Twin State Gas & Electric Co., 245, 262, 395
Humphreys v. Baird, 726
Humphreys v. Minnesota Clay Co., 91
Humphreys-Mexia Oil Co. v. Arseneaux, 72
Humphreys Oil Co. v. Liles, 642
Humphries v. Cousins, 547, 624
Hundley v. Louisville & Nashville Railroad Co., 1006
Hundley v. Martinez, 188
Hundt v. LaCrosse Grain Co., 220, 419, 425, 426
Hunkins v. Amoskeag Manufacturing Co., 442
Hunn v. Windsor Hotel Co., 442, 481
Hunnewell v. Duxbury, 744
Hunsucker v. High Point Bending & Chair Co., 340
Hunt v. Atlantic Coast Line Railroad Co., 245
Hunt v. Bates, 330
Hunt v. Bell, 791
Hunt v. Calacino, 66
Hunt v. Central Vermont Railway Co., 954
Hunt v. Chang, 929
Hunt v. City of Boston, 93
Hunt v. City Stores, Inc., 172
Hunt v. Goodimate Co., 763
Hunt v. Great Northern R. Co., 826
Hunt v. Hazen, 559
Hunt v. Hunt, 919, 930
Hunt v. Lane, 337
Hunt v. Portland Baseball Club, 485, 495
Hunt v. Silk, 730
Hunt v. Star Photo Finishing Co., 723
Hunt-Berlin Coal Co. v. Paton, 955
Hunt Oil Co. v. Berry, 972
Hunter v. Batton, 196, 463, 465
Hunter v. Board of Education of Montgomery County, 1049
Hunter v. Evergreen Presbyterian Vocational School, 410
Hunter v. Finnerty, 768
Hunter v. First State Bank of Morrilton, 524
Hunter v. Laurent, 50, 888
Hunter v. McLaughlin, 757
Hunter v. Mathis, 1058
Hunter v. Quality Homes, 723
Hunter v. Sharpe, 832
Hunter v. Shell Oil Co., 982
Hunter v. Wheate, 123
Huntingburgh, City of v. First, 183
Huntley v. Ward, 832
Hunziker v. Scheidemantle, 239
Hupe v. Sommer, 662
Huppert v. Morrison, 140
Hurd v. Lacy, 135
Hurdman v. North Eastern R. Co., 547
Hurlburt v. Planters National Bank & Trust Co., 952
Hurley v. Donovan, 965
Hurley v. Eddingfield, 375, 662
Hurley v. Lameraux, 674
Hurley v. Spokane, 518
Hurn v. Woods, 256

Huset v. J. I. Case Threshing Machine Co., 668, 681, 682, 684, 726
Hush v. Devilbiss Co., 908
Hush v. Reaugh, 738
Hushaw v. Dunn, 95
Huskie v. Griffin, 1006
Husky Refining Co. v. Barnes, 331, 336
Husovsky v. United States, 391
Husser v. Nogalusa Coca Cola Bottling Co., 519
Hussey, In re J.J., 133
Hussey v. Davis, 149
Hussey v. Flanagan, 105
Hussey v. Long Dock Railroad Co., 445
Husting Co., E. L. v. Coca Cola Co., 987
Huston v. Freemansburg Borough, 56
Hutchens v. Hankins, 199
Hutcherson v. Slate, 340
Hutcheson v. Misenheimer, 467
Hutcheson v. Peck, 922
Hutchings v. Tipsword, 736
Hutchins v. Hutchins, 1006
Hutchins v. Kimmell, 923
Hutchins v. Page, 841
Hutchinson v. Capeletti Brothers, Inc., 623
Hutchinson v. Dickie, 376
Hutchinson v. Merchants' & Mechanics' Bank of Wheeling, 93, 95
Hutchinson v. Mitchell, 460
Hutchinson v. New England Telephone & Telegraph Co., 830
Hutchinson v. Proxmire, 807, 988, 1057
Hutchinson v. Rubel Baking Co., 335
Hutchinson v. Schimmelfeder, 78
Hutchinson v. Stern, 65
Hutchinson v. Taylor, 919
Hutchinson v. Wenzel, 877
Hutchinson, Purity Ice Cream Co. v. Des Moines City Railway Co., 465
Huth v. Huth, 798
Hutsell v. Edens, 246
Hutto v. Southern Railway Co., 224
Hutton v. Davis, 955
Hutton v. State, 158
Hutton v. Watters, 324, 984, 985
Hutzler Brothers v. Taylor, 422
Hux v. Butler, 912
Huyck v. Hecla Mining Co., 394, 397, 433
Huydts v. Dixon, 198
Huyler v. Rose, 428
Huysman v. Kirsch, 661, 667
Hyatt v. McCoy, 928
Hyatt v. Murray, 304
Hyatt Creek Builders-Engineers Co. v. Board of Regents, 162
Hyde v. Avalon Air Transport, Inc., 457
Hyde v. Baggett Transportation Co., 505
Hyde v. Bryant, 436
Hyde v. City of Utica, 568
Hyde v. County of Rensselaer, 389
Hyde v. Greuch, 890, 892

TABLE OF CASES

Hyde v. Moffat, 379
Hyde v. Noble, 94, 536
Hyde v. Scyssor, 915, 931
Hyde v. Somerset Air Service, 81
Hyde v. Union Pacific Railroad Co., 398
Hyder v. Weilbaecher, 189, 256, 258
Hyett v. Northeastern Hospital for Women and Children, 574
Hygienic Fleeced Underwear Co. v. Way, 966
Hyland v. Southwell, 933
Hyma v. Lee, 750
Hyman v. Barrett, 515, 516
Hyman v. New York Central Railroad Co., 876
Hyman & Co., Julius v. Velsicol Corp., 1022
Hynding v. Home Accident Insurance Co., 588
Hynes v. New York Central Railroad Co., 389

I

I de S et ux. v. W de S, 42
Iaconio v. D'Angelo, 134
Iavazzo v. Rhode Island Hospital Trust Co., 91
Ibach v. Jackson, 114
Ibottson v. Peat, 1005
Ickes v. Brimhall, 949
Ideal Motor Co. v. Warfield, 829
Ideal Toy Corp. v. Plawner Toy Manufacturing Corp., 1018
Iden v. Evans Model Laundry, 834
Idlehour Development Co. v. City of St. Charles, 1063
Idleman v. Groves, 924
Iepson v. Noren, 496, 497
Iglesias v. Wells, 376
Ikeda v. Okada Trucking Co., 716
Ilford Urban District Council v. Beal and Judd, 547
Ilgenfritz v. Missouri Power & Light Co., 419
Illidge v. Goodwin, 328
Illinois Bell Telephone Co. v. Charles Ind Co., 74
Illinois Cent. Railroad Co. v. Hammer, 210
Illinois Central Railroad Co. v. Messina, 231
Illinois Central Railroad Co. v. Nelson, 468
Illinois Central Railroad Co. v. Oswald, 308
Illinois Central Railroad Co. v. Sanders, 674, 924
Illinois Central Railroad Co. v. Siler, 307, 491
Illinois Central Railroad Co. v. Sims, 532
Illinois Central Railroad Co. v. Wright, 266, 321
Illinois Farmers Insurance Co. v. Tapemark Co., 523
Illinois Minerals Co. v. McCarty, 92
Illinois Publishing & Printing Co. v. Industrial Commission, 575
Ilsley v. Nichols, 150
Imbler v. Pachtman, 1058, 1059
Imel v. Travelers Indemnity Co., 943
Imes v. Empire Hook & Ladder Co., 198
Imig v. March, 903
Immer v. Risko, 595, 902, 903
Imperial Brass Manufacturing Co. v. Industrial Commission, 573
Imperial Ice Co. v. Rossier, 981
Impervious Products Co. v. Gray, 768

Imre v. Riegel Paper Corp., 396
In re (see name of party)
INA Aviation Corp. v. United States, 467
Incolligno v. Ewing, 701
Indemnity Insurance Co. v. Koontz-Wagner Electric Co., 341
Indemnity Insurance Co. of North America v. Davis' Administrator, 587
Indemnity Insurance Co. of North America v. Smith, 588
Indian Towing Co. v. United States, 381, 1035, 1040, 1041, 1054
Indiana, Department of Natural Resources, State of v. Morgan, 223
Indiana Consolidated Insurance Co. v. Mathew, 172
Indiana Harbor Belt R. Co. v. Jones, 414, 422, 954
Indiana Service Corp. v. Johnston, 317
Indiana State Highway Commission v. Rickert, 223
Industrial Bank of Commerce v. Selling, 737
Industrial Commission v. Lambert, 575
Industrial Gas Antitrust Litigation, In re, 1029
Industrial Investment Co. v. King, 105
Information Control Corp. v. United Airlines, 483
Ingalls v. Bulkley, 100
Ingalls v. Hastings & Sons Publishing Co., 777
Ingalls v. Miller, 751
Ingersoll v. Liberty Bank, 270
Ingersoll v. Onondaga Hockey Club, 494
Ingerson v. Shattuck School, 486
Ingham v. Eastern Air Lines, Inc., 381, 1038
Inglehardt v. Mueller, 440
Inglis v. American Motors Corp., 657, 708, 749
Ingo v. Koch, 52
Ingram v. Root, 892
Ingram, State v., 44
Ingwaldson v. Skrivseth, 927
Inland Compress Co. v. Simmons, 483
Inland Power & Light Co. v. Grieger, 350
Inland Revenue Commissioners v. Hambrook, 998
Inman v. Baltimore & Ohio Railroad Co., 579
Inman v. Binghamton Housing Authority, 724
Innes v. Wylie, 41
Insull v. New York World Telegram Corp., 779, 801
Insurance Research Service v. Associates Finance Co., 780, 798, 799
Interborough Rapid Transit Co. v. Lavin, 994
Intermountain Building & Loan Association v. Casper Mutual Building and Loan Association, 756
International & Great Northern Railroad Co. v. Edmundson, 835
International & Great Northern Railroad Co. v. Greenwood, 1014
International & Great Northern Railroad Co. v. Slusher, 552
International Distributing Corp. v. American District Telephone Co., 502
International Longshoremen's Association, AFL–CIO v. Allied International Inc., 1026
International News Service v. Associated Press, 1020
International Oceanic Enterprises, Inc. v. Menton, 1064

International Products Co. v. Erie Railroad Co., 207, 382, 746
International Tailoring Co. of New York v. Lukas, 987
International Ticket Co. v. Wendrich, 1009
International Union United Auto., Aircraft and Agricultural Implement Workers of America v. Russell, 991, 1002, 1027
International Visible Systems Corp. v. Remington-Rand, 968
Interstate Amusement Co. v. Martin, 59
Interstate Dry Goods Stores v. Williamson, 8
Interstate Galloway Cattle Co. v. Kline, 544
Interstate Life & Accident Insurance Co. v. Brewer, 40, 41, 60, 63
Interstate National Bank v. McCormick, 102
Interstate Sash & Door Co. v. City of Cleveland, 550
Interstate Telephone & Telegraph Co. v. Public Service Electric Co., 998
Investigating Commission, In re, 822
Inwood Laboratories v. Ives Laboratories, Inc., 1015
Iowa Economic Heater Co. v. American Economics Heater Co., 744
Iowa Power & Light Co. v. Abild Construction Co., 340
Irby v. Wilde, 12
Ireland v. Complete Machinery & Equipment Co., 395, 412
Ireland v. McGarvish, 791, 792
Ireland v. Ward, 918
Irish v. Cloyes, 102
Iron City National Bank v. Anderson, Du Puy & Co., 737
Irvine v. City of Oelwein, 621
Irvine v. Gibson, 1074
Irvine v. Wood, 434
Irving v. United States, 381
Irwin v. Arrendale, 1062, 1066
Irwin v. Ashurst, 787, 812, 816, 817, 818
Irwin v. Jetter Brewing Co., 330
Irwin v. Murphy, 816
Irwin v. Yeagar, 147
Isaack v. Clark, 89
Isaacson v. Boston, Worchester & New York Street Railway Co., 521
Isaiah v. Great Atlantic & Pacific Tea Co., 141
Isham v. Dow's Estate, 289, 560
Island Air, Inc. v. LaBar, 982, 986, 987
Island Express v. Frederick, 464
Isle Royale Mining Co. v. Hertin, 75, 110
Isom v. Schettino, 530
Israel v. Portland News Publishing Co., 826, 835
Israel v. Wood Dolson Co., 1003
Iszler v. Jorda, 581
Ithaca Roller Mills v. Ann Arbor Railroad Co., 303
Itzkovitch v. Whitaker, 864
Iudica v. De Nezzo, 228
Iverson v. Frandsen, 834
Iverson v. Quam, 442
Iverson v. Solsbery, 224, 226
Iverson v. Vint, 634
Iverson, W.P. v. Dunham Manufacturing Co., 986, 996

Ives Laboratories, Inc. v. Darby Drug Co., 1018, 1021
Ivey, In the Interest of, 116
Ivey v. Wiggins, 943, 949
Ivie v. King, 825, 848
Ivy v. Security Barge Lines, Inc., 951
Iwata v. Champine, 238

J

J. P. M. & B. M. v. Schmid Laboratories, Inc., 372
J. & B. Development Co. v. King County, 1050, 1051
J. & C. Ornamental Iron Co. v. Watkins, 87
Jablonski v. United States, 384
Jack v. Torrant, 641
Jack Frost, Inc. v. Engineered Building Components Co., 478
Jackman v. Jones, 332
Jackovach v. Yocom, 117
Jackson v. Adams, 788
Jackson v. American Telephone & Telegraph Co., 11, 899
Jackson v. Associated Dry Goods Corp., 343
Jackson v. B. Lowenstein & Brothers, 288
Jackson v. Baker, 568
Jackson v. Beckham, 878
Jackson v. Brantley, 462
Jackson v. Central Torpedo Co., 661, 666
Jackson v. City of Biloxi, 172, 407
Jackson v. Coast Paint and Lacquer Co., 697, 701
Jackson v. Galveston, Harrisburg & San Antonio Railway Co., 307
Jackson v. Hopperton, 834
Jackson v. Innes, 101, 106
Jackson v. Knowlton, 154
Jackson v. Lowenstein & Brothers, 286
Jackson v. McCuiston, 181
Jackson v. McGrath, 821
Jackson v. Minidoka Irrigation District, 1029
Jackson v. New Jersey Manufacturers Insurance Co., 207
Jackson v. 919 Corp., 260, 434
Jackson v. Old Colony Street Railway Co., 126
Jackson v. O'Neill, 995
Jackson v. Pennsylvania Railroad Co., 416
Jackson v. Pettigrew, 75
Jackson v. Pike, 421
Jackson v. Pittsburgh, Cincinnati, Chicago & St. Louis Railway Co., 945
Jackson v. Record Publishing Co., 836
Jackson, Regina v., 157
Jackson v. Rupp, 63
Jackson v. Stanfield, 994, 1013
Jackson v. Train, 879, 885
Jackson v. United States Pipe Line, 581
Jackson v. Utica Light & Power Co., 300, 304
Jackson v. Virginia Hot Springs Co., 662
Jackson v. Wisconsin Telephone Co., 304, 306, 347
Jackson Atlantic, Inc. v. Wright, 182
Jacksonville, T. & K. W. R. Co. v. Lockwood, 84
Jacksonville Street Railway Co. v. Chappell, 665

Jacobs v. General Accident Fire & Life Assurance Corp., 339, 343
Jacobs v. Herlands, 823
Jacobs v. Jacobs, 521
Jacobs v. Mutual Mortgage & Investment Co., 386
Jacobs v. Southern Railway Co., 489
Jacobs, State v., 144
Jacobs v. Transcontinental & Western Air, 798
Jacobs v. Underwood, 821
Jacobs, Malcolm & Burtt v. Northern Pacific Railway Co., 663
Jacobsen v. Woerner, 331, 336
Jacobsen Construction Co. v. Structo-Lite Engineering, Inc., 497
Jacobson v. Siddal, 917, 923
Jacobson v. Sorenson, 47
Jacobson v. Van Boening, 27
Jacoby v. Town of City of Gillette, 549, 551, 564
Jaconne v. Schwegmann Brothers Giant Super Markets, Inc., 427
Jacova v. Southern Radio & Television Co., 859, 861
Jacquemin v. Bunker, 888
Jacques v. Childs Dining Hall Co., 49, 142
Jacques v. Parks, 48
Jaffe v. Stone, 874
Jaffee v. United States, 1037
Jaffray v. Hill, 323
Jaggar v. Winslow, 758
Jaggers v. Southeastern Greyhound Lines, 463
Jaillet v. Cashman, 1043
J'Aire Corp. v. Gregory, 997, 1001, 1002, 1008
Jakubiec v. Hasty, 176
Jakubowski v. Minnesota Mining and Manufacturing, 250
Jakway v. Proudfit, 766
James v. British Gen. Ins. Co., 586
James v. Campbell, 38
James v. Evans, 324
James v. Franks, 200
James v. Hayward, 642, 644
James v. Jane, 1062
James v. MacDougall & Southwick Co., 50
James v. Rutledge, 790
James v. Southwestern Insurance Co., 149
James, State v., 294
James v. United States, 381
James v. Wisconsin Power & Light Co., 404
James Music Co. v. Bridge, 675, 730
Jamestown Iron & Metal Co. v. Knofsky, 744
Jamieson v. Woodward & Lothrop, 686
Jamison v. Howard, 506
Jamison v. Moseley, 125
Jamison v. Rebenson, 775
Jammie v. Robinson, 769
Janiszewski v. Behrmann, 674
Janney v. Housekeeper, 115
Janofsky v. Garland, 382
Jansen v. Hilo Packing Co., 852
Janssen v. Carolina Lumber Co., 764
Janssen v. Mulder, 226

Janssen v. Neal, 231
Janusis v. Long, 457
Januszko v. State, 199
Janvier v. Sweeney, 61
Jaquith v. Stanger, 87
Jarboe v. Edwards, 914
Jardine v. Rubloff, 208
Jardine v. Upper Darby Lodge Co., 718
Jarman v. Offutt, 817, 818
Jarman v. Rea, 792
Jarmillo v. Hood, 167
Jarrahdale Timber Co. v. Temperley & Co., 963, 976
Jarrett v. Duncan Thecker Associates, 476
Jarrett v. Ross, 968
Jarrett v. Wills, 1047
Jarvis v. Hatheway, 830
Jarvis v. Howard, 411
Jarvis v. Manhattan Beach Co., 733
Jarvis v. Moy, Davies, Smith, Vanderwell & Co., 660
Jasper, United States v., 129
Jasperson v. Dominion Tobacco Co., 980
Javins v. First National Realty Corp., 722
Jay v. Walla Walla College, 419
Jays Creations, Inc. v. Hertz, 210
Jeck v. O'Meara, 762
Jeffcoat v. Caine, 1070
Jeffer v. Gifford, 621
Jefferies v. Duncombe, 786
Jefferson v. Derbyshire Farmers, Limited, 504
Jefferson v. Griffin Spalding County Hospital Authorities, 368
Jefferson v. Jameson & Morse Co., 445
Jefferson v. King, 393
Jefferson v. S. S. Kresge Co., 887
Jeffrey v. Copeland Flour Mills, 290
Jeffery v. Robbins, 899
Jeffries v. Great Western R. Co., 103
Jeffries v. Hargis, 111
Jeffries v. New York Evening Journal Publishing Co., 860
Jeffries v. Pankow, 101
Jekshewitz v. Groswald, 726
Jelleff, Inc., Frank R. v. Pollak Brothers, 342
Jellico Coal Co. v. Adkins, 575
Jenkins v. Atlantic Coast Line Railroad Co., 455
Jenkins v. City of Fort Wayne, 228
Jenkins v. Dell Publishing Co., 860, 861, 862, 867
Jenkins v. Fowler, 27
Jenkins v. General Motors Corp., 685, 696
Jenkins v. Holly, 102
Jenkins v. Jordon, 219
Jenkins v. Kentucky Hotel, Inc., 58
Jenkins v. Krieger, 254
Jenkins v. Midland Valley Railroad Co., 949
Jenkins v. North Carolina Department of Motor Vehicles, 462
Jenkins v. Parrish, 188
Jenkins v. Pennsylvania Railroad Co., 321, 349, 350
Jenkins v. State, 156
Jenne v. Sutton, 644

Jenner v. Collins, 620
Jenness v. Moses Lake Development Co., 751
Jenness v. Sheraton-Cadillac Properties, Inc., 383
Jenness v. Simpson, 918
Jennings v. Cooper, 920, 923
Jennings v. Fundeburg, 163
Jennings v. Glen Alden Coal Co., 404
Jennings v. Industrial Paper Stock Co., 429
Jennings v. Riddle, 154
Jennings v. Tacoma Railway & Motor Co., 183
Jennings v. United States, 514
Jennings Buick, Inc. v. City of Cincinnati, 245
Jensen v. Barnett, 52
Jensen v. Chicago, Milwaukee & St. Paul Railway Co., 518
Jensen v. Linner, 256
Jensen v. Lundorff, 990
Jensen v. Maine Eye & Ear Infirmary, 1070
Jenson v. Glemaker, 958
Jenson v. Olson, 818
Jentick v. Pacific Gas & Electric Co., 328
Jeppsen v. Jensen, 38, 65
Jergens Co., Andrew v. Woodbury, Inc., 1013, 1024
Jernigan v. Clark, 75
Jersey City Printing Co. v. Cassidy, 1006
Jesik v. Maricopa County Community College District, 1048
Jesionowski v. Boston & Maine Railroad Co., 578
Jesko v. Turk, 410
Jess v. Herrman, 472
Jess Edwards, Inc. v. Goergen, 309
Jessup v. Sloneker, 204
Jeune v. Del E. Webb Construction Co., 936
Jewel Tea Co. v. Grissom, 1023
Jewell v. Beckstine, 185
Jewell v. Colby, 1074
Jewell v. Kansas City Bolt & Nut Co., 484
Jewell v. Schmidt, 489
Jewell v. Shell Oil Co., 758
Jillson v. Caprio, 52, 155
Jiminez v. Zayre Corp., 200
Jivelekas v. City of Worland, 1055
Joannes v. Bennett, 828
Joannes v. Burt, 790
Joel v. Morrison, 503
Joest v. Clarendon & Rosedale Packet Co., 342
Joffre v. Canada Dry Ginger Ale, Inc., 249
Johns v. Associated Aviation Underwriters, 828
Johns v. Castles, 327
Johns v. Gittings, 840
Johns-Manville Products Corp. v. Contra Costa Superior Court, 577
Johns-Manville Sales Corp. v. Private Carriage Workers' Compensation Appeals Board, 214
John's Pass Seafood Co. v. Weber, 230, 435
Johnson v. Aetna Life Insurance Co., 988, 991
Johnson v. Allen, 922
Johnson v. Ashland Water Co., 569
Johnson v. Bathey, 401
Johnson v. Boeing Airplane Co., 867

Johnson v. Boston & Maine Railroad Co., 226, 232
Johnson v. Bradstreet Co., 829
Johnson v. Brant, 526
Johnson v. Brown, 819
Johnson v. Cadillac Motor Car Co., 683
Johnson v. Casetta, 718
Johnson v. Central Aviation Corp., 558
Johnson v. Chapman, 326, 346
Johnson v. Chesapeake & Ohio Railway Co., 156
Johnson v. Chicago, Milwaukee & St. Paul Railway Co., 348
Johnson v. Chicago, Rock Island & Pacific Railway Co., 507
Johnson v. Chicago & Northwestern Railway Co., 228
Johnson v. City of Fairmont, 326, 346, 349, 619
Johnson v. City of New York, 486
Johnson v. City of Rockford, 305
Johnson v. City of San Leandro, 724
Johnson v. Clark Equipment Co., 492, 712
Johnson v. Clay, 175
Johnson v. Clement F. Sculley Construction Co., 404, 410
Johnson v. Coca-Cola Bottling Co., 259
Johnson v. Commonwealth, 130, 786
Johnson v. Curtiss Northwest Airplane Co., 558
Johnson v. Delmarva Power & Light Co., 410
Johnson v. Dew, 557
Johnson v. Director General of Railroads, 206, 468
Johnson v. Dover, 817, 818
Johnson v. Drysdale, 620
Johnson v. Ebberts, 883
Johnson v. Elwood, 940
Johnson v. Farr, 93
Johnson v. General Motors Acceptance Corp., 59
Johnson v. Glidden, 914, 915
Johnson v. Granholm, 1058, 1059
Johnson v. Great Northern Railway Co., 56
Johnson v. Greenfield, 261
Johnson v. Gustafson, 987, 992, 1013
Johnson v. H. M. Bullard Co., 717
Johnson v. Harcourt, Brace, Jovanovich, Inc., 857
Johnson v. Harnisch, 334
Johnson v. Harris, 928
Johnson v. Harry Jarred, Inc., 194
Johnson v. Healy, 447
Johnson v. Hitchcock, 968, 975
Johnson v. Hockessin Tractor, Inc., 172
Johnson v. Horn, 15
Johnson v. Independent Life & Accident Insurance Co., 819
Johnson v. Irasburgh, 232, 457
Johnson v. J. I. Case Threshing Machine Co., 510
Johnson v. John Deere Plow Co., 201
Johnson v. Johnson, 126, 157, 255, 588
Johnson v. Johnson Publishing Co., 837
Johnson v. Kosmos Portland Cement Co., 277, 306, 316
Johnson v. Lambotte, 177, 1074
Johnson v. Langley, 831
Johnson v. Luhman, 929
Johnson v. McConnel, 37, 42

Johnson v. Maxwell, 642
Johnson v. Miller, 879
Johnson v. Misericordia Community Hospital, 384
Johnson v. Mobile & Ohio Railroad Co., 242
Johnson v. Monson, 506
Johnson v. Mount Ogden Enterprises, Inc., 895
Johnson v. Nielsen, 793
Johnson v. Norfolk & Western Railway Co., 51, 53, 121
Johnson v. O'Brien, 436
Johnson v. Ostrom, 254
Johnson v. Ottemeier, 906
Johnson v. Patterson, 136, 137
Johnson v. Pearce, 876
Johnson v. Peterson, 526
Johnson v. Plymouth Gypsum Plaster Co., 302
Johnson v. Powell, 464
Johnson v. Prange-Guessenhainer Co., 444
Johnson v. Reddy, 1068
Johnson v. Richards, 918
Johnson v. Robinson, 540
Johnson v. Rouchleau-Ray Iron Land Co., 165
Johnson v. Rudolph Wurlitzer Co., 829
Johnson v. Saint Paul City Railway Co., 182
Johnson v. Sampson, 56, 61
Johnson v. Sartain, 323
Johnson v. Schmitt, 993
Johnson v. Scott, 111
Johnson v. Scripps Publishing Co., 858, 868
Johnson v. Shields, 790
Johnson v. Southern Pacific Co., 876
Johnson v. Souza, 380
Johnson v. Spear, 716
Johnson v. Standard Brands Paint Co., 704
Johnson v. State, 73, 1047, 1048
Johnson, State v., 127
Johnson v. State of California, 1047
Johnson v. State of New York, 362
Johnson v. Straight's, Inc., 1047
Johnson v. Terminal Railroad Association, 308
Johnson v. Texas & Pacific Railway Co., 177, 178
Johnson v. Thompson, 457
Johnson v. Tilden, 479
Johnson v. Town of Oakland, 650
Johnson v. Weborg, 576
Johnson v. Webster Manufacturing Co., 488
Johnson v. Weedman, 90, 101
Johnson v. Weinberg, 506, 507
Johnson v. Weiner, 150
Johnson v. Williams, 405
Johnson v. Workmen's Compensation Appeals Board, 955
Johnson v. Zemel, 438
Johnson, State ex rel. v. Hash, 644
Johnson & Son, Inc., S. C. v. Johnson, 1017
Johnson Controls, Inc. v. Bowes, 588
Johnson Freight Lines, Inc. v. Tallent, 364
Johnson Gas Appliance Co. v. Reliable Gas Products Co., 1018
Johnson's Administrator v. Rutland R. Co., 180
Johnston v. Billot, 475

Johnston v. Cartwright, 819
Johnston v. De La Guerra Properties, 440
Johnston v. Disbrow, 918
Johnston v. Fargo, 482
Johnston v. Hare, 525
Johnston v. Harris, 202, 443
Johnston v. Long, 723
Johnston v. Mack Manufacturing Co., 540
Johnston v. Ohls, 565
Johnston v. Pierce Packing Co., 219
Johnston v. Rodis, 664
Johnston v. Schlarb, 818
Johnston v. Wilson, 137
Johnston v. Zale Corp., 870
Jolivette v. City of Lafayette, 466
Jolles v. 3720 Corp., 441
Jolley v. General Motors Corp., 242, 246
Jolley v. Powell, 176, 177, 178
Jolly v. General Accident Group, 944
Jolly v. Thornton, 105
Jolly v. Valley Pub. Co., 834
Jonas Glass Co., George v. Glass Bottle Blowers Association, 996
Jones v. Adams, 570, 575
Jones v. Adamson's, Inc., 525
Jones v. Adler, 626
Jones v. Asa G. Candler, Inc., 413
Jones v. Atlantic Coast Line Railroad Co., 57
Jones v. Atteberry, 501
Jones v. Billings, 400
Jones v. Boyce, 307
Jones v. Brown, 927, 934, 982
Jones v. Brownlee, 819
Jones v. Burgermeister Brewing Corp., 704
Jones v. Chappell, 621
Jones v. Chicago, Rock Island & Pacific Railway Co., 398
Jones v. Chicago Housing Authority, 444
Jones v. City of Birmingham, 1053
Jones v. City of Fort Dodge, 275
Jones v. City of Logansport, 511, 512
Jones v. Cody, 158, 985, 1010
Jones v. Cook, 526
Jones v. Czaza, 145
Jones v. Festiniog R. Co., 544, 547
Jones v. Fisher, 11
Jones v. Flaherty, 878
Jones v. Foutch, 212
Jones v. Harrisburg Polyclinic Hospital, 250, 253, 256, 257
Jones v. Hebdo, 48, 53
Jones v. Herald Post Co., 860, 861, 864
Jones v. Hittle Service, Inc., 208
Jones v. Hutchinson Manufacturing, Inc., 700
Jones v. Jones, 51, 792
Jones v. Kinney, 911
Jones v. Leslie, 984
Jones v. Littler, 791
Jones v. Llanrwst Urban District Council, 538, 547
Jones v. Louisville & Nashville Railroad Co., 405

Jones v. M. T. D. Products, Inc., 497
Jones v. Marshall, 156
Jones v. Matson, 941
Jones v. Monico, 821, 1057
Jones v. Morristown-Hamblen Hospital Association, 167
Jones v. Pulitzer Publishing Co., 838
Jones v. R. L. Polk & Co., 777, 810
Jones v. Randall, 674
Jones v. Raney Chevrolet Co., 206, 704
Jones v. Register & Leader Co., 795
Jones v. Rinehart & Dennis Co., 575
Jones v. Robertson, 551, 552
Jones v. Schmidt, 937
Jones v. Scofield Brothers, 596
Jones v. Spencer, 219
Jones v. Stanko, 206
Jones v. Stone, 98
Jones v. Tarleton, 100
Jones v. Tarrant Utility Co., 242, 240, 248
Jones v. Taylor, 532
Jones v. Trawick, 620
Jones v. Trice, 819
Jones v. United States, 1034
Jones v. Waterman Steamship Corp., 998
Jones v. West Side Buick Co., 10
Jones v. Williams, 642, 643
Jones v. Wilmington & Weldon Railroad Co., 881
Jones Co., Austin W. v. State, 314
Jonescue v. Jewel Home Shopping Service, 207, 233
Joopanenko v. Gavagan, 778, 794
Joos v. Auto-Owners Insurance Co., 189
Jordan v. Alabama Great Southern Railroad Co., 876
Jordan v. C.I.T. Corp., 150
Jordan v. Delta Drilling Co., 948
Jordan v. Empiregas, Inc. of Belle Mina, 894
Jordan v. Koerth, 329
Jordan v. United Verde Copper Co., 634
Jorgensen v. Meade Johnson Laboratories, Inc., 369
Joseph v. Baars, 830, 833, 834, 835
Joseph v. Meier & Frank Co., 53
Joseph v. Naylor, 919
Josephs v. Fuller (Club Dominicus), 186
Josephson v. Knickerbocker Broadcasting Co., 812
Joslyn v. Cadillac Automobile Co., 630
Joslyn v. Manship, 993
Joslyn v. St. Paul Distilling Co., 733
Jost v. Dairyland Power Co-operative, 625, 627, 629, 630
Journal of Commerce Publishing Co. v. Tribune Co., 1013, 1024
Jowett v. Wallace, 923
Joy v. Brown, 123
Joy v. Chau, 187
Joyce v. Great Northern Railway Co., 988
Joyce v. Massachusetts Real Estate Co., 334
Joyce v. Nash, 399, 417
Joyce, State v., 376
Jubb v. Maslanka, 621
Judd v. Rowley's Cherry Hill Orchards, Inc., 363
Judd v. Walker, 752
Judd v. Zupon, 417

Judge v. Rockford Memorial Hospital, 830
Judkins v. Sadler-MacNeil, 93, 98
Judson v. Giant Powder Co., 248, 255, 460
Judson v. Peoples Bank & Trust Co. of Westfield, 339, 340
Judy v. Belk, 433
Juhasz v. Quik Ships, Inc., 987
Jukes v. North American Van Lines, 334
Julian v. American Business Consultants, 832
Julian v. Kansas City Star Co., 800
Jumping Rainbow Ranch v. Conklin, 969
Juniata Acceptance Corp. v. Hoffman, 88, 104, 105
Junius Construction Co. v. Cohen, 738
Junkermann v. Tilyou Realty Co., 437, 438
Juragua Iron Co., United States v., 146
Jurovich v. Interstate Iron Co., 183
Justheim Petroleum Co. v. Hammond, 764
Justice v. Gatchell, 217
Just's, Inc. v. Arrington Construction Co., 1000
Justus v. Atchison, 370
Justus v. Wood, 314
Jutte v. Hughes, 552
Juzeler v. Buchli, 102

K

K., Stephen v. Roni L., 206, 910
Kaatz v. State, 471, 477
Kaatz, State v., 475
Kabatchnick v. Hanover-Elm Building Corp., 758
Kable v. Carey, 879, 884
Kacena v. George W. Bowers Co., 314
Kachman v. Blosberg, 197
Kaczer v. Marrero, 1072, 1073
Kaczkowski v. Bolubasz, 953
Kadylak v. O'Brien, 558
Kaempfe v. Lehn & Fink Products Corp., 687
Kahn v. Graper, 415
Kahn v. James Burton Co., 403, 407, 408
Kahn v. Urania Lumber Co., 338
Kaiser v. Nummerdor, 750, 752
Kaiserman v. Bright, 952
Kaje v. Chicago, St. Paul, Minneapolis & Omaha Railway Co., 648
Kajiya v. Dept. of Water Supply, 172
Kakluskas v. Somers Motor Lines, 398
Kalash v. Los Angeles Ladder Co., 683, 684
Kalberg v. Anderson Brothers Motor Co., 314
Kalechman v. Drew Auto Rental, Inc., 523, 528, 529
Kalinowski v. Smith, 409, 719
Kalkanes v. Willestoft, 154
Kall v. Carruthers, 549
Kamarath v. Bennett, 722
Kamm, Inc., Louis v. Flink, 981, 994, 1013
Kammerer v. Sachs, 790
Kamsler v. Chicago American Publishing Co., 774
Kane v. Hutchinson, 150
Kane v. Worcester Consolidated Street Railway Co., 196
Kansas, Oklahoma & Gulf Railway Co. v. Keirsey, 226
Kansas & Texas Coal Co. v. Galloway, 876

TABLE OF CASES

Kansas City, Fort Scott & Gulf Railroad Co. v. Kelly, 134
Kansas City, Memphis & Birmingham Railroad Co. v. Delaney, 774
Kansas City, Mexico & Orient Railway Co. of Texas v. Bell, 1007
Kansas City Southern Railway Co. v. Justis, 309
Kansas City Southern Railway Co. v. Leslie, 953
Kansas City Stockyards Co. v. Anderson, 576
Kansas Pacific Railway Co. v. Cutter, 954
Kansas Pacific Railway Co. v. Mihlman, 75
Kapalczynski v. Globe Construction Co., 723
Kapchuck v. Orlan, 476
Kapiloff v. Abington Plaza Corp., 737
Kapka v. Urbaszewski, 414
Kaplan v. Missouri-Pacific Railroad Co., 197, 487
Kaplan v. Stein, 717
Kaplan v. Suher, 753
Kapphahn v. Martin Hotel Co., 199
Kardas v. State, 952
Karelas v. Baldwin, 816
Karges Furniture Co. v. Amalgamated Woodworkers' Local Union No. 131, p. 1010
Karjavainean v. MacFadden Publications, 780, 841
Karl v. Juniata County, 176
Karlowski v. Kissock, 439
Karow v. Continental Insurance Co., 1073
Karpeles v. Heine, 461
Karpisek v. Cather & Sons Construction, Inc., 648
Karr v. Chicago, Rock Island & Pacific Railway Co., 286
Karr v. Parks, 932
Karr v. Sixt, 951
Karston, State ex rel. Williams v., 644
Kasal v. Picha, 893
Kasel v. Remington Arms Co., 707
Kasey v. Suburban Gas Heat, Inc., 703
Kassel Poultry Co. v. Sheldon Produce Co., 892
Kassowitz v. Sentinel Co., 790
Kasten v. Young Mens Christian Association, 1071
Katapodis v. Brooklyn Spectator, 773
Kath v. East St. Louis & Suburban Railway Co., 484
Kathan v. Comstock, 760
Katko v. Briney, 135
Katsonas v. W.M. Sutherland Building and Construction Co., 151
Katz v. Arundel-Brooks Concrete Co., 686
Katz v. Dunn, 764
Katz v. Helbing, 392, 403
Katz v. Kapper, 1010, 1013
Katz, People v., 127
Kaucher v. Blinn, 790
Kauffman v. A. H. Robins Co., 889, 991
Kauffman v. Bobo & Wood, 763
Kaufman v. Abramson, 62
Kaufman v. Boston Dye House, 564
Kaufman v. Clark, 928
Kaufman v. Kansas Power & Light Co., 45
Kaufman v. Taub, 167
Kaufman v. Western Union Telegraph Co., 362
Kavafian v. Seattle Baseball Club Association, 495
Kavanagh v. Barber, 622

Kavanagh v. New York, Ontario & Western Railway Co., 220
Kawamoto v. Yasutake, 351
Kawananakoa v. Polyblank, 1033
Kay v. Adams, 78
Kay v. Ludwick, 185
Kaye v. Newhall, 921
Kaylor v. Magill, 436
Kazales v. Minto Leasing, Inc., 239
Kearley v. Cowan, 52, 141
Kearney v. Clutton, 97, 111
Kearney v. London, B. & S. C. R. Co., 244
Kearney v. Mallon Suburban Motors, 874
Kearns v. Smith, 445
Keate v. Phillips, 733
Keates v. Earl of Cardogan, 737
Keating v. De Arment, 756
Keating v. Shell Chemical Co., 577
Keck v. Bairs, Inc., 248
Keck v. Jackson, 365
Keck v. Pozorski, 456
Keck v. Wacker, 508
Kee v. Armstrong, Byrd & Co., 782
Keeble v. Hickeringill, 27, 980, 1005
Keefe v. Hart, 152
Keefe v. State, 45
Keefer v. Lombardi, 666
Keegan v. Anchor Inns, Inc., 496, 497, 498
Keegan v. Minneapolis & St. Louis Railroad Co., 280, 291
Keel v. Hainline, 38, 42
Keel v. Titan Construction Corp., 1001, 1009
Keeler v. Fred T. Ley & Co., 755
Keeley v. Great Northern Railway Co., 817
Keeley v. Manor Park Apartments, 448
Keels v. Powell, 995
Keen v. Coleman, 902
Keen v. Dominick's Finer Foods, Inc., 719
Keena v. Scales, 250
Keenan v. Cherry & Webb, 757
Keene Lumber Co. v. Leventhal, 993
Keener v. Dayton Electric Manufacturing Co., 703, 946
Keep v. Otter Tail Power Co., 201, 394
Keep v. Quallman, 45, 110, 125, 126
Keesecker v. G. M. McKelvey Co., 76
Keffe v. Milwaukee & St. Paul Railway Co., 400
Keffer v. Logan Coca-Cola Bottling Works, Inc., 249
Kehl v. Abram, 760
Kehoe v. New York Tribune Co., 846
Keightlinger v. Egan, 561
Keiper v. Anderson, 665
Keith v. Tuttle, 150
Keith v. Wheeling & Lake Erie Railroad Co., 578
Keleher v. Putnam, 53, 155
Keleket X-Ray Corp. v. United States, 340
Kelite Products, Inc. v. Binzel, 10, 964
Keller v. Blasdel, 666
Keller v. Butler, 874
Keller v. City of St. Louis, 935
Keller v. Federal Bob Brannon Truck Co., 525

Keller v. Keidinger, 200
Keller v. Schwegmann Brothers, Inc., 426
Kellerman v. J. S. Durig Co., 462
Kelley v. Boettcher, 325
Kelley v. City of Columbus, 422
Kelley v. Hearst Corp., 836
Kelley v. Howard S. Wright Construction Co., 231, 511, 512
Kelley v. Kelley, 902
Kelley v. Lee, 933
Kelley v. Post Publishing Co., 861, 862
Kelley v. Schuyler, 150
Kelley v. Thibodeau, 523
Kellogg v. Chicago & North Western Railway Co., 460
Kellogg v. Viola, 635
Kellogg Co. v. National Biscuit Co., 1021
Kelly v. American Airlines, Inc., 247
Kelly v. Bemis, 149
Kelly v. Bennett, 135
Kelly v. Board of Education, 423
Kelly v. Carroll, 187
Kelly v. Central Hanover Bank & Trust Co., 982
Kelly v. Checker White Cab Co., 486
Kelly v. Chicago, Milwaukee & St. Paul and Pacific Railroad Co., 27
Kelly v. Daro, 820
Kelly v. Fine, 11
Kelly v. First State Bank, 967
Kelly v. Flaherty, 789, 793
Kelly v. Hoffman, 787, 812
Kelly v. Independent Publishing Co., 809
Kelly v. Johnson Publishing Co., 779
Kelly v. Laclede Real Estate & Investment Co., 437
Kelly v. Lang, 97, 98
Kelly v. Loew's, Inc., 787
Kelly v. Louisiana Oil Refining Co., 504
Kelly v. Malott, 212
Kelly v. Metropolitan St. R. Co., 660, 661
Kelly v. Morris County Traction Co., 1011
Kelly v. Ogilvie, 1067
Kelly v. Partington, 774
Kelly v. Peerless Insurance Co., 959
Kelly v. Retzer & Retzer, Inc., 201
Kelly v. Richards, 734
Kelly v. Robinson, 669
Kelly v. Schneller, 330
Kelly v. Trans Globe Travel Bureau, Inc., 504
Kelly v. Williams, 913
Kelly, State ex rel. Washington Motor Coach Co. v., 578
Kelman v. Wilen, 78
Kelsay v. Motorola, Inc., 1028
Kelsea v. Swett, 883
Kelsen v. Imperial Tobacco Co., 78
Kelsey-Seybold Clinic v. Maclay, 920
Kelso v. State, 527
Kemart Corp. v. Printing Arts Research Laboratories, Inc., 974
Kemline v. Simonds, 402
Kemmerlin v. Wingate, 188
Kemper v. Fort, 818

Kempf v. Boehrig, 226
Kempf v. Ranger, 751
Kendall v. City of Des Moines, 219
Kendall v. Drake, 30
Kendall v. Johnson, 554
Kendall v. Lively, 1009, 1014
Kendall v. Sears, Roebuck & Co., 907
Kendall v. Stone, 963, 974
Kendrick v. Ideal Holding Co., 571
Kendrick v. McCrary, 927
Keneally v. Orgain, 1029
Keneko v. Hilo Coast Processing Corp., 448, 478
Kenison v. Schaeffer, 465
Kennard, Commonwealth v., 150
Kennecott Copper Corp. v. McDowell, 549
Kennedy v. Burbidge, 876
Kennedy v. Cannon, 820
Kennedy v. Carter, 214
Kennedy v. Colt, 342
Kennedy v. Dashner, 588
Kennedy v. Davis, 945
Kennedy v. Flo-Tronics, Inc., 762
Kennedy v. Hedberg, 275
Kennedy v. Item Co., 831
Kennedy v. James Butler, Inc., 798
Kennedy v. Kennedy, 521, 935
Kennedy v. McAfee's Executrix, 941
Kennedy v. Mid-Continent Telecasting Co., 834
Kennedy v. Parrott, 118, 119
Kennedy v. Phillips, 421
Kennedy v. Press Publishing Co., 966
Kennedy v. Providence Hockey Club, Inc., 485
Kennedy v. Ricker, 240
Kennedy v. Shea, 926, 927
Kenner v. Harding, 762
Kenney v. Baltimore & Ohio Railroad Co., 925
Kenney v. Gurley, 827, 835
Kenney v. Hatfield, 773
Kenney v. Ranney, 96
Kenney v. Wong Len, 56
Kensinger Acceptance Corp. v. Davis, 139
Kent v. Bradley, 507
Kent v. Judkins, 146
Kent v. Southern Railway Co., 133
Kentucky & West Virginia Power Co. v. Anderson, 628
Kentucky Block Fuel Co. v. Roberts, 551
Kentucky Independent Oil Co. v. Schnitzler, 319
Kentucky Land & Immigration Co. v. Crabtree, 77
Kentucky Traction & Terminal Co. v. Roman's Guardian, 363
Kentucky Utilities Co. v. Garland, 404
Kentucky Utilities Co. v. McCarty's Administrator, 959
Kentucky West Virginia Gas Co. v. Lafferty, 639, 640
Kenworthy v. Kleinberg, 982
Kenyon v. F. M. C. Corp., 343
Kenyon v. Harford Accident & Indemnity Co., 48
Keogan v. Holy Family Hospital Service, 192
Kepler v. Chicago, St. Paul, Minneapolis & Omaha Railway Co., 519
Keppleman v. Upston, 159

TABLE OF CASES

Ker v. Bryan, 88
Kerby v. Chicago Motor Coach Co., 260
Kerby v. Hal Roach Studios, 852, 853, 863
Kermarec v. Compagnie Generale Transatlantique, 433
Kern v. Autman, 222
Kernan, In re Samuel, 98
Kernan v. American Dredging Co., 288
Kerner v. Employers Mutual Liability Insurance Co. of Wisconsin, 381
Kerns v. Couch, 664, 675
Kerr v. Connecticut Co., 176
Kerr v. Du Pree, 982, 1003
Kerr v. Shurtluff, 759
Kershaw v. McKown, 137
Kersting v. White, 830
Kesinger, United States v., 558
Kesner v. Trenton, 401
Kesterson v. California-Oregon Power Co., 395
Ketcham v. Miller, 660, 665
Ketchum v. Amsterdam Apartments Co., 106
Ketchum v. Catulin, 730
Ketelson v. Stilz, 330
Kett v. Graeser, 764
Kettelhut v. Edwards, 52
Keviczky v. Lorber, 981, 994
Kevorkian v. Bemis, 753
Kewanee Oil Co. v. Bicron Corp., 1022
Key v. Armour Fertilizer Works, 326, 349
Keys v. Alamo City Baseball Co., 494
Keys v. Romley, 390, 636
Keyser Canning Co. v. Klots Throwing Co., 544
Keystone Aeronautics Corp. v. R. J. Enstrom Corp., 709
Keystone-Fleming Transport v. City of Tahoka, 308
Keyworth v. Hill, 100
KGB, Inc. v. Giannoulas, 1021
Khanoyan v. All American Sports Enterprises, Inc., 247
Kidgill v. Moor, 621
Kientz v. Carlton, 686
Kiernan v. Van Schaik, 590
Kiess v. Armour & Co., 326
Kieszkowski v. Odlewany, 528
Kiff v. Youmans, 27
Kilbourn v. Thompson, 820, 1056, 1059
Kilgore v. Brown, 252
Kilgore v. Shepard Co., 249
Kilgour v. Evening Star Newspaper Co., 783
Kilian v. Doubleday & Co., 841, 842
Kilian v. Stackpole Sons, Inc., 801
Killebrew v. Carlisle, 888
Killen v. Olson, 872
Kilpack v. Wignall, 200
Kilpatrick v. Edge, 964
Kilts v. Supervisors of Kent County, 621, 622
Kim v. Anderson, 256
Kim v. Chinn, 11
Kimatian v. New England Telephone & Telegraph Co., 911
Kimball v. Bangs, 757
Kimball v. Post Publishing Co., 836
Kimbar v. Estis, 172

Kimbell v. DuBose, 527
Kimber v. Young, 742
Kimberly v. Ledbetter, 123
Kimble v. Kimble, 827
Kimble v. Mackintosh Hemphill Co., 304, 312
Kimery v. Public Service Co. of Oklahoma, 232, 454
Kimmerle v. New York Evening Journal, 773, 774
Kimmons v. Benson, 627, 641
Kimple v. Schafer, 539
Kinard v. Coats Co. Inc., 478
Kinaston v. Moore, 89
Kincaid v. Rusk, 1061
Kinchen v. Missouri Pacific Railway Co., 454
Kinderavich v. Palmer, 458, 463
Kindervater v. Motorists Casualty Insurance Co., 588
Kine v. Zuckerman, 367
King v. Apple River Power Co., 879
King v. Avtech Aviation, Inc., 358
King v. Blue Mountain Forest Association, 390, 539
King v. Carney, 117, 119
King v. Chicago, Milwaukee & St. Paul Railway Co., 290
King v. City of Seattle, 1045, 1047
King v. Columbian Carbon Co., 552
King v. Cope, 1015
King v. Douglas Aircraft Co., 703, 705
King v. Floding, 937
King v. Franklin, 159
King v. Hoare, 330
King v. Ilikai Properties, Inc., 443
King v. Investment Equities, Inc., 176
King v. Kline, 644
King v. Lake, 786
King v. Lamborn, 766
King v. Lennen, 408
King v. Livingston Manufacturing Co., 751, 752
King v. Martin, 872
King v. Moore, 328
King v. New Masonic Temple Association, 439
King v. Patrylow, 415
King v. Patterson, 829
King v. Robertson, 150
King v. Ruth, 348
King v. Southern Railway Co., 941
King v. State, 127
King v. Viscoloid Co., 937
King v. Williams, 188, 189
King v. Yarbray, 890
King, Inc., B. W. v. Town of West New York, 544
Kingkade v. Plummer, 964, 968
Kingman & Co. v. Stoddard, 770
Kings Laboratories v. Yucaipa Valley Fruit Co., 663
Kingsbery v. Phillips Petroleum Co., 988
Kingsbury v. Smith, 372
King-Seeley Thermos Co. v. Aladdin Industries, Inc., 1017
Kingsland v. Erie County Agricultural Society, 305, 318
Kingsley v. Noble, 738
Kingston v. Chicago & Northwestern Railway Co., 267
Kinikin v. Heupel, 191, 192
Kinkaid v. Rossa, 665, 764

Kinley v. Hines, 268
Kinmouth v. McDougall, 564
Kinnan v. Fidelity & Casualty Co., 586
Kinnare v. City of Chicago, 663
Kinney v. Hosea, 790
Kinney v. Smith, 952
Kinsey v. William Spencer & Son Corp., 329
Kinsey's Estate, In re, 557
Kinskier v. B. Goodman, Ltd., 723
Kinsley v. Von Atzingen, 312
Kinsman Transit, Co., Petition of, 297, 299, 1001
Kinter v. Kinter, 817
Kintz v. Galvin, 770
Kipper v. Vokolek, 925
Kirby v. Brown, Wheelock, Harris, Vought & Co., 380
Kirby v. Carlisle, 165
Kirby v. Foster, 139
Kirby v. Harker, 112
Kirby v. Hylton, 393, 404, 488, 489, 497
Kirby v. Jules Chain Stores Corp., 61, 64
Kirby v. Larson, 464, 531
Kirby v. Pittsburgh Courier Publishing Co., 847
Kirby v. Porter, 98
Kirby v. Smith, 790
Kirby Lumber Corp. v. Karpel, 73, 323
Kirby Lumber Corp. v. Walters, 326
Kiriluk v. Cohn, 581
Kirincich v. Standard Dredging Co., 265, 270
Kirk, In the Matter of, 778
Kirk v. Cassady, 77
Kirk v. Garrett, 112, 154
Kirk v. Gregory, 85
Kirk v. Middlebrook, 935
Kirk v. Vaccaro, 764
Kirkland v. Ensign-Bickford Co., 333
Kirkland v. General Motors Corp., 478, 497
Kirkman v. Philips' Heirs, 673
Kirkman v. Westchester Newspapers, 779
Kirkpatrick v. Crutchfield, 40
Kirkpatrick v. Damianakes, 395
Kirkpatrick v. Eagle Lodge No. Thirty-Two, 834
Kirkpatrick v. Parker, 928
Kirkpatrick v. Reeves, 742
Kirksey v. Jernigan, 63
Kirkwood v. Hickman, 141
Kirsch v. Barnes, 967
Kirschbaum v. Lowrey, 9
Kirshenbaum v. General Outdoor Advertising Co., 382, 445
Kitchens v. Barlow, 883
Kitchens v. Winter Co. Builders, Inc., 489, 492
Kitsap County Transportation Co. v. Harvey, 176
Kittell v. Vermont Weatherboard, Inc., 577
Kittle v. State, 418
Kitto v. Gilbert, 253
Klages v. General Ordinance Equipment Corp., 203
Klam v. Koppel, 101
Klaman v. Hitchcock, 317
Klassen v. Central Kansas Cooperative Creamery Association, 621

Klatz v. Pfeffer, 565
Klauder v. Cregar, 992
Klauder v. McGrath, 326, 346
Klaus v. Eden, 404
Kleber v. Allin, 920
Kleebauer v. Western Fuse & Explosives Co., 553, 564
Kleidon v. Glascock, 51
Klein v. Asgrow Seed Co., 749
Klein v. Catalano, 168
Klein v. Dow Corning Corp., 165
Klein v. Klein, 903, 904
Klein v. McGraw-Hill, Inc., 862
Klein, People v., 156
Klein v. United States, 304, 441
Kleinman v. Banner Laundry Co., 245
Kleinman v. Frank, 530
Kleinschmidt v. Matthieu, 801
Klenberg v. Russell, 561
Klepper v. Breslin, 959
Klepsch v. Donald, 554, 562
Klinck v. Colby, 826
Kline v. Abraham, 570
Kline v. Ansell, 917, 919, 930
Kline v. Burns, 722
Kline v. Eubanks, 981, 990
Kline v. Kline, 42, 43, 57
Kline v. Moyer, 277, 305
Kline v. 1500 Massachusetts Avenue Apartment Corp., 202
Kline v. Pennsylvania Railroad Co., 232
Kline v. Robert M. McBride & Co., 861, 862
Kling v. Torello, 946
Klingman v. Holmes, 932
Klingman v. Loew's, Inc., 259
Kloos v. Gatz, 93
Klor's, Inc. v. Broadway-Hale Stores, Inc., 1025
Klos v. Zahorik, 831
Klossner v. San Juan County, 948
Klous v. Hennessey, 1006
Kluender v. Semann, 781
Kluge v. Ries, 741
Klumph v. Dunn, 789
Knapp v. Barrett, 219
Knapp v. Connecticut Theatrical Corp., 419
Knapp v. Guyer, 97
Knapp v. Penfield, 986
Knapp v. Stanford, 174, 182, 197
Knauss v. Brua, 437
Kneece v. City of Columbia, 646
Kneiser v. Belasco-Blackwood Co., 413, 439
Knell v. Feltman, 337
Knickerbocker Ice Co. v. Gardiner Dairy Co., 981
Knierim v. Izzo, 65
Knight v. Atlantic Coast Line Railroad Co., 669
Knight v. Davis Carriage Co., 104
Knight v. Gibbs, 780
Knight v. Kaiser Co., 407
Knight v. Moore, 419
Knight v. Seney, 91
Knight v. United States, 164

Knight v. Western Auto Supply Co., 324
Knight v. Wilcox, 927
Knights v. Quarles, 667
Knippenberg v. Lord & Taylor, 343
Knippenberg v. Windemuth, 262
Knisley v. Pratt, 570, 573
Knockum v. Amoco Oil Co., 220, 224, 230
Knopfler v. Flynn, 758
Knott v. Litton, 323, 914
Knott v. Sargent, 874
Knowles v. Blue, 113
Knowles v. Knowles, 102
Knowles v. Pennsylvania Railroad Co., 650
Knowlton v. New York & New England Railway Co., 290
Knowlton v. Ross, 49, 50, 121
Knox v. Allen, 65
Knox v. Anderson, 750, 760
Knox v. Binkoski, 105
Knox v. Meehan, 775
Knox v. Moskins Stores, 92
Knoxville, City of v. Bailey, 596
Knoxville, City of v. Hargis, 437
Knoxville Traction Co. v. Lane, 57, 58
Knudsen v. Duffee-Freeman, Inc., 422
Knupp v. Esslinger, 52
Knutsen v. Brown, 331
Knutter v. Bakalarski, 182
Kobbe v. Chicago & North Western Railroad Co., 134
Kocan v. Garino, 431
Koch v. City of Chicago, 404
Koch v. Fox, 311
Koch v. Southern Pacific Transportation Co., 233
Koch v. Stone, 123
Koch v. Zimmermann, 310
Kocher v. Creston Transfer Co., 519
Kock v. Burgess, 991, 1003
Koehler v. Dubose, 819
Koehler v. Koehler, 922
Koehler v. Waukesha Milk Co., 291, 294, 950, 958, 959
Koelsch v. Philadelphia Co., 208
Koenig v. Patrick Construction Corp., 227
Koenig v. Patrick Construction Corp., 576
Koennecke v. Waxwing Cedar Products, Limited, 210
Koepf v. County of York, 905, 1048, 1063
Koetting v. Conroy, 561
Kofahl v. Delgado, 198
Kohl v. Taylor, 758
Kohler v. Wray, 428
Kohlhoss v. Mobley, 921
Kohn v. Clark, 270
Kohn v. United States, 1037, 1039
Kojic v. City of New York, 510
Kokesh v. Price, 517, 959
Kolakowski v. Voirs, 253
Kolb v. O'Conner, 855
Kolenko v. Certain-Teed Products Corp., 575
Kolka v. Jones, 894
Koll v. Manatt's Transportation Co., 164, 220, 221, 225
Koller v. Duggan, 86

Kolodkin v. Griffin, 511
Koltz v. Jahaaske, 329
Komar v. City of New York, 874
Kommerstad v. Great Northern Railway Co., 275, 284, 292
Kompass v. Light, 878
Konkle v. Haven, 802
Konskier v. Goodman, 83
Koogler v. Koogler, 522
Kool v. Lee, 897, 899
Koonce, State v., 156
Koontz v. Keller, 65
Kopaczski v. Eastern Air Lines, Inc., 183
Kopezak, People v., 1010
Kopka v. Bell Telephone Co., 76
Koplitz v. City of St. Paul, 530
Kopp v. R.S. Noonan, Inc., 418
Kopplin v. Quade, 560
Korach v. Loeffel, 665
Korbelik v. Johnson, 475
Korbin v. Berlin, 63
Korel v. United States, 242
Koris v. Norfolk & Western Railway, 870
Korn v. Rennison, 851
Kornoff v. Kingsburg Cotton Oil Co., 77, 84
Koroluck v. Giordano's Service Center, Inc., 521
Koroniotis v. La Porte Transit, Inc., 456
Korricks Dry Goods Co. v. Kendall, 388
Koseris v. J. R. Simplot Co., 631, 641
Kosich v. Poultrymen's Service Corp., 620
Kosminski v. Goldberg, 912
Koster & Wythe v. Massey, 549
Kosters v. The Seven-Up Co., 707
Kotler v. Lalley, 451
Kountze v. Kennedy, 740
Koursk, The, 322, 325, 328
Koussevitzky v. Allen, Towne & Heath, 860, 864
Kowal v. Hofher, 213
Kozan v. Comstock, 667
Kraaz v. La Quinta Motor Inns, Inc., 208
Kraft v. Lowe, 738
Krakowiak v. Sampson, 406
Kramer v. Lott, 54
Kramer v. Ricksmeier, 45, 56, 62
Kramer Service v. Wilkins, 269
Kramm v. Stockton Electric Railroad Co., 240
Kranda v. Houser-Norborg Medical Corp., 191, 192, 260
Krantz v. Nichols, 424
Krashes v. White, 889
Kraus v. Alamo National Bank of San Antonio, 511
Kraus v. National Bank of Commerce, 761
Krause v. Bucher, 10
Krause v. Home Mutual Insurance Co., 906
Krause v. Spiegel, 54
Kraushaar v. LeVin, 791
Krausnick v. Haegg Roofing Co., 528
Kraustrunk v. Chicago Housing Authority, 419, 428
Krauth v. Geller, 429
Krebiozen Research Foundation v. Beacon Press, 773, 977

Krebs v. Oliver, 788, 828
Kreider Truck Service, Inc. v. Augustine, 511
Kreifels v. Wurtele, 217
Kreisler, Inc., Charles v. Matusow, 94
Kremer v. Black, 921
Kremer v. Carr's Food Center, Inc., 428
Kremposky v. Mt. Jessup Coal Co., 414
Kresge Co., S. S. v. Kenney, 310
Kress & Co. v. Burkes, 575
Kress & Co., S.H. v. Bradshaw, 142
Kress & Co., S.H. v. Brashier, 40
Kress & Co., S.H. v. Musgrove, 138, 142
Kress & Co., S.H. v. Powell, 49, 54
Kress & Co., S.H. v. Telford, 194
Kressine v. Janesville Traction Co., 411
Kreuger v. Schmiechen, 596
Krieg v. Dayton-Hudson Corp., 882
Krieger v. Ownership Corp., 443
Krieger v. Popular Publications, 853
Krigbaum v. Sbarbaro, 1013
Krisovich v. John Booth, 723
Kristek v. Catron, 448
Krocker v. Westmoreland Planing Mill Co., 640
Kroeger v. Passmore, 53
Kroeger v. Safranek, 283
Kroger Co. v. Bowman, 695
Kroger Co. v. Thomas, 420
Kroger Grocery & Baking Co. v. Hamlin, 880
Kroger Grocery & Baking Co. v. Reddin, 960
Kroger Grocery & Baking Co. v. Reeves, 14
Kroger Grocery & Baking Co. v. Waller, 49, 141
Kroger Grocery & Baking Co. v. Woods, 183
Kroger Crocery & Baking Co. v. Yount, 833
Krol v. Plodick, 876
Krom v. Schoonmaker, 1072
Krone v. McCann, 420, 427
Kroon v. Beech Aircraft Corp., 475
Kropidlowski v. Pfister & Vogel Leather Co., 335
Kross v. Kelsey Hayes Co., 684
Krouse v. Graham, 952
Krueger v. City of Anaheim, 224
Krueger v. St. Joseph's Hospital, 166
Krueger v. State, 156
Krug v. Ward, 883
Krulic v. Petcoff, 842
Krump v. Highlander Ice Cream Co., 252
Kruse v. Rabe, 820, 826, 827, 833
Krutlies v. Bulls Head Coal Co., 581
Kryger v. Panaszy, 277
Kryszke v. Kamin, 895
Kubrick, United States v., 1035
Kuchlik v. Feuer, 915
Kuchynski v. Ukryn, 445
Kuehn, People v., 155
Kuehn v. White, 507
Kuelling v. Roderick Lean Manufacturing Co., 205, 206, 726, 737
Kuhlen v. Boston & Northern Street Railway Co., 383
Kuhn v. Bader, 271
Kuhn v. Brownfield, 941

Kuhn v. General Parking Corp., 440, 442, 444
Kuhn v. Jewett, 275, 283, 292, 294, 301
Kuhn v. Michael, 246
Kuhn v. P. J. Carlin Construction Co., 510
Kuhn v. Warner Brothers Pictures, 773
Kuhn v. Zabotsky, 177, 178, 1074
Kuhnhausen v. Stadelman, 878
Kuhnle v. Swedlund, 949
Kuhns v. Brugger, 1071
Kujek v. Goldman, 18
Kulaga v. State, 384
Kulesza v. Chicago Daily News, 832
Kulesza v. Wyhowski, 758
Kumkumian v. City of New York, 398, 465, 467
Kunan v. De Matteo, 515
Kundinger v. Bagnasco, 620
Kunz v. Johnson, 878
Kunzie v. Leeds, Inc., 244
Kupchinsky v. Vacuum Oil Co., 531
Kupferle Foundry Co., John C. v. St. Louis Merchants' Bridge Terminal Railway Co., 289
Kurpgeweit v. Kirby, 60
Kurtigian v. City of Worcester, 391
Kurtz v. Morse Oil Co., 232
Kuryer Publishing Co. v. Messmer, 985, 1010, 1025
Kvanli v. Village of Watson, 581
Kvenild v. Taylor, 990
Kwaitkowski v. Superior Trading Co., 202, 443
Kwass v. Kersey, 773
Kyle v. Chester, 673

L

L., Pamela v. Farmer, 384
La Bar v. Lindstrom, 748, 766
La Bella v. Brown, 329
La Crone v. Ohio Bell Telephone Co., 854
La Crosse Theaters Co., State ex rel. Cowie v., 644
La Faso v. La Faso, 717
La Follette, State ex rel. v. Hinkle, 852, 853, 863, 867
La France Electrical Construction & Supply Co. v. International Brotherhood of Electrical Workers, 994
La Freda v. Woodward, 439
La Hue v. Coca Cola Bottling, Inc., 691
La Londe v. Peake, 264, 312
La Plant v. E. I. Dupont de Nemours & Co., 684
La Porta v. Leonard, 817
La Rocco v. Fernandez, 252
La Salle Extension University v. Fogarty, 64
La Societe Anonyme de Remorquage a Helice v. Bennetts, 999
La Sota v. Philadelphia Transportation Co., 383
La Vine v. Clear Creek Skiing Corp., 185
Labarge v. Pere Marquette Railroad Co., 465
Labore v. Davison Construction Co., 401
Lacanfora v. Goldapel, 388, 389
LaCava v. City of New Orleans, 182
Lacey v. Laird, 115
Lacey v. United States, 1035
Lackey v. Brooks, 333

Lackner v. LaCroix, 874
Lacombe v. Greathouse, 403, 416
LaCount v. Hensel Phelps Construction Co., 509, 513, 514
Lacy v. Mitchell, 877
Lacy v. Reynolds, 781
Ladd v. Granite State Brick Co., 628
Lader v. Benkowitz, 899
Ladner v. Balsley, 752
Ladwig v. Heyer, 809
Lady Nelson, Limited v. Creole Petroleum Corp., 299
Laffin v. Apalucci, 125
Laflin & Rand Powder Co. v. Tearney, 619
Lafone v. Smith, 846
LaForge v. Fairchild Publications, 862
Lafourche Packet Co. v. Henderson, 570
Lafredo v. Bush Terminal Co., 440
LaFrenz v. Lake County Fair Board, 954
LaGorga v. Kroger Co., 710
Lahar v. Barnes, 628
Lahr v. Adell Chemical Co., 776, 851
Laidlaw v. Sage, 266
L'Aiglon Apparel, Inc. v. Lana Lobell, Inc., 1019
Laing v. Mitten, 817, 888
Laird v. Nelms, 558, 1036
Laird v. State Farm Insurance Co., 520
Laite v. Baxter, 163
Lake v. Emigh, 441
Lake v. King, 819, 820
Lake v. United States, 447
Lake Country Estates, Inc. v. Tahoe Regional Planning Agency, 1043, 1051
Lake Erie & Western Railroad Co. v. Halleck, 329
Lake Gateway Motor Inn v. Matt's Sunshine Gift Shops, Inc., 984, 986, 1011
Lake Shore & Michigan Southern Railway Co. v. Chicago, Lake Shore & South Bend Railway Co., 561, 628
Lake Shore & Michigan Southern Railway Co. v. Hession, 470
Lake Shore & Michigan Southern Railway Co. v. Lavalley, 569
Lake Shore & Michigan Southern Railway Co. v. Prentice, 12
Lalor v. Byrne, 883
Lamb v. Lamb, 904
Lamb v. Littman, 572
Lamb v. S. Cheney & Sons, 981
Lamb v. South Unit Jehovah's Witnesses, 511
Lamb v. Woodry, 40, 139
Lambach v. Lundberg, 760
Lambert v. Bessey, 21, 535
Lambert v. Breton, 897
Lambert v. Brewster, 65
Lambert v. Gearhart-Owen Industries, Inc., 261
Lambert v. Jones, 669
Lambert v. Pittsburgh Bridge & Iron Works, 517
Lambert v. Polen, 525
Lambert v. Robinson, 139
Lambert v. Sears, Roebuck & Co., 883, 884
Lambert v. Sistrunk, 679

Lambert v. Smith, 740
Lambert v. Village of Summit, 957
Lambertson v. Cincinnati Corp., 476
Lambrecht v. Schreyer, 36
Lambton v. Mellish, 354, 355, 634
Lamereaux v. Tula, 644
Lamine v. Dorrell, 672
Lamm v. Shingleton, 362
Lammers v. Pacific Electric Railway Co., 319
Lamont v. Commissioner of Motor Vehicles, 859
Lampe v. Lagomarcino-Grupe Co., 937
Lampert v. Reynolds Metals Co., 11
Lampesis v. Comolli, 763
Lamport v. 4175 Broadway, Inc., 990
Lampos v. Bazar, Inc., 870, 871, 881
Lanark, City of v. Dougherty, 210
Lancaster v. Hamburger, 841, 984, 985
Lancaster v. Montesi, 311
Lancaster & Love, Inc. v. Mueller Co., 894
Lance v. Senior, 170
Lancour v. Herald & Globe Association, 799
Land v. Bachman, 36
Landau v. City of New York, 552, 644
Landau v. Columbia Broadcasting System, 787, 809
Lander v. Seaver, 158, 159
Lander v. Wald, 790
Landerman v. Hamilton, 262
Landers v. East Texas Salt Water Disposal Co., 351
Landers v. School District No. 203, pp. 214, 383
Landesman v. Board of County Commissioners, 1055
Landman v. M. Susan & Associates, 406
Landon v. Watkins, 782, 1014
Landreth v. Phillips Petroleum Co., 669
Landreth v. Reed, 943
Landrum v. Ellington, 60
Landrum v. Wells, 53
Landry v. Hill, 125
Landry v. Hubert, 519
Landry v. Two R. Drilling Co., 946
Landstrom v. Thorpe, 972
Landy v. Olson & Serley Sash & Door Co., 303
Lane v. Atlantic Works, 304
Lane v. Capsey, 621
Lane v. Chatham, 914
Lane v. Dorney, 255
Lane v. F.W. Woolworth Co., 852
Lane v. Hampton, 269
Lane v. Hatfield, 952
Lane v. Mitchell, 3
Lane v. Schilling, 802
Lane v. Southern R. Co., 309
Lane v. Trenholm Building Co., 679
Lane v. United States, 1038
Lane v. Washington Daily News, 781
Laney v. Glidden Co., 872
Laney-Payne Farm Loan Co. v. Greenhaw, 746
Lang v. Amateur Softball Association of America, 494
Lang v. General Motors Corp., 708
Lang v. Stadium Purchasing Corp., 438
Lang v. United States Reduction Co., 570

Lang v. Wood, 821
Langabaugh v. Anderson, 564
Langazo v. San Joaquin Light & Power Corp., 395
Langdon v. Templeton, 77
Lange v. Hoyt, 183, 309
Lange v. Potter, 528
Langeland v. Farmers State Bank of Trimont, 984, 986, 1011
Langeland v. 78th & Park Ave. Corp., 260
Langer v. Goode, 390
Langford v. Boston & Albany Railroad Co., 54
Langford v. Mercurio, 425
Langford v. Vanderbilt University, 837, 858, 868
Langhorne Road Apartments, Inc. v. Bisson, 441
Langill v. First National Stores, 219
Langley v. Schumacker, 902
Langley Park Apartments v. Lund, 441
Langlinais v. Geophysical Service, Inc., 262
Langridge v. Levy, 205, 357, 668
Langston v. Chicago & North Western Railroad Co., 380
Langston v. Personal Service Insurance Co., 524
Langton v. Hagerty, 841
Lanier v. North Carolina State Highway Commission, 401, 407, 409
Lankford v. Mong, 214
Lankford, State v., 120
Lankford v. Sullivan, Long & Hagerty, 168
Lann v. Third National Bank in Nashville, 817
Lanning v. Sprague, 752
Lansing v. Stone, 544
Lanterman v. Delaware, Lackawanna & Western Railroad Co., 890, 892
Lantis v. Astec Industries, Inc., 448
Lantis v. Condon, 938
Lanza v. Poretti, 246, 248, 257
Lapentina v. Santangelo, 820
Lapique v. Dunnigan, 941
Laporta v. New York Central Railroad Co., 413
Lapp v. Stanton, 539
Larabee v. Traingle Steel, Inc., 461, 493
Larcher v. Wanless, 957
Larean v. La Compagnie d'Imprimerie de la Minerve, 778
Larimer & Weld Irrigation Co. v. Walker, 323
Larison v. Larison, 902
Larkin v. Noonan, 822
Larkin v. State, 187
Larkin v. Tsavaris, 624
Larmore v. Crown Point Iron Co., 414, 424
Larnel Builders v. Martin, 409
Larocque v. Dorsey, 871
Larrimore v. American National Insurance Co., 226
Larsen v. Credit Bureau, Inc. of Georgia, 898
Larsen v. Minneapolis Gas Co., 340
Larson v. Anderson, 331
Larson v. Boston Elevated Railway Co., 291, 302
Larson v. Calder's Park Co., 437, 438
Larson, Commonwealth v., 139
Larson v. Doner, 821
Larson v. Duluth, Missabe & Northern Railway Co., 312

Larson v. Independent School District No. 314, pp. 905, 1048
Larson v. New England Telephone & Telegraph Co., 648
Larson v. R. B. Wrigley Co., 59, 789, 794
Larson v. St. Francis Hotel, 248
Larson, Jr. Co., L. P. v. Lamont, Croliss & Co., 1016
Lartigue v. R. J. Reynolds Tobacco Co., 700
LaRue v. Russell, 77
Lary v. Cleveland, Columbus, Cincinnati, & Indianapolis Railway Co., 394
Las Vegas Sun, Inc. v. Franklin, 842
LaSalle Extension University v. Fogarty, 61
Lasecki v. Kabara, 905
Lashbrook v. Patten, 524
Lasiter, State v., 73
Laskowski v. Manning, 440
Lassiter v. Norfolk & Carolina R. R., 638
Laster v. Chaney, 154
Laswell v. Brown, 1037
Latendresse v. Marra, 239, 241
Latendresse v. Preskey, 577
Latham v. Des Moines Electric Light Co., 331
Latham v. Father Divine, 1007
Latham v. Karger, 923
Lathrop v. Sundberg, 832
Latimer v. City of Clovis, 398
Latimer v. Stubbs, 91
Latta v. New Orleans & Northwestern Railway Co., 147
Latta v. Robinson Erection Co., 732
Latta v. Siefke, 907
Latter v. Braddell, 121
Latzoni v. City of Garfield, 422
Laubach v. Morgan, 474
Laube v. Stevenson, 415
Laudati v. Stea, 809
Laugher v. Pointer, 509
Laughlin v. Hopkinson, 741
Laughlin v. St. Louis Union Trust Co., 894
Laun v. Union Electric Co. of Missouri, 817
Laurenzi v. Vranizan, 331
Laurie Co., William v. McCullough, 194
Lauson v. Town of Fond du Lac, 219
Lauzon v. Charroux, 890
Lavallee v. Pratt, 393, 398
Lave v. Neumann, 412, 429, 430, 454
Laver v. Kingston, 331
Laverrierre v. Casco Bank & Trust Co., 102
Laverty v. Snethen, 101
Lavery v. Crooke, 926, 927
Lavigne v. Lavigne, 918
Lavitch v. Smith, 424
Law v. Phillips, 511
Law v. Railway Express Agency, 395
Law v. Sidney, 758, 765
Law v. Visser, 289
Lawhorne v. Harlan, 1060
Lawler v. Earle, 826
Lawler v. Merritt, 824
Lawler v. Skelton, 550
Lawless v. Brotherhood of Painters, 985

Lawless v. Muller, 834
Lawrence v. Bamberger Railroad Co., 399
Lawrence v. Combs, 541
Lawrence v. Denver & Rio Grande Railroad Co., 518
Lawrence v. Eastern Air Lines, 635
Lawrence v. Grant Parish School Board, 488
Lawrence v. Spence, 926
Lawrence v. Womack, 44
Lawrence v. Ylla, 853
Lawrence Trust Co. v. Sun-America Publishing Co., 773
Laws v. Fisher, 938
Lawson v. Benjamin Ansehl Co., 687
Lawson v. Price, 68
Lawson v. State, 44
Lawter, United States v., 381
Lawton v. Herrick, 354
Lawyer v. Fritcher, 927
Lawyers' Mortgage Investment Corp. v. Paramount Laudries, 95
Lawyers Surety Corp. v. Snell, 164
Laxton v. Orkin Exterminating Co., 362, 363, 364
Layne v. International Brotherhood of Electrical Workers, 944
Layne v. Tribune Co., 810
Layton v. Harris, 803, 811
Lazar v. Cleveland Electric Illuminating Co., 469
Lazarus v. Eastern Air Lines, 247
Lazarus v. Phelps, 675
Lazenby v. Universal Underwriters Insurance Co., 13
Le Clear v. Perkins, 893
Le Fleur v. Vergilia, 486
Le Juene Road Hospital, Inc. v. Watson, 378
Le Laurin v. Murray, 345, 348
Le Lievre v. Gould, 357, 358
Le Massena v. Storm, 966
Le Moine v. Spicer, 789
Le Roux v. State, 423
Le Sage v. Pryor, 521
Leach v. Fosburgh Lumber Co., 75
Leach v. Francis, 132
Leach v. Leach, 60
Leach v. Woods, 77
Leachman v. Dougherty, 150
Leahan v. Cochran, 390, 450
Leahy, State ex rel. v. O'Rourke, 644
Leal v. C. C. Pitts Sand & Gravel, Inc., 368
Leame v. Bray, 30, 163
Leap v. Royce, 232
Lear Siegler, Inc. v. Ark-Ell Springs, Inc., 1022
Leavell & Co. v. Vilbig Bros., Inc., 659
Leavitt v. Gillaspie, 493
LeBeuf v. Atkins, 185
Lebourdais v. Vitrified Wheel Co., 681
Lebright v. Gentzlinger, 445
Lechman v. Hooper, 722
Ledbetter v. Thomas, 102
Ledbetter Bros., Inc. v. Holcomb, 638
Lederman v. Cunningham, 619
Ledford v. Pittsburgh & Lake Erie Railroad Co., 474
Ledford v. Smith, 899, 900

Ledger-Enquirer Co. v. Grimes, 782
Ledlie v. Wallen, 793
LeDoux v. Southern Farm Bureau Casualty Insurance Co., 525
Lee v. Atlantic Coast Line Railroad Co., 467
Lee v. Blessing, 269
Lee v. Brooklyn Union Publishing Co., 837
Lee v. Burk, 560
Lee v. Cannon Mills, 827
Lee v. Carwile, 265
Lee v. Cohrt, 680
Lee v. Comer, 907
Lee v. Crookston Coca-Cola Bottling Co., 250, 255, 696
Lee v. Hartford, 200
Lee v. Jerome Realty, Inc., 441
Lee v. National League Baseball Club of Milwaukee, 426, 489
Lee v. New River & Pocahontas Consolidated Coal Co., 958
Lee v. Salt River Valley Water Users' Association, 405
Lee v. Stewart, 76
Lee v. W. E. Fuetterer Battery & Supplies Co., 831
Lee v. Wilson and MacKinnon, 809
Lee Tung v. Burkhart, 96
Leece v. Griffin, 762
Leek v. Brasfield, 992
Leeseberg v. Builders Plumbers Supply Co., 890
Legac v. Vietmayer Brothers, 365
Leger v. Warren, 152
Legette v. Smith, 244
Legge v. Tucker, 663
Lehigh Structural Steel Co. v. Atlantic Smelting & Refining Works, 1024
Lehigh Valley Railroad Co. v. Kilmer, 198
Lehman v. Brooklyn City R. Co., 360
Lehman v. Goldin, 965
Lehmkuhl v. Junction City, 408
Lehmuth v. Long Beach Unified School District, 181
Lehner v. Berlin Publishing Co., 837, 838
Lehner v. Kelley, 795, 844
Lehnhard v. Robertson's Administratrix, 566
Lehre, State v., 840
Lehrer v. Elmore, 846
Lehrer v. Lorenzen, 951
Leibowitz v. Ortho Pharmaceutical Corp., 701
Leigh v. Wadsworth, 723
Leighton v. Dean, 421
Leininger v. New Orleans Item Publishing Co., 836
Leininger v. Stearns-Roger Manufacturing Co., 724
Leipske v. Guenther, 560
Leister v. Kelley, 315
Leisy v. Northern Pacific Railway Co., 233
Leisy v. United States, 558
Leitch & Co. v. Leydon, 87
Leite v. City of Providence, 212
LeJeune v. Allstate Insurance Co., 501
Lemarier v. A. Towle Co., 504
Lembeck v. Gerken, 743
Lemke v. Anders, 872
Lemle v. Breeden, 722

Lemley v. J & B Tire Co., 720
Lemley v. Penner, 435, 436
Lemmen v. Servais, 908
Lemmer v. The Tribune, 774
Lemmon v. King, 52
Lemon v. Edwards, 391
Lemon v. Simmons, 788
Lemons v. Kelly, 323
Len, Mark, State v., 125
Lenahan v. Pittston Coal Mining Co., 493
Lenark, City of v. Dougherty, 470
Lendino v. Fiorenza, 792
Lennane, Brown B., 571
Lennox v. White, 442
Lent v. Lent, 245
Lentz v. Gardin, 258
Lenz v. Ridgewood Associates, 238, 440, 441, 453
Leonard v. George, 875
Leonard v. North Dakota Co-op Wool Marketing Association, 524
Leonard v. Springer, 736, 744
Leonard v. Wilkins, 137
Leonard v. Wilson, 827
Leonardis v. Morton Chemical Co., 932
Leong v. Takasaki, 366
Leoni v. Reinhard, 312
Leon's Shoe Stores v. Hornsby, 52
LePelley v. Grefenson, 247, 256
Lepentina v. Santangelo, 826
Leposki v. Railway Express Agency, Inc., 298
Leppke v. Segura, 199
Lerentz v. R. K. O. Radio Pictures, 782
Leroy Fibre Co. v. Chicago, Milwaukee & St. Paul Railway Co., 460, 566
Lesch v. Great Northern Railway Co., 77, 289
Leslie v. Western Steel Co., 974
Leslie-Four Coal Co. v. Brock, 238
Lester v. Albers Super Markets, Inc., 49
Lester v. Magic Chef, Inc., 363
Letang v. Cooper, 163
Letang v. Ottawa Electric R. Co., 492
Letcher v. Derricott, 466
Leuck v. Goetz, 520
Leuthold v. Pennsylvania Railroad Co., 218
Leutholds v. Fairchilds, 98
Leveillee v. Wright, 305
Levelle, State v., 357
Leventhal v. Liberman, 726
Lever Brothers v. Jay's Chemical Corp., 1016
Leverett v. State, 1048
Leverton v. Curtis Publishing Co., 864
Levesque v. Levesque, 595
Levey v. Warner Bros. Pictures, 853
Levi v. Montgomery, 340
Levi v. Schwartz, 623
Levine v. Katz, 440
Levy v. Brannan, 883
Levy v. Gelber, 778
Levy v. Louisiana, 948
Levy v. McClintock, 143

Levy v. Ross, 995
Leward v. Baseley, 130
Lewis v. Baker, 701
Lewis v. Buckskin Joe's Inc., 164, 209
Lewis v. Chapman, 827
Lewis v. Corbin, 1006
Lewis v. Daily News Co., 775
Lewis v. Flint & P. M. Railway Co., 264
Lewis v. Fountain, 122
Lewis v. Hayes, 790, 795, 836
Lewis v. Huie-Hodge Lumber Co., 1010, 1013
Lewis v. I. M. Shapiro Co., 395
Lewis v. Lewis, 903, 907, 909
Lewis v. Montgomery Ward & Co., 53
Lewis v. Northern Illinois Gas Co., 179, 180
Lewis, People v., 267, 345
Lewis v. Physicians & Dentists Credit Bureau, 858
Lewis v. Piggly-Wiggly of Ferriday, Inc., 182
Lewis v. State, 1046
Lewis, State v., 154
Lewis v. Terry, 684
Lewis v. Timco, Inc., 478
Lewis v. United States Rubber Co., 696
Lewis v. Williams, 773, 877
Lewis v. Wolf, 200
Lewis v. Wolk, 262
Lewis v. Zell, 214
Lewis-Kures v. Edwards R. Walsh & Co., 423
Lewton v. Hower, 885
Leyenberger v. Paul, 875
Leyman Co., H. S. v. Short, 888
Li v. Yellow Cab Co., 471, 477, 496
Libbee v. Permanente Clinic, 370
Libby v. Berry, 902
Libby v. St. Louis, Iron Mountain & Southern Railroad Co., 665
Libby v. West Coast Rock Co., 396
Liber v. Flor, 208, 209, 1067
Liberty Mutual Insurance Co. v. Great Northern Railway Co., 304
Liberty National Life Insurance Co. v. Weldon, 202
Licciardi v. Molnar, 822, 831
Lichtenthal v. Gawoski, 200, 914
Lichter v. Fritsch, 203
Lichter v. Fulcher, 991
Liebel v. Montgomery Ward & Co., 792
Lieberman v. Township of Saddle River, 628
Liebhart v. Calahan, 462
Liesbosch Dredger v. S. S. Edison, 290, 1008
Life Printing & Publishing Co. v. Field, 779, 794
Lifer v. Raymond, 1050
Liff v. Schildkrout, 951
Liggett & Myers Tobacco Co. v. Cannon, 681, 682
Lightfoot v. Jennings, 794
Ligouri, People v., 127
Liljegren v. United Railways Co. of St. Louis, 42
Lilley, People v., 44
Lillie v. Thompson, 578
Lillie v. Warner Brothers Pictures, 867
Lilligren v. Burns International Detective Agency, 920

Lim, People v., 646
Limberg v. Glenwood Lumber Co., 569
Liming v. Illinois Central Railroad Co., 308
Limpus v. London General Omibus Co., 503, 505
Linares v. Edison Parking, Inc., 210
Lincenberg v. Issen, 476
Linch v. Carlson, 752
Lincoln v. Chadbourne, 642
Lincoln v. Grazer, 51
Lincoln v. Shea, 878
Lincoln City Lines, Inc. v. Schmidt, 463
Lind v. City of San Luis Obispo, 627, 648
Lind v. Schmid, 876
Lindauer v. Hill, 649
Lindberg Cadillac Co. v. Aron, 736
Linde v. Welch, 454
Lindekugel v. Spokane, Portland & Seattle Railway Co., 218
Linder v. Bidner, 915
Linder v. City of Payette, 310
Lindgren v. United States, 1040
Lindgren Plumbing Co. v. Doral Country Club, Inc., 11
Lindh v. Great Northern Railway Co., 64
Lindley v. Sink, 959
Lindquist v. Dilkes, 737
Lindquist v. Friedman's, Inc., 49, 142
Lindsay v. Acme Cement Plaster Co., 326, 346
Lindsay v. McDonnell Douglas Aircraft Co., 696
Lindsay-Strathmore Irrigation District v. Superior Court of Tulare County, 640
Line v. Spies, 780
Lineaweaver v. John Wanamaker Philadelphia, 511, 512
Linehan v. Linehan, 864
Linehan v. Nelson, 781, 783
Liney v. Chestnut Motors, Inc., 314
Lingard v. Kiraly, 989
Lingerfelt v. Winn-Dixie Texas, Inc., 419, 425, 426
Lininger v. Knight, 819
Linkenburger v. Owens, 337
Linn v. Rand, 199
Linnehan v. Sampson, 184, 198
Linney v. Maton, 846
Lion Oil Co. v. Sinclair Refining Co., 966
Lioni v. Marr, 389
Lipari v. Sears, Roebuck & Co., 384
Lipe v. Blackwelder, 137
Lipe v. Eisenlerd, 927, 928
Lipka v. United States, 1043
Lipman v. Atlantic Coast Line Railroad Co., 58
Lipman v. Brisbane Elementary School District, 823, 1046
Lipman, Wolfe & Co. v. Phoenix Assurance Co., 664
Lipnik v. Ehalt, 642
Lippold v. Kidd, 265
Lipscomb v. Shofner, 895
Lipsitz v. Schechter, 244
Lipson v. Superior Court of Orange County, 430, 431, 495, 496, 497
Liptak v. Karsner, 571
Lisle v. Lunch, 920

Lisowski v. Jaskiewicz, 855
Lister v. Campbell, 400, 405, 408, 409
Litchfield v. Browne, 730
Littell v. Argus Production Co., 723
Little v. Blue Goose Motor Coach Co., 955
Little v. Hackett, 530
Little v. Holmes, 924
Little v. McGraw, 513
Little v. McGuire, 541
Little v. Miles, 341
Little v. PPG Industries, Inc., 697
Little v. Sowers, 899
Little v. Williamson, 363
Little Rock, Mississippi River & Texas Railway Co. v. Brooks, 650
Little Rock Packing Co. v. Chicago, Burlington & Quincy Railroad Co., 315
Little Rock Traction & Electric Co. v. Morrison, 468
Little Schuylkill Navigation Railroad & Coal Co. v. Richards' Administrator, 350
Little Stores v. Isenberg, 141, 142
Littlefield v. Laughlin, 244
Littlehale v. E. I. DuPont de Nemours & Co., 184
Littlejohn v. Fitchburg Railroad Co., 5, 660
Littles v. Avis Rent-A-Car System, 524
Littman v. Bell Telephone Co. of Pennsylvania, 956
Liveright v. Max Lifsitz Furniture Co., 425
Livermore v. Batchelder, 137
Livermore v. Crane, 993
Livesey v. Stock, 15
Livezey v. Schmidt, 390
Livingston v. Adams, 549
Livingston v. Cunningham, 647
Livingston v. Davis, 626
Livingston v. Essex Investment Co., 445
Lloyd v. Farmers Coop. Store, 666
Lloyd v. Harris, 791
Lloyd v. Hough, 674
Lloyd v. Junkin, 758
Lloyd v. Loeffler, 925, 926, 928
Lloyd, Rex v., 645
Lloyd v. S.S. Kresge Co., 426
Lloyd v. State, 1048
Lloyds v. United Press International, Inc., 832
Lloyds of Minneapolis v. Smith, 337
Lo Castro v. Long Island Railroad Co., 134
Lo Rocco v. New Jersey Manufacturers Indemnity Insurance Co., 13
Lobdell v. Keene, 144
Local Dairymen's Cooperative Association v. Potvin, 990
Local Federal Savings and Loan Association of Oklahoma City v. Sickles, 968
Loch v. Confair, 253, 713
Locke v. Benton & Bowles, 780
Locke v. Johns Manville Corp., 165
Locke v. United States, 1036
Locker v. American Tobacco Co., 1013
Lockett v. Bi-State Transit Authority, 502
Lockett v. General Electric Co., 207

Lockett & Williams v. Gress Manufacturing Co., 894
Lockhart v. Bear, 899
Lockhart v. Besel, 951
Lockhart v. Western & Atlantic Railroad, 86
Lockowitz v. Melnyk, 516
Lockwood v. McCaskill, 291
Lockwood v. Setounis, 184
Lockwood v. Village of Buchanan, 1050
Lodge v. Pittsburgh & Lake Erie Railroad Co., 396
Loe v. Lenhardt, 549, 550
Loebig's Guardian v. Coca Cola Bottling Co., 247
Loesch v. R. P. Farnsworth & Co., 724
Loewer v. Harris, 738
Loewinthan v. Levine, 829
Loewnberg v. Rosenthal, 536
Loftsgaarden v. Reiling, 10
Loftus v. Dehail, 317
Loftus v. McCramie, 294
Logan v. Austin, 122
Logan v. Gardner, 734
Logan v. Hodges, 798, 833
Logan v. Reaves, 906
Logan v. St. Luke's General Hospital, 361
Logan's Super Markets, Inc. v. McCalla, 820
Loge v. United States, 1040, 1041
Loiseau v. Arp, 312
Loker v. Damon, 276
Lollar v. Dewitt, 519
Lomano v. Ideal Towel Supply Co., 314
Lomayestewa v. Our Lady of Mercy Hospital, 230, 461
Lombard v. Lennox, 794
Lombard v. Morse, 902
Lombard v. United States, 1037
Lomberg v. Renner, 414
Lomerson v. Johnston, 737
Lommori v. Milner Hotels, 444
Lomonte v. A & P Food Stores, 478
Lonardo v. Quaranta, 786
London Guarantee & Accident Co. v. Horn, 27, 989
London Iron & Metal Co. v. Abney, 430
Lone Star Gas Co. v. Kelly, 229
Lone Star Gas Co. v. Parsons, 403, 406
Loney v. McPhillips, 403
Long v. Ansell, 820
Long v. Burley State Bank, 888
Long v. City of New Boston, 183, 456
Long v. Crystal Refrigerator Co., 347
Long v. Decca Records, 867
Long v. Douthitt, 768
Long v. Forest-Fehlhaber, Joint Venture, 227, 461
Long v. Freeman, 761
Long v. International Vending Machine Co., 675, 730
Long v. Magnolia Hotel Co., 623
Long v. Mertz, 822
Long v. Moon, 515
Long v. New York Central Railroad Co., 617, 648
Long v. Omaha & Council Bluffs Street Railway Co., 311
Long v. Patterson, 379
Long v. Rucker, 967, 975

Long v. Seabrook, 1064
Long v. Sutherland-Backer Co., 404
Long v. United States, 557
Long v. Warren, 750
Long Beach, City of v. Bozek, 885, 890, 892
Long Island Jewish-Hillside Medical Center, In re Application of, 115, 116
Long-Lewis Hardware Co. v. Abston, 100
Longacre v. Reddick, 289
Longberg v. H.L. Green Co., 286
Longenecker v. Zimmerman, 75
Longmont, City of v. Swearingen, 423
Longo v. Reilly, 1006
Longo v. Tauriello, 819
Look v. Dean, 155
Loomis v. Terry, 136, 562
Looney v. McLean, 440
Loos v. Mountain Fuel Supply Co., 261
Lopard v. Symons, 99
Loper v. Askin, 920
Loper v. Morrison, 505
Lopes v. Connolly, 988
Lopes v. Narragansett Electric Co., 261
Lopez v. A/S D/S Svenborg, 510
Lopez v. Barreras, 526
Lopez v. Surchia, 38, 130
Lopez v. Townsend, 586
Lopez v. Waldrum's Estate, 935
Lopez v. Wigwam Department Stores No. 10, p. 50
Lorando v. Gethro, 588
Lorang v. Hays, 904, 911
L'Orange v. Medical Protective Co., 1028, 1029
Lord v. DeWitt, 628
Lord v. Guyot, 895
Lord, Stone & Co. v. Buchanan, 104
Lord Byron v. Johnston, 849, 863
Lord Electric Co. v. Barber Asphalt Paving Co., 661
Lord Leigh's Case, 157
Lord Mounteagle v. Countess of Worcester, 89
Lord Petre v. Heneage, 101
Lorenc v. Chemirad Corp., 363
Lorentz v. R.K.O. Radio Pictures, 781
Lorillard v. Field Enterprises, Inc., 790, 799
Lorshbough v. Township of Buzzle, 1050
Lorts v. McDonald, 717
Lorusso v. De Carlo, 404
Los Angeles & Salt Lake Railroad Co. v. Umbaugh, 959
Losee v. Buchanan, 548, 549, 550
Losi v. Natalicchio, 871
Lotan v. Cross, 88
Lothrop v. Adams, 836
Lotrich v. Life Printing & Publishing Co., 837
Lottman v. Barnett, 661
Loukz v. Hafner, 85
Louden v. City of Cincinnati, 553
Loudin v. Mohawk Airlines, Inc., 819, 992
Loudoun v. Eighth Avenue Railroad Co., 252
Lough v. John Davis & Co., 669
Lough v. Outerbridge, 1013
Loughran v. Flanders, 1049

Loui v. Oakley, 350, 351
Louis v. Blalock, 889
Louis v. Youngren, 511
Louisiana Oil Corp. v. Renno, 829
Louisville, City of v. Stuckenborg, 958
Louisville, Henderson & St. Louis Railway Co. v. Roberts, 84
Louisville & Cincinnati Packet Co. v. Rogers, 315
Louisville & E. Mail Co. v. Barnes' Administrator, 335
Louisville & Jefferson Co. v. Metropolitan Sewer District City of Louisville, 449
Louisville & Nashville Railroad Co. v. Anderson, 389
Louisville & Nashville Railroad Co. v. Arrow Transportation Co., 999
Louisville & Nashville Railroad Co. v. Bartee, 151
Louisville & Nashville Railroad Co. v. Blevins, 416
Louisville & Nashville Railroad v. Bogue, 946
Louisville & Nashville Railroad Co. v. Chapman's Administratrix, 471, 578
Louisville & Nashville Railroad Co. v. Dalton, 222
Louisville & Nashville Railroad Co. v. Daniels, 306
Louisville & Nashville Railroad Co. v. George, 482
Louisville & Nashville Railroad Co. v. Harrod's Administrator, 465
Louisville & Nashville Railroad Co. v. Jones, 291, 396
Louisville & Nashville Railroad Co. v. Joullian, 136
Louisville & Nashville Railroad Co. v. Logan's Administratrix, 14
Louisville & Nashville Railroad Co. v. McCoy, 212
Louisville & Nashville Railroad Co. v. Malone, 460
Louisville & Nashville Railroad Co. v. Patterson, 464
Louisville & Nashville Railroad Co. v. Roberts, 62
Louisville & Nashville Railroad Co. v. Scott's Administrator, 953
Louisville & Nashville Railroad Co. v. Scruggs & Echols, 375
Louisville & Nashville Railroad Co. v. Smith's Administrator, 553
Louisville & Nashville R. Co. v. Spinks, 2, 379
Louisville & Nashville Railroad Co. v. Spoonamore, 396
Louisville & Nashville Railroad v. Stephens, 951
Louisville & Nashville Railroad Co. v. Tomlinson, 529
Louisville & Nashville Railroad Co. v. Vanderpool, 398
Louisville & Nashville Railroad Co. v. Vaughn, 411
Louisville & Nashville Railroad Co. v. Weldon, 716
Louisville & Nashville Railroad Co. v. York, 570
Louisville & Nashville Railroad Co. v. Young, 570
Louisville Belt & Iron Co. v. Hart, 956
Louisville Press Co. v. Tennelly, 800
Louisville Railway Co. v. Sweeney, 68
Louisville Taxicab & Transfer Co. v. Ingle, 791
Louisville Times v. Stivers, 784
Louisville Trust Co. v. Horn, 395
Louisville Trust Co. v. Johns-Manville Product Corp., 167
Louisville Trust Co. v. Morgan, 270
Louisville Trust Co. v. Nutting, 408
Louka v. Park Entertainments, 776, 797
Love v. Cardwell, 455
Love v. Detroit, Jackson & Chicago Railroad Co., 958

Love Petroleum Co. v. Jones, 638
Lovejoy v. Murray, 330
Lovejoy v. Whitcomb, 830
Loveland v. Nelson, 242
Loveland Co., Petition of S.C., 999
Lovell v. Hammond Co., 91
Lovell v. Southern Railway Co., 407
Lovell Co., John W. v. Houghton, 826, 966
Lovick v. Marion, 388
Lovinger v. Hix Green Buick Co., 94
Low v. Bouverie, 733
Low v. Elwell, 144
Low v. Grand Trunk Railway Co., 429
Lowden v. Shoffner Mercantile Co., 307
Lowe v. City of Gastonia, 423
Lowe v. De Hoog, 790
Lowe v. General Motors Corp., 221
Lowe v. Kohn, 764
Lowe Foundation v. Northern Trust Co., 1008
Lowell v. Boston & L.R. Corp., 509
Lowen v. Hilton, 890
Lowenburg v. Rosenthal, 110
Lowery v. Dingmann, 767, 769
Lowery v. Louisville & Northwest Railroad Co., 105
Lowery v. McTier, 87
Lowery v. Manhattan R. Co., 198
Lowery v. Wade Hampton Co., 937
Lowney v. Knott, 99
Lowry v. Standard Oil Co., 46
Lowry v. Vedder, 834
Loyd v. Pearse, 794
Loynes v. Loring B. Hall Co., 490, 570
Lu May v. Van Drisse Motors, 576
Lubin v. Iowa City, 550
Lubitz v. Wells, 170
Lubore v. Pittsburgh Courier Publishing Co., 799
Luby v. Bennett, 891
Lucas v. Ambridge Yellow Cab Co., 532
Lucas v. City of Juneau, 310
Lucas v. Durrence, 96
Lucas v. Hamm, 1008
Lucas v. Long, 753
Lucas v. Southern Pacific Railroad, 218
Luce v. Hartman, 308
Luce, United States v., 354
Lucio v. Curran, 332
Luckett v. Cohen, 890
Luckey v. Roberts, 93, 94
Ludden v. Leavitt, 103
Ludowese v. Amidon, 766
Ludwick v. Penny, 899
Ludwig v. Johnson, 216
Ludwig v. Kirby, 574
Lueck v. Heisler, 150
Lueddecke v. Chevrolet Motor Co., 1021
Luedeke v. Chicago & North Western Railroad Co., 382
Luengene v. Consumers' Light, Heat & Power Co., 347
Lueptow v. Schraeder, 890
Luetzke v. Roberts, 767
Lufkin v. Cutting, 941

TABLE OF CASES

Lufkin v. Zane, 434, 437
Luger v. Windell, 587
Lugosi v. Universal Pictures, 1020
Luhmann v. Schaefer, 91
Luick v. Driscoll, 798, 824
Lujan v. Reed, 198
Luka v. Lowrie, 117
Lukas v. J.C. Penney Co., 47, 142
Lukas v. Tarpilauskas, 985, 996
Lukaszewicz v. Ortho Pharmaceutical Corp., 221
Luke v. Du Pree, 981
Luke v. Hill, 923
Luke v. Mercantile Acceptance Corp., 14
Lukus, State v., 147
Lumbermen's Mutual Casualty Co. v. United States Fidelity & Guarantee Co., 339
Lumbermen's Reciprocal Association v. Behnken, 572
Lumby v. Allday, 792
Lumley v. Gye, 980, 981, 983
Lumpkin v. Streifel, 420, 509
Lumsden v. L.A. Thompson Scenic Railway Co., 485
Luna v. Seattle Times Co., 846
Lunday v. Vogelmann, 1046
Lundberg v. Hagen, 958
Lunderberg v. Bierman, 342
Lundgren v. Western State Bank of Duluth, 896
Lundin v. Post Publishing Co., 799
Lundquist v. Kennecott Copper Co., 218
Lundy v. Whiting Corp., 453
Lunnie v. Gadapee, 752
Lurssen v. Lloyd, 621
Lusby v. Lusby, 904, 909
Lusitania, The, 318
Lusk v. Lusk, 595, 906
Lussan v. Grain Dealers Mutual Insurance Co., 163
Luster v. Luster, 595
Luthringer v. Moore, 550
Lutz v. Independent Construction Co., 11
Lutz v. Shelby Mutual Insurance Co., 197
Lutz v. United States, 220
Luzenberg v. O'Malley, 823
Lybrand v. State Co., 837
Lyda v. Cooper, 141
Lydecker v. Board of Chosen Freeholders of Passaic County, 724
Lykins v. Hamrick, 122, 124
Lyle v. Waddle, 802
Lyles v. State, 856, 861, 868
Lyman v. Dale, 542
Lyman v. Herrmann, 437
Lyman v. New England Newspaper Publishing Co., 775
Lynch v. Fisher, 280, 291, 292, 309
Lynch v. International Harvester Co., 695
Lynch v. Johnson, 1057, 1058
Lynch v. Knight, 55, 360, 795, 844, 916
Lynch v. Lyons, 774, 787
Lynch v. Metropolitan Elevated Railway Co., 142
Lynch v. Motel Enterprises, Inc., 410
Lynch v. Nurdin, 328, 400
Lynch v. Precision Machine Shop, Ltd., 250

Lynch v. Richardson, 715
Lynch v. Rosenthal, 178
Lynchard v. State, 149
Lynden Transport, Inc. v. Haragan, 244, 248
Lyne v. Nicholls, 966, 976
Lynn, Commonwealth v., 139
Lynn v. Hooper, 648
Lynn Mining Co. v. Kelly, 553
Lynn Open Air Theatre, Inc. v. Sea Crest Cadillac-Pontiac, Inc., 630
Lynott v. Pearson, 792
Lynwood v. Decatur Park District, 596
Lyon v. Barrett, 440, 441
Lyon v. Clark, 674
Lyon v. Daily Telegraph, 832
Lyon v. Izen, 924
Lyon v. Lash, 802
Lyons v. Davy-Pocahontas Coal Co., 875
Lyons v. Durocher, 334
Lyons v. Fairmont Real Estate Co., 83
Lyons v. Merrick, 540
Lyons v. Redding Construction Co., 496
Lyons v. Wagers, 438
Lyons v. Worley, 50, 51
Lyons v. Zale Jewelry Co., 62
Lyons Sons & Co. v. Gulliver, 645
Lyra Shipping Co., Limited, In re, 1001
Lysaght, Limited v. Lehigh Valley Railroad Co., 315
Lyshak v. City of Detroit, 398
Lyster v. Berberich, 744
Lytell v. Hushfield, 453
Lytton v. Baird, 874

M

MacArtor v. Graylyn Crest III Swim Club, 636
MacBeth v. Gerber's, Inc., 1013
MacBryde v. Burnett, 95
MacClure v. Accident & Casualty Insurance Co., 588
MacConnell v. Hill, 180
MacDonald v. MacDonald, 903
MacDonald v. Musick, 875
MacDonald v. Reich & Lievre, 736
MacDonough v. A.S. Beck Shoe Corp., 781
MacDonough v. F.W. Woolworth Co., 420
MacDougall v. Pennsylvania Power & Light Co., 195
MacFadden v. Anthony, 799
MacFadzen v. Olivant, 926
MacGibbon v. Robinson, 562
MacGregor v. Bradshaw, 521
MacInnis v. National Herald Printing Co., 776, 792
MacIntosh v. Dunn, 829
MacIntosh v. Great Northern Railway Co., 269
MacKenzie v. Fitchburg Paper Co., 550
MacKerron v. Madura, 991
MacLeod v. Tribune Publishing Co., 778, 781, 796
MacPherson v. Buick Motor Co., 357, 678, 682, 683, 685, 695
MacRae v. Afro-American Co., 775, 776, 781
McAbee v. Edwards, 1008

TABLE OF CASES

McAdams v. Chicago, Rock Island & Puget Sound Co., 349
McAdams v. Sutton, 348
McAdams v. Windham, 114
McAdoo v. Richmond & Danville Railroad Co., 210
McAfee v. Cargill, Inc., 690
McAfee, Commonwealth v., 157
McAfee v. Feller, 819
McAleavy v. Lowe, 581
McAleer v. Good, 49
McAllaster v. Bailey, 92
McAllister v. Pennsylvania Railroad Co., 321, 345, 348
McAllister v. Workmen's Compensation Appeals Board, 267
McAlpine v. AAMCO Automatic Transmissions, Inc., 990
McAndrew v. Scranton Republican Publishing Co., 778
McAndrews v. Collerd, 552, 644
McAndrews v. Roy, 867
McAnelly v. Chapman, 95
McArthur v. Johnson, 731
McAuley v. State, 132
McBee v. Fulton, 837
McBerry v. Ivie, 717
McBride v. Alles, 894
McBride v. Ledoux, 827
McBride v. Scott, 333
McBroom v. Wolsleger, 525
McCabe v. New Jersey Turnpike Authority, 1043
McCahill v. New York Transportation Co., 291
McCain Manufacturing Corp. v. Rockwell International Corp., 509
McCall v. Davis, 736
McCall v. McCall, 904
McCallie v. New York Cent. Railroad Co., 461
McCallion v. Missouri Pacific Railway Co., 717
McCane v. Wokoun, 743
McCann v. Anchor Line, 421
McCann v. Atlas Supply Co., 696
McCann v. Baton Rouge General Hospital, 189
McCann v. Chasm Power Co., 626
McCann v. New York Stock Exchange, 1010
McCann v. Sadowski, 176
McCants v. Chenault, 528
McCardle v. McGinley, 895
McCarthy v. Bunker Hill & Sullivan Mining & Coal Co., 631, 641
McCarthy v. Cincinnati Enquirer, 832
McCarthy v. Ference, 390
McCarthy v. Kenosha Auto Transport Corp., 251
McCarthy v. Kitchen, 878
McCarthy v. Maxon, 439
McCarthy v. Port of New York Authority, 432
McCarthy v. Thompson Square Theatre Co., 387
McCarthy v. Timmins, 505
McCarty v. Hosang, 251
McCarty v. Natural Carbonic Gas Co., 635
McCauley v. Logan, 170, 311
McCauley v. Steward, 504
McChargue v. Black Grading Contractors, Inc., 183

McChesney v. Wilson, 137
McClafferty v. Philp, 885
McClaim v. Harveston, 659
McClain v. Lewiston Interstate Fair & Racing Association, 539
McClallen v. Adams, 115
McClannan v. Chaplain, 151
McClarren v. Buck, 252
McClarty v. Bickel, 872
McClendon v. Citizens & Southern National Bank, 170, 201
McClendon v. Coverdale, 821
McClendon v. T.L. James & Co., 671
McClenny v. Inverarity, 898
McClinton v. White, 950
McClosky v. Martin, 621
McCloud v. Leavitt Corp., 723
McCluer v. Super Maid Cook-Ware Corp., 988
McClung v. Johnson, 166
McClung v. Louisville & Nashville Railroad Co., 620, 635
McClure v. Hoopeston Gas & Electric Co., 303
McClure v. Johnson, 661, 667, 941
McClure v. Stretch, 817
McClure, State ex rel. v. Dinwiddie, 338
McClusky v. Duncan, 425
McComb City v. Hayman, 403
McCombs v. Hegarty, 126
McComish v. DeSoi, 715
McConnell v. Herron, 228
McConville v. State Farm Mutual Auto Insurance Co., 210, 489, 493, 594
McCoombs v. Tuttle, 786
McCord v. Green, 459
McCord Rubber Co. v. St. Joseph Water Co., 550
McCordic v. Crawford, 428
McCormick v. Louis Weber & Co., 1003
McCown v. International Harvester Co., 712
McCoy v. Cornish, 576
McCoy v. Wesley Hospital & Nurse Training School, 664
McCracken v. West, 743
McCrary v. State, 154
McCrary v. United States, 342
McCrary Co., J.B. v. Phillips, 77
McCray v. City of Lake Louisville, 149
McCray v. Hunter, 526
McCready v. United Iron and Steel Co., 687
McCreary & Barlow v. Gaines, 94
McCreight v. Davey Tree Expert Co., 764
McCrillis v. Allen, 93
McCrory Stores Corp. v. Stachell, 142
McCrossen v. Moorhead, 914
McCuddin v. Dickinson, 841
McCue v. Deppert, 995
McCue v. Klein, 114, 124
McCullen v. Hereford State Bank, 94
McCulley v. Cherokee Amusement Co., 409, 411
McCulloch v. Goodrich, 126
McCullough v. Beech Aircraft Corp., 947

McCune v. Norwich City Gas Co., 27
McCurdy v. Hughes, 837
McCurdy v. Wallblom Furniture & Carpet Co., 96, 97
McCurry v. Young Men's Christian Association, 412, 413, 418
McDaniel v. Atlanta Coca-Cola Bottling Co., 855
McDaniel v. Bullard, 943
McDaniel v. Chicago, Rock Island & Pacific Railway Co., 570
McDaniel v. McNeil Laboratories, Inc., 701
McDavitt v. Boyer, 817
McDermott v. McClain, 317
McDermott v. Sway, 73
McDermott v. W.T. Grant Co., 52
McDevitt v. Standard Oil Co., 712
McDonald v. Bennett, 14
McDonald v. Camas Prairie Railroad Co., 661
McDonald v. Castle, 539
McDonald v. City of Red Wing, 146
McDonald v. First National Bank of McKeesport, 673
McDonald v. Franchere, 42
McDonald v. Fryberger, 199
McDonald v. Goodman, 759
McDonald v. Jodry, 539
McDonald v. Lastinger, 758, 761
McDonald v. Lee, 829
McDonald v. Louisville & Nashville Railroad Co., 572, 575
McDonald v. Massachusetts General Hospital, 1070
McDonald v. Milanecki, 448
McDonald v. Nugent, 790
McDonald v. Robinson, 268, 452
McDonald v. Snelling, 304
McDonald's Corp. v. Grissom, 419
McDonnell v. Cambridge Railroad Co., 621
McDonnell v. Pittsfield & North Adams Railroad Corp., 540
McDonnell v. Wasenmiller, 723
McDonough v. Gilman, 434
McDonough v. Williams, 738, 770
McDougall v. Claridge, 826
McDougall v. Snider, 564
McDowell v. Davis, 200, 267
McDowell v. Federal Tea Co., 227
McDowell v. Hurner, 526
McDowell, People v., 781
McDowell v. Village of Preston, 317
McEachern v. Richmond, 228
McElrath v. Electric Investment Co., 762, 763
McElroy v. Boise Cascade Corp., 461
McElroy v. Capron, 912, 913
McElroy v. Catholic Press Co., 882
McEntee v. New Jersey Steamboat Co., 100
McEvoy v. American Pool Corp., 304
McEvoy v. Helikson, 925
McFadden v. Bancroft Hotel Corp., 383
McFall v. Compagnie Maritime Belge, 341, 342
McFarland v. Hueners, 758
McFarland v. News & Observer Publishing Co., 332
McFarlane v. City of Niagara Falls, 566, 644, 651

McFarlin v. Hall, 384
McGann v. Allen, 897, 900
McGann v. Hamilton, 75
McGannon v. Chicago & North Western Railroad Co., 327, 329, 352
McGarr v. National & Providence Worsted Mills, 935
McGarrahan v. New York, New Haven & Hartford Railroad Co., 294
McGarry v. Missouri Pacific Railway Co., 880
McGaughey v. Haines, 410
McGee v. Board of Education, 485
McGee, State v., 128
McGehee v. Norfolk & Southern Railway Co., 562, 564
McGettigan v. National Bank of Washington, 318, 401, 403, 404
McGill v. Holman, 140
McGill v. Lazzaro, 944
McGlue v. Weekly Publications, Inc., 800
McGlynn v. Schultz, 93
McGonigle v. Victor H. Belleisle Co., 96, 97
McGovern, Commonwealth v., 643, 644
McGovern v. Martz, 820
McGovern v. Van Riper, 855, 864
McGowan v. Devonshire Hall Apartments, 208
McGrady v. Rosenbaum, 925, 929
McGranahan v. Dahar, 1058
McGrandy, People v., 128
McGrath v. American Cyanamid Co., 493
McGrath v. Sullivan, 920
McGrath Building Co. v. City of Bettendorf, 1053
McGregor v. Camden, 552
McGregor v. McGregor, 922, 1007
McGuffey v. Pierce-Fordyce Oil Association, 552
McGuffin v. Smith, 752
McGuinness v. Hargiss, 972
McGuire v. Adkins, 797
McGuire v. Almy, 1072
McGuire v. Amyx, 146
McGuire v. Armitage, 893
McGuire v. Bell Telephone Co. of Buffalo, 569
McGuire v. Dalton Co., 723
McGuire v. Gerstley, 995
McGuire v. Hartford Buick Co., 510
McGuire v. Rix, 117
McGuire v. United States, 151
McGuire v. Vaughan, 842
McHargue v. Fayette Coal & Feed Co., 757
McHenry v. Ford Motor Co., 550
McIlhenny Co. v. Gaidry, 974
McIlvoy v. Cockran, 133
McIntosh v. Brimmer, 640
McIntosh v. Bullard, Earnheart & Magness, 111
McIntosh v. Milano, 384
McIntyre v. Everest & Jennings, Inc., 686
McIntyre v. Kansas City Coca-Cola Bottling Co., 694
McIntyre v. McIntyre, 402, 404, 406, 407, 409
McIntyre v. Sholty, 1073
McIver v. Russell, 874
McKay v. Anheuser-Busch, Inc., 728

McKay v. Enid, 649, 650
McKay v. Southern Bell Telegraph & Telephone Co., 323, 355
McKay v. Syracuse Rapid Transit Railway Co., 958
McKee v. Delaware & H. Canal Co., 68
McKee v. Gratz, 114
McKee v. Hughes, 833, 989, 1011
McKee v. New Idea, Inc., 576
McKee v. Tourtellotte, 571
McKee v. Trisler, 539, 560
McKee v. Wilson, 789
McKeel v. Latham, 798
McKeesport Sawmill Co. v. Pennsylvania, 136, 642
McKelvey v. McKelvey, 904, 905
McKenna v. Allied Chemical & Dye Corp., 245
McKenna v. Austin, 334, 335, 339
McKenna v. Pacific Electric Railway Co., 554
McKenna v. Stephens, 199
McKenna v. Volkswagenwerk, A.G., 179
McKenry v. Western Union Telegraph Co., 1008
McKenzie v. Fairmont Food Co., 401
McKenzie v. Minis, 73
McKenzie v. Pacific Gas and Electric Co., 78, 550
McKenzie v. Soden Mineral Springs Co., 850, 853
McKenzie v. Wm. J. Burns International Detective Agency, 833
McKeon v. Chicago, Milwaukee & St. Paul Railway Co., 660
McKeon v. Goldstein, 532
McKeown v. Johnson, 912
McKern v. Beck, 904
McKibbin v. Pierce, 665
McKinney v. City and County of San Francisco, 568
McKinney v. Cooper, 818, 819
McKinney v. Frodsham, 254
McKinney v. Nash, 186, 192
McKinney v. Yelavich, 219
McKinnon v. Skil Corp., 225
McKinzie v. Huckaby, 59, 855
McKissick v. R. Connelly Jewelers, Inc., 239
McKnight v. Hasbrouck, 830
McKown v. Hunter, 882
McLain v. Boise Cascade Corp., 856
McLain v. McLain, 904
McLane v. Northwest Natural Gas Co., 551, 563, 567
McLaughlin v. Copeland, 1010
McLaughlin v. Cowley, 818
McLaughlin v. Fisher, 782
McLaughlin v. Siegel, 341
McLaughlin v. Waite, 103
McLean v. Andrews Hardwood Co., 471
McLean v. Brett, 560
McLean v. Colf, 138
McLean v. Goodyear Tire and Rubber Co., 695
McLean, People v., 150, 154
McLean v. Sanders, 48
McLearn v. Hill, 734
McLendon v. Hampton Cotton Mills Co., 411
McLennon v. Richardson, 156
McLeod v. American Publishing Co., 848

McLeod v. Grant County School District, 158, 202, 305
McLeod v. Jones, 140
McLeod v. Linde Air Products Co., 703
McLeod v. St. Aubyn, 803, 811
McLeod v. Whitten, 488
McLery v. McLery, 922
McLoughlin v. New York Edison Co., 142
McMahon v. Bergeson, 365
McMahon v. City of Virginia Beach, 379
McMahon v. May Department Stores Co., 892
McMahon v. Pearlman, 586
McManamon v. Hanover Township, 172
McManus v. Crickett, 505
McManus v. Getter Trucking Co., 456
McManus v. Rogers, 397
McManus v. Southern Railway Co., 648
McMartin v. Saemisch, 527
McMaster v. Ford Motor Co., 1010
McMillan v. Kuehnle, 644
McMillen v. Steele, 461
McMorries v. Hudson Sales Corp., 976
McMorris v. Simpson, 101
McMullen v. M. & M. Hotel Co., 425
McMurdie v. Underwood, 319
McMurrey Corp. v. Yawn, 133, 955
McNab v. Wallin, 441
McNair v. Goodwin, 335
McNall v. Farmers Insurance Group, 181
McNally v. Addis, 937
McNally v. Burleigh, 834
McNally v. Colwell, 265, 544
McNally v. Liebowitz, 184, 455, 460
McNally, State v., 149
McNamara v. Feihe, 734
McNamara v. Goldan, 782
McNamara v. Pabst, 872
McNamara v. Prather, 524
McNamee v. Hunt, 516
McNary v. Chamberlain, 991, 993
McNatt v. McRae, 127
McNaughton v. Smith, 665
McNayr v. Kelly, 821, 822
McNeely v. M. & M. Supermarkets, Inc., 169
McNeil v. Mullin, 122
McNeill v. Brooks, 101
McNeill v. Durham & Charlotte Railroad Co., 231
McNeill v. United States, 189
McNeill v. Wabash Railroad Co., 666
McNelis v. Bruce, 921
McNevins v. Lowe, 657
McNichol v. Grandy, 803
McNulty v. Hurley, 423
McNutt Oil & Refining Co. v. D'Ascoli, 1003, 1004
McPartland v. State, 590
McPherson v. Daniels, 799
McPherson v. Ellis, 187, 188, 189, 192
McPherson v. James, 539
McPherson v. McCarrick, 59
McPherson v. Sunset Speedway, Inc., 485
McPherson v. Tamiami Trail Tours, Inc., 202

McPherson v. Western Union Telegraph Co., 1000
McPheters v. Loomis, 393, 395
McPheters v. Page, 93, 101
McPike v. Scheuerman, 951
McQuacker v. Goddard, 543
McQuaide v. Bridgeport Brass Co., 690
McQuarters v. Ducote, 919
McQuiggan v. Ladd, 125
McQuillen v. Dobbs, 244
McQuire v. Western Morning News Co., 832
McRae v. Bandy, 94
McRae v. Brant, 874, 882
McSwain v. United States, 911
McVeigh v. Minneapolis & Rainy River Railroad Co., 960
McVey v. Marratt, 331
McWhorter v. City of New Smyrna Beach Utilities Commission, 245
Maahs v. Schultz, 920
Maas v. Perkins, 350
Mabardy v. McHugh, 751
Mabry v. Kettering, 855
Macard, People v., 127
Macartney v. Westbrook, 218
Macauley v. Tierney, 1013, 1024
Macbeth-Evans Glass Co. v. Schnelbach, 1022
Macca v. General Telephone Co. of Northwest, Inc., 653
Macdonald v. Roeth, 768
Macey v. James, 191
Macfadden's Publications, Inc. v. Turner, 809
Machesky v. Bizzell, 1026
Mack v. Hugger Brothers Construction Co., 504
Mack v. Precast Industries, Inc., 456
Mack, Miller Candle Co. v. MacMillan Co., 974
Mackay v. Benjamin Franklin Realty & Holding Co., 92
Mackin v. United States, 789
Maclean v. Scripps, 834
Maclenan v. Segar, 543
Macomber v. Kinney, 734
Macon, Succession of, 98
Macon v. Seaward Construction Co., 478, 938
Macon Coca-Cola Bottling Co. v. Chancey, 249
Macquarie, Regina v., 47
Macurda v. Lewiston Journal Co., 782
Maday v. Yellow Taxi Co., 475
Madda v. Reliance Insurance Co., 891
Madden v. Brown, 140
Madden v. Queens County Jockey Club, 662
Maddox v. Queen, 527
Maddran v. Mullendore, 132
Maddux v. Donaldson, 347, 351
Madget v. Madget, 902
Madho v. Akaji, 543
Madison v. Deseret Livestock Co., 366
Madison v. Ducktown Sulphur, Copper & Iron Co., 630, 631
Madison v. Neuberger, 920
Madison v. United States, 1040, 1041, 1042
Madisonville, City of v. Poole, 492
Madry v. State, 128

Madsen v. East Jordan Irrigation Co., 562
Maestas v. Overton, 903, 904
Maffei v. Incorporated Town of Kemmerer, 596
Magar v. Hammond, 397
Magay v. Claflin-Sumner Coal Co., 303, 388
Magee v. Holland, 924, 925
Magee v. Omansky, 649, 650
Magelo v. Roundup Coal Mining Co., 817
Magenheimer v. State ex rel. Dalton, 1067
Maggard v. McKelvey, 372
Magic City Steel & Metal Corp. v. Mitchell, 106
Magierowski v. Buckley, 930
Maglin v. Peoples City Bank, 438, 440
Maglio v. New York Herald Co., 966
Magmer v. Renk, 895
Magness v. Pledger, 819
Magnin v. Dinsmore, 99
Magnolia Coca Cola Bottling Co. v. Jordan, 367, 368
Magnuson v. O'Dea, 924
Magouirk v. Western Union Telegraph Co., 58
Magowan v. Rickey, 885
Magrine v. Krasnica, 720
Magrine v. Spector, 720
Maguire v. Maguire, 763
Mahaffey v. Ahl, 183, 200
Mahaffey v. McMahon, 894
Mahaffey v. Official Detective Stories, Inc., 778
Mahan v. Adam, 49
Mahan v. Doggett, 639
Mahan v. State of New York, to Use of Carr, 176
Mahaney v. Hunter Enterprises, 913
Mahan-Jellico Coal Co. v. Dulling, 445
Mahnke v. Moore, 64, 906
Mahone v. Autry, 635
Mahone v. McGraw-Edison Co., 340
Mahoney v. Beatman, 278, 459
Mahoney v. Belford, 848
Mahoney v. Roberts, 1003
Mahurin v. Harding, 740
Mahurin v. Lockhart, 391
Maichle v. Jonovic, 125
Maidman v. Jewish Publications, Inc., 791
Mail v. M.R. Smith Lumber & Shingle Co., 405
Mailand v. Mailand, 39, 41, 46
Mailhot v. Travelers Insurance Co., 20
Maille v. Lord, 505
Main v. Lehman, 425
Maine v. James Maine & Sons Co., 911
Mains v. Whiting, 791
Mainstee Bank & Trust Co. v. McGowan, 217
Maitland v. Twin City Aviation Corp., 81, 558
Major v. Burlington Cedar Rapids & Northern Railroad Co., 945
Major v. Waverly & Ogden, Inc., 227
Maki v. St. Luke's Hospital Association, 675, 730, 770
Makower v. Kinney System, 483
Malachy v. Soper, 963, 966, 971
Malatesta v. Lowry, 413, 424
Malco, Inc. v. Midwest Aluminum Sales, Inc., 15
Malcolm v. Little, 144

TABLE OF CASES 1189

Malcolmson v. Scott, 150
Malcom v. Spoor, 9, 151
Malczewski v. New Orleans Railway & Light Co., 58
Maldonado v. Southern Pacific Transportation Co., 381
Maleverer v. Spinke, 146
Malevich v. Hakola, 995
Malin v. Consolidated Rail Corp., 415, 422
Maliniemi v. Gronlund, 154
Mallett v. Taylor, 538
Malley v. Lane, 130
Malloy v. Chicago, Milwaukee & St. Paul Railway Co., 872, 885
Malloy v. Lane Construction Co., 553
Malloy v. New York Real Estate Association, 229
Malloy v. Starin, 542, 568
Malo v. Willis, 431, 432
Malone v. Belcher, 895, 898, 900
Malone v. Laksey, 621, 622
Malone v. Monongahela Valley Traction Co., 291
Malone v. St. Louis-San Francisco Railroad Co., 218
Malone v. Topfer, 928
Maloney v. Rath, 204, 228, 512
Maloof v. Post Publishing Co., 799
Maltman v. Sauer, 430
Man v. Warner Brothers, Inc., 832
Manasco v. Walley, 847
Manbeck v. Ostrowski, 830
Manchester Insurance & Indemnity Co. v. Ring, 504
Mancini, State v., 153
Mandal v. Hoffman Construction Co., 993, 997, 1001
Mandell v. Pivnick, 618, 619, 644
Manders v. Williams, 104
Mandolidis v. Elkins Industries, Inc., 211, 212, 214
Manfredonia v. American Airlines, Inc., 202
Mangan's Administrator v. Louisville Electric Light Co., 550
Manger v. Kree Institute of Electrolysis, Inc., 852, 863, 867
Mangini v. Southeastern Pennsylvania Transportation Authority, 202
Mangione v. Dimino, 418
Mangum, City of v. Brownlee, 542, 565, 568
Manhart v. Los Angeles, 954
Manhattan Egg Co. v. Seaboard Terminal & Refrigeration Co., 664
Manie v. Matson Oldsmobile-Cadillac Co., 361
Manila School District No. 15 v. Sanders, 314
Manion v. Jewel Tea Co., 801
Manitowoc Malting Co. v. Milwaukee Malting Co., 1016
Mankin v. Scala Theodrome Co., 998
Manks v. Moore, 490, 571
Manley v. Exposition Cotton Mills, 374, 662
Manley v. Horton, 517
Manley v. New York Telephone Co., 248
Manly v. Ohio Shoe Co., 744
Mann v. Cook, 525
Mann v. Leake & Nelson Co., 722
Mann v. Roosevelt Shop, 59, 776
Mann v. Stanley, 542
Mann v. State, 1051

Man Boudoir Car Co. v. Dupre, 291
Mannaugh v. J.C. Penney Co., 141
Manning v. Finn, 878
Manning v. Genesee River & Lake Ontario Steamboat Co., 572
Manning v. Grimsley, 38, 39
Manning v. Noa, 457
Manning v. 1234 Corp., 664
Manning v. Wells, 88
Manning v. Yokas, 581
Mannix v. Portland Telegram, 837
Manny v. Wilson, 95
Manola v. Stevens, 850
Mansell v. Webb, 544, 547, 548
Mansfield v. Wagner Electric Manufacturing Co., 226, 231
Mansfield, City of v. Brister, 634
Manson v. Wabash Railroad Co., 149
Mansur v. Eubanks, 436, 446
Mantia v. Kaminski, 212, 214
Mantle Lamp Co. v. Rucker, 756
Manton v. Brocklebank, 542, 561
Manufacturing Co., Rowe v. Curtis-Straub Co., 757
Manvell v. Thomson, 927, 928
Marathon Oil Co. v. Sterner, 245, 248
Marble v. Chapin, 780
Marble v. Jensen, 40
Marble v. Ross, 562
Marbury Lumber Co. v. Jones, 954
Marbury Lumber Co. v. Westbrook, 938
Marbury Management, Inc. v. Kohn, 503
March v. Cacioppo, 63
Marcuchi v. Norfolk & Western Railway Co., 153
Marcum, Commonwealth v., 156
Marcum v. State Automobile Mutual Insurance Co., 588
Marcum v. United States, 182
Marek v. Zanol Products Co., 867
Marengo v. Roy, 201
Marengo Cave Co. v. Ross, 82
Mares v. New Mexico Public Service Co., 245
Margaret Ann Super Markets v. Dent, 48
Margolis v. National Bellas Hess Co., 1021
Margosian v. United States Airlines, Inc., 73, 557
Mariani v. Nanni, 576
Marier v. Memorial Rescue Serv., Inc., 473
Marietta v. Cliffs Ridge, Inc., 194
Marietta Corp., Martin v. Evening Star Newspaper Co., 970
Marin Municipal Water District v. Northwestern Pacific Railroad Co., 551
Marine Insurance Co. v. Strecker, 723
Mariner, The, 304
Marinopoliski v. Irish, 426
Mariorenzi v. Joseph DiPonte, Inc., 433
Mark v. Merz, 872
Markarian v. Pagano, 249
Markart v. Zeimer, 119
Markel v. Scovil Manufacturing Co., 1019
Market State Bank v. Farmers' Savings Bank of Meservey, 91

TABLE OF CASES

Markland v. Baltimore & Ohio Railroad Co., 200
Markley v. Whitman, 42
Marks v. City of New York, 935
Marks v. Bell Telephone Co. of Pennsylvania, 855
Marks v. Hastings, 872, 879
Marks v. Jaffa, 850, 864
Marks v. Stein, 732, 770
Marlar v. Bill, 158
Marlatte v. Weickgenant, 898, 899
Marlin v. Drury, 763
Marlin Fire Arms Co. v. Shields, 965, 976
Marlor v. Ball, 542
Marlow v. Conway Iron Works, 483
Marlow v. Weekes, 84
Marlowe, State v., 128
Marohn v. Burnham Van Services, Inc., 484
Maroulis v. Elliot, 351
Marquart v. Toledo, Peoria & Western Railroad Co., 430
Marquet v. La Duke, 563
Marquis v. Benfer, 135, 136
Marriott v. Williams, 124, 329
Marron, State ex rel. v. Compere, 644
Marrone v. Washington Jockey Club, 47, 375, 662
Mars v. Delaware & Hudson Canal Co., 312
Mars v. Meadville Telephone Co., 317
Marsalis v. La Salle, 380
Marsh v. Billings, 970, 1016
Marsh v. Colby, 114
Marsh v. Hand, 539, 541
Marsh v. Hawkins, 1066
Marsh v. Interstate & Ocean Transportation Co., 456
Marsh v. Koons, 561
Marsh Wood Products Co. v. Babcock & Wilcox Co., 185, 195, 535, 684
Marshall v. Dehaven, 1008
Marshall v. Gunter, 819
Marshall v. Mastadon, Inc., 445
Marshall v. Michel Grain Co. v. Kansas City & Fort Scott & Memphis Railway Co., 95
Marshall v. National Police Gazette Corp., 781, 782
Marshall v. Nugent, 299, 308, 454
Marshall v. Ranne, 462, 491
Marshall v. Suburban Dairy Co., 245
Marshall v. Welwood, 548, 550
Marshfield Land & Lumber Co. v. John Week Lumber Co., 27
Martell v. White, 994
Martello v. Hawley, 336
Martens v. Reilly, 984
Martin v. Atlantic Coast Line Railroad, 950
Martin v. Ball, 920
Martin v. Bell, 210
Martin v. British Museum Trustees, 803, 810
Martin v. Carbide & Carbon Chemicals Corp., 120
Martin v. Castner-Knott Dry Goods Co., 142
Martin v. Cedar Lake Ice Co., 892
Martin v. City of Albany, 884, 895
Martin v. City of Asbury Park, 438
Martin v. City of New Orleans, 197
Martin v. Costa, 130

Martin v. Cunningham, 309
Martin v. Dorton, 859, 860
Martin v. Edwards Laboratories, 165
Martin v. F.I.Y. Theatre Co., 858
Martin v. George Hyman Construction Co., 461, 493
Martin v. Green, 94
Martin v. Hardesty, 123
Martin v. Hertz Corp., 453
Martin v. Herzog, 221, 230
Martin v. Houck, 50, 154
Martin v. Jansen, 42
Martin v. Johnson Publishing Co., 775, 862, 863, 864
Martin v. Jones, 398
Martin v. Lincoln Park West Corp., 47
Martin v. Maine Central Railroad Co., 734
Martin v. Mansfeldt, 949
Martin v. Martin, 643
Martin v. Mason, 101
Martin v. Morris, 123
Martin v. Nelson, 229
Martin v. New Metropolitan Fiction, 862
Martin v. New York & New England Railroad Co., 544
Martin v. North Star Iron Works, 304
Martin v. Payne, 926, 927
Martin, People v., 153
Martin v. Platt, 985, 990
Martin v. Puget Sound Electric Railway Co., 518
Martin v. Rexford, 890
Martin v. Reynolds Metals Co., 71, 245, 977
Martin v. Setter, 332, 334
Martin v. Shea, 418
Martin v. Sikes, 102
Martin, State v., 43
Martin v. Sterkx, 992, 1003
Martin v. Sutter, 793
Martin v. The Picayune, 809
Martin v. Union Pacific Railroad Co., 72
Martin v. United Security Services, 958
Martin v. United States, 207, 447
Martin v. Western Union Railroad Co., 460
Martin Theatres of Texas, Inc. v. Puryear, 419, 426
Martinez v. Dixie Carriers, Inc. 686
Martinez v. Gerber, 998
Martinez v. Lazaroff, 434
Martinez v. State, 1063
Martinez v. Teague, 245, 247, 363
Martinson v. Scherbel, 228
Marvin v. Marvin, 923
Marx v. Standard Oil Co., 438
Marx Productions, Inc., Groucho v. Day and Night Co., 1020
Maryland Casualty Co. v. Lamarre, 588
Maryland Casualty Co. v. Peppard, 587
Maryland Electric Railway Co., State ex rel. Cox v., 335
Maryland for Use of Pumphrey, State of v. Manor Real Estate & Trust Co., 269
Maryland Lumber Co. v. White, 339
Maryland Telephone & Telegraph Co. v. Ruth, 642, 643
Marzotto v. Gay Garment Co., 444
Maser v. Farmers' & Merchants' Bank, 98

TABLE OF CASES

Mask v. Rawls, 871
Mason v. Ditchbourne, 731
Mason v. Funderburk, 992
Mason v. Gerin Corp., 957
Mason v. Madson, 675, 766
Mason v. Mason, 902
Mason v. Moore, 744
Mason v. Russell, 528
Mason v. Western Pennsylvania Hospital, 186, 372, 373
Mason v. Wrightson, 40, 48, 1067
Masone v. Unishops of Modell's, Inc., 200
Masquat v. Maguire, 192
Massachusetts Bonding & Insurance Co. v. Arizona Concrete Co., 588
Massaletti v. Fitzroy, 215
Masse v. James H. Robinson Co., 575
Massee v. Williams, 848
Massengill v. Yuma County, 1049, 1060
Massey v. Jones, 817
Massey v. Scripter, 174, 209, 464, 519
Massey v. Tube Art Display, Inc., 501
Massie v. Copeland, 409
Massino v. Smaglick, 406
Mason v. Keeling, 539
Massuere v. Dickens, 775
Mastad v. Swedish Brethren, 419
Mastellone v. Argo Oil Corp., 91
Masters v. Alexander, 176
Masters v. Becker, 41
Masters v. Public Service Co. of New Hampshire, 177
Masterson v. Chesapeake & Potomac Telephone Co., 662
Matanuska Electric Association, Inc. v. Johnson, 510
Mathena v. Burchett, 590
Matheny v. Stonecutter Mills Corp., 411
Mathes, Estate of v. Ireland, 203
Matheson v. Harris, 968
Matheson v. Pearson, 213
Mathews v. Hogueland, 757
Mathews v. Mills, 351
Mathews v. Murray, 149
Mathewson v. Primeau, 626
Mathias v. Denver Union Terminal Railway Co., 418, 421
Mathine v. Kansas-Nebraska Natural Gas Co., 208
Mathis v. Granger Brick & Tile Co., 318
Mathis v. Stacy, 523
Mathis v. Virgin, 331
Matkovich v. Penn Central Transportation Co., 213
Matovina v. Hult, 51
Matson v. Margiotti, 821, 822
Matson v. United States, 82
Mattauch v. Walsh Brothers & Miller, 762
Matteawan Co. v. Bentley, 102
Matter of (see name of party)
Mattes v. City of Baltimore, 575
Matthow v. Cross, 772, 793, 794
Matthews v. Carolina & North Western Railway Co., 376
Matthews v. Coal, 323, 325, 329
Matthews v. Delaware, Lackawanna & Western Railroad Co., 327, 347
Matthews v. Hicks, 958
Matthews v. Kuwait Bechtel Corp., 660
Matthews v. Lawnlite Co., 703
Matthews v. Liberty Mutual Insurance Co., 381
Matthews v. MacLaren, 376
Matthews v. Missouri Pacific Railway Co., 450, 461, 565
Matthews v. Ollerton, 122
Matthews v. Porter, 306
Matthews v. Spiegel, 442
Matthews, United States v., 97
Matthis v. Kennedy, 818
Mattice v. Brinkman, 96, 98
Matts v. Homsi, 378
Mattson v. Minnesota & North Wisconsin Railroad Co., 411
Maturin v. Dronet, 531
Mau v. Rio Grande Oil Inc., 854, 858
Mauk v. Brundage, 11
Mauldin v. Sheffer, 661
Maulsby v. Cook, 140
Mauney v. Gulf Refining Co., 281
Maung Kyan Dun v. Ma Kyian, 543, 547
Maurer v. Harper, 219
Maurice v. Worden, 821, 822
Maurizi v. Western Coal & Mining Co., 576
Maus v. Pickens Sentinel Co., 244
Mautino v. Piercedale Supply Co., 303, 503
Mavity, State ex rel. v. Tyndall, 864
Mawe v. Piggott, 778
Mawson v. Eagle Harbor Transportation Co., 303
Mawson v. Vess Beverage Co., 78
Max v. Kahn, 992
Maxa v. Neidlein, 10
Maxey v. Freightliner Corp., 195, 487, 489
Maxfield v. Maxfield, 417, 418
Maxwell v. Colburn, 238
Maxwell v. Maxwell, 37, 55, 414, 424
Maxwell v. Olsen, 164
Maxwell Ice Co. v. Brackett, Shaw & Lunt Co., 745, 757
May v. Allied Chlorine and Chemical Products, Inc., 686
May v. Anderson, 975
May v. Baron, 41
May v. Bradford, 327
May v. Burdett, 541, 542
May v. Columbian Rope Co., 250
May v. Georger, 89, 101
May v. Goulding, 914
May v. Hrinko, 511
May v. Palm Beach Chemical Co., 911
May v. Phillips, 503
May v. Sharp, 572, 575
May v. Tidewater Power Co., 662
Mayberry v. Northern Pacific Railroad Co., 346
Maye v. Yappen, 75, 82, 110
Mayer v. Goodman, 879
Mayer v. Housing Authority of Jersey City, 441
Mayer v. Springer, 101
Mayer v. Studer & Manion Co., 675

Mayer v. Thompson-Hutchison Building Co., 670
Mayer v. Walter, 897
Mayfield Motor Co. v. Parker, 742
Mayflower Industries v. Thor Corp., 890
Mayhew v. Berrien County Road Commission, 335
Mayhew v. State, 130
Mayhew v. Sullivan Mining Co., 195
Maykut v. Plasko, 633
Mayle v. Pennsylvania Department of Highways, 1055
Maynard v. City of Madison, 1063
Maynard v. James, 102
Maynard v. Kenova Chemical Co., 501
Maynell v. Saltmarsh, 648
Mayo v. Goldman, 788
Mayo v. Sample, 822
Mayo v. Schumer, 649
Mayo Clinic v. Mayo's Drug & Cosmetic, Inc., 1016
Mayor and Council of Alpine v. Brewster, 643, 645
Mayor of Knoxville, State v., 146
Mayor of Manchester v. Williams, 780
Mayor of New York v. Lord, 146
Mayor of Paterson v. Erie Railroad Co., 7
Mays v. Stratton, 995
Maysville Transit Co. v. Ort, 859
Maytag v. Cummins, 795, 844
Maytag Co. v. Meadows Manufacturing Co., 779, 977, 1009
Mayweather v. State, 128
Mazzacco v. Purcell, 412, 414
Mazzera's Case, Francis, 786
Mazzucco v. North Carolina Board of Medical Examiners, 1057
Meacham v. Halley, 758
Mead v. Warner Pruyn Division, 706
Meade v. Montrose, 436
Meador v. Hotel Grover, 457
Meadows v. Grant, 879
Meadows v. Oates, 245, 249
Meads v. Dibble, 949
Meagher v. Garvin, 503
Mealey v. Bemidji Lumber Co., 988
Meaney v. Loew's Hotels, Inc., 780
Mears v. Accomac Banking Co., 761
Mears v. Alhadeff, 372
Mears v. Crocker First National Bank, 91, 669
Mears v. Dole, 550
Mears v. London & S.W.R. Co., 88, 104, 105
Meason v. Ralston Purina Co., 1003
Mecham v. Foley, 40
Mechler v. McMahon, 232
Medairy v. McAllister, 86
Medbury v. Watson, 762
Medcraft v. Merchants Exchange, 441
Medearis v. Miller, 499
Medeiros v. Kondo, 1059
Medford v. Levy, 624
Medford Housing Authority v. Marinucci Bros. & Co., 639
Medi-Clean Services, Inc. v. Hill, 398
Medina v. 187th Street Apartments, Limited, 443

Medley v. Trenton Investment Co., 514
Medlin v. United States, 406
Medved v. Doolittle, 277
Meek v. Harris, 60
Meeker v. Post Printing & Publishing Co., 837
Meeker v. Van Rensselaer, 642
Meeks v. Wood, 628
Meering v. Grahame-White Aviation Co., 48
Meese v. Brigham Young University, 174, 487, 488, 496, 498
Meetze v. Associated Press, 857, 858, 861
Megarry v. Norton, 777
Megeff v. Doland, 385
Mehigan v. Sheehan, 662
Mehrhof Brothers Brick Manufacturing Co. v. Delaware, Lackawanna & Western Railroad Co., 650
Meibus v. Dodge, 562
Meier v. Holt, 345
Meier v. Wilkens, 92
Meihost v. Meihost, 313
Mein v. Reed, 250
Meinecke v. Skaggs, 49
Meinhardt v. Vaughn, 527
Meints v. Huntington, 49, 121
Meistrich v. Casino Arena Attractions Inc., 493, 495
Meitzner v. Baltimore & Ohio Railroad Co., 413
Meixell v. Kirkpatrick, 331
Melbourne & Troy v. Louisville & Nashville Railroad Co., 379
Melcher v. Beeler, 823, 827
Meldrum v. Australian Broadcasting Co., 787
Meldrum v. State, 156
Melendres v. Soales, 478
Melgreen v. McGuire, 762
Melia v. Ford Motor Co., 478, 946
Melichar v. Frank, 327, 339
Melicharek v. Hill Bus Co., 383
Mellish v. Cooney, 313
Mellon v. Goodyear, 955, 956
Mellon v. Lehigh Valley Railroad Co., 287, 300
Mellott v. Louisville & Nashville Railroad Co., 488
Meloy v. City of Santa Monica, 434
Melton v. Allen, 364
Melton v. Rickman, 898
Melton, State v., 130
Melvin v. Pence, 891
Memel v. Feimer, 415
Memorial Hospital v. Scott, 176
Memphis & Charleston Railroad Co. v. Reeves, 316
Memphis Commercial Appeal v. Johnson, 810
Memphis Development Foundation v. Factors, Etc., Inc., 1020
Memphis Steam Laundry-Cleaners v. Lindsey, 1009, 1014
Menard v. Cashman, 440
Mencher v. Chesley, 778
Mendelson v. Blatz Brewing Co., 986, 995
Mendelson v. Davis, 280
Mendez v. Blackburn, 1067

Menefee v. Columbia Broadcasting System, Inc., 963, 966
Menke v. Peterschmidt, 467
Mennemeyer v. Hart, 949
Mennis v. Cheffings, 194
Menolascino v. Superior Felt & Bedding Co., 620
Mentesana v. LaFranco, 396
Mentzer v. New England Telephone & Telegraph Co., 662
Meraz v. Valencia, 872
Mercer v. Braswell, 466
Mercer v. Brown, 630
Mercer v. Corbin, 36
Merchant Shippers Association v. Kellogg Express & Draying Co., 342
Merchants' Cotton Press & Storage Co. v. Miller, 444
Merchants' & Miners' Transportation Co. v. Moore & Co., 665
Merchants' Mutual Automobile Liability Insurance Co. v. Smart, 586, 587
Merchants' National Bank v. Robison, 744
Mercier v. Naugatuck Fuel Co., 389
Mercury v. Mustachia, 888
Meredith v. Buster, 924
Meredith v. Reed, 208
Merenoff v. Merenoff, 903, 909
Meridian, City of v. Tingle, 648
Merle v. Sociological Research Film Corp., 786, 854, 964
Merlo v. Public Service Co., 312
Merriam v. McConnell, 390
Merrick v. Murphy, 447, 448
Merrick v. Sutterlin, 907
Merrigan, United States v., 999
Merrill v. City of Manchester, 1052
Merrill v. Post Publishing Co., 778, 780
Merrill Lynch, Pierce, Fenner & Smith v. Curran, 221, 222
Merriman v. Sea Pines Plantation Co., 455, 460
Merritt v. Cravens, 918
Merritt v. Reserve Insurance Co., 204
Merriweather v. Bell, 75
Merryweather v. Nixan, 336
Mersey Docks Trustees v. Gibbs, 1069
Mershon v. Gino's, Inc., 184
Mershon v. Williams, 144
Mertz v. J.M. Covington Corp., 151
Mertz v. Weibe, 526
Mesedahl v. St. Luke's Hospital Association, 199, 312
Meshbesher v. Channellene Oil & Manufacturing Co., 224, 304, 581
Mesher v. Osborne, 443
Mesite v. Kirchstein, 905
Messer v. City of Dickinson, 567
Messer v. United States, 1037
Messersmith v. American Fidelity Co., 586
Messick v. General Motors Corp., 712
Messing v. Judge & Dolph Drug Co., 270
Metallic Compression Casting Co. v. Fitchburg Railroad Co., 147, 382
Metcalf v. Chiprin, 444

Metcalf v. Times Publishing Co., 837, 838
Metcalfe, State v., 138
Meteye v. Times-Democrat Publishing Co., 836
Methodist Federation for Social Action v. Eastland, 820
Metropolitan Atlanta Rapid Transit v. Tuck, 227
Metropolitan Government of Nashville v. Counts, 400, 401, 402, 406, 410, 411
Metropolitan Life Insurance Co. v. James, 766
Metropolitan Life Insurance Co. v. Miller, 883
Metropolitan Opera Association v. Wagner-Nichols Recorder Corp., 1020
Metropolitan Paving Co. v. Brown-Crummer Investment Co., 763
Metropoulos v. Macpherson, 641
Mets v. Granrud, 245, 248, 258
Metter v. Los Angeles Examiner, 854, 859, 861
Metz v. Central Illinois Electric & Gas Co., 245
Metzger v. Baker, 758, 759
Metzger v. Dell Publishing Co., 862, 863, 864
Metzger v. Pennsylvania Ohio & Detroit Railroad Co., 71
Meunier v. Chemical Paper Co., 569
Mewhirter v. Hatten, 932
Meyer, In re Guardianship of, 1073
Meyer v. Cincinnati Street Railway Co., 326
Meyer v. Ewald, 878, 883
Meyer v. General Electric Co., 407
Meyer v. Kemper Ice Co., 628
Meyer v. Menominee & Marinette Light & Traction Co., 411
Meyer v. Nottger, 60
Meyer v. Parr, 819
Meyer v. Peter, 941
Meyer v. Ritterbush, 906
Meyer v. State, 937
Meyerle v. Pioneer Publishing Co., 846, 847
Meyers v. City of Louisiana, 468
Meyers v. Meyers, 1066
Meyers, State v., 127
Meyerson v. Hurlbut, 778, 791
Meyette v. Canadian Pacific Railway Co., 312
Memezullo v. Maletz, 817, 818
Mezyk v. National Repossessions, Inc., 314
MFA Mutual Insurance Co. v. Sailors, 588
M'Gibbon v. M'Curry, 564
Miami Beach, City of v. Bretagna, 889
Miami Coca-Cola Bottling Co. v. Reisinger, 249
Miami Herald Publishing Co. v. Brown, 847
Miami Herald Publishing Co. v. Tornillo, 1025
Micallef v. Miehle Co., 219
Micek v. Weaver-Jackson Co., 261
Micelli v. Hirsch, 271
Michael v. Dunkle, 918, 921
Michael v. Matson, 877
Michael v. St. Paul Mercury Indemnity Co., 595
Michael v. Warner/Chilcott, 207, 685
Michaels v. Brookchester, Inc., 443
Michaels v. New York Central Railroad Co., 315
Michaelsohn v. Smith, 526
Michaelson v. Denison, 159

Michaelson v. Turk, 60
Michalovic v. Genesee-Monroe Racing Association, Inc., 416
Michard v. Myron Stratton Home, 595
Micheletti v. Moidel, 666
Michelin Tire Co. v. Schulz, 757
Michelsen v. Dwyer, 649
Michigan Central Railroad v. Vreeland, 949, 951, 952
Michigan City v. Rudolph, 184, 535
Mick v. American Dental Association, 823, 830, 831, 833
Mickelson v. Forney, 251
Mid Continent Aircraft Corp. v. Curry County Service, Inc., 678, 709
Mid-West Chevrolet Corp. v. Noah, 666
Middlesboro Home Telegraph Co. v. Louisville & Nashville Railroad Co., 343
Middlesex Concrete Products & Excavating Corp. v. Carteret Industrial Association, 985
Middleton v. Cox, 215
Middleton v. Melbourne Tramway Co., 349
Middleton v. News Syndicate Co., 864
Middleton v. Nichols, 926
Middleton v. Whitridge, 376
Middletown Trust Co. v. Armour & Co., 466
Midkiff v. Midkiff, 906
Midland Empire Packing Co. v. Yale Oil Corp., 352
Midland Ins. Co. v. Smith, 982
Midland Valley Railroad Co. v. Littlejohn, 413
Midvale Coal Co. v. Cardox Corp., 999
Midwest Game Co. v. M. F. A. Milling Co., 690
Midwest Oil Co. v. City of Aberdeen, 550
Midwood & Co. v. Manchester Corp., 546, 548, 567
Mielenz v. Quasdorf, 780, 798
Mighell v. Stone, 927
Mikaelian v. Palaza, 395
Mike v. Borough of Aliquippa, 202
Mikula v. Balogh, 178
Milam v. Milam, 118
Milam v. Railway Express Agency, 809
Milburn v. Michel, 734
Mile High Fence Co. v. Radovich, 387, 388, 433
Miles v. A. Arena & Co., 513, 550
Miles v. Cuthbert, 928
Miles v. Forest Rock Granite Co., 547, 548, 552
Miles v. Harrison, 717
Miles v. Louis Wasmer, Inc., 787, 812
Miles v. McGrath, 821
Miles v. Record Publishing Co., 773, 790
Miles v. St. Regis Paper Co., 250
Miles v. Southeastern Motor Truck Lines, 305
Miles v. Stevens, 736
Milewski v. Kurtz, 921
Miley v. Foster, 829
Milford v. Bangor Railway & Electric Co., 671
Milissich v. Lloyd's, 838
Millard v. Miller, 348
Miller v. A. & R. Joint Venture, 435
Miller v. Alaska Steam Ship Co., 328
Miller v. Alvey, 164

Miller v. American National Bank in Little Falls, 879, 880
Miller v. Arnal Corp., 381, 382
Miller v. Ashcraft, 48
Miller v. Bahmmuller, 317
Miller v. Baker, 85
Miller v. Balthasser, 121
Miller v. Baltimore & Ohio South Western Railroad Co., 363
Miller v. Beck, 330, 332
Miller v. Bennett, 123, 954
Miller v. Blanton, 10, 13
Miller v. Board of Education, Union Free School District No. 1, p. 1048
Miller v. Chicago & North Western Railroad Co., 103
Miller v. Coleman, 619
Miller v. Cook, 366
Miller v. David, 777
Miller v. Derusa, 383
Miller v. Donovan, 786
Miller v. Duhart, 166
Miller v. Edison Electric Illuminating Co., 621
Miller v. Fano, 52
Miller v. Fenton, 337
Miller v. First National Bank of Gladbrook, 966, 974
Miller v. Fogleman Truck Lines, Inc., 240
Miller v. Foltis Fisher, Inc., 664
Miller v. Friedman's Jewelers, Inc., 59
Miller v. Gonzalez, 171
Miller v. Griesel, 200
Miller v. Highland Ditch Co., 325, 327, 349
Miller v. Hope, 816
Miller v. Howe, 826
Miller v. Hyde, 90
Miller v. Lambert, 208
Miller v. Levine, 922
Miller v. Long, 96
Miller v. McClelland, 78
Miller v. McGuire, 132
Miller v. Madison Square Garden Corp., 852
Miller v. Miller, 77
Miller v. Monson, 929
Miller v. Moran Brothers Co., 489
Miller v. Morse, 645
Miller v. Muscarelle, 669
Miller v. National Broadcasting Co., 853, 861
Miller v. Northern Pacific Railway Co., 347
Miller v. Nuckolls, 819, 941
Miller v. Oscar Schmidt, Inc., 134
Miller v. Osterlund, 759
Miller v. Pacific Constructors, 429
Miller v. Pelzer, 904
Miller v. Pennsylvania Railroad Co., 343
Miller v. Protrka, 757
Miller v. Prough, 348, 350
Miller, Regina v., 118
Miller v. Reiman-Wuerth Co., 503
Miller v. Robert Addie & Son's Collieries, 546
Miller v. Schenck, 649, 651
Miller v. Singer, 323, 328

Miller v. State, 181
Miller, State v., 134
Miller v. Sweitzer, 912
Miller v. Treat, 489
Miller v. Trinity Medical Center, 178
Miller v. Troy Laundry Machinery, 764
Miller v. Uhl, 101
Miller v. United States, 235
Miller v. United States Fidelity & Casualty Co., 586
Miller v. Van Newkirk, 190, 247
Miller v. Watkins, 206
Miller v. Wilson, 95, 941
Miller, Inc., Charles J. v. McClung-Logan Equipment Co., 240
Millers Mutual Casualty Co. v. Insurance Exchange Building Corp., 986
Millett v. Minnesota Crushed Stone Co., 621, 627, 639
Milligan v. Miller, 734
Milligan v. Wedge, 509
Milliken v. Heddesheimer, 123
Milliken v. Long, 927
Milliman, In re, 960
Millinery Creators' Guild v. Federal Trade Commission, 1025
Millington v. Southeastern Elevator Co., 932
Millirons v. Blue, 306
Millman v. Pratt, 965
Millman v. United States Mortgage & Title Guaranty Co., 311
Mills v. Armstrong (The Bernina), 530
Mills v. Bonanza International Corp., 434, 444
Mills v. Denny, 821
Mills v. Hall, 390, 620, 644
Mills v. Levine, 10
Millsap v. National Funding Corp., 121
Milner v. Hare, 894
Milner Hotels v. Dougherty, 58
Milostan v. City of Chicago, 264, 317
Milton v. Puffer, 83, 112
Milton v. State, 9
Milton Bradley Co. of Georgia, Inc. v. Cooper, 303
Milwaukee, City of v. Meyer, 7
Milwaukee & St. Paul Railroad Co. v. Arms, 10
Milwaukee & St. Paul Railway Co. v. Kellogg, 282
Milwaukee Insurance Co. v. Gas Service Co., 333
Mims v. Boland, 118
Mims v. Coleman, 517, 519, 520
Mims v. Metropolitan Life Insurance Co., 799, 823
Mindenberg v. Carmel Film Productions, 994
Miner v. Connecticut River Railroad Co., 481
Miner v. McNamara, 724
Mineral Industries, Inc. v. George, 998
Miniken v. Carr, 417
Mink, Commonwealth v., 357
Mink v. Majors, 336
Minkin v. Minkin, 906
Minneapolis Threshing Machine Co. v. Regier, 871
Minnesota Stove Co. v. Cavanaugh, 992
Minnesota Thresher Manufacturing Co. v. Gruben, 770

Minnesota Wheat Growers' Cooperative Marketing Association v. Radke, 989
Minor, Ex parte, 137
Minor v. Baldridge, 673
Minor v. Seliga, 52, 150
Minsky v. Satenstein, 985, 996
Minton v. Southern Railway Co., 466
Minutilla v. Providence Ice Cream Co., 262
Misco Leasing, Inc. v. Keller, 972
Misfeldt v. Hospital Authority of City of Marietta, 199
Mishkin v. Roreck, 793
Misiulis v. Milbrand Maintenance Corp., 512
Missio v. Williams, 912
Missoula Trust & Savings Bank v. Northern Pacific Railway Co., 545
Missouri v. National Organization for Women, Inc., 1012
Missouri-Kansas-Texas Railway Co. v. Canada, 948
Missouri, Kansas & Texas Railway Co. v. Central Railroad Co., 716
Missouri, Kansas & Texas Railway Co. of Texas v. Evans, 958
Missouri, Kansas & Texas Railway Co. v. Hawkins, 362
Missouri, Kansas & Texas Railway Co. v. Hunter, 106
Missouri, Kansas & Texas Railway Co. v. Merrill, 275
Missouri, Kansas & Texas Railway Co. v. Wood, 314
Missouri, State of v. National Organization for Women, Inc., 989, 1025
Missouri Pacific Railway Co. v. Burks, 716
Missouri Pacific Railway Co. v. Davis, 621
Missouri Pacific Railway Co. v. Gordon, 398
Missouri Pacific Railway Co. v. Lester, 409
Missouri Pacific Railway Co. v. Richardson, 311
Missouri Pacific Railway Co. v. Whitehead & Kales Co., 477
Missouri Veterinary Medical Association v. Glisan, 646
Misterek v. Washington Mineral Products, Inc., 390
Mitcham v. City of Detroit, 245
Mitchell v. Akers, 958
Mitchell v. Aldrich, 995
Mitchell v. Brady, 387
Mitchell v. Branch, 341
Mitchell v. C. & H. Transportation Co., 444
Mitchell v. Central Vermont Railway Co., 171
Mitchell v. Churches, 717
Mitchell v. Coca Cola Bottling Co., 269
Mitchell v. Donanski, 872
Mitchell v. Emblade, 231
Mitchell v. Friedman, 289
Mitchell v. Georgia & Alabama Railway Co., 103
Mitchell v. Harmony, 147
Mitchell v. Heaton, 486
Mitchell v. Hotel Berry Co., 233
Mitchell v. Langley, 1007
Mitchell v. Legarksy, 310
Mitchell v. Lonergran, 716, 717
Mitchell v. Miller, 704
Mitchell v. Mitchell, 73, 76
Mitchell v. Moore, 443
Mitchell v. Oklahoma Cotton Growers' Association, 147

Mitchell v. Ozan-Graysonia Lumber Co., 422
Mitchell v. Pettigrew, 307
Mitchell v. Randal, 14
Mitchell v. Raymond, 337
Mitchell, Regina v., 293
Mitchell v. Reitchick, 544
Mitchell v. Rochester Railway Co., 24, 55, 56, 360, 363
Mitchell v. Sigrest, 464
Mitchell v. Tarbutt, 325
Mitchell v. Volkswagenwerk, 352
Mitchell Realty Co. v. City of West Allis, 634
Mitchem v. Johnson, 721
Mitran v. Williamson, 61, 64
Mixon v. Dobbs House, Inc., 208, 380
Mize v. Rocky Mountain Bell Telephone Co., 283, 284, 302
Mizenis v. Sands Motel, Inc., 491
Moberg v. Scott, 938
Mobil Chemical Co. v. Bell, 250, 260, 261
Mobil Oil Corp. v. Higginbotham, 951, 952, 956
Mobil Oil Corp. v. Thorn, 443
Mobile Life Insurance Co. v. Brame, 38, 945, 982
Mobile Mechanical Contractors Association v. Carlough, 991
Mobley, State v., 154
Moch Co., H.R. v. Rensselaer Water Co., 24, 25, 357, 375, 662, 671
Mochen v. State, 1075
Mock v. Davies, 154, 861, 862
Mock v. Sears, Roebuck & Co., 419, 425
Mockowik v. Kansas City, St. Joseph & Council Bluffs, Railroad Co., 241
Mode v. Barnett, 929
Modec v. City of Eveleth, 488
Modisett v. McPike, 922
Modisette & Adams v. Lorenze, 780
Modlin v. City of Miami Beach, 1050
Moe v. Steenberg, 485
Moehlenbrock v. Parke Davis & Co., 304
Moelleur v. Moelleur, 920
Moen v. Hanson, 952, 954
Moens v. Heyworth, 737
Moffat v. Bateman, 215
Moffatt v. Buffums, Inc., 142
Moffatt v. Fisher, 895
Moffett v. Brewer, 641
Moffett v. Commerce Trust Co., 892, 898
Moffett, State v., 642
Moffitt v. Asheville, 1053
Moffitt v. Davis, 662
Moglen v. Varsity Pajamas, Inc., 854
Mogul S.S. Co. v. McGregor Gow & Co., 983, 1012, 1013
Mohler v. Owens, 126
Mohn, Commonwealth v., 645
Mohr v. Gault, 390
Mohr v. Williams, 40, 116, 118, 119
Molein v. Kaiser Foundation Hospitals, 206, 361, 364, 365
Molina v. Payless Foods, Inc., 180
Molino v. Asher, 503, 527

Molitor v. Kaneland Community Unit District No. 302, p. 596
Molony v. Boy Comics Publishers, 859, 860, 864
Moloso v. State, 510
Molski v. Bendza, 99
Molt v. Public Indemnity Co., 786
Momsen v. Nebraska Methodist Hospital, 187
Monach v. Koslowski, 1007
Monaco v. United States, 1037
Monaghan v. Cox, 879
Monaghan v. Globe Newspaper Co., 846
Monahan v. Clemons, 926
Monahan v. Devinny, 226
Monahan v. Weichert, 187, 188
Monarch Chemicals, Inc., State v., 437
Monarch Industrial Towel and Uniform Rental, Inc. v. Model Coverall Service, Inc., 989
Moncreif v. Wilkinson, 753
Mondrow v. Selwyn, 875, 879, 883
Mone v. Greyhound Lines, Inc., 370
Monell v. Department of Social Services, 1052, 1061
Moneyham v. Hamilton, 1007
Monge v. Beebe Rubber Co., 1028, 1029, 1030
Moning v. Alfono, 171, 200
Monize v. Begaso, 126
Monk v. Ehret, 52
Monkhouse v. Johns, 255
Monroe v. Razor Construction Co., 567
Monroe, State v., 36, 40, 120
Monsanto Chemical Works v. American Zinc, Lead & Smelting Co., 769
Monson v. Lathrop, 833
Monson v. Lewis, 138
Monson v. Lewis, 139
Monson v. Tussauds, 786, 798
Monsour v. Excelsior Tobacco Co., 227
Montambault v. Waterbury & Milldale Tramway Co., 457
Montega Corp. v. Hazelrigs, 76
Montegut v. Hickson, 1021
Monterosso v. Gaudette, 393
Montgomery v. City of Philadelphia, 822
Montgomery v. Crum, 924
Montgomery v. Jacob Brothers Co., 754
Montgomery v. Knox, 829
Montgomery, State v., 155
Montgomery Elevator Co. v. Gordon, 244, 250, 254, 479
Montgomery Ward & Co. v. Freeman, 141, 142
Montgomery Ward & Co. v. Keulemans, 888
Montgomery Ward & Co. v. McGraw-Hill Publishing Co., 774
Montgomery Ward & Co. v. Nance, 833
Montgomery Ward & Co. v. Ramirez, 407
Montgomery Ward & Co. v. South Dakota Retail Merchants' & Hardware Dealers' Association, 1013, 1024
Montgomery Ward & Co. v. Steele, 425
Montgomery Ward & Co. v. United Retail, Wholesale & Department Store Employees, 773, 976
Montgomery Ward & Co. v. Watson, 833

Montinieri v. Southern New England Telephone Co., 364
Montriou v. Jeffries, 759
Monumental Motor Tours v. Eaton, 328
Moodie v. Santoni, 451, 453
Moody v. Baker, 794
Moody v. Blake, 94
Moody v. Board of Supervisors of Niagara County, 642
Moody v. Drown, 91
Moody v. Kenny, 57
Moody v. Kirkpatrick, 340
Moody v. Martin Motor Co., 669
Moody v. Sindlinger, 106
Moon v. Northern Pacific Railway Co., 716
Moon v. United States, 188
Mooney v. Carter, 40
Mooney v. Johnson Cattle Co., 1003
Mooney v. Mull, 885
Moonie v. Lynch, 167
Moore v. Atchison, Topeka & Santa Fe Railway Co., 258
Moore v. Blanchard, 9
Moore v. Bowman, 112
Moore v. Burton Lumber & Hardware Co., 457, 480, 498
Moore v. Camden & Trenton Railway Co., 131
Moore v. Carey Bros. Oil Co., 105
Moore v. City of Bloomington, 552
Moore v. Clarke, 574
Moore v. Doerr, 913
Moore v. El Paso Chamber of Commerce, 41
Moore v. Ellis, 717
Moore v. Foster, 156, 323
Moore v. Francis, 773
Moore v. Gadsden, 390
Moore v. Horne, 1074
Moore v. Leaseway Transportation Corp., 502
Moore v. Meagher, 794
Moore v. Michigan National Bank, 897, 898
Moore v. Morse & Malloy Shoe Co., 569, 572
Moore v. Muntzel, 434
Moore v. New York Elevated Railroad Co., 855
Moore v. Palmer, 528
Moore v. Presnell, 162
Moore v. Robinson, 103
Moore v. Rolin, 967
Moore v. Rose-Hulman Institute of Technology, 181
Moore v. Savage, 62
Moore v. Skiles, 520
Moodie v. Standard Paint & Glass Co. of Pueblo, 390
Moore v. State, 211
Moore v. Thompson, 48
Moore v. Townsend, 317
Moore v. Wilson, 10
Moores v. Lucas, 372
Moorgate Merc. Co. v. Finch, 101
Moorman Manufacturing Co. v. National Tank Co., 708
Moos v. United States, 118, 1038
Mora v. Favilla, 229
Moraca v. Ford Motor Co., 696
Moragne v. State Marine Lines, Inc., 19, 945
Morain v. Devlin, 1073
Moran v. Corliss Steam Engine Co., 572

Moran v. Dunphy, 995
Moran v. Faberge, Inc., 207, 685
Moran v. Napolitano, 166
Moran v. Pittsburgh-Des Moines Steel Co., 723
Moran v. Quality Aluminum Casting Co., 933
Moran v. Raymond Corp., 487
Moran v. Valley Forge Drive-in Theatres, Inc., 428
Morash & Sons, Inc. v. Commonwealth, 1054, 1060
Morasse v. Brochu, 794
More v. Bennett, 775
More v. Weaver, 820
Moreau v. Moreau, 902
Morehouse v. Wanzo, 499
Morehouse College v. Russell, 1070
Moreland v. Atchison, 759
Moreno v. Herrera, 241
Moreno v. Los Angeles Transfer Co., 463
Moreno v. Marbil Productions, Inc., 990, 1003
Morey v. Fitzgerald, 146
Morey v. Lake Superior Terminal & Transfer Co., 297
Morey v. Thybo, 384
Morfessis v. Baum, 890
Morgan v. Andrews, 985, 986
Morgan v. Boyes, 77
Morgan v. Bucks Associates, 383
Morgan v. Cox, 163
Morgan v. Dun & Bradstreet, Inc., 834, 846
Morgan v. French, 10
Morgan v. Graham, 964
Morgan v. High Penn Oil Co., 625
Morgan v. Hodge, 767
Morgan v. Hudnell, 539, 560
Morgan v. Leuck, 906
Morgan v. Loyacomo, 40
Morgan v. Morgan, 763
Morgan v. Pennsylvania General Insurance Co., 235
Morgan v. Rosenberg, 188
Morgan, State v., 43
Morgan v. United States, 937
Morin v. Divide County Abstract Co., 768
Morin v. Hood, 97, 105
Morin v. Moreau, 879
Moritz v. Garnhart, 924
Moritz v. Pines Hotel, Inc., 507
Morley v. Chase, 110
Morley v. Post Printing & Publishing Co., 777
Morneau v. American Oil Co., 126
Morning v. Long, 921
Morningstar v. Lafayette Hotel Co., 3
Morrell v. Wiley, 767
Morril v. Morril, 236, 275, 311, 320
Morrill v. Hamel, 149
Morris v. Borough of Haledon, 648
Morris v. Cleveland Hockey Club, 488
Morris, Commonwealth v., 840
Morris v. Department of Labor and Industries, 575
Morris v. Diers, 332
Morris v. Evans, 789
Morris v. Graham, 650
Morris v. Granato, 425

TABLE OF CASES

Morris v. King Cole Stores, 441
Morris v. Kospelich, 339
Morris v. Lake Shore & Michigan Southern Railway Co., 307
Morris v. Lewis Manufacturing Co., 407
Morris v. MacNab, 12
Morris v. National Federation of the Blind, 847
Morris v. Owen, 938
Morris v. Platt, 128
Morris v. Robinson, 325, 330
Morris v. St. Paul City Railway Co., 353
Morris v. Scott, 871
Morris v. Third Ave. Railroad Co., 97
Morris v. Toy Box, 686
Morris v. Tuthill, 27
Morris v. Woodburn, 326
Morris & Co. v. Alvis, 570
Morris Run Coal Co. v. Barclay Coal Co., 324
Morrisey, State v., 156
Morrison v. Acton, 166
Morrison v. Carpenter, 416, 418
Morrison v. Davis & Co., 315
Morrison v. Harmer, 842
Morrison v. Kansas City Coca Cola Bottling Co., 195
Morrison v. Lawrence, 158
Morrison v. Le Tourneau Co., 246
Morrison v. Marquardt, 642
Morrison v. Medaglia, 199, 306, 352
Morrison v. National Broadcasting Co., 4, 964
Morrison v. Ritchie & Co., 796, 809
Morrison v. State, 134
Morrison-Jewell Filtration Co. v. Lingane, 1009
Morriss v. Marsden, 1074
Morrissette v. Beatte, 776, 781
Morrow v. Bonebrake, 752
Morrow v. Flores, 38
Morrow v. Southern Railway Co., 362
Morse v. Crawford, 1073
Morse v. Homer's, Inc., 203, 305
Morse v. Hurd, 93
Morse v. Liquor Control Commission, 648
Morse v. Piedmont Hotel Co., 1000
Morse v. Sinclair Automobile Service Co., 421
Morse v. Times-Republican Printing Co., 799
Mortensen v. Los Angeles Examiner, 837
Mortgage Commission Servicing Corp. v. Brock, 424
Mortimer v. Otto, 767
Mortin v. Shoppee, 43
Morton v. California Sports Car Club, 436
Morton v. Knipe, 827, 828
Morton v. Petitt, 1007
Morton v. Southwestern Telegraph & Telephone Co., 953
Morton v. Stack, 364
Morton v. United States, 1041, 1042
Morton v. Western Union Telegraph Co., 362, 665
Morton v. Young, 875
Mosca v. Middleton, 475
Moseley v. City of Kansas City, 410
Moseley v. J.G. McCrory, Co., 142

Mosely v. Johnson, 766
Moser v. Fulk, 871
Moser v. New York Life Insurance Co., 762
Moses v. Dubois, 52, 53
Moses v. Hoebel, 893
Moses v. Macferlan, 672, 673, 675
Moses v. Town of Morgantown, 323
Mosig v. Jersey Chiropodists, 1013
Mosler v. Whelen, 778
Mosler Safe Co. v. Ely-Norris Safe Co., 1019
Moss v. Atlanta Housing Authority, 427, 486, 488, 492, 497
Moss v. Cherdak, 335
Moss v. Fortune, 482
Moss v. Guarisco, 978
Moss v. Jones, 330
Moss v. Rishworth, 115
Mosseller v. Deaver, 77, 143, 144
Mossrud v. Lee, 304
Mothersill v. Voliva, 783
Motherway v. Wall, 759
Motiejaitis v. Johnson, 261
Motor Finance Co. v. Noyes, 105
Motor Improvements, Inc. v. A.C. Spark Plug Co., 1019
Motorists Mutual Insurance Co. v. Bill, 529
Motschenbacher v. R. J. Reynolds Tobacco Co., 853
Motsinger v. Sink, 888
Mott v. Scott, 541
Motyka v. City of Amsterdam, 1049, 1050
Moulin v. Monteleone, 918, 930
Moulton v. Gage, 488
Moulton v. Moore, 541
Moulton v. Moulton, 903
Moulton v. Norton, 746, 748
Mounsey v. Ellard, 432, 433
Mt. Healthy City School District Board of Education v. Doyle, 266
Mount Pleasant, Town of v. Van Tassell, 645
Mountain v. Wheatley, 484
Mountain Mobile Mix, Inc. v. Gifford, 474
Mountain States Telephone & Telegraph Co. v. Horn Tower Construction Co., 74
Mountain States Telephone & Telegraph Co. v. Kelton, 510
Mountain States Telephone & Telegraph Co. v. Vowell Construction Co., 74
Mouse v. Central Savings & Trust Co., 53
Mouse's Case, 146
Mowell v. Von Moschzisker, 879
Mowrer v. Ashland Oil & Refining Co., 556
Mowry v. Miller, 872
Mowry v. Raabe, 791, 975
Moyer v. Gordon, 143
Moyer v. Martin Marietta Corp., 1041
Moyer v. Phillips, 942, 943
Moyer Car Rental, Inc. v. Halliburton Co., 474, 524
Mozer v. Semenza, 318
Mozingo v. Cooley, 565
Mroczynski v. McGrath, 909
Mudrick v. Market Street Railway Co., 246

Mueller v. Fruen, 619
Mueller v. Hellrung Construction Co., 936
Mueller v. Technical Devices Corp., 99
Mueller v. Winston Brothers Co., 664, 947
Mueller & Co. v. Corley, 698
Muetze v. Tuteur, 775, 829
Muff v. Brainard, 575
Mugge v. Tampa Water Works Co., 671
Muhlmichl v. State, 311
Muirhead v. Gunst, 465
Mukasey v. Aaron, 517
Mulberry v. Fuellhart, 152
Mulchanock v. Whitehall Cement Manufacturing Co., 68, 553
Mulcrone v. Wagner, 429
Mulder v. Acme-Cleveland Corp., 476
Mulder v. Casho, 493
Mulderig v. St. Louis, Kansas City & Colorado Railroad Co., 340
Mulderig v. Wilkes-Barre Times Co., 834
Muldrow v. Weinstein, 576
Mulhall v. Fallon, 457
Mulherin v. Ingersoll-Rand Co., 478
Mulholland & Tedd, Ltd. v. Baker, 547
Mull v. Ford Motor Co., 312, 703
Mullane v. Crump, 667
Mullen v. Bruce, 1072, 1074
Mullen v. Eastern Trust & Savings Bank, 744
Mullen v. Lewiston Evening Journal, 834
Mullen v. St. John, 387
Mullen v. Wilkes-Barre Gas & Electric Co., 413
Muller v. McKesson, 565, 566
Muller v. Nebraska Methodist Hospital, 596
Muller v. West Jersey & Sea Shore Railroad Co., 232
Mulligan v. Atlantic Coast Line Railroad Co., 270
Mulligan v. Bailey, 737
Mullins v. Morgan, 640
Mullins v. Sanders, 898
Mulloy v. Hop Sang, 116, 119
Multer v. Knibbs, 922
Multerer, State ex rel. Trampe v., 644
Mulvehall v. Millward, 928
Mulvey v. Staab, 660
Muma v. Brown, 528
Mummaw v. Southwestern Telegraph & Telephone Co., 317
Munafo v. Helfand, 790
Munden v. Harris, 777
Mundon v. Taxicab Co., 1016
Mundy v. McDonald, 816
Munhall v. Pennsylvania Railroad Co., 1013
Municipal Metallic Bed Manufacturing Corp. v. Dobbs, 758
Muniz v. United Hospital Medical Center Presbyterian Hospital, 362
Muniz, United States v., 1036, 1037
Munn v. Hardee's Food Systems, Inc., 385
Munoz v. Olin, 478
Munro v. Williams, 79
Munro Hotel Co. v. Brough, 895

Munroe v. Beggs, 1007
Munsert v. Farmers Mutual Automobile Insurance Co., 906
Munsey v. Webb, 317
Munson v. Linnick, 883
Munson Line v. Green, 1009
Munster v. Lamb, 817
Munzer v. Blaisdell, 859
Murchison v. Powell, 304
Murdoch v. British Israel Fed., 311
Murdock v. Petersen, 415, 424
Murphey v. Caralli, 204
Murphy v. Ambassador East, 432
Murphy v. American Enka Corp., 575
Murphy v. Baltimore Gas & Electric Co., 386, 393, 394, 396, 397, 401, 433
Murphy v. Barlow Realty Co., 436
Murphy v. Board of Directors, 158
Murphy v. Boston & Maine Railroad, 954
Murphy v. Cartwright, 738
Murphy v. City of Carlsbad, 1053
Murphy v. City of Topeka-Shawnee County Department of Labor Services, 1064
Murphy v. Cory Pump & Supply Co., 686
Murphy v. Gillum, 564
Murphy v. Great Northern R. Co., 198, 304
Murphy v. Harty, 775
Murphy v. Hobbs, 11, 121, 736
Murphy v. Keating, 521
Murphy v. Kelly, 421
Murphy v. Larson, 879
Murphy v. Lincoln, 640
Murphy v. Martin Oil Co., 943, 950
Murphy v. Mitchell, 1007
Murphy v. Neely, 558
Murphy v. Sheftel, 766
Murphy v. Sioux City & Pacific Railroad Co., 86
Murphy v. Steeplechase Amusement Co., 485, 486
Murphy v. Taxicabs of Louisville, Inc., 271
Murray v. Alabama Power Co., 454
Murray v. Barncato, 816
Murray v. Cowherd, 670
Murray v. Eastern Maine Medical Center, 421, 428
Murray v. Fairbanks Morse, 479
Murray v. Lane, 393, 423, 426, 427, 440, 441, 442
Murray v. Lawson, 363
Murray v. Lehigh Valley Railroad Co., 511
Murray v. McAllister, 789
Murray v. McShane, 389
Murray v. O & A Express, Inc., 229, 230
Murray v. South Carolina R. Co., 571
Murray v. Templeton, 950
Murray v. United States, 205
Murray v. Wright, 314
Murrell v. Goodwill, 73, 725
Murrell v. Handley, 414
Murry Chevrolet Co. v. Cotten, 413
Musco v. Conte, 342
Musconetcong Iron Works v. Delaware, Lackawanna & Western Railroad Co., 765

Muse v. De Vito, 332, 333
Musgrove v. Pandelis, 265, 544
Muskogee Electric Traction Co. v. Tanner, 465
Muskopf v. Corning Hospital District, 1052, 1055
Musselman v. Borough of Hatfield, 172
Mussey v. Cahoon, 151
Mussey v. Scott, 144
Mustola v. Toddy, 90
Mutual Fire Insurance Co. v. Showalter, 1073
Mutual Life Insurance Co. v. Allen, 91
Muzychuk to Use and Benefit of Burns v. Yellow Cab Co., 947
Myer v. Minard, 628
Myers v. Afro-American Publishing Co., 867
Myers v. Arcadio, Inc., 1003
Myers v. Chicago, Rock Island & Pacific Railway Co., 229
Myers v. Hodges, 818
Myers v. Hoffman, 998
Myers v. Lennox Co-op Association, 489, 491
Myers v. Lowery, 759
Myers v. Reading Co., 578
Myers v. Shipley, 323
Myers v. Tranquility Irrigation District, 911
Myers, United States v., 43
Myers v. United States Camera Publishing Corp., 857
Myers & Myers v. United States Postal Service, 1041, 1042
Myhre v. Hessey, 874, 891
Myroft v. Sleight, 777

N

Nabors v. Keaton, 919
Nabozny v. Barnhill, 485
Naccash v. Burger, 362, 365, 371, 501
Nada Shah v. Sleeman, 543
Nadeau v. Dallaire, 921
Nadeau v. Fogg, 210
Nadeau v. Texas Co., 816
Nader v. General Motors Corp., 856
Nagel v. Landels, 204
Nager v. Lad 'n Dad Slacks, 982, 987
Nagle v. Nagle, 801
Nagy v. Manitoba Free Press, 970
Nahigian v. Belcher & Loomis Hardware Co., 248
Nahm v. J. R. Fleming & Co., 95
Nakashima v. Takase, 134
Nalepinski v. Durner, 397
Nall v. Alabama Utilities Co., 309
Nallan v. Helmsley-Spear, Inc., 202, 375, 381
Nally & Gibson v. Mulholland, 640
Nanace v. Mayflower Tavern, Inc., 59
Nance v. Flaugh, 799
Nance v. McClellan, 766
Nance v. Mayflower Tavern, 662
Nance v. Parks, 304
Nann v. Raimist, 968, 977
Nanson v. Jacob, 97
Napier v. First Congregational Church, 423

Napier v. Greenzweig, 657
Nappi v. Wilson, 53
Nappier v. Jefferson Standard Life Insurance Co., 858
Nardone v. Reynolds, 166
Nared v. School District of Omaha, 430, 432
Narramore v. Cleveland, Cincinnati, Chicago & St. Louis Railway Co., 569
Narsh v. Zirbser Brothers, Inc., 448, 449
Narup v. Benson, 750
Nary v. Parking Authority of Town of Dover, 421
Nash v. Atlantic White Tower System, Inc., 388
Nash v. City of North Platte, 210, 239
Nash v. Draughton Business School, 427
Nash v. Fisher, 809
Nash v. Lang, 105, 532
Nash v. Meyer, 123
Nash v. Minnesota Title Insurance & Trust Co., 736, 743, 745
Nash v. Page & Co., 662
Nash v. Sears, Roebuck & Co., 506
Nashua Gummed & Coated Paper Co. v. Noyes Buick Co., 513
Nashua Iron & Steel Co. v. Worcester & Nashua Railroad Co., 343
Nashville, Chattanooga & St. Louis Railway Co. v. Blackwell, 418
Nashville, Chattanooga & St. Louis Railway Co. v. Cleaver, 491, 570
Nashville, Chattanooga & St. Louis Railway Co. v. Miller, 55
Nashville, Chattanooga & St. Louis Railway v. White, 229
Nashville Interurban Railway Co. v. Gregory, 261
Nashville Lumber Co. v. Busbee, 958
Nashville Railway & Light Co. v. Trawick, 330
Nassif v. Goodman, 891
Nastasio v. Cinnamon, 308
Nataros v. Superior Court of Maricopa County, 874, 892
Natchez Times Publishing Co. v. Dunigan, 777
Nation v. District of Columbia, 642
National Airlines, Inc. v. Stiles, 950
National Association for Advancement of Colored People v. Claibourne Hardware Co., 989, 990, 991, 1005, 1010, 1012
National Association for the Advancement of Colored People v. Overstreet, 1009, 1026
National Association for Advancement of Colored People v. Webb's City, 1010, 1026
National Audubon Society v. Johnson, 647
National Bank of Bloomington v. Norfolk & Western Railway, 950
National Bank of Detroit v. Wayne Oakland Bank, 1012
National Bank of Savannah v. Kershaw Oil Mill, 744
National Ben Franklin Insurance Co. v. Careccta, 203
National Biscuit Co. v. Litzky, 575
National Bond & Investment Co. v. Whithorn, 50
National Coal Board v. Evans, 68, 74
National Copper Co. v. Minnesota Mining Co., 75, 83
National Disabled Soldier's League v. Haan, 823

National Dynamics Corp. v. Petersen Publishing Co., 964
National Farmers Union Property & Casualty Co. v. Frackelton, 476
National Glue Co. v. Thrash, 621
National Indemnity Co. v. Simmons, 588
National Leather Co. v. Roberts, 766
National Life & Accident Insurance Co. v. Anderson, 62
National Life & Accident Insurance Co. v. Wallace, 1010
National Manufacturing Co. v. United States, 1041, 1043
National Merchandising Corp. v. Leyden, 978, 987, 1004
National Novelty Import Co. v. Reed, 754
National Oil Co. v. Phillips Petroleum Co., 988, 996
National Oil Refining Co. v. Bush, 674
National Phonograph Co. v. Edison-Bell Phonograph Co., 996
National Protective Association of Steam Fitters & Helpers v. Cumming, 981
National Refining Co. v. Benzo Gas Motor Fuel Co., 964, 967, 968, 975, 976
National Refining Co., State ex rel. v. Seehorn, 941
National Savings Bank of the District of Columbia v. Ward, 667, 747
National Shawmut Bank of Boston v. Johnson, 744
National Spring Co. v. Pierpoint Associates, Inc., 1050
National Surety Co. v. Page, 891, 895
National Surety Corp. v. Applied Systems, Inc., 1022
National Tea Co. v. Gaylord Discount Department Stores, Inc., 248, 257, 434
National Tel. Co. v. Baker, 546, 552, 567
National Trailer Convoy, Inc. v. Oklahoma Turnpike Authority, 337
National Trucking & Storage Co. v. Driscoll, 528
Natnason v. Kline, 190
Natrona Power Co. v. Clark, 334, 335
Natvig's Sons, Inc., C. C. v. Summers, 474
Naudzius v. Lahr, 215
Naulty v. Bulletin Co., 783
Nave v. Hixenbaugh, 421
Navigazione Libera Triestina Societa Anonima v. Newtown Creek Towing Co., 266
Navy, State v., 644
Nazareno v. Urie, 199, 222, 225, 230
Neagle, In re, 155
Neal v. Bergland, 381
Neal v. Donahue, 1063
Neal v. Home Builders, 411
Neal v. Shiels, Inc., 200
Neal v. United States, 950
Neal, Estate of v. Friendship Manor Nursing Home, 258
Neall v. Hart, 54
Near v. Minnesota ex rel. Olson, 773
Nearpark Realty Corp. v. City Investing Co., 743
Neary v. Northern Pacific Railway Co., 212, 468
Neat v. Miller, 586
Neaton v. Lewis Apparel Stores, 775
Nebb v. Bell Syndicate, 809, 853
Necaise v. Chrysler Corp., 683
Nechodomu v. Lindstrom, 408, 409, 514

Neeb v. Hope, 10
Neel v. Magana, Olney, Levy, Cathcard & Gelfand, 167
Neeley v. Winn-Dixie Greenville, Inc., 798
Neely, State v., 43
Nees v. Hocks, 1028
Nees v. Minneapolis St. Railway Co., 347
Nees Brothers v. Minneapolis Street Railway Co., 268
Neese v. Toms, 523
Neff v. City of Cameron, 531
Neff v. Time, Inc., 856
Neff Lumber Co. v. First National Bank, 718
Negley v. Massey Ferguson, Inc., 474
Nehr v. Dobbs, 877
Nehring v. Connecticut Co., 276
Neibuhr v. Gage, 121, 736
Neill v. Shamburg, 738
Neiman-Marcus Co. v. Lait, 780, 784
Neis v. National Super Markets, Inc., 248, 250
Nelen v. Colwell, 99
Nelsen v. City of Gridley, 416
Nelson v. Amboni, 248
Nelson v. Berkner, 763
Nelson v. Busby, 937, 938
Nelson v. Chicago, Burlington & Quincy Railroad Co., 545
Nelson v. Comer, 1066
Nelson v. Crawford, 44, 63
Nelson v. Eastern Air Lines, 152
Nelson v. F.W. Woolworth Co., 420
Nelson v. Fruehauf Trailer Co., 717
Nelson v. Galveston, Harrisburg & San Antonio Railway Co., 959
Nelson v. Halvorson, 11
Nelson v. Hill, 54
Nelson v. Hokuf, 439
Nelson v. Illinois Central Railroad Co., 326, 328, 347
Nelson v. Kellogg, 48, 53
Nelson v. Leo's Auto Sales, Inc., 768
Nelson v. McKenzie-Hague Co., 567
Nelson v. McLellan, 411
Nelson v. Melvin, 923, 996
Nelson v. Miller, 891
Nelson v. Nason, 323
Nelson v. National Casualty Co., 875
Nelson v. Nelson, 486
Nelson v. Parker, 256
Nelson v. Peterman, 878
Nelson v. Rosenberg, 793
Nelson v. Schultz, 378
Nelson v. Staff, 965
Nelson v. State, 46
Nelson v. Swedish Evangelical Lutheran Cemetery Association, 640
Nelson v. Tanner, 540
Nelson v. Twin City Motor Bus Co., 349
Nelson v. United States, 514
Nelson v. Whitten, 823
Nelson v. William H. Ziegler Co., 303
Nelson v. Zamboni, 255
Nelson Manufacturing Corp., N.O. v. Dickson, 576

Nesalhouse v. Walker, 636
Nesbett v. Wilbur, 137
Nesbit v. Everette, 219
Nesmith v. Alford, 54, 870, 882, 883, 886
Nesmith v. Bowden, 220, 228
Nesmith v. Starr, 402, 441
Ness v. West Coast Airlines, Inc., 247
Nesta v. Meyer, 457
Netter v. New Orleans Public Service, Inc., 185
Nettles v. MacMillan Petroleum Corp., 782
Nettleton v. Cook, 878, 880
Nettleton v. James, 228
Netusil v. Novak, 561
Neu v. McCarthy, 159
Neuber v. Royalty Realty Co., 639
Neubrand v. Kraft, 717
Neufeld v. Rodeminski, 878
Neuhaus v. Daniels, 447
Neuman v. Shlansky, 181
Neumann v. Industrial Sound Engineering, Inc., 890
Neustadt, United States v., 1038
Neusus v. Sponholtz, 183
Nevada v. Hall, 1043
Nevada Credit Rating Bureau, Inc. v. Williams, 899
Neville v. American Barge Line Co., 937
Neville v. Higbie, 967, 973
Neville v. Mitchell, 346, 349
Nevin v. Pullman Palace Car Co., 662
New Brantner Extension Ditch Co. v. Ferguson, 550
New England Acceptance Corp. v. American Manufacturers Mutual Insurance Co., 508
New England Awl & Needle Co. v. Marlboro Awl & Needle Co., 1016
New England Cement Gun Co. v. McGivern, 1024
New England Foundation Co. v. Elliott A. Watrous, Inc., 666
New England Oil & Pipe Line Co. v. Rogers, 967, 968, 970
New Hampshire Board of Registration in Optometry v. Scott Jewelry Co., 1012
New Mexico Feeding Co. v. Keck, 239
New Mexico Water Quality Control Commission v. City of Hobbs, 1054
New Negro Alliance v. Sanitary Grocery Co., 1010
New Omaha Thompson Electric Light Co. v. Anderson, 413
New Orleans & N. E. Railroad Co. v. Burge, 266, 267, 268
New York, Chicago & St. Louis Railroad Co. v. Henderson, 260
New York, Chicago & St. Louis Railroad Co. v. McDougall, 489
New York, Lake Erie & Western Railway Co. v. Ball, 284, 457
New York, Lake Erie & Western Railway Co. v. Bennett, 58
New York, Lake Erie & Western Railroad Co. v. New Jersey Electric Ry. Co., 104, 532
New York, New Haven & Hartford Railroad Co. v. Henagan, 579
New York, New Haven & Hartford Railroad Co. v. Vizvari, 570
New York & Porto Rico S. Co. v. Garcia, 833, 834
New York Central Railroad Co. v. Chernew, 233
New York Central Railroad Co. v. Freedman, 93
New York Central Railroad Co. v. Grimstad, 265
New York Central Railroad Co. v. Lockwood, 210
New York Central Railroad Co. v. State, 673
New York Central Railroad Co. v. Thompson, 465
New York Central Railroad Co. v. Winfield, 578
New York Eskimo Pie Corp. v. Rataj, 283, 299
New York Life Insurance Co. v. Marotta, 732
New York Society for Suppression of Vice v. McFadden Publications, 779
New York Times v. Sullivan, 805, 815, 865, 887, 970, 971, 1011, 1012
New York Title & Mortgage Co. v. Hutton, 730, 743, 745
Newark, City of v. Eastern Airlines, 82
Newark Hardware & Plumbing Supply Co. v. Stove Manufacturers Corp., 992
Newark Trust Co. v. Bruwer, 834
Newberg, State v., 271, 323, 346
Newberger v. Pokrass, 246
Newberry v. Tarvin, 166
Newberry Co., J.J. v. Judd, 142
Newbury v. Vogel, 351
Newby v. Times-Mirror Co., 775
Newcastle, Town of v. Grubbs, 644
Newcomb v. Tisdale, 146, 148
Newcomb Hotel Co. v. Corbett, 854
Newell v. Randall, 738
Newell v. Whitcher, 44
Newhall v. Egan, 152
Newhall v. Kingsbury, 104
Newhart v. Pierce, 93
Newing v. Cheatham, 246, 248, 258
Newkirk v. Sabler, 140
Newlin v. New England Telephone & Telegraph Co., 997, 1000
Newman v. Christensen, 41
Newman v. City of Detroit, 367
Newman v. Fox West Coast Theatres, 417, 418
Newman v. Ligo Operating Co., 794
Newman v. Louisville & Nashville Railroad Co., 394
Newman v. Piazza, 462
Newman v. Southern Kraft Corp., 132
Newman v. Utility Trailer and Equipment Co., 700
Newport v. Hyde, 185
Newport, City of v. Fact Concerts, Inc., 12, 1044
Newsom v. Meyer, 76
Newsome v. Anderson, 68
Newsome, People v., 156
Newstead v. London Express Newspapers, 809
Newton v. Brook, 379
Newton v. Grubbs, 809
Newton v. Harland, 144
Newton v. McGowan, 881
Newton, State v., 46
Newton v. Weber, 902

Newton Co. v. Erickson, 324
Ney v. Yellow Cab Co., 224, 227, 313
Niagara Oil Co. v. Jackson, 550
Niagara Oil Co. v. Ogle, 552, 565
Nicholas v. Jenkins, 467
Nicholas v. Tri-State Fair & Sales Association, 419
Nicholls v. Colwell, 42, 118
Nicholls v. Ely Beet Sugar Factory, 69
Nichols v. Brabazon, 126
Nichols v. Consolidated Dairies, 411
Nichols v. Eaton, 835
Nichols v. English, 1072
Nichols v. Guy, 790
Nichols v. Item Publishers, 774
Nichols v. J. J. Newberry Co., 826
Nichols v. Lane, 756
Nichols v. Nashville Housing Authority, 958
Nichols v. Nold, 253, 695, 713
Nichols v. Severtsen, 892
Nichols v. Sonia, 151
Nichols & Shepard Co. v. Minnesota Threshing Manufacturing Co., 104
Nicholson v. American Fire & Casualty Insurance Co., 13
Nicholson v. Buffalo, Rochester & Pittsburgh Railway Co., 318
Nicholson v. Connecticut Half-Way House, Inc., 627, 629
Nicholson v. Hugh Chatham Memorial Hospital, Inc., 932, 933
Nicholson v. Roop, 881
Nickell v. Windsor, 423
Nickelsen v. Minneapolis, Northfield & Southern Railway Co., 438
Nickerson, Commonwealth v., 48, 114
Nickerson v. Hodges, 62, 725
Nickerson v. Massachusetts Title Insurance Co., 733
Nickerson v. Nickerson, 902, 904
Nickerson v. Thacher, 77
Nickerson v. Wheeler, 337
Nickleson v. Stryker, 928
Nickovich v. Mollart, 818
Nicks v. Joseph, 441, 443
Nicoletta v. North Jersey District Water Supply Commission, 1064
Nicoletti v. Westcor, Inc., 413, 423, 425
Nicoll v. Glennie, 325
Nicoll v. Long Island Railroad Co., 282
Nicolls v. Bastard, 103
Nicosia v. Guillory, 1071
Nidiffer v. Clinchfield Railroad Co., 382
Niebalski v. Pennsylvania Railroad Co., 252
Nieboer v. Detroit Electric Railway Co., 276
Nielsen v. Henry H. Stevens, Inc., 397
Nielsen v. Warner, 101
Nielson v. Eiler, 43
Niemann v. Vermilion County Housing Authority, 223, 401, 405, 406
Nienstedt v. Wetzel, 899, 900
Niernberg v. Gavin, 411

Nieting v. Blondell, 1055
Nifty Foods Corp. v. Great Atlantic & Pacific Tea Co., 1009
Nininger v. Norwood, 636
Nissen v. Cramer, 817
Nist v. Tudor, 212
Nitram Chemicals v. Parker, 638, 639
Nitroglycerine Case, The (Parrott v. Wells, Fargo & Co.), 559
Nixon v. Dispatch Printing Co., 837
Nixon v. Fitzgerald, 1061
Nixon v. Harris, 560
Nixon v. Herndon, 3
Nobility Homes v. Shivers, 708
Noble v. Fox, 739
Noble v. Harrison, 546, 547
Noble v. Johnson, 975
Noble v. Louisville Taxicab & Transfer Co., 42
Noble v. Marx, 444
Nobles v. Unruh, 299
Noce v. Ritchie, 48
Nocktonick v. Nocktonick, 907
Noe v. Chicago Great Western Railway Co., 468
Noe v. Meadows, 154
Noel v. Proud, 664
Noell v. Angle, 876
Noeninger v. Vogt, 792
Nohre v. Wright, 348
Noice v. Brown, 927
Nola v. Merollis Chevrolet Kansas City, Inc., 985, 990
Nolan v. Allstate Home Equipment Co., 892
Nolan v. Auto Transporters, 482, 483
Nolan v. Johns-Manville Asbestos, 167
Nolan v. Morelli, 581
Nolan v. Roberts, 398, 399
Nolan v. Standard Publishing Co., 791
Nolde Brothers, Inc. v. Wray, 206
Nonpareil Cork Manufacturing Co. v. Keasbey & Mattison Co., 965, 968, 975
Noonan v. Buick Co., 711
Noonan v. Orton, 827
Nopson v. Wockner, 261
Norden v. Jones, 675
Nordstrom v. Miller, 14
Nordstrom v. White Metal Rolling & Stamping Corp., 715
Norfolk & Portsmouth Belt Line Railroad Co. v. Barker, 179, 180
Norfolk & Western Railway Co. v. Amicon Fruit Co., 549
Norfolk & Western Railway Co. v. Henderson, 398
Norfolk & Western Railway Co. v. Holbrook, 218
Norfolk & Western Railway Co. v. Whitehurst, 283
Norfolk Southern Railroad Co. v. Beskin, 338
Norin v. Scheldt Manufacturing Co., 891
Norman v. City of Las Vegas, 855, 864
Normannia, The, 767
Norrell v. Vogel, 877
Norris v. Stoneham, 919
North v. Johnson, 264

North v. Williams, 140
North American Phillips Corp. v. Emery Air Freight Corp., 482
North Bend Lumber Co. v. City of Seattle, 460, 491
North Jellico Coal Co. v. Helton, 82
North Little Rock Transportation Co. v. Finkbeiner, 390
Northeast Airlines, Inc. v. World Airways, Inc., 987
Northern Assurance Co. v. New York Central Railroad Co., 147
Northern Commercial Co. v. United Airmotive, Inc., 379
Northern Pacific Railway Co. v. Gates, 650
Northern Pacific Railway Co. v. Lewis, 86
Northern States Contracting Co. v. Oakes, 290, 998
Northern Wisconsin Co-operative Tobacco Pool v. Bekkedal, 985, 989
Northup v. Eakes, 346, 354, 634
Northwestern Consolidated Milling Co. v. Chicago, Burlington & Quincy Railroad Co., 316
Northwestern Equipment Inc. v. Cudmore, 242
Northwestern National Casualty Co. v. McNulty, 13
Northwestern National Insurance Co. v. United States, 558
Northwestern Utilities v. London Guarantee & Accident Co., 546, 567
Norton v. Black, 403
Norton v. City of Easton, 405
Norton v. Jason, 926
Norton v. Kanouff, 963
Norton v. Payne, 915
Norton, State v., 780
Norton v. Wilbur Waggoner Equipment Rental & Excavating Co., 220
Norvell v. Safeway Stores Inc., 880, 881
Norvell v. Thompson, 75
Norwest v. Presbyterian Intercommunity Hospital, 936
Norwich, City of v. Breed, 389
Norwood v. Carolina Power & Light Co., 669
Norwood v. Eastern Oregon Land Co., 69
Norwood v. Lazarus, 440, 441
Norwood v. Sherwin-Williams Co., 182, 198, 426, 427, 454
Norwood v. Tellico River Lumber Co., 575
Norwood Trust Co. v. Twenty-Four Federal Street Corp., 99
Nosser v. Nosser, 959
Notarmuzzi v. Shevak, 776
Nothaus, People v., 601
Nounnan v. Sutter County Land Co., 754
Novak v. C. M. S. Builders & Developers, 408
Novak v. State, 532
Noved Realty Corp. v. A. A. P. Co., 738
Novick v. Becker, 890, 894
Novick v. Hearst Corp., 779
Novicki v. Blaw-Knox Co., 409
Nowak v. Nowak, 522, 531
Noyes v. Colby, 564
Noyes v. Shepherd, 148
Nuckolls v. Great Atlantic & Pacific Tea Co., 572
Nucor Corp. v. Tennessee Forging Steel Service, 1023
Nudd v. Matsoukas, 906, 959
Nuelle v. Wells, 907
Nugent v. Quam, 474
Nulsen v. Nulsen, 921
Nulty v. Hart-Bradshaw Lumber & Grain Co., 987
Nunan v. Bennett, 199, 280, 288, 294
Nunan v. Dudley Properties, 440
Nunez v. Nunez, 947
Nuyen v. Slater, 830
Nye v. Otis, 780
Nye v. Seymour, 506
Nye v. Western Union Tel. Co., 833
Nyer v. Carter, 894
Nyquist v. Foster, 764

O

Oak Haven Trailer Court, Inc. v. Western Wayne County Conservation Association, 630
Oakdale Building Corp. v. Smithereen Co., 255
Oakes v. Alexander, 816
Oakes v. Spaulding, 542
Oakland, City of v. Pacific Gas & Electric Co., 351
Oakland Meat Co. v. Railway Express Agency, Inc., 240
Oakley v. Lyster, 101, 102
Oates v. Glover, 765
Oates v. Taylor, 737
Oats v. Dublin National Bank, 342
Obanhein v. Arbuckle, 663
Oberempt v. Egri, 197
Oberlin v. Upson, 120, 926
Obert v. Dunn, 582
Obertoni v. Boston & Maine Railroad Co., 507
O'Boyle v. Avis Rent-A-Car System, 504
O'Brien v. American Bridge Co., 722
O'Brien v. Central Iron & Steel Co., 649
O'Brien v. Cunard S.S. Co., 113
O'Brien v. Fong Wan, 439
O'Brien v. Hazelet & Erdal, 168
O'Brien v. Louis K. Liggett, 247
O'Brien v. Luques, 753
O'Brien v. Pabst Sales Co., 854, 860, 867
O'Brien v. United States, 391
O'Brien v. Western Union Telegraph Co., 811, 984, 986
O'Callaghan v. Waller & Beckwith Realty Co., 482
O'Cana v. Espinosa, 790
Occhipinti v. Rheem Manufacturing Co., 370
Ocean Accident Co. v. Ilford Gas Co., 78
Ochampaugh v. City of Seattle, 394, 395, 397, 402, 407, 409
Ochoa, State v., 37
Ochs v. Borrelli, 372, 373
Ochs v. Woods, 754
Ockerman v. Faulkner's Garage, 413
O'Connell v. Chicago Park District, 94
O'Connell v. Walt Disney World Co., 484
O'Connor v. Altus, 447, 449
O'Connor v. Aluminum Ore Co., 621
O'Connor v. Benson Coal Co., 958
O'Connor v. Bloomer, 253

O'Connor v. Chicago, Milwaukee & St. Paul Railway Co., 317
O'Connor v. Corbitt, 940
O'Connor v. Donaldson, 1061
O'Connor v. Field, 846
O'Connor v. G & R Packing Co., 465
O'Connor v. Sill, 831
O'Connor v. United States, 252
O'Connor & Raque Co. v. Bill, 176
Odar v. Chase Manhattan Bank, 399
O'Day v. Shouvlin, 544, 551
Odden v. Union Indemnity Co., 586
Odegard v. Connolly, 591
O'Dell v. Cook's Market, Inc., 182
O'Dell v. Whitworth, 254
Oden v. Russell, 11
Odenwalt v. Zaring, 473
Odom v. East Ave. Corp., 662
O'Donnell v. Chase Hotel, Inc., 506
O'Donnell v. City of Chicago, 404
O'Donnell v. Elgin, Joliet & Eastern Railway Co., 227, 576, 581
O'Donnell v. Philadelphia Record Co., 834
O'Donohue v. Holmes, 145
Oehler v. L. Bamberger & Co., 63
Oestrike v. Neifert, 723
Oetjen v. Goff Kirby Co., 635
Official Aviation Guide Co. v. American Aviation Associates, Inc., 1023
Offshore Rental Co. v. Continental Oil Co., 998
O'Gara v. Philadelphia Electric Co., 395
Ogden v. Associated of the United States Army, 800
Ogden v. Claycomb, 126
Ogden v. Rabinowitz, 114
Ogden v. Riley, 788
Ogden v. Turner, 772
Oge v. Resolute Insurance Co., 96
Ogilvie v. Fotomat Corp., 14
Ogren v. Rockford Star Printing Co., 841
O'Hara v. Laclede Gaslight Co., 515
O'Hara v. Nelson, 552
O'Hara v. Western Seven Trees Corp. Intercoast Management, 442
O'Hearn v. Yorkshire Ins. Co., 586
Ohio & Mississippi Railway Co. v. Early, 382
Ohio & Mississippi Railway Co. v. Tindall, 955
Ohio Casualty Co. of Hamilton, Ohio v. Swan, 588
Ohio Casualty Insurance Co. v. Beckwith, 587
Ohio Casualty Insurance Co. v. Welfare Finance Co., 13
Ohio Farmers Insurance Co. v. Norman, 503
Ohio Finance Co. v. Berry, 87
Ohio Oil Co., State v., 7
Ohio Public Service Co. v. Myers, 786
Ohio Valley Bank v. Greenbaum Sons Bank & Trust Co., 330
Ohio Valley Contractors v. Board of Education of Wetzel Co., 1046
Ohio Valley Electric Railway Co. v. Scott, 642
Ohler v. Tacoma General Hospital, 167
Oil Belt Power Co. v. Touchstone, 413

Oil Conservation Engineering Co. v. Brooks Engineering Co., 974, 1011
Oil Well Core Drilling Co. v. Barnhart, 666
O'Keefe v. Kansas City Western Railway Co., 350, 459
O'Keefe v. South End Rowing Club, 409, 422
O'Keefe v. William J. Barry Co., 375
Oklahoma City v. Caple, 515
Oklahoma City v. West, 639
Oklahoma City Hotel Co. v. Levine, 483
Oklahoma Gas & Electric Co. v. Butler, 278
Oklahoma Gas & Electric Co. v. Hofrichter, 38
Oklahoma Natural Gas Co. v. Appel, 482
Oklahoma Natural Gas Co. v. Graham, 662
Oklahoma Natural Gas Co. v. Gray, 269
Oklahoma Publishing Co. v. Givens, 795, 809
Oklahoma Natural Gas Co. v. Pack, 667
Okmulgee, City of v. Hemphill, 305
Okun v. Superior Court, 1013
Olah v. Katz, 516
Olan Mills Inc. of Texas v. Dodd, 851, 852
O'Laughlin v. Minnesota Natural Gas Co., 207, 720
Old Dominion Branch No. 496, Letter Carriers v. Austin, 814
Old Town Development Co. v. Langford, 447, 722
Olderman v. Bridgeport-City Trust Co., 416
O'Leary v. Coenen, 433, 563
O'Leary v. State, 211
O'Leary v. Wangensteen, 137
Oles v. Pittsburg Times, 778
Olesen v. Beckanstin, 661
Olesen v. Fader, 132
Oleszczuk v. State, 223, 1050
Olfe v. Gordon, 189
Olivant v. Baring, 106
Oliver v. Aminoil, 183
Oliver v. Birmingham & Midland Omnibus Co., 531
Oliver v. City of Atlanta, 397
Oliver v. City of Worcester, 419
Oliver v. Haspil, 890
Oliver v. Kessler, 48
Oliver v. Miles, 271, 323
Oliver v. Union Transfer Co., 261
Oliver v. Williams, 334
Olney v. Boston & Maine Railroad, 570
Olschewski v. Hudson, 92
Olsen v. Kidman, 969
Olsen v. Macy, 422
Olsen v. Mading, 382, 445
Olsen Oil Co., R. v. Fidler, 968
Olsness v. State, 669
Olson v. A. W. Chesterton Co., 701
Olson v. Molland, 802, 803
Olson v. Pederson, 539
Olson v. Ratzel, 224, 230
Olson v. Riddle, 303
Oltmanns v. Driver, 490
Olwell v. Nye & Nissen Co., 674
Oma v. Hillman Periodicals, 860, 861, 862
Omaha National Bank v. Omaha Public Power District, 240

Omaha National Bank, State v., 90
O'Maley v. South Boston Gas Light Co., 570
O'Malley v. Laurel Line Bus Co., 305, 306
O'Malley v. Statesman Printing Co., 800
O'Malley-Kelley Oil & Auto Supply Co. v. Gates Oil Co., 894
Oman v. McIntyre, 296
O'Mara v. Pennsylvania Railroad Co., 249
Ominsky v. Charles Weinhagen & Co., 269, 292
Omni Flying Club, Inc. v. Cessna Aircraft Co., 484
Ondrey v. Shellmar Products Corp., 949
O'Neal v. Kellett, 441
O'Neal v. Southern Carbon Co., 349
O'Neil v. Bergan, 188
O'Neil v. Edmonds, 774
O'Neil v. National Oil Co., 335
O'Neil v. Sea Bee Club, 517, 522
O'Neil, State ex rel. Goff v., 645
O'Neill v. City of Port Jervis, 304, 306, 307
O'Neill v. Gray, 660
O'Neill v. Montfiore Hospital, 378
O'Neill v. New York, Ontario & Western Railway Co., 282
Ontario Ind. Loan Co. v. Lindsey, 968, 969, 970
Opal v. Material Service Corp., 552
Opelt v. Al. G. Barnes Co., 542, 563, 566
Opinion of the Justices, In re, 586, 602
Opple v. Ray, 223
Optivision v. Syracuse Shopping Center, 1010
O'Quin v. Baptist Memorial Hospital, 596, 1010
Orcutt v. Spokane County, 311
Order of Railway Conductors v. Jones, 983
Ordway v. Ferrin, 151
O'Regan v. Schermerhorn, 816
Ore-Ida Foods, Inc. v. Indian Head Cattle Co., 947
O'Reilly v. Curtis Publishing Co., 800
Organization for a Better Austin v. Keefe, 977
Orkin Exterminating Co. v. Culpepper, 203
Orlando v. Alamo, 929
Orient Overseas Line v. Globemaster Baltimore, Inc., 241
Orlando Executive Park, Inc. v. P. D. R., 202
Orleans, United States v., 1034
Orloff v. Los Angeles Turf Club, 663
Orlove v. Philippine Air Lines, 342
Ormsby v. Douglass, 827
O'Rourke v. Feist, 445
O'Rourke v. Walker, 158
O'Rourke, State ex rel. Leahy v., 644
Orr v. First National Stores, Inc., 532
Orr v. New Orleans Public Service, Inc., 209
Orr v. Saylor, 244
Orr v. United States, 513, 1034
Orrison v. City of Rapid City, 492
Orsini v. Eastern Wine Corp., 853
Orso v. City and County of Honolulu, 876
Ortega, United States v., 39, 41, 42
Ortho Pharmaceutical Corp. v. Chapman, 715
Orton v. Virginia Carolina Chemical Co., 266, 347, 634
Orwick v. Belshan, 293, 295

Osalek v. Baltimore & Ohio Railroad Co., 134
Osbekoff v. Mallory, 1057
Osborn v. Bank of United States, 1033
Osborn v. City of Whittier, 283, 292
Osborn v. Engleman, 920
Osborn v. Gene Teague Chevrolet Co., 736
Osborn v. Gillett, 945
Osborn v. Leach, 847
Osborn v. Leuffgen, 183
Osborn v. Veitch, 44
Osborne v. McMasters, 220, 224
Osborne v. Missouri Pacific Railroad Co., 750
Osborne v. Montgomery, 237, 291, 292
Osborne v. Morgan, 661, 669
Osborne v. Osmer, 540
Osborne v. Salvation Army, 576
Osborne, State ex rel. Clark v., 158
Osburn v. Pilgrim, 215
O'Shaughnessy v. Baxter, 150
O'Shea v. Lavoy, 489
Osinger v. Christian, 565
Osipoff v. City of New York, 505
Osmers v. Parade Publications, Inc., 800
Osterlind v. Hill, 375, 535
Ostro v. Safir, 798
Ostrofe v. H.S. Crocker Co., 1029
Ostroski v. Mount Prospect Shop-Rite, Inc., 403
Ostrowe v. Lee, 799, 833
Oswega Starch Factory v. Lendrum, 754
Otis v. Kolsky, 518
Otis Elevator Co. v. Embert to Use of South St. Corp., 670
Otis & Co. v. Grimes, 742
Otis Elevator Co. v. Robinson, 670
O'Toole v. Franklin, 889, 890, 891
O'Toole v. Pittsburgh & Lake Erie Railroad Co., 455
O'Toole v. Thousand Island Park Association, 437
O'Toole v. United States, 950
Ott v. Great Northern Railway Co., 30
Ott v. Washington Gas Light Co., 72
Otten v. Schutt, 830
Otter Tail Power Co. v. United States, 886
Otterbeck v. Lamb, 176
Otto v. Leany, 479, 527
Otto v. Levy, 508
Ottumwa, City of v. Nicholson, 84
Ouellette v. Blanchard, 433
Ouilette v. Theobald, 755
Oulighan v. Butler, 266, 347
Outcault v. New York Herald Co., 832
Over v. Schiffling, 826, 832, 834
Overbey v. Poteat, 540
Overhultz v. Row, 926, 985, 996
Overland Construction Co. v. Sirmons, 168
Overlock v. Ruedemann, 906
Overseas Tankship (U.K.) Ltd. v. Miller Steamship Co., 296
Overseas Tankship (U.K.) Ltd. v. Morts Dock & Engineering Co., Ltd., 296, 647
Oversmith v. Lake, 924, 925

TABLE OF CASES

Overson v. Lynch, 874
Overstreet v. New Nonpareil Co., 775, 783
Overstreet v. Ober, 252
Overton v. Combs, 894
Overton v. Overton, 921
Oviatt v. Camarra, 959
Oviatt v. Garretson, 348
Owen v. Beauchamp, 248
Owen v. Burcham, 180
Owen v. City of Independence, 1052, 1061, 1068
Owen v. Cook, 491
Owen v. Delano, 398
Owen v. Dix, 291
Owen v. Henman, 621, 855
Owen v. Ogilvie Publishing Co., 799
Owen v. Williams, 986
Owen v. Wilson, 166
Owens v. Cerullo, 329
Owens v. Elliott, 649
Owens v. Graetzel, 893
Owens v. Liverpool Corp., 362
Owens v. Mench, 963
Owens v. Norwood-White Coal Co., 762
Owens v. Scott Publishing Co., 804
Owens Brothers v. Chicago, Rock Island & Pacific Railway Co., 660
Owensboro Undertaking & Livery Association v. Henderson, 199, 717
Owl Drug Co. v. Crandall, 377, 381, 382
Ownby v. Kleyhammer, 904, 911
Oxford v. Berry, 53, 149, 152
Oxford v. Cross, 793
Oxner v. Seaboard Air Line Railway Co., 1004
Oyler v. Fenner, 919, 922
Ozark v. Wichita Manor, Inc., 250

P

P. v. Portadin, 372
P., Pamela v. Frank S., 910
Paar v. City of Prescott, 674
Pabon v. Hackensack Auto Sales, Inc., 206
Paccos v. Rosenthal, 98
Pacific Fire Ins. Co. v. Kenny Boiler & Manufacturing Co., 509
Pacific Indemnity Co. v. Thompson-Yaeger, Inc., 168
Pacific Live Stock Co. v. Murray, 348
Pacific Mutual Life Insurance Co. v. Tetirick, 62, 63
Pacific Packing Co. v. Bradstreet Co., 829
Pacific Typesetting Co. v. International Typographical Union, 991
Pack v. Wise, 858
Package Closure Corp. v. Sealright Co., 1013
Paderas v. Stauffer, 56
Padgett v. Boswell, 343
Padilla v. Chavez, 156
Padjen v. Shipley, 637
Padmore v. Lawrence, 826
Padmore v. Piltz, 159
Paducah Newspapers v. Wise, 775

Padula, State v., 125
Pagarigan v. Phillips Petroleum Co., 439
Page v. Green, 182
Page v. Hollingsworth, 538, 539
Page v. Mille Lacs Lumber Co., 650
Page v. Niagara Chemical Division of Food Machinery & Chem. Corp., 621, 640, 647
Page v. Parker, 751
Page v. Pilot Life Ins. Co., 763
Page v. Rose, 876, 879
Page v. Sloan, 245
Page v. Town of Bucksport, 278
Page v. Town of Newbury, 151
Pagelsdorf v. Safeco Insurance Co. of America, 446
Pagliero v. Wallace China Co., 1018
Paige v. North Oaks Partners, 402, 416
Paine v. Gamble Stores, 270
Paine v. Kelley, 48
Paint Products Co. v. Minwax Co., 1009, 1010
Painter v. City of Pittsburgh, 509
Painter v. E. W. Scripps Co., 836
Painter v. Gunderson, 646, 647
Painter v. Nichols, 570, 575
Painter v. TVA, 946
Painter, State v., 44
Pair v. Blakly, 200
Palatine Insurance Co. v. Griffin, 988
Palcsey v. Tepper, 906
Palermo v. Cottom, 870
Palestine Contractors, Inc. v. Perkins, 335
Palisades Citizens Association, Inc. v. Civil Aeronautics Board, 82
Pallet v. Sargent, 842
Pallikan v. Mark, 429
Palmateer v. International Harvester Co., 1029
Palmer v. Avery, 894
Palmer v. Baum, 928
Palmer v. Gordon, 397
Palmer v. Keene Forestry Association, 384
Palmer v. Mahin, 800, 846, 848
Palmer v. Maine Central Railroad Co. 48, 154
Palmer v. Mayo, 102
Palmer v. State, 465, 467
Palmer v. Thorpe, 772
Palmer v. Wick & Pultneytown Steam Shipping Co., 337
Palmeri v. Manhattan Railway Co., 506
Palmerlee v. Nottage, 780
Palmetto Bank & Trust Co. v. Grimsley, 764
Palmisano v. News Syndicate Co., 801
Palmiter v. Hackett, 738
Palmore v. Morris, Tasker & Co., 449
Palsgraf v. Long Island Railroad Co., 25, 284, 289, 293, 320
Paltey v. Egan, 512
Palumbo v. Harry M. Quinn, Inc., 91
Pamela Amusement Co. v. Scott Jewelry Co., 743
Pan American Petroleum Co. v. Byars, 622
Pan American Petroleum Corp. v. Like, 194
Panama Canal Co. v. Stockard & Co., 104
Panama Railroad Co. v. Johnson, 580

Panasuck v. Seaton, 343
Pandjiris v. Oliver Cadillac Co., 250
Pandolfo v. Bank of Benson, 775
Pangallo v. Murphy, 858
Pangburn v. Buick Motor Co., 328
Pangburn v. Bull, 893, 895
Panisko v. Dreibelbis, 49
Pankey v. Hiram Walker & Sons, 227
Panorama Resort v. Nichols, 541, 563
Pantazis v. Fidelity & Deposit Co. of Maryland, 957
Panther Coal Co. v. Looney, 351
Pantz v. Nelson, 99, 100
Pao Chen Lee v. Gregoriou, 764
Papakalos v. Shaka, 484
Papallo v. Meriden Savings Bank, 444
Pape, People v., 44
Pape v. Time, Inc., 838
Papenfus v. Shell Oil Co., 331
Papieves v. Lawrence, 63
Pappas v. Evans, 453
Pappenheim v. Metropolitan Elevated Railway Co., 84
Paquette v. Joyce, 388
Paquin v. Wisconsin Central Railway Co., 312
Paramount Pad Co. v. Baumrind, 994
Paramount Pictures v. Leader Press, 860, 966, 976
Paraska v. City of Scranton, 423
Parcell v. United States, 557
Parchefsky v. Kroll Brothers, 343
Pardee v. Nelson, 91
Parham v. Hughes, 948
Parham v. Taylor, 202
Parillo v. Giroux Co., 251
Paris v. Levy, 819, 832
Paris Air Crash, In re, 951
Park v. Chessin, 371
Park v. Detroit Free Press Co., 810, 837, 847
Park v. Security Bank & Trust Co., 888
Park, United States v., 227
Park & Sons Co., John D. v. National Wholesale Druggists' Association, 1013, 1024
Parke-Davis and Co. v. Stromsodt, 697
Parker v. American Woolen Co., 634
Parker v. Barnard, 220
Parker v. Brown, 1008
Parker v. City of Fort Worth, 644, 645
Parker v. Cushman, 563
Parker v. Dallas Hunting & Fishing Club, 885
Parker v. Flook, 1023
Parker v. Godin, 96
Parker v. Gordon, 918
Parker v. Highland Park, Inc., 497
Parker v. Kirkland, 818, 819
Parker v. Meek, 926, 928
Parker v. Middlebrook, 94
Parker v. Mise, 85
Parker v. Nelson Grain & Milling Co., 575
Parker v. Parker, 595
Parker v. Redden, 494
Parker v. Roberts, 52
Parker v. Roszell, 490
Parker v. Walrod, 112
Parker v. Warren, 705
Parker Co., Charles v. Silver City Crystal Co., 787, 832
Parkersburg & Marietta Sand Co. v. Smith, 673
Parkersburg Builders Material Co. v. Barrack, 626
Parking, Inc. v. Dalrymple, 421
Parkinson v. California Co., 270
Parkinson v. Shew, 675
Parks v. Allis-Chalmers Corp., 497
Parks v. Morris, Layfield & Co., 674
Parks v. Parks, 595
Parks v. Pere Marquette Railway Co., 384
Parks v. Starks, 283, 308
Parlato v. Connecticut Transit, 235
Parmenter v. Barstow, 330
Parmiter v. Coupland, 773
Parness v. City of Tempe, 202
Parr v. Helfrich, 94
Parratt v. Taylor, 1064
Parris v. St. Johnsbury Trucking Co., 12
Parrish v. Atlantic Coast Line Railroad Co., 377
Parrott v. Bank of America National Trust & Savings Association, 49
Parrott v. Wells Fargo & Co., 68
Parshall v. Lapeer Gas-Electric Co., 395
Parsons v. Age-Herald Co., 837
Parsons v. McKinley, 730
Parsons v. Manser, 542
Parsons v. Smithey, 913, 915
Partin v. Olney, 402
Partridge v. Sawyer, 879
Parvi v. City of Kingston, 199, 378, 381
Parzych v. Town of Branford, 181
Pashinian v. Haritonoff, 414, 415, 433
Pasierb v. Hanover Park Park District, 399, 406, 408, 411
Paskle v. Williams, 892
Pasley v. Freeman, 728, 755
Pasquale v. Chandler, 165
Passaic Print Works v. Ely & Walker Dry-Goods Co., 1010, 1013
Passman v. Commercial Credit Plan of Hammond, Inc., 62, 858
Pastene v. Adams, 317
Pastorelli v. Associated Engineers, 723
Patangall v. Mooers, 791
Pater v. Baker, 974, 975
Patnode v. Westenhaver, 323
Paton v. Great Northwestern Telegraph Co. of Canada, 799
Patrick v. Colerick, 139, 140
Patrick v. Smith, 554
Patrick v. Thomas, 798, 823
Patrol Valve Co. v. Farrell, 696
Patten v. Continental Casualty Co., 379
Patterson v. Adan, 586, 587
Patterson v. Brogan, 885
Patterson v. Correll, 762
Patterson v. Detroit, Lansing & Northern Railroad Co., 225

TABLE OF CASES

Patterson v. Henry, 126
Patterson v. Her Majesty Industries, Inc., 166
Patterson v. Hill, 921
Patterson v. Kasper, 666, 673
Patterson v. Kuntz, 130
Patterson v. Nutter, 158
Patterson v. Peabody Coal Co., 629
Patterson v. Prior, 673, 674
Patterson v. Rosenwald, 644
Patterson v. Standley, 125
Patterson, State v., 155
Patterson v. Tomlinson, 340
Patterson v. Tribune Co., 859
Patterson v. Weatherspoon, 170
Pattison v. Gulf Bag Co., 935
Pattison v. Jones, 828
Patton v. Brady, 940
Patton v. Cruce, 775
Patton v. Jacobs, 794
Patton v. Pickles, 259
Patton v. Texas Co., 439
Pattridge v. Youmans, 752
Patusco v. Prince Macaroni, Inc., 933
Paubel v. Hitz, 427, 429
Paul v. Davis, 867
Paul v. Hummel, 915
Paul v. N. L. Industries, 476
Paula v. Gagnon, 497
Pauley v. Combustion Engineering, Inc., 167
Paull v. Halferty, 965
Paulsen v. Gundersen, 118, 120
Paulsen v. Personality Posters, Inc., 832
Paulson v. Scott, 920
Pavelchak v. Finn, 449
Pavesich v. New England Life Insurance Co., 851, 863
Pavlik v. Kinsey, 1059, 1060
Pavlos v. Albuquerque National Bank, 521
Pavlovsky v. Board of Trade of San Francisco, 829
Pawhuska, City of v. Crutchfield, 56
Payless Discount Centers, Inc. v. 25–29 North Broadway Corp., 244, 250, 251
Payne v. Chicago & Alton Railroad Co., 458
Payne v. City of New York, 302
Payne v. M. Greenberg Construction, 248, 255, 393, 397
Payne v. Tancil, 790
Payson v. Macomber, 49, 121
Paysse v. Paysse, 793
Payton v. Abbott Labs, 361, 364, 365
Payton v. United States, 1040, 1041, 1042
Paxson, State v., 133
Paxton v. Alameda County, 723
Paxton v. Boyer 125, 128
Paxton v. Woodward, 775, 781
Peacock v. Retail Credit Co., 829
Peak v. Rhyno, 921
Pear v. Labiche's, Inc., 250
Pearce v. Brower, 822
Pearce v. Illinois Central Gulf Railroad Co., 412
Pearce v. Pearce, 924

Pearl Assurance Co., Limited v. National Insurance Agency, Inc., 8
Pearlman v. Garrod Shoe Co., 947
Pearlman v. W. O. King Lumber Co., 252
Pearlstein v. Leeds, 414
Pearson v. Dodd, 90, 856
Pearson v. Ehrich, 387
Pearson v. Inlow, 112
Pearson v. National Manufacture & Stores Corp., 959
Pearson v. Northland Transportation Co., 526
Pearson v. Skelton, 337
Pearson v. Taylor, 125
Pearson v. Wallace, 672
Pearson v. Wright, 821
Pearson & Son, S. v. Lord Mayor of Dublin, 764
Pease v. Brown, 750
Pease v. Shippen, 858
Pease v. Sinclair Refining Co., 171, 302
Pease v. Smith, 97
Pease & Elliman v. Wegeman, 665, 763
Peay v. Curtis Publishing Co., 862, 863, 864
Peck v. Brewer, 732
Peck v. Chouteau, 873
Peck v. Ellis, 337
Peck v. Newburgh Light, Heat & Power Co., 635
Peck v. Olian, 182, 454, 460
Peck v. Patterson, 98
Peck v. Smith, 83
Peck v. Tribune Co., 777, 804
Peck Iron & Metal Co. v. Seaboard Air Line Railway Co., 544
Peckham v. Warner Brothers Pictures, 152
Pecora v. Szabo, 970
Pecue v. West, 819, 835
Pecyk v. Semoncheck, 793
Pedernales Electric Cooperative, Inc. v. Schulz, 479
Pederson v. Dumouchel, 188
Pederson v. Eppard, 352
Pederson v. Jirsa, 919
Pederson v. Pederson, 574
Pedigo & Pedigo v. Croom, 352
Pedrick v. Raleigh & Pamlico Sound Railroad Co., 650
Pedroli v. Missouri Pacific Railway Co., 948
Peebler v. Olds, 890
Peed v. Washington Times, 859
Peek v. Derry, 767
Peek v. Gurney, 737
Peek v. Northern Pacific Railway Co., 1014
Peeples v. Brown, 85
Peeples v. Kawasaki Heavy Industries, Limited, 501
Peeples v. State, 822
Peerless Manufacturing Co. v. Bagley, 445, 512
Peerson v. Ashcraft Cotton Mills, 889, 891
Pegg v. Gray, 539
Pehowic v. Erie Lackawanna Railroad Co., 198
Pelavin v. Misner, 144
Pelham v. Griesheimer, 359
Pelkey v. Norton, 750
Pelletier v. Bilbiles, 505
Pellett v. Sonotone Corp., 334

Prosser & Keeton Torts 5th Ed. HB—27

Pellifigue v. Judice, 826
Peltola v. Western Workman's Publishing Society, 101
Pelton v. General Motors Acceptance Corp., 15
Pelton v. Markegard, 991
Pelzer v. Benish, 782
Pelzer v. Lange, 222
Pence v. Berry, 521
Pence v. Ketchum, 198, 199
Pendergrass v. Lovelace, 513
Pendergrass, State v., 158
Pendergrast, United States v., 557
Pendleton v. Time, Inc., 966, 972
Peneff v. Duluth, Missabe & Northern Railway Co., 716
Peneschi v. National Steel Corp., 514
Penfield v. Bennett Film Laboratories, 758
Penfold v. Westcote, 776
Penfolds Wines, Limited v. Elliott, 85, 100
Penick v. Ratcliffe, 817, 818
Penn v. Henderson, 133
Penn v. Inferno Manufacturing Corp., 705
Penn Central Transportation Co. v. Reddick, 504, 506
Penn Mutual Life Insurance Co. v. Crane, 754
Pennebaker v. Kimble, 736
Penney v. Pederson, 755
Penney Co., J.C. v. Chavez, 419, 427
Penney Co., J.C. v. Clark, 405
Penney Co., J.C. v. Cox, 141
Penney Co., J.C. v. McLaughlin, 504
Penney Co., J.C. v. Morris, 318
Penney Co., J.C. v. O'Daniell, 142
Pennington v. Davis-Child Motor Co., 717
Pennington v. Southern Pacific Co., 176
Pennington, State v., 645
Pennington's Administrator v. Pure Milk Co., 196
Penn-Ohio Steel Corp. v. Allis-Chalmers Manufacturing Co., 963
Pennsylvania Co. v. Roy, 209
Pennsylvania Co. v. West Penn Railways, 338
Pennsylvania Coal Co. v. Mahon, 645
Pennsylvania Coal Co. v. Sanderson, 551
Pennsylvania Fire Insurance Co. v. Levy, 100
Pennsylvania Railroad Co. v. Allen, 55
Pennsylvania Railroad Co. v. Hope, 283
Pennsylvania Railroad Co. v. Kerr, 283, 293
Pennsylvania Railroad Co. v. Miller, 636
Pennsylvania Railroad Co. v. Sagamore Coal Co., 552
Pennsylvania Railroad Co. v. Snyder, 716
Pennsylvania Railroad Co., State v., 545
Pennsylvania Railroad Co. v. Yingling, 382
Pennsylvania Steel Co. v. Elmore & Hamilton Contracting Co., 722
Pennsylvania Steel Co. v. Washington & Berkeley Bridge Co., 342
Pennsylvania Threshermen & Farmers Mutual Casualty Insurance Co. v. Thornton, 13
Penny v. Sears, Roebuck & Co., 426
Penny v. State, 44
Pennyman v. Rabanks, 962
Penry v. Dozier, 782
Pensacola Restaurant Supply Co. v. Davison, 182

Penthouse, Inc. v. Saba, 1057
Penthouse International, Limited v. Playboy Enterprises, 971
Penzin v. Stratton, 242
People v. _____ (see opposing party)
People ex rel. (see name of party)
People on Complaint of Maggio v. Charles Scribner's Sons, 853
People on Complaint of Stern v. Robert R. McBride & Co., 862
People's Finance & Thrift Co. v. Harwell, 60
Peoples Life Insurance Co. of Washington v. Talley, 829
People's National Bank v. Central Trust Co. of Kansas City, 742
Peoples National Bank v. Dixwell, 744
People's Service Drug Stores v. Somerville, 265
People's United States Bank v. Goodwin, 779
Peoria, City of v. Simpson, 327
Peoria Marine & Fire Insurance Co. v. Frost, 999
Pepper v. Morrill, 910
Perati v. Atkinson, 60
Perchell v. District of Columbia, 476
Percival v. General Motors Corp., 1028
Percival v. Hickey, 86
Pere Marquette Railroad Co. v. Chadwick, 622
Pereza v. Mark, 717
Perfection Paint & Color Co. v. Kouduris, 716
Perfetto v. Wesson, 525
Perham v. Coney, 102
Perham v. Portland General Electric Co., 945
Perkins v. Roberts, 214
Perkins v. Stein & Co., 30, 46
Perkins v. Vermont Hydro-Electric Corp., 292
Perks v. Firestone Tire & Rubber Co., 1028
Perlow v. AAAcon Auto Transport, Inc., 209
Perpich v. Leetonia Mining Co., 288
Perrenoud v. Helm, 880
Perricone, State v., 116
Perrigo, State v., 156
Perry v. Arsham, 891
Perry v. Bailey, 88
Perry v. Fredette, 175
Perry v. Hearst Corp., 841
Perry v. Hodgson, 119
Perry v. House of Refuge, 1070
Perry v. Hurdle, 876
Perry v. Jefferies, 22, 110, 536
Perry v. Kendrick's Transport, Ltd., 548, 564
Perry v. Northern Indiana Public Service Co., 381, 512, 513, 514
Perry v. Philadelphia, Baltimore & Washington Railroad Co., 956
Perry v. Rochester Lime Co., 312
Perry v. Ryback, 953
Perry v. St. Jean, 416
Perry Bros. Variety Stores v. Layton, 833
Perry's Administrator v. Louisville & Nashville Railroad Co., 955
Person v. Cauldwell-Wingate Co., 724

Personal Representative, Starling v. Fisherman's Pier, Inc., 426
Pescinski, In re Guardianship of, 115, 116
Pessl v. Bridger Bowl, 209
Pestlin v. Haxton Canning Co., 574
Petcoff v. Pestoret Lawrence Co., 322
Peter v. Chicago & North Western Railway Co., 461
Petermann v. International Brotherhood of Teamsters, Etc., 1028
Peters v. Hall, 873, 883
Peters v. Holiday Inns, Inc., 202
Peters v. Johnson, 268, 326, 668
Peters v. Jones, 928
Peters v. Lyons, 342
Peters v. Peters, 902
Peters v. Prince of Wales Theatre, 546
Peters v. Simmons, 167
Peterson v. American Grass Twine Co., 569
Peterson v. American Ice Co., 489
Peterson v. Balach, 433
Peterson v. Campbell, 455, 462
Peterson v. City and County of Honolulu, 907
Peterson v. City of Golden Valley, 514
Peterson v. Cleaver, 830
Peterson v. Conlan, 561
Peterson v. First National Bank, 759
Peterson v. Fulton, 278
Peterson v. Haffner, 38
Peterson v. Lutz, 149
Peterson v. Martin, 318
Peterson v. Minnesota Power & Light Co., 250, 454
Peterson v. Nielsen, 266
Peterson v. Rasmussen, 835
Peterson v. Richfield Plaza, 408
Peterson v. Robison, 154
Peterson v. Salt River Project Agricultural Improvement & Power District, 233
Peterson v. South & Western Railroad Co., 286
Peterson v. Standard Oil Co., 684
Peterson v. Steenerson, 821, 830
Peterson v. Taylor, 230, 401
Peterson, United States v., 128
Peterson v. Western Union Telegraph Co., 775, 786
Peterson v. Wolff, 101
Petit v. Cuneo, 986
Petition of (see name of party)
Petrak v. Cooke Contracting Co., 393
Petransky v. Repository Printing Co., 809
Petrey v. Liuzzi, 14
Petrich v. McDonald, 890
Petrie, In re, 573
Petrol Corp. v. Curtis, 569
Petroleum Marketing Corp. v. Metropolitan Petroleum Corp., 92
Petrone v. Margolis, 481
Petroski v. Northern Indiana Public Service Co., 410
Petry v. Childs & Co., 897
Pettengill v. Booth Newspapers, Inc., 506
Pettibone v. Simpson, 794
Petticolas v. City of Richmond, 330

Pettigrew v. W & H Development Co., 91
Pettingill v. Rideout, 8
Pettis v. State Department of Hospitals, 1066
Pett-Morgan v. Kennedy, 789
Pettway v. American Cast Iron Pipe Co., 1029
Petty v. General Accident Fire & Life Assurance Corp., 819
Pfaehler v. Ten Cent Taxi Co., 314
Pfaudler v. Pfaudler Co., 853
Pfeifer v. Standard Gateway Theater, 286, 288, 292, 321
Pfeiffer v. Grossman, 75
Pfeiffer v. Independent Plumbing & Heating Supply Co., 675
Pfeifly v. Henry, 782
Pfeiler v. Penn Allen Portland Cement Co., 587
Pfister v. Milwaukee Free Press Co., 848
Pfitzinger v. Dubs, 775
Pflugmacher v. Thomas, 527
Phelan v. Beswick, 15
Phelps, Commonwealth v., 156
Phelps v. Gilchrist, 99
Phenix Insurance Co. of Brooklyn v. New York Central & Hudson River Railroad Co., 382
Phez Co. v. Salem Fruit Union, 993, 1001
Phifer v. Foe, 835
Philadelphia, Baltimore & Washington Railroad Co. v. Mitchell, 516
Philadelphia, Baltimore & Washington Railroad Co. v. Roberts, 342
Philadelphia, City of v. Gilmartin, 650
Philadelphia, City of v. Philadelphia Rapid Transit Co., 998, 999
Philadelphia & Railroad Co. v. Derby, 5
Philadelphia & Reading Railway Co. v. Smith, 349, 350, 434, 459
Philadelphia Record Co. v. Leopold, 995
Philadelphia Wilmington & Baltimore Railroad Co. v. Quigley, 829
Philipp Co., Adolf v. New Yorker Staats-Zeitung Co., 965
Phillips v. ABC Builders, Inc., 168
Phillips v. Bradshaw, 834
Phillips v. Britannia Hygienic Laundry Co., 204, 228, 547
Phillips v. Bush, 413
Phillips v. Bynum, 540
Phillips v. Chicago Housing Authority, 443
Phillips v. Community Traction Co., 956
Phillips v. Dickerson, 65
Phillips v. Durham & C.R. Co., 283
Phillips v. Garner, 542
Phillips v. Goodyear Tire & Rubber Co., 1027
Phillips v. Gulf & South American Steamship Co., 348, 351
Phillips v. Hoefer, 791
Phillips v. Homestake Consolidated Placer Mines Co., 737, 738
Phillips v. Homfray, 940
Phillips v. International Association of Bridge, Structural & Ornamental Iron Workers, 886

TABLE OF CASES

Phillips v. J.F. Martin Cartage Co., 406, 407
Phillips v. J.L. Hudson Co., 715
Phillips v. Kimwood Machine Co., 693, 697, 701
Phillips v. Morrow, 53
Phillips v. Noble, 252
Phillips v. Pantages Theatre Co., 1006
Phillips v. Pickwick Stages, 148
Phillips v. Postal Telegraph Cable Co., 84
Phillips v. Soloway, 1074
Phillips, State v., 128, 156, 544
Phillips v. Sun Oil Co., 72, 74
Phillips v. Union Indemnity Co., 781
Phillips v. United States, 371, 373, 423
Phillips v. Wilpers, 133
Phillips & Benjamin Co. v. Ratner, 1003
Phillips Petroleum Co. v. Berry, 544
Phillips Petroleum Co. v. Hardee, 346, 351
Phillips Petroleum Co. v. Jenkins, 576
Phillips Petroleum Co. v. Vandergriff, 346, 634
Phillips Petroleum Co. v. West, 269
Phillips Sheet & Tin Plate Co. v. Griffith, 331
Philpot v. Brooklyn National League Baseball Club, 426
Philpot v. Kelley, 101
Philpott v. Kilpatrick, 921
Philpott v. Superior Court, 675
Phinney, State v., 150
Phipps v. General Motors Corp., 678, 693
Phipps v. Mitze, 409
Phipps v. Oregon Railroad & Navigation Co., 413
Phoenix, City of v. Camfield, 164
Phoenix, City of v. Johnson, 638, 645
Phoenix Insurance Co. v. Thomas, 380
Phoenix Newspapers v. Choisser, 836
Phoenix Refining Co. v. Powell, 228
Phoenix Title & Trust Co. v. Continental Oil Co., 747
Photographic Importing & Distributing Corp. v. Elgeet Optical Co., 1013, 1024
Pic Design Corp. v. Bearings Specialty Co., 1015
Picard v. McCormick, 761
Pickard v. City of Honolulu, 433
Pickard v. Sears, 733, 734
Pickens v. Hal J. Copeland Grocery Co., 965
Pickens v. Southern Railway Co., 404
Picker X-Ray Corp. v. General Motors Corp., 690
Pickering v. Dowson, 737
Pickett v. First American Savings & Loan Association, 239
Pickett v. Parks, 451
Pickett v. Waldorf System, 515, 516
Pickett v. Wilmington & Weldon Railroad Co., 396
Pickford Corp. v. De Luxe Laboratories, 91
Pickle v. Page, 924, 925
Pickwick Stages Corp. v. Messinger, 260
Pieczonka v. Pullman Co., 352, 353
Piedmont Cotton Mills, Inc. v. General Warehouse No. Two, Inc., 640
Piedmont Cotton Mills v. H.W. Ivey Construction Co., 991, 993
Piedmont Hotel Co. v. Henderson, 152
Pieh v. Flitton, 759

Piehl v. Dalles General Hospital, 204
Pier v. Schultz, 405
Pierce v. Albanese, 270, 288, 581
Pierce v. Carey, 740
Pierce v. Clemens, 495
Pierce v. Commonwealth, 135
Pierce v. Crisp, 917, 918, 921
Pierce v. DeGracia, 372
Pierce v. Doolittle, 884
Pierce v. Finerty, 140
Pierce v. Ford Motor Co., 684
Pierce v. Liberty Furniture Co., 706
Pierce v. Ortho Pharmaceutical Corp., 375, 1028, 1030
Pierce v. Thompson, 883
Pierce v. United States, 1041
Pierce v. Walters, 415
Pierce v. Yakima Valley Memorial Hospital Association, 596
Piercefield v. Remington Arms Co., 704
Pierpoint v. Hoyt, 91
Pierson v. Edstrom, 518
Pierson v. Pierson, 922
Pierson v. Ray, 1056, 1057, 1059, 1061
Pigg v. Brockman, 266
Piggly-Wiggly Alabama Co. v. Rickles, 39, 41
Piggott v. Miller, 928
Pigney v. Pointers Transport Service, 311
Pike v. Frank G. Hough Co., 678, 704, 946
Pike v. Grand Trunk Railway Co., 308
Pike v. Hanson, 50, 51
Pike v. United States, 950
Pilgrim Plywood Corp. v. Melendy, 644, 649, 651
Pilinko v. Merlau, 670
Pillars v. R.J. Reynolds Tobacco Co., 246, 258, 682
Pillsbury Flour Mills v. Miller, 590
Pilmore v. Hood, 738
Pilosky v. Dougherty, 340
Pilot Industries v. Southern Bell Telephone & Telegraph Co., 212
Pimpinello v. Swift & Co., 751
Pinal v. Ocean Ship Supply, Inc., 412, 413, 418
Pindell v. Rubenstein, 388, 401
Pine Bluff Natural Gas Co. v. Senyard, 515
Pine Grove Poultry Farm v. Newtown By-Products Manufacturing Co., 581, 683
Pines v. Perssion, 722
Pinette v. Pinette, 911
Pink v. Catanich, 793
Pinkerton National Detective Agency, Inc. v. Stevens, 855
Pinkham Lumber Co., J.E. v. Woodland State Bank, 332, 333
Pinn v. Lawson, 830
Pinnell v. Woods, 434
Pinnix v. Toomey, 661, 663
Pinoza v. Northern Chair Co., 461
Pion v. Caron, 794
Pioneer Construction Co. v. Bergeron, 937
Pioneer Hi-Bred Corn Co. v. Northern Illinois Gas Co., 207

Piper v. Menifee, 732
Pippin v. Chicago Housing Authority, 443
Piqua, City of v. Morris, 266
Piquet v. Wazelle, 526
Piracci v. Hearst Corp., 837
Piraccini v. Director General of Railroads, 544
Pirkle v. Oakdale Union Grammar School District, 377
Piscataqua Navigation Co. v. New York, New Haven & Hartford Railroad Co., 644, 650
Pitcher v. Lennon, 229
Pitman v. City of New York, 423
Pitney Bowes, Inc. v. Sirkle, 761
Pitre v. Bourgeois, 245
Pitrelli v. Cohen, 937
Pitt v. Donovan, 975
Pittman v. Cohn Communities, Inc., 1026
Pittman v. Pedro Petroleum Corp., 179, 407
Pittock v. Gardner, 948
Pitts v. Basile, 683
Pittsburg, Johnstown, Ebensburg & Eastern Railroad Co. v. Wakefield Hardware Co., 897, 898
Pittsburg Reduction Co. v. Horton, 318
Pittsburgh, Cincinnati, Chicago & St. Louis Ry. Co. v. Grom, 666
Pittsburgh, Cincinnati, Chicago & St. Louis Railway Co. v. Higgs, 660, 665
Pittsburgh, Cincinnati, Chicago & St. Louis Railway Co. v. Kinney, 482
Pittsburgh, Cincinnati, Chicago & St. Louis Railway Co. v. Lynch, 288
Pittsburgh, Cincinnati, Chicago & St. Louis Railway Co. v. Moore, 960
Pittsburgh, Cincinnati, Chicago & St. Louis Railway Co. v. Morton, 662
Pittsburgh, Fort Wayne, & Chicago Railway Co. v. Bingham, 394
Pittsburgh Athletic Club v. KQV Broadcasting Co., 1020
Pittsburgh Forge & Iron Co. v. Dravo Contracting Co., 297
Pittsburgh Steamship Co. v. Palo, 350, 357
Pittsfield Cottonwear Manufacturing Co. v. Pittsfield Shoe Co., 374
Pitzer v. M.D. Tomkies & Sons, 576
Pixley v. Clark, 552
Pixley v. Reed, 892
Pizitz Dry Goods Co., Louis v. Yeldell, 11
Pizzalotto v. Wilson, 256
Place v. Minster, 324
Placek v. City of Sterling Heights, 471
Plain v. Plain, 910
Plainview Realty, Inc. v. Board of Managers, 1026
Planchard v. Klaw & Erlanger New Orleans Theatres Co., 58
Plank v. Heirigs, 943
Plasikowski v. Arbus, 342
Plassan v. Louisiana Lottery Co., 876
Plate v. Southern Bell Telephone & Telegraph Co., 141
Platz v. City of Cohoes, 223, 232
Plaza Express Co. v. Galloway, 958

Pleasant v. Washington Sand & Gravel Co., 935
Plemmons v. Antles, 572
Plesko v. City of Milwaukee, 391
Plewes v. City of Lancaster, 425
Plimpton v. Friedberg, 761
Ploetz v. Big Discount Panel Center, Inc., 193, 194
Ploof v. Putnam, 147
Plonty v. Murphy, 43
Plotkin v. Plotkin, 902
Plough, Inc. v. Mason & Dixon Lines, 240
Plumb v. Richmond Light & Railroad Co., 252
Plumbing Connections, Inc. v. Kostelnik, 211
Plumlee, State v., 135, 155
Plumley v. Klein, 907
Plummer v. Dill, 413, 414
Plummer v. Reeves, 106
Plummer, State v., 430
Plunkett-Jarrell Grocery Co. v. Terry, 91
Plutshack v. University of Minnesota Hospitals, 191
Plyler v. Wheaton Van Lines, 213
PMP Associates, Inc. v. Globe Newspaper Co., 1024
Poche v. Maryland Casualty Co., 454
Pocholec v. Giustina, 405, 408, 409
Poe v. Voss, 751
Poeppers v. Missouri, Kansas & Texas Railway Co., 292
Pogany v. Chambers, 774, 778
Poggi v. Scott, 92, 93, 96, 97
Pohl v. Johnson, 665
Pokriefka v. Mazur, 1072
Polebitzke v. John Week Lumber Co., 140
Polemis, In re, 295, 296, 297, 302
Poleski v. Polish-American Publishing Co., 794
Poley v. Bender, 757
Polhill v. Walter, 741
Poling v. Ohio River Railroad Co., 413
Poliquin v. MacDonald, 368
Polk v. Trinity Universal Insurance Co., 915
Polk County v. Dodson, 1058
Polkinghorn v. Wright, 132
Pollack v. City of Newark, 50
Pollard v. Lyon, 793
Pollard v. Nicholls, 399
Pollard v. Oklahoma City Railway Co., 318
Pollard v. Phelps, 362
Pollard v. Photographic Co., 849
Pollard v. Ward, 921
Pollasky v. Minchener, 829, 832
Pollen v. Brewer, 143
Polley v. Boehck Equipment Co., 768
Polloni v. Ryland, 317
Polsky v. Levine, 496, 498
Pomeranz v. Class, 52
Pomfret v. Fletcher, 441
Pona v. Boulevard Arena, 494
Ponce v. Black, 251
Ponder v. Altura Farms Co., 770
Ponder v. Cobb, 830
Pontardawe R.D.C. v. Moore-Gwynn, 390
Pontarelli Trust v. City of McAllen, 1054
Ponticas v. K.M.S. Investments, 502

Pool, People v., 138
Poole v. Symonds, 103
Poor v. Oakman, 98
Pope v. Edward M. Rude Carrier Corp., 568
Pope v. Halpern, 518
Pope v. Reading Co., 387
Pope v. Willow Garages, 421
Popke v. Hoffman, 833
Popkin Brothers v. Volk's Tire Co., 342
Porell v. Cavanaugh, 93, 94
Poretsky & Sons, Harry v. Hurwitz, 423
Port Arthur, City of v. Wallace, 291
Portacci v. Moran Towing & Transportation Co., 471
Portee v. Jaffee, 365, 366
Porter v. Black, 229
Porter v. Delaware, Lackawanna Western Railroad Co., 364
Porter v. Department of Employment Security, 213
Porter v. King County Medical Society, 985
Porter v. Ritch, 155
Porter v. Stone, 754
Porter v. Stormont-Vail Hospital, 508
Porter v. United Railways Co. of St. Louis, 751
Porter, J.P. v. Bell, 547
Porubiansky v. Emory University, 185
Posin v. ABC Motor Court Hotel, 508
Posner Co., S.C. v. Jackson, 28, 981, 987, 990
Posnett v. Marble, 828
Posnien v. Rogers, 186
Post v. Munn, 85, 90
Postal Telegraph-Cable Co. v. Pacific Gas & Electric Co., 562, 628
Postal Telegraph-Cable Co. v. Warren-Godwin Lumber Co., 482
Postlewaite v. Morales, 251
Poston v. Home Insurance Co., 8
Posttape Associates v. Eastman Kodak Co., 484
Potashnick Truck Service v. City of Sikeston, 644
Potenburg v. Varner, 196, 197
Potomac Edison Co. v. Johnson, 244
Potomac Insurance Co. v. Nickson, 97
Potosi Zinc Co. v. Mahoney, 967
Potter v. Carolina Water Co., 671
Potter v. Crawford, 762
Potter Title & Trust Co. v. Young, 416, 425
Potts v. Amis, 416
Potts v. Chapin, 738
Potts v. Die, 832
Potts v. Krey, 197
Pottstown Daily News Publishing Co. v. Pottstown Broadcasting Co., 1020
Pouchan v. Godeau, 798
Poulin v. Colby College, 433
Poulos v. Dover Boiler & Plate Fabricators, 646, 647
Poulos v. Poulos, 836, 920, 922
Pound v. Augusta National, Inc., 183, 184, 419, 427, 456, 460, 488
Powell v. Barker, 338
Powell v. Benthall, 922
Powell v. Bentley & Gerwig Furniture Co., 629

Powell v. Champion Fiber Co., 49, 121
Powell v. Fall, 544, 547, 548
Powell v. Fletcher, 761
Powell v. Great Lakes Transit Corp., 421
Powell v. Heck, 486
Powell v. Langford, 717
Powell v. Ligon, 407
Powell v. Robinson, 100
Powell v. South Central Bell Telephone Co., 991
Powell v. Strickland, 917
Powell v. Superior Portland Cement, 636
Powell v. United Oil Corp., 434
Powell v. Village of Mount Zion, 220, 223
Powell v. Young, 826
Power v. Village of Hibbing, 311
Powers v. Clarkson, 77
Powers v. Durgin-Snow Pub. Co., 777
Powers v. Fisher, 92
Powers v. Kindt, 350
Powers v. Massachusetts Homeopathic Hospital, 1070
Powers v. Standard Oil Co., 266
Prager v. City of New York Housing Authority, 443
Prairie Creek Coal Mining Co. v. Kittrell, 956
Prairie Oil & Gas Co. v. Kinney, 981, 987
Prater v. Burns, 181, 200, 914
Prather v. H-K Corp., 419, 428
Pratt, Commonwealth v., 801
Pratt v. Daly, 938
Pratt v. Davis, 114, 115, 119
Pratt v. Duck, 12, 503
Pratt v. Freese's, Inc., 238
Pratt v. Higginson, 94, 98
Pratt v. Thompson, 746, 748
Pratt v. Western Pacific Railway Co., 484
Pratt Food Co. v. Bird, 1009
Praylou, United States v., 557
Preble v. Hanna, 99
Preble v. Johnson, 822
Preble, Town of v. Song Mountain, Inc., 644
Preece, State v., 127
Preferred Accident Insurance Co. v. Musante, Berman & Steinberg, 341, 343
Preissman v. D'Ornellas, 704
Prell Hotel Corp. v. Antonacci, 126, 507
Prendergast v. Allen, 526
Prentice v. Bertken, 874
Prentiss v. National Airlines, 557
President & Directors of Georgetown College, Application of, 116
President and Directors of Georgetown University v. Hughes, 596
President & Fellows of Harvard College v. Stearns, 650
President of Colby College v. Colby College-New Hampshire, 1017
Presley v. Cooper, 96
Press Co. v. Stewart, 832
Presson v. Mountain States Properties, Inc., 446
Prestenbach v. Sentry Insurance Co., 486
Preston v. Frey, 826, 848
Preston v. Hobbs, 825

Preston v. Hubbell, 117, 119
Preston v. Preston, 904
Preston v. Slezjak, 415
Preston, State ex rel. Anderson v., 649
Prettyman v. Shockley, 794
Prettyman v. Williamson, 921
Preuss v. Sambo's of Arizona, Inc., 426
Prewitt v. Clayton, 69, 78
Prewitt v. Wilson, 775, 780
Preyan v. United States Fidelity & Guaranty Co., 454
Pribonic v. Fulton, 491
Priboth v. Haveron, 123
Price v. Baker, 332, 333
Price v. Central Assembly of God, 422
Price v. Dickson, 639
Price v. Glosson Motor Lines, Inc., 162
Price v. Grose, 621
Price v. Jenkings, 780, 782
Price v. Johnson Cotton Co. of Wendell, 724
Price v. McDonald, 250
Price v. McNeill, 471, 576
Price v. New Castle Refractories Co., 575, 576
Price v. Seaboard Air Lines Railway Co., 532
Price v. Shell Oil Co., 719
Price v. Shepard, 117, 867, 1064
Price v. South Metropolitan Gas Co., 567
Price v. Wabash Railroad Co., 335, 336
Price v. Whitley, 775
Price v. Yellow Pine Paper Mill Co., 64
Price-Bass Co. v. Owen, 331
Prichard v. Veterans Cab Co., 181
Priddy v. Bunton, 50, 121
Pridgen v. Boston Housing Authority, 377, 398
Pries v. Atlanta Enterprises, 413
Priester v. Milleman, 87
Priestley v. Fowler, 480, 571
Priewe v. Fitzsimons & Connell Co., 642
Primeau, State v., 644
Primus v. Bellevue Apartments, 442
Prince v. Atchison, Topeka & Santa Fe Railway Co., 504
Prince v. Brackett, Shaw & Lunt Co., 756
Prince v. Pittston Co., 367
Prince v. Prince, 595
Prince v. Ridge, 45
Prince v. State Mutual Life Insurance Co., 10
Prince v. Wolf, 407, 409
Prince Albert v. Strange, 849
Princess Amusement Co. v. Smith, 143
Princeton Community Phone Book, Inc. v. Bate, 1063
Pringle v. Storrow, 732
Prins v. Holland-North America Mortgage Co., 798, 799
Prior v. White, 413, 424, 626, 632
Pritchard v. Liggett & Myers Tobacco Co., 269, 691, 700
Pritchett v. Board of Commissioners of Knox County, 855
Pritchett v. Kimberling Cove, Inc., 200
Proctor v. Adams, 147
Proctor v. Tilton, 140
Produce Trading Co. v. Norfolk Southern Railway Co., 342

Professional & B.M. Life Insurance Co. v. Bankers Life Co., 776
Progress Laundry Co. v. Hamilton, 1023
Prokey v. Hamm, 184
Prokop v. Becker, 558
Prooth v. Wallsh, 185, 188, 261, 262
Prosser v. City of Ottumwa, 647, 650
Provence v. Doolin, 485
Provenzo v. Sam, 308, 461
Provident Loan Trust Co. v. McIntosh, 753
Prowell v. City of Waterloo, 511
Prudential Society v. Ray, 199
Pruet v. Dugger-Holmes & Associates, 341
Pruitt v. Bethell, 552
Prutch v. Ford Motor Co., 253
Pryor v. Foster, 770
Pstragowski v. Metropolitan Life Insurance, 933
Public Motor Service Co. v. Standard Oil Co. of New Jersey, 732
Public Service Co. of New Hampshire v. Elliott, 175, 454
Public Service Electric & Gas Co. v. Waldroup, 343
Puchlopek v. Portsmouth Power Co., 68, 389
Puchta v. Rothman, 411
Puckett v. Sullivan, 623
Puckett v. Young, 540
Pudlo v. Dubiel, 303
Puffer v. Welch, 743
Puget Sound National Bank v. McMahon, 751
Puget Sound Navigation Co. v. Carter, 965
Puget Sound Traction, Light & Power Co. v. Frescoln, 957
Pugh v. Hassell, 88
Pugh v. Holmes, 435
Pugh, State v., 155
Pugsley v. Smyth, 920
Pulaski Gas Light Co. v. McClintock, 299
Pulaski Housing Authority v. Smith, 510
Pulka v. Edelman, 385
Pulliam v. Gentry, 760
Pulling v. Great Eastern R. Co., 941
Pullman v. Walter Hill & Co., 799
Pullman Palace-Car Co. v. Adams, 383
Pullman Palace Car Co. v. Bluhm, 309
Pullman Palace Car Co. v. Laack, 572
Pullman Standard Car Manufacturing Co. v. Local Union No. 2928, p. 779
Pulvermann v. A.S. Abell Co., 836
Pumphrey v. J.A. Jones Construction Co., 567
Pumphrey v. Manor Real Estate & Trust Co., 1034, 1040
Pumphrey v. Quillen, 742, 746
Purcell v. Davis, 627, 640
Purcell v. Macnamara, 882
Purcell v. St. Paul City Railway Co., 302, 360
Purcell v. Westinghouse Broadcasting Co., 838
Purchase v. Seelye, 310
Purdy v. Kerentoff, 954
Purdy v. Woznesensky, 65
Pure Milk Association v. Kraft, 990
Pure Milk Producers Association v. Bridges, 977
Pure Oil Co. v. Boyle, 1000

Purk v. Federal Press Co., 168
Purtle v. Shelton, 181
Putman v. Erie City Manufacturing Co., 705
Putnal v. Inman, 829
Putnam v. Payne, 146
Putnam v. Savage, 949
Putnam v. Stout, 443, 444
Putnam v. Wyley, 88
Putnam Memorial Hospital v. Allen, 327
Putney v. Keith, 211
Purofied Down Products Corp. v. National Association of Bedding Manufacturers, 974
Puroto v. Chieppa, 78
Purvis v. Busey, 649
Purvis v. Consolidated Energy Products Co., 708
Put and Hardy v. Rawsterne, 89
Putt v. Daussat, 199
Pyatt v. Engel Equipment, Inc., 715
Pyburn v. Fourseam Coal Co., 436
Pybus v. Grasso, 764
Pye v. Cardwell, 891
Pye v. Faxon, 515
Pyke v. City of Jamestown, 278
Pyle v. Waechter, 924, 928

Q

Quaker Oats Co. v. Grice, 278
Quaker Worsted Mills Corp. v. Howard Trucking Corp., 660, 666
Quarman v. Burnett, 509
Quatray v. Wicker, 337
Quattlebaum v. Wallace, 527
Quave v. Ray, 519, 521
Quebec R. Co. v. Vandry, 632
Quigley v. Clough, 135
Quigley v. Delaware & Hudson Canal Co., 307
Quill v. Empire State Telephone & Telegraph Co., 312
Quillen v. Quillen, 164, 183
Quillian v. Mathews, 229
Quimby v. Blackey, 8
Quina v. Roberts, 62
Quince, Commonwealth v., 998
Quinlan, In re, 116
Quinlivan v. Brown Oil Co., 986
Quinlivan v. Great Atlantic & Pacific Tea Co., 427
Quinn v. Crimmings, 551
Quinn v. Leathem, 1005
Quinn v. Nolan, 158
Quinn v. Sun Printing & Publishing Co., 775
Quinones v. Public Administrator, 458
Quinones v. United States, 1039

R

R. & L. Transfer Co. v. State for Use of Schmidt, 228
R and W Hat Shop v. Sculley, 981, 1003
Rabb v. Trevelyan, 836
Rabeke v. Baer, 928
Rabon v. Guardsmark, Inc., 506

Racer v. Utterman, 256, 260
Racine v. Morris, 389
Rackett v. Rackett, 126
Radburn v. Fir Tree Lumber Co., 349
Rade v. Press Publishing Co., 790
Radecki v. Schuckardt, 919, 920, 923, 1025
Raden v. City of Azusa, 1028
Rader v. Davis, 27
Rader v. Derby, 1018
Radigan v. W.J. Halloran Co., 286, 618
Radio Station KFH Co. v. Musicians Association Local No. 297, p. 985
Radle v. Hennepin Ave. Theatre & Realty Co., 421
Radoff v. Hunter, 562
Raefeldt v. Koenig, 30
Raflo v. Losantiville Country Club, 183
Rafter v. Dubrock's Riding Academy, 250
Rager v. McCloskey, 73, 1010
Ragnone v. Portland School District No. 1J, 416, 417
Ragsdale v. Ezell, 42
Rahn v. Milwaukee Electric Railway & Light Co., 83
Railroad Commission of Texas v. Manziel, 83
Railway Express Agency v. Goodman's New York & Connecticut Express Corp., 105
Raine v. Drasin, 887, 891
Raines v. Mercer, 911
Raines v. Southern Railway Co., 570
Rainham Chemical Works v. Belvedere Fish Guano Co., 546, 547, 548
Rainier's Dairies v. Raitan Valley Farms, 819
Rains v. Heldenfels Brothers, 377
Raisen v. Raisen, 903
Raleigh Fitkin-Paul Morgan Memorial Hospital v. Anderson, 116, 368
Ram v. Lamley, 826
Ramage v. Cohn, 660
Rambo v. Rambo, 905
Ramey v. Fassoulas, 372
Ramey v. Ramey, 217
Ramirez v. Chavez, 131, 324
Ramirez v. Deters, 455
Ramirez v. Redevelopment Agency of City & County of San Francisco, 340, 512
Rampell, Inc., A.S. v. Hyster Co., 986
Rampone v. Wanskuck Buildings, Inc., 443
Ramsby v. Beezley, 102
Ramsdell v. Pennsylvania R. Co., 832
Ramsey v. Arrott, 884
Ramsey v. Camp, 336
Ramsey v. Carolina-Tennessee Power Co, 284, 292, 348
Ramsey v. Cheek, 834
Ramsey v. Mading, 447
Ramsey v. Marutamaya Ogatsu Fireworks Co., 513
Ramsey v. Ramsey, 922
Ramsay v. Rimpley, 525
Ramstead v. Morgan, 819
Ranard v. O'Neil, 229
Rand v. Hearst Corp., 853
Randall v. Ridgley, 38
Randall v. Sanders, 77

TABLE OF CASES

Randall v. Shelton, 69, 171
Randall, Inc., Douglas W. v. AFA Protective Systems, Inc., 202, 203
Randol v. Kline's, Inc., 881
Randolf v. Town of Bloomfield, 349, 350
Randolph's Administrator v. Snyder, 375, 660, 662
Randy Knitwear, Inc. v. American Cyanamid Co., 749
Ranells v. City of Cleveland, 1053
Raney v. Honeywell, Inc., 699
Rangen, Inc. v. Sterling Nelson & Sons, Inc., 982, 1015
Ranger v. Goodrich, 789
Ranger Insurance Co. v. Hartford Steam Boiler Inspection & Insurance Co., 381
Raniak v. Krukowski, 143
Rank v. Kuhn, 918, 920, 922
Rankin v. Howard, 1057, 1058
Rankin v. Saenger, 874
Ranous v. Hughes, 822, 834
Ransmeier v. Camp Cody, Inc., 956
Ransom v. Grubbs, 415
Ranson v. Kitner, 111
Rapee v. Beacon Hotel Corp., 457
Raphael v. Goodman, 731
Rapid Sewing Center v. Sanders, 100
Rappaport v. Nichols, 303, 718
Rappaport v. Rappaport, 891
Rappenenecker v. United States, 382
Raschid, Al v. News Syndicate Co., 963
Rascoe v. Town of Farmington, 12
Rase v. Minneapolis, St. Paul & Sault Ste. Marie Railway Co., 570
Rasmussen v. Benson, 17, 289
Rasmussen v. National Tea Co., 423
Rasmussen v. Trico Feed Mills, 574
Rasmussen Buick-GMC, Inc. v. Roach, 893
Raspa, Commonwealth v., 36
Ratcliff v. Davies, 89
Ratcliffe v. Evans, 963, 972
Ratcliffe v. Walker, 836, 922
Rathmell v. Wesleyville Burough, 575
Rathvon v. Columbia Pacific Airlines, 247, 258, 259
Ratlief v. Yokum, 197, 464, 468, 477
Rau v. Kirschenman, 200
Rau v. Redwood City Woman's Club, 439
Rauch v. American Radiator & Standard Sanitary Corp., 704
Rauh & Sons Fertilizer Co., E. v. Shreffler, 625
Rausch v. McVeigh, 384
Raven v. Coates, 1053
Raven Red Ash Coal Co. v. Ball, 675
Ravndal v. Northfork Placers, 648
Rawe v. Richards, 956
Rawitzer v. St. Paul City Railway Co., 463
Rawlings Sporting Goods Co. v. Daniels, 686
Rawlins v. Hutchinson Publishing Co., 858
Rawlins v. Nelson, 575
Rawls v. Bennett, 876
Ray v. Ameri-Care Hospital, 186
Ray v. Dyer, 144
Ray v. Goldsmith, 220

Ray v. Hutchinson, 405
Ray v. Parsons, 922
Raycroft v. Tayntor, 27
Raymer v. United States, 382
Raymond v. Eli Lilly & Co., 167
Raymond v. General Motorcycle Co., 1072
Raymond v. Yarrington, 981, 1003
Raymond Syndicate v. Guttentag, 104
Rayonier, Inc. v. United States, 543
Ray's Administrator v. Standard Oil Co., 319
Razzano v. Kent, 84
RCA Manufacturing Co. v. Whiteman, 1020
Rea v. St. Louis-San Francisco Railroad Co., 260
Reach v. Quinn, 871
Read v. Case, 156
Read v. Coker, 43
Read v. J. Lyons & Co, 546, 548, 562
Read, Regina v., 772
Reading Finance & Security Co. v. Harley, 91
Reagan v. Guardian Life Insurance Co., 819
Reardon v. News-Journal Co., 864, 868
Reardon v. Thompson, 413
Reasnor, Town of v. Pyland Construction Co., 261
Reasoner v. Chicago Rock Island & Pacific Railway Co., 394
Reber v. Illinois Central Railroad Co., 621
Reboni v. Case Brothers, Inc., 576
Reckert v. Roco Petroleum Corp., 436
Recreation Centre Corp. v. Zimmerman, 423
Rector v. Smith, 816
Rector v. Southern Coal Co., 542
Redarowicz v. Ohlendorf, 659
Redd Chemical & Nitrate Co. v. W.T. Clay Mercantile Co., 105
Reddaway v. Banham, 1016
Redden v. James T. McCreery Co., 444
Reddick v. Newburn, 541
Reddie v. Scoolt, 928
Redding v. Redding, 905
Reddington v. Getchell, 389
Redgrave v. Hurd, 764
Redick v. Peterson, 363
Redman v. Hudson, 888
Redmond v. Columbia Pictures Corp., 860
Redway v. Gray, 792
Reece Construction Co. v. State Highway Commission, 239
Reed v. Cooke, 763
Reed v. Ford, 65
Reed v. Harper, 809
Reed v. Maley, 45
Reed v. Molnar, 225
Reed v. Orleans Parish Schoolboard, 858
Reed v. Pennsylvania Railroad Co., 577
Reed v. Peoria & Oquawka Railroad Co., 940
Reed v. Real Detective Publishing Co., 857
Reed v. Shreveport Furniture Co., 141
Reed Manufacturing Co., Evan L. v. Wurts, 380, 1008
Reeder v. Guaranteed Foods, Inc., 758
Reeder v. Western Gas & Power Co., 482

Reedie v. London & N.W.R. Co., 509
Reeg v. Shaughnessy, 188
Reek v. Lutz, 441
Reese v. Danforth, 1058
Reese v. Julia Sport Wear, 47
Reese v. Midland Empire Packing Co., 209, 240
Reese v. Reese, 906
Reeves v. Jackson, 75
Reeves v. Property Managers, Inc., 436
Reeves v. State, 130
Regan v. City of Seattle, 439
Regan v. Superb Theater, 937
Regas v. Helios, 102
Regent Co-op Equity Exchange v. Johnston's Fuel Liners, Inc., 328
Regester v. Lincoln Oil Refining Co., 649
Regez, State ex rel. v. Blumer, 644
Regina v. _____ (see opposing party)
Register Newspaper Co. v. Stone, 841
Regus v. Schartkoff, 761
Rehling v. Brainard, 921
Reich v. State Highway Department, 1046
Reichert v. Neacy, 894
Reichman v. Drake, 991, 992
Reichman v. Harris, 149
Reid v. Brodsky, 620
Reid v. Nichols, 846
Reid v. Spadone Machine Co., 938
Reid v. Swindler, 200
Reid v. True, 878
Reid v. Volkswagen of America, Inc., 729
Reiff v. Commonwealth, 1048
Reilly v. Curtiss, 792
Reiman v. Pacific Development Society, 777
Reiman Associates, Inc. v. R/A Advertising, Inc., 165
Reimann v. Monmouth Consolidated Water Co., 594, 671
Reimard v. Bloomsburg & Sullivan Railroad Co., 307
Reiner v. North American Newspaper Alliance, 994
Reinhardt v. Reitz, 884
Reininger v. Prickett, 830
Reiser v. Lohner, 192
Reiss v. Chicago, Milwaukee, St. Paul & Pacific Railroad Co., 218
Reiszel v. Fontana, 181
Reit v. Meyer, 874
Reitan v. Goebel, 793
Reiter v. Grober, 523, 530
Reitmeister v. Reitmeister, 867
Reitmeyer v. Sprecher, 443
Reliable Transfer Co., United States v., 471
Reliance Insurance Co. v. Barron's, 970
Reliance Insurance Co. v. Dickens, 162
Reliance Shoe Co. v. Manly, 744
Relle v. Western Union Telegraph Co., 362
Rembaugh v. Phipps, 98
Remeikis v. Boss & Phelps, Inc., 381
Remick Music Corp. v. American Tobacco Co., 970
Remington v. Bentley, 787, 792
Renaire Corp. v. Vaughn, 76, 141
Rendell v. Scott, 757

Renfro v. Fox, 237
Renfro Drug Co. v. Lawson, 779, 798, 800
Renfro Drug Co. v. Lewis, 422
Renfrow, State v., 357
Renner v. Canfield, 65
Rennick v. Fruehauf Corp., 363
Rennick v. Hoover, 393, 440
Renninger, Inc. v. Foremost Dairies, Inc., 695
Reno v. Bull, 768
Renslow v. Mennonite Hospital, 369
Renz v. Penn Central Corp., 396, 397, 479
Repke, People v., 129
Reporters' Association of America v. Sun Printing & Publishing Association, 779
Republic Gear Co. v. Borge-Warner Corp., 987
Republic Iron & Steel Co. v. Self, 45, 59
Republic of France v. United States, 281
Resag v. Washington National Insurance Co., 425, 426
Resavage v. Davies, 286, 365
Reserve Insurance Co. v. Gulf Florida Terminal Co., 239
Reservoir Manor Corp. v. Lumbermen's Mut. Insurance Casualty Co., 744
Respublica v. De Longchamps, 40, 41
Respublica v. Sparhawk, 148
Restaino v. Griggs Motor Sales, 387
Reste Realty Corp. v. Cooper, 722
Restifo v. McDonald, 339
Retail Credit Co. v. Garraway, 829
Retail Lumber Dealers' Association v. State, 1025
Retailers Commercial Agency, Inc., Petition of, 829, 835
Retherford v. Halliburton Co., 935
Reti v. Vaniska, Inc., 312
Reuck v. McGregor, 110, 154
Reugther v. Fowler & Williams, Inc., 1028
Reuille v. Bowers, 228, 230, 231
Reutenik v. Gibson Packing Co., 947
Reuter v. Iowa Trust & Savings Bank, 441
Reuter v. Kenmore Building Co., 424, 441
Reuter v. Swarthout, 541
Reuter v. United States, 240, 452
Reutkemeier v. Nolte, 11, 926, 927
Revell v. Deegan, 441
Rex v. _____ (see opposing party)
Reyes v. Wyeth Laboratories, 688
Reynolds v. City of Burlington, 175
Reynolds v. Clarke, 29, 30, 69, 622
Reynolds, Commonwealth v., 156
Reynolds v. Community Fuel Co., 626
Reynolds v. Fitzpatrick, 104, 105
Reynolds v. Pegler, 10, 15
Reynolds v. Pierson, 36, 40, 42
Reynolds v. Texas & Pacific Railway Co., 270, 321
Reynolds v. Thompson, 959
Reynolds v. Villines, 966
Reynolds v. W.H. Hinman Co., 549
Reynolds v. Willis, 950
Reynolds Metals Co. v. Martin, 71
Reynolds Metals Co. v. Yturbide, 245, 262
Rex Utilities, Inc. v. Gaddy, 454, 456, 459, 479
Rexroth v. Coon, 103

Rhea v. White, 337
Rhimer v. Davis, 176
Rhine v. Duluth, Missabe & Iron Range Railway Co., 195
Rhinehart v. Whitehead, 324
Rhoads v. Bryant, 523
Rhoads v. Service Machine Co., 492
Rhoades v. Bugg, 967
Rhoades v. Malta Vita Pure Food Co., 995
Rhoades v. Seidel, 436
Rhoda v. Aroostook General Hospital, 1070
Rhodes v. City of Kansas City, 407
Rhodes v. De Haan, 253
Rhodes v. Dunbar, 627, 640
Rhodes v. Fromenthal, 524
Rhodes v. Graham, 854
Rhodes v. Sperry & Hutchinson Co., 850, 854
Rhodes v. Star Herald Printing Co., 837
Rhodes, States v., 157
Riblet v. Spokane-Portland Cement Co., 70, 620, 639
Rice v. Argento, 411
Rice v. Coolidge, 872
Rice v. Eureka Paper Co., 571
Rice v. Forby 439
Rice v. Gilbreath, 766
Rice v. Jaskolski, 185, 188
Rice v. Lumberton, 1053
Rice v. Marler, 506
Rice v. Miller, 150
Rice v. Press, 760
Rice v. Price, 769
Rice v. Simmons, 776
Ricehill v. Brewer, 877
Rich v. City of Mobile, 1050
Rich v. Eason, 816
Rich v. Finley, 294
Rich v. McInerny, 54
Rich v. New York Central & Hudson River Railroad Co., 995
Rich v. Rogers, 887
Rich v. Scalio, 780, 798
Richard v. Gulf Theatres, 649
Richard v. Hunter, 14
Richard v. Nowlan, 103
Richard v. Richard, 903
Richard & Thalheimer, Ex parte, 730
Richards v. City of Lawton, 165
Richards v. Crocker, 184
Richards v. Daugherty, 634
Richards v. Ellis, 1059
Richards v. Foss, 742
Richards v. Gruen, 821
Richards v. Kansas Electric Power Co., 289, 308
Richards v. Marlow, 408, 409
Richards v. Stanley, 313, 314
Richards v. United States, 1034
Richards v. Washington Terminal Co., 632
Richardson, In re, 116
Richardson v. American Cotton Mills, 575
Richardson v. Anthony, 139, 140

Richardson v. Atkinson, 100
Richardson v. Bulk Petroleum Corp., 439
Richardson v. Dunbar, 223
Richardson v. Edgeworth, 1057
Richardson v. Fountain, 461
Richardson v. Gunby, 823, 827
Richardson v. Ham, 314
Richardson v. Hansen, 215
Richardson v. Murphy, 620
Richardson v. Pacific Power & Light Co., 334
Richardson v. Pridmore, 63
Richardson v. State Department of Roads, 958
Richardson v. Terry, 995
Richardson v. True, 526
Richardson v. United States, 208, 289, 308
Richardson, United States v., 43
Richardson, Allison, United States v., 45
Richardson, State ex rel. v. Edgeworth, 311
Richelieu Hotel Co. v. International Military Encampment Co., 731
Richenbacher v. California Packing Corp., 245, 247, 262
Richeson v. Kessler, 817
Richette v. Solomon, 995
Richey v. Kemper, 420
Richey & Gilbert Co. v. Northern Pacific Railway Co., 665
Richman Brothers Co. v. Miller, 513, 516
Richmond v. Employer's Fire Insurance Co., 485
Richmond v. Fiske, 42, 114
Richmond v. Knowles, 563
Richmond & Danville Railroad Co. v. Benson, 315
Richmond, City of v. House, 626
Richstein v. Roesch, 102
Richter v. Cordes, 143, 144
Richter v. Razore, 570
Richter v. Stolze, 793
Richtmyer v. Mutual Livestock Commission Co., 95, 98
Rickards v. Lothian, 546, 564, 567
Rickards v. Sun Oil Co., 1008
Rickbeil v. Grafton Deaconess Hospital, 799, 833
Ricker v. Freeman, 198, 307
Rickert v. Geppert, 246
Rickey v. Boden, 487, 488, 489, 491, 492, 497
Rickman v. Safeway Stores, Inc., 12
Ricky v. Chicago Transit Authority, 365, 366
Riddle v. McGinnis, 927
Ridenhour v. Oklahoma Contracting Co., 229
Rideout v. Winnebago Traction Co., 212
Rider v. Clarkson, 620
Riding v. Smith, 963, 966
Riding v. Travelers Insurance Co., 587
Ridley v. Grifall Trucking Co., 171
Ridley Investment Co. v. Croll, 724
Rieck v. Medical Protective Co. of Fort Wayne, Indiana, 372
Riedi v. Heinzl, 941
Riegel v. Hygrade Seed Co., 54
Riegel Textile Corp. v. Celanese Corp., 221
Riesbeck Drug Co. v. Wray, 177
Rieser v. District of Columbia, 203

Riess v. Sanford, 1022
Riexinger v. Ashton Co., 337
Rigby v. Hewitt, 281
Rigdon v. Rigdon, 907
Rightmire v. Shepard, 540
Riley v. Askin & Marine Co., 802, 803
Riley v. Baddour, 790
Riley v. Chicago Cougars Hockey Club, Inc., 485
Riley v. Davison Construction Co., 492, 497
Riley v. Gulf, Colorado & Santa Fe Railway Co., 375
Riley v. Holcomb, 181
Riley v. Industrial Finance Service Co., 329, 334, 351
Riley v. Johnson, 180
Riley v. Lissner, 445
Riley v. Marcus, 202, 443
Riley v. Standard Oil Co., 317, 544
Riley v. Standard Oil Co. of Indiana, 277
Riley v. White, 737
Rill v. Chiarella, 513
Rimer v. Rockwell International Corp., 225, 462
Rindge v. Sargent, 619
Rine v. Morris, 401
Rinehart v. Bills, 918
Riney v. Wray, 183
Ring v. Ogden, 3
Ringgold v. Land, 793
Ringhiser v. Chesapeake & Ohio Railway Co., 579
Rinzler v. Folsom, 71, 627
Ripps v. Herrington, 826
Rippy v. State, 126
Ripy v. Cronan, 758
Rischmiller v. Dahl, 950
Rise v. United States, 1037, 1042
Riser v. Riser, 911
Riser v. Smith, 229
Risley v. Lenwell, 510, 514
Risque's Administrator v. Chesapeake & Ohio Railway Co., 716
Riss v. City of New York, 1049, 1052
Ristan v. Frantzen, 352
Ritchie v. Arnold, 827
Ritchie v. Thomas, 259
Ritchie v. Widdemer, 828
Ritschy v. Garrels, 826
Rittenberry v. Robert E. McKee, Inc., 493
Ritter v. Beals, 493, 576
Ritter v. Ritter, 893, 902
Ritter v. Taucher, 523
Ritter Corp., T.E. v. Rose, 514
Rittmiller v. School District No. 84, p. 596
Rival v. Atchison, Topeka & Santa Fe Railroad Co., 376
Rivera v. Selfon Home Repairs & Improvements Co., 435, 444
Rivers, State v., 377
Riverside Cotton Mills v. Lainer, 328
Rives v. Atlanta Newspapers, Inc., 800
Riviello v. Waldron, 503
Rix v. Town of Alamogordo, 321, 349
Roach v. Damron, 140
Roach v. Harper, 855

Roach v. Kononen, 172
Roadman v. C.E. Johnson Motor Sales Co., 413
Roark v. St. Paul Fire & Marine Insurance Co., 246, 257
Roark v. Stone, 717
Robak v. United States, 371
Robalina v. Armstrong, 48, 114
Robbins v. Alberto-Culver Co., 687
Robbins v. City of Chicago, 515
Robbins v. Swift, 152
Robbins v. Treadway, 776
Roberson v. Rochester Folding Box Co., 24, 850, 852
Roberson v. State, 127
Roberson v. Stokes, 130
Roberts v. American Brewed Coffee, 200
Roberts v. Brown, 213, 214
Roberts v. Clark, 995
Roberts v. Cohen, 922
Roberts v. Commercial Standard Insurance Co., 588
Roberts v. Connelly, 928
Roberts v. Criss, 995
Roberts v. Gonzalez, 506
Roberts v. Griffith Co., 561
Roberts v. Harrison, 390
Roberts v. Hooper, 196
Roberts v. Indiana Gas & Water Co., 195, 378
Roberts v. Johnson, 210
Roberts v. Lisenbee, 912
Roberts v. Martin, 636
Roberts v. Messinger, 88
Roberts v. Mitchell Brothers Truck Lines, 239
Roberts, People v., 147
Roberts v. Ray, 249
Roberts v. Roberts, 794, 904
Roberts v. Rosenblatt, 429
Roberts v. Speck, 139
Roberts v. State, 175, 176
Roberts, State v., 127
Roberts v. Tardif, 186, 187, 188
Roberts v. Trans World Airlines, 209
Roberts v. Union Carbide Corp., 955
Roberts v. United States, 184, 460
Roberts v. Williams, 718
Roberts v. Yarboro & Wimberly, 98
Robertson v. Arnold, 636
Robertson v. Chicago, Burlington & Quincy Railroad Co., 326
Robertson v. Cincinnati, New Orleans & Tex. Pac. Ry., 638
Robertson v. Commonwealth, 153
Robertson v. Edelstein, 9
Robertson v. Industrial Insurance Co., 819
Robertson v. Parks, 324
Robertson v. Sichel, 1067
Robertson v. Smith, 752
Robertson v. Trammell, 335
Robertson v. Travis, 196
Robertson v. Wegmann, 944
Robidoux v. Busch, 542
Robillard v. P & R Racetracks, Inc., 485
Robillard v. Selah-Moxee Irrigation District, 346

Robillard v. Tillotson, 425
Robinette v. May Coal Co., 956
Robinette v. Price, 149
Robins v. Finestone, 664
Robins v. Franks, 790
Robins Dry Dock & Repair Co. v. Flint, 999
Robinson v. Baugh, 634
Robinson v. Bird, 104
Robinson v. Board of County Commissioners, 1059
Robinson v. Bruce Rent-A-Ford Co., 527
Robinson v. Butler, 309
Robinson v. City of Decatur, 130
Robinson v. Goudchaux's, 895, 896
Robinson v. Hartley, 525
Robinson v. Home Fire & Marine Insurance Co., 820
Robinson v. Howard Brothers of Jackson, Inc., 200
Robinson v. Johnson, 838
Robinson v. Jones, 798
Robinson v. Kerr, 540, 560
Robinson v. Kilvert, 562, 628
Robinson v. Lindsay, 181, 182, 1071
Robinson v. McNeil, 503
Robinson v. Moore, 927
Robinson v. Pediatric Affiliates Medical Group, Inc., 188
Robinson v. Pioche, Bayerque & Co., 176, 198
Robinson v. Robinson, 566
Robinson v. Shell Petroleum Corp., 528
Robinson v. Southern Railway Co., 383
Robinson v. Standard Oil Co., 284, 292
Robinson v. Threadgill, 661
Robinson v. Van Auken, 830
Robinson v. Warren, 532
Robinson v. Weaver, 166
Robinson & Co., C.N. v. Green, 47, 51, 141
Robison v. Robison, 554
Robison v. Texas Pine Land Association, 1013
Robson v. Jones, 140
Roby, In re, 574
Roby v. Auker, 211
Roche v. Llewellyn Ironworks Co., 590
Roche v. Meyler, 972
Rochester v. Anderson, 329
Rochester Brewing Co. v. Certa Bottling Works, 972
Rochester Civic Theater, Inc. v. Ramsey, 762
Rochester Gas & Electric Co. v. Dunlop, 68, 556, 557
Rochette v. Town of Newburgh, 392, 416
Rochin v. California, 866
Rockafellow v. Rockwell City, 390
Rockaway Boulevard Wrecking & Lumber Co. v. Raylite Electric Corp., 999
Rockford, Rhode Island & St. Louis Railroad Co. v. Heflin, 511
Rockingham Mutual Fire Insurance Co. v. Bosher, 39, 982
Rockwell v. Ortho Pharmaceutical Co., 166
Rockwell, People v., 38
Rod v. Farrell, 166
Roda v. Berko, 752, 737
Roddy v. Chicago & Northwestern Railroad, 246
Roddy v. Francis, 520

Roddy v. Missouri Pacific Railway Co., 716
Rodee v. Seaman, 761
Rodgers v. Bryan, 41
Rodgers v. Ferguson, 943
Rodgers v. Galindo, 339
Rodgers v. Missouri Pacific Railway Co., 315
Rodgers v. Wise, 829
Rodgers v. Yellow Cab Co., 303
Rodrigues v. Campbell Industries, 1000, 1001
Rodrigues v. State, 364, 365
Rodriguez v. Bethlehem Steel Corp., 932, 933, 938
Rodriguez v. City of New Haven, 455
Rodriguez v. Montgomery, 256
Rodriguez v. New York State Thruway Authority, 171, 197, 454
Rodriguez v. Patti, 368
Rodriguez v. Shell's City, Inc., 703
Rodwell v. Camel City Coach Co., 665
Roe v. Narragansett Electric Co., 395
Roe, People v., 130
Roe v. St. Louis Independent Packing Co., 413
Roe v. Wade, 369, 371, 867, 954
Roe & Co., Wm. G. v. Armour & Co., 349
Roebuck v. Wick, 754
Roehrich v. Holt Motor Co., 93
Roemer v. Retail Credit Co., 835
Roessler v. O'Brien, 442
Rogers v. Board of Road Commissioners for Kent County, 76
Rogers v. Brummet, 760
Rogers v. Butler, 596
Rogers v. Cato Oil & Grease Co., 430
Rogers v. Citizens Bank, 94
Rogers v. Coca Cola Bottling Co., 262
Rogers v. Doubleday & Co., 847
Rogers v. Elliott, 56, 628
Rogers v. Florence Printing Co., 10
Rogers v. Frush, 914
Rogers v. Hill, 873
Rogers v. Hime, 953
Rogers v. Kabakoff, 139
Rogers v. Karem, 703
Rogers v. Kent Board of County Road Commissioners, 73
Rogers v. Libbey, 674
Rogers v. Lumbermen's Mutual Casualty Co., 118
Rogers v. Missouri Pacific Railroad Co., 270, 578, 579
Rogers v. Newby, 913
Rogers v. Portland & Brunswick Street Railway Co., 750
Rogers v. Rogers, 911
Rogers v. Scyphers, 448, 723
Rogers v. Sells, 115
Rogers v. Smith, 932
Rogers v. Spady, 476
Rogers v. Thompson, 818
Rogers v. Toni Home Permanent Co., 690, 729
Rogers v. Toro Manufacturing Co., 532
Rogers v. Williard, 65, 66
Rogers v. Yellowstone Park Co., 903, 959

Roher Transfer & Storage Co., Earl E. v. Hutchinson Water Co., 671
Rohlfing v. Moses Akiona, Limited, 956
Rohlfs v. Weil, 513, 516
Rohr v. Riedel, 139, 848
Rohrabacher v. Woodward, 571
Rokusek v. Bertsch, 212
Roland v. Slesinger, 620
Rolater v. Strain, 116, 119
Roller v. Roller, 904, 905
Rollins Leasing Corp. v. Bakley, 532
Rollman v. Morgan, 464
Roman v. King, 492
Romana v. Boston Elevated Railway Co., 397
Romanik v. Toro Co., 908
Romano v. Birmingham Railway, Light & Power Co., 620
Romanoff Land & Mining Co. v. Cameron, 730
Romansky v. Cestaro, 228
Rome Sentinel Co. v. Boustedt, 859
Romedy v. Johnston, 429
Ronan v. Briggs, 929
Rookes v. Barnard, 9
Rooney v. New York, New Haven & Hartford Railroad Co., 345
Rooney v. Woolworth, 413
Roos v. Loeser, 223
Roper v. Commercial Fibre Co., 423
Roper v. Florida Public Utilities Co., 332
Rorer Iron Co. v. Trout, 763
Rosales v. Stewart, 392; 437
Rosario v. City of Lansing, 408
Roschmann v. Sanborn, 522
Roscoe v. Schoolitz, 827
Rose v. Borenstein, 778
Rose v. Daily Mirror, 779
Rose v. Gunn Fruit Co., 437
Rose v. Lundy, 19
Rose v. Pennsylvania Railroad Co., 283
Rose v. Peters, 288
Rose v. Port of New York Authority, 245
Rose v. Sapulpa Rural Water Co., 381
Rose v. Socony-Vacuum Corp., 549
Rose v. Sprague, 326
Rose v. Standard Oil Co. of New York, 619
Rose v. State, 567
Rose v. Tholborn, 827, 828
Rose Co. v. Lowery, 65, 141
Rosefield v. Rosefield, 911, 918, 925
Rosemont Enterprises, Inc. v. Irving, 853
Rosemont Enterprises, Inc. v. Random House, Inc., 897
Rosenau v. City of Estherville, 229
Rosenau v. Peterson, 461
Rosenbaum v. Roche, 828
Rosenberg v. Cryrowski, 761
Rosenberg v. Hartman, 199
Rosenberg v. Howle, 742
Rosenberg v. J.C. Penney Co., 506, 965
Rosenberg v. Mason, 834
Rosenberger v. Consolidated Coal Co., 412

Rosenblatt v. Baer, 806
Rosenblatt v. John F. Ivory Storage Co., 767
Rosenbloom v. Metromedia, Inc., 805
Rosenblum v. Ginis, 891
Roseneau v. City of Estherville, 410
Roseneau v. Empire Circuit Co., 981, 1024
Rosenkoff v.Mariani, 995
Rosenstrom v. North Bend Stage Line, 519
Rosewell, Rex v., 643
Roshto v. Hebert, 857
Ross v. Butler, 634
Ross v. Caunters, 980, 981, 987, 1001
Ross v. Cuthbert, 937
Ross v. Fitch, 794
Ross v. Hartman, 227, 313
Ross v. Kansas City General Hospital & Medical Center, 168
Ross v. Kirby, 389
Ross v. Michael, 43, 45, 133
Ross v. Nutt, 314
Ross v. Pennsylvania Railroad Co., 329
Ross v. Phillip Morris & Co., 700
Ross v. Sequatchie Valley Electric Co-op., 404
Ross v. United States, 1040
Ross v. Vereb, 180
Ross v. Williams Manufacturing Co., 73
Ross v. Wright, 1007, 1008
Rossell v. Cottom, 541
Rosser v. Atlantic Trust & Security Co., 265
Rossi v. Del Duca, 147
Rossiter v. Minnesota Bradner-Smith Paper Co., 892
Rossman v. La Grega, 469
Roswel v. Vaughan, 728
Roth v. First National Bank of New Jersey, 503
Roth v. Greensboro News Co., 847
Roth v. National Automobile Mutual Casualty Co., 587
Roth v. Palmer, 672
Roth v. Smith, 53
Rothberg v. Olenik, 721
Rothchild v. Schwarz, 92
Rothe v. Hull, 119
Rothenberg v. Aero Mayflower Transit Co., 484
Rothermel v. International Paper Co., 1024, 1029
Rothermel v. Phillips, 758
Rothman v. Metropolitan Casualty Insurance Co., 586
Rothstein Corp., R.L. v. Kerr S.S. Co., 91
Rotstain v. Lillis, 219
Rottkamp v. Young, 1063
Rotwein v. Gersten, 930
Rouleau v. Blotner, 266, 267
Rounds v. Phillips, 717
Rounds, People v., 153
Rountree v. Lerner Development Co., 441, 442
Roundtree v. Technical Welding and Fabrication Co., 943
Rourk v. Selvey, 347
Rourke v. Garza, 698, 706
Rouse v. Creech, 121
Rouse v. Gravelworks, Ltd., 547
Rouse v. Hornsby, 258

Rouse v. Twin Pines Sanitarium, Inc., 894
Rousseau, State v., 156
Routh v. Quinn, 223
Rovegno v. San Jose Knights of Columbus Hall Association, 270, 415
Rovinski v. Rowe, 308
Rovira v. Boget, 781
Row v. Home Savings Bank, 96, 112
Rowan v. Butler, 984, 1010
Rowe v. Ayer & Williams, 442
Rowe v. Hawkins, 132
Rowe v. Oscar Ewing Distributing Co., 262
Rowe v. Phillips, 760
Rowe v. Richards, 327, 956
Rowe v. United States, 127
Rowland v. Byrd, 394
Rowland v. Christian, 433
Rowland v. City of Corpus Christi, 393, 399, 412, 417
Roxana Petroleum Co. v. Cope, 937
Roy v. Goings, 879
Royal Aquarium v. Parkinson, 821
Royal Baking Powder Co. v. Wright, 949, 966, 969
Royal Finance Co. v. Schaefer, 1072
Royal Indemnity Co. v. Midland Counties Public Service Corp., 302
Royal Realty Co. v. Levin, 995
Royal-Liverpool Insurance Group v. Macarthy, 96
Royce v. Oakes, 101
Royer v. Belcher, 126
Rozell v. Northern Pacific Railway Co., 304
Rozewski v. Simpson, 564
Rozhon v. Triangle Publications, 853, 861
Rozumailski v. Philadelphia Coca Cola Bottling Co., 262
Rubalcava v. Gisseman, 902
Rubeck v. Huffman, 951
Rubenfeld, People v., 644, 645
Rubenstein v. United States, 207
Ruberg v. Skelly Oil Co., 374
Rubin v. Girard Trust Co., 446
Rubino v. Utah Canning Co., 667
Ruble v. Bunting, 776
Ruble v. Ruble, 921
Ruble v. Turner, 333
Ruby v. Casello, 441
Ruchinsky v. French, 488
Rucker v. Burke, 971
Rucker v. Frye, 525
Rude v. Nass, 828
Ruden v. Hansen, 186, 188
Ruderman v. Warner-Lambert Pharmaceutical Co., 691
Rudes v. Gottschalk, 222
Rudley v. Tobias, 929
Rudnay v. Corbett, 913
Rue v. State, Department of Highways, 461, 1073
Ruerat v. Stevens, 246
Ruff v. Eckerds Drugs, Inc., 885
Ruggles v. Sands, 78
Ruhs v. Pacific Power & Light, 511
Ruiz v. Bertolotti, 61
Ruiz v. Cold Storage & Insulation Contractors, Inc., 530

Ruiz v. Forman, 74
Rulane Gas Co. v. Montgomery Ward & Co., 313, 319
Rullis v. Jacobi, 40, 41
Rumbolz v. Wipf, 532
Rumetsch v. John Wanamaker, New York, Inc., 510
Rumsey v. Freeway Manor Minimax, 697
Rupert v. Stienne, 903, 907
Ruppel v. Ralston Purina Co., 11
Rush v. Buckley, 110, 149
Rush v. Cavenaugh, 791
Rush v. Commercial Realty Co., 492
Rush v. Miller, 191
Rush v. Plains Township, 405
Rush v. Smitherman, 718
Rush v. State Farm Mutual Automobile Insurance Co., 162
Rushing v. Hooper-McDonald, Inc., 71
Rushton v. Howle, 289, 308
Rushton v. Smith, 948
Rushton v. Winters, 207, 417
Rushworth v. Taylor, 99
Russ v. Western Union Telegraph Co., 362
Russell v. Aragon, 642
Russell v. Brown, 75
Russell v. Croteau, 984
Russell v. Ford Motor Co., 709
Russell v. Geis, 834
Russell v. Hamlett, 526
Russell v. Industrial Transportation Co., 752, 762, 766
Russell v. Jackson, 119
Russell v. Marboro Books, 864, 867
Russell v. Mayor of New York, 146
Russell v. Men of Devon, 1051
Russell v. Merchants & Miners Transportation Co., 265
Russell, Rex v., 377
Russell v. Salem Transportation Co., 936
Russell v. Tate, 1064
Russell v. Tomlinson, 325
Russell v. United States, 340
Russell v. Walker, 342
Russell Construction Co. v. Ponder, 717
Russell-Vaughn Ford, Inc. v. Rouse, 99
Russell's Case, 940
Russen v. Lucas, 51
Russick v. Hicks, 929
Russo v. Dinerstein, 307
Russo v. Texas & Pacific Railway Co., 399
Russo v. Williams, 746, 748
Rust v. Schaitzer, 333
Rustad v. Great Northern Railway Co., 583
Ruth v. Educational Films, 860, 861
Ruth v. Hutchinson Gas Co., 517
Ruth v. Ruth, 308
Rutherford v. Dougherty, 832
Rutherford v. Gray Line, Inc., 527
Rutherford v. Modern Bakery, 269
Rutherford v. Paddock, 841
Rutherford v. Rideout Bank, 505
Rutherford v. Smith, 525

Rutland & Washington Railroad Co. v. Bank of Middlebury, 106
Rutter v. Northeastern Beaver County School District, 487, 490, 491, 494, 496
Ruud v. Grimm, 351
Ryalls v. Leader, 778
Ryals v. Livingston, 766
Ryan v. Cameron, 219, 307
Ryan v. Chown, 96, 97, 663
Ryan v. City of Emmetsburg, 70, 552, 622
Ryan v. Cumberland Valley Railroad Co., 571
Ryan v. Donnelly, 155
Ryan v. Foster & Marshall, Inc., 478
Ryan v. Hearst Publications, 778, 783
Ryan v. Marren, 136, 562
Ryan v. New York Central Railroad Co., 25, 271, 275, 282, 284, 288, 293, 299, 594
Ryan v. St. Louis Transit Co., 722
Ryan v. State, 1049, 1050
Ryan v. Towar, 400
Ryan v. Western Pacific Insurance Co., 505
Ryan v. Wilson, 821, 822
Ryan v. Zweck-Wollenberg Co., 262
Ryan Gulch Reservoir Co. v. Swartz, 349
Ryan's Estate, In re, 342
Ryce v. Whitley, 445
Ryder, State ex rel. Wilcox v., 644
Ryerson v. American Surety Co. of New York, 891
Ryerson v. Carter, 138, 139, 140
Rylands v. Fletcher, 512, 549
Ryley v. Lafferty, 914
Ryon v. Shaw, 816

S

S.A. Empresa De Viacao Aerea Rio Grandense (Varig Airlines) v. United States, 381
Saad v. Pappageorge, 269
Saari v. State, 511
Saatzer v. Smith, 385, 428
Sabatinelli v. Butler, 200
Sabella v. Baton Rouge General Hospital, 244, 248
Saberton v. Greenwald, 11
Sabine & East Texas Railway Co. v. Johnson, 77
Sabo v. Delman, 763
Sabre v. Mott, 139
Sacco v. Herald Statesman, Inc., 970
Sachs v. Blewett, 763
Sachs v. Chiat, 550
Sackett v. Haeckel, 521, 523
Sacknoff v. Sacknoff, 911
Sacks v. Stecker, 817
Sacramento Suburban Fruit Lands Co. v. Melin, 758
Sadleir v. Knapton, 921
Sadler v. Great Western Railroad Co., 325, 328, 354, 634
Sadlier v. City of New York, 633
Sadowski v. Long Island Railroad Co., 579
Saenger Theatres Corp. v. Herndon, 59
Saetz v. Braun, 172

Safeco Insurance Co. of America v. City of Watertown, 182
Safety Cab Co. v. Fair, 334
Safety Investment Corp. v. State Land Office Board, 728
Safeway Stores, Inc. v. Amburn, 49, 50
Safeway Stores, Inc. v. Nest-Kart, 344, 477
Sage Club v. Hunt, 505, 507
Sager v. Sisters of Mercy, 77
Sage's Estate, In re, 590
Sahara v. Ragnar Benson, Inc., 405, 411
Said v. Butt, 985, 994
Sainsbury v. Pennsylvania Greyhound Lines, 761
St. Amant v. Thompson, 807
St. Charles Mercantile Co. v. Armour & Co., 28
St. Clair v. Douvas, 581
St. Clair v. McAllister, 252
St. Clair v. Smith, 154
St. George v. State, 314
St. Joseph Lead Co. v. Prather, 552, 562
St. Joseph Light & Power Co. v. Kaw Valley Tunneling, Inc., 387
St. Louis, Iron Mountain & Southern Railway Co. v. Fairbairn, 421
St. Louis, Iron Mountain & Southern Railway Co. v. Steel, 310
St. Louis, Iron Mountain & Southern Railway Co. v. Taylor, 227
St. Louis, Iron Mountain & Southern Railway Co. v. Waggoner, 406
St. Louis, Iron Mountain & Southern Railway Co. v. Wilson, 47
St. Louis, Iron Mountain & Southern Railway Co. v. Wirbel, 423
St. Louis & San Francisco Co. v. Goode, 957
St. Louis-San Francisco Railroad Co. v. Clark, 57
St. Louis-San Francisco Railroad Co. v. Ginn, 309
St. Louis & San Francisco Railroad Co. v. Madden, 513
St. Louis & San Francisco Railroad Co. v. Mathews, 544
St. Louis & San Francisco Railroad Co. v. Reed, 761
St Louis Cordage Co. v. Miller, 573
St. Louis Fixture & Show Case Co. v. F.W. Woolworth Co., 99, 100
St. Louis South Western Railway Co. v. White, 362
St. Louis Southwestern Railway Co. v. Pennington, 952
St. Louis Southwestern Railway Co. v. Williams, 227
St. Mary's Gas Co. v. Brodbeck, 550
St. Mary's Hosp., Inc. v. Bynum, 174
St. Onge v. Detroit & Mackinac Railway Co., 462
St. Paul Companies v. Capitol Office Supply Co., 509, 514
St. Petersburg, City of v. Collom, 1046
St. Petersburg Coca-Cola Bottling Co. v. Cuccinello, 76
St. Vincent's Hospital v. Stine, 1070
Saint-Pierre v. McCarthy, 271
Salanski v. Enright, 408
Salazar v. Bond Finance Co., 62
Salazar v. St. Vincent Hospital, 370
Salem Iron Co. v. Hyland, 630

TABLE OF CASES

Salgo v. Leland Stanford, Jr., University Board of Trustees, 190
Saliem v. Glovsky, 897, 898, 899, 900
Salin v. Kloempken, 359, 936
Salinas v. Kahn, 950
Salinero v. Pon, 168, 230, 514, 515, 516
Salinger v. Cowles, 835
Salis v. United States, 186, 187, 190
Salisbury v. Commonwealth, 155
Salisbury v. Crudale, 915
Salisbury v. Green, 140
Salisbury v. Poulson, 49, 53, 60, 141
Salisbury v. Union & Advertiser Co., 838
Salisbury, Regina v., 37
Sallies v. Johnson, 763
Sally v. Brown, 790
Salmon v. Delaware, L. & W.R. Co., 390
Salmon, Regina v., 271
Salmonson v. Horswill, 739
Salomone v. Yellow Taxi Corp., 503
Salsbury v. United Parcel Service, 644
Salsedo v. Palmer, 310
Salt River Valley Water Users' Association v. Cornum, 312
Salt Springs National Bank v. Wheeler, 92, 100
Salter v. Heiser, 768, 769
Salter v. Howard, 995, 1003
Salter Marine, Inc. v. Conti Carriers & Terminals, Inc., 464
Salvin v. North Brancepeth Coal Co., 628
Salvitti v. Throppe, 232
Salzman v. Maldaver, 736
Samms v. Eccles, 61, 64
Samp v. Long, 762
Sample v. Gulf Refining Co., 14
Samples v. Carnahan, 828
Samples v. Guyer, 675, 730
Sampson v. Henry, 143
Sampson v. Penney, 769
Sampson v. W.F. Enterprises, Inc., 451
Sams v. Gay, 251
Samson v. Saginaw Professional Building, Inc., 443
Samuel v. Curtis Publishing Co., 857, 861, 862, 863
Samuelson v. Chutich, 720
Samuelson v. Freeman, 166
San Angelo, City of v. Sitas, 437
San Antonio, City of v. Salvation Army, 626
San Antonio & Aransas Pass Railway Co. v. Behne, 305
San Antonio & Aransas Pass Railway Co. v. Long, 951
San Antonio & Aransas Pass Railway Co. v. Morgan, 406
San Antonio Gas Co. v. Singleton, 328
San Antonio River Authority v. Garrett Brothers, 1051
San Diego Building Trades Council v. Garmon, 1027
San Diego Gas & Electric Co. v. United States, 558
Sanborn v. Colman, 104
Sanborn v. Sturtevant, 73
Sanchez v. City of Espanola, 476
Sanchez v. J. Barron Rice, Inc., 195, 229
Sanchez v. Rice, 1049

Sanchez v. Rodriguez, 253
Sandberg v. Cavanaugh Timber Co., 544
Sandberg v. Hoogensen, 497
Sanders v. Frankfort Marine, Accident & Plate Glass Insurance Co., 587
Sanders v. Stutes, 419
Sanders v. Teape & Swan, 539
Sanders v. Wheaton, 454
Sanders-Clark v. Grosvenor Mansions Co., 620
Sanderson v. Beaugh, 392
Sanderson v. Northern Pacific Railway Co., 66
Sandford v. Chevrolet Division of General Motors, 478
Sandford v. Firestone Tire & Rubber Co., 422
Sandford v. Ware, 63
Sandlin v. Coyle, 992
Sandman v. Hagan, 507
Sandoval v. Sandoval, 908
Sandrock v. Taylor, 520
Sands v. American Railway Express Co., 484
Sands v. Robison, 818
Sandstrom v. Montana, 33, 36
Sandy v. Bushey, 565
Saner v. Bowker, 875
Sanford v. Boston Herald-Traveler Corp., 837
Sanford v. Pawtucket Street Railway Co., 511
Sankey v. Williamsen, 260
Sansonni v. Jefferson Parish School Board, 1048
Santee v. Haggart Construction Co., 590
Santiesteban v. Goodyear Tire & Rubber Co., 856, 858
Santor v. A & M Karagheusian, Inc., 708
Santora v. New York, New Haven & Hartford Railroad Co., 394
Sarat Lahiri v. Daily Mirror, 859
Sarat Lahiri v. Daily Mirror, 862
Sarch v. Blackburn, 562
Sard v. Hardy, 190, 191
Sardo v. Herlihy, 222
Sargeant v. Fedor, 912
Sargent v. Mathewson, 925
Sargent v. Robertson, 920
Sargent v. Ross, 440
Sargent v. Williams, 455
Sarkees v. Warner-West Corp., 782
Saros v. Avenue Theatre Co., 143
Sarraillon v. Stevenson, 619
Sarratt v. Holston Quarry Co., 288
Sartor v. Schaden, 1016
Sarwark Motor Sales, Inc. v. Husband, 736
Sarwark Motor Sales, Inc. v. Woolridge, 882
Satilla Manufacturing Co. v. Cason, 54
Sato v. Van Denburgh, 167
Satterfield v. McLellan Stores Co., 799
Satterlee v. Orange Glenn School District, 228
Sattler v. Neiderkorn, 666
Saucer v. Giroux, 779
Saugerties Bank v. Delaware & Hudson Co., 313
Saunders v. Gilbert, 12
Saunders v. Mills, 838
Saunders v. Mullinix, 121, 736
Saunders, Regina v., 293

Saunders and Archer, Queen v., 37
Saunders Drive-It Yourself Co. v. Walker, 717
Saunders System Birmingham Co. v. Adams, 267
Sauter v. New York Central & Hudson River Railroad Co., 352
Sauter v. New York Tribune, 506, 507
Savage v. Boies, 61, 64
Savage v. New York, New Haven & Hartford Railroad Co., 937
Savage v. Stover, 835
Savannah, Florida & Western Railway Co. v. Parish, 648
Savarese v. Bye, 388
Savignac v. Department of Transportation, 414, 417, 419
Sawdey v. R.W. Rasmussen Co., 329
Sawicki v. Connecticut Railway & Lighting Co., 389
Sawler v. Boston & Albany Railroad Co., 394
Sawyer v. Bailey, 932
Sawyer v. Davis, 632
Sawyer v. Gilmers, Inc., 795, 844
Sawyer v. McGillicuddy, 440
Sawyer v. Minneapolis & St. Louis Railroad Co., 716
Sawyer v. Pine Oil Sales Co., 686, 687
Sawyer v. Prickett, 762
Sawyer v. Sauer, 210
Saxby v. Southern Land Co., 753, 755
Saxon Motor Sales v. Torino, 976
Saxton v. Harris, 753
Sayadoff v. Warda, 123
Sayers v. Harlow U.D.C., 307
Sayre v. Davis, 938
Scalf v. Berkel, Inc., 168
Scalise v. National Utility Service, 14
Scanlon v. General Motors Corp., 250, 696
Scanlon v. Wedger, 484, 486
Scarlett v. Norwood, 928
Scarll v. Dixon, 827
Scarzella v. Saxon, 186
Scearce v. Mayor of Gainesville, 327
Scenic Hudson Preservation Conference v. Federal Power Commission, 647
Schaaf v. Coen, 465
Schaefer v. Hoffman, 582
Schaefer v. Washington Safety Deposit Co., 583
Schafer v. Ostmann, 329, 345
Schafer & Olson v. Varney, 310
Schaff v. Coyle, 544
Schaff v. R.W. Claxton, Inc., 313
Schaff v. Roach, 315
Schaffer v. Pennsylvania Railroad Co., 326, 346
Schaffner v. National Supply Co., 742
Schaffran v. Press Publishing Co., 837
Schagun v. Scott Manufacturing Co., 770
Schanafelt v. Seaboard Finance Co., 48, 50
Schantz v. Sears, Roebuck & Co., 141
Scharf v. Gardner Cartage Co., 716
Scharman v. Scharman, 734
Schatzky v. Harber, 445
Schaub v. Linehan, 164
Schauenberg, State v., 8

Schechter v. Friedman, 987
Scheele v. Union Loan & Finance Co., 762
Scheer v. Keown, 150
Scheffer v. Braverman, 409
Scheffer v. Washington City, Virginia Midland & Great Southern Railroad Co., 310
Scheibel v. Hillis, 398, 433
Scheibel v. Lipton, 415
Scheirman v. Pemberton, 941
Schelin v. Goldberg, 461
Schell v. Second National Bank, 387
Scheman v. Schlein, 62
Schenck v. Schenck, 798, 824
Schendel v. Chicago, Milwaukee & St. Paul Railway Co., 312
Schenk v. Schenk, 907
Schering & Glatz v. American Pharmaceutical Co., 977
Scheuer v. Rhodes, 1061
Scheuermann v. Scharfenberg, 135
Scheufele v. Newman, 133
Scheurich v. Empire District Electric Co., 69
Schichowski v. Hoffmann, 51
Schiele v. Hobart Corp., 957
Schiffahrt und Kohlen v. Chelsea Maritime Ltd., 1001
Schiffmann v. Hickey, 112
Schiller v. Strangis, 49, 50
Schilling v. Carl Township, 664
Schindler v. United States, 1035, 1042
Schippel v. Norton, 14
Schipper v. Levitt & Sons, Inc., 678
Schirmer v. Nethercutt, 667
Schiro v. Oriental Realty Co., 195
Schlaf v. State Farm Mutual Automobile Insurance Co., 848
Schlaks v. Schlaks, 417
Schlange v. Briggs Manufacturing Co., 575
Schlavick v. Manhattan Brewing Co., 955
Schleicher v. Western State Bank, 872
Schleifer v. Worcester North Sav. Inst., 666
Schlemmer v. Buffalo, Rochester & Pittsburgh Railway Co., 569
Schlender v. Andy Jansen Co., 438
Schlenger v. Weinberg, 486
Schlesinger Co., Louis v. Rice, 987
Schlessman v. Brainard, 41
Schlicht v. Thesing, 414, 424
Schlimmeyer v. Yurkiw, 464
Schlinkert v. Henderson, 822
Schlirf v. Loosen, 646
Schloendorff v. Society of New York Hospital, 116, 119, 190
Schlossman's v. Niewinski, 732
Schmartz v. Harger, 308
Schmeck v. City of Shawnee, 936
Schmeer v. Gas Light Co., 567
Schmeiser v. Trus Joist Corp., 686
Schmidt v. Fontaine Ferry Enterprises, 481
Schmidt v. George H. Hurd Realty Co., 423
Schmidt v. Landfield, 751
Schmidt v. Mesmer, 665, 770

Schmieding v. American Farmers Mutual Insurance Co., 867
Schmitt v. Jenkins Truck Lines, Inc., 519
Schmitt v. Kurrus, 40
Schmitt v. Ornes Esswein & Co., 756, 761
Schmitt v. Postal Telegraph Co., 666
Schmoldt v. Oakley, 976
Schmukler v. Ohio-Bell Telephone Co., 868
Schnabel v. Meredith, 861
Schnabl v. Ford Motor Co., 947
Schnader v. Brooks, 737
Schnathorst v. Williams, 879, 881
Schneider v. Baisch, 948, 949
Schneider v. Chrysler Motors Corp., 703
Schneider v. City Council of Augusta, 326
Schneider v. Heath, 737
Schneider v. Kessler, 150
Schneider v. Schneider, 759
Schock v. Ringling Brothers and Barnum & Bailey Combined Shows, 411
Schockey v. McCauley, 848
Schoedel v. State Bank of Newburg, 752
Schoen v. Gilbert, 184, 417
Schoen v. Washington Post, 794
Schoenly v. Nashville Speedways, Inc., 330
Schoepflin v. Coffey, 801
Schofield v. King, 251
Schofield v. Merrill, 394, 397, 433
Scholfield Gear & Pulley Co. v. Scholfield, 744
Scholl v. State, 127
Schomaker v. Havey, 459
Schonwald v. Ragains, 987
School Board of Lipps District No. 4 v. Saxon Lime & Lumber Co., 674
Schools v. Walker, 347
Schooner Catharine, The v. Dickinson, 471
Schoonmaker v. Kaltenbach, 266
Schreiber v. Walt Disney World Co., 419, 426
Schreiner v. Great Northern Railway Co., 275, 312
Schroder v. City of Lincoln, 646, 649
Schroeder v. Mauzy, 379
Schroeder v. Perkel, 371
Schrowang v. Von Hoffman Press, 97
Schubert v. August Schubert Wagon Co., 911
Schubert v. J.R. Clark Co., 206, 684
Schubert v. Sterling Trust Co., 548
Schubring v. Weggen, 486, 495
Schubkegel v. Gordino, 876
Schuer v. Veeder, 30
Schulte v. Florian, 101, 106
Schulte v. Willow River Power Co., 409
Schultz v. Brogan, 268, 278
Schultz v. Chicago & Northwestern Railway Co., 570
Schultz v. Frankfort Marine, Accident & Plate Glass Insurance Co., 786, 797
Schultz v. Gould Academy, 383
Schultz v. Strauss, 818, 820
Schultz v. Swift & Co., 528
Schulz v. Quintana, 386, 389

Schumacher v. Carl G. Neumann Dredging & Imp. Co., 723
Schumacher v. Shawhan Distillery Co., 11
Schumaker v. St. Paul & Duluth Railroad Co., 307
Schumann v. Crofoot, 177, 178, 1074
Schumpert v. Southern Railway Co., 346
Schupp v. Taendler, 99
Schuppin v. Unification Church, 919, 929
Schurk v. Christensen, 926
Schuster v. City of New York, 202, 383
Schuster v. Sutherland, 664
Schuyler v. Curtis, 850
Schwabacker v. Riddle, 751
Schwaller v. McFarland, 122
Schwartz v. Boswell, 877
Schwartz v. California Gas & Electric Corp., 312
Schwartz v. Cornell, 488
Schwartz v. Edrington, 853, 863
Schwartz v. Heffernan, 1064
Schwartz v. Macrose Lumber & Trim Co., 705
Schwartz v. Schwartz, 892
Schwartz v. Sears, Roebuck & Co., 212
Schwartz v. Thiele, 858
Schwartzmann v. Lloyd, 426
Schwarz Brothers Co. v. Evening News Publishing Co., 831
Schwingschlegl v. City of Monroe, 292
Schwinn v. Perkins, 145
Schwitters v. Des Moines Commercial College, 762
Sciandra v. Lynett, 836
Scibelli v. Pennsylvania Railroad Co., 410
Sclar v. Resnick, 847
Scofi v. McKeon Construction Co., 514
Scoggins v. Jude, 461, 487, 491, 493, 498
Scoggins v. Smith, 508
Scoggins v. Village of Hartford, 336
Scopel, State v., 644
Scott v. Aloha Beta Co., 469
Scott v. Bontekoe, 921
Scott v. Bradford, 190, 192
Scott v. Burnight, 761
Scott v. Chambers, 913
Scott v. City of Detroit, 381
Scott v. City of Opa Locka, 1049
Scott v. Commercial Union Insurance Co., 507
Scott v. Donald, 9
Scott v. Greene, 525
Scott v. Harrison, 794
Scott v. Huffman, 669
Scott v. Hull, 801
Scott v. Kopp, 370
Scott v. London & St. Katherine Docks Co., 244
Scott v. McDonnell Douglas Corp., 1057
Scott v. McGaugh, 519, 520, 521
Scott v. Min-Aqua Bats Water Ski Club, Inc., 502
Scott v. O'Brien, 11
Scott, People v., 444
Scott v. Prudential Outfitting Co., 988, 996
Scott v. Rizzo, 471
Scott v. Shepherd, 38, 307

Scott v. Stansfield, 816
Scott v. Texaco, Inc., 308
Scott v. University of Michigan Athletic Association, 419
Scott v. Watson, 202, 443
Scribner v. Beach, 132
Scribner v. Kelley, 542, 561
Scripps v. Foster, 848
Scrivani v. Dondero, 879
Scriven Co., J.A. v. Girard Co., 1016
Scudder v. Seaboard Coast Line Railroad, 938
Scurti v. City of New York, 410
Sea Land Industries, Inc. v. General Ship Repair Corp., 456, 457
Seaboard Air Line Railroad Co. v. American District Electric Protective Co., 341
Seaboard Air Line Railroad Co. v. Richmond-Petersburg Turnpike Authority, 390
Seaboard Air Line Railway Co. v. Branham, 416
Seaboard Air Line Railway Co. v. Horton, 578
Seaboard Air Line Railway Co. v. Martin, 951
Seaboard Air Line Railway Co. v. Mullin, 312, 315
Seaboard Air Line Railway Co. v. Oliver, 955
Seaboard Coast Line Railroad Co. v. Griffis, 238
Seaboard Coast Line Railroad Co. v. United States, 1041
Seaboard Coast Line R. Co. v. Zeigler, 226
Seabridge v. McAdam, 880
Seabrook v. Taylor, 914
Seago v. Roy, 434, 440
Seagraves v. ABCO Manufacturing Co., 205
Sea-Land Services, Inc. v. Gaudet, 952, 955, 956, 957
Seale v. Gulf, Colorado & Santa Fe Railway Co., 289
Seals v. Augusta Southern Railroad Co., 660
Seals v. Morris, 162
Seals v. Snow, 1073
Seaman v. Becar, 758
Seaman v. Cuppledick, 129
Seaman v. Dexter, 15
Seaman v. Henriques, 442
Seaman v. Netherclift, 817
Searcy v. Brown, 224
Searle v. Johnson, 989
Sears v. Mid-City Motors, Inc., 269
Sears v. Texas & New Orleans Railroad Co., 280
Sears, Roebuck & Co. v. American Plumbing & Supply Co., 982, 1015
Sears, Roebuck & Co. v. Devers, 361
Sears, Roebuck & Co. v. Donovan, 421
Sears, Roebuck & Co. v. Haven Hills Farms, Inc., 246
Sears, Roebuck & Co. v. Morris, 705
Sears, Roebuck & Co. v. Stiffel Co., 1018, 1021
Sears, Roebuck & Co. v. Young, 364
Seattle Taxicab Co. v. De Jarlais, 1016
Seavey v. New York, 1047
Seavey v. Preble, 146, 148, 642
Seavey Co. v. Union Transit Co., 315
Seavy v. New York, 1048
Seay v. Chrysler Corp., 478
Sebastian v. Kluttz, 919, 923
Sebastian v. Wood, 10

Sebring v. Colver, 479
Sebring v. Van Aken, 890
Seckerson v. Sinclair, 267, 347, 544
Secor v. Harris, 792
Securities and Exchange Commission v. Capital Gains Research Bureau, Inc., 739
Security Aluminum Window Manufacturing Corp. v. Lehman Associates, Inc., 12
Security Bank of Minnesota v. Fogg, 91
Security Building Co. v. Lewis, 441
Security National Bank v. Lish, 187
Security Sales Agency v. A.S. Abell Co., 778
Security Savings Bank v. Kellams, 761
Security Timber & Land Co. v. Reed, 228
Security Trust Co. v. O'Hair, 750, 752
Security Underwriters v. Rousch Motor Co., 586
Security-First National Bank of Los Angeles v. Lutz, 94
Sedleigh-Denfield v. O'Callaghan, 546
See v. Gosselin, 874
Seedkem, Inc. v. Safranek, 186
Seeds v. Seeds, 1007
Seeger v. Odell, 750
Seehorn, State ex rel. National Refining Co. v., 941
Seelbach, Inc. v. Mellman, 492
Seelenfreund v. Terminix of Northern California, Inc., 167
Seeley v. Combs, 246
Seelig v. Harvard Cooperative Society, 872
Seely v. White Motor Co., 709
Seffert v. Los Angeles Transit Lines, 255
Segal v. Horwitz Brothers, 305
Segal v. Justice Court Mutual Housing Cooperative, Inc., 435
Segall v. Piazza, 831
Seglinski v. Baltimore Copper Smelting & Rolling Co., 938
Sego v. Mains, 225
Seiber v. Pettitt, 917
Seidel v. Greenberg, 11, 18, 293, 873
Seiden v. Savings & Loan Association, 343
Seidenbach's, Inc. v. Williams, 361
Seidler v. Burns, 888
Seigel v. Long, 41
Seigle v. Bromley, 643
Seim v. Garavalia, 174, 220, 224, 230, 492
Seip v. Deshler, 773
Seith v. Commonwealth Electric Co., 317
Seitz v. Brewer's Refrigerating Machine Co., 756
Seitz v. Michel, 994
Selby v. Kuhns, 331
Selby Realty Co. v. City of San Buenaventura, 1050
Selchow & Righter Co. v. McGraw-Hill Book Co., 1017
Selengut, State v., 150
Selfe v. Smith, 365
Seligmann v. Hammond, 228
Selleck v. City of Janesville, 352
Seller v. Jenkins, 790
Sellers v. Cayce Mill Supply Co., 198
Sellers v. Henry, 853, 859, 868
Sellick v. Hall, 350

Sellinger v. Freeway Mobile Home Sales, Inc., 1020
Sellman v. Haddock, 222
Selma, City of v. Jones, 643
Selman v. Barnett, 925
Selman v. Shirley, 769
Selsman v. Universal Photo Books, Inc., 852
Seltzer v. Fields, 818
Semayne's Case, 150
Semeniuk v. Chentis, 718
Semler v. Psychiatric Institute of Washington, D.C., 943
Semple v. Morganstern, 100
Senator Cab Co. v. Rothberg, 528
Seneca Wire & Manufacturing Co. v. A.B. Leach & Co., 675, 729, 730, 731, 765
Seng v. American Stores Co., 427
Senior v. Ward, 955
Senner v. Danewolf, 438
Sentilles v. Inter-Caribbean Shipping Corp., 291
Sequin v. Eide, 1063
Serafino v. Palm Terrace Apartments, 987
Sergermeister v. Recreation Corp. of America, Inc., 209
Serota v. M. & M. Utilities, Inc., 75
Servis v. Servis, 921
7735 Hollywood Boulevard Venture v. Superior Court, 203, 443
Severance, People v., 643
Severin v. Kepple, 99
Severns v. Brainerd, 883
Seward v. Minneapolis Street Railway Co., 278
Seward v. Natural Gas Co., 684
Sewell v. Harrington, 87
Sexton v. American News Co., 803, 811
Sexton v. Commonwealth, 130
Sexton v. Ryder Truck Rental, Inc., 527
Seymour v. Chicago & Northwestern Railway Co., 756
Seymour National Bank v. State, 1060
Sezzin v. Stark, 442
Sforza v. Green Bus Lines, 1074
Shackett v. Bickford, 740, 741, 742
Shackett v. Schwartz, 434, 442
Shaefer v. Investor's Co. of Oregon, 442
Shaeffer v. O.K. Tool Co., 891
Shafer v. Grimes, 941
Shafer v. H.B. Thomas Co., 194
Shafer v. Keeley Ice Cream Co., 200, 305
Shafer v. Tacoma Eastern Railroad Co., 417, 486
Shaffer v. Rhyne, 762
Shafir v. Sieben, 305
Shaheen v. Knight, 372
Shahinian v. McCormick, 248, 254
Shahrokhfar v. State Farm Mutual Automobile Insurance Co., 479, 480, 487, 895
Shainberg Co. of Jackson v. Barlow, 706
Shaker v. Shaker, 906
Shakespeare v. City of Pasadena, 51
Shamhart v. Morrison Cafeteria, 645, 1015
Shanahan v. Monarch Engineering Co, 574
Shanander v. Western Loan & Building Co., 550
Shane v. Hoffmann, 448, 508
Shank v. Government Employees Insurance Co., 206

Shanley v. Wells, 156
Shannon v. Howard S. Wright Co., 454
Shannon v. Sims, 872
Shapiro v. Tchernowitz, 1074
Shapiro v. Toyota Motor Co., 388
Shapley v. Abbott, 758
Sharkey v. Burlingame Co., 764
Sharman v. C. Schmidt & Sons, Inc., 823
Sharon, Town of v. Anahama Realty Corp., 354
Sharp v. Johnston, 883
Sharp v. Ponce, 732
Sharpe v. Larson, 782
Sharpe v. Stephenson, 842
Sharpe v. Williams, 914
Shatterproof Glass Corp. v. James, 747
Shatz v. TEC Technical Adhesives, 230
Shaul v. Brown, 871
Shaw v. Boston American League Baseball Co., 485, 495
Shaw v. Butterworth, 445
Shaw v. Chicago, Milwaukee & St. Paul Railway Co., 377
Shaw v. Courtney, 152
Shaw v. Fulton, 897
Shaw v. Joyce, 541
Shaw v. Kaler, 103
Shaw v. Lord, 128, 129
Shaw v. North Pennsylvania R. Co., 94
Shaw v. Pacific Greyhound Lines, 245
Shaw v. Plunkett, 431
Shaw v. Time-Life Records, 1016
Shaw Cleaners & Dyers v. Des Moines Dress Club, 960, 966, 972, 975
Shaw's Jewelry Shop v. New York Herald Co., 645
Shea v. Cassidy, 132
Shea v. Cloquet Lumber Co., 880
Shea v. Kansas City, Fort Scott & Memphis Railroad Co., 488
Shea v. United States Fidelity & Casualty Co., 587
Shearing v. City of Rochester, 639
Shedd v. Patterson, 891, 941
Shedrick v. Lathrop, 1073
Sheehan v. Allred, 252
Sheehan v. Janesville Auto Transport, 220, 223, 225, 226
Sheehan v. Nims, 229
Sheehan v. St. Paul & Duluth Railroad Co., 393
Sheehan v. Sturges, 158
Sheehan v. Tobin, 830
Sheets v. Burleson, 389
Sheffield v. Central Freightlines, Inc., 507
Sheffield v. Turner, 1048
Sheffield Co. v. Phillips, 429
Sheffield Division Armco Steel Corp. v. Jones, 10
Sheffill v. Van Deusen, 798
Sheftall v. Central of Georgia R. Co., 832
Shehyn v. United States, 140
Shelburne, Inc., The v. Crossan Corp., 620
Shelby v. Sun Printing & Publishing Association, 775
Shelby Mutual Insurance Co. v. Kleman, 527
Shelden v. Wichita Railroad & Light Co., 226
Sheldon v. River Lines, 591

Sheldon v. Sherman, 140
Sheldon-Claire Co. v. Judson Roberts Co., 800
Sheldrick v. Abery, 85
Sheley v. Guy, 532
Shell Oil Co. v. Gutierrez, 711
Shell Oil Co. v. Mahler, 306
Shell Oil Co. v. Prestidge, 517
Shell Petroleum Corp. v. Liberty Gravel & Sand Co., 86
Shell Petroleum Corp. v. Scully, 675
Shell Petroleum Co. v. Wilson, 553
Shellabarger v. Morris, 60, 139
Shellburne, Inc. v. Roberts, 1057, 1059
Shellnut v. Central of Georgia Railroad Co., 95, 97
Shelton v. Barry, 49
Shelton v. Mullins, 532
Shelton v. Russell Pipe & Foundry Co., 366
Shelton v. Southern Railway, 885
Shelton v. Williams, 959
Shenkman v. O'Malley, 825
Shepard v. Merrill, 841
Shepherd v. Gardner Wholesale, Inc., 175
Shepherd v. Kendrick, 760
Shepherd v. Wakeman, 963, 996, 1007
Shepherd v. Woodson, 761
Sheppard v. Bryant, 820
Sheppard v. Dun & Bradstreet, 775
Sheppard v. Furniss, 54
Sheppard Publishing Co. v. Press Publishing Co., 963
Sheridan v. Aetna Casualty & Surety Co., 670
Sheridan v. Bean, 541
Sheridan v. Crisona, 822, 1064
Sheridan v. Great Atlantic & Pacific Tea Co., 426
Sheridan Drive-In Theatre v. State, 628
Sherin v. Eastwood, 780
Sherlock v. Manwaren, 327, 329
Sherlock v. Stillwater Clinic, 370, 372
Sherman v. Concourse Realty Corp., 443
Sherman v. Hartman, 260
Sherman v. Maine Central Railroad Co., 416
Sherman v. Platte County, 427, 428, 479
Sherman, State v., 127
Sherman v. Suburban Trust Co., 430
Sherman Gas & Electric Co. v. Belden, 349
Sherry v. Asing, 179
Sherwood v. Evening News Association, 837
Sherwood v. Salmon, 751
Sherwood v. Walker, 675
Shevak v. United States, 187
Shewalter v. Wood, 902
Sheward v. Magit, 130
Sheward v. Virtue, 683, 704
Shewmaker v. Clouiville & Nashville Railroad Co., 218
Shibuya v. Architects Hawaii, Limited, 168
Shideler v. Habiger, 281
Shields v. Wondries, 619
Shields v. Yonge, 945
Shiels v. Audette, 937
Shiffer v. Broadhead, 118
Shiffman v. Order of St. John, 547, 548
Shiles v. News Syndicate Co., 862

Shilkret v. Annapolis Emergency Hospital Association, 188
Shillady v. Elliot Community Hospital, 166
Shim v. Kikkoman International Corp., 8
Shine v. Wujick, 455
Shinglemeyer v. Wright, 823
Shinofield v. Curtis, 254
Shipe v. Schenk, 793, 794
Shipes v. Piggly Wiggly St. Andrews, Inc., 203
Shipherd v. Field, 661
Shipley v. Daly, 948
Shipley v. Fifty Associates, 550, 553
Shipley v. Ritter, 640
Shipp v. Autoville Limited, 870, 873
Shipp v. Davis, 718
Shipp v. McCraw, 788, 789
Shires v. Boggess, 8, 126
Shirley Cloak & Dress Co. v. Arnold, 206, 378
Shiroma v. Itano, 457
Shively, United States v., 313
Shiver v. Sessions, 906
Shockley v. Prier, 934
Shoe v. Hood, 520
Shoemaker v. Estate of Whistler, 519, 520
Shoemaker v. Friedberg, 833
Shoemaker v. Selnes, 885
Shoemaker v. Shoemaker, 881
Sholin v. Skamania Boom Co., 650
Shoninger Co., B. v. Mann, 484
Shonka v. Campbell, 339
Shook v. Crabb, 903
Shoop v. Hubbard, 214
Shor v. Billingsley, 787
Shor v. Paoli, 476
Shore v. Howard, 1058
Shore v. Town of Stonington, 357, 502
Short v. D.R.B. Logging Co., 260
Short v. News-Journal Co., 821, 822
Short Line, Inc. v. Perez, 476
Shorter v. People, 125
Shorter v. Retail Credit Co., 868
Shorter v. Shelton, 144
Shortt v. Hudson Supply & Equipment Co., 332, 334
Shoshone Coca-Cola Bottling Co. v. Dolinski, 245, 249
Shostakovitch v. Twentieth-Century Fox Film Corp., 868
Shramek v. General Motors Corp., 246
Shrewsbury v. Smith, 549
Shriver v. Marion County Court, 146
Shroades v. Rental Homes, Inc., 222, 435
Shrofe v. Rural Mutual Casualty Insurance Co., 340
Shubert v. Columbia Pictures Corp., 854
Shubert v. Nixon Amusement Co., 662
Shubert v. Variety, Inc., 782
Shubitz v. Consolidated Edison of New York, 663
Shuck v. Carney, 504
Shuck v. Means, 528
Shufelberger v. Worden, 487
Shulman v. Lerner, 113, 120
Shultz v. Barberton Glass Co., 364
Shuman v. Mashburn, 178

TABLE OF CASES

Shuman Estate v. Weber, 504
Shumate v. Johnson Publishing Co., 842
Shuput v. Heublein, Inc., 685
Shurtleff v. Stevens, 831, 836
Shutan v. Bloomenthal, 207
Shute v. Prom Motor Hotel, Inc., 208
Shute v. Shute, 890
Shuttler v. Brandfass, 760
Shypulski v. Waldorf Paper Products Co., 432
Sias v. General Motors Corp., 833
Sickra v. Small, 847
Sicola v. First National Bank of Altoona, 874
Sideman v. Guttman, 414
Sidis v. F-R Publishing Co., 800, 857, 860, 863
Sidle v. Humphrey, 441
Sidney Blumenthal & Co. v. United States, 992
Sidwell v. McVay, 375
Sieben v. Sieben, 475
Siebert v. Fowler, 187
Siegel v. Detroit City Ice & Fuel Co., 440
Siegel v. Spear & Co., 379, 1008
Siegfried v. Everhart, 565
Siegler v. Kuhlman, 556, 563
Sieling v. Clark, 736
Siesseger v. Puth, 214
Signal Oil and Gas Co. v. University Oil Products, 678
Signs v. Signs, 595, 907
Sikes v. McLean Trucking Co., 228
Sikes v. Tippins, 921
Silbernagel v. Voss, 307
Silesky v. Kelman, 907
Silkwood v. Kerr-McGee Corp., 559
Silliman v. Dobner, 28
Sills v. Forbes, 424
Sills v. Massey-Ferguson, Inc., 704
Sills v. Schneider, 586
Silva v. Mills, 926
Silva v. Silva, 907
Silva, State v., 1047
Silver v. Martin, 95
Silver v. Silver, 216
Silver Bridge Disaster Litigation, In re, 1035
Silver Falls Timber Co. v. Eastern & Western Lumber Co., 172, 283, 302, 303
Silverman v. General Motors Corp., 242, 245, 248, 254
Silverman v. Silverman, 911
Silverstein v. R.H. Macy & Co., 691
Silvia v. Pennock, 231
Sim v. Stretch, 774
Sim v. Weeks, 187
Simek v. Korbel, 311
Simmonds v. Richards, 675
Simmons v. Evans, 739
Simmons v. Everson, 326, 346
Simmons v. F.W. Woolworth Co., 254
Simmons v. J.C. Penney Co., 142
Simmons v. Lillystone, 101
Simmons v. Lollar, 308
Simmons Co. v. Hardin, 684
Simmel v. New Jersey Co-op Co., 405

Simmons v. Rhodes & Jamieson, 686
Simmons v. Sikes, 100
Simms v. D'Avillier, 125
Simon v. Goodyear Metallic Rubber Shoe Co., 665, 770
Simon v. Hudson Coal Co., 278
Simon v. Mullin, 368
Simon v. Noma Electric Corp., 1003
Simon v. Reilly, 91
Simon v. Solomon, 435
Simon v. Stim, 819
Simone v. Kirk, 569
Simone v. Rhode Island Co., 56, 360
Simons v. Kidd, 941
Simons v. United States, 1038
Simonsen v. Swenson, 827
Simpson v. Davis, 185
Simpson v. Doe, 427
Simpson v. Gray Line Co., 246, 252, 259
Simpson v. Grayson, 926, 927
Simpson v. Hill, 51
Simpson v. Logan Motor Co., 269
Simpson v. Miller, 229
Simpson v. Pere Marquette Railroad Co., 225
Simpson v. Plyler, 331
Simpson v. Powered Products of Michigan, Inc., 690
Simpson v. Press Publishing Co., 790
Simpson v. United States, 415, 416, 503
Simpson Co., C.W. v. Langley, 441
Simpson's Food Fair, Inc. v. City of Evansville, 1049
Sims v. Alford, 112
Sims v. Davis, 940
Sims v. Eleazar, 229
Sims v. Ferrill, 760
Sims v. Huntington, 465, 467
Sims v. Tigrett, 744
Sinclair v. Postal Telegraph & Cable Co., 867
Sinclair v. Stanley, 144
Sinclair Prairie Oil Co. v. Stell, 226, 549, 551
Sinclair Refining Co. v. Jones Super Service Station, 969, 974
Sinclair Refining Co. v. Meek, 49
Sindell v. Abbott Laboratories, 271, 713, 714
Singer v. Bander, 791
Singer v. I.A. Durbin, Inc., 202, 203
Singer v. Marx, 38
Singer v. Walker, 712
Singer Co. v. Stott & Davis Motor Express, Inc., 239
Singer Manufacturing Co. v. Bryant, 874
Singer Manufacturing Co. v. Clark, 96
Singer Manufacturing Co. v. Holdfodt, 11
Singer Manufacturing Co. v. King, 99
Singer Sewing Machine Co. v. Methvin, 41
Singer Sewing Machine Co. v. Phipps, 40, 139
Singler v. Journal Co., 787
Singletary v. Atlantic Coast Line Railroad Co., 176
Singletary v. National Railroad Passenger Corp., 531
Singleton v. Kubiak & Schmitt, 123
Singleton v. Wiley, 497, 498
Singleton Abbey v. Paludina, 277
Singley v. Bigelow, 941

Sink v. Sumrell, 466
Sinkler v. Kneale, 369
Sinkler v. Missouri Pacific Railway Co., 578
Sinn v. Burd, 365
Sinn v. Farmers' Deposit Savings Bank, 419
Sinram v. Pennsylvania Railroad Co., 286, 300, 999
Sinz v. Owens, 188
Sioux City & Pacific Railroad Co. v. Stout, 400
Sipe v. Helgerson, 248
Sipes, State v., 128
Sipp v. Coleman, 789
Sir Charles Stanley's Case, 323, 346
Sir John Heydon's Case, 323, 325, 329, 346
Sira v. Wabash Railroad Co., 313
Siragusa v. Swedish Hospital, 493, 576, 594
Sires v. Luke, 506
Sisemore v. Neal, 938
Sisk v. Crump, 135
Sitta v. American Steel & Wire Division, 684
Siverson v. Martori, 210, 524
Siverson v. Weber, 257
Six Carpenters Case, 151
Six Flags Over Georgia, Inc. v. Hill, 501
Skaggs v. Junis, 408, 410
Skaggs v. Stanton, 919
Skaja v. Andrews Hotel Co., 337
Skala v. Lehon, 327, 341
Skaling v. Sheedy, 135
Skalos v. Higgins, 460
Skapura v. Cleveland Electric Illuminating Co., 504
Skaria v. State, 443
Skehan v. Board of Trustees of Bloomsburg St. College, 1064
Skelly Oil Co. v. Jordan, 330
Skene v. Carayanis, 992, 1013
Skillings v. Allen, 206, 725
Skinn v. Reutter, 304
Skinner v. Reed-Prentice Division Package Machinery Co., 338, 344, 476, 477
Skipper v. Hartley, 323
Sklebar v. Downey, 8
Skog v. King, 137
Skoglund v. Minneapolis Street Railway Co., 932
Skollingsberg v. Brookover, 934, 935
Skousen v. Nidy, 42
Skrocki v. Stahl, 842
Skupienski v. Maly, 441
Slade v. City of Phoenix, 876, 882
Slagle v. United States, 1035, 1042
Slater v. Illinois Central Railroad Co., 378
Slater v. Kimbro, 892, 895
Slater v. Mersereau, 634
Slater v. Pacific American Oil Co., 350
Slater v. Swann, 85
Slater v. T.C. Baker Co., 275
Slater Trust Co. v. Gardiner, 736, 745
Slaton v. City of Chicago, 1055
Slattery v. Haley, 34
Slattery v. Marra Bro., 344
Slaven v. Germain, 353

Slawek v. Stroh, 928
Slawinski v. Mocettini, 384
Sleath v. Wilson, 504
Sledd v. Washington Metropolitan Area Transit Authority, 194
Sledge & Norfleet Co. v. Mann, 740
Sleeper v. Baker, 981
Slicer v. Quigley, 230
Slim v. Dailey Tel. Ltd., 804
Slimak v. Foster, 207
Slinker v. Wallner, 404, 411
Slitkin v. Avis Rent A Car System, Inc., 524
Sloan v. Butler, 106
Sloan v. City of Greenville, 617, 644
Sloan v. Gulf Refining Co. of Louisiana, 486
Sloan v. Pierce, 130
Slocinski v. Radwan, 830
Slocum v. Food Fair Stores of Florida, Inc., 59
Sloggy v. Dilworth, 323, 354, 355, 634
Sloss-Sheffield Steel & Iron Co. v. Johnson, 649
Sloss-Sheffield Steel & Iron Co. v. Long, 570
Sloss-Sheffield Steel & Iron Co. v. Wilkes, 669, 670
Slotkin v. Citizens Casualty Co. of New York, 508
Slotnick v. Cooley, 486
Slovensky v. Birmingham News Co., 933
Slusher v. State, 435, 440
Sluss v. Brown-Crummer Investment Co., 761
Smalich v. Westfall, 517, 529, 530
Small v. Boston & Maine Railroad Co., 570
Small v. Chronicle & Gazette Publishing Co., 847
Smalling v. LaSalle National Bank of Chicago, 428
Smart v. Aroostook Lumber Co., 649, 651
Smart v. Bissonette, 525
Smartt v. Lamar Oil Co., 239
Smedberg v. Moxie Dam Co., 647, 650
Smedberg v. Simons, 436
Smedley v. Piazzolla, 181
Smethurst v. Proprietors, Independent Congregational Church, 387
Smigrielski v. Nowak, 421
Smith v. Alameda County Social Services Agency, 1048
Smith v. Aldridge, 567
Smith v. American Employer's Insurance Co., 670
Smith v. Arbaugh's Restaurant, Inc., 433
Smith v. Ariens Co., 713
Smith v. Atlas Off-Shore Boat Service, Inc., 375, 1029
Smith v. Ayrault, 342
Smith v. Badlam, 742
Smith v. Baker & Sons, 571, 574
Smith v. Beatty, 737
Smith v. Bell & Stephens, 98
Smith v. Benson's Wild Animal Farm, 417
Smith v. Blakesburg Savings Bank, 121, 736
Smith v. Board of County Road Commissions of Chippewa County, 549, 552, 564
Smith v. Bolles, 768
Smith v. Boothe, 757
Smith v. Brennan, 369
Smith v. Byrd, 842
Smith v. California Department of Employment, 501

Smith v. Carlson, 307
Smith v. Castle, 489
Smith v. Chadwick, 736, 741, 750
Smith v. Chicago Housing Authority, 202
Smith v. City of Detroit, 952
Smith v. City of Sedalia, 645
Smith v. Clark, 52
Smith v. Clark Sherwood Oil Field Contractors, 959
Smith v. Claude Neon Lights, 250, 387
Smith v. Colgay, 940
Smith v. Conn, 335
Smith v. Connecticut Railway & Lighting Co., 465
Smith v. Cooper, 1046, 1065
Smith v. Coronado Foothills Estates Homeowners Association, Inc., 896
Smith v. Costello, 149, 646
Smith v. Crown-Zellerbach, Inc., 403
Smith v. Cumberland County Agricultural Society, 419, 428
Smith v. Dallas Utility Co., 84
Smith v. Delery, 131
Smith v. Dental Products Co., 1015
Smith v. Detroit Loan & Building Association, 144
Smith v. Diamond, 179, 229, 456, 461
Smith v. Doss, 861, 862
Smith v. Doyle, 525
Smith v. Dunlop Tire & Rubber Co., 823
Smith v. Durham, 99
Smith v. Erie Railroad Co., 569, 572
Smith v. Evans, 408
Smith v. Fiber Controls Corp., 184
Smith v. Fields, 880
Smith v. Ford Motor Co., 982, 986, 989, 996
Smith v. Fried, 460
Smith v. Gaffard, 793
Smith v. Gates, 151
Smith v. General Apartment Co., 443
Smith v. Gilbert, 674
Smith v. Golden State Hospital, 333
Smith v. Goldman, 396
Smith v. Goodman, Howell & Co., 1003
Smith v. Gorman, 902
Smith v. Great Western R. Co., 547, 564
Smith v. Hensley, 878, 880
Smith v. Higgins, 821, 829
Smith v. Hilton, 149
Smith v. Hobson, 790
Smith v. Hockenberry, 921
Smith v. Holst, 198
Smith v. Hubbard, 40
Smith v. Illinois Central Railroad Co., 407
Smith v. Insurance Co. of North America, 198, 460
Smith v. Inter-County Telephone Co., 514
Smith v. Jalbert, 542
Smith v. Johns, 766
Smith v. Johnson, 27
Smith v. Jordan, 526, 914
Smith v. Kaufman, 907
Smith v. Kenrick, 547
Smith v. Kidd, 883

Smith v. King, 876
Smith v. Kravitz, 445
Smith v. Lampe, 311
Smith v. Land & House Prop. Corp., 761
Smith v. Leech Brain & Co., Ltd., 296
Smith v. Leo, 58
Smith v. Levitt, 826
Smith v. Little, 248
Smith v. Lockheed Propulsion Co., 558
Smith v. London & S.W.R. Co., 275, 283, 292, 297
Smith v. Louisiana Cement Co., 488
Smith v. Lucky Stores, Inc., 516
Smith v. Lyons, 775
Smith v. McComb Infirmary Association, 957
Smith v. McDowell Furniture Co., 326
Smith v. McIntyre, 162
Smith v. Mann, 335
Smith v. Markensohn, 875
Smith v. Masten, 928
Smith v. Mill Creek Court, Inc., 183
Smith v. Miller, 376, 1067
Smith v. Monmaney, 447, 449
Smith v. Moran, 38
Smith v. Morse, 621, 624
Smith v. Moschetti, 1072
Smith v. Mottman, 419
Smith v. Munger, 208
Smith v. National Broadcasting Co., 861
Smith v. New England Aircraft Co., 79
Smith v. Newsam, 43
Smith v. Otto Hendrickson Post 212, American Legion, 403, 405
Smith v. Pate, 69
Smith v. Peerless Glass Co., 684, 704
Smith v. Pennsylvania-Reading Seashore Lines, 208
Smith v. Philadelphia & Reading Railway Co., 396
Smith v. Pierson, 876
Smith v. Pope, 738
Smith v. Portland Transaction Co., 226
Smith v. Prater, 299
Smith v. Regina Manufacturing Corp., 705
Smith v. Rengel, 437, 440, 441
Smith, Rex v., 377, 644
Smith v. Rice, 921
Smith v. Ryan, 731
Smith v. S.S. Kresge Co., 683
Smith v. Safeway Stores, Inc., 427
Smith v. Schoene, 912
Smith v. Selwyn, 8
Smith v. Shiflett, 91
Smith v. Simpson, 527
Smith v. Smith, 78, 451, 780, 781, 830, 836, 893, 904, 911, 922
Smith v. Southwest Missouri Railroad Co., 417
Smith v. Spirek, 523
Smith v. Staso Milling Co., 387, 625
Smith, State v., 153, 155, 156
Smith v. Stewart, 788
Smith v. Stone, 68, 72
Smith v. Suratt, 860

Smith v. Taylor, 912
Smith v. The Texan, Inc., 265
Smith v. Uffelman, 227
Smith v. Union Pacific Railroad Co., 218, 455
Smith v. United States, 423, 951, 952, 1037, 1038
Smith v. United States Casualty Co., 852
Smith v. United States Steel Corp., 406, 409
Smith v. Utley, 799
Smith v. Virginia Transit Co., 226
Smith v. Wade, 13
Smith v. Weber, 661
Smith v. West Suburban Transit Lines, Inc., 202
Smith v. WGN, Inc., 867
Smith v. Womack, 923
Smith v. Wright, 464
Smith v. Wunderlich, 78
Smith v. Yellow Cab Co., 327
Smith v. Zimbalist, 761
Smith, Kline & French Co. v. Smith, 758
Smith, State ex rel. v. Weinstein, 310
Smith Brothers & Co. v. W.C. Agee & Co., 829
Smith Co., F.H. v. Low, 761
Smith Lumber Co. v. Scott County Garbage Reducing & Fuel Co., 673
Smith Stage Co. v. Eckert, 586
Smitha v. Gentry, 1006
Smithhisler v. Dutter, 920
Smithpeter v. Mid-State Motor Co., 754
Smith's Administrator v. Corder, 718
Smith's Administratrix v. Middleton, 507
Smith's Case, 790
Smithson v. Garth, 323
Smithwick v. Hall & Upson Co., 457
Smyth v. Fidelity & Deposit Co. of Maryland, 105
Snavely v. City of Goldendale, 346, 349
Snead v. Bonnoil, 53
Snedaker v. King, 924
Snedecor v. Pope, 73
Sneeden v. Harris, 897
Sneesby v. Lancashire & Y. R. Co., 198, 304
Snelling, Commonwealth v., 840
Sneider v. Hyatt Corp., 199
Snider v. Bob Thibedeau Ford, Inc., 713
Snider v. Callahan, 178
Snider v. Newell, 927
Snider v. Northern States Power Co., 510
Snow v. Judy, 417
Snow v. Rudolph, 327
Snow v. Whitehead, 538, 546
Snowden v. Fort Lyon Canal Co., 674
Snowden v. Pearl River Broadcasting Corp., 812, 844
Snowden v. Sorenson, 982, 990
Snowhite v. State, 199
Snyder v. Fatherly, 827, 842
Snyder v. Fulton, 775
Snyder v. I. Jay Realty Co., 413, 440
Snyder v. Markham, 769
Snyder v. Moore, 435
Snyder v. Mutual Telegraph Co., 335
Snyder v. United States, 153

Soane v. Knight, 832
Soap Corp. of America v. Reynolds, 644, 645
Soby Construction, Inc. v. Skjonsby Truck Line Inc., 239
Socha v. Passino, 412, 413, 420
Sochacki v. Sas, 543, 546
Societa per Azioni de Navigazione Italia v. City of Los Angeles, 501
Sockett v. Gottlieb, 440
Socony-Vacuum Oil Co. v. Bailey, 74
Socony Vacuum Oil Co. v. Marvin, 458
Soderbach v. Townsend, 501, 509
Soderlin v. Marquette National Bank, 673
Soffos v. Eaton, 891
Sohn v. Katz, 395
Sohoro Pipeline Co. v. Harmon, 245
Soileau v. South Central Bell Telephone Co., 169, 173, 182, 454
Sokoloski v. Pugliese, 418
Sokolowske v. Wilson, 897
Soldano v. O'Danials, 382
Soles v. Ohio Edison Co., 409
Sollak v. State, 558
Sollinger v. Himchak, 455
Solmo v. Catholic Bishop of Chicago, 438
Solomon v. Branfman, 292
Solomon v. Warren, 950
Solomon v. White Motor Co., 696
Solosko v. Paxton, 794
Solozzi v. Casola, 746
Soltan v Shahboz, 751
Solverson v. Peterson, 775
Somers & Sons v. Le Clerc, 331
Somerset v. Hart, 204
Somerset Villa Inc. v. City of Lee's Summit, 349
Somerville v. Hawkins, 826
Sommermeyer v. Price, 521
Sonner v. Cordano, 948
Sonsee v. Jones & Green, 895
Soper v. Igo, Walker & Co., 924
Sorenson v. Balaban, 935
Sorenson v. Chevrolet Motor Co., 981, 987, 990
Sorenson v. Gardner, 760, 768
Sorenson v. Sorenson, 907
Sorenson v. Wood, 787, 812
Sorge v. Parade Publications, Inc., 800, 836
Soronen v. Olde Milford Inn, 461
Sorrell, In re, 913
Sorrell v. Smith, 1013, 1024
Sorrells v. Clifford, 755
Sorrells v. Matthews, 935
Sorrentino, State v., 132, 133
Sosa v. Coleman, 203, 384
Sosebee v. Hiott, 447
Soter v. Christoforacos, 817
Soter v. Griesedieck Brewery Co., 694
Soto v. Frankford Hospital, 207
Soto v. Greenpoint Hospital, 166
Souder v. Pendleton Detectives, Inc., 855
Soule v. Massachusetts Electric Co., 400, 401
Soulia v. Noyes, 443

Soulios v. Mills Novelty Co., 141
Sourbier v. Brown, 323
South v. A.B. Chance Co., 496
South v. Martin, 524
South v. National Railroad Passenger Corp. (AMTRAK), 196
South Brilliant Coal Co. v. Williams, 41
South Covington & Cincinnati Street Railway Co., Commonwealth v., 643
South Hetton Coal Co. v. North-Eastern News Association, 831
South Wales Miners' Federation v. Glamorgan Coal Co., 970, 983
Southard v. Forbes, Inc., 970
Southard v. Lira, 519
Southeastern Greyhound Lines v. Callahan, 669
Southeastern Greyhound Corp. v. Graham, 58
Southern v. Cowan Stone Co., 389
Southern Bell Telephone & Telegraph Co. v. Brackin, 405
Southern Bell Telephone & Telegraph Co. v. Martin, 388
Southern Bell Telephone & Telegraph Co. v. Spears, 265
Southern California Edison Co. v. Coleman, 557
Southern Cal. Investment Co. v. Wilshire, 636
Southern Car & Foundry Co. v. Adams, 874
Southern Cotton Oil Co. v. Anderson, 507
Southern Counties Ice Co. v. RKO Radio Pictures, 75, 76
Southern Development Co. v. Silva, 756
Southern Farm Bureau Casualty v. Wright Oil Co., 945
Southern Farm Bureau Casualty Insurance Co. v. Daniel, 13
Southern Farmers Association v. Whitfield, 878
Southern Idaho Realty of Twin Falls, Inc.—Century 21 v. Larry J. Hellhake and Associates, Inc., 994
Southern Indiana Gas & Electric Co. v. Indiana Insurance Co., 250
Southern Iron & Equipment Co. v. Bamberg, Ehrhardt & Walterboro Railway Co., 679
Southern Iron & Steel Co. v. Acton, 352
Southern Pacific Co. v. Cavin, 582
Southern Pacific Co. v. Gileo, 577
Southern Pacific Co. v. Morrison-Knudsen Co., 341
Southern Pacific Co. v. Raish, 334
Southern Pacific Railroad Co. v. Mitchell, 233
Southern Pacific Railroad Co. of Mexico v. Gonzales, 666
Southern Package Corp. v. Mitchell, 569
Southern Rail Co. v. White, 84
Southern Railway Co. v. Brunswick Pulp & Paper Co., 477
Southern Railway Co v. Campbell, 396
Southern Railway Co. v. Chambers, 992
Southern Railway Co. v. Drake, 466
Southern Railway Co. v. Grizzle, 374, 661
Southern Railway Co v. Hayes, 143
Southern Railway Co. v. Horine, 77
Southern Railway Co. v. Lee, 5
Southern Railway Co. v. Wahl, 398

Southern States Fire & Casualty Co. v. Cromartie, 743, 745
Southern Transportation Co. v. Harper, 312
Southport, City of v. Williams, 765
Southward v. Foy, 99
Southwest Drug Stores of Mississippi, Inc. v. Garner, 142, 833
Southwest Forest Industries, Inc. v. Westinghouse Electric Corp., 705
Southwestern Bell Telephone Co. v. Smith, 513
Southwestern Broadcasting Co. v. Oil Center Broadcasting Co., 1020
Southwestern Gas & Electric Co. v. Denney, 935
Southwestern Railroad Co. v. Mitchell, 895
Southwestern Telephone & Telegraph Co. v. Long, 795, 844
Southwestern Telephone & Telegraph Co. v. Luckett, 665
Souza v Corti, 528
Sovereign Pocohontas Co. v. Bond, 742
Sovine, State ex rel. v. Stone, 51
Sowder v. Nolan, 830
Sowles v. Moore, 265
Sox v. Hertz Corp., 327
Spackman v. Foster, 99
Spackman v. Ralph M. Parsons Co., 10
Spade v. Lynn & Boston Railroad Co., 24, 56, 360, 363
Spahn v. Guild Industries Corp., 502
Spain v. Kelland, 439
Spalding v. Oakes' Administrator, 337
Spalding v. Vilas, 821
Spall v. Janota, 387
Spanel v. Pegler, 778
Spannaus v. Otolaryngology Clinic, 253
Spano v. Perini Corp., 553
Sparger v. Worley Hospital, Inc., 204
Sparks v. Guaranty State Bank, 761
Sparks v. McCrary, 992, 1009, 1014
Sparks v. Porcher, 487
Sparks v. Rudy Fick, Inc., 764
Sparling v. Peabody Coal Co., 183, 449
Sparrow v. Vermont Savings Bank, 888
Spartan Aircraft Co. v. Jamison, 558
Spaulding v. Cameron, 619, 638, 640
Spear Stove & Heating Co., James v. General Electric Co., 757
Spearman v. University City Public School District, 1056
Speck v. Finegold, 371
Speece v. Browne, 424
Speed v. Transamerica Corp., 738
Speight v. Simonsen, 232
Spelina v. Sporry, 138
Spellens v. Spellens, 900
Spence v. American Oil Co., 312
Spence v. Three Rivers Builders & Masonry Supply, Inc., 690, 694
Spencer v. Amerton, 829
Spencer v. Burglass, 884, 890
Spencer v. Gedney, 460
Spencer v. Looney, 777

Spencer v. Madsen, 704
Spenser v. Fondry, 466
Sperier v. Ott, 66
Sperry Hutchinson Co. v. Louis Weber & Co., 987
Sperry Rand Corp. v. Hill, 780
Spherex, Inc. v. Alexander Grant & Co., 186
Spicer v. Smee, 546
Spidle v. Steward, 256
Spiegel v. Evergreen Cemetery Co., 63
Spiegel v. Metropolitan Life Insurance Co., 1001
Spielberg v. A. Kuhn & Bro., 829
Spier v. Barker, 352, 459
Spiering v. City of Hutchinson, 170, 311
Spiess v. Brandt, 760
Spike v. Sellett, 187, 256
Spiker v. Elkenberry, 392
Spillers v. Griffin, 464
Spillway Marina, Inc. v. United States, 1040
Spilotro v. Hugi, 186
Spinelli v. Golda, 434
Spitzer v. Spitzer, 924
Spivack v. Hara, 343
Spoehr v. Mittelstadt, 819
Spokane International Railway Co. v. United States, 564
Spokane Truck & Dray Co. v. Hoefer, 11
Spomer v. City of Grand Junction, 63
Spooner v. Holmes, 94, 98
Spooner v. Manchester, 102
Spoor v. Spooner, 52, 53
Sporleder, State ex rel. v. Staed, 99
Sporna v. Kalina, 310
Sporsem v. First National Bank, 483
Sports & General Press Agency v. "Our Dogs" Publishing Co., 859
Spradley v. Houser, 520
Spragins v. Jiffy Food Stores, Inc., 256
Sprague v. Bartlett, 532
Sprague v. Hauck, 486
Sprecher v. Adamson Companies, 386, 390, 391
Sprecher v. Roberts, 195
Spreckels v. Gorrill, 768
Spriggs v. Cheyenne Newspapers, 831
Springer v. Steiner, 155
Springer v. Swift, 824
Springfield Crystallized Egg Co. v. Springfield Ice & Refrigeration Co., 663
Springfield Gas & Electric Co., State ex rel. Wear v., 645
Sprinkle v. Lemley, 323
Sprogis v. Butler, 56
Spur Industries, Inc. v. Dell E. Webb Development Co., 635
Squadrito v. Griebsch, 154
Squibb & Sons, E.R. v. Ira J. Shapiro, Inc., 995
Squire v. Hill, 921
Squire v. Ordemann, 331
Squires v. Brooks, 275, 313
Squires v. Reynolds, 310
Squyres v. Christan, 760
Stacey v. Fidelity & Casualty Co., 587, 588

Stach v. Sears, Roebuck Co., 182, 460
Stackpole v. Healy, 539, 540, 565
Stacy v. Knickerbocker Ice Co., 265, 320
Stacy v. Shapiro, 441
Stadler v. Cross, 365, 366
Staed, State ex rel. Sporleder v., 99
Staehlin v. Hochdoerfer, 352
Stafford v. Chippewa Valley Electric Railroad Co., 222
Stahl v. Boston & Maine Railroad Co., 100
Stahl v. Kincade, 817
Stahlheber v. American Cyanamid Co., 685
Stahlin v. Hilton Hotels Corp., 380
Staley v. Turner, 873
Stallworth v. Doss, 87, 139
Stam v. Cannon, 518, 519
Stamat v. Merry, 214
Stamp v. Eighty-Sixth Street Amusement Co., 542, 568
Standard v. Shine, 179, 180
Standard Accident Insurance Co. of Detroit, Michigan v. Winget, 588
Standard & Poor's Corp., Inc. v. Commodity Exchange, Inc., 1022
Standard Brands v. Smidler, 1015
Standard Fruit & Steamship Co. v. Putname, 987
Standard Iron Works v. Southern Bell Telephone Co., 669
Standard Life & Accident Insurance Co. v. Bambrick Brothers Construction Co., 585
Standard Manufacturing Co. v. Slot, 732
Standard Motor Co. v. Blood, 705
Standard Nut Margarine Co. v. Mellon, 821
Standard Oil Co. v. Decell, 439
Standard Oil Co. v. Doyle, 1009, 1014, 1015
Standard Oil Co. v. Robins Dry Dock & Repair Co., 342
Standard Oil Co., United States v., 998
Standard Oil Co. v. Wakefield's Administrator, 716
Standard Oil Co. of Indiana v. Meissner, 413
Standard Paint Co. v. Rubberoid Roofing Co., 1016
Standard Printing Co. v. Fidelity & Deposit Co., 587
Standard Sanitary Manufacturing Co. v. Brian's Administrator, 334
Standefer v. United States, 1038
Standish v. Narragansett S.S. Co., 142
Standley v. Western Auto Supply Co., 893
Stanek v. Swierczek, 197
Stanfield v. Laccoarce, 502
Stanford v. A.F. Messick Grocery Co., 887
Stanfuturf v. Sipes, 381
Stanley v. Central Intelligence Agency, 1037
Stanley v. Chastek, 664, 666
Stanley v. City of Macon, 619
Stanley v. Fisher, 186, 188, 256
Stanley v. Prince, 841
Stanley, State v., 1060, 1065
Stanolind Oil & Gas Co. v. Bunce, 670
Stansbury v. Beckstrom, 977, 1026
Stansbury v. Fogle, 872
Stansfield v. Chesapeake & Potomac Telephone Co., 395
Stanton v. Hart, 879
Stanton v. Texas Co., 990

Stapler v. Parler, 323
Staples v. Smith, 88
Stapleton v. Butensky, 513
Stapleton v. Independent Brewing Co., 527
Star v. Rookesby, 67
Star Opera Co. v. Hylan, 644
Stark v. Equitable Life Assurance Society, 760
Stark v. Johnson, 917, 923
Stark v. Weeks Real Estate, 514, 515
Starkey v. Dameron, 135
Starks v. Comer, 795
Starling v. Fisherman's Pier, Inc., 419
Staroske v. Pulitzer Publishing Co., 1013, 1024
Starr v. Bartz, 734
Starr v. Clapp, 393, 394, 397
Starr v. Jackson, 78
Starr v. Philadelphia Transportation Co., 453
Stasiof v. Chicago Hoist & Body Co., 311
Stasulat v. Pacific Gas & Electric Co., 313
State v. ———— (see opposing party)
State ex rel. (see name of party)
State Farm Fire Insurance Co. v. Gregory, 995
State Farm Mutual Automobile Insurance Co. v. Anderson-Weber, Inc., 692, 694
State Farm Mutual Automobile Insurance Co. v. Bonacci, 588
State Farm Mutual Auto. Insurance Co. v. Continental Casualty Co., 339, 340
State Farm Mutual Automobile Insurance Co. v. Duran, 524, 525
State Farm Mutual Automobile Insurance Co. v. Fields, 1072
State Farm Mutual Automobile Insurance Co. v. Koval, 588
State Farm Mutual Automobile Insurance Co. v. Leary, 954, 955
State Farm Mutual Automobile Insurance Co. v. Westlake, 903
State for Use of Anderson v. Baltimore & Ohio Railroad Co., 396
State for Use of Bohon v. Feldstein, 436
State for Use of Little v. United States Fidelity & Guaranty Co., 898
State for use of Powell v. Moore, 49
State Highway Commission v. Empire Oil & Refining Co., 550
State Highway & Public Works Commission v. Cobb, 8
State National Bank of Iowa Park v. Rogers, 59
State Road Commission v. Oakes, 626
State Rubbish Collectors Association v. Siliznoff, 61, 64
State Stove Manufacturing Co. v. Hodges, 683
State to Use of Bond v. Consolidated Gas, Electric, Light & Power Co., 954
Stationers Corp. v. Dun & Bradstreet, Inc., 834
Staton v. Atlantic Coast Line Railroad, 635
Staub v. Van Benthuysen, 799, 800
Stavnezer v. Sage Allen & Co., 58, 59
Steadman v. Topham, 880
Steaks Unlimited, Inc. v. Deaner, 970
Stearn v. Prentice Bros., 390

Stearns v. Lindow, 522
Stearns v. Sampson, 44
Stebbins v. Edwards, 992
Stebbins v. North Adams Trust Co., 91
Steber v. Norris, 157, 158, 905
Steding v. Battistoni, 864
Steed v. Imperial Airlines, 948
Steed v. Knowles, 878
Steele v. Edwards, 798
Steele v. Marsicano, 97
Steele v. Rapp, 317
Steele v. St. Paul Fire & Marine Insurance Co., 366
Steele v. Southern Railway Co., 582
Steele, State v., 132
Steelman v. Lind, 430, 431, 432
Stees v. Kemble, 788
Stefanich v. Kuhns, 920
Steffan v. Zernes, 1000
Steffen v. McNaughton, 551
Steger v. Egyud, 336
Stehle v. Jaeger Automatic Machine Co., 220
Stehlek, State v., 601
Stein v. Beta Rho Alumni Association, Inc., 508
Stein v. Powell, 425
Stein v. Treger, 746, 748
Steinberg, People v., 120
Steiner v. Spencer, 575
Steinhardt v. Johns-Manville Corp., 165
Steinhauser v. Hertz Corp., 291
Steinke v. Bell, 189
Steinman v. Baltimore Antiseptic Steam Laundry Co., 42
Steinman v. Di Roberts, 774
Steinman v. Strobel, 470
Steinmeyer v. McPherson, 412, 417
Steitz v. Gifford, 100
Steketee v. Kimm, 798
Steljes v. Ingram, 660
Stemmler v. City of Pittsburgh, 304, 348
Stenberg v. Wilcox, 439
Stenbohn v. Brown-Corliss Engine Co., 587
Stencel Aero Engineering Corp. v. United States, 1034, 1037
Stepanek v. Kober Construction, 231, 512
Stepehnson v. Dreis & Krump Manufacturing Co., 184
Stepehson v. Triangle Publications, 800
Stephan v. Lynch, 478
Stephani v. City of Manitowoc, 172
Stephen v. City of Lincoln, 453
Stephens v. Collison, 760
Stephens v. Dulaney, 176
Stephens v. Elwall, 95, 536
Stephens v. Hubbard, 649
Stephens v. Mann, 463, 465
Stephens v. Mutual Lumber Co., 280, 295, 302
Stephens v. Myers, 43
Stephens v. Schadler, 349
Stephens v. Snyder Clinic Association, 168
Stephens v. United States, 153, 214
Stephens v. Waits, 63

Stephenson v. Little, 103
Stephenson v. State, 311
Steppacher & Brother, Walter M. v. Karr, 1015
Steppuhn v. Chicago Great Western Railway Co., 880
Sterchi Bros. Stores v. Castleberry, 684
Sterling v. New England Fish Co., 176
Sterling v. Warden, 118
Sterling Drug Co. v. Yarrow, 688, 697
Sterling Insurance Co. v. Hughes, 13
Stern v. Kaufman's Bakery, Inc., 92
Stern v. Miller, 370
Stern & Co., Edward v. Liberty Mutual Insurance Co., 586
Sternberg v. Hogg, 49
Sternberg Manufacturing Co. v. Miller, Du Brul & Peters Manufacturing Co., 825
Sternfels v. Metropolitan Street Railway Co., 950
Stertz v. Industrial Insurance Commission of Washington, 573
Sterud v. Chugach Electric Association, 510
Steudle v. Rentchler, 162
Stevens v. Adams, 156
Stevens v. City of Pittsburgh, 392
Stevens v. Dudley, 284
Stevens v. Eames, 96
Stevens v. Fassett, 158
Stevens v. Haering's Grocetorium, 802
Stevens v. Luther, 221
Stevens v. Moon, 619
Stevens v. Morse, 792, 834
Stevens v. Murphy, 904
Stevens v. O'Neill, 49
Stevens v. Parke, Davis & Co., 233
Stevens v. Sampson, 834
Stevens v. Siegel, 984
Stevens v. Snow, 775
Stevens v. Stevens, 215, 216
Stevens v. Union Memorial Hospital, 253
Stevens v. Van Deusen, 524
Stevens v. Wilber, 789, 790
Stevens-Salt Lake City, Inc. v. Wong, 550
Stevenson v. Baltimore Baseball Club, 828
Stevenson v. Belknap, 927, 928
Stevenson v. East Ohio Gas Co., 1000
Stevenson v. Love, 972
Stevenson v. Newnham, 27
Stevenson v. Northington, 835
Stevenson, State v., 127
Steward v. Borough of Magnolia, 911
Steward v. Gold Medal Shows, 924
Steward v. Gromett, 892
Stewart v. Cary Lumber Co., 507
Stewart v. Cooley, 54
Stewart v. Enterprise Co., & n, 842
Stewart v. F.A. North Co., 1-1
Stewart v. Feeley, 152
Stewart v. Ging, 830
Stewart v. Howe, 788
Stewart v. Jefferson Plywood Co., 169, 170, 308
Stewart v. Kroger Grocery Co., 278

Stewart v. Larkin, 764
Stewart v. Madison, 464, 470
Stewart v. 104 Wallace Street, Inc., 223, 388, 424
Stewart v. Rudner, 665
Stewart v. Sam Wallace Industrial Co., 509, 512
Stewart v. Schmieder Enterprises, 1050
Stewart v. Sonneborn, 876, 882, 888, 893, 895
Stewart v. Stearns, 752
Stewart v. Stephens, 527
Stewart v. Swartz, 914
Stewart v. Texas Co., 421
Stewart v. United States, 1037
Stewart v. Weiner, 376
Stewart v. Wyoming Cattle Ranche Co., 737
Stewart, State ex rel. v. Cozad, 553
Stewart & Co., James v. Newby, 572, 590
Stewart Dry Goods Co. v. Boone, 458
Stickel v. Atwood, 744
Stickel v. Riverview Sharpshooters' Park Co., 428
Stickney v. E.R. Squibb & Sons, Inc., 955
Stiers v. Marshall, 722
Stiles v. Kuriloff, 972
Stiles & Davis v. Laird, 643
Stillwell v. Rankin, 754, 766
Stimpson v. Sprague, 667, 941
Stine v. McShane, 348
Stinnett v. Commonwealth, 156
Stinson v. Atlantic Coast Line Railroad Co., 579
Stitt v. Gold, 666
Stober v. Embry, 486
Stock v. Fife, 517, 519, 521
Stockdale v. Midland Valley Railroad Co., 545
Stocker v. Stitt, 226
Stockett v. Watkins' Administrators, 674
Stocking v. Johnson Flying Service, 146, 255
Stockley v. Hornidge, 873
Stockman v. Marlowe, 213
Stockmen's National Bank v. Richardson, 379, 1008
Stockton v. Baker, 958
Stockwell v. Board of Trustees of Leland Stanford Jr. University, 270
Stockwell v. Gee, 43
Stoddard v. Ling-Temco-Vought, Inc., 253
Stodder v. Rosen Talking Machine Co., 628
Stodghill v. Chicago, Burlington & Quincy Railroad Co., 84
Stoecker v. Nathanson, 888
Stofer v. Montgomery Ward & Co., 427
Stoffer v. State, 127
Stogdon v. Charleston Transit Co., 229
Stohr v. Donahue, 881
Stokes v. Arey, 788
Stokes v. Carlson, 34, 35
Stokes v. Liberty Mutual Insurance Co., 368
Stoll v. Wellborn, 758
Stone v. Arizona Highway Commission, 1055
Stone v. Boston & Albany Railroad Co., 303
Stone v. C.I.T. Corp., 87
Stone v. Cheshire Railroad Corp., 509
Stone v. City of Philadelphia, 277

Stone v. Compton, 731
Stone v. Dickinson, 325
Stone v. First Wyoming Bank N.A., Lusk, 517
Stone v. Goss, 1022
Stone v. Foster, 192
Stone v. Hutchinson Daily News, 817, 818, 819
Stone v. Johnson, 379, 660, 663
Stone v. Knapp, 73
Stone v. Shaw Supply Co., 718
Stone v. Stevens, 876
Stone v. Textile Examiners & Shrinkers Employer's Association, 779
Stone v. United States, 93
Stone v. Van Noy Railroad News Co., 681, 682
Stone, State ex rel. Sovine v., 57
Stoner v. Carr, 166
Stoney Creek Woolen Co. v. Smalley, 758
Storch v. Gordon, 801
Storey v. Central Hide & Rendering Co., 631, 641
Storey v. Challands, 794
Storey v. State, 155, 156
Storey v. Wallace, 846
Storrs v. City of Utica, 511
Story v. Conger, 765
Story v. Howes, 490
Stotler v. Rochelle, 620, 629
Stott v. Gamble, 985
Stotzheim v. Djos, 487
Stouderman, State v., 156
Stout v. Madden, 704
Stovall v. Texas Co., 965
Stover v. Fechtman, 436
Stover v. Patrick, 521
Stowers v. Gilbert, 75
Stowers Furniture Co. v. Brake, 139
Strader v. Armstrong, 922
Strain v. Irwin, 48
Strakos v. Gehring, 724
Strand Enterprises v. Turner, 444
Strandholm v. Barbey, 650
Strange v. Cleveland, Cincinnati, Chicago & St. Louis Railway Co., 84
Stratford Theater v. Town of Stratford, 640
Straton v. Rastall, 675
Stratton, Commonwealth v., 40, 120, 725
Stratton v. Posse Normal School of Gymnastics, 59
Straube v. Larson, 985
Straus & Co., S.W., People v., 767
Strauss v. City of Louisville, 515
Strauss v. Hensey, 730
Strauss v. Hotel Continental Co., 502
Strawn v. Ingram, 122
Strayer v. Lindeman, 445, 512
Streenz v. Streenz, 907
Street v. Calvert, 464, 465, 474
Street v. Craig, 561
Street v. National Broadcasting Co., 859
Stribling v. deQuevedo, 372
Strick v. Stutsman, 242, 246, 252, 254, 257, 261
Stricker v. Hillis, 649, 651

Strickland v. Graybill, 758
Strickland v. King, 524
Strickland v. Roberts, 496, 497
Strickler v. National Broadcasting Co., 858, 861, 864
Stringer v. Zacheis, 256, 257
Strobeck v. Bren, 275, 312
Strobel v. Chicago, Rock Island & Pacific Railway Co., 266
Strode v. Gleason, 928, 929
Stroh Brewery Co. v. Grand Trunk Western Railway Co., 240
Stromer v. Yuba City, 999
Strong v. Adams, 88
Strong v. Campbell, 223
Strong v. Granite Furniture Co., 305
Strong v. Seattle Stevedore Co., 431, 432
Strother v. Hutchinson, 164
Strother v. Pacific Gas & Electric Co., 80
Strouse v. Leipf, 913
Strozzi v. Wines, 149
Strubing v. Mahar, 564
Struder v. Southern Pacific Co., 276
Strunk v. Strunk, 115, 116
Struve v. Tatge, 766
Stryk v. Mnichowicz, 726
Stryker v. Republic Pictures Corp., 852, 857, 858, 859, 860
Stuart v. Bell, 809, 833
Stuart v. Lester, 754, 766
Stuart v. News Publishing Co., 848
Stuart v. Wilkins, 218
Stubbs v. Mulholland, 877, 879, 883
Stubbs v. Pancake Corner of Salem, Inc., 455
Studdard v. Turner, 525
Student, The, 716
Studley, Inc., Julian J. v. Lefrak, 898
Stuempges v. Parke, Davis & Co., 845
Stufflebean v. Peaveler, 753
Stull v. Porter, 323
Stull v. Ragsdale, 531
Stultz v. Benson Lumber Co., 318
Stump v. Phillians, 228
Stump v. Sparkman, 1057, 1058, 1059
Stumpf v. Montgomery, 526
Sturm v. Boker, 758
Sturm, Ruger & Co. v. Bloyd, 184
Sturman v. Polito, 141
Sturtevant v. Pagel, 717
Stusser v. Mutual Union Insurance Co., 331
Stuyvesant v. Wilcox, 132, 140
Stuyvesant Insurance Co. v. Bournazian, 472
Su v. Perkins, 204
Suarez v. Dosky, 1049, 1051
Suarez v. Trans World Airlines, 209
Suburban Hospital Association v. Hadary, 256
Suburban Properties Management v. Johnson, 728
Succession of (see name of party)
Suchey v. Stiles, 883
Suchomajcz v. Hummel Chemical Co., 706
Suell v. Derricott, 946, 955

TABLE OF CASES

Suflas v. Cleveland Wrecking Co., 14
Suits v. Glover, 158
Sulhoff v. Everett, 420
Sulkowski v. Schaefer, 931, 933
Sullivan v. American Manufacturing Co. of Massachusetts, 648
Sullivan v. Associated Billposters and Distributors of United States and Canada, 941
Sullivan v. Boone, 265
Sullivan v. Boston Elevated Railway Co., 291
Sullivan v. Collins, 27
Sullivan v. County of Los Angeles, 1059, 1062, 1064
Sullivan v. Crabtree, 258, 259
Sullivan v. Davidson, 954
Sulivan v. Dunham, 553, 946
Sullivan v. H.P. Hood & Sons, 361
Sullivan v. Hamacher, 270
Sullivan v. Henry, 187, 188
Sullivan v. Montgomery, 117
Sullivan v. Moore, 734
Sullivan v. Philadelphia & Reading Railway Co., 259
Sullivan v. Ridgeway Construction Co., 485
Sullivan v. Stout, 660
Sullivan v. Strahorn-Hutton-Evans Comm. Co., 832
Sullivan v. Sullivan, 798
Sullivan v. United States, 530, 1040, 1042
Sullivan v. Valiquette, 918, 919
Sullivan & O'Brien v. Kennedy, 97
Summers v. Boston Safe Deposit Co., 941
Summers v. Tice, 271
Summerville v. Gillespie, 505
Summit County Development Corp. v. Bagnoli, 209
Summit Hotel Co. v. National Broadcasting Co., 787, 810, 812, 945
Summit View, Inc. v. W.W. Clyde & Co., 562
Sumner v. Amacher, 520, 521, 531
Sumner v. Beeler, 149
Sumner v. Utley, 792
Sumsion v. Streator-Smith, Inc., 660
Sumwalt Ice & Coal Co. v. Knickerbocker Ice Co., 991, 994
Sun Cab Co. v. Faulkner, 266
Sun-Maid Raisin Growers of Calif. v. Avis, 1009, 1015
Sun Printing & Publishing Association v. Schenck, 842, 848
Sunbeam Corp. v. Hall of Distributors, 994
Sunday v. Stratton Corp., 497, 498
Sunderland Brothers Co. v. Chicago, Burlington & Quincy Railroad Co., 315
Sunderlin v. Bradstreet, 829
Sunset Copper v. Zickrick, 333
Supchak v. United States, 1040, 1042
Superior Oil Co. v. Richmond, 308
Superwood Corp. v. Siempelkamp Corp., 708
Superx Drugs of Kentucky, Inc. v. Rice, 889
Surmanek v. State, 423
Surocco v. Geary, 146, 147, 148
Surratt v. Petrol, Inc., 398
Surratt v. Thompson, 903
Susquehanna Fertilizer Co. v. Malone, 550, 552
Susquehanna Power Co. v. Jeffress, 394
Sustin v. Fee, 1059
Suter v. San Angelo Foundry & Machine Co., 478, 701
Suter v. Wenatchee Water Power Co., 69
Sutherland v. Kroger Co., 854
Sutliff v. Sweetwater Water Co., 564
Sutor v. Wood, 871
Sutphen v. Hedden, 311
Sutterfield v. District Court, 326
Sutton v. Clarke, 325, 624
Sutton v. Greiner, 751
Sutton v. Public Service Interstate Transportation Co., 464
Sutton v. Huffman, 928
Sutton v. Penn, 429
Sutton v. Sutton, 183, 198, 921
Sutton and Ash v. Card, 546
Suttori v. Peckham, 103
Suzuki v. Small, 97
Svendsen v. State Bank of Duluth, 786
Swacker v. Wright, 853
Swager v. Couri, 983, 990, 1011
Swain v. Johnson, 981, 1003
Swain v. Tennessee Copper Co., 349
Swain & Son v. Chicago, Burlington & Quincy Railroad Co., 644
Swaine v. Great Norhtern Railway Co., 627, 640
Swan v. Tappan, 969, 974
Swaney v. Crawley, 1003
Swan-Finch Oil Corp. v. Warner-Quinlan Co., 147
Swann v. Rary, 842
Swanson v. City of Marquette, 404
Swanson v. Mississippi & Rum River Boom Co., 647, 650
Swartz v. United States Steel Corp., 932, 938
Swearingen v. Vik, 920
Swearsky v. Stanley Dry Goods Co., 515
Swede v. Passaic Daily News, 836
Sweenek v. Pathe News, 860, 861
Sweeney v. Abramovitz, 886
Sweeney v. Car/Puter International Corp., 246
Sweeney v. Carter, 1073
Sweeney v. Erving, 258
Sweeney v. F.W. Woolworth Co., 49, 50, 121
Sweeney v. Hartman, 528
Sweeney v. Patterson, 792
Sweeney v. Philadelphia Record Co., 792
Sweeney v. Schenectady Union Publishing Co., 778
Sweeney v. Smith, 990
Sweeney v. Tucker, 1057
Sweeney v. Winebuam, 183
Sweeney v. Young, 1059
Sweeny v. Old Colony & N.R. Co., 414
Sweet v. Kimball, 763
Sweet v. Post Publishing Co., 794, 810
Sweet v. Ringwelski, 206
Sweet v. Swangel, 250
Sweet Milk Co. v. Stanfield, 351
Sweeten v. Friedman, 142
Swenson v. Purity Baking Co., 262
Swenson v. Slawik, 440, 441

TABLE OF CASES

Swenson Trucking & Excavating, Inc. v. Truckweld Equipment Co., 174
Swerdfeger v. Krueger, 566
Swetland v. Curtiss Airports Corp., 79, 81
Swetnam v. F.W. Woolworth Co., 49
Swift v. Broyles, 639
Swift v. Rounds, 763
Swift & Co. v. Blackwell, 705
Swift & Co. v. Gray, 828
Swift & Co. v. St. Louis Transfer Railway Co., 218
Swift & Co. v. Schuster, 429
Swim v. Wilson, 97, 98
Swindell v. J. A. Tobin Construction Co., 517
Swine Flu Immunization Products Liability Litigation, In re, 191
Swiney v. Malone Freight Lines, 245
Swinton v. Whitinsville Savings Bank, 738
Switzer v. American Ry. Exp. Co., 835
Switzer v. Anthony, 809, 837
Switzer v. Detroit Investment Co., 464
Swoboda v. United States, 1034, 1035, 1042
Sworden v. Gross, 306
Swords v. Edgar, 438
Sworski v. Coleman, 581
Sworski v. Simons, 63
Sydenstricker v. Chicago & Northwestern Railway Co., 406
Sydney v. McFadden Newspaper Publishing Corp., 775
Sylva, People v., 46
Sylvester v. Northwestern Hospital of Minneapolis, 383
Sylvia v. Gobeille, 369
Symalla v. Dusenka, 132
Symphony Player Co. v. Hackstadt, 101
Syracuse Knitting Co. v. Blanchard, 763
System Auto Parks & Garages, Inc. v. American Economy Insurance Co., 483
System Operations, Inc. v. Scientific Games Development Corp., 963, 968, 971
Syas v. Nebraska Methodist Hospital Foundation, 421
Syah v. Johnson, 717
Sylvania Electric Products Co. v. Dura Electric Lamp Co., 1018
Symonds v. Hall, 150
Syverson v. Nelson, 575
Szabo v. Pennsylvania Railroad Co., 376
Szadiwicz v. Cantor, 123, 954
Szalatnay-Stacho v. Fink, 821
Szalay v. New York American, 809

T

T. & M. Homes, Inc. v. Township of Mansfield, 1051
Taafe v. Downes, 818
Taber v. Smith, 228
Tabor v. O'Grady, 462
Tabor v. Scobee, 119
Tabor v. Universal Exploration Co., 675
Tackaberry Co., William v. Sioux City Service Co., 349, 350, 619
Taft v. Taft, 59, 63
Taggart v. Shepherd, 675
Takoma Park Bank v. Abbott, 591
Talbert v. Talbert, 289, 308
Talbot v. Dr. W.H. Groves' Latter-Day Saints Hospital, Inc., 253
Talbot v. Sims, 490, 570
Talcott v. National Exhibition Co., 47, 51, 423
Taliaferro v. Sims, 817, 818
Tallbull v. Whitney, 188
Talley v. Alton Box Board Co., 818
Talley v. J. & L. Oil Co., 180, 409, 411
Talmage v. Smith, 38
Tamashiro v. DeGama, 595
Tameny v. Atlantic Richfield Co., 375, 1029
Tamiami Gun Shop v. Klein, 224, 461
Tampa Electric Co. v. Bryant, 471, 576
Tampa Electric Co. v. Larisey, 404
Tampa Union Terminal Co. v. Richards, 755
Tanana Trading Co. v. North American Trading & Transportation Co., 335
Taneian v. Meghrigian, 440
Tanner v. Gault, 821
Tanner v. Stevenson, 822, 823, 830, 834
Tanner-Brice Co. v. Sims, 867
TAO, Inc. v. Siebert, 996
Taplin v. Clark, 479
Taplan-Rice-Clerkin Co. v. Hower, 817, 872
Tappen v. Ager, 357
Tarantino v. Griebel, 882
Tarasoff v. Regents of University of California, 203, 359, 384, 1047
Taratino v. Allentown State Hospital, 1043
Tarleton v. McGawley, 970, 980, 1005, 1009, 1014
Tarman v. Southard, 505
Tarnowski v. Fite, 309
Tarpley v. Blabey, 786
Tarr v. General Electric Co., 994
Tarter v. Souderton Motor Co., 262
Tarzian, Inc., Sarkes v. Audio Devices, Inc., 1023
Tash v. Houston, 985, 990, 995
Tastor v. United States, 1038
Tate v. Canonica, 61, 62, 287, 293, 305, 311
Tate v. Ogg, 539
Taulbee v. Campbell, 491
Taulborg v. Andresen, 15
Tauscher v. Puget Sound Power & Light Co., 511, 514
Tavenner v. Morehead, 890
Tavernier v. Maes, 114, 485
Tavlinsky v. Ringling Brothers Circus Co., 925
Taxicab Motor Co. v. Pacific Coast Casualty Co., 587
Taylor v. Adams, 145
Taylor v. Armiger, 180
Taylor v. Arneill, 752
Taylor v. B. Heller & Co., 227
Taylor v. Baptist Medical Center, Inc., 364
Taylor v. Barnes, 646
Taylor v. Bennett, 626
Taylor v. Burr Printing Co., 732
Taylor v. Chambers, 830
Taylor v. Chesapeake & Ohio Railway Co., 148

Taylor v. City of Newport News, 1054
Taylor v. Centennial Bowl, Inc., 428
Taylor v. Costa Lines, Inc., 508
Taylor v. Cowit, 763
Taylor v. Glotfelty, 821
Taylor v. Granger, 539
Taylor v. Greiner, 889
Taylor v. Gumpert, 788
Taylor v. Hall, 790
Taylor v. Hearst, 536, 808, 846
Taylor v. Hocker, 203, 441, 443
Taylor v. Home Telephone Co., 307, 308
Taylor v. Hostetler, 574, 575, 576
Taylor v. Inhabitants of Plymouth, 146
Taylor v. K.T.V.B., Inc., 857
Taylor v. Kansas City, 423
Taylor v. Kinston Free Press Co., 801
Taylor v. Knox County Board of Education, 596
Taylor v. Leedy & Co., 435, 436
Taylor v. McCowat-Mercer Printing Co., 421
Taylor v. McDaniels, 823
Taylor v. Nashville Banner Publishing Co., 989, 1012
Taylor v. Neri, 998
Taylor v. New Jersey Highway Authority, 1043
Taylor v. Nohalty, 882
Taylor v. Olsen, 391
Taylor v. Paul O. Abbe, Inc., 705
Taylor v. Perkins, 790
Taylor v. S.H. Kress & Co., 932
Taylor v. Slaughter, 383
Taylor, State v., 134
Taylor v. Stimson, 435
Taylor v. Superior Ct., 178, 213
Taylor v. Thomas, 744
Taylor v. Vallelunga, 66
Taylor v. Western Pacific Railway Co., 949
Taylor v. Whitehead, 146
Taylor Motor Car Co. v. Hansen, 673
Teachout v. Van Hoesen, 760
Teagarden v. Russell's Administratrix, 407
Teakle v. San Pedro, Los Angeles & Salt Lake Railroad Co., 350, 464
Teall v. City of Cudahy, 380
Teasdale v. Beacon Oil Co., 199, 277, 303, 305, 317
Teche Lines v. Pope, 10
Tedescki v. Berger, 620, 644, 648
Tedesco v. Maryland Casualty Co., 9
Tedford v. Los Angeles Electric Co., 572
Tedla v. Ellman, 229
Teel v. May Department Stores Co., 141, 142
Teel v. Rio Bravo Oil Co., 551, 552
Teepen v. Taylor, 169
Teeters v. Frost, 122
Tehan v. United States ex rel. Shott, 866
Telechron, Inc. v. Telicon Corp., 1016
Tellefsen v. Fee, 150
Tempe v. Giacco, 459
Temperton v. Russel, 970, 983, 1005
Tempest v. Richardson, 418
Tempfer v. Joplin & Pittsburg Railway Co., 397, 465

Temple v. Congress Square Garage, 440
Temple v. Elvery, 542
Temple v. Wean United, Inc., 204, 711, 987
Templin v. Erkekedis, 363
Ten Broeck v. Journal Printing Co., 782
Tenant v. Goldwin, 624
Ten-Cate v. First National Bank, 737
Tennant v. Peoria & Pekin Union Railway Co., 579
Tennessee Central Railway Co. v. Doak, 935
Tennessee Coal, Iron & Railroad Co. v. Kimball, 85
Tenney v. Brandhove, 1056, 1061
Tenney v. Clement, 789
Tennyson v. Werthman, 790
Tenta v. Guraly, 982
Teolis v. Moscatelli, 118
Terhune v. Margaret Hague Maternity Hospital, 256
Terre Haute & I.R. Co. v. Buck, 310
Terre Haute & Indianapolis Railroad Co. v. Mason, 880
Terrell v. Lincoln Motel, Inc., 247
Terrell Hills Baptist Church v. Pawel, 734
Terrett v. Wray, 507
Territory v. Drennan, 132
Terry v. Dairymen's League Co-operative Association, 988
Terry v. Fellows, 820, 836
Terry v. Hooper, 791
Terry v. Hutchinson, 924, 926
Terry v. Linscott Hotel Corp., 373, 383
Terry v. Munger, 673
Terry v. New Orleans Great Northern Railroad Co., 225
Terry v. Zachry, 985
Terwilliger v. Wands, 794
Testa v. Katt, 1044
Testing Systems, Inc. v. Magnaflux Corp., 963, 964, 967, 968, 976
Teter v. Shultz, 751
Tetreault v. Campbell, 758
Tewksbury v. Bucklin, 541
Tex Smith, The Harmonica Man v. Godfrey, 790
Texas & New Orleans Railroad Co. v. Bean, 176
Texas & Pacific Railway Co. v. Behymer, 194, 195
Texas & Pacific Railway Co. v. Bigham, 289
Texas & Pacific Railway Co. v. Brick, 938
Texas & Pacific Railway Co. v. Bufkin, 660
Texas & Pacific Railway Co. v. Jones, 57, 58
Texas & Pacific Railway Co. v. McCleery, 268
Texas & Pacific Railway Co. v. Rigsby, 221
Texas & Pacific Railway Co. v. Tanskersley, 532
Texas Co. v. Haggard, 413
Texas Coca Cola Bottling Co. v. Lovejoy, 350
Texas Department of Corrections v. Herring, 1043
Texas Hotel Co. of Longview v. Cosby, 376
Texas Pacific Coal & Oil Co. v. Robertson, 10
Texas Power & Light Co. v. Burt, 409
Texas Public Utilities Corp. v. Edwards, 15
Texas Sling Co. v. Emanuel, 270
Texas-Louisiana Power Co. v. Daniels, 232
Texas-New Mexico Pipeline Co. v. Allstate Construction, Inc., 74
Tex-Jersey Oil Corp. v. Beck, 171

TG & Y Stores v. Atchley, 427
Thackery v. Union Portland Cement Co., 70
Thaggard v. Vafes, 947
Tharp v. Nolan, 789
Thate v. Texas & Pacific Railway Co., 501
Thayer v. Hutchinson, 103
Thayer v. Spear, 912
Thayer v. Worcester Post Co., 786, 867
Theaker v. Richardson, 798
Theil v. Cernin, 626
Thelen v. Spilman, 206, 378
Thellusson v. Woodford, 367
Themo v. New England Newspaper Publishing Co., 861
Theobald v. Angelos, 335
Theobald v. Kenney's Suburban House, Inc., 331
Theyer v. Purnell, 539, 560, 561
Thibodaux v. Town of Thibodeaux, 148
Thibodeau v. Cleff, 914
Thiel v. Cernin, 626
Thigpen v. Skousen & Hise, 549, 554
Thill v. Modern Erecting Co., 933
Thoirs v. Pounsford, 949
Thomas v. Atlantic Coast Line Railroad Co., 484
Thomas v. Barnes, 434, 435
Thomas v. Board of Township Trustees of Salem Township, Sedgwick County, 479
Thomas v. Boston & Providence Railroad Corp., 582
Thomas v. Bradbury, Agnew & Co., 776, 835
Thomas v. Carroll Construction Co., 493
Thomas v. Carter, 126
Thomas v. Casey, 308
Thomas v. Central Greyhound Lines, Inc., 209
Thomas v. Chicago Board of Education, 211
Thomas v. Cisneros, 878
Thomas v. Commercial Credit Corp., 10
Thomas v. Croswell, 838
Thomas v. D.C. Andrews & Co., 95
Thomas v. Doorley, 323
Thomas v. Dunne, 40
Thomas v. Gates, 369
Thomas v. General Electric Co., 868
Thomas v. Goodies Ice Cream Co., 200
Thomas v. Hanover Ins. Co., 183
Thomas v. Harrington, 513
Thomas v. Hinton, 878
Thomas v. Inman, 181, 200
Thomas v. Jacobs, 553
Thomas v. Kenyon, 459
Thomas v. Kinkead, 156
Thomas v. Malco Refineries, 341
Thomas v. Mississippi Valley Gas Co., 757
Thomas v. Ohio Coal Co., 634
Thomas v. Parker Rust Proof Co., 575
Thomas v. Quartermaine, 452
Thomas v. Sarrett, 474
Thomas v. State Highway Department, 1046
Thomas v. Thomas, 904
Thomas v. United States, 1041
Thomas v. Westbrook, 98
Thomas v. Williams, 376

Thomas v. Winchester, 682
Thomas' Administrator v. Maysville Street Railway & Transfer Co., 331
Thomas & Howard Co. v. Fowler, 764
Thomas-Kincannon-Elkin Drug Co. v. Hendrix, 507
Thomason v. Gray, 126
Thomason v. Sparkman, 982
Thompson v. Adelberg & Berman, 775, 786
Thompson v. Allstate Insurance Co., 1010
Thompson v. Ange, 385
Thompson v. Ashba, 210
Thompson v. Barry, 766
Thompson v. Beacon Valley Rubber Co., 883
Thompson v. Bohlken, 212, 213, 214, 381
Thompson v. Bridges, 791
Thompson v. Bronk, 674
Thompson v. Burke Engineering Sales Co., 723
Thompson v. City of Jacksonville, 854
Thompson v. County of Alameda, 384, 1047, 1048
Thompson v. Crocker, 75
Thompson v. Curtis Publishing Co., 858
Thompson v. Estate of Petroff, 942, 943
Thompson v. Fehlig Brothers Box & Lumber Co., 323
Thompson v. Fox, 309, 352
Thompson v. Gibson, 723
Thompson v. Harry C. Erb Co., 666
Thompson v. Havard, 914
Thompson v. Illinois Central Railroad Co., 84
Thompson v. Johnson, 323
Thompson v. Libby, 770
Thompson v. Lietz, 257
Thompson v. London County Council, 325, 328
Thompson v. Louisville & Nashville Railroad Co., 267, 345
Thompson v. Lupone, 291
Thompson v. Matthiasen, 832
Thompson v. Metropolitan Building Co., 91
Thompson v. Mobil Producing Co., 90
Thompson v. Modern School of Business and Correspondence, 741
Thompson v. National Railroad Passenger Corp., 482
Thompson v. Norfolk & Western Railway Co., 156
Thompson v. Phoenix Insurance Co., 759
Thompson v. Price, 877
Thompson v. Reedman, 703
Thompson v. St. Louis & San Francisco Railroad Co., 48
Thompson v. Seaboard Air Line Railway Co., 999
Thompson v. Shackell, 832
Thompson v. Southwestern Bell Telephone Co., 380
Thompson v. State, 130
Thompson v. Thompson, 901, 902
Thompson v. Tilton Electric Light & Power Co., 413
Thompson v. Town of Fort Branch, 953
Thompson v. United States, 434, 503, 1042
Thompson v. Upton, 775, 796
Thompson v. Vogue Co., 1016
Thompson v. Warehouse Corp. of America, Inc., 430
Thompson v. Weaver, 496
Thompson v. White, 388, 392, 965
Thompson v. Wold, 563

Thompson Co., John R. v. Vildibill, 43
Thoms v. D.C. Andrews & Co., 97
Thomsen v. Cayser, 1014
Thomson v. Deakin, 980
Thone v. Nicholson, 212
Thorburn v. Campbell, 544
Thoreson v. Milwaukee & Suburban Transport Co., 908, 909, 910
Thorley v. Lord Kerry, 786, 795
Thorn v. Moser, 823
Thornburg v. Long, 827
Thornburg v. Port of Portland, 82, 1043
Thorne v. Deas, 379
Thorne v. Tilbury, 100
Thorne v. United States, 514
Thornhill v. Alabama, 1025
Thornhill v. Carpenter-Morton Co., 685
Thornton v. Eneroth, 306, 352
Thornton v. Franklin Square House, 1070
Thornton v. Maine State Agricultural Society, 428
Thornton v. Mono Manufacturing Co., 168
Thornton v. Pender, 219
Thornton v. Rhoden, 817
Thornton v. Roosevelt Hospital, 167
Thornton v. Taylor, 126
Thornton v. Thornton, 502
Thornton v. Weaber, 283, 299
Thoroughgood's Case, 731
Thorp v. Burling, 95, 98
Thorpe v. Brumfitt, 354
Thorpe v. Cooley, 756
Thorogood v. Bryan, 530
Thorson v. Albert Lea Publishing Co., 810
Thrall v. Lathrop, 94
Thrash v. U-Drive-It Co., 705
Thrasher v. City of Atlanta, 79, 81
Thrasher v. Gerken, 420, 512, 514
Three Lakes Association v. Whiting, 898
3700 S. Kedzie Building Corp. v. Chicago Steel Foundry Co., 762
Throne v. Wandell, 119
Thropp v. Bache Halsey Stuart Shields, Inc., 195, 196
Thrower v. Smith, 251
Thrussell v. Handyside & Co., 491, 571
Thuringer v. Bonner, 661, 664
Thurman v. Etherton, 906
Thurmond v. Pepper, 172
Thurston v. Blanchard, 93, 672
Thurston v. Leno, 51, 1062
Thurston v. Wright, 883
Thweatt's Administrator v. Elder, 337
Thwing v. Hall & Ducey Lumber Co., 756
Tibbetts v. Nyberg, 251
Tibbits v. Crowell, 265
Tice v. Mandel, 918
Tichenor v. Hayes, 941
Tichenor v. Lohaus, 455, 460
Tidal Oil Co. v. Pease, 346, 551, 634
Tidal Western Oil Corp. v. Shackelford, 986
Tidd v. Skinner, 932

Tidewater Oil Co. v. Jackson, 83
Tidmore v. Mills, 801
Tiede v. Fuhr, 52
Tiene, Application of, 868
Tierney v. Ruppert, 826
Tierney v. State, 48
Tightmeyer v. Mongold, 673
Tiller v. Atlantic Coast Line Railroad Co., 578
Tillery v. Ellison, 260
Tillett v. Ward, 540
Tilley v. Stevenson, 546
Tillman v. Bellamy, 326
Tillman v. Public Belt Railroad Commission, 396
Tillotson v. Currin, 927
Timbrell v. Suburban Hospital, 256
Time, Inc. v. Firestone, 797, 805, 806, 892, 896
Time, Inc. v. Hill, 862, 865
Times Publishing Co. v. Carlisle, 799
Timken Roller Bearing Co. v. Leterstone Sales Co., 1015
Timmerman v. Gurnsey, 665, 770
Timmis v. Bennett, 819
Timmons v. Fulton Bag & Cotton Mills, 52
Timmons v. Reed, 219, 387
Timmons v. Williams Wood Products' Corp., 665
Timperley v. Chase Collection Service, 858
Tindle v. Birkett, 744
Tingle v. Chicago, Burlington & Quincy Railroad Co., 222, 275
Tinker v. Colwell, 917, 920
Tinkham v. Kole, 158
Tinkle v. Dunivant, 157
Tinkler v. Poole, 93
Tinline v. White Cross Ins. Ass'n, 586
Tinnerholm v. Parke-Davis & Co., 697
Tino v. Stout, 340
Tipaldi v. Riverside Memorial Chapel, 342
Tippecanoe Land & Trust Co. v. Jester, 669
Tipsword v. Potter, 133
Tipton v. Mullinix, 181
Tissot v. Great Southern Telephone & Telegraph Co., 642
Tittlebaum v. Boehmcke, 926, 928
Titus v. Bradford, Bordell & Kinzua Railroad Co., 194
Titus v. Montgomery Ward & Co., 53
Titus v. Morse, 734
Tjas v. Prochter, 393
Toadvine v. Cincinnati, New Orleans & Texas Pacific Railway Co., 375
Toal v. Zito, 790
Tobias v. Harland, 972
Tobin v. Alfred M. Best Co., 965
Tobin v. Deal, 95
Tobin v. Frankfort Water Co., 671
Tobin v. Grossman, 365, 366
Tobin v. Hoffman, 911
Tobin v. Seattle, 348
Toca v. Rojas, 913
Tocker v. Great Atlantic & Pacific Tea Co., 798
Todd v. Adams, 960
Todd v. Hargis, 525

Todd v. Hawkins, 827
Todd v. Weikle, 951, 952
Toetschinger v. Ihnot, 180
Tolbert v. Gerber Industries, Inc., 343, 344, 477
Toledo, City of v. Lowenberg, 50
Toledo, St. Louis & Kansas City Railroad Co. v. Loop, 642
Toledo, St. Louis & Western Railroad Co. v. Allen, 488
Toledo, Wabash & Western Railway Co. v. Harmon, 507
Toledo & Ohio Central Railway Co. v. S.J. Kibler & Brothers Co., 303, 316
Tolin v. Terrell, 184
Tollefson v. Price, 62, 841, 858
Tolley v. Engert, 328
Tolley v. J.S. Fry & Sons, Ltd., 776, 777
Tollisen v. Lehigh Valley Transportation Co., 198
Tom v. Days of '47, Inc., 208
Tom v. S.S. Kresge Co., 183, 427
Tomakian v. Fritz, 776
Tomassi v. Town of Union, 388
Tombigbee Electric Power Association v. Gandy, 269
Tomkins v. Northwestern Union Trust Co., 245
Tomko v. Sharp, 379
Tomlins, People v., 128
Tomlinson v. Sharpe, 504
Tompkins v. Hollister, 760
Tompkins v. Northwestern Union Trust Co., 246, 248, 251, 258
Tonawanda Railroad Co. v. Munger, 539
Tonkawa, City of v. Danielson, 542, 563
Tonkonogy v. Jaffin, 817, 818
Tonkovich v. South Florida Citrus Industries, Inc., 766
Toof v. Bently, 149
Toogood v. Spyring, 825
Tool Research & Engineering Corp. v. Henigson, 894
Toole v. Levitt, 442
Toole v. Morris-Webb Motor Co., 717
Toole v. Richardson-Merrell, Inc., 10, 205
Toombs v. Fort Pierce Gas Co., 704
Toomey v. Farley, 15, 778
Toomey v. Jones, 778
Toomey v. Sanborn, 429
Toone v. Adams, 313
Top Service Body Shop, Inc. v. Allstate Insurance Co., 983, 1011
Torette House v. Berkman, 546
Torgeson v. Missouri-Kansas-Texas Railway Co., 218
Toroian v. Parkview Amusement Co., 492
Torpey v. Red Owl Stores, 703
Torres v. Huner, 793
Torres v. Owens, 1065
Torres v. State, 362
Torski v. Mansfield Journal Co., 838
Toscani v. Hersey, 853
Toth v. Community Hospital at Glen Cove, 189
Totman, State v., 130
Tott v. Duggan, 746
Totten v. Sun Printing & Publishing Ass'n, 773
Tousley v. Board of Education, 112
Toussant v. Guice, 246, 259

Tout v. Hartford Accident & Indemnity Co., 385
Towaliga Falls Power Co. v. Sims, 304, 390, 620, 621, 639
Tower v. Camp, 327
Tower v. Crosby, 972
Towle v. St. Albans Publishing Co., 847
Town of (see name of town)
Towns v. Anderson, 364
Township of (see name of township)
Townsdin v. Nutt, 43
Towse v. State, 1059
Townsend v. Holderby, 922
Townsend v. Wathen, 400
Toy v. United States Cartridge Co., 569
Trabue v. Mays, 846
Tracey v. City of Minneapolis, 275, 311
Tracy v. Rublein, 326, 329
Tradesmen's National Bank v. Indiana Bicycle Co., 733
Trahan v. Smith, 914
Traill v. Ostermeir, 541
Trainor v. Frank Mercede & Sons, Inc., 386
Trainor v. Santana, 431
Trammell v. Bassett, 159
Trammell v. Citizens News Co., 858
Trammell v. Eastern Air Lines, 665
Trampe, State ex rel. v. Multerer, 644
Tranchina v. Arcinas, 899
Trans World Accounts, Inc. v. Associated Press, 970
Trans World Airlines, Inc. v. Alitalia-Linee Aeree Airlines, 241
Trans World Airlines v. Curtiss-Wright Corp., 709
Trans-American Van Service, Inc. v. Shirzad, 483
Transcontinental Gas Pipe Line v. Gault, 619, 627, 644
Transit Casualty Co. v. Puchalski, 239
Transylvania Casualty Insurance Co. v. Williams, 587
Trapani v. State, 311
Trapp v. Standard Oil Co., 303
Trapp v. Western Union Telegraph Co., 1000
Trascher v. Eagle Indemnity Co., 291
Traub v. Dinzler, 342
Trautwein v. Harbourt, 1006
Travelers Indemnity Co. v. Evans Pipe Co., 678
Travelers Insurance Co. v. Anderson, 379
Travis, Ex parte, 243, 246, 248
Travis v. Hay, 458
Traylor v. Coburn, 224
Traylor v. Horrall, 102
Traylor Engineering & Manufacturing Co. v. National Container Corp., 728, 758
Traynor v. Seiloff, 782, 829
Traywick v. Keeble, 94
Treadway v. Ebert Motor Co., 419, 422, 424, 426
Trebby v. Transcript Publishing Co., 837
Trebelhorn v. Bartlett, 742
Trebilcock v. Anderson, 821, 822
Treesh v. Stone, 10
Treloar v. Harris, 882
Tremblay v. Harmony Mills, 390
Tremblay v. J. Rudnick & Sons, 569
Trembley v. Carter, 932

Trentacost v. Brussel, 174, 202, 442
Trenton Mutual Life & Fire Insurance Co. v. Perrine, 972
Treptau v. Behrens Spa, 187
Treschman v. Treschman, 159, 905, 906
Tresise v. Ashdown, 219
Trevarton v. Trevarton, 907
Triangle Film Corp. v. Artcraft Pictures Corp., 988, 994, 996
Triangle Publications, Inc. v. Rohrlich, 1016, 1017
Tribble v. Gregory, 933
Trice v. Chicago Housing Authority, 201
Trico Coffee Co. v. Clemens, 397
Tricoli v. Centalanza, 323, 346
Triff v. National Bronze & Aluminum Foundry Co., 575
Triggs v. Sun Printing & Publishing Association, 809, 813
Trimarco v. Klein, 195
Trimble v. Exchange Bank, 342
Trimble v. Spears, 442
Trimboli v. Kinkel, 660
Trimming v. Howard, 667
Trinity & Brazos Valley Railway Co. v. Blackshear, 284
Triple-State Natural Gas & Oil Co. v. Wellman, 550
Triplett, State v., 46
Tritchler v. West Virginia Newspaper Publishing Co., 880
Trogden v. Terry, 10, 43, 45, 57
Trogrun v. Fruchtman, 190
Trojan Boat Co. v. Lutz, 704
Trombley v. Kolts, 377
Tromza v. Tecumseh Products Co., 342
Troop v. Dew, 323
Tropea v. Shell Oil Co., 299
Troppi v. Scarf, 185, 372
Troth v. Wills, 560, 561
Trotman v. Dunn, 817
Trottier v. West, 881
Trousil v. Bayer, 40
Trout v. Pennsylvania Railroad Co., 227
Trout v. Watkins Livery & Undertaking Co., 665
Troutman v. Modlin, 339, 340
Trowbridge v. Abrasive Co., 684
Trowell v. United States, 169, 183, 454, 460
Troy v. Long Island Jewish-Hillside Medical Center, 191
Truck Equipment Service Co. v. Fruehauf Corp., 1018, 1021
Truck Insurance Exchange v. Yardley, 501
Trudo v. Lazarus, 401
True v. Older, 123
True & True Co. v. Woda, 954
Truet v. State, 644
Truett Payne Co., J. v. Jackson, 11
Truhitte v. French Hospital, 189, 204, 506
Truman v. Fidelity & Casualty Co., 879
Truman v. Thomas, 190, 192, 219
Truman v. United Products Corp., 528
Trumbull v. Trumbull, 922
Trump v. Bluefield Waterworks & Improvement Co., 514

Trust v. Arden Farms Co., 249
Trust Co. of Norfolk v. Fletcher, 941
Trustees of First Baptist Church v. McElroy, 724
Trusty v. Patterson, 319, 715, 717
Truth Seeker Co. v. Durning, 106
Truxes v. Kenco Enterprises, Inc., 851
Try-Me Beverage Co. v. Harris, 262
Tryon v. Evening News Association, 831
Tsang v. Kan, 765
Tsuboi v. Cohn, 675
Tubbs v. Argus, 376, 377
Tubbs v. Commonwealth, 130
Tubbs v. Shears, 565
Tubbs v. Tukey, 152
Tubervil v. Stamp, 543, 563
Tuberville v. Savage, 45
Tubular Rivet & Stud Co. v. Exeter Boot & Shoe Co., 988, 991
Tuck v. Tuck, 726
Tuckachinsky v. Lehigh & Wilkesbarre Coal Co., 553, 564
Tucker v. American Employer's Insurance Co., 868
Tucker v. Bartlett, 880
Tucker v. Beazley, 738
Tucker v. Burt, 134
Tucker v. Collar, 286
Tucker v. Duncan, 868, 875, 886
Tucker v. State, 946
Tucker v. Tucker, 906
Tucker v. Union Oil Co. of California, 475, 476, 477
Tucker v. Wright, 106
Tucker Bros. v. Menard, 409
Tucker Oil Co. v. Matthews, 350
Tucson, City of v. Wondergem, 952
Tucson Rapid Transit Co. v. Tocci, 311
Tuell v. Marion, 650
Tuengel v. Stobbs, 259
Tuff v. Warman, 463
Tufty v. Sioux Transit Co., 951, 959
Tullay v. Reed, 132
Tullgren v. Amoskeag Manufacturing Co., 171, 270, 321
Tullidge v. Wade, 926
Tully v. Dasher, 888
Tulsa, City of v. Wells, 328
Tulsa Entertainment Co. v. Greenlees, 438, 439
Tunkl v. Regents of University of California, 483
Turbeville v. Mobile Light & Railroad Co., 377
Tureman v. Ketterlin, 620
Turley v. Tucker, 103
Turner v. ABC Jalousie Co., 63
Turner v. Atlantic Coast Line Railroad Co., 936
Turner v. Big Lake Oil Co., 549, 551
Turner v. Brien, 775
Turner v. Bucher, 529, 1074
Turner v. Caldwell, 1074
Turner v. Carter, 595
Turner v. Chicago, Rock Island & Pacific Railway Co., 317
Turner v. City of Spokane, 627, 641
Turner v. Estes, 922

TABLE OF CASES

Turner v. Gackle, 525
Turner v. General Motors Corp., 699
Turner v. Hall's Administratrix, 524, 525, 526
Turner v. Hearst, 810, 846
Turner v. Heavrin, 917
Turner v. International Harvester Co., 484
Turner v. Kent, 438
Turner v. Kirkwood, 339
Turner v. Manning, Maxwell & Moore, Inc., 194
Turner v. Maymott, 143
Turner v. Mellon, 52
Turner v. Minneapolis Street Railway Co., 291
Turner v. North American Van Lines, 251
Turner v. Page, 309
Turner v. Ridley, 450
Turner v. Silver, 229
Turner v. Staggs, 1055
Turner v. Stallibrass, 660, 663
Turner, State v., 128, 644, 645
Turner v. Thompson, 435, 441, 442
Turner v. Turner, 907
Turney v. Rhodes, 47
Turpen v. Booth, 1058
Turpin v. Sortini, 371
Turtenwald v. Aetna Casualty & Surety Co., 254
Turton v. New York Recorder Co., 810
Tuscaloosa, City of v. Fair, 329
Tushbant v. Greenfield's, 645
Tuttle v. Atlantic City Railroad Co., 307
Tuttle v. Buck, 1006, 1009, 1014
Tuttle v. Campbell, 674
Tuttle v. George H. Gilbert Manufacturing Co., 443
Tuttle v. Meyer Dairy Products Co., 361
Tuttle v. Short, 941
Tuttle v. Stovall, 770
Tutwiler v. I. Beverally Nalle, Inc., 423
Tweedy v. J.C. Penney Co., 870, 883
Tweedy v. Wright Ford Sales, Inc., 255
2310 Madison Avenue, Inc. v. Allied Bedding Manufacturing Co., 442, 443
Twin State Fruit Corp. v. Kansas, 752
Twitchell v. Glenwood-Inglewood Co., 982, 1000
Twitchell v. Nelson, 982, 991
Two Rivers Manufacturing Co. v. Day, 734
Tye v. Finkelstein, 996
Tyndall, State ex rel. Mavity v., 864
Tyra v. Cheney, 739
Tyree v. Tudor, 718
Tyson v. East Carolina Railroad Co., 399
Tyson v. Johns-Manville Sales Corp., 168

U

Uccello v. Laudenslayer, 384
Uhlein v. Cromack, 147
Uhlrig v. Shortt, 570
Ukiah City, Town of v. Ukiah Water & Implement Co., 671
Ullrich v. New York Press Co., 1074
Ulrich v. Kasco Abrasives Co., 205
Ulrich v. Schwarz, 127
Ultimate Computer Services v. Biltmore Realty Co., 435
Ultramares Corp. v. Touche, 742, 745, 747
Ulvig v. McKennan Hospital, 941
Ulwelling v. Crown Coach Corp., 670
Umberger v. Koop, 464
Unckles v. Hentz, 758
Underwood v. Gardner, 467
Unger v. Eagle Fish Co., 760
Union v. United Battery Service Co., 880
Union Bank & Trust Co. of Mt. Holley, New Jersey v. First National Bank & Trust Co. of Waynesboro, 906
Union Bus Co. v. Smith, 520
Union Car Advertising Co. v. Collier, 967, 968, 1006, 1010
Union Carbide Corp. v. Holton, 204
Union Carbide & Carbon Corp. v. Peters, 201, 285
Union Circulation Co. v. Hardel Publishers Service, 995
Union Depot & Railroad Co. v. Smith, 154
Union Oil Co. v. Oppen, 997
Union Oil Co. of California v. Hunt, 576
Union Pacific Railroad Co. v. Burke, 483
Union Pacific Railroad Co. v. Cappier, 375, 377
Union Pacific Railroad Co. v. Cogburn, 455
Union Pacific Railroad Co. v. Daniels, 572
Union Pacific Railroad Co. v. De Busk, 544
Union Pacific Railroad Co. v. Henry, 210, 470
Union Pacific Railroad Co. v. Lumbert, 218
Union Pacific Railroad Co. v. Vale Irrigation District, 78, 551
Union Stock Yards Co. v. Chicago, Burlington & Quincy Railroad Co., 337
Union Supply Co. v. Pust, 705
Union Trust Co. v. American Commercial Car Co., 528
Union Trust Co., United States v., 1040
United Airlines, Inc. v. Wiener, 343, 344, 1034
United Barge Co. v. Notre Dame Fleeting & Towing Service, Inc., 210
United Electric Light Co. v. Deliso Construction Co., 68, 74, 82
United Factories, State ex rel. v. Hostetter, 13
United Fuel Gas Co. v. Sawyers, 551
United Mine Workers of America v. Gibbs, 1027
United Mine Workers of America v. Pennington, 989, 1025
United Novelty Co. v. Daniels, 317
United Protective Workers v. Ford Motor Co., 662
United States v. _____ **(see opposing party)**
United States Aluminum Siding Corp. v. Dun & Bradstreet, 1009
United States Cities Corp. v. Sautbine, 91
United States Fidelity & Guaranty Co. v. Leon, 94
United States Fidelity & Guaranty Co. v. Millonas, 988, 995, 996, 1003, 1004
United States Fidelity & Guaranty Co. v. Peterson, 11
United States Fire Insurance Co. v. Cannon, 379
United States for Use and Benefit of Los Angeles Testing Laboratory v. Rogers & Rogers, 723
United States Smelting Co. v. Sisam, 621

United States Tire Co. v. Kirk, 893
United States to Use of Parravicino v. Brunswick, 821
United Verde Copper Co. v. Ralston, 619, 635
United Wild Rice, Inc. v. Nelson, 984, 988, 1011
United Zinc & Chemical Co. v. Britt, 401
Universal Athletic Sales Co. v. American Gym, Recreational & Athletic Equipment Corp., 1019
University Heights, City of v. Conley, 868
University of Louisville v. Hammock, 314
University of Notre Dame Du Lac v. Twentieth Century-Fox Film Corp., 854
Updegraff v. City of Ottumwa, 390, 437
Upham's Case, 309, 310
Uproar Co. v. National Broadcasting Co., 853
Ups N' Downs, Inc. v. Albina Enterprises, Inc., 209
Upton v. Hume, 775
Upton v. Times-Democrat Publishing Co., 777, 808
Uraneck v. Lima, 156
Urban v. Hartford Gas Co., 794
Urban v. Wait's Supermarket, Inc., 474
Urbano v. Meneses, 1051
Urchel v. Holy Cross Hospital, 166
Ure v. Maggio Brothers Co., 953
Urie v. Thompson, 957
Urseleo v. Rosengard, 440
Urton v. Price, 335
Urtz v. New York Central & Hudson River Railroad Co., 767
Ushirohira v. Stuckey, 349
Usill v. Hales, 837
USM Corp. v. Marson Fastener Corp., 1022
Usry v. Small, 289, 308
Utah State Farm Bureau Federation v. National Farmers Union Service Corp., 778, 779, 848
Utah State University v. Sutro & Co., 1059
Utley v. Hill, 744
Utz v. Mayes, 54

V

Vadyak v. Lehigh & New England Railroad Co., 507
Vail v. Pennsylvania Railroad Co., 826, 832
Vail v. Strong, 740
Vaillancourt v. Medical Center Hospital of Vermont, Inc., 365, 370
Valdes v. Karoll's Inc., 427
Valdez v. Gonzales, 3
Valentine v. Gonzalez, 786, 801
Valerni v. Hearst Magazines, 864
Vallen v. Fanjo Taxi Corp., 774
Vallis v. Canada Dry Ginger Ale, Inc., 695
Valton v. National Fund Life Assurance Co., 754
Valunas v. J.J. Newberry Co., 421
Valz v. Goodykoontz, 205, 726
Van Alstyne v. Rochester Telephone Corp., 68, 69, 76, 723
Van Ankin v. Westfall, 788
Van Arsdale v. Hollinger, 512, 514
Van Avery v. Platte Valley Land & Investment Co., 439
Van Blaricom v. Dodgson, 526

Van Boskirk v. Pinto, 589
Van Bronckhorst v. Taube, 166
Van Cleef v. City of Chicago, 317
Van Daele v. Vinci, 1028
Van Dorn v. Kimball, 48
Van Dresor v. King, 85
Van Dyke Productions, Inc., Willard v. Eastman Kodak Co., 484
Van Etten v. Noyes, 539
Van Gaasbeck v. Webatuck Central School District No. 1, p. 461
Van Hoose v. Blueflame Gas Co., 208, 209
Van Horn v. Stautz, 756
Van Horn v. Van Horn, 324, 1014
Van Horn v. William Blanchard Co., 473
Van Leuven v. Lyke, 561
Van Natta v. Snyder, 770
Van Products Co. v. General Welding and Fabricating Co., 1023
Van Sickel v. United States, 1037
Van Slyck v. Snell, 541
Van Vacter v. McKillip, 932
Van Vliet v. Vander Naald, 830
Van Vliet Fletcher Automobile Co. v. Crowell, 770
Van Wiginton v. Pulitzer Publishing Co., 778, 781
Van Winkle v. American Steam-Boiler Insurance Co., 206, 670
Van Zee v. Sioux Valley Hospital, 253, 256
Vanarsdale v. Laverty, 1011
Vance v. United States, 1034
Vance v. Vance, 364, 365, 891, 909
Vandenburgh v. Truax, 38, 72
Vander Linden v. Crews, 870, 873, 884
Vanderbilt v. Mathis, 883
Vanderbilt v. Mitchell, 852, 853
Vanderbilt, State v., 158
Vanderbloemen v. Suchosky, 520
Vanderdoes v. Rumore, 423
Vandermark v. Ford Motor Co., 692, 694
Vanderslice v. Shawn, 80
Vanlandingham v. Vanlandingham, 219
Vanloon v. Vanloon, 793
Vann v. Bowie Sewerage Co., 621
Vannah v. Hart Private Hospital, 507
Vanneman v. Powers, 913
Vanoni v. Western Airlines, 361
Vanover v. Wells, 799
Vantandillo, Rex v., 643
Vanthournout v. Burge, 211, 529
Vargus v. Pitman Mfg. Co., 478, 486, 492, 495, 497
Vargas v. Ruggiero, 63
Vargas, State v., 156
Varian Associates v. Compagnie Generale Transatlantique, 482
Varner v. Morton, 786
Varney v. Curtis, 90, 94
Vasser v. Berry, 877
Vassos v. Roussalis, 174, 189
Vaughan v. Industrial Silica Corp., 305
Vaughan v. Menlove, 169, 174, 177, 357, 543, 592

Vaughan v. Miller Brothers "101" Ranch Wild West Show, 541, 563
Vaughan v. Taff Vale R. Co., 543, 544, 546, 567
Vaughn v. Blackburn, 923
Vaughn v. Booker, 526
Vaughn v. Ellis, 966
Vaughn v. Glenn, 85
Vaughn v. Langmack, 165
Vaughn v. Mesch, 41, 142
Vaughn v. Missouri Power & Light Co., 387, 625
Vaughn v. United States, 1039
Vaughn v. Wright, 90, 91, 92
Vaught v. Jonathan L. Pettyjohn & Co., 992, 1003
Veach v. City of Phoenix, 1052
Veatch v. Wagner, 1020
Veazey v. Blair, 817
Vegelahn v. Guntner, 992, 1006
Vegich v. McDougal Hartmann Co., 461
Veltri v. City of Cleveland, 86
Vendrell v. School District No. 26C, p. 114
Venorick v. Revetta, 313
Ventresca v. Kissner, 788
Venzel v. Valley Camp Coal Co., 551
Verdis, State ex rel. v. Fidelity & Casualty Co., 154
Verheyen v. Dewey, 349, 634
Verhoeks v. Gillivan, 330
Verkamp Corp. of Kentucky v. Hubbard, 283
Verlinda v. Stone & Webster Engineering Corp., 346
Vermes v. American District Telegraph Co., 443
Vermillion v. Woman's College of Due West, 1070
Vermilye v. Western Union Telegraph Co., 483
Vermont Acceptance Corp. v. Wiltshire, 101, 666, 1072
Vermont Salvage Corp. v. Village of St. Johnsbury, 626
Verrett v. McDonough Marine Service, 458
Verrill v. Dewey, 1063
Verstraelen v. Kellog, 50
VerWys v. Vander Mey, 744
Veselenak v. Smith, 9
Vespe v. DiMarco, 164, 246
Vestal v. Gulf Oil Corp., 639
Vezina v. Souliere, 769
Vian v. Hilberg, 756
Vicars v. Wilcocks, 277, 778, 795, 844
Vicenty v. Eastern Air Lines, 382
Vicnire v. Ford Motor Credit Co., 364
Victorian Railway Commissioners v. Coultas, 55, 360, 363
Victorson v. Milwaukee & Suburban Transport Co., 937
Victory Sparkler & Specialty Co. v. Price, 226
Videan v. British Transport Commission, 288
Vidrine v. Missouri Farm Association, 184
Viebahn v. Board of Crow Wing Commissions, 650
Viehweg v. Mountain States Telephone & Telegraph Co., 331
Viera v. Atchison, Topeka & Santa Fe Railway Co., 243
Vierra v. Fifth Avenue Rental Service, 489
Vieths v. Ripley, 508
Vigil v. Rice, 834, 846
Vigilant Insurance Co. v. Bennett, 902
Vilas v. Mason, 99

Vilett v. Moler, 761
Village Development Co. v. Filice, 447
Village of (see name of village)
Villanueva v. Nowlin, 717
Villaret v. Villaret, 595, 904
Vincent v. Corbitt, 742
Vincent v. Riggi & Sons, Inc., 227, 230
Vincent v. Stinehour, 163
Vinal v. Core, 880
Vincer v. Ester Williams All-Aluminum Swimming Pool Co., 692
Vincioni v. Phelps Dodge Corp., 878
Vines v. Crescent Transit Co., 660
Vining v. Avis Rent-A-Car Systems, Inc., 203, 224
Vining v. Baker, 103
Vinson v. Flynn, 871
Vinson v. O'Malley, 792
Viou v. Brooks-Scanlon Lumber Co., 352
Virgil v. Time, Inc., 857
Virginia-Carolina Peanut Co. v. Atlantic Coast Line Railroad Co., 660
Virginia Dare Stores v. Schuman, 726
Virginia Electric & Power Co. v. Wynne, 883
Virginia State Board of Pharmacy v. Virginia Citizens Consumer Council, Inc., 977
Virginia Surety Co. v. Schlegel, 504
Virginia Transit Co. v. Simmons, 521
Virtue v. Creamery Package Manufacturing Co., 893, 1010
Viss v. Calligan, 794
Vitagraph Co. v. of America v. Ford, 965
Vitale v. Duerbeck, 445, 512
Vittorio v. St. Regis Paper Co., 149
Vittum v. Gilman, 941
Vizetelly v. Mudie's Select Library, 799, 803, 810
Vlases v. Montgomery Ward & Co., 706
Voelker v. Tyndall, 855
Vogel v. Bushnell, 779
Vogel v. Cobb, 664
Vogel v. Fetter Livestock Co., 420
Vogel v. Gruaz, 820
Vogel v. Sylvester, 919, 921, 923
Vogel v. W.T. Grant Co., 858
Vogreg v. Shepard Ambulance Co., 260
Vogue Co. v. Thompson-Hudson Co., 1015
Vogue Co. v. Vogue Hat Co., 1016
Vokal v. United States, 759
Volk v. Auto-Dine Corp., 867
Volk v. Baldzao, 370
Voll v. Butler, 145
Volz v. Williams, 439
Von Longerke v. City of New York, 515
Von Thodorovich v. Franz Josef Beneficial Association, 852
Vonault v. O'Rourke, 261
Voneye v. Turner, 858
Vonner v. State, 1048
Vosburg v. Putney, 37, 40, 42
Vosnos v. Perry, 177, 1072
Voss v. Bridwell, 250, 1065, 1066

Vossel v. Cole, 928
Votava v. Material Service Corp., 397, 398
Vowinckel v. N. Clark & Sons, 620
Vragnizan v. Savings Union Bank & Trust Co., 941
Vredenburg v. Behan, 542, 564
Vu v. Singer Co., 359
Vulcan Detinning Co. v. American Can Co., 1022
Vulcan Metals Co. v. Simmons Manufacturing Co., 757

W

W., Peter v. San Francisco Unified School District, 1049
W.C. Block, The, 105
W.K. Syson Timber Co. v. Dickens, 87
Wabash Railroad Co. v. Coker, 298
Wabash Railroad Co. v. Glass, 218
Wabash Railroad Co. v. Hartog, 716
Wabash Railroad Co. v. Henks, 210
Wabash Railroad Co. v. Walczak, 218
Wabash Railroad Co. v. Young, 774
Wachsmuth v. Merchants' National Bank, 821
Wachstein v. Christopher, 82
Wachtel v. National Alfalfa Journal, 1007
Waddell v. White, 763, 767
Wade v. Campbell, 648
Wade v. Culp, 987, 990
Wade v. Gennaro, 133
Wade v. Miller, 626, 628
Wadkins v. Digman, 883
Wadleigh v. City of Manchester, 553
Wagener v. Bill, 912
Wager v. Pro, 212, 463
Waggoner v. Midwestern Development, Inc, 721
Wagner v. American Family Mutual Insurance Co., 180
Wagner v. Bissell, 540
Wagner v. Coca-Cola Bottling Co., 249, 261
Wagner v. Coronet Hotel, 705, 719
Wagner v. International Railway Co., 196, 288, 308
Wagner v. Mittendorf, 310
Wagner v. Retail Credit Co., 815
Wagstaff v. City of Maplewood, 248
Wahl v. Strous, 989
Wahl v. Walton, 154
Wahlheimer v. Hardenbergh, 799
Waid v. Bergschneider, 591
Waier v. Peerless Oil Co., 633, 634
Wainwright v. Truckenmiller, 458
Waite v. North Eastern R. Co., 531
Waite v. Stockgrowers' Credit Corp., 795, 844
Wakefield v. Smithwick, 831
Wakelin v. London & S.W.R. Co., 452
Wakeman v. Wilbur, 650
Wakley v. Cooke, 841
Walden v. Coleman, 959
Walden v. Conn, 78, 992
Waldrop v. Nashville, Chattanooga & St. Louis Railway Co., 134
Wales v. Miner, 917
Wales Trucking Co. v. Stallcup, 625
Walgreen-Texas Co. v. Shivers, 427

Walinsky v. Kennedy, 1026
Walker v. Bee-News Publishing Co., 809
Walker v. Bignell, 174, 220, 223, 388
Walker v. Board of Education of Olean City School District, 1049
Walker v. Chanslor, 143
Walker v. Choate, 743
Walker v. City of New York, 463
Walker v. Clark Equipment Co., 366
Walker v. County of Randolph, 421
Walker v. Cronin, 985, 986, 1005
Walker v. D'Alesandro, 823
Walker v. Davis, 643
Walker v. First National Bank of Athena, 98
Walker v. Great Northern Railway, 367
Walker v. Hamby, 486, 488
Walker v. Ingram, 77
Walker v. L.B. Price Mercantile Co., 43
Walker v. Lamb, 855
Walker v. Lee, 221
Walker v. Nickerson, 560
Walker v. Rowe, 383
Walker v. St. Louis-San Francisco Railroad Co., 328
Walker v. Sheldon, 11
Walker v. Sprinkle, 404
Walker v. Strosnider, 582
Walker v. Tucker, 49, 789, 793
Walker v. Whittle, 854
Walker v. Williams, 414
Walker, Inc., Robert R. v. Burgdorf, 199, 305, 317
Walker Bank & Trust Co. v. First Security Corp., 1001
Walker Furniture Co., W.T. v. Dyson, 139
Walker Hauling Co. v. Johnson, 431
Walkoviak v. Hilton Hotels Corp., 202
Wall v. Brim, 120
Wall v. Colvard, Inc., 105, 106
Wall v. Trogdon, 79
Wallace v. A.H. Guion & Co., 549, 554
Wallace v. Bounds, 311
Wallace v. Der-Ohanian, 383
Wallace v. Garden City Osteopathic Hospital, 188
Wallace v. Jameson, 792
Wallace v. Lessard, 527, 528
Wallace v. Ludwig, 310
Wallace v. New York, New Haven & Hartford Railroad Co., 544
Wallace v. Norris, 260
Wallace v. Perry, 675
Wallace v. Schrier, 443
Wallace v. Shoreham Hotel Corp., 58, 59
Wallace v. Suburban Railway Co., 306
Wallace v. Wallace, 920, 922, 929
Wallach v. Bacharach, 854
Walldren Express & Van Co. v. Krug, 464
Wallin v. Eastern Railway Co., 298
Walling v. Fields, 48, 888
Wallinga v. Johnson, 305
Wallner v. Fidelity & Deposit Co. of Maryland, 154, 1063
Walls v. C.D. Smith & Co., 647

TABLE OF CASES

Walmsley v. Humenick, 163
Walmsley v. Rural Telephone Association, 280, 284, 292
Walrod v. Southern Pacific Co., 955
Walsh v. A.D. Conner, Inc., 454
Walsh v. Brown, 151
Walsh v. Eberlein, 872, 878
Walsh v. Ford Motor Co., 692
Walsh v. Hunt, 313
Walsh v. Madison Park Properties, Ltd., 430
Walsh v. United States Tent & Awning Co., 105
Walsh v. West Coast Mines, 480, 570
Walsh v. Zuisei Kaiun K.K., 376
Waltanen v. Wiitala, 495
Walter v. Davidson, 798
Walter v. Duncan, 791
Walter v. Wagner, 69
Walters v. Prairie Oil & Gas Co., 349, 350
Walters v. Sloan, 430, 431, 432
Walters v. Smith & Sons, 154
Walton v. Blauert, 267
Walton v. Sherwin-Williams Co., 684
Walton v. Will, 150
Walton, Witten & Graham Co. v. Miller's Administratrix, 326, 347
Walton Plow Co. v. Campbell, 731
Wampler v. Palmerton, 990
Wamsley v. Atlas S.S. Co., 92, 99
Wanamaker v. Lewis, 787
Wandt v. Hearst's Chicago American, 775, 781
Wangler Boiler & Sheet Metal Works v. Industrial Commission, 573
Wann v. Cullin, 753
Wannebo v. Gates, 314
Warchol v. City of Chicago, 408, 409
Ward v. Arnold, 760, 1008
Ward v. Avery, 421
Ward v. Brown, 541
Ward v. Egan, 47
Ward v. Forest Preserve District, 793
Ward v. Gee, 971, 972
Ward v. Jenson, 760
Ward v. League for Justice, 778
Ward v. Macauley, 88
Ward v. Painters' Local Union No. 300, p. 830
Ward v. Rogers, 1073
Ward v. St. Vincent's Hospital, 664
Ward v. West Jersey & Sea Shore Railroad Co., 56
Ward Cook, Inc. v. Davenport, 767
Warder-Bushnell & Glessner Co. v. Harris, 95
Wardman-Justice Motors v. Petrie, 14
Wardrop v. City of Manhattan Beach, 76
Wardrop v. Santi Moving & Express Co., 491
Ware v. Cattaneo, 423
Ware v. Garvey, 40
Ware v. Saufley, 452
Ware v. United States, 206
Ware v. Yellow Cab, Inc., 209, 211
Warfield, Ex parte, 923
Warfield v. Campbell, 873
Warfield v. Clark, 744

Waring v. Dunlea, 1020
Waring v. WDAS Broadcasting Station, 1020
Warnack v. State, 130
Warne v. Finseth, 752
Warner, Ex parte, 155, 156
Warner v. Capital Transit Co., 343
Warner v. City of Chicago, 171, 172
Warner v. Fry, 438
Warner v. Gulf Oil Corp., 894
Warner v. Kiowa County Hospital Authority, 1073
Warner v. Lockerby, 1074
Warner v. Lucey, 438, 439
Warner v. Martin, 94
Warner v. Press Pub. Co., 835
Warner v. Southwestern Bell Telephone Co., 663
Warner's Estate, In re, 730
Warren v. Cohen, 955
Warren v. Graham, 923
Warren v. Kelley, 149
Warren v. McLough Steel Corp., 514
Warren v. Parkhurst, 354, 355, 634
Warren v. Parrish, 62
Warren, People v., 150
Warren v. Pulitzer Publishing Co., 830
Warren v. T.G. & Y. Stores Co., 182
Warren v. Webb, 617
Warren v. Westrup, 329
Warren & Son Stone Co., Sam v. Gruesser, 619, 627
Warren Co. v. Dickson, 628
Warren Township School District No. 7 v. City of Detroit, 81
Warrener v. Federal Land Bank, 380
Warrior Manufacturing Co. v. Jones, 937
Warschauser v. Brooklyn Furniture Co., 988
Warshauer v. Lloyd Sabaudo S.A., 377
Warshaw v. Rockresorts, Inc., 715
Wartman v. Swindell, 114
Warwick v. Corbett, 761
Wary v. King, 246
Waschak v. Moffatt, 70, 71
Washburn v. Abrams, 924, 925
Washington v. Atlantic Richfield Co., 432
Washington v. Kemp, 305
Washington & Berkeley Bridge Co. v. Pennsylvania Steel Co., 205, 726
Washington & Georgetown R. Co. v. Hickey, 268, 317, 348
Washington & Old Dominion Railway Co. v. Zell's Administratrix, 518
Washington Annapolis Hotel Co. v. Riddle, 833
Washington Gaslight Co. v. District of Columbia, 342
Washington Loan & Trust Co. v. Hickey, 440
Washington Metropolitan Area Transit Authority v. L'Enfant Plaza Properties, Inc., 509, 513
Washington Motor Coach Co., State ex rel. v. Kelly, 578
Washington Post Co. v. Chaloner, 781
Washington Post Co. v. Kennedy, 536, 809
Washington Post Co. v. Keogh, 810
Washington Post Co. v. Sorrells, 754
Washington-Virginia Railway Co. v. Bouknight, 245

TABLE OF CASES

Wasik v. Borg, 704
Wason, Ex parte, 820
Wason v. Walter, 836
Wasson v. Brewer's Food Mart, Inc., 238, 427
Watch Tower Bible & Tract Society v. Dougherty, 986, 1025
Waterbury v. Byron Jackson, Inc., 235
Waterbury v. Lockwood, 151
Waterhouse v. McPheeters, 968
Waterman v. Hall, 85
Waters v. Anthony, 669
Waters v. Fleetwood, 853, 860
Waters v. McNearney, 620, 625
Waters v. Novak, 10
Waters-Pierce Oil Co. v. Deselms, 206, 684
Watford by Johnston v. Evening Star Newspaper Co., 423
Watkin v. Hall, 841
Watkins v. Gabriel Steel Co., 513, 516
Watkins v. Layton, 11
Watkins v. Lord, 918, 919
Watkins v. Sheppard, 189
Watkins Land Co. v. Clements, 636
Watson v. Adams, 590
Watson v. Adirondack Trailways, 202
Watson v. Burley, 525
Watson v. Cain, 884
Watson v. Chicago Transit Authority, 202
Watson v. Dilts, 60, 65, 77
Watson v. Gradzik, 913
Watson v. Kentucky & Indiana Bridge & Railroad Co., 199, 201, 277, 303, 305, 317, 348
Watson v. McSoud, 436
Watson v. M'Ewan, 820
Watson v. Mississippi River Power Co., 553
Watson v. Pyramid Oil Co., 346
Watson v. Reynolds, 974
Watson v. Rheinderknecht, 40, 138, 139, 292
Watson v. St. Annes Hospital, 1062, 1066
Watson v. Silsby, 765
Watson v. Southern Bus Lines, 219
Watson v. State, 154
Watson v. Wannamaker, 799
Watson v. Watson, 150
Watt v. Longsdon, 828
Watter v. Querry, 198
Watton v. Brinth, 659
Watts v. Aetna Casualty & Surety Co., 126
Watts v. Gerking, 1058
Watts v. Montgomery Traction Co., 232
Watts v. Smith, 347
Watts v. State, 128
Watzek v. Walker, 879
Watzig v. Tobin, 245, 251, 254, 257, 258
Waube v. Warrington, 286, 300, 365
Waugh v. Suburban Club Ginger Ale Co., 266
Wawak v. Stewart, 721
Way v. Tampa Coca Cola Bottling Co., 361
Way v. Waterloo, Cedar Falls & Northern Railroad Co., 326, 347

Waylander-Peterson Co. v. Great Northern Railway Co., 342
Wayne County v. Elk Spring Valley Turnpike Co., 674
Wayne-Oakland Bank v. Adams Rib, 911
Wayne Works v. Hicks Body Co., 779
Wear, State ex rel. v. Springfield Gas & Electric Co., 645
Weatherford v. Home Finance Co., 751
Weatherly v. Manatt, 144
Weatherly v. State, 186
Weaver v. Bank of America National Trust & Savings Association, 53, 305
Weaver v. Beneficial Finance Co., 795, 799, 844
Weaver v. Bush, 133
Weaver v. Cone, 750, 758
Weaver v. Lloyd, 841
Weaver v. McClintock-Trunkey Co., 278
Weaver v. O'Brien, 717
Weaver v. Ward, 163, 592, 1072
Weaver v. Winn-Dixie of La., Inc., 424
Weaver Mercantile Co. v. Thurmond, 549
Webb v. Beaven, 790
Webb v. Brown & Williamson Tobacco Co., 262
Webb v. Call Publishing Co., 846
Webb v. Cecil, 325
Webb v. Cerasoli, 207
Webb v. City of Sitka, 433
Webb v. Fox, 87
Webb v. Gray, 842
Webb v. Huffman, 519, 520, 521
Webb v. Moreno, 528
Webb v. Perry, 197
Webb v. Rome, Watertown & Ogdensburgh Railroad Co., 283
Webb v. Snow, 130
Webb v. State, 150, 314
Webb v. Youmans, 892
Webb v. Zern, 704
Webber v. Gray, 60
Webber v. Herkimer & Mohawk Street Railroad Co., 660
Webber v. Wright, 621
Webel v. Yale University, 439
Weber v. Aetna Casualty & Surety Co., 948
Weber v. Lane, 822
Weber v. Madison, 388, 390
Weber v. Stokely-Van Camp, Inc., 529
Weber-Stair Co. v. Fisher, 58
Webster v. Rome, Watertown & Ogdenburgh Railroad Co., 457
Webster Co. v. Steelman, 567
Weckerley v. Abear, 529
Weckert v. Wentworth & Irwin, 770
Weddle v. Phelan, 252
Wedel v. Johnson, 306, 561
Wedgwood Homes, Inc. v. Lund, 1018
Weeg v. Iowa Mutual Insurance Co., 663
Weeks v. City of Newark, 1054
Weeks v. Great Northern Railway Co., 307
Weeks v. Hackett, 103

Weeks v. McNulty, 265
Weeks v. Prostrollo Sons, Inc., 231
Weeks v. Sly, 143
Weeks-Thorn Paper Co. v. Glenside Woolen Mills, 649
Weggeman v. Seven-Up Bottling Co., 249
Weglein v. Golder, 787
Wegner v. Rodeo Cowboys Association, 15
Wegscheider v. Plastics, Inc., 498
Wehrhahn v. Fort Dearborn Casualty Underwriters, 587
Wehrman v. Liberty Petroleum Co., 14, 52
Weicker v. Weicker, 910
Weidberg v. La Guardia, 792
Weidman v. Consolidated Gas, Electric Light & Power Co., 389
Weidman v. Ketcham, 783, 803
Weidman Silk Dyeing Co. v. East Jersey Water Co., 634
Weigel v. McCloskey, 51
Weigel v. Reintjes, 422
Weikel v. Sterns, 737
Weil v. Lynds, 817
Weiler v. Herzfeld-Phillipson Co., 49, 121
Weinberg v. D–M Restaurant Corp., 239
Weinberg, People v., 73
Weinberg v. Underwood, 339, 906
Weinberg Co. v. Bixby, 323
Weingast v. State, 362
Weinstein v. Lake Pearl Park, Inc., 627, 648
Weinstein v. Powell, 218
Weinstein, State ex rel. Smith v., 310
Weinstock, Lubin & Co. v. Marks, 1016
Weintrob v. New York Life Insurance Co., 732
Weir v. Hoss, 803
Weirs v. Jones County, 184
Weirum v. RKO General, Inc., 200
Weis v. A.T. Hipke & Sons, 339
Weis v. Superior Court of San Diego County, 644
Weisbart v. Flohr, 38, 193
Weiss v. Axler, 259
Weiss v. Fote, 1043
Weiss v. Holman, 388, 389
Weissengoff v. Davis, 50
Weissman v. Wells, 361
Weitl v. Moes, 359, 370, 936
Weitzel v. Jukich, 769
Weitzman v. Nassau Electric Railroad Co., 350, 464
Weitzmann v. A.L. Barber Asphalt Co., 387
Welby v. Drake, 330
Welch v. Bancorp Management Advisors, 984
Welch v. Bergeron, 881
Welch v. Creech, 946
Welch v. Durand, 30
Welch v. Jenkins, 180
Welch & Son Contracting Co., J.H. v. Gardner, 305
Welch Veterinary Supply Co. v. Martin, 755
Weldon v. De Bathe, 902
Weldon v. Lehmann, 334
Weldon v. Times Book Co., 803, 811
Weller v. Chicago & Northwestern Railway Co., 309
Weller v. Foot and Mouth Disease Research Institute, 1000
Weller v. Home News Publishing Co., 943
Weller v. Worstall, 255
Wells v. Abrahams, 8
Wells v. Batts, 101
Wells v. Carter, 817, 818
Wells v. Cook, 743
Wells v. Coulter Sales, Inc., 461
Wells v. Englehart, 124
Wells v. Head, 137
Wells v. Howell, 539
Wells v. Knight, 553, 566
Wells v. McGehee, 117
Wells v. Parker, 874
Wells v. Toogood, 820
Wells v. Van Nort, 117, 119
Wells Amusement Co. v. Eros, 78
Wels v. Rubin, 818
Welsbach Light Co. v. American Incandescent Lamp Co., 965
Welsh v. Loomis, 331
Welsh v. Pritchard, 854
Welsh v. Todd, 624
Welsund v. Schueller, 926
Welter v. Curry, 476
Weltmer v. Bishop, 791
Welty v. Indianapolis & Vincennes Railroad Co., 461, 532
Wendelin v. Russell, 581
Wendell v. Conduit Machine Co., 867
Wendland v. Ridgefield Construction Services, Inc., 238
Wendt v. Lentz, 926, 927
Wenger v. Phillips, 883
Wenisch v. Hoffmeister, 532
Wenman v. Ash, 798, 824
Wennhak v. Morgan, 824
Wentworth v. McDuffie, 102
Wentworth v. Town of Waterbury, 518
Wenzell v. MTD Products, Inc., 711
Werline v. Aldred, 752
Werndli v. Greyhound Corp., 202
Werner v. Times-Mirror Co., 864
Werner v. Southern California Associated Newspapers, 847
Wernimont v. State, 455
Wertz v. Lawrence, 791, 792
Wertz v. Lincoln Liberty Life Insurance Co., 461
Wery v. Seff, 717
Wesbrock v. Colby, 425
Wesley v. Native Lumber Co., 984, 1014
West v. Baumgartner, 878
West v. Bristol Tramways, 546, 547
West v. Broderick & Bascom Rope Co., 686
West v. Cabell, 53, 150
West v. Cruz, 286
West v. Faurbo, 389
West v. McClure, 675
West v. Monroe Bakery, 588
West v. People's Banking & Trust Co., 828
West v. Poor, 215, 216
West v. Smallwood, 53

West v. Spratling, 376
West v. Troelstrup, 990
West v. United States Fidelity & Guaranty Co., 454
West Chicago Street Railroad Co. v. Liderman, 451
West Chicago St. Railroad Co. v. Liebig, 363
West Cumberland Iron & Steel Co. v. Kenyon, 547
West Edmond Salt Water Disposal Association v. Rosecrans, 83
West Jersey Railroad Co. v. Trenton Car Works Co., 101
West Kentucky Coal Co. v. Hazel's Administratrix, 670
West London Commercial Bank v. Kitson, 760
West Muncie Strawboard Co. v. Slack, 634
West Point Manufacturing Co. v. Detroit Stamping Co., 1018
West St. Auto Service, Inc. v. Schmidt, 675
West Texas Utilities Co. v. Harris, 268
West Tulsa Belt Railway Co. v. Bell, 106
West Virginia Cent. & P. Railway Co. v. Fuller, 68
West Virginia Transportation Co. v. Standard Oil Co., 28, 1010
Westaway v. Chicago, St. Paul, Minneapolis & Omaha Railway Co., 380
Westberg v. Willde, 504
Westby v. Itasca County, 511, 516
Westcliff Co. v. Wall, 743
Westerman v. Oregon Automobile Credit Corp., 139
Westerman v. Stout, 387
Western Assurance Co. v. Towle, 672
Western Auto Supply Co. v. Campbell, 428
Western Casualty & Surety Co. v. Shell Oil Co., 343
Western Coach Corp. v. Vaughn, 13
Western Counties Manure Co. v. Lawes Chem. Manure Co., 963, 969, 975
Western Engraving Co. v. Film Laboratories, Ltd., 546
Western Express Co. v. Smeltzer, 333
Western Geophysical Co. of America v. Mason, 554
Western Guaranty Loan Co. v. Dean, 64, 351
Western Loan & Savings Co. v. Silver Bow Abstract Co., 747
Western Railway of Alabama v. Milligan, 506
Western Stock Center, Inc. v. Sevit, Inc., 509, 510, 512, 514
Western Surety Co. v. Loy, 186
Western Union Telegraph Co. v. Bowman, 1008
Western Union Tel. Co. v. Brown, 833
Western Union Telegraph Co. v. Choteau, 665
Western Union Telegraph Co. v. Crall, 1006
Western Union Telegraph Co. v. Esteve Brothers, 663
Western Union Telegraph Co. v. Hill, 44
Western Union Telegraph Co. v. James, 482
Western Union Telegraph Co. v. Junker, 362
Western Union Telegraph Co. v. Lesesne, 811
Western Union Telegraph Co. v. McKibben, 1008
Western Union Telegraph Co. v. Mathis, 1000
Western Union Telegraph Co. v. Preston, 283, 957
Western Union Telegraph Co. v. Redding, 362
Western Union Telegraph Co. v. Speight, 362, 665
Western Union Telegraph Co. v. Thomasson, 881
Western Union Telegraph Co. v. Watson, 58
Westervelt v. Demarest, 760

Westhouton Coal & Cannel Co. v. Wigan Coal Corp., 547
Westinghouse Electric & Manufacturing Co. v. Diamond State Fibre Co., 990
Westinghouse Electric Corp. v. Nutt, 194, 195
Westlake v. Westlake, 922
Westlund v. Iverson, 224
Westminster Brymbo Coal & Coke Co. v. Clayton, 547
Westminster Laundry Co. v. Hesse Envelope Co., 1021
Weston v. Brown, 746
Weston Paper Co. v. Pope, 634
Westway Trading Corp. v. River Terminal Corp., 1004
Wetherbee v. Marsh, 848
Wetherby v. Retail Credit Co., 835
Wetmore v. Mellinger, 894
Wetumka, City of v. Crowell-Franklin Oil Co., 331
Wetzel v. Satterwhite, 76
Weyer v. Vollbrecht, 921
Weymouth v. Gile, 541
Whalen v. Bennett, 914
Whalen v. Roe, 867
Whalen v. Shivek, 437, 513
Whalen v. Union Bag & Paper Co., 632
Whaley v. Sloss-Sheffield Steel & Iron Co., 553
Whalley v. Lancashire R. Co., 146, 148
Wharam v. Investment Underwriters, 511
Wharton v. Chunn, 823
Whatley v. K-Mart Discount Stores, 62
Wheat v. Freeman Coal Mining Corp., 629
Wheat Culvert Co. v. Jenkins, 629
Wheelden v. Lowell, 140
Wheeler v. Darmochwat, 384
Wheeler v. Dell Publishing Co., 800
Wheeler v. Hanson, 888
Wheeler v. Lawson, 103
Wheeler v. Luhman, 929
Wheeler v. Norton, 68, 69
Wheeler v. P. Sorenson Manufacturing Co., 868
Wheeler v. Rudek, 590
Wheeler v. Satilla Rural Electric Membership Corp., 872
Wheeler-Stenzel Co. v. American Window Glass Co., 28, 984
Wheeler Terrace, Inc. v. Lynott, 200
Wheelock v. Noonan, 118
Wheelwright v. Vanderbilt, 743
Whelan v. Miller, 897
Whelan v. Van Natta, 425
Whellkin Coat Co. v. Long Branch Trust Co., 440
Whicher v. Phinney, 196
Whiles v. Grand Junction Mining and Fuel Co., 630
Whipple v. Brown Brothers Co., 732
Whipple v. Gorsuch, 878, 880
Whipple v. Grandchamp, 226
Whirl v. Kern, 51
Whitaker v. Poston, 664
Whitbourne v. Williams, 926
Whitby v. One-O-One Trailer Rental Co., 260
Whitcanock v. Nelson, 407
Whitcomb v. Hearst Corp., 809, 837
Whitcombe v. County of Yolo, 1048
White, In re Estate of, 802

White v. Apsley Rubber Co., 883
White v. Arizona Eastern Railroad Co., 327
White v. Atchison, Topeka & Santa Fe Railway Co., 949
White v. Atlanta Parking Service Co., 483
White v. Birmingham Post Co., 775
White v. Carr, 880
White v. C F, Industries, Inc., 510
White v. Cochrane, 493
White v. Consolidated Freight Lines, 569
White v. Dickerson, Inc., 304
White v. Eley, 664
White v. Fort, 8
White v. Greer, 197
White v. Griffin, 105
White v. Holmes, 717
White v. International Text Book Co., 875
White v. King, 214
White v. Lang, 277
White v. Longo, 921
White v. Lunder, 938
White v. McQueen, 111
White v. Massee, 992
White v. Mellin, 968, 975, 976
White v. Nellis, 926, 927
White v. Nicosia, 180
White v. Pacific Telephone & Telegraph Co., 878
White v. Safe Deposit & Trust Co. of Baltimore, 941
White v. Sander, 46
White v. Saunders, 532
White v. Scarritt, 897
White v. Schnoebelen, 165
White v. Seitz, 913
White v. Spence, 932, 933
White v. State, 138
White v. Sun Publishing Co., 846, 847
White v. Suncook Mills, 388, 648
White v. Teague, 590
White v. Thomson, 924
White v. United Mills Co., 819
White v. United States, 372, 1034
White v. Valenta, 776
White v. White, 324, 841
White v. Yup, 526
White Marble Lime Co. v. Consolidated Lumber Co., 986
White Sewing Machine Co. v. Conner, 140
White Mountain Freezer Co. v. Levesque, 649
Whitecross Wire & Iron Co. v. Savill, 148
Whiteford v. Henthorn, 883
Whitehead v. Keyes, 50
Whitehead v. Stringer, 49
Whitehead v. Zeiller, 76
Whiteley v. Adams, 833
Whiteley v. Foremost Dairies, 92
Whitewater Lumber Co., In re, 765
Whitfield v. Jessup, 691
Whitley v. Hix, 258
Whitman v Atchison, Topeka & Santa Fe Railway Co., 51, 121, 725
Whitman v. Campbell, 224
Whitman v. Mobile & Ohio Railroad Co., 309

Whitman v. W.T. Grant Co., 175
Whitmore v. Brown, 647
Whitney v. Brown, 144
Whitney v. California, 807
Whitney v. New York Casualty Insurance Association, 873
Whitney v. Ralph Myers Contracting Corp., 554, 567
Whitney v. Swett, 143
Whitney v. Tuttle, 329
Whitson v. May, 890
Whitson v. Oakland Unified School District, 385
Whitson Lumber Co., H.T. v. Upchurch, 309
Whittaker v. Sandford, 51
Whittaker v. Stangvick, 79
Whittemore v. Baxter Laundry Co., 552, 620
Whitten v. Bennett, 941
Whitten v. Miami-Dade Water & Sewer Authority, 430
Whittington v. Eli Lilly & Co., 372
Whittle v. Johnston, 532
Whittle v. Miller Lightning Rod Co., 648
Whittler v. Sharp, 106
Whittlesea v. Farmer, 334
Whittlesey v. Miller, 931, 932
Wholesale Laundry Board of Trade v. Tarrullo, 985
Wice v. Schilling, 744
Wichita & Western Railway Co. v. Davis, 210, 470
Wichita Coca-Cola Bottling Co. v. Tyler, 249
Wichita Falls v. Ramos, 388
Wick v. Wick, 905
Wick v. Widdell, 528
Wickenburg v. Minneapolis, St. Paul & Sault Ste. Marie Railway Co., 232, 286
Wickersham v. Johnson, 324
Widmer v. Fretti, 638
Widmyer v. Southeast Skyways, Inc., 209, 246, 255
Wiegand v. Meade, 154
Wieman v. Mabee, 831
Wiener v. United Airlines, 337
Wiener v. Weintraub, 819
Wiest v. City of Philadelphia, 326
Wiffin v. Kincard, 42, 114
Wiggins v. Boddington, 648
Wiggins v. Moskins Credit Clothing Store, 62, 620
Wiggs v. Farmer, 885
Wilbanks v. Brazil, 526
Wilbraham v. Snow, 89, 103
Wilbur v. Flood, 675, 730
Wilbur v. Kerr, 372
Wilbur v. Stokes, 149
Wilcox v. Gilmore, 893
Wilcox v. Hines, 436, 446
Wilcox v. Idaho Falls Latter Day Saints Hospital, 1070
Wilcox v. Moon, 802
Wilcox, People v., 134
Wilcox v. Warren Construction Co., 949
Wilcox, State ex rel. v. Ryder, 644
Wilcher v. Sharpe, 627, 637, 641
Wild v. Rarig, 992, 1027
Wilder v. General Motorcycle Sales Co., 310
Wilder v. Haworth, 667

Wilder v. Stanley, 304
Wildwood Mink Ranch v. United States, 81, 226
Wiley v. Campbell, 788
Wiley v. Simons, 742
Wiley v. West Jersey Railroad Co., 318
Wilfong v. Omaha & Council Bluffs Street Railway Co., 9
Wilhelm v. Globe Solvent Co., 686
Wilinski v. Belmont Builders, 411
Wilk v. Andrea Radio Corp., 868
Wilke v. Chicago Great Western Railway Co., 376
Wilkes v. Chicago, Rock Island & Pacific Railway Co., 660
Wilkie v. Roberts, 934
Wilkin v. Dana R. Pickup & Co., 166
Wilkins v. Leighton, 547
Wilkins v. Kane, 905
Wilkinson v. Detroit Steel & Spring Works, 512
Wilkinson v. Downton, 60, 61, 725
Wilkinson v. Hartford Accident & Indemnity Co., 451
Wilkinson v. Howell, 875
Wilkinson v. Powe, 987, 991, 994
Wilkinson v. Skinner, 1064
Wilkinson v. Stevison, 520
Wilkinson Live Stock Co., Anthony v. McIlquam, 647, 650
Wilko of Nashua, Inc. v. TAP Realty, Inc., 972
Wilks v. New York Telephone Co., 448, 565
Will v. Hughes, 12
Will v. Press Publishing Co., 842
Will v. Southern Pacific Co., 380
Willard v. City of Cambridge, 644, 647, 650
Willard v. Hagemeister, 185
Willard v. Press Publishing Co., 842
Willcox v. Harriman Securities Corp., 744
Willeford v. Bailey, 927
Willenbucher v. McCormick, 830
Willett v. Smith, 214
Willey v. Alaska Packers' Association, 663
Willey v. Fyrogas Co., 684, 704
Williams v. Adams, 986
Williams v. Adelman, 899
Williams v. Aetna Insurance Co., 388, 426
Williams v. Alioto, 1061
Williams v. American Mutual Liability Insurance Co., 303
Williams v. Bennett, 188
Williams v. Brennan, 294
Williams v. Byrd, 937
Williams v. California, 374
Williams v. Carolina & Northwestern Railroad Co., 662, 665
Williams v. Chick, 308
Williams v. City of Baton Rouge, 454
Williams v. Cobb, 198
Williams v. Consumers' Co., 590
Williams v. Crews, 884
Williams v. Davidson, 914
Williams v. Davis, 443
Williams v. Dickenson, 8

Williams v. Dougherty County, 759
Williams v. East Bay Motor Coach Lines, 172
Williams v. Equitable Credit Co., 833
Williams v. Field Transportation Co., 254
Williams v. Franzoni, 149
Williams v. Hays, 1073, 1074
Williams v. Hicks Printing Co., 846
Williams v. Holland, 30
Williams v. Horvath, 1061
Williams v. Houston Baseball Association, 485
Williams v. Illinois Central Railroad Co., 666
Williams v. Jefferson Hospital Association, 1070
Williams v. Jones, 504
Williams v. Journal Co., 837
Williams v. Kansas City Transit, Inc., 827
Williams v. Kerr, 766
Williams v. Knapp, 521
Williams v. Koehler & Co., 309
Williams v. Kroger Grocery & Baking Co., 833
Williams v. Kyes, 883
Williams v. Le Bar, 332
Williams v. Louisville & Nashville Railroad, 959, 960
Williams v. Marion Rapid Transit Co., 368
Williams v. Mickens, 314
Williams v. Minneapolis, St. Paul & Sault Ste. Marie Railway Co., 218
Williams v. Montgomery, 620
Williams v. Morristown Memorial Hospital, 424
Williams v. New York Central Railroad Co., 579
Williams v. New York Herald Co., 791
Williams v. Polger, 747
Williams v. Pomeroy Coal Co., 75, 83
Williams v. Powell, 53
Williams v. Primary School District No. 3, p. 402
Williams v. Rank & Son Buick, Inc., 750
Williams v. Riddle, 794
Williams v. Riley, 434
Williams v. Roberts, 95
Williams v. Safford, 146
Williams v. Sheldon, 325
Williams v. Smith, 100
Williams v. Spazier, 768, 769
Williams v. Spell, 465, 466, 467
Williams v. Spokane Falls & Northern Railway Co., 241, 582
Williams v. Springfield Gas & Electric Co., 412
Williams v. St. Louis Public Service Co., 260
Williams v. Standard-Examiner Publishing Co., 831, 835
Williams v. State, 18, 130, 314, 370
Williams, State v., 37
Williams v. Tripp, 650
Williams v. Underhill, 57
Williams v. United States, 203, 390, 558, 1034
Williams v. United States Fidelity & Guaranty Co., 381
Williams v. Wachovia Bank & Trust Co., 524, 527
Williams v. Walley, 1063
Williams v. Williams, 837, 907
Williams, State ex rel. v. Adams, 1062
Williams, State ex rel. v. Karston, 644
Williams's Case, 618

TABLE OF CASES

Williams Estate Co. v. Nevada Wonder Mining Co., 400
Williams Print. Co. v. Saunders, 835
Williamson v. Allen, 728
Williamson v. Allison, 740
Williamson v. Bennett, 365
Williamson v. Derry Electric Co., 492
Williamson v. Freer, 833
Williamson v. Garland, 180
Williamson v. McKenna, 212
Williamson v. Pacific Greyhound Lines, 660
Williamson v. Patterson, 743
Williamson v. Southern Railway Co., 389
Willing v. Mazzocone, 976, 1026
Willis v. Department of Conservation and Economic Development, 1055
Willis v. Duke Power Co., 948
Willis v. Midland Finance Co., 99
Willis v. O'Connell, 832
Willis v. San Bernardino Lumber & Box Co., 510
Willner v. Silverman, 1006
Wills v. Noyes, 895
Wilmerton v. Sample, 873
Wilmington General Hospital v. Manlove, 381
Wilmington Trust Co. v. Clark, 990
Wilmont Homes, Inc. v. Weiler, 640
Wilson v. Abilene Independent School District, 158
Wilson v. American Bridge Co., 395
Wilson v. Anderton, 100
Wilson v. Aylward, 920
Wilson v. Bowen, 887
Wilson v. Brett, 211
Wilson v. Brown, 860
Wilson v. Bryant, 917
Wilson v. Campbell, 143
Wilson v. Capital Automobile Co., 305
Wilson v. City of Kotzebue, 179, 1048
Wilson v. City of Long Beach, 394
Wilson v. City of Mineral Point, 640
Wilson v. City of New Bedford, 549
Wilson v. Claredon County, 959
Wilson v. Colonial Air Transport, 246
Wilson v. Cotterman, 794
Wilson v. Coulter, 921
Wilson v. Don LaCost, Inc., 530
Wilson v. Dowtin, 439
Wilson v. Dubois, 972
Wilson v. Farmers Chemical Ass'n, 638
Wilson v. Fitch, 831
Wilson v. Florida Processing Co., 430
Wilson v. Goscinske, 307
Wilson v. Great Northern Railway Co., 529
Wilson v. Gutschenritter, 1067
Wilson v. Hagins, 349
Wilson v. Hanley, 270
Wilson v. Hilske, 916, 918, 919
Wilson v. Jones, 741, 746, 748, 761
Wilson v. Lapham, 53, 54
Wilson v. Loew's, Inc., 1006
Wilson v. McLaughlin, 96
Wilson v. Mason, 755

Wilson v. Merry, 572
Wilson v. Missouri-Kansas-Texas Railway Co., 467
Wilson v. Nepstad, 1050
Wilson v. Northern Pacific Railway Co., 284
Wilson v. Oldroyd, 15
Wilson v. Orr, 40, 41
Wilson v. Parent, 644, 648
Wilson v. Piper Aircraft Corp., 231, 233
Wilson v. St. Louis & San Francisco Railroad Co., 63
Wilson v. Southern Traction Co., 463
Wilson v. Sponable, 385
Wilson v. State, 266, 345
Wilson v. Stilwill, 256, 257
Wilson v. Sun Publishing Co., 788, 845
Wilson v. Thermal Energy, Inc., 447
Wilson v. Townend, 620
Wilson v. Tumman, 325
Wilson v. Union Iron Works Dry Dock Co., 429
Wilson v. United States, 258
Wilson v. Waddell, 547
Wilson v. Walt, 1074
Wilson v. Western Union Telegraph Co., 1008
Wilson v. White, 349
Wilson v. Wilkins, 61, 64
Wilson v. Wright, 228
Wilson & Co. v. McGee, 575
Wilson Cypress Co. v. Logan, 101
Wilson Freight Forwarding Co. v. Cleveland, Columbus & Cincinnati Highway, 93
Wilson Motor Co. v. Dunn, 141
Wilton v. City of Spokane, 515
Wilton v. Middlesex Railroad Co., 932
Wimer v. Allbaugh, 782
Winchell v. Detroit & Mackinac Railway Co., 228
Winchester v. O'Brien, 661
Winchester Water Works Co. v. Holliday, 72
Windram v. French, 736
Windram Manufacturing Co. v. Boston Blacking Co., 737
Windsor Reservoir & Canal Co. v. Smith, 418
Wineman v. Carter, 937
Winfough v. Tri-State Insurance Co., 219
Winfrey v. S.S. Kresge Co., 256
Wing v. London General Omnibus Co., 547
Wingard v. Safeway Stores, Inc., 385, 420
Wingate v. Bunton, 138
Wingrove v. Home Land Co., 421, 458
Wink v. Western Maryland Railway Co., 265
Winkelman v. Boeing Airplane Co., 575
Winkfield, The, 104, 105
Winkler v. Lenoir & Blowing Rock Lines, 874
Winn v. City of Lowell, 176
Winn v. State, 144
Winn & Lovett Grocery Co. v. Archer, 10
Winn-Dixie Montgomery, Inc. v. Rowell, 246
Winn-Dixie Stores, Inc. v. Johnstoneaux, 383
Winnett v. Winnett, 710
Winnick v. Kupperman Construction Co., 911, 935
Winrod v. Time, Inc., 800
Winsette v. Hunt, 792

Prosser & Keeton Torts 5th Ed. HB—28

TABLE OF CASES

Winship v. Neale, 88
Winslow v. Mahfuz, 401
Winston, Inc., Samuel v. Charles James Services, Inc., 1021
Winter v. Atkinson, 137
Winter v. Bancks, 98
Winter v. Scherman, 245
Winterbottom v. Lord Derby, 650
Winterbottom v. Wright, 24, 357, 667, 681, 682
Winterbourne v. Morgan, 73
Winters v. Campbell, 52
Winters v. University District Building & Loan Association, 986
Wintersteen v. Semler, 269
Winterstein v. Wilcom, 482, 483
Wintringham v. Lafoy, 85, 87
Wirsing v. Smith, 12
Wirth v. Ehly, 403, 416
Wisconsin Central Railroad Co. v. Ross, 326, 346
Wisconsin Coca Cola Bottling Co. v. E.L. Husting Co., 987
Wisconsin Loan & Finance Corp. v. Goodnough, 666
Wisconsin Natural Gas Co. v. Ford, 473, 475
Wisconsin Power & Light Co. v. Columbia County, 69
Wisconsin River Improvement Co. v. Lyons, 650
Wise v. Brotherhood of Locomotive Firemen and Enginemen, 830
Wise v. Carter, 351
Wise v. Chicago, Rock Island & Pacific Railway Co., 396
Wise v. Crown Construction Co., 182
Wise v. Daniel, 9
Wise v. George C. Rothwell, Inc., 943
Wise v. Hayes, 684
Wise v. Roger Givens, Inc., 488, 489
Wise v. Western Union Telegraph Co., 964, 1009
Wise Bros. Pty. v. Commissioner for Railways, 546
Wisecarver & Stone v. Chicago, Rock Island & Pacific Railway Co., 328
Wisher v. Fowler, 390
Wishnick v. Frye, 740
Wishone v. Yellow Cab Co., 34
Wisniski v. Ong, 882
Wissman v. Wissman, 175, 198
With v. O'Flanagan, 738
Withers v. Henley, 51
Witherspoon v. Clegg, 103
Witte v. Bauderer, 923
Witte v. Haben, 155
Witthaus, State ex rel. Clemens v., 855
Wittkamp v. United States, 184
Woadson v. Nawton, 87
Wofford v. Rudick, 437
Wohlfort v. Wohlfort, 836, 922
Wojcik v. United Services Automobile Association, 952
Wojewoda v. Rybarczyk, 565
Wojtowicz v. Belden, 231
Wolcott v. Gaines, 123
Wolczek v. Public Service Co., 404
Wold v. Grozalsky, 340
Wolf v. Des Moines Elevator Co., 387

Wolf v. Fox, 726
Wolf v. Graber, 489
Wolf v. People of the State of Colorado, 866
Wolf v. Perry, 989
Wolf v. State, 150
Wolf & Sons, B.J. v. New Orleans Tailor-Made Pants Co., 989
Wolf Truck Lines, Ben v. Bailey, 578
Wolfe v. A.E. Kusterer & Co., 737
Wolfe v. Atlantic Coast Line Railroad Co., 488
Wolfe v. Beatty Motor Express, Inc., 219
Wolfe v. Checker Taxi Co., 284, 292
Wolfe v. Feldman, 246
Wolfe v. First National Bank, 733
Wolfe v. Lewisburg Trust & Safe Deposit Co., 100
Wolfenstein v. Fashion Originators' Guild of America, 1024
Wolff v. General Casualty Co. of America, 586
Wolff v. Lamann, 566
Wolfinger v. Shaw, 171, 308
Wolfmeyer v. Otis Elevator Co., 670
Wolfson v. Chelist, 415
Wolfson v. Syracuse Newspapers, 800
Wollaston v. Burlington Northern, Inc., 181
Wollenberger v. Hoover, 743
Wolston v. Reader's Digest Association, Inc., 806
Womack v. McDonald, 967, 972
Womack v. Preach, 958
Womack v. Willis-Knighton Clinic, 460
Wommack v. Orr, 194
Wonder v. Baltimore & Ohio Railroad Co., 569
Wood v. Balzano, 532
Wood v. Camp, 415
Wood v. Commonwealth, 46
Wood v. Cummings, 52, 53
Wood v. Dunlop, 960
Wood v. Geis Trucking Co., 246, 248
Wood v. Graves, 897
Wood v. Indemnity Insurance Co. of North America, 261
Wood v. Lane, 51
Wood v. Leadbitter, 73
Wood v. Mathews, 918
Wood v. Mobil Chemical Co., 931
Wood v. Palmer Ford, Inc., 872
Wood v. Pennsylvania Railroad Co., 284, 287, 300
Wood v. Phillips, 143
Wood v. Pierson, 100
Wood v. Posthuma, 189
Wood v. Prudential Insurance Co., 439
Wood v. Roeder, 759
Wood v. Rolfe, 328
Wood v. Saunders, 504
Wood v. Snider, 348, 350, 540
Wood v. Southwestern Public Service Co., 184
Wood v. State Through Dept. of Highways, 396
Wood v. Strickland, 1057, 1061
Wood v. United Airlines, 74, 557
Wood v. Wood, 907
Wood v. Young, 44

Woodard v. Des Moines, 933
Woodard v. Pacific Fruit & Produce Co., 963, 966, 969, 974
Woodbridge v. Marks, 136, 562
Woodbury v. Tampa Water Works Co., 671
Woodcock's Administrator v. Hallock, 308, 309
Wooden v. Hale, 905
Woodford v. McDaniels, 941
Woodham v. Allen, 121, 736
Woodhouse v. Powles, 829
Woodhouse v. Woodhouse, 918, 922
Woodland v. Portneuf-Marsh Valley Irrigation Co., 354, 355, 622, 634
Woodley v. Coker, 890
Woodling v. Knickerbocker, 801
Woodman v. Hubbard, 102
Woodman v. Metropolitan Railroad Co., 511
Woodruff v. North Bloomfield Gravel Mining Co., 325
Woodruff v. Tomlin, 186, 187
Woodruff v. Woodruff, 44
Woodruff v. Zaban & Son, 674
Woodruff & Sons v. Brown, 665
Woods v. Kansas City, Kaw Valley & Western Railroad Co., 347
Woods v. Lancet, 368
Woods v. Nichols, 524
Woods v. Scott, 763
Woodson v. Bailey, 918, 919
Woodson v. Huey, 119
Woodson v. State, 125
Woodville v. Pizatti, 789
Woodward v. Ashton, 672
Woodward v. Begbie, 271
Woodward v. Miller & Karwisch, 206
Woodward, State v., 126, 132
Woodward v. Washburn, 982
Woodward Iron Co. v. Goolsby, 394
Woodworth v. Mills, 877
Woody v. Brush, 992
Woodyear v. Schaefer, 354, 634
Woodzell v. Garzell Plastics Industries, 704
Wooley v. Batte, 337
Wooley v. Henderson, 190, 191
Woolf v. Chalker, 136, 562
Woolf v. City of Dallas, 403
Woolley's Laundry v. Silva, 1023
Woolridge Manufacturing Co. v. United States, 1008
Woolsey v. Judd, 849
Woolston v. Montana Free Press, 776, 782
Woolworth, F.W. v. Kirby, 183, 184, 383, 428
Wooten v. Martin, 789
Worcester County v. Ashworth, 348
Worden v. Davis, 48, 51
Work v. Campbell, 726
Workman v. City of San Diego, 520
World Publishing Co. v. Minahan, 799
World Publishing Co. v. Mullen, 781
Worldwide Commerce, Inc. v. Fruehauf Corp., 993
Worley v. Procter & Gamble Manufacturing Co., 690
Worrell v. Barnes, 724

Worrell v. Worrell, 595, 907
Worth v. Dortman, 523
Worth v. Dunn, 566
Worth v. Worth, 922
Worthington v. A.G. Rhodes & Sons Co., 104
Worthington v. Mencer, 535
Worthington v. Wade, 135
Wosika v. St. Paul City Railway Co., 520
Woy v. Turner, 807
Wozniczka v. McKean, 408
Wrabek v. Suchomel, 323, 328, 346
Wray v. Taylor, 145
Wright v. Caffey, 415
Wright v. Carter Products, Inc., 685, 688
Wright v. City of St. Cloud, 461
Wright v. Clark, 163
Wright v. Commonwealth, 155
Wright v. Concrete Co., 489
Wright v. Cooper, 325, 354
Wright v. Couch, 762
Wright v. Creative Corp., 724
Wright v. Davis, 906, 954
Wright v. Everett, 10
Wright v. Frank A. Andrews, 99
Wright v. Harris, 892
Wright v. Holland Furnace Co., 723
Wright v. Howe, 206
Wright v. Illinois & Mississippi Telephone Co., 459
Wright v. Lathrop, 820
Wright v. Lester, 918
Wright v. Moffitt, 222, 225
Wright v. Newman, 510
Wright v. O'Neal, 453
Wright v. Palmer, 1023
Wright v. Ramscot, 85
Wright v. Royse, 328
Wright v. School District, 92
Wright v. Southern Express Co., 137
Wright v. Southern Railway Co., 664
Wright v. Starr, 112, 122
Wright v. Syracuse, Binghamton & New York Railroad Co., 622
Wright v. Tate, 178
Wright v. Tudor City Twelfth Unit, 511, 513, 516
Wright v. United States, 1041
Wright v. White, 159
Wright v. Wilcox, 505
Wright v. Williams, 187, 188
Wright v. Wilson, 47
Wright & Taylor v. Smith, 441
Wright Bachman, Inc. v. Hodnett, 691
Wright Hepburn Webster Gallory Limited, State v., 645
Wright Titus, Inc. v. Swafford, 9
Wright's Estate, In re, 212
Wroblewski v. Otis Elevator Co., 670
Wyant v. Crouse, 76, 560
Wyatt v. Gilmore, 364
Wyatt v. Pacific Electric Railway Co., 246
Wycko v. Gnodtke, 952
Wyman v. Lehigh Valley Railroad Co., 569

Wyman v. Wallace, 930
Wynn v. Hale, 649
Wynnewood Lumber Co. v. Travelers Insurance Co., 661
Wyoming National Bank v. Security Bank & Trust Co., 1017
Wyseski v. Collette, 212
Wytupeck v. City of Camden, 404

Y

Y, Matter of Mario, 211
Yaffe v. City of Fort Smith, 620
Yakavicke v. Valentukevicius, 782
Yalowizer v. Husky Oil Co., 213, 393, 394, 397, 413, 433
Yamada v. Hilton Hotel Corp., 208
Yancey v. Gilespie, 831
Yancey, State v., 132
Yandell v. National Fireproofing Corp., 716
Yanhko v. Fane, 223
Yania v. Bigan, 375, 535
Yappel v. Mozina, 758
Yarborough v. Berner, 162
Yarbro v. Hilton Hotels Corp., 168
Yarmouth v. France, 491, 571
Yates v. Chappell, 242
Yates v. City of Milwaukee, 626, 632
Yates v. State, 154
Yates v. Tiffany, 649
Yates v. United States, 380, 1038
Yaun v. Allis-Chalmers Manufacturing Co., 686
Yazoo & Mississippi Valley Railroad Co. v. Aden, 307
Yazoo & Mississippi Valley Railroad Co. v. Gordon, 513, 542
Yazoo & Mississippi Valley Railroad Co. v. Lee, 399
Yazoo & Mississippi Valley Railroad Co. v. Leflar, 378
Yazoo & Mississippi Valley Railroad Co. v. Millsaps, 315
Yazoo & Mississippi Valley Railroad Co. v. Sanders, 11
Ybarra v. Spangard, 252, 253, 255
Yeager v. Wallace, 93, 672
Yeates v. Reed, 1074
Yekhtikian v. Blessing, 149
Yelk v. Seefeldt, 890
Yellow Cab Co. v. Becker, 1016
Yellow Cab Co. v. Dreslin, 339, 911
Yellow Cab Co. v. Hodgson, 252
Yellow Cab Co. of Nashville v. Pewitt, 327
Yellow Cab Co. of Rhode Island v. Anastasi, 1016
Yeomans v. Jones, 94
Yerkes v. Northern Pacific Railway Co., 175
Yianitsas v. Mercantile National Bank at Dallas, 872
Yin Sang Shum v. Venell, 387
Yocum v. Husted, 349
Yoder v. Nu-Enamel Corp., 768
Yoder v. Smith, 858
Yoder v. Yoder, 131
Yommer v. McKenzie, 549, 551
Yoos v. City of Rochester, 621
Yordon v. Savage, 934, 935
York v. Day's, Inc., 528

York v. Johnson, 830
Yost v. Grand Trunk Ry. Co., 924
Yost v. State, 476
Youl v. Harbottle, 97
Youmans v. Smith, 799, 818, 820
Young v. Andrews Hardwood Co., 54
Young v. Blaum, 542
Young v. Bynum, 519
Young v. Darter, 550
Young v. Dille, 329
Young v. Garwacki, 446
Young v. Geiske, 963
Young v. Gormley, 48
Young v. Grant, 179
Young v. Greneker Studios, 852
Young v. Jack Boring's, Inc., 887, 896
Young v. Macrae, 975
Young v. Masci, 527
Young v. Muhling, 1072
Young v. Park, 186, 187, 188
Young, People v., 130
Young v. Rankin, 904
Young v. Rothrock, 649
Young v. Saroukos, 441
Young v. Smith & Kelly Co., 722
Young v. State, 178, 335
Young, State v., 130
Young v. Western & Atlantic Railroad Co., 65, 854
Young v. Wiley, 904
Young v. Wlazik, 486
Young v. Young, 818
Younger v. Hoge, 763
Younger v. United States, 436
Youngquist v. American Railway Express Co., 966, 974
Yousling v. Dare, 798, 803
Youssoupoff v. Metro-Goldwyn-Mayer Pictures, 773, 783, 787, 795
Yovatt v. Winyard, 849
Yu v. New York, New Haven & Hartford Railroad Co., 376
Yukon Equipment, Inc. v. Fireman's Fund Insurance Co., 555
Yun Jeong Koo v. St. Bernard, 180
Yundt v. Hartrunft, 918

Z

Zabala Clemente v. United States, 381, 1034, 1035, 1041, 1042
Zabawa v. Eshenroeder, 954
Zabron v. Cunard Steamship Co., 662
Zaccari v. United States, 339, 532
Zacchini v. Scripps-Howard Broadcasting Co., 1021, 1022
Zacharias v. Nesbitt, 391
Zagar v. Union Pacific Railroad Co., 403
Zager v. Setzer, 742
Zahrte v. Sturm, Ruger & Co., 184, 497
Zajaczkowski v. State, 179
Zalewski v. Gallagher, 881

TABLE OF CASES

Zambito v. Southland Recreation Enterprises, 427
Zampos v. United States Smelting, Refining & Mining Co., 559
Zaninovich v. American Airlines, Inc., 953
Zank v. Chicago, Rock Island & Pacific Railway Co., 462
Zanley v. Hyde, 830
Zapfe v. Werner, 666
Zarcone v. Perry, 1057
Zarek v. Fredericks, 563
Zarling v. La Salle Coca Cola Bottling Co., 249
Zarrella v. Miller, 339
Zarrow v. Hughes, 992, 1000
Zartner v. Holzhauer, 941
Zaslow v. Kroenert, 85, 90, 96, 98
Zavala v. Regents of the University of California, 478
Zaye v. John Hancock Mut. Life Insurance Co., 379
Zayre of Georgia, Inc. v. Haynes, 162
Zayre of Virginia, Inc. v. Gowdy, 141, 142
Zeglen v. Minkiewicz, 339, 340
Zeidler v. Goelzer, 526, 914
Zeigler v. Ryan, 522
Zeinfeld v. Hayes Freight Lines, Inc., 827, 828
Zelenka v. Benevolent and Protective Order of Elks of the United States, 1006, 1028
Zelenko v. Gimbel Brothers, 381
Zeliff v. Jennings, 793
Zeliff v. Sabatino, 769
Zelinsky v. Chimics, 363
Zell v. Dunaway, 125
Zello v. Glover, 874
Zeni v. Anderson, 230
Zenik v. O'Brien, 873
Zenith Bathing Pavilion v. Fair Oaks Steamship Corp., 83
Zeno v. Lincoln General Hospital, 247, 256
Zentz v. Coca Cola Bottling Co., 250
Zepeda v. Zepeda, 18, 370, 909
Zerby v. Warren, 228

Zesch v. Abrasive Co. of Philadelphia, 185, 684, 704
Zettel v. City of West Bend, 647, 649
Zichler v. St. Louis Public Service Co., 252
Ziebarth v. Nye, 84
Ziegert v. South Chicago Community Hospital, 480
Ziegler v. Stinson, 766
Zier v. Hofflin, 795, 844
Zierer v. Daniels, 719
Zimmer v. Celebrities, Inc., 247, 260
Zimmer v. Stephenson, 71
Zimmerman v. Shreeve, 70
Zimmerman, State v., 781
Zimmerman Mfg. Co. v. Daffin, 78
Zimmermann v. Wilson, 855
Zimmern v. Blout, 758
Zingale v. Mills Novelty Co., 760
Zinn v. Hill Lumber & Investment Co., 439
Zinn v. Rice, 892, 898
Zinnel v. United States Shipping Board Emergency Fleet Corp., 265
Zion v. DeJonge, 93
Zito v. Friedman, 186
Znidersich v. Minnesota Utilities Co., 201
Zobel, State v., 377
Zoby v. American Fidelity Co., 1010
Zoll v. Allen, 842
Zontelli Brothers v. Northern Pacific Railway Co., 339
Zoski v. Gaines, 115
Zrust v. Spencer Foods, Inc., 487
Zuck v. Interstate Publishing Corp., 800
Zuckerberg v. Munzer, 914, 915
Zuckerbrod v. Burch, 181
Zumstein v. Shrumm, 561
Zumwalt v. Lindland, 493
Zurich Insurance Co. v. Missouri Edison Co., 245
Zuther v. Schild, 415
Zwink v. Burlington Northern, Inc., 206
Zylka v. Leikvoll, 377

Zambito v. Southland Recreation Enterprises, 427
Zamos v. United States Smelting, Refining & Mining
  Co., 859
Zankovich v. American Airlines, Inc., 958
Zank v. Chicago, Rock Island & Pacific Railway Co., 962
Zaubler v. Hyde, 529
Zaple v. Werner, 566
Zarcone v. Perry, 1037
Zaref v. Federico, 608
Zarling v. La Salle Coca Cola Bottling Co., 219
Zarrella v. Miller, 820
Zarrow v. Hughes, 992, 1000
Zartner v. Holzhauer, 941
Zasiov v. Kroenert, 85, 90, 98, 98
Zavala v. Regents of the University of California, 408
Zaye v. John Hancock Mut. Life Insurance Co., 878
Zayre of Georgia, Inc. v. Haynes, 162
Zayre of Virginia, Inc. v. Gowdy, 161, 412
Zeglen v. Minkiewicz, 839, 840
Zeidler v. Goelzer, 628, 914
Zeigler v. Ryan, 922
Zehfeld v. Hayes Freight Lines, Inc., 827, 828
Zelenka v. Benevolent and Protective Order of Elks of
  the United States 1000, 1028
Zelenko v. Gimbel Brothers, 851
Zellt v. Jennings, 703
Zellt v. Sabatino, 738
Zemaitis v. Childers, 202
Zell v. Dunaway, 156
Zello v. Glover, 874
Zent v. Anderson, 280
Zenn v. O'Brien, 873
Zenith Bathing Pavilion v. Bay Oaks Steamship Corp.,
  85
Zeno v. Lincoln General Hospital, 347, 556
Zenta v. Coca Cola Bottling Co., 250
Zepeda v. Zepeda, 18, 270, 605
Zerby v. Warren, 228

Zesch v. Abrasive Co. of Philadelphia, 183, 584, 704
Zettel v. City of West Bend, 847, 849
Ziemer v. St. Louis Public Service Co., 252
Ziebarth v. Nye, 842
Ziegert v. South Chicago Community Hospital, 180
Ziegler v. Stinson, 766
Zier v. Hoflin, 795, 841
Zierer v. Daniels, 719
Zimmer v. Celebrities, Inc., 247, 266
Zimmer v. Stephenson, 71
Zimmermann v. Shreeve, 70
Zimmerman, State v., 781
Zimmerman Mfg. Co. v. Pattim, 18
Zimmermann v. Wilson, 868
Zimmern v. Blout, 758
Zineale v. Milli Novelty Co., 780
Zinn v. Hill Lumber & Investment Co., 183
Zinn v. Rice, 592, 828
Zinnel v. United States Shipping Board Emergency
  Fleet Corp., 206
Zion v. Delonge, 98
Zito v. Friedman, 156
Zinderich v. Minnesota Utilities Co., 201
Zobel, State v., 877
Zoby v. American Fidelity Co., 1010
Zoll v. Allen, 842
Zorkail Brothers v. Northern Pacific Railway Co., 832,
  833
Zosla v. Gampe, 115
Zraus v. Spencer Foods, Inc., 487
Zuck v. Interstate Publishing Corp., 800
Zuckerberg v. Munzer, 914, 915
Zuckerbrod v. Burch, 181
Zunstein v. Shrumm, 561
Zurawski v. Lindland, 495
Zurich Insurance Co. v. Missouri Edison Co., 248
Zurheer v. Schild, 115
Zwirn v. Burlington Northern, Inc., 206
Zylka v. Leikvoll, 876

Index

References are to Pages

ABATEMENT
Of nuisance, 641.

ABDUCTION
Of wife or child, 917, 924.

ABUSE OF PROCESS
Elements of, 897.
Malicious prosecution distinguished, 897.

ACCIDENT
Liability for unavoidable, 162.
 Jury instructions, 163.
Mistake distinguished, 110.
Trespass to land, unforeseeable consequences, 73–77.

ACCORD AND SATISFACTION
See Release.

ACT
Misfeasance and nonfeasance, 373.
Necessity of voluntary, 34.

ACT OF GOD
Apportionment of damages between culpable cause and, 347.
As superseding cause, 314, 316.
Carriers, negligence of concurring with, 317.
Defense against, privilege of necessity, 145.
Strict liability, effect on, 564.

ADMINISTRATION
Convenience of, as factor in tort law, 23.

ADMIRALTY
Apportionment of damages in, 471.
Employers' liability, 471.
Wrongful death claim in, 945, 950, 956.

AERONAUTICS
Nuisance, flight through air space, 80.
Res ipsa loquitur, 246.
Strict liability for ground damage, 556.
Trespass, flight through air space, 79.

AGENCY
See Principal and Agent.

ALIENATION OF AFFECTIONS
Abolition of the action, 929.
Action for, 918.
Basis of liability, 919.
Defenses, 921.
Equitable relief, 923.
Of parent, 928.

ALIENATION OF AFFECTIONS—Cont'd
Privilege, 922.
Remedies, 923.
Statutory abolition of action, 930.
Wife's action for, 918.

ANIMALS
Dangerous, 541.
 Bailments, 541.
 Consequences, liability for, 561, 563.
 Keepers, liability of, 541.
 Scienter, 542.
 Wild animals, 542.
Invitees and licensees, injury to, 562.
Negligence, anticipating conduct, 198.
Strict liability for, 538.
Trespassers, injury to, 562.
Trespassing, 538.
 Bailor and bailee, 541.
 Consequences, liability for, 560.
 History, 539.
 Statutes regulating, 540.
 Straying from highway, 540.
Watchdog, defense of property by, 136.

ARMY AND NAVY
Discipline, 159.

ARREST
False. See False Imprisonment.
For breach of the peace, 154.
For felony, 154.
For misdemeanor, 154.
Legal process, privilege of, 149.
Mistake, 111.
Of lunatics, 155.
Reasonable force in making, 155.
Resistance to, 156.
Temporary detention of suspected thief, 141.
Trespass ab initio, 150.
With a warrant, 149.
Without a warrant, 153.

ASSAULT
 See also Battery.
Apprehension of battery, 43.
Damages, 43.
Distinguished from battery, 46.
Intent required for, 46.
Interest protected, 43.
Reasonable apprehension, 44.
Relation to battery, 46.
Self defense against, 124.
Transferred intent, 37.
Words, 45.

1263

ASSUMPSIT
See Restitution.

ASSUMPTION OF RISK
Abolition of defense, 493.
Alternative, existence of reasonable, 490.
Apart from contract, 484.
Appreciation of danger, 486.
Assurance of safety, 490.
Automobile guests, 486, 489.
Burden of proof, 495.
Comparative negligence statutes, 495.
Contributory negligence, relation to, 481.
Defense of, 480.
Duty of care, relation to, 481.
Economic pressure, 491.
Express agreement, 480, 482.
Federal Employers' Liability Act, 578.
Fellow servants. See Master and Servant.
Forms of, 480.
Implied acceptance of risk, 484.
Invitees, 485.
Knowledge of risk, 486.
   Minimum standard, 487.
Loss of services action, 937.
Master and servant. See Master and Servant.
Movement to abrogate defense, 493.
Promise to remedy condition, 490.
Rescuers, 491.
Strict liability, 566.
Theory of defense, 480.
Time sequence, 494.
Violation of statute, 492.
Voluntary acceptance of risk, 490.

ATTACHMENT
Wrongful, 896, 898.

ATTORNEYS
Negligence, standard of conduct, 182.

AUTHORITY OF LAW
See Legal Authority; Officers.

AUTOMOBILES
Accident, liability for unavoidable, 162.
Assured clear distance rule, 219.
Bailors,
   Gratuitous, liability, 717.
   Vicarious liability, 522.
Compensation systems, 584.
Compulsory liability insurance, 602.
Consent statutes, 527.
Donors, liability of gratuitous, 717.
Driver incapacitated, 162.
Duty to control driver, 384.
Entrusting to unsuitable driver, 523.
Family immunity, 905.
Family purpose doctrine, 524.
Guests,
   Assumption of risk, 486, 489.
   Statutes, 212, 215.
Imputed contributory negligence.
   Bailments, 532.
   Consent statutes, 527.
   Driver and passenger, 530.

AUTOMOBILES—Cont'd
   Husband and wife, 531.
   Joint enterprise, 529.
   Parent and child, 531.
Joint enterpise. See Joint Enterprise.
Liability insurance, impact, 589.
No-fault plans, 606.
Owner, vicarious liability, 522–529.
Present deficiencies of the law, 597.
   Attorneys, 599.
   Delay, 599.
   Fees, 599.
   Inadequate insurance coverage, 598.
   Liability only for fault, 598.
   Litigation, 598.
   Uninsured defendants, 597.
Remedies for deficiencies of law, 600.
   Columbia plan, 603.
   Compulsory insurance, 602.
   Financial responsibility laws, 601.
   First American statute, 606.
   Full aid insurance, 605.
   Keeton-O'Connell plan, 606.
   No-fault plans, 606.
   Saskatchewan plan, 604.
   Security responsibility laws, 601.
   Unsatisfied judgment funds, 603.
   Voluntary schemes, 600.
Unlocked car, injury by thief of, 203, 307.

AVIATION
See Aeronautics.

AVOIDABLE CONSEQUENCES
Contributory negligence distinguished, 458.

BAILMENTS
Automobiles,
   Consent statutes, 527.
   Entrusting to unsuitable driver, 523.
   Vicarious liability of bailor, 523.
   Vicarious liability of owner, 523.
Contract against liability for negligence, 483.
Conversion,
   Actions by bailor and bailee, 105.
   Misdelivery by bailee, 95.
   Misuse by bailee, 101.
   Receipt and transportation, 95.
   Redelivery by bailee, 98.
   Withholding chattel, 98.
Dangerous animals, 541.
Imputed contributory negligence, 532.
Negligence,
   Gratuitous bailor, liability to third person, 717.
   Liability of bailor to bailee, 718.
   Liability of bailor to third person, 715.
Strict tort liability of bailor, 715.
Trespassing animals, 541.

BATTERY
See also Assault.
Character of defendant's act, 41.
Consciousness of contact, 40.
Consent,
   As defense, 113.
   Necessity of absence of, 42.

INDEX

BATTERY—Cont'd
Distinguished from assault, 46.
Forcible entry, 144.
Intent required, 41.
Interest protected, 39.
Mistake, 111.
Offensive contact, 39.
Punitive damages, 40.
Relation to assault, 46.
Self-defense, 126.
Transferred intent, 37.
Unintended consequences, 40.

BLASTING
Strict liability, 69, 550, 552, 553.
Trespass or case, 553.

BOYCOTTS
See Interference; Unfair Competition.

BRIBERY
Interference with contract by, 982, 992, 1004.
Judges, bribery of not immune, 1057, 1058.
Tort liability, 872.

BURDEN OF PROOF
See Evidence.

BUSINESS VISITORS
See Invitees.

CAPACITY TO BEAR LOSS
As factor in determining tort liability, 24.

CARRIERS
Contract against liability for negligence, 482.
Driver and passenger, imputed contributory negligence, 530.
Duty of care, 208.
Duty to aid passenger in peril, 376.
Duty to serve, 374, 376.
Employees, liability to, 586.
Insult, liability for, 57.
Negligence concurring with act of God, 264.
Passenger, protection of, against attack, 383.
Presumption of negligence toward passenger, 243, 252.
Res ipsa loquitur, collisions with other vehicles, 252.
Supplying car, liability to third person for negligence, 715.

CASE
Blasting, trespass or case, 69.
Common law action on the, 29.

CAUSATION
See Proximate Cause.

CHARITIES
Abrogation of immunity, 1070.
Immunity of, 1069.
  Abrogation, 1070.
  Liability insurance and, 595.
  Public policy theory, 1070.
  Respondeat superior, 1070.
  State of the law, 1070.

CHARITIES—Cont'd
Trust fund theory, 1070.
Waiver theory, 1070.

CHATTELS
See also Products Liability.
Privilege of recapture, 137.
Trespass to, 85.

CHILDREN
See Infants.

CIVIL RIGHTS
Governmental action violating, 1034.
Malicious prosecution, claims for, 886.
Survival of actions, 944.

CLASS ACTIONS
Causation issues, 271, 351.

COMBINATION
Boycotts, 1023.
Interference with contract, 993.
Interference with prospective advantage, 1012, 1013, 1023.
Joint torts, 322.
Restraint of trade, 1023.

COMPARATIVE NEGLIGENCE
Admiralty rule, 471.
Apportionment of damages, 470.
Arguments in favor of, 469.
Assumption of risk, 495.
Causation, 474.
Joint tortfeasors, apportionment, 475.
Modified, 473.
Multiple parties, 471.
Pure, 471.
Res ipsa loquitur, effect on, 254.
Set-off, 472.
Slight and gross negligence, 470.
Statutes, 471, 495.
  Last clear chance under, 470.
Strict liability, effect on, 478.

COMPENSATION SYSTEMS
In general, 584.
No-fault insurance, 606.
No-fault plans, 606.
Present deficiencies of the law, 597.
Principles of compensation, 608.
Remedies for deficiencies of law. See Automobiles, Remedies for deficiencies of law, 600, and subheadings thereunder.
Social insurance and welfare, 612.
Strict accountability principle, 609.
Welfare principle, 612.

COMPUTER PROGRAMS
See Unfair Competition.

CONSENT
Absence of, necessity for battery, 42.
Automobile consent statutes, 527.
By conduct, 113.

CONSENT—Cont'd
Criminal act, consent to, 122.
 Age of consent statutes, 123.
Defamation, defense to, 823.
Defense to intentional torts, 112.
Duress, 119.
Exceeding consent, 118.
Fraud, 119.
Implied consent, 113.
Incapacity and surgical procedures, 115–118.
Incapacity to, 114.
Mistake, 119.
Privacy, defense to, 867.
Silence as, 113.
Surgical operations, 115–118.
Usage or custom, inferred from, 113.

CONSORTIUM
See Husband and Wife; Parent and Child; Unmarried Consorts.

CONSPIRACY
Tort liability, 324.

CONSTITUTIONAL LIMITATIONS
Damages,
 Presumed damage rule abrogated, 843.
Defamation,
 Fair comment, 831.
 Fault issues, 804, 808.
 Opinions, 813.
 Private figures and private defamation, 807.
 Public officials and public figures, 805.
 Public proceedings, report of, 836.
 Publishers and discriminators, 810.
 Punitive damages, 845.
 Reasons for privilege to defame, 804, 805.
Injurious falsehood, 968, 977.
Interference with contract claims, 988.
Interference with prospective advantage claims, 1011, 1025.
Malicious prosecution, 886.
Privacy,
 Public record, matters of, 862.
 Publication of truth, 862.
Unfair competition, 1025.
 Right to copy designs, 1021.

CONSTITUTIONAL PRIVILEGE
See Defamation, Privacy.

CONTRACT
Advantages of tort or contract action, 665.
Carrier supplying car, 715.
Election, tort or contract, 664.
Gravamen of action, tort or contract, 664.
Interference with. See Interference.
Lessors, agreement to repair, 443.
Misfeasance, 658, 660.
Misrepresentation of intent to perform, 763.
Negligence,
 Contract against liability, 482.
 Liability of contractor to third person for misperformance, 722.
 Liability of contractor to third person for nonperformance, 667.

CONTRACT—Cont'd
 Relation ot breach of contract, 655.
Nonfeasance, 658.
Physicians, contract to cure, 186.
Promise, breach of as negligence, 379.
Relation between tort and, 655.
Restitution. See Restitution.
Suppliers of chattels, see Products Liability.
Tort,
 Public utility services, 662.
 Relationships created by contract, 663.
Tort distinguished from, 4, 655.
Tort liability to third persons,
 Building contractors, 722.
 Electricity, 671.
 Gas, 671.
 History, 668.
 Misfeasance, 670.
 Nonfeasance, 668.
 Water companies, 671.
Warranty. See Warranty.

CONTRIBUTION
Immunity of family members, 910.
Joint tortfeasors, 336.
 Basis of division, 330.
 Intentional tortfeasors, 339.
 Liability insurers, 338, 339.
 Settlement, effect, 339.
 Statutes, 338.

CONTRIBUTORY NEGLIGENCE
Aggravated negligence, defense to, 462.
Apportionment of damages to causes, 459.
Assumption of risk, relation to, 460, 480, 495.
Avoidable consequences distinguished, 458.
Burden of proof, 451.
Causation and, 452.
Children, standard of conduct, 181.
Comparative negligence. See Comparative Negligence.
Definition, 451.
Dissatisfaction with, 452, 455.
Employees, common law defense against, 569.
Federal Employers' Liability Act, 471.
Imputed, 529.
 Automobile consent statutes, 527.
 Bailments, 532.
 Driver and passenger, 530.
 Family purpose doctrine, 524.
 Husband and wife, 531.
 Joint enterprise, 529.
 Loss of services, 937.
 Parent and child, 531.
 Wrongful death, 954, 958.
Insistence on legal right, 460.
Intentional torts, defense to, 462.
Joint enterprise, passenger versus driver, 521.
Known danger, negligence toward, 460.
Last clear chance, 462.
 Antecedent negligence of defendant, 468.
 Comparative fault, theory of, 462.
 Comparative negligence acts, 471.
 Continuing negligence of both parties, 467.
 Criticism, 468.

CONTRIBUTORY NEGLIGENCE—Cont'd
Discovered peril, 465.
Humanitarian doctrine, 467.
Origin of doctrine, 462.
Plaintiff helpless, 465.
Plaintiff inattentive, 466.
Proximate cause, relation to, 462.
Theories explaining, 462.
Unconscious last clear chance, 466.
Misrepresentation, defense to, 750.
Negligence, compared with, 453.
Of servants, 529.
Particular risk, limitation to, 457.
Proximate cause, relation to, 276, 452.
Reckless conduct, defense to, 462.
Rescue, unreasonable attempt, 307.
Scope of defense, 461.
Slightest degree, contribution in, 456.
Strict liability, defense to, 565.
Theories explaining defense, 452.
Violation of statute,
    By plaintiff, 230, 231.
    Defense to, 461.
Wrongful death,
    Beneficiaries, negligent, 958.
    Decedent, negligent, 954.

CONVERSION
Acquiring possession, 93.
Adverse claimants, 99.
Agent,
    Receiving possession, 95.
    Redelivery by, 98.
    Transferring possession, 97.
Asserting ownership, 102.
Bailee,
    Action by, 105.
    Receiving possession, 94.
    Redelivery, 98.
    Transferring possession, 97.
Bailor, action by, 105.
Bona fide purchaser, 93.
Character of defendant's act, 92.
Demand, necessity, 99.
Destruction or alteration, 100.
Development of modern law, 90.
Fraud,
    Acquisition of chattel by, 93.
    Bona fide purchase, 94.
Intangible rights, 91.
Jus tertii, 103.
Land, 90.
Major interferences, limitation to, 90.
Malicious prosecution compared, 896.
Mistake no defense, 93.
Nature, 90.
Plaintiff's interest, 102.
Possession, 102.
    Right to future, 104.
    Right to immediate, 104.
Removing the chattel, 95.
Restitution, 672.
Return of the chattel, 106.
Transferring possession, 96.
Trover, action of, 89.

CONVERSION—Cont'd
Using the chattel, 101.
What may be converted, 90.
Withholding possession, 98.

COST BENEFIT ANALYSIS
See Tort.

COVENANT
Not to sue, 334.

CRIME
Anticipating criminal acts, 201.
Consent to a criminal act, 122.
Proximate cause, intervening criminal acts, 201, 313.
Same act as tort and, 8.
Tort distinguished from, 7.

CRIMINAL CONVERSATION
Defenses, 921.
Husband's action for, 917, 919.
Statutory abolition of action, 930.
Wife's action for, 917, 919.

CUSTOM
Animal trespass, 539.
Consent by, 113.
Effect of, in negligence cases, 193.
Physicians and surgeons, 189.

DAMAGES
Acts innocent in themselves together cause harm, 354.
Apportionment among causes, 345.
    Alternative liability, 345.
    Burden of proof, 350.
    Common duty, 346.
    Comparative negligence, 468.
    Concerted action, 346.
    Contributory negligence cases, 459.
    Culpable and innocent causes, 347.
    Damages of same kind, 348.
    Difficulty of proof, 345, 350.
    Nuisances, 349.
    Plaintiff and defendant in nuisance cases, 459.
    Potential damage, 353.
    Single indivisible result, 347.
    Successive injuries, 352.
    Vicarious liability, 346.
Assault, 43.
Avoidable consequences,
    Contributory negligence distinguished, 458.
Comparative negligence. See Comparative Negligence.
Defamation, 793, 843.
    Nominal damages, 845.
    Presumed damage rule abrogated, 843.
    Punitive damages, 845.
False imprisonment, 48.
Injurious falsehood, special damage, 970.
Interference with contract, 1002.
Joint torts, entire liability, 328.
Malicious prosecution, 887.
Mental distress. See Mental Distress.
Misrepresentation, 765.
    Measure of damages, 766.
    Necessity of damage, 765.

INDEX

References are to Pages

DAMAGES—Cont'd
  Proximate cause, 767.
  Restitution, 765.
Negligence, necessity of damage, 165.
Nuisance, damages as remedy, 637.
Public nuisance, necessity of particular damage, 646, 648.
Punitive, 9.
  Battery, 40.
  Compensatory damages, relation, 14, 15.
  Discretion to deny, 14.
  Insurer's liability, 13.
  Intent as basis, 9.
  Mass disasters, 14.
  Nominal damages as basis, 14.
  Policy of, 11.
  Vicarious liability for, 13.
  Wilful or wanton conduct, 10, 213.
Survival of actions, damages recoverable, 950.
Trespass, necessity of damage,
  To chattels, 87.
  To land, 75.
Wrongful death, 949.

DANGEROUS THINGS AND ACTIVITIES
See Strict Liability.

DEAD BODIES
Intentional interference with, 63.
Negligent interference with 362.

DEATH
See Survival of Actions; Wrongful Death.

DECEIT
See Misrepresentation.

DEFAMATION
Abuse distinguished, 776.
Basis of liability, 797.
Broadcasting,
  Basis of liability, 812.
  Colloquium, 783.
  Libel or slander, 785.
  Political broadcasts, 824.
Consent as defense, 823.
Constitutional limitations,
  Fair comment on matters of public interest, 831.
  Fault issues, 804, 808.
  Private figures and private defamation, 807.
  Publishers and discriminators, 810.
  Punitive damages, 845.
Constitutional privilege, 804, 838.
  Fair comment, 831.
Construed as a whole, 780.
Corporation, defamation of, 777.
Damages, 793, 843.
  Nominal damages, 845.
  Presumed damage rule abrogated, 843.
Dead, defamation of the, 779.
Definition, 773.
Disparagement distinguished, 964.
External facts, meaning dependent upon, 780.
Fair comment, 831.
Fair construction, 780.
Fault issues in, 802.

DEFAMATION—Cont'd
Good motives as mitigating damages, 842.
Group or class, defamation of, 784.
History, 771.
Husband and wife, immunity, 824.
Immunities, absolute, 816.
Inducement, 780.
Injunction, 773.
Injurious falsehood distinguished, 964.
Innocent, strict liability for, 808.
Innuendo, necessity of, 780.
Interpretation, 780.
  Court or jury, 780.
Libel, 795.
  Distinguished from slander, 786.
  Proof of damage not required, 795.
  Proof of damage required, 796.
Malicious prosecution, relation to, 886.
Mental suffering, damages, 844.
Mitigation of damages, 842.
Municipal corporation, defamation of, 745, 780.
Negligence, liability based on, 802ff.
Opinion, 813.
Privacy, interrelation with, 864.
Privilege,
  Absolute, 815.
  Abuse of qualified, 832.
  Burden of proof, 835.
  Common interest, 828.
  Consent, 823.
  Court and jury, 835.
  Credit agencies, 829.
  Excessive publication, 833.
  Executive communications, 821.
  Fair comment, 831.
  Husband and wife, 824.
  Interest of publisher, 825.
  Interests of others, 826.
  Judicial proceedings, 816.
  Legislative proceedings, 820.
  Malice, 833.
  Motive or purpose, 833.
  Political broadcasts, 824.
  Public interest, 830.
  Public officers, 821.
  Public proceedings, report of, 836.
  Qualified or conditional, 824.
  Self-defense, 825.
Provocation, 842.
Proximate cause, 795.
Public figures, 805.
Public officials, 805.
Publication, 797.
  Appropriate to privilege, 833.
  By plaintiff, 803.
  By third person, 798.
  Intent or negligence, 803.
  Manner, 797.
  Necessity, 797.
  Negligent, 803.
  Repetition as, 799.
  Secondary distributors, 803, 810.
  Single publication rule, 800.
  To members of family, 798.
  Will, probate, 801.

INDEX

References are to Pages

DEFAMATION—Cont'd
Reference to plaintiff, 783.
Relational interest invaded, 771.
Repetition,
    Damages caused by, 795.
    Liability of republisher, 799.
Reputation, evidence, 846.
Retraction, 845.
Ridicule, 777.
Secondary distributors, 774, 803, 810.
Self-defense, 825.
Slander,
    Actionable without proof of damage, 788.
    Business, profession or office, 790.
    Crime, imputation, 788.
    Disease, imputation, 790.
    Homosexuality, 778.
    Libel distinguished, 786.
    Special damage, what is, 793.
    Unchastity, imputation, 792.
Slander of title. See Injurious Falsehood.
Special damage,
    Necessity of, 793.
    What is, 793.
Standard by which determined, 777.
Strict liability, 803.
Truth as defense, 839.
United States, 1038.
Who may be defamed, 778.
Will, probate, 801.

DEFENSE OF OTHERS
Mistake, 130.
Privilege, 129.
Reasonable force, 130.

DEFENSE OF PROPERTY
See Property, Defense of.

DISCIPLINE
Army and navy, 159.
Family, 157.
Privilege of, 157.
Schools, 158.

DISPARAGEMENT
See Injurious Falsehood.

DOGS
See Animals.

DOMESTIC RELATIONS
See Husband and Wife; Parent and Child.

DURESS
Consent obtained by, 121.
False imprisonment by duress against property, 50.

DUTY
See Negligence.

ECONOMIC ANALYSIS
See Tort.

ECONOMIC RELATIONS
See Interference.

ECONOMIC RETALIATION
See Interference.

EDUCATIONAL MALPRACTICE
See Governmental Liabilities.

ELECTION
Contract or tort, 664.

EMERGENCY
    See also Necessity.
Effect of, in negligence cases, 196.
Medical and surgical treatment in, 115–118.

EMPLOYERS
See Independent Contractors; Master and Servant.

ENTICEMENT
Of wife or child, 917, 924.

EQUITY
Misrepresentation, equitable relief, 729.
Nuisance, relief against, 640.

ESTOPPEL
Negligence, 733.
Strict responsibility, 733.

EVIDENCE
Burden of proof,
    Alternative liability, 271.
    Apportionment of damages, 350.
    Assumption of risk, 495.
    Contributory negligence, 451.
    Privilege in defamation, 835.
Causation in fact, proof, 269.
Expert testimony, necessity of in malpractice, 188.
Negligence,
    Burden of proof, 239.
    Circumstantial evidence, 242.
    Functions of court and jury, 235.
    Presumptions, 240.
    Proof, 235.
Res ipsa loquitur. See Res Ipsa Loquitur.
Sufficiency of evidence of facts, 235.
Weight of evidence of facts, 236.

EXPERIENCE
Minimum standard, 182.

EXPLOSIVES
Blasting, trespass or case, 69.
Strict liability for use of, 542, 552, 554.

FACTORS IN TORT LAW
See Tort.

FALSE ADVERTISING
See Unfair Competition.

FALSE IMPRISONMENT
Character of defendant's act, 49.
Confinement, 47.
    Consciousness of, 47.
Consent, 49.
Damages, 48.
Instigation, 52.

FALSE IMPRISONMENT—Cont'd
Intent and motive, 52.
Legal authority, assertion of, 50.
Malicious prosecution distinguished, 53, 885.
Non-action as basis, 52.
Participation, 52.
Property, duress against, 50.
Temporary detention for investigation, 141.

FAMILY RELATIONS
See Husband and Wife; Parent and Child.

FAULT
See also Strict Liability.
Fault principle, 608.
Historical development of concept, 21.
Legal distinguished from moral, 21, 22, 23.
Liability without, 534.
Meaning, 21, 534.

FEDERAL EMPLOYERS' LIABILITY ACT
See Master and Servant.

FEDERAL TORT CLAIMS ACT
See Governmental Liabilities.

FELLOW SERVANTS
See Master and Servant.

FIRE
Negligence, 382.
Preventing extinguishing, 382.
Strict liability for,
    Common law, 543.
    Statutes, 544.

FORCIBLE ENTRY
Force, use of, 143.
Possession, importance, 145.

FORESEEABILITY
See Negligence; Proximate Cause.

FRANCHISES
See Interference.

FRAUD
See Misrepresentation.

GOVERNMENTAL LIABILITIES
See also Officers.
Abrogation of immunities, 1055.
Assault and battery, 1038.
Basic policy immunity,
    Municipalities, 1052.
    States, 1046.
Civil rights claims, 1038.
Defamation, 1038.
Discretionary immunity,
    Municipalities, 1052.
    States, 1046.
    United States, 1039.
Educational malpractice, 1048.
False imprisonment, 1038.
Fire protection failures, 1049.

GOVERNMENTAL LIABILITIES—Cont'd
Immunities,
    Generally, 1032.
    Municipal Corporations, 1051.
        Abolition of immunities, 1052.
    States, 1043.
        Abrogation of immunity, 1045, 1055.
    United States, 1033.
Interference with contract, 1038.
Licensing, 1050.
Malicious prosecution, 1038.
Misrepresentation, 1038.
Mob action, 1055.
Municipal corporations,
    Basic policy immunity, 1052.
    Discretionary immunity, 1052.
    Governmental-proprietary distinction, 1053.
    Immunities, 1051.
        Abolition of immunity, 1052.
    Mob action, 1055.
    Notice required before suit, 1055.
    Nuisance, 1054.
    Trespass, 1054.
Notice required, 1055.
Nuisance, 1054.
Persons in custody, 1048.
Police failure, 1049.
Prisoner release, 1047.
Public duty doctrine, 1049.
States,
    Basic policy immunity, 1046.
    Children in custody injured, 1048.
    Discretionary immunity, 1046.
    Educational malpractice, 1048.
    Fire protection failure, 1049.
    Immunity, 1043.
    Licensing, 1050.
    Non-feasance, 1049.
    Person in custody injured, 1048.
    Police failure, 1049.
    Prisoner release programs, 1047.
    Procedural immunities, 1043.
    Public duty doctrine, 1049.
    Remedial immunities, 1044.
Strict liability, 1036.
Trespass, 1038, 1054.
United States,
    Armed forces, immunity to, 1036.
    Assault and battery, 1038.
    Civil rights claims, 1038.
    Civil rights violations, 1034.
    Defamation, 1038.
    Discretionary immunity, 1039.
    False imprisonment, 1038.
    Federal Tort Claims Act, 1034.
    Feres doctrine immunity, 1036.
    Immunities, 1033.
    Interference with contract, 1038.
    Law governing, 1034.
    Malicious prosecution, 1038.
    Misrepresentation, 1038.
    Omissions, 1035.
    Taking of property, 1033.
    Trespass, 1038.

References are to Pages

GROSS NEGLIGENCE
See Negligence.

HIGHWAYS
Animals straying from, 540.
Danger to, 388.
Lessors, danger to those outside premises, 437.
Natural conditions, 391.
Nuisance, public, 644, 645.
Trespasser straying from, 389.

HISTORY
Contractor's liability to third person, 658.
Duty in negligence cases, 356.
Factor in tort liability, 20, 21.
Husband and wife, 901.
Injuries falsehood, 962.
Interference with contract, 979.
Interference with prospective advantage, 1005.
Joint tortfeasors, 322.
Moral aspect of torts, 21.
Municipal corporations, immunity, 1051.
Negligence, development of, 160.
Nuisance, 617.
Res ipsa loquitur, 244.
Strict liability, 534.
Survival of actions, 940.
Trespass and case, 28.
Trover, action of, 89.
Vicarious liability, 499.
Warranty to consumer, 679.
Wrongful death, 940.

HUSBAND AND WIFE
Consortium, loss of,
    Husband's action, 931.
    Wife's action, 931.
Contribution claims against, 910.
Defamation, immunity in, 824.
Defenses to interference with relation, 937.
Discipline, 157.
Enticing or harboring wife, 917.
Family purpose doctrine, 524.
History, 901.
Husband,
    Abduction or enticement of wife, 917.
    Alienation of affections, 918.
    Criminal conversation, 917, 919.
    Defenses to action for injury to wife, 937.
    Injury to wife, action for, 931.
    Interference with interests of, 916.
    Loss of wife, 931.
Immunity,
    Generally, 901.
    Abolition of, 903.
    Effect of liability insurance on, 595.
Imputed contributory negligence, 531.
Intent to interfere with relation, 920.
Interference with relation, 915.
    Abolition of actions, 929.
    Basis of liability, 919.
    Equitable relief against, 923.
    Intent, necessity, 920.
    Statutes abolishing action, 930.
    Types of interference, 917.

HUSBAND AND WIFE—Cont'd
Loss of services, imputed contributory negligence, 937.
Married women's acts, 902.
Privilege to interfere with relation, 922.
Third parties, tort liability of, 910.
Tort actions between, 901.
    Abrogation of immunity, 903.
    Death, effect, 903.
    Duties, 907.
    History, 901.
    Immunity, 902.
    Liability insurance, 905.
    Vicarious liability, 912.
Vicarious liability for torts, 912.
Wife,
    Alienation of affections, 918.
    Criminal conversation, 917, 919.
    Injury to husband, 931.
    Interference with relational interest,
        Common law, 916.
Wrongful death, immunity in action for, 955.

IMMUNITIES
See Charities; Governmental Liabilities; Husband and Wife; Parent and Child; Officers.

IMPUTED NEGLIGENCE
See Contributory Negligence; Vicarious Liability.

INDEMNITY
Joint tortfeasors, 341.
    Imputed negligence, 341.
    Passive and active negligence, 343.
    Reliance, 342.
Liability insurance as form of, 585.
Public Officers, 1067.

INDEPENDENT CONTRACTORS
Building contractors, liability, 722.
"Collateral" negligence, 515.
"Inherently dangerous" activities, 512.
Lessors hiring, 445.
Liability for negligence,
    To third person for negligent performance, 722.
    To third person for nonperformance, 722.
Negligence of the employer, 510.
Non-delegable duty, 470, 511.
Servants, distinguished from, 501.
Vicarious liability for torts, 509.
Water companies, 671.

INDUCING BREACH OF CONTRACT
See Interference.

INFANTS
Anticipating negligence of, 200.
Contract, tort based on, 1071.
Custody, interference with, 925.
Immunity, 1071.
Incapacity to consent to tort, 114.
Misrepresentation by, 1072.
Negligence,
    Defendants and plaintiffs, 181.
    Engaging in adult activity, 181.
    Maximum and minimum ages, 180.

INDEX

References are to Pages

INFANTS—Cont'd
Prenatal injuries, 367.
Tort based on contract, 1071.
Tort liability of, 1071.
Trespassers. See Trespassers.

INJUNCTION
Alienation of affections, 923.
Defamation, 773.
Injurious falsehood, 976.
Nuisance, 630, 1643.

INJURIOUS FALSEHOOD
Comparative statements, 973.
Competition, 973.
Constitutional limits, 968, 977.
Disparagement of property, 964.
   Defamation distinguished, 964.
Elements of cause of action, 967.
History, 962.
Injunction against, 976.
Intent, necessity, 968.
Interests protected, 965.
Malice, 968.
Motive, 968.
Negligence, 969.
Opinion statements, 967–968.
Privilege, 973.
Proof of falsity, 967.
Prospective advantage, interference with, 1005.
Protection of defendant's interests, 973.
Remedies, 976.
Restitution for unjust enrichment, 973.
Reverse confusion, 971.
Scienter, 969.
Slander of title, 962.
Special damage, 969.

INSANITY
Arrest of lunatic, 155.
Consent to tort, incapacity to, 114.
Immunity of insane persons, 1072.
Immunity of mentally disabled, 1072.
Intent, 1074.
Negligence, 1074.
State compensation for acts of mentally disabled, 1075.

INSULTS
Liability, 4, 57.
Public utilities, 58.

INSURANCE
See Liability Insurance.

INTENT
Assault, intent required for, 46.
Battery, 41.
Consequences substantially certain to follow, 34.
Conversion, 92.
Crimes and torts, 33.
False imprisonment, 52.
Family relation, interference with, 920.
Injurious falsehood, 969.
Insane persons, 1074.
Interference with contract, 982.
Interference with prospective advantage, 1008.

INTENT—Cont'd
Meaning, 33.
Mental distress, acts directed at third person, 65.
Misrepresentation, intent to deceive, 741.
More extensive liability for, 26, 37.
Negligence distinguished, 36.
Nuisance, basis of liability for, 622.
Punitive damages based on, 9.
Transferred, 37.
Transition from trespass and case, 30.
Trespass to chattels, 86.
Wilful, wanton, reckless conduct distinguished, 36.

INTERFERENCE
Contract, interference with, 978.
   Basis of liability, 982.
   Bribery, 982, 992, 1004.
   Burden of proof, 983.
   Causation, 989.
   Combination, 993.
   Competition, 987.
   Constitutional limits, 988.
   Contract against public policy, 994.
   Damages, measure of, 1002.
   Defendant's interests, protection, 986.
   Disinterested motive, 985.
   Governmental liabilities, 1038.
   History, 979.
   Illegal means, 984.
   Intent required, 982.
   Intent to interfere, 982.
   Knowledge of relation, 982.
   Labor unions, 1002.
   Malice, 983, 984.
   Manner of interference, 989.
   Marry, contract to, 996.
   Medical Care Recovery Act, 999.
   Motive, 984.
   Nature of original contract, 994.
   Negligent interference, 997.
   Preventing performance, 991.
   Prima facie tort, 983.
   Privilege, 983.
   Proximate cause, 989.
   Public interest, action in, 985.
   Purpose, 964.
   Remedies, 1002.
   Restitution, 1003.
   Servant, injury to, 998.
   Subrogation compared, 999.
   Terminable at will, 995.
   Truth, 989.
   Unenforceable contract, 994.
   Yellow dog contract, 994.
Custody of children, 925.
Disparagement. See Injurious Falsehood.
Economic retaliation, 1027.
Employment, at will employees, 1027.
Family relations. See Husband and Wife; Parent and Child.
Franchises, termination, 1028.
Injunction, interference with rights under, 978.
Labor unions,
   Contract, interference with, 1002.
   Contract terminable at will, 995, 1002.
   Federal preemption of labor relations, 1025, 1026.

INDEX

References are to Pages

INTERFERENCE—Cont'd
  Federal regulation, 1027.
  Illegal means, 1026.
  Picketing, 1026.
  Public employee strike, 1027.
  Secondary boycotts, 1014, 1023, 1027.
  State law, remnants of, 1027.
  Statutes, 1026.
  Strikes, 1026.
  Strikes as interference, 1026.
  Prospective advantage, interference with, 1005.
    Basis of liability, 1008.
    Boycotts, 1023.
    Burden of proof, 1011.
    Combination, 1012, 1013, 1023.
    Competition, 1012.
    Constitutional limits, 1011, 1025.
    Franchisee protection, 1028.
    Franchises, termination, 1028.
    History, 1005.
    Illegal means, 1009.
    Intent, 1008.
    Legacies, 1007.
    Malice, 1009.
    Motive, 1009.
    Nature of relation, 1005.
    Non-commercial expectations, 1007.
    Political and social protests, 1025.
    Prima facie tort, 1010.
    Retaliatory discharge, 1027.
    Reverse confusion, 1015.
    Strikes and labor activities, 1026.
  Retaliatory discharge, 1027.
  Unfair competition, 1013.
    Appropriation of ideas, 1020.
    Imitation of appearance, 1015.
    Legal and illegal methods, 1002.
    Misrepresentation, 1015, 1018.
    Monopoly, 1013, 1024.
    Passing off, 1015.
    Restraint of trade, 1023.

INTOXICATION
  As negligence, 178.
  Dram Shop Acts, 581, 582.

INVITEES
  Area of invitation, 424.
  Assumption of risk, 485.
  Business interest theory, 420.
  Care required toward, 425.
  Categories, abolition of, 432.
  Duty to aid, 376, 383.
  Known and obvious dangers, 426, 427.
  Liability of occupier to, 419.
  Protection against third person, 383, 420.
  Public invitation theory, 422.
  Public officers and employees, 420.
  Strict liability to, 562.
  Who are, 420.

JOINT ENTERPRISE
  Actions between members of enterprise, 521.
  Common pecuniary interest, 519.
  Common property interest in vehicle, 519.

JOINT ENTERPRISE—Cont'd
  Common purpose, 518.
  Contributory negligence, imputed, 517.
  Criticism, 522.
  Defendant's liability, 529.
  Extension beyond business ventures, 517.
  Meaning, 516.
  Mutual right of control, 519.

JOINT TORTS
  Acts innocent in themselves together causing damage, 354.
  Apportionment of damages, 345.
    Common duty, 346.
    Concerted action 322, 345.
    Same kind, difficult to apportion, 350.
    Single indivisible result, 328, 347.
    Vicarious liability, 346.
  Concerted action, 346.
  Conspiracy, 324.
  Contribution, 336.
    Basis of division, 340.
    Intentional tortfeasors, 339.
    Liability insurers, 338, 339.
    Settlement, effect, 339.
    Statutes, 338.
  Covenant not to sue, 334.
  Entire liability, 328.
  History, 322.
  Indemnity, 341.
    Imputed negligence, 341.
    Passive and active negligence, 343.
    Reliance, 342.
  Joinder of defendants, 324.
  Judgment, 330.
  Jury, single verdict, 329.
  Meaning, 322.
  Release,
    As satisfaction, 332.
    Crediting payments made, 333, 335.
    Of one releasing others, 332.
  Satisfaction, 330, 332, 335.
  Separate verdicts, 329.
  Several liability, 327.

JOKES
  Liability for practical, 41.

JUDGMENTS
  Joint torts, 330.
  Satisfaction, 332, 335.

JURY
  Defamation, interpretation of, 780.
  Directed verdict, 236.
  Function of, in negligence cases, 235.
  Joint torts, single verdict, 329.
  Liability insurance,
    Effect on jury issues, 591.
    Effect on verdicts, 590.
  Malicious prosecution,
    Improper purpose, 882.
    Probable cause, 876.
  Punitive damages, discretion to deny, 14.

INDEX
References are to Pages

JURY—Cont'd
Res ipsa loquitur, evidence rebutting, 261.
Substantial causal factor, question for, 267.

KNOWLEDGE
Assumption of risk, 487.
Contributory negligence toward known danger, 460.
Duty to find out, 185.
Interference with contract, knowledge of relation, 982.
Negligence, minimum standard, 182.
Superior knowledge, skill and intelligence, 185.

LABOR UNIONS
See Interference.

LAND, OWNERS AND OCCUPIERS OF
Categories, abolition of, 432.
Conduct of others, duty to control, 391.
Invitees. See Invitees.
Landlord and tenant. See Landlord and Tenant.
Licensees. See Licensees.
Natural conditions, 390.
Nuisance. See Nuisance.
Outside of premises, injuries occurring, 385.
Straying from highway, liability to one, 389.
Trespass. See Trespass.
Trespassers. See Trespassers.
Vendor and vendee. See Vendors and Vendee.

LANDLORD AND TENANT
Activities of lessee, 434.
Agreement to repair, 443.
Attack on tenant, liability, 442.
Conditions dangerous outside of premises, 437.
Forcible entry, liability for, 144.
Known concealed conditions, 436.
Lessees, liability, 434.
Lessor's liability,
  Strict liability in tort, 722.
  Warranty, 722.
Negligence in making repairs, 445.
  Independent contractor, negligence of, 445.
  Necessity that situation be made worse, 445.
Non-liability of landlord, 435.
  Reversal of rule, 446.
Parts of premises retained in lessor's control, 440.
Premises leased for admission of public, 437.
Repairs, negligence in making, 445.
Trespass, necessity of possession in plaintiff, 70, 77.

LAST CLEAR CHANCE
See Contributory Negligence.

LAW
Misrepresentation, 758.
Rules of, 217.

LEGAL AUTHORITY
  See also Officers.
False imprisonment by assertion of, 50.
Mental distress, outrageous abuse of authority, 61.
Nuisance, defense to, 632.
Process, privilege of action under, 148.
Strict liability, defense to, 567.
Trespass ab initio, 150.

LIABILITY INSURANCE
Charity immunity, effect on, 595.
Contribution, 338, 339.
Cooperation clauses, 586.
Family immunities, effect on, 593.
Governmental immunity, effect on, 595.
Impact upon the law of torts, 589.
Indemnity, form, 585.
Injured plaintiff, no liability to, 586.
"Invisible" effects, 589.
Jury issues, effect on, 591.
Jury verdicts, effect on, 590.
Legality, 543, 585.
Misrepresentations by insured, 588.
Negligence, shift of emphasis in, 591.
"No action" clauses, 586.
Present deficiencies of the law, 597.
  Attorneys, 599.
  Delay, 599.
  Fees, 599.
  Inadequate coverage, 598.
  Liability only for fault, 598.
  Litigation, 598.
  Uninsured defendants, 597.
Punitive damages, 13.
Remedies for deficiencies of law, 600.
  Columbia plan, 603.
  Compulsory insurance, 602.
  Financial responsibility laws, 601.
  First American statute, 606.
  Full aid insurance, 605.
  Keeton-O'Connell plan, 606.
  Saskatchewan plan, 604.
  Security responsibility laws, 601.
  Unsatisfied judgment funds, 603.
  Voluntary schemes, 600.
Settlements, effect on, 590.
Specific mention, 593.
Terms of contract, 542, 584, 586.
Vicarious liability and, 593.
"Visible" effects, 593.
What it is, 584.

LIABILITY WITHOUT FAULT
See Strict Liability.

LIBEL
See Defamation.

LICENSEES
Activities endangering, 416.
Categories, abolition of, 432.
Change of conditions, 418.
Disclosure of known dangerous conditions, 416, 417.
Liability of occupier to, 412.
Liability of third person to, 412.
Naked, 412.
Persons included, 413.
Public officers and employees, 428.
  "Fireman's Rule," 429.
Recreational lands, 415.
Social guests, 413.
Strict liability to, 562.
Wilful or wanton conduct, 415.

LIMITATIONS, STATUTE OF
Negligence cases, 165.
Repose, statutes of, 167.
Trespass, 83.
Wrongful death, 957.

MALICE
Abuse of process, 897.
Defamation, meaning in, 833.
Injurious falsehood, 968.
Interference with contract, 983, 984.
Interference with prospective advantage, 1009.
Malicious civil proceedings, 894.
Malicious prosecution, 882.
Nuisance cases, 624.
Punitive damages in cases of, 10.
Qualified privilege in defamation, 832.

MALICIOUS PROSECUTION
Abuse of process distinguished, 897.
Civil proceedings, 889.
    Attachment, wrongful, 896.
    Compared with criminal, 892.
    Conversion compared, 896.
    Interference with person or property, 890.
    Malice, 894.
    Physicians counterattacks, 891.
    Probable cause, 893.
    Receivers, wrongful appointment, 896.
    Rejection by some courts, 889.
    Special damage, 896.
    Termination of proceeding, 894.
Civil rights claims for, 886.
Constitutional limits on action, 885, 886.
Damages recoverable, 869.
Defamation, relation to, 870, 886.
Defenses, 885.
Elements of cause of action, 871.
False imprisonment distinguished, 53, 885.
Guilt, defense of, 885.
Improper purpose, 882.
    Court or jury, 883.
Institution of proceedings, 871.
"Malice" in, 882.
Participation, 871.
Physician "counterattack" claims, 891.
Probable cause, 876.
    Advice of counsel, 879.
    Court or jury, 882.
    Disposition of case as evidence, 880.
    Meaning of, 876.
    Mistake of fact or law, 877.
    Reasonable belief, 876.
Prosecuting attorneys, 872.
Termination in favor of accused, 874, 880.
    Compromise, 875.
    Dismissal, 874, 880.
Witness' liability, 872.

MALPRACTICE
    See also Negligence; Physicians and Surgeons.
Doctors. See Physicians and Surgeons.
Professionals, other, 185.

MANUFACTURERS
See Products Liability.

MARRIAGE
Interference with contract, 996.

MASS ACCIDENTS
Market-share allocation, 271, 351.

MASTER AND SERVANT
Appliances, safe, 569.
Assumption of risk, 501.
Carrier employees, 577.
Common law defenses, 569.
Common law duties, 568.
Contract against liability for negligence, 482.
Contributory negligence of servant, 569.
Conversion by servant, 95, 97, 98.
Duty to aid servant in peril, 383.
Federal Employers' Liability Act, 577ff.
    Comparative negligence under, 471.
Fellow servants,
    Duty to provide suitable, 569.
    Non-liability for negligence, 569, 571.
    Related work, 570.
    Vice-principals, 571.
Independent contractors. See Independent Contractors.
Interference with relation. See Interference.
Joinder as defendants, 327.
Master's liability to servant, 568.
Place to work, safe, 569.
Rules, duty to make and enforce, 569.
Servants, who are, 501.
Statutory changes, 572, 577.
Vicarious liability,
    Damages not apportioned, 346.
    Dangerous instrumentalities, 507.
    Fellow servant rule, 569.
    Frolic and detour, 503.
    Intentional torts, 505.
    Justifications, 501.
    Nature, 501.
    Prohibited acts, 503.
    Punitive damages, 12.
    Scope of employment, 501.
Warning and instruction, 569.
Worker's compensation. See Worker's Compensation.

MENTAL DISTRESS
Abuse of defendant's power, 61.
Acts directed at a third person, 65.
Collecting creditors, 61.
Dead bodies,
    Intentional interference with, 63.
    Negligence toward, 362.
Defamation, damages in, 794, 844.
Extreme outrage, 60.
Fictitious claims, danger, 56, 361.
Impact requirement, 363.
Insult and indignity, 57.
    Carriers and public utilities, 57.
    Ordinary rule, 59.
    Shopkeepers, 58.
Intentional infliction, 57, 63.
    Extreme outrage, 60.
    Insult from public utilities, 58.
    Physical harm, necessity of, 64.

INDEX
References are to Pages

MENTAL DISTRESS—Cont'd
  Restatement of Torts, 64.
  Trivial offenses, 56, 59, 63.
  Type of injury redressed, 56.
Negligent infliction, 359.
Objections to compensation for, 360.
"Parasitic" damages for, 57, 363.
Peril or harm to another,
  Intentional torts, 65.
  Negligence, 365.
Physical injury,
  Mental distress with, 362.
  Mental distress without, 361.
Recovery without impact, 364.
Reluctance to redress, 55.
Special susceptibility of plaintiff, 62.
Telegraph, negligent transmission of message, 362.
Wilful or wanton conduct, 64.

MISAPPROPRIATION DOCTRINE
See Unfair Competition.

MISREPRESENTATION
Affirmance of transaction, effect of, 769.
Ambiguous statements, 736.
Basis of responsibility, 740.
Concealment, active, 737.
Conduct, by, 206, 736.
Conscious ignorance, 742.
Consent obtained by, 120.
Contributory negligence, 750.
Conversion by, 93.
  Bona fide purchase, 94.
Damages, 765.
  Measure of, 766.
  Necessity of, 765.
  Proximate cause, 767.
  Restitution, 765.
Deceit,
  Conscious ignorance, 727.
  Elements of cause of action, 728.
  History, 727, 740.
  Intent to deceive, 741.
  Interests protected, 726.
  Negligence distinguished, 742.
  Negligent misrepresentation, 745.
  Non-pecuniary injuries, 725.
  Persons protected, 743.
  Scienter, 741.
  Strict liability in action of, 748.
  Warranty distinguished, 729.
Defense, as a, 731.
Derry v. Peek, 740.
Estoppel,
  Positive representations, 733.
  Standing by, 733.
Equitable relief, 729.
Express warranty to consumer, 679.
Infant, liability of, 1071.
Insured, misrepresentations by, 588.
Intent to deceive, 741.
Intention, statements of, 755, 762.
Law, misrepresentations of, 758.
Materiality, 753.

MISREPRESENTATION—Cont'd
Mistake, equitable relief against, 729.
Negligence,
  Conduct, 206.
  Contributory negligence as defense, 750.
  Deceit action, 745.
  Estoppel, 733.
  Negligence action, 745.
  Persons protected, 745.
  Physical damage, 205, 725.
  Restitution, 730.
Nondisclosure. See Nondisclosure.
Opinion, statements of, 755.
  Justifiable reliance on, 760.
  Puffing, 757.
  Quality, 756.
  Restitution, 756.
  Value, 757.
Personal injuries, 726.
Physical injuries, 726.
Plaintiffs protected,
  Intentional misrepresentation, 743.
  Negligent misrepresentation, 745.
  Strict liability, 748.
Predictions, 743.
Promises, 763.
Proximate cause, 767.
Quasi-contract remedy, 672, 730.
Recoupment for, 732.
Reliance, 749.
  Contributory negligence, 750.
  Justifiable, 750.
  Known importance to plaintiff, 754.
  Materiality, 753.
  Necessity, 749.
  Substantial factor, 750.
Remedies for, 725.
  Summary of, 734.
Rescission for, 672, 729.
Restitution, 672, 730.
  At law, 730.
  Damage, necessity of, 765.
  Innocent misrepresentation, 748.
  Law, 758.
  Nondisclosure, 737.
  Opinion, 756.
  Reliance, 750.
"Sales talk", 757.
Scienter, 741.
Strict liability for, 748.
  Business transactions, 748.
  Deceit, action of, 748.
  Defense of fraud, 731.
  Estoppel, 733.
  Express warranty to consumer, 679.
  Restitution, 748.
Unfair competition by, 1015, 1018.
Value, statements of, 757.
Warranty. See Warranty.

MISTAKE
Arrest, 111.
As defense to intentional torts, 110.
Cause for, 727.
Consent given under, 119.

INDEX

References are to Pages

MISTAKE—Cont'd
Conversion, 93, 111.
Defense of others under, 130.
Defense of property under, 131.
Distinguished from accident, 110.
Equitable relief against, 729.
Induced by plaintiff's conduct, 112.
Necessity, 148.
Recapture of chattels under, 138.
Self-defense under, 125.
Trespass,
  To chattels, 86.
  To land, 74.

MONOPOLIES
See also Unfair Competition.
Prospective advantage, interference with, 1013, 1024.

MORALS
Peril, failure to aid one in, 375.
Tort and, 21.

MOTIVE
False imprisonment, 52.
Injurious falsehood, 968.
Interference with contract, 984.
Interference with prospective advantage, 1009.
Liability turning on, 25.
Nuisance, motive as factor in, 624.

MUNICIPAL CORPORATIONS
See also Governmental Liabilities.
Defamation of, 780.
Liability insurance and, 595.

NAMES
Appropriation of, 851.

NECESSITY
Damages inflicted under private, 147.
Mistake, 148.
Personal injury inflicted under, 148.
Private necessity, 146.
Privilege of, 145.
Public necessity, 146.

NEGLIGENCE
See also Proximate Cause.
Accident, unavoidable, 162.
  Jury instructions, 163.
Acts and omissions, 373.
Acts innocent in themselves together causing damage, 354.
Affirmative conduct, duty based on, 378.
Aged persons, standard of conduct, 182.
Aggravated negligence, 208.
Alternative course, 172.
Animals, anticipating conduct of, 198.
As conduct, 169.
Assumption of risk. See Assumption of Risk.
Attorneys, conduct required of, 186.
Automobiles,
  Assured clear distance rule, 219.
  Guests, 212, 215.
Balancing risk against utility of conduct, 171.

NEGLIGENCE—Cont'd
Burden of proof, 239.
  Double fault and alternative liability, 271.
Causation. See Proximate Cause.
Children,
  Anticipating negligence of, 200.
  Defendants and plaintiffs, 181.
  Engaging in adult activity, 181.
  Maximum and minimum ages, 180.
  Standard of conduct for, 179.
Circumstantial evidence of, 242.
Conduct of others, anticipating, 197.
Contract,
  Against liability for negligence, 482.
  Liability to third persons for misperformance, 722.
  Liability to third persons for nonperformance, 667.
  Misfeasance, 660.
  Nonfeasance, 668.
  Relation between tort and, 655.
Contractors, liability of, 722.
Contributory. See Contributory Negligence.
Controlling conduct of others, 383.
Court and jury, functions of, 235.
Criminal acts, anticipating, 201, 313.
Custom, 193.
Damage, necessity of, 165.
Degrees of care, 208.
Degrees of negligence, 208, 460.
Designs of products, 688.
Duty,
  Absolute wrong, theory of, 287.
  Assumption of, by conduct, 378.
  Assumption of risk, relation to, 481.
  Carrier to aid passenger, 376.
  Concept of relative, 357.
  Development of idea of, 358.
  For court, 236.
  History of, 358.
  Impossibility of formula for, 359.
  Invitor to aid invitee, 342, 376, 383.
  Limitations of, 359.
  Master and servant at common law, 568.
  Master to aid servant, 383.
  Palsgraf v. Long Island R. Co., 284.
  Particular interest of plaintiff, 289.
  Performance, entering upon, 379.
  Prenatal injuries, 367.
  Promise to aid, 379.
  Proximate cause, relation to, 274.
  Psychotherapists, 384.
  Reasons for limitations, 374.
  Relation to standard of conduct, 356.
  Res ipsa loquitur and, 255.
  Rescuers, to, 307.
  Scope of, 358.
  Unforeseeable consequences, 280.
  Unforeseeable plaintiffs, 284.
Elements of cause of action, 164.
Emergency, 196.
Employers of independent contractors, 509.
Entrustment, 197.
Experience, minimum standard of, 182.
Fire, 382.
Foreseeable intervening causes, 303.

NEGLIGENCE—Cont'd
Foreseeable risk, 169.
    Liability beyond, 290.
    Limitation to damages within, 281.
Forgetting, 182.
Gross negligence, 211.
Highway, danger to, 388.
Historical development, 160.
Infants, standard of conduct of, 179.
Injurious falsehood, 969.
Insane persons, 1074.
    Anticipating conduct of, 199.
Inspections, safety, by insurers, 381.
Intent distinguished, 36.
Interference with contract, 997.
Intoxication,
    As negligence, 179.
Invitees. See Invitees.
Knowledge,
    Duty to find out, 185.
    Minimum standard of, 182.
Landlord and tenant. See Landlord and Tenant.
Lessors, repairs made by, 445.
Liability insurance, effect on emphasis, 592.
Licensees. See Licensees.
Limitations, statute of, 165.
Making situation worse, necessity of, 378.
Malicious acts, anticipating, 201.
Memory, minimum standard of, 182.
Mental capacity, 176.
Mental distress. See Mental Distress.
Misfeasance, liability for, 373.
Misrepresentation,
    By conduct, 206, 736.
    Contributory negligence as defense, 750.
    Deceit action, 745.
    Estoppel, 733.
    Negligence action, 745.
    Persons protected, 745.
    Physical damage, 205, 725.
    Restitution, 745.
Negligence of others, anticipating 198, 328.
Nondisclosure, 205.
Nonfeasance, liability for, 373.
Nuisance, relation to, 652.
Per se, violation of statute, 227, 229.
Perception, minimum standard of, 182.
Performance, entering upon, 379.
Peril, duty to aid those in, 375.
Physical attributes of actor, 175.
Physicians and surgeons,
    Community, type of, 182.
    Customary methods, 189.
    Emergency, 116, 117.
    Expert testimony, necessity of, 188.
    Schools of medical thought, 187.
    Standard applied to, 185.
Pleading specific, res ipsa loquitur, 260.
Prenatal injuries,
    Liability for, 367.
        Viability, 368.
        Wrongful death, 368.
    Wrongful birth, 370.
    Wrongful life, 370.
    Wrongful pregnancy, 370.

NEGLIGENCE—Cont'd
Presumptions, 240.
Preventing aid by others, 382.
Products liability,
    Failure to warn, 685, 697.
    Flaws in products, 695.
Professional men, conduct required of, 185.
Promise to aid, breach of, 379.
Proof, 235.
Proximate cause. See Proximate Cause.
Reasonable person,
    Hypothetical character of, 175.
    Standard of, 173.
Recklessness. See Recklessness.
Res ipsa loquitur. See Res Ipsa Loquitur.
Risk-benefit analysis, 171.
Risk covered by statute, 225.
Rules of law, value of, 217.
Seller's liability for physical harm, 681.
Shifting responsibility, 203.
Slight negligence, 211, 470.
Standard of conduct, 173.
    Application, 193.
    Functions of court and jury, 235.
    General, for court, 236.
    Objective or subjective, 175.
    Particular, for jury, 237.
    Proximate cause, confusion with, 275.
    Rules of law, 217.
    Statute, effect of, 220.
    Variation with circumstances, 173.
Statute, compliance with as due care, 233.
Sufficiency of evidence of facts, 235.
Superior knowledge, skill and intelligence, 185.
Transition from trespass and case, 30.
Transitory incapacity, 162, 178.
Trespassers. See Trespassers.
Unreasonable risk, 169.
Vendors and vendees. See Vendors and Vendees.
Violation of statute. See Statute, Violation of.
Weight of evidence of facts for jury, 236.
Wilful and wanton. See Recklessness.

NEWSPAPERS
See Defamation; Privacy.

NO–FAULT INSURANCE
See Compensation Systems.

NONDISCLOSURE
Confidential relation, 738.
Duty to disclose, 738.
Lessors, 436.
Licensees, 416, 417.
New information, 738.
Non-liability for, 737.
Partial statements, 738.
Physical damage, 205.
Restitution, 730.
Vendors, 447.

NUISANCE
Abatement, summary, 641.
"Absolute" nuisance, 636.
Acts innocent in themselves together causing harm, 347, 354.

INDEX

NUISANCE—Cont'd
Aeronautics, flight through air space, 80.
Apportionment of damages,
  Among tortfeasors, 349.
  Between plaintiff and defendant, 459.
Assumption of risk as defense to, 633.
"Attractive" nuisance, 400.
Basis of liability, 619.
Coming to a nuisance, 634.
Conduct of others, 633.
Damages as remedy for, 637.
Defenses, 632.
Equity, relief in, 640.
Highway, danger to, 388, 644.
History, 617.
Injunction, relief by, 640.
Intent as basis of liability, 622.
Landowner's liability outside of premises, 385.
Legislation, effect of, 632.
Lessees, liability of, 434.
Lessors, liability of, 434, 437.
Meaning of, 616.
Mental effect, importance of, 627.
Municipal corporations, liability of, 1054.
Natural conditions, 391.
Negligence, relation to, 652.
Private nuisance, 618, 619.
  Distinguished from public, 618.
  Personal injuries from, 639.
  Property rights protected, 621.
  Reasonable use, 629, 630.
  Trespass distinguished, 622.
  Types of interference, 622.
Public nuisance, 643.
  Basis of tort liability, 646.
  Combined with private, 618.
  Crime of, 646.
  Distinguished from private, 618.
  Highway, danger to, 618.
  Necessity of public interest, 645.
  Particular damage, necessity of, 646.
  Pecuniary loss, 647, 651.
  Physical harm, 648.
  Statutory, 646.
  Types of interference, 643.
Reasonable use, 619ff, 626ff.
  Alternatives open, 630.
  Conflicting property rights, 629, 630.
  Factors affecting, 629, 630.
  Locality, nature of, 627, 633.
  Motive as a factor, 624.
  Utility of conduct, 630.
Reasonableness of defendant's conduct, 629.
Remedies, 637.
Sensitive use, 630.
Strict liability, relation to, 552, 554.
Substantial interference, 626.
Trivial interferences, 626.
Unreasonable interferences,
  Factors involved, 630.
  Mental annoyance, 627.
  Physical discomfort, 627.
  Physical harm to land or tangible property, 627.
Vendees, liability of, 449.

NUISANCE—Cont'd
Vendors, liability of, 447, 448.
Water, reasonable use of, 623.

OFFICERS
See also Arrest.
Abrogation of immunities, 1055.
Absolute immunity, 1056.
Administrative officers, see Executive officers, this topic.
Defamation, privileges in,
  Executive proceedings, 821.
  Judicial proceedings, 816.
  Legislative proceedings, 820.
Discretionary immunity, 1062, 1066.
Execution of civil process, 150.
Executive officers, 1057, 1059.
Federal officers,
  Federal claims against, 1060.
  State claims against, 1060.
Immunities of, 1056.
  Discretionary acts, 1062.
  Jurisdiction, exceeding, 1056.
  Ministerial acts, 1062.
  Superior and inferior, 1057.
Immunity, see particular topics.
Indemnity provisions for, 1067.
Invitees, 429.
Judicial officers, 1056.
  Jurisdiction, 1058.
Legal process, privilege of, 148.
Legislative officers, 1056.
Licensees, 429.
Privilege and immunity, 1066.
Privilege of legal authority, 148, 1066.
Prosecutors, 1058.
Quasi-judicial acts, 1057.
Remedies, alternatives affecting immunity, 1064.
Separation of powers considerations, 1065.
State officers,
  Federal claims against, 1061.
  State claims against, 1059.
Trespass ab initio, 150.
Types of claims against, 1062.

OWNERS AND OCCUPIERS OF LAND
See Land, Owners and Occupiers of.

PARENT AND CHILD
Abduction and enticement, 924.
Automobiles, family purpose doctrine, 524.
Child,
  Alienation of affections of parent, 929.
  Interference with interests of, 928.
Consortium,
  Child's claim, 935.
  Parents' claim, 934.
Contribution claims against, 910.
Custody, interference with, 925.
Discipline, 157.
Duty to control conduct of child, 384, 914.
Imputed contributory negligence, 531.
Injury to parent, 934.
Liability insurance, effect on immunity, 595.
Loss of services, imputed contributory negligence, 937.

INDEX

References are to Pages

PARENT AND CHILD—Cont'd
Mental distress at peril to child, 66, 366.
Parent,
  Action for interference with relation, 928.
  Defenses to action for injury to child, 937.
  Injuries to child, action for, 935.
Proximate cause, intervening negligence of parent, 199, 318.
Seduction, 926.
  Loss of services, necessity for, 926.
  Parent's action for, 926.
  Statutory abolition of action, 930.
Third parties, liability of, 910.
Tort actions between, 904.
  Abrogation of immunity, 907.
  Death, effect of, 906.
  Duties, 907.
  History, 904.
  Immunity, 904.
    Generally, 904.
    Abolished, 907.
  Liability insurance, 595.
Vicarious liability for torts, 912.
Wrongful death, immunity in action for, 955.

PARTIES
Joinder of defendants, 324.

PASSING OFF
See Unfair Competition.

PERIL
Duty to aid those in, 375.
Mental distress at peril to another, 65, 365.

PERJURY
Witness' tort immunity, 872.

PHYSICIANS AND SURGEONS
Community, type of, 187.
Consent to operation, incapacity, 115–118.
Contract to cure, 186.
Emergency, treatment in, 116, 117.
Informed consent, 120, 189.
Limitations, statute of, 166.
Malicious prosecution claims by, 891.
Negligent medical treatment, liability of original wrongdoer for, 309.
Res ipsa loquitur, 253, 256.
Schools of medical thought, 187.
Standard of conduct required of, 185.

PLEADING
Specific negligence pleaded, res ipsa loquitur, 260.

POLICY AND PROCESS
See Tort.

POSSESSION
Conversion, necessity of possession in plaintiff, 102.
Forcible entry, importance of possession, 145.
Trespass,
  To chattel, 87.
  To land, 70, 77.
  Vertical extent of possession, 78.

PRENATAL INJURIES
See Negligence.

PRESUMPTIONS
Carriers, negligence toward passenger, 243, 252.
Negligence, 240.
Res ipsa loquitur. See Res Ipsa Loquitur.
Strict liability through, 580.

PREVENTION
As factor in determining tort liability, 25.

PRIMA FACIE TORT
Interference with contract, 983.
Interference with prospective advantage, 1010, 1011.

PRINCIPAL AND AGENT
Vicarious liability,
  Agents other than servants, 508.
  Damages not apportioned, 346.
  Family immunity, 910.
  Nature of, 501.
  Reasons for, 499.

PRINCIPLES
Of compensation, 608.
Of tort law, 6.

PRIVACY
Appropriation of name or likeness, 851.
Consent of plaintiff, 867.
Constitutional limitations,
  Public record, matters of, 862.
Constitutional privilege, 862.
Constitutional right of, 866.
Defamation, interrelation with, 864.
Defenses, 867.
False light in the public eye, 863.
History, 849.
Intrusions, 854.
Lapse of time, 859.
News, privilege as to, 859.
Privileges, 867.
Public disclosure of private facts, 856.
Public figures, privilege as to, 859.
Recognition of right of, 849.

PRIVATE REMEDY, VIOLATION OF STATUTE
See Negligence; Statutes.

PRIVILEGE
Alienation of affections, 922.
Interference with contract, 983.
Meaning, 108.
Privacy, 867.
Strict liability, defense to, 567.

PROCESS
See Abuse of Process; Legal Authority.

PROCESS IN TORT LAW
See Tort.

PRODUCT SIMULATION
See Unfair Competition.

PRODUCTS LIABILITY
Bailors,
   Negligence liability, 715.
   Strict liability in tort, 715.
   Warranty liability, 715.
Builders, 722.
   Burden of proof, 712.
Causation,
   Identification of defendant as supplier of product, 713.
Component part sellers, 705.
   Contributory negligence, 710.
Dealers, 706.
Defect, meaning of, 694.
Defect of design,
   Meaning of, 698.
Defenses, 710.
   Discovery by intermediate party, 710.
Endorsers of products, 707.
Failure to warn,
   Intermediate party, negligence of, 710.
   Negligence, 685, 697.
   Strict liability, 697.
Liability to third person, 703.
   Altered product, 711.
   Care required, 684, 703.
   Class protected, 703.
   Defendants liable, 704.
   Directions and warning, 685ff.
   Disclaimers, 681, 691.
   Food and drink, 690.
   Interests protected, 693.
   Lapse of time, 712.
   MacPherson v. Buick Motor Co., 682.
   Negligence, 681, 703.
   Objections to warranty concept, 690.
   Pecuniary loss, 708.
   Plaintiffs protected, 703.
   Products beyond food, strict liability, 690.
   Products made by others, 705.
   Property damage, 708.
   Sellers liable for negligence, 705.
   Strict liability in tort, 692.
      Arguments for, 692.
Liability to those supplied,
   Warranty, 679.
License to use, 719.
Licensors of trademarks and patents, 707.
Losses, types of, 677.
Market share liability, 714.
Negligence,
   Designs, 688.
   Failure to warn, obvious dangers, 686.
   Negligence and physical harm, 681.
   Toxic and allergic reactions, failure to warn, 687.
Obvious dangers, failure to warn, 686.
Other than sellers,
   Extension of warranty to, 715.
   Liability to third persons, 715.
   Negligence, 715.
   Res ipsa loquitur, 255 n. 43, 695.
Services, 719.
State of the art,
   Designing out danger, 701.

PRODUCTS LIABILITY—Cont'd
   Discoverability of danger, 700.
Strict liability,
   Legal history, 690, 692.
Theories of recovery, 677.
Unsafe products, 694.
Warranty,
   Intangible economic losses, 679.

PROPERTY, DEFENSE OF
Apparent necessity, 131.
Destruction of property for, 136.
Mechanical devices, 134.
Mistake, 131.
Privilege of, 131.
Reasonable force, 132.
Watchdog, 136.

PROXIMATE CAUSE
See also Negligence.
Act of God, intervening, 314, 316.
Acts innocent in themselves together cause harm, 354.
Alternative liability, double fault and, 271.
Apportionment of damages, 345.
Alternative liability, 345.
Market-share allocation, 271, 351, 713.
Percentages, 272.
Proportional, 271, 345, 714.
Burden of proof,
   Common duty, 346.
   Concerted action, 346.
   Culpable and innocent causes, 347.
   Damages of same kind, 350.
   Difficulty of proof, 345, 350.
   Nuisance cases, 349.
   Plaintiff and defendant, 457.
   Potential damage, 353.
   Single indivisible result, 340.
   Successive injuries, 352.
   Vicarious liability, 346.
"But for" rule, 266.
Carriers, negligence concurring with act of God, 317.
Causation in fact, 263.
Concurring causes, either alone would produce result, 266.
Condition, cause and, 277.
Contributory negligence, relation to, 276, 452.
Dangerous animals, consequences, 561.
Defamation, 795.
Defenses to negligence, confusion with, 275, 452.
Direct causation, 293.
Duty, relation to, 274.
Foreseeable risk. See Unforeseeable consequences, infra, this title.
Functions of court and jury, 319.
Highly extraordinary consequences limitation, 298.
Interference with contract, 989.
Intervening causes, 301.
   Criminal acts, 201, 313.
   Disease, 310.
   Escaping danger, acts of one, 307.
   Foreseeable, 303.
   Foreseeable results of unforeseeable, 316.
   Increasing risk, necessity of, 305.
   Meaning of, 301.

INDEX

References are to Pages

PROXIMATE CAUSE—Cont'd
  Medical treatment, 309.
  Negligence of others, 199, 308.
  Normal, 306.
  Parents, negligence of, 318.
  Rescuers, 307.
  Second injury, 310.
  Suicide, 310.
  Unforeseeable results of unforeseeable, 311.
  Unlocked car, injury by thief, 203, 313.
  Justly attachable cause formula, 278.
  Last clear chance, relation to, 462.
  Last human wrongdoer, 277.
  Market-share allocation, 271, 351, 713.
  Misrepresentation, damages caused by, 767.
  Multiple causes, 266.
  Natural and probable consequences formula, 282.
  Nature of the problem, 264.
  Nearest cause formula, 276.
  Palsgraf v. Long Island R. Co., 284.
  Particular interest, liability limited to, 289.
  Personal injuries, consequences of, 291.
  Philosophical theories of causation, 263.
  Problems involved, 279.
  Products liability,
    Strict liability in tort, 711.
  Proof of causation in fact, 269.
  Proposed formulae, 276.
  Rescuers, 307.
  Role in principles, 612.
  Rules, systems of, 279.
  Same hazard formula, 283.
  Scope of the problem, 272.
  Shifting responsibility, 203, 318.
  Similar risk, limitation of liability to, 283.
  Standard of conduct, confusion with, 275.
  Statute, violation of, 223.
  Strict liability,
    Act of God, intervening, 564.
    Manner of occurrence, 564.
    Persons threatened, 562.
    Third party, intervening act of, 564.
    Type of harm threatened, 560.
  Substantial factor,
    General formula of, 278.
      Alternative to, 263.
    Test of causation in fact, 268.
  Time and space, limitations of, 282.
  Trespassing animals, consequences, 560.
  Unforeseeable consequences, 280.
    Direct causation, 293.
    Foresight,
      Anatomy of, 297.
      Flexibility of, 269.
    Fragmentation of risk, 298.
    Hindsight, 298.
    Intentional torts, 293.
    Liability beyond the risk, 290.
    Limitation of liability to risk, 281.
    Polemis case, 295.
    Same hazard formula, 283.
    Trespass to land, 73–77.
    Wagon Mound case, 296.
  Unforeseeable plaintiffs, 284.
  Violation of statute, 223.

PUBLIC FIGURES
See Defamation; Privacy.

PUBLIC OFFICERS
See Defamation; Officers; Privacy.

PUBLIC UTILITIES
Duty to serve, 374.
Insult, liability for, 58.

PUNITIVE DAMAGES
See Damages.

QUASI–CONTRACTS
See Restitution.

RAILROADS
Federal Employers' Liability Act, 577.
Stop, look and listen, 218.

RECAPTURE OF CHATTELS
Entry upon land for, 139.
Force or fraud, taking by, 138, 139.
Fresh pursuit, 138.
Mistake, 138.
Privilege of, 137.
Reasonable force, 138.
Temporary detention of suspected thief, 141.

RECEIVERS
Wrongful appointment, 896.

RECKLESSNESS
Automobile guest statutes, 212, 215.
Contributory negligence as defense, 462.
Gross negligence, relation to, 212.
Intent distinguished, 36.
Last clear chance, relation to, 462.
Licensees, 415.
Mental distress, 64.
Negligence distinguished, 36.
Punitive damages based on, 10, 213.
State of mind, 213.
Trespassers, 397.
Wilful and wanton conduct, 212.
  Misdefinition of, 214 n. 69, 397.

REFORM OF TORT LAW
Compensation systems, 600.
Lawmaking by courts, 17.
Overruling decisions, 18.
Policy and process, 15.

RELATIONAL INTERESTS
See Interference; Husband and Wife; Parent and Child.

RELEASE
Covenant not to sue, 334.
Joint tortfeasors,
  Crediting payments made, 333, 335.
  Effect of release of one, 332.
  Satisfaction, 330, 332, 335.
Wrongful death,
  Beneficiary's release, 959.
  Inter vivos release, 955.

INDEX

References are to Pages

RES IPSA LOQUITUR
Airplane accidents, 246.
Applications of, 244.
Burden of proof, 259.
Carrier and passenger, 243.
Collisions of vehicles, 251.
  Carriers with other vehicles, 252.
Defendant's duty, 255.
Eliminating the plaintiff, 254.
Evidence more accessible to defendant, 254.
Exclusive control in defendant, 249.
Expert testimony, necessity of, 256.
Exploding bottles, 247.
Inference from facts, 247.
Inference negligence was defendant's, 248.
Inference someone was negligent, 244.
Medical accidents, 252, 256.
Multiple defendants, 251.
Nature of the accident, 244.
Origin and history, 244.
Permissible inference, 257.
Physicians and surgeons, 252, 256.
Pleading specific negligence, 260.
Presumption, effect as, 258.
Procedural effect, 257.
Rebutting evidence, effect of, 261.
Specific evidence of plaintiff, 260.
Specific pleading, 260.
Suppliers of chattels, proof of negligence, 695, 712.

RESCISSION
See Restitution.

RESCUE
Assumption of risk, 491.
Contributory negligence, 491.
Duty, 307.
Proximate cause, 307.

RESTATEMENT OF TORTS, ROLE OF
See Tort.

RESTITUTION
Election to sue for, 672.
Goods, sale or use of, 673.
Land, use of, 674.
Misrepresentation, 730.
Real property, injuries to, 674.
Waiver of tort, 672.

RESTRAINT OF TRADE
Prospective advantage, interference with, 1023.

RETALIATORY DISCHARGE
See Interference.

RIGHT OF PRIVACY
See Privacy.

RISK
  See also Proximate Cause.
Bearing, 24, 596.
Distributing, 24, 596.
Foresight, anatomy of, 297.

RULES OF LAW
Proximate cause, systems of rules in, 279.
Value of, in negligence cases, 217.

SALES
See Products Liability; Warranty.

SATISFACTION
See Judgment; Release.

SCHOOLS
Discipline, 158.

SCIENTER
Dangerous animals, 542.
Deceit, 741.
Injurious falsehood, 969.

SEDUCTION
Age of consent statutes, 123.
Loss of services, necessity for, 926.
Parent's action, 926.
Statutory abolition of action, 930.

SELF-DEFENSE
Apparent necessity, 125.
Defamation, 825.
Illegal arrest, 128, 156.
Injury to third person, 128.
  Intentional, 129.
Killing in, 127.
Mistake, 125.
Privilege of, 124.
Reasonable force, 125.
Retreat, necessity of, 127.

SLANDER
See Defamation.

SLANDER OF TITLE
See Injurious Falsehood.

SOCIAL INSURANCE AND WELFARE
See Compensation Systems.

STATES
See Governmental Liabilities.

STATUTE, VIOLATION OF
Accident, unavoidable, 162.
Age of consent, 123.
Assumption of risk as defense, 492.
By plaintiff, 231.
Class of persons protected, 222, 224.
Consent to a criminal act, 123.
Contributory negligence as defense, 461.
Evidence of negligence, 230.
Excused violations, 227.
Negligence per se, 227, 229.
Proximate cause, 223.
Standard of conduct, statutory, 220.
Strict liability for, 227.
Type of risk covered, 225.
Unreasonable legislation, 229.

STATUTES
Abolishing "heart balm", 929.
Animal trespass, 540.
Automobiles,
    Consent statutes, 527.
Comparative negligence, 471, 495.
Compliance with, as due care, 233.
Contribution between tortfeasors, 338.
Court function as to, 19.
Fire, strict liability for, 544.
Forcible entry, 143.
Gaps in, 19.
Interpreting, 19, 20.
Married Women's Acts, 902.
Master and servant, 572, 577.
Nuisance,
    Legislative authority for, 632.
    Public, 643.
Private remedies, 19.
Strict liability, extension by statute, 580.
Survival of actions, 942.
Wrongful death acts, 945.

STRICT ACCOUNTABILITY PRINCIPLE
See Compensation Systems; Worker's Compensation.

STRICT LIABILITY
Abnormally dangerous activities, 545.
    American cases, 548.
    English cases, 545.
    Relation to surroundings, 546, 554.
    What is included, 546, 549, 555.
Act of God, intervening, 564.
Airplanes, ground damage from, 556.
Animals. See Animals.
Assumption of risk, 566.
Bailors, 715.
Basis of liability, 534.
Blasting, 69, 550, 552, 553.
Consent, defense of, 566.
Consumer, strict liability in tort to, 690.
Contributory negligence, 565.
Defamation, innocent, 808.
Development of, 534.
Dram Shop acts, 581, 582.
Employers' liability, 568.
Extension of principle into new fields, 522.
Extent of liability, 560.
    Manner of occurrence, 563.
    Persons endangered, 562.
    Type of harm threatened, 560.
Fault,
    Liability without, 534.
    Meaning of, 23, 534.
    Principle, 608.
Federal Tort Claims Act, 1034.
Fire,
    Common law, 543.
    Statutes, 544.
Legal authority, defense of, 567.
Misrepresentation, 748.
Natural use of land, 545.
Non-natural use, 545.
Nuclear energy, liability for shipping, producing, etc., 556.

STRICT LIABILITY—Cont'd
Nuisance, relation to, 552, 554.
Policy underlying, 536, 692.
Presumptions effecting, 580.
Privilege, defense of, 567.
Products liability,
    Defect, meaning of, 694.
    Defect of design, 698.
    Defenses, 710.
    Flaws in products, 695.
    Legal history, 690.
    Proximate cause, 711.
    State of the art, 700, 701.
Proximate cause, 559ff.
Rockets, ground damage from, 556.
Rylands v. Fletcher, 545.
Statutes imposing, 580.
Third party, intervening act of, 564.
To invitees, 562.
To licensees, 562.
To trespassers, 562.
Trespass to land, 68.
"Ultrahazardous activity", 551, 555.
Vicarious liability. See Vicarious Liability.
Violation of statute, 227.
Warranty. See Warranty.
Worker's compensation acts, 565, 572ff.

STRIKES
See Interference.

SUPPLIERS OF CHATTELS
See Products Liability.

SURVIVAL OF ACTIONS
Civil rights claims, 944.
Common law rules, 940.
Damages recoverable, 950.
Defenses, 954.
History, 940.
Personal torts, 942.
Property torts, 942.
Statutory provisions, 942.

THREATS
Mental distress, infliction of, 59.
Words not assault, 45.

TORT
Advantages of tort or contract action, 665.
Balancing interests, 16.
Capacity to bear loss as factor in, 24.
Characteristics of, 4.
Contract,
    Considerations relating to, distinguishing between, 656.
    Distinguished, 4, 655.
    Election, 664.
    Gravamen of action, 664.
    Misfeasance, 658, 660.
    Nonfeasance, 658.
    Public utility services, 662.
    Relation of tort to, 655.
    Relationships created by contract, 663.
    Restitution, 672.
    Tort liability to third persons, 667.

INDEX

References are to Pages

TORT—Cont'd
Convenience of administration, 23.
Cost benefit analysis, 16.
Crime,
    Distinguished, 7.
    Same act as both tort and, 8.
Definitions, 1.
Difficulty of definition, 1.
Duties, nature of, 5.
Economic analysis, 16.
Factors affecting liability in, 20.
Factors in tort law, 20.
Function of law of, 5.
Historical development, 20.
Law of tort, is there a, 3.
Liability insurance, "impact" of, 589.
Moral aspects of, 21.
Motive, liability turning on, 26.
Names, torts without, 3.
New torts, development of, 3.
Policy and process, 15.
Present deficiencies of law, 597.
Prevention and punishment in law of, 25.
Prima facie tort, 983, 1010.
Process in tort law, 16.
Punitive damages in, 9.
Purpose of law of, 5.
Remedies for deficiencies in law, 600.
Restatement of Torts, role of, 17.
Social engineering, 16.
Tripartite division of, 31.
Unreasonable conduct as basis of, 6.
Waiver of, 672.

TRADE SECRETS
See Unfair Competition.

TRADE UNIONS
See Interference.

TRADEMARKS
See Unfair Competition.

TRESPASS
Ab initio, 150.
Accident, liability for, 73.
Airplane, ground damage by, 74.
Animals, trespassing,
    Bailments, 541.
    Damages recoverable, 561.
    History, 539.
    Statutes regulating, 540.
    Straying from highway, 540.
Blasting, 68, 69.
Character of defendant's act, 72.
Chattels, trespass to, 85.
    Damage, necessity of, 87.
    Intent, 86.
    Possession, necessity of, 87.
Common law action of, 29.
Consequences, unforeseeable, 73–77.
Continuing, 73, 83.
Damage, necessity of, 75, 83.
Direct and indirect invasions, 69–71.
Flight over land, 79.
Forcible entry, liability for, 143.

TRESPASS—Cont'd
Invisible entry, 71.
Land, trespass to, 67.
Mistake as affecting liability, 74, 86.
Necessity, privilege of, 145.
Nuisance distinguished, 622.
Physical invasion, necessity of, 70, 77.
Pipelines, cables, and the like, 74, 86.
Possession, necessity of, 70, 77.
Recapture of chattels, entry for, 139.
Remaining on land, 73, 83.
Restitution, election to sue for, 674.
Statute of limitations, 83.
Strict liability for, 68.
Subsurface trespass, 82.
Vertical extent of possession, 78.

TRESPASSERS
Adults, 393.
Attractive nuisance, 400.
Basis of immunity toward, 394.
Categories, abolition of, 432.
Children, 399.
    Age, 408.
    Attraction, necessity of, 401.
    Balancing risk against utility, 392.
    Child's appreciation of danger, 408.
    Fixed rules as to particular conditions, 407.
    Foreseeability of trespass, 404.
    Natural conditions, 395.
    Negligence, rule of ordinary, 402.
    Risk of injury, foreseeable, 405.
    Special considerations affecting, 399.
    Third person, condition created by, 403.
    Very young children, reason to anticipate, 407.
Conditions, dangerous, 394, 398.
Continued toleration, 396.
Dangerous activities, 394.
Discovered, 396.
    Conditions on premises, 398.
Frequent trespass on limited area, 395.
Liability of occupiers to, 393.
Liability of third person to, 395.
Recreational lands, 415.
Straying from highway, 389.
Strict liability to, 562.
Wilful and wanton conduct, 397.

TROVER
See Conversion.

UNFAIR COMPETITION
    See also Injurious Falsehood.
Appropriation of ideas, 1020.
Boycott, 1023.
    Labor activities and strikes, 1025, 1026.
Computer programs, protection for, 1022.
Constitutional limits,
    Political protests, 1025.
    Right to copy designs, 1021.
False advertising, 1018.
Ideas, rights in, 1021.
Imitation of appearance, 1015.
Legal and illegal methods, 987, 1002.
Misappropriation, 1020.

INDEX

References are to Pages

UNFAIR COMPETITION—Cont'd
Misrepresentation, 1015, 1018.
Monopoly, 1013, 1024.
Motive, 1014.
Passing off, 1015.
Product simulation, 1015.
Restraint of trade, 1023.
Trade secrets, 1022.
Trademarks, 1015.

UNITED STATES
See Governmental Liabilities.

UNMARRIED CONSORTS
Consortium loss, 932.
Wrongful death, 947.

VENDORS AND VENDEES
Vendees, liability of, 449.
Vendors,
  Danger outside of premises, 447, 448.
  Known concealed dangers, 449.
  Liability of, 446.
Warranty, 679.

VICARIOUS LIABILITY
Agents other than servants, 508.
Automobiles,
  Consent statutes, 527.
  Entrusting to unsuitable driver, 523.
  Family purpose doctrine, 524.
  Liability of owners, 522.
Bailments, 523.
Damages not apportioned, 346.
Dangerous instrumentalities, 507.
Deviation from employment, 503.
Family, liability for torts of, 912.
Family immunity as affecting, 910.
Fellow servants, 571.
Frolic and detour, 503.
History, 499.
Husband and wife, 912.
Indemnity, 341.
Independent contractors,
  "Collateral" negligence of, 515.
  "Inherently dangerous" activities, 512.
  Negligence of employer, 510.
  Non-delegable duty, 511.
Intentional torts, 505.
Joinder of defendants, 324.
Joint enterprise. See Joint Enterprise.
Justifications, 499.
Liability insurance and, 593.
Meaning of, 499.
Nature of, 499.
Parent and child, 529, 912.
Prohibited acts, 503.
Punitive damages, 13.
Scope of employment, 501.
Servants, 501.

VIOLATION OF STATUTE
See Statute, Violation of.

WARRANTY
Consumer, warranty to,
  Beyond food, 690.
  Disclaimers, 691.
  Food and drink, 690.
  Objections to concept, 675.
  Products, beyond food and drink, 690.
Extension beyond sellers of chattels, 715.
History, 679.
Intangible economic losses, 679.
Sellers of chattels,
  Liability to those supplied, 679.
Services, 719.
Suppliers other than sellers, 715.
Tort character of, 690.

WATER
Failure to supply, 671.
Nuisance, reasonable use, 623, 625.
Strict liability, reservoirs, 546.

WELFARE PRINCIPLE
See Compensation Systems.

WILFUL AND WANTON MISCONDUCT
See Recklessness.

WITNESSES
Malicious prosecution, liability, 872.

WORKER'S COMPENSATION
Accident, injuries by, 573.
Arising out of employment, 572.
Common law remedy, effect on, 574.
Effect of statutes, 573ff.
History of legislation, 572.
Injuries not covered, 574.
Principle of strict accountability, 609.
Strict liability under, 573.
Theory of the acts, 573.

WRONGFUL BIRTH
See Negligence, Prenatal injuries.

WRONGFUL CIVIL PROCEEDINGS
See Malicious Prosecution.

WRONGFUL DEATH
Beneficiaries, 947.
  Defenses good against, 958.
Damages recoverable, 949.
Decedent, defenses good against, 954.
Family immunity in, 955.
Imputed contributory negligence, 954, 958.
Limitations, statute of, 957.
Plaintiffs in action for, 947.
Prenatal injuries, 367.
Release, beneficiary's release, 959.
Release by victim before death, 955.
Statutes, types of, 945.
Unmarried consorts, 947.

†